THE BOOK OF CATHOLIC QUOTATIONS

THE BOOK OF
CATHOLIC
QUOTATIONS

COMPILED FROM APPROVED SOURCES

ANCIENT, MEDIEVAL AND MODERN

Selected and Edited by

John Chapin

FARRAR, STRAUS AND CUDAHY

NEW YORK

Nihil obstat
John A. Goodwine, J.C.D.
Censor Librorum

Imprimatur
✠ Francis Cardinal Spellman
Archbishop of New York

The nihil obstat and imprimatur are official declarations that a book or pamphlet is free of doctrinal or moral error. No implication is contained therein that those who have granted the nihil obstat and the imprimatur agree with the contents, opinions or statements expressed.

September 7, 1956.

PUBLISHED SIMULTANEOUSLY IN CANADA BY AMBASSADOR BOOKS, LTD., TORONTO. DESIGNED BY ANDOR BRAUN. MANUFACTURED IN THE U.S.A. BY AMERICAN BOOK–STRATFORD PRESS, INC., NEW YORK

MATRI INTEMERATAE

SEDI SAPIENTIAE

PREFACE

The Book of Catholic Quotations represents a departure in the field of reference dictionaries devoted to quotations. As such, however, it scarcely needs any apology. Catholic readers have no doubt often felt the lamentable inadequacy of most standard works, from their point of view; the failure of such works to include authors and subjects of importance; the distortions, inaccuracies and even signs of prejudice which are reflected in many, in spite of laudable efforts to eliminate these defects. Clearly what is needed is a new work, conceived and compiled entirely from a Catholic viewpoint. But such a work ought not to be a mere supplement to existing works, in which the Catholic balance is redressed, as it were. A mere addendum could look forward to little life expectancy. What is needed is a comprehensive work, general in scope, in which the specifically Catholic element is allowed to play its proper part. *The Book of Catholic Quotations* is designed to fill this need.

Over 10,400 quotations on a multitude of subjects have been carefully selected from a list of approved Catholic sources representing the accumulated wisdom of centuries, from the earliest years of the Church down to the present time. Material of all kinds has been included. The reader will find maxims, proverbs, definitions; a selection of important pronouncements by the supreme pontiffs and other ecclesiastical authorities; typical statements of saints, doctors and mystics; quotations from poets and prose writers, all arranged in chronological order under hundreds of different subject headings. The Index of Sources lists all the authors, and the Index of Subjects is a copious concordance which will facilitate reference to key words, subjects and phrases. While most standard works are content with exploitation of the literary field, there is a tendency of late to recognize the usefulness of works which are broader in scope, compiled from many different kinds of sources. *The Book of Catholic Quotations* falls into this category. Intended primarily for the lay or average reader, it will also have its uses for the specialist.

A word should be said about sources, to forestall any misconception. The material that could be potentially exploited in compiling a work of this kind is of course enormous. An inspection of the Index of Sources will reveal the wide range of basic reference material consulted. But it will be apparent that a number of categories have been omitted. In the interest of limiting the scope of the work it has been necessary to impose certain restrictions and to choose with care. It was decided to exclude all biblical quotations, except as they are found in other quotations. The assumption is that these are more or less readily available in other works and that any partial selection would be unsatisfactory; it must not be thought that the editor intends to underestimate the great importance of biblical quotations. A somewhat more regrettable omission has been the exclusion of modern Continental Catholic sources. The supreme pontiffs, the Code of Canon Law, and a number of other writers have been excepted from this rule for obvious reasons, but on the whole, for this period, the work is largely confined to Catholic sources from the English-speaking world. Moreover, no particular effort has been made to tap contemporary, living Catholic authors on a large scale; quotations from some of the most notable have been included; others, equally deserving from every point of view, have had to be passed over. It is hoped that the reader will find some compensation for these losses in the generous quotations from the Fathers of the Church and other early sources.

The word "Catholic" is understood throughout the work in the sense in which it was used by Pope St. Gregory VII on page 114, namely as implying agreement with the Roman Church in matters of faith and morals. While the reader has a perfect right to assume that in *The Book of Catholic Quotations* proper standards of orthodoxy have been maintained in essential matters—many of the quotations, such as those from the creeds, the pronouncements of popes, the general councils, the Code of Canon Law, etc., leave one in no doubt on this score—he must be careful not to assume blindly that all quotations in the book, regardless of what they are about, are equally free from objections in all their implications. The reader must distinguish, as the Church does, between the authority of those who have a right to speak on matters of faith and morals, namely the hierarchy in its official capacity, and private individuals, no matter how illustrious or famous, who have no such right. Quotations are, by definition, phrases or sentences detached from context. In most works this presents no particular difficulty, because the author who cites them is able by a phrase or two to convey the proper atmosphere. But in a compilation of quotations this is quite impossible. Only in a few cases likely to be seriously misleading can explanatory notes be added. The editor must assume for the most part that his readers are generally familiar with the context, or can gather it from the quotation itself. It is important to bear these distinctions in mind, otherwise the poetical, rhetorical, and in some cases rather unrestrained language used by certain authors will be misinterpreted. It is also important to remember that the work is informal in nature. It does not pretend to offer a complete résumé of Catholic teaching, and is not a substitute for the catechism or other technical and official expositions of the faith. For the sake of completeness, a certain number of statements by non-Catholics, by dubious Catholics, or from works listed on the Index of Prohibited Books, have been included. All such authors or works have been marked with an asterisk (*) in the Index of Sources, and the quotations have been accompanied by explanatory notes where necessary. Obviously the ecclesiastical authorities cannot be held responsible for approving the sentiments or opinions expressed by these authors. Condemned Propositions, that is, citations from authors or sources which have been condemned by the Holy See for one reason or another, have also been included in a number of cases with an indication simply that the proposition was condemned. It is understood, of course, that the propositions were found to be objectionable on various grounds, which it has not been possible to reproduce here. Readers desiring fuller information must refer to such standard reference works as Denziger's *Enchiridion Symbolorum* (which will soon be published in an English translation), where these matters are properly set forth.

All books of this kind, like all anthologies, to some degree reflect the tastes and interests of the compiler. An absolute standard of objectivity is impossible of attainment. The editor is confident, however, that he has been reasonably successful in gathering together in one volume the more typical quotations which should find a place in such a collection.

Every effort has been made to render the translations as accurate and intelligible as possible, but the task admittedly has been difficult because of the many different sources from which the quotations have been culled. In some cases it has been necessary to have recourse to antiquated translations, and translations could not always be checked against the original text. In a few cases no reference has been given other than to author, because the quotation was taken from a work which did not indicate source. Needless to say, the reader's kind indulgence is requested, and any information with regard to defects of this kind, or defects in general, will be gratefully received.

The editor desires to express his gratitude to all who have cooperated in this work, especially to the staff of Farrar, Straus & Cudahy, who have facilitated the preparation and publication of the work in every possible way. Particular thanks are due to Mr. Daniel Duffin for his meticulous care in preparing the Index of Sources. Invaluable suggestions have been received from a number of different sources. The editor desires in particular to acknowledge helpful advice offered by the Reverend Elmer J. O'Brien, S.J., of Toronto, Canada; the Reverend Harold Charles Gardiner, S.J., literary editor of *America;* the Reverend J. Edgar Bruns, of St. Peter's, N. Y.; the Reverend John H. Ryder, of the Russian Center, Fordham University, N. Y.; the Reverend Christopher Huntington, of St. Aloysius, Great Neck, N. Y.; and Mr. James W. Lane, of St. James, N. Y. Thanks are also due to the staffs of the New York Public Library, St. Peter's Catholic Lending Library, the library of Union Theological Seminary, Fordham University library, the Library of Congress, and the library of Catholic University, for kind assistance.

J. C.

CONTENTS

Preface   vii

Quotations   1

Index of Subjects   933

Index of Sources   1057

A

Abandonment

Naked of friends and round beset with foes.

> Dryden: *Absalom and Achitophel.* (17th cent.)

Abbey

Adieu, sweet abbey of the tuneful dead! Fair vision of a time forever fled!

> E. Caswall: *A May Pageant.* (19th cent.)

Abbot

When anyone receives the name of abbot he ought to rule over his disciples with a double teaching: that is, let him show forth all good and holy things by deeds more than by words.

> St. Benedict: *Rule,* 2. (6th cent.)

An abbot who is worthy to rule a monastery should always remember what he is called and realize in his actions the name of a superior. For he is believed to be the representative cf Christ in the monastery, and for that reason is called by a name of His, according to the words of the apostle: *Ye have received the spirit of the adoption of sons, whereby we cry Abba, Father* (Rom. 8, 15).

> St. Benedict: *Rule,* 2. (6th cent.)

Abelard

I do not want to be a philosopher at the price of being rejected by Paul; nor yet an Aristotle at the price of being rejected by Christ, for there is no other name under heaven whereby I can be saved.

> Abelard. (12th cent.)

Ability

A few highly endowed men will rescue the world for centuries to come.

> Card. Newman: *Oxford University Sermons.* (19th cent.)

Abortion

You shall not kill an unborn child or murder a newborn infant.

> Teaching of the Twelve Apostles, 2. (2nd cent.)

For us murder is once for all forbidden; so even the child in the womb, while yet the mother's blood is still being drawn on to form the human being, it is not lawful for us to destroy. To forbid birth is only quicker murder. It makes no difference whether one takes away the life once born or destroy it as it comes to birth. He is a man, who is to be a man; the fruit is always present in the seed.

> Tertullian: *Apology,* 9, 8. (3rd cent.)

A woman who deliberately destroys a foetus is answerable for murder. And any fine distinction as to its being completely formed or unformed is not admissible amongst us.

> St. Basil: *Letters,* 188. (4th cent.)

Those who procure an abortion, including the mother, automatically incur an excommunication reserved to the ordinary (bishop). . . .

> Code of Canon Law, Canon 2350, 1 (20th cent.)

However we may pity the mother whose health and even life is imperiled by the performance of her natural duty, there yet remains no sufficient reason for condoning the direct murder of the innocent.

> Pope Pius XI: *Casti connubii*. (Dec. 31, 1930)

Absence

And when man is out of sight, quickly also he is out of mind.

> Thomas a Kempis: *The Imitation of Christ*, 1, 23. (15th cent.)

The farther off, the more desired; thus lovers tie their knot.

> Henry Howard, Earl of Surrey: *The Faithful Lover*. (16th cent.)

A boat at midnight sent alone
   To drift upon the moonless sea,
A lute, whose leading chord is gone,
A wounded bird, that hath but one
Imperfect wing to soar upon,
   Are like what I am, without thee.

> Thomas Moore: *Loves of the Angels: The Second Angel's Story*. (19th cent.)

Since you have waned from us,
   Fairest of women!
I am a darkened cage
   Songs cannot hymn in.
My songs have followed you,
   Like birds the summer;
Ah! bring them back to me,
   Swiftly, dear comer!

> Francis Thompson: *A Carrier Song*. (19th cent.)

Absolution

Absolve the sins of Thy people, we beseech Thee, O Lord, and may we be de-

livered by Thy goodness from the bonds of our sins which we have committed in our weakness.

> Roman Missal, Collect for Twenty-third Sunday after Pentecost. (Gregorian, 6th to 8th cent.)

I absolve you from your sins in the name of the Father, and of the Son, and of the Holy Ghost. (Ego te absolvo a peccatis tuis in nomine Patris, et Filii, et Spiritus Sancti.)

> Roman Ritual, Formula for Absolution. (ca. 10th cent.)

Nobody on his own authority can absolve persons who are not in some way his subjects. An act requires its proper matter on which to work; sacramental absolution is essentially a judicial act, which is effective only with subjects and subordinates. He who has no subjects cannot absolve. Jurisdiction settles what is the determinate material on which a priest can act.

> St. Thomas Aquinas: *Quodlibets*, 12, 19, 30. (13th cent.)

If any one saith that man is truly absolved from his sins and justified, because he assuredly believed himself absolved and justified; or that no one is truly justified but he who believes himself justified; and that by his faith alone absolution and justification are effected; let him be anathema.

> Council of Trent, Session 6, Canon 14. (Jan. 13, 1547)

The Lord instituted the Sacrament of Penance when, on being raised from the dead, He breathed upon His disciples, saying, Whose sins you shall forgive. . . .

> Decree of The Council of Trent, 14th Session. (1551)

See also Confession; Penance; Sin, Remission of

Absolutism

No reasonable ground can be adduced why subjects should control princes, or why power should be attributed to popular assemblies—except in the infancy, madness, or captivity of the prince, when a guardian or deputy may be created by the suffrages of the people. If princes were restrained by laws made by these assemblies or by the commands of the people, the power of the prince would be worthless and the royal name a vain thing.

Jean Bodin: *Republic,* 1, 8. (16th cent.)

If justice is the end of the law, and law is the command of the prince, and the prince is the image of the almighty God, then the laws of the prince should bear the stamp of divine laws.

Jean Bodin: *Republic,* 1, 8. (16th cent.)

All laws are vain, by which we right enjoy,
If kings unquestion'd can those laws destroy.

Dryden: *Absalom and Achitophel.* (17th cent.)

In modern times the absolute monarchy in Catholic countries has been, next to the Reformation, the greatest and most formidable enemy of the Church.

Lord Acton: *Political Thoughts on the Church.* (19th cent.)

Abstinence

Subdue your flesh by fasting and abstinence from meat and drink, as far as the health allows.

St. Augustine: *Letter 211* (His Rule). (5th cent.)

Total abstinence is easier than perfect moderation.

St. Augustine: *On the Good of Marriage.* (5th cent.)

And made almost a sin of abstinence.

Dryden: *The Character of a Good Parson.* (17th cent.)

The law of abstinence forbids taking as nourishment meat, meat juices, but not eggs, milk products, nor condiments of any kind though made from animal fats. The law of abstinence is to be observed on all Fridays.

Code of Canon Law, Canons 1250 and 1252, 1. (20th cent.)

See also Fasting

Abundance

All abundance which is not my God to me is neediness.

St. Augustine: *Confessions,* 13, 8. (5th cent.)

Abuse

Abuse is as great a mistake in controversy as panegyric in biography.

Card. Newman: *Letter to Fr. Coleridge, S.J.* (Ward, II, 114) (19th cent.)

Accident

Receive the accidents that befall thee as good, knowing that nothing happens without God.

Teaching of the Twelve Apostles, 3. (2nd cent.)

Accidie

Accidie is a shrinking of mind, not from any spiritual good, but from that to which it should cleave as in duty bound, namely the goodness of God.

St. Thomas Aquinas: *Disputations Concerning Evil,* 11, 3. (13th cent.)

Accord

It may rhyme but it accordeth not.

John Heywood: *Proverbs,* 1, 11. (16th cent.)

There is no good accord
Where every man would be a lord.

John Heywood: *Proverbs,* 2, 6. (16th cent.)

Acolyte

O almighty, eternal God, Fountain of light and Source of goodness, Who through Jesus Christ Thy Son, the true Light, didst illumine and by the mystery of His passion didst redeem the world, vouchsafe to bless these Thy servants whom we consecrate for the office of acolyte, beseeching Thy clemency to illumine their minds with the light of knowledge, and water them with the dew of Thy piety, that with Thine aid they may so fulfil the ministry which they have received as to deserve to attain to an everlasting reward.

Roman Pontifical, Ordination of Acolytes, Prayer *Omnipotens Sempiterne Deus.* (Gregorian, 6th to 8th cent.)

. . . It behoves the acolyte to carry the candlestick, to light the church lamps, and to bring the wine and water to the altar for the Eucharistic Sacrifice. . . .

Roman Pontifical, Ordination of Acolytes, Admonition. (ca. 10th cent.)

Act of God

An act of God does injury to no one. (Actus Dei nemini facit injuriam.)
Legal Maxim. (Medieval)

Acting

He doesn't act on the stage; he behaves.

Said of George Alexander by Oscar Wilde. (19th cent.)

Action

To keep constant guard over the actions of one's life.

St. Benedict: *Rule,* 4. (6th cent.)

The goodness of God knows how to use our disordered wishes and actions, often lovingly turning them to our advantage while always preserving the beauty of His order.

St. Bernard: *Letters,* 90, 6. (12th cent.)

Never do anything that thou canst not do in the presence of all.

St. Teresa of Jesus: *Maxims.* (16th cent.)

Great acts take time.

Card. Newman: *Apologia pro Vita Sua.* (19th cent.)

The greatest thing for us is the perfection of our own soul; and the saints teach us that this perfection consists in doing our ordinary actions well.

Archbp. Ullathorne: *Humility and Patience.* (19th cent.)

It is marvellous how our Lord sets His seal upon all that we do, if we will but attend to His working, and not think too highly upon what we do ourselves.

R. H. Benson: *The History of Richard Raynal Solitary.* (20th cent.)

See also Doing

Active and Contemplative Life

The one life, then, is in the arena, the other in a cave; the one is opposed to the confusion of the world, the other to the desires of the flesh; the one subdues, the other flees the pleasures of the body; the one more agreeable, the other safer; the one ruling, the other reigning in self; yet each denying herself that she may be Christ's, because to the perfect it was said: *If anyone wishes to come after Me, let him deny himself, and take up his cross, and follow Me* (Matth. 16, 24). He follows Christ who can say: *It is now no longer I that live, but Christ lives in me* (Gal. 2, 20).

St. Ambrose: *Letters,* 63. (396)

Now we are conscious of two powers in the human soul: the active and the contemplative; the former maps the way, the latter marks the journey's end; in the former we toil so that our hearts may be purified for the vision of God, in the latter we are at rest and see God; the former calls for the practice of the commandments of this life that passes away, in the latter we drink in the teachings of the life that will never pass away.

St. Augustine: *De Consensu Evangelistarum,* 1, 4, 8. (5th cent.)

In the active life a man makes progress though beset by the difficulties incident to our human life, he controls the rebellions of his bodily nature, curbing them by his reason. But the aim of the contemplative is to mount, through his desire of perfection, above merely human things; the active life means progress, the contemplative has reached the goal; the former makes a man holy, the latter makes him perfect.

Julianus Pomerius: *De Vita Contemplativa,* 2, 22. (5th cent.)

There are two kinds of lives in which Almighty God instructs us by His sacred word—namely, the active and the contemplative.

Pope St. Gregory I: *Hom. 14 in Ezechiel.* (5th cent.)

The contemplative life is more meritorious than the active, for the latter toils in the wear and tear of the present work by which it must needs help its neighbors; whereas the former, by a certain inward savor, already has a foretaste of the repose to come.

Pope St. Gregory I: *Hom. 3 in Ezechiel.* (5th cent.)

They who would hold the citadel of contemplation must first needs exercise themselves on the battlefield of toil.

Pope St. Gregory I: *Morals,* 6, 17. (5th cent.)

We ascend to the heights of contemplation by the steps of the active life.

Pope St. Gregory I: *Morals,* 31, 102. (5th cent.)

In the active life all the vices are first of all to be removed by the practice of good works, so that in the contemplative life a man may, with now purified mental gaze, pass to the contemplation of the divine Light.

St. Isidore of Seville: *Of the Supreme Good,* 3, 15. (7th cent.)

See also Contemplation; Contemplative Life

Activity

From stones and poets you may know,
That nothing so active is, as that which least seems so.

F. Thompson: *Contemplation.* (19th cent.)

Actor

The whole tribe of them is thrown out of all honor and privilege.

Tertullian: *De spectaculis.* (3rd cent.)

If a man be an actor or one who makes shows in the theater, either let him desist or let him be rejected.

St. Hippolytus: *The Apostolic Tradition,* 16. (With reference to pagan actors.) (3rd cent.)

What shall I say of the mimes who make a public profession of corruption? They teach men the tricks of adultery by representing them on the stage, and by pretence train to reality.

Lactantius: *Divinae institutiones,* 6. (4th cent.)

It shall not be lawful for any woman who is either in full communion or a probationer for baptism to marry or entertain any comedians or actors; whoever takes this liberty shall be excommunicated.

Decree of the Council of Elvira in Spain. (305)

Concerning players, we have thought fit to excommunicate them so long as they continue to act.

Decree of the First Council of Arles. (314)

I do not, however, assert that the actor is dishonorable when he follows his profession, although it is undoubtedly dishonorable to be an actor.

John of Salisbury *Policraticus*, 1, 8, 46. (12th cent.)

Peel'd, patch'd, and piebald, linsey-woolsey brothers
Grave mummers! sleeveless some and shirtless others.

Pope: *The Dunciad*, 3. (18th cent.)

Actress

There will, it is to be hoped, be great actresses in the future—actresses fired with the muses' madness and constrained to enlarge rather than to interpret the masterpieces of the world; but Providence (so economical, so generous!) never repeats an effect; and there will never be another Sarah Bernhardt.

Maurice Baring: *The Puppet Show of Memory*. (20th cent.)

Adam

The Lord my Maker, forming me of clay,
By His own breath the breath of life convey'd:
O'er all the bright new world He gave me sway,
A little lower than the angels made.
But Satan, using for his guile
The crafty serpent's cruel wile,
Deceiv'd me by the tree;
And sever'd me from God and grace,
And wrought me death and all my race,
As long as time shall be.
O Lover of the sons of men!
Forgive and call me back again!

Byzantine Triodion, Vespers of Quinquagesima. (Tr. Neale) (St. Theophanes, 8th cent.)

Adam, whiles he spake not, had paradise at will.

Wm. Langland: *Piers Plowman*, Passus 14. (14th cent.)

Adaptability

I shall cut my coat after my cloth.

John Heywood: *Proverbs*, 1, 8. (16th cent.)

Admiration

Fools admire, but men of sense approve.

Pope: *An Essay on Criticism*, 2. (18th cent.)

Admonition

We cannot deny that perseverance in good unto the end is a great gift of God, not to be had except from Him of Whom it is written: *Every good gift and every perfect gift is from above, coming down from the Father of Lights* (James 1, 17). Nevertheless, there is no reason for omitting the admonition of one who has not persevered; for it might be that God would give him repentance, and he would escape from the snare of the devil.

St. Augustine: *De Corruptione et Gratia*, 6, 10. (5th cent.)

Admonition is naturally bitter, but when mixed with the sugar of loving kindness, and warmed by the fire of charity, it becomes acceptable, gracious and very cordial.

Jean Pierre Camus: *The Spirit of St. Francis de Sales*, 2, 13. (17th cent.)

Adolescence

In adolescence . . . there is a curious mingling of refinement and brutality, stupidity and tenderness.

R. H. Benson: *By What Authority*. (20th cent.)

Adoption

Those who adopt children because they are unable to beget them in the flesh, beget them with greater chastity by their hearts.

St. Augustine: *Sermons*, 51. (5th cent.)

Adornment

Silk and purple and rouge and paint have beauty, but impart it not. Every such thing that you apply to the body exhibits its own loveliness, but leaves it not behind. It takes the beauty with it, when the thing itself is taken away. For the beauty that is put on with a garment and is put off with the garment, belongs without doubt to the garment, and not to the wearer of it.

> St. Bernard: *Letters,* 116, 4. (12th cent.)

Adulation

I would hardly dare to say who takes the palm in vice, he who defiles his tongue with adulation or he whose heart leaps with joy thereat.

> John of Salisbury: *Policraticus,* 3, 5, 183. (12th cent.)

Adulterer

The adulterer is a more grievous offender than the thief.

> St. John Chrysostom: *Homilies.* (4th cent.)

Adultery

The mind is guilty of adultery even if it merely pictures to itself a vision of carnal pleasure.

> Lactantius: *Divinae Institutiones,* 6. (4th cent.)

Everyone who puts away his wife, save on account of immorality, causes her to commit adultery (Matth. 5, 32). To such a degree is that nuptial pact which has been entered upon a kind of sacrament that it is not nullified by separation, since, as long as the husband, by whom she has been abandoned, is alive, she commits adultery if she marries another, and he who abandoned her is the cause of the evil.

> St. Augustine: *The Good of Marriage,* 7. (5th cent.)

A husband may murder his adulterous wife.

> Proposition condemned by Pope Alexander VII. (17th cent.)

Advent

Hark, a herald voice is calling;
"Christ is nigh," it seems to say;
"Cast away the dreams of darkness,
O ye children of the day."

. . . . . .

Lo, the Lamb, so long expected,
Comes with pardon down from heaven;
Let us haste with tears of sorrow,
One and all to be forgiven.

> Roman Breviary, Hymn *En clara vox redarguit* at Lauds. (Tr. Caswall) (Ambrosian, 5th cent.)

Stir up our hearts, O Lord, to prepare the ways of Thy only-begotten Son: that by His coming we may be able to serve Him with purified minds.

> Roman Missal, Collect for Second Sunday. (Gelasian, 5th to 7th cent.)

Mercifully hear, O Lord, the prayers of Thy people; that as they rejoice in the coming of Thine only-begotten Son according to the flesh, so when He cometh a second time in His majesty, they may receive the reward of eternal life.

> Gelasian Sacramentary, Collect for Advent. (5th to 7th cent.)

Celestial Word, to this our earth,
Sent down from God's eternal clime,
To save mankind by mortal birth
Into a world of change and time.

> Roman Breviary, Hymn *Verbum supernum prodiens* at Matins. (Tr. W. Courthope) (Ambrosian, ca. 6th cent.)

Bright Builder of the heavenly poles,
Eternal Light of faithful souls,
Jesus, Redeemer of mankind,
Our humble prayers vouchsafe to mind.

Who, lest the fraud of hell's black king
Should all men to destruction bring,

Didst, by an act of generous love,
The fainting world's Physician prove.

> Roman Breviary, Hymn *Creator alme
> siderum* (*Conditor alme siderum*) at
> Vespers. (Primer, 1685) (Much altered,
> Ambrosian, 7th cent.)

O Wisdom, that proceedest from the
mouth of the Most High, reaching from
end to end mightily, and sweetly disposing all things: come and teach us the way
of prudence.

> Roman Breviary, Great Antiphon at
> Vespers on December 17th. (ca. 7th cent.)

O Adonai, and Leader of the house of
Israel, Who didst appear unto Moses in
the burning bush, and gavest him the
law on Sinai: come and redeem us by
Thy outstretched arm.

> Roman Breviary, Great Antiphon at
> Vespers on December 18th. (ca. 7th cent.)

O Root of Jesse, Who standest as the
Ensign of the people, before Whom
kings shall not open their lips; to Whom
the gentiles shall pray: come and deliver
us, tarry now no more.

> Roman Breviary, Great Antiphon at
> Vespers on December 19th. (ca. 7th cent.)

O Key of David, and Scepter of the
house of Israel; Who openest, and no
man shutteth; Who shuttest, and no
man openeth: come and lead the captive
from the prison-house, and him that sitteth in darkness and in the shadow of
death.

> Roman Breviary, Great Antiphon at
> Vespers on December 20th. (ca. 7th cent.)

O Orient, Splendor of the eternal Light,
and Sun of justice: come and enlighten
them that sit in darkness and in the
shadow of death.

> Roman Breviary, Great Antiphon at
> Vespers on December 21st. (ca. 7th cent.)

O King of the gentiles, yea, and the desire thereof, the Cornerstone that makest
both one: come and save man, whom
Thou hast made out of the slime of the
earth.

> Roman Breviary, Great Antiphon at
> Vespers on December 22nd. (ca. 7th cent.)

O Emmanuel, our King and Lawgiver,
the expectation of all nations and their
Savior: come and save us, O Lord our
God.

> Roman Breviary, Great Antiphon at
> Vespers on December 23rd. (ca. 7th cent.)

There are three distinct comings of the
Lord of which I know, His coming to
men, His coming into men, and His
coming against men.

> St. Bernard: *Third Sermon for Advent.*
> (12th cent.)

O come, O come, Emmanuel,
And ransom captive Israel,
That mourns in lonely exile here,
Until the Son of God appear.
   Rejoice! rejoice! Emmanuel
   Shall come to thee, O Israel.

> Anonymous: *Veni veni Emmanuel.* (Tr. J.
> Neale) (13th cent.)

Hark! a glad exulting throng;
   Hark! the loud hosannas ring;
Glad hosannas loud and long
   Greet Messiah triumphing.

He, of Whom the prophets won
   Mystic visions faint and dim,
Comes, the All-Father's only Son,
   And redemption comes with Him.

> Anon: *Christi caterva clamitat.* (Tr. P.
> Onslow) (19th cent.)

Like the dawning of the morning,
   On the mountain's golden heights,
Like the breaking of the moonbeams
   On the gloom of cloudy nights.
Like a secret told by angels,
   Getting known upon the earth,
Is the Mother's expectation
   Of Messias' speedy birth.

> F. Faber: *Our Lady's Expectation.* (19th
> cent.)

No sudden thing of glory and fear
  Was the Lord's coming; but the dear
  Slow nature's days followed each
    other
  To form the Savior from His Mother
—One of the children of the year.

> Alice Meynell: *Advent Meditation.* (19th cent.)

Adventure

Adventure is the champagne of life.

> G. K. Chesterton: *Tremendous Trifles, 38.* (20th cent.)

Adversity

Those which are most happy are most sensible, and unless all things fall out to their liking, impatient of all adversity, every little cross overthrows them, so small are the occasions which take from the most fortunate the height of their happiness.

> Boethius: *De Consolatione Philosophiae,* 2, 4. (6th cent.)

For a man to rejoice in adversity is not grievous to him who loves; for so to joy is to joy in the Cross of Christ.

> Thomas a Kempis: *The Imitation of Christ,* 2, 6. (15th cent.)

No man is fit to comprehend heavenly things who hath not resigned himself to suffer adversities for Christ.

> Thomas a Kempis: *The Imitation of Christ,* 2, 12. (15th cent.)

Ye might have gone further and faren worse.

> John Heywood: *Proverbs,* 2, 4. (16th cent.)

There is no hell like to declined glory,
Nor is Prometheus' vulture half so fell
As the sad memory of a happy story
To him, that in adversity doth dwell.
Ah, let him die that is not as he was,
With ending bless break he the hour-glass.

> Anthony Copley: *A Fig For Fortune.* (Guiney, 334) (16th cent.)

Friendship, of itself a holy tie,
Is made more sacred by adversity.

> Dryden: *The Hind and the Panther, 3.* (17th cent.)

See also Prosperity and Adversity

Advice

I have often heard that it is more safe to hear and to take counsel than to give it.

> Thomas a Kempis: *The Imitation of Christ,* 1, 9. (15th cent.)

An honest man may take a fool's advice.

> Dryden. (17th cent.)

It is always a silly thing to give advice, but to give good advice is absolutely fatal.

> Oscar Wilde: *Portrait of Mr. W. H.* (19th cent.)

Adviser

Your choice should be of men approved, not to be proved.

> St. Bernard: *On Consideration,* 4, 4. (To Pope Eugenius III) (12th cent.)

Aesthetics

The poets complain of moralists. They themselves constantly confound art and morality to the detriment of both. A confusion of aesthetic values and ethical values, one of the scourges of our time.

> J. Maritain: *Art and Poetry.* (20th cent.)

Affection

Affection bends the judgment to her uses.

> Dante: *Inferno, Canto 13.* (14th cent.)

Affliction

We beseech Thee for those who are afflicted and in bonds and in poverty; give rest to each, free them from bonds, bringing them out of poverty; comfort

all, Thou Who art the Comforter and
Consoler.

> Sacramentary of Serapion, Prayer of the
> Faithful (27). (4th cent.)

God measures out affliction to our need.

> St. John Chrysostom: *Homilies.* (4th cent.)

One and the same violence of affliction
proves, purifies and melts the good, and
condemns, wastes and casts out the bad.

> St. Augustine: *The City of God,* 1. (5th
> cent.)

It is not enough to be afflicted because
God wills it; but we must be so as He
wills it, when He wills it, for as long as
He wills it, and exactly in the manner in
which it pleases Him.

> St. Francis de Sales: *Spiritual Conferences,*
> 21. (17th cent.)

The truly loving heart loves God's good
pleasure not in consolations only, but,
and especially, in afflictions also.

> St. Francis de Sales: *Treatise on the Love
> of God,* 9, 2. (17th cent.)

Many would be willing to have afflictions provided that they be not inconvenienced by them.

> St. Francis de Sales: *Introduction to the
> Devout Life,* 3, 3. (17th cent.)

Afternoon

The longer forenoon, the shorter afternoon.

> John Heywood: *Proverbs,* 1, 13. (16th
> cent.)

After-Thought

After-wits are dearly bought,
Let thy fore-wit guide thy thought.

> Bl. Robert Southwell: *Loss in Delay.* (16th
> cent.)

Agatha, Saint

Bright shall the day of St. Agatha rise,
Virgin and martyr, for lo! from the
skies,

Christ, as a lover, stooped tenderly
down,
Crowning her brow with His duplicate
crown.

. . . .

Glorious Agatha, now as a bride,
Raised by thy Savior, thou stand'st at
His side;
Hear us and plead for us, keeping thy
day,
Lift us and lead us to Jesus, we pray.

> Pope St. Damasus: *Martyris ecce dies
> Agathae.* (Tr. D. Donahoe) (4th cent.)

Age

Midway the journey of this life I was
'ware
That I had strayed into a dark forest,
And the right path appeared not anywhere.

> Dante: *Inferno, Canto 1.* (Opening lines
> of Divine Comedy) (Tr. L. Binyon) (14th
> cent.)

I loathe that I did love,
In youth that I thought sweet;
As time requires, for my behove,
Methinks they are not meet.

My lusts they do me leave,
My fancies all be fled,
And tract of time begins to weave
Grey hairs upon my head.

> Thomas, Lord Vaux: *The Aged Lover
> Renounceth Love.* (16th cent.)

For age, with stealing steps,
Hath clawed me with his crutch.

> Thomas, Lord Vaux: *The Aged Lover
> Renounceth Love.* (16th cent.)

Prime youth lasts not, age will follow
And make white these tresses yellow;
Wrinkled face for looks delightful
Shall acquaint the dame despiteful;
And when time shall date thy glory

Then too late thou wilt be sorry.
  Siren pleasant, foe to reason,
  Cupid plague thee for thy treason!

> Thomas Lodge: *Phillis.* (16th cent.)

Thou'lt find thy manhood all too fast—
Soon come, soon gone! and age at last
  A sorry *breaking up!*

> Thomas Moore: *Ode: Clapham Academy.*
> (19th cent.)

Now time has fled—the world is
  strange,
  Something there is of pain and change;
My books lie closed upon the shelf;
  I miss the old heart in myself.

> Adelaide Procter: *A Student.* (19th cent.)

Suffer, O silent one, that I remind thee
Of the great hills that stormed the sky
  behind thee,
Of the wild winds of power that have
  resigned thee.

> Alice Meynell: *A Letter from a Girl to her
> Old Age.* (19th cent.)

One should never trust a woman who
tells one her real age. A woman who
would tell one that would tell one anything.

> Oscar Wilde: *A Woman of No Importance.*
> (19th cent.)

As a white candle in a holy place,
So is the beauty of an aged face.

> Joseph Campbell: *The Old Woman.* (20th
> cent.)

I am older than dawn and sunset are.
I can think past the light of the oldest
star.
  .   .   .   .   .   .

How old am I? As days are told,
The earth is younger than I am old.

> Sister Madeleva: *You Ask My Age.* (20th
> cent.)

Age, Golden

The golden age only comes to men when
they have, if only for a moment, forgotten gold.

> G. K. Chesterton. (N. Y. Times
> Magazine, May 3, 1931.)

Age, Old

When men wish for old age for themselves, what else do they wish for but
lengthened infirmity?

> St. Augustine: *On Catechizing the
> Unlearned.* (5th cent.)

Let your old age be childlike, and your
childhood like old age; that is, so that
neither may your wisdom be with pride,
nor your humility without wisdom.

> St. Augustine: *In Ps. 112,* 2. (5th cent.)

The old may be out-run but not outreasoned.

> Chaucer: *The Knight's Tale.* (Tr. Coghill)
> (14th cent.)

A fond old man is often as full of words
as a woman.

> St. Thomas More: *English Works, 1169.*
> (16th cent.)

Childhood is ignorant, boyhood is lightheaded, youth is rash and old age is ill-
humored.

> Luis de Granada: *Guide for Sinners.* (16th
> cent.)

Bankrupt of life, yet prodigal of ease.

> Dryden: *Absalom and Achitophel.* (17th
> cent.)

Already I am worn with cares and age;
And just abandoning th' ungrateful
  stage;
Unprofitably kept at Heav'n's expense,
I live a rent-charge on His Providence.

> Dryden: *To Mr. Congreve.* (17th cent.)

Agnosticism

Do they really think that they have given me cause for rejoicing when they say that they consider that our soul is nothing but a little wind and smoke? Why should they say this in a tone of voice proud and content? Is it really a thing to say with such pride?

Pascal: *Pensées.* (17th cent.)

I do not see much difference between avowing that there is no God, and implying that nothing definite can for certain be known about Him.

Card. Newman: *Historical Sketches,* 3. (19th cent.)

Agnosticism solves not, but merely shelves, the mysteries of life. When agnosticism has done its withering work in the mind of man, the mysteries remain as before; all that has been added to them is a settled despair.

V. McNabb: *Thoughts Twice-dyed.* (20th cent.)

The chief function of agnosticism is to awake men from the dogmatic slumber of denial.

V. McNabb: *Thoughts Twice-dyed.* (20th cent.)

Agnosticism leads inevitably to moral indifference. It denies us all power to esteem or to understand moral values, because it severs our spiritual contact with God Who alone is the source of all morality and Who alone can punish the violation of moral laws with a sanction worthy of our attention.

Thomas Merton: *The Ascent to Truth.* (20th cent.)

Agreement

Ah, don't say that you agree with me. When people agree with me I always feel that I must be wrong.

Oscar Wilde: *The Critic as Artist,* 2; *Lady Windermere's Fan,* 2. (18th cent.)

Aid

Beasts are the subjects of tyrannic sway,
Where still the stronger on the weaker prey.
Man only of a softer mould is made;
Not for his fellows' ruin, but their aid.

Dryden: *The Hind and the Panther,* 1. (17th cent.)

Air

Let air you breathe be sunny, clear and light,
Free from disease, or cesspool's fetid blight.

School of Salerno, Code of Health. (11th cent.)

Wild air, world-mothering air,
Nestling me everywhere.

G. M. Hopkins: *The Bl. Virgin Compared to the Air We Breathe.* (19th cent.)

Alleluia

Alleluia, song of sweetness,
 Voice of joy, eternal lay:
Alleluia is the anthem
 Of the choirs in heavenly day,
Which the angels sing abiding
 In the house of God alway.

Anonymous: *Alleluia dulce carmen vox perennis gaudii.* (Tr. J. Neale) (9th or 10th cent.)

The strain upraise of joy and praise.
 Alleluia.
 To the glory of the King
Shall the ransomed people sing.
 Alleluia.
And the choirs that dwell on high
 Shall re-echo through the sky.
 Alleluia.

Godescalcus: *Cantemus cuncti.* (Tr. J. Neale) (10th cent.)

Alliance

[The Utopians] never enter into any alliance with any other state. They think leagues are useless things, and reckon that if the common ties of human nature do not knit men together the faith of promises will have no great effect on them.

> St. Thomas More: *Utopia.* (16th cent.)

Almsgiving

Almsgiving, therefore, is good as penance for sin; fasting is better than prayer, but almsgiving is better than both . . . for almsgiving relieves the burden of sin.

> So-called Second Letter of Clement I to the Corinthians, 16, 4. (ca. 2nd cent.)

Give to everyone that asks thee, and do not refuse, for the Father's will is that we give to all from the gifts we have received.

> Teaching of the Twelve Apostles, 1. (2nd cent.)

Offer your prayers and alms and do all things according to the gospel of our Lord.

> Teaching of the Twelve Apostles, 15. (2nd cent.)

He, therefore, who bestows food or raiment on the poor, but yet is stained with wickedness in his soul or body, offers the lesser to righteousness and the greater to sin, for to God he gives his possessions, but himself to the devil.

> Pope St. Gregory I: *Pastoral Care,* 3, 20. (6th cent.)

Alms are but the vehicles of pray'r.

> Dryden: *The Hind and the Panther,* 3. (17th cent.)

There is One alone Who cannot change;
Dreams are we, shadows, visions strange;
And all I give is given to One.
I might mistake my dearest son,
But never the Son Who cannot change.

> Alice Meynell: *San Lorenzo's Mother.* (19th cent.)

Alps

Alps on Alps in clusters swelling,
Mighty, and pure, and fit to make
The ramparts of a Godhead's dwelling.

> Thomas Moore: *Rhymes on the Road.* (19th cent.)

Altar

Altar against altar.

> St. Optatus: *De Schismate Donatistarum,* 1, 15. (4th cent.)

Women may not approach near the altar.

> Council of Laodicea, Can. 44. (365)

The altar is a type of the body, and the Body of Christ is on the altar.

> St. Ambrose: *On the Sacraments,* 4, 2, 7. (4th cent.)

Altars are God's theaters, where
In sacred scenery is shown
Love lifting red hands to the Over-throne.

> Clarence Walworth: *Andiatorocte.* (19th cent.)

Amateur

It is exceedingly hard for an amateur not to over-act his part.

> R. H. Benson: *An Average Man.* (20th cent.)

Ambition

The Church is full of ambitious men; the time is gone by for being shocked at the enterprising efforts of ambition; we think no more of it than a robber's cave thinks of the spoils of the wayfarers.

> St. Bernard: *On Consideration,* 1, 10. (12th cent.)

O ambition! the cross of the ambitious, how is it that though you torture all, you please all?

> St. Bernard: *On Consideration,* 3, 1. (12th cent.)

Ambition is the mother of hypocrisy and prefers to skulk in corners and dark places. It cannot endure the light of day. It is an unclean vice wallowing in the depths, always hidden, but with ever an eye to advancement.

St. Bernard: *Letters*, 129, 5. (12th cent.)

Distracted mortals! of what paltry worth
Are the arguments whereby ye are so prone
Senselessly to beat down your wings to earth!

Dante: *Paradiso, Canto 11.* (Tr. Binyon) (14th cent.)

Hew not too high lest the chip fall in thine eye.

John Heywood: *Proverbs*, 2, 7. (16th cent.)

Ambition is the mind's immodesty.

Sir William Davenant: *Gondibert.* (17th cent.)

Nor think ambition wise because 'tis brave.

Sir William Davenant: *Gondibert*, 1, 5. (17th cent.)

We are so presumptuous that we would be known by the whole world, and even by those who shall come when we shall be no more; and we are so vain that the esteem of five or six persons who surround us amuses and contents us.

Pascal: *Pensées.* (17th cent.)

But wild ambition loves to slide, not stand,
And fortune's ice prefers to virtue's land.

Dryden: *Absalom and Achitophel.* (17th cent.)

Desire of pow'r, on earth a vicious weed,
Yet, sprung from high is of celestial seed;
In God 'tis glory: and when men aspire,

'Tis but a spark too much of heavenly fire.

Dryden: *Absalom and Achitophel.* (17th cent.)

Desire of greatness is a god-like sin.

Dryden: *Absalom and Achitophel.* (17th cent.)

The same ambition can destroy or save,
And makes a patriot as it makes a knave.

Pope: *An Essay on Man*, 2. (18th cent.)

Certainly blessed are they that are ambitious; but the ambition must be pursued not by self-assertion, but by self-extinction.

R. H. Benson: *The Friendship of Christ.* (20th cent.)

Amendment

Let not your eyes enfeebled be with sin,
Cut short presumption for it will aspire:
Who takes advice, amendment doth begin,
Subdue your wills, and master your desire.

Thomas Lodge: *To All Young Gentlemen.* (16th cent.)

America

The Greek and Roman republics asserted the state to the detriment of individual freedom; modern republics either do the same, or assert individual freedom to the detriment of the state. The American republic has been instituted by Providence to realize the freedom of each with advantage to the other.

Orestes Brownson: *The American Republic.* (19th cent.)

From my heart, I say: America, with all thy faults, I love thee still.

Card. Gibbons: *The Faith of Our Fathers.* (19th cent.)

If there be any superior merit in the republican polity of the United States, it consists chiefly in this: that while it adds nothing and can add nothing to man's natural rights, it expresses them more clearly, guards them more securely, and protects them more effectually; so that man, under its popular institutions, enjoys greater liberty in working out his true destiny.

I. T. Hecker: *The Church and the Age.* (1887)

The form of government of the United States is preferable to Catholics above other forms. It is more favorable than others to the practice of those virtues which are the necessary conditions of the development of the religious life of man. This government leaves men a larger margin of liberty of action, and hence for cooperation with the guidance of the Holy Spirit, than any other government under the sun. With these popular institutions men enjoy greater liberty in working out their true destiny. The Catholic Church will therefore flourish all the more in this republican country in proportion as her representatives keep, in their civil life, to the lines of their republicanism.

I. T. Hecker. (Elliott's *Life,* 293) (19th cent.)

I have called America the providential nation. Even as I believe that God rules over men and nations, so do I believe that a divine mission has been assigned to the Republic of the United States. That mission is to prepare the world, by example and moral influence, for the universal reign of human liberty and human rights. America does not live for herself alone; the destinies of humanity are in her keeping.

Archb. Ireland: *Discourse on American Citizenship.* (Chicago, Feb. 22, 1895)

Americans, God has given you a great country; guard her well. He has made you a spectacle to all nations; He has confided to you humanity's highest des-

tiny; be not unworthy of Heaven's confidence.

Archb. Ireland: *American Citizenship.* (Chicago, Feb. 22, 1895)

The youth of America is their oldest tradition. It has been going on now for three hundred years.

Oscar Wilde: *A Woman of No Importance.* (19th cent.)

Of the American people this must be said—I say it from my heart, in full knowledge—a people more deeply penetrated with the sense of civic and political justice, more generous in concession of rights, where rights belong, more respectful of their every brother, their every fellow-citizen, is not in existence on the broad surface of the globe. This my tribute to the American people, the verdict my fifty years of private and public commingling compel me to pronounce.

Archbishop Ireland: *Catholicism and Americanism.* (Milwaukee, Aug. 11, 1913)

"My country, right or wrong," is a thing that no patriot would think of saying except in a desperate case. It is like saying, "My mother, drunk or sober."

G. K. Chesterton: *The Defendant.* (20th cent.)

America has invested her religion as well as her morality in sound income-paying securities. She has adopted the unassailable position of a nation blessed because it deserves to be blessed; and her sons, whatever other theologies they may affect or disregard, subscribe unreservedly to this national creed.

Agnes Repplier: *Times and Tendencies.* (20th cent.)

The American Constitution does resemble the Spanish Inquisition in this: that it is founded on a creed. America is the only nation in the world that is founded on a creed. That creed is set forth with dogmatic and even theological lucidity in the Declaration of Independence; perhaps the only piece of practical politics that is also theoretical politics and also great literature. It enunciates that all men are equal in their claim to justice, that their governments exist to give them that justice, and that their authority is for that reason just.

> G. K. Chesterton: *What I Saw in America.* (20th cent.)

The great American illusion is that of thinking of their country as a world apart, an Eden in a wicked universe. America is, whether it likes it or not, a part of the world, and particularly of European civilization. It came into being only because European ideas and European energy were carried to territories where they would have more adequate outlets. That these outlets were provided is America's glory, and that it took what Europe originated and gave it a new stamp and character. But 'isolation'—the kindred American illusion—was never anything but stupid and callous, as we now see it to be impossible.

> Theodore Maynard: *The Story of American Catholicism.* (20th cent.)

America and England

The old Anglo-American quarrel was much more fundamentally friendly than most Anglo-American alliances. Each nation understood the other enough to quarrel. In our time, neither nation understands itself even enough to quarrel.

> G. K. Chesterton: *Introduction to American Notes.* (20th cent.)

America and England can be far better friends when sharply divided than when shapelessly amalgamated.

> G. K. Chesterton: *What I Saw in America.* (20th cent.)

Most Englishmen know a good deal of American fiction, and nothing whatever of American history.

> G. K. Chesterton: *What I Saw in America.* (20th cent.)

It is the American, much more than the Englishman, who takes his pleasures sadly, not to say savagely.

> G. K. Chesterton: *What I Saw in America.* (20th cent.)

It is easy for an Englishman to confess that he never quite understood the American party system. It would perhaps be more courageous in him, and more informing, to confess that he never really understood the British party system.

> G. K. Chesterton: *What I Saw in America.* (20th cent.)

We are perpetually boring the world and each other with talk about the bonds that bind us to America. We are perpetually crying aloud that England and America are very much alike, especially England. We are always insisting that the two are identical in all things in which they most obviously differ. We are always saying that both stand for democracy, when we should not consent to stand their democracy for half a day.

> G. K. Chesterton: *What I Saw in America.* (20th cent.)

"Americanism"

It is too obvious to admit of denial that a people born and educated under the influence of popular institutions will tend to exalt reason, and emphasize the positive instincts of human nature, and be apt to look upon the intrinsic reason of things as the only criterion of truth. It is equally clear that the Catholic Church, if she is to keep within her fold those who have received her baptism, and to captivate an intelligent and energetic people like the Americans, will have to receive their challenge and be ready to answer satisfactorily the problems of reason; meet fully the demands of their special nature; bless and sanctify the imagination and senses and all man's God-given instincts.

> I. T. Hecker: *The Church and the Age.*

Natural virtues, practised in the proper frame of mind and heart, become supernatural. Each century calls for its type of Christian perfection. At one time it was martyrdom; at another it was the humility of the cloister. Today we need the Christian gentleman and the Christian citizen. An honest ballot and social decorum among Catholics will do more for God's glory and the salvation of souls than midnight flagellations or Compostellan pilgrimages.

> Archb. Ireland: *Introd. to Elliott's Hecker.* This and similar statements by Hecker and Ireland which seemed to overemphasize nature, activity, liberty, and were misunderstood in France, lay at the basis of the charge of "Americanism." (1891)

If by this name are to be understood certain endowments of mind which belong to the American people, just as other characteristics belong to other nations; and, if moreover, by it is designated your political conditions and laws and customs by which you are governed, there is no reason to take exception to the name.

> Pope Leo XIII: *Testem Benevolentiae.* (Condemning "Americanism") (Jan. 22, 1899)

In Europe "Americanism" was cradled as well as entombed; in America, it was unknown until it was condemned.

> Archb. Ireland: *The Genesis of Americanism.* (Art. appeared under name of J. St. Clair Etheridge, but is thought by some to have been written by the Archbishop.) (North American Review, May 1900.)

See also Modernism.

Americanism

Americanism is no doubt something more than a European ideal in surroundings favorable to it. But America is tied to the rest of the world, in its physical as well as its intellectual life; and of that

intellectual life the most catholic element is Catholicism.

> Theodore Maynard: *The Story of American Catholicism.* (20th cent.)

Americanization

We quarrel with no man for being a foreigner, but we recognize the moral right in no class of American citizens to train up their children to be foreigners, and then to claim for them all the rights, franchises, and immunities of American citizens.

> Orestes Brownson: *Public and Parochial Schools.* (Works, 12, 200ff.) (1859)

No encouragement must be given to social and political organizations or methods which perpetuate in this country foreign ideas and customs. An Irish-American, a German-American, or a French-American vote is an intolerable anomaly. We receive from America the right to vote as Americans, for America's weal, and if we cannot use our privilege as Americans we should surrender it. Efforts to concentrate immigrants in social groups and to retard their Americanization should be steadily frowned down.

> Archbishop Ireland: *American Citizenship.* (Chicago, Feb. 22, 1895)

Americans

There is nothing the matter with Americans except their ideals. The real American is all right; it is the ideal American who is all wrong.

> G. K. Chesterton. (*N. Y. Times,* Feb. 1, 1931.)

Most Americans are born drunk. . . . They have a sort of permanent intoxication from within, a sort of invisible champagne. . . . Americans do not need to drink to inspire them to do anything.

> G. K. Chesterton. (*N. Y. Times* Sunday Magazine, June 28, 1931.)

The American never imitates the Englishman in simply taking for granted both his own patriotism and his own superiority.

> G. K. Chesterton: *Generally Speaking.* (20th cent.)

If it comes to thinking, to questioning, to the use or abuse of speculation, no people have done it more than people sitting on the bare ground and staring at the stars. No people have done it less than people engaged in the applications of physical science to practical commerce. No people have done it less than the American people. The great mass of the American people remain, both for good and evil, stolidly, stubbornly, astonishingly conservative in their ideas.

> G. K. Chesterton: *Generally Speaking.* (20th cent.)

As no man is so dreadfully well-dressed as a well-dressed American, so no man is so terribly well-mannered as a well-mannered American.

> G. K. Chesterton: *Autobiography.* (Of Henry James) (20th cent.)

Amusement

Though it is lawful to play games, to dance, to adorn oneself, to be present at proper plays, and to feast, yet to have an affection to such things is contrary to devotion, and extremely hurtful and dangerous.

> St. Francis de Sales: *Introduction to the Devout Life,* 1, 23. (17th cent.)

Man is so wretched that he could be bored even without any cause of boredom, thanks to his natural constitution; and he is so futile that, although full of countless essential causes of boredom, the most trifling thing, such as a billiard table and a ball to push, is enough to amuse him.

> Pascal: *Pensées.* (17th cent.)

Anarchy

The Church cannot approve of that liberty which begets a contempt of the most sacred laws of God, and casts off the obedience due to lawful authority, for this is not liberty so much as license, and is most correctly styled by St. Augustine the *liberty of self-ruin,* and by the apostle St. Peter, the *cloak of malice.*

> Pope Leo XIII: *Immortale Dei.* (Nov. 1, 1885)

Ancestry

Full seldom human virtue rises through
  The branches.

> Dante: *Purgatorio, Canto* 7. (Tr. L. Binyon) (14th cent.)

You should study the Peerage, Gerald. . . . It is the best thing in fiction the English have ever done.

> Oscar Wilde: *A Woman of No Importance.* (19th cent.)

Angel

Every angel and demon is winged. Consequently they are everywhere in a moment; to them the whole world is one place.

> Tertullian: *The Christian Defence.* (3rd cent.)

Beauty is not necessary to God's angels.

> Tertullian: *Women's Dress.* (3rd cent.)

Angels may become men or demons, and again from the latter they may rise to be men or angels.

> Origen: *De Principiis.* (Latter opinion unorthodox) (4th cent.)

There are nine orders of angels, to wit, angels, archangels, virtues, powers, principalities, dominations, thrones, cherubim and seraphim.

> Pope Gregory the Great: *Homilies,* 34. (7th cent.)

Not Angles but angels. (Non Angli, sed angeli.)

> Reply of St. Gregory the Great, when certain blond British captives were pointed

out to him for sale as slaves at Rome, ca. 588. When he became pope, he sent St. Augustine of Canterbury to convert the island (597). (Bede, *Ecclesiastical History,* 2, 1) (6th cent.)

The word angel is the name of a function, not of a nature. For they are always spirits, but are called angels when they are sent.

St. Isidore: *Etymologies,* 7, 5. (7th cent.)

They take different forms at the bidding of their Master, God, and thus reveal themselves to men and unveil the divine mysteries to them.

St. John of Damascus: *Exposition of the Orthodox Faith,* 2, 3. (8th cent.)

They are mighty and prompt to fulfil the will of the Deity, and their nature is endowed with such celerity that wherever the divine glance bids them there they are straightway found.

St. John of Damascus: *Exposition of the Orthodox Faith,* 2, 3. (8th cent.)

An angel then is an intelligent essence, in perpetual motion, with freewill, incorporeal, ministering to God, having obtained by grace an immortal nature; and the Creator alone knows the form and limitation of its nature.

St. John of Damascus: *Exposition of the Orthodox Faith,* 2, 3. (8th cent.)

Christ, of the angels' praise and adoration,
Father and Savior Thou, of every nation,
Graciously grant us all to gain a station,
    Where Thou art reigning.

Roman Breviary, Feast of St. Michael (Sept. 29), Hymn *Christe sanctorum decus angelorum* at Lauds. (Tr. T. Ball) (Attr. to Bl. Rabanus Maurus, 9th cent.)

Thee, O Christ, the Father's splendor,
Life and virtue of the heart,
In the presence of the angels
Sing we now with tuneful art,

Meetly in alternate chorus
Bearing our responsive part.

Hymn *Tibi Christe splendor Patris.* (Tr. J. Neale) (Attr. to Bl. Rabanus Maurus, 9th cent.)

How many angels can dance upon the point of a needle?

Quodlibet ascribed to various medieval theologians. (Medieval)

They are intellectual natures, at the peak of creation.

St. Thomas Aquinas: *Contra Gentes,* 2, 42. (13th cent.)

Angels mean messengers and ministers. Their function is to execute the plan of divine providence, even in earthly things: *Who maketh His angels spirits; His ministers a flaming fire* (Ps. 103, 4).

St. Thomas Aquinas: *Contra Gentes,* 3, 79. (13th cent.)

Who ever try'd adventures like this
    knight,
Which, general of heaven, hell overthrew?
    For such a lady as God's spouse did
    fight,
    And such a monster as the devil subdue?

Henry Constable: *To St. Michael the Archangel.* (16th cent.)

Make yourself familiar with the angels, and behold them frequently in spirit; for, without being seen, they are present with you.

St. Francis de Sales: *Introduction to the Devout Life,* 16. (17th cent.)

You spirits! who have thrown away
That envious weight of clay,
    Which your celestial flight denied;
Who by your glorious troops supply
The winged hierarchy,
    So broken in the angel's pride!

W. Habington: *Laudate Dominum de Coelis.* (17th cent.)

Those who play at being angels, end up as animals. (Qui veut faire l'ange, fait la bête.)

Pascal. (17th cent.)

There written, all,
Black as the damning drops that fall
From the denouncing angel's pen
Ere Mercy weeps them out again.

Thomas Moore: *Lalla Rookh: Paradise and the Peri.* (19th cent.)

Hark! hark! my soul! angelic songs are swelling
O'er earth's green fields and ocean's wave-beat shore;
How sweet the truth those blessed strains are telling
Of that new life when sin shall be no more!
Angels of Jesus!
Angels of Light!
Singing to welcome
The pilgrims of the night.

F. Faber: *The Pilgrims of the Night.* (19th cent.)

Whenever we look abroad, we are reminded of those most gracious and holy beings, the servants of the Holiest, who deign to minister to the heirs of salvation. Every breath of air and ray of light and heat, every beautiful prospect, is, as it were, the skirts of their garments, the waving of the robes of those whose faces see God in heaven.

Card. Newman: *Parochial and Plain Sermons,* 2. (19th cent.)

It is a member of that family
Of wondrous beings, who, ere the worlds were made,
Millions of ages back, have stood around
The throne of God:—he never has known sin;
But through those cycles all but infinite,
Has had a strong and pure celestial life,
And bore to gaze on the unveil'd face of God,
And drank from the everlasting fount of truth,

And served Him with a keen ecstatic love.

Card. Newman: *The Dream of Gerontius.* (19th cent.)

No sceptre theirs, but they are kings:
Their forms and words are royal things.
Their simple friendship is a court,
Whither the wise and great resort.
No homage of the world they claim:
But in all places lives their fame.
Sun, moon, and stars; the earth, the sea;
Yea! all things, that of beauty be,
Honor their true divinity.

Lionel Johnson: *A Dream of Youth.* (19th cent.)

In highest heaven, at Mary's knee,
The cherubs sit with folded wings,
And beg her by St. Charity
To tell them tales of human things.
They throw their harps down on the floor,
And all their heavenly playthings leave,
And clamor to be told once more
The faerie tale of faulty Eve.

Enid Dinnis: *The Cherub-folk.* (20th cent.)

See also Michael the Archangel, Saint

Angel, Guardian

The angels must be entreated for us, who have been given us to guard us.

St. Ambrose: *Concerning Widows,* 55. (4th cent.)

The servants of Christ are protected by invisible, rather than visible, beings. But if these guard you, they do so because they have been summoned by your prayers.

St. Ambrose: *Sermo contra Auxent.* 11. (4th cent.)

O God, Who in a wonderful order hast established the ministry of angels and of men, mercifully grant that, as Thy holy angels ever do Thee service in heaven,

so they may at all times protect us on earth.

Roman Missal, Collect for Feast of St. Michael (Sept. 29). (Gregorian, 6th to 8th cent.)

They are the guardians of the divisions of the earth; they are set over nations and regions allotted to them by their Creator. They govern all our affairs and bring us help. And the reason surely is because they are set over us by the divine will and command and are ever in the vicinity of God.

St. John of Damascus: *Exposition of the Orthodox Faith*, 2, 3. (8th cent.)

Unworthy as we are, we pray to you, O leaders of the heavenly hosts, to cover us by your prayers with the protection of the wings of your immaterial glory, preserving us who come to you and earnestly cry, Deliver us from sorrows, O chiefs of the powers above.

Byzantine Parakletike, Troparion for Monday, Tone 4. (ca. 9th cent.)

God's universal providence works through secondary causes. . . . The world of pure spirits stretches between the Divine Nature and the world of human beings; because Divine Wisdom has ordained that the higher should look after the lower, angels execute the divine plan for human salvation: they are our guardians, who free us when hindered and help to bring us home.

St. Thomas Aquinas: *Commentary on the Sentences*, 2, 11, 1, 1. (13th cent.)

Angel-guardians of men, spirits and
    powers we sing,
Whom our Father hath sent, aids to
    our weakly frame,
Heavenly friends and guides, help
    from on high to bring,
Lest we fail through the foeman's wile.

Roman Breviary, Feast of Guardian Angels (Oct. 2), Hymn *Custodes hominum psallimus angelos* at Vespers. (Tr. A. McDougall) (Card. Bellarmine, 17th cent.)

Ruler of the dread immense!
Maker of this mighty frame!
Whose eternal providence
Guides it, as from Thee it came.

. . . .

King of kings, and Lord most High!
This of Thy dear love we pray:
May Thy guardian angel nigh,
Keep us from all sin this day.

Roman Breviary, Feast of Guardian Angels (Oct. 2), hymn *Aeterne Rector siderum* at Lauds. (Tr. Caswall) (Cardinal Bellarmine, 17th cent.)

Dear angel! ever at my side,
    How loving must thou be
To leave thy home in heaven to guard
    A guilty wretch like me.

F. Faber: *Hymn to My Guardian Angel*. (19th cent.)

I have no angels left
    Now, sweet, to pray to:
Where you have made your shrine
    They are away to.
They have struck heaven's tent,
    And gone to cover you:
Whereso you keep your state
    Heaven is pitched over you!

Francis Thompson: *A Carrier Song*. (19th cent.)

Our guardian spirits meet at prayer and
    play.
    Beyond pain, joy, and hope, an
    long suspense,
    Above the summits of our souls,
    hence,
An angel meets an angel on the way

Alice Meynell: *Thoughts in Separatic* (19th cent.)

Angels and Men

Herein then is the nature of ang
tinguished from the present cond
our own nature, that we are both
scribed by space, and straightene
blindness of ignorance; but the
angels are indeed bounded by
their knowledge extends far ab
yond comparison; for they

external and internal knowing, since they contemplate the very Source of knowledge Itself.

> Pope St. Gregory I: *Morals*, 2, 3. (6th cent.)

Angels are called intellectual because of their immediate and complete insight into all objects within their natural field. Human souls are called rational because their knowledge is acquired by a process of reasoning. Unlike the angels, they do not apprehend at once the full evidence of an object presented to them; they are convinced by formal argument, not by intuition.

> St. Thomas Aquinas: *Summa Theologica*, 1, 58, 3. (13th cent.)

Anger

Anger is a kind of temporary madness.

> St. Basil: *Against Anger*. (4th cent.)

Ordinary humanity would seem to require not merely that we refrain from exciting or increasing wrath among men by evil speaking, but that we study to extinguish wrath by kind speaking.

> St. Augustine: *Confessions*, 9, 9. (5th cent.)

There is no sin nor wrong that gives a man such a foretaste of hell in this life as anger and impatience.

> St. Catherine of Siena: *Letter to Monna Agnese*. (14th cent.)

Angry as a wasp.

> John Heywood: *Proverbs*, 1, 11. (16th cent.)

She frieth in her own grease.

> John Heywood: *Proverbs*, 1, 11. (16th cent.)

If she be angry, beshrew her angry heart.
        beshrew—plague take

> John Heywood: *Proverbs*, 1, 11. (16th cent.)

He that will be angry without cause,
Must be at one, without amends.
        at one—reconciled

> John Heywood: *Proverbs*, 2, 4. (16th cent.)

I wrestle not with rage,
  While fury's flame doth burn;
It is in vain to stop the stream
  Until the tide doth turn.
But when the flame is out,
  And ebbing wrath doth end,
I turn a late enraged foe
  Into a quiet friend.

> Bl. Robert Southwell: *Content and Rich*. (16th cent.)

Anger is quieted by a gentle word just as fire is quenched by water.

> J. P. Camus: *The Spirit of St. Francis de Sales*, 2, 13. (17th cent.)

There is a holy anger, excited by zeal, which moves us to reprove with warmth those whom our mildness failed to correct.

> St. Jean Baptiste de la Salle: *Les devoirs du Chrétien*, 14. (18th cent.)

Anglicanism

The panther sure the noblest, next the hind,
And fairest creature of the spotted kind:
Oh, could her in-born stains be wash'd away,
She were too good to be a beast of prey!
How can I praise, or blame, and not offend,
Or how divide the frailty from the friend?
Her faults and virtues lie so mix'd, that she
Nor wholly stands condemn'd nor wholly free.

> Dryden: *The Hind and the Panther*, 1. (17th cent.)

Such is her faith, where good cannot be had,
At least she leaves the refuse of the bad.

Nice in her choice of ill, though not of
best,
And least deform'd, because reform'd
the least.

> Dryden: *The Hind and the Panther,* 1.
> (17th cent.)

Sir Richard Steele has observed that there
is this difference between the Church of
Rome and the Church of England: the
one professes to be infallible—the other
to be never in the wrong.

> C. C. Colton: *Lacon.* (19th cent.)

When I see this Church thus treasuring
up and preserving from destruction the
accessories of our worship, so highly
prizing the very frame in which *our*
liturgy is but enclosed, I cannot but look
upon her as I would on one whom God's
hand hath touched, in whom the light of
reason is darkened, though the feelings
of the heart have not been seared—who
presses to her bosom and cherishes there
the empty locket which once contained
the image of all she loved on earth, and
continues to rock the cradle of her departed child!

> Card. Wiseman: *Lectures, 5.* (19th cent.)

O my mother, whence is this unto thee
that thou hast good things poured out
upon thee and canst not keep them, and
bearest children, yet darest not own
them? Why hast thou not the skill to
use their services, nor the heart to rejoice in their love? How is it that whatever is generous in purpose, and tender
or deep in devotion, thy flower and thy
promise, falls from thy bosom and finds
no home within thy arms?

> Card. Newman: *Sermon: The Parting of
> Friends.* (Last sermon preached as an
> Anglican) (19th cent.)

Securus judicat orbis terrarum! By those
great words of the ancient father [i.e. St.
Augustine], interpreting and summing
up the long and varied course of ecclesiastical history, the theory of the *Via
Media* was absolutely pulverized.

> Card. Newman: *Apologia pro Vita Sua, 3.*
> (The *Via Media* theory was to the effect
> that Anglicanism formed a sort of halfway
> house between Catholicism and
> Protestantism) (19th cent.)

And so I recognize in the Anglican
Church a time-honored institution, of
noble historical memories, a monument
of ancient wisdom, a momentous arm of
political strength, a great national organ,
a source of vast popular advantage, and,
to a certain point, a witness and teacher
of religious truth. . . . But that it is something sacred, that it is an oracle of revealed doctrine, that it can claim a share
in St. Ignatius or St. Cyprian, that it can
take the rank, contest the teaching, and
stop the path of the Church of St. Peter,
that it can call itself 'the bride of the
Lamb,' this is the view of it which simply disappeared from my mind on my
conversion, and which it would be almost a miracle to reproduce.

> Card. Newman: *Apologia pro Vita Sua,
> Note E.* (19th cent.)

And, as to its possession of an episcopal
succession from the time of the apostles,
well, it may have it, and, if the Holy See
ever so decide, I will believe it, as being
the decision of a higher judgment than
my own; but, for myself, I must have
St. Philip's gift, who saw the sacerdotal
character on the forehead of a gaily at-
tired youngster, before I can by my own
wit acquiesce in it, for antiquarian arguments are altogether unequal to the
urgency of the visible facts.

> Card. Newman: *Apologia pro Vita Sua,
> Note E.* (The bull *Apostolicae Curae* of
> Sept. 15, 1896, denying the validity of
> Anglican orders, subsequently confirmed
> the cardinal's impressions.) (19th cent.)

English Protestantism is the religion of
the throne: it is represented, realized,
taught, transmitted in the succession of
monarchs and an hereditary aristocracy.
It is religion grafted upon loyalty; and
its strength is not in argument, not in
fact, not in the unanswerable contro-
versialist, not in an apostolical succession, not in sanction of Scripture—but
in a royal road to faith, in backing up a

king whom men see, against a pope whom they do not see.

Card. Newman: *Present Position of Catholics in England*, 2. (19th cent.)

I do hereby profess, *ex animo,* with an absolute internal assent and consent, that Protestantism is the dreariest of possible religions; that the thought of the Anglican service makes me shiver, and the thought of the Thirty-Nine Articles makes me shudder. Return to the Church of England? No! *The net is broken and we are delivered.* I should be a consummate fool (to use a mild term) if in my old age I left *the land flowing with milk and honey,* for the city of confusion and the house of bondage.

Card. Newman: *Letter to the Editor of The Globe.* (19th cent.)

The divisibility of the Church is the cardinal doctrine of Anglicanism, and its most fundamental heresy. There are signs . . . that it is being relinquished by the most advanced school, but then this school professes to hold 'Anglicanism' in holy horror.

Abbot Chapman: *Bishop Gore and the Catholic Claims.* (20th cent.)

To tolerate everything is to teach nothing.

Dr. F. J. Kinsman: *Letter to the Rt. Rev. D. S. Tuttle, Presiding Bishop of the Protestant Episcopal Church.* (July 1, 1919)

The day of my consecration as bishop sealed my doom as an Anglican. While it was possible to maintain a purely theoretical view of the Anglican position, it was possible for me to believe in the essential catholicity of its inner spirit, of its tendencies, and of its ultimate achievements. . . . Most Anglicans assume that the special atmosphere about them represents the breath of the Church's truest life; and this is especially true of Catholic-minded Anglicans. They are themselves Catholics, and their special task is to 'Catholicize' the Church.

This feeling I shared until as bishop I felt the necessity of a Church to Catholicize me!

F. J. Kinsman: *Salve Mater.* (20th cent.)

Anguish

The tragedy of a child over a broken doll is not less poignant than the anguish of a worshipper over a broken idol, or of a king over a ruined realm.

R. H. Benson: *By What Authority.* (20th cent.)

Anne, Saint

Spotless Anna! Juda's glory!
    Through the Church from east to west,
Every tongue proclaims thy praises,
    Holy Mary's mother blest!

Anonymous: *Clarae diei gaudiis.* (Tr. Caswall) (17th cent.)

Annulment

See Marriage: Dissolution of Marriage

Annunciation of Our Lady

Today is the crowning of our salvation, and the manifestation of the mystery which was from eternity. The Son of God becometh the Son of the Virgin, and Gabriel giveth the good tidings of grace. Therefore with him let us cry to the Mother of God, Hail! full of grace, the Lord is with thee.

Byzantine Menaea, Troparion for the Feast (Mar. 25). (ca. 6th cent.)

Rejoice, O Virgin Mary, thou alone hast trampled down all heresies, because thou didst believe the archangel Gabriel's words: when thou a virgin didst give birth to God and Man, and after childbirth didst remain ever a virgin.

Roman Breviary, Responsory at Matins *Gaude Maria Virgo cunctas haereses sola interemisti.* (ca. 7th cent.)

O God, Who hast willed that Thy Word should take flesh, at the message of an angel, in the womb of the blessed Virgin Mary: grant to us Thy servants, that we who believe her to be truly the Mother of God may be helped by her intercession with Thee.

Roman Missal, Collect for the Feast. (Gregorian ca. 7th cent.)

So then, after the assent of the holy Virgin, the Holy Spirit descended on her, according to the word of the Lord which the angel spoke, purifying her, and granting her power to receive the divinity of the Word, and likewise power to bring forth.

St. John of Damascus: *Exposition of the Orthodox Faith*, 3, 2. (8th cent.)

Let heaven rejoice, and earth be glad,
    For He Who reigns above
With all His Father's glory clad,
    Hath shown His perfect love.

.   .   .   .   .   .

O wonder of surpassing might!
    With men dwells God the Son,
The womb contains the Infinite,
    Time holds the timeless One.

.   .   .   .   .   .

Hail! Mary, thou art full of grace,
    Blest evermore art thou,
The Lord, Whose mercies all embrace,
    Himself is with thee now.

Byzantine Menaea, Sticheron at Matins. (Tr. Littledale) (St. John of Damascus, 8th cent.)

Gabriel, from the heaven descending,
On the faithful Word attending,
Is in holy converse blending
    With the Virgin full of grace:
That good word and sweet he plighteth
In the bosom where it lighteth
And for EVA AVE writeth,
    Changing Eva's name and race.

Adam of St. Victor: *Missus Gabriel de coelis*. (Tr. J. Neale) (12th cent.)

One would swear he said *Ave!* for thereby
    Was she imagined and made manifest

Who turned the key to admit Love
    from on high.

Dante: *Purgatorio, Canto* 10. (Tr. Binyon) (14th cent.)

Spell EVA back and AVE shall you find,
    The first began, the last reversed our harms;
An angel's witching words did Eva blind,
    An angel's Ave disenchants the charms:
Death first by woman's weakness enter'd in,
In woman's virtue life doth now begin.

Bl. Robert Southwell: *The Virgin's Salutation*. (16th cent.)

Thrice happy day, which sweetly dost combine
Two hemispheres in th'equinoctial line:
The one debasing God to earthly pain,
The other raising man to endless reign.

Sir John Beaumont: *Annunciation and Resurrection*. (The Annunciation and Easter fell on the same day in 1627, March 25.)

What mortal tongue can sing thy praise,
    Dear Mother of the Lord?
To angels only it belongs
    Thy glory to record.

Jean Santeuil: *Quis te canat mortalium*. (Tr. Caswall) (18th cent.)

The angel spake the word—
Hail, thou of women blest!
From highest heaven the Godhead comes,
    And fills her virgin breast.

Jean Santeuil: *Supernus ales nuntiat*. (Tr. Caswall) (18th cent.)

A Word, a Word
Thou, Lord, didst utter which Thy willing handmaid heard,
And infinite, small Life within my own life breathed and stirred.

Sister Madeleva: *Dialogue*. (20th cent.)

Anonymity

To be anonymous is better than to be Alexander. Cowley said it engagingly, in his little essay on *Obscurity: Bene qui latuit, bene vixit:* he lives well that has lain well hidden.

L. I. Guiney: *Patrins.* (19th cent.)

Anticlericalism

Anticlericalism is not an article for export.

Saying attributed to Gambetta, of uncertain date. (19th cent.)

Antidote

The radish, pear, theriac, garlic, rue,
All potent poisons will at once undo.

School of Salerno, Code of Health. (11th cent.)

Antiquity

You are forever praising antiquity, and every day you improvise some new way of life.

Tertullian: *Apology,* 6, 9. (3rd cent.)

Anxiety

Beware of anxiety. Next to sin, there is nothing that so much troubles the mind, strains the heart, distresses the soul and confuses the judgment.

Archbp. Ullathorne: *Humility and Patience.* (19th cent.)

There is but one remedy for anxiety, and that is by using the firm force of patience to keep the objects of our solicitude in their proper place.

Archbp. Ullathorne: *Humility and Patience.* (19th cent.)

Ape

An ape is an ape, though clad in purple.

Erasmus: *In Praise of Folly.* (16th cent.)

Apologetics

A man who is well grounded in the testimonies of the Scripture is the bulwark of the Church.

St. Jerome: *In Isaiam,* 54, 12. (5th cent.)

When you debate with unbelievers, be warned to begin with, against striving to demonstrate the articles of faith. That would be to minimize their grandeur, for they surpass the minds of angels let alone of men. We believe them because God reveals them. Your intention should be to defend the faith, not to prove it up to the hilt.

St. Thomas Aquinas: *Concerning Reasons of Faith,* 2. (13th cent.)

A man should remind himself that an object of faith is not scientifically demonstrable lest, presuming to demonstrate what is of faith, he should produce inconclusive reasons and offer occasion for unbelievers to scoff at a faith based on such grounds.

St. Thomas Aquinas: *Summa Theologica,* 1, 46, 2. (13th cent.)

There are men who will build up a hundred weak and frivolous arguments against Catholicity, that they may have the easy pleasure of refuting them. They remind me of children who build up houses of tile-shards, such sport is it for them to cast them down again.

St. Thomas More. (16th cent.)

Brothers! spare reasoning;—men have settled long
That ye are out of date, and they are wise;
Use their own weapons; let your words be strong,
Your cry be loud, till each scared boaster flies;
Thus the apostles tamed the pagan breast,
They argued not, but preach'd; and conscience did the rest.

Card. Newman: *The Religion of Cain.* (1833)

Nothing is so difficult as to enter into the characters and feelings of men who have been brought up under a system of religion different from our own; and to discern how they may be most forcibly and profitably addressed, in order to win them over to the reception of divine truths, of which they are at present ignorant.

Card. Newman; *Historical Studies.* (Miscellanies, p. 65) (19th cent.)

The fact of revelation is in itself demonstrably true, but it is not therefore true irresistibly; else, how comes it to be resisted? There is a vast difference between what it is in itself, and what it is to us. Light is a quality of matter, as truth is of Christianity; but light is not recognized by the blind, and there are those who do not recognize truth, from the fault, not of truth, but of themselves. I cannot convert men, when I ask for assumptions which they refuse to grant me; and without assumptions no one can prove anything about anything.

Card. Newman: *Grammar of Assent,* 10. (19th cent.)

There is little use in arguing against the objections of non-Catholics, or in laboring directly for their refutation. We can effectually remove them only by correcting the premises from which the unbeliever reasons, and giving him first principles, which really enlighten his reason, and, as they become operative, expel his error by their own light and force.

Orestes Brownson: *The Convert.* (Works, 5, 1ff) (1857)

There are two things which it specially behooves every Catholic engaged in controversy to observe in his treatment of adversaries: that the discussion ought to be a means of converting them from error, instead of repelling them from truth by the fault of its defenders; and that no bitterness or personality should scandalize them by occasions of sin.

Lord Acton: *Ultramontanism.* (19th cent.)

Christian apologetics are only really useful in the mouth of one who realizes their entire inadequacy.

R. H. Benson: *The Light Invisible.* (20th cent.)

The reasoned arguments for the faith are not sufficiently strong to coerce the unwilling into faith, but they are stronger than any argument that can be brought against Christianity, and are quite sufficiently strong to reinforce and to strengthen the will to believe.

Arnold Lunn: *Now I See.* (20th cent.)

It is no use imploring people to try the Christian way of life until you have convinced them that Christianity is true. The attractions of this way of life are not self-evident. The Christian way of life is a way of self-denial and self-discipline, which are worth while if, and only if, Christianity is true. The first duty of the evangelist, therefore, is to prove that Christianity is true.

Arnold Lunn: *Now I See.* (20th cent.)

Christianity owes an immense debt to Hellenism, for the art of rational apologetics was a discovery of the Greeks.

Arnold Lunn: *The Revolt against Reason.* (20th cent.)

As an apologist I am the reverse of apologetic. So far as a man may be proud of a religion rooted in humility, I am very proud of my religion; I am especially proud of those parts of it that are most commonly called superstition. I am proud of being fettered by antiquated dogmas and enslaved by dead creeds (as my journalistic friends repeat with so much pertinacity), for I know very well that it is the heretical creeds that are dead, and that it is only the reasonable dogma that lives long enough to be called antiquated.

G. K. Chesterton: *Autobiography.* (20th cent.)

The brandishing of threats over the heads of those whose faith is imperfect is hardly the most effective way to win them to perfect faith. By telling them that they will be damned if they do not become Catholics, one is all too likely to draw the retort, "I'll be damned if I do!"

> Theodore Maynard: *Orestes Brownson.* (20th cent.)

We must make a start with modern man as he is, not as we should like to find him. Because our apologetic literature has missed this point, it is about fifty years behind the times. It leaves the modern soul cold, not because its arguments are unconvincing, but because the modern soul is too confused to grasp them.

> Bishop Sheen: *Peace of Soul.* (20th cent.)

See also Controversy; Economy

Apology

[Samuel] Johnson behaved very well. He understood (what so many faultlessly polite people do not understand) that a stiff apology is a second insult.

> G. K. Chesterton: *The Common Man.* (20th cent.)

Apostate

If any persons should betray the holy faith and should profane holy baptism, they shall be segregated from the community of all men, shall be disqualified from giving testimony, and, as we have previously ordained, they shall not have testamentary capacity. . . .

> Edict of the Emperors Valentinian, Theodosius, and Arcadius. (Theod. Code. 16, 7, 4.) (391)

Apostle

Th' eternal gifts of Christ the King,
The apostles' glory, let us sing;
And all with hearts of gladness raise
Due hymns of thankful love and praise.
For they the Church's princes are,
Triumphant leaders in the war,
The heavenly King's own warrior band,
True lights to lighten every land.

> Roman Breviary, Feasts of the Apostles, Hymn *Aeterna Christi munera* at Matins.

(Tr. based on Neale) (St. Ambrose, 4th cent.)

It is truly meet and just . . . to pray Thee, O Lord, the eternal Shepherd, not to abandon Thy flock; but through Thy blessed apostles to keep a continual watch over it, that it may be governed by those same rulers whom Thou didst set over it as Thy shepherds and vicars.

> Roman Missal, Preface of the Apostles. (Leonine, ca. 5th cent.)

O God, Who through Thy blessed apostles hast enabled us to come to the knowledge of Thy name; grant us to celebrate their everlasting glory by profiting thereby, and to profit thereby through our celebration.

> Roman Missal, Collect for Apostles. (Gelasian, 5th to 7th cent.)

Now let the earth with joy resound,
And heaven the chant re-echo round;
Nor heaven nor earth too high can raise
The great apostles' glorious praise.

O ye who, throned in glory dread,
Shall judge the living and the dead,
Lights of the world for evermore!
To you the suppliant prayer we pour.

Ye close the sacred gates on high;
At your command apart they fly:
Oh! loose for us the guilty chain
We strive to break, and strive in vain.

> Roman Breviary, Feasts of the Apostles, Hymn *Exultet orbis gaudiis* at Vespers and Lauds. (Tr. E. Caswall) (Author unknown, 10th cent.)

Laurelled with the stole victorious,
Is the Great King's senate glorious,
 Is the apostolic choir:
Heart and lips keep well in chorus,
With the pure soul's strains sonorous
 To angelic hymns aspire.

> Adam of St. Victor: *Stola regni laureatus.* (Tr. J. Neale) (12th cent.)

Appeal

An appeal is not a subterfuge, but a refuge.

> St. Bernard: *On Consideration*, 3, 2. (12th cent.)

Appearance

Boobies have looked as wise and bright
As Plato or the Stagyrite;
And many a sage and learned skull
Has peeped through windows dark and
  dull!

> Thomas Moore: *Nature's Labels.* (19th cent.)

It is only shallow people who do not judge by appearances.

> Oscar Wilde: *Picture of Dorian Gray.* (19th cent.)

Applause

Dost thou wish to be applauded? Applaud another.

> St. John Chrysostom: *Homilies.* (4th cent.)

Apple

All the evil in the world was brought into it by an apple. (Mala mali malo mala contulit omnia mundo.)

> Proverb. (Medieval)

Adam lay inbounden, bounden in a
  bond;
Four thousand winter thought he not
  too long;
And all was for an apple, an apple
  that he took,
As clerics finden written in their book;
Nor had the apple taken been, the
  apple taken been,
Nor had never our Lady been of heaven
  Queen.
Blessed be the time that apple taken
  was.
Therefore we must singen *Deo gratias.*

> Anonymous, untitled poem. (Sloane MS. 2593) (15th cent.)

Lost with an apple, and won with a nut.

> John Heywood: *Proverbs,* 1, 10. (16th cent.)

April

When that April with his showers sote
The drought of March hath pierced to
  the root,
And bathed every vine in such licour,
Of which virtue engendered is the
  flower.

> sote—sweet

> Chaucer: *Canterbury Tales: Prologue.* (Opening lines) (14th cent.)

When April rain had laughed the land
  Out of its wintry way,
And coaxed all growing things to greet
  With gracious garb the May.

> Shaemas O'Sheel: *While April Rain Went By.* (20th cent.)

Arbitration

    He was ever prompt
To arbitrate disputes on settling days
(For a small fee) in many helpful ways.

> Chaucer: *Canterbury Tales: Prologue.* (Tr. Coghill) (14th cent.)

Architecture

However my reason may go with Gothic, my heart has ever gone with Grecian.

> Card. Newman: *Letters.* (Written from Milan.) (19th cent.)

For myself, certainly, I think that that style which, whatever be its origin, is called Gothic, is endowed with a profound and a commanding beauty, such as no other style possesses with which we are acquainted, and which probably the Church will not see surpassed till it attain to the celestial city.

> Card. Newman: *Idea of a University,* 4. (19th cent.)

It is a remarkable fact . . . that Italy, the country of the arts, never had an architecture, and could never even adopt one from its neighbors without degrading or abolishing its character as a style. . . . Italy had great architects, but no great architecture.

> Coventry Patmore: *Principle in Art.* (19th cent.)

It has been said that Gothic architecture represents the soul aspiring to God, and that Renaissance or Romanesque architecture represents God tabernacling with men.

> R. H. Benson: *The Confessions of a Convert.* (20th cent.)

Christ prophesied the whole of Gothic architecture in that hour when nervous and respectable people (such people as now object to barrel-organs) objected to the shouting of the gutter-snipes of Jerusalem. He said, "If these were silent, the very stones would cry out." Under the impulse of His spirit arose like a clamorous chorus the façades of the medieval cathedrals, thronged with shouting faces and open mouths. The prophecy has fulfilled itself: the very stones cry out.

> G. K. Chesterton: *Orthodoxy.* (20th cent.)

One of the big problems for an architect in our time is that for a hundred and fifty years men have been building churches as if a church could not belong to our time. A church has to look as if it were left over from some other age. I think that such an assumption is based on an implicit confession of atheism—as if God did not belong to all ages and as if religion were really only a pleasant, necessary social formality, preserved from past times in order to give our society an air of respectability.

> Thomas Merton: *The Sign of Jonas.* (20th cent.)

Ardor

My faultless breast the furnace is, the fuel wounding thorns;
Love is the fire, and sighs the smoke, the ashes shame and scorns;

The fuel justice layeth on, and mercy blows the coals;
The metal in this furnace wrought are men's defiled souls;
For which, as now on fire I am to work them to their good,
So will I melt into a bath to wash them in My blood.

> Bl. Robert Southwell: *The Burning Babe.* (Poem much admired by Ben Jonson) (16th cent.)

Argument

Although the argument from authority based on human reason is the weakest, yet the argument from authority based on divine revelation is the strongest.

> St. Thomas Aquinas: *Summa Theologica,* I, I, 7. (13th cent.)

When we wish to reprove with profit, and show another that he is mistaken, we must observe on what side he looks at the thing, for it is usually true on that side, and to admit to him that truth, but to discover to him the side whereon it is false. He is pleased with this, for he perceives that he was not mistaken, and that he only failed to look on all sides.

> Pascal: *Pensées,* 8. (17th cent.)

A knock-down argument: 'tis but a word and a blow.

> Dryden: *Amphitryon,* I. (17th cent.)

Argument is not always able to command an assent though it be demonstration.

> Card. Newman. (Ward, II, 587) (19th cent.)

Men worry over an argument as a dog does over a bone. And put them away and pick them up again a few days later with just as much zest. That is one of the vital differences between men and women. It is only the unusually constituted woman who can pretend to like a troublesome thing that leads to nothing.

> Katharine T. Hinkson: *Three Fair Maids.* (20th cent.)

He's a man u'd argue the pope was a
Prodesan.

> Seumas MacManus: *Heavy Hangs the
> Golden Grain.* (20th cent.)

See also Apologetics

Aristocracy

The only real aristocracy is one of the
soul.

> Archb. Ireland. (Quoted in Moynihan's
> *Life,* 161.) (20th cent.)

Aristocracy is not a government, it is a
riot; that most effective kind of riot, a
riot of the rich.

> G. K. Chesterton: *What's Wrong with the
> World.* (20th cent.)

Aristotle

He was a man of excellent genius, though
inferior in eloquence to Plato.

> St. Augustine: *The City of God,* 8. (5th
> cent.)

> I saw the master of those who know:
>   he sate
> Amid the sons philosophy to him
>   bore.
> All do him honor, all eyes on him wait.

> Dante: *Inferno, Canto 4.* (Tr. Binyon)
> (14th cent.)

Army

The essence of an army is the idea of official inequality, founded on unofficial
equality. The colonel is not obeyed because he is the best man, but because he
is the colonel.

> G. K. Chesterton: *What's Wrong with the
> World.* (20th cent.)

> There is something gallantly great in the
>   banners of a foe,
> And the glory of arms and trumpets all
>   soldiers know.

> Sister Eleanore: *The Vocation of St.
> Francis.* (20th cent.)

Arrow

> Sweet hand! the sweet yet cruel bow
>   thou art,
>   From whence at one, five arrows fly,
>   So with five wounds at once I
>   wounded lie
>   Bearing in breast the print of every
> dart.

> Henry Constable: *Love's Franciscan.* (16th
> cent.)

Art

No art is ever learned without a master.

> St. Jerome: *Letters,* 125, 15. (5th cent.)

The composition of religious imagery
should not be left to the initiative of the
artists, but formed on principles laid
down by the Church and by religious traditions.

> Second Council of Nicaea. (787)

Art is simply a right method of doing
things. The test of the artist does not lie
in the will with which he goes to work,
but in the excellence of the work he produces.

> Thomas Aquinas: *Summa Theologica,* 1,
> 2, 57. (13th cent.)

A work of art represents the mind of the
maker.

> St. Thomas Aquinas: *Contra Gentes,* 2, 2.
> (13th cent.)

> Philosophy, to him who will attend,
>   Said he, in diverse places hath dis-
>   cerned
>   How nature her example and her end
> From Divine Intellect and Its art hath
>   learned.
>   And to thy Physics if good heed thou
>   pay
>   Thou wilt find, after but few pages
>   turned,
> That your art follows her, far as it may,
>   As scholar his master, so that your
>   art is

Of the Godhead the grandchild, so to say.

Dante: *Inferno, Canto 11*. (Tr. L. Binyon) (14th cent.)

God bred the arts, to make us more believe,
By seeking nature's covered mysteries,
His darker works; that faith might thence conceive
He can do more than what our reason sees.

Sir William Davenant: *The Christian's Reply to the Philosopher*. (17th cent.)

Art is only a prudent steward that lives on managing the riches of nature.

Pope: *Tr. of Homer, Iliad, Pref.* (18th cent.)

St. Thomas Aquinas writes, "Great riches are not required for the habit of magnificence; it is enough that a man should dispose of such as he possesses greatly, according to time and place." As in life, so in art, especially in architecture, greatness of style is quite independent of wealth of material; indeed, wealth of material is constantly found by true artists to be a fatal hindrance to grandeur of effect.

Coventry Patmore: *Principle in Art*. (19th cent.)

All loved Art in a seemly way
With an earnest soul and a capital A.

James J. Roche: *The V-a-s-e*. (19th cent.)

The secret of life is in art.

Oscar Wilde: *The English Renaissance*. (19th cent.)

Art never expresses anything but itself.

Oscar Wilde: *The Decay of Lying*. (19th cent.)

Art should never try to be popular.

Oscar Wilde: *The Soul of Man Under Socialism*. (19th cent.)

Master, thy enterprise,
Magnificent, magnanimous, was well done,
Which seized the head of art, and turned her eyes—
The simpleton—and made her front the sun.

Alice Meynell: *To Tintoretto in Venice*. (20th cent.)

The artistic temperament is a disease that afflicts amateurs. It is a disease which arises from men not having sufficient power of expression to utter and get rid of the element of art in their being. . . . Artists of a large and wholesome vitality get rid of their art easily, as they breathe easily, or perspire easily. But in artists of less force, the thing becomes a pressure, and produces a definite pain, which is called the artistic temperament.

G. K. Chesterton: *Heretics*. (20th cent.)

No kind of good art exists unless it grows out of the ideas of the average man.

G. K. Chesterton: *Evidence Before the Joint Select Committee on Stage Plays*. (20th cent.)

Art is the signature of man.

G. K. Chesterton: *The Everlasting Man*, 1, 1. (20th cent.)

The real question that is raised by Renaissance and especially Rococo art is not an artistic question but a religious question; the old religious question of Protestant protests against Catholic ornament or display. It would be absurd for me to pretend that I am impartial on the point; but I fancy I am rather more capable of seeing both sides of it than is generally supposed by those of the other side. Catholic history contains much more of Protestantism than Protestant history does of Catholicism.

G. K. Chesterton: *The Resurrection of Rome*. (20th cent.)

The Catholic Church, so often noted for its sleepy and hoary antiquity, has again and again been in the very vanguard of an advancing and changing world; and it is part of the joke that she has always suffered for it at the next change. She has filled the world with too many masterpieces when they were in the fashion; so there are too many of them to be pointed at as old-fashioned.

G. K. Chesterton: *The Resurrection of Rome.* (20th cent.)

It is right in all religious art that times should be telescoped together. Anachronism is only the pedantic word for eternity.

G. K. Chesterton: *Generally Speaking.* (20th cent.)

From the date of the emancipation of the Church under Constantine, A.D. 311, the Catholic Church took over the existing arts, smote them into its very body and soul, and began its great work of transforming them into its own spiritual image. What it did was to accept the arts as they then stood, give them a new content, give them little by little new and everchanging forms, give them finally a new work to do in that they became almost sacramental in character and were called upon to play their part in the symbolical expression of the loftiest and most tenuous spiritual values, and the communication of these amongst men.

Ralph Adams Cram: *The Catholic Church and Art.* (20th cent.)

As art has always been the product and the manifestation of a definite cultural period, so in its most highly specialized achievements and in certain of its most distinguished products it occurs, not synchronously with the crest of social and cultural attainment, but after the driving energy has ceased to function with power. This is particularly true of music and especially painting, the two most abstract and personal of the arts.

Ralph Adams Cram: *The Catholic Church and Art.* (20th cent.)

Art is a fundamental necessity in the human state. . . . Art teaches men the

pleasures of the spirit, and because it is itself sensitive and adapted to their nature, it is the better able to lead them to what is nobler than itself. In natural life it plays the same part, so to speak, as the "sensible graces" in the spiritual life: and from afar off, without thinking, it prepares the human race for contemplation, the spiritual joy of which surpasses every other joy.

J. Maritain: *Art and Scholasticism.* (20th cent.)

Art is beauty made a sacrament. Art is finite human expression made infinite by love.

V. McNabb: *Thoughts Twice-dyed.* (20th cent.)

Art is not sterile. Things come of it. Masterpieces are historical events.

V. McNabb: *Thoughts Twice-dyed.* (20th cent.)

"A man can be a very good Catholic in a factory." How true! But the fact remains that the factory-made art of the Catholic Repository is a very bad thing for making Catholics. If it be hard for a rich man to pass through the eye of a needle, it is no less hard for many men rich in culture to pass through the door of a modern church.

Eric Gill: *Beauty Looks after Herself.* (20th cent.)

The real distinction between art and nature is between those things which are the product of deliberate and voluntary acts and those that are done without thought and without consent. Between the two there is the innumerable multitude of things which people do and make without full deliberation and more or less involuntarily.

Eric Gill: *It All Goes Together.* (20th cent.)

Art is skill; that is what it has always been and what it has always been said to be. But it is a deliberate skill; and a work of art is the product of voluntary acts directed towards making. Hence art is a virtue of the intelligence—it is of the mind. Deliberation and volition are essential to the thing called art. An involuntary act or an act performed without intellection may be good or bad *in se;* it is not the act of an artist.

> Eric Gill: *It All Goes Together.* (20th cent.)

All art is propaganda, for it is in fact impossible to do anything, to make anything, which is not expressive of "value."

> Eric Gill: *It All Goes Together.* (20th cent.)

Art as a virtue of the practical intelligence is the well-making of what is needed—whether it be drain-pipes or paintings and sculptures and musical symphonies of the highest religious import—and science is that which enables us to deal faithfully with technique. As art is the handmaid of religion, science is the handmaid of art.

> Eric Gill: *It All Goes Together.* (20th cent.)

What is a work of art? A word made flesh. That is the truth, in the clearest sense of the text. A word, that which emanates from mind. Made flesh; a thing, a thing seen, a thing known, the immeasurable translated into terms of the measurable. From the highest to the lowest that is the substance of works of art. And it is a rhetorical activity; for whether by the ministry of angels or of saints or by the ministry of common workmen, gravers or gravediggers, we are all led heavenwards.

> Eric Gill: *It All Goes Together.* (20th cent.)

Picasso's art, in its present character, is the true art of atheism; I mean of that thorough defacement of contemporary man, which is mirrored in atheism. We are no more persons than the distorted, imbecile faces of those ferocious females are true human faces.

> J. Maritain: *The Range of Reason.* (20th cent.)

The value of earthly things is most clearly discerned from above, as contours hitherto invisible have been discovered and photographed from the air. It is from the aerial perspective of the supernatural, to which we are raised by Christian grace and truth, that we shall most clearly perceive the contours of culture and art spread out in the panorama of history, viewed thus *sub specie aeternitatis.*

> E. I. Watkin: *Catholic Art and Culture.* (20th cent.)

Modern art should be given free scope in the due and reverent service of the Church and the sacred rites, provided that they preserve a correct balance between styles tending neither to extreme realism nor to excessive symbolism, and that the needs of the Christian community are taken into consideration rather than the particular taste or talent of the individual artist.

> Pope Pius XII: *Mediator Dei.* (Nov. 20, 1947)

If there were no other proof of the infinite patience of God with men, a very good one could be found in His toleration of the pictures that are painted of Him and of the noise that proceeds from musical instruments under the pretext of being in His "honor."

> Thomas Merton: *Poetry and the Contemplative Life.* (In *Figures for an Apocalypse.*) (20th cent.)

The function of all art lies in fact in breaking through the narrow and tortuous enclosure of the finite, in which man is immersed while living here below, and in providing a window on the infinite for his hungry soul.

> Pope Pius XII: *The Function of Art.* (Apr. 8, 1952)

Artificiality

Nothing artificial is really pleasing.

> St. Ambrose: *On the Duties of the Clergy,* 1. (4th cent.)

Artist

Artists, like the Greek gods, are only revealed to one another.

> Oscar Wilde: *The English Renaissance.* (19th cent.)

An artist has liberty, if he is free to create any image in any material that he chooses.

> G. K. Chesterton: *Generally Speaking.* (20th cent.)

Artists are, or should be, not workers but wooers, of beauty.

> V. McNabb: *Thoughts Twice-dyed.* (20th cent.)

They were in the world and not of it— not because they were saints, but in a different way: because they were artists. The integrity of an artist lifts a man above the level of the world without delivering him from it.

> Thomas Merton: *The Seven Storey Mountain.* (20th cent.)

Arts, Liberal

For what else can we say to those who, although wicked and ungodly, believe themselves to be men of a liberal education, except what we read in the book that is truly liberal: *If the Son has made you free, then you shall be free indeed* (John, 8, 36)? For it is by His gift that whatever even those disciplines that are termed liberal by men who have not been called unto liberty, contain that is liberal, can be known at all. For they contain nothing consonant with liberty, unless what they contain is consonant with the truth.

> St. Augustine: *Letter 101.* (5th cent.)

Ascension of Our Lord

Since then Christ's Ascension is our uplifting, and the hope of the body is raised, whither the glory of the Head has gone before, let us exult, dearly beloved, with worthy joy and delight in the loyal paying of thanks. For today not only are we confirmed as possessors of paradise, but have also in Christ penetrated the heights of heaven.

> Pope St. Leo I: *Sermons,* 73, 4. (5th cent.)

Be present, O Lord, to our supplications; as we trust that the Savior of mankind is seated with Thee in majesty, so may we feel that, according to His promise, He abideth with us unto the end of the world.

> Collect from Leonine Sacramentary. (ca. 5th cent.)

Eternal Monarch, King most high,
Whose Blood hath brought redemption nigh,
By Whom the death of death was wrought,
And conquering grace's battle fought.

Ascending by the starry road,
This day Thou wentest home to God,
By Heaven to power unending called,
And by no human hand installed.

> Roman Breviary, Hymn *Aeterne Rex altissime* at Matins. (Tr. J. Neale) (Ambrosian, 5th cent.)

Grant, we beseech Thee, almighty God, that we who believe Thine only-begotten Son our Redeemer to have ascended this day into heaven, may ourselves dwell in spirit amid heavenly things.

> Roman Missal, Collect for the Feast. (Gregorian, 6th to 8th cent.)

God is gone up with a shout, Alleluia, Alleluia.
God is gone up with a shout, Alleluia, Alleluia.
And the Lord with the sound of a trumpet. Alleluia, Alleluia.
Glory be to the Father, and to the Son, And to the Holy Ghost.
God is gone up with a shout, Alleluia, Alleluia.
When Christ ascended up on high, Alleluia.
He led captivity captive, Alleluia.

> Roman Breviary, Responsory at Terce. (6th to 8th cent.)

O King of glory, Lord of hosts, Who hast this day exalted Thine own self, with great triumph, above all the heavens, leave us not orphans; but send unto us the Promise of the Father, even the Spirit of truth. Alleluia.

Roman Breviary, Antiphon at Second Vespers. (Liber Resp., 6th to 8th cent.)

Hail, Thou Who man's Redeemer art,
Jesu, the joy of every heart;
Great Maker of the world's wide frame,
And purest love's delight and flame.

. . . .

Our guide, our way to heavenly rest,
Be Thou the aim of every breast;
Be Thou the soother of our tears,
Our sweet reward above the spheres.

Roman Breviary, Hymn *Salutis humanae Sator* at Vespers and Lauds. (Tr. T. Potter) (Ambrosian, 7th or 8th cent.)

Jesus, Lord of life eternal,
    Taking those He lov'd the best,
Stood upon the Mount of Olives,
    And His own the last time blest:
Then, though He had never left it,
    Sought again His Father's breast.

. . . .

Knit is now our flesh to Godhead,
    Knit in everlasting bands:
Call the world to highest festal:
    Floods and oceans, clap your hands:
Angels, raise the song of triumph!
    Make response, ye distant lands!

Byzantine Pentekostarion, Canon at Matins. (Tr. Neale) (St. Joseph the Studite, 9th cent.)

Today above the sky He soared, alleluia.
The King of glory, Christ the Lord, alleluia.
He sitteth on the Father's hand, alleluia.
And ruleth sky and sea and land, alleluia.

Anonymous: *Coelos ascendit hodie*. (Tr. J. Neale) (13th cent.)

Rise—glorious Conqueror, rise,
Into Thy native skies,—
    Assume Thy right:

And where in many a fold
The clouds are backward roll'd—
Pass through those gates of gold,
    And reign in light!

M. Bridges: *Rise—glorious Conqueror, rise*. (19th cent.)

Why is thy face so lit with smiles,
    Mother of Jesus! why?
And wherefore is thy beaming look
    So fixed upon the sky?

F. Faber: *The Ascension*. (19th cent.)

Lift up, ye princes of the sky—
Lift up your portals, lift them high;
And you, ye everlasting gates,
Back on your golden hinges fly:
For lo, the King of glory waits
To enter victoriously.
Who is this King of glory? Tell,
O ye who sing His praise so well.

J. Aylward: *Arrangement of Psalm 23*. (19th cent.)

Ascetic

The true ascetic counts nothing his own save his harp.

Joachim of Flora: *Expositio in Apocalipsim*. (12th cent.)

Asceticism

The sacrifice most acceptable to God is complete renunciation of the body and its passions. This is the only real piety.

Clement of Alexandria: *Stromateis*, 5. (2nd cent.)

What greater pleasure can there be than to scorn being pleased, to contemn the world?

Tertullian: *De spectaculis*. (3rd cent.)

Blessed is the man, who for Thee, O Lord, letteth go all things created, who offereth violence to his nature, and through fervor of spirit crucifieth the lusts of the flesh: that so his conscience being cleared up, he may offer to Thee pure prayer, and may be worthy to be admitted among the choirs of angels, having excluded all things of the earth both from without and from within.

> Thomas a Kempis: *The Imitation of Christ,* 3, 48. (15th cent.)

Man was created to praise, honor and serve God. We therefore no more prefer health to sickness, riches to poverty, honor to disdain, long life to short, but desire and choose only that which more surely conduces toward the end for which we were created.

> St. Ignatius Loyola: *Spiritual Exercises.* (16th cent.)

There are two ways of conceiving the mastery of man over himself. Man can become master of his nature by imposing on the world of his own inner energies the law of reason, of reason assisted by grace. This work, which is the formation of oneself on love, requires that our branches be cut in order that we may bear fruit: which is mortification. Such a practice follows the ethics of asceticism. The heirs of rationalism seek to impose on us today an entirely different system of ethics, an anti-ascetic system that is exclusively technological. . . . Technique is good, machinery is good. . . . But if machinery and technical processes are not controlled and firmly subjugated to the well-being of mankind, that is to say, fully and vigorously subordinated to the ethics of religion and made the instruments of moral asceticism, mankind is irretrievably and literally lost.

> J. Maritain: *Freedom in the Modern World.* (20th cent.)

The only asceticism known to Christian history is one that multiplies desire, till the ascetic with something like divine avarice covets a kingdom beyond even the stars.

> V. McNabb: *Thoughts Twice-dyed.* (20th cent.)

See also Mortification

Ash Wednesday

Grant us, O Lord, to begin the service of our Christian warfare with holy fasting; that as we are about to fight against spiritual powers of wickedness, we may be fortified by the aid of self-denial.

> Roman Missal, Collect after Distribution of Ashes. (Leonine, ca. 5th cent.)

Grant, O Lord, to Thy faithful people, that they may enter on the venerable solemnity of this fast with fitting piety, and persevere to the end with steadfast devotion.

> Roman Missal, Collect. (Gregorian, 6th to 8th cent.)

Remember, man, that thou art dust, and into dust thou shalt return (Gen. 3, 19).

> Roman Missal, Formula for the Imposition of Ashes. (After 9th cent. ?)

Remember, man, that thou art dust
    And shalt to dust return:—
Then place not in the world thy trust,
    Its joys delusive spurn;
Prepare thee for the mighty change
    Impending over all;
Give to thy thoughts a loftier range—
    List to thy heavenward call.

> J. Beste: *Ash Wednesday.* (19th cent.)

Ashen cross traced on brow!
Iron cross hid in breast!
Have power, bring patience, now:
Bid passion be at rest.

> Lionel Johnson: *Ash Wednesday.* (19th cent.)

Aspen-Tree

Right as an aspes leaf she gan to quake.

> Chaucer: *Troilus and Criseyde.* (14th cent.)

And the wind, full of wantonness, wooes like a lover
    The young aspen-trees till they tremble all over.

> Thomas Moore: *Lalla Rookh: the Light of the Harem.* (19th cent.)

Aspiration

Men would be angels, angels would be gods.

Pope: *An Essay on Man, 1.* (18th cent.)

Ass

Fools! For I also had my hour;
  One far fierce hour and sweet:
There was a shout about my ears,
  And palms before my feet.

G. K. Chesterton: *The Donkey.* (20th cent.)

To me the wonderful charge was given,
  I, even a little ass, did go
Bearing the very weight of Heaven;
  So I crept cat-foot, sure and slow.

Katharine T. Hinkson: *The Ass Speaks.* (20th cent.)

Assertion

Never assert anything without first being assured of it.

St. Teresa of Jesus: *Maxims.* (16th cent.)

Assisi

A crown of roses and of thorns;
A crown of roses and of bay:
Each crown of loveliness adorns
Assisi, gleaming far away
On Umbrian heights, in Umbrian day.
        . . . .
O city on the Umbrian hills:
Assisi, mother of such sons!
What glory of remembrance fills
Thine heart, whereof the legend runs:
These are among my vanished ones.

Lionel Johnson: *Men of Assisi.* (19th cent.)

Association

Private societies, although they exist within the body politic, and are severally part of the commonwealth, cannot nevertheless be absolutely and as such prohibited by public authority. For to enter into a society of this kind is the natural right of man; and the state has for its office to protect natural rights, not to destroy them; and if it forbids citizens to form associations, it contradicts the very principle of its own existence, for both they and it exist in virtue of the like principle, namely, the natural tendency of man to dwell in society.

Pope Leo XIII: *Rerum Novarum.* (May 15, 1891)

We may lay it down as a general and lasting law that working-men's associations should be so organized and governed as to furnish the best and most suitable means for attaining what is aimed at, that is to say, for helping each individual member to better his condition to the utmost in body, soul, and property.

Pope Leo XIII: *Rerum Novarum.* (May 15, 1891)

Because social relations is one of man's natural requirements and since it is legitimate to promote by common effort decent livelihood, it is not possible without injustice to deny or to limit either to the producers or to the laboring and farming classes the free faculty of uniting in associations by means of which they may defend their property rights and secure the betterment of the goods of soul and body, as well as the honest comforts of life.

Pope Pius XII: *Sertum Laetitiae.* (Nov. 1, 1939)

Trade unions arose as a spontaneous and necessary consequence of capitalism, established as an economic system.

Pope Pius XII: *On Workers Organizations.* (Sept. 11, 1949)

Assumption

But there are two things most hard to bear with in the case of those who are in error, namely, hasty assumption before the truth has been made plain, and, when it has been made plain, defence of the falsehood thus hastily assumed.

St. Augustine: *De Trinitate, 2, 1.* (5th cent.)

There must ever be something assumed ultimately which is incapable of proof, and without which our conclusion will be as illogical as faith is apt to seem to men of the world.

Card. Newman: *Oxford University Sermons.* (19th cent.)

Assumption of Our Lady

O Mother of God, in thy childbirth thou didst retain thy virginity, in thy repose thou didst not forsake the world. Thou hast passed away unto life, being thyself the Mother of Life, and by thy intercession deliverest our souls from death.

Byzantine Menaea, Troparion for the Feast (Aug. 15). (ca. 6th cent.)

The grave and death could not retain the Mother of God, who is unceasing in prayers, our stalwart hope by her protection; for as she is the Mother of Life, He Who dwelt in the ever Virgin hath taken her away unto life.

Byzantine Menaea, Kontakion for the Feast. (ca. 6th cent.)

The festival of this day is venerable to us, O Lord, on which the holy Mother of God succumbed to earthly death; but she could not be held by the bonds of death, who bore of her own flesh Thine incarnate Son our Lord.

Gregorian Sacramentary, Collect for the Feast. (7th cent.)

Mary hath been taken to heaven; the angels rejoice; they praise and bless the Lord.

Roman Breviary, Antiphon at Lauds for the Feast. (Liber Respons., 7th cent.)

As the most glorious Mother of Christ, our Savior and God and the Giver of life and immortality, has been endowed with life by Him, she has received an eternal incorruptibility of the body together with Him Who has raised her up from the tomb and has taken her up to Himself in a way known only to Him.

Homily on the Assumption, 14. (Attr. to St. Modestus of Jerusalem) (7th cent.)

It was fitting that she, who had kept her virginity intact in childbirth, should keep her own body free from all corruption even after death. It was fitting that she, who had carried the Creator as a Child at her breast, should dwell in the divine tabernacles. It was fitting that the spouse, whom the Father had taken to Himself, should live in the divine mansions. It was fitting that she, who has seen her Son upon the Cross and who had thereby received into her heart the sword of sorrow which she had escaped in the act of giving birth to Him, should look upon Him as He sits at the right hand of the Father. It was fitting that God's Mother should possess what belongs to her Son, and that she should be honored by every creature as the Mother and as the Handmaid of God.

St. John of Damascus: *Hom. 2 on the Assumption,* 14. (8th cent.)

Thou art she who, as it is written, appearest in beauty, and thy virginal body is all holy, all chaste, entirely the dwelling place of God, so that it is henceforth completely exempt from dissolution into dust. Though still human, it is changed into the heavenly life of incorruptibility, truly living and glorious, undamaged and sharing in perfect life.

St. Germanus, Patriarch of Constantinople: *Sermon 1 on the Assumption.* (8th cent.)

Virgin, hail! alone the fairest!
Mother, who our Savior barest!
And the name of *Sea-Star* wearest,
   Star that leadeth not astray!
On the sea of this life never
Let us suffer wreck, but ever
To thy Savior, to deliver
   Those who travel o'er it, pray.

· · · · · ·

Thou by Him wast pre-elected,
By Whom all things are directed,
Who thy maiden-mark protected,
   When thy sacred womb He filled;
Parent of our Savior-brother!
Thou didst feel nor pain nor other
Sorrow, like to man's first mother,
   When thou broughtest forth that Child.

Mary! for thy merits wholly
Hast thou been uplifted solely,
O'er the choirs of angels holy,
  To a lofty throne above:
Joy is to this day pertaining,
When the heavens thou art gaining,
Then on us, below remaining,
  Look thou with maternal love!

Adam of St. Victor: *Ave Virgo singularis.*
(Tr. Wrangham) (12th cent.)

Glad thanks let us Godward carry,
For the assumption of holy Mary,
  Which distinguishes this day:
'Tis a day with gladness mated,
When she was with joy translated
  Up to heaven from earth away!

O'er angelic choirs uplifted,
She with higher rank was gifted
  Than all heaven's own home-born
    sons.
In His beauty she surveyeth
There her Son, and there she prayeth
For all true and faithful ones.

Adam of St. Victor: *Gratulemur in hac die.*
(12th cent.)

Weep, living things! of life the mother
  dies;
  The world doth lose the sum of all
    her bliss,
The queen of earth, the empress of the
  skies;
  By Mary's death mankind an orphan
    is.
Let nature weep, yea, let all graces
  moan;
  Their glory, grace, and gifts die all
    in one.

Bl. Robert Southwell: *The Death of Our
Lady.* (16th cent.)

Gem to her worth, spouse to her love
  ascends,
Prince to her throne, queen to her
  heavenly King,
Whose court with solemn pomp on her
  attends,
And choirs of saints with greeting notes
  do sing;
Earth rendereth up her undeserved
  prey,

Heaven claims the right, and bears the
  prize away.

Bl. Robert Southwell: *The Assumption of
Our Lady.* (16th cent.)

And who, I ask, could believe that the
ark of holiness, the dwelling place of the
Word of God, the temple of the Holy
Ghost, could be reduced to ruin? My
soul is filled with horror at the thought
that this virginal flesh which had begotten God, had brought Him into the
world, had nourished and carried Him,
could have been turned into ashes or
given over to be the food of worms?

St. Robert Bellarmine: *Sermons at Louvain*,
40. (17th cent.)

  Maria, men and angels sing,
  Maria, Mother of our King.
Live, rosy princess, live. And may the
  bright
Crown of a most incomparable light
Embrace thy radiant brows. O may the
  best
Of everlasting joys bathe thy white
  breast.
Live, our chaste love, the holy mirth
Of heav'n, the humble pride of earth.
Live, crown of women, Queen of men.
Live, mistress of our song. And when
Our weak desires have done their best,
Sweet angels, come, and sing the rest.

R. Crashaw: *The Glorious Assumption of
Our Bl. Lady, a Hymn.* (17th cent.)

Who is she that ascends so high,
Next the heavenly King,
Round about whom angels fly
And her praises sing?
Who is she that, adorned with light,
Makes the sun her robe,
At whose feet the queen of night
Lays her changing globe?

Sir John Beaumont: *The Assumption.*
(17th cent.)

Rejoice, O ye spirits and angels on
  high!
  This day the pure Mother of Love
By death was set free; and ascending
  the sky,

Was welcomed by Jesus, with triumph
  and joy,
  To the courts of His glory above.

Jean Santeuil: *O vos aetherei plaudite cives.*
(Tr. Caswall) (18th cent.)

Sing, sing, ye angel bands,
  All beautiful and bright;
For higher still, and higher,
  Through the vast fields of light,
Mary, your Queen, ascends,
  Like the sweet moon at night.

F. Faber: *The Assumption.* (19th cent.)

The rose is a mystery—where is it
  found?
Is it anything true? Does it grow upon
  ground?
It was made of earth's mould, but it
  went from men's eyes,
And its place is a secret and shut in the
  skies.
    In the gardens of God, in the day-
      light divine,
    Find me a place by thee, Mother of
      mine.

G. M. Hopkins: *Rosa Mystica.* (19th cent.)

Multitudinous ascend I,
  Dreadful as a battle arrayed,
For I bear you whither tend I;
  Ye are I: be undismayed!
I, the ark that for the graven
  Tables of the law was made;
Man's own heart was one; one, Heaven;
  Both within my womb were laid.
    For there Anteros with Eros,
      Heaven with man, conjoinèd
        was,—
    Twin-stone of the law, *Ischyros,*
      Agios Athanatos.

F. Thompson: *Assumpta Maria.* (19th
cent.)

The angel death from this cold tomb
  Of life did roll the stone away;
And He thou barest in thy womb
  Caught thee at last into the day,
Before the living throne of Whom
  The lights of heaven burning pray.

F. Thompson: *The Passion of Mary.* (19th
cent.)

As the immaculate conception was our
baptism, in Mary anticipated, so is the
assumption the resurrection of the body,
our resurrection, anticipated in Mary.

Joseph Rickaby: *An Old Man's Jottings.*
(20th cent.)

Mary, uplifted to our sight
In cloudy vesture stainless white,
Why are thine eyes like stars alight,
    Twin flames of charity?
Mine eyes are on His glorious face
That shone not on earth's darkened
    place,
But clothed and crowned me with His
    grace—
  The God Who fathered me.

Eleanor Downing: *On the Feast of the
Assumption.* (20th cent.)

By the authority of our Lord Jesus
Christ, of the blessed apostles Peter and
Paul, and by our own authority, we pronounce, declare and define it to be a
divinely revealed dogma: that the immaculate Mother of God, the ever Virgin Mary, having completed the course
of her earthly life, was assumed body
and soul into heavenly glory.

Pope Pius XII: *Munificentissimus Deus.*
(Nov. 1, 1950)

Astrology

Thus I saw it as obvious that such things
as happened to be said truly from the
casting of horoscopes were true not by
skill but by chance; and such things as
were false were not due to want of skill
in the art but merely that luck had fallen
the other way.

St. Augustine: *Confessions,* 7, 6. (5th
cent.)

In that large book that overhangs the
  earth
And people call the heavens, it well
  may be
That it was written in his stars at birth
Love was to be his death; for certainly
The death of every man is there to see

Patterned in stars, clearer than in a
  glass,
Could one but read how all will come
  to pass.

F. Chaucer: *The Man of Law's Tale.* (Tr.
Coghill) (14th cent.)

Astronomer

Starry amorist, starward gone,
Thou art—what thou didst gaze upon!
Passed through thy golden garden's
  bars,
Thou seest the Gardener of the stars!

F. Thompson: *A Dead Astronomer:
Stephen Perry, S.J.* (19th cent.)

Astronomy

Astronomy is the law of the stars, and it
traces with inquiring reason the courses
of the heavenly bodies, and their figures,
and the regular movements of the stars
with reference to one another and to the
earth.

St. Isidore: *Etymologies,* 3, 24. (7th cent.)

Asylum

See Sanctuary

Atheism

Pity atheists who seek; are they not piti-
able? Inveigh only against those who
make a boast of it.

Pascal: *Pensées.* (17th cent.)

Atheism is a sign of mental strength,
but only up to a certain point.

Pascal: *Pensées.* (17th cent.)

There are but two ways, the way to
Rome, and the way to atheism.

Card. Newman: *Apologia pro Vita Sua.*
(19th cent.)

Now who that runs can read it,
The riddle that I write
Of why this poor old sinner

Should sin without delight?
But I, I cannot read it
(Although I run and run)
Of them that do not have the faith
And will not have the fun.

G. K. Chesterton: *The Song of the Strange
Ascetic.* (20th cent.)

Who seeks perfection in the art
Of driving well an ass and cart,
Or painting mountains in a mist,
Seeks God although an atheist.

Francis Carlin: *Perfection.* (20th cent.)

'The people must have a religion': this
[bourgeois] formula expressed in an
exact though inverted form the same
conception as the phrase of Marx that
religion is the opiate of the people.
Atheist communism is only bourgeois
deism turned the other way round.

J. Maritain: *Freedom in the Modern
World.* (20th cent.)

It is significant that freedom of speech
and action has never been more ruth-
lessly suppressed than in the one great
European country which has officially
adopted atheism as the religion of the
state.

Arnold Lunn: *Now I See.* (20th cent.)

There are two kinds of atheists: those
who think they are atheists, and those
who are atheists.

J. Maritain: *The Range of Reason.* (20th
cent.)

Absolute atheism starts in an act of faith
in reverse gear and is a full-blown religious commitment. Here we have the
first internal inconsistency of contemporary atheism: it proclaims that all religion must necessarily vanish away, and it
is itself a religious phenomenon.

J. Maritain: *The Range of Reason.* (20th
cent.)

No man hates God without first hating
himself.

Bishop Sheen: *Peace of Soul.* (20th cent.)

The exile of God means the tyrannization of man.

> Bishop Sheen: *Life is Worth Living*. (20th cent.)

Athens

Athens, that home of all learning.

> Pope Leo XIII: *Aeterni Patris*. (Aug. 4, 1879)

Athlete

Be temperate, like an athlete of God; the prize is immortality and eternal life.

> St. Ignatius of Antioch: *Letter to Polycarp*, 2. (2nd cent.)

Thou wast anointed as Christ's athlete. . . . He who wrestles has something to hope for; where the contest is, there is the crown. Thou wrestlest in the world, but thou art crowned by Christ, and thou are crowned for contests in the world; for, though the reward is in heaven, yet the earning of the reward is placed here.

> St. Ambrose: *On the Sacraments*, 1, 2, 4. (4th cent.)

See also Sport

Atonement

And unless the first man has transgressed, the Second would never have come to the ignominies of the Passion. . . . For if Satan had not drawn the first Adam by wilful sin into the death of the soul, the second Adam, being without sin, would never have come into the voluntary death of the flesh. . . . For our Mediator deserved not to be punished for Himself, because He never was guilty of any defilement of sin. But if He had not Himself undertaken a death not due to Him, He would never have freed us from one that was justly due to us.

> Pope St. Gregory I: *Morals*, 3, 26-27. (6th cent.)

O almighty and everlasting God, Who art wonderful in the dispensation of all Thy works, let Thy servants whom Thou hast redeemed understand that the creation of the world in the beginning was not a more excellent thing than the immolation of Christ our Passover at the end of time.

> Roman Missal, Collect for Holy Saturday. (Gelasian, 5th to 7th cent.)

He willed to suffer death for our sins so that He might pay the price and free us from the charge of death, although He Himself was without crime. He also willed that His own death should not only make redress for us, but also be a sacrament of salvation, in that by the likeness of His death we may die to carnal life and be carried over into spiritual life: *Christ hath suffered once for our sins, the just for the unjust, that He might bring us to God, being put to death in the flesh, but quickened in the spirit* (1 Peter 3, 18).

> St. Thomas Aquinas: *Compendium of Theology*, 227. (13th cent.)

Although by His death Christ sufficiently merited salvation for the whole human race, each of us must there seek his own cure. Christ's death is like the universal cause of deliverance. . . . Nevertheless even a universal cause must be applied to be effective. The effects of original sin come to us through bodily birth; the effects of Christ's death come through the spiritual rebirth whereby we are incorporated in Christ.

> St. Thomas Aquinas: *Contra Gentes*, 4, 55. (13th cent.)

He is the Savior of all men, especially of the faithful (1 Tim. 4, 10). It is as the Head of all mankind that Christ saves and atones: *He is the propitiation for our sins, and not for ours only, but also for those of the whole world* (John 2, 2).

> St. Thomas Aquinas: *Summa Theologica*, 3, 8, 3. (13th cent.)

Strict satisfaction is rendered when the person offended is given what he loves as much as, or more than, he hated the offence. By suffering from charity, Christ offered to God more than what was demanded as recompense for the sin of the entire human race. First, from the greatness of His charity. Secondly, from the preciousness of the life He laid down, the life of a man Who was God. Thirdly, by the extent and depth of what was accepted. Christ's Passion was more than sufficient, it was superabundant.

> St. Thomas Aquinas: *Summa Theologica*, 3, 48, 2. (13th cent.)

Christ's Passion is the cause of our salvation in various ways—the efficient cause when related to His Godhead; the meritorious cause when related to His human will; the satisfying cause in that it liberates us from the debt of punishment; the redemptive cause in that it frees us from the bondage of sin; the sacrificial cause in that it reconciles us with God.

> St. Thomas Aquinas: *Summa Theologica*, 3, 48, 6. (13th cent.)

Christ's Passion is the true and proper cause of the forgiveness of sins.

> St. Thomas Aquinas: *Summa Theologica*, 3, 49, 1. (13th cent.)

The divine atonement whereby the new life of holiness with God has been gained for us in Christ, is not a merely passing act in the history of man's reconciliation with God, but the divine "world-form" of our human nature's redemption and reconciliation. So long as the world lasts, Christ's atoning life and death give the law to man's supernatural regeneration.

> Dom Cuthbert: *The Divine Atonement*. (In *God and the Supernatural*) (20th cent.)

See also Good Friday; Jesus Christ—High Priest and Mediator; Passion of our Lord; Redemption.

Augustine, Saint

Catholics venerate you as the restorer of the ancient faith, and while they look up to you, the heretics—an even more glorious testimony—detest you.

> St. Jerome: *Letter to St. Augustine* (*No. 195 among letters of St. Augustine*). (5th cent.)

We have ever had in communion with us Augustine of holy memory for the sake of his life and merits; never has the slightest breath of evil suspicion tarnished his name. We have always kept him in memory as a man of such great learning that my predecessors ranked him with the foremost masters. Unanimously they held him in high esteem, for all loved him and paid him honor.

> Pope St. Celestine I. (5th cent.)

Would you feast on delicious food, read the works of your countryman, the blessed Augustine, nor ask us to give you what, as compared with his white flour, is but our bran.

> Pope St. Gregory I: *Letter to Innocent, Prefect of Africa*. (6th cent.)

The greatest teacher of the churches after the apostles. (Maximus post apostolos ecclesiarum instructor.)

> Peter the Venerable: *Letter 229, 13* (To St. Bernard). (12th cent.)

Doctor of grace. (Doctor gratiae.)

> Official title of the bishop of Hippo. (In 1298 Boniface VIII named Sts. Ambrose, Jerome, Augustine and Gregory the Great, *Doctores Ecclesiae*.) (Before 13th cent.?)

What does the Christian world have more golden or august than this writer? (Quid habet orbis Christianus hoc scriptore magis aureum vel augustius?)

> Erasmus: *Praef. in Opera S. Augustini*. (16th cent.)

There's no pot without bacon in it, and no sermon without St. Augustine.

> Spanish Proverb. (Modern?)

A man than whom, by the verdict of history, past ages produced no greater or grander in all the world.

> Pope Pius XI: *Ad Salutem*. (Apr. 20, 1930)

Author

Authors are judged by strange capricious rules,
The great ones are thought mad, the small ones fools.

> Pope: *Prologue for Three Hours After Marriage*. (18th cent.)

A great author, gentlemen, is not merely one who has a *copia verborum*, whether in prose or verse, and can, as it were, turn on at his will any number of splendid phrases and swelling sentences; but he is one who has something to say and knows how to say it.

> Card. Newman: *Idea of a University*. (19th cent.)

The remark has been made that the history of an author is the history of his works; it is far more exact to say that, at least in the case of great writers, the history of their works is the history of their fortunes or their times.

> Card. Newman: *Idea of a University*. (19th cent.)

Great authors are always greater than their books.

> Coventry Patmore: *Principle in Art*. (19th cent.)

Go, songs, for ended is our brief, sweet play;
Go, children of swift joy and tardy sorrow:
And some are sung, and that was yesterday,
And some unsung, and that may be tomorrow.

> Francis Thompson: *Envoy*. (19th cent.)

The life of writing men has always been, since our remote fathers engaged upon it in the high Greek world, a bitter business. It is notoriously accompanied, for those who write well, by poverty and contempt; or by fatuity and wealth for those who write ill.

> Hilaire Belloc: *Gilbert Chesterton in English Letters*. (20th cent.)

Authority

Grant that we may be obedient to Thy almighty and excellent name, and to our rulers and governors on earth. Thou, Lord, hast given the authority of the kingdom to them through Thy all-powerful and unspeakable might, that we, acknowledging the glory and honor given them by Thee, may be subject to them and in no way resist Thy will. To them, Lord, give health, peace, concord, and firmness, that they may administer without offense the government which Thou hast given them.

> Pope St. Clement I: *Letter to the Corinthians*, 60, 4. (1st cent.)

It is right to submit to higher authority whenever a command of God would not be violated.

> St. Basil: *The Morals*, 79, 1. (4th cent.)

In the order of nature, when we learn anything, authority precedes reason. For a reason may seem weak, when, after it is given, it requires authority to confirm it.

> St. Augustine: *De Moribus Ecclesiae Catholicae*, 2, 3. (4th cent.)

When we offend those set over us, we oppose the ordinance of Him Who set them above us.

> Pope St. Gregory I: *Pastoral Care*, 3, 4. (6th cent.)

Under the king there are also free men and serfs, and they are subject to his power; all indeed are under him, but he is under no one, except it be God alone. He has no peer in his realm, otherwise he would lose the power of command, since peer has no authority over peer.

> Bracton: *On the Laws and Customs of England*, 1, 8, 5. (13th cent.)

Authority has the power to constrain spiritually as well as temporally, and to bind the conscience. Hence a Christian is bound to obey the authorities when their power is from God, but not otherwise.

> St. Thomas Aquinas: *Commentary on the Sentences*, 2, 44, 2, 2. (13th cent.)

In the field of human science the argument from authority is the weakest.

> St. Thomas Aquinas: *Summa Theologica*, 1, 1, 8. (13th cent.)

This right of dominion or authority can be justly done away with by the sentence or ordination of the Church which has the authority of God, since unbelievers in virtue of their unbelief deserve to forfeit their power over the faithful who are converted into children of God. This the Church does sometimes, and sometimes not.

> St. Thomas Aquinas: *Summa Theologica*, 2-2, 10, 10. (13th cent.)

Dominion and authority are institutions of human law, while the distinction between faithful and unbelievers arises from the divine law. Now the divine law which is the law of grace, does not do away with human law which is the law of natural reason. Wherefore the distinction between faithful and unbelievers, considered in itself, does not do away with dominion and authority of unbelievers over the faithful.

> St. Thomas Aquinas: *Summa Theologica*, 2-2, 10, 10. (13th cent.)

There can be no authority (*dominium*) with justice, whether it be authority over temporal things, or over lay persons, in which case there is even greater doubt, unless it has been instituted under the Church and by the Church.

> Egidius Colonna: *On Ecclesiastical Power*, 2, 7. (14th cent.)

No one is a civil ruler, no one is a prelate, no one is a bishop, while he is in mortal sin.

> Error of John Wyclif condemned by Pope Martin V, at Council of Constance, Session 8, May 4, 1415.

Men desire authority for its own sake that they may bear a rule, command and control other men, and live uncommanded and uncontrolled themself.

> St. Thomas More: *Dialogue of Comfort*. (16th cent.)

Authority is nothing else but mere numbers and the sum total of material forces.

> Proposition condemned by Pius IX in Syllabus of Errors. (1867)

To despise legitimate authority, no matter in whom it is invested, is unlawful; it is a rebellion against God's will.

> Pope Leo XIII: *Immortale Dei*. (Nov. 1, 1885)

The highest duty is to respect authority, and obediently to submit to just law.

> Pope Leo XIII: *Libertas Praestantissimum*. (June 20, 1888)

The right to command and to require obedience exists only in so far as it is in accordance with the authority of God, and is within the measure that He has laid down. But when anything is commanded which is plainly at variance with the will of God, there is a wide departure from this divinely constituted order, and at the same time a direct conflict with divine authority; therefore, it is right not to obey.

> Pope Leo XIII: *Libertas Praestantissimum*. (June 20, 1888)

Hallowed in the minds of Christians is the very idea of public authority, in which they recognize some likeness and symbol as it were of the Divine Majesty, even when it is exercised by one unworthy. A just and due reverence to the laws abides in them, not from force and threats, but from a consciousness of duty; *for God hath not given us the spirit of fear* (2 Tim. 1, 7).

> Pope Leo XIII: *Sapientiae Christianae*. (Jan. 10, 1890)

True and legitimate authority is void of sanction, unless it proceed from God, the supreme Ruler and Lord of all. The Almighty alone can commit power to a man over his fellow men.

> Pope Leo XIII: *Sapientiae Christianae.* (Jan. 10, 1890)

No authority has power to impose error, and if it resists the truth, the truth must be upheld until it is admitted.

> Lord Acton: *Conflicts with Rome.* (19th cent.)

Cast away authority, and authority shall forsake you!

> R. H. Benson: *By What Authority.* (20th cent.)

When the rulers of the people disdain the authority of God, the people in turn despise the authority of men.

> Pope Benedict XV: *Ad beatissimi apostolorum.* (Nov. 1, 1914)

Authority is not a short way to the truth; it is the only way to many truths; and for men on earth it is the only way to divine truths.

> V. McNabb: *Thoughts Twice-dyed.* (20th cent.)

There are three theories of power and therefore of authority, to wit: the robber theory that all power is for mastery; the hireling theory that all power is for wealth; the good shepherd theory that all power is for service.

> V. McNabb: *Thoughts Twice-dyed.* (20th cent.)

The nature of ecclesiastical authority has nothing in common with this "authoritarianism"; the latter can claim no point of resemblance to the hierarchical constitution of the Church.

> Pope Pius XII: *Judicial Jurisdiction of the Church.* (Oct. 2, 1945)

Educate youth to obedience and respect for authority. This is simple when man is submissive to God and recognizes the absolute value of His commandments.

For the unbeliever and the man who denies God, there cannot be any true, just and ordered authority because *there exists no authority except from God* (Rom. 13, 1). Man can neither rule nor be ruled by fear and force.

> Pope Pius XII: *Address to the Women of Italian Cath. Action,* July 24, 1949.

See also Catholic Church—Authority; Church and State; Government; Pope; State.

Autumn

The leaves are many under my feet,
    And drift one way.
Their scent of death is weary and sweet.
    A flight of them is in the grey
Where sky and forest meet.

> Alice Meynell: *In Autumn.* (19th cent.)

Again maternal autumn grieves,
As blood-like drip the maple leaves
    On nature's Calvary,
And every sap-forsaken limb
Renews the mystery of Him
    Who died upon a tree.

> J. B. Tabb: *Mater Dolorosa.* (19th cent.)

How are the veins of thee, Autumn,
        laden?
    Umbered juices, and pulpèd oozes
    Pappy out of the cherry-bruises,
Froth the veins of thee, wild, wild
        maiden!
        With hair that musters
        In globèd clusters,
    In tumbling clusters, like swarthy
        grapes.

> Francis Thompson: *A Corymbus for Autumn.* (19th cent.)

Sometimes when autumn's mellow sun-
        light spills
    On painted pomp of wooded heights
        the while,
My heart grows homesick for the eter-
        nal hills
    Bathed in the fadeless splendor of
        His smile.

> Sister M. Angelita: *Nostalgia.* (20th cent.)

The breeze that may be music
    When the summer lawns are fair
Will have no heart for singing
    In the autumn's mournful air.

Michael Earls: *An Autumn Rose-tree.*
(20th cent.)

Autumn days come swift like the running of a hound upon the moor.

Seumas MacManus: *Heavy Hangs the Golden Grain.* (20th cent.)

Avarice

Happy is the man who has been able to cut out the root of vices, avarice . . . what do superfluous riches profit in this world when they do not assist our birth or impede our dying? We are born into this world naked, we leave it without a cent, we are buried without our inheritance.

St. Ambrose: *Letters, 2.* (379)

Now, my son, see to what a mock are brought

The goods of Fortune's keeping,
    and how soon!
Though to possess them still is all
    man's thought.

Dante: *Inferno, Canto 7.* (Tr. Binyon)
(14th cent.)

I preach for nothing but for greed of
    gain
And use the same old text, as bold as
    brass,
Radix malorum est cupiditas.

Chaucer: *The Pardoner's Tale.* (Tr. Coghill) (14th cent.)

There are many definite methods, honest and dishonest, which make men rich; the only "instinct" I know of which does it is that instinct which theological Christianity crudely describes as "the sin of avarice."

G. K. Chesterton: *All Things Considered.* (20th cent.)

B

Baby

A baby of Belsabub's bower.

John Heywood: *Proverbs, 2, 4.* (16th cent.)

Bachelor

Lord of yourself, uncumber'd with a wife.

Dryden: *To John Dryden of Chesterton.* (17th cent.)

Badness

It is bad enough to be bad, but to be bad in bad taste is unpardonable.

Agnes Repplier: *Points of Friction.* (20th cent.)

Baldness

His head was bald and shone as any
    glass,
So did his face, as if it had been greased.

Chaucer: *Canterbury Tales: Prologue.* (Tr. Coghill) (14th cent.)

He was as ballid as a cote.

Lydgate: *Troy Book, 2.* (15th cent.)

Better a bald head than no head at all.

S. MacManus: *Heavy Hangs the Golden Grain.* (20th cent.)

Ball

All the boys of merry Lincoln
Were playing at the ball,

And by it came him sweet Sir Hugh,
And he play's o'er them all.

He kicked the ball with his right foot,
And catch'd it with his knee,
And through and through the Jew's
window
He gar'd the bonny ball flee.

> Anonymous: *Hugh of Lincoln.* (15th
> cent.)

Thou hast stricken the ball under the
line.

> John Heywood: *Proverbs,* 1, 11. (16th
> cent.)

Baptism

Baptize as follows: After first explaining all these points, baptize in the name
of the Father and of the Son and of the
Holy Spirit, in running water. But if
you have no running water, baptize in
other water; and if you cannot in cold,
then in warm. But if you have neither,
pour water on the head three times in
the name of the Father and of the Son
and of the Holy Spirit.

> Teaching of the Twelve Apostles, 7. (2nd
> cent.)

Happy is our sacrament of water, in that
by washing away the sins of our early
blindness, we are set free and admitted
into eternal life. . . . But we, little fishes,
after the example of our ICHTHYS
[Iesous Christos Theou Uios Soter: Jesus
Christ Son of God Savior] are born in
water, nor have we safety in any other
way than by permanently abiding in
water.

> Tertullian: *On Baptism,* 1. (The Greek
> word for fish is *ichthys.* Because the word
> spelled out the initial letters of the phrase
> referring to our Lord, the word was often
> used symbolically in early Christian
> iconography to represent the second Person
> of the Trinity.) (3rd cent.)

All waters, therefore, in virtue of the
pristine privilege of their origin, after
the invocation of God attain the sacramental power of sanctification; for the
Spirit immediately supervenes from the
heavens, and rests over the waters, sanctifying them from Himself; and being
thus sanctified, they imbibe at the same
time the power of sanctifying. Albeit the
similitude may be admitted to be suitable
to the simple act; that, since we are defiled by sins, as it were by dirt, we should
be washed from those stains in water.

> Tertullian: *On Baptism,* 4. (3rd cent.)

Thus too in our case the unction runs
carnally, but profits spiritually; in the
same way as the act of baptism itself too
is carnal, in that we are plunged in water,
but the effect spiritual, in that we are
freed from sins.

> Tertullian: *On Baptism,* 7. (3rd cent.)

There is to us one, and but one, baptism;
as well according to the Lord's Gospel as
according to the apostle's letters.

> Tertullian: *On Baptism,* 15. (3rd cent.)

Those therefore who receive this spiritual and saving seal, have need also of
the disposition akin to it. For as a writ-
ing-reed or a dart has need of one to use
it, so grace also has need of believing
minds.

> St. Cyril of Jerusalem: *Catechetical
> Discourses,* 1, 3. (4th cent.)

If any man receive not baptism, he hath
no salvation; except only martyrs, who
even without the water receive the kingdom.

> St. Cyril of Jerusalem: *Catechetical
> Discourses,* 3, 10. (4th cent.)

Thou, therefore, O bishop, according to
that type, shalt anoint the head of those
that are to be baptized, whether they be
men or women, with the holy oil, for a
type of the spiritual baptism. After that,
either thou, O bishop, or a presbyter that
is under thee, shall in the solemn form
name over them the Father, and Son, and
Holy Spirit, and shall dip them in the
water. . . . After that, let the bishop

anoint those that are baptized with ointment.

> Anonymous: *Constitutions of the Holy
> Apostles*, 3, 16. (4th cent.)

O God, the God of truth, the Artificer
of all, the Lord of all creation, bless this
Thy servant with Thy blessing: render
him clean in regeneration, make him
have fellowship with Thy angelic
powers, that he may no longer be named
flesh but spiritual, by partaking of Thy
divine and profitable gift. May he be
preserved until the end to Thee the
Maker of the world through Thine only-
begotten Jesus Christ.

> Sacramentary of Serapion, Prayer after
> Baptism (11). (4th cent.)

No athlete is admitted to the contest of
virtue, unless he has first been washed
of all stains of sins and consecrated with
the gift of heavenly grace.

> St. Ambrose: *Explanation of St. Luke*, 4,
> 4. (4th cent.)

The Father forgives sin, just as the Son
forgives; likewise also the Holy Ghost.
But He bade us be baptized in one name,
that is, *in the name of the Father and of
the Son, and of the Holy Ghost.* Wonder
not that He spoke of one name, when
there is one Substance, one Divinity, one
Majesty.

> St. Ambrose: *On the Sacraments*, 2, 7, 22.
> (4th cent.)

Wherefore recollect that thou hast received the spiritual seal, *the spirit of
wisdom, the spirit of prudence and
strength, the spirit of knowledge and
piety, the spirit of holy fear* (Is. 11, 2),
and preserve what thou hast received.
God the Father hath sealed thee, Christ
the Lord hath confirmed thee, and hath
given the foretaste of the Spirit in thy
heart (cf. 2 Cor. 1, 21-22), as thou hast
learned from the apostolic lesson.

> St. Ambrose: *On the Mysteries*, 7, 42. (4th
> cent.)

If, then, the Holy Ghost, coming upon
the Virgin effected conception, and fulfilled the work of regeneration, surely
we must not doubt that, coming upon
the font or upon those on whom baptism
is conferred, He effects the reality of regeneration.

> St. Ambrose: *On the Mysteries*, 9, 59. (4th
> cent.)

You [i.e. the schismatic Donatists] are
Christ's sheep; you bear the mark of the
Lord in the sacrament you have received,
but you have wandered away and are
lost.

> St. Augustine: *Letter 173.* (5th cent.)

If, however, in a case of extreme necessity a person cannot find a Catholic from
whom to receive Baptism, and if while
safeguarding his Catholic peace he approaches someone who is not in Catholic
unity with the object of receiving from
him what he would—had he been able—
have received in Catholic unity, then
were he to depart this life we could not
regard him as anything save a Catholic.

> St. Augustine: *De Baptismo contra
> Donatistas*, 1, 3. (5th cent.)

Outside the Church baptism can be in
you but it cannot avail you (inesse potuit,
non prodesse).

> St. Augustine: *Contra Cresconium*, 4, 76.
> (5th cent.)

For whatever unbaptized persons die
confessing Christ, this confession is of
the same efficacy for the remission of
sins as if they were washed in the sacred
font of baptism.

> St. Augustine: *The City of God*, 13, 7.
> (5th cent.)

Bow your head, proud Sicambrian, adore
what you have burned, and burn what
you have adored!

> Words attributed to St. Remigius, as he
> baptized (496) Clovis, king of the Franks
> (466–511). (According to Gregory of
> Tours, History of the Franks, 2, 21.)

O Lord and Master, our God, call Thy
servant N., to Thy holy illumination,

and make him worthy of this wondrous grace of Thy holy baptism; take from him the things of old, and renew him unto life eternal, and fill him with the power of Thy Holy Spirit unto union with Thy Christ, so that he may be no more a child of the body but a child of Thy kingdom. Through the favor and grace of Thine only-begotten Son with Whom Thou art blessed, with Thine all-holy, righteous, and life-giving Spirit, now and for ever, world without end. Amen.

> Byzantine Euchologion, Prayer after Profession of Faith. (ca. 5th cent.)

N., I baptize thee in the name of the Father, and of the Son, and of the Holy Spirit.

> Roman Ritual, Formula for Baptism. (Gregorian, ca. 5th cent.)

The servant of God N. is baptized in the name of the Father, Amen; and of the Son, Amen; and of the Holy Ghost. Amen.

> Byzantine Euchologion, Formula for Baptism. (ca. 5th cent.)

May almighty God, the Father of our Lord Jesus Christ, Who has given you a new birth by means of water and the Holy Spirit and forgiven all your sins, anoint you with the chrism of salvation in Christ Jesus our Lord, so that you may have everlasting life. Amen.

> Roman Ritual, Prayer at the Anointing. (Gelasian, ca. 5th cent.)

The servant of God N. is anointed with the oil of gladness, in the name of the Father, and of the Son, and of the Holy Ghost. Amen.

> Byzantine Euchologion, Formula at Anointing. (ca. 5th cent.)

But with respect to triple immersion in baptism, no truer answer can be given than what you have yourself felt to be right; namely that, where there is one faith, a diversity of usage does no harm to holy Church.

> Pope St. Gregory I: *Letters,* 1, 43. (To St. Leander, bishop of Seville.) (6th cent.)

Whoever says, then, that sins are not entirely put away in baptism, let him say that the Egyptians did not really die in the Red Sea. But if he acknowledges that the Egyptians really died, he must needs acknowledge that sins die entirely in baptism, since surely the truth avails more in our absolution than the shadow of the truth.

> Pope St. Gregory I: *Letters,* 11, 45. (6th cent.)

For every man that is not absolved by the water of regeneration, is tied and bound by the guilt of the original bond. But that which the water of baptism avails for with us, this either faith alone did of old in behalf of infants, or for those of riper years, the virtue of sacrifice, or for all that came of the stock of Abraham, the mystery of circumcision.

> Pope St. Gregory I: *Morals,* 4, Pref. (6th cent.)

O almighty and everlasting God, Who dost ever render Thy Church fruitful with new offspring, increase the faith and understanding of our catechumens; that, regenerated in the font of baptism, they may be united to the children of Thy adoption.

> Roman Missal, Collect for Good Friday. (Gelasian, ca. 6th cent.)

Baptism is not the work of man but of Christ, and this sacrament is so holy that it would not be defiled, even if the minister were a murderer.

> St. Isidore: *On the Offices of the Church,* 2, 25. (7th cent.)

Baptism in Greek means dipping in Latin; it is called dipping because man is thereby changed for the better by the spirit of grace, and becomes something far different from what he was. . . . Just as the outer body is cleansed by water, so by its mysterious effects the soul is secretly purified through the Holy Spirit.

> St. Isidore: *Etymologies,* 6, 19. (7th cent.)

Since man's nature is twofold, consisting of soul and body, He bestowed on us a twofold purification of water and of the Spirit: the Spirit renewing that part in us which is after His image and likeness, and the water by the grace of the Spirit cleansing the body from sin and delivering it from corruption, the water indeed expressing the image of death, but the Spirit affording the reward of life.

> St. John of Damascus: *Exposition of the Orthodox Faith,* 4, 9. (8th cent.)

In baptism Christ's passion works a regeneration; a person dies entirely to the old life and takes on the new. Therefore baptism washes away the whole guilt of punishment belonging to the past.

> St. Thomas Aquinas: *Commentary on Romans,* 11, lect. 4. (13th cent.)

Note three features in the sacrament of baptism: the mere sacrament, or outward sign, namely, the water which flows away; next, and this is part sign and part signified, namely, the character which remains; finally, the inner significance, namely, sanctifying grace, and this sometimes stays and sometimes goes away.

> St. Thomas Aquinas: *Commentary on the Sentences,* 4, 3, 1, 4. (13th cent.)

You have been baptized, but think not that you are straightway a Christian. . . . The flesh is touched with salt: what then if the mind remains unsalted? The body is anointed, yet the mind remains unanointed. But if you are buried with Christ within, and already practice walking with Him in newness of life, I acknowledge you as a Christian.

> Erasmus: *Enchiridion.* (16th cent.)

If any one saith that in the Roman church, which is the mother and mistress of all churches, there is not the true doctrine concerning the sacrament of baptism; let him be anathema.

> Council of Trent, Session 7, Canon 3. (Mar. 3, 1547)

If any one saith that the baptism which is even given by heretics in the name of the Father, and of the Son, and of the Holy Ghost, with the intention of doing what the Church doth, is not true baptism; let him be anathema.

> Council of Trent, Session 7, Canon 4. (Mar. 3, 1547)

If any one saith that baptism is optional, that is, not necessary to salvation; let him be anathema.

> Council of Trent, Session 7, Canon 5. (Mar. 3, 1547)

If any one saith that one who has been baptized cannot, even if he would, lose grace, let him sin ever so much, unless he will not believe; let him be anathema.

> Council of Trent, Session 7, Canon 6. (Mar. 3, 1547)

If any one saith that little children, since they have not actual faith, are not after having received baptism to be reckoned amongst the faithful; and that for this cause they are to be rebaptized when they have attained to years of discretion; or that it is better that the baptism of such be omitted, than that while not believing by their own act they should be baptized in the faith alone of the Church; let him be anathema.

> Council of Trent, Session 7, Canon 13. (Mar. 3, 1547)

Baptism, the door and foundation of the sacraments and necessary for the salvation of all in actual fact or at least by desire (*in voto*), is not validly conferred unless true and natural water is used with the prescribed formula of words.

> Code of Canon Law, Canon 737. (20th cent.)

Baptism of Desire (*In Voto*)

Consequently, apart from baptism by water, a person may obtain the grace of baptism from Christ's passion because he is made like to Christ in His sufferings. . . . For a similar reason a person who is baptized neither by water nor by blood may obtain the grace of baptism through the power of the Holy Spirit, because the Spirit moves his heart to believe God and love Him and be contrite for his sins. This is called the baptism of penitence [or desire].

> St. Thomas Aquinas: *Summa Theologica*, 3, 66, 11. (13th cent.)

Blood and desire, both are called baptisms, for they supply the place of baptism and produce its effect, though neither are sacraments, since they are not official signs.

> St. Thomas Aquinas: *Summa Theologica*, 3, 66, 11. (13th cent.)

Barbarism

What else is a barbarism but a word either spelled or pronounced other than was the custom of those who spoke Latin before our time?

> St. Augustine: *De Doctrina Christiana*, 2, 13, 19. (4th cent.)

A barbarism is the uttering of a word with an error in a letter or in a quantity. . . . It is called barbarism from the barbarian peoples, since they were ignorant of the purity of Latin speech; for each nation becoming subject to the Romans, transmitted to Rome along with their wealth their faults, both of speech and of morals.

> St. Isidore: *Etymologies*, 1, 32. (7th cent.)

Bashfulness

Unknown, unkissed.

> John Heywood: *Proverbs*, 1, 11. (16th cent.)

Bastard

From whatever source men be born, if they follow not the vices of their parents, and worship God aright, they shall be honest and safe.

> St. Augustine: *On the Good of Marriage*. (5th cent.)

Bath

Let the bathing of the body and the use of baths be not incessant, but be granted at the usual interval of time, that is, once a month.

> St. Augustine: *Letter 211* (his Rule). (5th cent.)

Fresh from the bath get warm.

> School of Salerno, Code of Health. (11th cent.)

Bean

Though beans will nourish, their husks are prone
To cause in all a constipated tone.

> School of Salerno, Code of Health. (11th cent.)

Like a bean in a monk's hood.

> John Heywood: *Proverbs*, 2, 6. (16th cent.)

Beard

Take a hair from his beard.

> John Heywood: *Proverbs*, 2, 7. (16th cent.)

You cannot grow a beard in a moment of passion.

> G. K. Chesterton: *Tremendous Trifles*, 19. (20th cent.)

Beauty

A holy woman may be beautiful by the gift of nature, but she must not give occasion to lust. If beauty be hers, so far from setting it off she ought rather to obscure it.

> Tertullian: *Women's Dress*. (3rd cent.)

All that loveliness which passes through men's minds into their skillful hands comes from that supreme Loveliness Which is above our souls, Which my soul sighs for day and night. From the Supreme Beauty those who make and seek after exterior beauty derive the measure by which they judge of it, but not the measure by which it should be used. Yet this measure too is there, and they do not see it: for if they did they would not wander far from it, but would preserve their strength only for Thee and would not dissipate it upon delights that grow wearisome.

St. Augustine: *Confessions*, 10, 34. (5th cent.)

Too late I loved Thee, O Beauty of ancient days, yet ever new! too late I loved Thee! And lo! Thou wert within, and I abroad searching for Thee. Thou wert with me, but I was not with Thee.

St. Augustine: *Confessions*, 10, 27. (5th cent.)

Beauty is indeed a good gift of God; but that the good may not think it a great good, God dispenses it even to the wicked.

St. Augustine: *The City of God*, 15, 22. (5th cent.)

What beauty lies hidden in the wisdom of God! From it alone do all things derive that beauty which appeals to our eyes. But to see that beauty, to embrace it, our hearts have to be purified.

St. Augustine: *In Ps. 32, Enarr. 1*, 7. (5th cent.)

No one is safe for whom everyone languishes.

John of Salisbury: *Policraticus*, 8, 11, 297. (12th cent.)

A beautiful woman is quick to inspire love; an ugly one's passions are easily stirred.

John of Salisbury: *Policraticus*, 8, 11, 297. (12th cent.)

Beauty and the beautiful—these are one and the same in God.

St. Thomas Aquinas: *Exposition of the De Divinis Nominibus*, 4, lect. 5. (13th cent.)

Beauty relates to the cognitive faculty; for beautiful things are those which please when seen. Hence beauty consists in due proportion; for the senses delight in things duly proportioned, as in what is after their own kind—because even sense is a sort of reason just as is every cognitive faculty.

St. Thomas Aquinas: *Summa Theologica*, 1, 5, 4. (13th cent.)

Sweet beauty with sour beggary.

John Heywood: *Proverbs*, 1, 13. (16th cent.)

The crow thinketh her own birds fairest in the wood.

John Heywood: *Proverbs*, 2, 4. (16th cent.)

Brittle beauty, that nature made so frail,
Whereof the gift is small, and short the season;
Flowering today, tomorrow apt to fail,
Fickle treasure, abhorred of reason.

Henry Howard, Earl of Surrey: *The Frailty and Hurtfulness of Beauty*. (16th cent.)

Of all chaste birds the phoenix doth excel,
Of all strong beasts the lion bears the bell,
Of all sweet flowers the rose doth sweetest smell,
Of all fair maids my Rosalynde is fairest.

Thomas Lodge: *Of Rosalynde*. (16th cent.)

Union in distinction makes order; order produces agreement; and proportion and agreement, in complete and finished things, make beauty.

St. Francis de Sales: *Treatise on the Love of God*, 1, 1. (17th cent.)

When beauty fires the blood, how love exalts the mind.

> Dryden: *Cymon and Iphigenia.* (17th cent.)

Old as I am, for ladies' love unfit,
The power of beauty I remember yet.

> Dryden: *Cymon and Iphigenia.* (17th cent.)

Beauties in vain their pretty eyes may roll;
Charms strike the sight, but merit wins the soul.

> Pope: *The Rape of the Lock,* 5. (18th cent.)

The love of the beautiful will not conquer the world, but, like the voice of Orpheus, it may for a while carry it away captive.

> Card. Newman: *Historical Sketches,* 3. (19th cent.)

Beauty's elixir vitae, praise.

> Coventry Patmore: *The Angel in the House: Bk. 2 Prologue.* (19th cent.)

Dost thou still hope thou shalt be fair,
When no more fair to me?

> F. Thompson: *The Fair Inconstant.* (19th cent.)

Beauty is the only thing that time cannot harm.

> Oscar Wilde: *The English Renaissance.* (19th cent.)

It is not in the features one by one that beauty lies, but rather in the coincidence of them all.

> R. H. Benson: *Come Rack! Come Rope!* (20th cent.)

Only intense self-importance makes men say that they are independent of exterior beauty. It's far more natural and simple to like beauty. Every child does.

> R. H. Benson: *The Dawn of All.* (20th cent.)

Her fairness wedded to a star,
Is fairer than all lilies are,
And flowers within her eyes more white
Than moonlight on an April night.

Her wonder like a wind doth sing,
Wedded to the heart of spring.
And April, dawning in her eyes,
Reflects the wonder of the skies.

Her beauty lights the April day
With radiance of her chastity,
And innocence doth slumber now
Upon her candid April brow.

> Edward J. O'Brien: *Her Fairness, Wedded to a Star.* (20th cent.)

Whose closed eyes find the face of God
In patient prayer,
Has looked, as Euclid never could,
On Beauty bare.

> Sister Miriam: *Beauty Bare.* (20th cent.)

Beauty is the radiance of truth; the fragrance of goodness.

> V. McNabb: *Thoughts Twice-dyed.* (20th cent.)

Bed

Till meat fall in your mouth, will ye lie in bed?

> John Heywood: *Proverbs,* 1, 9. (16th cent.)

The dust shall never be thy bed:
A pillow for thee will I bring,
Stuft with down of angels' wing.

> Richard Crashaw: *The Tear.* (17th cent.)

Bee

The bee is more honored than other animals, not because she labors, but because she labors for others.

> St. John Chrysostom: *Homilies.* (4th cent.)

Their heads be full of bees.

> John Heywood: *Proverbs,* 1, 12. (16th cent.)

The wild bee reels from bough to bough
  With his furry coat and his gauzy
    wing,
Now in a lily-cup, and now
  Setting the jacinth bell a-swing.

> Oscar Wilde: *Her Voice.* (19th cent.)

Beggar

Beggars should be no choosers.

> John Heywood: *Proverbs,* 1, 10. (16th
> cent.)

As well as the beggar knoweth his bag.

> John Heywood: *Proverbs,* 1, 11. (16th
> cent.)

Begging

The petition of an empty hand is dangerous.

> John of Salisbury: *Policraticus,* 5, 10.
> (12th cent.)

    Anywhere a profit might accrue
Courteous he was and lowly of service
    too.
Natural gifts like his were hard to
    match.
He was the finest beggar of his batch,
And, for his begging-district, payed a
    rent;
His brethren did no poaching where he
    went.

> Chaucer: *Canterbury Tales: Prologue.*
> (The wanton friar) (Tr. Coghill) (14th
> cent.)

Ye beg at a wrong man's door.

> John Heywood: *Proverbs,* 1, 9. (16th
> cent.)

Beginning

Who that well his work beginneth
The rather a good end he winneth.

> John Gower: *Confessio Amantis.* (14th
> cent.)

In Christ's name let us *begin,* for Christ
has finished.

> R. H. Benson: *Christ in the Church.* (20th
> cent.)

Beginning and End

A hard beginning maketh a good ending.

> John Heywood: *Proverbs,* 1, 4. (16th
> cent.)

Of a good beginning, there cometh a
  good eende:
Nay, Lucifer began well, and now a
  fiend.
But of good beginning and ending,
  truth to tell,
The best way to end well, is to begin
  well.

> John Heywood: *Three Hundred Epigrams.*
> (16th cent.)

The beginning of good things is good,
the progress better, the end best.

> St. Francis de Sales: *Treatise on the Love
> of God,* 2, 19. (17th cent.)

Behavior

Would to God we had behaved ourselves
well in this world, even for one day.

> Thomas a Kempis: *The Imitation of
> Christ,* 1, 23. (15th cent.)

Being

Being in the highest sense of the word
is that which ever continues the same,
which is throughout like itself, which
cannot in any part be corrupted or
changed, which is not subject to time,
which admits of no variation in its present as compared with its condition at any
other time. This is being in its truest
sense. For in this significance of the word
being there is implied a nature which is
self-contained and which endures immutably. This can be said only of God, to
Whom there is nothing contrary, strictly
speaking. For the contrary of being is
non-being.

> St. Augustine: *De Moribus Ecclesiae
> Catholicae,* 2, 1. (4th cent.)

Every being therefore, even though it be
imperfect, is good so far as it is a being;
so far as it is defective, it is evil.

> St. Augustine: *Enchiridion,* 13. (5th cent.)

Every being that is not God, is God's creature. Now every creature of God is good (I Tim. 4, 4): and God is the greatest good. Therefore every being is good.

> St. Thomas Aquinas: *Summa Theologica,* I, 5, 3. (13th cent.)

See also Existence; God: His Existence

Belief

If the thing believed is incredible, it is also incredible that the incredible should have been so believed.

> St. Augustine: *The City of God,* 22. (5th cent.)

A thing may indeed be known or believed, and yet not loved; but it is impossible that a thing can be loved which is neither known nor believed.

> St. Augustine: *De Spiritu et Littera,* 64. (5th cent.)

You can force a man to enter a church, to approach the altar, to receive the Sacrament; but you cannot force him to believe.

> St. Augustine: *In Joann. Evang. Tract.,* 26, 2. (5th cent.)

Understanding is the reward of faith. Therefore seek not to understand that thou mayest believe, but believe that thou mayest understand.

> St. Augustine: *In Joann. Evang. Tract.,* 39, 6. (5th cent.)

We cannot have full knowledge all at once. We must start by believing; then afterwards we may be led on to master the evidence for ourselves.

> St. Thomas Aquinas: *Disputations Concerning Truth,* 14, 10. (13th cent.)

Unbelievers who have never accepted the Faith should be subjected to no compulsion at all, for belief is an act of free-will. Given the power, however, the faithful may use force to prevent unbelievers from impeding the Faith by

blasphemy, or evil persuasion, or open persecution.

> St. Thomas Aquinas: *Summa Theologica,* 2-2, 10, 8. (13th cent.)

Whoever believes, assents to someone's words; so that in every form of belief, the person to whose words assent is given seems to hold the chief place and to be the end as it were; while the things by holding which one assents to that person hold a secondary place. Consequently he that holds the Christian faith aright, assents, by his will, to Christ, in those things which truly belong to His doctrine.

> St. Thomas Aquinas: *Summa Theologica,* 2-2, 11, 1. (13th cent.)

It is natural for the mind to believe, and for the will to love; so, failing real objects, they must fix on false ones.

> Pascal: *Pensées.* (17th cent.)

There are three roads to belief: reason, habit, revelation.

> Pascal: *Pensées.* (17th cent.)

It is absurd to argue men, as to torture them, into believing.

> Card. Newman: *Oxford University Sermons.* (19th cent.)

Thus, as regards the Catholic creed, if we really believe that our Lord is God, we believe all that is meant by such a belief; or, else, we are not in earnest, when we profess to believe the proposition. In the act of believing it all, we forthwith commit ourselves by anticipation to believe truths which at present we do not believe, because they have never come before us —we limit henceforth the range of our private judgment in prospect by the conditions, whatever they are, of that dogma.

> Card. Newman: *Grammar of Assent,* 5. (19th cent.)

It is the nature of man to believe the more because another believes, and to derive additional knowledge from an-other's mode of knowing.

Coventry Patmore: *Religio Poetae.* (19th cent.)

If any one shall say that the condition of the faithful and of those who have not yet attained to the only true faith is on a par, so that Catholics may have just cause for doubting with suspended assent the faith which they have already received under the teaching of the Church, until they shall have obtained a scientific dem-onstration of the credibility and truth of their faith; let him be anathema.

Vatican Council, Session 3, Canon 6. (Apr. 24, 1870)

When once one believes in a creed, one is proud of its complexity, as scientists are proud of the complexity of science. It shows how rich it is in discoveries. If it is right at all, it is a compliment to say that it's elaborately right. A stick might fit a hole or a stone a hollow by accident. But a key and a lock are both complex. And if a key fits a lock, you know it is the right key.

G. K. Chesterton: *Orthodoxy.* (20th cent.)

No one is to be forced against his will to embrace the Catholic faith.

Code of Canon Law, Canon 1351. (20th cent.)

There has always been a wall of division between the learned and the simple even in the acceptance of the same belief. The learned are accustomed to abstract ideas and use the sensible as a tuning-fork to keep their ideas in tune. The simple, on the other hand, do not grasp the meaning of these ideas unless they are translated into examples which can be seen or touched or handled. So sharply are these two classes separated that in certain phi-losophies and in certain religions the in-ner truth is supposed to be reserved for an *élite,* while the common people are left to amuse themselves with burlesques of the truth, what in fact often resolves itself into superstitious practices. That

the Christian religion has always escaped this danger would be a hazardous claim. But it is certainly true that Catholic au-thority tries to subordinate all devotion to doctrine and refuses to allow emotion or fancy to run away with the truth to be taught.

M. C. D'Arcy: *Death and Life.* (20th cent.)

See also Catholic Faith; Faith; Faith and Knowledge; Faith and Reason

Believer

The future belongs to believers and not to sceptics and doubters. The future be-longs to those who love, not to those who hate.

Pope Pius XII: *Address to the College of Cardinals.* (June 2, 1947)

Bell

The vesper bell from far,
That seems to mourn for the expiring day.

Dante: *Purgatorio, Canto 8.* (14th cent.)

She beareth the bell.

John Heywood: *Proverbs,* 1, 10. (16th cent.)

Hark, how chimes the passing bell,
There's no music to a knell.

James Shirley: *The Passing Bell.* (17th cent.)

Those evening bells! those evening bells!
How many a tale their music tells!
Of youth, and home, and that sweet time
When I last heard their soothing chime.

Thomas Moore: *Those Evening Bells.* (19th cent.)

With deep affection and recollection,
I often think of the Shandon bells,
Whose sounds so wild would, in days of childhood,
Fling round my cradle their magic spells—

On this I ponder, where'er I wander,
   And thus grow fonder, sweet Cork,
      of thee;
      With the bells of Shandon,
      That sound so grand on
The pleasant waters of the river Lee.

   F. Mahony (Fr. Prout): *The Bells of
   Shandon.* (19th cent.)

And every note of every bell
Sang Gabriel! rang Gabriel!
In the tower that is left the tale to tell
Of Gabriel, the archangel.

   Charles W. Stoddard: *The Bells of San
   Gabriel.* (19th cent.)

      Brief, on a flying night,
         From the shaken tower,
      A flock of bells take flight.
         And go with the hour.

   Alice Meynell: *Chimes.* (20th cent.)

Beloved

O pause between the sobs of cares;
   O thought within all thought that is;
Trance between laughters unawares:
   Thou art the shape of melodies,
And thou the ecstasy of prayers!

   Alice Meynell: *To the Beloved.* (19th
   cent.)

Benedictine Order

St. Benedict's true contribution to European civilization was not that his monks
were pioneers and builders and scholars
and guardians of the classical tradition.
These were only insignificant by-prod-
ucts of the wonderfully simple and
Christian communal life that was led in
the early Benedictine monasteries. The
influence and the example of that life
leavened, more than did anything else,
the Europe that had been invaded by
wave after wave of barbarian tribes. That
influence and example kept alive the central warmth of peace and unity among
men in a world that seemed to be wrestling with the ice of death.

   Thomas Merton: *The Waters of Siloe.*
   (20th cent.)

Benediction

See Blessed Sacrament; Blessing

Benefaction

We should not accept in silence the benefactions of God, but return thanks for
them.

   St. Basil: *The Morals,* 55, 1. (4th cent.)

Bereavement

Dear Lord, receive my son, whose win-
   ning love
To me was like a friendship, far above
The course of nature, or his tender age,
Could all my bitter griefs assuage;
Let his pure soul ordain'd sev'n years
   to be
In that frail body, which was part of me,
Remain my pledge in heav'n, as sent to
   shew,
How to this port at ev'ry step I go.

   Sir John Beaumont: *Of My Dear Son,
   Gervase Beaumont.* (17th cent.)

Best

The best is best cheap.

   John Heywood: *Proverbs,* 2, 7. (16th
   cent.)

   'Tis best by far,
   When best things are not possible,
   To make the best of those that are.

   Coventry Patmore: *L'Allegro.* (19th cent.)

Betrothal

As regards the marriage ceremony, you
inquire if a man may take in wedlock a
girl betrothed to another. We forbid this
absolutely, for the blessing which the
priest bestows upon her before marriage
is like a sacrilege among the faithful, if
it is marred by any such dishonor.

   Pope Siricius: *Decretal Letter to Himerius,
   Bishop of Tarragona,* 5. (Feb. 10, 385)

Betting

If the wager were but a butterfly I would never award him one wing.

St. Thomas More. (16th cent.)

Bible, Holy

The Scriptures of God, whether belonging to Christian or Jew, are much more ancient than any secular literature.

Tertullian: *The Testimony of the Christian Soul.* (3rd cent.)

Thanks be to the Gospel, by means of which we also, who did not see Christ when He came into this world, seem to be with Him when we read His deeds.

St. Ambrose: *Concerning Widows,* 62. (4th cent.)

Divine Scripture is the feast of wisdom, and the single books are the various dishes.

St. Ambrose: *On the Duties of the Clergy,* 1, 165. (4th cent.)

To be ignorant of the Scripture is not to know Christ.

St. Jerome: *In Isaiam, Prol.* (5th cent.)

Love the knowledge of the Scriptures and you will not love the errors of the flesh.

St. Jerome: *Letters,* 125, 11. (5th cent.)

Thus, since men had not the strength to discover the truth by pure reason and therefore we needed the authority of Holy Writ, I was coming to believe that You would certainly not have bestowed such eminent authority on those Scriptures throughout the world, unless it had been Your will that by them men should believe in You and in them seek You.

St. Augustine: *Confessions,* 6, 5. (5th cent.)

Indeed the authority of Scripture seemed to be more to be revered and more worthy of devoted faith in that it was at once a book that all could read and read easily, and yet preserved the majesty of its mystery in the deepest part of its meaning: for it offers itself to all in the plainest words and the simplest expressions, yet demands the closest attention of the most serious minds.

St. Augustine: *Confessions,* 6, 5. (5th cent.)

Marvellous is the profundity of Thy Scriptures. Their surface lies before us, flattering us as we flatter children. But marvellous is their profundity, O my God, marvellous is their profundity. To gaze into it is a shuddering, the shudder of awe, the shudder of love.

St. Augustine: *Confessions,* 12, 14. (5th cent.)

A letter from our fatherland.

St. Augustine: *In Ps. 64, Enarr,* 1, 2. (5th cent.)

It always was, and is today, the usual practice of Catholics to test the true faith by two methods: first, by the authority of the divine Canon, and then, by the tradition of the Catholic Church. Not that the Canon is insufficient in itself in each case. But, because most [false] interpreters of the Divine Word make use of their own arbitrary judgment and thus fall into various opinions and errors, the understanding of Holy Scripture must conform to the single rule of Catholic teaching—and this especially in regard to those questions upon which the foundations of all Catholic dogma are laid.

St. Vincent of Lerins: *Commonitoria,* 29. (5th cent.)

The Bible is a stream wherein the elephant may swim and the lamb may wade.

Pope St. Gregory I. (6th cent.)

Holy writ is set before the eye of the mind like a kind of mirror, that we may see our inward face in it; for therein we learn the deformities, therein we learn the beauties that we possess; there we are made sensible what progress we are making, there too how far we are from proficiency.

Pope St. Gregory I: *Morals,* 2, 1. (6th cent.)

Holy Writ by the manner of its speech transcends every science, because in one and the same sentence, while it describes a fact, it reveals a mystery.

Pope St. Gregory I: *Morals*, 20, 1. (5th cent.)

Whatever you read in the Old Testament, even though it actually happened, you must interpret spiritually and glean from the truth of history the sense of spiritual understanding.

St. Leander: *Rule*, 7. (6th cent.)

The New Testament is so called because it brings in the new. For men do not learn it, except those who have been renewed from their former state through grace and now belong to the New Testament, which is the kingdom of heaven.

St. Isidore: *Etymologies*, 6, 1. (7th cent.)

The Divine Law is to be understood in a triple manner: first, historically; second, tropologically; third, mystically. It is to be interpreted historically according to the letter, tropologically according to the moral sense, and mystically according to the spiritual significance.

St. Isidore: *Sentences*, 1, 18. (7th cent.)

The whole series of the divine Scriptures is interpreted in a fourfold way. In all holy books one should ascertain what everlasting truths are therein intimated, what deeds are narrated, what future events are foretold, and what commands or counsels are there contained.

St. Bede the Venerable: *De Tabernaculo*, 1. (8th cent.)

There can be no falsehood anywhere in the literal sense of Holy Scripture.

St. Thomas Aquinas: *Summa Theologica*, 1. (13th cent.)

All the senses of Holy Scripture are built on the literal sense, from which alone, and not from allegorical passages, can arguments be drawn. The spiritual sense brings nothing needful to faith which is not elsewhere clearly conveyed by the literal sense.

St. Thomas Aquinas: *Summa Theologica*, 1, 1, 10. (13th cent.)

Holy Writ expresses truth in two ways, first, through the literal sense, when things are signified by words; secondly, through the spiritual sense, when things are signified through other things.

St. Thomas Aquinas: 7 *Quodlibets*, 6, 14. (13th cent.)

Speech to your wit must needs be tempered so,
  Since but from things of sense it apprehends
  What it makes apt for the intellect to know.

Scripture to your capacity condescends
  For this cause, and a foot and hand will feign
  For God, yet something other it intends.

Dante: *Paradiso, Canto 4*. (Tr. Binyon) (14th cent.)

Yet even this to Heaven is less offence
  And more endurable than when Holy Writ
  Is cast aside or wrested from its sense.

They think not how much blood the sowing of it
  In the world cost, nor what blessed reward
  Is theirs, who humbly to its rule submit.

Each vies with the other to bring out a hoard
  Of fond inventions, which the preachers take
  And furbish: of the Gospel not a word.

Dante: *Paradiso, Canto 29*. (Tr. Binyon) (14th cent.)

If thou didst know the whole Bible by heart, and the sayings of all the philosophers, what would it all profit thee without the love of God and His grace?

> Thomas a Kempis: *The Imitation of Christ*, I, I. (15th cent.)

The Church was gathered and the faith was believed before ever any part of the New Testament was put in writing. And which writing was or is the true Scripture, neither Luther nor Tyndale knoweth but by the credence that they give to the Church. . . . Why should not Luther and Tyndale as well believe the Church, in that it telleth them this thing did Christ and his apostles say, as they must believe the Church (or else believe nothing) in that it telleth them this thing did Christ's evangelists and apostles write.

> St. Thomas More: *Apology*. (Works, 852. 1557) (1553)

And therefore if these men have now perceived so late, that the Scripture hath been misunderstanden all this while, and that of all those holy doctors no man could understand it; then am I too old at this age to begin to study it now. And trust these men's cunning, cousin, that dare I not, in nowise, sith I cannot see nor perceive no cause, wherefore I should think, that these men might not now in the understanding of Scripture, as well be deceived themself, as they bear us in hand, that all those other have been all this while before.

> St. Thomas More: *Dialogue of Comfort*. (With reference to the novel interpretations of the Reformers) (16th cent.)

In things of faith and morals belonging to the building up of Christian doctrine, that is to be considered the true sense of holy Scripture, which has been held and is held by our holy mother the Church, whose place it is to judge of the true sense and interpretation of the Scriptures; and, therefore . . . it is permitted to no one to interpret holy Scripture against such sense or also against the unanimous agreement of the fathers.

> Council of Trent, Session 3, chap. 2. (1546)

If anyone should not receive as sacred and canonical the entire books with all their parts, as they are wont to be read in the Catholic Church and are contained in the old Vulgate Latin edition, and if anyone should knowingly and of set purpose despise the aforesaid traditions, let him be anathema.

> Decree of the Council of Trent, Session 4, April 8, 1546.

The music of the gospel leads us home.

> F. Faber: *The Pilgrims of the Night*. (19th cent.)

[Scripture] cannot, as it were, be mapped, or its contents catalogued; but after all our diligence, to the end of our lives and to the end of the Church, it must be an unexplored and unsubdued land, with heights and valleys, forests and streams, on the right and left of our path and close about us, full of concealed wonders and choice treasures. Of no doctrine whatever, which does not actually contradict what has been delivered, can it be peremptorily asserted that it is not in Scripture; of no reader, whatever be his study of it, can it be said that he has mastered every doctrine which it contains.

> Card. Newman: *Development of Christian Doctrine*, 2. (19th cent.)

Reading, as we do, the Gospels from our youth up, we are in danger of becoming so familiar with them as to be dead to their force, and to view them as mere history.

> Card. Newman: *Grammar of Assent*, 4. (19th cent.)

A veil is spread between this world and the next. We, mortal men, range up and down in it, to and fro, and see nothing. . . . In the Gospel this veil is not removed: it remains; but every now and then marvelous disclosures are made to us of what is behind it.

> Card. Newman. (19th cent.)

A competent religious guide must be clear and intelligible to all, so that every one may fully understand the true meaning of the instructions it contains. Is the Bible a book intelligible to all? Far from it; it is full of obscurities and difficulties not only for the illiterate, but even for the learned.

> Card. Gibbons: *The Faith of Our Fathers,* 8. (19th cent.)

The language of the Bible is employed to express, under the inspiration of the Holy Ghost, many things which are beyond the power and scope of the reason of man—that is to say, divine mysteries and all that is related to them. There is sometimes in such passages a fulness and a hidden depth of meaning which the letter hardly expresses and which the laws of interpretation hardly warrant. Moreover, the literal sense itself frequently admits other senses, adapted to illustrate dogma or to confirm morality.

> Pope Leo XIII: *Providentissimus Deus.* (Nov. 18, 1893)

Seeing that the same God is the author both of the sacred books and of the doctrine committed to the Church, it is clearly impossible that any teaching can, by legitimate means, be extracted from the former which shall in any respect be at variance with the latter. Hence it follows that all interpretation is foolish or false which either makes the sacred writers disagree one with another, or is opposed to the doctrine of the Church.

> Pope Leo XIII: *Providentissimus Deus.* (Nov. 18, 1893)

Although the studies of non-Catholics, used with prudence, may sometimes be of use to the Catholic student, he should nevertheless bear well in mind . . . that the sense of holy Scripture can nowhere be found incorrupt outside the Church, and cannot be expected to be found in writers who, being without the true faith, only know the bark of sacred Scripture, and never attain the pith.

> Pope Leo XIII: *Providentissimus Deus.* (Nov. 18, 1893)

As it has been clearly shown by experience that, if the holy Bible in the vernacular is generally permitted without distinction, more harm than utility is thereby caused owing to human temerity: all versions in the vernacular, even by Catholics, are altogether prohibited, unless approved by the Holy See, or published under the vigilant care of the bishops with annotations taken from the fathers of the Church and learned Catholic writers.

> Pope Leo XIII: *Ap. Const. Officiorum ac Munerum.* (Jan. 25, 1897)

The Iliad is only great because all life is a battle, the Odyssey because all life is a journey, the Book of Job because all life is a riddle.

> G. K. Chesterton: *The Defendant.* (20th cent.)

Bible: Its Divine Inspiration

Only those books of Scripture which are called canonical have I learned to hold in such honor as to believe their authors have not erred in any way in writing them. But other authors I so read as not to deem anything in their works to be true, merely on account of their having so thought and written, whatever may have been their holiness and learning.

> St. Augustine: *Epist. ad Hieron.,* 19, 1. (5th cent.)

But who was the writer, it is very superfluous to inquire; since at any rate the Holy Spirit is confidently believed to have been the Author. He then Himself wrote them, Who dictated the things that should be written. He did Himself write them Who both was present as the Inspirer in that saint's work, and by the mouth of the writer has consigned to us His acts as patterns for our imitation.

> Pope St. Gregory I: *Morals, Pref.* (6th cent.)

The Emperor of heaven, the Lord of men and of angels, has sent you His epistles for your life's advantage—and yet you neglect to read them eagerly. Study them,

I beg you, and meditate daily on the words of your Creator. Learn the heart of God in the words of God, that you may sigh more eagerly for things eternal, that your soul may be kindled with greater longings for heavenly joys.

Pope St. Gregory I: *Letters*, 5, 46. (6th cent.)

But whoever understands Holy Scripture otherwise than according to the meaning of the Holy Spirit, by Whom it was written, although he may not withdraw from the Church, still he can be called a heretic.

St. Isidore: *Etymologies*, 8, 5. (7th cent.)

The abundant dew
Of the Holy Spirit Which is so outpoured
Upon the ancient parchments and the new
Is argument compelling my accord
With such precise proof that, compared with it,
All demonstration else appeareth blurred.

Dante: *Paradiso, Canto 24*. (Tr. Binyon) (14th cent.)

[The holy synod] following the examples of the orthodox fathers, receives and venerates with an equal affection of piety and reverence all the books both of the Old and of the New Testament—seeing that one God is the Author of both—as also the said traditions, those pertaining to faith as well as to morals, as having been dictated either by Christ's own word of mouth or by the Holy Ghost, and preserved in the Catholic Church by a continuous succession.

Decree of the Council of Trent, Session 4, Apr. 8, 1546.

If any one shall not receive as sacred and canonical the books of Holy Scripture entire with all their parts, as the holy synod of Trent has enumerated them, or shall deny that they have been divinely inspired; let him be anathema.

Vatican Council, Session 3, Canon 3. (Apr. 24, 1870)

For sacred Scripture is not like other books. Dictated by the Holy Ghost, it contains things of the deepest importance, which in many instances are most difficult and obscure. To understand and explain such things there is always required the "coming" of the same Holy Ghost; that is to say, His light and His grace.

Pope Leo XIII: *Providentissimus Deus*. (Nov. 18, 1893)

It is absolutely wrong and forbidden either to narrow inspiration to certain parts only of holy Scripture or to admit that the sacred writer has erred.... For all the books which the Church receives as sacred and canonical are written wholly and entirely, with all their parts, at the dictation of the Holy Ghost; and so far is it from being possible that any error can co-exist with inspiration, that inspiration is not only essentially incompatible with error, but excludes and rejects it as absolutely and necessarily as it is impossible that God Himself, the supreme Truth, can utter that which is not true.

Pope Leo XIII: *Providentissimus Deus*. (Nov. 18, 1893)

Let the interpreter use every care, and take advantage of every indication provided by the most recent research, in an endeavor to discern the distinctive genius of the sacred writer, his condition in life, the age in which he lived, the written or oral sources he may have used, and the literary forms he employed. He will thus be able better to discover who the sacred writer was and what he meant by what he wrote.

Pope Pius XII: *Divino Afflante*, 38. (Sept. 30, 1943)

Bigotry

Bigotry is the infliction of our own unproved first principles on others, and the treating others with scorn or hatred for not accepting them.

Card. Newman: *Present Position of Catholics in England*, 7. (19th cent.)

Bigotry does not consist in a man being convinced he is right; that is not bigotry, but sanity. Bigotry consists in a man being convinced that another man must be wrong in everything, because he is wrong in a particular belief; that he must be wrong, even in thinking that he honestly believes he is right.

G. K. Chesterton: *The Common Man.* (20th cent.)

Biography

Few deserve a biography, and to the undeserving none should be given.

Archb. Ireland: *Introd. to Elliott's Hecker.* (19th cent.)

The only biography that is really possible is autobiography.

G. K. Chesterton: *A Handful of Authors.* (20th cent.)

Bird

Better the bird in hand than ten in the wood.

John Heywood: *Proverbs,* 1, 11. (16th cent.)

It is a foul bird that defileth his own nest.

John Heywood: *Proverbs,* 2, 5. (16th cent.)

The birds are flown.

John Heywood: *Three Hundred Epigrams,* 280. (16th cent.)

O little bird, I'd be
  A poet like to thee,
Singing my native song—
Brief to the ear, but long
  To love and memory.

J. B. Tabb: *To a Songster.* (19th cent.)

The dear Lord God, of His glories weary—
  Christ our Lord had the heart of a boy—
Made Him birds in a moment merry,
  Bade them soar and sing for His joy.

Katharine T. Hinkson: *The Making of Birds.* (20th cent.)

Birth

If thou grievest for the dead, mourn also for those who are born into the world; for as the one thing is of nature, so is the other too of nature.

St. John Chrysostom: *Homilies.* (4th cent.)

Others have to be born, and the children of the citizens of today are born precisely in order to drive out their parents. For a boy is born so that he may one day say to his father: What are you doing here? Those who follow, those who are born, drive out those who preceded them. But there, in the hereafter, we shall all live on together. There will be no successors there, for neither will there be departures.

St. Augustine: *In Ps. 62 Enarr. 1, 14.* (5th cent.)

            Till skies be fugitives,
Till time, the hidden root of change, updries,
Are birth and death inseparable on earth;
For they are twain yet one, and death is birth.

F. Thompson: *Ode to the Setting Sun.* (19th cent.)

Birth, High

Men do not choose among navigators the one who is of highest birth to command a ship.

Pascal: *Pensées,* 6. (17th cent.)

Prodigious actions may as well be done
By weaver's issue, as by prince's son.

Dryden: *Absalom and Achitophel,* 1. (17th cent.)

Yet oh that fate, propitiously inclin'd,
Had rais'd my birth, or had debas'd my mind.

Dryden: *Absalom and Achitophel.* (17th cent.)

How happy had he been, if destiny
Had higher placed his birth, or not so
    high!

Dryden: *Absalom and Achitophel.* (17th
cent.)

Birth-Control

Everyone should remember that the
union of the two sexes is meant only for
the purpose of procreation.

Lactantius: *Divinae institutiones,* 6. (4th
cent.)

Intercourse with even a lawful wife is
unlawful and wicked if the conception
of offspring be prevented.

St. Augustine: *Conjugal Adultery,* 2.
(5th cent.)

Nuptial commerce, which is so holy, just
and commendable in itself, and so profitable to the commonwealth, is, nevertheless, in certain cases dangerous to
those that exercise it, as when the order
appointed for the procreation of children
is violated and perverted; in which case,
according as one departs more or less
from it, the sins are more or less abominable, but always mortal.

St. Francis De Sales: *Introduction to the
Devout Life,* 39. (17th cent.)

Any use whatsoever of matrimony exercised in such a way that the act is deliberately frustrated in its natural power to
generate life is an offence against the law
of God and of nature, and those who indulge in such are branded with the guilt
of a grave sin.

Pope Pius XI: *Casti Connubii.* (Dec. 31,
1930)

Those are not considered as acting against
nature who, in the married state, use their
right in the proper manner, even though,
on account of natural reasons, either of
time or of defect, new life cannot be
brought forth.

Pope Pius XI: *Casti Connubii.* (Dec. 31,
1930)

See also Abortion

Birthday

O God, the Life of the faithful, the Savior and Guardian of those that fear
Thee, Who, after the expiration of a
year, hast been pleased to bring Thy
servant N. to this his natural birthday;
increase in him the grace of the Protector
of life, and multiply his days with many
years; that having by Thy favor been carried through a happy life, he may be enabled to attain the height of heavenly
joys.

Gelasian Sacramentary, Collect. (5th to 7th
cent.)

My birthday!—what a different sound
    That word had in my youthful years;
And how each time the day comes
        round,
    Less and less white its mark appears.

Thomas Moore: *My Birthday.* (19th cent.)

Bishop

Our apostles also knew, through our
Lord Jesus Christ, that there would be
contention over the bishop's office. So,
for this cause, having received complete
foreknowledge, they appointed the
above-mentioned men, and afterwards
gave them a permanent character (*epi-
monen*), so that, as they died, other
approved men should succeed to their
ministry. Those, therefore, who were appointed by the apostles or afterwards by
other eminent men, with the consent of
the whole Church, and who ministered
blamelessly to the flock of Christ . . . we
consider are not justly deposed from
their ministry.

St. Clement I: *Letter to the Corinthians,*
44, 1-4. (1st cent.)

And let a man respect the bishop all the
more if he sees him to be a man of few
words. For, whoever is sent by the Master to run His house, we ought to receive
him as we would receive the Master Himself. It is obvious, therefore, that we
ought to regard the bishop as we would
the Lord Himself.

St. Ignatius of Antioch: *Letter to the
Ephesians,* 6. (2nd cent.)

Be obedient to your bishop and to one another, as Jesus Christ in His human nature was subject to the Father and as the apostles were to Christ and the Father. In this way there will be union of body and spirit.

> St. Ignatius of Antioch: *Letter to the Magnesians,* 13. (2nd cent.)

It is not lawful to baptize or to hold an agape without the consent of the bishop. On the other hand, whatever has his approval is pleasing to God. Thus, whatever you do will be safe and valid.

> St. Ignatius of Antioch: *Letter to the Smyrnaeans,* 8. (2nd cent.)

Elect therefore for yourselves, bishops and deacons worthy of the Lord, humble men and not covetous, and faithful and well tested; for they also serve you in the ministry of the prophets and teachers.

> Teaching of the Twelve Apostles, 15. (2nd cent.)

For the glory of the Church is the glory of the bishop.

> St. Cyprian: *Letters,* 6, 1. (3rd cent.)

Let the bishop be ordained, being in all things without fault, chosen by all the people.

> St. Hippolytus: *The Apostolic Tradition,* 2. (3rd cent.)

Father, *Who knowest the hearts of all,* grant this Thy servant Whom Thou hast chosen for the episcopate to feed Thy holy flock and serve as Thine high priest, that he may minister blamelessly by night and day, that he may unceasingly behold and propitiate Thy countenance and offer to Thee the gifts of Thy holy Church. And that by the high priestly Spirit he may have authority *to forgive sins* according to Thy command, *to assign lots* according to Thy bidding, to *loose every bond* according to the authority Thou gavest to the apostles, and that he may please Thee in meekness and a pure heart, *offering* to Thee a *sweet-smelling savor.*

> St. Hippolytus: *The Apostolic Tradition,* 3. (Excerpt from earliest known prayer for the consecration of a bishop.) (3rd cent.)

Do thou, therefore, O bishop, teach and rebuke, and loose by forgiveness. And know thy place, that it is that of God Almighty, and that thou hast received authority to forgive sins.

> Anonymous: *Didascalia Apostolorum,* 7. (3rd cent.)

For the bishops ought to be nourished from the revenues of the Church, but not to devour them.

> Anonymous: *Didascalia Apostolorum,* 8. (3rd cent.)

The bishop shall be appointed by all the bishops of the eparchy (province); if that is not possible on account of pressing necessity, or on account of the length of journeys, three bishops at the least shall meet, and proceed to the imposition of hands with the permission of those absent in writing. The confirmation of what has been done belongs by right, in each eparchy, to the metropolitan.

> Council of Nicaea, Can. 4. (325)

It is fitting that the possessions of the Church should be guarded with care and in all good conscience, with faith in God, Who sees and judges all. They must be managed under the supervision and direction of the bishop to whom the souls of the whole people in his diocese are entrusted.

> Council of Antioch, Can. 24. (341)

Thou Who didst send the Lord Jesus for the gain of the world, Thou Who through Him didst choose the apostles, Thou Who generation by generation dost ordain holy bishops, O God of truth, make this bishop also a living bishop, holy [*or* worthy] of the succession of the holy apostles, and give him grace and the divine Spirit, that Thou didst freely give to all Thy own servants and prophets and patriarchs: make him worthy to shepherd Thy flock and let him continue blamelessly and without offence in the bishopric through Thine only-begotten Jesus Christ.

Sacramentary of Serapion, Prayer for the Consecration of a Bishop (14). (4th cent.)

To be a bishop (*sacerdos*) is much, to deserve to be one is more.

St. Jerome: *Letters,* 49, 4. (4th cent.)

Be obedient to your bishop and welcome him as the parent of your soul.

St. Jerome: *Letters,* 52, 7. (4th cent.)

Let him understand that he is no bishop, who loves to rule and not be useful to his flock.

St. Augustine: *The City of God,* 19, 19. (5th cent.)

O holy Lord, Father almighty, eternal God, Honor of all dignities which serve unto Thy glory in sacred orders. O God, Who in the secret communings of familiar intercourse, giving instruction unto Thy servant Moses concerning, among other branches of divine worship, the nature of sacerdotal vesture, didst order that Thy chosen one Aaron should be clad in mystic robes during the sacred functions. . . . The adornment of our minds fulfils what was expressed by the outward vesture of that ancient priesthood, and now brightness of souls rather than splendor of raiment commends the pontifical glory unto us. Because even those things which were then sightly unto the eyes of the flesh, demanded rather that the eyes of the spirit should understand the things they signified. And therefore we beseech Thee, O Lord, grant bountifully this grace to this Thy servant, whom Thou hast chosen to the ministry of the high priesthood, so that whatever things those vestments signify by the refulgence of gold, the splendor of jewels, and the variety of diversified works, this may shine forth in his character and his actions. *Fill up in Thy priest the perfection of Thy ministry and sanc-*

tify with the dew of Thy heavenly ointment this Thy servant decked out with the ornaments of all beauty.

Roman Pontifical, Consecration of a Bishop, Prayer *Domine Sancte . . . honor omnium dignitatum.* (Leonine, ca. 5th cent.)

Grant to him, O Lord, the ministry of reconciliation in word and in deed, in the power of signs and of wonders. Let his speech and his preaching be not in the persuasive words of human wisdom, but in the showing of the Spirit and of power. Give to him, O Lord, the keys of the kingdom of heaven, so that he may make use of, not boast of the power which Thou bestowest unto edification, not unto destruction. Whatsoever he shall bind upon earth, let it be bound likewise in heaven and whatsoever he shall loose upon earth, let it likewise be loosed in heaven. Whose sins he shall retain, let them be retained, and do Thou remit the sins of whomsoever he shall remit. . . . Grant to him, O Lord, an episcopal chair for ruling Thy Church and the people committed to him. Be his authority, his power, his strength. Multiply upon him Thy blessing and Thy grace, so that by Thy gift he may be fitted ever to obtain Thy mercy, and by Thy grace may be faithful.

Roman Pontifical, Consecration of a Bishop, cont. of Prayer *Domine Sancte . . . honor omnium Dignitatum.* (First part Gelasian, ca. 6th cent.; last part Leonine, ca. 5th cent.)

O Master, Lord our God, who through thy glorious apostle Paul hast established orders and degrees for the dispensation of thy holy and pure mysteries before thy holy altar, who hast appointed apostles, prophets, and doctors; do thou, O Master of all, look upon this thy servant who has been chosen and deemed worthy to receive by the imposition of my hands, a sinner, and those of my colleagues and fellow-bishops here present, the heavy yoke of the gospel and the charge of a bishop. Strengthen him by the presence, the power and the grace of thy Holy Spirit, as thou didst strengthen the holy apostles and prophets, and as thou didst anoint the high priests. Make his ministry blameless and, adorning him with all gravity, make him holy, that he may be worthy to offer you prayers for the salvation of the people and be heard by you.

> Byzantine Euchologion, Prayer for the Consecration of a Bishop. (5th to 8th cent.)

The pontiff [bishop] is the chief of the priests. . . . For he ordains priests and levites [deacons]. He has power over all ranks of the clergy; he points out what each one should do.

> St. Isidore: *Etymologies,* 7, 12. (7th cent.)

Jesu, the world's Redeemer, hear;
Thy bishop's fadeless crown, draw near:
Accept with gentlest love today
The prayers and praises that we pay.

> Roman Breviary, Feasts of Confessor Bishops, Hymn *Jesu Redemptor omnium* at Lauds. (Tr. J. Chambers) (Ambrosian, 8th cent.)

Receive the Holy Spirit. (Accipe Spiritum Sanctum.)

> Roman Pontifical, Consecration of a Bishop, Formula pronounced by the consecrator and by the co-consecrators, as they lay their hands on the head of the person being consecrated. (ca. 10th cent.)

It is the duty of a bishop to judge, interpret, consecrate, ordain, offer sacrifice, baptize and confirm.

> Roman Pontifical, Consecration of a Bishop, Introductory Formula. (ca. 10th cent.)

If any one saith that bishops are not superior to priests; or that they have not the power of confirming and ordaining; or that the power which they possess is common to them and to priests . . . let him be anathema.

> Council of Trent, Session 23, Canon 7. (July 15, 1563)

Thou couldst a people raise, but couldst
    not rule:—
  So, gentle one,

Heaven set thee free,—for, ere thy
    years were full,
  Thy work was done;
According thee the lot thou lovedst
    best,
To muse upon the past,—to serve, yet
    be at rest.

> Card. Newman: *St. Gregory Nazianzen.* (19th cent.)

Each bishop on his throne, surrounded by his priests, judicially binding or loosing the souls of men by the power of the keys, is the judge of arbitration to avert the judgment of the last day.

> Card. Manning: *The Eternal Priesthood.* (19th cent.)

If the authority of Peter and his successors is plenary and supreme, it is not to be regarded as the sole authority. For He Who made Peter the foundation of the Church also *chose twelve, whom He called apostles* (Luke 6, 13); and just as it is necessary that the authority of Peter should be perpetuated in the Roman pontiff, so by the fact that the bishops succeed the apostles they inherit their ordinary power, and thus the episcopal order necessarily belongs to the essential constitution of the Church.

> Pope Leo XIII: *Satis Cognitum.* (June 20, 1896)

[Bishops] are not to be looked upon as vicars of the Roman pontiffs, because they exercise a power really their own, and are most truly called the ordinary pastors of the peoples over whom they rule.

> Pope Leo XIII: *Satis Cognitum.* (June 20, 1896)

Bishops are the successors of the apostles and by divine institution are placed over particular churches which they govern with ordinary jurisdiction under the authority of the Roman pontiff.

> Code of Canon Law, Canon 329, 1. (20th cent.)

All bishops in the year when they are bound to make their quinquennial report should betake themselves to Rome to venerate the tombs of the blessed apostles Peter and Paul and to visit the Roman pontiff. But bishops who are outside of Europe may visit Rome at alternate intervals, or every ten years.

> Code of Canon Law, Canon 341. (*Ad limina* visits) (20th cent.)

Bishops, whether individually or gathered together in special councils, are not infallible in doctrine; nevertheless, under the authority of the Roman pontiff, they are true doctors and teachers for the faithful committed to their charge.

> Code of Canon Law, Canon 1326. (20th cent.)

Everything suffers by translation except a bishop.

> Author unidentified, date unknown.

Black

He cometh out of Ethiope and Ind,
Black as is jet.

> Lydgate: *Troy Book,* 2. (15th cent.)

Blame

How strange it is that men are so rash as to dare to reprehend what they cannot possibly comprehend!

> St. Bernard: *On Consideration,* 2, 1. (12th cent.)

Blarney

There is a difference between blarney and boloney. Blarney is the varnished truth; boloney is the unvarnished lie. Blarney is flattery laid on so thin you love it; boloney is flattery laid on so thick you hate it.

> Bishop Sheen: *Life is Worth Living.* (20th cent.)

Blasphemy

There is nothing worse than blasphemy.

> St. John Chrysostom: *Homilies.* (4th cent.)

Blessed, The

You spirits! who have thrown away
That envious weight of clay,
    Which your celestial flight denied;
Who, by your glorious troops supply
The winged hierarchy,
    So broken in the angels' pride.

> W. Habington: *Laudate Dominum de Coelis.* (17th cent.)

See also Eternal Life

Blessed Sacrament of the Altar

Thou, Lord Almighty, hast created all things for the sake of Thy name and hast given food and drink for men to enjoy, that they may give thanks to Thee; but to us Thou hast vouchsafed spiritual Food and Drink and eternal life through (Jesus) Thy Servant. Above all, we give Thee thanks because Thou art mighty. To Thee be glory for evermore.

> Teaching of the Twelve Apostles, 10. (An early eucharistic prayer.) (2nd cent.)

And let all take care that no unbaptized person taste of the Eucharist nor a mouse or other animal, and that none of it at all fall and be lost. For it is the Body of Christ to be eaten by them that believe and not to be lightly thought of.

> St. Hippolytus: *The Apostolic Tradition,* 32. (3rd cent.)

Wherefore with full assurance let us partake as of the Body and Blood of Christ: for in the figure (*typos*) of Bread is given to thee His Body, and in the figure of Wine His Blood; that thou by partaking of the Body and Blood of Christ, may be made of the same body and the same blood with Him. For thus we come to bear Christ in us, because His Body and Blood are distributed through our members; thus it is that, according to blessed Peter, *we become partakers of the divine nature* (2 Peter 1, 4).

> St. Cyril of Jerusalem: *Catechetical Discourses,* 22, 3. (4th cent.)

Consider therefore the Bread and the Wine not as bare elements, for they are, according to the Lord's declaration, the Body and Blood of Christ; for even though sense suggest this to thee, yet let faith establish thee. Judge not the matter from the taste, but from faith be fully assured without misgiving, that the Body and Blood of Christ have been vouchsafed to thee.

St. Cyril of Jerusalem: *Catechetical Discourses,* 22, 6. (4th cent.)

For if in truth the Word has been made flesh and we in very truth receive the Word made flesh as food from the Lord, are we not bound to believe that He abides in us naturally, Who, born as a man, has assumed the nature of our flesh now inseparable from Himself, and has conjoined the nature of His own flesh to the nature of the eternal Godhead in the sacrament by which His Flesh is communicated to us?

St. Hilary of Poitiers: *On the Trinity,* 8, 13. (4th cent.)

As to the truth of the Flesh and Blood there is no room left for doubt. For both from the declaration of the Lord Himself and from our own faith, it is truly Flesh and truly Blood. And when These are eaten and drunk, it is brought to pass that we are both in Christ and Christ is in us. Is this not so?

St. Hilary of Poitiers: *On the Trinity,* 8, 14. (4th cent.)

I place before your eyes this Table where we communicate together, and the figures (*typoi*) of my salvation which I consecrate with the same mouth with which I present a request to you, this sacrament which raises us to heaven.

St. Gregory of Nazianzen: *Orations,* 17, 12. (4th cent.)

Do not neglect, O holy man of God, to pray and to intercede for me, when by your words you cause the divine Word to come down, and when by a bloodless cutting you separate the Body and Blood

of the Lord, your words serving as a knife.

St. Gregory of Nazianzen: *Letters,* 171. (4th cent.)

When you see It [the Body of Christ] exposed, say to yourself: Thanks to this Body, I am no longer dust and ashes, I am no more a captive but a free man: hence I hope to obtain heaven and the good things that are there in store for me, eternal life, the heritage of the angels, companionship with Christ; death has not destroyed this Body which was pierced with nails and scourged . . . this is that Body which was once covered with blood, pierced by a lance, from which issued saving fountains upon the world, one of blood and the other of water. . . . This Body He gave to us to keep and to eat, as a mark of His intense love.

St. John Chrysostom: *Hom. in I. Ep. ad Cor.,* 24, 4. (4th cent.)

Christ did this to bring us to a closer bond of friendship, and to signify His love toward us, giving Himself to those who desire Him, not only to behold Him, but also to handle Him, to eat Him, to embrace Him with the fulness of their whole heart. Therefore as lions breathing fire do we depart from that Table, rendered objects of terror to the devil.

St. John Chrysostom: *Homilies on St. John,* 46. (4th cent.)

But if a human blessing was powerful enough to change nature, what do we say of the divine consecration itself where the very words of the Lord and Savior act? For the Sacrament which thou receivest is consecrated by the word of Christ.

St. Ambrose: *On the Mysteries,* 9, 52. (4th cent.)

It is clear, therefore, that the Virgin gave birth contrary to the order of nature. And this Body which we consecrate is from the Virgin; why do you seek the natural order here in the case of the Body of Christ, when the Lord Jesus Himself was born of the Virgin contrary to nature? It was certainly the true flesh of Christ which was crucified, which was buried; truly, therefore, the Sacrament is a sacrament of that flesh.

St. Ambrose: *On the Mysteries, 9, 53.* (4th cent.)

Therefore you hear that as often as sacrifice is offered, the Lord's death, the Lord's resurrection, the Lord's ascension and the remission of sins is signified, and will you not take the Bread of life daily? He who has a wound needs medicine. The wound is that we are under sin; the medicine is the heavenly and venerable Sacrament.

St. Ambrose: *On the Sacraments, 5, 4, 25.* (4th cent.)

Even though you are weak, yet Christ cares for you. He says to His disciples, *Give them to eat.* You have the apostolic food [i.e. the lessons of Scripture], eat that, and you shall not faint. Eat that first, that afterwards you may come to the food of Christ, to the food of the Lord's Body, to the feast of the Sacrament, to that Cup wherein the souls of the faithful are inebriated.

St. Ambrose: *Explanation of Psalm 118, 15, 28.* (4th cent.)

Christ is food for me; Christ is drink for me; the Flesh of God is food for me, the Blood of God is drink for me. Christ is ministered to me daily.

St. Ambrose: *Explanation of Psalm 118, 18, 26.* (4th cent.)

Thine, O Christ, in endless sweetness:
    Thou art our celestial Bread;
Nevermore he knoweth hunger, who
    upon Thy Grace hath fed,
Grace whereby no mortal body but the
    soul is nourished.

Prudentius: *Tu cibus panisque noster.* (Tr. Pope and Davis) (From Cathemerinon, 4th cent.)

With the odor of the name of Christ, like a field, the world is filled; His is the blessing from the dew of heaven, that is, from the rain of divine words; and from the abundance of earth, that is from the gathering of peoples: His is the abundance of corn and wine, that is, the multitude which the corn and wine gathers together in the Sacrament of His Body and Blood.

St. Augustine: *The City of God, 16, 37.* (Commenting on the blessing invoked by Isaac on Jacob, Gen. 37, 27-29.) (5th cent.)

The Lord's Supper is the unity of the Body of Christ, not only in the Sacrament of the Altar, but in the bond of peace.

St. Augustine: *Letter 185, 24.* (5th cent.)

Let all this avail us to this end, that we eat not the Flesh and Blood of Christ in the Sacrament, as many evil men do, but that we eat and drink to the participation of the Spirit, that we abide as members of the Lord's body to be quickened by His spirit.

St. Augustine: *In Joan. Evang.* 27, 11. (5th cent.)

He Who suffered for us entrusted to us in His Sacrament His own Body and Blood, and this too He makes us also; for we are become His Body, and we are that which we receive through His mercy. Remember this, that you both were not and were created. You have been brought to the Lord's threshing-floor by the labors of the oxen, that is, of those preaching the gospel; you have been threshed. When as catechumens you were set apart, you were stored in the granary. You have your names: you began to be ground in the mill of fasting and exorcism. Afterwards you came to the water, and you were moistened, and were formed into one; by the heat of the Holy Spirit which came to you you were baked, and you became the bread of the Lord. Look what you have received. As then you see what was made one thing, so be you one, by loving one another, by holding one faith, one hope, undivided charity.

St. Augustine: *Sermon 109.* (5th cent.)

But when does flesh receive the bread which He calls his Flesh? The faithful know and receive the Body of Christ if they labor to be the Body of Christ. And they become the body of Christ, if they study to live by the spirit of Christ: for that which lives by the Spirit of Christ, is the body of Christ. This bread the apostle sets forth, where he says, *We being many are one body.* O sacrament of mercy, O sign of unity, O bond of love! Whoever wishes to live, let him draw near, believe, be incorporated, that he may be quickened.

St. Augustine: *In Joan. Ev. Tr. 26,* 13. (5th cent.)

Do Thou, O holy Sacrament, most divine of all the sacraments, lift the veils that envelope Thee with their symbols, reveal Thyself clearly to our sight, and fill the eyes of our mind with a unifying and clear light!

Pseudo-Dionysius: *Ecclesiastical Hierarchy,* 3, 3. (5th cent.)

The Good Shepherd laid down His life for His sheep, that He might convert His Body and Blood in our sacrament, and satisfy the sheep Whom He had redeemed with the nourishment of His own Flesh.

Pope St. Gregory the Great: *Homilies on the Gospels,* 14, 1. (6th cent.)

That body which is born of the holy Virgin is in truth body united with divinity, not that the body which was received up into the heavens descends, but that the bread itself and the wine are changed into God's Body and Blood.

St. John of Damascus: *Exposition of the Orthodox Faith,* 4, 13. (8th cent.)

Here, Lord Jesus, art Thou both Shepherd and Green Pasture.

St. Thomas Aquinas: *Sermon for Holy Thursday.* (13th cent.)

He has left His faithful His very Body for food and His very Blood for drink, nourishment for them under the appearance of bread and wine, and an abiding memorial of His noble engagement. O how precious then, how marvellous, how health-giving, how well-appointed His banquet! Nothing more precious, for in the Lord's Supper the food put before us is not the flesh of bulls and goats, as in olden times, but Christ Himself, our very God.

Roman Breviary, Feast of Corpus Christi, Lesson at Matins. (St. Thomas Aquinas, 13th cent.)

This sacrament is the everlasting *showing forth of His death until He come again* (1 Cor. 11, 26); the embodied fulfilment of all the ancient types and figures.

Roman Breviary, Feast of Corpus Christi, Lesson at Matins. (St. Thomas Aquinas, 13th cent.)

Christ's true Body, born from the Virgin Mary, is contained in the Sacrament of the altar. To profess the contrary is heresy, because it detracts from the truth of Scripture, which records our Lord's own words, *This is My body* (Matth. 26, 26).

St. Thomas Aquinas: *Commentary on the Sentences,* 4, 10, 1. (13th cent.)

That Christ's true Body and Blood are present in this Sacrament can be perceived neither by sense nor by reason, but by faith alone, which rests on God's authority.

St. Thomas Aquinas: *Summa Theologica,* 3, 75, 1. (13th cent.)

Every localized body is in place, after the manner of a thing with dimensions, commensurate by its quantity to the place it occupies. Christ's Body is not present in place in the sacrament of the Eucharist in this manner.

St. Thomas Aquinas: *Summa Theologica,* 3, 76, 5. (13th cent.)

Sing, my tongue, the Savior's glory,
Of His Flesh the mystery sing;
Of the Blood, all price exceeding,
Shed by our immortal King,
Destined, for the world's redemption,
From a noble womb to spring.

Of a pure and spotless Virgin
Born for us on earth below,
He, as Man, with man conversing,
Stayed, the seeds of truth to sow;
Then He closed in solemn order
Wondrously His life of woe.

On the night of that last Supper
Seated with His chosen band,
He, the Paschal victim eating,
First fulfills the Law's command;
Then as Food to His apostles
Gives Himself with His own hand.

Word-made-Flesh, the bread of nature
By His word to Flesh He turns;
Wine into His Blood He changes:—
What though sense no change discerns?
Only be the heart in earnest,
Faith her lesson quickly learns.

Roman Breviary and Missal, Feast of
Corpus Christi and Holy Thursday, Hymn
Pange lingua gloriosi Corporis mysterium.
(Tr. Caswall) (St. Thomas Aquinas, 13th
cent.)

Down in adoration falling,
Lo! the sacred Host we hail;
Lo! o'er ancient forms departing,
Newer rites of grace prevail;
Faith for all defects supplying,
Where the feeble senses fail.

Roman Breviary and Missal, Office of
Corpus Christi, Procession on Holy
Thursday, Benediction of the Blessed
Sacrament, *Tantum ergo Sacramentum.*
(Stanza from hymn *Pange lingua gloriosi;*
always sung kneeling.) (Tr. Caswall)
(St. Thomas Aquinas, 13th cent.)

Our solemn feast let holy joys attend;
Our hearts in hymns and praises blend;
With newer rites let former ages end,
  In heart, and voice, and deed.

Roman Breviary, Corpus Christi, Hymn
Sacris solemniis juncta sint gaudia. (Tr.

Chambers) (St. Thomas Aquinas, 13th
cent.)

Thus angels' Bread is made
The Bread of man today:
The living Bread from heaven
With figures doth away;
O wondrous gift indeed!
The poor and lowly may
Upon their Lord and Master feed.

Roman Breviary, Corpus Christi, *Panis
angelicus fit panis hominum.* (From hymn
Sacris solemniis juncta sint gaudia.) (Tr.
E. Caswall) (St. Thomas Aquinas, 13th
cent.)

The heavenly Word proceeding forth,
Yet leaving not the Father's side,
And going to His work on earth
Had reached at length life's eventide.
By false disciple to be given
To foemen for His blood athirst,
Himself, the Living Bread from heaven,
He gave to His disciples first.

Roman Breviary, Corpus Christi, Hymn
Verbum supernum prodiens at Lauds. (Tr.
Neale) (St. Thomas Aquinas, 13th cent.)

O saving Victim, opening wide
The gate of heaven to man below,
Our foes press on from every side,
Thine aid supply, Thy strength bestow.

Roman Breviary, Feast of Corpus Christi,
O salutaris hostia. (From hymn *Verbum
supernum prodiens.*) (Tr. Caswall) (St.
Thomas Aquinas, 13th cent.)

Praise, O Sion, praise thy Savior,
Shepherd, Prince, with glad behavior,
  Praise in hymn and canticle:
Sing His glory, without measure,
For the merit of your treasure
  Never shall your praises fill.

                . . . .

Sing His praise with voice sonorous;
Every heart shall hear the chorus
  Swell in melody sublime:
For this day the Shepherd gave us
Flesh and Blood to feed and save us,
  Lasting to the end of time.

Roman Missal, Feast of Corpus Christi,
Sequence *Lauda Sion Salvatorem* at Mass.
(Tr. H. Henry) (St. Thomas Aquinas,
13th cent.)

Hail, angelic Bread of heaven,
Now the pilgrim's hoping-leaven,
Yea, the Bread to children given
    That to dogs must not be thrown:
In the figures contemplated
'Twas with Isaac immolated,
By the Lamb 'twas antedated,
    In the Manna it was known.

Roman Missal, Feast of Corpus Christi,
Ecce panis angelorum. (From sequence
Lauda Sion Salvatorem.) (Tr. Henry)
(St. Thomas Aquinas, 13th cent.)

O God, Who in this wonderful Sacrament hast left us a memorial of Thy passion, grant us, we beseech Thee, so to venerate the sacred mysteries of Thy Body and Blood, that we may ever perceive within us the fruit of Thy redemption.

Roman Missal, Collect for Corpus Christi
(Thursday after Trinity Sunday) (St.
Thomas Aquinas, 13th cent.)

Godhead here in hiding, Whom I do adore
Masked by these bare shadows, shape and nothing more,
See, Lord, at Thy service low lies here a heart
Lost, all lost in wonder at the God Thou art.

Roman Missal, Hymn *Adoro te devote
latens Deitas* for thanksgiving after Mass.
(Tr. G. M. Hopkins) (St. Thomas
Aquinas, 13th cent.)

O memorial of my Savior dying,
Living Bread, that givest life to man;
May my soul, its life from Thee supplying,
Taste Thy sweetness, as on earth it can.

Deign, O Jesus, Pelican of heaven,
Me, a sinner, in Thy Blood to lave,
To a single drop of which is given
All the world from all its sin to save.

Roman Missal, Hymn *Adoro te devote
latens Deitas* for thanksgiving after Mass.
(Tr. Justice O'Hagan) (St. Thomas
Aquinas, 13th cent.)

Sanctify me wholly, Soul of Christ adored;

Be my sure salvation, Body of the Lord:
Fill and satisfy me, O Thou Blood unpriced:
Wash me, sacred water, from the side of Christ.
Passion of my Savior, be my strength in need:
Good and precious Jesus, to my prayer give heed:
In Thy wounds most precious let me refuge find:
All the power malignant of the foeman bind:
At death's final hour, call me to Thy face:
Bid me stand beside Thee in the heavenly place:
There with saints and angels I shall sing to Thee
Through the countless ages of eternity.

Hymn *Anima Christi sanctifica me.* (Tr.
T. Ball) (Anon., ca. 14th cent.)

Hail, true Body, truly born
Of the Virgin Mary mild,
Truly offered, racked and torn,
On the cross, for man defiled,
From Whose love-pierced, sacred side
Flowed Thy true Blood's saving tide:
Be a foretaste sweet to me
In my death's great agony,
O Thou loving, gentle One,
Sweetest Jesus, Mary's Son.

Hymn *Ave verum Corpus natum.* (Tr. E.
Garesché) (Probably by Pope Innocent
VI, 14th cent.)

Hail! Thou saving Victim, offered up for me and for all mankind upon the gibbet of the cross! Hail! Thou glorious and most precious Blood, That flowest from the wounds of Jesus Christ, my crucified Lord; to wash away the sins of the world! Forget not, O Lord, that I am one of those Whom Thou hast created, and with Thine own Blood redeemed.

Roman Missal, Prayer *Ad Mensam
Dulcissimi* before Mass. (ca. 15th cent.?)

Oh, the wonderful and hidden grace of this Sacrament, which only the faithful of Christ know; but unbelievers and such as are slaves to sin cannot experience. In this Sacrament is conferred spiritual grace; lost virtue is repaired in the soul; and beauty disfigured by sin returneth again.

Thomas a Kempis: *The Imitation of Christ,* 4, 1. (15th cent.)

If any one denieth that in the sacrament of the most holy eucharist are contained truly, really, and substantially, the Body and Blood together with the soul and divinity of our Lord Jesus Christ, and consequently the whole Christ; but saith that He is only therein as in a sign, or in a figure, or virtue; let him be anathema.

Council of Trent, Session 13, Canon 1. (Oct. 11, 1551)

If any one denieth that in the venerable sacrament of the eucharist the whole Christ is contained under each species, and under every part of each species, when separated; let him be anathema.

Council of Trent, Session 13, Canon 3. (Oct. 11, 1551)

If any one saith that after the consecration is completed the Body and Blood of our Lord Jesus Christ are not in the admirable sacrament of the eucharist, but are there only during the use, whilst it is being taken, and not either before or after; and that in the Hosts or consecrated particles, which are reserved or which remain after communion, the true Body of the Lord remaineth not; let him be anathema.

Council of Trent, Session 13, Canon 4. (Oct. 11, 1551)

If any one saith that in the holy sacrament of the eucharist Christ, the only-begotten Son of God, is not to be adored with the worship, even external, of latria; and is consequently neither to be venerated with a special festive solemnity nor to be solemnly borne about in processions, according to the laudable and universal rite and custom of holy Church; or is not to be proposed publicly to the people to be adored, and that the adorers thereof are idolaters; let him be anathema.

Council of Trent, Session 13, Canon 6. (Oct. 11, 1551)

If any one saith that it is not lawful for the sacred eucharist to be reserved in the sacristy, but that immediately after consecration it must necessarily be distributed amongst those present; or that it is not lawful that it be carried with honor to the sick; let him be anathema.

Council of Trent, Session 13, Canon 7. (Oct. 11, 1551)

If any one saith that Christ, given in the eucharist, is eaten spiritually only, and not also sacramentally and really; let him be anathema.

Council of Trent, Session 13, Canon 8. (Oct. 11, 1551)

If any one saith that faith alone is a sufficient preparation for receiving the sacrament of the most holy eucharist; let him be anathema. And for fear lest so great a sacrament may be received unworthily, and so unto death and condemnation, this holy synod ordains and declares that sacramental confession, when a confessor may be had, is of necessity to be made beforehand by those whose conscience is burdened by mortal sin, however contrite they may think themselves. . . .

Council of Trent, Session 13, Canon 11. (Oct. 11, 1551)

As Christ willed it and spake it
And thankfully blessed it and brake it,
And as the sacred words do make it
So I believe and take it.

My life to give therefor,
In earth to live no more.

Lines appearing in various Catholic sources, quoted by Princess Elizabeth when pressed to declare her opinion of the holy eucharist. She characteristically omitted the last two. (Guiney, 351) (16th cent.)

The God of hosts in slender Host doth
  dwell,
  Yea, God and Man with all to either
    due,
That God That rules the heavens and
  rifled hell,
  That Man Whose death did us to
    life renew;
That God and Man That is the angels'
  bliss,
In form of Bread and Wine our nur-
  ture is.

Bl. Robert Southwell: *Of the Blessed
Sacrament of the Aulter.* (16th cent.)

When Thee, O holy sacrificed Lamb,
  In severed signs I white and liquid
    see,
  As in Thy Body slain I think on
    Thee,
Which pale by shedding of Thy blood
  became.
  And when again I do behold the
    same
  Veil'd in white to be receiv'd of me,
  Thou seemest in Thy sindon wrapt
    to be
Like to a corpse, whose monument
  I am.
Buried in me, unto my soul appear,
  Prison'd in earth, and banisht from
    Thy sight,
  Like our forefathers who in limbo
    were,
Clear Thou my thoughts, as Thou didst
  give them light,
  And as Thou other freed from purg-
    ing fire
  Quench in my heart the flames of
    bad desire.

Henry Constable: *To the Blessed
Sacrament.* (16th cent.)

Now Lord, or never, they'll believe on
  Thee,
Thou to their teeth hast prov'd Thy
  Deity.

Richard Crashaw: *On the Miracle of
Loaves.* (17th cent.)

With all the pow'rs my poor heart hath
Of humble love and loyal faith,

Thus low, my hidden Life, I bow to
  Thee
Whom too much love hath bow'd more
  low for me.
Down, down proud sense! discourses
  die.
Keep close, my soul's inquiring eye!
Nor touch nor taste must look for more
But each sit still in his own door.

R. Crashaw: *Paraphrase of St. Thomas'
Hymn 'Adoro Te.'* (17th cent.)

Lord, to Thine altar let me go,
The child of weariness and woe,
  My home to find;
From sin and sense and self set free,
Absorbed alone in love of Thee,
Able to leave in liberty
  This world behind.

Jesus, be Thou my heavenly Food,
Sweet source divine of every good,
  Center of rest;
One with Thy heart let me be found,
Prostrate upon that holy ground,
Where grace and peace and life abound
  Drawn from Thy breast.

M. Bridges: *Lord, to Thine Altar Let Me
Go.* (19th cent.)

O Jesus Christ, remember,
  When Thou shalt come again,
Upon the clouds of heaven,
  With all Thy shining train;—
When every eye shall see Thee
  In Deity reveal'd,
Who now upon this altar
  In silence art conceal'd.

. . . .

Remember then, O Savior,
  I supplicate of Thee,
That here I bow'd before Thee
  Upon my bended knee;
That here I own'd Thy presence,
  And did not Thee deny;
And glorified Thy greatness
  Though hid from human eye.

E. Caswall: *O Jesus Christ remember.*
(19th cent.)

Rejoice! ye angels, and thou Church
  This day triumphant here below;

He comes in meekest emblems clad,
  Himself He cometh to bestow.
That Body Which thou gav'st, O earth,
  He giveth back—that Flesh, that
    Blood,
Born of the altar's mystic birth,
  At once thy worship and thy food.

Aubrey de Vere: *Corpus Christi.* (19th
cent.)

My God, my Life, my Love,
  To Thee, to Thee, I call;
O come to me from heaven above,
  And be my God my all.

My faith beholds Thee, Lord!
  Conceal'd in human food;
My senses fail, but in Thy word,
  I trust and find my God.

Anonymous: *Jesus in the Blessed
Sacrament.* (In Caswall's *Lyra Catholica*)
(19th cent.)

Jesus! my Lord, my God, my All!
  How can I love Thee as I ought?
And how revere this wondrous gift,
  So far surpassing hope or thought?

      .   .   .   .

Had I but Mary's sinless heart
  To love Thee with, my dearest King!
O, with what bursts of fervent praise
  Thy goodness, Jesus, would I sing!
    Sweet Sacrament! we Thee adore!
  O, make us love Thee more and
    more!

F. Faber: *Corpus Christi.* (19th cent.)

Thou that on sin's wages starvest,
Behold, we have the joy in harvest:
For us was gather'd the first-fruits
For us was lifted from the roots,
Sheaved in cruel bands, bruised sore,
Scourged upon the threshing-floor;
Where the upper mill-stone roof'd His
  head,
At morn we found the heavenly Bread,
And on a thousand altars laid,
Christ our sacrifice is made.

G. M. Hopkins: *Barnfloor and Winepress.*
(19th cent.)

Lo, in the sanctuaried east,
Day, a dedicated priest
In all his robes pontifical exprest,
Lifteth slowly, lifteth sweetly,
From out its orient tabernacle drawn,
Yon orbèd sacrament confest
Which sprinkles benediction through
  the dawn.

F. Thompson: *Orient Ode.* (19th cent.)

In the most holy eucharist under the appearances of bread and wine Christ the
Lord Himself is contained, offered, and
received.

Code of Canon Law, Canon 801. (20th
cent.)

I come before Thee, Lord, at close of
  day,
  My soul with fears and sad misgiv-
    ings stirred;
Too tired to pray, I kneel before Thy
  face
  And lay my burden down without a
    word.
I gaze in silence on the little door
  That keeps love's patient Prisoner in
    thrall,
Nor ask for more; my troubled heart
  has room
  For naught save this one thought,—
    Thou knowest all.

Sister M. Angelita: *An Evening Visit.*
(20th cent.)

See also Communion; Eucharist; Mass

Blessed Virgin Mary

I—*Holy Virgin of Virgins*

Oh, the richness of the virginity of
Mary!

St. Ambrose: *De Institutione Virginis*, 3,
19. (4th cent.)

But now that a Virgin has conceived in
the womb and has borne to us a Child of
Which the prophet says that *Government shall be upon His shoulder, and
His name shall be called the mighty God,
the everlasting Father* (Isa. 9, 6), now
the chain of the curse is broken. Death

came through Eve, but life has come through Mary. And thus the gift of virginity has been bestowed most richly upon women, seeing that it has had its beginning from a woman.

> St. Jerome: *Letters,* 22, 21. (4th cent.)

Indeed, her virginity was itself more beautiful and more pleasing, because Christ, in His conception, did not Himself take away that which He was preserving from violation by man; but, before He was conceived He chose one already consecrated to God of Whom He would be born.

> St. Augustine: *On Holy Virginity,* 4. (5th cent.)

For as a virgin she conceived, as a virgin she gave birth, a virgin she remained.

> St. Augustine: *Sermons,* 51. (5th cent.)

The dignity of virginity began with the Mother of the Lord.

> St. Augustine: *Sermons,* 51. (5th cent.)

A virgin who conceives, a virgin who gives birth; a virgin with Child, a virgin delivered of Child—a virgin ever virgin! Why do you marvel at these things, O man? When God vouchsafed to become man, it was fitting that He should be born in this way. He Who was made of her, had made her what she was.

> St. Augustine: *Sermons,* 186. (5th cent.)

For neither do we know the countenance of the Virgin Mary, from whom, untouched by a husband, nor tainted in the birth itself, He was wonderfully born.

> St. Augustine: *De Trinitate,* 8, 5. (5th cent.)

The gate which was shut (Ezech. 44, 2) was her virginity. Through it the Lord God of Israel entered; through it He advanced into this world from the Virgin's womb. And, because her virginity was preserved intact, the Virgin's gate has remained shut for ever.

> Rufinus: *Commentary on the Apostles' Creed,* 9. (5th cent.)

O Mary, how holy and how spotless is thy virginity! I am too dull to praise thee: for thou hast borne in thy breast Him whom the heavens cannot contain.

> Roman Breviary, Responsory at Matins. (Liber Responsalis, ca. 7th cent.)

Blessed art thou, O Virgin Mary, who hast carried the Lord, the Maker of the world. Thou hast borne Him Who created thee, and thou abidest a Virgin for ever.

> Roman Breviary, Responsory at Matins for Feasts of the Blessed Virgin. (Lib. Respons., ca. 7th cent.)

Men the most eloquent we see become as dumb fishes before thee, O Forthbringer; helpless to say in what way thou, being still a maid, wert able to bring forth. But we, marvelling at the mystery, cry out in faith: Hail! casket of God's wisdom; Hail! treasury of His providence. . . .

> Byzantine Triodion, Akathist Hymn, Oikos 9. (Tr. V. McNabb) (ca. 7th cent.)

For truly she was full of grace, to whom it had been granted by divine gift that she first among women should offer the most glorious gift of virginity to God.

> St. Bede the Venerable: *Homilies,* 1, 1. (8th cent.)

Just as He Who was conceived kept her who conceived still virgin, in like manner He Who was born preserved her virginity intact, only passing through her and keeping her closed. The conception, indeed, was through the sense of hearing, but the birth through the usual path by which children come.

> St. John of Damascus: *Exposition of the Orthodox Faith,* 4, 14. (8th cent.)

And thou that flow'r of virgines art alle,
Of whom that Bernard list so well to write,
To thee at my beginning first I calle;
Thou comfort of us wretches. . . .

> Chaucer: *The Second Nun's Prologue.* (14th cent.)

II—*Mother of God; Mother of Christ*

But the Son of God has a Mother touched by no impurity; yet she, whom He is seen to have, had never been a bride.

> Tertullian: *Apology,* 21, 9. (3rd cent.)

This Virgin became a mother, although her virginity was preserved and the seals were not broken; she bears a Child in her womb, although her integrity as a virgin is intact; and she has become Mother of God and handmaiden and work of His wisdom.

> St. Ephraem of Syria: *Hymns on the Blessed Virgin Mary,* 18, 20. (4th cent.)

But, O Virgin lady, immaculate Mother of God, my lady most glorious, most gracious, higher than heaven, much purer than the sun's splendor, rays or light . . . budding staff of Aaron, you appeared as a true staff, and the flower is your Son our true Christ, my God and Maker. You bore God and the Word according to the flesh, preserving your virginity before childbirth, a virgin after childbirth, and we have been reconciled with Christ God your Son.

> St. Ephraem of Syria: *Prayer to the most holy Mother of God.* (4th cent.)

If anyone believes that holy Mary is not the mother of God (*theotokos*), he has no share in the divine inheritance. If anyone says that Christ passed through the virgin as through a tube but was not formed in her in both a divine and human manner, divine without the assistance of man, human in accordance with the law of pregnancies, he likewise is ungodly.

> St. Gregory of Nazianzen: *Letters,* 101. (4th cent.)

What is greater than the Mother of God? What more glorious than she whom Glory Itself chose? What more chaste than she who bore a body without contact with another body? For why should I speak of her other virtues? She was a virgin not only in body but also in mind. . . .

> St. Ambrose: *Concerning Virgins,* 2, 7. (4th cent.)

Though she was the Mother of the Lord, yet she desired to learn the precepts of the Lord, and she who brought forth God, yet desired to know God.

> St. Ambrose: *Concerning Virgins,* 2, 13. (4th cent.)

Nor was Mary less than was befitting the Mother of Christ. When the apostles fled, she stood before the Cross and with reverent gaze beheld her Son's wounds, for she waited not for her Child's death, but the world's salvation.

> St. Ambrose: *Letters,* 63. (396)

Even her maternal relationship would have done Mary no good unless she had borne Christ more happily in her heart than in her flesh.

> St. Augustine: *On Holy Virginity,* 3. (5th cent.)

And on this account that one woman is both a Mother and a Virgin, not only in the spirit but also in the flesh. In the spirit, indeed, she is not the mother of our Head, Which is the Savior Himself, of Whom rather she was born after the Spirit—forasmuch as all, who have believed in Him, among whom she herself also is, are rightly called *children of the Bridegroom* (Matth. 9, 15)—but she is clearly the mother of His members, which we are, in that she cooperated by charity, that faithful ones should be born in the Church, who are members of that Head. In the flesh, however, she is the mother of the Head Himself. For it was meet that our Head should by means of an extraordinary miracle be born after the flesh of a virgin, that He might thereby signify that His members would be born after the spirit of a virgin, the Church.

> St. Augustine: *On Holy Virginity,* 6, 6. (5th cent.)

She is called full of grace and said to have found favor with God, for she was to become the Mother of her Lord, indeed, of the Lord of all.

> St. Augustine: *Enchiridion, 36.* (5th cent.)

Him Whom the heavens cannot contain, the womb of one woman bore. She ruled our Ruler; she carried Him in Whom we are; she gave milk to our Bread.

> St. Augustine: *Sermons,* 184. (5th cent.)

If anyone does not confess that Emmanuel is true God, and that therefore the holy Virgin is Mother of God (*Dei genetricem—Theotokon*), since she bore, after the flesh, the incarnate Word of God, let him be anathema.

> Council of Alexandria, Anathema 1 of St. Cyril. (430)

Nor was He first born of the holy Virgin as an ordinary man, in such a way that the Word only afterwards descended upon Him; rather was He united [with flesh] in the womb itself, and thus is said to have undergone birth according to the flesh, inasmuch as He makes His own the birth of His own flesh. . . . For this reason [the holy fathers] have boldly proclaimed the holy Virgin *Theotokos* (Mother of God).

> Council of Ephesus, Letter of St. Cyril to Nestorius (430). (Read and approved by the fathers of the council) (431)

Hail, from us, Mary, Mother of God, majestic common-treasure of the whole world, the lamp unquenchable, the crown of virginity, the staff of orthodoxy, the indissoluble temple, the dwelling of the Illimitable, Mother and Virgin, through whom He in the holy Gospels is called the *Blessed Who cometh in the name of the Lord.*

> St. Cyril of Alexandria: *Homilies,* 4. (5th cent.)

Therefore, may God forbid that anyone should attempt to defraud holy Mary of her privileges of divine grace and of her special glory. For by a unique favor of our Lord and God she is to be confessed to be the most true and most blessed Mother of God (*Theotokos*). She is truly the Mother of God, not merely in name . . . but rather because, as has already been said, in her sacred womb was accomplished the mystery that, by reason of a certain singular and unique Unity of person, even as the Word is flesh in flesh, so the man is God in God.

> St. Vincent of Lerins: *Commonitoria,* 15. (5th cent.)

The God Whom earth, and sea, and sky
Adore, and laud, and magnify,
Who o'er their threefold fabric reigns,
The Virgin's spotless womb contains.

    .   .   .   .   .   .

How blest that Mother, in whose shrine
The great Artificer divine,
Whose hand contains the earth and sky,
Vouchsafed, as in His ark, to lie.

> Roman Breviary, Feasts of the Blessed Virgin, Hymn *Quem terra pontus sidera* at Matins. (Tr. J. Neale) (Fortunatus, 6th cent.)

Remembering our all-holy, immaculate, most blessed and glorious Lady, the Mother of God and ever-virgin Mary, and all the saints, let us commend ourselves, each other, and all our life to Christ our God.

> Byzantine Rite, Concluding Petition of all Litanies. (ca. 6th cent.)

Thou who art more honorable than the cherubim, and incomparably more glorious than the seraphim, who without corruption didst bear God the Word, true Mother of God, we magnify thee.

> Byzantine Horologion, Troparion. (The *Timiotera* frequently occurs in Byz. liturgy and office. Composed by St. Cosmas the Melodist? Cf. hirmos of ode 9, Passion Service, Great Thursday.) (ca. 700?)

Hail! Mother of God, for thou didst have space in thy womb for Him Who in heaven is infinite. Hail! O Virgin, for thee the prophets did proclaim, and from thee Emmanuel shows forth; hail! Mother of Christ our God.

Byzantine Triodion, Great Thursday, Service of the Holy Passion. (ca. 6th-8th cent.)

Hail! Virgin Mother of God. O Mary, full of grace, the Lord is with thee. Blessed art thou among women, and blessed is the fruit of thy womb; for thou hast borne the Savior of our souls.

Byzantine Horologion, Troparion at Vespers. (ca. 6th to 8th cent.)

O most pure Mary, golden censer that became the tabernacle of the undivided Trinity; in thee the Father was well pleased, in thee the Son abode, and the Holy Ghost, overshadowing thee, declared thee, Maiden, Mother of God.

Byzantine Horologion, Exapostilarion at Matins. (ca. 6th to 8th cent.)

Let us mull over the words of the Gospel in frequent meditation, let us ever keep in mind the examples of Mary, the blessed Mother of God, so that we also may be found humble in the sight of God, that being subject in due honor also to our neighbor, we may deserve together with her to be exalted forever.

St. Bede the Venerable: *Homilies,* 1, 2. (8th cent.)

Hence it is with justice and truth that we call holy Mary the Mother of God. For this name embraces the whole mystery of the dispensation. For if she who bore Him is the Mother of God, assuredly He Who was born of her is God and likewise also Man.

St. John of Damascus: *Exposition of the Orthodox Faith,* 3, 12. (8th cent.)

Wherein does the Cross that typifies the Lord differ from a cross that does not do so? It is also just the same in the case of the Mother of the Lord. For the honor which we give to her is referred to Him Who was made incarnate of her.

St. John of Damascus: *Exposition of the Orthodox Faith,* 4, 16. (8th cent.)

Whenever I behold the image of the Virgin Mary, Mother of God, I cry: O immaculate Mother of God, pray to your Son and my God to have mercy on me, in goodness and in mercy, for the prayers of Mary are of great weight in gaining the clemency of the Master. Do not despise the prayer of a sinner, O all-venerable one, for He can save us Who deigned to suffer for us.

St. John of Damascus. (8th cent.)

Mother benign of our redeeming Lord,
Star of the sea and portal of the skies,
Unto thy fallen people help afford—
Fallen, but striving still anew to rise.
Thou who didst once, while wond'ring
      worlds adored,
Bear thy Creator, Virgin then as now,
O by thy holy joy at Gabriel's word,
Pity the sinners who before thee bow.

Roman Breviary, Antiphon of the Blessed Virgin *Alma Redemptoris mater* for Advent. (Tr. D. Hunter-Blair) (Hermann Contractus, 1013–1054)

Admire then both the benign condescension of the Son and the most excellent dignity of the Mother; and choose which one of the two is the more admirable. Each is a wonder, each a miracle. God is obedient to a woman, an unexampled humility! a woman is in the place of ancestor to God, a distinction without a sharer! When the praises of virgins are sung, it is said, that they follow the Lamb wherever He goes (Apoc. 14, 4), of what praise shall she be thought worthy, who even goes before Him?

St. Bernard: *Sermon 1 in Vigil. Nativ. Domini,* 7. (12th cent.)

The Mother of God was both a maid and espoused. Virginity and wedlock are honored in her person. She is a challenge to heretics who disparage either one or the other.

St. Thomas Aquinas: *Summa Theologica,* 3, 29, 1. (13th cent.)

Maiden and Mother, daughter of thine own Son,

Beyond all creatures lowly and lifted
   high,
Of the eternal design the corner-
   stone!

Thou art she who did man's substance
   glorify
So that its own Maker did not eschew
Even to be made of its mortality.

Dante: *Paradiso, Canto 33.* (Prayer of St.
Bernard) (Tr. Binyon) (14th cent.)

Thou Maid and Mother, daughter of
   thy Sone,
Thou well of mercy, sinful soules cure,
In whom that God, for bounty, chose
   to wone,
Thou humble, and high over every
   creature,
Thou nobledest so ferforth our nature,
That no disdain the Maker hadde of
   kinde,
His Son in blood and flesh to clothe
   and winde.

wone—dwell
ferforth—to such a degree

Chaucer: *The Second Nun's Tale.* (14th
cent.)

O Mother Mary, flower of all woman
   kind,
In beauty passing each earthly creature,
In whom the fiend no thought of sin
   could find;
O blessed Mother, remaining maiden
   pure,
O shining lamp, in light passing nature,
Most clear crystal, by clean virginity,
O holy Mother and Virgin, most de-
   mure—
Direct our life in this tempestuous sea.

Alexander Barclay: *Transl. of Brandt's
Ship of Fools.* (16th cent.)

   I sing of a maiden
   That is makeless,
   King of all kings
   To her Son she chose.

      .   .   .   .

   Mother and Maiden
   Was never none but she;

Well may such a lady
God's Mother be.

makeless—matchless

Anonymous: *Carol to Our Lady.* (15th
cent.)

Mother of almighty God!
   Suppliant at thy feet we pray;
Shelter us from Satan's fraud,
   Safe beneath thy wing this day.

Anonymous: *Te mater alma numinis.*
(Feast of the Motherhood of the Blessed
Virgin, Oct. 11.) (Tr. Caswall) (18th
cent.)

The Savior left high heaven to dwell
   Within the Virgin's womb;
And there arrayed Himself in flesh,
   Our Victim to become.

Anonymous: *Coelo Redemptor praetulit.*
(Feast of the Motherhood) (Tr. Caswell)
(18th cent.)

Hail, holy Virgin Mary—Hail!
Whose tender mercies never fail;
Mother of Christ, of grace divine,
Of purity the spotless shrine,—
Mother of God, with virtues crown'd,
Most faithful—pitiful—renown'd
Deign from thy throne to look on me,
And hear my mournful Litany.

M. Bridges: *Lady of Loretto.* (19th cent.)

Star of Jacob, ever beaming
   With a radiance all divine!
'Mid the stars of highest heaven
   Glows no purer ray than thine.

All in stoles of snowy brightness,
   Unto thee the angels sing;
Unto thee the virgin choirs,—
   Mother of th' eternal King!

Anonymous: *O stella Jacob fulgida.* (Tr.
Caswall) (19th cent.)

   As the sun
      O'er misty shrouds,
   When he walks
      Upon the clouds;

   Or as when
      The moon doth rise,

And refreshes
All the skies.

. . . . . .

Thus above
All mothers shone,
The Mother of
The blessed One.

Anonymous: *Ut sol decoro lumine*. (In
Caswall's *Lyra Catholica*) (19th cent.)

Mother! to thee myself I yield,
Console me in the hour of pain;
Be thou my life's support and shield,
And by me, at my death, remain!

Anonymous: *Offering to Our Lady*. (In
Caswall's *Lyra Catholica*) (19th cent.)

Say, did his sisters wonder what could
Joseph see
In a mild, silent little Maid like thee?
And was it awful, in that narrow house,
With God for Babe and Spouse?
Nay, like thy simple, female sort, each
one
Apt to find him in husband and in son,
Nothing to thee came strange in this.
Thy wonder was but wondrous bliss:
Wondrous, for, though
True virgin lives not but does know,
(Howbeit none ever yet confess'd,)
That God lies really in her breast,
Of thine He made His special nest!
And so
All mothers worship little feet,
And kiss the very ground they've trod;
But, ah, thy little Baby sweet
Who was indeed thy God!

Coventry Patmore: *Regina Coeli*. (19th
cent.)

The Church cannot insist too much on
the true position of Mary, for it is a
strong hedge round the doctrine of the
incarnation. Every grace of Mary's, every
prerogative, every dignity she has, is
hers simply because she is the Mother of
Christ; and it is wholly for His sake that
we honor her, nor do we give her any
honor which does not in consequence re-
dound to Him of necessity.

Abbot Chapman: *Bishop Gore and the
Catholic Claims*. (20th cent.)

III—*Ark of the Covenant; Mystical
Rose;
Tower of David; Tower of Ivory*

Holy of holies! rend the veil
Before thy throne of gold;
Ark of the covenant, all hail,—
The Virgin we behold!

M. Bridges: *Foederis Arca*. (19th cent.)

Daughter of David, ever fair,
In all thy gentle power,
Oh! let me find thy gracious care
An Ivory Tower!

M. Bridges: *Turris Eburnea*. (19th cent.)

Rose of the Cross, thou mystic flower!
I lift my heart to thee:
In every melancholy hour,
Mary! remember me.

M. Bridges: *Rosa mystica*. (19th cent.)

Ivory Tower! Star of the morning! Rose
Mystical! Tower of David, our De-
fence!
To thee our music flows,
Who makest music for us to thy Son.

Lionel Johnson: *A Descant upon the Litany
of Loretto*. (19th cent.)

IV—*Comforter of the Afflicted*

Thou art the delight of the angels, the
joy of the afflicted, the refuge of Christians, O Virgin Mother of the Lord. Help
us, and deliver us from eternal torment.

Byzantine Horologion, Exapostilarion at
Matins. (ca. 7th cent.)

O thou, who dost bless the world and
sanctify all, rest of those who are weary,
consolation of the afflicted, harbor for
the shipwrecked, pardon for sinners, relief for the burdened, prompt help for
those who call on thee.

St. John of Damascus: *First Homily on the
Falling Asleep of Our Lady*. (8th cent.)

O thou that art so fair and full of grace,
Be mine advocate in that high place
Thereas withouten end is sung Osanne,

Thou Christes Mother, daughter dear
of Anne!
And of thy light my soul in prison
lighte,
That troubled is by the contagion
Of my body, and also by the weighte
Of earthly lust and false affection;
O haven of refuge, O salvation
Of them that been in sorrow and dis-
tress.

Chaucer: *The Second Nun's Tale.* (14th
cent.)

V—*Compared with Eve*

The knot of Eve's disobedience was
loosed by the obedience of Mary. The
knot which the virgin Eve tied by her
unbelief, the Virgin Mary opened by
her belief.

St. Irenaeus: *Against the Heresies,* 3, 22, 3.
(2nd cent.)

And if the former [Eve] disobeyed God,
the latter [Mary] was persuaded to obey
God, so that the Virgin Mary became the
advocate of the virgin Eve. And thus, as
the human race fell into bondage to death
by means of a virgin, so it is rescued by
a virgin.

St. Irenaeus: *Against the Heresies,* 5, 19, 1.
(2nd cent.)

For the Lord came to seek back the lost
sheep, and it was man who was lost; and
therefore He did not become some other
formation, but He likewise, of her that
was descended from Adam, preserved
the likeness of formation; for Adam had
necessarily to be restored in Christ, that
mortality be absorbed in immortality,
and Eve in Mary, that a virgin, become
the advocate of a virgin, should undo
and destroy virginal disobedience by virginal obedience.

St. Irenaeus: *Proof of the Apostolic
Preaching,* 33. (2nd cent.)

For it was while Eve was yet a virgin,
that the ensnaring word had crept into
her ear which was to build the edifice of
death. Into a virgin's soul, in like manner, must be introduced that Word of

God which was to raise the fabric of life;
so that what had been reduced to ruin by
this sex, might by the selfsame sex be
recovered to salvation. As Eve had believed the serpent, so Mary believed the
angel. The delinquency which the one
occasioned by believing, the other by believing effaced.

Tertullian: *On the Flesh of Christ,* 17. (3rd
cent.)

If our first fall took place when the
woman received in her heart the venom
of the serpent, it is not to be wondered
at that our salvation was brought about
when a woman conceived the flesh of the
Almighty in her womb. . . . Through a
woman we were sent to destruction;
through a woman salvation was restored
to us.

St. Augustine: *Sermon 289,* 2. (5th cent.)

Thou, O Virgin, didst bring forth the
Giver of life, hast delivered Adam from
sin, and given joy to Eve instead of sorrow; for He That was incarnate from
thee, being God and Man, hath restored
life to them that had fallen from it.

Byzantine Horologion, Evlogitaria at
Matins on Sundays. (ca. 6th cent. ?)

She ministered to the Creator in that He
was created, to the Fashioner in that He
was fashioned, and to the Son of God and
God in that He was made flesh and became Man from her pure and immaculate
flesh and blood, satisfying the debt of the
first mother. For just as the latter was
formed from Adam without connection,
so also the former brought forth the new
Adam, Who was brought forth in accordance with the laws of parturition and
above the nature of generation.

St. John of Damascus: *Exposition of the
Orthodox Faith,* 4, 14. (8th cent.)

Eve sought the fruit, but did not find
there what she wished for. In her fruit
the blessed Virgin found all that Eve
had wanted.

St. Thomas Aquinas: *Exposition of the Hail
Mary.* (13th cent.)

VI—*Full of grace; Her sanctity*

Indeed full of grace, for to others it is given in portions, but on Mary its fulness is showered.

St. Jerome: *Letters,* 9. (4th cent.)

We must except the holy Virgin Mary, concerning whom I wish to raise no question when it touches the subject of sins, out of honor to the Lord; for from Him we know what abundance of grace for overcoming sin in every particular was conferred upon her who had the merit to conceive and bear Him Who undoubtedly had no sin.

St. Augustine: *De Natura et Gratia,* 42. (5th cent.)

But if she glories in her maternity, it is not in herself, but in Him Who was born of her. He Who was born of her is God; and He shall bestow upon His mother special glory in heaven, as she was prevented with special grace on earth, so that she conceived and bore miraculously and as a virgin.

St. Bernard: *Sermon 2 in Vigil. Nativ. Domini,* 1. (12th cent.)

I consider that the blessing of a fuller sanctification descended upon her, so as not only to sanctify her birth, but also to keep her life pure from all sin; which gift is believed to have been bestowed upon none other born of woman. This singular privilege of sanctity, to lead her life without any sin, entirely befitted the queen of virgins, who should bear the Destroyer of sin and death, who should obtain the gift of life and righteousness for all.

St. Bernard: *Letters,* 215, 4. (12th cent.)

Christ is the principle of grace, authoritatively in His Godhead, instrumentally in His manhood. But of all persons, the blessed Virgin Mary was closest to His manhood, which He received from her, and therefore fair it was that she should receive a greater measure of grace, above others.

St. Thomas Aquinas: *Summa Theologica,* 3, 27, 5. (13th cent.)

If anyone shall say that a man once justified . . . can through the whole of life avoid all sins, even though they be venial, except by a special privilege of God, as the Church holds to have been the case with the Blessed Virgin, let him be anathema.

Decree of the Council of Trent, Session 6, Canon 23. (Jan. 13, 1547)

VII—*Gate of Heaven*

Standing in the temple of thy glory, we think that we stand in heaven. O Mother of God, gate of heaven, open to us the gate of thy mercy.

Byzantine Horologion, Troparion at Matins. (ca. 7th cent.)

We sing unto thee, we praise thee, we worship thee, O God-bearer; for thou hast brought forth the one Son and God of the undivided Trinity, and hast opened to us on earth the heavens.

Byzantine Triodion, Great Canon of St. Andrew of Crete. (8th cent.)

Let us all praise the holy Virgin, as the gate of salvation and a garden enclosed, and as having been the cloud over the Everlasting Light: to her let us say: All Hail!

Byzantine Triodion, Great Thursday, Service of the Holy Passion. (ca. 6th to 8th cent.)

Gate of immortal bliss,—
  Whose sweet celestial ray
Comes shining o'er the vast abyss,
  That severs night from day.

M. Bridges: *Janua coeli.* (19th cent.)

VIII—*Help of Christians*

Refuge terrible in strength and that cannot be put to confusion, do not regard our prayers lightly, O Mother of God, good and worthy of all praise; confirm the estate of the orthodox, save those whom thou hast chosen to rule, and grant them victory from on high; for thou didst bring forth God, O most blessed one.

> Byzantine Horologion, Troparion at Matins. (ca. 6th to 8th cent.)

Hear us, holy Lord, almighty Father, eternal God, Who hast deigned to enlighten the whole world by the overshadowing of divine grace of the sacred womb of blessed Mary; we humbly implore Thy Majesty, that what we cannot obtain through our own merits, we may be able to obtain by her help.

> Gelasian Sacramentary, Collect for the Annunciation. (ca. 7th cent.)

O holy Mary, be thou a help to the helpless, a strength to the fearful, a comfort to the sorrowful; pray for the people, plead for the clergy, make intercession for all women vowed to God; may all that are keeping this thy holy feast day feel the might of thine assistance.

> Roman Breviary, Feasts of the Blessed Virgin, Antiphon at Vespers. (Lib. Respons., ca. 7th cent.)

O Virgin Mother of God, thou art an unassailable rampart, a fortress of salvation; we beseech thee, destroy the schemes of our enemies, turn the grief of thy people into joy, gather together those who belong to thee, strengthen our God-fearing rulers, intercede for the peace of the world; for thou, O Mother of God, art our hope.

> Byzantine Horologion, Troparion at Nocturns. (ca. 9th cent. ?)

O Mother of God, I have an unashamed trust in thee and shall be saved. I have thine help, most pure one, and have no fear. I shall put to flight my enemies and subdue them, with thy protection for my armor. Asking for thy mighty help I say, Save me, O Lady, by thy prayers, and rouse me from darkly sleep to praise thee, through the might of God the Son, Who took His flesh from thee.

> Byzantine Horologion, Troparion at Great Compline. (ca. 9th cent. ?)

Today we faithful hold a joyful festival, being o'ershadowed by thy presence, O Mother of God; and looking at thy most pure image, we humbly say, Cover us with thy honorable protection, and deliver us from all evil, praying thy Son, Christ our God, to save our souls.

> Byzantine Menaea, Troparion for Feast of the Protection of our Lady (Oct. 1) (After 9th cent. ?)

In dangers, in doubts, in difficulties, think of Mary, call upon Mary. Let not her name depart from thy lips, never suffer it to leave thy heart. And that thou mayest more surely obtain the assistance of her prayer, neglect not to walk in her footsteps.

> St. Bernard: *Second Sermon on the Virgin Mother*. (12th cent.)

Remember, holy Mary,
'Twas never heard or known
That anyone who sought thee
  And made to thee his moan—
That anyone who hastened
  For shelter to thy care
Was ever yet abandoned
  And left to his despair.

> Hymn *Memorare*, attr. to St. Bernard. (Tr. M. Russell) (12th cent.)

Immortal God, That savedst Susanne
Fro false blame, and thou, merciful maid,
Mary I mean, daughter to Saint Anne,
Before whose Child angels sing Osanne,
If I be guiltless of this felony,
My succour be, for else I shall die!

> Chaucer: *The Man of Law's Tale*, 639. (14th cent.)

Almighty and all-merciable queen,
To whom that all this world fleeth for socour,
To have release of sin, sorrow and tene,
Glorious Virgin, of all flowers flower,
To thee I flee, confounded in errour!
Help and relieve, thou mighty debonaire,
Have mercy on my perilous langour!
Vanquished m'hath my cruel adversaire.

>   tene—vexation, grief
> Chaucer: *An A.B.C.* (14th cent.)

O most blessed Virgin Mary, Mother most loving and merciful, I, a miserable sinner, come before thee with heartfelt prayer, that of thy loving kindness thou wouldst vouchsafe graciously to be near me and all who throughout the whole Church are to receive the Body and Blood of thy Son this day, even as thou wert near thy most dear Son as He hung bleeding on the Cross, that, aided by thy gracious help, we may worthily offer up a pure and acceptable sacrifice in the sight of the holy and undivided Trinity. Amen.

Roman Missal, Prayer *O Mater Pietatis et Misericordiae* before Mass. (Modern)

For, she waits till earth's aid forsakes us,
Till we know our own efforts are vain;
And we wait, in our faithless blindness,
Till no chance but her prayers remain.

Adelaide Procter: *The Shrines of Mary.* (19th cent.)

IX—*Her Immaculate Heart*

Mother of God! we hail thy heart,
Throned in the azure skies,
While far and wide within its charm
The whole creation lies.
O sinless heart, all hail!
God's dear delight, all hail!
Our home, our home is deep in thee,
Eternally, eternally.

F. Faber: *The Immaculate Heart of Mary.* (19th cent.)

Even as our predecessor of immortal memory, Leo XIII, at the dawn of the twentieth century saw fit to consecrate the whole human race to the most Sacred Heart of Jesus, so we have likewise, as the representative of the whole human family which He redeemed, desired to dedicate it in turn to the immaculate heart of the Virgin Mary.

Pope Pius XII: *Auspicia Quaedam.* (May 1, 1948)

X—*Her Humility*

Who is this virgin so worthy of reverence as to be saluted by an angel: yet so humble as to be betrothed to a carpenter? A beautiful combination is that of virginity with humility: and that soul singularly pleases God in which humility gives worth to virginity, and virginity throws a new luster on humility.

St. Bernard: *Sermon 1 in Vigil. Nativ. Domini,* 5. (12th cent.)

Reverence her, O you who are married, the purity of the flesh in incorruptible flesh: you also, holy virgins, admire the motherhood in a virgin: and all you who are men, imitate the humility of the Mother of God. Holy angels, honor the Mother of your King, you who adore the Son of a virgin of our race, Who is at once our King and yours, the Restorer of our race and the Founder of your state.

St. Bernard: *Sermon 1 in Vigil. Nativ. Domini,* 9. (12th cent.)

So the blessed Mother of God, the Virgin Mary, Mother of the Lord, who was above the law by a singular privilege, did not disdain for the sake of showing her humility to submit herself to the ordinances of the law.

Bracton: *On the Laws and Customs of England,* 1, 8, 5. (13th cent.)

XI—*Her Intercession*

O God, who, by the fruitful virginity of blessed Mary, hast given to mankind the rewards of eternal salvation: grant, we beseech thee, that we may experience her intercession for us, by whom we deserved to receive the Author of life, our Lord Jesus Christ.

Roman Missal, Feast of the Circumcision (Jan. 1), Collect. (Gregorian, ca. 7th cent.)

Rejoice, O Virgin Mary, thou alone hast destroyed all heresies. Who didst believe the words of the archangel Gabriel. Whilst a virgin thou didst bring forth God and man: and after childbirth thou didst remain a virgin. O Mother of God, intercede for us.

Roman Missal, Tract for Feasts of the B.V.M. (Gregorian, ca. 7th cent.)

Save those who hope in thee, O Mother of the Sun Which knows no setting, O Mother of God; by thy prayers ask thy divine Son, we beseech thee, to grant rest to him who has departed, where the souls of the just repose; make him a heir of the divine benefits in the halls of the just, unto everlasting memory, O immaculate one.

Byzantine Euchologion, Funeral Service, Farewell Troparion at the Grave. (ca. 8th cent. ?)

Do not despise, O most glorious one,
The prayers of those who faithfully be-
   seech thee,
But receive them and present them
To your Son God, O immaculate one,
To Him Who is our only Benefactor,
While we have you as our patron.

Attr. to St. John of Damascus. (8th cent.)

O Virgin, the prophet calls thee a cloud of perpetual light, for in thee the Logos of the Father came down like dew on fleece: He rises like the sun, illumines the world, and thus as Christ our God abolishes error. All-holy one, we beg thee do not cease to pray for us, who confess that you are the true Mother of God.

Attributed to St. John of Damascus. (8th cent.)

Daily, daily, sing to Mary,
   Sing, my soul, her praises due;
All her feasts, her actions worship,
   With the heart's devotion true.
      Lost in wond'ring contemplation
      Be her majesty confest:
      Call her Mother, call her Virgin,
      Happy Mother, Virgin blest.

She is mighty to deliver;
   Call her, trust her lovingly:
When the tempest rages round thee,
   She will calm the troubled sea.
      Gifts of heaven she has given,
      Noble Lady! to our race:

She, the Queen, who decks her
   subjects
With the light of God's own
   grace.

Bernard of Cluny: *Omni Die Dic Mariae.* (Tr. E. Caswall) (12th cent.)

Grant us Thy servants, we beseech Thee, O Lord our God, to enjoy perpetual health of mind and body; that through the glorious intercession of the blessed Mary ever Virgin, we may be delivered from present sorrow, and enjoy everlasting happiness.

Roman Missal, Collect for Feasts of the B.V.M. (ca. 14th cent.)

Remember, O most loving Virgin Mary, that never was it known that any one who fled to thy protection, implored thy help, and sought thy intercession, was left forsaken. Filled, therefore, with confidence in thy goodness, I fly to thee, O Mother, Virgin of virgins; to thee I come, before thee I stand a sorrowing sinner. Despise not my words, O Mother of the Word, but graciously hear and grant my prayer.

Prayer *Memorare O piissima Virgo Maria* in Raccolta. (Part of a longer prayer *Ave augustissima Regina pacis,* cf. Thurston, Prayers, 152) (ca. 15th cent.)

I consider it impossible then for those who believe the Church to be one vast body in heaven and earth, in which every holy creature of God has his place, and of which prayer is the life, when once they recognize the sanctity and dignity of the blessed Virgin, not to perceive immediately, that her office above is one of perpetual intercession for the faithful militant, and that our very relation to her must be that of clients to a patron, and that, in the eternal enmity which exists between the woman and the serpent, while the serpent's strength lies in being the tempter, the weapon of the second Eve and Mother of God is prayer.

Card. Newman: *Letter to the Rev. E. B. Pusey.* (19th cent.)

XII—*Mediatrix; Co-redemptrix; Dispensatrix*

[Mary] worked the salvation of the world and conceived the redemption of mankind.

> St. Ambrose: *Letters,* 49, 2. (4th cent.)

Mother of grace, O Mary blest,
To thee, sweet fount of love, we fly:
Shield us through life, and take us hence
To thy dear bosom when we die.

> Roman Breviary, Little Office of the Blessed Virgin, *Maria Mater gratiae.* (From Hymn *Quem terra pontus sidera.*) (Tr. E. Caswall) (Fortunatus. 6th cent.)

We beseech Thee, almighty God, may the glorious intercession of the blessed and glorious ever Virgin Mother of God Mary protect us, and lead us to life eternal.

> Gelasian Sacramentary, Collect for the Annunciation. (7th cent.)

O most pure Mother of God, thou art the hope and mediatrix and refuge of Christians, the wall that cannot be overthrown, the harbor of the helpless unagitated by storms; and since thou savest the world by thy ceaseless intercession, remember us also, O Virgin worthy of all praise.

> Byzantine Horologion, Troparion at Terce. (ca. 6th to 8th cent.)

O Mother of God, we make our boast in thee as a mediatrix with God. Stretch forth thy matchless hand, and overcome our foes; send to thy servants help from the holy place.

> Byzantine Horologion, Exapostilarion at Matins. (ca. 6th to 8th cent.)

Most blessed art thou, O Virgin Mother of God, for by Him That was incarnate of thee hell hath been led captive, Adam hath been recalled, the curse hath been made void, Eve hath been set free, death hath died, and we have been made to live. Wherefore praising thee we cry, Blessed art Thou, O Christ our God, Who so willed it, glory to Thee!

> Byzantine Horologion, Troparion at Matins. (ca. 6th to 8th cent.)

For she, being preordained by the prescient counsel of God and foreshadowed and proclaimed in different images and words of the prophets through the Holy Spirit, sprang at the predetermined time from the root of David, according to the promises that were made to him.

> St. John of Damascus: *Exposition of the Orthodox Faith,* 4, 14. (8th cent.)

All generations bless thee, O Virgin Mother of God; for in thee the Uncontainable vouchsafed to be contained, even Christ our God. We also are blessed who have thee for our mediatrix; for thou dost pray for us day and night and the scepter of kingdoms is strengthened by thy prayers. Praising thee, we cry, Hail! full of grace, the Lord is with thee.

> Byzantine Horologion, Troparion at Nocturns. (ca. 9th cent. ?)

O Lady, who art the door of grace, who dost open the gates of heaven to the faithful; open unto me the shining doors of repentance, and deliver me from the gates of death.

> Byzantine Euchologion, Penitential Canon, Third Ode. (ca. 9th cent. ?)

Through thee, O most blessed one, finder of grace, mother of life, mother of salvation, through thee let us have access to thy Son, so that through thee He may receive us Who was given us through thee.

> St. Bernard: *Second Sermon for Advent.* (12th cent.)

Our Lady, our mediatrix, our advocate, reconcile us, commend us, represent us to thy Son. Do so, O blessed one, by the grace which thou hast found by the prerogative which thou hast merited, by the mercy of which thou art mother; so that He Who has deigned to become by thy means a sharer of our weakness and our misery, Jesus Christ thy Son, our Lord, may at thy intercession make us sharers of His glory and blessedness, Who is above all God blessed for ever. Amen.

> St. Bernard: *Second Sermon for Advent.* (12th cent.)

O glorious Virgin! O rod sublime *from the root of Jesse!* To what a dizzy height dost thou lift thy crest! Even to Him That sitteth on the throne, even to the Lord of majesty! Yet this should not astonish us, seeing that thou hast struck so deep the roots of thy humility. O truly celestial plant, singularly holy, precious above all! Verily thou art the tree of life, which alone has been reputed worthy to bear the fruit of salvation.

> St. Bernard: *Second Sermon for Advent.* (12th cent.)

He willed us to have all through Mary. (Totum nos habere voluit per Mariam.)

> St. Bernard: *Sermon in Nativ. B.V.M., 7.* (12th cent.)

There is no reason why creatures should not be called mediators after a fashion, in that they co-operate in our reconciliation, disposing and ministering to men's union with God.

> St. Thomas Aquinas: *Summa Theologica,* 3, 26, 1. (13th cent.)

Lady, thou art so great and hast such might
  That whoso crave grace, nor to thee repair,
  Their longing even without wing seeketh flight.
Thy charity doth not only him up-bear
  Who prays, but in thy bounty's large excess
  Thou oftentimes dost even forerun the prayer.

> Dante: *Paradiso, Canto 33.* (Prayer of St. Bernard) (Tr. Binyon) (14th cent.)

O Mother-maid, Maid-mother, chaste and free!
O bush unburnt, burning in Moses' sight,

Thou that didst ravish down from Deity
Upon thy humbleness the Spirit's flight
That lit upon thy heart, and in whose might
The Word took flesh, help me to tell my story
In reverence of thee and of thy glory!

No tongue or knowledge can have confidence,
Lady, to tell thy great humility,
Thy bounty, virtue, and magnificence;
For sometimes, Lady, ere men pray to thee
Thou goest before in thy benignity
And through thy prayer thou gettest for each one
Light that may guide them to thy blessed Son.

> Chaucer: *The Prioress's Prologue.* (Tr. Coghill) (14th cent.)

Star of the morning, like an eye
  That beams upon the brow of love;
Oh! let thy lustrous radiancy
  Shine from above!

. . . .

Center, and source of endless grace
  For those who on thee humbly call
With the bright visions of thy face
  Illumine all!

> M. Bridges: *Stella Matutina.* (19th cent.)

Mary is only our mother by divine appointment, given us from the Cross; her presence is above, not on earth; her office is external, not within us.

> Card. Newman: *Letter to the Rev. E. B. Pusey.* (19th cent.)

May she, then, most holy mother of all Christ's members, to whose immaculate heart we have trustingly consecrated all men, her body and soul refulgent with the glory of heaven where she reigns with her Son—may she never cease to beg from Him that a continuous, copious flow of graces may pass from its glorious Head into all the members of the Mystical Body.

> Pope Pius XII: *Mystici Corporis.* (June 29, 1943)

He, the Son of God, reflects on His heavenly Mother the glory, the majesty and the dominion of His kingship; for, having been associated with the King of martyrs in the ineffable work of human redemption as Mother and co-operatrix, she remains forever associated with Him, with an almost unlimited power, in the distribution of the graces which flow from the redemption.

Pope Pius XII: *Radio Address on the Queenship.* (To Portugal) (May 13, 1946)

In the actual, living, human person who is the Virgin Mother of Christ are all the poverty and all the wisdom of all the saints. It all came to them through her, and is in her. The sanctity of all the saints is a participation in her sanctity, because in the order He has established God wills that all graces come to men through Mary.

Thomas Merton: *Seeds of Contemplation.* (20th cent.)

XIII—*Mother Most Chaste*

Let Mary's life be for you like the portrayal of virginity, for from her, as though from a mirror, is reflected the beauty of chastity and the ideal of virtue. See in her the pattern of your life, for in her, as though in a model, manifest teachings of goodness show what you should correct, what you should copy and what preserve. . . . She is the image of virginity. For such was Mary that her life alone suffices for the instruction of all.

St. Ambrose: *De Virginibus,* 2, 6. (4th cent.)

Mary bears the price of our redemption. The water which gushed out of the rock to refresh the people of Israel is her symbol (Numb. 20, 8). Hers is the integrity of maidenhood, the fruitfulness of wedlock, the purity of chastity. Let us bless her often, and sing her praises: *for behold, from henceforth all generations shall call me blessed* (Luke 1, 48).

St. Thomas Aquinas: *Sermon for the Fourth Sunday of Lent,* 47. (13th cent.)

And love my heart to chaste desires shall bring;
When fairest Queen looks on me from her throne,
And, jealous, bids me love but her alone.

Henry Constable: *Sonnet to our Blessed Lady.* (16th cent.)

Lily, O Lily of the valleys!
Lily, O Lily of Calvary hill!
White with the glory of all graces,
Earth with the breath of thy pure spirit fill;
Lily, O Lily of the valleys!
Lily, O Lily of Calvary Hill!

Lionel Johnson: *Flos florum.* (1894)

XIV—*Mother of All*

No one may understand the meaning of the Gospel [of St. John], if he has not rested on the breast of Jesus and received Mary from Jesus, to be his mother also.

Origen: *In Joh.* 1, 6. (3rd cent.)

Mary bore the Head of this body in the flesh; the Church bears the members of that Head in the spirit. In neither does virginity impede fecundity; in neither does fecundity destroy virginity.

St. Augustine: *On Holy Virginity,* 2. (5th cent.)

The Catholic Church, schooled by the Holy Ghost, has always most diligently professed, not only to venerate Mary most devoutly as the Mother of the Lord and Redeemer, the Queen of heaven and earth, but also to honor her with filial affection as the most loving Mother who was left to her with the last words of her dying Spouse.

Pope Benedict XIV: *Gloriosae Dominae.* (Sept. 27, 1748)

Mother, who lead'st me still by unknown ways,
Giving the gifts I know not how to ask,
Bless thou the work
Which, done, redeems my many wasted days,

Makes white the murk,
And crowns the few which thou wilt
not dispraise,
When clear my songs of lady's graces
rang,
And little guess'd I 'twas of thee I sang!

> Coventry Patmore: *The Child's Purchase.*
> (19th cent.)

All of us who are united with Christ
and are, as the apostle says, *Members of
His body, made from His flesh, and from
His bones* (Eph. 5, 30), have come
forth from the womb of Mary as a body
united to its head. Hence, in a spiritual
and mystical sense, we are called children
of Mary, and she is the mother of us all.

> Pope St. Pius X: *Ad diem illum.* (Feb. 2,
> 1904)

She, by the very fact that she brought
forth the Redeemer of the human race,
is also in a manner the most tender
mother of us all, whom Christ our Lord
deigned to have as His brothers (Rom.
8, 29).

> Pope Pius XI: *Lux Veritatis.* (Dec. 25,
> 1931)

We are all children of the same Mother,
Mary, who lives in heaven, the bond of
union for the Mystical Body of Christ
and new Eve, new Mother of the living,
who wishes to lead all men to the truth
and grace of her divine Son.

> Pope Pius XII: *Homily on the Assumption.*
> (AAS, 42, 1950, 781) (1950)

XV—*Queen of Sorrows*

Thy Mother seeing Thee, the Lamb
and Shepherd and Savior of the world,
upon the Cross, said with tears, Lo! the
world rejoiceth, for it gaineth deliverance; but my heart is broken, for I see
Thy crucifixion, which Thou endurest for
all, O my Son and my God.

> Byzantine Horologion, Troparion at None.
> (ca. 6th to 8th cent.)

Standing by Thy Cross, she that brought
Thee forth without seed, sorrowfully
cried, Alas! my sweetest Child, how dost
Thou fade away before mine eyes, how
art Thou numbered with the dead?

> Byzantine Horologion, Exapostilarion at
> Matins. (ca. 6th to 8th cent.)

But this blessed woman who was deemed
worthy of gifts that are supernatural, suffered those pains, which she escaped at
the birth, in the hour of the passion, enduring from motherly sympathy the
rending of the bowels, and when she beheld Him Whom she knew to be God by
the manner of His generation killed as
a malefactor, her thoughts pierced her as
a sword, and this is the meaning of this
verse: *A sword shall pierce through thy
own soul also* (Luke, 2, 35).

> St. John of Damascus: *Exposition of the
> Orthodox Faith,* 4, 14. (8th cent.)

At the Cross her station keeping,
Stood the mournful Mother weeping,
Close to Jesus to the last:
Through her heart, His sorrow sharing,
All His bitter anguish bearing,
Now at length the sword had passed.

· · · · · ·

Holy Mother! pierce me through;
In my heart each wound renew
Of my Savior crucified:
Let me share with thee His pain,
Who for all my sins was slain,
Who for me in torments died.

· · · · · ·

Virgin of all virgins blest!
Listen to my fond request:
Let me share thy grief divine;
Let me, to my latest breath,
In my body bear the death
Of that dying Son of thine.

> Roman Breviary, Feast of the Seven
> Sorrows of the Blessed Virgin (Lent).
> Hymn *Stabat Mater dolorosa.* (Tr. E.
> Caswall) (Attr. to Jacopone da Todi, 13th
> cent.)

O God, at Whose passion, according to
the prophecy of Simeon, a sword of sorrow pierced the sweet soul of the glorious Virgin and Mother Mary; grant in
Thy mercy that we, who call to mind

with veneration her soul pierced with
sorrow, through the glorious merits and
prayers of all the saints faithfully standing by Thy Cross, may obtain the blessed
result of Thy passion.

Roman Missal, Collect for Feast of Seven
Sorrows. (Friday before Palm Sunday).
(15th cent. ?)

Jesus, my love, my Son, my God,
  Behold Thy Mother wash'd in tears:
Thy bloody wounds be made a rod
  To chasten these my later years.

You cruel Jews, come work your ire
  Upon this worthless flesh of mine,
And kindle not eternal fire
  By wounding Him Who is divine.

Bl. Robert Southwell: *The Virgin Mary to
Christ*. (17th cent.)

In shade of death's sad tree
  Stood doleful she.
Ah she! now by none other
Name to be known, alas, but sorrow's
    Mother.
  Before her eyes
Hers, and the whole world's joys,
Hanging all torn she sees, and in His
    woes
And pains, her pangs and throes.
Each wound of His, from every part,
All, more at home in her own heart.

Richard Crashaw: *Sancta Maria Dolorum*.
(17th cent.)

  O Mother, turtle-dove!
  Soft source of love
That these dry lids might borrow
Something from thy full seas of sorrow!
  O in that breast
  Of thine (the noblest nest
Both of love's fires and floods) might
    I recline
This hard, cold heart of mine!
The chill lump would relent and prove
Soft subject for the siege of love.

Richard Crashaw: *Sancta Maria Dolorum*.
(17th cent.)

  Now let the darkling eve
  Mount suddenly on high,

The sun affrighted reave
His splendors from the sky,
While I in silence grieve
O'er the mocked agony
And the divine catastrophe.

Roman Breviary, Feast of the Seven
Sorrows of the Blessed Virgin (Sept. 15),
Hymn *Jam toto subitus vesper eat polo*.
(Tr. H. Henry) (Attr. to Callisto
Palumbella, 18th cent.)

What a sea of tears and sorrow
  Did the soul of Mary toss
To and fro upon its billows,
  While she wept her bitter loss;
In her arms her Jesus holding,
  Torn but newly from the Cross!

Roman Breviary, Feast of Seven Sorrows
(Sept. 15), Hymn *O quot undis
lachrymarum*. (Tr. Caswall) (Anonymous,
18th cent.)

God in Whom all grace doth dwell!
Grant us grace to ponder well
On the Virgin's dolors seven;
On the wounds to Jesus given.

Roman Breviary, Feast of Seven Sorrows,
Hymn *Summae Deus clementiae*. (Tr.
Caswall) (19th cent.)

O Queen of sorrows! raise thine eyes;
  See! the first light of dawn is there;
The hour is come, and thou must end
  Thy forty hours of lonely prayer.

. . . . . .

He comes! He comes! and will she run
  With freest love her Child to greet?
He came! and she, His creature, fell
  Prostrate at Her Creator's feet.

. . . . . .

O let not words be bold to tell
  What in the Mother's heart was
    done,
When for a moment Mary saw
  The unshrouded Godhead of her
    Son.

What bliss for us that Jesus gave
  To her such wondrous gifts and
    powers;

It is a joy the joys were hers,
  For Mary's joys are doubly ours!

F. Faber: *The Apparition of Jesus to our
Blessed Lady.* (19th cent.)

O Lady Mary, thy bright crown
  Is no mere crown of majesty;
For with the reflex of His own
  Resplendent thorns Christ circled
  thee.

The red rose of this Passiontide
  Doth take a deeper hue from thee,
In the five wounds of Jesus dyed,
  And in thy bleeding thoughts, Mary!

F. Thompson: *The Passion of Mary.*
(19th cent.)

Therefore, O tender Lady, Queen Mary,
  Thou gentleness that dost enmoss
  and drape
The Cross's rigorous austerity,
  Wipe thou the blood from wounds
  that needs must gape.

F. Thompson: *Ode to the Setting Sun.*
(19th cent.)

She that is heaven's Queen
  Her title borrows,
For that she, pitiful,
  Beareth our sorrows.
So thou, *Regina mi,*
  Spes infirmorum;
With all our grieving crowned
  Mater dolorum!

F. Thompson: *A Carrier Song.* (19th cent.)

XVI—*Name of Mary*

I'll sing a hymn to Mary,
  The Mother of my God,
The Virgin of all virgins,
  Of David's royal blood.
O teach me, holy Mary,
  A loving song to frame,
When wicked men blaspheme thee,
  To love and bless thy name.

Fr. Wyse: *Hymn to the Blessed Virgin.*
(19th cent.?)

XVII—*Queen of Heaven*

O glorious Lady! throned on high
Above the star-illumined sky;

Thereto ordained, thy bosom lent
To thy Creator nourishment.

Venantius Fortunatus: *Quem terra pontus
sidera* (*aethera*). (Tr. J. Doran and
M. Blacker) (6th cent.)

Assuredly she who played the part of the
Creator's servant and Mother is in all
strictness and truth in reality God's
Mother and Lady and Queen over all
created things.

St. John of Damascus: *Exposition of the
Orthodox Faith,* 4, 14. (8th cent.)

O thou, the world's most blessed Queen,
save them that from their soul confess
thee Mother of God; for thou art an invincible mediatrix, who truly didst bear
God.

Byzantine Oktoechos, Canon of Sixth Tone,
Fifth Ode. (ca. 9th cent.)

Hail to the Queen who reigns above,
Mother of clemency and love,
Hail, thou, our hope, life, sweetness;
  we
Eve's banished children cry to thee.

We from this wretched vale of tears
Send sighs and groans unto thy ears;
O, then, sweet Advocate, bestow
A pitying look on us below.

After this our exile, let us see
Our blessed Jesus, born of thee.
O merciful, O pious Maid,
O gracious Mary, lend thine aid.

Roman Breviary, Final Antiphon of the
Blessed Virgin after Pentecost, *Salve Regina
mater misericordiae* (Hail, Holy Queen,
Mother of mercy. . . .) (Primer, 1685)
(Attr. to Hermann Contractus, 1013–1054)

Hail, O Queen of heaven, enthroned!
Hail, by angels Mistress owned!
Root of Jesse, Gate of morn,
Whence the world's true Light was
  born:
Glorious Virgin joy to thee,
Loveliest whom in heaven they see:

Fairest thou where all are fair,
Plead with Christ our sins to spare.

Roman Breviary, Final Antiphon of Blessed
Virgin during Lent, *Ave Regina coelorum.*
(Tr. E. Caswall) (Authorship and date
uncertain, since 12th cent.)

Joy to thee, O Queen of heaven!
   Alleluia.
He Whom it was thine to bear;
   Alleluia.
As He promised, hath arisen;
   Alleluia.
Plead for us a pitying prayer;
   Alleluia.

Roman Breviary, Final Antiphon of Blessed
Virgin after Easter, *Regina coeli laetare
alleluia.* (Tr. E. Caswall) (Author
unknown, 14th cent. or earlier)

Doubt is there none, thou queen of
   misericorde,
That thou n'art cause of grace and
   mercy here;
God vouchsafed through thee with us
   t'acorde.
For certes, Christes blissful Mother
   dear,
Were now the bow bent in such manner,
As it was first, of justice and of ire,
The rightful God nolde of no mercy
   hear;
But through thee have we grace, as we
   desire.

t'acorde—to be reconciled
nolde—would not
Chaucer: *An A.B.C.* (14th cent.)

Sooth is, that God ne granteth no pity
Withoute thee; for God, of His good-
   nesse,
Forgiveth none, but it like unto thee.
He hath thee makèd Vicaire and Mais-
   tresse
Of all the world, and eek Governeresse
Of heaven, and He represseth His jus-
   tice
After thy will, and therefore in witnesse
He hath thee crowned in so royal wise.

eek—also
Chaucer: *An A.B.C.* (14th cent.)

Holy Queen! we bend before thee,
   Queen of purity divine!
Make us love thee, we implore thee,
   Make us truly to be thine.

St. Casimir: *Pulchra Tota sine Nota.* (Tr.
E. Vaughan) (15th cent.)

In that, O Queen of queens, thy birth
   was free
   From guilt, which others do of grace
      bereave,
   When, in their mother's womb they
      life receive,
   God, as His sole-borne Daughter,
      lovèd thee:
To match thee like thy birth's nobility,
   He thee His Spirit for thy Spouse did
      leave,
   Of Whom thou didst His only Son
      conceive;
   And so was linked to all the Trinity.

Cease, then, O queens, who earthly
   crowns do wear,
   To glory in the pomp of worldly
      things:
   If men such high respect unto you
      bear
Which daughters, wives and mothers
   are of kings;
   What honor should unto that Queen
      be done
   Who had your God for Father,
      Spouse and Son?

Henry Constable: *To Our Blessed Lady,
Sonnet I.* (17th cent.)

If love do follow worth and dignity,
   Thou all in thy perfections dost
      exceed;
   If love be led by hope of future meed,
   What pleasure more than thee in
      heaven to see?
An earthly sight doth only please the
   eye,
   And breeds desire, but doth not
      satisfy:
   Thy sight gives us possession of all
      joy;
And with such full delights each sense
   shall fill,

As heart shall wish but for to see
thee still,
And ever seeing, ever shall enjoy.

Henry Constable: *To Our Blessed Lady,*
Sonnet III. (17th cent.)

Hail, most high, most humble one!
Above the world; below thy Son,
Whose blush the moon beauteously
mars
And stains the timorous light of stars.
He that made all things had not done
Till He had made Himself thy Son.
The whole world's Host would be thy
Guest,
And board Himself at thy rich breast.
O boundless hospitality!
The Feast of all things feeds on thee.

Richard Crashaw: *The Hymn O Gloriosa*
Domina. (17th cent.)

This is why the blessed Virgin is called
powerful—nay, sometimes, all-powerful, because she has, more than anyone
else, more than all angels and saints, this
great, prevailing gift of prayer. No one
has access to the Almighty as His Mother
has; none has merit such as hers. Her
Son will deny her nothing that she asks;
and herein lies her power. While she
defends the Church, neither height nor
depth, neither men nor evil spirits,
neither great monarchs, nor craft of
man, nor popular violence, can avail to
harm us; for human life is short, but
Mary reigns above, a Queen forever.

Card. Newman: *Meditations and Devotions.*
(19th cent.)

She, about whose moonèd brows
Seven stars make seven glows,
Seven lights for seven woes;
She, like thine own galaxy,
All lusters in one purity.

F. Thompson: *A Dead Astronomer:*
Stephen Perry, S.J. (19th cent.)

Dipped in the instincts of heaven,
Robed in the garments of earth,
Maiden and Mother and Queen,
Wearing each crown at thy birth:
Threefold thy gift to the world,

Pluck'd from God's ripening sky,
Tending the altar of life,
Kindred to angels on high.

Thomas O'Hagan: *Woman.* (19th cent.)

O Flower of flowers, our Lady of the
May!
Thou gavest us the world's own
Light of light:
Under the stars, amid the snows, He
lay;
While angels, through the Galilean
night
Sang glory and sang peace.

Lionel Johnson: *Our Lady of the May.*
(19th cent.)

Hail Mary, pearl of grace,
Pure flower of Adam's race,
And vessel rare of God's election;
Unstained as virgin snow,
Serene as sunset glow—
We sinners crave thy sure protection.

Thou Queen of high estate,
Conceived immaculate
To form incarnate Love's pure dwell-
ing;
The Spirit found His rest
Within thy sinless breast,
And thence flow joys beyond all telling.

. . . .

Through His dear blood Who died,
By sinners crucified,
Art thou preserved, and we forgiven,
Help us to conquer sin,
That we may enter in,
Through thee, the golden gate, to
heaven.

Dom Bede Camm: *Hymn to Our Lady.*
(20th cent.)

Jesus is King throughout all eternity by
nature and by right of conquest; through
Him, with Him and subordinate to Him,
Mary is Queen by grace, by divine relationship, by right of conquest and by
singular election. And her kingdom is as
vast as that of her Son and God, since
nothing is excluded from her dominion.

And this queenship of hers is essentially maternal, exclusively beneficent.

Pope Pius XII: *Radio Address on the Queenship* (To Portugal). (May 13, 1946)

See also Mary

XVIII—*Refuge of Sinners*

O Mother of God, hope and protection of those who praise thee, remove from me the heavy yoke of my sins; and, chaste Mistress, receive me a penitent.

Byzantine Triodion, Great Canon of St. Andrew of Crete. (8th cent.)

Because of the multitude of my transgressions I come to thee, O pure Mother of God, asking for salvation. Visit thou my ailing soul, and beseech thy Son and our God to grant me remission of the sins I have wrought, O thou most blessed one.

Byzantine Euchologion, Prayer before Communion. (ca. 9th cent.?)

I am bowed down with many temptations and evil deeds, and with soul and body I bow down to thee, O pure one, and ceaselessly cry, Do thou convert me.

Byzantine Euchologion, Penitential Canon, First Ode. (ca. 9th cent.?)

O thou Virgin, spotless, undefiled, incorruptible, most chaste and pure, Lady, Bride of God, who by thy glorious giving birth hast united God the Word with men, and linked our apostate nature with heavenly things; who art the one hope of the hopeless, the helper of the oppressed, the ready protection of them that flee unto thee, and the refuge of all Christians; despise me not, a defiled sinner, who by my impious thoughts, words and deeds have made myself an unprofitable servant, and by reason of my sloth am become a slave of sensual pleasure. . . . Accept this my prayer offered unto thee with unhallowed lips, and using thy maternal influence with thy Son, our Lord and Master, beseech Him to open to me the loving tenderness of His grace. . . .

Byzantine Horologion, Prayer at Compline. (ca. 9th cent.?)

Since we dare not on account of our many sins, do thou, O Virgin Mother of God, pray Him That was born of thee. For thy maternal prayers avail much in gaining the Lord's mercy. Do not despise, O most pure one, the prayers of sinners, for He That vouchsafed to suffer for us is merciful and powerful to save.

Byzantine Horologion, Troparion at Great Compline. (ca. 9th cent.?)

So, Mary, they who justly feel the weight
   Of heaven's offended majesty, implore
   Thy reconciling aid with suppliant knee:
Of sinful man, O sinless advocate,
   To thee they turn, nor Him they less adore;
   'Tis still His light they love, less dreadful seen in thee.

Gerald Griffin: *The Nightingale*. (19th cent.)

XIX—*Seat of Wisdom*

We see the Blessed Virgin as a lamp of living light shining upon those in darkness; she kindleth an unearthly light to lead all unto divine knowledge; she, the radiance that enlighteneth the mind, is praised by our cry: Hail! ray of the spiritual Sun; Hail! ray-flash of never-waning light; Hail! lightning-flash illumining souls. . . .

Byzantine Triodion, Akathist Hymn, Oikos 11. (Tr. V. McNabb) (ca. 7th cent.)

XX—*Morning Star; Star of the Sea*

Hail, thou Star of ocean,
   Portal of the sky,
Ever-Virgin Mother
   Of the Lord most High!

Oh, by Gabriel's AVE
Uttered long ago,
EVA'S name reversing,
'Stablish peace below!

Tr. from Bute's Roman Breviary.

Ave, Star of ocean,
Child divine who barest,
Mother, ever-Virgin,
Heaven's Portal fairest.

Roman Breviary, Feasts of the Blessed
Virgin. Hymn *Ave maris stella* at Vespers.
(According to St. Jerome the name of
Mary meant "Star of the sea" or "Bitter
Sea." The more commonly accepted
meaning is "Lady." (Tr. A. Riley) (9th
cent.)

O thou, whosoever thou art, that knowest
thyself to be here not so much walking
upon firm ground as battered to and fro
by the gales and storms of this life's
ocean, if thou wouldst not be over-
whelmed by the tempest, keep thine eyes
fixed upon this star's shining. If the
hurricanes of temptation rise against
thee or thou art running upon the rocks
of trouble, look to the star, call on Mary.

Roman Breviary, Feast of the Holy Name
of Mary (Sept. 12), Lesson at Matins.
(St. Bernard, *Second Hom. on the Blessed
Virgin.*) (12th cent.)

Mary, Star of the Sea!
Look upon this little place:
Bless the kind fisher race,
Mary, Star of the Sea.

Lionel Johnson: *Cadgwith.* (19th cent.)

XXI—*Virgin Most Merciful*

We beseech Thee, O Lord, may the
merits of the blessed and glorious ever-
Virgin Mother of God Mary reach us,
and ever implore for us Thy mercy.

Gelasian Sacramentary, Collect for the
Annunciation. (ca. 7th cent.)

Thou that art the fountain of mercy,
vouchsafe to us thy sympathy, O Mother
of God. Look down on the people who
have sinned, show us thy wonted power;

for, trusting in thee, we cry, Hail! as did
formerly Gabriel, the captain of the incorporeal hosts.

Byzantine Horologion, Troparion at Sext.
(ca. 6th to 8th cent.)

Let us honor her and venerate her for her
mercy towards the needy. If nothing
glorifies God more than mercy, who will
deny that His mother is blessed with that
virtue. . . . She is the furnisher of all
good things.

St. John of Damascus (8th cent.)

O blessed Mother of God, open unto
us the gates of mercy, that, trusting in
thee, we may not perish, but be delivered
from evils by thee, for thou art the salvation of Christians.

Byzantine Horologion, Troparion at Great
Compline. (ca. 9th cent.?)

There is a glorious Lady in heaven who
hath ta'en
So great compassion on this soul dis-
trest
That the hard law she hath chosen to
restrain.

Dante: *Inferno, Canto 2.* (Tr. Binyon)
(14th cent.)

In thee is pity, in thee is tenderness,
In thee magnificence, in thee the sum
Of all that in creation most can bless.

Dante: *Paradiso, Canto 33.* (Prayer of
St. Bernard) (Tr. Binyon) (14th cent.)

Mother, quoth she, and maid bright
Mary,
Sooth is that through woman's egge-
ment
Mankind was lorn and damned aye to
die,
For which thy Child was on a cross
y-rent;
Thy blissful eyen saw all His torment;
Then is there no comparison between
Thy woe and any woe man may sustain.

· · · · · · ·

Now, lady bright, to whom all woeful
cryen,

Thou glory of womanhood, thou fair
may,
Thou haven of refuge, bright star of
day,
Rue on my child, that of thy gentillesse
Ruest on every rueful in distresse!

rue—have pity

Chaucer: *The Man of Law's Tale*, 841.
(14th cent.)

Why was I crowned and made queen?
Why was I called of mercy the well?
Why should an earthly woman been
So high in heaven above angel?
For thee, mankind, the truth I tell;
Thou ask me to help and I shall do
That I was ordained, keep thee from
hell,
Quia amore langueo.

Anonymous: *Quia Amore Langueo.* (14th
cent.)

Mother of mercy! day by day
My love of thee grows more and
more;
Thy gifts are strewn upon my way,
Like sands upon the great sea-shore.

. . . .

Jesus, when His three hours were run,
Bequeath'd thee from the Cross to
me,
And oh! how can I love thy Son,
Sweet Mother! if I love not thee.

F. Faber: *To our Blessed Lady.* (19th cent.)

XXII—*Virgin Most Powerful*

If thou seekest the dread throne of God
on earth,
marvel at the sight of the Virgin's temple.
For she beareth God in her arms
to this place's glory.
They who are set to be rulers on earth
believe that their scepters here retain
victory.
Here the sleepless patriarch
averts many a cosmic cataclysm.
When the barbarians were attacking
the city,
they saw her leading the army in the
field,

and straightway bent their unbending
necks.

Greek Anthology, 1, 120. (Tr. S. Leslie)
(Constantinople underwent a famous siege
by the Avars and Persians under the
Emperor Heraclius in 626 and was
allegedly saved by the miraculous
intervention of Our Lady of Blachernae;
the patriarch Sergius was active in
organizing the supplications.) (7th cent.)

Unto all maidens and unto all who fly to
thee thou art a wall, O maiden Forth-
bringer; the Maker of heaven and earth
has prepared thee unto this, dwelling in
thy womb and teaching all to sing unto
thee: Hail! pillar of purity; Hail! gate
of safety. . . .

Byzantine Triodion, Akathist Hymn,
Oikos 10. (Tr. V. McNabb) (ca. 7th cent.)

Hail! tent of the God and Word; hail!
holy beyond all holy ones; hail! ark
gilded by the Holy Ghost; hail! unfailing treasure-house of life; hail! precious
diadem of godly sovereigns; hail! worshipful honor of a worthy priesthood;
hail! the Church's unassailable tower;
hail! of the kingdom indestructible wall;
hail! whereby war-trophies are set up;
hail! whereby foes are stricken; hail!
my body's healing; hail! my soul's saving; hail! bride unbrided.

Byzantine Triodion, Akathist Hymn, 12.
(Tr. V. McNabb) (ca. 7th cent.)

O Mother of God, do thou preserve thy
servants from dangers, for all, after
God, flee for protection unto thee, as an
unconquerable bulwark.

Byzantine Triodion, Great Thursday,
Service of the Holy Passion. (ca. 6th to 8th
cent.)

It is through Mary alone that every impious heresy has been vanquished.

St. Bernard: *Sermon for Sunday within the
Octave of the Assumption.* (12th cent.)

See also Annunciation; Assumption;
Immaculate Conception; Nativity; Purification; Rosary

Blessed Virgin Mary: Devotion to Her

No worship of Mary is more gracious than if you imitate Mary's humility.

Erasmus: *Enchiridion.* (16th cent.)

One of those things that give me most consolation at the present moment is that I have been attached to the practice of devotion to the Blessed Virgin Mary, and that I have established it among the people under my care, and placed my diocese under her protection.

Archb. Carroll. (Among last remarks made to John Grassi) (1815)

The idea of the blessed Virgin was as it were *magnified* in the Church of Rome, as time went on,—but so were all the Christian ideas; as that of the blessed sacrament. The whole scene of pale, faint, distant apostolic Christianity is seen in Rome, as through a telescope or magnifier. The harmony of the whole, however, is of course what it was. It is unfair then to take one Roman idea, that of the Blessed Virgin, out of what may be called its context.

Card. Newman: *Apologia pro Vita Sua,* 4. (19th cent.)

Such devotional manifestations in honor of our Lady had been my great *crux* as regards Catholicism; I say frankly, I do not fully enter into them now; I trust I do not love her the less, because I cannot enter into them. They may be fully explained and defended; but sentiment and taste do not run with logic: they are suitable for Italy, but they are not suitable for England.

Card. Newman: *Apologia pro Vita Sua,* 4. (19th cent.)

I recollect one saying among others of my confessor, a Jesuit father, one of the holiest, most prudent men I ever knew. He said that we could not love the blessed Virgin too much, if we loved our Lord a great deal more.

Card. Newman: *Letter to the Rev. E. B. Pusey.* (19th cent.)

I fully grant that *devotion* towards the blessed Virgin has increased among Catholics with the progress of centuries; I do not allow that the *doctrine* concerning her has undergone a growth, for I believe that it has been in substance one and the same from the beginning.

Card. Newman: *Letter to the Rev. E. B. Pusey.* (19th cent.)

Now I say plainly, I never will defend or screen any one from your just rebuke, who, through false devotion to Mary, forgets Jesus. But I should like the fact to be proved first; I cannot hastily admit it. There is this broad fact the other way; —that if we look through Europe we shall find on the whole that just those nations and countries have lost their faith in the divinity of Christ, who have given up devotion to His Mother, and that those on the other hand who have been foremost in her honor have retained their orthodoxy.

Card. Newman: *Letter to the Rev. E. B. Pusey.* (19th cent.)

I will say plainly that I had rather believe (which is impossible) that there is no God at all, than that Mary is greater than God.

Card. Newman: *Letter to the Rev. E. B. Pusey.* (19th cent.)

Protestants have often said (I am not thinking of Dr. Gore) that we Catholics put our Lady in the place of Christ. I fear it is true that the place in which many Protestants put Christ is much the same as that in which we rightly put His Mother, that is to say, the highest place among creatures, but yet at an infinite distance from her Son and Creator.

Abbot Chapman: *Bishop Gore and the Catholic Claims.* (20th cent.)

It is good and useful to invoke in prayer the servants of God reigning with Christ in heaven and to venerate their relics and images; but all the faithful should honor the blessed Virgin Mary with filial devotion above all others.

> Code of Canon Law, Canon 1276. (20th cent.)

I do not want to be in a religion in which I am *allowed* to have a crucifix. I feel the same about the much more controversial question of the honor paid to the blessed Virgin. If people do not like that cult, they are quite right not to be Catholics. But in people who are Catholics, or call themselves Catholics, I want the idea not only liked but loved and loved ardently, and above all proudly proclaimed. I want it to be what the Protestants are perfectly right in calling it: the badge and sign of a papist. I want to be allowed to be enthusiastic about the existence of the enthusiasm; not to have my chief enthusiasm coldly tolerated as an eccentricity of myself.

> G. K. Chesterton: *Autobiography.* (With reference to certain Anglican tendencies) (20th cent.)

> Lovely Lady dressed in blue,
> Teach me how to pray!
> God was just your little Boy,
> And you know the way.
>
> Mary Dixon Thayer. (20th cent.)

Upon these two titles, Mary Mother of God, and Mary the Mother of mankind, the whole practice of the Catholic's devotion to the Blessed Virgin Mary is built.

> Archb. Goodier: *Inner Life of the Catholic.* (20th cent.)

All that has been written about the Virgin Mother of God proves to me that hers is the most hidden of sanctities. What people find to say about her generally tells us more about their own selves than it does about our Lady. For since God has revealed very little to us about her, men who know nothing of who and what she was only reveal themselves when they try to add something to what God has told us about her.

> Thomas Merton: *Seeds of Contemplation.* (20th cent.)

Blessedness

A blessed life may be defined as consisting simply and solely in the possession of goodness and truth.

> St. Ambrose: *Concerning Jacob,* 1, 32. (4th cent.)

Innocence and knowledge make a man blessed.

> St. Ambrose: *On the Duties of the Clergy,* 2, 9. (4th cent.)

The pursuit of God is the desire of beatitude, the attainment of God is beatitude. We pursue after Him by loving Him, we attain to Him, not indeed by becoming What He is, but by coming close to Him, as it were, in some marvelous intellectual fashion, wholly illumined and wholly embraced by His holiness. For He is Light itself and by that Light are we permitted to be illumined.

> St. Augustine: *De Moribus Ecclesiae Catholicae,* 18. (4th cent.)

In so far as concerns the nature of man, there is in him nothing better than the mind and reason. But he who would live blessedly ought not to live according to them; for then he would live according to man, whereas he ought to live according to God, so that he may attain to blessedness. And to accomplish this, our mind must not be content with itself, but must be subjected to God.

> St. Augustine: *Retractions,* 1, 1, 2. (5th cent.)

It is manifest that men are made blessed by the obtaining of divinity. And as men are made just by the obtaining of justice, and wise by the obtaining of wisdom, so they who obtain divinity must needs in like manner become gods. Wherefore everyone that is blessed is a god, but by nature there is only one God; but there may be many by participation.

> Boethius: *De Consolatione Philosophiae,* 3, 10. (6th cent.)

Condition, circumstance, is not the
thing;
Bliss is the same in subject or in king.

Pope: *An Essay on Man*, 4. (18th cent.)

O close my hand upon Beatitude!
Not on her toys.

Louise Imogen Guiney: *Deo Optimo
Maximo*. (19th cent.)

See also Eternal life; Happiness; Joy

Blessing

Out of God's blessing into the warm sun.

John Heywood: *Proverbs*, 2, 5. (16th cent.)

Blessings,
Flowers of never fading graces
To make immortal dressings
For worthy souls.

Richard Crashaw: *Prayer*. (17th cent.)

It is not God's way that great blessings
should descend without the sacrifice first
of great sufferings.

Card. Newman: *Sermons on Various
Occasions*. ("Second Spring" sermon,
preached before the first synod of
Westminster, July 13, 1852)

Lord, dismiss us with Thy blessing,
Hope and comfort from above;
Let us each, Thy peace possessing,
Triumph in redeeming love.

Robert Hawker: *Benediction*. (19th cent.)

Blindness

The very limit of human blindness is to
glory in being blind.

St. Augustine: *Confessions*, 3, 3. (5th
cent.)

The blind eat many a fly.

Lydgate: *Ballade*. (15th cent.)

In the country of the blind the one-eyed
man is king.

Erasmus: *Adagia*. (16th cent.)

The devil is ready to put out men's eyes
that are content willingly to wax blind.

St. Thomas More. (16th cent.)

Where the blind headeth the blind, both
fall in the dike.

John Heywood: *Proverbs*, 2, 5. (16th cent.)

Blind men should judge no colors.

John Heywood: *Proverbs*, 2, 5. (16th cent.)

Folk are ofttimes most blind in their
own cause.

John Heywood: *Proverbs*, 2, 5. (16th cent.)

Back to the primal gloom
Where life began,
As to my mother's womb
Must I a man
Return:
Not to be born again,
But to remain;
And in the school of darkness learn
What mean
'The things unseen.'

J. B. Tabb: *Going Blind*. (19th cent.)

Blockhead

The bookful blockhead, ignorantly
read,
With loads of learned lumber in his
head.

Pope: *An Essay on Criticism*, 3. (18th
cent.)

Blood

We multiply whenever we are mown
down by you; the blood of Christians is
seed (*semen est sanguis Christianorum*).

Tertullian: *Apology*, 50, 13. (3rd cent.)

The Church abhors bloodshed. (Ecclesia
abhorret a sanguine.)

The Council of Tours, 1163

For naturally blood will aye of kind
Draw unto blood, where he may it find.

Lydgate: *Troy Book*, 3 (15th cent.)

Bloodshed and persecution form no part of the creed of the Catholic Church. So much does she abhor the shedding of blood that a man becomes disqualified to serve as a minister at her altars who, by act or counsel, voluntarily sheds the blood of another.

Cardinal Gibbons: *The Faith of Our Fathers,* 18. (19th cent.)

Blood, Precious

Let us fix our gaze on the blood of Christ and realize how precious it is to the Father, seeing that it was poured out for our salvation and brought the grace of conversion to the whole world.

Pope St. Clement I: *Letter to the Corinthians,* 7, 4. (1st cent.)

Hail, holy wounds of Jesus, hail,
Sweet pledges of the saving Rood,
Whence flow the streams that never fail,
The purple streams of His dear Blood.

Roman Breviary, Feast of the Most Precious Blood (July 1), Hymn *Salvete Christi vulnera* at Lauds. (Tr. H. Oxenham) (Author unknown, 17th cent.)

He Who once, in righteous vengeance,
Whelmed the world beneath the flood,
Once again in mercy cleansed it
With the stream of His own Blood,
Coming from His throne on high
On the painful Cross to die.

Roman Breviary, Feast of the Most Precious Blood, Hymn *Ira justa Conditoris* at Matins. (Tr. E. Caswall) (Author unknown, 17th cent.)

They have left Thee naked, Lord, O that they had!
This garment too I would they had denied.
Thee with Thyself they have too richly clad;
Opening the purple wardrobe in Thy side.
O never could there be garment too good

For Thee to wear, but this, of Thine own blood.

Richard Crashaw: *Upon the Body of Our Bl. Lord. Naked and Bloody.* (17th cent.)

Hail! Jesus! hail! Who for my sake
Sweet blood from Mary's wounds didst take,
And shed it all for me;
O blessed be my Savior's Blood,
My life, my light, my only good,
To all eternity.

Viva, viva Gesu from the Raccolta. (Tr. F. Faber) (Modern)

Blood is the price of heaven;
All sin that price exceeds;
Oh come to be forgiven,—
He bleeds,
My Savior bleeds!
Bleeds!

F. Faber: *Blood is the Price of Heaven.* (19th cent.)

Blundering

Doeg, though without knowing how or why,
Made still a blund'ring kind of melody;
Spurr'd boldly on, and dash'd through thick and thin,
Through sense and nonsense, never out nor in;
Free from all meaning, whether good or bad,
And in one word, heroically mad.

Dryden: *Absalom and Achitophel.* (17th cent.)

Blushing

While, mantling on the maiden's cheek,
Young roses kindled into thought.

Thomas Moore: *Evenings in Greece.* (19th cent.)

Boar

She foameth like a boar.

John Heywood: *Proverbs,* 1, 11. (16th cent.)

Boasting

To shun vainglory.

> St. Benedict: *Rule,* 4. (One of his "tools of
> good works") (6th cent.)

> > Great boast and small roast
> > Maketh unsavory mouths
> > Wherever men host.

> John Heywood: *Proverbs,* 1, 11. (16th
> cent.)

Many a man speaketh of Robin Hood
That never shot in his bow.

> John Heywood: *Proverbs,* 2, 6. (16th
> cent.)

Boat

> Forth, to the alien gravity,
> Forth, to the laws of ocean, we
> > Builders on earth by laws of land
> > Entrust this creature of our hand
> Upon the calculated sea.

> Alice Meynell: *The Launch.* (20th cent.)

Body

Our body too might be said to be a
prison, not because it is a prison which
God hath made, but because it is under
punishment and liable to death. For
there are two things to be considered in
our body, God's handicraft and the punishment it has deserved.

> St. Augustine: *In Ps. 141,* 18. (5th cent.)

*The corruptible body weigheth down the
soul and the earthly habitation presseth
down the mind that museth upon many
things* (Wisdom 9, 15). Oh! Take
from me this body which weighs down
the soul, and then I will praise the Lord;
take from me this earthly habitation
which presseth down the mind musing
upon many things, and then I will gather
myself together into one compact whole
and praise the Lord.

> St. Augustine: *In Ps. 145 Enarr. 1,* 6. (5th
> cent.)

The tenement of clay.

> Dryden: *Absalom and Achitophel,* 1. (17th
> cent.)

> Creation's and Creator's crowning
> > good;
> > Wall of infinitude;
> > Foundation of the sky,
> > In heaven forecast
> And long'd for from eternity,
> > Though laid the last;
> > Reverberating dome,
> Of music cunningly built home
> Against the void and indolent disgrace
> > Of unresponsive space;
> > Little, sequester'd pleasure-house
> > For God and for His spouse.

> Coventry Patmore: *To the Body.* (19th
> cent.)

Body and Soul

The carnal cannot live a spiritual life,
nor can the spiritual live a carnal life,
any more than faith can act the part of
infidelity, or infidelity the part of faith.
But even the things you do in the flesh
are spiritual, for you do all things in
union with Jesus Christ.

> St. Ignatius of Antioch: *Letter to the
> Ephesians,* 8, 2. (2nd cent.)

It would suffice to say, indeed, that there
is not a soul that can at all procure salvation, except it believe whilst it is in the
flesh, so true is it that the flesh is the very
condition on which salvation hinges.
And since the soul is, in consequence of
its salvation, chosen to the service of
God, it is the flesh which actually renders it capable of such service. The flesh,
indeed, is washed, in order that the soul
may be cleansed; the flesh is anointed,
that the soul may be consecrated; the
flesh is signed (with the cross), that the
soul too may be fortified; the flesh is
shadowed with the imposition of hands,
that the soul also may be illuminated by
the Spirit; the flesh feeds on the Body
and Blood of Christ, that the soul may
likewise fatten on its God. They cannot

then be separated in their recompense, when they are united in their service.

> Tertullian: *On The Resurrection of The Flesh*, 8. (3rd cent.)

Despise the flesh, for it passes away; be solicitous for your soul which will never die.

> St. Basil: *Homily on the Words "Give Heed to Thyself."* (4th cent.)

The soul is the user, the body for use; hence the one is master, the other servant.

> St. Ambrose: *On the Good of Death*, 27. (4th cent.)

The eyes of the soul should not be hindered by the eyes of the body.

> R. H. Benson: *The History of Richard Raynal Solitary.* (20th cent.)

There was a look in his face which told that he was one of those who in keeping body and soul together have difficulties not only with the body, but also with the soul.

> G. K. Chesterton: *Alarms and Discursions.* (20th cent.)

Bohemia

I'd rather live in Bohemia than in any other land.

> J. B. O'Reilly: *Bohemia.* (19th cent.)

Boldness

The unlearned arise and take heaven itself by storm.

> St. Augustine: *Confessions,* 8, 8. (5th cent.)

For he who naught dare undertake,
By right he shall no profit take.

> John Gower: *Confessio Amantis,* 4. (14th cent.)

Fortune favors the bold.

> Erasmus: *Adagia.* (16th cent.)

Come what come would.

> John Heywood: *Proverbs,* 1, 11. (16th cent.)

Some in foul seasons perish through despair,
But more thro' boldness when the days are fair.

> Sir John Beaumont: *In Desolation.* (17th cent.)

Bonaventure, Saint

Seraphic Doctor.

> Title first given to the saint in 1333. Also known as *Doctor devotus.*

In writing he united to the highest erudition an equal amount of the most ardent piety; so that whilst enlightening his readers he also touched their hearts, penetrating to the inmost recesses of their souls.

> Pope Sixtus V: *Bull Triumphantis Jerusalem.* (16th cent.)

Having scaled the difficult heights of speculation in a most notable manner, he treated of mystical theology with such perfection that in the common opinion of the learned he is *facile princeps* in that field.

> Pope Leo XIII: *Allocution.* (October 11, 1890)

Book

Everywhere have I sought rest and found it not, except sitting apart in a nook with a little book.

> Thomas a Kempis: Inscription on his picture at Zwoll, Holland. (Said to have been composed by himself) (15th cent.)

While others are not hinder'd from their ends,
Delighting to converse with books or friends,
And living thus retir'd, obtain the pow'r
To reign as kings of every sliding hour.

> Sir John Beaumont: *Of True Liberty.* (17th cent.)

I never knew
More sweet and happy hours than I
    employ'd
Upon my books.

    James Shirley: *Lady of Pleasure*, 2, 1. (17th
    cent.)

The monument of vanish'd minds.

    Sir William Davenant: *Gondibert*, 2, 5.
    (17th cent.)

               Gold of the dead,
Which time does still disperse, but not
    devour.

    Sir William Davenant: *Gondibert*. (17th
    cent.)

The last thing one does in writing a book
is to know what to put first.

    Pascal: *Pensées*. (17th cent.)

It is our duty to live among books; especially to live by one book, and a very old one.

    Card. Newman: *Tracts for the Times*.
    (19th cent.)

            Dear, human books,
With kindly voices, winning looks!
Enchant me with your spells of art,
And draw me homeward to your heart.

    Lionel Johnson: *Oxford Nights*. (19th
    cent.)

Like every book I never wrote, it is by
far the best book I have ever written.

    G. K. Chesterton: *The Everlasting Man*,
    Introd. (20th cent.)

It is a good sign of health in a writer if
he thinks a book irrevocable. If the
writer is very healthy he will probably
regard the book as an irrevocable mistake. But in any case there is something
so sacred and final about the giving forth
of anything organic that most people
with sound instincts will always regard
it as something like the birth of a child:
a child who may grow up well or ill.
Like the birth of a child it is the giving
of liberty to something. Henceforth the

thing we have made is truly sundered
from us, as we are sundered from God.

    G. K. Chesterton: *A Handful of Authors*.
    (20th cent.)

When I am dead, I hope it may be said:
"His sins were scarlet, but his books
    were read."

    Hilaire Belloc: *On his Books*. (20th cent.)

Many a book is of less value than one
of its phrases.

    Frank Sheed. (20th cent.)

Book of Life

God's foreknowledge, which cannot be
deceived, is the book of life.

    St. Augustine: *The City of God*, 20, 15.
    (5th cent.)

Boredom

There is nothing so insupportable to man
as complete repose, without passion, occupation, amusement, care. Then it is
that he feels his nothingness, his isolation, his insufficiency, his dependence,
his impotence, his emptiness.

    Pascal: *Pensées*, 25. (17th cent.)

It is a tolerable definition of a bore, that
he is one who talks about himself when
you want to talk about yourself; but the
transposition of the sentence is not always true. A bore, certainly, always does
that; but he who does that is not always
a bore.

    R. H. Benson: *An Average Man*. (20th
    cent.)

Boredom is dangerously infectious; and
has a way of spreading across the footlights.

    G. K. Chesterton: *Generally Speaking*.
    (20th cent.)

Borgia

If plagues or earthquakes break not
    Heav'n's design,
Why then a Borgia or a Catiline?

    Pope: *An Essay on Man*, 1. (18th cent.)

Borrowing

Not so good to borrow, as be able to lend.

> John Heywood: *Proverbs,* 1, 10. (16th cent.)

I come to borrow what I'll never lend And buy what I'll never pay for.

> Sir William Davenant: *The Wits,* 1, 1. (17th cent.)

Bow

A long bow bent, at length must wear weak.

> John Heywood: *Proverbs,* 1, 11. (16th cent.)

Boy

Boys are always more or less inaccurate, and too many, or rather the majority, remain boys all their lives.

> Card. Newman: *Idea of a University.* (19th cent.)

Bracelet

Cease not to adorn yourself with good works—the true bracelets of a Christian woman.

> St. Jerome: *Letters,* 31, 2. (4th cent.)

Bravery

None but the brave deserve the fair.

> Dryden: *Alexander's Feast.* (17th cent.)

A really brave man doesn't allow himself to be dominated by his imagination—the kind of man who gets the V.C. His will rules him; or, rather, he rules himself through his will.

> R. H. Benson: *The Coward* (20th cent.)

Mere physical courage—the absence of fear—simply is not worth calling bravery. It's the bravery of the tiger, not the moral bravery of the man.

> R. H. Benson: *The Coward.* (20th cent.)

Bread

Nor fresh nor old be bread, but spongy, light,
Tasteful, well baked, of wheat freed from all blight.

> School of Salerno, Code of Health. (11th cent.)

Better is half a loaf than no bread.

> John Heywood: *Proverbs,* 1, 11. (16th cent.)

I know on which side my bread is buttered.

> John Heywood: *Proverbs,* 2, 7. (16th cent.)

Breviary

That most wonderful and most attractive monument of the devotion of the saints.

> Card. Newman: *Apologia pro Vita Sua, 2.* (19th cent.)

Bridge

First I gave you the bridge of My Son living and conversing in very deed amongst men, and when He the living Bridge left you, there remained the bridge and the road of His doctrine, as has been said, His doctrine being joined with My power and with His wisdom and with the clemency of the Holy Ghost. This power of Mine gives the virtue of fortitude to whoever follows this road, wisdom gives him light so that in this road he may recognize the truth, and the Holy Ghost gives him love which consumes and takes away all sensitive love out of the soul, leaving there only the love of virtue. Thus, in both ways, both actually and through His doctrine, He is the Way, the Truth, and the Life; that is, the Bridge which leads you to the height of heaven.

> St. Catherine of Siena: *The Dialogue.* (14th cent.)

Broadmindedness

Latitudinarians, while they profess charity towards all doctrines, nevertheless count it heresy to oppose the principle of latitude.

> Card. Newman: *Oxford University Sermons.* (19th cent.)

The first condition of broad-mindedness is to recognize that one is narrow; if one does not, one omits the most crucial fact of all.

> R. H. Benson: *The Sentimentalists.* (20th cent.)

A man so broad, to some he seem'd to be
Not one, but all Mankind in Effigy.

> Ronald Knox: *Absolute and Abitofhell.* (20th cent.)

Broom

The green new broom sweepeth clean.

> John Heywood: *Proverbs,* 2, 1. (16th cent.)

Brother

Sweet brother, if I do not sleep
My eyes are flowers for your tomb;
And if I cannot eat my bread,
My fasts shall live like willows where you died.
If in the heat I find no water for my thirst,
My thirst shall turn to springs for you, poor traveller.

. . . .

For in the wreckage of your April
Christ lies slain,
And Christ weeps in the ruins of my spring;
The money of whose tears shall fall
Into your weak and friendless hand,
And buy you back to your own land:
The silence of whose tears shall fall
Like bells upon your alien tomb.
Hear them and come: they call you home.

> Thomas Merton: *The Seven Storey Mountain.* (20th cent.)

Brown, John

Compassionate eyes had our brave John Brown,
And a craggy stern forehead, a militant frown;
He, the storm-bow of peace, give him volley on volley,
The fool who redeemed us once of our folly,
And the smiter that healed us, our right John Brown!

> Louise Imogen Guiney: *John Brown: A Paradox.* (19th cent.)

Browning, Robert

Yet few poets were so mated before and no poet was so mated afterward, until Browning stooped and picked up a fair-coined soul that lay rusting in a pool of tears.

> Francis Thompson: *Shelley.* (19th cent.)

He used poetry as a medium for writing in prose.

> Oscar Wilde: *The Critic as Artist,* 1. (19th cent.)

Brownson, Orestes

In lifting the countenances of Catholics from their time-out-of-mind cringing-ness to brute force, we are disposed to assign, as the chief instrument in God's hands, not his Grace of Baltimore (Archbishop Spalding), but Dr. Brownson himself. . . . At his feet, more than at those of any other man that taught in America, have the Catholic bishops sat. . . . Brownson's vocation has been to teach the teachers. . . . Brownson has been an eminently providential man.

> *Catholic Advocate* of Louisville. (Quoted in H. Brownson: *O. A. Brownson: Latter Life,* 587) (1874)

Bud

This bud showeth what fruit will follow.

> John Heywood: *Proverbs,* 1, 10. (16th cent.)

Bully

As a matter of fact, nobody in antiquity was less given to hectoring than Hector.

> G. K. Chesterton: *The Everlasting Man*, 1, 8. (20th cent.)

Burial of the Dead

Let there be no heavy charge for burying people in the cemetery for it is for all the poor; except they shall pay the hire of a workman to him who digs and the price of the tiles.

> St. Hippolytus: *The Apostolic Tradition*, 34. (3rd cent.)

All these things—the care of the funeral arrangements, the establishment of the place of burial, the pomp of the ceremonies—are more of a solace for the living than an aid for the dead.

> St. Augustine: *On the Care for the Dead*, 2. (5th cent.)

Bury her at even
That the stars may shine
Soon above her,
And the dews of twilight cover;
Bury her at even,
Ye that love her.

Bury her at even
In the wind's decline;
Night receive her
Where no voice can ever grieve her!
Bury her at even,
And then leave her!

> Michael Field: *Bury Her at Even*. (19th cent.)

Lay her in the mill-pond,
   Lay her in the sea;
Lay her where no sprig
   Of foliage will be.

Buried in the orchard
   Underneath a tree,
She would stir with yearning,
   Everlastingly.

> Gertrude Callaghan: *Burial*. (20th cent.)

The bodies of the deceased faithful shall be buried; it is forbidden to cremate them. If any person has in any way ordered that his body be cremated, it is illicit to carry out such instructions; if such a provision occur in a contract, last testament, or in any document whatsoever, it shall be disregarded.

> Code of Canon Law, Canon 1203. (20th cent.)

All baptized persons are to receive ecclesiastical burial unless they are expressly excluded from it by law.

> Code of Canon Law, Canon 1239, 3. (20th cent.)

See also Dead, The; Death

Businessman

This estimable merchant so had set
His wits to work, none knew he was in debt,
He was so stately in negotiation,
Loan, bargain, and commercial obligation.

> Chaucer: *Canterbury Tales: Prologue*. (Tr. Coghill) (14th cent.)

Busy

Though there was none so busy as was he
He was less busy than he seemed to be.

> Chaucer: *Canterbury Tales: Prologue*. (Tr. Coghill) (14th cent.)

None are so busy as the fool and knave.

> Dryden: *The Medal*. (17th cent.)

Buying and Selling

Make yourself a seller when you are buying, and a buyer when you are selling, and then you will sell and buy justly.

> St. Francis de Sales: *Introduction to the Devout Life*, 3, 36. (17th cent.)

C

Calm

An horrid stillness first invades the ear,
And in that silence we the tempest fear.

Dryden: *Astraea Redux.* (17th cent.)

Calvary, Mt.

Mount Calvary is the academy of love.

St. Francis de Sales: *Treatise on the Love of God,* 12, 13. (17th cent.)

See also Passion of our Lord

Candle

Sith nature thus gave her the praise,
    To be the chiefest work she wrought,
In faith, me thinks, some better ways
    On your behalf might well be sought,
Than to compare, as ye have done,
To match the candle with the sun.

Henry Howard, Earl of Surrey: *To the Fair Geraldine.* (16th cent.)

Some candle clear burns somewhere I came by.
I muse at how its being puts blissful back
With yellowy moisture mild night's blear-all black,
Or to-fro tender trambeams truckle at the eye.

G. M. Hopkins: *The Candle Indoors.* (19th cent.)

Candlelight

Lamps of God, on high that glow,
    Altar stars of earth below,
Starshine and candlelight,
    Light His way this Christmas night!

Sister M. Angelita: *Starshine and Candlelight.* (20th cent.)

Candor

To be intelligible is to be found out.

Oscar Wilde: *Lady Windermere's Fan.* (19th cent.)

Cannibalism

Most cannibalism is not a primitive or even a bestial habit. It is artificial and even artistic; a sort of art for art's sake. Men do not do it because they do not think it horrible. They wish, in the most literal sense, to sup on horrors.

G. K. Chesterton: *The Everlasting Man.* (20th cent.)

Canon Law

The Holy Roman Church dispenses justice and authority through the sacred canons, but is not bound by them. For it has the right of making canons in its capacity as the head and hinge of all the churches, from whose rule no one may dissent. Thus it imparts authority to the canons in such a way that it is not itself subject to them. But as Christ, Who gave the law, Himself fulfilled the law in the flesh . . . so the pontiffs of the Supreme See show regard for the canons they themselves have enacted or which have been enacted by their authority, and keep them by submitting themselves to them, that they may show that they are to be observed by others.

Gratian: *Decretum,* C. 25, Q. 7, P. 2. (12th cent.)

As the office of temporal princes is to enact legal precepts which are arbitrary applications of the natural law to temporal business affecting the commonwealth so also the office of ecclesiastical prelates is to command by statute matters which affect the common welfare of the faithful, that is, their spiritual welfare.

> St. Thomas Aquinas: *Summa Theologica*, 2-2, 147, 3. (13th cent.)

No human laws were ever devised which could so thoroughly succeed in making the arbitrary exercise of power impossible, as that prodigious system of canon law which is the ripe fruit of the experience and the inspiration of eighteen hundred years.

> Lord Acton: *Political Thoughts on the Church*. (19th cent.)

Laws which are purely ecclesiastical in their nature do not bind: unbaptized persons; baptized persons who do not have sufficient use of reason; baptized children who have the use of reason but are under seven years of age, unless the law explicitly rules otherwise.

> Code of Canon Law, Canon 12. (20th cent.)

Canticle of Canticles

The Canticle of Canticles is a spiritual delight of holy souls in the nuptial union of the King and Queen of the City, that is Christ and His Church. But this delight is wrapped up in veils of allegory, that it may be more ardently desired, and more agreeably exposed, and the Spouse may appear.

> St. Augustine: *The City of God*, 17, 20. (5th cent.)

Capital

Each needs the other: capital cannot do without labor, nor labor without capital.

> Pope Leo XIII: *Rerum novarum*. (May 15, 1891)

Capital has a right to a just share of the profits, but only to a just share.

> Cardinal O'Connell: *Pastoral Letter on the Laborer's Rights*. (1912)

By treating the laborer first of all as a man, the employer will make him a better working man; by respecting his own moral dignity as a man, the laborer will compel the respect of his employer and of the community.

> Pastoral Letter of the Catholic Archbishops and Bishops of the United States. (1919)

Capitalist

It is just that any man who does a service to society and increases the general wealth should himself have a due share of the increased public riches, provided always that he respects the laws of God and the rights of his neighbor, and uses his property in accordance with the dictates of faith and right reason.

> Pope Pius XI: *Quadragesimo anno*. (May 15, 1931)

Card-Playing

It is an old courtesy at the cards, perdy, to let the loser have his word.

> St. Thomas More: *English Works*, 1018. (16th cent.)

Cardinal

Accept the red hat, a special sign of the cardinal's dignity. This means that you should be ready to shed your blood and to die, if need be, in the fearless defence of our holy faith, for the preservation of quiet and peace among the Christian people. . . .

> Formula for Conferring the Red Hat. (Medieval)

Set he that hat on his head? Nay, chance so led
That by that time the hat came he had no head.

> John Heywood: *Epigrams*. (With ref. to St. John Fisher) (16th cent.)

You have not chosen me, but I have chosen you. (Non vos elegistis me, sed ego vos elegi.) (John, 15, 16.)

> Words inscribed by Urban VIII on a medal, when he had outlived all the cardinals created by his predecessors, a rare occurrence. (17th cent.)

The cardinals of the Holy Roman Church form the senate of the Roman pontiff and are his principal advisers and assistants in the government of the Church.

> Code of Canon Law, Canon 230. (20th cent.)

Care

He who watches out for his pennies and farthings, will be still more careful regarding crowns and pounds.

> St. Francis de Sales: *Letters to Persons in the World*, 4, 53. (17th cent.)

Restless anxiety, forlorn despair,
And all the faded family of care.

> Sir Samuel Garth: *The Dispensary*, 6. (17th cent.)

Career

Many girls want a mission in the world when they have plenty to do at home.

> Katharine T. Hinkson: *A Little Radiant Girl*. (20th cent.)

Carmelite

Madame Louise sleeps well o' nights,
Night is still at the Carmelites.

> Katharine T. Hinkson: *Aux Carmelites*. (20th cent.)

Carnal

In fine if anyone heard of what I may call 'carnalities,' he would not fail to attribute them to the carnal part of man; so no one doubts that 'animosities' belong to the soul of man.

> St. Augustine: *The City of God*, 14, 2. (5th cent.)

I learnt that in such restless violence blown
  This punishment the carnal sinners share
  Who let desire pull reason from her throne.

> Dante: *Inferno, Canto 5*. (Tr. Binyon) (14th cent.)

Cart

The best cart may overthrow.

> John Heywood: *Proverbs*, 1, 11. (16th cent.)

Carts well driven go along upright.

> John Heywood: *Proverbs*, 1, 11. (16th cent.)

Case

Clear out of the case.

> John Heywood: *Proverbs*, 1, 11. (16th cent.)

Castle

Castles in the air.

> Phrase. (Borrowed from St. Augustine: *in aere aedificare*.) (5th cent.)

Cat

When all candles be out all cats be grey.

> John Heywood: *Proverbs*, 1, 5. (16th cent.)

The cat would eat fish and would not wet her feet.

> John Heywood: *Proverbs*, 1, 11. (16th cent.)

Let the cat wink, and let the mouse run.

> John Heywood: *Proverbs*, 2, 4. (16th cent.)

A cat may look on a king.

> John Heywood: *Proverbs*, 2, 5. (16th cent.)

Catacomb

Rome, O Rome!
Surely thy strength is here! Three hundred years
The faithful people lived among the tombs;
The catacombs were their metropolis.
There in darkness thirty pontiffs ruled;
And died, save two, by martyrdom.

> Aubrey De Vere: *Mass in the Catacombs*. (19th cent.)

Catechism

It is the peculiar and grave responsibility especially of pastors of souls to see to the catechetical instruction of the Christian people.

> Code of Canon Law, Canon 1329. (20th cent.)

Catechumen

Let a catechumen be instructed for three years. But if a man be earnest and persevere well in the matter, let him be received, because it is not the time that is judged, but the conduct.

> St. Hippolytus: *The Apostolic Tradition*, 17. (3rd cent.)

Cathedral

I would that I had seen with my two
    eyes
The steeples of the Gothic Kingdom
    rise
Ere London grew too wealthy and too
    wise
To adore the Mother Maiden and her
    Child,
Ere greed and hate and frozen zeal de-
    filed,
And the great fire returned all to the
    wild,
When the cathedral crashed down into
    flames
With all her multitude of carven names,
Angels with harps and alabaster dames.
I would that I had seen those buttressed
    walls
Of that first towering splendid old St.
    Paul's.

> Wilfrid R. Childe: *The Former Glory*. (20th cent.)

Catherine of Siena, Saint

The light young man who was to die,
    Stopped in his frolic by the state,
Aghast, beheld the world go by;
    But Catherine crossed his dungeon
    gate.
    . . . .

She prayed, she preached him innocent;
    She gave him to the Sacrificed;
On her courageous breast he leant,
    The breast where beat the heart of
    Christ.

He left it for the block, with cries
    Of victory on his severed breath.
That crimson head she clasped, her
    eyes
Blind with the splendor of his death.

> Alice Meynell: *Saint Catherine of Siena*. (20th cent.)

Catholic

Christian is my name, and Catholic my surname. The former qualifies me, the latter manifests me for what I am. The latter demonstrates what the former signifies. And, if I finally must explain the word 'Catholic' and translate it from the Greek into the Roman idiom, Catholic means 'one everywhere,' or, as the more learned think, 'obedience to all the commandments of God.'

> St. Pacianus of Barcelona: *Letters*, 1, 4. (4th cent.)

We may say that a true and genuine Catholic is the man who loves the truth of God, the Church, and the Body of Christ; who does not put anything above divine religion and the Catholic faith—neither the authority, nor the affection, nor the genius, nor the eloquence, nor the philosophy of any other human being. He despises all that and, being firmly founded in the faith, is determined to hold and believe nothing but what the Catholic Church, as he has perceived, has held universally and from ancient times.

> St. Vincent of Lerins: *Commonitoria* 20. (5th cent.)

He cannot be accounted a Catholic who does not agree with the Roman Church. (Quod Catholicus non habeatur qui non concordat Romanae ecclesiae.)

> Pope St. Gregory VII: *Dictatus Papae*, 26. (11th cent.)

I am a Catholic, but not a papist.

> Daniel O'Connell. (19th cent.)

There are a great many people, honest people, but not over and above stocked with practical wisdom, who imagine that whatever is done or approved by Catholics in any age or country, in any particular time or locality, must needs be Catholic, and that opposition to it is necessarily opposition to Catholicity itself.

> Orestes Brownson: *Catholic Schools.*
> (Works, 12, 496ff) (1862)

Men cease to be Catholics, in the full sense of the term, by denying the universality of the idea or life the Church is living, the principle she is evolving and actualizing in the life of humanity, and alike whether they deny this universality in relation to space or in relation to time, in relation to the natural, or in relation to the supernatural.

> Orestes Brownson: *Catholic Schools.*
> (Works, 12, 496ff.) (1862)

The greatest thing about every Catholic is that he is one.

> John Ayscough: *Levia Pondera.* (20th cent.)

Catholic Action

As is well known, we have repeatedly and solemnly affirmed and protested that Catholic Action, both from its very nature and essence (the participation and collaboration of the laity with the apostolic hierarchy) and by our precise and categorical directions and dispositions, is outside and above every political party.

> Pope Pius XI: *Non Abbiamo Bisogno.*
> (June 29, 1931)

It was Jesus Christ Himself Who laid the first foundations of Catholic Action. It was Christ Himself Who, choosing and educating the apostles and disciples as collaborators in His divine apostolate, gave an example which at once was fol-lowed by the first holy apostles, as the sacred text itself substantiates.

> Pope Pius XI: *Non Abbiamo Bisogno.*
> (June 29, 1931)

The object of the new Catholic Action movements is not to widen the ecclesiastical function of the priest, but to Catholicize the secular function of the layman.

> M. de la Bedoyère: *Speech at a C.P.A. Rally.* (20th cent.)

Catholic and Protestant

I pray thee Protestant bear with me,
 To ask thee questions two or three,
And if an answer thou canst make,
 More of thy counsel I will take.

. . . .

You say your faith did appear,
 For the first six hundred year,
But tell me, if that you can,
 When papistry first began.
Where were the servants of the Lord,
 That none of them dost speak a word:
Where were the feeders of the sheep,
 What were they all so sound asleep,
That none of them could open mouth,
 Once to defend the known truth?

. . . .

> Gregory Martin: *Catholicke Questions to the Protestants.* (Guiney, 169) (16th cent.)

Herein is the strength of the Catholic Church; herein she differs from all Protestant mockeries of her. She professes to be built upon facts, not opinions; on objective truths, not on variable sentiments; on immemorial testimony, not on private judgment; on convictions or perceptions, not on conclusions. None else but she can make this profession.

> Card. Newman: *Difficulties of Anglicans,* 1.
> (19th cent.)

Protestants keep the exhibition of their faith for high days and great occasions, when it comes forth with sufficient pomp and gravity of language, and ceremonial of manner. Truths slowly totter out with Scripture texts at their elbow as unable to walk alone. . . . Protestants condemn

Catholics, because, however religious they may be, they are natural, unaffected, easy and cheerful in their mention of sacred things; and they think themselves never so real as when they are especially solemn.

> Card. Newman: *Difficulties of Anglicans,* I, 9. (19th cent.)

To the ordinary Protestant, religion is a detail, though an important detail; a part of life, but an interesting and consoling part. To the least practising Catholic, it it quite well known (even when the knowledge is thrust aside) that religion is the whole of life, embraces everything— that God's demands are paramount—that eternity is everything, this life nothing.

> Abbot Chapman: *Spiritual Letters.* (20th cent.)

Heresy and schism produce no saints. Protestantism, beginning most disreputably, has never attained a height greater than respectability: sanctity remains one of the four prerogatives of the Church.

> John Ayscough: *Saints and Places.* (20th cent.)

I have long thought that the real difference between the Catholic and Protestant view of Christianity is, or ought to be, this—that whereas we think of the Church as a sort of lucky bag which contains good bargains and bad, people who will be lost as well as people who will be saved, *real* Protestantism ought always to think of the Church as an assembly of the elect. I do not understand how a Christian can square this latter view with our Lord's parables, but I see its attractiveness on logical grounds.

> R. A. Knox: *Difficulties.* (20th cent.)

It has been said that Protestants are often better than their creed, and Catholics never so good as their own.

> C. C. Martindale: *The Gates of the Church.* (20th cent.)

It was not Catholic ceremonial, but Catholic continuity which appealed to me.

Catholicism was everywhere the same, branches of one great tree, the seed of which was sown in the catacombs. But Protestantism changed its shape from one valley to the next. Lutherans here, Zwinglians there, and Calvinists beyond the next hill barrier. Protestantism is a collection of sects, Catholicism the home of our race.

> Arnold Lunn: *Now I See.* (20th cent.)

Most Englishmen today are only Protestants in so far as they are not Catholics.

> Arnold Lunn: *Now I See.* (20th cent.)

Catholic Church

I—*Apostolic*

Fourthly, the Church is firm, solid as a house on massive foundations. The principal foundation is Christ Himself. . . . Secondary foundations are the apostles and apostolic teaching: hence the Church is called apostolic. . . . Its strength is signified by Peter, or Rock, who is its crown. A building is strong when it can never be overthrown though it may be shaken. The Church can never be brought down. Indeed it grows under persecution, and those who attack it are destroyed.

> St. Thomas Aquinas: *Exposition of the Apostles' Creed.* (13th cent.)

The true Church is also to be known from her origin, which she derives under the law of grace from the apostles; for her doctrines are neither novel nor of recent origin, but were delivered of old by the apostles, and disseminated throughout the world.

> Catechism of the Council of Trent, I. (16th cent.)

II—*Its Authority*

There are many other things which rightly keep me in the bosom of the Catholic Church. The consent of peoples and nations keeps me, her authority keeps me, inaugurated by miracles, nourished in hope, enlarged by love, and established by age. The succession of priests keeps me, from the very chair of the apostle Peter (to whom the Lord after His resurrection gave charge to feed His sheep) down to the present episcopate.

St. Augustine: *Contra Epistolam Manichaei.* (4th cent.)

This is the work of Divine Providence, achieved through the prophecies of the prophets, through the humanity and teaching of Christ, through the journeys of the apostles, through the suffering, the crosses, the blood and the death of the martyrs, through the admirable lives of the saints, and in all these, at opportune times, through miracles worthy of such great deeds and virtues. When, then, we see so much help on God's part, so much progress and such fruit, shall we hesitate to bury ourselves in the bosom of that Church? For starting from the apostolic chair down through successions of bishops, even unto the open confession of all mankind, it has possessed the crown of authority.

St. Augustine: *De Utilitate Credendi*, 17, 35. (4th cent.)

This Catholic Church, then, spread throughout the world, is known by three particular marks: whatever is believed and taught in it has the authority of the Scriptures, or of universal tradition, or at least of its own and proper usage. And this authority is binding on the whole Church as is also the universal tradition of the Fathers, while each separate Church exists and is governed by its private constitution and its proper rites according to difference of locality and the good judgment of each.

Boethius: *De Fide Catholica.* (6th cent.)

When our Lord sent forth His disciples, He enjoined three duties on them: to teach the faith, to give the sacraments to those imbued with faith, and to lead them on, so steeped, to the observance of divine precepts.

St. Thomas Aquinas: *Exposition of the First Decretal.* (13th cent.)

Concerning the power of punishing and ecclesiastical censure, it should be noted that the Church can exercise only a spiritual power directly, because it cannot impose any penalty in the external forum except a spiritual one, except conditionally or on occasion. For although the ecclesiastical judge has the responsibility of bringing men back to God, withdrawing them from sin, and punishing them, it only has this according to the way assigned by God, namely by separation from the sacraments, communion with the faithful, and in other ways pertaining to ecclesiastical censure.

John of Paris: *Concerning Royal and Papal Power*, 13. (14th cent.)

God has established in His Church a regime such as that which we have described . . . for in it there is the monarchy of the Holy See, the aristocracy of the bishops, who are true princes and not the mere vicars of the pope, and finally a form of democracy, inasmuch as there is no man in the entire body of the faithful who may not be called to the episcopate if he be judged worthy of that office.

St. Robert Bellarmine: *De Romano Pontifice*, 1, 3. (16th cent.)

Revelation has introduced a new law of divine governance over and above those laws which appear in the natural course of the world [i.e. in natural religion]; and in consequence we are able to argue for the existence of a standing authority in matters of faith on the analogy of nature, and from the fact of Christianity. Preservation is involved in the idea of creation. . . . As creation argues continual governance, so are apostles harbingers of popes.

Card. Newman: *Development of Christian Doctrine.* (19th cent.)

Moreover, it must be borne in mind that, as the essence of all religion is authority and obedience, so the distinction between natural and revealed lies in this, that the one has a subjective authority, and the other an objective. Revelation consists in the manifestation of the invisible divine Power, or in the substitution of the voice of a Lawgiver for the voice of conscience. The supremacy of conscience is the essence of natural religion; the supremacy of apostle, or pope, or Church, or bishop, is the essence of revealed.

Card. Newman: *Development of Christian Doctrine.* (19th cent.)

Catholic Christendom is no simple exhibition of religious absolutism, but presents a continuous picture of authority and private judgment alternately advancing and retreating as the ebb and flow of the tide;—it is a vast assemblage of human beings with wilful intellects and wild passions, brought together into one by the beauty and the majesty of a superhuman Power,—into what may be called a large reformatory or training-school, not as if into a hospital or into a prison, not in order to be sent to bed, not to be buried alive, but (if I may change my metaphor) brought together as if into some moral factory, for the melting, refining, and moulding, by an incessant, noisy process, of the raw material of human nature, so excellent, so dangerous, so capable of divine purpose.

Card. Newman: *Apologia pro Vita Sua, 5.* (19th cent.)

The Catholic Church claims, not only to judge infallibly on religious questions, but to animadvert on opinions in secular matters which bear upon religion, on matters of philosophy, of science, of literature, of history, and it demands our submission to her claim.

Card. Newman: *Apologia pro Vita Sua, 5.* (19th cent.)

Coming to you from the very time of the apostles, spreading out into all lands, triumphing over a thousand revolutions, exhibiting so awful a unity, glorifying in so mysterious a vitality; so majestic, so imperturbable, so bold, so saintly, so sublime, so beautiful, O ye sons of men can ye doubt that she is the divine messenger for whom you seek?

Card. Newman: *Sermons on Various Occasions.* (19th cent.)

Oh, long sought after, tardily found, desire of the eyes, joy of the heart, the truth after many shadows, the fulness after many foretastes, the home after many storms, come to her poor wanderers, for she it is and she alone, who can unfold the meaning of your being and the secret of your destiny. She alone can open to you the gate of heaven and put you on your way.

Card. Newman: *Sermons on Various Occasions.* (19th cent.)

The general sense of right and wrong, which is the first element in religion, is so delicate, so fitful, so easily puzzled, obscured, perverted, so subtle in its argumentative methods, so impressed by education, so biassed by pride and passion, so unsteady in its flight that in the struggle for existence amid various exercises and triumphs of the human intellect, this sense is at once the highest of all teachers, yet the least luminous; and the Church, the pope, the hierarchy, are in the divine purpose the supply of an urgent demand.

Card. Newman: *Difficulties of Anglicans, 2.* (19th cent.)

The obligation by which Catholic teachers and authors are strictly bound is confined only to those things which are proposed for universal belief as dogmas of faith by the infallible judgment of the Church.

Proposition condemned by Pius IX in Syllabus of Errors. (1867)

Let me never for an instant forget that thou hast established on earth a kingdom of Thy own, that the Church is Thy work, Thy establishment, Thy instrument; that we are under Thy will, Thy laws and Thy eye—that when the Church speaks Thou dost speak. Let not familiarity with this wonderful truth lead me to be insensitive to it—let not the weakness of

Thy human representations lead me to forget that it is Thou Who dost speak and art through them.

Card. Newman: *Meditations and Devotions.* (19th cent.)

The Church in and by itself, on account of its wonderful expansion, its eminent holiness and inexhaustible fruitfulness of all good, on account of its catholic unity and unconquerable stability, is a kind of great and abiding motive of credibility and an irrefutable witness to its divine commission.

Vatican Council, Session 3, Chap. 3. (April 24, 1870)

In faith and in the teaching of morality, God Himself made the Church a partaker of His divine authority, and through His heavenly gift she cannot be deceived. She is therefore the greatest and most reliable teacher of mankind, and in her swells an inviolable right to teach them.

Pope Leo XIII: *Libertas Praestantissimum.* (June 20, 1888)

Christ instituted in the Church a living, authoritative, and permanent magisterium, which He strengthened by His own power, taught by the Spirit of truth, and confirmed by miracles. He willed and ordered under the gravest penalties that its teachings should be received as if they were His own. As often therefore as it is declared on the authority of this teaching that this or that is contained in the deposit of divine revelation, it must be believed by everyone as true. If it could in any way be false, an evident contradiction follows; for then God Himself would be the author of error in man. *Lord, if we be in error, we are being deceived by Thee* (Richard of St. Victor: De Trin. 1, 2).

Pope Leo XIII: *Satis Cognitum.* (June 20, 1896)

Christ the Lord entrusted the deposit of faith to the Church, that under the constant guidance and assistance of the Holy Spirit she might sacredly guard and faithfully explain this divine revelation. The Church therefore has the right and duty, independently of any civil authority, to teach all nations the full doctrine of the gospel; and all men are bound by the law of God duly to learn this doctrine and to embrace the true Church of God.

Code of Canon Law, Canon 1322. (20th cent.)

The juridical mission of the Church, and the power to teach, govern and administer the sacraments derive their supernatural efficacy and force for the building up of the body of Christ from the fact that Jesus Christ, hanging on the Cross, opened up to His Church the fountain of divine graces, which protect it from ever teaching men false doctrine, and enable it to rule them for their soul's salvation through supernaturally enlightened pastors and to bestow on them abundantly heavenly graces.

Pope Pius XII: *Mystici Corporis.* (June 29, 1943)

God has given to His Church a living teaching authority to elucidate and explain what is contained in the deposit of faith only obscurely and implicitly. This deposit of faith our divine Redeemer has given for authentic interpretation not to each of the faithful, not even to theologians, but only to the teaching authority of the Church.

Pope Pius XII: *Humani Generis.* (Apr. 12, 1950)

III—*Catholic*

I believe . . . in one holy, Catholic and apostolic Church. . . .

Niceno-Constantinopolitan Creed. (4th cent.)

But the brightness of the Catholic and only true Church proceeded to increase in greatness, for it ever held to the same points in the same way, and radiated forth to all the race of Greeks and barbarians the reverent, sincere, and free nature, and the sobriety and purity of the divine teaching as to conduct and thought.

> Eusebius of Caesarea: *Ecclesiastical History*, 4, 7, 13. (4th cent.)

It is called Catholic then because it extends over all the world, from one end of the earth to the other; and because it teaches universally and completely one end and all the doctrines which ought to come to men's knowledge, concerning things both visible and invisible, heavenly and earthly; and because it brings into subjection to godliness the whole race of mankind, governors and governed, learned and unlearned; and because it universally treats and heals the whole class of sins, which are committed by soul and body, and possesses in itself every form of virtue which is named, both in deeds and words, and in every kind of spiritual gifts.

> St. Cyril of Jerusalem: *Catechetical Discourses*, 18, 24. (4th cent.)

But after the Jews for the plots which they made against the Savior were cast away from His grace, the Savior built out of the gentiles a second Holy Church, the Church of us Christians, concerning whom He said to Peter, *Upon this rock, etc.* (Matth. 16, 18).

> St. Cyril of Jerusalem: *Catechetical Discourses*, 18, 25. (4th cent.)

But we believe in Holy Church, assuredly the Catholic Church; for even heretics and schismatics style their assemblies 'churches.' But whereas heretics violate the faith by their false ideas about God, schismatics, by their wicked separation, cut themselves off from fraternal charity. Hence neither do heretics belong to the Catholic Church, for it loves God; nor do schismatics, for the Catholic Church loves its neighbor.

> St. Augustine: *De Fide et Symbolo*, 21. (4th cent.)

For this Catholic Church, vigorously spreading far and wide throughout the whole world, uses all who are in error to her own advancement, and to their amendment, when they shall wish to awaken from their error. She uses the heathen as material on which to work, heretics as a test of her teaching, schismatics as a proof of her stability, Jews as a comparison to show her beauty.

> St. Augustine: *De Vera Religione*, 6, 10. (4th cent.)

For whether they will or not, even heretics and schismatics when talking, not among themselves but with outsiders, call the Catholic Church nothing else but the Catholic Church. For otherwise they would not be understood unless they distinguished the Church by that name which she bears throughout the whole world.

> St. Augustine: *De Vera Religione*, 7, 12. (4th cent.)

You [i.e a schismatic] fancy that you have said something very clever when you explain the term 'Catholic' as meaning, not the being in communion with the 'Orbis terrarum,' but the keeping of all God's commandments and the possession of all the sacraments. You thereby seem to suggest that we rely on the term 'Catholic' when we wish to point to the Church spread throughout all nations; whereas what we rely on is God's promise and the number of patent prophecies emanating from the Truth itself, though I agree, of course, that the Church may also be justly termed 'Catholic' on the ground that it really does hold to the entire body of truth of which some shreds are discoverable in the various species of heresies.

> St. Augustine: *Letter 93, 23.* (5th cent.)

The Church grew, the nations believed, the princes of the earth have been conquered under the name of Christ, that they might be conquerors in the whole world. Their necks were placed under the yoke of Christ. Formerly they persecuted the Christians in defence of the idols, now they persecute the idols in defence of the Christians. All had recourse to the help of the Church in their every affliction, their every tribulation. That grain of mustard seed has grown and is become greater than all the herbs, and the birds of the air; the proud ones of the world come and find rest under its branches (Matt. 13, 31).

> St. Augustine: *Sermon 44, 1.* (5th cent.)

The Church is spread throughout the whole world: all nations have the Church. Let no one deceive you; it is the true, it is the Catholic Church. Christ we have not seen, but we have her; let us believe as regards Him. The apostles on the contrary saw Him, they believed as regards her. . . . They saw Christ, they believed in the Church which they did not see; and we who see the Church, let us believe in Christ, Whom we do not yet see.

> St. Augustine: *Sermon 238, 3.* (5th cent.)

Almighty and everlasting God, Who hast revealed Thy glory to all nations in Christ, preserve the works of Thy mercy; that Thy Church, spread over the whole world, may persevere with steadfast faith in the confession of Thy name.

> Roman Missal, Collect for Good Friday. (Gelasian, 5th to 7th cent.)

For it is the Church alone through which God willingly accepts a sacrifice, the Church alone which intercedes with confidence for those that are in error. The true sacrifice of the Redeemer is offered only in the one Catholic Church. It is the Church alone in which a good work is fruitfully carried on. It is the Church alone which guards those who are within it by the strong bond of charity. It is the Church alone in which we truly contemplate heavenly mysteries. For truth shines forth from the Catholic Church alone.

> Pope St. Gregory I: *Moralia in Job,* 35, 13. (6th cent.)

That Church is called universal which consists of all the churches, or in Greek *catholic.* According to this usage the Roman church is not the universal Church, but part of the universal Church, the first and chief part of course, as the head is to the body, because the plenitude of power resides in it, from which part of this authority flows to the others. That one Church which contains in it all the churches is called the universal Church. In this sense the Roman church alone is called the universal Church, because it alone by a privilege of remarkable dignity is above the others.

> Pope Innocent III: *Letter to the Patriarch of Constantinople.* (Reg. 2, 209) (13th cent.)

The Church is catholic, that is, universal: a) first with regard to place. . . . The Church has three parts, one on earth, a second in heaven, a third in purgatory: b) the Church is universal with regard to all conditions of human beings; nobody is rejected whether they be masters or slaves, men or women . . . : c) it is universal in time, and those are wrong who allow it a limited span of time, for it began with Abel and will last even to the end of the world.

> St. Thomas Aquinas: *Exposition of the Apostles' Creed.* (13th cent.)

Unlike republics of human institution, or the conventicles of heretics, [the Church] is not circumscribed within the limits of any one kingdom, nor confined to the members of any one society of men; but embraces within the amplitude of her love all mankind, whether barbarians or Scythians, slaves or freemen, male or female . . . She is also called universal, because all who desire eternal salvation must cling to and embrace her, like those who entered the ark to escape perishing in the flood.

> Catechism of the Council of Trent, 1. (16th cent.)

It seems to me, as I have been saying, that catholicity is not only one of the notes of the Church, but, according to the divine purposes, one of its securities.

> Card. Newman: *Apologia pro Vita Sua,* 5. (19th cent.)

There is no geography for the Catholic as a Catholic.

> Archbishop Hughes: *Lecture on St. Patrick.* (1861)

Founded on immutable and universal principles, the Church can never grow old or obsolete, but is the Church for all times and places, for all ranks and conditions of men. Man cannot change either the Church or the dogmas of faith, for they are founded in the highest reality, which is above him, over him, and independent of him.

> Orestes Brownson: *The American Republic.* (19th cent.)

A religion that merely dresses for church as it dresses for dinner, a religion that merely prays into a top-hat and calls a suit of funeral black its Sunday best—that does not express what is expressed either by a hermit or a hierarchy; does not express anything, except that its followers would have been equally contented with anything else. Whatever it is, the Church of Christ must not merely be what some of my Anglican friends used humorously to call mod. high. It must be very high, like the spire of Cologne cathedral or the tower of Salisbury; or else it must be very low, like the catacombs or the cave of Bethlehem.

> G. K. Chesterton: *The Resurrection of Rome.* (20th cent.)

The Church of Jesus Christ is neither Latin nor Greek nor Slav, but Catholic. Accordingly she makes no difference between her children, and Greeks, Latins, Slavs and members of all other nations are equal in the eyes of the Apostolic See.

> Pope Benedict XV. (20th cent.)

The Church, though she possesses all truth essentially, yet still awaits her accidental perfection. She has to be extended to all people in order that she may manifest all the riches of Christ. For Catholicism cannot be true to its name, if it is anything less than a universal religion, in which all truth is embodied and every form of piety and holiness is manifested in the unity of the one Body of Christ.

> Dom Griffiths: *The Golden String.* (20th cent.)

IV—*Christ, Head of the Church*

Wherever the bishop appears, there let the people be; as wherever Jesus Christ is, there is the Catholic Church.

> St. Ignatius of Antioch: *Letter to the Smyrnaeans,* 8. (2nd cent.)

All who from the beginning of the world have been righteous have Christ for their Head. For they believed that He was to come, Whom we believe to have now come; and it was in faith of Him in Whose faith we have been made whole, that they were made whole also; so that He should be in His own Person the Head of the whole of the City of Jerusalem. And all the faithful from the beginning unto the end were included in the number, to whom the legions and armies of angels were also joined, so that it might become one City under one King, and, as it were, one Province under one Governor, happy in perpetual peace and security, praising God eternally and happy eternally.

> St. Augustine: *In Ps. 36, Sermon 3,* 4. (5th cent.)

And since the whole Christ is head and body, which truth I do not doubt that you know well, the Head is our Savior Himself, Who suffered under Pontius Pilate, Who now, after He is risen from the dead, sits at the right hand of the Father; but His body is the Church: not this church or that, but diffused over all the world. . . . For the whole Church, made up of all the faithful . . . has its Head, which governs the body, situate in the heavens; though it is separated from sight, yet it is bound by love.

> St. Augustine: *In Ps. 56 Enarr.* (5th cent.)

Our Lord Jesus Christ is as one whole perfect Man, both head and body. We acknowledge the head in that Man Who was born of the Virgin Mary . . . The Body of this head is the Church, not the church of this country only, but of the whole world; not that of this age only, but from Abel himself down to those who shall be born to the end and shall believe in Christ, the whole assembly of saints belonging to one City, which City is Christ's body, of which Christ is the head.

St. Augustine: *In Ps. 90, Sermon 2,* 1. (5th cent.)

Think upon Christ our Head, by Whom the devil will without doubt in turn be conquered. Think also upon ourselves. Take care that you are in the Body, and you will be able to do all things in the Head. In yourself you are indeed exceedingly foolish; in Him you avail something.

Erasmus: *Enchiridion.* (16th cent.)

It is clear that the Son of God and of the blessed Virgin is to be called the Head of the Church for His singular pre-eminence. . . . Because Christ is so exalted, He alone by every right rules and governs the Church.

Pope Pius XII: *Mystici Corporis.* (June 29, 1943)

They walk the path of dangerous error who believe that they can accept Christ as the Head of the Church, while they reject genuine loyalty to His vicar on earth. They have taken away the visible head, broken the visible bonds of unity, and they leave the mystical body of the Redeemer in such obscurity and so maimed, that those who are seeking the haven of eternal salvation cannot see it and cannot find it.

Pope Pius XII: *Mystici Corporis.* (June 29, 1943)

V—*Church Militant, Suffering, and Triumphant*

Here it is the whole Church that is to be understood—not that part only which sojourns on earth, praising the name of the Lord from the rising of the sun to its setting and chanting a new song of deliverance from its ancient captivity; but that part also which always was in heaven, which always remained loyal to God, its Creator, and did not experience the woe that springs from a fall. This part, consisting of the holy angels, abides in perpetual bliss and helps, as it should, the other part which is still in exile; for both parts will be one in the fellowship of eternity, and even now are one in the bond of charity, the whole Church having been instituted for the purpose of worshipping God.

St. Augustine: *Enchiridion,* 56. (5th cent.)

Therefore, the temple of God, that is, of the sublime Trinity as a whole, is the Holy Church—everywhere, in heaven and on earth.

St. Augustine: *Enchiridion,* 56. (5th cent.)

The whole Church is one widow, whether in men or women, in married men or married women, in young men or in old, or in virgins. The whole Church is one widow, desolate in this world; if she feel this, if she is aware of her widowhood: then help is at hand for her.

St. Augustine: *In Ps. 131,* 23. (5th cent.)

The Church began at the place where the Holy Spirit descended from heaven and filled those who were sitting there together. In view of its present sojourn in strange parts the Church is called Sion, because from the distance of its sojourn it contemplates the promise of heavenly things; therefore it has received the name Sion, that is, contemplation. In view of the future peace of its home, it is called Jerusalem. For Jerusalem means the vision of peace.

St. Isidore: *Etymologies,* 8, 1. (7th cent.)

The Church consists principally of two parts, the one called the Church triumphant, the other the Church militant. The Church triumphant is that most glorious and happy assemblage of blessed spirits, and of those souls who have triumphed over the world, the flesh, and the devil, and, now exempt from the troubles of this life, are blessed with the fruition of everlasting bliss. The Church militant is the society of all the faithful still dwelling on earth, and is called militant, because it wages eternal war with those implacable enemies, the world, the flesh, and the devil. We are not however hence to infer that there are two Churches: they are two constituent parts of one Church.

Catechism of the Council of Trent, 1. (16th cent.)

VI—*City of God; Kingdom of God; Vessel, Ship, etc.*

As this broken bread was scattered over the hills and then, when gathered, became one mass, so may Thy Church be gathered from the ends of the earth into Thy kingdom. For Thine is the glory and power through Jesus Christ forevermore.

Teaching of the Twelve Apostles, 9. (Eucharistic prayer.) (2nd cent.)

The Catholic Church is the plantation of God, and His beloved vineyard; containing those who have believed in His unerring divine religion; who are the heirs by faith of His everlasting kingdom; who are partakers of His divine influence, and of the communication of the Holy Spirit; who are armed through Jesus, and have received His fear in their hearts; who enjoy the benefit of the sprinkling of the precious and innocent Blood of Christ; who have free liberty to call Almighty God, Father; being fellow-heirs and joint-partakers of His beloved Son.

Anonymous: *Constitutions of the Holy Apostles*, 1, 1. (4th cent.)

Faith is therefore the foundation of the Church; for it was not said of Peter's flesh, but of his faith, that the gates of hell should not prevail against it. But his confession conquered hell; and this confession has shut out more than one heresy. For whereas the Church like a goodly vessel is often beaten on by many waves,

the foundation of the Church must hold good against all heresies.

St. Ambrose: *On the Incarnation,* 33, 34. (4th cent.)

There are no more than two kinds of human society, which we may justly call two cities, according to the language of our Scriptures. The one consists of those who wish to live after the flesh, the other of those who wish to live after the spirit; and when they severally achieve what they wish, they live in peace, each after their kind.

St. Augustine: *The City of God,* 14, 2. (5th cent.)

We distribute the human race into two kinds of men, one living according to man, the other living according to God. Mystically, we call them two cities, or two societies of men: the one of which is predestined to reign eternally with God, the other to suffer eternal punishment with the devil.

St. Augustine: *The City of God,* 15, 1. (5th cent.)

These two Cities are made by two loves: the earthly City by love of oneself even to contempt of God; the heavenly City by love of God even to contempt of oneself. The one glories in itself, the other glories in God. The one seeks glory from men; to the other, God, witness of conscience, is its greatest glory. The one lifts up its head in its own glory: the other says to its God, *My glory and the lifter up of my head* (Ps. 3, 3).

St. Augustine: *The City of God,* 14, 28. (5th cent.)

Therefore the Church even now is the kingdom of Christ, and the kingdom of heaven. Accordingly, even now His saints reign with Him though otherwise than as they shall reign hereafter; and yet, though the tares grow in the Church along with the wheat, they do not reign with Him.

St. Augustine: *The City of God,* 20, 9. (5th cent.)

In truth, these two cities are entangled together in this world, and intermixed until the last judgment effect their separation.

St. Augustine: *The City of God*, 1, 35. (5th cent.)

So, too, as long as she is a stranger in the world, the city of God has in her communion, and bound to her by the sacraments, some who shall not eternally dwell in the lot of the saints.

St. Augustine: *The City of God*, 1, 35. (5th cent.)

True justice has no existence save in that republic Whose founder and ruler is Christ, if at least any choose to call this a republic; and indeed we cannot deny that it is the people's weal. But if perchance this name, which has become familiar in other connections, be considered alien to our common parlance, we may at all events say that in this city is true justice; the city of which Holy Scripture says, "Glorious things are said of thee, O city of God."

St. Augustine: *The City of God*, 2, 21. (5th cent.)

The Catholic Church is a mystery in the strict theological sense of the word. Her existence is not ultimately explainable in terms of human design and action; her total 'idea' is not discoverable by sheer philosophical and historical research. The existence of the Church hangs on a sovereignly free divine choice, whereby God *gave* to men this particular form for their religious life; and the 'idea' of the Church—what she ultimately is—is possessed, as a secret, by God alone.

J. C. Murray: *Address to Amer. Acad. of Political and Social Science.* (20th cent.)

As Christ was a full embodiment of all that Augustine meant by the City of God, so the Church may be described as a second embodiment of it. And as the life-principle of that City is *amor Dei usque ad contemptum sui*, a love for God so over-mastering that it destroys the deepest roots of selfishness, it follows that the 'typical' Christians are not prelates or theologians or canonists or administrators as such, but those in whom the love of God revealed in Christ has most fully won this all-controlling sway.

Dom Butler: *The Church and Infallibility.* (20th cent.)

Seen as a society living its life in the world, governed as societies of men must be governed, entering into relations with other human associations, the Church can be truly described as an institution. But *sub specie aeternitatis* she is the mysterious anticipation, beneath the veils of faith, of that kingdom of spirits whose full realization and glory are reserved to the 'age to come.'

Dom Butler: *The Church and Infallibility.* (20th cent.)

VII—*Extra ecclesiam nulla salus* (*Outside the Church there is no salvation*)

Whoso separates himself from the Church is joined to an adulterer and has cut himself off from the promises made to the Church; no one who quits the Church of Christ will attain to the rewards of Christ.

St. Cyprian: *De Unitate Ecclesiae, 6.* (3rd cent.)

Therefore it is the Catholic Church alone which retains true worship. This is the fountain of truth, this is the abode of the faith, this is the temple of God; into which if anyone shall not enter, or from which if any shall go out, he is estranged from the hope of life and eternal salvation.

Lactantius: *Divine Institutes*, 4, 30. (4th cent.)

It is the peculiar property of the Church that when she is buffeted she is triumphant, when she is assaulted with argument she proves herself in the right, when she is deserted by her supporters she holds the field. It is her wish that all men should remain at her side and in her bosom; if it lay with her, none would become unworthy to abide under the shelter of that august mother, none would be cast out or suffered to depart from her calm retreat. But when heretics desert her or she expels them, the loss she endures in that she cannot save them, is compensated by an increased assurance that she alone can offer bliss.

St. Hilary of Poitiers: *On the Trinity*, 7, 4. (4th cent.)

No one, indeed, attains to salvation and eternal life except he who has Christ as his Head. But no one can have Christ as Head, except he who is in His body, which is the Church.

St. Augustine: *Ep. ad Cath. contra Donat.*, 19, 49. (5th cent.)

No man can find salvation save in the Catholic Church. Outside the Catholic Church he can find everything save salvation.

St. Augustine: *Sermo ad Caesariensis Ecclesiae Plebem*, 6. (5th cent.)

Indeed, as long as you [i.e. the schismatic Donatists] remain outside the Church and severed from the fabric of unity and the bond of charity (*Foris autem ab ecclesia constitutus et separatus a compage unitatis et vinculo caritatis*), you would be punished with everlasting chastisement, even if you were burned alive for Christ's sake.

St. Augustine: *Letter 173*. (5th cent.)

How many that are not ours are yet, as it were, within; and how many that are ours are still, as it were, without. *The Lord knoweth who are His* (2 Tim. 2, 19). And they that are not ours, who are within, when they find their opportunities, go out, and they that are ours, who are without, when they find opportunities, return.

St. Augustine: *In Ps. 106*, 14. (5th cent.)

The holy universal Church proclaims that God cannot truly be worshipped save within herself, and asserts that all they who are without her pale shall never be saved.

Pope St. Gregory the Great: *Moralia in Job*, 14, 5. (6th cent.)

Church in Greek means convocation, or assembly in Latin, because all are called to [be members of] it.

St. Isidore: *Etymologies*, 8, 1. (7th cent.)

In a general way the whole congregation of the elect is called the Church. But now in a more particular manner by way of distinction, that part of the faithful which came before the time of the Lord's Incarnation is called the synagogue; that part which followed it is called the Church.

St. Bede the Venerable: *In Cantica Canticorum*, 2. (8th cent.)

Church means congregation. Holy Church is the congregation of believers of which each Christian is a member.

St. Thomas Aquinas: *Exposition of the Apostles' Creed*. (13th cent.)

As in one single human being there is one soul and one body but many members, so the Catholic Church has one body but many members. The soul animating this body is the Holy Ghost. Hence the Creed, after bidding us believe in the Holy Ghost, adds, *the Holy Catholic Church*.

St. Thomas Aquinas: *Exposition of the Apostles' Creed*. (13th cent.)

The Church is like the ark of Noah, outside of which nobody can be saved.

St. Thomas Aquinas: *Exposition of the Apostles' Creed*. (13th cent.)

That there is one holy catholic and apostolic Church we are compelled to believe and to hold, prompted by divine faith, and we do believe this firmly and confess it simply, outside of which there can be no salvation, or remission of sins. . . .

Boniface VIII: *Bull Unam Sanctam*, Nov. 18, 1302.

There is one holy universal Church, namely, all the predestined.

> Error of John Hus condemned by Pope Martin V at Council of Constance, Session 15, July 6, 1415.

Under the word 'Church' are comprehended no unimportant mysteries, for in this 'calling forth,' which the word 'church' (*ecclesia*) signifies, we at once recognize the benignity and splendor of divine grace, and understand that the Church is very unlike all other commonwealths: they rest on human reason and human prudence; this on the wisdom and councils of God; for He called us by the interior inspiration of the Holy Ghost, Who through the ministry and labor of His pastors and preachers penetrates into the hearts of men.

> Catechism of the Council of Trent, 1. (16th cent.)

Although the Catholic faith uniformly and truly teaches that the good and the bad belong to the Church, yet the same faith declares that the condition of both is very different: the wicked are contained in the Church, as the chaff is mingled with the grain on the threshing floor, or as dead members sometimes remain attached to a living body.

> Catechism of the Council of Trent, 1. (16th cent.)

No. 72: It is a note of the Christian Church that it is Catholic, comprising at once all the angels in heaven, and all the elect and just of earth, and of all ages.

No. 74: The Church, or the whole Christ, has the Word Incarnate for head, and all the saints as members.

No. 76: Nothing more roomy than the Church of God, because all the elect and righteous of all ages compose it.

> Propositions of P. Quesnel condemned by Pope Clement XI in his Bull, *Unigenitus,* September 10, 1713.

It is of faith that no man can be saved outside the apostolic Church of Rome, that this is the one ark of salvation and that anyone who does not board it will perish in the flood; but it is to be held as equally certain that those who are in a state of ignorance about the true religion, provided the ignorance be invincible, are not held in any way blameworthy in this matter in God's eyes.

> Pope Pius IX: *Allocution Singulari Quadam.* (December 9, 1854)

Hope must at least be entertained for all those who in no wise belong to the true Church of Christ.

> Proposition condemned by Pius IX in Syllabus of Errors. (1867)

To 'lose self' in a Society of some kind is the only means of saving self.

> R. H. Benson: *The Friendship of Christ.* (20th cent.)

It is by baptism that a man is made a member (*persona*) in the Church of Christ with all the rights and duties of Christians, unless, as regards rights, there exists some obstacle impeding the bond of ecclesiastical communion or a censure imposed by the Church.

> Code of Canon Law, Canon 87. (20th cent.)

Only those are *really* to be included as members of the Church who have been baptized and profess the true faith and who have not unhappily withdrawn from body-unity or for grave faults been excluded by legitimate authority.

> Pope Pius XII: *Mystici Corporis.* (June 29, 1943)

One must not imagine that the body of the Church, just because it bears the name of Christ, is made up during the days of its earthly pilgrimage only of members conspicuous for their holiness, or consists only of the group of those whom God has predestined to eternal happiness. It is the Savior's infinite mercy that allows place in His mystical body here for those whom He did not exclude from the banquet of old. For not every sin, however grave and enormous it be, is such as to sever a man automatically from the body of the Church, as does schism or heresy or apostasy.

Pope Pius XII: *Mystici Corporis.* (June 29, 1943)

Of those helps to salvation that are ordered to the last end only by divine decree, not by intrinsic necessity, God, in His infinite mercy, willed that such effects of those helps as are necessary to salvation can, in certain circumstances, be obtained when the helps are used only in *desire* or *longing.* . . . The same, in due proportion, should be said of the Church insofar as it is a general help to salvation. To gain eternal salvation it is not always required that a person be incorporated *in fact* as a member of the Church, but it is required that he belong to it at least in *desire* and *longing.*

Letter of the Holy Office to Archbishop Cushing of Boston. (Aug. 8, 1949)

VIII—*Holy*

For where the Church is, there is the Spirit of God; and where the Spirit of God is, there is the Church and every form of grace, for the Spirit is truth.

St. Irenaeus: *Against the Heresies*, 3, 24, 1. (2nd cent.)

For Christ is not simply in the head and not in the body, but Christ whole is in the head and in the body. What therefore His members are, that He is; but what He is, it does not follow that His members are.

St. Augustine: *In Joan. Evang.,* 28, 1. (5th cent.)

Then the Church is holy. . . . A church when consecrated is washed—so are the faithful cleansed by the blood of Christ. . . . A church is anointed too—so also the faithful receive a spiritual unction for their sanctification . . . Christ means the Anointed One. And His unction is the grace of the Holy Spirit. . . . More-

over the Church is holy by the indwelling of the Blessed Trinity. . . .

St. Thomas Aquinas: *Exposition of the Apostles' Creed.* (13th cent.)

The Church is called holy, because she is consecrated and dedicated to God. . . . The Church . . . is holy . . . because she is the body of Christ, by Whom she is sanctified, and in Whose blood she is washed (Eph. 1, 1; 1, 7; 5, 26).

Catechism of the Council of Trent, 1. (16th cent.)

It should not be deemed a matter of surprise that the Church, although numbering amongst her children many sinners, is called holy; for as those who profess any art, although they should depart from its rules, are called artists; so the faithful, although offending in many things and violating the engagements to the observance of which they had solemnly pledged themselves, are called holy, because they are made the people of God, and are consecrated to Christ by baptism and faith.

Catechism of the Council of Trent, 1. (16th cent.)

A milk white hind, immortal and unchang'd,
Fed on the lawns and in the forest rang'd;
Without unspotted, innocent within,
She fear'd no danger, for she knew no sin.

Dryden: *The Hind and the Panther*, 1. (17th cent.)

The Catholic Church has a way of growing saints which is shared by no other communion. They are not turned out all alike as by a machine, but have the most startling individualities, so that the world has constantly counted them as mad. In a well-managed garden flowers are healthier, larger, brighter, than in the fields, precisely because their idiosyncrasies are protected, encouraged, assisted to develop. And for this reason 'individualism' in the truest sense flourishes far more luxuriantly in the enclosed garden of the Catholic Church than in the uncultivated meadows and woods without.

> Abbot Chapman: *Bishop Gore and the Catholic Claims.* (20th cent.)

It is impossible that an individual or a society should 'be in Christ,' if it does not manifest the character of Christ in its own.

> R. H. Benson: *The Sanctity of the Church.* (20th cent.)

IX—*Infallible*

Clearly the person who accepts the Church as an infallible guide will believe whatever the Church teaches.

> St. Thomas Aquinas: *Summa Theologica,* 2-2, 5, 3. (13th cent.)

If Christianity is both social and dogmatic, and intended for all ages, it must humanly speaking have an infallible expounder. Else you will secure unity of form at the loss of unity of doctrine, or unity of doctrine at the loss of unity of form; you will have to choose between a comprehension of opinions and a resolution into parties, between latitudinarian and sectarian error.

> Card. Newman: *The Development of Christian Doctrine.* (19th cent.)

St. Paul says in one place that his apostolical power is given him to edification, and not to destruction. There can be no better account of the infallibility of the Church. It is a supply for a need, and it does not go beyond that need.

> Card. Newman: *Apologia pro Vita Sua,* 5. (19th cent.)

Such is the infallibility lodged in the Catholic Church . . . it is . . . supereminent prodigious power sent upon earth to encounter and master a giant evil.

> Card. Newman: *Apologia pro Vita Sua,* 5. (19th cent.)

The Roman pontiffs and oecumenical councils have gone beyond the limits of their powers, have usurped the rights of princes, and have erred in defining matters of faith and morals.

> Proposition condemned by Pius IX in Syllabus of Errors. (1867)

The appeal from the living voice of the Church to any tribunal whatsoever, human history included, is an act of private judgment and a treason, because that living voice is supreme; and to appeal from that supreme voice is also a heresy, because that voice, by divine assistance, is infallible.

> Card. Manning: *Letter to the London Daily Telegraph.* (19th cent.)

The Church is not susceptible of being reformed in her doctrines. The Church is the work of an Incarnate God. Like all God's works, it is perfect. It is, therefore, incapable of reform.

> Card. Gibbons: *The Faith of Our Fathers,* 7. (19th cent.)

Every man may err, but not the whole gathered together; for the whole hath a promise.

> R. H. Benson: *By What Authority.* (20th cent.)

X—*Mater Ecclesia, Spouse and Bride*

In saying, *Rejoice thou barren that bearest not,* He speaks of us, for our Church was barren before children were given her.

> So-called Second Letter of Clement to the Corinthians, 2, 1. (2nd or 3rd cent.)

He cannot have God for his Father who has not the Church for his mother.

> St. Cyprian: *De Unitate Ecclesiae,* 6. (3rd cent.)

The bride of Christ cannot be falsified: she is chaste and incorrupt. She knows but one home; she with scrupulous chastity keeps inviolate her one bride-chamber. She it is who preserves us for God;

she finds places in the Kingdom for the children she has begotten.

St. Cyprian: *De Unitate Ecclesiae, 6.* (3rd cent.)

So Holy Church, ignorant of wedlock, but fertile in bearing, is in chastity a virgin, yet a mother in offspring. . . . For what bride has more children than Holy Church, who is a virgin in her sacraments and a mother in her people?

St. Ambrose: *Concerning Virgins,* 1, 31. (4th cent.)

Rightly, O Catholic Church, most true mother of Christians, thou dost not only teach that God . . . must be worshipped in perfect purity and chastity . . . but thou dost also embrace love and charity to our neighbor in such a way that for the diverse diseases with which souls are afflicted for their sins, there is found with thee a medicine of prevailing efficacy. Thy training and teaching are childlike for children, forcible for youths, gentle for the aged, taking into account not only the age of the body but also that of the mind.

St. Augustine: *De Moribus Ecclesiae Catholicae,* 1, 30, 62. (4th cent.)

This Church, imitating His [i.e. Christ's] Mother, daily gives birth to His members, and likewise remains a virgin.

St. Augustine: *Enchiridion,* 34. (5th cent.)

Christ, designing to establish virginity in the heart of the Church, first preserved virginity in the body of Mary. When men and women marry, the woman is given to her spouse and she will no longer be a virgin; but the Church could not be a virgin if she had not found the Spouse to Whom she was given, to be the Son of a virgin.

St. Augustine: *Sermons,* 188. (5th cent.)

Moreover, why should you not be concerned in the Virgin's childbearing, seeing that you are the members of Christ? Mary gave birth to your Head; the Church gave birth to you. For the Church herself is also both mother and virgin: a mother through loving charity, a virgin through the soundness of her faith and sanctity. She gives birth to peoples, but her members belong to the One only of Whom she herself is the body of the Spouse. In this too she bears the likeness of that other Virgin, the fact that she is also the mother of unity among many.

St. Augustine: *Sermons,* 192. (5th cent.)

The Church, like blessed Mary ever Virgin, both espoused and immaculate, conceives us as a virgin by the Spirit, bears us as a virgin without pain, and both espoused as it were to one but made fruitful by another, through the single parts which compose the one Catholic Church is joined visibly to the pontiff set over it, but is increased through the invisible power of the Holy Spirit.

St. Bede the Venerable: *In Lucam,* 1. (8th cent.)

I have labored with all my might that holy Church, the bride of God, our mistress and our mother, should recover her honor and remain chaste, and free and Catholic.

Pope St. Gregory VII: *Letters.* (1084)

Though none of us would presume so far as to venture to say that his soul was the spouse of the Lord; yet, since we are members of the Church, which justly glories in that name, and in the fact which that name signifies, we may claim not unjustly a participation in that glory.

St. Bernard: *Sermons on the Canticle of Canticles,* 12, 11 (12th cent.)

First the planting and then the harvest. The Church is the garden: *my sister, my spouse is a garden enclosed* (Cant. 4, 12). Here are many plots, all different according to our callings, but all planted by God, and the whole is watered by the streams of Christ's sacraments flowing from His side. . . . The Church's ministers are like gardeners: *I have preached,*

Apollo watered (1 Cor. 3, 6). The fruits which wisdom has abundantly watered are the harvest. It is Christ Who brings us to glory, Christ Who brings to birth the Church's faithful . . . the fruits are the saints in glory. . . .

> St. Thomas Aquinas: *Commentary on the Sentences,* 1, Prol. (13th cent.)

There was a wedding feast, and the mother of Jesus was there (John 2, 1). Mystically the wedding feast means the Church: *this is a great sacrament, but I speak concerning Christ and the Church* (Eph. 5, 32). That marriage began in the Virgin's womb, where the Father espoused the Son to human nature in unity of person. . . . It was solemnized when the Church was joined to Him by faith. . . . It will be consummated when the bride, that is, the Church, shall be brought into the bridal chamber of heavenly glory.

> St. Thomas Aquinas: *Commentary on St. John,* 2, lect. 1. (13th cent.)

Thou to Thy spousal universe
Art Husband, she Thy wife and Church;
Who in most dusk and vidual church,
Her Lord being hence,
Keeps her cold sorrows by Thy hearse.

> F. Thompson: *Orient Ode.* (19th cent.)

XI—*Mystical Body of Christ*

Or have we not one God, and one Christ, and one Spirit of grace poured out upon us? And is there not one calling in Christ? Why do we divide and tear asunder the members of Christ, and raise up strife against our own body, and reach such a pitch of madness as to forget that we are members one of another?

> Pope St. Clement I: *Letter to the Corinthians,* 46, 5-7. (1st cent.)

Let us choose to belong to the Church of life, that we may win salvation. Now I imagine that you are not ignorant that the living *Church is the body of Christ* (Eph. 1, 23). For Scripture says, *God* *made man male and female;* the male is Christ, the female is the Church.

> So-called Second Letter of Clement to the Corinthians, 14, 2. (2nd or 3rd cent.)

In this very Sacrament our people are shown to be made one; so that just as many grains collected into one, and ground and mingled together make one loaf, so in Christ, Who is the heavenly Bread, we may know that there is one body, in which our whole company is joined and united.

> St. Cyprian: *Letters,* 62, 13. (253)

For He freed us from the slavery of our sins . . . restoring us to a new life, transforming us into a new man, establishing us in the body of His flesh. For He is Himself the Church, containing it entire in Himself by the sacrament of His Body. It was not Sion before it was liberated; but it is Sion which has been freed.

> St. Hilary of Poitiers: *Treatise on Ps. 125,* 6. (4th cent.)

But the Church is the body of Christ, whose members we in turn are, as the apostle testifies (Eph. 1, 23), for it is Sion the mountain of the Lord, the daughter of the king, the holy city, built with live stones on the foundation of the prophets and apostles.

> St. Hilary of Poitiers: *Treatise on Ps. 128,* 9. (4th cent.)

Thou [the Catholic Church] joinest together, not in society only, but in a sort of brotherhood, citizen with citizen, nation with nation, and the whole race of men, by reminding them of their common parentage. Thou teachest kings to look to the interests of their people, and dost admonish the people to be submissive to their kings. With all care dost thou teach all to whom honor is due, and affection, and reverence, and fear, consolation, and admonition and exhortation, and discipline, and reproach, and punishment. Thou showest that all these are not equally incumbent on all, but that charity is owing to all, and wrong-doing to none.

> St. Augustine: *De Moribus Ecclesiae*, 1, 30, 63. (4th cent.)

Christ and the Church are two in one flesh.

> St. Augustine: *In Ps. 142*, 3. (5th cent.)

One difference between an organic body and the Church's mystical body is this: the members of an organism are all knit together at one given period of time, whereas the members of the mystical body are dispersed throughout the ages, for the Church's body is made up of people of every century, from the beginning to the end of the world. They are not all contemporaries even in the world of grace. . . . Some are potential and will never be actual, others will be actual, either by faith, or by wayfarer's charity as well, or by the enjoyment of our heavenly home.

> St. Thomas Aquinas: *Summa Theologica*, 3, 8, 3. (13th cent.)

A natural body is a single organism composed of diverse members; likewise the whole Church, Christ's mystical body, is reputed to be one single person, of which the head is Christ.

> St. Thomas Aquinas: *Summa Theologica*, 3, 49, 1. (13th cent.)

Prompted by divine faith we are obliged to believe and to hold that there is one holy Catholic and apostolic Church, and this we firmly believe and simply confess, outside of which there is no salvation or remission of sins . . . which constitutes one mystical body, whose head is Christ. . . .

> Pope Boniface VIII: *Bull Unam Sanctam*, Nov. 18, 1302.

The Church is not something dead: it is the body of Christ endowed with supernatural life. As Christ, the head and exemplar, is not wholly in His visible human nature . . . nor wholly in the invisible divine nature . . . but is one, from and in both natures, visible and invisible; so the mystical body of Christ is the true Church only because its visible parts draw life and power from the supernatural gifts and other things whence spring their very nature and essence. But since the Church is such by divine will and constitution, such it must uniformly remain to the end of time.

> Pope Leo XIII: *Satis Cognitum*. (June 20, 1896)

Since the mystical body of Christ, that is to say, the Church, is, like the physical body, a unity, a compact thing closely joined together, it would be false and foolish to say that Christ's mystical body could be composed of separated and scattered members. Whoever therefore is not united with it is not a member of it nor does he communicate with its Head Who is Christ.

> Pope Pius XI: *Mortalium Animos*. (Jan. 6, 1928)

If we would define and describe this true Church of Jesus Christ—which is the one, holy, Catholic, apostolic, Roman Church—we shall find no expression more noble, more sublime or more divine than the phrase which calls it *the mystical body of Jesus Christ*. This title is derived from and is, as it were, the fair flower of the repeated teaching of Sacred Scripture and the holy fathers.

> Pope Pius XII: *Mystici Corporis*. (June 29, 1943)

Our Savior does not rule the Church directly in a visible manner, and so in carrying out the work of redemption He wishes to be helped by the members of His body. This is not because He is indigent and weak, but rather because He so willed it for the greater glory of His unspotted spouse. . . . Deep mystery this, subject of inexhaustible meditation; that the salvation of many depends on the prayers and voluntary penances which the members of the mystical body of Jesus Christ offer for this intention and on the assistance of pastors of souls and of the faithful, especially of fathers and mothers of families, which they must offer to our divine Savior as though they were His associates.

> Pope Pius XII: *Mystici Corporis*. (June 29, 1943)

We must accustom ourselves to see Christ in the Church. It is Christ Who lives in the Church, Who teaches, governs and sanctifies through her. It is Christ, too, Who manifests Himself differently in different members of His society.

> Pope Pius XII: *Mystici Corporis*. (June 29, 1943)

Genuine love of the Church is not satisfied with our being within this body members one of another, mutually careful one for another, rejoicing with Him Who glories, suffering with Him Who suffers; we must also recognize as brothers of Christ according to the flesh, destined together with us to eternal salvation, those others who have not yet joined us in the body of the Church.

> Pope Pius XII: *Mystici Corporis*. (June 29, 1943)

That the mystical body of Christ and the Catholic Church in communion with Rome are one and the same thing, is a doctrine based on revealed truth.

> Pope Pius XII: *Humani Generis*. (Aug. 12, 1950)

XII—*One*

We are a society with a common religious feeling, unity of discipline, a common bond of hope. (*Corpus sumus de conscientia religionis et disciplinae unitate et spei foedere.*)

> Tertullian: *Apology*, 39, 1. (3rd cent.)

Now we ought to hold fast and defend this unity—especially we bishops, who preside in the Church, that we may show that the episcopate too is itself one and undivided. . . . The episcopate, of which part is held by each severally and jointly,

is one. The Church, likewise, which is spread abroad far and wide into a multitude through the increase of her fruitfulness, is one. Just as the sun has many rays, but one light; and as a tree has many boughs, but one strength derived from its tenacious root; and as when many streams flow from one spring, though a multiplicity of waters is seen diffused in bountifulness as they gush forth—still unity is preserved in the source.

> St. Cyprian: *On the Unity of the Catholic Church*, 5. (3rd cent.)

God is one and Christ is one, and one is His Church, and the faith is one, and one His people welded together by the glue of concord into a solid unity of body. Unity cannot be rent asunder, nor can the one body, through the division of its structure, be divided into separate pieces—its outward members mangled and wrenched apart—torn into bits.

> St. Cyprian: *On the Unity of the Catholic Church*, 23. (3rd cent.)

God is one and Christ is one, His Church is one, His see is one, founded by the voice of the Lord on Peter. No other altar can be set up, no other priesthood instituted apart from that one altar and that one priesthood. Whoso gathers elsewhere, scatters.

> St. Cyprian: *Letters*, 40, 5. (3rd cent.)

The Church, which is Catholic and one, is not cut nor divided, but is indeed connected and bound together by the cement of the clergy (*sacerdotum*) who adhere to each other.

> St. Cyprian: *Letters*, 68, 8. (3rd cent.)

The Church, ordained by the Lord and established by His holy apostles, is one for all; but the frantic folly of discordant sects has severed them from her. . . . The hosts of heresy assemble themselves against her; each of them can defeat all the others, but not one can win a victory for itself. The only victory is the triumph which the Church celebrates over them all.

> St. Hilary of Poitiers: *On the Trinity,* 7, 4. (4th cent.)

Although there is one Church throughout the world, still each city has its own church; the Church is one in all these, although they are numerous, because it is considered to be one in many.

> St. Hilary of Poitiers: *Treatise on Ps. 14,* 3. (4th cent.)

All mankind is in Christ one man, and the unity of Christians is one Man.

> St. Augustine: *In Ps. 29, En.,* 2, 5. (5th cent.)

We beseech Thee, O Lord, mercifully receive the prayers of Thy Church; that all adversity and error being destroyed, it may serve Thee in security and freedom.

> Roman Missal, Collect for the Church. (Leonine, ca. 5th cent.)

Whereas cities are so-called from the people living together, the churches of the true faith are not improperly represented as 'cities,' since they are settled in different parts of the world and constitute one Catholic Church, in which all the faithful thinking what is right concerning God live together in harmony.

> Pope St. Gregory I: *Morals,* 16, 68. (6th cent.)

The unity of the Church is manifested in the mutual connection or communication of its members, and likewise in the relation of all the members of the Church to one head.

> St. Thomas Aquinas: *Summa Theologica,* 2-2, 9, 39, 1. (13th cent.)

This unity has a threefold cause; it comes from agreement of faith, of hope, and of charity.

> St. Thomas Aquinas: *Exposition of the Apostles' Creed.* (13th cent.)

The first mark of the true Church is described in the creed of the fathers, and

consists in unity: *My dove is one, my beautiful one is one* (Cant. 6, 8). So vast a multitude scattered far and wide is called one, for the reasons mentioned by St. Paul in his epistle to the Ephesians: *One Lord, one faith, one baptism* (Eph. 4, 5).

> Catechism of the Council of Trent, 1. (16th cent.)

One in herself, not rent by schism, but sound,
Entire, one solid shining diamond,
Not sparkles shattered into sects like you,
One is the Church, and must be to be true:
One central principle of unity.
As undivided, so from errors free,
As one in faith, so one in sanctity.

> Dryden: *The Hind and the Panther,* 2. (17th cent.)

The Church is the society of the faithful collected into one and the same body, governed by its legitimate pastors, of whom Jesus Christ is the invisible head —the pope, the successor of St. Peter, being His representative on earth.

> St. John Baptist de la Salle: *Les devoirs du chrétien,* 10. (18th cent.)

It is so evident from the clear and frequent testimonies of holy writ that the true Church of Jesus Christ is one, that no Christian can dare to deny it. But in judging and determining the nature of this unity many have erred in various ways. . . . We must investigate not how the Church may possibly be one, but how He, Who founded it, willed that it should be one.

> Pope Leo XIII: *Satis Cognitum.* (June 20, 1896)

These three bonds of unity, then, the symbolical, the liturgical, and the hierarchical, are all, according to the fathers, indispensable to the visible Church on earth. One faith, one communion, one spiritual government.

> Abbot Chapman: *Bishop Gore and the Catholic Claims.* (20th cent.)

The strength of the Church is her unity, which nothing is able to break, not because it is too strong, for humanly it is weak, but because it is a unity that is not of this earth.

> Archb. Goodier: *The Inner Life of the Catholic.* (20th cent.)

There is one Church, which was founded by Christ upon the rock of Peter, to be the way of salvation for all mankind. In this Church all those elements of truth which have been dispersed among the different peoples of the earth are gathered into unity; it is the center from which they derive their value and significance. The Church with her hierarchy and sacraments is the sole basis of unity for mankind, for it is this visible, hierarchical Church which constitutes the mystical Body of Christ on earth. Her ministers and her sacraments are simply the chosen instruments of divine grace, the means by which men are incorporated into the Body of Christ and made to participate in the light of His truth.

> Dom Griffiths: *The Golden String.* (20th cent.)

XIII—*Its Permanence*

This is holy Church, the one Church, the true Church, the Catholic Church, fighting against all heresies; she can fight, but she cannot be conquered. All heresies are expelled from her as if they were dead branches pruned from the vine; she herself, however, remains fixed in her root, in her vine, in her charity. The gates of hell shall not prevail against her.

> St. Augustine: *On the Creed, 6.* (4th cent.)

The Church has four marks, being one, holy, catholic or universal, and strong or lasting.

> St. Thomas Aquinas: *Exposition of the Apostles' Creed.* (13th cent.)

When [Christianity] dies, at least the world will die with it. The world's duration is measured by it. If the Church dies, the world's time is run. The world shall never exult over the Church. If the Church falls sick, the world shall utter a wail for its own sake; for, like Samson, the Church will bury all with it.

> Card. Newman: *Sermons on Subjects of the Day.* (19th cent.)

It is a peculiarity of the warfare between the Church and the world, that the world seems ever gaining on the Church, yet the Church is really ever gaining on the world.

> Card. Newman: *Sermons on Subjects of the Day.* (19th cent.)

One body, one spirit, one Lord,
  And one faith, for all ages was given;
One baptism in blessed accord,
  With one God, and one Father, in heaven.
One Church, the sole pillar and ground
  Of the truth, an immovable rock;
One Shepherd, by all to be own'd,
  And one fold, for that primitive flock!

. . . .

The Church that was built on the rock
  That for ages has stood, is the same!
Unshaken, endures every shock,
  And still baffles the enemy's aim.
Tho buffetted ever by foes
  From without and within it remains
Triumphant as first when it rose
  In its truth o'er idolatry's fanes.

> W. Young: *The Rock of Ages.* (19th cent.)

Who is she that stands triumphant,
  Rock in strength, upon the Rock,
Like some city crowned with turrets,
  Braving storm and earthquake shock?
Who is she her arms extending,
  Blessing thus a world restored:
All the anthems of creation
  Lifting to creation's Lord?
    Hers the kingdom, hers the scepter;
    Fall, ye nations, at her feet;
    Hers that truth whose fruit is freedom;
    Light her yoke, her burden sweet.

> Aubrey De Vere: *The Church.* (19th cent.)

I am not prepared to grant that the ancient Church was on the whole preferable to the modern. There were giants in those days: yet there is a fulness and richness in the Church of the twentieth century which was lacking in the fourth or fifth. I do not believe that the Church of God has been continually deteriorating ever since her foundation, but I believe that she has a divine life which increases in her without end.

> Abbot Chapman: *Bishop Gore and the Catholic Claims*. (20th cent.)

We see the ship of the Church today sailing merrily over very rough water. How often has she seemed to suffer shipwreck! Yet there she is, safe and sound. To investigate her past history is a most interesting, a most edifying study. The worse the scandals in the past, the greater the wonder of God's help that has made the Church survive. The Catholic historian can look difficulties in the face. He is not bound to any theory of the past. He has the New Testament at the one end of the history and the Church of today at the other, both manifestly divine, and with an admittedly unbroken sequence binding the one to the other. How the development has taken place is a matter for critical examination, not for theorizing.

> Abbot Chapman: *Bishop Gore and the Catholic Claims*. (20th cent.)

It was foreign to the mind of Christ to found a Church as a society which was to last on earth for a long course of centuries; nay, in the mind of Christ the kingdom of heaven together with the end of the world was about to come immediately.

> Proposition condemned by Decree of Holy Office, *Lamentabili*, June 3, 1907.

The organic constitution of the Church is not immutable; but Christian society like human society is subject to perpetual evolution.

> Proposition condemned by Decree of Holy Office, *Lamentabili*, June 3, 1907.

When Christ at a symbolic moment was establishing His great society, He chose for its corner-stone neither the brilliant Paul nor the mystic John, but a shuffler, a snob, a coward—in a word, a man. And upon this rock He has built His Church, and the gates of hell have not prevailed against it. All the empires and the kingdoms have failed because of this inherent and continual weakness, that they were founded by strong men and upon strong men. But this one thing—the historic Christian Church—was founded upon a weak man, and for that reason it is indestructible. For no chain is stronger than its weakest link.

> G. K. Chesterton: *Heretics*. (20th cent.)

We know, of course, that the Catholic Church cannot be destroyed. But what we do not know is the extent of the area over which it will survive; its power of revival or the power of the enemy to push it further and further back to its last defences until it may seem as though anti-Christ had come and the final issue was about to be decided. Of such moment is the struggle immediately before the world.

> H. Belloc: *The Great Heresies*. (20th cent.)

The Catholic Church is more than the sum of its parts. It is an organic and vital thing, like a nation. It has a life as vigorous as ever after twenty centuries. It is the thing which saved the world and in the weakening of which our general civilization may perish. To put that picture in a lively way before the mind of our generation is the chief task before us.

> H. Belloc: *Essays of a Catholic*. (20th cent.)

The myth of Rome's superb organization dies hard, but the more one sees of the Church from the inside the more convinced one becomes that the Church owes its success, and indeed its survival in a world of enemies, less to Henry Fordian organization than to supernatural assistance.

> Arnold Lunn: *Now I See*. (20th cent.)

The Catholic Church herself is an historic fact. Like a great mountain-range she bestrides the history of the past two thousand years. Whatever may be the attitude adopted towards her, it is impossible to escape her.

Pope Pius XII: *Allocution to the 10th Intern. Congress of Historical Sciences.* (1955)

XIV—*Visible*

But we teach that there is only one Church, and not two, and that the one and true Church is the assembly (*coetus*) of men bound together by the profession of the same Christian faith and by the communion of the same sacraments, under the rule of legitimate pastors, and especially of the one vicar of Christ on earth, the Roman pontiff.

St. Robert Bellarmine: *De Ecclesia Militante*, 2. (17th cent.)

The outward preaching of the Gospel; the promulgation from time to time of ecclesiastical discipline; the conversion of new provinces and nations from century to century during eighteen hundred years; the succession of pastors; the ordination of new levites for the recruiting [of the] sanctuary; the holding of councils, both general and provincial; the suffering martyrs; the founding of churches; the defections of heretics; the contentions against principalities and powers; the disputes—even the scandals of her members—all attest the visible perpetual existence of the Church as a continuation of the same Society instituted by our blessed Lord Himself.

Archbishop Hughes: *Letters on the Catholic Church.* (In reply to the Rev. Murray, a Presbyterian clergyman of Elizabethtown, N. J.) (1857)

If we consider the chief end of this Church and the proximate and efficient causes of salvation, it is undoubtedly *spiritual;* but in regard to those who constitute it, and to the things which lead to these spiritual gifts, it is *external* and necessarily visible.

Pope Leo XIII: *Satis Cognitum.* (June 20, 1896)

Those who arbitrarily conjure up and picture to themselves a hidden and invisible Church are in grievous and pernicious error, as also are those who regard the Church as a human institution which claims a certain obedience in discipline and external duties, but which is without the perennial communication of the gifts of divine grace, and without all that which testifies by constant and undoubted signs to the existence of that life which is drawn from God. It is assuredly as impossible that the Church of Christ can be the one or the other as that man should be a body alone or a soul alone. The connection and union of both elements is as absolutely necessary to the true Church as the intimate union of the soul and body is to human nature.

Pope Leo XIII: *Satis Cognitum.* (June 20, 1896)

The Church, like Her Master and His ordinances, must have an earthly as well as a divine nature, if she is to do His work.

R. H. Benson: *A City Set on a Hill.* (20th cent.)

They err in a matter of divine truth, who imagine the Church to be invisible, intangible, a something merely 'pneumatological,' as they say, by which many Christian communities, though they differ from each other in their profession of faith, are united by a bond that eludes the senses.

Pope Pius XII: *Mystici Corporis.* (June 29, 1943)

XV—*Aphorisms*

The Church is, as it were, the form of justice.

St. Ambrose: *On the Duties of the Clergy,* I, 142. (4th cent.)

Where the Church is, there is no death, but life eternal.

St. Ambrose: *In Ps. 40 Enarr. 30.* (4th cent.)

The Church does not die (Ecclesia non moritur.)

Legal maxim. (Medieval)

The nearer to the Church, the farther from God.

John Heywood: *Proverbs,* 1, 9. (Cf. French: Près de l'église, loin de Dieu; Italian: Piu presso la chiesa, piu lontano da Dio, etc.) (16th cent.)

The history of the Church should properly be called the history of truth.

Pascal: *Pensées.* (17th cent.)

I wish that you would crush this infamy. (Je voudrais que vous ecrasassiez l'infâme.)

Voltaire: *Letter to Jean d'Alembert.* (18th cent.)

If Rome dies, other churches may order their coffins.

G. Tyrrell. (20th cent.)

See also Catholic Faith; Christianity; Church and State; Clergy; Council, General; Hierarchy; Pope; Tradition, Ecclesiastical

Catholic Church and Civilization

The Latin church is the great fact which dominates the history of modern civilization.

H. C. Lea: *A History of Sacerdotal Celibacy,* 3. (19th cent.)

The Church can neither submit as a whole to the influence of a particular people, nor impose on one the features or the habits of another; for she is exalted in her catholicity above the differences of race, and above the claims of political power. At once the most firm and the most flexible institution in the world, she is all things to all nations—educating each in her own spirit, without violence to its nature, and assimilating it to herself without prejudice to the originality of its native character.

Lord Acton: *Döllinger on the Temporal Power.* (19th cent.)

This apostolic chair [of Rome] it was that gathered and held together the crumbling remains of the old order of things; this was the kindly light by whose help the culture of Christian times shone far and wide; this was an anchor of safety in the fierce storms by which the human race has been convulsed; this was the sacred bond of union that linked together nations distant in region and differing in character; in short, this was a common center from which was sought instruction in faith and religion, no less than guidance and advice for the maintenance of peace and the functions of practical life. In very truth it is the glory of the supreme pontiffs that they steadfastly set themselves up as a wall and a bulwark to save human society from falling back into its former superstition and barbarism.

Pope Leo XIII: *Inscrutabili.* (Apr. 21, 1878)

The Catholic Church, that imperishable handiwork of our all-merciful God, has for her immediate and natural purpose the saving of souls and securing our happiness in heaven. Yet in regard to things temporal, she is the source of benefits as manifold and great as if the chief end of her existence were to ensure the prospering of our earthly life. And indeed, wherever the Church has set her foot, she has straightway changed the face of things, and has attempered the moral tone of the people with a new civilization and with virtues before unknown. All nations which have yielded to her sway have become eminent by their gentleness, their sense of justice, and the glory of their high deeds.

Pope Leo XIII: *Immortale Dei.* (Opening words) (Nov. 1, 1885)

For learning is in itself good, and praise-worthy, and desirable; and further, all erudition which is the outgrowth of sound reason and in conformity with the truth of things serves not a little to confirm what we believe on the authority of God. The Church, truly, to our great benefit has carefully preserved the monuments of ancient wisdom; has opened everywhere homes of science, and has urged on intellectual progress by fostering most diligently the arts by which the culture of our age is so much advanced.

Pope Leo XIII: *Libertas Praestantissimum.* (June 20, 1888)

It is far from our intention to repudiate all that the genius of the time begets; nay, rather, whatever the search for truth attains, or the effort after good achieves, will always be welcome by us, for it increases the patrimony of doctrine and enlarges the limits of public prosperity. But all this, to possess real utility, should thrive without setting aside the authority and wisdom of the Church.

Pope Leo XIII: *Testem Benevolentiae.* (Jan. 22, 1899)

It is the teaching of history that when the Church pervaded with her spirit the ancient and barbarous nations of Europe, little by little the many and varied differences that divided them were diminished and their quarrels extinguished; in time they formed a homogeneous society from which sprang Christian Europe which, under the guidance and auspices of the Church, whilst preserving a diversity of nations, tended to a unity that favored its prosperity and glory.

Pope Benedict XV: *Pacem Dei Munus Pulcherrimum.* (May 23, 1920)

A Catholic culture does not mean or imply universality. A nation or a whole civilization is of the Catholic culture not when it is entirely composed of strong believers minutely practising their religion, nor even when it boasts a majority of such, but when it presents a deter-mining number of units—family institutions, individuals, inspired by and tenacious of the Catholic spirit.

H. Belloc: *The Crisis of Civilization.* (20th cent.)

This our European structure, built upon the noble foundations of classical antiquity, was formed through, exists by, is consonant to, and will stand only in the mold of, the Catholic Church. Europe will return to the faith, or she will perish. The faith is Europe. And Europe is the faith.

H. Belloc: *Europe and the Faith.* (20th cent.)

If Mr. Hilaire Belloc means that Europe would be nothing without the faith and that its *raison d'être* has been and remains to dispense the faith to the world, Mr. Belloc is right in saying that Europe is the faith. But speaking absolutely, no! Europe is not the faith and the faith is not Europe: Europe is not the Church and the Church is not Europe. Rome is not the capital of the Latin world. Rome is the capital of the world. *Urbs caput orbis.* The Church is universal because she is born of God, all nations are at home in her, the arms of her crucified Master are stretched above all races, above all civilizations. She does not bring nations the 'benefits of civilization,' but the blood of Christ and supernatural beatitude.

J. Maritain: *The Things That Are Not Caesar's.* (20th cent.)

The Church reminds us that, if our culture is Greco-Latin, our religion is not. The Church adopted such a culture, but did not subordinate herself to it. If the West, grown callous by the excess of prevarications and abuse of grace, refuses for a time her influence, she will boldly turn to cultures developed under other skies—she alone can do so without too great a risk, because she has in her hands the means of making all things right in hearts of good-will. She is the mother and nurse of civilization, and knows how to bring up a world.

> J. Maritain: *The Things That Are Not Caesar's.* (20th cent.)

The fundamental principles of Western civilization, individual liberty, human rights, the rights of private property, the integrity of human personality, derive from the doctrine now almost alone affirmed universally in the Western world by the Catholic church, that man at the core of his being is of a spiritual nature.

> *Resolution of the National Catholic Alumni Federation.* (1936)

The Church, from the beginning down to our own time, has always followed this wise practice: let not the Gospel on being introduced into any new land destroy or extinguish whatever its people possess that is naturally good, just or beautiful. For the Church, when she calls people to a higher culture and a better way of life, under the inspiration of the Christian religion, does not act like one who recklessly cuts down and uproots a thriving forest. No, she grafts a good scion upon the wild stock that it may bear a crop of more delicious fruit.

> Pope Pius XII: *Evangelii Praecones.* (June 2, 1951)

Our own civilization will pass, as those of the past have done; there is no need either to fear or to regret it. For the 'schema,' the *outward form* of this world, as St. Paul called it, is passing away; but beneath the outward form there is being built up continuously the Body of Christ, which is the unity of mankind in truth and charity. It is a hidden and mysterious process, which will only be realized in its fulness when this world of space and time has passed away altogether. Then we shall see the Church as it really is, as the fulfilment of the whole creation, the achievement of man's destiny by his participation in the life of God.

> Dom Griffiths: *The Golden String.* (20th cent.)

With regard to the future of humanity one can in the end do no more than offer conjectures. What concerns us is that the Church is aware of having received her mission and her task for all time to come, and for all men, and that in consequence she is not bound to any specific culture.

> Pope Pius XII: *Allocution to 10th Intern. Congress of Historical Sciences.* (1955)

See also Civilization

Catholic Church in England

. . . be it enacted by authority of this present parliament that the king, our sovereign lord . . . shall be taken, accepted, and reputed the only supreme head in earth of the Church of England called Anglicana Ecclesia, and shall have and enjoy, annexed and united to the imperial crown of this realm, as well the title and style thereof as all honors, dignities, pre-eminences, jurisdictions . . . to the said dignity of supreme head of the same Church belonging and appertaining; and that our said lord . . . shall have full power and authority from time to time to visit, repress, redress, reform . . . all such errors, heresies, abuses . . . which by any manner spiritual authority or jurisdiction ought or may lawfully be reformed . . . any usage, foreign laws, foreign authority . . . to the contrary notwithstanding.

> Henry VIII: *Supremacy Act.* (Abolishing papal authority and vesting same in crown.) (1534)

Suppose the parliament would make a law that God should not be God, would then you, Master Rich, say God were not God?

> St. Thomas More. (Reply to Sir Richard Rich, King's Solicitor, who was questioning him concerning the royal supremacy. Roper, Life.) (16th cent.)

Whereas, since the twentieth year of King Henry VIII . . . as well the spirituality as the temporality of your highness's realms and dominions have swerved from the obedience of the See

Apostolic and declined from the unity of Christ's Church . . . the pope's holiness and the See Apostolic sent hither unto your majesties [Mary and Philip] . . . and to the whole realm the most reverend father in God, the lord legate cardinal Pole, legate *de latere,* to call us home again into the right way . . . and we . . . seeing by the goodness of God our own errors, have acknowledged the same unto the said most reverend father, and by him have been . . . received and embraced into the unity and bosom of Christ's Church. . . .

Mary I: *Second Statute of Repeal.* (Restoring communion with the Holy See) (1555)

I, N., do utterly testify and declare in my conscience that the queen's highness is the only supreme governor of this realm, and of all other her highness's dominions and countries, as well in all spiritual or ecclesiastical things or causes as temporal, and that no foreign prince, person, prelate . . . hath or ought to have any jurisdiction, power, superiority . . . ecclesiastical or spiritual, within this realm; and therefore I do utterly renounce and forsake all foreign jurisdictions, powers, superiorities and authorities . . . and do promise that from henceforth I shall bear faith . . . to the queen's highness . . . and to my power shall assist and defend all jurisdictions . . . united or annexed to the imperial crown of this realm. . . .

Elizabeth I: *Act of Supremacy.* (Oath to be taken by all holding office in church or state. Catholics were thus debarred.) (1559)

No earthly commonwealth can give or confer [supremacy over the Church] to their prince, because they cannot give that which they have not by any natural faculty.

Cardinal Allen: *An Apology and True Declaration . . . of the Two English Colleges.* (1581)

There will never want in England men that will have care of their own salvation, nor such as shall advance other

men's; neither shall this Church here ever fail so long as priests and pastors shall be found for their sheep, rage man or devil never so much.

Bl. Edmund Campion: *Letters.* (16th cent.)

. . . be it enacted that . . . it shall be lawful for any person professing the Roman Catholic religion . . . to sit and vote in either house of parliament respectively, being in all other respects duly qualified . . . upon taking the following oath: . . . I do faithfully promise to maintain . . . the succession of the crown, which . . . stands limited to the princess Sophia . . . and the heirs of her body being Protestants . . . I do . . . declare that it is not an article of my faith . . . that princes excommunicated . . . by the pope . . . may be deposed or murdered by their subjects. . . . And I do declare that I do not believe the pope . . . hath or ought to have any temporal or civil jurisdiction, power . . . or pre-eminence, directly or indirectly, within this realm. I do swear that I will defend . . . the settlement of property within this realm as established by laws. . . . And I do hereby disclaim . . . any intention to subvert the present church establishment as settled by law. . . .

George IV: *Roman Catholic Emancipation Act.* (1829)

The great work is complete. Catholic England has been restored to its orbit in the ecclesiastical firmament. . . . Truly this is a day of joy and exultation. . . . Till such time as the Holy See shall think fit otherwise to provide, we govern and shall continue to govern the counties of Middlesex, Hertford, and Essex as ordinary thereof, and those of Surrey, Sussex, Hants, Berkshire, and Hampshire with the islands annexed as administrators with ordinary powers.

Card. Wiseman: *Pastoral Letter "From Out the Flaminian Gate of Rome."* (Announcing the restoration of the hierarchy in England. This letter immediately caused a storm of protest on the part of Protestants, who interpreted it as an attack on the Establishment) (1850)

The English Church was, and the English Church was not, and the English Church is once again. This is the portent, worthy of a cry. It is the coming in of a second spring; it is a restoration in the moral world, such as that which yearly takes place in the physical.

> Card. Newman: *Sermons on Various Occasions.* ("Second Spring" sermon, preached July 13, 1852 in St. Mary's, Oscott, before the first provincial synod of Westminster, following the restoration of the Catholic hierarchy in England)

Catholic Church in the United States

Their blood flowed as freely (in proportion to their numbers) to cement the fabric of independence as that of any of their fellow-citizens. They concurred with perhaps greater unanimity than any other body of men in recommending and promoting that government from whose influence America anticipates all the blessings of justice, peace, plenty, good order, and civil and religious liberty.

> Archb. Carroll: *Letters.* (June 10, 1789)

I presume that your fellow-citizens will not forget the patriotic part which you took in the accomplishment of their Revolution, and the establishment of your government, or the important assistance which they received from a nation in which the Roman Catholic faith is professed.

> George Washington: *To the Roman Catholics of the United States.* (March 12, 1790)

Notwithstanding the comparative poverty of the Catholic community—notwithstanding the embarrassed state of the Catholic churches—notwithstanding the hesitation which is felt at the idea of loaning money to churches of other denominations similarly circumstanced, there is one thing exceedingly glorious for our reputation, that, so far as I know, no man that ever had a just claim against a Catholic church ever lost one farthing of it.

> Archb. Hughes: *Address to the N.Y. Catholic Church Debt Association.* (1841)

It is not the union of Church and state—that is, the union, or identity rather, of religious and political principles—that it is desirable to get rid of, but the disunion or antagonism of Church and state. But this is nowhere possible out of the United States; for nowhere else is the state organized on Catholic principles, or capable of acting, when acting from its own constitution, in harmony with a really Catholic Church, or the religious order really existing, in relation to which all things are created and governed.

> Orestes Brownson: *The American Republic.* (19th cent.)

We are not among those who fancy that Catholicity can flourish here only by rooting out everything American, and completely revolutionizing American society and institutions. We believe American society, as natural society, is better organized and more in accordance with the needs of Catholic society, than is any other society on the face of the globe, and we are anxious to preserve and perfect it according to its original type.

> Orestes Brownson: *Works,* 12, 200ff. (1859)

So far as it is compatible with faith and piety, I am for accepting the American civilization with its usages and customs; leaving aside other reasons, it is the only way by which Catholicity can become the religion of our people. The character and spirit of our people, and their institutions, must find themselves at home in our Church in the way those of other nations have done; and it is on this basis alone that the Catholic religion can make progress in our country.

> Isaac T. Hecker. (Elliott's Life, p. 292) (19th cent.)

To the average looker-on Catholicity is what Catholics are, and Catholics in

America viewed from a standpoint of morality were then and still are a very mixed population. Why the fruits are worse than the tree is a sore perplexity even to expert controversialists.

Walter Elliott: *The Life of Father Hecker.* (19th cent.)

There is no conflict between the Catholic Church and America. I speak beneath this cathedral dome as an American citizen no less than as a Catholic bishop. The Church is the mother of my faith, the guardian of my hopes for eternity; America is my country, the protectress of my liberty and of my fortunes on earth. I could not utter one syllable that would belie, however remotely, either the Church or the Republic, and when I assert, as I now solemnly do, that the principles of the Church are in thorough harmony with the interests of the Republic, I know in the depths of my soul that I speak the truth.

Archb. Ireland: *Discourse on the Catholic Church and Civil Society.* (Baltimore, Nov. 10, 1884)

Woe to him my brethren, who would destroy or impair this blessed harmony that reigns among us! Woe to him who would sow tares of discord in the fair fields of the Church in America! Woe to him who would breed dissension among the leaders of Israel by introducing a spirit of nationalism into the camps of the Lord! Brothers we are, whatever may be our nationality, and brothers we shall remain. We will prove to our countrymen that the ties formed by grace and faith are stronger than flesh and blood. God and our country!—this our watchword. Loyalty to God's Church and to our country!—this our religious and political faith.

Card. Gibbons: *Sermon.* Milwaukee, August 20, 1891. (In *A Retrospect of Fifty Years,* 2, 151)

Thanks are due to the equity of the laws which obtain in America and to the customs of the well-ordered Republic. For the Church amongst you, unopposed by the constitution and government of your nation, fettered by no hostile legislation, protected against violence by the common laws and the impartiality of the tribunals, is free to live and act without hindrance.

Pope Leo XIII: *Longinque Oceani.* (Jan. 6, 1895)

It would be very erroneous to draw the conclusion that in America is to be sought the type of the most desirable status of the Church, or that it would be universally lawful or expedient for state and Church to be, as in America, dissevered and divorced.

Pope Leo XIII: *Longinque Oceani.* (Jan. 6, 1895)

All intelligent men are agreed, and we ourselves have with pleasure intimated it above, that America seems destined for greater things. Now it is our wish that the Catholic Church should not only share in, but help to bring about, this prospective greatness. We deem it right and proper that she should, by availing herself of the opportunities daily presented to her, keep equal step with the Republic in the march of improvement, at the same time striving to the utmost by her virtue and her institutions to aid in the rapid growth of the states.

Pope Leo XIII: *Longinque Oceani.* (Jan. 6, 1895)

Ours is the American Church, and not Irish, German, Italian, or Polish—and we will keep it American.

Card. Gibbons: *Speech at Meeting of Hierarchy,* Sept. 1920.

Catholic Faith

For the whole Church which is throughout the whole world possesses one and the same faith.

St. Irenaeus: *Against the Heresies,* 1, 10, 3. (2nd cent.)

Away with all attempts to produce a mottled Christianity, of Stoic, Platonic, and dialectic composition! We want no curious disputation after possessing Christ Jesus, no inquisition after enjoying the gospel! With our faith we desire no further belief. For this is our prior faith, that there is nothing which we ought to believe besides.

> Tertullian: *De praescriptione haereticorum,* 7. (3rd cent.)

But at the outset I lay down [this position] that there is some one, and therefore definite, thing taught by Christ, which the Gentiles are by all means bound to believe, and for that purpose to "seek," in order that they may be able, when they have "found" it, to believe. However there can be no indefinite seeking for that which has been taught as one only definite thing. You must "seek" until you "find," and believe when you have found; nor have you anything further to do but to keep what you have believed, provided you believe this besides, that nothing else is to be believed, and therefore nothing else is to be sought, after you have found and believed what has been taught by Him Who charges you to seek no other thing than that which He has taught.

> Tertullian: *De praescriptione haereticorum,* 9. (3rd cent.)

For whatever it shall be manifest that the true Christian rule and faith shall be, *there* will likewise be the true Scriptures and expositions thereof, and all the Christian traditions.

> Tertullian: *De praescriptione haereticorum,* 19. (3rd cent.)

Whosoever willeth to be saved, before all things it is necessary that he hold the Catholic faith; which faith, except every one do keep whole and undefiled, without doubt he shall perish eternally. Now the Catholic faith is this: that we worship one God in Trinity, and Trinity in Unity. . . .

> Athanasian Creed (*Quicumque vult*). (Formerly attr. to St. Athanasius) (Unknown authorship, ca. 4th or 5th cents.)

It is our will that all the peoples who are ruled by the administration of our clemency shall practice that religion which the divine Peter the apostle transmitted to the Romans, as the religion which he introduced makes clear even to this day. It is evident that this is the religion that is followed by the pontiff Damasus and by Peter, bishop of Alexandria, a man of apostolic sanctity. We command that those persons who follow this rule shall embrace the name of Catholic Christians. The rest, however, whom we adjudge demented and insane, shall sustain the infamy of heretical dogmas, their meeting places shall not receive the name of churches, and they shall be smitten first by divine vengeance and secondly by the retribution of our own initiative, which we shall assume in accordance with the divine judgment.

> Edict of the Emperors Gratian, Valentinian, and Theodosius to the People of Constantinople. (Theod. Code, 16, 1, 2) (Feb. 28, 380)

For while the hot restlessness of heretics stirs questions about many articles of the Catholic faith, the necessity of defending them forces us both to investigate them more accurately, to understand them more clearly, and to proclaim them more earnestly; and the question mooted by an adversary becomes the occasion of instruction.

> St. Augustine: *The City of God,* 16, 2. (5th cent.)

In the Catholic Church herself we must be careful to hold what has been believed everywhere, always and by all *quod ubique, quod semper, quod ab omnibus creditum est*); for that alone is truly and properly Catholic, as the word itself indicates, which embraces the universality of things. This will be brought about if we follow universality, antiquity, general consent. We shall follow universality if we confess as the sole truth the faith confessed by the whole Church throughout the world; antiquity, if we depart in nothing from the views of our holy predecessors and of our fathers; and lastly general consent, if, within this antiquity itself, we adopt the definitions and doctrines of all, or at least the greater part, of the bishops and doctors.

St. Vincent of Lerins: *Commonitorium,* 2, 5. (5th cent.)

O God, Who dost show to them that are in error the light of Thy truth, that they may return to the way of righteousness; grant to all those who profess themselves Christians that they may reject those things which are contrary to that name, and follow such things as are agreeable to the same.

Roman Missal, Collect for Third Sunday after Easter. (Leonine, ca. 5th cent.)

There are many who claim as theirs the dignity of the Christian religion; but that form of faith is valid and only valid which, both on account of the universal character of the rules and doctrines affirming its authority, and because the worship in which they are expressed has spread throughout the world, is called Catholic and universal.

Boethius: *De Trinitate,* 1. (6th cent.)

For he who believes not according to the tradition of the Catholic Church, or who has intercourse with the devil through strange works, is an unbeliever.

St. John of Damascus: *Exposition of the Orthodox Faith,* 4, 10. (8th cent.)

One Lord, one faith, one baptism (Eph. 4, 5). Hold firmly that our faith is identical with that of the ancients. Deny this, and you dissolve the unity of the Church.

St. Thomas Aquinas: *Disputations Concerning Truth,* 14, 12. (13th cent.)

The formal motive and object of faith is First Truth as manifested in Holy Scripture and the doctrine of the Church. A person who does not commit himself to the doctrine of the Church, as to a divine and unerring rule proceeding from the First Truth as revealed in the Holy Scriptures, is without the virtue of faith; he

assents to the truths of faith in some other manner.

St. Thomas Aquinas: *Summa Theologica,* 2-2, 5, 3. (13th cent.)

I, N., with firm faith believe and profess each and every article contained in the Symbol of faith which the holy Roman Church uses. . . . I resolutely accept and embrace the apostolic and ecclesiastical traditions and the other practices and regulations of that same Church. In like manner I accept Sacred Scripture according to the meaning which has been held by holy Mother Church and which she now holds. . . . I acknowledge the holy Catholic and apostolic Roman Church as the mother and teacher of all Churches; and I promise and swear true obedience to the Roman pontiff, vicar of Christ and successor of blessed Peter, prince of the apostles. . . .

Creed of Pope Pius IV (Council of Trent). (Bull *Injunctum nobis,* Nov. 13, 1564)

And this is certainly remarkable, that in every one who has embraced the Catholic religion, whatever was his difficulty in first receiving it, whatever may have been the first obstacles to his complete conviction, when once he has embraced and received it, it takes as strong a hold upon his affections and thoughts, as it could have done, if he had been educated in it from infancy.

Card. Wiseman: *Lectures,* 1. (19th cent.)

We allow no authority but the word of God, written or unwritten; and maintain that the control so necessary over the latter exists in its depository, that is, in the Church of Christ, which has been appointed by God to take charge of and keep safe those doctrines committed to her from the beginning, to be taught at all times to all nations.

Card. Wiseman: *Lectures,* 3. (19th cent.)

O that thy creed were sound!
For thou dost soothe the heart, thou
Church of Rome,

By thy unwearied watch and varied
round
Of service, in thy Savior's holy home.
I cannot walk the city's sultry streets,
But the wide porch invites to still
retreats,
Where passion's thirst is calm'd, and
care's unthankful gloom.

Card. Newman: *The Good Samaritan*.
(The cardinal has appended a note: "Of
course this is the exclamation of one who
was not in Catholic communion") (Pa-
lermo, 1833)

True Catholicity is commensurate with
the wants of the human mind; but persons are often to be found who are surprised that they cannot persuade all men
to follow them, and cannot destroy dissent, by preaching a portion of the divine
system, instead of the whole of it.

Card. Newman: *Oxford University Sermons*. (19th cent.)

Catholicism is a deep matter, you cannot
take it up in a tea-cup.

Card. Newman: *Letter to Spencer Noth-
cote*. (19th cent.)

[Catholic] doctrines are members of one
family, and suggestive, or correlative,
or confirmatory, or illustrative of each
other. One furnishes evidence to another, and all to each of them; if this is
proved, that becomes probable; if this
and that are both probable, but for
different reasons, each adds to the other
its own probability. . . . You must accept the whole or reject the whole; attenuation does but enfeeble, and ampu-
tation mutilate.

Card. Newman: *Development of Christian
Doctrine*. (19th cent.)

I believe the whole revealed dogma as
taught by the apostles, as committed by
the apostles to the Church, and as declared by the Church to me. I receive it,
as it is infallibly interpreted by the authority to whom it is thus committed,
and (implicitly) as it shall be, in like
manner, further interpreted by that same
authority till the end of time.

Card. Newman: *Apologia pro Vita Sua*, 5.
(19th cent.)

In the long run it will be found that
either the Catholic religion is verily and
indeed the coming in of the unseen
world into this, or that there is nothing
positive, nothing dogmatic, nothing real
in any of our notions as to whence we
come and whither we are going.

Card. Newman: *Discourse to Mixed
Congregations*. (19th cent.)

When once the mind is broken in, as it
must be, to the belief of a Power above it,
when once it understands, that it is not
itself the measure of all things in heaven
and earth, it will have little difficulty in
going forward. I do not say it will, or
can, go on to other truths, without conviction; I do not say it ought to believe
the Catholic faith without grounds and
motives; but I say that, when once it
believes in God, the great obstacle to
faith has been taken away—a proud,
self-sufficient spirit.

Card. Newman: *Discourse to Mixed Congregations*. (19th cent.)

The Church does not have the power of
defining dogmatically that the religion
of the Catholic Church is the only true
religion.

Proposition condemned by Pius IX in Syllabus of Errors. (1867)

The teaching of the Catholic Church is
inimical to the well-being and interests
of society.

Proposition condemned by Pius IX in Syllabus of Errors. (1867)

Faith of our fathers! living still
In spite of dungeon, fire, and sword:
Oh how our hearts beat high with joy
Whene'er we hear that glorious
word:
Faith of our fathers! holy faith!
We will be true to thee till death!

F. Faber: *Faith of Our Fathers*. (19th cent.)

Catholicity is that religion which links itself to all the faculties of the mind, appropriates all the instincts of human nature, and thus by concurring with the work of the Creator affirms its own divine origin.

Isaac T. Hecker. (Elliott's *Life,* 319) (19th cent.)

The Catholic Church alone teaches as matters of faith those things which the thoroughly sincere person of every sect discovers, more or less obscurely for himself, but dares not believe for want of external sanction.

Coventry Patmore. (19th cent.)

Catholicism is the sum of all religions and the queen of them.

R. H. Benson: *The Sentimentalists.* (20th cent.)

Modern Catholicism cannot be reconciled with true science unless it be transformed into a non-dogmatic Christianity, that is into a broad and liberal Protestantism.

Proposition condemned by Decree of Holy Office, *Lamentabili,* June 3, 1907.

The faithful are bound to profess their faith openly whenever under the circumstances silence, evasion, or their manner of acting would otherwise implicitly amount to a denial of the faith, or would involve contempt of religion, an offense to God, or scandal to their neighbor.

Code of Canon Law, Canon 1325, 1. (20th cent.)

No one is to be forced against his will to embrace the Catholic faith.

Code of Canon Law, Canon 1351. (20th cent.)

Now the faith is old and the devil is
    bold—
  Exceeding bold indeed;
And the masses of doubt that are float-
  ing about
  Would smother a mortal creed.

But we who sit in a sturdy youth
  And still can drink strong ale—
Let us put it away to infallible truth
  That always shall prevail.

H. Belloc: *Song of the Pelagian Heresy.* (20th cent.)

We are Christians and Catholics not because we worship a key, but because we have passed a door; and felt the wind that is the trumpet of liberty blow over the land of the living.

G. K. Chesterton: *The Everlasting Man,* 2, 4. (20th cent.)

Surely anybody's common sense would tell him that enthusiasts, who only met through their common enthusiasm for a leader whom they loved, would not instantly rush away to establish everything that he hated. No, if the 'ecclesiastical and dogmatic system' is as old as Pentecost it is as old as Christmas. If we trace it back to such very early Christians we must trace it back to Christ.

G. K. Chesterton: *The Everlasting Man,* 2, 4. (20th cent.)

I do not contend that everybody can be converted by reason, but I do contend that some people can be converted by reason. I do not regard Christianity purely as a system of thought; I regard Christianity as a way of life *and* a system of thought.

Arnold Lunn: *Now I See.* (20th cent.)

Perhaps even those who are most anti-Catholic are subconsciously aware of the fact that Catholicism is attractive because Catholicism is true. It is difficult, on any other hypothesis, to explain the widespread conviction that an interest in Rome is a danger signal, and that safety can only be assured by resolutely ignoring Catholicism.

Arnold Lunn: *Now I See.* (20th cent.)

The truth is that the Roman Catholic system, whether considered morally, intellectually or institutionally, is too strict for the careless, its standards too exacting for the slothful, and its concerns too wide for unresponsible individualists to be willing to shoulder.

> W. E. Orchard: *From Faith to Faith.* (20th cent.)

It would be a deadly error to confuse the universal cause of the Church with the particular cause of a civilization, to confuse, for example, Latinism with Catholicism, or Westernism with Catholicism. Catholicism is not linked to the culture of the West. Universality is not confined to one part of the world.

> J. Maritain: *The Things That Are Not Caesar's.* (20th cent.)

There is no other authentic and truly supranational universalism than Catholicism. The minds of men can only readjust themselves to the present needs of the world by adjusting themselves to the Catholic absolute. As their view so becomes more elevated, so also its horizon expands.

> J. Maritain: *The Things That Are Not Caesar's.* (20th cent.)

Only because it is inclusive can Catholicism be exclusive; only because it comprehends all religious truth can it be intolerant of all error. It is because it is the Catholic center that it cannot admit any other center, or regard as central any portion of the circumference.

> E. I. Watkin: *The Catholic Center.* (20th cent.)

It is possible to have the faith, and to do nothing about it. It is far commoner to have the faith and do next to nothing about it.

> R. Knox: *A Retreat for Lay People.* (20th cent.)

For centuries now Christianity has developed in a westerly direction, taking on an ever more western character of thought and expression. If it is ever to penetrate deeply into the East it will have to find a correspondingly eastern form, in which the genius of the peoples of the East will be able to find expression. For Christianity will never realize its full stature as a genuine Catholicism, that is, as the universal religion of mankind, until it has incorporated into itself all that is valid and true in all the different religious traditions. If we believe that in Christ is to be found the revelation of Truth itself, then we must recognize that all truth wherever it is to be found is contained implicitly in Christianity.

> Dom Griffiths: *The Golden String.* (20th cent.)

While we hold to the absolute universality of grace and believe that no one is deprived of it save by his own deliberate choice, we must hold with equal certainty that God chose to reveal Himself to one particular people and establish among them the unique way of salvation. All religious traditions contain some elements of the truth, but there is only one absolutely true religion; all religions have taught something of the way of salvation, but there is only one absolute way. Christ is the way, the truth and the life, and without Him no man comes to the Father.

> Dom Griffiths: *The Golden String.* (20th cent.)

See also Bible; Catholic Church; Christianity; Doctrine; Doctrine, Development of; Dogma; Faith; Faith and Reason; God; Good Works; Jesus Christ; Justification; Mystery; Religion; Revelation; Sacrament

Catholicity

True universalism, let it not be forgotten, is the very reverse of eclecticism. It does not marry the yea and the nay, heaven and hell. It presupposes a yea, but a yea vast enough to fill earth and sky—and excluding the nay for all eternity. The universality of truth and faith, which excludes error, is the indispensable condition of the universality of love, which excludes nothing that exists. Authentic universalism is centered. A city is at the center of the universe and makes its unity. AMOR is the same word as ROMA.

> J. Maritain: *The Things That Are Not Caesar's.* (20th cent.)

Cause

Were there no mediate causes, the universe would be made up only of effects, whereas it is a masterpiece of divine Providence, a plan executed through a chain of command.

> St. Thomas Aquinas: *Contra Gentiles,* 3, 77. (13th cent.)

Cause causeth.

> John Heywood: *Proverbs, 1, 9.* (16th cent.)

It becomes me not to draw my pen in defense of a bad cause, when I have so often drawn it for a good one.

> Dryden: *Fables, Preface.* (17th cent.)

The notion of causation is one of the first lessons we learn from experience.

> Card. Newman. (Ward, II, 587) (19th cent.)

It is to me a perplexity that grave authors seem to enunciate as an intuitive truth, that everything must have a cause.

> Card. Newman. (Ward, II, 587) (19th cent.)

When there is work to be done, a cause to be advanced, the unsafest men in the world to confide it to are those who are usually termed safe men.

> Orestes Brownson: *Works,* 11, 578. (1856)

Caution

Those who stumble on plain ground should shrink from approaching a precipice.

> Pope St. Gregory the Great: *Pastoral Rule,* 1, 3, 4. (6th cent.)

Look or ye leap.

> John Heywood: *Proverbs, 1, 2.* (16th cent.)

It is good to beware by other men's harms.

> John Heywood: *Proverbs,* 1, 11. (16th cent.)

Time quickly slips, beware how thou it spend,
Of wanton youth, repents a painful age:
Begin nothing without an eye to th'end,
Nor bow thine ear from counsel of the sage.

> Jasper Heywood: *Who Minds to Bring his Ship to Happy Shore, Must Care to Know the Lawes of Wysdomes Lore.* (16th cent.)

One must not run at one's spade or hoe; one must exercise a wearisome self-control. . . . Survey the work to be done, turn slowly, and after a pause begin.

> R. H. Benson: *None Other Gods.* (20th cent.)

An appearance of carelessness is vital in true caution.

> R. H. Benson: *An Average Man.* (20th cent.)

Cecilia, Saint

Let the deep organ swell the lay,
In honor of this festive day,
And let harmonious choirs proclaim
Cecilia's ever-blessed name.

> C. C. Pise: *Hymn to St. Cecilia.* (19th cent.)

Celibacy

I would be married, but I'd have no wife,
I would be married to a single life.

> Richard Crashaw: *On Marriage.* (17th cent.)

If a mistaken marriage can be purgatory, mistaken celibacy is hell.

> R. H. Benson: *The Conventionalists.* (20th cent.)

Celibacy, Clerical

Let bishops, priests, and deacons, and in general all the clergy who are specially employed in the service of the altar, abstain from conjugal intercourse with their wives and the begetting of children; let those who persist be degraded from the ranks of the clergy.

> Council of Elvira, Can. 33. (ca. 305)

If a priest marry, he shall be removed from the ranks of the clergy; if he commit fornication or adultery, he shall be excommunicated, and shall submit to penance.

> Council of Neocaesarea, Can. 1. (ca. 314–325)

Now the Lord Jesus, when He illumined us by His appearing, declared in the Gospel that He was come to fulfil the law, not to abolish it. And so He desired that the Church, whose Bridegroom He is, should have her visage shining with the splendor of chastity, that in the day of judgment, when He comes again, He may find her without spot or blemish, as He ordained by His apostle. Hence all we priests and Levites (deacons) are bound by the unbreakable law of those instructions to subdue our hearts and bodies to soberness and modesty from the day of our ordination, that we may be wholly pleasing to our God in the sacrifices which we daily offer.

> Pope Siricius: *Decretal Letter to Himerius, Bishop of Tarragona,* 10. (Feb. 10, 385)

We advise (*suademus*) that priests and Levites (deacons) should not live with their wives.

> Council of Rome, Can. 9. (According to decretal letter of Pope Siricius to bishops of Africa) (386)

Bishops, priests, and deacons must remain unmarried.

> Council of Rome, Can. 3. (402)

Although they who are not within the ranks of the clergy are free to take pleasure in the companionship of wedlock and the procreation of children, yet, for the sake of exhibiting the purity of complete continence, even subdeacons are not allowed carnal marriage; that *both they that have wives be as though they had none* (1 Cor. 7, 29), and they that have not may remain single. But if in this order, which is the fourth from the head, this is worthy to be observed, how much more is it to be kept in the first, second, and third, lest anyone be reckoned fit for either the deacon's duties or the presbyter's honorable position, or the bishop's pre-eminence, who is discovered as not yet having bridled his uxorious desires.

> Pope St. Leo I: *Letters,* 14. (Norm for Western Church.) (5th cent.)

Since it is declared in the apostolic canons that of those who are advanced to the clergy unmarried, only lectors and cantors are able to marry, we also, maintaining this, determine that henceforth it is in nowise lawful for any subdeacon, deacon, or presbyter after his ordination to contract matrimony; but if he shall have dared to do so, let him be deposed. And if any of those who enter the clergy wishes to be joined to a wife in lawful marriage before he is ordained subdeacon, deacon, or presbyter, let it be done.

> Quinisext Council of Constantinople, Can. 6. (Norm for Eastern Church.) (692)

If any one saith that clerics constituted in sacred orders or regulars who have solemnly professed chastity are able to contract matrimony, and that being contracted it is valid notwithstanding the ecclesiastical law or vow; and that the contrary is nothing else than to condemn marriage; and that all who do not feel that they have the gift of chastity, even though they have made a vow thereof, may contract marriage; let him be anathema: seeing that God refuses not that gift to those who ask for it rightly, neither does He *suffer us to be tempted above that which we are able* (1 Cor. 10, 13).

> Council of Trent, Session 24, Canon 9. (Nov. 11, 1563)

The clergy in major orders are forbidden to marry and are so bound by the obligation of observing chastity, that if they sin against it they are also guilty of sacrilege. . . . The minor clergy can contract marriage, but, unless the marriage is null because of force or fear applied to them, they fall *ipso iure* from the clerical state. A married man who without apostolic dispensation receives major orders, even in good faith, is forbidden to exercise those orders.

> Code of Canon Law, Canon 132. (Discipline of the Latin Church) (20th cent.)

The clergy must be careful not to have in their houses nor to associate habitually with women who might be objects of suspicion. They may live in the same house only with women who are beyond all suspicion of evil by reason of close relationship, such as mother, sister, or aunt, or who are above suspicion because of irreproachable character joined to a rather advanced age. . . . The clergy who are contumacious in this regard are presumed to be guilty of concubinage.

> Code of Canon Law, Canon 133. (20th cent.)

By his law of celibacy the priest, so far from losing the gift and duties of fatherhood, rather increases them immeasurably, for, although he does not beget progeny for this passing life of earth, he begets children for that life which is heavenly and eternal.

> Pope Pius XII: *Menti Nostrae.* (Sept. 23, 1950)

A priest's celibacy is a true fatherhood, as that of the woman dedicated to life in a religious community is a genuine motherhood. The priest is emphatically not just a pious bachelor. He is wedded to the Savior's work in this world, and celibacy is the obvious, congenial expression of the priest's relation to God and man.

> John LaFarge: *The Manner is Ordinary.* (20th cent.)

See also Priesthood; Virginity, Holy

Cemetery

For no other reason are those things which plainly become sepulchres of the dead said to be memorials or monuments, unless it is because of this: memorials admonish us to think of and to recall to our memory those who have been taken away by death from the eyes of the living, lest by forgetfulness they be removed from our hearts also.

> St. Augustine: *On the Care for the Dead,* 4. (5th cent.)

Censorship

The books of apostates, heretics, schismatics, and all writers whatsoever, defending heresy or schism, or in any way attacking the foundations of religion, are altogether prohibited. Moreover the books of non-Catholics, *ex professo* treating of religion, are prohibited, unless they clearly contain nothing contrary to the Catholic faith.

> Pope Leo XIII: *Officiorum ac Munerum.* (Jan. 25, 1897)

Books which professedly treat of, narrate, or teach lewd or obscene subjects are entirely prohibited, since care must be taken not only of faith but of morals, which are easily corrupted by the reading of such books.

> Pope Leo XIII: *Officiorum ac Munerum.* (Jan. 25, 1897)

The Church has the right to require that the faithful shall not publish books which she has not previously officially examined, and to prohibit their publication by anybody whatsoever for just cause. The provisions of this title also apply to daily publications, periodicals, and other published writings of whatever kind, unless the contrary appear.

> Code of Canon Law, Canon 1384. (20th cent.)

Unless previous ecclesiastical approval has been obtained, the following may not be published even by laymen: 1. books of the sacred Scriptures, or annotations or commentaries on them; 2. books which treat of holy Scripture, theology, church history, canon law, natural theology, ethics, or other similar religious and moral subjects; prayerbooks and books of devotion or instruction and training in religion, morals, asceticism, mysticism, and the like, even though they seem to favor piety; and in general all writings which contain anything of special importance to religion and good morals; 3. holy pictures, however they may be printed, whether with added prayers or not.

> Code of Canon Law, Canon 1385. (20th cent.)

The secular clergy are forbidden without the consent of their ordinaries, and religious without the permission of their major superiors and of the ordinary of the place, to publish books, even those which treat of profane subjects, and to contribute to or edit papers, magazines or reviews.

> Code of Canon Law, Canon 1386. (20th cent.)

Censure

For charity, most excellent and unassuming, gratefully accepts the dovelike eye; but for the dog's tooth nothing remains, save either to shun it by the most cautious humility, or to blunt it by the most solid truth; and far rather would I be censured by anyone whatsoever, than be praised by either the erring or the flatterer.

> St. Augustine: *De Trinitate*, 2, 1. (5th cent.)

Certitude

We love certainty. We like the pope to be infallible in faith, and the grave doctors to be infallible in morals, in order to have assurance.

> Pascal: *Pensées*. (17th cent.)

It seems then that on the whole there are three conditions of certitude: that it follows on investigation and proof, that it is accompanied by a specific sense of intellectual satisfaction and repose, and that it is irreversible.

> Card. Newman: *Grammar of Assent*, 7. (19th cent.)

He Who made us has so willed, that in mathematics indeed we should arrive at certitude by rigid demonstration, but in religious inquiry we should arrive at certitude by accumulated probabilities; —He has willed, I say, that we should so act, and, as willing it, He cooperates with us in our acting, and thereby enables us to do that which He wills us to do, and carries us on, if our will does but cooperate with His, to a certitude which rises higher than the logical force of our conclusions.

> Card. Newman: *Apologia pro Vita Sua*, 4. (19th cent.)

Certitude is a reflex action; it is to know that one knows.

> Card. Newman: *Apologia pro Vita Sua*, 4. (19th cent.)

> O the vague reality,
> The mysterious certainty!

> Alice Meynell: *Soeur Monique*. (19th cent.)

Cervantes

Cervantes on his galley sets the sword
  back in the sheath
(*Don Juan of Austria rides homeward
  with a wreath.*)
And sees across a weary land a straggling road in Spain,
Up which a lean and foolish knight
  forever rides in vain.

> G. K. Chesterton: *Lepanto*. (20th cent.)

Champion

Youth, beauty, graceful action seldom
  fail:
But common interest always will prevail:

And pity never ceases to be shown
To him, who makes the people's
  wrongs his own.

Dryden: *Absalom and Achitophel.* (17th
cent.)

Chance

We may define chance thus: it is an unexpected event of concurring causes in
those things which are done to some
end and purpose. Now the cause why
causes so concur and meet together, is
that order proceeding with inevitable
connexion, which, descending from the
fountain of Providence, disposeth all
things in their places and times.

Boethius: *De Consolation Philosophiae,*
5, 1. (6th cent.)

His own chance no man knoweth
But as fortune it on him throweth.

John Gower: *Confessio Amantis, 6.* (14th
cent.)

A chance may win that by mischance was
lost.

Bl. Robert Southwell: *Times Go By Turns.*
(16th cent.)

Revolving in his alter'd soul
  The various turns of chance below.

Dryden: *Alexander's Feast.* (17th cent.)

All nature is but art unknown to thee;
All chance, direction which thou canst
  not see.

Pope: *An Essay on Man,* 1. (18th cent.)

See also Fortune; Luck

Change

Times change and men deteriorate.
(Tempora mutantur et homines deteriorantur.)

Gesta Romanorum. (15th cent.)

As often change from hue to hue,
As doth the cocks of Ind.

John Heywood: *Proverbs,* 1, 11. (16th
cent.)

Would to God he and you had changed
places!

John Heywood: *Proverbs,* 2, 7. (16th cent.)

When mirth is full and free,
Some sudden gloom shall be;
When haughty power mounts high,
The watcher's axe is nigh.
All growth has bound; when greatest
  found,
  It hastes to die.

Card. Newman: *Reverses.* (19th cent.)

In a higher world it is otherwise; but
here below to live is to change, and to be
perfect is to have changed often.

Card. Newman: *Development of Christian
Doctrine.* (19th cent.)

We cannot unmake ourselves or change
our habits in a moment.

Card. Newman: *Apologia pro Vita Sua, 3.*
(19th cent.)

We can change, slowly and steadily, if
we set our will to it.

R. H. Benson: *The Coward.* (20th cent.)

Chaos

Lo, thy dread empire, chaos, is restored;
Light dies before thy uncreating word:
Thy hand, great anarch! lets the cur-
  tain fall,
And universal darkness buries all.

Pope: *The Dunciad, 4.* (18th cent.)

Character

Ye know what he hath been, but ye
know not what he is.

John Heywood: *Proverbs,* 1, 11. (16th
cent.)

God taketh me as I am, and not as I was.

John Heywood: *Proverbs,* 2, 9. (16th cent.)

A good cause proves less in a man's favor
than a bad cause against him. The final
judgment depends on the worst action.
Character is tested by true sentiments

more than by conduct. A man is seldom better than his word.

> Lord Acton: *Letter to M. Creighton.* ("Canons" for writing history) (Apr. 5, 1887)

At death, if at any time, we see ourselves as we are, and display our true characters.

> R. H. Benson: *Infallibility and Tradition.* (20th cent.)

It is strange, sometimes, to find that some silent old lady has a power for sounding human character, which far shrewder persons lack.

> R. H. Benson: *By What Authority.* (20th cent.)

The root of the matter does not lie in texts: it lies deeper: it lies in the character of every man.

> R. H. Benson: *An Average Man.* (20th cent.)

The encrusted character cannot be melted: it is too late. It has been fused, and has hardened again. It cannot be fused again. It must be all broken away.

> R. H. Benson: *The Sentimentalists.* (20th cent.)

Remember always that the world is not things, but persons, that no natural beauty of inanimate things can equal in interest the profound fascination of the human character.

> Katharine T. Hinkson: *The Castle of Dromore.* (20th cent.)

Charge

To flee charge, and find ease.

> John Heywood: *Proverbs,* 1, 11. (16th cent.)

Charity

Who can explain the bond of the charity of God? Who can express the splendor of its beauty? The height to which charity lifts us is inexpressible. Charity unites us to God, *Charity covers a multitude of sins;* charity bears all things, is long-suffering in all things. There is nothing mean in charity, nothing arrogant. Charity knows no schism, does not rebel, does all things in concord. In charity all the elect of God have been made perfect.

> Pope St. Clement I: *Letter to the Corinthians,* 49, 1-6. (1st cent.)

Without charity nothing is pleasing to God. In charity the Lord received us; out of the charity which He had for us, Jesus Christ our Lord gave His Blood for us by the will of God, and His Flesh for our flesh, and His life for our lives.

> Pope St. Clement I: *Letter to the Corinthians,* 49, 6. (1st cent.)

He who has charity is far from all sin.

> St. Polycarp: *Letter to the Philippians,* 3. (2nd cent.)

An illustrious and divine thing, dearest brethren, is the saving work of charity; a great comfort of believers, a wholesome guard of our security, a protection of hope, a safeguard of faith, a remedy of sin, a thing placed in the power of the doer, a thing both great and easy.

> St. Cyprian: *On Works and Alms,* 26. (3rd cent.)

Charity is the bond of brotherhood, the foundation of peace, the mainstay and security of unity, which is greater than both hope and faith, which excels both good works and martyrdom, which will abide with us always, eternal with God in the kingdom of heaven.

> St. Cyprian: *On Patience,* 15. (3rd cent.)

The bread that you store up belongs to the hungry; the cloak that lies in your chest belongs to the naked; and the gold that you have hidden in the ground belongs to the poor.

> St. Basil. (4th cent.)

Everyone must be loved equally; but, when you cannot be of assistance to all, you must above all have regard for those who are bound to you more closely by some accident, as it were, of location, circumstances, or occasions of any kind.

St. Augustine: *De Doctrina Christiana,* 1, 28, 29. (4th cent.)

I define charity as a motion of the soul whose purpose is to enjoy God for His own sake and oneself and one's neighbor for the sake of God.

St. Augustine: *De Doctrina Christiana,* 3, 10, 16. (4th cent.)

Nothing conquers except truth: the victory of truth is charity.

St. Augustine: *Sermon 358,* 1. (5th cent.)

To relieve the poor; to clothe the naked; to visit the sick; to bury the dead; to help the afflicted; to console the sorrowing; to avoid worldly conduct; to prefer nothing to the love of Christ.

St. Benedict: *Rule,* 4. (One of his "tools of good works") (6th cent.)

But what advantage is it to restrain the flesh by continence, if the mind is uninstructed to expand itself by compassion in the love of neighbor? For that chasteness of the flesh is as nothing, which is not recommended by sweetness of spirit.

Pope St. Gregory I: *Morals,* 6, 53. (6th cent.)

He that hath a talent, let him see that he hide it not; he that hath abundance, let him quicken himself to mercy and generosity; he that hath art and skill, let him do his best to share the use and the utility thereof with his neighbor.

Pope St. Gregory I: *Hom. in Evang.* 9, 7. (6th cent.)

Charity is a good disposition of the soul, which makes it prefer the knowledge of God to everything else.

St. Maximus the Confessor: *Centuries on Charity,* 1, 1. (7th cent.)

Even God lives by law, since I declared that this law was no other than charity. For what but charity preserves in the su-

preme and blessed Trinity, that lofty and unspeakable unity which it has? It is law, then, and charity the law of the Lord, which maintains in a wonderful manner the Trinity in Unity and binds it in the bond of peace. Yet let no one think that I here take charity for a quality or a certain accident in God, or otherwise to say that in God (which God forbid) there is something which is not God; but I say that it is the very substance of God. I say nothing new or unheard of, for St. John says *God is love* (I John 4, 16).

St. Bernard: *Letters,* 12, 4. (12th cent.)

The law of charity, then, is good and sweet, it is not only light and sweet to bear, but it renders bearable and light the laws even of slaves and mercenaries.

St. Bernard: *Letters,* 12, 7. (12th cent.)

When charity shall pull up on to the shore of eternity the net which she is now drawing through this vast and great sea so as to bring in without ceasing every sort of fish, she will then cast aside the bad and keep only the good. For in this life her net keeps every sort of fish within its ample folds and she accommodates herself to all making, in a sense, her own all the good and evil fortunes of everyone, not only so as to rejoice with the glad but also to weep with the afflicted. When she shall have come to shore everything that she has hitherto borne with sorrow she will cast aside as evil fish, retaining only what gives her pleasure and happiness.

St. Bernard: *Letters,* 12, 9. (12th cent.)

Because we cannot know for certain that we are in charity it does not follow that we cannot love from charity.

St. Thomas Aquinas: *Disputations concerning Charity,* 7. (13th cent.)

Charity brings to life again those who are spiritually dead.

St. Thomas Aquinas: *Disputations concerning Charity,* 1. (13th cent.)

Charity is the form, mover, mother, and root of all the virtues.

> St. Thomas Aquinas: *Disputations concerning Charity,* 3. (13th cent.)

We should love others truly, for their own sakes rather than our own.

> St. Thomas Aquinas: *Concerning the Two Precepts of Charity,* 5. (13th cent.)

Charity is love; not all love is charity.

> St. Thomas Aquinas: *Summa Theologica,* 1-2, 62, 2. (13th cent.)

We must look for the perfection of the Christian life in charity.

> St. Thomas Aquinas: *Summa Theologica,* 2-2, 184, 1. (13th cent.)

Help thy kin, Christ biddeth, for there beginneth charity.

> Langland: *Piers Plowman,* Passus 18. (14th cent.)

All other gifts of God and works of man are common to good and bad, to the elect and the reprobate, but the gift of charity belongs only to the good and the elect.

> Walter Hilton: *Scale of Perfection,* 1, 65. (14th cent.)

He is truly great who hath a great charity.

> Thomas a Kempis: *Imitation of Christ,* 1. (15th cent.)

Christian charity recognizes no property.

> Erasmus: *Enchiridion.* (E. was censured for this categorical statement, but he understood it in an orthodox sense.) (16th cent.)

A man is an adulterer, he commits sacrilege, he is a Turk—let the act of adultery be execrated, not the man; let the sacrilege, not the man, be despised. Let him kill the Turk, not the man.

> Erasmus: *Enchiridion.* (16th cent.)

True virtue has no limits, but goes on and on, and especially holy charity, which is the virtue of virtues, and which,

having an infinite object, would become infinite if it could meet with a heart capable of infinity.

> St. Francis de Sales: *Introduction to the Devout Life,* 1. (17th cent.)

Charity is much stronger and more assiduous than mere natural affection.

> St. Francis de Sales: *Spiritual Conferences,* 21. (17th cent.)

All is love's, and in love, for love, in holy Church.

> St. Francis de Sales: *Treatise on the Love of God,* Pref. (17th cent.)

All is made for charity, and charity for God.

> St. Francis de Sales: *Treatise on the Love of God,* 8, 6. (17th cent.)

Charity is a love of friendship.

> St. Francis de Sales: *Treatise on the Love of God,* 2, 22. (17th cent.)

Charity is both the means and the end, the one and only way by which we can attain that perfection which in truth is charity itself.

> J. P. Camus: *The Spirit of St. Francis de Sales,* 1, 1. (17th cent.)

Take it as a certain sign that your charity is not genuine if your words, no matter how true, are not charitable.

> J. P. Camus: *The Spirit of St. Francis de Sales,* 2, 12. (17th cent.)

Charity is the pure gold which makes us rich in eternal wealth.

> J. P. Camus: *The Spirit of St. Francis de Sales,* 5, 2. (17th cent.)

In faith and hope the world will disagree,
But all mankind's concern is charity.

> Pope: *An Essay on Man,* 3. (18th cent.)

Love is the gentle, tranquil, satisfied acquiescence and adherence of the soul in the contemplation of God; not only a preference of God before all things, but a delight in Him because He is God, and because His commandments are good; not only violent emotion or transport, but as St. Paul describes it, long-suffering, kind, modest, unassuming, innocent, simple, orderly, disinterested, meek, pure-hearted, sweet-tempered, patient, enduring.

Card. Newman: *Parochial and Plain Sermons*, 4. (19th cent.)

The organized charity, scrimped and iced,
In the name of a cautious, statistical Christ.

J. B. O'Reilly: *Bohemia*. (19th cent.)

Unarmed she goeth, yet her hands
Strike deeper awe than steel-caparisoned bands,
No fatal hurt of foe she fears,—
Veiled, as with mail, in midst of gentle tears.
'Gainst her thou canst not bar the door;
Like air she enters; where none dared before,
Even to the rich she can forgive
Their regal selfishness,—and let them live!

G. P. Lathrop: *Charity*. (19th cent.)

Charity gives peace to the soul. For whoever loves God above all things rests his heart in the eternal peace.

Archb. Ullathorne: *Humility and Patience*. (19th cent.)

If but the world would give to love
The crumbs that from its table fall,
'Twere bounty large enough for all
The famishing to feed thereof.

And love, that still the laurel wins
Of sacrifice, would lovelier grow,
And round the world a mantle throw
To hide its multitude of sins.

J. B. Tabb: *Charity*. (19th cent.)

The Power that lifts the leaf above
And sends the root below,
Sustains the heart in brother-love
And makes it heavenward grow.

J. B. Tabb: *Life*. (19th cent.)

The law of mutual charity perfects the law of justice.

Pope Leo XIII: *Graves de communi*. (Jan. 18, 1901)

No one is commanded to distribute to others that which is required for his own needs and those of his household; nor even to give away what is reasonably required to keep up becomingly his condition in life, *for no one ought to live other than becomingly* (St. Thomas: Summa T. 2-2, 32, 6). But, when what necessity demands has been supplied, and one's standing fairly taken thought for, it becomes duty to give to the indigent out of what remains over. *Of that which remaineth, give alms* (Luke 11, 41).

Pope Leo XIII: *Rerum Novarum*. (May 15, 1891)

The state can only give for economic reasons . . . while the Church gives for the love of God, and the love of God never yet destroyed any man's self-respect.

R. H. Benson: *The Dawn of All*. (20th cent.)

A half-light with charity must be nearer to God's heart than the glare of a desert.

R. H. Benson: *The Confessions of a Convert*. (20th cent.)

It has been said that charity is the pardoning of the unpardonable and the loving of the unlovable.

R. H. Benson: *Christ in the Church*. (20th cent.)

Let charity issue in good deeds. Let us be foremost in them.

R. H. Benson: *Lord of the World*. (20th cent.)

O my God, I love Thee with my whole heart above all things, because Thou art infinitely good and infinitely to be loved; and for Thy sake I love my neighbor as I love myself, and I forgive him if he has injured me in any way.

Act of Charity. (As printed in Catholic Catechism of Cardinal Gasparri, 1932.

Similar forms are to be found in all Catholic prayer books. The form is probably as old as the Council of Trent, or older.)

See also Love of God; Love of Neighbor

Charlemagne

To Charles Augustus, crowned by God, great and peace-loving emperor of the Romans, life and victory!

Acclamation when Charlemagne was crowned emperor in St. Peter's basilica on Christmas Day, 800.

Charles I

Vanquished in life, his death
By beauty made amends:
The passing of his breath
Won his defeated ends.

. . . .

King, tried in fires of woe!
Men hunger for thy grace:
And through the night I go,
Loving thy mournful face.

Lionel Johnson: *By the Statue of King Charles at Charing Cross.* (19th cent.)

Charm

She speaketh as she would creep into your bosom.

John Heywood: *Proverbs*, 1, 10. (16th cent.)

When men give up saying what is charming, they give up thinking what is charming.

Oscar Wilde: *Lady Windermere's Fan*, 2. (19th cent.)

Chastisement

See Punishment

Chastity

If anyone is able to persevere in chastity to the honor of the flesh of the Lord, let him do so in all humility.

St. Ignatius of Antioch: *Letter to St. Polycarp*, 5. (2nd cent.)

For Satan has discovered how to turn the cultivation of virtue itself to a man's destruction, and it makes no difference to him whether he ruins souls by lust or chastity.

Tertullian: *To His Wife*, 1, 6. (3rd cent.)

We Christians regard a stain upon our chastity as more dreadful than any punishment, or even than death itself.

Tertullian: *Apologeticus.* (2nd cent.)

We are taught that chastity has three forms—one that of married life, a second that of widowhood, and a third that of virginity. We do not so extol one form as to exclude the others. In this, indeed the Church is rich, in that it has those whom it can rank before others, but none whom it rejects.

St. Ambrose: *Concerning Widows*, 23. (4th cent.)

Let each one study his own powers, whether he can fulfil the precepts of virginal modesty. For of itself chastity is charming and attractive to all. But one's forces must be considered, that he who can may take it. The Lord's word is as it were an exhortation, stirring on His soldiers to the prize of purity. *He that can take it, let him take it:* let him who can, fight, conquer and receive his reward.

St. Jerome: *Comm. on St. Matthew*, 19, 12. (5th cent.)

The chastity of widows and virgins is above the chastity of marriage.

St. Augustine: *On the Good of Marriage.* (5th cent.)

Do not say that you have chaste minds if you have unchaste eyes, because an unchaste eye is the messenger of an unchaste heart.

St. Augustine: *Letter 211.* (His Rule.) (5th cent.)

To love chastity.

St. Benedict: *Rule*, 4. (One of his "tools of good works") (6th cent.)

Now, though the era of persecution is gone, yet our peace has its martyrdom, because though we bend not the neck to the sword, yet with a spiritual weapon we slay fleshly desires in our hearts.

> Pope St. Gregory I: *Hom. in Evang.* 1, 3, 4. (6th cent.)

Burn our reins and our heart, O Lord, with the fire of the Holy Ghost, that we may serve Thee with a chaste body and please Thee with a clean heart.

> Roman Missal, *Collect before Mass.* (Gelasian, before 8th cent.)

King of virgins and Lover of chastity and innocence, extinguish in my frame by the dew of Thy heavenly grace all flames of unlawful passion, that I may thus for evermore abide before Thee in innocency of body and soul.

> Roman Missal, Prayer *Summe Sacerdos* before Mass. (11th cent.)

After all what does a strict guard avail, as a lewd wife cannot be watched and a chaste one does not have to be?

> John of Salisbury: *Policraticus,* 8, 11, 297. (12th cent.)

Chastity without charity lies chained in hell,
It is but an unlighted lamp.
Many chaplains are chaste, but where is their charity?
There are no harder, hungrier men than men of holy Church.

> Langland: *Piers Plowman,* 2. (14th cent.)

O Christ, the glorious crown
Of virgins that are pure;
Who dost a love and thirst for Thee
Within their minds procure;
Thou art the Spouse of those
That chaste and humble be,
The hope, the life, the only help
Of such as trust in Thee.

> Bl. Philip Howard: *Hymn.* (16th cent.)

The virtue of chastity does not mean that we are insensible to the urge of concupiscence, but that we subordinate it to reason and the law of grace, by striving wholeheartedly after what is noblest in human and Christian life.

> Pius XII: *Sancta Virginitas.* (Mar. 25, 1954)

See also Continence

Chaucer, Geoffrey

Sith of our language he was the lode-star

. . . .

Sith he in Englishmaking was the best,
Pray unto God to give his soul good rest.

> Lydgate: *The Falls of Princes.* (15th cent.)

Chaucer, I confess, is a rough diamond; and must first be polish'd e'er he shines.

> Dryden: *Fables, Preface.* (17th cent.)

He is a perpetual fountain of good sense.

> Dryden: *Fables, Preface.* (17th cent.)

Cheating

'Tis no sin to cheat a cheater. (Fallere fallentem non est fraus.)

> Latin Proverb. (Medieval)

To wrest a thing from a friend is theft but to cheat the Church is sacrilege.

> St. Jerome: *Letters,* 52, 16. (4th cent.)

Cheek

To move the cheeks, puff them out, or slap them with the hands, are all exceedingly impolite, and entirely reprehensible.

> St. John Baptist de la Salle: *The Rules of Christian Manners and Civility,* 1. (17th cent.)

Cheerfulness

We may always rejoice, if we will only keep our head a little raised above the flood of human things.

> St. John Chrysostom. (5th cent.)

Christian cheerfulness is that modest, hopeful, and peaceful joy which springs from charity and is protected by patience. It is the well-regulated vigor of spiritual life that throws off all morbid humors and depressing influences, refusing them a lodgement in the soul devoted to God.

Archb. Ullathorne: *Humility and Patience.* (19th cent.)

Chesterton, Gilbert Keith

We are in some danger today of underestimating our debt to Mr. Chesterton, and of forgetting the impact which his books made on the minds of young men who were infected by the fallacy of Victorian rationalism. In those distant days many people still cherished the futile hope of reconstructing a positive ethical system on the basis of mere negation. Mr. Chesterton's destructive criticism of the Huxleys, Bradlaughs and Haeckels of our youth was as devastating as it was brilliant, and its value would be more widely appreciated today if it had not been so completely effective.

Arnold Lunn: *Now I See.* (20th cent.)

Chesterton is dead! That is to say and
   say
Englishry shrunken; death upon a day
   was not content with More but took
   his heir.

Robert Farren: *Chesterton.* (20th cent.)

His mind was oceanic, subject indeed to a certain restriction of repeated phrase and manner, but in no way restricted as to the action of the mind. He swooped upon an idea like an eagle, tore it with active beak into its constituent parts and brought out the heart of it. If ever a man analyzed finally and conclusively Chesterton did so.

H. Belloc: *Gilbert Chesterton in English Letters.* (20th cent.)

It seems to me that Gilbert Chesterton at his baptism was visited by three fairies. Two good and one evil. The two good fairies were the fairy of fecundity of speech and the fairy of wide apprecia-tion. The bad fairy was struck dead as she entered the church—and served her right. He was blessed in knowing nothing of the acerbities which bite into the life of writing men.

H. Belloc: *Gilbert Chesterton in English Letters.* (20th cent.)

Child

What is a child save a lower animal in the form of a man?

Luis de Granada: *Guide for Sinners.* (16th cent.)

There is nothing that more displeaseth God,
Than from their children to spare the rod.

John Skelton: *Magnyfycence.* (16th cent.)

Both the raven and the ape think their own young the fairest.

St. Thomas More: *Utopia.* (16th cent.)

The children of most renowned and noble personages be for most part destructions to a commonwealth.

Erasmus: *Adagia.* (16th cent.)

Children learn to creep ere they can go.

John Heywood: *Proverbs,* i, ii. (16th cent.)

It is a great honor to you that are married that God, designing to multiply souls, which may bless and praise Him to all eternity, makes you cooperate with Him in so noble a work, by the production of the bodies into which He infuses immortal souls, like heavenly drops, as He creates them.

St. Francis de Sales: *Introduction to the Devout Life,* 38. (17th cent.)

Children should never be taken to church in a dress which would not be thought good enough for appearing before company.

St. John Baptist de la Salle: *The Rules of Christian Manners and Civility,* 2. (17th cent.)

Behold the child, by nature's kindly law
Pleased with a rattle, tickled with a straw.

> Pope: *An Essay on Man,* 2. (18th cent.)

There oft are heard the tones of infant woe:
The short thick sob, loud scream, and shriller squall.

> Pope: *The Alley.* (18th cent.)

A child is a pledge of immortality, for he bears upon him in figure those high and eternal excellences in which the joy of heaven consists, and which would not thus be shadowed forth by the all-gracious Creator, were they not one day to be realized.

> Card. Newman: *Miscellanies,* 210. (19th cent.)

Children begin by loving their parents. After a time they judge them. Rarely, if ever, do they forgive them.

> Oscar Wilde: *A Woman of No Importance,* 2. (19th cent.)

Dear God, I wish I could have been
Among those girls and boys
You called to come and talk with You,
And who left all their toys,
And ran and climbed up on Your knee,
And held Your hand, and sat
Around You, learning lovely things.

> Mary D. Thayer: *Finding You.* (20th cent.)

Since life is but a play, we are none of us kings or cardinals or poor men in reality; we are all of us mere children of our Father.

> R. H. Benson: *The Mirror of Shalott.* (20th cent.)

When men otherwise capable of marriage enter upon it, it is wrong to stigmatize them as criminals because they will father only defective children.

> Pope Pius XI: *Casti connubii.* (Dec. 31, 1930)

Childbearing

And she who slays is she who bears, who bears.

> Alice Meynell: *Parentage.* (20th cent.)

Childhood

What was wonderful about childhood is that anything in it was a wonder. It was not merely a world full of miracles; it was a miraculous world.

> G. K. Chesterton: *Autobiography.* (20th cent.)

It is surely a tragedy that we have lost what the primitive Church seems to have had: a devotion precisely to the Boy-Christ. For He should stand, for the Christian, not of course for a nostalgic yearning after a vanished youth, not simply for a longing for an eternal recovery of youth, but again for something very matter-of-fact: for the preservation, or the recovery, here and now, of certain qualities of mind and soul which we associate with childhood, and which are part of the search for God, but which we all too easily lose.

> Gerald Vann: *The Water and the Fire.* (20th cent.)

Chivalry

A knight there was, and that a worthy man,
That from the time that he first began
To riden out, he loved chivalry,
Truth and honor, freedom and courtesy.
. . . .
And though that he was worthy, he was wise,
And of his port as meek as is a maid.
He never yet no villainy had said
In all his life, unto no manner wight.
He was a very parfit gentle knight.

> Chaucer: *Canterbury Tales: Prologue.* (14th cent.)

For knighthood is not in the feats of war,

As for to fight in quarrel right or
wrong,
But in a cause which truth can not de-
farre:
He ought himself for to make sure and
strong,
Justice to keep, mixt with mercy among:
And no quarrel a knight ought to take
But for a truth, or for a woman's sake.

> defarre—undo

Stephen Hawes: *The Pastime of Pleasure.*
(16th cent.)

The very name of the horse has been
given to the highest mood and moment
of the man; so that we might almost say
that the handsomest compliment to a
man is to call him a horse.

G. K. Chesterton: *The Everlasting Man,
Intr.* (20th cent.)

Choice

Of harmes two the less is for to choose.

Chaucer: *Troilus and Criseyde,* 2. (14th
cent.)

But it is said and ever shall,
Between two stools lieth the fall.

John Gower: *Confessio Amantis, Prol.*
(14th cent.)

Choir

Make of yourselves a choir, so that with
one voice and one mind, taking the keynote from God, you may sing in unison
with one voice [i.e. the bishop's] through
Jesus Christ to the Father, and He may
hear you and recognize you, in your good
works, as members of His Son.

St. Ignatius of Antioch: *Letter to the
Ephesians,* 4. (2nd cent.)

Chrism, Holy

But beware of supposing this to be plain
ointment. For as the bread of the Eucharist, after the invocation of the Holy
Ghost, is mere bread no longer, but the
Body of Christ, so also this holy ointment is no longer simple or common
ointment, after invocation, but is Christ's
gift of grace, and, by the advent of the
Holy Ghost, is made fit to impart His
divine Nature.

St. Cyril of Jerusalem: *Catechetical
Discourses,* 21, 3. (4th cent.)

Christ

See Jesus Christ

Christendom

The word Christendom relates to the
cultural order. It denotes a certain temporal regime that is common to peoples
educated by the Church. There is only
one Church; there may be divers types of
Christian civilization, different expressions of 'Christendom.'

J. Maritain: *Freedom in the Modern World.*
(20th cent.)

A new age of Christendom, if it is to
come, will be an age of reconciliation of
that which was disjoined, the age of a
'secular' Christian civilization, in which
temporal things, philosophical and scientific reason, and civil society, will enjoy
their autonomy and at the same time recognize the quickening and inspiring role
that spiritual things, religious faith, and
the Church play from their higher plane.

J. Maritain: *The Range of Reason.* (20th
cent.)

Christian

A Christian is not his own master, since
all his time belongs to God.

St. Ignatius of Antioch: *Letter to
St. Polycarp,* 7. (2nd cent.)

Christians do not commit adultery. They
do not bear false witness. They do not
covet their neighbor's goods. They honor
father and mother. They love their
neighbors. They judge justly. They avoid
doing to others what they do not wish

done to them. They do good to their enemies. They are kind.

> St. Aristides: *Apology for the Christian Faith.* (2nd cent.)

Hatred of the Christian name. (Odii erga nomen Christianorum.)

> Tertullian: *Apology,* 1, 4. (3rd cent.)

We are as many as we are alleged to be. (Sunt tanti quanti et denotamur.)

> Tertullian: *Apology,* 1, 6. (3rd cent.)

Christians are made, not born! (Fiunt, non nascuntur Christiani!)

> Tertullian: *Apology,* 18, 4. (3rd cent.)

"Look," they say, "how they love one another" (for themselves [i.e. the pagans] hate one another).

> Tertullian: *Apology,* 39, 7. (3rd cent.)

No one is wise, no one is faithful, no one excels in dignity, but the Christian; and no one is a Christian but he who perseveres even to the end.

> Tertullian: *De praescriptione haereticorum,* 3. (3rd cent.)

For all love those who love them; it is peculiar to Christians alone to love those that hate them.

> Tertullian: *To Scapula,* 1. (3rd cent.)

Christian is my name, Catholic my surname. (Christianus mihi nomen est, Catholicus cognomen.)

> St. Pacianus of Barcelona: *Contra Sympronianum,* 1, 4. (4th cent.)

In the lives of Christians we look not to the beginnings but to the endings.

> St. Jerome: *Letters,* 54, 6. (4th cent.)

To be a Christian is the great thing, not merely to seem one. And somehow or other those please the world most who please Christ least.

> St. Jerome: *Letters,* 58, 7. (4th cent.)

We are Christians, we belong to Christ.

> St. Augustine: *Sermon 130,* 4. (5th cent.)

O ye proud Christians, weary and sad of brow,
    Who, tainted in the vision of the mind,
    In backward steps your confidence avow,

Perceive ye not that we are worms, designed
    To form the angelic butterfly, that goes
    To judgment, leaving all defence behind?

Why doth your mind take such exalted pose,
    Since ye, disabled, are as insects, mean
    As worm, which never transformation knows.

> Dante: *Purgatorio, Canto 10.* (Tr. Binyon) (14th cent.)

He has a good part of Christianity who with certain mind has decided that he will become a Christian.

> Erasmus: *Enchiridion.* (16th cent.)

A very heathen in the carnal part,
Yet still a sad, good Christian at her heart.

> Pope: *Of the Characters of Women.* (18th cent.)

A true Christian may be almost defined as one who has a ruling sense of God's presence within him.

> Card. Newman: *Parochial and Plain Sermons,* 5. (19th cent.)

Christian and Pagan

One of the strange marks of the strength of Christianity is that, since it came, no pagan in our civilization has been able to be really human.

> G. K. Chesterton: *The Everlasting Man.* (20th cent.)

A pagan heart, a Christian soul had he.
He followed Christ, yet for dead Pan
  he sighed.
As if Theocritus in Sicily
  Had come upon the Figure Crucified.

  Maurice F. Egan: *Maurice de Guérin.*
  (20th cent.)

Christianity

It is not for nothing or any mere emptiness that the magnificence of the authority of the Christian faith is spread over
all the world. Such great and wonderful
things would never have been wrought
for us by God, if the life of the soul were
ended by the death of the body.

  St. Augustine: *Confessions,* 6, 11. (5th
  cent.)

The great part of Christianity is wholeheartedly to want to become a Christian.

  Erasmus: *Enchiridion.* (16th cent.)

Christianity teaches men these twin
truths together: that there is a God
Whom men can reach, and that there is
a corruption in their nature which renders them unworthy of Him.

  Pascal: *Pensées.* (17th cent.)

Other religions, such as heathenism, are
more popular, for they are all external;
but they are not for men of ability. A
purely intellectual religion would better
suit them; but it would not help the
commonalty. Christianity alone, with its
blend of external and internal, is suited
to all. It uplifts the commonalty inwardly, and humbles the proud outwardly; to be perfect it needs both; the
commonalty must understand the spirit
of the letter, the able submit their spirit
to the letter.

  Pascal: *Pensées.* (17th cent.)

For a religion to be true it must have
knowledge of our nature. It must know
its greatness and its meaning, and the
cause of both. What religion but Christianity knows that?

  Pascal: *Pensées.* (17th cent.)

Yes,—rather plunge me back in pagan
  night,
And take my chance with Socrates for
  bliss,
Than be the Christian of a faith like
  this,
Which builds on heavenly cant its
  earthly sway,
And in a convert mourns to lose a prey.

  Thomas Moore: *Intolerance.* (19th cent.)

It is indeed by no means clear that Christianity has at any time been of great spiritual advantage to the world at large. The
general temper of mankind, taking man
individually, is what it ever was, restless
and discontented, or sensual, or unbelieving. . . . But it has ever been a restraint on the world rather than a guide
to personal virtue and perfection on a
large scale; its fruits are negative.

  Card. Newman: *Oxford University
  Sermons.* (19th cent.)

Christianity has always been a learned
religion; it came into the world as the
offspring of an older system, to which
it was indebted for much which it contained, and which its professors were
obliged continually to consult.

  Card. Newman: *Oxford University
  Sermons.* (19th cent.)

Christianity, considered as a moral system, is made up of two elements, beauty
and severity; whenever either is indulged
to the loss or disparagement of the other,
evil ensues.

  Card. Newman: *Sermons on Subjects of the
  Day.* (19th cent.)

Thus it is that Christianity, even nega-
tively, and without contemplating its
positive influences, is the religion of
civilization.

  Card. Newman: *Historical Sketches,* 1.
  (19th cent.)

Does Gibbon think to sound the depths
of the eternal ocean with the tape and

measuring-rod of his merely literary philosophy?

Card. Newman: *Grammar of Assent*, 10. (19th cent.)

It is considered, and justly, as an evidence for Christianity, that the ablest men have been Christians; not that all sagacious or profound minds have taken up its profession, but that it has gained victories among them, such and so many, as to show that it is not the mere fact of ability or learning which is the reason why all are not converted.

Card. Newman: *Discourses to Mixed Congregations.* (19th cent.)

The prophecies and miracles set forth and recorded in the sacred Scriptures are the fiction of poets, and the mysteries of the Christian faith the result of philosophical investigations. In the books of the Old and New Testament there are contained mythical inventions, and Jesus Christ is Himself a myth.

Proposition condemned by Pius IX in Syllabus of Errors. (1867)

Civil society was renovated in every part by the teachings of Christianity. In the strength of that renewal the human race was lifted up to better things. Nay, it was brought back from death to life.

Pope Leo XIII: *Rerum novarum.* (May 15, 1891)

The failure of Christianity to unite all men one to another rested not upon its feebleness, but its strength; its lines met in eternity, not in time.

R. H. Benson: *Lord of the World.* (20th cent.)

That though you hunt the Christian man
Like a hare in the hill-side,
The hare has still more heart to run
Than you have heart to ride.

G. K. Chesterton: *Ballad of the White Horse.* (20th cent.)

The Christian ideal has not been tried and found wanting. It has been found difficult; and left untried.

G. K. Chesterton: *What's Wrong with the World.* (20th cent.)

If Christianity were only a new oriental fashion, it would never be reproached with being an old and oriental faith.

G. K. Chesterton: *The Everlasting Man,* Intr. (20th cent.)

To compare the Christian and Confucian religions is like comparing a theist with an English squire or asking whether a man is a believer in immortality or a hundred-per-cent American. Confucianism may be a civilization but it is not a religion.

G. K. Chesterton: *The Everlasting Man.* (20th cent.)

Christianity has died many times and risen again; for it had a God who knew the way out of the grave.

G. K. Chesterton: *The Everlasting Man.* (20th cent.)

There is and always has been the Church, and various heresies proceeding from a rejection of some of the Church's doctrines by men who still desire to retain the rest of her teaching and morals. But there never has been and never can be or will be a general Christian religion professed by men who all accept some central important doctrines, while agreeing to differ about others.

H. Belloc: *The Great Heresies.* (20th cent.)

Why is it that Europe alone among the civilizations of the world has been continually shaken and transformed by an energy of spiritual unrest that refuses to be content with the unchanging law of social tradition which rules the oriental cultures? It is because its religious ideal has not been the worship of timeless and changeless perfection but a spirit that strives to incorporate itself in humanity and to change the world.

> C. Dawson: *Christianity and the New Age.* (20th cent.)

Christianity is more than a doctrine. It is Christ Himself, living in those whom He has united to Himself in One Mystical Body. It is the mystery by which the incarnation of the Word of God continues and extends itself throughout the history of the world, reaching into the souls and lives of all men, until the final completion of God's plan. Christianity is the *re-establishment of all things in Christ* (Eph. 1, 10).

> Thomas Merton: *The Living Bread.* (20th cent.)

See also Catholic Church; Catholic Faith

Christmas

Hear, O Thou Shepherd of Israel,
Who dost above the cherubs dwell,
Appear within Thine ancient home,
Stir up Thy mighty power, and come!

Come, and display a virgin birth,
Redeem the nations of the earth;
Let every age the wonder see:
Such life befits a Deity.

> St. Ambrose: *Intende qui regis Israel.* (Tr. S. A. Hurlbut) (4th cent.)

O manifest infirmity, O wondrous humility, in which all the greatness of God lay hid! The mother to whom His infancy was subject, He ruled with His power; and to her at whose breasts He nursed, He gave the nourishment of truth. May He Who did not shrink from taking a beginning even like ours, perfect in us His gifts; and may He also make us children of God, He Who for our sakes wished to become a child of man.

> St. Augustine: *Sermons, 184.* (5th cent.)

Let us therefore be happy and celebrate the day on which Mary gave birth to the Savior—she, given in marriage, to the Creator of marriage; she, a virgin, to the Prince of virgins; espoused to a husband, but a mother not by her husband; a virgin before marriage, a virgin in marriage—a virgin with Child, a virgin nursing her Child! For indeed, when her omnipotent Son was born, He in no wise took away the virginity of His holy mother whom He had chosen when He was to be born.

> St. Augustine: *Sermons, 188.* (5th cent.)

Even though the succession of physical actions is now past, as it was preordained in the eternal design . . . nevertheless we unceasingly adore that birth from the Virgin who brought forth our salvation.

> Pope St. Leo I: *Ninth Sermon on the Nativity (Sermons, 28, 2).* (5th cent.)

O God, Who hast caused that those who come to be members of Thy Son through the child-bearing without human concupiscence of the blessed Virgin shall not be bound by the sins of their fathers; grant, we beseech Thee, that we who have put on the new creature may put off the corruption of the old.

> Leonine Sacramentary, Collect for Christmas. (ca. 5th cent.)

Almighty and everlasting God, Who hast willed that on the nativity of our Lord Jesus Christ, Thy Son, should depend the beginning and completion of all religion; grant us, we beseech Thee, to be reckoned as a portion of Him, on Whom is built the whole salvation of mankind.

> Leonine Sacramentary, Collect for Christmas. (ca. 5th cent.)

From lands that see the sun arise
To earth's remotest boundaries,
The Virgin-born today we sing,
The Son of Mary, Christ the King.
Blest Author of this earthly frame,
To take a servant's form He came,
That, liberating flesh by flesh,
Whom He had made might live afresh.

> Roman Breviary, Feast of Christmas, Hymn *A solis ortus cardine* at Lauds. (Tr. J. Neale) (Sedulius, 5th cent.)

O Christ our God, upon the world Thy birth hath shed the light of knowledge; for by it they that served the stars were taught by a star to worship Thee, the Sun of righteousness, and to know Thee, the Dayspring from on high. Glory to Thee, O Lord.

Byzantine Menaea, Troparion for Feast of the Nativity. (ca. 6-8th cent.)

Jesus, the Ransomer of man,
Who, ere created light began,
Didst from the sovereign Father spring,
His power and glory equalling.
The Father's light and splendor Thou,
Their endless hope to Thee that bow;
Accept the prayers and praise today
That through the world Thy servants
    pay.

Roman Breviary, Christmas, Hymn *Jesu Redemptor omnium* (*Christe Redemptor omnium*) at Vespers and Matins. (Tr. J. Neale and T. Potter) (Altered, Ambrosian, 6th cent.)

Remember, O Creator Lord,
That in the Virgin's sacred womb
Thou wast conceived, and of her flesh
Didst our mortality assume.

Roman Breviary, Little Office of the Blessed Virgin, Hymn *Memento rerum Conditor*. (From Hymn *Jesu Redemptor omnium* for Christmas Day.) (Tr. Caswall) (Ambrosian, 6th cent.)

Grant, we beseech Thee, almighty God, that as we are bathed in the new light of Thine Incarnate Word, that which shines by faith in our minds may blaze out likewise in our actions.

Roman Missal, Collect for Second Mass. (Gregorian 6th to 8th cent.)

It is truly meet and just . . . because by the mystery of the Word made flesh the light of Thy glory hath shown anew upon the eyes of our mind: that while we acknowledge Him to be God seen by men, we may be drawn by Him to the love of things unseen.

Roman Missal, Preface for Christmas. (Gregorian, 6th to 8th cent.)

The Mother brought forth the King, Whose name is called the Eternal; the joy of a Mother was hers, remaining a Virgin unsullied; neither before nor henceforth hath there been or shall be such another. Alleluia.

Roman Breviary, Christmas, Antiphon at Lauds. (Liber Resp., 6th to 8th cent.)

This day the Christ is born: this day the Savior is appeared: this day the angels sing praise in the earth and the archangels rejoice: this day the righteous are glad and say: Glory to God in the highest. Alleluia.

Roman Breviary, Christmas, Antiphon at Second Vespers. (cf. Liber Resp., 6th to 8th cent.)

Christ is born! Tell forth His fame!
Christ from heaven! His love pro-
    claim!
Christ on earth! Exalt His name!
Sing to the Lord, O world, with exulta-
    tion!
Break forth in thanksgiving, every na-
    tion!
For He hath triumphed gloriously!

Byzantine Menaea, Feast of the Nativity, Canon at Matins. (Tr. Neale) (St. Cosmas the Melodist, 8th cent.)

Magnify, my soul, her who is more honorable and glorious than the hosts above. I behold a mystery strange and wondrous. The cave is heaven, the Virgin is the throne of the cherubim, the manger is the place where the Incomprehensible is laid, Christ our God, Whom we magnify with song.

Byzantine Menaea, Feast of the Nativity, Canon at Matins, Ninth Ode. (8th cent.)

Shout! ye heavens, with laud and prais-
    ing,
    Shout in triumph, earth and sea,
Every voice its song upraising
    Loud proclaim the jubilee.
For the Lord of all creation
    Sees His creatures doomed to die,

And His right hand brings salvation,
  And His love brings liberty.

Peter the Venerable: *Coelum gaude, terra
plaude.* (Tr. P. Onslow) (12th cent.)

In her Lord His Church rejoices,
  Whom the host of heavenly voices
Welcome to His earthly throne:
  Peace from heaven their song re-
    citeth,
Earth to heaven it reuniteth,
  Church with angels now are one.

Adam of St. Victor: *Jubilemus Salvatori.*
(Tr. from Shipley's *Lyra Messianica*)
(12th cent.)

In the ending of the year
Light and Life to man appear:
And the holy Babe is here
  By the Virgin Mary.
For the Word becometh Flesh
  By the Virgin Mary.

What in ancient days was slain,
This day calls to life again:
God is coming here to reign
  By the Virgin Mary.

Anonymous: *In hoc anni circulo.* (Tr. J.
Neale) (German, 12th cent.?)

Let the faithful raise the lay
To the newborn King today:
That the Light of Light would come
From the Virgin's holy womb:
Purging Adam's guilt away,
Shedding joy and scattering gloom.

Anonymous: *Novi partus gaudium.* (Tr.
J. Neale) (14th cent.?)

I saw three ships come sailing in,
On Christmas Day, on Christmas Day,
I saw three ships come sailing in,
On Christmas Day in the morning.
And what was in those ships all three?
Our Savior Christ and his Lady.

Anonymous: *I Saw Three Ships.* (16th
cent.)

Rorate coeli desuper!
  Heavens, distil your balmy showers!
For now is risen the bright daystar,
  From the rose Mary, flower of
    flowers:

The clear Son, Whom no cloud de-
    vours,
Surmounting Phoebus in the east,
  Is comen of His heavenly towers:
    Et nobis Puer natus est.

William Dunbar: *On the Nativity of
Christ.* (16th cent.)

Behold, a silly tender Babe
  In freezing winter night
In homely manger trembling lies,
  Alas, a piteous sight!

The inns are full; no man will yield
  This little Pilgrim bed,
But forced He is with silly beasts
  In crib to shroud His head.

Bl. Robert Southwell: *New Prince, New
Pomp.* (16th cent.)

O dying souls; behold your living
    spring!
  O dazzled eyes! behold your Sun of
    grace!
Dull ears attend what word this Word
    doth bring!
  Up, heavy hearts, with joy your Joy
    embrace!
From death, from dark, from deafness,
    from despairs,
This Life, this Light, this Word, this
    Joy repairs.

Bl. Robert Southwell: *The Nativity of
Christ.* (16th cent.)

Come we shepherds whose blest sight
Hath met love's noon in nature's night;
Come, lift we up our loftier song,
And wake the Sun that lies too long.
To all our world of well-stol'n joy
He slept; and dreamt of no such thing.
While we found out heav'n's fairer eye
And kist the cradle of our King.

Richard Crashaw: *The Holy Nativity of
Our Lord, a Hymn.* (17th cent.)

Great King, from heaven's high throne
    descending low,
In Bethlehem's stable born in cold and
    woe,
Thou shiverest in a manger, Babe
    Divine,

Much hast Thou borne for sins: how
  much for mine!

St. Alphonso of Liguori: *Tu scendi dalle
Stelle.* (Tr. F. Husenbeth) (18th cent.)

See, amid the winter's snow,
Born for us on earth below,
See, the tender Lamb appears,
Promised from eternal years!

. . . . . .

Teach, O teach us, holy Child,
By Thy face so meek and mild,
Teach us to resemble Thee,
In Thy sweet humility!
  Hail, Thou ever-blessed morn!
  Hail, redemption's happy dawn!
  Sing through all Jerusalem,
  Christ is born in Bethlehem.

E. Caswall: *See, Amid the Winter's Snow.*
(19th cent.)

How can I keep my Christmas feast
  In its due festive show,
Reft of the sight of the High Priest
  From Whom its glories flow?

I hear the tuneful bells around,
  The blessed towers I see;
A stranger on a foreign ground,
  They peal a fast for me.

Card. Newman: *Christmas without Christ.*
(19th cent.)

Lacking samite and sable,
Lacking silver and gold,
The prince Jesus in the poor stable
Slept, and was three hours old.
As doves by the fair water,
Mary, not touched of sin,
Sat by Him,—the King's daughter,
All glorious within.

May Probyn: *A Christmas Carol.* (19th
cent.)

Now play through heaven the angel
  bell:
Make music of the angelus!
The King is come to Israel:
The Queen of heaven is found for us.

Lionel Johnson: *Christmas.* (19th cent.)

New every year,
New born and newly dear,
He comes with tidings and a song,
The ages long, the ages long.

Alice Meynell: *Unto Us a Son Is Given.*
(19th cent.)

You cannot visit the child without visiting the mother; you cannot in common
life approach the child except through
the mother. If we are to think of Christ
in this aspect at all, the other idea follows as it is followed in history. We
must either leave Christ out of Christmas, or Christmas out of Christ, or we
must admit, if only as we admit it in an
old picture, that those holy heads are too
near together for the haloes not to mingle and cross.

G. K. Chesterton: *The Everlasting Man.*
(20th cent.)

To us Christians, the first Christmas Day
is the solstice or bottle-neck of history.
Things got worse till then, ever since we
had lost Paradise; things are to get better since then, till we reach Paradise once
more. History is shaped like an X.

R. Knox: *Stimuli.* (20th cent.)

Christmas Eve

Bethlehem hath opened Eden,
  Come! let us behold:
Sweetness we have found once hidden,
  Pearl of price untold;
Gifts of Paradise all precious,
Stored within the cave refresh us.

. . . . . .

Now the Maid her Infant bearing
  Hasten we to greet;
He ere worlds the Godhead sharing,
  Little Child so sweet,
Born within this lowly place
Stays the thirst of Adam's race.

Byzantine Menaea, Feast of the Nativity,
Canon at Matins, Ikos. (Tr. W. Dix)
(St. Romanos the Melodist, 6th cent.)

O God, Who makest us glad with the
yearly expectation of our redemption;
grant that as we joyfully receive Thine

only-begotten Son as our Redeemer, we may also see Him without fear when He comes as our Judge.

> Roman Missal, Collect for the Vigil of Christmas. (Gelasian, ca. 6th cent.)

O God, Who hast made this most sacred night to shine with the illumination of the true Light; grant, we beseech Thee, that as we have known the mystery of that Light upon earth, we may also perfectly enjoy It in heaven.

> Roman Missal, Collect for Midnight Mass. (Gelasian, ca. 6th cent.)

The snow lay on the ground,
    The stars shone bright,
When Christ our Lord was born
    On Christmas night.

'Twas Mary, daughter pure
    Of holy Anne,
That brought into this world
    The God made Man.

> Old English Carol. (15th cent.?)

Come, all ye faithful,
    Joyful and triumphant,
O hasten, O hasten to Bethlehem;
    See in a manger
    The Monarch of angels.
    O come let us worship
    Christ the Lord.

> Hymn *Adeste fideles* for Christmastide. (Tr. Canon Oakeley) (Anon., 18th cent.)

· Lead me to Thy peaceful manger,
    Wond'rous Babe of Bethlehem;
Shepherds hail Thee, yet a stranger;
    Let me worship Thee with them.
I am vile, but Thou art holy;
    Oh, unite my heart to Thee;
Make me contrite, keep me lowly,
    Pure as Thou wouldst have me be.

> M. Bridges: *Lead me to Thy Peaceful manger.* (19th cent.)

At last Thou art come, little Savior!
    And Thine angels fill midnight with song;

Thou art come to us gentle Creator!
    Whom Thy creatures have sighed for so long.

> F. Faber: *Christmas Night.* (19th cent.)

Ah! no eve is like the Christmas eve!
Fears and hopes, and hopes and fears,
Tears and smiles, and smiles and tears,
Cheers and sighs, and sighs and cheers,
Sweet and bitter, bitter, sweet,
    Bright and dark, and dark and bright
All these mingle, all these meet,
    In this great and solemn night.

> Abram Ryan: *A Christmas Chant.* (19th cent.)

'Tis Christmas night! Again—
But not from heaven to earth—
Rings forth the old refrain
    'A Savior's birth!'
Nay, listen: 'tis below!
A song that soars above,
From human hearts aglow
    With heavenly love!

> J. B. Tabb: *Gloria in Excelsis.* (19th cent.)

'Tis Christmas night! the snow
    A flock unnumbered lies;
The old Judean stars aglow
    Keep watch within the skies.

An icy stillness holds
    The pulses of the night;
A deeper mystery enfolds
    The wondering hosts of light.

Till lo, with reverence pale
    That dims each diadem,
The lordliest, earthward bending, hail
    The Light of Bethlehem.

> J. B. Tabb: *The Light of Bethlehem.* (19th cent.)

There fared a mother driven forth
    Out of an inn to roam;
In the place where she was homeless
    All men are at home.
The crazy stable close at hand,
With shaking timber and shifting sand,

Grew a stronger thing to abide and
stand
Than the square stones of Rome.

G. K. Chesterton: *The House of Christmas.*
(20th cent.)

The Christmas stars at Bethlehem
Shone very clear and bright;
Oh, may they shine with light divine
For you this Christmas night!

Sister Madeleva: *Wishes.* (20th cent.)

Church (*Edifice*)

Thou heavenly, new Jerusalem,
Vision of peace in prophet's dream!
With living stones built up on high,
And rising to yon starry sky;
In bridal pomp thy form is crowned,
With thousand thousand angels round!

Roman Breviary, Dedication of Churches,
Hymn *Coelestis urbs Jerusalem.* (Tr. J.
Irons) (Greatly altered from hymn *Urbs
Jerusalem beata,* anon., 6th or 7th cent.)

O God, Who dost contain all things invisibly, and yet for the salvation of mankind dost visibly reveal signs of Thy
power: brighten this temple by the
power of Thy presence, and grant, that
all who gather here to beseech Thee or
to appeal to Thee for whatever reason,
may gain the benefit of Thy consolation.

Roman Missal, Collect for Dedication of a
Church. (Gregorian, 6th to 8th cent.)

The mother and head of all the churches
of the City and the world. (Omnium
urbis et orbis ecclesiarum mater et
caput.)

Inscription on the walls of the Lateran
Basilica in Rome. The Lateran is the
cathedral church of the popes and takes
precedence over all other churches.
(Medieval)

This peaceful seat my poverty secures,
War seldom enters but where wealth
allures.
Nor yet despise it, for this poor abode
Has oft receiv'd and yet receives a God;
A God, victorious of the stygian race,

Here laid His sacred limbs, and sanctified the place.

Dryden: *The Hind and the Panther,* 2.
(17th cent.)

Who builds a church to God and not to
fame
Will never mark the marble with his
name.

Pope: *Moral Essays,* 3. (18th cent.)

A church is understood to be a sacred
edifice devoted to divine worship which
is particularly used by all the faithful for
public divine worship.

Code of Canon Law, Canon 1161. (20th
cent.)

Church and State

I—*Antiquity: Basic Principles*

We are ever making intercession for all
the Emperors. We pray for them long
life, a secure rule, a safe home, brave
armies, a faithful senate, an honest people, a quiet world—and everything for
which a man and a Caesar can pray. All
this I cannot ask of any other but only
of Him, from Whom I know I shall receive it, since He it is Who alone gives.

Tertullian: *Apology,* 30, 4. (3rd cent.)

We must needs respect him [i.e. the
Roman Emperor] as the chosen of our
Lord. So I have a right to say, Caesar is
more ours than yours, appointed as he is
by our God. He is mine; and so I do
more for his safety . . . because I set the
majesty of Caesar below God and the
more commend him to God to Whom
alone I subordinate him.

Tertullian: *Apology,* 33, 2. (3rd cent.)

God has established you as priests, and
has given you power to judge us also,
and therefore we are rightly judged by
you. But you may not be judged by men.
Accordingly you must await the judgment of God alone among yourselves;
whatever your quarrels may be, they
should be reserved for examination by

Him. For you are indeed given to us as gods, and it is not right that man should judge gods, but only He, concerning Whom it is written: *God stood in the synagogue of gods; in the midst of them He judges the gods.*

> Speech attributed to the Emperor Constantine I. (In Rufinus; *Eccles. Hist.* 1, 2) (4th cent.)

Do not interfere in ecclesiastical affairs, and do not seek to give us orders concerning them, but rather learn from us what is to be done. God has granted you the empire; to us He has entrusted the affairs of the Church. Just as anyone revolting against your rule would be resisting the command of God, so you should also fear that by taking to yourself control of ecclesiastical affairs you will be responsible for a great wrong.

> Hosius, Bishop of Cordova: *Letter to the Emperor Constantius.* (In Athanasius, *History of the Arians,* 44.) (4th cent.)

How can you say that you have power to judge bishops; unless you are obedient to them, as to God, will you not be punished by the chastisement of death? Since this is so, how is it that you who are a profane person with regard to the household of God exact this penalty against the authority of the priests of God . . . ? Who are you, I say, who have usurped this authority which God has not given you, and if He should give it to you and permit you to have it, you would above all have to be a Christian [to exercise it], because it is a crime for a stranger to judge the servants of God, for an enemy of religion to judge the household of God.

> Lucifer of Cagliari: *On Behalf of St. Athanasius,* 1. (4th cent.)

By how much, therefore, the soul is more valuable than the body, so much the priestly office is beyond the kingly. For it binds and looses those that are worthy of punishment or of remission. Where-

fore you ought to love the bishop as your father, and fear him as your king.

> Anonymous: *Constitutions of the Holy Apostles,* 2, 34. (4th cent.)

Whosoever shall abuse the emperor or the governor unjustly, let him suffer punishment; and if he be a clergyman, let him be deprived; but if he be a layman, let him be suspended.

> Ecclesiastical Canons of the Holy Apostles, 84. (4th cent.)

The state is not in the Church, but the Church is in the state; that is, in the Roman Empire.

> St. Optatus: *De Schismate.* (4th cent.)

The emperor is within the Church, not above the Church.

> St. Ambrose: *Serm. contra Auxent,* 36. (4th cent.)

Bishops must not rashly assail kings, if there be no grave sins for which the latter deserve reproach; but, if there be grave sins, the bishop must not spare, that offenders may be corrected by his just remonstrances.

> St. Ambrose: *In Ps. 37 Enarr. 43.* (4th cent.)

Who is there who can deny that in matters of faith . . . bishops are wont to judge of Christian emperors, not emperors of bishops.

> St. Ambrose: *Letters,* 21, 4. (To the emperor Valentinian) (4th cent.)

Not only are all men under the sway of Rome subject to you, the emperors and princes of the earth, but you yourselves are also in the service of almighty God and our holy faith. Salvation will not be assured unless each one truly worships the true God, that is, the God of the Christians, by Whom all things are governed.

> St. Ambrose: *Letters,* 17. (To the emperor Valentinian) (384)

It is alleged that all things are permitted the emperor, that everything is his. To this I reply: Do not burden yourself with thinking that you have imperial power over things which are divine. Do not exalt yourself, but, if you wish to be emperor for a long time, be subject to God. Scripture says: *What things are God's to God, what are Caesar's to Caesar* (Matth. 22, 21). Palaces belong to the emperor, churches to the bishop.

> St. Ambrose: *Letters,* 20. (386)

The maintenance of civil law should be secondary to religion.

> St. Ambrose: *Letters,* 40. (To the emperor Theodosius) (388)

Cherish, therefore, the body of Christ, which is the Church. . . . Every member of Christ's body is necessary to the body. Do you, therefore, protect the whole body of the Lord Jesus, that He also of His divine mercy may preserve your kingdom.

> St. Ambrose: *Letters,* 41, 26. (To the emperor Theodosius) (4th cent.)

Priests alone, sir, are allowed to remain within the sanctuary. Depart, therefore, and stand with the rest of the laity. The purple makes princes, not priests.

> Sozomen: *Ecclesiastical History,* 7, 25.
> (Famous words attributed to St. Ambrose when the emperor Theodosius entered the sanctuary to receive Communion.) (4th cent.)

What more honorable designation can there be than for the emperor to be called the son of the Church? This designation is not concerned with sin, but with grace. For the emperor is within the Church, not above it; a good emperor seeks the help of the Church, he does not contemn it.

> St. Ambrose: *Letters,* 21. (4th cent.)

Two cities have been formed by two loves: the earthly by the love of self, even to the contempt of God; the heavenly by the love of God, even to the contempt of self. The former, in a word, glories in itself, the latter in the Lord. . . . In the one, the princes and the nations it subdues are ruled by the love of ruling; in the other, the princes and the subjects serve one another in love, the latter obeying, while the former take thought for all.

> St. Augustine: *The City of God,* 14, 28. (5th cent.)

These things being so, we do not attribute the power of giving kingdoms and empires to any save to the true God, Who gives happiness in the kingdom of heaven to the pious and the impious, as it may please Him, Whose good pleasure is always just.

> St. Augustine: *The City of God,* 5, 21. (5th cent.)

So, in availing ourselves of the terror of judges and laws, we desire their [i.e. heretics and schismatics] repentance, not their death, so that they may be saved from falling into the penalties of eternal judgment. We do not wish to see them quite absolved from punishment, nor, on the other hand, visited with the torments they deserve. Check their sins, therefore, in such a way as to produce repentance in at least a few.

> St. Augustine: *Letter 100.* (To Donatus, proconsul of Africa) (5th cent.)

Christian judge, fulfil the duty of a devoted father; be angry at wickedness, yet forget not humane considerations, and do not give rein to the desire to seek revenge for the atrocity of their sinful deeds, but exert your will to the curing of the sores of the sinners.

> St. Augustine: *Letter 133.* (To the tribune Marcellinus, with regard to the repression of the Circumcellions, heretics and malefactors) (5th cent.)

No person is to be compelled against his will to embrace the faith; yet unfaith is, in God's mercy, often severely chastised by the scourges of tribulation. Does it follow that because sound morals are to be chosen freely, bad morals are not to be punished by the law? At the same time corrective treatment of a disorderly life is out of place until a man has shown contempt for all attempts at teaching him how to live aright. When, then, laws are promulgated against you, they are not meant to compel you to be good but to prevent you from being bad.

> St. Augustine: *Contra Litt. Petiliani*, 2, 184. (5th cent.)

Besides your care for things temporal you so perseveringly exercise a religious foresight in the service of what is divine and eternal: to wit that the Catholic faith, which alone gives life to and alone hallows mankind, may abide in the one confession, and the dissensions which spring from the variety of earthly opinions may be driven away, most glorious emperor, from that solid rock, on which the city of God is built.

> Pope St. Leo I: *Letters*, 162, 1. (To the Emperor Leo) (458)

Since the Lord has enriched your clemency with such insight into His mystery, you ought unhesitatingly to consider that the kingly power has been conferred on you not for the governance of the world alone but more especially for the guardianship of the Church; that by quelling wicked attempts you may both defend that which has been rightly decreed, and restore true peace where there has been disturbance.

> Pope St. Leo I: *Letters*, 156, 3. (To the Emperor Marcian) (457)

There are indeed, most august emperor, two powers by which this world is chiefly ruled: the sacred authority of the popes and the royal power. Of these the priestly power is much more important, because it has to render account for the kings of men themselves at the divine tribunal. For you know, our very clement son, that although you have the chief place in dignity over the human race, yet you must submit yourself faithfully to those who have charge of divine things, and look to them for the means of your salvation. . . . For if in matters pertaining to the administration of public discipline, the bishops of the Church, knowing that the empire has been conferred upon you by divine instrumentality, are themselves obedient to your laws . . . with what willingness, I ask you, should you obey those to whom is assigned the administration of divine mysteries? . . . And if the hearts of the faithful ought to be submitted to all priests in general, who administer holy things in a right manner, how much more ought assent to be given to him who presides over that See which the Supreme Godhead Itself desired to be pre-eminent over all priests, and which the pious judgment of the whole Church has honored ever since?

> Pope Gelasius I: *Letter to the Emperor Anastasius I.* (Ep. 12) (Famous text) (494)

Christian emperors should defer to the rulers of the Church in their ordinances, not presume to give orders to them.

> Pope Gelasius I: *Letters*, 1, 10. (To Eastern bishops) (5th cent.)

The greatest gifts which God in His heavenly clemency bestows upon men are the priesthood and the imperial authority. The former ministers to divine things, the latter presides and watches over human affairs; both proceed from one and the same source and together they are the ornaments of human life. Therefore nothing is so close to the hearts of emperors as the moral wellbeing of the priesthood since priests have the task of perpetual prayer to God on behalf of emperors themselves. . . . We therefore have the greatest anxiety for the true doctrines of God and for the moral wellbeing of the priesthood by which, if it is preserved, we believe that the greatest gifts will be given to us by God. . . .

> Justinian I: *Edict*. (Corp. jur. civ., Nov. 6) (Apr. 17, 535.)

We follow whatever the emperor has done, if it is in accordance with the canons; but if it is not in accordance with them, we put up with it, in so far as we may without sin.

> Pope St. Gregory the Great: *Letters,* 11, 29. (6th cent.)

For that one and the same *Mediator between God and man, the Man Christ Jesus* (1 Tim. 2, 5) so separated the functions of the two authorities, giving each its own proper activities and distinct honors (desiring that these properties should be exalted by the medicine of humility and not brought down again to the depths by man's arrogance), that Christian emperors should have need of the pontiffs with regard to eternal life, while the pontiffs should make use of the emperor's laws with regard to the course of temporal affairs, and these alone: so that the activity of the spirit might be set free from carnal interruptions.

> Pope St. Nicholas I: *Letter* (*Proposueramus Quidem*) *to the Emperor Michael III.* (Ep. 8) (865)

II—*Middle Ages: Sacerdotium and Imperium*

Whence, that the summit of the priesthood may not be cheapened but that the dignity and power of its glory may be adorned even more than that of the earthly empire, behold, we turn over to our most blessed pontiff and universal pope Silvester both our aforesaid palace [i.e. the Lateran] and all the provinces, places and towns of the city of Rome, Italy, and the western regions, relinquishing them to his power and control and that of his successors, and by firm imperial censure we decree that this shall be done as a result of our divine, sacred and pragmatic constitution, and we likewise grant that these rights shall perpetually belong to the holy Roman church.

> Donation of Constantine. (8th cent.)

Whence we have considered it appropriate that our empire and the power of our kingdom should be transferred and changed to the eastern regions and that a city should be built bearing our name in the best location in the province of Byzantium, and that our empire should be established there, since it is just that where the principate of the priesthood and head of the Christian religion has been established by the heavenly Emperor, the earthly emperor should also not have his power.

> Donation of Constantine. (8th cent.)

2. The Roman pontiff alone deserves to be called universal.
8. He alone may use the imperial insignia.
9. The pope is the only person whose feet all princes kiss.
10. His name alone is pronounced in all the churches.
11. His name is unique in the world.
12. He may depose emperors.
18. His sentence cannot be revised by anyone, and he alone may revise those of others.
19. He may be judged by no one.
20. The pope may release subjects from their oath of fidelity to unjust princes.

> Pope St. Gregory VII: *Dictatus Papae.* (Inserted in his *Registrum* [2, 55] and representing his thought. Not an official document.) (1075)

Blessed Peter prince of the apostles, incline your pious ears to us, I beseech you, and hear me your servant, whom you have nourished from infancy. . . . The power of binding and loosing in heaven and on earth has been given to me by God especially through your grace and committed to me in your stead. Therefore, relying on this faith, for the honor and defense of your church, on behalf of God almighty, the Father, the Son and the Holy Ghost, by your power and authority I forbid the government of the entire kingdom of the Germans and of Italy to king Henry, son of the emperor Henry, who has risen against your church in unheard of pride; and I absolve all Christians from the bond of the oath which they have made or shall make; and I forbid that anyone should serve him as king. For it is fitting that he who strives to lessen the honor of your church, should lose the honor which he seems to have.

Pope St. Gregory VII: *Solemn Excommunication of Henry IV.* (Council of Rome, Feb. 1076.) (Ep. 3, 10 a)

Fear God, honor the king. But you do not fear God, who dishonor His ordinance in me. . . . You, therefore, condemned by the anathema [of St. Paul], by the judgment of all our bishops and by our own judgment, descend from, relinquish the apostolic throne which you have appropriated; let another ascend the chair of blessed Peter, who will not attempt to veil his violence in religion but will teach the sound doctrine of blessed Peter. I Henry, by the grace of God, king, with all our bishops, say to thee: Come down, come down, cursed for all eternity.

Henry IV: *Reply to Excommunication by Pope Gregory VII.* (1076)

So act now, I beseech you, holy fathers and princes, that all the world may know and recognize that, if you are able to bind and loose in heaven, you are able to take away and to grant earthly empires, kingdoms, principalities, dukedoms, marquisates, counties, and the possessions of every man according to merit. For you have frequently taken patriarchates, primacies, and archbishoprics from evil and unworthy men and conferred them on religious men. If you judge spiritual things, what is to be thought of your power to judge secular affairs . . . ! Let kings and all secular princes now learn how great you are, what power you have; and let them fear to despise the commands of your church.

Pope St. Gregory VII: *Allocution before Roman Council.* (When Henry IV was excommunicated the second time.) (1080)

When God gave to blessed Peter the princely power of binding and loosing in heaven and on earth, He made no ex-

ception, and withdrew nothing from his power. For he who denies that he can be bound by the sentence of the Church, must also deny that he can be absolved by its authority; and he who impudently denies this, separates himself from Christ altogether. But if the holy Apostolic See, having had the princely power divinely conferred on it, passes judgment on spiritual matters, why should it not also pass judgment on secular matters.

Pope St. Gregory VII: *Letters*, 4, 2. (To Hermann, bishop of Metz) (12th cent.)

The chief powers by which this world is ruled are two, the royal and the priestly. Both powers our Lord Jesus Christ willed to bear Himself in His person alone in a holy and mysterious way, for He is both King and Priest: King, because He governs us; Priest, because He has cleansed us by the immolation of His own body from the sordidness of our sins and reconciled us to His Father.

Hugh of Fleury: *Treatise on Royal Power and Priestly Dignity*, 1, 2. (12th cent.)

In my opinion the man who thinks it unworthy of apostles or apostolic men, to whom judgment over greater matters has been committed, to refrain from judging in these smaller ones, does not understand the relative value of things. Why should they not scorn to give judgment concerning men's poor earthly possessions, seeing that they shall judge heavenly things, and angels, too? Your jurisdiction, therefore, is over criminal cases, not over property.

St. Bernard: *On Consideration*, 1, 6. (To Pope Eugenius III.) (12th cent.)

Both swords therefore belong to the Church, the spiritual and the material. The material sword is to be drawn in defence of the Church, the spiritual by the Church; the spiritual by the hand of the priest, the material by the soldier, but at a sign from the priest, and on the order of the emperor.

St. Bernard: *On Consideration*, 4, 3. (12th cent.)

When kingdom and priesthood are at one, in complete accord, the world is well ruled, and the Church flourishes and brings forth abundant fruit. But when they are at variance, not only smaller interests prosper not, but even things of greatest moment fall into deplorable decay.

Ivo of Chartres: *Letter to Pope Paschal II.* (12th cent.)

The prince therefore receives this sword from the hand of the Church, since it may not itself have the sword of blood. Yet it has the sword, but uses it by the hand of the prince, on whom it has conferred the power of corporal punishment, reserving to itself the power over spiritual matters in the bishops. The prince is therefore a minister of the priestly power and one who exercises that part of the sacred functions which are unworthy of the hands of the priesthood.

John of Salisbury: *Policraticus*, 4, 3. (12th cent.)

Constantine, prince of the princes of this kingdom, was converted to the faith of Christ by Silvester, prince of the priests of the Church, and the whole world was clothed in the new rite of the Christian religion. Constantine placed the crown of the earthly kingdom on the Roman pontiff, and decreed by imperial authority that no one henceforth should assume the Roman empire without the consent of the pope.

Honorius of Augsburg: *Summa Gloria*, 17. (Concept based on false Donation of Constantine.) (12th cent.)

Therefore, the king is to be chosen by the priests of Christ, who are the true princes of the Church; only the consent of the laymen is required. Because the priestly power established the kingdom, the kingdom by law will be subject to the priestly power.

Honorius of Augsburg: *Summa Gloria*, 22. (12th cent.)

Inasmuch as the spiritual life is more worthy than the earthly, and the soul more worthy than the body, so the spiritual power exceeds the earthly in honor and dignity. For the spiritual power has to institute the earthly power that it may be, and to judge it if it is not good. However it was itself first instituted by God, and when it deviates can only be judged by God.

Hugh of St. Victor: *On the Sacraments*, 51, 2. (12th cent.)

In the same city and under the same king there are two peoples, among these peoples two ways of life, in these two ways of life two principates, and in these two principates a double order of jurisdiction. The city is the Church; the king of the city is Christ; the two peoples are the two orders in the Church, the clergy and the laity; the two lives are the spiritual and the carnal; the two principates are the sacerdotium and imperium; the double jurisdiction is the divine and human law. Give to each its own, and all will be well.

Stephen of Tournai: *Summa Decretorum, Introd.* (12th cent.)

Ecclesiastical liberty is nowhere better preserved than where the Roman church has full power in temporal as well as spiritual matters.

Pope Innocent III: *Letter to the Archbishop of Ravenna.* (Reg. 1, 27) (13th cent.)

To Peter He left the government not only of the whole Church but of the whole world (*seculum*).

Pope Innocent III: *Letter to the Patriarch of Constantinople.* (Reg. 2, 209) (13th cent.)

But princes should recognize, and certainly do recognize, as they have in our presence, that the right and authority of examining a person elected to be king and of promoting him to the empire belong to us, who anoint, consecrate, and crown him. For it is regularly and generally observed that the examination of the person should belong to him who does the consecrating.

Pope Innocent III: *Decretals,* 1, 6, 34. (13th cent.)

Therefore God has established two great lights in the firmament of heaven, which is the universal Church, He has established two great dignities, that is, the pontifical authority and the royal power. That which presides over the day, or spiritual matters, is the greater; that which presides over carnal matters (that is the night), is the lesser, so that, just as the sun is differentiated from the moon, so pontiffs may be differentiated from kings.

Pope Innocent III: *Decretals,* 1, 33, 6. (Letter to the Emperor Alexius) (13th cent.)

No one, surely, of sound mind is ignorant that it belongs to our office to reprove any Christian for mortal sin, and if he disregards our punishment, to compel him by ecclesiastical censure.

Pope Innocent III: *Decretals,* 2, 1, 13. (Intervention *ratione peccati*) (13th cent.)

Not only in the patrimony of the Church over which we exercise full authority in temporal matters, but also in other areas, in certain cases, we exercise temporal authority on occasion. . . .

Pope Innocent III: *Decretals,* 4, 17, 13. (Intervention *casualiter*) (13th cent.)

John, by the grace of God king of England. . . . We have in the first place granted to God and by this our present charter have confirmed, for us and our heirs forever, that the English Church shall be free and shall have its rights entire and its liberties inviolate. . . .

King John: *Magna Carta,* 1. (1215)

Spiritual power and secular power both derive from divine power. Consequently the secular power is subject to the spiritual power only to the extent that it is so subordinated by God, namely, in matters relating to the soul's salvation,

where the spiritual power is to be obeyed before the secular. In matters of political welfare, however, the temporal power should be obeyed before the spiritual: *render to Caesar,* etc. (Matth. 22, 21). That is the rule, unless historically it happens that secular power is joined to spiritual power, as in the pope, who occupies the peak of both powers, according to the dispensation of Christ, Who is both priest and king.

St. Thomas Aquinas: *Commentary on the Sentences,* 4, 44, 3, 4. (Last sentence probably has reference to pope as ruler of the States of the Church.) (13th cent.)

It is not within the competency of the Church to punish unbelief in those who have never received the faith, according to the saying of the Apostle (I Cor. 5, 12): *What have I to do to judge them that are without?* She can, however, pass sentence of punishment on the unbelief of those who have received the faith: and it is fitting that they should be punished by being deprived of the allegiance of their subjects: for this same allegiance might conduce to great corruption of the faith.

St. Thomas Aquinas: *Summa Theologica,* 2-2, 12, 2. (13th cent.)

Unbelief, in itself, is not inconsistent with dominion, since dominion is a device of the law of nations which is a human law; whereas the distinction between believers and unbelievers is of divine law, which does not annul human right. Nevertheless a man who sins by unbelief may be sentenced to the loss of his right of dominion, as also, sometimes, on account of other sins.

St. Thomas Aquinas: *Summa Theologica,* 2-2, 12, 2. (13th cent.)

In order that spiritual things might be distinguished from earthly things, the ministry of this kingdom [of Christ] has been entrusted not to earthly kings, but to priests, and in the highest degree to the chief priest, the successor of St. Peter, the vicar of Christ, the Roman

Pontiff, to whom all the kings of Christian peoples are to be subject as to our Lord Jesus Christ Himself. For those to whom pertains the care of intermediate ends should be subject to him to whom pertains the care of the ultimate end, and be directed by his rule.

St. Thomas Aquinas: *The Governance of Rulers,* 1, 14. (13th cent.)

Since the beatitude of heaven is the end of that virtuous life which we live at present, it pertains to the king's office to promote such good living among his people, as is suitable for the attainment of heavenly happiness, that is to say, he should command those things which lead to the happiness of heaven, and as far as possible, forbid the contrary. What conduces to true beatitude and what hinders it are learned from the law of God, the teaching of which belongs to the office of the priest.

St. Thomas Aquinas: *The Governance of Rulers,* 1, 15. (13th cent.)

In this Church and in its power there are two swords, the spiritual and the temporal, according to the words in the gospel. . . . Both therefore are in the power of the Church. . . . But one is to be exercised on behalf of the Church, the other by the Church. . . . But sword should be under sword, and the temporal authority should be subject to the spiritual authority. . . .

Pope Boniface VIII: *Bull Unam Sanctam,* Nov. 18, 1302.

For the material sword has its power from the supreme pontiff, since all power in the Church militant is derived from the supreme pontiff; for no one can have any power justly, or be the lord of anything with justice, as we have explained above at length, except through the Church, because he has been spiritually renewed and sacramentally absolved by it.

Egidius Colonna: *On Ecclesiastical Power,* 3, 3. (14th cent.)

[The pope] is superior in dignity and origin to every temporal power, and therefore it can be rightly concluded that in the supreme pontiff there pre-exists the fulness of pontifical and royal power.

James of Viterbo: *On Christian Government,* 9. (14th cent.)

When the king sins in spiritual matters, namely in faith, marriage, and other things which fall within the jurisdiction of the spiritual judge, the pope first of all has the responsibility of admonishing him, and if he finds that he is obstinate and incorrigible he can excommunicate him, but beyond this he may not go, except in unusual circumstances (*per accidens*) . . . when he may seek his deposition by the people.

John of Paris: *Concerning Royal and Papal Power,* 13. (Slightly rearranged.) (14th cent.)

Henceforward say that Rome's church,
  having willed
  Confusion of two rules, falls in a
    slough,
  And both she and her burden are
    defiled.

Dante: *Purgatorio, Canto 16.* (Tr. L. Binyon) (14th cent.)

Rome, that the good world made for
  man's abode,
  Was used to have two suns, by which
    were clear
  Both roads, that of the world and
    that of God.
One hath put out the other; to crozier
  Is joined the sword; and going in
    union
  Necessity compels that ill they fare,
Since, joined now, neither fears the
  other one.

Dante: *Purgatorio, Canto 16.* (Tr. Binyon) (14th cent.)

But ye perversely in religion place
  Him born to gird the sword upon his
    side,
  And make him king who should a
    pulpit grace;

Wherefore from the right road ye wander wide.

Dante: *Paradiso, Canto 8.* (Tr. Binyon) (14th cent.)

Similarly I say that temporal government does not owe its existence to the spiritual government, nor its power (which constitutes its authority), nor even its operation as such—though it certainly receives from the spiritual government the energy to operate more powerfully, by the light of grace which God infuses into it in heaven and which is dispensed to it on earth by the supreme pontiff.

Dante: *Monarchy, 3.* (14th cent.)

Two guides have been appointed for man to lead him to his twofold goal: there is the supreme pontiff who is to lead mankind to eternal life in accordance with revelation; and there is the emperor who, in accordance with philosophical teaching, is to lead mankind to temporal happiness.

Dante: *Monarchy, 3.* (14th cent.)

It belongs to the emperor to correct and appoint the pope, and to depose and punish him.

Error of Marsiglio of Padua and Jean of Jandun condemned by Pope John XXII in bull, *Licet iuxta doctrinam,* October 23, 1327.

The papal dignity derived from Caesar, and the election and institution of the pope arose from the power of Caesar.

Error of John Hus, condemned by Council of Constance, Session 15. (July 6, 1415)

III—*Modern Period*

The sovereign of a territory determines the religion of a territory. (Cujus regio, illius et religio.)

The Peace of Augsburg (1555) put an end to religious war in Germany by recognizing that Protestant (Lutheran) princes who had conformed to the Augsburg Confession should retain their lands and estates;

further changes were forbidden. Subjects who changed were obliged to quit the territory. The principle was hardly consistent with Catholic teaching.

The pope has not the same kind of right to depose temporal princes, even though they might deserve to be deposed, as he has to depose bishops, that is as their legitimate, ordinary judge. Nevertheless he may, as the supreme spiritual authority, dispose of kingdoms, taking away the power from one monarch and conferring it on another, if such a change be necessary for the salvation of souls.

St. Robert Bellarmine: *De Romano Pontifice,* 5, 6. (16th cent.)

We hold that the pope, as pope, although he does not have any purely temporal power, yet has in order for spiritual good (*in ordine ad bonum spirituale*) supreme power to dispose of the temporal affairs of all Christians.

St. Robert Bellarmine: *De Romano Pontifice,* 5, 6. (16th cent.)

It is quite true that all power is from God, but some power, such as that of the pope, comes from God immediately, while another kind of power, such as that of temporal princes, is derived from God not immediately but through the consent of human wills.

St. Robert Bellarmine: *Reply to Giovanni Marsiglio.* (17th cent.)

Two differences are observable between political and ecclesiastical power. One of these is connected with the subject in whom the power resides, political power being in the multitude, whereas ecclesiastical power is vested immediately in one person. The other difference is to be found in the sanction on which either power rests. Political power, taken in general, is of divine right, but in concrete instances it is based on the law of nations. Ecclesiastical power, on the other hand, is in every way divinely sanctioned and immediately from God.

St. Robert Bellarmine: *De Laicis, 6.* (16th cent.)

There does reside in the pope coercive power over temporal princes who are incorrigibly wicked, and especially over schismatics and stubborn heretics. He must possess this coercive weapon because directive force is inefficacious without coercive force . . . so that if the pope has directive power over temporal princes, he necessarily has coercive power also, in cases where they have been unwilling to obey the just direction laid down by laws or precepts.

> F. Suarez: *A Defence of the Catholic and Apostolic Faith,* 3, 23. (17th cent.)

As religion includes all that relates to communion with God, it must in some form be inseparable from every living act of man, both individually and socially; and, in the long run, men must conform either their politics to their religion or their religion to their politics. Christianity is constantly at work, moulding political society in its own image and likeness, and every political system struggles to harmonize Christianity with itself.

> Orestes Brownson: *The American Republic.* (19th cent.)

Religion is above and independent of the state, and the state has nothing to do with the Church or her dogmas, but to accept and conform to them as it does to any of the facts or principles of science, to a mathematical truth, or to a physical law.

> Orestes Brownson: *The American Republic.* (19th cent.)

The Church is not a true and perfect society, entirely free; nor is she endowed with proper and perpetual rights of her own, conferred upon her by her divine Founder; but it belongs to the civil power to define what the rights of the Catholic Church are, and the limits within which she may exercise those rights.

> Proposition condemned by Pius IX in Syllabus of Errors. (1867)

The ecclesiastical power ought not to exercise its authority without the permission and assent of the civil government.

> Proposition condemned by Pius IX in Syllabus of Errors. (1867)

The Church does not have the power to use force, nor does she have any temporal power direct or indirect.

> Proposition condemned by Pius IX in Syllabus of Errors. (1867)

In the case of conflicting laws enacted by the two powers, the civil law prevails.

> Proposition condemned by Pius IX in Syllabus of Errors. (1867)

Kings and princes are not only exempt from the jurisdiction of the Church, but are superior to the Church in deciding questions of jurisdiction.

> Proposition condemned by Pius IX in Syllabus of Errors. (1867)

The Church ought to be separated from the state, and the state from the Church.

> Proposition condemned by Pius IX in Syllabus of Errors. (1867)

The Catholic Church, while she is militant on earth, is compelled to wage an incessant conflict, both for the preservation of the purity of her doctrines and for her own liberty in proclaiming them. The political disputes are a part and a consequence of the dogmatic controversy, and the mission of the Church resides in both alike. All modern history is filled with this double contest; on the one hand with her successive victories over new forms of error, and on the other with her gradual emancipation from every earthly influence.

> Lord Acton: *The States of the Church.* (19th cent.)

The civil allegiance of no man is unlimited; and therefore the civil allegiance of all men who believe in God, or are governed by conscience, is in that sense divided. In this sense, and in no other, can it be said with truth that the civil allegiance of Catholics is divided. The civil allegiance of every Christian man in England is limited by conscience and the law of God; and the civil allegiance of Catholics is limited neither less nor more.

> Card. Manning: *Letter to the Times.* (In reply to Gladstone's *Expostulation.*) (Nov. 10, 1874)

The Church has a twofold work to do for mankind. Its first and primary, indeed, is to save souls, to lead men to eternal life. Its second, but no less true, is to ripen and to elevate the social and political life of men by its influences of morality and of law. As the Church is not a mere school of opinion for the enlightenment of the intellect, but a true kingdom for the government of the will, so its mission is not only to direct conscience and the will of individuals as units, but of fathers as the heads of households, and of princes or governors as the rulers of peoples and of nations. Hence, by the divine law of its mission to mankind, arises what is called the social and political status of the Church.

> Card. Manning: *Miscellanies,* 1. (19th cent.)

The only-begotten Son of God established on earth a society which is called the Church, and to it He handed over the exalted and divine office which He had received from His Father, to be continued through the ages to come. . . . This society is made up of men, just as the civil society is, and yet is supernatural and spiritual, on account of the end for which it was founded, and of the means by which it aims at attaining that end. Hence, it is distinguished and differs from civil society, and, what is of highest moment, it is a society chartered as of divine right, perfect in its nature and in its title, to possess in itself and by itself, through the will and loving kindness of its Founder, all needful provision for its maintenance and action. And just as the end at which the Church aims is by far the noblest of ends, so is its authority the most exalted of all authority, nor can

it be looked upon as inferior to the civil power, or in any manner dependent upon it.

> Pope Leo XIII: *Immortale Dei.* (Nov. 1, 1885)

The Almighty, therefore, has given the charge of the human race to two powers, the ecclesiastical and the civil, the one being set over divine, and the other over human things. Each in its kind is supreme, each has fixed limits within which it is contained, limits which are defined by the nature and special object of the province of each, so that there is, we may say, an orbit traced out within which the action of each is brought into play by its own native right. But, inasmuch as each of these two powers has authority over the same subjects, and as it might come to pass that one and the same thing—related differently, but still remaining one and the same thing— might belong to the jurisdiction and determination of both, therefore God, Who foresees all things, and Who is the Author of these two powers, has marked out the course of each in right correlation to the other. *For the powers that are, are ordained of God* (Rom. 13, 1).

> Pope Leo XIII: *Immortale Dei.* (Nov. 1, 1885)

There must, accordingly, exist between these two powers a certain orderly connection, which may be compared to the union of the soul and body in man. The nature and scope of that connection can be determined only . . . by having right regard to the nature of each power, and by taking account of the relative excellence and nobleness of their purpose. One of the two has for its proximate and chief object the well-being of this mortal life; the other, the everlasting joys of heaven. Whatever therefore in things human is of sacred character, whatever belongs either of its own nature or by reason of the end to which it is referred, to the salvation of souls, or to the worship of God, is subject to the power and judgment of the Church. Whatever is to be ranged under the civil and political order is rightly subject to the civil authority.

Pope Leo XIII: *Immortale Dei.* (Nov. 1, 1885)

To wish the Church to be subject to the civil power in the exercise of her duty is a great folly and a sheer injustice. Whenever this is the case, order is disturbed, for things natural are put above things supernatural.

Pope Leo XIII: *Immortale Dei.* (Nov. 1, 1885)

To attempt to involve the Church in party strife, and seek to bring her support to bear against those who take opposite views is only worthy of partisans. Religion should, on the contrary, be accounted by everyone as holy and inviolate.

Pope Leo XIII: *Sapientiae Christianae.* (Jan. 10, 1890)

Among us the Church is both old and new. We are a handful, but separate from the world, and from courts, and from the corrupt atmosphere of secular patronage and secular protection. The true protection of the Church is its own independence, and its true power is its own liberty.

Card. Manning: *The Eternal Priesthood.* (19th cent.)

It would be very erroneous to draw the conclusion that in America is to be sought the type of the most desirable status of the Church, or that it would be universally lawful or expedient for state and Church to be, as in America, dissevered and divorced.

Pope Leo XIII: *Longinque Oceani.* (Jan. 6, 1895)

Every Catholic, because he is at the same time a citizen, has the right and the duty, disregarding the authority of the Church and heedless of her wishes, counsel and demands, in defiance even of her rebukes, to pursue the public good in any way he thinks best. To prescribe a line of conduct for the citizen on any pretext whatever is an abuse of the ecclesiastical power which it is a duty to resist with all one's strength.

Proposition condemned by St. Pius X in Enc. *Pascendi Dominici.* (Sept. 8, 1907)

One may conceive two typically different modes of collaboration between the two powers. In the one case collaboration may be made effective by prominent use of the visible and external means that are proper to the temporal power, and finally by the use of force in its different manifestations. In the other case, collaboration will proceed with the use as principal means of the moral and spiritual activities that are proper to the Church, and primarily the power of Christian charity.

J. Maritain: *Freedom in the Modern World.* (20th cent.)

It is also clear that the interests of a durable social peace in a community which admits diversity of religious profession require that the collaboration of Church and state be effected by way of moral influence and amity rather than by legal constraint.

J. Maritain: *Freedom in the Modern World.* (20th cent.)

To ignore, on the plea of a 'separation' between State and Church wrongly and anti-politically understood, the religious traditions and schools of thought which are part of the heritage of the body politic, would simply mean for democracy to separate itself, and democratic faith, from the deepest of its living sources.

J. Maritain: *Man and the State.* (20th cent.)

Medieval man entered the State (what State there was) to become a 'citizen,' through the Church and his membership in the Church; modern man is a citizen with full civic rights whether he is a member of the Church or not.

J. C. Murray: *Governmental Repression of Heresy.* (1949)

There was a 'sacral' age, the age of medieval Christendom, mainly characterized on the one hand by the fact that the unity of faith was a prerequisite for political unity, and that the basic frame of reference was the unity of that social body, religio-political in nature, which was the *respublica Christiana,* on the other hand by the dominant dynamic idea of strength or fortitude at the service of justice. . . . In the Middle Ages not only the differentiation of the body politic as such was not completely achieved, but the Church had, as a matter of fact, to make up for a number of deficiencies in the civil order, and to take upon herself, because she was shaping civilization in her womb, many functions and responsibilities pertaining of themselves to political society. . . . The historical climate of modern civilization . . . is characterized by the fact that it is a 'lay' or 'secular,' not a 'sacral' civilization. On the one hand the dominant dynamic idea is not the idea of strength or fortitude at the service of justice, but rather that of the conquest of freedom and the realization of human dignity. On the other hand the root requirement for a sound mutual cooperation between the Church and the body politic is not the unity of a religio-political body . . . but the very unity of the human person, simultaneously a member of the body politic and of the Church, if he freely adheres to her. The unity of religion is not a prerequisite for political unity, and men subscribing to diverse religious or non-religious creeds have to share in and work for the same political and temporal common good.

J. Maritain: *Man and the State.* (20th cent.)

See also Authority; Catholic Church—Authority; Government; Politics; Pope

Church and State in the United States

General and equal toleration, by giving free circulation to fair argument, is a most effectual method to bring all denominations of Christians to an unity of faith.

Archb. Carroll: *An Address to the Roman Catholics of the United States of America.* (1784)

Congress shall make no law respecting an establishment of religion, or prohibiting the free exercise thereof; or abridging the freedom of speech, or of the press; or the right of the people peaceably to assemble, and to petition the Government for a redress of grievances.

Constitution of the United States, First Amendment. (1787)

Every religious denomination in this country, being obedient to the laws thereof, has a right to regulate, according to its own rules, the questions of ecclesiastical discipline appertaining to its government. Deny this right, and you destroy religious liberty.

Archb. Hughes: *Apology for his Pastoral.* (1842)

The United States have a religious as well as a political destiny, for religion and politics go together. Church and state, as governments, are separate indeed, but the principles on which the state is founded have their origin and ground in the spiritual order—in the principles revealed or affirmed by religion—and are inseparable from them.

Orestes Brownson: *The American Republic.* (19th cent.)

If I had the privilege of modifying the Constitution of the United States, I would not expunge or alter a single paragraph, a single line, or a single word of that important instrument. The Constitution is admirably adapted to the growth and expansion of the Catholic religion, and the Catholic religion is admirably adapted to the genius of the Constitution. They fit together like two links in the same chain.

Card. Gibbons: *Speech at the Installation of Fr. Conaty as Second Rector of Catholic University,* Jan. 19, 1897.

American Catholics rejoice in our separation of Church and state, and I can conceive no combination of circumstances likely to arise which would make a union desirable for either Church or state.

Card. Gibbons: *North American Review.* (March, 1909)

It cannot be too much emphasized that the religious liberty proclaimed by the First Amendment is not a piece of religious mysticism, but a practical political principle, ethically grounded in the obligations of the State to the consciences of its citizens and to its own end—social harmony, prosperity and peace.

J. C. Murray: *Separation of Church and State.* (In *America*, Dec. 7, 1946)

The American state does not recognize on the part of any Church the right to direct and authoritative intervention in its processes; to this extent it asserts its own autonomy as a political order. However, it does recognize in American society a 'spiritual power' that stands, as it were, not only over against it but above it—the Christian conscience, whose demands are acknowledged as relevant to the political order, whose right of moral judgment on all the processes of government is likewise acknowledged, guaranteed free expression and provided with institutional channels for it.

J. C. Murray: *Church and State in the Light of History.* (Theol. Studies, June, 1949)

Cigarette

A cigarette is the perfect type of a perfect pleasure. It is exquisite, and it leaves one unsatisfied. What more can you want?

Oscar Wilde: *The Picture of Dorian Gray*, 6. (19th cent.)

Circumstances

Circumstances are but the subject-matter, and not the rule of our conduct, nor in any sense the cause of it.

Card. Newman: *Oxford University Sermons.* (19th cent.)

Citizenship

No better citizen is there, whether in time of peace or war, than the Christian who is mindful of his duty; but such a one should be ready to suffer all things, even death itself, rather than abandon the cause of God or of the Church.

Pope Leo XIII: *Sapientiae Christianae.* (Jan. 10, 1890)

Morality is the very soul of good citizenship.

Archb. Ireland: *American Citizenship.* (Chicago, Feb. 22, 1895)

City

Crowded in cities man is crushed
By minor irregular motions,
Jarred by sharp sounds, and rushed
By fools who counterfeit vainglorious
    notions:
A thousand hollow Babels, tower
Two digits high at half a mile,
Swarming the blue with stone and
    clay—
Mute monuments of man's power
To conquer nature!—Oh smile
That men entomb themselves from
    night and day!

Frederic Thompson: *Heaven and Earth.* (20th cent.)

Civilization

Civilization is that state to which man's nature points and tends; it is the systematic use, improvement, and combination of those faculties which are his characteristic; and, viewed in its idea, it is the perfection, the happiness of our moral state. It is the development of art out of nature, and of self-government out of passion, and of certainty out of opinion, and of faith out of reason.

Card. Newman: *Historical Sketches*, 1. (19th cent.)

Considering, then, the characteristics of this great [western] civilized Society. . . . I think it has a claim to be considered as the representative society and civilization of the human race, as its perfect result and limit, in fact, those portions of the race which do not coalesce with it being left to stand by themselves as anomalies, unaccountable indeed, but for that very reason not interfering with what on the contrary has been turned to account and has grown into a whole. I call then this commonwealth pre-eminently and emphatically human society, and its intellect the human mind, and its decisions the sense of mankind, and its disciplined and cultivated state civilization in the abstract, and the territory on which it lies the *orbis terrarum,* or the world.

> Card. Newman: *The Idea of a University.* (19th cent.)

That civilization which conflicts with the doctrines of Holy Church is but a worthless imitation and a hollow name.

> Pope Leo XIII: *Inscrutabili.* (Apr. 21, 1878)

Civilization in the best sense merely means the full authority of the human spirit over all externals. Barbarism means the worship of those externals in their crude and unconquered state. Barbarism is the worship of nature.

> G. K. Chesterton: *All Things Considered.* (20th cent.)

There are many who insist on all that was dark or gross or negligent in the conditions of early barbarism, so that modern civilization may for one wild moment take on a fanciful semblance of decency. But old things have to be made very black indeed, if modern things are not to look blacker.

> G. K. Chesterton: *Generally Speaking.* (20th cent.)

Religion is the main determining element in the formation of a culture or civilization.

> H. Belloc: *The Crisis of Civilization.* (20th cent.)

Progress is the time-expression of an eternal plan. The past is the life-history of human souls, of their will and contribution to their heirs. By God's design the human race is knit together in a close and mysterious membership. Adam's fall affected all his children; the Son of Man took upon Himself the sins of all. The true meaning of civilization is growth in fellowship and common life.

> M. C. D'Arcy: *The Idea of God.* (In *God and the Supernatural*) (20th cent.)

We are faced with a spiritual conflict of the most acute kind, a sort of social schizophrenia which divides the soul of society between non-moral will to power served by inhuman techniques and a religious faith and a moral idealism which have no power to influence human life. There must be a return to unity—a spiritual integration of culture—if mankind is to survive.

> C. Dawson: *Gifford Lectures, 1947: Religion and Culture.*

The identification of religion with the particular cultural synthesis which has been achieved at a definite point of time and space by the action of historical forces is fatal to the universal character of religious truth. It is indeed a kind of idolatry—the substitution of an image made by man for the eternal transcendent reality.

> C. Dawson: *Gifford Lectures, 1947: Religion and Culture.*

The activity of the western mind, which manifested itself alike in scientific and technical invention as well as in geographical discovery, was not the natural inheritance of a particular biological type; it was the result of a long process of education which gradually changed the orientation of human thought and enlarged the possibilities of social action. In this process the vital factor was not the aggressive power of conquerors and capitalists, but the widening of the capacity of human intelligence and the development of new types of creative genius and ability.

> C. Dawson: *Gifford Lectures, 1948: Religion and the Rise of Western Culture.*

Even in the darkest periods of the middle ages this dynamic principle continued to operate. For what distinguishes western culture from the other world civilizations is its missionary character— its transmission from one people to another in a continuous series of spiritual movements.

> C. Dawson: *Gifford Lectures, 1948: Religion and the Rise of Western Culture.*

Our generation has been forced to realize how fragile and unsubstantial are the barriers that separate civilization from the forces of destruction. We have learnt that barbarism is not a picturesque myth or a half-forgotten memory of a long-passed stage of history, but an ugly underlying reality which may erupt with shattering force whenever the moral authority of a civilization loses its control.

> C. Dawson: *Gifford Lectures, 1948: Religion and the Rise of Western Culture.*

The beginnings of western culture are to be found in the new spiritual community which arose from the ruins of the Roman Empire owing to the conversion of the northern barbarians to the Christian faith. . . . The people of the north possessed no written literature, no cities, no stone architecture. They were, in short, 'barbarians'; and it was only by Christianity and the elements of a higher culture transmitted to them by the Church that western Europe acquired unity and form.

> C. Dawson: *Gifford Lectures, 1948: Religion and the Rise of Western Culture.*

See also Catholic Church and Civilization

Classes

The great mistake is to take up with the notion that class is naturally hostile to class, and that the wealthy and the workingmen are intended by nature to live in conflict. So irrational and so false is this view that the direct contrary is the truth.

> Pope Leo XIII: *Rerum novarum.* (May 15, 1891)

Just as the symmetry of the human frame is the result of the suitable arrangement of the different parts of the body, so in a state is it ordained by nature that . . . classes should dwell in harmony and agreement, so as to maintain the balance of the body politic. Each needs the other: capital cannot be without labor, nor labor without capital.

> Pope Leo XIII: *Rerum novarum.* (May 15, 1891)

Let Catholic writers take care when defending the cause of the proletariat and the poor not to use language calculated to inspire among the people aversion to the upper classes of society.

> Pope St. Pius X: *Letter to the Bishops of Italy on Catholic Social Action.* (Dec. 18, 1903)

Classic

By the classics of a national literature I mean those authors who have the foremost place in exemplifying the powers and conducting the development of its language.

> Card. Newman: *Idea of a University.* (19th cent.)

Cleanliness

If thou in health prolonged wouldst stay,
Wash frequently thy hands each day.

> School of Salerno, Code of Health. (11th cent.)

God requires corporal cleanliness in those that approach the altar.

> St. Francis de Sales: *Introduction to the Devout Life,* 25. (17th cent.)

Clergy

Those persons who devote the services of religion to divine worship, that is, those who are called clerics, shall be exempt from all compulsory public services whatever, lest, through the sacrilegious malice of certain persons, they should be called away from divine service.

> Edict of the Emperor Constantine I.
> (Theod. Code, 16, 2, 2) (Oct. 21, 319)

The great synod has stringently forbidden any bishop, presbyter, deacon, or any one of the clergy whatever, to have a woman (*subintroducta*) dwelling with him, except only his mother, sister, aunt, or such persons only as are beyond all suspicion.

> Council of Nicaea, Can. 3. (325)

According to the sanction which you are said to have obtained previously, no person shall obligate you and your slaves to new tax payments, but you shall enjoy exemption. Furthermore, you shall not be required to receive quartered persons, and if any of you, for the sake of a livelihood, should wish to conduct a business, they shall possess tax exemption.

> Edict of the Emperor Constantius to the Clergy. (Theod. Code, 2, 2, 8) (Aug. 27, 343)

By a law of our clemency we prohibit bishops to be accused in the courts. Therefore, if any person should lodge any complaint, such complaint must unquestionably be examined before other bishops, in order that an opportune and suitable hearing may be arranged for the investigation of all concerned.

> Edict of the Emperors Constantius and Constans. (Theod. Code, 16, 2, 12) (Oct. 7, 355)

Whatever is customary in the conduct of civil suits shall likewise be observed in ecclesiastical litigation, so that if there are any matters arising from certain dissensions and slight offenses pertaining to religious observance, they shall be heard in their own places and by the synods of their own dioceses, with the exception of those matters which criminal action has established shall be heard by ordinary and extraordinary judges or by the illustrious authorities.

> Edict of the Emperors Valens, Gratian, and Valentinian. (Theod. Code, 16, 2, 23) (May 17, 376)

Let not a bishop, a priest, or deacon undertake the cares of this world; but if he do, let him be deprived.

> Ecclesiastical Canons of the Holy Apostles, 7. (4th cent.)

He who has been married twice after his baptism, or has had a concubine, cannot be made a bishop, or presbyter, or deacon, or indeed any one of the sacerdotal catalogue.

> Ecclesiastical Canons of the Holy Apostles, 17. (4th cent.)

Of those who come into the clergy unmarried, we permit only the readers and singers, if they have a mind, to marry afterward.

> Ecclesiastical Canons of the Holy Apostles, 27. (4th cent.)

We do not permit slaves to be ordained into the clergy without their master's consent; for this would grieve those that owned them.

> Ecclesiastical Canons of the Holy Apostles, 82. (4th cent.)

Let a bishop, or presbyter, or deacon, who goes to the army, and desires to retain both the Roman government and the sacerdotal administration, be deprived. For *the things of Caesar belong to Caesar, and the things of God to God* (Matth. 22, 21).

> Ecclesiastical Canons of the Holy Apostles, 83. (4th cent.)

Your father of august memory not only gave his answer by word of mouth, but sanctioned by law this truth: In a matter of faith or of any Church regulation the decision should be given by him who is neither unsuited to the task nor disqualified by law . . . he wished priests to make judgments regarding priests. In fact, if a bishop were accused of any charge and the case of his character needed to be examined, he wished these matters to belong to the judgment of bishops.

St. Ambrose: *Letters,* 21. (To the emperor Valentinian.) (386)

Far be it from me to censure the successors of the apostles, who with holy words consecrate the Body of Christ, and who make us Christians. Having the keys of the kingdom of heaven, they judge men to some extent before the day of judgment, and guard the chastity of the bride of Christ.

St. Jerome: *Letters,* 14, 8. (4th cent.)

That clergyman soon becomes an object of contempt who being often asked out to dinner never refuses to go.

St. Jerome: *Letters,* 52, 15. (4th cent.)

Clerics must not be accused except before bishops. . . .

Edict of the Emperors Honorius and Theodosius. (Theod. Code, 16, 2, 41) (Dec. 11, 412)

Dearly beloved brethren, let us beseech our Lord Jesus Christ in behalf of these His servants, who hasten for His love to lay aside the hair of their heads, that He bestow upon them the Holy Ghost, Who shall keep them in the practice of religion forever, and protect their hearts from the stumbling blocks of the world and from worldly desires, so that even as they are changed in outward appearance, He may likewise grant them an increase of virtue, and, opening their eyes, deliver them from all spiritual and human blindness and bestow upon them the light of everlasting grace.

Roman Pontifical, Conferring of Clerical Tonsure, Prayer *Oremus Fratres Carissimi.* (Gregorian, 6th to 8th cent.)

Hearken, O Lord, to our supplications and vouchsafe to bless these Thy servants whom in Thy sacred name we invest with the habit of holy religion, that through Thy bounty, they may deserve to persevere devout in Thy Church, and attain to everlasting life.

Roman Pontifical, Making of Clerics, Prayer *Adesto Domine supplicationibus* for the Imposition of the Surplice. (Gregorian, 6th to 8th cent.)

Be ye clean, you that carry the vessels of the Lord (Isa. 52, 11). Those who carry the vessels of the Lord are those who undertake, in reliance on their way of living, to draw the souls of their neighbors to the everlasting holy places.

Pope St. Gregory I: *Pastoral Care,* 2, 2. (6th cent.)

Cleros in Greek means lot or inheritance. Therefore, the clergy are so called because they belong to the lot of the Lord, or because they have the share of the Lord. Generally, however, clergy means all who serve in the Church of Christ.

St. Isidore: *Etymologies,* 7, 12. (7th cent.)

May the Lord put on thee the new man, who, according to God, is created in justice and in the holiness of truth.

Roman Pontifical, Making of Clerics, Formula for Imposition of the Surplice. (13th cent.)

Long standing and small offering Maketh poor parsons.

John Heywood: *Proverbs,* 2, 9. (16th cent.)

The greatest clerks be not the wisest men.

John Heywood: *Proverbs,* 2, 5. (16th cent.)

There is nothing which draws others more readily to piety and the worship of God than the life and example of those who have dedicated themselves to the divine ministry. For when it is seen that they have withdrawn themselves from the affairs of the world to a loftier station, the others look at them as at a mirror and expect to find there the example they hope to follow.

Decree of the Council of Trent, Session 22. (Sept. 17, 1562)

My charge is, of free cost to preach the gospel, to minister the sacraments, to instruct the simple, to reform sinners, to confute errors—in brief, to cry alarm spiritual against foul vice and proud ignorance, wherewith many of my dear countrymen are abused.

Bl. Edmund Campion: *Campion's Brag.* (Addressed to the Lords of Queen Elizabeth's Privy Council) (16th cent.)

Religious vocations are not common, but special. It is a fatal mistake for religious to take the place of secular clergy.

Isaac T. Hecker. (Elliott's Life, 297) (19th cent.)

We enjoin upon our priests as a matter of strict precept, that both at home and abroad, and whether they are residing in their own diocese or outside of it, they should wear the Roman collar.

Decree of the Third Plenary Council of Baltimore. (1884)

Far, far from the clergy be the love of novelty! God hateth the proud and the obstinate mind.

Pope St. Pius X: *Pascendi.* (Sept. 8, 1907)

By divine law the clergy are distinct from the laity in the Church, although not all clerics are of divine institution; both however may be religious.

Code of Canon Law, Canon 107. (20th cent.)

Those who are dedicated to the divine service at least by the first tonsure are called clerics. They are not all of the same degree, but there is a sacred hierarchy among them in which some are subordinate to others. By divine institution the sacred hierarchy consists of bishops, priests and ministers as regards order; as regards jurisdiction, it consists of the supreme pontificate and the subor-

dinate episcopate; by ecclesiastical institution other degrees have also been added to these.

Code of Canon Law, Canon 108. (20th cent.)

All the faithful owe reverence to the clergy according to their various grades and offices; and they stain themselves with the sin of sacrilege if they do the clergy a real injury.

Code of Canon Law, Canon 119. (Privilegium Canonis) (20th cent.)

In all contentious or criminal cases the clergy should be summoned before an ecclesiastical judge, unless lawful provision to the contrary has been made for particular places.

Code of Canon Law, Canon 120, 1. (Privilegium Fori) (20th cent.)

All the clergy are immune from military service and from public civil charges and offices which are alien to the clerical state.

Code of Canon Law, Canon 121. (Privilegium Immunitatis) (20th cent.)

The clergy must lead a more holy life both interiorly and exteriorly than laymen, and must excel them in giving an example of virtue and good deeds.

Code of Canon Law, Canon 124. (20th cent.)

The clergy are forbidden to conduct business or trade, either personally or through agents, either for their own benefit or that of other persons.

Code of Canon Law, Canon 142. (20th cent.)

See also Bishop; Deacon; Episcopate; Hierarchy; Orders, Holy; Priest; Priesthood

Clergy and Laity

Each of us, brethren, must in his own place please God with a good conscience, reverently taking care not to deviate from the established rule of service (*leitourgia*).

> Pope St. Clement I: *Letter to the Corinthians,* 41, 1. (1st cent.)

What then is the Church but the multitude of the faithful, the aggregate of Christians? Now this aggregate embraces two orders, laymen and clerics, two sides, as it were, of one body. . . . Laymen who treat earthly things and the necessities of the earthly are the left part of the body of Christ. The clergy, indeed, since they dispense those things which pertain to the spiritual life are, as it were, the right part of the body of Christ. But the whole Body of Christ which is the universal Church consists of these two parts.

> Hugh of St. Victor: *On the Sacraments of the Christian Faith,* 2, 2, 2-3. (12th cent.)

Antiquity teaches us that laymen are in a high degree hostile to the clergy.

> Pope Boniface VIII: *Clericis laicos.* (13th cent.)

See also Church and State; Laity

Cloister

> Show me your cloister, asks the Lady
>   Poverty.
> Well, that were a cloister; for its bars
> Long strips of sunset, with corridors of
>   air
> Leading to chapel, and God everywhere.
> Earth beauteous and bare to lie upon,
> Lit by the little candle of the sun.
> The wind gone daily sweeping like a
>   broom—
> For these vast hearts it was a narrow
>   room.

> Charles L. O'Donnell: *Cloister.* (20th cent.)

Clothes

But let thy clothes be plain, not for adornment, but for a necessary covering:

not to minister to thy vanity, but to keep thee warm in winter, and to hide the unseemliness of the body.

> St. Cyril of Jerusalem: *Catechetical Discourses,* 4, 29. (4th cent.)

God sendeth cold after clothes.

> John Heywood: *Proverbs,* 1, 4. (cf. Gen. 3, 7-8) (16th cent.)

When clothing our body, we ought to remember that it bears the imprint of sin; we ought therefore to cover it with decency in accordance with the law of God.

> St. John Baptist de la Salle: *The Rules of Christian Manners and Civility,* 2. (17th cent.)

> Fortune in men has some small diff'-
>   rence made,
> One flaunts in rags, one flutters in bro-
>   cade;
> The cobbler apron'd, and the parson
>   gown'd,
> The friar hooded, and the monarch
>   crown'd.

> Pope: *An Essay on Man,* 4. (18th cent.)

Cloud

The cloud has been lifted from me for ever!

> Exclamation of J. H. Newman when informed that Pope Leo XIII wished to confer on him the cardinalate. (19th cent.)

> While the winds in their tricksome
>   courses
>   The snowy steeds vault upon
> That are foaled of the white sea-horses
> And washed in the streams of the
>   sun.

> F. Thompson: *Song of the Hours.* (19th cent.)

> I knew how the clouds arise
> Spumèd of the wild sea-snortings.

> F. Thompson: *The Hound of Heaven.* (19th cent.)

Coal

Let them that be a-cold blow at the coal.

John Heywood: *Proverbs*, 1, 10. (16th
cent.)

Cock

O wakeful bird! proclaimer of the day,
Whose piercing note doth daunt the
    lion's rage;
Thy crowing did myself to me bewray,
My frights and brutish heats it did as-
    suage.
But oh! in this alone, unhappy cock,
That thou to count my foils wert made
    the clock!

Bl. Robert Southwell: *St. Peter's Complaint.*
(16th cent.)

He is the sun's brave herald
    That, ringing his blithe horn,
Calls round a world dew-pearl'd
    The heavenly airs of morn.

Katharine T. Hinkson: *Chanticleer.* (20th
cent.)

Cocktail

Cocktails have all the disagreeability
without the utility of a disinfectant.

Shane Leslie: In the *London Observer.*
(20th cent.)

Coincidence

Coincidences are nothing to those who
have a great simplicity. The word is
only intended to explain away the methods by which the good God arranges the
affairs of His world.

Katharine T. Hinkson: *A Shameful
Inheritance.* (20th cent.)

Cold (Catarrh)

Fast well and watch. Eat hot your daily
    fare,
Work some, and breathe a warm and
    humid air;
Of drink be spare; your breath at times
    suspend,

These things observe if you your cold
    would end.

School of Salerno, Code of Health. (11th
cent.)

Collecting

My passion all my life has been non-
collecting.

Louise Imogen Guiney. (20th cent.)

Color

What value is given to cloth by adultera-
tion with false colors? God likes not that
which He Himself did not produce. Had
He not the power to order that sheep
should be born with purple or sky-blue
fleeces? He had the power, but He did
not wish; and what God did not wish
certainly ought not to be produced arti-
ficially.

Tertullian: *Women's Dress.* (3rd cent.)

Glory be to God for dappled things.

G. M. Hopkins: *Pied Beauty.* (19th cent.)

Combat

A hard foughten field where no man
scapeth unkilled.

John Heywood: *Proverbs,* 1, 11. (16th
cent.)

It is the fight alone that gives us pleasure,
not the victory.

Pascal: *Pensées.* (17th cent.)

Comedy

The debauching of virgins and the
amours of strumpets are the subject of
comedy.

Lactantius: *Divinae institutiones,* 6. (4th
cent.)

Of all dramatic writing, comic wit,
As 'tis the best, so 'tis most hard to hit.

Dryden: *The Wild Gallant, Epilogue.*
(17th cent.)

In a world where everything is ridiculous, nothing can be ridiculed. You cannot unmask a mask; when it is admittedly as hollow as a mask. You cannot turn a thing upside down, if there is no theory about when it is right way up. If life is really so formless that you cannot make head or tail of it, you cannot pull its tail; and you certainly cannot make it stand on its head.

> G. K. Chesterton: *Generally Speaking.*
> (20th cent.)

Comfort

All human comfort is vain and short.

> Thomas a Kempis: *The Imitation of Christ,*
> 3, 16. (15th cent.)

Let this be my consolation, to be willing to lack all human comfort.

> Thomas a Kempis: *The Imitation of Christ,*
> 3, 16. (15th cent.)

As the cure of the person is desperate who hath not the will to be cured, so is the discomfort of that person desperate who hath not the will to be comforted.

> St. Thomas More: *Dialogue of Comfort.*
> (16th cent.)

Comfort in tribulation can be secured only on the sure ground of faith holding as true the words of Scripture and the teaching of the Catholic Church.

> St. Thomas More: *Dialogue of Comfort.*
> (16th cent.)

Comic and Tragic

There are two things in which all men are manifestly and unmistakably equal. They are not equally clever or equally muscular or equally fat, as the sages of the modern reaction (with piercing insight) perceive. But this is a spiritual certainty, that all men are tragic. And this again is an equally sublime spiritual certainty, that all men are comic.

> G. K. Chesterton: *Charles Dickens.* (20th cent.)

Coming and Going

As fast as one goeth another cometh.

> John Heywood: *Proverbs,* 1, 3. (16th cent.)

Commandment

We should fulfill the commands of God with insatiable desire, ever pressing onward towards greater achievements.

> St. Basil: *The Morals,* 18, 4. (4th cent.)

God's precepts are light to the loving, heavy to the fearful.

> St. Thomas Aquinas: *Disputations Concerning Truth,* 24, 14. (13th cent.)

If any one saith that the commandments of God are, even for one that is justified and constituted in grace, impossible to keep; let him be anathema.

> Council of Trent, Session 6, Canon 18. (Jan. 13, 1547)

If any one saith that nothing beside faith is commanded in the Gospel; that other things are indifferent, neither commanded nor prohibited, but free; or that the ten commandments nowise appertain to Christians; let him be anathema.

> Council of Trent, Session 6, Canon 19. (Jan. 13, 1547)

If any one saith that the man who is justified and how perfect soever is not bound to observe the commandments of God and of the Church, but only to believe; as if indeed the Gospel were a bare and absolute promise of eternal life without the condition of observing the commandments; let him be anathema.

> Council of Trent, Session 6, Canon 20. (Jan. 13, 1547)

Common Law

While, however, they use laws and written law in almost all lands, in England alone there has been used within its boundaries an unwritten law and custom. In England legal right is based on an unwritten law which usage has approved. . . . For the English hold many things by customary law which they do not hold by law (*lex*).

Bracton: *On the Laws and Customs of England,* 1, 1, 2. (13th cent.)

The laws of England, though unwritten, it seems may be properly called laws (*leges*), (since this itself is a law—that which pleases the prince has the force of law) I mean those laws which it is evident were promulgated by the advice of the nobles and the authority of the prince, concerning doubts to be settled in their assembly.

Glanvill: *Treatise Concerning the Laws and Customs of England, Prol.* (13th cent.)

There is no pretence to say or insinuate to the contrary but that the laws and customs of England are not only good but the very best.

John Fortescue: *De laudibus legum Angliae.* (15th cent.)

Common Sense

It is extremely rare and original to be absolutely ordinary. . . . Didn't somebody say that there was nothing so uncommon as common sense?

R. H. Benson: *The Necromancers.* (20th cent.)

Communion, Holy

But let no one eat or drink of the Eucharist with you except those baptized in the name of the Lord, for it was in reference to this that the Lord said: *Do not give that which is holy to dogs.*

Teaching of the Twelve Apostles, 9. (2nd cent.)

We give Thee thanks, O Holy Father, for Thy holy name, which Thou hast enshrined in our hearts, and for the knowledge and faith and immortality which Thou hast made known to us

through Jesus Thy Servant. To Thee be glory for evermore.

Teaching of the Twelve Apostles, 10. (Eucharistic Prayer.) (2nd cent.)

Come together in common, one and all without exception in charity, in one faith and in one Jesus Christ, Who is of the race of David according to the flesh, the son of man and Son of God, so that with undivided mind you may obey the bishop and the priests, and break one Bread which is the medicine of immortality and the antidote against death, enabling us to live for ever in Jesus Christ.

St. Ignatius of Antioch: *Letter to the Ephesians,* 20. (2nd cent.)

And we ask that this bread should be given to us daily, that we who are in Christ and daily receive the Eucharist for the food of salvation, may not by the interposition of some heinous sin, by being prevented as withheld and not communicating from partaking of the heavenly Bread, be separated from Christ's Body, as He Himself predicts and warns: *I myself am the living bread that has come down from heaven. If anyone eats of this bread, he shall live for ever. And now, what is this bread which I am to give? It is My flesh, given for the life of the world* (John 6, 51-52).

St. Cyprian: *On the Lord's Prayer,* 18. (3rd cent.)

And let everyone of the faithful be careful to partake of the Eucharist before he eats anything else. For if he partakes with faith, even though some deadly thing were given to him, after this it cannot hurt him.

St. Hippolytus: *The Apostolic Tradition,* 32. (3rd cent.)

He who undertakes to receive Communion, without observing the manner in which participation in the Body and Blood of Christ has been granted, derives no benefit therefrom; and he who communicates unworthily is condemned.

St. Basil: *The Morals,* 21, 1. (4th cent.)

For this Blood moulds in us a royal image, it does not suffer our nobleness of soul to waste away, moreover it refreshes the soul, and inspires it with great virtue. This Blood puts to flight the devils, summons angels, and the Lord of angels. This Blood poured forth washed the world, and made heaven open. They that partake of it are built up with heavenly virtues, and arrayed in the royal robes of Christ; yea they are rather clothed by the King Himself. And if you come clean, you come healthfully; but if polluted by an evil conscience, you come to your destruction, to pain and torment. For if those who defile the imperial purple are visited with the same punishment as those who tear it, it is not unreasonable that those who receive Christ with an unclean heart should be beaten with the same stripes as those who pierced Him with nails.

St. John Chrysostom: *Homilies on St. John,* 46. (4th cent.)

We eat the Body of Christ that we may be able to be partakers of eternal life.

St. Ambrose: *Explanation of St. Luke,* 10, 49. (4th cent.)

This is the Bread of life; he, therefore, who eats life cannot die. For how can he die whose food is Life? How can he fail who has the Substance of Life?

St. Ambrose: *Explanation of Psalm 118,* 18, 28. (4th cent.)

If it is daily bread, why do you take it once a year, as the Greeks in the east are accustomed to do? Take daily what is to profit you daily. So live that you may deserve to receive it daily. He who does not deserve to receive it daily, does not deserve to receive it once a year.

St. Ambrose: *On the Sacraments,* 5, 4, 25. (4th cent.)

For are we not about to receive the Eucharist wherein we come to Christ Himself, and begin to reign with Him for ever? The Eucharist is our daily Bread. But let us so receive It as to be thereby refreshed, not in body merely but in mind. For the power which we know to be therein is the power of unity whereby we are brought into union with His Body and become His members. Let us be What we receive; for then It will be truly our daily bread.

St. Augustine: *Sermons,* 57. (5th cent.)

Draw nigh, and take the Body of the Lord,
And drink the holy Blood for you outpoured.
Saved by that Body, hallowed by that Blood,
Whereby refreshed, we render thanks to God.

Hymn *Sancti venite* from the Bangor Antiphonary (Irish). (Tr. J. Neale) (7th cent.)

His Flesh is eaten when the sacrament of His passion is received by the mouth unto cleansing, and is meditated upon by the heart unto imitation.

St. Bede the Venerable: *In Lucam,* 4. (8th cent.)

Let us draw near to it with an ardent desire, and with our hands held in the form of the Cross let us receive the Body of the Crucified One; and let us apply our eyes and lips and brows and partake of the Divine Coal, in order that the fire of the longing that is in us, with the additional heat derived from the Coal, may utterly consume our sins and illumine our hearts, and that we may be inflamed and deified by participation in the divine Fire (cf. Isa. 6, 6).

St. John of Damascus: *Exposition of the Orthodox Faith,* 4, 13. (8th cent.)

Let not the communion of Thy holy mysteries be unto my judgment, nor unto my condemnation, but unto the healing of my body and soul.

Byzantine Euchologion, Prayer before Communion. (ca. 8th cent.)

Behold I approach the divine communion!

My Creator, consume me not in the partaking of it;

For Thou art a consuming fire to the unworthy:

Purify me now from every stain.

Byzantine Euchologion, Prayer of St. Simeon before Communion. (ca. 8th cent.?)

May Thy holy Body, O Lord Jesus Christ our God, be unto me for eternal life, and Thy precious Blood for the remission of sins; and may this Eucharist be unto my joy, health and gladness. And at Thy terrible second-coming grant that I, a sinner, may stand at the right hand of Thy glory, through the prayers of Thy most pure Mother and of all the saints. Amen.

Byzantine Euchologion, Prayer after Communion. (ca. 8th cent.?)

O Thou holy Bread, Thou living Bread, Thou pure Bread, that, coming down from heaven, dost give life to the world, enter into my heart and wash away every stain both of flesh and of spirit. Choose my heart for Thy dwelling-place; heal me and cleanse me within and without; be Thou my sure defense; be Thou to me an abiding help for soul and body; scatter the crafty enemies that lie in wait to ruin me; may they flee from the dread presence of Thy majesty.

Roman Missal, Prayer *Summe Sacerdos* before Mass. (11th cent.)

O sweetest Lord Jesus Christ, I implore Thee, pierce the very marrow of my soul with the delightful, health-giving dart of Thy love, with true, tranquil, holy, apostolic charity, so that my whole soul may ever languish and faint for love of Thee and for desire of Thee alone.

Roman Missal, Prayer *Transfige Dulcissime Domine* of St. Bonaventure after Mass. (13th cent.)

Almighty and everlasting God, look down in mercy upon me, Thy servant, who now again draws near to the most holy sacrament of Thy only-begotten Son, our Lord Jesus Christ. I approach as one who is sick, to the Physician of life; as one unclean, to the Fountain of mercy; as one blind, to the Light of eternal brightness; as one poor and needy, to the Lord of heaven and earth.

Roman Missal, Prayer *Omnipotens Sempiterne Deus Ecce Accedo* of St. Thomas Aquinas before Mass. (13th cent.)

I give thanks to Thee, O Lord most holy, Father almighty, eternal God, that Thou hast vouchsafed, for no merit of my own, but out of Thy pure mercy, to appease the hunger of my soul with the precious Body and Blood of Thy Son, our Lord Jesus Christ. Humbly I implore Thee, let not this holy communion be to me an increase of guilt unto my punishment, but an availing plea for pardon and salvation.

Roman Missal, Prayer *Gratias tibi ago Domine* of St. Thomas Aquinas after Mass. (13th cent.)

If anybody knows from experience that daily Communion increases fervor without lessening reverence, then let him go every day. But if anybody finds that reverence is lessened and devotion not much increased, then let him sometime abstain, so as to draw nigh afterwards with better dispositions.

St. Thomas Aquinas: *Commentary on the Sentences*, 4, 12, 3, 1. (13th cent.)

While in a deep astonishment immersed
  My happy soul was tasting of that Food
  Which, itself sating, of itself makes thirst.

Dante: *Purgatorio, Canto* 31. (Tr. L. Binyon) (14th cent.)

If all the world should receive in communion the light and heat of this Sun, the Word, My only-begotten Son, would not be separated from Me—the true Sun, His eternal Father—because in His mystical body, the holy Church, He is administered to whoever will receive Him. He remains wholly with Me, and yet you have Him, whole God and whole Man, as I told thee, in the metaphor of the light, that, if all the world came to take light from it, each would have it entire, and yet it would remain whole.

St. Catherine of Siena: *The Dialogue.* (14th cent.)

What other nation is there so honored as the Christian people? Or what creature under heaven so beloved as a devout soul, to whom God cometh, that He may feed her with His glorious flesh? O unspeakable grace! O wonderful condescension! O infinite love, singularly bestowed upon man!

Thomas a Kempis: *The Imitation of Christ,* 4, 13. (15th cent.)

If any one denieth that all and each of Christ's faithful of both sexes are bound, when they have attained to years of discretion, to communicate every year at least at Easter, in accordance with the precept of holy mother Church; let him be anathema.

Council of Trent, Session 13, Canon 9. (Oct. 11, 1551)

If any one saith that by the precept of God or by necessity of salvation all and each of the faithful of Christ ought to receive both species of the most holy sacrament of the eucharist; let him be anathema.

Council of Trent, Session 21, Canon 1. (July 16, 1562)

If any one saith that the holy Catholic Church was not induced by just causes and reasons to communicate under the species of bread only, laymen and also clerics when not celebrating; let him be anathema.

Council of Trent, Session 21, Canon 2. (July 16, 1562)

If any one denieth that Christ whole and entire, the Fountain and Author of all graces, is received under the one species of bread, because, as some falsely assert, He is not received according to the institution of Christ Himself under both species; let him be anathema.

Council of Trent, Session 21, Canon 3. (July 16, 1562)

If any one saith that the communion of the eucharist is necessary for little children before they have arrived at years of discretion; let him be anathema.

Council of Trent, Session 21, Canon 4. (July 16, 1562)

O what could my Jesus do more,
    Or what greater blessing impart,
O silence, my soul, and adore,
    And press Him still near to thy heart.

Anonymous: *Holy Communion.* (In Caswall's *Lyra Catholica*) (19th cent.)

What happiness can equal mine?
    I've found the object of my love—
My Jesus dear—my King divine,
    Is come to me from heaven above!

.   .   .   .

I am my love's, and He is mine;
    In me He dwells; in Him I live;
What greater gifts could love combine?
    What greater could e'en heaven
        give?
O sacred banquet, heavenly feast!
    O overflowing source of grace!
Where God the food, and man the
        guest,
    Meet and unite in sweet embrace!

W. Young: *After Communion.* (19th cent.)

Jesus, gentlest Savior,
    God of might and power,
Thou Thyself art dwelling
    In us at this hour.
Nature cannot hold Thee,
    Heaven is all too strait
For Thine endless glory
    And Thy royal state.

F. Faber: *An Act of Thanksgiving.* (19th cent.)

Give us our daily Bread,
    O God, the Bread of strength;
For we have learnt to know
    How weak we are at length:

As children we are weak,
    As children must be fed;
Give us Thy grace, O Lord,
    To be our daily Bread.

    Adelaide A. Procter: *Our Daily Bread.*
(19th cent.)

Preserve, my Jesus, oh preserve
    My soul to everlasting life.
O, may this blest communion serve
    To aid my soul in passion's strife:
Oh, may Thy Body, may Thy Blood,
Be to my soul a saving food,
To fill it still with life and grace,
And every sinful stain efface.

    J. Beste: *Aspirations after Communion.*
(19th cent.)

I wish I were the little key
    That locks Love's Captive in,
And lets Him out to go and free
    A sinful heart from sin.

I wish I were the little bell
    That tinkles for the Host,
When God comes down each day to
    dwell
    With hearts He loves the most.
      . . . . . .

But, oh! my God, I wish the most
    That my poor heart may be
A home all holy for each Host
    That comes in love to me.

    A. Ryan: *A Child's Wish.* (19th cent.)

Palate, the hutch of tasty lust,
Desire not to be rinsed with wine:
The can must be so sweet, the crust
So fresh that come in fasts divine!

    G. M. Hopkins: *The Habit of Perfection.*
(19th cent.)

In every communion we are made flesh of
His flesh and bone of His bone; and if
our hearts are pure we are made also
heart of His heart, mind of His mind,
will of His will, spirit of His spirit. We
are not straitened in Him, but in ourselves. If our hearts were prepared as
they might and ought to be by contrition
and piety, the sacramental grace of even

one communion would suffice to sanctify
us in body, soul, and spirit.

    Card. Manning: *The Eternal Priesthood.*
(19th cent.)

I saw the throng, so deeply separate,
    Fed at one only board—
The devout people, moved, intent,
    elate,
    And the devout Lord.

O struck apart! not side from human
    side,
    But soul from human soul,
As each asunder absorbed the multi-
    plied,
    The ever unparted, whole.

    Alice Meynell: *A General Communion.*
(20th cent.)

Where God is not, there can be no communion with man, for the only reason by
which one perceives another's soul, or
understands that it is the soul of a man,
and has a likeness to one's own, is that
both are, in some measure, in God.

    R. H. Benson: *The History of Richard
Raynal Solitary.* (20th cent.)

Mother Mary, thee I see
Bringing Him, thy Babe, to me,
Thou dost say, with trusting smile:
Hold Him, dear, a little while.
Mother Mary, pity me,
For He struggles to be free!
My heart, my arms—He finds defiled:
I am unworthy of thy Child.
Mary, Mother, charity!
Bring thy Baby back to me!

    Caroline Giltinan: *Communion.* (20th
cent.)

There is a time wherein eternity
Takes rest upon the world; King
    Charity
Bowed to our fallen state, the God of
    grace
Made visible upon a human face.

    Leo Ward: *The Last Communion.* (20th
cent.)

The faithful should be urged to refresh themselves frequently with the eucharistic bread, even daily, according to the norms laid down in the decrees of the Apostolic See; and those who attend mass should not only communicate spiritually, but dispose themselves duly to receive the most holy eucharist sacramentally.

> Code of Canon Law, Canon 863. (20th cent.)

See also Blessed Sacrament; Eucharist; Mass

Communion of Saints

You must believe, therefore, that in this one Church you are gathered into the Communion of the Saints. You must know that this is the one Catholic Church established throughout the world, and with it you must remain in unshaken communion.

> Niceta of Remesiana: *De Symbolo,* 10. (5th cent.)

In that Mystical Body, thanks to the communion of saints, no good can be done, no virtue practiced by individual members, without its contributing something also to the salvation of all.

> Pope Pius XII: *Mystici Corporis.* (June 29, 1943)

Communism

So we, who are united in mind and soul, have no hesitation about sharing property. All is common among us—except our wives.

> Tertullian: *Apology,* 39, 11. (3rd cent.)

Communism is the Franciscan movement without the moderating balance of the Church.

> G. K. Chesterton: *The Thing.* (20th cent.)

Redistributions of property, jubilees, and agrarian laws occur at various intervals and in various forms; but that humanity inevitably passed through a communist stage seems as doubtful as the parallel proposition that humanity will inevitably return to it. It is chiefly interesting as evidence that the boldest plans for the future invoke the authority of the past; and that even a revolutionary seeks to satisfy himself that he is also a reactionary.

> G. K. Chesterton: *The Everlasting Man.* (20th cent.)

We have people who represent that all great historic motives were economic, and then have to howl at the top of their voices in order to induce the modern democracy to act on economic motives. The extreme Marxian politicians in England exhibit themselves as a small, heroic minority, trying vainly to induce the world to do what, according to their theory, the world always does.

> G. K. Chesterton: *Tremendous Trifles.* (20th cent.)

Communism is by its nature anti-religious. It considers religion as "the opiate of the people" because the principles of religion which speak of a life beyond the grave dissuade the proletariat from the dream of a soviet paradise which is of this world.

> Pope Pius XI: *Divini Redemptoris.* (March 19, 1937)

Communism is intrinsically wrong, and no one who would save Christian civilization may collaborate with it in any undertaking whatsoever. Those who permit themselves to be deceived into lending their aid towards the triumph of communism in their own country, will be the first to fall victims of their terror. And the greater the antiquity and grandeur of the Christian civilization in the regions where communism successfully penetrates, so much more devastating will be the hatred displayed by the godless.

> Pope Pius XI: *Divini Redemptoris.* (March 19, 1937)

The only way to rid the mind of a false idea is to replace it with a true idea. Communism must be criticized and exposed as a sham; it cannot be bludgeoned out of existence.

> Dom Aelred Graham: *Catholicism and the World Today.* (20th cent.)

The charge that twentieth-century Christianity is disturbed by a bad conscience is not without point. We are compelled to the sad conclusion that if professing Christians had always been ready to live up to the gospel, there would have been no room for the appearance of Marxian communism. The lesson of our deficiency is being dearly bought.

> Dom Aelred Graham: *Catholicism and the World Today.* (20th cent.)

There is no greater refutation of communism in the world than a mother.

> Bishop Sheen: *Life is Worth Living.* (20th cent.)

Company

> We went with the ten demons: ah, hideous company! but, 'In church with saints, and with guzzlers in the tavern.'
>
> Dante: *Inferno, Canto 22.* (14th cent.)

If I were to give advice, I would say to parents that they ought to be very careful whom they allow to mix with their children when young; for much mischief thence ensues, and our natural inclinations are unto evil rather than unto good.

> St. Teresa of Jesus: *Autobiography,* 2. (16th cent.)

Frequent not the company of immodest persons, especially if they be also impudent as is generally the case.

> St. Francis de Sales: *Introduction to the Devout Life,* 13. (17th cent.)

Comparison

Comparisons are odious.

> John Fortescue: *De laudibus legum Angliae.* (15th cent.)

Do not compare one person with another: it is a hateful thing to do.

> St. Teresa of Jesus: *Maxims.* (16th cent.)

Compassion

Although he that grieves with the grief-stricken is to be commended for his work of charity, yet the man who is fraternally compassionate would prefer to find nothing in others to need his compassion. . . . There is a kind of compassionate sorrow that is good, but there is no kind that we should rejoice to feel.

> St. Augustine: *Confessions,* 3, 2. (5th cent.)

For just as pure truth is seen only with a pure heart, so a brother's misery is truly felt with a miserable heart. But in order to have a miserable heart because of another's misery, you must first know your own; so that you may find your neighbor's mind in your own and know from yourself how to help him, by the example of our Savior, Who willed His passion in order to learn compassion; His misery, to learn commiseration.

> St. Bernard: *The Steps of Humility,* 3. (12th cent.)

Compensation

> If in one point a person be aggrieved, Then in another he shall be relieved.
>
> Chaucer: *The Reeve's Tale.* (Proverb) (14th cent.)

Competition

When competition ceases, effort ceases. Human nature is human nature, after all.

> R. H. Benson: *The Dawn of All.* (20th cent.)

It would be rash for a little shopkeeper of no particular ability to compete with Rothschild.

> R. H. Benson: *The Light Invisible.* (20th cent.)

All competition is in its nature only a furious plagiarism.

> G. K. Chesterton: *Charles Dickens.* (20th cent.)

Free competition, though within its limits it is productive of good results, cannot be the ruling principle of the economic world. It is necessary that economic affairs be brought once more into subjection to a true and effective guiding principle.

> Pope Pius XI: *Quadragesimo anno.* (May 15, 1931)

Complacency

Complacency is the one obstacle to progress—in finance, in art, in intellect, and in the things of the spirit.

> R. H. Benson: *Christ in the Church.* (20th cent.)

Just as in social things the essential bourgeois is one who, being tolerably well off, is completely complacent with his position, so in matter of mind *How hardly shall they who trust in riches,* says our Lord, *enter into the kingdom of heaven.*

> R. H. Benson: *Christ in the Church.* (20th cent.)

Complaint

He that complains or murmurs is not perfect, nor is he even a good Christian.

> St. John of the Cross: *Spiritual Sentences and Maxims.* (16th cent.)

Compliment

There is an Irish way of paying compliments as though they were irresistible truths which makes what otherwise would be an impertinence, delightful.

> Katharine T. Hinkson: *A Red, Red Rose.* (20th cent.)

Compline

Before the ending of the day,
Creator of the world we pray

That with Thy wonted favor Thou
Wouldst be our guard and keeper now.

From all ill dreams defend our eyes,
From nightly fears and fantasies;
Tread under foot our ghostly foe,
That no pollution we may know.

> Roman Breviary, Hymn *Te lucis ante terminum* for Compline. (Tr. Neale) (Ambrosian, 7th cent.)

Comrade

Christ, by Thine own darkened hour,
Live within me, heart and brain—
Let my hands slip not the rein!

Ah, how long ago it is
Since a comrade went with me!
Now a moment let me see

Thyself, lonely in the dark,
Perfect, without wound or mark!

> Padraic Colum: *Christ the Comrade.* (20th cent.)

Conceit

Of all speculations the market holds
    forth,
  The best that I know, for the lover
    of pelf,
Is to buy Marcus up at the price he is
    worth,
  And then sell him at that which he
    sets on himself.

> Thomas Moore: *A Speculation.* (19th cent.)

Conclusion

There is a great difference between a conclusion in the abstract and a conclusion in the concrete. A conclusion may be modified in fact by a conclusion from some opposite principle.

> Card. Newman: *Apologia pro Vita Sua.* (19th cent.)

One man, after a glance at a fragment of bone, will reconstruct Hercules; another, after the entire skeleton stands

before him, will even then question
whether it is Hercules at all.

> R. H. Benson: *An Average Man.* (20th
> cent.)

Concord

Concord is a harmonious movement of
several wills.

> Dante: *Monarchy*, 1. (14th cent.)

Concreteness

The unimaginative need concrete images.
There must be some channel for their
aspirations to flow through.

> R. H. Benson: *Lord of the World.* (20th
> cent.)

Concubinage

No Christian may marry his deceased
wife's sister, nor besides his wife have a
concubine.

> Council of Rome, Can. 9. (402)

So, concubines taken for a time, if they
have intercourse for the sake of children, do not justify their concubinage.

> St. Augustine: *The Good of Marriage*, 14.
> (5th cent.)

It is a grievous sin for married men to
have concubines; but it is a most grievous sin, and one committed in special
contempt of this great sacrament [of
matrimony], for married men also to
live in this state of damnation, and to
have the audacity at times to maintain
and keep them at their own homes even
with their own wives.

> Decree of the Council of Trent, Session,
> Chap. 8. (Nov. 11, 1563)

Condemnation

We ought not to condemn anyone, even
if his accusers be many, before making
a careful study of his case in his presence.

> St. Basil: *The Morals*, 54, 4. (4th cent.)

Confession

It is better for a man to confess his sins
than to harden his heart.

> Pope St. Clement I: *Letter to the
> Corinthians*, 51, 3. (1st cent.)

You shall confess your offences in
church, and shall not come forward to
your prayer with a bad conscience.

> Teaching of the Twelve Apostles, 4. (2nd
> cent.)

The narrower, then, the sphere of action of this second and only remaining
repentance, the more laborious is its
probation; in order that it may not be
exhibited in the conscience alone, but
may likewise be carried out in some external act. This act, which is more usually
expressed and commonly spoken of under a Greek name, is *exomologesis*
(confession), whereby we confess our
sins to the Lord, not indeed as if He
were ignorant of them, but inasmuch as
by confession satisfaction is settled, of
confession repentance is born; by repentance God is appeased.

> Tertullian: *On Repentance*, 9. (3rd cent.)

Since you know that after the first bul-
warks of the Lord's baptism there still
remains for you in confession a second
reserve of aid against hell, why do you
desert your own salvation? Why are you
tardy to approach what you know heals
you? Even dumb irrational animals recognize in their time of need the medicines which have been divinely assigned
them. . . . Shall the sinner, knowing that
confession has been instituted by the
Lord for his restoration, pass that by
which restored the Babylonian king to
his realms?

> Tertullian: *On Repentance*, 12. (3rd cent.)

I entreat you, beloved brethren, that
each one should confess his own sin,
while he who has sinned is still in this
world, while his confession may be received, while the satisfaction and remission made by the priests are pleasing to
the Lord. Let us turn to the Lord with

our whole heart, and expressing our repentance for our sin with true grief, let us entreat God's mercy.

> St. Cyprian: *On the Lapsed,* 29. (3rd cent.)

Even when one confesses his sins, he ought to do so with praise of God; nor is a confession of sins a pious one unless it be made without despair, and with a prayer for God's mercy.

> St. Augustine: *In Ps. 105,* 2. (5th cent.)

O God, Who purifiest the hearts of those who confess their sins unto Thee, and absolvest the self-accusing conscience from all bonds of iniquity; give pardon to the guilty, and vouchsafe healing to the wounded, that they may receive remission of all sins, and persevere henceforth in sincere devotion, and sustain no loss of everlasting redemption.

> Gelasian Sacramentary, Collect for Reconciling Penitents. (5th to 7th cent.)

Daily in one's prayer, with tears and sighs, to confess one's past sins to God; to amend those sins for the future.

> St. Benedict: *Rule,* 4. (One of his "tools of good works") (6th cent.)

In truth, where confession is, there is worship and there is honour. If there are sins, they are washed away in confession; if there are good works, they are commended by confession. When you confess your faults, it is a sacrifice to God of a troubled spirit; when you confess the benefits of God, you offer to God the sacrifice of praise. Confession is a fair ornament of the soul, which both cleanses a sinner and makes the righteous more thoroughly cleansed. Without confession the righteous is deemed ungrateful, and the sinner accounted dead.

> St. Bernard: *Letters,* 116, 4. (12th cent.)

The minister to whom confession is made is the delegate of Christ, Who is the judge of the living and the dead.

> St. Thomas Aquinas: *Contra Gentes,* 4, 72. (13th cent.)

A threefold confession is commended by the Scriptures. One is the confession of matters of faith, and this is a proper act of faith, since it is referred to the end of faith, as stated above. Another is the confession of thanksgiving or praise, and this is an act of *latria,* for its purpose is to give outward honor to God, which is the end of *latria.* The third is the confession of sins, which is ordained to the blotting out of sins, which is the end of penance, to which virtue it therefore belongs.

> St. Thomas Aquinas: *Summa Theologica,* 2-2, 3, 1. (13th cent.)

Full sweetly heard he confession,
And pleasant was his absolution.

> Chaucer: *Canterbury Tales: Prologue.* (15th cent.)

Under seal of the confessional. (Sub sigillo confessionis.)

> Latin Phrase. (Medieval)

If any one denieth either that sacramental confession was instituted or is necessary to salvation of divine right; or saith that the manner of confessing secretly to a priest alone, which the Church hath ever observed from the beginning and doth observe, is alien from the institution and command of Christ, and is a human invention; let him be anathema.

> Council of Trent, Session 14, Canon 6. (Nov. 25, 1551)

If any one saith that in the sacrament of penance it is not necessary of divine right for the remission of sins to confess all and singular the mortal sins which after due and diligent previous meditation are remembered, even those mortal sins which are secret, and those which are opposed to the last two commandments of the decalogue, as also the circumstances which change the species of a sin; but saith that such confession is only useful to instruct and console the penitent, and that it was of old only observed in order to impose a canonical satisfaction; or saith that they who strive to confess all their sins wish to leave nothing to the divine mercy to pardon; or finally that it is not lawful to confess venial sins; let him be anathema.

Council of Trent, Session 14, Canon 7. (Nov. 25, 1551)

If any one saith that the confession of all sins such as it is observed in the Church is impossible, and is a human tradition to be abolished by the godly; or that all and each of the faithful of Christ of either sex are not obliged thereunto once a year, conformably to the constitution of the great council of Lateran, and that for this cause the faithful of Christ are to be persuaded not to confess during Lent; let him be anathema.

Council of Trent, Session 14, Canon 8. (Nov. 25, 1551)

Though he who confesses every year is not bound to make a general confession, yet by making one there is secured greater profit and merit on account of the penitent's greater sorrow for all the sins and wickednesses of his whole life.

St. Ignatius of Loyola: *Spiritual Exercises.* (16th cent.)

It is an abuse to confess any kind of sin, whether mortal or venial, without a will to be delivered from it, since confession was instituted for no other end.

St. Francis de Sales: *Introduction to the Devout Life,* 19. (17th cent.)

The Catholic religion does not compel indiscriminate confession of sins; it allows us to remain hidden from the sight of all other men, save one to whom she bids us reveal the depths of our heart, and show ourselves as we are. There is only this one man in the world, whom she bids us undeceive, and him she binds to inviolable secrecy, so that this knowledge remains with him as if it were not.

Can anything be imagined more charitable, more tender?

Pascal: *Pensées.* (17th cent.)

Let the priest remember that in hearing confessions he assumes the role of a judge and a doctor and that he has been appointed by God to be a minister of divine justice as well as of mercy for the purpose of promoting the divine honor and the salvation of souls. Let him be careful never to ask for the name of the penitent, let him not detain him with curious and useless questions, especially concerning the sixth commandment, and let him be particularly careful not to ask the young imprudently about matters of which they are ignorant.

Code of Canon Law, Canon 888. (20th cent.)

The seal of the confessional is inviolable; let the confessor therefore take diligent care never to betray the sinner by word or sign or in any other way or for any reason. Interpreters are also bound by the obligation of maintaining the seal of the confessional and all others who may in any way have gained knowledge of a confession.

Code of Canon Law, Canon 889. (20th cent.)

Any one who has committed mortal sins after baptism, which have not yet been directly forgiven by the keys of the Church, is obliged to confess all such sins which he can remember after a careful examination of his conscience, and explain in confession any circumstances surrounding them which may alter the nature of the sin.

Code of Canon Law, Canon 901. (20th cent.)

Every one of the faithful after he has reached the age of discretion, that is, the use of reason, is faithfully bound to confess all his sins at least once a year.

Code of Canon Law, Canon 906. (20th cent.)

The precept of confessing sins is not satisfied by one who makes a sacrilegious or wilfully invalid confession.

Code of Canon Law, Canon 907. (20th cent.)

See also Mass: Prayers and Formulas; Penance; Sin, Remission of

Confessor of the Faith

Jesu, eternal Truth sublime,
Through endless years the same!
Thou crown of those who through all
      time
Confess Thy holy name.

Roman Breviary, Feasts of Confessors, Hymn *Jesu corona celsior* at Lauds. (Tr. E. Caswall) (Ambrosian, 6th cent.)

This confessor of the Lord Whose tri-
      umph
Now all the faithful celebrate, with
      gladness,
Erst on this feast day merited to enter
Into His glory.

Saintly and prudent, modest in be-
      havior,
Peaceful and sober, chaste was He, and
      lowly,
While that life's vigor, coursing
      through His members,
Quickened His being.

Roman Breviary, Feasts of Confessors, Hymn *Iste confessor Domini colentes* at Vespers and Matins. (Tr. from the Hymner) (Author unknown, 8th cent.)

Confessor

See Confession; Penance; Sin, Remission of

Confidence

See Trust

Confirmation

The bishop . . . after pouring oil and laying his hand on his head shall say: I anoint thee with holy oil in God the Father Almighty and Christ Jesus and the Holy Ghost. And sealing him on the forehead, he shall give him the kiss of peace and say: The Lord be with you. And he who has been sealed shall say: And with thy spirit.

St. Hippolytus: *The Apostolic Tradition,* 22. (3rd cent.)

Now as to the anointing of neophytes, it is clear that this cannot be done by any save the bishop. For even if the presbyters are priests of the second order, they still do not possess the plenitude of priestly office. Not only the custom of the Church shows that only the fulness of the priesthood can confirm, or can impart the sacred Paraclete, but even that passage of the Acts of the Apostles (8, 14-18) which asserts that Peter and John were sent to bestow the Holy Ghost on those already baptized.

Pope St. Innocent I: *Letter to Decentius, Bishop of Gubbio.* (416)

Almighty and everlasting God Who hast vouchsafed to regenerate these Thy servants by water and the Holy Ghost, and hast given unto them forgiveness of all their sins: send forth upon them Thy sevenfold Spirit, the Holy Paraclete from heaven. ℟ Amen. The Spirit of wisdom and understanding. ℟ Amen. The Spirit of counsel and fortitude. ℟ Amen. The Spirit of knowledge and godliness. ℟ Amen. Fill them with the Spirit of Thy fear and sign them with the sign of the cross in mercy unto life eternal, through Christ our Lord.

Roman Pontifical, Prayer Accompanying the Laying on of Hands. (Gelasian, 5th to 7th cent.)

The seal of the gift of the Holy Spirit. Amen.

Byzantine Euchologion, Formula at the Anointing. (5th to 8th cent.)

Thou art blessed, O Lord almighty, source of good, sun of justice, Who hast caused the light of salvation to shine on those who were in darkness by the appearance of Thy only Son and our God; Who hast granted us in spite of our unworthiness a blessed purification in the holy water, and a divine sanctification in the life-giving unction; Who hast now once again deigned to regenerate Thy servant who has just been enlightened by the water and the Spirit, and hast granted unto him the remission of his sins, voluntary and involuntary; do Thou, O Lord, universal and all-merciful King, grant him also the seal of the gift of Thy holy, all-powerful and adorable Spirit and the communion of the holy body and the precious blood of Thy Christ. Preserve him in Thy sanctification, strengthen him in the true faith, deliver him from the evil one and all his works, and preserve his soul in purity and justice by a holy fear, that, being pleasing to Thee in every deed and every word, he may become a son and heir of Thy kingdom.

> Byzantine Euchologion, Confirmation Prayer. (5th to 8th cent.)

For just as the remission of sins is granted through baptism, so the sanctification of the spirit is realized through unction. . . . While applied to the body, it is beneficial to the soul. . . . Hands are imposed, that the advocacy of the Holy Spirit may be brought down through benediction. For the Paraclete then willingly descends from the Father, when bodies have been made clean and blessed.

> St. Isidore: *Etymologies,* 6, 19.
> (Confirmation was conferred along with baptism in the Spanish church.) (7th cent.)

N., I sign thee with the sign of the cross, and I confirm thee with the chrism of salvation, in the name of the Father, and of the Son, and of the Holy Ghost.

> Roman Pontifical, Formula at the Anointing. (Originally Gelasian; present form ca. 9th cent.)

O God, Who didst give to Thine apostles the Holy Spirit, and through them and their successors didst will Him to be given to the rest of the faithful, look mercifully upon our humble service and grant to those whose foreheads we have anointed with holy chrism and signed with the sign of the holy cross, that the same Holy Spirit may come down upon them and by His gracious indwelling fashion their hearts to be a temple of His glory, Who with the Father, and the same Spirit, livest and reignest, God world without end. May the Lord give you blessing out of Sion, that you may see the good of Jerusalem all the days of your life and may inherit life eternal. Amen.

> Roman Pontifical, Blessing of Those Confirmed. (ca. 9th cent.)

The sacrament which gives strength to those who are reborn by baptism is for those who would fight for Christ . . . those who are confirmed are signed with the Cross of Christ. . . . They are sealed with a blend of oil and balsam, called chrism—oil, to symbolize the power of the Holy Ghost . . . balsam, to symbolize the good odor of those who profess Christ while mixing in the world. We are enrolled by bishops, who are like the leaders in Christ's army: the imposition of hands reminds us that virtue and strength come from Christ.

> St. Thomas Aquinas: *Contra Gentes,* 4, 60. (13th cent.)

If any one saith that the confirmation of those who have been baptized is an idle ceremony and not rather a true and proper sacrament; or that of old it was nothing more than a kind of catechism, whereby they who were near adolescence gave an account of their faith in the face of the Church; let him be anathema.

> Council of Trent, Session 7, Canon 1. (Mar. 3, 1547)

If any one saith that the ordinary minister of holy confirmation is not the bishop alone, but any simple priest soever; let him be anathema.

> Council of Trent, Session 7, Canon 3. (Mar. 3, 1547)

My God, accept my heart this day,
    And make it always Thine,—
That I from Thee no more may stray,
    No more from Thee decline.
            . . . . . .
Anoint me with Thy heavenly grace,
    Adopt me for Thine own,—
That I may see Thy glorious face,
    And worship at Thy throne!

> M. Bridges: *Hymn for Confirmation.* (19th cent.)

Signed with the Cross that Jesus bore,
We kneel, and tremblingly adore
    Our King upon His throne.
The lights upon the altar shine
Around His majesty divine,
    Our God and Mary's Son.

Now, in that presence dread and sweet,
His own dear Spirit we entreat,
    Who sevenfold gifts hath shed
On us, who fall before Him now,
Bearing the Cross upon our brow
    On which our Master bled.

> H. Rawes: *Confirmation Hymn.* (19th cent.)

Confirmation is the sacrament of the common priesthood of the laity.

> Gerald Vann: *The Divine Pity.* (20th cent.)

Conflict

All human conflict is ultimately theological.

> Card. Manning. (Belloc: *Cruise of the Nona,* p. 54) (19th cent.)

When a soul reaches a certain pitch of conflict, it ceases to be absolutely logical; it is rather a very tender, raw thing, with all its fibres stretched to agony, shrinking from the lightest touch, desiring to be dealt with only by hands that have been pierced.

> R. H. Benson: *The Confessions of a Convert.* (20th cent.)

Conformity

We should not conform with human traditions to the extent of setting aside the command of God.

> St. Basil: *The Morals,* 12, 1. (4th cent.)

When in Rome, do as the Romans do.

> Author unknown. (The saying is probably based upon some advice given to St. Augustine by St. Ambrose: "When I am at Rome I fast on Saturdays; when I am at Milan I do not. Follow the custom of the Church where you happen to be.") (4th cent.)

We cannot help conforming ourselves to what we love.

> St. Francis de Sales: *Treatise on the Love of God,* 8, 1. (17th cent.)

Confusion

Set the world on six and seven.

> Chaucer: *Troilus and Criseyde.* (14th cent.)

We make the fashion of Christendom to seem all turned quite up so down.

> St. Thomas More. (16th cent.)

Conqueror

I came, I saw, God conquered.

> John III Sobieski: Message to the pope after the defeat of the Turks at Vienna. (17th cent.)

Conquest

But even as Alexander when he knew
    His father's conquests wept, lest he
        should leave
No kingdom unto him for to subdue,
    So shall thy mother thee of praise
        bereave.
        So many hearts already she hath
            slain,
        As few behind to conquer shall
            remain.

> Henry Constable: *Of the Nativity of the Lady Rich's Daughter.* (16th cent.)

Conquest pursues where courage leads the way.

> Sir Samuel Garth: *The Dispensary*, 4. (17th cent.)

They'll wond'ring ask, how hands so vile
Could conquer hearts so brave.

> Thomas Moore: *Weep on, Weep on.* (19th cent.)

It is one thing to make conquests, another to consolidate an empire.

> Card. Newman: *Grammar of Assent*, 10. (19th cent.)

Conscience

A tranquil conscience and assured innocence produce a blessed life.

> St. Ambrose: *On the Duties of the Clergy*, 2, 1. (4th cent.)

Conscience and reputation are two things. Conscience is due to yourself, reputation to your neighbor.

> St. Augustine. (4th cent.)

Purify our consciences, O Lord, we beseech Thee, by Thy daily visitation; that when Thy Son our Lord cometh, He may find in us a mansion prepared for Himself.

> Roman Missal, Collect before Mass. (Gelasian, 5th to 7th cent.)

The testimony of a man's conscience is his only perfect and complete excuse.

> St. Bernard: *On Consideration*, 2, 1. (12th cent.)

A good conscience is a mine of wealth. And in truth what greater riches can there be, what thing more sweet than a good conscience?

> St. Bernard: *Letters*, 108, 3. (12th cent.)

Whatever is done against conscience, leads to perdition. (Quidquid fit contra conscientiam, aedificat ad gehennam.)

> Fourth Lateran Council. (1215)

By following a right conscience you not only do not incur sin but are also immune from sin, whatever superiors may say to the contrary.

> St. Thomas Aquinas: *Disputations Concerning Truth*, 17, 5. (13th cent.)

Therefore conscience is more to be obeyed than authority imposed from outside. For conscience obliges in virtue of divine command, whether written down in a code or instilled by natural law. To weigh conscience in the scales against obedience to legal authority is to compare the weight of divine and of human decrees. The first obliges more than the second, and sometimes against the second.

> St. Thomas Aquinas: *Disputations Concerning Truth*, 17, 5. (13th cent.)

Saving that conscience holdeth me secure,
  That good companion which doth fortify
  With a strong breastplate one who knows him pure.

> Dante: *Inferno, Canto 28*. (Tr. Binyon) (14th cent.)

O honorable conscience, clear and chaste,
How small a fault stings thee to bitter smart!

> Dante: *Purgatorio, Canto 3*. (Tr. L. Binyon) (14th cent.)

So may grace quickly sift away the scum
  Upon your conscience, so that through it clear
  The stream of memory down-flowing may come.

> Dante: *Purgatorio, Canto 13*. (Tr. L. Binyon) (14th cent.)

There be two things that are necessary and needful, and that is good conscience and good report; that is to say, good conscience in thine own person inward, and good report for thy neighbor outward.

> Chaucer: *Melibeus*, 52. (14th cent.)

No man securely rejoiceth unless he hath within him the testimony of a good conscience.

Thomas a Kempis: *The Imitation of Christ,* 1, 20. (15th cent.)

The testimony of a good conscience is the glory of a good man; have a good conscience and thou shalt ever have gladness. A good conscience may bear right many things and rejoices among adversities.

Thomas a Kempis: *The Imitation of Christ,* 2, 6. (15th cent.)

My conscience is my crown,
 Contented thoughts my rest;
My heart is happy in itself;
 My bliss is in my breast.

Bl. Robert Southwell: *Content and Rich.* (16th cent.)

The voice of God in man! which without rest
Doth softly cry within a troubled breast;
To all temptations is that soul left free
That makes not to itself a curb of me.

Sir Edward Sherburne: *Conscience.* (17th cent.)

Conscience is the royalty and prerogative of every private man.

Dryden: *The Hind and the Panther, Pref.* (17th cent.)

Immortal pow'rs the term of conscience know,
But int'rest is her name with men below.

Dryden: *The Hind and the Panther,* 3. (17th cent.)

Let us beware of trifling with conscience. It is often said that second thoughts are best; so they are in matters of judgment, but not in matters of conscience. In matters of duty first thoughts are commonly best—they have more in them of the voice of God.

Card. Newman: *Historical Studies.* (Miscellanies, p. 26) (19th cent.)

The feeling of conscience (being, I repeat, a certain keen sensibility, pleasant or painful,—self-approval and hope, or compunction and fear,—attendant on certain of our actions, which in consequence we call right or wrong) is twofold:—it is a moral sense, and a sense of duty; a judgment of the reason and a magisterial dictate.

Card. Newman: *Grammar of Assent,* 5. (19th cent.)

Conscience does not repose on itself, but vaguely reaches forward to something beyond self, and dimly discerns a sanction higher than self for its decisions, as is evidenced in that keen sense of obligation and responsibility which informs them.

Card. Newman: *Grammar of Assent,* 5. (19th cent.)

Conscience is nearer to me than any other means of knowledge.

Card. Newman: *Grammar of Assent,* 10. (19th cent.)

Certainly, I have always contended that obedience even to an erring conscience was the way to gain light, and that it mattered not where a man began, so that he began on what came to hand, and in faith; and that anything might become a divine method of truth; that to the pure all things are pure, and have a self-correcting virtue and a power of germinating.

Card. Newman: *Apologia pro Vita Sua,* 4. (19th cent.)

Conscience is the aboriginal vicar of Christ, a prophet in its informations, a monarch in its peremptoriness, a priest in its blessings and anathemas, and, even though the eternal priesthood throughout the Church could cease to be, in it the sacerdotal principle would remain and would have a sway.

Card. Newman: *Difficulties of Anglicans,* 2. (19th cent.)

Conscience has rights because it has duties.

> Card. Newman: *Difficulties of Anglicans,* 2. (19th cent.)

If I am obliged to bring religion into after-dinner toasts (which indeed does not seem quite the thing), I shall drink, —to the pope, if you please,—still, to conscience first, and to the pope afterwards.

> Card. Newman: *Letter to the Duke of Norfolk.* (19th cent.)

The Reformation was a great movement against the freedom of conscience—an effort to subject it to a new authority, the arbitrary initiative of a prince who might differ in religion from all his subjects.

> Lord Acton: *Döllinger on the Temporal Power.* (19th cent.)

Personal conscience is the ultimate asylum of the soul, in presence of civil or of ecclesiastical authority. Both Americanism and Catholicism bow to the sway of personal conscience.

> Archb. Ireland: *Catholicism and Americanism.* (Milwaukee, Aug. 11, 1913)

Conscience illuminated by the presence of Jesus Christ in the heart must be the guide of every man.

> R. H. Benson: *Christ in the Church.* (20th cent.)

There is nothing commoner than for people to try and kill their own conscience.

> R. H. Benson: *The Conventionalists.* (20th cent.)

You must not scold me, you must leave me my conscience.

> R. H. Benson: *The King's Achievement.* (20th cent.)

Consent

> He who is silent is supposed to consent.
> Legal maxim. (Corpus Juris Canonici, Reg. Juris 43 in Sexto.) (Medieval)

Conservatism

Be not the first by whom the new are tried,
Nor yet the last to lay the old aside.

> Pope: *An Essay on Criticism,* 2. (18th cent.)

Considerateness

We may be excused for not always being bright, but we are not excused for not being always gracious, yielding and considerate.

> St. Francis de Sales: *Treatise on the Love of God,* 11, 21. (17th cent.)

Consolation

We are easily consoled because we are easily distressed.

> Pascal: *Pensées.* (17th cent.)

When I sink down in gloom or fear,
  Hope blighted or delay'd,
Thy whisper, Lord, my heart shall cheer,
  ''Tis I; be not afraid!'

Or, startled at some sudden blow,
  If fretful thoughts I feel,
'Fear not, it is but I!' shall flow,
  As balm my wound to heal.

> Card. Newman: *Consolation.* (19th cent.)

Constancy

O live!, so rare a love! live! and in thee
The too frail life of female constancy.

> R. Crashaw: *Alexias, First Elegy.* (17th cent.)

As still to the star of its worship, though clouded,
  The needle points faithfully o'er the dim sea,
So dark when I roam in this wintry world shrouded,
  The hope of my spirit turns trembling to thee.

> Thomas Moore: *The Heart's Prayer.* (19th cent.)

I tempted all his servitors, but to find
My own betrayal in their constancy,
In faith to him their fickleness to me,
    Their traitorous trueness, and their
      loyal deceit.

> F. Thompson: *The Hound of Heaven.*
> (19th cent.)

Constantine the Great

O happy people, O glorious Ausonia! if
only the one who weakened the Empire
had never been born or had never been
misled by his own pious intentions.

> Dante: *Monarchy,* 2. (Reference is to false
> Donation of Constantine of 8th cent., which
> D. considered ill-advised and invalid,
> although authentic) (14th cent.)

Ah, Constantine, what evil fruit did
    bear
    Not thy conversion, but that dowry
    broad
    Thou on the first rich Father didst
    confer!

> Dante: *Inferno, Canto 19.* (Tr. Binyon)
> (14th cent.)

Contemplation

The soul in contemplation will arrive at
that most high and secret reward for
sake of which it has so labored; and in
which are such joys, such a full enjoyment of the highest and truest Good,
such a breath of serenity and eternity, as
are indescribable.

> St. Augustine: *On the Greatness of the
> Soul,* 76. (4th cent.)

No one who looks on God lives with that
life with which we mortals live in the
bodily senses; but unless he be in some
sort dead to this life, whether as having
wholly departed from the body, or as
rapt away from the bodily senses, he is
not uplifted to that vision.

> St. Augustine: *De Genesi ad Litt.* 12, 27.
> (5th cent.)

The contemplation of God is promised
to us as the goal of all our acts and the
eternal consummation of all our joys.

> St. Augustine: *De Trinitate,* 1, 8. (5th
> cent.)

Do thou, in the intent practice of mystic
contemplation, leave behind the senses
and the operations of the intellect, and
all things that the senses or the intellect
can perceive, and all things which are
not and things which are, and strain upwards in unknowing, as far as may be,
towards the union with Him Who is
above all being and knowledge. For by
unceasing and absolute withdrawal from
thyself and all things in purity, abandoning all and set free from all, thou
wilt be borne up to the ray of the divine
Darkness that surpasseth all being.

> Pseudo-Dionysius: *Mystical Theology,* 1.
> (5th cent.)

Trinity, which exceedeth all being, deity,
and goodness! Thou that instructeth
Christians in Thy heavenly wisdom!
Guide us to that topmost height of mystic lore which exceedeth light and more
than exceedeth knowledge, where the
simple, absolute, and unchangeable mysteries of heavenly Truth lie hidden in the
dazzling obscurity of the secret silence,
outshining all brilliance with the inten-
sity of their darkness, and surcharging
our blinded intellects with the utterly
impalpable and invisible fairness of
glories which exceed all beauty!

> Pseudo-Dionysius: *Mystical Theology,* 1.
> (5th cent.)

When with marvellous efforts it strives
to rise up from corporeal things and
images, it is a great thing indeed if the
soul, thrusting aside the bodily form, be
brought to the knowledge of itself, so
as to think of itself without bodily figure,
and by thus thinking of itself, to prepare
a pathway to contemplate the substance
of eternity. In this way it exhibits itself to itself as a kind of ladder, whereby
in ascending from outward things it may

pass into itself, and from itself may tend unto its Maker.

> Pope St. Gregory I: *Morals,* 5, 61-62. (6th cent.)

The Divinity never imparts Himself as He is to those that contemplate Him while still in this life, but shows forth His brightness scantily to the blinking eyes of our mind.

> Pope St. Gregory I: *Morals,* 5, 66. (6th cent.)

In contemplation it is the Principle— namely, God—Which is sought.

> Pope St. Gregory I: *Morals,* 6, 28. (5th cent.)

The mind by the force of its contemplation is carried out of the flesh, while by the weight of its corruption it is still held in the flesh.

> Pope St. Gregory I: *Morals,* 10, 13. (6th cent.)

For it very often happens that the spirit already lifts the mind on high, yet the flesh assails it with pressing temptations; and when the soul is led forward to the contemplation of heavenly things, it is struck back by the images of unlawful practice being presented. For the sting of flesh suddenly wounds him, whom holy contemplation was bearing away beyond the flesh.

> Pope St. Gregory I: *Morals,* 10, 17. (6th cent.)

Merely to love things above is already to mount on high.

> Pope St. Gregory I: *Morals,* 15, 53. (6th cent.)

If we wish to contemplate things within, let us rest from outward engagements. The voice of God, in truth, is heard as if in dreams, when with minds at ease we rest from the bustle of this world, and the divine precepts are pondered by us in the deep silence of the mind. For when the mind is at rest from outward employments, the weight of the divine precepts is more fully discerned.

> Pope St. Gregory I: *Morals,* 23, 37. (6th cent.)

The greatness of contemplation can be given to none but them that love.

> Pope St. Gregory I: *Homily 2 on Ezechiel.* (6th cent.)

Contemplation may be defined as the soul's true unerring intuition, or as the unhesitating apprehension of truth. But consideration is thought earnestly directed to research, or the application of the mind to the search for truth; though in practice the two terms are indifferently used for one another.

> St. Bernard: *On Consideration,* 2, 2. (12th cent.)

The first point in contemplation is to marvel at God's majesty; the second, at His judgments; the third, at His benefits; the fourth, at His promises.

> St. Bernard: *On Consideration,* 5, 14. (12th cent.)

The soul slumbering in contemplation dreams God; for through a mirror and in an enigma, and not face to face, does it behold Him; and it warms with the love of something conjectured rather than seen, momentarily, as if in the flash of a passing spark, and touched scantily and barely.

> St. Bernard: *On the Canticle of Canticles,* 18, 6. (12th cent.)

The grace of contemplation is granted only in response to a longing and importunate desire: Nevertheless He will not present Himself, even in passing, to every soul; but only to that soul which is shown, by great devotion, vehement desire, and tender affection, to be His bride, and to be worthy that the Word in all His beauty should visit her as a Bridegroom.

> St. Bernard: *On the Canticle of Canticles,* 22, 3. (12th cent.)

The perfect soul desires to be rapt by contemplation to the chaste embraces of her Spouse.

> St. Bernard: *Sermones de. div.*, 87, 2. (12th cent.)

Contemplation is the soul's clear, free, and attentive dwelling upon the truth to be perceived; meditation is the outlook of the soul occupied in searching for the truth; thought is the soul's glance, ever prone to distraction.

> Richard of St. Victor: *De Contemplatione*, 1, 4. (12th cent.)

In contemplation the mind is not at pause but fully active.

> St. Thomas Aquinas: *Summa Theologica*, 1, 58, 1. (13th cent.)

Better to light up than merely to shine, to deliver to others contemplated truths than merely to contemplate.

> St. Thomas Aquinas: *Summa Theologica*, 2-2, 188, 6. (13th cent.)

It is possible to contemplate God not only outside us and within us, but also above us. Outside we contemplate Him through His vestige, within us through His image, and above us through the light which is sealed on our minds. This light is the light of eternal Truth, since our very mind is immediately formed by Truth Itself.

> St. Bonaventure: *The Ascent of the Mind to God*, 5. (13th cent.)

Show me a soul whose eyes are opened by grace to the contemplation of God, a soul detached and withdrawn from the love of the world so that it has obtained purity and poverty of spirit, rest, interior silence and peace of conscience, elevation of thought, solitude and seclusion of heart, and the wakeful sleep of the spouse; a soul that has ceased to find pleasure and joy in the world, which is captivated by heavenly delights, and which is always thirsting and sighing gently for the presence of God, and I do not hesitate to say that such a soul is consumed with love and enveloped in spiritual light, worthy to be called and to be the spouse of Christ.

> Walter Hilton: *Scale of Perfection*, 2, 41. (14th cent.)

Contemplation is nothing else but a secret, peaceful, and loving infusion of God, which, if admitted, will set the soul on fire with the Spirit of love.

> St. John of the Cross: *The Dark Night of the Soul*. (16th cent.)

Seek in reading and thou shalt find in meditation; knock in prayer and it shall be opened to thee in contemplation.

> St. John of the Cross: *Spiritual Sentences and Maxims*. (16th cent.)

The acts of contemplation are four: to seek after God, to find Him, to feel His sacred touch in the soul, and to be united with Him and to enjoy Him.

> Archb. Ullathorne: *Humility and Patience*. (19th cent.)

When rocks fly homeward and shadows fall,
When roses fold on the hay-yard wall,
When blind moths flutter by door and tree,
Then comes the quiet of Christ to me.

> Joseph Campbell: *When Rooks Fly Homeward*. (20th cent.)

We become contemplatives when God discovers Himself in us.

> Thomas Merton: *Seeds of Contemplation*. (20th cent.)

Contemplative prayer is a deep and simplified spiritual activity in which the mind and will are fused into one. They rest in a unified and simple concentration upon God, turned to Him and intent upon Him and absorbed in His own light, with a simple gaze which is perfect adoration because it silently tells God that we have left everything else and desire even to leave our own selves for His sake, and that He alone is important to us, He alone is our desire and our life, and nothing else can give us any joy.

Thomas Merton: *Seeds of Contemplation.* (20th cent.)

See also Active and Contemplative Life; Meditation; Prayer

Contemplative Life

He who would attain to the life of contemplation must ever be turning to his Creator for illumination of his mind.

Julianus Pomerius: *De Vita Contemplativa,* 2, 8. (5th cent.)

Whoever has already subdued the insolencies of the flesh, has this task left him, to discipline his mind by the exercises of holy working; and whosoever opens his mind in holy works, has over and above to extend it to the secret pursuits of inward contemplation.

Pope St. Gregory I: *Morals,* 6, 56. (6th cent.)

It is necessary that whoever eagerly prosecutes the exercises of contemplation, first question himself with particularity, how much he loves. For the force of love is an engine of the soul, which, while it draws it out of the world, lifts it on high.

Pope St. Gregory I: *Morals,* 6, 58. (6th cent.)

The contemplative life has its most desirable sweetness which uplifts the soul above itself, opens the way to heavenly things, and makes spiritual things plain to the eyes of the soul.

Pope St. Gregory I: *Hom. 14 in Ezechiel.* (5th cent.)

The contemplative life means keeping of charity towards God and our neighbor, and fixing all our desires on our Creator.

Pope St. Gregory I: *Morals,* 6, 18. (5th cent.)

Contemplative [philosophy] is the name given that in which, passing beyond the visible, we enjoy some contemplation of the divine and celestial, and behold them with the mind alone, since they are beyond the bodily gaze.

St. Isidore: *Etymologies,* 2, 24. (7th cent.)

In a dark night,
With anxious love inflamed,
O, happy lot!
Forth unobserved I went,
My house being now at rest.

. . . .

O, guiding night;
O, night more lovely than the dawn;
O, night that hast united
The lover with his beloved,
And changed her into her love.

St. John of the Cross: *The Dark Night of the Soul.* (16th cent.)

I live, yet no true life I know,
And, living thus expectantly,
I die because I do not die.
Since this new death-in-life I've known
Estrang'd from self my life has been,
For now I live a life unseen:
The Lord has claim'd me as His own.
My heart I gave Him for His throne,
Whereon He wrote indelibly:
'I die because I do not die.'

St. Teresa of Jesus: *Poems.* (Tr. E. A. Peers) (16th cent.)

The poet enters into himself in order to create. The contemplative enters into God in order to be created.

Thomas Merton: *Seeds of Contemplation.* (20th cent.)

How many there must be who have smothered the first sparks of contemplation by piling wood on the fire before it was well lit.

Thomas Merton: *Seeds of Contemplation.* (20th cent.)

See also Active and Contemplative Life; Prayer

Contempt

Over-great homeliness engendereth dispraising.

Chaucer: *Melibeus.* (14th cent.)

Contentment

O God, Who hast forbidden us to be anxious about the supplies of this life; grant, we beseech Thee, that we may devoutly follow after what belongeth to Thee, and that all things salutary may be granted to us.

Gelasian Sacramentary, Collect. (5th to 7th cent.)

Content thyself with thine estate;
  Neither wish death, nor fear his might.

Henry Howard, Earl of Surrey: *Martial's Quiet Life.* (16th cent.)

When all is done and said, in the end thus shall you find,
He most of all doth bathe in bliss that hath a quiet mind;
And, clear from worldly cares, to deem can be content
The sweetest time in all his life in thinking to be spent.

Thomas, Lord Vaux: *Content.* (16th cent.)

Happy the man whose wish and care
  A few paternal acres bound,
Content to breathe his native air
  In his own ground.
Whose herds with milk, whose fields with bread,
  Whose flocks supply him with attire,
Whose trees in Summer yield him shade;
  In Winter fire.

Pope: *Ode to Solitude.* (18th cent.)

No eye to watch and no tongue to wound us,
All earth forgot, and all heaven around us.

Thomas Moore: *Come O'er the Sea.* (19th cent.)

See also Happiness; Joy

Continence

He who is chaste in flesh should not be proud, for he should know that he owes the gift of continence to another.

Pope St. Clement I: *Letter to the Corinthians,* 38, 2. (1st cent.)

We have been taught by the Lord and God of salvation that continence is a means of attaining eternal life, a proof of the faith that is in us, a pledge of the glory of that body which will be ours when we put on the garb of immortality, and, finally, an obligation imposed upon us by the will of God.

Tertullian: *To His Wife,* 1, 7. (3rd cent.)

I thought that continence was a matter of our own strength, and I knew that I had not the strength: for in my utter foolishness I did not know the word of Your Scripture that none can be continent unless You give it.

St. Augustine: *Confessions,* 6, 11. (5th cent.)

By continence we are collected and bound up into unity within ourself, whereas we had been scattered abroad in multiplicity. Too little does any man love Thee, who loves some other thing together with Thee, loving it not on account of Thee, O Thou Love, Who art ever burning and never extinguished! O Charity, my God, enkindle me! Thou dost command continence: grant what Thou dost command and command what Thou wilt.

St. Augustine: *Confessions,* 10, 29. (5th cent.)

Great are those two gifts, wisdom and continence: wisdom, forsooth, whereby we are formed in the knowledge of God; continence whereby we are not conformed to this world.

St. Augustine: *On the Good of Widowhood,* 15, 2, 21. (5th cent.)

It is praiseworthy that even during the life of her husband, by his consent, a female vow continence unto Christ.

> St. Augustine: *On the Good of Widowhood*. (5th cent.)

Wherefore, let not those who have chosen to remain unmarried flee marriage as a pitfall of sin, but let them surmount it as a hill of inferior blessing, that they may come to rest on the mountain of the greater blessing of continence.

> St. Augustine: *On Holy Virginity*, 18. (5th cent.)

O God, Who didst subdue the flames of fire for the three young men, mercifully grant that we Thy servants may not be consumed by the flames of vice.

> Roman Missal, Collect for Ember Saturday in September. (Gelasian, 5th to 7th cent.)

Contradiction

Do I contradict myself? Very well, then! I contradict myself!

> Savonarola. (15th cent.)

Regard the providence of God in the contradictions which are offered to you, for God permits them in order to detach you from all things and to unite you to Himself.

> St. Francis de Sales: *Letters to Persons in Religion*, 5, 5. (17th cent.)

Contrast

Contrast and oddness come not from chance, not from flaws in the material, not from interference with the divine plan, not from our deserts, but from God's own purpose, Who wills to impart His perfections to creatures, as much as each can stand.

> St. Thomas Aquinas: *Contra Gentes*, 2, 45. (13th cent.)

Contrition

Most holy God, my very soul
  With grief sincere is mov'd,

Because I have offended Thee,
  Whom I should e'er have lov'd.
Forgive me, Father; I am now
  Resolved to sin no more,
And by Thy holy grace to shun
  What made me sin before.

> Act of Contrition from *Hymns for the Year*, 1867.

Have mercy Thou, most gracious God!
  And my remittance sign;
The more Thy mercy shall accord,
  The greater glory Thine.

Thou surely hast not said in vain:
  "More joy in heaven is made,
For the lost sheep that's found again,
  Than those which never stray'd."

> Anonymous: *Prayer of the Contrite Sinner*. (In Caswall's *Lyra Catholica*) (19th cent.)

O my God, I am sorry with my whole heart for all my sins, and I hate them, not only because by sinning I have deserved the punishments appointed by Thee, but especially because I have offended Thee, the Supreme Good, Who art worthy to be loved above all things. Therefore I firmly resolve with the help of Thy grace not to sin again, and carefully to avoid the immediate occasions of sin.

> Act of Contrition. (As printed in Catholic Catechism of Cardinal Gasparri, 1932. Similar formulas are to be found in all Catholic prayer books. Form is probably as old as the Council of Trent, or older.)

See also Confession; Penance; Repentance

Controversy

We should not engage in fruitless or controversial discussions.

> St. Basil: *The Morals*, 25. (4th cent.)

In every dialogue and discourse we must be able to say to those who take offense: "What do you complain of?"

> Pascal: *Pensées*. (17th cent.)

When men understand each other's meaning, they see, for the most part, that controversy is either superfluous or hopeless.

> Card. Newman: *Oxford University Sermons.* (19th cent.)

You discharge your olive-branch as if from a catapult.

> Card. Newman: *Letter to the Rev. E. B. Pusey on his Eirenicon.* (19th cent.)

It will be a pity if, when other religions are vocal, the Catholic will keep silent and appear before the nations as dead. It is only the dying who do not love the noise of action.

> Archb. Ireland: *Le Matin,* Paris, September 25, 1895. (With regard to Catholic participation in the Paris World's Fair of 1900)

There can never be any clear controversy in a sceptical age.

> G. K. Chesterton: *The Victorian Age in Literature.* (20th cent.)

It never occurs to the critic to do anything so simple as to compare what is Catholic with what is non-Catholic. The one thing that never seems to cross his mind, when he argues about what the Church is like, is the simple question of what the world would be like without it. That is what I mean by being too narrow to see the house called the Church against the background called the cosmos.

> G. K. Chesterton: *The Thing.* (20th cent.)

People who are fond of remarking with sapient confidence, "Controversy does no good," should search their syllogisms for undistributed middles. For this conclusion does not follow from the premise, "Some people are not affected by controversy."

> Arnold Lunn: *Now I See.* (20th cent.)

Nothing dies harder than a theological difference.

> R. A. Knox: *The Listener,* Nov. 29, 1951.

It is not angry vociferations of members of warring factions that we need worry about, for I sometimes think that this type could be happily irate over any cause. But it is the men and women who live the Church's ways and yet who cannot see past the dream into the actuality —it is they who need our prayers.

> Katherine Burton: *The Next Thing.* (20th cent.)

See also Apologetics

Convention

There is nothing more conventional than the convention of unconventionality.

> R. H. Benson: *An Average Man.* (20th cent.)

Conventional people who think they have no limitations do more harm than any in the world; there is nothing more limiting.

> R. H. Benson: *The Sentimentalists.* (20th cent.)

The world would soon explode unless there were conventions to hold it together.

> R. H. Benson: *An Average Man.* (20th cent.)

The conventional view ruins more lives than all fanaticism put together.

> R. H. Benson: *The Coward.* (20th cent.)

No one in the world can become wholly conventional before he is thirty years old.

> R. H. Benson: *An Average Man.* (20th cent.)

No one in England under the rank of a peeress can afford to be unconventional. The English-woman who tries to be, only gives up one set of conventions for another.

> Katharine T. Hinkson: *Honey, My Honey.* (20th cent.)

Mr. Wells once held that the upper classes and the lower classes would be so much differentiated in the future that one class would eat the other. Certainly no paradoxical charlatan who had once found arguments for so startling a view would ever have deserted it except for something yet more startling. Mr. Wells has deserted it in favor of the blameless belief that both classes will be ultimately subordinated or assimilated to a sort of scientific middle class, a class of engineers. . . . He has come to the most dreadful conclusion a literary man can come to, the conclusion that the ordinary view is the right one. It is only the last and wildest kind of courage that can stand on a tower before ten thousand people and tell them that twice two is four.

> G. K. Chesterton: *Heretics.* (20th cent.)

Conversation

Be at peace regarding what is said or done in conversations: for if good, you have something to praise God for, and if bad, something in which to serve God by turning your heart away from it.

> St. Francis de Sales: *Letters to Persons in the World,* 2, 11. (17th cent.)

If you want to shine as a diner-out, the best way is to know something which others do not know, and not to know many things which everybody knows. This takes much less reading, and is doubly effective, inasmuch as it makes you a really good, that is, an interested listener, as well as a talker.

> Coventry Patmore: *Principle in Art.* (19th cent.)

Conversion

Almighty and everlasting God, convert us with our whole souls to Thyself; that as Thou dost grant such good gifts to the undeserving, Thou mayest bestow yet greater on the devout.

> Leonine Sacramentary, Collect. (ca. 5th cent.)

There are in truth three states of the converted: the beginning, the middle, and the perfection. In the beginning they experience the charms of sweetness, in the middle the contests of temptation, and in the end the plenitude of perfection.

> Pope St. Gregory I: *Morals,* 24, 28. (6th cent.)

Almighty and everlasting God, by Whom that begins to be which was not, and that which lay hid is made visible, cleanse away the folly of our heart, and purify us from our secret vices; that we may be able to serve Thee, O Lord, with a pure mind.

> Gelasian Sacramentary, Collect. (5th to 7th cent.)

First let a little love find entrance into their hearts, and the rest will follow.

> Rule of St. Philip Neri for dealing with sinners. (16th cent.)

'Tis not the work of force but skill
To find the way into man's will.
'Tis love alone can hearts unlock,
Who knows the word, he needs not knock.

> Richard Crashaw: *Non Vi.* (17th cent.)

What heav'n-entreated heart is this?
Stands trembling at the gate of bliss;
Holds fast the door, yet dares not venture
Fairly to open it, and enter.
Whose definition is a doubt
Twixt life and death, twixt in and out.

> Richard Crashaw: *To The Countess of Denby.* (17th cent.)

O dart of love! arrow of light!
O happy you, if it hit right,
It must not fall in vain, it must
Not mark the dry regardless dust.
Fair one, it is your fate; and brings
Eternal worlds upon its wings.
Meet it with wide-spread arms; and see
Its seat your soul's just center be.

> Richard Crashaw: *To the Countess of Denby.* (17th cent.)

All things swear friends to Fair and
  Good,
Yea, suitors; man alone is woo'd,
Tediously woo'd, and hardly won:
Only not slow to be undone.
As if the bargain had been driven
So hardly betwixt earth and heaven.

Richard Crashaw: *To the Countess of
Denby.* (17th cent.)

Men often mistake their imagination for
the promptings of their heart, and believe they are converted the moment they
think of conversion.

Pascal: *Pensées.* (17th cent.)

My thoughtless youth was wing'd with
  vain desires,
My manhood, long misled by wandring
  fires,
Follow'd false lights; and when their
  glimpse was gone,
My pride struck out new sparkles of her
  own.
Such was I, such by nature still I am,
Be Thine the glory and be mine the
  shame.
Good life be now my task: my doubts
  are done,
(What more could fright my faith,
  than Three in One?)

Dryden: *The Hind and the Panther,* 1.
(17th cent.)

The Church to be loved needs but to be
seen as she is; the truth to be believed
needs but to be presented to the mind
as it is in its real relations. . . . To convert a man it is necessary to enlighten
him, and all theologians teach us that
the grace which converts illustrates the
understanding at the same time that it
does the will.

Orestes Brownson: *Catholic Polemics.*
(Works, 20, 107 ff.) (1861)

God has not chosen every one to salvation: it is a rare gift to be a Catholic; it
may be offered to us once in our lives
and never again; and, if we have not
seized on the *accepted time,* nor know
in our day the things which are for our
peace, oh, the misery for us! What shall
we be able to say when death comes, and
we are not converted, and it is directly
and immediately our own doing that we
are not?

Card. Newman: *Discourses to Mixed
Congregations.* (19th cent.)

You must make a venture; faith is a
venture before a man is a Catholic. You
approach the Church in the way of reason, you enter it in the light of the
spirit.

Card. Newman. (19th cent.)

I have been in perfect peace and contentment; I never had one doubt. I was not
conscious to myself, on my conversion,
of any change, intellectual or moral,
wrought in my mind. I was not conscious
of firmer faith in the fundamental truths
of revelation, or of more self-command;
I had not more fervor; but it was like
coming into port after a rough sea; and
my happiness on that score remains to
this day without interruption.

Card. Newman: *Apologia pro Vita Sua,* 5.
(19th cent.)

A convert comes to learn, and not to
pick and choose. He comes in simplicity
and confidence, and it does not occur to
him to weigh and measure every proceeding, every practice which he meets
with among those whom he has joined.
He comes to Catholicism as to a living
stream, with a living teaching, and not
to a mere collection of decrees and
canons, which by themselves are of
course but the framework, not the body
and substance of the Church. And this
is a truth which concerns, which binds,
those also who never knew any other religion, not only the convert.

Card. Newman: *Letter to the Rev. E. B.
Pusey on his Eirenicon.* (19th cent.)

There is no happiness in the world comparable to that of the experience known
as conversion.

R. H. Benson: *An Average Man.* (20th
cent.)

Conversion has to materialize in small actions as well as in great.

> R. H. Benson: *An Average Man.* (20th cent.)

It will be by what we are, not by what we know, that we shall convert the Church's modern foes, if we ever do convert them.

> John Ayscough: *Levia Pondera.* (20th cent.)

It is impossible to be just to the Catholic Church. The moment men cease to pull against it they feel a tug towards it. The moment they cease to shout it down they begin to listen to it with pleasure. The moment they try to be fair to it they begin to be fond of it. But when that affection has passed a certain point it begins to take on the tragic and menacing grandeur of a great love affair.

> G. K. Chesterton: *The Catholic Church and Conversion.* (20th cent.)

The Church is a house with a hundred gates: and no two men enter at exactly the same angle.

> G. K. Chesterton: *The Catholic Church and Conversion.* (20th cent.)

This is one of the very queerest of the common delusions about what happens to a convert. In some muddled way people have confused the natural remarks of converts, about having found moral peace, with some idea of their having found mental rest, in the sense of mental inaction. . . . To become a Catholic is not to leave off thinking, but to learn how to think.

> G. K. Chesterton: *The Catholic Church and Conversion.* (20th cent.)

There must always remain . . . an element of mystery about conversion; partly, because it involves movements of the mind which remain obscure even to the acutest introspection, but still more because the workings of divine grace are secret; so that the most exhaustive controversy and the most penetrating anal-ysis have left theology baffled in its attempt to determine how grace influences the mind or co-operates with the will.

> W. E. Orchard: *From Faith to Faith.* (20th cent.)

Catholic suasions either break down all resistance and result in conversion, or tend to render all other avenues of religious approach impossible. One turns back from the threshold of the Church, but one does not return to the faith of one's youth.

> Arnold Lunn: *Now I See.* (20th cent.)

Those good people who imagine that conversions can be explained by the attractions of Catholic art and culture should read *The Stones of Venice.* If ever a man ought to have been a Catholic, that man was Ruskin, and the fact that he died outside the Church is a tribute to the enormous power of anti-Catholic dissuasions.

> Arnold Lunn: *Now I See.* (20th cent.)

Father Knox once remarked that the Church gets on by hook or crook, by the hook of the fisherman and the crook of the shepherd. Some priests are fishermen and others are shepherds by temperament. The former are mainly interested in the conversion of non-Catholics, the latter in the safeguarding of their own flock from corruption.

> Arnold Lunn: *Now I See.* (20th cent.)

The Catholic, if he makes a serious attempt to convert you, is a proselytiser; if he displays no particular interest in your conversion he is a Machiavellian Jesuit.

> Arnold Lunn: *Now I See.* (20th cent.)

I have always been latently and potentially a Catholic—there has been no swing round from a contradictory set of ideas. I joined the Church of Rome only because I found that it was impossible to be a Catholic in the church of my baptism.

> Sheila Kaye-Smith: *Three Ways Home.* (20th cent.)

Convert

Their busy teachers mingled with the Jews,
And raked for converts even the court and stews.

Dryden: *Absalom and Achitophel,* I. (17th cent.)

A convert is undeniably in favor with no party; he is looked at with distrust, contempt, and aversion by all. His former friends think him a good riddance, and his new friends are cold and strange; and as to the impartial public, their very first impression is to impute the change to some eccentricity of character, or fickleness of mind, or tender attachment, or private interest. Their utmost praise is the reluctant confession that 'doubtless he is very sincere.'

Card. Newman: *Essays Critical and Historical,* 2. (19th cent.)

The hardest thing, we apprehend, for converts from Protestantism to acquire, is the virtue of obedience: a virtue which we have never acquired, for it came natural to us . . . we were born to follow, not to lead; to obey, not to command.

Orestes Brownson: *Brownson's Quarterly Review, Last Series,* 3, 66. (1875)

That's the worst of these converts—they never can distinguish between faith and emotion!

R. H. Benson: *The Sentimentalists.* (20th cent.)

The Pope is barely Catholic enough for some converts.

John Ayscough: *Mezzogiorno.* (20th cent.)

Cooperation

Competition, founded upon the conflicting interests of individuals, is in reality far less productive of wealth and enterprise than cooperation, involving though it does the constant apparent sacrifice of the individual to the common interests.

R. H. Benson: *A City Set on a Hill.* (20th cent.)

Cooperation is the one hope of the world.

R. H. Benson: *Lord of the World.* (20th cent.)

Coquetry

Lesbia hath a beaming eye,
But no one knows for whom it beameth.

Thomas Moore: *Song: Lesbia Hath.* (19th cent.)

Corporation

History proves that, owing to a change in social conditions, functions that were once performed by small bodies can be performed to-day only by large corporations. Nevertheless, just as it is wrong to take from the individual and commit to the community functions that private enterprise and industry can perform, so it is an injustice, a grave evil and a violation of right order for a large organization to arrogate to itself functions which could be performed efficiently by smaller ones.

Pius XI: *Quadragesimo anno.* (May 15, 1931)

Corpus Christi (Feast)

See Blessed Sacrament

Corruption

For corruption is nothing but the destruction of good. Evil things therefore had their origin in good things, and unless they reside in good things, they do not exist at all.

St. Augustine: *Enchiridion,* 14. (5th cent.)

Cosmetics

Against Him those women sin who torment their skin with potions, stain their cheeks with rouge, and extend the line of their eyes with black coloring. Doubtless they are dissatisfied with God's plastic skill. In their own persons they convict and censure the Artificer of all things.

Tertullian: *Women's Dress.* (3rd cent.)

Such is the world that a little powder and gauze properly disposed secures a proper respect, and the neglect of it gives a *mauvais ton.*

Katharine T. Hinkson: *Rose of the Garden.* (20th cent.)

Council

The definition of a national council does not admit of any subsequent discussion, and the civil authority can assume this principle as the basis for its acts.

Proposition condemned by Pius IX in Syllabus of Errors. (1867)

Council, General

I confess that I receive and revere, as the four books of the Gospel, the four councils . . . the Nicene . . . the Constantinopolitan . . . the Ephesine . . . and the Chalcedonian. . . . These with full devotion I embrace and adhere to with most entire approval; since on them, as on a four-square stone, rises the structure of the holy Faith; and whosoever, of whatever life and behavior he may be, that does not hold fast to their solidity, even though he seem to be a stone, yet he lies outside the building.

Pope St. Gregory I: *Letters,* I, 25. (Synodical letter to John, Patriarch of Constantinople.) (6th cent.)

The canons of general councils began in the time of Constantine. For prior to that there was no opportunity for instructing the people [by this means], while the persecutions were raging.

St. Isidore: *Etymologies,* 6, 16. (7th cent.)

The Roman pontiff alone, as having authority over all councils, has full jurisdiction and power to summon, to transfer, to dissolve councils, as is clear not only from the testimony of holy writ, from the teaching of the fathers and of the Roman pontiffs, and from the decrees of the sacred canons, but from the teaching of the very councils themselves.

Pope Leo X: *Pastor Aeternus.* (Fifth Lateran Council) (Dec. 19, 1516)

The decrees of a general council do not have the definite force of binding, unless they have been confirmed by the Roman pontiff and promulgated by his order.

Code of Canon Law, Canon 227. (20th cent.)

An oecumenical council has supreme power over the entire Church. It is not permissible to appeal from the sentence of the Roman pontiff to a general council.

Code of Canon Law, Canon 228. (20th cent.)

See also Pope—Pope and General Council

Counsel

For what should I wade?
I was neither of court nor of counsel made.

John Heywood: *Proverbs,* I, II. (16th cent.)

'Tis not enough your counsel shall be true:
Blunt truths more mischief than nice falsehood do.

Pope: *An Essay on Criticism,* 3. (18th cent.)

Country

Nothing is sweeter than one's own country.

St. John Chrysostom: *Homilies.* (4th cent.)

How blessed is he, who leads a country life,
Unvex'd with anxious cares, and void of strife!

Dryden: *To John Dryden of Chesterton.* (17th cent.)

Anybody can be good in the country. There are no temptations there.

> Oscar Wilde: *Picture of Dorian Gray*, 19. (19th cent.)

Courage

The principal act of courage is to endure and withstand dangers doggedly rather than to attack them.

> St. Thomas Aquinas: *Summa Theologica*, 2-2, 123, 6. (13th cent.)

As little flowers, that by the chill of night
   Are closed, prick up their stems drooping and bent,
   And to the early ray re-open white,
So was it with my courage fallen and spent.

> Dante: *Inferno, Canto 2.* (Tr. Binyon) (14th cent.)

Stand like a tower whose summit never shakes
For the wind's blowing, and stays immovable.

> Dante: *Purgatorio, Canto 5.* (Tr. L. Binyon) (14th cent.)

Moreover, Christians are born for combat, whereof the greater the vehemence, the more assured, God willing, the triumph: *Have confidence; I have overcome the world* (John 16, 33).

> Pope Leo XIII: *Sapientiae Christianae.* (Jan. 10, 1890)

Courage is almost a contradiction in terms. It means a strong desire to live taking the form of a readiness to die.

> G. K. Chesterton: *Orthodoxy.* (20th cent.)

Courtesy

And to be rude to him was courteous.

> Dante: *Inferno, Canto 33.* (Tr. L. Binyon) (14th cent.)

She is a mirror of all courtesy.

> Chaucer: *Tale of the Man of Law.* (14th cent.)

Of courtesy, it is much less
Than Courage of Heart or Holiness,
Yet in my walks it seems to me
That the grace of God is in Courtesy.

> Hilaire Belloc: *Courtesy.* (20th cent.)

Covenant

Therefore, four Catholic covenants were given to mankind. The first, Noah's, was that of the rainbow after the flood; the second, Abraham's, being that of the circumcision. The third was the giving of the law in the time of Moses; and the fourth is that of the gospel given through our Lord Jesus Christ.

> St. Irenaeus: *Against the Heresies*, 3, 11, 8. (2nd cent.)

Covetousness

The devil rules over lovers of temporal goods belonging to this visible world, not because he is lord of this world, but because he is ruler of those covetous desires by which we long for all that passes away.

> St. Augustine: *De Agone Christiano*, 1, 1. (4th cent.)

He's no way covetous, but he'd fain have what is yours.

> Seumas MacManus: *Heavy Hangs the Golden Grain.* (20th cent.)

Cow

Many a good cow hath an evil calf.

> John Heywood: *Proverbs*, 1, 10. (16th cent.)

Crab

The greatest crabs be not the best meat.

> John Heywood: *Proverbs*, 1, 11. (16th cent.)

Creation

The rule of truth we hold is, that there is one God Almighty, Who made all things by His Word, and fashioned and formed that which has existence out of that which had none.

St. Irenaeus: *Against the Heresies,* 1, 22, 1. (2nd cent.)

I believe in one God, the Father almighty, Maker of heaven and earth, and of all things visible and invisible. . . .

Niceno-Constantinopolitan Creed. (4th cent.)

We are perfectly right in believing that God made the world from nothing, because even if the world was made from some kind of matter, that matter has itself been made from nothing.

St. Augustine: *On the Faith and the Creed,* 2. (4th cent.)

It is indeed a great thing for Him to have given us our very existence; but it will be a far greater thing for us to have found our rest in Him. For not because He performed these good works is He blessed, but because, since He had no need to do them, He rested in Himself rather than in them.

St. Augustine: *De Gen. ad Litt.* 4, 29. (5th cent.)

As in the seed there are invisibly and at one time all the things which in course of time will grow into a tree, so the universe must be conceived—since God created all things at the same time—as having had at the same time all the things which were made in it and with it, when the day of creation came.

St. Augustine: *De Gen. ad Litt.* 5, 23, 45. (5th cent.)

For it is one thing to form and direct the creature from the most profound and ultimate pole of causation, and He Who does this is alone the Creator, God; but it is quite another thing to apply some operation from without in proportion to the power and faculties assigned by Him, so that at this time or that, and in this or that way, the thing created may emerge. All these things, indeed, have originally and primarily already been created in a kind of web of the elements; but they make their appearance when they get the opportunity. For just as mothers are pregnant with their young, so the world itself is pregnant with things that are to come into being, things which are not created in it, except from the highest essence, where nothing either springs up or dies, has a beginning or an end.

St. Augustine: *De Trinitate,* 3, 9, 16. (5th cent.)

For things which are created are not known by God for the reason that they have been made; rather it is that they have been made, though they be mutable, because they are known immutably by Him.

St. Augustine: *De Trinitate,* 6, 10, 11. (5th cent.)

It is one thing to be, and another thing to be primarily (*principaliter*), one thing to be subject to change, and another thing to be independent of change. For all these things [i.e. creatures] are in being, but they are not maintained in being by themselves, and unless they are maintained by the hand of a governing agent, they could never be. . . . For all things were made out of nothing, and their being would again go into nothing, unless the Author of all things held it by the hand of governance.

Pope St. Gregory I: *Morals,* 16, 45. (6th cent.)

Since, then, God, Who is good and more than good, did not find satisfaction in self-contemplation, but in His exceeding goodness wished certain things to come into existence which would enjoy His benefits and share in His goodness, He brought all things out of nothing into being and created them, both what is invisible and what is visible.

St. John of Damascus: *Exposition of the Orthodox Faith,* 2, 2. (8th cent.)

There is a twofold going forth of God, the first where one Person proceeds from another—and so the divine Persons are distinct; the second whereby creatures proceed—and here the multiplying and diversifying of things is the common work of the whole Trinity.

> St. Thomas Aquinas: *Exposition of the De Divinis Nominibus*, 2, lect. 2. (13th cent.)

It is to be held with complete conviction that God brings creatures into existence of His own freewill, and is not bound by natural necessity.

> St. Thomas Aquinas: *Disputations Concerning Potency*, 3, 15. (13th cent.)

It is for this we are created: that we may give a new and individual expression of the absolute in our own peculiar character. As soon as the new is but the re-expression of the old, God ceases to live. Ever the mystery is revealed in each new birth; so must it be to eternity. The Eternal-Absolute is ever creating new forms of expressing Itself.

> Isaac T. Hecker. (Elliott's *Life*, p. 290) (19th cent.)

To create is to bring a thing into existence without any previous material at all to work on. *In the beginning God created the heaven and the earth* (Gen. 1, 1).

> St. Thomas Aquinas: *Contra Gentes*, 2, 16. (13th cent.)

Sing how the uncreated Light
Moved first upon the deep and night,
    And, at its *fiat lux*,
Created light unfurled, to be
God's pinions—stirred perpetually
    In flux and in reflux.

> F. Thompson: *Carmen Genesis*. (19th cent.)

Catholicism admits the presence of God in creation, which is a continual act, not a word once spoken or a careless wave of the hand. God is maintaining the creature in its existence; He is concurring with every act of movement, leaving us just room to be ourselves. The whole

earth is full of His glory. He fills every creature with benediction.

> M. C. D'Arcy: *The Idea of God*. (In *God and the Supernatural*) (20th cent.)

Creator

See God: Creator

Creature

Creatures are said to be in God in a twofold sense. In one way, so far as they are held together and preserved by the divine power; even as we say that things that are in our power are in us. In another sense things are said to be in God, as in Him Who knows them, in which sense they are in God through their proper ideas, which in God are not distinct from the divine essence. Hence things as they are in God are the divine essence. And since the divine essence is life and not movement, it follows that things existing in God in this manner are not movement, but life.

> St. Thomas Aquinas: *Summa Theologica*, 1, 18, 4. (13th cent.)

Ah! who would love a creature? who would place
His heart, his treasure, in a thing so base?
Which time consuming, like a moth destroys,
And stealing death will rob him of his joys.

> Sir John Beaumont: *Against Inordinate Love of Creatures*. (17th cent.)

We are not our own, any more than what we possess is our own. We did not make ourselves; we cannot be supreme over ourselves. We cannot be our own masters. We are God's property by creation, by redemption, by regeneration.

> Card. Newman: *Parochial and Plain Sermons*, 5. (19th cent.)

Credulity

The age of credulity is every age the world has ever known. Men have always turned from the ascertained, which is limited and discouraging, to the dubious, which is unlimited and full of hope for everybody.

Agnes Repplier: *Times and Tendencies.* (20th cent.)

Creed

I believe in God the Almighty, and in His only-begotten Son our Lord Jesus Christ, and in the Holy Spirit, and in the resurrection of the flesh, [in] the holy Catholic Church.

Creed. (An early form from Dêr-balyzeh papyrus.) (ca. 3rd cent.)

The rule of faith, indeed, is altogether one, alone immovable and irreformable; the rule, to wit, of believing in only one omnipotent God, Creator of the universe, and His Son Jesus Christ, born of the Virgin Mary, crucified under Pontius Pilate, raised again the third day from the dead, received in the heavens, sitting now at the right hand of the Father, destined to come to judge the living and dead through the resurrection of the flesh as well as of the spirit.

Tertullian: *On the Veiling of Virgins,* 1. (3rd cent.)

Dost thou believe in God the Father Almighty? Dost thou believe in Christ Jesus, the Son of God, Who was born of Holy Spirit and the Virgin Mary, Who was crucified in the days of Pontius Pilate, and died, and rose the third day living from the dead and ascended into heaven, and sat down at the right hand of the Father, and will come to judge the living and the dead? Dost thou believe in Holy Spirit in the holy Church, and the resurrection of the flesh?

St. Hippolytus: *The Apostolic Tradition,* 21. (Questions put to those being baptized.) (3rd cent.)

I believe in God the Father almighty *Creator of heaven and earth;* and in Jesus Christ His only Son our Lord; Who was *conceived* by the Holy Ghost, born of the Virgin Mary, *suffered* under Pontius Pilate, was crucified, *dead,* and

buried; *He descended into hell;* the third day He rose again from the dead; He ascended into heaven, sitteth at the right hand of *God* the Father *almighty;* from thence He shall come to judge the living and the dead. I believe in the Holy Ghost, the holy *Catholic* Church, *the communion of saints,* the forgiveness of sins, the resurrection of the body, *and life everlasting.*

Apostles Creed. (Received text as used in Western Church. Italicized words indicate main differences from Old Roman Creed, before 4th cent.) (ca. 5th to 8th cent.)

We believe (I believe, etc.) in one God, the Father almighty, Maker of heaven and earth, and of all things visible and invisible. And in one Lord Jesus Christ, the only begotten Son of God, and born of the Father before all ages. [God of God], light of light, true God of true God. Begotten not made, consubstantial to the Father, by Whom all things were made. Who for us men and for our salvation came down from heaven. And was incarnate of the Holy Ghost and of the Virgin Mary and was made man; was crucified also for us under Pontius Pilate, suffered and was buried; and the third day He rose again according to the Scriptures. And ascended into heaven, sitteth at the right hand of the Father, and shall come again with glory to judge the living and the dead, of Whose Kingdom there shall be no end. And in the Holy Ghost, the Lord and Giver of life, Who proceedeth from the Father [and the Son], Who together with the Father and the Son is to be adored and glorified, Who spake by the prophets. And one holy, Catholic and apostolic Church. We confess one baptism for the remission of sins. And we look for the resurrection of the dead and the life of the world to come. Amen.

Niceno-Constantinopolitan Creed. (Adopted by the Council of Nicaea, as modified by the Council of Constantinople. The bracketed words are later additions. Regularly used in the liturgy both in East and West: *Credo in unum Deum. . . .*) (325–381)

Whosoever willeth to be saved, before all things it is necessary that he hold the Catholic faith; which faith except every one do keep whole and undefiled, without doubt he shall perish eternally. Now the Catholic faith is this, that we worship one God in Trinity, and Trinity in Unity. . . .

> Athanasian Creed. (Formerly attr. to St. Athanasius, of unknown authorship. Recited at Prime on Sundays.) (ca. 4th or 5th cent.)

Let them believe the creed of the Apostles which the church of Rome keeps and guards in its entirety.

> St. Ambrose: *Letters,* 42, 5. (4th cent.)

Nothing is to be taken away from the apostolic writings, and nothing is to be added to them; in the same way we must expunge nothing from the Creed drawn up and handed down by the apostles, nor must we add anything to it. This is the Creed which the Roman church holds, where Peter, the first of the apostles, sat, and thither he brought the common decision (*sententiam*).

> St. Ambrose: *Explicatio Symboli ad Initiandos.* (4th cent.)

There is one true and only God,
  Our Maker and our Lord:
And He created everything
  By His almighty Word.
But in this one and only God
  There yet are Persons three;
The Father, Son, and Holy Ghost,—
  One blessed Trinity.
The second Person—God the Son—
  Came down on earth to dwell;
Took flesh and died upon the Cross,
  To save our souls from hell.
The good with God in heaven above
  Will ever happy be;
The wicked in the flames of hell
  Will burn eternally.
All this, and all the Church doth teach,
  My God, I do believe;
For Thou hast bid us hear the Church
  And Thou canst not deceive.

> Four Great Truths, in *Cantica Sacra,* 1865.

The chief articles of the Apostles' Creed had not for the Christians of the first ages the same sense they have for the Christians of our time.

> Proposition condemned by Decree of Holy Office, *Lamentabili,* June 3, 1907.

Creeds

Shall I ask the brave soldier who fights
    by my side
  In the cause of mankind, if our
    creeds agree?
Shall I give up the friend I have
    valued and tried,
  If he kneel not before the same altar
    with me?
From the heretic girl of my soul should
    I fly,
  To seek somewhere else a more
    orthodox kiss?
No! perish the hearts, and the laws
    that try
  Truth, valor, or love, by a standard
    like this!

> Thomas Moore: *Come Send Round the Wine.* (19th cent.)

Crime

No crime is rooted out once for all.

> Tertullian: *The Christian's Defence.* (3rd cent.)

So easy still it proves in factious times
With public zeal to cancel private
    crimes:
How safe is treason and how sacred ill,
Where none can sin against the people's will,
Where crowds can wink; and no offence
    be known,
Since in another's guilt they find their
    own.

> Dryden: *Absalom and Achitophel.* (17th cent.)

But treason is not owned when 'tis described;
Successful crimes alone are justified.

> Dryden: *The Medal.* (17th cent.)

Critic

No critic's verdict should, of right,
   stand good,
They are excepted all, as men of blood;
And the same law should shield him
   from their fury,
Which has excluded butchers from a
   jury.

   Dryden: *Secret Love, Second Prologue.*
   (17th cent.)

They who write ill, and they who ne'er
   durst write,
Turn critics out of mere revenge and
   spite.

   Dryden: *The Conquest of Granada,
   Prologue.* (17th cent.)

The generous critic fann'd the poet's
   fire,
And taught the world with reason to
   admire.

   Pope: *An Essay on Criticism*, 1. (18th
   cent.)

Criticism

Ye can see a mote in another man's eye,
But ye cannot see a balk in your own.

   John Heywood: *Proverbs*, 2, 7. (Cf. Matth.
   7, 3) (16th cent.)

To check young genius' proud career,
   The slaves who now his throne in-
   vaded,
Made criticism his prime vizier,
   And from the hour his glories faded.

   Thomas Moore: *Genius and Criticism.*
   (19th cent.)

Criticism has become an art, and exercises a continual and jealous watch over
the free genius of new writers. It is difficult for them to be original in the use
of their mother tongue without being
singular.

   Card. Newman: *Idea of a University.*
   (19th cent.)

Nothing would be done at all, if a man
waited till he could do it so well that
no one could find fault with it.

   Card. Newman. (19th cent.)

It would be well if the professed critic
would remember that criticism is not the
expression, however picturesque and
glowing, of the faith that is in him, but
the rendering of sound and intelligible
reasons for that faith.

   Coventry Patmore: *Principle in Art.* (19th
   cent.)

As sound philosophy is only sound sense
spread out, so true criticism of great
work is only right perception spread out;
and the use of criticism of such work is
not so much to teach men to enjoy it, as
to enable them to pronounce a prompt
and assured and demonstrable condemnation of bad or inferior work when
false or exaggerated claims are put forth
in its favor.

   Coventry Patmore: *Principle in Art.* (19th
   cent.)

When critics disagree the artist is in accord with himself.

   Oscar Wilde: *The Picture of Dorian Gray,
   Preface.* (19th cent.)

To disparage scenery as quite flat is of
course like disparaging a swan as quite
white, or an Italian sky as quite blue.

   G. K. Chesterton: *Robert Browning, 6.*
   (20th cent.)

A man is perfectly entitled to laugh at a
thing because he happens to find it incomprehensible. What he has no right
to do is to laugh at it as incomprehensible, and then criticize it as if he comprehended it.

   G. K. Chesterton: *What I Saw in America.*
   (20th cent.)

If a writer is so cautious that he never
writes anything that cannot be criticized,
he will never write anything that can be
read. If you want to help other people
you have got to make up your mind to
write things that some men will condemn.

   Thomas Merton: *Seeds of Contemplation.*
   (20th cent.)

Crocodile

Like the back of a gold-mailed saurian
Heaving its slow length from Nilotic slime.

F. Thompson: *Sister Songs.* (19th cent.)

Cromwell, Oliver

Cromwell was about to ravage all Christendom; the royal family was lost, and his own forever powerful, had it not been for a grain of sand that got into his ureter.

Pascal: *Pensées.* (17th cent.)

Cromwell, damned to everlasting fame.

Pope: *An Essay on Man,* 4. (18th cent.)

Cross, Holy

By this sign conquer. (*En touto nika. In hoc signo vinces.*)

These words accompanied a sign of the cross which appeared in the sky to the Emperor Constantine and his soldiers the day of the fateful battle of the Milvian Bridge. (According to Eusebius, *Vita Constantini.*) (312)

By the Cross death has been vanquished, Adam has returned to paradise, and has been made an heir of the kingdom, confounding the devil. The splendor and glory which Adam lost when he transgressed the commandment, the Lord gave back to him in baptism when He came; and He will come again at the end and raise him and his children up, and clothe them with glory in the bridal chamber of His light.

St. Ephraem of Syria: *Funeral Canons,* 53. (4th cent.)

Now, my soul, in liquid measures, let the sounding numbers flow;
Sing the trophy of His passion, sing the Cross triumphant now;
Sing the ensign of Christ's glory, marked on every faithful brow.

Prudentius: *Solve vocem mens sonoram.* (Tr. Pope and Davis) (From the Cathemerinon, 4th cent.)

On this Cross, indeed, throughout the whole of this life which is spent in the midst of trials and temptations, the Christian must continually hang. For there is no time in this life to draw out the nails, of which it is said in the psalm: "Pierce thou My flesh with the nails of thy fear" (Ps. 118, 120); the flesh is carnal concupiscence; the nails are the commandments of justice; with the latter the fear of the Lord pierces the former, and it crucifies us as an acceptable sacrifice to Him. Therefore in like manner the apostle says: "I beseech you, therefore, brethren, by the mercy of God, that you present your bodies a living sacrifice, holy, pleasing unto God" (Rom. 12, 1). This Cross, therefore, in which the servant of God is not only not confounded but even glories in the words: "God forbid that I should glory save in the Cross of our Lord Jesus Christ: by Whom the world is crucified to me, and I to the world" (Gal. 6, 14), this Cross, I say, is not merely for forty days but for the whole of this life.

St. Augustine: *Sermon 205,* 1. (5th cent.)

The cross of Christ symbolizes the true altar of prophecy, on which the oblation of man's nature should be celebrated by means of a salvation-bringing Victim. There the blood of the spotless Lamb blotted out the consequences of the ancient trespass: there the whole tyranny of the devil's hatred was crushed, and humiliation triumphed gloriously over the lifting up of pride.

Pope St. Leo I: *Sermons,* 55, 3. (5th cent.)

The cross of Christ is the true ground and chief cause of Christian hope.

Pope St. Leo I: *Sermons,* 56, 1. (5th cent.)

O the wonderful power of the cross! O the unspeakable glory of the Passion! in which is seen at once the Lord's judgment seat, the trial of the world and the power of the Crucified. For Thou, O Lord, didst draw all things unto Thee, and when Thou hadst spread forth Thy hands all day to a faithless and gainsaying people, the whole world took knowledge of undeniable Majesty. . . . For Thy cross is the source of all blessings, cause of all the gifts of grace; through it to them that believe is given strength out of weakness, glory out of shame, life out of death.

Pope St. Leo I: *Sermons,* 59, 7. (5th cent.)

The cross of Christ, which is granted for the salvation of mortals, is both a mystery and an example: a mystery by which the power of God is shown forth; an example, by which man's devotion is aroused.

Pope St. Leo I: *Sermons,* 72, 1. (5th cent.)

We worship Thy cross, O Lord, and we glorify Thy holy resurrection.

Byzantine Rite, Antiphon sung on Exaltation of Cross (Sept. 14) and during Adoration of Cross on Third Sunday in Lent. (ca. 6th cent.?)

The Cross is the watcher of the whole world, the Cross is the adornment of the Church, the Cross is the might of kings, the Cross is the strength of the faithful, the Cross is the glory of angels, and the wound of demons.

Byzantine Horologion, Exapostilarion at Matins. (ca. 6th cent.?)

Abroad the regal banners fly,
Now shines the Cross's mystery;
Upon it Life did death endure,
And yet by death did life procure.

Who, wounded with a direful spear,
Did, purposely to wash us clear
From stain of sin, pour out a flood
Of precious water mixed with blood.

That which the prophet-king of old
Hath in mysterious verse foretold,
Is now accomplisht, whilst we see
God ruling nations from a Tree.

Roman Breviary, Passion Sunday, Invention (May 3) and Exaltation of the Cross (Sept. 14), Hymn *Vexilla Regis Prodeunt* at Vespers. (Tr. Blount) (Venantius Fortunatus, 6th cent.)

O Cross, our only hope, all hail!
In this the time when woes assail.
To all the pious grant Thy grace,
And all the sinners' sins efface.

Roman Breviary, Invention and Exaltation of Cross, *O Crux Ave Spes Unica* at Vespers. (From hymn *Vexilla Regis Prodeunt*. Stanza is always sung kneeling.) (Fortunatus, 6th cent.)

Sing, my tongue, the glorious battle
With completed victory rife:
And above the Cross's trophy
Tell the triumph of the strife:
How the world's Redeemer conquered
By surrendering of His life.

Roman Breviary and Missal, Passion Sunday, Good Friday, Invention and Exaltation of the Cross, Hymn *Pange Lingua Gloriosi.* (Tr. Neale) (Fortunatus, 6th cent.)

Faithful Cross! above all other,
One and only noble Tree!
None in foliage, none in blossom,
None in fruit thy peers may be;
Sweetest Wood and Sweetest Iron!
Sweetest Weight is hung on thee.

Bend thy boughs, O Tree of glory!
Thy relaxing sinews bend;
For awhile the ancient rigor,
That thy birth bestowed, suspend;
And the King of heavenly beauty
On thy bosom gently tend!

Thou alone wast counted worthy
This world's ransom to uphold;
For a shipwrecked race preparing
Harbor, like the Ark of old;
With the sacred Blood anointed
From the smitten Lamb that rolled.

Roman Breviary, Invention and Exaltation of the Cross, *Crux fidelis inter omnes* at Lauds. (From hymn *Pange Lingua Gloriosi*) (Tr. Neale) (Fortunatus, 6th cent.)

O God, Who dost gladden us by the yearly festival of the exaltation of the holy Cross; we beseech Thee, grant unto us who on earth have known its mystery, to be found worthy to enjoy the rewards of its redemption in heaven.

Roman Missal, Collect for Exaltation of Cross (Sept. 14). (Gelasian, 7th cent.)

Hail, O Cross! Brighter than all the stars! Thy name is honorable upon earth! To the eyes of men thou art exceedingly lovely! Holy art thou among all things that are earthly! Thy transom made one only worthy balance whereon the price of the world was weighed! Sweetest wood and sweetest iron, Sweetest Weight is hung on thee! O that everyone who is here gathered this day to praise thee may find that thou art indeed salvation for him!

Roman Breviary, Exaltation of the Cross, Antiphon at Vespers. (Cf. Liber Respons., ca. 7th cent.)

O God, Who in the glorious finding of the Cross of salvation didst renew the wonders of Thy passion; grant us by the price of this life-giving wood to win the palm of eternal life.

Roman Missal, Collect for Invention of Cross (May 2). (Gelasian, 7th cent.)

O God, Whom all creatures obey and Who hast made all things in the wisdom of Thy Word, we humbly beseech Thine ineffable mercy, Thou Who art the tree of life and restorer of Paradise, that Thou wouldst blot out in all who believe in Thee, whom Thou hast condescended to redeem by the holy blood of Thy Son on the wood of the holy Cross, the dread poison of the serpent, and by the grace of Thy Holy Spirit wouldst ever pour out for them the cup of salvation.

Gelasian Sacramentary, Collect for Invention of Cross. (7th cent.)

O God, Who hast deigned to redeem mankind by the precious blood of our Lord Jesus Christ; graciously grant that those who come to adore the life-giving Cross may be freed from the bonds of their sins.

Gregorian Sacramentary, Collect for Sept. 14. (7th cent.)

In the midst of two thieves Thy Cross appeared as a balance of righteousness. On one side it sank to hell through the weight of blasphemy, on the other it rose from iniquity to divine knowledge. O Christ our God, glory to Thee.

Byzantine Horologion, Troparion at None. (ca. 8th cent.)

O Mother of God, thou art the mystical paradise, which, untilled, produced Christ, through Whom that life-bearing tree, the Cross, is planted on earth. Wherefore we now adore its exaltation, and magnify thee.

Byzantine Menaea, Exaltation of Cross (Sept. 14), Ninth Ode at Matins. (8th cent.)

This same truly precious and august Tree, on which Christ offered Himself as a sacrifice for our sakes, is to be worshipped as sanctified by contact with His holy body and blood; likewise the nails, the spear, the clothes, His sacred tabernacles which are the manger, the cave, Golgotha, which brings salvation, the tomb which gives life, Sion, the chief stronghold of the churches and the like, are to be worshipped. . . . Moreover we worship even the image of the precious and life-giving Cross, although made of another tree, not honoring the tree (God forbid) but the image as a symbol of Christ.

St. John of Damascus: *Exposition of the Orthodox Faith*, 4, 11. (8th cent.)

For no other thing has subdued death, expiated the sin of the first parent, despoiled Hades, bestowed the resurrection, granted the power to us of contemning the present and even death itself, prepared the return to our former blessedness, opened the gates of Paradise, given our nature a seat at the right hand of God, and made us the children and heirs of God, except the Cross of our Lord Jesus Christ.

St. John of Damascus: *Exposition of the Orthodox Faith*, 4, 11. (8th cent.)

O Cross, whereby the earth is blest,
Certain redemption, hope, and rest,
Once as the tree of torture known,
Now the bright gate to Jesus' throne.

St. Peter Damian: *Crux mundi benedictio.*
(Tr. J. Neale) (11th cent.)

Be the Cross our theme and story,
We who in the Cross's glory
    Shall exult for evermore.
By the Cross the warrior rises,
By the Cross the foe despises,
    Till he gains the heavenly shore.

Adam of St. Victor: *Hymn Laudes crucis
attollamus.* (Tr. J. Neale) (12th cent.)

Would'st thou dwell in joy abounding,
All thy life with light surrounding,
    Make the Cross thy constant care;
On the rood of thy Redeemer
Be thy soul an ardent dreamer,
    Bear it with thee everywhere.

Be thou toiling, be thou sleeping,
Be thou smiling, be thou weeping,
    Deep in grief or ecstasy;
Be thou coming, be thou going,
Pale with pain, with pleasure glowing,
    Let the Cross thy comrade be.

Every sin and every sorrow,
Every ill that life can borrow,
    In the Cross will gain surcease;
In the Cross, though sore and grieving,
He that humbly seeks relieving,
    Findeth refuge, findeth peace.

St. Bonaventure: *Recordare Sanctae Crucis.*
(Tr. D. Donahoe) (13th cent.)

O clear, O wealful alter, holy cross,
Reed of the Lamb's blood full of pity,
That wash the world fro the old iniq-
    uity,
Me fro the fiend, and fro his clawes
    keep,
That day that I shall drenchen in the
    deep.

Victorious tree, protection of true,
That only worthy were for to bear
The King of heaven with His woundes
    new,

The white Lamb, that hurt was with the
    spear,
Flemer of fiends out of him and her
On which thy limbs faithfully ex-
    tenden,
Me keep, and give me light my life
    t'amenden.

Flemer—driver

Chaucer: *The Man of Law's Tale,* 451.
(14th cent.)

If you rightly bear your cross, it will
bear you.

Thomas a Kempis: *The Imitation of Christ,*
2, 5. (15th cent.)

In the cross is salvation; in the cross is
life; in the cross is protection from thy
enemies. In the cross is infusion of heavenly sweetness; in the cross is strength
of mind; in the cross is joy of spirit. In
the cross is the height of virtue; in the
cross is the perfection of sanctity. There
is no health of the soul nor hope of eternal life but in the cross.

Thomas a Kempis: *The Imitation of Christ,*
2, 12. (15th cent.)

He that seeks not the cross of Christ
seeks not the glory of Christ.

St. John of the Cross: *Spiritual Sentences
and Maxims.* (16th cent.)

Do not desire crosses, save in proportion
to the measure wherewith you have
borne those that have already been sent
you.

St. Francis de Sales: *Introduction to the
Devout Life,* 3, 37. (17th cent.)

We have not to carry the cross of others,
but our own.

St. Francis de Sales: *Letters to Persons in
the World,* 2, 4. (17th cent.)

The crosses that we shape for ourselves
are always lighter than the ones laid
upon us.

Jean Pierre Camus: *The Spirit of St. Francis
de Sales,* 10, 11. (17th cent.)

Time has a day in store
When this so proudly poor
And self-oppressed spark, that has so
    long
By the love-sick world been made
Not so much their sun as shade,
Weary of this glorious wrong,
From them and from himself shall flee
For shelter to the shadow of Thy tree:
Proud to have gain'd this precious loss
And chang'd his false crown for Thy
    Cross.

R. Crashaw: *The Glorious Epiphany of Our
Lord, a Hymn.* (17th cent.)

Look up, languishing soul! Lo where
    the fair
Badge of thy faith calls back thy care,
    And bids thee ne'er forget
    Thy life is one long debt
Of love to Him, Who on this painful
    tree
Paid back the flesh He took for thee.

R. Crashaw: *Hymn of the Holy Cross.*
(17th cent.)

Our religion is wise and foolish. Wise,
in that it is the most learned, and the
best established through miracles, prophecies, etc. Foolish, because that is not
what makes us Christians; and brings
condemnation to those who do not belong, but not belief to those who do.
What makes them believe is the Cross.

Pascal: *Pensées.* (17th cent.)

Sweet the moments, rich in blessing,
    Which before the cross I spend;
Life, and health, and peace possessing
    From the sinner's dying Friend:
Here I'll sit, for ever viewing
    Mercy's streams in streams of blood;
Precious drops my soul bedewing
    Make my final peace with God!

M. Bridges: *Sub Cruce Christi.* (19th
cent.)

Jesus, I my cross have taken,
    All to leave and follow Thee;
I am poor, despised, forsaken,—
    Thou henceforth my all shall be:
Perish every fond ambition,—
    All I've sought, or hoped, or known;

Yet how rich is my condition,—
    God and heaven may be mine own!

M. Bridges: *Jesu, I My Cross Have Taken.*
(19th cent.)

The cross is the instrument of contrition
upon which the earthly man is broken to
be reformed upon the heavenly man.
The cross is the divine school of patience; the school of self-abnegation;
the school of penance; the school of
charity.

Archbp. Ullathorne: *Humility and
Patience.* (19th cent.)

The world is full of mysteries; the soul
is full of mysteries; heaven is all mystery
to us earthly creatures. But whoever embraces the cross with open heart finds
therein the explanation of a thousand
mysteries.

Archbp. Ullathorne: *Humility and
Patience.* (19th cent.)

We do not attach any instrinsic virtue to
the cross; this would be sinful and idolatrous. Our veneration is referred to
Him Who died upon it.

Card. Gibbons: *The Faith of Our Fathers,*
1. (19th cent.)

Even so, O Cross! thine is the victory.
    Thy roots are fast within our fair
    fields;
Brightness may emanate in heaven
    from thee,
    Here thy dread symbol only shadow
    yields.

F. Thompson: *Ode to the Setting Sun.*
(19th cent.)

Onward! onward!—'neath curse and
    blow,
    'Neath crushing cross in the darkling
    day,
With reeling sense, bruised knees that
    know
    The rocks and flints of Golgotha's
    way!

Joseph I. C. Clarke: *The Way of the Cross.*
(19th cent.)

It has been said that the cross is the symbol of absolutely endless expansion; it is never content. It points for ever and ever to four indefinitely receding points.

> R. H. Benson: *Christ in the Church.* (20th cent.)

Christ is laying his cross on you. It is a great honor.

> R. H. Benson: *An Average Man.* (20th cent.)

The Cross cannot be defeated for it is defeat.

> G. K. Chesterton: *The Ball and the Cross.* (20th cent.)

It is true, and even tautological, to say that the Cross is the crux of the matter.

> G. K. Chesterton: *The Everlasting Man.* (20th cent.)

Scorned, mocked, and spurned I've been,
    Derided and defied,
And I have been betrayed by one
    For whom I would have died.

One cross I thought so bitter
    No greater could befall,
Until I learned they suffer most
    Who have no cross at all.

> Sister Miriam: *Crosses.* (20th cent.)

See also Good Friday; Passion of our Lord

Cross, Sign of the

In all our actions when we come in or go out, when we dress, when we wash, at our meals, before retiring to sleep, we make on our foreheads the sign of the cross. These practices are not committed by a formal law of Scripture, but tradition teaches them, custom confirms them, faith observes them.

> Tertullian: *De Corona,* 3. (3rd cent.)

And when tempted always reverently seal thy forehead with the sign of the cross. For this sign of the Passion is displayed and made manifest against the devil if thou makest it in faith, not in order that thou mayest be seen of men, but by thy knowledge putting it forward as a shield.

> St. Hippolytus: *The Apostolic Tradition,* 37. (3rd cent.)

Let us, therefore, not be ashamed of the cross of Christ; but though another hide it, do thou openly seal it upon thy forehead, that the devils may behold the royal sign and flee trembling far away. Make then this sign at eating and drinking, at sitting, at lying down, at rising up, at speaking, at walking: in a word, at every act.

> St. Cyril of Jerusalem: *Catechetical Discourses,* 4, 14. (4th cent.)

Crow

The black crow thinketh her own birds white.

> Gavin Douglas: *Aeneis,* 9 Prol. (16th cent.)

Thrice and three times thrice his name;
(How cunning art Thou, Lord
To herald our perpetual shame
By this perennial bird.)

> Henry M. Robinson: *Cock-Crow: Woodstock.* (20th cent.)

Crown

The crown of victory is promised only to those who engage in the struggle.

> St. Augustine: *De Agone Christiano,* 1, 1. (4th cent.)

A monarch's crown with fate surrounded lies,
Who reach, lay hold on death that miss the prize.

> Dryden: *Absalom and Achitophel.* (17th cent.)

Crucifix

The world is my crucifix. (Mundus mihi crucifixus est.)

> Motto of the Carthusian Order. (Medieval)

On her white breast a sparkling cross
   she wore
Which Jews might kiss and infidels
   adore.

   Pope: *The Rape of the Lock,* 2. (18th
   cent.)

I saw the Crucifix bleeding:—
Ah! sweet it was, but solemn and dread,
To see the eyes turn in the holy head
So woeful and so pleading.
I felt, as never before,
That to pray is less than to adore;
That one vast mighty mystery
Comprises human history;
That these are one: Victim, High
   Priest,
And Lamb of a perpetual feast.

   Clarence Walworth: *Andiatorocte.* (19th
   cent.)

Cruelty

             Cruelty's a charm
In you that cannot mine enchantment
   harm,
Since cruelty is all perfection is.

   Rachel Annand: *To the Head of a Greek
   Boy.* (20th cent.)

Crusade

Kill them all, God will know His own!

   Words (probably apocryphal) attributed
   to the papal legate, Arnold of Cîteaux, at
   the siege of Béziers during the Albigensian
   crusade (1209). (According to Caesarius
   of Heisterbach, 1170–1240). (13th cent.)

Writers who point out and denounce the
evils of their times, even when they
themselves suggest no remedies, cannot
but help the unending work of the
Church. Writers who fight for noble
things always fight on the side of the
angels.

   Michael Williams: *Catholicism and the
   Modern Mind.* (20th cent.)

Cuckoo

And sweet to hear the cuckoo mock
   the spring

While the last violet loiters by the
   well.

   Oscar Wilde: *The Burden of Itys,* 10.
   (19th cent.)

Cuckoo, cuckoo!
In April skies were blue
As every hedgerow knew;
And there was you.
In April
The cuckoo shows his bill,
With wildflowers on vale and hill
   O, love!
Sweet was April, sweet was April!

   Katharine T. Hinkson: *Cuckoo, Cuckoo,*
   (20th cent.)

Culture

Those who find beautiful meanings in
beautiful things are the cultivated. For
these there is hope.

   Oscar Wilde: *The Picture of Dorian Gray,
   Preface.* (19th cent.)

The Catholic Church is not a cultured
set. She will never be a cultured set—a
set having a culture different from or
better than that in which she moves.

   Eric Gill: *Beauty Looks after Herself.*
   (20th cent.)

A social culture is an organized way of
life which is based on a common tradition and conditioned by a common environment. It is therefore not identical
with the concept of civilization which
involves a high degree of conscious ra-
tionalization nor with society itself, since
a culture normally includes a number of
independent social units.

   C. Dawson: *Gifford Lectures, 1947:
   Religion and Culture.*

See also Catholic Church and Civilization; Civilization

Cupidity

As for cupidity, it is then rightly directed by the charity which is joined with
it, since ceasing altogether to desire
things which are evil, it begins to prefer

those which are better, nor does it desire good things except in order to reach those which are better; which, when by the grace of God, it has fully obtained, the body and all the good things which belong to the body will be loved only for the sake of the soul, the soul for the sake of God, and God alone for Himself.

> St. Bernard: *Letters*. (12th cent.)

Curiosity

Free curiosity is of more value in learning than harsh discipline.

> St. Augustine: *Confessions*, 1, 14. (5th cent.)

Men are a race curious to know of other men's lives, but slothful to correct their own.

> St. Augustine: *Confessions*, 10, 3. (5th cent.)

This disease of curiosity (*cupiditatis*).

> St. Augustine: *Confessions*, 10, 35. (5th cent.)

Let curiosities alone.

> Thomas a Kempis: *The Imitation of Christ*, 1, 20. (15th cent.)

Be not curious about matters that do not concern thee; never speak of them, and do not ask about them.

> St. Teresa of Jesus: *Maxims*. (16th cent.)

Man's chief disease is curiosity about things he cannot know.

> Pascal: *Pensées*. (17th cent.)

Curiosity is only vanity. Most frequently we wish not to know, but to talk. We would not take a sea voyage for the sole pleasure of seeing without hope of ever telling.

> Pascal: *Pensées*, 2. (17th cent.)

You know what a woman's curiosity is. Almost as great as a man's!

> Oscar Wilde: *An Ideal Husband*, 1. (19th cent.)

Cursing

Pattering the devil's Pater Noster to herself.

> John Heywood: *Proverbs*, 1, 11. (16th cent.)

Custom

The customs of God's people and the institutions of our ancestors are to be considered as laws. And those who throw contempt on the customs of the Church ought to be punished as those who disobey the law of God.

> St. Augustine: *Letters*, 36. (5th cent.)

Custom (*consuetudo*) is a kind of law, having its origin in usage, which takes the place of law when law fails.

> St. Isidore: *Etymologies*, 5, 3. (7th cent.)

Customs are held from ancient times, approved by princes, and preserved by the people, determining whose anything is, or to whom it pertains. . . .

> Grand Coutumier de Normandie. (13th cent.)

Customs are binding in one of two ways. One of the ways is when the custom is general throughout the county and has been observed without dispute as long as man can remember. . . . The other way in which custom may be known and recognized is when there has been a dispute about some matter, and one of the parties appeals to a custom, and this custom is considered to be binding by judgment of the court. . . .

> Philippe de Beaumanoir: *Customs of Beauvaisis*, 24, 682. (13th cent.)

Men's customs change like leaves on the bough; some go and others come.

> Dante: *Paradiso, Canto 26*. (14th cent.)

Ancient custom has the force of law. (Vetustas pro lege semper habetur.)

> Legal Maxim. (Medieval?)

Custom may serve in place of law. (Consuetudo pro lege servatur.)

> Legal Maxim. (Medieval)

Custom rules the law. (Mos regit legem.)

> Legal Maxim. (Medieval)

Drops do pierce the stubborn flint,
  Not by force but often falling;
Custom kills with feeble dint,
  More by use than strength prevailing.

> Bl. Robert Southwell: *Loss in Delay.* (16th cent.)

Custom, that unwritten law,
By which the people keep even kings in
  awe.

> Sir William Davenant: *Circe,* 2, 3. (17th cent.)

I like to be as my fathers were,
  In the days ere I was born.

> W. S. Blunt: *The Old Squire.* (19th cent.)

Custom can obtain the force of law in
the Church only by the consent of the
competent ecclesiastical superior.

> Code of Canon Law, Canon 25. (20th cent.)

Custom is the best interpreter of laws.

> Code of Canon Law, Canon 29. (20th cent.)

See also Law; Tradition, ecclesiastical

Cynicism

The cynics, those canine philosophers....

> St. Augustine: *The City of God,* 14. (5th cent.)

Cecil Graham: What is a cynic?
Lord Darlington: A man who knows the
the price of everything, and the value of
nothing.

> Oscar Wilde: *Lady Windermere's Fan,* 3. (19th cent.)

D

Daffodil

O love-star of the unbeloved March,
  When cold and shrill,
Forth flows beneath a low, dim-lighted
  arch
    The wind that beats sharp crag and
    barren hill,
And keeps unfilmed the lately torpid
  rill!

> Aubrey de Vere: *Ode to the Daffodil.* (19th cent.)

There is a tiny yellow daffodil,
  The butterfly can see it from afar,

Although one summer evening's dew
  could fill
  Its little cup twice over, ere the star
Had called the lazy shepherd to his
  fold
And be no prodigal.

> Oscar Wilde: *The Burden of Itys.* (19th cent.)

Match not thy soul against the seraphim:
They are no more than moths blown
  to and fro
  About the tempest of the eternal
  will.

Rest undismay'd in field and forest dim
And, childlike, on some morning thou
   shalt know
   The certain faith of a March daffodil.

Compton Mackenzie: *The Lilies of the
Field.* (20th cent.)

Daisy

Of all the flowers in the mead,
Then love I most those flowers white
   and red,
Which that men callen daisies in our
   town.

Chaucer: *Legend of Good Women: Prologue.* (14th cent.)

That well by reason men it callë may
The day's-eye or else the eye-of-day,
The emperice and flower of flowers all.

Chaucer: *Legend of Good Women: Prologue.* (14th cent.)

Slight as thou art, thou art enough to
   hide
   Like all created things, secrets from
   me,
   And stand a barrier to eternity.

Alice Meynell: *To a Daisy.* (19th cent.)

Ah, drops of gold in whitening flame
Burning, we know your lovely name—
Daisies, that little children pull!

Francis Thompson: *To Daisies.* (19th
cent.)

Damnation

They who perish, perish by their own
negligence.

St. Ambrose: *Concerning Cain,* 2, 11. (4th
cent.)

For who does not know that man is not
damned unless for his evil will, nor, on
the other hand, granted deliverance, unless he has a good will?

St. Augustine: *Letter 173.* (5th cent.)

The damned are in the abyss of Hell, as
within a woeful city, where they suffer
unspeakable torments in all their senses

and members, because as they have employed all their senses and their members in sinning, so shall they suffer in
each of them the punishment due to sin.

St. Francis de Sales: *Introduction to the
Devout Life,* 15. (17th cent.)

Though the Church, in obedience to
God's Word, declares that unbaptized
infants are excluded from the Kingdom
of Heaven, it should not hence be concluded that they are consigned to the
place of the reprobate. . . . All that the
Church holds on this point is that unregenerate children are deprived of the
beatific vision, or the possession of God,
which constitutes the essential happiness
of the blessed.

Card. Gibbons: *The Faith of Our Fathers,*
19. (19th cent.)

See also Hell

Damned, The

They blasphemed God, blasphemed
   their mother's womb,
   The human kind, the place, the time,
   the seed
   Of their engendering, and their birth
   and doom;

Then weeping altogether in their sad
   need
   Betook themselves to the accursed
   shore
   Which awaits each who of God takes
   no heed.

Dante: *Inferno, Canto 3.* (Tr. Binyon)
(14th cent.)

Turn to thy science and be wise.
The more a thing perfected is, the
   more
It feels bliss, and in pain the sharper
   sighs.
Although the state of these accurst at
   core
   Never indeed in true perfection ends,
   They look then to be nearer than
   before.

Dante: *Inferno, Canto 6.* (D. refers to the
pious belief, unfounded, that after the last

judgment the lot of the damned will be somewhat alleviated.) (Tr. Binyon) (14th cent.)

Is the law of the abyss thus broken from?
  Or is there some new change in Heaven's decrees,
  That, being damned, unto my crags ye come?

Dante: *Purgatorio, Canto 1.* (Tr. Binyon) (14th cent.)

Damning

Damn with faint praise, assent with civil leer,
And without sneering teach the rest to sneer.

Pope: *An Epistle to Dr. Arbuthnot.* (18th cent.)

Dance

All be not merry that men see dance.

Lydgate: *Daunce of Machabree.* (15th cent.)

Shake off your heavy trance
And leap into a dance,
Such as no mortals use to tread,
  Fit only for Apollo
To play to, for the moon to lead,
  And all the stars to follow.

Francis Beaumont: *Masque of the Gentlemen of Gray's Inn and the Inner Temple.* (17th cent.)

That playing and dancing may be permissible, we should take part in such things for the sake of recreation and not merely from fondness of them.

St. Francis de Sales: *Introduction to the Devout Life,* 3, 34. (17th cent.)

Dear creature!—you'd swear
When her delicate feet in the dance twinkle round,
That her steps are of light, that her home is the air,

And she only *par complaisance* touches the ground.

Thomas Moore: *Fudge Family in Paris.* (19th cent.)

Fat wet bodies go waddling by,
Girdled with satin, though God knows why;
Gripped by satyrs in white and black,
With a fat wet hand on the fat wet back.

Alfred Noyes: *A Victory Dance.* (20th cent.)

Dandelion

With locks of gold today;
Tomorrow silver gray,
Then blossom-bald. Behold!
O man, thy fortune told!

John B. Tabb: *The Dandelion.* (19th cent.)

Dandy

A man who can dominate a London dinner-table can dominate the world. The future belongs to the dandy. It is the exquisites who are going to rule.

Oscar Wilde: *A Woman of No Importance,* 3. (19th cent.)

Danger

O God, Who knowest that we are set in the midst of dangers so great that, by reason of the frailty of our nature, we cannot always withstand them; grant us health of mind and body, that with Thy help we may overcome those things which we suffer for our sins.

Roman Missal, Collect for Fourth Sunday after Epiphany. (Gregorian, 6th to 8th cent.)

It be ill playing with short daggers.

John Heywood: *Proverbs,* 1, 12. (16th cent.)

Danger well past remembered works delight.

Henry Howard, Earl of Surrey: *Bonum est mihi quod humiliasti me.* (16th cent.)

Dante Alighieri

After they had talked together a little
while,
They turned to me and welcoming
signs displayed:
At which salute I saw my master
smile.
And yet more honor unto me they paid,
For me into their band did they invite,
So that I a sixth amid such wisdom
made.

Dante: *Inferno, Canto 4.* (Dante considered
himself a worthy successor of Virgil,
Homer, Horace, Ovid and Lucan.) (Tr.
Binyon) (14th cent.)

Dante was one who bare
Love in his deep heart, apprehended
there
When he was yet a child; and from
that day
The radiant love has never passed away.

Alice Meynell: *Two Boyhoods.* (20th
cent.)

Darkness

Whate'er my darkness be,
'Tis not, O Lord, of Thee:
The light is Thine alone;
The shadows, all my own.

J. B. Tabb: *Tenebrae.* (19th cent.)

Dawn

The dawn is sprinkling in the east
Its golden shower, as day flows in;
Fast mount the pointed shafts of light:
Farewell to darkness and to sin!

Roman Breviary, hymn *Aurora jam spargit
polum* for Saturday at Lauds. (Tr. E.
Caswall) (Ambrosian, 4th or 5th cent.)

O dawn, at last, long look'd for day!
Take thine own wings and come away.

Richard Crashaw: *The Name of Jesus.*
(17th cent.)

Behold, as from a silver horn,
The sacerdotal night

Outpours upon his latest-born
The chrism of the light;
And bids him to the altar come,
Whereon for sacrifice,
(A lamb before his shearers, dumb,)
A victim shadow lies.

J. B. Tabb: *Dawn.* (19th cent.)

All my stars forsake me.
And the dawn-winds shake me,
Where shall I betake me?

Whither shall I run
Till the set of sun,
Till the day be done?

Alice Meynell: *Song of the Night at
Daybreak.* (19th cent.)

East, oh, east of Himalay
Dwell the nations underground,
Hiding from the shock of day,
For the sun's uprising sound.

. . . .

So fearfully the sun doth sound,
Clanging up beyond Cathay;
For the great earth quaking sunrise
Rolling up beyond Cathay.

Francis Thompson: *The Mistress of Vision.*
(19th cent.)

And down the long and silent street,
The dawn with silver-sandalled feet,
Crept like a frightened girl.

Oscar Wilde: *The Harlot's House.* (19th
cent.)

Of all the fonts from which man's
heart has drawn
Some essence of the majesty of earth,

. . . .

I reckon first the sunset and the dawn.

George Sterling: *The Guerdon of the Sun.*
(20th cent.)

See also Lauds; Matins; Morning; Sunrise

Day

Be how so that the day be long,
The dark night cometh at last.

John Gower: *Confessio Amantis,* 6. (14th
cent.)

Now in his palace of the west,
    Sinking to slumber, the bright day,
Like a tired monarch fann'd to rest,
    'Mid the cool airs of evening lay;
While round his couch's golden rim
    The gaudy clouds like courtiers
        crept—
Struggling each other's light to dim,
    And catch his last smile e'er he slept.

Thomas Moore: *The Summer Fête.* (19th cent.)

And all the dying day might be
    Immortal in its dying!

Aubrey De Vere: *Evening Melody.* (19th cent.)

Daydreaming

I strongly wish for what I hope:
Like the daydreams of melancholy men,
I think and think on things impossible,
Yet love to wander in that golden maze.

Dryden: *The Rival Ladies,* 3, 1. (17th cent.)

Deacon

As ministers of the mysteries of Jesus Christ, the deacons should please all in every way they can; for they are not merely ministers of food and drink, but the servants of the Church of God. They must avoid all reproach as they would beware of fire.

St. Ignatius of Antioch: *Letter to the Trallians,* 2. (2nd cent.)

And a deacon when he is appointed shall be chosen according to what has been said before, the bishop alone laying hands on him in the same manner. . . . He is not ordained for a priesthood, but for the service of the bishop that he may do only the things commanded by him. . . . He does not receive the Spirit which is common to all the presbyterate . . . but that which is entrusted to him under the bishop's authority.

St. Hippolytus: *The Apostolic Tradition,* 9. (3rd cent.)

. . . O holy Lord . . . the Giver of honors, the Dispenser of orders, and Disposer of offices. . . . Look also we beseech Thee, O Lord, with kindly eye on these Thy servants whom we humbly dedicate to the office of deacon, for the service of Thy holy altars. . . . Thou art the Knower of secrets, the Searcher of hearts. With a heavenly discernment that never faileth, Thou art able to penetrate the mystery of their lives, wash away the faults that have crept into their souls, and grant them to do all things which it behoveth them to do. . . . *Send forth upon them, we beseech Thee, O Lord, the Holy Ghost, by Whom they may be strengthened by the gift of Thy seven-fold grace for the faithful performance of Thy ministry.* . . . In their conduct let Thy precepts shine forth, so that the people may follow in holy imitation the example of their chastity; and bearing before them the testimony of a good conscience, may they persevere firm and steadfast in Christ, and by merited successes deserve to rise by Thy grace from a lower grade to higher dignities.

Roman Pontifical, Ordination of Deacons, Consecration Prayer *Domine Sancte . . . honorum dator.* (Leonine, ca. 5th cent.)

O holy Lord, Father of faith, hope and grace, and Rewarder of all growth in virtue, Who in the heavenly and earthly ministrations of angels, everywhere appointed, dost diffuse the effect of Thy will through all the elements, vouchsafe to illumine also with spiritual love these Thy servants, that ready to do Thy bidding, they may grow up pure ministers at Thy holy altars; and purer through Thy favor, may they become worthy of the order of those seven, whom Thy apostles chose under the inspiration of the Holy Ghost, and of whom blessed Stephen was the leader and chief; and well formed in all the virtues by which they should serve Thee, may they be pleasing unto Thee.

Roman Pontifical, Ordination of Deacons, Prayer *Domine Sancte Pater Fidei.* (Gelasian, ca. 6th cent.)

O Lord our Savior, Who hast suggested to Thine apostles by Thine imperishable voice the institution of the diaconate, and hast chosen the protomartyr Stephen as the first of that order, fulfilling in him the words of Thy Gospel: He who would be the first among you, let him be your minister; do Thou, O Master of all, through the descent of Thy Holy and life-giving Spirit, fill with all faith, and love, and holiness, this Thy servant, whom Thou hast deemed worthy to enter the ministry of the diaconate; for it is not through the laying on of my hands, but through the visitation of Thy rich mercy that grace is given to those whom Thou makest worthy of serving Thee. Grant that being made free from all sin, he may stand blameless before Thee in the dreadful day of Thy judgment, and receive the unfailing reward of Thy promise.

> Byzantine Euchologion, Prayer for the Ordination of a Deacon. (ca. 5th to 7th cent.)

Deacon in Greek means minister in Latin. As priests are concerned with consecration, so deacons are charged with the ministry of dispensing. . . . Subdeacons are so called, because they are under the orders and office of the levites (deacons). They receive the offerings of the faithful in church, and bring them to the deacons to be placed on the altar.

> St. Isidore: *Etymologies*, 7, 12. (7th cent.)

. . . It is the duty of the deacon to minister at the altar, to baptize and to preach. . . .

> Roman Pontifical, Ordination of a Deacon, Admonition *Provehendi*. (ca. 10th cent.)

Receive the Holy Ghost, that you may have strength, and be able to resist the devil and his temptations. In the name of the Lord.

> Roman Pontifical, Ordination of Deacons. (Formula inserted in prayer of consecration before words "Send forth upon them. . . .") (13th cent.)

Dead, The

Each sorrowful mourner be silent!
Fond mothers give over your weeping:
None count those dear pledges as perished,
This death, it is life's reparation.

> Prudentius: *Jam moesta quiesce querela.* (From *Cathemerinon.*) (Tr. J. Neale) (4th cent.)

The souls of the dead, then, are in a place where they do not see the things that go on and transpire in this mortal life.

> St. Augustine: *On the Care for the Dead,* 13. (5th cent.)

One must not think, then, that any of the dead can intervene in the affairs of the living merely because the martyrs are present for the healing or aiding of certain ones. Rather, one should think this: the martyrs through divine power take part in the affairs of the living, but the dead themselves have no power to intervene in the affairs of the living.

> St. Augustine: *On the Care for the Dead,* 16. (5th cent.)

O lady, he is dead and gone;
  Lady, he's dead and gone;
And at his head a green grass turf;
  And at his heels a stone.

> Anon. *The Friar of Orders Gray.* (16th cent.)

He sleeps, and life's poor play is over.

> Pope: *Eloisa to Abelard.* (18th cent.)

"Weep not," ye mourners for the dead,
  But in this hope your spirits soar,
That ye can say of those ye mourn,
  They are not lost but gone before.

> Pope: *Epitaph for Elijah Fenton, East Hampstead, England.* (18th cent.)

Out of the depths to Thee, O Lord, I cry,
Lord! gracious turn Thine ear to suppliant sigh;
  If sins of man Thou scannest, who may stand

That searching eye of Thine, and chastening hand?
  Oh, hear our prayers and sighs, Redeemer blest,
And grant Thy holy souls eternal
rest.
And let perpetual light upon them
shine;
  For though not spotless, still these
  souls are Thine.

Anon. hymn inspired by Ps. 129, *De
Profundis*. (Westminster Hymnal) (19th
cent. ?)

Help, Lord, the souls which Thou hast
made,
The souls to Thee so dear,
In prison for the debt unpaid
Of sins committed here.

Those holy souls, they suffer on,
  Resign'd in heart and will,
Until Thy high behest is done,
  And justice has its fill.

For daily falls, for pardon'd crime,
  They joy to undergo
The shadow of Thy Cross sublime,
  The remnant of Thy woe.

Card. Newman: *All Souls*. (19th cent.)

They are at rest:
The fire has eaten out all blot and stain,
And, convalescent, they enjoy a blest
  Refreshment after pain;
Thus to the end, in Eden's grots they
lie,
And hear the fourfold river, as it
hurries by.

Card. Newman: *Refrigerium*. (19th cent.)

Weep not for me, when I am gone,
  Nor spend thy faithful breath
In grieving o'er the spot or hour
  Of all-enshrouding death;
    . . . .
But let it be thy best of prayers,
  That I may find the grace
To reach the holy house of toll,
  The frontier penance-place,—
To reach that golden palace bright,
  Where souls elect abide,

Waiting their certain call to heaven,
  With angels at their side;
    . . . . . .
So pray, that, rescued from the storm
  Of heaven's eternal ire,
I may lie down, then rise again,
  Safe, and yet saved by fire.

Card. Newman: *The Golden Prison*. (19th
cent.)

They cannot wholly pass away,
  How far soe'er above;
Nor we, the lingerers, wholly stay
  Apart from those we love:
For spirits in eternity,
  As shadows in the sun,
Reach backward into time, as we,
  Like lifted clouds, reach on.

J. B. Tabb: *The Departed*. (19th cent.)

Dead: Prayers for the Dead

We pray also for the holy fathers
and bishops who have fallen asleep before us, believing that it will be a very
great benefit to the souls for whom the
supplication is offered up, while that
holy and most awful sacrifice is set forth.

St. Cyril of Jerusalem: *Catechetical
Discourses*, 23, 9. (Of the prayers at mass
for the dead.) (4th cent.)

Let us pray for our brethren who sleep
in Christ, that God Who in His love for
men has received the soul of the departed one, may forgive him every fault,
and in mercy and clemency receive him
into the bosom of Abraham, with those
who in this life have pleased God.

Liturgy of the Apostolic Constitutions, 8.
(Syrian.) (4th cent.)

God, Who hast authority of life and
death, God of spirits and Master of all
flesh . . . we beseech Thee for the repose and rest of this Thy servant or
handmaid: give rest to his soul, his
spirit, in green places, in chambers of
rest with Abraham and Isaac and Jacob
and all Thy saints: and raise up his body
on the day which Thou hast ordained,
according to Thy promises. . . . Remem-

ber not his transgressions and sins: and cause his going forth to be peaceable and blessed. Heal the sorrow of those who belong to him, and grant unto us all a good end through Thine only-begotten Jesus Christ.

> Sacramentary of Serapion, Prayer for Commendation of the Dead (18). (4th cent.)

"Lay this body wherever it may be. Let no care of it disturb you: this only I ask of you that you should remember me at the altar of the Lord wherever you may be."

> St. Augustine: *Confessions*, 9, 11. (Words of St. Monica before her death.) (5th cent.)

It cannot be denied that the souls of the dead obtain relief through the piety of their living friends, when they have the Sacrifice of the Mediator offered for them, or when alms are given in the Church on their behalf. But these things benefit only those who during their lives merited that these services should one day help them.

> St. Augustine: *Enchiridion*, 110. (5th cent.)

We read in the book of Maccabees that sacrifice is offered for the dead. Yet, even if it were read nowhere in the Old Testament, the authority of the universal Church which clearly favors this practice is of great weight, where in the prayers of the priest which are poured forth to the Lord God at His altar the commemoration of the dead has its place.

> St. Augustine: *On the Care for the Dead*, 1. (5th cent.)

For if we had no care for the dead, we would not be in the habit of praying for them.

> St. Augustine: *On the Care for the Dead*, 14. (5th cent.)

If men's offences are such as can be remitted after death, the sacred oblation of the saving Victim is wont to be of great benefit to their souls even after death.

> Pope St. Gregory I: *Dialogues*, 4, 55. (6th cent.)

We commend to Thee, O Lord, the soul of Thy servant, N., and we beg Thee, O Lord Jesus Christ, Savior of the world, that Thou wouldst not refuse the welcoming embrace of the patriarchs to this soul for whose sake Thou didst, in Thy mercy, come down upon earth. . . .

> Roman Ritual, Commendation of the Departing Soul. (Gelasian, 5th to 7th cent.)

O God, the Creator and Redeemer of all the faithful, grant to the souls of Thy servants departed the remission of all their sins, that, by our devout prayers, they may obtain pardon for their sins which they have always desired.

> Roman Missal, All Souls (Nov. 2), Collect for First Mass. (Gelasian, 5th to 7th cent.)

Almighty and everlasting God, Who hast been pleased to breathe into man a soul according to Thy likeness, do Thou, while at Thy bidding dust returns to dust, command Thine image to be associated with Thy saints and elect in an everlasting home.

> Gelasian Sacramentary, Prayer for Dead. (5th to 7th cent.)

Thou That as God hast power over the living and the dead, and by Thy saints dost enlighten all the earth, Author of all things, save them that sing Thy praise.

> Byzantine Horologion, Exapostilarion at Matins. (ca. 5th to 9th cent.)

Where is earthly endeavor? Where is the vanity of temporal things? Where is gold and silver? Where is the crowd and tumult of household servants? All is dust, all ashes, all shadows! But come, let us cry to the immortal King: O Lord, endow with Thine eternal goods him who has departed from our midst, and grant him rest in everlasting bliss.

Byzantine Euchologion, Funeral Service, Troparion Idiomelon. (St. John of Damascus ?, 8th cent.)

I weep and grieve when I think of death and behold our comeliness within the tomb, created according to the image of God, lying formless and lifeless, bereft of all beauty. O wondrous woe! What is the meaning of this dread mystery? How can we be given over to decay, how can we be wedded to death? Indeed, this must be according to the will of God, as it is written of old; may He grant to the departed eternal rest.

Byzantine Euchologion, Funeral Service, Troparion Idiomelon. (St. John of Damascus ?, 8th cent.)

O God of spirit and all flesh, Who hast trampled down death, overthrown the devil, and granted life to the world; do Thou, O Lord, give rest to the soul of Thy departed servant, N., in a place of light, in a place of green pastures, in a place of repose, whence all pain and sorrow and grief have fled. O Thou gracious and merciful God, pardon every sin which he hath committed, whether by word, or deed, or thought, for there is no man who liveth and sinneth not. Thou alone art without sin, Thy righteousness is unto all eternity, and Thy word is truth. For Thou art the resurrection, and the life, and the repose of Thy departed servant, N., O Christ our God, and unto Thee we ascribe glory. . . .

Byzantine Euchologion, Funeral Service, Prayer. (8th cent.)

Come brethren, let us bid farewell to the departed and render thanks unto God. For he hath taken leave of his relatives, and presseth on the grave, and is no longer concerned about the vanities and sufferings of the flesh. Where now are his relatives and friends? We now must

be parted. Let us beseech the Lord to grant him eternal rest.

Byzantine Euchologion, Funeral Service, Farewell Troparia at the Grave. (8th cent.)

O Christ, rest the souls of Thy servants with the saints, where there is no sickness, nor sadness, nor sighing, but life without ending.

Byzantine Horologion, Troparion at Compline. (ca. 9th cent.)

Remember, O Lord, our fathers and brethren who sleep in the hope of resurrection to eternal life, and all who have departed in piety and faith. Forgive them their sins, voluntary and involuntary, which they have committed by deed, word, or intention. Place them in shining, tranquil and refreshing places, whence all sickness, sadness and sighing has been driven away, and where the light of Thy countenance shineth and gladdens all Thy saints for ever. . . .

Byzantine Horologion, Prayer for the Departed at Nocturns. (ca. 9th cent.)

O Lord, Jesus Christ, King of glory, deliver the souls of all the faithful departed from the pains of hell and from the deep pit: deliver them from the lion's mouth, that hell may not swallow them up, and may they not fall into darkness; but may Thy holy standard-bearer Michael lead them into the holy light, which Thou didst promise to Abraham and to his seed. We offer Thee sacrifices and prayers, O Lord: do Thou receive them on behalf of those souls whom we commemorate this day. Grant them, O Lord, to pass from death to life, as Thou hast promised to Abraham and his seed.

Roman Missal, All Souls Day, Offertory at Mass. (ca. 9th cent.)

O God, Whose property is ever to have mercy and to spare, we humbly beseech Thee on behalf of the soul of Thy servant N., whom Thou hast this day called out of the world, that Thou wouldst not deliver him into the hands of the enemy, nor forget him for ever, but command that he be taken up by Thy holy angels and borne to our home in paradise; that having put his hope and trust in Thee, he may not undergo the pains of hell, but may come to the possession of eternal joys.

Roman Missal, Collect for Funeral Mass. (ca. 9th cent.)

It is truly meet and just. . . . In Whom the hope of a blessed resurrection hath shone upon us, that those whom the certainty of dying afflicteth, may be consoled by the promise of future immortality. For unto Thy faithful, O Lord, life is changed, not taken away: and the abode of this earthly sojourn being dissolved, an eternal dwelling is prepared in heaven.

Roman Missal, Preface for Mass of the Dead. (ca. 9th cent.)

Deliver me, O Lord, from eternal death on that awful day: when the heavens and the earth shall be moved: when Thou shalt come to judge the world by fire. ℣ Fear and trembling have laid hold of me, and I am greatly afraid because of the judgment and the wrath to come: when the heavens and the earth shall be shaken. ℣ O that day, that day of wrath, of sore distress and misery, that great and exceeding bitter day: when Thou shalt come to judge the world by fire. ℣ Eternal rest grant unto them, O Lord, and let perpetual light shine upon them.

Roman Ritual, Burial Service, Responsory *Libera me, Domine.* (ca. 9th cent.)

I am the resurrection and the life; he who believes in Me, even if he die, shall live; and whoever lives and believes in Me, shall never die. (John 11, 25-26)

Roman Ritual, Burial Service, Antiphon at the Grave. (ca. 10th cent.)

That Thou wouldst vouchsafe to grant eternal rest to all the faithful deceased, we ask Thee, hear us.

Roman Missal, Litany of the Saints. (Present form, ca. 12th cent.)

See also Burial of the Dead

Death

Death ought to be our pleasure.

Tertullian: *De spectaculis.* (3rd cent.)

There is nothing dreadful in that which delivers from all that is to be dreaded.

Tertullian: *The Testimony of the Christian Soul.* (3rd cent.)

What is death at most? It is a journey for a season: a sleep longer than usual. If thou fearest death, thou shouldest also fear sleep.

St. John Chrysostom: *Homilies.* (4th cent.)

Death is the separation of soul and body.

St. Ambrose: *On the Good of Death,* 8. (4th cent.)

To the good man to die is gain.

St. Ambrose: *De Interpell. Job,* 2, 6. (4th cent.)

Death is not only not an evil but a good thing.

St. Ambrose: *On the Death of Satyrus,* 2, 39. (4th cent.)

During the time which intervenes between man's death and the final resurrection, the souls remain in places specially reserved for them, according as each is deserving of rest or tribulation for the disposition he has made of his life in the flesh.

St. Augustine: *Enchiridion,* 109. (5th cent.)

If the death that ends the toil of this life inspires such fear, how greatly that death is to be feared which casts men into everlasting pain!

St. Augustine: *Letter 122.* (5th cent.)

Of this at least I am certain, that no one has ever died who was not destined to die some time.

St. Augustine: *The City of God,* 1, 11. (5th cent.)

And of what consequence is it what kind of death puts an end to life, since he who has died once is not forced to go through the same ordeal a second time?

St. Augustine: *The City of God*, 1, 11. (5th cent.)

That death is not to be judged an evil which is the end of a good life; for death becomes evil only by the retribution which follows it. They, then, who are destined to die, need not be careful to inquire what death they are to die, but in what place death will usher them.

St. Augustine: *The City of God*, 1, 11. (5th cent.)

Wherefore, as regards bodily death, that is, the separation of the soul from the body, it is good unto none while it is being endured by those whom we say are in the article of death. For the very violence with which body and soul are wrenched asunder, which in the living had been conjoined and closely intertwined, brings with it a harsh experience, jarring horridly on nature so long as it continues, till there comes a total loss of sensation, which arose from the very interpenetration of spirit and flesh.

St. Augustine: *The City of God*, 13, 6. (5th cent.)

And regarding what happens after death, it is no absurdity to say that death is good to the good, and evil to the evil. For the disembodied spirits of the just are at rest; but those of the wicked suffer punishment till their bodies rise again— those of the just to life everlasting, and of the others to death eternal, which is called the second death.

St. Augustine: *The City of God*, 13, 8. (5th cent.)

For no sooner do we begin to live in this dying body, than we begin to move ceaselessly towards death. For in the whole course of this life (if life we must call it) its mutability tends towards death.

St. Augustine: *The City of God*, 13, 10. (5th cent.)

To keep death daily before one's eyes.

St. Benedict: *Rule*, 4. (6th cent.)

For a perfect life is an imitation of death, which the righteous so lead with care that they escape the snares of sin.

Pope St. Gregory I: *Morals*, 13, 33. (6th cent.)

O what terror in thy forethought,
    Ending scene of mortal life!
Heart is sickened, reins unloosened,
    Thrills each nerve with terror rife,
When the anxious heart depicteth
    All the anguish of the strife!

    .   .   .   .   .   .

Christ, unconquered King of glory!
    Thou my wretched soul relieve
In that most extremest terror
    When the body she must leave:
Let the accuser of the brethren
    O'er me then no power receive!

St. Peter Damian: *Gravi me terrore pulsas vitae dies ultima*. (Tr. J. Neale) (11th cent.)

Nothing is more certain than death, nothing more uncertain than its hour.

St. Anselm: *Meditations*, 7. (12th cent.)

Dead before death, alive after death. (Ante obitum mortuus, post obitum vivus.)

Epitaph of St. Francis. (13th cent.)

Blessed be God for our sister, the death of the body.

St. Francis. (13th cent.)

They have no hope of death: and their estate
    Is so abased in the blind life they own
    That they are envious of all others' fate.

Dante: *Inferno, Canto 3*. (Tr. L. Binyon) (14th cent.)

Death, alway cruel, pity's foe in chief,
Mother who brought forth grief,

Merciless judgment and without appeal!

> Dante: *La Vita Nuova,* 8. (14th cent.)

Then it is best, as for a worthy fame,
To dyen when that he is best of name.

> Chaucer: *The Knightes Tale.* (14th cent.)

Dead as a door nail.

> Langland: *Piers Plowman,* 2. (14th cent.)

A good death does honor to a whole life.

> Petrarch: *Canzoniere,* 16. (14th cent.)

Against death is worth no medicine.

> Lydgate: *Daunce of Machabree.* (15th
> cent.)

God: Where art thou, Death, thou
  mighty messenger?
Death: Almighty God, I am here at
  Your will,
  Your commandment to fulfil.

> Anonymous: *Everyman.* (16th cent.)

See me safe up: for my coming down, I
can shift for myself.

> St. Thomas More, as he ascended the
> scaffold. (16th cent.)

By god's body, master More, *Indignatio
principis mors est.*
  Is that all, my lord? quoth he. Then in
good faith is there no more difference
between your grace and me, but that I
shall die today, and you tomorrow.

> St. Thomas More, at his trial. (Roper,
> Life.) (16th cent.)

Death makes equal the high and low.

> John Heywood: *Be Merry, Friends.* (16th
> cent.)

Not Solomon, for all his wit,
  Nor Samson, though he were so
    strong,
No king nor person ever yet
  Could 'scape, but death laid him
    along:
    Wherefore I know that I must die,
    And yet my life amend not I.

> Bl. Robert Southwell: *Upon the Image of
> Death.* (16th cent.)

Happy are they who, being always on
their guard against death, find themselves always ready to die.

> St. Francis de Sales: *Letters to Persons in
> the World,* 3, 4. (17th cent.)

Only he
Dares welcome death, whose aims at
  virtue be.

> W. Habington: *To a Tomb.* (17th cent.)

What am I who dare to call Thee, God!
  And raise my fancy to discourse Thy
    power?
To whom dust is the period,
Who am not sure to farm this very
  hour?
For how know I the latest sand
In my frail glass of life, doth not now
  fall?
And while I thus astonish'd stand
I but prepare for my own funeral?
  Death doth with man no order keep:
It reckons not by the expense of years,
  But makes the queen and beggar
    weep.

> William Habington: *What Am I Who
> Dare to Call Thee, God?* (17th cent.)

The great decree of God
Makes every path of mortals lead
To this dark common period.
For what by-ways soe'er we tread,
We end our journey 'mong the dead.

> William Habington: *Welcome, Thou Safe
> Retreat!* (17th cent.)

No state of man is fortified
'Gainst the assault of th'universal
  doom:
But who the Almighty fear, deride
Pale death, and meet with triumph in
  the tomb.

> William Habington: *Who Am I Who
> Dare to Call Thee, God?* (17th cent.)

O harmless death! whom still the valiant brave,
  The wise expect, the sorrowful in-
    vite,

And all the good embrace, who know
    the grave
A short, dark passage to eternal light.

Sir William Davenant: *The Christian's
Reply to the Philosopher.* (17th cent.)

Why art thou slow, thou rest of trouble,
    death,
To stop a wretch's breath
That calls on thee, and offers her sad
    heart
A prey unto thy dart?

Philip Massinger: *The Emperor of the
East.* (17th cent.)

These death-seal'd lips are they dare
    give the lie
To the loud boasts of poor mortality;
These curtain'd windows, this retired
    eye
Outstares the lids of large-look'd ty-
    ranny.
This posture is the brave one this that
    lies
Thus low, stands up (methinks) thus,
    and defies
The world. All-daring dust and ashes!
    only you
Of all interpreters read nature true.

Richard Crashaw: *Death's Lecture at the
Funeral of a Young Gentleman.* (17th
cent.)

The glories of our blood and state
    Are shadows, not substantial things;
There is no armor against fate;
    Death lays his icy hand on kings:
      Scepter and crown
      Must tumble down,
And in the dust be equal made
With the poor crooked scythe and
    spade.

James Shirley: *A Dirge.* (17th cent.)

Devouring famine, plague, and war,
    Each able to undo mankind,
Death's servile emissaries are,
    Nor to these alone confin'd,
      He hath at will
    More quaint and subtle ways to kill.
A smile or kiss, as he will use the art,

Shall have the cunning skill to break a
    heart.

James Shirley: *Cupid and Death.* (17th
cent.)

Death quits all scores.

James Shirley: *Cupid and Death.* (17th
cent.)

All buildings are but monuments of
    death,
All clothes but winding-sheets for our
    last knell,
All dainty fattings for the worms be-
    neath,
All curious music but our passing bell:
Thus death is nobly waited on, for
    why?
All that we have is but death's livery.

James Shirley: *Death.* (17th cent.)

Death is easier to bear without thought
of it than the thought of death without
danger.

Pascal: *Pensées.* (17th cent.)

All human things are subject to decay,
And, when fate summons, monarchs
    must obey.

Dryden: *Mac Flecknoe.* (17th cent.)

She vanish'd, we can scarcely say she
    died;
For but a now, did heav'n and earth
    divide.

Dryden: *Eleonora.* (17th cent.)

Or break the eternal Sabbath of his rest.

Dryden: *The Spanish Friar,* 5, 2. (17th
cent.)

As a sweet odor, of a vast expense,
She vanished: we can scarcely say she
    died.

Dryden: *Ode to the Memory of Mrs. Anne
Killegrew.* (17th cent.)

To die is landing on some silent shore,
Where billows never break, nor tem-
    pests roar:

Ere well we feel the friendly stroke, 'tis o'er.

Sir Samuel Garth: *The Dispensary,* 3. (17th cent.)

The rest were vulgar deaths unknown to fame.

Pope: Tr. of Homer: *Iliad,* 22. (18th cent.)

How sweet is death to those who weep,
  To those who weep and long to die!

Thomas Moore: *Elegiac Stanzas.* (19th cent.)

Deep, deep—where never care or pain,
Shall reach her innocent heart again!

Thomas Moore: *Lalla Rookh: Prologue.* (19th cent.)

Die when you will, you need not wear
At heaven's court a form more fair
  Than beauty here on earth has given;
Keep but the lovely looks we see—
The voice we hear—and you will be
  An angel ready-made for heaven!

Thomas Moore: To ————. (Tr. of Lord Herbert's words to the beautiful nun at Murano: Moria pur quando vuol, non è bisogna mutar ni faccia ni voce per esser un angelo.) (19th cent.)

When true hearts lie wither'd
  And fond ones are flown,
Oh, who would inhabit
  This bleak world alone?

Thomas Moore: *The Last Rose of Summer.* (19th cent.)

Weep not for those whom the veil of the tomb,
  In life's happy morning, hath hid from our eyes,
Ere sin threw a blight o'er the spirit's young bloom,
  Or earth had profan'd what was born for the skies.

Thomas Moore: *Weep Not for Those.* (19th cent.)

Death chill'd the fair fountain ere sorrow had stain't it;
  'Twas frozen in all the pure light of its course,

And but sleeps till the sunshine of heaven has unchain'd it,
  To water that Eden where first was its source.

Thomas Moore: *Weep Not for Those.* (19th cent.)

I wish to have no wishes left,
  But to leave all to Thee;
And yet I wish that Thou shouldst will
  Things that I wish should be.

And these two wills I feel within,
  As on my death I muse:
But, Lord! I have a death to die,
  And not a death to choose.

F. Faber: *Wishes about Death.* (19th cent.)

The silver chord in twain is snapp'd
  The golden bowl is broken,
The mortal mould in darkness wrapp'd
  The words funereal spoken;
The tomb is built, or the rock is cleft,
  Or delved is the grassy clod,
And what for mourning man is left?
  O what is left—but God!

Anonymous: *God and Heaven.* (In Caswall's *Lyra Catholica*) (19th cent.)

After a little while,
When all the glories of the night and day
  Have fled for aye;
From friendship's glance and beauty's winsome smile,
  I pass away,
After a little while.

James R. Randall: *After a Little While.* (19th cent.)

And with the morn those angel faces smile
Which I have loved long since and lost awhile.

Card. Newman: *Pillar of the Cloud.* (19th cent.)

Whene'er goes forth Thy dread command,
  And my last hour is nigh,

Lord, grant me in a Christian land,
  As I was born, to die.

    Card. Newman: *Hora Novissima.* (19th
    cent.)

What he dieth that must he be forever;
as the tree falleth so must it lie.

    Card. Newman: *Miscellanies,* 178. (19th
    cent.)

Whilst I dwell, O my God, in this valley of tears,
    For refuge and comfort I fly unto
    Thee;
And when death's awful hour with its
  terrors appears,
    O merciful Jesus, have mercy on me.

    W. Young: *Bona Mors.* (19th cent.)

Sweet Savior! take me by the hand,
  And lead me through the gloom;
Oh it seems far to the other land,
  And dark in the silent tomb.

    F. Faber: *The Length of Death.* (19th
    cent.)

The shadow of the rock!
    Stay, pilgrim! stay!
Night treads upon the heels of day;
There is no other resting-place this way.
  The rock is near,
  The well is clear,
Rest in the shadow of the rock.

    F. Faber: *The Shadow of the Rock.* (19th
    cent.)

It is better to die, since death comes
  surely,
    In the full noon-tide of an honored
    name,
Than to lie at the end of years obscurely,
  A handful of dust in a shroud of
  shame.

    J. J. Roche: *Sir Hugo's Choice.* (19th
    cent.)

Hushed in the arms of death,
  Our young Marcellus sleeps.

    James R. Randall: *John Pelham.* (19th
    cent.)

Then the truth all creatures tell,
And His will Whom thou entreatest,
Shall absorb thee; there shall dwell
  Silence, the completest
Of thy poems, last and sweetest.

    Alice Meynell: *To Any Poet.* (19th cent.)

God laid His fingers on the ivories
Of her pure members as on smoothèd
  keys.
And there out-breathed her spirit's harmonies.

    Francis Thompson: *Her Portrait.* (19th
    cent.)

    Death, men say, is like a sea
    That engulfs mortality.

    Michael Field: *Death, Men Say, is Like a
    Sea.* (19th cent.)

Death is but a sharp corner near the beginning of life's procession down eternity.

    John Ayscough: *Outsiders—and In.* (20th
    cent.)

Oh, in some morning dateless yet
  I shall steal out in the sweet dark
And find my ship with sails all set
  By the dim quayside, and embark.

    Katharine T. Hinkson: *The Last Voyage.*
    (20th cent.)

When I am lying cold and dead,
With waxen taper at my head,
The night before my mass is said;
And friends that never saw my soul
Sit by my catafalque to dole
And all my life's good deeds unroll;
O Jesu, Jesu, will it be
That Thou wilt turn away from me?

    Hugh Francis Blunt: *What No Man
    Knoweth.* (20th cent.)

Babes now may smile into thy sunless
  eye
    And fear thee not, prone in thy kin-
    dred dust;
    No longer reck we thine insatiate
    lust
Of this our crumbling brief mortality.

Time is our bound no more; this nar-
row sky
  Metes not our visions; vaster is our
  trust
  Than all the regions of thy moth and
  rust,
Since passing now we know we do not
die.
For risen is our Christ, and with Him
we;
  And prostrate thou beside His open
  grave,
O ancient victor, in thy first defeat
And everlasting! Smiling now we see
Thou art but shadow with a broken
glaive,
  Within thy futile hands, His wind-
  ing-sheet.

Conde B. Pallen: *Christus Triumphans:
Mors Victa.* (20th cent.)

She lay asleep. We could not think her
dead.
That vivid spirit never knew eclipse.
The angel's kiss that loosed her prison
gates
  Had left a happy smile upon her lips.
Age, pain, and care fell from her like a
sheath
  That bursts its bond to set the flower
  free,
And on the quiet brow we saw instead
  The bloom of joyous immortality.

Sister M. Angelita: *The Quiet Heart.*
(20th cent.)

Death is no foeman, we were born to-
gether;
He dwells between the places of my
breath,
Night vigil at my heart he keeps and
whether
I sleep or no, he never slumbereth.
Though I do fear thee, knight of the
sable feather,
Thou wilt not slay me, death!

Sister Madeleva: *Knights Errant.* (20th
cent.)

Oh happy death, where life and fright,
Where love and loss are drawn apart
And stand, forever, separate,

While one by one the fragments of a
century
Disintegrate and fall in silence all
about us:
And these are news of peace, but not
dismay,
For heaven is builded deeper and
stronger everywhere
From the collapse of our neglected history.

Thomas Merton: *In April When Our Land
Last Died.* (20th cent.)

See also Burial of the Dead; Easter;
Eternal Life; Immortality; Resurrection

Death, Fear of

It is a poor thing for anyone to fear that
which is inevitable.

Tertullian: *The Testimony of the Christian
Soul.* (3rd cent.)

For it is for him to fear death who is not
willing to go to Christ. It is for him to
be unwilling to go to Christ who does
not believe that he is about to reign with
Christ.

St. Cyprian: *On Immortality,* 2. (3rd
cent.)

For man is by nature afraid of death and
of the dissolution of the body; but there
is this most startling fact, that he who
has put on the faith of the Cross despises
even what is naturally fearful, and for
Christ's sake is not afraid of death.

St. Athanasius: *On the Incarnation of the
Word of God,* 28. (4th cent.)

The foolish fear death as the greatest of
evils, the wise desire it as a rest after
labors and the end of ills.

St. Ambrose: *On the Good of Death,* 32.
(4th cent.)

If we fear death before it comes, we shall
conquer it when it comes.

Pope St. Gregory I: *Homilies on the
Gospels,* 13, 6. (6th cent.)

Sudden death is the only thing to dread, and that is why confessors dwell with the great.

> Pascal: *Pensées*. (17th cent.)

Death was denounc'd; that frightful sound
Which even the best can hardly bear.

> Dryden: *Threnodia Augustalis*. (17th cent.)

Death in itself is nothing; but we fear
To be we know not what, we know not where.

> Dryden: *Aurungzebe*, 4. (17th cent.)

Why fear thee, brother death,
That sharest, breath by breath,
This brimming life of mine?
Each draught that I resign
Into thy chalice flows.
Comrades of old are we;
All that the present knows
Is but a shade of me:
My self to thee alone
And to the past is known.

> J. B. Tabb: *My Messmate*. (19th cent.)

Death-Bed

A death-bed has scarcely a history; it is a tedious decline, with seasons of rallying and seasons of falling back; and since the end is foreseen, or what is called a matter of time, it has little interest for the reader, especially if he has a kind heart.

> Card. Newman: *Apologia pro Vita Sua*, 4. (Referring to his membership in the Anglican Church after 1841. He was received into the Catholic Church in 1845) (19th cent.)

Debt

Moreover, justice prescribes this order, that we should pay our debt first, and that only then we should, if we so decide, make a gift to our creditor in addition.

> St. Augustine: *Letter 110*. (5th cent.)

Alas, I am dying beyond my means.

> Oscar Wilde. (20th cent.)

A spendthrift never reveals all his debts.

> R. H. Benson: *The Sentimentalists*. (20th cent.)

Decadence

To be wrong, and to be carefully wrong, that is the definition of decadence.

> G. K. Chesterton: *A Miscellany of Men*. (20th cent.)

Decay

And all our chants but chaplet some decay.

> Francis Thompson: *Ode to the Setting Sun*. (19th cent.)

Deceit

Dost thou hate to be deceived? Do not deceive another.

> St. John Chrysostom: *Homilies*. (4th cent.)

Fraud, who so gnaweth at all men's conscience.

> Dante: *Inferno, Canto 11*. (Tr. L. Binyon) (14th cent.)

On such folk, plainly, is no trust
That fire and water holden in their fist.

> Lydgate: *Troy Book*, 4. (15th cent.)

To hold with the hare, and run with the hound.

> John Heywood: *Proverbs*, 1, 10. (16th cent.)

Fire in the tone hand, and water in the tother.

> John Heywood: *Proverbs*, 1, 10. (16th cent.)

A wolf in a lamb's skin.

> John Heywood: *Proverbs*, 1, 10. (16th cent.)

Indeed, it is not in human nature to deceive others for any long time, without in a measure deceiving ourselves also.

> Card. Newman: *Parochial and Plain Sermons*, 1, 10. (19th cent.)

Defeat

Fallen, fallen, fallen, fallen,
  Fallen from his high estate,
  And weltring in his blood:
Deserted at his utmost need
By those his former bounty fed;
On the bare earth expos'd he lies,
With not a friend to close his eyes.

Dryden: *Alexander's Feast.* (17th cent.)

Weep not the brave dead!
  Weep rather the living —
    On them lies the curse
  Of a doom unforgiving!
Each dark hour that rolls,
  Shall the memories they nurse,
Like molten hot lead,
Burn into their souls
  A remorse long and sore!
    They have helped to enthral a
  Great land evermore,
    They who fled from Cean-Salla.

J. C. Mangan: *Cean-Salla.* (Defeat of Kinsale, December 1601) (19th cent.)

It is remarkable that in so many great wars it is the defeated who have won. The people who were left worst at the end of the war were generally the people who were left best at the end of the whole business.

G. K. Chesterton: *Tremendous Trifles,* 20. (20th cent.)

Defect

Who is free from defects? He lacks everything who thinks he lacks nothing.

St. Bernard: *On Consideration,* 2, 7. (Addressed to Pope Eugenius III.) (12th cent.)

Defence

Even God Himself did not pass sentence upon Adam before he was called upon to make his defence. "Adam," says God, "where art thou? Hast thou not eaten of the tree whereof I commanded thee that thou shouldst not eat?" And the same question was put to Eve also.

John Fortescue: *De laudibus legum Angliae.* (15th cent.)

Defensive

An ingrained habit of the defensive is the prime condition of defeat. There is no such thing as a defensive battle or a defensive campaign, save in the sense that we may begin on the defensive, but only with the fixed object of turning to the offensive at the right moment.

H. Belloc: *Essays of a Catholic Layman in England.* (20th cent.)

Definition

Every definition is dangerous. (Omnis definitio periculosa est.)

Erasmus: *Adagia.* (16th cent.)

It is as easy to create as to define.

Card. Newman. (Ward, II, 587) (19th cent.)

Deification

For it is not by themselves being so that men are gods, but they become gods by participation in that one God Who is the true God.

St. Augustine: *In Ps. 118, Sermon 16,* 1. (5th cent.)

There can be no greater reward than that the earth-born sons of men should be made the sons of the Most High Who is in heaven.

St. Bede the Venerable: *In Lucam,* 2. (8th cent.)

Through His birth, that is, His incarnation, and baptism and passion and resurrection, He delivered our nature from the sin of our first parent and death and corruption, and became the first-fruits of the resurrection, and made Himself the way and image and pattern, in order that we too following in His footsteps may become by adoption what He Himself is by nature, sons and heirs of God and joint heirs with Him.

St. John of Damascus: *Exposition of the Orthodox Faith,* 4, 13. (8th cent.)

O love, holy and chaste! O sweet and pleasing affection! O pure and undefiled intention of the will! the more surely undefiled and purer, as there is now mixed with it nothing of its own; so much the sweeter and more pleasing, as its every feeling is wholly divine. To be thus affected is to become deified.

> St. Bernard: *On the Necessity of Loving God,* 10. (12th cent.)

Deism

Slave to no sect, who takes no private road,
But looks through nature up to nature's God.

> Pope: *An Essay on Man,* 4. (18th cent.)

Delay

To men prepared
Delay is injury and never friend.

> Dante: *Inferno, Canto 28.* (Tr. L. Binyon) (14th cent.)

Good is best when soonest wrought,
Lingered labors come to nought.

> Bl. Robert Southwell: *Loss in Delay.* (16th cent.)

Works adjourned have many stays,
Long demurs breed new delays.

> Bl. Robert Southwell: *Loss in Delay.* (16th cent.)

Delight

Life is not life at all without delight.

> Coventry Patmore: *Victory in Defeat.* (19th cent.)

Democracy

People's voice is God's voice, men say.

> Thomas Hoccleve: *De Regimine Principum,* 104. (15th cent.)

The American people will always be progressive as well as conservative; but they have learned a lesson, which they much needed, against false democracy: civil war has taught them that 'the sacred right of insurrection' is as much out of place in a democratic state as in an aristocratic or a monarchical state; and that the government should always be clothed with ample authority to arrest and punish whoever plots its destruction.

> Orestes Brownson: *The American Republic.* (19th cent.)

It is not of itself wrong to prefer a democratic form of government, if only the Catholic doctrine be maintained as to the origin and exercise of power. Of the various forms of government, the Church does not reject any that are fitted to procure the welfare of the subject; she wishes only—and this nature itself requires—that they should be constituted without involving wrong to any one, and especially without violating the rights of the Church.

> Pope Leo XIII: *Libertas Praestantissumum.* (June 20, 1888)

The citizens of America are her monarchs. No country deserves so well of its people as America, and none is so dependent upon them.

> Archb. Ireland: *The Church and Modern Society.* (19th cent.)

Democracy doesn't give the average man any real power at all. It swamps him among his fellows—that is to say, it kills his individuality; and his individuality is the one thing he has which is worth anything.

> R. H. Benson: *The Dawn of All.* (20th cent.)

All men are democrats when they are happy.

> G. K. Chesterton: *What's Wrong with the World.* (20th cent.)

Democracy in its human sense is not arbitrament by the majority; it is not even arbitrament by everybody. It can be more nearly defined as arbitrament by anybody: I mean that it rests on that club-habit of taking a total stranger for granted, of assuming certain things to be inevitably common to yourself and him.

G. K. Chesterton: *What's Wrong with the World.* (20th cent.)

Catholic theology has nothing to do with democracy, for or against, in the sense of a machinery of voting or a criticism of particular privileges. It is not committed to support what Whitman said for democracy, or even what Jefferson or Lincoln said for democracy. But it is absolutely committed to contradict what Mr. Mencken says against democracy. There will be Diocletian persecutions, there will be Dominican crusades, there will be rending of all religious peace and compromise, or even the end of civilization and the world, before the Catholic Church will admit that one single moron, or one single man, "is not worth saving."

G. K. Chesterton: *The Thing.* (H. L. Mencken remarked of certain ex-liberals, "They have come to realize that the morons whom they sweated to save do not want to be saved, and are not worth saving.") (20th cent.)

Democracy swept Europe with the sabre when it was founded on the Rights of Man. It has done literally nothing at all since it has been founded only upon the wrongs of man, or, more strictly speaking, its recent failure has been due to its not admitting the existence of any rights or wrongs, or indeed of any humanity.

G. K. Chesterton: *Charles Dickens.* (20th cent.)

That Christianity is identical with democracy, is the hardest of gospels; there is nothing that so strikes men with fear as the saying that they are all the sons of God.

G. K. Chesterton: *Twelve Types.* (20th cent.)

Democracy is a thing which is always breaking down through the complexity of civilization.

G. K. Chesterton: *The Everlasting Man.* (20th cent.)

If there be one thing more than another which is true of genuine democracy, it is that genuine democracy is opposed to the rule of the mob. For genuine democracy is based fundamentally on the existence of the citizen, and the best definition of a mob is a body of a thousand men in which there is no citizen.

G. K. Chesterton: *A Handful of Authors.* (20th cent.)

Democracy, that is, the government of the community by the community: a state wherein a man stands equal with his fellows, and has to suffer neither subservience nor the corruption of flattery and power; a state in which office alone commands, and not the being clothed with office—that is the ideal at the back of every man's mind who cares for right in public affairs, and who has within himself anything left of private honor. It is simplest put by saying that democracy is the noblest form of government.

H. Belloc: *The Cruise of the Nona.* (20th cent.)

Democracy means government by the uneducated, while aristocracy means government by the badly educated.

G. K. Chesterton: *N. Y. Times.* (Feb. 1, 1931.)

You can never have a revolution in order to establish a democracy. You must have a democracy in order to have a revolution.

G. K. Chesterton: *Tremendous Trifles.* (20th cent.)

Considering the extent and nature of the sacrifices demanded of all citizens, especially in our day when the activity of the state is so vast and decisive, the democratic form of government appears to many a postulate of nature imposed by reason itself.

> Pope Pius XII: *Christmas Message*. (Dec. 24, 1944)

Two rights which democracies guarantee to their citizens, as the very term democracy implies, are that they shall have full freedom to set forth their own views of the duties and sacrifices imposed upon them, and that they will not be compelled to obey without being heard. From the solidarity, harmony and good results produced by this understanding between the citizens and the government, one may decide when a democracy is really healthy and well balanced, and what is its life energy and power of expansion.

> Pope Pius XII: *Christmas Message*. (Dec. 24, 1944)

In the late 1920's men thought that democracy was inevitable; now they know that it is an achievement, always precarious.

> John Courtney Murray: *Address, Jesuit Philippine Bureau Dinner, NYC*. (Dec. 1, 1949)

Those who teach the democratic charter must believe in it with their whole hearts, and stake on it their personal convictions, their consciences, and the depths of their moral life. They must therefore explain and justify its articles in the light of the philosophical or religious faith to which they cling and which quickens their belief in the common charter.

> J. Maritain: *Man and the State*. (20th cent.)

True democracy cannot exist and thrive except in an atmosphere of respect for God and observance of His commandments, as well as for the Christian solidarity of brotherhood.

> Pope Pius XII: *Christmas Message*. (Dec. 24, 1953)

Demon

Demons are everywhere, and the cursing of them is universal.

> Tertullian: *The Testimony of the Christian Soul*. (3rd cent.)

Desire

Remove every evil desire and clothe yourself with good and holy desire. For if you are clothed with good desire, you will hate evil desire and bridle it as you please.

> Shepherd of Hermas, Mandate 12, 1. (2nd cent.)

For desire never ceases to pray even though the tongue be silent. If ever desiring, then ever praying.

> St. Augustine: *Sermon 80*, 7. (5th cent.)

I saw myself dying with a desire to see God, and I knew not how to seek that life otherwise than by dying.

> St. Teresa of Jesus: *Autobiography*, 20. (16th cent.)

Tender twigs are bent with ease,
  Aged trees do break with bending;
Young desires make little prease,
  Growth doth make them past amending.

> prease—press
> Bl. Robert Southwell: *Loss in Delay*. (16th cent.)

Do not desire not to be what you are, but desire to be very well what you are.

> St. Francis de Sales: *Letters to Persons in the World*, 6, 19. (17th cent.)

To desire something for any reason than for God is to desire God less.

> Jean Pierre Camus: *The Spirit of St. Francis de Sales*, 1, 3. (17th cent.)

To desire to love God is to love to desire Him, and hence to love Him; for love is the root of all desire.

> Jean Pierre Camus: *The Spirit of St. Francis de Sales*, 1, 3. (17th cent.)

O thou undaunted daughter of desires!
By all thy dower of lights and fires;
By all the eagle in thee, all the dove;
By all thy lives and deaths of love;
By thy large draughts of intellectual
    day,
And by thy thirsts of love more large
    than they;
By all thy brim-fill'd bowls of fierce de-
    sire,
By thy last morning's draught of liquid
    fire;
By the full kingdom of that final kiss
That seiz'd thy parting soul, and seal'd
    thee His;
By all the heav'ns thou hast in Him,
(Fair sister of the seraphim!)
By all of Him we have in thee;
Leave nothing of myself in me.
Let me so read thy life, that I
Unto all life of mine may die.

> Richard Crashaw: *The Flaming Heart.* (St.
> Teresa of Avila) (17th cent.)

And every little spark of beauty's burn-
    ing
Is but a fragment of the central fire,
Kindled of Thee, O Source of all our
    yearning!
    O Light! O Flame! Who art the
    world's desire.

> Sister M. Angelita: *Lesser Fires.* (20th
> cent.)

Desire and Will

Love celestial desires, and desire celestial love.

> St. Francis de Sales: *Letters to Persons in
> the World,* 1, 3. (17th cent.)

Desires, Evil

Grant unto us, we beseech Thee, O Lord,
the grace to quench within ourselves the
fire of evil desires; even as Thou didst
endow blessed Lawrence with strength
to triumph over the flames that tortured
him.

> Roman Missal, Collect after Mass.
> (Gregorian, 6th to 8th cent.)

Desolation

God hath created night
As well as days, to deck the varied
    globe;
Grace comes as oft clad in the dusky
    robe
Of desolation, as in white attire,
Which better fits the bright celestial
    choir.

> Sir John Beaumont: *In Desolation.* (17th
> cent.)

Despair

We need not despair of any man, so long
as he lives.

> St. Augustine: *In Ps. 36, Sermon 2, 11.*
> (5th cent.)

If anyone were to judge, in universal,
that God's mercy is not infinite, he
would be an unbeliever. But he who
despairs judges not thus, but that, for
him in that state, on account of some
particular disposition, there is no hope
of the Divine mercy.

> St. Thomas Aquinas: *Summa Theologica,*
> 2-2, 20, 2. (13th cent.)

A cry goes up of great despair,—
Miserere, Domine!

> Adelaide Procter: *The Storm.* (19th cent.)

Not, I'll not, carrion comfort, despair,
    not feast on thee;
Not untwist—slack they may be—these
    last strands of man
In me or, most weary, cry I can to
    more. I can;
Can something, hope, wish day come,
    not choose not to be.

> G. M. Hopkins: *Carrion Comfort.* (19th
> cent.)

That night, that year
Of now done darkness I wretch lay
    wrestling with (my God!) my
    God.

> G. M. Hopkins: *Carrion Comfort.* (19th
> cent.)

The golden wine is drunk, the dregs
remain,
Bitter as wormwood and as salt as
pain;
And health and hope have gone the
way of love
Into the dear oblivion of lost things.

Ernest Dowson: *Dregs*. (19th cent.)

Despair is the absolute extreme of self-
love. It is reached when a man deliberately turns his back on all help from
anyone else in order to taste the rotten
luxury of knowing himself to be lost.

Thomas Merton: *Seeds of Contemplation*.
(20th cent.)

It takes eternity to make a man despair.

Bishop Sheen: *Peace of Soul*. (20th cent.)

Despotism

Some races are like children, and require a despot to nurse, and feed, and
dress them, to give them pocket money,
and to take them out for airings.

Card. Newman: *Discussions and
Arguments*. (19th cent.)

The Christian notion of conscience im-
peratively demands a corresponding
measure of personal liberty. The feeling
of duty and responsibility to God is the
only arbiter of a Christian's actions.
With this no human authority can be
permitted to interfere. . . . The Church
cannot tolerate any species of government in which this right is not recognized. She is the irreconcilable enemy of
the despotism of the state, whatever its
name or its forms may be, and through
whatever instruments it may be exercised.

Lord Acton: *Political Thoughts on the
Church*. (19th cent.)

The sin and sorrow of despotism is not
that it does not love men, but that it
loves them too much and trusts them too
little.

G. K. Chesterton: *Robert Browning*. (20th
cent.)

If there is one fact we really can prove,
from the history that we do know, it is
that despotism can be a development,
often a late development and very often
indeed the end of societies that have
been highly democratic. A despotism
may almost be defined as a tired democracy.

G. K. Chesterton: *The Everlasting Man*.
(20th cent.)

Destiny

The destiny, minister general,
That executeth in the world over-all
The purveyance, that God hath seen be-
fore,
So strong it is, that, though the world
had sworn
The contrary of a thing, by yea or nay,
Yet sometime it shall fallen on a day
That faileth not eft within a thousand
year.
For certainly, our appetites here,
Be it of war, or peace, or hate, or love,
All is thus rulèd by the sight above.

Chaucer: *The Knightes Tale*. (14th cent.)

Where'er she lie,
Lock'd up from mortal eye,
In shady leaves of destiny.

Richard Crashaw: *Wishes to His
(Supposed) Mistress*. (17th cent.)

The one inexorable thing!

Louise Imogen Guiney: *A Friend's Song
for Simoisius*. (19th cent.)

See also Fate

Details

One should absorb the color of life, but
one should never remember its details.
Details are always vulgar.

Oscar Wilde: *The Picture of Dorian Gray*,
8. (19th cent.)

Detraction

He who could take away detraction from the world, would take away from it a great part of its sins and iniquities.

> St. Francis de Sales: *Introduction to the Devout Life,* 3, 29. (17th cent.)

Devil

The devil comes and tempts all the servants of God. Those who are strong in the faith resist him and he goes away from them, because he cannot find entrance. So, he goes then to the empty and, finding an entrance, he goes into them. Thus he accomplishes in them whatever he pleases and makes them his slaves.

> Shepherd of Hermas, Mandate 12, 5, 4. (2nd cent.)

Regarding the devil and his angels, and the opposing influences, the teaching of the Church has laid down that these beings exist indeed; but what they are, or how they exist, it has not explained with sufficient clearness. This opinion, however, is held by most, that the devil was an angel, and that having become an apostate he induced as many of the angels as possible to fall away with himself, and these up to the present time are called his angels.

> Origen: *De Principiis,* Proem. 6. (3rd cent.)

The devil's snare does not catch you, unless you are first caught by the devil's bait.

> St. Ambrose: *Explanation of Psalm 118,* 14, 37. (4th cent.)

The devil rules over lovers of temporal goods belonging to this visible world, not because he is lord of this world, but because he is ruler of those covetous desires by which we long for all that passes away.

> St. Augustine: *De Agone Christiano,* 1, 1. (4th cent.)

For there is more than one way of sacrificing to the fallen angels.

> St. Augustine: *Confessions,* 1, 17. (5th cent.)

When the devil is called the god of this world, it is not because he made it, but because we serve him with our worldliness.

> St. Thomas Aquinas: *Summa Theologica,* 1, 65, 1. (13th cent.)

Demons are intellectual without admixture of body, and therefore have no base inclinations.

> St. Thomas Aquinas: *Concerning Separate Substances,* 18. (13th cent.)

A liar and the father of lies.

> Dante: *Inferno, Canto* 23. (14th cent.)

O Satan, ever envious since the day
On which they chased you out of Paradise,
Our heritage! How soon you found the way
Through Eve to woman! Our bondage is the price.

> Chaucer: *The Man of Law's Tale.* (Tr. Coghill) (14th cent.)

For it is often said of him that yet lives,
He must needs go that the devil drives.

> Lydgate: *Assembly of Gods,* 3. (15th cent.)

The devil, they say, is dead, The devil is dead!

> John Skelton: *Colin Clout,* 36. (16th cent.)

Sin it were to believe the devil.

> St. Thomas More. (16th cent.)

In good faith, I rejoiced, son, quoth he, that I had given the devil a foul fall, and that with those lords I had gone so far, as without great shame I could never go back again.

> Words of St. Thomas More, after his doom had been sealed. (Roper, Life) (16th cent.)

To set up a candle before the devil.

> John Heywood: *Proverbs*, 1, 10. (16th cent.)

The devil in th'horloge.

> John Heywood: *Proverbs*, 2, 4. (16th cent.)

The devil is no falser than he is.

> John Heywood: *Proverbs*, 2, 5. (16th cent.)

I will not bear the devil's sack.

> John Heywood: *Proverbs*, 2, 5. (16th cent.)

Meet to set the devil on sale.

> John Heywood: *Proverbs*, 2, 7. (16th cent.)

The devil go with thee down the lane.

> John Heywood: *Proverbs*, 2, 7. (16th cent.)

Devils are not so black as they are painted.

> Thomas Lodge: *A Marguerite of America.* (16th cent.)

In all God's universe there is one, and only one, creature whom we know positively to be damned. And that creature is the devil. But remember, my dear young friends, though the devil is damned, he is no damn fool.

> J. B. Tabb. (Litz, *Father Tabb,* 38.) (19th cent.)

> Each in his proper gloom;
> Each in his dark, just place:
> The builders of their doom
> Hide, each his awful face.

> Lionel Johnson: *Visions.* (19th cent.)

Dark angel, with thine aching lust
To rid the world of penitence;
Malicious angel, who still dost
My soul such subtile violence!

.   .   .   .

Do what thou wilt, thou shalt not so,
Dark angel! triumph over me:

Lonely, unto the Lone I go;
Divine, to the Divinity.

> Lionel Johnson: *The Dark Angel.* (19th cent.)

To praise God is proper—but a wise one won't go on to blaguard the devil.

> Seumas MacManus: *Heavy Hangs the Golden Grain.* (20th cent.)

Don't bid the devil good-morra till you meet him.

> Seumas MacManus: *Heavy Hangs the Golden Grain.* (20th cent.)

Devotion

For Thee do I yearn, Justice and Innocence, Beautiful and Fair, in Thy beauteous light that satisfies and yet never sates! For with Thee is repose exceedingly and life without disquiet! He that enters into Thee enters into the joy of His Lord; for he shall know no fear, and in the Best shall be best. But I have deserted Thee and have wandered away, O Lord, my God! Too far have I wandered from Thee, the Steadfast One, in my youth, and I have become to myself a very land of want!

> St. Augustine: *Confessions*, 2, 10. (5th cent.)

Keep Thy household in continual godliness, we beseech Thee, O Lord; that it may be freed from all adversity by Thy protection, and devoted to Thy name in good works.

> Roman Missal, Collect for Twenty-first Sunday after Pentecost. (Gregorian, 6th to 8th cent.)

Devotion is a certain act of the will by which man gives himself promptly to the divine service.

> St. Thomas Aquinas: *Summa Theologica,* 2-2, 82, 3. (13th cent.)

Doctrinal instruction is nobler than chant as a method of rousing men to devotion.

> St. Thomas Aquinas: *Summa Theologica,* 2-2, 91, 2. (13th cent.)

I shall not believe that you are in the Spirit, unless I see the fruits of the Spirit.

> Erasmus: *Enchiridion.* (16th cent.)

True devotion is nothing else than good will by which a man holds himself ready for all that concerns the worship, honor and good pleasure of God.

> Louis de Blois (Blosius): *A Short Rule,* 3. (16th cent.)

Do not show signs of devotion outwardly when thou hast none within, but thou mayest lawfully hide the want thereof.

> St. Teresa of Jesus: *Maxims.* (16th cent.)

Let not thine inward devotion be visible unless in great necessity; St. Francis and St. Bernard used to say, *My secret is mine* (Is. 24, 16).

> St. Teresa of Jesus: *Maxims.* (16th cent.)

In so far as divine love beautifies our souls, and makes us pleasing to His divine majesty, it is called grace; in so far as it gives us strength to do good, it is called charity; but when it reaches such a degree of perfection, that it makes us not only do good, but do so carefully, frequently and readily, then it is called devotion.

> St. Francis de Sales: *Introduction to the Devout Life,* 1, 1. (17th cent.)

Charity and devotion differ no more, the one from the other, than the flame from the fire.

> St. Francis de Sales: *Introduction to the Devout Life,* 1, 1. (17th cent.)

One must not be so devoted to even the most pious practices as to be unable to break into them.

> Jean Pierre Camus: *The Spirit of St. Francis de Sales,* 8, 11. (17th cent.)

True devotion advances boldly, without stopping to worry about details.

> J. P. Camus: *The Spirit of St. Francis de Sales,* 20, 9. (17th cent.)

Genuine devotion is consistent with every state in life. Like liquid poured into a container, it adapts itself to any shape.

> J. P. Camus: *The Spirit of St. Francis de Sales,* 21, 3. (17th cent.)

Beads and prayer-books are the toys of age.

> Pope: *An Essay on Man,* 2. (18th cent.)

Men of reverential and religious tempers are apt to hide themselves from those who are not worthy of them.

> Card. Newman: *Essays Critical and Historical,* 2. (19th cent.)

Religion acts on the affections; who is to hinder these, when once aroused, from gathering in their strength and running wild?

> Card. Newman: *Letter to the Rev. E. B. Pusey.* (19th cent.)

I prefer English habits of belief and devotion to foreign, from the same causes, and by the same right, which justifies foreigners in preferring their own. In following those of my people, I show less singularity, and create less disturbance than if I made a flourish with what is novel and exotic. And in this line of conduct I am but availing myself of the teaching which I fell in with on becoming a Catholic; and it is a pleasure to me to think that what I hold now, and would transmit after me if I could, is only what I received then.

> Card. Newman: *Letter to the Rev. E. B. Pusey on his Eirenicon.* (19th cent.)

No soul can be lost by following the simple and well-beaten path of ordinary devotion and prayer.

> R. H. Benson: *The Light Invisible.* (20th cent.)

We have continually to test the reality of our devotion to Him by our practical devotion to one another.

> R. H. Benson: *The Friendship of Christ.* (20th cent.)

Dialectic

Dialectic is the discipline elaborated with a view to ascertaining the causes of things.

> St. Isidore: *Etymologies,* 2, 22. (7th cent.)

Dickens, Charles

Dickens was frequently horrible; he was never cruel. The art of Dickens was the most exquisite of arts: it was the art of enjoying everybody.

> G. K. Chesterton: *The Victorian Age in Literature.* (20th cent.)

Difficulty

Everything is plain and easy to the earnest; it is the double-minded who find difficulties.

> Card. Newman: *Parochial and Plain Sermons,* 1. (19th cent.)

Ten thousand difficulties do not make one doubt, as I understand the subject; difficulty and doubt are incommensurate.

> Card. Newman: *Apologia pro Vita Sua,* 5. (19th cent.)

Sometimes great difficulties are permitted only in order to strengthen character.

> R. H. Benson: *The Sentimentalists.* (20th cent.)

Digestion

Bitters will purge—crude things in all cause wind,
And salted meats the body dry and bind,
While crusts give rise to bile of darkest kind.

> School of Salerno, Code of Health. (11th cent.)

Fried meats do harm; while boiled give peptic peace;
And fragrant roasts, digestive powers increase.

> School of Salerno, Code of Health. (11th cent.)

The process of digestion in every organism separates the healthy and useful from the harmful and useless elements.

> R. H. Benson: *A City Set on a Hill.* (20th cent.)

Dignity

The two things that a healthy person hates most between heaven and hell are a woman who is not dignified and a man who is.

> G. K. Chesterton: *All Things Considered.* (20th cent.)

Dilettante

No man can be a true poet who writes for diversion only. These authors should be considered as versifiers and witty men rather than as poets.

> Pope: *Letter to Henry Cromwell.* (18th cent.)

Dimple

A dimple in the chin; a devil within.

> Irish Proverb. (Modern?)

Dining

In comparison with the stars, what is more trifling a matter than my dinner?

> St. Augustine: *Soliloquies,* 1. (4th cent.)

Great suppers will the stomach's peace impair.
Wouldst lightly rest? curtail thine evening fare.

> School of Salerno, Code of Health. (11th cent.)

Diners cannot be long where dainties want.

> John Heywood: *Proverbs,* 2, 1. (16th cent.)

After a good dinner, one can forgive anybody, even one's own relations.

> Oscar Wilde: *A Woman of No Importance,* 2. (19th cent.)

Director, Spiritual

Spiritual directors are not the chief workers, but rather the Holy Ghost; they are mere instruments, only to guide souls by the rule of faith and the law of God according to the spirit which God gives to each. Their object, therefore, should be not to guide souls by a way of their own, suitable to themselves; but to ascertain, if they can, the way which God Himself is guiding them.

St. John of the Cross: *The Ascent of Mt. Carmel.* (16th cent.)

Would you walk in earnest toward devotion? Seek some good man who will guide you; this is the greatest of all words of advice.

St. Francis de Sales: *Introduction to the Devout Life,* 1, 4. (17th cent.)

Disadvantage

Who had the worst end of the staff?

John Heywood: *Proverbs,* 2, 3. (16th cent.)

Disagreement

They two agreed like two cats in a gutter.

John Heywood: *Proverbs,* 2, 1. (16th cent.)

Disappointment

Blessed is he who expects nothing, for he shall never be disappointed.

Pope: *Letter to John Gay.* (18th cent.)

Like Dead-Sea fruits that tempt the eye
But turn to ashes on the lips.

Thomas Moore: *Lalla Rookh: The Fire-Worshippers.* (19th cent.)

Oh! ever thus from childhood's hour,
 I've seen my fondest hopes decay;
I never lov'd a tree or flow'r,
 But 'twas the first to fade away.
I never nurs'd a dear gazelle,
 To glad me with its soft black eye,

But when it came to know me well,
 And love me, it was sure to die!

Thomas Moore: *Lalla Rookh: The Fire-Worshippers.* (19th cent.)

Her hair was a waving bronze and her eyes
Deep wells that might cover a brooding soul;
And who, till he weighed it, could ever surmise
That her heart was a cinder instead of a coal?

John Boyle O'Reilly: *Disappointment.* (19th cent.)

Disapproval

If the worst fell, we could have but a nay.

John Heywood: *Proverbs,* 1, 11. (16th cent.)

Discipline

Therefore did You break my bones with the rod of Your discipline.

St. Augustine: *Confessions,* 6, 6. (5th cent.)

Discontent

Discontent is the first step in the progress of a man or nation.

Oscar Wilde: *A Woman of No Importance,* 2. (19th cent.)

Discretion

Without discretion virtue becomes vice and the natural impulses serve only to upset and wreck the personality.

St. Bernard: *Sermons on the Canticle of Canticles,* 50. (12th cent.)

Holy discretion ordains that the soul should direct all her powers to My service with a manly zeal, and that she should love her neighbor with such devotion that she would lay down a thousand times, if it were possible, the life of her body for the salvation of souls, enduring pains and torments so that her neighbor may have the life of grace, and giving her temporal substance for the profit and relief of his body. This is the supreme office of discretion which proceeds from charity.

> St. Catherine of Siena: *The Dialogue.* (14th cent.)

Discrimination

Discriminations and segregations in civil or political matters on lines of religion, of birthplace, of race, of language, of color, are wrong and un-American. Compel all to be Americans, in soul as well as in name: and then let the standard of their worth be their American citizenship.

> Archb. Ireland: *Discourse on Patriotism.* (New York, Apr. 4, 1894)

I would scorn to draw distinctions among Catholics because of race or language. I am, I must be, as Catholic as God's Church. I differ from men, I war with men on account of ideas, not on account of race.

> Archb. Ireland: *Freeman's Journal,* April 3, 1897.

Disdain

We often show more disdain by the expression of our mind than the expression of our face.

> St. Francis de Sales: *Letters to Persons in the World,* 1, 3. (17th cent.)

Disease

O God, Who dost not desire the death but the repentance of sinners: mercifully look upon Thy people who have turned to Thee; that as they are devoted to Thee, Thou mayest in Thy mercy remove from them the scourge of Thy anger.

> Roman Missal, Collect. (Gelasian, 5th to 7th cent.)

Disfavor

Cross thee quite out of my book.

> John Heywood: *Proverbs,* 1, 11. (16th cent.)

Dispensation

A dispensation is a relaxation of the law in a particular case: it can be granted by the legislator, by his successor in office, by a superior legislator and by a person delegated by the foregoing.

> Code of Canon Law, Canon 80. (20th cent.)

Disposition

To change one's disposition is greater than to change one's dress.

> St. Jerome: *Letters,* 77, 2. (4th cent.)

Dissimulation

To know how to dissemble is the knowledge of kings.

> Card. Richelieu: *Mirame.* (17th cent.)

Distance

As distant prospects please us, but when near
We find but desert rocks, and fleeting air.

> Sir Samuel Garth: *The Dispensary,* 3. (17th cent.)

A hair's breadth is sometimes a great distance.

> R. H. Benson: *The Confessions of a Convert.* (20th cent.)

Distrust

Here must thou all distrust behind thee leave.

> Dante: *Inferno, Canto 3.* (14th cent.)

I will not trust him though he were my brother.

> John Heywood: *Proverbs,* 1, 11. (16th cent.)

Divine Office

I think that variety and diversity in the prayers and psalms recited at appointed hours are desirable for the reason that routine and boredom, somehow, often cause distraction in the soul, while by change and variety of the psalmody and prayers said at the stated hours it is refreshed in devotion and renewed in sobriety.

St. Basil: *The Long Rules,* 37. (4th cent.)

What then is more blessed than to imitate on earth the anthems of angels' choirs; to hasten to prayer at the very break of day, and to worship our Creator with hymns and songs; then, when the sun shines brightly and we turn to our tasks, prayer attending us wherever we go, to season our labors with sacred song as food with salt? For that state of the soul in which there is joy and no sorrow is a boon bestowed by the consolation of hymns.

St. Basil: *Letters,* 2. (4th cent.)

If the psalm prays do you too pray; if it laments, so do you too; if it renders thanks, so do you also rejoice with it; if it hopes, so you too; if it speaks in the accents of fear, do you also tremble with it; for all that is written therein is meant to be a mirror for us.

St. Augustine: *Sermon on Ps. 30.* (5th cent.)

The work of God. (Opus Dei)

St. Benedict: *Rule,* 7. (6th cent.)

We believe that God is present everywhere and that *the eyes of the Lord in every place behold the good and the evil* (Prov. 15, 3); but let us especially believe this without any doubting when we are performing the divine office.

St. Benedict: *Rule,* 19. (6th cent.)

We decree that all the clergy attached to each church shall themselves sing the nocturnal, morning and evening prayers. For it is absurd that the clergy, on whom rests the duty of executing the psalmody, should hire people to sing in their stead. If many of the laity come to the churches and for the good of their souls take part in the psalmody, is it not absurd that the clergy who are specially appointed for that office should not fulfil it!

Decree of Justinian I. (Code, 1, 3, 4) (528)

Therefore that the face may be lifted up in prayer without spot (Job, 11, 13), it behoves that before the seasons of prayer everything that can possibly be reproved in the act of prayer be heedfully looked into, and that the mind when it stays from prayer as well should hasten to show itself such, as it desires to appear to the Judge in the very season itself of prayer.

Pope St. Gregory I: *Morals,* 10, 29. (6th cent.)

The divine office is a part of the divine tradition. It is a perpetual witness for God and for the faith. It has been wrought together by the hands of men; but those men were saints, and their work was wrought under the guidance of the Holy Ghost. The framing of the ritual may have been the work of human hands; but the materials of which it is composed are the words of the Spirit of God.

Card. Manning: *The Eternal Priesthood.* (19th cent.)

The psalms and scriptures of inspired men under the old law and the new, with the writings of the saints, are all interwoven into a wonderful texture of prayer and praise, of worship and witness of the kingdom of God, and of the communion of saints. The perpetual revolution of yearly solemnities and festivals—winter and spring, summer and autumn—brings round continually the whole revelation of faith. Prophets and apostles, evangelists and saints, speak to us with voices that never die. The whole history of the kingdom of God is always returning upon our sight.

Card. Manning: *The Eternal Priesthood.* (19th cent.)

The clergy who are in major orders . . . are bound to recite the canonical hours daily in their entirety according to the proper approved liturgical books.

Code of Canon Law, Canon 135. (20th cent.)

The divine office is the prayer of the mystical Body of Jesus Christ, offered to God in the name and on behalf of all Christians, when recited by priests and other ministers of the Church and by religious who are deputed by the Church for this.

Pope Pius XII: *Mediator Dei*. (Nov. 20, 1947)

See also Compline; Lauds; Liturgy; Matins; None; Prayer; Prime; Sext; Terce; Vespers; Vigil

Divorce

Divorce by now is prayed for, as if it were the proper sequel of marriage.

Tertullian: *Apology, 6, 6*. (3rd cent.)

Those whom God has joined together man must not put asunder (Matth. 19, 8), lest he act against the Lord's will. He alone may separate husband and wife Who has united them in marriage; and He will separate them, not by the harsh method of divorce, which He censures and outlaws, but by the destiny of death.

Tertullian: *On Monogamy, 9*. (3rd cent.)

A man is guilty of adultery if he marries a divorced woman; and so is he who divorces his wife, save on the ground of misconduct, in order to marry again.

Lactantius: *Divinae Institutiones, 6*. (4th cent.)

If any layman divorces his own wife, and takes another, or one divorced by another, let him be suspended.

Ecclesiastical Canons of the Holy Apostles, 48. (4th cent.)

It is wrong to leave a wife who is sterile in order to take another by whom children may be had. Anyone doing this is guilty of adultery.

St. Augustine: *Conjugal Adultery*, 1. (5th cent.)

If a man leaves his wife and she marries another, she commits adultery.

St. Augustine: *On the Good of Marriage*. (5th cent.)

For if they say that marriages should be dissolved for the sake of religion, be it known that, though human law has conceded this, yet divine law has forbidden it.

Pope St. Gregory I: *Letters, 11, 45*. (6th cent.)

If any one saith that on account of heresy, or irksome cohabitation, or the intentional absence of one of the parties, the bond of matrimony may be dissolved; let him be anathema.

Council of Trent, Session 24, Canon 5. (Nov. 11, 1563)

If any one saith that the Church has erred in that she hath taught, and doth teach, in accordance with evangelical and apostolical doctrine, that the bond of matrimony cannot be dissolved on account of the adultery of one of the married parties; and that both, or even the innocent one who gave not occasion to the adultery, cannot contract another marriage during the life-time of the other; and that he is guilty of adultery who, having put away the adulteress, shall take another wife, as also she who, having put away the adulterer, shall take another husband; let him be anathema.

Council of Trent, Session 24, Canon 7. (Nov. 11, 1563)

Divorce is born of perverted morals, and leads, as experience shows, to vicious habits in public and private life.

Pope Leo XIII: *Arcanum Divinae Sapientiae*. (Feb. 10, 1880)

The Romans of old are said to have shrunk with horror from the first examples of divorce, but ere long all sense of decency was blunted in their soul; the meager restraint of passion died out, and the marriage vow was so often broken that what some writers have affirmed would seem to be true—namely, women used to reckon years not by the change of consuls, but of their husbands.

> Pope Leo XIII: *Arcanum Divinae Sapientiae.* (Feb. 10, 1880)

Truly, it is hardly possible to describe how great are the evils that flow from divorce. Matrimonial contracts are by it made variable; mutual kindness is weakened; deplorable inducements to unfaithfulness are supplied; harm is done to the education and training of children; occasion is afforded for the breaking up of homes; the seeds of dissension are sown among families; the dignity of womanhood is lessened and brought low, and women run the risk of being deserted after having ministered to the pleasures of men.

> Pope Leo XIII: *Arcanum Divinae Sapientiae.* (Feb. 10, 1880)

This world is all one wild divorce court; nevertheless, there are many who still hear in their souls the thunder of the authority of human habit; those whom God hath joined together let no man sunder.

> G. K. Chesterton: *What's Wrong with the World.* (20th cent.)

Say, young man! if you've a wife,
  Kiss her.
Every morning of your life,
  Kiss her.
Every evening when the sun
Marks your day of labor done,
Get you homeward on the run—
  Kiss her!

        . . . .

If you think it's "soft," you're wrong.
  Kiss her.
Love like this will make you strong.
  Kiss her.
If you'd strike with telling force
At the evil of divorce,

Just adopt this simple course:
  Kiss her!

> T. A. Daly: *Kiss Her.* (20th cent.)

See also Marriage; Marriage: Dissolution; Marriage: Separation

Doctor

As usually happens, the man who has tried a bad doctor is afraid to trust even a good one.

> St. Augustine: *Confessions,* 6, 4. (5th cent.)

Knowledge not gratis comes. Nor without fees,
On sick men, would attend Hippocrates.
When any doctor first attends a call,
The patient would bestow the world and all;
But once relieved and safely out of bed,
The doctor's aid from memory has fled.

> School of Salerno, Code of Health. (11th cent.)

Good common sense and leechcraft cure disease,
Not empty words of boastful, lying quack.
(Sensus et ars medici curant, non verba sophistae.)

> School of Salerno, Code of Health. (11th cent.)

Shouldst doctors need? be these in doctors' stead—
Rest, cheerfulness, and table thinly spread.

> School of Salerno, Code of Health. (11th cent.)

Take your fee while the patient is still in pain.

> John of Salisbury: *Policraticus,* 2, 29, 168. (12th cent.)

Three faces wears the doctor: when first sought,
An angel's; and a god's, the cure half wrought;
But when, the cure complete, he seeks his fee,

The de'il looks then less terrible than he.

Saying. (Good's *Hist. Med.*, p. 227) (Medieval)

Good leech is he that can himself recure.

Lydgate: *Daunce of Machabree.* (15th cent.)

He is purse-sick, and lacketh a physician.

John Heywood: *Proverbs,* 1, 11. (16th cent.)

So liv'd our sires, ere doctors learn'd to kill,
And multiplied with theirs the weekly bill.

Dryden: *To John Dryden of Chesterton.* (17th cent.)

The first physicians by debauch were made:
Excess began, and sloth sustains the trade.

Dryden: *To John Dryden of Chesterton.* (17th cent.)

Speak, goddess! since 'tis thou that best canst tell,
How ancient leagues to modern discord fell;
And why physicians were so cautious grown
Of others' lives, and lavish of their own.

Sir Samuel Garth: *The Dispensary.* (17th cent.)

One doctor, singly like the sculler plies,
The patient struggles, and by inches dies;
But two physicians, like a pair of oars,
Waft him right swiftly to the Stygian shores.

Sir Samuel Garth: *The Dispensary.* (17th cent.)

How the doctor's brow should smile,
Crown'd with wreaths of camomile.

Thomas Moore: *Wreaths for Ministers.* (19th cent.)

Doctrine

In fact the refutation of heretics serves to bring into clearer light what Your Church holds and what sound doctrine is. *For there must be also heresies: that they who are approved may be made manifest among the weak.*

St. Augustine: *Confessions,* 7, 19. (5th cent.)

To announce to Catholic Christians a doctrine other than that which they have received was never permitted, is nowhere permitted, and never will be permitted. It was ever necessary, is everywhere necessary, and ever will be necessary that those who announce a doctrine other than that which was received once and for all be anathema.

St. Vincent of Lerins: *Commonitoria,* 9. (5th cent.)

'Tis said with ease, but never can be prov'd,
The Church her old foundations has remov'd,
And built new doctrines on unstable sands:
Judge that, ye winds and rains; you prov'd her, yet she stands.

Dryden: *The Hind and the Panther,* 2. (17th cent.)

We claim no pow'r, when heresies grow bold,
To coin new faith, but still declare the old.

Dryden: *The Hind and the Panther,* 2. (17th cent.)

Church doctrines are a powerful weapon; they were not sent into the world for nothing. God's word does not return to Him void.

Card. Newman: *Apologia pro Vita Sua,* 4. (19th cent.)

It is well known that, though the creed of the Church has been one and the same from the beginning, yet it has been so deeply lodged in her bosom as to be held by individuals more or less implicitly instead of being delivered from the first in those special statements, or what are called definitions, under which it is now presented to us, and which preclude mistake or ignorance. These definitions which are but the expression of portions of the one dogma which has ever been received by the Church, are the works of time; they have grown to their present shape and number in the course of eighteen centuries, under the exigency of successive events, such as heresies and the like, and they may of course receive still further definitions as time goes on.

> Card. Newman: *Difficulties of Anglicans,* 1. (19th cent.)

Why should ecclesiastical history, any more than the text of Scripture, contain in it 'the whole counsel of God'? Why should private judgment be unlawful in interpreting Scripture against the voice of authority, and yet be lawful in the interpretation of history . . . ? For myself I would simply confess that no doctrine of the Church can be rigorously proved by historical evidence: but at the same time that no doctrine can be simply disproved by it. Historical evidence reaches a certain way, more or less, towards a proof of the Catholic doctrines; often nearly the whole way; sometimes it goes only as far as to point in their direction; sometimes there is only an absence of evidence for a conclusion contrary to them; nay, sometimes there is an apparent leaning of the evidence to a contrary conclusion, which has to be explained; —in all cases there is a margin left for the exercise of faith in the word of the Church. He who believes the dogmas of the Church only because he has reasoned them out of history, is scarcely a Catholic. It is the Church's dogmatic use of history in which the Catholic believes; and she uses other informants also, Scripture, tradition, the ecclesiastical sense or phenomena, and a subtle ratiocinative power, which in its origin is a divine gift.

> Card. Newman: *Letter to the Duke of Norfolk.* (Against Dr. Döllinger and others) (19th cent.)

There is a certain number of ideas which the Christian irrefragably believes, with such a faith as no scientific man thinks of reposing in any of the progressive realizations of inductive science. And he feels that such ideas as the existence of God, the immortality of the soul, and the punishment of sin, can neither be destroyed by knowledge nor impede its acquisition. Not that he thinks these great religious ideas ought to remain in sterile isolation. Like other general principles, each of them is capable of being made the basis of a vast superstructure of doctrine, proceeding from it with logical necessity. The work of this development has been performed by the organic action of the Church, which in the course of centuries has worked out a consistent system of doctrine, altogether free from accidental or arbitrary elements, the inevitable result of the principles of faith reacting upon the strict laws of thought and historical growth. Every part of this system is equally certain, and, if not equally necessary to be known, yet equally incapable of being denied. No part of it can be destroyed by the progress of knowledge, the last defined dogma no more than the first, no more than the existence of God, or the immortality of the thinking being.

> Lord Acton: *Ultramontanism.* (19th cent.)

The Church must always put herself in harmony with existing ideas, and speak to each age and nation in its own language. A kind of amalgam between the eternal faith and temporal opinion is thus in constant process of generation, and by it Christians explain to themselves the bearings of their religion, so far as their knowledge allows. No wonder if, morally, this amalgam should be valued by its eternal rather than by its temporal element, and that its ideas should come to be regarded as almost equally sacred with the dogmas on which they are partly built. For they have the prestige of possession in their favor; they have come to be mixed up with social institutions and with philosophical speculation; and they form the outside line of defence in the controversial stronghold of Christendom.

> Lord Acton: *Ultramontanism.* (19th cent.)

From the beginning of the Church it has been a law of her nature, that the truths which eventually proved themselves the legitimate products of her doctrine, have had to make their slow way upwards through a phalanx of hostile habits and traditions, and to be rescued not only from open enemies, but also from friendly hands that were not worthy to defend them.

> Lord Acton: *Conflicts with Rome.* (19th cent.)

See also Catholic Faith; Dogma

Doctrine, Development of

Is then religion in the church of Christ incapable of progress? But surely there must be progress and that not a little! Who would be so much man's enemy and God's as to try to prevent it? We must make this reservation however, that the progress shall be a genuine progress and not an alteration of the faith. We have progress when a thing grows and yet remains itself; we have alteration when a thing becomes something else. Therefore let intelligence, knowledge, wisdom grow and make great progress, both those of individuals and those of the collectivity, those of a single man and those of the whole Church, down the ages, down the centuries, but on condition that this be exactly in accordance with their particular nature, that is to say continuing in the same dogma, the same meaning, the same thought.

> St. Vincent of Lerins, *Commonitorium,* 23, 1. (5th cent.)

In the same way, the dogma of the Christian religion ought to follow these laws of progress, so that it may be consolidated in the course of years, developed in the sequence of time, and sublimated by age—yet remain incorrupt and unimpaired, complete and perfect in all the proportions of its parts and in all its essentials (let us call them members and senses), so that it does not allow of any change, or any loss of its specific character, or any variation of its inherent form.

> St. Vincent of Lerins: *Commonitoria,* 23. (5th cent.)

Whatever has been planted in the husbandry of God's Church by the faith of the fathers should, therefore, be cultivated and guarded by the zeal of their children; it should flourish and ripen; it should develop and become perfect. For it is right that those ancient dogmas of heavenly philosophy should in the course of time be thoroughly cared for, filed, and polished; but it is sinful to change them, sinful to behead them or mutilate them. They may take on more evidence, clarity, and distinctness, but it is absolutely necessary that they retain their plenitude, integrity, and basic character.

> St. Vincent of Lerins: *Commonitoria,* 23. (5th cent.)

Regarding its substance, then, faith does not grow with the passage of time, for whatever has been believed since was contained from the start in the faith of the ancient fathers. As regards its explication, however, the number of articles has increased, for we moderns explicitly believe what they believed implicitly.

> St. Thomas Aquinas: *Summa Theologica,* 2-2, 2, 7. (13th cent.)

The life of doctrines may be said to consist in the law or principle which they embody. Principles are abstract and general, doctrines relate to facts; doctrines develop, and principles at first sight do not; doctrines grow and are enlarged; principles are permanent; doctrines are intellectual, and principles are more immediately ethical and practical. . . . Doctrines stand to principles, as the definitions to the axioms and postulates of mathematics.

> Card. Newman: *Development of Christian Doctrine.* (19th cent.)

I have maintained that modern Catholicism is nothing else but simply the legitimate growth and complement, that is, the natural and necessary development, of the doctrine of the early Church, and that its divine authority is included in the divinity of Christianity.

> Card. Newman: *Development of Christian Doctrine*, 5. (18th cent.)

Doctrines expand variously according to the mind, individual or social, into which they are received; and the peculiarities of the recipient are the regulating power, the law, the organization, or, as it may be called, the form of the development.

> Card. Newman: *Development of Christian Doctrine*, 5. (19th cent.)

. . . The increased expansion of the Christian creed and ritual, and the variations which have attended the process in the case of individual writers and churches, are the necessary attendants on any philosophy or polity which takes possession of the intellect and heart, and has had any wide or extended dominion . . . From the nature of the human mind; time is necessary for the full comprehension and perfection of great ideas; and . . . the highest and most wonderful truths, though communicated to the world once for all by inspired teachers, could not be comprehended all at once by the recipients, but, as being received and transmitted by minds not inspired and through media which were human, have required only the longer time and deeper thought for their full elucidation.

> Card. Newman: *The Development of Christian Doctrine*, 29 ff. (19th cent.)

Growth means the unfolding of interior capacities through the assimilation of external substances.

> R. H. Benson: *A City Set on a Hill.* (20th cent.)

The persistent witness of the Church to what she received from the Lord has ensured the identity of the teaching throughout, under the varying form of its expression, while her authority has been divinely assisted to decide what was in harmony with the original deposit and what was not. Yet it is probable that a Christian of the year 100 would have been puzzled by the Athanasian creed; he would have held implicitly all that it enunciates, but the fierce antitheses might well have surprised and shocked him. Judged by the standard of the first four oecumenical councils, scarcely a single ecclesiastical writer of the first three centuries is orthodox in expression.

> Abbot Chapman: *Bishop Gore and the Catholic Claims.* (20th cent.)

It is the divine assistance (not inspiration) which enables the Church to choose rightly, to obtain growth without change. An organism has this power of assimilation and rejection because it is living. The Catholic Church, by possessing it, shows that she lives. . . . The Anglican church, on the other hand, has the greatest facility for accepting new doctrine of any kind, but she lacks the faculty of discrimination which is the mark of life. She has no power of rejecting. She receives like a pail; she does not feed and digest like an organism.

> Abbot Chapman: *Bishop Gore and the Catholic Claims.* (20th cent.)

Dogmas, sacraments, hierarchy, both as regards the notion of them and the reality, are but interpretations and evolutions of the Christian intelligence which by external increments have increased and perfected the little germ latent in the Gospel.

> Proposition condemned by Decree of Holy Office, *Lamentabili,* June 3, 1907.

Dog

No creature is more sagacious than dogs, for they have more understanding than other animals. For they alone recognize their names, love their masters, guard their houses, risk their lives for them, do not abandon even their master's dead body. And finally their nature is such that they cannot exist without men. In dogs two things are to be regarded, courage and speed.

St. Isidore: *Etymologies,* 12, 2. (7th cent.)

Love me, love my dog. (Qui me amat, amat et canem meum.)

St. Bernard: *Sermons.* (12th cent.)

It is nought good a sleeping hound to wake.

Chaucer: *Troilus and Criseyde.* (14th cent.)

A gentle hound should never play the cur.

John Skelton: *Garland of Laurell.* (16th cent.)

What delight can there be, and not rather displeasure in hearing the barking and howling of dogs? Or what greater pleasure is there to be felt when a dog followeth a hare than when a dog followeth a dog?

St. Thomas More: *Utopia.* (16th cent.)

Hungry dogs will eat dirty puddings.

John Heywood: *Proverbs,* 1, 5. (16th cent.)

A poor dog that is not worth the whistling.

John Heywood: *Proverbs,* 1, 11. (16th cent.)

A hair of the dog that bit us last night.

John Heywood: *Proverbs,* 1, 11. (16th cent.)

An old dog biteth sore.

John Heywood: *Proverbs,* 2, 6. (16th cent.)

A dog will bark ere he bite.

John Heywood: *Proverbs,* 2, 7. (16th cent.)

It is hard to make an old dog stoop.

John Heywood: *Proverbs,* 2, 7. (16th cent.)

Histories are more full of examples of the fidelity of dogs than of friends.

Pope: *Letter to H. Cromwell.* (18th cent.)

Silence, ye wolves! while Ralph to Cynthia howls,
And makes night hideous.

Pope: *The Dunciad,* 3. (18th cent.)

I am his Highness's dog at Kew;
Pray tell me, sir, whose dog are you?

Pope: *On the Collar of a Dog.* (18th cent.)

He asks no angel's wing, no seraph's fire,
But thinks, admitted to that equal sky,
His faithful dog shall bear him company.

Pope: *An Essay on Man,* 1. (18th cent.)

Dogma

The Church of Christ, zealous and cautious guardian of the dogmas deposited with it, never changes any phase of them. It does not diminish them or add to them; it neither trims what seems necessary nor grafts things superfluous; it neither gives up its own nor usurps what does not belong to it. But it devotes all its diligence to one aim: to treat tradition faithfully and wisely; to nurse and polish what from old times may have remained unshaped and unfinished; to consolidate and to strengthen what already was clear and plain; and to guard what already was confirmed and defined.

St. Vincent of Lerins: *Commonitoria* 23. (5th cent.)

What is invidiously called dogmatism and system, in one shape or other, in one degree or another, is necessary to the human mind.

Card. Newman: *Oxford University Sermons.* (19th cent.)

The Catholic dogmas are, after all, but the symbols of a divine fact, which, far from being compassed by those very propositions, would not be exhausted, nor fathomed, by a thousand.

Card. Newman: *Oxford University Sermons.* (19th cent.)

No doctrine is defined till it is violated.

> Card. Newman: *Development of Christian Doctrine,* 4. (19th cent.)

From the age of fifteen, dogma has been the fundamental principle of my religion. I know of no other religion; I cannot enter into the idea of any other sort of religion; religion, as a mere sentiment, is to me a dream and a mockery.

> Card. Newman: *Apologia pro Vita Sua,* 2. (19th cent.)

Religion cannot but be dogmatic; it ever has been. All religions have had doctrines; all have professed to carry with them benefits which could be enjoyed only on condition of believing the word of a supernatural informant, that is, of embracing some doctrines or other.

> Card. Newman: *Discussions and Arguments.* (19th cent.)

All the dogmas of the Christian religion are indiscriminately the object of natural science or philosophy; and human reason, enlightened solely by history, is able by its own natural strength and principles to attain to the true knowledge of even the most abstruse dogmas; provided only that such dogmas be proposed to reason itself as its object.

> Proposition condemned by Pius IX in Syllabus of Errors. (1867)

If any one shall assert it to be possible that sometimes, according to the progress of science, a sense is to be given to doctrines propounded by the Church different from that which the Church has understood and understands; let him be anathema.

> Vatican Council, Session 3, Canon 3. (Apr. 24, 1870)

Dogma means the serious satisfaction of the mind. Dogma does not mean the absence of thought, but the end of thought.

> G. K. Chesterton: *The Victorian Age in Literature.* (20th cent.)

Truths turn into dogmas the moment they are disputed.

> G. K. Chesterton: *Heretics.* (20th cent.)

From ecclesiastical judgments and censures passed against free and more scientific exegesis, it may be gathered that the faith proposed by the Church contradicts history and that Catholic dogmas cannot really be reconciled with the true origins of the Christian religion.

> Proposition condemned by Decree of Holy Office, *Lamentabili,* June 3, 1907.

Some people do not like the word 'dogma.' Fortunately they are free, and there is an alternative for them. There are two things, and two things only, for the human mind, a dogma and a prejudice. The Middle Ages were a rational epoch, an age of doctrine. Our age is, at best, a poetical epoch, an age of prejudice. A doctrine is a definite point; a prejudice is a direction.

> G. K. Chesterton: *What's Wrong with the World.* (20th cent.)

All those truths must be believed with divine and Catholic faith which are contained in the written word of God or in tradition and which the Church proposes for acceptance as revealed by God, either by solemn definition or through her ordinary and universal teaching. It is the responsibility of an oecumenical council or the Roman pontiff speaking *ex cathedra* to pronounce a solemn definition of the faith. No doctrine is to be considered as dogmatically defined unless this is evidently proved.

> Code of Canon Law, Canon 1323. (20th cent.)

Instead of the liberty of dogma, you have the tyranny of taste.

> G. K. Chesterton: *A Miscellany of Men.* (20th cent.)

See also Catholic Faith; Doctrine; Doctrine, Development of

Dogmatist

For modes of faith let graceless zealots
fight;
His can't be wrong whose life is in the
right.

Pope: *An Essay on Man,* 3. (18th cent.)

There are two kinds of people in the
world: the conscious dogmatists and the
unconscious dogmatists. I have always
found myself that the unconscious dogmatists were by far the most dogmatic.

G. K. Chesterton: *Generally Speaking.*
(20th cent.)

Doing

Things done cannot be undone.

John Heywood: *Proverbs,* 1, 10. (16th
cent.)

Who will do less than they that may do
most?

John Heywood: *Proverbs,* 1, 11. (16th
cent.)

He that doeth as most men do,
Should be least wondered on.

John Heywood: *Proverbs,* 2, 2. (16th cent.)

It is as folk do, and not as folk say.

John Heywood: *Proverbs,* 2, 5. (16th cent.)

Saying and doing are two things.

John Heywood: *Proverbs,* 2, 5. (16th cent.)

Sooner said than done.

John Heywood: *Proverbs,* 2, 5. (16th cent.)

Better it be done than wish it had been
done.

John Heywood: *Proverbs,* 2, 5. (16th cent.)

As good undone, as do it too soon.

John Heywood: *Proverbs,* 2, 5. (16th cent.)

Do well, and have well.

John Heywood: *Proverbs,* 2, 9. (16th cent.)

Dominican Order (*Order of Preachers*)

Expecting the brethren of your order to
be the champions of the faith (*pugiles
fidei*) and true lights of the world, we
confirm your order.

Innocent III: *Letter confirming the Order.*
(Dec. 22, 1216)

Door

God never shuts one door but He opens
two.

Seumas MacManus: *Heavy Hangs the
Golden Grain.* (20th cent.)

Doorkeeper

At the gate of the monastery let there
be placed a wise old man, who understands how to give and receive a message, and whose years will keep him
from leaving his post. . . . As soon as
anyone knocks, or a poor man hails him,
let him answer *Thanks be to God* or
Blessed be.

St. Benedict: *Rule, 66.* (6th cent.)

Doorstep

Slippery the doorstep of the great house.

Seumas MacManus: *Heavy Hangs the
Golden Grain.* (20th cent.)

Doubt

Who doubts that he lives, and remembers, and understands, and wills, and
thinks, and knows, and judges? For indeed even if he doubts, he lives; if he
doubts, he remembers why he doubts;
if he doubts, he understands that he
doubts; if he doubts, he wishes to be
certain; if he doubts, he thinks; if he
doubts, he knows that he does not know;
if he doubts, he judges that he ought not
to give his consent rashly. Whosoever
therefore doubts about anything else,
ought not to doubt about all these
things; for if they were not, he would
not be able to doubt about anything.

St. Augustine: *De Trinitate,* 10, 14. (5th
cent.)

Doubt charms me no less than knowledge.

> Dante: *Inferno, Canto 11.* (14th cent.)

Time trieth truth in every doubt.

> John Heywood: *Proverbs,* 2, 5. (16th cent.)

Though thus, my friend, so long employed,
And so much midnight oil destroyed,
I must confess, my searches past,
I only learned to doubt at last.

> Thomas Moore: *Morality.* (19th cent.)

Fair hope is dead, and light
  Is quench'd in night.
What sound can break the silence of
    despair?
  O doubting heart!
  Thy sky is overcast,
  Yet stars shall rise at last,
  Brighter for the darkness past,
And angels' silver voices stir the air.

> Adelaide A. Procter: *A Doubting Heart.* (19th cent.)

Who can determine when it is, that the scales in the balance of opinion begin to turn, and what was a greater probability in behalf of a belief becomes a positive doubt against it?

> Card. Newman: *Apologia pro Vita Sua,* 4. (19th cent.)

  But the gods are dead—
Ay, Zeus is dead, and all the gods but
    Doubt,
And Doubt is brother devil to Despair!

> J. B. O'Reilly: *Prometheus: Christ.* (19th cent.)

She who, wise as she was fair,
For subtle doubts had simple clues.

> Coventry Patmore: *The Angel in the House.* (19th cent.)

Drama

All great amusements are a danger to the life of the Christian; but of all those which the world has invented there is none more to be feared than the play.

> Pascal: *Pensées.* (17th cent.)

Sure there's a fate in plays; and 'tis in
    vain
To write, while these malignant planets
    reign.
Some very foolish influence rules the
    pit,
Not always kind to sense, or just to wit.

> Dryden: *To Mr. Southern.* (17th cent.)

A problem play means a drama that plants its feet firmly along the very edge of the Ten Commandments, particularly of one of them that occurs towards the end.

> R. H. Benson: *An Average Man.* (20th cent.)

What makes the difference between the drama and all other kinds of art is that you crowd a mass of people together, not as you would crowd them in the streets, but as you would crowd them in a prison, in such a manner that it is humiliating for anybody present to make any protest.

> G. K. Chesterton: *Evidence before the Joint Select Committee on Stage Plays.* (20th cent.)

Dream

For whoever involves himself in the deception of dreams is not sufficiently awake to the law of God, suffers a loss of faith, and drowses to his own ruin.

> John of Salisbury: *Policraticus,* 2, 17, 97. (12th cent.)

Thou shalt make castles then in Spain,
And dream of joy all but in vain.

> Chaucer: *Romaunt of the Rose.* (14th cent.)

All dreams, as in old Galen I have read,
Are from repletion and complexion
    bred,
From rising fumes of indigested food,
And noxious humors that infect the
    blood.

> Dryden: *Fables Ancient and Modern.* (17th cent.)

At break of day dreams, they say, are true.

Dryden: *The Spanish Friar*, 3. (17th cent.)

One of those passing, rainbow dreams,
Half light, half shade, which fancy's beams
Paint on the fleeting mists that roll
In trance or slumber round the soul!

Thomas Moore: *Lalla Rookh: the Fire-Worshippers*. (19th cent.)

Oh! that a dream so sweet, so long enjoy'd,
Should be so sadly, cruelly destroy'd!

Thomas Moore: *Lalla Rookh: Veiled Prophet of Khorassan*. (19th cent.)

Oh! miserable power
To dreams allow'd, to raise the guilty past,
And back awhile the illumined spirit to cast
On its youth's twilight hour;
In mockery guiling it to act again
The revel or the scoff in Satan's frantic train!

Nay, hush thee, angry heart!
An angel's grief ill fits a penitent;
Welcome the thorn—it is divinely sent,
And with its wholesome smart
Shall pierce thee in thy virtue's palmy home,
And warn thee what thou art, and whence thy wealth has come.

Card. Newman: *Dreams*. (19th cent.)

Dreams grow holy put in action.

Adelaide Procter: *Philip and Mildred*. (19th cent.)

None thrives for long upon the happiest dream.

Coventry Patmore: *Tired Memory*. (19th cent.)

For another dream is mine,
And another dream is true,
    Sweeter even,
Of the little ones that shine
Lost within the light divine,—

Of some meekest flower, or you,
    In the fields of heaven.

Alice Meynell: *Soeur Monique*. (19th cent.)

The chambers in the house of dreams
Are fed with so divine an air,
That Time's hoar wings grow young therein,
    And they who walk there are most fair.

Francis Thompson: *Dream-Tryst*. (19th cent.)

A thousand creeds and battle-cries,
    A thousand warring social schemes,
A thousand new moralities,
    And twenty thousand dreams!

Alfred Noyes: *Forward*. (20th cent.)

Enough of dreams! no longer mock
    The burdened hearts of men!
Not on the cloud, but on the rock.

Alfred Noyes: *The Secret Inn*. (20th cent.)

He whom a dream hath possessed knoweth no more of doubting.

Shaemas O'Sheel: *He Whom a Dream Hath Possessed*. (20th cent.)

Dreamer

For a dreamer lives forever,
    And a toiler dies in a day.

J. B. O'Reilly: *The Cry of the Dreamer*. (19th cent.)

Dress

A woman's appearance depends upon two things: the clothes she wears and the time she gives to her toilet. . . . Against the first we bring the charge of ostentation, against the second of harlotry.

Tertullian: *Women's Dress*. (3rd cent.)

The desire to please by outward charms, which we know naturally invite lust, does not spring from a sound conscience. Why should you rouse an evil passion?

Tertullian: *Women's Dress*. (3rd cent.)

But there is a kind of matronly dress, befitting a person's station, distinct from the garments of a widow, which may become Christian wives without affronting Christian decorum.

> St. Augustine: *Letter 262.* (5th cent.)

Who is worse shod than the shoemaker's wife?

> John Heywood: *Proverbs,* 1, 11. (16th cent.)

Singularity in dress is ridiculous; in fact it is generally looked upon as a proof that the mind is somewhat deranged. The fashion of the country wherein one lives is the rule which should be followed in the choice and form of dress.

> St. John Baptist de la Salle: *The Rules of Christian Manners and Civility,* 2. (17th cent.)

So for thy spirit did devise
Its Maker seemly garniture,
Of its own essence parcel pure,

. . . .

Which woven vesture should subserve.
For outward robes in their ostents
Should show the soul's habiliments.

> F. Thompson: *Gilded Gold.* (19th cent.)

The essential thing for a necktie is style. A well-tied tie is the first serious step in life.

> Oscar Wilde: *A Woman of No Importance,* 3. (19th cent.)

When men wish to be safely impressive, as judges, priests or kings, they . . . wear skirts, the long, trailing robes of female dignity. The whole world is under petticoat government; for even men wear petticoats when they wish to govern.

> G. K. Chesterton: *What's Wrong with the World.* (20th cent.)

What women wear, in mid-July
On bathing beaches, who will care?
We've ceased to try to rectify
What women wear.

And yet, if—from my rolling-chair—
I heard somebody passing by
Say: "Look at those bold women there!"
I'm very much afraid that I
Would rise on tippy-toes to stare,
And you might hear my eager cry:
"What women? Where?"

> T. A. Daly: *Roundel by a Rounder.* (20th cent.)

Drinking

It is meet before we partake of food to bless the Maker of all things, and to sing when we drink.

> Clement of Alexandria: *Paedagogus.* (2nd cent.)

Art sick from vinous surfeiting at night?
Repeat the dose at morn, 'twill set thee right.

> School of Salerno, Code of Health. (11th cent.)

So was her jolly whistle well y-wet.

> Chaucer: *The Reeves Tale.* (14th cent.)

And who so wicked ale breweth,
Full oft he must the worse drink.

> John Gower: *Confessio Amantis,* 3. (14th cent.)

A man that boozed of that,
Fourpence a gallon.

> Langland: *Piers Plowman,* Passus 5. (14th cent.)

Dread the delight of drink and thou shalt do the better.
Though thou long for more, Measure is medicine.
What the belly asketh is not all good for the ghost,
What the soul loveth is not all food for the body.

> Langland: *Piers Plowman: The Vision of Holy Church.* (14th cent.)

"Much sweeter," she saith, "more acceptable

Is drink, when it is stolen privily,
Than when it is taken in form avow-
    able."

Lydgate: *The Remedy of Love.* (15th cent.)

When the wine were in and the wit out.

St. Thomas More. (16th cent.)

As I would needs brew, so must I drink.

John Heywood: *Proverbs,* 1, 8. (16th cent.)

Merry as cup and can could hold.

John Heywood: *Proverbs,* 2, 3. (16th cent.)

Like those that vainly hop'd kind
    Heav'n would wink,
While to excess on martyrs' tombs they
    drink.

Dryden: *Astraea Redux.* (17th cent.)

Bacchus' blessings are a treasure,
Drinking is the soldier's pleasure.

Dryden: *Alexander's Feast,* 1. (17th cent.)

Bacchus ever fair, ever young:
The jolly god in triumph comes.

Dryden: *Alexander's Feast.* (17th cent.)

The feast of reason and the flow of soul.

Pope: *The First Satire of the Second Book
of Horace.* (18th cent.)

Friend of my soul, this goblet sip,
    'Twill chase that pensive tear;
'Tis not so sweet as woman's lip,
    But, oh! 'tis more sincere.
Like her delusive beam,
    'Twill steal away thy mind:
But, truer than love's dream,
    It leaves no sting behind.

Thomas Moore: *Anacreontic.* (19th cent.)

If with water you fill up your glasses,
    You'll never write anything wise;
For wine is the horse of Parnassus,
    Which hurries a bard to the skies.

Thomas Moore: *Anacreontic.* (19th cent.)

Fill the bumper fair!
    Every drop we sprinkle

O'er the brow of care
    Smooths away a wrinkle.

Thomas Moore: *Fill the Bumper Fair.*
(19th cent.)

Wreath the bowl
    With flowers of soul,
The brightest wit can find us;
    We'll take a flight
    Tow'rds heaven tonight,
And leave dull earth behind us.

Thomas Moore: *Wreath the Bowl.* (19th
cent.)

The dipsomaniac and the abstainer are
not only both mistaken, but they both
make the same mistake. They both regard wine as a drug and not as a drink.

G. K. Chesterton: *George Bernard Shaw.*
(20th cent.)

In so far as drinking is really a sin it is
not because drinking is wild, but because
drinking is tame; not in so far as it is
anarchy, but in so far as it is slavery.
Probably the worst way to drink is to
drink medicinally. Certainly the safest
way to drink is to drink carelessly; that
is, without caring much for anything,
and especially not caring for the drink.

G. K. Chesterton: *All Things Considered.*
(20th cent.)

You ask me how I manage to consume
So many beers and whiskeys multi-
    plied;
Why I can stand as rigid as a broom
While others gently sway from side to
    side;
Why from the phrase 'ferriferous ver-
    micide'
My tongue, all unembarrassed, does not
    shrink?
—Hear then my city's boast, my call-
    ing's pride:
It was in Fleet Street that I learned to
    drink.

Cecil Chesterton: *Ballade of Professional
Pride.* (20th cent.)

It was the first drop that kilt me, the
last was harmless.

Seumas MacManus: *Heavy Hangs the
Golden Grain.* (20th cent.)

Have another drink—a bird can't fly on one wing.

> Seumas MacManus: *Heavy Hangs the Golden Grain.* (20th cent.)

Drop

A drop, one drop, how sweetly one fair drop
Would tremble on my pearl-tipt finger's top?
My wealth is gone, O go it where it will,
Spare this one jewel; I'll be Dives still.

> Richard Crashaw: *Dives Asking a Drop.* (17th cent.)

Drum

The double double double beat
Of the thundering drum
Cries, Hark! the foes come.

> Dryden: *A Song for St. Cecilia's Day.* (17th cent.)

Drunkenness

The drunken man is a living corpse.

> St. John Chrysostom: *Homilies.* (4th cent.)

The immoderate drinking of wine produces not fewer diseases of body and soul than much drinking of water, but far more and severer.

> St. John Chrysostom: *Homilies.* (4th cent.)

Drunkenness is the ruin of reason. It is premature old age. It is temporary death.

> St. Basil: *Homilies,* 14. (4th cent.)

Thou comest home as drunken as a mouse.

> Chaucer: *Wife of Bath's Prologue.* (14th cent.)

Where drunkenness reigneth in any route,
There is no counsel hid, withouten doubt.

> Chaucer: *Tale of the Man of Lawe.* (14th cent.)

For drunkenness is very sepulture
Of mannes wit and his discretion.

> Chaucer: *The Pardoneres Tale.* (14th cent.)

And drunkenness is eke a foul record
Of any man, and namely in a lord.

> Chaucer: *The Sumnour's Tale.* (14th cent.)

They lay and slept like drunken swine.

> Lydgate: *The Fall of Princes,* 3. (15th cent.)

Then hasten to be drunk,—the business of the day.

> Dryden: *Cymon and Iphigenia.* (17th cent.)

Dryden, John

Ev'n copious Dryden wanted, or forgot,
The last and greatest art—the art to blot.

> Pope: *The First Epistle of the Second Book of Horace.* (18th cent.)

Dryness, Spiritual

One single act done with dryness of spirit is worth more than many done with sensible devotion.

> St. Francis de Sales: *Spiritual Conferences,* 7. (17th cent.)

There is a difference between possessing the presence of God and having the feeling of His presence.

> St. Francis de Sales: *Spiritual Conferences,* 9. (17th cent.)

If God has stripped you of the sense of His presence, it is in order that even His presence may no longer occupy your heart, but Himself.

> St. Francis de Sales: *Letters to Persons in Religion,* 3, 5. (17th cent.)

The love that desires to walk to God's will through consolations walks ever in fear of taking the wrong path; but the love that strikes straight through dryness

toward the will of God walks in assurance.

> St. Francis de Sales: *Treatise on the Love
> of God,* 9, 2. (17th cent.)

Due

To everyone should be rendered what is
reasonably and fairly due him.

> St. Basil: *The Morals,* 32. (4th cent.)

Duelling

The detestable custom of duelling, introduced by the contrivance of the devil,
that by the bloody death of the body he
may accomplish the ruin of the soul,
shall be utterly exterminated from the
Christian world.

> Decree of the Council of Trent, Session 25.
> (Dec. 3, 1563)

A nobleman may accept a challenge to a
duel in order to avoid the imputation of
cowardice.

> Doctrine condemned by Pope Alexander
> VII. (17th cent.)

Dullness

The midwife laid her hand on his thick
skull,
With the prophetic blessing, "Be thou
dull."

> Dryden: *Absalom and Achitophel,* 2. (17th
> cent.)

Born a goddess, dullness never dies.

> Pope: *The Dunciad,* 1. (18th cent.)

Dunce

A wit with dunces and a dunce with wits.

> Pope: *The Dunciad,* 4. (18th cent.)

Dust

A heap of dust remains of thee:
'Tis all thou art, and all the proud shall
be.

> Pope: *Elegy to the Memory of an Unfor-
> tunate Lady.* (18th cent.)

When the heavens like a scroll,
At the voice of doom uproll,
When the earth and sky by fire
Melt in one vast funeral pyre,
Thou, O dust, sole earthly thing,
To eternal life shalt spring;
Leap to clothe the ransomed soul
With a garment rich and whole,
Weaving round the blanching bone
Living vesture all its own,
Glowing flesh all firm and fair,
Ruddy lip and gleaming hair,
And the thrilling crimson stain
Of each artery and vein.
Then, transfigured, glorified,
Kingly spirit's lowborn bride,
Raised unto his high degree,
Thou shalt reign immortally
In the bodies of the just,—
Apotheosis of dust.

> Sister M. Angelita: *Dust.* (20th cent.)

Duty

In doing what we ought we deserve no
praise, because it is our duty.

> St. Augustine: *Confessions.* 10. (5th cent.)

Honor and shame from no condition
rise;
Act well your part: there all the honor
lies.

> Pope: *An Essay on Man,* 4. (18th cent.)

Never think yourself safe because you
do your duty in ninety-nine points; it is
the hundredth which is to be the ground
of your self-denial.

> Card. Newman: *Parochial and Plain
> Sermons,* 1. (19th cent.)

And I read the moral—A brave en-
deavor
To do thy duty, whate'er its worth,
Is better than life with love forever,
And love is the sweetest thing on
earth.

> J. J. Roche: *Sir Hugo's Choice.* (19th cent.)

A man's duty to God must come before all else.

> R. H. Benson: *Come Rack! Come Rope!* (20th cent.)

It doesn't matter in the slightest what we do, so long as we've got to do it.

> R. H. Benson: *The Conventionalists.* (20th cent.)

Dying

What I pray you is dying? Just what it is to put off a garment. For the body is about the soul as a garment; and after laying this aside for a short time by means of death, we shall resume it again with more splendor.

> St. John Chrysostom: *Homilies.* (4th cent.)

Mere dying is too good for one whom it took seven strokes to kill.

> St. Jerome: *Letter,* 1, 13. (Said of a woman who persistently defied the executioner's efforts to dispatch her.) (4th cent.)

Father Abbot, I am come to lay my weary bones among you.

> Thomas Wolsey: On halting at Leicester Abbey on his way to London to answer a charge of treason. (16th cent.)

See my lips tremble and my eyeballs roll,
Suck my last breath, and catch my flying soul.

> Pope: *Eloisa to Abelard.* (18th cent.)

I am dying, sir, of a hundred good symptoms.

> Pope: *On his deathbed.* (18th cent.)

It's a strange thing now how people will know they're dying themselves when no one else could suspect anything wrong at all with them.

> Katharine T. Hinkson: *Per Istam Sanctam Unctionem (Countrymen All).* (20th cent.)

See also Death

E

Eagle

Like the young eagle who has lent his plume
To fledge the shaft by which he meets his doom,
See their own feathers pluck'd, to wing the dart
Which rank corruption destines for their heart!

> Thomas Moore: *Corruption.* (19th cent.)

Ear

And we shall speak of thee somewhat, I trow,

When thou art gone, to do thine ears glow!

> Chaucer: *Troilus and Criseyde.* (14th cent.)

Small pitchers have wide ears.

> John Heywood: *Proverbs,* 2, 5. (16th cent.)

See also Eyes and Ears

Earth

This congregated ball.

> Pope: *The First Epistle of the First Book of Horace.* (18th cent.)

They say, earth's beauty seems completest
  To them that on their death-beds rest;
Gentle lady! she smiles sweetest
  Just ere she clasps us to her breast.

F. Thompson: *Sister Songs.* (19th cent.)

Even the linked fantasies, in whose blossomy twist
I swung the earth a trinket at my wrist.

F. Thompson: *The Hound of Heaven.* (19th cent.)

Earthquake

Lord, Thou hast crushed Thy tender ones, o'erthrown
  Thy strong, Thy fair; Thy man Thou hast unmanned,
Thy elaborate works unwrought, Thy deeds undone,
  Thy lovely sentient human plan unplanned;
Destroyer, we have cowered beneath Thine own
  Immediate, unintelligible hand.

Alice Meynell: *Messina, 1908.* (20th cent.)

Ease

Take mine ease in mine inn.

John Heywood: *Proverbs,* 1, 5. (16th cent.)

East

Alway the longer east, the shorter west.

John Heywood: *Proverbs,* 1, 13. (16th cent.)

Easter

Many meetings and conferences with bishops were held on this point, and all unanimously formulated in their letters the doctrine of the Church for those in every country that the mystery of the Lord's Resurrection from the dead could be celebrated on no day save Sunday, and that on that day alone we should celebrate the end of the paschal fast.

Eusebius of Caesarea: *Ecclesiastical History,* 5, 23, 2. (Famous controversy under Pope Victor I, ca. 189–199 A.D.) (4th cent.)

Where is thy sting, O death? Where is thy victory, O hell? Christ hath risen, and thou art overthrown. Christ hath risen, and the demons have fallen. Christ hath risen, and the angels rejoice. Christ hath risen, and life reigneth. Christ hath risen, and not one dead resteth in the grave. For Christ having risen from the dead became the first-fruits of them that slept. To Him be glory and majesty to ages of ages. Amen.

Byzantine Pentecostarion, Holy Pascha, Catechetical Discourse of St. John Chrysostom at Matins. (4th cent.)

The morn had spread her crimson rays,
When rang the skies with shouts of praise;
Earth joined the joyful hymn to swell,
That brought despair to vanquished hell.
 . . . .
With Christ we died, with Christ we rose,
When at the font His name we chose;
Oh, let not sin our robes defile,
And turn to grief the Paschal smile.

Roman Breviary, Easter, Hymn *Aurora coelum purpurat (Aurora lucis rutilat)* at Lauds. (Tr. R. Campbell) (Much altered, Ambrosian, ca. 5th cent.)

O God, Who hast appointed the Paschal sacrifice for the world's salvation, be propitious to our supplications, that our supreme High Priest, interceding for us, may reconcile us, in that He is like unto us, in that He is equal to Thee, even Jesus Christ our Lord.

Gelasian Sacramentary, Collect for Easter Wednesday. (5th to 7th cent.)

Hail! Festal day! for evermore ador'd,
Wherein God conquered hell, and upward soar'd!

Fortunatus: *Salve festa dies toto venerabilis aevo.* (Tr. Neale) (6th cent.)

O thou, the heavens' eternal King,
Creator, unto Thee we sing,
With God the Father ever One,
Co-equal, co-eternal Son.

. . . . . .

Eternal Shepherd, Thou dost lave
Thy flock in pure baptismal wave—
That mystic bath, that grave of sin,
Where ransomed souls new life begin.

. . . . . .

Grant, Lord, in Thee each faithful
     mind
Unceasing Paschal joy may find;
And from the death of sin set free
Souls newly born to life by Thee.

> Roman Breviary, Easter, Hymn *Rex
> sempiterne coelitum (Rex aeterne Domine)*
> at Matins. (Britt, Hymns, p. 147) (Much
> altered, Ambrosian, 6th cent.)

O God, Who on this day hast overcome
death and opened to us the gate of everlasting life through Thine only-begotten
Son; follow with Thy help the desires
which Thou dost put into our minds and
by continual assistance give effect to the
same.

> Roman Missal, Collect for Easter.
> (Gregorian, ca. 6th cent.)

It is truly meet and just, right and availing unto salvation, that at all times, but
especially on this day, we should extol
Thy glory, O Lord, when Christ our
Passover was sacrificed. For He is the
true Lamb that hath taken away the sins
of the world, Who by dying hath overcome our death, and by rising again hath
restored our life.

> Roman Missal, Preface for Easter.
> (Gregorian, ca. 6th cent.)

This is the day which the Lord hath
made. This day is the most solemn of all
solemnities. This day is our Passover.
Upon this day our Savior Jesus Christ,
according to the flesh, rose again from
the dead.

> Roman Breviary, Easter at Prime. (cf.
> Liber Resp., 6th to 8th cent.)

The Lord is risen from the grave, Alleluia, Alleluia.
The Lord is risen from the grave, Alleluia, Alleluia.
Who hung for us upon the Tree, Alleluia, Alleluia.
Glory be to the Father, and to the Son,
     and to the Holy Ghost.
The Lord is risen from the grave, Alleluia, Alleluia.

> Roman Breviary, Easter, Responsory at
> Terce. (6th to 8th cent.)

At the Lamb's high feast we sing
Praise to our victorious King,
Who hath washed us in the tide
Flowing from His pierced side.

. . . .

Christ, the Lamb Whose Blood was
     shed,
Paschal Victim, Paschal Bread;
With sincerity and love
Eat we manna from above.

. . . .

Paschal triumph, Paschal joy,
Only sin can this destroy;
From the death of sin set free,
Souls reborn, dear Lord, in Thee.

> Roman Breviary, Hymn *Ad regias Agni
> dapes (Ad coenam Agni providi)* at
> Vespers (Tr. R. Campbell) (Much altered,
> Ambrosian, 7th cent.)

Thy resurrection, O Savior Christ, angels
sing in heaven. Grant unto us also on
earth to extol Thee with pure heart.

> Byzantine Pentekostarion, Sticheron at
> Matins. (6th to 8th cent.)

Christ is risen from the dead, death by
death down doth He tread, and on those
within the tombs He bestoweth life.

> Byzantine Pentekostarion, Troparion for
> Easter. (6th to 8th cent.)

Today the sacred Passover is made manifest to us, the new and holy Passover,
the mystic Passover, the Passover worthy
of all honor, the Passover which is Christ
the Redeemer, the spotless Passover, the
mighty Passover, the Passover of the
faithful, the Passover that openeth unto

us the gates of Paradise, the Passover that sanctifieth all the faithful.

Byzantine Pentekostarion, Sticheron at Matins. (ca. 6th to 8th cent.)

The night of Easter is spent in keeping the vigil (*pervigilia*) because of the coming of our King and Lord, that the time of His resurrection may not find us sleeping, but awake. The reason for this night is twofold: either because He then received back His life when He suffered, or because He is later to come for judgment at the same hour at which He arose.

St. Isidore: *Etymologies,* 6, 17. (7th cent.)

We celebrate Easter as not merely to re-call to memory the death and resurrection of Christ but also to have before our eyes the rest that is told about Him with reference to its mystic meaning. For on account of the new life and the new man which we are bidden to put on, while putting off the old, purging away the old ferment that we may be a new sprinkling, since Christ is sacrificed as our Pasch; on account of this newness of life, then, the first month in the months of the year is mystically assigned to the celebration of Easter.

St. Isidore: *Etymologies,* 6, 17. (7th cent.)

Having seen the resurrection of Christ, we adore the holy Lord Jesus, Who alone is without sin. We worship Thy Cross, O Master, and sing and glorify Thy resurrection; for Thou art our God, we know no other beside Thee, we call upon Thy name. O come, all ye faithful, let us adore Christ's holy resurrection; for, by the Cross, great joy is come into all the world. Ever praising the Lord, let us sing His resurrection; for, enduring crucifixion, He overthrew death by His death.

Byzantine Horologion, Matins, Troparion after Gospel. (ca. 6th to 8th cent.)

'Tis the day of resurrection:
    Earth! tell it out abroad!
The Passover of gladness!
    The Passover of God!

From death to life eternal,
    From this world to the sky,
Our Christ hath brought us over,
    With hymns of victory.

Byzantine Pentekostarion, Holy Pascha, Golden Canon. (St. John Chrysostom, 8th cent.)

Shine, shine, O new Jerusalem; for the glory of the Lord hath shone on thee. Rejoice and exult, O Sion. And thou, pure Mother of God, be glad for the resurrection of thy Son.

Byzantine Pentekostarion, Holy Pascha, Golden Canon. (8th cent.)

Come, ye faithful, raise the strain
    Of triumphant gladness!
God hath brought his Israel
    Into joy from sadness:
Loos'd from Phar'oh's bitter yoke
    Jacob's sons and daughters;
Led them with unmoisten'd foot
    Through the Red Sea waters.

'Tis the spring of souls today;
    Christ hath burst His prison;
And from three days' sleep in death,
    As a sun hath risen.
All the winter of our sins,
    Long and dark, is flying
From His Light, to Whom we give
    Laud and praise undying.

Byzantine Pentekostarion, St. Thomas Sunday (Low), Canon. (Tr. J. Neale) (St. John Chrysostom, 8th cent.)

Christ the Lord is risen today:
Christians, hasten your vows to pay;
Offer ye your praises meet
At the Paschal Victim's feet;
For the sheep the Lamb hath bled,
Sinless in the sinner's stead.
Christ the Lord is risen on high;
Now He lives, no more to die.

Roman Missal, Easter Week, Sequence *Victimae Paschali* at Mass. (Tr. J. Leeson) (Attr. to Wipo, 11th cent.)

Alleluia! Alleluia! Alleluia!
Ye sons and daughters of the King

Whom heavenly hosts in glory sing,
Today the grave hast lost its sting!
                    Alleluia!

Anonymous: *O filii et filiae.* (Tr. J. Neale)
(12th cent.)

Purge we out the ancient leaven,
That the feast of earth and heaven
    We may celebrate aright:
On today our hope stands founded:
Moses teacheth how unbounded
    Is its virtue and its might.

Adam of St. Victor: *Zyma vetus expurgetur.*
(Tr. J. Neale) (12th cent.)

Hail the much-remembered day!
Night from morning flies away,
    Life the chains of death hath burst:
Gladness, welcome! grief, begone!
Greater glory draweth on
    Than confusion at the first.
Flies the shadow from the hue:
Flies the ancient from the new:
    Comfort hath each tear dispersed.

Adam of St. Victor: *Ecce dies celebris.* (Tr.
J. Neale) (12th cent.)

Today the Victor o'er His foes
For human consolation rose. Alleluia.

Anonymous: *Surrexit Christus hodie.* (Tr.
J. Neale) (13th cent.)

    Alleluia! Alleluia!
Finished is the battle now;
The crown is on the Victor's brow!
    Hence with sadness,
    Sing with gladness,
                    Alleluia!

Anonymous: *Finita jam sunt proelia.* (Tr.
J. Neale) (13th cent.)

The cloud of night is passed away:
Mary, rejoice, rejoice today! Alleluia.
He that abhorred not thy womb
Hath risen victorious from the tomb.
    Alleluia.

Anonymous: *Jam pulsa cedunt nubila.* (Tr.
J. Neale) (13th cent.)

All mortal men this day rejoice,
In Christ that you redeemed hath:

By death, with death sing we with
    voice,
To Him that hath appeas'd God's
    wrath.
Due unto man for sinful path,
Wherein before he went astray:
Give thanks to Him with perfect faith,
That for mankind hath made this glo-
    rious day.

Jasper Heywood: *Easter Day.* (16th cent.)

Rise, Heir of fresh eternity,
    From Thy virgin tomb:
Rise mighty Man of wonders, and Thy
    world with Thee
    Thy tomb, the universal east,
    Nature's new womb,
Thy tomb, fair immortality's perfumed
    nest.

Richard Crashaw: *Easter Day.* (17th cent.)

All hail! dear Conqueror! all hail!
    O what a victory is Thine!
How beautiful Thy strength appears,
    Thy crimson wounds, how bright
    they shine!

F. Faber: *Jesus Risen.* (19th cent.)

Break the box and shed the nard;
Stop not now to count the cost;
Hither bring pearl, opal, sard;
Reck not what the poor have lost;
Upon Christ throw all away:
Know ye, this is Easter Day.

G. M. Hopkins: *Easter.* (19th cent.)

Behold, the night of sorrow gone,
Like Magdalen the tearful dawn
Goes forth with love's anointing sweet,
To kiss again the Master's feet!

J. B. Tabb: *Easter Morning.* (19th cent.)

All night had shout of men and cry
    Of woeful women filled His way;
Until that noon of somber sky
    On Friday, clamor and display
Smote him; no solitude had He,
No silence, since Gethsemane.

Public was death; but power, but might,
    But life again, but victory,

Were hushed within the dead of night,
The shutter'd dark, the secrecy.
And all alone, alone, alone
He rose again behind the stone.

Alice Meynell: *Easter Night.* (20th cent.)

In very deed,
Washed with new fire to their irra-
diant birth,
Reintegrated are the heavens and earth;
From sky to sod,
The world's unfolded blossom smells
of God.

F. Thompson: *An Ode after Easter.* (19th
cent.)

Eating

Eat not again till thou dost certain feel
Thy stomach freed of all its previous
meal.
This mayest thou know from hunger's
teasing call,
Or mouth that waters—surest sign of
all!

School of Salerno, Code of Health. (11th
cent.)

He that gapeth till he be fed
May fortune to fast and famish for
hunger.

John Heywood: *Proverbs,* 1, 9. (16th cent.)

Feed by measure, and defy the physician.

John Heywood: *Proverbs,* 2, 7. (16th cent.)

It is a greater virtue to eat without choice
what is set before you, than always to
choose the worst.

St. Francis de Sales: *Introduction to the
Devout Life,* 3, 23. (17th cent.)

Persons of honor never think of eating
but at sitting down at table, and after
dinner wash their hands and their
mouths, that they may neither retain the
taste nor the scent of what they have
been eating.

St. Francis de Sales: *Introduction to the
Devout Life,* 39. (17th cent.)

He needs no more than birds and beasts
to think,
All his occasions are to eat and drink.

Dryden: *Absalom and Achitophel.* (17th
cent.)

Thus vulgar dishes are by cooks disguis'd,
More for their dressing than their substance priz'd.

Dryden: *To Sir Robert Howard.* (17th
cent.)

Echo

How sweet the answer Echo makes
To music at night,
When, roused by lute or horn, she
wakes,
And far away, o'er lawns and lakes,
Goes answering light.

Thomas Moore: *Echo.* (19th cent.)

It seemed the harmonious echo
From our discordant life.

Adelaide Procter: *The Lost Chord.* (19th
cent.)

Economic Order

Economic life must be inspired by Christian principles.

Pope Pius XI: *Quadragesimo Anno.* (May
15, 1931)

The mutual relations between capital
and labor must be determined according
to the laws of the strictest justice, called
commutative justice, supported however
by Christian charity. Free competition
and still more economic domination
must be kept within just and definite
limits, and must be brought under the
effective control of the public authority,
in matters appertaining to this latter's
competence. The public institutions of
the nations must be such as to make the
whole of human society conform to the
common good, i.e. the standard of social
justice. If this is done, the economic system, that most important branch of so-

cial life, will necessarily be restored to sanity and right order.

> Pope Pius XI: *Quadragesimo Anno.* (May 15, 1931)

The national economy, as it is the product of the men who work together in the community of the State, has no other end than to secure without interruption the material conditions in which the individual life of the citizens may fully develop.

> Pope Pius XII: *The Social Question in the New Order.* (June 1, 1941)

Economy

As almighty God did not all at once introduce the gospel to the world, and thereby gradually prepared men for its profitable reception, so, according to the doctrine of the early Church, it was a duty, for the sake of the heathen among whom they lived, to observe a great reserve and caution in communicating to them the knowledge of *the whole counsel of God.* This cautious dispensation of the truth, after the manner of a discreet and vigilant steward, is denoted by the word 'economy.' It is a mode of acting which comes under the head of prudence, one of the four cardinal virtues.

> Card. Newman: *Apologia pro Vita Sua, Note F.* (19th cent.)

The principle of economy is familiarly acted on among us every day. When we would persuade others, we do not begin by treading on their toes. Men would be thought rude who introduced their religious notions into mixed society, and were devotional in a drawing-room.

> Card. Newman: *Apologia pro Vita Sua, Note F.* (19th cent.)

Ecstasy

Ecstasy is naught but the going forth of a soul from itself and its being caught up in God, and this is what happens to the soul that is obedient, namely, that it

goes forth from itself and from its own desires, and thus lightened, becomes immersed in God.

> St. John of the Cross: *Spiritual Sentences and Maxims.* (16th cent.)

I wish I could explain with the help of God, wherein union differs from rapture, or from transport, or from flight of the spirit, as they say, or from a trance, which are all one. I mean that all these are only different names for one and the same thing, which is also called ecstasy.

> St. Teresa of Jesus: *Autobiography,* 20. (16th cent.)

Rapture, for the most part, is irresistible. It comes, in general, as a shock, quick and sharp, before you can collect your thoughts, or help yourself in any way, and you see and feel it as a cloud, or a strong eagle rising upwards, and carrying you away on its wings.

> St. Teresa of Jesus: *Autobiography,* 20. (16th cent.)

The height of love's ecstasy is to have our will not in its own contentment but in God's.

> St. Francis de Sales: *Treatise on the Love of God,* 6, 11. (17th cent.)

There was never a saint but has had the ecstasy of life and operation.

> St. Francis de Sales: *Letters to Persons in the World,* 6, 57. (17th cent.)

See also Contemplation; Prayer

Eden, Garden of

> This is the spot, of men believed to be
>   Earth's center, and the place of
>   Adam's grave,
> And here a slip that from a barren tree
>   Was cut, fruit sweet and salutary
>   gave—
> Yet not unto the tillers of the land;
> That blessed fruit was culled by other
>   hand.

> Victorinus: *De Ligno Vitae.* (Tr. Trench) (4th or 5th cent.)

Education

What greater work is there than training the mind and forming the habits of the young?

> St. John Chrysostom: *Hom. 60 in Matth.,* 18. (4th cent.)

It is the duty of good education to arrive at wisdom by means of a definite order.

> St. Augustine: *Soliloquia,* 1, 13, 23. (4th cent.)

Let whatever should be acquired through human means be acquired humbly, and let anyone who is instructing another pass on to him whatever he has received without haughtiness or grudging.

> St. Augustine: *De Doctrina Christiana,* Prol. 5. (4th cent.)

By education most have been misled;
So they believe, because they so were bred.

> Dryden: *The Hind and the Panther,* 3. (17th cent.)

'Tis education forms the common mind;
Just as the twig is bent the tree's inclined.

> Pope: *Moral Essays,* 1. (18th cent.)

Mutual education, in a large sense of the word, is one of the great and incessant occupations of human society, carried on partly with set purpose, and partly not. One generation forms another; and the existing generation is ever acting and reacting upon itself in the persons of its individual members.

> Card. Newman: *Historical Sketches.* (19th cent.)

The problem for statesmen of this age is how to educate the masses, and literature and science cannot give the solution.

> Card. Newman: *Discussions and Arguments.* (19th cent.)

Christianity, and nothing short of it, must be made the element and principle of all education. . . . Where revealed truth has given the aim and direction to knowledge, knowledge of all kinds will minister to revealed truth. But if in education we begin with nature before grace, with evidences before faith, with science before conscience, with poetry before practice, we shall be doing much the same as if we were to indulge the appetites and passions, and turn a deaf ear to the reason. In each case we misplace what in its place is a divine gift.

> Card. Newman: *Discussions and Arguments.* (19th cent.)

Education is a high word; it is the preparation for knowledge, and it is the imparting of knowledge in proportion to that preparation.

> Card. Newman: *Idea of a University.* (19th cent.)

This process of training, by which the intellect, instead of being formed or sacrificed to some particular or accidental purpose, some specific trade or profession, or study or science, is disciplined for its own sake, for the perception of its own proper object, and for its own highest culture, is called liberal education.

> Card. Newman: *Idea of a University.* (19th cent.)

As health ought to precede labor of the body, and as a man in health can do what an unhealthy man cannot do, and as of this health the properties are strength, energy, agility, graceful carriage and action, manual dexterity, and endurance of fatigue, so in like manner general culture of mind is the best aid to professional and scientific study, and educated men can do what illiterate cannot.

> Card. Newman: *Idea of a University.* (19th cent.)

All things now are to be learned at once, not first one thing, then another, not one well but many badly. Learning is to be without exertion, without attention, without toil; without grounding, without advance, without finishing.

> Card. Newman: *Idea of a University.*
> (19th cent.)

Recreations are not education; accomplishments are not education. Do not say, the people must be educated, when after all you only mean, amused, refreshed, soothed, put into good spirits and good humor, or kept from vicious excesses. I do not say that such amusements, such occupations of mind, are not a great gain; but they are not education.

> Card. Newman: *Idea of a University, 6.*
> (19th cent.)

I say then, if a liberal education be good, it must necessarily be useful too.

> Card. Newman: *Idea of a University, 7.*
> (19th cent.)

Why do we educate, except to prepare for the world . . . ? Will it much matter in the world to come whether our bodily health or whether our intellectual strength was more or less, except of course as this world is in all its circumstances a trial for the next?

> Card. Newman: *Idea of a University*
> (19th cent.)

Catholic education must recognize the catholicity of truth under all its aspects, and tend to actualize it in all the relations of life, in religion and civilization. Its tendency is to aid the Church in the fulfillment of her mission, which is the continuous evolution and actualization of the idea, or the life of the Word made flesh, in the life of humanity, or completion in mankind of the incarnation completed in the individual man . . . assumed by the Word.

> Orestes Brownson: *Catholic Schools.*
> (Works, 12) (1862)

No amount of pious training or pious culture will protect the faithful, or preserve them from the contamination of the age, if they are left inferior to non-Catholics in secular learning and intellectual development. The faithful must be guarded and protected by being trained and disciplined to grapple with the errors and false systems of the age. They must be not only more religiously, but also more intellectually educated. They must be better armed than their opponents,—surpass them in the strength and vigor of their minds, and in the extent and variety of their knowledge. They must, on all occasions and against all adversaries, be ready to give a reason for the hope that is in them.

> Orestes Brownson: *Catholic Polemics.*
> (Works, 20) (1861)

In educating the young it is not sufficient that religious instruction be given to them at fixed times; it is necessary also that every other subject that is taught to them be permeated with Christian piety. If this is wanting, little good can be expected from any kind of learning.

> Pope Leo XIII: *Militantis ecclesiae.* (1897)

No man who worships education has got the best out of education; no man who sacrifices everything to education is even educated. . . . What is wrong is a neglect of principle; and the principle is that without a gentle contempt for education, no gentleman's education is complete.

> G. K. Chesterton: *The Common Man.*
> (20th cent.)

To train a citizen is to train a critic. The whole point of education is that it should give a man abstract and eternal standards, by which he can judge material and fugitive conditions.

> G. K. Chesterton: *All is Grist.* (20th cent.)

A great curse has fallen upon modern life with the discovery of the vastness of the word 'education.' Men have discovered that singing and wandering, the toys that are broken and the flowers that are plucked and thrown away, the dreams that have no archetype and the projects that have no fulfilment, are parts of one great thing that is called 'education'—education which in older and somewhat plainer language would have been called 'the saving of the soul.' But in many modern educationists the effect of this great discovery has been precisely the opposite to that which it should have been. Instead of making Greek and geography as healthy as 'hunt-the-slipper' they have set to work to make 'hunt-the-slipper' as mechanical, as coercive, as meanly conscientious as Greek and geography.

> G. K. Chesterton: *A Handful of Authors.* (20th cent.)

Parents are bound by a most serious obligation to provide to the best of their ability for the religious and moral as well as the physical and civil education of their children, and also to provide for their temporal welfare.

> Code of Canon Law, Canon 1113. (20th cent.)

All the faithful are to be instructed in such a way from their youth that not only nothing contrary to the Catholic faith and sound morals is taught them, but that particular place may be given to religious and moral instruction.

> Code of Canon Law, Canon 1372, 1. (20th cent.)

The state has a right to insist that its citizens shall be educated.

> Pastoral Letter of the American Catholic Hierarchy. (1919)

The fundamental theory of liberty upon which all governments in this Union repose excludes any general power of the State to standardize its children by forcing them to accept instruction from public teachers only. The child is not the mere creature of the State; those who nurture him and direct his destiny have the right coupled with the high duty, to recognize, and prepare him for additional duties.

> U.S. Supreme Court Decision in Oregon School Case, June 1, 1925.

It is the inalienable right as well as the indispensable duty of the Church, to watch over the entire education of her children, in all institutions, public or private, not merely in regard to the religious instruction there given, but in regard to every other branch of learning and every regulation in so far as religion and morality are concerned.

> Pope Pius XI: *Divinus Illius Magistri.* (Dec. 31, 1929)

The family holds directly from the Creator the mission and hence the right to educate the offspring, a right inalienable because inseparably joined to a strict obligation, a right anterior to any right whatever of civil society and of the state, and therefore inviolable on the part of any power on earth.

> Pope Pius XI: *Divinus Illius Magistri.* (Dec. 31, 1929)

It must never be forgotten that the subject of Christian education is man whole and entire, soul united to body in unity of nature, with all his faculties natural and supernatural, such as right reason and revelation show him to be.

> Pope Pius XI: *Divinus Illius Magistri.* (Dec. 31, 1929)

In countries of mixed creeds . . . a heavy burden weighs upon Catholics, who under the guidance of their bishops and with the indefatigable cooperation of the clergy, secular and regular, support Catholic schools for their children entirely at their own expense; to this they feel obliged in conscience, and with a generosity and constancy worthy of all praise, they are firmly determined to make adequate provision for what they openly profess as their motto: "Catholic education in Catholic schools for all the Catholic youth." If such education is not aided from the public funds, as distributive justice requires, certainly it may not be opposed by any civil authority ready to recognize the rights of the family, and the irreducible claims of legitimate liberty.

> Pope Pius XI: *Divinus Illius Magistri.* (Dec. 31, 1929)

Since education consists essentially in preparing man for what he must be and for what he must do here below, in order to attain the sublime end for which he was created, it is clear that there can be no true education which is not wholly directed to man's last end, and that in the present order of Providence, since God has revealed Himself to us in the Person of His only begotten Son, Who alone is *the way, the truth and the life,* there can be no ideally perfect education which is not Christian education.

> Pope Pius XI: *Divinus Illius Magistri.* (Dec. 31, 1929)

Every method of education founded wholly or in part, on the denial or forgetfulness of original sin and of grace, and relying on the sole powers of human nature, is unsound.

> Pope Pius XI: *Divinus Illius Magistri.* (Dec. 31, 1929)

The United States is a country of diverse theologies and one creed, of many churches and one temple, of a thousand theories and one conviction. The creed is education, the temple is the schoolhouse, the conviction is the healing power of knowledge.

> Agnes Repplier: *Times and Tendencies.* (20th cent.)

The period during which I was being instructed by somebody I did not know, about something I did not want to know.

> G. K. Chesterton: *Autobiography.* (20th cent.)

If we accept the religious view of man's nature, we are compelled to take a very different, a radically different view of education. No longer can we think merely of *getting on* in the commercial and materialistic sense. We must now think of getting on in the sense of getting heavenwards. And in everything we learn and in everything we teach to our children or our pupils, we must bear this fact in mind. We must learn to get on in the world—not as an end in itself,

but as a means to getting heavenwards. Any education which neglects this fact, and to the extent to which it neglects it, is false education, because it is false to man. It is untrue; it is not in accordance with his nature as child of God and heir also.

> Eric Gill: *It All Goes Together.* (20th cent.)

Every form of education that mankind has known, from the savage tribe to the highest forms of culture, has always involved two elements—the element of technique and the element of tradition; and hitherto it has always been the second that has been the more important. In the first place education teaches children how to do things—how to read and write, and even at a much more primitive level how to hunt and cook, and plant and build. But besides all these things, education has always meant the initiation of the young into the social and spiritual inheritance of the community: in other words education has meant the transmission of culture.

> Christopher Dawson: *Understanding Europe.* (20th cent.)

See also Learning; School

Education and Religion

Rightly or wrongly, we believe that the best safeguard, aside from purely Catholic instruction and the sacraments, of the faith and morals of our children, is not in building up a wall of separation, not required by Catholic doctrine, between them and the non-Catholic community, but in training them to feel, from the earliest possible moment, that the American nationality is their nationality, that Catholics are really and truly an integral portion of the great American people.

> Orestes Brownson: *Public and Parochial Schools.* (Works, 12) (1859)

Education is not omnipotent, and can never be a substitute for the sacraments.

No system of schools ever devised, can be completely successful in making or keeping a people moral and religious.

Orestes Brownson: *Public and Parochial Schools*. (Works, 12) (1859)

In a word, religious truth is not only a portion, but a condition of general knowledge. To blot it out is nothing short, if I may so speak, of unravelling the web of university teaching. It is, according to the Greek proverb, to take the spring from out of the year; it is to imitate the preposterous proceeding of those tragedians who represented a drama with the omission of its principal part.

Card. Newman: *Idea of a University*, 3. (19th cent.)

Every education teaches a philosophy; if not by dogma then by suggestion, by implication, by atmosphere. Every part of that education has a connection with every other part. If it does not all combine to convey some general view of life, it is not education at all. And the modern educationalists, the modern psychologists, the modern men of science, all agree in asserting and reasserting this —until they begin to quarrel with Catholics over Catholic schools.

G. K. Chesterton: *The Common Man*. (20th cent.)

The truth is that the modern world has committed itself to two totally different and inconsistent conceptions about education. It is always trying to expand the scope of education; and always trying to exclude from it all religion and philosophy. But this is sheer nonsense. You can have an education that teaches atheism because atheism is true, and it can be, from its own point of view, a complete education. But you cannot have an education claiming to teach all truth, and then refusing to discuss whether atheism is true.

G. K. Chesterton: *The Common Man*. (20th cent.)

Eel

As sure to hold as an eel by the tail.

John Heywood: *Proverbs*, 1, 10. (16th cent.)

Effort

God only asks you to do your best.

R. H. Benson: *The Religion of the Plain Man*. (20th cent.)

Egg

The vulgar boil, the learned roast an egg.

Pope: *The Second Epistle of the Second Book of Horace*. (18th cent.)

Yet who can help loving the land that has taught us
Six hundred and eighty-five ways to dress eggs?

Thomas Moore: *The Fudge Family in Paris*. (19th cent.)

Egypt

Sound the loud timbrel o'er Egypt's dark sea!
Jehovah has triumph'd—his people are free.

Thomas Moore: *Sound the Loud Timbrel*. (19th cent.)

Elect, The

If Adam had not sinned, it seems probable that as many men as women would have been born. God alone knows the number of the elect; we cannot guess whether more men than women are saved, or whether they equal one another.

St. Thomas Aquinas: *Quodlibets*, 3, 11, 25. (13th cent.)

O chosen band, to the great supper called
Of the blessed Lamb Who giveth you to feast

So that desire in you is still fore-
stalled.

Dante: *Paradiso, Canto 24.* (Tr. Binyon)
(14th cent.)

Elephant

When people call this beast to mind,
    They marvel more and more
At such a little tail behind,
    So large a trunk before.

Hilaire Belloc: *The Elephant.* (20th cent.)

Elizabeth I

She hath abused her body, against God's
laws, to the disgrace of princely majesty
and the whole nation's reproach, by unspeakable and incredible variety of lust,
which modesty suffereth not to be remembered.

Card. Allen: *Admonition to the Nobility
and People of England and Ireland.* (16th
cent.)

Eloquence

He who is educated and eloquent must
not measure his saintliness merely by his
fluency. Of two imperfect things holy
rusticity is better than sinful eloquence.

St. Jerome: *Letters,* 52, 9. (4th cent.)

From you then I learned that a thing
was not bound to be true because uttered
eloquently, nor false because the utterance of the lips is ill-arranged; but that
on the other hand a thing is not necessarily true because badly uttered, nor
false because spoken magnificently. For
it is with wisdom and folly as with
wholesome and unwholesome food; just
as either kind of food can be served
equally well in rich dishes or simple, so
plain or beautiful language may clothe
either wisdom or folly indifferently.

St. Augustine: *Confessions,* 5, 6. (5th
cent.)

Eloquence is the painting of thought.

Pascal: *Pensées,* 24. (17th cent.)

Eloquence is the art of saying things in
such a way that those whom we address
can understand them easily and pleas-
urably; they feel attracted by them, so
that self-interest induces a more willing
reflexion thereon.

Pascal: *Pensées.* (17th cent.)

Emotion

Emotions should be servants, not masters—or at least not tyrants.

R. H. Benson: *The Sentimentalists.* (20th
cent.)

Human emotion has a power of influencing or saturating inanimate nature.

R. H. Benson: *The Light Invisible.* (20th
cent.)

The only objection to being where all
the keenest emotions meet is that you
feel none of them.

G. K. Chesterton: *The Victorian Age in
Literature.* (20th cent.)

Emotionalism

The emotional revivalist often produces
valuable effects, but all revivalist movements are subject to the law of diminish-
ing returns. It is impossible for men to
live for ever on the heights. A religion
which equates the emotional state with
salvation is a broken reed when the temperature drops. Much misery has been
caused by the evangelical doctrine that
Christianity is worthless unless it is the
product of a conversion which is always
represented as a vivid religious experience.

Arnold Lunn: *Now I See.* (20th cent.)

Emperor

The man denies he is emperor, who says
he is God. Unless he is a man, he is not
emperor.

Tertullian: *Apology,* 33, 3. (3rd cent.)

Thou art the head of the world, while thy head is the Ruler of Olympus, whose members thou dost rule with the just order of the law.

> Wippo: *Panegyric of the Emperor Henry III.* (11th cent.)

Encyclopedia

For it is the test of a good encyclopedia that it does two rather different things at once. The man consulting it finds the thing he wants; he also finds how many thousand things there are that he does not want.

> G. K. Chesterton: *The Common Man.* (20th cent.)

End

Indifferent acts are judged by their ends; sins are judged by themselves.

> St. Augustine: *Against Lying.* (5th cent.)

Some time an end there is of every deed.

> Chaucer: *The Knightes Tale.* (14th cent.)

Everything hath end.

> Chaucer: *Troilus and Criseyde.* (14th cent.)

The end proveth everything.

> John Gower: *Confessio Amantis, 6.* (14th cent.)

All is well that ends well.

> John Heywood: *Proverbs, 1, 10.* (16th cent.)

If you will the end, you must will the means.

> Saying of St. Thérèse. (19th cent.)

We were sent into the world to fulfil some end.

> R. H. Benson: *The Conventionalists.* (20th cent.)

Endurance

Patient endurance is the perfection of charity.

> St. Ambrose: *Explanation of St. Luke, 5, 60.* (4th cent.)

What can't be cured must be endured.

> English Proverb. (14th cent.)

Enemy

Everyone is his own enemy.

> St. Bernard. (12th cent.)

Every wise man dreadeth his enemy.

> Chaucer: *Melibeus.* (14th cent.)

For in this world is no worse pestilence
Than homely foe all day in thy presence.

> Chaucer: *The Marchantes Tale.* (14th cent.)

I choose my friends for their good looks, my acquaintances for their good characters, and my enemies for their intellects. A man cannot be too careful in the choice of his enemies.

> Oscar Wilde: *The Picture of Dorian Gray,* 1. (19th cent.)

How could I know he was my enemy,
    I who had never met with hate before?
I told him one great sorrow of my life;
    He wept. He was my enemy no more.

> Sister Miriam: *The Solvent.* (20th cent.)

See also Friend and Enemy

England

O sweet the time, when neither folly might
Mislead your hopes, nor alter old decrees.
O happy truth when as with sweet delight,
She labored still for conscience not for fees.
O blessed time, when zeal with bended knees,
'Gan bless the heavens, that bent their powers divine,
The English hearts to wisdom to incline.

> Thomas Lodge: *Truth's Complaint over England.* (16th cent.)

Tyre of the west, and glorying in the
name
More than in faith's pure fame!
O trust not crafty fort nor rock re-
nown'd
Earn'd upon hostile ground;
Wielding trade's master-keys, at thy
proud will
To lock or loose its waters, England!
trust not still.
Dread thine own power! Since haughty
Babel's prime,
High towers have been man's crime.

Card. Newman: *England.* (After visiting
Gibraltar) (19th cent.)

England, surely, is the paradise of little
men, and the purgatory of great ones.

Card. Newman: *Discussions and
Arguments.* (19th cent.)

O, season strange for song!
And yet some timely power persuades
my lips.
Is't England's parting soul that nerves
my tongue,
As other kingdoms, nearing their
eclipse,
Have, in their latest bards, uplifted
strong
The voice that was their voice in ear-
lier days?
Is it her sudden, loud and piercing cry,
The note which those that seem too
weak to sigh
Will sometimes utter just before they
die?

Coventry Patmore: *The Unknown Eros:
Proem.* (19th cent.)

O royal England! happy child
Of such a more than regal line.

F. Thompson: *Ode for the Diamond Jubilee
of Queen Victoria, 1897.* (19th cent.)

Bright Hellas lies far hence,
Far the Sicilian sea:
But England's excellence
Is fair enough for me.

Lionel Johnson: *In England.* (19th cent.)

Tartuffe has emigrated to England and
opened a shop.

Oscar Wilde: *The Picture of Dorian Gray,*
17. (19th cent.)

Set in this stormy northern sea,
Queen of these restless fields of tide,
England! what shall men say of thee,
Before whose feet the world divide?

Oscar Wilde: *Ave Imperatrix.* (19th cent.)

England has a wonderful central heart,
but its circulation is not of the best, for
all that.

R. H. Benson: *An Average Man.* (20th
cent.)

The earth is a place on which England
is found,
And you will find it however you twirl
the globe round;
For the spots are all red and the rest is
all grey,
And that is the meaning of Empire
Day.

G. K. Chesterton: *Songs of Education.*
(20th cent.)

England has been divided into three
classes: Knaves, Fools, and Revolutionists.

G. K. Chesterton: *Victorian Age in English
Literature.* (20th cent.)

It is so obvious and jolly to be optimistic
about England, especially when you are
an optimist—and an Englishman.

G. K. Chesterton: *Tremendous Trifles,* 26.
(20th cent.)

But London, London has become
A heavenly symbol and the sum
Of all the world can give.
And English air that was my breath
Remains my mortal life, till death
Shall set me free to live.

Theodore Maynard: *Exile.* (20th cent.)

English Language

I have endeavor'd to write English as
near as I could distinguish it from the

tongue of pedants and that of affected travelers. Only I am sorry that (speaking so noble a language as we do) we have not a more certain measure for it, as they have in France, where they have an Academy erected for that purpose.

Dryden: *The Rival Ladies, Dedication.* (17th cent.)

English Literature

The literature of England is no longer a mere letter, printed in books, and shut up in libraries, but it is a living voice, which has gone forth in its expressions and its sentiments into the world of men, which daily thrills upon our ears and syllables our thoughts, which speaks to us through our correspondents, and dictates when we put pen to paper.

Card. Newman: *Idea of a University.* (19th cent.)

Englishmen

But we, brave Britons, foreign laws despised,
And kept unconquer'd and uncivilized.

Pope: *An Essay on Criticism,* 3. (18th cent.)

I consider, indeed, Englishmen the most suspicious and touchy of mankind; I think them unreasonable, and unjust in their seasons of excitement; but I had rather be an Englishman, (as in effect I am), than belong to any other race under heaven. They are as generous, as they are hasty and burly; and their repentance for their injustice is greater than their sin.

Card. Newman: *Apologia pro Vita Sua, Preface.* (19th cent.)

It is not at all easy (humanly speaking) to wind up an Englishman to a dogmatic level.

Card. Newman: *Apologia pro Vita Sua,* 4. (19th cent.)

Those things which the English public never favors—youth, power, and enthusiasm.

Oscar Wilde: *The English Renaissance.* (19th cent.)

The idea that there is something English in the repression of one's feelings is one of those ideas which no Englishman ever heard of until England began to be governed exclusively by Scotchmen, Americans, and Jews.

G. K. Chesterton: *Heretics.* (20th cent.)

We, the English nation, have an ethic, a morality, and if we had not we should never have been a nation at all.

G. K. Chesterton: *Evidence before the Joint Select Committee on the Stage Plays.* (20th cent.)

The English are a modest people; that is why they are entirely ruled and run by the few of them that happen to be immodest.

G. K. Chesterton: *A Miscellany of Men.* (20th cent.)

Three things to beware of: The hoof of a horse, the horn of a bull, and the smile of an Englishman.

Seumas MacManus: *Heavy Hangs the Golden Grain.* (20th cent.)

You never find an Englishman among the under-dogs—except in England, of course.

Evelyn Waugh: *The Loved One.* (20th cent.)

Enmity

To pray for one's enemies in the love of Christ; to make peace with one's adversary before sundown.

St. Benedict: *Rule,* 4. (One of his "tools of good works") (6th cent.)

Hostility is as indefinable as love, and as unmistakable.

R. H. Benson: *The Conventionalists.* (20th cent.)

Enough

Who has enough, of no more has he need.

Robert Henryson: *Town and Country Mouse.* (15th cent.)

He that knoweth when he hath enough
is no fool.

> John Heywood: *Proverbs,* 2, 7. (16th cent.)

Here is enough and too much.

> John Heywood: *Proverbs,* 2, 8. (16th
> cent.)

Enough is enough.

> John Heywood: *Proverbs,* 2, 11. (16th
> cent.)

Entertainment

That is the essence of decadence, the
effacement of five people who do a thing
for fun by one person who does it for
money.

> G. K. Chesterton: *Heretics.* (20th cent.)

Envy

Not to give way to envy.

> St. Benedict: *Rule,* 4. (One of his "tools
> of good works") (6th cent.)

For when the foul sore of envy corrupts
the vanquished heart, the very exterior
itself shows how forcibly the mind is
urged by madness.

> Pope St. Gregory I: *Morals,* 5, 85. (6th
> cent.)

Better be envied than pitied.

> John Heywood: *Proverbs,* 1, 11. (16th
> cent.)

Envy, that does with misery reside,
The joy and the revenge of ruined
pride.

> Dryden. (17th cent.)

Envy is a criminal sorrow for the welfare of our neighbor.

> St. John Baptist de la Salle: *Les devoirs du
> chrétien,* 14. (18th cent.)

Envy will merit as its shade pursue,
But like a shadow proves the substance
true.

> Pope: *An Essay on Criticism,* 2. (18th
> cent.)

Envy, to which th' ignoble mind's a
slave,
Is emulation in the learn'd or brave.

> Pope: *An Essay on Man,* 2. (18th cent.)

Epiphany

Bethlehem, of noblest cities
None can once with thee compare;
Thou alone the Lord from heaven
Didst for us incarnate bear.

. . . .

Solemn things of mystic meaning:
Incense doth the God disclose;
Gold a royal Child proclaimeth;
Myrrh a future tomb foreshows.

> Roman Breviary, Epiphany, Hymn *O sola
> magnarum urbium* at Lauds. (Tr. E.
> Caswall) (Prudentius, Cathemerinon, 4th
> cent.)

Why impious Herod, vainly fear
That Christ the Savior cometh here?
He takes no earthly realms away
Who gives the crown that lasts for aye.

. . . .

In holy Jordan's purest wave
The heavenly Lamb vouchsafed to
lave;
That He, to whom was sin unknown,
Might cleanse His people from their
own.

New miracle of power divine!
The water reddens into wine:
He spake the word: and poured the
wave
In other streams than nature gave.

> Roman Breviary, Epiphany, Hymn *Crudelis
> Herodes Deum* at Vespers. (Tr. J. Neale)
> (Sedulius, 5th cent.)

That day, beloved children, on which
Christ, the Savior of the world, for the
first time appeared to the gentiles, is to
be venerated with a most holy honor by
us also. . . . For that day is not past in
such a way that the power of the work
which was then revealed should be past
as well.

> Pope St. Leo I: *Sixth Sermon on the
> Epiphany.* (5th cent.)

Magnify, my soul, her who is more honorable and glorious than the hosts above. O most pure Virgin, blessed Mother, the mystery of thy childbirth passeth understanding, and by it we have gained full salvation. We worthily praise thee as our benefactress, and bring thee songs as a thank-offering.

> Byzantine Menaea, Theophany, Canon at Matins, Ninth Ode. (ca. 6th cent.)

Today, O Lord, Thou didst manifest Thyself to the whole world, and Thy light hath come upon us who in understanding sing to Thee, Thou didst come, Thou didst appear, O Light inaccessible.

> Byzantine Menaea, Theophany, Kontakion. (ca. 6th cent.)

O God, Who on this day didst reveal Thine only-begotten Son to the gentiles by the leading of a star; mercifully grant, that we who know Thee now by faith, may be brought to the contemplation of the beauty of Thy majesty.

> Roman Missal, Epiphany, Collect. (Gregorian, ca. 6th cent.)

This day the Church is joined unto the heavenly Bridegroom, since Christ hath washed away her sins in Jordan; the wise men hasten with gifts to the marriage supper of the King; and they that sit at meat together make merry with water turned into wine. Alleluia.

> Roman Breviary, Epiphany, Antiphon at Lauds. (Liber Resp. ca. 6th cent.)

Fair eastern star, that art ordain'd to run
Before the sages, to the rising Sun,
Here cease thy course, and wonder that the cloud
Of this poor stable can thy Maker shroud.

> Sir John Beaumont: Of the Epiphany. (17th cent.)

Look up, sweet Babe, look up and see
    For love of Thee
    Thus far from home
    The east is come

To seek herself in Thy sweet eyes;
We, who strangely went astray,
    Lost in a bright
    Meridian night,
A darkness made of too much day,
    Beckon'd from far
    By Thy fair star,
Lo at last have found our way.

> Richard Crashaw: The Glorious Epiphany of Our Lord, a Hymn. (17th cent.)

Episcopate

For one must obey the presbyters in the Church, who have their succession from the apostles, who with the succession to the episcopate have received the sure charisma of truth according to the Father's pleasure.

> St. Irenaeus: Against the Heresies, 4, 26, 2. (2nd cent.)

The episcopate, of which part is held by each severally and jointly, is one.

> St. Cyprian: On the Unity of the Catholic Church, 5. (3rd cent.)

There is one Church, divided by Christ throughout the whole world into many members, and also one episcopate diffused through a harmonious multitude of many bishops.

> St. Cyprian: Letters, 51, 24. (3rd cent.)

Whence you ought to know that the bishop is in the Church, and the Church in the bishop; and if anyone be not with the bishop, that he is not in the Church.

> St. Cyprian: Letters, 68, 8. (3rd cent.)

See also Bishop; Hierarchy

Epitaph

All hope of never dying here lies dead.

> Richard Crashaw: On the Death of Mr. Herrys. (17th cent.)

Equality

For we are all by nature equal as men, but by an additional dispensation of

God some men are set over or are inferior to others.

Pope St. Gregory I: *Morals,* 21, 15. (6th cent.)

Wherefore, all who are superiors should not regard in themselves the power of their rank, but the equality of their nature; and they should find their joy not in ruling over men, but in helping them. . . . By nature a man is made superior to the beasts (Gen. 9, 1), but not to other men; it is therefore said to him that he should be feared by beasts, but not by men. Evidently, to wish to be feared by an equal is to lord it over others, contrary to the natural order.

Pope St. Gregory I: *Pastoral Care,* 2, 6. (6th cent.)

From the time of the first fairy-tales men had always believed ideally in equality; they had always thought that something ought to be done, if anything could be done, to redress the balance between Cinderella and the ugly sisters. The irritating thing about the French was not that they said this ought to be done: everybody said that. The irritating thing about the French was that they did it.

G. K. Chesterton: *Introduction to Hard Times.* (20th cent.)

The equality existing among the various social members consists only in this: that all men have their origin in God the Creator, have been redeemed by Jesus Christ, and are to be judged and rewarded or punished by God exactly according to their merits or demerits.

Pope St. Pius X: *Letter to the Bishops of Italy on Catholic Social Action.* (1903)

Equity

Equity is the agreement of things, which desires equal rights in equal cases. So God, according to that which He desires, is called equity: equity is nothing else than God. If this equity is found perpetually in the will of man, it is called justice; such will, reduced to the form of precepts, whether in written form or customary is called law (*jus*).

Fragmentum Pragense, 4, 2. (In Carlyle, *Med. Political Theory,* II, 8.) (11th cent.)

Error

It is human to err; it is devilish to remain wilfully in error.

St. Augustine: *Sermon 164,* 14. (5th cent.)

He errs only when he thinks he knows what he does not know, for he accepts what is false as true, and herein lies the essence of error.

St. Augustine: *Enchiridion,* 17. (5th cent.)

For to fall into error in many matters is but human weakness, while to know naught but reality is the divine perfection of angels.

John of Salisbury: *Policraticus,* 2, 12, 86. (12th cent.)

Man is a being filled with error. This error is natural, and, without grace, ineffaceable. Nothing shows him the truth; everything deceives him.

Pascal: *Pensées,* 4. (17th cent.)

Errors, like straws, upon the surface flow;
He who would search for pearls must dive below.

Dryden: *All for Love,* prologue. (17th cent.)

To err is human, to forgive divine.

Pope: *An Essay on Criticism,* 2. (18th cent.)

For his was the error of head, not of heart.

Thomas Moore: *The Irish Slave.* (19th cent.)

All aberrations are founded on, and have their life in, some truth or other.

Card. Newman: *Apologia pro Vita Sua.* (19th cent.)

Nothing carried on by human instruments, but has its irregularities, and affords ground for criticism, when minutely scrutinized in matters of detail.

> Card. Newman: *Apologia pro Vita Sua*, 5. (19th cent.)

A wavering or shallow mind does perhaps as much harm to others as a mind that is consistent in error.

> Card. Newman: *Discussions and Arguments*. (19th cent.)

Most mistaken people mean well, and all mistaken people mean something. There is something to be said for every error, but, whatever may be said for it, the most important thing to be said about it is that it is erroneous.

> G. K. Chesterton: *All is Grist*. (20th cent.)

Escape

The birds were flown.

> John Heywood: *Proverbs*, 1, 12. (16th cent.)

Men, not having been able to cure death, misery, and ignorance, have imagined to make themselves happy by not thinking of these things.

> Pascal: *Pensées*, 2. (17th cent.)

Essence

Other things that are called essences or substances admit of accidents, whereby a change, whether great or small, is produced in them. But there can be no accident of this kind in respect of God: and therefore He Who is God is the only immutable substance or essence, to Whom certainly Being itself, whence is derived the term essence, most especially and most truly belongs.

> St. Augustine: *De Trinitate*, 5, 2, 3. (5th cent.)

Esteem

As the esteem of good men cannot be taken away by false accusations, so it cannot be won by the attentions of flattery.

> St. Bernard: *Letters*. (12th cent.)

Esteem is in particular a noble and delicate sentiment which scorns all that is not becoming.

> John of Salisbury: *Policraticus*, 3, 5, 182. (12th cent.)

Man's deepest abasement is his pursuit of glory; but it is likewise the greatest mark of his excellence; for, whatever possessions he may have, whatever health and essential comfort, he is not content unless he have the esteem of his fellows.

> Pascal: *Pensées*. (17th cent.)

Eternal Life

We measure everything by the standard of the future, rather than the present, and define as useful only that which will be of service to us with reference to the grace of eternal life.

> St. Ambrose: *On the Duties of the Clergy*, 1, 28. (4th cent.)

Eternal life is the actual knowledge of truth. How wrongheaded and preposterous they are who imagine that their teaching about the knowledge of God will make us perfect, when this is the reward of those who are actually perfect.

> St. Augustine: *De Moribus Ecclesiae Catholicae*, 1, 25, 47. (4th cent.)

Now he lives in Abraham's bosom. . . . For what other place is there for such a soul?

> St. Augustine: *Confessions*, 9, 3. (5th cent.)

Show me one who loves; he will understand what I say. Show me one who yearns and hungers; show me one who during his pilgrimage in this wilderness thirsts and sighs after the Fount of that eternal fatherland; show me one such, he will understand what I say.

> St. Augustine: *In Joann. Evang. Tract.*, 26, 4. (5th cent.)

Almighty and merciful God, unto Whose everlasting blessedness we ascend, not by the frailty of the flesh, but by the activity of the soul; make us ever by Thine inspiration to seek after the courts of the heavenly City, and by Thy mercy confidently to enter them.

> Leonine Sacramentary, Collect. (ca. 5th cent.)

To desire eternal life with all spiritual longing.

> St. Benedict: *Rule*, 4. (One of his "tools of good works") (6th cent.)

Forasmuch as there is to us in this life a difference in works, doubtless there will be in the future life a difference in degrees of dignity, that whereas here one surpasses another in desert, there one may excel another in reward. . . . *In my Father's house there are many mansions* (John, 14, 2).

> Pope St. Gregory I: *Morals*, 4, 70. (6th cent.)

To the fount of life eternal
  cries the soul with longing thirst,
And the spirit, flesh imprisoned,
  seeks the bars of flesh to burst;
Strives to gain that heavenly country,
  exiled now and sin-accurst.

> St. Peter Damian: *Ad perennis vitae fontem mens sitivit arida.* (Tr. S. A. Hurlbut) (11th cent.)

Nobody is excluded from the kingdom of heaven except through human fault.

> St. Thomas Aquinas: *Contra Gentes*, 4, 50. (13th cent.)

O happy, whom He chooseth for that bliss!

> Dante: *Inferno, Canto 1*. (Tr. Binyon) (14th cent.)

There shall be seen that unto which we cleave
  By faith, not proven in argument; self-shown
As is the simple truth that all believe.

> Dante: *Paradiso, Canto 2*. (Tr. Binyon) (14th cent.)

Then saw I how each heaven for every soul
  Is paradise, though from the Supreme Good
  The dews of grace not in one measure fall.

> Dante: *Paradiso, Canto 3*. (Tr. Binyon) (14th cent.)

On His Son gazing, with the Love that still
  From one and from the other's breath proceeds,
The Power primordial and ineffable
Made with such order all that circling speeds
  Through mind or space, that he who looks on it
  Cannot but taste Him, as thereon he feeds.

> Dante: *Paradiso, Canto 10*. (Tr. Binyon) (14th cent.)

None ever rose to see
This realm who had not the belief in Christ
After or before the nailing on the tree.

> Dante: *Paradiso, Canto 19*. (Tr. Binyon) (14th cent.)

We by apostolic authority define that . . . the souls of all the saints who departed from this world before the passion of our Lord Jesus Christ, as also the souls of the holy apostles, martyrs, confessors, virgins and of the rest of the faithful who have departed this life after receiving Christ's baptism, in whom there is found nothing calling for purification when they died . . . as also the souls of children who have been regenerated by the said Christian baptism and who die before attaining the use of freewill— these, straightway upon their death, or after purification in the case of those who need it, even before the resurrection of their bodies and the general judgment, have been, are, and will be, since the Ascension of our Lord . . . gathered into heaven . . . and have . . .

seen and do see the Divine Essence with an intuitive vision, face to face. . . .

> Pope Benedict XII: *Benedictus Deus.* (June 29, 1336)

What does heaven mean for a rational soul? Nothing else than Jesus, God. For if that is heaven which is above everything else, then only God is heaven to the human soul, for He alone is above the nature of the soul. And if a soul is able through grace to know the divine nature of Jesus, then indeed it sees heaven, for it sees God.

> Walter Hilton: *Scale of Perfection,* 2, 33. (14th cent.)

For a small living men run a great way, for eternal life many will scarce move a single foot from the ground.

> Thomas a Kempis: *The Imitation of Christ,* 3, 3. (15th cent.)

It is no small matter to lose or gain the kingdom of heaven.

> Thomas a Kempis: *The Imitation of Christ,* 3, 47. (15th cent.)

O most happy mansion of the city above! O most bright day of eternity, which knows no night, but is always enlightened by the sovereign Truth! A day always joyful, always secure, and never changing its state for the contrary. O that this day would shine upon us, and all those temporal things would come to an end!

> Thomas a Kempis: *The Imitation of Christ,* 3, 48. (15th cent.)

The way to heaven out of all places is of like length and distance.

> St. Thomas More: *Utopia.* (16th cent.)

Remember, that into God's vineyard there goeth no man, but he that is called thither.

> St. Thomas More: *Dialogue of Comfort.* (16th cent.)

Is not this house as nigh heaven as my own?

> St. Thomas More, with reference to the Tower of London. (Roper, Life) (16th cent.)

Soar up, my soul, unto thy rest, cast off this loathsome load,
Long is the date of thy exile, too long the strict abode.
Graze not on worldly wither'd weed, it fitteth not thy taste,
The flowers of everlasting spring, do grow for thy repast.

> Bl. Robert Southwell: *Seeke Flowers of Heaven.* (16th cent.)

For how dare mortals here their thoughts erect
To taste those joys, which they in heav'n expect?

> Sir John Beaumont: *In Spiritual Comfort.* (17th cent.)

Little does passing time matter to a soul which aspires to eternity, and which only takes notice of perishing moments in order to pass by them into immortal life.

> St. Francis de Sales: *Letters to Persons in Religion,* 4, 8. (17th cent.)

The world is only peopled to people heaven.

> St. Francis de Sales: *Letters to Persons in the World,* 2, 32. (17th cent.)

The shortest life is the best if it leads us to the eternal.

> St. Francis de Sales: *Letters to Persons in the World,* 2, 33. (17th cent.)

Let them sleep, let them sleep on;
Till this stormy night be gone,
Till the eternal morrow dawn;
Then the curtains will be drawn,
And they awake into a light,
Whose day shall never die in night.

> Richard Crashaw: *An Epitaph Upon a Young Married Couple.* (17th cent.)

Thou wilt have time enough for hymns
   divine,
Since heav'n's eternal year is thine.

> Dryden: *Ode to the Memory of Mrs.
> Killigrew.* (17th cent.)

A Persian's heav'n is easily made,
'Tis but black eyes and lemonade.

> Thomas Moore: *Intercepted Letters, 6.*
> (19th cent.)

Earth has no sorrow that Heaven cannot
heal.

> Thomas Moore: *Come, Ye Disconsolate.*
> (19th cent.)

This world is all a fleeting show,
For man's illusion given;
The smiles of joy, the tears of woe,
Deceitful shine, deceitful flow,—
There's nothing true but Heaven.

> Thomas Moore: *This World is All a
> Fleeting Show.* (19th cent.)

Take all the pleasures of all the spheres,
And multiply each through endless
   years,—
One minute of heaven is worth them
   all.

> Thomas Moore: *Lalla Rookh: Paradise and
> the Peri.* (19th cent.)

Joy, joy for ever!—my task is done—
The gates are pass'd, and heaven is
   won!

> Thomas Moore: *Lalla Rookh: Paradise and
> the Peri.* (Concluding lines) (19th cent.)

O Paradise! O Paradise!
   Who doth not crave for rest?
Who would not seek the happy land,
   Where they that loved are blest;
      Where loyal hearts and true,
         Stand ever in the light,
      All rapture through and through
         In God's most holy sight?

> F. Faber: *Paradise.* (19th cent.)

A sea before
The throne is spread;—its pure still
   glass

Pictures all earth-scenes as they pass.
   We, on its shore,
Share, in the bosom of our rest,
God's knowledge, and are blest.

> Card. Newman: *A Voice from Afar.* (19th
> cent.)

Love of heaven is the only *way* to
heaven.

> Card. Newman: *Parochial and Plain
> Sermons,* 8. (19th cent.)

Ah, well! it is a purchase and a prize.
Buy then! Bid then!—What?—Prayer,
   patience, alms, vows.—
Look, look! a May-mess, like on orchard
   bows;
Look! March-bloom, like on mealed-
   with-yellow sallows.—
These are indeed the barn: within-
   doors house
The shocks. This piece-bright paling
   hides the Spouse
Christ, and the Mother of Christ and
   all His hallows.

> G. M. Hopkins: *The Starlight Night.*
> (19th cent.)

Beautiful habitations, auras of delight!
Who shall bewail the crags and bitter
   foam
And angry sword-blades flashing left
   and right
Which guard your glittering height,
That none thereby may come!

> Coventry Patmore: *Auras of Delight.* (19th
> cent.)

   Love makes the life to be
   A fount perpetual of virginity;
      For, lo, the elect
Of generous love, how named soe'er,
   affect
      Nothing but God,
      Or mediate or direct,
      Nothing but God,
   The Husband of the heavens:
And who Him love, in potence great
   or small,

Are, one and all,
Heirs of the palace glad,
And thinly clad
With the bridal robes of ardor virginal.

Coventry Patmore: *Deliciae Sapientiae De Amore*. (19th cent.)

The heavens that seemed so far away
    When old-time grief was near,
Beyond the vista seen today,
    Close o'er my life appear;
For there, in reconcilement sweet,
    The human and divine,
The loftiest and the lowliest, meet
    On love's horizon-line.

       J. B. Tabb: *Restrospect*. (19th cent.)

Short arm needs man to reach to heaven,
    So ready is heaven to stoop to him.

Francis Thompson: *Grace of the Way*. (19th cent.)

Cruel, to take from a
Sinner his heaven!

   F. Thompson: *A Carrier Song*. (19th cent.)

Look for me in the nurseries of heaven.

   F. Thompson: *To My Godchild*. (19th cent.)

O world invisible, we view thee:
    O world intangible, we touch thee,
O world unknowable, we know thee,
    Inapprehensible, we clutch thee!

   F. Thompson: *In No Strange Land*. (19th cent.)

Upon the eternal borders let
My still too fearful soul be set:
    Then wait the will of God,
    A loving period.
Closer I dare not come, nor see
The face of Him, Who died for me.
    Child! Thou shalt dwell apart:
    But in My sacred heart.

   Lionel Johnson: *Visions*. (19th cent.)

The temper of mind with which we regard eternity is of considerable importance as illustrating our view of the past.

   R. H. Benson: *The Death-beds of Bloody Mary and Good Queen Bess*. (20th cent.)

For Catholics it is a fundamental dogma of the faith that all human beings, without any exception whatever, were specially made, were shaped and pointed like shining arrows, for the end of hitting the mark of beatitude. It is true that the shafts are feathered with free will, and therefore throw the shadow of all the tragic possibilities of free will; and that the Church (having been aware for ages of that darker side of truth, which the new sceptics have just discovered) does also draw attention to the darkness of that potential tragedy. But that does not make any difference to the gloriousness of the potential glory. In one aspect it is even a part of it; since the freedom is itself a glory. In that sense they would still wear their haloes even in hell.

   G. K. Chesterton: *The Thing*. (20th cent.)

This is the song of the empire builder,
    Who built not of wasted lands,
But who builded a kingdom of golden deeds
    And of things not made by hands.

     ·   ·   ·   ·   ·   ·

The mind cannot measure its boundaries,
    All space is its outer gate:
It is broader than ever a man conceived
    And more durable than fate.

     ·   ·   ·   ·   ·   ·

This is the kingdom our brother built:
    It is good: it hath sufficed;—
For who can measure the glory he keeps
    With our elder brother, Christ?

   John J. Rooney: *The Empire Builder (On the Death of a Catholic Gentleman)*. (20th cent.)

Lo, comfort blooms on pain, and peace on strife,
    And gain on loss!
What is the key to everlasting life?
    A blood-stained Cross.

       Joyce Kilmer: *Pennies*. (20th cent.)

Time is but God's contrivance for giving us the opportunity to know Him. Through that time gleams the skein of eternity; all that is past and gone is rescued from the tomb by belonging to the eternal purpose. How idle and foolish beside this is the worship of mere progress, of the Nietzschean ideal of man passing to superman. Men are not mere dung to fructify the seed of the future; they cannot wait for the colophon, for the pages of their lives are being written in the sweat of their brow. No! there is one unchanging and abiding God giving permanence to the fleeting acts of man.

> M. C. D'Arcy: *The Idea of God.* (In *God and the Supernatural*) (20th cent.)

See also Death; Jerusalem, Heavenly; Judgment, Last; Paradise; Vision of God

Eternity

As eternity is the proper measure of permanent being, so time is the proper measure of movement.

> St. Thomas Aquinas: *Summa Theologica,* 1, 10, 4. (13th cent.)

Eternity, when I think thee
(Which never any end must have
Nor knewest beginning) and foresee
Hell is designed for sin a grave.

My frighted flesh trembles to dust,
My blood ebbs fearfully away:
Both guilty that they did to lust
And vanity my youth betray.

> William Habington: *Quoniam Ego in Flagella Paratus Sum.* (17th cent.)

Time is short, eternity is long.

> Card. Newman: *Development of Christian Doctrine.* (19th cent.)

An alien ear,
Homesick for harpings of eternity.

> C. L. O'Donnell: *The Dead Musician.* (20th cent.)

So must outlive we even earth and sky,
Thou, God, and I, in one persistent now.

And when eternity is old then Thou
Shalt still be young, but how much
younger I!

> Edwin Essex: *Epigram.* (20th cent.)

Ethics

Socrates first established ethics with a view to correcting and regulating conduct, and he devoted all his attention to the discussion of right living, dividing it into the four virtues of the soul, namely, prudence, justice, fortitude, and temperance.

> St. Isidore: *Etymologies,* 2, 24. (7th cent.)

As regards ethics, we cannot discuss what we ought to do unless we know what we can do.

> St. Thomas Aquinas: *Commentary on the De Anima,* 1, lect. 1, 2. (13th cent.)

See also Morality

Eucharist, Holy

The sacrament (*mystery*) of sacraments.

> Pseudo-Dionysius: *Ecclesiastical Hierarchy,* 3. (5th cent.)

The noblest sacrament, consequently, is that wherein His Body is really present. The Eucharist crowns all the other sacraments.

> St. Thomas Aquinas: *Disputations concerning Truth,* 27, 4. (13th cent.)

How I hate this folly of not believing in the Eucharist, etc.! If the gospel be true, if Jesus Christ be God, what difficulty is there?

> Pascal: *Pensées.* (17th cent.)

See also Blessed Sacrament; Communion; Liturgy; Mass; Sacrament

Eucharist: Sacrifice

It will be no small sin for us, if we depose from the episcopacy men who have blamelessly and in holiness offered up sacrifice (*ta dora*).

> Pope St. Clement I: *Letter to the Corinthians,* 44, 4. (1st cent.)

And on the Lord's Day, after you have come together, break bread and offer the Eucharist, having first confessed your offences, so that your sacrifice may be pure.

> Teaching of the Twelve Apostles, 14. (2nd cent.)

However, no one quarreling with his brother may join your meeting until they are reconciled; your sacrifice must not be defiled. For here we have the saying of the Lord: *In every place and time offer Me a pure sacrifice; for I am a mighty King, says the Lord; and My name spreads terror among the nations.* (Mal. 1, 10)

> Teaching of the Twelve Apostles, 14. (2nd cent.)

Let that Eucharist be held valid which is offered by the bishop or by one to whom the bishop has committed this charge.

> St. Ignatius of Antioch: *Letter to the Smyrnaeans,* 8. (2nd cent.)

He would have us offer our gift at the altar frequently and without interruption.

> St. Irenaeus: *Against the Heresies,* 4, 18, 6. (2nd cent.)

It is quite evident that this prophecy [Isaiah 33, 13-19] also alludes to the bread which our Christ gave us to offer in remembrance of the Body which He assumed for the sake of those who believe in Him, for whom He also suffered, and also to the cup which He taught us to offer in the Eucharist, in commemoration of His Blood.

> St. Justin Martyr: *Dialogue with Trypho,* 70. (2nd cent.)

Thou art a Priest for ever, after the order of Melchizedek (Ps. 109). . . . For who is more a Priest of the most high God than our Lord Jesus Christ, Who offered a sacrifice to God the Father, and offered that very same thing which Melchizedek had offered, that is, bread and wine, to wit, his Body and Blood?

> St. Cyprian: *Letters,* 62, 4. (3rd cent.)

That priest truly discharges the office of Christ, who imitates what Christ did; he offers a true and full sacrifice in the Church to God the Father, when he proceeds to offer it according to the way in which he sees Christ Himself to have offered it.

> St. Cyprian: *Letters,* 62, 14. (3rd cent.)

After the spiritual sacrifice, the bloodless service, is completed [i.e. the consecration of the elements], we entreat God over that sacrifice of propitiation for the common peace of the churches, for the welfare of the world; for kings; for soldiers and allies; for the sick; for the afflicted; and, in a word, for all who stand in need of succor we all pray and offer this sacrifice.

> St. Cyril of Jerusalem: *Catechetical Discourses,* 23, 8. (4th cent.)

When you behold the Lord sacrificed and prostrate, and the priest standing over the sacrifice and praying, and all who are stained with that precious Blood, do you then suppose you are among men, and standing upon earth? Are you not immediately transported to heaven?

> St. John Chrysostom: *On the Priesthood,* 3, 4. (4th cent.)

It follows beyond all doubt that the whole redeemed City, the congregation and fellowship of saints, is offered as a universal sacrifice to God by the High Priest, who in the form of a servant has offered Himself in His Passion for us that we might be members of so venerable a Head. This *form of a servant* it was that He offered, in this was He offered, because in this respect He is Mediator; in this, Priest; in this Sacrifice. According to the apostle (Rom. 12, 1-5) . . . this whole sacrifice, of which he speaks, we ourselves are. This is the sacrifice of Christians: *many, one body in Christ.* And this the Church re-enacts (*frequentat*) in the Sacrament of the Altar known to the faithful, to the end that it may be shown to her that in the oblation which she offers she herself is offered.

> St. Augustine: *The City of God,* 10, 6. (5th cent.)

He also is a priest, Himself the offerer and the oblation. Of this truth He wished there to be a daily sacred sign (*sacramentum*) in the sacrifice of the Church, which being the Body whereof He is the Head, learns to offer herself through Him. The ancient sacrifices of the saints were manifold and various signs of this true sacrifice. And to this supreme and true sacrifice all false sacrifices have given place.

> St. Augustine: *The City of God,* 10, 20. (5th cent.)

Nor do we set up altars, to sacrifice to the martyrs, but to God alone, God of the martyrs and our God. In this sacrifice all the men of God, who in confession of their allegiance to Him have overcome the world, are named in due place and order, but are not invoked by the sacrificing priest. The reason is, because he is sacrificing to God, not to them, because he is God's priest, not theirs, although it is in their memorial shrine that he sacrifices. The sacrifice itself is the Body of Christ, which is not offered to them, because it is what they themselves are.

> St. Augustine: *The City of God,* 22, 10. (5th cent.)

When sacrifices either of the altar or of alms of any kind are offered for all the baptized dead, they are thank offerings for the good; for those who were not very bad they are propitiatory offerings; and, though for the very bad they have no significance as helps for the dead, they do bring a measure of consolation to the living. And those who actually receive such profit, receive it in the form either of a complete remission of sin, or of at least an amelioration of their sentence.

> St. Augustine: *Enchiridion,* 110. (5th cent.)

We ought to immolate to God the daily sacrifices of our tears, the daily offerings of his Flesh and Blood. For this Victim peculiarly preserves the soul from eternal death, as it renews to us in a mystery the death of the Only-begotten; Who, although being risen from the dead He dies no more and death shall have no more dominion over Him, yet, while in Himself He lives immortal and incorruptible, for us is immolated again in this mystery of the sacred oblation. For it is His Body that is there taken, His Flesh that is divided for the salvation of the people, His Blood that is poured, not as before into the hands of unbelievers, but into the mouths of the faithful. Hence let us estimate the importance of this sacrifice for us, which for our absolution ever imitates the Passion of the only-begotten Son. For what Christian can doubt that at the very hour of the offering, at the words of the priest, the heavens are opened, the choirs of angels are present in that mystery of Jesus Christ, the lowest things are knit with the highest, the earthly things are united with the heavenly, the visible and the invisible are made one?

> Pope St. Gregory the Great: *Dialogues,* 4, 58. (6th cent.)

Sacrifice is so called from being 'made sacred,' because by mystical prayer it is consecrated on our behalf in memory of the Lord's passion; whence, at His command, we call this the Body and Blood of Christ. Consisting of the fruits of the earth, it is sanctified and becomes the Sacrament, by the invisible operation of the Holy Spirit. The sacrament of the bread and chalice is called by the Greeks the Eucharist, which means thanksgiving in Latin. What is better than the Blood and Body of Christ?

> St. Isidore: *Etymologies,* 6, 19. (7th cent.)

We celebrate the solemn ceremonies of the mass, we immolate to God the most sacred Body and precious Blood of our Lamb by Whom we have been redeemed from sins unto the attainment of our salvation.

St. Bede the Venerable: *Homilies, 2, 1.* (8th cent.)

Not only do the priests offer the sacrifice, but also all the faithful: for what the priest does personally by virtue of his ministry, the faithful do collectively by virtue of their intention.

Pope Innocent III: *De Sacro Altaris Mysterio, 3, 6.* (13th cent.)

There is one Christ, not many offered by Christ and by us. For Christ was offered once, and His sacrifice was the original of ours. There is one body, not many, and so, wherever He is offered, the sacrifice is one and the same with His.

St. Thomas Aquinas: *Summa Theologica, 3, 83, 1.* (13th cent.)

For two reasons the celebration of the Eucharist is called the immolation of Christ. First, because, as Augustine observes, the usage is to call images by the names of the things they represent. . . . The celebration of this sacrament, the holy mass, is an image representing Christ's Passion. That was the real immolation. . . . The host was offered once in Christ, powerful for everlasting salvation. What then about us? Do we not offer it every day, in record of His death? Secondly, through this sacrament we are made partakers of the fruit of our Lord's Passion.

St. Thomas Aquinas: *Summa Theologica, 3, 83, 1.* (13th cent.)

If any one saith that in the mass a true and proper sacrifice is not offered to God; or that to be offered is nothing else but that Christ is given us to eat; let him be anathema.

Council of Trent, Session 22, Canon 1. (Sept. 17, 1562)

If any one saith that by those words, *Do this for a commemoration of Me* (Luke 22, 19), Christ did not institute the apostles priests (*sacerdotes*); or did

not ordain that they and other priests should offer His own body and blood; let him be anathema.

Council of Trent, Session 22, Canon 2. (Sept. 17, 1562)

If any one saith that the sacrifice of the mass is only a sacrifice of praise and of thanksgiving; or that it is a bare commemoration of the sacrifice consummated on the Cross, but not a propitiatory sacrifice; or that it profits him only who receives; and that it ought not to be offered for the living and for the dead for sins, pains, satisfactions, and other necessities; let him be anathema.

Council of Trent, Session 22, Canon 3. (Sept. 17, 1562)

If any one saith that by the sacrifice of the mass a blasphemy is cast upon the most holy sacrifice of Christ consummated on the Cross; or that it is thereby derogated from; let him be anathema.

Council of Trent, Session 22, Canon 4. (Sept. 17, 1562)

We, therefore, confess that the sacrifice of the mass is one and the same sacrifice with that of the Cross: the Victim is one and the same, Christ Jesus, Who offered Himself once only, a bloody sacrifice on the altar of the Cross. The bloody and unbloody victim is still one and the same, and the oblation of the Cross is daily renewed in the eucharistic sacrifice in obedience to the command of our Lord: *Do this for a commemoration of Me.*

Catechism of the Council of Trent, 2. (16th cent.)

The lips of the Church are never silent, but from the four winds the breath of the Sacrifice goes up for ever from many lands in one eternal tongue.

John Ayscough: *Saints and Places.* (20th cent.)

Priests alone have the power of offering the sacrifice of the mass.

Code of Canon Law, Canon 802. (20th cent.)

It is an unquestionable fact that the work of our redemption is continued, and that its fruits are imparted to us, during the celebration of the liturgy, notably in the august sacrifice of the altar. Christ acts each day to save us, in the sacraments and in His holy sacrifice. By means of them He is constantly atoning for the sins of mankind, constantly consecrating it to God.

> Pope Pius XII: *Mediator Dei.* (Nov. 20, 1947)

Let the souls of Christians be like altars on each one of which a different phase of the sacrifice, offered by the High Priest, comes to life again, as it were: pains and tears which wipe away and expiate sin; supplication to God which pierces heaven; dedication and even immolation of oneself made promptly, generously and earnestly; and, finally, that intimate union by which we commit ourselves and all we have to God, in Whom we find our rest.

> Pope Pius XII: *Mediator Dei.* (Nov. 20, 1947)

Eucharist: Transubstantiation

The bread and wine of the eucharist before the invocation of the holy and adorable Trinity were simple bread and wine, while after the invocation the bread becomes the Body of Christ, and the wine the Blood of Christ.

> St. Cyril of Jerusalem: *Catechetical Discourses,* 19, 7. (4th cent.)

The word of Christ could make out of nothing that which was not; can it then not change the things which are into that which they were not? For to give new natures to things is quite as wonderful as to change their natures.

> St. Ambrose: *On the Mysteries,* 9, 52. (4th cent.)

You say perhaps, 'My bread is of the usual kind.' But that bread is bread before the words of the sacraments; when

consecration has been added, from bread it becomes the Flesh of Christ. Let us therefore prove this. How can that which is bread be the Body of Christ? By consecration. But in what words and in whose language is the consecration? Those of the Lord Jesus.

> St. Ambrose: *On the Sacraments,* 4, 4, 14. (4th cent.)

Now we, as often as we receive the Sacraments, which by the mystery of holy prayer are transformed (*transfigurantur*) into Flesh and Blood, proclaim the Lord's death.

> St. Ambrose: *Concerning Faith,* 4, 124. (4th cent.)

He washes us from our sins daily in His Blood, when the memory of His blessed passion is repeated at the altar, when the creature of bread and wine is transferred into the sacrament of His Flesh and Blood by the ineffable sanctification of His Spirit: and thus His Body and Blood is poured out and killed, not by the hands of infidels unto their destruction, but is assumed by the mouth of the faithful unto their salvation.

> St. Bede the Venerable: *Homilies,* 1, 14. (8th cent.)

Just as in nature the bread by the eating and the wine and the water by the drinking are changed into the body and blood of the eater and drinker, and do not become a different body from the former one, so the bread of the altar (*prothesis*) and the wine and water are supernaturally changed by the invocation and presence of the Holy Spirit into the Body and Blood of Christ, and are not two but one and the same.

> St. John of Damascus: *Exposition of the Orthodox Faith,* 4, 13. (8th cent.)

The bread and the wine are not merely figures of the Body and Blood of Christ (God forbid!) but the deified Body of the Lord itself, for the Lord has said: *This is My body,* not, this is a figure of my body; and *My blood,* not, a figure of my blood.

> St. John of Damascus: *Exposition of the Orthodox Faith,* 4, 13. (8th cent.)

I, Berengarius, firmly believe and confess with my mouth, that the bread and wine which are laid on the altar, by the mystery of sacred prayer and the words of our Redeemer, are substantially converted into the very flesh and blood of our Lord Jesus Christ, true and life-giving; and that after consecration it is the true Body of Christ which was born of the Virgin, which was offered as a sacrifice on the cross for the salvation of the world, and which sits at the right hand of the Father, and the very Blood of Christ which flowed from His side; and that the sacrament is to be understood not merely as a sign and virtually, but actually and really, as I have read it and you understand it to be set forth in this brief statement.

> Statement of Berengarius at Sixth Council of Rome. (1079)

There is one holy universal Church of the faithful outside which absolutely no one is saved, in which Jesus Christ Himself is both Priest and Victim, Whose Body and Blood are truly contained in the sacrament of the altar under the appearances of bread and wine, the bread and the wine being by divine power transubstantiated into His body and blood, so that for the perfecting of the mystery of unity we may receive of Him what He took from us. And no one may consecrate this sacrament except a priest who has been duly ordained according to the keys of the Church, which Jesus Christ Himself granted to the apostles and their successors.

> Fourth Lateran Council, Chap. 1, De Fide Catholica. (1215)

The whole substance of bread is converted into the whole substance of Christ's Body, the whole substance of wine into the whole substance of His Blood. This is not a transmutation or transformation; it is not catalogued under the ordinary physical processes, but is given the special name of transubstantiation.

> St. Thomas Aquinas: *Summa Theologica,* 3, 75, 4. (13th cent.)

It is evident to the senses that all the accidents of bread and wine remain after consecration. Such is the reasonable course of divine Providence, for it is abominable to eat human flesh and drink human blood. That is why Christ's Body and Blood are offered to us under the species of what we are accustomed to take, namely, bread and wine.

> St. Thomas Aquinas: *Summa Theologica,* 3, 75, 5. (13th cent.)

Does any unbeliever profess that the changing of bread and wine into the Body and Blood of the Lord is impossible? Then let him consider God's omnipotence. Admit that nature can transform one thing into another, then with greater reason should you admit that God's almighty power, which brings into existence the whole substance of things, can work, not as nature does, by changing forms in the same matter, but by changing one whole thing into another whole thing.

> St. Thomas Aquinas: *Concerning Reasons of Faith,* 8. (13th cent.)

If any one saith that in the sacred and holy sacrament of the eucharist the substance of the bread and wine remains conjointly with the Body and Blood of our Lord Jesus Christ, and denieth that wonderful and singular conversion of the whole substance of the bread into the Body, and of the whole substance of the wine into the Blood—the species only of the bread and wine remaining—which conversion indeed the Catholic Church most aptly calls transubstantiation; let him be anathema.

> Council of Trent, Session 13, Canon 2. (Oct. 11, 1551)

People say that the doctrine of transubstantiation is difficult to believe; I did not believe the doctrine till I was a Catholic. I had no difficulty in believing it as soon as I believed that the Catholic Roman Church was the oracle of God, and that she had declared this doctrine to be part of the original revelation. It is difficult, impossible to imagine, I grant; —but how is it difficult to believe?

> Card. Newman: *Apologia pro Vita Sua,* 5. (19th cent.)

Sir Thomas More is one of the choice specimens of wisdom and virtue; and the doctrine of transubstantiation is a kind of proof charge. A faith which stands that test, will stand any test.

> Card. Newman's version of what Lord Macaulay said, quoted in *Apologia,* chap. 5. (19th cent.)

Eunuch

Let not him who has disabled himself be made a clergyman; for he is a self-murderer, and an enemy to the creation of God.

> Ecclesiastical Canons of the Holy Apostles, 22. (4th cent.)

Europe

We shall never have a common peace in Europe till we have a common principle in Europe. People talk of the United States of Europe; but they forget that it needed the very doctrinal Declaration of Independence to make the United States of America. You cannot agree about nothing any more than you can quarrel about nothing.

> G. K. Chesterton: *All Things Considered.* (20th cent.)

Europe is not a political creation. It is a society of peoples who shared the same faith and the same moral values. The European nations are parts of a wider spiritual society.

> Christopher Dawson: *Understanding Europe.* (20th cent.)

Evening

Now was the hour which longing backward bends
   In those that sail, and melts their heart in sighs,
   The day they have said farewell to their sweet friends,
And pricks with love the outsetting pilgrim's eyes
   If the far bell he hears across the land
   Which seems to mourn over the day that dies.

> Dante: *Purgatorio, Canto 8.* (Tr. L. Binyon) (14th cent.)

Sweet Savior! bless us ere we go;
   Thy word into our minds instil;
And make our lukewarm hearts to glow
   With lowly love and fervent will.
Through life's long day and death's dark night,
O gentle Jesus! be our light.

> F. Faber: *Evening Hymn at the Oratory.* (19th cent.)

When evening's last faint beams are gone
And cheerless night comes stealing on,
The gentle moon grows kindly bright,
And brightest shines in deepest night.

And thus when worldly hope departs,
When sadness shades our lonely hearts,
Thy love, dear Lord, begins to shine,
And cheers those hearts with joy divine.

> Canon Scannell: *Hymn.* (19th cent.)

In ashes from the wasted fires of noon,
   Aweary of the light,
Comes evening, a tearful novice, soon
   To take the veil of night.

> J. B. Tabb: *The Postulant.* (19th cent.)

I was heavy with the even,
When she lit her glimmering tapers
Round the day's dead sanctities.

> F. Thompson: *The Hound of Heaven.* (19th cent.)

See also Vespers; Twilight

Event

Events often cut the knots which appear insoluble to theory.

Lord Acton: *Döllinger on the Temporal Power.* (19th cent.)

Everything

All cometh to one.

John Heywood: *Proverbs*, 1, 13. (16th cent.)

Evidence

Two equally sincere and intelligent souls may encounter the same external evidences and draw mutually exclusive conclusions from them.

R. H. Benson: *The Confessions of a Convert.* (20th cent.)

Evil

Nature throws a veil either of fear or shame over all evil.

Tertullian: *Apology*, 1. (3rd cent.)

Although it be with truth thou speakest evil, this is also a crime.

St. John Chrysostom: *Homilies.* (4th cent.)

There is nothing evil save that which perverts the mind and shackles the conscience.

St. Ambrose: *Hexaem*, 1, 31. (4th cent.)

What is that which is called evil, but the privation of good?

St. Augustine: *Enchiridion*, 11. (5th cent.)

Every being therefore is good, since He who is the Creator of all being whatever is supremely good. But because unlike their Creator they are not perfectly and unalterably good, the good which is in them can be both lessened and increased. But to lessen the good is to give rise to evil.

St. Augustine: *Enchiridion*, 12. (5th cent.)

For corruption is nothing but the destruction of good. Evil things therefore had their origin in good things, and unless they reside in good things, they do not exist at all.

St. Augustine: *Enchiridion*, 14. (5th cent.)

We cannot doubt at all that the cause of the good things which are ours is God's goodness alone, and that the cause of evil is the defection of the will in a being mutably good—first it was the will of an angel, then that of man—from the immutable good.

St. Augustine: *Enchiridion*, 23. (5th cent.)

For He [i.e. God] deemed it better to bring good out of evil than not to permit any evil to exist at all.

St. Augustine: *Enchiridion*, 27. (5th cent.)

For, were it not good that evil things should also exist, the omnipotent God would most certainly not allow evil to be, since beyond doubt it is just as easy for Him not to allow what He does not will, as it is for Him to do what He wills.

St. Augustine: *Enchiridion*, 96. (5th cent.)

Evil, therefore, is that which falls away from essence and tends to non-being. . . . It tends to make that which is to cease to be.

St. Augustine: *De Moribus Ecclesiae Catholicae*, 2, 2, 2. (4th cent.)

But God, as He is the supremely good Creator of good natures, so is He of evil wills the most just Ruler; so that, while they make an ill use of good natures, He makes a good use of even evil wills.

St. Augustine: *The City of God*, 11, 17. (5th cent.)

For God would not create, I do not say of angels, but even of men, any individual whom He foresaw would be evil, unless He foresaw all along to what uses of His good servants He would apply these evil servants, and so adorn the order of the ages like a beautiful poem with antitheses.

> St. Augustine: *The City of God*, 11, 18. (5th cent.)

And since no one is evil by nature, but whoever is evil is evil by vice, he who lives according to God ought to cherish towards evil men a perfect hatred, so that he shall neither hate the man because of his vice, nor love the vice because of the man, but hate the vice and love the man.

> St. Augustine: *The City of God*, 14, 6. (5th cent.)

There cannot be a nature in which there is no good. Not even the devil's nature is an evil thing inasmuch as it is a nature, but perversity makes it evil. God does not take away all that He has given to nature, but He takes something away and leaves something.

> St. Augustine: *The City of God*, 19, 13. (5th cent.)

It is He who, when He foreknew that man would in his turn sin by abandoning God and breaking His law, did not deprive him of the power of free will, because He at the same time foresaw what good He Himself would bring out of the evil, and how from this mortal race, deservedly and justly condemned, He would by His grace collect, as now He does, a people so numerous, that He thus fills up and repairs the blank made by the fallen angels, and that thus that beloved and heavenly city is not defrauded of the full number of its citizens, but perhaps may even rejoice in a still more overflowing population.

> St. Augustine: *The City of God*, 22, 1. (5th cent.)

Highest Providence often worketh that wonderful miracle, that evil men make those which are evil good.

> Boethius: *De Consolatione Philosophiae*, 4, 6. (6th cent.)

A thing essentially evil cannot exist. The foundation of evil is always a good subject.

> St. Thomas Aquinas: *Compendium of Theology*, 117. (13th cent.)

Evil as such cannot be desired.

> St. Thomas Aquinas: *Disputations concerning Evil*, 1, 1. (13th cent.)

Now we can begin to recognize what evil is: it is not a real substance, for evil things are good by their substance, but a deficiency of some good which a thing should possess, but does not.

> St. Thomas Aquinas: *Exposition of the De Divinis Nominibus*, 4, lect. 14. (13th cent.)

That God permits evil to happen in this world He governs does not derogate from His goodness. In the first place, divine Providence does not change the natures of things out of recognition, but respects them. The perfection of the universe requires that some should be indefectible, while others should suffer changes according to their nature. Were evil swept away entirely, divine Providence could not regenerate and restore the integrity of things, and this would be a greater evil than the particular ills they suffer.

> St. Thomas Aquinas: *Compendium of Theology*, 142. (13th cent.)

Take away all evil, and much good would go with it. God's care is to bring good out of the evils which happen, not to abolish them.

> St. Thomas Aquinas: *Compendium of Theology*, 142. (13th cent.)

The more of kindly strength is in the soil,
So much doth evil seed and lack of culture
Mar it the more, and make it run to wildness.

> Dante: *Purgatorio, Canto 26*. (Tr. Cary) (14th cent.)

Of two evils we should always choose the less.

> Thomas a Kempis: *Imitation of Christ,* 3. (2nd cent.)

If evils come not, then our fears are vain;
And if they do, fear but augments the pain.

> St. Thomas More: *On Fear.* (16th cent.)

If any man saith that it is not in man's power to make his ways evil, but that the works that are evil God worketh as well as those that are good, not permissively only but properly and of Himself, in such wise that the treason of Judas is no less His own proper work than the vocation of Paul; let him be anathema.

> Council of Trent, Session 6, Canon 6. (Jan. 13, 1547)

Never listen to or say evil of any one except of thyself, and when that gives thee pleasure thou art making great progress.

> St. Teresa of Jesus: *Maxims.* (16th cent.)

> In the rising stifle ill,
> Lest it grow against thy will.

> Bl. Robert Southwell: *Loss in Delay.* (16th cent.)

The real mystery is, not that evil should never have an end, but that it should ever have had a beginning. . . . How are we to explain it, the existence of God being taken for granted, except by saying that another will, besides His, has had a part in the disposition of His work, that there is a quarrel without remedy, a chronic alienation, between God and man?

> Card. Newman: *Grammar of Assent,* 10. (19th cent.)

Universal evils are not cured by specifics.

> I. T. Hecker: *The Church and the Age.* (1887)

In the government of states it is not forbidden to imitate the Ruler of the world; and, as the authority of man is powerless to prevent every evil, it has (as St. Augustine says) to overlook and leave unpunished many things which are punished, and rightly, by divine providence. But if, in such circumstances, for the sake of the common good (and this is the only legitimate reason), human law may or even should tolerate evil, it may not and should not approve or desire evil for its own sake; for evil of itself, being a privation of good, is opposed to the common welfare which every legislator is bound to desire and defend to the best of his ability.

> Pope Leo XIII: *Libertas Praestantissimum.* (June 20, 1888)

Your resolution should be to trust God, and to believe no evil lightly.

> R. H. Benson: *The Queen's Tragedy.* (20th cent.)

God did not make evil. But He would not even have permitted it, says St. Augustine, were He not so great that He can bring good out of it.

> Abbot Chapman: *Spiritual Letters.* (20th cent.)

See also Good and Bad; Sin

Evildoing

Men never do evil so completely and cheerfully as when they do it from religious conviction.

> Pascal: *Pensées.* (17th cent.)

Evolution

> Out of the dusk a shadow,
>   Then, a spark;
> Out of the cloud a silence,
>   Then, a lark;
> Out of the heart a rapture,
>   Then, a pain;
> Out of the dead, cold ashes,
>   Life again.

> John B. Tabb: *Evolution.* (19th cent.)

The evolutionists seem to know everything about the missing link except the
fact that it is missing.

> G. K. Chesterton: *Evolution.* (20th cent.)

I am too fat to climb a tree,
  There are no trees to climb;
Instead, the factory chimneys rise,
  Unscalable, sublime.

The past was bestial ignorance:
  But I feel a little funky,
To think I'm further off from heaven
  Than when I was a monkey.

> G. K. Chesterton: *Race-Memory (By a
> Dazed Darwinian).* (20th cent.)

The Victorian secularists were 'dawnists,' to borrow Hugh Kingsmill's excellent term. Mr. Wells, for instance, never
tired of prophesying the rosy dawn
which would dispel the shadows of
superstition. But the dawnists are a di-
minishing sect today, for the world is
ceasing to believe in the inevitability of
progress or in the automatic beneficence
of evolution.

> Arnold Lunn: *Now I See.* (20th cent.)

The teaching authority of the Church
does not forbid that in conformity with
the present state of human science and
sacred theology research and discussions
on the part of men experienced in both
fields take place with regard to the doctrine of evolution in so far as it inquires
into the origin of the human body as
coming from pre-existent and living
matter—for Catholic faith obliges us to
hold that souls are immediately created
by God. However, this must be done in
such a way that reasons for both opinions, that is, those favorable and those
unfavorable to evolution, be weighed
and judged with the necessary seriousness, moderation and measure and provided that all are prepared to submit to
the judgment of the Church to whom
Christ has given the mission of interpreting authentically the Sacred Scripture and of defending dogmas of faith.

> Pope Pius XII: *Humani Generis.* (Apr. 12,
> 1950)

The faithful cannot embrace that opinion which maintains either that after
Adam there existed on this earth true
men who did not take their origin
through natural generation from him as
from the first parent of all, or that Adam
represents a certain number of first parents. Now it is in no way apparent how
such an opinion can be reconciled with
that which the sources of revealed truth
and the documents of teaching authority
of the Church propose with regard to
original sin, which proceeds from sin
actually committed by an individual
Adam and which through generation is
passed on to all and is in everyone as his
own.

> Pope Pius XII: *Humani Generis.* (Apr. 12,
> 1950)

Exaggeration

Never exaggerate, but utter thy mind
with simplicity.

> St. Teresa of Jesus: *Maxims.* (16th cent.)

Example

This noble example to his sheep he
  gave,
That first he wrought, and afterward
  he taught.
Out of the gospel he the wordes
  caught;
And this figure he added eke thereto,
That if gold rust, what shall iron do?
For if a priest be foul, on whom we
  trust,
No wonder is a lewd man to rust.

> Chaucer: *Canterbury Tales: Prologue.*
> (14th cent.)

He that biddeth other fold do well, and
giveth evil example with the contrary
deed himself, fareth even like a foolish
weaver, that would weave a part with
his one hand and unweave a part with
his other.

> St. Thomas More. (16th cent.)

The example of Alexander's chastity has not made so many continent as that of his drunkenness has made intemperate.

> Pascal: *Pensées*, 8. (17th cent.)

No force the free-born spirit can constrain,
But charity and great example gain.

> Dryden. (17th cent.)

Excommunication

But if thou see that a man will not repent, but has altogether abandoned himself, then with grief and sorrow cut him off and cast him out of the Church.

> Anonymous: *Didascalia Apostolorum*, 10. (3rd cent.)

Sit anathema. (Let him be accursed) (I Cor. 16, 22)

> Expression, from the time of the council of Elvira [ca. 300], usually appended to solemn ecclesiastical canons or pronouncements de fide, signifying that all who opposed them should be considered accursed or beyond the pale. Word "anathema" gradually came to mean same thing as excommunication, especially if pronounced with solemn rites according to the Roman Pontifical. [cf. Code of Canon Law, can. 2257, 2].

As regards the excommunicated, the sentence passed by the bishops of each province shall have the force of law, in conformity with the canon which says: He who has been excommunicated by some should not be admitted by others. . . .

> Council of Nicaea, *Can.* 5. (325)

If any brother shall be found contumacious, or disobedient, or proud, or a murderer, or in any way despising and contravening the holy rule and the order of his superiors: let such a one . . . be admonished secretly . . . for a first and second time. If he do not amend, let him be rebuked publicly before all. But if even then he do not correct his life, let him suffer excommunication, pro-

vided that he understands the gravity of that penalty. If, however, he be perverse, let him undergo corporal punishment.

> St. Benedict: *Rule*, 23. (6th cent.)

The measure of excommunication and punishment should be proportioned to the gravity of the fault.

> St. Benedict: *Rule,* 24. (6th cent.)

And oftentimes such cursing wrongfully returneth again to him that curseth, as a bird that returneth again to his own nest.

> Chaucer: *The Personnes Tale*. (14th cent.)

"From the Church Militant and Triumphant we sever thee."
"Nay! from the Church Triumphant thou canst not!"

> Savonarola: *Reply to the Sentence of Excommunication*. (Strictly speaking, this is contrary to Catholic teaching. Sav. held that he was unjustly excomm. for political reasons.) (15th cent.)

Although the sword of excommunication is the chief weapon of ecclesiastical discipline, and very useful for keeping the people to their duties, it is to be used only with sobriety and circumspection, for experience teaches that if it be used rashly and for small reason it will be more despised than feared, and will work more evil than good.

> Decree of the Council of Trent, 25th Session. (Dec. 4, 1563)

Excuse

We often do ill and do worse in excusing it.

> Thomas a Kempis: *The Imitation of Christ,* 2, 5. (15th cent.)

Execution

By the dial of the clock
'Twas day in the dark above her lonely head.

This day thou shalt be with Me. Ere the cock
Announced the day she met the Immortal Dead.

> Alice Meynell: *Nurse Edith Cavell.* (20th cent.)

Exegesis

We must be on guard against giving interpretations of Scripture that are far-fetched or opposed to science, and so exposing the word of God to the ridicule of unbelievers.

> St. Augustine: *De Genesi ad litteram.* (5th cent.)

Study and pains were now no more their care;
Texts were explained by fasting and by prayer.

> Dryden: *Religio Laici.* (17th cent.)

Exercise

Better to hunt in fields, for health unbought,
Than fee the doctor for a nauseous draught.
The wise for cure, on exercise depend;
God never made His work, for man to mend.

> Dryden: *To John Dryden of Chesterton.* (17th cent.)

Exercises, Religious

The time that really matters is the time between our religious exercises.

> R. H. Benson: *The Light Invisible.* (20th cent.)

Exile

I have loved justice and hated iniquity; therefore I die in exile.

> Pope Gregory VII. (On his deathbed.) (11th cent.)

Thou shalt leave all that thou hast loved most dear;

This is the arrow, shooting from the bow
Of banishment, which thou hast first to fear.
How bitter another's bread is, thou shalt know
By tasting it; and how hard to the feet
Another's stairs are, up and down to go.

> Dante: *Paradiso, Canto 17.* (Tr. L. Binyon)

He made all countries where he came his own.

> Dryden: *Astraea Redux.* (17th cent.)

By foreign hands thy dying eyes were clos'd,
By foreign hands thy decent limbs compos'd,
By foreign hands thy humble grave adorn'd,
By strangers honor'd, and by strangers mourn'd!

> Pope: *To the Memory of an Unfortunate Lady.* (18th cent.)

And more true joy Marcellus exiled feels
Than Caesar with a senate at his heels.

> Pope: *An Essay on Man,* 4. (18th cent.)

In Siberia's wastes
No tears are shed,
For they freeze within the brain.
Nought is felt but dullest pain,
Pain acute, yet dead.
Pain as in a dream,
When years go by
Funeral-paced, yet fugitive,
When man lives, and doth not live,
Doth not live—nor die.

> J. C. Mangan: *Siberia.* (19th cent.)

Existence

We exist because God is good.

> St. Augustine: *De Doctrina Christiana, 1,* 31. (4th cent.)

This appears as a wonder but yet as a truth to our minds: that this world could not be known to us, if it were not existing, but it could not have existed at all unless God had known it.

> St. Augustine: *The City of God*, 11, 10, 3. (5th cent.)

When I say 'I understand that I am,' do I not signify by this one word 'I understand' three inseparable things? For I prove that I am, that I can understand that I am, and that I do understand that I am.

> John Scotus Eriugena: *On the Division of Nature*, 1, 50. (9th cent.)

No rational mind can doubt that all creatures live and continue to exist, so long as they do exist, by the sustenance afforded by that very Being through Whose creative act they are endowed with the existence that they have.

> St. Anselm: *Monologium*, 13. (11th cent.)

Doing is only of value so far as it contributes to being. This is the point of existence—to be.

> R. H. Benson: *The Conventionalists*. (20th cent.)

See also God: His Existence

Expectation

Blessed is he who expects nothing, for he shall never be disappointed.

> Pope: *Letter to John Gay*. (18th cent.)

Experience

Not sweet son, nor revered old father, nor
   The long-due love which was to have made glad
   Penelope for all the pain she bore,

Could conquer the inward hunger that I had
   To master earth's experience, and to attain
   Knowledge of men's mind, both the good and bad.

> Dante: *Inferno, Canto 26*. (With reference to Ulysses) (Tr. Binyon) (14th cent.)

Who heeds experience, trust him not.

> J. B. O'Reilly: *Rules of the Road*. (19th cent.)

What man would be wise, let him drink of the river
   That bears on its bosom the record of time;
A message to him every wave can deliver
   To teach him to creep till he knows how to climb.

> J. B. O'Reilly: *Rules of the Road*. (19th cent.)

Necessity has no law, and experience is often one form of necessity.

> Card. Newman: *Idea of a University*. (19th cent.)

A burnt child loves the fire.

> Oscar Wilde: *The Picture of Dorian Gray*, 17. (19th cent.)

Experience and conflict, whether it end in victory or defeat, give the years to a man far more than the passing of time.

> R. H. Benson: *Come Rack! Come Rope!* (20th cent.)

'Inherited experience' is only a rather clumsy phrase—a piece of paper gummed up to cover a crack in the world.

> R. H. Benson: *The Necromancers*. (20th cent.)

In a controversial argument the appeal to religious experience is dangerous, but religious experience is undoubtedly effective—when it is silent. It is certainly communicable. "One loving soul," says St. Augustine, "sets another on fire." Christianity can sometimes be caught no less than taught.

> Arnold Lunn: *Now I See*. (20th cent.)

Exploitation

It violates right order whenever capital so employs the working or wage-earning classes as to divert business and economic activity entirely to its own arbitrary will and advantage, without any regard to the human dignity of the workers, the social character of economic life, social justice, and the common good.

Pope Pius XI: *Quadragesimo anno.* (May 15, 1931)

Exploration

Of all who since have used the open sea,
Than the bold English none more fame have won;
Beyond the year, and out of heav'n's highway,
They make discoveries where they see no sun.

Dryden: *Annus Mirabilis.* (17th cent.)

Extravagance

In squandering wealth was his peculiar art:
Nothing went unrewarded, but desert.
Begger'd by fools, whom still he found too late:
He had his jest, and they had his estate.

Dryden: *Absalom and Achitophel.* (17th cent.)

Extreme Unction

We invoke Thee Who hast all authority and power, Savior of all men, Father of our Lord and Savior Jesus Christ, and pray Thee to send the healing power of Thine Only-begotten from heaven upon this oil . . . that it may become to those who are being anointed with it . . . a throwing off of every sickness and infirmity . . . for good grace and remission of sins, for a medicine of life and salvation, for health and soundness of soul, body, spirit, and for perfect strengthening. . . .

Sacramentary of Serapion, Prayer. (17) (4th cent.)

Why therefore do you lay on hands and believe it to be an effect of the blessing if any of the sick happen to recover?

St. Ambrose: *On Penitence,* 8. (With reference to the Novatians.) (4th cent.)

Is one of you sick? Let him send for the presbyters of the church, and let them pray over him, anointing him with the oil in the Lord's name. Prayer offered in faith will restore the sick man, and the Lord will give him relief; if he is guilty of sins, they will be pardoned (James, 5, 14). There is no doubt that this text must be received or understood of the sick faithful, who may be anointed with the holy oil of chrism; which, having been blessed by the bishop, it is permitted not only to priests but to all Christians to use for anointing in their own need or that of their families. . . . This unction may not be given to penitents [i.e. canonical penitents], seeing that it is a kind of sacrament (*genus sacramenti*). For how is it imagined that one kind may be given to those to whom the other sacraments are denied?

Pope Innocent I: *Letters, 25.* (To Decentius of Eugubium.) (416)

O Lord, Who in Thy pity and mercy dost heal the torments of our souls and bodies; O Master, do Thou bless this oil that it may become a remedy for those who are anointed with it, and that it may cause every suffering, every bodily and spiritual defilement, and every evil, to cease; that Thy most holy name may be glorified thereby, Father, Son, and Holy Ghost, now and forever, world without end. Amen.

Byzantine Euchologion, Service of the Holy Oil, Prayer. (ca. 6th to 8th cent.)

O holy Father, physician of souls and of bodies, Who didst send Thine only-begotten Son our Lord Jesus Christ to heal every ill and deliver us from death; heal this servant of Thine, N., from all corporal and spiritual infirmities, and quicken him by the grace of Thy Christ; through the intercession of our most holy Lady, Mother of God and ever-Virgin, Mary . . . and all the saints. For Thou art the source of healing, O Christ our God, and unto Thee we give glory,

Father, Son, and Holy Ghost, now and forever, world without end. Amen.

> Byzantine Euchologion, Service of the Holy Oil, Prayer at the Anointing. (ca. 6th to 8th cent.)

We implore Thee, O Lord, look with kindness on Thy servant, N., who is growing weak as his body fails. Cherish and revive the soul which Thou didst create, so that, purified and made whole by his sufferings, he may find himself restored by Thy healing.

> Roman Ritual, Last Anointing, Prayer after the Anointing. (Gregorian, ca. 6th to 8th cent.)

Now the custom of the Church is that the sick should be anointed by the priests with consecrated oil and through the accompanying prayer restored to health. If therefore the sick be in sins and shall have confessed these to the priests of the Church and shall have sincerely undertaken to relinquish and amend them, they shall be remitted to them. For sins can not be remitted without the confession of amendment.

> Venerable Bede: *Commentary on St. James.* (8th cent.)

In the name of the Father, and of the Son, and of the Holy Ghost. May any power that the devil has over you be utterly destroyed, as I place my hands on you and call upon the help of the glorious and holy Mother of God, the Virgin Mary, and of her illustrious spouse St. Joseph, and of all the holy angels, archangels, patriarchs, prophets, apostles, martyrs, confessors, virgins, and all the saints. Amen. By this holy anointing and His most loving mercy may the Lord forgive you whatever wrong you have done by the use of your (sight, hearing, sense of smell, sense of taste and power of speech, sense of touch, power to walk). Amen.

> Roman Ritual, Last Anointing, Prayer and Formula for Anointing. (Priest varies last formula as he anoints the eyes, ears, nose, mouth, hands, and feet of sick person.) (ca. 9th cent.?)

If any one saith that extreme unction is not truly and properly a sacrament instituted by Christ our Lord and promulgated by the blessed apostle James; but is only a rite received from the fathers, or a human figment; let him be anathema.

> Council of Trent, Session 14, Canon 1. (Nov. 25, 1551)

If any one saith that the sacred unction of the sick does not confer grace, nor remit sin, nor comfort the sick; but that it has now ceased, as though it were formerly only the grace of working cures; let him be anathema.

> Council of Trent, Session 14, Canon 2. (Nov. 25, 1551)

Upon the eyes, the lips, the feet,
On all the passages of sense,
The atoning oil is spread with sweet
Renewal of lost innocence.

· · · · · · ·

Vials of mercy, sacring oils,
I know not where nor whence I come,
Nor through what wanderings and toils,
To crave of you viaticum.

Yet, when the walls of flesh grow weak,
In such an hour it well may be,
Through mist and darkness, light will break,
And each anointed sense will see.

> Ernest Dowson: *Extreme Unction.* (19th cent.)

Extremism

Our senses can grasp nothing that is extreme. Too much noise deafens us; too much light blinds us; too far or too near prevents us seeing; too long or too short is beyond understanding; too much truth stuns us.

> Pascal: *Pensées,* 1. (17th cent.)

So over violent, or over civil,
That every man, with him, was God or devil.

> Dryden: *Absalom and Achitophel.* (17th cent.)

Eye

Paradise stood formed in her eye.

> Chaucer: *Troilus and Criseyde*. (14th cent.)

His bright eyes rolled, they never
  seemed to settle,
And glittered like the flames beneath
  a kettle.

> Chaucer: *Canterbury Tales: Prologue*. (Tr.
> Coghill) (14th cent.)

Better eye out than always ache.

> John Heywood: *Proverbs*, 1, 8. (16th cent.)

What the eye sees not, the heart rues not.

> John Heywood: *Proverbs*, 2, 7. (16th cent.)

O sacred eyes, the springs of living
  light,
The earthly heavens, where angels joy
  to dwell:
How could you deign to view my
  dreadful plight,
Or let your heavenly beams look on my
  hell?
But those unspotted eyes encountered
  mine,
As spotless sun doth on the dunghill
  shine.

> Bl. Robert Southwell: *St. Peter's Complaint*.
> (16th cent.)

Her eyes are sapphires set in snow,
  Refining heaven by every wink;
The gods do fear whenas they glow,
And if do tremble when I think,
  Heigh ho, would she were mine.

> Thomas Lodge: *Rosalynde*. (16th cent.)

Eyes, that displace
The neighbor diamond, and out-face
That sunshine by their own sweet
  grace.

> Richard Crashaw: *Wishes to his (Supposed)
> Mistress*. (17th cent.)

Why has not man a microscopic eye?
For this plain reason: man is not a fly.

> Pope: *An Essay on Man*, 1. (18th cent.)

Nothing is lost on him who sees
  With an eye that feeling gave;—
For him there's a story in every breeze,
And a picture in every wave.

> Thomas Moore: *Boat Glee*. (19th cent.)

Man for his glory
To ancestry flies,
While woman's bright story
Is told in her eyes.

> Thomas Moore: *Desmond's Song*. (19th
> cent.)

Those eyes, whose light seem'd rather
  given
To be ador'd than to adore—
Such eyes as may have looked *from*
  heaven,
But ne'er were raised to it before!

> Thomas Moore: *Loves of the Angels*.
> (19th cent.)

The light that lies
In women's eyes,
Has been my heart's undoing.

> Thomas Moore: *The Time I've Lost in
> Wooing*. (19th cent.)

And the world's so rich in resplendent
  eyes,
'Twere a pity to limit one's love to a
  pair.

> Thomas Moore: *'Tis sweet to Think*. (19th
> cent.)

And violets, transform'd to eyes,
Enshrin'd a soul within their blue.

> Thomas Moore: *Evenings in Greece:
> Second Evening*. (19th cent.)

Eyes of most unholy blue.

> Thomas Moore: *By That Lake*. (19th cent.)

How blue were Ariadne's eyes
  When, from the sea's horizon line,
At eve, she raised them to the skies!
My Psyche, bluer far are thine.

> Aubrey De Vere: *Psyche*. (19th cent.)

Across what calm of tropic seas,
  'Neath alien clusters of the nights,

Looked, in the past, such eyes as these!
    Long-quenched, relumed, ancestral
        lights!

> Alice Meynell: *To O_____, Of Her Dark Eyes.* (20th cent.)

Eyes and Ears

Fields have eyes and woods have ears.

> John Heywood: *Proverbs,* 2, 5. (16th cent.)

F

Face

And where thou hast most matter to
    complain,
Make the good face and glad in port
    thee feign.

> Lydgate: *Troy Book,* 2. (15th cent.)

Men speak of some that bear two faces
in one hood.

> St. Thomas More. (16th cent.)

Give place, you ladies, and be gone,
    Boast not yourselves at all,
For here at hand approacheth one,
    Whose face will stain you all.

The virtue of her lively looks
    Excels the precious stone;
I wish to have none other books
    To read or look upon.

> John Heywood: *On the Princess Mary.* (16th cent.)

A face that's best
By its own beauty drest,
And can alone commend the rest.

A face made up
Out of no other shop,
Than what nature's white hand sets
    ope.

> Richard Crashaw: *Wishes to His (Supposed) Mistress.* (17th cent.)

If to her share some female errors fall
Look on her face, and you'll forget 'em
    all.

> Pope: *The Rape of the Lock,* 2. (18th cent.)

Facts

It is of great importance in order to gain
assured knowledge of things, to rely on
exact acquaintance with facts, rather
than on the uncertain testimony of
public rumor; and then what we have
proved for certain we may proclaim
without hesitation.

> St. Bernard: *Letters.* (12th cent.)

Much is said in this day by men of
science about the duty of honesty in
what is called the pursuit of truth,—by
'pursuing truth' being meant pursuit of
facts.

> Card. Newman: *Via Media,* 1. (19th cent.)

Men must have facts first and explanations afterwards.

> R. H. Benson: *Introduction to the Mustard Tree.* (20th cent.)

Facts depend for their interpretation
upon the point of view.

> R. H. Benson: *The Dawn of All.* (20th cent.)

Faculties

The intellect is the most superficial of our faculties; there are simply scores of things that we cannot understand in the least, but of which, for all that, we are as certain as of our own existence. Next to that comes the emotion; it is certainly nearer to us than intellect, though not much; and thirdly comes the will.

R. H. Benson: *The Mirror of Shalott.* (20th cent.)

Failure

> To fear not sensible failure,
> Nor covet the game at all,
> But fighting, fighting, fighting,
> Die, driven against the wall.

Louise Imogen Guiney: *The Kings.* (19th cent.)

You will fail sometimes, but not finally.

R. H. Benson: *The King's Achievement.* (20th cent.)

> Their wreaths are willows and their tribute, tears;
> Their names are old sad stories in men's ears;
> Yet they will scatter the red hordes of hell,
> Who went to battle forth and always fell.

Shaemas O'Sheel: *They Went Forth to Battle, But They Always Fell.* (20th cent.)

Faint-Heartedness

This fault of pusillanimity and timorous mind letteth a man also many times from the doing of many good things, which (if he took a good stomach to him in the trust of God's help) he were well able to do: but the devil casteth him in a cowardice, and maketh him take it for humility, to think himself innocent and unable thereto, and therefore to leave the good thing undone, whereof God offereth him occasion, and had made him meet and convenient thereto.

St. Thomas More: *Dialogue of Comfort.* (16th cent.)

Fair

> Though every man may not sit in the chair,
> Yet alway the grace of God is worth a fair.

John Heywood: *Proverbs,* I, 12. (16th cent.)

Fairy-Tales

Fairy-tales do not give a child his first idea of bogy. What fairy-tales give the child is his first clear idea of the possible defeat of the bogy. The baby has known the dragon intimately ever since he had an imagination. What the fairy-tale provides for him is a St. George to kill the dragon.

G. K. Chesterton: *Tremendous Trifles.* (20th cent.)

Faith

For faith is the beginning and the end is love, and God is the two of them brought into unity. After these comes whatever else makes up a Christian gentleman.

St. Ignatius of Antioch: *Letter to the Ephesians,* 14. (2nd cent.)

For the name of faith is one in speech, but has two distinct meanings. For there is one kind of faith, dogmatic, involving an assent of the soul to some particular point. . . . But there is a second kind of faith, which is bestowed by Christ as a gift of grace.

St. Cyril of Jerusalem: *Catechetical Discourses,* 5, 10-11. (4th cent.)

Faith is a whole-hearted assent to aural doctrine with full conviction of the truth of what is publicly taught by the grace of God.

St. Basil: *Concerning Faith.* (4th cent.)

Faith means battles; if there are no contests, it is because there are none who desire to contend.

St. Ambrose: *Explanation of Psalm 118,* 11, 21. (4th cent.)

First it is necessary to believe that God's oracles in the Scriptures are true. Faith is the beginning of a Christian man.

> St. Ambrose: *Explanation of Psalm 118,* 20, 56, 57. (4th cent.)

Faith is the firm foundation of all the virtues.

> St. Ambrose: *In Ps. 40 Enarr. 4.* (4th cent.)

It is faith which delivers through the blood of Christ.

> St. Ambrose: *Letters,* 73, 11. (4th cent.)

No one who believes, whatever may have been his condition, however great may have been his fall, need fear that he will perish. When anyone believes, the wrath of God departs and life comes.

> , St. Ambrose: *On Penitence,* 1, 51. (4th cent.)

My faith, Lord, cries to Thee, the faith that Thou hast given me, that Thou hast inbreathed in me, through the humanity of Thy Son and by the ministry of Thy Preacher.

> St. Augustine: *Confessions,* 1, 1. (5th cent.)

What is faith save to believe what you do not see? (Quid est enim fides, nisi credere quod non vides?)

> St. Augustine: *Sermons,* 40. (5th cent.)

Faith, which is the foundation of all righteousness, which is not preceded by good works but from which all good works flow, purifies us from all sin, illuminates our minds, reconciles us to God and admits us to fellowship with all who share in the Divine nature; it fills us with hope of future reward, increases in us all the virtues and establishes us in the possession of them.

> Julianus Pomerius: *De Vita Contemplativa,* 3, 21. (5th cent.)

We beseech Thee, O Lord, in Thy compassion to increase Thy faith in us; because Thou wilt not deny the aid of Thy loving kindness to those on whom Thou bestowest a steadfast belief in Thee.

> Leonine Sacramentary, Collect. (ca. 5th cent.)

Faith is a sure foretaste by the exercise of the will of truth not yet manifested.

> St. Bernard: *On Consideration,* 5, 3. (12th cent.)

Faith does not quench desire, but inflames it.

> St. Thomas Aquinas: *Contra Gentes,* 3, 40. (13th cent.)

This is eternal life, that they may know Thee, the only true God (John, 17, 3). This supernatural knowledge is now entered into by faith, which believes, through infused light, truths exceeding our natural wits.

> St. Thomas Aquinas: *Disputations concerning Truth,* 14, 2. (13th cent.)

Faith is a habit of mind, which begins eternal life in us, and induces a reasonable assent to things unseen.

> St. Thomas Aquinas: *Disputations concerning Truth,* 14, 2. (13th cent.)

The author of faith is he who produces the believer's assent to the truth declared. Mere hearing is not a sufficient cause. The assent is caused by the will, not by any reason of necessity. And therefore a preacher or herald cannot produce faith. God is the cause of faith, for He alone can alter our wills.

> St. Thomas Aquinas: *Disputations concerning Truth,* 27, 3. (13th cent.)

The infused light of the habit of faith discovers the meaning of the articles of the Creed just as the mind's natural power of abstraction discovers the first evidences of reason.

> St. Thomas Aquinas: *Commentary on the Sentences,* 3, 23, 2, 1. (13th cent.)

By faith the Christian soul enters, as it were, into marriage with God: *I will espouse thee to me in faith* (Hos. 2, 20).

> St. Thomas Aquinas: *Exposition of the Apostles' Creed.* (13th cent.)

The virtue of faith causes the mind to assent to a truth which, transcending human understanding, is held in divine knowledge. . . . Men accept God's knowledge by faith and are joined thereby to Him. Faith's principal object is God Himself; other things are subsidiary and dependent.

> St. Thomas Aquinas: *Disputations concerning Truth*, 14, 8. (13th cent.)

The light of faith makes us see what we believe. For just as, by the habits of the other virtues, man sees what is becoming to him in respect of that habit, so, by the habit of faith, the human mind is directed to assent to such things as are becoming to a right faith, and not to assent to others.

> St. Thomas Aquinas: *Summa Theologica*, 2-2, 1, 4. (13th cent.)

Unbelievers are in ignorance of things that are of faith, for neither do they see or know them in themselves, nor do they know them to be credible. The faithful, on the other hand, know them, not as by demonstration, but by the light of faith which makes them see that they ought to believe them.

> St. Thomas Aquinas: *Summa Theologica*, 2-2, 1, 5. (13th cent.)

The reasons employed by holy men to prove things that are of faith, are not demonstrations; they are either persuasive arguments showing that what is proposed to our faith is not impossible, or else they are proofs drawn from the principles of faith, i.e., from the authority of Holy Writ. Whatever is based on these principles is as well proved in the eyes of the faithful, as a conclusion drawn from self-evident principles is in the eyes of all.

> St. Thomas Aquinas: *Summa Theologica*, 2-2, 1, 5. (13th cent.)

By faith we hold many truths about God, which the philosophers were unable to discover by natural reason, for instance His providence and omnipo-

tence, and that He alone is to be worshipped, all of which are contained in the one article of the unity of God.

> St. Thomas Aquinas: *Summa Theologica*, 2-2, 1, 8. (13th cent.)

The formal object of faith is the First Truth, as manifested in Holy Writ and the teaching of the Church, which proceeds from the First Truth.

> St. Thomas Aquinas: *Summa Theologica*, 2-2, 5, 3. (13th cent.)

After grace had been revealed, both learned and simple folk are bound to explicit faith in the mysteries of Christ, chiefly as regards those which are observed throughout the Church, and publicly proclaimed, such as the articles which refer to the incarnation. As to other minute points in reference to the articles of the incarnation, men have been bound to believe them more or less explicitly according to each one's state and office.

> St. Thomas Aquinas: *Summa Theologica*, 2-2, 2, 7. (13th cent.)

Faith is the substance of things hoped, and proof
Of things invisible to mortal sight.

> Dante: *Paradiso, Canto 24*. (Quoting Hebr. 11, 1.) (Tr. Binyon) (14th cent.)

It is a fatal error to mistake mere historical belief for saving faith. A man may firmly believe his religion historically, and yet have no part nor portion therein practically and savingly. He must not only believe his faith, he must believe *in* his faith.

> St. Thomas More: *Meditations and Devotions*. (16th cent.)

A faint faith is better than a strong heresy.

> St. Thomas More. (16th cent.)

Believe that you have it, and you have it.

> Erasmus: *Letter to St. Thomas More*. (16th cent.)

If any one saith that, grace being lost through sin, faith also is always lost with it; or that the faith which remains, though it be not a lively faith, is not a true faith; or that he who has faith without charity is not a Christian; let him be anathema.

Council of Trent, Session 6, Canon 28. (Jan. 13, 1547)

Faith declares what the senses do not see, but not the contrary of what they see. It is above them, not contrary to them.

Pascal: *Pensées*. (17th cent.)

For my salvation must its doom receive
Not from what others, but from what
I believe.

Dryden: *Religio Laici*. (17th cent.)

Faith is not built on disquisitions vain;
The things we must believe are few and
plain.

Dryden: *Religio Laici*. (17th cent.)

The extremes of too much faith, and none.

Thomas Moore: *Fables*. (19th cent.)

Faith is the dawning of day
Where darkness was before,
To rising of a solar ray
To set in night no more.

Faith lights an eye within the soul
From earth to heaven that turns,
And there, where wheels of glory roll,
Admires, adores, and burns.

M. Bridges: *Faith*. (19th cent.)

Great God, whatever through Thy
Church
Thou teachest to be true,
I firmly do believe it all,
And will confess it too.
Thou never canst deceived be,
Thou never canst deceive,
For Thou art Truth itself, and Thou
Dost tell me to believe.

Act of Faith from *Hymns for the Year*, 1867.

O gift of gifts! O grace of faith!
My God! How can it be
That Thou, Who hast discerning love,
Shouldst give that gift to me?

F. Faber: *Conversion*. (First line: *O faith, thou workest miracles*) (19th cent.)

The word of life is offered to a man; and, on its being offered, he has faith in it. Why? On these two grounds,—the word of its human messenger, and the likelihood of the message.

Card. Newman: *Oxford University Sermons*. (19th cent.)

Faith then is not a conclusion from premises, but the result of an act of the will, following upon a conviction that to believe is a duty.

Card. Newman: *Letter to Mrs. Froude*. (June 27, 1848)

Faith is illuminative, not operative; it does not force obedience, though it increases responsibility; it heightens guilt, it does not prevent sin; the will is the source of action.

Card. Newman: *Difficulties of Anglicans*, I. (19th cent.)

No one is a martyr for a conclusion, no one is a martyr for an opinion; it is faith that makes martyrs.

Card. Newman: *Discourses to Mixed Congregations*. (19th cent.)

I come then to this conclusion;—if I must submit my reason to mysteries, it does not much matter whether it is a mystery more or a mystery less, when faith anyhow is the very essence of all religion, when the main difficulty to an inquirer is to hold that there is a living God, in spite of the darkness which surrounds Him, the Creator, Witness, and Judge of men.

Card. Newman: *Discourses to Mixed Congregations*. (19th cent.)

Faith is that supernatural virtue by which, through the help of God and through the assistance of His grace, we believe what He has revealed to be true, not on account of the intrinsic truth perceived by the natural light of reason, but because of the authority of God Himself, the Revealer, Who can neither deceive nor be deceived.

> Vatican Council, Session 3, Chap. 3. (Apr. 24, 1870)

If any one shall say that divine revelation cannot be made credible by outward signs, and therefore that men ought to be moved to faith solely by the internal experience of each, or by private inspiration; let him be anathema.

> Vatican Council, Session 3, Canon 3 de Fide. (Apr. 24, 1870)

Faith must be sincere. When defended by sin it is not sincere; theologically, it is not faith. God's grace does not operate by sin.

> Lord Acton: *Letter to M. Creighton.* (Apr. 5, 1887)

Faith, after all, is a divine operation wrought in the dark, even though it may seem to be embodied in intellectual arguments and historical facts.

> R. H. Benson: *The Confessions of a Convert.* (20th cent.)

Faith is a gift which can be given or withdrawn; it is something infused into us, not produced by us.

> R. H. Benson: *A Mirror of Shalott.* (20th cent.)

Faith depends not on intellectual, but on moral conditions.

> R. H. Benson: *The Light Invisible.* (20th cent.)

Sometimes faith is far more beautiful unadorned, and it is quite possible to crush a delicate and growing faith with a weight of learned arguments intended to adorn and perfect it.

> R. H. Benson: *The Light Invisible.* (20th cent.)

Those who have the faith of children have also the troubles of children.

> R. H. Benson: *The Light Invisible.* (20th cent.)

Faith is the door through which we enter the supernatural order. It opens into heaven. It tells us: *We have not here a lasting city, but we seek one that is to come* (Hebr. 13, 14).

> Abbot Chapman: *Spiritual Letters.* (20th cent.)

Who looks with love upon the flower
  Will contemplate the root;
Nor can he well forget the tree
  Who relishes the fruit.

Dull-hued, indeed, am I, the flower,
  If faith, the root, be dry;
But nourished with the precious blood,
  The fruit is Christ, not I.

> Sister Miriam: *The Root of Jesse.* (20th cent.)

Without a heritage of faith I'd be
A far less stalwart friend of men than
  he.
Who follows all the night the darkness
  gives
Deserves to see the sun by which love
  lives.

> Sister Miriam: *I Pray for One I Love.* (20th cent.)

A living Christianity is necessary to the world. Faith must be actual, practical, existential faith. To believe in God must mean to live in such a manner that life could not possibly be lived if God did not exist. For the practical believer, gospel justice, gospel attentiveness to everything human must inspire not only the deeds of the saints, but the structure and institutions of common life, and must penetrate to the depths of terrestrial existence.

> J. Maritain: *The Range of Reason.* (20th cent.)

For, from the beginning of the world,
How few of us have heard the silver of
  thy creed

Or paid our hearts for hours of emptiness
With gold of thy belief?

Thomas Merton: *Figures for an
Apocalypse.* (20th cent.)

The deep secret of the mystery of faith
lies in the fact that it is a "baptism" in
the death and sacrifice of Christ. We
can only give ourselves to God when
Christ, by His grace, "dies" and rises
again spiritually within us.

Thomas Merton: *The Ascent to Truth.*
(20th cent.)

Ultimately faith is the only key to the
universe. The final meaning of human
existence, and the answers to the questions on which all our happiness depends cannot be found in any other way.

Thomas Merton: *Seeds of Contemplation.*
(20th cent.)

See also Belief; Bible; Catholic Faith;
Christianity; Dogma; Doctrine; God:
His Existence; God: Man's Knowledge of God; Grace; Justification; Mystery; Religion; Revelation

Faith, Articles of

As regards the primary points or articles
of faith, man is bound to believe them,
just as he is bound to have faith; but as
to other points of faith, man is not
bound to believe them explicitly, but
only implicitly, or to be ready to believe
them, in so far as he is prepared to believe whatever is contained in the Divine
Scriptures. Then alone is he bound to
believe such things explicitly, when it is
clear to him that they are contained in
the doctrine of faith.

St. Thomas Aquinas: *Summa Theologica,*
2-2, 2, 5. (13th cent.)

As regards the substance of the articles
of faith, they have not received any increase as time went on: since whatever
those who lived later have believed, was
contained, albeit implicitly, in the faith
of those Fathers who preceded them.
But there was an increase in the number
of articles believed explicitly, since to
those who lived in later times some were
known explicitly which were not known
explicitly by those who lived before
them.

St. Thomas Aquinas: *Summa Theologica,*
2-2, 1, 7. (13th cent.)

Articles of faith in Christian theology
are like self-evident principles in philosophy, being so arranged that some are
implicit in others. All rational principles
can be taken back to the principle of contradiction. Similarly the articles of faith
are based on certain primary principles
of faith.

St. Thomas Aquinas: *Summa Theologica,*
2-2, 2, 7. (13th cent.)

See also Creed; Doctrine, Development
of

Faith, Confession of

It is not necessary for salvation to confess one's faith at all times and in all
places, but in certain places and at certain times, when, namely, by omitting
to do so, we would deprive God of due
honor, or our neighbor of a service that
we ought to render him: for instance,
if a man, on being asked about his faith,
were to remain silent, so as to make people believe either that he is without
faith, or that the faith is false, or so as
to turn others away from the faith; for
in such cases as these, confession of
faith is necessary for salvation.

St. Thomas Aquinas: *Summa Theologica,*
2-2, 3, 2. (13th cent.)

Faith and Charity

There is no love without hope, no hope
without love, and neither hope nor love
without faith.

St. Augustine: *Enchiridion,* 8. (5th cent.)

Faith itself is of no avail without charity. For without charity faith can indeed
be, but can profit nothing.

St. Augustine: *De Trinitate,* 15, 18, 32.
(5th cent.)

Christ dwells in our head through the faith of our mind; we can be certain He does when we know that we believe what the Catholic Church holds and teaches. He dwells in our hearts through faith quickened by charity; we cannot be certain about this, or that we have charity, unless a special grace or revelation be granted us.

> St. Thomas Aquinas: *Commentary on 2 Corinthians*, 13, lect. 2. (13th cent.)

It is love makes faith, not faith love.

> Card. Newman: *Parochial and Plain Sermons*, 4. (19th cent.)

The safeguard of faith is a right state of heart. This it is that gives it birth; it also disciplines it. This is what protects it from bigotry, credulity, and fanaticism. It is holiness, or dutifulness, or the new creation, or the spiritual mind, however we word it, which is the quickening and illuminating principle of true faith, giving it eyes, hands, and feet.

> Card. Newman: *Oxford University Sermons*. (19th cent.)

Love and faith are as much realities as artistic faculties, and need similar cultivation.

> R. H. Benson: *Lord of the World*. (20th cent.)

Faith and Devotion

Faith and devotion are as distinct in fact, as they are in idea. We cannot, indeed, be devout without faith, but we may believe without feeling devotion.

> Card. Newman: *Letter to the Rev. E. B. Pusey*. (19th cent.)

Faith and Hope

Faith has to do with things that are not seen and hope with things that are not in hand.

> St. Thomas Aquinas: *Summa Theologica*, 1-2, 57. (13th cent.)

Faith and Knowledge

We cannot deny that believing and knowing are different things, and that in matters of great importance, pertaining to divinity, we must first believe before we seek to know.

> St. Augustine: *On Free Will*, 2, 6. (4th cent.)

There is nothing we would rather know than what we already know by faith. When the veil shall have been utterly removed from the things of which we are now assured by faith, the cup of bliss will be full.

> St. Bernard: *On Consideration*, 5, 3. (12th cent.)

Between knowledge through science and knowledge through faith there is this difference: science shines only in the mind, showing that God is the cause of everything, that He is one and wise, and so forth. Faith enlightens the mind and also warms the affections, telling us not merely that God is first cause, but also that He is Savior, Redeemer, loving, made flesh for us.

> St. Thomas Aquinas: *Commentary on 2 Corinthians*, 2, lect. 3. (13th cent.)

Faith is a kind of knowledge, inasmuch as the intellect is determined by faith to some knowable object. But this determination to one object does not proceed from the vision of the believer, but from the vision of him who is believed.

> St. Thomas Aquinas: *Summa Theologica*, 1, 12, 13. (13th cent.)

If any one shall say that divine faith is not distinguished from natural knowledge of God and of moral truths, and therefore that it is not requisite for divine faith that revealed truth be believed because of the authority of God Who reveals it; let him be anathema.

> Vatican Council, Session 3, Canon 2 de Fide. (Apr. 24, 1870)

The realities discerned by faith are susceptible of infinite corroboration, for God is "infinitely visible and infinitely credible," and, since the knowledge of God is the one end of life, the sum of human wisdom consists in the accumulation of such corroborations.

Coventry Patmore: *Religio Poetae.* (19th cent.)

Religion can be made intelligible if we take the pains to make it so; its proofs may be found, its laws ascertained, and the conscience and reason constrained to acknowledge them. And Catholics are the only persons who can enter on this field of labor with perfect freedom; for they alone have a religion perfectly defined, clearly marked off from all other spheres of thought; they alone therefore can enter these spheres free from all suspicion of doubt, and from all fear of discord between faith and knowledge. If this clear distinction has ever been forgotten by Catholics, defeat was sure to follow, and that defeat was the victory of truth. Authority may put itself in opposition to its own code; but that code is vindicated by the defeat of authority.

Lord Acton: *Ultramontanism.* (19th cent.)

Faith and Miracles

The authority of faith derives from the revelation of the Father through the Son and the Holy Ghost, not from angels or miracles, though in certain cases truths of faith have been disclosed through angels . . . and many miracles have been wrought to support them.

St. Thomas Aquinas: *Against the Errors of the Greeks,* 30. (13th cent.)

Faith and Reason

If the work of God could be comprehended by reason, it would be no longer wonderful, and faith would have no merit if reason provided proof.

Pope St. Gregory I: *Homilies on the Gospels,* 26, 1. (6th cent.)

For I do not seek to understand that I may believe, but I believe in order to understand. For this also I believe,— that unless I believe, I should not understand.

St. Anselm: *Proslogium,* 1. (11th cent.)

For what is more against reason than by reason to attempt to transcend reason? And what is more against faith than to be unwilling to believe what reason cannot attain?

St. Bernard: *Letters,* 125, 1. (12th cent.)

We must not attempt to prove what is of faith, except by authority alone, to those who receive the authority; while as regards others it suffices to prove that what faith teaches is not impossible.

St. Thomas Aquinas: *Summa Theologica,* I, 32, 1. (13th cent.)

It is philosophically impossible for divine faith to profess what the reason must regard as false: not even divine omnipotence can make this otherwise.

St. Thomas Aquinas: *On the Unity of the Intellect.* (13th cent.)

Human reason is weak, and may be deceived, but true faith cannot be deceived.

Thomas a Kempis: *The Imitation of Christ,* 4, 18. (15th cent.)

For in this, Christian philosophy and human wisdom differ much; that guided solely by the light of nature, and having made gradual advances by reasoning on sensible objects and effects, human wisdom, after long and laborious investigation, at length reaches with difficulty the contemplation of the invisible things of God, discovers and understands the first cause and author of all things; whilst on the contrary Christian philosophy so enlightens and enlarges the human mind, that at once and without difficulty it pierces the heavens, and illumined with the splendors of the divinity contemplates first the eternal source of light, and in its radiance all created things.

Catechism of the Council of Trent, 1. (16th cent.)

If we surrender everything to reason, our religion will lose all mystery and the supernatural. If we offend against the principles of reason, our religion will be absurd and ridiculous.

> Pascal: *Pensées*. (17th cent.)

Few minds in earnest can remain at ease without some sort of rational grounds for their religious belief; to reconcile theory and fact is almost an instinct of the mind.

> Card. Newman: *Apologia pro Vita Sua*, 5. (19th cent.)

Life is not long enough for a religion of inferences.

> Card. Newman: *Discussions and Arguments*. (19th cent.)

The natural man holds divine truths merely as an opinion, and not as a point of faith; grace believes, reason does but opine; grace gives certainty, reason is never decided.

> Card. Newman: *Discourses to Mixed Congregations*. (19th cent.)

Right reason, that is, reason rightly exercised, leads the mind to the Catholic faith, and plants it there, and teaches it in all its religious speculations to act under its guidance.

> Card. Newman: *Idea of a University*, 8. (19th cent.)

Reason is one thing and faith is another, and reason can as little be made a substitute for faith, as faith can be made a substitute for reason.

> Card. Newman: *Discourses to Mixed Congregations*. (19th cent.)

All the truths of religion proceed from the innate strength of human reason; hence reason is the ultimate standard by which man can and ought to arrive at the knowledge of all truths of every kind.

> Proposition condemned by Pius IX in Syllabus of Errors. (1867)

The faith of Christ is in opposition to human reason, and divine revelation not only is not useful, but is even hurtful to the perfection of man.

> Proposition condemned by Pius IX in Syllabus of Errors. (1867)

Every man is free to embrace and profess that religion which, guided by the light of reason, he considers to be true.

> Proposition condemned by Pius IX in Syllabus of Errors. (1867)

If any one shall say that the assent of Christian faith is not a free act, but necessarily produced by the arguments of human reason; or that the grace of God is necessary for that living faith only *which worketh by charity;* let him be anathema.

> Vatican Council, Session 3, Canon 5 de Fide. (Apr. 24, 1870)

If any one shall say that in divine revelation there are no mysteries truly and properly so called, but that all the doctrines of faith can be understood and demonstrated from natural principles by properly cultivated reason; let him be anathema.

> Vatican Council, Session 3, Canon 1 de Fide et Ratione. (Apr. 24, 1870)

If any one shall say that human sciences are to be so freely treated that their assertions, although opposed to revealed doctrine, can be held as true, and cannot be condemned by the Church; let him be anathema.

> Vatican Council, Session 3, Canon 2 de Fide et Ratione. (Apr. 24, 1870)

Who can express the magnificence of the light of faith as compared with the light of reason? In the things of God and the soul, reason but gropes among the shadows reflected here below; whilst faith, with its light direct from God, opens out the infinite and eternal prospect of divine truth, which, though obscurely seen, is yet surely seen by the

humble mind, giving a breadth and firmness to the mind that nothing can explain but the action of God in the soul.

> Archb. Ullathorne: *Humility and Patience.*
> (19th cent.)

The man who says, Unless I *feel,* I will
not believe, is as narrow and foolish as
the man who says, Unless I understand,
I will not believe.

> R. H. Benson: *Christ in the Church.* (20th
> cent.)

Faith can and does exist, quite apart
from intellect, and to increase or develop the one often means the decrease
and incoherence of the other.

> R. H. Benson: *The Light Invisible.* (20th
> cent.)

If faith did not exist apart from intellect,
clever people would have a better hope
of salvation than stupid people; and
that is absurd—as absurd as if rich
people should be nearer God than poor
people.

> R. H. Benson: *The Light Invisible.* (20th
> cent.)

Intellect has nothing more to do with
faith really than jewels have to do with
a beautiful woman.

> R. H. Benson: *The Light Invisible.* (20th
> cent.)

It is a very dangerous matter to hold the
Catholic faith as a matter of 'the religious consciousness.' It is a matter of
truth or falsehood.

> Abbot Chapman: *Spiritual letters.* (20th
> cent.)

Simple secularists still talk as if the
Church had introduced a sort of schism
between reason and religion. The truth
is that the Church was actually the first
thing that ever tried to combine reason
and religion.

> G. K. Chesterton: *The Everlasting Man.*
> (20th cent.)

A saint is no less effective as a saint because, like St. Augustine or St. Thomas
Aquinas, he can give a reason for the
faith which is the driving force behind
his sanctity. It is the glory of the Catholic Church that it can produce not only
saints, but also great thinkers.

> Arnold Lunn: *Now I See.* (20th cent.)

Faith and Understanding

Faith opens the door to understanding,
unbelief closes it.

> St. Augustine: *Letter 137, 15.* (5th cent.)

Faith merely assents to what is proposed,
but the gift of understanding brings
some insight into the truth, and this,
where our ultimate end is concerned,
supposes sanctifying grace.

> St. Thomas Aquinas: *Summa Theologica,*
> 2-2, 8, 5. (13th cent.)

Such are the two gifts which will be
found to lie at the beginning and at the
end of our new life, both intellectual
in their nature, and both divinely imparted; faith being an exercise of the
reason, so spontaneous, unconscious,
and unargumentative, as to seem at first
sight even to be a moral act, and wisdom
being that orderly and mature develop-
men of thought, which in earthly language goes by the name of science and
philosophy.

> Card. Newman: *Oxford University
> Sermons.* (19th cent.)

Faith and Works

God chose that man should seek salvation by faith rather than by works, lest
anyone should glory in his deeds and
thereby incur sin.

> St. Ambrose: *In Ps. 43 Enarr. 14.* (4th
> cent.)

For faith without works cannot please,
nor can good works without faith.

> St. Bede the Venerable: *De Temporum
> Ratione.* (8th cent.)

You do right when you offer faith to God; you do right when you offer works. But if you separate the two, then you do wrong. For faith without works is dead; and lack of charity in action murders faith, just as Cain murdered Abel, so that God cannot respect your offering.

> St. Bernard: *Sermons on the Canticle of Canticles,* 24. (12th cent.)

Faith, Hope and Charity

Almighty and everlasting God, grant unto us an increase of faith, hope, and charity; and that we may obtain what Thou dost promise, cause us to love that which Thou dost command.

> Roman Missal, Collect for Thirteenth Sunday after Pentecost. (Leonine, ca. 5th cent.)

St. Paul instructs us that our entire perfection is contained at present under three concise headings: *and now there remain faith, hope, charity, these three* (I Cor. 13, 13). Such is the apostle's order, such the order of reason, for we cannot love unless we have good reason to hope, and we cannot hope unless we have knowledge.

> St. Thomas Aquinas: *Compendium of Theology,* 1. (13th cent.)

The law the lawyers know about
  Is property and land;
But why the leaves are on the trees,
And why the winds disturb the seas,
Why honey is the food of bees,
Why horses have such tender knees,
Why winters come and rivers freeze,
Why faith is more than what one sees,
And hope survives the worst disease,
And charity is more than these,
  They do not understand.

> Douglas Pepler: *The Law the Lawyers Know About.* (20th cent.)

Falcon

I caught this morning morning's minion, king-

Dom of daylight's dauphin, dapple-dawn-drawn Falcon. . . .

> G. M. Hopkins: *The Windhover.* (19th cent.)

Fall

'Tis human fate sometime to slip and fall,
But to ingrovel in dirt is beastly base.

> Anthony Copley: *A Fig for Fortune.* (16th cent.)

For low they fall whose fall is from the sky.

> F. Thompson: *The Dread of Height.* (19th cent.)

Fall of Man

The envy of the devil then was the reason of man's fall. For that same demon, so full of envy and with such hatred of good, would not suffer us to enjoy the pleasures of heaven, when he himself was kept below on account of his arrogance, hence the false one tempts miserable man with hope of Godhead, and leading him up to as great a height of arrogance as himself, he hurls him down into a pit of destruction just as deep.

> St. John of Damascus: *Exposition of the Orthodox Faith,* 2, 30. (8th cent.)

The Fall had its beginning in the accurst
  Arrogance of him whom thou didst see compressed
  With all the world's weights down upon him forced.

> Dante: *Paradiso, Canto 29.* (D. imagined the devil at the center of the earth in the bottom of hell) (Tr. Binyon) (14th cent.)

See also Adam; Sin, Original

Falseness

As false as God is true.

> John Heywood: *Proverbs,* 2, 7. (16th cent.)

See also Error; Truth and Error

Fame

The desire for fame tempts even noble minds.

> St. Augustine: *The City of God,* 5. (5th cent.)

Wherefore, every man must be content with that glory which he may have at home, and that noble immortality of fame must be comprehended within the compass of one nation.

> Boethius: *De Consolatione Philosophiae,* 2, 7. (6th cent.)

Naught but a wind's breath is the world's acclaim,
    Which blows now hence, now thence, as it may hap,
And when it changes quarter, changes name.

> Dante: *Purgatorio, Canto 11.* (Tr. L. Binyon) (14th cent.)

For not on downy plumes, nor under shade
Of canopy reposing, fame is won.

> Dante: *Inferno, Canto 24.* (Tr. Cary) (14th cent.)

Your fame is like the summer flower
Which blooms and dies in one short hour;
The sunny warmth which brings it forth
Soon slays with parching power.

> Dante: *Purgatorio, Canto 11.* (14th cent.)

For what is fame in itself but the blast of another man's mouth as soon passed, as spoken?

> St. Thomas More: *Dialogue of Comfort.* (16th cent.)

What men call fame is, after all, but a very windy thing. A man thinks that many are praising him, and talking of him alone, and yet they spend but a very small part of the day thinking of him, being occupied with things of their own.

> St. Thomas More. (16th cent.)

This gift alone I shall her give,
    When death doth what he can;
Her honest fame shall ever live
    Within the mouth of man.

> John Heywood: *On the Princess Mary.* (16th cent.)

No earthly gift lasts after death, but fame;
This governs men more careful of their name
Than of their souls, which their ungodly taste
Dissolves to nothing, and shall prove at last
Far worse than nothing: praises come too late,
When man is not, or is in wretched state.

> Sir John Beaumont: *Of the Miserable State of Man.* (17th cent.)

We are so presumptuous that we wish to be known by all the world, and even by people who will live after we are gone; and we are so vain that the good opinion of five or six persons near us delights and contents us.

> Pascal: *Pensées,* 2. (17th cent.)

What's fame? A fancied life in others' breath;
A thing beyond us, ev'n before our death . . .
All that we feel of it begins and ends
In the small circle of our foes or friends.

> Pope: *An Essay on Man,* 4. (18th cent.)

And what is fame? The meanest have their day;
The greatest can but blaze and pass away.

> Pope: *The First Epistle of the First Book of Horace.* (18th cent.)

To the quick brow fame grudges her best wreath
While the quick heart to enjoy it throbs beneath:
On the dead forehead's sculptured marble shown,

Lo, her choice crown—its flowers are
also stone.

John J. Piatt: *The Guerdon.* (19th cent.)

Their noonday never knows
What names immortal are:
'Tis night alone that shows
How star surpasseth star.

J. B. Tabb: *Fame.* (19th cent.)

See also Glory

Familiarity

We must have charity for all, but familiarity is not expedient.

Thomas a Kempis: *The Imitation of
Christ,* 1, 8. (15th cent.)

Family

The family may be regarded as the cradle of civil society, and it is in great
measure within the circle of family life
that the destiny of states is fostered.

Pope Leo XIII: *Sapientiae Christianae.*
(Jan. 10, 1890)

No human law can abolish the natural
and original right of marriage, nor in
any way limit the chief and principal
purpose of marriage ordained by God's
authority from the beginning: *Increase
and multiply.* Hence we have the family,
the society of a man's house—a society
very small, one must admit, but none
the less a true society, and one older
than any state. Consequently, it has
rights and duties peculiar to itself which
are quite independent of the state.

Pope Leo XIII: *Rerum Novarum.* (May
15, 1891)

The union of the family lies in love; and
love is the only reconciliation of authority and liberty.

R. H. Benson: *The Dawn of All.* (20th
cent.)

We can say that the family is the unit of
the state; that it is the cell that makes
up the formation. Round the family do

indeed gather the sanctities that separate men from ants and bees. Decency
is the curtain of that tent; liberty is the
wall of that city; property is but the
family farm; honor is but the family
flag.

G. K. Chesterton: *The Everlasting Man.*
(20th cent.)

The family is more sacred than the state,
and men are begotten not for the earth
and for time, but for heaven and eternity.

Pope Pius XI: *Casti connubi.* (Dec. 31,
1930)

Fanatic

'Gainst form and order they their
power employ,
Nothing to build and all things to destroy.

Dryden. (17th cent.)

Fancy

There are no rules of architecture for a
castle in the clouds.

G. K. Chesterton: *The Everlasting Man.*
(20th cent.)

Farewell

Farewell again, thou lamp of light
Vicegerent of my heart,
He that takes leave so oft, I think,
He likes not to depart.

Francis Tregian: *Letter from Prison to his
Wife.* (Guiney, 196) (16th cent.)

Farewell, farewell to thee, Araby's
daughter!
Thus warbled a Peri beneath the dark
sea.

Thomas Moore: *Lalla Rookh: The Fire-
Worshippers.* (19th cent.)

Good-bye, dear heart. Be thou, as I am,
glad.
Glad for the grace of loneliness and
yearning

My heart, far faring from thee, shall
    have had
      Ere its returning.
Pluck future joy from out this present
    pain;
    Rejoice to know that these small
      seeds of sorrow
Shall be love's harvest when we meet
    again,
    Some bright tomorrow.

> T. A. Daly: *The Journey's End.* (20th
> cent.)

See also Parting

Farmer

And farmers fatten most when famine
reigns.

> Sir Samuel Garth: *The Dispensary,* 2.
> (17th cent.)

Fashion

Be not the first by whom the new are
    tried,
Nor yet the last to lay the old aside.

> Pope: *An Essay on Criticism,* 2. (18th
> cent.)

Fashion is what one wears oneself. What
is unfashionable is what other people
wear.

> Oscar Wilde: *An Ideal Husband,* 3. (19th
> cent.)

After all, what is fashion? From the
artistic point of view, it is usually a form
of ugliness so intolerable that we have
to alter it every six months.

> Oscar Wilde: *Suitable Dress for Women
> Workers.* (19th cent.)

See also Clothes; Dress

Fasting

Fasting is better than prayer.

> So-called Second Epistle of St. Clement to
> Corinthians. (2nd cent.)

Here is the fast you must keep for God:
Do not commit any wicked deed in your
life and serve the Lord with a pure
heart; keep His commandments by walking according to His directions and do
not let any evil desire enter your heart;
have faith in God.

> Shepherd of Hermas, Parable 5, 1, 4-5.
> (2nd cent.)

Let not your fasts be with hypocrites, for
they fast on Mondays and Thursdays,
but do you fast on Wednesdays and Fridays.

> Teaching of the Twelve Apostles, 8, 1.
> (2nd cent.)

Widows and virgins shall fast often
and pray on behalf of the Church. The
presbyters when they wish and the laity
likewise shall fast.

> St. Hippolytus: *The Apostolic Tradition,*
> 25. (3rd cent.)

No one shall taste anything at the Pascha
before the offering is made, for if anyone does so the fast is not reckoned to
him. But if anyone is pregnant or sick
and cannot fast the two days, let them
fast on the Saturday, taking bread and
water if necessary.

> St. Hippolytus: *The Apostolic Tradition,*
> 29. (Reference to the strict pre-Easter fast
> of the early Church.) (3rd cent.)

If anyone of the clergy be found to fast
on the Lord's Day, or on the Sabbath,
except only one [Holy Saturday], let
him be deprived; but if he be one of
the laity, let him be suspended.

> Ecclesiastical Canons of the Holy Apostles,
> 64. (4th cent.)

Fasting is a medicine.

> St. John Chrysostom: *Homilies.* (4th cent.)

The mystic Table is obtained by fasting,
is acquired at the price of hunger. To
that venerable Table holy fasts lead us,
by that hunger we purchase the things
which are eternal.

> St. Ambrose: *Concerning Elias,* 33. (4th
> cent.)

Subdue your flesh by fasting and abstinence from meat and drink, as far as the health allows.

> St. Augustine: *Letter 211* (his Rule). (5th cent.)

O almighty and everlasting God, Who by salutary abstinence dost heal us both in soul and body; we humbly beseech Thy majesty, that appeased by the fervent devotion of those who fast, Thou wouldst grant us help now and in time to come.

> Roman Missal, Collect for Ember Saturday in September. (Gelasian, ca. 5th cent.)

To love fasting.

> St. Benedict: *Rule,* 4. (One of his "tools of good works") (6th cent.)

As long as he who fasts, fasts for God, and he who fasts not, also fasts not for God, devotion is as well satisfied with one as with the other.

> St. Francis de Sales: *Spiritual Conferences,* 1. (17th cent.)

It is better not to fast and be thereby humbled, than to fast and to be self-satisfied therewith.

> Pascal: *Pensées.* (17th cent.)

The law of fasting prescribes that not more than one full meal be taken per day; but it does not forbid that some food be taken in the morning and evening, provided the approved custom of the place as regards the quantity and kind of food is observed.

> Code of Canon Law, Canon 1251, 1. (20th cent.)

See also Almsgiving; Mortification; Penance

Fasting and Abstinence

All persons who have completed their seventh year are bound by the law of abstinence. All persons from the completion of their twenty-first year to the beginning of their sixtieth year are bound by the law of fast.

> Code of Canon Law, Canon 1254. (20th cent.)

The law of abstinence and fast together is to be observed on Ash Wednesday, the Fridays and Saturdays of Lent, the Ember Days, and on the vigils of Pentecost, the Assumption, All Saints and Christmas. The law of fast alone is to be observed on the other days of Lent. On Sundays or holidays of obligation the law of abstinence, or of abstinence and fast, or of fast alone, ceases, except on a feast of obligation during Lent; vigils are not anticipated; likewise the law ceases on Holy Saturday at noon.

> Code of Canon Law, Canon 1252, 4. (These general rules are sometimes modified by dispensation according to time and place.) (20th cent.)

See also Abstinence

Fat

All the gruel is in the fire.

> Chaucer: *Troilus and Criseyde.* (14th cent.)

She was made like a beer-pot, or a barrel.

> John Heywood: *Proverbs,* 2, 1. (16th cent.)

A swine overfat is cause of his own bane.

> John Heywood: *Proverbs,* 2, 7. (16th cent.)

I am resolved to grow fat and look young till forty, and then slip out of the world with the first wrinkle and the reputation of five-and-twenty.

> Dryden: *Secret Love,* 3, 1. (17th cent.)

Fatalism

Fatalism is the refuge of a conscience-stricken mind, maddened at the sight of evils which it has brought upon itself, and cannot remove.

> Card. Newman: *Oxford University Sermons.* (19th cent.)

Fate

If by fate anyone means the will or power of God, let him keep his meaning but mend his language: for fate commonly means a necessary process which will have its way apart from the will of God and of men.

> St. Augustine: *The City of God,* 5. (5th cent.)

What profits it to butt against the Fates?

> Dante: *Inferno, Canto 9.* (14th cent.)

Alas! what port can such a pilot find, Who in the night of fate must blindly steer.

> Dryden: *Annus Mirabilis.* (17th cent.)

Man may, as Pinkerton [Sir Jonas Pinkerton] writes, be master of his fate, but he has a precious poor servant. It is easier to command a lapdog or a mule for a whole day than one's own fate for half an hour.

> H. Belloc: *The Path to Rome.* (20th cent.)

See also Destiny

Father

Like father, like son: every good tree maketh good fruits.

> Wm. Langland: *Piers Plowman,* 3. (14th cent.)

Father, God the

The Father is the principle of the whole Deity.

> St. Augustine: *De Trinitate,* 4, 20. (5th cent.)

God is therefore truly the Father, inasmuch as He is Father of truth; He does not create the Son from outside Himself, but generates Him from His own substance. That is to say, being wise, He generates Wisdom, being just, Justice, being eternal, the Eternal, being immortal, the Immortal, being invisible, the Invisible. Because He is Light, He gen-erates Brightness, and because He is Mind, the Word.

> Rufinus: *Commentary on the Apostles' Creed,* 4. (5th cent.)

[We believe] in one Father, the beginning and cause of all: begotten of no one: without cause or generation, alone subsisting: creator of all: but Father of one only by nature, His only-begotten Son and our Lord and God and Savior Jesus Christ, and producer of the most Holy Spirit. . . . For there never was a time when the Father was and the Son was not, but always the Father and always the Son, Who was begotten of Him, existed together. For He could not have received the name Father apart from the Son.

> St. John of Damascus: *Exposition of the Orthodox Faith,* 1, 8. (8th cent.)

Great God! within Whose simple essence we
Nothing but that which is Thyself can find:
When on Thyself Thou didst reflect Thy mind,
Thy thought was God, which took the form of Thee.
And when this God, thus born, Thou lov'st, and He
Lov'd Thee again with passion of like kind,
(As lovers' sighs which meet become one wind,)
Both breath'd one Spright of equal Deity.
Eternal Father! whence these Two do come
And whil'st the title of *my* Father have,
An heavenly knowledge in my mind engrave,
That it Thy Son's true image may become;
And sense my heart with sighs of holy love,
That it the temple of the Spright may prove.

> Henry Constable: *Sonnet to God the Father.* (16th cent.)

Thee, sovereign God, our grateful accents praise;
We own Thee Lord, and bless Thy
wondrous ways;
To Thee, eternal Father, earth's whole
frame
With loudest trumpets sounds immortal fame.

Dryden: *Translation of Te Deum
Laudamus.* (17th cent.)

Father of all! in every age,
In every clime adored,
By saint, by savage, and by sage,
Jehovah, Jove, or Lord!

Pope: *Universal Prayer.* (18th cent.)

Father! the sweetest, dearest name,
That men or angels know!
Fountain of life, that had no fount
From which itself could flow!

Thy life is one unwearing day;
Before its 'now' thou hast
No varied future yet unlived,
No lapse of changeless past.

Thou comest not, Thou goest not;
Thou wert not, wilt not be;
Eternity is but a thought
By which we think of Thee.

F. Faber: *The Eternal Father.* (19th cent.)

My God! how wonderful Thou art,
Thy Majesty how bright,
How beautiful Thy mercy-seat
In depths of burning light!

How dread are Thine eternal years,
O everlasting Lord!
By prostrate spirits day and night
Incessantly adored!

F. Faber: *Our Heavenly Father.* (19th
cent.)

See also God

Fathers of the Church

Only those opinions of the Fathers are
to be brought forward which were expressed by those who lived, taught and
persevered in the holy Catholic faith and
communion, and who deserved either to
die faithfully in Christ or to be martyred
gloriously for Him. Those men are to
be believed, moreover, in accordance
with the following rule: Only that is to
be held as certain, valid and beyond
doubt, which either all or most of them
have confirmed in one and the same
sense—manifestly, frequently, and persistently, as though a council of masters
stood in agreement—and which they
have accepted, kept, and handed on. On
the other hand, what some saint, learned
man, bishop, confessor, or martyr has
individually thought outside of, or even
contrary to, the general opinion must be
considered his personal, particular, and
quite private opinion, entirely removed
from the common, public and general
opinion.

St. Vincent of Lerins: *Commonitoria,* 28.
(5th cent.)

The writings of the fathers of the
Church are also proper sources [for the-
ology], yet their authority is not final.
Faith rests on divine revelations made
through the prophets and apostles and
set down in the canonical Scriptures, not
on revelations, if there be any, made to
other holy teachers.

St. Thomas Aquinas: *Summa Theologica,*
I, I, 8. (13th cent.)

Among men, the knowledge of faith had
to proceed from imperfection to perfection; and, although some men have been
after the manner of active causes,
through being doctors of the faith,
nevertheless the manifestation of the
Spirit is given to such men for the common good so that the knowledge of
faith was imparted to the Fathers who
were instructors in the faith, so far as
was necessary at the time for the instruction of the people, either openly or in
figures.

St. Thomas Aquinas: *Summa Theologica,*
2-2, I, 7. (13th cent.)

For myself, hopeless as you consider it,
I am not ashamed still to take my stand
upon the fathers, and do not mean to

budge. The history of their times is not yet an old almanac to me. Of course I maintain the value and authority of the 'schola', as one of the *loci theologici;* nevertheless I sympathize with Petavius in preferring to the 'contentious and subtle theology' of the middle age, that 'more elegant and fruitful teaching which is moulded after the image of erudite antiquity'. The fathers made me a Catholic, and I am not going to kick down the ladder by which I ascended into the Church.

> Card. Newman: *Letter to the Rev. E. B. Pusey.* (19th cent.)

Fault

As Augustine says, fault is the evil we perform, punishment the evil we undergo (*De Libero Arbitrio,* 1, 2).

> St. Thomas Aquinas: *Disputations concerning Evil,* 1, 4. (13th cent.)

When it seems that God shows us the faults of others, keep on the safer side—it may be that thy judgment is false. On thy lips let silence abide. And any vice which thou mayest ascribe to others, do thou ascribe at once to them and to thyself, in true humility. If that vice really exists in a person, he will correct himself better, seeing himself so gently understood, and will say of his own accord the thing which thou wouldst have said to him.

> St. Catherine of Siena: *Letter to Sister Daniella.* (14th cent.)

We would willingly have others perfect, and yet we amend not our own faults. We would have others severely corrected, and will not be corrected ourselves. The large liberty of others displeaseth us, and yet we will not have our own desires denied us. We will have others kept under by strict laws, but in no sort will ourselves be restrained. And thus it appeareth how seldom we weigh our neighbor in the same balance with ourselves.

> Thomas a Kempis: *The Imitation of Christ,* 1, 16. (15th cent.)

Hard is for any man all faults to mend.

> John Heywood: *Proverbs,* 1, 11. (16th cent.)

He hath but one fault, he is nought.

> John Heywood: *Proverbs,* 1, 11. (16th cent.)

Do not think of the faults of others but of what is good in them and faulty in thyself.

> St. Teresa of Jesus: *Maxims.* (16th cent.)

It seems no fault to do that all have done;
The number of offenders hides the sin;
Coach drawn with many horse doth easily run,
Soon followeth one where multitudes begin.

> Bl. Robert Southwell: *St. Peter's Complaint.* (16th cent.)

The business of finding fault is very easy, and that of doing better very hard.

> St. Francis de Sales: *Letters to Persons in Religion,* 3, 1. (17th cent.)

What faults he had (for who from faults is free?)
His father could not or he would not see.

> Dryden: *Absalom and Achitophel.* (17th cent.)

They judge but half who only faults will see.

> Dryden. (17th cent.)

Faultlessness

He is lifeless that is faultless.

> John Heywood: *Proverbs,* 1, 11. (16th cent.)

Whoever thinks a faultless piece to see,
Thinks what ne'er was, nor is, nor e'er shall be.

> Pope: *An Essay on Criticism,* 2. (18th cent.)

Favor

From plots and treasons heav'n pre-
  serve my years,
But save me most from my petitioners.
Unsatiate as the barren womb or grave;
God cannot grant as much as they can
  crave.

> Dryden: *Absalom and Achitophel.* (17th
> cent.)

Fear

Fear is the foundation of safety.

> Tertullian: *Women's Dress.* (3rd cent.)

If fear were not a good thing, fathers
would not have set schoolmasters over
their children, nor lawgivers magistrates
for cities.

> St. John Chrysostom: *Homilies.* (4th cent.)

The weight of fear is the anchor of the
heart.

> Pope St. Gregory I: *Morals,* 6, 58. (6th
> cent.)

More afraid than hurt.

> John Heywood: *Proverbs,* 1, 4. (16th cent.)

Ah fear! abortive imp of drooping
  mind;
Self-overthrow, false friend, root of
  remorse;
Sighted in seeing ills, in shunning
  blind,
Foil'd without field, by fancy not by
  force;
Ague of valor, frenzy of the wise,
Fine honor's stain, love's frost, the
  mint of lies.

> Bl. Robert Southwell: *St. Peter's Complaint.*
> (16th cent.)

It will be quite enough to receive the
evils which come upon us from time to
time, without anticipating them by the
imagination.

> St. Francis de Sales: *Letters to Persons in
> Religion,* 4, 2. (17th cent.)

We must not fear fear.

> St. Francis de Sales: *Letters to Persons in
> the World,* 4, 13. (17th cent.)

Fear is a greater evil than the evil itself.

> St. Francis de Sales: *Letters to Persons in
> the World,* 6, 12. (17th cent.)

Those who love to be feared, fear to be
loved; they themselves are of all people
the most abject; some fear them, but
they fear everyone.

> Jean Pierre Camus: *The Spirit of St. Francis
> de Sales,* 7, 3. (17th cent.)

The clouds dispell'd, the sky resum'd
  her light,
And nature stood recover'd of her
  fright.
But fear, the last of ills, remain'd behind,
And horror heavy sat on every mind.

> Dryden: *Theodore and Honoria.* (17th
> cent.)

I shall not be afraid any more,
  Either by night or day;
What would it profit me to be afraid
  With you away?

> Aline Kilmer: *I Shall Not Be Afraid.*
> (20th cent.)

At the root of all war is fear: not so
much the fear men have of one another
as the fear they have of everything. It is
not merely that they do not trust one another: they do not even trust themselves.
If they are not sure when someone else
may turn around and kill them, they are
still less sure when they may turn around
and kill themselves. They cannot trust
anything, because they have ceased to believe in God.

> Thomas Merton: *Seeds of Contemplation.*
> (20th cent.)

Fear of God

So, by keeping God's commandments,
you will be powerful in every action,
and your action will be beyond criticism.

Fear the Lord, then, and you will do everything well.

> Shepherd of Hermas, Mandate 7, 1. (2nd cent.)

For I have learnt for a fact that nothing so effectively obtains, retains and regains grace, as that we should always be found not high-minded before God, but filled with holy fear.

> St. Bernard: *Sermons on the Canticle of Canticles,* 53. (12th cent.)

There is no true liberty, nor solid joy, but in the fear of God with a good conscience.

> Thomas a Kempis: *The Imitation of Christ,* 1, 21. (15th cent.)

Fear God, and thou shalt have no need of being afraid of man.

> Thomas a Kempis: *The Imitation of Christ,* 3, 36. (15th cent.)

We must fear God through love, not love Him through fear.

> Jean Pierre Camus: *The Spirit of St. Francis de Sales,* 1, 16. (17th cent.)

Feast

The feast of reason, and the flow of soul.

> Pope: *The First Satire of the Second Book of Horace.* (18th cent.)

February

Rich meanings of the prophet-Spring adorn,
  Unseen, this colorless sky of folded showers,
  And folded winds; no blossom in the bowers;
A poet's face asleep in this grey morn.

Now in the midst of the old world forlorn
  A mystic child is set in these still hours,
  I keep this time, even before the flowers,
Sacred to all the young and the unborn.

> Alice Meynell: *In February.* (19th cent.)

Feeling

Trust not to thy feeling, for whatever it be now, it will quickly be changed into another thing.

> Thomas a Kempis: *The Imitation of Christ,* 1, 13. (15th cent.)

It may be that the heart has reasons of which the head knows nothing, but, for the life of me, I have never been able to see why the reasons of the heart which lead so many people into the wrong bed, should lead anybody to the right conclusions.

> Arnold Lunn: *Now I See.* (20th cent.)

Not to show one's feelings is as much a drawback sometimes as the wearing of the heart upon the sleeve.

> R. H. Benson: *By What Authority.* (20th cent.)

Fellowship

They cleave together like burrs.

> John Heywood: *Proverbs,* 2, 5. (16th cent.)

Individuals cannot cohere closely unless they sacrifice something of their individuality.

> R. H. Benson: *A City Set on a Hill.* (20th cent.)

Few

The few the better fare.

> John Heywood: *Proverbs,* 2, 7. (16th cent.)

Fiction

The only real people are the people who have never existed.

> Oscar Wilde: *The Decay of Lying.* (19th cent.)

Truth must necessarily be stranger than fiction; for fiction is the creation of the human mind and therefore congenial to it.

> G. K. Chesterton: *The Club of Queer Trades.* (20th cent.)

Literature and fiction are two entirely different things. Literature is a luxury; fiction is a necessity.

> G. K. Chesterton: *A Defence of Penny Dreadfuls*. (20th cent.)

Fidelity

Thou dost never depart from us, yet with difficulty do we return to Thee.

> St. Augustine: *Confessions*, 8, 3. (5th cent.)

Piteous, sad, wise, and true as steel.

> Chaucer: *Legend of Good Women*. (14th cent.)

> For this proverb is ever new
> That strong locks maken true.

> John Gower: *Confessio Amantis*, 5. (14th cent.)

Thou, O Lord, Thou alone art most faithful in all things, and besides Thee there is no other such.

> Thomas a Kempis: *The Imitation of Christ*, 3, 45. (15th cent.)

They who wish to live happily and in perfect fidelity, must accustom themselves to live according to reason, rule and obedience, not according to their own inclinations.

> St. Francis de Sales: *Spiritual Conferences*, 1. (17th cent.)

To love God in sugar—little children would do as much; but to love Him in wormwood, that is the test of our fidelity.

> St. Francis de Sales: *Letters to Persons in the World*, 5, 5. (17th cent.)

Lay a garland on my hearse of the dismal yew;
Maidens, willow branches bear; say I died true:
My love was false, but I was firm from my hour of birth;
Upon my buried body lay lightly gentle earth.

> Francis Beaumont: *Aspatia's Song from the Maid's Tragedy*, 2, 2. (17th cent.)

Fight

See Combat

Finding

Fast bind, fast find.

> John Heywood: *Proverbs*, 1, 3. (16th cent.)

He findeth that seeks.

> John Heywood: *Proverbs*, 1, 10. (16th cent.)

Find things ere they be lost.

> John Heywood: *Proverbs*, 1, 11. (16th cent.)

Finger

At my finger's end.

> John Heywood: *Proverbs*, 1, 6. (16th cent.)

Fire

Burnt child fire dreadeth.

> John Heywood: *Proverbs*, 2, 2. (16th cent.)

No fire without some smoke.

> John Heywood: *Proverbs*, 2, 5. (16th cent.)

Leap out of the frying pan into the fire.

> John Heywood: *Proverbs*, 2, 5. (16th cent.)

The fire that kindles also burns.

> R. H. Benson: *The Conventionalists*. (20th cent.)

Fish

When fish are soft, the largest you should prize;
When hard, the most healthy those of smallest size.

> School of Salerno, Code of Health. (11th cent.)

The great fish [eat] the small.

> Alexander Barclay: *The Ship of Fools*. (16th cent.)

Nother fish, nor flesh, nor good red herring.

> John Heywood: *Proverbs,* 1, 10. (16th cent.)

Fish is cast away that is cast in dry pools.

> John Heywood: *Proverbs,* 1, 11. (16th cent.)

All is fish that cometh to net.

> John Heywood: *Proverbs,* 1, 11. (16th cent.)

The fish with ease into the net doth glide,
But to get out the way is not so wide.

> Bl. Robert Southwell: *Lewd Love is Loss.* (16th cent.)

Fishing

It is ill fishing before the net.

> John Heywood: *Proverbs,* 1, 11. (16th cent.)

Flag

Furl that banner! True, 'tis gory,
Yet 'tis wreathed around with glory,
And 'twill live in song and story,
    Though its folds are in the dust.

> Abram Ryan: *The Conquered Banner.* (19th cent.)

They say I do not love thee,
    Flag of my native land;
Whose meteor folds above me,
    To the free breeze expand;
Thy broad stripes proudly streaming,
And thy stars so brightly gleaming.

> C. C. Pise: *The American Flag.* (19th cent.)

Up to the breeze of the morning I fling you,
    Blending your folds with the dawn in the sky;
There let the people behold you, and bring you
    Love and devotion that never shall die.
        Proudly, agaze at your glory, I stand,
        Flag o' my land! flag o' my land!

> T. A. Daly: *Flag o' My Land.* (20th cent.)

Lift up the banner red
With the blood of heroes shed
In victory!
Lift up the banner blue
As heaven, and as true
In constancy!
Lift up the banner white
As sea foam in the light
Of liberty;
The banner of the triple hue,
The banner of the red and white and blue,
Bright ensign of the free!

> Conde B. Pallen: *The Raising of the Flag.* (20th cent.)

This is the song of the wind as it came
Tossing the flags of the nations to flame.

> Alfred Noyes: *The Avenue of the Allies.* (20th cent.)

Flattery

What cannot praise effect in mighty minds,
When flattery soothes and when ambition blinds!

> Dryden: *Absalom and Achitophel.* (17th cent.)

Flesh

Let our flesh die, that in it all that is sinful may die; and, as though living again from the dead, let us rise to new works and a new life.

> St. Ambrose: *On the Duties of the Clergy,* 1, 185. (4th cent.)

The flesh is the apparel of the soul, which is clothed with a body as a garment.

> St. Ambrose: *Hexaem.* 6, 39. (4th cent.)

For the flesh is not life to itself, but the soul is the life of the flesh. The soul is not life to itself, but God is the life of the soul. . . . And if the soul live after God, then doth the flesh live rightly after the soul.

> St. Augustine: *Sermon 156,* 6, 6. (5th cent.)

Not to fulfil the desires of the flesh.

> St. Benedict: *Rule,* 4. (One of his "tools of good works") (6th cent.)

For men have ever a likerous appetite
On lower thing to perform their de-
light
Than on their wives, be they never so
fair,
Nor never so true, nor so debonair.
Flesh is so newfangel, with mis-
chaunce,
That we can in no thing have plesaunce
That tendeth unto virtue any while.

> Chaucer: *The Maunciples Tale.* (14th cent.)

The fraile flesh, whose nature is
Ay ready for the sporne and fall,
The firste foeman is of all.
It warreth night, it warreth day,
So that a man hath never rest.

> John Gower: *Confessio Amantis,* 5. (14th cent.)

See also Body and Soul

Flight

He would fain flee, but he wanteth
feathers.

> John Heywood: *Proverbs,* 1, 11. (16th cent.)

To all swift things for swiftness did I
sue;
Clung to the mane of every whistling
wind.

> F. Thompson: *The Hound of Heaven.* (19th cent.)

Flock

But we, O Lord, are Thy little flock: do
Thou keep possession of us. Spread
forth Thy wings, and let us shelter under
them. Be Thou our glory; let us be loved
because of Thee and let Thy word be
feared in us.

> St. Augustine: *Confessions,* 10, 36. (5th cent.)

Florence, Italy

Rejoice, Florence, because thy fame is
flown
Over earth and sea, winging the
heavenly vault,
And even through hell's regions it is
known.

> Dante: *Inferno, Canto 26.* (Tr. Binyon) (14th cent.)

Many love justice, yet haste not to shoot
The word, being well advisèd, from
the bow;
But on thy people's lips it leapeth
out.

Many to bear the common burden are
slow;
But thy folk answer to the call un-
bid,
Crying, I gird me to the task and go.

Rejoice now, thou hast reason, thou
amid
Thy riches, thou at peace, thou wise
of will!
That I speak truth, the event cannot
keep hid.

> Dante: *Purgatorio, Canto 6.* (Poet's eulogy of the city that banished him) (Tr. Binyon) (14th cent.)

Flower

But when they had unloosed the linen
band
Which swathed the Egyptian's body,
—lo! was found
Closed in the wasted hollow of her
hand
A little seed, which sown in English
ground
Did wondrous snow of starry blossoms
bear,
And spread rich odors through our
springtide air.

> Oscar Wilde: *Athanasia.* (19th cent.)

Antonio Sarto ees buildin' a wall,
But maybe he nevva gon' feenish at all.
Eet sure won'ta be
Teell flower an' tree

An' all kinda growin' theengs sleep een
   da fall.

> T. A. Daly: *The Blossomy Barrow.* (20th
> cent.)

Flute

The soft complaining flute.

> Dryden: *A Song for St. Cecilia's Day.*
> (17th cent.)

Fog

The yellow fog came creeping down
The bridges, till the houses' walls
Seemed changed to shadows, and St.
   Paul's
Loomed like a bubble o'er the town.

> Oscar Wilde: *Impression du Matin.* (19th
> cent.)

Fold

Behold
The time is now! Bring back, bring
   back
Thy flocks of fancies, wild of whim.
O lead them from the mountain-track
   Thy frolic thoughts untold,
O bring them in—the fields grow
   dim—
And let me be the fold.

> Alice Meynell: *The Fold.* (20th cent.)

Folklore

There is something about peasant traditions, and even about peasant legends,
which knows how to keep close to the
earth. It is a mark of true folklore that
even the tale that is evidently wild is
eminently sane.

> G. K. Chesterton: *The Common Man.*
> (20th cent.)

Folly

We were deceived by the wisdom of the
serpent, but we are freed by the foolishness of God.

> St. Augustine: *De Doctrina Christiana,* 1,
> 14, 13. (4th cent.)

It were a folly to put my finger too far
in the fire.

> John Heywood: *Proverbs,* 2, 2. (16th cent.)

Shoot folly as it flies.

> Pope: *An Essay on Man,* 1. (18th cent.)

When I am old and tutored by
   The grim experience of days;
When I have proved men in their
      ways,
Oh, do not let the dreamer die.

When I have learned aside to toss
   The foolish things that wise men
      hate,
Lest littleness should hold me great,
Be mine the folly of the Cross.

> Enid Dinnis: *A Franciscan Prayer.* (20th
> cent.)

Food

Eggs newly laid and broths of richest
   juice,
With ruby wine, increase of strength
   produce.

> School of Salerno, Code of Health. (11th
> cent.)

God never sendeth mouth but He
sendeth meat.

> John Heywood: *Proverbs,* 1, 4. (16th cent.)

Where coin is not common, commons
must be scant.

> John Heywood: *Proverbs,* 2, 1. (16th cent.)

Old fish and young flesh doth men best
feed.

> John Heywood: *Proverbs,* 2, 4. (16th cent.)

See also Dining; Eating; Meal

Fool

Well, well, try anything once, come
   hot, come cold,
If we're not foolish young, we're foolish old.

> Chaucer: *The Knight's Tale.* (Tr. Coghill)
> (14th cent.)

Fools cannot hold their tongue.

> Chaucer: *Romaunt of the Rose.* (14th cent.)

A fool may eke a wise man often guide.

> Chaucer: *Troilus and Criseyde.* (14th cent.)

For by his tongue a fool is often known.

> Lydgate: *Troy Book,* 2. (15th cent.)

I never saw fool yet that thought himself other than wise. For as it is one spark of soberness left in a drunken head, when he perceiveth himself drunk and getteth him fair to bed, so if a fool perceive himself a fool, that point is no folly, but a little spark of wit.

> St. Thomas More. (16th cent.)

There is no fool to ten old fool.

> John Heywood: *Proverbs,* 2, 2. (16th cent.)

A fool's bolt is soon shot.

> John Heywood: *Proverbs,* 2, 3. (16th cent.)

They that think none ill, are soonest beguiled.

> John Heywood: *Proverbs,* 2, 5. (16th cent.)

Fools are more hard to conquer than persuade.

> Dryden: *Absalom and Achitophel.* (17th cent.)

You'll ne'er convince a fool himself is so.

> Sir Samuel Garth. (18th cent.)

Fools rush in where angels fear to tread.

> Pope: *An Essay on Criticism,* 3. (18th cent.)

You beat your pate, and fancy wit will come;
Knock as you please, there's nobody at home.

> Pope: *Epigram.* (18th cent.)

The fool is happy that he knows no more.

> Pope: *An Essay on Man,* 2. (18th cent.)

No creature smarts so little as a fool.

> Pope: *An Epistle to Dr. Arbuthnot.* (18th cent.)

Foot

He thinketh his feet be where his head shall never come.

> John Heywood: *Proverbs,* 1, 11. (16th cent.)

It is the feet of clay that make the gold of the image precious.

> Oscar Wilde: *The Picture of Dorian Gray,* 15. (19th cent.)

Fop

True fops help nature's work, and go to school,
To file and finish God-Almighty's fool.

> Dryden: *The Man of Mode,* Epilogue. (17th cent.)

Force

What force cannot effect, fraud shall devise.

> Richard Crashaw: *Sospetto d'Herode.* (17th cent.)

Force rules the world, and not opinion; but opinion is that which makes use of force.

> Pascal: *Pensées,* 24. (17th cent.)

In the kingdom of scholars force is powerless; force is only master of external action.

> Pascal: *Pensées.* (17th cent.)

Material force is the *ultima ratio* of political society everywhere. Arms alone can keep the peace.

> Card. Newman: *Discussions and Arguments.* (19th cent.)

Foreigner

A foreigner is a man who laughs at everything except jokes. He is perfectly entitled to laugh at anything, so long as he realizes, in a reverent and religious spirit, that he himself is laughable.

> G. K. Chesterton: *What I Saw in America.* (20th cent.)

Foresight

One good forewit is worth two after wits.

> John Heywood: *Proverbs,* 1, 8. (16th cent.)

Forgiveness

There are many kinds of alms the giving of which helps us to obtain pardon for our sins; but none is greater than that by which we forgive from our heart a sin that some one has committed against us.

> St. Augustine: *Enchiridion,* 72. (5th cent.)

And is He not more ready to pardon than we to sin? And is He not the Physician and we the sick, the Bearer of our iniquities?

> St. Catherine of Siena: *Letter to Neri di Landoccio.* (14th cent.)

Forgiven and forgotten.

> John Heywood: *Proverbs,* 2, 3. (16th cent.)

Not light of credit to reports,
  Revenge he never sought,
But would forgive, and did forget
  The wrongs that were him wrought.

> Thomas Prideaux: *Elegy for Stephen Gardiner, Lord Bishop of Winchester.* (16th cent.)

How easy 'tis for parents to forgive!
With how few tears a pardon might be won
From nature, pleading for a darling son!

> Dryden: *Absalom and Achitophel.* (17th cent.)

She hugg'd the offender, and forgave the offence.

> Dryden: *Cymon and Iphigenia.* (17th cent.)

Kings can forgive, if rebels can but sue.

> Dryden: *Prologue to His Royal Highness.* (17th cent.)

And, dying, bless the hand that gave the blow.

> Dryden: *The Spanish Friar,* 2, 2. (17th cent.)

To err is human, to forgive divine.

> Pope: *An Essay on Criticism,* 2. (18th cent.)

No true penitent forgets or forgives himself: an unforgiving spirit towards himself is the very price of God's forgiving him.

> Card. Newman: *Sermons on Subjects of the Day.* (19th cent.)

  Only Heaven
Means crowned, not conquered, when
    it says
  "Forgiven."

> Adelaide Procter: *A Legend of Provence.* (19th cent.)

Yet what returns of love did I endure,
When to be pardon'd seem'd almost more sweet
Than aye to have been pure!

> Coventry Patmore: *Victory in Defeat.* (19th cent.)

So humble things, Thou hast borne for us, O God,
Left'st Thou a path of lowliness untrod?
Yes, one, till now; another Olive-Garden.
For we endure the tender pain of pardon,—
One with another we forbear. Give heed,
Look at the mournful world Thou hast decreed.
The time has come. At last we hapless men
Know all our haplessness all through.
  Come, then,

Endure undreamed humility: Lord of
heaven,
Come to our ignorant hearts and be
forgiven.

Alice Meynell: *Veni Creator.* (19th cent.)

My patient God, forgive!
Praying Thy pardon sweet
I lay a lonely heart
Before Thy feet.

Ethna Carbery: *Mea Culpa.* (19th cent.)

See also Sin, Remission of

Forgotten

Out of sight, out of mind.

John Heywood: *Proverbs,* 1, 3. (16th cent.)

Seldom seen, soon forgotten.

John Heywood: *Proverbs,* 1, 11. (16th
cent.)

Form

For everything owes its being to form.
(Omne namque esse ex forma est.)

Boethius: *De Trinitate,* 2. (6th cent.)

All things, whatever their abode,
Have order among themselves; this
form it is
That makes the universe like unto God.

Dante: *Paradiso, Canto 1.* (Tr. Binyon).
(14th cent.)

Fornication

Fornication is a lapse from one marriage
into many.

Clement of Alexandria: *Stromateis.* (2nd
cent.)

A man who is unmarried let him be
taught not to commit fornication but
either to marry lawfully or to abide
steadfast.

St. Hippolytus: *The Apostolic Tradition,*
16, 7. (3rd cent.)

Fortitude

Fortitude is the disposition of soul which
enables us to despise all inconveniences
and the loss of things not in our power.

St. Augustine: *On Free Will,* 1, 27. (4th
cent.)

See also Courage

Fortune

The pride of fickle fortune spareth
none,
And, like the floods of swift Euripus
borne,
Oft casteth mighty princes from their
throne,
And oft the abject captive doth adorn.

Boethius: *De Consolatione Philosophiae,*
2, 1. (6th cent.)

For I think that fortune, when she is
opposite, is more profitable to men than
when she is favorable. For in prosperity,
by a show of happiness and seeming to
caress, she is ever false, but in adversity
when she showeth herself inconstant by
changing, she is ever true.

Boethius: *De Consolatione Philosophiae,*
2, 8. (6th cent.)

The Wisdom that transcendeth all, and
made
The heavens and gave them guides
to rule them right,
So that each splendor should the
other aid

With equal distribution of the light
In like sort also a general minister
Set over this world's glory and fond
delight,

From time to time those vain goods to
transfer
From people to people, and from
class to class,
Beyond cunning of mortals to deter.

Dante: *Inferno, Canto 7.* (Tr. Binyon)
(14th cent.)

Gifts of fortune,
That pass as a shadow on the wall.

Chaucer: *The Marchantes Tale.* (14th cent.)

For sure it is, if fortune wills to flee,
No man may stay her course or keep his hold;
Let no one trust a blind prosperity.

Chaucer: *The Monk's Tale.* (Tr. Coghill) (14th cent.)

Fortune hath in her honey gall.

Chaucer: *The Monk's Tale.* (14th cent.)

Variant fortune was; aye in short space
Her wheel was ready to turn without let.

Lydgate: *Assembly of Gods.* (15th cent.)

Fortune is stately, solemn, proud, and high:
And riches giveth, to have service therefor.
The needy beggar catcheth an half-penny:
Some man a thousand pound, some less some more.
But for all that she keepeth ever in store,
From every man some parcel of his will,
That he may pray therefor and serve her still.

St. Thomas More: *Against My Lady Fortune.* (16th cent.)

No change of fortune's calms
Can cast my comforts down;
When fortune smiles, I smile to think
How quickly she will frown.

Bl. Robert Southwell: *Content and Rich.* (16th cent.)

The sea of fortune doth not ever flower,
She draws her favours to the lowest ebb;
Her tides hath equal times to come and go,
Her loom doth weave the fine and coarsest web.

No joy so great, but runneth to an end;
No hap so hard, but may in fine amend.

Bl. Robert Southwell: *Times Go By Turns.* (16th cent.)

No wind so changeable, no sea so wavering,
As giddy fortune in reeling vanities;
Now mad, now merciful, now fierce, now favoring,
In all things mutable but mutabilities.

Bl. Robert Southwell: *Fortune's Falsehood.* (16th cent.)

Here on earth nothing is stable,
Fortune's changes well are known;
Whilst as youth doth then enable,
Let your seeds of joy be sown:
After death, when you are gone,
Joy and pleasure is there none.

Thomas Lodge: *Robert, Second Duke of Normandy.* (16th cent.)

When fortune favors, none but fools will dally.

Dryden: *The Duke of Guise, Epilogue.* (17th cent.)

Ill fortune seldom comes alone.

Dryden: *Cymon and Iphigenia.* (17th cent.)

See also Chance; Luck

Fox

When the fox preacheth then beware your geese.

John Heywood: *Proverbs,* 2, 7. (16th cent.)

France

I know nothing about whether God loves or hates the English, but this I do know that they will all be driven from France, except those who perish here.

St. Jeanne d'Arc. (Reply to question at her interrogation.) (15th cent.)

France has always been at the point of dissolution. She has found the only method of immortality. She dies daily.

G. K. Chesterton: *Tremendous Trifles,* 9. (20th cent.)

Francis of Assisi, Saint

The Assisian, who kept plighted faith
    to three,
To song, to sanctitude, and poverty.

> F. Thompson: *To My Godchild*. (19th cent.)

Francis De Sales, Saint

He the sweet Sales, of whom we
    scarcely ken
How God he could love more, he so
    loved men.

> F. Thompson: *To My Godchild*. (19th cent.)

Francis Xavier, Saint

Lo! on the slope of yonder shore
    Beneath that lonely shed,—
A saint hath found his conflicts o'er,
    And laid his dying head!

. . . .

Oh! to be one, through life and death,
    In Christ, with such as thee:
And when I yield my latest breath,
    Do thou remember me!

> M. Bridges: *St. Francis Xavier*. (19th cent.)

Franciscan Order

The rule and life of the Minor Brothers
is this, namely, to observe the holy gospel of our Lord Jesus Christ by living in
obedience, without property, and in
chastity.

> St. Francis of Assisi: *Rule*. (1223)

The brothers shall appropriate nothing
to themselves, neither a house nor place
nor anything. And as pilgrims and
strangers in this world . . . let them go
confidently in quest of alms. . . . This,
my dearest brothers, is the height of the
most sublime poverty, which has made
you heirs and kings of the kingdom of
heaven: poor in goods but exalted in
virtue.

> St. Francis of Assisi: *Rule, ch. 6*. (1223)

These are the arms of our service. (Haec
sunt arma militiae nostrae.)

> Motto of the Franciscan Order. (Cross)
> (Medieval)

Silent, lonely, and with no company,
    One before and one after, as on their
        way
    Journey the Minor Friars, journeyed
        we.

> Dante: *Inferno, Canto 23*. (Tr. Binyon)
> (14th cent.)

Franks

Have the Franks for friends, but not for
neighbors.

> Emperor Nicephorus I. (9th cent.)

Fraternity

For all we are Christ's creatures, and
    of His coffers rich,
And brethren as of one blood, as well
    beggars as earls.
For on Calvary of Christ's blood, Chris-
    tendom gan spring,
And blood brethren we became there,
    of one body won,
As *quasimodo geniti*, and gentlemen
    each one,
No beggar or serving-boy among us,
    save sin made us so.

> Wm. Langland: *Vision of Piers Plowman*
> (B. 11, 192-7). (Tr. C. Dawson) (14th cent.)

We all know the important things,
though we all violate and neglect them.
Gigantic industry, abysmal knowledge
are needed for the discovery of the tiny
things—the things that seem hardly
worth the trouble. Generally speaking,
the ordinary man should be content with
the terrible secret that men are men—
which is another way of saying that they
are brothers.

> G. K. Chesterton: *Illustrated London News*.
> (20th cent.)

What is required of those who believe
in God is a witness of God; and what

the world demands and expects of the Christian is first and foremost to see the love of truth and brotherly love made genuinely present in and through man's personal life—to see a gleam of the gospel shining in the one place where the crucial test and crucial proof are to be found, namely the obscure context of relations between person and person.

> J. Maritain: *The Range of Reason.* (20th cent.)

Fraud

> But since fraud is a vice of man's alone,
>> It more offends God: so are lowest set
>> The fraudulent, and the heavier is their groan.
>
> Dante: *Inferno, Canto II.* (Tr. Binyon) (14th cent.)

Freedom

Canst thou ever imperiously impose anything upon a free mind? Canst thou remove a soul settled in firm reason from the quiet state which it possesseth?

> Boethius: *De Consolatione Philosophiae,* 2, 6. (6th cent.)

For there is this difference between the kings of nations and the Roman emperor, that the former have slaves for their subjects, the latter free men. And therefore, in all your acts, your first object should be to maintain justice, your second to preserve a perfect liberty. You ought to value the liberty of those whom you are appointed to judge as jealously as though it were your own; and if you would not be wronged yourself by your superiors, you should guard with respect the liberty of your inferiors.

> Pope St. Gregory the Great: *Letters,* 11, 4. (To the imperial official Leontius) (6th cent.)

This liberty, or this principle of all our liberty, is God's most precious gift to human nature, for by it we are made happy here as men, and happy as gods in the beyond.

> Dante: *Monarchy,* 1. (Referring to the gift of freewill) (14th cent.)

Ah! Freedom is a noble thing.
Freedom makes man to have liking:
Freedom all solace to man gives:
He lives at ease that freely lives.

> John Barbour: *The Bruce.* (14th cent.)

Freedom which in no other land will thrive,
Freedom an English subject's sole prerogative.

> Dryden: *Threnodia Augustalis.* (17th cent.)

I am as free as nature first made man,
Ere the base laws of servitude began,
When wild in woods the noble savage ran.

> Dryden: *The Conquest of Granada,* 1. (17th cent.)

It is not good to be too free. It is not good to have everything one wants.

> Pascal: *Pensées,* 25. (17th cent.)

O freedom! once thy flame hath fled,
It never lights again.

> Thomas Moore: *Weep on, Weep on.* (19th cent.)

Oh! remember life can be
No charm for him who lives not free.

> Thomas Moore: *Before the Battle.* (19th cent.)

The most certain test by which we judge whether a country is really free is the amount of security enjoyed by minorities.

> Lord Acton: *The History of Freedom in Antiquity.* (19th cent.)

No freedom is so great as that of the children of God who are fast bound by the perfect law of love and liberty.

> R. H. Benson: *The Friendship of Christ.* (20th cent.)

To the bulk of mankind the absence of law appears freedom; it is only a minority that has ever willingly recognized that in the most perfect law is the most perfect liberty.

John Ayscough: *The Universe.* (20th cent.)

What matters death, if freedom be not dead?
    No flags are furled, if freedom's flag be furled.
Who fights for freedom, goes with joyful tread
    To meet the fires of hell against him hurled,
And has for captain Him whose thorn-wreathed head
    Smiles from the Cross upon a conquered world.

Joyce Kilmer: *The Peacemaker.* (20th cent.)

We should be grateful to St. Gregory VII, to Innocent III, to Gregory IX, to Boniface VIII, for having given this unhappy world the strongest testimony of the rights and power of the spirit. Canossa will always remain the consolation of free minds.

J. Maritain: *The Things That Are Not Caesar's.* (20th cent.)

See also Liberty

Freedom and Slavery

Hardest servitude has he
That's jailed in arrogant liberty;
And freedom, spacious and unflawed,
Who is walled about with God.

F. Thompson: *To the English Martyrs.* (19th cent.)

Freedom of Religion

It is a fundamental human right, a privilege of nature, that every man should worship according to his own convictions: one man's religion neither harms nor helps another man. It . . . is certainly no part of religion to compel religion.

Tertullian: *To Scapula,* 2. (Proconsul of Africa.) (3rd cent.)

You do not compel a man to worship what he does not wish, being unwilling . . . each one should be free to defend faithfully and keep his own principles.

St. Ambrose: *Letters,* 17. (To the emperor Valentinian.) (384)

And whereas the enforcing of the conscience in matters of religion hath frequently fallen out to be of dangerous consequence in those commonwealths where it has been practised, and for the more quiet and peaceful government of this province, and the better to preserve mutual love and amity among the inhabitants, no person within this province, professing to believe in Jesus Christ, shall be anyways troubled, molested, or discountenanced for his or her religion, or in the free exercise thereof.

Toleration Act of the Colonial Assembly of Maryland. (1649)

Religious liberty is not the negative right of being without any particular religion, just as self-government is not anarchy. It is the right of religious communities to the practice of their own duties, the enjoyment of their own constitution, and the protection of the law, which equally secures to all the possession of their own independence.

Lord Acton: *The Protestant Theory of Persecution.* (19th cent.)

Religious liberty, therefore, is possible only where the coexistence of different religions is admitted, with an equal right to govern themselves according to their own several principles. Tolerance of error is requisite for liberty; but freedom will be most complete where there is no actual diversity to be resisted, and no theoretical unity to be maintained, but where unity exists as the triumph of truth, not of force, through the victory of the Church, not through the enactment of the state.

Lord Acton: *The Protestant Theory of Persecution.* (19th cent.)

The Church indeed deems it unlawful to place the various forms of divine wor-

ship on the same footing as the true religion, but does not on that account
condemn those rulers who, for the sake
of securing some great good or of hin-
dering some great evil, patiently allow
custom or usage to be a kind of sanction
for each kind of religion having its place
in the state. In fact, the Church is wont
to take earnest heed that no one shall be
forced to embrace the Catholic faith
against his will, for as St. Augustine
wisely reminds us, *Man cannot believe
otherwise than of his own freewill.*

> Pope Leo XIII: *Immortale Dei.* (Nov. 1,
> 1885)

Another liberty is widely advocated,
namely, liberty of conscience. If by this
is meant that everyone may, as he
chooses, worship God or not, it is sufficiently refuted by the arguments already
adduced. But it may also be taken to
mean that every man in the state may
follow the will of God and, from a consciousness of duty and free from every
obstacle, obey His commands. This indeed is true liberty, a liberty worthy of
the sons of God, which nobly maintains
the dignity of man and is stronger than
all violence or wrong—a liberty which
the Church has always desired and held
most dear.

> Pope Leo XIII: *Libertas Praestantissimum.*
> (June 20, 1888)

See also Church and State in the United
States; Toleration

Freedom of Speech

It is not fitting for an emperor to deny
freedom of speech, or for a bishop not
to say what he thinks. There is no quality in emperors so popular and estimable
as the willingness to cherish freedom
even in those whom you have subdued
on the battlefield. The difference between good and bad emperors is that the
good love freedom; the bad slavery.

> St. Ambrose: *Letters*, 40. (To the emperor
> Theodosius.) (388)

Men have a right freely and prudently
to propagate throughout the state what
things soever are true and honorable, so
that as many as possible may possess
them; but lying opinions, than which
no mental plague is greater, and vices
which corrupt the heart and moral life,
should be diligently repressed by public
authority, lest they insidiously work the
ruin of the state.

> Pope Leo XIII: *Libertas Praestantissimum.*
> (June 20, 1888)

In regard . . . to all matters of opinion
which God leaves to man's free discussion, full liberty of thought and of
speech is naturally within the right of
everyone; for such liberty never leads
men to suppress the truth, but often to
discover it and make it known.

> Pope Leo XIII: *Libertas Praestantissimum.*
> (June 20, 1888)

It is not by any means self-evident upon
the face of it that an institution like the
liberty of speech is right or just. . . .
The theory of free speech, that truth is
so much larger and stranger and more
many-sided than we know of, that it is
very much better at all costs to hear every
one's account of it, is a theory which has
been justified upon the whole by experi-
ment, but which remains a very daring
and even a very surprising theory. It is
really one of the great discoveries of the
modern time; but once admitted, it is a
principle that does not merely affect
politics, but philosophy, ethics, and finally, poetry.

> G. K. Chesterton: *Robert Browning.* (20th
> cent.)

Freewill

If man does not have the free faculty to
shun evil and to choose good, then,
whatever his actions may be, he is not
responsible for them.

> St. Justin Martyr: *First Apology*, 43. (2nd
> cent.)

Not only in works, but also in faith, God has given man freedom of the will.

> Iranaeus: *Adversus haereses,* 4. (2nd cent.)

I find, then, that man was by God constituted free, master of his own will and power; indicating the presence of God's image and likeness in him by nothing so well as by this constitution of his nature. For it was not by his face, and by the lineaments of his body, though they were so varied in his human nature, that he expressed his likeness to the form of God; but he showed his stamp in that essence which he derived from God Himself (that is the spiritual, which answered to the form of God), and in the freedom and power of his will.

> Tertullian: *Tertullian Against Marcion,* 2, 5. (3rd cent.)

This also is clearly defined in the teaching of the Church, that every rational soul is possessed of freewill and volition; that it has a struggle to maintain with the devil and his angels, and opposing influences, because they strive to burden it with sins; but if we live rightly and wisely, we should endeavor to shake ourselves free of a burden of that kind.

> Origen: *De Principiis, Proem.* 5. (3rd cent.)

The power of choosing good and evil is within the reach of all.

> Origen: *De Principiis,* 2. (3rd cent.)

We are not constrained by servile necessity, but act with freewill, whether we are disposed to virtue or incline to vice.

> St. Ambrose: *Concerning Jacob,* 1, 1. (4th cent.)

But it does not follow that, though there is for God a certain order of all causes, there must therefore be nothing depending on the free exercise of our own wills, for our wills themselves are included in that order of causes which is certain to God, and is embraced by His foreknowledge, for human wills are also causes of human actions; and He Who foreknew all the causes of things would certainly among those causes not have been ignorant of our wills.

> St. Augustine: *The City of God,* 5, 9. (5th cent.)

The freedom of the will is then true freedom, when it does not serve vices and sins.

> St. Augustine: *The City of God,* 12, 6. (5th cent.)

Let us then first of all lay down this proposition and see whether it satisfies the question before us: that freewill, naturally assigned by the Creator to our rational soul, is such a neutral power, as can either incline towards faith, or turn towards unbelief. Consequently a man cannot be said to have even that will with which he believes in God, without having received it; since this rises at the call of God out of the freewill which he received naturally when he was created. God no doubt wishes all men to be saved and to come into the knowledge of the truth; but yet not so as to take away from them freewill, for the good or evil use of which they may be most righteously judged.

> St. Augustine: *De Spiritu et Littera,* 58. (5th cent.)

But can these members of the human race to whom God promised deliverance and a place in the eternal kingdom be saved by the merits of their works? That is out of the question. For what good work can one do who is ruined, except so far as he has been delivered from his ruin? Can he do so by the free determination of his will? That, too, is out of the question. For it was by the evil use of his freewill that man destroyed both himself and his freewill.

> St. Augustine: *Enchiridion,* 30. (5th cent.)

Each of these, namely, faith and good works, is ours because it is the result of the free choice of our will, and yet each is the gift of the Spirit of faith and of charity to us.

St. Augustine: *Retractions,* 1, 23, 2. (5th cent.)

There can be no reasonable nature, unless it be endued with freewill. For that which naturally hath the use of reason hath also judgment by which it can discern of everything by itself, wherefore of itself it distinguisheth betwixt those things which are to be avoided, and those which are to be desired.

Boethius: *De Consolatione Philosophiae,* 5, 2. (6th cent.)

Freedom of will is nothing else than volition.

St. John of Damascus: *Exposition of the Orthodox Faith,* 3, 14. (8th cent.)

Man is master of his acts and of his willing or not willing, because of his deliberate reason, which can be bent to one side or another. And although he is master of his deliberating or not deliberating, yet this can only be by a previous deliberation; and since it cannot go on to infinity, we must come at length to this, that man's free will is moved by an extrinsic principle, which is above the human mind, to wit by God.

St. Thomas Aquinas: *Summa Theologica,* 1-2, 109, 2. (13th cent.)

Every Christian is bound to hold that acts which issue from a man's own will, namely all his human acts properly so called, are not subject to determinism.

St. Thomas Aquinas: *Letter to Reginald of Piperno.* (13th cent.)

A light is given you to know good
    and ill,
And freewill which, though oft dis-
    comfited
  In its first battlings with the stars'
      decree,
  Wins in the end all, be it but rightly
      bred.

Dante: *Purgatorio, Canto 16.* (Tr. Binyon) (14th cent.)

Of all the gifts God in His bounty ex-
    treme
  Made when creating, most conform-
    able
  To His own goodness, and in His
      esteem
Most precious, was the liberty of the
    will,
  With which creatures that are intel-
    ligent
  Were all endowed, they only, and
      are so still.

Dante: *Paradiso, Canto 5.* (Tr. Binyon) (14th cent.)

If any one saith that man's freewill moved and excited by God, by assenting to God exciting and calling, nowise cooperates towards disposing and preparing itself for obtaining the grace of justification; that it cannot refuse its consent, if it would, but that as something inanimate it does nothing whatever and is merely passive; let him be anathema.

Council of Trent, Session 6, Canon 4. (Jan. 13, 1547)

If any one saith that since Adam's sin the freewill of man is lost and extinguished; or that it is a thing with only a name, yea a name without a reality, a figment in fine, introduced into the Church by Satan; let him be anathema.

Council of Trent, Session 6, Canon 5. (Jan. 13, 1547)

We have freedom to do good or evil; yet to make choice of evil, is not to use, but to abuse our freedom.

St. Francis de Sales: *Treatise on the Love of God,* 12, 10. (17th cent.)

God presses us but does not oppress our liberty.

St. Francis de Sales: *Treatise on the Love of God,* 2, 12. (17th cent.)

There are no galley slaves in the royal vessel of divine love—every man works his oar voluntarily.

Jean Pierre Camus: *The Spirit of St. Francis de Sales,* 7, 3. (17th cent.)

That our will is free is self-evident.

> René Descartes: *Principles of Philosophy*, 1. (17th cent.)

As the Catholic Church declares in the strongest terms the simplicity, spirituality, and immortality of the soul, so with unequaled constancy and publicity she ever asserts its freedom also. These truths she has always taught, and has sustained them as a dogma of faith, and whenever heretics or innovators have attacked the liberty of man, the Church has defended it and protected this noble possession from destruction.

> Pope Leo XIII: *Libertas Praestantissimum*. (June 20, 1888)

According to most philosophers, God in making the world enslaved it. According to Christianity, in making it He set it free. God had written, not so much a poem, but rather a play; a play He had planned as perfect, but which had necessarily been left to human actors and stage-managers, who had since made a great mess of it.

> G. K. Chesterton: *Orthodoxy*. (20th cent.)

It must be remembered that the modern world has done deep treason to the eternal intellect by believing in the swing of the pendulum. A man must be dead before he swings. It has substituted an idea of fatalistic alternation for the medieval freedom of the soul seeking truth.

> G. K. Chesterton: *What's Wrong with the World*. (20th cent.)

See also Grace and Freewill

French Language

> And French she spake full fair and fetishly,
> After the school of Stratford-atte-Bowe,
> For French of Paris was to her unknowe.
>
> Chaucer: *Canterbury Tales: Prologue*. (14th cent.)

Friar

> A barefoot friar all in brown,
> Weather-beat face and storm-rent gown,
> Tattered hood over shaven crown,
> Travelled as the sun goes down.
>
> Rosa Mulholland (Lady Gilbert): *The Irish Franciscan*. (19th cent.)

Friday

> And on a Friday fell all this mischance.
>
> Chaucer: *The Nonne Preestes Tale*. (14th cent.)

Friend

> For herein especially does a friend differ from a flatterer; the flatterer speaks to give pleasure, but the friend refrains from nothing, even that which gives pain.
>
> St. Basil: *Letters*, 20. (4th cent.)

> Rightly has a friend been called 'the half of my soul.'
>
> St. Augustine: *Confessions*, 4, 6. (5th cent.)

> O God, Who by the grace of the Holy Ghost hast poured the gifts of charity into the hearts of Thy faithful people; grant unto Thy servants NN., for whom we beseech Thy mercy, health of body and soul; that they may love Thee with all their strength, and with perfect affection fulfil thy pleasure.
>
> Roman Missal, Collect for Devoted Friends (Gregorian, 6th to 8th cent.)

> My son, keep well thy tongue, and keep thy friend.
>
> Chaucer: *The Maunciples Tale*. (14th cent.)

> A fresh, a free, a friendly man.
>
> John Gower: *Confessio Amantis*, 5. (14th cent.)

> Prove thy friend ere thou have need.
>
> John Heywood: *Proverbs*, 1, 11. (16th cent.)

Love's sweetest mark, laud's highest
    theme, man's most desired light,
To love Him, life; to leave Him, death;
    to live in Him, delight.
He mine, by gift; I His, by debt; thus
    each, to other's due.
First friend He was; best friend He is;
    all times will try Him true.

Bl. Robert Southwell: *A Child, my Choyse.*
(16th cent.)

A friend in words, where deeds be
    dead,
Is like a well that water wants;
And he that with fair words is fed,
    Doth look for fruits of wither'd
    plants.
But there as words and deeds agree,
    Accept that friend and credit me.

Anonymous: *Untitled Poem.* (Add. MS.
15, 225; possibly by Robert Southwell)
(Guiney, 282) (16th cent.)

My guide, philosopher, and friend.

Pope: *An Essay on Man,* 4. (18th cent.)

When I remember all
    The friends, so link'd together,
I've seen around me fall,
    Like leaves in wintry weather,
I feel like one who treads alone
    Some banquet-hall deserted,
Whose lights are fled, whose garlands
    dead,
    And all but he departed!

Thomas Moore: *Oft in the Stilly Night.*
(19th cent.)

The friends, who in our sunshine live,
    When winter comes, are flown;
And he who has but tears to give,
    Must weep those tears alone.

Thomas Moore: *Oh, Thou! Who Dry'st
the Mourner's Tear.* (19th cent.)

From quiet homes and first beginning,
    Out to the undiscovered ends,
There's nothing worth the wear of
    winning
    But laughter and the love of friends.

Hilaire Belloc: *Sonnets and Verse:
Dedicatory Ode.* (20th cent.)

Friend and Enemy

Just as the flattery of a friend can pervert, so the insult of an enemy can sometimes correct.

St. Augustine: *Confessions,* 9, 8. (5th cent.)

For if good fortune makes your friends
    for you
Ill fortune makes them enemies for
    sure.

Chaucer: *The Monk's Tale.* (Tr. Coghill)
(14th cent.)

The world is large when its weary
    leagues two loving hearts divide;
But the world is small when your
    enemy is loose on the other side.

J. B. O'Reilly: *Distance.* (19th cent.)

Friendship

True friendship ought never to conceal
what it thinks.

St. Jerome: *Letters,* 81, 1. (4th cent.)

For there is no true friendship unless
you weld it between souls that cleave
together through that charity which is
shed in our hearts by the Holy Ghost
Who is given to us.

St. Augustine: *Confessions,* 4, 4. (5th cent.)

Blessed is the man that loves thee, and
his friend in thee and his enemy for
thee. For he alone never loseth a friend,
to whom all men are dear for His sake
who is never lost.

St. Augustine: *Confessions,* 4, 9. (5th cent.)

I want my friend to miss me as long as
I miss him.

St. Augustine: *Letter* 2. (4th cent.)

Friendship is more than is catell.

Chaucer: *The Romaunt of the Rose.* (14th
cent.)

A faithful friend I fain would find,
    To find him there he might be found,
But now is the world wext so unkind,
    That friendship is fall to the ground.

Juliana Berners. (15th cent.)

Be merry, man! and take not far in
mind
  The wavering of this wretched world
    of sorrow;
To God be humble, and to thy friend
    be kind,
  And with thy neighbors gladly lend
    and borrow.

William Dunbar: *No Treasure Without
Gladness.* (16th cent.)

Of all the heavenly gifts, that mortal
men commend,
What trusty treasure in the world can
countervail a friend?
            . . . . . .
O friendship, flower of flowers: O
lively sprite of life,
O sacred bond of blissful peace, the
stalwart staunch of strife.

Nicholas Grimald: *Of Friendship.* (Guiney,
96) (16th cent.)

Friendship requires the exchange of
good, not evil.

St. Francis de Sales: *Introduction to the
Devout Life,* 3, 22. (17th cent.)

Friendships begun in this world will be
taken up again, never to be broken off.

St. Francis de Sales: *Letters to Persons in
the World,* 3, 4. (17th cent.)

It is absolutely necessary for friendship
that reciprocity should exist between the
two who love each other, and that this
friendship should be contracted through
the action of reason.

St. Francis de Sales: *Spiritual Conferences,*
4. (17th cent.)

For 'tis the bliss of friendship's holy
state
To mix their minds, and to communicate;
Though bodies cannot, souls can penetrate.

Dryden: *Eleonora.* (17th cent.)

For friendship, of itself a holy tie,
Is made more sacred by adversity.

Dryden. (17th cent.)

A friendship that like love is warm;
A love like friendship, steady.

Thomas Moore: *How Shall I Woo?* (19th
cent.)

Oh, call it by some better name,
For friendship sounds too cold.

Thomas Moore: *Oh Call It by Some Better
Name.* (19th cent.)

It is mutual respect which makes friendship lasting.

Card. Newman: *Parochial and Plain
Sermons,* 1. (19th cent.)

It was not I who sought friends, but
friends who sought me.

Card. Newman: *Apologia pro Vita Sua,* 1.
(19th cent.)

I thank eternal God that you are mine,
Who are His too: courageous and
divine
Must friendship be, through this great
grace of God;
And have eternity for period.

Lionel Johnson: *To Certain Friends.* (19th
cent.)

In a true friendship, the weaker of the
two must always, little by little, become
conformed not only to the habits of life,
but to the habits of thought, of the
stronger.

R. H. Benson: *The Friendship of Christ.*
(20th cent.)

The essence of a perfect friendship is
that each friend reveals himself utterly
to the other, flings aside his reserves,
and shows himself for what he truly is.

R. H. Benson: *The Friendship of Christ.*
(20th cent.)

Human friendships usually take their
rise in some external detail. We catch
a phrase, we hear an inflection of a voice,
we notice the look of the eyes, or a
movement in walking; and the tiny experience seems to us like an initiation
into a new world.

R. H. Benson: *The Friendship of Christ.*
(20th cent.)

Humility, obedience, simplicity—these are the virtues on which the divine friendship, as well as mere human friendships, alone can thrive.

> R. H. Benson: *Christ in the Church.* (20th cent.)

Sometimes a fragile word
  A friendship breaks or seals.
Who knows the word that hurts
  Must know its twin that heals.

The heart whose god is God,
  Though it has many foes,
Is kept by friendly thorns
  More upright than a rose.

> Sister Miriam: *Sometimes a Fragile Word.* (20th cent.)

Frivolity

Religion might approximately be defined as the power which makes us joyful about the things that matter. Fashionable frivolity might, with a parallel propriety, be defined as the power which makes us sad about the things that do not matter.

> G. K. Chesterton: *The Common Man.* (20th cent.)

Frugality

Let those reckon themselves richer who in enduring frugality have been stronger; It is better to want less than to receive more (*melius est enim minus egere quam plus habere*).

> St. Augustine: *Letter 211* (his *Rule*). (5th cent.)

Frugality is a handsome income.

> Erasmus: *Colloquia.* (16th cent.)

The frugal crone, whom praying priests attend,
Still strives to save the hallow'd taper's end,

Collects her breath, as ebbing life retires.

> Pope: *Moral Essays,* 1. (18th cent.)

Frustration

While I beat the bush,
Other men catch the birds.

> John Heywood: *Proverbs,* 1, 3. (16th cent.)

Fullness

As full as a tun.

> John Heywood: *Proverbs,* 1, 11. (16th cent.)

Fundamentalism

The fundamentalists are funny enough, and the funniest thing about them is their name. For, whatever else the fundamentalist is, he is not fundamental. He is content with the bare letter of Scripture—the translation of a translation, coming down to him by the tradition of a tradition—without venturing to ask for its original authority.

> G. K. Chesterton: *All is Grist.* (20th cent.)

Funeral

See Burial; Dead, The; Death

Fur

The fur that warms a monarch warmed a bear.

> Pope: *An Essay on Man,* 3. (18th cent.)

Future

Most men prefer and strive for the present, we for the future.

> St. Ambrose: *On the Duties of the Clergy,* 1, 217. (4th cent.)

G

Gain

All the gain of this world is the loss of souls.

> St. Ambrose: *Letters*, 2. (379)

Not venture, not have.

> John Heywood: *Proverbs*, 1, 11. (16th cent.)

Evil gotten good never proveth well.

> John Heywood: *Proverbs*, 1, 11. (16th cent.)

Soon gotten, soon spent; ill gotten, ill spent.

> John Heywood: *Proverbs*, 2, 6. (16th cent.)

Gaity

A very merry, dancing, drinking,
Laughing, quaffing, and unthinking time.

> Dryden: *The Secular Masque*. (17th cent.)

Children are not gay and lighthearted, except now and then—just as men and women are not serious, except now and then.

> R. H. Benson: *Come Rack! Come Rope!* (20th cent.)

Gambling

Let a bishop, or presbyter, or deacon who indulges himself in dice, or drinking, either leave off those practices, or let him be deprived. If a sub-deacon, a reader, or a singer does the like, either let him leave off, or let him be suspended; and so for one of the laity.

> Ecclesiastical Canons of the Holy Apostles, 42-43. (4th cent.)

The devil invented gambling.

> St. Augustine: *The City of God*, 4. (5th cent.)

Hazard is very mother of lyings
And of deceit, and cursed forswearings.

> Chaucer: *The Pardoneres Tale*. (14th cent.)

Nought lay down, nought take up.

> John Heywood: *Proverbs*, 1, 11. (16th cent.)

Nought won by the tone, nought won by the tother.

> John Heywood: *Proverbs*, 1, 11. (16th cent.)

I might put my winning in mine eye,
And see never the worse.

> John Heywood: *Proverbs*, 1, 11. (16th cent.)

Such and such a man spends his life playing every day for a small stake. Give him every morning the money that he may gain during the day, on condition that he will not play—you will make him unhappy. It will perhaps be said that what he seeks is the amusement of play, not gain. Let him play then for nothing; he will lose his interest and be wearied.

> Pascal: *Pensées*, 5. (17th cent.)

And once or twice to throw the dice
Is a gentlemanly game,
But he does not win who plays with sin
In the Secret House of Shame.

> Oscar Wilde: *The Ballad of Reading Gaol*, 3. (19th cent.)

Garden

My heart shall be my garden. Come my
    own,
    Into thy garden; thine be happy
    hours
    Among my fairest thoughts, my
    tallest flowers,
From root to crowning petal thine
    alone.

> Alice Meynell: *The Garden.* (19th cent.)

Generosity

O almighty and everlasting God, Who
in the abundance of Thy loving kindness art wont to grant beyond the deserts
and desires of those who humbly pray to
Thee; pour down upon us Thy mercy,
forgiving us those things for which our
conscience is afraid, and adding those
things for which we dare not pray.

> Roman Missal, Collect for Eleventh Sunday
> after Pentecost. (Gelasian, 5th to 7th cent.)

Genius

Great geniuses have their empire, their
renown, their greatness, their victory,
and their lustre, and have no need of
material grandeurs, with which they
have no relation. They are not seen with
the eyes, but with the mind; that is
enough.

> Pascal: *Pensées,* 19. (17th cent.)

Great wits are sure to madness near
    allied
And thin partitions do their bounds
    divide.

> Dryden: *Absalom and Achitophel.* (17th
> cent.)

Time, place, and action may with pains
    be wrought;
But genius must be born, and never
    can be taught.

> Dryden: *To Mr. Congreve.* (17th cent.)

One science only will one genius fit,
So vast is art, so narrow human wit.

> Pope: *An Essay on Criticism,* 1. (18th
> cent.)

Strange power of genius, that can
    throw
Round all that's vicious, weak, and low,
Such magic lights, such rainbow dyes
As dazzle ev'n the steadiest eyes.

> Thomas Moore: *Rhymes on the Road.*
> (19th cent.)

What an impostor genius is;
How, with that strong, mimetic art,
    Which forms its life and soul, it
    takes
All shapes of thought, all hues of
    heart,
    Nor feels, itself, one throb it wakes;
How like a gem its light may smile
    O'er the dark path by mortals trod,
Itself a mean worm the while,
    As crawls at midnight o'er the sod.

> Thomas Moore: *Rhymes on the Road.*
> (19th cent.)

Great things are done by devotion to one
idea; there is one class of geniuses, who
would never be what they are, could they
grasp a second.

> Card. Newman: *Historical Sketches, 3.*
> (19th cent.)

It is difficult to say how far an absolute
moral courage in acknowledging intui-
tions may not be of the very nature of
genius: and whether it may not be described as a sort of interior sanctity
which dares to see and confess to itself
that it sees, though its vision should
place it in a minority of one. Everybody
feels that genius is, in a sort, infallible.

> Coventry Patmore: *Religio Poetae.* (19th
> cent.)

A commonplace about men of genius
is that they usually have religious dispositions. It would be strange were it
otherwise, seeing that genius is nothing
but the power of discerning the things
of the spirit.

> Coventry Patmore: *Religio Poetae.* (19th
> cent.)

I have nothing to declare except my genius.

> Statement of Oscar Wilde to the customs officers when he landed in America, 1882. (19th cent.)

Genius is the ability to think in a very large number of categories.

> A Saying of H. Belloc. (20th cent.)

Gentleman

He never yet a boorish thing had said
In all his life to any, come what might;
He was a true, a perfect gentle-knight.

> Chaucer: *Canterbury Tales: Prologue.* (Tr. Coghill) (14th cent.)

Look who that is most virtuous alway,
Prive and apart, and most intendeth aye
To do that gentle deedes that he can,
And take him for the greatest gentle man.

> Chaucer: *Tale of the Wyf of Bathe.* (14th cent.)

His tribe were God Almighty's gentle-men.

> Dryden: *Absalom and Achitophel,* 1. (17th cent.)

Ours are a sort of modest, inoffensive people, who neither have sense nor pretend to any, but enjoy a jovial sort of dullness; they are commonly known in the world by the name of honest, civil gentlemen.

> Pope: *Letter to William Wycherley.* (18th cent.)

It is almost a definition of a gentleman to say he is one who never inflicts pain.

> Card. Newman: *Idea of a University.* (19th cent.)

If a man is a gentleman, he knows quite enough, and if he is not a gentleman, whatever he knows is bad for him.

> Oscar Wilde: *A Woman of No Importance,* 3. (19th cent.)

If a man's mind is erroneously possessed with the idea that he is a great violinist, that need not prevent his being a gentleman and an honest man. But if once his mind is possessed in any strong degree with the knowledge that he is a gentleman, he will soon cease to be one.

> G. K. Chesterton: *All Things Considered.* (20th cent.)

There is no such thing as being a gentleman at important moments; it is at unimportant moments that a man is a gentleman. At important moments he ought to be something better.

> G. K. Chesterton: *A Handful of Authors.* (20th cent.)

Gentleness

If there be any good in gentleness, I trowe it to be only this, that it seemeth a manner imposed to gentle men, that they should not disgrace or degenerate from the virtues of their noble kindred.

> Chaucer: *Boethius,* 3. (14th cent.)

Nothing appeases an enraged elephant so much as the sight of a little lamb.

> St. Francis de Sales: *Introduction to the Devout Life,* 3, 8. (17th cent.)

When you encounter difficulties and contradictions, do not try to break them, but bend them with gentleness and time.

> St. Francis de Sales: *Letters to Persons in Religion,* 1, 6. (17th cent.)

He who can preserve gentleness amid pains, and peace amid worry and multitude of affairs, is almost perfect.

> St. Francis de Sales: *Letters to Persons in Religion,* 2, 25. (17th cent.)

It takes more oil than vinegar to make a good salad.

> Jean Pierre Camus: *The Spirit of St. Francis de Sales,* 2, 13. (17th cent.)

Geometry

The science of geometry is said to have been discovered first by the Egyptians, because when the Nile overflowed and and all their lands were overspread with mud, its origin in the division of the land by lines and measurements gave the name to the art. Later, being carried further by the keenness of philosophers, it measured the spaces of the seas, the heavens, and the air.

> St. Isidore: *Etymologies*, 3, 10. (7th cent.)

Ghost

They who see the Flying Dutchman never, never reach the shore.

> J. B. O'Reilly: *The Flying Dutchman*. (19th cent.)

A grey haunted wind is blowing in the hall,
And stirring through the shadowy spears upon the wall,
The drinking horn goes round from shadowy lip to lip—
And about the golden methers shadowy fingers slip.

> Ethna Carbery: *The Shadow House of Lugh*. (19th cent.)

The dreamy little villages, where by the fires at night,
Old sanachies with ghostly tale the boldest hearts affright;
The crooning of the windblast is the wailing banshee's cry,
And when the silver hazels stir they say the fairies sigh.

> James B. Dollard: *Song of the Little Villages*. (20th cent.)

I do not see ghosts; I only see their inherent probability.

> G. K. Chesterton: *Tremendous Trifles*. (20th cent.)

Giant

Theirs was the giant race before the flood.

> Dryden: *To Mr. Congreve*. (17th cent.)

Gibbons, James Cardinal

Often have I thanked God that in this latter quarter of the nineteenth century Cardinal Gibbons has been given to us as a primate, as a leader. Catholic of Catholics, American of Americans, a bishop of his age and of his country, he is to America what Leo is to Christendom. . . . He has made the Church known to the people of America; he has demonstrated the fitness of the Church for America, the natural alliance existing between the Church and the freedom-loving democratic institutions of America.

> Archbishop Ireland. (1893)

Gift

It is the intention which makes a gift rich or poor, and gives things a value.

> St. Ambrose: *On the Duties of the Clergy*, 1, 149. (4th cent.)

For whoso giveth a gift, or doth a grace,
Does it betimes, his thank is well the more.

> Chaucer: *Legend of Good Women: Prologue*. (14th cent.)

Throw no gift again at the giver's head.

> John Heywood: *Proverbs*, 1, 11. (16th cent.)

For gifts are scorn'd where givers are despis'd.

> Dryden: *The Hind and the Panther*, 3. (17th cent.)

Take gifts with a sigh: most men give to be paid.

> J. B. O'Reilly: *Rules of the Road*. (19th cent.)

Gift-Horse

Never look a gift horse in the mouth. (Equi donati dentes non inspiciuntur.)

> St. Jerome: *On the Epistle to the Ephesians*. (5th cent.)

Gifts of God

How blessed and wonderful are the gifts of God, beloved. Life in immortality, joyousness in justice, truth in confidence, faith in trustfulness, continence in holiness. And all these things fall within our understanding. And what shall we say of the things that are being prepared for those who persevere. Only the Creator and Father of the ages, the all-holy One, knows their greatness and beauty.

> Pope St. Clement I: *Letter to the Corinthians*, 35, 1-4. (1st cent.)

Thanks be to Thee, my Joy and my Glory and my Hope and my God: thanks be to Thee for Thy gifts: but do Thou preserve them in me. Thus Thou wilt preserve me, and the things Thou hast given me shall increase and be made perfect, and I shall be with Thee: because even that I exist is Thy gift.

> St. Augustine: *Confessions*, 1, 20. (5th cent.)

Out of God's gifts, then, we make gifts to God, and from us He receives what He first gave us. Our state of beggarhood would, unless He first gave us something, remain absolute emptiness.

> St. Augustine: *Sermon 115*, 1. (5th cent.)

It is easy to want things from the Lord and yet not want the Lord Himself; as though the gift could ever be preferable to the Giver!

> St. Augustine: *In Ps. 76, Enarr. 1, 2.* (5th cent.)

Gift better than Himself God doth not know,
  Gift better than his God no man can see;
This gift doth here the giver given bestow,
  Gift to this gift let each receiver be:
God is my gift, Himself He freely gave me,
God's gift am I, and none but God shall have me.

> Bl. Robert Southwell: *The Nativity of Christ.* (16th cent.)

Lift up your hearts! Yes, I will lift
  My heart and soul, dear Lord, to Thee,
Who every good and perfect gift
  Vouchsaf'st so lavishly and free.

All that is best, from Thee comes down
  On us, with rich and ample store,
Thy bounteous hands our wishes crown
  With good, increasing more and more.

> Anonymous: *Sursum Corda.* (In Caswall's *Lyra Catholica*) (19th cent.)

My soul! what hast thou done for God?
  Look o'er thy misspent years and see;
Sum up what thou hast done for God,
  And then what God hath done for thee.

He made thee when He might have made
  A soul that would have loved Him more;
He rescued thee from nothingness,
  And set thee on life's happy shore.

> F. Faber: *The Gifts of God.* (19th cent.)

Gifts of the Holy Ghost

The gift of the Holy Ghost, by coming into the soul endows it with prudence, temperance, justice, and fortitude, and at the same time strengthens it against every kind of temptation by his sevenfold gift.

> Pope St. Gregory I: *Moralia in Job*, 2, 26. (5th cent.)

The Holy Ghost gives wisdom against folly, understanding against dullness, counsel against rashness, fortitude against fears, knowledge against ignorance, piety against hardness of our heart, and fear against pride.

> Pope St. Gregory I: *Moralia in Job*, 2, 26. (5th cent.)

The gifts excel the virtues, not in what they do, but in how they do it.

> St. Thomas Aquinas: *Summa Theologica*, 1-2, 68, 2. (13th cent.)

Giving

> So that the more she gave away,
> The more, y-wis, she had alway.

Chaucer: *The Romaunt of the Rose.* (14th cent.)

Better to give than take.

John Heywood: *Proverbs,* 1, 5. (16th cent.)

He giveth oft who gives what's oft refused.

Richard Crashaw: *Epigrammata Sacra.* (17th cent.)

God to His promise, not our practice, gives.

John Dryden: *Britannia Rediviva.* (17th cent.)

Gladstone, William Ewart

The faculty of concealing his thoughts in words, of separating conviction from argument, was not the least striking of the great statesman's talents.

Agnes Repplier: *Article in Life.* (20th cent.)

Glory

Glory is wont to exalt, not to humble.

Tertullian: *Women's Dress.* (3rd cent.)

For if, contrary to our belief, men wholly perish, there is no glory at all, since he to whom it is said to belong is nowhere extant.

Boethius: *De Consolatione Philosophiae,* 2, 7. (6th cent.)

To the greater glory of God. (Ad majorem Dei gloriam.)

Pope St. Gregory the Great: *Dialogues,* 1. (Motto of the Jesuits) (6th cent.)

How swiftly passes away the glory of the world!

Thomas a Kempis: *The Imitation of Christ,* 1, 3. (15th cent.)

Short is the glory that is given and taken by men; and sorrow followeth ever the glory of the world.

Thomas a Kempis: *The Imitation of Christ,* 2, 6. (15th cent.)

But true glory and holy joy is to glory in Thee and not in one's self; to rejoice in Thy name, and not to be delighted in one's own virtue, nor in any creature, save only for Thy sake.

Thomas a Kempis: *The Imitation of Christ,* 3, 40. (15th cent.)

To God alone be glory. Soli Deo gloria.

Latin phrase. (Medieval)

The greatest baseness of man is his seeking for glory: but even this is the greatest indication of his excellence; for, whatever possession he may have on earth, whatever health and essential comfort he may have, he is not satisfied without the esteem of men.

Pascal: *Pensées,* 2. (17th cent.)

> Who pants for glory finds but short repose;
> A breath revives him, or a breath o'erthrows.

Pope: *The First Epistle of the Second Book of Horace.* (18th cent.)

Solomon! where is thy throne? It is gone in the wind.
Babylon! where is thy might? It is gone in the wind.
Like the swift shadows of noon, like the dreams of the blind,
Vanish the glories and pomps of the earth in the wind.

James C. Mangan: *Gone in the Wind.* (19th cent.)

> Go where glory waits thee:
> But, while fame elates thee,
> O, still remember me!

Thomas Moore: *Go Where Glory Waits Thee.* (19th cent.)

See also Fame

Gluttony

Greediness closed Paradise; it beheaded John the Baptist.

Pope Innocent III: *De Contemptu Mundi,* 2, 18. (12th cent.)

To kindle and blow the fire of lechery, That is annexed unto gluttony.

Chaucer: *The Pardoneres Tale.* (14th cent.)

O gluttony, full of cursedness, O cause first of our confusion, O original of our damnation.

Chaucer: *The Pardoneres Tale.* (14th cent.)

Herodes, (whoso well the story sought,)
When he of wine was réplete at his feast,
Right at his own table he gave his hest
To slay the baptist John full guiltless.

Chaucer: *The Pardoneres Tale.* (14th cent.)

Gluttony is no sin if it doesn't injure health.

Doctrine condemned by Pope Alexander VII. (17th cent.)

Fill the capacious squire and deep divine.

Pope: *Moral Essays, 3.* (18th cent.)

Goad

Folly it is to spurn against a prick.

John Heywood: *Proverbs,* 2, 5. (16th cent.)

God

I—Blessed Trinity

Baptize in the name of the Father, and of the Son, and of the Holy Spirit, in running water.

Teaching of the Twelve Apostles, 7. (2nd cent.

O Lord, almighty God . . . I bless You, I glorify You through the eternal and heavenly High Priest Jesus Christ, Your beloved Son, through Whom be glory to You together with Him and the Holy Spirit, both now and for the ages to come. Amen.

Anonymous: *The Martyrdom of St. Polycarp.* (His prayer before death) (ca. 156)

Thou unbegotten God, the Sire,
And Thou, the sole-begotten Son,
Who, with the Spirit's sacred fire,
Art everlasting, three in one.

St. Hilary of Poitiers: *Deus Pater Ingenite.* (Tr. D. Donahoe) (4th cent.)

Sweet Lord, O love Thy holy name;
I hear my mother Church proclaim
The Spirit, Sire and Son the same,
One God eternal.

St. Hilary of Poitiers: *Ad Coeli Clara.* (Tr. D. Donahoe) (4th cent.)

Now the Catholic faith is this: that we worship one God in Trinity, and Trinity in Unity, neither confounding the Persons, nor dividing the substance, for there is one Person of the Father, another of the Son, and another of the Holy Ghost; but the godhead of the Father, of the Son, and of the Holy Ghost is one, the glory equal, the majesty co-eternal. . . .

Athanasian Creed. (Formerly attr. to St. Athanasius, of unknown authorship) (ca. 4th or 5th cent.)

It is not easy to find a term which appropriately defines such great excellence, unless it is better to say that this Trinity is one God from Whom, through Whom, and in Whom all things exist. (Cf. Rom. 11, 36)

St. Augustine: *De Doctrina Christiana,* 1, 5, 5. (4th cent.)

In the Father resides unity, in the Son equality, and in the Holy Ghost the perfect union of unity and equality. These three qualities are all one because of the Father, all equal because of the Son, and all united because of the Holy Ghost.

St. Augustine: *De Doctrina Christiana,* 1, 5, 5. (4th cent.)

For the Christian it is enough to believe that the cause of all created things, in heaven and on earth, visible or invisible, is none other than the goodness of the Creator, Who is the one and true God; that there is no being whatsoever but God Himself or what comes from Him; that God is a Trinity, that is to say, the Father, the Son begotten of the Father, and the Holy Spirit proceeding from the same Father, but one and the same Spirit of the Father and the Son.

St. Augustine: *Enchiridion, 9.* (5th cent.)

Since the Father is God, the Son is God, and the Holy Spirit is God, and since there are in God no points of difference distinguishing Him from God, He differs from none of the others. But where there are no differences there is no plurality; where there is no plurality there is unity.

Boethius: *De Trinitate, 5.* (6th cent.)

O Trinity of blessed light,
O Unity of princely might,
The fiery sun now goes his way;
Shed Thou within our hearts Thy ray.

Roman Breviary, Trinity Sunday, Hymn *O lux beata Trinitas* at Vespers. (Tr. J. Neale) (Adaptation of hymn *Jam sol recedit igneus* by St. Ambrose) (4th cent.)

O Thou Who dost all nature sway,
Dread Trinity in Unity,
Accept the trembling praise we pay
To Thy eternal majesty.

Roman Breviary, Trinity Sunday, Hymn *Tu Trinitatis Unitas* at Lauds. (Tr. E. Caswall) (Adaptation of hymn attributed to Pope St. Gregory) (6th cent.)

Great God of boundless mercy hear;
Thou ruler of this earthly sphere;
In substance one, in persons three,
Dread Trinity in Unity!

Roman Breviary, Hymn *Summae Parens clementiae* for Saturday at Matins. (Tr. J. Chambers) (Ambrosian, 7th cent.)

O God, by Whose command is swayed
This ordered world which Thou hast made;

Parent of heavenly clemency,
In nature One, in persons Three;
Assist us while our minds we raise,
Inflamed with Thy immortal praise;
That with our sober thoughts, we may
Forever our thanksgiving pay.

Roman Breviary, Trinity Sunday, Hymn *Summae Parens clementiae* at Matins (Tr. from Primer, 1706) (Adaptation of two preceding) (after 8th cent.)

O most holy Trinity, have mercy upon us. O Lord, cleanse our sins. O Master, forgive our transgressions. Visit us, O holy One, and heal our infirmities, for Thy name's sake.

Byzantine Horologion, Troparion. (ca. 6th to 8th cent.)

The Father is my trust, the Son is my refuge, the Holy Ghost is my protection. O holy Trinity, glory to Thee.

Byzantine Horologion, Troparion at Nocturns. (ca. 6th to 8th cent.)

O most holy Trinity, that art Might in one substance and Kingdom undivided, be gracious to me a sinner. Confirm and instruct my heart, and take from me all defilement. Illumine my thoughts that I may ever praise, sing and worship, and say, One holy, one Lord Jesus Christ, unto the glory of God the Father. Amen.

Byzantine Horologion, Troparion at Vespers. (ca. 6th to 8th cent.)

For no other generation is like to the generation of the Son of God, since no other is Son of God. For though the Holy Spirit proceeds from the Father, yet this is not generative in character but processional. This is a different mode of existence, alike incomprehensible and unknown, just as is the generation of the Son.

St. John of Damascus: *Exposition of the Orthodox Faith,* 1, 8. (8th cent.)

For we recognize one God, but only in the attributes of Fatherhood, Sonship, and Procession, both in respect of cause and effect and perfection of subsistence, that is, manner of existence, do we perceive difference.

St. John of Damascus: *Exposition of the Orthodox Faith*, 1, 8. (9th cent.)

It is very fitting to praise the Trinity, supremely divine, the eternal Father Who has created all things, the coeternal Word who was begotten by the Father before all time and without being separated from Him, and the Holy Ghost Who proceeds from the Father from eternity.

Byzantine Horologion, Troparion Triadikon at Nocturns. (Metrophanes, 9th cent.)

First and last of faith's receiving,
Source and Sea of man's believing,
God, Whose might is all potential,
God, Whose truth is truth's essential,
Good supreme in Thy subsisting,
Good in all Thy seen existing,
Over all things, all things under,
Touching all, from all asunder.
Center Thou, but not intruded,
Compassing and yet included.

Hildebert of Lavardin: *Prayer to the Holy Trinity*. (Tr. H. Kynaston) (11th cent.)

The Catholic Faith confesses that the 'properties' of the Persons are identical with the Persons themselves; and that the Persons themselves are nothing else than one God, one divine Substance, one divine Nature, one divine and supreme Majesty.

St. Bernard: *De Consideratione*, 5, 8. (12th cent.)

How can plurality consist with unity, or unity with plurality? To examine the fact closely is rashness, to believe it is piety, to know it is life, and life eternal.

St. Bernard: *De Consideratione*, 5, 8. (12th cent.)

Among all things called one, the Unity of the Divine Trinity holds the first place.

St. Bernard: *De Consideratione*, 5. (12th cent.)

Confess we all the Unity,
Adoring still the Trinity
     With equal reverence,
Asserting ever Persons three,
Differing each personally,
     With mutual difference.

Adam of St. Victor: *Profitentes Unitatem*. (Tr. anon. from *Paradise of the Soul*) (12th cent.)

The manner whereby God is in Himself as known in knower is described by the terms *generation, father, son, word,* all of which imply a specific likeness. But the manner whereby God is in Himself as beloved in lover is described by the terms *breath* or *spirit:* in this sense the Creed bids us believe in the Spirit.

St. Thomas Aquinas: *Compendium of Theology*, 46. (13th cent.)

The term *procession* within the Blessed Trinity signifies a coming forth from a principle and not necessarily a going out to an object, though the coming forth of the Holy Spirit, a coming forth of love, does imply a going out to another, namely to the beloved. And because the eternal comings forth are the cause and type of all creation, so it is that the begetting of the Son is the exemplar of all making, and the Father's loving of the Son is the exemplar of all granting of love to creatures. Hence the Holy Spirit Who is the love whereby the Father loves the Son, is also the love whereby God loves creatures and imparts to them his goodness.

St. Thomas Aquinas: *Commentary on the Sentences*, 1, 14, 1, 1. (13th cent.)

The divine nature is really and entirely identical with each of the three persons, all of whom can therefore be called one: *I and the Father are one* (John, 10, 30).

St. Thomas Aquinas: *Disputations concerning the Union of the Word Incarnate*, 2. (13th cent.)

That One and Two and Three Who ever shall
     Live and reign ever as Three and Two and One,

Not circumscribed but circumscrib-
ing all,
Thrice by those spirits, by each and
every one,
Was hymned with such melodious
acclaim,
'Twere full reward for all good ever
done.

Dante: *Paradiso, Canto 14.* (Tr. Binyon)
(14th cent.)

O triple Light, which in a single star
Shining on them their joy can so expand,
Look down upon this storm wherein
we are!

Dante: *Paradiso, Canto 31.* (Tr. Binyon)
(14th cent.)

O almighty and everlasting God, Who
hast given to Thy servants grace, in the
confession of the true faith, to acknowledge the glory of the eternal Trinity,
and in the power of Thy majesty, to
worship the Unity; grant that by steadfastness in the same faith we may evermore be defended from all adversities.

Roman Missal, Collect for Trinity Sunday.
(First Sunday after Pentecost) (Feast was
extended to Latin Church by Pope John
XXII in 14th cent.) (10th cent.)

Trinity blessed, Deity coequal,
Unity sacred, God one eke in essence,
Yield to Thy servant, pitifully calling
Merciful hearing.

Virtuous living did I long relinquish,
Thy will and precepts miserably scorn-
ing,
Grant to me, sinful patient, repenting,
Healthful amendment.

Richard Stanyhurst: *To the Trinity.*
(Guiney, 190) (16th cent.)

Whence shall we then begin
To sing, or write of this,
Where no beginning is?
Or if we enter in,
When shall we end? The end is endless
bliss;

Thrice happy we, if well so rich a
thread we spin.

Sir John Beaumont: *Ode to the Blessed
Trinity.* (17th cent.)

O Thou immortal Light divine!
Dread Trinity in Unity!
Almighty One! almighty Trine!
Give ear to Thy creation's cry.

. . . .

Three Persons!—one Immensity
Encircling utmost space and time!
One Greatness, Glory, Sanctity,
One everlasting Truth sublime!

Anonymous: *Aeterna Lux, Divinitas.* (Tr.
E. Caswall) (Modern)

O blessed Trinity!
Thy children dare to lift their hearts to
Thee,
And bless Thy triple Majesty!
Holy Trinity!
Blessed equal Three,
One God, we praise Thee.

F. Faber: *The Holy Trinity.* (19th cent.)

Father! Creator! Lord Most High!
Sweet Jesus! Fount of clemency!
Blest Spirit! Who dost sanctify!
God ruling over all!

F. Faber: *The Life of our Lord.* (19th
cent.)

Have mercy on us, God most High!
Who lift our hearts to Thee,
Have mercy on us worms of earth,
Most holy Trinity!

Most ancient of all mysteries!
Before Thy throne we lie;
Have mercy now, most merciful,
Most holy Trinity!

F. Faber: *God.* (19th cent.)

The Church is accustomed most fittingly
to attribute to the Father those works of
the divinity in which power excels, to
the Son those in which wisdom excels,
and those in which love excels to the
Holy Ghost. Not that all perfections and
external operations are not common to
the divine Persons; for *the operations of*

the Trinity are indivisible, even as the essence of the Trinity is indivisible (St. Augustine: *De Trin.* 1, 4). But by a certain comparison and a kind of affinity between the operations and the properties of the Persons these operations are attributed or, as it is said, 'appropriated' to one Person rather than to the others.

Pope Leo XIII: *Divinum Illud.* (May 4, 1897)

In God there can be no selfishness, because the Three Selves of God are three subsistent relations of selflessness, overflowing and superabounding in joy in the perfection of their gift of their one life to one another.

Thomas Merton: *Seeds of Contemplation.* (20th cent.)

II—*Creator; First Cause; Lord*

It has been the universal opinion of mankind from ancient times, from the earliest tradition of the protoplast, that there is one God the Maker of heaven and earth. . . . For nature reveals its Author, the work suggests the Artist, and the world manifests its Designer. But the whole Church throughout the world has received this tradition from the apostles.

St. Irenaeus: *Against the Heresies,* 2, 9, 1. (2nd cent.)

Now nobody denies what nobody is ignorant of—for nature herself is teacher of it—that God is the Maker of the universe, and that it is good, and that it is man's by free gift of its Maker.

Tertullian: *De Spectaculis,* 2. (3rd cent.)

I believe in one God, the Father almighty, Maker of heaven and earth. . . .

Niceno-Constantinopolitan Creed. (4th cent.)

God is the only one who has no beginning.

St. Jerome: *Letters.* (4th cent.)

We praise Thee, O God; we acknowledge Thee to be the Lord. (Te Deum laudamus; te Dominum confitemur.)

St. Nicetas (?): *Te Deum laudamus.* (ca. 400)

You are—and You are the God and Lord of all that You have created: and before Your face stand the causes of all things transient and the changeless principles of all things that change, and the eternal reasons of all the things of unreason and of time.

St. Augustine: *Confessions,* 1, 6. (5th cent.)

The cause of things, therefore, which makes but is not made, is God; but all other causes both make and are made.

St. Augustine: *The City of God,* 5, 9. (5th cent.)

The very order, disposition, beauty, change, and motion of the world and of all visible things proclaim that it could only have been made by God, the ineffably and invisibly great and the ineffably and invisibly beautiful.

St. Augustine: *The City of God,* 11, 4, 2. (5th cent.)

O Thou, That dost the world in lasting
  order guide,
Father of heaven and earth, Who makest time swiftly slide,
And, standing still, Thyself, yet fram'st all moving laws,
Who to Thy work wert moved by no external cause:
But by a sweet desire, where envy hath no place,
Thy goodness moving Thee to give each thing his grace,
Thou dost all creatures' forms from highest patterns take,
From Thy fair mind the world fair like Thyself doth make.

Boethius: *De Consolatione Philosophiae,* 3, 9. (Poetic abridgment of the first part of Plato's *Timaeus.*) (6th cent.)

Neither would the course of nature continue so certain, nor would the different parts hold so well-ordered motions in due places, times, causality, spaces and qualities, unless there were One Who, Himself remaining quiet, disposeth and ordereth this variety of motions. This, Whatsoever it be, by Which things created continue and are moved, I call God, a name Which all men use.

Boethius: *De Consolatione Philosophiae,* 3, 12. (6th cent.)

Earth's mighty Maker, Whose command
Raised from the sea the solid land;
And drove each billowy heap away,
And bade the earth stand firm for aye.

Roman Breviary, Hymn *Telluris alme Conditor* for Tuesday at Vespers. (Tr. anon., from the Hymnal Noted) (Attr. to Pope St. Gregory I, 6th cent.)

O sovereign Lord of nature's might,
Who bad'st the water's birth divide;
Part in the heavens to take their flight,
And part in ocean's deep to hide.

Roman Breviary, Hymn *Magnae Deus potentiae* for Thursday at Vespers. (Tr. W. Courthope) (Attr. to Pope St. Gregory I, 6th cent.)

Maker of man, Who from Thy throne
Dost order all things, God alone;
By Whose decree the teeming earth
To reptile and to beast gave birth.

Roman Breviary, Hymn *Hominis superne Conditor* for Friday at Vespers. (Tr. J. Chambers) (Attr. to Pope St. Gregory I, 6th cent.)

God operates through secondary causes, but beyond shadow of doubt is quite able to manage without them.

St. Thomas Aquinas: *Disputations concerning Potency,* 6, 1. (13th cent.)

God works throughout all activity after the manner of all these three causes, final, efficient, and formal. First, He is end, aim, purpose. . . . Second, He is efficient cause. . . . All things act by

God's power, and He, therefore, is the efficient cause of all activity. . . . Third . . . the formal cause . . . He is the cause, not merely as providing the active form . . . but also as sustaining the form and power of everything.

St. Thomas Aquinas: *Summa Theologica,* 1, 105, 5. (13th cent.)

All events that take place in this world, even those apparently fortuitous or casual, are comprehended in the order of divine Providence, on which fate depends.

St. Thomas Aquinas: *Summa Theologica,* 1, 105, 5. (13th cent.)

Among all the causes, the end holds the primacy. From it the others take their actual causality, for no activity is without purpose. Since a final purpose is the cause of a proximate purpose, the ultimate end is the first of all causes.

St. Thomas Aquinas: *Contra Gentes,* 3, 17. (13th cent.)

Thou Great First Cause least understood,
    Who all my sense confin'd
To know but this, that Thou art good,
    And that myself am blind.

Alexander Pope: *Universal Prayer.* (18th cent.)

Thou art, O God, the life and light
    Of all this wondrous world we see,
Its glow by day, its smile by night,
    Are but reflections caught from Thee—
        Where'er we turn, Thy glories shine,
        And all things fair and bright are Thine.

Anonymous: *Thou Art O God the Life and Light.* (In Caswall's *Lyra Catholica*) (19th cent.)

Thou liv'st in all things, and around;
    To Thee external is their nought;
Thou of the boundless art the bound;
    And still creation is Thy thought.

In vain, O God, our wings we spread;
  So distant art Thou—yet so nigh.
Remains but this, when all is said,
  For Thee to live; in Thee to die.

Aubrey De Vere: *May Carols*, 3, 12. (19th cent.)

I admire Thee, Master of the
    tides,
  Of the yore-flood, of the year's
    fall;
The recurb and the recovery of the
    gulf's sides,
  The girth of it and the wharf
    of it and the wall;
Stanching, quenching ocean of a
    motionable mind;
Ground of being, and granite of it:
    past all
Grasp God, throned behind
Death with a sovereignty that heeds
  but hides, bodes but abides.

G. M. Hopkins: *The Wreck of the Deutschland*, 32. (19th cent.)

III—*His Eternity*

God's beginning in time to be called what He was not called before [sc. Lord], is manifestly a temporal denomination (*manifestum est relative dici*), not implying any accident in God, as though anything happened to Him, but decidedly implying accident in that in relation to which God begins to have some denomination.

St. Augustine: *De Trinitate*, 5, 16. (5th cent.)

God alone is completely immutable; for that reason true and proper eternity is His alone. Other things share in His eternity to the degree that His stillness possesses them.

St. Thomas Aquinas: *Summa Theologica*, I, 10, 3. (13th cent.)

O Lord! my heart is sick,
Sick of this everlasting change;
  And life runs tediously quick
Through its unresting race and
    varied range:

Change finds no likeness to itself in
    Thee,
And wakes no echo in Thy mute eternity.

F. Faber: *The Eternity of God*. (19th cent.)

IV—*His Existence*

For it is one thing to be persuaded of the existence of a thing, and quite another to know what it is.

St. Gregory of Nazianzen: *Orations*, 28, 5. (4th cent.)

Could any man be his own maker? Or is there any other channel through which being and life should flow into us, save that we are made by You, Lord, to Whom 'being' and 'being alive' are not two separate things, since infinite Being is identical with infinite Life?

St. Augustine: *Confessions*, 1, 6. (5th cent.)

For God is more truly thought than expressed; and He exists more truly than He is thought.

St. Augustine: *De Trinitate*, 7, 4, 7. (5th cent.)

God always is, nor has He been and is not, nor is but has not been, but as He never will not be; so He never was not.

St. Augustine: *De Trinitate*, 14, 15, 21. (5th cent.)

The whole nature of the universe itself which surrounds us, and to which we also belong, proclaims that it has a most excellent Creator, Who has given to us a mind and natural reason, whereby to see that things living are to be preferred to things that are not living; things that have sense to things that have not; things that have understanding to things that have not; things immortal to things mortal; things powerful to things impotent; things righteous to things unrighteous; things beautiful to things deformed; things good to things evil; things incorruptible to things corruptible; things unchangeable to things changeable; things invisible to things visible; things incorporeal to things corporeal; things blessed to things miserable.

> St. Augustine: *De Trinitate,* 15, 4. (5th cent.)

For the knowledge of God's existence has been implanted by Him in all my nature.

> St. John of Damascus: *Exposition of the Orthodox Faith,* 1, 1. (8th cent.)

For He does not belong to the class of existing things: not that He has no existence, but that He is above all existing things, nay even, above existence itself.

> St. John of Damascus: *Exposition of the Orthodox Faith,* 1, 4. (8th cent.)

Things then that are mutable are also wholly created. But things that are created must be the work of some maker, and the maker cannot have been created. For if He had been created, He also must surely have been created by someone, and so on until we arrive at something uncreated. The Creator, then, being uncreated, is also wholly immutable. And what could this be other than Deity?

> St. John of Damascus: *Exposition of the Orthodox Faith,* 1, 3. (8th cent.)

Even the very continuity of the creation and its preservation and government, teach us that there exists a Deity, Who supports and maintains and preserves and ever provides for this universe.

> St. John of Damascus: *Exposition of the Orthodox Faith,* 1, 3. (8th cent.)

For everything that is moved is moved by another thing. And who again is it that moves that? and so on to infinity until we at length arrive at something motionless. For the first mover is motionless, and that is the Deity.

> St. John of Damascus: *Exposition of the Orthodox Faith,* 1, 4. (8th cent.)

For everything that is, exists either through something or through nothing. But nothing exists through nothing. For it is altogether inconceivable that anything should not exist by virtue of something. Whatever is, then, does not exist except through something. Since this is true, either there is one Being, or there are more than one, through Which all things that are exist. . . . Since truth altogether excludes the supposition that there are more beings than one, through which all things exist, that Being through Which all exist must be one. . . . There is, then, some one Being Which alone exists in the greatest and highest degree of all. . . .

> St. Anselm: *Monologium,* 3. (Ontological argument) (11th cent.)

That than which nothing greater can be conceived, cannot exist in the understanding alone. For, suppose it exists in the understanding alone: then it can be conceived to exist in reality; which is greater. Therefore, if that than which nothing greater can be conceived exists in the understanding alone, the very Being than Which nothing greater can be conceived, is one than Which a greater can be conceived. But obviously this is impossible. Hence, there is no doubt that there exists a Being, than Which nothing greater can be conceived, and it exists both in the understanding and in reality.

> St. Anselm: *Proslogium,* 2. (11th cent.)

If you say that God is good, great, blessed, wise, or any such thing, the starting point is this: God is.

> St. Bernard: *On Consideration,* 5, 6. (12th cent.)

To look for the Most High beneath the summit of man's thought is absurd; to place Him there is impious. He must be sought beyond it, not on this side of it.

> St. Bernard: *On Consideration,* 5, 7. (12th cent.)

In fact he who questions whether God exists and whether He is powerful, wise, and good is not merely irreligious; he is lacking in faith and deserves to be taught his lesson by punishment.

John of Salisbury: *Policraticus*, 7, 7, 115. (12th cent.)

God's first effect is existence. All other effects presuppose and are based on that. He is pure existence. The existence of all other things partakes of His.

St. Thomas Aquinas: *Compendium Theologiae*, 68. (13th cent.)

To know that God exists in a general and confused way is implanted in us by nature, inasmuch as God is man's beatitude. For man naturally desires happiness, and what is naturally desired by man must be naturally known to him. This, however, is not to know absolutely that God exists.

St. Thomas Aquinas: *Summa Theologica*, 1, 2, 1. (13th cent.)

The existence of God, in so far as it is not self-evident to us, can be demonstrated from those of His effects which are known to us.

St. Thomas Aquinas: *Summa Theologica*, 1, 2, 2. (13th cent.)

That God exists, and other such theological truths which can be known by natural reason, are not articles of faith, but preambles to the Creed; faith presupposes reason as grace presupposes nature, or as any perfection supposes a subject capable of betterment. Nevertheless nothing bars a truth which is demonstrable in itself and open to scientific knowledge from being accepted as a matter of belief before its proof has been grasped.

St. Thomas Aquinas: *Summa Theologica*, 1, 2, 2. (13th cent.)

God so lives that He has no principle of life.

St. Thomas Aquinas: *Summa Theologica*, 1, 18, 3. (13th cent.)

Metaphysical proofs of God are so remote from man's range of reason and so involved that they fail to grip; and even if they were of service to some it would only be during the moment of demonstration; an hour afterwards men fear they have been wrong.

Pascal: *Pensées*. (17th cent.)

God is proved not only by the zeal of those who seek Him, but by the blindness of those who seek Him not.

Pascal: *Pensées*. (17th cent.)

Our idea of God implies necessary and eternal existence; the manifest conclusion then is that God does exist.

René Descartes: *Principles of Philosophy*, 1. (17th cent.)

For a man of religious mind is he who attends to the rule of conscience, which is born with him, which he did not make for himself, and to which he feels bound in duty to submit. And conscience immediately directs his thoughts to some Being exterior to himself, Who gave it, and Who evidently is superior to him; for a law implies a lawgiver, and a command implies a superior.

Card. Newman: *Parochial and Plain Sermons*, 2. (19th cent.)

I am a Catholic by virtue of my believing in God; and if I am asked why I believe in a God, I answer that it is because I believe in myself, for I feel it impossible to believe in my own existence (and of that fact I am quite sure) without believing also in the existence of Him, Who lives as a personal, all-seeing, all-judging Being in my conscience.

Card. Newman: *Apologia pro Vita Sua*, 4. (19th cent.)

Every one spontaneously embraces the doctrine of the existence of God, as a first principle, and a necessary assumption. It is not so much proved to him, as borne in upon his mind irresistibly, as a truth which it does not occur to him, nor is possible for him, to doubt; so various and so abundant is the witness for it contained in the experience and the conscience of every one.

Card. Newman: *Discourses to Mixed Congregations.* (19th cent.)

There exists no supreme, all-wise, all-provident divine Being, distinct from the universe, and God is identical with the nature of things, and is therefore subject to changes. In effect, God is produced in man and in the world, and all things are God and have the very substance of God, and God is one and the same thing with the world, and therefore spirit with matter, necessity with liberty, good with evil, justice with injustice.

Proposition condemned by Pius IX in Syllabus of Errors. (1867)

If any one shall deny that there is one true God, Creator and Lord of all things visible and invisible; let him be anathema.

Vatican Council, Session 3, Canon 1. (Apr. 24, 1870.)

I don't know what further proof anyone wants of Who our Lord is than that men and women find the keenest, and, in fact, their only joy, in serving Him and belonging to Him.

R. H. Benson: *The Light Invisible.* (20th cent.)

You can, by arguments, draw a number of lines that converge towards God, and render His existence and His attributes probable; but you cannot reach Him along those lines.

R. H. Benson: *The Light Invisible.* (20th cent.)

The hierarchy of beauty and goodness visible in the world point beyond themselves to a consummate beauty—the Master and Interpreter of fate. The universe is too significant to be anonymous, and if it has a meaning and an owner, then all in it, earth and body and spirit,

are protected by, and ensconced within, Infinite care.

M. C. D'Arcy: *The Idea of God.* (In *God and the Supernatural*) (20th cent.)

Mankind's belief in God is a rebuke to, and a condemnation of, the careless atheist. For it is the height of rashness or of pride to assume without investigation that so large a part of the race is giving credit to an illusion, for the existence of which no rational grounds can be assigned.

R. A. Knox: *The Belief of Catholics.* (20th cent.)

Belief in God is the unshaken foundation of all social order and of all responsible action on earth.

Pope Pius XI: *Caritate Christi compulsi.* (May 3, 1932)

To discover God is not to discover an idea but to discover oneself. It is to awake to that part of one's existence which has been hidden from sight and which one has refused to recognize. The discovery may be very painful; it is like going through a kind of death. But it is the one thing which makes life worth living.

B. Griffiths: *The Golden String.* (20th cent.)

V—*His Glory, Greatness, Majesty*

Though our lips can only stammer, we yet chant the high things of God.

Pope St. Gregory I: *Moralia in Job,* 5, 26, 29. (5th cent.)

The glory of Him Who moveth all that is
    Pervades the universe, and glows more bright
    In the one region, and in another less.

Dante: *Paradiso, Canto 1.* (Tr. Binyon) (14th cent.)

Provided that God be glorified, we must not care by whom.

St. Francis de Sales: *Spiritual Conferences,* 8. (17th cent.)

Full of glory, full of wonders,
  Majesty divine!
Mid Thine everlasting thunders
  How Thy lightnings shine!
Shoreless Ocean! who shall sound
    Thee?
Thine own eternity is round Thee,
  Majesty divine!

F. Faber: *Majesty Divine.* (19th cent.)

O Majesty unspeakable and dread!
  Wert Thou less mighty than Thou
    art,
Thou wert, O Lord! too great for our
    belief,
  Too little for our heart.

Thy greatness would seem monstrous
    by the side
  Of creatures frail and undivine;
Yet they would have a greatness of
    their own
  Free and apart from Thine.

F. Faber: *The Greatness of God.* (19th
cent.)

God's majesty speaks to us by the works
of His almighty hands.

R. H. Benson: *The History of Richard
Raynal Solitary.* (20th cent.)

Trumpeter sound for the splendor of
God! .

Alfred Noyes: *Trumpet Call.* (20th cent.)

VI—*His Goodness; Supreme Good*

You are God, omnipotent and good,
even if You had done these things
alone: for none other can do them save
You, the One, Who are the exemplar of
all things, the All-Beautiful, Who form
and set in order all things by Your law.

St. Augustine: *Confessions,* 1, 7. (5th
cent.)

The highest good, than which there is
no higher, is God, and consequently He
is unchangeable good, hence truly eternal and truly immortal. All other good
things are only from Him, not of Him.
For what is of Him, is Himself.

St. Augustine: *De Natura Boni,* 1. (5th
cent.)

Since nothing can be imagined better
than God, who doubteth but that is
good than which is nothing better? And
reason doth in such sort demonstrate
God to be good that it convinceth Him
to be perfectly good. For unless He were
so, He could not be the Chief of all
things.

Boethius: *De Consolatione Philosophiae,*
3, 10. (6th cent.)

We may then securely conclude that the
substance (*substantiam*) of God con-
sisteth in nothing else but goodness.

Boethius: *De Consolatione Philosophiae,*
3, 10. (6th cent.)

It follows, therefore, that all other goods
are good through another being than
which they themselves are, and this being alone is good through itself. Hence,
this alone is supremely good, which is
alone good through itself. For it is supreme, in that it so surpasses other beings, that it is neither equalled nor ex-
celled. But that which is supremely good
is also supremely great. There is, therefore, some one Being Which is supremely good, and supremely great, that
is, the Highest of all existing beings.

St. Anselm: *Monologium,* 1. (11th cent.)

A man turning from an evil life is bound
to be rendered desperate by the knowledge of his sins, if he does not also know
how good God is, how kind and gentle,
and how ready to forgive.

St. Bernard: *Sermons on the Canticle of
Canticles,* 36. (12th cent.)

The Good ineffable and infinite
  That is on high so runneth unto love
  As a beam comes to a body that is
    bright.
So much It gives as warmth It findeth
    of,
  So that, how far soever love be
    poured,
  The eternal Goodness doth Its best
    improve.

Dante: *Purgatorio, Canto 15.* (Tr. Binyon)
(14th cent.)

VII—*His Holiness*

Scripture says: *Ten thousand times ten thousand stood by Him, and thousand thousands ministered to Him, and they cried, Holy, Holy, Holy is the Lord of Sabaoth, the whole creation is full of His glory* (Dan. 7, 10; Is. 6, 3). Therefore, we too must gather together in concord and a good conscience and cry earnestly to Him, as it were with one mouth, that we may share in His great and glorious promises.

Pope St. Clement I: *Letter to the Corinthians,* 34. (This hymn of praise, or a variation of it, is found repeated in every liturgy, from the earliest apostolic times.) (1st cent.)

Holy God, holy Strong One, holy Immortal One, have mercy on us.

Chant, called Trisagion, sung during Byzantine Liturgy. (Allegedly introduced by Patriarch Proclus, 434–446; but form is probably older.)

For Thou art holy, our God, and dost rest among the holy, and to Thee we give glory, Father, Son, and Holy Ghost, now and for ever, world without end. Amen.

Byzantine Horologion, Doxology at Matins. (ca. 4th cent.)

Praise to the Holiest in the height,
    And in the depth be praise:
In all His words most wonderful;
    Most sure in all His ways!

Card. Newman: *Hymn from The Dream of Gerontius.* (19th cent.)

O God! Thy power is wonderful,
    Thy glory passing bright;
Thy wisdom, with its deep on deep,
    A rapture to the sight.

Thy justice is the gladdest thing
    Creation can behold;
Thy tenderness so meek, it wins
    The guilty to be bold.

Yet more than all, and ever more,
    Should we Thy creatures bless,

Most worshipful of attributes,
    Thine awful holiness.

F. Faber: *My Father.* (19th cent.)

VIII—*His Immanence, Omnipresence, Indwelling*

For You, O highest and nearest, most hidden and most present, have not parts greater and smaller; You are wholly everywhere, yet nowhere limited within space, nor are You of any bodily form.

St. Augustine: *Confessions,* 6, 3. (5th cent.)

It must therefore be acknowledged that God is everywhere by the presence of His Divinity but not everywhere by the indwelling of His grace.

St. Augustine: *Letter 187.* (5th cent.)

God Who made things is more nigh to us than are those many things which He has made.

St. Augustine: *De Gen. ad Litt.,* 5, 24. (5th cent.)

God by a common mode is in all things by His presence, power and substance; still He is said to be present more familiarly in some by grace.

Pope St. Gregory I: *Hom. 8 in Ezech.* (5th cent.)

For whereas the same Being abides within all things, without all things, above all things, beneath all things, He is both above by virtue of His dominion, and beneath by virtue of His upholding; without, by His immensity, and within, by His subtlety; ruling from on high, holding together from below; encompassing without, penetrating within; not abiding by one part above, by another beneath, or by one part without, and by another part within, but One and the Same, and wholly everywhere, upholding in ruling, ruling in upholding; penetrating in encompassing, encompassing in penetrating.

Pope St. Gregory I: *Morals,* 2, 20. (6th cent.)

O supreme and unapproachable Light! O whole and blessed Truth, how far art Thou from me, who am so near to Thee! How far removed art Thou from my vision, though I am so near to Thine! Everywhere Thou art wholly present, and I see Thee not. In Thee I move, and in Thee I have my being; and I cannot come to Thee. Thou art within me, and about me, and I feel Thee not.

> St. Anselm: *Proslogium,* 16. (11th cent.)

God is in all things; not, indeed, as part of their essence, nor as an accident; but as an agent is present to that upon which it works.

> St. Thomas Aquinas: *Summa Theologica,* 1, 8, 1. (13th cent.)

God is always with us, why should we not always be with God?

> Archb. Ullathorne: *Humility and Patience.* (19th cent.)

It is only in the affirmation of the divine transcendence and of the incarnation that the values of immanence can be saved.

> J. Maritain: *Freedom in the Modern World.* (20th cent.)

God is an all-powerful Cause because He gives to all things their being and their very nature and acts in them, more intimate to them than they are to themselves, in the way that is proper to their essential being; thus assuring from within the free action of those creatures that are by nature free.

> J. Maritain: *Freedom in the Modern World.* (20th cent.)

IX—*His Immutability*

You are the Life of souls, the Life of lives, Livingness itself, and You shall not change, O Life of my soul.

> St. Augustine: *Confessions,* 3, 6. (5th cent.)

God alone is immutable; and whatever things He has made, being from nothing, are mutable.

> St. Augustine: *De Natura Boni,* 1. (5th cent.)

Other things that are called essences or substances admit of accidents, whereby a change, whether great or small, is produced in them. But there can be no accident of this kind in respect of God: and therefore He Who is God is the only immutable substance or essence, to Whom certainly Being itself, whence is derived the term essence, most especially and most truly belongs.

> St. Augustine: *De Trinitate,* 5, 2, 3. (5th cent.)

The world is marked with the imprint of mutability, of a beginning and an end in time; and with cogent and irresistible voice it bespeaks a Creator, completely distinct from the world itself, and by His very nature immutable.

> Pope Pius XII: *Address to Italian Catholic Action,* Sept. 12, 1948.

X—*His Infiniteness, Incomprehensibility*

For of God we do not speak as we should (for that is known only to Him), but in accordance with the capacity of human nature and our weakness. We do not explain what God is but candidly confess that we do not have exact knowledge concerning Him. For with respect to God to confess our ignorance is the best knowledge.

> St. Cyril of Jerusalem: *Catechetical Discourses,* 6, 2. (4th cent.)

What then are we to say of God? If you have understood what you are trying to say, it is not God.

> St. Augustine. (5th cent.)

We can know what God is not, but we cannot know what He is.

> St. Augustine: *De Trinitate.* (5th cent.)

Thou thinkest of the earth; this is not God: thou thinkest of the sea; this is not God: of all things which are on the earth, men and beasts; this is not God: of all things which are in the sea, which fly through the air; this is not God: of whatever shines in the sky, the stars, the sun, and the moon; this is not God: of heaven itself; this is not God. Think of the angels, virtues, powers, archangels, thrones, principalities, dominations; this is not God. What is He then? I could only tell thee what He is not. Dost thou ask what He is? "Eye hath not seen, nor ear heard: neither hath it entered into the heart of man" (1 Cor. 2, 9). Why seekest thou That Which hath not risen up to the heart should rise up to the tongue?

St. Augustine: *In Ps. 85*, 12. (5th cent.)

God then is infinite and incomprehensible: and all that is comprehensible about Him is His infinity and incomprehensibility. All that we can affirm concerning God does not explain God's nature, but only the qualities of His nature.

St. John of Damascus: *Exposition of the Orthodox Faith*, 1, 4. (8th cent.)

God is incomprehensible; but you have apprehended not a little if you have ascertained this much about Him, that He is nowhere Who is not enclosed by space, and that He is everywhere Who is not shut out by space. In His own sublime and incomprehensible way, as all things are in Him, so He is in all things.

St. Bernard: *On Consideration*, 5, 6. (12th cent.)

To realize that God is far beyond anything we think, that is the mind's achievement.

St. Thomas Aquinas: *Exposition of the De Divinis Nominibus*, 1, lect. 3. (13th cent.)

Oh, wayward man! discontented first that thy God is far from thee, discontented again when He has drawn near,—complaining first that He is high, complaining next that He is low;—unhumbled being, when wilt thou cease to make thyself thine own center, and learn that God is infinite in all He does, infinite when He reigns in heaven, infinite when He serves on earth, exacting our

homage in the midst of His angels, and winning homage from us in the midst of sinners?

Card. Newman: *Discourses to Mixed Congregations*. (19th cent.)

O my Lord God . . . I adore Thee, because Thou art so mysterious, so incomprehensible. Unless Thou wert incomprehensible, Thou wouldst not be God. For how can the Infinite be other than incomprehensible to me.

Card. Newman: *Meditations and Devotions*. (19th cent.)

The living God, the God Who is God and not a philosopher's abstraction, lies infinitely beyond the reach of anything our eyes can see or our minds can understand. No matter what perfection you predicate of Him, you have to add that He is not what we conceive by that term.

Thomas Merton: *Seeds of Contemplation*. (20th cent.)

XI—*His Justice*

Let the guilty weigh
This well: God fears no sops to avert
    His stroke.

Dante: *Purgatorio, Canto 33*. (Tr. Binyon) (14th cent.)

Wherefore the sight that your world
    liveth by
Penetrates not the eternal justice
    more
Than into the ocean penetrates the
    eye.

Dante: *Paradiso, Canto 19*. (Tr. Binyon) (14th cent.)

Lord Christ, quoth he, how may this
    world endure?
So full of sin is many a creature!
O mighty God, if that it be Thy will,
Sith Thou art rightful judge, how may
    it be
That Thou wilt suffren innocence to
    spill,
And wicked folk reign in prosperity?

Chaucer: *The Man of Law's Tale*, 811. (14th cent.)

God's justice is a bed where we
    Our anxious hearts may lay,
And, weary with ourselves, may sleep
    Our discontent away.

F. Faber: *The Right Must Win.* (First line: O it is hard to work for God) (19th cent.)

Now conscience suggests to us many things about that Master, Whom by means of it we perceive, but its most prominent teaching, and its cardinal and distinguishing truth, is that He is our Judge. In consequence, the special attribute under which it brings Him before us, to which it subordinates all other attributes, is that of justice—retributive justice.

Card. Newman: *Grammar of Assent,* 10. (19th cent.)

Thou art indeed just, Lord, if I contend
With Thee; but, sir, so what I plead is
    just.
Why do sinners' ways prosper? and
    why must
Disappointment all I endeavor end?

G. M. Hopkins: *Thou Art Indeed Just, Lord.* (19th cent.)

XII—*His Knowledge, Omniscience, Wisdom*

Therefore, just as in this sun one may remark three certain things, namely, that it is, that it shines, and that it illumines, so also in that most hidden God Whom you wish to know there are three things, namely, that He is, that He is known, and that He makes other things to be known.

St. Augustine: *Soliloquia,* 1, 8, 15. (4th cent.)

Let your mercies, O God, confess to You from the very depths of my soul. For Who else recalls us from the death that all error is, except the Life Which cannot die, and the Wisdom Which illumines the minds that need it and needs no illumination from any other, by

Which the world is governed even to the windblown leaves of the trees?

St. Augustine: *Confessions,* 7, 6. (5th cent.)

But it does not follow that, though there is for God a certain order of all causes, there must therefore be nothing depending on the free exercise of our own wills, for our wills themselves are included in that order of causes which is certain to God, and is embraced by His foreknowledge, for human wills are also causes of human actions; and He Who foreknew all the causes of things would certainly among those causes not have been ignorant of our wills.

St. Augustine: *The City of God,* 5, 9. (5th cent.)

To confess that God exists, and at the same time to deny that He has foreknowledge of future things, is the most manifest folly.

St. Augustine: *The City of God,* 5, 9. (5th cent.)

It cannot rightly be said of any human artist that he works blindly; neither has God wrought anything in ignorance of what He was making. He has made all things with knowledge: things that He knew beforehand, such things He has made. Hereupon occurs a thought, wonderful but true; this world could not be known to us unless it existed; but it could not exist unless it were known beforehand to God.

St. Augustine: *The City of God,* 11, 10. (5th cent.)

Plato was not so foolish as to suppose God made happier by the knowledge of His work, but he wished to signify that the same work pleased the Artificer, when done, which had pleased Him as a work of art to do, not that God's knowledge changes in any way, as though things not yet done, or being done, or already done, impress Him differently; His knowledge is not couched in three tenses, nor does the aspect of His mind pass from thought to thought.

St. Augustine: *The City of God,* 11, 21. (5th cent.)

What man is there who can comprehend that wisdom' by which God knows all things, in such wise that neither what we call things past are past therein, nor what we call things future are therein looked for as coming, as though they were absent; but both past and future things together with those actually present are all present.

St. Augustine: *De Trinitate,* 15, 7, 13. (5th cent.)

He knew beforehand, without any beginning, all things to come in time, and among them also what we should ask of Him and when, and to whom He would listen or not listen, and on what subjects. And with respect to all His creatures, both spiritual and corporeal, it is not because they are that He knows them, but they are because He knows them.

St. Augustine: *De Trinitate,* 15, 13, 22. (5th cent.)

If we consider the immensity and singleness of God's wisdom, it is one, simple, and indivisible; if the great number of things with which it has to do, it is manifold and diverse.

John of Salisbury: *Policraticus,* 2, 21, 117. (12th cent.)

For this is what the highest wisdom does: it manifests the hidden truths of divinity; it produces the works of creation, and furthermore restores them at need; it brings them to the completion of achieving their own proper and perfect purpose.

St. Thomas Aquinas: *Commentary on the Sentences,* Prol. (13th cent.)

God alone knows the depths and the riches of His Godhead, and divine wisdom alone can declare His secrets.

St. Thomas Aquinas: *Commentary on the Sentences,* Prol. (13th cent.)

Since God's act of understanding, which is His being, is measured by eternity; and since eternity is without succession, comprehending all time, the present glance of God extends over all time, and to all things which exist in any time, as to objects present to Him. But there are other things in God's power, or the creature's, which nevertheless are not, nor will be, nor were; and as regards these He is said to have the knowledge, not of vision, but of simple intelligence.

St. Thomas Aquinas: *Summa Theologica,* I, 14, 9. (13th cent.)

It cannot be granted that God can know more than He knows; because such a proposition implies that first of all He did not know, and then afterwards knew.

St. Thomas Aquinas: *Summa Theologica,* I, 14, 15.

The knowledge of God is the cause, not indeed of Himself, but of other things. He is actually the cause of some, that is, of things that come to be in some period of time; and He is virtually the cause of others, that is, of things which He can make and which nevertheless are never made.

St. Thomas Aquinas: *Summa Theologica,* I, 14, 16. (13th cent.)

It is necessary to suppose ideas in the divine mind.

St. Thomas Aquinas: *Summa Theologica,* I, 15, 1. (13th cent.)

God's living is His knowing. His power of understanding, the object understood, and His act of understanding are all identical.

St. Thomas Aquinas: *Summa Theologica,* I, 18, 4. (13th cent.)

Although bad things are in God's knowledge, as being comprised under that knowledge, yet they are not in God as created by Him, or preserved by Him, or as having their type in Him. They are known by God through the types of good things.

St. Thomas Aquinas: *Summa Theologica,* I, 18, 4. (13th cent.)

As by one act God understands all things in His essence, so by one act He wills all things in His goodness.

St. Thomas Aquinas: *Summa Theologica,* I, 19, 5. (13th cent.)

O Light, Who in Thyself alone
  Dwell'st and Thyself know'st, and
    self-understood,
  Self-understanding, smilest on Thine
    own!

Dante: *Paradiso, Canto 33.* (Tr. Binyon) (14th cent.)

Who sees with equal eye, as God of all,
A hero perish or a sparrow fall,
Atoms or systems into ruin hurled
And now a bubble burst, and now a
  world.

Pope: *An Essay on Man,* I. (18th cent.)

XIII—*His Love, Charity*

Even if Thou, O Lord, dost turn Thy face away from us, yet the light of Thy countenance is imprinted within us.

St. Ambrose: *In Ps. 43 Enarr. 88.* (4th cent.)

God loves all things that He has made, and amongst them rational creatures more, and of these especially those who are members of His only-begotten Son; and much more than all, His only-begotten Son Himself.

St. Augustine: *Tract. in Joann,* 110. (5th cent.)

God's love for us is not greater in heaven than it is now.

St. Thomas Aquinas: *Quodlibets,* 5, 3, 6. (13th cent.)

The holy ardor that irradiates all
Lives most in what most like to itself
  is proved.

Dante: *Paradiso, Canto 7.* (Tr. Binyon) (14th cent.)

When did God's love for you begin? When He began to be God. When did He begin to be God? Never, for He has always been without beginning and without end, and so He has always loved you from eternity.

St. Francis de Sales: *Introduction to a Devout Life,* 5, 14. (17th cent.)

The Christian's God is not a God Who is simply author of mathematical truths and of the order of the elements; that is the lot of the heathen and of the Epicureans. He is not merely a God Who employs His providence upon the life and well-being of men, in order to bestow on His worshippers a long and prosperous life; that is the heritage of the Jews. But the God of Abraham, the God of Isaac, the God of Jacob, the Christian's God, is a God of love and consolation, a God Who fills the soul and heart of those whom He hath purchased, a God Who makes them deeply conscious of their misery and of His infinite mercy; Who makes His home in their heart, filling it with humility, joy, confidence and love; Who renders them incapable of any other object than Himself.

Pascal: *Pensées.* (17th cent.)

Jesus! why dost Thou love me so?
  What hast Thou seen in me
To make my happiness so great,
  So dear a joy to Thee?

Wert Thou not God, I then might think
  Thou hadst no eye to read
The badness of that selfish heart,
  For which Thine own did bleed.

But Thou art God, and knowest all;
  Dear Lord! Thou knowest me;
And yet Thy knowledge hinders not
  Thy love's sweet liberty.

F. Faber: *The Pain of Love.* (19th cent.)

My child, give Me thy heart!
For I have loved thee with a love
No mortal heart can show;
A love so deep, My saints in heaven
Its depths can never know:

When pierced and wounded on the
Cross,
Man's sin and doom were Mine,
I lov'd thee with undying love;
Immortal and divine.

Adelaide Procter: *Give Me Thy Heart*.
(19th cent.)

The magnet calls the steel:
Answers the iron to the magnet's
breath;
What do they feel
But death!
The clouds of summer kiss in flame and
rain,
And are not found again;
But the heavens themselves eternal are
with fire
Of unapproach'd desire,
By the aching heart of love, which can-
not rest,
In blissfulest pathos so indeed pos-
sess'd.

Coventry Patmore: *Deliciae Sapientiae de
Amore*. (19th cent.)

I fled Him, down the nights and down
the days;
I fled Him, down the arches of the
years;
I fled Him, down the labyrinthine ways
Of my own mind; and in the midst
of tears
I hid from Him, and under running
laughter.
Up vistaed hopes I sped;
And shot precipitated,
Adown titanic glooms of chasmèd
fears,
From those strong feet that followed
after.

. . . .

(For, though I knew His love Who
followèd,
Yet was I sore adread
Lest having Him, I must have not
beside.)

. . . .

Still with unhurrying chase,
And unperturbèd pace,
Deliberate speed, majestic instancy,
Came on the following feet,

And a Voice above their beat—
Naught shelters thee, who wilt not
shelter Me.

F. Thompson: *The Hound of Heaven*.
(19th cent.)

It is not only we who thirst and knock:
it is God Who, thirsting for our love,
died upon the Cross that He might open
the kingdom of heaven to all believers.

R. H. Benson: *The Confessions of a
Convert*. (20th cent.)

Surely the King of love needed no herald
when Himself was near.

R. H. Benson: *By What Authority*. (20th
cent.)

I have lived too much in the sweetness
of God and forgotten His sorrows!

R. H. Benson: *The Light Invisible*. (20th
cent.)

The love of Christ is a deeper thing than
the mere presents He makes to his new
friends.

R. H. Benson: *The Friendship of Christ*.
(20th cent.)

XIV—*His Mercy*

The mercy of God may be found between the bridge and the stream.

St. Augustine: *Confessions*. (Of a man
falling into a river.) (5th cent.)

He therefore will be guilty unto condemnation under God's power, who
shall think too contemptuously of His
mercy to believe in Him. But whosoever
shall put his trust in Him, and yield
himself up to Him, for the forgiveness
of all his sins, for the cure of all his corruption, and for the kindling and illumination of his soul by His warmth and
light, shall have good works by His
grace; and by them he shall be even in
his body redeemed from the corruption
of death, crowned, satisfied with blessings—not temporal, but eternal—above
what we can ask or understand.

St. Augustine: *De Spiritu et Littera*, 58.
(5th cent.)

And never to despair of God's mercy.

> St. Benedict: *Rule,* 4. (One of his 'tools of good works') (6th cent.)

If God had not created man He would still indeed have been perfect in goodness, but He would not have been actually merciful, since mercy can only be exercised toward the miserable.

> St. Francis de Sales: *Spiritual Conferences,* 2. (17th cent.)

God's fair were guessed scarce but for opposite sin;
Yea, and His mercy, I do think it well,
Is flashed back from the brazen gates of hell.

> F. Thompson: *Sister Songs.* (19th cent.)

XV—*His Nature, Name, Attributes*

God, therefore, is not to be thought of as being either a body or as existing in a body, but as an uncompounded intellectual nature (*simplex intellectualis natura*), admitting within Himself no addition of any kind; so that He cannot be believed to have within Him a greater and a less, but is such that He is in all parts, a monad and henad, and is the mind and source from which all intellectual nature or mind takes its beginning.

> Origen: *De Principiis,* 1, 1, 6. (3rd cent.)

First then let there be laid as a foundation in your soul the doctrine concerning God; that God is one, alone unbegotten, without beginning, change or variation; neither begotten of another, not having another to succeed Him in His life; Who neither began to live in time, nor endeth ever: and that He is both good and just.

> St. Cyril of Jerusalem: *Catechetical Discourses,* 4, 4. (4th cent.)

God is Spirit, and has nothing corporeal in His substance, but is wholly Spirit.

> St. Ambrose: *In Ps. 43 Enarr. 65.* (4th cent.)

Some names there are which express evidently the property of the divinity, and some which express the clear truth of the divine majesty, but others there are which are applied to God metaphorically by way of similitude.

> St. Ambrose: *De Fide,* 2. (4th cent.)

The nature of God is a circle whose center is everywhere and its circumference nowhere.

> St. Augustine. (5th cent.)

O thou, the greatest and the best, mightiest, almighty, most merciful and most just, utterly hidden and utterly present, most beautiful and most strong, abiding yet mysterious, suffering no change and changing all things: never new, never old, making all things new, *bringing age upon the proud and they know it not;* ever in action, ever at rest, gathering all things to Thee and needing none; sustaining, fulfilling and protecting, creating and nourishing and making perfect; ever seeking though lacking nothing.

> St. Augustine: *Confessions,* 1, 4. (5th cent.)

All things can be said of God, yet is nothing worthily said of God. Nothing is wider than this utter want. Thou seekest a name befitting Him and findest none; thou seekest in what way soever to speak of Him and thou findest Him in all things.

> St. Augustine: *In Joan. Evang.,* 13, 5. (5th cent.)

But God is truly called in manifold ways, great, good, wise, blessed, true, and whatsoever other things seem to be said of Him not unworthily; but His greatness is the same as His wisdom; for He is not great by bulk, but by power; and His goodness is the same as His wisdom and greatness, and His truth the same as all those things; and in Him it is not one thing to be blessed, and another to be great, or wise, or true, or good, or in a word to be Himself.

> St. Augustine: *De Trinitate,* 6, 7. (5th cent.)

'God' so far as human intelligence can conceive, is the designation of the absolutely supreme nature or substance. . . . When 'God' is uttered, you are to understand a substance without beginning or end, simple, uncompounded, invisible, incorporeal, ineffable, incomprehensible: a substance in which there is nothing accidental, nothing creaturely. For He Who is the Originator of all things is Himself without origin.

> Rufinus: *Commentary on the Apostles' Creed*, 4. (5th cent.)

He who is, is the principal of all names applied to God; for comprehending all in itself, it contains existence itself as an infinite and indeterminate sea of substance.

> St. John of Damascus: *Exposition of the Orthodox Faith*, 1. (8th cent.)

It is evident that He is incorporeal, For how could that possess body which is infinite, and boundless, and formless, and intangible and invisible, in short, simple and not compound?

> St. John of Damascus: *Exposition of the Orthodox Faith*, 1, 4. (8th cent.)

Everything said of God signifies not His substance, but rather shows forth what He is not; or expresses some relation, or something following from His nature or operation.

> St. John of Damascus: *Exposition of the Orthodox Faith*, 1, 9. (8th cent.)

God is Eternity. God is Love; He is length without extension, breadth without distension. In both cases alike He exceeds the narrow limits of space and time, but in virtue of His unfettered nature, not through the vastness of His substance. In such wise He is immeasurable Who hath made all things by measure; and although He be immeasurable, His very immensity must be thus 'measured.'

> St. Bernard: *On Consideration*, 5, 13. (12th cent.)

God is not confined in time, for He is eternal, and without beginning or end. His being is constant, ever present, never altering from past to future. Nothing can be taken away from Him, nothing added. And his name is *He Who Is* (Exod. 3, 13).

> St. Thomas Aquinas: *Exposition of the First Decretal.* (13th cent.)

No human emotions can be strictly attributed to God, with the exception of love and joy, and even these then carry no counterpart to the organic changes which take place in human affection and pleasure.

> St. Thomas Aquinas: *Contra Gentes*, 1, 91. (13th cent.)

God is most happy, and therefore supremely conscious.

> St. Thomas Aquinas: *Commentary on the Metaphysics*, 3, lect. 11. (13th cent.)

Since divine truths are incomprehensible and beyond definition, it is more appropriate to keep to broad terms, and avoid very pointed ones.

> St. Thomas Aquinas: *Against the Errors of the Greeks*, 1. (13th cent.)

His perfect fruitfulness.

> St. Thomas Aquinas: *Summa Theologica*, 1, 27, 5. (13th cent.)

Person signifies what is noblest in nature, namely a complete substance of an intellectual kind, and therefore, with all due safeguards, the term should be applied to God, Whose nature embraces every perfection.

> St. Thomas Aquinas: *Summa Theologica*, 1, 29, 3. (13th cent.)

Person in God signifies a relation subsisting in the divine nature.

> St. Thomas Aquinas: *Summa Theologica*, 1, 30, 1. (13th cent.)

To Him no high, no low, no great, no small;

He fills, He bounds, connects and equals all!

Pope: *An Essay on Man*, 1. (18th cent.)

The word 'God' is a theology in itself, indivisibly one, inexhaustibly various, from the vastness and the simplicity of its meaning. Admit a God, and you introduce among the subjects of your knowledge, a fact encompassing, closing in upon, absorbing, every other fact conceivable.

Card. Newman: *Historical Sketches*, 3. (19th cent.)

Of all points of faith, the being of God is, to my own apprehension, encompassed with most difficulty, and yet borne in upon our minds with most power.

Card. Newman: *Apologia pro Vita Sua*, 5. (19th cent.)

The attributes of God, though intelligible to us on their surface,—for from our own sense of mercy and holiness and patience and consistency, we have general notions of the All-merciful and All-holy and All-patient, and of all that is proper to His essence,—yet, for the very reason that they are infinite, transcend our comprehension, when they are dwelt upon, when they are followed out, and can only be received by faith.

Card. Newman: *Discourses to Mixed Congregations*. (19th cent.)

XVI—*His Omnipotence*

What is impossible to God? Not that which is difficult to His power, but that which is contrary to His nature.

St. Ambrose: *Letters*, 50, 1. (4th cent.)

He is called Almighty for no other reason than that He can do whatever He wills, and because the effectiveness of His almighty will cannot be thwarted by the will of any creature whatsoever.

St. Augustine: *Enchiridion*, 96. (5th cent.)

For He is called omnipotent on account of His doing what He wills, not on account of His suffering what He wills not; for if that should befall Him, He would by no means be omnipotent. Wherefore, He cannot do some things for the very reason that He is omnipotent.

St. Augustine: *The City of God*, 5, 10. (5th cent.)

> God's might to direct me,
> God's power to protect me,
> God's wisdom for learning,
> God's eye for discerning,
> God's ear for my hearing,
> God's word for my clearing.

Early Gaelic Hymn. (Attr. to St. Patrick.) (Tr. Sigerson) (ca. 6th cent.?)

God is called omnipotent because He can do all things that are possible absolutely.

St. Thomas Aquinas: *Summa Theologica*, 1, 25, 3. (13th cent.)

XVII—*His Providence*

For there is no one so uncivilized, and of such an uncultivated disposition, who, when he raises his eyes to heaven, although he knows not by the providence of what God all this visible universe is governed, does not understand from the very magnitude of the objects, from their motion, arrangement, constancy, usefulness, beauty, and temperament, that there is some Providence, and that that which exists with wonderful method must have been prepared by some greater intelligence.

Lactantius: *Divine Institutes*, 1, 2. (4th cent.)

For, if the providence of God does not preside over human affairs, there is no point in busying oneself about religion.

St. Augustine: *De Utilitate Credendi*, 16, 34. (4th cent.)

That divine Providence which is wont to reform the depraved manners of men by chastisement, and which exercises with similar afflictions the righteous and praiseworthy.

> St. Augustine: *The City of God*, 1, 1. (5th cent.)

To the divine Providence it has seemed good to prepare in the world to come for the righteous good things, which the unrighteous shall not enjoy; and for the wicked evil things, by which the good shall not be tormented. But as for the good things of this life, and its ills, God has willed that these shall be common to both; that we might not too eagerly covet the things which wicked men are seen equally to enjoy, nor shrink with an unseemly fear from the ills which even good men often suffer.

> St. Augustine: *The City of God*, 1, 8. (5th cent.)

Providence is the divine type itself, seated in the Supreme Ruler; which disposeth all things.

> Boethius: *De Consolatione Philosophiae*, 4, 6. (6th cent.)

For Providence is the very divine reason itself, seated in the highest Prince, which disposeth all things. But Fate is a disposition inherent in changeable things, by which Providence connecteth all things in their due order. For Providence embraceth all things together, though diverse, though infinite; but Fate putteth every particular thing into motion being distributed by places, forms, and time; so that this unfolding of temporal order being united into the foresight of God's mind is Providence, and the same uniting, being digested and unfolded in time, is called Fate.

> Boethius: *De Consolatione Philosophiae*, 4, 6. (6th cent.)

The acts of our Maker ought always to be reverenced without examining, for they can never be unjust.

> Pope St. Gregory I: *Morals*, 9, 22. (6th cent.)

Alas, why is it people so dispraise
God's providence or fortune and her ways,
That can so often give in many a guise
Far better things than ever they devise?

> Chaucer: *The Knight's Tale*. (Tr. Coghill) (14th cent.)

In all created things discern the providence and wisdom of God, and in all things give Him thanks.

> St. Teresa of Jesus: *Maxims*. (16th cent.)

That God can do impossibilities—this position is not heretical, though I am convinced it is untenable.

> St. Thomas Aquinas: *On the Eternity of the World*. (13th cent.)

Not God alone in the still calm we find;
He mounts the storm, and walks upon the wind.

> Pope: *An Essay on Man*, 2. (18th cent.)

Now it has never been a firm article of Christian faith, that His providence is in fact not general merely, but is, on the contrary, thus particular and personal; and that, as there is a particular providence, so of necessity that providence is secretly concurring and cooperating with that system [of the visible world] which meets the eye, and which is commonly recognized among men as existing.

> Card. Newman: *Essays Critical and Historical*, 2. (19th cent.)

When we confess God as omnipotent only, we have gained but a half-knowledge of Him: His is an omnipotence which can at the same time swathe itself in infirmity and can become the captive of its own creatures. He has, if I may so speak, the incomprehensible power of even making Himself weak. We must know Him by His names, Emmanuel and Jesus, to know Him perfectly.

> Card. Newman: *Sermons Preached on Various Occasions*. (19th cent.)

There is no place in the world but contains some trace of God; He has left His secret marks everywhere and they only need to be found.

J. Maritain: *The Things That Are Not Caesar's.* (20th cent.)

XVIII—*His Transcendence*

We confess the Lord *high and lifted up* (Isa. 6, 1), Who is *above all* (Rom. 9, 5). Were He the existence of things, He would be within the universe, not above it.

St. Thomas Aquinas: *Contra Gentes,* 1, 26. (13th cent.)

God is both transcendent and the cause of everything. Accordingly theologians sometimes confess that He is beyond all speech, while at other times they attribute many and various names to Him.

St. Thomas Aquinas: *Exposition of the De Divinis Nominibus,* 1, lect. 3. (13th cent.)

May you see God in all, through all, and above all. May the divine transcendence and the divine immanence be the two poles of your life.

Isaac T. Hecker. (Elliott's *Life,* 304) (19th cent.)

If God is a cause *like* other causes, a person *like* other persons, a king *like* other kings, these terms being simply carried to their absolute meaning, it follows that He is an all-powerful cause only because He uses compulsion against every creature; that He is sovereign freedom only because He determines good and evil by an act of arbitrary will; that He is worthy of adoration only because He annihilates man as He goes. All this is for us nonsense, since it is to make created things the measure of the uncreated God and totally to misunderstand His transcendence.

J. Maritain: *Freedom in the Modern World.* (20th cent.)

It is dangerous to talk glibly about the infinite God. It is sometimes dangerous to talk about Him at all, unless talking of Him brings you deeper into His mystery, and finally flattens you into silence in the face of His transcendence!

Thomas Merton: *The Ascent to Truth.* (20th cent.)

XIX—*His Truth*

In God existence is not an accidental quality, but subsisting truth.

St. Hilary of Poitiers: *De Trinitate.* (4th cent.)

O eternal Truth, and true Charity, and lovely Eternity, Thou art my God, to Thee do I sigh day and night.

St. Augustine: *Confessions,* 7, 10, 16.

O splendor of God, by Whose largess I saw
    With these mine eyes Truth realmed in triumph, fill
    My lips with power to re-tell how I saw.

Dante: *Paradiso, Canto* 30. (Tr. Binyon) (14th cent.)

God is not only true, but Truth Itself.

Pope Leo XIII: *Aeterni patris.* (Aug. 4, 1879)

If God be Truth, and God be Love, is it not absolutely inevitable that the love of God should bring the truth of God down to the level of the very simplest.

R. H. Benson: *Christ in the Church.* (20th cent.)

XX—*His Unity, Simplicity*

We acknowledge one God, uncreated, eternal, invisible, impassible, uncomprehensible, illimitable, Who is apprehended by the understanding only and the reason, Who is encompassed by light, and beauty, and spirit, and power ineffable, by Whom the universe has been created through His Logos, and set in order, and is kept in being.

Athenagoras: *Supplication,* 10. (2nd cent.)

God is not, if He is not one; because we more properly believe that that has no existence which is not as it ought to be. In order, however, that you may know that God is one, ask What God is, and you will find Him to be not otherwise than one. So far as a human being can form a definition of God, I adduce one which the conscience of all men will also acknowledge,—that God is the great Supreme, existing in eternity, unbegotten, unmade, without beginning, without end.

> Tertullian: *Against Marcion,* 1, 3. (3rd cent.)

God is truly and absolutely simple.

> St. Augustine: *De Trinitate,* 4, 6, 7. (5th cent.)

If we say, then, that there are many Gods, we must recognize difference among the many. For if there is no difference among them, they are one rather than many. But if there is difference among them, what becomes of the perfectness? For that which falls short of perfection, whether it be in goodness, or power, or wisdom, or time, or place, could not be God. But it is this very identity in all respects that shows that the Deity is one and not many.

> St. John of Damascus: *Exposition of the Orthodox Faith,* 1, 5. (8th cent.)

One God! one Majesty!
There is no God but Thee!
Unbounded, an extended Unity!

Awful in unity,
O God! we worship Thee,
More simply One, because supremely Three!

> F. Faber: *The Unity of God.* (19th cent.)

XXI—*His Will*

It is the duty of those who are zealous for God's good pleasure to make inquiry as to what it is right for them to do.

> St. Basil: *The Morals,* 9, 2. (4th cent.)

No one may prefer his own will to the will of God, but in everything we must seek and do the will of God.

> St. Basil: *The Morals,* 12, 3. (4th cent.)

As regards the will of God, even if some take scandal, we must not let this hamper our freedom of action.

> St. Basil: *The Morals,* 33, 4. (4th cent.)

The will of God is the measure of things.

> St. Ambrose: *Hexaem.* 2, 4. (4th cent.)

Nothing, therefore, happens unless the Omnipotent wills it to happen: He either permits it to happen, or He brings it about Himself.

> St. Augustine: *Enchiridion,* 95. (5th cent.)

In His supreme will resides the power which acts on the wills of all created spirits, helping the good, judging the evil, controlling all, granting power to some, not granting it to others. For, as He is the creator of all natures, so also is He the bestower of all powers, not of all wills; for wicked wills are not from Him, being contrary to nature, which is from Him.

> St. Augustine: *The City of God,* 5, 9. (5th cent.)

Philosophers in their vanity have thought fit to attribute contingent effects to other causes, being utterly unable to perceive the cause that is shown above all others, the will of God.

> St. Augustine: *De Trinitate,* 3, 2. (5th cent.)

And so it comes to pass that the will of God is the first and supreme cause of all corporeal forms and movements. For nothing is done visibly or sensibly, unless either by command or permission from the inner judgment hall, invisible and intelligible, of the supreme Ruler, according to the ineffable justice of rewards and punishments, of grace and retribution, in that abounding and boundless commonwealth of the whole creation.

> St. Augustine: *De Trinitate*, 3, 4, 9. (5th cent.)

Grant, we beseech Thee, almighty God, that, ever meditating on Thy reasonable commands, we may effectively accomplish in word and deed that which is pleasing to Thee.

> Roman Missal, Collect for Sixth Sunday after Epiphany. (Gelasian, 5th to 7th cent.)

We must hold that the will of God is the cause of things; and that He acts by the will, and not, as some have supposed, by a necessity of His nature.

> St. Thomas Aquinas: *Summa Theologica*, 1, 19, 4. (13th cent.)

God therefore neither wills evil to be done, nor wills it not to be done, but wills to permit evil to be done; and this is good.

> St. Thomas Aquinas: *Summa Theologica*, 1, 19, 9. (13th cent.)

I worship Thee, sweet will of God!
  And all Thy ways adore,
And every day I live I seem
  To love Thee more and more.

Thou wert the end, the blessed rule
  Of Jesu's toils and tears;
Thou wert the passion of His heart
  Those three and thirty years.

> F. Faber: *The Will of God*. (19th cent.)

  Nathless, discern'd may be,
By listeners at the doors of destiny,
The fly-wheel swift and still
Of God's incessant will,
Mighty to keep in bound, tho' powerless to quell,
The amorous and vehement drift of
  man's herd to hell.

> Coventry Patmore: *Crest and Gulf*. (19th cent.)

A broken heart and God's will done would be better than that God's will should be avoided.

> R. H. Benson: *Come Rack! Come Rope!* (20th cent.)

It needs a very pure intention, as well as great spiritual discernment, always to recognize the divine voice.

> R. H. Benson: *The Friendship of Christ*. (20th cent.)

Life is nothing but a play and a pretence, and His will must be done, however much we rebel at it.

> R. H. Benson: *The History of Richard Raynal Solitary*. (20th cent.)

God's will is as energetic in the bewildering rush of the current as in the quiet, sheltered backwater.

> R. H. Benson: *The King's Achievement*. (20th cent.)

XXII—*Man's Knowledge of God*

Although God is invisible to man by reason of His eminence, as regards His providence He can by no means be unknown. *Although no man knows the Father except the Son*, yet all things are aware of the fact of His existence, because the reason implanted in their minds moves them and reveals to them that there is one God the Lord of all.

> St. Irenaeus: *Against the Heresies*, 2, 6, 1. (2nd cent.)

As regards His greatness it is impossible to know Him, but as touching His love we may, for it is this that leads us to God through His Word. When we obey Him always we learn that there is so great a God, and that it is He Who has by Himself established, arranged, and ordered all things, and Who now contains both ourselves and this world of ours.

> St. Irenaeus: *Against the Heresies*, 4, 20, 1. (2nd cent.)

From the beginning knowledge of God is the dowry of the soul, one and the same for Egyptians, Syrians, and the tribes of Pontus. For their souls call the God of the Jews their God.

Tertullian: *Against Marcion,* 1, 10 (3rd cent.)

For things which are worthy of God will prove the existence of God. We maintain that God must first be known from *nature,* and afterwards be authenticated by *instruction:* from nature by His works; by instruction, through His revealed announcements.

Tertullian: *Against Marcion,* 1, 18. (3rd cent.)

To the great Moses God first appeared in light. Afterwards God spoke to him through a cloud. Finally, when he had ascended to greater and more perfect heights, Moses saw God in darkness. All this signifies that our passage from false and errant notions of God is a passage from darkness to light. A closer consideration of hidden things through things which can be seen leads the soul to that nature which cannot be seen: and this is like a cloud overshadowing all that has outward appearances, in order to lead the soul on and accustom it to the dark. The soul that thus climbs into the heights, leaving behind everything that human nature can attain by itself, enters into the sanctuary of the knowledge of God, surrounded on every side by the divine darkness. And there, everything that can be seen or understood having been left outside, nothing is left for the soul to see but that which is invisible and incomprehensible. And therein God is hidden, for Scripture says of the lawgiver: *Moses entered into the darkness where God was* (Exod. 24, 18).

St. Gregory of Nyssa: *Hom. 11 on the Cant. of Canticles.* (4th cent.)

O God, Who art ever the same, let me know myself, let me know Thee.

St. Augustine: *Soliloquies,* 2, 1, 1. (4th cent.)

The Most High God, Who is better known by knowing what He is not (*scitur melius nesciendo*).

St. Augustine: *De Ordine,* 2, 44. (4th cent.)

No one has ever seen God either in this life, as He is, nor in the angelic life, as visible things are seen by corporeal vision.

St. Augustine: *De Videndo Deum,* Ep. 147. (5th cent.)

For the mind to attain to God in some degree is great beatitude.

St. Augustine: *De Verbo Domini,* Serm. 38. (5th cent.)

For God is, and truly and supremely is. And this, so I think, we must not only hold to by faith as a fact beyond doubt, but by a sure, though as yet slender, form of cognition, we attain to it.

St. Augustine: *De Libero Arbitrio,* 15, 39. (4th cent.)

If therefore thou art unable to apprehend either by the senses of the body or by meditation in the mind whatever mutable thing thou seest, unless it be held in some rhythmic form, which if it lost, it would fall back into nothingness, doubt not that, in order that these mutable things may not be checked in their course, but by measured motions and by distinctive variety of forms bring time to a close as a poem's ending, there must be some eternal and immutable Form, Which is neither contained nor, as it were, diffused in place, neither extended nor varied in time, and through Which all mutable things can receive a form and according to their kind fulfil and accomplish their ordered rhythms in space and time.

St. Augustine: *De Libero Arbitrio,* 16, 44. (4th cent.)

When first I knew Thee Thou didst raise me up, that I might see there was something for me to see, though as yet I was not fit to see it.

St. Augustine: *Confessions,* 7, 10, 16. (5th cent.)

God does not increase owing to the fact that He is known, but he who knows God increases by his knowledge of God.

St. Augustine: *Sermon 117, 5.* (5th cent.)

His divinity can in no wise be seen by human sight, but is seen by that sight with which those who see are no longer men, but beyond men.

St. Augustine: *De Trinitate, 1, 6.* (5th cent.)

Besides the knowledge of God obtained by processes of philosophical and theological speculation, there is that most divine knowledge of God which takes place through ignorance, in the union which is above intelligence, when the intellect, quitting all things that are, and then leaving itself also, is united to the superlucent rays, being illuminated thence and therein by the unsearchable depth of wisdom.

Pseudo-Dionysius: *On the Divine Names, 7, 3.* (5th cent.)

Unto this Darkness which is beyond light we pray that we may come, and through loss of sight and knowledge may see and know that which transcends sight and knowledge, by the very fact of not seeing and knowing; for this is real sight and knowledge.

Pseudo-Dionysius: *Mystical Theology, 2.* (5th cent.)

What do they not see, who see Him Who sees all things?

Pope St. Gregory I: *Dialogues, 4.* (5th cent.)

We do not know God in His essence but by the grandeur of His creation and the action of His Providence, which present to us, as in a mirror, the reflection of His infinite goodness, wisdom, and power.

St. Maximus the Confessor: *Centuries on Charity, 1, 96.* (7th cent.)

It is not within our capacity, therefore, to say anything about God or even to think of Him, beyond the things which have been divinely revealed to us, whether by word or by manifestation, by the divine oracles both of the Old Testament and the New Testament.

St. John of Damascus: *Exposition of the Orthodox Faith, 1, 2.* (8th cent.)

Lord, if Thou art not here, where shall I seek Thee, being absent? But if Thou art everywhere, why do I not see Thee present? Truly Thou dwellest in unapproachable light. But where is unapproachable light, or how shall I come to it? Or who shall lead me to that light and into it, that I may see Thee in it?

St. Anselm: *Proslogium, 1.* (11th cent.)

Demonstrative knowledge about God leaves so much unsaid, and is therefore not final happiness.

St. Thomas Aquinas: *Contra Gentes, 3, 39.* (13th cent.)

The knowledge of God is naturally implanted in all.

St. Thomas Aquinas: *Summa Theologica, 1, 2, 1.* (13th cent.)

A created mind may see God, but cannot know all that He has done and can do: that would be to comprehend His power.

St. Thomas Aquinas: *Summa Theologica, 1, 12, 8.* (13th cent.)

Those who see the divine essence see what they see in God not by any likeness, but by the divine essence itself united to their intellect. For each thing is known is so far as its likeness is in the one who knows.

St. Thomas Aquinas: *Summa Theologica, 1, 12, 9.* (13th cent.)

God cannot be seen in His essence by a mere human being, except he be separated from this mortal life.

St. Thomas Aquinas: *Summa Theologica, 1, 12, 11.* (13th cent.)

As the knowledge of God's essence is by grace, it belongs only to the good;

but the knowledge of Him by natural reason can belong to both good and bad.

> St. Thomas Aquinas: *Summa Theologica,* 1, 12, 12. (13th cent.)

We know God better through grace than through unaided reason.

> St. Thomas Aquinas: *Summa Theologica,* 1, 12, 13. (13th cent.)

He is mad who hopes that reason in its
  sweep
    The infinite way can traverse back
    and forth
  Which the three Persons in one substance keep.
With the *quia* stay content, children of
  earth!
    For if the whole before your eyes
    had lain,
    No need was there for Mary to give
    birth.

> Dante: *Purgatorio, Canto 3.* (Tr. Binyon) (14th cent.)

For that abysmal Good which we taste and possess, we can neither grasp nor understand; neither can we enter into it by ourselves or by means of our exercises. And so we are poor in ourselves, but rich in God.

> Bl. John of Ruysbroeck: *The Sparkling Stone,* 9. (14th cent.)

  To win to the knowledge of all,
  Wish not to know anything.
  To win to the tasting of all,
  Wish not to taste anything.
  To come to the possession of all,
  Wish not to possess anything.
  To win to the being of all,
  Wish not to be anything.

> St. John of the Cross. (16th cent.)

The difference between knowledge of God and love of Him!

> Pascal: *Pensées.* (17th cent.)

There are only two classes of men who can be called rational—those who serve God with all their hearts because they know Him, and those who seek Him

wholeheartedly because they know Him not.

> Pascal: *Pensées.* (17th cent.)

God of Abraham, God of Isaac, God
  of Jacob,
Not of the philosophers and the
  learned.
Certitude. Certitude. Feeling. Joy.
  Peace.
. . . . . .
Forgetfulness of the world and of all
  outside God.
. . . . . .
Righteous Father, the world hath not
  known Thee,
But I have known Thee.
Joy, joy, joy, tears of joy.
. . . . . .
My God, wilt Thou leave me?
Let me not be separated from Thee for
  ever!

> Pascal: *Memorial.* (Record of mystical experience inscribed on scrap of paper found stitched inside his doublet) (1654)

How can the less the greater comprehend?
Or finite reason reach Infinity?
For what could fathom God were
  more than he.

> Dryden: *Religio Laici.* (17th cent.)

As we have our initial knowledge of the universe through sense, so do we in the first instance begin to learn about its Lord and God from conscience; and, as from particular acts of that instinct, which makes experiences, mere images (as they ultimately are) upon the retina, the means of our perceiving something real beyond them, we go on to draw the general conclusion that there is a vast external world, so from the recurring instances in which conscience acts, forcing upon us importunately the mandate of a Superior, we have fresh evidence of the existence of a sovereign Ruler, from Whom those particular dictates which we experience proceed.

> Card. Newman: *Grammar of Assent,* 4. (19th cent.)

If any one shall say that the one true God our Creator and Lord cannot be certainly known by the light of human reason through created things; let him be anathema.

Vatican Council, Session 3, Canon 1. (Apr. 24, 1870)

God Whom none may live and mark!

F. Thompson: *Orient Ode.* (19th cent.)

It was the man in the street who understood our Lord, and the doctor of the law who was perplexed and offended.

R. H. Benson: *The Religion of the Plain Man.* (20th cent.)

To have a knowledge of the Creator is incalculably a more noble thing than to have knowledge of His creation.

R. H. Benson: *The Friendship of Christ.* (20th cent.)

It is in silence that God is known, and through mysteries that He declares Himself.

R. H. Benson: *The Confessions of a Convert.* (20th cent.)

There is but one thing in the world really worth pursuing—the knowledge of God.

R. H. Benson: *Introduction to Lady Lovat's Life of St. Teresa.* (20th cent.)

Intellect has not much to do with the knowledge of God, and the things which He hides from the wise and prudent He reveals to babes.

R. H. Benson: *The Light Invisible.* (20th cent.)

Whatever else there was, there was never any such thing as the evolution of the idea of God. The idea was concealed, was avoided, was almost forgotten, was even explained away; but it was never evolved.

G. K. Chesterton: *The Everlasting Man,* I, 4. (20th cent.)

Often the western wind has sung to me,
There have been voices in the streams and meres,
And pitiful trees have told me, God, of Thee:
And I heard not. Oh! open Thou mine ears.

Lord Alfred Douglas: *A Prayer.* (20th cent.)

The book of God no man can write; he must lay down his pen. This is the streak of agnosticism in Catholic theology.

M. C. D'Arcy: *The Idea of God.* (In *God and the Supernatural*) (20th cent.)

Plato's flight to God is not the highest Catholic conception. It may be necessary, it often is necessary to leave the creature to find the Creator; but the perfect ideal is the synoptic vision of all reality as included within the divine Love, and therefore most lovable in itself. And it is this ideal which is at the back of progress and civilization, and has been raised to a still higher plane by the union of all Catholics in Christ.

M. C. D'Arcy: *The Idea of God.* (In *God and the Supernatural*) (20th cent.)

Our discovery of God is, in a way, God's discovery of us. We cannot go to heaven to find Him because we have no way of knowing where heaven is or what it is. He comes down from heaven and finds us. He looks at us from the depths of His own infinite actuality, which is everywhere, and His seeing us gives us a superior reality in which we also discover Him. We only know Him in so far as we are known by Him, and our contemplation of Him is a participation of His contemplation of Himself.

Thomas Merton: *Seeds of Contemplation.* (20th cent.)

The more one discovers of God, the more one finds one has to learn. Every step in advance is a return to the beginning, and we shall not really know Him as he is, until we have returned to our beginning, and learned to know Him as both the beginning and the end of our journey.

> Dom Griffiths: *The Golden String.* (20th cent.)

XXIII—*God and Man*

There is an enmity between What is of God and what is of man.

> Tertullian: *The Christian's Defence.* (3rd cent.)

God is to be estimated, not by human statements, but by His own words.

> St. Ambrose: *On Penitence,* 1, 21. (4th cent.)

Laugh where we must, be candid where we can,
But vindicate the ways of God to man.

> Pope: *An Essay on Man,* 1. (18th cent.)

XXIV—*Aphorisms, etc.*

God willing. (Deo favente.)

> Phrase occurs in Virgil, *Aeneid,* 1, 303.

Man thinks, God directs. (Homo cogitat, Deus indicat.)

> Alcuin: *Epistles.* (8th cent.)

Man proposes, but God disposes. (Homo proponit, sed Deus disponit.)

> Thomas a Kempis: *The Imitation of Christ,* 1, 19. (Based on Proverbs, 16, 9: *The heart of man must plan his course, but his steps will fall as the Lord directs.*) (15th cent.)

To God, most good, most great. (Deo optimo maximo.)

> Legend, used especially in dedications. (16th cent.)

God is where He was.

> John Heywood: *Proverbs,* 1, 12. (16th cent.)

Here is God in th'ambry.

> ambry—wall tabernacle

> John Heywood: *Proverbs,* 2, 4. (16th cent.)

Every man for himself and God for us all.

> John Heywood: *Proverbs,* 2, 9. (16th cent.)

See also Father, God the; Gifts of God; Holy Ghost; Jesus Christ; Love of God; Serving God; Trust in God; Union with God; Vision of God

Gods

A god does not change his ways.

> Tertullian: *The Christian's Defence.* (3rd cent.)

Gods meet gods, and justle in the dark.

> Dryden and Nathaniel Lee: *Oedipus,* 4. (17th cent.)

Gold

All is not gold that shines like gold. (Non teneas aurum totum quod splendet ut aurum.)

> Alain de Lille: *Parabolae,* 3. (13th cent.)

All is not gold that glitters.

> John Heywood: *Proverbs,* 1, 10. (16th cent.)

A man may buy gold too dear.

> John Heywood: *Proverbs,* 2, 7. (16th cent.)

Man was made the standing jest of Heav'n,
And gold but sent to keep the fools in play,
For some to heap and some to throw away.

> Pope: *Moral Essays,* 3. (18th cent.)

Golden Rule

All things whatsoever that thou wouldst not wish to be done to thee, do thou also not to another.

> Teaching of the Twelve Apostles. (2nd cent.)

Whatever the Christians do not wish to be done to them they do not do to another.

> St. Aristides: *Apology for the Christian Faith*, 15. (2nd cent.)

Good, Goodness

Inasmuch as we exist, we are good.

> St. Augustine: *De Doctrina Christiana*, 1, 42. (4th cent.)

For that which every man seeketh most after, is by him esteemed his greatest good. Which is all one with happiness.

> Boethius: *De Consolatione Philosophiae*, 3, 1. (6th cent.)

All things but God are good by participation.

> Boethius: *De Hebdomadibus*. (6th cent.)

Goodness and being are really the same, and differ only in idea.

> St. Thomas Aquinas: *Summa Theologica*, 1, 5, 1. (13th cent.)

The essence of goodness consists in this, that it is in some way desirable.

> St. Thomas Aquinas: *Summa Theologica*, 1, 5, 1. (13th cent.)

Whatsoever is called good is good by the divine goodness, which is its first exemplar cause, its effective cause, and its final cause.

> St. Thomas Aquinas: *Summa Theologica*, 1, 6, 4. (13th cent.)

Each one confusedly doth apprehend
A longed-for good, wherein the mind may rest;
And there each one strives to attain that end.

> Dante: *Purgatorio, Canto 17*. (Tr. L. Binyon) (14th cent.)

Be a good child, and God will help you.

> St. Jeanne d'Arc. (Advice she claimed to have received from St. Michael.) (15th cent.)

There is no creature so little and contemptible as not to manifest the goodness of God.

> Thomas a Kempis: *The Imitation of Christ*, 2, 4. (15th cent.)

Sometimes we so much occupy ourselves with being good angels that we neglect to be good men and women.

> St. Francis de Sales: *Letters to Persons in the World*, 1, 5. (17th cent.)

All that is good *in* us, is not *of* us.

> Jean Pierre Camus: *The Spirit of St. Francis de Sales*, 19, 3. (17th cent.)

They say everything in the world is good for something.

> Dryden: *The Spanish Friar*, 3, 2. (17th cent.)

Hard was their lodging, homely was their food,
For all their luxury was doing good.

> Sir Samuel Garth: *Claremont*. (18th cent.)

Though the useful is not always good, the good is always useful.

> Card. Newman: *Idea of a University*, 7. (19th cent.)

The personal is not a mere figure for the impersonal: rather the impersonal is a clumsy term for something more personal than common personality. God is not a symbol of goodness. Goodness is a symbol of God.

> G. K. Chesterton: *William Blake*. (20th cent.)

See also Being; God—His Goodness

Good and Bad

The power of choosing good and evil is within the reach of all.

> Origen: *De Principiis*, 2. (3rd cent.)

For my good deeds are Your act and Your gift, my ill deeds are my own faults and Your punishments.

> St. Augustine: *Confessions*, 10, 4. (5th cent.)

He that is good is free, though he be a slave; he that is evil is a slave, though he be a king.

> St. Augustine: *The City of God,* 4. (5th cent.)

God, it is true, foresaw the evil that man would do (foreseeing it, of course, He did not force man to do it), but at the same time He knew the good that He would Himself make come out of it.

> St. Augustine: *De Correptione et Gratia,* 12, 37. (5th cent.)

To attribute to God, and not to self, whatever good one sees in oneself; but to recognize always that the evil is one's own doing, and to impute it to oneself.

> St. Benedict: *Rule,* 4. (One of his 'tools of good works') (6th cent.)

Every existent, whatsoever and howsoever, is from God, Who is the perfect good. Since evil cannot be the direct effect of good, no being as such can be evil: *every creature of God is good* (I Tim. 4, 4).

> St. Thomas Aquinas: *Contra Gentes,* 3, 7. (13th cent.)

Man knows not how either to rejoice aright or how to grieve aright, for he understands not the distance that there is between good and evil.

> St. John of the Cross: *Spiritual Sentences and Maxims.* (16th cent.)

In working well, if travail you sustain,
Into the wind shall lightly pass the pain;
But of the deed the glory shall remain,
And cause your name with worthy wights to reign.
In working wrong, if pleasure you attain,
The pleasure soon shall fade, and void as vain;
But of the deed throughout the life the shame
Endures, defacing you with foul defame.

> Nicholas Grimald: *Musonius the Philosopher's Sayings.* (16th cent.)

In this perishable life, good is never to be found without evil following in its train.

> St. Francis de Sales: *Spiritual Conferences,* 3. (17th cent.)

Where good and ill, together blent,
Wage an undying strife.

> Card. Newman: *A Martyr Convert.* (19th cent.)

Nothing emboldens the wicked so greatly as the lack of courage on the part of the good.

> Pope Leo XIII: *Sapientiae Christianae.* (Jan. 10, 1890)

Good Friday

Come, let us praise Him, Who was crucified for us. For Mary beheld Him on the tree and said: Even if Thou dost endure the cross, Thou art my Son and my God.

> Byzantine Triodion, Matins, Kontakion. (St. Romanos the Melodist, 6th cent.)

Jerusalem, Jerusalem, be converted to the Lord thy God.

> Roman Breviary, Tenebrae. (Versicle repeated after each lesson at matins on Holy Thursday, Good Friday and Holy Saturday) (Before 7th cent.)

Thou didst ransom us from the curse of the law by Thy Precious Blood; Thou didst shed forth immortality upon mankind by being nailed to the cross and pierced with a spear. O our Savior, glory to Thee.

> Byzantine Triodion, Kathisma at Matins (Service of Holy Passion). (ca. 6th to 8th cent.)

Thou that didst clothe Thyself with light as with a garment didst stand naked at the judgment seat, and didst receive blows on the cheek from hands which Thou didst make. Yea, the wicked people nailed the Lord of glory to the Cross. Then was the veil of the temple rent in twain, the sun was darkened, unable to behold outraged God, Whom all things fear. Let us worship Him.

Byzantine Triodion, Tenth Antiphon at Matins. (ca. 6th to 8th cent.)

Thus saith the Lord to the Jews, My people, what have I done unto thee, or in what have I hindered thee? I gave sight to the blind, I cleansed thy lepers, I restored the paralytic. My people, what have I done unto thee, and what hast thou done in return for Me? For manna, thou hast returned hyssop; for water, vinegar; for My love thou hast nailed Me to the Cross. But no longer will I withhold Myself from others: I will call the gentiles Mine, and these shall glorify Me, with the Father and the Spirit, and I will give them eternal life.

Byzantine Triodion, Twelfth Antiphon at Matins. (ca. 6th to 8th cent.)

Today is suspended on the tree He That suspendeth the earth upon the waters (*thrice*). He That is the King of angels is crowned with thorns. He That covereth the heavens with clouds is covered with derisive purple. He That freed Adam in the Jordan is buffeted. The Bridegroom of the Church is pierced with nails. The Son of the Virgin is wounded with a spear. We adore Thy passion, O Christ (*thrice*). Let us also behold Thy glorious resurrection.

Byzantine Triodion, Fifteenth Antiphon at Matins. (ca. 6th to 8th cent.)

All creation was changed by fear, when it saw Thee, O Christ, hanging upon the cross; the sun was darkened, and the foundations of the earth were shaken. All things suffered with the Creator of all things. O Lord, Who for us didst willingly endure, glory to Thee.

Byzantine Triodion, Aposticha at Matins. (ca. 6th to 8th cent.)

Behold the wood of the Cross on which hung the Savior of the world. Come let us adore.
We adore Thy Cross, O Lord: and we praise and glorify Thy holy resurrection;

for behold by the wood of the Cross joy came into the whole world.

Roman Missal, Antiphons sung during Adoration of Cross on Good Friday. (Liber Resp., ca. 7th cent.)

O My people, what have I done to thee? or in what have I afflicted thee? answer Me. ℣ Because I led thee out of the land of Egypt, thou hast prepared a cross for Thy Savior. . . .
What more ought I to do for thee, and have not done? I planted thee, indeed, My most beautiful vineyard: and thou art become to Me exceeding bitter; for thou hast given Me vinegar in My thirst; and with a spear thou hast pierced the side of thy Savior.

Roman Missal, Good Friday, Reproaches (Improperia) sung during Adoration of Cross. (ca. 7th cent.)

Our Shepherd, the fount of living water, is gone, at Whose passing the sun was darkened: For He is taken, Who took captive the first man: today our Savior burst asunder both the gates and the bolts of death. ℣ He destroyed the prisons of hell, and overthrew the might of the devil. . . .

Roman Breviary, Matins of Holy Saturday, Responsory. (ca. 6th-8th cent.)

When Thou, the deathless Life, didst come down to death, then didst Thou slay hades through the dazzling brightness of Thy Godhead; and when Thou didst raise up the dead from the abyss, all the powers of heaven cried aloud: Christ, our God, Giver of life, glory to Thee.

Byzantine Triodion, Epitaphy (Matins of Holy Saturday). (ca. 6th to 8th cent.)

Come, let us behold our life lying in the grave in order that He may give life to those who lie in their graves. Come, and let us see today Him of Judea, Who sleeps; to Him we will prophetically cry: Who shall raise Thee up, O King, Thou Who didst as a lion fall asleep? But of Thine own power rise up, Thou

Who didst willingly give Thyself for us.
O Lord, glory to Thee.

> Byzantine Triodion, Sticheron at Matins.
> (ca. 6th to 8th cent.)

> This day eternal Love, for me
> Fast nail'd unto a cursed tree,
> Rending His fleshly veil, did through
>   His side
> A way to paradise provide.
> This day Life dy'd; and dying, over-
>   threw
> Death, sin, and Satan too.
>   O happy day!
>   May sinners say:
> But day can it be said to be,
>   Wherein we see
> The bright Sun of celestial light
> O'ershadowed with so black a night?

> Sir Edward Sherburne: *Good Friday.*
> (17th cent.)

See also Cross; Palm Sunday; Passion of
Our Lord

Good Works

Let us consider that all the saints have
been adorned with good works; and the
Lord Himself, adorning Himself with
good works [i.e. the works of creation],
rejoiced. Holding this pattern, then, let
us follow out His will without hesitation; let us do the work of justice with
all our strength.

> Pope St. Clement I: *Letter to the
> Corinthians,* 33, 7-8. (1st cent.)

Let your baptism be ever your shield,
your faith a helmet, your charity a spear,
your patience a panoply. Let your works
be deposits, so that you may receive the
sum that is due to you.

> St. Ignatius of Antioch: *Letter to St.
> Polycarp,* 6. (2nd cent.)

Our prayers and fastings are of less
avail, unless they are aided by almsgiving . . . entreaties alone are of little force
to obtain what they seek, unless they
be made sufficient by the addition of
deeds and good works.

> St. Cyprian: *On Works and Alms,* 5. (3rd
> cent.)

He who would obey the gospel must first
be purged of all defilement of the flesh
and the spirit that so he may be acceptable to God in the good works of holiness.

> St. Basil: *The Morals,* 2, 1. (4th cent.)

To be active in works and unfaithful in
heart is like raising a beautiful and lofty
building on an unsound foundation.
The higher the building, the greater the
fall. Without the support of faith good
works cannot stand.

> St. Ambrose: *On the Duties of the Clergy,*
> 2, 7. (4th cent.)

How speedily are the prayers of people
who do good works heard! For it is
precisely in fasting, almsdeeds and
prayer that our righteousness in this life
consists. Would you have your prayers
fly to God, equip them with the two
wings of fasting and almsdeeds.

> St. Augustine: *In Ps. 42 Enarr. 1,* 8. (5th
> cent.)

We do the works, but God works in us
the doing of the works.

> St. Augustine: *De Dono Perseverentiae,*
> 13, 33. (5th cent.)

A work is then truly excellent, when the
intention of the workman is struck out
from the love of God, and returns again
and again to rest in charity.

> St. Augustine. (5th cent.)

Let Thy grace always precede and follow
us, we beseech Thee, O Lord; and make
us ever intent upon good works.

> Roman Missal, Collect for Sixteenth
> Sunday after Pentecost. (Gregorian, 6th
> to 8th cent.)

Stir up the wills of Thy faithful people,
we beseech Thee, O Lord; that seeking
the fruit of good works more earnestly,
they may receive more abundantly the
gifts of Thy loving kindness.

> Roman Missal, Collect for Twenty-fourth
> Sunday after Pentecost. (Gregorian, 6th to
> 8th cent.)

And as a man, by feeling hour by hour
In the doing of good works increased
    delight,
Perceives his virtue growing more
    and more.

Dante: *Paradiso, Canto 18.* (Tr. Binyon)
(14th cent.)

I would ween that good works were not
so deadly poison, but (taking not too
much at once, for dosing of the stomach,
no more at once, lo! than I see the world
wont to do), many drams of such treacle,
mixed with one scruple of dread, were
able enough, for ought I can see, to preserve the soul from presumption, that
one spoonful of good works should no
more kill the soul than a potager of
good worts kill or destroy the body.

St. Thomas More: *Confutation of Tindale.*
(16th cent.)

Men's chief study nowadays, seems to
be how they may best do without good
works. They will go hanging and idling
about God's vineyard, rather than come
up, and be hired into it.

St. Thomas More. (16th cent.)

If any one saith that all works done
before justification, in whatsoever way
they be done, are truly sins or merit the
hatred of God; or that the more earnestly
one strives to dispose himself for grace,
the more grievously he sins; let him be
anathema.

Council of Trent, Session 6, Canon 7.
(Jan. 13, 1547)

If any one saith that the justice received
is not preserved and also increased before God through good works; but that
the said works are merely the fruits and
signs of justification obtained, but not a
cause of the increase thereof; let him be
anathema.

Council of Trent, Session 6, Canon 24.
(Jan. 13, 1547)

If any one saith that in every good work
the just sins venially at least, or—what
is more intolerable still—mortally, and

consequently deserves eternal punishments; and that for this cause only he
is not damned, that God does not impute those works unto damnation; let
him be anathema.

Council of Trent, Session 6, Canon 25.
(Jan. 13, 1547)

If any one saith that the just ought not
for their good works done in God to expect and hope for eternal recompense
from God through His mercy and the
merit of Jesus Christ, if so be that they
persevere to the end in well doing and
in keeping the divine commandments;
let him be anathema.

Council of Trent, Session 6, Canon 26.
(Jan. 13, 1547)

If any one saith that the good works of
one that is justified are in such manner
the gifts of God, as that they are not
also the good merits of him that is justified; or that the said justified by the
good works which he performs through
the grace of God and the merit of Jesus
Christ, Whose living member he is, does
not truly merit increase of grace, eternal
life, and the attainment of that eternal
life,—if so be however that he depart
in grace,—and also an increase of glory;
let him be anathema.

Council of Trent, Session 6, Canon 32.
(Jan. 13, 1547)

Think not that pleasing God lies so
much in performing good works as in
performing them with good will, and
without attachment and respect to persons.

St. John of the Cross: *Spiritual Sentences
and Maxims.* (16th cent.)

All thy good works which went before
And waited for thee at the door,
Shall own thee there; and all in one
Weave a constellation
Of crowns, with which the King thy
    Spouse
Shall build up thy triumphant brows.

Richard Crashaw: *Hymn to St. Teresa.*
(17th cent.)

Good actions still must be maintained
    with good,
As bodies nourished with resembling
    food.
>   Dryden. (17th cent.)

Goodwill

Goodwill is increased by the gathering
together of the Church, by fellowship
in faith, by association in baptism, by
the bond of grace received, by communion in the sacraments. The bond of
grace tends mightily to increase good-
will.

> St. Ambrose: *On the Duties of the Clergy,*
> 1, 170. (4th cent.)

Goose

When the rain raineth and the goose
    winketh,
Little wots the gosling what the goose
    thinketh.

> John Skelton: *Garland of Laurell.* (16th
> cent.)

As deep drinketh the goose as the gander.

> John Heywood: *Proverbs,* 2, 7. (16th
> cent.)

While man exclaims, "See all things
    for my use!"
"See man for mine!" replies a pam-
    pered goose.

> Pope: *An Essay on Man,* 3. (18th cent.)

Gospel

All is not gospel that thou dost speak.

> John Heywood: *Proverbs,* 2, 2. (16th
> cent.)

Gossip

Let us then join with those to whom
grace is given from God; let us put on
concord in meekness of spirit and in
self-control, keeping ourselves far from

all gossip and evil speaking, being justified by works and not by words.

> Pope St. Clement I: *Letter to the
> Corinthians,* 30, 3. (1st cent.)

To tell tales out of school.

> John Heywood: *Proverbs,* 1, 10. (16th
> cent.)

Blab it wist, and out it must.

> John Heywood: *Proverbs,* 1, 10. (16th
> cent.)

>   Her ears might well glow,
> For all the town talked of her.

> John Heywood: *Proverbs,* 2, 1. (16th
> cent.)

If all men knew what others say of them,
there would not be four friends in the
world.

>   Pascal: *Pensées,* 8. (17th cent.)

And all who told it added something
    new,
And all who heard it made enlarge-
    ments too;
In ev'ry ear it spread, on ev'ry tongue
    it grew.

> Pope: *The Temple of Fame.* (18th cent.)

Government

Whatsoever moveth is stronger than that
which is moved, and whatsoever governeth is stronger than that which is
governed.

> St. Aristides: *Apology for the Christian
> Faith.* (2nd cent.)

It seems to me that to rule men is the art
of arts, and the science of sciences, for
man is a being diverse and manifold in
character.

> St. Gregory of Nazianzen: *Orations,* 2, 16.
> (4th cent.)

But there could be nothing more fortunate for human affairs than that, by
the mercy of God, they who are endowed with true piety of life, if they

have the skill for ruling people, should also have the power. But such men, however great virtues they may possess in this life, attribute it solely to the grace of God that He has bestowed it on them —willing, believing, seeking. And at the same time they understand how far they are short of that perfection of righteousness which exists in the society of those holy angels for which they are striving to fit themselves.

> St. Augustine: *The City of God*, 5, 19. (5th cent.)

It is a common experience that in the school of adversity the heart is forced to discipline itself; but when a man has achieved supreme rule, it is at once changed and puffed up by the experience of his high estate.

> Pope St. Gregory I: *Pastoral Care*, 1, 3. (6th cent.)

If all were without fear, who could possibly restrain anyone from doing evil? Hence princes and kings are chosen among the nations, that they may coerce the people from evil through the fear in which they are held, and subdue them to right living through laws.

> St. Isidore: *Sentences*, 3, 47. (7th cent.)

The best form of government is in a state or kingdom, wherein one is given the power to preside over all, while under him are others having governing powers: and yet a government of this kind is shared by all, both because all are eligible to govern, and because the rulers are chosen by all. For this is the best form of polity, being partly kingdom, since there is one at the head of all; partly aristocracy, in so far as a number of persons are set in authority; partly democracy, i.e. government by the people, and the people have the right to choose their rulers.

> St. Thomas Aquinas: *Summa Theologica*, 1-2, 105, 1. (13th cent.)

If, therefore, it is natural for man to live in the society of many, it is necessary that there exist among men some means by which the group may be governed. For where there are many men together, and each one is looking after his own interest, the group would be broken up and scattered unless there were also someone to take care of what appertains to the common weal.

> St. Thomas Aquinas: *The Governance of Rulers*, 1, 1. (13th cent.)

If, therefore, a group of free men is governed by their ruler for the common good of the group, that government will be right and just, as is suitable to free men. If, however, the government is organized, not for the common good of the group but for the private interest of the ruler, it will be an unjust and perverted government.

> St. Thomas Aquinas: *The Governance of Rulers*, 1, 1. (13th cent.)

Now, the welfare and safety of a multitude formed into a society is the preservation of its unity, which is called peace, and which, if taken away, the benefit of social life is lost and moreover the multitude in its disagreement becomes a burden to itself. The chief concern of the ruler of a multitude, therefore, should be to procure the unity of peace.

> St. Thomas Aquinas: *The Governance of Rulers*, 1, 2. (13th cent.)

Since man is by nature a social animal living in a group, a likeness of the divine rulership is found in him, not only in this, that a single man is ruled by reason, but also in that a multitude is governed through the reason of one man.

> St. Thomas Aquinas: *The Governance of Rulers*, 1, 12. (13th cent.)

Just as the laws are made for the sake of the body politic rather than the body politic for the laws, likewise those living under the law do not exist for the sake of the legislator but he for them. . . . From which it is evident that although the consul or the king are lords over others in regard to means, they are them-

selves ministers towards others in regard
to ends.

> Dante: *Monarchy*, 1. (14th cent.)

By divine ordinance the ecclesiastical
order is subject to one person; but there
is no obligation by divine law for the
faithful, as laymen, to be subject to one
supreme monarchy in temporal matters.
By the natural law, which is from God,
they are permitted to live in civil communities, and that they may obviously
order their lives properly in these communities, to choose different rulers in
accordance with the nature of the community.

> John of Paris: *Concerning Royal and Papal
> Power*, 3. (14th cent.)

A prince is set up in authority not
through knowledge of the laws or
through practical wisdom or moral virtue, although these are the qualities of
a perfect governor. For many may have
these qualities who, lacking the authority, are not governors, unless perchance
they are near to power. The effective
power in the institution of a governing
body, that is, in election, pertains to the
legislator—that is, to the whole body of
citizens. The latter likewise have the
power of correcting the government, and
even the power of deposition, should
such become expedient for the common
interest.

> Marsiglio of Padua: *Defensor Pacis*, 1, 15.
> (14th cent.)

No man securely governeth but he who
would willingly live in subjection.

> Thomas a Kempis: *The Imitation of Christ*,
> 1, 20. (15th cent.)

Since by nature all men are free, all government—whether based on written law
or on law embodied in a ruler through
whose government the subjects are restrained from evil deeds and their liberty regulated, for a good end, by
fear of punishment—arises solely from
agreement and consent of the subjects.
For if men are by nature powerful and
equally free, a valid and ordained authority of any one person, whose power
is by nature like that of any of the rest,
cannot be created save by election and
consent of the others, just as law is established by consent.

> Cardinal Nicholas of Cusa: *De
> Concordantia Catholica*, 2, 14. (15th cent.)

There be two kinds of kingdoms, of the
which that one is a lordship called in
Latin *dominium regale,* and that other is
called *dominium politicum et regale.*
And they differ in that the first king
may rule his people by such laws as he
maketh himself. . . . The second king
may not rule his people by other laws
than such as they assent unto.

> Sir John Fortescue: *Governance of
> England*, 1. (The author considered
> France an example of the first kind, and
> England, with its Parliament, an instance
> of the second.) (15th cent.)

Political rule is so natural and necessary
to the human race that it cannot be withdrawn without destroying nature herself; for the nature of man is such that
he is a social animal.

> St. Robert Bellarmine: *De Laicis*, 5. (16th
> cent.)

Individual forms of government in specific instances derive from the law of
nations, not from the natural law, for,
as is evident, it depends on the consent
of the people to decide whether kings,
or consuls, or other magistrates are to
be established in authority over them;
and if there be a legitimate cause, the
people can change a kingdom into an
aristocracy, or an aristocracy into a democracy, and vice versa, as we read was
done in Rome.

> St. Robert Bellarmine: *De Laicis*, 6. (16th
> cent.)

Political power, considered in general,
not descending in particular to monarchy, aristocracy, or democracy, comes
directly from God alone; for this follows of necessity from the nature of

man, since that nature comes from Him Who made it. Besides, this power derives from the natural law, since it does not depend upon the consent of men; for, willing or unwilling, they must be ruled over by some one, unless they wish the human race to perish, which is against a primary instinct.

> St. Robert Bellarmine: *De Laicis,* 6. (16th cent.)

[Political] power resides, as in its subject, immediately in the whole state, for this power is by divine law, but divine law gives this power to no particular man, therefore divine law gives this power to the collected body.

> St. Robert Bellarmine: *De Laicis,* 6. (16th cent.)

Political power is delegated by the multitude to one or several, for the state cannot of itself exercise this power, therefore it is held to delegate it to some individual, or to several, and this authority of rulers considered thus in general is both by natural law and by divine law, nor could the entire human race assembled together decree the opposite, that is, that there should be neither rulers nor leaders.

> St. Robert Bellarmine: *De Laicis,* 6. (16th cent.)

A civil magistracy accompanied by temporal power for human government is just and in complete harmony with human nature. This conclusion is certainly true, and a matter of faith.

> F. Suarez: *On Laws and God the Lawgiver,* 3, 1. (17th cent.)

All empire is no more than pow'r in trust.

> Dryden: *Absalom and Achitophel.* (17th cent.)

For forms of government let fools contest:
Whate'er is best administer'd is best.

> Pope: *An Essay on Man,* 3. (18th cent.)

No government, whose workings are entrusted to men, ever is or can be practically perfect—secure all good, and guard against all evil. In all human governments there will be defects and abuses, and he is no wise man who expects perfection from imperfection. But the American constitution, taken as a whole, and in all its parts, is the least imperfect that has ever existed, and under it individual rights, personal freedom and independence, as well as public authority or society, are better protected than under any other.

> Orestes Brownson: *The American Republic.* (19th cent.)

Christianity introduced no new forms of government, but a new spirit, which totally transformed the old ones.

> Lord Acton: *Political Thoughts on the Church.* (19th cent.)

The Church approves of every one devoting his services to the common good, and doing all that he can for the defence, preservation, and prosperity of his country.

> Pope Leo XIII: *Libertas Praestantissimum.* (June 20, 1888)

A society can neither exist nor be conceived in which there is no one to govern the wills of individuals, in such a way as to make, as it were, one will out of many, and to impel them rightly and orderly to the common good; therefore, God has willed that in a civil society there should be some to rule the multitude. And this also is a powerful argument, that those by whose authority the state is administered must be able so to compel the citizens to obedience that it is clearly a sin in the latter not to obey. But no man has in himself or of himself the power of constraining the freewill of others by fetters of authority of this kind. This power resides solely in God, the Creator and Legislator of all things; and it is necessary that those who exercise it should do so as having received it from God.

> Pope Leo XIII: *Diuturnum.* (June 20, 1881)

Government should be administered for the welfare of the citizens, because they who govern others possess authority solely for the welfare of the state.

> Pope Leo XIII: *Immortale Dei.* (Nov. 1, 1885)

That the king can do no wrong was never anything but a legal fiction; and it is a legal fiction still. The doctrine of divine right was not a piece of idealism, but rather a piece of realism, a practical way of ruling amid the ruin of humanity; a very pragmatic piece of faith. The religious basis of government was not so much that people put their trust in princes, as that they did not put their trust in any child of man.

> G. K. Chesterton: *What's Wrong with the World.* (20th cent.)

The party system in England is an enormous and most efficient machine for preventing political conflicts.

> G. K. Chesterton: *George Bernard Shaw.* (20th cent.)

There are only two kinds of social structure conceivable—personal government and impersonal government. If my anarchic friends will not have rules, they will have rulers. Preferring personal government, with its tact and flexibility, is called royalism. Preferring impersonal government, with its dogmas and definitions, is called republicanism. Objecting broadmindedly both to kings and creeds is called Bosh—at least, I know no more philosophic word for it.

> G. K. Chesterton: *What's Wrong with the World.* (20th cent.)

It is said that modern government makes life safer; and the claim is very tenable. But at least it is certain that modern government makes life for the governing classes safer; and never before in the history of the world has it been so safe a business to govern.

> G. K. Chesterton: *Generally Speaking.* (20th cent.)

It is idle to talk against representative government or for it. All government is representative government until it begins to decay. Unfortunately (as is also evident) all government begins to decay the instant it begins to govern.

> G. K. Chesterton: *A Miscellany of Men.* (20th cent.)

The most successful government is that which leads its subjects to the highest aim by means of the greatest freedom.

> V. McNabb: *Thoughts Twice-dyed.* (20th cent.)

Justice requires that to lawfully constituted authority there be given that respect and obedience which is its due; that the laws which are made shall be in wise conformity with the common good; and that, as a matter of conscience, all men shall render obedience to these laws.

> Pope Pius XII: *Easter Message of Peace.* (Apr. 9, 1939)

See also Authority; Democracy; Despotism; King; Law; Politics; Republic; Ruler; Sovereignty; State; Totalitarianism; Tyranny

Grace

Since we are hindered by the devil from obeying with our thought and deed God's will in all things, we pray and ask that God's will may be done in us; and that it may be done in us we have need of God's good will, that is, of His help and protection, since no one is strong in his own strength, but he is safe by the grace and mercy of God.

> St. Cyprian: *On the Lord's Prayer,* 14. (3rd cent.)

For God has not only made us out of nothing; but He gave us freely, by the

grace of the Word, a life in correspondence with God.

> St. Athanasius: *On the Incarnation of the
> Word of God,* 5. (4th cent.)

Cleanse thy vessel, that thou mayest receive grace more abundantly. For though
remission of sins is given equally to all,
the communion of the Holy Ghost is bestowed in proportion to each man's faith.

> St. Cyril of Jerusalem: *Catechetical
> Discourses,* 1, 5. (4th cent.)

Every holy thought is the gift of God,
the inspiration of God, the grace of God.

> St. Ambrose: *Concerning Cain,* 1, 45. (4th
> cent.)

God calls those whom He deigns to call,
and whom He wills to make religious.

> St. Ambrose: *Explanation of St. Luke,* 7,
> 27. (4th cent.)

Thou wouldst not have been called to
grace, had not Christ thought thee
worthy of His grace.

> St. Ambrose: *On the Sacraments,* 1, 1, 1.
> (4th cent.)

The law detects, grace alone conquers,
sin.

> St. Augustine: *Of Continence.* (5th cent.)

As the eye of the body cannot see unless
it is helped by the brightness of light,
so, neither can a man, even if he is most
righteous, live righteously unless he be
helped by the eternal light of justice.

> St. Augustine: *De Natura et Gratia,* 26.
> (5th cent.)

Whoever denies that we ought to say the
prayer "Lead us not into temptation"
(and they deny it who maintain that the
help of God's grace is not necessary to
man for salvation, but that the gift of
the law is enough for the human will)
ought without doubt to be removed beyond all hearing, and to be anathema-
tized by the tongue of all.

> St. Augustine: *De Perfect. Just.,* 21.
> (5th cent.)

Do not be disturbed at His saying that
they do by nature those things that are
of the Law; for the Spirit of grace works
this, in order to restore in us the image
of God, after which we were naturally
made.

> St. Augustine: *De Spiritu et Littera,* 27.
> (5th cent.)

This grace of Christ without which
neither infants nor adults can be saved,
is not rendered for any merits, but is
given *gratis,* on account of which it is
also called *grace.*

> St. Augustine: *De Natura et Gratia,* 4.
> (5th cent.)

There is no method whereby any persons
arrive at absolute perfection, or whereby
any man makes the slightest progress to
true and godly righteousness, but by the
assisting grace of our crucified Savior
Christ, and the gift of His Spirit; and
whosoever shall deny this cannot rightly,
I almost think, be reckoned in the number of any kind of Christians at all.

> St. Augustine: *De Natura et Gratia,* 70.
> (5th cent.)

This is the right understanding of the
grace of God through Jesus Christ our
Lord, by which alone men are freed
from evil and without which they do no
good whatsoever either in thought or in
will and love or in action; not only do
men know by its showing what they are
to do, but by its power they do with love
what they know is to be done.

> St. Augustine: *De Correptione et Gratia,*
> 2, 3. (5th cent.)

God so works in the hearts of men and
in freewill itself that holy thought, good
counsel and every desire of goodwill is
of God, since through Him alone we
are capable of anything good, without
Whom we can do nothing.

> St. Prosper of Aquitaine: *Indiculus on
> Grace,* 6. (5th cent.)

Grace . . . not actually freely given is not
grace at all.

> Pope St. Leo I: *Letters,* 1, 3. (5th cent.)

O Lord, we beseech Thee, mercifully hear the prayers of Thy people who call upon Thee; and grant that they may both perceive what they ought to do, and may have the strength to fulfill the same.

> Roman Missal, Collect for First Sunday after Epiphany. (Gregorian, 6th to 8th cent.)

Let grace be the beginning, grace the consummation, grace the crown.

> St. Bede the Venerable: *In Cant. Cant.* 1. (8th cent.)

We are prepared for grace in that we are turned to God. For this we need the help of divine grace.

> St. Thomas Aquinas: *Quodlibets,* 1, 4, 7. (13th cent.)

A positive reality is put into a person who receives grace: there is, first, the gift freely given him, and next, his response and acknowledgment.

> St. Thomas Aquinas: *Summa Theologica,* 1-2, 110, 1. (13th cent.)

According to the common manner of speech, grace is usually taken in three ways: First for anyone's love, as we are accustomed to say that the soldier is in the good graces of the king, i.e., the king looks on him with favor. Secondly, it is taken for any gift freely bestowed, as we are accustomed to say: I do you this act of grace. Thirdly, it is taken for the recompense of a gift given *gratis,* inasmuch as we are said to be *grateful* for benefits.

> St. Thomas Aquinas: *Summa Theologica,* 1-2, 110, 1. (13th cent.)

Grace is a certain beauty of soul, which wins the divine love.

> St. Thomas Aquinas: *Summa Theologica,* 1-2, 110, 2. (13th cent.)

Grace has five effects in us: first, our soul is healed; second, we will good; third, we work effectively for it; fourth, we persevere; fifth, we break through to glory.

> St. Thomas Aquinas: *Summa Theologica,* 1-2, 111, 3. (13th cent.)

As the soul is the life of the body, God is the life of the soul by His gracious presence. And yet however vivid the experience of grace may be, it is only in faith, and it is not that which we shall have of God Himself in the happiness of heaven.

> Walter Hilton: *Scale of Perfection,* 2, 41. (14th cent.)

When the grace of God cometh to a man then he is strong and powerful for all things; and when it departeth then he is poor and weak, left as it were only to stripes.

> Thomas a Kempis: *The Imitation of Christ,* 2, 8. (15th cent.)

He rideth at ease that is carried by the grace of God.

> Thomas a Kempis: *The Imitation of Christ,* 2, 9. (15th cent.)

This grace is so excellent that neither the gift of prophecy, nor the working of miracles, nor any speculation, how sublime soever, is of any value without it. Nor even faith, nor hope, nor any other virtues, are acceptable to Thee without charity and grace.

> Thomas a Kempis: *The Imitation of Christ,* 3, 55. (15th cent.)

For the gifts of nature are common to the good and bad; but grace or divine love is the proper gift of the elect, and they that are adorned with it are esteemed worthy of eternal life.

> Thomas a Kempis: *The Imitation of Christ,* 3, 55. (15th cent.)

Grace is the mistress of truth, the teacher of discipline, the light of the heart, the comforter of affliction, the banisher of sorrow, the expeller of fears, the nurse of devotion, the producer of tears. What am I without it but a piece of dry wood, and an unprofitable stock, fit for nothing but to be cast away.

> Thomas a Kempis: *The Imitation of Christ,* 3, 55. (15th cent.)

If any man marvel that God made all His creatures such as they should always need aid of His grace, let him know that God did it out of His double goodness. First, to keep them from pride by causing them [to] perceive their feebleness, and to call upon Him; and secondly, to do His creatures honor and comfort.

> St. Thomas More: *Treatise on the Passion.* (16th cent.)

In space cometh grace.

> John Heywood: *Proverbs,* 1, 4. (16th cent.)

God does not command the impossible, but in commanding serves notice that one do what he can, and pray for what he cannot (St. Augustine: *De natura et gratia,* 43, 50), and He helps us to accomplish it.

> Council of Trent, Session 6, Canon 2. (Jan. 13, 1547)

If any one saith that the grace of God through Jesus Christ is given only for this, that man may be able more easily to live justly and to merit eternal life, as if by freewill without grace he were able to do both, though hardly indeed and with difficulty; let him be anathema.

> Council of Trent, Session 6, ch. II. (Jan. 13, 1547)

All grace to God, from Whom all graces run.

> Bl. Robert Southwell: *Lewd Love is Loss.* (16th cent.)

My good, O Lord, Thy gift; Thy strength, my stay;
Give what Thou bidst, and then bid what Thou wilt.

> Bl. Robert Southwell: *St. Peter's Complaint.* (Last line translates St. Augustine: *Da quod jubes: jube quod vis.* Conf. 10, 29) (16th cent.)

When God calls anyone to Christianity He obliges Himself to furnish him with all that is required for being a good Christian.

> St. Francis de Sales: *Letters to Persons in Religion,* 5, 8. (17th cent.)

The grace of concealing a grace is in itself not slight.

> Jean Pierre Camus: *The Spirit of St. Francis de Sales,* 8, 11. (17th cent.)

A little reed in the hand of grace becomes a mighty staff.

> Jean Pierre Camus: *The Spirit of St. Francis de Sales,* 14, 7. (17th cent.)

This then must be the med'cine for my woes,
To yield to what my Saviour shall dispose:
To glory in my baseness, to rejoice
In mine afflictions, to obey His voice,
As well when threatenings my defects reprove,
As when I cherisht am with words of love,
To say to Him, in ev'ry time and place,
Withdraw Thy comforts, so Thou leave Thy grace.

> Sir John Beaumont: *In Desolation.* (17th cent.)

The burden of life is from ourselves, its lightness from the grace of Christ and the love of God.

> Archb. Ullathorne: *Humility and Patience.* (19th cent.)

Only the power of God can bear us up to God. Our will is free, and if we follow the divine attraction, the grace of that attraction will bring us to His presence.

> Archb. Ullathorne: *Humility and Patience.* (19th cent.)

I have been groping in darkness, seeking where Thou wast not, and I have found Thee not. But, O Lord my God, *Thou hast found me*—leave me not.

> Isaac T. Hecker: *Prayer.* (1844)

Whom God does once with heart to
heart befriend,
He does so till the end:
And having planted life's miraculous
germ,
One sweet pulsation of responsive love,
He sets him sheer above,
Not sin and bitter shame
And wreck of fame,
But hell's insidious and more black at-
tempt,
The envy, malice, and pride,
Which men who share so easily con-
done
That few ev'n list such ills as these to
hide.
From these unalterably exempt,
Through the remember'd grace
Of that divine embrace,
Of his sad errors none,
Though gross to blame,
Shall cast him lower than the cleansing
flame,
Nor make him quite depart
From the small flock named 'after
God's own heart,'
And to themselves unknown.

Coventry Patmore: *Remembered Grace.*
(19th cent.)

A balanced soul, alight with tranquil
grace within, is not afraid to look at the
darkness without.

R. H. Benson: *The King's Achievement.*
(20th cent.)

It would seem that grace has a certain
power, accumulating through the centuries, of saturating even physical objects with its force, however men may
rebel.

R. H. Benson: *A Mirror of Shalott.* (20th
cent.)

Grace is given or offered to all, but in
odd ways. We cannot judge. Fortunately
it is not our business just now. Our
business is on the contrary, *not* to judge,
and we shall not be judged.

Abbot Chapman: *Spiritual Letters.* (20th
cent.)

The Church is not taught by theologians,
they are taught by her. The Church is
not sanctified by her saints; she sanctifies them, with the grace of Christ.

Thomas Merton: *The Ascent to Truth.*
(20th cent.)

Grace, Sanctifying

Divine grace may be similarly divided.
In one sense it is called grace freely bestowed, *gratia gratis data,* which in technical theology usually stands for the
special gifts of prophecy, wisdom, and
the like. . . . In the second sense, grace
is called sanctifying grace, *gratia gratum
faciens . . .* which renders a man agreeable to God. . . .

St. Thomas Aquinas: *Disputations
Concerning Truth,* 27, 1. (13th cent.)

One ounce of sanctifying grace is worth
more than a hundred pounds of those
graces which theologians call 'gratuitous,' of which the gift of miracles is
one.

Jean Pierre Camus: *The Spirit of St.
Francis de Sales,* 5, 3. (17th cent.)

Grace and Freewill

Let us not defend grace in such a way
as to seem to make away with freewill.
On the other hand we may not assert
freedom of will in such manner as in our
impious pride to be judged ungrateful
for the grace of God.

St. Augustine: *De Peccatorum Meritis et
Remissione,* 2, 18, 28. (5th cent.)

In man there is both freewill and divine
grace, without the aid of which free
will can neither be turned to God nor
make any advance towards God.

St. Augustine: *Letter 214.* (5th cent.)

Actually, the effect of this grace of God
in us is that, in recovering and holding
on to good, we not only are able to do
what we will, but we also will to do what
we are able to do.

St. Augustine: *De Correptione et Gratia,*
11, 32. (5th cent.)

Since there is no perseverance without the power and the will to persevere, both the possibility and the will to persevere are given to them [the saints] by the bounty of divine grace. Their will is so roused by the Holy Spirit that they are able to persevere, because they will to do so; and they will to do so, because God effects this will. If in the weakness of this life . . . their will were to be left to itself to keep faithful if it wished to that aid of God without which they could not persevere, and if God did not effect in them the will itself, their will would in its weakness be overcome amid life's many and severe temptations. . . . Consequently an aid was given to the weakness of the human will, with the result that it is unwaveringly and invincibly influenced by divine grace.

St. Augustine: *De Correptione et Gratia,* 12, 38. (5th cent.)

Rational natures are poised between alternatives. God moves the human spirit to good; nevertheless it could resist. It is God's doing, then, that a man prepares himself to receive grace. If he lacks grace, then the cause of the failure lies in him, not in God.

St. Thomas Aquinas: *Quodlibets,* 1, 4, 7. (13th cent.)

Grace and Nature

Human nature is not completely corrupt or entirely destitute of good, and without supernatural help—though never without the divine help pervading all activity—a man can contrive particular good ends . . . but not his entire well-being. He will fail somewhere. . . . Fallen nature, therefore, needs grace, first to be healed, and next, to act supernaturally and deserve everlasting life.

St. Thomas Aquinas: *Summa Theologica,* 1-2, 109, 2. (13th cent.)

Hence man, by his natural endowments, cannot produce meritorious works proportionate to everlasting life; and for this a higher force is needed, viz., the force of grace. And thus without grace man cannot merit everlasting life; yet he can perform works conducing to a good which is natural to man, as to toil in the fields, to drink, to eat, or to have friends, and the like.

St. Thomas Aquinas: *Summa Theologica,* 1-2, 109, 5. (13th cent.)

Grace is nature's perfection, and therefore impairs nothing natural.

St. Thomas Aquinas: *Against Those Who Impugn the Worship of God,* 6. (13th cent.)

Since the aptness for grace is part of human nature's good estate, we can now appreciate how sin diminishes nature. And because grace perfects nature, heightening mind and will and the sensitive parts which serve reason, we can appreciate also how sin, by depriving us of grace and clogging our natural abilities, also hurts nature. The results of sin are ignorance, malice, and concupiscence, and these are called the wounds of nature.

St. Thomas Aquinas: *Disputations concerning Evil,* 11, 11. (13th cent.)

Nature looks upon the outward things of man, but grace turns herself to the interior. Nature is often deceived, but grace has her trust in God that she may not be deceived.

Thomas a Kempis: *The Imitation of Christ,* 3, 31. (15th cent.)

The grace of God supplies the void, and where there is less nature there is more grace.

St. Francis de Sales: *Letters to Persons in Religion,* 5, 9. (17th cent.)

Grammar

Grammar is the science of speaking correctly, and is the source and foundation of literature.

St. Isidore: *Etymologies,* 1, 5. (7th cent.)

Grammar, that ground is of all.

> Langland: *Piers Plowman*, Passus 18. (14th cent.)

God does not much mind bad grammar, but He does not take any particular pleasure in it.

> Erasmus. (16th cent.)

Gratitude

> What is gladness without gratitude,
> And where is gratitude without a God?
>
> Coventry Patmore: *Amelia.* (19th cent.)

Grave

> A pick-axe and a spade,
> And eke a shrouding-sheet,
> A house of clay for to be made
> For such a guest most meet.
>
> Henry, Lord Vaux: *The Aged Lover Renounceth Love.* (16th cent.)

For as yourselves your empires fall,
And every kingdom hath a grave.

> William Habington: *Nox Nocti Indicat Scientiam.* (17th cent.)

The grave unites; where e'en the great find rest,
And blended lie th' oppressor and th' oppressed.

> Pope: *Windsor Forest.* (18th cent.)

Yet shall thy grave with rising flow'rs be dressed,
And the green turf lie lightly on thy breast;
There shall the morn her earliest tears bestow,
There the first roses of the year shall blow.

> Pope: *Elegy to the Memory of an Unfortunate Lady.* (18th cent.)

> Tread lightly, she is near
> Under the snow,
> Speak gently, she can hear
> The daisies grow.
>
> All her bright golden hair
> Tarnished with rust,
> She that was young and fair
> Fallen to dust.
>
> .   .   .   .

> Peace, peace, she cannot hear
> Lyre or sonnet,
> All my life's buried here,
> Heap earth upon it.
>
> Oscar Wilde: *Requiescat.* (19th cent.)

Graveyard

> Here's an acre sown indeed,
> With the richest royalest seed.
>
> Francis Beaumont: *On the Tombs in Westminster Abbey.* (17th cent.)

Tired of the tempest and racing wind,
Tired of the spouting breaker,
Here they come at the end, to find
Rest in the silent acre.

> Charles W. Stoddard: *A Nantucket Grave.* (19th cent.)

Gravity, Force of

Gravity is nothing else than a natural force implanted by the Creator of the world into its parts, so that, coming together in the shape of a sphere, they might form a unified whole.

> Nicolaus Copernicus: *De revolutionibus orbium coelestium.* (16th cent.)

Grease

Thus is he fried in his own grease.

> Lydgate: *Temple of Glass,* 14. (15th cent.)

Great and Small

Many small make a great.

> John Heywood: *Proverbs,* 1, 11. (16th cent.)

He that high growth on cedars did bestow,
Gave also lowly mushrumps leave to grow.

> Bl. Robert Southwell: *Great and Small.* (16th cent.)

Great and small have the same accidents, and the same vexations, and the same passions; but one is at the circumference of the wheel and the other near the center, and thus less agitated by the same movements.

Pascal: *Pensées*, 8. (17th cent.)

Greatness

For it is the part of a truly great man not merely to be equal to great things, but also to make little things great by his own power.

St. Basil: *Letters*, 98. (4th cent.)

The compass of the whole earth compared to the scope of heaven is no bigger than a pin's point, which is as much as to say that, if it be conferred with the greatness of the celestial sphere, it hath no bigness at all.

Boethius: *De Consolatione Philosophiae*, 2, 7. (6th cent.)

Who climbeth highest most dreadful is his fall.

Lydgate: *Minor Poems*, p. 120. (15th cent.)

He who stays not in his littleness, loses his greatness.

St. Francis de Sales: *Letters to Persons in Religion*, 3, 43. (17th cent.)

Gods where e'er they go
Bring their heaven with them, their
    great footsteps place
An everlasting smile upon the face,
Of the glad earth they tread on.

Richard Crashaw: *Upon the Duke of York, His Birth, A Panegyric.* (17th cent.)

They that are great, and worthy to be so,
Hide not their rays, from meanest plants that grow.
Why is the Sun set in a throne so high,
But to give light to each inferior eye?
His radiant beams distribute lively grace
To all, according to their worth and place.

Sir John Beaumont: *Of True Greatness, to my Lord Marquis of Buckingham.* (17th cent.)

His grandeur he derived from Heav'n alone,
For he was great, e'er fortune made him so;
And wars, like mists that rise against the sun,
Made him but greater seem, not greater grow.

Dryden: *Heroic Stanzas to the Memory of Oliver, Late Lord Protector.* (17th cent.)

Who noble ends by noble means obtains,
Or, failing, smiles in exile or in chains,
Like good Aurelius let him reign, or bleed
Like Socrates—that man is great indeed.

Pope: *An Essay on Man*, 4. (18th cent.)

Persons and things look great at a distance, which are not so when seen close.

Card. Newman: *Apologia pro Vita Sua*, 4. (Letter of Nov. 25, 1845 to Card. Acton, following his conversion) (19th cent.)

For so it is with all greatness, that, because it is great, it cannot be comprehended by ordinary minds at once; but time, and distance, and contemplation are necessary for its being recognized by beholders.

Card. Newman: *Discourses to Mixed Congregations.* (19th cent.)

Great men are something different from an enlarged repetition of average and familiar types, and the working and motive of their minds is in many instances the exact contrary of ordinary men, living to avoid contingencies of danger, and pain, and sacrifice, and the weariness of constant thinking and far-seeing precaution.

Lord Acton: *Döllinger's Historical Work.* (19th cent.)

The world is charged with the grandeur of God.

G. M. Hopkins: *God's Grandeur.* (19th cent.)

The first-rate great man is equal with other men, like Shakespeare. The second-rate great man is on his knees to other men, like Whitman. The third-rate great man is superior to other men, like Whistler.

G. K. Chesterton: *Heretics.* (20th cent.)

We are able to answer the question, 'Why have we no great men?' We have no great men chiefly because we are always looking for them. We are connoisseurs of greatness, and connoisseurs can never be great; we are fastidious—that is, we are small.

G. K. Chesterton: *Charles Dickens.* (20th cent.)

Dear Lord, but once before I pass away
Out of this hell into the starry night
Where still my hopes are set in death's despite,
Let one great man be good, let one pure ray
Shine through the gloom of this my earthly day
From one tall candle set upon a height.

Lord Alfred Douglas: *Lighten our Darkness.* (20th cent.)

Greece

Where are the islands of the blest?
They stud the Aegean sea;
And where the deep Elysian rest?
It haunts the vale where Peneus strong
Pours his incessant streams along,
While craggy ridge and mountain bare
Cut keenly through the liquid air,
And, in their own pure tints array'd,
Scorn earth's green robes which change and fade,
And stand in beauty undecay'd,
Guards of the bold and free.

Card. Newman: *Heathen Greece.* (19th cent.)

Let heathen sing thy heathen praise,
Fall'n Greece! the thought of holier days
In my sad heart abides;

For sons of thine in truth's first hour
Were tongues and weapons of His power,
Born of the Spirit's fiery shower,
Our fathers and our guides.

Card. Newman: *The Greek Fathers.* (19th cent.)

Greed

It is an excellent rule to banish greed beyond the reach of scandal, and not only to be innocent of it.

St. Bernard: *On Consideration,* 4, 6. (12th cent.)

O covetousness, so hasty to submerge
Mortals, that each and all are powerless
To draw their eyes forth from thy blinding surge!

Dante: *Paradiso, Canto 27.* (Tr. Binyon) (14th cent.)

See also Avarice; Covetousness

Green

All thing is gay that is green.

John Heywood: *Proverbs,* 2, 1. (16th cent.)

Grief

Grief and death were born of sin, and devour sin.

St. John Chrysostom: *Homilies.* (4th cent.)

There is no greater grief than, in misery, to recall happier times.

Dante: *Inferno, Canto 5.* (14th cent.)

I did not know that thou wert dead before;
I did not feel the grief I did sustain;
The greater stroke astonisheth the more;
Astonishment takes from us sense of pain.
I stood amazed when others' tears begun,

And now begin to weep when
they have done.

Henry Constable: *On the Death of Sir
Philip Sidney.* (16th cent.)

Nothing speaks our grief so well
As to speak nothing.

Richard Crashaw: *Upon the Death of a
Gentleman.* (17th cent.)

Thus long my grief has kept me dumb:
   Sure there's a lethargy in mighty
     woe,
   Tears stand congeal'd, and cannot
     flow;
And the sad soul retires into her in-
     most room:
Tears, for a stroke forseen, afford re-
     lief;
   But, unprovided for a sudden blow,
Like Niobe we marble grow;
   And petrify with grief.

Dryden: *Threnodia Augustalis.* (17th
cent.)

Mute and magnificent, without a tear.

Dryden: *Threnodia Augustalis.* (17th
cent.)

Weep on! and as thy sorrows flow,
I'll taste the luxury of woe.

Thomas Moore: *Anacreontic.* (19th cent.)

See how time makes all grief decay.

Adelaide Procter: *Life in Death.* (19th
cent.)

My bankrupt heart has no more tears to
   spend.
Else I am well assured I should offend
With fiercer weepings of these desperate eyes
For poor love's failure than his hopeless rise.

G. M. Hopkins: *The Beginning of the
End.* (19th cent.)

   The dream is over,
   The vision has flown,
   Dead leaves are lying
   Where roses have blown;

   Withered and strown
   Are the hopes I cherished,—
   All hath perished
   But grief alone.

Denis F. McCarthy: *Lament.* (19th cent.)

I know you: solitary griefs,
Desolate passions, aching hours,
I know you; tremulous beliefs,
Agonized hopes, and ashen flowers!

Lionel Johnson: *The Precept of Silence.*
(19th cent.)

You must not grieve too much. God almighty can set all right.

R. H. Benson: *The King's Achievement.*
(20th cent.)

See also Sorrow

Guest

Every guest who comes to the monastery
shall be received as if he were Christ
Himself.

The Rule of St. Benedict. (6th cent.)

An unbidden guest knoweth not where
to sit.

John Heywood: *Proverbs,* 1, 9. (16th
cent.)

Welcome the coming, speed the parting
guest.

Pope: *Tr. of Homer: Odyssey,* 15. (18th
cent.)

Guidance

O God, the Bestower of peace and the
Lover of charity, grant to Thy servants
a true agreement with Thy will, that we
may be delivered from all the temptations that beset us.

Leonine Sacramentary, Collect. (ca. 5th
cent.)

Mercifully regard, O Lord, the prayers
of Thy family, and while they submit
themselves to Thee with their whole
heart, do Thou prosper, support, and

encompass them; that relying on Thee as their Guide, they may be entangled in no evils, and replenished with all good.

> Leonine Sacramentary, Collect. (ca. 5th cent.)

Direct our hearts in Thy tender mercy, we beseech Thee, O Lord; because without Thee we are not able to please Thee.

> Roman Missal, Collect for Eighteenth Sunday after Pentecost. (Gelasian, 5th to 7th cent.)

Guilt

The act of sin may pass, and yet the guilt remain.

> St. Thomas Aquinas: *Summa Theologica,* 1-2, 109, 7. (13th cent.)

If any one saith that after the grace of justification has been received by every penitent sinner the guilt is remitted, and the debt of eternal punishment is blotted out in such wise that there remains not any debt of temporal punishment to be discharged either in this world or in the next in purgatory, before the entrance to the kingdom of heaven can be opened to him; let him be anathema.

> Council of Trent, Session 6, Canon 30. (Jan. 13, 1547)

For secret guilt by silence is betray'd.

> Dryden: *The Hind and the Panther,* 3. (17th cent.)

Gypsy

Whither, O gypsy wagon
Lumbering by?
This night so soft with summer,
So dim and shy.

Wild headlong creatures, whither
This night of rest?
O whining axle, whither
In endless quest?

> Daniel Corkery: *The Gypsies.* (20th cent.)

H

Habit

But habits of any kind are so strong in their possession of the minds of men that, even in the case of those that are evil (and these usually come from the dominant passions), we can more quickly condemn and detest them than we can abandon or change them.

> St. Augustine: *De Utilitate Credendi,* 17, 35. (4th cent.)

A habit is that whereby something is done when necessary.

> St. Augustine: *De Bono Conjugali,* 21. (5th cent.)

A habit is a settled disposition.

> St. Thomas Aquinas: *Summa Theologica,* 1-2, 49, 2. (13th cent.)

By a faculty we are able to do something, but by a habit we are expert at acting well or ill according to the faculty, that is the difference between ability and habit.

> St. Thomas Aquinas: *Contra Gentes,* 4, 77. (13th cent.)

Form small habits and make them laws!

> R. H. Benson: *The Sentimentalists.* (20th cent.)

Habits, Evil

But oftentimes if we brace ourselves
with strong energy against the incite-
ments of evil habits, we turn even those
very evil habits to the account of virtue.

Pope St. Gregory I: *Morals*, 3, 70. (6th
cent.)

Hair

Long hair and short wit.

John Heywood: *Proverbs*, 2, 7. (16th
cent.)

Tresses, that wear
Jewels, but to declare
How much themselves more precious
are.

Richard Crashaw: *Wishes to his
(Supposed) Mistress.* (17th cent.)

Fair tresses man's imperial race insnare,
And beauty draws us with a single hair.

Pope: *The Rape of the Lock*, 2. (18th
cent.)

Half

That's just, if the half shall judge the
whole.

John Heywood: *Proverbs*, 1, 13. (16th
cent.)

Half-Truth

The thing from which the world suffers
just now more than from any other evil
is not the assertion of falsehoods, but the
endless and irrepressible repetition of
half-truths.

G. K. Chesterton: *G. F. Watts.* (20th
cent.)

Half-Wit

Half-wits are fleas, so little and so light,
We scarce could know they live, but
that they bite.

Dryden: *All for Love, Prologue.* (17th
cent.)

Hand

Things past my hands I cannot call
again.

John Heywood: *Proverbs*, 1, 10. (16th
cent.)

With empty hands men may no hawks
allure.

John Heywood: *Proverbs*, 2, 5. (16th
cent.)

Have both their hands full.

John Heywood: *Proverbs*, 2, 5. (16th
cent.)

The hands of the king are soft and
fair—
They never knew labor's strain.
The hands of the robber redly wear
The bloody brand of Cain.
But the hands of the Man are hard and
scarred
With the scars of toil and pain.

James J. Roche: *The Way of the World.*
(19th cent.)

Never extend your hand farther than you
can withdraw it.

Seumas MacManus: *Heavy Hangs the
Golden Grain.* (20th cent.)

Handshake

To offer one's hand to a superior would
be impolite; but if they choose to give
that proof of good-will, it should be
received with respect and gratitude, inclining the head.

St. John Baptist de la Salle: *The Rules of
Christian Manners and Civility*, 1. (17th
cent.)

Hanging

Suits hang half a year in Westminster
hall;
At Tyburn half an hour's hanging
endeth all.

John Heywood: *Epigrams.* (16th cent.)

Happiness

No one is really happy merely because he has what he wants, but only if he wants things he ought to want.

> St. Augustine: *In Ps. 26, Enarr.*, 2, 7. (5th cent.)

Whoever possesses God is happy.

> St. Augustine: *De Vita Beata*, 2, 11. (4th cent.)

This, then, is the full satisfaction of souls, this the happy life: to recognize piously and completely the One through Whom you are led into the truth, the nature of the truth you enjoy, and the bond that connects you with the supreme measure.

> St. Augustine: *De Vita Beata*, 4, 35. (4th cent.)

Following after God is the desire of happiness; to reach God is happiness itself.

> St. Augustine: *De Moribus Ecclesiae Catholicae*, 11, 18. (4th cent.)

If then we ask what it is to live well—that is, to strive after happiness by living well—it must assuredly be to love virtue, to love wisdom, to love truth, and to love with all the heart, with all the soul, and with all the mind: virtue which is inviolable and immutable, wisdom which never gives place to folly, truth which knows no change or variation from its uniform character.

> St. Augustine: *De Moribus Ecclesiae Catholicae*, 13, 22. (4th cent.)

Some (angels and men alike) steadily set up their rest in the good that is common to them all, in God Himself, His eternity, truth, love. Others (angels and men) choose rather to delight in their own power, as though they were their own sufficient good, and so have drifted away from the higher general good and source of happiness to purposes of their own. . . . If it is asked why the one are happy, the right answer is, Because they cleave to God. If it is asked why the others are miserable, the right answer is, Because they do not cleave to God. There is no good capable of making any rational or intellectual creature happy except God.

> St. Augustine: *The City of God*, 12, 1. (5th cent.)

Wherefore, it is manifest that blessedness is an estate replenished with all that is good. This, as we said, all men endeavor to obtain in divers ways. For there is naturally ingrafted in men's minds an earnest desire of that which is truly good; but deceitful error withdraweth it to that which falsely seemeth such.

> Boethius: *De Consolatione Philosophiae*, 3, 1. (6th cent.)

For strength and greatness give ability; beauty and swiftness, fame; and health yieldeth pleasure. By all which we manifestly seek for nothing else but happiness.

> Boethius: *De Consolatione Philosophiae*, 3, 1. (6th cent.)

Since every reward is therefore desired because it is thought to be good, who can judge him to be devoid of reward, who hath goodness for his possession . . . ? Since that goodness itself is happiness, it is manifest that all good men even by being good are made happy.

> Boethius: *De Consolatione Philosophiae*, 4, 3. (6th cent.)

The sight of an effect rouses a natural desire to know the cause. The human mind can view the whole range of things, and therefore instinctively craves to know their cause, which, ultimately, is God alone. Happiness is not attained until this natural appetite is at rest . . . only knowing God will produce the state where restlessness is stilled.

> St. Thomas Aquinas: *Contra Gentes*, 3, 25. (13th cent.)

Felicity is the pure contemplation of the noblest Truth (Aristotle, Ethics, 10, 7).

> St. Thomas Aquinas: *Contra Gentes*, 3, 25. (13th cent.)

Happiness is the ultimate achievement of rational nature.

St. Thomas Aquinas: *Quodlibets*, 10, 8, 1. (13th cent.)

Better to be happy than wise.

John Heywood: *Proverbs*, 2, 6. (16th cent.)

Your happiness consists not now alone
In those high comforts, which are often thrown
In plenteous manner from our Savior's hand,
To raise the fall'n, and cause the weak to stand;
But ye are blest, when, being trodden down,
Ye taste His cup, and wear His thorny crown.

Sir John Beaumont: *Transfiguration of Our Lord*. (17th cent.)

The past and present are only our means; the future is always our end. Thus we never really live, but only hope to live. Always looking forward to being happy, it is inevitable that we should never be so.

Pascal: *Pensées*, 3. (17th cent.)

O happiness! our being's end and aim!
Good, pleasure, ease, content! whate'er thy name:
That something still which prompts th' eternal sigh,
For which we bear to live, or dare to die.

Pope: *An Essay on Man*, 4. (18th cent.)

The thought of God, and nothing short of it, is the happiness of man.

Card. Newman: *Parochial and Plain Sermons*, 5. (19th cent.)

Happiness is not a matter of events; it depends upon the tides of the mind.

Alice Meynell: *The Rhythm of Life*. (19th cent.)

Happiness is the shadow of things past,
Which fools shall take for that which is to be.

F. Thompson: *An Ode after Easter*. (19th cent.)

There are two kinds of happiness for mortal men: there is that which is carnal and imperfect, and hangs on circumstances, and the health of the body and suchlike things; and there is that which is spiritually perfect, which hangs on nothing else than the doing of the will of God almighty.

R. H. Benson: *The History of Richard Raynal Solitary*. (20th cent.)

Happiness is a mystery like religion, and should never be rationalized.

G. K. Chesterton: *Heretics*. (20th cent.)

The false optimism, the modern happiness, tires us because it tells us we fit into this world. The true happiness is that we don't fit. We come from somewhere else. We have lost our way.

G. K. Chesterton: *Tremendous Trifles*, 38. (20th cent.)

See also Blessedness; Contentment; Eternal Life; Joy; Joy and Sorrow

Hard-Heartedness

That heart alone is hard which does not shudder at itself for not feeling its hardness.

St. Bernard: *On Consideration*, 1, 2. (12th cent.)

Hardy, Thomas

Mr. Hardy is anthropomorphic out of sheer atheism. He personifies the universe in order to give it a piece of his mind. But the fight is unequal for the old philosophical reason: that the universe had already given Mr. Hardy a piece of *its* mind to fight with.

G. K. Chesterton: *The Victorian Age in Literature*. (20th cent.)

Harlot

The harlot knows not how to love but only to ensnare; her kiss hath poison, and her mouth a pernicious drug.

> St. John Chrysostom: *Homilies.* (4th cent.)

Phryne had talents for mankind;
Open she was and unconfin'd,
  Like some free port of trade.

> Pope: *Phryne.* (18th cent.)

Harm

No one is harmed except by himself.

> St. John Chrysostom: *Expos. in Ps. 139.* (4th cent.)

I deny that to be good which hurteth the possessor.

> Boethius: *De Consolatione Philosophiae,* 2, 5. (6th cent.)

O almighty and merciful God, in thy goodness keep us from all harm; that, being ready both in body and soul, we may freely accomplish Thy will.

> Roman Missal, Collect for Nineteenth Sunday after Pentecost. (Gelasian, 5th to 7th cent.)

She can no more harm than can a she ape.

> John Heywood: *Proverbs,* 1, 10. (16th cent.)

There is no harm done in all this fray.

> John Heywood: *Proverbs,* 1, 11. (16th cent.)

Dear God, though Thy all-powerful hand
Should so direct my earthly fate
That I may seem unfortunate
To them who do not understand
That all things follow Thy decree,
Staunchly I'll bear whate'er's Thy will—
Praying Thee but to grant me still

That none shall come to harm through me.

> Conal O'Riordan: *Care is Heavy.* (20th cent.)

See also Danger

Harmony

For even the universe itself is said to have been put together with a certain harmony of sounds, and the very heavens revolve under the guidance of harmony.

> St. Isidore: *Etymologies,* 3, 17. (7th cent.)

So in our life the different degrees
Render sweet harmony among these wheels.

> Dante: *Paradiso, Canto 6.* (Tr. Cary) (14th cent.)

So did I see the glorious wheel roll on
  And render voice to voice, in harmony
  And in a sweetness never to be known
Save where joy tastes its own eternity.

> Dante: *Paradiso, Canto 10.* (Tr. Binyon) (14th cent.)

Harp

Ye harp on the string that giveth no melody.

> John Heywood: *Proverbs,* 2, 4. (16th cent.)

The harp that once through Tara's halls
  The soul of music shed,
Now hangs as mute on Tara's walls
  As if that soul were fled.
So sleeps the pride of former days,
  So glory's thrill is o'er;
And hearts, that once beat high for praise,
  Now feel that pulse no more.

> Thomas Moore: *The Harp That Once Through Tara's Halls.* (19th cent.)

If the pulse of the patriot, soldier, or lover,

Have throbb'd at our lay, 'tis thy glory
  alone;
I was but as the wind, passing heed-
  lessly over,
And all the wild sweetness I wak'd was
  thy own.

  Thomas Moore: *Dear Harp of my
  Country.* (19th cent.)

'Tis believ'd that this harp which I
  wake now for thee
Was a siren of old who sung under the
  sea.

  Thomas Moore: *Origin of the Harp.*
  (19th cent.)

Harvest

A long harvest for a little corn.

  John Heywood: *Proverbs,* 1, 12. (16th
  cent.)

Each mindful plant has't to make good
The hope and promise of his bud.
Seed-time's not all: there should be
  harvest too.

  Richard Crashaw: *To the Countess of
  Denby against Irresolution in Religion.*
  (17th cent.)

Haste

There is no workman, what-so-ever he
  be,
That may both worken well and hastily.

  Chaucer: *The Marchantes Tale.* (14th
  cent.)

He hasteth well that wisely can abide.

  Chaucer: *Troilus and Criseyde.* (14th
  cent.)

For hasty man he wanteth never care.

  Chaucer: *Troilus and Criseyde.* (14th
  cent.)

Haste maketh waste.

  John Heywood: *Proverbs,* 1, 2. (16th
  cent.)

The more haste the less speed.

  John Heywood: *Proverbs,* 1, 2. (16th
  cent.)

The hasty man never wanteth woe.

  John Heywood: *Proverbs,* 1, 2. (16th
  cent.)

Folks show much folly, when things
  should be sped,
To run to the foot that may go to the
  head.

  John Heywood: *Proverbs,* 2, 5. (16th
  cent.)

Hurry ruins saints as well as artists.

  Thomas Merton: *Seeds of Contemplation.*
  (20th cent.)

Hat

Mine old hat must have a new band.

  John Heywood: *Proverbs,* 2, 1. (16th
  cent.)

All good hats are made out of nothing.

  Oscar Wilde: *The Picture of Dorian
  Gray,* 17. (19th cent.)

Hate

You shall not hate any man; but some
you shall admonish, and pray for others,
and still others you shall love more than
your own life.

  Teaching of the Twelve Apostles, 2.
  (2nd cent.)

For what is there more unfair than to
hate a thing of which you know nothing,
even though it deserve to be hated?
Hatred is only merited when it is *known*
to be merited. But without that knowledge, whence is its justice to be vindicated?

  Tertullian: *Apology,* 1. (3rd cent.)

To hate no man.

  St. Benedict: *Rule,* 4. (6th cent.)

Hate cannot wish thee worse
Than guilt and shame have made thee.

  Thomas Moore: *When First I Met Thee.*
  (19th cent.)

High above hate I dwell, O storms! farewell.

> Louise Imogen Guiney: *The Sanctuary.*
> (19th cent.)

Hawk

The first point of hawking is hold fast.

> John Heywood: *Proverbs,* 2, 4. (16th
> cent.)

Head

When the head acheth all the body is
worse.

> John Heywood: *Proverbs,* 2, 7. (16th
> cent.)

Head and Heart

The heart has its reasons which reason
cannot know.

> Pascal: *Pensées,* 4. (17th cent.)

Healing

They that are whole can heal others;
but in my case it was, *Physician, heal thyself.*

> Card. Newman: *Apologia pro Vita Sua,*
> 4. (19th cent.)

Health

At early dawn, when first from bed you
  rise,
Wash in cold water, both your hands
  and eyes,
With comb and brush then cleanse your
  teeth and hair,
And thus refreshed, your limbs outstretch with care.

> School of Salerno, Code of Health. (11th
> cent.)

If thou to health and vigor wouldst attain,
Shun weighty cares—all anger deem
  profane,
From heavy suppers and much wine
  abstain.

Nor trivial count it, after pompous
  fare,
To rise from table and to take the air.

> School of Salerno, Code of Health. (11th
> cent.)

Ye may write to your friends that ye are
in health.

> John Heywood: *Proverbs,* 2, 4. (16th
> cent.)

Take care of your health, that it may
serve you to serve God.

> St. Francis de Sales: *Letters to Persons in
> Religion,* 1, 12. (17th cent.)

Health of body and mind is a great blessing, if we can bear it.

> Card. Newman: *Parochial and Plain
> Sermons,* 1. (19th cent.)

Health—silliest word in our language,
and one knows so well the popular idea
of health. The English country gentleman galloping after a fox—the unspeakable in full pursuit of the uneatable.

> Oscar Wilde: *A Woman of No
> Importance,* 1. (19th cent.)

Heart

The heart is the most noble of all the
members of our body.

> St. John Chrysostom: *Homilies.* (4th
> cent.)

Let us learn to cast our hearts into God.

> St. Bernard. (12th cent.)

I am he who held both keys of Fred-
    erick's heart
  And to their wards so softly did
    apply,
  Locking and then unlocking with
    such art.

> Dante: *Inferno, Canto 13.* (Pier delle
> Vigne, the ill-fated chancellor of
> Frederick II) (Tr. Binyon) (14th cent.)

He hath the sore which no man healeth,
The which is known as lack of heart.

> John Gower: *Confessio Amantis,* 4. (14th
> cent.)

There is nothing in this world that
agreeth worse
Than doth a lady's heart and a beggar's
purse.

> John Heywood: *Proverbs,* 1, 10. (16th
> cent.)

To set at my heart that thou settest at
thy heel.

> John Heywood: *Proverbs,* 1, 11. (16th
> cent.)

A heart, a heart, sweet Saviour,
  A heart vouchsafe to send:
A heart to bid me take good heart,
  My heavy heart to mend.

> Anonymous: *The Harty Wyshes of a
> Penytent Synner.* (Guiney, 356) (16th
> cent.)

O heart! the equal poise of love's both
  parts,
Big alike with wounds and darts,
Live in these conquering leaves; live
  all the same,
And walk through all tongues one triumphant flame.
Live here, great heart; and love and
  die and kill,
And bleed and wound; and yield and
  conquer still.

> Richard Crashaw: *The Flaming Heart.*
> (Ref. is to St. Teresa of Avila and her
> works) (17th cent.)

Who knows my heart's woes so well
as I?

> R. Crashaw: *Alexias, First Elegy.* (17th
> cent.)

How hollow and full of ordure is the
heart of man!

> Pascal: *Pensées,* 5. (17th cent.)

And the heart that is soonest awake to
  the flowers,
  Is always the first to be touch'd by
  the thorns.

> Thomas Moore: *Oh! Think Not My
> Spirits.* (19th cent.)

Heart speaketh unto heart. (Cor ad cor
loquitur)

> Motto chosen by Card. Newman for his
> shield when he became a cardinal. (19th
> cent.)

Lift up your hearts! We lift
  Them up
To God, and to God's gift,
  The passion cup.
Lift up your hearts! Ah, so
  We will:
Through storm of fire or snow,
  We lift them still.

> Lionel Johnson: *Sursum Corda.* (19th
> cent.)

Hearts live by being wounded.

> Oscar Wilde: *A Woman of No
> Importance,* 3. (19th cent.)

The heart is as divine a gift as the mind;
and to neglect it in the search for God is
to seek ruin.

> R. H. Benson: *Lord of the World.* (20th
> cent.)

Speak from your heart. Be bold, yet not
overbold.

> R. H. Benson: *By What Authority.* (20th
> cent.)

God breaks hearts to remake them.

> K. T. Hinkson: *Julia.* (20th cent.)

"Right as a   Ribstone Pippin!" But it
lied.

> Hilaire Belloc: *For False Heart.* (20th
> cent.)

Yea, Lord, I too—
Only in this insatiate torment like to
  you:
For love, that still must give, and ask,
  the whole,
That may not rest short of the flame-
  wrapped goal,
Nor find surcease in any timorous part:
I am the human heart!

> Katherine Bregy: *I Thirst . . .* (20th cent.)

Heathen

In heathen parts. (In partibus infidelium.)

> Words formerly added to the name of sees
> conferred on nonresidential or titular
> bishops in the Latin Church. The phrase
> has not been used since 1882. The present
> custom is to join the name of the district
> or country to that of the see.

Heaven

Most dear pause in a mellow lay!
  Thou art inwoven with every air.
With thee the wildest tempests play,
  And snatches of thee everywhere
Make little heavens throughout a day.

> Alice Meynell: *To the Beloved.* (19th
> cent.)

See also Eternal Life; Paradise

Heaven and Earth

Grant us, O Lord, not to mind earthly
things, but to love things heavenly; and
even now, while we are placed among
things that are passing away, to cleave
to those that shall abide.

> Leonine Sacramentary, Collect. (ca. 5th
> cent.)

Heaven is far, the world is nigh.

> J. Gower: *Confessio Amantis, Prol.* (14th
> cent.)

Heaven and Hell

They that be in hell ween there is none
other heaven.

> John Heywood: *Proverbs*, 1, 11. (16th
> cent.)

So help me God, and none otherwise
but I verily think, that a man buyeth hell
here with so much pain, that he might
have heaven with less than the one-half.

> St. Thomas More: *Dialogue of Comfort.*
> (16th cent.)

The fairest flowers have not the sweetest smell,

A seeming heaven proves oft a damning hell.

> Bl. Robert Southwell: *Lewd Love is Loss.*
> (16th cent.)

Hell could not fright me with immortal
  fire,
Were it not arm'd with Thy forsaking
  ire:
Nor should I look for comfort and delight
In heav'n, if heav'n were shadow'd
  from Thy sight.

> Sir John Beaumont: *An Act of Contrition.*
> (17th cent.)

Hell was built on spite, and heav'n on
pride.

> Pope: *An Essay on Man*, 3. (18th cent.)

Beholding heaven, and feeling hell.

> Thomas Moore: *Lalla Rookh: the
> Fire-Worshippers.* (19th cent.)

Heaven would be hell to an irreligious
man.

> Card. Newman: *Miscellanies*, 309. (19th
> cent.)

'Tis said there were no thought of hell,
  Save hell were taught; that there
    should be
A heaven for all's self-credible.
  Not so the thing appears to me.
'Tis heaven that lies beyond our sights,
  And hell too possible that proves;
For all can feel the God that smites,
  But ah, how few the God that loves!

> F. Thompson: *Heaven and Hell.* (19th
> cent.)

The Catholic Church will have no phi-
losophies. She will permit no comforts;
the cry of the martyrs is in her far voice;
her eyes that see beyond the world present us heaven and hell to the confusion
of our human reconciliations, our happy
blending of good and evil things.

> H. Belloc: *The Path to Rome.* (20th
> cent.)

The devil is no fool. He can get people feeling about heaven the way they ought to feel about hell. He can make them fear the means of grace the way they do not fear sin. And he does so, not by light but by obscurity, not by realities but by shadows; not by clarity and substance, but by dreams and the creatures of psychosis. And men are so poor in intellect that a few cold chills down their spine will be enough to keep them from ever finding out the truth about anything.

> Thomas Merton: *The Seven Storey Mountain.* (20th cent.)

Hell is full of the talented, but heaven, of the energetic.

> Bishop Sheen: *Life is Worth Living.* (20th cent.)

Hedge

Where the hedge is lowest man may soonest over.

> John Heywood: *Proverbs,* 2, 5. (16th cent.)

Heel

Show a fair pair of heels.

> John Heywood: *Proverbs,* 2, 7. (16th cent.)

Heiress

All heiresses are beautiful.

> Dryden: *King Arthur,* 1, 1. (17th cent.)

Hell

And ever-burning gehenna will burn up the condemned, and a punishment devouring with living flames; nor will there be any source whence at any time they may have either respite or end to their torments. Souls with their bodies will be reserved in infinite tortures for suffering. . . . The pain of punishment will then be without the fruit of penitence; weeping will be useless, and prayer ineffectual. Too late they will believe in eternal punishment who would not believe in eternal life.

> St. Cyprian: *To Demetrianus the Proconsul of Africa,* 24. (3rd cent.)

The perpetual death of the damned, that is, their separation from the life of God, will go on without end and will be their common lot, regardless of what people prompted by human sentiments may conjure up about different kinds of punishment or a mitigation or interruption of their torments.

> St. Augustine: *Enchiridion,* 113. (5th cent.)

To dread hell.

> St. Benedict: *Rule,* 4. (6th cent.)

Is there one fire in hell, or, according to the diversity of sinners, are there as many kinds of fire prepared in that place? The fire of hell is one, but it does not torment all sinners in the same way. Everyone there, according to the quantity of his sin, has the measure of his pain.

> Pope St. Gregory I: *Dialogues,* 4, 42-43. (6th cent.)

The pit of hell is as deep as despair.

> Abbot William of St. Thierry: *On Contemplating God.* (12th cent.)

The best man in hell hath such comfort as if the whole world were on fire, even to the firmament on high, and he were in the midst of that fire in his shirt or stark naked. But another man may have it tenfold worse, or thirtyfold, or sixtyfold, or an hundredfold, or a thousandfold, or sixty thousandfold worse, for the more his sins the deeper his place in hell and the hotter his fire.

> Berthold of Regensburg: *Sermon.* (13th cent.)

Concerning the inquiry whether hell is at or near the center of the earth, my opinion is that nothing should be rashly asserted, not least because Augustine reckoned that nobody knows where hell is. . . . For myself I do not believe that man can know the position of hell.

> St. Thomas Aquinas: *Opusculum* 21. (13th cent.)

Hell is ruled by time, not by true eternity.

> St. Thomas Aquinas: *Summa Theologica,* 1, 10, 3. (13th cent.)

That the saints may enjoy their beatitude and the grace of God more abundantly they are permitted to see the punishment of the damned in hell.

> St. Thomas Aquinas: *Summa Theologica,* 3. (13th cent.)

Through me the way is to the city of
   woe:
   Through me the way into the eternal
   pain;
   Through me the way among the lost
   below.

Righteousness did my Maker on high
   constrain.
Me did divine authority uprear;
Me supreme Wisdom and primal
   Love sustain.

Before I was, no things created were
   Save the eternal, and eternal I abide.
   Relinquish all hope, ye who enter
   here.

> Dante: *Inferno, Canto 3.* (Inscription over the gate of hell) (Tr. Binyon) (14th cent.)

Here sighs, plaints, and voices of the deepest woe resounded through the starless sky. Strange languages, horrid cries, accents of grief and wrath, voices deep and hoarse, with hands clenched in despair, made a commotion which whirled forever through that air of everlasting gloom, even as sand when whirlwinds sweep the ground.

> Dante: *Inferno, Canto 3.* (14th cent.)

There is in hell a place stone-built
   throughout,
Called Malebolge, of an iron hue,
Like to the wall that circles it about.

> Dante: *Inferno, Canto 18.* (14th cent.)

It is good however, that if love as yet reclaim thee not from evil, at least the fear of hell restrain thee.

> Thomas a Kempis: *The Imitation of Christ,* 1, 24. (15th cent.)

If any one saith that the fear of hell, whereby by grieving for our sins we flee unto the mercy of God or refrain from sinning, is a sin, or makes sinners worse; let him be anathema.

> Council of Trent, Session 6, Canon 8. (Jan. 13, 1547)

Represent to yourself a city involved in darkness, burning with brimstone and stinking pitch, and full of inhabitants who cannot make their escape.

> St. Francis de Sales: *Introduction to the Devout Life,* 15. (17th cent.)

From this time I have held with a full inward assent and belief the doctrine of eternal punishment, as delivered by our Lord Himself, in as true a sense as I hold that of eternal happiness; though I have tried in various ways to make that truth less terrible to the imagination.

> Card. Newman: *Apologia pro Vita Sua,* 1. (19th cent.)

For God is everywhere.
Go down to deepest hell, and He is
   there,
And, as a true but quite estranged
   friend,
He works, 'gainst gnashing teeth of
   devilish ire,
With love deep hidden lest it be blasphemed,
If possible, to blend
Ease with the pangs of its inveterate
   fire;
Yea, in the worst
And from His face most wilfully
   accurst
Of souls in vain redeem'd,
He does with potions of oblivion kill
Remorse of the lost love that helps them
   still.

> Coventry Patmore: *Tristitia.* (19th cent.)

O mighty house of hate!
Stablished and grounded so,
Love cannot pass the gate,
Even to dull its woe!

> Lionel Johnson: *Visions*. (19th cent.)

The second death that never dies,
That cannot die, when time is dead:
Live death, wherein the lost soul cries,
Eternally uncomforted.

> Lionel Johnson: *The Dark Angel*. (19th cent.)

They order things so damnably in hell.

> H. Belloc: *To Dives*. (20th cent.)

They're very strict on etiquette in hell.

> H. Belloc: *To Dives*. (20th cent.)

Hell is where no one has anything in common with anybody else except the fact that they all hate one another and cannot get away from one another and from themselves.

> Thomas Merton: *Seeds of Contemplation*. (20th cent.)

See also Damned, The; Heaven and Hell; Purgatory

Hell, The Descent into

Christ, our captain, for a season
    deigned to dwell in death's domain,
That the dead, long time imprisoned,
    might return to life again,
Breaking by His great example ancient
    sin's enthralling chain.

> Prudentius: *Ad brevem se mortem*. (Tr. Pope and Davis) (From the Cathemerinon, 4th cent.)

It was fitting that Christ should have descended into hell. First, because He came to bear our burden that He might free us from punishment. . . . Because of sin our lot was hell. And as Christ died to deliver us from death, so He went down to hell that we might not have to stay there. . . . Secondly, that the devil might be conquered and his captives rescued.

. . . Thirdly, that He might show forth His power by visiting and enlightening hell as well as by living and dying on earth. . . .

> St. Thomas Aquinas: *Summa Theologica*, 3, 52, 1. (St. Thomas is speaking of the limbo of the fathers.) (13th cent.)

Help

We beseech Thee, O Lord, guard Thy Church by Thy perpetual favor; and because without Thee the frailty of human nature cannot but fall, let it ever be kept from things harmful by Thy help, and drawn to things profitable to salvation.

> Roman Missal, Collect for Fourteenth Sunday after Pentecost. (Gelasian, 5th to 7th cent.)

Direct our actions, we beseech Thee, O Lord, by Thy inspiration, and further them with Thy continual help; that every prayer and work of ours may always begin from Thee and through Thee likewise be ended.

> Roman Missal, Collect for Ember Saturday in Lent. (Gregorian, 6th to 8th cent.)

No one is so rich that he does not need another's help; no one so poor as not to be useful in some way to his fellow man; and the disposition to ask assistance from others with confidence, and to grant it with kindness, is part of our very nature.

> Pope Leo XIII: *Graves de communi*. (Jan. 18, 1901)

Heresy

I exhort you, then, to leave alone the foreign fodder of heresy and keep entirely to Christian food. . . . For heretics mingle poison with Jesus Christ, as men might administer a deadly drug in sweet wine . . . so that without thought or fear of the fatal sweetness a man drinks his own death.

> St. Ignatius of Antioch: *Letter to the Trallians*, 6. (2nd cent.)

Ignorance is the mark of the heathen, knowledge of the true Church, and conceit of the heretics.

> Clement of Alexandria: *Stromateis*, 1. (2nd cent.)

The order of time shows that that is divine and true which has been handed down from the beginning; that that is alien and false which has been added later. That is the prescription which disposes of all heresies started in later days —they can make no assured claim to the truth.

> Tertullian: *De praescriptione haereticorum*, 31, 3. (3rd cent.)

Whoever has been separated from the Church is yoked with an adulteress, is separated from the promises made to the Church. Nor shall he who leaves Christ's Church arrive at Christ's rewards. He is a stranger, he is sacrilegious, he is an enemy. Who has not the Church for mother can no longer have God for father.

> St. Cyprian: *On the Unity of the Catholic Church*, 6. (3rd cent.)

Nevertheless, the Lord allows and suffers these things to be, while each man's will remains free, so that while our hearts and minds are tested in the crucible of truth, the sound faith of those that are approved may shine forth clear and undimmed.

> St. Cyprian: *On the Unity of the Catholic Church*, 10. (3rd cent.)

All heresies are forbidden by both divine and imperial laws and shall forever cease. . . .

> Edict of the Emperors Gratian, Valentinian, and Theodosius. (Theod. Code, 16, 5, 5) (Aug. 20, 379)

But we believe in Holy Church, assuredly the Catholic Church; for even heretics and schismatics style their assemblies 'churches.' But whereas heretics violate the faith by their false ideas about God, schismatics, by their wicked separation, cut themselves off from fraternal charity. Hence neither do heretics belong to the Catholic Church, for it loves God; nor do schismatics, for the Catholic Church loves its neighbor.

> St. Augustine: *De Fide et Symbolo*, 21. (4th cent.)

For, of course, you cannot have a schism, unless those who cause it adhere to divergent opinions—whereas heresy is a schism grown old.

> St. Augustine: *Contra Cresconium*, 9. (5th cent.)

For you are not to suppose, brethren, that heresies could be produced through any little souls. None save great men have been the authors of heresies.

> St. Augustine: *In Ps. 124*, 5. (5th cent.)

Who ever introduced a heresy who had not previously separated from the common agreement prevailing in the universal and traditional Catholic Church?

> St. Vincent of Lerins: *Commonitoria*, 24. (5th cent.)

The toleration of heretics is more injurious than the devastation of the provinces by the barbarians.

> Pope St. Gelasius I. (5th cent.)

Therefore, heresy is so called from the Greek word meaning 'choice,' by which each chooses according to his own will what he pleases to teach or believe. But we are not permitted to believe whatever we choose, nor to choose whatever someone else has believed. We have the apostles of God as authorities, who did not themselves of their own will choose what they would believe, but faithfully transmitted to the nations the teaching received from Christ. So, even if an angel from heaven should preach otherwise, he shall be called anathema.

> St. Isidore: *Etymologies*, 8, 3. (7th cent.)

Heresy is of its very nature opposed to faith, but schism is of its very nature opposed to the unity of ecclesiastical charity. Since, then, faith and charity are different virtues—although whoso lacks faith lacks charity—so, too, schism and heresy are distinct vices; and while a man who is a heretic is also a schismatic, the converse is not true.

St. Thomas Aquinas: *Summa Theologica,* 2a 2ae, 39, 1 ad 3. (13th cent.)

If forgers and malefactors are put to death by the secular power, there is much more reason for excommunicating and even putting to death one convicted of heresy.

St. Thomas Aquinas: *Summa Theologica,* 2. (13th cent.)

It is a shorter thing, and sooner done, to write heresies, than to answer them.

St. Thomas More: *Apology.* (16th cent.)

I would not give the paring of a pear for his prayer, putting away the true faith therefrom as he doth.

St. Thomas More. (16th cent.)

Here is the badge of heresy: its dogmas are unfruitful; it has no theology. Deduct its remnants of Catholic theology, and what remains? Polemics, explanations, protests.

Card. Newman: *Oxford University Sermons.* (19th cent.)

In reading ecclesiastical history, when I was an Anglican, it used to be forcibly brought home to me, how the initial error of what afterwards became heresy was the urging forward some truth against the prohibition of authority at an unseasonable time.

Card. Newman: *Apologia pro Vita Sua,* 5. (19th cent.)

It is not enough to avoid heresy, but one must also carefully shun all errors which more or less approach it; hence all must observe the constitutions and decrees by which the Holy See has proscribed and forbidden dangerous opinions of that sort.

Code of Canon Law, Canon 1324. (20th cent.)

The denial of a scheme wholesale is not heresy, and has not the creative power of a heresy. It is of the essence of heresy that it leaves standing a great part of the structure it attacks. On this account it can appeal to believers and continues to affect their lives through deflecting them from their original characters. Wherefore it is said of heresies that "they survive by the truth they retain."

Hilaire Belloc: *The Great Heresies.* (20th cent.)

Arianism was a typical example on the largest scale of that reaction against the supernatural which, when it is fully developed, withdraws from religion all that by which religion lives.

Hilaire Belloc: *The Great Heresies.* (20th cent.)

See also Schism

Heretics

They [i.e. heretics] especially accuse the Catholic Church that it commands its adherents to believe, while they boast that they do not impose the yoke of believing on their followers, but rather reveal the source of their teaching.

St. Augustine: *De Utilitate Credendi,* 9, 21. (4th cent.)

The privileges that have been granted in consideration of religion must benefit only the adherents of the Catholic faith. It is our will, moreover, that heretics and schismatics not only be alien from these privileges but shall also be bound and subjected to various compulsory public services.

Edict of the Emperor Constantine I. (Theod. Code, 16, 5, 1) (Sept. 1, 326)

Lest heretics should in their crazy folly continue to perpetrate [the enormities] which they are found to have committed, they are to be forbidden to teach or to learn their false precepts, nor are their bishops to dare to promulgate a faith which they have not got or to ordain ministers which themselves are not.

Decree of the Emperors Valentinian, Theodosius and Arcadius. (Codex Theodosianus, 16, 5, 24) (July, 394)

Under the heading 'heretic' and subject to all the penalties enacted against them, come all such as are found deviating from the norm and rule of the Catholic religion (*judicio Catholicae religionis et tramite*) even on minor points.

Decree of the Emperors Valentinian, Theodosius and Arcadius. (Codex Theodosianus, 16, 5, 28) (Sept., 395)

Although it is customary for crimes to be expiated by punishment, it is our will, nevertheless, to correct the depraved desires of men by an admonition to repentance. Therefore, if any heretics, whether they are Donatists or Manichaeans . . . should embrace, by a simple confession, the Catholic faith and rites, which we wish to be observed by all men . . . we decree that they shall be absolved from all guilt. . . .

Decree of the Emperors Arcadius and Honorius. (Theod. Code, 16, 5, 41) (Nov. 15, 407)

Originally my opinion was that no one should be coerced into the unity of Christ, that we must act only by words, fight only by arguments, and prevail only by force of reason, lest we should have those whom we knew to be avowed heretics feigning themselves to be Catholics. But this opinion of mine was overcome not by the words of those who controverted it, but by conclusive examples to which they could point.

St. Augustine: *Letter 93*, 5, 17. (5th cent.)

So, in availing ourselves of the terror of judges and laws, we desire their [i.e. heretics and schismatics] repentance, not

their death, so that they may be saved from falling into the penalties of eternal judgment. We do not wish to see them quite absolved from punishment, nor, on the other hand, visited with the torments they deserve. Check their sins, therefore, in such a way as to produce repentance in at least a few.

St. Augustine: *Letter 100* (to Donatus, proconsul of Africa). (5th cent.)

They are heretics who in the Church of God entertain some unwholesome and perverse opinion, and on being rebuked refuse to alter it and square it to sound and right doctrine, but are contumacious in their resistance, refuse to amend their pestilential and deadly creed, and persist in defending the same.

St. Augustine: *The City of God*, 18, 51. (5th cent.)

For if he holds false beliefs about God or on some point of doctrine which concerns the substance (*aedificationem*) of the faith, so that his mental attitude is not simply that of a man who hesitates because he is still searching for the truth but rather that of one holding firmly to his beliefs, in fact differing in no way from the opinions and errors of the sort of man who knows everything—then he is a heretic and is really outside the Church, though so far as external appearances go, he may seem to be in it. As a matter of fact the Church has many hidden heretics in her midst, people, that is, who do not obstinately maintain their false views as to draw the attention of others to the fact—if they do so they are, of course, expelled.

St. Augustine: *Quaestionum Septemdecem in Matth.*, 11, 1. (5th cent.)

O almighty and everlasting God, who savest all, and willest not that anyone should perish: look down on the souls of those deceived by the wiles of the devil; that the evil of heresy being removed from their hearts, the erring may repent and return to the unity of thy truth.

Roman Missal, Collect for Good Friday. (Gelasian, ca. 5th cent.)

We should detest and prohibit in heretics not those common beliefs in which they are with us and not against us, but those divisions of peace contrary to truth by which they are against us and do not follow the Lord with us.

St. Bede the Venerable: *In Marcam*, 3. (8th cent.)

A heretic who pertinaciously disbelieves one article is not prepared to follow the teaching of the Church in all matters. If he is not pertinacious he is not in heresy, but only in error. A pertinacious heretic, however, is without divine faith in all the other articles of the Creed, but assents to them from his own opinion.

St. Thomas Aquinas: *Summa Theologica,* 2-2, 5, 3. (13th cent.)

For a person is not to be called a heretic so soon as he errs in matters of faith: then only is he to be so called, when in defiance of the authority of the Church he maintains impious opinions with unyielding pertinacity.

Catechism of the Council of Trent, 1. (16th cent.)

So oft with heretics such terms we use,
As they can brook, not such as we would choose.

Sir John Beaumont: *Against Abused Love.* (17th cent.)

God's and king's rebels have the same good cause,
To trample down divine and human laws:
Both would be call'd reformers, and their hate,
Alike destructive both to Church and state.

Dryden: *The Hind and the Panther,* 1. (17th cent.)

Have not all heretics the same pretence,
To plead the Scriptures in their own defence?

Dryden: *The Hind and the Panther,* 2. (17th cent.)

Any one who after baptism, while remaining nominally a Christian, pertinaciously denies or doubts any one of the truths which must be believed with divine and Catholic faith, is a heretic; if he falls away entirely from the Christian faith, he is an apostate; finally if he rejects the authority of the supreme pontiff or refuses communion with the members of the Church, he is a schismatic.

Code of Canon Law, Canon 1325, 2. (20th cent.)

The heretic (who is also the fanatic) is not a man who loves truth too much; no man can love truth too much. The heretic is a man who loves his truth more than truth itself. He prefers the half-truth that he has found to the whole truth which humanity has found. He does not like to see his own precious little paradox merely bound up with twenty truisms into the bundle of the wisdom of the world.

G. K. Chesterton: *The Common Man.* (20th cent.)

See also Church and State

Hero

Heroes are much the same, the point's agreed,
From Macedonia's madman to the Swede;
The whole strange purpose of their lives, to find
Or make an enemy of all mankind.

Pope: *An Essay on Man,* 4. (18th cent.)

Calculation never made a hero.

Card. Newman: *Development of Christian Doctrine.* (19th cent.)

Heroism

Christian heroism has not the same sources as heroism of other kinds. It has its source in the heart of a God scourged and turned to scorn and crucified outside the city gate.

J. Maritain: *Freedom in the Modern World.* (20th cent.)

Hierarchy

For the high priest [*archiereus,* i.e. the bishop] has been allotted his proper ministrations (*leitourgiai*), and to the priests their proper place has been assigned, and on the Levites their own duties are laid. The lay man is bound by the lay ordinances.

> Pope St. Clement I: *Letter to the Corinthians,* 40, 5. (1st cent.)

I exhort you to be careful to do all things in the harmony of God, the bishops having the primacy after the model of God and the priests after the model of the council of the apostles, and the deacons (who are so dear to me) having entrusted to them the ministry of Jesus Christ.

> St. Ignatius of Antioch: *Letter to the Magnesians,* 6. (2nd cent.)

Our Lord, Whose precepts and admonitions we ought to observe, describing the honor of a bishop and the order of His Church, speaks in the Gospel and says to Peter: *I say unto thee, That thou art Peter, and upon this rock,* etc. (Matth. 16, 18-19). Thence, through the changes of times and successions, the ordination of bishops and plan of the Church flows onward; so that the Church is founded upon the bishops, and every act of the Church is controlled by these same rulers. Since this then is founded on the divine law, I marvel that some with daring temerity have chosen to write to me as if they wrote in the name of the Church; when the Church is established in the bishop and clergy and all who stand in the faith.

> St. Cyprian: *Letters,* 26, 1. (3rd cent.)

Though they [i.e. priests] have a common dignity, yet they have not uniform rank; inasmuch as even among the blessed apostles, notwithstanding the similarity of their honorable estate, there was a certain distinction of power, and while the election of them all was equal, yet it was given to one to take the lead of the rest. From which model has

arisen a distinction between bishops also, and by an important ordinance it has been provided . . . that there should be in each province one whose opinion should have the priority among the brethren; and again that a certain one should be appointed in the greater cities to undertake a fuller responsibility, through whom the care of the universal Church should converge towards Peter's one seat, and nothing anywhere should be separated from its head.

> Pope St. Leo I: *Letters,* 14, 12. (5th cent.)

There is a difference between the secular and the ecclesiastical order: the apostolical origin of a church, its being founded by an apostle, gives it a right to a higher hierarchical rank.

> Pope St. Leo I: *Letters,* 104, 3. (5th cent.)

O almighty and everlasting God, by whose Spirit the whole body of the Church is sanctified and governed: hear our supplications for all the orders thereof, that by the assistance of Thy grace all in their several degrees may render Thee faithful service.

> Roman Missal, Collect for Good Friday. (Gelasian, ca. 5th cent.)

The order of bishops is four-fold, namely, patriarchs, archbishops, metropolitans, and bishops.

> St. Isidore: *Etymologies,* 7, 12. (7th cent.)

The diversity of states and offices in the Church serves, first, the integrity of the Church, second, the carrying out of the Church's action, third, the dignity and beauty of the Church.

> St. Thomas Aquinas: *Summa Theologica,* 2-2, 183, 2. (13th cent.)

All priests, whether pope, archbishop, or simple priest, are of equal authority and jurisdiction according to the institution of Christ.

> Error of Marsiglio of Padua and Jean of Jandun condemned by Pope John XXII in bull, *Licet Iuxta Doctrinam,* October 23, 1327.

If any one saith that in the Catholic Church there is not a hierarchy by divine ordination instituted, consisting of bishops, priests, and ministers; let him be anathema.

> Council of Trent, Session 23, Canon 6. (July 15, 1563)

Those who are designated as members of the ecclesiastical hierarchy are not chosen by the consent or calling of the people or the secular authority; but they are constituted in the degrees of the power of order by holy ordination; in the supreme pontificate once the conditions for a legitimate election and acceptance of the office have been fulfilled by divine law, and in the remaining degrees of the power of jurisdiction by canonical appointment.

> Code of Canon Law, Canon 109. (20th cent.)

See also Acolyte; Bishop; Clergy; Deacon; Episcopate; Orders, Holy; Pastor; Patriarch; Pope; Priest; Priesthood; Succession, Apostolic; Tradition, Ecclesiastical

Hill

Hills peep o'er hills, and Alps on Alps arise.

> Pope: *An Essay on Criticism*, 2. (18th cent.)

Green hills are blue from a distance.

> Irish Proverb. (Modern ?)

History

History is the story of what has been done, and by its means what has taken place in the past is perceived.

> St. Isidore: *Etymologies*, 1, 41. (7th cent.)

The most profitable thing in the world for the instruction of human life is history.

> Froissart. (14th cent.)

In truth, every event of this world is a type of those that follow, history proceeding forward as a circle ever enlarging.

> Card. Newman: *Discussions and Arguments*. (19th cent.)

Experience slowly taught him that he who takes all history for his province is not the man to write a compendium.

> Lord Acton: *Döllinger's Historical Work*. (19th cent.)

The first law of history is not to dare to utter falsehood; the second, not to fear to speak the truth.

> Pope Leo XIII: *On the Opening of the Vatican Archives*, August 18, 1883.

The inflexible integrity of the moral code is, to me, the secret of the authority, the dignity, the utility of history.

> Lord Acton: *Letter to M. Creighton*, Apr. 5, 1887.

The ethics of history cannot be denominational.

> Lord Acton: *Letter to M. Creighton*, Apr. 5, 1887.

History is better written from letters than from histories: let a man criminate himself. No public character has ever stood the revelation of private utterance and correspondence.

> Lord Acton: *Letter to M. Creighton*, Apr. 5, 1887.

Anybody can make history. Only a great man can write it.

> Oscar Wilde: *Aphorisms*. (19th cent.)

History is not written in the interests of morality.

> Agnes Repplier: *Times and Tendencies*. (20th cent.)

Truth lies in proportion. You do not tell an historical truth by merely stating a known fact; nor even by stating a number of facts in a certain and true order.

You can tell it justly only by stating the known things in the order of their values.

Hilaire Belloc: *The Crisis of Civilization.* (20th cent.)

The evidence on which we base our historical conclusion must include much more than documents; much more than recorded statements. We have also tradition. Memories passed on from one generation to another tend of course to be distorted, and if they are written down very late will often contain false elements of mere legend. But, on the other hand, tradition is sincere (which the written evidence of one witness very often is not) and it is broad-based. Over and over again a tradition which the learned, depending upon documents alone, have ridiculed turns out upon the discovery of further corroboration to be true.

Hilaire Belloc: *The Crisis of Civilization.* (20th cent.)

Now the most difficult thing in the world in connection with history, and the rarest of achievement, is the seeing of events as contemporaries saw them, instead of seeing them through the distorting medium of our later knowledge.

Hilaire Belloc: *The Great Heresies.* (20th cent.)

We can know nothing of any nation unless we know its history; and we can know nothing of the history of any nation unless we know something of the history of all nations. The book of the world is full of knowledge we need to acquire, of lessons we need to learn, of wisdom we need to assimilate.

Agnes Repplier: *Points of Friction.* (20th cent.)

We are not cooperators with change; we are cooperators with God. To absent oneself from history is to seek death. Eternity does not vacate time; but possesses it from on high. Our duty is to act on history to the limit of our power, God being first served; but to be re-

signed if it often works against us: it will not happen against the will of God. Thus, the chief thing for us, from the point of view of existence in history, is not to succeed, for success does not endure for ever; but to have been there, in it, for this is indelible.

J. Maritain: *Freedom in the Modern World.* (20th cent.)

The tree is known by its fruits. If you want to understand the social and political history of modern nations, study hell. And yet the world, with all its wars, is not yet hell. And history, however terrible, has another and a deeper meaning. For it is not the evil of history that is its significance and it is not by the evil of our time that our time can be understood. In the furnace of war and hatred, the City of those who love one another is drawn and fused together in the heroism of charity under suffering, while the city of those who hate everything is scattered and dispersed and its citizens are cast out in every direction, like sparks and smoke and flame.

Thomas Merton: *Seeds of Contemplation.* (20th cent.)

Holiness

For our Leader, the Divine Word, does not demand a strong body and beautiful countenance, or high and noble birth, but a pure soul, well-grounded in holiness. He demands the password of our King, namely, divine deeds, for the power to perform such deeds is transmitted to the soul through the Word.

St. Justin Martyr: *Discourse to the Greeks.* (2nd cent.)

Not to wish to be called holy before one is holy; but first to be holy, that one may more truly be called so.

St. Benedict: *Rule,* 4. (One of his 'tools of good works') (6th cent.)

Public welfare which fosters the state and its individual citizens consists in sanctity of life, for life is man's most cherished possession and its sanctity his greatest blessing.

> John of Salisbury: *Policraticus*, 3, 1, 171. (12th cent.)

Sanctity, then, is said to be that whereby a man's mind and its acts are applied to God. Hence sanctity does not differ from religion essentially, but in idea only.

> St. Thomas Aquinas: *Summa Theologica*, 2, 2, 81, 8. (13th cent.)

Not to go along the way to God is to go back.

> St. Thomas Aquinas: *Commentary on Ephesians*, 4, lect. 5. (13th cent.)

He who would fully and feelingly understand the words of Christ, must study to make his whole life conformable to that of Christ.

> Thomas a Kempis: *The Imitation of Christ*, 1, 1. (15th cent.)

Only the actions of the just
Smell sweet and blossom in the dust.

> James Shirley: *A Dirge.* (17th cent.)

This is what Christianity has done in the world; such is the result of Christian teaching; viz., to elicit, foster, mature the seeds of heaven which lie hid in the earth, to multiply (if it may be said) images of Christ, which, though they be few, are worth all else that is among men, and are an ample recompense and *a crown of rejoicing* for apostles and evangelists *in the presence of our Lord Jesus Christ at his coming* (1 Thess. 2, 19).

> Card. Newman: *Parochial and Plain Sermons*, 4. (19th cent.)

Holiness rather than peace.

> One of Card. Newman's Mottoes. (19th cent.)

To obtain the gift of holiness is the work of *a life*.

> Card. Newman: *Miscellanies*, 313. (19th cent.)

The Holy Spirit is the immediate guide of the soul in the way of salvation and sanctification; and the criterion, or test, that the soul is guided by the Holy Spirit, is its ready obedience to the authority of the Church.

> I. T. Hecker: *The Church and the Age.* (19th cent.)

Personal experience proves the lesson of history, that what religion needs is not so much holy states of life as holy men and women.

> Isaac T. Hecker. (Elliott's *Life*, 299) (19th cent.)

To attain to the spiritual estate of the conscious guidance of the indwelling Holy Spirit, the practice of asceticism and of the natural and Christian moral virtues are the preparatory means.

> Isaac T. Hecker. (Elliott's *Life*, 307) (19th cent.)

One of the many points in which Catholic philosophy shows itself superior to the philosophy of Protestant religionists in the knowledge of the human mind is its distinct recognition of the fact that there are as many degrees of human capacity for holiness as for any other kind of eminence, and that for most men a very moderate degree of spirituality is the utmost for which they are entitled to hope.

> Coventry Patmore: *Principle in Art.* (19th cent.)

But not all height is holiness,
Nor every sweetness good.

> Coventry Patmore: *Let Be.* (19th cent.)

Holiness consists not in doing uncommon things, but in doing all common things with an uncommon fervor.

> Card. Manning: *The Eternal Priesthood.* (19th cent.)

Holiness seeks to propagate itself, becoming love as it does so, and cries out, Be holy, for I am holy.

> R. H. Benson: *The Sanctity of the Church.* (20th cent.)

Is it not high time that sanctity should descend from the heaven of cloistered life that four centuries of the Baroque spirit had reserved for it, descend to the world of secular culture and labor in social and political affairs with a view to the reform of the temporal order of mankind? Yes, indeed; on condition that it retains its sanctity and does not lose its character on the way. There is the rub.

> J. Maritain: *Freedom in the Modern World.* (20th cent.)

What a travesty and a tragedy to paint Christianity simply in terms of character-building—the stiff upper lip, the straight bat, the categorical imperative! It is a travesty because it is likely to end in smugness of self-made morality, in the arrogant self-reliance, self-complacency and scorn of the sinner which it is precisely the purpose of religion to destroy. It is a tragedy because at best, if this is what we teach the young, we give them the prose of Christianity without the poetry, the dry bones instead of the living flesh and blood—and how then shall we expect them to be set on fire?

> Gerald Vann: *The Water and the Fire.* (20th cent.)

One of the merits of Christianity, and an indication of its exuberant vitality, is the fact that the goal which God has fixed for every soul, namely sanctity, can be reached by diverse ways. The spirit breathes how and where it wills: hence the manifold variety of saints who shine like stars in the firmament of the Church and preach the richness of divine gifts.

> Pope Pius XII: *Address to the Italian St. Vincent de Paul Society.* (Apr. 27, 1952)

Nothing is more suspicious, in a man who seems holy, than an impatient desire to reform other men.

> Thomas Merton: *Seeds of Contemplation.* (20th cent.)

You cannot have supernatural perfection unless you have first (by God's grace) perfected your own nature on its own level. Before you can be a saint you have got to become human. An animal cannot be a contemplative.

> Thomas Merton: *Seeds of Contemplation.* (20th cent.)

Because virginity should be esteemed as something more perfect than marriage, it does not follow that it is necessary for Christian perfection. Holiness of life can really be attained even without a chastity that is consecrated to God. Witness to this are the many holy men and women who are publicly honored by the Church, and who were faithful spouses and stood out as an example of excellent fathers and mothers; indeed it is not rare to find married people who are very earnest in their efforts for Christian perfection.

> Pius XII: *Sancta Virginitas.* (Mar. 25, 1954)

See also Blessed Virgin Mary; Catholic Church—Holy; Contemplative Life; Gifts of the Holy Ghost; God—His Holiness; Grace; Perfection; Prayer; Saint; Virtue

Holy Family

O house of Nazareth the blest,
Fair hostess of the Lord,
The Church was nurtured at thy breast
And shared thy scanty board.

In all the spreading lands of earth
The wandering sun may see
No dearer spot, no ampler worth
Than erst was found in thee!

> Roman Breviary, Feast of the Holy Family (First Sunday after Epiphany), Hymn *O gente felix hospite* at Lauds. (Tr. H. Henry) (Pope Leo XIII, 19th cent.)

A thousand lights their glory shed
On shrines and altars garlanded;
While swinging censers dusk the air
    With perfumed prayer.

> Roman Breviary, Feast of Holy Family, Hymn *Sacra jam splendent decorata lychnis* at Matins. (Tr. H. Henry) (Pope Leo XIII, 19th cent.)

O highest Hope of mortals,
Blest Light of saints above,
O Jesu, on whose boyhood
Home smiled with kindly love;

And thou whose bosom nursed Him,
O Mary, highly graced,
Whose breast gave milk to Jesus,
Whose arms thy God embraced;

And thou of all men chosen
To guard the Virgin's fame,
To whom God's Son refused not
A father's gracious name.

> Roman Breviary, Feast of the Holy
> Family, Hymn *O Lux beata coelitum* at
> Vespers. (Tr. from the Marquess of
> Bute's Roman Breviary) (Pope Leo XIII,
> 19th cent.)

O Lord Jesus Christ, Who when Thou
wast subject to Mary and Joseph didst
sanctify home life with ineffable virtues:
grant that by their assistance, we may be
instructed by the example of Thy holy
family and become partakers of their
eternal happiness.

> Roman Missal, Collect for Feast of the
> Holy Family. (Feast extended to Latin
> Church by Pope Benedict XV) (20th
> cent.)

The old trinity was of father and
mother and child and is called the human family. The new is of Child and
mother and father and has the name of
the Holy Family. It is in no way altered
except in being entirely reversed; just
as the world which is transformed was
not in the least different, except in being turned upside-down.

> G. K. Chesterton: *The Everlasting Man*,
> 1, 2. (20th cent.)

Holy Ghost, God the

The Holy Spirit Himself, which also
operates in the prophets, we assert to be
an effluence of God, flowing from Him
and returning back again like a beam of
the sun.

> Athenagoras: *Supplication*, 10. (2nd
> cent.)

The Holy Ghost is a Power most mighty,
a Being divine and unsearchable; for
He is living and intelligent, a sanctifying principle of all things made by God
through Christ. . . . There is one God the
Father . . . and one Lord, Jesus Christ
. . . and one Holy Ghost, Who through
the prophets preached of Christ, and
when Christ was come, descended, and
manifested Him.

> St. Cyril of Jerusalem: *Catechetical
> Discourses*, 16, 3. (4th cent.)

The Holy Ghost is not of an inferior nature to the Father and the Son, but, so to
say, consubstantial and coeternal.

> St. Augustine: *Of the Faith and the Creed*.
> (4th cent.)

Now what the soul is to the body of
man, the Holy Spirit is in the body of
Christ, which is the Church. The Holy
Spirit does that in the whole Church,
which the soul does in all the members
of a single body.

> St. Augustine: *Sermon 267*, 4, 4. (5th
> cent.)

As "to be born" is, for the Son, to be
from the Father, so, for the Holy Ghost,
"to be the Gift of God" is to proceed
from Father and Son.

> St. Augustine: *De Trinitate*, 4, 20. (5th
> cent.)

May the power of the Holy Ghost be
with us, we beseech Thee, O Lord, mercifully cleansing our hearts and defending them from all harm.

> Roman Missal, Collect before Mass.
> (Leonine, ca. 5th cent.)

Every soul is quickened by the Holy
Ghost, is elevated by His purity, and is
mystically enlightened by the threefold
Unity.

> Byzantine Horologion, Anavathmi at
> Matins. (ca. 6th to 8th cent.)

Heavenly King, Paraclete, Spirit of
truth, Who art everywhere present and
fillest all things, the Treasury of good

things and the Bestower of life, come and dwell in us, and purify us from every stain, and save our souls in Thy goodness.

> Byzantine Horologion, Prayer. (ca. 6th to 8th cent.)

For to conceive of the Spirit Who dwells in God as after the likeness of our own spirit, would be to drag down the greatness of the divine nature to the lowest depths of degradation. But we must contemplate Him as an essential power, existing in His own proper and peculiar subsistence, proceeding from the Father and resting in the Word, and showing forth the Word, neither capable of disjunction from God in Whom He exists, and the Word Whose companion He is, nor poured forth to vanish into nothingness, but being in subsistence in the likeness of the Word . . . having no beginning and no end. For never was the Father at any time lacking in the Word, nor the Word in the Spirit.

> St. John of Damascus: *Exposition of the Orthodox Faith,* 1, 7. (8th cent.)

Likewise we also believe in one Holy Spirit, the Lord and Giver of life, Who proceeds from the Father and rests in the Son; the object of equal adoration and glorification with the Father and Son, since He is co-essential and co-eternal: the Spirit of God, direct, authoritative, the fountain of wisdom, and life, and holiness.

> St. John of Damascus: *Exposition of the Orthodox Faith,* 1, 8. (8th cent.)

O God, Who didst teach the hearts of the faithful by the light of the Holy Ghost, grant that in the same Spirit we may be truly wise and ever rejoice in His consolation.

> Roman Missal, Collect before Mass. (Before 10th cent.)

From both proceeding, as from one,
The Father, and the eternal Son,
    Thou Spirit Paraclete:
Give tongues to speak, but first inspire

Our hearts with love's all-quickening fire,
    Thy own true genial heat.

> Adam of St. Victor: *Qui procedis ab utroque.* (Tr. anon.) (12th cent.)

Love can be used either as an essential name of the divine nature or as a personal name of a divine person—then it is the proper name of the Holy Ghost, as *Word* is the proper name of the Son.

> St. Thomas Aquinas: *Summa Theologica,* 1, 37, 1. (13th cent.)

A gift is freely given, and expects no return. Its reason is love. What is first given is love; that is the first gift. The Holy Ghost comes forth as the substance of love, and *Gift* is His proper name.

> St. Thomas Aquinas: *Summa Theologica,* 1, 38, 2. (13th cent.)

Eternal Spright! which art in heaven the Love
    With which God and his Son each other kiss;
    And Who, to shew who God's Beloved is,
    The shape and wings took'st of a loving Dove.
When Christ ascending, sent Thee from above
    In fiery tongues; Thou camst down unto his,
    That skill in uttering heavenly mysteries
    By heat of zeal both faith and love might move.
True God of love! from Whom all true love springs,
    Bestow upon my love Thy wings and fire,
    My soul and spirit is, and with Thy wings
Make like an angel fly from earth's desire,
    And with Thy fire and heart inflamm'd may bear,
    And in Thy sight a seraphim appear.

> Henry Constable: *Sonnet to God the Holy Ghost.* (16th cent.)

Creator Spirit, by Whose aid
The world's foundations were laid,
Come visit every pious mind;
Come pour Thy joys on human kind;
From sin and sorrow set us free,
And make Thy temples worthy Thee.

Dryden: *Transl. of Hymn Veni Creator.*
(Rabanus Maurus, 9th cent.) (17th cent.)

O let us fall and worship Him,
The love of Sire and Son,
The consubstantial Breath of God,
The coeternal One!

Ah! see how like the incarnate Word,
His blessed Self He lowers,
To dwell with us invisible,
And make His riches ours.

Most humble Spirit! mighty God!
Sweet must Thy presence be,
If loss of Jesus can be gain,
So long as we have Thee!

F. Faber: *The Descent of the Holy Ghost.*
(First line: O mighty Mother! why that
light) (19th cent.)

Fountain of love! Thyself true God!
Who through eternal days
From Father and from Son hast flowed
In uncreated ways!

O Majesty unspeakable!
O Person all divine!
How in the threefold Majesty
Doth Thy procession shine!

Fixed in the Godhead's awful light
Thy fiery breath doth move;
Thou art a wonder by Thyself
To worship and to love.

F. Faber: *The Eternal Spirit.* (19th cent.)

Holy Ghost! come down upon Thy
children,
Give us grace, and make us Thine;
Thy tender fires within us kindle,
Blessed Spirit! Dove divine!

F. Faber: *Holy Ghost, Come Down Upon
Thy Children.* (19th cent.)

Because the Holy Ghost over the
bent

World broods with warm breast and
with ah! bright wings.

G. M. Hopkins: *God's Grandeur.* (19th
cent.)

The whole future of the human race depends on bringing the individual soul
more completely and perfectly under the
sway of the Holy Spirit.

Isaac T. Hecker. (Elliott's Life, 307)
(19th cent.)

What society most needs today is the
baptism of the Holy Spirit.

I. T. Hecker. (Elliott's Life, 307) (19th
cent.)

Whatever we are, that we are by the divine goodness; and this goodness is specially attributed to the Holy Ghost.

Pope Leo XIII: *Divinum Illud.* (May 4,
1897)

You cannot trace the guidance of the
Spirit of God, or diagnose His operations
in the secret rooms of the soul. He seems
at times to let good go, and to bring instead good out of evil, and light into
voluntary darkness.

R. H. Benson: *The Confessions of a
Convert.* (20th cent.)

See also Gifts of the Holy Ghost; God;
Pentecost

Holy Innocents

With terror doth the tyrant hear
The King of kings hath come to dwell
Where David's court shall widely rear
A sceptered reign o'er Israel.
Then cries out, raging, at the word:
"He comes to stand where we have
stood:
Hence, soldier, and with ruthless sword
Deluge the cradles deep with blood!"

Roman Breviary, Feast of the Holy
Innocents (Dec. 28), Hymn *Audit
tyrannus anxius* at Matins. (Tr. H. Henry)
(Prudentius, from Cathemerinon, 4th
cent.)

All hail, ye little martyr flowers,
Sweet rosebuds cut in dawning hours!
When Herod sought the Christ to find
Ye fell as blooms before the wind.
First victims of the martyr bands,
With crowns and palms in tender
    hands,
Around the very altar, gay
And innocent, ye seem to play.

> Roman Breviary, Feast of the Holy
> Innocents, Hymn *Salvete flores martyrum*
> at Lauds. (Tr. A. Riley.) (Prudentius,
> from Cathemerinon, 4th cent.)

O God, whose praise the martyred Innocents confessed today not in speech but
by their death; mortify within us all
vices, that our lives may also confess by
our actions Thy faith which our tongues
profess.

> Roman Missal, Feast of the Holy
> Innocents, Collect. (Gelasian, 5th to 7th
> cent.)

O blessed babes! first flowers of
    Christian spring,
    Who though untimely cropp'd fair
      garlands frame,
With open throats and silent mouths
    you sing
    His praise whom age permits you not
      to name;
Your tunes are tears, your instruments
    are swords,
Your ditty death, and blood in lieu of
    words!

> Robert Southwell: *The Flight into Egypt.*
> (16th cent.)

Holy Saturday (*Vigil of Easter*)

You shall come together and watch and
keep vigil all the night with prayers and
intercessions, and with reading of the
prophets, and with the Gospel and with
psalms, with fear and trembling and
with earnest supplication, until the third
hour in the night after the Sabbath; and
then break your fasts.

> Anonymous: *Didascalia Apostolorum,* 21.
> (3rd cent.)

Let the angelic choirs of heaven now rejoice; let the divine mysteries be celebrated with joy; and let the trumpet of
salvation resound for the victory of so
great a King. Let the earth also rejoice,
illumined with such resplendent rays;
and enlightened with the brightness of
the eternal King, let it feel that the darkness of the whole world is dispersed. Let
our mother the Church also rejoice,
adorned with the brightness of such a
great light; and may this temple resound with the joyful voices of the
people.

> Roman Missal, Easter Vigil, *Exultet* at
> Blessing of Paschal Candle. (Gregorian,
> ca. 6th cent.)

O God, the supreme Father of all believers, Who throughout the world dost
multiply the children of Thy promise by
diffusing the grace of Thy adoption, and
by this Paschal sacrament makest Thy
servant Abraham, according to Thy oath,
the father of all nations; grant Thy people worthily to enter into the grace of
Thy calling.

> Roman Missal, Easter Vigil, Collect.
> (Gelasian, ca. 7th cent.)

O almighty and everlasting God, mercifully look upon Thy people who are about
to be reborn and pant like the hart after
the fountain of Thy waters; graciously
grant that the thirst of their faith may,
by the sacrament of baptism, sanctify
their souls and bodies.

> Roman Missal, Easter Vigil, Collect.
> (Gelasian, ca. 7th cent.)

O God, Who makest this most sacred
night bright with the glory of the resurrection of our Lord; preserve in the
new offspring of Thy family the spirit
of adoption which Thou hast given
them; that, renewed in body and spirit,
they may render Thee an exemplary
service.

> Roman Missal, Easter Vigil, Collect.
> (Gelasian, ca. 7th cent.)

By Thy passion, Christ, we have been
freed from passions, and by Thy resur-

rection delivered from corruption. Glory to Thee, O Lord.

Today hell groans and cries, my might is sacrificed. The Shepherd is crucified and Adam raised. I have lost those that I ruled. I have disgorged all those I devoured in my power. The crucified One hath opened the graves, and the power of death hath no avail. Glory to Thy Cross, O Lord, and to Thy resurrection.

Byzantine Triodion, Stichera at Vespers. (ca. 6th to 8th cent.)

The Sabbath is so called in Hebrew from the word meaning rest, because the Lord rested on this day after completing the world. On this day also the Lord rested in the tomb, that He might confirm the mystery of that rest; what the Jews were ordered to observe foreshadowed what was to come. But when Christ had fulfilled the figure by His burial, the observance of the Sabbath lapsed.

St. Isidore: *Etymologies,* 6, 18. (7th cent.)

See also Easter; Passion of our Lord

Holy Thursday

O God, from Whom Judas received the punishment of his guilt, and the thief the reward of his confession, grant us the effect of Thy clemency: that as our Lord Jesus Christ in His passion gave to each a different recompense according to his merits, so may He deliver us from our old sins and grant us the grace of His resurrection.

Roman Missal, Collect for Holy Thursday and Good Friday. (Gelasian, 5th to 7th cent.)

Holy Thursday (*Coena Dominica,* Lord's Supper) is so called, because on that day the Savior celebrated the pasch with His disciples; and this is also celebrated today in accordance with the tradition, and the holy chrism is consecrated on this day, and the end of the Old Testament and the beginning of the New is declared.

St. Isidore: *Etymologies,* 6, 18. (7th cent.)

Oh the mystery, passing wonder,
When, reclining at the board,
Eat, Thou saidst to Thy disciples,
That true Bread with quick'ning stor'd:
Drink in faith the healing Chalice
From a dying God outpour'd.

. . . .

Christ is now our mighty Pascha,
Eaten for our mystic bread:
Take we of His broken Body,
Drink we of the Blood He shed,
As a lamb led out to slaughter,
And for this world offered.

Byzantine Triodion, Canon at Compline. (Tr. Neale) (St. Andrew of Crete, 8th cent.)

Christ for our sake became obedient unto death, even to the death of the cross. For which cause God also hath exalted Him, and hath given Him a name which is above all names. (Phil. 2, 8)

Roman Breviary, Tenebrae (Matins-Lauds). (Versicle repeated on last three days of Holy Week.) (ca. 8th cent.)

A new commandment I give you: that you love one another, as I have loved you, saith the Lord (John 13, 34). . . . .

After the Lord was risen from supper, He put water into a basin, and began to wash the feet of His disciples: this was the example He gave unto them. . . .

Where charity and love are, there is God. ℣. The love of Christ has gathered us together. ℣. Let us rejoice in Him and be glad. ℣. Let us fear and love the living God. ℣. And let us love one another with a sincere heart.

Roman Missal, Antiphons at Washing of the Feet. (Gelasian, ca. 7th cent.)

Assist, O Lord, we beseech Thee, this performance of our service; and since Thou didst vouchsafe to wash the feet of Thy disciples, despise not the work of Thy hands, which Thou hast commanded us to imitate: that as here the outward stains are washed away for us and by us, so likewise may the inward stains of all be blotted out by Thee.

Roman Missal, Collect at Washing of the Feet. (Before 10th cent. ?)

At the Supper with the twelve
Thou, O Christ, wast seated;
And hast prophesied Thy death
Soon to be completed;
And hast pointed Judas out
By the morsel meted:
And unto Gethsemane,
After, hadst retreated.

Hymn from Sarum Missal. (Tr. J. Neale) (12th cent.)

See also Blessed Sacrament; Good Friday

Homage

For when we more than human homage pay,
The charming cause is justly snatched away.

Dryden. (17th cent.)

Home

Home is homely though it be poor.

John Heywood: Proverbs, 1, 4. (16th cent.)

The home is not a convent.

Jean Pierre Camus: The Spirit of St. Francis de Sales, 21, 6. (17th cent.)

Happy the man whose wish and care
A few paternal acres bound,
Content to breathe his native air,
In his own ground.

Pope: Ode on Solitude. (18th cent.)

Who has not felt how sadly sweet
The dream of home, the dream of home,
Steals o'er his heart, too soon to fleet,
When far o'er sea or land we roam?

Thomas Moore: The Dream of Home. (19th cent.)

The bird, let loose in eastern skies,
When hast'ning fondly home,
Ne'er stoops to earth her wing, nor flies
Where idle warblers roam;
But high she shoots through air and light,
Above all low delay,
Where nothing earthly bounds her flight,
Nor shadow dims her way.

Thomas Moore: The Bird, Let Loose. (19th cent.)

Nor has the world a better thing,
Though one should search it round,
Than thus to live one's own sole king,
Upon one's own sole ground.

W. S. Blunt: The Old Squire. (19th cent.)

The sense of home-coming—that strange passion for a particular set of inanimate things; or, at the most, for an association of ideas—has no parallel in human emotions.

R. H. Benson: By What Authority. (20th cent.)

The eagle nests near the sun;
The dove's low nest for me!—
The eagle's on the crag; sweet one,
The dove's in our green tree!
For hearts that beat like thine and mine
Heaven blesses humble earth;—
The angels of our heaven shall shine
The angels of our hearth!

John J. Piatt: A Song of Content. (19th cent.)

God looks down well pleased to mark
In earth's dusk each rosy spark,
Lights of home and lights of love,
And the child the heart thereof.

Katharine T. Hinkson: A Night Thought. (20th cent.)

Homer

The lord of the sublimest song soaring over the others like an eagle.

Dante: Inferno, Canto 4. (14th cent.)

Honesty

The less time it takes anyone to be led away from honesty, the more wicked he is.

> Erasmus: *Enchiridion.* (16th cent.)

The modest front of this small floor,
Believe me, reader, can say more
Than many a braver marble can,—
Here lies a truly honest man.

> Richard Crashaw: *Epitaph upon Mr. Ashton.* (17th cent.)

An honest man's the noblest work of God.

> Pope: *An Essay on Man,* 4. (18th cent.)

Honey

A fly followeth the honey.

> Thomas Hoccleve: *De regimine principum.* (15th cent.)

One can catch more flies with a spoonful of honey than with a hundred barrels of vinegar.

> Jean Pierre Camus: *The Spirit of St. Francis de Sales,* 2, 13. (17th cent.)

Honor

Vain honor is a play of divers parts,
Where feignèd words and gestures please our hearts;
The flatter'd audience are the actors' friends;
But lose that title when the fable ends.

> Sir John Beaumont: *Of the Miserable State of Man.* (17th cent.)

Be not with honor's gilded baits beguiled.

> Sir William Davenant: *Gondibert,* 1, 5. (17th cent.)

Whoever would not die to preserve his honor would be infamous.

> Pascal: *Pensées,* 3. (17th cent.)

The brave man seeks not popular applause,
Nor overpower'd with arms, deserts his cause;
Unsham'd, though foil'd, he does the best he can;
Force is of brutes, but honor is of man.

> Dryden: *Palamon and Arcite,* 3. (17th cent.)

When honor's lost, 'tis a relief to die;
Death's but a sure retreat from infamy.

> Sir Samuel Garth: *The Dispensary,* 5. (17th cent.)

Honor and shame from no conditions rise;
Act well your part, there all the honor lies.

> Pope: *An Essay on Man,* 4. (18th cent.)

True, conscious honor is to feel no sin;
He's armed without that's innocent within.

> Pope: *The First Epistle of the First Book of Horace.* (18th cent.)

Great objects exact a venture, and a sacrifice is the condition of honor.

> Card. Newman: *Oxford University Sermons.* (19th cent.)

When honor comes to you be ready to take it;
But reach not to seize it before it is near.

> J. B. O'Reilly: *Rules of the Road.* (19th cent.)

Honors

The honors of this world, what are they but puff, and emptiness and peril of falling?

> St. Augustine: *On Catechizing the Unlearned.* (5th cent.)

What should people desire for themselves and for those dear to them, honors and high station, something more, that is, than mere temporal prosperity? Yes, emphatically; but provided always, that in planning and contriving such things for those of whom they have charge, they are not enamored of honors and such like for their own sake, but for the sake of Something else which alone renders positions of honor and dignity good.

St. Augustine: *Letter 130* (to Proba on prayer). (5th cent.)

Honors and privileges are worth nothing if everyone has them. If we all wore crowns, the kings would go bareheaded.

R. H. Benson: *The Dawn of All.* (20th cent.)

Hook

By hook or crook.

John Heywood: *Proverbs,* 1, 11. (16th cent.)

Hope

What can be hoped for which is not believed?

St. Augustine: *On Faith, Hope, and Charity.* (5th cent.)

No man is able of himself to grasp the supreme good of eternal life; he needs divine help. Hence there is here a twofold object, the eternal life we hope for, and the divine help we hope by.

St. Thomas Aquinas: *Disputations concerning Hope,* 1. (13th cent.)

Hope, said I,
Is certain expectation that the heart
Has of the future glory; the effect
Of divine grace and precedent desert.

Dante: *Paradiso, Canto 25.* (Tr. Binyon) (14th cent.)

But now of hope the calends begin.

Chaucer: *Troilus and Criseyde.* (14th cent.)

Sweet hope is sovereign comfort of our life:
Our joy in sorrow, and our peace in strife.

Sir John Beaumont: *An Act of Hope.* (17th cent.)

O Thou Who art our Author and our End,
On Whose large mercy chains of hope depend;
Lift me to Thee by Thy propitious hand:
For lower I can find no place to stand.

Sir John Beaumont: *An Act of Hope.* (17th cent.)

Dear hope! earth'd dowry, and heav'n's debt!
The entity of those that are not yet.
Subtlest, but surest being! Thou by whom
Our nothing has a definition!

R. Crashaw: *M. Crashaw's Answer for Hope.* (17th cent.)

When I consider life, 'tis all a cheat,
Yet, fooled with hope, men favor the deceit;
Trust on, and think to-morrow will repay;
Tomorrow's falser than the former day;
Lies worse, and, while it says we shall be blest
With some new joys, cuts off what we possessed.

Dryden: *Aurengzebe,* 4. (17th cent.)

Hope springs eternal in the human breast;
Man never is, but always to be, blest.

Pope: *An Essay on Man,* 1. (18th cent.)

My God, I firmly hope in Thee,
For Thou art great and good;
Thou gavest us Thine only Son
To die upon the Rood.
I hope through Him for grace to live
As Thy commandments teach,
And through Thy mercy, when I die
The joys of heaven to reach.

Act of Hope from *Hymns for the Year,* 1867.

The hopes that lost in some far distance seem,
May be the truer life, and this the dream.

Adelaide Procter: *A Legend of Provence.* (19th cent.)

We did not dare to breathe a prayer
    Or to give our anguish scope!
Something was dead in each of us,
    And what was dead was hope.

Oscar Wilde: *The Ballad of Reading
Gaol*, 3. (19th cent.)

As long as matters are really hopeful,
hope is a mere flattery or platitude; it
is only when everything is hopeless that
hope begins to be a strength at all. Like
all the Christian virtues, it is as unreasonable as it is indispensable.

G. K. Chesterton: *Heretics.* (20th cent.)

Youth is pre-eminently the period in
which a man can be lyric, fanatical,
poetic; but youth is the period in which
a man can be hopeless. The end of every
episode is the end of the world. But the
power of hoping through everything, the
knowledge that the soul survives its adventures, that great inspiration comes to
the middle-aged. God has kept that good
wine until now.

G. K. Chesterton: *Charles Dickens.* (20th
cent.)

See also Faith

Hope and Fear

Before sinning, let man fear God's justice, but after sinning let him presume
on His mercy. And let him not so fear
His justice as not to be strengthened by
the consolation of hope; nor so confident
of His mercy as to neglect to apply to his
wounds the medicine of adequate penance.

Pope St. Gregory I: *Morals,* 33, 23. (6th
cent.)

Art thou righteous? Then fear lest thou
fall. Art thou a sinner? Then believe in
His mercy, that thou mayest rise.

Pope St. Gregory I: *Homilies on the
Gospel,* 34, 15. (6th cent.)

Horace

Horace still charms with graceful neg-
    ligence,

And without method talks us into
sense.

Pope: *An Essay on Criticism,* 3. (18th
cent.)

Horizon

There's a magic in the distance, where
the sea-line meets the sky.

Alfred Noyes: *Forty Singing Seamen.*
(20th cent.)

Horn

All are not hunters that blow the horn.

Latin Proverb. (Medieval)

Horse

The horse is the only creature that weeps
for man and feels the emotion of grief.

St. Isidore: *Etymologies,* 12, 1. (7th cent.)

His palfrey was as brown as is a berry.

Chaucer: *Canterbury Tales: Prologue.*
(Tr. Coghill) (14th cent.)

    When the great steed
Is stole, then he taketh heed
And maketh the stable-door fast.

John Gower: *Confessio Amantis,* 4.
(14th cent.)

Here were we fallen in a great question of the law, whether the grey mare
may be the better horse or not.

St. Thomas More: *Dialogue of Comfort,*
2, 5. (16th cent.)

It be a good horse that never stumbleth.

John Heywood: *Proverbs,* 1, 8. (16th
cent.)

A short horse is soon curried.

John Heywood: *Proverbs,* 1, 10. (16th
cent.)

A man may well bring a horse to the
    water,
But he cannot make him drink.

John Heywood: *Proverbs,* 1, 11. (16th
cent.)

How can the foal amble if the horse and mare trot?

> John Heywood: *Proverbs,* 1, 11. (16th cent.)

While the grass groweth the horse starveth.

> John Heywood: *Proverbs,* 1, 11. (16th cent.)

A scald horse is good enough for a scabbed squire.

> scald—scaly
>
> John Heywood: *Proverbs,* 1, 11. (16th cent.)

The common horse is worst shod.

> John Heywood: *Proverbs,* 1, 11. (16th cent.)

Set the cart before the horse.

> John Heywood: *Proverbs,* 2, 7. (16th cent.)

I hear in my heart, I hear in its ominous pulses
All day, on the road, the hoofs of invisible horses,
All night, from their stalls, the importunate pawing and neighing.

> Louise Imogen Guiney: *The Wild Ride.* (19th cent.)

They're knowledgable crathurs, but terrible aisy frightened. Horses is like women—they require the soothin' word an' the strong gentle touch. But there's not many has the sense to give it to them.

> Katharine T. Hinkson: *The Forge* (*Countrymen All*). (20th cent.)

Thunder on, you silver stallions,
Let your plunging, flying hooves
Strike and ring against the sky;
Let your hoof-beats wake the old gods
Sleeping on the hills of glory;
Let your cruel breath chill the night stars;
Fly, stallions, fly!

> William Berry: *Thunder On, You Silver Stallions.* (20th cent.)

It's only the Lord can make a race horse out of a jackass.

> Seumas MacManus: *Heavy Hangs the Golden Grain.* (20th cent.)

Hospitality

The Christian should offer his brethren simple and unpretentious hospitality.

> St. Basil: *The Morals,* 38. (4th cent.)

He that cometh every day, shall have a cockney;
He that cometh now and then, shall have a fat hen.

> cockney—cock's egg
>
> John Heywood: *Proverbs,* 1, 11. (16th cent.)

Host

Reckoners without their host must reckon twice.

> John Heywood: *Proverbs,* 1, 8. (16th cent.)

Hot

Hot as a toast.

> John Heywood: *Proverbs,* 2, 1. (16th cent.)

Hour

It happeth in one hour that happeth not in seven year.

> John Heywood: *Proverbs,* 1, 11. (16th cent.)

Hours are golden links, God's token,
Reaching heaven; but, one by one,
Take them, lest the chain be broken
Ere the pilgrimage be done.

> Adelaide Procter: *One by One.* (19th cent.)

Yet, if the roots of the truth were bare,
Our transience is only a mortal seeming;

Fond men, we are fixed as a still despair,
And we fleet but in your dreaming.

F. Thompson: *Song of the Hours.* (19th cent.)

House

Three things damn a house: a leaky roof, an evil woman, and smoke. (Sunt tria damna domus: imber, mala femina, fumus.)

Latin Proverb. (Medieval)

Oh, to have a little house!
To own the hearth and stool and all!
The heaped-up sods upon the fire,
The pile of turf against the wall!

To have a clock with weights and chains
And pendulum swinging up and down!
A dresser filled with shining delph,
Speckled and white and blue and brown!

Padraic Colum: *An Old Woman of the Roads.* (20th cent.)

I went back to a place I knew
When I was very, very small;
The same old yellow roses grew
Against the same old wall.

. . . .

And yet the place seemed changed and still;
The house itself had shrunk, I know.
And then my eyes began to fill—
For I had always loved it so!

Aline Kilmer: *Remembrance.* (20th cent.)

House without hound, cat, or child, house without love or affection.

Seumas MacManus: *Heavy Hangs the Golden Grain.* (20th cent.)

Household

Let your household love you; if they do not, make them fear you.

St. Bernard: *On Consideration,* 4, 6. (To Pope Eugenius III) (12th cent.)

Housekeeping

The care of a smallish house resembles a telescope. It may be reduced to a very small compass and yet remain intact; or it may be prolonged to an almost incredible extent.

R. H. Benson: *An Average Man.* (20th cent.)

Hughes, Archbishop John

His natural gifts of mind and heart, independent of his education, were of a high order and made him pre-eminent in leadership; not only was he a great ruler of an important diocese in a hierarchy remarkable for distinguished bishops, but also a master-builder of the Church in the United States and one of the most helpful and sagacious of the makers of America.

Card. Hayes: *John Hughes.* (In Catholic Encyclopedia, vol. 7.) (20th cent.)

Human Nature

Let the human race take hope and rediscover its own nature. Let it see what an important place it occupies among the works of God. Men! do not despise yourselves—the Son of God assumed manhood. Women! do not despise yourselves—the Son of God was born of a woman. Yet, do not love things carnal, for in the sight of the Son of God, we are neither male nor female. Do not love things temporal; for, if it were right to love them, the human nature assumed by the Son of God would have loved them. Do not be afraid of insults and crosses and death, for, if these were harmful to man, the human nature assumed by the Son of God would not have suffered them.

St. Augustine: *De Agone Christiano,* 11, 12. (4th cent.)

Left to itself, human nature tends to death, and utter apostasy from God, however plausible it may look externally.

Card. Newman: *Sermons on Subjects of the Day.* (19th cent.)

There is nothing so irrepressible as human nature; nothing that so yearns to push itself forward.

> R. H. Benson: *The Friendship of Christ.* (20th cent.)

Human Race

For there is nothing so social by nature, so unsocial by its corruption, as this race.

> St. Augustine: *The City of God,* 12, 27. (5th cent.)

Humanism

The debate that divides our contemporaries and that compels us all to make an election is between two conceptions of humanism: a *theocentric* conception, which is the Christian conception; and an *anthropocentric* conception, which has its first origins in the spirit of the Renaissance. The first conception may be described as authentic humanism; the second conception may be called inhuman humanism.

> J. Maritain: *Freedom in the Modern World.* (20th cent.)

Humanitarianism

Humanitarianism is as hard as inhumanity.

> G. K. Chesterton: *Tremendous Trifles,* 32. (20th cent.)

The modern humanitarian can love all opinions, but he cannot love all men; he seems sometimes, in the ecstasy of his humanitarianism, even to hate them all. He can love all opinions, including the opinion that men are unlovable.

> G. K. Chesterton: *Introduction to Hard Times.* (20th cent.)

There is no opposition between the laws that govern the life of faithful Christians and the postulates of a genuine humane humanitarianism, but rather unity and mutual support.

> Pope Pius XII: *Summi Pontificatus.* (Oct. 20, 1939)

True religion and profound humaneness are not rivals. They are sisters.

> Pope Pius XII: *On the Republic of Liberia.* (Feb. 28, 1951)

Humiliation

Humility which humiliation teaches us to practise, is the foundation of the entire spiritual fabric. Thus humiliation is the way to humility, as patience to peace, as reading to knowledge. If you long for the virtue of humility, you must not flee from the way of humiliation. For if you do not allow yourself to be humiliated, you cannot attain to humility.

> St. Bernard: *Letters.* (12th cent.)

I have been honor'd and obey'd,
    I have met scorn and slight;
And my heart loves earth's sober shade,
    More than her laughing light.

For what is rule but a sad weight
    Of duty and a snare?
What meanness, but with happier fate
    The Savior's Cross to share?

> Card. Newman: *Humiliation.* (19th cent.)

Humility

Let us, therefore, brethren, be of a humble frame of mind, ridding ourselves of all arrogance and haughtiness and foolishness and passion.

> Pope St. Clement I: *Letter to the Corinthians,* 13. (1st cent.)

For it is to the humble-minded that Christ belongs, not to those who exalt themselves above His flock. The Scepter of the divine majesty, the Lord Jesus Christ, did not, for all His power, come clothed in boastful pomp and overweening pride, but in a humble frame of mind.

> Pope St. Clement I: *Letter to the Corinthians,* 16. (1st cent.)

There is something in humility which strangely exalts the heart.

> St. Augustine: *The City of God,* 14. (5th cent.)

Lord and Master of my life, give me not the spirit of indolence, despair, ambition and vain speaking; but rather the spirit of chastity, humble-mindedness, patience and love do Thou grant unto me, Thy servant. Yea, O Lord King, let me see mine own faults, and let me not judge my brother; for Thou art blessed to ages of ages. Amen.

> Byzantine Horologion, Prayer of St. Ephraem at Vespers. (Before 5th cent.?)

Wherefore, brethren, if we wish to attain to the summit of humility and desire to arrive speedily at that heavenly exaltation to which we ascend by the humility of the present life, then we must set up a ladder of our ascending actions like unto that which Jacob saw in his vision, whereon angels appeared to him, descending and ascending. By that descent and ascent we must surely understand nothing else than this, that we descend by self-exaltation and ascend by humility.

> St. Benedict: *Rule,* 7. (6th cent.)

The first degree of humility, then, is that a man keep the fear of God before his eyes. . . . The second degree . . . is that a man love not his own will. . . . The third degree is that a man for the love of God subject himself to his superior in all obedience. . . . The fourth degree . . . is that meeting in this obedience with difficulties . . . he should with a quiet mind hold fast to patience. . . . The fifth degree . . . is that he humbly confess and conceal not from his abbot any evil thoughts that enter his heart and any secret sins that he has committed. . . . The sixth degree . . . is that a monk be content with the meanest and worst of everything. . . . The seventh degree . . . is that he should not only in his speech declare himself . . . of less account than all others, but should in his own inmost heart believe it. . . .

> St. Benedict: *Rule,* 7. (6th cent.)

For then only is a praiseworthy work displayed to men without harm, when the praise awarded is genuinely trodden under in the mind's contempt.

> Pope St. Gregory I: *Morals,* 8, 84. (6th cent.)

For he is less in need who is without a garment, than he who is without humility.

> Pope St. Gregory I: *Morals,* 21, 30. (6th cent.)

A man is quite incapable of learning humility in a position of superiority, if he does not refrain from acting proudly when he was in a position of subjection.

> Pope St. Gregory I: *Pastoral Care,* 1, 9. (6th cent.)

O God, Who dost resist the proud and give Thy grace to the humble, grant us the virtue of true humility after the pattern revealed to the faithful by Thy only-begotten Son in His own person; that we may never arouse Thy indignation by our pride, but may always receive the gifts of Thy grace in perfect subjection.

> Roman Missal, Collect. (Gelasian, ca. 6th cent.)

When I look at the condition of my human weakness my strength is shattered, but when I raise my eyes to the grace of divine assistance I am confident that I can accomplish virtuous deeds.

> St. Bede the Venerable: *Commentary on Habacuc.* (8th cent.)

Great graces cannot be obtained without humility; so those who are to have them must be humiliated, that they may be made worthy by humility to receive grace. When you yourself experience humiliation, you should take it as a sure sign that some grace is in store.

> St. Bernard: *Sermons on the Canticle of Canticles,* 34. (12th cent.)

Humility is the mother of salvation.

> St. Bernard: *Sermons on the Canticle of Canticles,* 36. (12th cent.)

Humility is that thorough self-examination which makes a man contemptible in his own sight. It is acquired by those who set up a ladder in their hearts whereby to ascend from virtue to virtue, that is, from step to step, until they attain the summit of humility, from where, as from the Sion of speculation, they can see the truth.

> St. Bernard: *The Steps of Humility,* 1. (12th cent.)

He alone is truly humble who restrains his own soul, who is even afraid to let the excellency that is in him be known, that he may not be thought to be what he is not.

> St. Bernard: *Letters,* 11. (12th cent.)

Meekness in itself is nought else but a true knowing and feeling of a man's self as he is.

> Anonymous: *The Cloud of Unknowing,* 13. (14th cent.)

This is the highest science and most profitable lesson, truly to know and despise ourselves.

> Thomas a Kempis: *The Imitation of Christ,* 1, 2. (15th cent.)

Esteem not thyself better than others, lest, perhaps, thou be accounted worse in the sight of God, Who knoweth what is in man.

> Thomas a Kempis: *The Imitation of Christ,* 1, 7. (15th cent.)

Be not proud of thy own works: for the judgments of God are different from the judgments of men; and oftentimes that displeaseth Him which pleaseth men.

> Thomas a Kempis: *The Imitation of Christ,* 1, 7. (15th cent.)

If thou hast anything of good, believe better things of others, that thou mayest preserve humility.

> Thomas a Kempis: *The Imitation of Christ,* 1, 7. (15th cent.)

It is better to have little knowledge with humility and a weak understanding, than greater treasures of learning with self-conceit.

> Thomas a Kempis: *The Imitation of Christ,* 3, 7. (15th cent.)

Learn, O dust, to obey; learn to humble thyself, thou that art but dirt and mire, and to cast thyself down under the feet of all men.

> Thomas a Kempis: *The Imitation of Christ,* 3, 13. (15th cent.)

The whole world will not move him whom truth hath established in humility. Neither will he be moved with the tongues of all that praise him who hath settled his whole hope in God.

> Thomas a Kempis: *The Imitation of Christ,* 3, 14. (15th cent.)

Humble thyself in all things.

> Thomas a Kempis: *The Imitation of Christ,* 3, 24. (15th cent.)

> When thou art oppressed with pain,
> Think that 'tis no loss, but gain;
> Suffering with humility
> Yields a shower of good to thee.
>
> Thou shalt honor thus the Lord,
> Duplicate thine own reward,
> Please the angel hosts on high,
> And thy neighbors edify.
>
> Thomas a Kempis: *Quum a malis molestaris.* (Tr. D. Donahoe) (15th cent.)

Never mention anything concerning thyself which men account praiseworthy, such as learning, goodness, birth, unless with the hope of doing good thereby, and then let it be done with humility, remembering that these are gifts of God.

> St. Teresa of Jesus: *Maxims.* (16th cent.)

Shall I be humble? Yes, if you will it. But I will it. You are then. But I feel distinctly that I am not. So much the better, for this serves to make it more certain.

> St. Francis de Sales: *Letters to Persons in Religion*, 4, 25. (17th cent.)

True humility makes no pretence of being humble, and scarcely ever utters words of humility.

> St. Francis de Sales: *Introduction to the Devout Life*, 3, 5. (17th cent.)

Professions of humility are the very cream, the very essence of pride; the really humble man wishes to be, and not to appear so. Humility is timorous, and starts at her shadow; and so delicate that if she hears her name pronounced it endangers her existence.

> Ascribed to St. Francis de Sales. (17th cent.)

Humility is a descending charity and charity is an ascending humility.

> Jean Pierre Camus: *The Spirit of St. Francis de Sales*, 8, 1. (17th cent.)

A man who despises himself in true humility is happy to discover others who agree with him.

> Jean Pierre Camus: *The Spirit of St. Francis de Sales*, 19, 3. (17th cent.)

Golden deeds kept out of sight, are most laudable.

> Pascal: *Pensées.* (17th cent.)

Humility, that low, sweet root,
From which all heavenly virtues shoot.

> Thomas Moore: *Loves of the Angels: Third Angel's Story.* (19th cent.)

This is true humility, to feel and to behave as if we were low; not, to cherish a notion of our importance, while we affect a low position.

> Card. Newman: *Idea of a University.* (19th cent.)

Humility is one of the most difficult of virtues both to attain and to ascertain. It lies close upon the heart itself, and its tests are exceedingly delicate and subtle. Its counterfeits abound.

> Card. Newman: *Idea of a University*, 8. (19th cent.)

The science of humility rests upon the knowledge of God and of oneself.

> Archb. Ullathorne: *Humility and Patience.* (19th cent.)

God loves to be resisted in His displeasure, and to be restrained by the humble from inflicting punishment. One saint will often save a nation; so true is it that humble souls are the hinges on which God moves the world.

> Archb. Ullathorne: *Humility and Patience.* (19th cent.)

The least known among the virtues, and consequently the most misunderstood, is the virtue of humility, and yet it is the very groundwork of the Christian religion.

> Archb. Ullathorne: *Humility and Patience.* (19th cent.)

From the wise heavens I half shall smile to see
How little a world, which owned you, needed me.

> F. Thompson: *To My Godchild.* (19th cent.)

Bear to be last, though the world's fools were first.

> Lionel Johnson: *Mastery.* (19th cent.)

Humility in oneself is not attractive, though it is attractive in others.

> Dom Chapman: *Spiritual Letters.* (20th cent.)

To feel extraordinarily small and unimportant is always a wholesome feeling.

> R. H. Benson: *The Conventionalists.* (20th cent.)

The truth is, that all genuine appreciation rests on a certain mystery of humility and almost of darkness. . . . Blessed is he that expecteth nothing, for he shall possess the cities and the mountains; blessed is the meek, for he shall inherit the earth. Until we realize that things might not be, we cannot realize that things are. Until we see the background of darkness we cannot admire the light as a single and created thing. As soon as we have seen that darkness, all light is lightning, sudden, blinding, and divine. Until we picture nonentity we underrate the victory of God, and can realize none of the trophies of His ancient war. It is one of the million wild jests of truth that we know nothing until we know nothing.

G. K. Chesterton: *Heretics.* (20th cent.)

The old humility made a man doubtful about his efforts, which might make him work harder. But the new humility makes a man doubtful about his aims, which will make him stop working altogether.

G. K. Chesterton: *Orthodoxy.* (20th cent.)

Humility is the luxurious art of reducing ourselves to a point, not to a small thing or a large one, but to a thing with no size at all, so that to it all the cosmic things are what they really are—of immeasurable stature.

G. K. Chesterton: *The Defendant.* (20th cent.)

Rest on the lower bough,
Whose wings are frail,
Nor seek the riotous tops
Lashed by the gale.

Let not ambition tempt
To flutter where
The eagle's iron wing
May scarcely dare.

Conde B. Pallen: *The Lower Bough.* (20th cent.)

If there were no humility in the world, everybody would long ago have committed suicide.

Thomas Merton: *Seeds of Contemplation.* (20th cent.)

Humility is the surest sign of strength.

Thomas Merton: *Seeds of Contemplation.* (20th cent.)

Hummingbird

A flash of harmless lightning,
A mist of rainbow dyes,
The burnished sunbeams brightening
From flower to flower he flies.

John B. Tabb: *The Humming Bird.* (19th cent.)

Humor

It is pleasant and not in the least unbecoming for a man of honor to indulge occasionally in reasonable mirth, but it is disgraceful to lower personal dignity by excessive indulgence in it.

John of Salisbury: *Policraticus,* 1, 8, 48. (12th cent.)

It is quite useless to talk about profane jesting. All jesting is in its nature profane, in the sense that it must be the sudden realization that something which thinks itself solemn is not so very solemn after all.

G. K. Chesterton: *Heretics.* (20th cent.)

If there is one thing more than another which any one will admit who has the smallest knowledge of the world, it is that men are always speaking gravely and earnestly and with the utmost possible care about the things that are not important, but always talking frivolously about the things that are. Men talk for hours with the faces of a college of cardinals about things like golf, or tobacco, or waistcoats, or party politics. But all the most grave and dreadful things in the world are the oldest jokes in the world—being married; being hanged.

G. K. Chesterton: *Heretics.* (20th cent.)

Giacobbe Finelli so funny, O! My!
By tweestin' hees face an' by weenkin' hees eye

He maka you laugh teell you theenk
    you weell die.
  He don't gotta say som'theeng; all
      he ees do
  Ees maka da face an', how moocha
      you try,
  You can no help laugh w'en he
      lookin' at you—
    Giacobbe Finelli so funny, O!
      My!

> T. A. Daly: *Da Comica Man.* (20th cent.)

Nature is inferior to man in many
things, but most of all in respect of the
human specialty of humor.

> G. K. Chesterton: *All is Grist.* (20th
> cent.)

Wit is lower than humor; but sham
humor is much easier than sham wit.
You can pretend that you have made an
atmosphere; you cannot pretend that
you have made a pun.

> G. K. Chesterton: *A Handful of Authors.*
> (20th cent.)

Hunger

Hunger maketh hard beans sweet.

> John Heywood: *Proverbs,* I, 10. (16th
> cent.)

Hunger pierceth stone wall.

> John Heywood: *Proverbs,* I, 12. (16th
> cent.)

Hunger is insolent.

> Pope: Tr. of Homer: *Odyssey,* 7. (18th
> cent.)

Hunter

His head was like a nut, his face was
    brown.
He knew the whole of woodcraft up
    and down.

> Chaucer: *Canterbury Tales: Prologue.*
> (Tr. Coghill) (14th cent.)

Hunting

Hunting is indeed a silly and very trying
business and never balances the losses of
its extravagance by the advantages of its
success.

> John of Salisbury: *Policraticus,* I, 4.
> (12th cent.)

Greyhounds he had, as swift as birds,
    to course.
Hunting a hare or riding at a fence
Was all his fun, he spared for no ex-
    pense.

> Chaucer: *Canterbury Tales: Prologue.*
> (Tr. Coghill) (14th cent.)

Proud Nimrod first the bloody chase
    began,
A mighty hunter, and his prey was
    man.

> Pope: *Windsor Forest.* (18th cent.)

Assassins find accomplices. Man's merit
Has found him three, the hawk, the
    hound, the ferret.

> W. S. Blunt: *Assassins.* (19th cent.)

I like the hunting of the hare
    Better than that of the fox;
I like the joyous morning air,
    And the crowing of the cocks.

I like the calm of the early fields,
    The ducks asleep by the lake,
The quiet hour which nature yields,
    Before mankind is awake.

> W. S. Blunt: *The Old Squire.* (19th cent.)

Husband

For certainly, whatever we may say,
All women long—and O that it might
    be!—
For husbands tough, dependable and
    free,
Secret, discreet, no niggard, not a fool
That boasts and then will find his cour-
    age cool
At every trifling thing!

> Chaucer: *The Nun's Priest's Tale.* (Tr.
> Coghill) (14th cent.)

There is only one real tragedy in a woman's life. The fact that her past is always her lover, and her future invariably her husband.

> Oscar Wilde: *An Ideal Husband*, 3. (19th cent.)

Husband and Wife

Every husband exacts chastity from his wife; but beauty a believing Christian does not require.

> Tertullian: *Women's Dress*. (3rd cent.)

Let a woman show deference, not being a slave to her husband; let her show she is ready to be guided, not coerced. She is not worthy of wedlock who is worthy of chiding. Let the husband, too, manage his wife like a steersman, pay honor to her as his life partner, share with her as the co-heir of grace.

> St. Ambrose: *Letters*, 63. (396)

A knowing wife if she is worth her salt
Can always prove her husband is at
  fault.

> Chaucer: *The Wife of Bath's Prologue*. (Tr. Coghill) (14th cent.)

Under the yoke of matrimony bowed,
The heart, in bliss abounding, sings
  aloud.
For who is so obedient as a wife?
Who is so true, so careful for his life
Whether in health or sickness as a
  mate?
For weal or woe she tends upon his
  state,
Never forsakes him in her love or tires
Though he lie bedridden till he expires.

> Chaucer: *The Merchant's Tale*. (Tr. Coghill) (14th cent.)

Husbands are in heaven, whose wives scold not.

> John Heywood: *Proverbs*, 2, 7. (16th cent.)

To make a good husband, make a good wife.

> John Heywood: *Proverbs*, 2, 8. (16th cent.)

O wives! love tenderly and cordially the husband whom God has given you, but with a respectful love and full of reverence; for therefore did God create them of a sex more vigorous and predominant.

> St. Francis de Sales: *Introduction to the Devout Life*, 38. (17th cent.)

How sweet the mutual yoke of man
  and wife,
When holy fires maintain love's heavenly life!

> R. Crashaw: *Alexias, Third Elegy*. (17th cent.)

To these, whom death again did wed,
This grave's their second marriage-bed.
For though the hand of fate could force
'Twixt soul and body a divorce,
It could not sunder man and wife,
'Cause they both lived but one life.

> Richard Crashaw: *An Epitaph Upon a Young Married Couple*. (17th cent.)

A man's friend likes him but leaves him as he is: his wife loves him and is always trying to turn him into somebody else. Women who are utter mystics in their creed are utter cynics in their criticism.

> G. K. Chesterton: *Orthodoxy*. (20th cent.)

There is no hope for men who do not boast that their wives bully them.

> G. K. Chesterton: *Alarms and Discursions*. (20th cent.)

The whole value of the normal relations of man and woman lies in the fact that they first begin really to criticize each other when they first begin really to admire each other. And a good thing, too, I say, with a full sense of the responsibility of the statement, that it is better that the sexes should misunderstand each other until they marry. It is better that they should not have the knowledge until they have the reverence and charity.

> G. K. Chesterton: *The Common Man*. (20th cent.)

The subjection of the wife to the husband may vary in its degree and manner according to the conditions of person, place and time. If the husband neglect his duty, it falls to the wife to take his place as directing head of the family.

Pope Pius XI: *Casti connubii* (Dec. 31, 1930)

See also Wife

Hymn

See Divine Office; Liturgy

Hypocrisy

Thou shalt hate all hypocrisy, and everything that is not pleasing to the Lord.

Teaching of the Twelve Apostles, 4. (2nd cent.)

She looketh as butter would not melt in her mouth.

John Heywood: *Proverbs,* 1, 10. (16th cent.)

Hypocritic zeal
Allows no sins but those it can conceal.

John Dryden: *The Medall.* (17th cent.)

Who point, like finger-posts, the way They never go.

Thomas Moore: *Song: For the Poco-Curante Society.* (19th cent.)

The foolish, fashionable air
Of knowing all, and feeling nought.

Coventry Patmore: *The Angel in the House.* (19th cent.)

I hope you have not been leading a double life, pretending to be wicked, and being really good all the time. That would be hypocrisy.

Oscar Wilde: *The Importance of Being Earnest,* 2. (19th cent.)

Hypocrite

That man is rightly accounted a hypocrite, who diverts the ministry of government to purposes of domination.

Pope St. Gregory I: *Pastoral Care,* 2, 6. (6th cent.)

Let it never be forgotten that a hypocrite is a very unhappy man; he is a man who has devoted himself to a most delicate and arduous intellectual art in which he may achieve masterpieces which he must keep secret, fight thrilling battles and win hair-breadth victories for which he cannot have a whisper of praise. A really accomplished impostor is the most wretched of geniuses: he is a Napoleon on a desert island.

G. K. Chesterton: *Robert Browning.* (20th cent.)

I

Iconoclast

An iconoclast may be indignant; an iconoclast may be justly indignant; but an iconoclast is not impartial.

G. K. Chesterton: *The Everlasting Man,* Intr. (20th cent.)

Idea

Ideas are certain principal forms, or permanent and immutable types of things, they themselves not being formed. Thus they are eternal, and existing always in the same manner, as being contained in the divine intelligence. Whilst, however, they themselves neither come into being nor decay, yet we say that in accordance with them everything is formed that can arise or decay, and all that actually does so.

> St. Augustine: *De Diversis Quaestionibus,* 46. (4th cent.)

False ideas may be refuted indeed by argument, but by true ideas alone are they expelled.

> Card. Newman: *Apologia pro Vita Sua, Preface.* (19th cent.)

Living movements do not come of committees, nor are great ideas worked out through the post, even though it had been the penny post.

> Card. Newman: *Apologia pro Vita Sua,* 2. (19th cent.)

Ideal

There is only one really startling thing to be done with the ideal, and that is to do it.

> G. K. Chesterton: *What's Wrong with the World.* (20th cent.)

Idealism

To say that a man is an idealist is merely to say that he is a man.

> G. K. Chesterton: *Heretics.* (20th cent.)

Ideology

An ideology in the modern sense of the word is very different from a faith, although it is intended to fulfil the same sociological functions. It is the work of man, an instrument by which the conscious political will attempts to mold the social traditions to its purpose. But faith looks beyond the world of man and his works; it introduces man to a higher and more universal range of reality than the finite and temporal world to which the state and the economic order belong. And thereby it introduces into human life an element of spiritual freedom which may have a creative and transforming influence on man's social culture and historical destiny as well as on his inner personal experience.

> C. Dawson: *Gifford Lectures, 1948: Religion and the Rise of Western Culture.*

Idleness

Idleness is the enemy of the soul.

> St. Benedict: *Rule,* 48. (6th cent.)

Sloth brings in all woe.

> J. Gower: *Confessio Amantis,* 4. (14th cent.)

Mother of vices, called idleness.

> Lydgate: *Fall of Princes,* 2. (15th cent.)

What heart can think, or tongue express,
The harm that groweth of idleness?

> John Heywood: *Idleness.* (16th cent.)

And heard thy everlasting yawn confess
The pains and penalties of idleness.

> Pope: *The Dunciad,* 4. (18th cent.)

To have too much to do is for most men safer than to have too little.

> Card. Manning: *The Eternal Priesthood.* (19th cent.)

Idol

There's a one-eyed yellow idol to the north of Khatmandu,
There's a little marble cross below the town,
There's a broken-hearted woman tends the grave of Mad Carew,
And the yellow god forever gazes down.

> J. M. Hayes: *The Green Eye of the Yellow God.* (20th cent.)

Idolatry

But idolaters are so called because they offer to their idols things belonging to men, and this not as outward signs which may excite them in spiritual affections, but as being acceptable by those idols for their own sake. And especially because they offered them empty and vile things.

St. Thomas Aquinas: *Summa Theologica,* 2, 2, 81, 7. (13th cent.)

Whatever a man seeks, honors, or exalts more than God, that is the god of his idolatry.

Archb. Ullathorne: *Humility and Patience.* (19th cent.)

The Catholic Church exists on earth for the sole purpose of insisting, in season and out of season, that God be recognized for what He is, and as so recognized, worshipped. The Church is society's permanent rampart against idolatry. This is the ultimate, in a sense it is the only, sin, the root of all disorder.

Dom Aelred Graham: *Catholicism and the World Today.* (20th cent.)

Ignatius of Antioch, Saint

Please let me be thrown to the wild beasts; through them I can reach God. I am God's wheat; I am ground by the teeth of the wild beasts that I may end as the pure bread of Christ. If anything, coax the beasts on to become my sepulcher and to leave nothing of my body undevoured so that, when I am dead, I may be no bother to anyone.

St. Ignatius of Antioch: *Letter to the Romans,* 4. (2nd cent.)

Ignorance

It is no small gain to know your own ignorance.

St. Jerome: *Letters,* 61, 3. (4th cent.)

There is, then, in us something which we must term 'learned ignorance' (*docta ignorantia*); ignorance it is, yet an 'ignorance' instructed by the Spirit of God Who helps our weakness.

St. Augustine: *Letter 130* (to Proba on prayer). (5th cent.)

For in other living creatures the ignorance of themselves is nature, but in men it is vice.

Boethius: *De Consolatione Philosophiae,* 2, 5. (6th cent.)

Better unborn than untaught.

John Heywood: *Proverbs,* 1, 10. (16th cent.)

The fool is happy that he knows no more.

Pope: *An Essay on Man,* 2. (18th cent.)

We must make up our minds to be ignorant of much, if we would know anything.

Card. Newman: *Discussions and Arguments.* (19th cent.)

There are no limits to invincible ignorance.

Baron von Huegel: *Letters.* (Quoted) (20th cent.)

Illumination

The striving after God is therefore the desire of beatitude, the attainment of God is beatitude itself. We seek to attain God by loving Him; we attain to Him, not by becoming entirely what He is, but in nearness to Him, and in wonderful and sensible contact with Him, and in being inwardly illuminated and occupied by His truth and holiness. He is Light itself; it is given to us to be illuminated by that Light.

St. Augustine: *De Moribus Ecclesiae Catholicae,* 1, 11, 18. (4th cent.)

If the life of the spirit is the illumination of knowledge, and if this knowledge is the love of God Who produces it, we are right in saying: There is nothing beyond the love of God.

St. Maximus the Confessor: *Centuries on Charity,* 1, 9. (7th cent.)

See also Contemplation; God—Man's Knowledge of God.

Illusion

We cannot do without a view, and we put up with an illusion, when we cannot get a truth.

> Card. Newman: *Idea of a University*, 4. (19th cent.)

For every age is fed on illusions, lest men should renounce life early, and the human race come to an end.

> Joseph Conrad. (20th cent.)

Image

The Holy Synod commands that images of Christ, of the Mother of God and of the other saints be kept in churches, and that due honor and reverence be paid to them, not because it is believed that there is any divinity in them, or that anything may be asked of them, but because the honor which is done to them is done to the prototypes they represent.

> Decree of the Council of Trent, Session 25. (1564)

The pagans looked upon an idol as a god endowed with intelligence and the other attributes of the Deity. Catholic Christians know that a holy image has no intelligence or power to hear and help them.

> Card. Gibbons: *The Faith of Our Fathers*, 15. (19th cent.)

See also Saints, Veneration of

Imagination

How fancy throws us into perturbation!
People can die of mere imagination.

> Chaucer: *The Miller's Tale*. (Tr. Coghill) (14th cent.)

The greatest philosopher in the world, standing on the brink of a precipice, on an amply wide plank, and convinced by his reason that he was perfectly safe, would be undone by his imagination. Many would be unable even to think of such a thing without breaking into a cold sweat.

> Pascal: *Pensées*. (17th cent.)

That fairy kind of writing which depends only upon the force of imagination.

> Dryden: *King Arthur, Dedication*. (17th cent.)

Never yet was shape so dread,
But fancy, thus in darkness thrown,
And by such sounds of horror fed,
Could frame more dreadful of her own.

> Thomas Moore: *Lalla Rookh: The Fire-Worshippers*. (19th cent.)

In recent times genius and imagination have come to be widely regarded as one and the same thing. They are not so, however, though they are perhaps indissolubly connected. The most peculiar and characteristic mark of genius is insight into subjects which are dark to ordinary vision and for which ordinary language has no adequate expression. Imagination is rather the language of genius: the power which traverses at a single glance the whole external universe, and seizes on the likenesses and images, and their combinations, which are best able to embody ideas and feelings otherwise inexpressible; so that the *things which are unseen are known by the things which are seen*.

> Coventry Patmore: *Religio Poetae*. (19th cent.)

It seems chiefly the function of the imagination to visualize facts, and it is an abuse of that faculty to employ it chiefly in visualizing fancies.

> R. H. Benson: *The Light Invisible*. (20th cent.)

Immaculate Conception of the Blessed Virgin

Indeed You, O Lord, and Your Mother are the only ones who are in every respect completely beautiful. For there is no corruption in Thee, O Lord, nor any stain in Thy Mother.

> St. Ephraem of Syria: *Nisibene Songs*, 27, 8. (4th cent.)

Now with the exception of the holy Virgin Mary in regard to whom, out of respect for the Lord, I do not propose to have a single question raised on the subject of sin after all, how do we know what greater degree of grace for a complete victory over sin was conferred on her who merited to conceive and bring forth Him Who all admit was without sin. . . .

> St. Augustine: *De Natura et Gratia*, 42. (5th cent.)

Moreover, the Virgin, from whom that Man was taken of whom we are speaking, was of the number of those who were cleansed from their sins before His birth, and He was born of her in her purity.

> St. Anselm: *Cur Deus Homo*, 16. (A common early, medieval view was that Mary was conceived in original sin, but, by a special privilege, her soul was sanctified before her birth.) (11th cent.)

If before her conception she could not possibly be sanctified, since she did not exist, nor in the conception itself, because of the sin which adhered in it, it remains to be believed that she received sanctification when existing in the womb after conception, which, by excluding sin, made her birth holy, but not her conception. . . . But what I have said is in submission to the judgment of whosoever is wiser than myself; and especially I refer the whole of it, as of all matters of a similar kind, to the authority and decision of the See of Rome, and I am prepared to modify my opinion if in anything I think otherwise than that See.

> St. Bernard: *Letter to the Canons of Lyons*. (12th cent.)

All men sinned in Adam (cf. Rom. 5, 12). This statement is certainly true, and I declare it would be impious to deny it.

But when I consider the eminence of God's grace in you, I find that in a truly remarkable way you were placed not among but above all other creatures; hence I conclude that in your conception you were not bound by the law of nature like others, but by the extraordinary power and operation of Divinity, in a way transcending human reason, you were preserved free from all taint of sin.

> Eadmer of Canterbury: *De Conceptione Beatae Mariae*, 12. (This view ultimately prevailed.) (PL 159, 306B) (12th cent.)

If the Blessed Virgin had been sanctified in any way before her conception (*animatio*), she would not have incurred the stain of original sin and would thus not have needed redemption and salvation by Christ, according to Matth. 1, 21: *He will save His people from their sins.* The difficulty is that Christ would not be the Savior of all men, as is said in I Tim. 4.—Whence it follows that the sanctification of the Blessed Virgin occurred after her conception.

> St. Thomas Aquinas: *Summa Theologica*, 3, 27, 2. (13th cent.)

By the crib wherein reposing,
With His eyes in slumber closing,
Lay serene her Infant-boy,
Stood the beauteous Mother feeling
Bliss that could not bear concealing,
So her face o'erflowed with joy.

Oh, the rapture naught could smother
Of that most immaculate Mother
Of the sole-begotten One;
When with laughing heart exulting,
She beheld her hopes resulting
In the great birth of her Son.

. . . .

Fount of love, forever flowing,
With a burning ardor glowing,
Make me, Mother, feel like thee;
Let my heart with graces gifted
All on fire, to Christ be lifted,
And by Him accepted be.

> Hymn *Stabat Mater speciosa*. (Imitation of *Stabat Mater dolorosa*, probably by same author.) (Tr. D. MacCarthy) (Attr. to Jacopone da Todi, 13th cent.)

Mary most assuredly needed Christ as a Redeemer, for she would have incurred original sin in the usual way from her parents, if she had not been preserved by the grace of the Mediator. Just as others needed Christ that sin already incurred might be forgiven by His merit, so she needed the preventive action of the Mediator all the more, that there might not be any sin to be incurred [original sin], and that she might not incur any [ordinary sin].

Duns Scotus: *Comm. in Lib. III Sentent., Dist. 3, Quaest. 1.* (13th cent.)

. . . This holy Synod declares that it is not its intention to comprise in this decree, which deals with original sin, the blessed and immaculate Virgin Mary, the Mother of God. . . .

Decree of the Council of Trent, Session 5. (June 17, 1546)

Our second Eve puts on her mortal
    shroud,
    Earth breeds a heaven for God's new
        dwelling-place;
Now riseth up Elias' little cloud,
    That growing shall distil the showers
        of grace;
Her being now begins, who, ere she
    ends,
Shall bring our good that shall our evil
    mend.

Bl. Robert Southwell: *The Virgin Mary's Conception.* (16th cent.)

Blest guardian of all virgin souls,
Portal of bliss to man forgiven,
Pure Mother of almighty God,
Thou hope of earth and joy of heaven!

Fair lily found among the thorns,
Most beauteous dove with wings of
    gold,
Rod from whose tender root upsprang
That healing Flower so long foretold.

Thou tower against the dragon proof,
Thou star to storm-tossed voyagers
    dear;

Our course lies o'er a treacherous deep,
Thine be the light by which we steer.

Roman Breviary, Feast of the Immaculate Conception, Hymn *Praeclara custos virginum* at Matins. (Tr. E. Caswall) (Author unknown, 17th cent.)

O purest of creatures! sweet Mother!
    sweet Maid!
The one spotless womb wherein Jesus
    was laid!
Dark night hath come down on us,
    Mother! and we
Look out for thy shining, sweet Star of
    the Sea!

Deep night hath come down on this
    rough-spoken world,
And the banners of darkness are boldly
    unfurl'd;
And the tempest-tost Church—all her
    eyes are on thee,
They look to thy shining, sweet Star
    of the Sea!

Anonymous: *Sine labe concepta.* (Tr. F. Faber) (19th cent. ?)

Hail, Queen of the heavens!
    Hail, Mistress of earth!
Hail, Virgin most pure,
    Of immaculate birth!
Clear star of the morning,
    In beauty enshrined!
O Lady, make speed
    To the help of mankind!

Anonymous: *Salve mundi domina.* (Tr. Caswall) (19th cent.)

We pronounce, declare and define, unto the glory of the holy and indivisible Trinity, the honor and ornament of the holy Virgin, the Mother of God, for the exaltation of the Catholic faith and the increase of the Christian religion by the authority of our Lord Jesus Christ and the blessed apostles Peter and Paul, and in our own authority, that the doctrine which holds the blessed Virgin Mary to have been from the first moment of her conception by a singular grace and privilege of almighty God, in view of the merits of Jesus Christ the Savior of mankind, preserved free from all stain of original sin was revealed by God, and is therefore to be firmly and constantly believed by all the faithful.

Pope Pius IX: *Ineffabilis Deus*. (Dec. 8, 1854.)

O God, Who by the immaculate conception of the Virgin didst make her a worthy habitation for Thy Son, and didst by His foreseen death preserve her from all stain of sin; grant, we beseech Thee, that through her intercession we may be cleansed from sin and come with pure hearts to Thee.

Roman Missal, Collect for the Feast of the Immaculate Conception (Dec. 8). (The feast originated in the East ca. the 7th cent. as the Conception of St. Anne, and reached the West via the Normans and England. Sixtus IV extended it to the entire Latin church in 1476.) (19th cent.)

Pure as the snow, we say. Ah! never flake
  Fell through the air
  One-tenth as fair
As Mary's soul was made for Christ's dear sake.
  Virgin Immaculate,
The whitest whiteness of the Alpine snows,
Beside thy stainless spirit, dusky grows.

Eleanor C. Donnelly: *Mary Immaculate*. (19th cent.)

I am the Immaculate Conception.

Words of our Lady to St. Bernadette Soubirous on the occasion of her appearance to the latter in the grotto at Lourdes, March 3, 1858.

Lo! Mary is exempt from stain of sin,
Proclaims the pontiff high;
And earth applauding celebrates with joy
  Her triumph far and high.

Unto a lowly timid maid she shows
Her form in beauty fair,
And the Immaculate Conception truth
  Her sacred lips declare.

O honored cave, by Mary's smile adorned!
O hallowed rock, whence spring
The living waters of a gushing stream,
  The gifts of life to bring.

And thither from the farmost bounds of earth
The pilgrims wend their way,
And suppliant around the Virgin's shrine
  Her powerful help they pray.

Roman Breviary, Feast of the Apparition of the Immaculate Virgin Mary at Lourdes (Feb. 11), Hymn *Omnis expertem maculae Mariam*. (Tr. by Benedictines of Stanbrook) (Anonymous, 19th cent.)

O rosy dawn! thou dost proclaim
Salvation's happy day,
To thee, O Virgin, 'mid night's shades
Thy people humbly pray.

. . . .

O loving Mother, hear our prayer,
As suppliant we cry;
Protect us in our strife with hell
Who dost its power defy.

Roman Breviary, Feast of the Apparition (Feb. 11), Hymn *Aurora soli praevia* at Lauds. (Tr. by the Benedictines of Stanbrook) (Anon., 19th cent.)

O Virgin Mother of our God,
While we thy matchless glories chant,
Do thou, in answer to our praise,
To us abundant graces grant.

We Adam's guilty children are,
A sin-infected progeny,
Thou art, O Virgin, we believe,
Alone from his infection free.

Roman Breviary, Feast of the Apparition (Feb. 11), Hymn *Te dicimus praeconio* at Matins. (Tr. Archb. Bagshawe) (anon., 19th cent.)

O glorious childbearer,
O secret womb,
O gilded bridechamber, from which hath come the sightly
  Bridegroom forth,
O amber veil,

Thou sittest in heaven, the white love
  of the Gael.
Thy head is crowned with stars, thy
  radiant hair
Shines like a river thro' the twilight
  air;
Thou walkest by trodden ways and
  trackless seas,
Immaculate of man's informities.

Joseph Campbell: *O Glorious Childbearer.*
(20th cent.)

Ah me! Unworthy I to sing
The stainless Mother of my King,
My King and Lord,
The incarnate Word,
Heaven itself comprest
Within her virgin breast!
How may my faltering rhyme
Sing of eternity in time,
Omnipotence in human frailty exprest,
Our earthly garden fragrant with celes-
  tial thyme.

Conde B. Pallen: *Maria Immaculata.* (20th
cent.)

Immortality

To be immortal is to share in Divinity.

Clement of Alexandria: Stromata, 5, 10.
(2nd cent.)

We maintain that after life has passed
away thou still remainest in existence,
and lookest forward to a day of judgment, and according to thy deserts art
assigned to misery or bliss.

Tertullian: *The Soul's Testimony.* (3rd
cent.)

Who at this day is without the desire
that he may be often remembered when
he is dead? Who does not give all endeavor to preserve his name by works
of literature, or by the simple glory of
his virtues, or by the splendour even of
his tomb? How is it the nature of the
soul to have these posthumous ambitions
and with such amazing effort to prepare
the things it can only use after decease?

It would care nothing about the future,
if the future were quite unknown to it?

Tertullian: *The Soul's Testimony,* 4. (3rd
cent.)

After the royal throne comes death;
after the dunghill comes the Kingdom
of Heaven.

St. John Chrysostom: *Homilies.* (4th
cent.)

After the resurrection of the body shall
have taken place, being set free from
the condition of time, we shall enjoy
eternal life, with love ineffable and
steadfastness without corruption.

St. Augustine: *Of Faith and the Creed.*
(4th cent.)

We also are made partakers of this eternal life, and become in our own measure,
immortal. But the eternal life itself, of
which we are made partakers, is one
thing; we ourselves, who by partaking
of it shall live eternally, are another.

St. Augustine: *De Trinitate,* 1, 6, 10. (5th
cent.)

But ask not bodies doomed to die
To what abode they go;
Since knowledge is but sorrow's spy,
It is not safe to know.

Sir William Davenant: *The Just Italian,*
5, 1. (17th cent.)

The immortality of the soul is a matter
which concerns us so strongly, which
touches us so closely, that a man must
have lost all feeling not to care to know
about it. All our acts and thoughts must
follow such different lines, according as
there is or is not eternal bliss to look for
that no step can be taken with sense and
judgment unless we keep our eyes steadily fixed on this point which must be our
final aim.

Pascal: *Pensées.* (17th cent.)

And doom'd to death, though fated not
to die.

Dryden: *The Hind and the Panther,* 1.
(17th cent.)

E'en now the spirit moves
  In visions yet to be,
Whereof the present proves
  A dream and prophecy.
For still, the shadows gone,
  With light forever new,
Behold, another dawn
  Proclaims the promise true.

> J. B. Tabb: *Immortality.* (19th cent.)

I come from nothing; but from where
  Come the undying thoughts I bear?
Down, through long links of death
  and birth,
From the past poets of the earth,
My immortality is there.
    . . . .
Before this life began to be,
The happy songs that wake in me
  Woke long ago and far apart.
  Heavily on this little heart
Presses this immortality.

> Alice Meynell: *A Song of Derivations.*
> (19th cent.)

I shall take flight as a bird wings
  Into the infinite blue—
What if my song comes ringing
  Down through the stars and the
  dew?

> Charles L. O'Donnell: *Immortality.* (20th
> cent.)

How many there are who show themselves most sensitive to their reputation
after death; they assume that they will
somehow or other be affected by what
people say of them; they burn their letters and write their memorial. Even the
universal desire for an immortality of
fame shows the depth of the belief in
immortality of life.

> M. C. D'Arcy: *Death and Life.* (20th
> cent.)

The world cannot reconcile itself to the
silence of the grave; it is haunted, and
in idle moments when it is taken off its
guard it shows itself thoroughly committed to some kind of belief in an afterlife.

> M. C. D'Arcy: *Death and Life.* (20th
> cent.)

It would be a supreme delusion to seek
in time, and in history, and in the results
of our deeds here below, to seek, that is,
in subjective immortality, any adequate
fulfilment of that irrepressible aspiration
to survival which inhabits the depths of
our substances.

> J. Maritain: *The Range of Reason.* (20th
> cent.)

Primitive men did not philosophize; but,
for all that, they had their own way, an
instinctive, non-conceptual way, of believing in the soul's immortality. It was
a belief rooted in an obscure experience
of the self, and in the natural aspirations
of the spirit in us to overcome death.

> J. Maritain: *The Range of Reason.* (20th
> cent.)

Immortality is not a more or less precarious, successful or unsuccessful survival in other men, or in the ideal waves
of the universe. Immortality is a nature-
given, inalienable property of the human soul as a spiritual substance. And
grace makes eternal life possible to all,
to the most destitute as well as to the
most gifted.

> J. Maritain: *The Range of Reason.* (20th
> cent.)

See also Eternal life; Soul

Immunity

The immunity of the Church and of
ecclesiastical persons derived its origin
from the civil law.

> Proposition condemned by Pius IX in
> Syllabus of Errors. (1867)

Imperfection

For all that is said to be imperfect is so
termed for the want it hath of perfection.

> Boethius: *De Consolatione Philosophiae,*
> 3, 10. (6th cent.)

We must be prepared to see weeds growing in our garden and also have the courage to pull them up.

> St. Francis de Sales: *Spiritual Conferences,* 9. (17th cent.)

Imperialism

So that Lancashire merchants whenever they like
Can water the beer of a man in Klondike,
Or poison the beer of a man in Bombay;
And that is the meaning of Empire Day.

> G. K. Chesterton: *Songs of Education.* (20th cent.)

Impiety

What more impiety can he avow
Whose heart rebelleth at God's judgment dread?

> Dante: *Inferno, Canto 20.* (Tr. Binyon) (14th cent.)

Impiety! of harden'd mind,
Gross, dull, presuming, stubborn, blind,
Unmov'd amid this mighty all,
Deaf to the universal call.

> William Hamilton: *Contemplation.* (18th cent.)

Importance

No one in the world except a mortified saint is actually displeased at the fact of becoming rather important.

> R. H. Benson: *An Average Man.* (20th cent.)

Impossible

No one can be obliged to do the impossible. (Nemo potest ad impossibilia obligari.)

> Legal maxim. (cf. Reg. Juris 6 Lib. Sexti of Corpus Juris Canonici) (Medieval)

Imprisonment

The first step in punitive action, the arrest, must not be done wantonly, but must respect juridical norms. It is not admissible that even the most culpable citizen should be liable to arbitrary arrest and to disappear without a word into prison. To send someone into a concentration camp and keep him there without any regular trial is a mockery of law.

> Pope Pius XII: *Address to the 6th Int. Congr. of Penal Law.* (Oct. 3, 1953)

Impudence

For bold knaves thrive without one grain of sense,
But good men starve for want of impudence.

> Dryden: *Constantine the Great, Epilogue.* (17th cent.)

Impulsiveness

To be impulsive certainly leads to troublesome times, but also, sometimes it prevents them.

> R. H. Benson: *None Other Gods.* (20th cent.)

Impunity

Impunity, the child of carelessness, the mother of insolence, the root of impudence, the nurse of transgressions.

> St. Bernard: *On Consideration,* 3, 5. (12th cent.)

Incarnation of Our Lord

The Word of God, Jesus Christ, on account of His great love for mankind, became what we are in order to make us what He is Himself.

> Irenaeus: *Adversus haereses,* 5. (2nd cent.)

For by His becoming Man, the Savior was to accomplish two works of love; first, in putting away death from us and renewing us again; secondly, being unseen and invisible, in manifesting and making Himself known by His works to be the Word of the Father, and the Ruler and King of the universe.

> St. Athanasius: *On the Incarnation of the Word of God,* 16. (4th cent.)

For He was made Man that we might be made God.

> St. Athanasius: *On the Incarnation of the Word of God,* 54. (4th cent.)

Believe then that this only-begotten Son of God came down from heaven upon earth for our sins, and took upon Him this human nature of like passions with us, and was begotten of the Holy Virgin and of the Holy Ghost, and was made Man, not in seeming and mere show, but in truth; nor yet by passing through the Virgin as through a channel; but was of her made truly flesh, and truly nourished with milk, and did truly eat as we do, and truly drink as we do. For if the Incarnation was a phantom, salvation is a phantom also.

> St. Cyril of Jerusalem: *Catechetical Discourses,* 4, 9. (4th cent.)

Believe that the Son of God, the eternal Word, who was begotten of the Father before all ages and without body, was in these latter days for your sake also made Son of Man, born of the Virgin Mary ineffably and stainlessly (for nothing can be stained where God is, and by which salvation comes), in his own Person at once entire Man and perfect God.

> St. Gregory of Nazianzen: *Orations,* 40, 45. (4th cent.)

He alone was conceived and born of a virgin without any of that defilement which inheres in the origin of ordinary men. For it was fitting that He Who was not to share through His body in the sin of the fall, should be without experience of the contagion that is normal in generation.

> St. Ambrose: *Apologia David,* 57. (4th cent.)

What was the purpose of the Incarnation but this—that the flesh which had sinned should be redeemed by itself?

> St. Ambrose: *On the Incarnation,* 56. (4th cent.)

The grace of God could not have been more graciously commended to us than thus, that the only Son of God, remaining unchangeable in Himself, should assume humanity, and should give us the hope of His love, by means of the mediation of a human nature, through which we, from the condition of men, might come to Him Who was so far off—the immortal from the mortal; the unchangeable from the changeable; the just from the unjust; the blessed from the wretched.

> St. Augustine: *The City of God,* 10, 29. (5th cent.)

The one thoroughly laid down and safe way to avoid all going wide of truth is the doctrine of the incarnation—that one and the same Person is God and Man; as God, the end of our going; as Man, the way we are to go (*ut idem ipse sit Deus et homo, quo itur Deus, qua itur homo*).

> St. Augustine: *The City of God,* 11, 2. (5th cent.)

God died, that a kind of celestial exchange might be made, that men might not see death. . . . Forasmuch as He is both God and Man, wishing that we should live by that which was His, He died by that which was ours. For He had nothing Himself whereby He could die, nor had we anything whereby we could live. . . . What an exchange!

> St. Augustine: *Sermon* 80, 5. (5th cent.)

By joining to us the likeness of His humanity, He took away the unlikeness of our unrighteousness; and by being made partaker of our mortality, He made us partakers of His divinity.

> St. Augustine: *De Trinitate,* 4, 2. (5th cent.)

For the motive behind the mystery of the incarnation, which I previously explained, was just this: the divine power of the Son of God, like a hook wrapped in a covering of human flesh and, as the apostle Paul said, *in habit found as man,* was to lure on the Prince of the world to a conflict, and while Christ offered him His human flesh as a bait, the Deity concealed within Him was to hold Him fast with a hook, as a result of the shedding of His immaculate blood.

Rufinus: *Commentary on the Apostles' Creed,* 16. (5th cent.)

If anyone does not confess that the flesh of the Lord is life-giving, and belongs to the divine Word as His own, but says that it belongs to another external to Him, Who is united with him only in dignity, or only participates in the divine indwelling; and does not rather hold it to be life-giving, for this reason, as we have said, that it belongs to the Word, Who can make all things live, let him be anathema.

Council of Alexandria, Anathema 11 of St. Cyril. (430)

If anyone does not confess that the Word of God suffered in the flesh, was crucified in the flesh, and tasted death in the flesh, and became the first-born from the dead, since He as God is Life and the Life-giver; let him be anathema.

Council of Alexandria, Anathema 12 of St. Cyril. (430)

Weakness is assumed by strength, lowliness by majesty, mortality by immortality, in order that one and the same Mediator between God and men might die in the one and rise in the other.

Pope St. Leo I: *Sermons,* 21, 2. (5th cent.)

This only-begotten eternal Son of the eternal Father was born by the Holy Ghost of the Virgin Mary. This birth in time has taken nothing from, and added nothing to, the eternal birth [from the Father], and its only end is the redemption of men. For we could

not overcome sin and the author of death, unless our nature had been assumed and made His own by Him Whom neither sin could stain nor death hold. He was conceived by the Holy Ghost in the womb of the Virgin, and she bore Him without injury to her virginity, even as she conceived Him without loss of the same.

Pope St. Leo I: *Dogmatic Epistle to Flavian, Bishop of Constantinople.* (Ep. 28, 2) (June 13, 449)

He participated in our infirmities, but not in our sins. He took upon Him the form of a servant without the stain of sin, and He raised the human without impairing the divine. The emptying of Himself (Phil. 2, 7) . . . was no loss of power, but a working of compassion.

Pope St. Leo I: *Dogmatic Epistle.* (Ep. 28, 3) (June 13, 449)

This day is set forth a wonderful mystery, a new thing hath been created in the earth—God is made Man. That which He was He remaineth, and that which He was not He taketh, suffering therein neither confusion nor division.

Roman Breviary, Feast of the Circumcision (Jan. 1), Antiphon at Lauds. (Liber Resp., ca. 6th to 8th cent.)

Herein is a great mystery of heirship; the womb of her that knew not a man is become the temple of God: in taking of her flesh He was not defiled: all nations shall come and say, Glory to Thee, O Lord!

Roman Breviary, Feast of the Circumcision, Antiphon at Vespers. (Liber Resp., ca. 6th to 8th cent.)

For by the good pleasure of our God and Father, the only-begotten Son and Word of God and God, Who is in the bosom of the God and Father, of like essence with the Father and the Holy Spirit, Who was before the ages, Who is without beginning and was in the beginning, Who is in the presence of the God and Father, and is God and

made in the form of God, bent the
heavens and descended to earth: that is
to say, He humbled without humiliation
His lofty station which could not be
humbled, and condescends to His servants, with a condescension ineffable and
incomprehensible (for that is what the
descent signifies).

> St. John of Damascus: *Exposition of the
> Orthodox Faith,* 3, 1. (8th cent.)

For what greater thing is there than that
God should become man?

> St. John of Damascus: *Exposition of the
> Orthodox Faith,* 3, 1. (8th cent.)

Wherefore we speak not of man as having become God, but of God as having
become Man. For being by nature perfect God, He naturally likewise became
perfect Man.

> St. John of Damascus: *Exposition of the
> Orthodox Faith,* 3, 2. (8th cent.)

Indeed I think myself that the chief
reason why the unseen God willed to
appear in flesh and mix with men was
that He might draw to Himself in flesh
the love of those who were not yet able
to love save in a carnal manner, and so
to lead them gradually on to spiritual
love.

> St. Bernard: *Sermons on the Canticle of
> Canticles,* 20. (12th cent.)

From Christ's fulness grace is outpoured
on us. The Son of God was made Man
that men might be made gods and become the children of God.

> St. Thomas Aquinas: *Compendium of
> Theology,* 214. (13th cent.)

Not from necessity was Christ a debtor
to death, but from love of God and man.

> St. Thomas Aquinas: *Commentary on the
> Sentences,* 2, 20, 1, 5. (13th cent.)

By His divine nature Christ is simple,
by His human nature He is complex.

> St. Thomas Aquinas: *Disputations
> concerning the Union of the Word
> Incarnate,* 2. (13th cent.)

The Catholic faith professes that Christ's
body is of the same kind as ours, and
with this body goes a true rational soul,
and simultaneously the perfect Deity, all
three substantial and together in one
Person, not in one nature.

> St. Thomas Aquinas: *Compendium of
> Theology,* 209. (13th cent.)

The greatness of God was not cast off,
but the slightness of human nature was
put on.

> St. Thomas Aquinas: *Disputations
> concerning the Union of the Word
> Incarnate,* 1. (13th cent.)

Indeed, the Incarnation is a unique
union, surpassing every communion
known to us. . . . Augustine says about
this mystery that, if explanation be
sought, let us acknowledge that it is a
marvel, and, if precedent, then that
there was nothing like it before; what
God can do let us own we cannot probe,
for in such cases the whole reason of
the fact lies in the might of the Maker.
(Ad Volusianum, 2)

> St. Thomas Aquinas: *Disputations
> concerning the Union of the Word
> Incarnate,* 1. (13th cent.)

It is safer to teach that the Incarnation
was ordained by God as a remedy for
sin, and that if no sin had come in the
Incarnation would not have taken place.
Nevertheless, God's power should not
be circumscribed: He might have become incarnate even if sin had never
entered.

> St. Thomas Aquinas: *Summa Theologica,*
> 3, 1, 3. (13th cent.)

The Son of God assuming human
breath,
Becomes a subject to His vassal death,
That graves and hell laid open by His
strife,
May give us passage to a better life.
See for this work how things are newly
styl'd,
Man is declar'd almighty! God, a
Child!

> Sir John Beaumont: *Annunciation and
> Resurrection.* (17th cent.)

When love of us call'd Him to see
If we'd vouchsafe His company,
He left His Father's court, and came
Lightly as a lambent flame,
Leaping upon the hills, to be
The humble King of you and me.
Nor can the cares of His whole crown
(When one poor sigh sends for Him
    down)
Detain Him, but He leaves behind
The late wings of the lazy wind,
Spurns the tame laws of time and
    place,
And breaks through all ten heavens
    to our embrace.

Richard Crashaw: *To the Countess of
Denby.* (17th cent.)

Man is God, is the popular mode of
speech; God is man, is the Catholic.

Card. Newman: *Essays Critical and
Historical,* I. (19th cent.)

For this to earth the Savior came
    In flesh: in part for this He died;
That man might have, in soul and
    frame,
    No faculty unsanctified.
That fancy's self—so prompt to lead
    Through paths disastrous or de-
    filed—
Upon the Tree of Life might feed;
    And sense with soul be reconciled.

Aubrey de Vere: *May Carols,* 2, 10.
(19th cent.)

The idea of the incarnation is the idea
of Providence capitalized; and at the
same time raised to the infinite.

Aubrey de Vere. (19th cent.)

Let Christians leave off thinking of the
incarnation as a thing past, or a figure
of speech, and learn to know that it consists for them in their becoming the
intimately and humanly beloved of a
divine and yet human Lover; and His
local paradise and heaven of heavens.

Coventry Patmore: *The Rod, the Root and
the Flower.* (19th cent.)

God clothes himself actually and literally with His whole creation. Herbs

take up and assimilate minerals, beasts
assimilate herbs, and God, in the Incarnation and its proper sacrament, assimi-
lates us, who, as St. Augustine says, 'are
God's beasts.'

Coventry Patmore: *The Rod, the Root and
the Flower.* (19th cent.)

Since God is approaching man, it is not
a degradation, but a triumph of His love,
that He should come so far down to
meet him.

R. H. Benson: *A City Set on a Hill.* (20th
cent.)

Every thought, word, action, silence, and
self-repression in the incarnate life of
the Word of God is full of spiritual significance and effectiveness.

R. H. Benson: *Preface to Bonds of Love.*
(20th cent.)

The incarnation is not an event; but an
institution. What Jesus once took up He
never laid down.

V. McNabb: *Thoughts Twice-dyed.* (20th
cent.)

The incarnation is but God's emphatic
statement that He cannot be a mere
tribal deity, a mere God of Abraham,
Isaac and Jacob. He is the Light of the
world. This Light of lights cannot be
quenched under the bushel of nationality.

V. McNabb: *Thoughts Twice-dyed.* (20th
cent.)

See also Advent; Atonement; Christmas; Jesus Christ; Redemption

Inconsistency

T'abhor the makers, and their laws ap-
    prove,
Is to hate traitors and their treason
    love.

Dryden: *The Hind and the Panther,* 3.
(17th cent.)

Indecision

> But now I cast that finer sense
> And sorer shame aside:
> Such dread of sin was indolence,
> Such aim at heaven was pride.

Card. Newman: *Sensitiveness.* (19th cent.)

Indians

By our Apostolic authority we define and proclaim that the Indians, or any other peoples who may be hereafter discovered by Catholics, although they be not Christian, must in no way be deprived of their liberty or their possessions.

Pope Paul III: *Bull 'Sublimis Deus.'*

Indifference, Holy

The indifferent heart is as a ball of wax in the hands of its God, receiving with equal readiness all the impressions of the divine pleasure.

St. Francis de Sales: *Treatise on the Love of God,* 9, 4. (17th cent.)

Remain in indifference as to having or not having spiritual goods.

St. Francis de Sales: *Letters to Persons in Religion,* 5, 5. (17th cent.)

Holy indifference goes beyond resignation: for it loves nothing except for the love of God's will.

St. Francis de Sales: *Treatise on the Love of God,* 9, 4. (17th cent.)

Indifferentism

Conscience has rights because it has duties; but in this age, with a large portion of the public, it is the very right and freedom of conscience to dispense with conscience, to ignore a Lawgiver and Judge, to be independent of unseen obligations. It becomes a license to take up any or no religion, to take up this or that and let it go again, to go to church, to go to chapel, to boast of being above all religions and to be impartial critic of each of them.

Card. Newman: *Difficulties of Anglicans,* 2. (19th cent.)

Individualism

What is modern individualism? A misunderstanding, a blunder; the exaltation of individuality camouflaged as personality, and the corresponding degradation of personality.

J. Maritain: *Three Reformers.* (20th cent.)

Individual liberty, freed from all bonds and all laws, all objective and social values, is in reality only a death-dealing anarchy.

Pope Pius XII: *Address to the World Federal Government Movement.* (Apr. 6, 1951)

Individuality

> Each the known track of sage philosophy
> Deserts, and has a byway of his own:
> So much the restless eagerness to shine,
> And love of singularity prevail.

Dante: *Paradiso, Canto 29.* (Tr. Cary) (14th cent.)

Indulgence

Whereas the power of conferring indulgences was granted by Christ to the Church, and she has, even in the most ancient times, used the said power delivered unto her of God; the sacred holy synod teaches and enjoins that the use of indulgences, most salutary for Christian people and approved of by the authority of sacred councils, is to be retained in the Church; and it condemns with anathema those who either assert that they are useless, or who deny that there is in the Church the power of granting them.

Decree of the Council of Trent, Session 25. (Dec. 4, 1563)

Let all value indulgences or the remission before God of the temporal punishment due for sins whose guilt has already been forgiven, which ecclesiastical authority grants from the treasury of the Church, by way of absolution for the living and by way of suffrage for the departed.

> Code of Canon Law, Canon 911. (20th cent.)

Industrialism

Dead matter leaves the factory ennobled and transformed, whereas men are corrupted and degraded.

> Pope Pius XI: *Quadragesimo anno.* (May 15, 1931)

This is the fundamental evil of industrialism. It has depersonalized work. It has disintegrated the worker. It has made the work the least interesting, because the least personal part of his life. It has created a state of things in which nothing is expected from work, but the pay for doing it, and all the happiness of living is relegated to the time when we are not working.

> Eric Gill: *It All Goes Together.* (20th cent.)

Inequality

Inequality of rights and of power proceeds from the very Author of nature, *from whom all paternity in heaven and earth is named.*

> Pope Leo XIII: *Quod Apostolici Muneris.* (Dec. 28, 1878)

Infallibility

See Catholic Church: Infallible; Pope: His Infallibility

Infidelity

He who is unfaithful to God cannot be truly a friend to man.

> St. Ambrose: *On the Duties of the Clergy,* 3, 132. (4th cent.)

Infinity

Although we cannot number the infinite, nevertheless it can be comprehended by Him Whose knowledge has no bounds.

> St. Augustine: *The City of God,* 12. (5th cent.)

See also God: His Infiniteness

Influence

Moreover, it is but the truth to say, that it had ever been an annoyance to me to seem to be the head of a party; and that even from fastidiousness of mind, I could not bear to find a thing done elsewhere, simply or mainly because I did it myself, and that, from distrust of myself, I shrank from the thought, whenever it was brought home to me, that I was influencing others.

> Card. Newman: *Apologia pro Vita Sua,* 4. (19th cent.)

Ingratitude

Ingratitude is the soul's enemy; it empties it of merit, scatters its virtues, and deprives it of graces. Like a hot, parching wind, it dries up the well-spring of holiness, the dew of mercy, and the streams of grace.

> St. Bernard: *Sermons on the Canticle of Canticles,* 51. (12th cent.)

Men use, if they have an evil turn, to write it in marble, and whoso doth us a good turn, we write it in dust.

> St. Thomas More: *Richard III.* (16th cent.)

Ingratitude's a weed of every clime,
It thrives too fast at first, but fades in time.

> Sir Samuel Garth: *Epistle to the Earl of Godolphin.* (18th cent.)

Inheritance

Man's natural right of possessing and transmitting property by inheritance must remain intact and cannot be taken away by the state.

> Pope Pius XI: *Quadragesimo anno.* (May 15, 1931)

Injury

Most injuries are more happily met by the indifference which is shown for them than by any other means.

> St. Francis de Sales: *Letters to Persons in the World,* 1, 11. (17th cent.)

Forgiveness to the injured does belong,
But they ne'er pardon who have done the wrong.

> Dryden: *The Conquest of Granada,* 2. (17th cent.)

Injustice

Injustice swift, erect and unconfin'd,
Sweeps the wide earth, and tramples o'er mankind.

> Pope: Tr. of Homer: *Iliad,* 9. (18th cent.)

The injustice of an act when successful does no injury to the sanctity of the law.

> Proposition condemned by Pius IX in Syllabus of Errors. (1867)

Ink

Ink is black, and hath an ill smack.
No man will it drink nor eat.

> John Heywood: *Proverbs,* 2, 4. (16th cent.)

Inn

He knew the taverns well in every town.

> Chaucer: *Canterbury Tales: Prologue.* (14th cent.)

Innocence

Hold fast to simplicity of heart and innocence. Yes, be as infants who do not know the wickedness that destroys the life of men.

> Shepherd of Hermas, Mandate 2, 1. (2nd cent.)

Joy, infant saints, whom in the tender flower
A happy storm did free from fear of sin!
Long is their life that die in blissful hour;
Joyful such ends as endless joys begin:
For long they live that live till they be nought:
Life saved by sin, is purchase dearly bought!

> Bl. Robert Southwell: *St. Peter's Complaint.* (16th cent.)

His passport is his innocence and grace,
Well known to all the natives of the place.

> Dryden: *On the Death of Amyntas.* (17th cent.)

A sight like innocence when one has sinned!

> F. Thompson: *Sister Songs.* (19th cent.)

The hills look over on the south,
And southward dreams the sea;
And, with the sea-breeze hand in hand,
Came innocence and she.

> F. Thompson: *Daisy.* (19th cent.)

Nothing looks so like innocence as an indiscretion.

> Oscar Wilde: *Lady Windermere's Fan,* 2. (19th cent.)

Innocence of a fault does not entirely do away with the distress and stigma of its punishment.

> R. H. Benson: *None Other Gods.* (20th cent.)

Nothing is too difficult for the innocent.

> Eric Gill: *It All Goes Together.* (20th cent.)

Innovation

Innovations to which we are not committed are illuminating things.

> Agnes Repplier: *Points of Friction.* (20th cent.)

Inquisition

I heartily pray that religious intolerance may never take root in our favored land. May the only king to force our conscience be the King of kings; may the only prison erected among us for the sin of unbelief be the prison of a troubled conscience; and may our only motive for embracing truth be not the fear of man, but the love of truth and of God.

> Card. Gibbons: *The Faith of Our Fathers.* (19th cent.)

There was once . . . a most ambitious program of governmental censorship of thought and utterance. It was the Spanish Inquisition. Some say that this program saved Spain from Protestantism. If it did so, it did so at a high price which Spain and the rest of the Catholic world is still paying. The price in Spain was the loss of the intellectuals, anti-clericalism, and the rise of that peculiarly militant type of unbelief which, on the evidence of history, tends to ensue upon governmental efforts to suppress unbelief. The price in the rest of the world has been a shadow, still unerased, upon the Catholic name.

> J. C. Murray: *Government and the Order of Culture.* (French rationalism was largely responsible for anti-clericalism, not the Inquisition.) (Theol. Studies, Mar. 1954)

Insanity

Men are so hopelessly insane that (by one of insanity's tricks) it would be insane to guard one's sanity.

> Pascal: *Pensées.* (17th cent.)

There is a pleasure sure
In being mad which none but madmen know.

> Dryden: *The Spanish Friar,* 3. (17th cent.)

If Nietzsche had not ended in imbecility, Nietzscheism would end in imbecility. Thinking in isolation and with pride ends in being an idiot. Every man who will not have softening of the heart must at last have softening of the brain.

> G. K. Chesterton: *Orthodoxy.* (20th cent.)

The mind that finds its way to wild places is the poet's; but the mind that never finds its way back is the lunatic's.

> G. K. Chesterton: *What's Wrong with the World.* (20th cent.)

Insincerity

For they wish to be humble, without being despised; to be content with their own, yet without mortification of the body; to be patient, yet without undergoing insults; and when they seek to make virtuous attainments, yet eschew the toils thereof, what else is this than that at one and the same time to know nothing of the conflicts of war in the field, and to desire to have the triumphs for war in the city.

> Pope St. Gregory I: *Morals,* 7, 34. (6th cent.)

Insolence

Now, we best reprove the insolent, when we show them that what they believe they have done well has been ill-done, so that a wholesome confusion may ensue from what they believe won glory for them.

> Pope St. Gregory I: *Pastoral Care,* 3, 8. (6th cent.)

Inspiration

What is talk? It is feeling that matters— inspiration, not expression.

> R. H. Benson: *The Sentimentalists.* (20th cent.)

Instinct

How instinct varies in the grov'ling swine,
Compar'd, half-reasoning elephant, with thine!

'Twixt that and reason what a nice barrier!
Forever sep'rate, yet forever near.

Pope: *An Essay on Man,* 1. (18th cent.)

We know very little indeed about the inner working of our own selves. There's instinct, for instance. We know nothing about that, except that it is so.

R. H. Benson: *The Necromancers.* (20th cent.)

Instruction

See Education

Insult

An insult is either sustained or destroyed, not by the disposition of those who insult, but by the disposition of those who bear it.

St. John Chrysostom: *Homilies.* (4th cent.)

You should not show greater courage than in despising insults.

St. Francis de Sales: *Letters to Persons in the World,* 1, 12. (17th cent.)

A harvest of virtues should be reaped from a crop of insults and injuries.

J. P. Camus: *The Spirit of St. Francis de Sales,* 14, 8. (17th cent.)

Intellectuals

If there is one class of men whom history has proved especially and supremely capable of going quite wrong in all directions, it is the class of highly intellectual men. I would always prefer to go by the bulk of humanity; that is why I am a democrat.

G. K. Chesterton: *All Things Considered.* (20th cent.)

Intention

Man beholdeth the face, but God looketh upon the heart. Man consid-

ereth the actions, but God weigheth the intentions.

Thomas a Kempis: *The Imitation of Christ,* 2, 6. (15th cent.)

One of the most excellent intentions that we can possibly have in all our actions, is to do them because our Lord did them.

St. Francis de Sales: *Spiritual Conferences,* 18. (17th cent.)

God looks at the intention of the heart rather than the gifts He is offered.

Jean Pierre Camus: *The Spirit of St. Francis de Sales,* 15, 9. (17th cent.)

Intercourse, Sexual

For, what food is to the health of man, intercourse is to the health of the race, and both are not without carnal pleasure, which, however, when modified and put to its natural use with a controlling temperance, cannot be a passion [i.e. evil passion].

St. Augustine: *The Good of Marriage,* 16. (5th cent.)

Intercourse, Social

I exhort you, therefore, to cast from your mind the thought that you have no need of communion with another. For it does not befit the character of one who walks in charity, nor of one who fulfills the command of Christ, to cut himself off from all connexion with his brethren.

St. Basil: *Letters,* 65. (4th cent.)

Interference

It is an extraordinarily difficult problem as to how much one must interfere, and how far refrain.

R. H. Benson: *The Conventionalists.* (20th cent.)

International Community

The Catholic doctrine on the state and civil society has always been based on the principle that in keeping with the will of God, the nations form together a community with a common aim and common duties. Even when the proclamation of this principle and its practical consequences gave rise to violent reactions, the Church denied her assent to the erroneous concept of an absolutely autonomous sovereignty divested of all social obligations.

> Pope Pius XII: *Christmas Message*. (Dec. 24, 1948)

Internationalism

Oh, how I love humanity,
  With love so pure and pringlish,
And how I hate the horrid French,
  Who never will be English!

The international idea,
  The largest and the clearest,
Is welding all the nations now,
  Except the one that's nearest.

> G. K. Chesterton: *The World State*. (20th cent.)

Ireland

The judgment hour must first be nigh,
Ere you shall fade, ere you can die,
  My dark Rosaleen!

> James C. Mangan: *Dark Rosaleen*. (19th cent.)

Sweet Innisfallen, long shall dwell
In memory's dream that sunny smile,
Which o'er thee on that evening fell,
When first I saw thy fairy isle.

> Thomas Moore: *Sweet Innisfallen*. (19th cent.)

And blest for ever is she who relied
Upon Erin's honor and Erin's pride.

> Thomas Moore: *Rich and Rare*. (19th cent.)

Island of saints, still constant, still allied
To the great truths opposed to human pride;
Island of ruins, towers, cloisters grey,

Whence palmer kings with pontiffs once did stray
To Rome and Sion, or to kindle fire
Which amid later darkness can inspire
Lands that in fondest memory and song
Thy pristine glory fearlessly prolong.

> Kenelm H. Digby: *Erin*. (19th cent.)

For grandeur, nations, kingdoms have their day,
But faith like thine will never pass away.

> Kenelm H. Digby: *Erin*. (19th cent.)

If will had wings,
  How fast I'd flee
To the home of my heart
  O'er the seething sea!
If wishes were power,
  If words were spells,
I'd be this hour
  Where my own love dwells.

My own love dwells
  In the storied land,
Where the holy wells
  Sleep in yellow sand;
And the emerald lustre
  Of paradise beams,
Over homes that cluster
  Round singing streams.

> Thomas D'Arcy McGee: *Home Thoughts*. (19th cent.)

Mother of tears! sweet mother of sad sons!
All mourners of the world weep Irish, weep
Ever with thee: while burdened time still runs,
Sorrows reach God through thee, and ask for sleep.

> Lionel Johnson: *To Weep Irish*. (19th cent.)

Thy sorrow, and the sorrow of the sea,
Are sisters; the sad winds are of thy race:
The heart of melancholy beats in thee,
And the lamenting spirit haunts thy face,
Mournful and mighty mother!

> Lionel Johnson: *Ireland*. (19th cent.)

The wail of Irish winds,
The cry of Irish seas:
Eternal sorrow finds
Eternal voice in these.

Lionel Johnson: *Parnell.* (19th cent.)

Everything about Ireland, her mountains, her streams, her clouds and mist, her dew and sunshine, her music that is the expansion of them all, is made for allurement, especially for the allurement of her conquerors.

Katharine T. Hinkson: *The Adventures of Alicia.* (20th cent.)

Ireland is a country in which the political conflicts are at least genuine: they are about something. They are about patriotism, about religion, or about money: the three great realities.

G. K. Chesterton: *George Bernard Shaw.* (20th cent.)

Ah, sweet is Tipperary in the springtime of the year.

Denis A. McCarthy: *Ah, Sweet is Tipperary.* (20th cent.)

Whether on the scaffold high
Or on the battle-field we die,
Oh, what matter, when for Erin dear
we fall!

T. D. Sullivan: *God Save Ireland.* (20th cent.)

Ireland and England

A mirror faced a mirror: ire and hate
Opposite ire and hate.

Alice Meynell: *Reflections in Ireland.* (20th cent.)

Irish, The

Irishman he mak' me seeck!
He ees gat excit' so queeck,
    An' so queeck for fightin', too,
An', baysides, you neva know
How you gona please heem. So
    W'ata deuce you gona do?

T. A. Daly: *Da Fightin' Irishman.* (20th cent.)

"Who says that the Irish are fighters
    be birth?"
    Says little Dan Crone.
"Faix, there's not a more peaceable
    race on th'earth,
    If ye l'ave 'em alone."

T. A. Daly: *The Peaceable Race.* (20th cent.)

An Englishman sets up an English home wherever he goes. An Irishman takes root in the soil of his own country. Even if he makes a home in another it has no real permanence. His dream is always to come back.

Katharine T. Hinkson: *A Union of Hearts.* (20th cent.)

The average autochthonous Irishman is close to patriotism because he is close to the earth; he is close to domesticity because he is close to the earth; he is close to doctrinal theology and elaborate ritual because he is close to the earth. In short, he is close to the heavens because he is close to the earth.

G. K. Chesterton: *George Bernard Shaw.* (20th cent.)

For the great Gaels of Ireland
    Are the men that God made mad,
For all their wars are merry
    And all their songs are sad.

G. K. Chesterton: *The Ballad of the White Horse.*

Iron

The iron of the soul never gets a sharp point unless it be filed down by the malice of enemies.

Pope St. Gregory I: *Homilies on the Gospels,* 38, 7. (6th cent.)

The iron hot, time is for to smite.

Lydgate: *Troy Book,* 2. (15th cent.)

We must beat the iron while it is hot, but we may polish it at leisure.

Dryden: *Dedication to the Aeneis.* (17th cent.)

Irreligion

There is no such thing, of course, really as irreligion—except by a purely conventional use of the word. The 'irreligious' man is one who has made up his mind either that there is no future world, or that it is so remote, as regards effectivity, as to have no bearing upon this. And that is a religion—at least it is a dogmatic creed—as much as any other.

R. H. Benson: *The Dawn of All.* (20th cent.)

Irritation

One is none the less liable to irritability in the east wind, however much one may assert that an immortal soul ought to be impervious to atmospheric conditions.

R. H. Benson: *An Average Man.* (20th cent.)

Island

Fairest isle, all isles excelling,
Seat of pleasures, and of loves;
Venus here will choose her dwelling,
And forsake her Cyprian groves.

Dryden: *King Arthur,* 5. (17th cent.)

Italy

Ah, slavish Italy! thou inn of grief!
Vessel without a pilot in loud storm!
Lady no longer of fair provinces,
But brothel-house impure!

Dante: *Purgatorio, Canto 6.* (Tr. Cary) (14th cent.)

The primacy of Italy is Christian and Catholic, or it has none. Alas for your fair land and for your noble race if, forgetting its true greatness, it covet false glory which is not its own. In that hour it abdicates its mission—the greatest a people ever had—and descends from its primacy among the nations of the world. A vocation lost is a prelude to a fall.

This is not to increase, but to decrease before God and man.

Card. Manning: *Discourse before the Accademia of the Quiriti, Rome,* April 21, 1863.

But O the unfolding south! the burst
    Of summer! O to see
Of all the southward brooks the first!
    The travelling heart went free
With endless streams; that strife was
    stopped;
And down a thousand vales I dropped,
    I flowed to Italy.

Alice Meynell: *The Watershed: Lines Written between Munich and Verona.* (20th cent.)

O'er the Campagna it is dim warm
    weather;
    The spring comes with a full heart
        silently,
    And many thoughts; a faint flash of
        the sea
Divides two mists; straight falls the
    falling feather.

With wild spring meanings hill and
    plain together
    Grow pale, or just flush with a dust
        of flowers.
    Rome in the ages, dimmed with all
        her towers,
Floats in the midst, a little cloud at
    tether.

Alice Meynell: *Spring on the Alban Hills.* (19th cent.)

Ivy

The creeping, dirty, courtly ivy.

Pope: *The Dunciad,* 1. (18th cent.)

On my velvet couch reclining,
Ivy leaves my brow entwining,
While my soul expands with glee,
What are kings and crowns to me?

Thomas Moore: *Odes of Anacreon.* (19th cent.)

J

Jack

What availeth lordship, yourself for to kill
With care and with thought how Jack shall have Jill.

> John Skelton: *Magnyfycence.* (16th cent.)

Jack would be a gentleman if he could speak French.

> John Heywood: *Proverbs,* 1, 11. (16th cent.)

I have been common Jack to all that whole flock.

> John Heywood: *Proverbs,* 1, 11. (16th cent.)

Jaundice

The jaundice of the soul.

> Dryden: *The Hind and the Panther,* 3. (17th cent.)

All looks yellow to the jaundiced eye.

> Pope: *An Essay on Criticism,* 2. (18th cent.)

Jealousy

Not to be jealous.

> St. Benedict: *Rule,* 4. (One of his 'tools of good works') (6th cent.)

For jealous folk are dangerous, you know,
At least they want their wives to think them so.

> Chaucer: *The Reeve's Tale.* (Tr. Coghill) (14th cent.)

Fool that I was, upon my eagle's wings
I bore this wren, till I was tired with soaring,
And now he mounts above me.

> Dryden: *All for Love,* 2, 1. (17th cent.)

Thou tyrant, tyrant jealousy,
Thou tyrant of the mind!

> Dryden: *Love Triumphant: Song of Jealousy.* (17th cent.)

Plain women are always jealous of their husbands, beautiful women never are!

> Oscar Wilde: *A Woman of No Importance,* 1. (19th cent.)

Jerome, Saint

Asked who and what I was I replied: I am a Christian. But he who presided said: Thou liest, thou art a follower of Cicero and not of Christ. For *where thy treasure is, there will thy heart be also.*

> St. Jerome: *Letter* 22, 30. (Famous words which the saint believed that he heard when he was transported 'in the spirit' before the eternal Judge and condemned for his inordinate love of classical literature.) (4th cent.)

Jerusalem, Heavenly

Blessed city, heavenly Salem,
Vision dear of peace and love,
Who, of living stones upbuilded,
Art the joy of heaven above,
And, with angel cohorts circled,
As a bride to earth dost move.

> Anonymous: *Urbs Jerusalem beata.* (Tr. J. Neale) (6th or 7th cent.)

Mine be Sion's habitation,
Sion, David's sure foundation:
Form'd of old by light's Creator,
Reach'd by Him, the Mediator:
An apostle guards the portal
Denizen'd by forms immortal,
On a jasper pavement builded,
By its Monarch's radiance gilded.

Hildebert of Tours: *Me receptet Sion illa.*
(Tr. J. Neale) (First line: *Extra portam
jam delatum,* 12th cent.)

Jerusalem the golden,
With milk and honey blest,
Beneath thy contemplation
Sink heart and voice oppressed.
I know not, O I know not
What joys await us there,
What radiancy of glory,
What light beyond compare.

Bernard of Cluny: *Urbs Sion aurea.*
(From poem *De Contemptu mundi.*)
(Tr. J. Neale) (12th cent.)

Jerusalem, my happy home,
  When shall I come to thee;
When shall my sorrows have an end
  Thy joys when shall I see?

O happy harbor of the saints,
  O sweet and pleasant soil;
In thee no sorrow may be found,
  No grief, no care, no toil.

In thee no sickness may be seen,
  No hurt, no ache, no sore;
There is no death, nor ugly deuil,
  There is life for evermore.

Anonymous: *Jerusalem, my Happy Home.*
(Variously attributed; in Add. MS.
15,225) (Guiney, 278) (16th cent.)

Jerusalem, thy joys divine,
  No joys may be compar'd to them,
No people blessèd so as thine,
  No city like Jerusalem.

Bl. Henry Walpole: *The Description of
Heavenly Jerusalem.* (Guiney, 259)
(16th cent.)

Sing me the men ere this
Who, to the gate that is
A cloven pearl unwrapt,

The big white bars between
With dying eyes have seen
The sea of jasper, lapt
About with crystal sheen;
And all the far pleasance
Where linkèd angels dance,
With scarlet wings that fall
Magnificial, or spread
Most sweetly overhead,
In fashion musical
Of cadenced lutes instead.

Digby M. Dolben: *He Would Have His
Lady Sing.* (19th cent.)

The world has narrow gates and wide;
Men seek their loves through all of
  them
And I have come here seeking mine,
  Jerusalem, Jerusalem!

Sister Madeleva: *Gates.* (20th cent.)

Jesuits (Society of Jesus)

We may easily suffer ourselves to be surpassed by other religious orders in fasting, watching and other austerities of
diet and clothing, which they practise
according to their rule, but in true and
perfect obedience and the abnegation of
our will and judgment, I greatly desire,
most dear brethren, that those who
serve God in this Society should be conspicuous.

St. Ignatius Loyola: *Letter to Members of
the Society in Portugal.* (1553)

And touching our Society, be it known
to you that we have made a league—
all the Jesuits in the world, whose succession and multitude must overreach
all the practices of England—cheerfully
to carry the cross you shall lay upon us,
and never to despair your recovery,
while we have a man left to enjoy your
Tyburn, or to be racked with your torments, or consumed with your prisons.
The expense is reckoned, the enterprise
is begun; it is of God, it cannot be withstood. So the faith was planted: so it
must be restored.

Bl. Edmund Campion: *Campion's Brag.*
(Addressed to the 'Lords of her
Majesty's Privy Council') (16th cent.)

I never had mind, and am strictly forbidden by our father that sent me, to deal in any respect with matter of state or policy of this realm, as things which appertain not to my vocation, and from which I do gladly restrain and sequester my thoughts.

Bl. Edmund Campion: *Campion's Brag.* (16th cent.)

Jesuits are nothing but Puritan-papists.

King James I. (The king was unable to stomach either Jesuit [St. Robert Bellarmine] or Calvinist opposition to the royal absolutism.) (17th cent.)

The logical outcome of the existence of the Society founded by St. Ignatius of Loyola was the dogmatic definition of papal infallibility; for this was the final word of victory of divine truth over the specific error which the Jesuits were specially called to combat.

I. T. Hecker: *The Church and the Age.* (1887)

Jesus Christ

I—*Son of God; Word of God; Lord; Master; God and Man*

Thou dost multiply nations upon earth and hast chosen from them all those that love Thee through Jesus Christ Thy beloved Child, and through Him Thou hast taught us, made us holy, and brought us to honor.

Pope St. Clement I: *First Letter to the Corinthians,* 59, 3. (1st cent.)

There is one Doctor active in both body and soul, begotten and yet unbegotten, God in man, true Life in death, Son of Mary, and Son of God, first able to suffer and then unable to suffer, Jesus Christ, our Lord.

St. Ignatius of Antioch: *Letter to the Ephesians,* 6. (2nd cent.)

But the Son of God is the Logos (Word) of the Father, in idea and in operation; for after the pattern of Him and by Him were all things made, the Father and the Son being One. And, the Son being in the Father and the Father in the Son, in oneness and power of spirit, the understanding and reason of the Father is the Son of God.

Athenagoras: *Supplication,* 10. (2nd cent.)

I believe in God the Father almighty, and in Jesus Christ, His only Son, our Lord. . . .

Old Roman Creed. (Before 4th cent.)

We hold for certain that Jesus, our Lord, is God the Son of God, King the Son of the King, Light of Light, Creator, Counsellor, Leader, Way, Savior, Shepherd, Gatherer, Gate, Pearl, and Lamp. He is thus called by many names. But leaving aside all the rest, let us show that He is Son of God, Himself God Who came forth from God.

St. Aphraates: *Proofs,* 17, 2. (4th cent.)

Believe also in the Son of God, one and only, our Lord Jesus Christ, Who was begotten God of God, begotten Life of Life, begotten Light of Light, who is in all things like to Him that begat, Who received not His being in time, but was before all ages eternally and incomprehensibly begotten of the Father: the Wisdom and the Power of God, and His Righteousness personally subsisting: Who sitteth on the right hand of the Father before all ages.

St. Cyril of Jerusalem: *Catechetical Discourses,* 4, 7. (4th cent.)

Many, my beloved, are the true testimonies concerning Christ. The Father bears witness from heaven of His Son: the Holy Ghost bears witness, descending bodily in the likeness of a dove: the archangel Gabriel bears witness, bringing good tidings to Mary: the Virgin Mother of God (*Theotokos*) bears witness. . . .

St. Cyril of Jerusalem: *Catechetical Discourses,* 10, 19. (4th cent.)

He does not cease to be God because He becomes Man, nor fail to be Man, because He remains for ever God. This is the true faith for human blessedness, to preach at once the Godhead and the manhood, to confess the Word and the flesh, neither forgetting the God, because He is man, nor ignoring the flesh, because He is the Word.

St. Hilary of Poitiers: *On the Trinity*, 9, 3. (4th cent.)

The Son is the Image of the invisible God. All things that belong to the Father He expresses as the Image; all things that are the Father's He illumines as the splendor of His glory and manifests to us.

St. Ambrose: *Hexaem.* 2, 19. (4th cent.)

The Son is the Face of the Father, for he who sees the Son sees the Father also.

St. Ambrose: *Explanation of Psalm 118*, 17, 28. (4th cent.)

I beseech it by our Lord Jesus Christ Thy Son, *the Man of Thy right hand, the Son of Man, Whom Thou hast confirmed for Thyself* as Mediator between Thyself and us: by Whom Thou didst seek us when we sought Thee not, didst seek us indeed that we might seek Thee.

St. Augustine: *Confessions*, 11, 2. (5th cent.)

Just as every human being is one person, that is, a rational soul and body, so, too, is Christ one Person, the Word and Man.

St. Augustine: *Enchiridion*, 36. (5th cent.)

This then is Christ Jesus, the only Son of God, who is also our Lord. 'Only' can be applied to him both as Son and as Lord. For Jesus Christ is 'only' both as God's authentic Son and as our sole Lord. All other sons of God, though designated sons, have that title by the grace of adoption, not as a result of any natural relationship.

Rufinus: *Commentary on the Apostles' Creed*, 8. (5th cent.)

If anyone does not confess that the Word (*Logos*) from God the Father hypostatically united Himself with the flesh, and with that which has become His own flesh is one Christ, God and Man together, let him be anathema.

Council of Alexandria, Anathema 2 of St. Cyril. (430)

If anyone divides the expressions which are used in the evangelical and apostolic writings or by the saints, in reference to Christ, or which are by Him applied to himself, between two Persons or Hypostases, and specially ascribes the one class to the Man, separated from the divine Word, and the other as divine merely to the Word, let him be anathema.

Council of Alexandria, Anathema 4 of St. Cyril. (430)

If anyone ventures to say that Christ is a man who bears God (*theophoron*), and not rather, that He is true God, as the one Son in nature, in accordance with the expressions *The Word was made flesh* and *He too shared a common inheritance of flesh and blood* with us, let him be anathema.

Council of Alexandria, Anathema 5 of St. Cyril. (430)

All the faithful confess that they believe in God, the Father Almighty, and in Jesus Christ His only Son our Lord, Who was born by the Holy Ghost of the Virgin Mary. By these three propositions almost every heresy is overthrown. For, if one believes in God the Father Almighty, then is the Son declared to be co-eternal with Him, differing in nothing from the Father, because He is God of God, Almighty of the Almighty, Co-eternal of the Eternal, not later in time, not inferior in power, not unequal in glory, not divided in essence.

Pope St. Leo I: Dogmatic Epistle to Flavian Bishop of Constantinople. (Ep. 28, 2) (June 13, 449)

Moreover, the Word appropriates to Himself the attributes of humanity, for all that pertains to His holy flesh is His, and He imparts to the flesh His own attributes by way of the communication of properties in virtue of the interpenetration of the parts one with another, and the oneness according to subsistence, and inasmuch as He Who lived and acted both as God and as Man, taking to Himself either form and holding intercourse with the other form, was one and the same.

St. John of Damascus: *Exposition of the Orthodox Faith*, 3, 3. (8th cent.)

Christ, therefore, is one, perfect God and perfect Man; and Him we worship along with the Father and the Spirit, with one obeisance, adoring even His immaculate flesh, and not holding that the flesh is not worthy of worship; for in fact it is worshipped in the one person of the Word, which indeed became person for it. But in this we do not do homage to that which is created. For we worship Him not as mere flesh, but as flesh united with Divinity, and because His two natures are brought under the one Person and one subsistence of God the Word.

St. John of Damascus: *Exposition of the Orthodox Faith*, 3, 8. (8th cent.)

For there never was a time when God was not Word (*logos*): but He ever possesses His own Word, begotten of Himself, not as our word is, without a subsistence and dissolving into air, but having a subsistence in Him and life and perfection, not proceeding out of Himself but ever existing within himself.

St. John of Damascus: *Exposition of the Orthodox Faith*, 1, 6. (8th cent.)

Only-begotten Son and Word of God, Who art immortal and didst vouchsafe for our salvation to take flesh of the holy Mother of God and ever Virgin Mary, and without change didst become Man, and wast crucified, Christ God, and by death didst overcome death, being one of the holy Trinity and glori-

fied with the Father and the Holy Ghost: save us!

Byzantine Horologion, Prayer at the Office of the Typika. (Before 9th cent. ?)

God the Son is equal with the Father. He was subject to death, not in His divine nature, which is the living fountainhead of all things, but in our nature which he assumed into the unity of His person.

St. Thomas Aquinas: *Concerning Reasons of Faith*, 5. (13th cent.)

God the Son was not made by God, but was naturally born of God. Consequently he is not subject to Divine providence or to the eternal law: but rather is Himself the eternal law by a kind of appropriation, as Augustine explains (*De Vera Religione*, 31). But He is said to be subject to the Father by reason of His human nature, in respect of which also the Father is said to be greater than He.

St. Thomas Aquinas: *Summa Theologica*, 1-2, 93, 4. (13th cent.)

One difference between Christ and other men is this: they do not choose when to be born, but He, the Lord and Maker of history, chose His time, His birthplace, and His mother.

St. Thomas Aquinas: *Summa Theologica*, 3, 35, 8. (13th cent.)

Theological tradition ascribes to Christ a threefold grace. First, the grace of hypostatic union, whereby a human nature is united in person to the Son of God. Second, sanctifying grace, the fulness of which distinguishes Christ above all others. Third, His grace as Head of the Church.

St. Thomas Aquinas: *Compendium of Theology*, 214. (13th cent.)

We profess two wisdoms in Christ, the uncreated wisdom of God and the created wisdom of man.

St. Thomas Aquinas: *Compendium of Theology*, 216. (13th cent.)

Great Prince of heaven! begotten of that
King
  Who rules the kingdom that himself
    did make,
  And of that Virgin Queen man's
    shape did take,
  Which from king David's royal
    stock did spring;
No marvel, though thy birth made
  angels sing,
  And angels' ditties shepherds' pipes
    awake,
  And kings, like shepherds, humbled
    for Thy sake,
  Kneel at Thy feet, and gifts of
    homage bring:
For heaven and earth, the high and
  low estate
  As partners of Thy birth make equal
    claim;
  Angels, because in heaven God Thee
    begat.
Shepherds and kings, because Thy
  Mother came
  From princely race, and yet by
    poverty
Made glory shine in her humility.

    Henry Constable: *Sonnet to God the Son.*
    (16th cent.)

Amid the eternal silences
  God's endless Word was spoken;
None heard but He who always spake,
  And the silence was unbroken.

    F. Faber: *The Eternal Word.* (19th cent.)

The divinity of Jesus Christ is not proved
from the Gospels; but is a dogma which
the Christian conscience has derived
from the notion of the Messias.

    Proposition condemned by Decree of Holy
    Office, *Lamentabili,* June 3, 1907.

It is lawful to believe that the Christ of
history is far inferior to the Christ who
is the object of faith.

    Proposition condemned by Decree of
    Holy Office, *Lamentabili,* June 3, 1907.

When the grasp upon Christ's divinity
is sure and unfaltering, there is no
danger that an intimate affection for
His humanity will lead souls astray.

    R. H. Benson: *A Book of the Love of
    Jesus.* (20th cent.)

We must affirm our Son
From the ambiguous nature's difficult
  speech,
Gather in darkness that resplendent
  One,
  Close as our grasp can reach.

Nor shall we ever rest
From this our task. An hour sufficed
  for thee,
Thou innocent! He lingers in the
  breast
  Of our humanity.

    Alice Meynell: *To the Mother of Christ,
    the Son of Man.* (20th cent.)

Rationalists renounce reason in their attempt to solve the problem of Christ.
Either Christ was God or He was mad.
The rationalist will not accept the former alternative, he dare not suggest the
latter.

    Arnold Lunn: *Now I See.* (20th cent.)

II—*Eternal Judge*

Hail! Thou Judge of souls departed!
  Hail of all the loving King!
On the Father's right hand throned,
  through His courts Thy praises ring,
Till at last for all offenses righteous
  judgment shalt Thou bring.

    Prudentius: *Macte Judex mortuorum.*
    (Tr. Pope and Davis) (From the
    Cathemerinon, 4th cent.)

My soul, my soul, awake, why dost thou
sleep? The end is near, and thou wilt
be troubled. Awake, then, that Christ
God, who is everywhere and filleth all
things, may spare thee.

    Byzantine Triodion, Great Canon,
    Kontakion. (8th cent.)

Righteous Judge! for sin's pollution
Grant Thy gift of absolution,
Ere that day of retribution.

    Thomas of Celano: *Dies Irae.* (13th cent.)

III—*Good Shepherd; Friend of Man*

The Savior of our souls and helmsman of our bodies, the Shepherd of the Catholic Church throughout the world.

> Martyrdom of St. Polycarp, 19. (2nd cent.)

Thou art the Good Shepherd; seek me, a lamb, and do not overlook me in my wanderings.

> Byzantine Triodion, Great Canon of St. Andrew of Crete. (8th cent.)

He is the Good Shepherd, Who gives His life for the sheep—His life for them, His flesh to them, the one for their redemption, the other for their food. O mighty marvel! He is Himself the Shepherd of the sheep, their Pasturage and their redemption's Price.

> St. Bernard: *Sermons on the Canticle of Canticles,* 31. (12th cent.)

O gracious Shepherd! for Thy simple flock
  By guileful goats to ravening wolves misled,
  Who Thine own dear heart's precious blood didst shed,
  And lamb-like offered to the butcher's block:
O gracious Shepherd! unremoving Rock
  Of succor to all such as thither fled,
  Respect one of thy flock which followèd
These cursèd goats, and doth repentant knock,
  To be with mercy taken to Thy fold.
I know Thy grace doth still for wanderers look;
  I was a lost sheep once: dear Lord! behold,
And in compassion take me with Thy hook.
  In one lost sheep new found, Thou dost rejoice;
  Then know Thy sheep, which knows his Shepherd's voice.

> Henry Constable: *O Gracious Shepherd.* (16th cent.)

I met the good Shepherd,
  But now on the plain,
As homeward He carried
  His lost one again.
I marvell'd how gently
  His burden He bore;
And, as He pass'd by me,
  I knelt to adore.

> E. Caswall: *The Good Shepherd.* (19th cent.)

I saw the shepherd fold the sheep,
With all the little lambs that leap.

O Shepherd Lord, so I would be
Folded with all my family.

> Wilfrid Meynell: *The Folded Flock.* (19th cent.)

Christ comes to each soul, all trusting as a friend, and in each He is betrayed over and over again.

> R. H. Benson: *Christ in the Church.* (20th cent.)

IV—*High Priest and Mediator*

We praise Thee through Jesus Christ, High Priest and Guardian of our souls, through Whom be glory and majesty to Thee, both now and for ever and ever. Amen.

> Pope St. Clement I: *Letter to the Corinthians,* 61, 3. (1st cent.)

A priest must offer something and in accordance with the law enter into the holy places by means of blood. Therefore, since God has rejected the blood of bulls and goats, it was needful for this Priest to enter into the supreme holy of holies in heaven by means of His own Blood, that the offering for our sins might be for ever. Therefore the Priest and Victim are one and the same. . . . He was led as a Lamb to the slaughter and He is a Priest after the order of Melchizedek.

> St. Ambrose: *Concerning Faith,* 3, 87. (4th cent.)

Other priests offered for themselves and for their people; this Priest, not having sin that He should offer for Himself, offered Himself for the whole world, and by His own Blood entered into the holy places. He, then, is the new Priest and the new Victim, not of the law but above the law, the universal Advocate.

St. Ambrose: *Letters,* 44, 16, 17. (4th cent.)

Now clearly a Mediator between God and men should have something in common with God, something in common with men; if He were in both points like men, He would be too far from God; if He were in both points like God, He would be too far from men: and in neither event could He be a mediator.

St. Augustine: *Confessions,* 10, 42. (5th cent.)

For He was to Thee both Victor and Victim, and Victor because Victim: for us He was to Thee both Priest and Sacrifice, and Priest because Sacrifice: turning us from slaves into Thy sons, by being Thy Son and becoming a Slave.

St. Augustine: *Confessions,* 10, 43. (5th cent.)

I beseech it by our Lord Jesus Christ Thy Son, *the Man of Thy right hand, the Son of man, Whom Thou hast confirmed for Thyself* as Mediator between Thyself and us: by Whom Thou didst seek us when we sought Thee not, didst seek us indeed that we might seek Thee: Thy Word, by which Thou hast made all things and me among them: Thy only One, by Whom Thou hast called the people of the faithful, and me among them, unto adoption.

St. Augustine: *Confessions,* 11, 2. (5th cent.)

It follows truly that the whole body of the redeemed, that is the congregation and society of the saints, be offered to God by that great Priest, for He offered Himself as an oblation for us, that we might be members of so great a Head in the form of a servant. . . . This is the Christian sacrifice that "we, being many, are one body in Christ" (Rom. 12, 5). This the Church celebrates in the sacrament of the altar, so well known to the faithful, wherein is shown that in that oblation the Church is offered.

St. Augustine: *The City of God,* 10, 6. (5th cent.)

Our faith is sound if we believe that no man, old or young, is delivered from the contagion of death and the bonds of sin, except by the one Mediator of God and men, Jesus Christ.

St. Augustine: *De Correptione et Gratia,* 7. (5th cent.)

For we shall then contemplate God, the Father and the Son and the Holy Spirit, when the Mediator between God and man, the Man Christ Jesus, shall have delivered up the kingdom to God, even the Father, so as no longer to make intercession for us, as our Mediator and Priest, Son of God and Son of man; but that He himself too, in so far as He is a Priest that has taken the form of a Servant for us, shall be put under Him who has put all things under Him, and under Whom He has put all things: so that, in so far as He is God, He with Him will have put us under Himself; in so far as He is a Priest, He with us will be put under Him.

St. Augustine: *De Trinitate,* 1, 10. (5th cent.)

In such wise that, whereas four things are to be considered in every sacrifice— to whom it is offered, by whom it is offered, what is offered, for whom it is offered—the same one and true Mediator himself, reconciling us to God by the sacrifice of peace, might remain one with Him to Whom He offered, might make those one in Himself for whom He offered, Himself might be in one both the Offerer and the Offering.

St. Augustine: *De Trinitate,* 4, 14. (5th cent.)

For two reasons He is called a Priest: first, because He offered up His body as an oblation and victim to God the Father for us; second, because through us He condescends day after day to be offered up. He is the Way along which we journey to our salvation; the Truth, because He rejects what is false; the Life, because He destroys death. He is the Vine, because He spread out the branches of His arms that the world might pluck in clusters the grapes of consolation from the cross.

> St. Niceta of Remesiana: *De Diversis Appellationibus.* (5th cent.)

If anyone says that it was not the divine Word Himself, when He was made flesh and man, like us, but another than He, a man distinct from Him, who became our High Priest and Apostle; or says that He gave himself for a sacrifice not for us alone, but also for Himself, although He as the sinless one needed no sacrifice, let him be anathema.

> Council of Alexandria, Anathema 10 of St. Cyril. (430)

For He is our true and eternal High Priest, Whose governance can have neither change nor end, He Whose type was shown by the priest Melchizedek, not offering Jewish victims to God, but offering the sacrifice of that mystery, which our Redeemer consecrated in His own body and blood.

> Pope St. Leo I: *Sermons,* 5, 3. (5th cent.)

O great High Priest, our true Pontiff, Jesus Christ, Who didst offer Thyself to God the Father a pure and spotless Victim upon the altar of the cross for us miserable sinners, and didst give us Thy Flesh to be our meat and Thy Blood to be our drink. . . .

> Roman Missal, Prayer *Summe Sacerdos* before Mass. (11th cent.)

The proper office of a mediator is to join opposed parties, for extremes meet in a middle. To achieve our union with God is Christ's work. . . . He alone is the perfect Mediator between God and men, forasmuch as the human race was brought into agreement with God through His death.

> St. Thomas Aquinas: *Summa Theologica,* 3, 26, 1. (13th cent.)

This I know full well now, and did not know then, that the Catholic Church allows no image of any sort, material or immaterial, no dogmatic symbol, no rite, no sacrament, no saint, not even the blessed Virgin herself, to come between the soul and its Creator. It is face to face, *solus cum solo,* in all matters between man and his God. He alone creates; He alone has redeemed; before His awful eye we go in death; in the vision of Him is our eternal beatitude.

> Card. Newman: *Apologia pro Vita Sua.* (19th cent.)

V—*Infant Jesus; Christ Child*

O Christ, whose glory fills the heaven,
Our only hope, in mercy given;
Child of a Virgin meek and pure;
Son of the Highest evermore.

> Roman Breviary Hymn *Aeterna coeli gloria* for Friday at Lauds. (Tr. J. Julian) (Ambrosian, 5th cent.)

As I in hoary winter's night stood shivering in the snow,
Surprised I was with sudden heat which made my heart to glow;
And lifting up a fearful eye to view what fire was near,
A pretty Babe all burning bright did in the air appear;
Who, scorched with excessive heat, such floods of tears did shed,
As though His floods should quench His flames which with His tears were fed.

> Bl. Robert Southwell: *The Burning Babe.* (Greatly admired by Ben Jonson) (16th cent.)

His chilling cold doth heat require,
Come seraphims in lieu of fire;
This little Ark no cover hath,
Let cherubims' wings His body swathe.
Come Raphael, this Babe must eat,
Provide our little Tobie meat.

Let Gabriel be now His groom,
That first took up His earthly room;
Let Michael stand in His defence,
Whom love hath link'd to feeble sense.
Let graces rock when He doth cry,
Let angels sing His lullaby.

Bl. Robert Southwell: *New Heaven, New War.* (16th cent.)

My soul with Christ join thou in fight,
Stick to the tents that He hath dight;
Within His crib is surest ward,
This little Babe will be thy guard.
If thou wilt foil thy foes with joy,
Then flit not from the heavenly Boy.

Bl. Robert Southwell: *New Heaven, New War.* (16th cent.)

Thou young, yet wise; though small,
    yet strong; though Man, yet God
    He is.
As wise, He knows; as strong, He can;
    as God, He loves to bliss.
His knowledge rules; His strength,
    defends; His love, doth cherish all.
His birth, our joy; His life, our light;
    His death, our end of thrall.

Bl. Robert Southwell: *A Child, My Choyse.* (16th cent.)

Welcome, all wonders in one sight!
Eternity shut in a span.
Summer in winter. Day in night.
Heaven in earth, and God in Man.
Great little One! whose all-embracing
    birth
Lifts earth to heaven, stoops heaven to
    earth.

Richard Crashaw: *The Holy Nativity of Our Lord, a Hymn.* (17th cent.)

Love! Love! Infinite love!
    The lowly Lady of grace
Bows underneath the o'ershadowing
    Dove,
    Her eternal Son to embrace!
For God is there, the Ancient of Days,
    And Infant of human years:
Whilst angels around them incessantly
    gaze,
    And nature is wrapt in tears!

M. Bridges: *Domus Aurea.* (19th cent.)

Dear little One! how sweet Thou art,
    Thine eyes how bright they shine,
So bright they almost seem to speak
    When Mary's look meets Thine!

F. Faber: *Hymn to the Infant Jesus.* (19th cent.)

O see how Jesus trusts Himself
    Unto our childish love,
As though by His free ways with us
    Our earnestness to prove!

God gives Himself as Mary's Babe
    To sinners' trembling arms,
And veils His everlasting light
    In childhood's feeble charms.

F. Faber: *True Love.* (19th cent.)

Sleep, holy Babe,
    Upon Thy Mother's breast!
Great Lord of earth and sea and sky,
How sweet it is to see Thee lie
    In such a place of rest.

. . . .

Sleep, holy Babe!
    While I with Mary gaze
In joy upon that face awhile,
Upon the loving infant smile,
    Which there divinely plays.

E. Caswall: *Sleep, Holy Babe.* (19th cent.)

O sing a joyous carol
    Unto the holy Child,
And praise with gladsome voices
    His Mother undefiled:
Our infant voices greeting
    Shall hail our infant king;
And our sweet Lady listens
    When infant voices sing.

Hymn of Sister M.B. in Westminster Hymnal. (19th cent.?)

All joy is young, and new all art,
And He, too, whom we have by heart.

Alice Meynell: *Unto Us a Son is Given.* (19th cent.)

Little Jesus, wast Thou shy
Once, and just so small as I?

And what did it feel like to be
Out of heaven, and just like me?

Francis Thompson: *Ex Ore Infantium.*
(19th cent.)

Vines branching stilly
    Shade the open door,
In the house of Zion's lily,
    Cleanly and poor.
Oh, brighter than wild laurel
    The Babe bounds in her hand,
The King, who for apparel
    Hath but a swaddling-band,
And sees her heavenlier smiling than
    stars in His command!

Louise Imogen Guiney: *A Carol.* (19th
cent.)

The Christ-child stood at Mary's knee,
    His hair was like a crown,
And all the flowers looked up at Him,
    And all the stars looked down.

G. K. Chesterton: *A Christmas Carol.*
(20th cent.)

O Jesus, coeternal with the Father,
    Son of His love to all eternity,
"Playing before Him in the world at all
    times,"
    A Child in very truth Thou seemest
    to me.

Sister M. Angelita: *The Child Eternal.*
(20th cent.)

Ah, Bethlehem, I needs must come to
    thee;
Needs must I tread thy rock and feel
    thy cold,
And follow sense across thought's in-
    finite night;
And kiss the hem of God's humility,
Touch the tired hands that God's frail
    flesh enfold:
To speak those names, to rest me in
    that sight.

C. C. Martindale: *Sancta Dei Genetrix.*
(20th cent.)

VI—*Jesus*

Thou art sweet Jesus, Thou art my Creator; in Thee, O Savior, will I be justified.

Byzantine Triodion, Great Canon of St.
Andrew of Crete. (8th cent.)

Jesu! the very thought of Thee
With sweetness fills my breast;
But sweeter far Thy face to see,
And in Thy presence rest.

Nor voice can sing, nor heart can frame,
Nor can the memory find,
A sweeter sound than Thy blest name,
O Savior of mankind!

Anonymous English Cistercian: *Hymn
'Jesu dulcis memoria.'* (Tr. J. Neale)
(Formerly attributed to St. Bernard of
Clairvaux) (12th cent.)

To know Jesus and Him crucified is my
philosophy, and there is none higher.

St. Bernard: *Sermons on the Canticle of
Canticles,* 44. (12th cent.)

We ought rather choose to have the
whole world against us than to offend
Jesus.

Thomas a Kempis: *The Imitation of
Christ,* 2, 8. (15th cent.)

It is a great art to know how to converse
with Jesus, and to know how to keep
Jesus is great wisdom. Be humble and
peaceable, and Jesus will be with thee.

Thomas a Kempis: *The Imitation of
Christ,* 2, 8. (15th cent.)

Whosoever findeth Jesus findeth a good
treasure, yea, good above all gods. And
he that loseth Jesus loseth exceedingly
much, and more than if he lost the
whole world.

Thomas a Kempis: *The Imitation of
Christ,* 2, 8. (15th cent.)

To be without Jesus is a grievous hell,
and to be with Jesus a sweet paradise.

Thomas a Kempis: *The Imitation of
Christ,* 2, 8. (15th cent.)

Jesus is God! The glorious bands
    Of golden angels sing
Songs of adoring praise to him,
    Their Maker and their King.
He was true God in Bethlehem's crib,
    On Calvary's Cross true God,

He who in heaven eternal reigned,
  In time on earth abode.

F. Faber: *Jesus is God.* (First line: Jesus
is God! The solid earth) (19th cent.)

O Jesus, Jesus! dearest Lord!
  Forgive me if I say
For very love Thy sacred name
  A thousand times a day.

I love Thee so, I know not how
  My transports to control;
Thy love is like a burning fire
  Within my very soul.

F. Faber: *Jesus my God and my All.*
(19th cent.)

VII—*King*

Eighty-six years I have served Him, and
He has done me no wrong. How can I
blaspheme my King Who has saved me?

Martyrdom of St. Polycarp, 9. (Answer of
the saint when he was told to revile
Christ.) (2nd cent.)

The true Christ, the divine and heavenly
Logos, the only High Priest of the world,
the only King of all creation, the only
Archprophet of prophets of the Father.

Eusebius of Caesarea: *Ecclesiastical
History,* 1, 3, 8. (4th cent.)

Let me chant in sacred numbers, as I
  strike each sounding string,
Chant in sweet melodious anthems,
  glorious deeds of Christ our King;
He, my Muse, shall be Thy story; with
  His praise my lyre shall ring.

Prudentius: *Da puer plectrum.* (Tr. Pope
and Davis) (From Cathemerinon, 4th
cent.)

He takes no earthly realms away
Who gives the crown that lasts for aye.

Non eripit mortalia,
Qui regna dat caelestia.

Sedulius: *Hymn Crudelis Herodes.* (5th
cent.)

No hymn that seeks to weave into one
Thy many mercies is worthy of Thee;
were we to bring Thee, O holy King,
odes many as the sea sand we should do
nothing worthy of what Thou hast given
to us who sing to Thee: Alleluia.

Byzantine Triodion, Akathist Hymn,
Kontakion 11. (Tr. V. McNabb) (ca. 7th
cent.)

Almighty and everlasting God, Who in
Thy beloved Son, King of the whole
world, hast willed to restore all things
anew; grant in thy mercy that all the
families of nations, rent asunder by the
wound of sin, may be made subject to
His gentle rule.

Roman Missal, Collect, for Feast of Christ
the King. (last Sunday in Oct.) (Feast
extended to Latin Church by Pius XI,
Encyclical *Quas Primas,* Dec. 11, 1925.)
(20th cent.)

It is truly meet and just. . . . Who with
the oil of gladness hast anointed Thine
only-begotten Son, our Lord Jesus Christ,
as eternal High Priest and universal
King; that offering Himself on the altar
of the cross as an immaculate host and
peace-offering, He might fulfil the mystery of human redemption; and all
creation being made subject to His dominion, He might deliver into the hands
of Thine infinite majesty a kingdom eternal and universal, a kingdom of truth
and life, a kingdom of holiness and
grace, a kingdom of justice, love and
peace. . . .

Roman Missal, Preface for Feast of Christ
the King. (20th cent.)

In the recognition of the royal prerogatives of Christ and in the return of individuals and of society to the law of
His truth and of His love lies the only
way to salvation.

Pope Pius XII: *Summi Pontificatus.*
(October 20, 1939)

VIII—*Lamb of God*

Behold the Lamb!
Oh! Thou for sinners slain,—
Let it not be in vain,
  That Thou hast died:

Thee for my Savior let me take,—
Thee,—Thee alone my refuge make,—
Thy pierced side!

M. Bridges: *Ecce Agnus Dei.* (19th cent.)

Crown Him with many crowns,
The Lamb upon His throne:
Hark how the heavenly anthem drowns
All music but its own.
Awake my soul, and sing
Of Him who died for thee;
And hail Him as thy matchless King
Through all eternity.

M. Bridges: *Song of the Seraphs.* (19th cent.)

Blessed Lamb—on Calvary's mountain
Slain to take our sins away,
Let the drops of that rich fountain
Our tremendous ransom pay:
Sacred Savior! Sacred Savior!
Lowly at Thy feet we pray.

M. Bridges: *Dona nobis pacem.* (19th cent.)

IX—*Light of the World*

Christ, the true Light which enlightens
and sanctifies every man that comes into
the world; let the light of Thy countenance shine upon us that in it we may
behold the unapproachable light. And
make straight our ways in the doing
of Thy commandments; through the
prayers of Thy Mother, and of all the
saints. Amen.

Byzantine Horologion, Prayer at Prime. (ca. 8th cent.)

Lead, kindly Light, amid the encircling
gloom,
Lead thou me on!
The night is dark, and I am far from
home—
Lead thou me on!
Keep thou my feet; I do not ask to see
The distant scene,—one step enough
for me.

Card. Newman: *Light in the Darkness.* (19th cent.)

Thou art the incarnated Light
Whose Sire is aboriginal, and beyond

Death and resurgence of our day and
night;
From Him is thy vicegerent wand
With double potence of the black and
white.
Giver of love, and beauty, and desire,
The terror, and the loveliness, and
purging,
The deathfulness and lifefulness of
fire!

F. Thompson: *Orient Ode.* (19th cent.)

X—*Savior; Redeemer*

Neither the kingdoms of this world nor
the bounds of the universe have any use
for me. I would rather die for Jesus
Christ than rule the last reaches of the
earth. My search is for Him Who died
for us; my love is for Him Who rose for
our salvation.

St. Ignatius of Antioch: *Letter to the Romans,* 6. (2nd cent.)

From this hell upon earth there is no
escape, save through the grace of the
Savior Christ, our God and Lord. The
very name Jesus shows this, for it means
Savior; and He saves us especially from
passing out of this life into a more
wretched and eternal state, which is
rather a death than a life.

St. Augustine: *The City of God,* 22, 22. (5th cent.)

Christ is never conquered. . . . He hath
conquered in thy behalf, and he hath
conquered for thee, and He hath conquered in thee.

St. Augustine: *In Ps. 149,* 10. (5th cent.)

Dear Jesus, Savior of the world,
Our Savior be today;
Protect our hearts in darkness hurled,
And guide us in Thy way.

Pope St. Gregory I: *Salvator Mundi Domine.* (Tr. D. Donahoe) (Attr. to him, 6th cent.)

Jesus, our love, our Savior,
The joy of every heart,
Thou bringest light unto our night,
For Light itself Thou art.

What wealth of love o'ercame Thee
  That Thou shouldst will to die
Upon the tree of Calvary
  To save mankind thereby!

The night of sin is broken,
  The power of hell o'erthrown,
The heavenly door made wide once
    more
    By Thee, most holy One.

Anonymous: *Jesu Nostra Redemptio.* (Tr.
D. Donahoe) (Ambrosian, 7th or 8th
cent.)

O Jesu; our redemption!
  Loved and desired with tears!
God, of all worlds Creator!
  Man, in the close of years!

What wondrous pity moved Thee
  To make our cause thine own!
And suffer death and torments,
  For sinners to atone!

Hymn *Jesu Nostra Redemptio.* (Tr.
Caswall) (Ambrosian, 7th or 8th cent.)

A Helper and a Protector He has become to me unto salvation, my God, and
I will glorify Him; He is the God of my
father, and I will exalt Him, for He has
triumphed gloriously.

Byzantine Triodion, Great Canon of St.
Andrew of Crete. (8th cent.)

Hail! O Christ, the Word and Wisdom
and Power of God, and God omnipotent! What can we helpless ones give
Thee in return for all these good gifts
of thine? For all are Thine, and Thou
askest nothing from us except our salvation, Thou Who art Thyself the Giver
of this, and yet art grateful to those who
receive it through Thine unspeakable
goodness. Thanks be to Thee Who gave
us life, and granted us the grace of a
happy life, and restored us to that, when
we had gone astray, through Thine unspeakable condescension.

St. John of Damascus: *Exposition of the
Orthodox Faith,* 4, 4. (8th cent.)

I do not want to be a philosopher at the
price of being rejected by Paul; nor yet
an Aristotle at the price of being rejected by Christ, for there is no other
name under heaven whereby I can be
saved. I adore Christ reigning at the
Father's right hand. With the arms of
faith I embrace Him working divinely
in that glorious virginal flesh which He
received of the Holy Ghost.

Abelard. (12th cent.)

Christ, the Son of God Most High,
Suppliants unto Thee we cry;
By Thy love for her who bore Thee,
And with tenderest care watched o'er
    Thee,
Hearken to our lowly prayer;
Thou, our two-fold Savior, spare,
Fountain of our earthly pleasure,
And the soul's eternal treasure.
Though defiled by sin, we pray,
Wash Thou all our guilt away.

Pope Innocent III: *Christe fili summi
Patris.* (Tr. G. Cox) (12th cent.)

By a Carpenter mankind was created and
made, and by a Carpenter meet it was
that man should be repaired.

Erasmus: *Paraphrase of St. Mark.* (16th
cent.)

Christ, health of fever'd soul, heaven
  of the mind,
Force of the feeble, nurse of infant
  loves,
Guide to the wandring foot, light of
  the blind,
Whom weeping wins, repentant sorrow
  moves.
Father in care, mother in tender heart!
Revive and save me, slain with sinful
  dart.

Bl. Robert Southwell: *St. Peter's
Complaint.* (16th cent.)

O blessed God, O Savior sweet,
  O Jesus, look on me!
O Christ, my King, refuse me not,
  Though late I come to Thee!

I come to Thee, confounded quite
  With sorrow and with shame,
When I beheld Thy bitter wounds
  And knew I did the same.

Ven. Nicholas Postgate: *Hymn.* (17th
cent.)

Rock of ages, rent for me,
Let me hide myself in Thee;
Let the water and the blood,
From Thy riven side which flowed,
Be of sin the double cure;
Cleanse me from its guilt and power.

Anonymous: *Jesus pro me perforatus.*
(Tr. in Caswall's *Lyra Catholica*)
(Modern, ?)

We come to Thee, sweet Savior;
Just because we need Thee so:
None need Thee more than we do;
Nor are half so vile or low.

F. Faber: *We come to Thee sweet Savior.*
(19th cent.)

Every passage in the history of our Lord
and Savior is of unfathomable depth,
and affords inexhaustible matter of contemplation. All that concerns Him is infinite, and what we first discern is but
the surface of that which begins and
ends in eternity.

Card. Newman: *Discourses to Mixed
Congregations.* (19th cent.)

Come down, O Christ, and help me!
reach Thy hand,
For I am drowning in a stormier sea
Than Simon on Thy Lake of Galilee:
The wine of life is spilled upon the
sand.
My heart is as some famine-murdered
land
When all good things have perished
utterly,
And well I know my soul in hell
must lie
If I this night before God's throne
should stand.

Oscar Wilde: *E Tenebris.* (19th cent.)

Never to have known Jesus Christ in
any way is the greatest of misfortunes,
but it involves no perversity or ingratitude. But, after having known Him, to
reject or forget Him, is such a horrible
and mad crime as to be scarcely credible.
For He is the origin and source of all
good, and just as mankind could not be
freed from slavery but by the sacrifice

of Christ, so neither can it be preserved
but by His power.

Pope Leo XIII: *Tametsi.* (Nov. 1, 1900)

With this ambiguous earth
His dealings have been told us. There
abide:
The signal to a Maid, the human birth,
The lesson, and the young Man cruci-
fied.

Alice Meynell: *Christ in the Universe.*
(20th cent.)

Better God beaten and denied, than all
the world beside in prosperity.

R. H. Benson: *The Mirror of Shalott.*
(20th cent.)

To restore all things in Christ. (Instaurare omnia in Christo.) (Eph. 1, 10)

Motto of Pope St. Pius X for his
pontificate. (*E Supremi Apostolatus
Cathedra,* Oct. 4, 1903)

I see His blood upon the rose
And in the stars the glory of His eyes,
His body gleams amid eternal snows,
His tears fall from the skies.

Joseph M. Plunkett: *I See His Blood.*
(20th cent.)

XI—*The Way*

When we have traveled all ways, we
shall come to the End of all ways, who
says, *I am the way.*

St. Ambrose: *Explanation of Psalm 118,
5, 22.* (4th cent.)

Christ as God is the fatherland where
we are going, Christ as Man is the way
by which we go.

St. Augustine: *Sermon 124, 3.* (5th cent.)

The very acts of Christ are precepts.

Pope St. Gregory I: *Homilies on the
Gospels, 17, 1.* (6th cent.)

Christ's manner of life was shaped to
the purpose of His incarnation. He came
into the world, first, that He might pro-

claim the truth. . . . Secondly, He came that He might free men from sin. . . . Thirdly, He came that we might have *access to God* (Rom. 5, 2).

St. Thomas Aquinas: *Summa Theologica,* 3, 40, 1. (13th cent.)

Thou art the Way.
Hadst thou been nothing but the goal, I cannot say
If thou hadst ever met my soul.

I cannot see—
I, child of process—if there lies An end for me,
Full of repose, full of replies.

I'll not reproach
The road that winds, my feet that err, Access, Approach
Art thou, Time, Way, and Wayfarer.

Alice Meynell: *I am the Way.* (19th cent.)

You never attained to him? If to attain Be to abide, then that may be.
Endless the way, followed with how much pain!
The Way was He.

Alice Meynell: *Via, et Veritas, et Vita.* (20th cent.)

See also Advent; Ascension; Atonement; Blessed Sacrament; Christmas; Dead, The; Death; Easter; Eucharist; God; Good Friday; Grace; Hell, Descent into; Holy Family; Holy Saturday; Holy Thursday; Incarnation; Judgment (After Death); Judgment, Last; Mass; Name of Jesus; Passion of our Lord; Redemption; Resurrection; Salvation

Jews

The race of the Hebrews is not new but is honored among all men for its antiquity and is itself well known to all.

Eusebius of Caesarea: *Ecclesiastical History,* 1, 4, 5. (4th cent.)

O almighty and everlasting God, Who drivest not away from Thy mercy even the unbelieving Jews: hear our prayers which we offer for the blindness of that people; that acknowledging the light of Thy truth, which is Christ, they may be delivered from their darkness.

Roman Missal, Collect for Good Friday. (Gelasian, 5th to 7th cent.)

The Jews, a headstrong, moody, murm'ring race
As ever tried th' extent and stretch of grace;
God's pamper'd people, whom, debauch'd with ease,
No king could govern nor no God could please.

Dryden: *Absalom and Achitophel.* (17th cent.)

O piteous race!
Fearful to look upon,
Once standing in high place,
    Heaven's eldest son.
    O aged blind
Unvenerable! as thou flittest by,
I liken thee to him in pagan song,
    In thy gaunt majesty,
The vagrant king, of haughty-purposed mind
    Whom prayer nor plague could bend;
Wrong'd, at the cost of him who did the wrong,
Accursed himself, but in his cursing strong,
    And honor'd in his end.

Card. Newman: *Judaism.* (Reference is to Oedipus) (1833)

John the Apostle, Saint

John the Evangelist, among his fellows and companions the other Evangelists, received this special and peculiar gift from the Lord . . . that he should tell those things concerning the Son of God which may perhaps rouse the attentive minds of little ones, but cannot fill them since they are as yet not capable of receiving them; while to minds of somewhat larger growth, which have reached man's estate in the interior life, he gives with his words something whereby they may be both exercised and fed.

> St. Augustine: *In Joan. Evang.* 18, 1. (5th cent.)

Illumine Thy Church, O Lord, in thy goodness, that being enlightened by the teachings of Thy apostle and evangelist blessed John, it may attain to everlasting gifts.

> Roman Missal, Feast of St. John (Dec. 27), (Collect. Gregorian, similar prayer in Leon. Sacr., ca. 5th cent.)

The life which God's incarnate Word
   Lived here below with men,
Three blessed evangelists record,
   With heaven-inspired pen:

John penetrates on eagle wing
   The Father's dread abode;
And shows the mystery wherein
   The Word subsists with God.

            .   .   .   .

Oh, dear to Christ!—to thee upon
   His Cross, of all bereft,
Thou virgin soul! the Virgin Son
   His Virgin Mother left.

> Anonymous: *Quae dixit, egit, pertulit.* (Tr. Caswall) (17th cent.)

God is love! And of all men he knew
   best,
Who lay upon that breast,
And heard the beating of the heart of
   God:
Who Calvary trod,
And stood,
With Mary in her mourning mother-
   hood,
Beneath the rood.

> Lionel Johnson: *De Amicitia.* (19th cent.)

John the Baptist, Saint

O God, who hast made this day honorable for us by the birth of blessed John;
pour forth upon Thy people the grace
of spiritual joys, and direct the souls of
all the faithful into the ways of eternal
salvation.

> Roman Missal, Nativity of John the Baptist (June 24), Collect. (Leonine, ca. 5th cent.)

The great forerunner of the morn
The herald of the Word, is born:
And faithful hearts shall never fail
With thanks and praise his light to
   hail.

> St. Bede the Venerable: *Praecursor altus luminis.* (Tr. J. Neale) (8th cent.)

O for thy spirit, holy John, to chasten
Lips sin-polluted, fettered tongues to
   loosen;
So by thy children might thy deeds of
   wonder
   Meetly be chanted.

> Roman Breviary, Nativity of John the Baptist, Hymn *Ut queant laxis resonare fibris* at Vespers. (Tr. W. Blew) (Paul the Deacon, 8th cent.)

O sylvan prophet! whose eternal fame
Echoes from Judah's hills and Jordan's
   stream,
The music of our numbers raise,
And tune our voices to thy praise.

> Dryden: *Hymn for the Nativity of St. John the Baptist.* (17th cent.)

Jonson, Ben

Great Jonson needs no architect of
   wit;
Who forc'd from art, receiv'd from
   nature more
Than doth survive him, or e're liv'd
   before.

> William Habington: *Elegy Upon the Death of Ben Jonson.* (17th cent.)

He invades authors like a monarch; and
what would be theft in other poets, is
only victory in him.

> Dryden: *Essay of Dramatic Poesy.* (17th cent.)

Joseph, Saint

The Lord, then, was not of the seed of Joseph, though this was thought to be so; but yet to the piety and love of Joseph a Son was born of the Virgin Mary—He Who was also the Son of God.

St. Augustine: *Sermons,* 51. (5th cent.)

There is no doubt then that this Joseph, to whom the mother of the Savior was espoused, was a man good and preeminently faithful. A prudent and faithful servant he was, I say, whom the Lord placed beside Mary to be her protector, the nourisher of His human body, and the single and most trusty assistant on earth in His great design.

St. Bernard: *Sermon 2 in Vigil. Nativ. Domini,* 16. (12th cent.)

Though thou hast recourse to many saints as thine intercessors, go especially to St. Joseph, for he has great power with God.

St. Teresa of Jesus: *Maxims.* (16th cent.)

May we be helped by the merits of the spouse of Thy most holy Mother, we beseech thee, O Lord; so that what we cannot obtain of ourselves, may be given us through his intercession.

Roman Missal, Collect for Feast of St. Joseph (Mar. 19). (16th cent.)

Joseph, the praise and glory of the heavens,
Sure pledge of life, and safety of the wide world,
As in our joy we sing to thee, in kindness
List to our praises.

Roman Breviary, Feast of St. Joseph (Mar. 19), Hymn *Coelitum Joseph decus atque nostrae.* (Tr. A. McDougall) (Author unknown, 17th cent.)

Worshipped throughout the Church to earth's far ends
With prayer and solemn rite,

Joseph this day triumphantly ascends
Into the realms of light.

. . . .

There throned in power, let us his loving aid
With fervent prayers implore;
So may he gain us pardon in our need,
And peace for evermore.

Roman Breviary, Feast of St. Joseph, Hymn *Iste quem laeti colimus fideles.* (Tr. E. Caswall) (Unknown author, 17th cent.)

Let angels chant thy praise, pure spouse of purest bride,
While Christendom's sweet choirs the gladsome strains repeat,
To tell thy wondrous fame, to raise the peeling hymn,
Wherewith we all thy glory greet.

Roman Breviary, Feast of St. Joseph, Hymn *Te Joseph celebrent agmina coelitum.* (Tr. T. Potter) (Author unknown, 17th cent.)

To all, who would holily live,
To all, who would happily die,
St. Joseph is ready to give
Sure guidance and help from on high.

Anonymous: *Quicunque sanus vivere.* (Tr. Caswall) (19th cent.)

Dear husband of Mary! dear nurse of her Child!
Life's ways are full weary, the desert is wild;
Bleak sands are all round us, no home can we see;
Sweet spouse of our Lady! we lean upon thee.

F. Faber: *The Patronage of St. Joseph.* (19th cent.)

Hail! holy Joseph, hail!
Husband of Mary, hail!
Chaste as the lily flower
In Eden's peaceful vale.

Hail! holy Joseph, hail!
Father of Christ esteem'd!

Father be thou to those
Thy Foster-Son redeem'd.

F. Faber: *Hymn to St. Joseph*. (19th cent.)

O guardian and father of virgins, holy Joseph, to whose faithful care was committed Christ Jesus, very innocence itself, and Mary, the Virgin of virgins, I beg and beseech thee through this doubly dear pledge of Jesus and Mary, that, preserved from all uncleanness, thou mayest make me with an undefiled mind, a pure heart and a chaste body, to serve Jesus and Mary ever most chastely.

Roman Missal, Prayer after Mass. (19th cent.?)

O God, Who hast given us a royal priesthood, vouchsafe, we beseech Thee, that as blessed Joseph was found worthy to touch His hands and to bear in his arms Thy only-begotten Son, born of the Virgin Mary, so may we be made fit, by cleanness of heart and blamelessness of life, to minister at Thy holy altar; may we this day with reverent devotion partake of the sacred Body and Blood of Thy only-begotten Son, and may we in the world to come be accounted worthy to receive an everlasting reward.

Roman Missal, Prayer before Mass. (19th cent.?)

O God, Who in Thine unspeakable providence didst vouchsafe to choose blessed Joseph for Thy most holy Mother's spouse; grant, we beseech Thee, that we who revere him as our protector on earth, may be worthy to have him for our intecessor in heaven.

Roman Missal, Patronage of St. Joseph (Wed. after 2nd Sunday after Easter), Collect. (1847)

Joseph, honored from sea to sea,
This is your name that pleases me,
Man of the house.

. . . .

Father of Jesus, husband of Mary,
Hold up your lilies for sanctuary!

Joseph, honored from sea to sea,
Guard me mine and my own rooftree.
Man of the house!

Katharine Tynan Hinkson: *The Man of the House*. (20th cent.)

Journalism

As the great man's guest must produce his good stories or songs at the evening banquet, as the platform orator exhibits his telling facts at midday, so the journalist lies under the stern obligation of extemporizing his lucid views, leading ideas and nutshell truths for the breakfast table.

Card. Newman: *Idea of a University*, Pref. (19th cent.)

It is always the unreadable that occurs.

Oscar Wilde: *The Decay of Lying*. (19th cent.)

In America the president reigns for four years, and journalism governs for ever and ever.

Oscar Wilde: *The Soul of a Man under Socialism*. (19th cent.)

In old days men had the rack. Now they have the press.

Oscar Wilde: *The Soul of a Man under Socialism*. (19th cent.)

We do not need a censorship of the press. We have a censorship by the press.

G. K. Chesterton: *Orthodoxy*. (20th cent.)

What is really the matter with almost every paper is that it is much too full of things suitable to the paper.

G. K. Chesterton: *Autobiography*. (20th cent.)

Joy

Clothe yourself with cheerfulness, which always finds favor with God and is acceptable to Him.

Shepherd of Hermas, Mandate 10, 3, 1. (2nd cent.)

All seek joy, but it is not found on earth.

> St. John Chrysostom: *Homilies*. (4th cent.)

Grant us, we beseech Thee, O Lord our God, ever to rejoice in devotion to Thee; because our happiness is perpetual and full, if we are continually serving the Author of all good.

> Leonine Sacramentary, Collect. (ca. 5th cent.)

Joy is heightened by the contrast of torment, as the black background of a picture makes the white or red stand out more clearly.

> Pope St. Gregory I: *Homilies on the Gospels*, 40, 8. (6th cent.)

Let the brothers ever avoid appearing gloomy, sad, and clouded, like the hypocrites; but let one ever be found joyous in the Lord, gay, amiable, gracious, as is meet.

> St. Francis. (13th cent.)

For ever the latter end of joy is woe,
God wot that worldly joy is soon ago.

> Chaucer: *The Nonne Preests Tale*. (14th cent.)

Your heart hangeth on a joly pin.

> Chaucer: *The Marchantes Tale*. (14th cent.)

As merry as three chips.

> John Heywood: *Proverbs*, 1, 7. (16th cent.)

Merry as a cricket.

> John Heywood: *Proverbs*, 1, 11. (16th cent.)

Merry as a pie.

> John Heywood: *Proverbs*, 2, 3. (16th cent.)

The mo the merrier.

> John Heywood: *Proverbs*, 2, 7. (16th cent.)

It is merry in hall when beards wag all.

> John Heywood: *Proverbs*, 2, 7. (16th cent.)

Better is one month's cheer, than a churl's whole life.

> John Heywood: *Proverbs*, 2, 7. (16th cent.)

No joy so great, but runneth to an end;
No hap so hard, but may in fine amend.

. . . .

Unmedled joys here to no man befall;
Who least, hath some, who most, hath never all.

> Bl. Robert Southwell: *Times Go by Turns*. (16th cent.)

Be merry and be wise.

> Sir William Davenant: *Man's the Master, Prol.* (17th cent.)

For present joys are more to flesh and blood
Than a dull prospect of a distant good.

> Dryden: *The Hind and the Panther*, 3. (17th cent.)

Joy rul'd the day, and love the night.

> Dryden: *The Secular Masque*. (17th cent.)

Oh stay! oh stay!
Joy so seldom weaves a chain
Like this tonight, that oh 'tis pain
To break its links so soon.

> Thomas Moore: *Fly not Yet*. (19th cent.)

And joy, like a mew sea-rocked apart,
Tossed on the waves of his troubled heart.

> F. Thompson: *The Poppy*. (19th cent.)

The *carpe diem* religion is not the religion of happy people, but of very unhappy people. Great joy does not gather the rose buds while it may; its eyes are fixed on the immortal rose which Dante saw. Great joy has in it the sense of immortality; the very splendor of youth is the sense that it has all space to stretch its legs in.

> G. K. Chesterton: *Heretics.* (20th cent.)

Joy, which was the small publicity of the pagan, is the gigantic secret of the Christian. . . . The tremendous figure which fills the Gospels towers in this respect, as in every other, above all the thinkers who ever thought themselves tall. His pathos was natural, almost casual. The Stoics, ancient and modern, were proud of concealing their tears; He showed them plainly on His open face at any daily sight, such as the far sight of His native city. Yet He concealed something. . . . There was something that He hid from all men when He went up a mountain to pray. There was something that He covered constantly by abrupt silence or impetuous isolation. There was some one thing that was too great for God to show us when He walked upon our earth; and I have sometimes fancied that it was His mirth.

> G. K. Chesterton: *Orthodoxy.* (20th cent.)

See also Contentment; Happiness

Joy and Sorrow

To everyone of us joy or sorrow pays its respects in turn.

> John of Salisbury: *Policraticus,* 3, Pref. (12th cent.)

But, ah! how unsincere are all our joys!
Which, sent from heav'n, like lightning, make no stay:
Their palling taste the journey's length
  destroys,
Or grief, sent post, o'ertakes them on
  the way.

> Dryden: *Annus Mirabilis.* (17th cent.)

Joy is life's tree—grief but its leaf.

> Abram Ryan: *Lines.* (19th cent.)

Man is more himself, man is more man-like, when joy is the fundamental thing in him, and grief the superficial. Mel-ancholy should be an innocent interlude, a tender and fugitive frame of mind; praise should be the permanent pulsation of the soul. Pessimism is at best an emotional half-holiday; joy is the uproarious labor by which all things live.

> G. K. Chesterton: *Orthodoxy.* (20th cent.)

Jubilee

> Though no high-hung bells or din
> Of braggart bugles cry it in—
>   What is sound? Nature's round
> Makes the Silver Jubilee.
>
> Five and twenty years have run
> Since sacred fountains to the sun
>   Sprang, that but now were shut,
> Showering Silver Jubilee.
>
> G. M. Hopkins: *The Silver Jubilee.* (19th cent.)

Judaism

It is out of place to preach Jesus Christ and to practise Judaism. For Christianity did not believe in Judaism, but Judaism in Christianity; it was in the latter that men of every tongue believed and were gathered together in God.

> St. Ignatius of Antioch: *Letter to the Magnesians,* 10. (2nd cent.)

See also Jews

Judas

> Judas he japed with Jewen silver,
> And sithen on an elder hanged himself.
>
> Langland: *Piers Plowman,* Passus 1. (14th cent.)

It does seem to me that one of the reasons why our Lord chose Judas to be an apostle was because He wanted us to be prepared, from the first, against every possible shock to our consciences. If Judas could be described as our Lord's apostle, I don't quite see why Alexander VI should not be His vicar.

> R. A. Knox: *Difficulties.* (20th cent.)

Judge

Christian judge, fulfil the duty of a devoted father; be angry at wickedness, yet forget not humane considerations, and do not give rein to the desire to seek revenge for the atrocity of their sinful deeds, but exert your will to the curing of the sores of the sinners.

St. Augustine: *Letter 133* (to the tribune Marcellinus, with regard to the repression of the Circumcellions, heretics and malefactors). (5th cent.)

See also Jesus Christ—Eternal Judge; Judgment, Last

Judgment

Hear the other side. (Audi alteram partem.)

St. Augustine: *De Duabus Animabus,* 14, 22. (Proverb) (4th cent.)

O mortal men, be wary how ye judge.

Dante: *Paradiso, Canto* 20. (14th cent.)

Often, if we followed our own impressions, the devil would make us see many truths to lead us into falsehood; and this, because we make ourselves judges of the minds of our fellow creatures, which are for God alone to judge.

St. Catherine of Siena: *Letter to Sister Daniella.* (14th cent.)

A man should hear all parts ere he judge any.

John Heywood: *Proverbs,* 1, 13. (16th cent.)

If we judge ourselves, we will not be judged by God.

Jean Pierre Camus: *The Spirit of St. Francis de Sales,* 2, 14. (17th cent.)

Those who look well after their own consciences rarely fall into the sin of judging others.

Jean Pierre Camus: *The Spirit of St. Francis de Sales,* 2, 15. (17th cent.)

'Tis with our judgment as with our watches: none
Go just alike, yet each believes his own.

Pope: *An Essay on Criticism,* 1. (18th cent.)

It is one of the conditions inseparable from a public career to be often misunderstood, and sometimes judged unfairly even when understood the best.

Lord Acton: *Cardinal Wiseman.* (19th cent.)

We are not here to judge, but to give our own account.

R. H. Benson: *The King's Achievement.* (20th cent.)

It is manifestly most unreasonable that intelligent men should be divided upon the absurd modern principle of regarding every clever man who cannot make up his mind as an impartial judge, and regarding every clever man who can make up his mind as a servile fanatic. As it is, we seem to regard it as a positive objection to a reasoner that he has taken one side or the other. We regard it (in other words) as a positive objection to a reasoner that he has contrived to reach the object of his reasoning. We call a man a bigot or a slave of dogma because he is a thinker who has thought thoroughly and to a definite end.

G. K. Chesterton: *All Things Considered.* (20th cent.)

Judgment, Private

Private judgment in matters of faith is nothing else than the beginning of disintegration.

R. H. Benson: *Lord of the World.* (20th cent.)

The Catholic does not appeal to authority to support his belief in authority, among other reasons because the great medieval theologians had learned from Aristotle not to argue in a circle. It is only when the Catholic has established by reason the existence of an infallible

Church that he surrenders his private judgment to the judgment of the Church, on those points, and on those points only, on which the Church speaks with the voice of God. In all other questions private judgment still remains supreme.

Arnold Lunn: *Now I See.* (20th cent.)

Judgment, Particular

O Lord, do not bring Thy servant to trial, for no man becomes holy in Thy sight unless Thou dost grant him forgiveness of all his sins. We implore Thee therefore do not let the verdict of Thy judgment go against him, whom the loyal prayer of Christian faith is commending to Thy mercy, but rather by the help of Thy grace may he escape the sentence which he deserves, for during his earthly life he was signed with the seal of the Holy Trinity; Who livest and reignest forever. Amen.

Roman Ritual, Burial Service, Prayer *Non intres in judicium.* (Gregorian, 6th to 8th cent.)

You see me lying speechless and breathless before you. Weep over me, O brethren, friends, relatives, and acquaintances. For yesterday I was conversing with you, but the dread hour of death came upon me all of a sudden. But, now, all my friends who have loved me and held me dear, give me your last farewell kiss; for I shall no longer walk with you, or talk with you. I go before the Judge, Who knows no favorites. Both slave and master stand before Him, king and soldier, rich and poor, equal in all respects. Each shall be rewarded with glory or shame according to his deeds. So I beseech you all, pray to Christ our God for me without ceasing, that I may not be sentenced to the place of punishment for my sins, but that I may be established in the light of eternal life.

Byzantine Euchologion, Funeral Service, Farewell Troparion at the Grave. (St. John of Damascus ?, 8th cent.)

O God, Who alone art ever merciful and sparing of punishment, we pray Thee humbly in behalf of Thy servant, N., whom Thou hast commanded to go forth today from this world. Do not hand him over to the power of the enemy and do not forget him forever; but command that his soul be taken up by the holy angels and brought home to paradise, so that, since he hoped and believed in Thee, he may not undergo the punishments of hell, but rather possess everlasting joys.

Roman Ritual, Burial Service, Prayer *Deus qui proprium.* (ca. 10th cent. ?; similar Gelasian collect, ca. 6th cent.)

Immediately after death the soul stands before the tribunal of Christ, to face the particular judgment. . . . At the particular judgment the soul will be judged about every single thing—its thoughts, words, deeds, and omissions. The sentence then passed on the soul will be ratified at the General Judgment, when it will be made publicly manifest.

Card. Gasparri: *The Catholic Catechism.* (20th cent.)

Judgment, Last

The prophets have foretold two comings of Christ: the one, which has already taken place, was that of a dishonored and suffering Man; the other coming will take place, as it is predicted, when He shall gloriously come from heaven with His angelic army, when He shall also raise to life the bodies of all the men that ever were, shall cloak the worthy with immortality, and shall relegate the wicked, subject to sensible pain for all eternity, into the eternal fire with the evil demons.

St. Justin Martyr: *First Apology,* 52. (2nd cent.)

What exultation will that be of the angels, what glory that of the saints as they rise again! What the reign of the righteous thereafter! What a city, the New Jerusalem! Yes, and there are still to come other spectacles—that last, that eternal Day of Judgment, that Day which the Gentiles never believed would come, that Day they laughed at, when this old world and all its generations shall be consumed in one fire.

Tertullian: *De Spectaculis*, 30. (ca. 197)

Dost thou believe in Christ Jesus, the Son of God, Who . . . ascended into heaven, and sat down at the right hand of the Father, and will come to judge the living and the dead?

St. Hippolytus: *The Apostolic Tradition*, 21. (Question put to those being baptized; still part of baptism ritual.) (3rd cent.)

Oh, what and how great will that day be at its coming, beloved brethren, when the Lord shall begin to count up His people, and to recognize the merits of each one by the inspection of His divine knowledge, to send the guilty to gehenna, and to set on fire persecutors with the perpetual burning of a penal fire, but to pay to us the reward of our faith and devotion!

St. Cyprian: *Letters*, 55, 10. (3rd cent.)

Believe . . . that He is to return, glorious and illustrious, to exercise judgment on the living and the dead, not indeed in His former fleshly form, nor yet without a body, but with a body more august and more divine such as He alone knew.

St. Gregory Nazianzen: *Oratio 45.* (4th cent.)

But when we shall have come to that judgment, the date of which is called peculiarly the day of judgment, and sometimes the day of the Lord, we shall then recognize the justice of all God's judgments, not only of such as shall then be pronounced, but of all which take effect from the beginning, or may take effect before that time.

St. Augustine: *The City of God*, 20, 2. (5th cent.)

To fear the day of judgment.

St. Benedict: *Rule*, 4. (One of his 'tools of good works') (6th cent.)

O God, when Thou shalt come on earth with glory, when all shall quake, when a fiery river shall draw all before Thy judgment seat, when the books shall be opened and all secrets revealed; then do Thou save me from the unquenchable fire, and grant that I may stand at Thy right hand, O righteous Judge.

Byzantine Triodion, Apokreos Sunday (Sexagesima), Kontakion. (St. Romanos the Melodist, 6th cent.)

That great day of wrath and terror,
   The last day of woe and doom,
Like a thief that comes at midnight,
   On the sons of men shall come.

Anonymous: *Apparebit repentina dies magna Domini.* (Tr. J. Neale) (6th cent.)

Day of the King most righteous,
   The day is nigh at hand,
The day of wrath and vengeance,
   And darkness on the land.

Day of thick clouds and voices,
   Of mighty thundering,
A day of narrow anguish
   And bitter sorrowing.

The love of women's over,
   And ended is desire,
Men's strife with men is quiet,
   And the world lusts no more.

St. Columba: *Regis regum rectissimi.* (Tr. H. Waddell) (Irish Liber Hymnorum, 6th cent.)

That fearful day, that day of speech-
      less dread,
When Thou shalt come to judge the
      quick and dead—
   I shudder to foresee,
   O God! what then shall be!

When Thou shalt come, angelic legions
      round,
With thousand thousands, and with
      trumpet sound,
   Christ, grant me in the air
   With saints to meet me there!

         .   .   .   .

God comes;—and who shall stand be-
      fore his fear?

Who bide His presence, when He
    draweth near
My soul, my soul, prepare
To kneel before Him there!

Haste,—weep,—be reconcil'd to Him
    before
The fearful judgment knocketh at the
    door:
    Where, in the Judge's eyes,
    All, bare and naked, lies.

> Byzantine Triodion, Canon for Sexagesima
> Sunday. (Tr. J. Neale) (St. Theodore of
> the Studium) (9th cent.)

How fearful shall Thy judgment be, O
Lord, when angels stand around and
men be there, when the books be opened
and our actions shown, and our intentions tried. What then shall be Thy sentence, for I was born in sin? Who shall
quench the flame for me? Who shall
make my darkness light, if Thou, O
Lord, the Lover of mankind, do not have
mercy on me?

> Byzantine Horologion, Troparion at Great
> Compline (ca. 9th cent. ?)

Deliver me, O Lord, from everlasting
death on that day of terror: When the
heavens and the earth will be shaken:
As Thou dost come to judge the world
by fire. ℣. I am in fear and trembling at
the judgment and the wrath that is to
come, when the heavens and the earth
will be shaken. ℣. That day will be a
day of wrath, of misery, and of ruin: a
day of grandeur and great horror: As
Thou dost come to judge the world by
fire. ℣. Eternal rest grant unto them, O
Lord, and let perpetual light shine upon
them. Deliver me. . . .

> Roman Ritual, Burial Service, Responsory
> *Libera me Domine.* (Based on Soph. 1, 15.
> Cf. hymn *Dies Irae.*) (ca. 10th cent. ?)

The world is very evil;
The times are waxing late;
Be sober and keep vigil,
The Judge is at the gate;

The Judge that comes in mercy,
The Judge that comes with might,

To terminate the evil,
And diadem the right.

> Bernard of Cluny: *Hora novissima!* (From
> poem *'De Contemptu Mundi'*) (Tr. J.
> Neale) (12th cent.)

Judgment cannot be pronounced on a
man until he has run his course.

> St. Thomas Aquinas: *Summa Theologica,*
> 3, 59, 5. (13th cent.)

Day of wrath and doom impending,
David's word with Sibyl's blending!
Heaven and earth in ashes ending!

O, what fear man's bosom rendeth,
When from heaven the Judge de-
    scendeth,
On Whose sentence all dependeth!

Wondrous sound the trumpet flingeth,
Through the earth's sepulchers it
    ringeth,
All before the throne it bringeth.

> Roman Missal, Requiem Mass, Sequence
> *Dies irae dies illa.* (Tr. W. Irons)
> (Thomas of Celano, 13th cent.)

No more from that bed
He wakes until the angel trumpet
    sounds
When the stern Power shall make
    His advent dread.
They shall revisit then their sad grave-
    mounds,
    And each his flesh and his own
        shape resume,
    And hear what through eternity re-
        sounds.

> Dante: *Inferno, Canto 6.* (Tr. Binyon)
> (14th cent.)

No sorrow then shall enter in
With pity the great Judge's ears.
This moment's ours. Once dead, his sin
Men cannot expiate with tears.

> William Habington: *Quoniam Ego in
> Flagella Paratus Sum.* (17th cent.)

The day that is past must not judge the
day present, nor the present day judge

that which is past; it is only the last day that judges all.

St. Francis de Sales: *Introduction to the Devout Life*, 3, 29. (17th cent.)

When rattling bones together fly
From the four corners of the sky.

John Dryden: *Ode to the Memory of Mrs. Anne Killegrew*. (17th cent.)

Rise, O Lord, in all Thy glory
  On the last and dreadful day:
Lo! the lofty hills are hoary
  Trembling ere they melt away:
Come to judgment, come to judgment,
  Let Thy wheels no longer stay.

Hymn *Dies finalis*. (Tr. M. Bridges) (Modern ?)

That day of doom,
One and the same for the collected
  world—
That solemn consummation for all
  flesh,
Is, in the case of each, anticipate
Upon his death.

Card. Newman: *The Dream of Gerontius*. (19th cent.)

Souls are like wax waiting for a seal. By themselves they have no special identity. Their destiny is to be softened and prepared in this life, by God's will, to receive, at their death, the seal of their own degree of likeness to God in Christ. And this is what it means, among other things, to be judged by Christ. The wax that has melted in God's will can easily receive the stamp of its identity, the truth of what it was meant to be. But the wax that is hard and dry and brittle and without love will not take the seal: for the seal, falling upon it, grinds it to powder.

Thomas Merton: *Seeds of Contemplation*. (20th cent.)

There is a certain false mysticism which likes to gloat over the prospect of a last judgment in which the whole history of mankind will fall into oblivion under the anathema of an enraged God. But the true Christian viewpoint is that which looks forward to the last judgment as the clarification and vindication of human history.

Thomas Merton: *The Living Bread*. (20th cent.)

June

        The fair
Tanned face of June, the nomad gypsy,
  laughs
Above her widespread wares, the while
  she tells
The farmers' fortunes in the fields, and
  quaffs
The water from the spider-peopled
  wells.

Francis Ledwidge: *June*. (20th cent.)

O you poor folks in cities,
A thousand thousand pities!
Heaping the fairy gold that withers
  and dies;
One field in the June weather
Is worthy all the gold ye gather,
One field in June weather—one Paradise.

Katharine T. Hinkson: *June Song*. (20th cent.)

Jury

The man who laugh'd but once, to see
  an ass
Mumbling to make the cross-grain'd
  thistles pass;
Might laugh again, to see a jury chaw
The prickles of an unpalatable law.

Dryden: *The Medal*. (17th cent.)

The hungry judges soon the sentence
  sign,
And wretches hang that jurymen may
  dine.

Pope: *The Rape of the Lock*, 3. (18th cent.)

Our civilization has decided, and very justly decided, that determining the guilt or innocence of men is a thing too important to be trusted to trained men.

It wishes for light upon that awful matter, it asks men who know no more law than I know, but who can feel the things that I felt in the jury-box. When it wants a library catalogued, or the solar system discovered, or any trifle of that kind, it uses up its specialists. But when it wishes anything done which is really serious, it collects twelve of the ordinary men standing round. The same thing was done, if I remember right, by the Founder of Christianity.

> G. K. Chesterton: *Tremendous Trifles*, 11. (20th cent.)

Just

What is against truth cannot be just.

> St. Augustine: *To Consentius, Against Lying.* (5th cent.)

Whatever is, is in its causes just.

> Dryden: *Oedipus*, 3, 1. (17th cent.)

Justice

The piety of justice is first exercised towards God; secondly, towards one's country; next, towards parents; lastly, towards all.

> St. Ambrose: *On the Duties of the Clergy,* 1, 127. (4th cent.)

The rule of justice is plain, namely, that a good man ought not to swerve from the truth, not to inflict any unjust loss on anyone, nor to act in any way deceitfully or fraudulently.

> St. Ambrose: *On the Duties of the Clergy,* 3, 73. (4th cent.)

Justice . . . is the virtue that gives to each his due.

> St. Augustine: *On Freewill*, 1, 27. (Quoting a maxim of Roman law.) (4th cent.)

Let justice be done though the world perish.

> St. Augustine. (5th cent.)

I have loved justice and hated iniquity; therefore I die an exile.

> Pope St. Gregory VII. (Last words) (11th cent.)

Justice is the will to attribute to each his due. It is full and complete in God, but in us is called justice by participation.

> Fragmentum Pragense, 3, 9. (In Carlyle, Med. Polit. Theory, II 10.) (11th cent.)

Justice is a certain rectitude of mind whereby a man does what he ought to do in the circumstances confronting him.

> St. Thomas Aquinas: *Summa Theologica,* 61. (13th cent.)

Two main reasons why men fall short of justice—deference to magnates, deference to the mob.

> St. Thomas Aquinas: *Commentary on Job,* 34, lect. 2. (13th cent.)

For justice is not brought down from its height,
  Because in an instant burning love can here
  Redeem the debt these souls have to requite.

> Dante: *Purgatorio, Canto 6.* (Tr. Binyon) (14th cent.)

  The Primal Will,
  In itself good, to its own self, which is
  The Sovereign Good, forever cleaveth still,
All then is just which is attuned to this;
  To no created good does it adhere,
  But from its radiance is that good's increase.

> Dante: *Paradiso, Canto 19.* (Tr. Binyon) (14th cent.)

Justice is what is established.

> Pascal: *Pensées*, 7. (17th cent.)

A prince's favors on but few can fall,
But justice is a virtue shared by all.

> Dryden. (17th cent.)

Justice and Equity

Justice differs from equity, for equity is observed in things themselves; when equity leaves the will and takes form, it becomes justice.

> Irnerius: *Gloss on the Digest,* 1, 1. (12th cent.)

Justification

And we also, having been called through His will in Christ Jesus, are not justified by ourselves, or by our own wisdom or understanding or piety or the works we have done in holiness of heart, but through the faith, by which Almighty God has justified all men from the beginning; to Whom be glory for all ages. Amen.

> Pope St. Clement I: *Letter to the Corinthians,* 32, 4. (1st cent.)

We shall then be made truly free when God fashions us, that is, forms and creates us, not as men, which He has already done, but as good men, which He now does by his grace, in order that we may be *a new creature in Christ* according to the words: *Create a clean heart in me, O God.*

> St. Augustine: *Enchiridion,* 31. (5th cent.)

The sinner is justified by God moving him to righteousness; *it is God that justifieth the ungodly* (Rom. 4, 5). Now God moves all things according to the mode of each. . . . In those who can exercise their freewill the motion from God to righteousness is not without a motion of freewill; He infuses justifying grace in such wise that He moves at the same time the freewill to accept the gift.

> St. Thomas Aquinas: *Summa Theologica,* 1-2, 113, 3. (13th cent.)

If any one saith that man may be justified before God by his own works, whether done through the teaching of human nature or that of the law, without the grace of God through Jesus Christ; let him be anathema.

> Council of Trent, Session 6, Canon 1. (Jan. 13, 1547)

If any one saith that without the prevenient inspiration of the Holy Ghost and without His help man can believe, hope, love, or be penitent as he ought, so as that the grace of justification may be bestowed upon him; let him be anathema.

> Council of Trent, Session 6, Canon 3. (Jan. 13, 1547)

If any one saith that by faith alone the impious is justified, in such wise as to mean that nothing else is required to cooperate in order to the obtaining the grace of justification, and that it is not in any way necessary that he be prepared and disposed by the movement of his own will; let him be anathema.

> Council of Trent, Session 6, Canon 9. (Jan. 13, 1547)

If any man saith that men are justified either by the sole imputation of the justice of Christ or by the sole remission of sins to the exclusion of the grace and *the charity which is poured forth in their hearts by the Holy Ghost* (Rom. 5, 5), and is inherent in them; or even that the grace whereby we are justified is only the favor of God; let him be anathema.

> Council of Trent, Session 6, Canon 11. (Jan. 13, 1547)

If any man saith that justifying faith is nothing else but confidence in the divine mercy which remits sins for Christ's sake; or that this confidence alone is that whereby we are justified; let him be anathema.

> Council of Trent, Session 6, Canon 12. (Jan. 13, 1547)

If any one saith that he who has fallen after baptism is not able by the grace of God to rise again; or that he is able indeed to recover the justice which he has lost, but by faith alone without the sacrament of penance, contrary to what the holy Roman and universal Church—instructed by Christ and His apostles—has hitherto professed, observed, and taught; let him be anathema.

> Council of Trent, Session 6, Canon 29. (Jan. 13, 1547)

In like manner *Christ in us* is said to be *the hope of glory.* Christ then is our righteousness by dwelling in us by the Spirit: He justifies us by entering into us, He continues to justify us by remaining in us. This is really and truly our justification, not faith, not holiness, not (much less) a mere imputation; but through God's mercy, the very presence of Christ.

> Card. Newman: *Lectures on Justification.* (19th cent.)

Justinian I, Emperor

Caesar I was, and am Justinian,
    Who by the will of Primal Love possessed
Pruned from the laws the unneeded and the vain.

> Dante: *Paradiso, Canto 6.* (With reference to his codification of Roman law) (Tr. Binyon) (14th cent.)

K

Keys, Power of the

See Confession; Penance; Peter, Saint; Sin, Remission of

Kicking

It is contrary to decency and to Christian mildness to kick anyone, no matter who it may be.

> St. John Baptist de la Salle: *The Rules of Christian Manners and Civility,* 1. (17th cent.)

Don't kick till you're spurred.

> Seumas MacManus: *Heavy Hangs the Golden Grain.* (20th cent.)

Kindness

Be kind to all and severe to thyself.

> St. Teresa of Jesus: *Maxims.* (16th cent.)

One kind word wins more willing service than a hundred harsh orders or stern reproofs.

> J. P. Camus: *The Spirit of St. Francis de Sales,* 7, 9. (17th cent.)

Kind as kings upon their coronation day.

> Dryden: *The Hind and the Panther,* 1. (17th cent.)

Who does a kindness is not therefore kind;
Perhaps prosperity becalmed his breast;
Perhaps the wind just shifted from the East.

> Pope: *Moral Essays,* 2. (18th cent.)

Then within my bosom
Softly this I heard:
Each heart holds the secret;
Kindness is the word.

> J. B. O'Reilly: *What is Good?* (19th cent.)

The kind need kindness most of all.

Katharine T. Hinkson: *The Daughter of the Manor.* (20th cent.)

King

. . . Kings [i.e. of the Jews] also, at the bidding of God, were made christs in a certain symbolism by the prophets who anointed them, inasmuch as they also bore in themselves the types of the royal and sovereign power of the only true Christ, the divine Logos Who reigns over all.

Eusebius of Caesarea: *Ecclesiastical History,* 1, 3, 7. (4th cent.)

We beseech thee, almighty God, that Thy servant N., our king, who by Thy mercy has assumed the government of the kingdom, may also be granted an increase in all the virtues; worthily adorned with them, may he succeed in avoiding the enormity of all vices and with Thy favor attain to Thee, Who art the Way, the Truth, and the Life.

Roman Missal, Collect for the King. (Gregorian, 6th to 8th cent.)

O God, the Protector of all kingdoms and especially of the Christian empire; grant to Thy servants our kings NN. to cultivate the triumph of Thy virtue by their knowledge, that as they have been constituted princes by Thy disposition, so may they always be powerful by Thy gift.

Gregorian Sacramentary, Collect. (6th to 8th cent.)

King is so called from ruling. But he does not rule who does not correct. The name of king therefore is held by him who does right, and is lost by him who sins. Whence there was this proverb among the ancients: You will be king if you do right; but you will not be if you do not. The royal virtues are principally two: justice and piety. Piety is the more praised in kings, for justice is of itself a severer virtue.

St. Isidore: *Etymologies,* 9, 3. (7th cent.)

What are impious kings but the great robbers of the earth, fierce as lions, ravening like wolves; but they are great today and perish tomorrow, and of them God has said: *They reigned, but not by Me; they arose as princes, but I knew it not.*

Sedulius Scotus: *On Christian Rulers,* 8. (9th cent.)

It is the king's chief duty to govern the people of God and rule them with equity and justice, and to strive that they may have peace and concord. For he must first of all be a defender of the churches and servants of God. Kings have a duty to look out for the safety and work of the clergy, and the Church of Christ should be guarded by their arms and protection; the want of widows, orphans, the poor, and indeed all the needy should be warded off.

Jonas of Orleans: *On the Institution of Kings,* 4. (9th cent.)

Therefore, O king, love justice and judgment, the royal road, which has been trodden by former kings from of old. . . . But temper justice and diligently guard against left-handed cruelty. . . . If you wish your throne to be firmly established by the Lord, O king, do not cease to do justice to the poor and the orphaned.

Smaragdus: *The Royal Way,* 8-9. (9th cent.)

Therefore, as the royal dignity and power excels all other earthly powers, so the most wicked and disgraceful should not be chosen to exercise it, but he who in rank and dignity as well as in wisdom, justice and piety surpasses all others. It is necessary that he who is to have the care of all, who is to rule over all, should be resplendent with the grace of virtues above others, that he may administer the power entrusted to him with the highest measure of equity. For the people do not exalt him above themselves, that he may be given free rein to exercise tyranny over them, but that he may defend them from the tyranny and wrongdoing of others.

Manegold of Lauterbach: *Ad Gebehardum,* 30. (11th cent.)

This is the only or greatest difference between a prince and a tyrant, that the prince obeys the law and governs the people, whose servant he reckons himself to be, according to the rule of law. . . . The power of all his subjects is rightfully conferred on him, that he may be empowered to seek out and to do what is best for the welfare of each and all, and that he may make the best dispositions with regard to the human commonwealth. . . . According to the emperor [Justinian] it is a saying worthy of the majesty of a ruler for a prince to acknowledge that he is bound by the laws. For the authority of the prince depends on the authority of the law; and it is a greater thing than empire to submit the princely authority to the laws (Code, 1, 14, 4).

John of Salisbury: *Policraticus,* 4, 1. (12th cent.)

The prince is said to be freed from the bonds of the law, not that he may do evil, but because it is his essential responsibility to do justice not from fear of any penalty but from love of justice, to further the welfare of the state, and in everything to prefer the wellbeing of others to his own private will. . . . The prince is the minister of the public utility and servant of equity, and in himself represents the person of the state, because he punishes all injuries, damages, and crimes with equity.

John of Salisbury: *Policraticus,* 4, 2. (12th cent.)

But the king should not be under any man, only under God and the law, for the law makes the king. Let the king therefore attribute to the law what the law attributes to him, namely lordship and power, for there is no king where will rules and not law.

Bracton: *On the Laws and Customs of England,* 1, 8, 5. (13th cent.)

The king should swear by oath at his coronation in the name of Jesus Christ to promise these three things to the people under him. First, that he will see to it and do what in him lies that true peace may be enjoyed by the Church of God and all Christian people in his time; secondly, that he will forbid rapine and all wrongdoing among all classes; thirdly, that in all his judgments he will ordain equity and mercy, that God in His mercy and clemency may show him mercy and that all may enjoy lasting peace through his justice.

Bracton: *On the Laws and Customs of England,* 3, 9, 2. (13th cent.)

The idea of king implies that he be one man who is chief and that he be a shepherd who seeks the common good of the multitude and not his own advantage.

St. Thomas Aquinas: *The Governance of Rulers,* 1, 1. (13th cent.)

How many above there deem themselves great kings
   Now, who shall lie wallowing in mire like swine,
   Leaving a name that with dishonor rings!

Dante: *Inferno, Canto 8.* (Tr. Binyon) (14th cent.)

The king never dies. (Rex numquam moritur.)

Legal Maxim. (Medieval)

The king is dead, long live the king! (Le roi est mort, vive le roi!)

Formula used by herald at arms under the *ancien régime,* when he announced the death of the king and the accession of his successor from the balcony of the palace. (Medieval)

The king can do no wrong. (Rex non potest peccare.)

Legal Maxim. (Medieval)

In counsel giving unto his grace, ever tell him what he ought to do, but never tell him what he is able to do, so shall you shew yourself a true faithful servant, and a right worthy counsellor. For if the lion knew his own strength, hard were it for any man to rule him.

St. Thomas More: *Advice to Thomas Cromwell.* (Roper's *Life*) (16th cent.)

This hath not offended the king.

St. Thomas More. (As he drew his beard aside before placing his head on the block.) (16th cent.)

This is the first duty that must be found in the heart of princes, to love their subjects as sons, to procure peace and plenty for them, to protect them from unjust treatment at the hands of officials.

St. Robert Bellarmine: *The Duty of a Christian Prince.* (17th cent.)

No king can have political authority immediately from God, but only from a human ordinance.

F. Suarez: *Adversus Anglicanae Sectae Errores,* 3, 3. (17th cent.)

See what a full and certain blessing flows
From him that, under God, the earth commands:
For kings are types of God, and by their hands
A world of gifts and honors he bestows.

Sir John Beaumont: *Of His Majesty's Vow.* (17th cent.)

O gracious Maker! on whose smiles or frowns
Depends the fate of scepters and of crowns;
Whose hand not only holds the hearts of kings,
But all their steps are shadow'd with Thy wings.

Sir John Beaumont: *A Thanksgiving.* (17th cent.)

Who finds himself unhappy is not being a king, except a king dethroned.

Pascal: *Pensées,* 2. (17th cent.)

Kings are the publick pillars of the state,
Born to sustain and prop the nation's weight.

Dryden: *Absalom and Achitophel.* (17th cent.)

The people have a right supreme
To make their kings; for kings are made for them.

Dryden: *Absalom and Achitophel,* 1. (17th cent.)

But kings too tame are despicably good.

Dryden. (17th cent.)

From the beginning of history the king has been distinguished from the tyrant, the magistrate or the official by the possession of a charisma or divine mandate which sets him apart from other men; so that even today the crown and scepter which are the symbols of this sacred character remain the emblem of royalty as they were 5,000 years ago.

C. Dawson: *Gifford Lectures, 1947: Religion and Culture.*

See also Church and State; Government; Monarchy; Tyranny

Kingdom

Justice being taken away, then, what are kingdoms but great robberies? For what are robberies themselves, but little kingdoms? The band itself is made up of men; it is ruled by the authority of a prince, it is knit together by the pact of the confederacy; the booty is divided by the law agreed on. If, by the admittance of abandoned men, this evil increases to such a degree that it holds places, fixes abodes, takes possession of cities, and subdues peoples, it assumes the more plainly the name of a kingdom, because the reality is now manifestly conferred on it, not by the removal of covetousness, but by the addition of impunity.

St. Augustine: *The City of God,* 4, 4. (5th cent.)

These things being so, we do not attribute the power of giving kingdoms and empires to any save to the true God, Who gives happiness in the kingdom of heaven to the pious and the impious, as it may please Him, whose good pleasure is always just.

St. Augustine: *The City of God,* 5, 21. (5th cent.)

A kingdom is the government of a self-sufficient (*perfectae*) multitude ordered toward the common good by one person.

John of Paris: *Concerning Royal and Papal Power,* 1. (14th cent.)

Kingdom of Heaven

See Eternal life

Kiss

How can she give a kiss, sour or sweet?
Her chin and her nose within half an
  inch meet.

John Heywood: *Proverbs,* 2, 1. (16th cent.)

Many kiss the child for the nurse's sake.

John Heywood: *Proverbs,* 2, 7. (16th cent.)

One kiss, the maiden gives, one last,
Long kiss, which she expires in giving.

Thomas Moore: *Lalla Rookh: Paradise and the Peri.* (19th cent.)

I saw you take his kiss! 'Tis true.
  Oh, modesty! 'Twas strictly kept:
He thought I slept; at least, I knew
  He thought I thought he thought I
    slept.

Coventry Patmore: *Epigram.* (19th cent.)

How should great Jove himself do else
  than miss
  To win the woman he forgets to kiss.

Coventry Patmore: *De Natura Deorum.* (19th cent.)

Not a kiss which I have given,
But shall triumph upon my lips in
  heaven,
Or cling a shameful fungus there in
  hell.

F. Thompson: *Orient Ode.* (19th cent.)

The subtle sanctities which dart
From childish lips' unvalued precious
  brush.

F. Thompson: *Sister Songs.* (19th cent.)

Oh, what a kiss
With filial passion overcharged is this!
To this misgiving breast
This child runs, as a child ne'er ran to
  rest
Upon the light heart and the unop-
  pressed.

Alice Meynell: *The Modern Mother.* (20th cent.)

Kiss of Peace

The baptized shall embrace one another,
men with men and women with women.
But let not men embrace women.

St. Hippolytus: *The Apostolic Tradition,* 18. (Speaking of liturgical functions) (3rd cent.)

See also Mass: prayers

Knave

Two false knaves need no broker.

John Heywood: *Proverbs,* 1, 11. (16th cent.)

It is merry when knaves meet.

John Heywood: *Proverbs,* 1, 11. (16th cent.)

An old knave is no child.

John Heywood: *Proverbs,* 2, 2. (16th cent.)

Knight

In fifteen mortal battles he had been
And jousted for our faith at Tramissene

Thrice in the lists, and always killed his man.

> Chaucer: *Canterbury Tales: Prologue.* (Tr. Coghill) (14th cent.)

Knowledge

This only I know, that I know not the things which I cannot know.

> St. Ambrose: *On the Incarnation,* 21. (4th cent.)

We judge all things according to the divine truth.

> St. Augustine: *De Vera Religione,* 30. (4th cent.)

Whereas knowledge and action make a man happy, as in knowledge error must be guarded against, so must wickedness be avoided in action. Now whosoever supposes that he can know truth while he is still living iniquitously, is in error.

> St. Augustine: *De Agone Christiana* 13, 14. (4th cent.)

For those therefore who are ascending upwards [i.e. in the degrees of knowledge] the first action may be called, for the sake of instruction, quickening; the second, sensation; the third, art; the fourth, virtue; the fifth, tranquillity; the sixth, entry; the seventh, contemplation. They may also be thus named: of the body, through the body, about the body, the soul towards itself, the soul in itself, towards God, with God.

> St. Augustine: *De Quantitate Animae,* 35, 79. (4th cent.)

Let knowledge be applied to a kind of scaffolding, making it possible for the edifice of charity to rise, to endure for ever, even when knowledge is done away with.

> St. Augustine. (5th cent.)

Thus by stages I passed from bodies to the soul which uses the body for its perceiving, and from this to the soul's inner power, to which the body's senses present external things, as indeed the beasts are able; and from there I passed on to the reasoning power, to which is referred for judgment what is received from the body's senses. This too realized that it was mutable in me, and rose to its own understanding. It withdrew my thought from its habitual way, abstracting from the confused crowds of fantasms that it might find what light suffused it, when with utter certainty it cried aloud that the immutable was to be preferred to the mutable, and how it has come to know the immutable itself: for if it had not come to some knowledge of the immutable, it could not have known it as certainly preferable to the mutable. Thus in the thrust of a trembling glance my mind arrived at that which is.

> St. Augustine: *Confessions,* 7, 17. (5th cent.)

Our knowledge compared with Thine, is ignorance.

> St. Augustine: *Confessions,* 11, 4. (5th cent.)

It would be good if men would meditate upon three things to be found in themselves. . . . The three things of which I speak are existence, knowledge, will. For I am, and I know, and I will.

> St. Augustine: *Confessions,* 13, 11. (5th cent.)

We are, and we know that we are, and we love that being and knowledge. On those three facts no possible likeness of falsehood to truth troubles us. . . . On these truths I dread no arguments of Academics, saying, What if you are mistaken? For if I am mistaken, I am in being (*sum*). He that is not cannot be mistaken, and if I am mistaken, by that very fact I exist. He who is not in existence surely cannot be mistaken; and if I am mistaken, by that very fact I am an existent being.

> St. Augustine: *The City of God,* 11, 26. (5th cent.)

The knowledge of Divine things may be properly called wisdom, and the knowledge of human affairs may properly receive the name of knowledge.

St. Augustine: *De Trinitate,* 14, 1. (5th cent.)

All that is known is not comprehended according to the force which it has in itself, but according to the faculty of those who know it. (Omne enim quod cognoscitur non secundum sui vim sed secundum cognoscentium potius comprehenditur facultatem.)

Boethius: *De Consolatione Philosophiae,* 5, 4. (Aristotle) (6th cent.)

Nothing is more excellent than knowledge.

St. John of Damascus: *Dialectica,* 1. (8th cent.)

There are some who desire knowledge merely for its own sake; and that is shameful curiosity. And there are others who desire to know, in order that they may themselves be known; and that is vanity, disgraceful too. Others, again, desire knowledge in order to acquire money or preferment by it; that too is a discreditable quest. But there are also some who desire knowledge, that they may build up the souls of others with it; and that is charity. Others, again, desire it that they may themselves be built up thereby; and that is prudence. Of all these types, only the last two put knowledge to the right use.

St. Bernard: *Sermons on the Canticle of Canticles,* 36. (12th cent.)

Things are known in the knower after the manner of the knower, not after their own manner of existence.

St. Thomas Aquinas: *Exposition of the De Divinis Nominibus,* 2, lect. 4. (13th cent.)

A scrap of knowledge about sublime things is worth more than any amount about trivialities.

St. Thomas Aquinas: *Summa Theologica,* 1, 1, 5. (13th cent.)

Intelligent beings are distinguished from non-intelligent beings in that the latter possess only their own form; whereas the intelligent being is naturally adapted to have also the form of some other thing; for the idea of the thing known is in the knower. Hence it is manifest that the nature of a non-intelligent being is more contracted and limited; whereas the nature of intelligent beings has a greater amplitude and extension.

St. Thomas Aquinas: *Summa Theologica,* 1, 14, 1. (13th cent.)

Now man has different kinds of knowledge, according to the different objects of his knowledge. He has *intelligence* as regards the knowledge of principles; he has *science* as regards knowledge of conclusions; he has *wisdom,* according as he knows the highest cause; he has *counsel* or *prudence,* according as he knows what is to be done.

St. Thomas Aquinas: *Summa Theologica,* 1, 14, 1. (13th cent.)

For God the whole fulness of intellectual knowledge is contained in one object, namely the divine Essence, in which He knows all things. Rational creatures achieve a lower and less simple completeness. What He knows in single simplicity they know in many forms.

St. Thomas Aquinas: *Summa Theologica,* 1, 55, 3. (13th cent.)

A truth may be accepted as evident either in itself or through another truth. What is self-evident is like a first principle; the quality of mind perfecting knowledge at this stage is termed understanding, or sense of principle. What is evident through another truth is not perceived immediately but arrived at by inference.

St. Thomas Aquinas: *Summa Theologica,* 1-2, 57, 2. (13th cent.)

Hence we must say that for the knowledge of any truth whatsoever man needs divine help, that the intellect may be moved by God to its act. But he does not need a new light added to his natural light, in order to know the truth in all things, but only in some that surpass his natural knowledge.

> St. Thomas Aquinas: *Summa Theologica,*
> 1-2, 109, 1. (13th cent.)

With the *quia* stay content, children of
    earth!
  For if the whole before your eyes
    had lain,
  No need was there for Mary to give
    birth.

> Dante: *Purgatorio, Canto 3.* (Tr. L.
> Binyon) (14th cent.)

  Knowledge comes
Of learning well retain'd, unfruitful
    else.

> Dante: *Paradiso, Canto 5.* (14th cent.)

The greatest clerks be not the wisest men.

> Chaucer: *The Reeves Tale.* (14th cent.)

All men naturally desire to know, but what doth knowledge avail without the fear of God?

> Thomas a Kempis: *The Imitation of Christ,*
> 1, 2. (15th cent.)

There are many things the knowledge of which is of little profit to the soul.

> Thomas a Kempis: *The Imitation of Christ,*
> 1, 2. (15th cent.)

Because many make it more their study to know than to live well, therefore are they often deceived, and bring forth none, or very little fruit.

> Thomas a Kempis: *The Imitation of Christ,*
> 1, 3. (15th cent.)

He said he knew what was what.

> John Skelton: *Why Come Ye Not To
> Courte?* (16th cent.)

Inordinate appetite of knowledge is a means to drive many a man out of his paradise, as it did Adam and Eve of old.

> St. Thomas More. (16th cent.)

But that great ever-Goodness from
    above,
To make Himself discerned, did bestow
On our desire of knowledge such a
    love,
That all men seek all what they may to
    know;
Yea time in His own courts to undergo;
  And to observe what He would over-
    pass,
  Do make a mirror of His hour-glass.

> Richard Verstegan: *Verses.* (From *A
> Restoration of Decayed Intelligence,* 1605)
> (Guiney, 219) (17th cent.)

Frail life! in which through mists of
    human breath
  We grope for truth and make our
    progress slow,
Because by passion blinded, till by
    death,
  Our passions ending, we begin to
    know.

> Sir William Davenant: *The Christian's
> Reply to the Philosopher.* (17th cent.)

And some to such a height of learning
    grow,
They die persuaded, that they nothing
    know.

> Sir John Beaumont: *Of the Miserable
> State of Man.* (17th cent.)

O knowledge! if a heav'n on earth
    could be,
I would expect to reap that bliss in
    thee:
But thou art blind, and they that have
    thy light,
More clearly know, they live in dark-
    some night.

> Sir John Beaumont: *Of the Miserable
> State of Man.* (17th cent.)

Is it not one of the most common excuses made by the poor for being ir-religious, that they have had no educa-tion? as if to know much was a neces-sary step for right practice.

> Card. Newman: *Parochial and Plain
> Sermons,* 1, 3. (19th cent.)

The conclusions of one generation are the truths of the next.

> Card. Newman: *Grammar of Assent*, 7. (19th cent.)

We know, not by a direct and simple vision, not at a glance, but, as it were, by piecemeal and accumulation, by a mental process, by going round an object, by the comparison, the combination, the mutual correction, the continual adaptation, of many partial notions, by the employment, concentration, and joint action of many faculties and exercises of mind.

> Card. Newman: *Idea of a University*. (19th cent.)

Really know what you say you know: know what you know and what you do not know; get one thing well before you go on to a second.

> Card. Newman: *Idea of a University*. (19th cent.)

Truth has two attributes—beauty and power; and while useful knowledge is the possession of truth as powerful, liberal knowledge is the apprehension of it as beautiful. Pursue it either as beauty or as power, to its furthest extent and its true limit, and you are led by either road to the Eternal and Infinite, to the intimations of conscience and the announcements of the Church.

> Card. Newman: *Idea of a University*. (19th cent.)

Knowledge is capable of being its own end.

> Card. Newman: *Idea of a University*, 5. (19th cent.)

That only is true enlargement of mind which is the power of viewing many things at once as one whole, of referring them severally to their true place in the universal system, of understanding their respective values, and determining their mutual dependence.

> Card. Newman: *Idea of a University*. (19th cent.)

Our notions of things are never simply commensurate with the things themselves.

> Card. Newman. (Ward, II, 587) (19th cent.)

No one can completely define things which exist externally to the mind, and which are known to him by experience.

> Card. Newman. (Letter to W. Froude, Ward, II, 587) (19th cent.)

I am chargeable with no paradox when I speak of a knowledge which is its own end, when I call it liberal knowledge, or a gentleman's knowledge, when I educate for it, and make it the scope of a university.

> Card. Newman: *Idea of a University*. (19th cent.)

You must be above your knowledge, not under it, or it will oppress you; and the more you have of it the greater will be the load.

> Card. Newman: *Idea of a University*. (19th cent.)

Knowledge comes of doing. Never to act is never to know.

> Bishop John L. Spalding: *Education and the Higher Life*. (19th cent.)

It is one of the signs of reality in the spiritual world that no one can ever describe so much as he knows.

> R. H. Benson: *The Light Invisible*. (20th cent.)

We suck out of all things a kind of essence that abides with us always.

> R. H. Benson: *The History of Richard Raynal Solitary*. (20th cent.)

It is possible for spiritual facts to represent themselves vividly and clearly to the intellect, so that the person to whom the intellectual vision is given does not, so to speak, 'see' anything, but only 'apprehends' something to be true.

R. H. Benson: *The Light Invisible.* (20th cent.)

No man could bear to live if he knew all that was happening in the world at one time.

R. H. Benson: *The History of Richard Raynal Solitary.* (20th cent.)

To go behind knowledge in order to criticize it is an impossible feat, for our criticism is an intellectual act; we might as well turn out the light in order to study our appearance in the dark.

M. C. D'Arcy: *The Idea of God.* (In *God and the Supernatural*) (20th cent.)

The end of learning is knowledge, and the mind is uneasy until it attains certitude.

M. C. D'Arcy: *The Nature of Belief.* (20th cent.)

The difference between the discursive reason and the intuition of the contemplative is not the same as the difference between the natural and the supernatural (in the technical, theological sense of the words)—between reason and faith;

it is simply a question of the different levels of consciousness which are equally parts of human nature.

C. Dawson: *Gifford Lectures, 1947: Religion and Culture.*

See also Mind; Reason; Understanding

Knowledge and Wisdom

If therefore this is the right distinction between wisdom and knowledge, that the intellectual cognizance of eternal things belongs to wisdom, but the rational cognizance of temporal things to knowledge, it is not difficult to judge which is to be preferred or postponed to which.

St. Augustine: *De Trinitate,* 12, 15. (5th cent.)

The gift of knowledge makes for the correct management of temporal matters and shows us how to lead good lives in the midst of wicked persons; understanding enables us to study the Creator and His invisible creation; wisdom affords us the contemplation solely of eternal truth and a delight in it.

St. Thomas Aquinas: *In III Sententiarum,* 35, Proemium. (13th cent.)

L

Labor

Labor is a powerful medicine.

St. John Chrysostom: *Homilies.* (4th cent.)

Labor is our portion lest we should make this world our rest and not hope for the hereafter.

St. John Chrysostom: *Homilies.* (4th cent.)

To labor is to pray. (Laborare est orare.)

Motto of the Benedictines. (6th cent.)

O Lord God, King of heaven and earth, vouchsafe this day to direct and sanctify, to rule and govern our hearts and bodies, our thoughts, words and deeds, in Thy law, and in the works of Thy commandments: that now and ever we may, by

Thy help, attain salvation and freedom,
O Savior of the world.

> Roman Breviary, Prayer *Dirigere et sanctificare* at Prime. (Originally said by monks in chapter before they began day's work.) (ca. 7th cent.)

That labor is safe which no failure can render void.

> St. Bernard: *On Consideration,* 4, 2. (12th cent.)

He who labors as he prays lifts his heart to God with his hands.

> St. Bernard: *Ad sororem.* (12th cent.)

For he that is true of his tongue, and of his two hands,
And doth his work therewith, and willeth no man ill,
He is a god by the gospel.

> Langland: *Piers Plowman,* Passus 2. (14th cent.)

Why seekest thou rest, since thou art born to labor?

> Thomas a Kempis: *The Imitation of Christ,* 2, 10. (15th cent.)

> Small is life's labor;
> Soon comes the close;
> Great the reward is,—
> Endless repose.
> Oft as thou bearest
> With patience the rod
> Thy spirit becometh
> A martyr to God.

> Thomas a Kempis: *Labor parva est.* (Tr. D. Donahoe) (15th cent.)

Labor, as well as fasting, serves to mortify and subdue the flesh. Provided the labor you undertake contributes to the glory of God and your own welfare, I would prefer that you should suffer the pain of labor rather than that of fasting.

> St. Francis de Sales: *Introduction to the Devout Life,* 23. (17th cent.)

To labor is the lot of man below;
And when Jove gave us life, he gave us woe.

> Pope: Tr. of Homer: *Iliad,* 10. (18th cent.)

Labor itself is but a sorrowful song,
The protest of the weak against the strong.

> F. Faber: *The Sorrowful World.* (19th cent.)

According to natural reason and Christian philosophy working for gain is creditable, not shameful, to a man, since it enables him to earn an honorable livelihood; but to misuse men as though they were things in the pursuit of gain, or to value them solely for their physical powers—that is truly shameful and inhuman.

> Pope Leo XIII: *Rerum Novarum.* (May 15, 1891)

The employer must never tax his workers beyond their strength, or employ them in work unsuited to their sex and age. His great and principal duty is to give every one what is just.

> Pope Leo XIII: *Rerum Novarum.* (May 15, 1891)

Justice demands that the interests of the working classes should be carefully watched over by the administration, so that they who contribute so largely to the advantage of the community may themselves share in the benefits which they create—that being housed, clothed and bodily fit, they may find their life less hard and more endurable. It follows that whatever shall appear to prove conducive to the well-being of those who work should obtain favorable consideration.

> Pope Leo XIII: *Rerum Novarum.* (May 15, 1891)

Hail to thee, laborer! Upon whose face
God set his seal of grace!
Whose might hath built the Pyramids; whose hands
Feed all the hungry lands;
Lift thy proud head, and bear thy flag unfurled,
Above the foremost rank of our advancing world!

> Mary Elizabeth Blake: *The Laborer.* (20th cent.)

I cannot conceive any thought better calculated to ease the yoke and to lighten the burden of the Christian toiler than the reflection that the highest type of Manhood has voluntarily devoted Himself to manual labor.

> Card. Gibbons: *Letter to the American Federation of Labor.* (Baltimore, June 28, 1920.)

The great scandal of the nineteenth century is that the Church lost the working class.

> Pope Pius XI. (As reported by the Abbé Cardijn, founder of J.O.C.) (20th cent.)

The only kind of labor which gives the workingman a title to all its fruits is that which he does as his own master.

> Pope Pius XI: *Quadragesimo anno.* (May 15, 1931)

No labor is so cheap as that of men who own nothing but their bodily strength.

> Eric Gill: *It All Goes Together.* (20th cent.)

The leisure state is founded upon a false angelism, a false notion of the fitness of men to enjoy themselves without the direct responsibility of each one to earn his living and that of his wife and children by his own work. This false angelism was, fifteen hundred years ago, called Manicheeism. It is the same illusion today. It is the notion that matter is essentially evil and therefore work essentially degrading.

> Eric Gill: *It All Goes Together.* (20th cent.)

We must return again and again to the simple doctrine: physical labor, manual work, is not in itself bad. It is the necessary basis of all human production and, in the most strict sense of the words, physical labor directed to the production of things needed for human life is both honorable and holy.

> Eric Gill: *It All Goes Together.* (20th cent.)

For work is not only, for every man, a means of decent livelihood, but it is the means through which all those manifold powers and faculties with which nature, training and art have endowed the dignity of the human personality, find their necessary expression.

> Pope Pius XII: *Easter Message of Peace.* (Apr. 9, 1939)

Lady

To be called 'Madam' is a glorious
   thought,
And so is going to church and being
   seen
Having your mantle carried like a
   queen.

> Chaucer: *Canterbury Tales: Prologue.* (Tr. Coghill) (14th cent.)

Laggard

Charon, the demon, beckoning before,
   With eyes of glowing coal, assem-
   bles all:
   Whoever lags, he beats him with his
   oar.

> Dante: *Inferno, Canto 3.* (Tr. Binyon) (14th cent.)

Laity

The layman is bound by the lay ordinances.

> Pope St. Clement I: *Letter to the Corinthians,* 40, 5. (1st cent.)

Hear these things, then, laymen also, the elect Church of God. For the former people [the Jews] also was called a church; but you are the Catholic Church, the holy and perfect, *a royal priesthood, a holy multitude, a people for inheritance,* the great Church, the bride adorned for the Lord God.

> Anonymous: *Didascalia Apostolorum, 9.* (3rd cent.)

Layfolk are united spiritually to Christ through faith and charity, but not by active sacramental power. Theirs is a spiritual priesthood, to offer spiritual sacrifices.

St. Thomas Aquinas: *Summa Theologica,* 3, 82, 1. (13th cent.)

"The laymen, what are they?" an angry bishop once grumbled to Newman. And the great cardinal answered, "Well, without them the Church would look rather foolish!"

Card. Newman. (Quoted) (19th cent.)

I want a laity, not arrogant, not rash in speech, not disputatious, but men who know their religion, who enter into it, who know just where they stand, who know what they hold, and what they do not, who know their creed so well that they can give an account of it, who know so much of history that they can defend it. I want an intelligent, well-instructed laity.

Card. Newman: *Present Position of Catholics in England.* (19th cent.)

I have as much right to make my suggestions, and offer my advice to the bishops or to the supreme pontiff as had Charlemagne and St. Louis, or as has Louis Napoleon or Francis Joseph to offer theirs. Before the Church, if not before the state, all laymen are equal.

Orestes Brownson: *Lacordaire.* (Works, 20, 249ff.) (1862)

Laymen have the right of receiving from the clergy, according to the norm of ecclesiastical discipline, spiritual goods and especially aids necessary for salvation.

Code of Canon Law, Canon 682. (20th cent.)

Indeed let this be clearly understood, especially in these our days: the fathers and mothers of families, and those who are spiritual parents through baptism, and in particular those members of the laity who assist the ecclesiastical hierarchy in spreading the kingdom of the divine Redeemer, occupy an honorable, even though often lowly, place in the Christian community. Under the impulse of God and with His help they can reach the peak of holiness; and such holiness, Jesus Christ has promised, will never be wanting to the Church.

Pope Pius XII: *Mystici Corporis.* (June 29, 1943)

See also Priesthood of the Faithful

Lamb

As soon goeth the young lambskin to the market as the old ewe's.

John Heywood: *Proverbs,* 2, 4. (16th cent.)

Lameness

If you will walk with lame men you'll soon limp yourself.

Seumas MacManus: *Heavy Hangs the Golden Grain.* (20th cent.)

Language

Man is the one name belonging to every nation on earth; there is one soul and many tongues, one spirit and many sounds; every country has its own speech, but the subjects of speech are common to all.

Tertullian: *The Testimony of the Christian Soul.* (3rd cent.)

Though a knowledge of all languages is difficult for anyone, still no one is so sluggish that, situated as he is in his own nation, he should not know his own nation's language. For what else is he to be thought except lower than the brute animals? For they make the sound that is proper to them, but he is worse who lacks a knowledge of his own language.

St. Isidore: *Etymologies,* 9, 1. (7th cent.)

Sydneian showers
Of sweet discourse, whose powers
Can crown old winter's head with flowers.

Richard Crashaw: *Wishes to his (Supposed) Mistress.* (17th cent.)

Examples of past times our deeds
should sway;
But we must speak the language of the
day.

Sir John Beaumont: *Against Abused Love.*
(17th cent.)

I trade both with the living and the dead,
for the enrichment of our native language.

Dryden: *Dedication of the Aeneis.* (17th
cent.)

A thing well said will be wit in all languages.

Dryden: *Essay of Dramatic Poesy.* (17th
cent.)

Oh, but the heavenly grammar did I
hold
Of that high speech which angels'
tongues turn gold!
So should her deathless beauty take no
wrong,
Praised in her own great kindred's fit
and cognate tongue:
Or if that language yet with us abode
Which Adam in the garden talked with
God!
But our untempered speech descends—
poor heirs!
Grimy and rough-cast still from
Babel's bricklayers:
Curse on the brutish jargon we inherit,
Strong but to damn, not memorize, a
spirit!

F. Thompson: *Her Portrait.* (19th cent.)

Lark

When the sky falleth we shall have larks.

John Heywood: *Proverbs,* 1, 4. (16th
cent.)

The lark now leaves his watery nest,
And climbing, shakes his dewy
wings.

Sir William Davenant: *Morning Song.*
(17th cent.)

When leaves turn outward to the light,
And all the roads are fringed with
green,

When larks are pouring, high, unseen,
The joy they find in song and flight,
Then I, too, with the lark would wing
My little flight, and, soaring, sing.

Mary Ainge De Vere: *Poet and Lark.*
(20th cent.)

Last Words

I am the wheat of Christ; I am going to
be ground with the teeth of wild beasts,
that I may be found pure bread.

St. Ignatius of Antioch. (2nd cent.)

Thanks be to God.

St. Cyprian. (When the judge condemned
him to be beheaded.) (3rd cent.)

Let this word of mine be kept by you, so
that no one shall know in what place my
body reposes, for I shall receive it incorruptible from my Savior in the resurrection of the dead. And distribute my
garments thus: To Athanasius the bishop
give one of my sheepskins, and the
cloak under me which was new when
he gave it to me, and has become old by
my use of it; and to Serapion the bishop
give the other sheepskin; and do you
have the haircloth garment. And for the
rest, children, farewell, for Anthony is
going, and is with you no more.

St. Anthony. (ca. 355)

I have not so behaved myself that I
should be ashamed to live; nor am I
afraid to die, because I have so good a
Master.

St. Ambrose. (397)

Glory to God for all things, Amen.

St. John Chrysostom. (407)

Oh, Lord, shall I die at all? Shall I die
at all? Yes! Why, then, oh Lord, if ever,
why not now?

St. Augustine. (430)

Glory be to the Father, and to the Son,
and to the Holy Ghost.

St. Bede the Venerable. (ca. 735)

Lord, into Thy hands I commend my spirit.

> Charlemagne. (814)

I commend myself to the blessed Lady Mary, hoping by her intercessions to be reconciled to her most dear Son, our Lord Jesus Christ.

> King William I of England. (The Conqueror) (1087)

I have loved justice and hated iniquity; therefore I die an exile.

> Pope St. Gregory VII. (11th cent.)

I shall gladly obey His call; yet I would also feel grateful if He would grant me a little longer time with you, and if I could be permitted to solve a question on the origin of the soul.

> St. Anselm. (1109)

In death at last let me rest with Abelard.

> Héloïse. (1164)

For the name of Jesus and the defence of the Church I am willing to die.

> St. Thomas a Becket. (1170)

Under the feet of my friars.

> St. Dominic. (When asked where he would like to be buried.) (Others report: Possess poverty.) (1221)

I have done my part, may Christ teach you to do yours.

> St. Francis of Assisi. (Others report: The righteous wait expectant till I receive my recompense.) (1226)

I will enter now into the house of the Lord.

> King St. Louis IX of France. (Others report: We will go to Jerusalem.) (1270)

I receive Thee, Ransom of my soul. For love of Thee have I studied and kept vigil, toiled, preached, and taught. Never have I said word against Thee.

> St. Thomas Aquinas. (1274)

Carry my bones before you on your march, for the rebels will not be able to endure the sight of me, alive or dead.

> King Edward I of England. (While advancing against Robert Bruce.) (1307)

Thou, O Lord, callest me, and I come to Thee, not through my merits, but through Thy mercy alone, which I ask of Thee in virtue of Thy blood! Blood, blood. . . . Father, into Thy hands I commend my soul and my spirit.

> St. Catherine of Siena. (From letter of Ser Barduccio di Piero Carnigiani) (1380)

Now, O God, Thou dost let Thy servant depart in peace! The soul that is accompanied to eternity by the prayers of three hundred children, may advance with humble hope into the presence of their Father and their God.

> Jean Charlier de Gerson. (When he realized that the children whom he had specially cared for were praying for him.) (1429)

Jesus! Jesus!

> St. Jeanne d'Arc. (1431)

Oh Gabriele, how much better would it have been for thee, and how much more would it have promoted thy soul's welfare, if thou hadst never been raised to the pontificate, but hadst been content to lead a quiet and religious life in the monastery.

> Pope Eugenius IV (Gabriele Condolmero). (1447)

My Lord has suffered as much for me.

> Savonarola. (Others report: O Florence, what hast thou done today?) (1498)

I die unprepared.

> Cesare Borgia. (Killed at the siege of the Castle of Biano.) (1507)

This is death.

> Cardinal Ximénes de Cisneros. (1517)

Had I but served God as diligently as I have served my king, He would not have given me over in my grey hairs. But this is the just reward that I must receive for my indulgent pains and study, not regarding my service to God, but only to my prince.

Cardinal Wolsey. (1530)

That is enough to last till I get to heaven.

William Warham, Archbishop of Canterbury. (When told by his servants that he still had thirty pounds.) (1532)

O Lord! O Lord! make an end! make an end!

Erasmus. (1536)

Monks! monks! monks!

King Henry VIII of England. (1547)

I have erred with Peter, but I have not wept with Peter. (Erravi cum Petro, sed non flevi cum Petro.)

Stephen Gardiner, Bishop of Winchester. (1555)

After I am dead, you will find Calais written in my heart.

Queen Mary I of England. (1558)

My soul I resign to God, my body to the earth, and my worldly possessions to my relations; admonishing them that through their lives and in the hour of death they think upon the sufferings of Jesus Christ. And I do desire that my body be taken to the city of Florence for its last rest.

Michelangelo Buonarotti. (1563)

Over my spirit flash and float in divine radiancy the bright and glorious visions of the world to which I go.

St. Teresa of Jesus. (Uncertain) (1582)

O Lord, into Thy hands I commend my spirit.

Mary, Queen of Scots. (1587)

I die like a good Catholic, in faith and obedience to the holy Roman Church.

King Philip II of Spain. (1598)

God's will be done! Jesus, my God and my all!

St. Francis de Sales. (1622)

Absolutely, and I pray God to condemn me, if I had any other aim than the welfare of God and of the state.

Cardinal Richelieu. (When asked whether he forgave his enemies.) (1642)

I suffer the violence of pain and death, but I know whom I have believed.

Jacques Bénigne Bossuet, Bishop of Méaux. (1704)

"Dear gentlemen, let me die a natural death."

"I am going on my journey: they have greased my boots already."

Sir Samuel Garth, physician. (The first words were spoken after he saw the doctors gathering in consultation about him; the second after he had been administered extreme unction.) (1719)

I am dying, sir, of a hundred good symptoms.

Alexander Pope. (1744)

"I repose all my confidence in the goodness of God and the merits of our dear Lord Jesus Christ. I recommend myself to the powerful intercession of His Blessed Mother and of all the saints, in the hope that they will obtain for me the pardon of my offenses."

"Sir, my hopes have always been fixed on the cross of Christ."

Archb. John Carroll. (The last remark was made to a Protestant minister who observed that his hopes must now be fixed on another world.) (1815)

Soul of Christ, sanctify me; body of Christ, save me; blood of Christ, inebriate me; water from the side of Christ, strengthen me . . . Jesus, Mary, Joseph.

Mother Elizabeth Seton. (1821)

Guard the Church I have loved so well
and sacredly.

> Pope Pius IX. (Others report the
> following words: Death wins this time.)
> (1878)

I love you, dear, but the Lord is my Life
and my Light.

> Coventry Patmore. (To his wife) (1896)

Lateness

Better late than never.

> John Heywood: *Proverbs,* 1, 10. (16th
> cent.)

He was always late on principle, his
principle being that punctuality is the
thief of time.

> Oscar Wilde: *The Picture of Dorian Gray,*
> 3. (19th cent.)

Latitudinarianism

So, Freedom reign'd; so, Priests, dismay'd by naught,
Thought what they pleas'd, and mention'd what they thought.

> Ronald Knox: *Absolute and Abitofhell.*
> (20th cent.)

Lauds

Maker of all, eternal King,
Who day and night about dost bring:
Who weary mortals to relieve,
Dost in their times the seasons give:
Now the shrill cock proclaims the day,
And calls the sun's awakening ray—
The wand'ring pilgrim's guiding light,
That marks the watches night by night.

> Roman Breviary, Hymn *Aeterne rerum
> conditor* for Sunday. (Tr. W. Copeland)
> (St. Ambrose, 4th cent.)

O splendor of God's glory bright,
O thou that bringest light from light,
O Light of Light, light's living Spring,
O Day, all days illumining.

> Roman Breviary, Hymn *Splendor paternae
> gloriae* for Monday. (Tr. from the
> Yattendon Hymnal) (St. Ambrose, 4th
> cent.)

As the bird, whose clarion gay
Sounds before the dawn is grey,
Christ, who brings the spirit's day,
Calls us, close at hand.
"Wake!" He cries, "and for my sake,
From your eyes dull slumbers shake!
Sober, righteous, chaste, awake!
At the door I stand!"

> Roman Breviary, Hymn *Ales diei nuntius*
> for Tuesday. (Tr. W. Courthope)
> (Prudentius, from Cathemerinon, 4th
> cent.)

Day is breaking, dawn is bright:
Hence, vain shadows of the night!
Mists that dim our mortal sight,
Christ is come! Depart!

> Roman Breviary, Hymn *Nox et tenebrae et
> nubila* for Wednesday. (Tr. W.
> Courthope) (Prudentius, from
> Cathemerinon, 4th cent.)

See the golden sun arise!
Let no more our darkened eyes
Snare us, tangled by surprise
In the maze of sin!

> Roman Breviary, Hymn *Lux ecce surgit
> aurea* for Thursday. (Tr. W. Courthope)
> (Prudentius, from Cathemerinon, 4th
> cent.)

Lo, the dim shadows of the night are
waning;
Lightsome and blushing, dawn of day
returneth;
Fervent in spirit, to the world's Creator
Pray we devoutly.

> Roman Breviary, Hymn *Ecce jam noctis
> tenuatur umbra* for Sunday. (Post-
> Pentecostal season) (Tr. M. Blacker
> adapted by M. Britt) (Attr. to Pope St.
> Gregory I, 6th cent.)

See also Dawn; Matins; Morning

Laughter

Laughter does not seem to be a sin, but
it leads to sin.

> St. John Chrysostom: *Homilies.* (4th
> cent.)

Not to speak vain words or such as move to laughter; not to love much or violent laughter.

> St. Benedict: *Rule,* 4. (One of his 'tools of good works') (6th cent.)

He laugheth but from the lips forward.

> St. Thomas More: *Confutation.* (16th cent.)

In thy mirth refrain from immoderate laughter, and let it be humble, modest, kindly, and edifying.

> St. Teresa of Jesus: *Maxims.* (16th cent.)

The sense of humor has other things to do than to make itself conspicuous in the act of laughter.

> Alice Meynell: *Laughter.* (19th cent.)

Laughter has something in it in common with the ancient winds of faith and inspiration; it unfreezes pride and unwinds secrecy; it makes men forget themselves in the presence of something greater than themselves; something (as the common phrase goes about a joke) that they cannot resist.

> G. K. Chesterton: *The Common Man.* (20th cent.)

Laughter and love are everywhere. The cathedrals, built in the ages that loved God, are full of blasphemous grotesques. The mother laughs continually at the child, the lover laughs continually at the lover, the wife at the husband, the friend at the friend.

> G. K. Chesterton: *Napoleon of Notting Hill.* (20th cent.)

Cleanse us from ire of creed or class,
    The anger of the idle kings;
Sow in our souls, like living grass,
    The laughter of all lowly things.

> G. K. Chesterton: *A Hymn for the Church Militant.* (20th cent.)

A laugh is like a love affair in that it carries a man completely off his feet; a laugh is like a creed or a church in that it asks that a man should trust himself to it.

> G. K. Chesterton: *A Handful of Authors.* (20th cent.)

Lavishness

For lavish grants suppose a monarch tame
And more his goodness than his wit proclaim.

> Dryden: *Absalom and Achitophel.* (17th cent.)

Law

I—*Definitions*

Law is twofold—natural and written. The natural law is in the heart, the written law on tables. All men are under the natural law. First of all, nature herself teaches us to do what is good; afterwards came the law that was given through Moses.

> St. Ambrose: *De Fuga,* 15. (4th cent.)

Where, therefore, there is no true justice there can be no right (*jus*). For that which is done by right (*jure*) is justly done, and what is unjustly done cannot be done by right.

> St. Augustine: *The City of God,* 19, 21. (5th cent.)

The precepts of the law are these: to live honorably, to injure no other man, to render to every man his due.

> Institutes of Justinian. (6th cent.)

What has pleased the prince has the force of law. . . . (Quod principi placuit, legis habet vigorem. . . .)

> Institutes of Justinian, 1, 2, 6. (Famous statement of Ulpian, 3rd cent.) (6th cent.)

All laws are either divine or human. Divine laws are manifest in nature, human laws in customs; and so the latter differ, since different laws please different peoples. Divine law is called *fas,* human law *jus.* To pass through another's property is of divine law, but not of human law.

> St. Isidore of Seville: *Etymologies,* 5, 2. (7th cent.)

Law (*jus*) is either natural, or civil, or universal (*gentium*).

> St. Isidore of Seville: *Etymologies,* 5, 4, 1. (7th cent.)

Natural law is what is common to all peoples, and what is observed everywhere by the instinct of nature rather than by any ordinance, as the marriage of man and woman, the begetting and rearing of children, the common possession of all things, the one freedom of all, and the acquisition of those things that are taken in the air, or on land, or on sea. Likewise the restoring of property entrusted or lent, and the repelling of violence by force. For this, or anything like this, is not considered unjust but natural and fair.

> St. Isidore: *Etymologies,* 5, 4, 1-2. (7th cent.)

Civil law is what each people or state has enacted as its own law, for human and divine reasons.

> St. Isidore: *Etymologies,* 5, 5. (7th cent.)

Public law has to do with sacred things, the priests, and magistrates.

> St. Isidore: *Etymologies,* 5, 8. (7th cent.)

A law is an enactment of the people, by which the elders together with the plebeians passed some law.

> St. Isidore: *Etymologies,* 5, 10. (7th cent.)

Plebiscites are what the plebeians alone enact. . . .

> St. Isidore: *Etymologies,* 5, 11. (7th cent.)

A decree of the senate (*senatusconsultum*) is what the senators alone determine in council for the people.

> St. Isidore: *Etymologies,* 5, 12. (7th cent.)

A constitution or edict is what the king or emperor has enacted or proclaims.

> St. Isidore: *Etymologies,* 5, 13. (7th cent.)

Privileges are laws applying to individuals, as it were, private laws. For privilege is so called it is applied to a private person.

> St. Isidore: *Etymologies,* 5, 18. (7th cent.)

Every law either permits something, as that a brave man should compete for a prize, or forbids something, as that no one should be allowed to ask for the sacred maidens in marriage, or punishes, as that he who has committed murder should suffer capital punishment. For human life is governed by the reward or punishment of law.

> St. Isidore: *Etymologies,* 5, 19. (7th cent.)

Laws were made in order that the boldness of men might be checked by the fear of them, and innocence be safe among the wicked, and the power of harm bridled among the wicked by the dread of punishment.

> St. Isidore: *Etymologies,* 5, 20. (7th cent.)

A law should be honest, just, possible, according to nature, according to the customs of the country, adapted to the place and time, necessary, useful, clear also, lest it contain anything obscure tending to fraud, for the common good of all citizens.

> St. Isidore: *Etymologies,* 5, 21. (7th cent.)

Everything that is *fas* may be given the name of divine or human law, while human customs duly written and handed down are known as law (*lex*).

> Gratian: *Decretum,* D. 1. (12th cent.)

But it ought to be remembered that law promulgated in fear by a spirit of slavery is one thing; and that given sweetly and gently by the spirit of liberty is another. Those who are sons are not obliged to submit to the first, but they are always under the rule of the second.

> St. Bernard: *Letters,* 12, 6. (12th cent.)

This is the definition of law by its four essential parts: an ordinance of reason for the sake of the common good, commanded by the authority who has charge of the community, and promulgated.

St. Thomas Aquinas: *Summa Theologica,* 1-2, 90, 4. (13th cent.)

Particular arrangements instituted by human art which fit in with the principles of natural law are called human laws, given the presence of the four essential conditions of law.

St. Thomas Aquinas: *Summa Theologica,* 1-2, 91, 3. (13th cent.)

The light of natural reason, whereby we discern what is good and what is evil, which is the function of the natural law, is nothing else than an imprint on us of the divine light. It is therefore evident that the natural law is nothing else than the rational creature's participation of the eternal law.

St. Thomas Aquinas: *Summa Theologica,* 1-2, 91, 2. (13th cent.)

A tyrannical law, through not being according to reason, is not a law, absolutely speaking, but rather a perversion of law; and yet in so far as it is something in the nature of a law, it aims at the citizens' being good.

St. Thomas Aquinas: *Summa Theologica,* 1-2, 92, 1. (13th cent.)

Laws are called just on the three counts of end, author, and form. By their end, when ordained to the common welfare; by their author, when the legislator does not go outside the bounds of his authority; by their form, when the burdens imposed on subjects are fairly distributed and promote the common good. Legislation is illegal when it conflicts with human goodness according to the three norms given above, and is immoral when it conflicts with divine goodness and the eternal law. . . . Ordinances of this sort offer violence rather than reasonable direction. . . . They do not bind in conscience, except on occasion, when it may

be necessary to avoid public disorder or scandal.

St. Thomas Aquinas: *Summa Theologica,* 1-2, 96, 4. (13th cent.)

Law is not right exactly (*ipsum jus*), but the norm of right (*aliqualis ratio juris*).

St. Thomas Aquinas: *Summa Theologica,* 2-2, 57, 1. (13th cent.)

No one is obliged to obey a precept unless he be reasonably informed about it.

St. Thomas Aquinas: *Disputations concerning Truth,* 17, 3. (13th cent.)

Law is a common, just, and stable precept, which has been sufficiently promulgated.

F. Suarez: *On Laws,* 1, 12. (17th cent.)

II—*Eternal law*

What about that law which is called supreme reason, which must always be obeyed, by which the evil deserve an unhappy life and the good a blessed life, by which the law we have agreed to call temporal is rightly laid down and rightly changed? Can any intelligent person not see that it is unchangeable and eternal?

St. Augustine: *On Freewill,* 1, 15. (4th cent.)

No man loses Thee, unless he goes from Thee; and in going from Thee, where does he go or where does he flee save from Thee to Thee?—from God well-pleased to God angered? For where shall he not find Thy law fulfilled in his punishment? Thy law is truth and truth is Thou.

St. Augustine: *Confessions,* 4, 9. (5th cent.)

For this is the property of that eternal and just law of God, that he who would not be ruled with gentleness by God should be ruled as a punishment by his own self; and that all those who have willingly thrown off the gentle yoke and light burden of charity would bear unwillingly the insupportable burden of their own will.

St. Bernard: *Letters,* 12, 5. (12th cent.)

The whole universe is governed by divine reason. God is the Prince of the Universe, the plan of government He has in His mind bears the character of law, and because it is conceived in eternity and not in time is rightly called the eternal law.

St. Thomas Aquinas: *Summa Theologica,* 1-2, 91, 1. (13th cent.)

No one can know the eternal law, as it is in itself, except the blessed who see God in His essence. But every rational creature knows it in its reflection, greater or less. For every knowledge of truth is a kind of reflection and participation of the eternal law, which is the unchangeable truth.

St. Thomas Aquinas: *Summa Theologica,* 1-2, 93, 2. (13th cent.)

Since the eternal law is the plan of government in the Chief Governor, all the plans of government in the inferior governors must be derived from the eternal law. But these plans of inferior governors are all other laws besides the eternal law. Therefore all laws, in so far as they partake of right reason, are derived from the eternal law.

St. Thomas Aquinas: *Summa Theologica,* 1-2, 93, 3. (13th cent.)

Even an unjust law, in so far as it retains some appearance of law, though being framed by one who is in power, is derived from the eternal law; since all power is from the Lord God.

St. Thomas Aquinas: *Summa Theologica,* 1-2, 93, 3. (13th cent.)

Laws come before men live together in society, and have their origin in the natural and consequently in the eternal law.

Pope Leo XIII: *Libertas Praestantissimum.* (June 20, 1888)

The eternal law of God is the sole standard and rule of human liberty, not only in each individual man, but also in the community and civil society which men constitute when united.

Pope Leo XIII: *Libertas Praestantissimum.* (June 20, 1888)

III—*Divine law*

In order that we should not be held up by doubts as to what we should do and what to avoid, our human behavior is regulated by a divinely given law, which, if we follow, we are assured we cannot go wrong.

St. Thomas Aquinas: *Summa Theologica,* 1-2, 91, 4. (13th cent.)

Bear in mind that human and divine law differ in their immediate aims. Human law, the purpose of which is the tranquillity of the state, operates by policing external acts which could break the public peace. The purpose of divine law, on the other hand, is to lead us through to eternal happiness, the obstacles to which are sins, internal as well as external. The effective putting down of crime and the enforcement of sanctions suffices for human law, but not for divine law, which would adapt the whole man to everlasting joy.

St. Thomas Aquinas: *Summa Theologica,* 1-2, 98, 1. (13th cent.)

As the leading purpose of human law is to bring about the friendship of men among themselves, so divine law is chiefly intended to establish men in friendship with God.

St. Thomas Aquinas: *Summa Theologica,* 1-2, 99, 2. (13th cent.)

IV—*Natural law*

What else are the laws of God written in our hearts but the very presence of the Holy Ghost?

St. Augustine: *Concerning the Spirit and the Letter,* 24. (5th cent.)

Natural law is superior in dignity to customs and enactments. For whatever has been either received through usage or written down that is contrary to natural law, is to be considered void and invalid.

Gratian: *Decretum*, D. 8, Part 2. (12th cent.)

There can be no dispensation from the natural law, except perhaps in the case of two evils, when it is necessary to choose one or the other.

Gratian: *Decretum*, D. 13, Pt. 1. (12th cent.)

Ignorance of the natural law is one thing, ignorance of civil law another. Ignorance of the natural law is never excusable in the case of adults; ignorance of the civil law is sometimes permissible, sometimes not.

Gratian: *Decretum*, C. 1, Q. 4, P. 4. (12th cent.)

Thus natural law is a certain quality (*vis*) planted in mankind by nature, which leads men to do what is good and to avoid what is evil. Natural law consists of three parts, namely, commands, prohibitions, and demonstrations. It commands men to do what is useful, as: *Thou shalt love the Lord Thy God;* it forbids that which is harmful, as: *Thou shalt not kill;* and it points out what is expedient, as: all things should be held in common, there should be one liberty for all mankind, and so forth.

Rufinus: *Summa Decretorum*, D. 1. Dict. Grat. ad cap. 1. (12th cent.)

Whatever there may be in the laws of the emperors, in the writings of authors, in the examples of the saints, contrary to natural law, we hold to be null and void.

Rufinus: *Summa Decretorum*, D. 8. (12th cent.)

Custom has added to and taken away from the natural law. It has added to it such things as the canonical ceremonies with inspection of the suitability of persons constituting marriage, in the union of man and wife. It has taken away from it, not with regard to precepts and prohibitions, but with respect to its demonstrations, as in the matter of liberty, for by the law of nations slavery has been introduced.

Stephen of Tournai: *Summa Decreti*, D. 1. (12th cent.)

We must say that the natural law, as to general principles, is the same for all, both as to rectitude and as to knowledge. But as to certain matters of detail, which are conclusions, as it were, of those general principles, it is the same for all in the majority of cases, both as to rectitude and as to knowledge; and yet in some few cases it may fail, both as to rectitude, by reason of certain obstacles (just as natures subject to generation and corruption fail in some few cases on account of some obstacle), and as to knowledge, since in some the reason is perverted by passion, or evil habit, or an evil disposition of nature.

St. Thomas Aquinas: *Summa Theologica*, 1-2, 94, 4. (13th cent.)

The written law is said to be given for the correction of the natural law, either because it supplies what was wanting in the natural law; or because the natural law was perverted in the hearts of some men, as to certain matters, so that they esteemed those things good which are naturally evil, which perversion stood in need of correction.

St. Thomas Aquinas: *Summa Theologica*, 1-2, 94, 5. (13th cent.)

The natural law dates from the creation of the rational creature. It does not vary according to time, but remains unchangeable.

St. Thomas Aquinas: *Summa Theologica*, 1-2, 94, 5. (13th cent.)

For where God governeth immediate,
The natural law runs not, and hath no
  sway.

Dante: *Paradiso, Canto* 30. (Tr. Binyon) (14th cent.)

The law of nature is the same thing as the eternal law implanted in rational creatures, and inclining them to their right action and end; and can be nothing else but the eternal reason of God, the Creator and Ruler of all the world.

Pope Leo XIII: *Libertas Praestantissimum.* (June 20, 1888)

The laws of nature and of the Gospel, which by right are superior to all human contingencies, are necessarily independent of all particular forms of civil government, while at the same time they are in harmony with everything that is not repugnant to morality and justice. They are, therefore, and they must remain absolutely free from the passions and the vicissitudes of parties, so that, under whatever political constitution, the citizens may and ought to abide by those laws which command them to love God above all things, and their neighbors as themselves. This has always been the policy of the Church.

Pope Leo XIII: *Graves de Communi.* (Jan. 18, 1901)

V—*Human or positive law*

The emperor makes laws which he is himself the first to keep.

St. Ambrose: *Letters,* 21, 9. (4th cent.)

So true is it that, where there is most law, there is also most injustice.

St. Jerome: *Letters,* 1, 14. (Quoting a Latin proverb: *Summum jus, summa injuria.*) (4th cent.)

In temporal law there is nothing just and lawful, but what man has drawn from the eternal law.

St. Augustine: *De libero arbitrio,* 1, 6. (4th cent.)

A temporal law, however just, may be justly changed in course of time.

St. Augustine: *De libero arbitrio,* 1, 6. (4th cent.)

It is just that a prince should obey his own laws. For he may then rightly consider that his laws are to be kept by all, when he also shows them proper respect. Princes are bound by their own laws and should not violate in their own persons laws which they establish for subjects. For the voice of their authority is just, if they do not allow themselves to do what they prohibit the people from doing.

St. Isidore: *Sentences,* 3, 51. (7th cent.)

Laws are confirmed when they are approved by the customs of those who use them.

Gratian: *Decretum,* Can. 3, post D. 4. (12th cent.)

But the king should not be under any man, only under God and the law, for the law makes the king. Let the king therefore attribute to the law what the law attributes to him, namely lordship and power, for there is no king where will rules and not the law.

Bracton: *On the Laws and Customs of England,* 1, 8, 5. (13th cent.)

The practical reason is concerned with practical matters, which are singular and contingent: but not with necessary things, with which the speculative reason is concerned. Wherefore human laws cannot have the inerrancy that belongs to the demonstrated conclusions of sciences.

St. Thomas Aquinas: *Summa Theologica,* 1-2, 91, 3. (13th cent.)

Human authority, which can legislate only about matters it is competent to judge, cannot extend to interior acts which are hidden, but is restricted to exterior acts which are manifest.

St. Thomas Aquinas: *Summa Theologica,* 1-2, 91, 4. (13th cent.)

Human legislation, which is enacted for a group composed for the greater part of human beings who are not of consummate virtue, does not forbid all vices, from which the virtuous abstain, but only those grave ones which most people can avoid, those especially which damage others, and which have to be put down if civilized intercourse is to be maintained.

> St. Thomas Aquinas: *Summa Theologica,* 1-2, 96, 2. (13th cent.)

All law is directed to the common well-being. From this it draws its force and meaning, and to the extent that it falls short of this it does not oblige in conscience.

> St. Thomas Aquinas: *Summa Theologica,* 1-2, 96, 6. (13th cent.)

Law has the power to compel; indeed the ability to enforce is a condition of the ability to command.

> St. Thomas Aquinas: *Summa Theologica,* 1-2, 100, 9. (13th cent.)

It is of the essence of a nation that the mutual relations of the citizens be ordered by just laws.

> St. Thomas Aquinas: *Summa Theologica,* 1-2, 105, 2. (13th cent.)

By common consent human will can institute juridical rights so long as they are not contrary to natural justice. These matters make up the field of positive law.

> St. Thomas Aquinas: *Summa Theologica,* 2-2, 57, 2. (13th cent.)

For nations, kingdoms and cities have different characteristics which demand different laws for their government, law being intended as a concrete rule of life.

> Dante: *Monarchy,* 1. (14th cent.)

For such law as man giveth other wight, He should him-selven usen it by right.

> Chaucer: *Man of Law's Prologue.* (14th cent.)

The law is so lordly and loth to maken end.

> Langland: *Piers Plowman,* Passus 4. (14th cent.)

Do law away, what is a king?
Where is the right of anything?

> John Gower: *Confessio Amantis,* 7. (14th cent.)

Human laws are no other than rules whereby the perfect notion of justice can be determined.

> Sir John Fortescue: *On the Laws of England,* 4. (15th cent.)

Know, then, that all human laws are either the law of nature, customs, or statutes which are also called constitutions; but the two former, when they are reduced to writing and made public by a sufficient authority of the prince and commanded to be observed, they then pass into the nature of and are accepted as constitutions or statutes, and in virtue of such promulgation and command oblige the subject to the observance of them under a greater penalty than otherwise they could do.

> Sir John Fortescue: *On the Laws of England,* 15. (15th cent.)

The laws of England, as far as they agree with, and are deduced from, the law of nature, are neither better nor worse in their decisions than the laws of other states or kingdoms in similar cases.

> Sir John Fortescue: *On the Laws of England,* 16. (15th cent.)

All laws are promulgated for this end: that every man may know his duty; and therefore the plainest and most obvious sense of the words is that which must be put on them.

> St. Thomas More: *Utopia.* (16th cent.)

The object of civil legislation is the natural welfare of the community and of its individual members, in order that they may live in peace and justice, with a sufficiency of those goods that are necessary for physical conservation and comfort, and with those moral conditions which are required for private well-being and public prosperity.

> F. Suarez: *De Legibus,* 3, 11. (17th cent.)

No written laws can be so plain, so
pure,
But wit may gloss and malice may obscure.

> Dryden: *The Hind and the Panther,* 2.
> (17th cent.)

For laws are only made to punish those
Who serve the king, and to protect his
foes.

> Dryden: *Absalom and Achitophel.* (17th
> cent.)

The net of law is spread so wide,
No sinner from its sweep may hide.
Its meshes are so fine and strong,
They take in every child of wrong.
O wondrous web of mystery!
Big fish alone escape from thee!

> J. J. Roche: *The Net of Law.* (19th cent.)

Moral laws do not stand in need of the
divine sanction, and it is not at all necessary that human laws should be made
conformable to the laws of nature, and
receive their power of binding from
God.

> Proposition condemned by Pius IX in
> Syllabus of Errors. (1867)

Law is order in liberty, and without order liberty is social chaos. The highest
test of a people's fitness for free institutions is their willingness to obey law.

> Archbishop Ireland: *American Citizenship.*
> (Chicago, Feb. 22, 1895)

What reason and the natural law do for
individuals, that human law, promulgated for their good, does for the citizens of states.

> Pope Leo XIII: *Libertas Praestantissimum.*
> (June 20, 1888)

Laws are instituted when they are promulgated. Laws are presumed to be not
personal but territorial, unless the law
indicates that it is a personal law.

> Code of Canon Law, Canon 8. (20th cent.)

Laws affect future, not past acts, unless
it is explicitly declared they are retro-
active.

> Code of Canon Law, Canon 10. (20th
> cent.)

VI—*International law*

The law of nations (*jus gentium*) is the
seizing, building, and fortifying of settlements, wars, captivities, servitudes,
the right of recovery (*postliminia*),
treaties, truces, the obligation not to
violate an ambassador, the prohibition
of intermarriage with aliens. And it is
called jus gentium because almost all
nations observe it.

> St. Isidore: *Etymologies,* 5, 6. (7th cent.)

The law of nations is indeed, in some
way, natural to man, in so far as he is a
reasonable being, because it is derived
from the natural law by way of a conclusion that is not very remote from its
premises. Wherefore men easily agree
thereto.

> St. Thomas Aquinas: *Summa Theologica,*
> 1-2, 95, 4. (13th cent.)

The idea which credits the state with
unlimited authority is not simply an
error harmful to the eternal life of nations, to their prosperity, and to the
larger and well-ordered increase in their
well-being, but likewise it injures the
relations between peoples, for it breaks
the unity of supranational society, robs
the law of nations of its foundation and
vigor, leads to violation of others' rights
and impedes agreement and peaceful intercourse.

> Pope Pius XII: *Summi Pontificatus.*
> (October 20, 1939)

The human race is bound together by
reciprocal ties, moral and juridical, into
a great commonwealth directed to the
good of all nations and ruled by special
laws which protect its unity and promote its prosperity.

> Pope Pius XII: *Summi Pontificatus.*
> (October 20, 1939)

There is nothing more necessary for the national or international community than respect for the majesty of the law and the salutary thought that the law is also sacred and protected, so that whoever breaks it is punishable and will be punished.

Pope Pius XII: *Address to the 6th Int. Congr. of Penal Law.* (Oct. 3, 1953)

The right to existence, the right to respect from others and to one's good name, the right to one's own culture and national character, the right to develop oneself, the right to demand observance of international treaties, and other like rights, are exigencies of the law of nations, dictated by nature herself.

Pope Pius XII: *The World Community.* (Dec. 6, 1953)

See also Authority; Canon Law; Church and State; Commandment; Common Law; God; Government; Justice; King; Power; Revelation; Tyranny

Lawsuit

To go to law and not be out of one's mind is scarcely granted to the saints.

St. Francis de Sales: *Letters to Persons in Religion,* 4, 5. (17th cent.)

Lawyer

A sergeant at the law who paid his calls,
Wary and wise, for clients at St. Paul's
There also was, of noted excellence.

Chaucer: *Canterbury Tales: Prologue.* (Tr. Coghill) (14th cent.)

Ye who plead for the poor, and take money at their hands,
Ye lawyers, ye advocates, be sure of this:
When ye draw near to death, and pray for pardon,
Your pardon at your parting hence will be but small.
Saint Matthew bids me tell you this, and if I lie, blame him.

Langland: *Piers Plowman: God's Bull of Pardon.* (14th cent.)

The man of law who never saw
The way to buy and sell,
Weening to rise by merchandise,
I pray God speed him well!

St. Thomas More: *A Merry Jest.* (16th cent.)

[The Utopians] have no lawyers among them, for they consider them as a sort of people whose profession it is to disguise matters.

St. Thomas More: *Utopia.* (16th cent.)

The mere sight of an advocate in cap and cassock induces a high opinion of his competence.

Pascal: *Pensées.* (17th cent.)

It is a horrible demoralizing thing to be a lawyer. You look for such low motives in everyone and everything.

Katharine T. Hinkson: *The Love of Sisters.* (20th cent.)

Laxity

When the head languishes, the members have no vigor.

Pope St. Gregory I: *Pastoral Care,* 2, 7. (6th cent.)

Lazarus

Bright were the mornings first impearl'd
O'er earth, and sea, and air;
The birthdays of a rising world—
For power divine was there.

But fairer shone the tears of God,
For Lazarus, o'er his grave;
Since love divine bedew'd the sod
Of one He sought to save.

M. Bridges: *And Jesus Wept.* (19th cent.)

Learning

What is wrong with us? What is this that you heard? The unlearned arise and take heaven by force, and here are we with all our learning, stuck fast in flesh and blood! Is there any shame in following because they have gone before us, would it not be a worse shame not to follow at once?

> St. Augustine: *Confessions*, 8, 8. (5th cent.)

Let there be no doubt in the mind of the man who has benefited from the common heritage but does not trouble to contribute to the common good that he is failing sadly in his duty. For he is not *a tree beside the running waters bearing fruit in due season* (Ps. 1, 3) but rather a vicious whirlpool, for ever swallowing things but never throwing them up again.

> Dante: *Monarchy*, 1. (14th cent.)

Learning is not to be blamed, nor the mere knowledge of anything which is good in itself and ordained by God; but a good conscience and a virtuous life are always to be preferred before it.

> Thomas a Kempis: *The Imitation of Christ*, 1, 3. (15th cent.)

Never read anything that thou mayest appear more learned or more wise. Study rather to mortify thy vices, for this will avail thee more than being able to answer many hard questions.

> Thomas a Kempis: *The Imitation of Christ*, 3, 43. (15th cent.)

A little learning is a dangerous thing;
Drink deep, or taste not the Pierian spring:
There shallow draughts intoxicate the brain,
And drinking largely sobers us again.

> Pope: *An Essay on Criticism*, 2. (18th cent.)

Ask of the learn'd the way: the learn'd are blind.

> Pope: *An Essay on Man*, 4. (18th cent.)

The longer one lives the more he learns.

> Thomas Moore: *Dream of Hindoostan*. (19th cent.)

There is a mission of genius, of intelligence in the Church, which is not necessarily restricted to the clergy, and may be committed to laymen, or to clergymen in a sense outside of their sacerdotal character, for the Church has a right to the service of the genius, the intelligence, the learning, the good-will and the zeal of all her members, of laymen as well as of clergymen.

> Orestes Brownson: *Lacordaire*. (*Works*, 20, 249ff.) (1862)

A man may have learned a dozen languages, and have the whole circle of the sciences at his fingers' ends, and may know nothing worthy of being called knowledge; indeed, there is nothing which seems to be a greater hindrance to the acquisition of living knowledge rather than an engrossing devotion to the acquisition of words, facts, logical methods, and natural laws. It requires little learning to make a wise or truly knowing man, but much learning may not impossibly spoil one.

> Coventry Patmore: *Religio Poetae*. (19th cent.)

It is obvious that in the existing keen competition of talents, and the widespread and in itself noble and praiseworthy passion for knowledge, Catholics ought to be not followers but leaders. It is necessary therefore that they should cultivate every refinement of learning, and zealously train their minds to the discovery of truth and the investigation, so far as it is possible, of the entire domain of nature.

> Pope Leo XIII: *Longinque Oceani*. (Jan. 6, 1895)

It is easy enough to say the cultured man should be the crowd's guide, philosopher and friend. Unfortunately, he has nearly always been a misguiding guide, a false friend and a very shallow philosopher. And the actual catastrophes we have suffered, including those we are now suffering, have not in historical fact been due to the prosaic practical people who are supposed to know nothing, but almost invariably to the highly theoretical people who knew that they knew everything. The world may learn by its mistakes; but they are mostly the mistakes of the learned.

> G. K. Chesterton: *The Common Man.* (20th cent.)

A little learning leads men away from the truth; a large learning confirms the truth.

> Hilaire Belloc: *Essays of a Catholic.* (20th cent.)

See also Education; Knowledge; School

Leaven

Put away, therefore, the bad leaven which is old and stale, and be converted into the new leaven which is Jesus Christ. Be salted in Him, lest any of you lose your savor, for by your savor will you be judged. It is out of place to preach Jesus Christ and to practise Judaism.

> St. Ignatius of Antioch: *Letter to the Magnesians,* 10. (2nd cent.)

How can the lump be leavened if the leaven be withdrawn!

> R. H. Benson: *The Light Invisible.* (20th cent.)

Lecture

British audiences do not as a rule go to lectures to be entertained. They go more or less as students, to acquire information. Therefore very few of them go.

> Sheila Kaye-Smith: *Kitchen Fugue.* (20th cent.)

Leg

His legs were lean,
Like sticks they were, no calf was to be seen.

> Chaucer: *Canterbury Tales: Prologue.* (Tr. Coghill) (14th cent.)

But long be thy legs, and short be thy life.

> John Heywood: *Proverbs,* 2, 7. (16th cent.)

Legislation

What has pleased the prince has the force of law, inasmuch as by a *lex regia* which has been enacted concerning his imperium the people grants to and bestows upon him all its power and authority. (Quod principi placuit, legis habet vigorem: utpote cum lege regia quae de imperio eius lata est, populus ei et in eum omne suum imperium et potestatem conferat.)

> Institutes of Justinian, 1, 2, 6. (Also Dig. 1, 4, 1.) (Quoting Ulpian, 3rd cent.) (6th cent.)

Law (*lex*) is made by the consent of the people and the ordinance of the king.

> Edictum Pistense of Charles the Bald. (864)

For as a king is the minister and vicar of God he can do nothing on earth which is not according to law, nor is this contrary to the saying *what pleases the prince has the force of law* (Justinian's Digest, 1, 4, 1), since there follows at the end of the law *in conjunction with the lex regia which has been passed concerning his imperium;* and this is presumed to be not every rash expression of the king's will, but what shall have been duly defined with the counsel of his great men, the king warranting its authority after deliberation and consultation upon it.

> Bracton: *On the Laws and Customs of England,* 3, 9, 3. (Bracton apparently deliberately distorts or mistranslates the Latin of Justinian in favor of medieval theory: the king under law.) (13th cent.)

In order that the volition of what is commanded may have the nature of law, it needs to be in accord with some rule of reason. And in this sense is to be understood the saying that the will of the sovereign has the force of law; otherwise the sovereign's will would savor of lawlessness rather than of law.

> St. Thomas Aquinas: *Summa Theologica,* 1-2, 90, 1. (13th cent.)

That which touches all should be approved by all. (Quod omnes tangit, debet ab omnibus approbari.)

> Legal maxim. (cf. Reg. juris 29 lib. sexti) (Medieval)

Let us say, in accordance with the truth and the counsel of Aristotle in *Politics,* Bk. 3, ch. 6, that the legislator, or the primary and proper efficient cause of the law, is the people or the whole body of citizens, or the weightier part thereof, by its choice or will expressed orally in a general gathering of the citizens, commanding or determining certain things to be done or omitted with regard to man's civil actions, under threat of temporal penalty or punishment. I say weightier part, taking into consideration both the number of persons and their quality in the community for which the law is enacted.

> Marsilius of Padua: *Defensor Pacis,* 1, 12, 3. (14th cent.)

The highest privilege of sovereignty consists primarily in giving laws not only to individuals but also to the people as a whole, without their consent.

> Jean Bodin: *Republic,* 1, 8. (Theory of absolutism) (16th cent.)

The human legislator must attain to that balance, that keen sense of moral responsibility, without which it is easy to mistake the boundary between the legitimate use and the abuse of power. Thus only will his decisions have internal consistency, noble dignity and religious sanction, and be immune from selfishness and passion.

> Pope Pius XII: *Summi Pontificatus.* (October 20, 1939)

See also Government; Law

Leisure

In leisure a man ought not to revel in the luxury of having nothing to do; he should be occupied with either the investigation or the discovery of truth; one should advance in truth, hold fast what one finds, and not grudge communicating it to another. The thing to love in an active life is not honor or power, for *all things are vanity under the sun,* but the work itself.

> St. Augustine: *The City of God,* 19, 19. (5th cent.)

The modern world is killing leisure.

> Gerald Vann: *The Water and the Fire.* (20th cent.)

Lent

If any bishop, or presbyter, or deacon, or reader, or singer, does not fast the fast of forty days, or the fourth day of the week, and the day of the Preparation (Friday), let him be deprived, except he be hindered by weakness of body. But if he be one of the laity, let him be suspended.

> Ecclesiastical Canons of the Holy Apostles, 69. (4th cent.)

O kind Creator, bow Thine ear
To mark the cry, to know the tear
Before Thy throne of mercy spent
In this Thy holy fast of Lent.

> Roman Breviary, Hymn *Audi benigne Conditor* for Vespers. (Tr. T. Lacey) (Pope St. Gregory I, 6th cent.)

The fast, as taught by holy lore,
We keep in solemn course once more:
The fast to all men known, and bound
In forty days of yearly round.
The law and seers that were of old
In divers ways this Lent foretold,
Which Christ, all seasons' King and Guide,
In after ages sanctified.

> Roman Breviary, Hymn *Ex more docti mystico* for Matins. (Tr. J. Neale) (Attr. to Pope St. Gregory I, 6th cent.)

Jesu, salvation's Sun divine,
Within our inmost bosoms shine,
With light all darkness drive away
And give the world a better day.

Roman Breviary, Hymn *O Sol salutis intimis* for Lauds. (Tr. from Primer of 1706) (Ambrosian, 6th cent.)

In these days, therefore, let us add something beyond the wonted measure of our service, such as private prayers and abstinence in food and drink. Let each one, over and above the measure prescribed for him, offer God something of his own freewill in the joy of the Holy Spirit.

St. Benedict: *Rule,* 49. (6th cent.)

Let Thy gracious favor, we beseech Thee, O Lord, carry us through the fast which we have begun; that as we observe it by bodily discipline, so we may be able to fulfil it with sincerity of mind.

Roman Missal, Collect for Friday after Ash Wednesday. (Gelasian, 5th to 7th cent.)

O God, Who dost purify Thy Church by the yearly observance of forty days; grant to Thy household, that what we strive to obtain from Thee by self-denial, we may secure by good works.

Roman Missal, Collect for First Sunday in Lent. (Gregorian, 6th to 8th cent.)

O supersubstantial Trinity, That art adored in Unity, remove from me the heavy yoke of my sins, and in Thy mercy grant me the tears of repentance.

Byzantine Triodion, Great Canon of St. Andrew. (Thursday before Passion Sunday.) (8th cent.)

Now are the days of humblest prayer,
When consciences to God lie bare,
And mercy most delights to spare.
    Oh hearken when we cry,
        Chastise us with Thy fear;
    Yet, Father! in the multitude
        Of Thy compassions, hear!

F. Faber: *Lent.* (19th cent.)

The fare in Lent should be austere.
No cakes and ale, no kraut and beer;
    No fatted goose, with heavy wines,
    That Croesus fancies when he dines—
They're all taboo this time o' year.

T. A. Daly: *The Fare in Lent.* (20th cent.)

In a dear rout of loneliness
how life again sang sweet
when fasting arms knew banqueting
and avid eyes could feast;
and the long Lent of love was eased
for one Laetare Day.

But afterwards came Lent again:
again the fasting way.

Robert Farren: *Laetare.* (20th cent.)

Leo I, Pope Saint

From the tomb his call to the Church still rings out: *Watch lest the wolf rend God's flock.* Like a true lion (*leo*) he roared, and all the wild beasts trembled; but the sheep gathered close around their shepherd.

Inscription on tomb of Pope. (Composed by Pope Sergius I, 688)

Leo XIII, Pope

Leo! Vicar of Christ,
His voice, his love, his sword:
Leo! Vicar of Christ,
Earth's angel of the Lord.

.   .   .   .   .   .

Leo! God grant this thing:
Might some, so proud to be
Children of England, bring
Thine England back to thee!

Lionel Johnson: *To Leo XIII.* (19th cent.)

Leper

Oh, a leper must be a terrible thing to see
When one is beautiful, young, and free!

Sister Eleanore: *The Vocation of St. Francis.* (20th cent.)

Letter

I have made this letter longer than usual because I lack the time to make it shorter.

Pascal: *Provincial Letters,* 16. (17th cent.)

I listen and my hand thy letter presses;
I, time-worn woman, touch it with caresses,
I kiss the faded ink of its addresses.

Susan L. Emory: *An Old Woman's Answer to a Letter from Her Girlhood.* (19th cent.)

Libel

For oh, 'twas nuts to the father of lies,
(As this wily fiend is nam'd in the Bible)
To find it settled by laws so wise
That the greater the truth, the worse the libel!

Thomas Moore: *A Case of Libel.* (19th cent.)

Liberalism

You cannot halve the gospel of God's grace;
Men of presumptuous heart! I know you well.
You are of those who plan that we should dwell,
Each in his tranquil home and holy place;
Seeing the Word refines all natures rude,
And tames the stirrings of the multitude.
And ye have caught some echoes of its lore,
As heralded amid the joyous choirs;
Ye mark'd it spoke of peace, chastised desires,
Good-will and mercy,—and ye heard no more;
But, as for zeal and quick-eyed sanctity,
And the dread depths of grace, ye pass'd them by.
And so ye halve the truth; for ye in heart,
At best, are doubters whether it be true,

The theme discarding, as unmeet for you,
Statesmen or sages. O new-encompass'd art
Of the ancient foe!—but what, if it extends
O'er our own camp, and rules amid our friends?

Card. Newman: *Liberalism.* (Written as an Anglican, with reference to a growing trend in Protestant thought) (1833)

When I was young, I knew the word first as giving name to a periodical, set up by Lord Byron and others. . . . Afterwards, liberalism was the badge of a theological school, of a dry and repulsive character, not very dangerous in itself, though dangerous as opening the door to evils which it did not itself either anticipate or comprehend. At present it is nothing else than that deep, plausible scepticism, which I spoke of above, as being the development of human reason, as practically exercised by the natural man.

Card. Newman: *Apologia pro Vita Sua,* 5. (19th cent.)

By liberalism I mean false liberty of thought, or the exercise of thought upon matters, in which, from the constitution of the human mind, thought cannot be brought to any successful issue, and therefore is out of place. Among such matters are first principles of any kind; and of these the most sacred and momentous are especially to be reckoned the truths of revelation.

Card. Newman: *Apologia pro Vita Sua,* Note A. (19th cent.)

No one can dislike the democratic principle more than I do. No one mourns, for instance, more than I, over the state of Oxford, given up, alas! to 'liberalism and progress,' to the forfeiture of her great medieval motto, 'Dominus illuminatio mea,' and with a consequent call on her to go to Parliament or to the Herald's College for a new one; but what can we do? All I know is that

Toryism, that is, loyalty to persons, 'springs immortal in the human breast'; that religion is a spiritual loyalty; and that Catholicity is the only divine form of religion. And thus in centuries to come there may be found out some way of uniting what is free in the new structure of society with what is authoritative in the old, without any base compromise with 'progress' and 'liberalism.'

> Card. Newman: *Letter to the Duke of Norfolk.* (19th cent.)

Liberalism in religion is the doctrine that there is no positive truth in religion, but that one creed is as good as another, and this is the teaching which is gaining substance and force daily. It is inconsistent with any recognition of any religion, as *true*. It teaches that all are to be tolerated, for all are matters of opinion.

> Card. Newman: *'Biglietto Speech,' on being raised to the Cardinalate.* (19th cent.)

The mistake of bourgeois liberalism has been to conceive democratic society to be a kind of lists or arena in which all the conceptions of the bases of common life, even those most destructive to freedom and law, merely meet with no more than the pure and simple indifference of the body politic, while they compete before public opinion in a kind of free market of the mother-ideas, healthy or poisoned, of political life.

> J. Maritain: *Man and the State.* (20th cent.)

Liberty

There is no true liberty except the liberty of the happy who cleave to the eternal law.

> St. Augustine: *On Freewill,* 1, 32. (4th cent.)

For what is liberty but the unhampered translation of will into act?

> Dante: *Letters,* 6. (14th cent.)

Liberty of spirit is a detachment of the Christian heart from all things to follow the known will of God.

> St. Francis de Sales: *Letters to Persons in the World,* 3, 11. (17th cent.)

I leave you the spirit of liberty—not that which excludes obedience, for that is the liberty of the flesh; but that which excludes restraint, scruple and worry.

> St. Francis de Sales: *Letters to Persons in the World,* 3, 11. (17th cent.)

Blessed are the hearts which can bend; they shall never be broken.

> Jean Pierre Camus: *The Spirit of St. Francis de Sales,* 7, 1. (17th cent.)

More liberty begets desire of more,
The hunger still increases with the store.

> Dryden: *The Hind and the Panther,* 1. (17th cent.)

Give me again my hollow tree,
A crust of bread, and liberty.

> Pope: *The Sixth Satire of the Second Book of Horace.* (18th cent.)

His safety must his liberty restrain.

> Pope: *An Essay on Man,* 3. (18th cent.)

Oh! if there be, on this earthly sphere,
A boon, an offering heaven holds dear,
'Tis the last libation liberty draws
From the heart that bleeds and breaks in her cause!

> Thomas Moore: *Lalla Rookh: Paradise and the Peri.* (19th cent.)

The tribute most high to a head that is royal,
Is love from a heart that loves liberty too.

> Thomas Moore: *The Prince's Day.* (19th cent.)

God makes no man a slave, no doubter free;
Abiding faith alone wins liberty.

> J. J. Roche: *Washington.* (19th cent.)

Liberty, the highest of natural endowments, being the portion of intellectual or rational natures only, confers on man this dignity: that he is *in the arbitrament of his own will* (Ecclesiasticus 15, 14) and has power over his actions.

> Pope Leo XIII: *Libertas Praestantissimum.* (June 20, 1888)

The true liberty of human society does not consist in every man doing what he pleases, for this would simply end in turmoil and confusion, and bring on the overthrow of the state; but rather in this, that through the injunctions of the civil law all may more easily conform to the prescriptions of the eternal law.

> Pope Leo XIII: *Libertas Praestantissimum.* (June 20, 1888)

Liberty is not a means to a higher political end. It is itself the highest political end.

> Lord Acton: *Lectures on Modern History.* (19th cent.)

Man must have liberty—he was made for it; but what liberty would that be which he has not learned to use?

> R. H. Benson: *The Dawn of All.* (20th cent.)

The idea of liberty has ultimately a religious root; that is why men find it so easy to die for and so difficult to define. It refers finally to the fact that, while the oyster and the palm tree have to save their lives by law, man has to save his soul by choice.

> G. K. Chesterton: *A Miscellany of Men.* (20th cent.)

See also Freedom

License

Liberty will ever be more free and secure, in proportion as license is kept in restraint.

> Pope Leo XIII: *Libertas Praestantissimum.* (June 20, 1888)

Life

Blessed is he that hath a short life.

> Pope St. Clement I: *Epistle to the Corinthians.* (2nd cent.)

The sole purpose of life in time is to gain merit for life in eternity.

> St. Augustine: *Letter 130* (to Proba on prayer). (5th cent.)

It is no great thing to live long, nor even to live for ever; but it is a great thing to live well.

> St. Augustine: *Sermons,* 127, 2. (5th cent.)

If a man live according to himself, that is according to man, not according to God, assuredly he lives according to a lie. . . . For man not to live as he was created to live is a lie.

> St. Augustine: *The City of God,* 14, 4, 1. (5th cent.)

Life is an abstract term, signifying the very living of what is alive.

> St. Thomas Aquinas: *Contra Gentes,* 1, 97. (13th cent.)

Of divers voices is sweet music made:
So in our life the different degrees
Render sweet harmony among these wheels.

> Dante: *Paradiso, Canto 6.* (Tr. Cary) (14th cent.)

The life of every brute and plant on earth
  Is by the quick beams of the sacred fires
  From its combining potencies drawn forth.
But the Supreme Benignity inspires
  Directly your life, making it to love
  Itself, and kindling it to fresh desires.

> Dante: *Paradiso, Canto 7.* (Tr. Binyon) (14th cent.)

This world is but a thoroughfare full of woe,

And we but pilgrims passing to and
fro.
Death is an end of every worldly sore.

St. Chaucer: *The Knightes Tale.* (14th cent.)

And therefore let us never make our
reckoning of long life. Keep it while we
may, because God hath so commanded.
But if God gives the occasion that with
His good will we may go, let us be glad
thereof, and long to go to Him.

St. Thomas More: *Dialogue of Comfort.*
(16th cent.)

Life is a wandering course to doubtful
rest;
As oft a cursed rise to damning leap,
As happy race to win a heavenly crest;
None being sure what final fruits to
reap:
And who can like in such a life to
dwell,
Whose ways are strict to heaven, but
wide to hell?

Bl. Robert Southwell: *Life is But Loss.*
(16th cent.)

We in this life are walking, as it were,
on ice.

St. Francis de Sales: *Spiritual Conferences,*
3. (17th cent.)

From length of life no happiness can
come.

Sir John Beaumont: *Of the Miserable State
of Man.* (17th cent.)

Between us and hell or heaven there is
nothing but life, which of all things is
the frailest.

Pascal: *Pensées,* 1. (17th cent.)

O, that I less could fear to lose this
being,
Which, like a snow-ball, in my coward
hand
The more 'tis grasped, the faster melts
away.

Dryden: *All for Love.* (17th cent.)

When I consider life, 'tis all a cheat;
Yet, fooled with hope, men favor the
deceit.

Dryden: *Aurengzebe,* 4. (17th cent.)

But life can never be sincerely blest;
Heaven punishes the bad, and proves
the best.

Dryden. (17th cent.)

A mighty maze but not without a plan.

Pope: *An Essay on Man,* 1. (18th cent.)

Life can little more supply
Than just to look about us and to die.

Pope: *An Essay on Man,* 1. (18th cent.)

This speck of life in time's great wilderness
This narrow isthmus 'twixt two boundless seas,
The past, the future, two eternities!

Thomas Moore: *Lalla Rookh: The Veiled
Prophet of Khorassan.* (19th cent.)

Life is a waste of wearisome hours,
Which seldom the rose of enjoyment
adorns,
And the heart that is soonest awake to
the flowers,
Is always the first to be touch'd by
the thorns.

Thomas Moore: *Oh! Think Not My
Spirits.* (19th cent.)

This life is all chequer'd with pleasures
and woes.

Thomas Moore: *This Life is All
Chequer'd.* (19th cent.)

They may rail at this life—from the
hour that I began it,
I found it a life full of kindness and
bliss;
And until they can show me some happier planet,
More social and bright, I'll content
me with this.

Thomas Moore: *They May Rail.* (19th
cent.)

Half my life is full of sorrow,
    Half of joy, still fresh and new;
One of these lives is a fancy,
    But the other one is true.

Adelaide Procter: *Dream-Life.* (19th
cent.)

To suffer and to endure is the lot of
humankind. Let them strive as they may,
they will never summon up enough
strength and cunning to throw off the
ills and troubles which beset them.

Pope Leo XIII: *Rerum novarum.* (May 15,
1891)

A well-spent life is the only passport to
heaven.

Pope Leo XIII: *Immortale Dei.* (Nov. 1,
1885)

How light the touches are that kiss
The music from the chords of life!

Coventry Patmore: *By the Sea.* (19th cent.)

For life is the mirror of king and slave,
    'Tis just what we are and do;
Then give to the world the best you
    have,
    And the best will come back to you.

Madeleine Bridges: *Life's Mirror.* (19th
cent.)

Columbus-like, I sailed into the night,
    The sunset-gold to find:
Alas! 'twas but the phantom of the
    light!
Life's Indies lay behind!

J. B. Tabb: *The Voyager.* (19th cent.)

Life is coquetry
Of death, which wearies me,
    Too sure
    Of the amour.

F. Thompson: *To the Dead Cardinal of
Westminster.* (19th cent.)

What expiating agony
May for him, damned to poesy,
Shut in that little sentence be—
What deep austerities of strife—
He 'lived his life.' 'He lived *his* life.'

F. Thompson: *A Judgment in Heaven:
Epilogue.* (19th cent.)

To have lived enchanted years
Free from sorrows, free from fears.

Lionel Johnson: *Winchester.* (19th cent.)

Life is far too important a thing ever
to talk seriously about.

Oscar Wilde: *Lady Windermere's Fan,* 1.
(19th cent.)

One's real life is so often the life that
one does not lead.

Oscar Wilde: *Rose-Leaf and Apple-Leaf:
Envoi.* (19th cent.)

Ah! somehow life is bigger after all
Than any painted angel could we see
The God that is within us!

Oscar Wilde: *Humanitad.* (19th cent.)

No life is perfect that has not been lived
youth in feeling, manhood in battle, old
age in meditation.

W. S. Blunt: *The Perfect Life.* (19th
cent.)

Three times have I beheld
Fear leap in a babe's face, and take his
    breath,
    Fear, like the fear of eld
That knows the price of life, the name
    of death.

What is it justifies
This thing, this dread, this fright that
    has no tongue,
    The terror in those eyes
When only eyes can speak—they are
    so young?

· · · · · ·

Life: There's nought else to seek;
Life only, little prized; but by design
    Of nature prized. How weak,
How sad, how brief! O how divine,
    divine!

Alice Meynell: *The Treasure.* (20th cent.)

From golden dawn to purple dusk,
Piled high with bales of smiles and
    tears,
The caravans are dropping down
Across the desert-sands of years.

J. C. Miller: *The March of Humanity.*
(20th cent.)

A dead thing can go with the stream, but only a living thing can go against it.

> G. K. Chesterton: *The Everlasting Man,* 2, 6. (20th cent.)

Life is not void or stuff for scorners:
We have laughed loud and kept our love,
We have heard singers in tavern corners
And not forgotten the birds above:
We have known smiters and sons of thunder
And not unworthily walked with them,
We have grown wiser and lost not wonder;
And we have seen Jerusalem.

> G. K. Chesterton: *To F. C.* (20th cent.)

The full value of this life can only be got by fighting; the violent take it by storm. And if we have accepted everything we have missed something—war. This life of ours is a very enjoyable fight, but a very miserable truce.

> G. K. Chesterton: *Charles Dickens.* (20th cent.)

The perplexity of life arises from there being too many interesting things in it for us to be interested properly in any of them; what we call its triviality is really the tag-ends of numberless tales; ordinary and unmeaning existence is like ten thousand thrilling detective stories mixed up with a spoon.

> G. K. Chesterton: *Tremendous Trifles,* 3. (20th cent.)

Life is a thing too glorious to be enjoyed.

> G. K. Chesterton: *George Bernard Shaw.* (20th cent.)

The law of life is the law of sacrifice and discipline.

> C. Dawson: *Gifford Lectures, 1947.*

Life and Death

For no sooner do we begin to live in this dying body, than we begin to move ceaselessly towards death. For in the whole course of this life (if life we must call it) its mutability tends towards death.

> St. Augustine: *The City of God,* 13, 10. (5th cent.)

O almighty and everlasting God, Who dost rule both the living and the dead, and hast mercy on all whom Thou dost foreknow shall be Thine in faith and in deed: we humbly beseech Thee; that all those for whom we intend to pray, whether still living in the flesh or gone to their reward, may obtain the forgiveness of all their sins by Thy divine clemency, through the intercession of all Thy saints.

> Roman Missal, Collect for Living and Dead. (ca. 10th cent.)

Remember that thou hast but one soul; that thou canst die but once; that thou hast but one life, which is short and peculiar to thyself; that there is but one blessedness, and that for ever; and thou wilt despise many things.

> St. Teresa of Jesus: *Maxims.* (16th cent.)

How can the tree but waste and wither away
That hath not sometime comfort of the sun?
How can that flower but fade and soon decay
That always is with dark clouds overrun?
Is this a life? Nay, death you may it call,
That feels each pain and knows no joy at all.

> Thomas, Lord Vaux: *Death in Life.* (16th cent.)

I sought my death, and found it in my womb;
I looked for life, and saw it was a shade;
I trod the earth, and knew it was my tomb;
And now I die, and now I am but made.

The glass is full, and now my glass is run,
And now I live, and now my life is done.

Chidiock Tichborne: *Elegie.* (Martyred 1586)

O life! what lets thee from a quick decease?
O death! what draws thee from a present pray?
My feast is done, my soul would be at ease,
My grace is said; O death! come take away.

I live, but such a life as ever dies;
I die, but such a death as never ends;
My death to end, my dying life denies,
And life my giving death no whit amends.

Bl. Robert Southwell: *I Die Alive.* (16th cent.)

One that lives by other's breath,
Dieth also by his death.

Bl. Robert Southwell: *Mary Magdalen's Complaint.* (16th cent.)

O true Life! sith thou hast left me,
Mortal life is tedious;
Death it is to live without thee,
Death of all most odious:
Turn again or take me to thee,
Let me die or live thou in me.

Bl. Robert Southwell: *Mary Magdalen's Complaint.* (16th cent.)

Life is but loss where death is deemèd gain,
And loathèd pleasures breed displeasing pain.

Bl. Robert Southwell: *Life is But Loss.* (16th cent.)

All ye that fix your eyes upon this tomb,
Remember this, that beauty fadeth fast,
That honors are enthrall'd to hapless doom,
That life hath nothing sure, but soon doth waste:

So live you then, that, when your years are fled,
Your glories may survive when you are dead.

Thomas Lodge: *Diana's Epitaph.* (16th cent.)

She'll bargain with them, and will give
Them God; teach them how to live
In Him; or if they this deny,
For Him she'll teach them how to die.

Richard Crashaw: *Hymn to the Name and Honor of St. Teresa.* (17th cent.)

So I may gain thy death, my life I'll give.
(My life's thy death, and in thy death I live.)
Or else, my life, I'll hide thee in his grave,
By three days' loss eternally to save.

R. Crashaw: *Whosoever Shall Lose His Life.* (Matth. 16, 25) (17th cent.)

Since ev'ry man who lives is born to die,
And none can boast sincere felicity,
With equal mind, what happens, let us bear,
Nor joy, nor grieve too much for things beyond our care.
Like pilgrims to th' appointed place we tend;
The world's an inn, and death the journey's end.

Dryden: *Palamon and Arcite,* 3. (17th cent.)

Life can little more supply
Than just to look about us and to die.

Pope: *An Essay on Man,* 1. (18th cent.)

Life is short; death is certain; and the world to come is everlasting.

Card. Newman: *Miscellanies,* 324. (19th cent.)

                    All
Life death does end and each day dies with sleep.

G. M. Hopkins: *No Worst, There is None.* (19th cent.)

They are not long, the days of wine
    and roses:
  Out of a misty dream
Our path emerges for a while, then
    closes
  Within a dream.

  Ernest Dowson: *Vitae Summa Brevis.*
  (19th cent.)

  For there is nothing lives but some-
    thing dies,
And there is nothing dies but some-
    thing lives.

  F. Thompson: *Ode to the Setting Sun.*
  (19th cent.)

The fairest things in life are death and
    birth,
  And of these two the fairer thing is
    death.

  F. Thompson: *Ode to the Setting Sun.*
  (19th cent.)

Life is a play acted by dying men,
  Where, if its heroes seem to foot it
    well
And go light-tongued without grimace
    of pain,
  Death will be found anon. And who
    shall tell
Which part was saddest, or in youth
    or age,
When the tired actor stops and leaves
    the stage?

    W. S. Blunt: *Esther, 1.* (19th cent.)

A life of noise! a restless death:
The sanctities of life's last breath
Profaned with ritual pride and state;
Last pageant of the little great.

  Lionel Johnson: *Laleham.* (19th cent.)

None knew so well as I:
For he who lives more lives than one
  More deaths than one must die.

  Oscar Wilde: *The Ballad of Reading Gaol,*
  3. (19th cent.)

Unlike the youth that all men say
  They prize—the youth of abounding
    blood,
In love with the sufficient day,
  And gay in growth, and strong in
    bud;

Unlike was mine! Then my first slum-
    ber
  Nightly rehearsed my last; each
    breath
Knew itself one of the unknown num-
    ber.
  But life was urgent with me as
    death.

  Alice Meynell: *The Unexpected Peril.*
  (20th cent.)

One day of life, One soul to save,
One weary strife, One wayside grave.
One solemn knell, One trampled sod,
One way to hell, One way to God.

  Hugh Francis Blunt: *All of it.* (20th cent.)

To go to death, however painful, with
honor and applause, or at least with the
silence of respect, were easy. It is not
hard to die upon a throne; but to live
on a dunghill with Job, that is bitterness.

  R. H. Benson: *By What Authority.* (20th
  cent.)

Death, after all, reveals what life cannot, for at death we take not only a review of our past, but a look into the
future.

  R. H. Benson: *The Death-beds of Bloody
  Mary and Good Queen Bess.* (20th cent.)

Light

Light, even though it passes through
pollution, is not polluted.

  St. Augustine: *Tract. in Joannem,* 1, 5, 15.
  (5th cent.)

Then sorrow, touch'd by thee, grows
    bright
  With more than rapture's ray;
As darkness shows us worlds of light
  We never saw by day.

  Thomas Moore: *Oh, Thou Who Dry'st the
  Mourner's Tears.* (19th cent.)

Likeness

No more like together is than is chalk
to coals.

  St. Thomas More: *English Works, 674.*
  (16th cent.)

No more like than an apple to an oyster.

St. Thomas More: *English Works*, 724. (16th cent.)

Lilac

Go down to Kew in lilac-time, in lilac-
time, in lilac-time;
Go down to Kew in lilac-time (it
isn't far from London!)
And you shall wander hand in hand
with love in summer's wonder-
land;
Go down to Kew in lilac-time (it
isn't far from London!)

Alfred Noyes: *The Barrel-Organ*. (20th cent.)

Lily

But lilies, stolen from grassy mold,
No more curled state unfold,
Translated to a vase of gold;
In burning throne though they keep
still
Serenities unthawed and chill.

F. Thompson: *Gilded Gold*. (19th cent.)

O lily of the King! low lies thy silver
wing,
And long has been the hour of thine
unqueening;
And thy scent of Paradise on the night-
wind spills its sighs,
Nor any take the secrets of its meaning.

F. Thompson: *Lilium Regis*. (19th cent.)

Long from their purpled heights,
Their reign of high delights,
The queens have wended down death's
mildewed stair,
Leaving the scent of lilies on the air,
To gladden earth through all her days
and nights,
That once she cherished anything so
fair.

Eleanor R. Cox: *Dreaming of Cities Dead*. (20th cent.)

Limbo

These sinned not: but the merit that
they achieve
Helps not, since baptism was not
theirs, the gate
Of that faith, which was given to
thee to believe.

Dante: *Inferno, Canto 4*. (Tr. Binyon) (14th cent.)

Down there a place is that no torments
try
But only darkness grieves, where the
lament
Hath not the sound of wail, but is a
sigh.

There dwell I with the babies innocent
Who bitten by the tooth of Death
expired
Before they were from human guilt
exempt.

There dwell I among those never at-
tired
In the three holy virtues; without sin
All the others they both followed
and desired.

Dante: *Purgatorio, Canto 7*. (Dante holds that those in limbo do not know the theological virtues, but they know the cardinal virtues.) (Tr. Binyon) (14th cent.)

Lineage

There is nothing men more pride themselves on than birth, for this very reason,
that it is irrevocable; it can neither be
given to those who have it not, nor
taken away from those who have.

Card. Newman: *Historical Sketches*, 1. (19th cent.)

Lion

If there is famine, if there is plague, the
cry is at once: "The Christians to the
lion!" What! all of them to one lion?

Tertullian: *Apology*, 40, 2. (3rd cent.)

Tremble ye nations who secure before,
Laught at those arms that 'gainst our-
  selves we bore;
Rous'd by the lash of his own stubborn
  tail,
Our lion now will foreign foes assail.

> Dryden: *Astraea Redux.* (17th cent.)

Lips

My lady's presence makes the roses red,
Because to see her lips they blush for
  shame.

> Henry Constable: *Sonnets to Diana, 9.*
> (16th cent.)

Listening

He listens to good purpose who takes
note.

> Dante: *Inferno, Canto 15.* (14th cent.)

Listeners hear no good of themselves:
and I suppose that's true of the other
senses as well.

> R. H. Benson: *The Necromancers.* (20th
> cent.)

Literature

The safe and cautious thing to do is to
read only Catholic books. It is somewhat
dangerous to expose the unsophisticated
to pagan literature; but a training in
both is very useful to those safe in the
faith, for accurate reading on a wide
range of subjects makes the scholar;
careful selection of the better makes the
saint.

> John of Salisbury: *Policraticus,* 7, 10, 133.
> (12th cent.)

A literary religion is so little to be
depended upon; it looks well in fair
weather, but its doctrines are opinions,
and, when called to suffer for them, it
slips them between its folios, or burns
them at its hearth.

> Card. Newman: *Discussions and*
> *Arguments.* (19th cent.)

Literature is to man in some sort what
autobiography is to the individual; it is
his life and remains.

> Card. Newman: *Idea of a University.*
> (19th cent.)

If literature is to be made a study of
human nature, you cannot have a Christian literature. It is a contradiction in
terms to attempt a sinless literature of
sinful man.

> Card. Newman: *Idea of a University.*
> (19th cent.)

On the whole all literatures are one;
they are the voices of the natural man.

> Card. Newman: *Idea of a University.*
> (19th cent.)

First-rate excellence in literature, as in
other matters, is either an accident or
the outcome of a process; and in either
case demands a course of years to secure.
We cannot reckon on a Plato, we cannot
force an Aristotle, any more than we can
command a fine harvest, or create a coal
field. If a literature be, as I have said,
the voice of a particular nation, it requires a territory and a period, as large
as that nation's extent and history, to
mature in.

> Card. Newman: *Idea of a University.*
> (19th cent.)

Human nature is in all ages and in all
countries the same; and its literature,
therefore, will ever and everywhere be
one and the same also. Man's work
will savor of man; in his elements and
powers excellent and admirable, but
prone to disorder and excess, to error
and sin. Such too will be his literature; it
will have the beauty and the fierceness,
the sweetness and the rankness, of the
natural man.

> Card. Newman: *Idea of a University.*
> (19th cent.)

Man is a being of genius, passion, intellect, conscience, power. He exercises
these various gifts in various ways, in
great deeds, in great thoughts, in heroic

acts, in hateful crimes. He founds states, he fights battles, he builds cities, he ploughs the forest, he subdues the elements, he rules his kind. He creates vast ideas, and influences many generations. He takes a thousand shapes, and undergoes a thousand fortunes. Literature records them all to the life.

> Card. Newman: *Idea of a University*, 9. (19th cent.)

Not till the whole human race is made new will its literature be pure and true. If you would in fact have a literature of saints, first of all have a nation of them.

> Card. Newman: *Idea of a University*. (19th cent.)

The primary duty of a literary man is to have clear conceptions, and to be exact and intelligible in expressing them.

> Card. Newman: *Grammar of Assent*, 3. (19th cent.)

Literature always anticipates life. It does not copy it, but moulds it to its purpose.

> Oscar Wilde: *The Decay of Lying*. (19th cent.)

Literature and fiction are two entirely different things. Literature is a luxury; fiction is a necessity.

> G. K. Chesterton: *A Defence of Penny Dreadfuls*. (20th cent.)

Nothing is important except the fate of the soul; and literature is only redeemed from an utter triviality, surpassing that of naughts and crosses, by the fact that it describes not the world around us, or the things on the retina of the eye, or the enormous irrelevancy of encyclopedias, but some condition to which the human spirit can come.

> G. K. Chesterton: *Introduction to The Old Curiosity Shop*. (20th cent.)

Little

A little thing comforts us because a little thing afflicts us.

> Pascal: *Pensées*, 6. (17th cent.)

Liturgy

I wept at the beauty of Your hymns and canticles, and was powerfully moved at the sweet sound of Your Church's singing. Those sounds flowed into my ears, and the truth streamed into my heart: so that my feeling of devotion overflowed, and the tears ran from my eyes, and I was happy in them.

> St. Augustine: *Confessions*, 9, 6. (5th cent.)

The remembrance of the things done by the Savior of mankind, dearly beloved children, is most useful to us, if these things we honor by believing, we take upon ourselves by imitating. For in the dispensation of Christ's mysteries there is at once the power of grace and the encouragement of teaching, so that He Whom we confess in the spirit of faith, we may follow in the example of our work.

> Pope St. Leo I: *Seventh Sermon on the Epiphany*. (5th cent.)

Let the law of prayer determine the law of belief. (Legem credendi lex statuat supplicandi.)

> St. Prosper of Aquitaine: *Indiculus on Grace*, 8. (5th cent.)

The holy founders who first elaborated the form of our rites, considering it wise to organize our sacred hierarchy on the model of the heavenly hierarchies which are not of this world, clothed these immaterial hierarchies in a variety of material symbols and forms in order to represent them to us, so that we might rise in an analogous way from these sacred signs to the simple and ineffable spiritual realities of which they are only the image. It is impossible, as a matter of fact, for our human minds to attain in an immaterial way to the imitation and contemplation of the heavenly hierarchies without the use of material means capable of guiding us, proportionate to our nature.

> Pseudo-Dionysius: *Heavenly Hierarchy*, 1. (5th cent.)

The Greeks led us to the edifices where they worship their God and we knew not whether we were in heaven or on earth. For on earth there is no such splendor or such beauty, and we are at a loss how to describe it. We only know that God dwells there among men and their service is fairer than the ceremonies of other nations. For we cannot forget that beauty.

> Alleged report of envoys sent by St. Vladimir (978–1015) to Germany, Bulgaria and Constantinople. As a result, the Russians adopted the Byzantine rite. (Story probably apocryphal, 11th cent.)

If any one says that the received and approved rites of the Catholic Church wont to be used in the solemn administration of the sacraments may be contemned, or without sin be omitted at pleasure by the ministers or be changed by every pastor of the churches into other new ones; let him be anathema.

> Council of Trent, Session 7, Canon 13. (Mar. 3, 1547)

It is superstition to found your hopes on ceremonies, but it is pride to refuse to submit to them.

> Pascal: *Pensées*. (17th cent.)

Her whole system of language and rites proves either that the Church, who can speak her mind plainly enough when there is occasion for plainness, wantonly and habitually indulges in the folly of delivering a large part of her message in a language that few can understand, or that there is a body of knowledge which ought not to be and cannot be effectually communicated to all; and that in her reticence she is but obeying the command: *Tell not the vision to any man till Christ be risen* in him.

> Coventry Patmore: *Religio Poetae*. (19th cent.)

The rule of life which is laid down for Catholics is not of such a nature as not to admit modifications according to the diversity of time and place. . . . The history of all past ages is witness that the Apostolic See . . . has constantly adhered *to the same doctrine, in the same sense and in the same mind* (Vat. Council, de fide Cath. c. 4): but it has always been accustomed to so modify the rule of life that, while keeping the divine right inviolate, it has never disregarded the manners and customs of the various nations which it embraces.

> Pope Leo XIII: *Testem Benevolentiae*. (Jan. 22, 1899)

If I had to indicate in two or three words the main characteristics which go to make up the genius of the Roman rite, I should say that those characteristics were essentially soberness and sense.

> Edmund Bishop: *The Genius of the Roman Rite*. (*Liturgica Historica*) (20th cent.)

The clergy shall not presume to induce those belonging to the Latin rite to transfer to an Eastern rite, nor those belonging to Eastern rites to transfer to the Latin rite. No one may transfer to another rite without the permission of the Apostolic See, or, after legitimate transfer, return to his old rite.

> Code of Canon Law, Canon 98, 2-3. (20th cent.)

It belongs exclusively to the Apostolic See to regulate the sacred liturgy and to approve liturgical books.

> Code of Canon Law, Canon 1257 (20th cent.)

Great liturgies cannot be manufactured; they grow.

> Arnold Lunn: *Within that City*. (20th cent.)

The sacred liturgy is the public worship which our Redeemer as Head of the Church renders to the Father, as well as the worship which the community of the faithful renders to its Founder, and through Him to the heavenly Father. It is, in short, the worship rendered by the Mystical Body of Christ in the entirety of its Head and members.

> Pope Pius XII: *Mediator Dei*. (Nov. 20, 1947)

It is an error and a mistake to think of the sacred liturgy as merely the outward or visible part of divine worship or as an ornamental ceremonial. No less erroneous is the notion that it consists solely in a list of laws and prescriptions according to which the ecclesiastical hierarchy orders the sacred rites to be performed. It should be clear to all, then, that God cannot be honored worthily unless the mind and heart turn to Him in quest of the perfect life, and that the worship rendered to God by the Church in union with her divine Head is the most efficacious means of achieving sanctity.

> Pope Pius XII: *Mediator Dei*. (Nov. 20, 1947)

The sacred liturgy, as a matter of fact, includes divine as well as human elements. The former, instituted as they have been by God, cannot be changed in any way by men. But the human components admit of various modifications, as the needs of the age and the good of souls may require, and as the ecclesiastical hierarchy, under the guidance of the Holy Spirit, may have authorized.

> Pope Pius XII: *Mediator Dei*. (Nov. 20, 1947)

Certainly the Church is a living organism, and therefore in those things which pertain to the sacred liturgy it grows and develops and conforms itself to the circumstances and requirements of various times, saving and guarding nevertheless the integrity of doctrine.

> Pope Pius XII: *Mediator Dei*. (Nov. 20, 1947)

The most pressing duty of Christians is to live the liturgical life, and increase and cherish its supernatural spirit.

> Pope Pius XII: *Mediator Dei*. (Nov. 20, 1947)

The centuries which followed the fall of the Empire in the West, in spite of the impoverishment of their material culture, were from the liturgical point of view a great creative age, and it is remarkable that this is no less true of the semi-barbarian West than of the stable and comparatively prosperous Byzantine world. All these ages possessed of poetry, music and art found expression in the liturgy—an expression no later age has been able to surpass.

> C. Dawson: *Gifford Lectures, 1948: Religion and the Rise of Western Culture.*

The liturgy is . . . not only a school of literary taste and a mine of marvelous subjects, but it is infinitely more; it is a great sacramental built around the six sacraments which surround the greatest sacrament who is Christ Himself dwelling among us even unto the consummation of the world.

> Thomas Merton: *Poetry and the Contemplative Life*. (In *Figures for an Apocalypse*.) (20th cent.)

The prayers of the Church are the age-long poetry of mankind, lifted above the perfection of poetry, for they are the prayer of Christ on earth. That is what the ritual means, with its ordered movements, its wide encircling gestures of love, its kiss of peace, its extended arms of sacrifice.

> Caryll Houselander: *Guilt*. (20th cent.)

Without the worship of the heart liturgical prayer becomes a matter of formal routine; its technically finished performance may give aesthetic pleasure, but the spirit has gone out from it. That is why the Church has been at pains to curb the ardor of its own liturgical enthusiasts.

> Dom Aelred Graham: *Catholicism and the World Today*. (20th cent.)

The secret of Catholicism's capacity to harmonize liturgical worship with the demands of personal devotion lies in the fact that both the one and the other are a response to the same reality. Each is focused on the God who reveals Himself in faith, Who attracts the mind by being unalloyed truth and the heart in virtue of His infinite goodness.

> Dom Aelred Graham: *Catholicism and the World Today.* (20th cent.)

See also Advent; Ash Wednesday; Blessed Sacrament; Blessed Virgin Mary; Christmas; Dead, The; Divine Office; Easter; Epiphany; Eucharist; Good Friday; Holy Saturday; Holy Thursday; Lent; Mass: Prayers and Formulas; Mass: Rites and Ceremonies; Palm Sunday; Pentecost; Religion; Saint; Worship

Livelihood

> Our laws for such affronts have fore-feits made:
> He takes his life, who takes away his trade.

> Dryden: *Absalom and Achitophel.* (17th cent.)

Living

> Let us live then, and be glad
> While young life's before us
> After youthful pastime had,
> After old age hard and sad,
> Earth will slumber o'er us.
> (Gaudeamus igitur,
> Juvenes dum sumus
> Post jucundam juventutem,
> Post molestam senectutem,
> Nos habebit humus.)

> Medieval students' song. (ca. 13th century, but revised in 18th century.)

While we live, let us live. (Dum vivimus vivamus.)

> Latin Proverb. (Medieval)

Logic

A student should address himself to logic before the other sciences, because it deals with their common procedure.

> St. Thomas Aquinas: *Commentary on the Metaphysics,* 2, lect. 5. (13th cent.)

There was an Oxford cleric too, a student,
Long given to logic, longer than was prudent.

> Chaucer: *Canterbury Tales: Prologue.* (Tr. Coghill) (14th cent.)

She choppeth logic.

> John Heywood: *Proverbs,* 2, 4. (16th cent.)

Logic makes but a sorry rhetoric with the multitude.

> Card. Newman: *Discussions and Arguments.* (19th cent.)

While we talk logic, we are unanswerable; but then, on the other hand, this universal living scene of things is after all as little a logical world as it is a poetical; and, as it cannot without violence be exalted into poetical perfection, neither can it be attenuated into a logical formula.

> Card. Newman: *Grammar of Assent,* 8. (19th cent.)

We proceed as far indeed as we can, by the logic of language, but we are obliged to supplement it by the more subtle and elastic logic of thought; for forms by themselves prove nothing.

> Card. Newman: *Grammar of Assent,* 10. (19th cent.)

London

People-pestered London.

> Nicholas Grimald: *The Lover to His Dear.* (16th cent.)

Go where we may, rest where we will, Eternal London haunts us still!

> Thomas Moore: *Rhymes on the Road,* 9. (19th cent.)

Loneliness

> When you go,
> There's loneliness in loneliness.

> Alice Meynell: *The Visiting Sea.* (19th cent.)

My soul has solitudes Where no pace
falls;
Thy silent trespassings No man fore-
stalls.

My soul has silences No voice can
break;
Only thy hidden words Its echoes wake.

But oh, the solitudes Shouldst thou not
come!
The stricken silences, When thou art
dumb!

> Edwin Essex: *Loneliness.* (20th cent.)

See also Solitude

Lord

I will frankly call the emperor lord
(*dominum*), but only in the ordinary
way, but only when force is not brought
to bear on me to call him Lord in the
sense of God.

> Tertullian: *Apology,* 34, 1. (3rd cent.)

A king may spill, a king may save;
A king may make a lord a knave;
And of a knave a lord also.

> John Gower: *Confessio Amantis,* 7. (14th
> cent.)

Henceforth a series of new time began,
The mighty years in long procession
ran:
Once more the God-like David was
restor'd,
And willing nations knew their lawful
lord.

> Dryden: *Absalom and Achitophel.* (17th
> cent.)

Lord of humankind.

> Dryden: *The Spanish Friar,* 2, 2. (17th
> cent.)

Losing

Always to let the losers have their words.

> John Heywood: *Proverbs,* 2, 6. (16th
> cent.)

Far better is a little loss than a long
sorrow.

> Langland: *Piers Plowman,* Passus 1. (14th
> cent.)

All that's bright must fade,—
    The brightest still the fleetest;
All that's sweet was made
    But to be lost when sweetest.

> Thomas Moore: *All That's Bright Must
> Fade.* (19th cent.)

Loss and Gain

Measure thy life by loss instead of
gain;
Not by the wine drunk, but by the wine
poured forth;
For love's strength standeth in love's
sacrifice;
And whoso suffers most hath most to
give.

> Eleanor Hamilton King: *The Disciples.*
> (19th cent.)

Lourdes

See Immaculate Conception

Love

Love knows no rule (Amor ordinem
nescit).

> St. Jerome: *Letter to Chromatius.* (4th-5th
> cent.)

You had pierced our hearts with the
arrow of Your love, and our minds were
pierced with the arrows of Your words.

> St. Augustine: *Confessions,* 9, 2. (5th
> cent.)

There is no greater invitation to love
than loving first, and that soul is sterner
than it ought which, even if it were unwilling to bestow love, is also unwilling
to repay it.

> St. Augustine: *On Catechizing the
> Unlearned.* (5th cent.)

That is to be called love which is
true, otherwise it is desire; so that those
who desire are said improperly to love,
just as they who love are said improperly

to desire. But that is true love, that cleaving to the truth we may live righteously, and so may despise all mortal things in comparison with the love of men, whereby we wish them to live righteously.

> St. Augustine: *De Trinitate,* 8, 7. (5th cent.)

The principal effect of love is to unite the wills of those who love, so as to make of them but one and the same will.

> Pseudo-Dionysius: *On the Divine Names,* 4. (5th cent.)

By it [i.e. divine love] all holy laws
  are made and marriage rites are tied,
By it is faithful friendship joined.
  How happy mortals were,
If that pure love did guide their minds,
  which heavenly spheres doth guide!

> Boethius: *De Consolatione Philosophiae,* 2, 8. (6th cent.)

Love is a gift of the Holy Ghost by which those who have already attained the first step of truth through humility under the Son's training may advance to the second through sympathy for neighbor under the Holy Ghost's teaching.

> St. Bernard: *The Steps of Humility,* 7. (12th cent.)

Carnal love is that love by which man loves himself, for his own sake and before all else.

> St. Bernard: *On the Necessity of Loving God,* 8, 23. (12th cent.)

The beloved may be absent or present, but love stays on.

> St. Thomas Aquinas: *Summa Theologica,* 1-2, 28, 1. (13th cent.)

Love can deny nothing to love.

> Andreas Capellanus: *De Amore.* (13th cent.)

Love, which insists that love shall mutual be.

> Dante: *Inferno, Canto 5.* (14th cent.)

Love, that all gentle hearts so quickly know.

> Dante: *Inferno, Canto 5.* (14th cent.)

Nor creature nor creator ever yet,
  My son, was without love, continued he,
  Natural, or of the mind: thou knowest it.

The natural always is from error free;
  But the other may, through a bad object, err
  By too much force or its deficiency.

> Dante: *Purgatorio, Canto 17.* (Tr. Binyon) (14th cent.)

A lord of terrible aspect.

> Dante: *La Vita Nuova,* 3. (14th cent.)

All ye that pass along love's trodden way,
  Pause ye awhile and say
  If there be any grief like unto mine:
  I pray you that you harken a short space
  Patiently, if my case
  Be not a piteous marvel and a sign.

> Dante: *La Vita Nuova,* 7. (14th cent.)

The god of love, a! *benedicite,*
How mighty and how great a lord is he!

> Chaucer: *The Knightes Tale.* (14th cent.)

For ever it was, and ever it shall befal,
That love is he that alle thing may bind.

> Chaucer: *Troilus and Criseyde.* (14th cent.)

Full sooth is said that love nor lordship
Will not, his thankes, have no fellowship.

          his thankes—willingly

> Chaucer: *The Knightes Tale.* (14th cent.)

For love is blind all day and may not see.

> Chaucer: *The Marchantes Tale.* (14th cent.)

Wist thou not the old clerkes saw,
That who shall give a lover any law?

> Chaucer: *The Knightes Tale.* (14th cent.)

Love is a thing aye full of busy dread.

> Chaucer: *Troilus and Criseyde.* (14th cent.)

Among the holy books wise,
I find writ in such wise,
Who loveth nought is here as dead.

> John Gower: *Confessio Amantis,* 4. (14th cent.)

It hath and shall be evermore
The love is master where he will.

> John Gower: *Confessio Amantis,* 1. (14th cent.)

And netheles there is no man
In all this world so wise, that can
Of love temper the measure.

> John Gower: *Confessio Amantis,* 1. (14th cent.)

Love's law is out of rule.

> John Gower: *Confessio Amantis,* 1. (14th cent.)

Love is the leech of life, next to our Lord,
It is the graft of peace, the nearest road to heaven.

> Langland: *Piers Plowman,* Passus 2. (14th cent.)

There is no living in love without suffering.

> Thomas a Kempis: *The Imitation of Christ,* 3, 5. (15th cent.)

Love is swift, sincere, pious, pleasant, gentle, strong, patient, faithful, prudent, long-suffering, manly and never seeking her own; for wheresoever a man seeketh his own, there he falleth from love.

> Thomas a Kempis: *The Imitation of Christ,* 3, 5. (15th cent.)

Love is more than great richesse.

> Lydgate: *The Story of Thebes,* 3. (15th cent.)

He that loveth is void of all reason.

> Alexander Barclay: *The Ship of Fools.* (16th cent.)

If love be strong, hot, mighty, and fervent,
There may no trouble, grief, or sorrow fall,
But that the lover would be well content
All to endure, and think it eke too small,
Though it were death, so he might there withal
The joyful presence of that person get,
On whom he hath his heart and love yset.

> St. Thomas More: *The Measure of Love.* (16th cent.)

Hot love soon cold.

> John Heywood: *Proverbs,* 1, 2. (16th cent.)

In love is no lack.

> John Heywood: *Proverbs,* 1, 4. (16th cent.)

Love lives by love, as larks live by leeks.

> John Heywood: *Proverbs,* 1, 10. (16th cent.)

Love me little, love me long.

> John Heywood: *Proverbs,* 2, 2. (16th cent.)

They do not love that do not show their love.

> John Heywood: *Proverbs,* 2, 9. (16th cent.)

But oft the words come forth awrye of him that loveth well.

> Henry Howard, Earl of Surrey: *Pangs and Sleights of Love.* (16th cent.)

Misdeeming eye! that stoopest to the lure
Of mortal worths, not worth so worthy love;
All beauty's base, all graces are impure

That do thy erring thoughts from God
remove.
Sparks to the fire, the beams yield to
the Sun,
All grace to God, from Whom all
graces run.

> Bl. Robert Southwell: *Lewd Love is Loss.*
> (16th cent.)

Glean not in barren soil these offal-
ears,
Sith reap thou mayst whole heavens of
delight;
Base joys with griefs, bad hopes do end
in fears,
Lewd love with loss, evil peace with
deadly fight:
God's love alone doth end with endless
ease,
Whose joys in hope, whose hope concludes in peace.

> Bl. Robert Southwell: *Lewd Love is Loss.*
> (16th cent.)

O loathe that love whose final aim is
lust,
Moth of the mind, eclipse of reason's
light;
The grave of grace, the mole of nature's
rust,
The wreck of wit, the wrong of every
right.
In sum, an evil whose harms no tongue
can tell;
In which to live is death, to die is hell.

> mole—fleshly mass
>
> Bl. Robert Southwell: *Lewd Love is Loss.*
> (16th cent.)

May was never the month of love
For May is full of flowers;
But rather April, wet by kind,
For love is full of showers.

> Bl. Robert Southwell: *Love's Servile Lot.*
> (16th cent.)

Plough not the seas, sow not the sands,
Leave off your idle pain;
Seek other mistress for your minds;
Love's service is in vain.

> Bl. Robert Southwell: *Love's Servile Lot.*
> (16th cent.)

First shall the heavens want starry
light,
The seas be robbed of their waves,
The day want sun, the sun want bright,
The night want shade, the dead men
graves,
The April, flowers and leaf and tree,
Before I false my faith to thee.

> Thomas Lodge: *Love's Protestation.* (16th
> cent.)

Love lurks as soon about a sheepcote as
a palace.

> Thomas Lodge: *Rosalynde.* (16th cent.)

To tread a maze that never shall have
end;
  To burn in sighs and starve in daily
  tears;
To climb a hill and never to descend;
  Giants to kill, and quake at childish
  fears;
To pine for food, and watch the Hes-
perian tree;
  To thirst for drink, and nectar still
  to draw;
To live accurst, whom men hold blest
to be;
  And weep those wrongs which never
  creature saw;
If this be love, if love in these be
founded,
My heart is love, for these in it are
grounded.

> Henry Constable: *Diana.* (16th cent.)

Let wilder youths, whose soul is sense,
Profane the temple of delight,
And purchase endless penitence
With the stolen pleasure of one night.

Time's ever ours, while we despise
The sensual idol of our clay,
For though the sun do set and rise
We joy one everlasting day.

> William Habington: *The Reward of
> Innocent Love.* (17th cent.)

Love is the movement, effusion and advancement of the heart toward the good.

> St. Francis de Sales: *Treatise on the Love
> of God,* 1, 7. (17th cent.)

Love desires secrecy.

> St. Francis de Sales: *Treatise on the Love of God*, 6, 1. (17th cent.)

Love is bittersweet, and while we live in this world it never has a sweetness perfectly sweet, because it is not perfect, nor ever purely satisfied.

> St. Francis de Sales: *Treatise on the Love of God*, 6, 13. (17th cent.)

Love is a magistrate who exercises his authority without noise, without policemen or sergeants.

> St. Francis de Sales: *Treatise on the Love of God*, 8, 1. (17th cent.)

How can ardor of love possibly make one desire to be separated from grace, since love is grace itself?

> St. Francis de Sales: *Treatise on the Love of God*, 10, 16. (17th cent.)

Love's great artillery.

> R. Crashaw: *Prayer.* (17th cent.)

And I, what is my crime I cannot tell,
Unless it be a crime t'have lov'd too well.

> R. Crashaw: *Alexias.* (17th cent.)

Love too, that leads the way, would
    lend the wings
To bear me harmless through the hardest things.
And where love lends the wing, and
    leads the way,
What dangers can there be dare say me
    nay?

> R. Crashaw: *Alexias.* (17th cent.)

Love knows no nonage, nor the mind.
'Tis love, not years or limbs, that can
Make the martyr or the man.

> R. Crashaw: *Hymn to St. Teresa.* (17th cent.)

Love, thou art absolute sole lord
Of life and death.

> R. Crashaw: *Hymn to St. Teresa.* (17th cent.)

Unconstant, frail,
In nothing sure, but sure to fail:
Which, if we lose it, we bewail;
And when we have it, still we bear
The worst of passions, daily fear.

> Sir John Beaumont: *A Description of Love.* (17th cent.)

Love is like youth, he thirsts for age,
He scorns to be his mother's page:
But when proceeding times assuage
The former heat, he will complain,
And wish those pleasant hours again.

> Sir John Beaumont: *A Description of Love.* (17th cent.)

Love is a region full of fires,
And burning with extreme desires,
An object seeks, of which possest,
The wheels are fixt, the motions rest,
The flames in ashes lie opprest:
This meteor, striving high to rise,
(The fuel spent) falls down and dies.

> Sir John Beaumont: *A Description of Love.* (17th cent.)

Love one too much, thou art a slave to all.

> Sir John Beaumont: *Against Inordinate Love of Creatures.* (17th cent.)

My love's a noble madness.

> Dryden: *All for Love*, 2, 1. (17th cent.)

Pains of love be sweeter far
Than all other pleasures are.

> Dryden: *Tyrannic Love*, 4. (17th cent.)

Love on pity cannot live.

> Dryden: *A Song.* (17th cent.)

Love's the noblest frailty of the mind.

> Dryden: *The Indian Emperor*, 2. (17th cent.)

For, heav'n be thank'd, we live in such
    an age,
When no man dies for love, but on the
    stage.

> Dryden: *Mithridates, Epilogue.* (17th cent.)

But love's a malady without a cure.

> Dryden: *Palamon and Arcite,* 2. (17th cent.)

Fool, not to know that love endures no tie,
And Jove but laughs at lover's perjury.

> Dryden: *Palamon and Arcite,* 2. (17th cent.)

Antony, who lost the world for love.

> Dryden: *Palamon and Arcite,* 2. (17th cent.)

Love is love's reward.

> Dryden: *Palamon and Arcite,* 2. (17th cent.)

Love either finds equality or makes it;
Like death he knows no difference in degrees,
But planes and levels all.

> Dryden: *Marriage à la Mode,* 3. (17th cent.)

She ne'er loved who durst not venture all.

> Dryden: *Aurengzebe,* 5. (17th cent.)

Love is no more a violent desire,
'Tis a mere metaphor, a painted fire.

> Dryden. (17th cent.)

Tell me, what's love? said youth, one day,
To drooping age, who crost his way—
It is a sunny hour of play,
For which repentance dear doth pay,
Repentance! repentance!
And this is love, as wise men say.

> Thomas Moore: *Youth and Age.* (19th cent.)

There's nothing half so sweet in life
As love's young dream.

> Thomas Moore: *Love's Young Dream.* (19th cent.)

Is there on earth a space so dear
As that within the blessed sphere
Two loving arms entwine?

> Thomas Moore: *To Fanny.* (19th cent.)

No, the heart that has truly lov'd never forgets,
But as truly loves on to the close,
As the flower turns on her god, when he sets,
The same look which she turned when he rose.

> Thomas Moore: *Believe Me, If All Those Endearing Young Charms.* (19th cent.)

Howe'er man rules in science and in art,
The sphere of woman's glories is the heart.

> Thomas Moore: *Epilogue to the Tragedy of Ina.* (19th cent.)

I know not, I ask not, if guilt's in that heart,
I but know that I love thee, whatever thou art.

> Thomas Moore: *Come, Rest in This Bosom.* (19th cent.)

Love is life, and death at last
Crowns it eternal and divine.

> Adelaide Procter: *Life in Death.* (19th cent.)

O thou whose light is in thy heart,
Love-taught submission! without thee
Science may soar a while; but art
Drifts barren o'er a shoreless sea.

> Aubrey de Vere: *Prologue to May Carols.* (19th cent.)

The warrior for the true, the right,
Fights in love's name;
The love that lures thee from that fight
Lures thee to shame:
That love which lifts the heart, yet leaves
The spirit free,—
That love, or none, is fit for one
Man-shaped like thee.

> Aubrey de Vere: *Song.* (19th cent.)

To love it is and love alone
That life or luxury is known.

> John B. Tabb: *The Test.* (19th cent.)

What makes love's dawning glow
Changeless through joy and woe?
Only the constant know!—
　　Eileen Aroon!

Gerald Griffin: *Eileen Aroon.* (19th cent.)

Everyone who has loved and reflected on
love for an instant, knows very well that
what is vulgarly regarded as the end of
that passion, is, as the Church steadfastly maintains, no more than its accident. The flower is not for the seed, but
the seed for the flower. And yet what
is that flower, if it be not the rising bud
of another flower, flashed for a moment
of eternal moment before our eyes, and
at once withdrawn, lest we should misunderstand the prophecy, and take it for
our final good?

Coventry Patmore: *Religio Poetae.* (19th
cent.)

Love is not love which does not sweeter
　　live
For having something dreadful to for-
　　give.

Coventry Patmore: *De Natura Deorum.*
(19th cent.)

The moods of love are like the wind,
And none knows whence or why they
　　rise.

Coventry Patmore: *The Angel in the
House.* (19th cent.)

　Love, light for me
Thy ruddiest blazing torch,
That I, albeit a beggar by the porch
Of the glad palace of virginity,
May gaze within, and sing the pomp I
　　see;
For crown'd with roses all,
'Tis there, O love, they keep thy fes-
　　tival!

Coventry Patmore: *Deliciae Sapientiae de
Amore.* (19th cent.)

Though love is all of earth that's dear,
Its home, my children, is not here;
The pathos of eternity
Does in its fullest pleasure sigh.

Coventry Patmore. (19th cent.)

My fair, no beauty of thine will last
Save in my love's eternity.
Thy smiles, that light thee fitfully,
Are lost for ever—their moment past—
Except the few thou givest to me.

Alice Meynell: *The Lover Urges the
Better Thrift.* (19th cent.)

With the first dream that comes with
　　the first sleep
I run, I run, I am gathered to thy
　　heart.

Alice Meynell: *Renouncement.* (19th
cent.)

Last night, ah, yesternight, betwixt her
　　lips and mine
There fell thy shadow, Cynara! thy
　　breath was shed
Upon my shoulder between the kisses
　　and the wine;
And I was desolate and sick of an old
　　passion,
Yea, I was desolate and bowed my
　　head:
I have been faithful to thee, Cynara! in
　　my fashion.

Ernest Dowson: *Non Sum Qualis Eram
Bonae Sub Regno Cynarae.* (19th cent.)

　　I, who loved with all my life,
　　　Love with all my death.

F. Thompson: *Messages.* (19th cent.)

Why do you so clasp me,
　　And draw me to your knee?
Forsooth, you do but chafe me,
　　I pray you let me be:
I will be loved but now and then
　　When it liketh me!

F. Thompson: *Love and the Child.* (19th
cent.)

Love, love! your flower of withered
　　dream
In leavèd rhyme lies safe, I deem,
Sheltered and shut in a nook of rhyme,
From the reaper man, and his reaper
　　time.

F. Thompson: *The Poppy.* (19th cent.)

I fear to love thee, sweet, because
Love's the ambassador of loss.

F. Thompson: *To Olivia.* (19th cent.)

Bianca: Canst tell me what love is?
Guido: It is consent. The union of two
minds, two souls, two hearts
In all they think, and hope, and feel.

Oscar Wilde: *A Florentine Tragedy.* (19th
cent.)

One pulse of passion—youth's first
fiery glow,—
Is worth the hoarded proverbs of the
sage:
Vex not thy soul with dead philosophy;
Have we not lips to kiss with, hearts to
love, and eyes to see?

Oscar Wilde: *Panthea.* (19th cent.)

The only difference between a caprice
and a life-long passion is that the caprice
lasts a little longer.

Oscar Wilde: *The Picture of Dorian Gray,*
2. (19th cent.)

When one is in love one begins to deceive oneself. And one ends by deceiving
others.

Oscar Wilde: *A Woman of No
Importance,* 3. (19th cent.)

Men always want to be a woman's first
love. That is their clumsy vanity. We
women have a more subtle instinct about
things. What we like is to be a man's
last romance.

Oscar Wilde: *A Woman of No
Importance,* 2. (19th cent.)

In love respect should come first and
ardor second.

R. H. Benson: *Come Rack! Come Rope!*
(20th cent.)

Every soul that loves is a treasure-house
of all that she has ever loved.

R. H. Benson: *The History of Richard
Raynal Solitary.* (20th cent.)

The cruellest nickname ever given to a
really beautiful thing is that of calf-love.

Certainly it has its clumsiness and its
crudeness, but these result simply from
the fact that the instruments of expression are not adequate.

R. H. Benson: *The Coward.* (20th cent.)

Self-sacrifice and chivalry, and even art,
all come from the heart.

R. H. Benson: *Lord of the World.* (20th
cent.)

When a man falls in love suddenly, his
whole center changes. Up to that point
he has, probably, referred everything
to himself—considered things from his
own point. When he falls in love the
whole thing is shifted; he becomes a
part of the circumference, perhaps even
the whole circumference; someone else
becomes the center. For example, things
he hears and sees are referred in future
instantly to this other person; he ceases
to be acquisitive. His entire life, if it is
really love, is pulled sideways; he does
not desire to get, but to give. That is
why it is the noblest thing in the world.

R. H. Benson: *The Mirror of Shalott.*
(20th cent.)

The heart sometimes finds out things
that reason cannot.

R. H. Benson: *Lord of the World.* (20th
cent.)

It is only the souls that do not love that
go empty in this world.

R. H. Benson: *The History of Richard
Raynal Solitary.* (20th cent.)

To love is to wish the other's highest
good.

R. H. Benson: *Come Rack! Come Rope!*
(20th cent.)

Real love seeks not to possess, but to be
possessed; not, so to speak, to devour
the beloved, to satisfy self with the beloved, but the exact contrary—to be devoured and to satisfy.

R. H. Benson: *Christ in the Church.* (20th
cent.)

My love is like a bird—
A bird with shining wings;
Like a bird in the dusk, it flies,
Like a bird in the dusk, it sings.

Mary D. Thayer: *Bird-song.* (20th cent.)

You cannot love a thing without wanting to fight for it.

G. K. Chesterton: *Introduction to Nicholas
Nickleby.* (20th cent.)

Love is not blind; that is the last thing
it is. Love is bound; and the more it is
bound the less it is blind.

G. K. Chesterton: *Orthodoxy.* (20th
cent.)

Love is cruel, love is sweet,
Cruel sweet!
Lovers sigh till lovers meet,
Sigh and meet.
Sigh and meet and sigh again,
Cruel sweet! O sweetest pain!

Love is blind, but love is shy,
Blind and shy;
Thoughts are bold but words are shy,
Bold and shy.
Bold and shy and bold again,
Sweet is boldness, shyness, pain.

Thomas MacDonagh: *Song.* (20th cent.)

Tho' the sun in heaven desert you,
'Love will find out the way.'

Alfred Noyes: *Love Will Find Out the
Way.* (20th cent.)

Heart of my heart, the world is young;
Love lies hidden in every rose.

Alfred Noyes: *Unity.* (20th cent.)

Some tell us bitterly that true love
dies—
And speak too quickly, waiting not the
rise
Of strong returning tides to greet their
eyes.
For love, though deep and fickle, like
the sea

Obeys the uncomprehended moon.
And we
Observe its ebb and flow bewilderedly.

Theodore Maynard: *Tides.* (20th cent.)

See also Charity; God; Love of God;
Love of Neighbor

Love and Death

She never undertook to know
What death with love should have to
do;
Nor has she e'er yet understood
Why to show love, she should shed
blood.
Yet though she cannot tell you why,
She can love, and she can die.

Richard Crashaw: *Hymn to St. Teresa.*
(17th cent.)

Scarce has she blood enough to make
A guilty sword blush for her sake;
Yet has she a heart dares hope to prove
How much less strong is death than
love.

Richard Crashaw: *Hymn to St. Teresa.*
(17th cent.)

O how oft shalt thou complain
Of a sweet and subtle pain;
Of intolerable joys,
Of a death, in which who dies
Loves his death, and dies again;
And lives, and dies, and knows not why
To live, but that he thus may never
leave to die.

Richard Crashaw: *Hymn to St. Teresa.*
(17th cent.)

If I be shipwreck'd, love shall teach to
swim;
If drown'd, sweet is the death endur'd
for him.

Richard Crashaw: *Alexias, First Elegy.*
(17th cent.)

Between death and love there is no alternative.

St. Francis de Sales: *Letters to Persons in
Religion,* 6, 24. (17th cent.)

Well blest is he who has a dear one
  dead;
A friend he has whose face will never
  change—
A dear communion that will not grow
  strange;
The anchor of a love is death.

> J. B. O'Reilly: *Forever.* (19th cent.)

Love and Friendship

When Psyche's friend becomes her
  lover,
  How sweetly these conditions blend!
But, oh, what anguish to discover
  Her lover has become—her friend!

> Madeleine Bridges: *Friend and Lover.*
> (19th cent.)

Friendship and love differ mainly in
this: that, whereas the felicity of friendship consists in a mutual interchange of
benefits, intellectual and otherwise, that
of love is in giving on one part and
receiving on the other, with a reciprocal
perception of how sweet it is to the en-
dower to endow and the receiver to receive.

> Coventry Patmore: *Religio Poetae.* (19th
> cent.)

Love and friendship both refuse
The boundaries men set to use.
Nor can the subtlest gods define
Their tenuous dividing line.
Their precincts in the realm of mind
A man is impotent to find.
No wonder then the upright will
Is mystified and volatile.

> Sister Miriam: *Border Mystery.* (20th
> cent.)

Love and Hate

Whoever entertains in his heart any
trace of hatred for anyone, regardless
of what the offence may have been, is a
complete stranger to the love of God.
Love of God and hatred of any man are
absolutely incompatible with one another.

> St. Maximus the Confessor: *Centuries on
> Charity,* 1, 15. (7th cent.)

If hate were none, would love burn
lowlier bright?

> F. Thompson: *Sister Songs.* (19th cent.)

Love and Marriage

Let those about to enter into wedlock
pray diligently for divine help, so that
they may make their choice in accordance with Christian prudence, not led by
the blind and unrestrained impulse of
lust, nor by any desire for riches, nor by
any other base influence, but by a true
and noble love and sincere affection for
the future partner.

> Pope Pius XI: *Casti connubii.* (Dec. 31,
> 1930)

Love of God

First, thou shalt love the God Who
made thee, secondly, thy neighbor as
thyself; and whatsoever thou wouldst
not have done to thyself, do not thou to
another.

> Teaching of the Twelve Apostles, 1. (2nd
> cent.)

Thou hast made us for Thyself, and the
heart of man is restless until it finds its
rest in Thee.

> St. Augustine: *Confessions,* 1, 1. (5th
> cent.)

Late have I loved thee, O Beauty so ancient and so new; late have I loved
Thee! For behold Thou wert within me,
and I outside; and I sought Thee outside and in my unloveliness fell upon
those lovely things that Thou hast made.
Thou wert within me and I was not
with Thee.

> St. Augustine: *Confessions,* 10, 27. (5th
> cent.)

But I am divided up in time, whose
order I do not know, and my thoughts
and the deepest places of my soul are
torn with every kind of tumult until the
day when I shall be purified and melted

in the fire of Thy love and wholly joined to Thee.

> St. Augustine: *Confessions,* 11, 29. (5th cent.)

He who loves his neighbor must needs also love above all else love itself. But *God is love; and he that dwelleth in love, dwelleth in God* (1 John 4, 6). Therefore he must needs above all else love God.

> St. Augustine: *De Trinitate,* 8, 7. (5th cent.)

For it is no small thing that God is going to give to those who thus yearn; no half-efforts will get them to that goal. What God is going to give them is not something He has made; He is going to give them Himself, Himself, Who made all things. Toil, then, to lay hold of God; yearn long for what you are going to possess for ever.

> St. Augustine: *In Ps. 83 Enarr.,* 1, 3. (5th cent.)

Though we are born and die here, let us not love this world; let us ever, through love of God, pass on hence; let us by charity dwell among the heights, by that charity wherewith we love God. Let us during this our earthly pilgrimage be ever occupied with the thought that we shall not always be here, and then, by leading good lives, we shall be preparing for ourselves a place whence we shall never pass on.

> St. Augustine: *In Joann. Evang. Tract.,* 32, 9. (5th cent.)

We sin by that part of us which loves God less; whereas did we wholly love God there would be nought in us which induce us to serve the allurements of sin. For what do we understand by loving God save that our souls are wholly occupied with Him and that our one and only desire is to enjoy the vision of God, while we hate sin and abhor the world.

> Julianus Pomerius: *De Vita Contemplativa,* 3, 15, 1. (5th cent.)

O God, Who hast taught Thy Church to keep all Thy heavenly commandments by loving Thy Godhead and our neighbor; grant us the spirit of peace and grace, that Thy universal family may be both devoted to Thee with their whole heart, and united to each other with a pure will.

> Leonine Sacramentary, Collect. (ca. 5th cent.)

In the first place, to love the Lord God with all one's heart, all one's soul, and all one's strength.

> St. Benedict: *Rule,* 4. (First of his 'tools of good works') (6th cent.)

Grant, O Lord, that we may have a perpetual fear of Thy holy name; for Thou never failest to direct and govern by Thy grace those whom Thou dost bring up in the steadfastness of Thy love.

> Roman Missal, Collect for Second Sunday after Pentecost. (Gelasian, 5th to 7th cent.)

O God, Who hast prepared for those who love Thee such good things as eye hath not seen; pour into our hearts love of Thee, that, loving Thee in and above all things, we may obtain Thy promises which surpass all that we can desire.

> Roman Missal, Collect for Fifth Sunday after Pentecost. (Gelasian, 5th to 7th cent.)

He who fixes his mind firmly on the love of God despises the visible world, and even his own body, as if it belonged to another.

> St. Maximus the Confessor: *Centuries on Charity,* 1, 6. (7th cent.)

It is therefore most obvious that the rational creature was created for this purpose, that it might love the supreme Being above all other goods, as this Being is itself the supreme good; nay, that it might love nothing except it, unless because of it; since that Being is good through itself, and nothing else is good except through it.

St. Anselm: *Monologium,* 68. (11th cent.)

There is a twofold reason, I should say, why God should be loved for His own sake: because nothing else can be more justly or more profitably loved.

St. Bernard: *On the Necessity of Loving God,* 1. (12th cent.)

Love is sufficient by itself, it pleases by itself, and for its own sake. It is like a merit, and itself its own recompense. Love seeks neither cause nor fruit beyond itself. Its fruit is its use. I love because I love; I love that I may love. Love, then, is a great reality. It is the only one of all the movements, feelings and affections of the soul in which the creature is able to respond to its Creator, though not upon equal terms, and to repay like with like.

St. Bernard: *On the Canticle of Canticles,* 83. (12th cent.)

The true spouse of our soul is God, and then are we truly coupled unto Him, when we draw near Him by hope and soothfast love.

Richard of St. Victor: *Benjamin Minor,* 5. (12th cent.)

O Love! how can I be
Afraid of foolishness,
If through it I possess
And am possessed by Thee?

St. Francis. (13th cent.)

Love of our neighbor is included in the love of God.

St. Thomas Aquinas: *Commentary on Galatians,* 5, lect. 3. (13th cent.)

Now to love God above all things is natural to man and to every nature, not only rational but irrational, and even to inanimate nature according to the manner of love which can belong to each creature. And the reason of this is that it is natural to all to seek and love things according as they are naturally fit (to be sought and loved) since *all things act according as they are naturally fit.* Now it is manifest that the good of the part is for the good of the whole; hence everything, by its natural appetite and love, loves its own proper good on account of the common good of the whole universe, which is God.

St. Thomas Aquinas: *Summa Theologica,* 1-2, 109, 3. (13th cent.)

That heart is free which is held by no love other than the love of God.

St. Bonaventure. (13th cent.)

All things are sweet to holy love.

St. Bonaventure. (13th cent.)

For it is of the nature of love, to love when it feels itself loved, and to love all things loved of its beloved. So when the soul has by degrees known the love of its Creator toward it, it loves Him, and, loving Him, loves all things whatsoever that God loves.

St. Catherine of Siena: *Letter to Messer Ristoro Canigiani.* (14th cent.)

Thus should of God the lover be content
Any distress or sorrow to endure,
Rather than to be from God absent,
And glad to die, so that he may be sure
By his departing hence for to procure,
After this valley dark, the heavenly light,
And of his love the glorious blessed sight.

St. Thomas More: *The Measure of Love.* (16th cent.)

Grant, I pray thee, such heat into mine heart,
That to this love of thine may be egal:
Grant me fro Satan's service to astart,
With whom me rueth so long to have be thrall.

Grant me good Lord, and Creator of
  all,
The flame to quench of sinful desire,
And in Thy love set all mine heart a
  fire.

> St. Thomas More: *A Prayer of Pico Della
> Mirandola.* (16th cent.)

Sweet Jesu, if it be Thy will: unto my
  plaints attend;
Grant grace I may continue still: Thy
  servant to the end.
Grant, blessed Lord, grant Saviour
  sweet: grant Jesu King of bliss,
That in Thy love I live and die: sweet
  Jesu, grant me this.

> Anonymous Poem, possibly by Bl. Henry
> Walpole. (Guiney, 275) (16th cent.)

My God, I love Thee, not because
  I hope for heaven thereby;
Nor because they, who love Thee not,
  Must burn eternally.

Thou, O my Jesus, Thou didst me
  Upon the Cross embrace;
For me didst bear the nails and spear,
  And manifold disgrace.

> St. Francis Xavier: *O Deus, ego amo te.*
> (Tr. Caswall) (16th cent.)

If, Lord, Thy love for me is strong
As this which binds me unto Thee,
What holds me from Thee, Lord, so
  long,
What holds Thee, Lord, so long from
  me?

> St. Teresa of Jesus: *Poems.* (Tr. A.
> Symons) (16th cent.)

I saw an angel close by me, on my left
side, in bodily form. . . . I saw in his
hand a long spear of gold, and at the
iron's point there seemed to be a little
fire. He appeared to me to be thrusting
it at times into my heart, and to pierce
my very entrails; when he drew it out,
he seemed to draw them out also, and to
leave me all on fire with a great love of
God.

> St. Teresa of Jesus: *Autobiography,* 20.
> (16th cent.)

I gave myself to Love divine,
And lo! my lot so changèd is
That my Beloved One is mine
And I at last am surely His.
When that sweet Huntsman from
    above
First wounded me and left me prone,
Into the very arms of Love
My stricken soul forthwith was thrown.
Since then my life's no more my own
And all my lot so changèd is
That my Beloved One is mine
And I at last am surely His.

> St. Teresa of Jesus: *Poems.* (Tr. E. A.
> Peers) (16th cent.)

Withhold thy heart from all things: seek
God, and thou shalt find Him.

> St. Teresa of Jesus: *Maxims.* (16th cent.)

Make many acts of love, for they set the
soul on fire and make it gentle.

> St. Teresa of Jesus: *Maxims.* (16th cent.)

Then shall my love of pleasure have his
  fill,
    When Beauty self, in Whom all
      pleasure is,
    Shall my enamored soul embrace
      and kiss,
And shall new loves and new delight
  distil,
    Which from my soul shall gush into
      my heart,
    And through my body flow to every
      part.

> Henry Constable: *Sonnet to Our Blessed
> Lady.* (16th cent.)

Man has a natural inclination to love
God above all things.

> St. Francis de Sales: *Treatise on the Love
> of God,* 1, 16. (17th cent.)

We are not drawn to God by iron chains,
but by sweet attractions and holy inspirations.

> St. Francis de Sales: *Treatise on the Love
> of God,* 2, 12. (17th cent.)

The love of men toward God takes its being, progress and perfection from the eternal love of God toward men.

St. Francis de Sales: *Treatise on the Love of God*, 4, 6. (17th cent.)

The most certain sign that we love God only in all things is when we love Him equally in all things.

Jean Pierre Camus: *The Spirit of St. Francis de Sales*, 1, 8. (17th cent.)

Lord, when the sense of Thy sweet
  grace
Sends up my soul to seek Thy face,
Thy blessed eyes breed such desire,
I die in love's delicious fire.

        .   .   .   .   .   .

Still live in me this loving strife
Of living death and dying life.
For while Thou sweetly slayest me,
Dead to myself, I live in Thee.

Richard Crashaw: *A Song.* (17th cent.)

Eternal Love! what 'tis to love Thee
  well,
None but himself, who feels it, none
  can tell.
But oh, what to be lov'd of Thee as
  well,
None, not himself who feels it, none
  can tell.

Richard Crashaw: *In Amorem Divinum.*
(17th cent.)

    Live, Jesus, live! and let it be
    My life to die for love of Thee.

Motto of Richard Crashaw. (17th cent.)

God alone is to be loved, self alone to be hated.

Pascal: *Pensées.* (17th cent.)

For few would love their God unless they feared.

Dryden. (17th cent.)

He alone is sufficient for the heart Who made it.

Card. Newman: *Miscellanies,* 220. (19th cent.)

With all my heart and soul and strength
  I loved Thee, O my Lord,
For Thou art perfect, and all things
  Were made by Thy blest Word.
Like me to Thine own image made,
  My neighbor Thou dost make,
And as I love myself, I love
  My neighbor for Thy sake.

Act of Love from *Hymns for the Year,*
1867.

O God! Thou wert my childhood's
  love,
  My boyhood's pure delight,
A presence felt the livelong day,
  A welcome fear at night,—

Oh let me speak to thee, dear God!
  Of those old mercies past,
O'er which new mercies day by day
  Such lengthening shadows cast.

F. Faber: *The God of my Childhood.*
(19th cent.)

O Jesus! Jesus! sweetest Lord!
  What art Thou not to me?
Each hour brings joy before unknown,
  Each day new liberty!

        .   .   .   .   .   .

O love of Jesus! Blessed love!
  So will it ever be;
Time cannot hold Thy wondrous
  growth,
  No, nor eternity!

F. Faber: *Jesus my God and my All.* (19th cent.)

Why dost thou beat so quick, my heart?
  Why struggle in thy cage?
What shall I do for thee, poor heart!
  Thy throbbing heat to swage?

        .   .   .   .   .   .

Dear Comforter! Eternal Love!
  If Thou wilt stay with me,
Of lowly thoughts and simple ways
  I'll build a nest for Thee.

        .   .   .   .   .   .

Who made this beating heart of mine,
  But Thou, my heavenly guest?
Let no one have it then but Thee,
  And let it be Thy nest.

F. Faber: *Sweetness in Prayer.* (19th cent.)

It is the maddening joy of the conscious companionship of Jesus Christ that has produced the lovers, and therefore the giants, of history.

R. H. Benson: *The Friendship of Christ.* (20th cent.)

The end and lesson is the same—that Christ purges His friends of all that is not of Him; that He leaves them nothing of themselves, in order that He may be wholly theirs; for no soul can learn the strength and the love of God until she has cast her weight upon Him.

R. H. Benson: *The Friendship of Christ.* (20th cent.)

Lord, let me seek, with sturdy heart and mind,
  In passion of desire and longingly.
Let me desire Thee, seeking Thee; and find—
  Loving Thee, find Thee; love Thee, finding Thee.

John Gray: *Lord, if Thou art not Present.* (20th cent.)

  All we know is trust,
And trust is born of love, and love of God,
And we were given what we call our reason
In order thus to reason back to love;
For all the child knows is the love he feels
For those who gave him being, and all man knows
Is that God gave him being, and Him he loves,
And reverences, and forever seeks,
  His Father, and his God.

Louise Morgan Sili: *Faith.* (20th cent.)

Love, you have struck me straight, my Lord!
  Past innocence, past guilt,
I carry in my soul the sword
  You buried to the hilt.

And though to eyes in terrible pain
  Heaven and earth may reel,

For fear you may not strike again
  I will not draw the steel.

Charles L. O'Donnell: *Resolution.* (20th cent.)

So I fare on the deific pathway my Love has travelled
As I fashion the web that Penelope could not have spun,
And ravel the heavenly robe of delay that she could not have ravelled
Under the sun.

Sister Madeleva: *Penelope.* (20th cent.)

Afraid? Of you, strong proxy lover, you, God's sea?
I give you my small self ecstatically,
To be caught, held, or buffeted; to rest
Heart to your heart, and breast to breathing breast;
To know on arms and cheeks, on brow and lips the bliss,
The stinging madness of one infinite kiss;
Daring your most exquisite, sweet alarms
In the safe compass of the everlasting arms.

Sister Madeleva: *The Swimmer.* (20th cent.)

My lover is a fool more wise Than Solomon;
My lover is a bird that flies Into the Sun.
He is a lighted lamp, my love, A midnight cry,
A mortal worm that died to prove He could not die.
My lover is a cedar tree With branches spread;
A sweet and bitter fruit is he, Alive and dead.
My lover is a quiet rain Falling onfleece;
My lover is or endless pain Or endless peace,
Or sometime an instinctive mole Breaking the Clod;
My lover is a thief who stole The name of God.

Sister Madeleva: *Riddles, One, Two, and Three.* (20th cent.)

The love of God is not a mild benevolence; it is a consuming fire. To those who resist it it becomes an eternal torment; to those who are willing to face its demands, it becomes a fire that cleanses and purifies; those whom it has once penetrated, it transforms into itself.

> Dom Griffiths: *The Golden String.* (20th cent.)

There is no dart in the quiver of the godly soul for anything but the Divine Target.

> Bishop Sheen: *Peace of Soul.* (20th cent.)

See also Charity

Love of Neighbor

We must be free from all enmity toward all men and love our enemies; and, when necessity requires, lay down our life for our friends with a love like that which God and His Christ had for us.

> St. Basil: *The Morals,* 5. (4th cent.)

Confirm, O Lord, we pray Thee, the hearts of Thy children, and strengthen them with the power of Thy grace; that they may both be devout in prayer to Thee, and sincere in love for each other.

> Leonine Sacramentary, Collect. (ca. 5th cent.)

Happy is the man who is able to love all men alike.

> St. Maximus the Confessor: *Centuries on Charity,* 1, 17. (7th cent.)

He alone loves the Creator perfectly who manifests a pure love for his neighbor.

> St. Bede the Venerable: *Homilies,* 3, 31. (8th cent.)

He that loves not his neighbor abhors God.

> St. John of the Cross: *Spiritual Sentences.* (16th cent.)

To love our neighbor in charity is to love God in man.

> St. Francis de Sales: *Treatise on the Love of God,* 10, 11. (17th cent.)

It is not for the creature's sake that you submit yourself to the creature, but for the love of the Creator Whom you acknowledge in the creature.

> St. Francis de Sales: *Letters to Persons in Religion,* 5, 12. (17th cent.)

It is to those who have the most need of us that we ought to show our love more especially.

> St. Francis de Sales: *Spiritual Conferences,* 4. (17th cent.)

We can never love our neighbor too much.

> St. Francis de Sales: *Spiritual Conferences,* 4. (17th cent.)

No man can be a friend of Jesus Christ who is not a friend to his neighbor.

> R. H. Benson: *The Friendship of Christ.* (20th cent.)

Lover

Love equalizes lovers.

> St. Francis de Sales: *Treatise on the Love of God,* 5, 5. (17th cent.)

Of all afflictions taught a lover yet,
'Tis sure the hardest science to forget.

> Pope: *Eloisa to Abelard.* (18th cent.)

There are always lovers in the working classes. It is only in our class, the middle-class, there are not enough men to go around.

> Katharine T. Hinkson: *A Midsummer Rose.* (20th cent.)

Perhaps there are things that are too great to happen, and too big to pass through the narrow doors of birth. For this world is too small for the soul of man; and, since the end of Eden, the very sky is not large enough for lovers.

> G. K. Chesterton: *The Common Man.* (20th cent.)

Loyalty

We should be low and love-like, and
  leal, each man to other,
And patient as pilgrims, for pilgrims
  are we all.

Langland: *Piers Plowman*, Passus 13.
(14th cent.)

Cursed be that loyalty which reaches so
far as to go against the law of God.

St. Teresa of Jesus: *Autobiography*, 5.
(16th cent.)

Luck

Now for good luck, cast an old shoe
after me.

John Heywood: *Proverbs*, 1, 9. (16th
cent.)

God sendeth fortune to fools.

John Heywood: *Proverbs*, 2, 6. (16th
cent.)

There's no good love without good luck.

Oliver St. John Gogarty: *Good Luck*.
(20th cent.)

Three unluckiest things to meet first
thing in the morning: a mad dog, a man
who lent you money, and a red-haired
girl.

Seumas MacManus: *Heavy Hangs the
Golden Grain*. (20th cent.)

See also Chance; Fortune

Lucy, Saint

We watch'd, as she linger'd all the day
  Beneath the torturer's skill;
And we pray'd that the spirit might
    pass away,
  And the weary frame be still.
'Twas a long sharp struggle from dark-
    ness to light,
  And the pain was fierce and sore;
But she, we knew, in her latest fight
  Must be more than conqueror!

J. Neale: *Martyrdom of St. Lucy*. (19th
cent.)

Lullaby

Upon my lap my Sovereign sits,
And sucks upon my breast,
Meanwhile His love sustains my life,
And gives my body rest.
    Sing lullaby, my little Boy,
    Sing lullaby, my life's joy.

Richard Verstegan: *Our Blessed Lady's
Lullaby*. (Guiney, 211) (16th cent.)

Lunatic

Whence comes it that a cripple does not
irritate us, and a crippled mind does
irritate us? Because a cripple recognizes
that we go straight, and a crippled spirit
says that it is we who limp; were it not
for this we should have pity for him
and not anger.

Pascal: *Pensées*, 6. (17th cent.)

Lust

By lust I mean that affection of the mind
which aims at the enjoyment of one's
self and one's neighbor without reference to God.

St. Augustine: *De Doctrina Christiana*, 3,
10. (4th cent.)

Sinful lust is not nature, but a disease of
nature.

St. Augustine: *Of Continence*. (5th cent.)

Foul lust of lechery, behold thy due!
Not only dost thou darken a man's
  mind,
But bringest destruction on his body
  too.
In their beginning all thy works are
  blind
And in their end are grief. How many
  find
That not the act alone, but even the will
To set about it can deprave and kill!

Chaucer: *The Man of Law's Tale*. (Tr.
Coghill) (14th cent.)

Lute

If thou would'st have me sing and play
  As once I play'd and sung,

First take this time-worn lute away,
  And bring me one freshly strung.

Thomas Moore: *If Thou Would'st Have Me Sing and Play.* (19th cent.)

Luther, Martin

The jolly Luther, reading him, began
T'interpret Scriptures by his Alcoran;
To grub the thorns beneath our tender feet
And make the paths of paradise more sweet:
Bethought him of a wife, ere half way gone,
(For 'twas uneasy travailing alone),
And in this masquerade of mirth and love,
Mistook the bliss of heav'n for bacchanals above.

Dryden: *The Hind and the Panther,* 1. (17th cent.)

Lying

Lying is wrong even to save chastity.

St. Augustine: *On Lying.* (4th cent.)

He who says that some lies are just, must be judged to say no other than that some sins are just, and therefore some things are just which are unjust: than which what can be more absurd?

St. Augustine: *Against Lying.* (5th cent.)

It seems to me that every lie is truly a sin, although it makes a great difference with what intention and in what matter a man lies.

St. Augustine: *Enchiridion,* 18. (5th cent.)

Every lie must be called a sin because it is man's duty, not only when he knows the truth but also when, being human, he errs or is deceived, to speak what is in his mind, whether this be really true or only thought to be true, whereas it is not.

St. Augustine: *Enchiridion,* 22. (5th cent.)

No one can be so bold—I mean no man—
At lies and swearing as a woman can.

Chaucer: *The Wife of Bath's Prologue.* (Tr. Coghill) (14th cent.)

He spinneth that fine lie with flax, fetching it out of his own body, as the spider spinneth her cobweb.

St. Thomas More. (16th cent.)

Children and fools cannot lie.

John Heywood: *Proverbs,* 1, 11. (16th cent.)

It is a sovereign remedy against lying to unsay the lie on the spot.

St. Francis de Sales: *Introduction to the Devout Life,* 3, 8. (17th cent.)

M

Machine

The unbreathing engine marks no tune,
Steady at sunrise, steady at noon,
  Inhuman, perfect, saving time,
  And saving measure, and saving rhyme—
And did our Ruskin speak too soon?

No noble strength on earth, he sees,
Save Hercules' arm; his grave decrees
  Curse wheel and steam. As the wheels ran
  I saw the other strength of man,
I knew the brain of Hercules.

Alice Meynell: *The Threshing Machine.* (20th cent.)

Madness

Mad as a March hare.

John Heywood: *Proverbs*, 2, 5. (16th cent.)

Men are mad so unavoidably that not to be mad would constitute one a madman of another order of madness.

Pascal: *Pensées*, 6. (17th cent.)

For those whom God to ruin has design'd,
He fits for fate, and first destroys their mind.

Dryden: *The Hind and the Panther*, 3. (17th cent.)

Great wits are sure to madness near alli'd
And thin partitions do their bounds divide.

John Dryden: *Absalom and Achitophel*, 1. (17th cent.)

There is a pleasure sure
In being mad which none but madmen know.

John Dryden: *The Spanish Friar*, 2. (17th cent.)

Magi, The

Who are these that ride so fast o'er the desert's sandy road,
That have tracked the Red Sea shore, and have swum the torrents broad;
Whose camels' bells are tinkling through the long and starry night—
For they ride like men pursued, like the vanquished of a fight?

F. Faber: *The Three Kings.* (19th cent.)

Magnanimity

For to keep the rebellious under one's hand is truly the part of a strong man and a ruler, but to be kind and gentle to the fallen is the mark of one who surpasses all men in magnanimity and kindness.

St. Basil: *Letters*, 112. (4th cent.)

Maiden

When once the young heart of a maiden is stolen,
The maid herself will steal after it soon.

Thomas Moore: *Ill Omens.* (19th cent.)

Majority and Minority

To be in the weakest camp is to be in the strongest school.

G. K. Chesterton: *Heretics.* (20th cent.)

Malice

Much malice mingl'd with a little wit
Perhaps may censure this mysterious
writ.

Dryden: *The Hind and the Panther,* 3.
(17th cent.)

Man

It is the glory of man to continue and
remain in the service of God.

St. Irenaeus: *Against the Heresies,* 4, 14,
1. (2nd cent.)

Cursed is everyone who placeth his hope
in man.

St. Augustine: *On the Christian Conflict.*
(4th cent.)

Man is a noble being created to the
image and likeness of God, not insofar
as he is housed in a mortal body, but in
that he is superior to brute beasts because of the gift of a rational soul.

St. Augustine: *De Doctrina Christiana,* 1,
22, 20. (4th cent.)

Man, then, as viewed by his fellow man,
is a rational soul with a mortal and
earthly body in its service.

St. Augustine: *De Moribus Ecclesiae
Catholicae,* 27, 52. (4th cent.)

An earthly animal, to be sure, but
worthy of heaven (*terrenum quidem
animal, sed coelo dignum*).

St. Augustine: *The City of God,* 22, 1.
(5th cent.)

Man is nothing else than . . . a sack of
dung, the food of worms.

St. Bernard: *Meditationes piissimae.* (12th
cent.)

God's likeness in men can be compared
to that of Hercules in marble—a semblance of form, a disparity of nature.

St. Thomas Aquinas: *Contra Gentes,* 4, 26.
(13th cent.)

Man is said to be after the image of
God, not as regards his body, but as regards that whereby he excels other animals. Now man excels all animals by his
reason and intelligence; hence it is according to his intelligence and reason,
which are incorporeal, that man is said
to be according to the image of God.

St. Thomas Aquinas: *Summa Theologica,*
1, 3, 1. (13th cent.)

What a man is in the sight of God, so
much he is and no more.

Saying of St. Francis of Assisi. (13th
cent.)

Creature of God, immortal man!
    Poor vessel wrought of clay!
Whose present life is but a span,
    So quick it fleets away!

Dionysius the Carthusian: *Homo Dei
creatura.* (Tr. Caswall) (15th cent.)

Man is a noble animal, for whose sake
alone God fashioned this wonder machine of the world. He is likewise a fellow citizen of the angels, a son of God,
an heir of immortality, a member of
Christ, a member of the Church.

Erasmus: *Enchiridion.* (16th cent.)

Thy name, O Lord, how great
    Is found before our sight,
It fills the earth and spreads the air,
    The great works of Thy might.

But yet among all these
    I ask what thing is man;
Or what is Adam's son,
    That bears his father's mark,
For whose delight and comfort eke
    Thou hast wrought all this work.

I see Thou mind'st him much,
    That dost reward him so:
Being but earth to rule the earth,
    Whereon himself doth go.

Henry Howard, Earl of Surrey: *The
Greatness of God.* (Guiney, 75) (16th
cent.)

Then as thereat I mus'd,
It came into my thought,
How God even from one mass of clay,
All human kind had wrought.

As well the silly wretch,
That lives in low degree,
As any mighty emperor,
How puissant so he be.

Richard Verstegan: *The Substance of
Humaine Flesh.* (Guiney, 216) (17th
cent.)

Lord, what is man? why should he
    cost Thee
So dear? what had his ruin lost Thee?
Lord, what is man? that Thou hast over-
    bought
    So much a thing of nought?
          . . . . . .
Alas, sweet Lord, what wer't to Thee
If there were no such worms as we?
Heav'n ne'er the less still heav'n would
    be,
    Should mankind dwell
    In the deep hell.
What have his woes to do with Thee?

Richard Crashaw: *Caritas Nimia.* (17th
cent.)

Man is an epitome of the world; he is
a little world in himself, in which all
that is to be found in the great world of
the universe is to be found.

St. Francis de Sales: *Spiritual Conferences,*
3. (17th cent.)

Man is not worthy of God; but he is not
incapable of being made worthy of Him.

Pascal: *Pensées.* (17th cent.)

Man is but a reed, the most feeble thing
in nature, but he is a thinking reed. The
entire universe need not arm itself to
crush him. A vapor, a drop of water
suffices to kill him. But if the universe
were to crush him man would still be
more noble than that which killed him,
because he knows that he dies, and the
advantage which the universe has over
him: the universe knows nothing of this.

Pascal: *Pensées.* (17th cent.)

Man is naturally credulous and incred-
ulous, timid and rash.

Pascal: *Pensées.* (17th cent.)

Man is neither an angel nor a brute, and
the very attempt to raise him to the level
of the former sinks him to that of the
latter.

Pascal: *Pensées.* (17th cent.)

What is man in nature? A nothing when
compared to infinity; a whole when
compared to nothing; a middle point
between nothing and whole.

Pascal: *Pensées.* (17th cent.)

Man, to himself, is the most prodigious
object in nature.

Pascal: *Pensées.* (17th cent.)

What a monster then is man! What a
novelty, what a portent, what a chaos,
what a contradiction, what a prodigy!
Universal judge and helpless worm;
trustee of truth, and sink of uncertainty
and error; glory and off-scouring of the
universe.

Pascal: *Pensées.* (17th cent.)

How dull, and how insensible a beast
Is man.

Dryden: *Discourse Concerning the Origin
and Progress of Satire,* 1. (17th cent.)

Men are but children of a larger
    growth;
Our appetites as apt to change as theirs,
And full as craving too, and full as
    vain.

Dryden: *All for Love,* 4, 1. (17th cent.)

What dust we dote on when 'tis man we
love.

Alexander Pope: *Eloisa to Abelard.* (18th
cent.)

Each beast, each insect, happy in its
    own,
Is Heav'n unkind to man, and man
    alone?

Shall he alone whom rational we call
Be pleased with nothing if not blessed
  with all?

> Alexander Pope: *An Essay on Man,* 2.
> (18th cent.)

Great lord of all things, yet a prey to
  all;
Sole judge of truth, in endless error
  hurled;
The glory, jest and riddle of the world!

> Alexander Pope: *An Essay on Man,* 2.
> (18th cent.)

The proper study of mankind is man.

> Alexander Pope: *An Essay on Man,* 2.
> (18th cent.)

Men may be read, as well as books, too
much.

> Alexander Pope: *Moral Essays,* 1. (18th
> cent.)

O man, strange composite of heaven
    and earth!
  Majesty dwarf'd to baseness! fra-
    grant flower
Running to poisonous seed! and seem-
  ing worth
  Cloaking corruption! weakness mas-
    tering power!
Who never art so near to crime and
  shame,
As when thou hast achieved some deed
    of name!

> Card. Newman: *The Dream of Gerontius,*
> 291. (19th cent.)

The ideal man! Oh, the ideal man
should talk to us as if we were goddesses,
and treat us as if we were children. He
should refuse all our serious requests, and
gratify every one of our whims. He
should encourage us to have caprices,
and forbid us to have missions. He
should always say much more than he
means, and always mean much more
than he says.

> Oscar Wilde: *A Woman of No
> Importance,* 2. (19th cent.)

Never has there been so little discussion
about the nature of men as now, when,
for the first time, anyone can discuss it.

> G. K. Chesterton: *Heretics.* (20th cent.)

Man is an exception, whatever else he
is. If he is not the image of God, then
he is a disease of the dust. If it is not
true that a divine being fell, then we can
only say that one of the animals went
entirely off his head.

> G. K. Chesterton: *All Things Considered.*
> (20th cent.)

It is not funny that anything else should
fall down; only that a man should fall
down. . . . Why do we laugh? Because
it is a grave religious matter: it is the
fall of man. Only man can be absurd:
for only man can be dignified.

> G. K. Chesterton: *All Things Considered.*
> (20th cent.)

For human beings, being children, have
the childish wilfulness and the childish
secrecy. And they never have from the
beginning of the world done what the
wise men have seen to be inevitable.

> G. K. Chesterton: *The Napoleon of
> Notting Hill.* (20th cent.)

Individually men may present a more or
less rational appearance, eating, sleeping, and scheming. But humanity as a
whole is changeful, mystical, fickle, delightful. Men are men, but Man is a
woman.

> G. K. Chesterton: *The Napoleon of
> Notting Hill.* (20th cent.)

Man is not merely an evolution but
rather a revolution.

> G. K. Chesterton: *The Everlasting Man,* 1,
> 1. (20th cent.)

The more we really look at man as an
animal, the less he will look like one.

> G. K. Chesterton: *The Everlasting Man,* 1,
> 1. (20th cent.)

Whether we are highbrows or lowbrows, the definition of man which is

accepted today comes to the same thing: in either case it means that we have no idea of man except that his only reason for existence is to get on in this world and have as good a time as possible.

Eric Gill: *It All Goes Together.* (20th cent.)

Man and Woman

Woman is the confusion of man.

Vincent of Beauvais: *Speculum historiale,* 10. (13th cent.)

There can no man in humbless him acquit
As woman can, nor can he be half so true,
As woman been.

Chaucer: *The Clerkes Tale.* (14th cent.)

Woman is for mannes help y-wrought.

Chaucer: *The Merchant's Tale.* (14th cent.)

In men we various ruling passions find;
In women two almost divide the kind;
Those only fix'd, they first or last obey,
The love of pleasure and the love of sway.

Pope: *Moral Essays, 2.* (18th cent.)

Female and male God made the man,
His image is the whole, not half.

Coventry Patmore: *The Angel in the House.* (19th cent.)

Women are never disarmed by compliments. Men always are.

Oscar Wilde: *An Ideal Husband, 3.* (19th cent.)

Women represent the triumph of matter over mind, just as men represent the triumph of mind over morals.

Oscar Wilde: *The Picture of Dorian Gray,* 4. (19th cent.)

I like men who have a future, and women who have a past.

Oscar Wilde: *The Picture of Dorian Gray,* 15. (19th cent.)

You never can tell about women; the older they are the greater fools they are about men.

Katharine T. Hinkson: *A Daughter of the Fields.* (20th cent.)

There is nothing women hate so much as to see men selfishly enjoying themselves without the solace of feminine society.

Katharine T. Hinkson: *Cousins and Others.* (20th cent.)

A man's good work is effected by doing what he does; a woman's by being what she is.

G. K. Chesterton: *Robert Browning.* (20th cent.)

If the man is the head of the family, the woman is the heart, and as he occupies the chief place in ruling, so she may and ought to claim for herself the chief place in love.

Pope Pius XI: *Casti connubii.* (Dec. 31, 1930)

Man, Old

Most men in years, as they are generally discouragers of youth, are like old trees that being past bearing themselves, will suffer no young plants to flourish beneath them.

Pope: *Letter to William Wycherley.* (18th cent.)

Manna

The manna falls, yet that celestial bread
Like Jews you munch, and murmur while you feed.

Dryden: *Britannia Rediviva.* (17th cent.)

Manners

At meat her manners were well taught withal;
No morsel from her lips did she let fall,
Nor dipped her fingers in the sauce too deep;

But she could carry a morsel up and
  keep
The smallest drop from falling on her
  breast.

> Chaucer: *Canterbury Tales: Prologue.*
> (Tr. Coghill) (14th cent.)

Manners before morals!

> Oscar Wilde: *Lady Windermere's Fan,* 4.
> (19th cent.)

It's bad manners to talk about ropes in
the house of a man whose father was
hanged.

> Seumas MacManus: *Heavy Hangs the
> Golden Grain.* (20th cent.)

Manning, Henry Edward Cardinal

> Anchorite, who didst dwell
> With all the world for cell!

> Francis Thompson: *To the Dead Cardinal
> of Westminster.* (19th cent.)

Marigold

The God above, for man's delight,
Hath here ordained every thing.
Sun, moon, and stars, shining so bright,
With all kind fruits that here doth
  spring,
And flowers that are so flourishing.
  Amongs all which that I behold,
As to my mind best contenting,
  I do commend the marigold.

> William Forrest: *A New Ballade of the
> Marigolde.* (Guiney, 149) (16th cent.)

The marigold abroad her leaves doth
  spread,
Because the sun's and her power is the
  same.

> Henry Constable: *Sonnets to Diana.* (16th
> cent.)

Market

Men know how the market goeth by the
market men.

> John Heywood: *Proverbs,* 1, 11. (16th
> cent.)

Marriage

It is better to marry only because it is
worse to burn. It is still better neither to
marry nor to burn.

> Tertullian: *To his Wife.* (3rd cent.)

And when will there be an end of marrying? I suppose, when there is an end of
living!

> Tertullian: *An Exhortation to Chastity,*
> 10. (3rd cent.)

I praise wedlock, I praise marriage: but
it is because they produce virgins.

> St. Jerome: *De Virginitate.* (5th cent.)

There as my heart is set, there will I
wive.

> Chaucer: *The Clerkes Tale.* (14th cent.)

And such a bliss is there betwixt them
  two
That, save the joy that lasteth evermo,
There is none like, that any creature
Hath seen or shall, while that the
  world may dure.

> Chaucer: *Tale of the Man of Lawe.* (14th
> cent.)

We wedded men live in sorrow and care.

> Chaucer: *The Merchant's Prologue.* (14th
> cent.)

> For it ne sits not unto fresh May
> Forto be coupled to cold January.

> Lydgate: *Temple of Glas.* (15th cent.)

Who weddeth or he be wise, shall die
or he thrive.

> John Heywood: *Proverbs,* 1, 8. (16th
> cent.)

It is hard to wife and thrive both in a
year.

> John Heywood: *Proverbs,* 1, 11. (16th
> cent.)

> When men will needs marry,
> Wisdom and haste may vary.

> John Heywood: *Proverbs,* 1, 13. (16th
> cent.)

It is better to be an old man's darling
Than a young man's warling.

> John Heywood: *Proverbs*, 2, 7. (16th cent.)

Peace and silence be the guide
To the man, and to the bride:
If there be a joy yet new
In marriage, let it fall on you,
    That all the world may wonder:
If we should stay, we should do worse,
And turn our blessings to a curse,
    By keeping you asunder.

> Francis Beaumont: *Masque of the Gentleman of Gray's Inn and the Inner Temple*. (17th cent.)

I am to be married within these three days; married past redemption.

> Dryden: *Marriage à la Mode*, 1. (17th cent.)

The woes of wedlock with the joys, we mix;
'Tis best repenting in a coach and six.

> Sir Samuel Garth: *Cato: Prologue*. (18th cent.)

Grave authors say, and witty poets sing,
That honest wedlock is a glorious thing,
But depth of judgment most in him appears
Who wisely weds in his maturer years.

> Alexander Pope: *January and May*. (18th cent.)

They dream in courtship, but in wedlock wake.

> Alexander Pope: *The Wife of Bath*. (18th cent.)

Most of the failures in marriage come of the man's not having manhood enough to assert the prerogatives which it is the woman's more or less secret delight to acknowledge. She knows her place, but does not know how to keep it unless he knows it also; and many an otherwise amiable woman grows restless and irritable under the insupportable doubt as to whether she has got her master.

> Coventry Patmore: *Religio Poetae*. (19th cent.)

Some dish more sharply spiced than this
Milk-soup men call domestic bliss.

> Coventry Patmore: *Olympus*. (19th cent.)

There's nothing in the world like the devotion of a married woman. It's a thing no married man knows anything about.

> Oscar Wilde: *Lady Windermere's Fan*, 3. (19th cent.)

Twenty years of romance make a woman look like a ruin; but twenty years of marriage make her something like a public building.

> Oscar Wilde: *A Woman of No Importance*, 1. (19th cent.)

Nowadays, all the married men live like bachelors, and all the bachelors like married men.

> Oscar Wilde: *The Picture of Dorian Gray*, 15. (19th cent.)

If Americans can be divorced for "incompatibility of temper" I cannot conceive why they are not all divorced. I have known many happy marriages, but never a compatible one. The whole aim of marriage is to fight through and survive the instant when incompatibility becomes unquestionable. For a man and a woman, as such, are incompatible.

> G. K. Chesterton: *What's Wrong with the World*. (20th cent.)

I gravely doubt whether women ever were married by capture. I think they pretended to be; as they still do.

> G. K. Chesterton: *What's Wrong with the World*. (20th cent.)

The revolt against vows has been carried in our day even to the extent of a revolt against the typical vow of marriage. It is most amusing to listen to the opponents of marriage on this subject. They appear to imagine that the ideal of constancy was a joke mysteriously imposed on mankind by the devil, instead of being as it is a yoke consistently imposed on all lovers by themselves. They have invented a phrase, a phrase that is a black vs. white contradiction in two words—"free love"—as if a lover ever had been or could be free.

> G. K. Chesterton: *The Defendant.* (20th cent.)

Sane marriage is an untheatrical thing; it is therefore not surprising that most modern dramatists have devoted themselves to insane marriage.

> G. K. Chesterton: *George Bernard Shaw.* (20th cent.)

A young man is bothered till he's married—and after that he's bothered entirely.

> Seumas MacManus: *Heavy Hangs the Golden Grain.* (20th cent.)

Marry a mountain woman and you marry the mountain.

> Seumas MacManus: *Heavy Hangs the Golden Grain.* (20th cent.)

Marriage: Sacrament

When men and women marry, the union should be made with the consent of the bishop, so that the marriage may be according to the Lord and not merely out of lust. Let all be done to the glory of God.

> St. Ignatius of Antioch: *Letter to Polycarp,* 5. (2nd cent.)

Tell my sisters to love the Lord and be satisfied with their husbands in flesh and spirit. In the same way tell my brothers in the name of Jesus Christ to love their wives as the Lord does the Church (cf. Eph. 5, 25).

> St. Ignatius of Antioch: *Letter to Polycarp,* 5. (2nd cent.)

How shall we ever be able adequately to describe the happiness of that marriage which the Church arranges, the Sacrifice strengthens, upon which the blessing sets a seal, at which the angels are present as witnesses, and to which the Father gives His consent.

> Tertullian: *To His Wife.* (3rd cent.)

No wedding or birthday feast shall be celebrated during Lent.

> Council of Laodicea, Can. 52. (365)

It is not permitted to marry the wife or the son of an uncle.

> Council of Rome, Can. 11. (402)

Since every man is a part of the human race, and human nature is something social and possesses the capacity for friendship as a great and natural good, for this reason God wished to create all men from one, so that they might be held together in their society, not only by the similarity of race, but also by the bond of blood relationship. And so it is that the first natural tie of human society is man and wife.

> St. Augustine: *The Good of Marriage,* 1. (5th cent.)

The marriage of male and female is something good. This union divine Scripture so commands that it is not permitted a woman who has been dismissed by her husband to marry again, as long as her husband lives, nor is it permitted a man who has been dismissed by his wife to marry again, unless she who left has died.

> St. Augustine: *The Good of Marriage,* 3. (5th cent.)

Marriage itself among all races is for the one purpose of procreating children, whatever will be their station and character afterwards; marriage was instituted for this purpose, so that children might be born properly and decently.

> St. Augustine: *The Good of Marriage,* 17. (5th cent.)

Marriage is a good in which the married are better in proportion as they fear God more chastely and more faithfully, especially if they also nourish spiritually the children whom they desire carnally.

St. Augustine: *The Good of Marriage,* 19. (5th cent.)

Be propitious, O Lord, unto our humble prayers, and graciously further Thy institution which Thou hast ordained for the increase of the human race; so that what is joined together by Thy authority, may be maintained by Thy help.

Roman Missal, Special Nuptial Collect after Lord's Prayer. (Leonine, ca. 5th cent.)

O God, Who by Thy mighty power didst make all things out of nothing, Who having set in order the elements of the universe and made man to God's image, didst appoint woman to be his inseparable helpmeet, in such wise that the woman's body took its beginning out of the flesh of man, thereby teaching that what Thou hadst been pleased to institute from one principle might never lawfully be put asunder; O God Who hast hallowed wedlock by a mystery so excellent that in the marriage bond Thou didst foreshadow the union of Christ with His Church . . . look in Thy mercy upon this Thy handmaid, who is to be joined in wedlock and entreats protection and strength from Thee.

Roman Missal, Special Prayer for Bride in Nuptial Mass. (Gregorian, ca. 7th cent.)

The servant of God N. is betrothed unto the servant of God N., in the name of the Father, and of the Son, and of the Holy Ghost. Ṙ. Amen.

Byzantine Euchologion, Betrothal Service. (Formula of priest as he gives a gold ring to the groom and a silver ring to the bride.) (Before 8th cent. ?)

The servant of God N. is crowned unto the servant of God N., in the name of the Father, and of the Son, and of the Holy Ghost. Ṙ. Amen.

Byzantine Euchologion, Service of Crowning. (Formula used by priest as he places crowns on bride and groom.) (Before 8th cent. ?)

Priest: N., will you take N., here present, for your lawful wife (husband) according to the rite of our holy mother the Church?
Groom (Bride): I will.
Groom (Bride): I, N., take you, N., for my lawful wife (husband), to have and to hold, from this day forward, for better, for worse, for richer, for poorer, in sickness and in health, until death do us part.

Roman Ritual, Marriage Rite, The Exchange of Vows. (Essential rite is ancient; formulas date from ca. 9th cent. ?)

In the name of the Father, and of the Son, and of the Holy Ghost. Take and wear this ring as a pledge of my fidelity.

Roman Ritual, Marriage Rite, Formula for Exchange of Rings. (Rite is ancient; formula dates from ca. 9th cent. ?)

May the God of Abraham, the God of Isaac, and the God of Jacob be with you, and may he fulfil his blessing in you: that you may see your children's children even to the third and fourth generation, and thereafter may you have life everlasting, by the grace of our Lord Jesus Christ, who with the Father and the Holy Ghost liveth and reigneth God for ever and ever. Amen.

Roman Missal, Blessing at end of Nuptial Mass. (ca. 9th cent. ?)

I join you in matrimony: In the name of the Father, and of the Son, and of the Holy Ghost. Ṙ. Amen.

Roman Ritual, Marriage Rite, Confirmation of Marriage Bond by Priest. (Formula introduced in middle ages, ca. 12th cent. ?)

Holy Scripture speaks of four marriages. The first in its historical and literal sense, the bodily union of a man and woman; the second allegorical, the union of Christ with His Church; the third tropological or moral, the union of God with the soul; the fourth anagogical or eschatological, the union of God with the Church Triumphant.

St. Thomas Aquinas: *Sermons, First Sunday after Epiphany*, 20. (13th cent.)

The efficient cause of matrimony is the mutual consent of the partners expressed in words about their undertaking here and now. Marriage has three blessings. The first is children, to be received and raised for God's service. The second is the loyal faith whereby each serves the other. The third is the sacrament, which signifies the inseparable union of Christ with His Church.

St. Thomas Aquinas: *Concerning the Articles of Faith and Sacraments of the Church*, 2.

The form of matrimony consists in an inseparable union of minds; a couple are pledged to one another in faithful friendship. The end is the begetting and upbringing of children, through marriage intercourse and shared duties in which each helps the other to rear children.

St. Thomas Aquinas: *Summa Theologica*, 3, 19, 2. (13th cent.)

The first parent of the human race, under the influence of the divine Spirit, pronounced the bond of matrimony perpetual and indissoluble, when he said: *This now is bone of my bones, and flesh of my flesh. Wherefore a man shall leave father and mother, and shall cleave to his wife, and they shall be two in one flesh* (Gen. 2, 23-24). But that by this bond two only are united and joined together, our Lord taught more plainly, when rehearsing those last words as having been uttered by God, he said: *therefore now they are not two, but one flesh* (Matth. 19, 6); and straightway confirmed the firmness of that tie, proclaimed so long before by Adam, by these words: *What therefore God hath*

joined together, let no man put asunder (Matth. 19, 6).

Decree of the Council of Trent, Session 24. (Nov. 11, 1563)

If any one saith that matrimony is not truly and properly one of the seven sacraments of the evangelic law, instituted by Christ the Lord; but that it has been invented by men in the Church; and that it does not confer grace; let him be anathema.

Council of Trent, Session 23, Canon 1. (Nov. 11, 1563)

If any one saith that it is lawful for Christians to have several wives at the same time, and that this is not prohibited by any divine law; let him be anathema.

Council of Trent, Session 24, Canon 2. (Nov. 11, 1563)

If any one saith that only those degrees of consanguinity and affinity which are set down in Leviticus can hinder matrimony from being contracted, and dissolve it when contracted; and that the Church cannot dispense in some of those degrees, or establish that others may hinder and dissolve it; let him be anathema.

Council of Trent, Session 23, Canon 3. (Nov. 11, 1563)

If any one saith that the Church could not establish impediments dissolving marriage; or that she has erred in establishing them; let him be anathema.

Council of Trent, Session 24, Canon 4. (Nov. 11, 1563)

If any one saith that the prohibition of the solemnization of marriages at certain times of the year is a tyrannical superstition derived from the superstition of the heathen; or condemns the benedictions and other ceremonies which the Church makes use of therein; let him be anathema.

Council of Trent, Session 24, Canon 11. (Nov. 11, 1563)

If any one saith that matrimonial causes do not belong to ecclesiastical judges; let him be anathema.

Council of Trent, Session 24, Canon 12. (Nov. 11, 1563)

The state of marriage is one that requires more virtue and constancy than any other; it is a perpetual exercise of mortification.

St. Francis de Sales: *Letters to Persons in the World,* 1, 8. (17th cent.)

Marriage is an order in which the profession must be made before the noviciate.

Jean Pierre Camus: *The Spirit of St. Francis de Sales,* 7, 10. (17th cent.)

It is clear that marriage, even in the state of nature and certainly long before it was raised to the dignity of a sacrament, was divinely instituted in such a way that it should be a perpetual and indissoluble bond, which cannot therefore be dissolved by any civil law.

Pope Pius VI: *Rescript to the Bishop of Agria.* (18th cent.)

Marriage is the most inviolable and irrevocable of all contracts that were ever formed. Every human compact may be lawfully dissolved but this.

James Cardinal Gibbons: *The Faith of Our Fathers,* 31. (19th cent.)

It should be known that no power can dissolve the bond of Christian marriage whenever this has been ratified and consummated; and that, of a consequence, those husbands and wives are guilty of a manifest crime who plan, for whatever reason, to be united in a second marriage before the first one has been ended by death.

Pope Leo XIII: *Arcanum Divinae Sapientiae.* (Feb. 10, 1880)

Marriage is a sacrament, because it is a holy sign which gives grace, showing forth an image of the mystical nuptials of Christ with the Church. But the form and image of these nuptials is shown precisely by the very bond of that most close union in which man and woman are bound together in one; which bond is nothing else but the marriage itself. Hence it is clear that among Christians every true marriage is, in itself and by itself, a sacrament; and that nothing can be further from the truth than to say that the sacrament is a certain added ornament, or outward endowment, which can be separated and torn away from the contract at the caprice of man.

Pope Leo XIII: *Arcanum Divinae Sapientiae.* (Feb. 10, 1880)

Marriage has God for its Author, and was from the very beginning a kind of foreshadowing of the incarnation of His Son; and therefore there abides in it a something holy and religious; not extraneous, but innate; not derived from men, but implanted by nature.

Pope Leo XIII: *Arcanum Divinae Sapientiae.* (Feb. 10, 1880)

Christ our Lord raised the contract itself of marriage between baptized persons to the dignity of a sacrament. Therefore it is impossible for a valid contract of marriage between baptized persons to exist without being by that very fact a sacrament.

Code of Canon Law, Canon 1012. (20th cent.)

The primary end of marriage is the procreation and education of children; its secondary end is mutual help and to serve as a remedy for concupiscence. The essential properties of marriage are unity and indissolubility, which acquire a peculiar firmness in Christian marriage by reason of its sacramental character.

Code of Canon Law, Canon 1013. (20th cent.)

1. The valid marriage of baptized persons is said to be ratified (*ratum*) if it has not yet been completed by consummation; it is said to be ratified and consummated (*ratum et consummatum*)

if the conjugal act has taken place between the parties for which the marriage contract is by its nature ordained and by which husband and wife are made one flesh. 2. After the celebration of the marriage, if the parties have cohabited together, the consummation of the marriage is presumed, until the contrary is proved. 3. The marriage of non-baptized persons, validly celebrated, is said to be legitimate (*legitimum*). 4. An invalid marriage is said to be putative (*putativum*) if it was celebrated in good faith on the part of at least one of the parties, until both parties are certainly informed of its nullity.

> Code of Canon Law, Canon 1015. (20th cent.)

The marriage of baptized persons is governed not only by divine law but also by canon law, without prejudice to the competency of the civil power as regards the merely civil effects of such marriage.

> Code of Canon Law, Canon 1016. (20th cent.)

To declare authoritatively when the divine law forbids or invalidates a marriage belongs solely to the supreme authority of the Church. The same supreme authority has the exclusive right to establish for baptized persons impeding or diriment impediments either by way of general or particular law.

> Code of Canon Law, Canon 1038. (20th cent.)

Marriage is effected by the consent of the parties, lawfully expressed between persons who are capable according to law; and this consent no human power can supply. Matrimonial consent is an act of the will by which each party gives and accepts a perpetual and exclusive right over the body, for acts which are of themselves suitable for the generation of children.

> Code of Canon Law, Canon 1081. (20th cent.)

By a valid marriage there is produced between the parties a bond which is by nature perpetual and exclusive; moreover Christian marriage confers grace upon the parties if they place no obstacle to it.

> Code of Canon Law, Canon 1110. (20th cent.)

To take away from man the natural and primeval right of marriage, to circumscribe in any way the principal ends of marriage laid down in the beginning by God himself in the words *Increase and multiply* (Gen. 1, 28), is beyond the power of any human law.

> Pope Pius XI: *Casti Connubii*. (Dec. 31, 1930)

Christian parents must also understand that they are destined not only to propagate and preserve the human race on earth, indeed not only to educate any kind of worshippers of the true God, but children who are to become members of the Church of Christ, to raise up fellow-citizens of the saints, and members of God's household, that the worshippers of God and our Savior may daily increase.

> Pope Pius XI: *Casti Connubii*. (Dec. 31, 1930)

Marriage: Dissolution of Marriage

If any one saith that matrimony contracted, but not consummated, is not dissolved by the solemn profession of religion by one of the married parties; let him be anathema.

> Council of Trent, Session 24, Canon 6. (Nov. 11, 1563)

Defender of marriage (defensor vinculi).

> Officer appointed by Pope Benedict XIV to oppose suits for annulment. (18th cent.)

Marriage which is ratified and consummated cannot be dissolved by any human power, nor by any cause save death.

> Code of Canon Law, Canon 1118. (20th cent.)

Legitimate marriage between non-baptized persons, even though it has been consummated, is dissolved in favor of the faith by virtue of the Pauline privilege. This privilege does not apply in the case of a marriage between a baptized and an unbaptized person which was entered into with a dispensation from the impediment of disparity of cult.

> Code of Canon Law, Canon 1120. (20th cent.)

See also Divorce; Marriage: Separation of Husband and Wife

Marriage: Mixed Marriage

Christians shall not marry heretics. They shall neither take them nor their children in marriage, nor shall they give their sons or daughters in marriage to them, until they promise to become Christians.

> Council of Laodicea, Can. 31. (365)

Everywhere and with the greatest strictness the Church forbids marriage between baptized persons, one of whom is a Catholic and the other a member of a schismatical or heretical sect. If there is any danger of the falling away of the Catholic party and the perversion of the children such a marriage is forbidden by the divine law also.

> The Code of Canon Law, Canon 1060. (20th cent.)

Marriage: Second Marriage

First marriages are of better desert than second.

> St. Augustine: *On the Good of Widowhood.* (5th cent.)

No pious Christian ought to marry twice.

> Alexander Pope: *The Wife of Bath.* (18th cent.)

Marriage: Separation of Husband and Wife

If a woman leaves her husband and separates herself from an abhorrence of the married state, let her be anathema.

> Council of Gangra, Can. 14. (ca. 365)

If anyone says that the Church is in error when she decides that for many reasons husband and wife may separate from bed and board or from cohabitation for a definite period of time or even indefinitely: let him be anathema.

> Council of Trent, Session 24, Canon 8. (Nov. 11, 1563)

Husband and wife are obliged to observe community of conjugal life unless a just reason excuses them.

> Code of Canon Law, Canon 1128. (20th cent.)

Martha, Saint

As Jesus sought His wandering sheep,
  With weary toil oppress'd,
He came to Martha's lowly roof,
  A loved and honored guest.

O bless'd art thou, whose threshold poor,
  Those holy feet have trod,
To wait on so divine a guest,
  And to receive thy God!

> Anonymous: *Flagrans amore perditos.* (In Caswall's *Lyra*) (Parisian Brev., 17th cent.)

Martyr

For let him that is condemned for the name of the Lord God be esteemed by you as a holy martyr, an angel of God, or God upon earth, even one that is spiritually clothed with the Holy Spirit of God; for through him you see the Lord our Savior, inasmuch as he has been found worthy of the incorruptible crown, and has renewed again the witness of His passion.

> Anonymous: *Didascalia Apostolorum, 19.* (3rd cent.)

We do not set up temples, priesthoods, and sacrifices for our martyrs, because they are not our gods, but their God is our God. We do certainly honor their shrines (*memorias*) as shrines of holy men of God, who have fought for the truth even to bodily death, that true religion might be known and false and fictitious religions confuted . . . what is offered at their shrines is offered to God, Who made them both men and martyrs, that by such celebration we may return thanks to God for their victories, and call God to aid, that by the renewal of their memory we may be incited to imitation of such crowns and palms of martyrdom.

St. Augustine: *The City of God,* 8, 27. (5th cent.)

The martyrs were bound, imprisoned, scourged, racked, burnt, rent, butchered —and they multiplied.

St. Augustine: *The City of God,* 22, 6. (5th cent.)

The death of the martyrs blossoms in the faith of the living.

Pope St. Gregory I: *Homilies on the Gospels,* 38, 4. (6th cent.)

O God, of Thy soldiers the portion and crown,
Spare Thy people, who hymn the praise of the blest;
Earth's bitter joys, its lures and its frown,
He scanned them and scorned, and so is at rest.

Thy martyr he ran all valiantly o'er
An highway of blood for the prize Thou hast given.
We kneel at Thy feet and meekly implore,
That our pardon may wait on his triumph in heaven.

Roman Breviary, Feast of One Martyr, hymn *Deus tuorum militum* at Vespers. (Tr. Card. Newman) (Ambrosian, 6th cent.)

O glorious King of martyr hosts,
Thou crown that each confessor boasts,
Who leadest to celestial day
Those who have cast earth's joys away.

Roman Breviary, Feast of Many Martyrs, hymn *Rex gloriose martyrum* at Lauds. (Tr. R. Littledale and G. Palmer) (Ambrosian, 6th cent.)

There are two kinds of martyrs, one in open suffering, the other in the hidden virtue of the spirit. For many, enduring the snares of the enemy and resisting all carnal desires, because they have sacrificed themselves in their hearts to almighty God, have also become martyrs in time of peace, and if they had lived in time of persecution, they could have been martyrs in reality.

St. Isidore: *Etymologies,* 7, 11. (7th cent.)

The hymn for conquering martyrs raise:
The victor innocents we praise:
Whom in their woe earth cast away,
But heaven with joy received today.
Whose angels see the Father's face
World without end, and hymn His grace:
And while they chant unceasing lays,
The hymn for conquering martyrs raise.

St. Bede the Venerable: *Hymnum canentes martyrum.* (Tr. J. Neale) (8th cent.)

Sing, O sons of the Church sounding the martyrs' praise!
God's true soldiers applaud, who, in their weary days,
Won bright trophies of good, glad be the voice ye raise,
While these heroes of Christ ye sing!

Roman Breviary, Feast of Many Martyrs, hymn *Sanctorum meritis inclyta gaudia* at Vespers. (Tr. D. Donahoe) (Author unknown, 8th cent.)

Thy Church, clad in beautiful raiment with the blood of thy martyrs in all the world, as with purple and fine linen, crieth unto Thee through them, O Christ our God, Send down Thy bounties upon

Thy people, give peace to the state, and great mercy to our souls.

Byzantine Horologion, Kontakion at Compline. (Before 9th cent.)

Martyr of unconquered might,
Follower of the incarnate Son!
Who, victorious in the fight,
Hast celestial glory won;

By the virtue of thy prayer,
Let no evil hover nigh;
Sin's contagion drive afar;
Waken drowsy lethargy.

Roman Breviary, Feast of One Martyr, hymn *Invicte martyr unicum* at Lauds. (Tr. E. Caswall) (Author unknown, 10th cent. or later)

God knows it is not force nor might,
Nor war nor warlike band,
Nor shield and spear, nor dint of sword,
That must convert the land:
It is the blood of martyrs shed,
It is that noble train,
That fight with word and not with sword,
And Christ their capitaine.

Thomas Pounde (?): *Complaynt of a Catholike for the Death of M. Edmund Campion.* (Guiney, 181) (16th cent.)

O that it were as it was wont to be!
When Thy old friends of fire, all full of Thee,
Fought against frowns with smiles; gave glorious chase
To persecutions; and against the face
Of death and fiercest dangers, durst with brave
And sober pace march on to meet a grave.
On their bold breasts about the world they bore Thee
And to the teeth of hell stood up to teach Thee,
In center of their inmost souls they wore Thee,
Where racks and torments striv'd, in vain, to reach Thee.

Richard Crashaw: *The Name of Jesus.* (17th cent.)

Those thy old soldiers, great and tall,
Ripe men of martyrdom, that could reach down
With strong arms, their triumphant crown;
Such as could with lusty breath
Speak loud into the face of death
Their great Lord's glorious name.

Richard Crashaw: *Hymn to St. Teresa.* (17th cent.)

This may not be the age of saints, but all times are the age of martyrs.

Card. Newman: *Present Position of Catholics in England.* (19th cent.)

No one is a martyr for a conclusion, no one is a martyr for an opinion; it is faith that makes martyrs.

Card. Newman: *Discourses to Mixed Congregations.* (19th cent.)

First fearless witness to his belief
In Jesus crucified,
The red-robed martyrs' noble chief,
Thus for his Master died.
And to the end of time his name
Our Holy Church shall e'er proclaim,
And with a mother's pride shall tell
How her great proto-martyr fell.

Abram Ryan: *Saint Stephen.* (19th cent.)

Behold a great high priest with rays
Of martyrdom's red sunset crowned;
None other like him, in the days
Wherein he trod the earth, was found.
The swords of men unholy met
Above that just one, and he bled:
But God, the God he served, hath set
A wreath unfading on his head.

Aubrey de Vere: *St. Thomas of Canterbury.* (19th cent.)

Ah, see the fair chivalry come, the companions of Christ!
White horsemen, who ride on white horses, the knights of God!
They, for their Lord and their Lover who sacrificed

All, save the sweetness of treading
    where He first trod!

Lionel Johnson: *Te Martyrum Candidatus*.
(19th cent.)

The fire was no match for thee,
Who burned with an intenser glow.
It did but help thine ardor free,
That was too trammeled here below.
The splendor of thy keen desire
Shamed the wild flames and paled the
    fire.

Edward Garesché: *To a Martyr*. (20th
cent.)

Martyrdom

Those martyrdoms are blessed and noble, then, which take place according to
the will of God, for we must be careful to ascribe to God the power over all
occurrences.

Martyrdom of St. Polycarp, 2. (2nd cent.)

Fire and cross and battling with wild
beasts, their clawing and tearing, the
breaking of bones and mangling of
members, the grinding of my whole
body, the wicked torments of the devil—
let them assail me, so long as I get to
Jesus Christ.

St. Ignatius of Antioch: *Letter to the
Romans*, 5. (2nd cent.)

To all our persecutors we say: "You are
our brethren; apprehend, rather, the
truth of God." But when neither they
nor you will listen to us, but you do all
in your power to force us to deny Christ,
we resist you and prefer to endure death,
confident that God will give us all the
blessings which He promised us through
Christ.

St. Justin Martyr: *Dialogue with Trypho*,
96. (2nd cent.)

We multiply whenever we are mown
down by you; the blood of Christians is
seed (*semen est sanguis Christianorum*).

Tertullian: *Apology*, 50, 13. (3rd cent.)

The Lord has willed that we should
even rejoice over persecutions because,
when persecutions occur, then the faith
is crowned, God's soldiers are put to the
test and heaven is opened to martyrs.
We have not enlisted in an army merely
to think of peace and to decline battle,
seeing that the Lord, the master of humility, endurance and suffering, has
taken the first place in the conflict, that
He might first do what He taught us to
do and that He might himself first endure for us what He exhorts us to endure.

St. Cyprian: *Letters*, 66. (3rd cent.)

Baptism by fire.

Eusebius of Caesarea: *Ecclesiastical
History*, 6, 4, 3. (Expression used by early
Christians for martyrdom.) (4th cent.)

The ashes of martyrs drive away demons.

St. John Chrysostom: *Homilies*. (4th
cent.)

I came from martyrdom unto this peace.

Dante: *Paradiso, Canto 15*. (14th cent.)

As for me, I have no inclination to risk
my life for the truth. . . . Popes and emperors must settle the creeds. If they
settle them well, so much the better; if,
ill, I shall keep on the safe side.

Erasmus: *Letter to Archbishop Warham of
Canterbury*. (16th cent.)

It was not our death that ever we feared.
But we knew that we were not lords of
our own lives, and therefore for want of
answer would not be guilty of our
deaths. The only thing that we have now
to say is, that if our religion do make us
traitors, we are worthy to be condemned;
but otherwise are, and have been, as
good subjects as ever the Queen had.

Bl. Edmund Campion: *Statement at Trial*.
(16th cent.)

England look up, thy soil is stain'd
    with blood,

Thou hast made martyrs many of thine
own;
If thou hast grace their deaths will do
thee good,
The seed will take which in such blood
is sown,
And Campion's learning fertile so before,
Thus watered too, must needs of force
be more.

Bl. Henry Walpole (?): *Upon the Death
of M. Edmund Campion.* (Guiney, 178)
(16th cent.)

Discomfort not, whatever your foes do
threat,
Reck not of racks, their torments are
but toys,
The more they do, upon your bodies
set,
The more with me, they shall increase
your joys:
Yea and the greater, that your torments
be,
The greater comfort shall you have of
me.

Thomas Pounde: *A Consolation to
Afflicted Catholykes.* (Guiney, 186) (16th
cent.)

Farewell, then, all the world! Adieu.
Teresa is no more for you.
Farewell, all pleasures, sports and joys,
(Never till now esteemed toys)
Farewell, whatever dear may be,
Mother's arms, or father's knee,
Farewell, house, and farewell, home!
She's for the Moors and martyrdom.

Richard Crashaw: *Hymn to St. Teresa.*
(17th cent.)

For all have not the gift of martyrdom.

Dryden: *The Hind and the Panther,* 2.
(17th cent.)

A martyrdom is a season of God's espe-
cial power in the eye of faith, as great as
if a miracle were visibly wrought.

Card. Newman: *Historical Studies.*
(Miscellanies, p. 118) (19th cent.)

Mary Magdalen, Saint

His sacred feet with tears of agony
She bathes; and prostrate on the ground
adores;
Steeps them in kisses chaste, and wipes
them dry
With her own hair; then forth her
precious ointment pours.

Roman Breviary, Feast (July 22), *Maria
castis osculis (Nardo Maria pistico).*
(From hymn *Magno salutis gaudio*) (Tr.
E. Caswall) (Much altered, attr. to Pope
St. Gregory I, 6th cent.)

Son of the Highest, deign to cast
On us a pitying eye;
Thou, who repentant Magdalen
Didst call to endless joy.

. . . . . .

O Jesus, balm of every wound!
The sinner's only stay!
Wash Thou in Magdalen's pure tears
Our guilty spots away.

Roman Breviary, Feast (July 22), hymn
Summi Parentis Unice at Lauds. (Tr. E.
Caswall) (St. Odo of Cluny, 10th cent.)

Exalt, O mother Church, today
The clemency of Christ the Lord;
By sevenfold grace who wipes away
The guilt of sevenfold crimes abhorred.

St. Odo of Cluny: *Lauda mater ecclesia.*
(Tr. J. Neale) (10th cent.)

Blessed offender! who thyself hast try'd
How far a sinner differs from a
saint;
Join thy wet eyes, with tears of my
complaint,
While I sigh for that grave for which
thou cry'd.
No longer let my sinful soul abide
In fever of thy first desire's feint;
But let thy love, which last did taint,
With pangs of thy repentance, pierce
my side.
So shall my soul no foolish virgin be
With empty lamp; but, like a Mag-
dalen, bear
For ointment-box a breast with oil of
grace:

And so the zeal, which then shall burn
  in me,
May make my heart like to a lamp
  appear,
And in my spouse's palace give me
  place.

Henry Constable: *To Saint Mary
Magdalen.* (16th cent.)

If short delights entice my heart to
  stray,
Let me by thy long penance learn to
  know
How dear I should for trifling pleas-
  ures pay;
And if I virtue's rough beginning shun,
Let thy eternal joys unto me show
What high reward by little pain is
  won.

Henry Constable: *To St. Mary Magdalen.*
(16th cent.)

Father of lights! one glance of thine,
Whose eyes the universe control,
Fills Magdalen with holy love,
And melts the ice within her soul.

Roman Breviary, Feast (July 22), hymn
Pater superni luminis at Vespers. (Tr. E.
Caswall) (Card. Bellarmine, 1542–1621)

The proud Egyptian queen, her Roman
  guest,
(T'express her love in height of state
  and pleasure)
With pearl dissolv'd in gold, did feast,
Both food and treasure.

And now (dear Lord!) Thy lover, on
  the fair
And silver tables of Thy feet, behold!
Pearl, in her tears and in her hair,
Offers Thee gold.

Sir Edward Sherburne: *The Magdalen.*
(17th cent.)

To the hall of that feast came the sinful
  and fair;
She heard in the city that Jesus was
  there;
She mark'd not the splendor that blazed
  on their board;

But knelt silently at the feet of her
  Lord.

J. J. Callanan: *Mary Magdalen.* (19th
cent.)

There of virgins none
  Is fairer seen,
  Save one,
Than Mary Magdalen.

Coventry Patmore: *Deliciae Sapientiae De
Amore.* (19th cent.)

Maryland

Here the Roman Catholic and the Protestant Episcopal, whom the world
would persuade have proclaimed open
wars against each other, contrariwise
concur in an unanimous parallel of
friendship.

George Alsop: *The Character of the
Province of Maryland.* (17th cent.)

The despot's heel is on thy shore,
  Maryland!
His torch is at thy temple door,
  Maryland!
Avenge the patriotic gore
That flecked the streets of Baltimore,
And be the battle queen of yore,
  Maryland, my Maryland!
      .   .   .   .

Remember Carroll's sacred trust,
Remember Howard's warlike thrust,
And all thy slumberers with the just,
  Maryland, my Maryland.

J. R. Randall: *Maryland, My Maryland.*
(19th cent.)

Mass, Holy

The worthiest thing, most of goodness,
In all this world, it is the mass.

Lay Folk's Mass Book. (13th cent.)

Paris is well worth a mass. (Paris vaut
bien une messe.)

Saying attributed to Henri IV of France,
but probably not his in this form. (See
Guerlac, Les Citations Françaises, ed. 1933,
p. 260.) (17th cent.)

To me nothing is so consoling, so piercing, so thrilling, so overcoming, as the mass. . . . It is not a mere form of words —it is a great action, the greatest action that can be on earth. It is, not the invocation merely, but, if I dare use the word, the evocation of the Eternal.

> Card. Newman: *Loss and Gain,* 20. (19th cent.)

Thou Who hast made this world so
    wondrous fair,—
  The pomp of clouds; the glory of
    the sea;
  Music of waters;song-birds' melody;
The organ of Thy thunder in the air;
Breath of the rose; and beauty every-
    where—
  Lord, take this stately service done to
    Thee,
The grave enactment of Thy Calvary
In jewelled pomp and splendor pic-
    tured there!
Lord, take the sounds and sights; the
    silk and gold;
  The white and scarlet; take the rev-
    erent grace
  Of ordered step; window and glow-
    ing wall—
Prophet and prelate, holy men of old;
  And teach us, children of the holy
    place
  Who love Thy courts, to love Thee
    best of all.

> Robert H. Benson: *At High Mass.* (20th cent.)

The mass was low and short—they are a Christian people.

> H. Belloc: *The Path to Rome.* (20th cent.)

Mass must be heard on feast days of obligation; and one must abstain from servile labor, from judicial proceedings, and also, unless legitimate customs or special permission allows, from public trafficking, public gathering of buyers and sellers, and all other public buying and selling.

> Code of Canon Law, Canon 1248. (20th cent.)

It is desirable that all the faithful should be aware that to participate in the eucharistic sacrifice is their chief duty and supreme dignity, and that not in an inert and negligent fashion, giving way to distractions and day-dreaming, but with such earnestness and concentration that they may be united as closely as possible with the High Priest, according to the apostle, *Let this mind be in you which was also in Christ Jesus* (Phil. 2, 5). And together with Him and through Him let them make their oblation, and in union with Him let them offer up themselves.

> Pope Pius XII: *Mediator Dei.* (Nov. 20, 1947)

Mass: Prayers and Formulas

I—*Mass: Preparation*

Incline the ears of Thy loving kindness, most gracious God, unto our prayers, and enlighten our heart with the grace of the Holy Ghost, that we may worthily celebrate Thy mysteries and love Thee with an everlasting love.

> Roman Missal, Prayer before Mass. (Recited privately by celebrant) (Before 10th cent.)

O God, to Whom every heart is open, every desire known, and from Whom no secrets are hidden; cleanse the thoughts of our hearts by the inspiration of Thy Holy Spirit, that we may perfectly love Thee, and worthily praise Thy name.

> Roman Missal, Prayer before Mass. (Recited privately by celebrant) (Before 10th cent.)

O great High Priest, our true Pontiff, Jesus Christ, who didst offer Thyself to God the Father a pure and spotless Victim upon the altar of the Cross for us miserable sinners, and didst give us Thy Flesh to be our meat and Thy Blood to be our drink, and didst ordain this mystery in the might of Thy Holy Spirit. . . . Make me by Thy grace, always so to believe and understand, to conceive and firmly to hold, to think and to speak, of this same deep mystery, as shall please Thee and be good for my soul. (Summe Sacerdos et vere Pontifex. . . .)

Roman Missal, Prayer before Mass. (Recited privately by celebrant) (11th cent.)

Thou shalt sprinkle me with hyssop, O Lord, and I shall be cleansed; Thou shalt wash me, and I shall be made whiter than snow. (Asperges me, Domine, hyssopo, et mundabor: lavabis me, et super nivem dealbabor.) (Ps. 50, 3)

Roman Missal, Asperges. (Antiphon sung before high mass as celebrant sprinkles people with holy water.) (ca. 10th cent.)

I saw water flowing from the right side of the temple, Alleluia; and all to whom that water came were saved, and they shall say: Alleluia, alleluia. (Vidi aquam egredientem de templo a latere dextro, alleluia; et omnes ad quos pervenit aqua ista salvi facti sunt, et dicent: alleluia, alleluia.)

Roman Missal, Vidi Aquam. (Antiphon sung in place of Asperges during Eastertide.) (ca. 10th cent.)

II—*Mass: Introductory Prayers and Chants*

In the name of the Father, and of the Son, and of the Holy Ghost. Amen. (In nomine Patris, et Filii, et Spiritus Sancti. Amen.)

Roman Missal, Ordinary of Mass. (The sign of the cross at the beginning of mass was apparently in use from the earliest times, but the present formula cannot be traced before the 14th cent. Cf. Jungmann, I, 296)

Blessed be the kingdom of the Father, of the Son, and of the Holy Ghost, now and forever, world without end. Amen.

Byzantine Euchologion, Blessing at beginning of Liturgy. (Before 8th cent.)

Judge me, O God, and distinguish my cause from the nation that is not holy; deliver me from the unjust and deceitful man. . . . Send forth Thy light and Thy truth: they have led me and brought me into Thy holy hill, and into Thy tabernacles. And I will go into the altar of God: unto God, Who giveth joy to my youth. . . . (Ps. 42). (Judica me, Deus. . . . Et introibo ad altare Dei: ad Deum qui laetificat juventutem meam . . .)

Roman Missal, Ordinary of Mass, *Judica me.* (Originally recited privately by celebrant on way to altar; now said at foot of altar) (Introduced ca. 1000)

I confess to almighty God, to blessed Mary ever Virgin, to blessed Michael the archangel, to blessed John the Baptist, to the holy apostles Peter and Paul, to all the saints, and to you, father, that I have sinned exceedingly in thought, word, and deed, through my fault, through my fault, through my most grievous fault. Therefore I beseech blessed Mary ever Virgin, blessed Michael the archangel, blessed John the Baptist, the holy apostles Peter and Paul, all the saints, and you, father, to pray to the Lord our God for me. (Confiteor Deo omnipotenti, beatae Mariae semper Virgini. . . .)

Roman Missal, Ordinary of Mass, *Confiteor.* (ca. 11th cent.)

May almighty God have mercy upon you, forgive you your sins and bring you to life everlasting. Amen. (Misereatur vestri omnipotens Deus. . . .)

Roman Missal, Ordinary of Mass, *Misereatur.* (ca. 11th cent.)

May the almighty and merciful Lord grant us pardon, absolution, and remission of our sins. (Indulgentiam, absolutionem et remissionem peccatorum nostrorum tribuat nobis omnipotens et misericors Dominus. Amen.)

Roman Missal, Ordinary of Mass, *Indulgentiam.* (ca. 11th cent.)

Take away from us our iniquities, we beseech thee, O Lord, that we may enter into Thy holy of holies with pure souls.

(Aufer a nobis, quaesumus Domine, iniquitates nostras. . . .)

Roman Missal, Ordinary of Mass, *Aufer a nobis.* (Leonine, ca. 5th cent.; recited as priest ascends altar steps, ca. 9th cent.)

We beseech Thee, O Lord, by the merits of Thy saints, whose relics are here, and of all the saints, that Thou wouldst vouchsafe to pardon all my sins. Amen. (Oramus te, Domine, per merita sanctorum tuorum. . . .)

Roman Missal, Ordinary of Mass, *Oramus te.* (Recited as priest kisses the altar, 11th cent.)

Kyrie eleison (*3 times*); Christe eleison (*3 times*); Kyrie eleison (*3 times*). (Lord have mercy; Christ have mercy; Lord have mercy.)

Roman Missal, Ordinary of Mass, *Kyrie eleison.* (Introduced ca. 5th cent.)

In peace let us pray to the Lord.
For the peace from on high, and for the salvation of our souls, let us pray to the Lord.
For the peace of the whole world, for the good estate of the holy churches of God, and for the union of all, let us pray to the Lord. . . .

Byzantine Euchologion, Divine Liturgy, Litany of Peace. (*Kyrie eleison* is sung after each petition.) (ca. 4th cent.)

Glory be to the Father, and to the Son, and to the Holy Ghost; as it was in the beginning, is now, and ever shall be, world without end. Amen. (Gloria Patri, et Filio, et Spiritui Sancto, sicut erat in principio, et nunc, et semper, et in saecula saeculorum. Amen.)

Roman Missal, Ordinary of Mass. (Lesser Doxology regularly sung at conclusion of all psalms. The psalm said or sung at this point in the mass is called the Introit, and varies for each mass. In Byzantine rite three antiphons sung at this point. Doxology dates from 4th cent.; singing of introit psalm from ca. 5th cent.)

Glory to God in the highest, and on earth peace to men of good will. We praise Thee. We bless Thee. We adore Thee. We glorify Thee. We give thanks to Thee for Thy great glory. O Lord God, heavenly King, God the Father almighty. O Lord, the only-begotten Son, Jesus Christ. O Lord God, Lamb of God, Son of the Father. Thou Who takest away the sins of the world, have mercy upon us. Thou Who takest away the sins of the world, receive our prayer. Thou Who sittest at the right hand of the Father, have mercy upon us. For Thou only art holy. Thou only art the Lord. Thou only, O Jesus Christ, art most High. With the Holy Ghost, in the glory of God the Father. Amen.

Roman Missal, Ordinary of Mass, *Gloria in Excelsis Deo.* (Originally Greek, ca. 4th cent.; chant was sung only by bishop on certain festive days; from 11th cent., by every celebrant.)

O only-begotten Son and Word of God, Who being immortal didst vouchsafe to take flesh for our salvation of the holy Mother of God, and ever-Virgin Mary; Thou Who without change didst become Man and wast crucified, O Christ our God, by death trampling upon death; Thou Who wast Thyself one of the Holy Trinity, Who art glorified with the Father and the Holy Spirit, save us.

Byzantine Euchologion, Divine Liturgy, Chant *Monogenes.* (Sung between second and third antiphon) (Attr. to Justinian, 6th cent.)

℣. The Lord be with you. ℟. And with thy spirit. (Dominus vobiscum. Et cum spiritu tuo.)

Roman Missal, Ordinary of Mass. (Formula of salutation, of Jewish origin, used to introduce the Prayer or Collect.) (Before 5th cent.)

℣. Peace be unto you. ℟. And with thy spirit. (Pax vobiscum. Et cum spiritu tuo.)

Roman Missal, Ordinary of Mass. (Formula of salutation used by bishops) (Before 5th cent.)

III—*Mass: The Lessons*

Wisdom! Stand!

Come, let us adore and bow down before Christ. Save us, O Son of God, Who didst rise again from the dead, we who sing to Thee: Alleluia.

> Byzantine Euchologion, Divine Liturgy, Little Entrance. (Entrance with book of gospels) (ca. 6th cent.)

Holy God, holy Strong One, holy Immortal One, have mercy on us (*thrice*). Glory be to the Father, and to the Son, and to the Holy Ghost, now and for ever, world without end. Amen. Holy Immortal One, have mercy on us. (Agios o Theos, agios ischyros, agios athanatos, eleison imas. . . .)

> Byzantine Euchologion, Divine Liturgy, *Trisagion.* (Chant frequently sung in Byzantine rite; in Roman rite only on Good Friday.) (5th cent.)

℞. Thanks be to god. (Deo gratias.)

> Roman Missal, Ordinary of Mass. (Response after reading of Epistle.) (Before 5th cent.)

Cleanse my heart and my lips, O almighty God, who didst cleanse the lips of the prophet Isaias with a burning coal: vouchsafe through Thy gracious mercy so to cleanse me that I may worthily proclaim Thy holy Gospel.

> Roman Missal, Ordinary of Mass, Prayer *Munda cor meum.* (Said before the Gospel) (14th cent.)

Alleluia! Alleluia! Alleluia!

> Chant sung between Epistle and Gospel in almost all rites. (In Roman rite, preceded by chanting of Gradual psalm.) (Before 4th cent.)

℣. The Lord be with you. ℞. And with thy spirit.
℣. The beginning (or continuation) of the holy Gospel according to. . . . (Initium, vel Sequentia sancti Evangelii secundum. . . .)
℞. Glory be to Thee, O Lord. (Gloria tibi, Domine)

. . . .

℞. Praise be to Thee, O Christ. (Laus tibi, Domine)

> Roman Missal, Ordinary of Mass. (Chants accompanying the singing or recitation of the Gospel. Before the Gospel the sign of the cross is made on the forehead, mouth and breast.) (Before 8th cent.)

IV—*Mass: Offertory*

All the catechumens go out! Catechumens, go out! All catechumens go out! Let not any of the catechumens remain!

> Byzantine Euchologion, Divine Liturgy, Dismissal of Catechumens. (Before 4th cent.)

I believe in one God, the Father almighty, Maker of heaven and earth, and of all things visible and invisible. And in one Lord Jesus Christ, the only begotten Son of God, born of the Father before all ages. . . . (Credo in unum Deum, Patrem omnipotentem, Factorem coeli et terrae, visibilium omnium, et invisibilium. Et in unum Dominum Jesum Christum, Filium Dei unigenitum. Et ex Patre natum ante omnia saecula. . . .)

> Roman Missal, Ordinary of Mass, Creed. (The Nicean-Constantinopolitan creed is regularly used in the Roman rite at mass, but was not recited at Rome before the 11th cent. Cf. Jungmann, i, 469. In Byzantine rite, creed recited immediately before Preface, and preceded by Kiss of Peace.)

We who mystically represent the cherubim, who sing to the life-giving Trinity the hymn Holy, Holy, Holy, let us now lay aside all earthly cares; that we may receive the King of the world who comes borne by unseen armies of angels. Alleluia, Alleluia, Alleluia.

> Byzantine Euchologion, Divine Liturgy, Cherubikon Hymn. (Sung as holy gifts are borne in procession to the altar at the Great Entrance.) (6th cent.)

Receive, O holy Father, almighty and eternal God, this spotless host, which I, Thy unworthy servant, offer unto Thee, my living and true God, for mine own countless sins, offences and negligences, and for all here present; as also for all faithful Christians living and dead, that it may avail both for my own and for their salvation unto life eternal. Amen.

> Roman Missal, Ordinary of Mass, Prayer *Suscipe Sancte Pater.* (9th cent.)

We offer Thee, O Lord, the chalice of salvation, beseeching Thy clemency, that it may ascend in the sight of Thy divine majesty with a sweet savor, for our own salvation and that of the whole world. Amen.

> Roman Missal, Ordinary of Mass, Offering of Chalice *Offerimus tibi Domine.* (Mozarabic, before 11th cent.)

O God, Who hast marvellously created human nature, and still more marvellously renewed it; grant that by the mystery of this water and wine we may be made partakers of His divinity, Who vouchsafed to share in our humanity, Jesus Christ Thy Son, our Lord; Who liveth, etc.

> Roman Missal, Ordinary of Mass, Mixture of Water and Wine, *Deus qui humanae substantiae.* (Originally Leonine ca. 5th cent.)

Come, O Sanctifier, almighty and eternal God, and bless this sacrifice in Thy holy name.

> Roman Missal, Ordinary of Mass, Invocation of Holy Ghost on Gifts, *Veni Sanctificator.* (Before 11th cent.)

Through the intercession of blessed Michael the archangel standing at the right hand of the altar of incense, and of all his elect, may the Lord vouchsafe to bless this incense, and to receive it in an odor of sweetness.

> Roman Missal, Ordinary of Mass, Incensation of Gifts, *Per intercessionem beati Michaelis.* (ca. 11th cent.)

I will wash my hands among the innocent: and will encompass Thy altar, O Lord: That I may hear the voice of Thy praise, and tell of all Thy wondrous works. (Lavabo inter innocentes manus meas: et circumdabo altare tuum, Domine: Ut audiam vocem laudis, et enarrem universa mirabilia tua.) (Ps. 25, 6)

> Roman Missal, Ordinary of Mass, the *Lavabo.* (Ceremonial washing of hands.) (ca. 9th cent.)

Receive, O holy Trinity, this oblation, which we offer Thee in remembrance of the passion, resurrection, and ascension of our Lord Jesus Christ, and in honor of blessed Mary ever Virgin, of blessed John the Baptist, the holy apostles Peter and Paul, of these and of all the saints, that it may avail to their honor and our salvation: and that they may vouchsafe to intercede for us in heaven, whose memory we now keep on earth.

> Roman Missal, Ordinary of Mass, Prayer to blessed Trinity, *Suscipe Sancta Trinitas.* (ca. 9th cent.)

Lord, God almighty, Who alone art holy, Who dost accept the sacrifice of praise from those who call upon Thee with their whole heart, also accept the prayer of us sinners, and draw us to Thy holy altar. Enable us to offer Thee gifts, and a spiritual sacrifice for our sins and for the negligences of the people, and deign that we may find grace before Thee, that our sacrifice may be well-pleasing to Thee. And let the good Spirit of Thy grace rest upon us and upon these gifts here set forth, and upon Thy whole people.

> Byzantine Euchologion, Divine Liturgy, Prayer of the Prothesis. (5th to 8th cent.)

Brethren, pray that my sacrifice and yours may be acceptable to God the Father almighty. ℟. May the Lord receive the sacrifice from Thy hands, to the praise and glory of His name, for our benefit and that of all His holy Church. (Orate fratres: ut meum ac vestrum sacrificum acceptabile fiat apud Deum Patrem omnipotentem. ℟. Suscipiat Dominus sacrificium de manibus tuis, ad laudem et gloriam nominis sui, ad utilitatem quoque nostram, totiusque Ecclesiae suae sanctae. Amen.)

Roman Missal, Ordinary of Mass, *Orate fratres*. (Exhortation and response before Secret Prayers.) (8th to 12th cent.)

V—*Mass: Canon or Anaphora*

℣. The Lord be with you. ℟. And with thy spirit.

℣. Lift up your hearts. (Sursum corda)

℟. We lift them up to the Lord. (Habemus ad Dominum)

℣. Let us give thanks to the Lord our God. (Gratias agamus, Domino Deo nostro)

℟. It is meet and right. (Dignum et justum est)

It is truly meet and just, right and availing unto salvation, that we should at all times and in all places give thanks unto Thee, O holy Lord, Father almighty and everlasting God. Who with Thine only-begotten Son and the Holy Ghost art one God, one Lord; not in the oneness of a single person, but in the Trinity of one substance. For that which we believe from Thy revelation concerning Thy glory, that same we believe also of Thy Son, and of the Holy Ghost, without difference or separation. So that in confessing the true and everlasting Godhead, we shall adore distinction in persons, oneness in being, and equality in majesty. Which the angels and archangels; the cherubim also and seraphim do praise, nor cease to cry out with one voice:

Holy, Holy, Holy, Lord God of Hosts. Heaven and earth are full of Thy glory. Hosanna in the highest. Blessed is He that cometh in the name of the Lord. Hosanna in the highest. (. . . Sanctus, sanctus, sanctus Dominus Deus Sabaoth. Pleni sunt caeli et terra gloria tua. Hosanna in excelsis. Benedictus, qui venit in nomine Domini. Hosanna in excelsis.)

Roman Missal, Ordinary of Mass, Preface of the Trinity. (Preface varies according to the mass; this form is Gelasian, ca. 6th cent. Basic formulas at beginning and end in use from apostolic times.)

We therefore humbly pray and beseech Thee, O most merciful Father, through Jesus Christ Thy Son our Lord, that Thou wouldst vouchsafe to receive and bless these gifts, these offerings, these holy and unblemished sacrifices. Which we offer Thee in the first place for Thy holy Catholic Church, that it may please Thee to grant her peace, to protect, unite and govern her throughout the world, together with Thy servant N. our pope [N. our bishop, and all true believers and professors of the Catholic and Apostolic faith].

Be mindful, O Lord, of Thy servants and handmaids, NN. and of all here present, whose faith and devotion are known to Thee, for whom we offer, or who offer up to Thee this sacrifice of praise for themselves and all those dear to them, for the redemption of their souls, the hope of their safety and salvation: who now pay their vows to Thee, the eternal, living, and true God.

Roman Missal, Canon of Mass, Prayers *Te igitur* and *Memento Domine*. (ca. 5th cent.; words in brackets added later.)

In communion with, and venerating the memory, above all of the glorious ever Virgin Mary, Mother of our God and Lord Jesus Christ; also of Thy blessed apostles and martyrs, Peter and Paul, Andrew, James, John, Thomas, Philip, Bartholomew, Matthew, Simon and Thaddeus, Linus, Cletus, Clement, Sixtus, Cornelius, Cyprian, Laurence, Chrysogonus, John and Paul, Cosmas and Damian, and of all Thy saints; by whose merits and prayers grant that we may be defended in all things by the help of Thy protection.

Roman Missal, Canon of Mass, Prayer *Communicantes*. (Present form, ca. 500)

This oblation, therefore, of our service and that of Thy whole family, we beseech Thee, O Lord, graciously to accept [and to order our days in Thy peace, and bid us to be delivered from eternal damnation and numbered among the flock of Thy elect. Through Christ our Lord]. Amen.

Which oblation do Thou, O God, vouchsafe in all things to bless, approve, ratify, make worthy and acceptable: that it may become for us the Body and Blood of Thy most beloved Son our Lord Jesus Christ.

Roman Missal, Canon of Mass, Prayers *Hanc igitur Oblationem* and *Quam oblationem*. (Present form and place, 5th cent. for first; 4th cent. for second; bracketed words said to have been added by Pope St. Gregory I, 6th cent.)

Who the day before He suffered took bread into His holy and venerable hands, and with His eyes lifted up to heaven, unto Thee, God, His almighty Father, giving thanks to Thee, He blessed, broke and gave it to His disciples, saying: *Take and eat ye all of this, for this is my Body.*

In like manner after He had supped, taking also this excellent chalice into His holy and venerable hands, and giving thanks to Thee, He blessed and gave it to His disciples, saying: *Take and drink ye all of this, for this is the chalice of my Blood, of the new and eternal testament: the mystery of faith: which shall be shed for you and for many unto the remission of sins.* As often as ye shall do these things, ye shall do them in remembrance of me.

Roman Missal, Canon of Mass, Prayers *Qui Pridie* and *Simili Modo*. (Words of Institution) (Present form, ca. 4th cent.)

Wherefore, O Lord, we Thy servants, and likewise Thy holy people, calling to mind the blessed passion of the same Christ Thy Son our Lord, and also His resurrection from hell and His glorious ascension into heaven, offer unto Thy most excellent majesty, of Thy gifts and presents, a pure Victim, a holy Victim, a spotless Victim, the holy Bread of eternal life, and the Chalice of everlasting salvation.

Upon which vouchsafe to look with a propitious and serene countenance, and to accept them as Thou wert pleased to accept the gifts of Thy just servant Abel, and the sacrifice of our patriarch Abraham, and that which Thy high priest Melchisedec offered to Thee, a holy sacrifice, a spotless Victim.

Roman Missal, Canon of Mass, Prayers *Unde et memores* and *Supra quae propitio*. (Anamnesis) (Present form, ca. 5th cent.)

We most humbly beseech Thee, almighty God, command these things to be carried up by the hands of Thy holy angel to Thine altar on high, in the sight of Thy divine majesty, that as many of us who, by participation at this altar, shall receive the most sacred Body and Blood of thy Son may be filled with every heavenly blessing and grace. Through the same Christ our Lord. Amen.

Roman Missal, Canon of Mass, Prayer *Supplices te rogamus*. (Held by some to be equivalent to an epiclesis) (ca. 5th cent.)

Moreover, we offer unto Thee this reasonable and unbloody sacrifice, and we call upon Thee, we pray Thee and beseech Thee, send down Thy Holy Ghost upon us and upon these gifts here present. And make this bread the precious Body of Thy Christ. And that which is in this chalice, the precious Blood of Thy Christ. Changing them by Thy Holy Spirit. Amen.

Byzantine Euchologion, Divine Liturgy, Epiclesis. (Present form, 4th or 5th cent.)

Be mindful also, O Lord, of Thy servants and handmaids, NN., who have gone before us with the sign of faith and repose in the sleep of peace.

Grant to them O Lord, and to all who repose in Christ a place of refreshment, light and peace, we beseech Thee. Through the same Christ our Lord. Amen.

Vouchsafe also to grant to us sinners, Thy servants, who have hope in the abundance of Thy mercy, some share in the fellowship of Thy holy apostles and martyrs: John, Stephen, Matthias, Barnabas, Ignatius, Alexander, Marcellinus, Peter, Felicitas, Perpetua, Agatha, Lucy, Agnes, Cecilia, Anastasia, and all

Thy saints, into whose company admit us, we beseech Thee, not regarding our merits but pardoning our offenses. Through Christ our Lord.

Roman Missal, Canon of Mass, Prayers *Memento etiam Domine* and *Nobis quoque Peccatoribus.* (Present form, ca. 5th cent.)

Moreover, we offer Thee this reasonable sacrifice for our forefathers who rest in the faith, our fathers, patriarchs, prophets, apostles, preachers, evangelists, martyrs, confessors, ascetics, and for every just spirit made perfect in the faith.

Above all for the most holy, immaculate, praiseworthy and glorious Lady, the Mother of God and ever Virgin Mary.

For holy John the prophet, forerunner and baptist, for the holy, glorious and famous apostles, for N. whose memory we keep, and for all Thy saints, through whose prayers look down upon us, O God.

Remember also all those who have fallen asleep in the hope of the resurrection unto life eternal, NN., and grant them rest where the light of Thy countenance shines upon them. . . .

Remember above all, O Lord, our bishop N. (or the pope of Rome), preserve him to thy churches in peace, in safety, in honor, in health, in length of days, and faithfully dispensing the word of Thy truth.

Byzantine Euchologion, Divine Liturgy, Intercessions for Living and Dead. (Present form, ca. 5th to 8th cent.)

It is indeed fitting to bless thee, Mother of God, ever blessed and most sinless Mother of our God. More honored than the cherubim, infinitely more glorious than the seraphim, who without stain didst bear God the Word, true Mother of God, we magnify thee.

Byzantine Euchologion, Divine Liturgy, Chant sung during Intercessions. (ca. 7th cent.)

Through whom, O Lord, Thou dost always create, sanctify, quicken, bless, and bestow upon all these Thy gifts.

Through Him, and with Him, and in Him, be unto Thee, O God the Father almighty, in the unity of the Holy Ghost, all honor and glory, world without end. Amen.

Roman Missal, Canon of Mass, Blessing *Per quem haec omnia* and Doxology *Per ipsum.* (Present form, ca. 5th cent.)

VI—*Mass: Communion*

Our Father, Who art in heaven, hallowed be Thy name; Thy kingdom come; Thy will be done on earth as it is in heaven. Give us this day our daily bread; and forgive us our trespasses, as we forgive them that trespass against us. And lead us not into temptation. ℟. But deliver us from evil. (Matth. 6, 9)

Roman Missal, Ordinary of Mass, *Pater Noster.* (ca. 4th cent.)

Deliver us, O Lord, we beseech Thee, from all evils, past, present, and to come; and by the intercession of the blessed and glorious Mary ever a Virgin and Mother of God, and of Thy holy apostles Peter and Paul, and of Andrew, and of all the saints, mercifully grant peace in our times, that through the help of Thy bountiful mercy we may always be free from sin and safe from all trouble. Through the same.

Roman Missal, Ordinary of Mass, Prayer *Libera nos quaesumus Domine* after *Our Father.* (Gelasian, 5th to 7th cent.)

Look down, O Lord Jesus Christ our God, from Thy holy dwelling-place, from the throne of glory of Thy kingdom, and come to sanctify us, Thou who dost sit in high with the Father and art here with us, though unseen. And grant that from Thy almighty hand there may be given to us Thy spotless Body and precious Blood, and through us to all the people.

Holy Things for the holy!

Byzantine Euchologion, Divine Liturgy. (Priest elevates Holy Bread as he pronounces last formula aloud.) (5th to 8th cent.)

One only is holy, one only is Lord, Jesus Christ in the glory of God the Father. Amen.

> Byzantine Euchologion, Divine Liturgy. (Sung by choir after the above.) (5th to 8th cent.)

Broken and distributed is the Lamb of God, Son of the Father, Who is broken but not divided, ever eaten and never consumed, and Who sanctifies those who participate.

> Byzantine Euchologion, Divine Liturgy, Formula at Fraction of Host. (5th to 8th cent.)

The peace of the Lord be with you always. (Pax Domini sit semper vobiscum.) ℟. And with thy spirit. (Et cum spiritu tuo.)

> Roman Missal, Ordinary of Mass, Formula at the Fraction. (Before 8th cent.)

May this mixture and consecration of the Body and Blood of our Lord Jesus Christ avail us that receive it unto life everlasting. Amen. (Haec commixtio et consecratio Corporis et Sanguinis Domini nostri Jesu Christi, fiat accipientibus nobis in vitam aeternam. Amen.)

> Roman Missal, Ordinary of Mass, Prayer at Commingling. (A particle of the Host is dropped into the chalice at this point.) (About 8th cent.; words slightly altered in 16th cent.)

Lamb of God, who takest away the sins of the world, have mercy on us. (Agnus Dei, qui tollis peccata mundi, miserere nobis.)

Lamb of God, who takest away the sins of the world, have mercy on us. (Agnus Dei, qui tollis peccata mundi, miserere nobis.)

Lamb of God, who takest away the sins of the world, give us peace. (Agnus Dei, qui tollis peccata mundi, dona nobis pacem.)

> Roman Missal, Ordinary of Mass, *Agnus Dei*. (Chant sung after the fraction.) (Introduced by Pope Sergius I, 687–701.)

Lord Jesus Christ, Who saidst to Thy apostles, Peace I leave with you, my peace I give unto you; look not upon my sins, but upon the faith of Thy Church; and vouchsafe to grant her peace and unity according to Thy will: who livest and reignest God for ever and ever. Amen.

> Roman Missal, Ordinary of Mass, Prayer *Domine Jesu Christe, qui dixisti apostolis.* (11th cent.)

Peace be with thee. (Pax tecum.)

> Roman Missal, Ordinary of Mass, Kiss of Peace. (Formula used by priest imparting kiss of peace at High Mass. The kiss at this point in the Roman rite is anomalous. Other rites have it before the Canon.)

O Lord, Jesus Christ, Son of the living God, who according to the will of Thy Father didst by Thy death, through the cooperation of the Holy Ghost, give life to the world, deliver me by this Thy most holy Body and Blood from all my transgressions and from every evil; and make me always cleave to Thy commandments, and never suffer me to be separated from Thee, who livest, etc.

Let not the reception of Thy Body, O Lord Jesus Christ, which I, though unworthy, presume to take, turn against me unto judgment and damnation; but through Thy loving kindness may it avail me for a safeguard and healing remedy for my soul and body; who with God, etc.

> Roman Missal, Ordinary of Mass, Prayers *Domine Jesu Christe* and *Perceptio Corporis tui.* (Before communion of celebrant) (ca. 10th cent.)

I believe, O Lord, and confess that Thou art truly Christ, the Son of the living God, who didst come into the world to save sinners, of whom I am the greatest. And I believe that this is Thy most pure Body, and this Thy most precious Blood. I therefore pray Thee, have mercy on me, and forgive my sins, voluntary and involuntary, in word and in deed, committed in knowledge or in ignorance. Deem me worthy without condemnation to partake of Thy most pure mysteries for the remission of my sins and life eternal. Amen.

> Byzantine Euchologion, Divine Liturgy, Prayer before Communion. (Attr. to St. John Chrysostom, ca. 4th cent. ?)

Make me this day a sharer in thy mystic supper, O Son of God. For I will not reveal Thy mysteries to Thy enemies, nor will I, like Judas, give Thee a kiss, but like the thief, I say to Thee: Remember me, O Lord, in Thy kingdom.

> Byzantine Euchologion, Divine Liturgy, Communion Chant. (From liturgy for Holy Thursday.) (5th to 8th cent.)

I will take the Bread of Heaven, and call upon the name of the Lord. (Panem coelestem accipiam, et nomen Domini invocabo.)

Lord, I am not worthy that Thou shouldest enter under my roof; say but the word and my soul shall be healed (Matth. 8, 8). (Domine, non sum dignus, ut intres sub tectum meum: sed tantum dic verbo et sanabitur anima mea.)

May the Body of our Lord Jesus Christ preserve my soul to life everlasting. Amen. (Corpus Domini nostri Jesu Christi custodiat animam meam in vitam aeternam. Amen.)

> Roman Missal, Ordinary of Mass, Communion Formulas. (As the celebrant consumes the Host.) (From about 10th cent.)

What shall I render to the Lord for all the things that He hath rendered to me? I will take the chalice of salvation, and I will call upon the name of the Lord (Ps. 115, 3, 4). (Quid retribuam Domino pro omnibus quae retribuit mihi? Calicem salutaris accipiam, et nomen Domini invocabo.)

Praising, I will call upon the Lord, and I shall be saved from my enemies (Ps. 17, 4). (Laudans invocabo Dominum, et ab inimicis meis salvus ero.)

May the Blood of our Lord Jesus Christ preserve my soul to life everlasting. Amen. (Sanguis Domini nostri Jesu Christi custodiat animam meam in vitam aeternam. Amen.)

> Roman Missal, Ordinary of Mass, Communion Formulas. (As the celebrant consumes the Precious Blood.) (From about 10th cent.)

Behold the Lamb of God, behold Him Who taketh away the sins of the world. (Ecce Agnus Dei: ecce qui tollit peccata mundi.)

> Roman Missal, Ordinary of Mass, Communion of the Faithful. (Formula recited by priest as he holds up the Sacred Host.) (16th cent.)

Grant, O Lord, that what we have taken with our mouth, we may receive with a clean mind, and that from a temporal gift it may become for us an everlasting remedy.

May Thy Body, O Lord, which I have received, and Thy Blood which I have drunk, cleave to my bowels; and grant that no stain of sin may remain in me, whom Thy pure and holy sacraments have refreshed: who livest, etc.

> Roman Missal, Ordinary of Mass, Prayers after Communion, *Quod ore sumpsimus* and *Corpus tuum Domine quod sumpsi.* (First, Leonine, ca. 5th cent.; second, Gallican, 7th cent.)

We thank Thee, O Lord and Lover of men, Benefactor of our souls, that Thou hast deigned to give us this day Thy heavenly and immortal mysteries. Make straight our path, strengthen us all in Thy fear, guard our life, guide our steps, by the prayers and supplications of the glorious Mother of God and ever-Virgin Mary and of all Thy saints.

> Byzantine Euchologion, Divine Liturgy, Prayer of Thanksgiving. (5th to 8th cent.)

VII—*Mass: Blessing and Dismissal*

Go, you are dismissed. (Ite, missa est.)

℟. Thanks be to God. (Deo gratias.)

May almighty God bless you, the Father, the Son, and the Holy Ghost.

℟. Amen. (Benedicat vos omnipotens

Deus, Pater et Filius et Spiritus Sanctus.
Amen.)

> Roman Missal, Ordinary of Mass,
> Dismissal and Blessing. (First formula
> probably antedates 5th cent.; latter, a
> shortened form, does not seem to be older
> than 11th cent. Cf. Jungmann, 2, 441)

Let us bless the Lord. (Benedicamus
Domino.)

℟. Thanks be to God. (Deo gratias.)

> Roman Missal, Ordinary of Mass, Formula
> of Dismissal. (Used during Advent and
> Lent in place of *Ite;* ca. 11th cent.)

May they rest in peace. (Requiescant in
pace)

> Roman Missal, Ordinary of Mass,
> Dismissal for Requiem Masses. (ca. 13th
> cent.)

May my worship and bounden duty be
pleasing unto Thee, O holy Trinity; and
grant that the sacrifice which I have
offered all unworthy in the sight of Thy
majesty may be received by Thee and
win forgiveness from Thy mercy for
me and for all those for whom I have
offered it up.

> Roman Missal, Ordinary of Mass, Prayer
> *Placeat tibi Sancta Trinitas.* (Recited
> between dismissal and blessing.)
> (Gallican, ca. 11th cent.)

O Lord, Who dost bless them that bless
Thee, and dost sanctify them that trust
in Thee, save Thy people and bless
Thine inheritance. Guard the company
of Thy Church, sanctify those who love
the beauty of Thy house. Give them
honor by Thy divine power, and forsake
us not who hope in Thee. Give peace to
Thy world, to Thy churches, to the
priests, to our rulers, to the army, and
to all Thy people. For every good gift
and every perfect gift is from above,
and cometh down from Thee, the
Father of lights, and to Thee we render
glory and thanksgiving and worship,
Father, Son, and Holy Ghost, now and
for ever, world without end. Amen.

> Byzantine Euchologion, Divine Liturgy,
> Prayer behind the Ambo. (5th to 8th
> cent.)

In the beginning was the Word, and the
Word was with God, and the Word was
God. . . . (John 1, 1)

> Roman Missal, Ordinary of Mass, Last
> Gospel. (First said among thanksgiving
> prayers after mass, ca. 13th cent.; later
> incorporated in reformed missal of Pope
> St. Pius V in 1570.)

Mass: Rites and Ceremonies

We ought in proper order to do all
things which the Lord has commanded
us to perform at appointed times. He
has commanded the offerings (*pros-
phoras*) and services (*leitourgias*) to be
carried out, not carelessly or disorderly,
but at fixed times and seasons. He has
Himself fixed according to His surpassing counsel where and by whom He desires them to be performed, in order that
all things may be done in holy fashion
according to His good pleasure and acceptable to His will.

> Pope St. Clement I: *Letter to the
> Corinthians,* 40, 1-4. (1st cent.)

Be zealous, then, in the observance of
one Eucharist. For there is one Flesh of
our Lord, Jesus Christ, and one Chalice
that brings union in His Blood. There
is one altar, as there is one bishop with
the priests and deacons, who are my
fellow workers. And so, whatever you
do, let it be done in the name of the
Lord.

> St. Ignatius of Antioch: *Letter to the
> Philadelphians,* 4. (2nd cent.)

For because Christ bore us all, in that
He also bore our sins, we see that in the
water is understood the people, but in
the wine is showed the Blood of Christ.
But when the water is mingled in the
cup with wine, the people is made one
with Christ, and the assembly of believers is associated and conjoined with
Him in Whom it believes; which association and conjunction of water and
wine is so mingled in the Lord's cup,
that that mixture cannot any more be

separated. Whence, moreover, nothing can separate the Church.

> St. Cyprian: *Letters, 62*, 13. (3rd cent.)

For all the other things which are said in the earlier parts of the service are said by the priest . . . when it comes to the consecration of the venerable sacrament, the priest no longer uses his own language, but he uses the language of Christ. Therefore, the word of Christ consecrates this sacrament.

> St. Ambrose: *On the Sacraments,* 4, 4, 14. (4th cent.)

The Lord Jesus Himself cries, *This is my body.* Before the blessing of the heavenly words another kind of thing is named, after the consecration it is designated Body. He Himself speaks of His blood. Before consecration it is spoken of as something else, after consecration, it is named Blood. And thou sayest, *Amen,* that is, so be it.

> St. Ambrose: *On the Mysteries,* 9, 54. (4th cent.)

At the Sacrament of the Body and Blood of Christ, nothing shall be offered but bread and wine mixed with water.

> Council of Hippo, Can. 23. (393)

The Sacrament of the Altar shall always be celebrated fasting, except on the anniversary of its institution, *Coena Domini* (Holy Thursday).

> Council of Hippo, Can. 28. (393)

The Sacrament of this thing, that is of the unity of the Body and Blood of Christ [i.e. understood as the fellowship of His body and members, holy Church], is prepared on the Lord's Table in some places every day, in some places at certain intervals of days, and from the Lord's Table it is taken by some unto life, by some unto destruction. But the thing itself of which it is the Sacrament is for every man unto life, for none unto destruction, whosoever shall have been partaker thereof.

> St. Augustine: *In Joan. Evang.* 26, 17. (5th cent.)

The mass takes place at the time of sacrifice, when the catechumens are put out, as the levite (deacon) cries: If there is any catechumen inside, let him go forth; then the mass [proper begins], for they cannot be present at the sacraments of the altar who are known to be as yet unbaptized.

> St. Isidore: *Etymologies,* 6, 19. (7th cent.)

Great is this mystery, and great the dignity of priests, to whom that is given which is not granted to angels. For priests alone, rightly ordained in the Church, have power to celebrate and to consecrate the body of Christ.

> Thomas a Kempis: *The Imitation of Christ,* 4, 5. (15th cent.)

When a priest celebrateth, he honoreth God, he rejoiceth the angels, he edifieth the Church, he helpeth the living, he obtaineth rest for the dead, and maketh himself partaker of all that is good.

> Thomas a Kempis: *The Imitation of Christ,* 4, 5. (15th cent.)

If any one saith that the canon of the mass contains errors and is therefore to be abrogated; let him be anathema.

> Council of Trent, Session 22, Canon 6. (Sept. 17, 1562)

If any one saith that the ceremonies, vestments, and outward signs, which the Catholic Church makes use of in the celebration of masses, are incentives to impiety rather than offices of piety; let him be anathema.

> Council of Trent, Session 22, Canon 7. (Sept. 17, 1562)

If any one saith that the rite of the Roman Church, according to which a part of the canon and the words of consecration are pronounced in a low tone, is to be condemned; or that the mass ought to be celebrated in the vulgar tongue only; or that water ought not to be mixed with the wine that is to be offered in the chalice, since it is contrary to the institution of Christ; let him be anathema.

> Council of Trent, Session 22, Canon 9. (Sept. 17, 1562)

If any one saith that masses wherein the priest alone communicates sacramentally are unlawful, and are therefore to be abrogated; let him be anathema.

> Council of Trent, Session 22, Canon 8. (Sept. 17, 1562)

The sound of a low, sweet whisper
   Floats over a little bread,
And trembles around a chalice,
   And the priest bows down his head!
O'er a sign of white on the altar—
   In the cup—o'er a sign of red.

> A. Ryan: *Feast of the Sacred Heart.* (19th cent.)

See also Blessed Sacrament; Communion; Eucharist; Liturgy; Sacrament

Master

He who has not one master, has many.

> St. Ambrose: *Explanation of St. Luke,* 9, 6. (4th cent.)

Such captain, such retinue.

> John Gower: *Confessio Amantis,* 3. (14th cent.)

Materialism

No other forces are to be recognized except those which reside in matter, and the whole science and excellence of morality is bound up with the accumulation and increase of wealth by whatever means possible, and with the gratification of pleasure.

> Proposition condemned by Pius IX in Syllabus of Errors. (1867)

If any one shall not be ashamed to assert that, except for matter, nothing exists; let him be anathema.

> Vatican Council, Session 3, Canon 2. (Apr. 24, 1870)

The Christian admits that the universe is manifold and even miscellaneous, just as a sane man knows that he is complex. Nay, the really sane man knows that he has a touch of the madman. But the materialist's world is quite simple and solid, just as the madman is quite sure he is sane. The materialist is sure that history has been simply and solely a chain of causation, just as the interesting person before mentioned is quite sure that he is simply and solely a chicken. Materialists and madmen never have doubts.

> G. K. Chesterton: *Orthodoxy.* (20th cent.)

The materialist theory of history, that all politics and ethics are the expressions of economics, is a very simple fallacy indeed. It consists simply of confusing the necessary conditions of life with the normal preoccupations of life, that are quite a different thing. It is like saying that because a man can walk about on two legs, therefore he never walks about except to buy shoes and stockings.

> G. K. Chesterton: *The Everlasting Man,* 1, 7. (20th cent.)

In one sense, to do him justice, this melancholy materialist is the most disinterested of men. The mystic is one who will serve something invisible for his own reasons. The materialist is one who will serve anything visible for no reason.

> G. K. Chesterton: *All is Grist.* (20th cent.)

Nobody is more parochial than the materialist, for it is the essence of parochialism to assume that nothing exists outside one's own parish. The materialist, like John Wesley, takes the world for his parish. Unlike Wesley, he does not realize that there are other parishes.

> Arnold Lunn: *Now I See.* (20th cent.)

Mathematics

Mathematics comes midway between physics and metaphysics, and is more certain than either of them.

> St. Thomas Aquinas: *Exposition of the De Trinitate,* 6, 1. (13th cent.)

Matins

And at the hour when the cock crows,
likewise rise and pray, because at the
hour of cockcrow the children of Israel
denied Christ Whom we have known by
faith, daily awaiting in hope the appearing of the eternal light at the resurrection of the dead.

> St. Hippolytus: *The Apostolic Tradition,*
> 36. (3rd cent.)

Our limbs refreshed with slumber now,
And sloth cast off, in prayer we bow;
And while we sing Thy praises dear,
O Father, be Thou present here.

> Roman Breviary, hymn *Somno refectis*
> *artubus* for Monday. (Tr. J. Neale) (St.
> Ambrose, 4th cent.)

O Light of Light, O Dayspring bright,
Co-equal in Thy Father's light:
Assist us, as with prayer and psalm
Thy servants break the twilight calm.

> Roman Breviary, hymn *Consors paterni*
> *luminis* for Tuesday. (Tr. J. Chadwick
> and J. Chambers) (St. Ambrose, 4th
> cent.)

Who madest all and dost control,
  Lord, with Thy touch divine,
Cast out the slumbers of the soul,
  The rest that is not Thine.

> Roman Breviary, hymn *Rerum Creator*
> *optime* for Wednesday. (Tr. Card.
> Newman) (Attr. Pope St. Gregory I, 6th
> cent.)

The dusky veil of night hath laid
The varied hues of earth in shade;
Before Thee, righteous Judge of all,
We contrite in confession fall.

> Roman Breviary, hymn *Nox atra rerum*
> *contegit* for Thursday. (Tr. J. Chadwick)
> (Attr. to Pope St. Gregory I, 6th cent.)

O Three in One, and One in Three,
Who rulest all things mightily:
Bow down to hear the songs of praise
Which, freed from bonds of sleep, we
  raise.

> Roman Breviary, hymn *Tu Trinitatis*
> *Unitas* for Friday. (Tr. G. Palmer and J.

Chadwick) (Attr. to Pope St. Gregory I,
6th cent.)

See also Dawn; Lauds; Morning; Sunrise

Matrimony

See Marriage

Matter

All matter depends on motion.

> René Descartes: *Principles of Philosophy,*
> 2. (17th cent.)

Concrete matter does not admit of demonstration.

> Card. Newman. (Ward, II, 587) (19th
> cent.)

Maturity

Men come to their meridian at various
periods of their lives.

> Card. Newman: *Idea of a University,* 7.
> (19th cent.)

May

He was as fresh as is the month of May.
> Chaucer: *Canterbury Tales: Prologue.*
> (14th cent.)

Which May had painted with his softe
  showers
This garden full of leaves and of
  flowers.
> Chaucer: *The Frankeleyns Tale.* (14th
> cent.)

For May will have no slogardye a-night.
The season pricketh every gentle heart.
> Chaucer: *The Knightes Tale.* (14th cent.)

May, that mother of monthes glad.
> Chaucer: *Troilus and Criseyde.* (14th
> cent.)

The green, green grass, the glittering
  grove,
  The heaven's majestic dome,

They image forth a tenderer bower,
  A more refulgent home;
They tell us of that Paradise
  Of everlasting rest,
And that high Tree, all flowers and
      fruit,
  The sweetest, yet the best.
    O Mary, pure and beautiful,
      Thou art the Queen of May:
    Our garlands wear about thy hair,
      And they will ne'er decay.

Card. Newman: *Hymn: Green are the
Leaves.* (19th cent.)

This is the image of the Queen
  Who reigns in bliss above;
Of her who is the hope of men,
  Whom men and angels love!
    Most holy Mary! at thy feet
      I bend a suppliant knee;
    In this thy own sweet month of
      May,
    Dear Mother of God I pray,
      Do thou remember me.

E. Caswall: *Hymn to the Blessed Virgin.*
(19th cent.)

In vain thy altars do they heap
  With blooms of violated May
Who fail the words of Christ to keep;
  Thy Son who love not, nor obey.

  . . . .

Who loveth Thee must love Thy Son.
  Weak love grows strong Thy smile
    beneath;
But nothing comes from nothing; none
  Can reap love's harvest out of death.

Aubrey de Vere: May Carol. (19th cent.)

Maid yet Mother as May hath been—
To thee we tender the beauties all
Of the month by men called virginal.
And, where thou dwellest in deep-
    groved Aidenn,
  Salute thee, mother, the maid-
    month's Queen!

G. M. Hopkins: *Ad Mariam.* (19th cent.)

May is Mary's month, and I
Muse at that end and wonder why:

Her feast follow reason,
Dated due to season—

G. M. Hopkins: *The May Magnificat.*
(19th cent.)

Ah! my heart is weary waiting,
  Waiting for the May—
Waiting for the pleasant rambles,
Where the fragrant hawthorn brambles,
  With the woodbine alternating,
    Scent the dewy way.
  Ah! my heart is weary waiting,
    Waiting for the May.

Denis F. McCarthy: *Waiting for the May.*
(19th cent.)

God ripes the wines and corn, I say,
And wenches for the marriage-day,
And boys to teach love's comely play.
  By Goddes fay, by Goddes fay!
It is the month, the jolly month,
It is the jolly month of May.

F. Thompson: *A May Burden.* (19th cent.)

Meal

Bless us, O Lord, and these Thy gifts
which we are about to receive from Thy
bounty.

Roman Ritual, Blessing before Meals.
(Originally Gelasian, 5th to 7th cent.)

Two hungry meals make the third a
glutton.

John Heywood: *Proverbs,* 1, 11. (16th
cent.)

Better are meals many than one too
merry.

John Heywood: *Proverbs,* 2, 7. (16th
cent.)

See also Dining; Eating; Food; Wine

Meanness

For little souls on little shifts rely,
And coward arts of mean expedients
  try.

Dryden: *The Hind and the Panther,* 3.
(17th cent.)

Measure

In everything, I wot, there lieth measure.

> Chaucer: *Troilus and Criseyde.* (14th cent.)

Meat

Look not on the meat, but look on the man.

> John Heywood: *Proverbs,* 2, 4. (16th cent.)

Medal

A medal of St. Christopher he wore
Of shining silver on his breast.

> Chaucer: *Canterbury Tales: Prologue.* (Tr. Coghill) (14th cent.)

Meddling

We should not busy ourselves with matters which do not concern us.

> St. Basil: *The Morals,* 9, 1. (4th cent.)

Have an oar in every man's barge.

> John Heywood: *Proverbs,* 1, 10. (16th cent.)

Of little meddling cometh great rest.

> John Heywood: *Proverbs,* 2, 2. (16th cent.)

Who meddleth in all thing may shoe the gosling.

> John Heywood: *Proverbs,* 2, 3. (16th cent.)

Medicine

From laws of health and sickness learn disease;
Who studies life, her laws more wisely sees.
The greatest duty of the healing art
Is first to know whence all diseases start.

> School of Salerno, Code of Health. (11th cent.)

Alas! no herb in any garden grows
That can avert grim death's unerring throes.

> School of Salerno, Code of Health. (11th cent.)

Some fell by laudanum, and some by steel,
And death in ambush lay in every pill.

> Sir Samuel Garth: *The Dispensary,* 4. (17th cent.)

Learn from the beasts the physic of the field.

> Pope: *An Essay on Man,* 3. (18th cent.)

Medievalism

Now a knightlier sort you'll never find
Than the university modern mind;
Generous even to serious fault—
When not directly under assault.
To the glories of elder Christian days
It gives no end of its choicest praise.
Of course the loveliest things are said
Provided the past stays decently dead;
It must never be hinted to ears polite
That the ancient faith is not moribund, quite.

> W. M. T. Gamble: *Medieval Appreciations.* (20th cent.)

Mediocrity

This miserable fate
Suffer the wretched souls of those who lived
Without praise or blame.

> Dante: *Inferno, Canto 3.* (Tr. Cary) (14th cent.)

Too much wit, like too little, is charged with madness. Mediocrity alone is good.

> Pascal: *Pensées.* (17th cent.)

Meditation

Let your consideration begin with yourself, lest, while you neglect yourself, you waste your energies on other things. . . .

Though you know all mysteries, though you know the breadth of the earth, the height of the heavens, the depth of the sea, if you know not yourself, you will be like a man building without a foundation, and will not succeed in rearing an edifice but in making a ruin.

St. Bernard: *On Consideration,* 2, 3. (12th cent.)

First of all, consideration purifies the very fountain, that is the mind, from which it springs. Then it governs the affections, directs our actions, corrects excesses, softens the manners, adorns and regulates the life, and lastly bestows the knowledge of things divine and human alike.

St. Bernard: *On Consideration,* 1, 7. (12th cent.)

To meditate on the life and sufferings of Jesus Christ I have called wisdom; in these I have placed the perfection of righteousness for me, the fulness of knowledge, the abundance of merits, the riches of salvation. There is among them for me sometimes a draught of salutary bitterness, sometimes, again, a sweet unction of consolation. In adversities they raise me up, and in prosperity my exuberant delight. . . . It is for these reasons that I have them frequently in my mouth, as you know, and always in my heart, as God knoweth. . . . In a word, my philosophy is this, and it is the loftiest in the world, to know Jesus and Him crucified.

St. Bernard: *On the Canticle of Canticles,* 43, 4. (12th cent.)

The purpose of a book of meditations is to teach you how to think and not to do your thinking for you.

Thomas Merton: *Seeds of Contemplation.* (20th cent.)

See also Contemplation; Prayer

Meekness

And of his port as meek as is a maid.

Chaucer: *Canterbury Tales: Prologue.* (14th cent.)

Be meek, and bear adversity
In Jesus' sacred name;
There's danger in prosperity;
It brings a scorching flame.

Thomas a Kempis: *Adversa mundi tolera.* (Tr. D. Donahoe) (15th cent.)

Meeting

And doth not a meeting like this make amends
For all the long years I've been wand'ring away?

Thomas Moore: *And Doth Not a Meeting?* (19th cent.)

There's a feast undated, yet
    Both our true lives hold it fast,—
Even the day when first we met.
    What a great day came and passed,
—Unknown then, but known at last.

Alice Meynell: *An Unmarked Festival.* (19th cent.)

Melancholy

Cleanse yourself, then, of this wicked melancholy and you will live to God. So, also, will they live to God who cast away melancholy and clothe themselves in complete cheerfulness.

Shepherd of Hermas, Mandate 10, 3, 4. (2nd cent.)

The earth, late choked with showers,
    Is now arrayed in green;
Her bosom springs with flowers,
    The air dissolves her teen:
The heavens laugh at her glory,
Yet bide I sad and sorry.

Thomas Lodge: *Scilla's Metamorphosis.* (16th cent.)

Memory

Great is this power of memory, exceedingly great, O my God, a spreading limitless room within me. Who can reach its uttermost depth? Yet it is a faculty of my soul and belongs to my nature.

St. Augustine: *Confessions,* 10, 8. (5th cent.)

No grief surpasses this
(And that my teacher knows full
  well)—
In the midst of misery to remember
bliss.

Dante: *Inferno, Canto 5.* (Tr. L. Binyon)
(14th cent.)

For of fortune's sharp adversity
The worst kind of infortune is this,
A man to have been in prosperity,
And it remember, when it passèd be.

Chaucer: *Troilus and Criseyde.* (14th
cent.)

Memory is necessary for all operations
of the reason.

Pascal: *Pensées.* (17th cent.)

Long, long be my heart with such
  memories fill'd!
Like the vase in which roses have once
  been distill'd:
You may break, you may shatter the
  vase if you will,
But the scent of the roses will hang
  round it still.

Thomas Moore: *Farewell! But Whenever.*
(19th cent.)

When time, who steals our years away,
  Shall steal our pleasures, too,
The mem'ry of the past will stay,
  And half our joys renew.

Thomas Moore: *Song.* (19th cent.)

Oft, in the stilly night,
  Ere slumber's chain has bound me,
Fond memory brings the light
  Of other days around me.

Thomas Moore: *The Light of Other Days.*
(19th cent.)

Memory, in widow's weeds, with naked
feet stands on a tombstone.

Aubrey de Vere: *Widowhood.* (19th
cent.)

A great memory does not make a philosopher, any more than a dictionary can
be called a grammar.

Card. Newman: *Knowledge in Relation to
Culture.* (19th cent.)

A place in thy memory, dearest!
  Is all that I claim:
To pause and look back when thou
  hearest
  The sound of my name.

Gerald Griffin: *A Place in Thy Memory.*
(19th cent.)

Mercy

Dost thou wish to receive mercy? Show
mercy to thy neighbor.

St. John Chrysostom: *Homilies.* (4th
cent.)

Mercy, also, is a good thing, for it makes
men perfect, in that it imitates the perfect Father. Nothing graces the Christian soul so much as mercy.

St. Ambrose: *On the Duties of the Clergy,*
1, 38. (4th cent.)

O God, if Thou shouldst determine to
render to us what we deserve, we must
sooner perish than endure our deserved
punishment; we therefore pray Thee
mercifully to forgive our wanderings;
and that we may be able to be converted
to Thy commandments, do Thou go before us with abundant mercy.

Leonine Sacramentary, Collect. (ca. 5th
cent.)

Wouldst thou give due desert to all?
Love then the good, and pity thou the
  ill.

Boethius: *De Consolatione Philosophiae,*
4, 4. (6th cent.)

O God, Who dost reveal Thy almighty
power chiefly in showing mercy and
pity; increase Thy mercy towards us;
that we, seeking the way of Thy
promises, may be made partakers of Thy
heavenly treasures.

Roman Missal, Collect for Tenth Sunday
after Pentecost. (Gelasian, 5th to 7th
cent.)

O God, who desirest not the death, but
the repentance of sinners, reject not
from Thy tender love my wretched self,

a frail sinner; nor look to my sins and crimes, and my unclean and base thoughts, whereby I am woefully disunited from Thy will; but look Thou to Thine own mercy.

> Gregorian Sacramentary, Collect. (ca. 7th cent.)

Happy is the soul who has made it her business to collect miseries, to pour on them the oil of mercy and heat them on the fire of love!

> St. Bernard: *Sermons on the Canticle of Canticles,* 11. (12th cent.)

For there is no greater proof of pitying mercy possible, than that a man should lay down his own life for those condemned to death.

> St. Bernard: *Sermons on the Canticle of Canticles,* 61. (12th cent.)

Mercy is the fulfilment of justice, not the abolition.

> St. Thomas Aquinas: *Summa Theologica,* I, 21, 3. (13th cent.)

For mercy is a greater thing than right.

> Chaucer: *The Knight's Tale.* (Tr. Coghill) (14th cent.)

Mercy of mercy must needs arise.

> Langland: *Piers Plowman,* Passus 12. (14th cent.)

Reason to rule, but mercy to forgive: The first is law, the last prerogative.

> Dryden: *The Hind and the Panther,* 1. (17th cent.)

Merit

Reward is what you receive, merit what you do. The first is in the mind, the second in the will through charity.

> St. Thomas Aquinas: *Disputations concerning Truth,* 14, 5. (13th cent.)

Any deliberate act without exception done from a state of grace is meritorious.

> St. Thomas Aquinas: *Commentary on the Sentences,* 2, 40, 1, 5. (13th cent.)

No one should judge that he has greater perfection because he performs great penances and gives himself in excess to the slaying of his body than he who does less, inasmuch as neither virtue nor merit consists therein; for otherwise he would be in an evil case, who from some legitimate reason was unable to do actual penance. Merit consists in the virtue of love alone, flavored with the light of true discretion, without which the soul is worth nothing.

> St. Catherine of Siena: *The Dialogue.* (14th cent.)

The Catholic doctrine of merit, laid down by the council of Trent, is that every good work, done in the state of grace, is rewarded by God with a title to an increase of happiness in heaven. God is the great Employer, and He pays for every human deed of goodness, done by any servant and child of His in grace.

> Joseph Rickaby: *An Old Man's Jottings.* (20th cent.)

Merriment

See Joy

Metaphor

She sees a mob of metaphors advance, Pleas'd with the madness of the mazy dance.

> Pope: *The Dunciad,* 1. (18th cent.)

Metaphysics

Not to be a metaphysician is no sin; it is only an inconvenience when one insists on writing or talking about metaphysics.

> Orestes Brownson. (Quoted in H. Brownson: *O. A. Brownson: Middle Life,* p. 454.) (19th cent.)

Metaphysics for the most part are justly open to the objection that they attempt to explain things which Aristotle declares to be too simple to be intelligible —things which we cannot see with definiteness, not because they are beyond the focus of the mind's eye, but because they are too much within it.

> Coventry Patmore: *Religio Poetae.* (19th cent.)

Metaphysics is the only thoroughly emotional thing.

> G. K. Chesterton: *Tremendous Trifles*, 5. (20th cent.)

Michael the Archangel, Saint

O Jesu! Life-spring of the soul!
The Father's power and glory bright!
Thee with the angels we extol;
From Thee they draw their life and light.
Thy thousand thousand hosts are spread
Embattled o'er the azure sky;
But Michael bears Thy standard dread,
And lifts the mighty Cross on high.

> Roman Breviary, Feast (Sept. 29), hymn *Te splendor et virtus Patris* (*Tibi Christe splendor Patris*) at Vespers. (Tr. E. Caswall) (Altered, attr. to Bl. Rabanus Maurus, 9th cent.)

Let our love break forth in praises,
And the hymn our choir upraises
In the holy angels' sight!
Praise is pleasant, praise befitting,
When our hearts, no sin committing,
With our lips in praise unite.

Michael let all men be lauding,
None of us ourselves defrauding
Of the gladness of today;
Happy days, for ever telling
Of the triumph all-excelling
Of the angels' bright array!

> Adam of St. Victor: *Laus erumpat ex affectu.* (Tr. Wrangham) (12th cent.)

Middle Ages

The most absurd thing that could be said of the Church is the thing we have all heard said of it. How can we say that the Church wishes to bring us back to the Dark Ages? The Church was the only thing that ever brought us out of them.

> G. K. Chesterton: *Orthodoxy.* (20th cent.)

The Middle Ages sleep in alabaster
A delicate fine sleep. They never knew
The irreparable hell of that disaster
That broke with hammers heaven's fragile blue.

> Wilfrid R. Childe: *The Last Abbot of Gloucester.* (20th cent.)

The Middle Ages were not the ages of faith in the sense of unquestioning submission to authority and blind obedience. They were ages of spiritual struggle and social change, in which the existing situation was continually being modified by the reforming energy and the intellectual activity that were generated by the contact between the living stream of Christian tradition and the youthful peoples of the west.

> Christopher Dawson: *Medieval Essays.* (20th cent.)

I do not maintain that the general level of religious life was higher than at other times or that the state of the Church was healthier, still less that scandals were rarer or moral evils less obvious. What one can assert is that in the middle ages more than at other periods in the life of our civilization the European culture and the Christian religion were in a state of communion: the highest expressions of medieval culture, whether in art, in literature or in philosophy, were religious, and the greatest representatives of medieval religion were also the leaders of medieval culture.

> Christopher Dawson: *Medieval Essays.* (20th cent.)

Medieval culture was the matrix in which the western type was formed and the ultimate source of the new forces that have moved and transformed the world.

> C. Dawson: *Gifford Lectures, 1948.*

But even the culture of the Middle Ages itself cannot be characterized as the Catholic culture; although closely bound to the Church, it drew its elements from different sources also. Even the religious unity that was a mark of the Middle Ages was not peculiar to them: it was already a characteristic note of Christian antiquity.

Pope Pius XII: *Allocution to the 10th Intern. Congress of Historical Sciences.* (1955)

Midnight

It was evening there,
But here the very noon of night.

Dante: *Purgatorio, Canto 15.* (14th cent.)

Might

Might overcometh right.

John Heywood: *Proverbs,* 2, 5. (16th cent.)

Militarism

My life's amusements have been just the same
Before and after standing armies came.

Pope: *The Second Satire of the Second Book of Horace.* (18th cent.)

Military Service

Do not think that it is impossible for anyone to please God while engaged in military service.

St. Augustine: *Letter 189* (to Count Boniface, Governor of Africa). (5th cent.)

Miller

Much water goeth by the mill
That the miller knoweth not of.

John Heywood: *Proverbs,* 2, 5. (16th cent.)

Every honest miller has a golden thumb.

* Chaucer: *Canterbury Tales.* (An old saying with reference to the merchant who keeps his thumb on the scales when weighing anything) (14th cent.)

Milton, John

Three poets, in three distant ages born,
Greece, Italy, and England did adorn.
The first in loftiness of thought surpass'd,
The next in majesty, in both the last:
The force of nature could no further go;
To make a third she join'd the former two.

Dryden: *Lines under the Portrait of Milton.* (1688)

Milton's strong pinion now not Heaven can bound,
Now serpent-like, in prose he sweeps the ground,
In quibbles, angel and archangel join,
And God the Father turns a school-divine.

Pope: *The First Epistle of the Second Book of Horace.* (18th cent.)

Mind

For the intellect of man, his mind and thought and intention, and other things of that nature, are nothing apart from the soul. But they are the motions and operations of the soul, having no existence apart from or without the soul.

St. Irenaeus: *Against the Heresies,* 2, 29, 3. (2nd cent.)

Nothing is greater than the mind of man, except God.

St. Augustine: *De Trinitate,* 15, 1. (5th cent.)

In so far as concerns the nature of man, there is in him nothing better than the mind and reason. But he who would live blessedly ought not to live according to them; for then he would live according to man, whereas he ought to live according to God, so that he may attain to blessedness. And to accomplish this, our mind must not be content with itself, but must be subjected to God.

St. Augustine: *Retractions,* 1, 1, 2. (5th cent.)

The spark of reason cannot be extinguished so long as the light of mind remains; and sin can never make away with the mind.

> St. Thomas Aquinas: *Commentary on the Sentences*, 2, 39, 3, 1. (13th cent.)

There is nothing that the divine mind does not understand actually, nor the human mind potentially.

> St. Thomas Aquinas: *Disputations concerning Truth*, 2. (13th cent.)

Thy mind reverting still to things of earth,
Strikes darkness from true light.

> Dante: *Purgatorio, Canto 15.* (Tr. Cary) (14th cent.)

So many heads, so many wits.

> John Heywood: *Proverbs,* 1, 3. (16th cent.)

Two heads are better than one.

> John Heywood: *Proverbs,* 1, 9. (16th cent.)

Untilled ground, however rich, will bring forth thistles and thorns; so also the mind of man.

> St. Teresa of Jesus: *Maxims.* (16th cent.)

I feel no care of coin;
    Well-doing is my wealth;
My mind to me an empire is,
    While grace affordeth health.

> Bl. Robert Southwell: *Content and Rich.* (16th cent.)

Man's mind a mirror is of heavenly sights,
A brief wherein all marvels summed lie,
Of fairest forms and sweetest shapes the store,
Most graceful all, yet thought may grace them more.

> Bl. Robert Southwell: *Look Home.* (16th cent.)

The mind must be persuaded, it cannot be constrained.

> Jean Pierre Camus: *The Spirit of St. Francis de Sales,* 20, 4. (17th cent.)

The more mind we have, the more original men do we discover there are. Common people find no difference between men.

> Pascal: *Pensées,* 9. (17th cent.)

All bodies, the firmament, the stars, the earth and its kingdoms, are not equal to the lowest mind; for mind knows all these and itself; and these bodies nothing.

> Pascal: *Pensées.* (17th cent.)

Of all the tyrannies on human kind
The worst is that which persecutes the mind.

> Dryden: *The Hind and the Panther,* 1. (17th cent.)

Love, hope and joy, fair pleasure's smiling train,
Hate, fear and grief, the family of pain,
These mix'd with art, and to due bounds confin'd
Make and maintain the balance of the mind.

> Pope: *An Essay on Man,* 2. (18th cent.)

No prelate's lawn, with hair-shirt lined,
Is half so incoherent as my mind.

> Pope: *The First Epistle of the First Book of Horace.* (18th cent.)

I have the mind of an archangel in the body of a rhinoceros.

> W. G. Ward. (19th cent.)

Son of immortal seed, high-destined man!
Know thy dread gift,—a creature, yet a cause:
Each mind is its own center, and it draws
Home to itself, and moulds in its thought's span

All outward things, the vassals of its will,
Aided by heaven, by earth unthwarted still.

Card. Newman: *Substance and Shadow.* (19th cent.)

The bodily eye, the organ for apprehending material objects, is provided by nature; the eye of the mind, of which the object is truth, is the work of discipline and habit.

Card. Newman: *Idea of a University.* (19th cent.)

Great minds need elbow-room, not indeed in the domain of faith, but of thought.

Card. Newman: *Idea of a University.* (19th cent.)

When the intellect is cultivated, it is as certain that it will develop into a thousand various shapes, as that infinite hues and tints and shades of color will be reflected from the earth's surface, when the sunlight touches it; and in matters of religion the more, by reason of the extreme subtlety and abstruseness of the mental action by which they are determined.

Card. Newman: *Letter to the Duke of Norfolk.* (19th cent.)

Thou inmost, ultimate
Council of judgment, palace of decrees,
Where the high senses hold their spiritual state,
Sued by earth's embassies,
And sign, approve, accept, conceive, create.

Alice Meynell: *To the Body.* (20th cent.)

There are few differences in this drab-colored world so startling as those between various kinds of minds.

R. H. Benson: *An Average Man.* (20th cent.)

The brute-tamer stands by the brutes, a head's breadth only above them.
A head's breadth? Ay, but therein is

hell's depth, and the height up to heaven,
And the thrones of the gods and their halls, their chariots, purples and splendors.

Padraic Colum: *The Plougher.* (20th cent.)

There is no salvation save in truth, and the royal road of truth is by the mind.

M. C. D'Arcy: *The Nature of Belief.* (20th cent.)

An open scent bottle soon loses its scent.
An open mind is often a vacant mind.
There is something to be said for corks.

Arnold Lunn: *Within that City.* (20th cent.)

There will always be a tendency, more marked in transitional times, for Christians to demand a faith free from the trammels of theology, the processes, starled and camel-borne, of the human reason. But an unintellectual salvation means an unsaved intellect. The Child grew in wisdom, as well as in stature.

R. Knox: *Stimuli.* (20th cent.)

Our minds are like crows. They pick up everything that glitters, no matter how uncomfortable our nests get with all that metal in them.

Thomas Merton: *Seeds of Contemplation.* (20th cent.)

Minute

Still work for the minute and not for the year.

J. B. O'Reilly: *Rules of the Road.* (19th cent.)

Miracle

I should not be a Christian but for the miracles.

St. Augustine. (5th cent.)

And I call a miracle anything which appears arduous or unusual, beyond the expectation or abilities of the one who marvels at it; of which kind there is nothing better suited for the people and in general for fools than what affects the senses.

St. Augustine: *De Utilitate Credendi*, 16, 34. (4th cent.)

Although, therefore, the standing miracle of this visible world is little thought of, because always before us, yet, when we arouse ourselves to contemplate it, it is a greater miracle than the rarest and most unheard of marvels. For man himself is a greater miracle than any miracle done through his instrumentality.

St. Augustine: *The City of God*, 10, 12. (5th cent.)

Why, they ask, do not those miracles, which you preach of as past events, happen nowadays? I might reply that they were necessary before the world believed, to bring the world to believe; but whoever is still looking for prodigies to make him believe is himself a great prodigy for refusing to believe where the world believes.

St. Augustine: *The City of God*, 22. (5th cent.)

But when such things [i.e. manifestations of the divine will] happen in as it were a continuous stream ·of everflowing succession, passing from the hidden to the visible, and from the visible to the hidden, by a regular and beaten track, then they are called natural; but when for the admonition of men they are intruded by an unusual form of change, they are called miracles.

St. Augustine: *De Trinitate*, 3, 6. (5th cent.)

Since the wickedness of the evil one has prevailed so mightily against man's nature as even to drive some into denying the existence of God . . . the disciples of the Lord and His apostles, enlightened by the Holy Spirit and working wonders in His power and grace, took them captive in the net of miracles and drew them up out of the depths of ignorance to the light of the knowledge of God.

St. John of Damascus: *Exposition of the Orthodox Faith*, 1, 3. (8th cent.)

The faith of Christ believed by the saints and handed down to us has been marked by the seal of God shown in works no creature can perform. These are the miracles by which Christ has confirmed holy apostolic doctrine.

St. Thomas Aquinas: *Exposition of the Apostles' Creed*. (13th cent.)

If you say, but no one has seen miracles performed, then I answer, that once upon a time everybody worshipped false gods and persecuted Christians, and then afterwards all were converted including the wise, noble, powerful, by a few poor and unlettered preachers. Either this was miraculous or not. If so, then the point is granted; if not, then I ask, what greater miracle could there have been than to convert so many without miracles?

St. Thomas Aquinas: *Exposition of the Apostles' Creed*. (13th cent.)

Miracles demonstrate the veracity of the announcer, not directly the truth of what he preaches.

St. Thomas Aquinas: *Commentary on the Sentences*, 3, 24, 1, 4. (13th cent.)

Augustine speaks of a miracle as an event unusual and abrupt, above the faculty of nature, a surprise to the expectation of the wondering onlooker (In Joann. Evang. Tract. 8).

St. Thomas Aquinas: *Disputations concerning Potency*, 6, 2. (13th cent.)

From these three premises, that God is the complete cause of natural realities, that He has distinct knowledge of each and all, and that, uncompelled by natural necessity, He works voluntarily, it follows that He can produce particular effects apart from the ordinary run of nature.

St. Thomas Aquinas: *Disputations concerning Potency*, 6, 1. (13th cent.)

Above nature, against nature, besides nature—that is the traditional division applied to God's miraculous works. Above nature . . . the effect can never be produced by natural forces . . . for example, the Incarnation of the Word. . . . Against nature . . . God's action interrupts the trend of natural forces . . . for example, when He . . . caused a Virgin to bring forth a child. Besides nature . . . nature can produce the effect, but not in the same way . . . as for example when Christ changed water into wine. . . .

St. Thomas Aquinas: *Disputations concerning Potency*, 6, 2. (13th cent.)

Miracles are signs *not to them that believe, but to them that believe not* (1 Cor. 14, 22).

St. Thomas Aquinas: *Summa Theologica*, 3, 43, 2. (13th cent.)

If the world, said I, without miracles
    Turned Christian, then a miracle is
        born
    That all the rest a hundred times
        excels.

Dante: *Paradiso, Canto 24.* (Tr. Binyon) (14th cent.)

It is impossible on reasonable grounds to disbelieve miracles.

Pascal: *Pensées.* (17th cent.)

A miracle may be considered as an event inconsistent with the constitution of nature, that is, with the established course of things in which it is found. Or, again, an event in a given system which cannot be referred to any law, or accounted for by the operation of any principle, in that system. It does not necessarily imply a violation of nature, as some have supposed,—merely the interposition of an external cause, which, we shall hereafter show, can be no other than the agency of the Deity. And the effect produced is that of an unusual or increased action in the parts of the system.

Card. Newman: *Essays on Miracles*, 1, 1. (19th cent.)

A miracle is no argument to one who is deliberately, and on principle, an atheist.

Card. Newman: *Essays on Miracles*, 1, 1. (19th cent.)

Miracles are not only not unlikely, they are positively likely; and for this simple reason, because, for the most part, when God begins He goes on. . . . If the divine Being does a thing once, He is, judging by human reason, likely to do it again.

Card. Newman: *Present Position of Catholics in England*, 7. (19th cent.)

The Incarnation is the most stupendous event which ever can take place on earth; and after it and henceforth, I do not see how we can scruple at any miracle on the mere ground of its being unlikely to happen.

Card. Newman: *Present Position of Catholics in England*, 7. (19th cent.)

If any one shall say that miracles are impossible, and therefore that all the accounts regarding them, even those contained in Holy Scripture, are to be dismissed as fabulous or mythical; or that miracles can never be known with certainty, and that the divine origin of Christianity is not rightly proved by them; let him be anathema.

Vatican Council, Session 3, Canon 4. (Apr. 24, 1870)

Presumably the Creator—as He is evidently, in relation to the whole, a magnified freewill, inventive, arbitrary— also acts within the world in the same way; not necessarily by adding new force by His action, but by directing forces, as human beings do. . . . And in this way He manifests Himself; just as I can prove my existence to you by speaking to you, or writing to you, or knocking you down (if I could). Except by "miracles," external or internal, God has no means of making Himself known in His own world. The "impossibility" of miracles is another way of saying that everyone can act in the world except the Creator.

Abbot Chapman: *Spiritual Letters,* p. 208. (20th cent.)

The only thing still old-fashioned enough to reject miracles is the New Theology.

G. K. Chesterton: *Orthodoxy.* (With reference to a school of Protestant theology) (20th cent.)

If miracles cannot happen, they cannot happen in the twentieth century or in the twelfth. If they can happen, nobody can prove that there is a time when they cannot happen. The best that can be said for the sceptic is that he cannot say what he means, and therefore, whatever else he means, he cannot mean what he says. But if he only means that miracles can be *believed* in the twelfth century, but cannot be believed in the twentieth, then he is wrong again, both in theory and in fact. He is wrong in theory, because an intelligent recognition of possibilities does not depend on a date but on a philosophy. An atheist could disbelieve in the first century and a mystic could continue to believe in the twenty-first century. And he is wrong in fact because there is every sign of there being a great deal of mysticism and miracle in the twenty-first century; and there is quite certainly an increasing mass of it in the twentieth.

G. K. Chesterton: *The Common Man.* (20th cent.)

Mere repetition does not prove reality or inevitability. We must know the nature of the thing and the cause of the repetition. If the nature of the thing is a creation, and the cause of the thing a creator, in other words if the repetition itself is only the repetition of something willed by a person, then it is *not* impossible for the same person to will a different thing. If a man is a fool for believing in a Creator, then he is a fool

for believing in a miracle; but not otherwise.

G. K. Chesterton: *The Common Man.* (20th cent.)

I cannot understand people having historical difficulties about miracles. For, once you grant that miracles *can* happen, all the historical evidence at our disposal bids us believe that sometimes they do.

R. A. Knox: *The Belief of Catholics.* (20th cent.)

Miracles are important, and are only important because they provide evidence of the fact that the universe is not a closed system, and that effects in the natural world can be produced by the reactions of non-human will.

Arnold Lunn: *Now I See.* (20th cent.)

For those who believe in God no explanation is needed; for those who do not believe in God no explanation is possible.

John LaFarge: *The Manner is Ordinary.* (Of miraculous cures at Lourdes) (20th cent.)

Mirror

See now the eternal Virtue's breadth
    and height,
    Since it hath made itself so vast a
    store
    Of mirrors upon which to break its
    light,
Remaining in itself one, as before.

Dante: *Paradiso, Canto 29.* (Tr. Binyon) (14th cent.)

As a man more readily sees spots on his face when he looks in a mirror, so the soul who with true knowledge of self rises with desire and gazes with the eye of the intellect at herself in the sweet mirror of God knows better the stains of her own face by the purity which she sees in Him.

St. Catherine of Siena: *The Dialogue.* (14th cent.)

'Tis the last rub that polishes the mirror.

> C. Patmore: *De Natura Deorum*. (19th cent.)

No mirror keeps its glances.

> Alice Meynell: *Your Own Fair Youth.* (19th cent.)

> A wandering world of rivers,
> A wavering world of trees,
> If the world grow dim and dizzy
> With all changes and degrees,
> It is but our Lady's mirror
> Hung dreaming in its place,
> Shining with only shadows
> Till she wakes it with her face.

> G. K. Chesterton: *The Trinkets*. (20th cent.)

Misanthropy

A misanthrope I can understand—a womanthrope never.

> Oscar Wilde: *The Importance of Being Earnest*, 2. (19th cent.)

The misanthropic idea, as in Byron, is not a truth, but it is one of the immortal lies. As long as humanity lasts it can be hated.

> G. K. Chesterton: *Uses of Adversity*. (20th cent.)

Miser

> A miser with an eager face
> Sees that each roseleaf is in place.
> He keeps beneath strong bolts and bars
> The piercing beauty of the stars.
> The colors of the dying day
> He hoards as treasure—well he may!

> Theodore Maynard: *The World's Miser*. (20th cent.)

Misery

I am miserable from no cause save that of my ignorance, and if knowledge also shall cause me misery, then misery is eternal.

> St. Augustine: *Soliloquies*, 2. (4th cent.)

> Alas, how thy dull mind is headlong cast
> In depths of woe, where, all her light once lost,
> She doth to walk in utter darkness haste,
> While cares grow great with earthly tempests tost.

> Boethius: *De Consolatione Philosophiae*, 1, 2. (6th cent.)

So true it is that nothing is miserable but what is thought so, and contrariwise, every estate is happy if he that bears it be content.

> Boethius: *De Consolatione Philosophiae*, 2, 4. (6th cent.)

No misery is more genuine than false joy.

> St. Bernard: *Concerning Grace and Freewill*, 5. (12th cent.)

It is good to have companions in misery.

> John Gower: *Confessio Amantis*, 2. (14th cent.)

Our misery is the throne of God's mercy.

> St. Francis de Sales: *Letters to Persons in the World*, 6, 12. (17th cent.)

Man alone is miserable.

> Pascal: *Pensées*. (17th cent.)

Mission

My object is not to drive anyone into the Catholic communion against his will, but to have the naked truth made known to all who are astray and revealed by God's help through my ministry, commending itself so well that they may embrace and follow it.

> St. Augustine: *Letter 34*. (4th cent.)

The missions are an unequaled school for learning men. All men and women in a parish are made known to the missionary, for they walk or stumble through his very soul.

> W. Elliott: *Life of Father Hecker*. (19th cent.)

To practical people like Americans there is no oral or written evidence of the true religion so valid as the spectacle of its power to change bad men into good ones. Such a people will accept arguments from history and from Scripture, but those of a moral kind they demand; they must see the theories at work. A mission is a microcosm of the Church as a moral force.

W. Elliott: *Life of Father Hecker.* (19th cent.)

It is as clear to me as noonday light that countries and peoples have each their peculiar needs and aspirations as they have their peculiar environments, and that, if we would enter into souls and control them, we must deal with them according to their conditions. . . . The Savior prescribed timeliness in pastoral caring. The master of a house, He said, *bringeth forth out of his treasury new things and old,* as there is demand for one kind or the other.

Archb. Ireland: *Introd. to Elliott's Hecker.* (1891)

No one is to be forced against his will to embrace the Catholic faith.

Code of Canon Law, Canon 1351. (20th cent.)

The Church is not willing at any price to be enlisted in the work of colonization of any power, for such work belongs in the order of civilization or of culture. She meets opposition on this score not only at the hands of governments but also on the part of many Catholics who are badly educated in these matters and whose thought of the contemporary world is conditioned by a mass of fictitious images which represent a degenerate form of cultural ethic that was proper to the period of the Crusade.

J. Maritain: *Freedom in the Modern World.* (20th cent.)

The great hour of the Christian conscience has struck. May this conscience of Christianity be awakened to a full and virile appreciation of its mission of help and salvation for a mankind wavering in its spiritual framework.

Pope Pius XII: *Address on Easter Sunday,* March 28, 1948.

The fact of the missions reveals the Church's faith in herself as the Catholic unity of mankind.

J. C. Murray: *Address, Jesuit Philippine Dinner NYC.* (Dec. 1, 1949)

The Church's aim is not the domination of peoples or the gaining of temporal dominions; she is eager only to bring the supernatural light of faith to all peoples, and to promote the interests of civilization and culture, and fraternal concord among nations.

Pope Pius XII: *Letter to Prefect of S. Congr. of Propaganda Fide.* (Apr. 9, 1950)

The object of missionary activity, as all know, is to bring the light of the Gospel to new races and to form new Christians. However, the ultimate goal of missionary endeavor, which should never be lost sight of, is to establish the Church on sound foundations among non-Christian peoples, and place it under its own native hierarchy.

Pope Pius XII: *Evangelii Praecones.* (June 2, 1951)

The herald of the Gospel and messenger of Christ is an apostle. His office does not demand that he transplant European civilization and culture, and no other, to foreign soil, there to take root and propagate itself. His task in dealing with these peoples, who sometimes boast of a very old and highly developed culture of their own, is to teach and form them so that they are ready to accept willingly and in a practical manner the principles of Christian life and morality; principles, I might add, that fit into any culture, provided it be good and sound, and which give that culture greater force in safeguarding human dignity and in gaining human happiness. Catholic inhabitants of missionary countries, although they are first of all citizens of the kingdom of God and members of His great family, do not for all that cease to be citizens of their earthly fatherland.

Pope Pius XII: *Evangelii Praecones.* (June 2, 1951)

Missionary

A drill-master makes but an indifferent apostle.

V. McNabb: *Thoughts Twice-dyed.* (20th cent.)

Mistake

Mistakes are made on two counts: an argument is either based on error or incorrectly developed.

St. Thomas Aquinas: *Disputations concerning Truth,* 17, 2. (13th cent.)

The only things one never regrets are one's mistakes.

Oscar Wilde: *The Picture of Dorian Gray,* 3. (19th cent.)

Mistress

The character of the mistress is judged by that of the maid.

St. Jerome: *Letters,* 79, 9. (5th cent.)

Moderation

Measure is a merry mean.

John Heywood: *Proverbs,* 2, 7. (16th cent.)

Moderation is always good in all exercises, except in that of loving God.

St. Francis de Sales: *Letters to Persons in Religion,* 3, 20. (17th cent.)

This is the height of virtue: to correct immoderation moderately.

St. Francis de Sales: *Letters to Persons in the World,* 4, 3. (17th cent.)

Modernism

The basis of these new ideas . . . may be said to be this: in order that dissidents may be brought more readily to acknowledge Catholic truth the Church should show itself more sympathetic to the tolerant spirit of the present age, and, relaxing its former strictness, be more indulgent toward modern views and methods. Many think that this should be so not only with regard to disciplinary matters, but also with regard to doctrinal matters affecting the deposit of faith. . . .

Pope Leo XIII: *Testem Benevolentiae.* (The pope's prophetic letter to Cardinal Gibbons described an attitude of mind which could probably not be attributed to any American ecclesiastic, but which was shortly to be recognized as the heresy of modernism on the Continent.) (Jan. 22, 1899)

Undoubtedly, were anyone to attempt the task of collecting together all the errors that have been broached against the faith and to concentrate into one the sap and substance of them all, he could not succeed in doing so better than the Modernists have done. Nay, they have gone farther than this, for . . . their system means the destruction not of the Catholic religion alone, but of all religion.

Pope St. Pius X: *Pascendi Dominici Gregis.* (Sept. 8, 1907)

Modernity

To be merely modern is to condemn oneself to an ultimate narrowness; just as to spend one's last earthly money on the newest hat is to condemn oneself to the old-fashioned. The road of the ancient centuries is strewn with dead moderns.

G. K. Chesterton: *The Common Man.* (20th cent.)

Modesty

To Christian modesty it is not enough to be so, but to seem so too.

Tertullian: *On Women's Dress,* 2, 13. (3rd cent.)

Modesty in human beings is praised because it is not a matter of nature, but of will.

> Lactantius: *Divinae institutiones,* 6. (4th cent.)

Even for this I liked him better: the modesty of a mind admitting incapacity is a finer thing than the knowledge I was in search of.

> St. Augustine: *Confessions,* 5, 7. (5th cent.)

Be modest in all thy words and works.

> St. Teresa of Jesus: *Maxims.* (16th cent.)

Moment

> One by one the sands are flowing,
> One by one the moments fall;
> Some are coming, some are going;
> Do not strive to grasp them all.

> Adelaide Procter: *One by One.* (19th cent.)

Monarchy

The rule of one man is therefore to be preferred to the rule of many, although perils follow from both.

> St. Thomas Aquinas: *The Governance of Rulers,* 1, 5. (13th cent.)

Now the end and aim of all good government is the union and peace of the citizens, a union which chiefly consists of common ideals and common endeavors. Such, without doubt, will be pursued much more surely and easily if one man rather than many has to be obeyed, for it could hardly be that many men who were in no wise dependent on one another should judge alike about the same things.

> St. Robert Bellarmine: *De Romano Pontifice,* 1, 2. (16th cent.)

God has implanted a natural tendency to the monarchical form of government not only in the hearts of men but in practically all things.

> St. Robert Bellarmine: *De Romano Pontifice,* 1, 2. (16th cent.)

Monastic Life

These are the rules we lay down for your observance, who have entered upon monastic life. Firstly, to fulfil the end for which you have gathered into one community, dwell together in the house as single-minded sisters, and have *one mind and one heart* towards God. And call not anything your own, but let everything be common property.

> St. Augustine: *Letter 211.* (His famous rule) (5th cent.)

Therefore must we establish a school of the Lord's service; in founding which we hope to ordain nothing that is harsh or burdensome. But if, for good reason, for the amendment of evil habit or the preservation of charity, there be some strictness of discipline, do not be at once dismayed and run away from the way of salvation, of which the entrance must needs be narrow. But, as we progress in our monastic life and faith, our hearts shall be enlarged, and we shall run with unspeakable sweetness of love in the way of God's commandments; so that, never abandoning His rule but persevering in His teaching in the monastery until death, we shall share by patience in the sufferings of Christ, that we may deserve to be partakers also of His kingdom. Amen.

> St. Benedict: *Rule; Prologue.* (6th cent.)

> Bernardus valles, montes Benedictus amabat,
> Oppida Franciscus, celebres Dominicus urbes.

> (Bernard loved the valleys, Benedict the mountains,
> Francis the towns, Dominic the populous cities.)
>   Medieval saying.

Monasticism is not godliness, but a kind of life, either useful or useless to anyone depending on one's habit of body or of temperament. Certainly just as I do not urge you to it so do I not urge you against it.

> Erasmus: *Enchiridion.* (16th cent.)

I believe that monastic piety grows cold, languishes, disappears on every side for no other reason than that the monks grow old and gray in the letter, and do not escape to the spiritual understanding of the Scriptures.

Erasmus: *Enchiridion*. (16th cent.)

St. Benedict found the world, physical and social, in ruins, and his mission was to restore it in the way not of science, but of nature, not as if setting about to do it, not professing to do it by any set time, or by any rare specific, or by any series of strokes, but so quietly, patiently, gradually, that often till the work was done, it was not known to be doing. It was a restoration rather than a visitation, correction or conversion.

Card. Newman: *Historical Studies*, 2. (19th cent.)

O beatific life! Who is there shall gainsay
  Your great refusal's victory, your little loss,
Deserting vanity for the more perfect way,
  The sweetest service of the most dolorous Cross?

Ernest Dowson: *Carthusians*. (19th cent.)

  I have desired to go
  Where springs not fail,
To fields where flies no sharp and sided hail
  And a few lilies blow.
  And I have asked to be
  Where no storms come,
Where the green swell is in the havens dumb,
  And out of the swing of the sea.

G. M. Hopkins: *Heaven-Haven* (*A Nun Takes the Veil*). (19th cent.)

The chaos of habits that always goes with males when left entirely to themselves has only one honorable cure; and that is the strict discipline of a monastery. Anyone who has seen our unhappy young idealists in East End settlements losing their collars in the wash and liv-ing on tinned salmon will fully under-stand why it was decided by the wisdom of St. Bernard or St. Benedict, that if men were to live without women, they must not live without rules.

G. K. Chesterton: *What's Wrong with the World*. (20th cent.)

Oh, the banks of May are fair,
  Charm of sound and sight,
Breath of heaven fills the air,
  To the world's delight.

Far more wondrous is a bower,
  Fairer than the May,
Love-of-God it wears in flower,
  Blooming night and day.

   · · · · · ·

Carmel by the western sea
  Holds your blessed bower:
Love-of-God eternally
  Keeps your heart a-flower.

Michael Earls: *To a Carmelite Postulant*. (20th cent.)

For the modern historian the great im-portance of monasticism may seem to lie in its services to culture, in its preserva-tion of the tradition of letters and of classical literature. But from the point of view of medieval religion it is the essential monastic ideals of asceticism and otherworldliness and fidelity to the Rule that are the important matters, for it was these that gave it its spiritual in-dependence, its powers to resist the pres-sure of its environment and to initiate movements of religious reform.

Christopher Dawson: *Medieval Essays*. (20th cent.)

The best religious order is the one which performs most faithfully and exactly its own particular function in the Church, sanctifying its members and saving souls in the precise way laid down for it in the designs of God and by the dispositions of the Holy See. This means that the best orders are the ones which are able to cling most closely to the ideal of their founders and to live their lives most perfectly according to their own particular rules.

> Thomas Merton: *The Waters of Siloe.* (20th cent.)

Perfection is not something you can acquire like a hat—by walking into a place and trying on several and walking out again ten minutes later with one on your head that fits. Yet people sometimes enter monasteries with that idea.

> Thomas Merton: *Seeds of Contemplation.* (20th cent.)

A monastery can never be merely an escape from the world. Its very purpose is to enable us to face the problems of the world at their deepest level, that is to say, in relation to God and eternal life. Everything in the monastic life down to the minutest detail has to be viewed from this angle.

> Dom Griffiths: *The Golden String.* (20th cent.)

Money

Nothing that is God's is obtainable by money.

> Tertullian: *The Christian's Defence.* (3rd cent.)

But one thing is, ye know it well enow,
Of chapmen, that their money is their plough.

> chapman—trader, merchant
> Chaucer: *The Shipmannes Tale.* (14th cent.)

A penny can do no more than it may.

> Lydgate: *The London Lyckpenny.* (15th cent.)

A little wanton money, which burned out the bottom of his purse.

> St. Thomas More: *Works,* 195. (16th cent.)

> Be it better, be it worse,
> Do ye after him
> That beareth the purse.

> John Heywood: *Proverbs,* 1, 5. (16th cent.)

To bring a shilling to sixpence quickly.

> John Heywood: *Proverbs,* 2, 5. (16th cent.)

He had not one penny to bless him.

> John Heywood: *Proverbs,* 2, 8. (16th cent.)

For my own part, I believe that honor and money nearly always go together, and that he who desires honor never hates money, while he who hates money cares little for honor.

> St. Teresa of Jesus: *Way of Perfection,* 2. (16th cent.)

Two mites, two drops (yet all her house and land)
Falls from a steady heart, though trembling hand:
The other's wanton wealth foams high, and brave,
The other cast away, she only gave.

> Richard Crashaw: *Upon the Sepulcher of our Lord.* (17th cent.)

The chief and most excellent rule for the right use of money is one which the heathen philosophers hinted at, but which the Church has traced out clearly, and has not only made known to men's minds, but has impressed upon their lives. It rests on the principle that it is one thing to have a right to the possession of money and another to have a right to use money as one wills.

> Pope Leo XIII: *Rerum Novarum.* (May 15, 1891)

God! what a little accident of gold
Fences our weakness from the wolves of old!

> W. S. Blunt: *Prison Sonnet.* (19th cent.)

In these days, when there is so much enterprise, money has become, as it were, a living thing that grows; or, at the least, a tool that can be used.

> R. H. Benson: *By What Authority.* (20th cent.)

Money is power, and power is an attribute: it must surely be taken into account then.

R. H. Benson: *The Average Man.* (20th cent.)

He married the money and bade the wife to the weddin'.

Seumas MacManus: *Heavy Hangs the Golden Grain.* (20th cent.)

If you have money, consider that perhaps the only reason God allowed it to fall into your hands was in order that you might find joy and perfection by throwing it away.

Thomas Merton: *Seeds of Contemplation.* (20th cent.)

Monk

First and foremost, the monk should own nothing in this world, but he should have as his possessions solitude of the body, modesty of bearing, a modulated tone of voice, and a well-ordered manner of speech.

St. Basil: *A Discourse on Ascetical Discipline.* (4th cent.)

[The monk] should work with his hands, be ever mindful of his last end, joyful in hope, patient in adversity, unceasingly prayerful, giving thanks in all things, humble toward everyone, hating pride, sober and watchful to keep his heart from evil thoughts. He ought to heap up treasure in heaven by observing the commandments, examining himself as to his daily thoughts and actions, not entangling himself in the occupations and superfluities of the world.

St. Basil: *A Discourse on Ascetical Discipline.* (4th cent.)

The common people say that a bad accompanist makes a good singer; do we want these same common people to laugh at us in the same way and say that a bad monk makes a good clergyman?

St. Augustine: *Letter 60.* (5th cent.)

There are two classes a monk should avoid: women and bishops.

Johannes Cassianus: *De institutis coenobiorum.* (5th cent.)

There are evidently four kinds of monks. The first are the cenobites, that is those who live in monasteries, serving under a rule and an abbot. The second are the anchorites or hermits, that is those . . . who go out well-armed from the ranks of the community to the solitary combat of the desert. They are able now to live without the help of others, and by their own strength and God's assistance to fight against the temptations of mind and body. The third kind of monks is that detestable one of the Sarabaites. . . . In their actions they still conform to the standards of the world. . . . Their law is their own pleasure. . . . The fourth kind of monks are those called gyrovagues. They spend their whole lives wandering from province to province . . . worse in all respects than the Sarabaites.

St. Benedict: *Rule,* 1. (6th cent.)

Let them sleep clothed and girt with girdles or cords, but not with their belts, so that they may not have their knives at their sides while they are sleeping, and be cut by them in their sleep.

St. Benedict: *Rule,* 22. (The reason for thus sleeping was that they might repair without delay to night prayer) (6th cent.)

Let no one presume to give or receive anything without the abbot's leave, or to have anything as his own, anything whatever, whether book or tablets or pen or whatever it may be; for monks should not have even their bodies and wills at their disposal.

St. Benedict: *Rule,* 33. (6th cent.)

The life of a monk ought at all times to be lenten in its character.

St. Benedict: *Rule,* 49. (6th cent.)

He is a monk who has separated his soul from the material world in order to attach himself firmly to God by means of self-control, charity, the singing of psalms, and prayer.

> St. Maximus the Confessor: *Centuries on Charity,* 2, 54. (7th cent.)

A monk out of his monastery is like a fish out of water.

> Gratian: *Decretum.* (12th cent.)

But the cowl hideth such a bird within
  That, if the crowd could see it as it is,
  They'd see what pardon they con-
    fided in;
Through which this folly on earth hath
    such increase
  That without warrant of authority
  They rush to catch at any promises.

> Dante: *Paradiso, Canto 29.* (D. refers to certain dissolute orders of his day) (Tr. Binyon) (14th cent.)

Merry sang the monks who in Ely fare
When Canute the king came rowing
    there
—Row, knights, nearer to the land
And hear we the song of monken band.

> Anonymous: *The Monks of Ely.* (14th cent.)

If thou wouldst be a monk thou must be content, for Christ's sake, to be esteemed a fool in this world. (cf. I Cor. 4, 10)

> Thomas a Kempis: *Imitation of Christ,* 1. (15th cent.)

A monk is a man who has given up everything in order to possess every-thing. . . . The monk's business is to empty himself of all that is selfish and turbulent and make way for the unap-prehended Spirit of God.

> Thomas Merton: *The Waters of Siloe.* (20th cent.)

Monogamy

For after He had formed man and saw that he must needs have a companion like himself, He took one of his ribs and made of it one woman, although obvi-ously matter for others was not lacking nor was the Artisan unequal to the task of making more. Adam had many ribs, and the hands of God are tireless; yet more wives than one God did not create. And, therefore, the man whom God made, Adam, and the woman whom God made, Eve, living in monogamy, fixed this as an inviolable law for man-kind, a law based on God's original de-cree and the precedent set in the begin-ning.

> Tertullian: *An Exhortation to Chastity,* 5. (3rd cent.)

Monotheism

There is but one God, to Whom the name of God alone belongs, from Whom all things come, and Who is Lord of the whole universe.

> Tertullian: *The Testimony of the Christian Soul.* (3rd cent.)

According to the teaching of monothe-ism, God is an individual, self-depend-ent, all-perfect, unchangeable Being; intelligent, living, personal and present; almighty, all-seeing, all-remembering; between Whom and His creatures there is an infinite gulf; Who has no origin, Who is all-sufficient for Himself; Who created and upholds the universe; Who will judge every one of us, sooner or later, according to that law of right and wrong which He has written in our hearts.

> Card. Newman: *Idea of a University.* (19th cent.)

Monster

Neither in the case of monsters which are born and live, how quickly soever they die, will it be denied that they will rise again, or is it to be believed that they will rise again so, and not rather with their nature corrected and freed from fault.

> St. Augustine: *On Faith, Hope and Charity.* (5th cent.)

Monuments

To seek to leave monuments of our dignity in the prison of this world, is like causing a coat of arms to be sculptured over our prison gate.

St. Thomas More. (16th cent.)

Mood

Sometimes we are foolish and identify our emotion with ourselves; and think that our moods are our character.

R. H. Benson: *The Mirror of Shalott.* (20th cent.)

Moon

Make me believe that the moon is made of a green cheese.

John Heywood: *Proverbs,* 2, 7. (16th cent.)

And on the lunar world securely pry.

Dryden: *Annus Mirabilis.* (17th cent.)

Like moonlight o'er a troubled sea,
Brightening the storm it cannot calm.

Thomas Moore: *The Loves of the Angels.* (19th cent.)

The moon looks
On many brooks,
The brook can see no moon but this.

Thomas Moore: *While Gazing on the Moon's Light.* (19th cent.)

Behold, whatever wind prevail,
Slow westering, a phantom sail—
The lonely soul of yesterday—
Unpiloted, pursues her way.

John B. Tabb: *The Mid-Day Moon.* (19th cent.)

The stranded moon lay quivering like a lustrous
Medusa newly washed up from the tide.

F. Thompson: *Sister Songs.* (19th cent.)

Pale ports o' the moon.

F. Thompson: *The Hound of Heaven.* (19th cent.)

And suddenly the moon withdraws
Her sickle from the lightning skies,
And to her somber cavern flies,
Wrapped in a veil of yellow gauze.

Oscar Wilde: *La Fuite de la Lune.* (19th cent.)

The moon was a ghostly galleon tossed upon cloudy seas.

Alfred Noyes: *The Highwayman.* (20th cent.)

Moralist

To wisest moralists 'tis but given
To work rough border-law of heaven.

F. Thompson: *A Judgment in Heaven: Epilogue.* (19th cent.)

Moralists are unhappy people. When they insist on the immutability of moral principles, they are reproached for imposing unlivable requirements on us. When they explain the way in which those immutable principles are to be put into force, taking into account the diversity of concrete situations, they are reproached for making morality relative. In both cases, however, they are only upholding the claims of reason to direct life.

J. Maritain: *Man and the State.* (20th cent.)

Morality

There is nothing which is more of a help to a good life than to believe that God will be our Judge, Whom hidden things do not escape, Whom unseemly things offend, and Whom good things delight.

St. Ambrose: *On the Duties of the Clergy,* 1, 124. (4th cent.)

Moral science is better occupied when treating of friendship than of justice.

St. Thomas Aquinas: *Commentary on the Ethics,* 8, lect. 1. (13th cent.)

Since moral activity is concerned with particular occasions, sweeping moral judgments partly miss the point.

St. Thomas Aquinas: *Summa Theologica,* 2-2, Prol. (13th cent.)

Strive we then to think aright: that is the first principle of moral life.

Pascal: *Pensées.* (17th cent.)

Physical science will not, when I am in distress, make up to me for want of moral practice. But moral science will always make up for ignorance of physical science.

Pascal: *Pensées.* (17th cent.)

I find the doctors and the sages
Have differ'd in all climes and ages,
And two and fifty scarce agree
On what is pure morality.

Thomas Moore: *Morality.* (19th cent).

Never did moral thought occur
    In more unlucky hour than this;
For oh! I just was leading her
    To talk of love and think of bliss.

Thomas Moore: *The Snake.* (19th cent.)

In ethics—'tis you that can check,
    In a minute, their doubts and their quarrels;
Oh! show but that mole on your neck,
    And 'twill soon put an end to their morals.

Thomas Moore: *To Fanny.* (19th cent.)

There is something in moral truth and goodness, in faith, in firmness, in heavenly-mindedness, in meekness, in courage, in lovingkindness, to which this world's circumstances are quite unequal, for which the longest life is insufficient, which makes the highest opportunities of this world disappointing, which must burst the prison of this world to have its appropriate range.

Card. Newman: *Miscellanies,* 125. (19th cent.)

The Catholic church holds it better for the sun and moon to drop from heaven, for the earth to fail, and for all the many millions in it to die of starvation in extremest agony, as far as temporal affliction goes, than that one soul, I will not say, should be lost, but should commit one single venial sin, should tell one wilful untruth, or should steal one poor farthing without excuse.

Card. Newman: *Apologia pro Vita Sua,* 5. (19th cent.)

The moral code, in its main lines, is not new; it has long been known; it is not universally accepted in Europe, even now. The difference in moral insight between past and present is not very large.

Lord Acton: *Letter to M. Creighton.* (1887)

Modern morality consists in accepting the standards of one's own age.

Oscar Wilde: *The Picture of Dorian Gray,* 6. (19th cent.)

Moral conviction—that conviction on which a man acts—does not always coincide with the intellectual process. Occasionally it outruns it, occasionally lags behind, and the first sign of its arrival is cessation of strain. The intellect may still be busy, arranging, sorting, classifying; but the thing itself is done, and the soul leans back.

R. H. Benson: *The Necromancers.* (20th cent.)

Much has been said, and said truly, of the monkish morbidity, of the hysteria which has often gone with the visions of hermits or nuns. But let us not forget that this visionary religion is, in one sense, necessarily more wholesome than our modern and reasonable morality. It is more wholesome for this reason, that it can contemplate the idea of success or triumph in the hopeless fight towards the ethical ideal, in what Stevenson called, with his usual startling felicity, "the lost fight of virtue." A modern morality, on the other hand, can only point with absolute conviction to the horrors that follow breaches of law; its only certainty is a certainty of ill. It can only point to imperfection. It has no perfection to point to.

G. K. Chesterton: *Heretics.* (20th cent.)

Modern realists are indeed terrorists, like the dynamiters; and they fail just as much in their effort to create a thrill. Both realists and dynamiters are well-meaning people engaged in the task, so obviously ultimately hopeless, of using science to promote morality.

G. K. Chesterton: *Heretics.* (20th cent.)

The Jesuits, especially in their capacity of casuists, suffered almost entirely from being two hundred years before their time. They tried to start in a cautious way what is now surging up on every side of us in a chaotic way. . . . In other words, they recognized that there really are problems in moral conduct; not problems about whether the moral law should be obeyed, but problems about how in a particular case the moral law really applies.

G. K. Chesterton: *The Thing.* (20th cent.)

Neither Catholicism nor any other form of Christianity pretends to have a special morality of its own; religion is meant to enforce, not to supersede, the natural code of morals.

R. A. Knox: *The Belief of Catholics.* (20th cent.)

For the preservation of the moral order neither the laws and sanctions of the temporal power are sufficient nor the beauty of virtue and the expounding of its necessity. A religious authority must enter in to enlighten the mind, to direct the will, and to strengthen human frailty by the aid of divine grace.

Pope Pius XI: *Casti connubii.* (Dec. 31, 1930)

We cannot have ethics without religion; neither can we have religion without ethics.

V. McNabb: *Thoughts Twice-dyed.* (20th cent.)

The modern world forgets that the greatest exponents of practical Christianity have been the Christians who held most firmly to the central doctrines of their faith. Christian ethics will not long survive the Christian creed.

Arnold Lunn: *Now I See.* (20th cent.)

That man and nature are the creation of God, that they are wholly dependent on Him both in their existence and their activities, is Christianity's first premise. It is this, and this alone, that makes sense of civilized man's respect for absolute values, his conviction that there exist intellectual and moral standards which no amount of wishful thinking can alter.

Dom Aelred Graham: *Catholicism and the World Today.* (20th cent.)

The whole happiness of man and even his sanity depend on his moral condition. And since society does not exist all by itself in a void, but is made up of the individuals who compose it, the problems of society cannot ultimately be solved except in terms of the moral life of individuals. If the citizens are sane, the city will be sane. If the citizens are wild animals, the city will be a jungle.

Thomas Merton: *The Ascent to Truth.* (20th cent.)

Morning

The bounds of night are safely past,
And slumber's bars asunder cast,
While morn uprises on the blue
And bathes the skies in radiance new.

Soon as the earliest light we see
We lift our souls, O Lord, to Thee;
To Thee, sweet source of living light,
In song and prayer our hearts unite.

St. Hilary of Poitiers: *Jam Meta Noctis Transit.* (Tr. D. Donahoe) (4th cent.)

O wondrous Giver of the light!
  By whose eternal ray serene,
After the lingering hours of night,
  The glory of the morn is seen.

St. Hilary of Poitiers: *Lucis Largitor Splendide.* (Tr. D. Donahoe) (4th cent.)

The morning is a friend to the muses.

> Erasmus: *Colloquia.* (16th cent.)

Rise, thou best and brightest morning!
  Rosy with a double red;
With thine own blush thy cheeks
    adorning
  And the dear drops this day were
    shed.

All the purple pride that laces
  The crimson curtains of thy bed,
Guilds thee not with so sweet graces,
  Nor sets thee in so rich a red.

> Richard Crashaw: *New Year's Day.*
> (17th cent.)

I love my love in the morning,
  For she like morn is fair—
Her blushing cheek its crimson streak,
  Its clouds her golden hair,
Her glance its beam so soft and kind,
  Her tears its dewy showers,
And her voice the tender whispering
    wind
  That stirs the early bowers.

> Gerald Griffin: *I Love My Love in the
> Morning.* (19th cent.)

Belovèd, it is morn!
  A redder berry on the thorn,
  A deeper yellow on the corn,
For this good day new-born.
  Pray, sweet, for me
  That I may be
  Faithful to God and thee.

> Emily H. Hickey: *Beloved, it is Morn.*
> (19th cent.)

Forsaking now her dark and dreadful
    past,
  A lovely Magdalen, she laves earth's
    feet
With tears of dew and perfume of the
    rose,
  Then dries them with her long-
    tressed sunbeams sweet.

> Sister M. Angelita: *Morning.* (20th cent.)

See also Dawn; Lauds; Matins

Mortality

It is generall,
To be mortall.

> J. Skelton: *Gift of a Skull.* (16th cent.)

Sad mortality may hide
In his ashes all her pride,
With this inscription o'er his head:
All hope of never dying here lies dead.

> Richard Crashaw: *On the Death of
> Mr. Herrys, No. 3.* (17th cent.)

Mortality, behold, and fear!
What a change of flesh is here!
Think how many royal bones
Sleep within this heap of stones:
Here they lie had realms and lands,
Who now want strength to stir their
    hands:
Where from pulpits seal'd with dust
They preach: In greatness is no trust.

> Francis Beaumont: *On the Tombs in
> Westminster Abbey.* (17th cent.)

Why have we longings of immortal
    pain,
And all we long for mortal?

> F. Thompson: *To the Setting Sun.* (19th
> cent.)

The immortal could we cease to con-
    template,
The mortal part suggests its every trait.

> F. Thompson: *Her Portrait.* (19th cent.)

It knows but will not tell.
Awake, alone, it counts its father's
    years—
  How few are left—its mother's. Ah,
    how well
It knows of death, in tears.

> Alice Meynell: *Intimations of Mortality:
> from Recollections of Early Childhood.*
> (20th cent.)

Mortification

For perfection does not consist in macerating or killing the body, but in killing
our perverse self-will.

> St. Catherine of Siena: *Letter to Sister
> Daniella.* (14th cent.)

May we be annihilated in ourselves to live wholly to God!

St. Francis de Sales: *Letters to Persons in Religion,* 2, 1. (17th cent.)

We do not become perfect by the multiplication of exercises, penances and austerities, but rather by the purity of love with which we do them.

St. Francis de Sales: *Spiritual Conferences,* 13. (17th cent.)

It is a thousand times better to die with our Lord than to live without Him.

St. Francis de Sales: *Letters to Persons in the World,* 6, 21. (17th cent.)

It is far better to mortify the body through the spirit, than the spirit through the body.

J. P. Camus: *The Spirit of St. Francis de Sales,* 15, 4. (17th cent.)

So long as the enemy can enter into our souls and torment us, he does not care how much we mortify our bodies.

J. P. Camus: *The Spirit of St. Francis de Sales,* 15, 3. (17th cent.)

Never practise any mortification of a considerable character without counsel. The devil, when he can no longer keep us back, aims at driving us too far and too fast.

Isaac T. Hecker. (Elliott's *Life,* 320) (19th cent.)

See also Fasting; Penance

Mother

What tigress is there that does not purr over her young ones, and fawn upon them in tenderness.

St. Augustine: *The City of God,* 15. (5th cent.)

No mother more indulgent but the true.

Dryden: *The Hind and the Panther,* 1. (17th cent.)

Lord Illingworth: All women become like their mothers. That is their tragedy.
Mrs. Allonby: No man does. That is his.

Oscar Wilde: *A Woman of No Importance,* 2. (19th cent.)

One wept whose only child was dead,
New-born, ten years ago.
Weep not; he is in bliss, they said.
She answered, Even so,

Ten years ago was born in pain
A child, not now forlorn.
But oh, ten years ago, in vain,
A mother, a mother was born.

Alice Meynell: *Maternity.* (20th cent.)

Sweet creatures who make the home-places
As cheerful and bright as they may,
Whose feminine beauty embraces
A heart to illumine the way,
Though skies may be ever so gray;
Good mothers, whose children caress them
And hail them as chums at their play—
We sing the plain "women," God bless them!

T. A. Daly: *Ballade to the Women.* (20th cent.)

What is a mother? Who shall answer this?
A mother is a font and spring of life,
A mother is a forest in whose heart
Lies hid a secret ancient as the hills,
For men to claim and take its wealth away;
And like the forest shall her wealth renew
And give, and give again, that men may live.

Card. Spellman: *Mary, Mother of Mankind.* (20th cent.)

Motion

Whatever moves is moved by another.

St. Thomas Aquinas: *Summa Theologica,* 1. (13th cent.)

Our nature lies in motion; absolute rest is death.

Pascal: *Pensées.* (17th cent.)

Motive

In vain the sage, with retrospective eye,
Would from th' apparent what con-
    clude the why,
Infer the motive from the deed, and
    show
That what we chanced was what we
    meant to do.

> Alexander Pope: *Moral Essays,* 1. (18th
> cent.)

Mountain

Hills peep o'er hills, and Alps on Alps
arise.

> Alexander Pope: *An Essay on Criticism,*
> 2. (18th cent.)

The mountains from their heights reveal
to us two truths. They suddenly make us
feel our insignificance, and at the same
time they free the immortal mind, and
let it feel its greatness, and they release
it from the earth.

> H. Belloc: *The Path to Rome.* (20th cent.)

Mountain-Climbing

If there is any value in scaling the mountains, it is only that from them one can
behold the plains.

> G. K. Chesterton: *Daily News.* (20th
> cent.)

That school of stern but voluntary discipline which is the essence of all serious
mountaineering, is a fine school for the
natural virtues.

> Arnold Lunn: *Now I See.* (20th cent.)

Mourning

The house of mourning teaches charity
and wisdom.

> St. John Chrysostom: *Homilies.* (4th
> cent.)

Mourning ruined joy's estate.

> F. Thompson: *Buona Notte.* (19th cent.)

Mouse

It is a wily mouse
That can build his dwelling-house
    Within the cattes ear.

> John Skelton: *Why Come Ye Not To
> Courte?* (16th cent.)

Mouth

That shall not stop my mouth.

> John Heywood: *Proverbs,* 2, 4. (16th
> cent.)

As a pomegranate, cut in twain,
White-seeded in her crimson mouth.

> Oscar Wilde: *La Bella Donna della mia
> Mente.* (19th cent.)

Murder

Murder will out, that see we day by day.

> Chaucer: *The Nonne Preestes Tale.* (14th
> cent.)

He that killeth a man when he is drunk,
Shall be hanged when he is sober.

> John Heywood: *Proverbs,* 1, 10. (16th
> cent.)

The greatest crime is homicide. The accomplice is no better than the assassin;
the theorist worse.

> Lord Acton: *Letter to M. Creighton.*
> (1887)

Music

Music is the science of melodizing
(*modulandi*) well.

> St. Augustine: *De Musica,* 1, 2. (4th cent.)

Music is the practical knowledge of
melody (*peritia modulationis*), consisting of sound and song; it is called music
by derivation from the Muses.

> St. Isidore: *Etymologies,* 3, 15. (7th cent.)

Music rouses the emotions, it calls the
senses to a different quality. In battles,
the music of the trumpet fires the war-

riors, and the more impetuous its loud sound the braver is the spirit for fighting. . . . Music also comforts the mind in the enduring of labors, and singing lightens weariness in solitary tasks. Music also calms overwrought minds. . . . Whatever we say or whatever emotions we feel within from the beating of our impulses, it is proven that they are brought into communion with the virtues through the musical rhythms of harmony.

St. Isidore: *Etymologies,* 3, 17. (7th cent.)

And after shewed he him the nine
   spheres,
And after that the melody heard he
That cometh of those spheres thrice
   three,
That well is of music and melody
In this world here, and cause of harmony.

Chaucer: *The Parlement of Foules.* (14th cent.)

What passion cannot music raise and quell?

Dryden: *A Song for St. Cecilia's Day.* (17th cent.)

From harmony, from heavenly harmony
   This universal frame began:
   From harmony to harmony
Through all the compass of the notes
   it ran,
The diapason closing full in man.

Dryden: *A Song for St. Cecilia's Day.* (17th cent.)

The trumpet shall be heard on high,
The dead shall live, the living die,
And music shall untune the sky.

Dryden: *A Song for St. Cecilia's Day.* (17th cent.)

Warriors she fires with animated
   sounds,
Pours balm into the bleeding lover's
   wounds.

Pope: *Ode for Musick on St. Cecilia's Day.* (18th cent.)

Music resembles poetry; in each
Are nameless graces which no methods
   teach,
And where a master-hand alone can
   reach.

Pope: *An Essay on Criticism,* 1. (18th cent.)

Music has charms alone for peaceful minds.

Pope: *Sappho to Phaon.* (18th cent.)

Light quirks of music, broken and uneven,
Make the soul dance upon a jig to
   heav'n.

Pope: *Moral Essays,* 4. (18th cent.)

This must be the music, said he, of the
   spears,
For I am curst if each note of it doesn't
   run through one!

Thomas Moore: *Fudge Family in Paris.* (19th cent.)

Seated one day at the organ,
   I was weary and ill at ease,
And my fingers wandered idly
   Over the noisy keys.

I do not know what I was playing,
   Or what I was dreaming then,
But I struck one chord of music
   Like the sound of a great Amen.

Adelaide Procter: *The Lost Chord.* (19th cent.)

Music is in all growing things;
And underneath the silky wings
   Of smallest insects there is stirred
   A pulse of air that must be heard;
Earth's silence lives, and throbs, and
   sings.

George P. Lathrop: *Music of Growth.* (19th cent.)

And if sad the music is,
It is sad with mysteries
Of a small immortal thing
That the passing ages sing,—
Simple music making mirth

Of the dying and the birth
Of the people of the earth.

Alice Meynell: *Soeur Monique: a Rondeau by Couperin.* (19th cent.)

A quality
Which music sometimes has, being the art
Which is most nigh to tears and memory.

Oscar Wilde: *The Burden of Itys.* (19th cent.)

Her ivory hands on the ivory keys
Strayed in a fitful fantasy,
Like the silver gleam when the poplar trees
Rustle their pale leaves listlessly.

Oscar Wilde: *In the Golden Room: A Harmony.* (19th cent.)

Sacred music, being a complementary part of the solemn liturgy, participates in the general scope of the liturgy, which is the glory of God and the sanctification of the faithful . . . and since its principal office is to clothe with suitable melody the liturgical text proposed for the understanding of the faithful, its proper aim is to add greater efficacy to the text, in order that through it the faithful may be the more easily moved to devotion.

Pope St. Pius X: *Motu Proprio on Sacred Music.* (Nov. 22, 1903)

The more closely a composition for the Church approaches in its movement, inspiration and savor the Gregorian form, the more sacred and liturgical it becomes; and the more out of harmony it is with that supreme model, the less worthy it is of the temple.

Pope St. Pius X: *Motu Proprio on Sacred Music.* (Nov. 22, 1903)

Take them, you, that smile on strings, those nobler sounds than mine,
The words that never lie, or brag, or flatter, or malign.

G. K. Chesterton: *To M. E. W.* (20th cent.)

Music, whether instrumental from an organ or other instruments, or vocal, in which there is any tinge of the lascivious or impure, must be entirely excluded from churches; and the liturgical laws regarding sacred music must be observed.

Code of Canon Law, Canon 1264. (20th cent.)

The Harper draws his golden string,
And over-head, like birds awing—
That soar and flutter as they sing—
    The music floats
    In liquid notes,
    And all is still.

Sister Imelda: *An Etching.* (20th cent.)

There's a barrel-organ carolling across a golden street
In the city as the sun sinks low;
And the music's not immortal; but the world has made it sweet
And fulfilled it with the sunset glow.

Alfred Noyes: *The Barrel-Organ.* (20th cent.)

Musician

He was an organ where God kept the stops.

C. L. O'Donnell: *The Dead Musician.* (20th cent.)

Mutability

For the mutability of mutable things is simply their capacity for all the forms into which mutable things can be changed.

St. Augustine: *Confessions,* 12, 6. (5th cent.)

Mystery

For just as in the case of things which appear to our eyes experience seems better than a theory of causation, so too in the case of dogmas which transcend our comprehension faith is better than apprehension through processes of reasoning, for faith teaches us to understand that which is separated in person but at the same time united in substance.

> St. Basil: *Letters*, 38. (4th cent.)

If the works of God were such as might be easily comprehended by human reason, they could not be called wonderful or unspeakable.

> Thomas a Kempis: *The Imitation of Christ*, 4, 18. (15th cent.)

A revelation is religious doctrine viewed on its illuminated side; a mystery is the selfsame doctrine viewed on the side unilluminated.

> Card. Newman: *Essays Critical and Historical*, 1. (19th cent.)

Mysteries in religion are measured by the proud according to their own capacity; by the humble, according to the power of God: the humble glorify God for them, the proud exalt themselves against them.

> Card. Newman: *Miscellanies*, 131. (19th cent.)

The mysteries of God are unveiled by those who carry them first by assault.

> R. H. Benson: *The Light Invisible*. (20th cent.)

Mysteries revealed by God cannot be harmful to men; nor should they remain as treasures hidden in a field, useless. They have been given from on high precisely to help the spiritual progress of those who study them in a spirit of piety.

> Pope Pius XII: *Mystici Corporis*. (June 29, 1943)

Wonder is one of the faculties most easy to lose: we have it in childhood, undiscriminating no doubt but vivid and deep; we all too easily lose it as we grow older and become immersed in our daily concerns; and so, unless we are very careful, not beauty only but life itself passes us by. For inevitably life loses its meaning when it loses its mystery.

> Gerald Vann: *The Water and the Fire*. (20th cent.)

Mysticism

Never did any spiritual mystical writer pretend to receive any new or formerly unknown lights or revelations in matters of faith, beyond what have been known and universally received in the Church. But they have a clearer sight of ordinary mysteries.

> Augustine Baker: *Sancta Sophia*. (17th cent.)

It is really a distressing fact that so much should be written on mysticism by those who do not seem to be aware of the state of the question. There is an immense literature stretching down the ages, and this and the carefully thought out science of the spiritual life in the Catholic Church, with its vast evidence, its carefully drawn distinctions, have been completely ignored.

> M. C. D'Arcy: *The Nature of Belief*. (20th cent.)

The mystic condition is not a common condition, and it is mere confusion to identify it with what is ordinarily meant by the religious experience.

> M. C. D'Arcy: *The Nature of Belief*. (20th cent.)

Mysticism keeps men sane. As long as you have mystery you have health; when you destroy mystery you create morbidity. The ordinary man has always been sane because the ordinary man has always been a mystic. He has permitted the twilight. He has always had one foot in earth and the other in fairyland. He has always left himself free to doubt his gods; but (unlike the agnostic of today) free also to believe in them. He has always cared more for truth than consistence.

> G. K. Chesterton: *Orthodoxy*. (20th cent.)

For the mystic especially it is important that theology should flourish and good theologians abound, for in the guidance which objective theology supplies lies the mystic's sole certainty of escaping self-delusion.

> Philip Hughes. (20th cent.)

One of the greatest paradoxes of the mystical life is this: that a man cannot enter into the deepest center of himself and pass through that center into God, unless he is able to pass entirely out of himself and empty himself and give himself to other people in the purity of a selfless love.

> Thomas Merton: *Seeds of Contemplation.* (20th cent.)

The simplicity of the Gospels, if kept in mind, makes false mysticism impossible. Christ has delivered us forever from the esoteric and strange. He has brought the light of God to our own level to transfigure our ordinary existence.

> Thomas Merton: *The Living Bread.* (20th cent.)

See also Contemplation; Contemplative Life

Myth

It seems strangely forgotten nowadays that a myth is a work of imagination and therefore a work of art.

> G. K. Chesterton: *The Everlasting Man.* (20th cent.)

N

Nail

Leave me as I am, for He who gives me the power to endure the fire will grant me also to remain in the flames unmoved, even without the security which nails give.

> Martyrdom of St. Polycarp, 13. (2nd cent.)

Name

Do not concern yourself with anxiety for the show of a great name.

> Thomas a Kempis: *The Imitation of Christ,* 3, 24. (15th cent.)

O name forever sad, forever dear.

> Pope: *Eloisa to Abelard.* (18th cent.)

Oh, breathe not his name! let it sleep in
    the shade,
  Where cold and unhonor'd his relics
    are laid.

> Thomas Moore: *Oh, Breathe Not His Name.* (19th cent.)

I speak your name—a magic thing—
Jocund April takes my hand,
Golden birds begin to sing,
Laughter fills the silver land.

> Eleanor R. Cox: *To a Dead Poet.* (20th cent.)

Name of Jesus, Holy

For the name of Christ is on the lips of all: it is invoked by the just man in the service of justice, by the perjurer for the sake of deceiving, by the king to con-firm his rule, by the soldier to nerve himself for battle, by the husband to establish his authority, by the wife to confess her submission . . . all invoke the name of Christ, the Christian with true reverence, the pagan with feigned respect; and they shall all undoubtedly give to that same Person Whom they invoke an account both of the spirit and of the language in which they repeat His name.

St. Augustine: *Letter 232, 4.* (5th cent.)

Nothing restrains anger, curbs pride, heals the wound of malice, bridles self-indulgence, quenches the passions, checks avarice and puts unclean thoughts to flight, as does the name of Jesus.

St. Bernard: *Sermons on the Canticle of Canticles,* 18. (12th cent.)

> Jesu, the very thought of Thee
> With sweetness fills my breast;
> But sweeter far Thy face to see,
> And in Thy presence rest.
>
> . . . .
>
> O Jesu, King most wonderful
> Thou conqueror renowned,
> Thou sweetness most ineffable,
> In Whom all joys are found.
>
> . . . .
>
> O Jesu, Thou the beauty art
> Of angel-worlds above;
> Thy name is music to the heart,
> Enchanting it with love.

Roman Breviary, Feast of Holy Name of Jesus, Hymn *Jesu dulcis memoria.* (Tr. E. Caswall) (12th cent.)

Thy name, O Lord, is for me oil poured out. For the grace of Thy visitation makes me fully understand the true meaning of Thy name, which is Jesus, Savior. For it is Thy gracious presence that saves me from sorrow and from sin.

Walter Hilton: *Scale of Perfection,* 2, 41. (14th cent.)

> I sing the name which none can say
> But touch'd with an interior ray:

> The name of our new peace; our good:
> Our bliss: and supernatural blood:
> The name of all our lives and loves.

Richard Crashaw: *The Name of Jesus.* (17th cent.)

> Come, holy name! appear from forth the bright
> Regions of peaceful light
> Look from Thine own illustrious home,
> Fair king of names, and come.
> Leave all Thy native glories in their gorgeous nest,
> And give Thyself a while the gracious guest
> Of humble souls, that seek to find
> The hidden sweets
> Which man's heart meets
> When Thou art Master of the mind.

Richard Crashaw: *The Name of Jesus.* (17th cent.)

> Welcome dear, all-adored name!
> For sure there is no knee
> That knows not Thee.
> Or if there be such sons of shame,
> Alas what will they do
> When stubborn rocks shall bow
> And hills hang down their heav'n-saluting heads
> To seek for humble beds
> Of dust, where in the bashful shades of night
> Next to their own low nothing they may lie,
> And couch before the dazzling light of Thy dread majesty.

Richard Crashaw: *The Name of Jesus.* (17th cent.)

O God, Who didst appoint Thine only-begotten Son to be the Savior of mankind, and didst bid that He should be called Jesus; mercifully grant that we, who venerate His holy name on earth, may also enjoy the vision of Him in heaven.

Roman Missal, Feast of the Holy Name of Jesus (Sunday after New Year's), Collect. (18th cent.)

O Jesus, Jesus! dearest Lord!
  Forgive me if I say
For very love Thy sacred name
  A thousand times a day.

F. Faber: *Jesus My God and My All.*
(19th cent.)

Nap

Post-prandial sleep, ye mortals, put
  afar,
In any month whose name includes
  an R.
Post-prandial sleep's alone salubrious,
In months whose names their ending
  have in US.

School of Salerno, Code of Health. (i.e.
the summer months) (11th cent.)

Let noontide sleep be brief, or none at
  all;
Else stupor, headache, fever, rheums
  will fall
On him who yields to noontide's
  drowzy call.

School of Salerno, Code of Health. (11th
cent.)

Napoleon

Grand, gloomy, and peculiar, he sat
upon the throne a sceptered hermit,
wrapped in the solitude of his own
originality.

Charles Phillips: *The Character of
Napoleon.* (19th cent.)

Narrow-Mindedness

You haven't any business to say that anybody is narrow-minded just because he
doesn't agree with your conception of
the universe.

R. H. Benson: *The Conventionalists.*
(20th cent.)

Every man is dangerous who only cares
for one thing.

G. K. Chesterton: *Napoleon of Notting
Hill.* (20th cent.)

Nation

A nation (*populus*) is a multitude of
men joined together in society by an
agreement of law, and harmonious fellowship.

St. Isidore: *Etymologies,* 9, 4. (7th cent.)

Better one suffer, than a nation grieve.

Dryden: *Absalom and Achitophel.* (17th
cent.)

Every living nation has an idea given it
by Providence to realize, and whose realization is its special work, mission, or
destiny.

Orestes Brownson: *The American
Republic.* (19th cent.)

The development of a nation is strangely
paralleled by the development of an individual. There comes in both a period
of adolescence, of the stirring of new
powers, of an increase of strength, of
the dawn of new ideals, of the awakening of self-consciousness.

R. H. Benson: *By What Authority.* (20th
cent.)

The Nation is a community, not a society. The Nation is one of the most important, perhaps the most complex and
complete community engendered by civilized life. . . . It is something ethico-
social: a human community based on the
fact of birth and lineage, yet with all
the moral connotations of those terms:
birth to the life of reason and the activities of civilization, lineage in familial
traditions, social and juridical formation,
cultural heritage, common conceptions
and manners, historical recollections,
sufferings, claims, hopes, prejudices, and
resentments. An ethnic community, generally speaking, can be defined as a community of patterns of feeling rooted in
the physical soil of the origin of the
group as well as in the moral soil of history; it becomes a nation when this fac-
tual situation enters the sphere of self-
awareness, in other words when the
ethnic group becomes conscious of the

fact that it constitutes a community of patterns of feeling . . . and possesses its own unity and individuality, its own will to endure in existence.

J. Maritain: *Man and the State*. (20th cent.)

Nationality

Nationality exists, and has nothing in the world to do with race. Nationality is a thing like a church or a secret society; it is a product of the human soul and will; it is a spiritual product.

G. K. Chesterton: *Heretics*. (20th cent.)

Rome conquered nations, but Ireland has conquered races. The Norman has gone there and become Irish, the Scotchman has gone there and become Irish, the Spaniard has gone there and become Irish, even the bitter soldier of Cromwell has gone there and become Irish. Ireland, which did not even exist politically, has been stronger than all the races that existed scientifically. . . . Ireland, unrecognized and oppressed, has easily absorbed races, as such trifles are easily absorbed. She has easily disposed of physical science, as such superstitions are easily disposed of. Nationality in its weakness has been stronger than ethnology in its strength. Five triumphant races have been absorbed, have been defeated by a defeated nationality.

G. K. Chesterton: *Heretics*. (20th cent.)

Nativity of the Blessed Virgin

We beseech Thee, O Lord, grant to Thy servants the gift of Thy heavenly grace; as the child-bearing of the blessed Virgin was the beginning of salvation, so may the joyful festival of her nativity bring us an increase of peace.

Roman Missal, Collect for the Feast. (Sept. 8) (Gregorian, ca. 7th cent.)

Thou art blessed and venerable, O Virgin Mary, who with purity unstained wast found to be the Mother of our Savior. Virgin Mother of God, He

Whom the whole world was unable to contain enclosed Himself in thy womb, being made flesh.

Roman Missal, Gradual for the Feast. (ca. 7th cent.)

May the humanity of Thine only-begotten Son be our help, O Lord; may He, Who by being born of a Virgin did not diminish but hallowed the integrity of His Mother, deliver us on this festival of her nativity from our sins.

Roman Missal, Secret at Mass. (Gregorian, ca. 7th cent.)

Thy birth, O Virgin Mother of God, was a message of joy to the whole world, for out of thee rose the Sun of righteousness, even Christ our God, Who hath taken away the curse and brought a blessing, confounded death, and given unto us everlasting life.

Roman Breviary, Antiphon at Second Vespers. (Liber Respons., ca. 7th cent.)

Beyond all doubt the Mother of the Lord also was holy before birth; nor is holy Church at all in error in accounting the day of her nativity holy, and celebrating it each year with solemn and thankful joy.

St. Bernard: *Letters*. (12th cent.)

Sweet Morn! thou Parent of the Sun!
  And Daughter of the same!
What joy and gladness, through thy
  birth,
This day to mortals came!

Clothed in the Sun I see thee stand,
  The moon beneath thy feet;
The stars above thy sacred head
  A radiant coronet.

Jean Santeuil: *Aurora quae solem paris*. (Tr. Caswall) (18th cent.)

Natural

That is natural to each thing which is caused by Him from Whom is all mode, number, and order in nature.

St. Augustine: *Contra Faustum*. (5th cent.)

Nature

The whole realm of nature is his who has God for his portion.

> St. Ambrose: *Explanation of Psalm 118,* 8, 5. (4th cent.)

Let us imitate nature: conformity with nature provides us with a formula of discipline and a standard of rectitude.

> St. Ambrose: *On the Duties of the Clergy,* 1, 84. (4th cent.)

Nature is nothing else than that which a thing is understood to be in its own kind.

> St. Augustine: *De Moribus Manichaeorum,* 2, 2. (4th cent.)

All nature is good.

> St. Augustine: *On Continence.* (5th cent.)

Nature is the principle of movement inherent in and not accidentally attached to bodies.

> Boethius: *Contra Eutychen,* 1. (Quoting Aristotle) (6th cent.)

Nature is the specific difference that gives form to anything. (Natura est unam quamque rem informans specifica differentia.)

> Boethius: *Contra Eutychen,* 1. (6th cent.)

What is natural cannot wholly perish.

> St. Thomas Aquinas: *Summa Theologica,* 2-2, 126, 1. (13th cent.)

Nature, as well as God, works effects contrary to particular natures. . . . No part of nature, however, acts against the universal order of nature.

> St. Thomas Aquinas: *Disputations concerning Potency,* 6, 1. (13th cent.)

Nature is the art of God eternal.

> Dante: *De monarchia.* (14th cent.)

We may by our endeavors raise nature somewhat above her frailty, but never triumph over her till death.

> John Habington: *Life and Reign of Edward IV.* (17th cent.)

We must not measure nature by ourselves, but by itself.

> Pascal: *Pensées.* (17th cent.)

Nature has some perfections, to show that she is the image of God; and some defects, to show that she is only His image.

> Pascal: *Pensées.* (17th cent.)

Nature, like liberty, is but restrained
By the same laws which first herself ordained.

> Pope: *An Essay on Criticism,* 1. (18th cent.)

Nature is not inanimate; its daily toil is intelligent; its works are duties.

> Card. Newman: *Parochial and Plain Sermons,* 2. (19th cent.)

Nature loves, as lady bright,
  In gayest guise to shine,
All forms of grace, all tints of light,
  Fringe her robe divine.

> Card. Newman: *My Lady Nature and her Daughters.* (19th cent.)

Nature 'mid the spheres holds sway,
Ladies rule where hearts obey.

> Card. Newman: *My Lady Nature and her Daughters.* (19th cent.)

What makes this earth so wondrous fair?
The will of God inhabits there,
For at creation each thing did
The simple thing that it was bid.

.   .   .   .   .   .

It's only in the heart of man
That God's frustrated in his plan.
Man's little wisdom, yours and mine,
Alone upsets the great design—
The workings of the human heart,
So scornful of the wild thyme's art.

If trees and flowers were wise as men
Oh! nature would be ugly then!

Enid Dinnis: *A Ditty of Creation*. (20th cent.)

It is His garment; and to them
Who touch in faith its upmost hem
He, turning, says again, I see
That virtue hath gone out of me.

J. B. Tabb: *Nature*. (19th cent.)

Indeed nature is at best merely a female name we give to providence, when we are not treating it very seriously; a piece of feminist mythology. There is a sort of fireside fairytale, more fitted for the hearth than for the altar; and in that what is called nature can be a sort of fairy godmother. But there can only be fairy godmothers because there are godmothers, and there can only be godmothers because there is a God.

G. K. Chesterton: *Autobiography*. (20th cent.)

This is the gateway to the promised
land.
Here, in God's own cathedral, wherein
stand
Vast mountain altars, incalculably old,
Lit by the kindling tapers of the dawn,
With pomp unrivalled goes forever on,
Majestic, nature's solemn ritual
Of changing seasons, summer, winter,
fall,
In vestments emerald, white, or bur-
nished gold.

Sister M. Angelita: *The Canyon*. (20th cent.)

Nature and Art

Nature varies and imitates; art imitates and varies.

Pascal: *Pensées*. (17th cent.)

Neatness

Be neat, but be on your guard against affectation, vanity and singularity.

St. Francis de Sales: *Introduction to the Devout Life*, 3, 25. (17th cent.)

Be quite clean and neat, but not particular and dainty.

St. Francis de Sales: *Letters to Persons Living in the World*, 6, 14. (17th cent.)

Necessity

What necessity proffers necessity cheapens.

Tertullian: *To His Wife*, 1, 3. (3rd cent.)

You make a virtue of necessity.

St. Jerome: *Apologeticum*, 3. (5th cent.)

Necessity has no law. (Legem non habet necessitas.)

St. Augustine: *Soliloquium*, 2. (5th cent.)

It is necessity and not pleasure that compels him.

Dante: *Inferno, Canto 12*. (12th cent.)

That shall be, shall be.

John Heywood: *Proverbs*, 2, 1. (16th cent.)

Neck

Pluck up thy spirits, man, and be not afraid to do thine office; my neck is very short: take heed therefore thou strike not awry, for saving of thine honesty.

St. Thomas More, to the executioner. (Roper, *Life*) (16th cent.)

They wove the lotus band to deck
And fan with pensile wreath each neck.

Thomas Moore: *Odes of Anacreon*. (19th cent.)

Needle

To go look for a needle in a meadow.

St. Thomas More: *Works*, 838. (16th cent.)

Neighbor

The love of our neighbor hath its bounds in each man's love of himself.

St. Augustine: *On Lying*. (4th cent.)

Not one will change his neighbor with himself.

> Pope: *An Essay on Man*, 2. (18th cent.)

Neighborliness

> They're neighborly in Ireland,
>   and if they've little store,
> They'd share it with a neighbor
>   and there's still the open door.
> For him that turns the poor away
>   may turn away unfed
> The very Son of God Himself as
>   He begs for bread.

> Katharine T. Hinkson: *The Philosopher.*
> (20th cent.)

Nerves

> Silence is the best treatment for over-strained nerves.

> R. H. Benson: *An Average Man.* (20th cent.)

Neutrality

> I can pray for opposite parties, and for opposite religions, with great sincerity.

> Pope: *Letter to William Trumbull.* (18th cent.)

Newman, John Henry Cardinal

> Mr. Newman has stood for several years before the public as a man of rare gifts and acquirements; he was at the head of a very influential party in the Anglican communion, and appears to have enjoyed a personal esteem, and exerted a personal influence, which seldom fall to the lot of any but the master minds of their age or country. We may well, then, look upon his conversion with more than ordinary gratitude to the great Head of the Church, and as an event of more than ordinary significance.

> Orestes Brownson: *Newman's Development of Christian Doctrine.* (*Works,* 14, 1ff) (1846)

> The history of our land will hereafter record the name of John Henry New-man among the greatest of our people, as a confessor for the faith, a great teacher of men, a preacher of justice, of piety, and of compassion. May we all follow him in his life, and may our end be painless and peaceful like his.

> Cardinal Manning: *Eulogy of Cardinal Newman.* (The Oratory, South Kensington, Aug. 20, 1890)

> The freedom of the living dead;
> The service of a living pain:
> He chose between them, bowed his head
>   And counted sorrow gain.
>
>   .   .   .   .
>
> Ah, sweetest soul of all! Whose voice
> Hailed morning, and the sun's increase:
> We of the restless night rejoice,
>   We also, at thy peace.

> Lionel Johnson: *In Falmouth Harbour*, 2. (1887)

> As St. Philip [Neri], by his love for those who leant upon him, and by his personal character, drew all men to him for guidance and advice, winning respect and esteem from Jews and infidels as well as members of the Church, so did Newman, by the power of his personality, find himself the center of influence among vast numbers, priests and laymen, non-Catholics as well as Catholics. The simple priest was by the popular voice called the apostle of Rome; the English Oratorian was, as a representative critic has expressed it, canonized at his death by the voice of the English people.

> Wilfrid Ward: *Witnesses to the Unseen.* (19th cent.)

> Whatever else is right, the theory that Newman went over to Rome to find peace and an end of argument, is quite unquestionably wrong. He had far more quarrels after he had gone over to Rome. But, though he had far more quarrels, he had far fewer compromises: and he was of that temper which is tortured more by compromise than by quarrel. He was a man at once of abnormal energy and abnormal sensibility: nobody

without that combination could have written the *Apologia*. If he sometimes seemed to skin his enemies alive, it was because he himself lacked a skin. In this sense his *Apologia* is a triumph far beyond the ephemeral charge on which it was founded; in this sense he does indeed (to use his own expression) vanquish not his accuser but his judges.

> G. K. Chesterton: *The Victorian Age in Literature.* (20th cent.)

Both Newman and Gladstone often seemed, in their mildness and restraint, a long time coming to the point, but the point was deadly sharp.

> G. K. Chesterton: *A Handful of Authors.* (20th cent.)

News

In order that you may always give good news, entertain others as if you came from the other world, for if you talk to them in the language of the parts where they live, it will be no great news to them.

> St. Francis de Sales: *Letters to Persons in Religion*, 4, 35. (17th cent.)

Nice

As nice as a nun's hen.

> John Heywood: *Proverbs*, 2, 1. (16th cent.)

Night

Maker of all things! God most High! Great ruler of the starry sky! Who, robing day with beauteous light, Hast clothed in soft repose the night.

> St. Ambrose: *Deus Creator omnium.* (Tr. J. Chambers) (4th cent.)

Blest Lord, Creator of the glowing light,
    At Whose behest the hours successive move,
    The sun has set: black darkness broods above:

Christ! light Thy faithful through the coming night.

> Prudentius: *Inventor rutili dux bone luminis.* (Tr. Pope and Davis) (From Cathemerinon, 4th cent.)

And the best of all ways
To lengthen our days
Is to steal a few hours from the night, my dear.

> Thomas Moore: *The Young May Moon.* (19th cent.)

The night is dark, and I am far from home.

> Card. Newman: *Lead, Kindly Light.* (19th cent.)

The star-usurping battlements of night.

> George Sterling: *In Extremis.* (20th cent.)

Most holy night, that still dost keep
The keys of all the doors of sleep,
To me when my tired eyelids close
    Give thou repose.

> Hilaire Belloc: *The Night.* (20th cent.)

Nightingale

There's a bower of roses by Bendemeer's stream,
And the nightingale sings round it all day long.

> Thomas Moore: *Lalla Rookh: The Veiled Prophet of Khorassan.* (19th cent.)

Nihilism

I am very fond of revolutionists, but not very fond of nihilists. For nihilists, as their name implies, have nothing to revolt about.

> G. K. Chesterton: *The Thing.* (20th cent.)

Nobility

True nobility means to despise empty nobility. True nobility means to be a servant of Christ.

> Erasmus: *Enchiridion.* (16th cent.)

What can ennoble sots, or slaves, or cowards?
Alas, not all the blood of all the Howards.

> Pope: *An Essay on Man,* 4. (18th cent.)

Non-Denominationalism

It is a good deal more fashionable, and considered a great deal more 'spiritual,' to stand outside creeds and churches than within them.

> R. H. Benson: *Christ in the Church.* (20th cent.)

None (Ninth Hour)

And at the ninth hour also let prayer be protracted and praise be sung that is like to the souls of the righteous glorifying God Who lieth not, Who remembered His saints and sent to them His Word to enlighten them. For in that hour Christ was pierced in His side with a lance and shed forth blood and water and brought the rest of the time that day in light to evening. Whereby He made the dawn of another day at the beginning of His sleep, fulfilling the type of His resurrection.

> St. Hippolytus: *The Apostolic Tradition,* 36. (3rd cent.)

O strength and stay upholding all creation,
Who ever dost thyself unmoved abide,
Yet day by day the light in due gradation
From hour to hour through all its changes guide.

> Roman Breviary, Hymn *Rerum Deus tenax vigor* for None. (Tr. J. Ellerton and F. Hort.) (Possibly by St. Ambrose, 4th cent.)

Thou that at the ninth hour didst in Thy flesh taste death for us; mortify the lusts of our flesh, O Christ our God, and save us.

> Byzantine Horologion, Troparion at None. (ca. 6th to 8th cent.)

Nonsense

To die for faction is a common evil,
But to be hang'd for nonsense is the devil.

> Dryden: *Absalom and Achitophel.* (17th cent.)

Normality

In thought there is something pleasant in a wholesome normality acquiesced in, not because of a lack of personal originality; but because it has been deliberately discovered to be the highest art of living.

> R. H. Benson: *The Sentimentalists.* (20th cent.)

It is a question whether it is better to be normal and imperceptive and conventional, or to be abnormal and intuitive and passionate.

> R. H. Benson: *The Conventionalists.* (20th cent.)

Nose

Hold their noses to grindstone.

> John Heywood: *Proverbs,* 1, 5. (16th cent.)

Your heart is in your nose.

> John Heywood: *Proverbs,* 1, 11. (16th cent.)

Your nose betrays what porridge you love.

> Thomas Lodge: *Rosalynde.* (16th cent.)

If the nose of Cleopatra had been a little shorter the whole face of the world would have been changed.

> Pascal: *Pensées.* (17th cent.)

In cleaning the nose, the rules of cleanliness and decency should be exactly followed, always turning a little to one side, and making use of a handkerchief.

> St. John Baptist de la Salle: *The Rules of Christian Manners and Civility,* 1. (17th cent.)

Nothing

O mighty Nothing! unto thee,
Nothing, we owe all things that be.
God spake once when He all things
    made,
He sav'd all when He *Nothing* said.
The world was made of nothing then;
'Tis made by *Nothing* now again.

> Richard Crashaw: *And He Answered
> Them Nothing*. (17th cent.)

Blessed be he who expects nothing, for
he shall never be disappointed.

> Pope: *Letter to John Gay*. (18th cent.)

Notoriety

Notoriety, or, as it may be called, newspaper fame, is to the many what style
and fashion, to use the language of the
world, are to those who are within or
belong to the higher circles; it becomes
to them a sort of idol, worshipped for
its own sake, and without any reference
to the shape in which it comes before
them.

> Card. Newman: *Discourses to Mixed
> Congregations*. (19th cent.)

Novel

People put the matter wrong when they
say that the novel is a study of human nature. Human nature is a thing that even
men can understand. Human nature is
born of the pain of a woman; human
nature plays at peep-bo when it is two
and at cricket when it is twelve; human
nature earns its living and desires the
other sex and dies. What the novel deals
with is what women have to deal with;
the differentiations, the twists and turns
of this eternal river.

> G. K. Chesterton: *The Victorian Age in
> Literature*. (20th cent.)

A good novelist always has a philosophy; but a good novel is never a book
of philosophy.

> G. K. Chesterton: *A Handful of Authors*.
> (20th cent.)

Novelist

Novelists are generally great liars.

> St. John Baptist de la Salle: *The Rules of
> Christian Manners and Civility*, 2. (17th
> cent.)

They find life crude and leave it raw.

> Oscar Wilde: *The Decay of Lying*. (19th
> cent.)

Novelty

Novelty is often error for those who are
unprepared for it, from the refraction
with which it enters into their conceptions.

> Card. Newman. (Ward, II, 476) (19th
> cent.)

The one thing that the public dislikes is
novelty.

> Oscar Wilde: *The Soul of Man under
> Socialism*. (19th cent.)

Novice

Let us not be troubled at finding ourselves novices in the exercise of virtues,
for in the monastery of a devout life
everyone considers himself always a
novice.

> St. Francis de Sales: *Treatise on the Love
> of God*, 9, 7. (17th cent.)

While yet a young probationer,
    And candidate of heav'n.

> Dryden: *Ode to the Memory of Mrs.
> Killigrew*. (17th cent.)

Who knows what days I answer for
    today?
Giving the bud I give the flower. I
    bow
This yet unfaded and a faded brow;
Bending these knees and feeble knees,
    I pray.

> Alice Meynell: *The Young Neophyte*.
> (19th cent.)

Nun

They are the flower of the Church, the beauty and ornament of spiritual grace, a subject of joy, a perfect and unsullied homage of praise and honor, the image of God corresponding to the sanctity of the Lord, the most illustrious portion of Christ's flock. In them the glorious fecundy of our mother, the Church, finds expression and she rejoices; the more the number of virgins increases, the greater is this mother's joy.

St. Cyprian: *On the Dress of Virgins,* 3. (3rd cent.)

A virgin ought not only to be so, but also to be perceived and believed to be so: no one on seeing a [consecrated] virgin should be in any doubt as to whether she is one.

St. Cyprian: *On the Dress of Virgins,* 5. (3rd cent.)

Hold fast, O virgins! hold fast what you have begun to be; hold fast what you shall be. A great reward awaits you, a great recompense of virtue, the immense advantage of chastity.

St. Cyprian: *On the Dress of Virgins,* 22. (3rd cent.)

What we are to be, you have already commenced to be. You already possess in this world the glory of the resurrection; you pass through the world without suffering its contagion. In preserving virgin chastity, you are the equals of the angels of God.

St. Cyprian: *On the Dress of Virgins,* 22. (3rd cent.)

A virgin does not have an imposition of hands, for personal choice alone is that which makes a virgin.

St. Hippolytus: *The Apostolic Tradition,* 13. (Nuns are blessed or consecrated, not ordained.) (3rd cent.)

You yourself, O Christ, are my all. For You I keep myself chaste, and holding aloft my shining lamp I run to meet You, my Spouse.

St. Methodius of Olympus: *The Banquet or On Virginity,* 11, 2. (ante 311)

Therefore, since most embrace virginity while still young and unformed in understanding, this before anything else should be their employment, to search out a fitting guide and master of this way, lest, in their present ignorance, they should wander from the direct route, and strike out new paths of their own in trackless wilds.

St. Gregory of Nyssa: *On Virginity,* 23. (4th cent.)

She is a virgin who is married to God.

St. Ambrose: *De Virginibus,* 1, 8. (4th cent.)

You have heard, parents, that a virgin is a gift of God, the oblation of parents, the priesthood of chastity. The virgin is a mother's victim, by whose daily sacrifice divine anger is appeased.

St. Ambrose: *De Virginibus,* 7, 32. (4th cent.)

Jesu, the virgins' crown, do Thou
Accept us as in prayer we bow;
Born of that Virgin, whom alone
The Mother and the Maid we own.

Amongst the lilies Thou dost feed,
By virgin choirs accompanied—
With glory decked, the spotless brides
Whose bridal gifts Thy love provides.

They, whereso'er Thy footsteps bend,
With hymns and praises still attend:
In blessed troops they follow Thee,
With dance, and song, and melody.

Roman Breviary, Feasts of Holy Virgins, Hymn *Jesu corona virginum.* (Tr. J. Neale) (Attr. to St. Ambrose, 4th cent.)

We do not praise in virgins the fact that they are virgins, but that they are virgins dedicated to God by holy chastity.

St. Augustine: *On Holy Virginity,* 11. (5th cent.)

Love with all your hearts Him Who is the most beautiful of the sons of men: you are free, your hearts are not fettered by conjugal bonds. . . . If then you would owe your husbands great love, how great is that love you owe Him because of Whom you have willed to have no husbands? Let Him Who was fastened to the cross be securely fastened to your hearts.

St. Augustine: *On Holy Virginity,* 54. (5th cent.)

Wherever they have to go, let there not be less than three; and the sister who requires to go somewhere is not to go along with those she chooses herself, but with those the superior orders.

St. Augustine: *Letter 211.* (His Rule) (5th cent.)

What you admire in the flesh of Mary, do in the inner chamber of your soul. He who believes with the heart unto justice conceives Christ. He who *confesses by mouth unto salvation* (cf. Rom. 10, 10) gives birth to Christ. In this manner may your spirits be blessed with both bounteous fecundity and persevering virginity.

St. Augustine: *Sermons,* 191. (5th cent.)

. . . O God the gracious dweller in chaste bodies, and God the lover of holy souls . . . look down, O Lord, on these Thy servants, who, placing the vow of their continence in Thy hand, offer their devotion to Thee from Whom these vows first derived . . . this gift also has flowed to certain minds from the fount of Thy bounty that, while no obstacles may lessen the honor of marriage and the nuptial blessing continues to grace the state of holy matrimony, still there are certain lofty souls who wish to avoid the carnal bond of husband and wife in matrimony, long for the sacrament, and would not imitate what is done in marriage but love that which is signified by the institution. Holy virginity has recognized its Author, and desirous of imitating the purity of the angels, has vowed

itself to the bridal-chamber and marriage bed of Him who is the Spouse of perpetual virginity, even as He is the Son of perpetual virginity. Grant Thy protection to those who implore Thy aid and desire to be confirmed by the consecration of Thy blessing. . . .

Roman Pontifical, Blessing and Consecration of Holy Virgins, Prayer *Deus Castorum Corporum.* (Leonine, 5th to 6th cent.)

Son of a Virgin, Maker of Thy Mother,
Thou, Rod and Blossom from a stem unstained,
Now while a virgin fair of fame we honor,
  Hear our devotion!

Roman Breviary, Feasts of Holy Virgins, Hymn *Virginis proles, opifexque Matris.* (Tr. L. Housman) (Author unknown, 8th cent.)

The kingdom of this earth and all worldly trappings I have valued as worthless for love of our Lord Jesus Christ, Whom I have seen, loved, believed and preferred above all else.

Roman Pontifical, Blessing and Consecration of Holy Virgins, Antiphon Sung as Candidates Range themselves around the Bishop for Consecration. (ca. 10th cent. ?)

Receive the sacred veil, that it may be known you have despised the world and submitted yourself truly and humbly, with your entire heart, to Jesus Christ, as His bride forever; may He defend you from all evil, and lead you to life eternal.

Roman Pontifical, Blessing and Consecration of Holy Virgins, Formula for the Imposition of the Veil. (ca. 10th cent. ?)

There was also a nonne, a prioresse,
That of her smiling was full simple and coy.

Chaucer: *Canterbury Tales: Prologue.* (14th cent.)

How happy is the blameless vestal's lot
The world forgetting, by the world
forgot.

> Pope: *Eloisa to Abelard.* (18th cent.)

Quiet form of silent nun,
What has given you to my inward eyes?
What has marked you, unknown one,
In the throng of centuries
That mine ears do listen through?
This old master's melody
That expresses you;
This admired simplicity,
Tender, with a serious wit;

And two words the name of it,
'Soeur Monique.'

> Alice Meynell: *Soeur Monique: a Rondeau by Couperin.* (19th cent.)

Nurse

And always keep a-hold of nurse
For fear of finding something worse.

> H. Belloc: *Jim.* (20th cent.)

Nut

For oh, 'twas nuts to the father of lies.

> Thomas Moore: *A Case of Libel.* (19th cent.)

O

Oath

The abolishing of oaths is more useful than any fasting; it is more profitable than any austerity.

> St. John Chrysostom: *Homilies.* (4th cent.)

Not to swear, lest perchance one forswear oneself.

> St. Benedict: *Rule,* 4. (One of his 'tools of good works') (6th cent.)

One must not swear, neither by Creator nor by creature, unless it be with truth, necessity, and reverence.

> St. Ignatius of Loyola: *Spiritual Exercises.* (16th cent.)

An oath, that is, the invocation of the name of God in witness to the truth, may be made only in truth, in judgment, and in justice.

> Code of Canon Law, Canon 1316, 1. (20th cent.)

Obedience

Let us consider those who are enrolled under our rulers [i.e. the Roman Emperors], how well ordered, and how readily, how obediently they carry out commands. Not all are prefects, or tribunes, or centurions, or in charge of bands of fifty, and so forth; but each one in his own rank carries out the commands issued by the emperor and the officers.

> Pope St. Clement I: *Letter to the Corinthians,* 37, 2-4. (1st cent.)

The head without the feet is nothing, and so also the feet without the head are nothing. The smallest members of our body are necessary and useful to the whole body. But all conspire together and unite in a single obedience, so that the whole body may be saved. Therefore, let our whole body be saved in Christ Jesus, and let each be subject to his neighbor, according to the position which grace bestowed on each.

> Pope St. Clement I: *Letter to the Corinthians*, 37, 5-38, 2. (1st cent.)

In a state it is lawful for the reigning monarch to command something which none had ever commanded before him and he himself had never commanded before; and obedience in this event is not against the fellowship of the state: indeed disobedience would be against the fellowship, for it is the general agreement of all societies of men to obey their kings.

> St. Augustine: *Confessions*, 3, 8. (5th cent.)

Let the superior be obeyed like a mother, with all due honor, so that you offend not God through offending her; much more should you obey the priest who has charge of you all.

> St. Augustine: *Letter 211* (His Rule). (5th cent.)

To obey in all things the commands of the abbot, even though he himself (which God forbid) should act otherwise: remembering the Lord's precept: *What they say, do ye; but what they do, de ye not* (Matth. 23, 3).

> St. Benedict: *Rule*, 4. (One of his 'tools of good works') (6th cent.)

The first degree of humility is obedience without delay.

> St. Benedict: *Rule*, 5. (6th cent.)

From these it appears clearly that those who command things evil are not to be obeyed, especially when in yielding to wrong commands, in which you appear to obey man, you show yourself plainly disobedient to God, Who has forbidden everything that is evil. For it is altogether unreasonable to profess yourself obedient when you know that you are violating obedience due to the superior on account of the inferior, that is, to the Divine on account of the human.

> St. Bernard: *Letters*. (12th cent.)

Faith does not detract from the order of justice, but rather establishes it more firmly. The order of justice requires that subordinates should be obedient to their superiors; otherwise civilization could not be kept going. Therefore, the faithful are not excused from the obligation of obedience to their rulers.

> St. Thomas Aquinas: *Summa Theologica*, 2-2, 104, 6. (13th cent.)

It is a very great thing to stand in obedience, to live under a superior, and not to be at our own disposal.

> Thomas a Kempis: *The Imitation of Christ*, 1, 9. (15th cent.)

No man securely commands but he who has learned to obey.

> Thomas a Kempis: *The Imitation of Christ*, 1, 20. (15th cent.)

They that are bound must obey.

> John Heywood: *Proverbs*, 2, 5. (16th cent.)

Our Lord makes much of this submission, and with perfect justice; for it is by means of it that we make Him master of the freewill He has given us. We practise it sometimes quickly and completely, thereby winning an immediate self-conquest; at other times it is only after a thousand struggles that we succeed, constantly thinking that the decisions made by superiors in our case are nothing but folly. But finally, being drilled and practised by this painful exercise, we conform to what is commanded—painfully or not, we do it. Upon this our Lord, having helped us all the time, now seeing that we submit our will and our reason for His sake, gives us the grace to become masters of both.

> St. Teresa of Jesus: *Book of Foundations*, 5. (16th cent.)

When God puts inspirations into a heart, the first he gives is obedience.

> St. Francis de Sales: *Treatise on the Love of God*, 8, 13. (17th cent.)

The devil does not fear austerity but holy obedience.

> St. Francis de Sales: *Letters to Persons in Religion,* 3, 8. (17th cent.)

In proportion to our affection and esteem for the maker of the law, is the exactness of our observance of it.

> St. Francis de Sales: *Spiritual Conferences,* 13. (17th cent.)

Blessed are the obedient, for God will never suffer them to go astray.

> St. Francis de Sales: *Introduction to the Devout Life,* 3, 11. (17th cent.)

Impassioned thoughts, high aspirations, sublime imaginings, have no strength in them. They can no more make a man obey consistently, than they can move mountains.

> Card. Newman: *Parochial and Plain Sermons,* 1. (19th cent.)

As obedience to conscience, even supposing conscience ill-informed, tends to the improvement of our moral nature, and ultimately of our knowledge, so obedience to our ecclesiastical superior may subserve our growth in illumination and sanctity, even though he should command what is extreme or inexpedient, or teach what is external to his legitimate province.

> Card. Newman: *Development of Christian Doctrine.* (19th cent.)

I never have resisted, nor can resist, the voice of a lawful superior speaking in his own province.

> Card. Newman: *Letter to Healy Thompson.* (1859)

Obedience is not servitude of man to man, but submission to the will of God, Who governs through the medium of men.

> Pope Leo XIII: *Immortale Dei.* (Nov. 1, 1885)

Obedience to the will of God—or even what is merely believed to be the will of God—is actually more meritorious not less, when it is unaccompanied by emotional consolations and sensible fervor.

> R. H. Benson: *The Confessions of a Convert.* (20th cent.)

The virtue of obedience is an exalted virtue, eminently reasonable; it is not in the least servile or blind, but requires on the contrary the greatest freedom of spirit and the strongest discernment.

> J. Maritain: *The Things that are not Caesar's.* (20th cent.)

Oblivion

Where high the tombs of royal Egypt heave,
The vulture shadows with arrested wings
The indecipherable boasts of kings,
Till Arab children hear their mother's cry
And leave in mockery their toy—they leave
The skull of Pharaoh staring at the sky.

> George Sterling: *Three Sonnets on Oblivion.* (20th cent.)

Obscenity

Do not use obscene language, or let your eye wander, for from all these come adulteries.

> Teaching of the Twelve Apostles, 3. (2nd cent.)

Obscurity

Now, in our opinion no author should be blamed for obscurity, nor should any pains be grudged in the effort to understand him, provided that he has done his best to be intelligible. Difficult thoughts are quite distinct from difficult words. Difficulty of thought is the very heart of poetry.

> Alice Meynell: *Robert Browning.* (In *The Pen,* 1880.) (19th cent.)

Obstinacy

Never be obstinate, especially in things of no moment.

St. Teresa of Jesus: *Maxims*. (16th cent.)

There is no obstinacy like religious obstinacy, for the spiritual man encourages himself in his wrong course by a conviction that he is following divine guidance.

R. H. Benson: *Christ in the Church*. (20th cent.)

O'Connell, Daniel

Daniel O'Connell was not a bigot in religion—he was a liberal Catholic. Do not misunderstand me—my idea of a liberal Catholic is one who is sincere and faithful in the profession of his faith, but who recognizes in every other human being the same right that he claims for himself; but in modern times a liberal Catholic has come to be understood as a man who makes no distinctions between one creed and another. O'Connell was none of these; he believed in his religion, and from the period of his unfortunate duel to the close of his life he combined the dedication of a practical Catholic in his private moral life with the highest duties of a politician and a statesman, and that is what scarcely any other public man that I have read of has ever accomplished before.

Archbishop Hughes: *Lecture on Daniel O'Connell*. (1856)

Offender

And love the offender, yet detest the offence.

Pope: *Eloisa to Abelard*. (18th cent.)

Offering

Whatever thou doest, offer it up to God, and pray it may be for His honor and glory.

St. Teresa of Jesus: *Maxims*. (16th cent.)

Offer everything to the Father everlasting, in union with the merits of His Son Jesus Christ.

St. Teresa of Jesus: *Maxims*. (16th cent.)

Office

The papist only has his writ of ease.
No gainful office gives him the pretence
To grind the subject or defraud the prince.
Wrong conscience, or no conscience may deserve
To thrive, but ours alone is privileg'd to sterve.

Dryden: *The Hind and the Panther*, 3. (With ref. to the Test Act, 1673, debarring Catholics from office holding.) (17th cent.)

On-Looker

In worldly works degrees are three,
Makers, doers, and lookers-on:
The lookers on have liberty,
Both the others to judge upon.
Wherefore in all, as men are bent,
See all, say nought, hold thee content.

Jasper Heywood: *Looke or You Leape*. (16th cent.)

Open-Mindedness

I think he thought that the object of opening the mind is simply opening the mind. Whereas I am incurably convinced that the object of opening the mind, as of opening the mouth, is to shut it again on something solid.

G. K. Chesterton: *Autobiography*. (Of H. G. Wells) (20th cent.)

Opinion

Opinion is holding something to be provisionally true which you do not know to be false.

St. Bernard: *On Consideration*, 5, 3. (12th cent.)

Never come forward to give thine own opinion about anything unless asked to do so, or charity requires it.

St. Teresa of Jesus: *Maxims.* (16th cent.)

We must never so form our opinions as not to be ready, if necessary, willingly to give them up.

St. Francis de Sales: *Spiritual Conferences,* 14. (17th cent.)

An intellectual man, as the world now conceives of him, is one who is full of "views" on all subjects of philosophy, on all matters of the day. It is almost thought a disgrace not to have a view at a moment's notice on any question from the personal Advent to the cholera or mesmerism.

Card. Newman: *Idea of a University, Pref.* (19th cent.)

Opinion, Public

Rulers who prefer popular opinion to truth have as much power as robbers in the desert.

St. Justin Martyr: *First Apology,* 12. (2nd cent.)

To stifle the opinions of citizens, to reduce them forcibly to silence, is, in the eyes of every Christian, an outrage on the natural rights of man, a violation of the order of the world as established by God.

Pope Pius XII: *Allocution to International Convention of Catholic Press.* (Feb. 18, 1950)

Opportunism

A man who is perpetually thinking whether this race or that race is strong, of whether this cause or that cause is promising, is the man who will never believe in anything long enough to make it succeed. The opportunist politician is like a man who should abandon billiards because he was beaten at billiards, and abandon golf because he was beaten at golf. There is nothing which is so weak for working purposes as this enormous importance attached to immediate victory. There is nothing that fails like success.

G. K. Chesterton: *Heretics.* (20th cent.)

Opportunity

He who will not when he may, may not when he will. (Quia qui non vult cum potest, non utique poterit cum volet.)

John of Salisbury: *Policraticus,* 8, 17. (12th cent.)

He that will not when he may,
When he would he shall have nay.

John Heywood: *Proverbs,* 1, 3. (16th cent.)

When the sun shineth make hay.

John Heywood: *Proverbs,* 1, 3. (16th cent.)

When the iron is hot, strike.

John Heywood: *Proverbs,* 1, 3. (16th cent.)

The tide tarrieth no man.

John Heywood: *Proverbs,* 1, 3. (16th cent.)

That one will not another will.

John Heywood: *Proverbs,* 1, 3. (16th cent.)

Time wears all his locks before,
    Take thou hold upon his forehead;
When he flies, he turns no more,
    And behind his scalp is naked.
Works adjourned have many stays,
Long demurs breed new delays.

Bl. Robert Southwell: *Loss in Delay.* (16th cent.)

Hoist up sail while gale doth last,
    Tide and wind stay no man's pleasure;
Seek not time when time is past,
    Sober speed is wisdom's leisure.

Bl. Robert Southwell: *Loss in Delay.* (16th cent.)

Heav'n has to all allotted, soon or late,
Some lucky revolution of their fate;
Whose motions, if we watch and guide
with skill,
(For human good depends on human
will),
Our fortune rolls as from a smooth
descent
And, from the first impression, takes
the bent;
But, if unseiz'd, she glides away like
wind;
And leaves repenting folly far behind.

> Dryden: *Absalom and Achitophel.* (17th
> cent.)

Thou strong seducer, opportunity!

> Dryden: *The Conquest of Granada,* 1, 4,
> 3. (17th cent.)

Opposite

Nature refuseth to have contraries joined.
(Natura respuit ut contraria quaeque
jungantur.)

> Boethius: *De Consolatione Philosophiae,*
> 2, 6. (6th cent.)

Opposition

For opposition makes a hero great.

> Dryden. (17th cent.)

I have had all my life-time to fight
against powerful odds, but I have never
seen any way to do, but to keep on
fighting. No man ever yet stood up for
truth and justice, God and heaven, but
he had to complain of opposition from
all quarters.

> Orestes Brownson: *Letter to
> Count de Montalembert.* (1851)

Optimism

I wot well clerks will say, as them leste
By arguments, that all is for the best.

leste—pleases

> Chaucer: *The Frankeleyns Tale.* (14th
> cent.)

One truth is clear: whatever is, is right.

> Pope: *An Essay on Man,* 1. (18th cent.)

Nothing contributes more to cheerfulness than the habit of looking at the
good side of things. The good side is
God's side of them.

> Archb. Ullathorne: *Humility and
> Patience.* (19th cent.)

For you who believe in God and the
Catholic Church, and one or two other
things, a convinced optimism is the
only reasonable philosophy.

> R. H. Benson: *Dedication to the
> Sentimentalists.* (20th cent.)

The noble temptation to see too much
in everything.

> G. K. Chesterton: *Robert Browning,* 1.
> (20th cent.)

Popular optimism—the kind which is
hawked about like shoe-strings—is the
apotheosis of superficiality. The obvious
is its support, the inane is its ornament.

> Agnes Repplier: *Points of Friction.* (20th
> cent.)

Orange

If I were yonder orange-tree
   And thou the blossom blooming
   there,
I would not yield a breath of thee
   To scent the most imploring air!

> Thomas Moore: *If I Were Yonder Wave.*
> (19th cent.)

Orange-trees
Whose fruit and blossoms in the breeze
Were wantoning together free,
Like age at play with infancy.

> Thomas Moore: *Lalla Rookh: Paradise and
> the Peri.* (19th cent.)

Orator

There are those who speak well, and do
not write well. It is because the place,
the audience, warms them, and elicits

from their mind more than they find in it without this warmth.

> Pascal: *Pensées,* 9. (17th cent.)

Orchard

> Good is an orchard, the saint saith,
> To meditate on life and death.
>
> Katharine T. Hinkson: *Of an Orchard.* (20th cent.)

Order

Order is an arrangement of components equal and unequal, assigning the proper place to each.

> St. Augustine: *The City of God,* 19, 13. (5th cent.)

Order is heaven's first law.

> Pope: *An Essay on Man,* 4. (18th cent.)

Orders, Holy

He cannot have the ordination of the Church who does not hold the unity of the Church.

> St. Cyprian: *Letters,* 51, 8. (With regard to the consecration of bishops.) (3rd cent.)

For which reason you must diligently observe and keep the practice delivered from divine tradition and apostolic observance, which is also maintained among us and practically in every province; that for the proper celebration of ordinations [i.e. consecration of bishops] all the neighboring bishops of the same province should assemble with that people for which a prelate is ordained. And the bishop should be chosen in the presence of the people, who have most fully known the life of each one, and have looked into the doings of each one as respects his habitual conduct.

> St. Cyprian: *Letters,* 77, 5. (3rd cent.)

For the presbyter has authority only for this one thing, to receive. But he has no authority to give holy orders. Wherefore he does not ordain a man to orders, but by laying on hands at the ordination of a presbyter he only blesses [lit. seals], while the bishop ordains (*cheirotonein*).

> St. Hippolytus: *The Apostolic Tradition,* 9. (3rd cent.)

Let a bishop be ordained by two or three bishops, a presbyter by one bishop, as also a deacon, and the rest of the clergy.

> Ecclesiastical Canons of the Holy Apostles, 1-2. (4th cent.)

Those men are received by the Church as its rulers whom the Holy Ghost prepares: so that in the people of God's adoption, the whole body of which is priestly and royal, it is not the prerogative of earthly origin which obtains the unction, but the condescension of divine grace which creates the bishop.

> Pope St. Leo I: *Sermons,* 3, 1. (5th cent.)

Once upon a time there was no difference of style between bishops and priests. Bishops were those who superintended, as Augustine notes (*De Civitate Dei,* 19, 19), while priests, or presbyters in Greek, meant elders. . . . Nevertheless a real distinction of rank existed between them. . . . The difference was afterwards expressed in name and style, and the denial of the difference is reckoned a heretical tenet by Augustine (*De Haeresibus,* 53).

> St. Thomas Aquinas: *Summa Theologica,* 2-2, 184, 6. (13th cent.)

Such is its dignity that the sacrament of the eucharist is not consecrated save in the person of Christ. Whoever acts for another must have power conferred by the other. By baptism Christ grants the power of receiving this sacrament, by holy orders the power of consecrating it, for ordination places a man in the ranks of those to whom Christ said, *Do this for a commemoration of me* (Luke 22, 19).

> St. Thomas Aquinas: *Summa Theologica,* 3, 82, 1. (13th cent.)

If any one saith that there is not in the New Testament a visible and external priesthood; or that there is not any power of consecrating and offering the true Body and Blood of the Lord, and of forgiving and retaining sins; but only an office and bare ministry of preaching the gospel; or that those who do not preach are not priests at all; let him be anathema.

> Council of Trent, Session 23, Canon 1.
> (July 15, 1563)

If any one saith that besides the priesthood there are not in the Catholic Church other orders, both greater and minor, by which as by certain steps advance is made unto the priesthood; let him be anathema.

> Council of Trent, Session 23, Canon 2.
> (July 15, 1563)

If any one saith that order or sacred ordination is not truly and properly a sacrament instituted by Christ the Lord; or that it is a kind of human figment devised by men unskilled in ecclesiastical matters; or that it is only a kind of rite for choosing ministers of the word of God and of the sacraments; let him be anathema.

> Council of Trent, Session 23, Canon 3.
> (July 15, 1563)

If any one saith that by sacred ordination the Holy Ghost is not given; and that vainly therefore do the bishops say, *Receive ye the Holy Ghost;* or that a character is not imprinted by that ordination; or that he who has once been a priest can again become a layman; let him be anathema.

> Council of Trent, Session 23, Canon 4.
> (July 15, 1563)

If any one saith that in the Catholic Church there is not a hierarchy by divine ordination instituted, consisting of bishops, priests, and ministers; let him be anathema.

> Council of Trent, Session 23, Canon 6.
> (July 15, 1563)

If any one saith that bishops are not superior to priests; or that they have not the power of confirming and ordaining; or that the power which they possess is common to them and to priests; or that orders, conferred by them, without the consent or vocation of the people or of the secular power are invalid; or that those who have neither been rightly ordained, nor sent by ecclesiastical and canonical power but come from elsewhere, are lawful ministers of the word and of the sacraments; let him be anathema.

> Council of Trent, Session 23, Canon 7.
> (July 15, 1563)

Strictly adhering in this matter to the decrees of the pontiffs our predecessors, and confirming them most fully, and, as it were, renewing them by our own authority, of our own motion and certain knowledge we pronounce and declare that ordinations carried out according to the Anglican rite have been and are absolutely null and utterly void.

> Pope Leo XIII: *Apostolicae Curae.* (Sept. 13, 1896)

By the institution of Christ the sacrament of orders distinguishes the clergy from the laity in the Church for the government of the faithful and for the ministry of divine worship.

> Code of Canon Law, Canon 948. (20th cent.)

The ordinary minister of holy ordination is a consecrated bishop; the extraordinary minister is a priest who, though lacking episcopal consecration, has received the power of conferring certain orders either by law or by special permission from the Apostolic See.

> Code of Canon Law, Canon 951. (20th cent.)

A bishop who is to consecrate another bishop must be assisted in the consecration by two other bishops, unless a dispensation has been expressly obtained from the Apostolic See.

> Code of Canon Law, Canon 954. (20th cent.)

It is a grave wrong to force anyone, in any way or for any reason, to embrace the clerical state or to prevent anyone who is canonically qualified from embracing the clerical state.

> Code of Canon Law, Canon 971. (20th cent.)

For anyone to be licitly ordained, the following are required: reception of holy confirmation; moral habits suitable to the order to be received; canonical age; proper training; reception of inferior orders; observance of the proper intervals between them; canonical title, if it is a question of major orders.

> Code of Canon Law, Canon 974. (20th cent.)

[Barred from receiving holy orders are the following, called] irregular by defect (*irregulares ex defectu*): those who are illegitimate . . . unless they have been legitimatized or professed solemn vows; those having physical defects who could not perform the ministry of the altar, either safely because of weakness or decently because of some deformity . . . epileptics or insane persons . . . those who have been twice married . . . those who have been branded with infamy by the law; a judge who has imposed the death sentence; those who have exercised the office of public executioner as well as their immediate and voluntary assistants in carrying out the death sentence.

> Code of Canon Law, Canon 984. (20th cent.)

See also Acolyte; Bishop; Clergy; Deacon; Episcopate; Hierarchy; Pastor; Pope; Priest; Priesthood; Sacrament

Organ

> But oh! what art can teach
> What human voice can reach

> The sacred organ's praise?
> Notes inspiring holy love,
> Notes that wing their heavenly ways
> To mend the choirs above.

> Dryden: *A Song for St. Cecilia's Day.* (17th cent.)

Origen

It is better to err with Origen than to be right with others.

> St. Vincent of Lerins: *Commonitoria,* 17 (cited as the saying of those who exalted Origen unduly). (5th cent.)

When he writes well, no one writes better; when he writes badly, no one writes worse.

> Cassiodorus: *Institutiones,* 1, 1, 8. (6th cent.)

Orthodoxy

> A song, a song of gladness!
>   A song of thanks and praise!
> The horn of our salvation
>   Hath God vouchsaf'd to raise!
> A monarch true and faithful,
>   And glorious in her might,
> To champion Christ's own quarrel,
>   And orthodoxy's right!

> Byzantine Triodion, Orthodox Sunday (First of Lent), Canon. (Tr. Neale) (St. Theodore the Studite, 9th cent.)

A man must be orthodox upon most things, or he will never even have time to preach his own heresy.

> G. K. Chesterton: *George Bernard Shaw.* (20th cent.)

This is the thrilling romance of orthodoxy. People have fallen into a foolish habit of speaking of orthodoxy as something heavy, humdrum, and safe. There never was anything so perilous or so exciting as orthodoxy. It was sanity: and to be sane is more dramatic than to be mad. It was the equilibrium of a man behind madly rushing horses, seeming to stoop this way and that, yet in every attitude having the grace of statuary and the accuracy of arithmetic. The Church in its early days went fierce and fast with any warhorse; yet it is utterly unhistoric to say that she merely went mad along one idea, like a vulgar fanaticism. She swerved to left and right, so exactly as to avoid enormous obstacles. . . . To have fallen into any one of the fads from Gnosticism to Christian Science would indeed have been obvious and tame. But to have avoided them all has been one whirling adventure; and in my vision the heavenly chariot flies thundering through the ages, the dull heresies sprawling and prostrate, the wild truth reeling but erect.

> G. K. Chesterton: *Orthodoxy.* (20th cent.)

Oh, he thwacked them hard and he
    thwacked them long
  On each and all occasions,
Till they bellowed in chorus loud and
    strong
  Their orthodox persuasions.

> H. Belloc: *Song of the Pelagian Heresy.*
> (20th cent.)

There is, properly speaking, no liberalism in Catholic theology. What does exist, even among the most orthodox of theologians, is a certain amount of difference of opinion, of a minor character. There are strict and less strict statements of the same doctrines. The point to remember, however, is that they are always the same doctrines. To be a Catholic at all a man must be orthodox.

> Theodore Maynard: *Orestes Brownson.*
> (20th cent.)

Oven

No man will another in the oven seek
Except that himself have been there
  before.

> John Heywood: *Proverbs,* 2, 7. (16th cent.)

Over-Eating

Nothing is so unfitting for a Christian as surfeiting, according to our Lord's words: *Take heed lest your hearts be overcharged with surfeiting and drunkenness* (Luke 21, 34).

> St. Benedict: *Rule,* 39. (6th cent.)

Overconfidence

In this life, which is rightly called one continuing trial, no man ought to be oversure that though he is capable of becoming better instead of worse, he is not actually becoming worse instead of better.

> St. Augustine: *Confessions,* 10, 32. (5th cent.)

Oxford

Oxford's a place where wit can never sterve.

> Dryden: *The University of Oxford,*
> *Prologue.* (17th cent.)

Oxford to him a dearer name shall be,
Than his own mother university.
Thebes did his green unknowing youth
  engage,
He chooses Athens in his riper age.

> Dryden: *The University of Oxford,*
> *Prologue.* (17th cent.)

P

Pacifism

Pacifism is a positive faith; it is the faith of those who believe that men are made for peace and that peace is not only natural to men but is that state of affairs in which alone men can fulfil themselves or (what is only another way of saying the same thing) properly serve their fellow-men and love and praise God.

Eric Gill: *It All Goes Together.* (20th cent.)

Paganism

A pagan is a person who can do what hardly any person for the last two thousand years could do: a person who can take nature naturally.

G. K. Chesterton: *The Victorian Age in Literature.* (20th cent.)

Since Christianity broke the heart of the world and mended it, one cannot really be a pagan; one can only be an anti-Christian.

G. K. Chesterton: *A Handful of Authors.* (20th cent.)

Meredith was not a pantheist; he was a pagan. The difference consists in this tremendous fact; that a pagan always has sacraments, while a pantheist has none.

G. K. Chesterton: *A Handful of Authors.* (20th cent.)

A pagan is not an atheist: he is religious in so far as he does his best to placate the gods. But his religious observances are inspired not by a passion for righteousness, but by a practical desire to obtain solid benefits from the gods.

Arnold Lunn: *Now I See.* (20th cent.)

Pain

The more a thing perfected is, the more
It feels bliss, and in pain the sharper sighs.

Dante: *Inferno, Canto 6.* (Tr. L. Binyon) (14th cent.)

Pain and sorrow are the almost necessary medicines of the impetuosity of nature. Without these, men though men, are like spoilt children; they act as if they considered everything must give way to their own wishes and conveniences.

Card. Newman: *Parochial and Plain Sermons,* 5. (19th cent.)

O, pain, love's mystery,
Close next of kin
To joy and heart's delight,
Low pleasure's opposite,
Choice food of sanctity
And medicine of sin,
Angel, whom even they that will pursue
Pleasure with hell's whole gust
Find that they must
Perversely woo,
My lips, thy live coal touching, speak thee true.

Coventry Patmore: *Pain.* (19th cent.)

Nothing begins, and nothing ends,
That is not paid with moan;
For we are born in other's pain,
And perish in our own.

F. Thompson: *Daisy.* (19th cent.)

Painting

Painting can do for the illiterate what writing does for those who can read.

Pope St. Gregory I. (6th cent.)

His colors laid so thick on every place,
As only shew'd the paint, but hid the
  face.

Dryden: *To Sir Robert Howard.* (17th
cent.)

But poets are confin'd in narrower
  space,
To speak the language of their native
  place;
The painter widely stretches his command;
Thy pencil speaks the tongue of ev'ry
  land.

Dryden: *To Sir Godfrey Kneller.* (17th
cent.)

You only paint to live, not live to paint.

Dryden: *To Sir Godfrey Kneller.* (17th
cent.)

Religious paintings are the catechism of
the ignorant.

Card. Gibbons: *The Faith of Our Fathers,*
15. (19th cent.)

Palm Sunday

Almighty and everlasting God, Who
didst will that our Savior should take
upon Him our flesh and suffer death
upon the Cross, that all mankind might
follow the example of His great humility; mercifully grant that we may
follow the example of His patience, and
also be made partakers of His resurrection.

Roman Missal, Collect. (Gregorian, ca.
6th cent.)

Bless, we beseech Thee, O Lord, these
branches of palm or olive; and grant
that what Thy people this day bodily
perform for Thy honor, they may perfect spiritually with the greatest of devotion, by gaining a victory over the
enemy, and ardently loving every work
of mercy.

Roman Missal, Prayer for the Blessing of
Palms. (One of several.) (ca. 9th cent.)

The Hebrew children bearing branches
of olives, went forth to meet the Lord,
crying out and saying, Hosanna in the
highest! (cf. Matth. 21, 9)

Roman Missal, Antiphon sung during
Distribution of Palms. (ca. 9th cent.)

All glory, laud and honor
To Thee, Redeemer, King,
To Whom the lips of children
Made sweet hosannas ring.

. . . . . .

The people of the Hebrews
With psalms before Thee went;
Our praise and prayer and anthems
Before Thee we present.

Roman Missal, Hymn *Gloria laus et honor
tibi sit Rex Christe Redemptor* sung during
Procession. (Tr. J. Neale) (Theodulf,
Bishop of Orleans, 9th cent.)

Pantheism

All are but parts of one stupendous
  whole,
Whose body nature is, and God the
  soul.

Pope: *An Essay on Man,* 1. (18th cent.)

If any one shall say that the substance
and essence of God and of all things is
one and the same; let him be anathema.

Vatican Council, Session 3, Canon 3. (Apr.
24, 1870)

If any one shall say that finite things,
both corporeal and spiritual, or at least
spiritual, have emanated from the divine
substance; or that the divine essence by
the manifestation and evolution of itself
becomes all things; or lastly that God is
universal or indefinite being, which by
determining itself constitutes the universality of things, distinct according to
genera, species and individuals; let him
be anathema.

Vatican Council, Session 3, Canon 4. (Apr.
24, 1870)

If any one shall not confess that the
world and all things which are contained in it, both spiritual and material,

have been in their whole substances produced by God out of nothing; or shall say that God created, not by his will free from all necessity, but by a necessity equal to the necessity whereby he loves himself; or shall deny that the world was made for the glory of God; let him be anathema.

> Vatican Council, Session 3, Canon 4. (Apr. 24, 1870)

The fact is that pure mysticism is but pantheism; and that pantheism is, on principle and incurably, a non-moral, a supra-moral and non-personalist position, within which there is really no place for a distinct and definite God, for sin, for contrition, for the sense of our being creatures, and for adoration.

> Baron von Hügel: *The Life of Prayer.* (20th cent.)

Whatever the merits or demerits of the pantheistic sentiment of melting into nature of 'oneness' (I think they call it) with seas and skies, it is not and it never has been a popular sentiment. It has been the feeling of a few learned aesthetes and secluded naturalists. Popular poetry is all against pantheism and quite removed from immanence. . . . Ballads and carols do not go to the tune of 'One with the Essence of the Boundless World.' Ballads and carols go to the tune of 'Over the Hills and Far Away'; the sense that life leads by a strange and special path to something sacred and separate.

> G. K. Chesterton: *Daily News.* (20th cent.)

Papacy

See Pope

Papalism

I should like a new papal bull every morning with my *Times* at breakfast.

> Saying of William G. Ward. (Ward, *Newman*, II, 213) (19th cent.)

Paradise

Not in mine eyes alone is Paradise.

> Dante: *Paradiso, Canto 18.* (14th cent.)

She is an all-pure soul who cannot love the paradise of God, but only the God of paradise.

> St. Francis de Sales: *Treatise on the Love of God,* 10, 5. (17th cent.)

> One morning a Peri at the gate
> Of Eden stood disconsolate.

> Thomas Moore: *Lalla Rookh: Paradise and the Peri.* (19th cent.)

> O Paradise! O Paradise!
> Who doth not crave for rest?
> Who would not seek the happy land
> Where they that love are blest?

> F. Faber: *Paradise.* (19th cent.)

> There is no expeditious road
> To pack and label men for God,
> And save them by the barrel-load.
> Some may perchance, with strange surprise,
> Have blundered into Paradise.

> F. Thompson: *A Judgment in Heaven: Epilogue.* (19th cent.)

> If Paradise be yet more fair
> Than earth in tender April guise,
> Poor soul, how shall thy frailty bear
> God's great and ultimate surprise?

> Sister M. Benvenuta: *Easter Thought.* (20th cent.)

See also Eternal Life

Paradox

After all, what was a paradox but a statement of the obvious so as to make it sound untrue?

> R. A. Knox: *A Spiritual Aeneid.* (20th cent.)

Pardon

See Forgiveness; Sin, Remission of

Parent

O God, Who has commanded us to honor our father and our mother, have mercy on the souls of my father and mother, and forgive them their sins; grant that I may see them in the joy of eternal glory.

> Roman Missal, Prayer for Deceased Parents. (ca. 11th cent.)

Parnell, Charles Stewart

> Not his, to hail the dawn:
> His but the herald's part.
> Be ours to see withdrawn
> Night from our mother's heart.
>
> Lionel Johnson: *Parnell.* (19th cent.)

Parting

Take it not to heart when thou art forsaken by a friend; knowing that one time or other we all must part.

> Thomas a Kempis: *The Imitation of Christ,* 2, 9. (15th cent.)

And soon, too soon, we part with pain, To sail o'er silent seas again.

> Thomas Moore: *The Meeting of the Ships.* (19th cent.)

> Adieu! such is the word for us,
>   'Tis more than word—'tis prayer;
> They do not part, who do part thus,
>   For God is everywhere.
>
> Abram Ryan: *Parting.* (19th cent.)

> They are so sad to say: no poem tells
> The agony of hearts that dwells
> In lone and last farewells.
>
> Abram Ryan: *Farewells!* (19th cent.)

> With all my will, but much against my
>   heart,
>   We two now part.
>   My very dear,
> Our solace is the sad road lies so clear.
>   It needs no art,
>   With faint, averted feet
>   And many a tear,

In our opposed paths to persevere. Go thou to east, I west.

> Coventry Patmore: *A Farewell.* (19th cent.)

Parting's well-paid with soon again to meet.

> Coventry Patmore: *The Azalea.* (19th cent.)

> And they that part too early
>   May meet again too late.
>
> F. Thompson: *Absence.* (19th cent.)

> She went her unremembering way,
>   She went and left in me
> The pang of all the partings gone,
>   And partings yet to be.
>
> F. Thompson: *Daisy.* (19th cent.)

Party

Party-spirit at best is but the madness of many for the gain of a few.

> Pope: *Letter to Martha Blount.* (18th cent.)

A *Catholic* political party ordained by its very constitution (as a political party) to temporal things and differentiated by religion (as a *Catholic* party) runs a twofold risk; in the first place of compromising the welfare of Catholicism and of individual souls in the affairs of the world, of degrading the things of the spirit and of reducing them to the level of the temporal and of the particular; of confounding religion with politics and of the conduct of a particular party; and in the second place of failing at certain times in the duty it owes to the temporal interests it is formed to serve, by hesitating to involve the glory of a great name in risks and enterprises of a purely terrestrial order which are often (even to the point of hazard) essential for the protection of those interests.

> J. Maritain: *Freedom in the Modern World.* (20th cent.)

Taken separately indeed the interests of Catholicism (*secundum hominem dico*) would seem to be not that all Catholics should be grouped as far as possible in a single party (however powerful it might appear) but rather that there should be a majority of Catholics in all the decent political parties—assuming always that modern states will continue to allow the normal rule of plurality of political parties and political bodies within their territory.

> J. Maritain: *Freedom in the Modern World.* (20th cent.)

Passion

A movement of the soul contrary to nature in the sense of disobedience to reason, that is what passions are.

> Clement of Alexandria: *Stromateis,* 2, 13. (2nd cent.)

True quietness of heart is won by resisting our passions, not by obeying them.

> Thomas a Kempis: *The Imitation of Christ,* 3, 25. (15th cent.)

No envy, no revenge, no rage, no pride,
No lust, no rapine, should his courses
  guide:
Though all the world conspires to do
  him grace,
Yet he is little, and extremely base,
If in his heart these vices take their
  seat;
(No pow'r can make the slave of pas-
  sions great.)

> Sir John Beaumont: *Of True Greatness, to my Lord Marquis of Buckingham.* (17th cent.)

Any sudden gust of passion, as an ecstasy of love in an unexpected meeting, cannot better be expressed than in a word and a sigh, breaking one another. Nature is dumb on such occasions; and to make her speak would be to represent her unlike herself.

> Dryden: *Of Dramatic Poesy.* (17th cent.)

Passion makes us cowards grow,
What made us brave before.

> Dryden: *An Evening's Love,* 2. (17th cent.)

What reason weaves, by passion is undone.

> Pope: *An Essay on Man,* 2. (18th cent.)

And you, brave Cobham! to the latest
  breath,
Shall feel your ruling passion strong
  in death.

> Pope: *Moral Essays,* 1. (18th cent.)

Madness lies in every passion—in human love and music and idealism—in fact, in everything that is not what is called normal, in everything as soon as it looms larger than other interests.

> R. H. Benson: *The Conventionalists.* (20th cent.)

Passion of Our Lord

O God, Whom to love above all is righteousness, multiply in us the gifts of Thine ineffable grace; and since in the death of Thy Son Thou hast given us the hope for those things in which we believe, grant us through His resurrection to attain the end for which we long.

> Roman Missal, Collect for Palm Sunday. (Gelasian, 5th to 7th cent.)

O God, Who for us hast willed Thy Son to undergo the ignominy of the Cross, that Thou mightest drive away from us the power of the enemy; grant to us Thy servants to attain the grace of resurrection.

> Roman Missal, Collect for Wednesday in Holy Week. (Gregorian, 6th to 8th cent.)

Thirty years among us dwelling,
His appointed time fulfilled,
Born for this, He meets his Passion,
For that this He freely willed:

On the Cross the Lamb is lifted,
Where His life-blood shall be spilled.

Roman Breviary, Passion Sunday and
Invention and Exaltation of the Cross,
hymn *Lustra sex qui jam peregit.* (From
hymn *Pange lingua glorioso*) (Tr. Neale)
(Fortunatus, 6th cent.)

We adore Thy most pure image, O
Christ our God, entreating forgiveness
for our sins; for Thou wast pleased of
Thy own will to ascend the Cross in Thy
flesh, that Thou mightest deliver from
the slavery of the enemy those whom
Thou didst create. Therefore we exclaim
to Thee with thanks, Thou hast filled all
things with joy, O our Savior, Thou that
camest to save the world.

Byzantine Horologion, Troparion at Sext.
(ca. 6th to 8th cent.)

Lord, Thy death upon the tree
Brings uplifting thought to me,
Calm of mind and holy fire,
Love of God and pure desire.

O to bear in memory
All Thy grief and obloquy,
Holy Christ, Thy thorny wreath,
Spear and nails and crucial death!

All these blessed wounds of Thine,
Witness of Thy love divine,
Cruel scourging and distress,
O the mortal bitterness!

St. Bonaventure: *In Passione Domini.* (Tr.
D. Donahoe) (13th cent.)

Oh, what shame and desolation,
Working out the world's salvation,
    Deigns the King of heaven to bear!
See Him bowed with sorrows endless,
Hungry, thirsty, poor and friendless,
    Even to the Cross repair.

St. Bonaventure: *Quam despectus quam
dejectus.* (Tr. P. Worsley) (13th cent.)

Mary Mother, come and see:
Thy Son is nailèd on a tree.

His body is wrappèd all in woe,
Hand and foot; He may not go;

Thy Son, Lady, that thou lovest so,
    Naked is nailèd upon a tree.

Anonymous: *Mary Mother, Come and See.*
(15th cent.)

O Christ, my Lord, which for my sins
    didst hang upon a tree,
Grant that Thy grace in me poor wretch
    may still ingrafted be.

Grant that Thy naked hanging there,
    may kill in me all pride
And care of wealth, sith Thou didst
    then in such poor state abide.

Bl. Philip Howard: *Poem.* (Guiney, 227)
(16th cent.)

O cruel death, O wounds most deep,
O guiltless blood, O bitter pain;
Alas who can forbear to weep
To see God's Son so cruelly slain?

. . . .

O Saviour sweet, hear my request,
Make me partner of Thy pain;
In solace let me never rest,
Sith Thou in sorrow dost remain.

And if it be Thy glorious will,
That I shall taste of this Thy cup,
Lo, here Thy pleasure to fulfil,
Myself I wholly offer up.

Bl. Swithin Wells: *To Christ Crucified.*
(Guiney, 174) (16th cent.)

Jesus! all hail, Who for my sin
Didst die, and by that death didst win
    Eternal life for me;
Send me Thy grace, good Lord! that I
Unto the world and flesh may die,
    And hide my life with Thee.

Jesus! from out Thine open side
Thou hast the thirsty world supplied
    With endless streams of love;
Come ye who would your sickness
    quell,
Draw freely from that sacred well,
    Its heavenly virtues prove.

Anonymous: *Jesu, nostros ob reatus.*
(From *Paradisus Animae* of Horstius.)
(Tr. F. Faber) (ca. 17th cent.)

I beseech Thee, O most sweet Lord Jesus Christ, that Thy passion be to me a source of strength whereby I may be fortified, protected, and defended; that Thy wounds may be to me food and drink wherewith I may be fed, filled, and satisfied; that the sprinkling of Thy blood may be to me the washing away of all my sins; that Thy death may be to me unfailing life; that Thy Cross may be to me unending glory. In these be my refreshment, rejoicing, health, and the desire of my heart, who liveth and reigneth for ever and ever. Amen.

Roman Missal, Prayer *Obsecro Te Dulcissime Domine Jesu.* (Modern)

Look down upon me, good and gentle Jesus, while before Thy face I humbly kneel, and with burning soul pray and beseech Thee to fix deep in my heart lively sentiments of faith, hope, and charity, true contrition for my sins, and a firm purpose of amendment; while I contemplate with great love and tender pity Thy five wounds, pondering over them within me, and calling to mind the words which David the prophet said of Thee, my Jesus: They have pierced my hands and my feet; they have numbered all my bones.

Roman Missal, Prayer *En Ego O Bone et Dulcissime Jesu.* (Modern)

O'erwhelmed in depths of woe,
 Upon the Tree of scorn
Hangs the Redeemer of mankind,
 With racking anguish torn.

. . . .

Come! fall before His Cross,
 Who shed for us His Blood;
Who died the Victim of pure love,
 To make us sons of God.

Jesu! all praise to Thee,
 Our joy and endless rest!
Be Thou our guide while pilgrims here,
 Our crown amid the blest.

Anonymous: *Saevo Dolorum Turbine.* (Tr. E. Caswall) (19th cent.)

Jesu! as though Thyself were here,
I draw in trembling sorrow near;
And, hanging o'er Thy form divine,
Kneel down to kiss these wounds of
 Thine.

Hail, awful brow! hail, thorny wreath!
Hail, countenance now pale in death!
Whose glance so late but brightly
 blazed,
That angels trembled as they gazed.

. . . .

Oh, by those sacred hands and feet
For me so mangled! I entreat,
My Jesu, turn me not away,
But let me here for ever stay.

Anonymous: *Jesu dulcis amor meus.* (Tr. E. Caswall) (19th cent.)

Behold the Man! Who wore
 A crown of thorns for me:
And in His sacred Person bore
 Our sins upon the tree:
Our sins upon the tree,
 Thus full of honor made,
Through Him Whose love beyond de-
 gree
 Our ransom paid.

M. Bridges: *Ecce Homo.* (19th cent.)

O Calvary! Calvary!
 Mountain of love,
Lo, here is the Victim
 Who came from above:
One, One with the Father
 Enthroned in the sky:
Yet now He had rather
 In agony die.

See! see as His altar
 The Cross is displayed,
And He, the great sacrifice,
 On it is laid:
The Sovereign of nature
 Submits to His Sire,
And God for the creature
 Can bear to expire.

M. Bridges: *Calvary.* (19th cent.)

The winepress, the winepress—
 The voice is from God:

The floor of His fury
  Is now to be trod;
The sins of all nations
  Are full to o'erflowing;
And the blast of His anger
  From heaven is blowing.

. . . . . .

The Victim, the Victim,
  Behold He is here;
He looks on the tempest,
  Its clouds disappear:
In the red robe of scourging
  Triumphant He stands,
And blots out the sentence
  With blood on His hands.

M. Bridges: *The Purple Robe.* (19th cent.)

Man of sorrows, wrapt in grief,
Bow Thine ear to our relief:
Thou for us the path hast trod
Of the dreadful wrath of God;
Thou the cup of fire hast drained
Till its light alone remained.
Lamb of God! we look to Thee:
Hear our mournful litany.

M. Bridges: *Man of Sorrows.* (19th cent.)

O come and mourn with me awhile;
  See, Mary calls us to her side;
O come and let us mourn with her,—
  Jesus, our Love, is crucified!

. . . . . .

Come, take thy stand beneath the Cross,
  And let the Blood from out that side
Fall gently on thee drop by drop;—
  Jesus, our Love, is crucified!

. . . . . .

O love of God! O sin of man!
  In this dread act your strength is
    tried;
And victory remains with love,
  For he, our Love, is crucified.

F. Faber: *Jesus Crucified.* (19th cent.)

O soul of Jesus, sick to death!
Thy blood and prayer together plead;
My sins have bowed Thee to the
  ground,
As the storm bows the feeble reed.

F. Faber: *The Agony.* (19th cent.)

There was silence in the heavens
  When the Son of man was led
From the garden to the judgment;
  Sudden silence, strange, and dread!
All along the empyreal coasts
On their knees the immortal hosts
Watched, with sad and wondering eyes,
That tremendous sacrifice.

Aubrey de Vere: *Stanzas.* (19th cent.)

O Captain of the wars, whence won Ye
  so great scars?
  In what fight did Ye smite, and what
    manner was the foe?
Was it on a day of rout they compassed
  Thee about,
  Or gat Ye these adornings when Ye
    wrought their overthrow?

'Twas on a day of rout they girded Me
  about,
  They wounded all my brow, and they
    smote Me through the side:
My hand held no sword when I met
  their armèd horde,
  And the conqueror fell down, and
    the Conquered bruised His pride.

F. Thompson: *The Veteran of Heaven.*
(19th cent.)

At one small house of Nazareth;
  And Golgotha
Saw Breath to breathlessness resign its
  breath,
And Life do homage for its crown to
  death.

F. Thompson: *Sister Songs.* (19th cent.)

Where Life was slain and Truth was
  slandered
On that one holier hill than Rome.

G. K. Chesterton: *To F. C. in Memoriam
Palestine.* (20th cent.)

See also Atonement; Cross; Good Friday; Hell, Descent into; Holy Saturday; Holy Thursday; Jesus Christ; Redemption

Past

To improve the future needs human care and application; to break with the past needs divine power.

> St. Ambrose: *Explanation of Psalm 118, 22, 3.* (4th cent.)

Raked up in th' ashes, and covered again.

> John Heywood: *Proverbs, 2, 2.* (16th cent.)

For hope shall brighten days to come,
And memory gild the past!

> Thomas Moore: *Song.* (19th cent.)

O there are voices of the past,
  Links of a broken chain,
Wings that can bear me back to times
  Which cannot come again;
Yet God forbid that I should lose
  The echoes that remain!

> Adelaide Procter: *Voices of the Past.* (19th cent.)

For all the past, read true, is prophecy.

> F. Thompson: *An Ode after Easter.* (19th cent.)

We live in time, and the past must always be the most momentous part of it.

> Lionel Johnson: *Post Liminium.* (19th cent.)

All day I watch the stretch of burning
  sand;
  All night I brood beneath the golden
    stars;
Amid the silence of a desolate land,
  No touch of bitterness my reverie
    mars.
Built by the proudest of a kingly line,
  Over my head the centuries fly fast;
The secrets of the mighty dead are
    mine;
  I hold the key of a forgotten past.

> Agnes Repplier: *Le Repos En Egypte: The Sphinx.* (19th cent.)

Oh! leave the past to bury its own dead.

> W. S. Blunt: *To One Who Would Make a Confession.* (19th cent.)

Even if that were possible, it's foolish merely to regret things that are passed. There is always a best to be got out of them.

> R. H. Benson: *The Coward.* (20th cent.)

We lose nothing of what is good and sweet in the past.

> R. H. Benson: *The History of Richard Raynal Solitary.* (20th cent.)

The past is a dead king who makes no peers, and rewards his living courtiers with no ribbons or stars: he has not a penny in his pocket.

> John Ayscough: *Levia Pondera.* (20th cent.)

The truth is that all feeble spirits naturally live in the future, because it is featureless; it is a soft job; you can make it what you like. The next age is blank, and I can paint it freshly with my favorite color. It requires real courage to face the past, because the past is full of facts which cannot be got over; of men certainly wiser than we and of things done which we could not do.

> G. K. Chesterton: *George Bernard Shaw.* (20th cent.)

Pastor

The government of souls is the art of arts.

> Pope St. Gregory I: *Pastoral Care, 1, 1.* (6th cent.)

For no one does more harm in the Church than he, who having the title or rank of holiness, acts evilly. No one presumes to take to task such a delinquent, and the offence, serving as an example, has far-reaching consequences, when the sinner is honored out of respect paid to his rank.

> Pope St. Gregory I: *Pastoral Care, 1, 2.* (6th cent.)

The conduct of a prelate should so far surpass the conduct of the people, as the life of a pastor sets him apart from his flock. For one who is so regarded that the people are called his flock, must carefully consider how necessary it is for him to maintain a life of rectitude. It is necessary, therefore, that he should be pure in thought, exemplary in conduct, discreet in keeping silence, profitable in speech, in sympathy a near neighbor to everyone, in contemplation exalted above all others, a humble companion to those who lead good lives, erect in his zeal for righteousness against the vice of sinners. He must not be remiss in his care for the inner life by preoccupation with the external; nor must he in his solicitude for what is internal, fail to give attention to the external.

Pope St. Gregory I: *Pastoral Care*, 2, 1. (6th cent.)

It is evidently necessary that they who devote themselves to the office of preaching should never depart from the occupation of sacred reading . . . when subjects consult the pastor in any spiritual matter, it is most disgraceful if he should then seek to learn at a time when he ought to solve their problem.

Pope St. Gregory I: *Pastoral Care*, 2, 11. (6th cent.)

For almighty God perfects in great measure the minds of those who rule, but leaves them partially imperfect, for this reason, that when they are resplendent with extraordinary attainments, they may grieve with disgust for their imperfections, and, least of all, exalt themselves for great things, when they have to labor and struggle against very small matters.

Pope St. Gregory I: *Pastoral Care*, 4. (6th cent.)

Pastors today need one to hold them up
  On this side and on that, and one to
    lead
  (So heavy are they), and one behind
    to prop.

Dante: *Paradiso, Canto 21*. (Tr. Binyon) (14th cent.)

Happy the priest who loves his pastor's lot and lives wholly in it, fulfilling day by day the slight and despised acts of charity to all who need his care, and laying up in heaven unconsciously the gold dust of a humble life, looking only for his eternal reward.

Card. Manning: *The Eternal Priesthood.* (19th cent.)

A pastor is a priest or moral person upon whom a parish is conferred in his own right with the care of souls to be exercised under the authority of the ordinary of the place.

Code of Canon Law, Canon 451, 1. (20th cent.)

Pastorate

Supreme rank is, therefore, well-administered, when the superior lords it over vices rather than over brethren. When rulers correct their delinquent subjects, it is incumbent on them to observe carefully that, while they smite faults with due discipline in virtue of their authority, they acknowledge, by observing humility, that they are only the equals of the brethren whom they correct.

Pope St. Gregory I: *Pastoral Care*, 2, 6. (6th cent.)

Close under the Abbey of Westminster there lie concealed labyrinths of lanes and courts, and alleys and slums, nests of ignorance, vice, depravity, and crime, as well as squalor, wretchedness and disease; whose atmosphere is typhus, whose ventilation is cholera; in which swarms a huge and almost countless population, nominally, at least, Catholic; haunts of filth which no Sewage Commission can reach, dark corners which no Lighting Board can brighten. This is the part of Westminster which alone I covet, and which I shall be glad to claim and visit as a blessed pasture in which sheep of Holy Church are to be tended, in which a bishop's godly work has to be done.

Card. Wiseman: *Letter to 'The Times.'* (19th cent.)

Pasture

Change of pasture maketh fat calves.

> John Heywood: *Proverbs*, 2, 4. (16th cent.)

Pater Noster (Our Father)

Pray thus three times a day.

> Teaching of the Twelve Apostles, 8. (2nd cent.)

He may be in my Pater noster indeed;
But be sure, he shall never come in my Creed.

> John Heywood: *Proverbs*, 2, 9. (16th cent.)

Patience

Be long-suffering and prudent, and you will obtain the mastery over wickedness and accomplish all justice.

> Shepherd of Hermas, Mandate 5, 1. (2nd cent.)

Patience is the companion of wisdom.

> St. Augustine: *On Patience.* (5th cent.)

It is a common experience even among patient people that at the moment when they suffer adversity or are made to bear contumely, they are not affected by any vexation. . . . But when after a time they recall what they have suffered, they become inflamed with resentment and seek out reasons for revenge.

> Pope St. Gregory I: *Pastoral Care*, 3, 9. (6th cent.)

Patience is the root and guardian of all the virtues.

> Pope St. Gregory I: *Homilies on the Gospels*, 35, 4. (6th cent.)

O God, Who by the patience of Thine only-begotten Son didst crush the pride of the ancient enemy; grant us, we beseech Thee, to have a worthy recollection ot the things which He devoutly endured on our behalf, and thus, by His example, patiently to bear with our adversities.

> Roman Missal, Collect. (ca. 9th cent.?)

Patience is not good, if when you may be free you allow yourself to become a slave.

> St. Bernard: *On Consideration*, 1, 3. (12th cent.)

Patience is a high virtue, certain,
For it vanquisheth, as this clerk seyn,
Things that regour should never attain.

> Chaucer: *The Frankeleyns Tale.* (14th cent.)

Patience, which is the leech of all offence.

> John Gower: *Confessio Amantis*, 3. (14th cent.)

Sufferance is a sovereign virtue.

> Langland: *Piers Plowman*, Passus 11. (14th cent.)

Be plastered with patience.

> Langland: *Piers Plowman*, Passus 20. (14th cent.)

All men commend patience, although few be willing to practise it.

> Thomas a Kempis: *Imitation of Christ*, 3. (15th cent.)

At the least bear patiently, if thou canst not joyfully.

> Thomas a Kempis: *The Imitation of Christ*, 3, 57. (15th cent.)

Let patience grow in your garden alway.

> John Heywood: *Proverbs*, 1, 11. (16th cent.)

The virtue of patience is the one which most assures us of perfection.

> St. Francis de Sales: *Letters to Persons in the World*, 1, 5. (17th cent.)

Have patience with all the world, but first of all with yourself.

> St. Francis de Sales: *Letters to Persons in the World*, 6, 17. (17th cent.)

Beware the fury of a patient man.

> Dryden: *Absalom and Achitophel.* (17th cent.)

Patience is the queen of the soul. She is seated on the rock of fortitude. She conquers and is never conquered.

> Archbp. Ullathorne: *Humility and Patience.* (19th cent.)

Patmore, Coventry

> This strong
> Sad soul of sovereign song.
>
> F. Thompson: *A Captain of Song.* (19th cent.)

Patriarch

The old custom in use in Egypt, in Libya, and in Pentapolis, should continue to exist, that is, that the bishop of Alexandria should have jurisdiction over all these provinces; for there is a similar relation for the bishop of Rome. The rights which they formerly possessed must also be preserved to the churches of Antioch and the other provinces.

> Council of Nicaea, Can. 6. (325)

Wherefore, though there were many apostles, yet in respect of the principate the See of the prince of the apostles alone has grown strong in authority, which, though in three places, is yet the See of one. For he himself exalted the See in which he deigned to rest and end his life [Rome]. He himself adorned the See to which he sent his disciple as evangelist [Alexandria]. He himself established the See over which he presided for seven years [Antioch]. Since then it is the See of one and one See, over which by divine authority three bishops now preside, whatever good I hear of you, that I impute to myself. And if you believe anything good of me, impute that to your merits, for we are one in him who says: *that they may be one, as we are one* (John 17, 11).

> Pope St. Gregory the Great: *Letters, 6, 58.* (To Eulogius, Patriarch of Alexandria) (6th cent.)

After the Roman church, which by the disposition of God has a primacy of ordinary power over all other churches . . . the church of Constantinople shall have the first place, that of Alexandria the second, that of Antioch the third, and that of Jerusalem the fourth.

> Fourth Lateran Council. (1215)

Patrick, Saint

Hear ye all, lovers of God, the holy merits
Of the man blessed in Christ, Patrick the bishop,
How for his good ways he is likened to the angels,
And because of his perfect life is deemed equal to the apostles.

> St. Secundinus: *Audite Omnes.* (Hymn in honor of St. Patrick.) (5th cent.)

Hibernia's champion saint, all hail!
   With fadeless glory crown'd;
The offspring of your ardent zeal,
   This day your praise shall sound.

> Anonymous: *Hymn to St. Patrick.* (In Caswall's *Lyra Catholica*) (19th cent.)

Grateful notes to heaven ascending,
   To the world new joys proclaim,
Faith and love together blending,
   We revere our Patrick's name.
Happy saint! in bliss adoring,
   Jesus, Savior of mankind,
Hear Thy children Thee imploring;
   May we Thy protection find.

> Sinnott: *St. Patrick.* (19th cent.)

Saint Patrick, for our country pray,
   Our ever-faithful land,
Whose martyred hosts so gloriously
   Before God's great throne stand;
Look down upon thy children here,
   Look down upon our race,
And bless, dear saint, this little isle
   And each one's native place.

> Anon. Hymn from *Hymns for the Ecclesiastical Year.* (19th cent.)

Patriot

Never was patriot yet, but was a fool.

Dryden: *Absalom and Achitophel.* (17th cent.)

Good heav'ns, how faction can a patriot paint!

Dryden: *Absalom and Achitophel.* (17th cent.)

Patriotism

Far, dearer, the grave or the prison,
Illumed by one patriot name,
Than the trophies of all who have risen
On liberty's ruins to fame.

Thomas Moore: *Forget Not the Field.* (19th cent.)

Incivism—will Catholic apologists never learn it?—is the heaviest stone flung at the Church in all free lands today.

W. Elliott: *Life of Father Hecker,* 339. (19th cent.)

There is a higher love than love of country—the love of truth, the love of justice, the love of righteousness; and he alone is a patriot who is willing to suffer obliquy and the loss of money and friends, rather than betray the cause of truth, justice, and righteousness, for only by being faithful to this can he rightly serve his country.

Archb. J. L. Spalding: *Opportunity and Other Essays.* (1899)

Patriotism, like charity, begins at home.

Archb. Spalding: *Opportunity and Other Essays.* (1899)

The Catholic Church commands and consecrates patriotism. The true Catholic must needs be the true patriot. In the eyes of the Church loyalty to country is loyalty to God; patriotism is a heavenly virtue, a high and holy form of obedience; the patriot dying for his country wears the halo of the martyr.

Archb. Ireland: *Disc. on the Catholic Church and Civil Society.* (Baltimore, Nov. 10, 1884)

We are bound to love dearly the country whence we have received the means of enjoyment this mortal life affords, but we have a much more urgent obligation to love with ardent soul the Church to which we owe the life of the soul, a life that will endure forever.

Pope Leo XIII: *Sapientiae Christianae.* (Jan. 10, 1890)

Next to God is country, and next to religion is patriotism. Patriotism is a Catholic virtue. I would have Catholics be the first patriots of the land.

Archb. Ireland: *The Church and Modern Society.* (19th cent.)

A number of young Englishmen have obviously got into their minds the extraordinary notion that the greatness of England ought to make an Englishman proud. The truth is just the reverse, the greatness of England ought to make an Englishman humble. One ought not to swagger about being the fellow citizen of Shakespeare; rather one ought to feel that Shakespeare might have had a better fellow citizen. In other words, an Englishman ought to feel unworthy of his country; it is only fools or aliens who feel worthy of it.

G. K. Chesterton: *A Handful of Authors.* (20th cent.)

Patriotism and religion. These always have been and always will be the only things for which men will sacrifice themselves, their possessions, their money.

Eric Gill: *It All Goes Together.* (20th cent.)

Paul, Saint

Through jealousy and strife Paul demonstrated how to win the prize of patient endurance. Seven times he was imprisoned, he was forced to leave and stoned, he preached in the east and in the west; and, finally, won the splendid renown which his faith had earned. He taught the right manner of life to the whole world, traveled as far as the western boundary [Spain?], and, when he had given testimony before the authorities, ended his earthly career and was taken up into the holy place as the greatest model of patient endurance.

Pope St. Clement I: *Letter to the Corinthians*, 5. (1st cent.)

O God, Who didst teach the multitude of the gentiles by the preaching of blessed Paul the apostle; grant, we beseech Thee, that we who celebrate his heavenly birthday, may also enjoy his patronage with Thee.

Roman Missal, Collect. (Gelasian, 5th to 7th cent.)

Lead us, great teacher Paul, in wisdom's ways,
And lift our hearts with thine to heaven's high throne;
Till faith beholds the clear meridian blaze;
And sunlike in the soul reigns charity alone.

Roman Breviary, Feast of St. Paul's Conversion, *Egregie doctor Paule mores instrue.* (From hymn *Beate pastor Petre*) (Tr. E. Caswall) (Attr. to Elpis, wife of Boethius, 6th cent.)

O God, Who seest that we put no trust in anything that we do, mercifully grant that we may be defended against all adversity by the protection of the doctor of the gentiles.

Roman Missal, Collect for Sexagesima. (Gregorian, 6th to 8th cent.)

Paul is made one of the chiefest among the saints, and a chosen vessel; verily he is worthy to be glorified, for he was made worthy to sit upon one of the twelve thrones.

Roman Breviary, Antiphon at Matins for Feast of Commemoration (June 30). (Liber Respons. ca. 6th to 8th cent.)

O God, Who hast taught the whole world by the preaching of blessed Paul the apostle; grant that we, who this day

celebrate his conversion, may by following his example be drawn unto Thee.

Roman Missal, Collect for Feast of St. Paul's Conversion (Jan. 25). (ca. 8th cent.)

Afterwards too the Chosen Vessel went
The confirmation of that faith to bring
Which is for way of our salvation sent.

Dante: *Inferno, Canto* 2. (Tr. Binyon) (14th cent.)

All ye who groan beneath
A load of ills oppress'd!
Entreat St. Paul, and he will pray
The Lord to give you rest.

Anonymous: *Pressi malorum pondere.* (Tr. Caswall) (18th cent.)

Payment

To rob Peter and pay Paul.

John Heywood: *Proverbs,* 1, 11. (16th cent.)

Misreckoning is no payment.

John Heywood: *Proverbs,* 2, 4. (16th cent.)

Even reckoning maketh long friends.

John Heywood: *Proverbs,* 2, 4. (16th cent.)

Peace

Thou didst touch me and I burned for Thy peace.

St. Augustine: *Confessions,* 10, 27. (5th cent.)

This peace is sought after by laborious wars, and attained by what is accounted glorious victory. When victory falls to the side that had the juster cause for fighting, who doubts that such victory is matter of congratulation, and the peace that has come of it desirable? Such victory and peace are good things, and beyond doubt are the gifts of God.

St. Augustine: *The City of God,* 15, 4. (5th cent.)

Belligerents are not reluctant to have peace, but they want a peace to their own liking.

> St. Augustine: *The City of God,* 19, 12. (5th cent.)

Peace of mortal man with God is well-ordered obedience in faith under the eternal law. The peace of mankind is a well-ordered concord. The peace of a household is a well-ordered concord of the members of the community in the matter of command and obedience. The peace of a city is the well-ordered concord of the citizens in the matter of command and obedience. The peace of the heavenly City is social life in thorough good order and concord for the enjoyment of God and of one another's company in God. The peace of all things is the tranquillity of order. Order is an arrangement of components equal and unequal, assigning the proper place to each.

> St. Augustine: *The City of God,* 19, 13. (5th cent.)

Grant, we beseech Thee, O Lord, that the course of this world may be so peaceably governed by Thee, that Thy Church may joyfully serve Thee in quiet devotion.

> Roman Missal, Collect for Fourth Sunday after Pentecost. (Leonine, ca. 5th cent.)

Not to make a feigned peace.

> St. Benedict: *Rule,* 4. (One of his "tools of good works") (6th cent.)

Dispose our days in Thy peace, and command us to be rescued from eternal damnation, and numbered in the flock of Thy elect.

> Words added to Canon of the Mass by Pope St. Gregory I. (6th cent.)

O God, from Whom all holy desires, right counsels, and just works proceed: grant to Thy servants that peace which the world cannot give; that our hearts may be devoted to Thy commandments, and, the fear of the enemy being re-moved, our times may be peaceful under Thy protection.

> Roman Misssal, Collect. (Gelasian, 5th to 7th cent.)

Peace and good. (Pax et bonum.)

> Motto of the Franciscan Order. (13th cent.)

In His will is perfected our peace.

> Dante: *Paradiso, Canto 3.* (14th cent.)

Universal peace is the most excellent means of securing our happiness.

> Dante: *Monarchy,* 1. (14th cent.)

We should have much peace if we would not busy ourselves with the sayings and doings of others.

> Thomas a Kempis: *The Imitation of Christ,* 1, 11. (15th cent.)

Thy peace shall be in much patience.

> Thomas a Kempis: *The Imitation of Christ,* 3, 25. (15th cent.)

Peace is better than a fortune.

> St. Francis de Sales: *Letters to Persons in the World,* 21, 10. (17th cent.)

You virgins, that did late despair
To keep your wealth from cruel men,
Tie up in silk your careless hair;
Soft peace is come again.

> James Shirley: *Piping Peace.* (17th cent.)

That peace which made thy prosperous reign to shine,
That peace thou leav'st to thy imperial line,
That peace, oh happy shade, be ever thine!

> Dryden: *Threnodia Augustalis.* (17th cent.)

When first the ark was landed on the shore,
And Heav'n had vowed to curse the ground no more,
When tops of hills the longing patri-arch saw,

And the new scene of earth began to
draw,
The dove was sent to view the waves'
decrease,
And first brought back to man the
pledge of peace.

Dryden: *The Unhappy Favorite, Prologue.*
(17th cent.)

Peace, the loathed manna which hot
brains despise.

Dryden. (17th cent.)

I knew by the smoke, that so gracefully
curl'd
Above the green elms, that a cottage
was near,
And I said, If there's peace to be found
in the world,
A heart that was humble might hope
for it here!

Thomas Moore: *Ballad Stanzas.* (Refers to
the old Redfield farm at Batavia, N. Y.,
where the poet spent a night in 1804)
(19th cent.)

I do not ask, O Lord, that Thou
shouldst shed
Full radiance here;
Give but a ray of peace that I may tread
Without a fear;
I do not ask my cross to understand,
My way to see—
Better in darkness just to feel Thy hand
And follow Thee.
Joy is like restless day; but peace divine
Like quiet night:
Lead me on, O Lord—till perfect day
shall shine
Through peace to Light.

Adelaide Procter: *Per Pacem ad Lucem.*
(19th cent.)

For peace do not hope; to be just you
must break it.

J. B. O'Reilly: *Rules of the Road.* (19th
cent.)

O England, how hast thou forgot,
In dullard care for undisturb'd increase
Of gold, which profits not,

The gain which once thou knew'st was
for thy peace!
Honor is peace, the peace which does
accord
Alone with God's glad word:
'My peace I send you, and I send a
sword.'

Coventry Patmore: *Peace.* (19th cent.)

I shall not hold my little peace; for me
There is no peace but one.

Alice Meynell: *The Poet to the Birds.*
(20th cent.)

Picture the peace of the ransomed soul,
that knows itself safe in the arms of
God; that rejoices, even in this world,
in the light of His face and the ecstasy
of His embrace; that dwells by waters of
comfort, and lies down in the green
pastures of the heavenly love; while,
round this little island of salvation in an
ocean of terror, the thunders of wrath
sound only as the distant surge on a far-
off reef.

R. H. Benson: *By What Authority.* (20th
cent.)

To serve the cause of peace is to serve
justice. To serve the cause of peace is to
serve the interests of the people, especially the lowly and dispossessed. To
serve the cause of peace is to face the
future with serene and unruffled countenance. To serve the cause of peace is to
hasten the day when all nations without exception shall lay aside their rival-
ries and feuds, and embrace one another as brothers. To serve the cause of
peace is to serve civilization.

Pope Pius XII: *Now is the Time for
Action.* (Sept. 7, 1947)

The Christian order, since its purpose is
peace, is essentially an order of liberty.
It is the cooperative effort of men and
peoples toward the progressive realization in all spheres of life of the ends
God has assigned to humanity.

Pope Pius XII: *Christmas Address.* (Dec.
24, 1951)

Peacock

She is a peacock in everything but beauty.

> Oscar Wilde: *The Picture of Dorian Gray,* 1. (19th cent.)

Pearl

A pearl will shine in the midst of squalor and a gem of the first water will sparkle in the mire.

> St. Jerome: *Letters, 66,* 7. (4th cent.)

Men should not put pearles white
To-fore rude swine.

> Lydgate: *Minor Poems,* p. 188. (15th cent.)

Has a pearl less whiteness
Because of its birth?

> Thomas Moore: *Desmond's Song.* (19th cent.)

Pedant

The boastful blockhead ignorantly read,
With loads of learned lumber in his head.

> Pope: *An Essay on Criticism,* 3. (18th cent.)

Pen

The pen wherewith thou dost so heavenly sing
Made of a quill from an angel's wing.

> Henry Constable: *Sonnets.* (16th cent.)

Penance (Sacrament)

Let us also intercede for those who fall into any transgression, that meekness and humility may be granted them, so that they may yield not to us but to God's will. For in this way there will be for them a fruitful, perfect, and compassionate remembrance (*mneia*) with God and the saints.

> Pope St. Clement I: *Letter to the Corinthians,* 56, 1. (1st cent.)

I entreat you, beloved brethren, that each one should confess his own sin, while he who has sinned is still in this world, while his confession may be received, while the satisfaction and remission made by the priests are pleasing to the Lord. Let us turn to the Lord with our whole heart, and expressing our repentance for our sin with true grief, let us entreat God's mercy.

> St. Cyprian: *On the Lapsed,* 29. (3rd cent.)

As thou baptizest a heathen and then receivest him, so also lay hand upon this man, while all pray for him, and then bring him in and let him communicate with the Church. For the imposition of hand shall be to him in the place of baptism: for whether by the imposition of hand or by baptism, they receive the communication of the Holy Spirit.

> Anonymous: *Didascalia Apostolorum,* 10. (3rd cent.)

They who believe in the Lord must first do penance according to the preaching of John and of our Lord Jesus Christ Himself; for they who do not penance now will receive a harsher sentence than those who were condemned before the time of the gospel.

> St. Basil: *The Morals,* 1. (4th cent.)

Mere renouncement of sin is not sufficient for the salvation of penitents, but fruits worthy of penance are also required of them.

> St. Basil: *The Morals,* 1, 3. (4th cent.)

Sins are forgiven by the Holy Ghost. . . . Men discharge a ministry for the remission of sins; they do not exercise any power of their own. For they forgive sins not in their own name but in that of the Father and of the Son and of the Holy Ghost. They ask, the Godhead gives; the service is man's, the reward is of the Power on high.

> St. Ambrose: *On the Holy Spirit,* 3, 137. (4th cent.)

Where punishment for sins is prescribed there ought to be penance; where remission is given to sinners there also is grace. Penance precedes; grace follows. There is neither penance without grace nor grace without penance, for penance should first condemn the sin so that grace can do away with it.

> St. Ambrose: *Letters*, 26. (4th cent.)

Within the Church sins are forgiven in three ways: by baptism, by prayer, and by the greater humility of penance.

> St. Augustine: *On the Creed*, 8. (4th cent.)

In Holy Church the remission of even crimes themselves, no matter how great they may be, by God's mercy need not be despaired of by those who do penance according to the gravity of their sins.

> St. Augustine: *Enchiridion*, 65. (5th cent.)

To do penance is to bewail the evil we have done, and to do no evil to bewail.

> Pope St. Gregory I: *Homilies on the Gospels*, 34, 15. (6th cent.)

Graciously hear the prayers of Thy people, we beseech Thee, O Lord; that we who are justly afflicted for our sins, may be mercifully delivered by Thy goodness for the glory of Thy name.

> Roman Missal, Collect for Septuagesima. (Gregorian, 6th to 8th cent.)

Graciously hear our prayers, we beseech Thee, O Lord; that, being freed from the chains of our sins, we may be defended by Thee against all adversity.

> Roman Missal, Collect for Quinquagesima. (Gregorian, 6th to 8th cent.)

O God, Who art offended by sin and appeased by penance, mercifully regard the prayers of Thy suppliant people, and turn aside the scourge of Thy anger, which we deserve for our sins.

> Roman Missal, Collect for Thursday after Ash Wednesday. (Gregorian, 6th to 8th cent.)

Through the office of priests those should be reconciled to Holy Church by doing penance, who have departed from its society by sinning.

> St. Bede the Venerable: *In Marcam*, 4. (8th cent.)

The Church's ministers do not remit sin of their own authority as principal efficient causes. Only God can do that. . . . They should not be called givers of grace, for that implies authority, but rather ministers of the granting of Christ's grace.

> St. Thomas Aquinas: *Commentary on the Sentences*, 1, 14, 3. (13th cent.)

Not any priest can absolve from sin, as some have mistakingly thought, but only that priest who has duly received jurisdiction.

> St. Thomas Aquinas: *Contra Gentes*, 4, 72. (13th cent.)

Good is penance and maceration of the body; but do not present these to me as a rule for everyone. If either for ourselves or others, we made penance our foundation . . . we should be ignorant, and should fall into a critical attitude, and become weary and very bitter: for we should strive to give a finite work to God Who is infinite Love, and demands from us only infinite desire.

> St. Catherine of Siena: *Letter to Sister Daniella*. (14th cent.)

If any one saith that in the Catholic Church penance is not truly and properly a sacrament, instituted by Christ our Lord for reconciling the faithful unto God, as often as they fall into sin after baptism; let him be anathema.

> Council of Trent, Session 14, Canon 1. (Nov. 25, 1551)

If any one denieth that for the entire and perfect remission of sins there are required three acts in the penitent, which are as it were the matter of the sacrament of penance, to wit, contrition, confession, and satisfaction, which are called the three parts of penance; or saith that they are two parts only of penance, to wit, the terrors with which the conscience is smitten upon being convinced of sin, and the faith generated by the gospel or by the absolution, whereby one believes that his sins are forgiven him through Christ; let him be anathema.

Council of Trent, Session 14, Canon 4. (Nov. 25, 1551)

If any one saith that the sacramental absolution of the priest is not a judicial act, but a bare ministry of pronouncing and declaring sins to be forgiven to him who confesses; provided only he believes himself to be absolved, or even though the priest absolve not in earnest but in joke; or saith that the confession of the penitent is not required, in order that the priest may be able to absolve him; let him be anathema.

Council of Trent, Session 14, Canon 9. (Nov. 25, 1551)

If any one saith that God always remits the whole punishment together with the guilt, and that the satisfaction of penitents is no other than the faith whereby they apprehend that Christ has satisfied for them; let him be anathema.

Council of Trent, Session 14, Canon 12. (Nov. 25, 1551)

If any one saith that satisfaction for sins as to their temporal punishment is nowise made to God through the merits of Jesus Christ by the punishments inflicted by him and patiently borne, or by those enjoined by the priest, nor even by those voluntarily undertaken, as by fastings, prayers, almsdeeds, or by other works also of piety; and that therefore the best penance is merely a new life; let him be anathema.

Council of Trent, Session 14, Canon 13. (Nov. 25, 1551)

If any one saith that the keys are given to the Church only to loose, not also to bind; and that therefore priests act con-

trary to the purpose of the keys and contrary to the institution of Christ, when they impose punishments on those who confess; and that it is a fiction that, after the eternal punishment has by virtue of the keys been removed, there remains for the most part a temporal punishment to be discharged; let him be anathema.

Council of Trent, Session 14, Canon 15. (Nov. 25, 1551)

Shun not the shelf of most deserved shame,
Stick in the sands of agonizing dread;
Content thee to be storms' and billows' game,
Divorced from grace, thy soul to penance wed:
Fly not from foreign ills, fly from the heart,
Worse than the worst of ills is that thou art.

Bl. Robert Southwell: *St. Peter's Complaint.* (16th cent.)

Be a lion in the pulpit, but a lamb in the confessional.

Saying of St. Alphonso of Liguori. (18th cent.)

So long as there is sin in the world so long must there be penance.

R. H. Benson: *The Dawn of All.* (20th cent.)

In the sacrament of penance sins committed after baptism are forgiven, if the penitent has the proper disposition, by means of the judicial absolution pronounced by a legitimate minister.

Code of Canon Law, Canon 870. (20th cent.)

Penance is a recognition and reestablishment of the moral order in the world, which is founded on the eternal law, that is, on the living God.

Pope Pius XI: *Caritate Christi compulsi.* (May 3, 1932)

See also Absolution; Confession; Sin, Remission of

Pentecost

Round roll the weeks our hearts to
  greet,
With blissful joy returning;
For lo! the Holy Paraclete
On twelve bright brows sits burning.

Roman Breviary, Pentecost, Hymn *Beata
nobis gaudia* at Lauds. (Tr. W. Blew)
(Attr. to St. Hilary of Poitiers, 4th cent.)

Now Christ, ascending whence He
  came,
Had mounted o'er the starry frame,
The Holy Ghost on man below,
The Father's promise, to bestow.

. . . .

When the third hour shone all around,
There came a mighty rushing sound,
And told the apostles, while in prayer,
That, as was promised, God was there.

Roman Breviary, Pentecost, Hymn *Jam
Christus astra ascenderat* at Matins. (Tr.
J. Neale) (Ambrosian, 4th cent.)

This operation, visibly exhibited, and
presented to mortal eyes, is called the
sending of the Holy Spirit; not that His
very substance appeared, in which He
Himself also is invisible and unchangeable, like the Father and the Son, but
that the hearts of men, touched by things
seen outwardly, might be turned from
the manifestation in time of Him as
coming to His hidden eternity as ever
present.

St. Augustine: *De Trinitate*, 2, 5. (5th
cent.)

Grant, we beseech Thee, almighty God,
that the splendor of Thy brightness may
shine upon us, and the light of Thy light
confirm with the illumination of the
Holy Spirit the hearts of those who have
been born again through Thy grace.

Roman Missal, Collect for Vigil of
Pentecost. (Gregorian, 6th to 8th cent.)

O God, Who on this day didst teach the
hearts of Thy faithful people by the
light of the Holy Spirit; grant us by
the same Spirit to have right judgment

in all things and ever rejoice in His holy
consolation.

Roman Missal, Collect. (Gregorian, 6th to
8th cent.)

Blessed art Thou, O Christ our God,
Who didst make the fishermen wise,
sending the Holy Ghost on them, and by
them netting the whole world. Glory to
Thee, O Lover of mankind.

Byzantine Pentekostarion, Troparion. (ca.
6th to 8th cent.)

Come, Holy Ghost, Creator, come,
From Thy bright heavenly throne!
Come, take possession of our souls,
And make them all Thy own!

Thou who art called the Paraclete,
Best gift of God above,
The living Spring, the living Fire,
Sweet Unction and true Love!

. . . .

Through Thee may we the Father
  know—
Through Thee the eternal Son—
And Thee the Spirit of them both—
Thrice-blessed Three in One.

Roman Breviary, Pentecost, Hymn *Veni
creator Spiritus* at Vespers. (Tr. from
Garden of the Soul) (Probably by Bl.
Rabanus Maurus, 9th cent.)

This day the day of Pentecost is fully
come, Alleluia. This day the Holy Ghost
appeared in fire unto the disciples, and
gave unto them gifts of grace: He sent
them into all the world to preach and to
testify: he that believeth, and is baptized, shall be saved. Alleluia.

Roman Breviary, Antiphon at Second
Vespers. (ca. 9th cent.)

Day delightful! day most noted!
When o'er Christ's disciples floated
  Fire sent from the throne on high,
Filling hearts, and tongues endowing,
And on hearts and tongues bestowing
  Words and thoughts in harmony.

Adam of St. Victor: *Lux jucunda lux
insignis.* (Tr. Wrangham) (12th cent.)

Holy Spirit, come and shine
On our souls with beams divine,
Issuing from Thy radiance bright.
Come, O Father of the poor,
Ever bounteous of Thy store,
Come, our heart's unfailing light.

Roman Missal, Pentecost, Sequence *Veni Sancte Spiritus* at Mass. (Tr. J. Aylward) (Probably by Pope Innocent III, 13th cent.)

Descend, then, Spirit of the eternal King!
To Thee, to Him, to His avenging Son,
The Triune of God, in boundless trust we cling:
His help once ours, our nationhood is won.
    We watch the time
    Till that sublime
Event shall thrill the free of every clime.
Speed, mighty Spirit! speed its march,
And thus complete for earth mankind's triumphal arch.

James C. Mangan: *Hymn for Pentecost.* (19th cent.)

People

The voice of the people is the voice of God. (Vox populi, vox Dei.)

Alcuin: *Epistles.* (Proverb) (9th cent.)

O stormy people, unsad and ever untrue,
And indiscreet, and changing as a vane,
Delighting ever in rumble that is new,
And like the moon ay waxe ye and wane!

Chaucer: *The Clerkes Tale.* (14th cent.)

If by the people you understand the multitude, the *hoi polloi,* 'tis no matter what they think; they are sometimes in the right, sometimes in the wrong; their judgment is a mere lottery.

Dryden: *Of Dramatic Poesy.* (17th cent.)

Nor is the people's judgment always true;
The most may err as grossly as the few.

Dryden: *Absalom and Achitophel,* 1. (17th cent.)

The people are a many-headed beast.

Pope: *The First Epistle of the First Book of Horace.* (18th cent.)

Perception

Philosophers tell us that the value of existence lies not in the objects perceived, but in the powers of perception.

R. H. Benson: *By What Authority.* (20th cent.)

Perfection

If thou canst bear the whole yoke of the Lord, thou wilt be perfect, but if thou canst not, do what thou canst.

Teaching of the Twelve Apostles, 6. (2nd cent.)

No one is suddenly made perfect.

St. Bede the Venerable: *In Lucam,* 4. (Echoing St. Gregory I.) (8th cent.)

Each and everything is said to be perfect in so far as it attains to its proper end; and this is its ultimate perfection.

St. Thomas Aquinas: *Summa Theologica,* 2-2, 184, 1. (13th cent.)

Thou shalt love the Lord thy God with thy whole heart. (Deut. 6, 5) *Thou shalt love thy neighbor as thyself* (Lev. 19, 18). These are the two commandments of which our Lord spoke: *on these two commandments hang all the law and the prophets* (Matth. 22, 40). The perfection of the Christian life, therefore, consists in keeping these precepts.

St. Thomas Aquinas: *Summa Theologica,* 2-2, 184, 3. (13th cent.)

Everything is at its best and most perfect when in the condition intended for it by the First Cause, which is God.

Dante: *Monarchy,* 1. (14th cent.)

If thou wilt be perfect, sell thy will and give it to the poor in spirit; come to Christ through meekness and humility; and follow Him to Calvary and the grave.

St. John of the Cross: *Spiritual Sentences and Maxims.* (16th cent.)

We can never attain to perfection while we have an affection for any imperfection.

> St. Francis de Sales: *Spiritual Conferences,* 8. (17th cent.)

Perfection does not lie in not seeing the world, but in not tasting or relishing it.

> St. Francis de Sales: *Letters to Persons in the World,* 6, 52. (17th cent.)

Whoever thinks a faultless piece to see,
Thinks what ne'er was, nor is, nor e'er shall be.

> Pope: *Essay on Criticism,* 2. (18th cent.)

O keep thy conscience sensitive;
  No inward token miss;
And go where grace entices thee;—
  Perfection lies in this.

> F. Faber: *Perfection.* (First line: O how the thought of God attracts) (19th cent.)

One only among the sons of men has carried out a perfect work, and satisfied and exhausted the mission on which He came. One alone has with His last breath said *Consummatum est.*

> Card. Newman: *Idea of a University.* (19th cent.)

That soul is perfect which is guided habitually by the instinct of the Holy Spirit.

> Isaac T. Hecker. (Elliott's *Life,* 307) (19th cent.)

No man can advance three paces on the road of perfection unless Jesus Christ walks beside him.

> R. H. Benson: *The Friendship of Christ.* (20th cent.)

Perplexity

The surest manner to perplex a man is to suggest to him that his brain is clouded.

> R. H. Benson: *The History of Richard Raynal Solitary.* (20th cent.)

Persecution

Ah, my brother, you are mistaken, you are mistaken, if you suppose that there is ever a time when the Christian does not suffer persecution.

> St. Jerome: *Letters,* 14, 4. (4th cent.)

Oh! that it were as it was wont to be,
When thy old friends of fire, all full of thee,
Fought against frowns with smiles! gave glorious chase
To persecutions, and against the face
Of death and fiercest dangers durst, with brave
And sober pace, march on to meet a grave.

> R. Crashaw: *Most Holy Name of Jesus.* (17th cent.)

The instance cannot be found in the history of mankind, in which an anti-Christian power could long abstain from persecution.

> Card. Newman: *Oxford University Sermons.* (19th cent.)

The general law of persecution is the conversion of the persecutors.

> I. T. Hecker: *The Church and the Age.* (1887)

If the Lord wishes that other persecutions should be suffered, the Church feels no alarm; on the contrary, persecutions purify her and confer upon her a fresh force and a new beauty. There are, in truth, in the Church certain things which need purification, and for this purpose those persecutions answer best which are launched against her by great politicians.

> Pope Pius IX. (Roussel, Actes et Paroles de Pie IX, Paris, 1874)

If the old priests forced a statement on mankind, at least they previously took some trouble to make it lucid. It has been left for the modern mobs of Anglicans and Nonconformists to persecute for a doctrine without even stating it.

> G. K. Chesterton: *Heretics.* (20th cent.)

Perseverance

A tree is shown by its fruit, and in the same way those who profess to belong to Christ will be seen by what they do. For what is needed is not mere present profession, but perseverance to the end in the power of faith.

> St. Ignatius of Antioch: *Letter to the Ephesians,* 14. (2nd cent.)

O God, Who hast willed that the gate of mercy should stand open to the faithful; look on us, and have mercy upon us; that we who by Thy grace are following the path of Thy will, may never turn aside from the ways of eternal life.

> Gelasian Sacramentary, Collect. (5th to 7th cent.)

We cannot command our final perseverance, but must ask it from God.

> St. Thomas Aquinas: *Disputations concerning Truth,* 24, 14. (13th cent.)

If any one saith that he will for certain, of an absolute and infallible certainty, have that great gift of perseverance unto the end, unless he have learned this by special revelation; let him be anathema.

> Council of Trent, Session 6, Canon 16. (Jan. 13, 1547)

If any man saith that the justified either is able to persevere without the special help of God in the justice received; or that with that help he is not able; let him be anathema.

> Council of Trent, Session 6, Canon 22. (Jan. 13, 1547)

Though perseverance does not come from our power, yet it comes within our power.

> St. Francis de Sales: *Treatise on the Love of God,* 3, 4. (17th cent.)

He greatly deceives himself who thinks that prayer perfects one without perseverance and obedience.

> St. Francis de Sales: *Letters to Persons in Religion,* 3, 44. (17th cent.)

Persistence

Nothing is so hard that it does not yield to that which is harder.

> St. Bernard: *On Consideration,* 4, 3. (12th cent.)

Person

Wherefore if person belongs to substances alone, and these rational, and if every nature is a substance, existing not in universals but in individuals, we have found the definition of persons, viz.: The individual substance of a rational nature (naturae rationabilis individua substantia).

> Boethius: *Contra Eutychen,* 3. (6th cent.)

Person denotes that which is the highest perfection in the whole realm of nature.

> St. Thomas Aquinas: *Summa Theologica,* I, 29, 3. (13th cent.)

Personality

Personality should reside in the will as in a castle, and issue orders to the passions and intellectual apprehensions, who, in their turn, should inform their master of external happenings and await his decision.

> R. H. Benson: *The Sentimentalists.* (20th cent.)

It is a very significant fact that the idea of human personality and also the practical recognition of the dignity of human personality developed only during those centuries in which the dogmas of the Trinity and of the Incarnation were teaching Christendom the truths of divine personality.

> J. Maritain: *Freedom in the Modern World.* (20th cent.)

Persuasion

Anything pleasant easily persuades, and while it gives pleasure it fixes itself in the heart.

> Lactantius: *Divinae institutiones,* 6. (4th cent.)

We are more easily persuaded, in general, by the reasons we ourselves discover than by those which are given to us by others.

> Pascal: *Pensées*. (17th cent.)

Minds in our day are to be governed by respecting their freedom, not by restraining it, and men in authority must be more ready to convince than to command.

> Orestes Brownson: *Works*, 20, 107ff. (1861)

Pessimism

Pessimism is regnant, if not supreme amongst us.

> R. H. Benson: *Dedication to the Sentimentalists*. (20th cent.)

Pessimism is a thing unfit for a white man; a thing like opium, that may often be a poison and sometimes a medicine, but never a food for us, who are driven by an inner command not only to think but to live, not only to live but to grow, and not only to grow but to build.

> G. K. Chesterton: *Victorian Age in Literature*. (20th cent.)

Peter, Saint

Let us take the noble examples of our own generation. It was due to jealousy and envy that the greatest and most holy pillars were persecuted and fought to the death. Let us pass in review the good apostles: Peter, who through unmerited jealousy underwent not one or two, but countless hardships and after thus giving testimony, departed to the place of glory that was his due.

> Pope St. Clement I: *Letter to the Corinthians*, 5. (1st cent.)

For though you think that heaven is still shut up, remember that the Lord left the keys of it to Peter here, and through him to the Church, which keys everyone will carry with him, if he has been questioned and made confession [of faith].

> Tertullian: *Scorpiace*, 10. (3rd cent.)

For first of all the Lord gave that power [i.e. to remit sins] to Peter, upon whom He built His Church, and whence He appointed and showed the source of unity—the power, namely, that whatsoever He loosed on earth should be loosed in heaven.

> St. Cyprian: *Letters*, 72, 7. (3rd cent.)

And when all were silent, for it was beyond man's reach to learn, Peter, leader of the apostles, and chief herald of the Church, uttering no refinement of his own, nor persuaded by man's reasoning, but having his mind enlightened by the Father, says to him: *Thou art the Christ*.

> St. Cyril of Jerusalem: *Catechetical Discourses*, 11, 3. (4th cent.)

Simon, My disciple, I have made thee a foundation of holy Church. I called thee Rock on a previous occasion, because thou shalt be the support of all the buildings; thou art the overseer of those who will build My Church on earth. If they try to build anything evil, thou, the foundation, shalt reprimand them. Thou art the head of the fountain from which My doctrine shall be drunk, thou art the head of My disciples; I will give all people to drink through thee; yours is that life-giving sweetness I pour forth; I have chosen thee to be as it were the firstborn in My establishment and thou shalt become the heir of My treasures. The keys of My kingdom I have given thee. Lo, I have established thee prince over all My treasures.

> St. Ephraem of Syria: *Sermons on Holy Week*, 4, 1. (4th cent.)

O foundation of the Church blessed in calling him by this new name, O rock worthy to be built upon, which will dissolve the laws of hell, the gates of Tartarus, and all the bonds of death! O blessed doorkeeper of heaven, to whose judgment the keys of access to eternity are committed, whose earthly sentence is binding authority in heaven: whatsoever is either bound or loosed on earth, has the same binding force in heaven.

St. Hilary of Poitiers: *Commentary on St. Matthew,* 16, 7. (4th cent.)

The first See of the apostle Peter is therefore the Roman church, *without stain, without wrinkle, or anything of the kind* (Eph. 5, 27). But the second See was consecrated at Alexandria, in the name of blessed Peter, by his disciple Mark the evangelist; and he, being directed by St. Peter into Egypt, preached the word of truth, and perfected a glorious martyrdom. And the third See of the most blessed apostle Peter is at Antioch, which is held in honor because he lived there before he came to Rome, and there, first, the name of the new race of Christians arose.

Council of Rome under Pope Damasus. (From *Decretum Gelasianum,* a composition of the sixth century.) (382)

Peter, the leader of the choir, the mouth of all the apostles, the head of that tribe, the ruler of the whole world, the foundation of the Church, the ardent lover of Christ.

St. John Chrysostom: *Homily on 2 Timothy,* 3, 1. (4th cent.)

When the Lord was about to ascend into heaven, He left us, as it were, a vicegerent of His love. Because Peter alone of all others professes His love, he is preferred to all . . . that being the more perfect he should govern the perfect.

St. Ambrose: *Explanation of St. Luke,* 10, 175, 176. (4th cent.)

At length Peter is set over the Church, after being tempted by the devil. And so the Lord signified beforehand what came to pass afterwards, in that He chose him to be the shepherd of the Lord's flock. For He said to him, *When thou art converted, strengthen thy brethren* (Luke 22, 31-32).

St. Ambrose: *In Ps. 43 Enarr. 40.* (4th cent.)

But you say that the Church was founded upon Peter: although elsewhere the same is attributed to all the apostles, and they all receive the keys of the kingdom of heaven, and the strength of the Church depends on them all alike, yet one among the twelve is chosen so that when a head has been appointed, there may be no occasion for schism.

St. Jerome: *Against Jovinianus,* 1. (4th cent.)

The Savior confided to this man, as some special trust, the whole universal Church, after having asked him three times: *Dost thou love me?* And he received the world in charge, as one flock one shepherd, having heard, *Feed my lambs;* and the Lord gave, well nigh in His own stead, that most faithful disciple to the proselytes as a father, and shepherd, and instructor.

St. Asterius of Amasea: *On the Chief Holy Apostles, Peter and Paul.* (395)

It is not without reason that, among all the apostles, it is Peter who represents the Catholic Church. For the keys of the kingdom of heaven were given to this Church when they were given to Peter. And when it was said to him, it was said to all: *Lovest thou me? Feed my sheep* (Cf. John 21, 17).

St. Augustine: *De Agone Christiano,* 30, 32. (4th cent.)

You see the most eminent dignitary of this noble Empire lay aside his crown and bow in supplication before the tomb of the fisherman Peter.

St. Augustine: *Letter 232.* (With reference perhaps to the submission of the Emperor Theodosius before St. Ambrose.) (5th cent.)

To Peter alone was it given to play the part of the whole Church, and because of his part, which of the whole Church he alone took, it was given to him to hear the words: *I will give to thee the keys of the kingdom of heaven* (Matth. 16, 19). Now it was not one man but the unity of the Church that received those keys. By this fact the pre-eminence of Peter was proclaimed, in that he bore the figure of the very universality and unity of the Church.

> St. Augustine: *Sermon 245, 2, 2.* (5th cent.)

As Christ is the Shepherd, is Peter not a shepherd? On the contrary, Peter is also shepherd, and so are all of such kind without any doubt shepherds. For if he be not shepherd, why should it be said to him: *Feed my sheep?* Yet it is the true shepherd who feeds his own sheep. Now it was said to Peter, not, Feed thy sheep, but *my* sheep. Hence Peter is shepherd not in himself, but in the body of the Shepherd. For if he fed his own sheep, they would immediately become goats which he was feeding.

> St. Augustine: *Sermon 285, 5.* (5th cent.)

I suppose there is no slight to Cyprian in comparing him with the apostle Peter in respect of his crown of martyrdom; rather I ought to be afraid lest I am slighting Peter. Who can be ignorant that the chief apostolate is to be preferred to any episcopate? But even if the dignity of their sees differs, the glory of martyrdom is one. . . .

> St. Augustine: *Concerning Baptism, 2, 2.* (5th cent.)

Some things are said which seem to relate especially to the apostle Peter, and yet are not clear in their meaning unless referred to the Church, which he is acknowledged to have represented in a figure, on account of the primacy which he bore among the disciples.

> St. Augustine: *In Ps. 108 Enarratio.* (5th cent.)

Who is ignorant that the first of the apostles is the most blessed Peter?

> St. Augustine: *In Joannis Evang. Tr., 56.* (5th cent.)

In Peter the courage of them all is strengthened, and the assistance of divine grace is so disposed that the steadfastness, which is imparted through Christ to Peter, is conveyed through Peter to the other apostles.

> Pope St. Leo I; *Sermons, 4, 3.* (5th cent.)

He was ordained before the rest in such a way that from his being called the rock, from his being pronounced the foundation, from his being constituted the doorkeeper of the kingdom of heaven, from his being set as the umpire to bind and to loose, whose judgments shall retain their validity in heaven, from all these mystical titles we might know the nature of his association with Christ. And still today he more fully and effectually performs what is entrusted to him, and carries out every part of his duty and charge in Him and with Him, through Whom he has been glorified. And so if anything is rightly done and rightly decreed by us, if anything is won from the mercy of God by our daily supplications, it is of his work and merits whose power lives and whose authority prevails in his See.

> Pope St. Leo I: *Sermons, 3, 3.* (5th cent.)

Admittedly there was conveyed also to the other apostles the right of that authority, and the office established by this pronouncement [Matth. 18, 18] was handed on to all the chiefs of the Church: but it was not in vain that the gift which was imparted to them all was entrusted to one in particular. For it was for this reason that this power was specially attributed to Peter, namely because the person of Peter is set at the head of all the rulers of the Church.

> Pope St. Leo I: *Sermons, 4, 3.* (5th cent.)

One Peter is chosen from the whole world, who is placed in charge both of the calling of all nations and all the apostles and all the fathers of the Church; so that, although there are many priests and many pastors in the people of God, Peter may properly rule all whom Christ also rules as the head (*principaliter*).

Pope St. Leo I: *Sermons*, 4, 2. (5th cent.)

When the twelve apostles, after receiving from the Holy Ghost the power of speaking with all tongues, had distributed the world into parts among themselves, and undertaken to instruct it in the gospel, the most blessed Peter, chief of the apostolic band, was appointed to the citadel of the Roman Empire, that the light of truth which was being displayed for the salvation of all nations, might spread itself more effectively throughout the body of the world from the head itself.

Pope St. Leo I: *Sermons*, 82, 3. (5th cent.)

O God, Who by conferring the keys of the kingdom of heaven didst grant to Thy blessed apostle Peter the pontifical power of binding and loosing; grant that by the help of his intercession we may be freed from the bonds of our sins.

Gelasian Sacramentary, Collect. (5th to 7th cent.)

Thou art the shepherd of the sheep and the prince of the apostles, and unto thee are given the keys of the kingdom of heaven.

Roman Breviary, Feast of Apostles Peter and Paul (June 29), Antiphon at Lauds. (Liber Respons., ca. 6th cent.)

Peter, blest shepherd, hearken to our cry,
And with a word unloose our guilty chain;
Thou! who hast power to ope the gates on high
To men below, and power to shut them fast again.

Roman Breviary, Peter's Chairs at Rome and Antioch (Jan. 18 & Feb. 22), Hymn *Beate pastor Petre clemens accipe*. (Tr. E. Caswall) (Attr. to Elpis, 6th cent.)

To all the Church of the elect authority of binding and loosing . . . is given. But blessed Peter who confessed Christ with a true faith and was attached to Him with a true love, received in a special way the keys of the kingdom of heaven and the primacy of judicial power (*principatus judiciariae potestatis*), so that all believers throughout the world might understand that those who separate themselves from the unity of his faith and society cannot be absolved from the chains of sin, nor enter the door of the heavenly kingdom.

St. Bede the Venerable: *Homilies*, 2, 16. (8th cent.)

Peter, whatever thou shalt bind on earth,
The same is bound above the starry sky;
What here thy delegated power doth loose,
Is loosed in heaven's supremest court on high:
To judgment shalt thou come, when the world's end is nigh.

Roman Breviary, Peter's Chair at Rome (Jan. 18), Hymn *Quodcumque in orbe nexibus revinxeris*. (Tr. E. Caswall) (Attr. to St. Paulinus of Aquileia, 8th cent.)

In wondrous mode set free, lo, at the Lord's command
The galling iron chain doth fall from Peter's hand,
From Peter, shepherd blest, who doth with gentle sway,
His faithful children lead in virtue's fragrant way,
And e'er with watchful love the temper drive away.

Roman Breviary, Feast of St. Peter's Chains (Aug. 1), *Miris modis repente liber ferrea*. (From hymn *Quodcumque in orbe nexibus revinxeris*) (Tr. T. Potter) (Attr. to St. Paulinus of Aquileia, 8th cent.)

Eternal light of that great man
To whom our Lord the keys at parting gave,

Which He brought down, of joy's
supreme domain.

Dante: *Paradiso, Canto 24.* (Tr. Binyon)
(14th cent.)

Seek ye a patron to defend
   Your cause?—then, one and all,
Without delay upon the prince
   Of the apostles call.

Anonymous: *Si vis patronum quaerere.*
(Tr. Caswall) (19th cent.)

If any one therefore shall say that blessed
Peter the apostle was not appointed the
prince of the apostles and the visible
head of the whole Church militant, or
that the same directly and immediately
received from the same our Lord Jesus
Christ a primacy of honor only, and not
of true and proper jurisdiction; let him
be anathema.

Vatican Council, Session 4, Dogmatic
Constitution 1. (July 18, 1870)

It is necessary to bear this in mind: nothing was conferred on the apostles apart
from Peter, but several things were
conferred upon Peter apart from the
apostles.

Pope Leo XIII: *Satis Cognitum.* (June 20,
1896)

He rose, he heard—
Our father, our St. Peter, in his tears—
The crowing, twice, of the prophetic
   bird,
The saddest cock-crow of our human
   years.

Alice Meynell: *The Voice of a Bird.* (20th
cent.)

See also Pope

Peter and Paul, Saints

In these ways you also, by such an admonition, have united the planting that
came from Peter and Paul, of both the
Romans and the Corinthians. For indeed
both planted also in our Corinth, and
likewise taught us; and likewise they
taught together also in Italy, and were
martyred at the same time.

Dionysius of Corinth: *Letter to the
Romans.* (In Eusebius, *Eccl. Hist.* 2, 25,
8.) (171)

It is related that in his [i.e. Nero's]
time Paul was beheaded in Rome itself,
and that Peter likewise was crucified,
and the title of 'Peter and Paul,' which
is still given to the cemeteries there,
confirms the story, no less than does a
writer of the Church named Caius, who
lived when Zephyrinus was bishop of
Rome [c. 198–217 A.D]. Caius in a
written discussion with Proclus, the
leader of the Montanists, speaks as follows of the places where the sacred
relics of the apostles in question were
deposited: *But I can point out the
trophies of the apostles, for if you will
go to the Vatican or to the Ostian Way
you will find the trophies of those who
founded this church. . . .*

Eusebius of Caesarea: *Ecclesiastical
History,* 2, 25, 5-8. (4th cent.)

The heaven is not so bright, when the
sun sends forth his rays, as is the city
of Rome, sending out these two lights
into all the world. Thence Paul will be
caught up, thence Peter. . . . What two
crowns has the city about it, with what
golden chains it is girded about, what
fountains it has! Therefore I admire the
city, not for its much gold, not for its
columns, not for any other phantasy, but
for these pillars of the Church.

St. John Chrysostom: *Homilies on
Romans,* 32. (4th cent.)

O God, Who hast made this day holy
with the martyrdom of Thy apostles
Peter and Paul; grant that Thy Church
spread throughout the world may always
be governed by their authority (*magisterium*), from whom it first received the
faith.

Leonine Sacramentary, Collect for June 29.
(Gregorian collect presently used in
Roman Missal has variation: 'that Thy
Church may in all things follow the
precepts of those from whom. . . .') (ca.
5th cent.)

It is truly meet and just . . . because it is a result of Thy work and Thy power that the glorious confession of Thy blessed apostles Peter and Paul, the annual solemnity of which we are now celebrating, is never prevailed against by false teaching nor shaken by adversity, but the faithful structure of Thy body everywhere, by Thy disposition, receives that which that See has deemed right, which Thou wished to have the primacy over the whole Church.

Leonine Sacramentary, Feast of Apostles (June 29), Preface. (ca. 5th cent.)

The beauteous light of God's eternal majesty
Streams down in golden rays to grace this holy day
Which crowned the princes of the apostles' glorious choir,
And unto guilty mortals showed the heavenward way.

The teacher of the world and keeper of heaven's gate,
Rome's founders twain and rulers too of every land,
Triumphant over death by sword and shameful cross,
With laurel crowned are gathered to the eternal band.

O happy Rome! who in thy martyr princes' blood,
A twofold stream, art washed and doubly sanctified.
All earthly beauty thou alone outshinest far,
Empurpled by their outpoured lifeblood's glorious tide.

Roman Breviary, Feast of Peter and Paul, Hymn *Decora lux aeternitatis auream* (*Aurea luce et decore roseo*) at Vespers. (Tr. L. Hall) (Altered, attr. to Elpis, wife of Boethius, 5th cent.)

O God, Whose right hand upheld blessed Peter walking upon the waves, lest he should sink, and delivered his fellow-apostle Paul when shipwrecked for the third time from the depth of the sea; hear us in Thy mercy, and grant that through their merits we may obtain the glory of everlasting life.

Roman Missal, Collect. (Gelasian, ca. 6th cent.)

The earth's wide bounds the honored festival
Of blessed Peter and holy Paul
Is kept in happy memory, and maintained
To grace whom Christ's redeeming blood ordained
Among the apostles princes over all.

St. Paulinus of Aquileia: *Felix per Omnes Festum.* (Tr. D. Donahoe) (8th cent.)

O three times happy two! O golden pair!
Who with your blood did lay the Church's ground
Within the fatal town which twins did found,
And settled there the Hebrew fisher's chair,
Where first the Latin shepherd rais'd his throne,
And since the world and Church were rul'd by one.

Henry Constable: *Sonnet to Saints Peter and Paul.* (16th cent.)

The world has to be saved by hook or by crook; it is well for the Church when anglers and shepherds do not fall out.
R. Knox: *Stimuli.* (20th cent.)

Pheasant

See! from the brake the whirring pheasant springs,
And mounts exulting on triumphant wings:
Short is his joy; he feels the fiery wound,
Flutters in blood, and panting beats the ground.

Pope: *Windsor Forest.* (18th cent.)

Philanthropy

There is an old proverb, quoth she, sayeth, that the goodness that thou mayest do this day, do it, and abide not nor delay it not till tomorrow.

> Chaucer: *The Tale of Melibeus.* (14th cent.)

Philip Neri, Saint

Saint Philip! I have never known
  A saint as I know thee;
For none have made their wills and
  ways
  So plain for men to see!

> F. Faber: *Saint Philip's Picture.* (19th cent.)

Philosopher

Man existed before the philosopher.

> Tertullian: *The Testimony of the Christian Soul.* (3rd cent.)

But all be that he was a philosopher,
Yet had he but little gold in coffer.

> Chaucer: *Canterbury Tales: Prologue.* (14th cent.)

To ridicule philosophy: that is to be a real philosopher.

> Pascal: *Pensées,* 7. (17th cent.)

Philosophers astonish ordinary men—
Christians astonish philosophers.

> Pascal: *Pensées.* (17th cent.)

Oh, wondrous creature! mount where
  science guides,
Go measure earth, weigh air, and state
  the tides;
Instruct the planets in what orbs to run,
Correct old Time, and regulate the sun;
Go teach eternal wisdom how to rule,
Then drop into thyself, and be a fool!

> Pope: *An Essay on Man,* 2. (18th cent.)

Philosophy

Is this not the task of philosophy to inquire about the divine?

> St. Justin Martyr: *Dialogue with Trypho,* 1. (2nd cent.)

Philosophy is the knowledge of that which exists, and a clear understanding of the truth; and happiness is the reward of such knowledge and understanding.

> St. Justin Martyr: *Dialogue with Trypho,* 3. (2nd cent.)

Philosophy is the knowledge of things human and divine, united with a zeal for right living.

> St. Isidore: *Etymologies,* 2, 24. (7th cent.)

Philosophy is the meditation on death; this definition is better suited to Christians who, trampling on worldly ambition, live in the intercourse of discipline, after the likeness of their future country.

> St. Isidore: *Etymologies,* 2, 24. (7th cent.)

Philosophy is called natural when the nature of each and every thing is discussed, since nothing arises contrary to nature in life, but each thing is assigned to those uses for which it was intended by the Creator, unless perchance by God's will it is shown that some miracle has intervened.

> St. Isidore: *Etymologies,* 2, 24. (7th cent.)

Philosophy is the art of arts and science of sciences.

> St. John of Damascus: *Dialectica,* 3. (8th cent.)

It is indeed a great step in advance, for one aspiring to philosophy, to deplore the lack of virtue in himself.

> John of Salisbury: *Policraticus,* 7, Prol. (12th cent.)

Because philosophy arises from awe a philosopher is bound in his way to be a lover of myths and poetic fables. Poets and philosophers are alike in being big with wonder.

> St. Thomas Aquinas: *Commentary on the Metaphysics,* 1, lect. 3. (13th cent.)

Science and philosophy, in their elementary idea, are nothing else but this habit of viewing, as it may be called, the objects which sense conveys to the mind, of throwing them into system, and uniting and stamping them with one form.

> Card. Newman: *Idea of a University*, 4. (19th cent.)

What has philosophy taught men but to promise without practising, and to aspire without attaining? What has the deep and lofty thought of its disciples ended in but eloquent words?

> Card. Newman: *Idea of a University*. (19th cent.)

The method and principles by which the doctors of scholastic philosophy cultivated theology of old are no longer suitable to the demands of our times and the progress of the sciences.

> Proposition condemned by Pius IX in Syllabus of Errors. (1867)

Philosophy is merely thought that has been thought out. It is often a great bore. But man has no alternative, except between being influenced by thought that has been thought out and being influenced by thought that has not been thought out. The latter is what we commonly call culture and enlightenment.

> G. K. Chesterton: *The Common Man*. (20th cent.)

Philosophy is not the concern of those who pass through Divinity and Greats, but of those who pass through birth and death. Nearly all the more awful and abstruse statements can be put in words of one syllable, from 'A child is born' to 'A soul is damned.' If the ordinary man may not discuss existence, why should he be asked to conduct it?

> G. K. Chesterton: *George Bernard Shaw*. (20th cent.)

The Catholic philosophy is a universal philosophy found to fit anywhere with human nature and the nature of things. But even when it does not fit in with human nature it is found in the long run to favor something yet more fitting. It

generally suits us, but where it does not suit us we learn to suit it, so long as we are alive enough to learn anything.

> G. K. Chesterton: *The Catholic Church and Conversion*. (20th cent.)

Philosophy and Christianity

The philosopher aspires towards a divine principle; the Christian, towards a divine Agent.

> Card. Newman: *Oxford University Sermons*. (19th cent.)

The Church not only ought never to pass judgment on philosophy, but ought to tolerate the errors of philosophy, leaving it to correct itself.

> Proposition condemned by Pius IX in Syllabus of Errors. (1867)

Philosophy is to be expounded without taking any account of supernatural revelation.

> Proposition condemned by Pius IX in Syllabus of Errors. (1867)

Philosophy, if rightly made use of by the wise, in a certain way tends to smooth and fortify the road to true faith, and to prepare the souls of its disciples for the fit reception of revelation; for which reason it is well called by ancient writers sometimes a stepping-stone to the Christian faith, sometimes the prelude and help of Christianity, sometimes the Gospel teacher.

> Pope Leo XIII: *Aeterni Patris*. (Aug. 4, 1879)

Philosophy does not seek to overthrow revelation; it seeks rather to defend it against assailants.

> Pope Leo XIII: *Inscrutabili*. (Apr. 21, 1878)

Philosophy is the science of the limitations of the human mind. When you know philosophy, you know what you cannot know.

> Joseph Rickaby: *An Old Man's Jottings*. (20th cent.)

Truth and its philosophic expression cannot change from day to day, least of all where there is a question of the self-evident principles of the human mind or of those propositions which are supported by the wisdom of the ages and by divine revelation. Whatever new truths the sincere human mind is able to find certainly cannot be opposed to truth already acquired, since God, the Highest Truth, has created and guides the human intellect, not that it may daily oppose new truths to rightly established ones, but rather that having eliminated errors which may have crept in, it may build truth upon truth in the same order and structure that exist in reality, the source of truth. Let no Christian therefore, whether philosopher or theologian, embrace eagerly and lightly whatever novelty happens to be thought up from day to day, but rather let him weigh it with painstaking care and a balanced judgment, lest he lose or corrupt the truth he already has, with grave danger and damage to his faith.

Pope Pius XII: *Humani Generis.* (Apr. 12, 1950)

Piety

See Devotion; Love of God; Serving God

Pilgrim

O Christ, our King, give ear!
O Lord and Maker, hear!
And guide our footsteps lest they stray.
O ever Three and One,
Protect our course begun,
And lead us on our holy way!

Chorus

Have mercy on us, Lord:
Have mercy on us, Lord,
And guide our footsteps lest they stray.

Anonymous: *Audi nos Rex Christe.* (Tr. J. Neale) (Pilgrims' song) (11th cent.)

When the sweet showers of April fall and shoot

Down through the drought of March to pierce the root,

. . . .

Then people long to go on pilgrimages
And palmers long to seek the stranger strands
Of far-off saints, hallowed in sundry lands,
And specially, from every shire's end
In England, down to Canterbury they wend
To seek the holy blissful martyr, quick
In giving help to them when they were sick.

Chaucer: *Canterbury Tales: Prologue.* (Tr. Coghill) (14th cent.)

The pilgrim who spends all his time counting his steps will make little progress.

Jean Pierre Camus: *The Spirit of St. Francis de Sales,* 12, 3. (17th cent.)

The pilgrim to Rome brings back from Rome what he brought to Rome.

Seumas MacManus: *Heavy Hangs the Golden Grain.* (20th cent.)

Pity

Now when a man suffers himself, it is called misery; when he suffers in the suffering of another, it is called pity.

St. Augustine: *Confessions,* 3, 2. (5th cent.)

All feel pity for those like themselves.

Claudianus: *In Eutropium,* 1. (5th cent.)

Let Thy continual pity cleanse and defend Thy Church, we beseech Thee, O Lord; and because it cannot continue in safety without Thee, govern it continually with Thy help.

Roman Missal, Collect for Fifteenth Sunday after Pentecost. (Gelasian, 5th to 7th cent.)

Here pity most doth show herself alive, When she is dead.

Dante: *Inferno, Canto 20.* (14th cent.)

For pity runneth soon in gentle heart.

> Chaucer: *The Knightes Tale.* (14th cent.)

To pity the unhappy is not contrary to selfish desire; on the other hand, we are glad of the occasion to thus testify friendship and attract to ourselves the reputation of tenderness, without giving anything.

> Pascal: *Pensées,* 8. (17th cent.)

See also Mercy

Plagiarism

But this our age such authors does afford,
As make whole plays, and yet scarce write one word;
Who, in this anarchy of wit, rob all,
And what's their plunder, their possession call.

> Dryden: *Albumazar, Prologue.* (17th cent.)

Platitude

In modern life nothing produces such an effect as a good platitude. It makes the whole world kin.

> Oscar Wilde: *An Ideal Husband,* 1. (19th cent.)

Plausibility

Anything will become plausible, if you read all that can be said in its favor, and exclude all that can be said against it.

> Card. Newman: *Present Position of Catholics in England,* 1. (19th cent.)

Playfulness

Let me twine with you caresses,
Wantoning
With our Lady-Mother's vagrant tresses,
Banqueting
With her in her wind-walled palace,
Underneath her azured daïs.

> F. Thompson: *The Hound of Heaven.* (19th cent.)

Pleasing

In men for the sake of women, just as in women for the sake of men, there is implanted, by a defect of nature, the desire to please.

> Tertullian: *Women's Dress.* (3rd cent.)

There is a short precept: He pleaseth God whom God pleaseth.

> St. Augustine: *In Ps. 32, Enar. 2, Sermo 1,* 1. (5th cent.)

Whate'er he did was done with so much ease,
In him alone, 'twas natural to please.

> Dryden: *Absalom and Achitophel.* (17th cent.)

Pleasure

The Epicureans had the liberty to state the notion, and determine the object of pleasure. Why can't we Christians have the same privilege? What offence is it if we differ from you in the idea of satisfaction? If we won't brighten our humor, and live pleasantly, where's the harm? If anybody has the worst of it, it is only ourselves.

> Tertullian: *Apologeticus.* (2nd cent.)

No display of virtue gives an act distinction if its origin is rooted in pleasure.

> John of Salisbury: *Policraticus,* 1, 4, 33. (12th cent.)

The mind which is created apt to love,
Soon as by pleasure it is stirred to act,
To every pleasing thing is quick to move.

> Dante: *Purgatorio, Canto 18.* (Tr. Binyon) (14th cent.)

For he was Epicurus owen son.

> Chaucer: *Canterbury Tales: Prologue.* (14th cent.)

Who will, in time present, pleasure refrain

Shall, in time to come, the more pleasure obtain.

John Heywood: *Proverbs*, 1, 11. (16th cent.)

Follow pleasure, and then will pleasure flee;
Flee pleasure, and pleasure will follow thee.

John Heywood: *Proverbs*, 1, 11. (16th cent.)

Dame Pleasure's drugs are steep'd in sin,
Their sugar'd taste doth breed annoy;
O fickle sense! beware her gin,
Sell not thy soul for brittle joy!

Robert Southwell: *Man's Civil War.* (16th cent.)

Pluck the fruit and taste the pleasure,
    Youthful lordlings of delight;
Whilst occasion gives you seizure,
    Feed your fancies and your sight:
        After death, when you are gone,
        Joy and pleasure is there none.

Thomas Lodge: *Robert, Second Duke of Normandy.* (16th cent.)

We must be able to find pleasure in ourselves when alone, and in our neighbor when in his company.

J. P. Camus: *The Spirit of St. Francis de Sales*, 21, 5. (17th cent.)

Admirers of false pleasures must sustain
The weight and sharpness of ensuing pain.

Sir John Beaumont: *Against Inordinate Love of Creatures.* (17th cent.)

Large scope of pleasure drowns us like a flood,
To rest in little, is our greatest good.

Sir John Beaumont: *Of True Liberty.* (17th cent.)

Sweet is pleasure after pain.

Dryden: *Alexander's Feast.* (17th cent.)

I take my pleasures without change
And as I lived I live.

W. S. Blunt: *The Old Squire.* (19th cent.)

Pleasure and Pain

Take a pain for a pleasure all wise men can.

John Heywood: *Proverbs*, 1, 5. (16th cent.)

For all the happiness man can gain
Is not in pleasure, but in rest from pain.

Dryden: *The Indian Emperor*, 4, 1. (17th cent.)

Self-love and reason to one end aspire;
Pain their aversion, pleasure their desire.

Pope: *An Essay on Man*, 2. (18th cent.)

The intensest pain and the intensest joy lie close together.

R. H. Benson: *The Light Invisible.* (20th cent.)

The moment a soul recognizes that there may be a joy in pain which is absent from pleasure, she has taken the first step towards the practical solution of the problem of pain.

R. H. Benson: *Christ in the Church.* (20th cent.)

Plenty

Plenty is no dainty.

John Heywood: *Proverbs*, 2, 4. (16th cent.)

Plot

Plots, true or false, are necessary things,
To raise up commonwealths and ruin kings.

Dryden: *Absalom and Achitophel.* (17th cent.)

Poe, Edgar Allan

A certain tyrant, to disgrace
The more a rebel's resting place,
Compelled the people every one
To hurl, in passing there, a stone,
Which done, behold, the pile became
A monument to keep the name.
And thus it is with Edgar Poe;
Each passing critic has his throw,
Nor sees, defeating his intent,
How lofty grows the monument.

John B. Tabb: *Poe's Critics.* (19th cent.)

Poet

The more rhetoric, the more mischief;
and the best poets are the worst citizens.

Lactantius: *Divinae institutiones, 6.* (4th cent.)

He could songs make and well indite.

Chaucer: *Canterbury Tales: Prologue.* (14th cent.)

The first happiness of the poet's imagination is properly invention, or finding
of the thought; the second is fancy, or
the variation, deriving or molding of
that thought as the judgment represents
it proper to the subject; the third is
elocution, or the art of clothing and
adorning that thought so found and
varied, in apt, significant and sounding
words.

John Dryden: *Annus Mirabilis.* (17th cent.)

Poets, like lovers, should be bold and
dare,
They spoil their business with overcare;
And he, who servilely creeps after
sense,
Is safe, but ne'er will reach an excellence.

Dryden: *Tyrannic Love, Prologue.* (17th cent.)

A poet is not born in every race.

Dryden: *To John Dryden of Chesterton.* (17th cent.)

The employment of a poet is like that
of a curious gunsmith or watchmaker:
the iron or silver is not his own, but
they are the least part of that which gives
the value; the price lies wholly in the
workmanship.

Dryden: *An Evening's Love,* Pref. (17th cent.)

Poets, like painters, thus unskill'd to
trace
The naked nature and the living grace,
With gold and jewels cover every part,
And hide with ornaments, their want
of art.

Pope: *An Essay on Criticism, 2.* (18th cent.)

Poets are the only poor fellows in the
world whom anybody will flatter.

Pope: *Letter to William Trumbull.* (18th cent.)

Pensive poets painful vigils keep,
Sleepless themselves to give their readers sleep.

Pope: *The Dunciad, 1.* (18th cent.)

We poets are (upon a poet's word)
Of all mankind the creatures most
absurd;
The season when to come, and when
to go,
To sing, or cease to sing, we never
know.

Pope: *The First Epistle of the Second Book of Horace.* (18th cent.)

Tell thou the world, when my bones
lie whitening
Amid the last homes of youth and
eld,
That there was one whose veins ran
lightning
No eye beheld.

And tell how trampled, derided, hated,
And won by weakness, disease, and
wrong,
He fled for shelter to God, who mated
His soul with song.

James C. Mangan: *The Nameless One.* (19th cent.)

The poet is great nature's own high priest,
Ordained from very birth
To keep for hearts an everlasting feast—
To bless or curse the earth.

Abram Ryan: *Poets.* (19th cent.)

The poet is par excellence the perceiver, nothing having any interest for him unless he can, as it were, see and touch it, with the spiritual senses, with which he is preeminently endowed.

Coventry Patmore: *Religio Poetae.* (19th cent.)

A double life the poet lived,
And with a double burthen grieved;
The life of flesh and life of song,
The pangs to both lives that belong.

F. Thompson: *A Judgment in Heaven: Epilogue.* (19th cent.)

And ah, we poets, I misdoubt,
Are little more than thou!
We speak a lesson taught we know not how,
And what it is that from us flows
The hearer better than the utterer knows.

F. Thompson: *Sister Songs.* (19th cent.)

I would not, if I could, be called a poet.
I have no natural love of the 'chaste muse'.
If aught be worth the doing I would do it;
And others, if they will, may tell the news.

W. S. Blunt: *Love Sonnets of Proteus, 95.* (19th cent.)

A poet mused upon the dusky height,
Between two stars towards night,
His purpose in his heart. I watched, a space,
The meaning on his face:
There was the secret, fled from earth and skies,
Hid in his grey young eyes.

My heart and all the summer wait his choice,

And wonder for his voice.
Who shall foretell his songs, and who aspire
But to divine his lyre?
Sweet earth, we know thy dimmest mysteries,
But he is lord of his.

Alice Meynell: *In Early Spring.* (19th cent.)

A poet of one mood in all my lays,
Ranging all like to sing one only love,
Like a west wind across the world I move,
Sweeping my harp of floods mine own wild ways.

Alice Meynell: *A Poet of One Mood.* (19th cent.)

It is the very difference between the artistic mind and the mathematical that the former sees things as they are in a picture, some nearer and larger, some smaller and farther away: while to the mathematical mind everything, every inch in a million, every fact in a cosmos must be of equal value. That is why mathematicians go mad, and poets scarcely ever do.

G. K. Chesterton: *G. F. Watts.* (20th cent.)

Any common scientific philosopher can have small ideas so long as he is not called upon to have large ideas as well. But great poets use the telescope as well as the microscope. Great poets are obscure for two opposite reasons; now, because they are talking about something too large for any one to understand, and now again because they are talking about something too small for any one to see.

G. K. Chesterton: *All Things Considered.* (20th cent.)

Poets will tend towards Christian orthodoxy for a perfectly plain reason: because it is about the simplest and freest thing now left in the world.

G. K. Chesterton: *All Things Considered.* (20th cent.)

To poets, Lord, Thou givest neither drink
Nor raiment, fire nor peace nor food;
Enhungered, thirsting as they daily sink
Beneath the trampling multitude.

> Sir Shane Leslie: *Priest or Poet.* (20th cent.)

A Catholic poet should be an apostle by being first of all a poet, not try to be a poet by being first of all an apostle. For if he presents himself to people as a poet, he is going to be judged as a poet and if he is not a good one his apostolate will be ridiculed.

> Thomas Merton: *Seeds of Contemplation.* (20th cent.)

Poet and His Poetry

From me, my art, thou canst not pass away;
    And I, a singer though I cease to sing,
        Shall own thee without joy in thee or woe.

Through my indifferent words of every day,
    Scattered and all unlinked the rhymes shall ring,
        And make my poem; and I shall not know.

> Alice Meynell: *Unlinked.* (19th cent.)

Who looked for thee, thou little song of mine?
    This winter of a silent poet's heart
    Is suddenly sweet with thee. But what thou art,
Mid-winter flower, I would I could divine.

> Alice Meynell: *To One Poem in a Silent Time.* (19th cent.)

Surely there was a time I might have trod
The sunlit heights, and from life's dissonance
Struck one clear chord to reach the ears of God.

> Oscar Wilde: *Hélas!* (Prefixed to Paris edition of his poems, 1903) (19th cent.)

Poetess

A maudlin poetess.

> Pope: *An Epistle to Dr. Arbuthnot.* (18th cent.)

Poetry

A well-made poem is a powerful piece of imposture. It masters the fancy, and hurries it nobody knows whither.

> Lactantius: *Divinae institutiones, 6.* (4th cent.)

Poetry is devils' wine (Poesis est vinum daemonum.)

> St. Augustine: *Contra Academicos, 1.* (4th cent.)

Prophane conceits and feignèd fits I fly;
Such lawless stuff doth lawless speeches fit.
With David, verse to virtue I apply,
Whose measure best with measured words doth fit:
It is the sweetest note that men can sing
When grace in virtue's key tunes nature's string.

> Bl. Robert Southwell: *To the Reader.* (From *St. Peter's Complaint*) (16th cent.)

Not orators so much with flowing words
Can sway the hearts of men, and whet their swords
Or blunt them at their pleasure, as our strains,
(Whose larger sphere the orb of prose contains),
Can men's affections lessen or increase,
And guide their passions, whisp'ring war or peace.

> Sir John Beaumont: *Of the Excellent Use of Poems.* (17th cent.)

He makes sweet music, who in serious lines,
Light dancing tunes, and heavy prose declines:

When verses like a milky torrent flow,
They equal temper in the poet show.

> Sir John Beaumont: *To His Late Majesty concerning the True Form of English Poetry.* (17th cent.)

Kings may
Find proud ambition humbled at the sea,
Which bounds dominion: But the nobler flight
Of poesie hath a supremer right
To empire, and extends her large command
Where ere th' invading sea assaults the land.

> William Habington: *To William Davenant.* (17th cent.)

To vulgar eyes the sacred truth I write,
May seem a fancy. But the eagle's sight
Of saints and poets miracles oft view,
Which to dull heretics appear untrue.

> William Habington: *Castara.* (17th cent.)

So poetry, which is in Oxford made
An art, in London only is a trade.

> Dryden: *The University of Oxford, Prologue.* (17th cent.)

Wit will shine
Through the harsh cadence of a rugged line.

> Dryden: *To the Memory of Mr. Oldham.* (17th cent.)

Should men be rated by poetic rules,
Lord, what a poll would there be rais'd from fools!

> Dryden: *The True Widow, Prologue.* (17th cent.)

O gracious God how far have we
Profaned thy heav'nly gift of poesy!
Made prostitute and profligate the muse,
Debased to each obscene and impious use,
Whose harmony was first ordained above

For tongues of angels and for hymns of love!

> Dryden: *To the Memory of Mrs. Anne Killigrew.* (17th cent.)

What praise soe'er the poetry deserve,
Yet every fool can bid the poet starve.

> Dryden. (17th cent.)

Delight is the chief if not the only end of poesy: instruction can be admitted but in the second place, for poetry only instructs as it delights.

> Dryden: *An Essay of Dramatic Poesy.* (17th cent.)

Happy who in his verse can gently steer,
From grave to light; from pleasant to severe.

> Dryden: *The Art of Poetry,* 1, 75. (17th cent.)

No muse is proof against a golden shower.

> Sir Samuel Garth: *Claremont.* (18th cent.)

Monosyllabic lines, unless very artfully managed, are stiff or languishing, but may be beautiful to express melancholy, slowness or labor.

> Pope: *Letter to William Walsh.* (18th cent.)

'Tis not enough no harshness gives offence;
The sound must seem an echo to the sense.

> Pope: *An Essay on Criticism,* 2. (18th cent.)

With Christians, a poetical view of things is a duty,—we are bid to color all things with hues of faith, to see a divine meaning in every event, and a superhuman tendency.

> Card. Newman: *Essays Critical and Historical,* 1. (19th cent.)

The Church herself is the most sacred and august of poets. Poetry . . . is a method of relieving the over-burdened mind; it is a channel through which emotion finds expression, and that a safe, regulated expression. Now what is the Catholic Church, viewed in her human aspect, but a discipline of the affections and passions? What are her ordinances and practices but the regulated expression of keen, or deep, or turbid feeling, and thus a 'cleansing,' as Aristotle would word it, of the sick soul?

Card. Newman: *Essays Critical and Historical*, 2. (19th cent.)

Like as a brook that all night long
Sings, as at noon, a bubble-song
    To sleep's unheeding ear,
The poet to himself must sing,
When none but God is listening
    The lullaby to hear.

J. B. Tabb: *In Solitude*. (19th cent.)

Nothing has so much injured modern art as the artist's ambition to show off his 'breadth'; and many an immortal lyric or idyll has been lost because the lyric or idyllic poet has chosen to forsake his line for the production of exceedingly mortal epics or tragedies. . . . Poets, whose 'works' are always collectively exhibited, should beware how they betray the inevitable fact of the narrowness of genius. Not only should they never leave their own line for another which is not their own, but they should be equally careful not to go over it again when they have once got to the end of it.

Coventry Patmore: *Religio Poetae*. (19th cent.)

The poet always treats spiritual realities as the concrete and very credible things they truly are. He has no slipshod notions about the immeasurable and infinite. He knows, as Plato knew, that God himself is most falsely described as infinite. God is the synthesis, as Proclus declares in his treatise on the fables of Homer, of infinite and boundary, and is excellently intelligible, though for ever unutterable, by those who love him.

Coventry Patmore: *Religio Poetae*. (19th cent.)

Neither in ancient nor in modern times has there been a poet, worthy of that sacred name, who would not have been horrified had he fancied that the full meaning of some of his sayings could be discerned by more than ten in ten thousand of his readers.

Coventry Patmore: *Religio Poetae*. (19th cent.)

All things sing to me—cry: laughter, or tears, or music.
The storm hath its rhythmical beat; the day its musical cadence:
Ever an ebb or a flow—a flame, or a mournful nightfall,
A rivulet bearded with moss, to me is Theocritus singing;
A violet, bursting in spring, thrills me with exquisite music;
A child's voice, heard in the dusk, shakes me with infinite pathos,
The flash of the daybreak's sword, the march of the midnight planets,
The sweep of the mighty winds, the shout of the prophet-voiced thunder,
Restlessly throb in my soul, and shale themselves into measure.

Charles J. O'Malley: *The Poet's Harvesting*. (19th cent.)

And so my touch, to golden poesies
Turning love's bread, is bought at hunger's price.

F. Thompson: *Sister Songs*. (19th cent.)

It is the supreme proof of a man being prosaic that he always insists on poetry being poetical.

G. K. Chesterton: *The Everlasting Man*. (20th cent.)

There is nothing more artificial than the cry of artificiality as directed against the old pastoral poetry. We have entirely missed all that our fathers meant by looking at the externals of what they wrote. People have been so much amused with the mere fact that the china shepherdess was made of china that they have not even asked why she was made at all.

> G. K. Chesterton: *The Everlasting Man.* (20th cent.)

Poetry is only the algebra of life; passion is its arithmetic.

> G. K. Chesterton: *A Handful of Authors.* (20th cent.)

To ransom one lost moment with a rhyme,
Or, if fate cries and grudging gods demur,
To clutch life's hair, and thrust one naked phrase
Like a lean knife between the ribs of time.

> Lord Alfred Douglas: *The City of the Soul.* (20th cent.)

Nay, what is poetry? A bright-winged bird
    Singing the songs of our lost Eden days;
'Tis beauty, caught in rapturous midflight,
    And caged in some brief, deathless line or phrase;
The voice of David singing to his harp,
    While earth, a weary Saul with guilt oppressed,
Forgets a space its sordid griefs and cares,
    And feels a thrill of hope within its breast.

> Sister M. Angelita: *Poetry (to the Rhetoricians).* (20th cent.)

Verse is a slow thing to create; nay, it is not really created: it is a secretion of the mind, it is a pearl that gathers round some irritant and slowly expresses the very essence of beauty and desire that has lain long, potential and unexpressed, in the mind of the man who secretes it.

> Hilaire Belloc: *On Nothing, and Kindred Subjects.* (20th cent.)

Poetic experience is distinct in nature from mystical experience. Because poetry emanates from the free creativity of the spirit, it is from the very start oriented toward expression, and terminates in a word proffered, it wants to speak; whereas mystical experience, because it emanates from the deepest longing of the spirit bent on knowing, tends of itself toward silence and internal fruition.

> J. Maritain: *The Range of Reason.* (20th cent.)

No Christian poetry worthy of the name has been written by anyone who was not in some degree a contemplative.

> Thomas Merton: *Poetry and the Contemplative Life.* (In *Figures for an Apocalypse.*) (20th cent.)

Poetry and Prose

It is not poetry, but prose run mad.

> Pope: *An Epistle to Dr. Arbuthnot.* (18th cent.)

Alas, what are we doing all through life, both as a necessity and as a duty, but unlearning the world's poetry, and attaining to its prose!

> Card. Newman: *Idea of a University.* (19th cent.)

Poison

Venom destroys venom.

> Langland: *Piers Plowman,* Passus 21. (14th cent.)

I know too well the poison and the sting
    Of things too sweet.

> Adelaide Procter: *Per Pacem ad Lucem.* (19th cent.)

What is one man's poison is another man's drug.

> R. A. Knox: *The Belief of Catholics.* (20th cent.)

Poisoning

To assimilate blindfold will sooner or later end in poisoning.

> R. H. Benson: *A City Set on a Hill.* (20th cent.)

Pole, Reginald Cardinal

Failure to perform an impossible task has, more than once in history, been the occasion of a startling personal success.

R. H. Benson: *Introduction to the Angelical Cardinal.* (20th cent.)

Politeness

One should be affable in conversation and agreeable in social intercourse, not resorting to wit as a means of gaining popularity, but depending upon the charm which comes from gracious politeness.

St. Basil: *Letters,* 2. (4th cent.)

It is true there are many very polite men, but none that I ever heard of who were not either fascinating women or obeying them.

G. K. Chesterton: *What's Wrong with the World.* (20th cent.)

Politician

The privilege that statesmen ever claim;
Who private interest never yet pursu'd,
But still pretended 'twas for others' good:
What politician yet e'er scap'd his fate
Who saving his own neck not sav'd the state?

Dryden: *Absalom and Achitophel.* (17th cent.)

For politicians neither love nor hate.

Dryden: *Absalom and Achitophel.* (17th cent.)

In friendship false, implacable in hate,
Resolved to ruin or to rule the state.

Dryden: *Absalom and Achitophel,* 1. (17th cent.)

What we need, as the ancients understood, is not a politician who is a business man, but a king who is a philosopher.

G. K. Chesterton: *The Common Man.* (20th cent.)

Politics

With the rashness of ignorance the uninitiated dare to dabble in affairs of state.

John of Salisbury: *Policraticus,* 1, 4, 35. (12th cent.)

There is no leisure about politics, for they are ever seeking an end outside political practice, for instance power or fame. Political life neither provides our final end nor contains the happiness we seek for ourselves or others. . . . The purpose of temporal tranquillity, which well-ordered policies establish and maintain, is to give opportunities for contemplating truth.

St. Thomas Aquinas: *Commentary on the Ethics,* 10, lect. 11. (13th cent.)

To place and power all public spirit tends,
In place and power all public spirit ends;
Like hardy plants, that love the air and sky,
When out, 'twill thrive—but taken *in,* 'twill die!

Thomas Moore: *Corruption.* (19th cent.)

The Catholic Church is not a party in the politics of any nation, at home or abroad. Her mission is to all nations, and to all parties in each, except as either may be divided from the other by the eternal principles of right and wrong. She can never give up her mission and her message to all for the sake of *only* some.

Archb. Hughes: *Letters.* (Works, 2, 471) (1852)

It is common to advise Catholics to make up their minds to accept the political doctrines of the day; but it would be more to the purpose to recall the ideas of Catholic times.

> Lord Acton: *Political Thoughts on the Church.* (19th cent.)

The Church can no more identify her cause with scientific error than with political wrong. Her interests may be impaired by some measure of political justice, or by the admission of some fact or document. But in neither case can she guard her interests at the cost of denying the truth.

> Lord Acton: *Conflicts with Rome.* (19th cent.)

A civil ruler dabbling in religion is as reprehensible as a clergyman dabbling in politics. Both render themselves odious as well as ridiculous.

> Card. Gibbons: *The Faith of Our Fathers,* 12. (19th cent.)

The best men for the office, whatever the religious creed of the man. To put a Catholic into office, merely because he is a Catholic, though otherwise unworthy and incapable, is a crime against America, a sin against almighty God.

> Archb. Ireland: *Catholicism and Americanism.* (Milwaukee, Aug. 11, 1913)

It is a calumny that we deeply resent, to say that in civic and political matters Catholic voters are under the influence of the Church. Priests and bishops do not dictate the politics of Catholics; if they strove to do so their interference would be promptly repulsed. It is of public knowledge that the Catholic vote is distributed among several political parties of the country.

> Archb. Ireland: *Catholicism and Americanism.* (Milwaukee, Aug. 11, 1913)

He thinks like a Tory and talks like a Radical, and that's so important nowadays.

> Oscar Wilde: *Lady Windermere's Fan,* 2. (19th cent.)

Politicians have no politics.

> G. K. Chesterton: *Autobiography.* (20th cent.)

The hazards of politics come not from campaigns and elections, as might be supposed, but rather from the nature of the creature that engages in politics. Ambition, love, jealousy, hate and the many emotions and reactions man is heir to frequently affect the course of nation and world more than principles or circumstances or events.

> James A. Farley. (In *The Sign,* Aug. 1948.)

See also Church and State; Democracy; Government; State

Pomposity

> A vile conceit in pompous words express'd,
> Is like a clown in regal purple dress'd.

> Pope: *An Essay on Criticism,* 2. (18th cent.)

Pomposity is only the failure of pomp.

> G. K. Chesterton: *A Handful of Authors.* (20th cent.)

Pope

I—Pope: Successor of St. Peter

They have not the heritage of Peter who have not the see of Peter, rent by their impious division.

> Tertullian: *De Poenitentia,* 1, 7. (3rd cent.)

There is one God, and Christ is one, and there is one Church, and one chair founded upon Peter by the word of the Lord. Another altar cannot be constituted nor a new priesthood be made, except the one altar and the one priesthood.

St. Cyprian: *Letters,* 39, 5. (3rd cent.)

The Lord speaks to Peter and says: *And I tell thee this in my turn, that thou art Peter, and it is upon this rock that I will build my Church; and the gates of hell shall not overcome it; and I will give to thee the keys of the kingdom of heaven; and whatsoever thou shalt bind on earth shall be bound in heaven, and whatever thou shalt loose on earth shall be loosed in heaven* (Matth. 16, 18-20). He builds his Church upon one [or, After his resurrection he again says to him: *Feed my sheep.* Upon him alone he builds his Church, and to him he commits his sheep to be fed], and although he gives equal authoritative power to all the apostles after his resurrection and says to them: *As the Father sent me, so do I send you. Receive the Holy Spirit: whose sins you shall forgive, they shall be forgiven them, whose sins you shall retain, they shall be retained* (John 20, 21-23), still, that he might show forth unity, he [made one chair, and] provided by his authority that the origin (*originem*) [and principle (*rationem*)] of this unity should begin from one. The other apostles were, of course, what Peter was, endowed with a like fellowship both of office and power, but the beginning proceeds from unity [and a primacy is given to Peter], so that the single Church of Christ [and a single chair] may be visibly set forth. [Moreover, they are all shepherds, but it is shown that the flock is one, to be fed by all the apostles with unanimous agreement. He who does not maintain this unity of the Church, does he believe that he retains the faith? He who deserts the chair of Peter on whom the Church has been founded, does he still believe that he is in the Church?] Does he who strives against and resists the Church, believe that he is in the Church . . . ?

St. Cyprian: *On the Unity of the Catholic Church,* 4. (Famous text on the primacy. The words in brackets appear to be authentic, but it is not certain whether they belong to a first or second revision of the work.) (3rd cent.)

Run over the apostolic churches, in which the very thrones of the apostles are still pre-eminent in their places, in which their own authentic writings are read, uttering the voice and representing the face of each of them severally. . . . Since, moreover, you are close upon Italy, you have Rome, from which there comes even into our own hands the very authority (of the apostles themselves). How happy is its church, on which apostles poured forth all their doctrines along with their blood! where Peter endures a passion like his Lord's! where Paul wins his crown in a death like John's! where the Apostle John was first plunged, unhurt, into boiling oil, and thence remitted to his island—exiled!

Tertullian: *On Prescription of Heretics,* 36. (3rd cent.)

For this will appear best and fittest, that the priests of the Lord from all the provinces should report to the head (*caput*), that is to the See of Peter the apostle.

Letter of the Council of Sardica to Pope Julius I. (342)

You cannot deny that you know that upon Peter first in the city of Rome was conferred the episcopal chair, on which sat Peter, the head of all the apostles, whence he is called Cephas, that in this one chair unity should be preserved by all, lest the other apostles might uphold each for himself separate chairs, so that he who should set up a second chair against the unique chair would already be a schismatic and a sinner. Well, then, on the one chair, which is the first of the endowments, Peter sat first, to whom succeeded Linus . . . to Damasus Siricius, who today is our colleague, and he with the whole world agrees with us in one bond of communion through the intercourse of letters.

> St. Optatus of Mileve: *On the Schism of Donatists*, 2, 2-3. (4th cent.)

Although all the Catholic churches diffused throughout the world are but one bridal chamber of Christ, yet the holy Roman church has been set before the rest by no conciliar decrees, but has obtained the primacy by the voice of our Lord and Savior in the gospel: *Thou art Peter, etc.* (Matth. 16, 18 ff).There is added also the society of the most blessed apostle Paul, a *chosen vessel,* who was crowned on one and the same day, suffering a glorious death, with Peter in the city of Rome, under Caesar Nero; and they alike consecrated the above-named Roman church to Christ the Lord, and set it above all others in the whole world by their presence and venerable triumph.

> Council of Rome under Pope Damasus. (From *Decretum Gelasianum,* a composition of the sixth century) (382)

A victim I implore the priest for salvation, a sheep the shepherd for protection. Away with jealousy of the Roman preeminence, away with ambition! I speak to the successor of the fisherman and to the disciple of the cross. I follow no one as chief save Christ but I am joined in communion with your blessedness, that is, with the See of Peter. Upon that rock I know the Church is built.

> St. Jerome: *Letters,* 15. (To Pope Damasus) (4th cent.)

. . . we will not deny you a full reply to each detail of your inquiry, as the Lord deigns to inspire us, for in view of our office we have no right to dissemble and none to keep silence, since it is our duty more than anyone's to be zealous for the Christian faith. We bear the burdens of all who are heavy laden; nay, rather, the blessed apostle Peter bears them in us and protects and

watches over us, his heirs, as we trust, in all the cares of his ministry.

> Pope Siricius: *Decretal Letter to Himerius, Bishop of Tarragona,* 1. (Feb. 10, 385)

Reckon up the priests from the days that Peter sat, and in their ancestral ranks note who succeeded whom; for that is the rock over which the gates of hell shall never prevail.

> St. Augustine: *Psalmus contra Partem Donati.* (4th cent.)

The universal ordering of the Church at its birth took its origin from the office of blessed Peter, in which is found both its directing power and its supreme authority. From him as from its source, at the time when our religion was in the stage of growth, all churches received their common order. This much is shown by the injunctions of the council of Nicaea, since it did not venture to make a decree in his regard, recognizing that nothing could be added to his dignity: in fact it knew that all had been assigned to him by the word of the Lord. So it is clear that this church is to all churches throughout the world as the head is to the members, and that whoever separates himself from it becomes an exile from the Christian religion, since he ceases to belong to its fellowship.

> Pope Boniface I: *Letters,* 14. (To the bishops of Thessaly.) (422)

No one can doubt, nay, it is known to all the ages, that holy and blessed Peter, prince and head of the apostles, pillar of the faith, and foundation-stone of the Catholic Church, received from our Lord Jesus Christ, the Savior and Redeemer of the human race, the keys of the kingdom, and that the power of binding and loosing sins was given to him; and that he continues to live and exercise judgment even to this day in the person of his successors.

> Council of Ephesus (Third General Council), Speech of the papal legate Philip before the Third Session. (431)

We exhort you, honorable brother, that you obediently listen to what has been written by the blessed pope of the city of Rome, since blessed Peter, who lives and presides in his own See, offers the truth of the faith to those who seek. For we in our zeal for peace and faith cannot decide questions of faith apart from the consent of the bishop of Rome.

St. Peter Chrysologus: *Letter to Eutyches.* (In Letters of Pope Leo, 25) (449)

The most holy church of Rome through blessed Peter prince of the apostles holds the leadership (*principatus*) over all the churches of the whole world.

Letter from the Bishops of the Province of Arles to Pope Leo I. (Among the Letters of Pope Leo I, Ep. 65, 2.) (5th cent.)

And He [Christ] too rejoices over your good feeling and welcomes your respect for the Lord's own institution as shown towards the partners of His honor, commending the well-ordered love of the whole Church, which ever finds Peter in Peter's see, and from affection for so great a shepherd grows not lukewarm even over so inferior a successor as myself.

Pope St. Leo I: *Sermons*, 2, 2. (5th cent.)

I vow and promise to you, and through you to St. Peter, the chief of the apostles, and to his vicar, the most blessed Gregory and his successors, that I will never be persuaded by anyone in any way to return to that schism from which I have been set free by the mercy of our Redeemer, but I will ever remain under all circumstances in the unity of the Holy Catholic Church, and in communion with the Roman pontiff. Therefore I swear by almighty God and by these four holy Gospels which I hold in my hands, and by the life and genius of our sovereigns who rule the commonwealth, that I will always faithfully abide in the unity of the Catholic Church, to which by the goodness of God I have returned, and in the communion of the Roman pontiff.

Confession of Firminus, Bishop of Trieste. (Among letters of Gregory I, 12, 13) (602)

Just as the Lord enjoined the care of His whole flock, that is the Church, on blessed Peter, so Peter rightfully commands those shepherds of the Church who succeed him to guard the flock of God which has been committed to each one with careful governance.

St. Bede the Venerable: *In Ep. 1 Petr.* (8th cent.)

But the primacy is given to Peter, that the unity of the Church may be proclaimed. All are shepherds, but one flock is indicated, which was then shepherded by all the apostles with unanimous consent, and is henceforth shepherded by their successors under a common care.

St. Bede the Venerable: *Homilies*, 2, 15. (8th cent.)

The Roman pontiffs successors of Peter and vicars of Jesus Christ, succeeding each other in a remarkable line of succession through the ages, have received from the Lord the primacy and authority (*magisterium*) over all the churches and all the prelates of the Church, nay over all the faithful. As others are called to have a share in responsibility, so the plenitude of power resides in them. For that remarkable privilege did not expire in Peter and with Peter, which the Lord granted in his person to all his successors until the end of the world. Apart from sanctity of life and miraculous manifestations, the jurisdictional power of his successors is alike in all.

Pope Innocent III: *Letter to the King of the Armenians.* (Reg. 2, 220) (13th cent.)

As in each diocese there is one bishop who is the head of the Church among that people, so in the whole Church and over all Christian people there is one supreme bishop, namely the Roman pope, successor of Peter, that the Church militant may bear the likeness of the Church triumphant, where One presides over the whole universe.

> John of Paris: *Concerning Royal and Papal Power*, 3. (14th cent.)

Blessed Peter the apostle did not have more authority than the other apostles had, and was not the head of the apostles. And Christ left no head for the Church, and did not appoint anyone his vicar.

> Errors of Marsiglio of Padua and Jean of Jandun condemned by Pope John XXII in bull *Licet iuxta doctrinam,* October 23, 1327.

We define that the holy Roman see and the Roman pontiff has the primacy over the whole Church, and the Roman pontiff is himself the successor of blessed Peter, prince of the apostles, and true vicar of Christ, head of the whole Church and father and teacher of all Christians; and to him in blessed Peter was delivered by our Lord Jesus Christ the full power of feeding, ruling, and governing the universal Church; as is also set forth in the acts and sacred canons of the general councils.

> Decree of the Council of Florence, *Laetentur Coeli.* (July 6, 1439)

This indictment is . . . directly repugnant to the laws of God and His holy Church, the supreme government of which, or of any part thereof, may no temporal prince presume by any law to take upon him as rightfully belonging to the See of Rome, a spiritual pre-eminence by the mouth of our Savior Himself, personally present upon the earth, to St. Peter and his successor bishops of the same See, by special prerogative, granted. . . .

> Reply of St. Thomas More to indictment charging him with treason for denying the king's supremacy. (16th cent.)

This Church also has but one ruler and one governor, the invisible one Christ, whom the eternal Father *hath made head over all the Church, which is His body*

(Eph. 1, 22); the visible one him who, as legitimate successor of Peter the prince of the apostles, fills the apostolic chair. That this visible head is necessary to establish and preserve unity in the Church is the unanimous accord of the fathers.

> Catechism of the Council of Trent, 1. (16th cent.)

If any one then shall say that it is not by the institution of Christ the Lord, or by divine right, that blessed Peter has a perpetual line of successors in the primacy over the universal Church; or that the Roman pontiff is not the successor of blessed Peter in this primacy; let him be anathema.

> Vatican Council, Session 4, Dogmatic Constitution 2. (July 18, 1870)

The primacy is the bulwark, or rather the corner-stone, of Catholicism; without it, there would be as many churches as there are nations or states. Not one of those who have denounced the papacy as a usurpation has ever attempted to show that the condition which its absence necessarily involves is theologically desirable, or that it is the will of God.

> Lord Acton: *Döllinger on the Temporal Power.* (19th cent.)

The rejection of the primacy of St. Peter has driven men on to a slippery course, where all the steps are downwards.

> Lord Acton: *Döllinger on the Temporal Power.* (19th cent.)

II—*Pope: Universal Pontiff*

But if some be disobedient to the words which have been spoken by him through us, let them understand that they will entangle themselves in transgression and no little danger. But we shall be guiltless of their sin. . . . For you will give us joy and gladness, if you render obedience to the things written by us through the Holy Spirit.

> Pope St. Clement: *Letter to the Corinthians,* 59, 1-2 and 63, 2. (1st cent.)

Ignatius Theophorus to the church on which the majesty of the most high Father and of Jesus Christ, His only Son, has had mercy; to the church beloved and enlightened by the faith and charity of Jesus Christ, our God, through the will of Him Who has willed all things that exist—the church in the place of the country of the Romans that holds the primacy [or *possibly:* the church that holds the primacy in the place of Christ]. I salute you in the name of Jesus Christ, the Son of the Father. You are a church worthy of God, worthy of honor, felicitation and praise, worthy of attaining to God, a church without blemish, which holds the primacy of the community of love, obedient to Christ's law, bearing the Father's name. To you who are united, outwardly and inwardly, in the whole of His commandment and filled with grace, in union with God and with every alien stain filtered out, I wish every innocent joy in Jesus Christ, our God.

St. Ignatius of Antioch: *Salutation of Letter to the Romans.* (2nd cent.)

I hear that there has even been an edict set forth, and a peremptory one too. The sovereign pontiff, that is the bishop of bishops, pronounces: I remit the crimes of adultery and fornication, to those who have done penance.

Tertullian: *On Modesty,* 1. (Opinion differs as to whether he is here referring derisively to popes Zephyrinus or Callistus, or to some African bishop. Dates from his Montanist or later heretical period.) (3rd cent.)

When in the time of this Clement [Pope St. Clement I, c. 90–99 A.D.] no little dissension arose among the Christians at Corinth, the church in Rome sent a most powerful letter to the Corinthians urging them to peace and renewing their faith and the tradition which they had recently received from the apostles.

Eusebius of Caesarea: *Ecclesiastical History,* 5, 6, 3. (4th cent.)

Upon this, Victor [ca. 189–199] who presided at Rome, immediately tried to cut off from the common unity the dioceses of all Asia, together with the adjacent churches, on the grounds of heterodoxy, and he indited letters announcing that all the Christians there were absolutely excommunicated. But they were by no means pleased by this and issued counter-requests to him to consider the cause of peace and unity. . . .

Eusebius of Caesarea: *Ecclesiastical History,* 5, 24, 9-10. (With reference to the famous controversy over the date of Easter.) (4th cent.)

Suppose, you insist, that some guilt had lain upon them, their cases should have been tried according to the rule of the Church, not in this way. You should have written to us all, that a just sentence might be issued by us all. For the sufferers were bishops and churches of no ordinary sort but those which the apostles themselves once governed in their own persons. And why was no word sent to us particularly concerning the church of the Alexandrians? Are you ignorant that the custom has been for word to be sent to us first and then for a just decision to be proclaimed from this spot?

Pope Julius I: *Letter to Eusebian Bishops at Antioch.* (341)

Bishop Hosius said: If a bishop has had sentence pronounced against him in some action, and thinks that he has a good cause for the judgment to be reconsidered, let us, if you agree, do honor to the memory of the holy apostle Peter; let letters be written to the bishop of Rome, either by those who have conducted the examination or by the bishops living in the nearest province; if he decides that the sentence must be reconsidered, let it be reconsidered and let him appoint judges; but if he concludes that the case is such that it is inexpedient to reopen old wounds by raking up the past, his [own] decision shall stand confirmed.

Council of Sardica, Canon 3. (342)

Bishop Gaudentius said: A rider, if you agree, to this very holy decision has been made: When a bishop has been deposed by the judgment of the bishops living in neighboring places and has announced that he must transact business in the city of Rome, let another bishop on no account be ordained in his stead in the same see after the appeal of him who appears to have been deposed, except the case shall have been determined by the judgment of the bishop of Rome.

Council of Sardica, Canon 4. (342)

Bishop Hosius said: If the bishop of Rome has thought it just that the inquiry should be reopened: let him vouchsafe to write to the bishops in the adjacent . . . province to search out all things with diligence and make decision according to fidelity of truth. But if anyone asks for his case to be heard again, and by his own petition has moved the bishop of Rome to send a presbyter with a special mission, it shall be in the bishop's power to say what he wishes or what he judges best. . . .

Council of Sardica, Canon 5. (342)

The bishop of Constantinople shall hold the first rank after the bishop of Rome, because Constantinople is the New Rome.

Council of Constantinople (Second General Council), Can. 3. (381)

. . . the Roman Church, head of the whole Roman world, and that sacred trust of the apostles, whence flow all the rights of venerable communion upon persons.

St. Ambrose: *Letters,* 11, 4. (To the emperors Gratian, Valentinian, and Theodosius.) (381)

We think, too, that you should consult our holy brother, bishop of the church at Rome, for we presume that what you determine will in no wise displease him.

St. Ambrose: *Letters,* 56, 7. (To Theophilus of Alexandria) (4th cent.)

We have, I think, dearest brother, disposed of all the questions which . . . you reported . . . to the Roman church as to the head of your body. Now we do once again urge you, brother, bend your mind to observing the canons and keeping the decretals that have been ordained . . . no priest of the Lord is free to be ignorant of the statutes of the Apostolic See and the venerable provisions of the canons. . . .

Pope Siricius: *Decretal Letter to Himerius, Bishop of Tarragona,* 20. (Feb. 10, 385)

You have . . . preserved the customs of the fathers and have not spurned that which they decreed by a divine and not human sentence, that whatsoever is done, even though it be in distant provinces, should not be ended without being brought to the knowledge of this See, that by its authority the whole just pronouncement should be strengthened, and that from it all other churches (like water flowing from the natal source and flowing through the different regions of the world, the pure streams of one incorrupt head), should receive what they ought to enjoin.

Pope Innocent I: *Letters,* 29. (In reply to Council of Carthage confirming their sentence condemning Pelagianism.) (417)

We also wrote to the late Pope Innocent, in addition to the reports of the councils, a private letter, in which we dealt more fully with the same question. To all he wrote back to us in the manner that was right and proper for the pontiff of the Apostolic See.

St. Augustine: *Letters,* 186. (5th cent.)

For it has never been lawful to reconsider what has once been settled by the Apostolic See.

Pope Boniface I: *Letters,* 13. (To Rufinus, bishop of Thessalonica) (422)

Moreover because our care extends throughout all the churches, since the

Lord demands this of us, who entrusted to the most blessed Peter the primacy of apostolic honor in reward for his faith, establishing the universal Church on his firmness as a foundation, we share the duty of responsibility which we possess with these who are joined with us in love of the fraternity.

> Pope St. Leo: *Letters*, 5, 2. (5th cent.)

It is certain that for us the only defence lies in the favor of the God of heaven; and to deserve it our first care is to support the Christian faith and its venerable religion. Inasmuch then as the primacy of the Apostolic See is assured, by the merit of Saint Peter, who is chief of the episcopal order, by the rank of the city of Rome, and also by the authority of a sacred synod, let no one presume to attempt any illicit act contrary to the authority of that See. For then at length will the peace of the churches be maintained everywhere, if the whole body acknowledges its ruler.

> Rescript of Emperors Theodosius II and Valentinian III to Aetius. (445)

Since the authoritative decision of the sacred synod itself has confirmed the primacy of the Apostolic See as appropriate to holy Peter . . . it shall not be lawful for any bishop, whether in Gaul or in other provinces, in violation of ancient custom to undertake anything without the authority of the venerable pope of the eternal city. For them and all men the force of law shall belong to whatever the Apostolic See has ordained or shall ordain: so that whosoever shall fail to appear when summoned to judgment by the bishop of Rome, shall be compelled to present himself by the governor of that province. . . .

> Rescript of the Emperors Theodosius II and Valentinian III to Aetius. (Among Letters of Pope Leo I, 11) (5th cent.)

I have delegated to you, my beloved, the vicegerency of my authority, so that you may share the care for which by divine appointment we ourselves are chiefly responsible in regard to all the churches.

> Pope St. Leo I: *Letters*, 14, 1. (To Anastasius, Bishop of Thessalonica.) (5th cent.)

As in all things we follow the ordinances of the holy fathers, and know the recently read canon of the 150 bishops [Second Council of Constantinople, can. 3], so we decree the same in regard to the privileges of the most holy church of Constantinople, the New Rome. Rightly have the fathers rendered to the see of Old Rome the first honors on account of its character as the imperial city, and moved by the same considerations the 150 bishops have accorded equal honors to the most holy see of New Rome, judging with good reason that the city which is the seat of the imperial power and the senate, and which enjoys the same honor as the old imperial city, should also in ecclesiastical matters be exalted, and hold the second place after her.

> Council of Chalcedon, Canon 28. (This famous canon was not confirmed by the Holy See because it appeared to be derogatory to the primacy of the pope *jure divino,* although the Holy See later acquiesced in Constantinople's claim to have the second place, *jure ecclesiastico.*) (451)

. . . but secular affairs are one thing, and the divine another, and there is no other firm foundation but upon the rock which the Lord laid as a foundation-stone. To the before-named [Anatolius, bishop of Constantinople] it ought to suffice that, with the help of thy piety and by my consent, he has received the bishopric of so great a city. He should not esteem lightly the imperial city; but he cannot make it an apostolic see; nor must he hope to increase by injury done to others, for the privileges of the churches, which are defined by the canons of the holy fathers, and fixed by the decrees of the venerable synod of Nicaea, must be destroyed by no injustice and altered by no innovation. On this point I must, by the help of Christ, persistently discharge my duties, because this care (*dispensatio*) is committed to me, and it would involve me in blame if the regulations drawn up, under the teaching of the Holy Spirit, at Nicaea were violated with my consent—be that far from me—and if the wish of one brother [Anatolius] had more weight with me than the common good of the whole house of God. . . .

> Pope St. Leo I: *Letters,* 104. (To the Emperor Marcian) (May 22, 452)

Nor is it permitted anyone to pass judgment on its [i.e. the Holy See's] decisions . . . no one however may appeal from this See.

> Pope Gelasius I: *Letters,* 26, 5. (5th cent.)

Nobody at any time and for whatever human pretext may haughtily set himself above the office of him who by Christ's order was set above all and everyone and whom the universal Church had always recognized as its head.

> Pope Gelasius I: *Letters,* 12, 3. (5th cent.)

. . . therefore to this Thy servant N., whom Thou has appointed as bishop of the apostolic see and primate of all priests throughout the world and teacher of Thy universal Church, and chosen for the ministry of the high priesthood, we beseech Thee, O Lord, grant this grace; invest him with pontifical authority (*cathedram*) to rule Thy Church and all Thy people. . . .

> Gregorian Sacramentary, Prayer for Consecration of the Pope. (ca. 6th cent.)

It is clear to everyone who knows the Gospel that the care of the whole Church has been committed to the blessed Peter, chief of the apostles. For him it is said: *Peter, dost thou love me? Feed my sheep* . . . Behold he receives the keys of the kingdom of heaven; to him is given the power of binding and loosing; to him the care and primacy of the whole Church is committed; and yet he is never called the Universal Apostle. But that most holy man, my fellow-bishop John

[patriarch of Constantinople] wishes to be called the universal bishop! I am compelled to exclaim, O tempora! O mores!

> Pope St. Gregory the Great: *Letter to the Emperor Maurice.* (Ep. 5, 37) (6th cent.)

As regards the church of Constantinople, who can doubt that it is subject to the Apostolic See? Why, both our most religious lord the emperor, and our brother the bishop of Constantinople continually acknowledge it.

> Pope St. Gregory the Great: *Letters,* 9, 26. (6th cent.)

It is evident that the judgment of the Apostolic See, than which there is no authority greater, may be rejected by no one, nor is it lawful for anyone to pass judgment on its judgment.

> Pope Nicholas I: *Letter to the Emperor Michael III.* (9th cent.)

If any one shall despise the dogmatic decisions, injunctions, interdicts, sanctions or decrees which have been wisely published by the one who presides over the Apostolic See on behalf of the Catholic faith, ecclesiastical discipline, the correction of the faithful, the punishment of the wicked, or the forbidding of present or future evils, let him be anathema.

> Pope St. Nicholas I: Roman Council of 861, chap. 5.

O God, the Shepherd and Ruler of all the faithful, favorably look upon Thy servant N., whom Thou hast been pleased to appoint pastor over Thy Church; grant, we beseech Thee, that he may benefit both by word and example those over whom he has been set, and thus attain unto life eternal, together with the flock committed to his care.

> Roman Missal, Collect for the Pope. (ca. 10th cent.)

1. The Roman church has been founded by Christ alone.
2. The Roman pontiff may alone be called universal.

3. He alone may depose or absolve bishops.

8. He alone may use the imperial insignia.

9. The pope is the only one whose feet are kissed by all princes.

10. His name is alone pronounced in all the churches.

12. He may depose emperors.

16. No council may be called general without his consent.

18. His judgment may not be revised by anyone, and he alone may revise the judgments of others.

19. He may not be judged by anyone.

20. No one may condemn a decision of the Apostolic See.

21. The important matters of each church should be referred to him.

26. He who does not agree with the Roman church may not be considered a Catholic.

27. The pope may release subjects from their oath of fealty to wicked rulers.

Pope St. Gregory VII: *Dictatus Papae*.
(Famous document found among letters of the pope. Uncertain for what purpose it was composed, but apparently represents the pope's own view of his high office.) (ca. 1075)

Does Peter's chair flatter you? It is a watch-tower whence, in a word, you exercise supervision; the very name of 'bishop' reminds you not of lordship, but of duty. How fitting it is that you are set on high where you can view all things, inasmuch as you are appointed watchman over all.

St. Bernard: *On Consideration*, 2, 6.
(Addressed to Pope Eugenius III) (12th cent.)

For I do not think that you have inherited the world absolutely, but with certain limitations; as it seems to me you have been entrusted with a stewardship over it, not put in possession of it.

St. Bernard: *On Consideration*, 3, 1.
(Addressed to Pope Eugenius III) (12th cent.)

For the prophet's saying applies to me: *I have established thee above nations and kingdoms, that you may uproot and destroy and ruin and dissipate, and build and plant* . . . others are called to a share in responsibility, but only Peter was charged with the fulness of power. Now therefore you see who that servant is, who has been set over the household, namely the vicar of Jesus Christ, the God of Pharaoh: he has been made a mediator between God and man, below God, but higher than man, less than God, but greater than man; who judges all things, and is judged by no one; announcing with the voice of the apostle: *He who judges me, is the Lord.* . . .

Pope Innocent III: *Sermon preached at his consecration. (Sermones de diversis*, 2) (12th cent.)

Christ left to Peter not only the universal Church, but the whole world to govern.

Pope Innocent III: *Letters.* (13th cent.)

The pope possesses such plenitude of power within the Church that he can dispense from purely ecclesiastical regulations, which are ordinances which belong to positive law, that is, human law. But he can give no dispensation from the precepts of the divine law and the natural law; their force comes from divine decree.

St. Thomas Aquinas: *Quodlibets*, 4, 8, 13. (13th cent.)

Therefore there is one body of this one and only Church, and one head, not two heads, like a monster, namely, Christ and Christ's vicar Peter, and Peter's successor. . . . For if the earthly power deviates, it will be judged by the spiritual power; but if a lesser spiritual power deviates, it will be judged by its superior, but if it deviates in its head, it can only be judged by God alone, not by man. For its authority, although given to man and exercised by man, is not human but divine, in accordance with the words of our Lord to Peter (Matth. 16, 19). . . . Accordingly we declare, affirm, define and pronounce that it is altogether necessary for salvation for every creature to be subject to the Roman pontiff.

> Pope Boniface VIII: *Bull Unam Sanctam.* (Nov. 18, 1302)

If a pope sins in spiritual matters, by granting benefices through simony, dissipating the goods of the churches, depriving ecclesiastical persons and bodies of their rights, or entertaining or teaching things which are not in accordance with faith or morals, he is first of all to be admonished by the cardinals, who stand for all the clergy. But if he is incorrigible and they are unable to remove this scandal from the Church by themselves, then as an aid to justice they must implore the help of the secular arm.

> John of Paris: *Concerning Royal and Papal Power,* 13. (14th cent.)

Take care that I do not have to complain about you to Jesus crucified. There is no one else I can complain to, for you have no superior on earth.

> St. Catherine of Siena: *Letter to Pope Gregory XI.* (14th cent.)

Sitting in that chair in which Peter the prince of the apostles sat to the close of his life, the Catholic Church recognizes in the person of the supreme pontiff the most exalted degree of dignity and the full amplitude of jurisdiction; a dignity and a jurisdiction not based upon synodal or other human constitutions, but emanating from no less an authority than God Himself. As the successor of St. Peter, and the true and legitimate vicar of Jesus Christ, he therefore presides over the universal Church, the father and governor of all the faithful, of bishops also, and of all other prelates, be their station, rank, or power what they may.

> Catechism of the Council of Trent, 2. (16th cent.)

Full in the panting heart of Rome,
Beneath the apostle's crowning dome,
From pilgrims' lips that kiss the ground,
Breathes in all tongues one only sound:

God bless our pope, the great, the good.

> Card. Wiseman: *Hymn.* (19th cent.)

The papacy, that unique institution, the crown of the Catholic system, exhibits in its history the constant working of that law which is at the foundation of the life of the Church, the law of continuous organic development.

> Lord Acton: *Döllinger on the Temporal Power.* (19th cent.)

As the Church advances towards fulness and maturity in her forms, bringing forward her exhaustless resources, and calling into existence a wealth of new elements,—societies, corporations, and institutions,—so is the need more deeply felt for a powerful supreme guide to keep them all in health and harmony, to direct them in their various spheres, and in their several ways towards the common ends and purposes of all, and thus to provide against decay, variance, and confusion. Such an office the primacy alone can discharge, and the importance of the papacy increases as the organization of the Church is more complete.

> Lord Acton: *Döllinger on the Temporal Power.* (19th cent.)

What is the Holy See in its relation to the masses of Catholics, and where does its strength lie? It is the organ, the mouth, the head of the Church. Its strength consists in its agreement with the general conviction of the faithful. When it expresses the common knowledge and sense of the age, or of a large majority of Catholics, its position is impregnable. The force it derives from this general support makes direct opposition hopeless, and therefore disedifying, tending only to division and promoting reaction rather than reform. The influence by which it is to be moved must be directed first on that which gives it strength, and must pervade the members in order that it may reach the head.

> Lord Acton: *Conflicts with Rome.* (19th cent.)

If any one then shall say that the Roman pontiff has the office merely of inspection or direction, and not full and supreme power of jurisdiction over the universal Church, not only in things which belong to faith and morals, but also in those things which relate to the discipline and government of the Church spread throughout the world; or assert that he possesses merely the principal part, and not all the fulness of this supreme power; or that this power which he enjoys is not ordinary and immediate, both over each and all the churches and over each and all the pastors of the faithful; let him be anathema.

Vatican Council, Session 4, Dogmatic Constitution 3. (July 18, 1870)

We cannot take as much as we please, and no more, of an institution which has a monadic existence. We must either give up the belief in the Church as a divine institution altogether, or we must recognize it at this day in that communion of which the pope is the head. With him alone and round him are found the claims, the prerogatives, and duties which we identify with the kingdom set up by Christ. We must take things as they are; to believe in a Church, is to believe in the pope. And thus this belief in the pope and his attributes, which seems so monstrous to Protestants, is bound up with our being Catholics at all; as our Catholicism is bound up with our Christianity.

Card. Newman: *Letter to the Duke of Norfolk*. (19th cent.)

The Roman church became the head of all the churches not through the ordinance of Divine Providence but through merely political conditions.

Proposition condemned by Decree of Holy Office, *Lamentabili*, June 3, 1907.

The Roman pontiff, when legitimately elected, enjoys by divine right immediately following the acceptance of the election full authority of supreme jurisdiction.

Code of Canon Law, Canon 219. (20th cent.)

The first See is judged by no one.

Code of Canon Law, Canon 1556. (20th cent.)

There have been times, under a Leo, or a Gregory, or a Hildebrand, when it looked as if the papacy was a match for all comers. But in ordinary circumstances, although it has never ceased to preserve the tradition of doctrine and of moral theory which (we believe) was handed down from the apostles, it has only succeeded partially and with great difficulty in combating the bad traditions of its own more worldly supporters.

R. A. Knox: *Difficulties*. (20th cent.)

The medieval papacy combined two distinct but related functions. It was the ruler of the Church in the strict sense, the representative of Peter and the head of the ecclesiastical hierarchy, but it was also the leader and judge of Christian society in the widest sense—the president of a kind of European league of nations and the supreme authority in international law.

Christopher Dawson: *Medieval Essays*. (20th cent.)

The action and the theory of the modern papacy are the outcome of an agelong growth, and we must seek in the pages of history less for a proof of the papal claims than for the evidence that they have shared in, and been central to, the general development of that society, which is our only historical link with the origins of Christianity.

Dom Butler: *The Church and Infallibility*. (20th cent.)

III—*Pope: Teacher of the Church; His Infallibility*

But since it would take too long to set out here the successions of all the churches, we shall turn to that great, ancient and universally known church founded and organized at Rome by the two most glorious apostles Peter and Paul, and we shall show that the tradition it has received of the apostles and the faith that it preaches to men has come down to our time through the regular succession of its bishops; and thus we shall confute all those who, in whatever way, whether by self-complacency, vainglory, blindness or error, enter into unauthorized assemblies. For it is with this Roman church, by reason of its more powerful pre-eminence [*or possibly,* the preeminent authority of its foundation: *propter potentiorem principalitatem*], that every other church, that is to say all the faithful everywhere, ought to agree, inasmuch as in this church the apostolic tradition has been preserved continuously by those who come from everywhere (*ab his qui sunt undique*).

> St. Irenaeus: *Against the Heresies,* 3, 3, 1. (Famous text.) (2nd cent.)

After such things as these, moreover, they still dare . . . to set sail and to bear letters from schismatic and profane persons to the throne of Peter, and to the chief church (*ecclesiam principalem*) whence priestly unity takes its source; and not to consider that these were the Romans whose faith was praised in the preaching of the apostle, to whom faithlessness could have no access.

> St. Cyprian: *Letters,* 54, 14. (3rd cent.)

Truly nature has not given us two suns; but she has given us two Romans, as lights of the whole world, an old dominion and a new [Constantinople]; the one differs from the other as the latter outshines the East and the former the West. But the beauty of the one balances exactly in the scales with the beauty of the other. Regarding the faith which they uphold, the ancient Rome has kept a straight course from of old, and still does so, uniting the whole West by sound teaching, as is just, since she pre-

sides over all and guards the universal divine harmony.

> St. Gregory of Nazianzen: *Poem on His Life,* 1, 567-572. (4th cent.)

It is therefore with due care and fitness that you consult the secrets of the Apostolic office (that office, I mean, to which belongs, besides those things that are outside, the care of all the churches) as to what opinion should be held on doubtful matters, following the form of the ancient rule which, you and I know, has ever been kept in the whole world. . . . Especially as often as questions of faith are to be ventilated, I think all our brothers and fellow bishops ought to refer to none but Peter, that is to the author of their name and office. . . . We declare that Pelagius and Celestius . . . inventors of new doctrines . . . should by the authority of apostolic vigor be deprived of ecclesiastical communion, until they recover from the snares of the devil. . . .

> Pope St. Innocent I: *Letters,* 30. (To the Council of Mileve) (417)

And so, for the establishment of the grace of God . . . we believe to be quite enough whatever the writings of the Apostolic See have taught us . . . so that we absolutely regard as not Catholic anything that is seen to be contrary to the decisions we have just quoted.

> St. Prosper of Aquitaine: *Indiculus on Grace,* 15. (ca. 435)

This is the faith of the fathers; this is the faith of the apostles! So we all believe; so the orthodox believe! Anathema to him who does not so believe! Peter has spoken these things through Leo! So taught the apostles! Piously and truly did Leo teach; so taught Cyril; the eternal memory of Cyril! Leo and Cyril taught the same; anathema to him who does not so believe! This is the truth faith!

> Council of Chalcedon, Session 2. (Exclamation of the fathers after the reading of Pope Leo's tome to Flavian.) (451)

You have indeed safeguarded the faith, which is likened to a golden stream coming down to us by command of Him Who first gave it being, you were an interpreter of the words of blessed Peter to all mankind, and poured forth on all the blessing pronounced on his faith; wherefore we regarded you as the captain of our religion with great gain to our salvation. . . .

Letter from the Council of Chalcedon to Pope Leo I requesting his Approbation. (Among the Letters of Pope Leo I, 98.) (5th cent.)

Although He has delegated the care of his sheep to many shepherds, yet He has not Himself abandoned the guardianship of His beloved flock. And from His overruling and eternal protection we have received the support of the apostle's aid also, which assuredly does not cease from its operation: and the strength of the foundation on which the whole superstructure of the Church is reared, is not weakened by the weight of the temple that rests upon it. For the solidity of that faith which was praised in the chief of the apostles is perpetual: and as that remains which Peter believed in Christ, so that endures which Christ instituted in Peter.

Pope St. Leo I: *Sermons,* 3, 2. (5th cent.)

The beginning of salvation is to preserve the rule of a correct faith and to deviate in no respect from the constitutions of the fathers. And because the teaching of our Lord Jesus Christ cannot be allowed to fall, Who said: *Thou art Peter,* etc. (Matth. 16, 18), these things which were said are proved by the effects of things, because in the Apostolic See religion has always been preserved without spot or blemish. Desiring in no respect to be separated from this hope and faith, and following the constitutions of the fathers, we anathematize all heretics. . . . We receive and approve . . . all the universal epistles of pope Leo which he wrote concerning the Christian religion. And therefore, as we

have said, following in all things the Apostolic See and approving all of its constitutions, I trust that I may be deemed worthy to be in communion with you, in which as the Apostolic See declares there is complete and true the totality of the Christian religion.

Pope Hormisdas: *Formula, subscribed by John II, Patriarch of Constantinople.* (519)

The Roman Church has never erred, and, according to Scripture, never shall err.

Pope St. Gregory VII: *Dictatus Papae,* 22. (Unofficial document) (ca. 1075)

We believe that the holy Roman Church enjoys supreme and full primacy and preeminence over the whole Catholic Church, which it truly and humbly recognizes that it has received with the plenitude of power from our Lord Himself in the person of blessed Peter, prince or head of the apostles, whose successor the Roman pontiff is; and as the apostolic see is bound before all others to defend the truth of faith, so also if any questions regarding faith shall arise, they must be defined by its judgment.

Second Oecumenical Council of Lyons, Profession of Faith of Michael Palaeologus. (1274)

Only the Church of Peter, to whose lot fell Italy when the disciples were sent out to preach, has always stood fast in the faith. While the faith has disappeared or has partly decayed in other regions, the church of Peter still flourishes in faith and free from heresy.

St. Thomas Aquinas: *Exposition of the Apostles' Creed.* (13th cent.)

I am moved to obedience to that See not only by what learned and holy men have written, but by this fact especially, that we shall find that on the one hand every enemy of the Christian faith makes war on that See, and that, on the other hand, no one has ever declared himself an enemy of that See who has not also shortly shown most evidently that he was the enemy of the Christian religion.

> St. Thomas More: *Letter to John Bugenhagen.* (16th cent.)

It is a misrepresentation often repeated, that Catholics imagine the supreme pontiff to be free from all liability to moral transgression, as though they believed that no action performed by him could be sinful. It can hardly be necessary for me to deny so gross and so absurd an imputation.

> Card. Wiseman: *Lectures,* 8. (1835)

He for eighteen hundred years has lived in the world; he has seen all fortunes, he has encountered all adversaries, he has shaped himself for all emergencies. If ever there was a power on earth who had an eye for the times, who has confined himself to the practicable, and has been happy in his anticipations, whose words have been facts, and whose commands prophecies, such is he in the history of ages, who sits from generation to generation in the chair of the apostles, as the vicar of Christ, and the doctor of his Church.

> Card. Newman: *Idea of a University,* 1. (19th cent.)

A certitude is directed to this or that particular proposition; it is not a faculty or gift, but a disposition of mind relatively to a definite case which is before me. Infallibility, on the contrary, is just that which certitude is not; it *is* faculty or gift, and relates, not to some one truth in particular, but to all possible propositions in a given subject matter. We ought in strict propriety, to speak, not of infallible acts, but of acts of infallibility.

> Card. Newman: *Grammar of Assent,* 7. (19th cent.)

A man is infallible, whose words are always true; a rule is infallible, if it is unerring in all its possible applications. An infallible authority is certain in every particular case that may arise; but a man who is certain in some definite case, is not on that account infallible.

> Card. Newman: *Grammar of Assent,* 7. (19th cent.)

We teach and define that it is a dogma divinely revealed: that the Roman pontiff, when he speaks *ex cathedra,* that is, when in discharge of the office of pastor and doctor of all Christians, by virtue of his supreme apostolic authority he defines a doctrine regarding faith or morals to be held by the universal Church, by the divine assistance promised to him in blessed Peter, is possessed of that infallibility with which the divine Redeemer willed that his Church should be endowed for defining doctrine regarding faith or morals: and that therefore such definitions of the Roman pontiff are irreformable of themselves, and not from the consent of the Church.

> Vatican Council, Session 4, Dogmatic Constitution *Pastor Aeternus* 4. (July 18, 1870)

For myself, ever since I was a Catholic, I have held the pope's infallibility as a matter of theological opinion; at least, I see nothing in the definition which necessarily contradicts Scripture, tradition, or history; and the 'Doctor ecclesiae' (as the pope is styled by the Council of Florence) bids me accept it. In this case I do not receive it on the word of the council, but on the pope's self-assertion.

> Card. Newman: *Letter of July 27, 1870.* (In *Letter to the Duke of Norfolk*) (1874)

What is the real doctrine of infallibility? It simply means that the pope, as successor of St. Peter, Prince of the Apostles, by virtue of the promises of Jesus Christ, is preserved from error of judgment when he promulgates to the Church a decision on faith or morals.

> Card. Gibbons: *The Faith of Our Fathers,* 11. (19th cent.)

All true followers of Christ believe in the infallibility of the Roman pontiff in the sense defined by the Vatican Council with the same faith as they believe the incarnation of our Lord.

Pope Pius XI: *Mortalium animos.* (Jan. 6, 1928)

IV—*Pope and Episcopate*

For although every shepherd presides over his own flocks with a particular responsibility . . . we have a duty which is shared with them all; in fact the function of each one is a part of our work: so that when men resort to the See of the blessed apostle Peter from all quarters of the world, and seek from our bounty his love of the whole Church entrusted to him by the Lord, the greater our duty to everyone, the heavier we feel the burden to be which rests on our shoulders.

Pope St. Leo I: *Sermons,* 5, 2. (5th cent.)

My honor is the honor of the whole Church. My honor is the solid strength of my brothers. I am truly honored when due honor is paid to each and every one.

Pope St. Gregory I: *Letter to Eulogius, Patriarch of Alexandria.* (6th cent.)

You are he to whom the keys have been committed, and the sheep entrusted. There are indeed other doorkeepers of heaven, and other shepherds of flocks, but as you have received both names in a manner different from the rest, so for you they bear a more glorious meaning. Other pastors each have their several flocks assigned to them; to you all the flocks have been entrusted, one flock under one shepherd. Do you ask for proof of that? It is the Lord's word.

St. Bernard: *Consideration,* 2, 8. (Addressed to Pope Eugenius III) (12th cent.)

Above all, consider that the holy Roman Church of which God has made you the head, is the mother of churches, not their mistress; but that you are not sovereign lord of the bishops, but one of them,

the brother, too, of those who love God, and a partaker with them that fear Him.

St. Bernard: *On Consideration,* 4, 7. (To Pope Eugenius III) (12th cent.)

The power of the supreme pontiff is far from standing in the way of the power of the ordinary and immediate episcopal jurisdiction by which the bishops who, under appointment of the Holy Spirit, succeeded in the place of the apostles, feed and rule individually, as true shepherds, the particular flock assigned to them.

Vatican Council, Session 4, Dogmatic Constitution *de Ecclesia,* ch. 3. (July 18, 1870)

The power of the Roman pontiff is supreme, universal, and absolutely independent, whereas the power of the bishops is fixed within definite limits and is not absolutely independent.

Pope Leo XIII: *Satis Cognitum.* (1896)

See also Bishop

V—*Pope and General Council*

Wherefore the most holy and blessed Leo, archbishop of the great and elder Rome, through us and through this present most holy council, together with the thrice blessed and all glorious Peter the apostle, who is the rock and support of the Catholic Church and the foundation of the orthodox faith, has stripped him of the episcopal and priestly dignity.

Council of Chalcedon, 3rd Session. (Sentence of deposition and degradation pronounced against Dioscorus, Patriarch of Alexandria by the legates of the Holy See and the members of the council.) (451)

Indeed resolutions of bishops which are repugnant to the rules of the holy canons composed at Nicaea . . . we dismiss as invalid, and by the authority of Peter, the blessed apostle, we absolutely disannul by a general decree in all ecclesiastical cases, obeying those laws which the Holy Ghost defined by the 318 bishops [at Nicaea] for the pacific observance of all priests, in such sort that even if a greater number were to pass a different decree from theirs, whatever was opposed to their constitution would have to be held in no respect.

> Pope St. Leo I: *Letters,* 105. (To the empress Pulcheria, with regard to canon 28 of the council of Chalcedon, which the pope refused to accept.) (452)

On the return of our brothers and fellow priests whom the See of blessed Peter sent to the holy council, we ascertained, beloved, the victory you and we together had won, by help from above, over the blasphemy of Nestorius and the madness of Eutyches. Wherefore we glory in the Lord . . . Who has allowed us to sustain no harm in our brethren, but has corroborated, by the irrevocable assent of the whole brotherhood, what He had before defined by our ministry, to show that what had before been enacted by the first See of all, and received by the judgment of the whole Christian world, had truly proceeded from Himself, that in this too the members may agree with the head.

> Pope St. Leo I: *Letters,* 120. (To Theodoret of Cyrus.) (453)

There has sprung up in our time an execrable abuse, unheard of in earlier ages, namely that some men, imbued with the spirit of rebellion, presume to appeal to a future council from the Roman pontiff, the vicar of Jesus Christ . . . not from a desire for a sounder judgment but to escape the penalties of their misdeeds. . . . We condemn appeals of this kind and denounce them as erroneous and detestable. . . .

> Pope Pius II: *Execrabilis.* (Jan. 1460)

I then affirm that this unfailing guide
In pope and gen'ral councils must reside;
Both lawful, both combin'd; what one decrees
By numerous votes, the other ratifies:

On this undoubted sense the Church relies.

> Dryden: *The Hind and the Panther,* 2. (17th cent.)

There is nothing to prevent the decree of a general council, or the act of all peoples, from transferring the supreme pontificate from the bishop and city of Rome to another bishop and another city.

> Proposition condemned by Pius IX in Syllabus of Errors. (1867)

A council may not be considered oecumenical which has not been summoned by the Roman pontiff. It belongs to the same Roman pontiff to preside over an oecumenical council either in person or through others, to determine and designate the matters to be discussed there and the order of discussing them, to transfer, suspend or dissolve the council, and to confirm its decrees.

> Code of Canon Law, Canon 222. (20th cent.)

See also Council, General

VI—*Pope: Temporal Sovereign*

The sovereignty of the pope over his own dominions is no essential portion of his dignity: his supremacy was not the less before it was acquired, and should the unsearchable decrees of Providence in the lapse of ages deprive the Holy See of its temporal sovereignty, as happened to the seventh Pius, through the usurpation of a conqueror, its dominion over the Church and over the consciences of the faithful would not thereby be impaired.

> Card. Wiseman: *Lectures,* 8. (1835)

Italy recognizes the sovereignty of the Holy See in the international field, as a right naturally belonging to it, according to its tradition and the requirements of its mission in the world. Italy recognizes as belonging to the Holy See full right of ownership, absolute power, and sovereign jurisdiction over the Vatican, as at present constituted, with all its dependencies and endowments, thus creating Vatican City for the special purposes and with the means provided by the present treaty.

> Lateran Treaty, Arts. 2 and 3. (Feb. 11, 1929)

VII—*Pope: Titles, Aphorisms, etc.*

Where Peter is, there is the Church. (Ubi Petrus, ibi ecclesia.)

> St. Ambrose: *In Ps. 40 Enarr.* (A medieval variation of this is: *Ubi papa, ibi Roma.*) (4th cent.)

The cause is finished; would that the error were as speedily finished. (Causa finita est: utinam aliquando finiatur error.)

> St. Augustine: *Sermon* 131, 10. (St. Augustine informed his people of the papal condemnation of the Pelagian heresy. His words undoubtedly gave rise to the popular saying, usually attributed to him: *Roma locuta est, causa finita est.*) (5th cent.)

The first See is judged by no one. (Prima sedes a nemine judicatur.)

> So-called Constitution of Silvester I. (Document apparently forged about 490, but similar phrases occur in authentic letters of early popes, cf. Gelasius I, above.)

Bishop of Rome, Archbishop, Patriarch, Pope. (Episcopus Romanus, Archiepiscopus, Patriarcha, Papa.)

> The first was the usual designation during most of antiquity. The pope was not differentiated from other bishops by any special title. He shared the second and third with other prelates from about the 5th cent., i.e. Alexandria, Antioch, Jerusalem, Constantinople, Aquileia, etc. The title pope was at first not applied exclusively to him, not until the 11th cent., but it became usual in the West to apply it to him from ca. the 4th cent. In the East it has been used generally of all priests to the present day.
> The pope signs documents with his assumed name followed by the letters PP, standing for *Papa*.

Servant of the servants of God. (Servus servorum Dei.)

> Title first assumed by Pope St. Gregory I, and in regular use by the popes since his time. (6th cent.)

Supreme pontiff and universal pope. (Summus pontifex et universalis papa.)

> Title applied to Pope St. Nicholas I by his legate Arsenius, and frequently used thereafter. (9th cent.)

Apostolic See, Holy See, Chair of Peter. (Sedes apostolica, cathedra apostolica, sancta sedes, cathedra Petri.)

> Terms applied to the Holy See from about the 4th cent. Rome was not the only see to be called apostolic, but the term 'Apostolic See' came to be used almost exclusively of Rome because the latter was the only see in the West founded by an apostle and because of the universal jurisdiction of the pope. Hence the pope was sometimes designated as 'The Apostolic' or 'Apostolic Lord' (apostolicus, domnus apostolicus) in the Middle Ages.

Pontifex Maximus.

> Title of the high priest or chief of pontiffs in pagan Rome. Although title was perhaps applied ironically by Tertullian to one of the popes in his day (3rd cent.), it was apparently not generally used by the popes until the Renaissance.

Health and apostolic benediction. (Salutem et apostolicam benedictionem.)

> Phrase appearing at the beginning of certain pontifical communications, from about the 8th cent. (Pope Constantine, 707–715).

During the vacancy of the Holy See. (Sede vacante.)

> Term used of the Holy See following the death of one pope and the election of another. The formula is also used with reference to any see or bishopric. (Medieval)

I announce to you a great joy: we have a pope: his eminence the most reverend lord cardinal N., who choose the follow-

ing name N. . . . (Annuntio vobis gaudium magnum: habemus papam: eminentissimum ac reverendissimum dominum cardinalem N., qui sibi nomen N. imposuit.)

> Formula used by senior cardinal deacon as he announces the election of a new pope from the balcony of St. Peter's to the people assembled in the Piazza di San Pietro. (Medieval)

Thus passes the glory of the world! (Sic transit gloria mundi!)

> As the pope proceeds to his coronation, he puts a handful of flax three times in the flames of a little burner. As he does so each time, the master of ceremonies pronounces these words. (Medieval)

For the city and for the world. (Urbi et orbi.)

> Formula refers to solemn blessing with plenary indulgence which the pope imparts on certain occasions, usually from the balcony of St. Peter's, to the city of Rome and the Catholic world. (Medieval)

O in beginning once so bright,
To what ignoble ending dost thou sink!

> Dante: *Paradiso, Canto 27.* (Tr. Binyon) (Dante deplored the growing worldliness of the popes and curia.) (14th cent.)

He who eats from the pope, dies of it! (Qui mange du pape, en meurt!)

> French Proverb. (Signifying that those who act against the pope invariably suffer for it.) (Medieval ?)

He who has the pope for a cousin can easily become a cardinal. (Wer den Papst zum Vetter hat, kann leicht Kardinal werden.)

> German Proverb. (Medieval ?)

Your holiness holds the place of God on earth.

> Savonarola. (Words addressed to Pope Alexander VI.) (15th cent.)

If Rome be against me, know that she is not against me, but Christ.

> Savonarola. (15th cent.)

Let us enjoy the papacy, since God has given it to us. (Godiamoci il papato, poichè Dio ce l'ha dato.)

> Leo X is reported to have said this to his brother Giuliano Medici, following his election. (16th cent.)

Accept, receive, take, are words pleasing to the pope. (Accipe, sume, cape, sunt verba placentia papae.)

> Rabelais: *Pantagruel,* 3, 42. (Quoting medieval saying.) (16th cent.)

Being a man I may come to be pope.

> Cervantes: *Don Quixote,* 2, 47. (17th cent.)

St. Peter is very well at Rome. (Bien se está San Pedro en Roma.)

> Cervantes: *Don Quixote,* 2, 41. (17th cent.)

You may not sit in Rome and strive with the pope.

> Ferguson: *Scottish Proverbs.* (Medieval saying.) (16th cent.)

The pope may act outside the law, above the law, and against the law. (Papa potest extra jus, super jus et contra jus.)

> St. Robert Bellarmine: *De Summo Pontifice.* (17th cent.)

"You will not live to see the days of Peter." (Non videbis dies Petri.)

"This is not de fide." (Non est de fide.)

> When a domestic murmured that Urban VIII would not live longer than the pontificate of St. Peter (25 years), the acute pope overheard him and replied in kind. Pius IX used the same phrase: Non videbis annos Petri. (17th cent.)

No popery!

> Cry of the London mob in 1681, and frequently thereafter.

To be more papal than the pope.

> Saying modeled on the French: *One must not be more royalist than the king (Il ne faut pas être plus royaliste que le roi),*

which, according to Chateaubriand, was coined under Louis XVI. (19th cent. ?)

If you would be a pope, you must think of nothing else.

> H. Bohn: *Handbook of Proverbs,* 422. (1855)

The rock of St. Peter on its summit enjoys a pure and serene atmosphere, but there is a great deal of Roman malaria at the foot of it.

> Card. Newman: *Letter to the Duke of Norfolk.* (Apropos deliberate misrepresentation of the Syllabus of Pius IX) (19th cent.)

More Catholic than the pope.

> Bismarck. (1887)

Dear me, how strange it would be to have someone guessing infallibly.

> Reply of Card. Gasquet to an English lady who asked him whether the next Pope would be an American. (1914)

Poppy

Summer set lipt to earth's bosom bare,
And left the flushed print in a poppy there.

> F. Thompson: *The Poppy.* (19th cent.)

The poppy opes her scarlet purse of dreams.

> Scharmel Iris: *Early Nightfall.* (20th cent.)

Portrait

Good heav'n! that sots and knaves should be so vain,
To wish their vile resemblance may remain!
And stand recorded at their own request,
To future days, a libel or a jest.

> Dryden: *To Sir Godfrey Kneller.* (17th cent.)

Every portrait that is painted with feeling is a portrait of the artist, not of the sitter.

> Oscar Wilde: *The Picture of Dorian Gray,* 1. (19th cent.)

Possessing

He that hath plenty of goods shall have more;
He that hath but a little, he shall have less;
He that hath right nought, right nought shall possess.

> John Heywood: *Proverbs,* 1, 11. (16th cent.)

Better to have than wish.

> John Heywood: *Proverbs,* 2, 4. (16th cent.)

The pleasure of possessing
Surpasses all expressing;
But 'tis too short a blessing,
And love too long a pain.

> Dryden: *Farewell, Ungrateful Traitor.* (17th cent.)

Possessions

Be not anxious about what you have, but about what you are.

> Pope St. Gregory I: *Homilies on the Gospels,* 13, 6. (6th cent.)

Man should not consider his material possessions as his own, but as common to all, so as to share them without hesitation when others are in need. Whence the apostle says: *Command the rich of this world . . . to offer with no stint, to apportion largely.*

> St. Thomas Aquinas: *Summa Theologica,* 2-2, 66, 2. (13th cent.)

For well you know that nor life nor health nor riches nor honor nor dignity nor lordship is your own. Were they yours, you could possess them in your own way. But in such an hour a man wishes to be well, he is ill; or living, and he is dead; or rich, and he is poor; or a lord, and he is made a servant and vassal. All this is because these things are not his own, and he can only hold them in so far as may please him who has lent them to him.

> St. Catherine of Siena: *Letter to Charles V, King of France.* (14th cent.)

It is easier to renounce worldly possessions than it is to renounce the love of
them.

> Walter Hilton: *Scale of Perfection*, 1, 71.
> (14th cent.)

To have an attachment for and actually
to possess more than you reasonably need
is a great fault. To be attached to something of which you do not have need
is also a fault, but a lesser one, but to
possess and make use of what you need
without being attached to it is blameless.

> Walter Hilton: *Scale of Perfection*, 1, 71.
> (14th cent.)

See also Property; Wealth

Possibility

I admit the case as possible, but yet as
such a case, as, I trust in God, this
good man shall see the sky fall first and
catch larks ere it happen.

> St. Thomas More. (16th cent.)

Pot

Little pot, soon hot.

> John Heywood: *Proverbs*, 1, 11. (16th
> cent.)

Poverty

Neither the wealth of Darius nor the
riches of Croesus would suffice to satisfy
the wants of the world's poor.

> St. Jerome: *Letters*, 118, 5. (5th cent.)

I wish you to be the friend of the poor,
but especially their imitator. The one is
the grade of beginner, the other of the
perfect, for the friendship of the poor
makes us the friend of kings, but the
love of poverty makes us kings ourselves. The kingdom of heaven is the
kingdom of the poor, and one of the
marks of royal power is to do good to
friends according to our will.

> St. Bernard: *Letters*. (12th cent.)

No one should commend poverty save
the poor.

> St. Bernard: *Sermons*. (12th cent.)

Poverty I love, but not dirt.

> St. Bernard (12th cent.)

Possess poverty.

> St. Dominic. (Dying words) (13th cent.)

Poverty is an odious blessing.

> Vincent of Beauvais: *Speculum historiale.*
> (13th cent.)

If thou be poor, thy brother hateth thee,
And all thy friends do flee from thee,
    alas!

> Chaucer: *Man of Lawes Tale.* (14th cent.)

A poor man, that beareth no riches on
him by the way, may boldly sing before
thieves.

> Chaucer: *Boethius,* Bk. 2, prose 5. (14th
> cent.)

Poverty, often, when heart is lowly,
Brings one to God and teaches what is
    holy,
Gives knowledge of oneself and even
    lends
A glass by which to see one's truest
    friends.

> Chaucer: *The Wife of Bath's Tale.* (Tr.
> Coghill) (14th cent.)

As poor as Job.

> John Gower: *Confessio Amantis,* 5. (14th
> cent.)

I had rather be poor for Thee than rich
without Thee.

> Thomas a Kempis: *The Imitation of
> Christ,* 3, 59. (15th cent.)

Light gain makes heavy purses.

> John Heywood: *Proverbs,* 1, 11. (16th
> cent.)

As rich as a new shorn sheep.

> John Heywood: *Proverbs,* 1, 11. (16th
> cent.)

Though love decree departure death to be,
Poverty parteth fellowship, we see.

John Heywood: *Proverbs,* 1, 12. (16th cent.)

To desire to be poor but not to be inconvenienced by poverty, is to desire the honor of poverty and the convenience of riches.

St. Francis de Sales: *Introduction to the Devout Life,* 3, 16. (17th cent.)

As for those who possess not the gifts of fortune, they are taught by the Church that in God's sight poverty is no disgrace, and that there is nothing to be ashamed of in earning their bread by labor.

Pope Leo XIII: *Rerum Novarum.* (May 15, 1891)

Neither must it be supposed that the solicitude of the Church is so preoccupied with the spiritual concerns of her children as to neglect their temporal and earthly interests. Her desire is that the poor, for example, should rise above poverty and wretchedness, and better their condition in life; and for this she makes a strong endeavor. By the very fact that she calls men to virtue and forms them to its practice she promotes this in no slight degree.

Pope Leo XIII: *Rerum Novarum.* (May 15, 1891)

The Lady Poverty was fair:
But she has lost her look of late,
With change of times and change of air.
Ah slattern! she neglects her hair,
Her gown, her shoes; she keeps no state
As once when her pure feet were bare.

Alice Meynell: *The Lady Poverty.* (19th cent.)

The poor I saw at the cloister gate
    Mutely beg with their patient eyes
An alms, for the love of Him Who sate

And supped with the poor in humble guise.

Speer Strahan: *The Poor.* (20th cent.)

It is easy enough to tell the poor to accept their poverty as God's will when you yourself have warm clothes and plenty of food and medical care and a roof over your head and no worry about the rent. But if you want them to believe you—try to share some of their poverty and see if you can accept it as God's will yourself!

Thomas Merton: *Seeds of Contemplation.* (20th cent.)

Power

For the human mind is prone to pride even when not supported by power; how much more, then, does it exalt itself when it has that support! But he disposes his power aright, who knows how with great care both to derive from it what is profitable and to subdue the temptations which it creates, and how, though in possession of it, to realize equality with others, and at the same time set himself above sinners in his zeal for retribution.

Pope St. Gregory I: *Pastoral Care,* 2, 6. (6th cent.)

Envy of a foreign tyrant
    Threateneth kings, not shepherds humble;
Age makes silly swains delirant,
    Thirst of rule gars great men stumble.

gars—makes

Thomas Lodge: *Old Damon's Pastoral.* (17th cent.)

That prince who yields the least of royal sway,
So far his people's freedom does betray.
Right lives by law, and law subsists by pow'r;
Disarm the shepherd, wolves the flock devour.

Dryden: *Absalom and Achitophel.* (17th cent.)

They who possess the prince possess the laws.

> John Dryden: *Absalom and Achitophel,* 1. (17th cent.)

How fatal 'tis to be too good a king!

> Dryden: *Absalom and Achitophel.* (17th cent.)

Yes, I am proud; I must be proud to see Men, not afraid of God, afraid of me.

> Pope: *Epilogue to the Satires,* 2. (18th cent.)

Power to be powerful, and strength to be strong, must be exerted only now and then.

> Card. Newman: *Letter to Lord Acton.* (1858)

All public power proceeds from God.

> Pope Leo XIII: *Immortale Dei.* (Nov. 1, 1885)

Power tends to corrupt and absolute power corrupts absolutely. Great men are almost always bad men, even when they exercise influence and not authority: still more when you superadd the tendency or the certainty of corruption by authority. There is no worse heresy than that the office sanctifies the holder of it.

> Lord Acton: *Letter to M. Creighton.* (1887)

Praise

Behold, O Truth, in You I see that I should be moved by praise of myself, not for my own sake but for the good of my neighbor.

> St. Augustine: *Confessions,* 10, 37. (5th cent.)

It is a great matter not to rejoice in human praise and honors but to discard all empty ostentation, and, if any of it must be kept, to turn it all to the use and the well-being of those who honor us.

> St. Augustine: *Letter 22.* (4th cent.)

Our meditation in this present life should be in the praise of God; for the eternal exultation of our life hereafter will be the praise of God; and none can become fit for the future life, who hath not practiced himself for it now.

> St. Augustine: *In Ps. 148,* 1. (5th cent.)

He does not know how to flee from praise when it abounds, if he yearned for it when it was absent.

> Pope St. Gregory I: *Pastoral Care,* 1, 9. (6th cent.)

It is the nature of this universal vanity which is in us to wish for praise when we deserve blame, and to be loath to praise others when we know them to be praiseworthy.

> St. Bernard: *Letters,* 19, 3. (12th cent.)

Be sparing in praise and more so in blaming.

> Langland: *Piers Plowman.* (14th cent.)

Thou art not more holy if thou art praised nor anything the worse if thou art dispraised.

> Thomas a Kempis: *The Imitation of Christ,* 2, 6. (15th cent.)

Ye praise the wine before ye taste of the grape.

> John Heywood: *Proverbs,* 1, 10. (16th cent.)

What creature, O sweet Lord,
    From praising Thee can stay,
What earthly thing but fill'd with joy,
    Thine honor doth bewray.

bewray—betray

> Richard Verstegan: *Hymn.* (Guiney, 220) (16th cent.)

No laurel wreath about my brow!
    To Thee, my God! all praise! Whose law
The conquered doth and conqueror bow:

For both dissolve to air, if Thou
  Thy influence withdraw.

W. Habington: *Non Nobis Domine.*
(17th cent.)

Praise is devotion fit for mighty minds,
  The differing world's agreeing sacrifice,
Where Heaven divided faiths united
  finds.

Sir William Davenant: *Gondibert.* (17th
cent.)

Be thou the first true merit to befriend,
His praise is lost who stays till all commend.

Pope: *An Essay on Criticism,* 2. (18th
cent.)

Praise undeserv'd is satire in disguise.

Pope: *An Essay on Man,* 1. (18th cent.)

And hearts that once beat high for
  praise
Now feel that pulse no more.

Thomas Moore: *The Harp That Once
Through Tara's Halls.* (19th cent.)

Speak not the word that turns the
  flower to ashes,
  Praise not the beauty passing as you
  gaze.
Let your eyes drink of loveliness in
  silence:
  It will but wither even as you praise.

Aline Kilmer: *Favete Linguis.* (20th
cent.)

The humble man receives praise the way
a clean window takes the light of the
sun. The truer and more intense the light
is, the less you see of the glass.

Thomas Merton: *Seeds of Contemplation.*
(20th cent.)

See also Self-praise

Praise and Blame

Now God bless all true workers, let us
  pray:
The night time cometh, when we all
  must rest:

Strive we, and do, lest by and by we sit
In that blind life to which all other fate
Is cause for envy; with the naked souls
Who never lived, knowing nor praise
  nor blame,
But kept themselves in mean neutrality,
Hateful alike to God and to his foes.

Emily H. Hickey: *Michael Villiers,
Idealist.* (19th cent.)

Prayer

Prayer is conversation with God.

Clement of Alexandria: *Stromateis,* 7.
(2nd cent.)

And let every faithful man and woman
when they rise from sleep at dawn before
they undertake any work wash their
hands and pray to God, and so let them
go to their work.

St. Hippolytus: *The Apostolic Tradition,*
35. (3rd cent.)

Pray also before thy body rests upon thy
bed.

St. Hippolytus: *The Apostolic Tradition,*
36. (3rd cent.)

We meet in gathering and congregation
to approach God in prayer, massing our
forces to surround Him. This violence
that we do Him pleases God.

Tertullian: *Apology,* 39, 2. (3rd cent.)

When we stand praying, beloved brethren, we ought to be watchful and earnest
with our whole heart, intent on our
prayers. Let all carnal and worldly
thoughts pass away, nor let the soul at
that time think on anything except the
object of its prayer.

St. Cyprian: *On the Lord's Prayer,* 31.
(3rd cent.)

Those who pray should not come to God
with fruitless or naked prayers. Petition is ineffectual when it is barren entreaty that beseeches God.

St. Cyprian: *On the Lord's Prayer,* 32.
(3rd cent.)

Those prayers quickly ascend to God which the merits of our works urge upon God.

> St. Cyprian: *On the Lord's Prayer, 33.* (3rd cent.)

We do not say *my* Father, but *our* Father, neither do we say give *me,* but give *us;* and this because the Teacher of unity did not wish prayer to be made privately, viz., that each should pray for himself alone; for He wished one to pray for all since He in his single Person had borne all.

> St. Cyprian: *On the Lord's Prayer.* (3rd cent.)

As some kneel on the Lord's Day and on the days of Pentecost, the holy synod has decided that, for the observance of a general rule, all shall offer their prayers to God standing.

> Council of Nicaea, Can. 20. (325)

He prays best who does not know that he is praying.

> St. Anthony. (4th cent.)

Prayer is to be commended, for it engenders in the soul a distinct conception of God. And the indwelling of God is this—to hold God ever in memory, His shrine established within us.

> St. Basil: *Letters,* 2. (4th cent.)

Reflect what great happiness is bestowed upon you, what glory is given to you, namely, to converse in your prayers with God, to join in colloquy with Christ, and to beg for what you wish or desire.

> St. John Chrysostom: *Hom. 2. On Prayer.* (4th cent.)

Where prayer is poured forth, sins are covered.

> St. Ambrose: *De Interpel. Job,* 2, 8. (4th cent.)

Our Father, Who hast exhorted us to pray, Who also bringest about what Thou hast asked of us; since we live better when we pray to Thee and are better: hear me as I tremble in this darkness and reach out Thy hand to me. Hold Thy light before me and recall me from my strayings, that with Thee as my guide I may return to myself and to Thee. Amen.

> St. Augustine: *Soliloquies,* 2, 6, 9. (4th cent.)

Nor should we imagine, as some do, that prolonged prayer is the same thing as 'much-speaking'; many words are one thing; long-continued feelings of devotion quite another.

> St. Augustine: *Letter 130.* (To Proba on prayer) (5th cent.)

It is lawful to pray for what it is lawful to desire.

> St. Augustine: *Letters,* 130, 12. (To Proba.) (5th cent.)

When you pray to God with psalms and hymns, meditate in your heart upon that which you utter with your voice.

> St. Augustine: *Letter 211.* (His *Rule.*) (5th cent.)

The daily prayers of the faithful make satisfaction for those daily, tiny, light faults from which this life cannot be free.

> St. Augustine: *Enchiridion,* 71. (5th cent.)

How speedily are the prayers of people who do good works heard! For it is precisely in fasting, almsdeeds and prayer that our righteousness in this life consists. Would you have your prayers fly to God equip them with the two wings of fasting and almsdeeds.

> St. Augustine: In *Ps. 42 Enarr. 1,* 8. (5th cent.)

For God does not hear us as man hears. Unless you shout with your lungs and chest and lips, a mere man does not hear; whereas to God your very thoughts shout.

> St. Augustine: In *Ps. 141 Enarr. 1,* 2. (5th cent.)

He knows how to live well who knows how to pray well. (Recte novit vivere qui recte novit orare.)

> Anonymous sermon. (Among sermons of St. Augustine, 55, 1.) (5th cent. ?)

He who asks of God in faith things needful for this life is sometimes mercifully heard and sometimes mercifully not heard. For the Physician knows better than the patient what will avail for the sick man.

> St. Prosper of Aquitaine: *Sententiae ex Augustino delibatae,* 212. (5th cent.)

In a single day I have prayed as many as a hundred times, and in the night almost as often.

> St. Patrick: *Confessio.* (5th cent.)

But before all things it is good to begin with prayer, as thereby giving ourselves up to and uniting ourselves with God.

> Pseudo-Dionysius: *On the Divine Names,* 6, 1. (5th cent.)

To apply oneself frequently to prayer.

> St. Benedict: *Rule,* 4. (One of his 'tools of good works.') (6th cent.)

If we wish to prefer a petition to men of high station, we do not presume to do it without humility and respect; how much more ought we to supplicate the Lord God of all things with all humility and pure devotion. And let us be sure that we shall not be heard for our much speaking, but for purity of heart and tears of compunction. Our prayer, therefore, ought to be short and pure, unless it chance to be prolonged by the impulse and inspiration of divine grace.

> St. Benedict: *Rule,* 20. (6th cent.)

Let Thy merciful ears, O Lord, be open to the prayers of Thy suppliant people; and that Thou mayest grant them their petitions, do Thou cause them to ask for such things as shall please Thee.

> Roman Missal, Collect for Ninth Sunday after Pentecost. (Gelasian, 5th to 7th cent.)

The lips' reasoning. (Oris ratio.)

> Cassiodorus: *Comm. in Ps. 38.* (6th cent.)

For with God both of these of necessity match each other exactly: practice should be sustained by prayer, and prayer by practice.

> Pope St. Gregory I: *Morals,* 18, 10. (6th cent.)

He causes his prayers to be of more avail to himself, who offers them also for others.

> Pope St. Gregory I: *Morals,* 35, 21. (6th cent.)

Men by petitioning may merit to receive what almighty God arranged before the ages to give them.

> Pope St. Gregory I: *Dialogue,* 1, 8. (6th cent.)

To pray is the same thing as to speak. (Orare idem est ac dicere.)

> St. Isidore of Seville: *Etymologies,* 10. (7th cent.)

All the virtues assist the soul to attain to a burning love of God, but, above all, pure prayer. By means of it the soul escapes completely from the midst of creatures, carried to God, as it were, on wings.

> St. Maximus the Confessor: *Centuries on Charity,* 1, 11. (7th cent.)

The highest state of prayer, it is said, is when the soul leaves the flesh and the world and, by means of the act of prayer, leaves behind all matter and form. He who can maintain this condition without injury is in reality capable of continual prayer.

> St. Maximus the Confessor: *Centuries on Charity,* 2, 61. (7th cent.)

Those only seek in the name of the Savior who seek the things which pertain to eternal salvation.

> St. Bede the Venerable: *Homilies,* 2, 7. (8th cent.)

Prayer is a raising up of the mind to God or a petitioning of God for what is fitting.

> St. John of Damascus: *Exposition of the Orthodox Faith*, 3, 24. (8th cent.)

Prayer is a wine which makes glad the heart of man . . . it moistens the dry soil of the conscience, it brings about the perfect absorption of the food of good actions, and distributes them into all the members of the soul; strengthening faith, giving vigor to hope, rendering charity active and yet well ordered, and shedding an unction over the whole character.

> St. Bernard: *Sermons on the Canticle of Canticles*, 18, 6. (12th cent.)

Pray and work. (Ora et labora.)

> Motto of the Cistercians. (ca. 12th cent. ?)

For prayer to be effective our petitions should be for benefits worthily to be expected from God. *Ye ask, and receive not, because ye ask amiss* (James 4, 3).

> St. Thomas Aquinas: *Compendium of Theology*, 252. (13th cent.)

But it is not necessary for us to set forth our petitions before God in order to make known to him our needs or desires, but rather that we ourselves may realize that in these things it is needful to have recourse to the divine assistance.

> St. Thomas Aquinas: *Summa Theologica*, 2, 2, 83, 2. (13th cent.)

What profits pleading that Heaven will not hear?

> Dante: *Purgatorio, Canto 4.* (14th cent.)

We little know the things for which we pray.

> Chaucer: *Canterbury Tales: The Knight's Tale.* (Tr. Coghill) (14th cent.)

Prayer in itself properly is nought else but a devout intent directed unto God, for the getting of good and the removing of evil.

> Anonymous: *The Cloud of Unknowing*, 39. (14th cent.)

Not only pleasure will withdraw men from prayer, but also affliction sometimes; but there is this difference: affliction will sometimes extort a short prayer from the wickedest man alive, but pleasure stifles it altogether.

> St. Thomas More: *Meditations and Devotions.* (16th cent.)

All that should be sought for in the exercise of prayer is conformity of our will with the divine will, in which consists the highest perfection.

> St. Teresa of Jesus. (16th cent.)

He that flees from prayer flees from all that is good.

> St. John of the Cross: *Spiritual Sentences.* (16th cent.)

Oh! fortress of the faithful, sure defence,
In which doth Christians' cognizance consist;
Their victory, their triumph come from thence,
So forcible, hell-gates cannot resist:
A thing whereby both angels, clouds and stars,
At man's request fight God's revengeful wars.

Nothing more grateful in the highest eyes,
Nothing more firm in danger to protect us,
Nothing more forcible to pierce the skies,
And not depart till mercy do respect us:
And, as the soul life to the body gives,
So prayer revives the soul, by prayer it lives.

> Bl. Robert Southwell: *Verses Prefixed to 'Short Rules of Good Life.'* (16th cent.)

When thou dost talk with God—by prayer I mean—
Lift up pure hands, lay down all lust's desires;
Fix thoughts on heaven, present a conscience clean:

Since holy blame to mercy's throne
    aspires,
Confess faults' guilt, crave pardon for
    thy sin,
Tread holy paths, call grace to guide
    therein.

Bl. Robert Southwell: *Preparative to
Prayer.* (16th cent.)

If you have the gift for mental prayer,
always reserve for that the principal
place above private vocal prayers.

St. Francis de Sales: *Introduction to the
Devout Life,* 2, 1. (17th cent.)

Holy Church does not teach us to pray
for ourselves in particular, but always
for ourselves and for our Christian
brethren.

St. Francis de Sales: *Letters to Persons in
the World,* 3, 11. (17th cent.)

The chief exercise of prayer is to speak
to God and to hear God speak in the
bottom of your heart.

St. Francis de Sales: *Treatise on the Love
of God,* 6, 1. (17th cent.)

Two went to pray? O, rather say,
One went to brag, the other to pray;
One stands up close and treads on
    high,
Where the other dares not lend his eye;
One nearer to God's altar trod,
The other to the altar's God.

Richard Crashaw: *Two Went Up To the
Temple to Pray.* (17th cent.)

Our vows are heard betimes! and
    Heaven takes care
To grant, before we can conclude the
    pray'r:
Preventing angels met it half the way,
And sent us back to praise, who came
    to pray.

Dryden: *Britannia Rediviva.* (17th cent.)

As down in the sunless retreats of the
    ocean,
    Sweet flowers are springing no mor-
    tal can see,

So, deep in my soul the still prayer of
    devotion
    Unheard by the world rises silent to
    thee.

Thomas Moore: *As Down in the Sunless
Retreats.* (19th cent.)

This is the highest excellence to which
we ordinarily attain; to understand our
own hypocrisy, insincerity, and shallow-
ness of mind,—to own, while we pray,
that we cannot pray aright,—to repent
of our repentings,—and to submit ourselves wholly to His judgment, Who
could indeed be extreme with us, but has
already shown His loving-kindness in
bidding us to pray.

Card. Newman: *Parochial and Plain
Sermons,* 1. (19th cent.)

He who gives up regularity in prayer
has lost a principal means of reminding
himself that spiritual life is obedience
to a Lawgiver, not a mere feeling or
taste.

Card. Newman: *Parochial and Plain
Sermons,* 1. (19th cent.)

O for the happy days gone by,
    When love ran smooth and free,
Days when my spirit so enjoy'd
    More than earth's liberty!

O for the times when on my heart
    Long prayer had never pall'd,
Times when the ready thought of God
    Would come when it was call'd!

F. Faber: *Dryness in Prayer.* (19th cent.)

Ah! dearest Lord! I cannot pray,
    My fancy is not free;
Unmannerly distractions come,
    And force my thoughts from Thee.

The world that looks so dull all day
    Glows bright on me at prayer,
And plans that ask no thought but then
    Wake up and meet me there.

F. Faber: *Distractions in Prayer.* (19th
cent.)

If we leave religion as a subject of thought for all hours of the day equally, it will be thought of in none.

> Card. Newman: *Miscellanies.* (19th cent.)

As speech is the organ of human society, and the means of human civilization, so is prayer the instrument of divine fellowship and divine training.

> Card. Newman: *Miscellanies,* 203. (19th cent.)

Who can really pray to a Being, about whose existence he is seriously in doubt?

> Card. Newman: *Apologia pro Vita Sua, 1.* (19th cent.)

> Pray, sweet, for me, that I may be Faithful to God and thee.

> E. H. Hickey: *Beloved, It is Morn.* (19th cent.)

The path of prayer is the King's highway from earth to heaven.

> Archbp. Ullathorne: *Humility and Patience.* (19th cent.)

Prayer is the noblest and most exalted action of which man is capable through the grace of God.

> Archbp. Ullathorne: *Humility and Patience.* (19th cent.)

As God created all things by His word, so man by prayer obtains whatever he wills. Nothing has so great a power to obtain grace for us as prayer when rightly made; for it contains the motives by which God easily allows Himself to be appeased and to incline to mercy.

> Pope Leo XIII: *Exeunte Jam Anno.* (Dec. 25, 1888)

In reading, our minds terminate upon a book; in meditation, our intelligence and our heart terminate upon God. Prayer is a vital act of faith and desire to attain a fuller knowledge of God and a closer union with Him in affection and in resolution—that is, in heart and will.

> Card. Manning: *The Eternal Priesthood.* (19th cent.)

Master of spirits! hear one: King of souls!
I kneel before Thine altar, the long night,
Besieging Thee with penetrable prayers.

> Lionel Johnson: *The Darkness.* (19th cent.)

We all win from God exactly what we deserve. We all get from God exactly what we really want of Him.

> R. H. Benson: *Christ in the Church.* (20th cent.)

The fact that the single occupation of prayer appears idle or grotesque, or at the best mistaken, to men of our day, is but one more sign of how spiritual faculties are beginning to decay.

> R. H. Benson: *A Book of the Love of Jesus.* (20th cent.)

It is Christ that prays in every soul in whom He lives.

> R. H. Benson: *Preface to Bands of Love.* (20th cent.)

Pray a good deal; one must be supple.

> R. H. Benson: *The Sentimentalists.* (20th cent.)

Pray as you can and do not try to pray as you can't.

> Dom Chapman: *Spiritual Letters.* (20th cent.)

The only way to pray is to pray; and the way to pray well is to pray much. If one has no time for this, then one must at least pray regularly. But the less one prays, the worse it goes.

> Dom Chapman: *Spiritual Letters.* (20th cent.)

The most fundamental need, duty, honor and happiness of man, is not petition, nor even contrition, nor again even thanksgiving; these are three kinds of prayer which indeed must never disappear out of our spiritual lives; but adoration.

> Baron von Hügel: *The Life of Prayer.* (20th cent.)

I take these to be the seven great facts and doctrines concerning God—His richness; His double action, natural and supernatural; His perfect freedom; His delightfulness; His otherness; His adorableness; and His prevenience. These seven facts, vividly apprehended, will even singly and how much more if seen conjointly, each penetrating and calling forth the others, bring much depth and breadth, much variety and elasticity into our prayer.

Baron von Hügel: *The Life of Prayer.* (20th cent.)

Prayer will remove the fundamental cause of present day difficulties.

Pope Pius XI: *Caritate Christi compulsi.* (May 3, 1932)

People who only know how to think about God during certain fixed periods of the day will never get very far in the spiritual life. In fact they will not even think of Him in the moments they have religiously marked off for 'mental prayer.'

Thomas Merton: *Seeds of Contemplation.* (20th cent.)

See also Contemplation; Divine Office; Liturgy; Meditation; Worship

Preacher

Vainly does the preacher utter the word of God exteriorly unless he listens to it interiorly.

St. Augustine: *Sermons,* 179, 1. (5th cent.)

For that cock, too, which the Lord in his figure of speech [cf. Job, 38, 2] took as a symbol of the good preacher, when he is preparing to crow, first shakes his wings, and beating himself with them, makes himself more alert. So, it is obviously necessary that they who give utterance to words of holy preaching, should first be awake in the earnest practice of good works, lest, being them-selves slack in performing them, they stir up others by words only.

Pope St. Gregory I: *Pastoral Care,* 3, 40. (6th cent.)

But it is the peculiar way with haughty preachers, that they are more desirous of strictly reproving their hearers even when distressed, than to cherish them in a kindly manner. For they are more anxious to chide and reprove faults, than to encourage goodness with praise. They are anxious to appear superior to other people, and they are better pleased when anger raises their feelings than when charity brings them down. They ever wish to find something to smite sharply with reproof.

Pope St. Gregory I: *Morals,* 24, 40. (6th cent.)

Do you know how I test the value of a preacher? If the listeners go away striking their breasts, saying: Today I will do better; not by their saying: What a wonderful sermon.

Jean Pierre Camus: *The Spirit of St. Francis de Sales,* 19, 12. (17th cent.)

His preaching much, but more his practice wrought;
A living sermon of the truths he taught.

Dryden: *The Character of a Good Parson.* (17th cent.)

Those preachers are foolish and improvident who, in speaking of religion and proclaiming the things of God, use no words but those of human science and human prudence, trusting to their own reasonings rather than to those of God. Their discourses may be brilliant and fine, but they must be feeble and they must be cold, for they are without the fire of the utterance of God (Jerem. 23, 29).

Pope Leo XIII: *Providentissimus Deus.* (Nov. 18, 1893)

The world runs after pulpit orators. They please the ear, and do not disturb the conscience. They move the emotions, but do not change the will. The world suffers no loss for them, nor is it humbled, nor wounded.

Card. Manning: *The Eternal Priesthood.* (19th cent.)

The simple, the humble, and the faithful instinctively detect the preacher who preaches himself; even men of the world, accustomed to the brief and peremptory language of earnest life, at once find out the unreal and the professional. They will listen to an honest preacher, though he be rude and rough. The fewer of his own words and the more of God's words the surer he is to command the hearing and the respect of men.

Card. Manning: *The Eternal Priesthood.* (19th cent.)

Preaching

He gathers abundant fruits from his preaching, who sows before the seeds of welldoing.

Pope St. Gregory I: *Morals,* 6, 54. (6th cent.)

Nobody, however learned or holy, should preach unless commissioned by God and ecclesiastical authority. . . . Preaching, exhorting, teaching, which are the public concern and care of the Church, are committed to the bishops, who only can exercise this official authority.

St. Thomas Aquinas: *Quodlibets,* 12, 18, 27. (13th cent.)

Christ said not to His first assembly: Go and preach trifles to the world; but gave to them the true foundation.

Dante: *Paradiso, Canto* 29. (14th cent.)

For with the princes of pride the preachers dwelleth.

Langland: *Piers Plowman.* (14th cent.)

The best meditation before preaching is prayer. We must, indeed, meditate what we preach, and make meditations in our sermons, but not sermons in our meditations; for our meditations are for our own sanctification, and we cannot more surely reach the hearts of other men than by teaching what has first been realized in our own.

Card. Manning: *The Eternal Priesthood.* (19th cent.)

The responsibility of preaching the Catholic faith is entrusted chiefly to the Roman pontiff for the whole Church, and to the bishops for their own dioceses. Bishops are bound to preach the gospel personally unless excused by some legitimate reason; moreover they should employ not only the pastors of parishes but other suitable persons, in order that this responsibility may be properly carried out.

Code of Canon Law, Canon 1327. (20th cent.)

Preaching is heady wine. It is pleasant to tell people exactly where they get off.

Arnold Lunn: *Now I See.* (20th cent.)

The world is waiting for those who love it; if you don't love the world, don't preach to it: preach to yourself.

Vincent McNabb. (20th cent.)

Predestination

Between grace and predestination there is only this difference, that predestination is the preparation for grace, while grace is the donation itself.

St. Augustine: *De Praedestinatione Sanctorum,* 19. (5th cent.)

Therefore God chose us in Christ before the foundation of the world, predestinating us to the adoption of children, not because we were going to be ourselves holy and immaculate, but He chose and predestinated us that we might be so.

St. Augustine: *De Praedestinatione Sanctorum,* 37. (5th cent.)

The number of the predestined is certain, and can neither be increased nor diminished.

> St. Augustine: *De Correptione et Gratia,* 13. (5th cent.)

So long as this mortal life endures, no one of the faithful may presume that he belongs to the number of the predestined.

> St. Augustine: *De Correptione et Gratia,* 13, 40. (5th cent.)

Why should grace deliver this one and that, why not this one and that; I would not that thou inquire of me. I am a man. I consider the depth of the Cross. I do not penetrate it. I stand in awe. I do not search into it. Incomprehensible are His judgments, unsearchable His ways.

> St. Augustine: *Sermon 165,* 7, 9. (5th cent.)

Why He draws one, and another He draws not, seek not to judge, if thou dost not wish to err.

> St. Augustine: *Tract. in Joann.,* 26. (5th cent.)

It must be borne in mind that God foreknows but does not predetermine everything, since He foreknows all that is in us, but does not predetermine it all.

> St. John of Damascus: *De Fide Orthodoxa,* 2, 30. (8th cent.)

God our Savior will have all men to be saved, and to come to the knowledge of the truth (1 Tim. 2, 4) . . . God antecedently wills all men to be saved, but consequently wills some to be damned, according to the requirements of His justice. . . . Whatsoever God simply wills, that He does; whatsoever He wishes, that may not come about.

> St. Thomas Aquinas: *Summa Theologica,* 1, 19, 6. (13th cent.)

The causality of reprobation is unlike that of predestination. For predestination is the cause both of what is awaited in the future, namely glory, and of what is received in the present, namely grace. Whereas reprobation is not the cause of present fault, but of future result, namely, of being abandoned by God. Fault is born of the freewill of the person who deserts grace.

> St. Thomas Aquinas: *Summa Theologica,* 1, 23, 4. (13th cent.)

The reason for the predestination of some, and reprobation of others, must be sought for in the goodness of God.

> St. Thomas Aquinas: *Summa Theologica,* 1, 23, 5. (13th cent.)

When things are directed to an end we may distinguish between the plan and its outcome: not everything directed to an end succeeds in reaching it. Providence supplies the plan, and directs all human beings to happiness. Predestination, however, relates to the success of the plan, and applies only to those who will actually reach heaven.

> St. Thomas Aquinas: *Disputations concerning Truth,* 6, 1. (13th cent.)

From all eternity some are preordained and directed to heaven; they are called the predestined. . . . From all eternity, too, it has been settled that others will not be given grace, and these are called the reprobate or rejected ones.

> St. Thomas Aquinas: *Contra Gentes,* 3, 164. (13th cent.)

Predestination! how remote and dim
  Thy root lies hidden from the intellect
  Which only glimpses the First Cause Supreme!
And you, ye mortals, keep your judgment checked,
  Since we, who see God, have not therefore skill
  To know yet all the number of the elect.
To us such wanting is delectable
  Because our good in this good is refined,

That, what God willeth, that we also
will.

Dante: *Paradiso, Canto 20*. (Tr. L.
Binyon) (14th cent.)

Ask any scholar of discerning;
He'll say the schools are filled with
altercation
On this vexed matter of predestination,
Long bandied by a hundred thousand
men.
How can I sift it to the bottom then?

Chaucer: *The Nun's Priest's Tale*. (Tr.
Coghill) (14th cent.)

If any one saith that a man who is born
again and justified is bound of faith to
believe that he is assuredly in the number
of the predestinate; let him be anathema.

Council of Trent, Session 6, Canon 15.
(Jan. 13, 1547)

If any one saith that the grace of justification is only attained to by those who
are predestined unto life; but that all
others who are called are indeed called,
but receive not grace as being by the
divine power predestined unto evil; let
him be anathema.

Council of Trent, Session 6, Canon 17.
(Jan. 13, 1547)

That God has foreordained everything
is self-evident.

Descartes: *Principles of Philosophy*, 1.
(17th cent.)

For how can that eternal Power be just
To punish man who sins because he
must?
Or how can he reward a virtuous deed
Which is not done by us, but first de-
creed?

Dryden. (17th cent.)

Preparedness

We ought not to be sanguine about anything; the right rule is to hope nothing,
to fear nothing, to expect nothing, to be
prepared for everything.

Card. Newman: *Essays Critical and
Historical*, 1. (19th cent.)

The time is coming, it will soon be
come
When those who dare not fight
For God or for the right,
Shall fight for peace.

Aubrey de Vere: *Liberalism*. (19th cent.)

Present and Future

Oh, the dullness and hardness of the
human heart, which thinketh only of
present things and provideth not more
for things to come.

Thomas a Kempis: *The Imitation of
Christ*, 1, 23. (15th cent.)

Such is; what is to be?
The pulp so bitter, how shall taste the
rind?

F. Thompson: *The Hound of Heaven*.
(19th cent.)

Presumption

Huntsmen push into brambles, and often
return more injured than the animal they
intend to injure.

St. Francis de Sales: *Letters to Persons in
the World*, 4, 3. (17th cent.)

We usually know what we ought to do,
but we rarely know what we should do;
it is always a sign of presumption to
imagine ourselves able to handle hot
coals without burning ourselves.

Jean Pierre Camus: *The Spirit of St.
Francis de Sales*, 16, 6. (17th cent.)

Prevention

Prevention is better than cure.

Erasmus: *Adagia*. (16th cent.)

Pride

Arrogance and boldness belong to those
that are accursed of God.

Pope St. Clement I: *Epistle to the
Corinthians*. (2nd cent.)

For every other kind of iniquity prompts the doing of evil deeds, but pride lurks even in good deeds to their undoing.

> St. Augustine: *Letter 211.* (5th cent.)

Pride strives for perverse excellence, a very special sin when God is despised, but also present whenever our neighbor is despised.

> St. Thomas Aquinas: *Disputations concerning Evil,* 8, 2. (13th cent.)

Pride, envy, avarice—these are the sparks
Have set on fire the hearts of all men.

> Dante: *Inferno, Canto 6.* (14th cent.)

Pride is the cause of alle woe.

> John Gower: *Confessio Amantis,* 1. (14th cent.)

I counsel every man and woman to beware even of the very least spice of pride, which seemeth to be the bare delight and liking of ourselves, for anything that either is in us or outwardly belonging to us. Let every man lie well in wait of ourselves, and let us mark well when the devil first casteth any proud, vain thought into our mind, and let us forthwith make a cross on our breast, and bless it out by-an-by, and cast it at his head again.

> St. Thomas More: *Treatise on the Passion.* (16th cent.)

Pride will have a fall; for pride goeth before and shame cometh after.

> John Heywood: *Proverbs,* 1, 10. (16th cent.)

Every cock is proud on his own dunghill.

> John Heywooa: *Proverbs,* 1, 11. (16th cent.)

He beareth a dagger in his sleeve, trust me,
To kill all that he meeteth prouder than he.

> John Heywood: *Proverbs,* 1, 11. (16th cent.)

I clip high-climbing thoughts,
   The wings of swelling pride;
Their fall is worst, that from the height
   Of greatest honor slide.

> Bl. Robert Southwell: *Content and Rich.* (16th cent.)

Of all the causes which conspire to blind
Man's erring judgment, and misguide the mind,
What the weak head with strongest bias rules
Is pride, the never failing vice of fools.

> Pope: *An Essay on Criticism,* 2. (18th cent.)

Thus unlamented pass the proud away,
The gaze of fools and pageant of a day;
So perish all, whose breast ne'er learned to glow
For others' good, or melt at others' woe.

> Pope: *Elegy to the Memory of an Unfortunate Lady.* (18th cent.)

I was not ever thus, nor pray'd that Thou
   Shouldst lead me on;
I loved to choose and see my path, but now
   Lead Thou me on!
I loved the garish day, and, spite of fears,
Pride ruled my will: remember not past years.

> Card. Newman: *The Pillar of the Cloud.* (19th cent.)

Living on pride is windy diet.

> R. H. Benson: *The Sentimentalists.* (20th cent.)

There are various kinds of pride—the noisy pride of the self-made man, the eloquent pride of the enthusiast, the steady, assertive pride of the sovereign —but there is no pride in the universe such as that dead, silent pride, claiming nothing, yet certain of everything.

> R. H. Benson: *The Coward.* (20th cent.)

One of the thousand objections to the sin of pride lies precisely in this, that self-consciousness of necessity destroys self-revelation. A man who thinks a great deal about himself will try to be many-sided, attempt a theatrical excellence at all points, will try to be an encyclopedia of culture, and his own real personality will be lost in that false universalism. Thinking about himself will lead to trying to be the universe; trying to be the universe will lead to ceasing to be anything.

> G. K. Chesterton: *Heretics.* (20th cent.)

O God of earth and altar,
Bow down and hear our cry,
Our earthly rulers falter,
Our people drift and die;
The walls of gold entomb us,
The swords of scorn divide,
Take not Thy thunder from us,
But take away our pride.

> G. K. Chesterton: *A Hymn.* (20th cent.)

Nothing wears like pride.

> John Ayscough: *Mezzogiorno.* (20th cent.)

Who can escape the secret desire to breathe a different atmosphere from the rest of men? Who can do good things without seeking to taste in them some sweet distinction from the common run of sinners in this world?

> Thomas Merton: *Seeds of Contemplation.* (20th cent.)

When a proud man thinks he is humble his case is hopeless.

> Thomas Merton: *Seeds of Contemplation.* (20th cent.)

Priest

For your priests, who are worthy of the name and worthy of God, like the strings of a lyre, are in harmony with the bishop.

> St. Ignatius of Antioch: *Letter to the Ephesians,* 4. (2nd cent.)

And when a presbyter is ordained the bishop shall lay his hand upon his head,

the presbyters also touching him. And he shall pray over him.

> St. Hippolytus: *The Apostolic Tradition,* 8. (3rd cent.)

Be you the priest and the sacrifice of God; do not lose that which has been given to you by the authority of God. Clothe yourself with the garment of sanctity, gird yourself with the cincture of chastity; let Christ be the covering for your head; let the cross of Christ be the protection for your face; instil in your breast the sacrament of divine wisdom; let the odor of your prayers always ascend upon high; let your heart be, as it were, an altar, on which you may safely offer your body as a victim to God.

> St. Peter Chrysologus: *Sermons,* 108. (5th cent.)

. . . O holy Lord. . . . Source of every honor and Dispenser of all dignities . . . having appointed bishops to rule Thy people, Thou didst choose, as their companions and helpers, men next in rank and dignity. . . . With the same foresight, O Lord, Thou didst associate with the apostles of Thy Son, teachers of the faith, through whom they have filled the whole world with their successful preaching. Wherefore, we beseech Thee, O Lord, grant the same helps also to our weakness, which, inasmuch as it is greater than theirs, stands so much the more in need of such assistance. *Bestow then, we beseech Thee, almighty Father, the dignity of the priesthood upon these Thy servants; renew in them the spirit of holiness, that they may receive from Thee, O God, this office next to ours in dignity, and that the example of their lives may be for others an incentive to virtue. . . .*

> Roman Pontifical, Ordination of Priests, Consecration Prayer *Domine Sancte . . . honorum auctor et distributor.* (Leonine, ca. 5th cent.)

O God, Who art great in Thy power and inscrutable in Thy wisdom, Who art admirable in Thy plans with regard to men; do Thou, O Lord, fill with the gift of Thy Holy Spirit this Thy servant, whom Thou hast been pleased to promote to the order of priest; make him worthy to stand blameless before Thy holy altar, to proclaim the gospel of Thy kingdom, to minister the word of Thy truth, to offer thee gifts and spiritual sacrifices, to renew the people through the laver of regeneration. Grant that at the second coming of our Lord and Savior Jesus Christ, he may receive the reward of the good steward through Thy mercy and loving kindness.

> Byzantine Euchologion, Prayer for Ordination of a Priest. (ca. 5th cent.)

Vouchsafe, O Lord, to consecrate and sanctify these hands by this unction, and by our blessing, that whatsoever they shall bless may be consecrated and sanctified; in the name of our Lord, Jesus Christ.

> Roman Pontifical, Ordination of Priests, Anointing of Hands. (Gelasian, ca. 6th cent.)

As a king is so called from ruling, so a priest is so called from sacrificing. For he consecrates and sanctifies. . . . Presbyter in Greek means elder in Latin. Presbyters are so called, not on account of years or decrepit old age, but on account of the honor and dignity which they have received. Presbyters, therefore, are called priests, because they offer sacrifice, as bishops do, but although they are priests, they have not reached the fulness of the episcopate, for they do not sign on the forehead with chrism, or give the Holy Ghost, which only bishops can do as the Acts of the Apostles plainly indicates.

> St. Isidore: *Etymologies,* 7, 12. (7th cent.)

Dearly beloved children, who are about to be consecrated to the office of the priest, strive to receive it worthily, and to discharge its functions in a praiseworthy manner. For it is the duty of a priest to offer sacrifice, to bless, to govern, to preach and to baptize. . . .

> Roman Pontifical, Ordination of Priests, Admonition, *Consecrandi.* (ca. 10th cent.)

As you, therefore, beloved children, have been chosen by the voice of our brethren to be consecrated as our coadjutors, preserve the purity of your lives in unspotted holiness. Bear in mind what you do. Let your conduct be in conformity with the action you perform, so that celebrating the mystery of the Lord's death, you take heed to mortify your members from all vices and lusts. Let your doctrine be spiritual medicine for the people of God; let the odor of your life be the delight of the Church of Christ, so that by your preaching and example you may build up the house, that is, the family of God.

> Roman Pontifical, Ordination of Priests, Admonition *Consecrandi.* (ca. 10th cent.)

Receive power to offer sacrifice to God and to celebrate mass for the living as well as for the dead, in the name of the Lord.

> Roman Pontifical, Ordination of Priests, Formula *Accipe Potestatem.* (ca. 10th cent.)

Receive the Holy Ghost; whose sins thou shalt forgive they are forgiven them; and whose sins thou shalt retain they are retained.

> Roman Pontifical, Ordination of Priests, Formula *Accipe Spiritum Sanctum.* (13th cent.)

A holy-minded man of good renown
There was, and poor, the parson to a town,
Yet he was rich in holy thought and work.
He also was a learned man, a clerk.

> Chaucer: *Canterbury Tales: Prologue.* (Tr. Coghill) (14th cent.)

Christ and his twelve apostles and their lore
He taught, but followed it himself before.

> Chaucer: *Canterbury Tales: Prologue.* (Tr. Coghill) (14th cent.)

A priest clad in his sacred vestments is Christ's vicegerent, to pray to God for himself, and for all the people, in a suppliant and humble manner.

> Thomas a Kempis: *The Imitation of Christ,* 4, 5. (15th cent.)

The priest should be adorned with all the virtues, and give an example to others of a righteous life. Let his conversation be not according to the common and vulgar ways of men, but with the angels and with men that are perfect.

> Thomas a Kempis: *The Imitation of Christ,* 4, 5. (15th cent.)

But now I see well the old proverb is true:
That parish priest forgetteth that ever he was clerk!

> John Heywood: *Tyb.* (16th cent.)

A priest has the primacy of Abel, the patriarchate of Abraham, the government of Noe, the order of Melchisedech, the dignity of Aaron, the authority of Moses, the perfection of Samuel, the power of Peter, the unction of Christ.

> Bl. Peter of Blois: *Sermons to Priests,* 60. (16th cent.)

The scandal that is given by particular priests reflects not on the sacred function. A satirical poet is the check of the layman on bad priests. When a clergyman is whipped, his gown is first taken off, by which the dignity of his office is secured.

> Dryden: *Fables, Intro.* (17th cent.)

To the carnal eye the priest looks like other men, but to the eye of faith he is exalted above the angels, because he exercises powers not given even to angels.

> Card. Gibbons: *The Faith of Our Fathers,* 28. (19th cent.)

A priest ought to be in no place where his Master would not go, nor employ in anything which his Master would not do.

> Card. Manning: *The Eternal Priesthood.* (19th cent.)

The end of man is the glory of God. The end of a Christian is the greater glory of God. The end of a priest is the greatest glory of God.

> Card. Manning: *The Eternal Priesthood.* (19th cent.)

Clerics ought to lead a holier life than lay people and they should be an example to them by their virtue and their actions.

> Code of Canon Law, can. 124. (20th cent.)

The first striving of a priestly soul should be the closest union with the divine Redeemer by accepting humbly and entirely the Christian doctrine and by diligently applying it in every moment of his life so that his faith illumines his conduct and his conduct is the reflection of his faith.

> Pope Pius XII: *Menti Nostrae.* (Sept. 23, 1950)

Priesthood

The work of the ministry is an exalted work and leads to the kingdom of heaven.

> St. Basil: *On Renunciation of the World.* (4th cent.)

Neither do we permit any of the laity to perform any of the offices belonging to the priesthood; as, for instance, neither the sacrifice, nor baptism, nor the laying on of hands, nor the blessing. . . . For such sacred offices are conferred by the laying on of hands of the bishop.

> Anonymous: *Constitutions of the Holy Apostles,* 3, 10. (4th cent.)

The priestly office is discharged upon earth, but holds the rank of heavenly things; and very rightly so. For not man, nor angel, nor archangel nor any other created power, but the Paraclete Himself, instituted this order, and induced those who yet abode in the flesh to make manifest the ministry of angels. Wherefore it behooves him that is consecrated to be as pure as one who stands in heaven itself among those powers.

St. John Chrysostom: *On the Priesthood,* 3, 4. (4th cent.)

For those [i.e. priests] who dwell upon earth and make their abode therein, have been commissioned to dispense things which are in heaven, and have received an authority such as God has not given either to angels or to archangels. For it has not been said to them, *All that you bind on earth shall be bound in heaven, and all that you loose on earth shall be loosed in heaven* (Matth. 18, 18). Those who rule upon earth, indeed, have authority to bind, but bodies only; whereas this bond takes hold of the soul itself, and reaches heaven; what priests execute below, God ratifies above, and the Master confirms the judgment of His servants.

St. John Chrysostom: *On the Priesthood,* 3, 5. (4th cent.)

The priesthood requires a great soul; for the priest has many harassing troubles of his own, and has need of innumerable eyes on all sides.

St. John Chrysostom: *Homilies on the Acts of the Apostles,* 3. (4th cent.)

If I were to meet at the same moment one of the blessed come down from heaven and a poor priest, I should go first to the priest in order to honor him, and I should hasten to kiss his hands because they handle the Word of Life and are something superhuman.

Thomas of Celano: *Legenda 2, pt. 2.* (13th cent.)

The priesthood is the spiritual power conferred on the ministers of the Church by Christ for the purpose of dispensing the sacraments to the faithful.

John of Paris: *Concerning Royal and Papal Power,* 2. (14th cent.)

They are My anointed ones, and I call them My Christs, because I have given them the office of administering Me to you, and have placed them like fragrant flowers in the mystical body of holy Church. The angel himself has no such dignity, for I have given it to those men whom I have chosen for My ministers, and whom I have appointed as earthly angels in this life. In all souls I demand purity and charity, that they should love Me and their neighbor. . . . But far more do I demand purity in My ministers, and love towards Me and towards their fellow-creatures, administering to them the Body and Blood of My only-begotten Son, with the fire of charity and a hunger for the salvation of souls, for the glory and honor of My name.

St. Catherine of Siena: *The Dialogue.* (14th cent.)

Sacrifice and priesthood are, by the ordinance of God, in such wise conjoined, as that both have existed in every law. Whereas therefore in the New Testament the Catholic Church has received from the institution of Christ the holy visible sacrifice of the eucharist; it must needs also be confessed that there is in that Church a new, visible, and external priesthood, into which the old has been *translated* (Hebr. 7, 12).

Decree of the Council of Trent, Session 23, Chap. 1 (July 15, 1563)

In service o'er the mystic feast I stand;
   I cleanse Thy victim-flock, and bring
      them near
   In holiest wise, and by a bloodless
      rite.
   O Fire of love! O gushing Fount of
      light!
(As best I know, who need Thy cleansing hand)
   Dread office this, bemired souls to
      clear
   Of their defilement, and again make
      bright.

Card. Newman: *The Priestly Office.* (Paraphrase from St. Greg. Nazianzen) (19th cent.)

Are we not priests, whose ministry
   The power of salt must show?

A light for all the world to see
And brighten in its glow;
A city on a hill, to be
The joy of men below?

Thomas Bridgett: *Lyra Hieratica*. (19th cent.)

O wondrous is the lot of him who stands
A Christian priest, within a Christian fane,
And binds with pure and consecrated hands,
Round earth and heaven, a festal, flowery chain;
Even as between the blue arch and the main,
A circling western ring of golden light
Weds the two worlds, or as the sunny rain
Of April makes the cloud and clay unite,
Thus links the priest of God the dark world and the bright.

Denis F. McCarthy: *The Priest's Work*. (19th cent.)

A blot upon a layman's coat is little seen; a spot upon an alb cannot be hid.

Card. Manning: *The Eternal Priesthood*. (19th cent.)

Only to the apostles, and thenceforth to those on whom their successors have imposed hands, is granted the power of the priesthood, in virtue of which they represent the person of Jesus Christ before their people, acting at the same time as representatives of their people before God. This priesthood is not transmitted by heredity or human descent. It does not emanate from the Christian community. It is not a delegation from the people. Prior to acting as representative of the community before the throne of God, the priest is the ambassador of the divine Redeemer.

Pope Pius XII: *Mediator Dei*. (Nov. 20, 1947)

The visible, external priesthood of Jesus Christ is not handed down indiscrimi-

nately to all members of the Church in general, but is conferred on designated men, through what may be called the generation of holy orders.

Pope Pius XII: *Mediator Dei*. (Nov. 20, 1947)

Priesthood of the Faithful, Royal

What is the people itself but priestly? To whom it was said, *You are a chosen race, a royal priesthood, a consecrated nation* (1 Peter, 2, 9), as the apostle Peter says. Everyone is anointed to the priesthood, is anointed to the kingdom also; but it is a spiritual kingdom and a spiritual priesthood.

St. Ambrose: *On the Sacraments*, 4, 1, 3. (4th cent.)

They will be priests of God and Christ, and will reign with Him a thousand years (Apoc. 20, 6); this refers not to bishops alone and presbyters, who are now specially called priests in the Church; but as we call all believers Christians (*christos*) on account of the mystical chrism, so we call all priests (*sacerdotes*), because they are members of the one Priest.

St. Augustine: *The City of God*, 20, 10. (5th cent.)

O God, Who hast made all who are reborn in Christ a royal and priestly race; grant unto us both to desire and to be able to do what Thou dost command, that, having called Thy people to eternal life, the faith of their hearts and the devotion of their actions may be one.

Gelasian Sacramentary, Collect for Easter. (ca. 5th cent.)

But after our Lord, the true King and eternal Priest, was anointed by God the Father with a mystic and heavenly unction, not only priests and kings but the whole Church is consecrated by the unction of chrism, because each is a member of the eternal King and Priest. Therefore because we are a royal and priestly race, after baptism we are anointed that we may be called by the name of Christ.

> St. Isidore: *On the Offices of the Church,* 2, 26. (7th cent.)

By the waters of baptism, as by common right, Christians are made members of the mystical Body of Christ the Priest, and by the 'character' which is imprinted on their souls, they are appointed to give worship to God; thus they participate, according to their condition, in the priesthood of Christ.

> Pope Pius XII: *Mediator Dei.* (Nov. 20, 1947)

See also Laity

Prime

> Now in the sun's new dawning ray,
> Lowly of heart, our God we pray
> That he from harm may keep us free
> In all the deeds this day shall see.
>
> Roman Breviary Hymn *Jam Lucis Orto Sidere* for Prime. (Tr. A. G. McDougall) (Ambrosian, 5th cent.)

O Lord God almighty, Who hast brought us to the beginning of this day; defend us in the same by Thy power; that we may not fall this day into any sin, but that all our thoughts, words and works may be directed to the fulfilment of Thy will.

> Roman Breviary, Prayer at Prime. (Gregorian, ca. 7th cent. ?)

Principle

Aristotle notes that principles cannot be rigorously demonstrated, but they can be defended by exposing the effects of denying them, and recommended by bringing out their analogies with the ways things work (Metaphysics, 4, 4).

> St. Thomas Aquinas: *Exposition of the De Trinitate,* 2, 2. (13th cent.)

Manners with fortunes, humors turn with climes,
Tenets with books, and principles with times.

> Pope: *Moral Essays,* 1. (18th cent.)

It is to the living mind that we must look for the means of using correctly principles of whatever kind.

> Card. Newman: *Grammar of Assent,* 10. (19th cent.)

Principle is always respectable; even a bad man is more respected, though he may be more hated, if he owns and justifies his actions, than if he is wicked by accident.

> Card. Newman: *Difficulties of Anglicans,* 1. (19th cent.)

Printing

Providence . . . permitted the invention of printing as a scourge for the sins of the learned.

> Pope: *The Dunciad,* proem. (18th cent.)

Prison

> I know not whether laws be right,
> Or whether laws be wrong;
> All that we know who lie in gaol
> Is that the wall is strong;
> And that each day is like a year,
> A year whose days are long.
>
> Oscar Wilde: *The Ballad of Reading Gaol,* 5. (19th cent.)

> This too I know—and wise it were
> If each could know the same—
> That every prison that men build
> Is built with bricks of shame,
> And bound with bars, lest Christ should see
> How men their brother maim.
>
> Oscar Wilde: *The Ballad of Reading Gaol,* 5. (19th cent.)

Privilege

Privileges may be acquired not only by the direct concession of the competent authority and by communication, but also by legitimate custom or by prescription. Possession of a privilege for one hundred years or from time immemorial justifies the presumption that a privilege has been granted.

> Code of Canon Law, Canon 63. (20th cent.)

Procrastination

By and by never comes. (Modo et modo non habebant modum.)

> St. Augustine: *Confessions*, 8, 5. (5th cent.)

Procreation

The crown of marriage, then, is the chastity of procreation and faithfulness in rendering the carnal debt.

> St. Augustine: *The Good of Marriage*, 11. (5th cent.)

Proficiency

A really high degree of proficiency in any particular subject invariably leads to atrophy in other directions.

> R. H. Benson: *None Other Gods*. (20th cent.)

Profit

O God, Whose providence in the ordering of all things never fails; we humbly beseech Thee, put away from us all harmful things, and give us those things which are profitable for us.

> Roman Missal, Collect for Seventh Sunday after Pentecost. (Gelasian, ca. 6th cent.)

Nothing is less profitable than to spend much labor on that by which one profits little.

> John of Salisbury: *Policraticus*, 1, 5, 36. (12th cent.)

To put pressure upon the destitute for the sake of gain and to make a profit out of the need of another is condemned by all laws, human or divine.

> Pope Leo XIII: *Rerum novarum*. (May 15, 1891)

Progress

The Roman pontiff can and ought to reconcile himself, and come to terms, with progress, liberalism, and modern civilization.

> Proposition condemned by Pius IX in Syllabus of Errors. (1867)

Progress is the realization of utopias.

> Oscar Wilde: *The Soul of Man under Socialism*. (19th cent.)

'Progress' is meaningless unless there is to the mind of him who uses it some ideal standard or goal to which his idea of progress is related.

> R. H. Benson: *Infallibility and Tradition*. (20th cent.)

Progress is not an illegitimate word, but it is logically evident that it is illegitimate for us. It is a sacred word, a word that could only rightly be used by rigid believers and in the ages of faith.

> G. K. Chesterton: *Heretics*. (20th cent.)

Progress, properly understood, has indeed a most dignified and legitimate meaning. But as used in opposition to precise moral ideals, it is ludicrous. So far from it being the truth that the ideal of progress is to be set against that of ethical or religious finality, the reverse is the truth. Nobody has any business to use the word progress unless he has a definite creed and a cast-iron code of morals. Nobody can be progressive without being infallible—at any rate, without believing in some infallibility. For progress by its very name indicates a direction; and the moment we are in the least doubtful about the direction, we become in the same degree doubtful about the progress.

> G. K. Chesterton: *Heretics*. (20th cent.)

In the thought of the Christian the enemy of God is at the service of God. God has His adversaries, not in the metaphysical but in the moral order. Yet his adversaries are always at His service. He is served by the martyrs, and by the executioners who made them martyrs. Everything that happens in the history of the world serves in one way or another the progress of the Church and, in a more or less obscure way, some kind of progress in the world.

> J. Maritain: *Freedom in the Modern World.* (20th cent.)

It is above all a clear principle of wisdom that all progress is truly such if it knows how to add new conquests to old, to join new benefits to those acquired in the past—in a word, if it knows how to make capital out of experience.

> Pope Pius XII: *Christmas Address.* (Dec. 24, 1952)

Prohibition

Forbid us thing, that thing desyren we.

> Chaucer: *Wife of Bath's Prologue.* (14th cent.)

Proletariat

In dirt and darkness hundreds stink content.

> Pope: *First Epistle of the First Book of Horace.* (18th cent.)

See also Property

Promise

> You never bade me hope, 'tis true;
>   I asked you not to swear:
> But I looked in those eyes of blue,
>   And I read a promise there.

> Gerald Griffin: *You Never Bade Me Hope.* (19th cent.)

Proof

[Absolute proof] can never be furnished to us by the logic of words, for as certitude is of the mind, so is the act of inference which leads to it. Every one who reasons is his own center.

> Card. Newman: *Grammar of Assent, 9.* (19th cent.)

Property

Nature has poured forth all things for the common use of all men. And God has ordained that all things should be produced that there might be food in common for all, and that the earth should be the common possession of all. Nature created common rights, but usurpation has transformed them into private rights.

> St. Ambrose: *On the Duties of the Clergy,* 1, 132. (4th cent.)

And call not anything your own, but let everything be common property.

> St. Augustine: *Letter 211.* (From his famous *Rule*) (5th cent.)

Those who neither crave what belongs to others, nor give away what they have, are to be admonished to consider seriously that the earth, out of which they were taken, is common to all men, and therefore, too, brings forth nourishment for all in common. In vain, therefore, do those think themselves guiltless, who arrogate to themselves alone the common gift of God. . . . For when we administer necessities to the needy, we give them what is their own, not what is ours; we pay a debt of justice, rather than do a work of mercy.

> Pope St. Gregory I: *Pastoral Care,* 3, 21. (6th cent.)

Property (*res*) is so called from possessing rightly; right (*jus*) from possessing justly. . . . What is wrongly possessed, is not the owner's. He possesses wrongly who either uses his own things improperly or takes possession of someone else's improperly.

> St. Isidore: *Etymologies,* 5, 25. (7th cent.)

The law of nature differs from custom or enactments. For by the law of nature all things are the common property of all men. This was true not only in the case of [the primitive Church] . . . but in Plato's [ideal] city, regulated according to justice, in which no one had any affects of his own. But by customary law or enactments this is said to be mine, and that someone else's.

> Gratian: *Decretum,* D. 8, Pt. 1. (12th cent.)

Unbelief in itself is not incompatible with the rights to own and to rule, which derive from the *jus gentium,* or human law common to many nations. The distinction between believers and unbelievers is a matter of divine law, which does not abrogate human law.

> St. Thomas Aquinas: *Summa Theologica,* 2-2, 12, 2. (13th cent.)

The property of the Church belongs to the pope as the principal dispenser, but does not belong to him as lord or possessor.

> St. Thomas Aquinas: *Summa Theologica,* 2-2, 100, 1. (13th cent.)

He who is not subject to God, justly loses and unjustly possesses all that he has from God.

> Egidius Colonna: *On Ecclesiastical Power,* 2, 8. (14th cent.)

That dog is mine, said those poor children; that place in the sun is mine. Such is the beginning of usurpation throughout the earth.

> Pascal: *Pensées,* 7. (17th cent.)

The Church has no innate and legitimate right to acquire and possess property.

> Proposition condemned by Pius IX in Syllabus of Errors. (1867)

The church . . . enjoins that the right of property and of its disposal, which are derived from nature, should in every case remain inviolate.

> Pope Leo XIII: *Quod apostolici muneris.* (Dec. 28, 1878)

It is surely undeniable that, when a man engages in remunerative labor, the impelling reason and motive of his work is to obtain property, and thereafter to hold it as his very own. If one man hires out to another his strength or skill, he does so for the purpose of receiving in return what is necessary for the satisfaction of his needs; he therefore expressly intends to acquire a right full and real, not only to the remuneration, but also to the disposal of such remuneration, just as he pleases.

> Pope Leo XIII: *Rerum Novarum.* (May 15, 1891)

Every man has a right by nature to possess property as his own.

> Pope Leo XIII: *Rerum Novarum.* (May 15, 1891)

The fact that God has given the earth for the use and enjoyment of the whole human race can in no way be a bar to the owning of private property. For God has granted the earth to mankind in general, not in the sense that all without distinction can deal with it as they like, but rather that no part of it was assigned to anyone in particular, and that the limits of private possession have been left to be fixed by man's own industry, and by the laws of individual races.

> Pope Leo XIII: *Rerum Novarum.* (May 15, 1891)

Men always work harder and more readily when they work on that which belongs to them; nay, they learn to love the very soil that yields in response to the labor of their hands, not only food to eat, but an abundance of good things for themselves and those that are dear to them.

> Pope Leo XIII: *Rerum Novarum.* (May 15, 1891)

The Church may acquire temporal property by every just means allowed by the natural or the positive law.

> Code of Canon Law, Canon 1499. (20th cent.)

The Roman pontiff is the supreme administrator and dispenser of all Church property.

> Code of Canon Law, Canon 1518. (20th cent.)

The Christian conscience cannot admit as just a social order which either denies in principle or renders impossible or negatory in practice, the natural right to property whether over consumptive goods or by means of production. But neither can it accept those systems which recognize the right to private property according to a completely false concept of it and which are therefore opposed to a true and healthy social order.

> Pope Pius XII: *Fifth Anniversary of the Outbreak of War.* (Sept. 1, 1944)

Though the owners of industrial enterprises are given to boasting their close attachment to the institution of property, the effect of their politics has been the proletarianization of the masses of workers, and in the minds of the majority of persons today the idea of property is not ownership of the means of production, but simply ownership of a share of the money profits of industry and of the mass-produced furniture and pleasure-things (cars, wireless sets, etc.) which money can buy.

> Eric Gill: *It All Goes Together.* (20th cent.)

A proletarian is one who owns nothing but his power to labor and that of his children; children are his only 'real property.' At all times and in all countries there have been proletarians, but in no previous society has the property-less man been politically free!

> Eric Gill: *It All Goes Together.* (20th cent.)

Prophecy

The best interpretation of a prophecy is the history of its fulfilment.

> Card. Wiseman: *Lectures,* 8. (19th cent.)

Prophet

But not everyone who speaks in the spirit is a prophet, but only if he follows the conduct of the Lord.

> Teaching of the Twelve Apostles, 11. (2nd cent.)

The prophet ill sustains his holy call,
Who finds not heav'n to suit the tastes of all.

> Thomas Moore: *Lalla Rookh: The Veiled Prophet of Khorassan.* (19th cent.)

Proportion

People in ignoble circumstances never do have any sense of proportion, or of their own impertinence.

> R. H. Benson: *An Average Man.* (20th cent.)

Prose

The fact of a man being a poisoner is nothing against his prose.

> Oscar Wilde: *Intentions.* (19th cent.)

Prosperity

The remembrance of past wants makes present prosperity more pleasant.

> St. John Chrysostom: *Homilies.* (14th cent.)

Though the prosperity of some men be but a very short summer day, Lord! how lusty and how proud they will be, buzzing about like a bumble-bee in sunny weather; not aware that one winter day will spoil all their lightsomeness.

> St. Thomas More. (16th cent.)

Prosperity and Adversity

In adversity I desire prosperity, in prosperity I fear adversity. Yet what middle place is there between the two, where man's life may be other than trial? There is woe and woe again in the prosperity of this world, woe from the fear of adversity, woe from the corruption of joy. There is woe in the adversity of this world, and a second woe and a third, from the longing for prosperity, and because adversity itself is hard, and for fear that endurance may break. Is not man's life upon earth trial without intermission?

St. Augustine: *Confessions*, 10, 28. (5th cent.)

The good neither take the blessings offered them here below as anything great, nor dread very much the ills brought upon them. While they use present advantages, they point to the inconvenient things to come, and when they lament over present evils, they are comforted in the love of the good things to follow.

Pope St. Gregory I: *Morals*, 8, 92. (6th cent.)

He is a great man who, when he falls into adversity, does not fall away at least a little from his wisdom; and he is as great who has been favored by the smiles of fortune without becoming the butt of her ridicule.

St. Bernard: *On Consideration*, 2, 12. (12th cent.)

If things always went wrong, no one could endure it; if they always went well, everyone would become arrogant.

St. Bernard: *Letters*, 149. (12th cent.)

He is hardly human who is not shaken by his own material losses, while he is not quite a man who remains unmoved by what happens to others.

John of Salisbury: *Policraticus*, 3, Pref. (12th cent.)

If God sends you adversity, accept it with patience and give thanks for it to our Lord, realizing that you have deserved it and that it will be for your own good. If He gives you prosperity, thank Him humbly for it, so that the gift which should improve you may not, through pride or in any other way, make you

worse; for one should not use God's gifts to war against Him.

St. Louis IX, King of France. (In Joinville's Life, 741.) (13th cent.)

See also Adversity

Protection

Almighty and everlasting God, mercifully look upon our infirmity, and stretch forth the right hand of Thy majesty to protect us.

Roman Missal, Collect for Third Sunday after Epiphany. (Gregorian, ca. 6th cent.)

In Thine infinite goodness, we beseech Thee, O Lord, watch over Thy household: as it relies solely upon the hope of Thy heavenly grace, so may it ever be defended by Thy protection.

Roman Missal, Collect for Fifth Sunday after Epiphany. (Gregorian, ca. 6th cent.)

O God, the protector of all that trust in Thee, without whom nothing is strong, nothing is holy: multiply Thy mercies upon us; that having Thee for our ruler and guide, we may so pass through things temporal, that we finally not lose those things which are eternal.

Roman Missal, Collect for Third Sunday after Pentecost. (Gregorian, ca. 6th cent.)

Protestantism

Religion shows a rosy color'd face,
Not hatter'd out with drudging works of grace;
A down-hill Reformation rolls apace.
What flesh and blood would crowd the narrow gate,
Or, till they waste their pamper'd paunches, wait?
All would be happy at the cheapest rate.

Dryden: *The Hind and the Panther*, 1. (17th cent.)

What one can plead, the rest can plead as well;

For amongst equals lies no last appeal,
And all confess themselves are fallible.

> Dryden: *The Hind and the Panther*, 2.
> (17th cent.)

Protestantism, viewed in its more Catholic aspect, is doctrine without active principle; viewed in its heretical, it is active principle without doctrine.

> Card. Newman: *Development of Christian Doctrine*, 5. (19th cent.)

If nothing is to be held as revealed but what every one perceives to be in Scripture, there is nothing that can be so held, considering that in matter of fact there is no universal agreement as to what Scripture teaches and what it does not teach: and why are one man's opinions to be ruled by the readings of another?

> Card. Newman: *Essays Critical and Historical*, 1, 3. (19th cent.)

England is the head of Protestantism, the center of its movements, and the stronghold of its power. Weakened in England, it is paralyzed everywhere; conquered in England, it is conquered throughout the world.

> Card. Manning: *Speech at the Third Provincial Council of Westminster.* (1859)

Such, then, is popular protestantism, considered in its opposition to Catholics. Its truth is establishment by law; its philosophy is theory; its faith is prejudice; its facts are fiction; its reasonings fallacies; and its security is ignorance about those whom it is opposing. The law says that white is black; ignorance says, why not? Theory says it ought to be; fallacy says it must be; fiction says it is, and prejudice says it shall be.

> Card. Newman: *Present Position of Catholics.* (19th cent.)

Protestantism is nothing else than another form of the same true Christian religion, in which form it is possible to please God equally as much as in the Catholic Church.

> Proposition condemned by Pius IX in Syllabus of Errors. (1867)

The nature of Protestantism may be defined as the exaggerated development of personal independence, directed to the negation of the divine authority of the Church, and chiefly aiming at its overthrow in the person of its supreme representative, the pope.

> Isaac T. Hecker: *The Church and the Age.* (1887)

The whole edifice of the Protestant church and theology reposes . . . on two principles, one material, the other formal—the doctrine of imputation, and the sufficiency of the Bible. But the material principle is given up by exegesis and by dogmatic theology; and as to the formal principle, for the sufficiency of the Bible, or even for the inspiration of the writings of the disciples of the apostles, not the shadow of a scriptural argument can be adduced.

> Lord Acton: *Döllinger on the Temporal Power.* (19th cent.)

A soul cannot be eternally satisfied with kindness, and a soothing murmur, and the singing of hymns.

> R. H. Benson: *The Confessions of a Convert.* (20th cent.)

The Reformation is always described as a protest against the power of the pope. I should rather describe it as a protest against the impotence of the pope. It did not come in a time like that of Innocent III, when the pope was really powerful. It came at the end of a long trail of tragi-comedy and bathos, in which the central power, so far from being too central, had been hopelessly decentralized and divided. It was not until people had had the absurd experience of having three popes that they completed the absurdity of having three or four religions.

> G. K. Chesterton: *The Resurrection of Rome.* (20th cent.)

Protestants are Catholics gone wrong; that is what is really meant by saying they are Christians. Sometimes they have gone very wrong; but not often have they gone right ahead with their own particular wrong. Thus a Calvinist is a Catholic obsessed with the Catholic idea of the sovereignty of God. But when he makes it mean that God wishes particular people to be damned, we may say with all restraint that he has become a rather morbid Catholic.

> G. K. Chesterton: *The Catholic Church and Conversion.* (20th cent.)

The Protestant world in England today is a very curious and subtle thing, which it would not become me to criticize; but this may be said of it without offence, that while it is naturally a little disturbed by a Protestant accepting Catholicism, it is far more terribly disturbed by any Protestant who still preserves Protestantism.

> G. K. Chesterton: *Autobiography.* (20th cent.)

All churches, howsoever named or formed, ultimately derive from the primitive Church, the old Church, the historical Church, the great Church, the mother Church, which, however called, has come down and still continues unbroken only in the Roman Church. However corrupt, or however much a failure others may judge that Church to be, their existence depends upon its historical continuity, and, more than they realize, upon its still continuing to exist. Even the merely and most militant Protestant Church would lose its *raison d'être* if the Catholic Church ceased to exist. Whatever truth other churches retain, they have derived from the Catholic Church, and so have to thank it for having preserved it for them Moreover, it has every truth that any one of them possesses, and more than all of them taken together.

> W. E. Orchard: *The Way of Simplicity.* (20th cent.)

Protestantism is not merely negative, or to be regarded as nothing but a historical remnant of Catholicism; it may be regarded as a kind of parasite living upon the Church—one that would die should the Church die, one also that draws all its nutriment from the Church. To that extent it is positive; to that extent it is Catholic.

> Theodore Maynard: *Orestes Brownson.* (20th cent.)

Pure Protestantism might be defined as the rejection of every non-spiritual element or aid in religion, and if it exists at all it is to be sought outside the Christian bodies altogether.

> Dom Butler: *The Church and Infallibility.* (20th cent.)

See God—His Providence

Prudence

He who flees will fight again.

> Tertullian: *De fuga in Persecutione.* (3rd cent.)

No man is prudent who is ignorant of God.

> St. Ambrose: *On the Duties of the Clergy,* I, 117. (4th cent.)

The first course of duty is prudence. Piety is the foundation of all the virtues.

> St. Ambrose: *On the Duties of the Clergy,* I, 126. (4th cent.)

Prudence is the knowledge of what is to be sought and avoided.

> St. Augustine: *On Freewill,* I, 27. (4th cent.)

Few pay attention to prudence because few possess it.

> St. Bernard: *On Consideration,* I, 8. (12th cent.)

Prudence is the application of right reason to moral practice.

> St. Thomas Aquinas: *Disputations concerning the Cardinal Virtues*, 2. (13th cent.)

Advisement is good before the deed.

> Chaucer: *Troilus and Criseyde*. (14th cent.)

It is great wisdom not to be rash in our doings; nor to maintain too obstinately our own opinion.

> Thomas a Kempis: *The Imitation of Christ*, 1, 4. (15th cent.)

Prudence, my lord, is the virtue of those who command, not of those who obey.

> St. Ignatius Loyola. (Thompson, *Loyola*) (16th cent.)

Psalm

If the psalm prays do you too pray; if it laments, so do you too; if it renders thanks, so do you also rejoice with it; if it hopes, so you too; if it speaks in the accents of fear, do you also tremble with it; for all that is written therein is meant to be a mirror for us.

> St. Augustine: *Sermon in Ps. 30.* (5th cent.)

Christ, his Cross shall be my speed!
Teach me, Father John, to read:
That in church on holy day
I may chant the psalm and pray.

> Robert S. Hawker: *A Christ-Cross Rhyme.* (19th cent.)

Psychoanalysis

Psychoanalysis is the confessional without the safeguards of the confessional.

> G. K. Chesterton: *The Thing.* (20th cent.)

The psychoanalyst tends to regard what he calls the unconscious as of more importance than the conscious. The unconscious is the Stock Exchange, and the conscious is little more than the newspaper report of its proceedings, with the inner history of what has happened left out.

> M. C. D'Arcy: *The Nature of Belief.* (20th cent.)

Psychoanalysis is the probing of mind by mind; confession is the communion of conscience and God.

> Bishop Sheen: *Peace of Soul.* (20th cent.)

There are many souls stretched out on a psychoanalytic couch today who would be far better off if they brought their consciences to the confessional box.

> Bishop Sheen: *Peace of Soul.* (20th cent.)

Psychology

Man is an ordered unit and whole, a microcosm, a sort of state whose charter, determined by the end of the whole, subordinates to this end the activity of the parts according to the true order of their value and function. This charter is, in the final analysis, of an ontological and metaphysical origin, not a psychological and personal one. There are those who have thought it necessary to accentuate the opposition between the metaphysical and the psychological. A completely wrong approach! The psychic itself belongs to the domain of the ontological and metaphysical.

> Pope Pius XII: *Address to 5th Int. Congr. of Psychotherapy and Clinical Psychology.* (Apr. 13, 1953.)

Public

Nor is the people's judgment always true:
The most may err as grossly as the few.

> Dryden: *Absalom and Achitophel.* (17th cent.)

Punctuality

Punctuality is the thief of time.

> Oscar Wilde: *The Picture of Dorian Gray,* 3. (19th cent.)

Punishment

Sin is a suppurating wound; punishment is the surgeon's knife.

> St. John Chrysostom: *Homilies*. (4th cent.)

When the bad are punished, others become better.

> St. John Chrysostom: *Homilies*. (4th cent.)

For if every sin were now visited with manifest punishment, nothing would seem to be reserved for the final judgment; on the other hand, if no sin received now a plainly divine punishment, it would be concluded that there is no divine providence at all.

> St. Augustine: *The City of God*, 1, 8. (5th cent.)

The reason why everlasting punishment appears hard and unjust to human ideas is because in this infirmity of our mortal state we have no adequate grasp of that exceeding high and pure wisdom which would enable us to form an idea of the enormity of man's first transgression. The higher man's enjoyment of God, the greater his impiety in forsaking God: destroying in himself a good gift that might have lasted for ever, he became deserving of evil to last for ever.

> St. Augustine: *The City of God*, 21, 12. (5th cent.)

Every age and degree of understanding should have its appropriate measure of discipline.

> St. Benedict: *Rule*, 30. (6th cent.)

For to be made to feel annoyance from heat and cold, from hunger and thirst, to be afflicted with diseases, and one day even to be put out of existence, what else are all these, but the scourges of sin?

> Pope St. Gregory I: *Morals*, 13, 36. (6th cent.)

The sword of heaven is not in haste to smite,
Nor yet doth linger.

> Dante: *Paradiso, Canto 22.* (14th cent.)

Bishops and other ordinaries should remember that they are shepherds and not slave-drivers, and that they must so rule over their subjects as not to domineer over them but to love them as sons and brothers; they should endeavor by exhortation and admonition to deter them from wrongdoing lest they be obliged to administer due punishment after faults have been committed.

> Council of Trent, Session 13, Ch. 1. (Oct. 11, 1551)

Though some punishments are more human than others there is no such thing as humane punishment.

> G. K. Chesterton: *What's Wrong with the World.* (20th cent.)

The Church has a constitutional and proper right, independent of any human authority, to punish delinquents subject to her both by spiritual and temporal penalties.

> Code of Canon Law, Canon 2214. (20th cent.)

Purgatory

In short, inasmuch as we understand the prison pointed out in the Gospel to be hades, and as we also interpret the uttermost farthing to mean the very smallest offence which has to be recompensed there before the resurrection, no one will hesitate to believe that the soul undergoes in hades some compensatory discipline, without prejudice to the full process of the resurrection, when the recompense will be administered through the flesh besides.

> Tertullian: *Treatise on the Soul*, 58. (3rd cent.)

For if on the foundation of Christ you have built not only gold and silver and precious stones (1 Cor. 3) but also wood and hay and stubble, what do you expect when the soul shall be separated from the body? Would you enter into heaven with your wood and hay and stubble and thus defile the kingdom of God . . . ? It remains then that you be committed to the fire which will burn the light materials. . . . But this fire consumes not the creature, but what the creature has himself built. . . . It is manifest that the fire destroys the wood of our transgressions, and then returns to us the reward of our good works.

Origen. (PG 13, 445, 448) (3rd cent.)

When he has quitted his body and the difference between virtue and vice is known he cannot approach God till the purging fire shall have cleansed the stains with which his soul was infested. That same fire in others will cancel the corruption of matter, and the propensity to evil.

St. Gregory of Nyssa. (PG 46, 524) (4th cent.)

There is not one baptism only. One is that which the Church administers here by water and the Holy Ghost. Another is the baptism of suffering, whereby each is cleansed by his own blood. There is also a baptism at the entrance of Paradise. This last baptism did not exist in the beginning; but after the sinner was driven out of Paradise, God set there a fiery sword. . . . But though there be a purgation here, there must be a second purification there, that each of us, burnt but not burnt up by that fiery sword, may enter into the delight of Paradise. But this fire whereby involuntary and casual sins are burnt away . . . is different from that which the Lord has assigned to the devil and his angels, of which he says, Enter *into everlasting fire.*

St. Ambrose: *Explanation of Psalm 118,* 3, 14-17. (4th cent.)

The question whether such is the case, is justified and may yield to a solution or remain in doubt: the question whether some of the faithful are saved by a sort of purgatorial fire, and this sooner or later according as they have loved more or less the goods that perish.

St. Augustine: *Enchiridion,* 69. (5th cent.)

During the time which intervenes between man's death and the final resurrection, the souls remain in places specially reserved for them, according as each is deserving of rest or tribulation for the disposition he has made of his life in the flesh.

St. Augustine: *Enchiridion,* 109. (5th cent.)

Evidently, then, it is in this life that the basis is laid on which a person deserves to have his condition in the afterlife alleviated or aggravated; and therefore let no one hope that what he neglected to do here he will merit with God when he dies.

St. Augustine: *Enchiridion,* 110. (5th cent.)

Not all who suffer temporal punishment after death come in for the everlasting punishment which is to be after judgment. To some, what is not remitted in this world is remitted in the world to come.

St. Augustine: *The City of God,* 21, 13. (5th cent.)

There is then a certain kind of life, which is neither, on the one hand, so bad that those who adopt it are not helped towards the kingdom of heaven by any bountiful almsgiving by which they may relieve the wants of the saints, and make friends who could receive them into eternal habitations, nor on the other hand, so good that it of itself suffices to win for them that great blessedness, if they do not obtain mercy through the merit of those whom they have made their friends.

St. Augustine: *The City of God,* 21, 27. (5th cent.)

It is to be believed that before the judgment there is a purgatorial fire for certain minor sins. For the Truth says that if anyone blasphemes against the Holy Ghost, it shall not be forgiven him, either in this world or in the next. From which we learn that certain sins may be forgiven in this world and certain in the next . . . the apostle (1 Cor. 3, 12) holds out the possibility of being saved by fire, not to him who builds on the foundation iron, brass, or lead, that is, the greater and harder sins that are no longer remissible in purgatory, but to the builder of wood, hay, and stubble, that is, the least and lightest sins, which the fire easily consumes. We must know, however, that a man will not be cleansed in purgatory of even the least sins, unless during his lifetime he deserved by his good works to receive such favor.

Pope St. Gregory I: *Dialogue*, 4, 39. (6th cent.)

And thou shalt see those who in fire refrain
  From sorrow, since their hope is in the end,
  Whensoever it be, to the blessèd to attain.

Dante: *Inferno, Canto 1*. (Tr. Binyon) (14th cent.)

Now hoisteth sail the pinnace of my wit
  For better waters, and more smoothly flies
  Since of a sea so cruel she is quit,
And of that second realm, which purifies
  Man's spirit of its soilure, will I sing,
  Where it becometh worthy of Paradise.

Dante: *Purgatorio, Canto 1*. (Tr. Binyon) (14th cent.)

True it is that whoso, though he at last repent,
  In contumacy of Holy Church hath died,
  Must stay without this bank, refused the ascent,
For thirty-fold the time that in the pride

Of his presumption he remained, unless
  In prayers to abridge that term he may confide.

Dante: *Purgatorio, Canto 3*. (D. conceives of purgatory as a mountain) (Tr. Binyon) (14th cent.)

Enter, but we warned that he who is found
Looking behind him is again out-cast.

Dante: *Purgatorio, Canto 9*. (Tr. Binyon) (14th cent.)

Naught on this sacred slope
Can happen which its order overrides,
Nor is aught suffered outside custom's scope.

Dante: *Purgatorio, Canto 21*. (Tr. Binyon) (14th cent.)

Yet there is more, for added to my load,
I am to pay the duties that are owed
To God. . . .
A dead beast has no punishment or pain,
But after death a man must weep again
That living has endured uncounted woe;
I have no doubt that it may well be so.
I leave the answer for divines to tell,
But that there's pain on earth I know too well.

Chaucer: *The Knight's Tale*. (Tr. Coghill) (14th cent.)

Furthermore, if [souls] have departed this life repenting of their sins and with love of God, but before they have by fruits worthy of penance made satisfaction for things they have done or omitted, then after death their souls are purified by the punishments of purgatory; also that for their relief from such punishments, the suffrages of the faithful still living avail, namely the sacrifice of the mass, prayers and almsdeeds and other offices of piety. . . .

Decree of the Council of Florence, *Laetentur Coeli*. (Agreed to by Greeks and Latins.) (1439)

Gold which has been purified to a certain point ceases to suffer any diminution from the action of fire, however great it be; for the fire does not destroy gold, but only the dross that it may chance to have. In like manner, the divine fire acts on souls: God holds them in the furnace until every defect has been burnt away and He has brought them each in his own degree to a certain standard of perfection. Thus purified, they rest in God without any alloy of self, they become impassible because there is nothing left to be consumed.

> St. Catherine of Genoa: *Treatise on Purgatory*, 10. (15th cent.)

Whereas the Catholic Church, instructed by the Holy Ghost, has from the sacred writings and the ancient tradition of the fathers taught in sacred councils and very recently in this oecumenical synod that there is a purgatory, and that the souls there detained are helped by the suffrages of the faithful, but principally by the acceptable sacrifice of the altar; the holy synod enjoins on bishops that they diligently endeavor that the sound doctrine concerning purgatory, transmitted by the holy fathers and sacred councils, be believed, maintained, taught, and everywhere proclaimed by the faithful of Christ.

> Decree of the Council of Trent, Session 25. (Dec. 3, 1563)

If purgatory is a species of hell as regards suffering, it is even more a species of paradise as regards heavenly love and sweetness.

> Jean Pierre Camus: *The Spirit of St. Francis de Sales*, 6, 6. (17th cent.)

O turn to Jesus, Mother! turn,
    And call Him by His tenderest names;
Pray for the holy souls that burn
    This hour amid the cleansing flames.

> F. Faber: *Hymn to our Blessed Lady for the Souls in Purgatory.* (19th cent.)

Help, Lord, the souls which Thou hast made,
    The souls to Thee so dear,
In prison, for the debt unpaid
    Of sins committed here.

Those holy souls, they suffer on,
    Resign'd in heart and will,
Until Thy high behest is done,
    And justice has its fill.

For daily falls, for pardon'd crime,
    They joy to undergo
The shadow of Thy Cross sublime,
    The remnant of Thy woe.

> Card. Newman: *Hymn: For the Dead.* (19th cent.)

Now let the golden prison ope its gates,
Making sweet music, as each fold revolves
Upon its ready hinge. And ye, great powers,
Angels of purgatory, receive from me
My charge, a precious soul, until the day,
When, from all bond and forfeiture released,
I shall reclaim it for the courts of light.
    .   .   .   .   .   .
Farewell, but not for ever! brother dear,
    Be brave and patient on thy bed of sorrow;
Swiftly shall pass thy night of trial here,
    And I will come and wake thee on the morrow.

> Card. Newman: *The Dream of Gerontius.* (Concluding lines addressed by the angel to the soul of Gerontius.) (19th cent.)

> How long, O Lord, how long
> These penal fires among?
> Till love with fiercer flame
> The strength of torture tame.

> J. B. Tabb: *Purgatory.* (19th cent.)

> O plan of happy pains,
> And land of dear desires!
> Where love divine detains
> Glad souls among sweet fires.

> Lionel Johnson: *Visions.* (19th cent.)

The Reformation may be said to have begun with a revolt against the doctrine of purgatory; yet while, despite Christ's clear teaching, the modern revolt is rather against hell as unthinkable, and heaven as unattractive, the one condition of the after-life now found widely acceptable, may be characterized as a kind of universal perpetual and progressive purgatory, which, however, never attains, or eventually arrives at perfection.

W. E. Orchard: *The Necessity for the Church.* (20th cent.)

The doctrine of purgatory is supported by the spontaneous convictions of a large portion of mankind. Men do not really believe that death ends all things; they are much more inclined to imagine a final scene in which all will end well. But between the happy state of human beings and their characters, as we knew them on earth, there is a chasm. Sentimentalists like to think of the chasm, or better, period, as a kind of rest-house or sanatorium. . . . In this way purgatory, which had been denied for religious reasons, comes back in *bourgeois* disguise.

M. C. D'Arcy: *Death and Life.* (20th cent.)

Purification

There is no cleansing process which has not within it a certain destructive power.

R. H. Benson: *The Friendship of Christ.* (20th cent.)

Purification of the Blessed Virgin

O almighty and everlasting God, we humbly beseech Thy majesty; as Thine only-begotten Son was this day presented in the temple in the substance of our flesh, so grant unto us to be presented unto Thee with purified souls.

Roman Missal, Collect. (Gregorian, 7th cent.)

O Sion, adorn thy bridal chamber, and welcome Christ the King: embrace Mary, for she who is the very gate of heaven, bringeth to thee the glorious King of the new light. Remaining ever-Virgin, in her arms she bears her Son before the day-star, Whom Simeon, receiving into his arms declared unto all peoples to be the Lord of life and death and the Savior of the world.

Roman Missal, Antiphon sung during Procession (Feb. 2). (From Greek Liturgy, by St. Cosmas) (Liber Antiphonarius, 7th-8th cents.)

O Sion! open wide thy gates;
  Let figures disappear;
A Priest and Victim both in one,
  The Truth himself is here.

Jean Santeuil: *Templi sacratas pande Sion fores.* (Tr. Caswall) (18th cent.)

Joy! joy! the mother comes,
  And in her arms she brings
The Light of all the world.
  The Christ, the King of kings;
And in her heart the while
  All silently she sings.

F. Faber: *The Purification.* (19th cent.)

Puritans

A numerous host of dreaming saints succeed;
Of the true old enthusiastick breed:
'Gainst form and order they their pow'r employ.
Nothing to build, and all things to destroy.

Dryden: *Absalom and Achitophel.* (17th cent.)

A puritan is a person who pours righteous indignation into the wrong things.

G. K. Chesterton: (*N.Y. Times, Nov. 21, 1930.*)

Puritanism

Amid all the great work of Puritanism the damning indictment of it consists in one fact, that there was one only of the fables of Christendom that it retained and renewed, and that was the belief in witchcraft. It cast away the generous and wholesome superstition, it approved only of the morbid and the dangerous. In their treatment of the great national fairy-tale of good and evil, the Puritans killed St. George but carefully preserved the dragon.

> G. K. Chesterton: *The Common Man.* (20th cent.)

Puritanism is only a paralysis, which stiffens into Stoicism when it loses religion.

> G. K. Chesterton: *Autobiography.* (20th cent.)

When the medieval Catholic was not lax he was a Puritan frowning on dances, on the drama, even religious drama, on secular literature and amusements generally. Puritanism was not made in Geneva, or in Edinburgh for that matter. The Protestant Puritans did but discover its nakedness and display its inhumanity by isolating it from the poetry and humanity of Catholic devotion and worship and by seeking to impose it by force on the entire community.

> E. I. Watkin: *Catholic Art and Culture.* (20th cent.)

Purity

To sow the seeds of perfect purity and to arouse a desire for virginity has always belonged to the function of the priesthood.

> St. Ambrose: *De Virginitate,* 5, 26. (4th cent.)

Purity of soul cannot be lost without consent.

> St. Augustine: *On Lying.* (4th cent.)

Pour out, O Lord, we beseech Thee, the Spirit of grace upon Thy family, and cast out from them whatever they have incurred by the fraud of the devil or by earthly corruption; that being cleansed within and without, they may ever render unto Thee a pure worship, and may the more readily obtain what they fitly and reasonably ask.

> Leonine Sacramentary, Collect. (ca. 5th cent.)

A pure heart penetrates heaven and hell.

> Thomas a Kempis: *The Imitation of Christ,* 2, 4. (15th cent.)

Yes—for a spirit, pure as hers,
Is always pure, even while it errs;
As sunshine, broken in the rill,
Though turned astray, is sunshine still.

> Thomas Moore: *Lalla Rookh: The Fire-Worshippers.* (19th cent.)

The impure then cannot love God; and those who are without love of God cannot really be pure. Purity prepares the soul for love, and love confirms the soul in purity.

> Card. Newman: *Discourses to Mixed Congregations.* (19th cent.)

Purpose

But natheless his purpose held he still,
As lordes do, when they will have their will.

> Chaucer: *The Clerkes Tale.* (14th cent.)

Purse

There was no one else there but the priest and the parson—yet I lost my purse.

> Seumas MacManus: *Heavy Hangs the Golden Grain.* (20th cent.)

Q

Quarreling

Not to love contention.

> St. Benedict: *Rule*, 4. (One of his 'tools of good works.') (6th cent.)

One ill word axeth (asketh) another.

> John Heywood: *Proverbs*, 1, 9. (16th cent.)

Come together by the ears.

> John Heywood: *Proverbs*, 2, 1. (16th cent.)

Dissensions, like small streams, are first begun,
Scarce seen, they rise, but gather as they run:
So lines that from their parallel decline,
More they proceed the more they still disjoin.

> Sir Samuel Garth: *The Dispensary*, 8. (17th cent.)

Queen

Cease, then, O queens, who earthly crowns do wear,
    To glory in the pomp of worldly things:
If men such high respect unto you bear
Which daughters, wives and mothers are of kings;
    What honor should unto that Queen be done
    Which had your God for Father, Spouse and Son?

> Henry Constable: *To Our Blessed Lady, Sonnet I.* (17th cent.)

Question

Questions are never indiscreet. Answers sometimes are.

> Oscar Wilde: *An Ideal Husband*, 1. (19th cent.)

Quiet

He is as quiet as a lamb.

> Langland: *Piers Plowman*, Passus 6. (14th cent.)

Quickness

Quick as a bee.

> John Heywood: *Proverbs*, 1, 9. (16th cent.)

R

Race

Prizes would be for legs of slowest pace,
Were cripples made the judges of the race.

Dryden. (17th cent.)

Racism

He who takes the race, or the people, or the state, or the form of government, the bearers of the power of the state or other fundamental elements of human society—which in the temporal order of things have an essential and honorable place—out of the system of their earthly valuation, and makes them the ultimate norm of all, even of religious values, and deifies them with an idolatrous worship, perverts and falsifies the order of things created and commanded by God. Such a one is far from true belief in God and a conception of life corresponding to true belief.

Pope Pius XI: *Mit Brennender Sorge.* (March 14, 1937)

Only superficial minds can lapse into the heresy of speaking of a national God, of a national religion; only such can make the mad attempt of trying to confine within the boundaries of a single people, within the narrow bloodstream of a single race, God the Creator of the world, the King and Lawgiver of all peoples before Whose greatness all peoples are small as a drop in a bucket.

Pope Pius XI: *Mit Brennender Sorge.* (March 14, 1937)

Rainbow

Whatso looks lovelily
Is but the rainbow on life's weeping rain.

F. Thompson: *Ode to the Setting Sun.* (19th cent.)

An arch of God's great temple fair thou art,
Wrought by some airy builder of the skies;
The sunbeam's secret, wrested from its heart,
And blazed abroad in hues of paradise.
A flaming screed across the heavens flung,
The jeweled autograph of the Most High,
Writ on the sky's wide scroll when the earth was young
To seal His oath to centuries gone by.

Sister M. Angelita: *To the Rainbow.* (20th cent.)

Rank

Dost thou wish to enjoy the first rank? First concede that place to another.

St. John Chrysostom: *Homilies.* (4th cent.)

It is not ecclesiastical rank that makes a man a Christian.

St. Jerome: *Letters,* 14, 9. (4th cent.)

Rashness

Circumcise the lips of my mouth and the lips of my mind of all rash speech and lying.

St. Augustine: *Confessions,* 11, 2. (5th cent.)

Rat

If they smell a ratt
They grisely chide and chatt.

John Skelton: *The Image of Hypocrisy.* (16th cent.)

Rationalism

Unbelievers call themselves rational; not because they decide by evidence, but because, after they have made their decision, they merely occupy themselves in sifting it.

> Card. Newman: *Oxford University Sermons.* (19th cent.)

It is rationalism to accept the revelation, and then to explain it away; to speak of it as the word of God, and to treat it as the word of man; to refuse to let it speak for itself; to claim to be told the *why* and the *how* of God's dealings with us, as therein described, and to assign to Him a motive and scope of our own; to stumble at the partial knowledge which He may give us of them; to put aside what is obscure, as if it had not been said at all; to accept one half of what has been told us, and not the other half; to assume that the contents of revelation are also its proof; to frame some gratuitous hypothesis about them, and then to garble, gloss, and color them, to trim, clip, pare away, and twist them, in order to bring them into conformity with the idea to which we have subjected them.

> Card. Newman: *Essays Critical and Historical,* 1. (19th cent.)

The rationalist makes himself his own center, not his Maker; he does not go to God, but he implies that God must come to him.

> Card. Newman: *Essays Critical and Historical,* 2. (19th cent.)

The fundamental doctrine of rationalism is the supremacy of the human reason, which, refusing due submission to the divine and eternal reason, proclaims its own independence, and constitutes itself the supreme principle and source and judge of truth.

> Pope Leo XIII: *Libertas Praestantissimum.* (June 20, 1888)

Rationalism owes much of its success not only to its name, but also to the folly of Christians who should never have described their opponents as rationalists, thus labelling themselves by implication as anti-rational.

> Arnold Lunn: *The Revolt against Reason.* (20th cent.)

Raven

The raven's house is built with reeds,—
Sing woe, and alas is me!
And the raven's couch is spread with weeds,
High on the hollow tree;
And the raven himself, telling his beads
In penance for his past misdeed,
Upon the top I see.

> Thomas D'Arcy McGee: *The Penitent Raven.* (19th cent.)

Reading

Take and read, take and read. (Tolle lege, tolle lege.)

> St. Augustine: *Confessions,* 8, 12. (Words heard by him in the garden at the time of his conversion) (5th cent.)

To listen gladly to holy reading.

> St. Benedict: *Rule,* 4. (One of his 'tools of good works.') (6th cent.)

If thou wouldst profit by thy reading, read humbly, simply, honestly, and not desiring to win a character for learning.

> Thomas a Kempis: *Imitation of Christ,* 1. (15th cent.)

There is a great deal of difference between the eager man who wants to read a book, and the tired man who wants a book to read.

> G. K. Chesterton: *Charles Dickens.* (20th cent.)

Realism

Realism is simply romanticism that has lost its reason.

> G. K. Chesterton: *Alarms and Discursions.* (20th cent.)

Women are the only realists; their whole object in life is to pit their realism against the extravagant, excessive, and occasionally drunken idealism of men.

> G. K. Chesterton: *A Handful of Authors.* (20th cent.)

There is no realism like the insatiable realism of love.

> G. K. Chesterton: *A Handful of Authors.* (20th cent.)

Reason

Can you, I pray, find anything in human nature higher than reason?

> St. Augustine: *On Freewill,* 2, 13. (4th cent.)

Reason is the vision of the mind by means of which it beholds the true, by itself and without the help of the body; or the contemplation itself of the true, without the aid of the body; or the true itself, which it beholds.

> St. Augustine: *De Immortalitate Animae,* 6, 10. (4th cent.)

Reason (*ratio*), you might say, is the sight of the mind, but reasoning (*ratiocinatio*) is reason's search, that is, the actual moving of the sight of the mind over the things that are to be seen. Hence, by reasoning, we search; by reason we see.

> St. Augustine: *De Quantitate Animae,* 27, 52. (4th cent.)

Reason in man is rather like God in the world.

> St. Thomas Aquinas: *Opusc.* 11, 1 *de Regno,* 12. (13th cent.)

And this I know, for kind wit me taught,
That reason shall reign and realms govern.

> Langland: *Piers Plowman,* Passus 4. (14th cent.)

O youth, alas! why wilt thou not incline
And unto rulèd reason bowe thee,
Since reason is the very straight line
That leadeth folk into felicity?

> Thomas Hoccleve: *La Male Regle.* (15th cent.)

As for that, reason runneth to halves.

> John Heywood: *Proverbs,* 2, 4. (16th cent.)

Natural reason is a good tree which God has planted in us; the fruits which spring from it cannot but be good.

> St. Francis de Sales: *Treatise on the Love of God,* 11, 1. (17th cent.)

Reason rules us far more imperiously than a master, for if you disobey him you suffer, while if you disobey it you are a fool.

> Pascal: *Pensées.* (17th cent.)

Two excesses: reason excluded, only reason allowed.

> Pascal: *Pensées.* (17th cent.)

Dim as the borrowed beams of moon and stars
To lonely, weary, wand'ring travelers,
Is reason to the soul.

> Dryden: *Religio Laici.* (17th cent.)

All men have a reason, but not all men can give a reason.

> Card. Newman: *Oxford University Sermons.* (19th cent.)

Reason can but ascertain the profound difficulties of our condition, it cannot remove them.

> Card. Newman: *Oxford University Sermons.* (19th cent.)

Human reason, without any reference whatsoever to God, is the sole arbiter of truth and falsehood, and of good and evil; it is law to itself, and suffices by its natural force to secure the welfare of men and of nations.

> Proposition condemned by Pius IX in Syllabus of Errors. (1867)

If any one shall say that human reason is so independent that faith cannot be enjoined upon it by God; let him be anathema.

> Vatican Council, Session 3, Canon 1. (Apr. 24, 1870)

I can stand brute force, but brute reason is quite unbearable. There is something unfair about its use. It is hitting below the intellect.

> Oscar Wilde: *The Picture of Dorian Gray*, 3. (19th cent.)

Those who most confidently appeal to reason are usually the very persons most controlled by imagination.

> R. H. Benson: *Introduction to the Mustard Tree*. (20th cent.)

The abhorrence of Latinity is as worthless as the idolatry of it; for many minds it is merely an ornamental façade for concealing a fundamental intolerance of the form of reason.

> J. Maritain: *The Things that are not Caesar's*. (20th cent.)

It is well known how highly the Church regards human reason, for it stands to reason to demonstrate with certainty the existence of God, personal and one; to prove beyond doubt from divine signs the very foundations of the Christian faith; to express properly the law which the Creator has imprinted in the hearts of men; and finally to attain to some notion, indeed a very fruitful notion, of mysteries.

> Pope Pius XII: *Humani Generis*. (Apr. 12, 1950)

See also Faith and Reason; Mind; Understanding

Reason and Will

It is always the case with men whose will runs ahead of their rational insight that their affections become perverted through their having put the light of reason behind them, and they are then drawn along by these affections like blind men who obstinately deny their blindness.

> Dante: *Monarchy*, 3. (14th cent.)

There are two main ways of settling questions that come up for decision, and both ways are possible to a religious man. One way is to lay stress on the intellectual side, to weigh the arguments carefully, and decide, as it were, by reasoning alone; the other is to lay comparatively little stress on the arguments and the intellectual side generally, and to make the main effort lie in the aspiration of the will towards God for guidance.

> R. H. Benson: *The Light Invisible*. (20th cent.)

Reasoning

How a man reasons is as much a mystery as how he remembers.

> Card. Newman: *Oxford University Sermons*. (19th cent.)

Clearness in argument certainly is not indispensable to reasoning well. Accuracy in stating doctrines or principles is not essential to feeling and acting upon them. The exercise of analysis is not necessary to the integrity of the process analyzed. The process of reasoning is complete in itself, and independent.

> Card. Newman: *Oxford University Sermons*. (19th cent.)

To most men argument makes the point in hand only more doubtful, and considerably less impressive. After all, man is *not* a reasoning animal; he is a seeing, feeling, contemplating, acting animal.

> Card. Newman: *Discussions and Arguments*. (19th cent.)

Our most natural mode of reasoning is, not from proposition to proposition, but from things to things, from concrete to concrete, from wholes to wholes.

> Card. Newman: *Grammar of Assent,* 8. (19th cent.)

Rebel

> Of these the false Achitophel was first,
> A name to all succeeding ages curst.
> For close designs and crooked counsels fit,
> Sagacious, bold, and turbulent of wit,
> Restless, unfixt in principles and place,
> In pow'r unpleased, impatient of disgrace.
>
> Dryden: *Absalom and Achitophel.* (17th cent.)

Rebels in Cork are patriots at Madrid.

> Thomas Moore: *The Sceptic.* (19th cent.)

Rebuke

On all occasions abjure asperity, even when it is necessary to administer a rebuke; for if you first abase yourself and show humility, you will easily find your way to the heart of him who needs your ministrations.

> St. Basil: *Letters,* 2. (4th cent.)

Never rebuke anyone but with discretion, and humility, and self-abasement.

> St. Teresa of Jesus: *Maxims.* (16th cent.)

When rebuked for anything receive the rebuke with inward and outward humility, and pray to God for the person who gives the rebuke.

> St. Teresa of Jesus: *Maxims.* (16th cent.)

Reconciliation

The reconciling of a soul to God is a greater thing than the reconciling of east to west.

> R. H. Benson: *Lord of the World.* (20th cent.)

Recreation

If you have no need of recreation for yourself, you must help to make recreation for those who do need it.

> St. Francis de Sales: *Spiritual Conferences,* 13. (17th cent.)

Redemption

For no one is redeemed except through unmerited mercy, and no one is condemned except through merited judgment.

> St. Augustine: *Enchiridion,* 94. (5th cent.)

But once sin had created a wide rift between the human race and God, it was necessary that a mediator, who alone was born and lived and was put to death without sin, should reconcile us with God even to the extent of obtaining for us the resurrection of the body unto life everlasting, in order that the pride of man might be rebuked and cured through the humility of God; that man might be made to see how far he had departed from God, when the incarnate God came to summon him back; that man in his stubbornness might receive an example of obedience from the God-Man; that the fountain of grace might be opened by the Only-Begotten taking the form of a servant, a form which had no antecedent merits; that the resurrection also of the body, promised to the redeemed, might be presaged in the resurrection of the Redeemer; that the devil might be conquered by that same nature which he rejoiced to have deceived, without man, however, taking glory in himself, lest pride spring up anew.

> St. Augustine: *Enchiridion,* 108. (5th cent.)

For it is by this grace of God through Jesus Christ our Lord that all those who are delivered, are delivered, since no one can be delivered in any other way than through it.

> St. Augustine: *Letter 179.* (5th cent.)

O God, Who hast marvelously created man, and more marvelously redeemed him: grant us, we beseech Thee, to resist the allurements of sin with a strong mind, that we may be able to attain to eternal joys.

Roman Missal, Collect for Holy Saturday. (Gregorian, ca. 6th cent.)

Now because Christ's passion was the sufficient and superabundant satisfaction for human guilt and the consequent debt of punishment, His passion was a kind of price, which paid the cost of freeing us from both obligations. . . . Christ rendered satisfaction, not by giving money or anything of the sort, but by spending for us what was of the highest value. He gave Himself, and therefore His passion is called our redemption.

St. Thomas Aquinas: *Summa Theologica*, 3, 48, 4. (13th cent.)

The Divine Goodness, whereof all
    things bear
    The seal, designed then all its paths
      to assay
    That it might lift you up where once
      ye were;
Nor 'twixt the final night and the first
    day
    Did aught of such grandeur come to
      pass
Nor ever shall, on one or the other
    way.
God gave Himself with larger boun-
    teousness
    To enable man to lift himself again
    Than if he had only pardoned of his
      grace;
And justice must all other modes dis-
    dain
    Except the Son of God humbled
      Him so
    That He became incarnated in man.

Dante: *Paradiso, Canto 7.* (Dante held that there were only two ways in which man could recover his former status after the Fall: either God forgave the fault, or man by his own will and deed achieved satisfaction [which he could not do by himself]). (Tr. Binyon) (14th cent.)

This decree, brother, is not to be shown
    To the eyes of him whose unper-
      fected wit
    Hath not in love's flame into ripe-
      ness grown.

Dante: *Paradiso, Canto 7.* (Tr. Binyon) (14th cent.)

If any one saith that Christ Jesus was given of God to men as a Redeemer in Whom to trust, and not also as a Legislator Whom to obey; let him be anathema.

Council of Trent, Session 6, Canon 21. (Jan. 13, 1547)

God might have redeemed the world by a manifestation of His glory; but He chose to do it by shame. Jesus was rejected of men, and they hid their faces from Him as if ashamed to own Him. This lot He has bequeathed to us.

Card. Manning: *The Eternal Priesthood.* (19th cent.)

It is a greater act to restore than to create, to bring the disobedient will back to obedience than to will it into existence, to reconcile enemies than to create worshippers, to redeem than to make.

R. H. Benson: *The Friendship of Christ.* (20th cent.)

See also Atonement; Grace; Jesus Christ; Passion of our Lord; Sacrament; Salvation

Reform

Truths would you teach, or save a sink-
    ing land?
All fear, none aid you, and few under-
    stand.

Pope: *An Essay on Man,* 4. (18th cent.)

It is not of much use to be entreated to turn over a new leaf, when you see no kind of reason for doing so.

R. H. Benson: *None Other Gods.* (20th cent.)

Reformation

But 'tis the talent of our English nation,
Still to be plotting some new Reformation.

Dryden: *Sophonisba, Prologue.* (17th cent.)

It cannot be denied that corruption of morals prevailed in the sixteenth century to such an extent as to call for a sweeping reformation, and that laxity of discipline invaded even the sanctuary.

Card. Gibbons: *The Faith of Our Fathers*, 3. (19th cent.)

Refuge

O God, our refuge and strength, the Author of all godliness, hear the devout prayers of Thy Church, and grant that we may effectively obtain what we ask for in confidence.

Roman Missal, Collect for Twenty-second Sunday after Pentecost. (Gregorian, 6th to 8th cent.)

Refusal

When I had marked some few among the press,
  I chanced the shade of him to recognize
  Who made the great refusal, from meanness.

Dante: *Inferno, Canto 3.* (Tr. L. Binyon) (Thought to refer to the abdication of Pope St. Celestine V in 1294) (14th cent.)

  Why wilt thou chide,
Who hast attained to be denied?
  O learn above
All price is my refusal, Love.
  My sacred Nay
Was never cheapened by the way.
Thy single sorrow crowns thee lord
Of an unpurchasable word.

Alice Meynell: *Why Wilt Thou Chide?* (19th cent.)

It needs more courage to refuse than to be foolhardy.

R. H. Benson: *The Coward.* (20th cent.)

Regeneration

For wisdom is lifeless without grace; but when wisdom has received grace, then its work begins to be perfect. This is called regeneration.

St. Ambrose: *On the Sacraments*, 3, 1, 1. (4th cent.)

See also Baptism; Grace

Regret

I desire rather to feel compunction than to know its definition.

Thomas a Kempis: *The Imitation of Christ*, 1, 1. (15th cent.)

As, when the seaward ebbing tide doth pour
  Out by the low sand spaces,
The parting waves slip back to clasp the shore
  With lingering embraces,—

So in the tide of life that carries me
  From where thy true heart dwells,
Waves of my thoughts and memories turn to thee
  With lessening farewells.

Alice Meynell: *Regrets.* (19th cent.)

Relatives

O Christ, my Creator and Redeemer, almighty Lord God, forgive all their sins to all who are joined to me by friendship or blood, and for whom I am desired to pray, or have resolved to pray, and to all Thy faithful people. Deliver them from all evil, preserve them in all good, and bring them to everlasting joy.

Roman Missal, Collect for Friends and Relatives. (ca. 9th cent.)

Many kins folk and few friends.

John Heywood: *Proverbs*, 1, 11. (16th cent.)

Relativity

When we see an effect always taking place in the same manner, we conclude that there is a natural necessity for it, as, that the sun will rise to-morrow, etc.; but nature often deceives us, and does not bow to her own laws.

> Pascal: *Pensées*, 4. (17th cent.)

Religion

Wisdom precedes, religion follows; for the knowledge of God comes first, His worship is the result of knowledge.

> Lactantius: *Divine Institutes*, 4, 4. (4th cent.)

For we are created on this condition, that we pay just and due obedience to God who created us, that we should know and follow Him alone. We are *bound* and *tied* to God by this *chain of piety;* from which *religion* itself received its name.

> Lactantius: *Divine Institutes*, 4, 28. (4th cent.)

For true religion is that by which the soul is united to God so that it binds itself again by reconciliation to Him from Whom it had broken off, as it were, by sin.

> St. Augustine: *De Quantitate Animae,* 36, 80. (4th cent.)

No one doubts that he who seeks true religion either already believes the soul to be immortal if that religion is to be of any profit to him, or that it is just that very truth he wishes to discover in this same religion. It is for the sake of the soul that all religion exists; for, how it may be with the nature of the body causes no worry or solicitude, especially after death, to one whose soul possesses that by which it may be happy.

> St. Augustine: *De Utilitate Credendi,* 7, 14. (4th cent.)

If the providence of God does not preside over human affairs, there is no point in busying oneself about religion.

> St. Augustine: *De Utilitate Credendi,* 16, 34. (4th cent.)

Let religion bind us once more to the one almighty God.

> St. Augustine: *De Vera Religione,* 55. (4th cent.)

For He is the fountain of our happiness, He is the end of all our desires. Choosing Him, or rather choosing Him again (*Hunc eligentes vel potius religentes*), Whom we had lost through our negligence—choosing Him again, I say, whence *religion* is said to be derived from *religere* (choose again), we tend towards Him by love that we may rest in Him, and find our happiness by attaining that end.

> St. Augustine: *The City of God,* 10, 3. (5th cent.)

Religion is so called, because by it we bind our souls to the one God for divine worship with a bond of service.

> St. Isidore: *Etymologies,* 8, 2. (7th cent.)

A religious man is, as Cicero remarks, so called from *religion,* for he is occupied with, and, as it were, reads through again and again (*relegit*) the things that concern divine worship.

> St. Isidore of Seville: *Etymologies,* 10. (7th cent.)

Religion too has certain first principles which universal reason or piety has dictated, and these, in the service of God and in training character, contribute to the attainment of blessedness. There is one principle that all religions have, and that is that there is a God, powerful, wise, good, awe-inspiring, and lovable.

> John of Salisbury: *Policraticus,* 7, 7, 116. (12th cent.)

God has no need for our worship. It is we who need to show our gratitude for what we have received.

> St. Thomas Aquinas: *Commentary on the Sentences,* 3, 9, 1, 3. (13th cent.)

Religion, in its original sense, meant binding yourself to God's due service through faith. Everybody undertakes this on entering the Christian religion by baptism when Satan and all his pomps are renounced. But religion also has a narrower meaning, namely, of binding yourself to certain deeds of charity, deeds which in some special manner serve God and renounce the world: it is in this sense that we speak of the religious life, or the life of religion.

> St. Thomas Aquinas: *Against those who impugn the Worship of God,* 1. (13th cent.)

But whether religion be so called from frequent *reading,* or from *fresh election* of him whom we have negligently lost, or from *rebinding,* it properly implies a certain relation to God. For it is He to Whom we ought to be especially bound as our indefectible principle; to Him must we assiduously direct our choice as our ultimate end; He it is Whom we negligently lose by sin and Whom we must regain by believing in Him and by professing our faith in Him.

> St. Thomas Aquinas: *Summa Theologica,* 2, 2, 81, 1. (13th cent.)

Religion is the virtue by which men show God due worship and reverence.

> St. Thomas Aquinas: *Summa Theologica,* 2, 2, 81, 1. (13th cent.)

Now the human mind needs—if it would be united to God—the guidance of the things of sense; for as the apostle says to the Romans (1, 20): *The invisible things of him are clearly seen, being understood by the things that are made.* Hence in divine worship it is necessary to make use of certain corporal acts, so that by their means, as by certain signs, man's mind may be stirred up to those spiritual acts whereby it is knit to God. Consequently religion has certain interior acts which are its chief ones and which essentially belong to it; but it has also external acts which are secondary and which are subordinated to the interior acts.

> St. Thomas Aquinas: *Summa Theologica,* 2, 2, 81, 7. (13th cent.)

If the laws of God and man are at variance, the former are to be obeyed in derogation of the latter. (Summa ratio est quae pro religione facit.)

> Legal Maxim. (Broom, Legal Maxims) (Medieval ?)

Religion is directly concerned with those things which specially pertain to divine worship—ceremonies, for example, sacrifices, oblations, etc. Whereas sanctity directly regards the mind, and through the mind the other virtuous works, including those of religion . . . for it makes use of them so as thereby to apply the mind—and by consequence all acts that proceed from the human mind—to God. Thus we see that many religious people are not saints, whereas all saints are religious.

> Card. Cajetan: *Comm. in Summa Theol.* 2, 2, 81, 8. (16th cent.)

The nearer to the Church, the farther from God.

> John Heywood: *Proverbs,* 1, 9. (16th cent.)

Rise, then, immortal maid! religion, rise!
Put on thyself in thine own looks: t'our eyes
Be what thy beauties, not our blots, have made thee,
Such as (e're our dark sins to dust betray'd thee)
Heav'n set thee down new drest; when thy bright birth
Shot thee like lightning, to th'astonisht earth.

> Richard Crashaw: *On A Treatise of Charity.* (17th cent.)

Every religion is false which in its creed fails to worship one God as source of all things, and in its practice fails to love one only God as the end of all.

> Pascal: *Pensées.* (17th cent.)

The truth of religion lies in its very obscurity, in the little light we have on it, and in our indifference to that light.

> Pascal: *Pensées,* 8. (17th cent.)

If we submit everything to reason, our religion will have nothing in it mysterious or supernatural. If we violate the principles of reason, our religion will be absurd and ridiculous.

> Pascal: *Pensées*, 14. (17th cent.)

Men have contempt for religion, and fear that it is true. To cure this it is necessary to commence by showing that religion is not contrary to reason; then that it is venerable, and worthy of respect; next to make it amiable, and make the good wish that it were true; and finally to show that it is true.

> Pascal: *Pensées*, 24. (17th cent.)

For, with my country's pardon be it said,
Religion is the least of all our trade.

> Dryden: *The Hind and the Panther*, 2. (17th cent.)

Religion is not a theory, a subjective view, an opinion, but is, objectively, at once a principle, a law, and a fact, and, subjectively, it is, by the aid of God's grace, practical conformity to what is universally true and real.

> Orestes Brownson: *The American Republic*. (19th cent.)

It is no necessary mark of a true religion that it is rational in the common sense of the word; nor is it any credit to a man to have resolved only to take up what he considers rational. The true religion is in part altogether above reason, as in its mysteries.

> Card. Newman: *Parochial and Plain Sermons*, 2. (19th cent.)

Religion is for practice, and that immediate.

> Card. Newman: *Essays Critical and Historical*, 2. (19th cent.)

A man who is religious, is religious morning, noon, and night; his religion is a certain character, a mould in which his thoughts, words, and actions are cast, all forming parts of one and the same whole.

> Card. Newman: *Parochial and Plain Sermons*, 7. (19th cent.)

Is not this the error, the common and fatal error, of the world, to think itself a judge of religious truth without preparation of heart?

> Card. Newman: *Oxford University Sermons*. (19th cent.)

For I never could understand how a man could be of two religions at once.

> Card. Newman: *Apologia pro Vita Sua*, 4. (19th cent.)

How is it that men, when left to themselves, fall into such various forms of religion, except that there are various types of mind among them, very distinct from each other?

> Card. Newman: *Apologia pro Vita Sua*, 5. (19th cent.)

A religion is not a proposition, but a system; it is a rite, a creed, a philosophy, a rule of duty, all at once; and to accept a religion is neither a simple assent to it nor a complex, neither a conviction nor a prejudice, neither a notional assent nor a real, not a mere act of profession, nor of credence, nor of opinion, nor of speculation, but it is a collection of all these various kinds of assents, at once and together, some of one description, some of another.

> Card. Newman: *Grammar of Assent*, 7. (19th cent.)

No religion is from God which contradicts our sense of right and wrong.

> Card. Newman: *Grammar of Assent*, 10. (19th cent.)

Who was ever consoled in real trouble by the small beer of literature or science?

> Card. Newman: *Discussions and Arguments*. (19th cent.)

The essence of religion is the idea of a moral Governor and a particular providence.

Card. Newman: *Discussions and Arguments.* (19th cent.)

Man, a being endued with reason, cannot on that very account live altogether at random; he is obliged in some sense to live on principle, to live by rule, to profess a view of life, to have an aim, to set up a standard, and to take to him such examples as seem to him to fulfill it. His reason does not make him independent (as men sometimes speak); it forces on him a dependency on definite principles and laws, in order to satisfy its own demands. He must, by the necessity of his nature, look up to something; and he creates, if he cannot discover, an object for his veneration.

Card. Newman: *Discourses to Mixed Congregations.* (19th cent.)

Man may in the observance of any religion whatever find the way of salvation and arrive at eternal salvation.

Proposition condemned by Pius IX in Syllabus of Errors. (1867)

The religion of the multitude is ever vulgar and abnormal, it will ever be tinctured with fanaticism and superstition, while men are what they are. A people's religion is ever a corrupt religion, in spite of the provisions of Holy Church. If she is to be Catholic, you must admit within her net fish of every kind, guests good and bad, vessels of gold, vessels of earth. You may beat religion out of men, if you will, and then their excesses will take a different direction; but if you make use of religion to improve them, they will make use of religion to corrupt it.

Card. Newman: *Letter to the Rev. E. B. Pusey.* (19th cent.)

All things are to be viewed and valued as they bear on the destiny of man. Religion is the solution of the problem of man's destiny. Religion, therefore, lies at the root of everything which concerns man's true interest.

I. T. Hecker: *The Church and the Age.* (1887)

A civil ruler dabbling in religion is as reprehensible as a clergyman dabbling in politics. Both render themselves odious as well as ridiculous.

Card. Gibbons: *The Faith of Our Fathers,.* 12. (19th cent.)

Religion is the key of history.

Lord Acton. (19th cent.)

When two do not agree about religion, it is nearly always futile to hope for agreement in other things.

Pope Leo XIII: *Arcanum divinae sapientae.* (Feb. 10, 1880)

Religion of its essence is wonderfully helpful to the state. For since it derives the prime origin of all power directly from God Himself, with grave authority it charges rulers to be mindful of their duty, to govern without injustice or severity, to rule their people kindly and with almost paternal charity; it admonishes subjects to be obedient to lawful authority, as to the ministers of God; and it binds them to their rulers not merely by obedience, but by reverence and affection, forbidding all seditions and venturesome enterprises calculated to disturb public order and tranquillity, and cause greater restrictions to be put upon the liberty of the people.

Pope Leo XIII: *Libertas Praestantissimum..* (June 20, 1888)

Religion is not religion until it has become, not only natural, but so natural that nothing else seems natural in its presence; and until the whole being of man says, *Whom have I in heaven but thee, and what on earth in comparison of thee?* and *To whom shall we go if we leave thee?*

Coventry Patmore: *The Rod, the Root and the Flower.* (19th cent.)

It is scarcely likely that men on fire with success, whether military or commercial, will be patient of the restraints of religion.

> R. H. Benson: *By What Authority.* (20th cent.)

Today, as in Bethlehem, the bourgeois sits at home and discusses the census, while shepherds and kings adore in the stable.

> R. H. Benson: *Christ in the Church.* (20th cent.)

All good comes simply and solely from religion.

> R. H. Benson: *The Conventionalists.* (20th cent.)

Religion always is, and always has been, at the root of every world movement.

> R. H. Benson: *The Dawn of All.* (20th cent.)

If religion were small enough for our intellects, it could not be great enough for our soul's requirements.

> R. H. Benson: *The Mirror of Shalott.* (20th cent.)

Religion . . . must at least touch the will; for however small our will may be, it is always large enough to be united to the will of God.

> R. H. Benson: *Christ in the Church.* (20th cent.)

Religion is not one department of life (like art or biology) ; it cannot be segregated from the rest of our experience without ceasing to be true to itself: it is, on the contrary, either the sum of the whole of life, affecting and being affected by every single incident of life, or it is not true religion at all.

> R. H. Benson: *Introduction to Lady Lovat's Life of St. Teresa.* (20th cent.)

If a person's conscience tells him a certain religion is true, he's bound to follow it, whatever happens.

> R. H. Benson: *An Average Man.* (20th cent.)

The object of religion is that the soul should serve God, not that God should serve the soul.

> R. H. Benson: *The Friendship of Christ.* (20th cent.)

Religion is ever, *qua* religion, authoritative and absolute. What constitutes religion is not simply to hold a view and to try to live a life with respect to the unseen and the Deity as possibly or even certainly beautiful or true or good: but precisely that which is over and above this, the holding this view and this life to proceed somehow from God Himself, so as to bind my innermost mind and conscience to unhesitating assent. Not simply that I think it, but that in addition I feel bound to think it transforms a thought about God into a religious act.

> Baron von Hügel: *The Mystical Element of Religion,* I, I. (20th cent.)

Religion is at all times more or less both traditional and individual, both external and internal, both institutional, rational, and volitional. It always answers more or less to the needs of authority and society, of reason and proof, of interior sustenance and purification. I believe because I am told, because it is true, because it answers to my deepest interior experiences and needs. And, everything else being equal, my faith will be at its richest and deepest and strongest, in so far as all these three motives are most fully and characteristically operative within me, at one and the same time, and towards one and the same ultimate result and end.

> Baron von Hügel: *The Mystical Element of Religion,* I, I. (20th cent.)

When religion is banished, human authority totters to its fall.

> Pope Benedict XV: *Ad beatissimi apostolorum.* (Nov. I, 1914)

I cannot understand why something which is unpopular because of what it means should become frightfully popular because it no longer means anything.

G. K. Chesterton: *All is Grist.* (20th cent.)

I have been in many churches, chapels, and halls where a confident pride in having got beyond creeds was coupled with quite a paralyzed incapacity to get beyond catchwords. But wherever the falsity appears it comes from neglect of the same truth: that men should agree on a principle, that they may differ on everything else; that God gave men a law that they might turn it into liberties.

G. K. Chesterton: *A Miscellany of Men.* (20th cent.)

Pessimism says that life is so short that it gives nobody a chance; religion says that life is so short that it gives everybody his final chance.

G. K. Chesterton: *Introduction to Nicholas Nickleby.* (20th cent.)

A cosmic philosophy is not constructed to fit a man; a cosmic philosophy is constructed to fit a cosmos. A man can no more possess a private religion than he can possess a private sun and moon.

G. K. Chesterton: *Introduction to the Book of Job.* (20th cent.)

But even in our quiet life I think we can feel the great fact that is the core of all religion. However quiet may be the skies, or however cool the meadows, we always feel that if we did know what they meant the meaning would be something mighty and shattering. About the weakest weed there is still a sensational difference between understanding and not understanding. We stare at a tree in an infinite leisure; but we know all the time that the real difference is between a stillness of mystery and an explosion of explanation. We know all the time that the question is whether it will always continue to be a tree or turn suddenly into something else.

G. K. Chesterton: *The Common Man.* (20th cent.)

So far from it being irreverent to use silly metaphors on serious questions, it is one's duty to use silly metaphors on serious questions. It is the test of one's seriousness. It is the test of a responsible religion or theory whether it can take examples from pots and pans and boots and butter-tubs. It is the test of a good philosophy whether you can defend it grotesquely. It is the test of a good religion whether you can joke about it.

G. K. Chesterton: *All Things Considered.* (20th cent.)

Religion is the sense of ultimate reality, of whatever meaning a man finds in his own existence or the existence of anything else.

G. K. Chesterton: *Come to Think of It.* (20th cent.)

I realized that ritual will always mean throwing away something; *destroying* our corn and wine upon the altar of our gods.

G. K. Chesterton: *Tremendous Trifles.* (20th cent.)

It is the root of all religion that a man knows that he is nothing in order to thank God that he is something.

G. K. Chesterton: *The Resurrection of Rome.* (20th cent.)

I have heard modern people talk of the needlessness of all the old rituals and reliquaries and the need for a simple religion of the heart. But their demand is rather dangerous, especially to themselves. If we really had a simple religion of the heart we should all be loaded with relics, and rituals would be going on all day long. If our creed were only of the higher emotions, it would talk of nothing else but special shrines, sacred spots, indispensable gestures, and adorable rags and bones. In short, religion of pure good feeling would be a positive orgy of superstition.

G. K. Chesterton: *A Handful of Authors.* (20th cent.)

It is the business of the historical science of religion to show how religion has fulfilled this task: how the vital relation has been maintained between the depths of the Unconscious and the surface of the social order: how religion asserts its internal spiritual autonomy and how it is moulded and conditioned by the influences of environment and social function.

C. Dawson: *Gifford Lectures, 1947: Religion and Culture.*

Religion has its origins in the depths of the soul and it can be understood only by those who are prepared to take the plunge.

C. Dawson: *Gifford Lectures, 1947: Religion and Culture.*

All religion is based on the recognition of a superhuman Reality of which man is somehow conscious and towards which he must in some way orientate his life. The existence of the tremendous transcendent reality that we name God is the foundation of all religion in all ages and among all peoples.

C. Dawson: *Gifford Lectures, 1947: Religion and Culture.*

The complete secularization of social life is a relatively modern and anomalous phenomenon. Throughout the greater part of mankind's history, in all ages and states of society, religion has been the great central unifying force of culture. It has been the guardian of tradition, the preserver of the moral law, the educator and the teacher of wisdom.

C. Dawson: *Gifford Lectures, 1947: Religion and Culture.*

Every historic religion from the lowest to the highest agrees on two fundamental points;—first in the belief in the existence of divine or supernatural powers whose nature is mysterious but which control the world and the life of man; and secondly in the association of these powers with particular men, or things, or places or ceremonies, which act as channels of communication or means of access between the human and the divine worlds.

C. Dawson: *Gifford Lectures, 1947: Religion and Culture.*

See also Belief; Faith; God; Liturgy; Worship

Religion and Art

Religion and art are older than agriculture and industry. In the beginning was the word, and man was a seer and an artist before he was a producer.

C. Dawson: *Gifford Lectures, 1947: Religion and Culture.*

Religion and Science

Many a man will live and die upon a dogma: no man will be a martyr for a conclusion.

Card. Newman: *Discussions and Arguments.* (19th cent.)

I consider, then, that intrinsically excellent and noble as are scientific pursuits, and worthy of a place in a liberal education, and fruitful in temporal benefits to the community, still they are not, and cannot be, *the instrument* of an ethical training; that physics do not supply a basis, but only materials for religious sentiment; that knowledge does but occupy, does not form the mind; that apprehension of the unseen is the only known principle capable of subduing moral evil, educating the multitude, and organizing society; and that, whereas man is born for action, action flows not from inferences, but from impressions,—not from reasonings, but from faith. . . .

Card. Newman: *Discussions and Arguments.* (19th cent.)

I believe that the study of nature, when religious feeling is away, leads the mind, rightly or wrongly, to acquiesce in the atheistic theory, as the simplest and easiest. . . . To those who are conscious of matter, but not conscious of mind, it seems more rational to refer all things to one origin, such as they know, than to assume the existence of a second origin such as they know not.

> Card. Newman: *Discussions and Arguments.* (19th cent.)

It is religion, then, which suggests to science its true conclusions; the facts come from knowledge, but the principles come from faith.

> Card. Newman: *Discussions and Arguments.* (19th cent.)

As to physical science, of course there can be no real collision between it and Catholicism. Nature and grace, reason and revelation, come from the same divine Author, Whose works cannot contradict each other.

> Card. Newman: *Idea of a University, 9.* (19th cent.)

Religion admits the heart and the whole man to the witness-box, while science only admits the head—scarcely even the senses.

> R. H. Benson: *The Light Invisible.* (20th cent.)

Religious

Religious are persons who have taken vows in a religious society; religious with simple vows are those who have taken vows in a religious congregation; regulars are those who have taken vows in an order; sisters are religious women with simple vows; nuns are religious women with solemn vows. . . .

> Code of Canon Law, Canon 488, 7. (20th cent.)

Religious Life

Three stages have to be passed in order to reach perfect friendship with God. External goods have to be renounced. Carnal thoughts have to be left behind. Life has to be given up, either by suffering death for Christ or by denying one's own will. Whosoever binds his whole life by vow to these works of perfection assumes the status of perfection. Such is the religious life.

> St. Thomas Aquinas: *Concerning the Perfection of the Spiritual Life,* 16. (13th cent.)

The habit and the tonsure contribute little; but a change of manners, and an entire mortification of the passions, make a truly religious man.

> Thomas a Kempis: *The Imitation of Christ,* 1, 17. (15th cent.)

O how great was the fervor of all religious in the beginning of their holy institution!

> Thomas a Kempis: *The Imitation of Christ,* 1, 18. (15th cent.)

It is commendable for a religious man to go seldom abroad, to fly being seen, and not to desire to see men.

> Thomas a Kempis: *The Imitation of Christ,* 1, 20. (15th cent.)

The life of a good religious man ought to be eminent in all virtues, that he may be such interiorly as he appears to men in his exterior.

> Thomas a Kempis: *The Imitation of Christ,* 1, 19. (15th cent.)

All who bind themselves by profession to the religious state are obliged to tend towards perfection with all their strength, although they are not bound to arrive at that perfection at which they aim.

> Bl. Louis of Blois: *A Short Rule.* (16th cent.)

Religious orders are not formed for the purpose of gathering together perfect people, but those who have the courage to aim at perfection.

> St. Francis de Sales: *Spiritual Conferences,* 16. (17th cent.)

When God calls anyone to be a religious, he binds Himself to bestow on that person all that is needed for perfection in his vocation.

St. Francis de Sales: *Spiritual Conferences,* 17. (17th cent.)

Those who desire to live according to nature should stay in the world, and only those should enter religion who are determined to live according to grace.

St. Francis de Sales: *Spiritual Conferences,* 20. (17th cent.)

One can be a good religious without reciting in choir, without wearing this or that particular habit, without abstinence from such or such things; but without poverty and community of goods, no one can be so.

St. Francis de Sales: *Letters to Persons in Religion,* 1, 1. (17th cent.)

The religious life is not a natural life; it is above nature, and its soul is given and formed by grace.

St. Francis de Sales: *Letters to Persons in Religion,* 4, 20. (17th cent.)

The religious state or fixed manner of living together in common by which the faithful undertake to observe, in addition to the usual precepts, the evangelical counsels by vows of obedience, chastity and poverty, is to be held in honor by all.

Code of Canon Law, Canon 487. (20th cent.)

A religious society [is one that has been] approved by legitimate ecclesiastical authority, in which the members (*sodales*) make a profession of public vows, either perpetual or temporary, the latter to be renewed at fixed intervals of time, according to the laws proper to the society, and thus strive after evangelical perfection. A religious order [is one] in which solemn vows are taken. . . . A religious congregation or simply congregation is one in which only simple vows are taken, either perpetual or temporary. . . .

Code of Canon Law, Canon 488, 1-2. (20th cent.)

Any Catholic who is not debarred by a legitimate impediment and is prompted by a right intention and is fit to bear the burdens of a religious life may be admitted into religion.

Code of Canon Law, Canon 538. (20th cent.)

The Church stands suppliant before the throne of God, dressed, like the King's daughter in the psalm, *in gilded clothing surrounded with variety.* The variety —that is, the designs and ornaments which add beauty to the comely garments of the Church—consists of all the different ways and states of life in which Christians can serve God and give Him glory. Chief among these ways are those which are followed by the different religious orders and congregations.

Thomas Merton: *The Waters of Siloe.* (20th cent.)

The final end proposed to the religious orders is nothing else but God Himself: which means that their function is to bring their numbers, in one way or another, to the vision and possession of God, Who is the summit of all reality and the perfection of infinite truth and the unending fulness of all joy.

Thomas Merton: *The Waters of Siloe.* (20th cent.)

See also Monastic Life

Remedy

Go now, and with some daring drug
Bait thy disease. And whilst they tug,
Thou to maintain their precious strife,
Spend the dear treasures of thy life.
    Go, take physic,
    Doat upon
Some big-nam'd composition:
Th'oraculous doctor's mystic bills,
Certain hard words made into pills;
And what at last shalt gain by these?
    Only a costlier disease.
That which makes us have no need
Of physic, that's physic indeed.

Richard Crashaw: *Temperance, or the Cheap Physician.* (17th cent.)

Remembrance

Those we love truly never die
Though year by year the sad memorial
    wreath,
A ring and flowers, types of life and
    death,
    Are laid upon their graves.

> J. B. O'Reilly: *Forever.* (19th cent.)

How larger is remembrance than de-
    sire!
    How deeper than all longing is re-
    gret!

> Michael Field: *Ebbtide at Sundown.* (19th cent.)

Sometime it may be pleasing to remem-
    ber
The curls about your brow,
To talk about your eyes, your smile,
    your dearness,
    But it is anguish now.

> Aline Kilmer: *Olim Meminisse Juvabit.* (20th cent.)

Remorse

I wealthiest am when richest in remorse.

> Bl. Robert Southwell: *St. Peter's Complaint.* (16th cent.)

A torture kept for those who know,
Know everything, and—worst of all—
Know and love virtue while they fall!

> Thomas Moore: *Loves of the Angels: the Second Angel's Story.* (19th cent.)

Renegade

Still violent, whatever cause he took,
But most against the party he forsook:
For renegades, who ne'er turn by
    halves,
Are bound in conscience to be double
    knaves.

> Dryden: *Absalom and Achitophel.* (17th cent.)

Renouncement

I must not think of thee; and, tired yet
    strong,
    I shun the thought that lurks in all
    delight—
    The thought of thee—and in the
    blue heaven's height,
And in the sweetest passage of a song.
Oh, just beyond the fairest thoughts
    that throng
    This breast, the thought of thee waits
    hidden yet bright;
    But it must never, never come in
    sight;
I must stop short of thee the whole day
    long.

> Alice Meynell: *Renouncement.* (19th cent.)

Repentance

Let us also intercede for those who fall
into any transgression, that meekness
and humility may be granted them, so
that they may yield not to us but to God's
will. For in this way there will be for
them a fruitful, perfect, and compassionate remembrance with God and the
saints.

> Pope St. Clement I: *First Letter to the Corinthians,* 56, 1. (1st cent.)

So let us also, while we are still in this
world, repent with our whole heart of
the evil things we have done in the flesh,
that we may be saved by the Lord while
we have time for repentance. For, after
leaving the world, we cannot there confess or repent any more.

> So-called Second Letter of Clement I to the Corinthians, 8, 2-3. (ca. 2nd cent.)

How inconsistent it is to expect pardon
of sins to be granted to a repentance
which they have not fulfilled. This is to
hold out your hand for merchandise, but
not produce the price. For repentance is
the price at which the Lord has determined to award pardon.

> Tertullian: *On Repentance,* 6. (3rd cent.)

Repeated sickness must have repeated medicine. You will show your gratitude to the Lord by not refusing what the Lord offers you. You have offended but still can be reconciled. You have One Whom you may satisfy, and Him willing.

Tertullian: *On Repentance*, 7. (3rd cent.)

To him who still remains in this world no repentance is too late. The approach to God's mercy is open, and the access is easy to those who seek and apprehend the truth . . . pardon is granted to the man who confesses, saving mercy is given from the divine goodness to the believer, and a passage is opened to immortality even in death itself.

St. Cyprian: *To Demetrianus Proconsul of Africa*, 25. (3rd cent.)

I am not worthy, Lord, mine eyes
  To turn unto Thy starry skies;
But bowed in sin, with moans and
      sighs,
  I beg Thee, hear me.

St. Hilary of Poitiers: *Ad Coeli Clara.* (Tr. D. Donahoe) (4th cent.)

Properly speaking, there are especially two kinds of compunction: for the soul that thirsts for God is first sorry in his heart from fear, and then from love.

Pope St. Gregory I: *Dialogue*, 3, 34. (6th cent.)

Whence shall I begin to bewail the deeds of my miserable life? What beginning shall I make, O Christ, of my present complaint? Do Thou, O Merciful One, grant me the forgiveness of my trespasses.

Byzantine Triodion, Great Canon of St. Andrew of Crete. (Thursday before Passion Sunday) (8th cent.)

Repentance is the returning from the unnatural to the natural state, from the devil to God, through discipline and effort.

St. John of Damascus: *Exposition of the Orthodox Faith*, 2, 30. (8th cent.)

O most sweet Jesus Christ, open to me, O Jesus, the gates of repentance, O Jesus Lover of mankind, and receive me who fall down before Thee and earnestly beseech Thee, O Jesus my Savior, for the forgiveness of my sins!

Byzantine Parakletike, Suppliant Canon of Our Lord. (Theoctistus, 9th cent.)

Give me tears, O God, as Thou once gavest them to the sinful woman, and let me wash Thy feet therewith, Thy feet that saved me from the path of sin. And let me cleanse my life with penitence, and so bring Thee fragrant myrrh. And let me hear Thy sacred words, *Go in peace, thy faith hath made thee whole.*

Byzantine Horologion, Troparion at Great Compline. (ca. 9th cent.)

No power can the impenitent absolve.

Dante: *Inferno, Canto 27.* (14th cent.)

Therefore I rede you this counsel take, Forsaketh sin, ere sin you forsake.

Chaucer: *The Phisiciens Tale.* (14th cent.)

Harm done, too late followeth repentance.

Lydgate: *The Fall of Princes*, 3. (15th cent.)

All worldly honor now farewell,
  All worldly wealth adieu,
Pride and vainglory, pack you hence,
  Too long I servèd you.

In you I dream'd my joy had been,
  But I deceivèd was,
And now, broad waking, I do see,
  That it hangs on the Cross.

Anonymous untitled poem, possibly by Bl. Henry Walpole. (Guiney, 276) (16th cent.)

Where sin was hatch'd, let tears now wash the nest,
Where life was lost, recover life with cries;
Thy trespass foul, let not thy tears be few,

Baptize thy spotted soul in weeping
dew.

Bl. Robert Southwell: *St. Peter's
Complaint.* (16th cent.)

Tell me naked wretch of sin,
My gates are shut, how cam'st thou in,
. . . .

Go to (sirra), get you gone,
Let an aged man alone,
All retirèd as you see
To record repentingly
His youth's amisses.

Anthony Copley: *Love's Owl.* (16th cent.)

Time! where didst thou those years
inter
Which I have seen decrease?
My soul's at war, and truth bids her
Find out their hidden sepulcher,
To give her troubles peace.
. . . .

I have infected with impure
Disorders my first years.
But I'll to penitence inure
Those that succeed. There is no cure
Nor antidote but tears.

William Habington: *Time, Where Didst
Thou Those Years Inter?* (17th cent.)

He that on his pillow lies
Tear-enbalmed before he dies,
Carries like a sheep his life,
To meet the sacrificer's knife,
And for eternity is prest,
Sad bell-wether to the rest.

James Shirley: *The Passing Bell.* (17th
cent.)

For while my former flames remain
within,
Repentance is but want of pow'r to sin.

Dryden: *Palamon and Arcite,* 3. (17th
cent.)

Repentance is the virtue of weak minds.

Dryden: *The Indian Emperor,* 3, 1. (17th
cent.)

I view my crime, but kindle at the view,
Repent old pleasures, and solicit new.

Pope: *Eloisa to Abelard.* (18th cent.)

Remorse is easy enough, but repentance
means love; and a soul that has lost her
lover has lost her own power of loving.

R. H. Benson: *Christ in the Church.* (20th
cent.)

Reprobation

As men are ordained to eternal life
through the providence of God, it likewise is part of that providence to permit
some to fall away from that end; this is
called reprobation.

St. Thomas Aquinas: *Summa Theologica,*
1, 23, 3. (13th cent.)

See also Predestination

Republic

For I mean in its own place to show
that . . . Rome never was a republic, I
grant there was a republic of a certain
kind, and certainly much better administered by the more ancient Romans than
by their modern representatives.

St. Augustine: *The City of God,* 2, 21.
(5th cent.)

For the people, according to his [i.e.
Cicero's] definition, is an assemblage
associated by a common acknowledgment of right and by a community of
interests.

St. Augustine: *The City of God,* 19, 21.
(5th cent.)

Consequently, if the republic is the weal
of the people, and there is no people if
it be not associated by a common acknowledgment of right, and if there is
no right where there is no justice, then
most certainly it follows that there is no
republic where there is no justice.

St. Augustine: *The City of God,* 19, 21.
(5th cent.)

But if we discard this definition of a
people, and, assuming another, say that
a people is an assemblage of reasonable
beings bound together by a common
agreement as to the objects of their love,

then, in order to discover the character of any people, we have only to observe what they love. . . . And it will be a superior people in proportion as it is bound together by higher interests, inferior in proportion as it is bound together by lower. According to this definition of ours, the Roman people is a people, and its weal is without doubt a commonwealth or republic.

> St. Augustine: *The City of God*, 19, 24. (5th cent.)

For in some soils republics will not grow.

> Dryden. (17th cent.)

Catholicity in religion sanctions republicanism in politics, and republicanism in politics favors Catholicity in religion.

> I. T. Hecker: *The Church and the Age.* (1887)

Republics live by virtue. Monarchies and empires may rely on physical force, or on the wisdom and goodness of the one or the few. Republics are ruled by the many, and the virtue of the people is the life of the nation.

> Archb. Ireland: *American Citizenship.* (Chicago, Feb. 22, 1895)

See also Catholic Church in the United States; Church and State in the United States; Democracy; Government; State

Reputation

A woman's reputation is a tender plant; it is like a fair flower which withers at the slightest blast and fades away at the first breath of wind.

> St. Jerome: *Letters*, 79, 8. (5th cent.)

Conscience and reputation are two things. Conscience is due to yourself, reputation to your neighbor.

> St. Augustine. (5th cent.)

If you aim at perfection you should shun not only things bad in themselves, but things that have the appearance of evil. In the one case you have regard to your conscience, in the other to your reputation.

> St. Bernard: *On Consideration*, 3, 4. (12th cent.)

It sometimes happens that a person, when not known, shines by a good reputation, who, when he is present, is disagreeable to them that see him.

> Thomas a Kempis: *The Imitation of Christ*, 1, 8. (15th cent.)

He that hath an ill name is half hanged.

> John Heywood: *Proverbs*, 2, 6. (16th cent.)

When thoughts as to whether people like you or not come into your mind, do not even look at them, for they will always like you as much as God wills.

> St. Francis de Sales: *Letters to Persons in Religion*, 5, 5. (17th cent.)

Reputation is but a signboard to show where virtue lodges.

> St. Francis de Sales: *Introduction to the Devout Life*, 3, 7. (17th cent.)

Excessive fear of losing a good name indicates a great distrust of its foundation, which is the truth of a good life.

> St. Francis de Sales: *Introduction to the Devout Life*, 3, 7. (17th cent.)

Trouble not yourself about human judgments.

> St. Francis de Sales: *Letters to Persons in the World*, 4, 1. (17th cent.)

If you wish nothing to cross your life, desire not the reputation or the glory of the world.

> St. Francis de Sales: *Letters to Persons in the World*, 4, 1. (17th cent.)

So long as God is served, what does it matter whether it be by the exaltation or by the defamation of our good reputation?

> J. P. Camus: *The Spirit of St. Francis de Sales*, 8, 8. (17th cent.)

Would you have men think well of you? Hold your tongue.

> Pascal: *Pensées.* (17th cent.)

Requiem

Eternal rest grant unto them, O Lord; and let perpetual light shine upon them. A hymn, O God, becometh Thee in Sion; and a vow shall be paid to Thee in Jerusalem. Hear my prayer: all flesh shall come to Thee (4 Esdr. 2, 34; Ps. 64, 2). (Requiem aeternam dona eis, Domine; et lux perpetua luceat eis. . . .)

> Roman Missal, Introit of Masses for the Dead. (Lib. Antiph., ca. 7th cent.)

Request

Suspect the man on whose behalf you are entreated: the man who asks for himself is already judged.

> St. Bernard: *On Consideration*, 4, 4. (To Pope Eugenius III) (12th cent.)

> Honorable request
> By silence and performance should be paid.

> Dante: *Inferno, Canto 24.* (Tr. Binyon) (14th cent.)

Requirement

We must not be unjust and require from ourselves what is not in ourselves.

> St. Francis de Sales: *Letters to Persons in the World*, 2, 17. (17th cent.)

Resignation

Blessed are they who do not their own will on earth, for God will do it in heaven above.

> St. Francis de Sales: *Letters to Persons in Religion*, 3, 17. (17th cent.)

Whosoever takes pleasure in God desires faithfully to please God, and in order to please Him, desires to resign himself to Him.

> St. Francis de Sales: *Treatise on the Love of God*, 8, 1. (17th cent.)

The readiness to keep his eyes blindfolded, to follow the divine call wherever it may lead him, was not, for [Cardinal] Newman, the caprice of a moment; it was the inspiration of a long, and in some ways a difficult life. It is an attitude God loves to find in the soul; must (humanly speaking) find in a soul if He is to do anything with it. His 'sacrament of the present moment,' keeping all your mind concentrated on the thing you ought to be doing here and now, because it is His will, blindfolding yourself to what the future has in store, never wasting yourself on day-dreams and unnecessary alarms—that is the key-attitude of Christian resignation. And it will never be more justly phrased than it was, by a great and sensitive soul, a hundred years ago.

> R. Knox: *Stimuli.* (Reference is to hymn: *Lead, Kindly Light*) (20th cent.)

Resoluteness

Through thick and thin.

> Chaucer: *The Reeves Tale.* (14th cent.)

> Give me the man that with undaunted spirit
> Dares give occasion of a tragedy,
> And be content for his more after-merit
> To be down beaten from felicity:
>> To th'end that with a fierce amount he may
>> Re-bless himself in spite of fortune's day.

> Anthony Copley: *A Fig For Fortune.* (16th cent.)

> How easy 'tis when destiny proves kind,
> With full spread sails to run before the wind,

But those that 'gainst stiff gales laveer-
ing go
Must be at once resolv'd and skilful
too.

> Dryden: *Astraea Redux.* (17th cent.)

Pride at having been resolute compen-
sates for lost comfort.

> R. H. Benson: *The Sentimentalists.* (20th
> cent.)

Resolution

No one likes his own good resolutions
noised about, both from mere common
delicacy, and from fear lest he should
not be able to fear them.

> Card. Newman: *Apologia pro Vita Sua,* 4.
> (19th cent.)

Every broken resolution leaves the mark
of its teeth on us.

> John Ayscough: *The Universe.* (20th
> cent.)

Responsibility

If there is any truth brought home to
us by conscience, it is this, that we are
personally responsible for what we do,
that we have no means of shifting our
responsibility, and that dereliction of
duty involves punishment.

> Card. Newman: *Grammar of Assent,* 10.
> (19th cent.)

We are responsible for doing what we
can.

> R. H. Benson: *The Sentimentalists.* (20th
> cent.)

Rest

Rest comes at length, though life be
long and dreary;
The day must dawn, and darksome
night be past.

> F. Faber: *The Pilgrims of the Night.*
> (19th cent.)

Restraint

No man loveth his fetters, be they made
of gold.

> John Heywood: *Proverbs,* 1, 8. (16th
> cent.)

Resurrection

Let us consider, beloved, how the Lord
is continually revealing to us the resurrection that is to be. Of this He has constituted the Lord Jesus Christ the first-
fruits, by raising Him from the dead.

> Pope St. Clement I: *Letter to the
> Corinthians,* 24, 1. (1st cent.)

Let none of you say that this flesh is not
judged and does not rise again . . . for as
you were called in the flesh, you shall
also come in the flesh.

> So-called Second Epistle to the Corinthians.
> (2nd cent.)

The root of all good works is the hope
of the resurrection; for the expectation
of the reward nerves the soul to good
works.

> St. Cyril of Jerusalem: *Catechetical
> Discourses,* 18, 1. (4th cent.)

Faith therefore in the resurrection of the
dead, is a great commandment and doctrine of the Holy Catholic Church; great
and most necessary, though gainsaid by
many, yet surely warranted by the truth.

> St. Cyril of Jerusalem: *Catechetical
> Discourses,* 18, 1. (4th cent.)

Faith maintains this principle and we
must believe it: Neither the soul nor the
human body suffers complete annihila-
tion; the wicked arise again for punishment beyond imagination, while the
good rise again for everlasting life.

> St. Augustine: *De Doctrina Christiana,* 1,
> 21, 19. (4th cent.)

The bodies of the saints will therefore
rise again free from every defect, from
every deformity, as well as from every
corruption, encumbrance, or hindrance.

In this respect their freedom of action will be as complete as their happiness; and for this reason their bodies have been called 'spiritual,' though undoubtedly they will be bodies and not spirits.

St. Augustine: *Enchiridion,* 91. (5th cent.)

"Nothing is far from God, and I have no fear that He will not know at the end of the world from what place He is to raise me up."

St. Augustine: *Confessions,* 9, 11. (Words of St. Monica before death, when asked whether she was afraid to die in a foreign country.) (5th cent.)

As, then, there are two regenerations, of which I have already made mention, —the one according to faith, and which takes place in the present life by means of baptism; the other according to the flesh, and which shall be accomplished in its incorruption and immortality by means of the great and final judgment— so are there also two resurrections—the one the first and spiritual resurrection, which has place in this life, and preserves us from coming into the second death; the other the second, which does not occur now, but in the end of the world, and which is of the body, not of the soul, and which by the last judgment shall dismiss some into the second death, others into that life which has no death.

St. Augustine: *The City of God,* 20, 6. (5th cent.)

Some say that women shall not rise again in the female sex, but all in the male; but they seem to me wiser who have no hesitation in affirming that all shall rise again in their own sex.

St. Augustine: *The City of God,* 22. (5th cent.)

For the human soul is immortal, and continues after its separation from the body. Yet union with body is essential to it, for by its very nature soul is form of body. Without body it is in an unnatural condition; and what is unnatural cannot go on for ever. Therefore the soul, which is perpetual, is not for ever apart from the body, but will be reunited with it. The soul's immortality, therefore, seems to demand the eventual resurrection of the body.

St. Thomas Aquinas: *Contra Gentes,* 3, 79. (13th cent.)

True Christian hearts cease to lament,
  For grief it is in vain,
For Christ you know was well content
  To suffer bitter pain
That we may come to heaven's bliss,
  There joyfully to sing.
Who doth believe shall never miss
  To have a joyful rising!

Ven. John Thewlis: *The Song of a Happy Rising.* (17th cent.)

    This only can be said:
    He loved us all; is dead;
      May rise again.
But if He rise not? Over the far
      main,
The sun of glory falls indeed: the stars
      are plain.

Lionel Johnson: *A Burden of Easter Vigil.* (19th cent.)

All you that weep, all you that mourn,
  All you that grieving go,
Lift up your eyes, your heads adorn,
  Put off your weeds of woe.
The sorrows of the Passion week
  Like tearful dreams are fled.
For He hath triumphed Whom you seek,
  Is risen—that was dead.

Henry Longan Stuart: *Resurrexit.* (20th cent.)

See also Easter

Reticence

We all keep back lots of things. We don't shout out in the morning from our windows that we've slept very tolerably, and are just going to have our bath.

R. H. Benson: *The Sentimentalists.* (20th cent.)

Retirement

Thus let me live, unseen, unknown,
  Thus unlamented let me die
Steal from the world, and not a stone
  Tell where I lie.

Pope: *Ode on Solitude.* (18th cent.)

Walk sober off before the sprightlier
  age
Comes titt'ring on, and shoves you from
  the stage.

Pope: *Second Epistle of the Second Book
of Horace.* (18th cent.)

Retribution

Such as ye have sown must ye needs reap.

Lydgate: *Assembly of Gods.* (15th cent.)

Reunion of Christians

Imitate the Good Shepherd, Who seeks
for the lost sheep and brings it back on
His shoulder. . . . In thy zeal for the
service of God, aim at winning back to
Him, by the prayers of the Church, all
those who have in any way strayed from
it.

Pope St. Leo I: *Letters,* 171. (5th cent.)

In short, in doctrine, or in discipline
Not one Reform'd, can with another
  join:
But all, from each, as from damnation
  fly;
No union they pretend, but in non-
  popery.

Dryden: *The Hind and the Panther,* 2.
(17th cent.)

See how his Church, adorn'd with ev'ry
  grace,
With open arms, a kind forgiving face,
Stands ready to prevent her long-lost
  sons' embrace.
Not more did Joseph o'er his brethren
  weep,
Nor less himself could from discovery
  keep,
When in the crowd of suppliants they
  were seen,

And in their crew his best-belov'd Benjamin.

Dryden: *The Hind and the Panther,* 2.
(17th cent.)

Our mouth is open to you, to you all of
Greek or other oriental rites who are
separated from the Catholic Church. We
earnestly desire that each and every one
of you should meditate upon the words,
so full of gravity and love, addressed by
Bessarion to your forefathers: "What
answer shall we give to God when He
comes to ask why we have separated from
our brethren: to Him Who, to unite us
and bring us into one fold, came down
from heaven, was incarnate, and was
crucified? What will our defence be in
the eyes of posterity? Oh, my venerable
fathers, we must not suffer this to be, we
must not entertain this thought, we must
not thus so ill provide for ourselves and
for our brethren."

Pope Leo XIII: *Praeclara Gratulationis.*
(June 20, 1894)

It is not for any human motive, but im-
pelled by divine charity and a desire for
the salvation of all, that we advise reconciliation and union with the Church of
Rome; and we mean a perfect and complete union, such as could not subsist in
any way if nothing else was brought
about but a certain kind of agreement in
the tenets of belief and an intercourse of
fraternal love. The true union between
Christians is that which Jesus Christ, the
Author of the Church, instituted and desired, and which consists in a unity of
faith and a unity of government.

Pope Leo XIII: *Praeclara Gratulationis.*
(June 20, 1894)

Nor is there any reason for you to fear
. . . that we or any of our successors will
ever diminish your rights, the privileges
of your patriarchs, or the established
ritual of any one of your churches. It
has been and always will be the intent
and tradition of the Apostolic See to
make a large allowance, in all that is

right and good, for the primitive traditions and special customs of every nation.

> Pope Leo XIII: *Praeclara Gratulationis.*
> (June 20, 1894)

How can hearts be united in perfect charity where minds do not agree in faith?

> Pope Leo XIII: *Praeclara Gratulationis.*
> (June 20, 1894)

Far be it for anyone to diminish or for any reason whatever to pass over anything of this divinely delivered doctrine; whosoever would do so, would rather wish to alienate Catholics from the Church than to bring over to the Church those who dissent from it. Let them return; indeed, nothing is nearer to our heart; let all whose who are wandering far afield from the sheepfold of Christ return; but let it not be by any other road than that which Christ has pointed out.

> Pope Leo XIII: *Testem Benevolentiae.*
> (Jan. 22, 1899)

Jesus Christ is moving His chalice from one place to another throughout the world, extending the frontiers of the Church, augmenting everywhere within her labor and desire in distant preparation for the return of the Christian East to unity, or the end of the fratricidal schisms provoked by the Reformation, or imploring Heaven to make the scales fall from the eyes of the elder race, or extending the secular effort of the missions and solemnly inviting the nations of Asia to share in the plenitude of the priesthood and the government of the churches.

> J. Maritain: *The Things that are not Caesar's.* (20th cent.)

The chief obstacle to union lies in a misunderstanding, a confusion between the spiritual temperament and the culture of one or the other and the Church which is universal. The spirit of Orthodoxy is not the same thing as the Russian spirit; the spirit of Catholicism is not the same

thing as the Latin spirit. Once these things are well and truly realized on both sides, unity will not be far to seek.

> J. Maritain: *The Things that are not Caesar's.* (20th cent.)

The work of reconciliation can be attempted with a firm hope of success only on three conditions; we must rid ourselves of current errors accumulated in the course of centuries with regard to the beliefs and institutions of the Oriental churches. The Easterns, on the other hand, must devote themselves to considering the identity of teaching of the Greek and Latin fathers. Thirdly, there must be an exchange of views between both sides in a high spirit of charity.

> Pope Pius XI: *Consistorial Address.* (Dec. 18, 1924)

A federation of Christians is inconceivable in which each member retains his own opinions and private judgment in matters of faith.

> Pope Pius XI: *Mortalium Animos.* (Jan. 6, 1928)

The unity of Christians cannot otherwise be obtained than by securing the return of the separated to the one true Church of Christ from which they once unhappily withdrew. To the one true Church of Christ, we say, that stands forth before all and that by the will of its Founder will remain forever the same as when He himself established it for the salvation of all mankind.

> Pope Pius XI: *Mortalium Animos.* (Jan. 6, 1928)

The Catholic Church takes no actual part in 'oecumenical' conventions and other assemblies of a similar character. Yet, as numerous pontifical documents show, she has, despite this fact, never ceased, nor will she ever cease to pursue with deepest concern and promote with assiduous prayers to God every endeavor to bring about what was so close to the heart of Christ the Lord, that all who believe in Him *may be made perfect in one* (John, 17, 23).

> Instruction of the Holy Office, *De Motione Oecumenica,* Dec. 20, 1949.

The work of 'reunion' belongs above all to the office and charge of the Church. Hence, it behooves bishops, whom *the Holy Ghost hath placed to rule the Church of God,* to bestow upon it their special attention. They should therefore not only carefully and efficaciously keep this movement under vigilant observation, but also prudently foster and guide it unto the twofold end of assisting those who are in search of the truth and the true Church, and of shielding the faithful from the perils which readily follow in the tread of the movement.

> Instruction of the Holy Office, *De Motione Oecumenica,* Dec. 20, 1949.

Non-Catholics may certainly be told that, in returning to the Church, they will forfeit none of the good that the grace of God had hitherto wrought in their souls, but that the return will bring this to its perfection and final consummation. Yet this must not be represented in such fashion as to create in them the impression that by their return they were making a contribution to the Church of something essential that she lacked in the past. All this must be truly set forth clearly and intelligibly for the double reason that they are really seeking the truth and that outside of the truth no true union can ever be attained.

> Instruction of the Holy Office, *De Motione Oecumenica,* Dec. 1, 1949.

See also Catholic Church; Schism

Revelation, Divine

Knowing all things, therefore, and providing for what is profitable for each one, He revealed that which it was to our profit to know; but what we were unable to bear He kept secret.

> St. John of Damascus: *Exposition of the Orthodox Faith,* 1, 1. (8th cent.)

Human salvation demands the divine disclosure of truths surpassing reason.

> St. Thomas Aquinas: *Summa Theologica,* 1, 1, 1. (13th cent.)

Truths above reason can be believed on authority alone; where that is lacking we have to take hints from the workings of nature.

> St. Thomas Aquinas: *Summa Theologica,* 1-2, 101, 1. (13th cent.)

As prayer is the voice of man to God, so revelation is the voice of God to man.

> Card. Newman: *Grammar of Assent,* 10. (19th cent.)

Divine revelation is imperfect, and therefore subject to a continual and indefinite progress corresponding with the advancement of human reason.

> Proposition condemned by Pius IX in Syllabus of Errors. (1867)

If any one shall say that it is impossible or inexpedient that man should be taught by divine revelation concerning God and the worship to be paid to Him; let him be anathema.

> Vatican Council, Session 3, Canon 2. (Apr. 24, 1870)

If any one shall say that man cannot be raised by divine power to a higher than natural knowledge and perfection, but can and ought by continuous progress to arrive at length of himself at the possession of all that is true and good; let him be anathema.

> Vatican Council, Session 3, Canon 3. (Apr. 24, 1870)

Revelation brings its own solution with it, and we doubt, if men had never had a supernatural revelation, that they would ever have felt either its necessity, or seen its possibility. It is the fact of revelation that stimulates thought, quickens the faculties, and directs the mind to the facts which prove its necessity and possibility.

> O. Brownson: *Brownson's Quarterly Review, Last Series,* 1, 155. (1873)

A Christian cannot live by philosophy. Only the light of Christian revelation gives the end as well as the means of life. It is the same for you as for me and the man in the street. If one has more learning, another has more grace, it is all one.

> Abbot Chapman: *Spiritual Letters.* (20th cent.)

Revelation, constituting the object of Catholic faith, was not completed with the apostles.

> Proposition condemned by Decree of Holy Office, *Lamentabili,* June 3, 1907.

That the Christian revelation is the last supernatural revelation the world can expect, is the verdict not only of theology, but of experience. Bethlehem has exhausted the world's capacity for worship. Only one great religion has arisen since; a palpable throw-back to the Old Testament. All our other adventures have been variations of the Christian theme; the dead gods do not rise.

> R. Knox: *Stimuli.* (20th cent.)

The truths that have to do with God and the relations between God and men completely surpass the sensible order and demand self-surrender and self-abnegation in order to be put into practice and to influence practical life. Now the human intellect in gaining the knowledge of such truths is hampered both by the activity of the senses and the imagination, and by evil passions arising from original sin. Hence men easily persuade themselves in such matters that what they do not wish to believe is false or at least doubtful. It is for this reason that divine revelation must be considered morally necessary so that those religious and moral truths which are not of their nature beyond the reach of reason in the present condition of the human race may be known with a firm certainty and with freedom from all error.

> Pope Pius XII: *Humani Generis.* (Apr. 12, 1950)

Revelation, Private

I can no more . . . I cannot; such things have been revealed to me that what I have written seems but straw.

> St. Thomas Aquinas. (Reply to his companion Reginald, who urged the saint to continue with his writing.) (ca. 1274)

Every revelation of truth felt with interior savor and spiritual joy is a secret whispering of God in the ear of a pure soul.

> Walter Hilton: *Scale of Perfection,* 2, 46. (14th cent.)

Revenge

Vengeance is not cured by another vengeance, nor a wrong by another wrong; but each increaseth and aggreggeth the other.

> Chaucer: *The Tale of Melibeus.* (14th cent.)

Tit for tat.

> John Heywood: *Proverbs,* 2, 4. (16th cent.)

Prompt to revenge, not daring to forgive,
Our lives unteach the doctrines we believe.

> Dryden. (17th cent.)

Reverence

Let us fear the Lord Jesus, Whose blood was given for us; let us respect our leaders; let us honor the presbyters; let us teach the young in the school of the fear of God.

> Pope St. Clement I: *Letter to the Corinthians,* 21, 6. (1st cent.)

Revolution

Furthermore, it rather seems, that to proceed against the cruelty of tyrants is an action to be undertaken, not through the private presumption of a few, but by public authority. First of all, if to provide itself with a king belongs to the right of the multitude, it is not unjust that the king set up by that multitude be destroyed or his power restricted, if he tyrannically abuse the royal power. It must not be thought that such a multitude is acting unfaithfully in deposing the tyrant, even though it has previously subjected itself to him in perpetuity; because he himself has deserved that the covenant with his subjects should not be kept, since, in ruling the multitude, he did not act faithfully as the office of a king demands.

> St. Thomas Aquinas: *The Governance of Rulers*, 1, 6. (13th cent.)

If a lawful king rules tyrannically, and there is no other way for the kingdom to protect itself except to depose him, it is lawful for the whole community by a solemn act to do so. This action is sanctioned by the law of nature, which always allows us to repel force by force, as well as by the terms of the original contract under which the first king accepted sovereignty from the people.

> F. Suarez: *De Juramento Fidelitatis Regis Angliae*, 4. (17th cent.)

The art of revolutionizing and overturning states is to undermine established customs, by going back to their origin, in order to mark their want of justice.

> Pascal: *Pensées*, 4. (17th cent.)

Inciting to revolution is treason, not only against man, but also against God.

> Pope Leo XIII: *Immortale Dei*. (Nov. 1, 1885)

To wish to change the face of the earth without first changing one's heart (which no man can do of his own strength) is to undertake a work that is purely destructive. Perhaps indeed if omnipotent love did truly transform our hearts, the exterior work of reform would already be half done.

> J. Maritain: *Freedom in the Modern World*. (20th cent.)

A Christian revolution can succeed only by the use of just those means which are beyond the ability of others to use. If faith is able to move mountains, is it powerless to shift the mighty from their seats? If Christians, who live by faith in their private lives, lay aside their faith when they approach the things of political and social life, they must be content to be towed like slaves in the wake of history.

> J. Maritain: *Freedom in the Modern World*. (20th cent.)

The revolutions of men change nothing. The only influence that can really upset the injustice and iniquity of men is the power that breathes in Christian tradition, renewing our participation in the life that is the light of men.

> Thomas Merton: *Seeds of Contemplation*. (20th cent.)

Reward

Requital for more important works is based on prudent management of lesser ones.

> St. Basil: *The Morals*, 18, 3. (4th cent.)

You must lovingly leave some work to others, and not seek to have all the crowns.

> St. Francis de Sales: *Letters to Persons in Religion*, 2, 6. (17th cent.)

Rhetoric

Rhetoric is the science of speaking well in civil questions for the purpose of persuading to what is just and good.

> St. Isidore: *Etymologies*, 2, 1. (7th cent.)

Rhyme

Yea, marry, now it is somewhat, for now it is rhyme, whereas before it was neither rhyme nor reason.

> Saying of St. Thomas More. (To a friend who had rendered in verse an indifferent book.) (16th cent.)

Rhyme is the rock on which thou art to wreck.

> Dryden: *Absalom and Achitophel.* (17th cent.)

Rich

The rich in this world cannot be made useful for the Lord, unless their riches have been cut out of them.

> Shepherd of Hermas, Vision 3, 6, 6. (2nd cent.)

The rich man is not one who is in possession of much, but one who gives much.

> St. John Chrysostom: *Homilies.* (4th cent.)

> The guarantee
From Lambeth that the rich can never burn,
And even promising a safe return.

> Hilaire Belloc: *To Dives.* (20th cent.)

Rich and Poor

He is rich enough who is poor with Christ.

> St. Jerome: *Letters,* 14, 1. (4th cent.)

He was at an ebb, though he be now afloat.

> John Heywood: *Proverbs,* 1, 11. (16th cent.)

Every man basteth the fat hog we see;
But the lean shall burn ere he basted be.

> John Heywood: *Proverbs,* 1, 11. (16th cent.)

Be poor in folly, rich in all but sin;
So by your death your glory shall begin.

> Thomas Lodge: *A Solitary Life Commended.* (16th cent.)

He is rich in spirit who has his riches in his spirit or his spirit in his riches; he is poor in spirit who has no riches in his spirit, nor his spirit in his riches.

> St. Francis de Sales: *Introduction to the Devout Life,* 3, 14. (17th cent.)

He who seeks only the glory of God finds it in poverty and in abundance.

> St. Francis de Sales: *Letters to Persons in Religion,* 3, 15. (17th cent.)

The poor man, rich in faith, who toils for the love of God and is generous of the little fruit of his labors, is much nearer to heaven than the rich man who spends a fortune in good works from no higher motive than his natural inclination to benevolence.

> Archb. Ullathorne: *Humility and Patience.* (19th cent.)

That which is large enough for the rich to covet is large enough for the poor to defend.

> G. K. Chesterton: *The Napoleon of Notting Hill.* (20th cent.)

Riches

Riches are not forbidden, but the pride of them is.

> St. John Chrysostom: *Homilies.* (4th cent.)

Just as riches are an impediment to virtue in the wicked, so in the good they are an aid of virtue.

> St. Ambrose: *Explanation of St. Luke,* 8, 85. (4th cent.)

If you lack earthly riches, let them not be sought in the world by evil works; but if you possess them, let them be laid up in heaven by good works. The manly Christian spirit (*animum virilem et Christianum*) ought neither to be elated by their accession nor depressed by their departure.

> St. Augustine: *Letter 189.* (5th cent.)

Although the rich man from his mines of gold
Dig treasure which his mind can never fill,
And lofty neck with precious pearls enfold,
And his fat fields with many oxen till,

Yet biting cares will never leave his head,
Nor will his wealth attend him being dead.

Boethius: *De Consolatione Philosophiae,* 3, 3. (6th cent.)

Woe also to the rich, who have their consolation here, for when the poor shall go into the kingdom of God they shall stand lamenting without.

Thomas a Kempis: *The Imitation of Christ,* 3, 58. (15th cent.)

If he be called stout that hath fortitude, he wise that hath wisdom, he learned that hath the gift of languages, why not he rich in goodness, who hath riches? I must, therefore, conclude that riches are not to be numbered among good things.

St. Thomas More. (16th cent.)

Riches bringeth oft harm, and never fear.

John Heywood: *Proverbs,* 1, 12. (16th cent.)

Riches prick us with a thousand troubles in getting them, as many cares in preserving them, and with yet more anxieties in spending them, and with grief in losing them.

J. P. Camus: *The Spirit of St. Francis de Sales,* 16, 4. (17th cent.)

It is not a sin to have riches, but it is a sin to fix our hearts upon them.

St. John Baptist de la Salle: *Les devoirs du chrétien,* 14. (18th cent.)

To whom can riches give repute or trust
Content or pleasure, but the good and just?

Pope: *An Essay on Man,* 4. (18th cent.)

It is certainly true of intellectual, as of all other riches, that they who possess them shall find difficulty in entering into the kingdom of God.

R. H. Benson: *The Light Invisible.* (20th cent.)

See also Possessions; Wealth

Ridicule

Yes, I am proud; I must be proud to see
Men, not afraid of God, afraid of me;
Safe from the bar, the pulpit and the throne,
Yet touch'd and shamed by ridicule alone.

Pope: *Epilogue to the Satires,* 2. (18th cent.)

All fools have still an itching to deride,
And fain would be upon the laughing side.

Pope: *An Essay on Criticism,* 1. (18th cent.)

Right

Grant to us, O Lord, we beseech Thee, the spirit always to think and do such things as are right; that we who cannot exist without Thee, may be able to live according to Thy will.

Roman Missal, Collect for Eighth Sunday after Pentecost. (Leonine, ca. 5th cent.)

O God, from Whom all good things come: grant to us Thy suppliants that by Thy inspiration we may think those things that are right, and do them under Thy guidance.

Roman Missal, Collect for Fifth Sunday after Easter. (Gelasian, 5th to 7th cent.)

Right (*jus*) is a relation existing between human beings in their dealings with each other and in their dealings with things. When right is maintained, human society is preserved, but when it is neglected society is corrupted.

Dante: *Monarchy,* 2. (14th cent.)

For who can be secure of private right,
If sovereign sway may be dissolv'd by might?

Dryden: *Absalom and Achitophel.* (17th cent.)

Whatever is, is right.

Pope: *An Essay on Man,* 1. (18th cent.)

For modes of faith let graceless zealots
  fight;
His can't be wrong whose life is in the
  right.

> Pope: *An Essay on Man,* 3. (18th cent.)

For right is right, since God is God;
  And right the day must win;
To doubt would be disloyalty,
  To falter would be sin!

> F. Faber: *The Right must Win.* (19th
> cent.)

Right consists in material fact. Human
duties are an empty word, and all human
facts have the force of right.

> Proposition condemned by Pius IX in
> Syllabus of Errors. (1867)

To do and dare, and die at need,
  But while life lasts, to fight—
For right or wrong a simple creed,
  But simplest for the right.

> J. J. Roche: *Gettysburg.* (19th cent.)

Anyone who possesses a natural right
may make use of all legitimate means to
protect it, and to safeguard it from violation.

> Card. O'Connell: *Pastoral Letter on the
> Laborer's Rights.* (1912)

We must not be so insistent upon demanding our rights as in discharging our
obligations.

> Pope Benedict XV: *Letter to the Bishop
> of Bergamo.* (1920)

Who has not known how pleasant 'tis
  to sigh,
"Others, thank God, are less correct
  than I?"

> Ronald Knox: *Absolute and Abitofhell.*
> (20th cent.)

Righteousness

The life of good men is a living study.

> Pope St. Gregory I: *Morals,* 24, 16. (6th
> cent.)

It is a small thing to keep righteousness,
unless you love it as well.

> St. Bernard: *On Consideration,* 3, 2. (12th
> cent.)

Ripe

Soon ripe, soon rotten.

> John Heywood: *Proverbs,* 1, 10. (16th
> cent.)

Rising

Awake, awake, the morn will never
  rise,
Till she can dress her beauty at your
  eyes.

> Sir William Davenant: *Morning.* (17th
> cent.)

Rite

See Divine Office; Liturgy; Mass—Rites
and Ceremonies

Ritual

I come of Anglo-Irish stock, and like
most Anglo-Irishmen I have some difficulty in understanding the Englishman's
passion for ritual. The Englishman not
only enjoys ritual; he is extremely good
at it.

> Arnold Lunn: *Now I See.* (20th cent.)

River

Rivers are roads that move.

> Pascal: *Pensées,* 7. (17th cent.)

The river ran on—and on—and on—
  Day and night, and night and day;
Going and going, and never gone.

> Abram Ryan: *Song of the River.* (19th
> cent.)

Wide waters in the waste; or, out of
  reach,
  Rough Alpine falls where late a gla-
    cier hung;
Or rivers groping for the alien beach,
  Through continents, unsung.

Nay, not these nameless, these remote,
 alone;
  But all the streams from all the water-
    sheds—
Peneus, Danube, Nile—are the un-
 known
  Young in their ancient beds.

> Alice Meynell: *Rivers Unknown to Song.*
> (20th cent.)

Here, in the midnight of the solemn
 wood,
  He heard a roar as of a mighty wind,
  The onward rush of waters unconfined
Trampling in legions through the solitude.
Then lo! before him swept the conquering flood,
  Free as the freedom of the truthstrong mind
  Which hills of doubt could neither
 hide nor bind,
Which, all in vain, the valley mounds
 withstood!

> John J. Rooney: *Marquette on the Shores
> of the Mississippi.* (20th cent.)

Road

Before the Roman came to Rye or out to
 Severn strode,
The rolling English drunkard made the
 rolling English road.
A reeling road, a rolling road, that ram-
 bles round the shire,
And after him the parson ran, the sex-
 ton and the squire.
A merry road, a mazy road, and such as
 we did tread
That night we went to Birmingham by
 way of Beachy Head.

> G. K. Chesterton: *The Rolling English
> Road.* (20th cent.)

The road was a ribbon of moonlight over
the purple moor.

> Alfred Noyes: *The Highwayman.* (20th
> cent.)

Robe

At the foot of the Cross on Calvary
 The soldiers sat and diced,
And one of them was the devil
 And he won the robe of Christ.

> Joyce Kilmer: *The Robe of Christ.* (20th
> cent.)

Robin

The Savior, bowed beneath His Cross,
 climbed up the dreary hill,
And from the agonizing wreath ran
 many a crimson rill;
The cruel Roman thrust Him on with
 unrelenting hand,
Till, staggering slowly 'mid the crowd,
 He fell upon the sand.
A little bird that warbled near, that
 memorable day,
Flitted around and strove to wrench one
 single thorn away;
The cruel spike impaled his breast,—
 and thus 'tis sweetly said,
The robin has his silver vest incarna-
 dined with red.

> J. R. Randall: *Why the Robin's Breast
> Was Red.* (19th cent.)

Roman Church

See Catholic Church; Peter, Saint; Pope

Roman Empire

The Empire of which you are ministers
is the rule of citizens, not of tyrants.

> Tertullian: *Apology,* 2, 14. (3rd cent.)

We know that the great force which
threatens the whole world, the end of the
age itself with its menace of hideous suffering, is delayed by the respite which
the Roman Empire means for us. We do
not wish to experience all that; and
when we pray for its postponement we
are helping forward the continuance of
Rome.

> Tertullian: *Apology,* 32, 1. (3rd cent.)

A Christian is enemy to none, least of all to the Emperor of Rome, whom he knows to be appointed by his God, and so cannot but love and honour; and whose well-being moreover, he must needs desire, with that of the empire over which he reigns so long as the world shall stand—for so long as that shall Rome continue.

Tertullian: *To Scapula,* 2. (3rd cent.)

We have long felt that God is angry, yet we do not try to appease Him. It is our sins which make the barbarians strong, it is our vices which vanquish Rome's soldiers: and, as if there were here too little material for carnage, civil wars have made almost greater havoc among us than the swords of foreign foes. . . . Unhappy are we who are so displeasing to God that He uses the fury of the barbarians to execute His wrath against us.

St. Jerome: *Letters,* 60, 17. (4th cent.)

Thus it was not only that worldly reward might be rendered to worldly men that the Roman Empire was raised to such a height of human glory, but also that the citizens of that everlasting City, during their pilgrimage here, may diligently and soberly consider those examples, and reflect how much love is due to their heavenly country in view of life everlasting, if an earthly city was so much loved by Roman citizens in view of human glory.

St. Augustine: *The City of God,* 5, 16. (5th cent.)

Lo, all mankind has bowed to the kingdom of Remus, different rites say the same and think the same. Thus it is destined that Christian law should bind all the earth in one bond.

Prudentius: *Peristephanon,* 2, 429. (5th cent.)

But that the result of this unspeakable grace might be spread abroad throughout the world, God's providence made ready the Roman Empire, whose growth has reached such limits that the whole multitude of nations are brought into close connexion. For the divinely planned work particularly required that many kingdoms should be leagued together under one empire, so that the preaching of the world might quickly reach to all people, when they were held beneath the rule of one state.

Pope St. Leo I: *Sermons,* 82, 2. (Feast of the Apostles Peter and Paul, June 29) (5th cent.)

Be merciful, O Lord, to the people who hope in Thee, and show the right hand of Thy protection for the defense of the Roman name; that the kingdom which is devoted to Thy majesty may always be defended by Thy power.

Leonine Sacramentary, Collect. (ca. 5th cent.)

Is there anything in history more notorious than the wantonness and pride of the Romans? A race unaccustomed to peace, familiar with tumult; a race to this very day fierce and intractable; who will never submit except when they have no power to resist.

St. Bernard: *On Consideration,* 4, 2. (12th cent.)

The Roman Empire was begotten in the womb of piety.

Dante: *Monarchy,* 2. (Saying adopted by defenders of the empire towards the end of the 12th cent.) (14th cent.)

The Roman people were ordained to rule by nature.

Dante: *Monarchy,* 2. (14th cent.)

Men lived as citizens of one state which they took for granted and which they even regarded as eternal. . . . There was plenty of conflict between armies and individuals as to who should have the advantage of ruling, but never any doubt as to the type of function which the 'emperor' filled, nor as to the type of universally despotic action which he exercised. There were any number of little local liberties and customs which were the pride of the separate places to which they attached, but there was no conception of such local differences being antagonistic to the one life of the one state. That state was, for the men of that time, the world.

> Hilaire Belloc: *Europe and the Faith.* (20th cent.)

Romance

Romance should never begin with sentiment. It should begin with science and end with a settlement.

> Oscar Wilde: *An Ideal Husband,* 3. (19th cent.)

When one is in love, one always begins by deceiving oneself, and one always ends by deceiving others. That is what the world calls a romance.

> Oscar Wilde: *The Picture of Dorian Gray,* 4. (19th cent.)

Apes and ivory, skulls and roses, in junks of old Hong-Kong,
Gliding over a sea of dreams to a haunted shore of song.

> Alfred Noyes: *Apes and Ivory.* (20th cent.)

Rome

Nothing deathless there is in the whole fabric of this universe; neither this sphere nor the kingdoms of men, nor golden Rome, nor sea nor land, nor the fiery stars of the heavens.

> Juvencus: *Gospel Epic.* (Tr. Kuhnmuench) (4th cent.)

The city which had taken the whole world was itself taken.

> St. Jerome: *Letters,* 127, 12. (With reference to the capture of Rome by Alaric in 410 A.D.) (5th cent.)

My mother, having joined me at Milan, found that the church there did not fast on Saturdays as at Rome, and was at a loss what to do. I consulted St. Ambrose, of holy memory, who replied: "When I am at Rome, I fast on a Saturday; when I am at Milan, I do not. Follow the custom of the church where you are."

> St. Augustine: *Letter 2,* 18. (Origin of saying: When at Rome, do as the Romans do [?]) (4th cent.)

For these are the men, through whom the light of Christ's gospel shone on thee, O Rome, and through whom thou, who wast the teacher of error, wast made the disciple of truth. . . . These are they who promoted thee to such glory, that being made a holy nation, a chosen people, a priestly and royal state [cf. 1 Peter 2, 9], and the head of the world through the blessed Peter's holy See thou didst attain a wider sway by the worship of God than by earthly government.

> Pope St. Leo I: *Sermons,* 82, 1. (Feast of the Apostles Peter and Paul) (5th cent.)

O happy Rome! thou art empurpled by
The precious blood of princes; thou canst vie
  In beauty with the world; not by thine own,
  But by their merits, is thy glory known,
Whose blessed bones beneath thy pavement lie.

> St. Paulinus of Aquileia: *Felix per Omnes Festum.* (Tr. D. Donahoe) (8th cent.)

O Rome illustrious, of the world empress!
Over all cities thou queen in thy goodliness!
Red with the roseate blood of the martyrs, and
White with the lilies of virgins at God's right hand!
Welcome we sing to thee; ever we bring to thee
Blessings, and pay to thee praise for eternity.

> Anonymous: *O Roma nobilis orbis et domina.* (Tr. J. A. Symonds) (Pilgrim song) (9th or 10th cent.)

Rome is the capital of the world.

> Pope Innocent II. (In letter to the Second Lateran Council.) (12th cent.)

A thousand roads lead men forever to Rome.

> Alain de Lille: *Book of Parables,* 591. (12th cent.)

Right as diverse paths lead diverse folk the right way to Rome.

> Chaucer: *A Treatise on the Astrolabe.* (14th cent.)

Rome was not built in one day.

> John Heywood: *Proverbs,* 1, 11. (16th cent.)

Make the most of Rome. Do you see the dead corpse of that imperial city? What can be glorious in life, if such wealth and beauty has come to nothing? But who has stood firm in these wretched changes—what survives? The relics of the saints and the chair of the Fisherman.

> Bl. Edmund Campion: *Letter to Gregory Martin.* (16th cent.)

See the wild waste of all-devouring years,
How Rome her own sad sepulchre appears,
With nodding arches, broken temples spread,
The very tombs now vanish'd like their dead.

> Pope: *Moral Essays,* 5. (18th cent.)

O Mary! Mother Mary! our tears are flowing fast,
For mighty Rome, St. Philip's home, is desolate and waste;
There are wild beasts in her palaces far fiercer and more bold
Than those that lick'd the martyrs' feet in heathen days of old.

> F. Faber: *St. Philip's Home.* (19th cent.)

At last, the dream of youth
Stands fair and bright before me,
The sunshine of the home of truth
Falls tremulously o'er me.

And tower, and spire, and lofty dome
In brightest skies are gleaming;
Walk I, today, the ways of Rome,
Or am I only dreaming?

> A. Ryan: *In Rome.* (19th cent.)

The eternity of Rome, then, if it be not an exact truth, is nevertheless no mere rhetorical exaggeration. It denotes the fact that Rome has been chosen of God as the center of His kingdom, which is eternal, as the depository of His eternal truths, as the fountain of His graces which lead men to a higher life, as the witness and guardian of law and principles of which the sanction and the fruit are eternal.

> Card. Manning: *Discourse before the Accademia of the Quiriti.* (1863)

All roads lead to Rome, which is one reason why many people never get there.

> G. K. Chesterton: *Orthodoxy.* (20th cent.)

Rome, the herald, the mother and guardian of civilization and the eternal values of life; this Rome which its greatest historian already called, as if by divine instinct, *caput orbis terrarum* (capital of the world, Livy, 1, 16) and whose destiny is a mystery which is unfolded through the centuries. . . .

> Pope Pius XII: *Address on Easter Sunday.* (March 28, 1948)

See also Peter, Saint; Peter and Paul, Saints; Pope

Rosary

She wore a coral trinket on her arm,
A set of beads, the gaudies tricked in green,
Whence hung a golden brooch of brightest sheen
On which there first was graven a crowned A,
And lower, *Amor vincit omnia.*

> Chaucer: *Canterbury Tales: Prologue.* (Tr. Coghill) (14th cent.)

The messenger from God's high throne
His secret counsel making known
Hails Mary, child of David's race,
God's Virgin Mother, full of grace.

Roman Breviary, Feast of the Holy Rosary
(Oct. 7), hymn *Coelestis aulae nuntius* at
Vespers. (Tr. A. McDougall) (Fr. A.
Ricchini, 18th cent.)

O God, Whose only-begotten Son, by His
life, death, and resurrection, hath purchased for us a reward of eternal salvation; grant, we beseech Thee, that meditating on these mysteries in the most holy
rosary of the blessed Virgin Mary, we
may both imitate what they contain and
obtain what they promise.

Roman Missal, Collect for the Feast
(Oct. 7). (18th cent.)

Sweet, blessed beads! I would not part
With one of you for richest gem
That gleams in kingly diadem;
Ye know the history of my heart.

Abram Ryan: *My Beads.* (19th cent.)

Some people do not like to take the medicine that would heal them, and call it
nonsense. The rosary is exactly that medicine which cures an amazing deal of nonsense. Call it spiritual homeopathy if
you like. Many a proud spirit has been
brought down by it—many a faddy spirit
has been made patient by it. Many a
queasy spirit has been made strong by
it. Many a distracted spirit has become
recollected by it. *The weak things of this
world hath God chosen to confound the
strong.*

Archb. Ullathorne: *Letters in the Oscation.*
(19th cent.)

And I see you where you stand
With your life held in your hand
As a rosary of days.
And your thoughts in calm arrays,
And your innocent prayers are told
On your rosary of days.
And the young days and the old
With their quiet prayers did meet
When the chaplet was complete.

Alice Meynell: *Soeur Monique: a Rondeau
by Couperin.* (19th cent.)

Rose

With sweetness fresh as any rose.

Lydgate: *Troy Book,* 5. (15th cent.)

When I admire the rose,
That nature makes repose
In you the best of many,
More fair and blest than any,
And see how curious art
Hath decked every part,
I think with doubtful view
Whether you be the rose, or the rose
is you.

Thomas Lodge: *William Longbeard.*
(16th cent.)

It is only weak heads that are made to
ache with the scent of roses.

Jean Pierre Camus: *The Spirit of St.
Francis de Sales,* 8, 3. (17th cent.)

What would the rose with all her pride
be worth,
Were there no sun to call her brightness forth?

Thomas Moore: *Love Alone.* (19th cent.)

Rose of the desert! thus should woman
be
Shining uncourted, lone and safe, like
thee.

Thomas Moore: *Rose of the Desert.* (19th
cent.)

Rose of the garden! such is woman's
lot—
Worshipp'd while blooming—when
she fades, forgot.

Thomas Moore: *Rose of the Desert.* (19th
cent.)

Rose, thou art the sweetest flower
That ever drank the amber shower;
Rose, thou art the fondest child
Of dimpled spring, the wood-nymph
wild.

Thomas Moore: *Odes of Anacreon,* 45.
(19th cent.)

A rose I marked, and might have
  plucked; but she
Blushed as she bent, imploring me to
  spare her,
Nor spoil her beauty by such rivalry.

> Aubrey de Vere: *Flowers I Would Bring.*
> (19th cent.)

The fairest things have fleetest end;
  Their scent survives their close,
But the rose's scent is bitterness
  To him that loved the rose!

> F. Thompson: *Daisy.* (19th cent.)

The red rose whispers of passion,
  And the white rose breathes of love;
Oh, the red rose is a falcon,
  And the white rose is a dove.

But I send you a cream-white rosebud
  With a flush on its petal tips;
For the love that is purest and sweetest
  Has a kiss of desire on the lips.

> J. B. O'Reilly: *A White Rose.* (19th
> cent.)

  It seemed too late for roses
    When I walked abroad today,
  October stood in silence,
    By the hedges all the way:
  Yet did I hear a singing,
    And I saw a red rose-tree:
  In fields so gray with autumn
    How could song or roses be?

> Michael Earls: *An Autumn Rose-tree.*
> (20th cent.)

Though spring come late, and summer
  soon,
And June make summer's gift com-
  plete,
The life of a rose is sadly fleet,
And fleet are the dancing feet of June.
If you will listen when the wind is
  sweet,
You'll hear the roses speak to the moon.

> J. Corson Miller: *Roses.* (20th cent.)

Or risen from play at your pale raiment's hem
  God, grown adventurous from all
  time's repose,

Of your tall body climbed the ivory
  Tower
  And kissed upon your mouth the
  mystic Rose.

> G. K. Chesterton: *A Little Litany.* (20th
> cent.)

Rosemary

  The humble rosemary
Whose sweets are so thanklessly shed
To scent the desert and the dead.

> Thomas Moore: *Lalla Rookh: Light of the
> Harem.* (19th cent.)

Rowing

Faintly as tolls the evening chime,
Our voices keep tune and our oars keep
  time.

> Thomas Moore: *A Canadian Boat-song.*
> (19th cent.)

Ruin

We build with strength the deep tower
  wall
  That shall be shattered thus and thus.
And fair and great are court and hall,
  But *how* fair—this is not for us,
Who know the lack that lurks in all.

> Alice Meynell: *Builders of Ruins.* (19th
> cent.)

Rule

Every rule is adapted to a certain class of
things. If it be transferred to another its
truth is immediately exposed to distor-
tion.

> John of Salisbury: *Policraticus,* 2, 19, 111.
> (12th cent.)

Nay, if riches rule the roast,
Behold what cause I have to boast!

> John Heywood: *Four Plays.* (16th cent.)

The rule is far from plain, where all dissent.

> Dryden: *The Hind and the Panther,* **2.**
> (17th cent.)

Ruler

Rulers are custodians of the decrees of God.

> St. Basil: *The Morals,* 79. (4th cent.)

We pray for all rulers, may they have a peaceable life; and for the rest of the Catholic Church.

> Sacramentary of Serapion, Prayer of the Faithful (27). (4th cent.)

But we say that they [Christian Emperors] are happy if they rule justly; if they are not lifted up amid the praises of those who pay them sublime honors, and the obsequiousness of those who salute them with an excessive humility, but remember that they are men; if they make their power the handmaid of His majesty by using it for the greatest possible extension of His worship; if they fear, love, worship God; if more than their own kingdom they love that kingdom in which they are not afraid to have partners; if they are slow to punish, ready to pardon; if they apply that punishment as necessary to government and defence of the republic, and not in order to gratify their own enmity; if they grant pardon, not that iniquity may go unpunished, but with the hope that the transgressor may amend his ways; if they compensate with the lenity of mercy and the liberality of benevolence for whatever severity they may be compelled to decree; if their luxury is as much restrained as it might have been unrestrained; if they prefer to govern depraved desires rather than any nation whatever; and if they do all these things, not through ardent desire of empty glory, but through love of eternal felicity, not neglecting to offer to the true God, Who is their God, for their sins, the sacrifices of humility, contrition, and prayer.

> St. Augustine: *The City of God,* 5, 24. (5th cent.)

In this world no one rules by mere love; if you are but amiable, you are no hero; to be powerful, you must be strong, and to have dominion you must have a genius for organizing.

> Card. Newman: *Historical Sketches,* 3. (19th cent.)

The essential function of authority is to safeguard and develop freedom. In Plato's golden phrase, rulers should be 'craftsmen of freedom.'

> V. McNabb: *Thoughts Twice-dyed.* (20th cent.)

See also Government; King; State

Rumor

Even when it brings some truth with it, rumor is not free from the flaw of falsehood, for it ever takes away from, adds to, and alters the truth.

> Tertullian: *The Christian's Defence.* (3rd cent.)

The flying rumors gather'd as they roll'd,
Scarce any tale was sooner heard than told;
And all who told it added something new,
And all who heard it made enlargements too.

> Pope: *The Temple of Fame.* (18th cent.)

When rumors increase, and when there is abundance of noise and clamor, believe the second report.

> Pope: *Letter to William Trumbull.* (18th cent.)

S

Sabbath

O what their joy and their glory must
be,—
Those endless sabbaths the blessed ones
see!
Crown to the valiant: to weary ones
rest:
God shall be all, and in all ever blest.

Abelard: *O quanta qualia sunt illa sabbata.*
(Tr. J. Neale) (12th cent.)

And never broke the Sabbath, but for
gain.

Dryden: *Absalom and Achitophel,* 1.
(17th cent.)

See Christians, Jews, one heavy Sabbath
keep,
And all the western world believe and
sleep.

Pope: *The Dunciad,* 3. (18th cent.)

See also Sunday

Sack

An old sack axeth (asketh) much patch-
ing.

John Heywood: *Proverbs,* 2, 2. (16th
cent.)

It is a bad sack that will abide no clouting.

John Heywood: *Proverbs,* 2, 4. (16th
cent.)

Sacrament

With these sacraments [i.e. baptism and
the eucharist] Christ feeds His Church;
by them the soul's very being is strengthened.

St. Ambrose: *On the Mysteries,* 9, 55.
(4th cent.)

And suddenly there came a sound. . . .
What does this mean, but the descent of
the Holy Spirit, who wished to show
Himself to unbelievers in bodily form
also; that is in bodily form by a sign,
spiritually by a sacrament. . . . For in the
beginning signs were shown for unbelievers; now in the fulness of the Church
we must gather truth not by a sign, but
by faith.

St. Ambrose: *On the Sacraments,* 2, 5, 15.
(4th cent.)

The mysteries of the Christians are older
than those of the Jews, and the sacraments of the Christians are more divine
than those of the Jews.

St. Ambrose: *On the Sacraments,* 4, 3, 10.
(4th cent.)

But at the present time [i.e. under the
new dispensation], after the proof of
our liberty has shown forth so clearly in
the resurrection of our Lord, we are not
oppressed with the heavy burden of attending even to those signs which we
now understand, but there have been
handed down to us by our Lord Himself
and by apostolic practice a few rites in
place of many, and those at once very
easy to perform, most august in their significance, and most pious in their observance. Such for example are the sacrament
of baptism and the celebration of the
Body and Blood of the Lord.

St. Augustine: *De Doctrina Christiana,* 3,
9. (4th cent.)

A sacrament is the performance in any
ceremony of an act whereby some holy
thing is signified.

St. Augustine: *Letters,* 40, 2. (5th cent.)

The Church unreservedly acknowledges the existence among you [i.e. the schismatic Donatists] of sacraments which are really her own; they do not cease to be hers because they happen to be with you. Remember that with you those sacraments are adventitious (*aliena*); but when the Church to which they really belong shall have received you, amended, then those sacraments which, when merely adventitious, made for your destruction, will make for your salvation.

> St. Augustine: *Contra Epistolam Parmeniani,* 2, 28. (5th cent.)

The spiritual virtue of a sacrament is like light: although it passes among the impure, it is not polluted.

> St. Augustine: *In Joannis Evang.,* 1, 15. (5th cent.)

That ceremony is called a sacrament in which that which is done is understood to signify something in a holy sense. Baptism, chrism [confirmation], and the Body and Blood of the Lord are called sacraments. They are sacraments, because the divine power secretly brings about the salutary effects of these sacraments under cover of corporeal things; whence they are called sacraments from secret power or from mysteries. Whence also, whether they are dispensed in the Church of God by good or by bad ministers, because the Holy Spirit mysteriously works in them, although He once appeared in apostolic times in visible works, these gifts have nothing added to them by the qualities of good ministrants, nor anything taken from them by bad ministrants.

> St. Isidore: *Etymologies,* 6, 19. (7th cent.)

A sacrament is a material object sanctified and consecrated by the Word of God.

> Peter Lombard: *Book of Sentences,* 4, 1, 2. (12th cent.)

The Church's seven sacraments have common and proper features. Common to all is the giving of grace, common to all their being made up' of words and things. Christ is their author; He is the Word made flesh, and as His flesh was sanctified and given sanctifying virtue because of the Word united to it, so sacramental things are sanctified and have sanctifying virtue because of the words uttered in them. . . . Hence these sanctifying words are called the form of the sacraments, and the sanctified elements the matter. . . . Every sacrament, too, requires a minister who confers it with the intention of bestowing and doing what the Church bestows and does. If any of these three be defective . . . then no sacrament is celebrated.

> St. Thomas Aquinas: *On the Articles of Faith and Sacraments of the Church,* 2. (13th cent.)

Christ's death is the world-wide cause of salvation. All the same, any universal cause needs to be applied to produce particular effects; consequently determinate remedies need to be applied to men if they are to be brought into the blessings flowing from Christ's death. These remedies, which are the sacraments of the Church, come to us in portions and are bound up with what we can experience.

> St. Thomas Aquinas: *Contra Gentes,* 4, 56. (13th cent.)

What is there awkward about visible and bodily things ministering to spiritual health? Are they not the instruments of God, Who was made flesh for us and suffered in this world? An instrument's virtue is not its own, but is imparted by the principal cause which sets it to work. Hence, the sacraments do not act from the properties of their natural elements, but because they have been adopted by Christ to communicate His strength.

> St. Thomas Aquinas: *Contra Gentes,* 4, 56. (13th cent.)

Remember that the purpose of the sacraments is to help us on our way to our last end.

> St. Thomas Aquinas: *Contra Gentes,* 4, 70. (13th cent.)

Grace is in the sacraments like an effect in a cause, not like an accident in a substance. . . . So when the sacraments are classed as instruments we should not entertain the notion that grace resides in them.

St. Thomas Aquinas: *Disputations Concerning Truth*, 26, 7. (13th cent.)

We are bound to profess that the sacraments of the new law in some manner confer grace, and not merely because they are liturgically instructive. . . . Neither the sacraments nor any other creature can be the principal causes of grace, which is produced solely by divine power, but . . . they are instrumental causes.

St. Thomas Aquinas: *Disputations Concerning Truth*, 27, 4. (13th cent.)

A sacrament is a remembrance of the past [Christ's Passion], a proof of the present [grace], and a promise of the future [eternal life].

St. Thomas Aquinas: *Summa Theologica*, 3, 60, 3. (13th cent.)

Grace should not be reputed to be in the sacraments as though they were receptacles or vessels.

St. Thomas Aquinas: *Summa Theologica*, 3, 62, 3. (13th cent.)

A character is a kind of seal, which marks a thing as being set apart for some particular purpose. . . . The faithful are deputed to a twofold end. First and principally to the enjoyment of glory; for this purpose they are sealed with grace. . . . But secondly, each of the faithful is commissioned to receive, or bestow on others, activities appropriate to God's worship. This, properly speaking, is where sacramental character plays its role. All Christian ritual derives from Christ's priesthood. Consequently the sacramental character manifests Christ's character, and configures the faithful to His priesthood.

St. Thomas Aquinas: *Summa Theologica*, 3, 63, 3. (13th cent.)

If any one saith that the sacraments of the new law were not all instituted by Jesus Christ, our Lord; or that they are more or less than seven, to wit, baptism, confirmation, the eucharist, penance, extreme unction, order, and matrimony; or even that any one of these seven is not truly and properly a sacrament; let him be anathema.

Council of Trent, Session 7, Canon 1. (Mar. 3, 1547)

If any one saith that the sacraments of the new law are not necessary unto salvation, but superfluous; and that without them or without the desire thereof, men obtain of God through faith alone the grace of justification, though all [the sacraments] are not indeed necessary for every individual; let him be anathema.

Council of Trent, Session 7, Canon 4. (Mar. 3, 1547)

If any one saith that the sacraments of the new law do not contain the grace which they signify; or that they do not confer that grace on those who do not place an obstacle thereto; as though they were merely outward signs of grace or justice received through faith, and certain marks of Christian profession whereby believers are distinguished amongst men from unbelievers; let him be anathema.

Council of Trent, Session 7, Canon 6. (Mar. 3, 1547)

If any one saith that by the said sacraments of the new law grace is not conferred through the act performed (*ex opere operato*), but that faith alone in the divine promise suffices for the obtaining of grace; let him be anathema.

Council of Trent, Session 7, Canon 8. (Mar. 3, 1547)

If any one saith that in the three sacraments of baptism, confirmation, and order, there is not imprinted in the soul a character, that is, a certain spiritual and indelible sign on account of which they cannot be repeated; let him be anathema.

Council of Trent, Session 7, Canon 9. (Mar. 3, 1547)

If any one saith that all Christians have power to administer the word and all the sacraments; let him be anathema.

Council of Trent, Session 7, Canon 10. (Mar. 3, 1547)

If any one saith that in ministers, when they effect and confer the sacraments, there is not required the intention at least of doing what the Church does; let him be anathema.

Council of Trent, Session 7, Canon 11. (Against Protestant error) (Mar. 3, 1547)

The holy synod declares that this power has ever been in the Church, that in the dispensation of the sacraments, their substance being untouched, it may ordain or change what things soever it may judge most expedient for the profit of those who receive or for the veneration of the said sacraments according to the difference of circumstances, times, and places.

Decree of the Council of Trent, Session 21, Chap. 2. (July 16, 1562)

The Church has seven sacraments,
　As we must all believe:
But three there are more requisite
　To know and to receive.
Baptism washes out the sin
　Which Adam did commit:
The sins which we ourselves have done
　Confession will remit.
The Eucharist we know to be
　The Body and Blood divine
Of Jesus Christ, both God and Man,
　In form of bread and wine.
In Confirmation we believe
　The Holy Ghost is given;
In Extreme Unction we get strength
　To die and go to heaven.
By Holy Orders priests are made,
　And get both power and grace:
And Matrimony blesses those
　Who married life embrace.
All praise and thanks to Jesus be,
　And to His holy Blood,
By Him we have the sacraments,
　The source of every good.

The Seven Sacraments, in *Cantica Sacra,* 1865.

O earth, maternal earth, and thou, O heaven,
And night, first born, who now, e'en now, dost waken
The host of stars, thy constellated train,
Tell me if those can ever be forgiven,
Those abject, who together have partaken
These sacraments of nature—and in vain.

Aubrey de Vere: *The Sacraments of Nature.* (19th cent.)

Since the sacraments of the New Law instituted by Christ our Lord are all special means of sanctification and salvation, the greatest care and reverence should be used in administering and receiving them at appropriate times and with the proper rites. It is forbidden to administer the sacraments of the Church to heretics or schismatics, even to those who err in good faith and ask for them, unless they have previously renounced their errors and been reconciled to the Church.

Code of Canon Law, Canon 731. (20th cent.)

See also Baptism; Blessed Sacrament; Communion; Confirmation; Eucharist; Extreme Unction; Marriage; Mass; Orders, Holy; Penance

Sacramental

We should not profane holy things by mingling them with those meant for ordinary use.

St. Basil: *The Morals,* 30. (4th cent.)

That which is consecrated to God should be honored as holy as long as the will of God is fulfilled in it.

St. Basil: *The Morals,* 31, 1. (4th cent.)

Sacred Heart

O Christ, the world's Creator bright,
Who didst mankind from sin redeem,
Light from the Father's glorious light,
True God of God, in bliss supreme.

· · · · · · ·

O Savior, let Thy potent love
Flow ever from Thy bounteous heart;
To nations that pure fount above
The grace of pardon will impart.

Roman Breviary, Feast of the Sacred Heart
(Friday after Octave of Corpus Christi),
hymn *Auctor beate saeculi* at Vespers.
(Tr. F. Husenbeth) (Author unknown,
18th cent.)

Lo, how the savage crew
Of our proud sins hath rent
The heart of our all-gracious God,
That heart so innocent.

. . . . . .

O wounded heart, whence sprang
The Church, the Savior's bride;
Thou door of our salvation's Ark
Set in its mystic side.

Thou holy fount, whence flows
The sacred sevenfold flood,
Where we our filthy robes may cleanse
In the Lamb's saving Blood.

Roman Breviary, Feast of Sacred Heart,
hymn *En ut superba criminum* at Matins.
(Tr. E. Caswall) (Unknown author, 18th
cent.)

Jesus, behind Thy temple's veil,
Hid in an ark of gold,
On stones engraven, lay the law
Thy finger wrote of old.

But in Thy body's temple new,
Thy life-blood's throbbing shrine,
Held, upon fleshly tables graved,
The law of love divine.

Roman Breviary, Feast of the Sacred Heart,
hymn *Cor arca legem continens* at Lauds.
(Tr. Marquess of Bute's Roman Breviary)
(Author unknown, 18th cent.)

All ye who seek a comfort sure
In trouble and distress,
Whatever sorrow vex the mind,
Or guilt the soul oppress:

Jesus, Who gave Himself for you
Upon the Cross to die,

Opens to you His sacred heart;
O to that heart draw nigh.

Hymn *Quicumque certum quaeritis*. (Tr.
E. Caswall) (Author unknown, 18th
cent.)

O Thou, the Son of God most High,
Thou Father of the life to be,
O Prince of peace, to Thee we cry,
We bring our song of praise to Thee.

. . . . . .

Lord, keep us ever in Thy heart,
Thy tender love to feel and know,
The joys of heaven to us impart,
When we shall leave these walks below.

Hymn *Summi Parentis Filio*. (Tr. D.
Donahoe) (Author unknown, 18th cent.)

O heart of Jesus, purest heart,
Altar of holiness Thou art,
Cleanse Thou my heart, so sordid, cold,
And stained by sins so manifold.

Take from me, Lord, this tepid will,
Which doth Thy heart with loathing
fill;
And then infuse a spirit new—
A fervent spirit, deep and true.

Anonymous: *Cor Jesu cor purissimum*.
(Tr. M. Russell) (19th cent. ?)

I need Thee, precious Jesus,
I need a friend like Thee;
A friend to soothe and sympathize,
A friend to care for me.

I need Thy heart, sweet Jesus,
To feel each anxious care;
I long to tell my every want,
And all my sorrows share.

. . . . . .

I'll need Thee, sweetest Jesus,
When death's dread hour draws
nigh,
To hide me in Thy sacred heart,
Till wafted safe on high.

Anonymous: *Hymn to the Sacred Heart*.
(In *Hymns for the Year*, 1867) (19th
cent.)

O God, Who in the heart of Thy Son,
wounded by our transgressions, dost

mercifully vouchsafe to bestow upon us the infinite treasures of Thy love; grant, we beseech Thee, that revering it with fitting devotion, we may make a worthy reparation for our sins.

Roman Missal, Collect for the Feast. (19th cent. ?)

It is truly meet and just. . . . Who didst will that Thine only-begotten Son should be pierced by the soldier's lance as He hung upon the Cross: that from His opened heart, as from a sanctuary of divine bounty, might be poured out upon us streams of mercy and grace; and that in His heart always burning with love for us, the devout may find a haven of rest and the penitent a refuge of salvation.

Roman Missal, Preface for the Feast. (19th cent.)

O heart of Jesus, heart of God,
  O source of boundless love,
By angels praised, by saints adored,
  From their bright thrones above.

The poorest, saddest heart on earth,
  May claim Thee for its own;
O burning, throbbing heart of Christ,
  Too late, too little known.

Lady G. Fullerton: *The Sacred Heart.* (19th cent.)

I sit tonight by the firelight,
  And I look at the glowing flame,
And I see in the bright red flashes
  A Heart, a Face, and a Name.

A. Ryan: *Nocturne.* (19th cent.)

Oh! love that is deep and deathless!
  Oh! faith that is strong and grand!
Oh! hope that will shine forever,
  O'er the wastes of a weary land!
Christ's heart finds an earthly heaven
  In the palm of the priest's pure hand.

A. Ryan: *Feast of the Sacred Heart.* (19th cent.)

Then leave thy vain attempts
  To seek for peace;
The world can never give
  One soul release:

But in thy Savior's heart
  Securely dwell,
No pain can harm thee, hid
  In that sweet cell.
Then fly, O coward soul,
  Delay no more,
What words can speak the joy
  For thee in store?
What smiles of earth can tell
  Of peace like thine?
Silence and tears are best
  For things divine.

Adelaide A. Procter: *The Sacred Heart.* (19th cent.)

A heart that hath a Mother, and a treasure of red blood,
A heart that man can pray to, and feed upon for food!

F. Faber: *The Sacred Heart.* (First line: Unchanging and unchangeable, before angelic eyes) (19th cent.)

Since there is in the sacred heart a symbol and a sensible image of the infinite love of Jesus Christ which moves us to love one another, therefore it is fitting and proper that we should consecrate ourselves to His most sacred heart—an act which is nothing else than an offering and a binding of one's self to Jesus Christ, seeing that whatever honor, veneration, and love is given to His divine heart is really and truly given to Christ Himself.

Pope Leo XIII: *Annum Sacrum.* (May 25, 1899)

To choose the heart for emblem is to dedicate oneself to the only heart which does not lie, and it is encircled with thorns.

J. Maritain: *Art and Poetry.* (20th cent.)

Sacrifice

A sacrifice is the visible sacrament or sacred sign of an invisible sacrifice.

St. Augustine: *The City of God,* 10, 5. (5th cent.)

Thus a true sacrifice is every work which is done that we may be united to God in holy fellowship, and which has a reference to that supreme good and end in which alone we can be truly blessed.

> St. Augustine: *The City of God,* 10, 6. (5th cent.)

To Thee, meek Majesty! soft King
Of simple graces and sweet loves.
Each of us his lamb will bring
Each his pair of silver doves;
Till burnt at last in fire of Thy fair eyes,
Ourselves become our own best sacrifice.

> Richard Crashaw: *The Holy Nativity of Our Lord, a Hymn.* (17th cent.)

Good is never done except at the expense of those who do it: truth is never enforced except at the sacrifice of its propounders.

> Card. Newman: *Present Position of Catholics in England,* 9. (19th cent.)

A willing sacrifice she takes
   The burden of our fall within;
Holy she stands; while on her breaks
   The lightning of the wrath of sin;
She drinks her Savior's cup of pain,
And, one with Jesus, thirsts again.

> Robert H. Benson: *The Teresian Contemplative.* (20th cent.)

See also Eucharist: Sacrifice; Self-sacrifice

Sacrilege

Those persons who through ignorance confuse or through negligence violate and offend the sanctity of the divine law commit sacrilege.

> Edict of the Emperors Gratian, Valentinian, and Theodosius. (Theod. Code, 16, 2, 25) (380)

If anyone shall have committed such a sacrilege as to break into Catholic churches, deal violently with the clergy and ministers, or treat the service or the place itself injuriously . . . such a one must be brought before the chief authorities. . . . Those convicted of or pleading guilt to such injuries done to the priests and ministers of the Catholic Church and to the service and place itself must suffer capital punishment.

> Decree of the Emperors Arcadius and Honorius. (Codex Theodosianus, 16, 2, 31.) (398)

Sadness

He who in pleasing God displeases man, has no grounds for sadness. But he who in pleasing men displeases God or who thinks that he displeases both God and man, if sadness does not come upon him, is far from the virtue of wisdom.

> Pope St. Gregory I: *Morals,* 15, 42. (6th cent.)

On no account give way to sadness, the enemy of devotion.

> St. Francis de Sales: *Letters to Persons in Religion,* 4, 29. (17th cent.)

Dreary! weary!
Weary! dreary!
Sighs my soul this lonely night.
   Farewell gladness!
   Welcome sadness!
Vanished are my visions bright.

> Abram Ryan: *At Night.* (19th cent.)

Mostly men's many-featured faces wear
Looks of fixed gloom, or else of restless care;
The very babes, that in their cradle lie,
Out of the depths of unknown trouble cry.

> Aubrey de Vere: *Mundus Morosus.* (19th cent.)

The great enemy of the soul is not trial but sadness, which is the bleeding wound of self-love.

> Archb. Ullathorne: *Humility and Patience.* (19th cent.)

She left me marvelling why my soul
   Was sad that she was glad;

At all the sadness in the sweet,
The sweetness in the sad.

> F. Thompson: *Daisy.* (19th cent.)

See also Melancholy

Safety

Seeing the coast clear . . . he sate him down.

> Thomas Lodge: *Rosalynde.* (16th cent.)

Sailor

O God, Who led our fathers through the Red Sea, and guided them among the mighty waters while they sang praises to Thy name; we humbly beseech Thee, watch over Thy servants in this ship, ward off all dangers, favor them with a tranquil passage, and grant that they may attain their desired port.

> Roman Missal, Collect for Sailors. (Gregorian, 6th to 8th cent.)

Seafaring men range from one end of the earth to the other; but the multiplicity of external objects which they have encountered forms no symmetrical and consistent picture upon their imagination; they see the tapestry of human life as if it were on the wrong side, and it tells no story.

> Card. Newman: *Idea of a University.* (19th cent.)

They say who saw one sea-corpse cold
He was all of lovely manhood mould,
Every inch a tar,
Of the best we boast our sailors are.

> G. M. Hopkins: *The Loss of the Eurydice.* (19th cent.)

Saint

What saint has ever won his crown without first contending for it?

> St. Jerome: *Letters,* 22, 39. (4th cent.)

But, somehow or other, I find more delight in considering the saints when I

regard them as the teeth of the Church. They bite off men from their heresies and carry them over to the body of the Church, when their hardness of heart has been softened as if by being bitten off and chewed.

> St. Augustine: *De Doctrina Christiana,* 2, 6, 7. (4th cent.)

And if among all the saints some are more saintly than others, it is only because God dwells in them more abundantly.

> St. Augustine: *Letter 187.* (5th cent.)

The glorious company of the apostles praise Thee. The goodly fellowship of the prophets praise Thee. The white-robed army of martyrs praise Thee. All Thy saints and elect with one voice do acknowledge Thee, O Blessed Trinity, one God!

> Roman Breviary, Feast of All Saints (Nov. 1), Antiphon at Lauds. (From *Te Deum,* 5th cent.)

Grant, we beseech Thee, almighty God, that the intercession of holy Mary Mother of God, of all Thy saints, apostles, martyrs, confessors and virgins, and of all Thy elect, may gladden us everywhere; that as we revere their merits, we may enjoy their patronage.

> Roman Missal, Feast of All Saints, Collect for Votive Mass. (Gregorian, 6th to 8th cent.)

O Lord, if we did not have Thy saints to pray for us and Thy goodness so merciful unto us, how should we have dared, O Savior, to sing to Thee Whom angels glorify without ceasing? O Searcher of hearts, spare our souls.

> Byzantine Euchologion, Sticheron from Penitential Office. (Before 9th cent. ?)

O Christ, Thy guilty people spare!
Lo, kneeling at Thy gracious throne,
Thy Virgin Mother pours her prayer,
Imploring pardon for her own.

. . . .

Ye prophets and apostles high!
Behold our penitential tears;
And plead for us when death is nigh,
And our all-searching Judge appears.

> Roman Breviary, Feast of All Saints,
> hymn *Placare Christe servulis* (*Christe
> Redemptor omnium*) at Vespers. (Tr.
> Caswall) (Altered, Bl. Rabanus Maurus ?,
> 9th cent.)

Giver of life, eternal Lord!
Thy own redeemed defend;
Mother of grace! thy children save,
And help them to the end.

                .   .   .   .

All ye who high above the stars
In heavenly glory reign!
May we through your prevailing prayers
Unto your joys attain.

> Roman Breviary, Feast of All Saints, hymn
> *Salutis aeternae dator* (*Jesu Salvator
> saeculi*) at Lauds. (Tr. Caswall) (Attr.
> to Bl. Rabanus Maurus, 9th cent.)

Defend us, we beseech Thee, O Lord,
from all dangers of soul and body, and
by the intercession of the blessed and
glorious ever Virgin Mary Mother of
God, blessed Joseph, the blessed apostles Peter and Paul, blessed N., and all
the saints, graciously grant us protection
and peace; that all adversities and errors
being overcome, Thy Church may serve
Thee in security and freedom.

> Roman Missal, Collect. (ca. 11th cent.)

Oh, if thou hadst seen the everlasting
crown of the saints in heaven, and in
how great glory they now triumph who
appeared contemptible heretofore to this
world, and in a manner even unworthy
of life, doubtless thou wouldst immediately cast thyself down to the very earth,
and wouldst rather seek to be under the
feet of all, than to have command over
so much as one.

> Thomas a Kempis: *The Imitation of
> Christ*, 3, 47. (15th cent.)

It is much more acceptable to God for
a man to think of the greatness of his
own sins, and how little he is advanced
in virtue, and at how great a distance he
is from the perfection of the saints, than
to dispute which of them is greater or
less.

> Thomas a Kempis: *The Imitation of
> Christ*, 3, 58. (15th cent.)

In honor of the holy and undivided
Trinity, for the exaltation of the Catholic faith and the growth of the Christian religion, by the authority of our
Lord Jesus Christ, of the blessed Apostles Peter and Paul, and by our own,
after mature deliberation, after offering
many prayers to God, after having conferred with our venerable brethren, the
Cardinals of the Holy Roman Church,
and with the Patriarchs and Bishops
present in Rome, we declare that the
blessed—is a Saint and we inscribe his/
her name in the list of Saints, in the
name of the Father, and of the Son and
of the Holy Ghost. Amen.

> Formula used by the popes in proclaiming
> the canonization of a saint. (17th cent. ?)

To make a man a saint, it must indeed
be by grace; and whoever doubts this
does not know what a saint is, or a man.

> Pascal: *Pensées,* 24. (17th cent.)

The worst of madmen is a saint run mad.

> Pope: *The First Epistle of the First Book
> of Horace.* (18th cent.)

The saint's is not the hero's praise;—
    This I have found, and learn
Nor to malign heaven's humblest ways,
    Nor its least boon to spurn.

> Card. Newman: *The Saint and the Hero.*
> (19th cent.)

It never surprises me to read anything
extraordinary in the devotions of a saint.
Such men are on a level very different
from our own, and we cannot understand them. I hold this to be an important canon in the lives of the saints, according to the words of the apostles, *The
spiritual man judges all things, and he
himself is judged of no one.* But we may

refrain from judging, without proceeding to imitate.

> Card. Newman: *Letter to the Rev. E. B.
> Pusey.* (19th cent.)

Teach us, O Lord, and enable us to live
the life of saints and angels!

> Card. Newman. (19th cent.)

Nature designed me for a life above
The mere discordant dreams in which
  I live.
If I now go a beggar on the earth,
I was saint of heaven by right of birth.

> W. S. Blunt: *The Sinner-Saint.* (19th
> cent.)

The saint is simply a person who has so
strong and clear a sight of the truth
which concerns him individually, and
such courage to confess his vision, that
he is always ready to become a 'confessor' under any extremity of persecution.

> Coventry Patmore: *Religio Poetae.* (19th
> cent.)

Heaven were not heaven, and they not
    there;
Heaven were no heaven, my friends
    away:
  O saints and angels! hear the prayer,
  I pray you every day.

> Lionel Johnson: *Friends.* (19th cent.)

It is said that a saint is one who always
chooses the better of the two courses
open to him at every step.

> R. H. Benson: *The Light Invisible.* (20th
> cent.)

Every saint is a little looking-glass of
God: a facet of the jewel which constitutes the Catholic Church.

> John Ayscough: *Address to the Catholic
> Women's League.* (1914)

Earth's saints are those who to the last
Cling to beauty's broken mast
Then striking boldly seaward, reach
The smooth-stoned slope of heaven's
  beach.

> Henry M. Robinson: *Earth-Canonized.*
> (20th cent.)

The saints have ever been, are, and ever
will be the greatest benefactors of society, and perfect models for every class
and profession, for every state and condition of life, from the simple and un-
cultured peasant to the master of science
and letters, from the humble artisan to
the commander of armies, from the
father of a family to the ruler of peoples
and nations, from simple maidens and
matrons of the domestic hearth to
queens and empresses.

> Pope Pius XI: *Divinus Illius Magistri.*
> (Dec. 31, 1929)

One is a saint only after death. Before,
one is on the way.

> J. Maritain: *Art and Poetry.* (20th cent.)

Sainthood is not the negation of human
life. Saints have been kings, artisans,
preachers, doctors, priests, painters,
poets. Why should they not be novelists?

> J. Maritain: *Art and Poetry.* (20th cent.)

The eyes of the saint make all beauty
holy and the hands of the saint consecrate everything they touch to the glory
of God, and the saint is never offended
by anything and is scandalized at no
man's sin because he does not know sin.
He knows nothing but the love and the
mercy of God and he is on earth to bring
that love and that mercy to all men.

> Thomas Merton: *Seeds of Contemplation.*
> (20th cent.)

A man cannot be a perfect Christian—
that is, a saint,—unless he is also a communist. This means that he must either
absolutely give up all right to possess
anything at all, or else only use what he
himself needs, of the goods that belong
to him, and administer the rest for other
men and for the poor: and in his determination of what he needs he must be
governed to a great extent by the gravity
of the needs of others.

> Thomas Merton: *Seeds of Contemplation.*
> (20th cent.)

Saints, Veneration of

We always offer sacrifices for them, as you remember, as often as we celebrate the passions and days of the martyrs in annual commemoration.

St. Cyprian: *Letters,* 33, 3. (3rd cent.)

If the apostles and martyrs, when they were still in the body, and had still to be solicitous on their own account, prayed for others, how much more when they have won the crown, when they have gained the victory and the triumph?

St. Jerome: *Contra Vigilantium,* 6. (5th cent.)

Nor do we set up altars, to sacrifice to the martyrs, but to God alone, God of the martyrs and our God. In this sacrifice all the men of God, who in confession of their allegiance to Him have overcome the world, are named in due place and order, but are not invoked by the sacrificing priest. The reason is, because he is sacrificing to God, not to them, because he is God's priest, not theirs, although it is in their memorial shrine that he sacrifices. The sacrifice itself is the Body of Christ, which is not offered to them, because it is what they themselves are.

St. Augustine: *The City of God,* 22, 10. (5th cent.)

To the saints honor must be paid as friends of Christ, as sons and heirs of God . . . if the Creator and Lord of all things is also called King of kings and Lord of lords and God of gods, surely the saints also are gods and lords and kings. For God is God and Lord and King of these.

St. John of Damascus: *Exposition of the Orthodox Faith,* 4, 15. (8th cent.)

Are not those then worthy of honor who are the patrons of the whole race, and make intercession to God for us? Truly we ought to give honor to them by raising temples to God in their name, bringing them first-fruits, honoring their memories and taking spiritual delight in them, in order that the joy of those who call on us may be ours, that in our attempts at worship we may not on the contrary cause them offence. For those who worship God will take pleasure in those things whereby God is worshipped, while his shield-bearers will be angry at those things at which God is angry.

St. John of Damascus: *Exposition of the Orthodox Faith,* 4, 15. (8th cent.)

. . . we define with all care and diligence that there may be set up, in the same way as the figure of the precious and life-giving cross, venerable and holy images (*ikones*) . . . of our Lord God and Savior Jesus Christ, also of our Lady the holy and immaculate Mother of God, of the glorious angels, of all the saints, and of good men. . . . For so often as such imaginative representations are looked on, men who contemplate them feel their minds uplifted by such reminders of those who have proceeded them, they feel a desire to imitate them, they are moved to kiss them and exhibit towards them due reverence (*proskynesis*) ; not indeed the true worship of faith (*latria*), which pertains only to the Divine Nature. . . . For the honor which is paid to the image passes to that which the image represents, and he who reveres the image reveres in it the subject represented. . . .

Second Council of Nicaea, De Sacris Imaginibus, Actio 7. (787)

Do you account it a great thing if, wrapped up in Francis' cowl, you are carried into the tomb? Like clothing will bestow no benefit upon you in death if your morals were unlike his in life.

Erasmus: *Enchiridion.* (16th cent.)

No devotion to the saints is more acceptable and more proper than if you strive to express their virtue.

Erasmus: *Enchiridion.* (16th cent.)

If any one saith that it is an imposture to celebrate masses in honor of the saints and for obtaining their intercession with God, as the Church intends; let him be anathema.

> Council of Trent, Session 22, Canon 5. (Sept. 17, 1562)

The holy synod enjoins on all bishops and others who sustain the office and charge of teaching that . . . they especially instruct the faithful diligently concerning the intercession and invocation of saints; the honor paid to relics; and the legitimate use of images: teaching them that the saints, who reign together with Christ, offer up their own prayers to God for men; that it is good and useful suppliantly to invoke them, and to have recourse to their prayers, aid, and help for obtaining benefits from God, through his Son Jesus Christ our Lord, Who alone is our Redeemer and Savior. . . . Also that the holy bodies of holy martyrs and others now living with Christ . . . are to be venerated by the faithful, through which bodies many benefits are bestowed by God on men. . . .

> Decree of the Council of Trent, Session 25. (Dec. 3, 1563)

The devotions then to angels and saints as little interfered with the incommunicable glory of the Eternal, as the love which we bear our friends and relations, our tender human sympathies, are inconsistent with that supreme homage of the heart to the Unseen, which really does but sanctify and exalt, not jealously destroy, what is of earth.

> Card. Newman: *Apologia pro Vita Sua,* 4. (19th cent.)

A heart tenderly attached to the saints will give vent to its feelings in the language of hyperbole, just as an enthusiastic lover will call his future bride his adorable queen, without any intention of worshipping her as a goddess.

> Card. Gibbons: *The Faith of Our Fathers,* 13. (19th cent.)

Only those servants of God may be honored with public worship, who are by authority of the Church numbered among the saints and blessed.

> Code of Canon Law, Canon 1277, 1. (20th cent.)

Salesmanship

There's always chance to fear, and many a slip
Makes for anxiety in salesmanship.

> Chaucer: *The Shipman's Tale.* (Tr. Coghill) (14th cent.)

Salt

Salt-cellars ever should stand at the head
Of dishes, wheresoe'er a table's spread.
Salt will all poisons expurgate with haste,
And to insipid things impart a taste.

> School of Salerno, Code of Health. (11th cent.)

Salt and Sugar

It is a well-regulated mixture of both sugar and salt which produces a good flavor in a salad dressing.

> Jean Pierre Camus: *The Spirit of St. Francis de Sales,* 17, 3. (17th cent.)

Salt and sugar are both excellent things, but too much of either spoils the dish.

> Jean Pierre Camus: *The Spirit of St. Francis de Sales,* 19, 2. (17th cent.)

Salvation

While the Savior does not reject the willing, He does not constrain the unwilling; while He does not deny Himself to those who seek Him, He does not strive with those who cast Him out.

> St. Ambrose: *Explanation of St. Luke,* 4, 55. (4th cent.)

It is one thing to see the land of peace from a wooded mountaintop, yet not find the way to it and struggle hopelessly far from the way, with hosts of those fugitive deserters from God, under their leader the Lion and the Dragon, besetting us about and ever lying in wait; and quite another to hold to the way that leads there, a way guarded by the care of our heavenly General, where there are no deserters from the army of heaven to practice their robberies—for indeed they avoid that way as a torment.

St. Augustine: *Confessions,* 7, 21. (5th cent.)

O loving God, what is it in men that makes them rejoice more for the salvation of a soul that was despaired of or one delivered from a major peril, than if there had always been hope or the peril had been less?

St. Augustine: *Confessions,* 8, 3. (5th cent.)

As to the manner and time, however, in which anything that pertains to the one salvation common to all believers and pious persons is brought about, let us ascribe wisdom to God, and for our part submit ourselves to His will.

St. Augustine: *Letter 102.* (5th cent.)

God wills all men to be saved that are saved, not because there is no man whom He does not wish saved, but because there is no man saved whose salvation He does not will.

St. Augustine: *De Praedestinatione Sanctorum,* 1, 8. (5th cent.)

O God, unchangeable power and light eternal, mercifully look upon the wonderful mystery of Thy whole Church, and peacefully bring about the salvation of mankind by Thy eternal decree; that all the world may know and see that what has fallen down has been raised up, what is old has been made new, and that all things are restored through Him from Whom they received their beginning, even our Lord Jesus Christ.

Roman Missal, Collect for Holy Saturday. (Gelasian, 5th to 7th cent.)

God's original wish was that all should be saved and come to His kingdom. For it was not for punishment that He formed us but to share in His goodness, inasmuch as He is a good God. But inasmuch as He is a just God, His will is that sinners should suffer punishment. The first then is called God's antecedent will and pleasure, and springs from Himself, while the second is called God's consequent will and permission, and has its origin in us.

St. John of Damascus: *Exposition of the Orthodox Faith,* 2, 29. (8th cent.)

If a man born among infidels and barbarians does what lies in his power God will reveal to him what is necessary for salvation, either by inward inspiration or by sending him a preacher of the faith.

St. Thomas Aquinas: *Summa Theologica,* 2. (13th cent.)

Divine care supplies everybody with the means necessary for salvation, so long as he on his part does not put up obstacles.

St. Thomas Aquinas: *Disputations concerning Truth,* 14, 11. (13th cent.)

Believe that you are chosen by the mercy of God to be saved as one of His elect. Never depart from this hope, whatever you see or hear, or whatever temptations come upon you. And even though you think yourself a sinner only worthy of hell, because you do no good and do not serve God as you ought, hold fast to this faith and hope, ask mercy, and all shall be well.

Walter Hilton: *Scale of Perfection,* 1, 21. (14th cent.)

Salvation by the cross. (In cruce salus.)

St. Thomas a Kempis: *Imitation of Christ,* 2. (15th cent.)

See also Catholic Church; Catholic Faith; Grace; Jesus Christ; Justification; Redemption

Sanctity

See Holiness

Sanctuary (Asylum)

The temples of the Most High God shall be open to those persons who are afraid. Not only do we sanction that the altars and the surrounding oratory of the temple . . . but also the space up to the outside doors of the church, which people desiring to pray enter first, we order to be an altar of safety for those who seek sanctuary. . . . We also command that those persons who seek sanctuary shall not have within the churches any arms at all. . . .

> Edict of the Emperors Theodosius and Valentinian. (Theod. Code, 9, 45, 4) (431)

Sand

> Single sands have little weight,
> Many make a drowning freight.

> Bl. Robert Southwell: *Loss in Delay.* (16th cent.)

Sanity

Of a sane man there can be only one definition. He is a man who can have tragedy in his heart and comedy in his head.

> G. K. Chesterton: *Tremendous Trifles,* 32. (20th cent.)

Satan

See Devil

Satire

The true end of satire is the amendment of vices by correction.

> John Dryden: *Absalom and Achitophel, Pref.* (17th cent.)

If any fool is by our satire bit,
Let him hiss loud, to show you all he's hit.

> Pope: *Prologue for Three Hours After Marriage.* (18th cent.)

Satire's my weapon, but I'm too discreet
To run amuck, and tilt at all I meet.

> Pope: *The First Satire of the Second Book of Horace.* (18th cent.)

Savage

When wild in the woods the noble savage ran.

> John Dryden: *The Conquest of Granada,* 1. (17th cent.)

Saving

Better spare at brim than at bottom.

> John Heywood: *Proverbs,* 2, 5. (16th cent.)

Ever spare and ever bare.

> John Heywood: *Proverbs,* 2, 5. (16th cent.)

Savior

The people's pray'r, the glad diviners theme,
The young men's vision and the old man's dream!
Thee, savior, Thee the nation's vows confess;
And, never satisfied with seeing, bless.

> Dryden: *Absalom and Achitophel.* (17th cent.)

See also Jesus Christ—Savior

Savonarola, Girolamo

A very wonderful man, you will allow, my brethren, was this Savonarola: for years he had his own way; at length his innocence, sincerity and zeal were the ruin of his humility.

> Card. Newman. (19th cent.)

Scandal

Whatever is opposed to the will of the Lord is scandal.

> St. Basil: *The Morals,* 33, 1. (4th cent.)

To avoid scandal even that which is not of necessity should be done.

> St. Basil: *The Morals,* 33, 3. (4th cent.)

It is then certain that except when the necessary interests of the truth require, it is not permitted to any one to give any scandal, neither to order it, nor to consent to it.

> St. Bernard: *Letters.* (12th cent.)

Of unknown duchesses lewd tales we tell.

> Pope: *The Temple of Rome.* (18th cent.)

Gossip is charming! History is merely gossip. But scandal is gossip made tedious by morality.

> Oscar Wilde: *Lady Windermere's Fan,* 3. (19th cent.)

The basis of every scandal is an absolutely immoral certainty.

> Oscar Wilde: *A Woman of No Importance,* 1. (19th cent.)

Scepticism

Our inability to prove quite forbids dogmatism. Our instinct for truth quite forbids scepticism.

> Pascal: *Pensées.* (17th cent.)

It is idle to talk always of the alternative of reason and faith. Reason is itself a matter of faith. It is an act of faith to assert that our thoughts have any relation to reality at all. If you are merely a sceptic, you must sooner or later ask yourself the question, 'Why should anything go right; even observation or deduction? Why should not good logic be as misleading as bad logic? They are both movements in the brain of a bewildered ape.' The young sceptic says, 'I have a right to think for myself.' But the old sceptic, the complete sceptic, says, 'I have no right to think for myself. I have no right to think at all.'

> G. K. Chesterton: *Orthodoxy.* (20th cent.)

He had found the thing which the modern people call impressionism, which is another name for that final scepticism which can find no floor to the universe.

> G. K. Chesterton: *The Man Who Was Thursday.* (20th cent.)

What matter, whether two and two be four,
So long as none account them to be more?
What difference, whether black be black or white,
If no officious Hand turn on the Light?
Whether our Fact is Fact, no Man can know,
But Heav'n preserve us, we will treat it so.

> Ronald Knox: *Absolute and Abitofhell.* (20th cent.)

Schism

Why are there quarrels and ill will and dissensions and schisms and fighting among you? Do we not have one God and one Christ, and one Spirit of grace poured out upon us? And is there not one calling in Christ? Why do we wrench and tear apart the members of Christ, and revolt against our own body, and reach such folly as to forget that we are members of one another?

> Pope St. Clement I: *Letter to the Corinthians,* 46, 5-8. (1st cent.)

For a man ought to suffer anything and everything, rather than divide the Church of God, and it is no less glorious to incur martyrdom to avoid schism than to avoid idolatry; in fact in my opinion it is more so. For in the one case a man is a martyr for the sake of his own single soul, but in the other for the sake of the whole Church.

> Dionysius of Alexandria: *Letter to Novatian.* (In Eusebius, *Eccl. Hist.* 6, 45.) (252)

For this has been the source from which heresies and schisms have arisen, that God's priest is not obeyed, nor do people reflect that there is for the time one priest in the Church, who for the time is judge instead of Christ, and if the whole brotherhood would obey him, according to divine teaching, no one would stir up anything against the college of priests. . . .

St. Cyprian: *Letters*, 54, 5. (To Pope Cornelius) (252)

No one shall pray in common with heretics and schismatics.

Council of Laodicea, Can. 33. (365)

Secede not from the Church: for nothing is stronger than the Church. Thy hope is the Church; thy salvation is the Church; thy refuge is the Church. It is higher than the heavens and wider than the earth. It never grows old, but is ever full of vigor. Wherefore holy writ pointing to its strength and stability calls it a mountain.

St. John Chrysostom: *Hom. De Capto Eutropio*, 6. (4th cent.)

I say and protest that it is as wrong to divide the Church as to fall into heresy.

St. John Chrysostom: *Hom. 11 in Ep. ad Eph.*, 5. (4th cent.)

We think that this difference exists between heresy and schism: heresy has no perfect dogmatic teaching, whereas schism, through some episcopal dissent, also separates from the Church.

St. Jerome: *Comm. in Ep. ad Titum*, 3, 10. (5th cent.)

As though anyone forbade you to quit your error! It was your pride that bound you fast *in the seat of scorning*.

St. Augustine: *Psalmus contra Partem Donati*. (5th cent.)

Well you know what the Catholic Church is, and what it is to be cut off from the Vine; are there any thoughtful men among you? Let them come and find life in the Root.

St. Augustine: *Psalmus contra Partem Donati*. (4th cent.)

You [i.e. the schismatic Donatists] are Christ's sheep; you bear the mark of the Lord in the sacrament you have received, but you have wandered away and are lost. There is no reason why you should be angry with us for recalling you from wandering and seeking you when you were lost, for it is better for us to carry out the will of the Lord, Who gave us the injunction to compel you to return to His fold, than to acquiesce in the will of the wandering sheep and allow you to be lost.

St. Augustine: *Letter 173*. (5th cent.)

Whosoever shall have separated himself from the Catholic Church, no matter how praiseworthy such a person may fancy his life has been, yet for that one crime of having cut himself off from the unity of Christ he shall not have eternal life, but the wrath of God shall abide with him for ever.

St. Augustine: *Letter 141*. (5th cent.)

It happens that, as in the human body, some member may be cut off—a hand, a finger, a foot. Does the soul follow the amputated member? As long as it was in the body it lived; separated, it forfeits its life. So the Christian is a Catholic as long as he lives in the body: cut off from it he becomes a heretic—the life of the spirit follows not the amputated member.

St. Augustine: *Sermons*, 267, 4. (5th cent.)

Schism, unless I am mistaken, means that men think the same and follow the same rites as others; but they prefer to split up the congregation. Whereas a sect means that its followers think very differently from the rest and have set up for themselves a very different form of divine worship.

St. Augustine: *Contra Faustum*, 20, 3. (5th cent.)

Heresy is of its very nature opposed to faith, but schism is of its very nature opposed to the unity of ecclesiastical

charity. Since, then, faith and charity
are different virtues—although whoso
lacks faith lacks charity—so, too, schism
and heresy are distinct vices; and while
a man who is a heretic is also a schismatic, the converse is not true. . . . At
first sight and from one angle schism
appears to be a different thing from
heresy; yet there is no schism which does
not fashion for itself some heresy—for
example, that it is right to have left the
Church.

> St. Thomas Aquinas: *Summa Theologica,*
> 2a, 2ae, 39, 1 ad 3. (13th cent.)

If I am once absolutely convinced that
our Church is in schism, there is, according to the doctrine (I believe) of every
age, no safety for me in it.

> Card. Newman: *Letter to E. Coleridge.*
> (Newman was reconciled to the Catholic
> Church, Oct. 9, 1845) (1844)

O Eastern Church! imperial schism
Swept from thy forehead crown and
    chrism:
Loose from the fold thy Caesars broke:
Thy penance came—the Moslem yoke!
O Eastern Church, so great of old,
    What art thou at this hour?
God called thee! why thy backward
    gaze
    Servile to mortal power?
Thou stand'st amid the salt sand-waste
A queenly statue, fire-defaced;
A pillar wrecked of sentenced pride,
A dead faith's image petrified!

> Aubrey de Vere: *Hymns and Poems.*
> (19th cent.)

See also Catholic Church; Heresy; Reunion of Christians

Scholar

His only care was study, and indeed
He never spoke a word more than was
    need,
Formal at that, respectful in the ex-
    treme,
Short, to the point, and lofty in his
    theme.

> Chaucer: *Canterbury Tales: Prologue.*
> (Tr. Coghill) (14th cent.)

School

For one and one make two, two and
two make four, I found a loathsome refrain; but such empty unrealities as the
Wooden Horse with its armed men, and
Troy on fire, and Creusa's ghost, were
sheer delight.

> St. Augustine: *Confessions,* 1, 13. (5th
> cent.)

We are, and always have been, decidedly
in favor of really Catholic schools, that
is, schools in which our children are sure
to be taught, and well taught, their religion, and we cannot understand how
any Catholic at all worthy of the name
can be otherwise than earnestly in favor
of such schools. . . .

> Orestes Brownson: *Public and Parochial
> Schools.* (*Works,* 12) (1859)

No schools, not even our Catholic
schools, are perfect.

> Brownson: (*Works,* 12) (1859)

The district school system is an American pet; it is the pride of the American
people, their boast, and really their
glory. It is dear to their hearts, and we
cannot strike them in a tenderer point
than in striking this system, or do anything more effectual in stirring up their
wrath against us, or in confirming their
prejudices against our religion—a system devised and adopted for themselves
without any view favorable or unfavorable to Catholics, for it was devised and
adopted when there were scarcely any
Catholics in the country.

> Orestes Brownson: *Public and Parochial
> Schools.* (*Works,* 12) (1859)

Free schools! Blest indeed is the nation
whose vales and hillsides they adorn,
and blest the generations upon whose
souls are poured their treasures! No tax
is more legitimate than that which is
levied in order to dispel mental darkness, and build up within the nation's

bosom intelligent manhood and womanhood.

> Archb. Ireland: *Discourse on State Schools
> and Parish Schools.* (St. Paul, 1890)

The free school of America! Withered
be the hand raised in sign of its destruction!

> Archb. Ireland: *Discourse on State Schools
> and Parish Schools.* (St. Paul, 1890)

Catholic children should not attend non-
Catholic, neutral, or mixed schools, that
is, those which are open also to non-
Catholics. It pertains exclusively to the
ordinary of the place to decide, in accordance with instructions of the Holy
See, under what circumstances and with
what safeguards against the danger of
perversion of the faith, attendance at
such schools may be tolerated.

> Code of Canon Law, Canon 1374. (20th
> cent.)

The Church has the right to establish for
every branch of learning, not only elementary but intermediate and higher
schools.

> Code of Canon Law, Canon 1375. (20th
> cent.)

The faithful must not fail to help with
the founding and maintenance of Catholic schools.

> Code of Canon Law, Canon 1379, 3. (20th
> cent.)

See also Education

Schoolmaster

> When the night shall lift from Erin's
>   hills, 'twere shame if we forget
> One band of unsung heroes whom
>   freedom owes a debt.
> When we brim high cups to brave ones
>   then, their memory let us pledge
> Who gathered their ragged classes be-
>   hind a friendly hedge.
>
> Seumas MacManus: *The Hedge
> Schoolmasters.* (19th cent.)

Science

For science is the knowledge of all
things. (*Est enim disciplina quarum-
cumque rerum scientia.*)

> St. Augustine: *De Immortalitate Animae,*
> 1, 1. (4th cent.)

Practical sciences proceed by building
up; theoretical sciences by resolving into
components.

> St. Thomas Aquinas: *Commentary on the
> Ethics,* 1, lect. 3. (13th cent.)

A science is a system of principles and
conclusions.

> St. Thomas Aquinas: *Exposition of the De
> Trinitate,* 2, 2. (13th cent.)

True science is about things which really
exist.

> St. Thomas Aquinas: *Exposition of 'The
> Divine Names,'* 1, lect. 2. (13th cent.)

Is it not evident, in these last hundred
years, that more errors of the school have
been detected, more useful experiments
in philosophy have been made, more
noble secrets in optics, medicine, anat-
omy, astronomy, discovered, than in all
those credulous and doting ages, from
Aristotle to us? So true it is, that nothing spreads more fast than science, when
rightly and generally cultivated.

> Dryden: *Of Dramatic Poesy.* (17th cent.)

[Scientists] are ever inquiring *whence*
things are, not *why;* referring them to
nature, not to mind; and thus they tend
to make a system a substitute for a
God. . . .

> Card. Newman: *Discussions and
> Arguments.* (19th cent.)

The decrees of the Apostolic See and
the Roman congregations impede the
true progress of science.

> Proposition condemned by Pius IX in
> Syllabus of Errors. (1867)

Put by the telescope!
Better without it man may see,
Stretch'd awful in the hush'd midnight,
The ghost of his eternity.

> Coventry Patmore: *The Unknown Eros.*
> (19th cent.)

There are philosophers who teach an invariable uniformity in the laws of nature; I do not see on what ground of experience or reason they take up this position.

> Card. Newman. (Ward, II, 587) (19th cent.)

The Church has shown herself to be hostile to the progress of natural and theological sciences.

> Proposition condemned by Decree of Holy Office, *Lamentabili,* June 3, 1907.

Science in the modern world has many uses; its chief use, however, is to provide long words to cover the errors of the rich.

> G. K. Chesterton: *Heretics.* (20th cent.)

'Scientism' is the philosophy of those who believe that science confirms the supremacy of natural law, and refutes the belief in the supernatural.

> Arnold Lunn: *The Revolt against Reason.* (20th cent.)

Man learns from two books: the universe, for the human study of the things created by God; and the Bible, for the study of God's superior will and truth. One belongs to reason, the other to faith. Between them there is no clash.

> Pope Pius XII: *Address to the Pontifical Academy of Science.* (Dec. 3, 1939)

Science which has apostatized from the life of the spirit, while it deluded itself into thinking that it has acquired full liberty and autonomy in denying God, finds itself today punished by a servitude more humiliating than ever before. For it has become the slave and the almost blind follower of policies and orders which take no account of the rights of truth or of the human person.

> Pope Pius XII: *Christmas Message.* (Dec. 24, 1943)

Scientist

Apparently a scientist is a man who surveys all the sciences, without any particular study of them, and then gives expression to his own moral principles or prejudices.

> G. K. Chesterton: *All is Grist.* (20th cent.)

Scorn

We trample grass, and prize the flowers
  of May;
Yet grass is green, when flowers do fade
  away.

> Bl. Robert Southwell: *Scorn Not the Least.* (16th cent.)

Scorn springs easily to the essentially vulgar-minded.

> G. K. Chesterton: *Alarms and Discursions.* (20th cent.)

Scruple

The reason why scruples are a mischief is that they are a forgetfulness of God's kindness.

> John Ayscough: *Marotz.* (20th cent.)

Sea

The sea, unmated creature, tired and
  lone,
Makes on its desolate sands eternal
  moan.

> F. Faber: *The Sorrowful World.* (19th cent.)

Strange sea! why is it that you never
  rest?
  And tell me why you never go to
  sleep?
Thou art like one so sad and sin-oppressed—

(And the waves are the tears you
    weep)—
And thou didst never sin—what ails
    the sinless deep?

Abram Ryan: *Sea Reverie.* (19th cent.)

O sea, forever calling to the shore
    With menace or caress,—
A voice like his unheeded that of yore
    Cried in the wilderness;
A deep forever yearning unto deep,
    For silence out of sound,—
Thy restlessness the cradle of a sleep
    That thou hast never found.

J. B. Tabb: *Vox Clamantis.* (19th cent.)

But, visiting sea, your love doth press
    And reach in further than you know,
    And fills all these; and when you go
There's loneliness in loneliness.

Alice Meynell: *The Visiting Sea.* (19th
cent.)

Search

It is lost that is unsought.

John Heywood: *Proverbs,* 1, 11. (16th
cent.)

As good seek nought, as seek and find
nought.

John Heywood: *Proverbs,* 1, 11. (16th
cent.)

Seasickness

Seasickness its full gripe in none will
    fix,
Who wisely with their wine salt water
    mix,
And to each threatened qualm this
    draught prefix.

School of Salerno, Code of Health. (11th
cent.)

Secret

Men should keep counsel, and not tell
    their wives
Secrets that it concerns them to retain,
Touching the safety of their limbs and
    lives.

Chaucer: *The Monk's Tale.* (Tr. Coghill)
(14th cent.)

For secrets are edged tools,
And must be kept from children and
    from fools.

Dryden: *Sir Martin Mar-all,* 2, 2. (17th
cent.)

Sect

A thousand daily sects rise up and die;
A thousand more the perished race supply.

Dryden: *Religio Laici.* (17th cent.)

Secularism

To wish to draw an exact line of separation between religion and life, between
the natural and the supernatural, between the Church and the world, as if
they had nothing to do with each other,
as if the rights of God were valueless in
all the manifold realities of daily life,
whether human or social, is entirely foreign to Catholic thought and is positively
anti-Christian.

Pope Pius XII: *On Christian Rebirth.*
(Jan. 22, 1947)

Self

We are more troublesome to ourselves
than anyone else is to us.

St. Francis de Sales: *Letters to Persons in
the World,* 6, 52. (17th cent.)

Who can know himself, and the multitude of subtle influences which act upon
him?

Card. Newman: *Apologia pro Vita Sua.*
(19th cent.)

So long as self reigns . . . our whole instinct is, obviously, in some manner towards self-assertion.

R. H. Benson: *The Friendship of Christ.*
(20th cent.)

Self is the Gorgon. Vanity sees it in the
mirror of other men and lives. Pride
studies it for itself and is turned into
stone.

G. K. Chesterton: *Heretics.* (20th cent.)

I'm myself but who are you?

> Seumas MacManus: *Heavy Hangs the Golden Grain.* (20th cent.)

Self-Approval

One self-approving hour whole years
   outweighs
Of stupid starers and of loud huzzas.

> Pope: *An Essay on Man,* 4. (18th cent.)

Self-Confidence

'Tis with our judgments as our watches,
   none
Go just alike, yet each believes his own.

> Pope: *An Essay on Criticism,* 1. (18th cent.)

Self-Consciousness

As a rule one realizes self-consciousness, as philosophers tell us, by self-differentiation from what is not self.

> R. H. Benson: *The Mirror of Shalott.* (20th cent.)

Self-Contempt

It is a thing to be especially borne in mind, that each individual soul is rendered the more precious in the sight of God in proportion as it is the more despised in its own eyes for the love of Truth.

> Pope St. Gregory I: *Morals,* 18, 59. (6th cent.)

Self-Control

Who has a harder fight than he who is striving to overcome himself?

> Thomas a Kempis: *The Imitation of Christ,* 1, 3. (15th cent.)

Self-Criticism

Perhaps the only sound criticism is self-criticism.

> G. K. Chesterton: *The Thing.* (20th cent.)

Self-Defence

Self-defence is nature's eldest law.

> Dryden: *Absalom and Achitophel.* (17th cent.)

Self-Deception

It is of course an evil to be full of faults, but it is an even greater evil to be full of them and unwilling to recognize them, since that is to add the further fault of self-delusion.

> Pascal: *Pensées.* (17th cent.)

It is extremely easy to deceive oneself; and it is extremely hard not to be self-conscious and complacent—not to see only what one would wish to see.

> R. H. Benson: *The Confessions of a Convert.* (20th cent.)

The mind of an average man—above all when he is scarcely more than just a man —is all but infinitely complex. Yet if there is one thing that rises dominant and rigid out of the myriad motives and desires and faculties that twine and intertwine beneath, it is the power of an astonishing self-deception.

> R. H. Benson: *An Average Man.* (20th cent.)

Self-Knowledge

Full wise is he that can himselven know.

> Chaucer: *The Monkes Tale.* (14th cent.)

The soul, who is lifted by a very great and yearning desire for the honor of God and the salvation of souls, begins by exercising herself for a certain space of time in the ordinary virtues, remaining in the cell of self-knowledge, in order to know better the goodness of God towards her. This she does because knowledge must precede love, and only when she has attained love can she strive to follow and to clothe herself with truth.

> St. Catherine of Siena: *The Dialogue.* (14th cent.)

The humble knowledge of thyself is a surer way to God than the deepest search after science.

> Thomas a Kempis: *The Imitation of Christ*, 1, 3. (15th cent.)

We know ourselves so little that many think they are going to die when they are well, and many think they are well when they are near dying.

> Pascal: *Pensées*, 25. (17th cent.)

All our knowledge is ourselves to know.

> Pope: *An Essay on Man*, 4. (18th cent.)

Self-Love

Self-love is cunning, it pushes and insinuates itself into everything, while making us believe it is not there at all.

> St. Francis de Sales: *Letters to Persons in Religion*, 1, 1. (17th cent.)

And thou, self-love! who tak'st from earth
With the vile, crawling worm, by birth,
Untouch'd with others' joy or pain,
The social smile, the tear humane;
Thyself thy sole, intemperate guest,
Uncall'd thy neighbor to the feast;
As if—Heaven's universal heir—
'Twas thine to seize, and not to share.

> William Hamilton: *Contemplation*. (18th cent.)

Self-Praise

Let our praise be with God, and not from ourselves, for God hates those who praise themselves.

> Pope St. Clement I: *Letter to the Corinthians*, 30, 6. (1st cent.)

Fondly we think we honor merit then,
When we but praise ourselves in other men.

> Pope: *An Essay on Criticism*, 2. (18th cent.)

Self-Sacrifice

Self-sacrifice is good in its way, but we must take care that we don't sacrifice to the detriment of others.

> Katharine T. Hinkson: *The Way of a Maid*. (20th cent.)

Man's highest life does not consist in self-expression, but in self-sacrifice.

> R. H. Benson: *Christ in the Church*. (20th cent.)

Self-Service

Self do, self have.

> John Heywood: *Proverbs*, 1, 8. (16th cent.)

Self-Will

Self-will should be so completely poured out of the vessel of the soul into the ocean of the will of God, that whatever God may will, that at once the soul should will; and that whatever God may allow, that the soul should at once willingly embrace, whether it may be in itself sweet or bitter.

> Louis de Blois (Blosius): *A Short Rule*, 1. (16th cent.)

Selfishness

Each man for himself, there is none other.

> Chaucer: *The Knightes Tale*. (14th cent.)

Every man for himself, and God for us all.

> John Heywood: *Proverbs*, 2, 9. (16th cent.)

Self is the medium through which Judgment's ray
Can seldom pass without being turned astray.

> Thomas Moore: *The Sceptic*. (19th cent.)

It is an appalling fact that again and again those who claim to be enjoying the most intimate friendship with God are distinguished by selfishness and a lack of charity towards their neighbors.

> R. H. Benson: *The Friendship of Christ.* (20th cent.)

Sense

The frontiers between sense and spirit are the devil's hunting-grounds.

> Coventry Patmore: *Memoirs.* (19th cent.)

It is one of the most dangerous things in the world to think oneself sensible; it is even more dangerous than to be told so.

> R. H. Benson: *None Other Gods.* (20th cent.)

Sensibility

Man's sensibility to trifles and insensibility to great things shows a strange reversal of values.

> Pascal: *Pensées.* (17th cent.)

Sensuality

If a soul lives long enough on the plane of sensuality or of ambition, she finds that Christ is worth less than nothing there.

> R. H. Benson: *Christ in the Church.* (20th cent.)

Sentiment

She was all sentiment and tender heart.

> Chaucer: *Canterbury Tales: Prologue.* (Tr. Coghill) (14th cent.)

Nature has cast men in so soft a mold,
That but to hear a story, feigned for pleasure,
Of some sad lover's death, moistens my eyes,
And robs me of my manhood.

> Dryden: *All for Love,* 4, 1. (17th cent.)

This is the essence of the sentimentalist, that he seeks to enjoy every idea without its sequence, and every pleasure without its consequence.

> G. K. Chesterton: *Alarms and Discursions.* (20th cent.)

Sermon

The literary point of view is not the most important in judging a sermon.

> R. H. Benson: *The Light Invisible.* (20th cent.)

"O the pastor'd a sermon was splendid this mornin',"
    Said Nora O'Hare,
"But there's some in the parish that must have had warnin'
An' worshiped elsewhere;
But wherever they were, if their ears wasn't burnin',
    Troth, then, it is quare!"

> T. A. Daly: *Applying the Sermon.* (20th cent.)

People are frightened by tracts and they don't like lay-sermons, even sugar-coated ones.

> Katherine Burton: *The Next Thing.* (20th cent.)

Serpent

Some flow'rets of Eden ye still inherit,
But the trail of the serpent is over them all!

> Thomas Moore: *Lalla Rookh: Paradise and the Peri.* (19th cent.)

Servant

Servants as a class are full of complaints; and no matter what you give them it is always too little.

> St. Jerome: *Letters,* 117, 8. (5th cent.)

The Christian should blush who cannot trust a Christian with his property.

> St. Bernard: *On Consideration,* 4, 6. (12th cent.)

Let us treat our servants as ourselves, or rather as we should wish to be treated if we were in their position.

> Jean Pierre Camus: *The Spirit of St. Francis de Sales,* 7, 9. (17th cent.)

Service

He in truth desires to imitate God who administers his high position with a view to the benefit of others, and is not elated with his own praises; when placed above others, he desires to serve, and not to rule over them.

> Pope St. Gregory I: *Morals*, 26, 48. (6th cent.)

Had I but served God as diligently as I have served my king, he would not have given me over in my grey hairs. But this is the just reward that I must receive for my indulgent pains and study, not regarding my service to God, but only to my prince.

> Card. Wolsey, to Sir William Kingston, Constable of the Tower, at Leicester Abbey, Nov. 5, 1530. (Accused of high treason, the Cardinal was on his way to London, but fell sick and died at the abbey.)

The individual saves his life by losing it, and realizes the meaning of his own identity only by merging it in the commonwealth.

> R. H. Benson: *A City Set on a Hill*. (20th cent.)

What is the matter with the cult of service is that, like so many modern notions, it is an idolatry of the intermediate, to the oblivion of the ultimate. It is like the jargon of the idiots who talk about efficiency without any criticism of effect. The sin of service is the sin of Satan: that of trying to be first where it can only be second. A word like service has stolen the sacred capital letter from the thing which it was once supposed to serve. There is a sense in serving God, and an even more disputed sense in serving man; but there is no sense in serving Service.

> G. K. Chesterton: *The Thing*. (20th cent.)

Serving God

Ready service, according to our ability, even in very small things and even if rendered by women, is acceptable to God.

> St. Basil: *The Morals*, 37. (4th cent.)

All men consult Thee about what they will, but they do not always hear what they will by way of answer. He is Thy best servant who endeavoreth not to hear from Thee that which he desireth, but rather desireth that which he heareth from Thee.

> St. Augustine: *Confessions*, 10, 26, 37. (5th cent.)

Almighty and merciful God, by Whose gift it comes about that Thy faithful people render Thee true and laudable service; grant, we beseech Thee, that we may run without hindrance toward the goal of Thy promises.

> Roman Missal, Collect for Twelfth Sunday after Pentecost. (Leonine, ca. 5th cent.)

To fulfil God's commandments daily in one's deeds.

> St. Benedict: *Rule*, 4. (One of his 'tools of good works') (6th cent.)

O pleasant and delightful service of God, which makes a man truly free and holy! O sacred state of religious bondage, which makes men equal to angels, pleasing to God, terrible to the devils and commendable to all the faithful.

> Thomas a Kempis: *The Imitation of Christ*, 3, 10. (15th cent.)

Imagine thyself always to be the servant of all, and look upon all as if they were Christ our Lord in person; and so shalt thou do Him honor and reverence.

> St. Teresa of Jesus: *Maxims*. (16th cent.)

Often it is required to leave God for God, renouncing his sweetness to serve Him in His sorrows and travails.

> St. Francis de Sales: *Letters to Persons in Religion*, 2, 23. (17th cent.)

There is nothing small in the service of God.

> St. Francis de Sales: *Letters to Persons in Religion*, 3, 26. (17th cent.)

What matters it to a truly loving soul whether God be served by this means or by another?

St. Francis de Sales: *Letters to Persons in Religion*, 3, 25. (17th cent.)

God has created me to do Him some definite service; he has committed some work to me which He has not committed to another. I have my mission—I never may know it in this life, but I shall be told it in the next.

Card. Newman: *Meditations and Devotions.* (19th cent.)

Every soul that tries, however poorly, to serve God knows by experience those heavinesses by which our Lord tests and confirms His own.

R. H. Benson: *The Light Invisible.* (20th cent.)

We may serve God by digging with the hands, or by talking friendly with our neighbor.

R. H. Benson: *The History of Richard Raynal Solitary.* (20th cent.)

The object of religion is that the soul should serve God, not that God should serve the soul.

R. H. Benson: *The Friendship of Christ.* (20th cent.)

It is not true that it is only with the soul that God is perceived or served.

R. H. Benson: *The History of Richard Raynal Solitary.* (20th cent.)

Sex

Each loves itself, but not itself alone,
Each sex desires alike, till two are one,
Nor ends the pleasure with the fierce
  embrace;
They love themselves a third time in
  their race.

Pope: *An Essay on Man*, 3. (18th cent.)

About sex especially men are born unbalanced; we might almost say men are born mad. They scarcely reach sanity till they reach sanctity.

G. K. Chesterton: *The Everlasting Man.* (20th cent.)

One thing only in the whole world is more absurd than the convention of the fig leaf, and that is the pretence that sex is not uniquely significant.

Eric Gill: *It All Goes Together.* (20th cent.)

The evil of immorality in sex is not merely that of self-indulgence, but the profanation of something sacred, the desecration of a holy instinct which arises from the depths of our unconscious being and is the bearer of life or death.

Dom Griffiths: *The Golden String.* (20th cent.)

Sext (Sixth Hour)

Pray also at the sixth hour, for at that hour when Christ had been hanged upon the wood of the Cross the daylight was divided and it became darkness. And so let them pray at that hour a prevailing prayer, likening themselves to the cry of Him Who prayed and caused all creation to be made dark for the unbelieving Jews.

St. Hippolytus: *The Apostolic Tradition,* 36. (3rd cent.)

O God of truth, O Lord of might,
Who orderest time and change aright,
Who send'st the early morning ray,
And light'st the glow of perfect day.

Roman Breviary, Hymn *Rector potens verax Deus* for Sext. (Tr. Neale) (Possibly by St. Ambrose, 4th cent.)

Thou that at the sixth day and hour didst nail to the cross the sin Adam committed in Paradise; tear asunder also the bill of our offences, O Christ our God, and save us.

Byzantine Horologion, Troparion for Sext. (ca. 5th to 8th cent.)

Shadow

If picture more, more should the pattern please;
No shadow can with shadowed thing compare.

Bl. Robert Southwell: *Lewd Love is Loss.*
(16th cent.)

Under thy shadow may I lurk awhile,
Death's easy search I'll easily beguile:
Thy shadow Peter, must shew me the Sun,
My light's thy shadow's shadow, or 'tis done.

Richard Crashaw: *The Sick Implore St. Peter's Shadow.* (17th cent.)

Shakespeare, William

Those hands, which you so clapped, go now and wring,
You Britons brave; for done are Shakespeare's days;
His days are done, that made the dainty plays,
Which made the Globe of heaven and earth to ring.

Hugh Holland: *Shakespeare Dead.* (From first folio) (17th cent.)

Heav'n, that but once was prodigal before,
To Shakespeare gave as much; she could not give him more.

Dryden: *To Mr. Congreve.* (17th cent.)

Shakespeare, thy gift, I place before my sight;
With awe I ask his blessing ere I write;
With rev'rence look on his majestic face;
Proud to be less, but of his godlike race.

Dryden: *To Sir Godfrey Kneller.* (17th cent.)

He was the man who of all modern, and perhaps ancient poets, had the largest and most comprehensive soul. . . . He was naturally learned; he needed not the spectacles of books to read nature; he looked inwards, and found her there. . . .

He is many times flat, insipid; his comic wit degenerates into clenches, his serious swelling into bombast. But he is always great, when some occasion is presented to him.

Dryden: *Essay of Dramatic Poesy.* (17th cent.)

When he describes anything you more than see it; you feel it.

Dryden: *Essay of Dramatic Poesy.* (17th cent.)

Shakespeare (whom you and every playhouse bill
Style the divine, the matchless, what you will)
For gain, not glory, wing'd his roving flight,
And grew immortal in his own despite.

Pope: *The First Epistle of the Second Book of Horace.* (18th cent.)

And one wild Shakespeare, following nature's lights,
Is worth whole planets, fill'd with Stagyrites.

Thomas Moore: *The Sceptic.* (19th cent.)

Shakespeare is English in everything, above all in his weaknesses.

G. K. Chesterton: *The Common Man.* (20th cent.)

Shame

When we sin, we are all ashamed at the presence of our inferiors.

St. John Chrysostom: *Homilies.* (4th cent.)

There smites nothing so sharp, nor smelleth so sour
As shame.

Langland: *Piers Plowman,* Passus 11. (14th cent.)

It is in almost every country become a common proverb, that shame is as it is taken.

St. Thomas More. (16th cent.)

Shameful craving must have shameful nay.

> John Heywood: *Proverbs,* 1, 11. (16th cent.)

Women—for they are more bound to purity than men,—if once they have lost all shame before God, are in nothing whatever to be trusted; and that in exchange for the gratification of their will, and of that affection which the devil suggests, they will hesitate at nothing.

> St. Teresa of Jesus: *Autobiography,* 5. (16th cent.)

Love taught him shame; and shame, with love at strife,
Soon taught the sweet civilities of life.

> Dryden: *Cymon and Iphigenia.* (17th cent.)

In the shadow of the rood
Love and shame together stood;
Love, that bade him bear the blame
Of her fallen sister shame;
Shame, that by the pangs thereof
Bade him break his heart for love.

> J. B. Tabb: *On Calvary.* (19th cent.)

Of all sweet passions shame the loveliest.

> Alfred Douglas: *In Praise of Shame.* (20th cent.)

What would shame him would turn back a funeral.

> Seumas MacManus: *Heavy Hangs the Golden Grain.* (20th cent.)

Shamrock

O, the shamrock, the green, immortal shamrock!
Chosen leaf of bard and chief,
Old Erin's native shamrock.

> Thomas Moore: *Oh the Shamrock.* (19th cent.)

Sharpness

All thing that is sharp is short.

> John Heywood: *Proverbs,* 2, 2. (16th cent.)

She

Whoe'er she be—
That not impossible she
That shall command my heart and me.

> Richard Crashaw: *Wishes to His Supposed Mistress.* (17th cent.)

Sheep

Your sheep, that were wont to be so meek and tame, and so small eaters, now, as I hear say, be become so great devourers, and so wild, that they eat up and swallow down the very men themselves.

> St. Thomas More: *Utopia.* (16th cent.)

Shelley, Percy Bysshe

Few men in the world's history had more faith than Shelley. He had faith in the end of the most earthquake speculations, in the licence of the most confounding passions. Indeed, he could bring himself to have faith in anything except in the faiths of everybody else.

> G. K. Chesterton: *A Handful of Authors.* (20th cent.)

Shepherd

The first holy men were shepherds.

> St. Augustine: *The City of God,* 15. (5th cent.)

Poor shepherds, home-spun things,
Whose wealth's their flock; whose wit, to be
Well read in their simplicity.

> Richard Crashaw: *The Holy Nativity of Our Lord, a Hymn.* (17th cent.)

Shepherdess

She walks—the lady of my delight—
A shepherdess of sheep.
Her flocks are thoughts. She keeps them white;
She guards them from the steep;
She feeds them on the fragrant height,
And folds them in for sleep.

> Alice Meynell: *The Shepherdess.* (20th cent.)

Ship

By viewing nature, nature's handmaid
    art
Makes mighty things from small things
    grow:
Thus fishes first to shipping did impart,
Their tail the rudder, and their head
    the prow.

> Dryden: *Annus Mirabilis.* (17th cent.)

More than once a ship has sunk in harbor.

> Seumas MacManus: *Heavy Hangs the Golden Grain.* (20th cent.)

Shipwreck

Like ships that have gone down at sea,
When heaven was all tranquillity.

> Thomas Moore: *Lalla Rookh: the Light of the Harem.* (19th cent.)

What matter in what wreck we reached
    the shore,
    So we both reached it?

> W. S. Blunt: *To One Who Would Make a Confession.* (19th cent.)

Shoe

But I wot best where wringeth me my shoe.

> Chaucer: *The Marchantes Tale.* (14th cent.)

The shoe will hold with the sole.

> John Heywood: *Proverbs,* 2, 5. (16th cent.)

Shrew

Every man can rule a shrew, save he that hath her.

> John Heywood: *Proverbs,* 2, 6. (16th cent.)

When all shrews have dined,
Change from foul weather to fair is oft
    inclined.

> John Heywood: *Proverbs,* 1, 13. (16th cent.)

Shrine

Weep, weep, O Walsingham,
    Whose days are nights,
Blessings turned to blasphemies,
    Holy deeds to despites:
Sin is where our Lady sat,
    Heaven turned is to hell;
Satan sits where our Lord did sway,
    Walsingham, O farewell!

> Anonymous, untitled poem. (Rawl. Poet. MS. 219) (16th cent.)

Sickness

O Lord God of compassions, stretch out Thine hand and grant that all the sick may be healed. Grant them to be counted worthy of health. Free them from the sickness that lies upon them. Let them be healed in the name of Thine Only-begotten. May His holy name be to them a medicine for health and soundness.

> Sacramentary of Serapion, Blessing of the Sick (30). (4th cent.)

Before all things and above all things care must be taken of the sick, so that they may be served in very deed as Christ himself. . . . But let the sick on their part consider that they are being served for the honor of God, and not provoke their brethren who are serving them by their unreasonable demands. Yet they should be patiently borne with, because from such as these is gained a more abundant reward.

> St. Benedict: *Rule,* 36. (6th cent.)

The sick on the other hand are to be admonished to realize that they are sons of God by the very fact that the scourge of discipline chastises them. For unless it were His plan to give them an inheritance after their chastisements, He would not trouble to school them in affliction.

> Pope St. Gregory I: *Pastoral Care,* 3, 12. (6th cent.)

Almighty and everlasting God, the eternal Salvation of believers, hear us on behalf of Thy ailing servants, NN., for whom we implore the aid of Thy mercy; that their health may be restored to them, and they may give thanks to Thee in Thy church.

> Roman Missal, Collect for the Sick. (Gelasian, 5th to 7th cent.)

O almighty and merciful God, Who hast vouchsafed to mankind both the remedies that bring salvation and the gifts of eternal life; graciously regard Thy servant, N., who is suffering from bodily sickness, and restore his soul, which Thou hast created; that in the hour of his death it may worthily be presented by the hands of holy angels to its Creator, without any stain of sin.

> Roman Missal, Collect for one near death. (Originally Gelasian, 5th to 7th cent.)

Make sickness itself a prayer.

> St. Francis de Sales: *Letters to Persons in the World*, 2, 31. (17th cent.)

God's will is as much in sickness as in health.

> St. Francis de Sales: *Treatise on the Love of God*, 9, 10. (17th cent.)

Long illnesses are good schools of mercy for those who tend the sick, and of loving patience for those who suffer.

> J. P. Camus: *The Spirit of St. Francis de Sales*, 9, 7. (17th cent.)

Ungrateful men, why do you sickness loathe,
Which blessings give in heaven, or earth, or both?

> Sir John Beaumont: *Of Sickness*. (17th cent.)

Sidney, Sir Philip

Sidney, whom we yet admire
Lighting our little torches at his fire.

> Sir Aston Cokain: *Funeral Elegy on Mr. Michael Drayton*. (17th cent.)

Sighing

Not such sorrowful sighs as men make
For woe, or else when that folk be sick,
But easy sighs, such as been to like.

> Chaucer: *Troilus and Criseyde*. (14th cent.)

To sigh, yet feel no pain.

> Thomas Moore: *The Blue Stocking*. (19th cent.)

Sight

I see much, but I say little, and do less.

> John Heywood: *Proverbs*, 1, 11. (16th cent.)

Sign

A sign is a thing which, apart from the impression that it presents to the senses, causes of itself some other thing to enter our thoughts.

> St. Augustine: *De Doctrina Christiana*, 2, 1, 1. (4th cent.)

Silence

It is easier to be altogether silent than not to exceed in words.

> Thomas a Kempis: *The Imitation of Christ*, 1, 20. (15th cent.)

Three may keep counsel, if two be away.

> John Heywood: *Proverbs*, 2, 5. (16th cent.)

I will say nought but mum, and mum is counsel.

> John Heywood: *Proverbs*, 2, 5. (16th cent.)

Fear oftentimes restraineth words, but makes not thoughts to cease;
And he speaks best that hath the skill when for to hold his peace.

> Thomas, Lord Vaux: *Content*. (16th cent.)

Mere silence is not wisdom, for wisdom consists in knowing when and how to speak and when and where to keep silent.

> J. P. Camus: *The Spirit of St. Francis de Sales,* 20, 2. (17th cent.)

Silence is the greatest persecution.

> Pascal: *Pensées,* 24. (17th cent.)

The parson's cant, the lawyer's sophistry,
Lord's quibble, critic's jest, all end in
thee;
All rest in peace at last, and sleep eternally.

> Pope: *Silence.* (Imitation of the Earl of Rochester.) (18th cent.)

Be silent and safe—silence never betrays
you.

> J. B. O'Reilly: *Rules of the Road.* (19th cent.)

Elected silence, sing to me
And beat upon my whorlèd ear,
Pipe me to pastures still and be
The music that I care to hear.

> G. M. Hopkins: *The Habit of Perfection.* (19th cent.)

I walk down the valley of silence—
Down the dim, voiceless valley—
alone!
And I hear not the fall of a footstep
Around me, save God's and my own;
And the hush of my heart is as holy
As hovers where angels have flown.

> A. Ryan: *Song of the Mystic.* (19th cent.)

Thou art like silence all unvexed,
Though wild words part my soul
from thee.
Thou art like silence unperplexed,
A secret and a mystery
Between one footfall and the next.

> Alice Meynell: *To the Beloved.* (19th cent.)

He knew the precise psychological moment when to say nothing.

> Oscar Wilde: *The Picture of Dorian Gray,* 2. (19th cent.)

Not, silence, for thine idleness I raise
My silence-bounded singing in thy
praise,
But for thy moulding of my Mozart's
tune,
Thy hold upon the bird that sings the
moon,
Thy magisterial ways.

> Alice Meynell: *To Silence.* (20th cent.)

Silence is the unbearable repartee.

> G. K. Chesterton: *Charles Dickens.* (20th cent.)

I know a wind-swept hill where all day
long
Comes never footfall nor the sound of
word,
Only by swallow's wing or woodlark's
song
Is that immense and brooding stillness
stirred.

> Blanche Mary Kelly: *Silentium Altum.* (20th cent.)

Have you heard silence singing in the
twilight,
When all was hushed and grey,
When black and still across white pools
unrippled
The shadows lay?
When from the marshlands rose the
mists upcurling,
And not a wind-breath stirred,
And not a cricket quavered from the
meadow,
Nor note of bird—
Have you not heard silence murmur-
ously singing
Into your ear,
A magic music wrung from depth of
shadow
And of fear?

> Eleanor Downing: *Transmutation.* (20th cent.)

Nothing delicate or fine
Seems to find this soul of mine;
Only heavy harmonies
Sudden chords that jar;
Winds blowing through a forest,
Waves breaking on a bar.

So I seek for silence
Where the secrets are:
Silence like the moonlight
Or a falling star.

Caroline Giltinan: *The Seeker*. (20th cent.)

The silent mouth is melodious.

Seumas MacManus: *Heavy Hangs the Golden Grain*. (20th cent.)

Simony

If any bishop obtains that dignity by money, or even a presbyter or deacon, let him and the person that ordained him be deprived; and let him be entirely cut off from communion, as Simon Magus was by me Peter.

Ecclesiastical Canons of the Holy Apostles, 30. (4th cent.)

O Simon Magus, O lost wretches led
    By thee, who prostitute the things
        that need,
    Being things of God, with goodness
        to be wed;
Who gape for gold and silver, mouths
    of greed!

Dante: *Inferno, Canto 19*. (Tr. Binyon) (14th cent.)

For he was qualified to hear confessions,
Or so he said, with more than priestly scope;
He had a special license from the pope.
Sweetly he heard his penitents at shrift
With pleasant absolution, for a gift.

Chaucer: *Canterbury Tales: Prologue*. (The wanton friar) (Tr. Coghill) (14th cent.)

Simplicity

How blessed are the simple, aye, indeed,
That only know enough to say their creed!

Chaucer: *The Miller's Tale*. (Tr. Coghill) (14th cent.)

Though I have spent years in reading and prayer, yet I could never find anything more efficacious, nor, for attaining to mystical theology, more direct than that the spirit should become like a little child and a beggar in the presence of God.

J. Gerson. (15th cent.)

Blessed are the simple, for they shall have much peace.

Thomas a Kempis: *The Imitation of Christ*, 1, 11. (15th cent.)

There is no artifice as good and desirable as simplicity.

St. Francis de Sales: *Introduction to the Devout Life*, 3, 30. (17th cent.)

In everything I love simplicity.

St. Francis de Sales: *Letters to Persons in Religion*, 1, 1. (17th cent.)

We are all very simple; it is when we forget that, that we go wrong.

R. H. Benson: *The Sentimentalists*. (20th cent.)

The only simplicity that matters is the simplicity of the heart. If that be gone, it can be brought back by no turnips or cellular clothing; but only by tears and terror and the fires that are not quenched.

G. K. Chesterton: *Heretics*. (20th cent.)

Sin

For God alone is without sin; and the only man without sin is Christ, since Christ is also God.

Tertullian: *Treatise on the Soul*, 41. (3rd cent.)

Sin then, as we have said, is a fearful evil, but not incurable; fearful for him who clings to it, but easy of cure for him who by repentance puts it from him.

St. Cyril of Jerusalem: *Catechetical Discourses*, 2, 1. (4th cent.)

The condemnation of those who know and do not apply their knowledge is the more severe; but even sin committed in ignorance is not without risk.

> St. Basil: *The Morals*, 9, 4. (4th cent.)

The end of sin is death.

> St. Basil: *The Morals*, 10. (4th cent.)

Committing sin estranges us from the Lord and leagues us with the devil.

> St. Basil: *The Morals*, 22. (4th cent.)

Sins that are easiest to amend bring the greatest punishment.

> St. John Chrysostom: *Homilies*. (4th cent.)

Everyone who commits sin is the slave of sin.

> St. Ambrose: *Concerning Joseph*, 4. (4th cent.)

The human race is subject to three kinds of sin, for when we sin it is either by thought, or word, or deed.

> St. Jerome: *Letters*. (4th cent.)

Sin is nothing else than to neglect eternal things, and seek after temporal things.

> St. Augustine: *De Libero Arbitrio*, 1. (4th cent.)

No one sins by an act he cannot avoid.

> St. Augustine: *De Libero Arbitrio*, 3. (4th cent.)

So true is it that every sin is voluntary, that, unless it be voluntary, it is no sin at all.

> St. Augustine: *De Libero Arbitrio*, 3, 18. (4th cent.)

Since human nature is inclined to appraise sins not by the measure of their malice, but, instead, by the measure of its own customs, it often happens that a man considers as reprehensible only those acts which the men of his own country and age usually protest against and denounce; and he holds as accepta-ble and commendable only those allowed by the usage of those with whom he lives.

> St. Augustine: *De Doctrina Christiana*, 3, 10, 15. (4th cent.)

Every sin is more injury to him who does than to him who suffers it.

> St. Augustine: *Enchiridion*. (5th cent.)

He who is the servant of sin is free to sin. And therefore he will not be free to do what is right until, freed from sin, he begins to be the servant of justice.

> St. Augustine: *Enchiridion*, 30. (5th cent.)

We commit sin because of one of two reasons: either we do not as yet see what we ought to do, or we do not do what we know ought to be done. The first of these is the evil of ignorance; the latter, that of weakness.

> St. Augustine: *Enchiridion*, 81. (5th cent.)

All sin is a kind of lying.

> St. Augustine: *Against Lying*. (5th cent.)

We may not sin in order to prevent another's sinning.

> St. Augustine: *Against Lying*. (5th cent.)

My sin was all the more incurable because I thought I was not a sinner; and my iniquity was more execrable in that I would rather have You, God Almighty, vanquished in me to my destruction than myself vanquished by You for my salvation.

> St. Augustine: *Confessions*, 5, 10. (5th cent.)

For the law of sin is the fierce force of habit, by which the mind is drawn and held even against its will, and yet deservedly because it had fallen wilfully into the habit.

> St. Augustine: *Confessions*, 8, 5. (5th cent.)

If every sin were now visited with manifest punishment, nothing would seem to be reserved for the final judgment; on the other hand, if no sin received now a plainly divine punishment, it would be concluded that there is no divine providence at all.

St. Augustine: *The City of God,* 1, 8. (5th cent.)

Men are punished by God for their sins often visibly, always secretly, either in this life or after death, although no man acts rightly save by the assistance of divine aid; and no man or devil acts unrighteously save by the permission of the divine and most just judgment.

St. Augustine: *The City of God,* 20, 1. (5th cent.)

Man will be altogether lost unless, through the grace of the Mediator, he be forgiven those things which are deemed mere sins of thought, since without the will to do them, he desires nevertheless to enjoy them.

St. Augustine: *De Trinitate,* 12, 12. (5th cent.)

A sin that is not quickly blotted out by repentance, is both a sin and a cause of sin.

Pope St. Gregory I: *Hom.,* 11. (5th cent.)

Therefore God never spares him that offends, in that he never leaves his sin without taking vengeance on it. For either man himself in doing penance punishes it in himself, or God in dealing with man in vengeance for it, visits it with His rod, and thus there is never any sparing of sin, in that it is never remitted without vengeance.

Pope St. Gregory I: *Morals,* 9 54. (6th cent.)

For we must understand that a sin is committed in three ways. For it is perpetrated either through ignorance, or infirmity, or of set purpose. And we sin more grievously from infirmity than through ignorance, but much more grievously of set purpose than from infirmity.

Pope St. Gregory I: *Morals,* 25, 28. (6th cent.)

Sin becomes much more scandalous when the sinner is honored for his position.

Pope St. Gregory I: *Regula Pastoralis,* 1, 2. (5th cent.)

Man is said to sin against himself, against God, and against his neighbor.

St. Isidore of Seville: *De Summo Bono.* (7th cent.)

For wickedness is nothing else than the withdrawal of goodness, just as darkness is nothing else than the withdrawal of light.

St. John of Damascus: *Exposition of the Orthodox Faith,* 2, 30. (8th cent.)

To sin is nothing else than not to render to God His due.

St. Anselm: *Cur Deus Homo.* (11th cent.)

Every one who sins ought to pay back the honor of which he has robbed God; and this is the satisfaction which every sinner owes to God.

St. Anselm: *Cur Deus Homo.* (11th cent.)

Theologians hold that in fact no deliberate act is morally neutral: if directed to God by grace then it is meritorious; if it cannot be so directed it is sin; if it is not directed then it is vanity, which amounts to sin.

St. Thomas Aquinas: *Commentary on the Sentences,* 1, 1, 3. (13th cent.)

We commit a sinful act by turning to a temporal attraction without being duly directed to our last end. . . . There is a turning to, and a turning away; the first, the self-indulgence and wasteful love, represents the material element in sin; the second, the aversion and hate, represents the formal element, formal because morality is defined with reference to our last end.

> St. Thomas Aquinas: *Disputations Concerning Evil,* 4, 2. (13th cent.)

There are two sides to every sin, the turning to transient satisfaction and the turning away from everlasting value. As regards the first, the principle of all sins can be called lust—lust in its most general sense, namely, the unbridled desire for one's own pleasure. As regards the second, the principle is pride, pride in its general sense, the lack of submission to God.

> St. Thomas Aquinas: *Disputations Concerning Evil,* 8, 1. (13th cent.)

Sin, the direct opposite of an act of virtue, is a disordered activity; vice, the direct opposite of virtue, is the condition of a thing out of its proper natural bearings.

> St. Thomas Aquinas: *Summa Theologica,* 1-2, 71, 1. (13th cent.)

The cause of sin is the will's not holding to the rule of reason and divine law.

> St. Thomas Aquinas: *Summa Theologica,* 1-2, 75, 1. (13th cent.)

Unless he be his partner in crime, a son is not blamed for his father's wrongdoing.

> St. Thomas Aquinas: *Summa Theologica,* 1-2, 81, 1. (13th cent.)

Sin is a human act gone bad. . . . The rule for human acts is twofold, one proximate and of a piece with man, namely his conscience, the other ultimate, primary, and transcendent, namely the eternal law.

> St. Thomas Aquinas: *Summa Theologica,* 1-2, 81, 6. (13th cent.)

To do sin is mannish, but certes to persevere long in sin is the work of the devil.

> mannish—the lot of man
>
> Chaucer: *The Tale of Melibeus.* (14th cent.)

Old sin, new shame.

> John Gower: *Confessio Amantis.* (14th cent.)

It would be better to eschew sin than to flee death.

> Thomas a Kempis: *The Imitation of Christ,* 1, 23. (15th cent.)

If any one saith that a man once justified can sin no more, nor lose grace, and that therefore he that falls and sins was never truly justified; or on the other hand that he is able during his whole life to avoid all sins, even those that are venial, except by a special privilege from God as the Church holds in regard of the Blessed Virgin; let him be anathema.

> Council of Trent, Session 6, Canon 23. (Jan. 13, 1547)

Ah! sin, the nothing that doth all things file,
Outcast from heaven, earth's curse, the cause of hell;
Parent of death, author of our exile,
The wreck of souls, the wares that fiends do sell;
That men to monsters, angels turn to devils,
Wrong of all rights, self-ruin, root of evils.

> Bl. Robert Southwell: *St. Peter's Complaint.* (16th cent.)

O sin! how huge and heavy is thy weight,
That weighest more than all the world beside;
Of which when Christ had taken in His freight,
The poise thereof His flesh could not abide.
Alas; if God himself sink under sin,
What will become of man that dies therein?

> Bl. Robert Southwell: *Sin's Heavy Load.* (16th cent.)

Who is mad enough to think it possible to sin more than God can forgive?

Jean Pierre Camus: *The Spirit of St. Francis de Sales*, 6, 3. (17th cent.)

Search thro' the world, we shall not
  know a thing,
Which may to reason's eye more horror
  bring,
Than disobedience to the highest
  Cause,
And obstinate aversion from His laws.

Sir John Beaumont: *Of Sin.* (17th cent.)

But, when to sin our bias'd nature leans,
The careful devil is still at hand with
  means.

Dryden: *Absalom and Achitophel.* (17th cent.)

O what are the wages of sin,
  The end of the race we have run?
We have slaved for the master we
    chose,
  And what is the price we have won?

We gave away all things for him,
  And in truth it was much that was
    given,—
The love of the angels and saints,
  And the chance of our getting to
    heaven.

F. Faber: *The Wages of Sin.* (19th cent.)

The world has cycles in its course, when
    all
  That once has been, is acted o'er
    again:—
Not by some fated law, which need
    appal
  Our faith, or binds our deeds as with
    a chain;
But by men's separate sins, which
    blended still
  The same bad round fulfil.

Card. Newman: *Faith against Sight.* (19th cent.)

A man must be far gone in degradation, and has lost even that false independence of mind which is often a substitute for real religion in leading to exertion, who,

while living in sin, steadily and contentedly holds the opinion that he is born for sin.

Card. Newman: *Parochial and Plain Sermons*, 1, 7. (19th cent.)

Sins in the regenerate are only the breaking forth of leaves in the trunk that is felled.

Coventry Patmore: *Memoirs.* (19th cent.)

O the success of his redeeming!
  O child, it is a rescued sin!

Alice Meynell: *Beyond Knowledge.* (20th cent.)

O murdering sin, O sin
Could I begin again,
Alas, what might have been!

Hugh Francis Blunt: *The Condemned Soul.* (20th cent.)

The fetters of sin are harder to slip than any that religion and conscience and virtue can forge.

Katharine T. Hinkson: *The Lost Angel.* (20th cent.)

When the world goes wrong, it proves rather that the Church is right. The Church is justified, not because her children do not sin, but because they do.

G. K. Chesterton: *The Everlasting Man, Intr.* (20th cent.)

The devil makes many disciples by preaching against sin. He convinces them of the great evil of sin, induces an emotional crisis which persuades them that God ignores their sins, and after that he lets them spend the rest of their lives meditating on the intense sinfulness and evident reprobation of other men.

Thomas Merton: *Seeds of Contemplation.* (20th cent.)

To be a Christian is to accept the responsibility for sin not only in oneself but in others also. It is to recognize that we all bear the responsibility for one another.

Dom Griffiths: *The Golden String.* (20th cent.)

Sin, Mortal and Venial

A distinction must be made according to the gravity of the case: it does not hold that because every crime is a sin, therefore every sin is a crime (*crimen*).

St. Augustine: *Enchiridion*, 64. (5th cent.)

The division of sin into mortal and venial sins is not like the division of a genus into two species; they are not specifically different kinds of sin, determined by the objects to which they turn. The difference between mortal and venial sin is decided by the stage reached by the disordered turning away from God. . . . When our acts are so deranged that we turn away from our last end, namely God, to whom we should be united by charity, then the sin is mortal. Short of that, the sin is venial.

St. Thomas Aquinas: *Summa Theologica*, 1-2, 72, 5. (13th cent.)

A sin may be venial in three ways. First, through its cause, i.e. through having cause to be forgiven, which cause lessens the sin; thus a sin that is committed through weakness or ignorance is said to be venial. Secondly, through its issue; thus every sin, through repentance, becomes venial, i.e. receives pardon (*veniam*). Thirdly, by its genus, e.g. an idle word.

St. Thomas Aquinas: *Summa Theologica*, 1-2, 77, 8. (13th cent.)

Although a man who commits a venial sin does not actually refer his act to God, nevertheless he still keeps God as his habitual end. He does not decisively set himself on turning away from God, but from overfondness for a created good he falls short of God. He is like a man who loiters, but without leaving the way.

St. Thomas Aquinas: *Commentary on the Sentences*, 1, 1, 3. (13th cent.)

In order that a sin should be mortal it is necessary that a man should act against the witness of his conscience, or else that his conscience is so blinded that he does not hold it a mortal sin to act deliberately in a way which God and the Church condemn as such.

Walter Hilton: *Scale of Perfection*, 2, 41. (14th cent.)

The Catholic Church holds it better for the sun and moon to drop from heaven, for the earth to fail, and for all the many millions in it to die of starvation in extremest agony, as far as temporal affliction goes, than that one soul, I will not say, should be lost, but should commit one single venial sin, should tell one wilful untruth, or should steal one poor farthing without excuse.

Card. Newman: *Apologia pro Vita Sua*, 5. (19th cent.)

Venial sins may torment a soul like hell.

R. H. Benson: *The Queen's Tragedy*. (20th cent.)

Sin, Original

The kingdom of death dominated mankind to such an extent as to drive all, by due penalty, headlong into the second death, of which there is no end, except that the undue grace of God has delivered some.

St. Augustine: *The City of God*, 14, 1. (5th cent.)

The whole clay of humanity is a condemned clay.

St. Augustine: *The City of God*, 21. (5th cent.)

God made man good at the beginning of the human creation, and there is no iniquity with God. For this reason the initial perversity, whereby God is not obeyed, is from man, because he fell by his own bad will from the goodness in which God originally constituted him, and became perverse.

St. Augustine: *De Correptione et Gratia*, 6, 9. (5th cent.)

Original sin is a racial sin, not a personal sin.

> St. Thomas Aquinas: *Disputations concerning Evil,* 4, 1. (13th cent.)

Original sin fastens on the whole human race. It is first of all found in the soul, which, although direct from God, is part of human nature. When human nature is transmitted, so also is original sin.

> St. Thomas Aquinas: *Disputations concerning Evil,* 4, 1. (13th cent.)

If any one does not confess that the first man, Adam, when he had transgressed the commandment of God in Paradise, immediately lost the holiness and justice wherein he had been constituted; and that he incurred through the offence of that sin the wrath and indignation of God, and consequently, death, with which God had previously threatened him, and together with death, captivity under his power who thenceforth *had the empire of death, that is to say, the devil* (Hebr. 2, 14), and that the entire Adam, through that offence of sin, was changed in body and soul for the worse, let him be anathema.

> Decree of the Council of Trent, Session 5. (Repeating language of Council of Orange, 529) (June 17, 1546)

If any one asserts that the sin of Adam injured himself alone, and not his posterity; and that the holiness and justice received of God, which he lost, he lost for himself alone, and not for us also; or that he, being defiled by the sin of disobedience, has only transfused death and pains of the body into the whole human race but not sin also, which is the death of the soul; let him be anathema.

> Decree of the Council of Trent, Session 5. (June 17, 1546)

Carlyle said that men were mostly fools. Christianity, with its surer and more reverent realism, says that they are all fools. This doctrine is sometimes called the doctrine of original sin. It may also be described as the doctrine of the equality of men.

> G. K. Chesterton: *Heretics.* (20th cent.)

Oh, he didn't believe in Adam or Eve—
　He put no faith therein;
His doubts began with the fall of man,
　And he laughed at original sin.

> H. Belloc: *Song of the Pelagian Heresy.* (20th cent.)

Sin, Remission of

For first of all the Lord gave that power [i.e. to remit sins] to Peter, upon whom He built His Church, and whence He appointed and showed the source of unity—the power, namely, that whatsoever He loosed on earth should be loosed in heaven.

> St. Cyprian: *Letters,* 72, 7. (3rd cent.)

The Lord is loving unto man, and swift to pardon, but slow to punish. Let no man therefore despair of his own salvation.

> St. Cyril of Jerusalem: *Catechetical Discourses,* 2, 19. (4th cent.)

With good reason does Peter, out of all the apostles, act in the person of the Catholic Church—for to this Church were the keys of the kingdom of heaven given when bestowed on Peter (Matth., 16, 19). Hence when the Lord asked him: *Dost thou love Me?* (John, 21, 15) that question was put to all. The Catholic Church, then, ought readily to pardon her children when they repent and are re-established in devotion to her.

> St. Augustine: *De Agone Christiano,* 32. (4th cent.)

For outside the Church there is no remission of sins. She received as her very own the pledge of the Holy Spirit, without whom no sin whatever is remitted, so that those to whom sins are remitted receive life everlasting.

> St. Augustine: *Enchiridion,* 65. (5th cent.)

But as to what your sweetness has added in your letters, that you will continue to be urgent with me until I write that it has been revealed to me that your sins are forgiven, you have demanded a difficult, nay an unprofitable thing; difficult, because I am unworthy of having a revelation made to me; unprofitable, because you ought not to become secure about your sins, except on the last day of your life when you are no longer able to bewail them. But until that day comes, you ought, ever suspicious and fearful, to be afraid of faults and wash them away with daily tears.

Pope St. Gregory I: *Letters,* 7, 25. (To Gregoria, a lady of the court at Constantinople.) (6th cent.)

Graciously grant unto Thy faithful pardon and peace, we beseech Thee, O Lord; that being cleansed from all their sins, they may serve Thee with a reassured conscience.

Roman Missal, Collect for Twentieth Sunday after Pentecost. (Gelasian, 5th to 7th cent.)

We beseech Thee, O Lord, hear the prayers of Thy suppliants, and spare the sins of those who confess unto Thee; graciously grant us both pardon and peace.

Roman Missal, Collect for Remission of Sins. (Gregorian, ca. 6th cent.)

For not without confession of amendment can sins be remitted.

St. Bede the Venerable: *In Ep. Jacob.* (8th cent.)

Remember Thy servants, O Lord, in Thy goodness, and forgive them the sins they have committed during the course of their lives; for there is none sinless save Thee, Who art able to give rest even to the departed.

Byzantine Horologion, Troparion at Nocturns. (Before 8th cent. ?)

Judicial power has two parts, the authority to pass a verdict, and the authority to pronounce sentence. These are called the two keys of the Church, namely, the power of discerning and the power of binding and loosing. They were committed by our Lord to Peter: *I will give thee the keys of the kingdom of heaven* (Matth. 16, 19). Do not misunderstand, this power was not restricted to him personally, but was meant to spread out from him to others, otherwise the welfare of the faithful would not be sufficiently provided for.

St. Thomas Aquinas: *Contra Gentes,* 4, 72. (13th cent.)

If any one saith that it is necessary for every one, in order to obtain the remission of sins, that he believe for certain and without any wavering arising from his own infirmity and indisposition, that his sins are forgiven him; let him be anathema.

Council of Trent, Session 6, Canon 13. (Jan. 13, 1547)

See also Absolution; Confession; Penance

Sin Against the Holy Ghost

Not every sin in word or deed is to be called the sin against the Holy Spirit, but only some sin that is definite and peculiar, namely that hardness of heart whereby to the close of his days a man refuses to obtain remission of his sins in the unity of that Body of Christ which is quickened by the Holy Spirit.

St. Augustine: *Letter 185,* 49. (5th cent.)

Singularity

Always avoid singularity to the utmost of thy power, for it does great harm in a community.

St. Teresa of Jesus: *Maxims.* (16th cent.)

Sinner

Prosperous sinners fare worst of all in the end.

St. John Chrysostom: *Homilies.* (4th cent.)

The sinner is not cast out, he casts himself out.

St. Ambrose: *In Ps. 43 Enarr. 25.* (4th cent.)

They pull to pieces every profession of religion, and think that they have found a remedy for their own doom, if they can disprove the holiness of others, if they can detract from everyone, if they can show that those who perish are many, and sinners a great multitude.

St. Jerome: *Letters,* 45, 4. (4th cent.)

With love of the sinner and hatred of the sin. (Cum dilectione hominum et odio vitiorum.)

St. Augustine: *Letter 211.* (A favorite thought of St. Augustine's) (5th cent.)

Master, God, Father almighty; Lord, only-begotten Son, Jesus Christ, and Holy Ghost, one Godhead, one Might! be gracious unto me a sinner; and by ways Thou knowest save me, Thine unworthy servant; for Thou art blessed to ages of ages. Amen.

Byzantine Horologion, Prayer at Terce. (ca. 6th to 8th cent.)

The body of a sinner is a tomb, covering a soul dead by sin. . . . Inside a corpse, though outside sometimes an effigy of the living.

St. Thomas Aquinas: *Commentary on St. Matthew,* 23. (13th cent.)

Young saint, old sinner.

John Heywood: *Proverbs,* 1, 10. (16th cent.)

Since the goodness of God is so great that one single moment suffices to obtain and receive His grace, what assurance can we have that a man who was a sinner yesterday is so today?

St. Francis de Sales: *Introduction to the Devout Life,* 3, 29. (17th cent.)

There are only two sorts of men: the one the just, who believe themselves sinners;

the other sinners, who believe themselves just.

Pascal: *Pensées,* 25. (17th cent.)

My spirit longeth for Thee
  To dwell within my breast;
Although I am unworthy
  Of so divine a Guest!

Of so divine a Guest—
  Unworthy though I be;
Yet hath my heart no rest
  Until it come to Thee!

  . . . .

Cheer up, desponding soul,
  Thy longing pleased I see:
'Tis part of that great whole,
  Wherewith I long'd for Thee!

M. Bridges: *Peccator ad Christum* and *Christus ad Peccatorem.* (19th cent.)

We are sinners, but we do not know how great. He alone knows Who died for our sins.

Card. Newman: *Parochial and Plain Sermons,* 1, 4. (19th cent.)

To recognize Christ in the sinner is not only to Christ's service, but to the sinner's as well.

R. H. Benson: *The Friendship of Christ.* (20th cent.)

Sinners are people who hate everything, because their world is necessarily full of betrayal, full of illusion, full of deception. And the greatest sinners are the most boring people in the world because they are also the most bored and the ones who find life most tedious.

Thomas Merton: *Seeds of Contemplation.* (20th cent.)

To be a sinner is our distress, but to know it is our hope.

Bishop Sheen: *Peace of Soul.* (20th cent.)

Sitting

Better sit still than rise and fall.

John Heywood: *Proverbs,* 2, 5. (16th cent.)

Sky

O great Creator of the sky,
Who wouldst not the floods on high
With earthly waters to confound,
But mad'st the firmament their bound.

Roman Breviary, Hymn *Immense coeli Conditor* for Monday at Vespers. (Tr. J. Neale) (Attr. to Pope St. Gregory I, 6th cent.)

O God, Whose hand hath spread the sky,
And all its shining hosts on high,
And painting it with fiery light,
Made it so beauteous and so bright.

Roman Breviary Hymn *Coeli Deus sanctissime* for Wednesday at Vespers. (Tr. J. Neale) (Attr. to Pope St. Gregory I, 6th cent.)

When I survey the bright
    Celestial sphere;
So rich with jewels hung, that night
    Doth like an Ethiop bride appear:
My soul her wings doth spread
    And heavenward flies,
The Almighty's mysteries to read
    In the large volume of the skies.

W. Habington: *Nox Nocti Indicat Scientiam.* (17th cent.)

For the bright firmament
    Shoots forth no flame
So silent, but is eloquent
    In speaking the Creator's name.

W. Habington: *Nox Nocti Indicat Scientiam.* (17th cent.)

I never saw a man who looked
    With such a wistful eye
Upon that little tent of blue
    Which prisoners call the sky,
And at every drifting cloud that went
    With sails of silver by.

Oscar Wilde: *The Ballad of Reading Gaol,* 1. (19th cent.)

Slander

Far better not be born than to be one
That people slander and say cheap
    things about.

Chaucer: *The Shipman's Tale.* (Tr. Coghill) (14th cent.)

It may be a slander, but it is no lie.

John Heywood: *Proverbs,* 2, 7. (16th cent.)

Too often do we call the truths which offend us by the name of slander.

J. P. Camus: *The Spirit of St. Francis de Sales,* 8, 10. (17th cent.)

A slanderer cannot succeed unless he has a reputation for hating slander.

Pascal: *Provincial Letters,* 16. (17th cent.)

Slang

All slang is metaphor, and all metaphor is poetry.

G. K. Chesterton: *A Defence of Slang.* (20th cent.)

Slavery

But do you who are slaves be subject to your master, as to God's representative, in reverence and fear.

Teaching of the Twelve Apostles, 4. (2nd cent.)

Should any one say: Are there not among you some poor, some rich, some slaves, some who are masters; is there no difference between different persons? I answer: There is none, nor is there any other cause why we call each other by the name of brother than that we consider ourselves to be equals; for, when we measure all human things, not by the body but by the spirit, although their corporal condition may be different from ours, yet in spirit they are not slaves to us, but we esteem and call them brethren, fellow workers in religion.

Lactantius: *Divine Institutes,* 5, 16. (4th cent.)

Those who from motives of religion shall give deserved liberty to their slaves in the midst of the Church shall be regarded as having given the same with the same legal force as that by which

Roman citizenship has been customarily given with the traditional solemn rites. But this is permitted only to those who give this liberty in the presence of the priest.

> Edict of the Emperor Constantine I.
> (Theod. Code, 4, 7, 1.) (321)

The peculiar characteristic of slavery is to be always in fear.

> St. Ambrose: *Concerning Joseph,* 20.
> (4th cent.)

The prime cause of slavery is sin, which brings man under the dominion of his fellow, that which does not happen save by the judgment of God, with Whom is no unrighteousness, and Who knows how to award fit punishments to every variety of offence. . . . But by nature, as God first created us, no one is the slave either of man or of sin. This servitude is however penal, and is appointed by that law which enjoins the preservation of the natural order and forbids its disturbance; for if nothing had been done in violation of that law, there would have been nothing to restrain by penal servitude.

> St. Augustine: *The City of God,* 19, 15.
> (5th cent.)

Whether slaves or freemen, we are all one in Christ, and have to serve alike in the army of the same Lord.

> St. Benedict: *Rule,* 2. (6th cent.)

Since our Redeemer, the creator of all creatures, for this reason graciously willed to assume human flesh, that, by the grace of His divinity and breaking asunder the bonds of slavery in which we were held captive, He might restore us to our former liberty, it is well done when men whom nature brought forth in the beginning as children and on whom the law of nations has imposed the yoke of slavery are restored to that liberty in which they were born, through the benefit of manumission.

> Pope St. Gregory I: *Letters,* 5, 12. (6th cent.)

Slaves are to be admonished not to despise their masters, lest they offend God by their proud opposition to His ordinances. Masters also are to be admonished that they offend God by priding themselves on His gift to them, and not realizing that they who are held in subjection by reason of their state of life, are their equals in virtue of their common nature. The former are to be admonished to bear in mind that they are servants of masters; the latter, that they are to acknowledge themselves to be fellow servants of servants.

> Pope St. Gregory I: *Pastoral Care,* 3, 5.
> (6th cent.)

Because of the sin of the first man the punishment of slavery was divinely imposed on the human race, so that He might inflict slavery more mercifully on those who He perceives are not suited to liberty. Although original sin was remitted for all the faithful by the grace of baptism, yet God in His justice has so ordered the lives of men, establishing some as slaves, others as masters, that the power of slaves to do evil is restrained by the power of those who rule over them. For if all were without any fear, who could restrain anyone from evil?

> St. Isidore: *Sentences,* 3, 47. (7th cent.)

As in Jesus Christ there is neither free nor slave, and no slave is to be kept from the sacraments of the Church, so also the marriage of slaves must in no wise be prohibited. Even if they have contracted marriages contrary to the will of their masters, these are in no wise to be dissolved by the authority of the Church; but they must continue to discharge their lawful and accustomed services to their own masters.

> Pope Hadrian IV: *Decretals,* 4, 9, 1.
> (12th cent.)

Either be wholly slaves or wholly free.

> Dryden: *The Hind and the Panther,* 2.
> (17th cent.)

The blow that liberates the slave
But sets the master free.

> J. J. Roche: *Gettysburg.* (19th cent.)

Would that all who hold high positions
in authority and power, or who desire
the rights of nations and of humanity to
be held sacred, or who earnestly devote
themselves to the interests of the Catholic religion, would all, everywhere acting
on our exhortations and wishes, strive together to repress, forbid, and put an end
to that kind of traffic, than which nothing is more base and wicked.

> Pope Leo XIII: *Letter 'In Plurimis' to the
> Bishops of Brazil.* (With ref. to slave
> trade) (May 5, 1888)

It is however chiefly to be wished that
this may be prosperously accomplished,
which all desire, that slavery may be banished and blotted out without any injury
to divine or human rights, with no political agitation, and so with the solid
benefit of the slaves themselves, for
whose sake it is undertaken.

> Pope Leo XIII: *Letter 'In Plurimis'.*
> (May 5, 1888)

When, amid the slave multitude whom
she has numbered among her children,
some, led astray by some hope of liberty,
have had recourse to violence and sedi-
tion, the church has always condemned
these unlawful efforts, and through her
ministers has applied the remedy of patience.

> Pope Leo XIII: *Letter 'In Plurimis'.*
> (May 5, 1888)

Sleep

Lord, Thou knowest the watchfulness
of my invisible enemies, and Thou Who
madest me dost see the weakness of my
flesh. Therefore into Thy hands I commend my spirit. Keep me under the
shadow of the wings of Thy goodness,
lest I sleep the sleep of death. Enlighten
the eyes of my mind with Thy divine

words, and in due course awaken me to
praise Thee, O good Lover of mankind.

> Byzantine Horologion, Troparion at Great
> Compline. (ca. 8th cent. ?)

When birds shall roost,
Who shall appoint their hour—
The cock, or the hen?

> John Heywood: *Proverbs,* 2, 2. (16th
> cent.)

Sleep, death's ally, oblivion of tears,
Silence of passions, balm of angry sore,
Suspense of loves, security of fears,
Wrath's lenitive, heart's ease, storm's
calmest shore,
Sense's and soul's reprieval from all
cumbers,
Benumbing sense of ill with quiet slum-
bers.

> Bl. Robert Southwell: *St. Peter's
> Complaint.* (16th cent.)

Let not the sluggish sleep
Close up thy waking eye,
Until with judgment deep
Thy daily needs thou try:
He that one sin in conscience keeps
When he to quiet goes,
More venturesome is than he that sleeps
With twenty mortal foes.

> William Byrd: *Songs.* (16th cent.)

I shall sleep like a top.

> Sir William Davenant: *The Rivals,* 3.
> (17th cent.)

Softly, O midnight hours!
Move softly o'er the bowers
Where lies in happy sleep a girl so fair:
For ye have power, men say,
Our hearts in sleep to sway
And cage cold fancies in a moonlight
snare.

> Aubrey de Vere: *Softly, O Midnight
> Hours.* (19th cent.)

Sleep! the spirits that attend
On thy waking hours are fled.
Heaven thou canst not now offend
Till thy slumber-plumes are shed;

Consciousness alone doth lend
  Life its pain, and death its dread;
Innocence and peace befriend
  All the sleeping and the dead.

  J. B. Tabb: *Slumber-Song.* (19th cent.)

But sleep stole on me unawares,
  Even on me at last;
Though drop by drop the minutes faint,
  Like hours at midnight passed.

  Eleanor Hamilton King: *The First of June.*
  (19th cent.)

But when sleep comes to close each dif-
    ficult day,
  When night gives pause to the long
      watch I keep,
    And all my bonds I needs must
        loose apart,
Must doff my will as raiment laid away.

  Alice Meynell: *Renouncement.* (19th
  cent.)

Dreams, who loves dreams! forget all
    grief;
Find in sleep's nothingness relief.

  Lionel Johnson: *Oxford Nights.* (19th
  cent.)

The dovecote doors of sleep.

  Alice Meynell: *At Night.* (19th cent.)

Dear fool, be true to me!
I know the poets speak thee fair, and I
    Hail thee uncivilly.
But O I call with a more urgent cry!
    . . . .
Come and release me; bring
My irresponsible mind; come in thy
    hours.
Draw from my soul the sting
Of wit that trembles, consciousness that
    cowers.

For if night comes without thee
She is more cruel than day. But thou,
    fulfil
  Thy work, thy gifts about thee—
Liberty, liberty, from this weight of
    will.

  Alice Meynell: *To Sleep.* (20th cent.)

Sleep falls like snowflakes, and it seems
'Tis always drifting into dreams;
But death falls like the snow at sea,
And drifts into eternity.

  Francis Carlin: *Sleep.* (20th cent.)

Sleeplessness

Suffered the trampling hoof of every
    hour
  In night's slow-wheelèd car;
Until the tardy dawn dragged me at
    length
From under those dread wheels.

  F. Thompson: *Sister Songs.* (19th cent.)

Smile

What I saw seemed a smile of the uni-
    verse;
  So that the intoxicating ecstasy
  Entered me both by the eyes and by
    the ears.

  Dante: *Paradiso, Canto* 27. (Tr. L.
  Binyon) (14th cent.)

Eternal smiles his emptiness betray,
As shallow streams run dimpling all the
    way.

  Pope: *An Epistle to Dr. Arbuthnot.* (18th
  cent.)

A scornful smile lay keen
On lips that, living, prophesied of
    doom.

  F. Thompson: *Ode for the Diamond
  Jubilee of Queen Victoria, 1897.* (19th
  cent.)

Snapdragon

Trinity had never been unkind to me.
There used to be much snapdragon growing on the walls opposite my freshman's
rooms there, and I had for years taken it
as the emblem of my own perpetual resi-
dence even unto death in my university.

  Card. Newman: *Apologia pro Vita Sua,* 4.
  (19th cent.)

Sneezing

Sneezing absorbs all the faculties of the soul.

> Pascal: *Pensées*, 25. (17th cent.)

Sudden, with starting tears each eye o'erflows,
And the high dome reechoes to his nose.

> Pope: *The Rape of the Lock*, 5. (18th cent.)

Snare

And why, it is asked, are there so many snares? That we may not fly low, but seek the things that are above.

> St. John Chrysostom: *Homilies*. (4th cent.)

Snobbishness

It isn't decent, nothing good can come
Of having truck with slum-and-gutter dwellers,
But only with the rich and victual-sellers.

> Chaucer: *Canterbury Tales: Prologue*. (Tr. Coghill) (14th cent.)

She was a sneering woman and she thought
That ladies should respect her, so they ought,
What with her well-connected family,
And education in a nunnery.

> Chaucer: *The Reeve's Tale*. (Tr. Coghill) (14th cent.)

Snow

O tender mountain-tops and delicate,
Where summer-long the westering sun-light sate!
Within that fastness darkened from the sun,
What solitary things were done?

The clouds let go, they rose, they winged away;
Snow-white the altered mountains faced the day,

As saints who keep their counsel sealed and fast,
Their anguish over-past.

> Alice Meynell: *The First Snow*. (20th cent.)

Snowflake

So purely, so palely,
Tinily, surely,
Mightily, frailly,
Insculped and embossed,
With his hammer of wind,
And his grave of frost.

> F. Thompson: *To a Snowflake*. (20th cent.)

Sobriety

'Tis a madness to be sober alone, while the nation continues drunk.

> Dryden: *Religio Laici*, Pref. (17th cent.)

Socialism

Socialists, Communists, and Nihilists . . . strive to uproot the foundations of civilized society.

> Pope Leo XIII: *Quod apostolici muneris*. (Dec. 28, 1878)

The main tenet of socialism, namely, the community of good, must be rejected without qualification, for it would injure those it pretends to benefit, it would be contrary to the natural rights of man, and it would introduce confusion and disorder into the commonwealth.

> Pope Leo XIII: *Rerum novarum*. (May 15, 1891)

No one can be, at the same time, a sincere Catholic and a true socialist.

> Pope Pius XI: *Quadragesimo anno*. (May 15, 1931)

Socialism appears to be afraid of its own principles, and of the conclusions drawn from them by the communists. In consequence, it is drifting toward truths which the Christian tradition has always supported. Indeed it cannot be denied that its program often comes close to the just demands of Christian reformers.

> Pope Pius XI: *Quadregesimo anno*. (May 15, 1931)

Society

To seek the society of others and to shun it are two blameworthy extremes in the devotion of those who live in the world.

> St. Francis de Sales: *Introduction to the Devout Life*, 3, 24. (17th cent.)

Gerald: I suppose society is wonderfully delightful?
Lord Illingworth: To be in it is merely a bore. But to be out of it is simply a tragedy.

> Oscar Wilde: *A Woman of No Importance*, 3. (19th cent.)

Human society, as established by God, is composed of unequal elements, just as parts of the human body are unequal; to make them all equal is impossible, and would mean the destruction of human society itself.

> Pope St. Pius X: *Letter to the Bishops of Italy on Catholic Social Action*. (1903)

Society is a rational process, and its rationality consists essentially in its progress—never rectilinear, always interrupted by regressions—towards an ideal of human community, structured after the demands of social justice and the equality of man with man, and informed by the spirit of social charity and the solidarity of all men.

> J. C. Murray: *Address to Amer. Acad. of Political and Social Science*. (1948)

To say that the Church has a mission in the temporal order is not to defend what is called 'clericalism.' It is simply to say that the virtualities of Christian faith are not exhausted by personal piety; they demand an attack on organized injustice in all its forms; they demand positive action to establish and secure such institutions in the temporal order as will be favorable to the growth of the seed of eternal life planted in baptism.

> J. C. Murray: *Address to Amer. Academy of Political and Social Science*. (1948)

The origin and primary scope of social life is the conservation, development and perfection of the human being, helping him to realize accurately the demands and values of religion and culture set by the Creator for every man and for all mankind, both as a whole and in its natural ramifications.

> Pope Pius XII: *Christmas Message*. (Dec. 24, 1942)

Society of Jesus

See Jesuits

Soldier

Brothers, let us be His soldiers, therefore in all earnestness, under His faultless commands.

> Pope St. Clement I: *Letter to the Corinthians*, 37, 1. (1st cent.)

I am a soldier of Christ: combat is not permitted me.

> Sulpicius Severus: *Life of St. Martin*, 4. (Quoting the saint's words when the latter refused further service as a Roman soldier) (4th cent.)

Drinking is the soldier's pleasure.

> Dryden: *Alexander's Feast*. (17th cent.)

Soldiers of Christ! arise
  And put your armor on,
Strong in the strength which God supplies
    Through His eternal Son;
Strong is the Lord of hosts,
  And in His mighty power,
Who in the strength of Jesus trusts,
  Is more than conqueror.

> Anonymous: *Soldiers of Christ! Arise.* (In Caswall's *Lyra Catholica*) (19th cent.)

When falls the soldier brave,
  Dead at the feet of wrong,
The poet sings and guards his grave
  With sentinels of song.

> Abram J. Ryan: *Sentinel Songs.* (19th cent.)

Young as the youngest who donned the
    Gray,
  True as the truest that wore it,
Brave as the bravest he marched away,
(Hot tears on the cheeks of his mother
    lay),
Triumphant waved our flag one day—
  He fell in the front before it.

> A. Ryan: *In Memory of My Brother.* (19th cent.)

God! to hear the shrill
Sweet treble of her fifes upon the
    breeze,
And at the summons of the rock gun's
    roar
To see her red coats marching from the
    hill!

> W. S. Blunt: *Gibraltar.* (19th cent.)

The sunshine streaming upon Salmon's
    height
  Is not so sweet and white
As the most heretofore sin-spotted soul
  That darts to its delight
Straight from the absolution of a faith-
    ful fight.

> Coventry Patmore: *Peace.* (19th cent.)

In a wood they call the Rouge Bouquet,
There is a new-made grave today,
Built by never a spade nor pick,
Yet covered with earth ten meters thick.
There lie many fighting men,
  Dead in their youthful prime.
Never to laugh nor love again
  Nor taste the summertime.

> Joyce Kilmer: *Rouge Bouquet.* (20th cent.)

From softness only softness comes;
Urged by a bitterer shout within,
Men of the trumpets and the drums
Seek, with appropriate discipline,
That glory past the pit or wall

Which contradicts and stops the breath,
And with immortalizing gall
Builds the most stubborn things on
    earth.

> Oliver Gogarty: *Marcus Curtius.* (20th cent.)

But off with your hats and three times
    three for Columbia's true-blue sons:
The men below who batter the foe—the
    men behind the guns!

> John J. Rooney: *The Men Behind the Guns.* (20th cent.)

Solemnity

Why are little children always supposed
to be gay? There is no solemnity in the
world to be compared to the solemnity of
a little boy or of his sister who has charge
of him.

> R. H. Benson: *The Light Invisible.* (20th cent.)

It is so easy to be solemn; it is so hard to
be frivolous.

> G. K. Chesterton: *All Things Considered.* (20th cent.)

Solitude

The wise saith, Woe him that is alone,
For, and he fall, he hath no help to rise.

> Chaucer: *Troilus and Criseyde.* (14th cent.)

The greatest saints avoided the company
of men as much as possible, and chose to
live to God in secret.

> Thomas a Kempis: *The Imitation of Christ,* 1, 20. (15th cent.)

O well are you that have subdued,
The force of world's desire,
And in the fort of solitude,
For safety do retire.
  Retir'd from freedom so suppos'd,
In straightness freedom find,
Because true freedom is enclos'd
In circuit of the mind.
  The world and fortune you deprive,
From doing you despite:

Dead unto men, to God alive,
That gives life's true delight.

> Richard Verstegan: *Of the State of Solitary Life*. (Guiney, 215) (16th cent.)

Sweet solitary life, thou true repose,
  Wherein the wise contemplate heaven
    aright,
In thee no dread of war or worldly foes,
  In thee no pomp seduceth mortal
    sight,
In thee no wanton cares to win with
    words,
No lurking toys, which city life affords.

> Thomas Lodge: *A Solitary Life Commended*. (16th cent.)

The only justification for a life of deliberate solitude is the conviction that it will help you to love not only God but also other men. Otherwise, if you go into the desert merely to get away from crowds of people you dislike, you will not find peace or solitude either: you will only isolate yourself with a tribe of devils. Go into the desert not to escape other men but in order to find them in God.

> Thomas Merton: *Seeds of Contemplation*. (20th cent.)

There is no true solitude except interior solitude.

> Thomas Merton: *Seeds of Contemplation*. (20th cent.)

Something

Something is better than nothing.

> John Heywood: *Proverbs*, 1, 10. (16th cent.)

Son

That unfeather'd two-legged thing, a son.

> Dryden: *Absalom and Achitophel*, 1. (17th cent.)

Son, God the

See Jesus Christ

Song

Song is the leap of mind in the eternal breaking out into sound.

> St. Thomas Aquinas: *Exposition of the Psalms, Prol.* (13th cent.)

Our lady sings magnificat
  With tune surpassing sweet,
And all the virgins bear their parts,
  Sitting above her feet.

> Anonymous: *Jerusalem, My Happy Home*. (Guiney, 281) (16th cent.)

And heaven had wanted one immortal song.

> Dryden: *Absalom and Achitophel*. (17th cent.)

What will a child learn sooner than a song?

> Pope: *The First Epistle of the Second Book of Horace*. (18th cent.)

None knew whether
The voice or lute was most divine,
So wondrously they went together.

> Thomas Moore: *Lalla Rookh: Prologue*. (19th cent.)

Roll forth, my song, like the rushing
    river
  That sweeps along to the mighty sea;
God will inspire me while I deliver
    My soul of thee!

> James Mangan: *The Nameless One*. (19th cent.)

Swift, swift, and bring with you
Song's Indian summer!

> F. Thompson: *A Carrier Song*. (19th cent.)

My human song must be
  My human thought. Be patient till
    'tis done.
I shall not hold my little peace; for me
  There is no peace but one.

> Alice Meynell: *The Poet to the Birds*. (20th cent.)

He sits at the foot of Golgotha,
  And out of his singing soul
He fashions songs to make his Lord
  A shining aureole.
But all the songs he sings are vain,
  And all his singing dross—
For he sits at the foot of Golgotha
  While Christ hangs on the Cross.
And yet his Lord may deem his songs
  Were better sung than not,
For they, at least, remembered Him
  While other songs forgot.

> Myles Connolly: *Lament for a Poor Poet.*
> (20th cent.)

It is the best of all trades to make songs,
and the second best to sing them.

> Hilaire Belloc: *On Song.* (20th cent.)

The very best songs that ever are
  sung
Are sung while the heart is bleeding.

> Joyce Kilmer: *Daw's Dinner.* (20th cent.)

Because the road was steep and long
  And through a dark and lonely land,
God set upon my lips a song
  And put a lantern in my hand.

> Joyce Kilmer: *Love's Lantern.* (20th
> cent.)

Give me the sun, a bird, a flower,
  And I shall spin you a song
    That will live an hour.

Give me a heart, a joy, a tear,
  And I shall weave you a song
    That will live a year.

But give me a love death cannot sever,
  And I will build you a song
    To live forever.

> Sister Miriam: *Give Me the Sun.* (20th
> cent.)

God has so many singing birds
To lilt from sunny throats,
Proud birds with slow strong notes,
Like stately Dons of Spain:
God has full many singing birds
To mock on hill and plain
The tabor of the wind,
The viol of the rain.

God has so many troubadours
With songs of March and May
On pipe and flageolet
To flute of flower and seed,
God has so many troubadours
To sing in court and train,
He will not miss my bitter reed,
I shall not sing again.

> Eileen Duggan: *The Last Song.* (20th
> cent.)

But I can only offer you, my sweet,
The songs I made on many a night of
  stars.
Yet have I worshipped honor, loving
  you.

> Theodore Maynard: *If I Had Ridden
> Horses.* (20th cent.)

Sophistry

The most sophistical of all sophists are
the gymnosophists.

> G. K. Chesterton: *The Everlasting Man,*
> I, I. (20th cent.)

Mere light sophistry is the thing that I
happen to despise most of all things, and
it is perhaps a wholesome fact that this
is the thing of which I am generally accused.

> G. K. Chesterton: *Orthodoxy.* (20th cent.)

Sore

It is ill healing of an old sore.

> John Heywood: *Proverbs,* 2, 8. (16th
> cent.)

Sorrow

Take sorrow out of your heart, for it is
the sister of divided purpose and violent
anger.

> Shepherd of Hermas, Mandate 10, 1. (2nd
> cent.)

Sorrow is given us on purpose to cure us
of sin.

> St. John Chrysostom: *Homilies.* (4th
> cent.)

And where was I to find such pleasures save in You, O Lord, You Who use sorrow to teach, and wound us to heal, and kill us lest we die to You.

> St. Augustine: *Confessions,* 2, 2. (5th cent.)

Make not two sorrows of one, if thou can:
Lest making of two sorrows, mar one man.

> John Heywood: *Three Hundred Epigrams.* (16th cent.)

Sorrow, the smart of ill, sin's eldest child;
Best, when unkind in killing whom it bred;
A rack for guilty thoughts, a bit for wild;
The scourge that whips, the salve that cures offence:
Sorrow, my bed and home, while life hath sense.

> Bl. Robert Southwell: *St. Peter's Complaint.* (16th cent.)

Nothing but sin should sadden us, and to this sorrow for sin it is necessary that holy joy should be attached.

> St. Francis de Sales: *Letters to Persons in Religion,* 4, 29. (17th cent.)

Earth hath no sorrow that heaven cannot heal.

> Thomas Moore: *Come, Ye Disconsolate.* (19th cent.)

When heaven sends sorrow,
    Warnings go first,
    Lest it should burst
    With stunning might
    On souls too bright
        To fear the morrow.

> Card. Newman: *Warnings.* (19th cent.)

God hath his ways
For every soul here sorrow-tossed.

> Abram Ryan: *Nocturne.* (19th cent.)

When I was young, I said to sorrow,
    Come, and I will play with thee!
He is near me now all day,
And at night returns to say,
I will come again tomorrow—
    I will come and stay with thee.

> Aubrey de Vere: *When I was Young.* (19th cent.)

Do not cheat thy heart and tell her
    Grief will pass away,
Hope for fairer times in future,
    And forget today.
Tell her, if you will, that sorrow
    Need not come in vain;
Tell her that the lesson taught her
    Far outweighs the pain.

> Adelaide Procter: *Friend Sorrow.* (19th cent.)

Sorrow, my friend,
I owe my soul to you.
And if my life with any glory end,
Of tenderness for others, and the words are true,
Said, honoring, when I'm dead,—
Sorrow, to you, the mellow praise, the funeral wreath, are due.

> Mother M. Alphonsa: *A Song before Grief.* (19th cent.)

Yet Christian sadness is divine
    Even as thy patient sadness was:
The salt tears in our life's dark wine
    Fell in it from the saving Cross.

Bitter the bread of our repast;
    Yet doth a sweet the bitter leaven:
Our sorrow is the shadow cast
    Around it by the light of heaven.

> F. Thompson: *L'Envoy.* (19th cent.)

Sorrow, O sister Sorrow, O mine own!
    Whither away hast flown?
Without thee, fiery is the flowery earth,
    A flowing dance of mirth.

> Lionel Johnson: *Before the Cloister.* (19th cent.)

Where there is sorrow, there is holy ground.

> Oscar Wilde: *De Profundis.* (19th cent.)

Our Lord does not leave us comfortless when He sends us sorrow.

R. H. Benson: *The History of Richard Raynal Solitary*. (20th cent.)

Sorrow, borne with resentment and bitterness, isolates the soul not only from God, but from her own fellows.

R. H. Benson: *The Friendship of Christ*. (20th cent.)

Sweet sorrow, play a grateful part,
Break me the marble of my heart
And of its fragments pave a street
Where, to my bliss, myself may meet
One hastening with pierced feet.

Helen Parry Eden: *Sorrow*. (20th cent.)

O Sower of sorrow,
From the seed of your sowing
Tomorrow the mower
The wheat will be mowing.

O Reaper of ruth,
'Mid the roots of your reaping
Springs the truth that in sleep
Bears the fruit of all sleeping.

O Binder of sheaves,
That are loose for your binding,
Withered leaves you shall find
And shall lose after finding.

J. M. Plunkett: *O Sower of Sorrow*. (20th cent.)

Only by sorrow's ladder shall we rise,
For joy is an abbreviated stair,
We come upon its threshold unaware—
High sorrow's ladder reaches to the skies!

Gertrude Callaghan: *Sorrow's Ladder*. (20th cent.)

An erstwhile sinner knocked at heaven's gate,
Without the password dread.
I know no countersign, save sorrow, Lord,—
Pass in, our Savior said.

Charles J. Quirk: *The Countersign*. (20th cent.)

I cannot cast away my cross,
Nor thorns about my brow untwine,
But I can knock at heaven's gate
When sorrow knocks at mine.

Sister Miriam: *Sanctuary*. (20th cent.)

The darts of toil and sorrow, sent
Against your peaceful beauty, are
As foolish and as impotent
As winds that•blow against a star.

Joyce Kilmer: *As Winds That Blow Against A Star*. (20th cent.)

Soul

O the witness of the soul, in its very nature Christian! (O testimonium animae naturaliter Christianae!)

Tertullian: *Apology*, 17, 6. (3rd cent.)

God is everywhere, and the goodness of God is everywhere; demons are everywhere, and the cursing of them is everywhere; the invocation of divine judgment is everywhere, death is everywhere, and the sense of death is everywhere, and all the world over is found the witness of the soul.

Tertullian: *The Soul's Testimony*, 6. (3rd cent.)

The soul we define to be sprung from the breath of God, immortal, possessing body, having form, simple in its substance, intelligent in its own nature, developing its power in various ways, free in its determinations, subject to the changes of accident, in its faculties mutable, rational, supreme, endued with an instinct of presentiment, evolved out of one.

Tertullian: *Treatise on the Soul*, 22. (3rd cent.)

Let not our soul become flesh, but let our flesh, being obedient to the soul's direction, become soul.

St. Ambrose: *Explanation of Psalm 118*, 4, 7. (4th cent.)

If you wish a definition of what the soul (*animus*) is, I have a ready answer. It seems to me to be a certain kind of substance, sharing in reason, fitted to rule the body.

> St. Augustine: *De Quantitate Animae, 13, 22.* (4th cent.)

To teach these grades [i.e. of the soul] to anyone, let the acts of the soul from the lowest to the highest be called, first, animation; second, sensation; third, art; fourth, virtue; fifth, tranquillity; sixth, approach; seventh, contemplation. They can be named also in this way: of the body; through the body; about the body; towards itself; in itself; towards God; in God. Or again in this way: beautifully of another; beautifully through another; beautifully about another; beautifully towards a beautiful; beautifully in a beautiful; beautifully towards Beauty; beautifully in Beauty.

> St. Augustine: *De Quantitate Animae, 35, 79.* (4th cent.)

The life whereby we are joined unto the body is called the soul.

> St. Augustine: *On Faith and the Creed.* (4th cent.)

No one doubts that he who seeks true religion either already believes the soul to be immortal if that religion is to be of any profit to him, or that it is just that very truth he wishes to discover in this same religion. It is for the sake of the soul that all religion exists; for, how it may be with the nature of the body causes no worry or solicitude, especially after death, to one whose soul possesses that by which it may be happy.

> St. Augustine: *De Utilitate Credendi, 7, 14.* (4th cent.)

If, again, we were so to define man as to say, Man is a rational substance consisting of mind and body, then without doubt man has a soul that is not body, and a body that is not soul.

> St. Augustine: *De Trinitate, 15, 7.* (5th cent.)

For the flesh is not life to itself, but the soul is the life of the flesh. The soul is not life to itself, but God is the life of the soul. . . . And if the soul live after God, then doth the flesh live rightly after the soul.

> St. Augustine: *Sermon 156, 6, 6.* (5th cent.)

For the soul is the inner face of man, by which we are known, that we may be regarded with love by our Maker.

> Pope St. Gregory I: *Morals, 10, 27.* (6th cent.)

The soul, accordingly, is a living essence, simple, incorporeal, invisible in its proper nature to bodily eyes, immortal, reasoning and intelligent, formless, making use of an organized body, and being the source of its powers of life and growth and sensation and generation, mind being but its purest part and not in any wise alien to it; (for as the eye to the body, so is the mind to the soul); further it enjoys freedom and volition and energy, and is mutable, that is, it is given to change, because it is created.

> St. John of Damascus: *Exposition of the Orthodox Faith, 2, 12.* (8th cent.)

Every holy soul is itself heaven in a sense —a heaven with understanding for its sun, faith for its moon, and virtues for its stars, a heaven where God dwells, according to His faithful promise, *We will come unto him and make our abode with him.*

> St. Bernard: *Sermons on the Canticle of Canticles, 28.* (12th cent.)

The soul is not fattened out of frying pans!

> St. Bernard: *Letters, 1, 11.* (12th cent.)

God is the life of the soul—as the efficient cause, not the formal cause.

> St. Thomas Aquinas: *Disputations Concerning Charity, 1.* (13th cent.)

The human soul is the actuality of an organism, which is its instrument—not, however, for every activity, for some activities of the soul surpass the range of the body.

St. Thomas Aquinas: *Disputations Concerning the Soul,* 2. (13th cent.)

The mind is a subsisting form, and is consequently immortal. Aristotle agrees that the mind is divine and perpetual (*De Anima,* 1, 5).

St. Thomas Aquinas: *Disputations Concerning the Soul,* 14. (13th cent.)

The soul is that through which we have communion with animals, spirit that through which we have intercourse with spiritual substances. Nevertheless it is one and the same substance which quickens body and which, by its power called mind, is able to understand.

St. Thomas Aquinas: *Commentary on Hebrews,* 4, lect. 2. (13th cent.)

For I am that Lord of life, love is my
drink,
And for that drink today, I died upon
earth.
But I will drink of no ditch, nor of no
deep learning,
But of the common cup, of all Christian souls;
Though the drink was death, and hell
the deep bowl.
I fought so that yet I thirst, for man's
soul's sake;
  Sitio.

Langland: *Piers Plowman* (B, 18, 363-6).
(Tr. C. Dawson) (14th cent.)

In the most noble part of the soul, the domain of our spiritual powers, we are constituted in the form of a living and eternal mirror of God; we bear in it the imprint of His eternal image and no other image can enter there.

Bl. John Ruysbroeck: *The Mirror of Eternal Salvation,* 8. (14th cent.)

I began to think of the soul as if it were a castle made of a single diamond or of very clear crystal, in which there are many rooms, just as in heaven there are many mansions.

St. Teresa of Jesus: *Interior Castle,* 1, 1.
(16th cent.)

A happy soul, that all the way
To heaven hath a summer day

          .   .   .   .   .   .

And, when life's sweet fable ends,
Soul and body part like friends:—
No quarrels, murmurs, no delay;
A kiss, a sigh, and so away.

Richard Crashaw: *In Praise of Lessius'
Rules of Health.* (17th cent.)

O fly my soul, what hangs upon
  Thy drooping wings,
  And weighs them down,
With love of gaudy mortal things.

James Shirley: *O Fly My Soul.* (17th
cent.)

I reflected how soon in the cup of
  desire
The pearl of the soul may be melted
  away;
How quickly, alas, the pure sparkle of
  fire
  We inherit from heav'n, may be
  quench'd in the clay.

Thomas Moore: *Stanzas.* (19th cent.)

The greatness of the soul is her capacity for God.

Archb. Ullathorne: *Humility and Patience.*
(19th cent.)

Let it be plainly understood that we cannot return to God unless we enter first into ourselves. God is everywhere, but not everywhere to us. There is but one point in the universe where God communicates with us, and that is the center of our own soul.

Archb. Ullathorne: *Humility and Patience.*
(19th cent.)

Darkness and solitude shine, for me.
  For life's fair outward part are rife
The silver noises; let them be.
  It is the very soul of life
Listens for thee, listens for thee.

Alice Meynell: *To the Beloved.* (19th
cent.)

Her soul from earth to heaven lies,
  Like the ladder of the vision,
    Whereon go
    To and fro,
In ascension and demission,
Star-flecked feet of Paradise.

> F. Thompson: *Scala Jacobi Portaque
> Eburnea.* (19th cent.)

How should I gauge what beauty is her
  dole,
Who cannot see her countenance for her
  soul,
As birds see not the casement for the
  sky?
And as 'tis check they prove its presence by,
I know not of her body till I find
My flight debarred the heaven of her
  mind.

> F. Thompson: *Her Portrait.* (19th cent.)

The surfaces of the soul are a little raw
on Monday mornings.

> R. H. Benson: *The Sentimentalists.* (20th
> cent.)

Each soul is as great as the world, and in
each soul there is room for all the tragedies of the world to be re-enacted, as
every puddle is great enough to hold the
sun.

> R. H. Benson: *Christ in the Church.* (20th
> cent.)

The huge modern heresy of altering the
human soul to fit its conditions, instead
of altering human conditions to fit the
human soul.

> G. K. Chesterton: *What's Wrong with the
> World.* (20th cent.)

When on the grass a frail, crushed egg
  I find,
  While from the blue the thrush's
    wild notes ring,
I think, this mortal shell once left be-
  hind,
  How my freed spirit, too, shall soar
    and sing.

> Sister M. Angelita: *Portents.* (20th cent.)

The primacy of the spirit is a fact of our
experience. We know ourselves as persons and therefore as governed, ruled, ordered and led (however often we have
been or are misled) by our personal
selves. We may and must allow its due
weight to the physical and material world
which conditions our lives, and all its
geological, geographical, climatic, racial
and economic forces and circumstances;
but those things did not make us; they
are simply the conditions under and in
which we live. We neglect or deny them
at our peril; but to deny our spiritual
nature and its primacy is not merely dangerous, it is man's damnation. The integrity of the individual means exactly that
—the realization of man's dual nature
and the primacy of the spirit.

> Eric Gill: *It All Goes Together.* (20th
> cent.)

Souls are like athletes, that need opponents worthy of them, if they are to be
tried and extended and pushed to the
full use of their powers, and rewarded
according to their capacity.

> Thomas Merton: *The Seven Storey
> Mountain.* (20th cent.)

The soul is feminine to God. An activist
world is a world which thinks it can be
masculine to reality without first being
feminine. It cannot. Gender is a much
wider term than sex: whether human
beings are male or female they have to
learn the same essential lesson: that they
must be feminine before they can hope
with success to be masculine: they must
be contemplative before they can hope to
be wisely and graciously active: they
must receive before they attempt to give.

> Gerald Vann: *The Water and the Fire.*
> (20th cent.)

What constitutes man is principally the
soul, the substantial form of his nature.
From it, ultimately, flows all the vital activity of man. In it are rooted all the
psychic dynamisms with their own proper
structure and their organic law. It is the
soul which nature charges with the gov-

ernment of all man's energies, in so far as these have not yet acquired their final determination.

Pope Pius XII: *Address to 5th Int. Congr. of Psychotherapy and Clinical Psychology.* (Apr. 13, 1953)

See also Body and Soul; Eternal Life; Immortality; Resurrection

Sovereignty

Sovereignty is supreme power over citizens and subjects, unrestrained by laws.

Jean Bodin: *Republic,* 1, 8. (16th cent.)

He has sovereignty who, after God, acknowledges no one greater than himself.

Jean Bodin: *Republic,* 1, 8. (16th cent.)

Sovereignty, under God, inheres in the organic people, or the people as the republic; and every organic people fixed to the soil, and politically independent of every other people, is a sovereign people, and, in the modern sense, an independent sovereign nation.

Orestes Brownson: *The American Republic.* (19th cent.)

[The Englishman] has that instinctive veneration for the law, that he can worship it even in the abstract, and thus is fitted to go shares with others all around him in that political sovereignty, which other races are obliged to concentrate in one ruler.

Card. Newman: *Discussions and Arguments.* (19th cent.)

It is one of the most pernicious of modern illusions to think that there can be no sovereignty, liberty or independence which is not absolute. If such were the case, no man would be free or a king unless he were God.

J. Maritain: *The Things That Are Not Caesar's.* (20th cent.)

In the eyes of a sound political philosophy there is no sovereignty, that is, no natural and inalienable right to *tran-scendent* or *separate* supreme power in political society. Neither the prince nor the king nor the emperor were really sovereign, though they bore the sword and the attributes of sovereignty. Nor is the state sovereign; nor are even the people sovereign. God alone is sovereign.

J. Maritain: *Man and the State.* (20th cent.)

Sow

As meet as a sow to bear a saddle.

¶ meet—fitting, suitable

John Heywood: *Proverbs,* 2, 1. (16th cent.)

Spanish

O 'tis not Spanish, but 'tis heaven she speaks!

Richard Crashaw: *Apology for Hymn to St. Teresa.* (17th cent.)

Speech

Her speech is silent and her silence is speech.

St. Jerome: *Letters,* 24, 5. (4th cent.)

To keep one's mouth from evil and depraved talk; not to love much speaking.

St. Benedict: *Rule,* 4. (One of his 'tools of good works') (6th cent.)

The carl spake one thing, but he thought another.

carl—man, rustic

Chaucer: *The Freres Tale.* (14th cent.)

Spare to speak, spare to speed.

John Heywood: *Proverbs,* 1, 11. (16th cent.)

Let thy words be few when in the midst of many.

St. Teresa of Jesus: *Maxims.* (16th cent.)

In speaking of others always be calm and cheerful.

St. Teresa of Jesus: *Maxims.* (16th cent.)

Bend thyself to the temper of whomsoever is speaking to thee: be merry with the mirthful, sorrowful with the sad: in a word, make thyself all things to all, to gain all.

> St. Teresa of Jesus: *Maxims*. (16th cent.)

In all talking and conversation let something always be said of spiritual things, and so shall all idle words and evil-speaking be avoided.

> St. Teresa of Jesus: *Maxims*. (16th cent.)

If we say less than we should it is easy to add, but having said too much it is hard to take it off.

> St. Francis de Sales: *Letters to Persons in the World,* 4, 3. (17th cent.)

Be brief when you cannot be good.

> St. Francis de Sales: *Letters to Persons in Religion,* 4, 33. (17th cent.)

If charity does not draw us to speak of ourselves and of what belongs to us, we ought to keep silent on the subject.

> St. Francis de Sales: *Letters to Persons in Religion,* 5, 2. (17th cent.)

Here is a fellow who, when he is silent, will never begin to speak; and when he once begins to speak, will never stop.

> Card. Newman: *Apologia pro Vita Sua,* 1. (Reported as having been said about himself) (19th cent.)

Grant me the power of saying things
Too simple and too sweet for words.

> Coventry Patmore: *The Angel in the House.* (19th cent.)

Do not trust all who talk smoothly. Listen much and speak little.

> R. H. Benson: *The Queen's Tragedy.* (20th cent.)

Spending

Spend, and God shall send.

> John Heywood: *Proverbs,* 2, 5. (16th cent.)

Spinning

Spin, daughter Mary, spin,
Twirl your wheel with silver din;
Spin, daughter Mary, spin,
Spin a tress for Viola.

> F. Thompson: *The Making of Viola.* (19th cent.)

Spinster

My soul abhors the tasteless dry embrace
Of a stale virgin with a Winter face.

> Pope: *January and May.* (18th cent.)

Spirit

He must have little spirit who thinks that a spirit is nothing.

> St. Bernard. (12th cent.)

The philosopher thinks that the spiritual lies very far beyond the material, like a remote landmark behind a plain. The mystic thinks that the spiritual is very close behind the material, like a brigand hiding behind a bush. Science is always saying that the other world, if it exists, is too distant to be seen. Religion is always saying that it is too close to be seen. The kingdom of heaven is at hand.

> G. K. Chesterton: *A Handful of Authors.* (20th cent.)

See also Soul

Spiritual Life

For what is more consoling to a soul on earth than to be withdrawn by grace from the trouble of worldly affairs, from the defilement of desiring and the vanity of loving creatures, into the peace and sweetness of spiritual love, where it inwardly perceives God's presence and is satisfied with the light of His countenance?

> Walter Hilton: *Scale of Perfection,* 2, 41. (14th cent.)

The more a man is united within himself, and interiorly simple, the more and higher things doth he understand without labor; because he receiveth the light of understanding from above.

> Thomas a Kempis: *The Imitation of Christ*, 1, 3. (15th cent.)

Whoever desires to please God, to make any progress in spiritual life, and at length to arrive at perfection, must as a first step detest all heresies and schisms, adhering firmly to the Church Catholic, and subjecting himself humbly to her.

> Louis de Blois (Blosius): *A Short Rule*, 1. (16th cent.)

He who aspires to heavenly love, must sedulously reserve for it his leisure, his spirit and his affections.

> St. Francis de Sales: *Treatise on the Devout Life*, 12, 3. (17th cent.)

To live according to the spirit is to think, speak and act according to the virtues that are in the spirit, and not according to the sense and sentiments which are in the flesh.

> St. Francis de Sales: *Letters to Persons in Religion*, 3, 47. (17th cent.)

There is no soil so barren but that diligent tenderness brings forth some fruit.

> Jean Pierre Camus: *The Spirit of St. Francis de Sales*, 2, 13. (17th cent.)

He who believes himself to be far advanced in the spiritual life has not even made a good beginning.

> Jean Pierre Camus: *The Spirit of St. Francis de Sales*, 13, 5. (17th cent.)

The man who knows best how to control his natural inclinations is more open to supernatural inspirations.

> Jean Pierre Camus: *The Spirit of St. Francis de Sales*, 15, 8. (17th cent.)

What are all the petty interests of this mortal life, that they should absorb the soul, compared with the wonderful things above us that hang on the tree of life, and are always ready for the soul that is willing to reach up to them.

> Archb. Ullathorne: *Humility and Patience.* (19th cent.)

It belongs to the man who is in quest of his supreme good to draw as near to divine things as his condition of life will allow.

> Archb. Ullathorne: *Humility and Patience.* (19th cent.)

The whole design of God's beneficent government of souls is to draw them out of themselves and to bring them to His truth and good.

> Archb. Ullathorne: *Humility and Patience.* (19th cent.)

Spiritual natures are on the summits of creation; there is nothing but God above them.

> Archb. Ullathorne: *Humility and Patience.* (19th cent.)

The whole aim of the science of Christian perfection is to instruct men how to remove the hindrances in the way of the action of the Holy Spirit, and how to cultivate those virtues which are most favorable to His solicitations and inspirations. Thus the sum of spiritual life consists in observing and yielding to the movements of the Spirit of God in our soul, employing for this purpose all the exercises of prayer, spiritual reading, the practice of virtues, and good works.

> Isaac T. Hecker. (Elliott's Life, 312) (19th cent.)

The action of the Holy Spirit embodied visibly in the authority of the Church, and the action of the Holy Spirit dwelling invisibly in the soul form one inseparable synthesis; and he who has not a clear conception of this two-fold action of the Holy Spirit is in danger of running into one or the other, and sometimes into both, of these extremes, either of which is destructive of the end of the Church. The Holy Spirit, in the external authority of the Church, acts as the infallible interpreter and criterion of the divine revelation. The Holy Spirit in the soul acts as the divine Life-giver and Sanctifier. It is of the highest importance that these two distinct offices of the Holy Spirit should not be confounded.

Isaac T. Hecker. (Elliott's Life, 313.) (19th cent.)

The way of the spiritual path is strewn with the wrecks of souls that might have been friends of Christ.

R. H. Benson: *The Friendship of Christ.* (20th cent.)

Every advance in spiritual life has its corresponding dangers; every step that we rise nearer God increases the depth of the gulf into which we may fall.

R. H. Benson: *The Friendship of Christ.* (20th cent.)

It is the oldest temptation in the world, and the most fruitful parent of sins, and the most dangerous temptation—in that it contains so much of truth—to regard self rather than God as the center in which spiritual effort must originate.

R. H. Benson: *Preface to Bands of Love.* (20th cent.)

When Frederick William Faber preached the panegyric of St. Ignatius Loyola on the occasion of the feast of the founder of the Jesuits in the Jesuit church at Farm Street, he spent an hour in unbroken, sympathetic, indeed fervent exposition of this saint's spirituality, and only in the last sentence did he introduce the necessary limitation and expansion: "This, then, my dear brethren, is St. Ignatius's way to heaven; and, thank God, it is not the only way!"

Baron von Hügel: *The Life of Prayer.* (20th cent.)

It is easy to count up the proprieties in a watchful world; but exceedingly hard to put the spiritual life on a paying basis.

Agnes Repplier: *Times and Tendencies.* (20th cent.)

Every moment and every event of every man's life on earth plants something in his soul. For just as the wind carries thousands of invisible and visible winged seeds, so the stream of time brings with it the germs of spiritual vitality that come to rest imperceptibly in the minds and wills of men.

Thomas Merton: *Seeds of Contemplation.* (20th cent.)

There are no plains in the spiritual life; we are either going uphill or coming down.

Bishop Sheen: *Peace of Soul.* (20th cent.)

Spiritualism

It is forbidden to publish, read, or keep books in which sorcery, divination, magic, the evocation of spirits, and other superstitions of this kind are taught or commended.

Pope Leo XIII: *Ap. Const. Officiorum ac Munerum.* (Jan. 25, 1897)

Good intentions don't protect us in the least. To go to seances with good intentions is like holding a smoking-concert in a powder-magazine on behalf of an orphan asylum. It's not the least protection to open the concert with a prayer. We've got no business there at all. So we're blown up just the same.

R. H. Benson: *The Necromancers.* (20th cent.)

Spitting

When in a holy place, in the presence of superiors, or in clean apartments, one should always spit into a handkerchief. Children are guilty of unpardonable rudeness when they spit in the face of a companion; neither are they excusable who spit from windows, or on the walls or furniture.

St. John Baptist de la Salle: *The Rules of Christian Manners and Civility.* I. (17th cent.)

Sport

Sport is necessary for some natures. After all, the killing of creatures is necessary for man's food, and sport . . . is a survival of man's delight in obtaining food, and it requires certain noble qualities of endurance and skill.

R. H. Benson: *The Light Invisible*. (20th cent.)

The Church does not forbid sport on Sunday. She looks upon it kindly, provided that Sunday remains the Lord's Day, the day for repose of body and soul.

Pope Pius XII: *Address to Int. Assoc. of Sport Writers*. (Nov. 10, 1951)

What end do men pursue with so vast and diffused an activity? It is the use, the development, the control—by means of man and for the service of man—of the energies enclosed within the body; the joy which comes from this power and action, is not unlike that which the artist experiences when he is using, and is master of, his instrument.

Pope Pius XII: *Sports and Gymnastics*. (Nov. 8, 1952)

To elevate gymnastics, sport, rhythm, with all their associations, to the supreme scope of life would in truth be too little for man, whose primary greatness consists in much more elevated aspirations, tendencies and endowments.

Pope Pius XII: *Sports and Gymnastics*. (Nov. 8, 1952)

Spring

Spring returns with jubilation,
When the Tree of our salvation,
Chiefest of the forest nation,
Wrought the work of reparation,
Fallen man redeeming.

Anonymous: *Ecce tempus est vernale*. (Tr. J. Neale) (13th cent.)

The sweet season, that bud and bloom forth brings,

With green hath clad the hills, and eke the vale.

Henry Howard, Earl of Surrey: *Description of Spring*. (16th cent.)

Eternal spring, with smiling verdure here
Warms the mild air, and crowns the youthful year.

Sir Samuel Garth: *The Dispensary*, 4. (17th cent.)

The English Church was, and the English Church was not, and the English Church is once again. This is the portent, worthy of a cry. It is the coming in of a second spring; it is the restoration in the moral world, such as that which yearly takes place in the physical.

Card. Newman: *Second Spring Sermon (Sermons on Various Occasions)*. (1852)

Who knows not spring? who doubts when blows
Her breath, that spring is come indeed?
The swallow doubts not; nor the rose
That stirs, but wakes not; nor the weed.

Aubrey de Vere: *Spring*. (19th cent.)

O, baby spring,
That flutter'st sudden 'neath the breast of earth
A month before the birth;
Whence is the peaceful poignancy,
The joy contrite,
Sadder than sorrow, sweeter than delight,
That burthens now the breath of everything,
Though each one sighs as if to each alone
The cherish'd pang were known?

Coventry Patmore: *Saint Valentine's Day*. (19th cent.)

O spring! I know thee. Seek for sweet surprise
In the young children's eyes.

But I have learnt the years, and know
  the yet
Leaf-folded violet.

> Alice Meynell: *In Early Spring.* (19th
> cent.)

Spring is come home with her world-
  wandering feet,
And all things are made young with
  young desires.

> F. Thompson: *An Ode after Easter.* (19th
> cent.)

There she sat amid her ladies,
  Where the shade is
Seen as Enna mead ere Hades'
  Gloom fell 'thwart Persephone.

> F. Thompson: *Sister Songs.* (19th cent.)

This is the time when bit by bit
The days begin to lengthen sweet
And every minute gained is joy—
And love stirs in the heart of a boy.

> Katharine T. Hinkson: *Turn o' the Year.*
> (20th cent.)

But the men that live in the south coun-
  try
  Are the kindest and most wise,
They get their laughter from the loud
  surf,
  And the faith in their happy eyes
Comes surely from our sister the spring
  When over the sea she flies;
The violets suddenly bloom at her feet,
  She blesses us with surprise.

> Hilaire Belloc: *The South Country.* (20th
> cent.)

Die, Boreas,
And drown your ruins in the gaudy sea,
December, clash your cymbals once
  again
And put them away.
The crops come thronging from the
  ground.
The land is green with strength.
The harvests sing like confidence
In the ascetic earth.
Let there be no more patience
With your iron music, death:

Stand, continents, and wear the spring
  your crown!

> Thomas Merton: *Canticle for the Blessed
> Virgin.* (20th cent.)

Stage

The world is a great stage on which God
displays His many wonders.

> Jean Pierre Camus: *The Spirit of St.
> Francis de Sales,* 19, 3. (17th cent.)

The stage being the representation of the
world and its actions in it, how can it be
imagined that the picture of human life
can be more exact than life itself is?

> Dryden: *The Rival Ladies, Dedication.*
> (17th cent.)

Stake

> So is it an ill stake
That cannot stand one year in a hedge.

> John Heywood: *Proverbs,* 2, 4. (16th
> cent.)

Star

If thou, he answered, follow but thy
  star,
Thou canst not miss at last a glorious
  haven.

> Dante: *Inferno, Canto 15.* (14th cent.)

Thus those celestial fires,
  Though seeming mute,
The fallacy of our desires
  And all the pride of life confute:

For they have watched since first
  The world had birth;
And found sin in itself accursed,
  And nothing permanent on earth.

> W. Habington: *Nox Nocti Indicat
> Scientiam.* (17th cent.)

But soon, the prospect clearing,
  By cloudless starlight on he treads,
And thinks no lamp so cheering
  As that light which Heaven sheds.

> Thomas Moore: *I'd Mourn the Hopes.*
> (19th cent.)

When twilight dews are falling soft
  Upon the rosy sea, love,
I watch the star, whose beam so oft
  Has lighted me to thee, love.

Thomas Moore: *When Twilight Dews.*
(19th cent.)

No star is ever lost we once have seen,
We always may be what we might have
  been.

Adelaide Procter: *A Legend of Provence.*
(19th cent.)

Look at the stars! look, look up at the
  skies!
O look at all the fire-folk sitting in the
  air!
The bright boroughs, the circle-citadels
  there!

G. M. Hopkins: *The Starlight Night.*
(19th cent.)

Bells that from night's great bell-tower
  hang in gold,
Whereon God rings his changes manifold.

F. Thompson: *To Stars.* (19th cent.)

O'er the wake of the white-sailed moon,
  Which to men is the galaxy.

F. Thompson: *Song of the Hours.* (19th
cent.)

When the stars pitch the golden tents
Of their high encampment on the
  plains of night.

F. Thompson: *To a Child heard Repeating
her Mother's Verses.* (19th cent.)

About the whole cosmos there is a tense
and secret festivity—like preparations
for Guy Fawkes' day. Eternity is the eve
of something. I never look up at the
stars without feeling that they are the
fires of a schoolboy's rocket, fixed in their
everlasting fall.

G. K. Chesterton: *Heretics.* (20th cent.)

Among all the strange things that men
have forgotten, the most universal and
catastrophic lapse of memory is that by
which they have forgotten that they are
living on a star.

G. K. Chesterton: *The Defendant.* (20th
cent.)

God be thanked for the Milky Way
  that runs across the sky.
That's the path that my feet would
  tread whenever I have to die.

Some folks call it a Silver Sword, and
  some a Pearly Crown.
But the only thing I think it is, is
  Main Street, Heaventown.

Joyce Kilmer: *Main Street.* (20th cent.)

The stars make no noise.

Seumas MacManus: *Heavy Hangs the
Golden Grain.* (20th cent.)

State

Here too is laudable security for the
commonwealth; for a state is neither
founded nor preserved perfectly save in
the foundation and by the bond of faith
and of firm concord, when the highest
common good is loved by all, and this
highest and truest thing is God.

St. Augustine: *Letters,* 137, 5. (5th cent.)

What is a state (*civitas*) but a multitude
of men, brought together into some
bond of agreement?

St. Augustine: *Letters,* 138, 2. (5th cent.)

A society of men is just, only if it obeys
You.

St. Augustine: *Confessions,* 3, 9. (5th
cent.)

The state (*civitas*) is a multitude of men
joined together by the bond of society.

St. Isidore: *Etymologies,* 15, 2. (7th cent.)

Who does not know that kings and
dukes had their origin from those who,
ignorant of God, in pride, rapine, per-
fidy, homicide, and finally by almost
every kind of crime, at the instigation of
the prince of this world, the devil, that

is, have arrogated to themselves in blind cupidity and insufferable presumption the lordship over equals, that is, other men.

> Pope St. Gregory VII: *Letters,* 8, 21. (To Hermann, bishop of Metz.) (11th cent.)

It is not the ultimate end of an assembled multitude to live virtuously, but through virtuous living to attain to the possession of God.

> St. Thomas Aquinas: *The Governance of Rulers,* 1, 14. (13th cent.)

Thus it is obvious that the temporal monarch receives his authority directly, and without intermediary [i.e. the pope], from the Source of all authority, which Source (though utterly indivisible in the citadel of its simplicity) flows out into manifold channels through its abounding goodness.

> Dante: *Monarchy,* 3. (14th cent.)

A state is an association of families and their common affairs, governed by a supreme power and by reason.

> Jean Bodin: *Republic,* 1, 1. (16th cent.)

In our conviction the true view of the origin and nature of the state . . . is that which recognizes in the state the same divine origin and the same ends as in the Church, which holds that it belongs as much to the primitive essence of a nation as its language, and that it unites men together by a moral, not, like family and society, by a natural and sensible, bond.

> Lord Acton: *The Rambler,* 2. (1860)

The state, as the origin and source of all rights, is endowed with a certain right not circumscribed by any limits.

> Proposition condemned by Pius IX in Syllabus of Errors. (1867)

To exclude the Church, founded by God Himself, from life, from laws, from the education of youth, from domestic society is a grave and fatal error. A state

from which religion is banished can never be well regulated.

> Pope Leo XIII: *Immortale Dei.* (Nov. 1, 1885)

Now a state chiefly prospers and thrives through moral rule, well-regulated family life, respect for religion and justice, the moderation and fair imposing of public taxes, the progress of the arts and of trade, the abundant yield of the land —through everything, in fact, which makes the citizens better and happier.

> Pope Leo XIII: *Rerum Novarum.* (May 15, 1891)

The State does not contain in itself and does not mechanically bring together in a given territory a shapeless mass of individuals. It is and should be in practice the organic and organizing unity of a real people. The people and a shapeless multitude (or, as it is called, 'the masses') are two distinct concepts.

> Pope Pius XII: *Christmas Message.* (Dec. 24, 1944)

We have to distinguish clearly between the State and the Body Politic. These do not belong to two diverse categories, but they differ from each other as a part differs from the whole. The Body Politic or the Political Society is the whole. The State is a part—the topmost part—of this whole.

> J. Maritain: *Man and the State.* (20th cent.)

The body politic . . . contains . . . the family units, whose essential rights and freedoms are anterior to itself, and a multiplicity of other particular societies which proceed from the free initiative of citizens and should be as autonomous as possible. Such is the element of pluralism inherent in every true political society. Family, economic, cultural, educational, religious life matter as much as does political life to the very existence and prosperity of the body politic. . . . Since in political society authority comes from below, through the people, it is normal that the whole dynamism of authority in the body politic should be made up of particular and partial authorities rising in tiers above one another, up to the top authority of the State.

> J. Maritain: *Man and the State.* (20th cent.)

The State is only that part of the body politic especially concerned with the maintenance of law, the promotion of the common welfare and public order, and the administration of public affairs. The State is a part which specializes in the interests of the whole.

> J. Maritain: *Man and the State.* (20th cent.)

When we say that the State is the superior part in the body politic, this means that it is superior to the other organs or collective parts of this body, but it does not mean that it is superior to the body politic itself. The part as such is inferior to the whole. The State is inferior to the body politic as a whole, and is at the service of the body politic as a whole. Is the State even the *head* of the body politic? Hardly, for in the human being the head is an instrument of such spiritual powers as the intellect and the will, which the whole body has to serve; whereas the functions exercised by the State are for the body politic, and not the body politic for them.

> J. Maritain: *Man and the State.* (20th cent.)

The community is the great means intended by nature and God to regulate the exchange of mutual needs and to aid each man to develop his personality fully according to his individual and social abilities.

> Pope Pius XII: *The Moral Limits of Medical Research.* (Sept. 14, 1952)

See also Authority; Church and State; Government; Republic; Ruler; Sovereignty

State (*Status*)

> To rise by others' fall
> I deem a losing gain;
> All state with others' ruin built
> To ruin runs amain.
>
> Bl. Robert Southwell: *Content and Rich.* (16th cent.)

Statesman

> Statesman, yet friend to truth; of soul sincere,
> In action faithful, and in honor clear;
> Who broke no promise, serv'd no private end,
> Who gain'd no title, and who lost no friend.
>
> Pope: *On James Craggs.* (18th cent.)

See also Politician

Station

It matters not in what station a man renders himself approved; the object of a good man is to render himself approved in any station. The crucial thing is, not that station should dignify character, but that character should dignify station. The lower the station, the more lofty is the virtue of him who occupies it worthily.

> St. Ambrose: *Letters,* 2, 19. (4th cent.)

Stations of the Cross

> From pain to pain, from woe to woe,
> With loving hearts and footsteps slow,
> To Calvary with Christ we go.
> See how His precious blood
> At every station pours!
> Was ever grief like His?
> Was ever sin like ours?
>
> F. Faber: *From Pain to Pain.* (19th cent.)

Stephen, Saint

> Yesterday with exultation
> Joined the world in celebration
> Of her promised Savior's birth;

Yesterday the angel nation
Poured the strains of jubilation
   O'er the Monarch born on earth.

But today, o'er death victorious,
By his faith and actions glorious,
   By his miracles renowned,
Dared the deacon protomartyr
Earthly life for heaven to barter,
   Faithful midst the faithless found.

> Adam of St. Victor: *Heri mundus
> exsultavit.* (Tr. J. Neale) (12th cent.)

O captain of the martyr host!
   O peerless in renown!
Not from the fading flowers of earth
   Weave we for thee a crown.
The stones that smote thee, in thy blood
   Made glorious and divine,
All in a halo heavenly bright
   About thy temples shine.

> Jean Santeuil: *O qui tuo dux martyrum.*
> (Tr. Caswall) (18th cent.)

See also Martyr

Stillness

There is in stillness oft a magic power
To calm the breast when struggling
   passions lower;
Touched by its influence, in the soul
   arise
Diviner feelings, kindred with the
   skies.

> Card. Newman: *Solitude.* (19th cent.)

Stinginess

As free of gift as a poor man of his eye.

> John Heywood: *Proverbs,* 1, 11. (16th
> cent.)

His dole is soon done.

> John Heywood: *Proverbs,* 1, 11. (16th
> cent.)

She will not part with the paring of her
nails.

> John Heywood: *Proverbs,* 1, 11. (16th
> cent.)

In that house a man shall as soon break
his neck as his fast.

> John Heywood: *Proverbs,* 1, 11. (16th
> cent.)

Stoics

And if some with a vanity all the more
monstrous for its being so rare, have
made it their hobby never to be roused
and excited, bent or inclined by any
emotion, they are in a way rather to lose
all humanity than to attain to true tranquillity. For a policy is not right by the
mere fact of its being hard, nor sound by
the fact of its being unfeeling.

> St. Augustine: *The City of God,* 14, 9.
> (5th cent.)

Stomach

An empty stomach, calling loud for
   food,
To hear long tales is in no willing
   mood.

> School of Salerno, Code of Health. (11th
> cent.)

When the belly is full, the bones would
be at rest.

> John Heywood: *Proverbs,* 2, 2. (16th
> cent.)

Stone

The rolling stone never gathereth moss.

> John Heywood: *Proverbs,* 1, 11. (16th
> cent.)

Storm

After a storm comes a calm.

> Sir William Davenant: *Cruel Brother,* 1.
> (17th cent.)

Straight

As right as a line.

> John Heywood: *Proverbs,* 1, 11. (16th
> cent.)

Strength

When Thou art our strength, it is strength indeed, but when our strength is our own it is only weakness.

> St. Augustine: *Confessions,* 4, 16. (5th cent.)

O God of all power and might, Who art the Giver of all good things; implant in our hearts the love of Thy name, increase in us true religion, nourish us with all goodness, and by Thy mercy keep us in the same.

> Roman Missal, Collect for Sixth Sunday after Pentecost. (Gelasian, 5th to 7th cent.)

When we feel us too bold, remember our own feebleness. When we feel us too faint, remember Christ's strength.

> St. Thomas More: *Dialogue of Comfort.* (16th cent.)

Strike

The worker has the right to refuse to work, that is, to strike, and to induce by peaceful and lawful methods others to strike with him.

> Card. O'Connell: *Pastoral Letter on the Laborer's Rights.* (1912)

Study

In the study of created things we must not exercise a mere idle and passing curiosity, but must make them a stepping-stone to things that are immortal and that abide for ever.

> St. Augustine: *De Vera Religione,* 29. (4th cent.)

For it is a patent fact that a person makes speedy progress as a result of his good studies precisely in proportion as he is prompt to do what his studies prompt him to do.

> St. Augustine: *De Opere Monachorum,* 20. (5th cent.)

Prefer to arrive at knowledge over small streamlets, and do not plunge immediately into the ocean, since progress must go from the easier to the more difficult.

. . . Consider not from whom you hear anything, but impress upon your mind everything good that is said. Make an effort thoroughly to understand whatever you read and hear. In all doubt seek to penetrate to the truth. Try always to store away as much as possible in the chambers of your mind. What is too far above strive not after for the present. If so be you follow these directions you will produce useful flowers and fruits in the vineyard of the Lord of hosts, as long as you live.

> St. Thomas Aquinas: *Letters.* (Grabmann, Thomas Aquinas, p. 51) (13th cent.)

What! Study until reason lost dominion
Poring on books in cloisters? Must he toil
As Austin bade and till the very soil?
Was he to leave the world upon the shelf?
Let Austin have his labor to himself.

> Chaucer: *Canterbury Tales: Prologue.* (The worldly monk) (Tr. Coghill) (14th cent.)

Nothing is more common in an age like this, when books abound, than to fancy that the gratification of a love of reading is real study.

> Card. Newman: *Idea of a University.* (19th cent.)

Stupidity

The rest to some faint meaning make pretence,
But Shadwell never deviates into sense.
Some beams of wit on other souls may fall,
Strike through and make a lucid interval;
But Shadwell's genuine night admits no ray,
His rising fogs prevail upon the day.

> Dryden: *Mac Flecknoe.* (17th cent.)

Whenever a man does a thoroughly stupid thing, it is always from the noblest motives.

> Oscar Wilde: *The Picture of Dorian Gray,* 6. (19th cent.)

Style

When we encounter a natural style we are always astonished and delighted, for we expected to see an author, and found a man.

> Pascal: *Pensées,* 7. (17th cent.)

It is the least pardonable fault in an orator to fail in clearness of style, and the most pardonable fault of a poet.

> Card. Newman: *Grammar of Assent,* 3. (19th cent.)

We might as well say that one man's shadow is another's as that the style of a really gifted mind can belong to any but himself. It follows him about as a shadow. His thought and feeling are personal, and so his language is personal.

> Card. Newman: *Idea of a University.* (19th cent.)

That pomp of language, that full and tuneful diction, that felicitousness in the choice and exquisiteness in the collocation of words, which to prosaic writers seem artificial, is nothing else but the mere habit and way of a lofty intellect.

> Card. Newman: *Idea of a University.* (19th cent.)

As to patterns for imitation, the only master of style I have ever had (which is strange, considering the differences of the languages) is Cicero. I think I owe a great deal to him, and as far as I know to no one else.

> Card. Newman: *Letters,* 2, 426. (19th cent.)

Style may be called a living form which the live spirit wraps around itself.

> John La Farge: *Considerations on Painting.* (19th cent.)

His style is chaos illumined by flashes of lightning. As a writer, he has mastered everything except language.

> Oscar Wilde: *The Decay of Lying.* (With reference to George Meredith) (19th cent.)

The style is the man; and some will add that, thus unsupported, it does not amount to much of a man. It is a sort of fighting and profane parody of the Old Testament.

> G. K. Chesterton: *Victorian Age in Literature.* (Referring to Swinburne.) (20th cent.)

Subdeacon

Hands shall not be laid on subdeacon, but he shall be named that he may serve the deacon.

> St. Hippolytus: *The Apostolic Tradition,* 14. (3rd cent.)

O holy Lord, Father almighty, eternal God, vouchsafe to bless these Thy servants whom Thou hast deigned to choose for the office of subdeacon, that they may be tireless and watchful sentinels of the heavenly army in Thy sanctuary, that they may faithfully minister at Thy holy altars; and let the Spirit of wisdom and understanding, the Spirit of counsel and fortitude, the Spirit of knowledge and piety rest upon them and fill them with the Spirit of Thy fear, and confirm them in the divine ministry, so that obedient to Thee both in word and deed they may obtain Thy grace.

> Roman Pontifical, Ordination of Subdeacons, Prayer *Domine Sancte Pater Omnipotens.* (Gelasian, 5th to 7th cent.)

O Lord our God, Who by one and the same Holy Spirit dost distribute Thy gifts to Thy chosen ones, Who hast granted to Thy Church divers orders and disposed in them degrees of ministry for the service of Thy holy and immaculate mysteries; Thou Who in Thine unspeakable foreknowledge hast also appointed Thy servant here to be worthy to serve Thy holy Church; do Thou, O Master, preserve him blamelessly in all things, and grant him to love the splendor of Thy house, to stand before the gate of Thy holy temple and to light the lamp of the tabernacle of Thy glory. Plant him in Thy holy Church as a fruitful olive tree that he may bear the fruit of justice; grant that on the day of Thy coming Thy servant may be found perfect and may enjoy the reward of those who have pleased Thee.

> Byzantine Euchologion, Prayer for Ordination of a Subdeacon. (ca. 5th to 8th cent.)

. . . it behooves the subdeacon to prepare water for the service of the altar, to wash the altar cloths and the corporals, to assist the deacon and present him the chalice and paten used in the sacrifice. . . .

> Roman Pontifical, Ordination of Subdeacons, Admonition. (ca. 10th cent.)

Subjectivism

Subjectivism is, I believe, the principal barrier to the universal acceptance of the Christian revelation. People are not prepared to accept a deity who does not conform to the standards of behavior which they lay down in advance.

> Arnold Lunn: *Now I See.* (20th cent.)

Submission

The real and only satisfactory motive for submission does not lie in superficial things, but in the deep, still current of faith that comes from God direct, and bears the soul along.

> R. H. Benson: *A City Set on a Hill.* (20th cent.)

Submission to a weak man is discipline. Submission to a strong man is only servility.

> G. K. Chesterton: *What's Wrong with the World.* (20th cent.)

Substance

See Being; Essence; God

Subtle

The subtle man is immeasurably easier to understand than the natural man.

> G. K. Chesterton: *Robert Browning, 1.* (20th cent.)

Success

The religious man is the only successful man.

> F. Faber. (19th cent.)

Every really great achievement is inspired by motives of the heart, and not of the head; by feeling and passion, not by a calculation of probabilities.

> R. H. Benson: *The Light Invisible.* (20th cent.)

To chivalrous souls a pathetic failure often appeals more than an excellent success.

> R. H. Benson: *The King's Achievement.* (20th cent.)

It is a great mistake to become so successful that one has no time to keep up with the times.

> Katharine T. Hinkson: *Dick Pentreath.* (20th cent.)

Succession, Apostolic

The apostles received the gospel for us from the Lord Jesus Christ; Jesus Christ was sent from God. Christ, therefore, is from God and the apostles are from Christ. Both, accordingly, came in proper order by the will of God. Receiving their orders, therefore, and being filled with confidence because of the resurrection of the Lord Jesus Christ, and confirmed in the word of God, with full assurance of the Holy Spirit, they went forth preaching the gospel of the kingdom of God that was about to come. Preaching, accordingly, throughout the country and cities, they appointed their first-fruits, after testing them by the Spirit, to be bishops and deacons of those who should believe.

> Pope St. Clement I: *Letter to the Corinthians,* 42, 1-5. (1st cent.)

Let them produce the original records of their churches; let them unfold the roll of their bishops, running down in due succession from the beginning in such a manner that the first bishop of theirs shall be able to show for his ordainer and predecessor some one of the apostles or of apostolic men,—a man, moreover, who continued steadfast with the apostles. For this is the manner in which the apostolic churches transmit their registers: as the church of Smyrna, which records that Polycarp was placed therein by John; as also the church of Rome, which makes Clement to have been ordained in like manner by Peter.

> Tertullian: *On the Prescription of Heretics*, 32. (3rd cent.)

See also Hierarchy; Tradition, Ecclesiastical

Suffering

Torture us, rack us, condemn us, crush us; your cruelty only proves our innocence. That is why God suffers us to suffer all this.

> Tertullian: *Apology*, 50, 12. (3rd cent.)

This, in short, is the difference between us and others who know not God, that in misfortune they complain and murmur, while adversity does not call us away from the truth of virtue and faith, but strengthens us by its suffering.

> St. Cyprian: *On Immortality*, 13. (3rd cent.)

Bodily suffering makes wicked souls miserable, but borne with fortitude it purifies souls that are good.

> St. Augustine: *De Agone Christiano*, 7, 8. (4th cent.)

How is it, that almighty God so utterly disregards in this present state of being those whom He chose so exaltedly before the worlds, saving this, which is plain to the religious sense of the faithful, that it is for this reason He thus presses them below, because He sees how to recompense them on high? And He casts them down without to the level of things contemptible, because He leads them on within to the height of things incomprehensible.

> Pope St. Gregory: *Morals*, 3, 11. (6th cent.)

He who knoweth how to suffer will enjoy much peace. Such a one is a conqueror of himself and lord of the world, a friend of Christ, and an heir of heaven.

> Thomas a Kempis: *The Imitation of Christ*, 2, 3. (15th cent.)

All recommend patience, but alas! how few there are that desire to suffer.

> Thomas a Kempis: *The Imitation of Christ*, 2, 12. (15th cent.)

Nothing, how little soever, that is suffered for God's sake, can pass without merit in the sight of God.

> Thomas a Kempis: *The Imitation of Christ*, 3, 19. (15th cent.)

Of sufferance cometh ease.

> John Heywood: *Proverbs*, 1, 9. (16th cent.)

All thing may be suffered saving wealth.

> John Heywood: *Proverbs*, 2, 4. (16th cent.)

The purest suffering bears and carries in its train the purest understanding.

> St. John of the Cross: *Spiritual Sentences and Maxims*. (16th cent.)

Desire earnestly always to suffer for God in every thing and on every occasion.

> St. Teresa of Jesus: *Maxims*. (16th cent.)

One ounce of patient suffering is worth far more than a pound of action.

> J. P. Camus: *The Spirit of St. Francis de Sales*, 9, 9. (17th cent.)

Take the cross *He sends*, as it is, and not as *you* imagine it to be.

> Mother Cornelia Connelly. (19th cent.)

Better a day of strife
Than a century of sleep.

> A. Ryan: *The Rosary of My Tears.* (19th
> cent.)

Who does not see that to bear pain well
is to meet it courageously, not to shrink
or waver, but to pray for God's help,
then to look at it steadfastly, to summon
what nerve we have of mind and body,
to receive its attack, and to bear up
against it (while strength is given us)
as against some visible enemy in close
combat?

> Card. Newman: *Parochial and Plain
> Sermons,* 3. (19th cent.)

We all suffer for each other, and gain
by each other's sufferings; for man never
stands alone here, though he will stand
by himself one day hereafter; but here
he is a social being, and goes forward to
his long home as one of a large company.

> Card. Newman: *Grammar of Assent,* 10.
> (19th cent.)

There is nothing that we suffer for the
honor of God, however little it may be,
that is not more serviceable to us than if
we possessed the dominion of the world.

> Archb. Ullathorne: *Humility and Patience.*
> (19th cent.)

The consequences of sin are bitter and
hard to bear, and they must accompany
man as long as life lasts. To suffer and
to endure, therefore, is the lot of humanity; let them strive as they may, no
strength and no artifice will ever succeed
in banishing from human life the ills
and troubles which beset it.

> Pope Leo XIII: *Rerum Novarum.* (May
> 15, 1891)

Oh, man's capacity
For spiritual sorrow, corporal pain!
Who has explored the deepmost of that
sea,
With heavy links of a far-fathoming
chain?

. . . .

Only One has explored
The deepmost; but He did not die of it.
Not yet, not yet He died. Man's human
Lord
Touched the extreme; it is not infinite.

> Alice Meynell: *The Crucifixion.* (20th
> cent.)

The whole of nature exists on the principle of vicarious suffering; and to reject
Christianity because of the doctrine of
the atonement is to reject nature itself
on the same account.

> R. H. Benson: *Christ in the Church.* (20th
> cent.)

Suicide

Parricide is more wicked than homicide,
but suicide is the most wicked of all.

> St. Augustine: *On Patience.* (5th cent.)

For if it is not lawful to take the law into
our own hands, and slay even a guilty
person, whose death no public sentence
has warranted, then certainly he who
kills himself is a homicide, and so much
the guiltier of his own death, as he was
more innocent of that offence for which
he doomed himself to die.

> St. Augustine: *The City of God,* 1, 17.
> (5th cent.)

Brutus and Cato might discharge their
souls,
And give them furloughs for another
world;
But we, like sentries, are obliged to
stand
In starless nights, and wait the 'pointed
hour.

> Dryden: *Don Sebastian,* 2, 1. (17th cent.)

Not only is suicide a sin, it is the sin. It
is the ultimate and absolute evil, the refusal to take an interest in existence; the
refusal to take the oath of loyalty to life.
The man who kills a man, kills a man.
The man who kills himself, kills all
men; as far as he is concerned he wipes
out the world.

> G. K. Chesterton: *Orthodoxy.* (20th
> cent.)

Those who lay violent hands on themselves, if death ensue, shall be deprived
of ecclesiastical burial. . . .

> Code of Canon Law, Canon 2350, 2. (20th
> cent.)

Suitor

The last suitor wins the maid.

> Seumas MacManus: *Heavy Hangs the*
> *Golden Grain.* (20th cent.)

Summer

In summer season when soft was the sun.

> Langland: *Piers Plowman,* Prol. (14th
> cent.)

One swallow maketh not summer.

> John Heywood: *Proverbs,* 2, 5. (16th
> cent.)

When summer took in hand the winter to assail,
With force of might, and virtue great,
his stormy blast to quail,
And when he clothèd fair the earth
about with green,
And every tree new garmented, that
pleasure was to seen:
Mine heart gan new revive, and
changèd blood did stir
Me to withdraw my winter woe, that
kept within the door.
Abroad, quoth my desire: assay to
set thy foot,
Where thou shalt find the savour sweet:
for sprung is every root.

> Henry Howard, Earl of Surrey: *Complaint*
> *of a Lover.* (Guiney, 79) (16th cent.)

The summer looks out from her brazen
tower,
Through the flashing bars of July.

> F. Thompson: *A Corymbus for Autumn.*
> (19th cent.)

Like a matron grown jaded—
Fat, forty, and fair—
In a nook cool and shaded,
Who nods in her chair;
Then, sudden, aware

Of the eyes of the masses,
Feigns a wide-awake air,
Summer smiles as she passes.

> T. A. Daly: *Ballade of Summer's Passing.*
> (20th cent.)

Sun

The sun is very beautiful, but it is too
imbecile and weak to be a god.

> St. John Chrysostom: *Homilies.* (4th
> cent.)

Be Thou praised, my Lord, with all
Thy creatures,
above all Brother Sun
who gives the day and lightens us
therewith.
And he is beautiful, and radiant with
great splendor,
of Thee, Most High, he bears similitude.

> St. Francis of Assisi: *Canticle of the Sun.*
> (13th cent.)

And see—the sun himself!—on wings
Of glory up the east he springs.
Angel of light! who from the time
Those heavens began their march sub-
lime,
Hath first of all the starry choir
Trod in his Maker's steps of fire!

> Thomas Moore: *Lalla Rookh: the*
> *Fire-Worshippers.* (19th cent.)

As the full moon shining there
To the sun that lighteth her
Am I unto thee for ever,
O my secret glory-giver!
O my light, I am dark but fair,
Black but fair.

> Alice Meynell: *The Moon to the Sun! The*
> *Poet Sings to her Poet.* (19th cent.)

Sunday

Sunday, indeed, is the day on which we
hold our common assembly because it is
the first day on which God, transforming
the darkness and matter, created the
world; and our Savior Jesus Christ arose
from the dead on the same day. For they

crucified Him on the day before, that of Saturn, and on the day after, Sunday, He appeared to His apostles and disciples, and taught them the things which we have passed on to you also for consideration.

St. Justin Martyr: *First Apology, 67.* (2nd cent.)

Hail day! whereon the One in Three
First formed the earth by sure decree,
The day its Maker rose again,
And vanquished death, and burst our
   chain.

Roman Breviary, Hymn *Primo die quo Trinitas* for Sunday at Matins. (Tr. J. M. Neale) (Attributed to Pope St. Gregory I, 6th cent.)

The Lord's Day is so called, because on that day the joy of our Lord's resurrection is celebrated. This day the Jews did not observe, but it was declared by the Christians in honor of the Lord's resurrection, and the celebration began from that time.

St. Isidore: *Etymologies, 6, 18.* (7th cent.)

God ended all the world's array,
And rested on the seventh day:
His holy voice proclaimed it blest,
And named it for the sabbath rest.

St. Bede the Venerable: *Post facta celsa Conditor.* (Tr. J. Neale) (8th cent.)

Sunday is not a day for judicial proceedings. (Dies Dominicus non est juridicus)

Legal Maxim. (Broom, Legal Maxims) (Medieval ?)

See also Sabbath

Sunrise

Soil not thy plumage, gentle dove,
   With sublunary things,—
Till in the fount of light and love,
   Thou shalt have bathed thy wings.

. . . .

See—where the Sun of righteousness,
   Unfolds the gates of day:
Go,—meet him in his glorious dress,
   And quaff the orient ray!

M. Bridges: *The Christian to his Soul at Sunrise.* (19th cent.)

Golden
Earthquake in the east.

F. Thompson: *Song of the Hours.* (19th cent.)

Sunset

O setting sun, that as in reverent days
   Sinkest in music to thy smoothèd
      sleep,
Discrowned of homage, though yet
      crowned with rays,
   Hymned not at harvest more, though
      reapers reap.

F. Thompson: *Ode to the Setting Sun.* (19th cent.)

Nobody of any real culture ever talks nowadays about the beauty of a sunset. Sunsets are quite old-fashioned. They belong to the time when Turner was the last note in art.

Oscar Wilde: *The Decay of Lying.* (19th cent.)

Sunshine

As thick as motes in the sunbeam.

Chaucer: *The Wife of Bath's Tale.* (14th cent.)

Blest power of sunshine!—genial day,
What balm, what life is in thy ray!
To feel thee is such real bliss,
That had the world no joy but this,
To sit in sunshine calm and sweet,—
It were a world too exquisite
For man to leave it for the gloom,
The deep, cold shadow of the tomb.

Thomas Moore: *Lalla Rookh: the Fire-Worshippers.* (19th cent.)

Superfluities

Superfluities do not hurt. (Superflua non nocent.)

> St. Augustine: *The City of God*. (5th cent.)

Superior

Let her [i.e. the mother superior] be cheerful in maintaining discipline and fearful to impose it; and although both are necessary, yet let her endeavor to be more loved by you than feared, always bearing in mind that she has to render an account of you to God.

> St. Augustine: *Letter 211* (his *Rule*). (5th cent.)

If the goal of Christianity is the imitation of Christ according to the measure of his incarnation, insofar as is conformable with the vocation of each individual, they who are entrusted with the guidance of many others are obliged to animate those still weaker than themselves, by their assistance, to the imitation of Christ.

> St. Basil: *The Long Rules*, 43. (4th cent.)

Supernatural

With us the super-human is the only place where you can find the human. Human nature is hunted, and has fled into sanctuary.

> G. K. Chesterton: *Tremendous Trifles*, 30. (20th cent.)

For the next twenty-four hours I remained in the mental condition of the modern world. I mean the condition in which all natural explanations have broken down and no supernatural explanation has been established.

> G. K. Chesterton: *Tremendous Trifles*, 39. (20th cent.)

Nature is always looking for the supernatural.

> G. K. Chesterton: *The Everlasting Man*. (20th cent.)

Superstition

Neither the higher clergy nor the lower clergy may be magicians, conjurors, mathematicians, or astrologers, nor shall they make so-called amulets, which are chains for their own souls. And those who wear these amulets shall be shut out from the Church.

> Council of Laodicea, Can. 36. (365)

Superstition is the cruellest thing in the world. Faith is to live in the sun. Superstition is to sit in darkness.

> Katharine T. Hinkson: *The House of the Foxes*. (20th cent.)

Superstition recurs in all ages, and especially in rationalistic ages.

> G. K. Chesterton: *The Everlasting Man*. (20th cent.)

Surgery

All practice is theory; all surgery is practice; ergo, all surgery is theory.

> Lanfranc: *Chirurgia magna*. (13th cent.)

Surprise

The fool of nature stood with stupid eyes
And gaping mouth, that testified surprise.

> Dryden: *Cymon and Iphigenia*. (17th cent.)

Swan

The jealous swan, against his death that singeth.

> Chaucer: *The Parlement of Foules*. (14th cent.)

When mild Favonius breathes, with warbling throat
The milk-white swan chants with a sweeter note,
But sweeter yet her music far excels
When death approaches, which her tune foretells.

> Henry Hawkins: *Hoc Cygno Vinces*. (17th cent.)

Swearing

A man who desires to live in accordance with the gospel must not swear by anyone, for if it is not allowed to swear, neither is it allowed to swear by anyone.

> Origen: *Tract. 35 in Matth.* (3rd cent.)

Swearing is worse than theft.

> St. John Chrysostom: *Homilies.* (4th cent.)

In elder times an ancient custom t'was,
To swear in weighty matters by the mass.
But when mass was put down, as old men note,
They swore then by the cross of this gray grote.
And when the cross was held likewise in scorn
Then faith, and truth, for common oaths were sworn.
But now men banisht have both faith and truth,
So that God damn me is the common oath.
So custom keeps decorum by gradation,
Losing mass, cross, faith, truth, followeth damnation.

> Henry Fitzsimon: *Untitled Poem.* (From *The Justification and Exposition of the Divine Sacrifice of the Mass,* Douay, 1611.) (Guiney, 326) (17th cent.)

See also Oath

Sweet and Bitter

> With thy speech a question is entwined,
> How a sweet seed a bitter fruit may bear.

> Dante: *Paradiso, Canto 8.* (14th cent.)

Sweet and Sour

Sweet meat will have sour sauce.

> John Heywood: *Proverbs,* 1, 8. (16th cent.)

Take the sweet with the sour.

> John Heywood: *Proverbs,* 2, 4. (16th cent.)

Sweetness

Short and sweet if I were judge, a piece surely worthy praise.

> Thomas Lodge: *A Defence of Play.* (16th cent.)

And sweet is sweet, though purchasèd with sorrow.

> F. Thompson: *Envoy.* (19th cent.)

Swimming

He must needs swim, that is hold up by the chin.

> John Heywood: *Proverbs,* 1, 5. (16th cent.)

It is not the way to learn to swim in troubled waters, never to have gone into them.

> Card. Newman: *Idea of a University.* (19th cent.)

Swine

Though he love not to buy the pig in the poke.

> John Heywood: *Proverbs,* 1, 9. (16th cent.)

Sword

He that striketh with the sword, shall be stricken with the scabbard.

> John Heywood: *Proverbs,* 2, 7. (16th cent.)

Sycamore

As I sat under a sycamore tree,
A sycamore tree, a sycamore tree,
I looked me out upon the sea
On Christ's Sunday at morn.

I saw three ships a-sailing there,
A-sailing there, a-sailing there,

Jesus, Mary, and Joseph they bare
On Christ's Sunday at morn.

> Anonymous: *I Saw Three Ships.* (15th
> cent.)

Sympathy

Better than grandeur, better than gold,
Than rank and titles a thousand fold,

Is a healthy body and a mind at ease,
And simple pleasures that always
please.
A heart that can feel for another's woe,
With sympathies large enough to en-
fold
All men as brothers, is better than gold.

> Abram Ryan: *Better than Gold.* (19th
> cent.)

T

Tale

Refrain from listening to worldly tales,
that you may not in any way stain your
soul with the spattering of mud.

> St. Basil: *On Renunciation of the World.*
> (4th cent.)

Say forth thy tale, and tarry not the time.

> Chaucer: *The Reeves Prologue.* (14th
> cent.)

This is a fair tale of a tub told us of his
election.

> St. Thomas More: *Confutation of Tyndale.*
> (16th cent.)

A tale that fleeth far is sure to catch many
new feathers; but pluck them off again,
and the thing remains as bald as a coote.

> St. Thomas More. (16th cent.)

A good tale ill told, in the telling is
marred.

> John Heywood: *Proverbs,* 2, 7. (16th
> cent.)

Talent

No one respects a talent that is concealed.

> Erasmus: *Adagia.* (16th cent.)

Talents are distributed unevenly, it is
true: to one ten, and to another five; but
each has one pound, all alike.

> R. H. Benson: *The Light Invisible.* (20th
> cent.)

Talk

But far more numerous was the herd of
such,
Who think too little, and who talk too
much.

> Dryden: *Absalom and Achitophel.* (17th
> cent.)

Talk to every woman as if you loved her,
and to every man as if he bored you.

> Oscar Wilde: *A Woman of No
> Importance,* 3. (19th cent.)

I suspect that the real reason that an Englishman does not talk is that he cannot
leave off talking. I suspect that my solitary countrymen, hiding in separate rail-

way compartments, are not so much retiring as a race of Trappists as escaping from a race of talkers.

> G. K. Chesterton: *What I Saw in America.* (20th cent.)

Don't say all you'd like to say lest you hear something you wouldn't like to hear.

> Seumas MacManus: *Heavy Hangs the Golden Grain.* (20th cent.)

Talkativeness

Much talkativeness is the sign of a feeble mind, and an undisciplined will.

> Archb. Ullathorne: *Humility and Patience.* (19th cent.)

Taste

To enjoy is, as it were, to create; to understand is a form of equality, and the full use of taste is an act of genius.

> John La Farge: *Considerations on Painting.* (19th cent.)

Taxation

Kings cannot reign unless their subjects give;
And they who pay the taxes bear the rule.

> Dryden: *To Sir Godfrey Kneller.* (17th cent.)

The right to possess private property is derived from nature, not from man; and the state has the right to control its use in the interests of the public good alone, but by no means to absorb it altogether. The state would therefore be unjust and cruel if under the name of taxation it were to deprive the private owner of more than is fair.

> Pope Leo XIII: *Rerum Novarum.* (May 15, 1891)

Te Deum

We praise Thee, O God: we acknowledge Thee to be the Lord.

Thee, the eternal Father, all the earth doth worship.
To Thee all the angels, to Thee the heavens, and all the powers therein:
To Thee the cherubim and seraphim with unceasing voice cry aloud:
Holy, holy, holy, Lord God of Sabaoth.

> Roman Breviary, Hymn *Te Deum laudamus* at Matins. (Tr. Msgr. H. Henry) (Attr. to St. Nicetas, 335–415)

Teacher

The teacher of youth, whether in a public or a private school, has no absolute rights of his own. All that he exercises have been given to him by others. Every Christian child has an inalienable right to instruction that is in harmony with the teachings of the Church, the pillar and foundation of all truth.

> Pope Pius XI: *Divini illius magistri.* (Dec. 31, 1929)

Teaching

The master loseth his time to learn
When the disciple will not hear.

> Chaucer: *The Romaunt of the Rose.* (14th cent.)

Better fed than taught.

> John Heywood: *Proverbs,* 1, 10. (16th cent.)

Bachelor's wives and maid's children be well taught.

> John Heywood: *Proverbs,* 2, 6. (16th cent.)

Men must be taught as if you taught them not,
And things unknown proposed as things forgot.

> Pope: *An Essay on Criticism,* 3. (18th cent.)

To discover and to teach are distinct functions; they are also distinct gifts, and are not commonly found united in the same person.

> Card. Newman: *Idea of a University.* (19th cent.)

Everybody who is incapable of learning has taken to teaching.

> Oscar Wilde: *The Decay of Lying.* (19th cent.)

Tears

Go your way; as sure as you live, it is impossible that the son of these tears should perish.

> St. Augustine: *Confessions,* 3, 12. (Words of the bishop to St. Monica with reference to St. Augustine's eventual conversion) (5th cent.)

Tears gain everything, and one drop of water attracts another.

> St. Teresa of Jesus: *Autobiography,* 19. (16th cent.)

> O 'tis a tear,
> Too true a tear; for no sad eyn,
> How sad so e're
> Rain so true a tear as thine;
> Each drop leaving a place so dear,
> Weeps for itself, is its own tear.

> Richard Crashaw: *The Tear.* (17th cent.)

Man is a creature, born and nurst in tears,
He through his life the marks of sorrow bears;
And dying, thinks he can no off'ring have
More fit than tears distilling on his grave.

> Sir John Beaumont: *Of Tears.* (17th cent.)

It is only to the happy that tears are a luxury.

> Thomas Moore: *Lalla Rookh: Prologue.* (19th cent.)

Some reckon their age by years,
Some measure their life by art;
But some tell their days by the flow of their tears,
And their lives by the moans of their heart.

> Abram J. Ryan: *The Rosary of My Tears.* (19th cent.)

The tears that trickled down our eyes,
They do not touch the earth today;
But soar like angels to the skies,
And, like the angels, may not die;
For ah! our immortality
Flows thro' each tear—sounds in each sigh.

> A. J. Ryan: *Tears.* (19th cent.)

Crying is the refuge of plain women, but the ruin of pretty ones.

> Oscar Wilde: *Lady Windermere's Fan,* 1. (19th cent.)

'Tis those who have no tears for Time that must weep in Eternity.

> John Ayscough: *The Ave Maria.* (20th cent.)

Tears on my pillow—witnesses in vain
Of half-remembered pain!
Her vision draws away unto eternal day,
Leaving the noon for my content
But holding a lament
To slake the moon and stars of our commune,—
Tears on my pillow—tears against the moon.

> Thomas Walsh: *Tears against the Moon.* (20th cent.)

Tediousness

It were as soon done to weave a new web of cloth as to sew up every hole in a net.

> St. Thomas More. (16th cent.)

E'en wit's a burden when it talks too long.

> Dryden. (17th cent.)

Temperance

Temperance is a disposition that restrains our desires for things which it is base to desire.

> St. Augustine: *On Freewill,* 1, 27. (4th cent.)

Temperance is simply a disposition of the mind which sets bounds to the passions.

> St. Thomas Aquinas: *Summa Theologica,* 57. (13th cent.)

Temporal and Eternal

But not all solicitude about temporal affairs is forbidden, only such as is superfluous and out of due order.

> St. Thomas Aquinas: *Summa Theologica*, 2, 2, 83, 6. (13th cent.)

Let temporal things serve thy use, but the eternal be the object of thy desire.

> Thomas a Kempis: *The Imitation of Christ*, 3, 16. (15th cent.)

We should enjoy spiritual things but only use corporal things.

> St. Francis de Sales: *Introduction to the Devout Life*, 3, 39. (17th cent.)

Temptation

The devil cannot lord it over those who are servants of God with their whole heart and who place their hope in Him. The devil can wrestle with, but not overcome them.

> Shepherd of Hermas, Mandate 12, 5, 2. (2nd cent.)

The devil tempts that he may ruin; God tempts that He may crown.

> St. Ambrose: *Concerning Abraham*, 1, 66. (4th cent.)

For the devil does not seduce or influence anyone, unless he finds him ready in some part similar to himself. He finds him coveting something, and cupidity opens the door for the devil's suggestion to enter.

> St. Augustine: *Sermon 32*, 11, 11. (5th cent.)

Grant unto Thy people, we beseech Thee, O Lord, the grace to withstand the temptations of the devil, and with pure minds to follow Thee the only God.

> Roman Missal, Collect for Seventeenth Sunday after Pentecost. (Gelasian, 5th to 7th cent.)

O God, Who dost justify the ungodly and dost not desire the death of sinners:

we humbly beseech Thy majesty; that Thou wouldst graciously protect Thy servants who trust in Thy mercy by Thy heavenly assistance, and preserve them by Thy continual protection; that they may both serve Thee and not be separated from Thee by temptation.

> Roman Missal, Collect. (Gregorian, 6th to 8th cent.)

O almighty and most merciful God, graciously regard our prayers, and free our hearts from the temptation of evil thoughts; that we may become a fitting dwelling-place for Thy Holy Spirit.

> Roman Missal, Collect. (ca. 9th cent.)

God does not punish people for what they would have done, but for what they do.

> St. Thomas Aquinas: *Disputations concerning Evil*, 2, 2. (13th cent.)

No man is so perfect and holy as not to have sometimes temptations; and we cannot be wholly without them.

> Thomas a Kempis: *The Imitation of Christ*, 1, 13. (15th cent.)

There is no order so holy, nor place so retired, where there are not temptations and adversities.

> Thomas a Kempis: *The Imitation of Christ*, 1, 13. (15th cent.)

Inconstancy of mind, and small confidence in God, is the beginning of all evil temptations.

> Thomas a Kempis: *The Imitation of Christ*, 1, 13. (15th cent.)

We must be watchful, especially in the beginning of temptation, because then the enemy is more easily overcome, if he is not suffered to come in at all at the door of the soul, but is kept out and resisted at his first knock. Whence a certain man said, Withstand the beginning: after-remedies come too late.

> Thomas a Kempis: *The Imitation of Christ*, 1, 13. (15th cent.)

Fire tries iron, and temptation tries a just man.

> Thomas a Kempis: *The Imitation of Christ,* 1, 13. (15th cent.)

All the temptations of hell cannot stain a soul that does not love them.

> St. Francis de Sales: *Letters to Persons in the World,* 6, 6. (17th cent.)

Let the enemy rage at the gate, let him knock, let him push, let him cry, let him howl, let him do worse; we know for certain that he cannot enter save by the door of our consent.

> St. Francis de Sales: *Letters to Persons in Religion,* 1, 8. (17th cent.)

Our Lord permits us to fail in little occasions, that we may humble ourselves and know that if we overcome certain great temptations it is not by our own strength.

> St. Francis de Sales: *Letters to Persons in Religion,* 4, 32. (17th cent.)

Internal Cerberus, whose griping fangs,
That gnaw the soul are the mind's secret pangs,
Thou greedy vulture that dost gorging tire
On hearts corrupted by impure desire.

> Sir Edward Sherburne: *Conscience.* (17th cent.)

Satan now is wiser than of yore,
And tempts by making rich, not making poor.

> Pope: *Moral Essays,* 3. (18th cent.)

There is no sin in temptation, and there can be no temptation without a lively image being presented to the mind.

> R. H. Benson: *The Queen's Tragedy.* (20th cent.)

And hath it come to this, my daughter dear,
—My little daughter dearer than myself!—
That thou dost come to tempt thy father's soul

And play the serpent, even as mother Eve
Did'st serve old Adam! Verily I deemed
That if all others doubting looked askance
And held me cursed with pride, and little wit,
Thou, bonny Meg, would'st read my heart aright,
And know me for the man I know myself.

> Mary Elizabeth Blake: *In the Tower (St. Thomas More).* (20th cent.)

Tenderness

As for her sympathies and tender feelings,
She was so charitably solicitous
She used to weep if she but saw a mouse
Caught in a trap, if he were dead or bleeding.

> Chaucer: *Canterbury Tales: Prologue.* (Tr. Coghill) (14th cent.)

Tennyson, Alfred Lord

He [Tennyson] had a great deal to say; but he had much more power of expression than was wanted for anything he had to say. He could not think up to the height of his own towering style.

> G. K. Chesterton: *Victorian Age in Literature.* (20th cent.)

Terce (Third Hour)

And if indeed thou art at home pray at the third hour and praise God; but if thou art elsewhere and that time comes, pray in thy heart to God. For in this hour Christ was seen nailed upon the tree. And therefore in the Old Testament the law bade the shewbread always to be offered at the third hour as a type of the Body and Blood of Christ; and the dumb lamb was slain which was a type of the perfect Lamb. For Christ is the Shepherd, and He is also the Bread which came down from heaven.

> St. Hippolytus: *The Apostolic Tradition,* 36. (3rd cent.)

Come, Holy Ghost, who ever One
Art with the Father and the Son,
It is the hour, our souls possess
With Thy full flood of holiness.

Roman Breviary, hymn *Nunc Sancte nobis Spiritus* for Terce. (Tr. Card. Newman.) (Possibly by St. Ambrose, 4th cent.)

Lord, Who didst send down Thy most holy Spirit at the third hour upon Thine apostles; take Him not away from us, O blessed One, but renew Him in us who pray to Thee.

Byzantine Horologion, Troparion at Terce. (ca. 6th to 8th cent.)

Thanksgiving

O God, Whose mercy is without measure and Whose bountiful goodness knows no end: we give thanks to Thy gracious majesty for the gifts conferred upon us, ever beseeching Thy clemency; that even as Thou dost grant the wishes of Thy suppliants, Thou wouldst not abandon them but dispose them to receive still further rewards.

Roman Missal, Collect. (After 9th cent.)

Give thanks frequently to God for all the benefits He has conferred on you, that you may be worthy to receive more.

St. Louis IX, King of France. (As reported in Joinville's *Life,* 746.) (13th cent.)

One act of thanksgiving, when things go wrong with us, is worth a thousand thanks when things are agreeable to our inclinations.

Bl. John of Avila. (16th cent.)

Yea, though I sin each day times seven,
And dare not lift the fearfullest eye to
heaven,
Thanks must I give
Because that seven times are not eight
or nine,
And that my darkness is all mine,
And that I live
Within this oak-shade one more min-
ute even,

Hearing the winds their Maker magnify.

Coventry Patmore: *Faint Yet Pursuing.* (19th cent.)

Theatre

A certain woman went to the theatre and brought the devil home with her. And when the unclean spirit was pressed in the exorcism and asked how he durst attack a Christian, "I have done noth-ing," says he, "but what I can justify, for I seized her upon my own ground."

Tertullian: *De Spectaculis.* (3rd cent.)

The higher and inferior clergy shall not join in witnessing any dramatic perform-ance at weddings or feasts, but before the actors appear they shall rise and go out.

Council of Laodicea, Can. 54. (365)

In the theatre the demon of impurity displays his pomp with so many charms and seductive graces that the most solid virtue can hardly withstand it.

St. John Baptist de la Salle: *Les devoirs du chrétien,* 7. (18th cent.)

Theologian

A theologian is one who has mastered theology—one who can say how many opinions there are on every point, what authors have taken which, and which is the best—who can discriminate exactly between proposition and proposition, argument and argument, who can pro-nounce which are safe, which allowable, which dangerous—who can trace the his-tory of doctrines in successive centuries, and apply the principles of former times to the conditions of the present.

Card. Newman: *Letter to Sister Maria Pia.* (19th cent.)

Theology

To this science alone belongs that whereby saving faith is begotten, nour-ished, protected and strengthened.

St. Augustine: *De Trinitate,* 14, 1. (5th cent.)

Philosophy is called divine when we discuss the ineffable nature of God, or beings that are spiritual to some extent and of most profound nature.

St. Isidore: *Etymologies,* 2, 24. (7th cent.)

There are two kinds of theology. One follows the reasonable course of inferring divine truths from meanings governing the physical world: it is thus that philosophers, claiming for fundamental philosophy, or metaphysics, the title of the divine science, have discussed theological truths. The other, while appreciating that at present when we are wayfarers we cannot see for ourselves the supreme evidence of divine truths, already begins through infused faith to take after and share in God's knowledge by cleaving to His fundamental truth for its own sake.

St. Thomas Aquinas: *Exposition of the De Trinitate,* 2, 2. (13th cent.)

The purpose of theology is threefold: to refute error, to teach sound morals, and to contemplate truth.

St. Thomas Aquinas: *On the Sentences I,* Prol. 1, 5. (13th cent.)

Theology deserves to be called the highest wisdom, for everything is viewed in the light of the first cause.

St. Thomas Aquinas: *Contra Gentes,* 2, 4. (13th cent.)

The premises of Christian theology are revealed truths, accepted on the word of the teacher who reveals them. Consequently its typical method is the appeal to authority. This does not impair its scientific dignity, for though to cite human authority is the poorest form of argument, the appeal to divine authority is the highest and most cogent.

St. Thomas Aquinas: *Summa Theologica,* 1, 1, 8. (13th cent.)

Christian theology also avails itself of human reasoning to illustrate the truths of faith, not to prove them. Grace does not scrap nature, but improves it; reason subserves faith, and natural love runs through charity.

St. Thomas Aquinas: *Summa Theologica,* 1, 1, 8. (13th cent.)

The principles of reason are the foundations of philosophy, the principles of faith are the foundations of Christian theology. The truths of philosophy are more restricted; they cannot be contrary to the truths of faith, but instead offer likenesses and anticipations of them. Nature is the prelude to grace.

St. Thomas Aquinas: *Exposition of the De Trinitate,* 2, 3. (13th cent.)

Theology teaches of God, is taught by God, and leads to God. (Theologia Deum docet, a Deo docetur, ad Deum ducit.)

Scholastic adage. (Medieval)

Ye other few, who have raised your
    necks for boon
  Of the angels' bread betimes, given
    to sustain
  The life lived here (and surfeit none
    hath known).

Dante: *Paradiso, Canto 2.* (Tr. Binyon) (14th cent.)

Theology hath vexed me ten score
    times;
The more I muse thereon the mistier it
    seemeth,
And the deeper I divine, the darker me
    thinketh it.

Langland: *Piers Plowman,* Passus 12. (14th cent.)

Love is the abridgment of all theology.

St. Francis de Sales: *Treatise on the Love of God,* 8, 1. (17th cent.)

Since human reason is placed on a level with religion itself, theological science must be treated exactly like the philosophical sciences.

Proposition condemned by Pius IX in Syllabus of Errors. (1867)

University education without theology is simply unphilosophical. Theology has at least as good a right to claim a place there as astronomy.

> Card. Newman: *Idea of a University.* (19th cent.)

Theology . . . is the most noble of studies.

> Pope Leo XIII: *Aeterni patris.* (Aug. 4, 1879)

Theology is only articulate religion.

> G. K. Chesterton: *The Common Man.* (20th cent.)

In the higher cultures the existence of religion has always involved the existence of theology—that is to say, a rational system of religious knowledge. All the higher religions do in fact assert the existence of divine truth and base their teaching upon it. And it is obvious that if there is no true knowledge of the object of religious experience, religion loses its validity, and even its social coherence, and becomes an irrational impulse like any other delusional form of psychosis.

> Christopher Dawson: *Gifford Lectures, 1947: Religion and Culture.*

It is the traditional teaching of natural theology that the elements of religious truth are common to the human race and accessible to every rational creature—that the divine Being is the transcendent end towards which all the different ways of life converge and the divine law the universal norm by which all different patterns of human behavior can be coordinated.

> C. Dawson: *Gifford Lectures, 1947: Religion and Culture.*

Theologians must always return to the source of divine revelation; for it belongs to them to point out how the doctrine of the living teaching authority is to be found either explicitly or implicitly in the Scriptures and in tradition. Besides, each source of divinely revealed doctrine contains so many rich treasures

of truth that they can really never be exhausted. Hence it is that theology, through study of its sacred sources, remains ever fresh.

> Pope Pius XII: *Humani Generis.* (Apr. 12, 1950)

Theory

None of us can go a little way with a theory; when it once possesses us, we are no longer our own masters. It makes us speak its words, and do violence to our nature.

> Card. Newman: *Essays Critical and Historical,* 2. (19th cent.)

Thief

Your law, O Lord, punishes theft; and this law is so written in the hearts of men that not even the breaking of it blots it out: for no thief bears calmly being stolen from—not even if he is rich and the other steals through want.

> St. Augustine: *Confessions,* 2, 4. (5th cent.)

He that is once a thief is ever more in danger.

> Langland: *Piers Plowman,* Passus 15. (14th cent.)

As meet as a rope for a thief.

> John Heywood: *Proverbs,* 1, 10. (16th cent.)

Where be no receivers, there be no thieves.

> John Heywood: *Proverbs,* 1, 12. (16th cent.)

Thirst

> The natural thirst which is unquenchable
> Save by the water the Samaritan
> Poor woman asked the boon of at the well.

> Dante: *Purgatorio, Canto 21.* (Tr. Binyon) (14th cent.)

Thomas Aquinas, Saint

The teaching of Blessed Thomas is the true and Catholic doctrine.

> Pope Urban V: *Letter to the University of Toulouse.* (14th cent.)

Reason, as borne on the wings of Thomas, can scarcely rise higher.

> Pope Leo XIII: *Aeterni patris.* (Aug. 4, 1879)

Thomas of Canterbury, Saint

Joy, O Sion! and rejoice thou;
With both vow and lifted voice now,
  With a holy joy be glad!
For Christ's sake assassinated,
Is thy Thomas immolated,
  A most precious victim made.

> Adam of St. Victor: *Gaude Sion et laetare.* (Tr. Wrangham) (12th cent.)

Thomas More, Saint

If we had been master of such a servant, of whose doings ourselves have had these many years no small experience, we would rather have lost the best city of our dominions, than have lost such a worthy counsellor.

> Emperor Charles V. (To Sir Thomas Eliott, English ambassador, when informed that the saint had been executed.) (16th cent.)

Ah, happy fool of Christ, unawed
By familiar sanctities,
You served your Lord at holy ease!
Dear jester in the courts of God.

> F. Thompson: *To the English Martyrs.* (19th cent.)

Thomism

It is a mistake to think that you have in Thomism a comfortable house replete with every modern philosophical convenience, so that one has only to understand what St. Thomas said to answer any modern difficulty. St. Thomas was not raised up to save posterity the trouble of thinking for themselves. His philosophy is a starting-point; it will take you a long way; but you may have to continue the journey by yourself.

> Joseph Rickaby: *An Old Man's Jottings.* (20th cent.)

It is not Catholicism which is Thomist, it is Thomism which is Catholic and it is Catholic because it is universalist.

> J. Maritain: *The Things That Are Not Caesar's.* (Quoting Père H. Woroniecki) (20th cent.)

Thought

Men have the power of thinking that they may avoid sin.

> St. John Chrysostom: *Homilies.* (4th cent.)

Thought is a kind of sight of the mind.

> St. Augustine: *De Trinitate,* 15, 9. (5th cent.)

To attempt in verse things scarce to thought assured.

> Dante: *Purgatorio, Canto 29.* (14th cent.)

I have heard said that thought is free.

> John Gower: *Confessio Amantis,* 5. (14th cent.)

Occupy your minds with good thoughts, or the enemy will fill them with bad ones: unoccupied they cannot be.

> St. Thomas More: *Meditations and Devotions.* (16th cent.)

A penny for your thought.

> John Heywood: *Proverbs,* 2, 4. (16th cent.)

Companion none is like unto the mind alone,
For many have been harmed by speech; through thinking few or none.

   .   .   .   .   .   .

Our wealth leaves us at death, our kinsmen at the grave;

But virtues of the mind unto the heavens with us we have.
Wherefore, for virtue's sake, I can be
well content
The sweetest time of all my life to deem
in thinking spent.

> Thomas, Lord Vaux: *Content.* (16th
> cent.)

One single thought of a man is of greater
worth than the whole world; wherefore
God alone is worthy of him.

> St. John of the Cross: *Spiritual Sentences
> and Maxims.* (16th cent.)

The mind a creature is, yet can create,
To nature's patterns adding higher skill;
Of finest works wit better could the
state
If force of wit had equal power of will:
Device of man in working hath no end;
What thought can think another
thought can mend.

> Bl. Robert Southwell: *Look Home.* (16th
> cent.)

Man's greatness lies in his power of
thought.

> Pascal: *Pensées.* (17th cent.)

Man is but a reed, the weakest thing in
nature; but a thinking reed.

> Pascal: *Pensées.* (17th cent.)

By space the universe embraces me and
swallows me up like an atom, by thought
I embrace the universe.

> Pascal: *Pensées.* (17th cent.)

I can easily conceive of a man without
hands, feet, head, for it is only experience
that teaches us that the head is more necessary than the feet. But I cannot conceive of a man without thoughts,—it
would be a stone or a brute.

> Pascal *Pensées.* (17th cent.)

It is mere chance that suggests thoughts;
it is mere chance that obliterates them
from the world; there is no particular

method by which they may be preserved
or acquired.

> Pascal: *Pensées.* (17th cent.)

Second thoughts are best.

> Dryden: *The Spanish Friar,* 2. (Proverb)
> (17th cent.)

In the present day mistiness is the mother
of wisdom.

> Card. Newman: *Essays Critical and
> Historical,* 1, 7. (19th cent.)

There is but one thought greater than
that of the universe, and that is the
thought of its Maker.

> Card. Newman: *Idea of a University.*
> (19th cent.)

It is the very energy of thought
Which keeps thee from thy God.

> Card. Newman: *Dream of Gerontius,*
> 363. (19th cent.)

It is often said that second thoughts are
best. So they are in matters of judgment,
but not in matters of conscience. In matters of duty, first thoughts are commonly
best. They have more in them of the
voice of God.

> Card. Newman. (19th cent.)

'They toil not, neither do they spin'—
The blossom-thoughts that here within
The garden of my soul arise,
Alike unheeding wintry skies;
Or sun or rain, or night or day,
And never hence to pass away.

> J. B. Tabb: *Immortelles.* (19th cent.)

She walks—the lady of my delight—
A shepherdess of sheep.
Her flocks are thoughts. She keeps them
white;
She guards them from the steep;
She feeds them on the fragrant height,
And folds them in for sleep.

> Alice Meynell: *The Shepherdess.* (20th
> cent.)

My heart has thoughts, which, though
　　thine eyes hold mine,
　　Flit to the silent world and other
　　　　summers,
With wings that dip beyond the silver
　　seas.

> Alice Meynell: *The Garden.* (19th cent.)

I come from nothing; but from where
Come the undying thoughts I bear?

> Alice Meynell: *A Song of Derivations.*
> (19th cent.)

Beauty ends where an intellectual expression begins. Intellect destroys the harmony of any face. The moment one sits
down to think, one becomes all nose.

> Oscar Wilde: *The Picture of Dorian Gray,*
> 1. (19th cent.)

In a tremendous climax of anxiety there
is no consecutiveness of thought, and
very little orderly consideration at all.

> R. H. Benson: *The Coward.* (20th cent.)

The modern world with its modern
movements is living on its Catholic capital. It is using, and using up, the truths
that remain to it out of the treasury of
Christendom; including, of course, many
truths known to pagan antiquity but crys-
stallized in Christendom.

> G. K. Chesterton: *The Thing.* (20th
> cent.)

All human thought, even the highest,
has its horizons; there are realms which
it cannot encompass and mirror in its nature, be it the most candid and clear.
God alone measures reality by what He
is, and in His essence sees all things vividly or faintly resembling His truth.

> M. C. D'Arcy: *The Nature of Belief.*
> (20th cent.)

The ultimate heresy is not the denial of
the existence of God but the denial, implicit or explicit, of the law of contradiction—a thing cannot be and not be—for
the man who repudiates the law of contradiction repudiates the very basis of
thought and commits himself to a scepticism even more fundamental than
atheism.

> Arnold Lunn: *The Revolt against Reason.*
> (20th cent.)

Three things that shouldn't be let rust—
a sword, a spade, and a thought.

> Seumas MacManus: *Heavy Hangs the
> Golden Grain.* (20th cent.)

Thoughts, Evil

When evil thoughts come into one's
heart, to dash them at once on the rock
of Christ and to manifest them to one's
spiritual father.

> St. Benedict: *Rule,* 4. (One of his 'tools of
> good works') (6th cent.)

Thrift

As great a craft is keep well as win.

> Chaucer: *Troilus and Criseyde.* (14th
> cent.)

When thrift and you fell first at a fray,
You played the man, for ye made thrift
　　run away.

> John Heywood: *Proverbs,* 1, 11. (16th
> cent.)

In choice of thrift let honor be your
　　gain,
　　Win it by virtue and by manly might;
In doing good esteem thy toil no pain,
　　Protect the fatherless and widow's
　　　　right:
Fight for thy faith, thy country, and
　　thy king;
For why? this thrift will prove a blessed
　　thing.

> Thomas Lodge: *A Solitary Life
> Commended.* (16th cent.)

We men have so much encouraged each
other in throwing money right and left,
that there has come at last to be a sort
of chivalrous and poetical air about losing sixpence. But on a broader and more
candid consideration the case scarcely
stands so. Thrift is the really romantic
thing; economy is more romantic than

extravagance. Heaven knows I for one speak disinterestedly in the matter; for I cannot clearly remember saving a half-penny ever since I was born.

> G. K. Chesterton: *What's Wrong with the World*. (20th cent.)

Thrush

Hush! With sudden gush
As from a fountain sings in yonder bush
The hermit thrush.

> John B. Tabb: *Overflow*. (19th cent.)

A voice peels in this end of night
  A phrase of notes resembling stars,
Single and spiritual notes of light.
    What call they at my window-bars?
    The south, the past, the day to be,
    An ancient infelicity.

> Alice Meynell: *A Thrush before Dawn*. (20th cent.)

Sing clear, O throstle,
Thou golden-tongued apostle
And little brown-frocked brother
Of the loved Assisian!

> T. A. Daly: *To a Thrush*. (20th cent.)

Thunder

Heaven's great artillery.

> R. Crashaw: *The Flaming Heart*. (17th cent.)

Tide

Hoist up sail while gale doth last,
Tide and wind stay no man's pleasure.

> Bl. Robert Southwell: *Loss in Delay*. (16th cent.)

As the inhastening tide doth roll,
Home from the deep, along the whole
  Wide shining strand, and floods the caves,
  —Your love comes filling with happy waves
The open sea-shore of my soul.

> Alice Meynell: *The Visiting Sea*. (19th cent.)

Tiger

The tiger, on the other hand, is kitten-ish and mild;
He makes a pretty playfellow for any little child;
And mothers of large families (who claim to common sense)
Will find a tiger will repay the trouble and expense.

> Hilaire Belloc: *The Tiger*. (20th cent.)

If a man proves too clearly and convincingly to himself that the tiger is an optical illusion—well, he will find out that he is wrong. The tiger will himself intervene in the discussion.

> G. K. Chesterton: *Illusions*. (20th cent.)

Time

Time takes no holiday.

> St. Augustine: *Confessions*, 4, 8. (5th cent.)

What then *is* time . . . ? I do not know. But at any rate this much I dare affirm that I know: that if nothing passed there would be no past time; if nothing were approaching, there would be no future time; if nothing were, there would be no present time.

> St. Augustine: *Confessions*, 11, 14. (5th cent.)

We can affirm that time *is* only in that it tends towards non-being.

> St. Augustine: *Confessions*, 11, 14. (5th cent.)

At any rate it is now quite clear that neither future nor past actually exists. Nor is it right to say there are three times, past, present and future. Perhaps it would be more correct to say: there are three times, a present of things past, a present of things present, and a present of things future. For these three exist in the mind, and I find them nowhere else.

> St. Augustine: *Confessions*, 11, 20. (5th cent.)

For if eternity and time are rightly distinguished by this, that time does not exist without some movement and transition, while in eternity there is no change, who does not see that there could have been no time had not some creature been made, which by some motion could give birth to change,—the various parts of which motion and change, as they cannot be simultaneous, succeed one another,—and thus, in these shorter or longer intervals of duration, time would begin?

> St. Augustine: *The City of God,* 11, 6. (5th cent.)

It is the wisest who grieve most at loss of time.

> Dante: *Purgatorio, Canto 3.* (14th cent.)

> For time y-lost, this knowen ye,
> By no way may recovered be.

> Chaucer: *The Hous of Fame.* (14th cent.)

As time him hurt, a time doth him cure.

> Chaucer: *Troilus and Criseyde.* (14th cent.)

Bide for time who will, for time will no man bide.

> John Skelton: *Works,* 1, 137. (16th cent.)

Time is tickle.

> John Heywood: *Proverbs,* 1, 3. (16th cent.)

> Time is a treasure worthy high esteem,
> But time once lost no treasure can redeem;
> Wherefore in time whilst now fit time thou hast,
> Spend well thy time before thy time be past,
> Else out of time thou shalt be sure of this:
> To rue the time that now thou spend'st amiss.

> Peter Mowle: *How Precious a Thing is Time.* (Guiney, 358) (16th cent.)

> The lopped tree in time may grow again,

> Most naked plants renew both fruit and flower;
> The sorriest wight may find release of pain,
> The driest soil suck in some moist'ning shower.
> Times go by turns, and chances change by course;
> From foul to fair, from better hap to worse.

> Bl. Robert Southwell: *Times Go By Turns.* (16th cent.)

> Now I see, and seeing sorrow,
> That the day, consumed, returns not.
> Who dare trust upon tomo. :ow,
> ' When nor time nor life sojourns not?

> Thomas Lodge: *Old Damon's Pastoral.* (17th cent.)

> Time overwears what erst his license wrought,
> And also seeks remembrance to deface,
> Of what himself hath to destruction brought,
> In that long tract of his all alt'ring space;
> That none might of his ruins view the place:
> And as he all beginnings seeks to end,
> So all his endings to oblivion tend.

> Richard Verstegan: *Verses.* (From *A Restoration of Decayed Intelligence,* 1605) (Guiney, 218) (17th cent.)

The enemy is glad to make you lose time when he cannot make you lose eternity.

> St. Francis de Sales: *Letters to Persons in Religion,* 2, 13. (17th cent.)

Time is short, eternity is long.

> Card. Newman: *Development of Christian Doctrine.* (19th cent.)

Time hath a taming hand.

> Card. Newman: *Persecution.* (19th cent.)

> Time, eternity's fountain, whose waters
> Fall back thither from whence they rose.

> F. Thompson: *Song of the Hours.* (19th cent.)

I dimly guess what time in mists con-
  founds;
Yet ever and anon a trumpet sounds
From the hid battlements of eternity;
Those shaken mists a space unsettle,
  then
Round the half-glimpsèd turrets slowly
  wash again.

> F. Thompson: *The Hound of Heaven.*
> (19th cent.)

Time his glass sits nodding by;
  'Twixt its turn and turn a spawn
Of universes buzz and die
  Like the ephemeris of the dawn.

> F. Thompson: *An Echo of Victor Hugo.*
> (19th cent.)

Next to grace time is the most precious
gift of God. Yet how much of both we
waste. We say that time does many
things. It teaches us many lessons, weans
us from many follies, strengthens us in
good resolves, and heals many wounds.
And yet it does none of these things.
Time does nothing. But time is the condition of all these things which God does
in time. Time is full of eternity. As we
use it so shall we be. Every day has its
opportunities, every hour its offer of
grace.

> Card. Manning: *The Eternal Priesthood.*
> (19th cent.)

Time, the messenger of fate!
Cunning master of debate,
Cunning soother of all sorrow,
Ruthless robber of tomorrow;
Tyrant to our dallying feet,
Though patron of a life complete.

> Mother M. Alphonsa: *A Protean Glimpse.*
> (19th cent.)

  What are the years of time?
A little space of day, and then the
  night;
A little span of sorrow and delight;
  Of dirges tolling and of joy-bells
  chime.
Yet can their calm, slow-moving, noise-
  less feet
Marshal the world to glory of defeat;

Lure forceful wrong behind the prison
  bars,
And leash triumphant right beyond the
  morning stars!
Or, swift as winds, and aimless too as
  they,
Bid heedless moments fleet and pass
  away.

> Mary Elizabeth Blake: *A Jubilee Ode.*
> (20th cent.)

Time must always ultimately teach.

> H. Belloc: *First and Last.* (20th cent.)

Stay your haste: the Man who made time
made plenty of it.

> Seumas MacManus: *Heavy Hangs the
> Golden Grain.* (20th cent.)

Timeliness

Time and place give best advice,
Out of season, out of price.

> Bl. Robert Southwell: *Loss in Delay.*
> (16th cent.)

Timidity

Where heart has failed
There shall no castle be assailed.

> John Gower: *Confessio Amantis.* (14th
> cent.)

Title

And nobler is a limited command,
Giv'n by the love of all your native
  land,
Than a successive title, long, and dark,
Drawn from the mouldy rolls of Noah's
  ark.

> Dryden: *Absalom and Achitophel.* (17th
> cent.)

Today

Let me get through today, and I shall
not fear tomorrow.

> St. Philip Neri. (16th cent.)

Rise! for the day is passing,
  And you lie dreaming on;

Happy the man, and happy he alone,
  He who can call today his own;
  He who, secure within, can say,
Tomorrow, do thy worst, for I have
    liv'd today.

Dryden: *Imitations of Horace,* 3. (17th
cent.)

The others have buckled their armor,
  And forth to the fight are gone:
A place in the ranks awaits you,
  Each man has some part to play;
The past and the future are nothing,
  In the face of the stern today.

Adelaide Procter: *Now.* (19th cent.)

Toleration

It is a fundamental human right, a privilege of nature, that every man should worship according to his own convictions: one man's religion neither harms nor helps another man. It . . . is certainly no part of religion to compel religion.

Tertullian: *To Scapula,* 2. (Proconsul of
Africa.) (3rd cent.)

We, Constantine and Licinius the emperors, having met in concord at Milan and having set in order everything which pertains to the common good and public security, are of the opinion that among the various things which we perceived would profit men . . . was to be found the cultivation of religion; we should therefore give both to Christians and to all others free facility to follow the religion which each may desire, so that by this means whatever divinity is enthroned in heaven may be gracious and favorable to us. . . . Therefore we are of the opinion that the following decision is in accordance with sound and true reasoning: that no one who has given his mental assent to the Christian persuasion or to any other which he feels to be suitable to him should be compelled to deny his conviction. . . .

Famous Edict granting Toleration to
Christianity and other Religions. (313)

Human government is derived from the divine government, and should imitate it. Now although God is all-powerful and supremely good, nevertheless He allows certain evils to take place in the universe which He might prevent, lest, without them, greater good might be forfeited or greater evils ensue. Accordingly in human government also, those who are in authority rightly tolerate certain evils lest certain good be lost, or certain evils incurred. Hence though unbelievers sin in their rites they may be tolerated, either on account of some good that ensues therefrom, or because of some evil avoided.

St. Thomas Aquinas: *Summa Theologica,*
2-2, 10, 11. (13th cent.)

Oh happy regions, Italy and Spain,
Which never did those monsters entertain!
The wolf, the bear, the boar, can there
    advance
No native claim of just inheritance.
And self-preserving laws, severe in
    show,
May guard their fences from th' invading foe.
Where birth has plac'd 'em, let 'em
    safely share
The common benefit of vital air;
Themselves unharmful, let them live
    unharm'd;
Their jaws disabl'd, and their claws disarm'd.

Wolf, bear, boar—various Protestant
    sects

Dryden: *The Hind and the Panther,* 1.
(17th cent.)

There can be no question but that the remnants of the old system of polity [i.e. constitutional principles]—the utter disappearance of which keeps the rest of Christendom in a state of continual futile revolution—exist more copiously in this country than in any other. Instead of the revolutions and the religious wars by which, in other Protestant countries, Catholics have obtained toleration, they

have obtained it in England by the force
of the very principles of the constitution.

> Lord Acton: *Political Thoughts on the
> Church.* (19th cent.)

If Catholics were in power tomorrow in
England, not a penal law would be proposed, nor the shadow of constraint be
put upon the faith of any man. We would
that all men fully believed the truth; but
a forced faith is a hypocrisy hateful to
God and man. . . . If the Catholics were
tomorrow the 'imperial race' in these
kingdoms they would not use political
power to molest the divided and hereditary religious state of our people. We
would not shut one of their churches, or
colleges, or schools. They would have the
same liberties we enjoy as a minority.

> Card. Manning: *The Vatican Decrees.*
> (In reply to Mr. Gladstone) (1875)

The modern theory that you should
always treat the religious convictions of
other people with profound respect finds
no support in the Gospels. Mutual tolerance of religious views is the product not
of faith, but of doubt.

> Arnold Lunn: *Now I See.* (20th cent.)

The ever-increasing contacts and indiscriminate mingling of various religious
denominations within the same national
groups have induced the civil courts to
apply the principle of 'tolerance' and
'freedom of conscience.' In such circumstances, let us add, Catholics are in duty
bound to practical political, civic and social tolerance with respect to the faithful of other denominations.

> Pope Pius XII: *Address to Members of
> the Rota.* (Oct. 6, 1946)

See also Church and State in the United
States, Freedom of Religion

Tomb

> How life and death in Thee
> Agree!
> Thou hadst a virgin womb,
> And tomb.

A Joseph did betroth
Them both.

> R. Crashaw: *To Our Lord Upon the
> Choice of His Sepulcher.* (17th cent.)

The Sabbath of the tomb.

> Pope: *To Mrs. M.B. on Her Birthday.*
> (18th cent.)

Now is come a darker thing,
And is come a colder sting,
Unto us, who find the womb
Opes on the courtyard of the tomb.

> F. Thompson: *Past Thinking of Solomon.*
> (19th cent.)

Tongue

> The tongue breaketh bone,
> Though itself have none.

> Proverbs of Alfred, 425. (13th cent.)

My son, keep well thy tongue and keep
thy friend.
A wicked tongue is worse than a fiend.

> Chaucer: *The Maunciples Tale.* (14th
> cent.)

Her tongue is no edge tool, but yet it
will cut.

> John Heywood: *Proverbs,* 1, 10. (16th
> cent.)

Your tongues run before your wits.

> John Heywood: *Proverbs,* 2, 4. (16th
> cent.)

His tongue, the Spirit's two-edged
sword,
Had magic in its blade,—
For while it smote with every word,
It heal'd the wounds it made!

> M. Bridges: *St. Francis Xavier.* (19th
> cent.)

Many a man's tongue broke his nose.

> Seumas MacManus: *Heavy Hangs the
> Golden Grain.* (20th cent.)

Too Much

Too much noise deafens us; too much light dazzles us; too much distance or too much proximity impedes vision; too much length or too much brevity of discourse obscures it; too much truth astonishes us.

Pascal: *Pensées*, 2. (17th cent.)

Tooth

In spite of his teeth.

J. Skelton: *Why Come Ye Not To Courte?* (16th cent.)

Totalitarianism

The Catholic Church is the best defence against state absolutism just because it stands for the absolute; it is a defence against totalitarianism just because it is the only tolerable totalitarianism, that of religion with its claims over all, and its power to regulate every instinct, inspire every ideal, and secure the highest happiness of mankind.

W. E. Orchard: *The Necessity for the Church.* (20th cent.)

See also Absolutism; Despotism

Town

The serried town whose small street tortuously
Led darkling to the dazzling sea.

Alice Meynell: *The First Snow.* (20th cent.)

Golden towns, where golden houses are.
Joyce Kilmer: *Roofs.* (20th cent.)

Toy

Ah, when at last we lie with tranced breath,
Not vexing thee in death,
And thou rememberest of what toys
We made our joys,
How weakly understood,

Thy great commanded good,
Then fatherly not less
Than I whom thou hast moulded from the clay,
Thou'lt leave thy wrath, and say,
I will be sorry for their childishness.

Coventry Patmore: *The Toys.* (19th cent.)

Tradition, Ecclesiastical

This preaching (*kerygma*) and this faith the Church, although scattered over the whole world, diligently observes, as if it occupied but one house, and believes as if it had but one mind, and preaches and teaches as if it had but one mouth. And although there are many dialects in the world, the meaning of the tradition is one and the same.

St. Irenaeus: *Against the Heresies,* 1, 10, 2. (2nd cent.)

If there was a question about any trifling matter would it not be necessary to have recourse to the oldest churches, in which the apostles lived, and obtain from them some clear and definite ruling on the present subject of dispute? And if the apostles had not left us the Scriptures, should we not need to follow the order of tradition which they handed on to those to whom they entrusted the churches?

St. Irenaeus: *Against the Heresies,* 3, 4, 1. (2nd cent.)

The teaching of the apostles is the true gnosis. We have the ancient constitution (*systema*) of the Church throughout the world, and the character of the body of Christ in the successions of bishops to whom they [the apostles] entrusted the Church in each place, which has come down to us with its safeguard of the Scriptures in the fulness and soundness of their interpretation, without addition or subtraction.

St. Irenaeus: *Against the Heresies,* 4, 33, 8. (2nd cent.)

If then these things are so, it is the same degree manifest that all doctrine which agrees with the apostolic churches—those moulds and original sources of the faith—must be reckoned for truth, as undoubtedly containing that which the churches received from the apostles, the apostles from Christ, Christ from God. Whereas all doctrine must be prejudged as false which savors of contrariety to the truth of the churches and apostles of Christ and God.

Tertullian: *On the Prescription of Heretics*, 21. (3rd cent.)

Now it ought to be known that the holy apostles, in preaching the faith of Christ, delivered themselves with the utmost clearness on certain points which they believed to be necessary to everyone, even to those who seemed somewhat dull in the investigation of divine knowledge; leaving, however, the grounds of their statements to be examined into by those who should deserve the excellent gifts of the Spirit, and who, especially by means of the Holy Spirit Himself, should obtain the gift of language, wisdom, and knowledge: while on other subjects they merely stated the fact that things were so, keeping silence as to the manner or origin of their existence.

Origen: *De Principiis, Proem.* 3. (3rd cent.)

Let them innovate in nothing, but keep the traditions. (Nihil innovetur nisi quod traditum est.)

Pope St. Stephen I: *Letter to St. Cyprian.* (Ep. Cypr. 74) (3rd cent.)

And now, *through the love which He had for all the saints,* having come to our most important topic, we turn to the subject of the tradition which is proper for the churches, in order that those who have been rightly instructed may hold fast to that tradition which has continued until now, and fully understanding it from our exposition may stand the more firmly therein. . . . The Holy Ghost bestows the fulness of grace on those who believe rightly that they may

know how those who are at the head of the Church should teach the tradition and maintain it in all things.

St. Hippolytus: *The Apostolic Tradition,* 1. (3rd cent.)

We should observe everything without exception which has been handed down by the Lord through the gospel and the apostles.

St. Basil: *The Morals,* 12, 2. (4th cent.)

In all things I desire to follow the Roman church. Yet we too are not without discernment; and what other places have done well to retain, we too do well to maintain.

St. Ambrose: *On the Sacraments,* 3, 1, 5. (4th cent.)

The best advice that I can give you is this. Church traditions—especially when they do not run counter to the faith—are to be observed in the form in which previous generations have handed them down; and the use of one church is not to be annulled because it is contrary to that of another.

St. Jerome: *Letters,* 71, 6. (4th cent.)

Only those opinions of the Fathers are to be brought forward which were expressed by those who lived, taught and persevered in the holy Catholic faith and communion, and who deserved either to die faithfully in Christ or to be martyred gloriously for Him. Those men are to be believed, moreover, in accordance with the following rule: Only that is to be held as certain, valid and beyond doubt, which either all or most of them have confirmed in one and the same sense—manifestly, frequently, and persistently, as though a council of masters stood in agreement—and which they have accepted, kept, and handed on. On the other hand, what some saint, learned man, bishop, confessor, or martyr has individually thought outside of, or even contrary to, the general opinion must be considered his personal, particular, and quite private opinion, entirely removed from the common, public and general opinion.

St. Vincent of Lerins: *Commonitoria*, 28. (5th cent.)

With regard to the tradition of the Church, two precautions had to be rigorously and thoroughly observed, adhered to by everyone who does not wish to become a heretic: first, it must be ascertained whether there exists from ancient times a decree established by all the bishops of the Catholic Church with the authority of a universal council, and second, should a new question arise for which no decree can be found, one must revert to the opinions of the holy fathers;—to be more precise, of those fathers who remained in their own times and places in the unity of communion and of faith and who were therefore held as teaching 'probable' doctrine.

St. Vincent of Lerins: *Commonitoria*, 29. (5th cent.)

This Catholic Church spread throughout the world is known by three particular marks: whatever is believed and taught in it has the authority of the Scriptures, or of universal tradition, or at least of its own and proper usage. And this authority is binding on the whole Church as is also the universal tradition of the Fathers.

Boethius: *De Fide Catholica.* (6th cent.)

With these things let us be satisfied, and let us abide by them, not removing everlasting boundaries, nor overpassing the divine tradition.

St. John of Damascus: *Exposition of the Orthodox Faith*, 1, 1. (8th cent.)

The weightiest authority is the Church's custom. It should be constantly and punctiliously observed. Ecclesiastical writings draw their warrant from the Church's authority. We should take our stand on the Church's traditional teaching, rather than on the pronouncements

of Augustine or Jerome or any other doctor.

St. Thomas Aquinas: *Quodlibets,* 2, 4, 7. (13th cent.)

Since it has been shown that the Church's traditions are subsequent to the Church, it follows that the Church does not derive its authority from the traditions but that the traditions derive their authority from the Church.

Dante: *Monarchy,* 3. (14th cent.)

Must all tradition then be set aside?
This to affirm were ignorance or pride.
Are there not many points, some needful sure
To saving faith, that Scripture leaves obscure?
Which every sect will wrest a several way
(For what one sect interprets, all sects may.)

Dryden: *Religio Laici.* (17th cent.)

Faith is not built on disquisitions vain;
The things we must believe, are few and plain:
But since men will believe more than they need;
And every man will make himself a creed,
In doubtful questions 'tis the safest way
To learn what unsuspected ancients say.

Dryden: *Religio Laici.* (17th cent.)

Before the word was written, said the hind,
Our Savior preached His faith to human kind;
From His apostles the first age receiv'd
Eternal truth, and what they taught, believ'd.
Thus by tradition faith was planted first;
Succeeding flocks succeeding pastors nurs'd.
This was the way our wise Redeemer chose,
(Who sure could all things for the best dispose,)

To fence His fold from their encroaching foes.

> Dryden: *The Hind and the Panther, 2.*
> (17th cent.)

The mind of the Spirit, the thoughts,
the principles which are like the breathing of the Church, the way in which
habitually and, as it were, inconsciously,
she looks at things, rather than any set
of dogmas, static and systematic.

> Card. Newman: *Via Media,* vol. 1, p. 249.
> (19th cent.)

Tradition has its legitimate place and its
true service. By tradition is meant, what
has ever been held, as far as we know,
though we do not know how it came to
be held, and for that very reason think
it true, because else it would not be held.

> Card. Newman: *Present Position of
> Catholics in England.* (19th cent.)

Catholics hold that the apostles made
over the divine revelation to the generation after them, not only in writing, but
by word of mouth, and in the ritual of
the Church. We consider that the New
Testament is not the whole of what they
left us; that they left us a number of doctrines, not in writing at all, but living
in the minds and mouths of the faithful.

> Card. Newman: *Present Position of
> Catholics in England.* (19th cent.)

A Church that appeals merely to ancient
written words can be no more at the best
than an antiquarian society.

> R. H. Benson: *The Confessions of a
> Convert.* (20th cent.)

The biggest paradox about the Church is
that she is at the same time essentially
traditional and essentially revolutionary.
But that is not as much of a paradox as
it seems, because Christian tradition, unlike all others, is a living and perpetual
revolution. . . . The presence of a strong
element of human conservatism in the
Church should not obscure the fact that
Christian tradition, supernatural in its
source, is something absolutely opposed

to human traditionalism. For the living
tradition of Catholicism is like the
breath of a physical body. It renews life
by repelling stagnation. It is a constant,
quiet, peaceful revolution against death.

> Thomas Merton: *Seeds of Contemplation.*
> (20th cent.)

See also Catholic Faith; Doctrine, Development of; Fathers of the Church;
Succession, Apostolic

Tradition, Human

We should not conform with human
traditions to the extent of setting aside
the command of God.

> St. Basil: *The Morals,* 12, 1. (4th cent.)

Tragedy

There is no theatre in the world has anything so absurd as the English tragi-
comedy. Here, a course of mirth; there,
another of sadness and passion; a third
of honor; and the fourth a duel. Thus
in two hours and a half we run through
all the fits of Bedlam.

> Dryden: *Of Dramatic Poesy.* (17th cent.)

Trance

O fantasy, that dost at time so rout
  Our senses that a man stays negligent
  Although a thousand trumpets sound
    about,
Who moves thee, if senses naught to
    thee present?
  There moves thee a light which of
    itself is shaped
  In heaven, or by a will wherefrom 'tis
    sent.

> Dante: *Purgatorio, Canto 17.* (Tr. Binyon)
> (14th cent.)

Transcendentalism

The essential mistake of the transcendentalists is the taking for their guide
the instincts of the soul instead of the
inspirations of the Holy Spirit.

> Isaac T. Hecker. (Elliott's *Life,* 308)
> (19th cent.)

Transfiguration of Our Lord

All ye who would the Christ descry,
Lift up your eyes to Him on high:
There mortal gaze hath strength to see
The token of His majesty.

A wondrous sign we there behold,
That knows not death nor groweth old,
Sublime, most high, that cannot fade,
That was ere earth and heaven were
  made.

Roman Breviary, Feast of the
Transfiguration (Aug. 6), hymn
Quicumque Christum quaeritis. (Tr. A.
McDougall) (Prudentius, from
Cathemerinon, 4th cent.)

Among His twelve apostles
  Christ spake the words of life,
And show'd a realm of beauty
  Beyond a world of strife:
When all My Father's glory
  Shall shine express'd in Me,
Then praise Him, then exalt Him,
  For magnified is He!

Upon the mount of Tabor
  The promise was made good;
When, baring all the Godhead,
  In light itself He stood:
And they, in awe beholding,
  The apostolic three,
Sang out to God their Savior,
  For magnified was He!

Byzantine Menaea, Feast of the
Transfiguration (Aug. 6), Canon. (Tr.
Neale) (St. Cosmas, 8th cent.)

Light of the anxious heart,
Jesus Thou dost appear,
To bid the gloom of guilt depart,
And shed Thy sweetness here.

Roman Breviary, Feast of the
Transfiguration, *Lux alma Jesu mentium*
(*Amor Jesu dulcissime*). (Tr. Card.
Newman) (From hymn *Jesu dulcis
memoria*) (Anon., 12th cent.)

At His Transfiguration Christ showed
His disciples the splendor of His beauty,
to which He will shape and color those
who are His: *he will reform the body of
our lowness configured to the body of
his glory* (Phil. 3, 21).

St. Thomas Aquinas: *Summa Theologica,*
3, 45, 1. (13th cent.)

O God, Who in the glorious transfiguration of Thine only-begotten Son didst
confirm the mysteries of the faith by the
testimony of the fathers, and Who by
their voice from the shining cloud, didst
in wondrous manner foreshadow the
perfect adoption of sons: grant us, in
Thy loving kindness, we beseech Thee,
to be co-heirs with Him Who is the
King of glory, and in that very glory
call us in the end to share.

Roman Missal, Collect for the Feast.
(Feast celebrated in East from ca. 6th
cent., but only extended to West by
Callixtus III in 1457.) (15th cent. ?)

Translation

It is difficult in following lines laid
down by others not sometimes to diverge
from them, and it is hard to preserve
in a translation the charm of expressions
which in another language are most felic-
itous. Each particular word conveys a
meaning of its own, and possibly I have
no equivalent by which to render it, and
if I make a circuit to reach my goal, I
have to go many miles to cover a short
distance. To these difficulties must be
added the windings of hyperbata, differences in the use of cases, divergencies of
metaphor; and last of all the peculiar
and if I may so call it, inbred character
of the language. If I render word for
word, the result will sound uncouth, and
if compelled by necessity I alter anything in the order or wording, I shall
seem to have departed from the function of a translator.

St. Jerome: *Preface to His Translation of
the Chronicle of Eusebius of Caesarea.*
(4th cent.)

A skilled translator's job, therefore,
when rendering Catholic theology from
one language to another, is to keep the

sense while changing the turn of speech in accordance with native idiom.

> St. Thomas Aquinas: *Against the Errors of the Greeks, Prol.* (13th cent.)

No literal translation can be just to an excellent original in a superior language; but it is a great mistake to imagine (as many have done) that a rash paraphrase can make amends for this general defect.

> Pope: Tr. of Homer: *Iliad, Pref.* (18th cent.)

Transubstantiation

See Eucharist: Transubstantiation

Travel

We beseech Thee for those who are travelling from home, grant them an angel of peace as their fellow-traveller, that they may receive no hurt from anyone, that they may finish their voyage and their travels in much cheerfulness.

> Sacramentary of Serapion, Prayer of the Faithful (27). (4th cent.)

And men go abroad to admire the heights and mountains, the mighty billows of the sea, the long courses of rivers, the vast compass of the ocean, and the circular motion of the stars, and yet pass themselves by.

> St. Augustine: *Confessions,* 10, 8. (5th cent.)

Hear our humble prayers, O Lord, and order the paths of Thy servants according to the welfare of Thy watchful eye; that among all the vicissitudes of their journey and this present life, they may always be protected by Thy help.

> Roman Missal, Collect for Pilgrims and Travelers. (Gelasian, 5th to 7th cent.)

A class of men who are exceedingly tiresome are those who, having traveled, talk of nothing but their adventures, the countries which they have seen or traversed, the dangers whether real or fictitious, which they have encountered, repeating the same things an hundred times over.

> St. John Baptist de la Salle: *The Rules of Christian Manners and Civility,* 2. (17th cent.)

Led by my hand, he saunter'd Europe round,
And gather'd ev'ry vice on Christian ground.

> Pope: *The Dunciad,* 4. (18th cent.)

I sometimes think it is a pity that people travel in foreign countries; it narrows their minds so much.

> G. K. Chesterton: *Daily News.* (20th cent.)

Half the trouble about the modern man is that he is educated to understand foreign languages and misunderstand foreigners. The traveller sees what he sees; the tripper sees what he has come to see.

> G. K. Chesterton: *Autobiography.* (20th cent.)

Treachery

The smiler with the knife under the cloak.

> Chaucer: *The Knightes Tale.* (14th cent.)

We dipped our hands in the dish together.
I kissed the face I loved so well.
And here is a halter that will tether
Another ass in the fields of hell.

> James L. Duff: *Iscariot.* (20th cent.)

Treason

The slander of majesty shall not be punished, for if it proceed from levity it is to be despised; if from madness, to be pitied; if from malice forgiven.

> Codex Theodosianus. (Contrary to the usual Roman practice) (5th cent.)

If anyone shall presume out of contumacy and pride to contradict or resist the royal power, which, according to the apostle, can only be from God, and shall refuse to obey its just and reasonable decrees which are in accordance with God, the ecclesiastical law, and the civil law, let him be anathema.

> Council of Toledo. (Cited in Regino of Prum, *De Synod. Causis,* 2, 301.) (6th cent.)

There are many forms of treason, but none is graver than that which is exercised against the whole body of justice.

> John of Salisbury: *Policraticus,* 3, 15. (12th cent.)

What king, what crown from treason's reach is free,
If Jove and heaven can violated be?

> Dryden: *Astraea Redux.* (17th cent.)

During his office, treason was no crime.
The sons of Belial had a glorious time.

> Dryden: *Absalom and Achitophel.* (17th cent.)

Oh for a tongue to curse the slave
Whose treason, like a deadly blight,
Comes o'er the councils of the brave
And blasts them in their hour of might!

> Thomas Moore: *Lalla Rookh: the Fire-Worshippers.* (19th cent.)

Treasure

Better is the possession of a small treasure found than the expectation of a greater which is to find.

> St. Francis de Sales: *Treatise on the Love of God,* 8, 12. (17th cent.)

Tree

Ye cannot see the wood for the trees.

> John Heywood: *Proverbs,* 2, 4. (16th cent.)

Quiet through the streets with silver sound
The flood of life doth flow;

Upon whose banks on every side
The wood of life doth grow.
There trees for evermore bear fruit,
And evermore do spring,
There evermore the angels sit,
And evermore do sing.

> Anonymous: *Jerusalem, My Happy Home.* (Guiney, 281) (16th cent.)

Tender twigs are bent with ease,
Aged trees do break with bending.

> Bl. Robert Southwell: *Loss in Delay.* (16th cent.)

I will bend the tree while it is a wand.

> Thomas Lodge: *Rosalynde.* (16th cent.)

Old trees! old trees! in your mystic gloom
There's many a warrior laid,
And many a nameless and lonely tomb
Is sheltered beneath your shade.
Old trees! old trees! without pomp or prayer
We buried the brave and the true,
We fired a volley and left them there
To rest, old trees, with you.

> Abram Ryan: *Old Trees.* (19th cent.)

I think that I shall never see
A poem lovely as a tree.

A tree whose hungry mouth is pressed
Against the earth's sweet-flowing breast.

. . . .

Poems are made by fools like me,
But only God can make a tree.

> Joyce Kilmer: *Trees.* (20th cent.)

There's no tree but has enough rotten wood to burn it.

> Seumas MacManus: *Heavy Hangs the Golden Grain.* (20th cent.)

Trial

For as the toils of the contests bring athletes their crowns, so the test which comes to Christians through their tribulations leads them on to perfection, if with fitting patience in all thanksgiving we accept the Lord's dispensations.

> St. Basil: *Letters*, 101. (4th cent.)

O almighty and everlasting God, the comfort of the afflicted and the strength of those that labor: let the prayers of those who call upon Thee in any tribulation be heard by Thee; that all may rejoice that Thy mercy has relieved them in their necessities.

> Roman Missal, Collect for Good Friday. (Gelasian, 5th to 7th cent.)

Tribulation meriteth in patience, and in the obedient conforming of the man's will unto God, and in thanks given to God for His visitation.

> St. Thomas More: *Dialogue of Comfort.* (16th cent.)

All trying and painful things afflicting either soul or body, however or from whatever source they may arise, are to be taken by the servant of God as coming only from the hand of our Lord. Such things we should endure for the love of God with a resigned and patient spirit, to the end, yea, even to the last extremity, firmly persuaded that they are most useful to him, most profitable for his salvation, although it may seem to him quite otherwise.

> Louis de Blois: *A Short Rule*, 3. (16th cent.)

What do you think the bed of tribulation is? It is simply the school of humility.

> St. Francis de Sales: *Letters to Persons in Religion*, 1, 8. (17th cent.)

We must measure our trials by ourself, and not ourselves by our trials.

> St. John of the Cross: *Spiritual Sentences and Maxims.* (16th cent.)

God never permits anything to come upon us as a trial or test of our virtue without desiring that we should profit by it.

> St. Francis de Sales: *Spiritual Conferences*, 17. (17th cent.)

Trifles

From little spark may burst a mighty flame.

> Dante: *Paradiso, Canto* 1. (14th cent.)

For the proverb saith that many small maken a great.

> Chaucer: *The Persones Tale.* (14th cent.)

Small things are best: grief and unrest
   To rank and wealth are given;
But little things on little wings
   Bear little souls to heaven.

> F. Faber: *Written in a Little Lady's Little Album.* (19th cent.)

One dark cloud can hide the sunlight;
Loose one string, the pearls are scattered;
Think one thought, a soul may perish;
Say one word, a heart may break.

> Adelaide Procter: *Philip and Mildred.* (19th cent.)

Trinity, Blessed

See God—Blessed Trinity

Triumph

The greater the danger in battle, the greater the joy in triumph.

> St. Augustine: *Confessions*, 8, 3. (5th cent.)

Trouble

There is no man in the world without some trouble or affliction, though he be a king or a pope.

> Thomas a Kempis: *The Imitation of Christ*, 1, 22. (15th cent.)

The fat is in the fire.

> John Heywood: *Proverbs*, 1, 3. (16th cent.)

In dock, out nettle.

> John Heywood: *Proverbs*, 2, 1. (16th cent.)

There's trouble in every house, and some on the street.

> Seumas MacManus: *Heavy Hangs the Golden Grain.* (20th cent.)

True

It must needs be true that every man sayeth.

> John Heywood: *Proverbs,* 1, 11. (16th cent.)

Truism

There is only one thing that it requires real courage to say, and that is a truism.

> G. K. Chesterton: *G. F. Watts.* (20th cent.)

Perhaps there are no things out of which we get so little of the truth as the truisms; especially when they are really true.

> G. K. Chesterton: *The Everlasting Man.* (20th cent.)

Trumpet

> The trumpet's loud clangor
> Excites us to arms,
> With shrill notes of anger,
> And mortal alarms.

> Dryden: *A Song for St. Cecilia's Day.* (18th cent.)

> Let the loud trumpet sound
> Till the roofs all around
> The shrill echoes rebound.

> Pope: *Ode for Music on St. Cecilia's Day.* (18th cent.)

Trust

In trust is treason.

> John Heywood: *Proverbs,* 2, 5. (16th cent.)

To trust a friend is not to believe that he can do no wrong; we must trust no man like that; for all fall at times.

> R. H. Benson: *The Queen's Tragedy.* (20th cent.)

Trust in God

Cast off indecision and doubt not in the least, when asking anything from God. . . . Those who are divided in purpose are they who waver before the Lord and altogether fail to obtain any of their requests. But those who are wholly perfect in the faith ask everything with reliance on the Lord and they receive.

> Shepherd of Hermas, Mandate 9, 1-6. (2nd cent.)

We must needs abide in the Lord and not depart from Him. For, if the Lord be our protector and helper, we are able firmly to endure every contest; but if we neglect and forsake the Lord, we make our adversary stronger.

> St. Ambrose: *In Ps. 43 Enarr. 94.* (4th cent.)

O God, the strength of all those who put their trust in Thee, mercifully hear our prayers; and because through the weakness of our mortal nature we can do nothing without Thee, grant us the help of Thy grace, that in fulfilling Thy commandments, we may please Thee both in will and in deed.

> Roman Missal, Collect for First Sunday after Pentecost. (Gelasian, 5th to 7th cent.)

> Always place in God thy trust,
> Will and do what's right and true;
> Let thy soul be brave and just;
> Show thy Lord a humble mind;
> Thou shalt thus His favor find;
> Love but few and simple things;
> Simple life much comfort brings.

> Thomas a Kempis: *In Domino Semper Spera.* (Tr. D. Donahoe) (15th cent.)

In short, I cannot fully trust to anyone to bring me seasonable help in my necessities, save only to Thee, my God. Thou art my hope, Thou art my confidence, Thou art my comforter, and most faithful above all.

> Thomas a Kempis: *The Imitation of Christ,* 3, 59. (15th cent.)

Let nothing disturb thee,
Nothing affright thee;
All things are passing;
God never changeth;
Patient endurance
Attaineth to all things;
Who God possesseth
In nothing is wanting;
Alone God sufficeth.

St. Teresa of Jesus: *Poems*. (Tr. Henry
W. Longfellow) (Lines written in her
breviary) (16th cent.)

Consider seriously how quickly people
change, and how little trust is to be had
in them; and cleave fast unto God, Who
changeth not.

St. Teresa of Jesus: *Maxims*. (16th cent.)

If once thy hope be anchor'd in God
No wave, no bluster can endanger thee,
Thy foot from falling is securely shod,
He corresponding to thy fidelity.
    If God thy center be and thy defence,
    Be hell, be devil thy circumference.

Anthony Copley: *A Fig for Fortune*.
(16th cent.)

O ever living Lord of lords,
    O mighty King of kings,
O solace of the sorrowful,
    O glass, who gladness brings:
O puissant Prince, O passing Power,
    O Regent of all rule,
My guide, my guard, expel from me
    All foolish fear and dule:

                .   .   .   .   .   .

Let not my sins me cause, O Lord,
    To wander from the rock,
But grant I may be found in fold
    Of Thine afflicted flock.

dule—dole

Francis Tregian: *A Prayer in Prison*.
(Guiney, 197) (16th cent.)

While Thou, O my God, art my help
    and my defender,
No cares can o'erwhelm me, no ter-
    rors appall;
The wiles and the snares of this world
    will but render

More lively my hope in my God and
    my all.

Joh. Landspergius: *Deus meus et omnia*.
(Tr. W. Young) (19th cent.)

What is more elevating and transport-
ing, than the generosity of heart which
risks everything on God's word.

Card. Newman: *Parochial and Plain
Sermons*, 2. (19th cent.)

All is dreary till we believe—what our
hearts tell us—that we are all subjects of
God's governance; nothing is dreary, all
inspires hope and trust, directly we understand that we are under His hand,
and that whatever comes to us is from
Him as a method of discipline and
guidance.

Card. Newman: *Oxford University
Sermons*. (19th cent.)

Plan not, nor scheme—but calmly wait;
    His choice is best:
While blind and erring in thy sight,
His wisdom sees and judges right,
    So trust and rest.

Adelaide A. Procter: *Confido et
Conquiesco*. (First line: Fret not, poor
soul, while doubt and fear) (19th cent.)

Nothing is so bad as not trusting God.

R. H. Benson: *By What Authority*. (20th
cent.)

Whenever your soul begins to be disturbed and anxious, put yourself in His
hands, and refuse to decide for yourself.
It is so easy.

R. H. Benson: *By What Authority*. (20th
cent.)

All things work together for good, if
one will but trust God.

R. H. Benson: *An Average Man*. (20th
cent.)

Truth

Love truth and let nothing but truth
issue from your mouth, in order that the

spirit which God has settled in this flesh of yours may be found to be truthful in the sight of all men.

> Shepherd of Hermas, Mandate, 3, 1. (2nd cent.)

All truth wherever it is found belongs to us as Christians.

> St. Justin Martyr: *Second Apology*, 13. (2nd cent.)

That is true which is.

> St. Augustine: *Soliloquies*, 2, 5. (4th cent.)

Hence thou must in no manner deny that there is an immutable truth, embracing all such things as are immutably true; a truth which thou canst not call thine, or mine, or any man's, but which is present to all and gives itself to all alike who discern the things that are immutably true, as a light which in some miraculous way is both secret and yet open to all.

> St. Augustine: *De Libero Arbitrio*, 2, 12, 33. (4th cent.)

Everyone who knows that he is in doubt about something, knows a truth, and in regard to this that he knows he is certain. Therefore he is certain about a truth. Consequently everyone who doubts if there be a truth, has in himself a true thing on which he does not doubt; nor is there any true thing which is not true by truth. Consequently whoever for whatever reason can doubt, ought not to doubt that there is truth.

> St. Augustine: *De vera Religione*, 39, 73. (4th cent.)

That it was You who taught me, I believe: for it is the truth, and there is no other teacher of truth save You, no matter where or when it may happen to shine.

> St. Augustine: *Confessions*, 5, 6. (5th cent.)

Nothing conquers except truth: the victory of truth is charity.

> St. Augustine: *Sermon 358*, 1. (5th cent.)

To utter truth from heart and mouth.

> St. Benedict: *Rule*, 4. (One of his 'tools of good works') (6th cent.)

Since there are therefore three states or steps of truth, we ascend to the first by the toil of humility, to the second by the emotion of compassion, to the third by the ecstasy of contemplation.

> St. Bernard: *The Steps of Humility*, 6. (12th cent.)

Truth is the equation of thought and thing.

> St. Thomas Aquinas: *Summa Theologica*, 1, 16, 1. (13th cent.)

If we speak of truth as it exists in the intellect, according to its proper nature, then there are many truths in many created intellects. . . . But if we speak of truth as it is in things, then all things are true by one primary truth; to which each one is assimilated according to its own entity. Thus, although the essences of forms or things are many, yet the truth of the divine intellect is one, in conformity to which all things are said to be true.

> St. Thomas Aquinas: *Summa Theologica*, 1, 16, 6. (13th cent.)

Every truth without exception—and whoever may utter it—is from the Holy Ghost.

> St. Thomas Aquinas: *Summa Theologica*, 1-2, 109, 1. (13th cent.)

> Ever to that truth,
> Which but the semblance of a falsehood wears,
> A man, if possible, should bar his lip.
> > Dante: *Inferno, Canto 16*. (14th cent.)

Every truth that is not itself a first principle must be demonstrated by means of some truth that is a first principle.

> Dante: *Monarchy*, 1. (14th cent.)

Truth is the highest thing that man may keep.

> Chaucer: *The Frankeleyns Tale.* (14th cent.)

Teach it to the simple, the learned know it well:
Truth is treasure, the best tried on earth.

> Langland: *Piers Plowman,* Passus 2. (14th cent.)

But there are seven sisters ever serving truth,
Porters of the posterns; one called abstinence,
Humility, charity, chastity be the chief maidens there;
Patience and peace help many a one;
Lady Almsgiving lets in full many.

> Langland: *Piers Plowman,* Passus 8. (14th cent.)

Truth, the discovery made by traveling minds.

> Sir William Davenant: *Gondibert.* (17th cent.)

We arrive at the truth, not by the reason only, but also by the heart.

> Pascal: *Pensées,* 10. (17th cent.)

For truth has such a face and such a mien,
As, to be loved, needs only to be seen.

> Dryden: *The Hind and the Panther.* (17th cent.)

For oh, 'twas nuts to the father of lies,
(As this wily fiend is nam'd in the Bible)
To find it settled by laws so wise
   That the greater the truth, the worse the libel!

> Thomas Moore: *A Case of Libel.* (19th cent.)

Gentlest and bravest in the battle-brunt—
The champion of the truth.

> James R. Randall: *John Pelham.* (19th cent.)

Catholic truth is simply truth, all truth in the intelligible order and in the super-intelligible, in religion and civilization, in time and eternity, in God and in His creative act.

> Orestes Brownson: *Catholic Schools.* (Works, 12) (1862)

Still is the might of truth, as it has been:
Lodg'd in the few, obey'd, and yet unseen.
Rear'd on lone heights, and rare,
His saints their watch-flame bear,
And the mad world sees the wide-circling blaze,
Vain searching whence it streams, and how to quench its rays.

> Card. Newman: *The Course of Truth.* (19th cent.)

No truth can really exist external to Christianity.

> Card. Newman: *Oxford University Sermons.* (19th cent.)

From shadows and symbols to the truth.
(Ex umbris et imaginibus in veritatem.)

> Epitaph of Cardinal Newman. (Chosen by himself, ultimately derives from Plato's *Republic,* Bk. 7) (19th cent.)

The truth is great, and shall prevail,
When none cares whether it prevail or not.

> Coventry Patmore: *Magna est Veritas.* (19th cent.)

The defence of a thesis is far easier than the discovery of truth.

> Lord Acton: *Ultramontanism.* (19th cent.)

Truths and principles are divine; they govern the world; to suffer for them is the greatest glory of man.

> Card. Manning: *Miscellanies,* 1. (19th cent.)

Youth must with time decay,
   Eileen aroon!
Beauty must fade away,
   Eileen aroon!

Castles are sacked in war,
Chieftains are scattered far,
Truth is a fixed star,
    Eileen aroon!

Gerald Griffin: *Eileen Aroon.* (19th cent.)

Truth is a maid, whom men woo diversely;
This, as a spouse; that, as a light-o'-love,
To know, and having known, to make his brag.

F. Thompson: *Whereto art thou come?* (19th cent.)

Divine truth must always be extreme; it must, so to speak, always overlap at both ends, just because it is divine, and therefore much too big for this world.

R. H. Benson: *Christ in the Church.* (20th cent.)

Truth is not any more immutable than man himself, since it is evolved with him, in him, and through him.

Proposition condemned by Decree of Holy Office, *Lamentabili,* June 3, 1907.

Truths turn into dogmas the moment they are disputed.

G. K. Chesterton: *Heretics.* (20th cent.)

The old religionists tortured men physically for a moral truth. The new realists torture men morally for a physical truth.

G. K. Chesterton: *Tremendous Trifles.* (20th cent.)

The Catholic is much more certain about the fixed truths than about the fixed stars.

G. K. Chesterton: *The Common Man.* (20th cent.)

Truth springs infernal in the human breast.

Michael Williams: *Catholicism and the Modern Mind.* (20th cent.)

Truth and Error

And I looked upon other things, and I saw that they owed their being to You

and that all finite things are in You: but in a different manner, being in You not as in a place, but because You are and hold all things in the hand of Your truth, and all things are true inasmuch as they are: nor is falsehood anything, save that something is thought to be which is not.

St. Augustine: *Confessions,* 7, 15. (5th cent.)

Truth on one side of the Pyrenees; error on the other.

Pascal: *Pensées,* 3. (17th cent.)

Blunt truths more mischief than nice falsehoods do.

Pope: *An Essay On Criticism,* 3. (18th cent.)

Truth is one and invariable, but error is variable and manifold. It is always the same truth that we must oppose to error, but it is seldom the same error for two successive moments to which we must oppose it.

Orestes Brownson: *Protestantism in a Nutshell.* (Brownson's Quarterly Rev., October, 1849)

Error may flourish for a time, but truth will prevail in the end. The only effect of error ultimately is to promote truth.

Card. Newman: *Idea of a University.* (19th cent.)

Fact and argument are the tests of truth and error.

Card. Newman: *Present Position of Catholics in England,* 3. (19th cent.)

Truth-Telling

It is better to remain silent than speak the truth ill-humoredly, and so spoil an excellent dish by covering it with bad sauce.

J. P. Camus: *The Spirit of St. Francis de Sales.* (17th cent.)

Tuberose

The tuberose, with her silvery light,
    That in the gardens of Malay
Is call'd the Mistress of the Night,

So like a bride, scented and bright;
    She comes out when the sun's away.

> Thomas Moore: *Lalla Rookh: Light of
> the Harem.* (19th cent.)

Turn

One good turn asketh another.

> John Heywood: *Proverbs,* 1, 11. (16th
> cent.)

Twilight

Spirit of twilight, through your folded
    wings
    I catch a glimpse of your averted
    face,
And rapturous on a sudden my soul
    sings,
    Is not this common earth a holy
    place?

> Olive Custance: *Twilight.* (20th cent.)

Our Lady of the twilight,
    She hath such gentle hands,
So lovely are the gifts she brings
    From out the sunset-lands,
So bountiful, so merciful,
    So sweet of soul is she;
And over all the world she draws
    Her cloak of charity.

> Alfred Noyes: *Our Lady of the Twilight.*
> (20th cent.)

Tyrannicide

It is not merely lawful to slay a tyrant
but even right and just. He that taketh
the sword is worthy of perishing with
the sword (Cicero, *De Off.* 3, 6, 32).
But the words *by taking the sword* refer
to one who usurps it in his temerity, not
to him who receives from God the right
to use it.

> John of Salisbury: *Policraticus,* 3, 15.
> (12th cent.)

For if in the case of treason anyone may
act as prosecutor, how much more in the
case of that crime which attacks the laws
which command even the emperors. Assuredly no one will avenge a public
enemy [tyrant], but he who does not

attack him is guilty of a crime against
himself and the whole body of the commonwealth.

> John of Salisbury: *Policraticus,* 3, 15.
> (12th cent.)

Tyranny

Tyrants in Greek are the same as kings
in Latin; for of old there was no difference between tyrant and king. . . . Later
on it came about that the worst and most
wayward kings who exhibited a desire
for power and oppressed the people by
their rule were known as tyrants.

> St. Isidore: *Etymologies,* 9, 3. (7th cent.)

Especially is he who receives power from
God the slave of the laws and the
servant of right and justice; but he who
usurps power oppresses justice, and
makes the laws slaves to his own will.
Therefore it is fitting that justice arm
herself against him who disarms the
laws, and that the power of the state
treat him with severity who strives to
palsy the hand of the state.

> John of Salisbury: *Policraticus,* 3, 15.
> (12th cent.)

The end of tyrants is confusion; destruction, if they persevere in their wickedness; pardon, if they are recalled from
wickedness.

> John of Salisbury: *Policraticus,* 8, 21.
> (12th cent.)

The government of tyrants cannot last
long because it is hateful to the multitude, and what is against the wishes of
the multitude cannot be long preserved.

> St. Thomas Aquinas: *The Governance of
> Rulers,* 1, 10. (13th cent.)

For not a city lacks its tyrant brood.

> Dante: *Purgatorio, Canto 6.* (Dante's
> contemptuous remark about Italian
> city-states other than Florence) (Tr.
> Binyon) (14th cent.)

Tyranny is a universal and extravagant
desire for domination.

> Pascal: *Pensées.* (17th cent.)

U

Ugliness

As comely as a cow in a cage.

> John Heywood: *Proverbs,* 2, 1. (16th cent.)

Unbelief

O almighty and everlasting God, Who desireth not the death but the life of sinners, mercifully hear our prayer, and deliver them [pagans] from the worship of idols, and gather them in Thy holy Church to the praise and glory of Thy name.

> Roman Missal, Collect for Good Friday. (Gelasian, 5th to 7th cent.)

To have the faith is not part of human nature, but it is part of human nature that man's mind should not thwart his inner instinct, and the outward preaching of the truth. Hence in this way unbelief is contrary to nature.

> St. Thomas Aquinas: *Summa Theologica,* 2-2, 10, 1. (13th cent.)

Unbelief in itself is not incompatible with the rights to own and to rule, which derive from the *jus gentium,* or human law common to many nations. The distinction between believers and unbelievers is a matter of divine law, which does not abrogate human law.

> St. Thomas Aquinas: *Summa Theologica,* 2-2, 12, 2. (13th cent.)

If any one saith that there is no mortal sin but that of infidelity; or that grace once received is not lost by any other sin, however grievous and enormous, save by that of infidelity; let him be anathema.

> Council of Trent, Session 6, Canon 27. (Jan. 13, 1547)

Begin by pitying unbelievers, miserable enough through their very condition. Strong language should be used only where there is chance of doing good; here it would do harm.

> Pascal: *Pensées.* (17th cent.)

Unconventionality

Unconventionality is all very well in thought; in fact, it is the spice of life. But it must be a philosophy to think by and not a rule to act by.

> R. H. Benson: *The Sentimentalists.* (20th cent.)

Understanding

Understanding is the reward of faith. Therefore seek not to understand that thou mayest believe, but believe that thou mayest understand.

> St. Augustine: *In Joan. Evang.,* 39, 6. (5th cent.)

Understand what it is that thou dost not understand, lest thou understand nothing, and do not despise any man who, in order that he may truly understand, understands that he does not understand that which he does not understand.

> St. Augustine: *De anima et ejus origine,* 4, 11, 15. (5th cent.)

Understanding is the sure and clear knowledge of some invisible thing.

> St. Bernard: *On Consideration,* 5, 3. (12th cent.)

Thus understanding and love, that is, the knowledge of and delight in the truth, are, as it were, the two arms of the soul, with which it embraces and comprehends with all saints the length and breadth, the height and depth, that is the eternity, the love, the goodness, and the wisdom of God.

> St. Bernard: *Letters*. (12th cent.)

Since human knowledge begins with the outside of things as it were, it is evident that the stronger the light of the understanding, the further can it penetrate into the heart of things. Now the natural light of our understanding is of finite power; wherefore it can reach to a certain fixed point. Consequently man needs a supernatural light, in order to penetrate further still so as to know what it cannot know by its natural light: and this supernatural light which is bestowed on man is called the gift of understanding.

> St. Thomas Aquinas: *Summa Theologica*, 2-2, 8, 1. (13th cent.)

A reaction, of course, or, rather, a series of them, is always to be found in every soul that is making any advance in the intellectual region.

> R. H. Benson: *The Religion of the Plain Man*. (20th cent.)

See also Reason

Understanding (Agreement)

A clever man had warned me against 'understandings' some thirteen years before: I have hated them ever since.

> Card. Newman: *Apologia pro Vita Sua*, 2. (19th cent.)

Union with God

I pray that in them there may be a union based on the flesh and spirit of Jesus Christ, Who is our everlasting life, a union of faith and love, to which nothing is to be preferred, but especially a union with Jesus and the Father.

> St. Ignatius of Antioch: *Letter to the Magnesians*, 1, 2. (2nd cent.)

Let us therefore do all things in the conviction that He dwells in us. Thus we shall be His temples and He will be our God within us. And this is the truth, and it will be made manifest before our eyes. Let us, then, love Him as He deserves.

> St. Ignatius of Antioch: *Letter to the Ephesians*, 15, 3. (2nd cent.)

You all are fellow-travellers, God-bearers (*theophoroi*) and temple-bearers (*naophoroi*), Christ-bearers (*Christophoroi*).

> St. Ignatius of Antioch: *Letter to the Ephesians*, 9, 2. (2nd cent.)

The soul seeks the Word in order to yield to It for correction, to be enlightened by It for knowledge, to rely upon It for virtue, to be reformed by It for wisdom, to be conformed to It for beauty, to be married to It for fecundity, to enjoy It for bliss.

> St. Bernard: *Sermons on the Canticle of Canticles*, 85. (12th cent.)

Man's perfection is to be like God . . . in unity of spirit, whereby man not only becomes one with God in the sense that he wills the same things as God, but in the sense that he is unable to will what God does not will.

> William of St. Thierry: *Epistola ad Fratres de Monte Dei*, 2, 16. (12th cent.)

Every rational soul ought with all its strength to desire to approach God and to be united to Him through the perception of His invisible presence.

> Walter Hilton: *Scale of Perfection*, 2, 41. (14th cent.)

The soul that is united with God is feared by the devil as though it were God Himself.

> St. John of the Cross: *Spiritual Sentences and Maxims*. (16th cent.)

> This union of divinest love
> By which I live a life above,
> Setting my heart at liberty
> My God to me enchains;
> But then to see His majesty

In such a base captivity
It so my spirit pains,
That evermore I weep and sigh,
Dying because I do not die.

St. Teresa: *Vivo, fin vivir en mi.* (Tr. E.
Caswall) (16th cent.)

The end of love is no other thing than
the union of the lover and the thing
loved.

St. Francis de Sales: *Treatise on the Love
of God,* 1, 9. (17th cent.)

The union to which love aspires is
spiritual.

St. Francis de Sales: *Treatise on the Love
of God,* 1, 10. (17th cent.)

It is not only by the imitation of Christ,
but by actual union with Him, that love
becomes and remains the driving force
of the soul.

R. H. Benson: *An Average Man.* (20th
cent.)

It would be an incalculable relief to cease
from striving, and to let self be merged
in that Personality so amazingly strong
and compelling.

R. H. Benson: *The Necromancers.* (20th
cent.)

In a soul's union with God nothing is
lost which she unites with Him.

R. H. Benson: *The Friendship of Christ.*
(20th cent.)

To live is to commune with God; to
find
His will, be nailed to it as to a cross
By arms, though bound, caressing
all mankind;
To merge myself in Him nor call it loss.
For, dying thus I live; and yet not I
But Christ in me, Who not again can
die.

Sister Miriam: *Young Frassati Meditates.*
(20th cent.)

The only true joy on earth is to escape
from the prison of our own self-hood (I
do not say the body, because the body is

God's temple and therefore it is holy)
and enter by love into union with the
Life Who dwells and sings within the
essence of every creature and in the core
of our own souls.

Thomas Merton: *Seeds of Contemplation.*
(20th cent.)

Union, Labor

See Association

Unity

Form all together one choir, so that, with
the symphony of your feelings and having all taken the tone of God, you may
sing with one voice to the Father through
Jesus Christ, that He may listen to you
and know you from your chant as the
canticle of His only Son.

St. Ignatius of Antioch: *Letter to the
Ephesians,* 4, 2. (2nd cent.)

From many to make one. (Ex pluribus
unum facere.)

St. Augustine: *Confessions,* 4, 8. (5th
cent.)

There are three unions in this world:
Christ and the Church, husband and
wife, spirit and flesh.

St. Augustine: *On Continence.* (5th cent.)

O humanity, in how many storms must
you be tossed, how many shipwrecks
must you endure, so long as you turn
yourself into a many-headed beast lust-
ing after a multiplicity of things . . . !
You pay no heed . . . to the sweetness of
divine counsel when it is breathed into
you through the trumpet of the Holy
Spirit: *Behold how good and pleasant it
is for brethren to dwell together in unity*
(Ps. 132, 1).

Dante: *Monarchy,* 1. (14th cent.)

None understand better the nature of
real distinction than those who have entered into unity.

John Tauler. (14th cent.)

Our hearts, my love, were form'd to be
The genuine twins of sympathy,
   They live with one sensation:
In joy or grief, but most in love,
Like chords in unison they move,
   And thrill with like vibration.

> Thomas Moore: *Sympathy: To Julia.*
> (19th cent.)

Universality

Universality is a contradiction in terms. You cannot be everything if you are anything. If you wish to be white all over, you must austerely resist the temptation to have green spots or yellow stripes. If you wish to be good all over, you must resist the spots of sin or the stripes of servitude. It may be great fun to be many-sided; but however many sides one has there cannot be one of them which is complete and rounded innocence. A polygon can have an infinite number of sides; but no one of its sides can be a circle.

> G. K. Chesterton: *A Handful of Authors.*
> (Apropos of Oscar Wilde) (20th cent.)

Universe

The entire universe pre-exists in the Godhead, which is its primordial cause. Father, Son, and Holy Ghost are all in all, because in their divinity every other thing is anticipated and possessed.

> St. Thomas Aquinas: *Exposition of the De Divinis Nominibus,* 2, lect. 1. (13th cent.)

The entire universe is one dominion and realm, governed by one ruler, who is the first mover, the first truth, the first good —God, blessed for ever and ever.

> St. Thomas Aquinas: *Commentary on the Metaphysics,* 12, lect. 2. (13th cent.)

God is an artist and the universe is His work of art.

> St. Thomas Aquinas: *Summa Theologica,* 1, 45, 6. (13th cent.)

There is but one thought greater than that of the universe, and that is the thought of its Maker.

> Card. Newman: *Idea of a University.*
> (19th cent.)

Wonderful, indeed, is this universe come from the omnipotent love of the Creator; wonderful are its elements which allow God's human creatures to mingle their voices in glorifying Him despite the apparent barriers of time and space.

> Pope Pius XII: *Radio Message to Eucharistic Congress in St. Paul, Minn.* (June 29, 1941)

See also Creation; God: Creator; World

University

A university is, according to the usual designation, an *alma mater,* knowing her children one by one, not a foundry, or a mint, or a treadmill.

> Card. Newman: *Idea of a University.*
> (19th cent.)

A university, I should lay down, by its very name professes to teach universal knowledge.

> Card. Newman: *Idea of a University,* 2.
> (19th cent.)

A university training is the great ordinary means to a great but ordinary end; it aims at raising the intellectual tone of society, at cultivating the public mind, at purifying the national taste, at supplying true principles to popular enthusiasm and fixed aims to popular aspiration, at giving enlargement and sobriety to the ideas of the age, at facilitating the exercise of political power, and refining the intercourse of private life.

> Card. Newman: *Idea of a University.*
> (19th cent.)

If then a practical end must be assigned to a university course, I say it is that of training good members of society. Its art is the art of social life, and its end is fitness for the world.

> Card. Newman: *Idea of a University.*
> (19th cent.)

Unseasonableness

We should avoid unseasonable intrusions and discover the appropriate time for each word and deed.

St. Basil: *The Morals,* 14. (4th cent.)

Unselfishness

Most of us have suffered from a certain sort of lady, who by her perverse unselfishness, gives more trouble than the selfish; who almost clamors for the unpopular dish and scrambles for the worst seat. Most of us have known parties or expeditions full of this seething fuss of self-effacement.

G. K. Chesterton: *What's Wrong with the World.* (20th cent.)

Usefulness

If you have real ambitions to be of use in the world, it is impossible to regret one's increased sphere of usefulness.

R. H. Benson: *An Average Man.* (20th cent.)

Usury

Since many clerics, filled with avarice and with the spirit of usury, forget the sacred words . . . and demand usuriously (that is, every month) a rate of interest, the great and holy synod declares that if any-one, after the publication of this law, takes interest, no matter on what grounds, or carries on the business of usurer, no matter in what way . . . he must be turned out of the clergy, and his name struck off the list.

Council of Nicaea, Can. 17. (325)

Let a bishop, or presbyter, or deacon who requires usury of those he lends to, either leave off doing so, or let him be deprived.

Ecclesiastical Canons of the Holy Apostles, 44. (4th cent.)

Usury is the taking of any interest whatever upon an unproductive loan.

Hilaire Belloc: *Economics for Helen.* (20th cent.)

Utilitarianism

Many a man is acting on utilitarian principles, who is shocked at them in set treaties, and disowns them.

Card. Newman: *Oxford University Sermons.* (19th cent.)

Utopia

The weakness of all utopias is this, that they take the greatest difficulty of man and assume it to be overcome, and then give an elaborate account of the overcoming of the smaller ones. They first assume that no man will want more than his share, and then are very ingenious in explaining whether his share will be delivered by motor-car or balloon.

G. K. Chesterton: *Heretics.* (20th cent.)

V

Vacuum

A vacuum is repugnant to reason.

> Descartes: *Principles of Philosophy*, 2.
> (17th cent.)

Valentine's Day, Saint

For this was on St. Valentine's Day,
When every fowl cometh there to
choose his mate.

> Chaucer: *The Parlement of Foules*. (14th
> cent.)

Vanity

All the preoccupation of men with the things of this life is but the game of children on the sands. For children take delight in the activity of their play and as soon as they have finished building what they build, their pleasure ends. For as soon as their labor is completed, the sand falls down and nothing is left of their buildings.

> St. Gregory of Nyssa: *Homily 1 on
> Ecclesiastes*. (4th cent.)

A man often glories the more for his very contempt of vainglory: for which reason he does not really glory in his contempt of glory; in that he glories in it, he does not contemn it.

> St. Augustine: *Confessions*, 10, 38. (5th
> cent.)

She wore no chain or crownet set with stones,
No gaudy skirt nor broidered belt, to gather
All eyes with more charm than the wearer owns.

> Dante: *Paradiso, Canto 15*. (Tr. Binyon)
> (14th cent.)

Those who write against vanity wish to have the glory of having written well, and those who read them wish to have the glory of reading well, and I who write this have the same desire, and maybe also those who read this.

> Pascal: *Pensées*, 2. (17th cent.)

The greatest magnifying glasses in the world are a man's own eyes when they look upon his own person.

> Pope: *Letter to William Wycherley*.
> (18th cent.)

Vanity, or vainglory, is the offspring of pride, and the eldest daughter of that detestable vice. Pride is her father, self-love is her mother, and cobwebs are her clothing. She is such a light, fond thing, that were it not that her seductions weaken and undermine the best-formed minds and hearts both of men and women, for her own sake she would be unworthy of any serious consideration.

> Archb. Ullathorne: *Humility and Patience*.
> (19th cent.)

Variety

Distinction and variety in the world is intended by the First Cause. God brings things into existence in order that His goodness may be communicated and manifested. One solitary creature would not suffice. Therefore He makes creatures many and diverse, that what is wanting in one may be supplied by another.

> St. Thomas Aquinas: *Summa Theologica*,
> 1, 47, 1. (13th cent.)

Veil

Moreover let all the women have their heads veiled with a scarf but not with a veil of linen only, for that is not a sufficient covering.

> St. Hippolytus: *The Apostolic Tradition,*
> 18. (3rd cent.)

As when a piece of wanton lawn,
A thin, aerial veil, is drawn
O'er a beauty's face; seeming to hide
More sweetly shows the blushing bride.

> Richard Crashaw: *Temperance, or the*
> *Cheap Physician.* (17th cent.)

Venture

He that never climbed, never fell.

> John Heywood: *Proverbs,* 1, 12. (16th
> cent.)

Veronica's Veil

My Lord Christ Jesus, very God, is this
Indeed Thy likeness in such fashion
wrought?

> Dante: *Paradiso, Canto 31.* (Tr. Binyon)
> (14th cent.)

Versatility

Ye have many strings to the bow.

> John Heywood: *Proverbs,* 1, 11. (16th
> cent.)

A man so various, that he seem'd to be
Not one, but all mankind's epitome.
Stiff in opinions, always in the wrong;
Was everything by starts, and nothing
    long;
But, in the course of one revolving
    moon,
Was chemist, fidler, statesman, and buffoon.

> Dryden: *Absalom and Achitophel.* (17th
> cent.)

Verse

And this unpolish'd, rugged verse I
    chose;
As fittest for discourse, and nearest
prose.

> Dryden: *Religio Laici.* (17th cent.)

Imagination in a poet is a faculty so wild
and lawless that, like an high-ranging
spaniel, it must have clogs tied to it lest
it outrun the judgment. The great easiness of blank verse renders the poet too
luxuriant.

> Dryden: *The Rival Ladies, Pref.* (17th
> cent.)

I chose verse, and even rhyme, for two
reasons. The one will appear obvious:
that principles, maxims or precepts, so
written, both strike the reader more
strongly at first and are more easily retained by him afterward. The other may
seem odd, but it is true: I found I could
express them more shortly this way than
in prose.

> Pope: *An Essay on Man, Pref.* (18th
> cent.)

Vespers

Joyful light of the holy glory of the immortal, the heavenly, the holy and blessed
Father, O Jesus Christ!
   Now that the sun is setting and the
evening lights are kindled, we hymn the
Father, and the Son, and the Holy Spirit
of God.
   Worthy art Thou at all times to be
praised with holy voices, O Son of God,
that livest life! Therefore all the world
doth glorify Thee!

> Byzantine Euchologion, Vespers, hymn
> *Phos Hilaron.* (Before 3rd cent.)

O blest Creator of the light,
Who mak'st the day with radiance
    bright,
And o'er the forming world didst call
The light from chaos first of all.
Whose wisdom joined in meet array
The morn and eve, and named them
    day:
Night comes with all its darkling fears;
Regard Thy people's prayers and tears.

> Roman Breviary, hymn *Lucis Creator*
> *optime* for Sunday at Vespers. (Tr. E.
> Caswall) (Attr. to Pope St. Gregory I, 6th
> cent.)

As fades the glowing orb of day,
To Thee, great source of light, we pray;
Blest Thee in One, to every heart
Thy beams of life and love impart.

Roman Breviary, hymn *Jam sol recedit
igneus* for Saturday at Vespers. (Tr. T.
Potter) (St. Ambrose, 4th cent.)

Be the day never so long,
Evermore at last they ring to evensong.

John Heywood: *Proverbs*, 2, 7. (16th
cent.)

Vestal

How happy is the blameless vestal's lot,
The world forgetting, by the world forgot.

Pope: *Eloisa to Abelard.* (18th cent.)

Viaticum, Holy

With respect to the dying, the old rule of
the Church should continue to be observed, which forbids that anyone who is
on the point of death should be deprived
of the last and most necessary Viaticum. . . .

Council of Nicaea, Can. 13. (325)

We all have a common ending of temporal life in the certitude of one and the
same hope, as we close our eyes in death:
having previously received the Viaticum
of the heavenly mystery, we trust that we
shall be found immediately in the true
life and shall remain in this forever.

St. Bede the Venerable: *De Tabernaculo,*
2. (8th cent.)

Receive, my brother, this Food for your
journey, the Body of our Lord Jesus
Christ, that He may guard you from the
malicious enemy and lead you into everlasting life. Amen.

Roman Ritual, Administration of Viaticum.
(Formula of priest as he gives Sacrament
to the dying.) (ca. 13th cent.)

Vice

The first is unbelief, the second is incontinence, the third disobedience, and the
fourth deceit. Their companions are
called: grief, wickedness, licentiousness,
irascibility, lying, foolishness, slander,
and hatred.

Shepherd of Hermas, Parable 9, 15, 3.
(2nd cent.)

This is the definition of vice: the wrong
use, in violation of the Lord's command,
of what has been given us by God for a
good purpose.

St. Basil: *The Long Rules,* 2. (4th cent.)

Since vice is contrary to nature, a vice is
the more grievous according as it diminishes the integrity of nature.

St. Augustine: *De Libero Arbitrio,* 3, 14.
(4th cent.)

The greatest virtues are only splendid
vices.

St. Augustine: *Confessions.* (5th cent.)

We make a ladder of our vices, if we
trample those same vices underfoot.

St. Augustine: *Sermon on the Ascension.*
(5th cent.)

There is no vice so clean contrary to nature that it obliterates even the faintest
traces of nature.

St. Augustine: *The City of God,* 19, 12.
(5th cent.)

In other living creatures the ignorance of
themselves is nature, but in men it is vice.

Boethius: *De Consolatione Philosophiae,*
2, 5. (6th cent.)

Vice to forsake is better late than never.

Lydgate: *Assembly of Gods.* (15th cent.)

Vice is a monster of so frightful mien
As to be hated needs but to be seen;
Yet seen too oft, familiar with her
face,
We first endure, then pity, then em-
brace.

Pope: *An Essay on Man,* 2. (18th cent.)

You do not get rid of vice by human expedients; you can but use them according to circumstances, and in their place, as making the best of a bad matter. You must go to a higher source for renovation of the heart and of the will. You do but play a sort of 'hunt the slipper' with the fault of our nature, till you go to Christianity.

> Card. Newman: *Discussions and Arguments.* (19th cent.)

When people impute special vices to the Christian Church, they seem entirely to forget that the world (which is the only other thing there is) had these vices much more. The Church has been cruel; but the world has been much more cruel. The Church has plotted; but the world has plotted much more. The Church has been superstitious; but it has never been so superstitious as the world is when left to itself.

> G. K. Chesterton: *All Things Considered.* (20th cent.)

That vice never tires men, might be a tenable and entertaining lie; that the individual instrument of vice never tires them is not, even as a lie, tenable enough to be entertaining.

> G. K. Chesterton: *A Handful of Authors.* (20th cent.)

See also Virtue and Vice

Victory

Unless the battle has preceded, there cannot be a victory . . . for the helmsman is recognized in the tempest; the soldier is proven in warfare.

> St. Cyprian: *On Immortality,* 12. (3rd cent.)

If Christ is with us, who is against us? You can fight with confidence where you are sure of victory. With Christ and for Christ victory is certain.

> St. Bernard: *Letters,* 1, 13. (12th cent.)

Son Roper, I thank our Lord the field is won.

> St. Thomas More, after his condemnation. (Roper, *Life*) (16th cent.)

E'en victors are by victories undone.

> Dryden. (17th cent.)

To conquer a motive or tame an imagination is at once more arduous and more far-reaching in its effects than a victory in merely outward matters.

> R. H. Benson: *The King's Achievement.* (20th cent.)

Vigil

And at midnight rise and wash thy hands with water and pray . . . truly those men of holy memory who handed on the tradition to us taught us thus: because in this hour every creature hushes for a brief moment to praise the Lord; stars and plants and waters stand still in that instant; all the hosts of the angels ministering unto him together with the souls of the righteous praise God.

> St. Hippolytus: *The Apostolic Tradition,* 36. (3rd cent.)

The quiet and solitude of the night make it a favorable time for prayer and most suitable for those who watch. With worldly occupations put aside and the attention undivided, whole man, at night, stands in the divine presence.

> St. Niceta of Remesiana: *De Vigiliis Servorum Dei,* 8. (5th cent.)

Now, from the slumbers of the night arising,
Chant we the holy psalmody of David,
Hymns to our Master, with a voice concordant,
> Sweetly intoning.

> Roman Breviary, hymn *Nocte surgentes vigilemus omnes* for Sunday at Matins. (Post-Pentecostal season) (Tr. from *Hymner*) (Altered, attr. to Pope St. Gregory I, 6th cent.)

Behold! the Bridegroom cometh in the
middle of the night,
And blest is he whose loins are girt,
whose lamp is burning bright;
But woe to that dull servant, whom the
Master shall surprise
With lamp untrimmed, unburning,
and with slumber in his eyes.

Do thou, my soul, beware, beware, lest
thou in sleep sink down,
Lest thou be given o'er to death and
lose the golden crown;
But see that thou be sober, with watchful eyes, and thus
Cry—Holy, holy, holy God, have
mercy upon us.

Byzantine Horologion, Troparion at
Nocturns. (Tr. G. Moultrie) (ca. 9th
cent. ?)

Village

The pleasant little villages that grace
the Irish glynns
Down among the wheatfields—up amid
the whins,
The little white-walled villages crowd-
ing close together,
Clinging to the Old Sod in spite of
wind and weather.

James B. Dollard: Song of the Little
Villages. (20th cent.)

Violet

Twice happy violets! that first bad birth
In the warm spring, when no frosts nip
the earth;
Thrice happy now; since you trans-
planted are
Unto the sweeter bosom of my fair.

Sir Edward Sherburne: Violets in
Thaumantia's Bosom. (17th cent.)

In this secluded shrine,
O miracle of grace,
No mortal eye but mine
Hath looked upon thy face.

. . . .
Whereof—as shade to shade
Is wedded in the sun—

A moment's glance hath made
Our souls forever one.

John B. Tabb: To a Wood-Violet. (19th
cent.)

Virgil

There is Virgil . . . this most famous and
approved of all poets.

St. Augustine: The City of God, 1, 3. (5th
cent.)

And art thou then that Virgil, and that
well
Which pours abroad so ample a
stream of song?
. . . .
O glory and light of all the poets'
throng!
May the ardent study and great love
serve me now
Which made me to peruse thy book
so long!
Thou art my master and my author thou.
Thou only art he from whom the
comely style
I took, wherein my merit men avow.

Dante: Inferno, Canto 1. (Tr. L. Binyon)
(14th cent.)

Virgin

I will say it boldly, though God can do
all things, He cannot raise a virgin up
after she has fallen.

St. Jerome: De Virginitate. (5th cent.)

Thou youngest virgin-daughter of the
skies,
Made in the last promotion of the
blest.

Dryden: Ode to the Memory of Mrs.
Killigrew. (17th cent.)

See also Nun

Virginity, Holy

In other sciences men have devised certain practical methods for cultivating the
particular subject; and so, I take it, vir-

ginity is the practical method in the science of the divine life, furnishing men with the power of assimilating themselves with spiritual natures.

> St. Gregory of Nyssa: *On Virginity*, 5. (4th cent.)

Virginity stands as far above marriage as the heavens above the earth.

> St. John Chrysostom: *On Virginity*, 9. (4th cent.)

The root, and the flower, too, of virginity is a crucified life.

> St. John Chrysostom: *On Virginity*, 80. (4th cent.)

Virginity is natural and marriage came after the Fall.

> St. Jerome: *On Virginity*. (5th cent.)

Virginity can be lost even by a thought.

> St. Jerome: *On Virginity*. (5th cent.)

The gift of virginity has been poured most abundantly upon women, seeing that it was from a woman it began.

> St. Jerome: *On Virginity*. (5th cent.)

Virginity has a special reward hereafter.

> St. Augustine: *On Holy Virginity*. (5th cent.)

Christ, in being born of a virgin who, before she knew Who was to be born of her, had resolved to remain a virgin, chose rather to approve holy virginity than to impose it. So, even in that woman in whom He took upon himself the nature of a slave, He desired virginity to be free.

> St. Augustine: *On Holy Virginity*, 4. (5th cent.)

Not because it is virginity is it held in honor, but because it is consecrated to God.

> St. Augustine: *On Holy Virginity*, 8. (5th cent.)

Because perpetual continence, and virginity above all, is a great good in the saints of God, extreme vigilance must be exercised lest it be corrupted by pride. . . . The more clearly I see the greatness of this gift, the more truly do I fear lest it be plundered by thieving pride. No one therefore protects virginity but God himself who bestowed it: and *God is charity*. The guardian therefore of virginity is charity; the habitat of this guardian is humility.

> St. Augustine: *On Holy Virginity*, 33, 51. (5th cent.)

For if it is a great and excellent thing to blazon the pages of this world's history with high-sounding names, how immeasurably greater and more glorious to trample this world under foot by integrity of body and soul!

> St. Augustine: *Letter 150*. (To Proba and Juliana.) (5th cent.)

Let them that are married regard the unmarried as above themselves; let them acknowledge them to be better; let them love in them what they themselves have not, and let them love Christ in them.

> St. Augustine: *Sermon 96*, 8, 10. (5th cent.)

The Mother bore Him in her womb, let us bear Him in our hearts. The Virgin was pregnant by the incarnation of Christ; let our hearts be pregnant by our faith in Christ. The Virgin gave birth to the Savior; let our souls give birth to salvation, and let us bring forth praise. Let us not be sterile; let our souls be fertile to God.

> St. Augustine: *Sermon 189*, 3, 3. (5th cent.)

Holy virginity is a better thing than conjugal chastity. . . . A mother will hold a lesser place in the kingdom of heaven, because she has been married, than the daughter, seeing that she is a virgin. . . . But if thy mother has been humble and thou proud, she will have some sort of a place, but thou none.

> St. Augustine: *Sermon 354*, 9, 9. (5th cent.)

This is the only-begotten Son of God,
the only-begotten Son of a virgin also,
the only Spouse of all holy virgins, the
fruit, the glory, the gift of holy virginity,
Whom holy virginity brought forth
physically, to Whom holy virginity is
wedded spiritually, by Whom holy virginity is made fruitful and kept inviolate,
by Whom she is adorned, to remain ever
beautiful, by Whom she is crowned, to
reign forever glorious.

St. Fulgentius: *Letters,* 3, 4, 6. (6th cent.)

Renounce marriage, and imitate the angels.

John of Damascus: *Dialectica.* (8th cent.)

Virginity is the rule of life among the
angels, the property of all incorporeal
nature.

St. John of Damascus: *Exposition of the
Orthodox Faith,* 4, 24. (8th cent.)

If our Redeemer so loved the flower of
unimpaired modesty that not only was
He born from a virginal womb, but was
also cared for by a virgin nurse even
when He was still an infant crying in the
cradle, by whom, I ask, does He wish his
Body to be handled now that He reigns,
immense, in heaven?

St. Peter Damian: *De Coelibatu
Sacerdotum,* 3. (11th cent.)

If any one saith that the marriage state
is to be placed above the state of virginity or of celibacy, and that it is not better
and more blessed to remain in virginity
or in celibacy than to be united in matrimony; let him be anathema.

Council of Trent, Session 24, Canon 10.
(Nov. 11, 1563)

Behold my soul, shut in my body's jail,
   The which the drake of hell gapes to
     devour:
   Teach me, O virgin! how thou didst
     prevail?
Virginity, thou sayest, was all thy aid:
   Give me then purity, instead of
     power,

And let my soul made chaste, pass
   for a maid.

drake—dragon

Henry Constable: *Sonnet to St. Margaret.*
(16th cent.)

Neither widowhood nor virginity has
any place in heaven but that which is assigned to them by humility.

St. Francis de Sales: *Introduction to the
Devout Life,* 3, 40. (17th cent.)

No happier vows I know
Than to a virgin grave untouch'd to go.

R. Crashaw: *Alexias, Third Elegy.* (17th
cent.)

Holy virginity and that perfect chastity
which is consecrated to the service of God
are without doubt the most precious
treasures which the Founder of the
Church has left in heritage to the society
which He established.

Pope Pius XII: *Sacra Virginitas.* (Mar.
25, 1954)

Virginity is not a Christian virtue unless
we embrace it *for the kingdom of
heaven;* that is, unless we take up this
way of life precisely to be able to devote
ourselves more freely to divine things to
attain heaven more surely, and with skillful efforts to lead others more readily to
the kingdom of heaven. . . . This is the
primary purpose, this the central idea of
Christian virginity: to aim only at the
divine, to turn thereto the whole mind
and soul; to want to please God in everything, to think of Him continually, to
consecrate body and soul completely to
Him.

Pope Pius XII: *Sacra Virginitas.* (Mar. 25,
1954)

Virginity is a difficult virtue. That one be
able to embrace it there is needed not
only a strong and declared determination
of abstaining completely and perpetually
from those legitimate pleasures derived
from marriage; but also a constant vigilance and struggle to contain and dominate rebellious movements of body and

soul, a flight from the importunings of the world, a struggle to conquer the wiles of Satan.

Pope Pius XII: *Sacra Virginitas.* (Mar. 25, 1954)

Virtue

Continence is the daughter of faith, simplicity of continence, innocence of simplicity, reverence of innocence, knowledge of reverence, love of knowledge. Their acts then are pure, reverent and divine. Whoever serves them and succeeds in mastering their acts will have a dwelling in the tower, along with God's saints.

Shepherd of Hermas, Vision 3, 8, 7-8. (2nd cent.)

A Christian's virtue is the only possession that cannot be conquered or destroyed.

Eusebius of Caesarea: *Ecclesiastical History,* 8, 14, 17. (4th cent.)

The definition of the virtue which God requires of us is: the use with a good conscience of these same gifts [of God] in accordance with the Lord's command.

St. Basil: *The Long Rules,* 2. (4th cent.)

Where virtue is, there are many snares.

St. John Chrysostom: *Homilies.* (4th cent.)

So good a thing is virtue that even its enemies applaud and admire it.

St. John Chrysostom: *Homilies.* (4th cent.)

He who quits himself and cleaves to virtue, loses his own and gains what is eternal.

St. Ambrose. (5th cent.)

It is certain that virtue is the only and highest good, and that it alone abounds in the fruit of a blessed life; and that a blessed life, by means of which eternal life is won, depends on virtue only.

St. Ambrose: *On the Duties of the Clergy,* 2, 18. (4th cent.)

I hold virtue to be nothing else than perfect love of God.

St. Augustine: *De Moribus Ecclesiae Catholicae,* 15, 25. (4th cent.)

Let this therefore in the first place be laid down as an unassailable position, that the virtue which makes the life good has its throne in the soul, and thence rules the members of the body, which becomes holy in virtue of the holiness of the will; and that while the will remains firm and unshaken, nothing that another person does with the body, or upon the body, is any fault of the person who suffers it, so long as he cannot escape it without sin.

St. Augustine: *The City of God,* 1, 16. (5th cent.)

For there is no true virtue except that which is directed towards that end in which is the highest and ultimate good of man.

St. Augustine: *The City of God,* 5, 12. (5th cent.)

Virtue hath a proper dignity of her own, which she presently endueth her possessors withal.

Boethius: *De Consolatione Philosophiae,* 3, 4. (6th cent.)

For there is no man who masters that degree of goodness which he desires, in that almighty God, Who discerns the inward parts, sets bounds to the very spiritual attainments themselves, so that man may not exalt himself in those things in which he is able, by reason of that which he tries to apprehend and cannot.

Pope St. Gregory I: *Morals,* 12, 3. (6th cent.)

We prepare ourselves with great anxiety to undertake our own improvement, when we observe in others that virtue which we have not ourselves.

Pope St. Gregory I: *Morals,* 24, 19. (6th cent.)

Charity arises from inner peace (*apatheia*); inner peace from hope in God;

hope from patience and longsuffering; the latter from studious self-control; self-control from fear of God; and fear of God from faith in Christ.

> St. Maximus the Confessor: *Centuries on Charity,* 1, 2. (7th cent.)

Virtues demand discretion, and all excess is vice.

> St. Bede the Venerable: *On the Proverbs of Salomon.* (8th cent.)

Virtue is a gift from God implanted in our nature.

> St. John of Damascus: *Exposition of the Orthodox Faith,* 2, 30. (8th cent.)

This seems to me the only real safeguard of life: that the mind, by the life-giving power of the spirit, be illuminated for the acquisition of knowledge and be inspired with the love of honor and zeal for virtue.

> John of Salisbury: *Policraticus,* 3, 1, 173. (12th cent.)

Virtue seeks the esteem of the good and even of all men, if that be possible, but scorns to attain it by degrading means.

> John of Salisbury: *Policraticus,* 3, 5, 182. (12th cent.)

Virtue is what happiness deserves and happiness is the reward of virtue. These then are the two *summa bona,* the one of the journey, the other of the homecoming. For nothing takes precedence of virtue while the exile is estranged from God; nothing is better than felicity while the citizen enjoys his rights and rejoices with his Lord.

> John of Salisbury: *Policraticus,* 7, 8, 118. (12th cent.)

Augustine defines virtue as a good quality of mind, whereby life is lived aright, which no one uses ill, and which God works in us apart from sin.

> St. Thomas Aquinas: *Disputations concerning the Virtues in Common,* 2. (Actually from Peter Lombard, based upon St. Augustine.) (13th cent.)

A virtuous act has four characteristics. First, it is a measured kind of operation, appropriate to the circumstances of its situation. Secondly, it evinces a certain steadiness in acting that way; there is a reliability about the person who does it. Thirdly, it is well adapted to achieve an end which is not merely his own self-betterment. Fourthly, it is done deliberately. (Aristotle)

> St. Thomas Aquinas: *Disputations concerning the Cardinal Virtues,* 1. (13th cent.)

The nature of virtue is that it should direct man to good.

> St. Thomas Aquinas: *Summa Theologica,* 1-2, 64, 1. (13th cent.)

The theological virtues join the human mind to God; the intellectual virtues are good qualities rendering the reason ready to know the truth; the moral virtues are perfections bringing the appetites under the control of right reason; the gifts of the Holy Ghost are dispositions whereby every power of the soul can be played on by God.

> St. Thomas Aquinas: *Summa Theologica,* 1-2, 68, 8. (13th cent.)

The essence of virtue consists in the doing rather of what is good than of what is difficult.

> St..Thomas Aquinas: *Summa Theologica,* 2-2, 123, 12. (13th cent.)

Ye were not formed to live the life of brutes,
But virtue to pursue, and knowledge high.

> Dante: *Inferno, Canto 26.* (14th cent.)

Natural goodness comes of God, no strain
Of blood can give it, no, nor ancestor.

> Chaucer: *The Clerk's Tale.* (Tr. Coghill) (14th cent.)

Virtue is nought else but an ordered and measured affection, plainly directed unto God for Himself.

> Anonymous: *The Cloud of Unknowing,* 12. (Quoting Richard of St. Victor: *Benjamin Minor,* cap. 7) (14th cent.)

Oh, glorious virtue! Who would not give himself to death a thousand times, and endure any suffering through desire to win thee? Thou art a queen, who dost possess the entire world; thou dost inhabit the enduring life; for while the soul that is arrayed in thee is yet mortal, thou makest it abide by force of love with those who are immortal.

> St. Catherine of Siena: *Letter to Monna Agnese.* (14th cent.)

God does not ask the impossible, but instructs you to do what you are able, and to pray for aid in doing what you are not able to do yourself, that He may help you.

> Decree of the Council of Trent, 6th Session, Chap. 11. (Jan. 13, 1547)

What one art thou, thus in torn weed yclad?
Virtue, in price whom ancient sages had.
Why poorly 'rayed? For fading goods past care.
Why double-faced? I mark each fortune's fare.
This bridle, what? Mind's rages to restrain.
Tools why bear you? I love to take great pain.
Why wings? I teach above the stars to fly.
Why tread you death? I only cannot die.

> Nicholas Grimald: *Virtue.* (16th cent.)

I dwell in grace's court,
Enrich'd with virtue's rights;
Faith guide my wit, love leads my will,
Hope all my mind delights.

> Bl. Robert Southwell: *Content and Rich.* (16th cent.)

If virtue be thy guide,
True comfort is thy path,

And thou secure from erring steps,
That lead to vengeance wrath.

Not widest open door,
Nor spacious ways she goes;
To straight and narrow gate and way,
She calls, she leads, she shows.

> Bl. Robert Southwell: *To the Christian Reader.* (16th cent.)

Prevent the time, the days are full of danger,
Whilst youthful vigor yields you furtherance,
Make reason guide, let folly be a stranger,
Virtue is perfected by art and usance.
Enrich your minds with skill, for why they must,
Remain eterne when body is but dust.

> Thomas Lodge: *To All Young Gentlemen.* (16th cent.)

And virtue can as well
In cottages remain,
As honor may in high estate,
In courts of princes reign.

> Richard Verstegan: *The Substance of Humaine Flesh.* (Guiney, 216) (17th cent.)

Everyone argues in favor of the virtue he practices easily, and exaggerates the difficulties of the virtues which are contrary to it.

> St. Francis de Sales: *Letters to Persons in Religion,* 2, 25. (17th cent.)

True virtue has no limits.

> St. Francis de Sales: *Treatise on the Love of God,* 3, 1. (17th cent.)

Love virtue rather than fear sin.

> Jean Pierre Camus: *The Spirit of St. Francis de Sales,* 19, 1. (17th cent.)

The power of a man's virtue should not be measured by his special efforts, but by his ordinary doing.

> Pascal: *Pensées.* (17th cent.)

And when in glory, through the public place,

The spoils of conquered nations were
to pass,
And but one day for triumph was
allowed,
The consul was constrained his pomp to
crowd;
And so the swift procession hurried on,
That all, though not distinctly, might
be shown:
So, in the straitened bounds of life con-
fined,
She gave but glimpses of her glorious
mind,
And multitudes of virtues passed along,
Each pressing foremost in the mighty
throng,
Ambitious to be seen, and then make
room
For greater multitudes that were to
come.

> Dryden: *Eleonora.* (18th cent.)

Oh, let us still the secret joy partake,
To follow virtue even for virtue's sake.

> Pope: *The Temple of Fame,* 1. (18th
> cent.)

Know then this truth (enough for man
to know):
Virtue alone is happiness below.

> Pope: *An Essay on Man,* 4. (18th cent.)

Mere natural virtue wears away when
men neglect to deepen it into religious
principle.

> Card. Newman: *Historical Studies.*
> (Miscellanies, p. 39) (19th cent.)

The whole labor of virtue consists in
transferring the will from the attractions
of nature to the attractions of grace, and
in getting out of that narrow selfishness
and away from those morbid sensibili-
ties, to reach the divine atmosphere of
truth and justice.

> Archb. Ullathorne: *Humility and Patience.*
> (19th cent.)

The Christian virtues are the feet and
wings whereby the soul moves in the direction of her final end.

> Archb. Ullathorne: *Humility and Patience.*
> (19th cent.)

The chief assertion of religious morality
is that white is a color. Virtue is not the
absence of vices or the avoidance of
moral dangers; virtue is a vivid and
separate thing, like pain or a particular
smell.

> G. K. Chesterton: *Tremendous Trifles,* 2.
> (20th cent.)

Our virtue springs from freedom and
comes to its strength by trial and effort.
A make-believe trial could never succeed
in generating the virtues we love most
and a real trial means risks and failure.
In sighing, therefore, for a halcyon world
and a release from the strain of our days
we are really asking for a museum and
not a world, a museum in which we
would lie like desiccated mummies sans
strength and sans happiness.

> M. C. D'Arcy: *The Pain of this World.*
> (20th cent.)

Some of the most virtuous men in the
world are also the bitterest and most unhappy, because they have unconsciously
come to believe that all their happiness
depends on their being more virtuous
than other men.

> Thomas Merton: *Seeds of Contemplation.*
> (20th cent.)

Virtue and Vice

No vice is found but in the shadow of
some virtue.

> John Scotus Eriugena: *On the Division of
> Nature,* 1, 68. (9th cent.)

The life of sin is a fall from coherence
to chaos; the life of virtue a climb from
the many to the One.

> St. Thomas Aquinas: *Summa Theologica,*
> 1-2, 72, 1. (13th cent.)

Human virtue, which renders a man good
in himself and in his deeds, is in accordance with human, that is, rational nature.
Vice is contrary to human nature, because
against the order of reason.

> St. Thomas Aquinas: *Summa Theologica,*
> 1-2, 71, 2. (13th cent.)

When we are assailed by some vice, we must, as far as possible, embrace the practice of the contrary virtue.

St. Francis de Sales: *Introduction to the Devout Life,* 3, 1. (17th cent.)

The diff'rence is too nice
Where ends the virtue or begins the vice.

Pope: *An Essay on Man,* 2. (18th cent.)

Virtuous and vicious ev'ry man must be,
Few in th' extreme, but all in the degree.

Pope: *An Essay on Man,* 2. (18th cent.)

There is no subtle spiritual evil in the fact that people always brag about their vices; it is when they begin to brag about their virtues that they become insufferable.

G. K. Chesterton: *Tremendous Trifles,* 27. (20th cent.)

Virtues, Cardinal

Prudence is concerned with things, and by it evil is distinguished from good. Fortitude is the virtue by which adversity is endured with calmness. Temperance the virtue by which lust and concupiscence are bridled. Justice the virtue by which in a right decision each is given his due.

St. Isidore: *Etymologies,* 2, 24. (7th cent.)

Virtues, Theological

To be well adjusted to an end we must know and desire it; the desire demands that we are in love with this end and are confident we can attain it. The theological virtues are therefore three—faith, which makes us know God; hope, which makes us look forward to joining Him; charity, which makes us His friends.

St. Thomas Aquinas: *Disputations concerning the Virtues in General,* 12. (13th cent.)

Vision of God, Beatific

God now appears as He wishes, not as He is. No wise man, no saint, no prophet, is able to see Him as He is, nor has been able in this mortal body.

St. Bernard: *On the Canticle of Canticles,* 31, 2. (12th cent.)

The final aim of rational creatures is nothing short of the vision of God, the seeing of His very self.

St. Thomas Aquinas: *Compendium of Theology,* 104. (13th cent.)

When this end is attained the natural desire is stilled, for God's essence united to the mind is the principle of knowing all things and is the fount of all goodness.

St. Thomas Aquinas: *Compendium of Theology,* 106. (13th cent.)

Sweet volumes, stored with learning fit for saints,
Where blissful choirs imparadise their minds;
Wherein eternal study never faints,
Still finding all, yet seeking all it finds:
How endless is your labyrinth of bliss,
Where to be lost the sweetest finding is!

Bl. Robert Southwell: *St. Peter's Complaint.* (16th cent.)

I scorn thy foolish fears with sweet derision;
Each year but brought us nearer to the vision
Of God Himself in His own fields elysian.

Susan L. Emory: *An Old Woman's Answer to a Letter from her Childhood.* (19th cent.)

The ultimate perfection of the contemplative life is not a heaven of separate individuals, each one viewing his own private vision of God: it is a sea of love which flows through the one person of all the elect, all the angels and saints, and their contemplation would be incomplete if it were not shared, or if it were shared with fewer souls, or with spirits capable of less vision and less joy.

> Thomas Merton: *Seeds of Contemplation.* (20th cent.)

Vocation

A good vocation is simply a firm and constant will in which the called person has to serve God in the way and in the places to which almighty God has called him.

> St. Francis de Sales: *Letters to Persons in Religion,* 5, 8. (17th cent.)

If a person shows a firm and persevering determination to serve God in the manner and place to which His divine majesty calls her, she gives the best proof we can have that she has a true vocation.

> St. Francis de Sales: *Spiritual Conferences,* 17. (17th cent.)

The most important thing in life is the choice of a calling: it is left to chance.

> Pascal: *Pensées.* (17th cent.)

It seems to me that it is the right thing for a director to discourage people who think they have a vocation. If it is real, it will vanquish all obstacles, and will stand out, not as a mere invitation, but as a categorical imperative.

> Abbot Chapman: *Spiritual Letters.* (20th cent.)

Voting

The casting of the ballot is the supreme act of citizenship. Ballot in hand, the citizen is a sovereign, and with his fellow-citizens he decides the destiny of the Republic.

> Archb. Ireland: *American Citizenship.* (Chicago, Feb. 22, 1895)

The ballot is the pride of the true American; the proper use of it is a sacred duty.

The American who does not care to vote on election day, deserves disenfranchisement or exile: the American who boasts of his political indolence proclaims his own shame.

> Archb. Ireland: *American Citizenship.* (Chicago, Feb. 22, 1895)

Vow

Oh happy prince whom Heav'n hath taught the way
By paying vows to have more vows to pay!

> Dryden: *Astraea Redux.* (17th cent.)

A vow, that is, a deliberate and free promise made to God of a good which is possible and better, must be fulfilled by reason of the virtue of religion. All persons who have a sufficient use of reason are capable of making a vow, unless they are forbidden to do so by law. A vow which is made as the result of grave and unjust fear is null by law.

> Code of Canon Law, Canon 1307. (20th cent.)

See also Monastic Life; Nun; Religious Life

Vulgarity

Vulgarity is simply the conduct of other people.

> Oscar Wilde: *An Ideal Husband,* 3. (19th cent.)

Let no man deceive himself; if by vulgarity we mean coarseness of speech, rowdiness of behavior, gossip, horseplay, and some heavy drinking: vulgarity there always was, wherever there was joy, wherever there was faith in the gods.

> G. K. Chesterton: *Heretics.* (20th cent.)

Wage

Let the working man and the employer make free agreements, and in particular let them agree freely as to wages; nevertheless, there underlies a dictate of natural justice more imperious and ancient than any bargain between man and man, namely, that wages ought not to be insufficient to support a frugal and well-behaved wage-earner.

> Pope Leo XIII: *Rerum Novarum*. (May 15, 1891)

The wage paid to the working man must be sufficient for the support of himself and of his family.

> Pope Pius XI: *Quadragesimo Anno.* (May 15, 1931)

If a business be unprofitable on account of bad management, want of enterprise, or out-worn methods, that is not a just reason for reducing the wages of its workers.

> Pope Pius XI: *Quadragesimo Anno.* (May 15, 1931)

Whenever possible the wage-contract should be modified by a partnership-contract, whereby the wage-earner is made to share in the ownership, the management or the profits.

> Pope Pius XI: *Quadragesimo Anno.* (May 15, 1931)

Waiting

For evermore I wait, and longer too.

> Robert Henryson: *Town and Country Mouse.* (15th cent.)

Who waiteth for dead men shoes shall go long barefoot.

> John Heywood: *Proverbs,* 1, 11. (16th cent.)

Wall

Further than the wall he cannot go.

> John Heywood: *Proverbs,* 2, 5. (16th cent.)

Wants

What can a man want that it is not in God's power to give?

> St. Augustine: *In Ps. 146 Enarr. 1,* 1. (5th cent.)

Things three, no more; but three are needful.
The one is clothing, to save thee from chill,
The one is meat, for thy health's sake,
The third is drink when thou driest.

> Langland: *Piers Plowman,* Passus 1. (14th cent.)

So blind is our mortality, and so unaware what will fall, so unsure also what manner of mind we will have tomorrow, that God could not lightly do man a more vengeance than in this world to grant him his own foolish wishes.

> St. Thomas More: *Dialogue of Comfort.* (16th cent.)

My wishes are but few,
All easy to fulfil;
I make the limits of my power
The bonds unto my will.

> Bl. Robert Southwell: *Content and Rich.* (16th cent.)

In this world there are only two tragedies. One is not getting what one wants, and the other is getting it. The last is the real tragedy.

> Oscar Wilde: *Lady Windermere's Fan,* 3. (19th cent.)

Wantonness

Your Cleopatra; Dolabella's Cleopatra;
every man's Cleopatra.

> Dryden: *All for Love,* 4, 1. (17th cent.)

War

But those wars also are just, without
doubt, which are ordained by God Himself, in Whom is no iniquity, and Who
knows every man's merits. The leader
of the army in such wars, or the people
itself, are not so much the authors of the
war as the instruments.

> St. Augustine: *Quaestiones in
> Heptateuchum.* (4th cent.)

Nor was God ignorant that man would
sin, and that mortal men would go so
far on their monstrous course of sinning
that beasts devoid of rational will would
live together according to their kind on
a footing of greater peace and security
than men; for never have lions or drag-
ons waged such wars with one another
as men with men.

> St. Augustine: *The City of God,* 12, 23.
> (5th cent.)

If the Christian teaching condemned
wars of every kind, the injunction given
in the Gospel to the soldiers seeking
counsel as to salvation, would rather be
cast away their arms and withdraw themselves wholly from military service,
whereas what was said to them was: "Do
violence to no man, neither calumniate
any man; and be content with your pay"
(Luke 3, 14).

> St. Augustine: *Letter 138,* 2. (5th cent.)

Yet if human peace is so sweet for procuring the temporal salvation of men,
how much sweeter is peace with God for
procuring the eternal salvation of the
angels! So let it be your necessity and
not your choice that slays the enemy who
is fighting against you. Just as violence
is the portion of him who rebels and
resists, so mercy is the due of him who
has been conquered or captured, especially when a disturbance of the peace
is not to be feared.

> St. Augustine: *Letter 189.* (To Count
> Boniface, Governor of Africa.) (5th
> cent.)

O God, Who dost crush wars, and subdue the assailants of those who hope in
Thee by the power of Thy defence:
grant help to Thy servants who implore
Thy mercy; that having put down the
fierceness of their enemies, we may
praise Thee with a ceaseless thanksgiving.

> Roman Missal, Collect. (Originally
> Gelasian, 5th to 7th cent.)

For a war to be just three conditions are
necessary—public authority, just cause,
right motive.

> St. Thomas Aquinas: *Summa Theologica,*
> 2-2, 40, 1. (13th cent.)

O spirit that there enshrouded dost
  abide,
Not now is thy Romagna, and was not
  e'er,
  Without war in her tyrants' hearts.

> Dante: *Inferno, Canto 27.* (Tr. Binyon)
> (14th cent.)

War is sweet to those who don't know it.

> Erasmus: *Adagia.* (16th cent.)

Civil wars are the greatest of all evils.

> Pascal: *Pensées.* (17th cent.)

Can anything be more ridiculous than
that a man has a right to kill me because
he dwells the other side of the water,
and because his prince has a quarrel
with mine, although I have none with
him?

> Pascal: *Pensées.* (17th cent.)

War makes the valiant of his right secure,
And gives up fraud to be chastis'd with
  ease.

> Dryden: *Annus Mirabilis.* (17th cent.)

All delays are dangerous in war.

> Dryden: *Tyrannic Love*, 1. (Cf. Silius Italicus, 1st cent.) (17th cent.)

War is the trade of kings.

> Dryden: *King Arthur*, 2. (17th cent.)

War, he sung, is toil and trouble;
Honor but an empty bubble.

> Dryden: *Alexander's Feast*. (17th cent.)

Of old, between two nations was great war:
  Its cause, no mortal knew; nor when begun;
Therefore they combated so much the more,
  The sire his sword bequeathing to his son.

> Aubrey de Vere: *Infant Bridal*. (19th cent.)

As long as war is regarded as wicked it will always have its fascinations. When it is looked upon as vulgar, it will cease to be popular.

> Oscar Wilde: *The Critic as Artist*. (19th cent.)

And while this rose made round her cup,
  The armies died convulsed. And when
This chaste young silver sun went up
  Softly, a thousand shattered men,
One wet corruption, heaped the plain,
After a league-long throb of pain.

> Alice Meynell: *Summer in England, 1914*. (20th cent.)

Man pays that debt with new munificence,
  Not piecemeal now, not slowly, by the old:
Not grudgingly, by the effaced thin pence,
  But greatly and in gold.

> Alice Meynell: *Lord, I Owe Thee a Death*. (20th cent.)

Ye that follow the vision
  Of the world's weal afar,
Have ye met with derision
  And the red laugh of war?

> Alfred Noyes: *Love Will Find Out the Way*. (20th cent.)

Child of God, therefore children of God, therefore brothers. All wars are civil wars. The doctrine of sovereign states is superstition.

> Eric Gill: *It All Goes Together*. (20th cent.)

The community of nations must reckon with unprincipled criminals who, in order to realize their ambitious plans, are not afraid to unleash total war. This is the reason why other countries, if they wish to preserve their very existence and their most precious possessions, and unless they are prepared to accord free action to international criminals, have no alternative but to get ready for the day when they must defend themselves. This right to be prepared for self-defense cannot be denied, even in these days, to any state. That however does not in any way alter the fact that unjust war is to be accounted as one of the very gravest crimes which international penal law must proscribe, must punish with the heaviest penalties, and the authors of which are in every case guilty and liable to the punishment that has been agreed upon.

> Pope Pius XII: *Address to the 6th Int. Congr. of Penal Law*. (Oct. 3, 1953)

War and Peace

The purpose of all war is peace.

> St. Augustine: *The City of God*, 15. (5th cent.)

The most disadvantageous peace is better than the most just war.

> Erasmus: *Adagia*. (16th cent.)

Peace itself is war in masquerade.

> Dryden: *Absalom and Achitophel*, 1. (17th cent.)

Warning

Half warned, half armed.

John Heywood: *Proverbs,* 2, 6. (16th cent.)

Washington, George

The last act of his supreme magistracy was to inculcate in most impressive language on his countrymen . . . his deliberate and solemn advice; to bear incessantly in their minds that nations and individuals are under the moral government of an infinitely wise and just Providence; that the foundations of their happiness are morality and religion; and their union amongst themselves their rock of safety. . . .

May these United States flourish in pure and undefiled religion, in morality, peace, union, liberty and the enjoyment of their excellent Constitution, as long as respect, honor, and veneration shall gather around the name of Washington; that is, whilst there still shall be any surviving record of human events!

Archb. Carroll: *Eulogy of George Washington.* (1799)

His work well done, the leader stepped aside,
Spurning a crown with more than kingly pride,
Content to wear the higher crown of worth,
While time endures, First Citizen of earth.

J. J. Roche: *Washington.* (19th cent.)

A nobleness to try for,
A name to live and die for.

George P. Lathrop: *The Name of Washington.* (19th cent.)

Waste

A duchess may ruin a duke for a diamond necklace; but there is the necklace.

G. K. Chesterton: *What's Wrong with the World.* (20th cent.)

Water

Who water drinks at meals hath mischief brewed;
The stomach chilled voids undigested food.

School of Salerno, Code of Health. (11th cent.)

They drank the water clear,
Instead of wine, but yet they made good cheer.

Robert Henryson: *The Town and Country Mouse.* (15th cent.)

Foul water as soon as fair will quench hot fire.

John Heywood: *Proverbs,* 1, 5. (16th cent.)

The conscious water saw its God, and blushed.

R. Crashaw: *Upon the Water Made Wine.* (17th cent.)

Way

See Jesus Christ: The Way

Way of Life

In the Church there are three ways of life for the members of Christ: wedlock, widowhood, and virginity.

St. Augustine: *Sermons,* 196. (5th cent.)

Weakness

My grace is enough for thee; my strength finds its full scope in thy weakness (2 Cor. 12, 9). Thus by the plain voice of God it is shown that the guardian of power is weakness. For we are then kept to good effect within, when by God's appointment we are tempted to a bearable degree without, sometimes by bad propensities, sometimes by pressing misfortunes.

Pope St. Gregory I: *Morals,* 19, 12. (6th cent.)

The weaker hath the worse.

> John Heywood: *Proverbs,* 1, 10. (16th cent.)

Faint not, and fret not, for threaten'd
woe,
Watchman on truth's grey height!
Few though the faithful, and fierce
though the foe,
Weakness is aye heaven's might.

> Card. Newman: *The Watchman.* (19th cent.)

Wealth

The bread that you store up belongs to
the hungry; the cloak that lies in your
chest belongs to the naked; and the gold
that you have hidden in the ground belongs to the poor.

> St. Basil: *Homilies,* 2. (4th cent.)

Nothing is more fallacious than wealth.
Today it is for thee, tomorrow it is
against thee. It arms the eyes of the
envious everywhere. It is a hostile comrade, a domestic enemy.

> St. John Chrysostom: *Homilies.* (4th cent.)

The friends of Job, who railed at him
before,
Came cap in hand, when he had three
times more.

> Dryden. (17th cent.)

The golden lure
Of wealth, insatiate and unsure.

> Lionel Johnson: *Laleham.* (19th cent.)

Certainly it is our theory, that wealth
will be a protection against political
corruption. The English statesman is
bribed not to be bribed. He is born with
a silver spoon in his mouth, so that he
may never afterwards be found with the
silver spoons in his pocket.

> G. K. Chesterton: *What's Wrong with the World.* (20th cent.)

Wealth which is constantly being aug-
mented by social and economic progress,
must be so distributed amongst the various individuals and classes of society
that the common good of all . . . be
thereby promoted.

> Pope Pius XI: *Quadragesimo Anno.* (May 15, 1931)

Each class must receive its due share,
and the distribution of created goods
must be brought into conformity with
the demands of the common good and
social justice, for every sincere observer
is conscious that the vast differences between the few who hold excessive wealth
and the many who live in destitution
constitute a grave evil in modern society.

> Pope Pius XI: *Quadragesimo Anno.* (May 15, 1931)

Justice requires that all men acknowledge and defend the sacrosanct rights
of human freedom and human dignity,
and that the infinite wealth and resources
with which God has endowed the whole
of the earth, shall be distributed, in conformity with right reason, for the use
of all His children.

> Pope Pius XII: *Easter Message of Peace.* (Apr. 9, 1939)

Wear

All thing is the worse for the wearing.

> John Heywood: *Proverbs,* 2, 1. (16th cent.)

Weather

After clouds black, we shall have
weather clear.

> John Heywood: *Proverbs,* 1, 11. (16th cent.)

There's much afoot in heaven and earth
this year;
The winds hunt up the sun, hunt up
the moon,
Trouble the dubious dawn, hasten the
drear
Height of a threatening noon.

> Alice Meynell: *The Rainy Summer.* (20th cent.)

Wedding

Christians, when they attend weddings, shall not jump and dance, but shall partake of the meal or breakfast with a modesty becoming Christians.

Council of Laodicea, Can. 53. (365)

Wedding is destiny
And hanging likewise.

John Heywood: *Proverbs*, 1, 3. (16th cent.)

It is meet that a man be at his own bridal.

John Heywood: *Proverbs*, 1, 6. (16th cent.)

The time approached; to church the parties went,
At once with carnal and devout intent.

Pope: *January and May*. (18th cent.)

See also Marriage

Weed

Ill weed groweth fast.

John Heywood: *Proverbs*, 1, 10. (16th cent.)

Weeping

I wept not, so to stone within I grew.

Dante: *Inferno, Canto 33*. (14th cent.)

Better children weep than old men.

John Heywood: *Proverbs*, 1, 11. (16th cent.)

Weeping is the ease of woe.

Richard Crashaw: *The Weeper*. (17th cent.)

Welfare

Stretch forth, O Lord, the right hand of heavenly assistance to Thy faithful servants; that they may seek Thee with their whole heart, and obtain what they rightly ask for.

Roman Missal, Collect. (Gregorian, ca. 7th cent.)

Well

There is a well, a willow-shaded spot,
Cool in the noon-tide gleam,
With rushes nodding in the little stream,
And blue forget-me-not.

F. W. Faber: *The Cherwell Water Lily*. (19th cent.)

Beyond the four seas of Eire, beyond the sunset's rim,
It lies half forgot, in a valley deep and dim;
Like a star of fire from the skies' gold tire,
And whoso drinks the nine drops shall win his heart's desire—
At the Well o' the World's End.

Ethna Carberry: *Well o' the World's End*. (19th cent.)

Wheat

I am God's wheat; I am ground by the teeth of the wild beasts that I may end as the pure bread of Christ.

St. Ignatius of Antioch: *Letter to the Romans*, 4. (Describing himself.) (2nd cent.)

Wheel

Call upon the wheels, master, call upon the wheels,
Steel is beneath your hand, stone beneath your heels—
Men of tact that arbitrate, slow reform that heals—
Save the stinking grease, master, save it for the wheels.

G. K. Chesterton: *The Song of the Wheels*. (20th cent.)

Whistling

He trudg'd along unknowing what he sought,
And whistled as he went, for want of thought.

Dryden: *Cymon and Iphigenia*. (17th cent.)

Whistling to keep myself from being afraid.

> Dryden: *Amphitryon*, 3, 1. (17th cent.)

White

What is white?
  The soul of the sage, faith-lit,
The trust of age,
  The infant's untaught wit.
What more white?
  The face of Truth made known,
The voice of youth
  Singing before her throne.

> Thomas MacDonagh: *What is White?* (20th cent.)

Wickedness

I am Juniper and I am wicked.
  That's as sure as steel is blue,
Juniper, the fool, is wicked,
  Little Father, it is true.

> Eileen Duggan: *Juniper.* (20th cent.)

Widow

Teach widows to be prudent in the faith of the Lord, and to pray without ceasing for all, to keep far from all calumny, slander, false witness, love of money, and every evil, knowing that they are an altar of God, that He inspects all things, and that not one of their calculations or thoughts or *the hidden things of the heart* (1 Cor. 14, 25) escapes Him.

> St. Polycarp: *Letter to the Philippians*, 4. (2nd cent.)

Second marriages are lawful, but holy widowhood is better.

> St. Augustine: *On the Good of Widowhood.* (5th cent.)

The devout widow never desires to be esteemed either beautiful or comely, contenting herself with being such as God desires her to be, that is to say, humble and abject in her own eyes.

> St. Francis de Sales: *Introduction to the Devout Life*, 40. (17th cent.)

A virgin widow and a mourning bride.

> Dryden: *Palamon and Arcite*, 3. (17th cent.)

No crafty widows shall approach my bed:
They are too wise for bachelors to wed.

> Pope: *January and May.* (18th cent.)

What's all the world to a man when his wife's a widow?

> Seumas MacManus: *Heavy Hangs the Golden Grain.* (20th cent.)

Life's pleasantest three: A cat's kitten, a goat's kid, and a young widow.

> Seumas MacManus: *Heavy Hangs the Golden Grain.* (20th cent.)

It's bad manners to begin courting a widow before she gets home from the funeral.

> Seumas MacManus: *Heavy Hangs the Golden Grain.* (20th cent.)

Wife

Let us teach our wives to remain in the faith taught them and in charity and purity to cherish their husbands in all truth, loving all others impartially in complete chastity, and to bring up their children in the fear of God.

> St. Polycarp: *Letter to the Philippians*, 4. (2nd cent.)

Have no fear, blessed sisters; no wife is ugly to her own husband.

> Tertullian: *Women's Dress.* (3rd cent.)

It involves less misery to possess an unattractive than to keep under surveillance a beautiful wife.

> John of Salisbury: *Policraticus*, 8, 11, 297. (12th cent.)

It is arrogant for one who has taken a second wife to accuse Venus of hostility.

> John of Salisbury: *Policraticus*, 8, 11, 299. (12th cent.)

This flower of wifely patience.

> Chaucer: *The Clerkes Tale*. (14th cent.)

I have a wife, the worste that may be;
For though the fiend to her y-coupled
were,
She would him overmatch, I dare well
swear.

> Chaucer: *The Marchantes Tale: Prologue*.
> (14th cent.)

One shouldn't be too inquisitive in life
Either about God's secrets or one's
wife.

> Chaucer: *The Miller's Tale*. (Tr. Coghill)
> (14th cent.)

But who may have a more ungracious
life
Than a child's bird and a knave's wife?

> J. Skelton: *Garlande of Laurell*. (16th
> cent.)

He that will thrive must ask leave of
his wife.

> John Heywood: *Proverbs*, 1, 11. (16th
> cent.)

Oh! what choice may compare to the
devil's life
Like his that have chosen a devil to his
wife?

> John Heywood: *Proverbs*, 2, 6. (16th
> cent.)

Bachelors boast how they will teach their
wives good.

> John Heywood: *Proverbs*, 2, 6. (16th
> cent.)

The devil with his dam hath more rest
in hell
Than I have here with thee.

> John Heywood: *Proverbs*, 2, 7. (16th
> cent.)

Down Theseus went to hell, Pirith his
friend to find:
O that wives in these our days were to
their mates as kind!

> Nicholas Grimald: *Of Friendship*. (16th
> cent.)

Here lies my wife: here let her lie!
Now she's at rest, and so am I.

> Dryden: *Epitaph Intended for his Wife*.
> (17th cent.)

All other goods by fortune's hands are
given:
A wife is the peculiar gift of heav'n.

> Pope: *January and May*. (18th cent.)

Horses (thou sayest) and asses men
may try,
And ring suspected vessels ere they
buy;
But wives, a random choice, untried
they take;
They dream in courtship, but in wedlock wake.

> Pope: *The Wife of Bath*. (18th cent.)

No man should have a secret from his
wife. She invariably finds it out.

> Oscar Wilde: *An Ideal Husband*, 2. (19th
> cent.)

When you go forth to find a wife, leave
your eyes at home but take both ears
with you.

> Seumas MacManus: *Heavy Hangs the
> Golden Grain*. (20th cent.)

There's only one thing in the world
better than a good wife—no wife.

> Seumas MacManus: *Heavy Hangs the
> Golden Grain*. (20th cent.)

Never make a toil of a pleasure, as Billy
Ban said when he dug his wife's grave
only three feet deep.

> Seumas MacManus: *Heavy Hangs the
> Golden Grain*. (20th cent.)

See also Husband and Wife

Wilde, Oscar

Queerly enough, it was the very multitude of his falsities that prevented him
from being entirely false. Like a many-
colored humming top, he was at once a
bewilderment and a balance. He was so

fond of being many-sided that among his sides he even admitted the right side. He loved so much to multiply his souls that he had among them one soul at least that was saved. He desired all beautiful things—even God.

> G. K. Chesterton: *A Handful of Authors.* (20th cent.)

I heard his golden voice and marked
  him trace
Under the common thing the hidden
  grace,
And conjure wonder out of emptiness,
Till mean things put on beauty like a
  dress
And all the world was an enchanted
  place.

> Lord Alfred Douglas: *The Dead Poet.* (20th cent.)

Wilderness

What would the world be, once bereft
Of wet and of wildness? Let them be
  left,
O let them be left, wildness and wet;
Long live the weeds and the wilderness
  yet.

> G. M. Hopkins: *Inversnaid.* (19th cent.)

Wilfulness

We loath our manna, and we long for
  quails;
Ah, what is man, when his own wish
  prevails!
How rash, how swift to plunge himself
  in ill;
Proud of his pow'r and boundless in
  his will!

> Dryden: *The Medall.* (17th cent.)

Will

It is therefore no monstrousness, partly to will, and partly not to will, but a sickness of the soul to be so weighted down by custom that it cannot wholly rise even with the support of truth. Thus there are two wills in us, because neither

of them is entire: and what is lacking to the one is present in the other.

> St. Augustine: *Confessions,* 8, 9. (5th cent.)

It is certain that we keep the commandments if we so will; but because the will is prepared by the Lord, we must ask Him for such a force of will as suffices to make us act by willing. It is certain that it is we who will when we will, but it is He who makes us will what is good.

> St. Augustine: *De Gratia et Libero Arbitrio,* 17, 32. (5th cent.)

It is by the will that we sin, and live righteously.

> St. Augustine: *Retractiones,* 1, 9. (5th cent.)

To hate one's own will.

> St. Benedict: *Rule,* 4. (One of his 'tools of good works') (6th cent.)

For this is the property of that eternal and just law of God, that he who would not be ruled with gentleness by God, should be ruled as a punishment by his own self; and that all those who have willingly thrown off the gentle yoke and light burden of charity would bear unwillingly the insupportable burden of their own will.

> St. Bernard: *Letters.* (12th cent.)

To will change is not the same as to change will.

> St. Thomas Aquinas: *Summa Theologica,* 1, 19, 7. (13th cent.)

Like will to like.

> John Heywood: *Proverbs,* 1, 4. (16th cent.)

Will will have will though will woe win.

> J. Heywood: *Proverbs,* 1, 11. (16th cent.)

It is the will only that God desires, but all the other powers run after it to be united to God with it.

> Francis de Sales: *Treatise on the Love of God,* 7, 2. (17th cent.)

He who could walk the waters could also ride triumphantly upon what is still more fickle, unstable, tumultuous, treacherous—the billows of human wills, human purposes, human hearts.

> Card. Newman. (19th cent.)

All that God asks of us is our will; when given to Him, in whatever condition, He will make it good.

> Archb. Ullathorne: *Humility and Patience.* (19th cent.)

Thy will is the sovereign measure
And only event of things:
The puniest heart, defying,
Were stronger than all these kings.

> Louise Imogen Guiney: *The Kings.* (19th cent.)

The will is the lynch-pin of the faculties.

> Francis Thompson. (19th cent.)

The way the will becomes strong is . . . by doing small things you've made up your mind to do, however much you don't want to do them at the time.

> R. H. Benson: *The Coward.* (20th cent.)

The will is quite close to us; it is that through which we consciously act, after having heard the reasons for or against action suggested by the other faculties. But the will is, after all, a faculty of itself—not self itself.

> R. H. Benson: *The Mirror of Shalott.* (20th cent.)

You've got to live by your will, and not by your imagination—in quite small things.

> R. H. Benson: *The Coward.* (20th cent.)

Religion . . . must at least touch the will; for however small our will may be, it is always large enough to be united to the will of God.

> R. H. Benson: *Christ in the Church.* (20th cent.)

Starve the imagination and feed the will. It's for want of that, in these days of nervous systems and rush and excitement, that so many people break down.

> R. H. Benson: *The Coward.* (20th cent.)

The worship of will is the negation of will. To admire mere choice is to refuse to choose. If Mr. Bernard Shaw comes up to me and says, "Will something," that is tantamount to saying, "I do not mind what you will," and that is tantamount to saying, "I have no will in the matter." You cannot admire will in general, because the essence of will is that it is particular.

> G. K. Chesterton: *Orthodoxy.* (20th cent.)

Will (*Testament*)

Every person shall have the liberty to leave at his death any property that he wishes to the most holy and venerable council of the Catholic Church. Wills shall not become void. There is nothing which is more due to men than that the expression of their last will, after which they can no longer will anything, shall be free and the power of choice, which does not return again, shall be unhampered.

> Edict of the Emperor Constantine I. (Theod. Code, 16, 2, 4) (321)

Happy who never trust a stranger's will,
Whose friendship's in his interest understood!
Since money giv'n but tempts him to be ill,
When pow'r is too remote to make him good.

> Dryden: *Annus Mirabilis.* (17th cent.)

Willingness

Nothing is impossible to a willing heart.

> John Heywood: *Proverbs,* 1, 4. (16th cent.)

Wind

I know, and knew, which way the wind
blew and will blow.

John Heywood: *Proverbs*, 2, 9. (16th
cent.)

The wind was fair, but blew a mackrel
gale.

Dryden: *The Hind and the Panther*, 3.
(17th cent.)

O wind, thou hast thy kingdom in the
      trees,
    And all thy royalties
Sweep through the land today.
    It is mid-June,
And thou with all thy instruments in
      tune,
    Thine orchestra
Of heaving fields and heavy swinging
      fir,
    Strikest a lay
    That doth rehearse
Her ancient freedom to the universe.

Michael Field: *A Summer Wind*. (19th
cent.)

O what a miracle wind is this
    Has crossed the English land today
With an unprecedented kiss,
    And wonderfully found a way!

Alice Meynell: *A Wind of Clear Weather
in England*. (20th cent.)

    The wind is blind,
Is blind alone. How has he hurled
His ignorant lash, his aimless dart,
His eyeless rush upon the world,
    Unseeing, to break his unknown
      heart!

Alice Meynell: *The Wind is Blind*. (20th
cent.)

A flock of winds came winging from
    the north,
Strong birds with fighting pinions driv-
    ing forth
    With a resounding call:—

Where will they close their wings and
    cease their cries —

Between what warming seas and con-
    quering skies —
    And fold, and fall?

Alice Meynell: *The Roaring Frost*. (20th
cent.)

Another day awakes. And who—
    Changing the world—is this?
He comes at whiles, the winter through,
    West wind! I would not miss
His sudden tryst: the long, the new
    Surprises of his kiss.

Vigilant, I make haste to close
    With him who comes my way,
I go to meet him as he goes;
    I know his note, his lay,
His color and his morning-rose,
    And I confess his day.

Alice Meynell: *West Wind in Winter*.
(20th cent.)

There sits a piper on the hill
    Who pipes the livelong day,
And when he pipes both loud and
      shrill,
    The frightened people say:
"The wind, the wind is blowing up
    'Tis rising to a gale,"
The women hurry to the shore
    To watch some distant sail.
The wind, the wind, the wind, the
    wind
    Is blowing to a gale.

Dora Sigerson Shorter: *The Piper on the
Hill*. (20th cent.)

The wind was a torrent of darkness
among the gusty trees.

Alfred Noyes: *The Highwayman*. (20th
cent.)

Wine

Wine was given us of God, not that we
might be drunken, but that we might be
sober; that we might be glad, not that
we get ourselves pain.

St. John Chrysostom: *Homilies*. (4th
cent.)

Wine is for mirth, and not for madness.

St. John Chrysostom. (4th cent.)

Ripe, good old wine imparts a richer
blood
To him who daily tastes its tonic flood.

School of Salerno, Code of Health. (11th
cent.)

Whoe'er of too much ruby wine partakes,
Himself, forsooth, both hoarse and
costive makes.

School of Salerno, Code of Health. (11th
cent.)

Rich, heavy wines that are both sweet
and white,
The body's size increase, and e'en its
might.

School of Salerno, Code of Health. (11th
cent.)

The taste of wines, their clearness,
odor, shade,
Are living proofs of their specific
grade;
You'll find all those that are of highest
source,
Fragrant, frigid, fair, fuming high with
force.

School of Salerno, Code of Health. (11th
cent.)

Wine taken with excess,
As Scripture doth express,
Causeth great heaviness
Unto the mind.

But they that take pleasure
To drink it with measure
No doubt a great treasure
They shall it find.

Anonymous: *Temperance.* (14th cent.)

Ye praise the wine before ye taste of
the grape.

John Heywood: *Proverbs,* 1, 10. (16th
cent.)

Let the King
Me ever into these his cellars bring
Where flows such wine as we can have
of none
But him who trod the wine-press all
alone:

Wine of youth, life, and the sweet
deaths of love;
Wine of immortal mixture, which can
prove
Its tincture from the rosy nectar; wine
That can exalt weak earth, and so refine
Our dust, that at one draught, mortality
May drink itself up, and forget to die.

Richard Crashaw: *Apology for Hymn to
St. Teresa.* (17th cent.)

The modest nymph [i.e. water] saw its
God and blushed. (Nympha pudica
Deum vidit, et erubuit.)

Richard Crashaw: *Epigrammatum
Sacrorum.* (Of the miracle at Cana.)
(17th cent.)

Inflaming wine, pernicious to mankind,
Unnerves the limbs, and dulls the noble
mind.

Pope: *Tr. of Homer: Iliad,* 6. (18th
cent.)

Wine can of their wits the wise beguile,
Make the sage frolic, and the serious
smile.

Pope: *Tr. of Homer: Odyssey,* 14. (18th
cent.)

And Noah he often said to his wife
when he sat down to dine,
"I don't care where the water goes if it
doesn't get into the wine."

G. K. Chesterton: *The Flying Inn.* (20th
cent.)

Our souls shall be leviathans
In purple seas of wine
When drunkenness is dead with death,
And drink is all divine;
Learning in those immortal vats
What mortal vineyards mean;
For only in heaven we shall know
How happy we have been.
. . . .
Measure is here, and law, to learn,
When honor rules it so,
To lift the glass and lay it down
Or break the glass and go.
But when the world's new deluge boils

From the new Noah's vine,
Our souls shall be leviathans
In sanguine seas of wine.

> G. K. Chesterton: *The Red Sea.* (20th cent.)

When Horace wrote his noble verse,
His brilliant, glowing line,
He must have gone to bed the worse
For good Falernian wine.
No poet yet could praise the rose
In verse that so serenely flows
Unless he dipped his Roman nose
In good Falernian wine.

> Theodore Maynard: *A Tankard of Ale.* (20th cent.)

Wing

O, unknown Eros? What this breeze
Of sudden wings
Speeding at far returns of time from
interstellar space
To fan my very face,
And gone as fleet,
Through delicatest ether feathering
soft their solitary beat,
With ne'er a light plume dropp'd, nor
any trace
To speak of whence they came, or
whither they depart?

> Coventry Patmore: *To the Unknown Eros.* (19th cent.)

Winking

He winketh with the tone eye and
looketh with the tother.

> John Heywood: *Proverbs,* 1, 11. (16th cent.)

Winning

He laugheth that winneth.

> John Heywood: *Proverbs,* 1, 5. (16th cent.)

There is no such thing as fighting on the
winning side: one fights to find out
which is the winning side.

> G. K. Chesterton: *What's Wrong with the World.* (20th cent.)

Winter

But hasty winter, with one blast, hath
brought
The hopes of autumn, summer, spring,
to nought.

> Dryden: *Upon the Death of Lord Hastings.* (17th cent.)

Wisdom

Wisdom is the foundation, and justice
the work without which a foundation
cannot stand.

> St. Ambrose: *On the Duties of the Clergy,* 1, 251. (4th cent.)

Dost thou hold wisdom to be anything
other than truth, wherein we behold and
embrace the supreme good?

> St. Augustine: *De Libero Arbitrio,* 2, 9, 27. (4th cent.)

There are not many wisdoms, or orders
of truth; there is but one wisdom, one
order of truth; and in that there are immense and unchangeable treasures of
things intelligible, including all invisible and unchangeable ideals (*rationes*),
even of things visible and changeable
which by this wisdom are made.

> St. Augustine: *The City of God,* 11, 10. (5th cent.)

Let your old age be childlike, and your
childhood like old age; that is, so that
neither may your wisdom be with pride,
nor your humility without wisdom.

> St. Augustine: *In Ps. 112,* 2. (5th cent.)

Great are those two gifts, wisdom and
continence: wisdom, forsooth, whereby
we are formed in the knowledge of
God; continence whereby we are not
conformed to this world.

> St. Augustine: *De Bono Viduitatis,* 15, 2, 21. (5th cent.)

Whatever you depend on in yourself of
wisdom or power, attribute it to Him
Who is the Wisdom and Power of God
—that is, to Christ.

> St. Bernard: *Sermons on the Canticle of Canticles,* 13. (12th cent.)

The first task of man aspiring to wisdom is the consideration of what he himself is: what is within him, what without, what below, what above, what opposite, what before, and what after.

> John of Salisbury: *Policraticus,* 3, 2, 174. (12th cent.)

This is the greatest wisdom, by despising the world to tend to heavenly kingdoms.

> Thomas a Kempis: *The Imitation of Christ,* 1, 1. (15th cent.)

There is a great difference between the wisdom of an illuminated and devout man, and the knowledge of a learned and studious scholar.

> Thomas a Kempis: *The Imitation of Christ,* 3, 31. (15th cent.)

Fruitless is the wisdom of him who has no knowledge of himself.

> Erasmus: *Enchiridion.* (16th cent.)

It is great folly to wish to be wise with an impossible wisdom.

> St. Francis de Sales: *Treatise on the Love of God,* 1, 3. (17th cent.)

The assembled souls of all that men held wise.

> Sir William Davenant: *Gondibert,* 2, 5. (17th cent.)

Ask, who is wise?—You'll find the self-same man
A sage in France, a madman in Japan;
And here some head beneath a mitre swells,
Which there had tingled to a cap and bells.

> Thomas Moore: *The Sceptic.* (19th cent.)

Wisdom is the clear, calm, accurate vision and comprehension of the whole course, the whole work of God; and though there is none who has it in its fulness but he who *searcheth all things, yea, the deep things* of the Creator, yet *by the Spirit* they are in a measure *revealed unto us.*

> Card. Newman. (19th cent.)

So still the ruler by the ruled takes rule,
And wisdom weaves itself i' the loom
o' the fool.

> F. Thompson: *Sister Songs.* (19th cent.)

He may die of wind but he'll never die of wisdom.

> Seumas MacManus: *Heavy Hangs the Golden Grain.* (20th cent.)

Wishing

Wishers and woulders be no good householders.

> John Heywood: *Proverbs,* 1, 11. (16th cent.)

For not to wish is not to be deceived.

> Dryden. (17th cent.)

I'd rather be handsome than homely;
I'd rather be youthful than old;
If I can't have a bushel of silver
I'll do with a barrel of gold.

> J. J. Roche: *Contentment.* (19th cent.)

Wit

Two have more wit than one.

> John Gower: *Confessio Amantis.* (14th cent.)

When they were driven to their wits' end.

> Lydgate: *Assembly of Gods.* (15th cent.)

A professional wit—a bad character.

> Pascal: *Pensées.* (17th cent.)

When our great monarch into exile went,
Wit and religion suffer'd banishment.

> Dryden: *To My Lord Chancellor.* (17th cent.)

Wit may be defined as justness of thought and a facility of expression, or (in the midwives' phrase) a perfect conception with an easy delivery.

Pope: *Letter to William Wycherley.* (18th cent.)

True wit is nature to advantage dress'd,
What oft was thought, but ne'er so well expressed.

Pope: *An Essay on Criticism,* 2. (18th cent.)

Whose wit, in the combat, as gentle as bright,
Ne'er carried a heart-stain away on its blade.

Thomas Moore: *Lines on the Death of Sheridan.* (19th cent.)

A man may enjoy humor all by himself; he may see a joke when no one else sees it; he may see the point and avoid it. But wit is a sword; it is meant to make people feel the point as well as see it. All honest people saw the point of Mark Twain's wit. Not a few dishonest people felt it.

G. K. Chesterton: *A Handful of Authors.* (20th cent.)

Witchcraft

I am absolutely certain that there is such a thing as witchcraft. I impute a belief in it to common sense, to experience and the records of experience, and to a broad view of humanity as a whole. I impute disbelief in it to inexperience, to provincial ignorance, to local limitations, and all the vices that balance the virtues of [Upper] Tooting. Common sense will show that the habit of invoking evil spirits, often because they were evil, has existed in far too vast a variety of different cultures, classes and social conditions to be a chance piece of childish credulity. Experience will show that it is *not* true that it disappears everywhere before the advance of education; on the contrary, some of its most evil ministers have been the most highly educated.

G. K. Chesterton: *The Common Man.* (20th cent.)

Woe

That bank of woe
Wherein all the evil of the world is penned.

Dante: *Inferno, Canto 7.* (Tr. Binyon) (14th cent.)

O sudden woe, that ever art successor
To worldly bliss!

Chaucer: *The Man of Law's Tale.* (14th cent.)

Wolf

To keep the wolf from the door.

John Heywood: *Proverbs,* 2, 7. (16th cent.)

Woman

The judgment of God upon your sex endures even today; and with it inevitably endures your position of criminal at the bar of justice. You are the gateway of the devil.

Tertullian: *Women's Dress,* 1. (3rd cent.)

And let the women stand in the assembly by themselves apart from the men, both the baptized women and the women catechumens.

St. Hippolytus: *The Apostolic Tradition,* 18. (3rd cent.)

The beauty of women is the greatest snare. Or rather, not the beauty of woman, but unchastened gazing.

St. John Chrysostom: *Homilies.* (4th cent.)

Nothing so much casts down the mind of man from its citadel as do the blandishments of women, and that physical contact without which a wife cannot be possessed.

St. Augustine: *Soliloquies,* 1. (4th cent.)

Woman is a thrall
Disposed and ruled over by men in all!

Chaucer: *The Man of Law's Tale.* (Tr. Coghill) (14th cent.)

For women, speaking generally, are prone
To follow fortune's favors, once they're known.

Chaucer: *The Knight's Tale.* (Tr. Coghill) (14th cent.)

For half so boldly can there no man
Swear and lyen as a woman can.

Chaucer: *The Wife of Bath's Prologue.* (14th cent.)

Deceit, weeping, spinning, God hath give
To women kindly, while we may live.

Chaucer: *Wife of Bath's Prologue.* (Tr. of Latin Proverb: Fallere, flere, nere, Dedit Deus in muliere.) (14th cent.)

For take my word for it, there is no libel
On women that the clergy will not paint,
Except when writing of a woman-saint,
But never good of other women, though.

Chaucer: *The Wife of Bath's Prologue.* (Tr. Coghill) (14th cent.)

Nothing is to man so dear
As woman's love in good manner.
A good woman is man's bliss,
Where her love right and steadfast is.

Robert Mannyng: *The Handling of Sins.* (14th cent.)

If women might be suffered to begin once in the congregation to fall in disputing, those aspen leaves of theirs would never leave wagging.

St. Thomas More. (16th cent.)

A woman hath nine lives like a cat.

John Heywood: *Proverbs,* 2, 4. (16th cent.)

I believe that all men must have a greater affection for those women whom they see disposed to be good: and even for the attainment of earthly ends, women must have more power over men because they are good.

St. Teresa of Jesus: *Autobiography,* 5. (16th cent.)

O women! woe to men; traps for their falls;
Still actors in all tragical mischances;
Earth's necessary ills, captiving thralls,
Now murdering with your tongues, now with your glances;
Parents of life and love, spoilers of both,
The thieves of hearts, false, do you love or loath!

Bl. Robert Southwell: *St Peter's Complaint.* (16th cent.)

Whoe'er she be,
That not impossible she,
That shall command my heart and me.

R. Crashaw: *Wishes to his (Supposed) Mistress.* (17th cent.)

Heaven, when it strives to polish all it can
Its last best work, but forms a softer man.

Pope: *Moral Essays,* 2. (18th cent.)

In men we various ruling passions find;
In women two almost divide the kind;
Those only fixed, they first or last obey,
The love of pleasure, and the love of sway.

Pope: *Moral Essays,* 2. (18th cent.)

Most women have no characters at all.

Pope: *Moral Essays,* 2. (18th cent.)

When the father of gods and men presented the newly created woman to the council of Olympus, we know that she was greeted with peals of laughter; and to this day there is nothing that a woman of well-balanced mind hates more in a man than his taking her too much *au grand sérieux.*

Coventry Patmore: *Religio Poetae.* (19th cent.)

A woman, like the Koh-i-noor,
Mounts to the price that's put on her.

Coventry Patmore: *The Angel in the House.* (19th cent.)

Ah, wasteful woman, she who may
  On her sweet self set her own price,
Knowing man cannot choose but pay,
  How has she cheapen'd Paradise;
How given for nought her priceless
    gift,
  How spoil'd the bread and spill'd
    the wine,
Which, spent with due respective thrift,
  Had made brutes men and men di-
    vine.

> Coventry Patmore: *The Angel in the
> House.* (19th cent.)

A woman is a foreign land,
  Of which, though there he settle
    young
A man will ne'er quite understand
  The customs, politics, and tongue.

> Coventry Patmore: *The Angel in the
> House.* (19th cent.)

I am on the side of the Trojans. They
fought for a woman.

> Oscar Wilde: *The Picture of Dorian Gray,*
> 17. (19th cent.)

Describe us as a sex, was her challenge.
Sphinxes without secrets.

> Oscar Wilde: *The Picture of Dorian Gray,*
> 17. (19th cent.)

Many a woman has a past; but I am told
that she has a dozen, and that they all fit.

> Oscar Wilde: *Lady Windermere's Fan,* 1.
> (19th cent.)

A woman with a past has no future.

> Oscar Wilde: *Lady Windermere's Fan.*
> (19th cent.)

The history of women is the history of
the worst form of tyranny the world has
ever known. The tyranny of the weak
over the strong. It is the only tyranny
that lasts.

> Oscar Wilde: *A Woman of No
> Importance,* 3. (19th cent.)

There is no limit to the power of a good
woman.

> R. H. Benson: *The Sentimentalists.* (20th
> cent.)

The women have a lot to bear. I do be
thinkin' often God must be sorry He
didn't make them harder.

> Katharine T. Hinkson: *The Dear Irish
> Girl.* (20th cent.)

Women generally make up in heat what
they lack in debating power.

> K. T. Hinkson: *A Daughter of Kings.*
> (20th cent.)

There is nothing a woman so dislikes as
to have her old opinions quoted to her,
especially when they confute new ones.

> Katharine T. Hinkson: *Her Ladyship.*
> (20th cent.)

Variability is one of the virtues of a
woman. It obviates the crude requirements of polygamy. If you have a good
wife you are sure to have a spiritual
harem.

> G. K. Chesterton: *Daily News.* (20th
> cent.)

There are only three things in the world
that women do not understand: and they
are Liberty, Equality and Fraternity.

> G. K. Chesterton: *On Women.* (20th
> cent.)

Right wise it was of our Colm (Columba) when founding in Iona his famous
sixth century school and colony of
monks and scholars, he forbade the
bringing in of a cow. "Where comes a
cow," the wise man laid down, "there
follows a woman; and where comes a
woman follows trouble."

> Seumas MacManus: *Heavy Hangs the
> Golden Grain.* (20th cent.)

Womanhood

I love thee, dear, for what thou art,
  Nor would I wish thee otherwise,
For when thy lashes lift apart
  I read, deep-mirrored in thine eyes,
The glory of a modest heart.

Wert thou as fair as thou art good,
  It were not given to any man,

With daring eyes of flesh and blood,
  To look thee in the face and scan
The splendor of thy womanhood.

> T. A. Daly: *To a Plain Sweetheart.* (20th
> cent.)

Women, Holy

High let us all our voices raise
In that heroic woman's praise
Whose name, with saintly glory bright,
Shines in the starry realms of light.

> Roman Breviary, Feasts of Holy Women,
> hymn *Fortem virili pectore.* (Tr. E.
> Caswall) (Card. S. Antoniano, 1540–
> 1603)

Wonder

This wonder lasted nine days.

> John Heywood: *Proverbs,* 2, 1. (16th
> cent.)

Wonder is especially proper to childhood, and it is the sense of wonder above
all that keeps us young.

> Gerald Vann: *The Water and the Fire.*
> (20th cent.)

Woods

Midway the journey of this life I was
    'ware
  That I had strayed into a dark forest,
  And the right path appeared not any-
    where.

> Dante: *Inferno, Canto* 1. (Opening lines
> of *Divine Comedy,* tr. Binyon) (14th
> cent.)

Wooing

            Nigh and sly
Wins against Fair and Square who isn't
  there.

> Chaucer: *The Miller's Tale.* (Tr. Coghill)
> (14th cent.)

A man shall win us best with flattery.

> Chaucer: *Wife of Bath's Tale.* (14th
> cent.)

As ancient ladies do
That courted long at length are forc'd
  to woo.

> Dryden: *To My Lord Chancellor.* (17th
> cent.)

But as men say, Where heart is failed,
There shall no castle be assailed.

> John Gower: *Confessio Amantis,* 5. (14th
> cent.)

The time I've lost in wooing,
  In watching and pursuing
    The light that lies
    In woman's eyes,
Has been my heart's undoing.

> Thomas Moore: *The Time I've Lost in
> Wooing.* (19th cent.)

If I speak to thee in friendship's name,
  Thou think'st I speak too coldly;
If I mention love's devoted flame,
  Thou say'st I speak too boldly.

> Thomas Moore: *How Shall I Woo?* (19th
> cent.)

Ah, whither shall a maiden flee,
  When a bold youth so swift pursues,
And siege of tenderest courtesy,
  With hope perseverant, still renews?

> Coventry Patmore: *The Angel in the
> House.* (19th cent.)

Forward and backward all in one; that
is the way a woman loves to be wooed.

> R. H. Benson: *By What Authority.* (20th
> cent.)

Word

What is word but wind?

> Anonymous: *Ancrene Riwle,* 122. (13th
> cent.)

No less flattering in her word,
That purely, her simple record
Was found as true as any bond.

> Chaucer: *Book of the Duchesse.* (14th
> cent.)

A glutton of words.

> Langland: *Piers Plowman,* Passus 1. (14th cent.)

To the intelligent man a word is enough.

> Thomas a Kempis: *The Imitation of Christ,* 3, 34. (Latin proverb.) (15th cent.)

It hurteth not the tongue to give fair words.

> John Heywood: *Proverbs,* 1, 9. (16th cent.)

Fair words make fools fain.

> John Heywood: *Proverbs,* 2, 5. (16th cent.)

Such distance is between high words
and deeds!
In proof, the greatest vaunter seldom
speeds.

> Bl. Robert Southwell: *St. Peter's Complaint.* (16th cent.)

What things have we seen
Done at the Mermaid! heard words
that have been
So nimble and so full of subtle flame
As if that every one from whence they
came
Had meant to put his whole wit in a
jest,
And resolved to live a fool the rest
Of his dull life.

> Francis Beaumont: *Letter to Ben Jonson.* (17th cent.)

And torture one poor word ten thousand
ways.

> Dryden: *Mac Flecknoe.* (17th cent.)

Harsh words, though pertinent, uncouth
appear;
None please the fancy who offend the
ear.

> Sir Samuel Garth: *The Dispensary,* 4. (17th cent.)

A barren superfluity of words.

> Sir Samuel Garth: *The Dispensary,* 2. (17th cent.)

Nothing is more common than for men
to think that because they are familiar
with words, they understand the ideas
they stand for.

> Card. Newman: *Parochial and Plain Sermons,* 1. (19th cent.)

Every word man's lips have uttered
Echoes in God's skies.

> Adelaide Procter: *Words.* (19th cent.)

Deep in my heart subsides the infre-
quent word,
And there dies slowly throbbing like a
wounded bird.

> F. Thompson: *Her Portrait.* (19th cent.)

He's as good as his word—and his word's
no good.

> Seumas MacManus: *Heavy Hangs the Golden Grain.* (20th cent.)

A kind word never broke a tooth.

> Seumas MacManus: *Heavy Hangs the Golden Grain.* (20th cent.)

Wordsworth, William

He found in stones the sermons he had
already hidden there.

> Oscar Wilde: *The Decay of Lying.* (19th cent.)

And one was Wordsworth; he
Conceived the love of nature childishly
As no adult heart might; old poets sing
That exaltation by remembering.

> Alice Meynell: *Two Boyhoods.* (20th cent.)

Work

They must hunger in frost that will not
work in heat.

> John Heywood: *Proverbs,* 1, 11. (16th cent.)

Ye run to work in haste as nine men
held ye.

> John Heywood: *Proverbs,* 1, 11. (16th cent.)

As good play for nought as work for nought.

> John Heywood: *Proverbs,* 1, 11. (16th cent.)

Many hands make light work.

> John Heywood: *Proverbs,* 2, 5. (16th cent.)

See also Labor

World

This world and the future world are two enemies. This world talks of adultery and corruption and love of money and deceit, but that world says farewell to these things. We cannot, then, be friends of both, but we must say farewell to this to possess the other.

> So-called Second Letter of St. Clement to the Corinthians, 6. (2nd cent.)

This also is a part of the Church's teaching, that the world was made and took its beginning at a certain time, and is to be destroyed on account of its wickedness. But what existed before this world, or what will exist after it, has not become clearly known to the many, for there is no clear statement regarding it in the teaching of the Church.

> Origen: *De Principiis, Proem.* 7. (3rd cent.)

Hence the one peaceful and trustworthy tranquillity, the one solid and firm and constant security, is this, for a man to withdraw from these eddies of a distracting world, and, anchored on the ground of the harbor of salvation, to lift his eyes from earth to heaven; and having been admitted to the gift of God, and being already very near to his God in mind, he may boast, that whatever in human affairs others esteem lofty and grand, lies altogether beneath his consciousness.

> St. Cyprian: *Letters,* 1, 14. (3rd cent.)

To flee from the world is to abstain from sins.

> St. Ambrose: *De Fuga,* 17. (4th cent.)

The verdict of the world is conclusive. (Securus judicat orbis terrarum.)

> St. Augustine: *Contra Litt. Parmeniani,* 3, 24. (5th cent.)

The very order, disposition, beauty, change, and motion of the world and of all visible things proclaim that it could only have been made by God, the ineffably and invisibly great and the ineffably and invisibly beautiful.

> St. Augustine: *The City of God,* 11, 4, 2. (5th cent.)

Let us look sideways, as it were, on all that is done in this world.

> Pope St. Gregory I: *Homilies on the Gospels,* 36, 11. (6th cent.)

That the world has not always existed is to be held by faith alone, and cannot be demonstratively proved.

> St. Thomas Aquinas: *Summa Theologica,* 1, 46, 2. (13th cent.)

The world is blind.

> Dante: *Purgatorio, Canto 16.* (14th cent.)

So go'th the world; now woe, now weal.

> John Gower: *Confessio Amantis,* 8. (14th cent.)

In the world there must be of all sorts.

> J. Skelton: *Quixote,* 2, 6. (16th cent.)

Grant me Thy grace, good Lord, to set the world at naught; to set my mind fast upon Thee; and not to hang upon the blast of men's mouths.

> St. Thomas More: *Meditations and Prayers.* (16th cent.)

Let the world wag.

> John Heywood: *Proverbs,* 1, 5. (16th cent.)

The world runneth on wheels.

> J. Heywood: *Proverbs,* 2, 7. (16th cent.)

Let the world slide, let the world go;
A fig for care and a fig for woe!

> J. Heywood: *Be Merry, Friends.* (16th cent.)

Leave to the worldly their world.

> St. Francis de Sales: *Letters to Persons in the World,* 1, 10. (17th cent.)

All the world together is not worth one soul.

> St. Francis de Sales: *Introduction to the Devout Life,* 5, 14. (17th cent.)

We must make use of this world as though we were not making use of it at all.

> Jean Pierre Camus: *The Spirit of St. Francis de Sales,* 16, 4. (17th cent.)

He who does not see the world's futility is himself most futile.

> Pascal: *Pensées.* (17th cent.)

> Give, you gods,
Give to your boy, your Caesar,
The rattle of a globe to play withal,
This gewgaw world, and put him cheaply off:
I'll not be pleased with less than Cleopatra.

> Dryden: *All for Love,* 2, 1. (17th cent.)

They alone are able truly to enjoy this world, who begin with the world unseen. They alone enjoy it, who have first abstained from it. They alone can truly feast, who have first fasted; they alone are able to use the world, who have learned not to abuse it; they alone inherit it, who take it as a shadow of the world to come, and who for that world to come relinquish it.

> Card. Newman: *Parochial and Plain Sermons,* 6. (19th cent.)

The one peculiar and characteristic sin of the world is this, that whereas God would have us live for the life to come, the world would make us live for this life.

> Card. Newman: *Sermons on Subjects of the Day,* 7. (19th cent.)

You must either conquer the world or the world will conquer you. You must be either master or slave.

> Card. Newman: *Sermons on Subjects of the Day.* (19th cent.)

Unveil, O Lord, and on us shine
In glory and in grace;
This gaudy world grows pale before
The beauty of Thy face.

Till Thou art seen, it seems to be
A sort of fairy ground,
Where suns unsetting light the sky
And flowers and fruits abound.

But when Thy keener, purer beam
Is pour'd upon our sight,
It loses all its power to charm,
And what was day is night.

> Card. Newman: *The Two Worlds.* (19th cent.)

Three worlds there are:—the first of sense—
That sensuous earth which round us lies;
The next of faith's intelligence;
The third of glory, in the skies.

The first is palpable, but base;
The second heavenly, but obscure;
The third is star-like in the face—
But ah! remote that world as pure.

> Aubrey de Vere: *May Carols,* 2, 9. (19th cent.)

There is no other reason for the existence of this world than the charity of God and the communication of His charity. The world was made for man, man for the soul, the soul for charity, and charity unites the soul with God.

> Archb. Ullathorne: *Humility and Patience.* (19th cent.)

An idle poet, here and there
Looks round him, but for all the rest,
The world, unfathomably fair,
Is duller than a whitling's jest.

> Coventry Patmore: *The Revelation.* (19th cent.)

To me
Thy world's a morning haunt,
A bride whose zone no man hath slipt
But I, with baptism still bedript
Of the prime water's font.

> F. Thompson: *Carmen Genesis.* (19th cent.)

The true mystery of the world is the visible, not the invisible.

> Oscar Wilde: *The Picture of Dorian Gray,* 2. (19th cent.)

I have my beauty,—you your art—
Nay, do not start:
One world was not enough for two
Like me and you.

> Oscar Wilde: *Her Voice.* (19th cent.)

All who set not their minds on this world are accounted fools; but who will be the merrier in the world that is to come?

> R. H. Benson: *The History of Richard Raynal Solitary.* (20th cent.)

Only religion, only revelation, can explain things. Only God, Who made the kosmos, can say what He made it for, what end it is to serve.

> Abbot Chapman: *Spiritual Letters.* (20th cent.)

For nothing is more certain than that though this world is the only world that we have known, or of which we could ever dream, the fact does remain that we have named it 'a strange world.' In other words, we have certainly felt that this world did not explain itself, that something in its complete and patent picture has been omitted.

> G. K. Chesterton: *Robert Browning.* (20th cent.)

The world is not to be justified as it is justified by the mechanical optimists; it is not to be justified as the best of all possible worlds. . . . Its merit is precisely that none of us could have conceived such a thing; that we should have rejected the bare idea of it as miracle and unreason. It is the best of all impossible worlds.

> G. K. Chesterton: *Charles Dickens.* (20th cent.)

With all the multiplicity of knowledge there is one thing happily that no man knows: whether the world is old or young.

> G. K. Chesterton: *The Defendant.* (20th cent.)

The story of the universe is another Person's, and we are part of the story, its characterization, not its author.

> M. C. D'Arcy: *The Idea of God.* (In *God and the Supernatural*) (20th cent.)

The world may be divided into those who take it or leave it and those who split the difference.

> R. A. Knox. (20th cent.)

This outer world is but the pictured scroll
Of worlds within the soul;
A colored chart, a blazoned missal-book,
Whereon who rightly look
May spell the splendors with their mortal eyes,
And steer to Paradise.

> Alfred Noyes: *The Two Worlds.* (20th cent.)

Atlas held the firmament But could not see the sun;
He had the world between his hands But did not have its fun.

· · · · · · ·

He knelt for aeons, burdened With the whole unwieldy scheme
And he missed the point entirely Of the grand, deific theme.

> Sister Madeleva: *Meditation on Atlas.* (20th cent.)

World, End of the

God postpones the collapse and dissolution of the universe (through which the bad angels, the demons, and men would cease to exist), because of the Christian seed, which He knows to be the cause in nature [of the world's preservation].

> St. Justin Martyr: *Second Apology, 7.* (2nd cent.)

For when the judgment is finished, this heaven and earth shall cease to be, and there will be a new heaven and a new earth. For this world shall pass away by transmutation, not by absolute destruction.

> St. Augustine: *The City of God,* 20, 14. (5th cent.)

Pellucid thus in saintly trance,
    Thus mute in expectation,
What waits the earth? Deliverance?
    Ah, no! Transfiguration.

> Aubrey de Vere. (19th cent.)

See also Judgment, Last

Worldliness

It is wickedness to love the world, and those things that come into being and pass away, and to lust after these things, and to labor for them in order to acquire them, and to rejoice when they are abundant, and to fear lest they perish, and to be saddened when they perish. Such a life cannot see that pure, and undefiled, and immutable Truth, and cleave to it, to be for evermore unmoved.

> St. Augustine: *De Agone Christiano,* 13, 14. (4th cent.)

For my part, when I look upon those who love this world, I know not at what moment wisdom can most opportunely undertake the healing of their souls, for when things apparently are prosperous with them, they scornfully disdain her wholesome warnings and deem them but a kind of old wives' tale; but when they are in the pangs of adversity, they rather think of escaping the source of their present pangs than of seizing the things that may provide a cure and a haven of ref-

uge, in which their pangs may be completely prevented.

> St. Augustine: *Letter 203.* (5th cent.)

There was a monk, a leader of the fashions;
Inspecting farms and hunting were his passions,
A manly man, to be an abbot able,
Many the dainty horses in his stable;
. . . .
The rule of good St. Benet or St. Maur
As old and strict he tended to ignore.

> Chaucer: *Canterbury Tales: Prologue.* (Tr. Coghill) (14th cent.)

There was a friar, a wanton one and merry,
A limiter, a very festive fellow.
In all four orders there was none so mellow
As he in flattery and dalliant speech.

> Chaucer: *Canterbury Tales: Prologue.* (Tr. Coghill) (14th cent.)

Worm

Worms' food is fine end of our living.

> Lydgate: *Daunce of Machabree.* (15th cent.)

Tread a worm on the tail, and it must turn again.

> John Heywood: *Proverbs,* 2, 4. (16th cent.)

Worry

There is no annoyance so great as the annoyance which is composed of many trifling, but continuous worries.

> St. Francis de Sales: *Letters to Persons in Religion,* 4, 32. (17th cent.)

Worship

For men invariably worship what they like best.

> St. Jerome: *Letters,* 22, 10. (4th cent.)

God is to be worshipped by faith, hope, and love.

> St. Augustine: *On Faith, Hope, and Charity.* (5th cent.)

It is the highest duty of religion to imitate Him Whom thou adorest.

> St. Augustine: *The City of God,* 8, 17. (5th cent.)

Surely to obey in simple tranquillity and unsolicitous confidence, is the noblest conceivable worship he can pay to the Creator.

> Card. Newman: *Sermons Preached on Various Occasions.* (19th cent.)

Christianity is eminently an objective religion. For the most part it tells us of persons and facts in simple words, and leaves that announcement to produce its effect on such hearts as are prepared to receive it.

> Card. Newman: *Letter to the Rev. E. B. Pusey.* (19th cent.)

The temple I would build should be all white,
Each stone the record of a blameless day;
The souls that entered there should walk in light,
Clothed in high chastity and wisely gay.
Lord, here is darkness. Yet this heart unwise,
Bruised in thy service, take in sacrifice.

> W. S. Blunt: *How Shall I Build?* (19th cent.)

The worship due to the most holy Trinity, to each of the divine Persons, to our Lord Jesus Christ, even under the sacramental species, is called *cultus latriae* [highest kind of worship, adoration]; that which is due to the blessed Virgin Mary is called *cultus hyperduliae* [special veneration or worship]; that which is due to the others who reign with Christ in heaven is called *cultus duliae* [veneration or worship]. To sacred relics and images there is also due a veneration and worship which is relative to the person to whom the relics and images refer.

> Code of Canon Law, Canon 1255. (20th cent.)

It is illicit for Catholics in any way to assist actively or take part in sacred worship of non-Catholics. Passive or merely material presence, for the sake of civil courtesy, duty, or respect, for a grave reason which in case of doubt should have the approval of the bishop may be tolerated, at funerals, weddings, and other such celebrations of non-Catholics, provided there is no danger of perversion or scandal.

> Code of Canon Law, Canon 1258. (20th cent.)

Men who assist at divine worship whether in the church or outside should have their heads uncovered, unless the approved practice among the people or special circumstances require the contrary; women should have their heads covered and should be modestly dressed, especially when they approach the holy table.

> Code of Canon Law, Canon 1262, 2. (20th cent.)

Human society as such is bound to offer to God public and social worship. It is bound to acknowledge in Him its supreme Lord and first beginning, and to strive toward Him as to its last end, to give Him thanks and offer Him propitiation.

> Pope Pius XI: *Ad Catholici Sacerdotii.* (Dec. 20, 1935)

It is a law of man's nature, written into his very essence, and just as much a part of him as the desire to build houses and cultivate the land and marry and have children and read books and sing songs, that he should want to stand together with other men in order to acknowledge their common dependence on God, their Father and Creator.

> Thomas Merton: *The Seven Storey Mountain.* (20th cent.)

Worship, then, is not a part of the Christian life: it is the Christian life.

> Gerald Vann: *The Divine Pity.* (20th cent.)

To worship ourselves is to worship nothing. And the worship of nothing is hell.

> Thomas Merton: *Seeds of Contemplation.* (20th cent.)

See also Divine Office; Liturgy

Worth

Not the worth of a bean.

> John Heywood: *Proverbs,* 1, 10. (16th cent.)

Wound

No one heals himself by wounding another.

> St. Ambrose: *In Ps. 37 Enarr.* 46. (4th cent.)

O pleasant port, O place of rest,
  O royal rift, O worthy wound;
Come, harbor me a weary guest,
  That in the world no ease have
    found.

>   .   .   .   .

O happy soul that flies so high,
  As to attain this sacred cave;
Lord, send me wings that I may fly,
  And in this harbor quiet have.

> Bl. Robert Southwell: *Man to the Wound in Christ's Side.* (16th cent.)

For in love's field was never found
A nobler weapon than a wound.
Love's passives are his activ'st part:
The wounded is the wounding heart.

> Richard Crashaw: *The Flaming Heart.* (St. Teresa of Avila) (17th cent.)

My wound is great because it is so small.

> Dryden: *All for Love,* 1. (17th cent.)

Wrath

The purple winepress of the wrath of God.

> Lionel Johnson: *Ireland.* (19th cent.)

Wreath

The wreath of brightest myrtle wove
With brilliant tears of bliss among it,
And many a rose leaf cull'd by love
To heal his lips when bees have stung it.

> Thomas Moore: *The Wreath and the Chain.* (19th cent.)

Wretchedness

The wretched have no friends.

> Dryden: *All for Love,* 3, 1. (17th cent.)

Writing

I confess then, that I attempt to be one of those who write because they have made some progress, and who, by means of writing, make further progress.

> St. Augustine: *Letter 143,* 2. (5th cent.)

When he writes well, no one writes better; when he writes badly, no one writes worse.

> Cassiodorus: *Institutiones,* 1, 1, 8. (Said of Origen) (6th cent.)

Learn to write well, or not to write at all.

> Dryden: *Essay on Satire.* (17th cent.)

To writing bred, I knew not what to say.

> Dryden: *Saying.* (17th cent.)

To write upon all is an author's sole chance
For attaining, at last, the least knowledge of any.

> Thomas Moore: *Literary Advertisement.* (19th cent.)

Wrong

Let us be assured that to do no wrong is really superhuman, and belongs to God alone.

> St. Gregory of Nazianzen: *Orations,* 16, 14. (4th cent.)

This is ever the case with men who do wrong; they quiet the voice within them by the imagination that all others are pretty much what they are themselves.

> Card. Newman: *Present Position of Catholics in England.* (19th cent.)

Y

Year

For many years! (Ad multos annos!)
For many years, O Lord! (Is polla eti,
  Despota.)

> Liturgical Acclamations. (First, chanted at
> consecration of bishop, Roman Pontifical,
> ca. 8th-10th cent.; second, regularly
> chanted by choir in pontifical mass
> according to Byzantine rite, before 8th
> cent.)

Yesterday

Yesterday will not be called again.

> J. Skelton: *Magnyfycence.* (16th cent.)

Yielding

It is better to bow than break.

> John Heywood: *Proverbs,* 1, 9. (16th
> cent.)

Young and Old

To reverence the old; to love the young.

> St. Benedict: *Rule,* 4. (Among his 'tools
> of good works') (6th cent.)

The young cock croweth, as he the old
heareth.

> John Heywood: *Proverbs,* 1, 10. (16th
> cent.)

Young Man

He had his son with him, a fine young
  squire,

A lover and cadet, a lad of fire
With curly locks, as if they had been
  pressed.

> Chaucer: *Canterbury Tales: Prologue.*
> (Tr. Coghill) (14th cent.)

Youth

You yourself know how slippery is the
path of youth—a path on which I myself
have fallen, and which you are now trav-
ersing not without fear.

> St. Jerome: *Letters,* 7, 4. (4th cent.)

Force of juventus, hardy as lion.

> Lydgate: *Minor Poems,* p. 198. (15th
> cent.)

My prime of youth is but a frost of
  cares,
My feast of joy is but a dish of pain,

. . . . . .

The spring is past, and yet it hath not
  sprung;
The fruit is dead, and yet the leaves are
  green;
My youth is gone, and yet I am but
  young.

> Chidiock Tichborne: *Elegie.* (Martyred,
> 1586)

Youth should watch joys and shoot them
as they fly.

> Dryden: *Aurengzebe,* 3. (17th cent.)

Only one youth, but life was still God-
given!

Only one youth, but life sped on to
  heaven!

Susan L. Emory: *An Old Woman's
Answer to a Letter from her Childhood.*
(19th cent.)

Youth is a disease that must be borne
with patiently! Time, indeed, will cure
it: yet, until the cure is complete, elders
must bear it as well as they can, and not
seem to pay too much attention to it. A
rigorous and prudent diet, long hours of
sleep, plenty of occupation—these are
the remedies for the fever!

R. H. Benson: *Come Rack! Come Rope!*
(20th cent.)

Not often, when the carnal dance is
    mad—
  Not often, in our youth's audacity,
  Shall one, aware, have final faith in
    thee,
O soul, for he that knows thee shall be
    sad
Betimes, and youth would be forever
    glad.
    Then, craving freedom, never are we
    free;
    Through many-colored mists we call
    or flee,
And in illusion's raiment are we clad.

George Sterling: *The Final Faith.* (20th
cent.)

If you could influence the young it would
turn earth into heaven.

Katharine T. Hinkson: *The French Wife.*
(20th cent.)

Youth but lives for the hour. If it did not
it would not be youth.

K. T. Hinkson: *The Story of Clarice.*
(20th cent.)

God, Who had made you valiant,
    strong and swift,
And maimed you with a bullet long ago,
And cleft your riotous ardor with a rift,
And checked your youth's tumultuous
    overflow,
Gave back your youth to you,
And packed in moments rare and few
Achievements manifold
And happiness untold,
And bade you spring to death as to a
    bride,
In manhood's ripeness, power and
    pride,
And on your sandals the strong wings
    of youth.

Maurice Baring: *In Memoriam, A. H.
1916.* (20th cent.)

The young don't know what age is, and
the old forget what youth was.

Seumas MacManus: *Heavy Hangs the
Golden Grain.* (20th cent.)

Z

Zeal

No sacrifice is more acceptable to God
than zeal for souls.

Pope St. Gregory I: *Hom. 12 in Ezechiel.*
(5th cent.)

Zeal without knowledge is always less
useful and effective than regulated zeal,
and very often it is highly dangerous.

St. Bernard: *Sermons on the Canticle of
Canticles,* 50. (12th cent.)

We are often moved with passion, and we think it to be zeal.

> Thomas a Kempis: *The Imitation of Christ,* 2, 5. (15th cent.)

Christ bade His followers take the
    sword;
And yet He chid the deed,
When hasty Peter seized his word,
    And made a foe to bleed.

The gospel creed, a sword of strife,
    Meek hands alone may rear;
And ever zeal begins its life
    In silent thought and fear.

Ye, who would weed the vineyard's soil,
    Treasure the lesson given;
Lest in the judgment-books ye toil
    For Satan, not for heaven.

> Card. Newman: *Zeal and Meekness.* (1833)

There are few catastrophes so great and irremediable as those that follow an excess of zeal.

> R. H. Benson: *A Winnowing.* (20th cent.)

INDEX OF SUBJECTS

The references are to the page of the text. The letter "a" denotes the left-hand column of the page, "b" the right-hand column.

The order of the index is strictly alphabetical. To save space, the key word or key phrase is replaced by its initial letter. For the sake of uniformity all references to Our Lord as either JESUS or CHRIST are grouped together under the one heading JESUS CHRIST. References to Our Lady will be found principally under the headings BLESSED VIRGIN MARY, LADY, MARY, and MOTHER OF GOD. The abbreviation BVM stands for Blessed Virgin Mary and may represent either the whole phrase or a part of it.

Foreign words and biblical quotations have been italicized. The definite and indefinite articles and other unessential words have generally been omitted.

A

Aaron budding staff of A., 80a; chosen, clad in mystic robes, 68a
Abandonment My God, wilt Thou leave me?, 395b; naked of friends, 1a; With not a friend to close his eyes, 254a
Abasement man's deepest a., pursuit of glory, 301b
Abbey Adieu, sweet a. of tuneful dead, 1a
Abbot ought to rule with double teaching 1a; A., representative of Christ in monastery, 1a; A manly man, to be an a. able, 927b; Father A., I am come, 282b; Let no one give or receive anything without a.'s leave, 618b; live in monasteries, under an a., 618b; To obey commands of a., 642a
Abel beginning of Church, 123a; Church began with A., 121b; Thy just servant A., 592a
Abelard, 520a
Aberrations All a., founded on some truth, 300b
Abide He hasteth well that wisely can a., 422a; to cleave to those that shall a., 425a; We must needs a. in the Lord, 881b
Abideth Savior a. with us unto end, 35b
Abiding a. in house of God alway, 12b; a. yet mysterious, 386b
Ability difference between a. and habit, 417b; few highly endowed will rescue world, 1b; men of a. and Christianity, 164a; strength and greatness give a., 419b
Abnegation in obedience and a., I desire Society be conspicuous, 479b
Abnormal question, whether better to be normal or a., 637b
Abode *make our a. with him*, 835b
Abortion no reason for condoning direct murder, 2a; those who procure a., excomm., 2a; To forbid birth, only quicker murder, 1b; woman destroying foetus, answerable for murder, 1b; You shall not kill unborn child, 1b
Abraham, 223b; A. and to his seed, 245b; A., father of all na-

tions, 441b; bosom of A., 243b; chambers of rest with A., 243b; God of A., Isaac, Jacob, 384b, 395b; May God of A., 576b; now he lives in A.'s bosom, 301b; sacrifice of our patriarch A., 592a; welcoming embrace of patriarchs, 244b
Abroad A. the regal banners fly, 230a
Absence farther off, more desired, 2a; man out of sight, out of mind, 2a; Since you have waned from us, 2a
Absent Rather than to be from God a., 561b
Absolute a. monarchy in Catholic countries, 3a; a. power corrupts absolutely, 714a; Eternal A. is ever creating new forms, 225a
Absolution essentially judicial act, 2b, 669b; from the a. of a faithful fight, 830a; May the Lord grant us pardon a., 587b; pleasant a., for a gift, 203b, 815a; Righteous Judge! for sin's pollution Grant a., 483b; true a. in baptism, 51b
Absolutionem Indulgentiam, a. et remissionem peccatorum, 587b
Absolutism canon law safeguard against a., 112a; Church, best defence against a., 873a; ecclesiastical authority, not authoritarianism, 47a; If kings unquestion'd can laws destroy, 3a; most formidable enemy of Church, 3a; prince, image of almighty God, 3a; theory of a., 534a
Absolve confession required, in order that priest may a., 669a; I a. you from your sins, 2b; No power can the impenitent a., 764b; Not any priest can a. from sin, 668b; the sins of Thy people, 2a
Absolved by the water of regeneration, 51b
Absolvo Ego te absolvo a peccatis tuis, 2b
Absorbed in love of Thee, 77b
Abstainer dipsomaniac and the a., 279b
Abstinence law of a. and fast together, 338b; made almost a sin of a., 3a; persons who have completed seventh year, bound by a., 338a; salutary a., 338a; subdue

flesh by a., 3a, 338a; to be observed on all Fridays, 3b
Abstract difference, conclusion in a., conclusion in concrete, 201b
Abundance All a. not God, neediness, 3b; a. of Thy loving kindness. 363a; glory of God in poverty and a., 775b; he that hath a., 155a
Abuse great mistake in controversy, 3b
Abyss Thou didst raise up dead from a., 400b; Is the law of the a. thus broken from? 239a; vast a. severs night from day, 86b
Academy Mt. Calvary is a. of our love, 111a
Accept A., receive, take, 710b
Access A., Approach Art thou, 493a; *a. to God*, 493a; no one has access, as His Mother, 97a
Accidents a. of bread and wine remain after consecration, 311b; essences or substances admit of a., 301a, 380b; eucharistic a., 71a; Receive a. that befall thee, 3b; veils enveloping Sacrament, 73a
Accidie A., a shrinking of mind, 3b
Accipe A. Spiritum Sanctum, 69a
Accompanist bad a. makes a good singer, 618a
Accomplice a. is no better than assassin, 625b
Accomplishments a., not education, 290a
Accord There is no good a., 3b
Accordeth may rhyme, but a. not, 3b
Accursed A. himself, but in his cursing strong, 493b; Let him be a., 317a
Acerbities which bite writing men, 160b
Ache Better eye out than always a., 322a
Achievement Every great a., inspired by motives of heart, 850b
Achitophel, 751a
Acolyte behoves a. to carry candlestick, 4a; illumine minds with light of knowledge, 4a
Acre Here's an a. sown indeed, 413b; Rest in the silent a., 413b
Act a. done from state of grace, meritorious, 604a; a. of God

933

does injury to no one, 4a; *all things a. as they are naturally fit,* 561b; by an a. of generous love, 8a; He doesn't a., he behaves, 4a; liberty, translation of will into a., 537a; Never to a. is never to know, 514b; no deliberate a. is morally neutral, 817b

Action flows, not from reasonings, but from faith, 760b; knowledge and a. make a man happy, 511a; only dying do not love noise of a., 217a

Actions confess by our a. Thy faith, 441a; Direct our a. by Thy inspiration, 428b; God uses our disordered a., 4a; keep constant guard over a., 4a; light may blaze in our a., 167a; perfection, doing ordinary a. well, 4b; Prodigious a., 65b; we must set up ladder of ascending a., 450a

Active nothing so a., as that which least seems so, 5b

Active Life A. is in the arena, 4b; ascend to contemplation by steps of a., 5a; battlefield of toil, 5a; calls for practice of commandments, 4b; contemplative, more meritorious than a., 5a; in a., body curbed by reason, 5a; in a., God instructs by His word, 5a; in a., vices removed by good works, 5a; in a. we toil to be purified, 4b; makes man holy, 5a; maps way, 4b; opposed to confusion of world, 4b; rules in self, 4b

Activity no a. is without purpose, 373b

Actor not dishonorable, following profession, 5b; dishonorable to be a., 6a; When tired a. stops and leaves stage, 543a

Actors excommunicated so long as act, 5b; Peel'd, patch'd, and piebald, 6a; women marrying a., excommunicated, 5b

Actresses fired with muses' madness, 6a

Acts Great a. take time, 4b; Indifferent a. judged by ends, 395a; Man is master of his a., 357a; no man a. rightly, save by divine aid, 817a; rule for human a. twofold, 818a; very a. of Christ are precepts, 492b; voluntary and involuntary a., 33b

Actus A. Dei nemini facit injuriam, 4a

Ad A. majorem Dei gloriam, 367a; *A. multos annos!* 930a

Ad limina a. visits of bishops to pope, 70a

Adam *All men sinned in A.,* 186b, 460a; A. and existence of other first parents, 316b; A. and transmission of original sin, 316b, 821a; A. lay inbounden, 29a; by Him, A. recalled, 90a; called upon to make his defence, 254a; Christ is new A., 85b; entire A., changed in body and soul for worse, 821a; had many ribs, 619b; had to be restored in Christ, 85a; has returned to paradise, 229a; nail to cross sin A. committed, 809b; O'er bright new world He gave me ways, 6a; Oh, he didn't believe in A. or Eve, 821b; Or what is A.'s son, 569b; pronounced bond of matrimony indissoluble, 577a; Pure flower of A.'s race, 97b; Purging A.'s guilt away, 168a; Satan drew A. into death, 43a; Shepherd is crucified, A. raised, 442a; Stays thirst of A.'s race, 169b; that language Which A. talked, 519a; Virgin

delivered A. from sin, 85b; We A.'s guilty children are, 462b

Adaptability cut coat after cloth, 6b

Adieu A.! such is the word for us, 654a

Administer a. high position for benefit of others, 808a

Administered Whate'er is best a., is best, 406a

Admire Fools a., men of sense approve, 6b; I a. Thee, Master of the tides, 374a

Admonished a. secretly, 317a

Admonition mixed with kindness, acceptable, 6b; naturally bitter, 6b; of those who do not persevere, 6b

Adolescence a., mingling of refinement and brutality, 6b

Adonai O Adonai, Leader of Israel, 8a

Adopt A. me for Thine own, 207a

Adopted adopted children begotten by heart, 6b

Adoption called faithful unto a., 485a; diffusing grace of Thy a., 441b; grace of a., 481a; people of God's a., 647b; spirit of a., 441b

Adoration a. of Blessed Sacrament by people, 76b; Down in a falling, 74a, 77b; here I bow'd before Thee, 77b; I come before Thee at close of day, 78b; Lost, all lost in wonder, 75a

Adore Come, let us a. before Christ, 589a; Godhead, Whom I do a., 75a; I knelt to a., 484b; O silence, my soul, and a., 197b; shepherds, and kings a. in the stable, 758a; to pray is less than to a., 235a; what you have burned, 50b

Adorest imitate Him Whom thou a., 928a

Adornment little powder and gauze properly disposed, 222a

Adulation he who defiles tongue with a., 7a

Adulterer more grievous offender than thief, 7a

Adulteress separated from Church, yoked with a., 429a

Adulterous husband may not murder adulterous wife, 7b

Adultery a. be execrated, not man, 156a; bond of matrimony not dissolved on account of a., 267b; Christians do not commit a., 162b; divorce and a., 267a; *Everyone who causes her to commit a.,* 7a; marrying while first husband alive, 7a; mind picturing vision, guilty of a., 7a; nuptial pact not nullified by a., 7a

Advancement with ever an eye to a., 14a

Advantage source of vast popular a., 23b

Advent Deliver us, tarry now no more, 8a; Hark, a herald voice is calling, 7b; His coming to men, 8b; No sudden thing of glory and fear, 9a; prepare ways of only-begotten Son, 7b; when He cometh second time in majesty, 7b

Adventure the champagne of life, 9a

Adversaries God has a., in moral order, 733a; treatment of a. in controversy, 27a

Adversary Vanished m'hath my cruel adversaire, 87b

Adversities all a. and errors overcome, 134a, 793a; good conscience rejoices among a., 209a; resigned to suffer a. for Christ, 9a

Adversity Be meek, bear a., 602b;

freed from all a., 261b; Friendship, more sacred by a., 9b; gone further and faren worse, 9a; great man and a., 736a; If God sends you a., accept it, 736a, In a. I desire prosperity, 735b; in school of a., heart forced to discipline itself, 404a; No hap so hard, but may in fine amend, 351b; no hell like declined glory, 9a; rejoicing in a., to him who loves, 9a; sensible, impatient of all a., 9a; strengthens us by its suffering, 851a; to love Him in wormwood, 344a

Advice ever tell him what he ought to do, 508b; honest man may take fool's a., 9b; more safe to hear than give, 9b; Time and place give best a., 870b; to give good a., absolutely fatal, 9b; Who takes a., doth amendment begin, 14b

Advisement A. is good before the deed, 739a

Adviser choice should be of men approved, 9b

Advocate Be mine a. in that high place, 84b; mere sight of a., induces high opinion of competence, 531b; new Priest, universal A., 485a; Of sinful man, O sinless A., 98b; our mediatrix, our a., 90b; then, sweet A., bestow, 95b

Advocates Ye lawyers, ye a., be sure of this, 531a

Affable One should be a. in conversation, 691a

Affairs uninitiated dare to dabble in a. of state, 691b

Affection bends judgment to her uses, 9b; Charity, much stronger than natural a., 156b; With deep a. and recollection, 58b

Affections Catholic Church, discipline of a. and passions, 689a

Afflicted afflicted because God wills it, 10a; God, comfort of a., 880a; joy of a., 84b; justly a. for our sins, 668a; rejoice with glad but weep with a., 155b; to help the a., 155a; We beseech Thee for those a., 9b; we must be a. as it pleases God, 10a

Affliction measured out to our need, 10a; no man in world without some a., 880b; proves, purifies, melts good, 10a; will sometimes extort a short prayer, 718b

Afflictions In mine a., to obey His voice, 410b; loving heart loves God in a., 10a; provided no inconvenience, 10a

Afraid I shall not be a. any more, 342b; More a. than hurt, 342a; ''Tis I; be not a.!' 210b

Afterlife condition in a., based on this life, 741b; world committed to some kind of belief in a. 464a

Afternoon longer forenoon, shorter a., 10a

After-thought After-wits are dearly bought, 10a

After-wits A. are dearly bought, 10a

Against If Christ is with us, who is a. us? 895a

Agamus Gratias a., Domino Deo Nostro, 591a

Agape not lawful hold a. without bishop, 67a

Agatha, Saint, 10a

Age A. hath clawed me with his crutch, 10b; *bringing a. upon the proud,* 386b; canonical a., 649a; Church must speak to each a., 270b; every a. is fed on illusions, 459a; Let your old a. be childlike,

917b; Like a. at play with infancy, 646b; Never trust woman who would tell a., 11a; Of wanton youth, repents a painful a., 149b; premature old a., 280a; Some reckon their a. by years, 859a; The a. of credulity is every a., 225b

Age, Golden comes to men who forget gold, 11b

Age, Middle Midway the journey of this life, 10b

Age, Old a sorry breaking up, 11a; Grey hairs upon my head, 10b; lengthened infirmity, 11b; Let your o. be childlike, 11b; men who wish for o., 11b; O. is ill-humored, 11b; Worn with cares and age, 11b

Aged beauty of an a. face, 11a

Ages like a beautiful poem, 314a; Millions of a. back, 20a; The a. long, the a. long, 169b

Aggrieved If in one point person be a., 200b

Agios A. o Theos, ischyros, a-thanatos, 41a, 589a

Agnosticism a., or Catholic faith, 146b; chief function to awake men, 12a; leads to moral indifference, 12a; solves not merely shelves mysteries, 12a; streak of a. in Catholic theology, 396b

Agnostics say soul nothing but wind and smoke, 12a; them that do not have the faith, 42b

Agnus A. Dei, qui tollis peccata mundi, 594a; Ecce A. Dei, 595b

Agony In my death's great a., 75b

Agrarian a. laws, 199a

Agree When people a. with me, 12a; You cannot a. about nothing, 312a

Agreement order produces a., 54b; Where every man would be lord, 3b

Agreeth nothing in this world a. worse, 424a

Agriculture Religion and art, older than a., 760b

Aesthetics confounded with morality, 9b

Aeternitatis viewed sub specie a., 34b

Aid man, made for fellows' a., 12b; Thine a. supply, Thy strength bestow, 74b

Aim Be Thou the a. of every breast, 36a; final a. of rational creatures, vision of God, 903b

Air autumn's mournful a., 48a; Content to breathe his native a., 443a; English a. that was my breath, 296b; Let a. you breathe be sunny, 12b; Like a. she enters; where none dared, 157a; rise from table and take the a., 423a; the waving of angels' robes, 20a; Wild a., world-mothering a., 12b

Alaric, 780a

Alarm to cry a. spiritual against foul vice, 190a

Alb a spot upon an a., cannot be hid, 730a

Ale And who so wicked a. breweth, 278b

Alexander VI, Pope, 498b

Alexander, 26a, 207b, 317a

Alexandria, 662a, 662b, 675a

Algebra Poetry is only the a. of life, 690a

All A. cometh to one, 313a; A. is made for charity, 156b; Every man for himself and God for us a., 397b

Allegiance civil a. of Christian, limited by conscience, 182a

Allegorical a. passages of Scripture, 61a

Alleluia Alleluia! Alleluia!, 286a, 589a; song of sweetness, 12b

Alliance Utopians never enter into a., 12b

Alliances Anglo-American a., 16a

Allurements resist a. of sin with strong mind, 752a

Alma Mater university, an a., not a foundry, 890b

Almighty A. of A., Co-eternal of Eternal, 481b; called A., because He can do whatever He wills, 388a

Alms A. are but vehicles of pray'r, 13a; help dead, 244a; many kinds of a., 349a; Of that which remaineth, give a., 157b

Almsdeeds in fasting, a. and prayer, righteousness consists, 401b

Almsgiving Give to everyone that asks thee, 13a

Alone Woe him that is a., 830b

Alps, 13b, 434a, 625a

Altar A. against a., 13b; a. of life, 97b; a type of the body, 13b; Born of the a.'s mystic birth, 78a; bring wine and water to a., 4a; corporal cleanliness in those that approach a., 187b; draw us to Thy holy a., 590b; fit to minister at Thy holy a., 496a; holy mysteries before a., 68b; I will go into the a. of God, 587b; let your heart be an a., 726b; Lord, to Thine a. let me go, 77b; No other a. apart from that one a., 133b; O God of earth and a., bow down, 726a; one a., one bishop with priests and deacons, 597b, 692b; remember me at a. of the Lord, 244a; Sacrament of a., 72b, 73b; Thine a. on high, 592b; Thyself, spotless Victim upon a. of cross, 486a; Women may not approach a., 13b; you can force man to approach a., 57a

Altare introibo ad a. Dei, 587b

Altars a. are God's theaters, 13b; Let souls of Christians be like a., 310a; Nor do we set up a. to martyrs, 795a; on a thousand a. laid, 78a

Alteram Audi a. partem, 499a

Altruism bee honored because labors for others, 55b

Am I a., I know, I will, 511b

Amalgam between eternal faith and temporal opinion, 270b

Amat Qui me a., a. et canem meum, 273a

Amateur hard for a. not to over-act, 13b

Amateurs temperament, disease that afflicts a., 32b

Ambition A. is mind's immodesty, 14a; cannot endure light of day, 14a; Desire of greatness, god-like sin, 14b; enterprising efforts of a., 13b; Hew not too high, 14a; In God 'tis glory, 14a; Let not a. tempt, 453a; makes patriot and knave, 14b; Men would be angels, 38a; A., mother of hypocrisy, 14a; must be persued by self-extinction, 14b; Nor think a. wise because brave, 14a; O a.! the cross of the ambitious, 13b; Perish every fond a., 233a; same a. can destroy or save, 14b; tortures all, 13b; When flattery soothes and a. blinds!, 345b; wild a. loves to slide, 14a

Ambitious Church is full of a. men, 13b

Ambrose, Saint, 44b, 207b

Ambry Here is God in th' a., 397a

Amen Like the sound of a great A., 626b

Amend And yet my life a. not I, 248a; my life t' amenden, 232b

Amendment Who takes advice, doth a. begin, 14b

America A. is my country, 143a; A.'s glory, 16a; A., with thy faults, I love thee still, 14b; better organized than other society, 142b; blessed because deserves to be blessed, 15b; called providential nation, 15a; citizens of A. are her monarchs, 255b; does not understand England enough, 16a; England and A., much alike, 16b; gave new stamp to European civilization, 16a; in accordance with needs of Catholic society, 142b; invested religion in securities, 15b; Loyalty to God's Church and country!, 143a; no conflict between Catholic Church and A., 143a; No country deserves so well of people as A., 255b; part of European civilization, 16a; seems destined for greater things, 143b; The free school of A.!, 802a; youth of A., their oldest tradition, 15b

American A. civilization and Catholic Church, 142b; A. constitution, least imperfect, 406b; A. history unknown to Englishmen, 16a; A. illusion, their country world apart, 16a; A. party system, not understood by Englishmen, 16b; A. people always progressive and conservative, 255a; A. republic realizes freedom, 14b; A. society better organized, 142b; my tribute to American people, 15b; never takes for granted own patriotism, 18a; no man so well-dressed or mannered, 18a; Ours is A. Church not Irish, 143b; real A. all right; ideal A. all wrong, 17b; takes pleasures savagely, 16b; tied to rest of world, 17a; worthy of their A. citizenship, 265a

Americanism Both A. and Catholicism bow to sway of conscience, 210a; something more than European ideal, 17a; understood as endowments, 17a

"Americanism" cradled and entombed in Europe, 17a; unknown in America, until condemned, 17a

Americanization efforts to retard A. frowned down, 17b

Americans A., and practical effects of religion, 613a; be not unworthy of Heaven's confidence, 15b; Compel all to be A., 265a; demands of their special nature, 16b; do not need drink to inspire them, 17b; endowments belonging to American people, 17a; intelligent and energetic people, 16b; nothing the matter with them except ideals, 17b; not given to speculation, 18a; not to be trained up as foreigners, 17b; spectacle to all nations, 15a; stolidly conservative in ideas, 18a

Amor a. Dei usque ad contemptum sui, 125a; AMOR is the same word as ROMA, 149a; A. vincit annia, 781b; A. ordinem nescit, 550b

Amore Quia a. langueo, 100a

Amorist Starry a., starward gone, 42a

Amorous The a. drift of man's herd to hell, 392a

Amour Too sure Of the a., 540a

Amours debauching of virgins, a. of strumpets, 192b

Amuse billiard ball enough to a. man, 18a

Amuses esteem, a. and contents us, 14a

Amusement a., not education, 290a

Amusements affection for a., contrary to devotion, 18a; great a., danger to life of Christian, 276a

Anachronism only pedantic word for eternity, 33a

Analysis He swooped upon idea like an eagle, 160a

Anamnesis, 592b

Anarch Thy hand, great a.! 153b

Anarchy *liberty of self-ruin*, 18b; self-government is not a., 354b

Anathema he shall be called a., 429b; *Sit a.*, 317a

Anatolius, Patriarch, 699b

Ancestor woman in place of a. of God, 82b

Ancestry Man for his glory To a. flies, 322b; seldom cause of human virtue, 18b

Anchorite A., who didst dwell, 573a

Anchorites a. or hermits, solitary combat in desert, 618b

Ancient Flies the a. from the new, 286a; God is there, the A. of Days, 487a; road of a. centuries, strewn with dead moderns, 614b

Ange Qui veut faire l'ange, 20a

Angel An a. meets an a. on the way, 21b; An a.'s Ave disenchants charms, 25b; An a.'s grief ill fits a penitent, 277a; a.'s kiss that loosed her prison gates, 252a; carried up by hands of Thy holy a., 592b; Dear a.! ever at my side, 21b; Dark a., with thine aching lust, 261a; denouncing a.'s pen, 20a; even if a. from heaven should preach otherwise, 429b; Every a. and demon winged, 18b; gaz'd on unveil'd face of God, 20a; intelligent essence with free-will, 19a; I saw an a. close by me, 562a; limitation of its nature, 19a; Man, neither a. nor a brute, 570b; May Thy guardian a. nigh, 21b; served Him with keen ecstatic love, 20b; Sing, sing, ye a. bands, 41a; The a. spake the word, 19b; with the morn those a. faces smile, 250b; word a., name of function, 19a; word of Lord which a. spoke, 25a

Angel-guardians A. of men, 21a

Angeli Non Angli, sed angeli, 18b

Angelic a. songs are swelling, 20a; fellowship with a. powers, 50a; Let a. choirs now rejoice, 441b

Angelism leisure state, founded upon false a., 517a

Angels A little lower than a. made, 6a; abiding in house of God always, 12b; admitted among choirs of a., 37a; aids to our weakly frames, 21a; all heaven's own home-born sons, 40a; all things honor their true divinity, 20b; A.s' knowledge, far above us, 21b; A. are everywhere, 18b; A. of Jesus! 20a; a. sing praise in the earth, 167b; a. take up dead, 246a; A. with harps and alabaster dames, 114a; a. would be gods, 38a; Beauty not necessary to a., 18b; apprehend at once full evidence, 22a; between God and man, 21a; bright celestial choir, 258b; Church with a. now are one, 168a; contemplate Source of knowledge, 22a; cover us by your prayers, 21a; Deliver us from sorrows, 21a; devotions to a. and saints, 796a; ever do God service, 20b; execute divine plan for salvation, 21a; fill up blank made by

fallen a., 313a; fight on the side of the a., 235a; Fools rush in where a. fear to tread, 348a; found wherever divine glance bids, 19a; function to execute plan of Providence, 19b; govern all our affairs, 21a; have been given us as guardians, 20b; have struck heaven's tent, 21b; have thrown away weight of clay, 19b; Heavenly friends and guides, 21a, 241b; help bring us home, 21a; honor Mother of your King, 88b; How many a. can dance on a needle, 19b; incorporeal hosts, 99b; intellectual natures, at peak of creation, 19b; invisible beings that guard, 20b; King of world, borne by unseen armies of a., 589b; legions and armies of a., 487a; Like a secret told by a., 8b; make yourself familiar with a., 19b; Maria, men and a. sing, 40b; mean messengers and ministers, 19b; ministry of a., 20b, 34a; minister to heirs of salvation, 20a; must be entreated for us, 20b; nine orders of a., 18b; No scepter theirs, but they are kings, 20b; Not Angles, but angels, 18b; O'er the choirs of a. holy, 40a; Of the a.' bright array! 605a; our guardian spirits, 21b; O ye who sing His praise so well, 36b; perfection of society of holy a., 404a; Rejoice, ye spirits and a. on high, 40b; Renounce marriage, imitate the a., 898a; Round about whom a. fly, 40b; servants of the Holiest, 20a; set over nations and regions, 21a; some truths revealed through a., 331a; stood Around throne of God, 20a; Stuft with down of a.' wing, 55b; summoned by your prayers, 20b; Sweet a., come and sing the rest, 40b; take different forms, 19a; Their simple friendship a court, 20b; Thine a. fill midnight with song, 170a; Those who play at being a., 20a; Thy thousand thousand hosts are spread, 605a; unveil divine mysteries to men, 19a; Virginity is rule of life among a., 898a; Where linkèd a. dance, 479b; Which a. and archangels, do praise, 591a; *Who maketh His a. spirits*, 19b; whose faces see God in heaven, 20a; wings of your immaterial glory, 21a; With thousand thousand a. round! 171a; world of pure spirits, 21a; ye princes of the sky, 36b

Angelus, 169a, 312b

Anger all a. deem profane, 423a; A. is quieted by gentle word, 22b; Beware the fury of a patient man, 662a; gives man foretaste of hell, 22a; holy a., excited by zeal, 22b; kind of temporary madness, 22a; Nothing restrains a. as does name of Jesus, 630a; scourge of Thy a., 668a; She frieth in her own grease, 22a

Angles Not A., but angels, 18b

Angli Non A., sed angeli, 18b

Anglican A. orders invalid, 648b; A. service makes me shiver, 24a

Anglicana A. ecclesia, 140b

Anglicanism as a halfway house, 23a; attitude toward devotion to BVM, 102a; bearest children, darest not own them, 23a; belief in its essential catholicity, 24a; cherishes an empty locket, 23a; city of confusion and house of bondage, 24a; divisibility of

Church, cardinal doctrine, 24a; does not possess apostolic succession, 23b; English Protestantism, religion of throne, 23b; its facility for accepting new doctrine, 272b; its most fundamental heresy, 24a; mod. high, 122a; Nice in her choice of ill, 23a; no power of rejecting, she receives like pail, 272b; one whom God's hand hath touched, 23a; preserves accessories of Catholic worship, 23a; religion grafted upon loyalty, 23b; repudiated papal authority, 141a; school holds 'Anglicanism' in holy horror, 24a; special atmosphere of A., 24a; strength not in argument, 23b; The panther sure the noblest, 22b; thou hast good things, canst not keep them, 23a; To tolerate everything is to teach nothing, 24a; transmitted in succession of kings and aristocracy, 23b

Anglicans Catholic-minded A., 24a; persecute for doctrine without even stating it, 672b

Anglo-American A. quarrel, more friendly than alliance, 16a

Anglo-Catholics (Anglicans), 24a

Angry a. as a wasp, 22a; beshrew her a. heart, 22a; He that will be a. without cause, 22b

Anguish a. of child over broken doll, 24b

Animae testimonium a. naturaliter Christianae! 834b

Animal man, an earthly a., worthy of heaven, 569a; man, a seeing, contemplating, acting a., 750b; man is *not* a reasoning a., 750b

Animam Corpus Domini nostri custodiat a. meam, 595a

Animosities belong to soul of man, 113a

Announce I a. to you a great joy, 709b

Anoint A. me with heavenly grace, 207a

Anne, St., 24b, 85a, 87b, 170a, 462a

Annos Ad multos a.!, 930a

Annulment, 579a

Annunciation A word Thy willing handmaid heard, 25b; crowning of our salvation, 24b; good tidings of grace, 24b; Holy Spirit descended on her, 25a; In woman's virtue, life doth begin, 25b; manifestation of mystery from eternity, 24b; Oh, by Gabriel's AVE, 99a; O wonder of surpassing might! 25a; Spirit's flight lit upon thy heart, 91b; thou didst believe angel Gabriel's words, 24b, 88b; womb overshadowed by grace, 87a

Anointed each a. sense will see, 321b; flesh is a. that soul may be consecrated, 105b; servant of God is a. with oil of gladness, 51a

Anointing with chrism of salvation, 51a; with holy oil at baptism, 49b

Anonymous To be a., better than to be Alexander, 26a

Ante A. obitum mortuus, 247b

Antecedent God's a. will, 797b

Anteros For there Anteros with Eros, 41a

Anthem a. of choirs in heavenly day, 12b

Anthems Chant in sweet melodious a., 489a

Anthony, St., 519b

Anti-Catholic enormous power of a. dissuasions, 220b

Anti-Christ it may seem as though a. had come, 136b

Anti-Christian, 651a

Anticlericalism a. and rise of militant unbelief, 473a; A., not article for export, 26a

Antidote, 26a

Antioch, 662a, 662b, 675a

Antiphons, 588a

Antiquarian a. arguments unequal to facts, 23b; Church not an a. society, 876a

Antiquated reasonable dogma lives to be a., 27b

Antiquity hoary a. of Catholic Church, 32b; You are forever praising a., 26a

Anti-religious Communism is by its nature a., 199b

Antony A. lost world for love, 555a

Anxiety but one remedy for a., 26a; climax of a., no consecutiveness of thought, 867a; Restless a., forlorn despair, 113a

Anxious a. about supplies of this life, 215a

Apatheia, 899b

Ape An a. is an a., 26a; Both raven and a. think own young fairest, 160b; no more harm than a she a., 421a

Apes A. and ivory, skulls and roses, 780a

Apollo *I have preached A. watered,* 130b

Apologetic a. literature, fifty years behind times, 28a; As apologist, I am reverse of a., 27b

Apologetics art of rational a., 27b; defend faith rather than prove it to hilt, 26b; difficult, enter into characters others, 27a; discovery of Greeks, 27b; expel error by light of first principles, 27a; first prove Christianity is true, 27b; how to address others forcibly, 27a; men who live Church's ways, 217b; must deal with modern man, 28a; occasion of instruction, 144b; useful to one who realizes inadequacy, 27b; Use their own weapons, 26b; weak arguments, houses of tile-shards, 26b

Apology stiff a., second insult, 28a

Apostacy severs man from body of Church, 128a

Apostate if he falls away entirely, a., 432b; our a. nature, 98a

Apostates books of a., heretics, prohibited, 151b; persons who betray holy faith, 28a; segregated from community, 28a

Apostle divine Word Himself, 486a; drill-master makes but indifferent a., 614a; herald of Gospel and messenger of Christ, 613b

Apostles all receive keys of kingdom of heaven, 675b; Among His twelve a., 877a; among a., distinction of power, 433a; a. and martyrs pray for others, 795a; appointed first-fruits, bishops and deacons, 850b; authority of loosing given a., 67a; believed in Church they did not see, 121a; chosen as collaborators, 67b, 115a; delivered themselves with utmost clearness, 874a; distributed world into parts among themselves, 677a; doctrines delivered of old by a., 116b; endowed with a like fellowship of office and power, 693a; episcopal succession from a., 23b; foresaw contention over bishop's office, 66b; From a. the first age receiv'd, 875b; given three duties, 117a; given to one to

take lead of rest, 433a, 676b; glorious and famous a., 593a; Great King's senate glorious, 28b; harbingers of popes, 117b; have successors in bishops, 66b, 69b; His chosen band, 74a; Laurelled with the stole victorious, 28b; Let them believe creed of A., 227a; Lights of the world for evermore, 28b; made priests by Christ, 309a; most holy pillars, 674a; nothing conferred on a. apart from Peter, 678a; Oh! loose for us the guilty chain, 28b; obedient to Christ and Father, 67a; one flock shepherded by all a., 695b; O ye who throned in glory dread, 28b; Peter, leader of the choir, mouth of a., 675a; profit by celebrating a.'s glory, 28b; received gospel from Christ, 850b; rulers set over Thy flock, 28b; St. Augustine greatest teacher after a., 44b; secondary foundations of Church, 116b; Shall judge the living and the dead, 28b; strength of Church depends on them all, 675b; successors of the a., 189a; teaching of a., true gnosis, 873b; the Church's princes, 28a; The glorious company of the a. praise Thee, 792b; their everlasting glory, 28b; through Thy blessed a. keep watch, 28b; Thus a. tamed pagan breast, 26b; Thy shepherds and vicars, 28b; transmitted to nations teaching received from Christ, 429b; True lights to lighten every land, 28a; twelve, whom He called a., 69b

Apostolate chief a., preferred to any episcopate, 676a; His divine a., 115a

Apostolic a. choir, 28b; a. Christianity, seen through telescope, 101a; a. churches, moulds and sources of faith, 874a; A. Lord, 709b; A. See, Holy See, Chair of Peter, 709b; churches which apostles themselves once governed, 697b; church of Constantinople, subject to A. See, 700b; Health and a. benediction, 709b; If any one shall despise decisions of A. See, 700b; in A. See, religion always preserved without spot, 705a; judgment of A. See, than which no authority greater, 700b; never lawful reconsider what once settled by A. See, 698b; No one may condemn a decision of A. See, 701a; primacy of A. See, 699a

Apostolicae Curae, Bull, 23b

Apostolical a. origin of church, gives right to higher rank, 433b

Apostolicity A. of Catholic Church, 116b

Apostolicus domnus a., 709b

Apostolos Maximus post a. ecclesiarum instructor, 44b

Apotheosis A. of dust, 281b

Apparel The flesh is the a. of the soul, 345b

Apparition A. of Jesus to our Lady, 94b

Appeal a. to future council from Roman pontiff, 708a; custom has been for word to be sent to us first, 697b; not subterfuge, but refuge, 29a

Appeals from living voice of Church, 129b

Appearance Boobies have looked as wise, 29a; woman's a. depends upon two things, 277b

Appearances only shallow people

do not judge by a., 29a; under a. of bread and wine, 78b, 311a

Appetite For men have ever a lecherous a., 346a

Applauded Dost thou wish to be a.? 29a

Applause The brave man seeks not popular a., 444a

Apple all was for an apple, 29a; Lost with a., won with nut, 29b; No more like, than a. to oyster, 544a

Appreciation fairy of wide a., 160a

Apprehension vision and a. in spiritual experience, 515a

Appropriate a. time for each word and deed, 891a

Approve Fools admire, men of sense a., 6b

Approved choice of men a., not to be proved, 9b; That which touches all, should be a. by all, 534a

April A., dawning in her eyes, 55b; In A. skies were blue, 235b; in the wreckage of your A., 109a; Sweet was A., sweet was A.! 235b; When that April with his showers, 29b; When A. rain had laughed the land, 29b

Aquam Vidi a. egredientem de templo, 587a

Arbitrariness canon law effective guard against a., 112a

Arbitrate Men of tact that a., 910b; prompt to a. disputes, 29b

Arcanum discipline of a., 288a

Archangels one of nine orders of angels, 18b

Archbishop appointed in greater cities, 433b; confirms episcopal consecration, 67b

Archbishops bishops four-fold, patriarchs, a., metropolitans, and bishops, 433b

Archiereus, 433a

Architect one of problems for a. our time, 30a

Architects Italy had great a., 30a

Architecture Christ prophesied Gothic a., 30a; Gothic endowed with profound beauty, 29b; Italy, no great a. of its own, 30a; my reason may go with Gothic, 29b

Archprophet A. of prophets of the Father, 489a

Ardor as now on fire I am, 30b; holy a. that irradiates all, 384a; In love, respect first, a. second, 557a

Arena active life is in arena, 4b

Argue absurd to a. men into believing, 57b; a. pope was a Prodesan, 31a

Arguing little use in a. against non-Catholics, 27a

Argument a. from authority based on reason, 30b; a. from authority, weakest in human science, 46a; a. from revelation, strongest, 30b; Begin by pitying unbelievers, 887b; care not to offend, 216b; Clearness in a., not indispensable to reasoning, 750b; Fact and a., tests of truth and error, 885b; inadequacy of apologetics, 27b; knock-down a., 30b; man convinced by a., not intuition, 22a; Men worry over an a., 30b; not always able to command assent, 30b; The feast of reason, 279a; to cite human authority, poorest form of a., 863a; To most, a. makes point more doubtful, 750b; troublesome thing that leads to nothing, 30b; Women generally make up in heat, 921b

Arguments antiquarian a. unequal

to facts, 23b; a. cannot coerce unwilling, 27b; of what paltry worth Are a., 14a; possible to crush faith with learned a., 328a; weak a. against Catholicity, 26b; weak a., like houses of tile-shards, 26b

Arianism, 430b

Arise wicked a. again for punishment, 768b

Aristocracy means government by badly educated, 256b; not government, but riot, 31a; only real a., one of soul, 31a

Aristotle, 1b, 29a, 31a

Ark a. of holiness, 40b; a. of the covenant, 84b; Catholic Church is like a. of Noah, 126b; for tables of law, 41a; gilded by Holy Ghost, 100b; Harbor, like the A. of old, 230b; This little A. no cover hath, 486b; Vouchsafed, as in His a., to lie, 81b; When first the a. was landed on the shore, 665b

Arm momentous a. of political strength, 23b

Arma Haec sunt a. militiae nostrae, 352b

Armed Half warned, half a., 908a

Armies Before and after standing a. came, 606a; The a. died convulsed, 907a

Armor There is no a. against fate, 249a

Arms A. alone can keep peace, 348b; glory of a. and trumpets, 31a; reach down With strong a., 582a; safe compass of the everlasting a., 564b; These are the a. of our service, 352b

Army essence of a., official inequality, 31a; serve alike in a. of same Lord, 825a

Arrest no arbitrary a., 465b

Arrogance A. and boldness, belong to those accursed of God, 724b

Arrow O dart of love! a. of light! 218b; pierced our hearts with the a. of Your love, 550b

Arrows From whence at one, five a. fly, 31b; our minds, pierced with a. of Your words, 550b

Ars Sensus et a. medici curant, 268b

Art All a. is propaganda, 34a; All joy is young, and new all a., 487b; All loved A. in a seemly way, 32a; always product of cultural period, 33a; a. is a virtue of intelligence, 34a; A. is beauty made a sacrament, 33b; A. is finite expression made infinite, 33b; A. is handmaid of religion, 34a; A. is not sterile, 33b; a. is skill, 33b; A. is the signature of man, 32b; a. of enjoying everybody, 263a; breaks through enclosure of finite, 34b; Church has filled world with masterpieces, 33a; confusion of art and morality, 9b; contours of culture and art, 34b; difference between drama and other kinds of a., 276b; distinction between a. and nature, 33b; factory-made a. bad thing, 33b; From me, my a., thou canst not pass away, 687a; fundamental necessity to man, 33a; government of souls, is a. or arts, 659b; grows out of ideas of average man, 32b; imbecile faces of Picasso's a., 34a; in religious a., times telescoped, 33a; leads heavenwards, 34a; myth, work of imagination and of a., 629b; Nature is the a. of God eternal, 633a; Nature varies and imitates, a. imitates and varies, 634a; no a.

learned without master, 31b; Of the Godhead the grandchild, 32a; patience of God in tolerating bad a., 34b; Picasso's a., true a. of atheism, 34a; Philosophy is a. of arts, 680b; prepares man for contemplation, 33b; principles laid down by Church, 31b; provides window on infinite, 34b; prudent steward, 32a; Religion and a., older than agriculture, 760b; represents mind of maker, 31b; Rococo art, 32b; secret of life is in a., 32a; should never try to be popular, 32a; should preserve balance, 34b; simply right method of doing things, 31b; So vast is a., so narrow human wit, 363a; teaches pleasures of spirit, 33b; that strong, mimetic a., 363b; the a. to blot, 281b; Things come of it, 33b; to rule men is a. of arts, 403b; virtue of practical intelligence, 34a; With earnest soul and capital A., 32a; work of art is a word made flesh, 34a

Article those in a. of death, 247a

Articles, Thirty-Nine, 24a

Artificer, A. of all, 50a; great A. divine, 81b

Artificial Nothing a. really pleasing, 34b

Artificiality God does not like a., 192b

Artillery Heaven's great a., 868a; Love's great a., 554a

Artist a.'s acts cannot be involuntary, 34a; a.'s ambition to show off his 'breadth,' 689a; Every portrait painted with feeling, portrait of a., 711a; God is an a., 890a; has liberty if free to create, 35a; no human a. works blindly, 382b; taste or talent of individual a., 34b; test of a. in excellence of work, 31b; the work suggests the A., 372a

Artistic a. temperament, disease, 32b; difference between a. mind and mathematical, 686b

Artists get rid of their art easily, 32b; Hurry ruins saints as well as a., 422b; in world, but not of it, 35a; only revealed to one another, 35a; religious imagery not left to a., 31b; should be wooers of beauty, 35a; true a. and wealth of material, 32a

Arts became sacramental under Constantine, 33a; Church took over existing a., 33a; flower after cultural peak, 33a; God bred a. to make us believe, 32a

Ascension Christ's A., our uplifting, 35a; confirms us as possessors of paradise, 35a; God is gone up with a shout, 35b; He led captivity captive, 35b; His glorious a. into heaven, 592a; Now Christ, ascending whence He came, 670a; Sought again His Father's breast, 36a; Today above the sky He soared, 36a

Ascertained Men have always turned from the a., 226a

Ascetic letteth go all things created, 36b; true a. counts nothing his own, 36b; with divine avarice, covets kingdom, 37a

Asceticism desire only that which conduces toward end, 37a; mastery of man over himself, 37a; only one a. known to Christian history, 37a; renunciation, only real piety, 36b

Ashamed I have not so behaved that I should be a. to live, 519b; When we sin, we are all a., 810b

Ashen A. cross trace on brow, 37b;

Agonized hopes, and a. flowers!, 416b

Ashes All is dust, a., shadows!, 244b; a. of martyrs drive away demons, 583b; how could BVM become a.?, 40b; Raked up in th' a., 659a

Ash Wednesday, 37b

Ask a. for such things as shall please Thee, 717a; those wholly perfect in the faith, a. everything, 881b; Ye a., and receive not, 718a

Asks man who a. for himself, always judged, 767a

Asleep fallen a. in hope of resurrection, 593a; She lay a., 252a

Aspen Right as an aspes leaf, 37b

Asperges A. me, Domine, hyssopo, 587a

Asperity On all occasions, abjure a., 751a

Aspiration irrepressible a. to survival, 464b; Men would be angels, 38a

Aspirations Impassioned thoughts, high a., 643a

Ass art of driving an a. and cart, 42b; Fools! I also had my hour, 38a; I, even a little a., did go, 38a; The man who laugh'd but once, to see an a., 503b

Assassin The accomplice is no better than the a., 625b

Assassins A. find accomplices, 454b

Assemble right of people to a., 184b

Assemblies power should not be attributed to a., 3a

Assent argument not always able to command a., 30b; a. with civil leer, 239a; Church does not need a. of State, 181b; to accept religion, neither simple a. nor complex, 756b; to Christian doctrine and faith, 57b; with absolute internal a. and consent, 24a

Assert Never a. anything without being assured, 38a

Assimilate To a. blindfold, will end in poisoning, 690b

Assisi O city on the Umbrian hills, 38a

Assistance by continual a. give effect, 284a; grace of divine a., 450b; might of assistance of BVM, 87a; Stretch forth right hand of heavenly a., 910a

Association right of a., natural right of man, 38a

Associations cannot be prohibited by public authority, 38a

Assumed must ever be something a. ultimately, 39a

Assumption hasty a., before truth made plain, 38b

Assumption of Our Lady BVM, assumed body and soul into glory, 41b; By Mary's death mankind an orphan is, 40a; divinely revealed dogma, 41b; festival of this day, venerable, 39a; Gem to her worth, spouse to her love, 40a; grave and death could not retain her, 39a; bear you whither tend I, 41a; in way known only to Him, 39a; in thy repose thou didst not forsake world, 39a; Mary hath been taken to heaven, 39a; Mary, uplifted to our sight, 41b; Mary, your Queen, ascends, 41a; Multitudinous ascend I, 41a; O'er the choirs of angels holy, 40a; our resurrection in Mary anticipated, 41b; Round about whom angels fly, 40b; thou hast passed away to life, 39a; Who is she that ascends so high?, 40b

Assumptions without a. no one can prove anything, 27a

Assured Never assert anything without being a., 38a

Astonishment takes from us sense of pain, 415b

Astrology, 41b

Astronomer Starry amorist, 42a

Astronomy investigates movements of stars, 42a

Asunder *What God hath joined, let no man put a.*, 577a

Asylum churches, altar of safety for those who seek sanctuary, 798a

Athanasius, St., 519b

Athanatos Agios o Theos, ischyros, a., 41a, 589a

Atheism absolute a., religious phenomenon, 42b; adopted as religion of state, 42b; a. and education, 393a; avowing there is no God, 12a; exile of God, 43a; implicit confession of a., 30a; inconsistency of contemporary a., 42b; mirrors defacement of contemp. man, 34a; Picasso's art, true art of a., 34a; scepticism are more fundamental than a., 867a; science and a., 760b; way to Rome, and way to a., 42a; withering work of agnosticism, 12a

Atheist A pagan is not an a., 651a; A., communism is bourgeois deism, 42b; Mankind's belief in God, rebuke to careless a., 377b; miracle, no argument to a., 610b; Seeks God, although an a., 42b

Atheists Pity a. who seek, 42a; two kinds of a., 42b

Athens, 43a, 650b

Athlete Be temperate, like a. of God, 43a; no a. admitted to contest, 50a; Thou wast annointed as Christ's a., 43a

Athletes Souls are like a., 837b; toils of contests bring a. their crowns, 879b

Atlas A. held the firmament, 926b

Atone For sinners to a.!, 491a

Atonement Christ's passion reconciles us with God, 44a; Christ's passion, superabundant, 44a; divine world-form of redemption, 44a; He cleansed us by immolation of His own body, 176b; His death, sacrament of salvation, 43b; His passion, a kind of price, which paid cost, 752a; immolation of Christ our Passover, 43b; Mediator freed us from death, 43a; not merely passing act, 44a; pride of man, rebuked through humility of God, 751b; to reject Christianity because of doctrine of a., 852b

Atones as head of mankind, Christ a., 43b

Atoning Christ, constantly atoning for sins, 310a; Christ's a. life and death, 44a

Attain a. to Him, in being inwardly illuminated, 458b

Attenuation a. does but enfeeble, 146a

Attractions sweet a. and holy inspirations, 562b

Attributes a. of God transcend our comprehension, 388a

Audi A. alteram partem, 499a

Audience Some very foolish influence rules the pit, 276b

Aufer A. a nobis, 588a

Augsburg Confession, 180a

Augsburg, Peace of, 180a

Augustine, St., 23a; all loved and paid him honor, 44b; breath of suspicion never tarnished name, 44b; detested by heretics, 44b; Doctor of grace, 44b; greatest teacher after apostles, 44b; Let Austin have his labor to himself,

848b; no sermon without S., 44b; past ages produced no greater or grander, 44b; pronouncements of A. or any other doctor, 875a; What more golden or august?, 44b

Augustine of Canterbury, St., 19a

Aunt not permitted, to marry wife or son of uncle, 575b

Auras Beautiful habitations, a. of delight!, 304b

Aurelius, Emperor Marcus, 414b

Aureum hoc scriptore magis aureum, 44b

Ausonia O happy people, O glorious A.!, 211a

Austerities a. of diet and clothing, 479b; purity of love with which we do them, 624a

Austerity devil does not fear a., but holy obedience, 643a

Author A. of all things, 224b, 244b; A. of life, our Lord Jesus Christ, 88b; Blest A. of this earthly frame, 166b; expected to see a., found man, 849a; Fountain and A. of all graces, 197a; great a., one who has something to say, 45a; history of a., history of his works, 45a; nature reveals its A., 372a; O Thou, our A. and our End, 445b

Authoritarianism ecclesiastical authority, not a., 47a

Authorities must be obeyed, when power from God, 45b

Authority appeal to a. to support a., 499b; appeal to divine a., highest and most cogent argument, 863a; argument from a. based on reason, 30b; argument from a., weakest in human science, 46a; a. and wisdom of Church, 139a; A. may put itself in opposition to code, 331a; a. of bishop, unto edification, 68b; a. of governments is just, 16a; A. of kingdoms, from God, 45b; a. of popes and bishops contrasted, 69b; a. of prince depends on a. of law, 508a; a. of rulers, by natural law and by divine law, 45b, 406a; a. unto edification, 129a; By a. of our Lord Jesus Christ, 41b; Cast away a., a. shall forsake you!, 47a; Church teaches submission to a., 131b; despising legitimate a., rebellion against God, 46b; divine law gives power to collected body, 406a; eccles. a., vested immediately in one person, 180b; Eccles. power in every way immediately from God, 180b; Educate youth to respect for a., 47a; essential function of a., to safeguard freedom, 784b; greater than empire, to submit princely a. to laws, 508a; highest duty, to respect a., 46b; in political society, a. comes from below, 845b; institution of human law, 46a; love is only reconciliation of a. and liberty, 336a; men desire a. for its own sake, 46b; nature of ecclesiastical a., 117a; necessity of a. in religion, 118b; *no a., except from God*, 47b; no a. has power to impose error, 47a; no a. if in mortal sin, 46a; No king can have political a. immediately from God, 509a; nothing but mere numbers, 46b; no true a., if man denies God, 47b; only way to many truths, 47a; peer has no a. over peer, 45b; people despise a. of men, 47a; in general, comes directly from God alone, 405b; power to constrain spiritually and temporally, 45b; precedes reason in learning, 45b; public a., symbol of Divine Majesty, 46b; secular a. can be abol-

ished by Church, 46a; three theories of power, 47a; To all Church, a. of binding and loosing given, 677b; to cite human a., poorest form of argument, 863a; unbelievers forfeit a. over faithful, 46a; When religion is banished, a. totters, 758b; When rulers disdain authority of God, 47a; without sanction, unless from God, 46b

Authors acerbities which bite writing men, 160b; Catholic a. and dogmas, 118b; great a., greater than their books, 45a; holiness of a., no guarantee against error, 63b; judged by capricious rules, 45a

Autobiography Literature is to man, what a. is to individual, 545b; only biography possible, a., 65a

Autumn Again maternal a. grieves, 47b; A. days come swift, 48a; How are veins of thee, A., laden, 47b; In the a.'s mournful air, 48a; nature's Calvary, 47b; when a.'s mellow sunlight spills, 47b; wild, wild maiden!, 47b

Avail in Him you a. something, 123a

Avarice sin of a., instinct for riches, 48b; the root of vices, 48a; with something like divine a., 37a

Ave And for EVA AVE writeth, 25a, 25b; Ave, star of ocean, 99a; Oh, by Gabriel's AVE, 99a; One would swear he said Ave!, 25a

Average good art and a. man, 32b

Awake A. a., the morn will never rise, 777b; My soul, my soul, a., why dost thou sleep?, 483b

Award I would never a. him one wing, 60a

Azured Underneath her a. daïs, 683a

B

Babe A pretty B. all burning bright, 486b; Behold, a silly tender B., 168b; Fear leap in a b.'s face, 540b; God gives Himself as Mary's B., 487b; Look up, sweet B., 299a; Sleep, holy B., 487b; The B. bounds in her hand, 488a; the holy B. is here, 168a; This little B. will be thy guard, 487a; Thou shiverest in a manger, B. Divine, 168b; With God for B. and Spouse, 84a; Won'drous B. of Bethlehem, 170b

Babel rough-cast from B.'s bricklayers, 519a; Since haughty B.'s prime, 296a

Babels A thousand hollow B. tower, 185b; B. now may smile into thy sunless eye, 251b; O blessed b.! first flowers of Christian spring, 441a

Baby b. of Belsabub's bower, 48a; oft are heard the tones of infant woe, 161a; thy little B. sweet, 84a

Babylon B.! where is thy might?, 367b

Bacchus B.'s blessings are a treasure, 279a; B. ever fair, ever young, 279a

Bachelor priest, not just pious b., 151a; uncumber'd with wife, 48a

Bachelorhood be married to a single life, 149b

Bachelors all the married men live like b., 574b; boast how they will teach their wives, 912a

Bacon There's no pot without b., 44b

Bad b. in b. taste, unpardonable, 48a; b. things are in God's knowledge, 383b; condemned, wasted, by affliction, 10a; evil is slave, though he be king, 399a; Evil, that which tends to non-being, 313b; Evil things had origin in good things, 313b; Heaven punishes b., proves best, 539a; known by God through types of good things, 384a; no one is evil by nature, 314a; tares grow in Church, 124b; What is evil, but privation of good?, 313a; When the b. are punished, 740a; whoever is evil is evil by vice, 314a

Bag As well as bagger knoweth his b., 56a

Bait caught by the devil's b., 260a

Baits with honor's gilded b. beguiled, 444a

Bald Better a b. head than no head, 48b; blossom-bald, 239b; He was as ballid as a cote, 48b

Ball He kicked the b. with his right foot, 49a; This congregated b., 282b

Ballot b. is pride of true American, 904a; casting of b., supreme act of citizenship, 904a; honest b. and social decorum, 17a

Balm As b. my wound to heal, 210b; O Jesus, b. of every wound!, 584b

Baltimore, Maryland, 101a, 585b

Bands Knit in everlasting b., 36a

Bane swine overfat is cause of his own b., 338b

Banishment b., which thou hast first to fear, 318b

Bankrupt B. of life, prodigal of ease, 11b

Banner b. of the red and white and blue, 345b; Furl that b.! True, 'tis gory, 345a

Banners Abroad the regal b. fly, 230a; something gallantly great in b. of foe, 31a

Banquet O sacred b., heavenly feast!, 197b

Banqueting B. in her wind-walled palace, 683a

Banshee the wailing b.'s cry, 365a

Baptism actual or by desire (in voto), 52b; anointing with holy oil in b., 49b; b. and forgiveness of sins, 51a; b. and membership in Church, 127b; B. by fire, 583b; b. by immersion, 49b; b. of heretics, true b., 52b; b. of martyrdom, 49b, 50b; b. of non-Catholics valid, 50b; buried with Christ within, 52a; By b., Christians participate in priesthood of Christ, 731a; by suffering or martyrdom, 53a; by this Paschal sacrament, 441b; changes man for better by grace, 51b; cleanses flesh and soul, 51b, 105b; diffusing grace of Thy adoption, 441b; disposition proper to b., 49b; door and foundation of sacraments, 52b; fellowship with angelic powers through b., 50a; fills with power of Holy Spirit, 51a; he that believeth, and is b., shall be saved, 670b; holy illumination, 50b; how sanctification takes place, 52a; leaves character which remains, 52a; Let Your b. be your shield, 401a; makes us children of the kingdom, 51a; mark of the Lord, 50b; minister cannot defile sacrament, 51b; means dipping in Latin, 51b; natural water must be used with formula, 52b; necessary for salvation, 52b; new birth by means of water and Spirit, 51a; no b., no salvation, 49b; not optional, 52b; of blood and desire, 53a; of penitence or desire, 53a; One Lord, one faith, one b., 145a; our b., anticipated in Mary, 41b; prefigured by drowning of Egyptians,

51b; prescribed formula must be used, 52b; purifies soul through Holy Spirit, 51b; regenerated in font of b., 51b; regeneration, effected by Holy Ghost, 50b; remission of sins through b., 206a; renews unto life eternal, 51a; signed with seal of Holy Trinity, 500a; spiritual and saving seal, 49b; spiritual effect of unction, 49b; there is to us but one b., 49b; three features in sacrament of b., 52a; Thy divine and profitable gift, 50a; triple immersion in b., 51a; true doctrine of b. in Roman church, 52b; twofold purification of body and soul, 52a; validity of non-Catholic b., 50b; washes away guilt of punishment, 50a, 52a; washes away sins, 49a; washes out sin Which Adam did commit, 788a; water of regeneration, 51b; waters imbibe power of sanctifying, 49b; What society needs, b. of Holy Spirit, 440b; When at the font His name we chose, 283b; wondrous grace of holy b., 51a; work not of man but of Christ, 51b; In pure b. wave, 284a; That mystic bath, that grave of sin, 284a

Baptize b. in name of Father, 49a, 368a; b. in running water, 49a; I b. thee in name of the Father, 51a; non-Catholics sometimes b. Catholics, 50b; not lawful to. without bishop, 67a; thy spotted soul in weeping dew, 765a

Baptized all reborn in Christ, royal and priestly race, 730b; anointed as Christ's athlete, 43a; children of Thy adoption, 51b; may not go on sinning, 52b; new offspring of Thy family, 441b; Questions put to those being b., 226a; servant of God is b. in the name, 51a; those born again through Thy grace, 670a; we are b. in only one name, 50a

Barbarians b. and influence of Church, 139a; conversion to Christian faith, 187a; ignorant of purity of Latin, 53a; our sins, which make b. strong, 779a; toleration of heretics, more injurious than b., 429b; transmitted faults to Romans, 53a; when b. were attacking city, 100a

Barbarism fragile barriers separate civilization from b., 187a; misspelled or mispronounced word, 53a; modern civilization and early b., 186a; so-called from barbarians, 53a; worship of nature, 186a

Bards in their latest b., 296a

Bargain b. betwixt earth and heaven, 219a

Barge Have an oar in every man's b., 601a

Bark b. of Scripture known to non-Catholics, 63a

Baroque four centuries of B. spirit, 437a

Barren Rejoice thou b. that bearest not, 129b

Barrel She was made like a b., 338b

Bashfulness Unknown, unkissed, 53a

Bastards shall be honest and safe, 53b

Bath Fresh from b., get warm, 53b; let b. not be incessant, 53b; once a month, 53b

Battle conquering grace's b. fought, 35b; Dreadful as a b. arrayed, 41a; Finished is the b. now, 286a; no such thing as defensive b., 254b; only dying do not love noise,

217a; Sing, my tongue, the glorious b., 230b; Unless b. has preceded, cannot be victory, 895a; Who went to b. forth and always fell, 324a

Battle-cries A thousand creeds and b., 277b

Battlefield active life, b. of toil, 5a

Battlements The star-usurping b. of night, 636b

Battles Faith means b., 324b

Bay crown of roses and of b., 38a

Be not choose not to b., 258b; one thing to b., another to b. primarily, 224b; Wish not to b. anything, 395a

Beads A set of b., the gaudies tricked in green, 781b; B. and prayer-books, toys of age, 262b; Sweet, blessed b.! I would not part, 782a; telling his b. In penance for past misdeed, 748b

Bean Like a b. in a monk's hood, 53b; Not the worth of a b., 929a

Beans cause constipated tone, 53b; Hunger maketh hard b. sweet, 454a

Bear By Sacrament we b. Christ in us, 70b; fur that warms a monarch warmed a b., 361b; let us b. Him in our hearts, 897b

Beard cannot be grown in moment, 53b; Take a hair from his b., 53b; This hath not offended the king, 509a

Beards It is merry in hall when b. wag all, 497b

Bearer B. of our iniquities?, 349a

Bearing of his port as meek as is a maid, 161b

Bears she who slays is she who b., 161b

Beast too good to be a b. of prey, 22b

Beasts By nature, man made superior to b., 300a; I am ground by teeth of wild b., 458a; subjects of tyrannic sway, 12b

Beatific unregenerate children deprived of b. vision, 238b

Beatitude arrows hitting the mark of b., 305b; attainment of God is b., 102b, 393b, 458b; in vision of Him is our eternal b., 486b; O close my hand upon B.!, 103a; pursuit of God is desire of b., 102b

Beauties B. in vain their pretty eyes may roll, 55a

Beautiful All b. and bright, 41a; b. things please when seen, 54b; b. woman quick to inspire love, 54a; beauty and b., same in God, 54b; For Thee do I yearn, Justice, Innocence, B., 261b; From Thy fair mind, world fair like Thyself doth make, 372b; love of b. will not conquer world, 55a; the All-B., 378a; You, and Your Mother, only ones completely b., 459b

Beauty all b. derived from God, 54a; all things that of beauty be, 20b; artists wooers, not workers, of b., 35a; balance of b. and severity in Christianity, 164b; beautifully in B., 835a; b. and beautiful, same in God, 54b; b. and goodness point beyond themselves, 377a; b. and intellectual expression, 867a; B.'s elixir vitae, praise, 55a; B. self, in Whom all pleasure is, 562b; believing Christian does not require, 455a; BVM, thou appearest in b., 39b; Brittle b., nature made so frail, 54b; chiefest work wrought by nature, 111a; consists in due proportion, 54b; disfigured by sin, 76a; dispensed even to wicked, 54a;

draws us with a single hair, 418a; every child likes b., 55a; every little spark of b.'s burning, 258a; Fickle treasure, abhorred of reason, 54b; Flowering today, tomorrow apt to fail, 54b; gift is small, short the season, 54b; Giver of love, and b., and desire, 490b; God is measure of beauty, 54a; good gift of God, 54a; Has looked On B. bare, 55b; hearts have to be purified to see b., 54a; Her b. lights the April day, 55b; holy woman ought to obscure b., 53b; How should I gauge what b. is her dole, 837a; lies in coincidence of features, 55a; little powder and gauze properly disposed, 222a; love of b. may captivate but not conquer, 55a; My fair, no b. of thine will last, 556b; natural and simple to like b., 55a; not imparted by silk, 7a; not necessary to angels, 18b; O B. so ancient and so new, 559b; O Jesu, Thou the b. art, 630a; of women is the greatest snare, 919b; only thing time cannot harm, 55a; order, b. of world, proclaim made by God, 372b; profound and commanding b., 29b; proportion and agreement make b., 54b; put on with a garment, 7a; radiance of truth, fragrance of goodness, 55b; relates to cognitive faculty, 54b; She is a peacock in everything but b., 667a; should be used for God, 54a; Sweet b. with sour beggary, 54b; the b. of an aged face, 11a; The piercing b. of the stars, 612a; The power of b. I remember yet, 55a; Too late have I loved Thee, O B., 54a; When b. fires blood, 55a; Youth, b., graceful action seldom fail, 152b

Becomingly *no one ought to live .other than b.,* 157b

Bed dust shall never be thy b., 55b; for reasons, husband and wife may separate from b., 580b; will ye lie in b.? 55b

Bedridden Though he lie b. till he expires, 455a

Bee labors for others, 55b; more honored than other animals, 55b; Quick as a b., 746b; wild b. reels from bough to bough, 56a

Beers So many b. and whiskeys multiplied, 279b

Bees Their heads be full of b., 55b

Before B. the ending of the day, 201a

Befriend Whom God does once with heart b., 411a

Beg Ye b. at wrong man's door, 56a

Beggar As well as b. knoweth his bag, 56a; He was finest b. of his batch, 56a; lady's heart and a b.'s purse, 424a

Beggars b. should be no choosers, 56a

Beggary sweet beauty with sour b., 54b

Begging petition of empty hand dangerous, 56a

Begin after a pause, b., 149b; B. nothing without eye to th'end, 149b; Best way to end well is to b. well, 56b; every prayer and work may b. from Thee, 428b; In Christ's name let us b., 56a

Beginning God, b. of all things, 218b, 372a; hard b. maketh good ending, 56b; *In the b. God created heaven and earth,* 225a; *In the b. was the Word,* 596b; Of good b., cometh good eende, 56b; O in b. once so bright, 710a; O Lord, Who hast brought us to b. of this day, 731a; Who that well his work beginneth, 56a

Beginnings In Christians, we look not to b. but to endings, 163a

Begotten men, b. for heaven and eternity, 336b

Beguiled They that think none ill, soonest b., 348a

Behaved I have not so b. that I should be ashamed to live, 519b; Would to God we had b. ourselves, 56b

Behaves He doesn't act, he behaves, 4a

Behavior good b. even for one day, 56b

Behold B. the Man! who wore A crown of thorns, 657b

Being b. belongs especially to God, 301a; b. self-contained and enduring, 56b; B., than Which nothing greater can be conceived, 375b; cannot be corrupted or changed, 56b; divine B., transcendent end towards which life converges, 864a; eternity, proper measure of permanent b., 306a; every b. is good, 56b, 57a, 313a; every b. not God is God's creature, 57a; everything owes its b. to form, 350a; God, all-perfect, unchangeable B., 619b; Goodness and b., really the same, 398a; Ground of b. and granite of it, 374a; infinite B. is identical with infinite Life, 374b; no b. as such can be evil, 399a; one B. alone exists in highest degree, 375b; rational creature created, that it might love supreme B., 560b; that which continues the same, 56b; to Whom 'b.' and 'b. alive,' not separate things, 374b

Belief assent given to someone's words, 57b; authority of Scriptures leads to b., 60a; b. and acquisition of knowledge, 270b; b. and credibility, 57a; b., and limitation of private judgment, 57b; from b. to mastery of knowledge, 57a; fulness of Catholic b., 144a; implications of b. in Catholic creed, 57b; implicit and explicit b., 271b; is act of freewill, 57a; Let law of prayer determine law of b., 546b; No one forced against will to embrace Catholic faith, 613a; rational grounds for their religious b., 332a; three roads to belief, 57b; wall of division between learned and simple, 58a; we take hints from workings of nature, 772b; With gold of thy b.? 329a

Believe b. faith, b. *in* faith, 326b; b. that thou mayest understand, 57a; B. that you have it, and you have it, 326b; Dost thou b. in God the Father Almighty? 226a; God bred arts, to make us b., 32a; Holy Ghost bestows fulness of grace on those who b. rightly, 874a; I, b. and profess, 145b; I b. in God, because I b. in myself, 376b; I b. in God, the Father almighty, 226a; I b. in Jesus Christ, His only Son, 480b; I b. in one God, 224a, 589b; I believe in one holy, Catholic, 119b; *Man cannot b. otherwise than of his own freewill,* 355a; natural for mind to b., 57b; nature of man to b. from others' example, 57b; *not to them that b.,* 610a; possible to b., but not love, 57a; reasoned arguments strengthen will to believe, 27b; required of those who b. in God, witness of God, 352b; So they b., because they so were bred, 289a; Spirit moves heart to b., 53a; that thou mayest understand, 887b; The things we must b., are few and plain, 327a, 875b; unless I b., I should not understand, 331b; Unless I *feel,* I will not b., 333a; Unless I understand, I will not b., 333a; we are not permitted to b. whatever we choose, 429b; we may b. without feeling devotion, 330a; we must first b. before we seek to know, 330b; What makes them b. is the Cross, 233a; will to b., received from God, 356b; you cannot force man to b., 57a

Believed impossible to love what is not b., 57a

Believers all true b. and professors of the Catholic faith, 591b; future belongs to b., not doubters, 58b; supreme Father of all b., 441b

Believes b. with heart unto justice, 640a; he who b. in Me, even if he die, 246a, 670b

Believing absurd to argue men into b., 57b; b. and knowing are different things, 330b; we must start by b., 57a

Bell every note of every b., 59a; Hark, how chimes the passing b., 58b; If the far b. he hears across the land, 312b; I wish I were the little b., 198a; Now play through heaven the angel b., 169a; Of all strong beasts lion bears the b., 54b; Setting the jacinth b. a-swing, 56a; she beareth the b., 58b; That vesper b. from afar, 58b

Belligerents want peace to their liking, 665a

Bells A flock of b. take flight, 59a; I hear the tuneful b. around, 169a; I often think of the Shandon b., 58b; they call you home, 109a; Those evening b.! 58b; Though no high-hung b. or din, 498b

Bell-wether Sad b. to the rest, 765a

Belly What b. asketh, not all good for ghost, 278b; When b. is full, bones would be at rest, 847b

Belong We are Christians, we b. to Christ, 163b

Beloved B., it is morn! 623a; my B. One is mine, 562b; to love all things loved of its b., 561b

Belsabub baby of the B.'s. bower, 48a

Bending Aged trees do break with b., 257b

Bene *B. qui latuit, b. vixit,* 26a

Benedicamus *B. Domino,* 596a

Benedicat *B. vos omnipotens Deus,* 595b

Benedict, St., 59a, 615b, 616a

Benedictine, 59a

Benediction Health and apostolic b., 709b; He fills every creature with b., 225b; sprinkles b. through the dawn, 78b

Benedictus *Bernardus valles, montes B. amabat,* 615b

Benefactions return thanks for b. of God, 59b

Benefactor Lover of men, B. of our souls, 595b; our only B., 89a

Benefactress We praise thee as our b., 299a

Benefits Give thanks frequently to God for all b., 862a; God's b., 212b

Benet, St., 927b
Benevolence love of God, not mild b., 565a
Benignity Thou goest before in thy benignity, 91b
Benjamin, 770b
Bent Tender twigs are b. with ease, 257b
Bereavement Dear Lord, receive my son, 59b
Bernard, St., 79b, 91a, 615b
Bernardus B. valles, montes Benedictus amabat, 615b
Bernhardt, Sarah, 6a
Berry His palfrey, brown as is a b., 446b
Beshrew b. her angry heart, 22a
Bessarion, 770b
Best all is for the b., 646a; All that is b., from Thee comes down, 366b; b. cart may overthrow, 113b; b. is b. cheap, 59b; give to world b. you have, 540a; God only asks you to do your b., 293b; Good is b. when soonest wrought, 255a; greatest crabs be not b. meat, 223b; Heaven punishes bad, proves b., 539a; in the B. shall be b., 261b; None but b. deserve the fair, 108a; O thou, the greatest and the b., 386b; 'Tis b. by far, 59b; To make the b. of those that are, 59b; Whate'er is b. administr'd, is b., 406a
Bestower Treasury of good things, B. of life, 439a
Bête l'ange, fait la bête, 20a
Bethlehem Ah, B., I needs must come to thee, 488a; B. of noblest cities, 298b; He was true God in B.'s crib, 488b; has exhausted world's capacity for worship, 773a; hath opened Eden, 169b; In B.'s stable born in cold, 168b; low like cave of B., 122a; O hasten, O hasten to B., 170a; The Christmas stars at B., 171a; The Light of B., 170b; Wond'rous Babe of B., 170a
Better believe b. things of others, 451a; Esteem not thyself b. than others, 451a; nothing can be imagined b. than God, 378b
Betterment b. of workers, 38b
Betting If wager were but one butterfly, 60a
Betrayed He is b. over and over again, 484b
Betrothal The servant of God N. is betrothed, 576a; violation of b., sacrilege, 59b
Beware b. by other men's harms, 149b; Three things to b. of, 297b
Bible a book all can read, 60a; all senses built on literal sense, 61a; all written therein, meant to be mirror for us, 63b, 739a; authority of B. and tradition of Church, 60b; authors have not erred, 63b; book that is truly liberal, 35a; cannot be fully fathomed, 62b; canonical books received by Trent, 64a; Catholic faith and true interpretation, 144a; contains facts and mysteries, 61a; demands closest attention, 60b; we derive spiritual sense from history, 61a; divine canon, 60b; divine law, 61a; divinely inspired, 64a; divine word, 60b; error cannot coexist with inspiration, 64b; foolish oppose teaching of B. and Church, 63a; full of obscurities, 63a; God, Author both Testaments, 64a; heart of God in words of God, 64a; how much blood sowing of it cost, 61b; helps us to be with Him, 60a; illustrates

morality, 63a; inspiration guaranteed by Church, 62a, 64a; interpretation and private judgment, 60b; is B. intelligible to all? 63a; language of B. expresses mysteries, 63a; let interpreter use research, 64b; letter from our fatherland, 60b; like a mirror wherein we see progress, 60b; literal and spiritual sense, 61b; literal sense often admits others, 63a; meditate daily on words of Creator, 64a; men needed authority of Holy Writ, 60a; modern methods of interpretation, 64b; mysteries of B. beyond reason, 63a; not correctly interpreted outside Church, 63a; Old Testament must be spiritually read, 61a; our duty to live by one book, 107a; preserves majesty of mystery, 60a; profundity is marvelous, 60b; reveals disclosures behind veil, 62b; sacred writers cannot disagree, 63a; senses illustrate dogma, 63a; stream wherein elephant may swim, 60b; studies of non-Catholics sometimes useful, 63a; sufficiency of B., 737b; teachings of B. not contrary to Church, 63a; vernacular versions authorized, 63b; what would B. profit without love? 62a; whether doctrines contained therein, 62b
Bibles must have *imprimatur*, 152a
Bid Give what Thou bidst, and b. what Thou wilt, 410a
Bigot b. or slave of dogma, 499b
Bigotry belief others wrong in everything, 65a; infliction of unproved first principles, 64b
Bile b. of darkest kind, 263a
Billiard billiard ball enough to amuse man, 18a
Bind *All that you b. on earth*, 729a; Fast b., fast find, 344b; whatsoever bishop shall b. on earth, 68b; *whatsoever thou shalt b. on earth*, 693a
Binder O B. of sheaves, 834a
Binding pontifical power of b. and loosing, 175b, 677a; To all Church, authority of b. and loosing given, 677b
Biography few deserve b., 65a; only b., autobiography, 65a; panegyric, mistake in b., 3b
Bird a b. can't fly on one wing, 280a; better b. in hand than ten in wood, 65a; foul b. defileth own nest, 65a; My love is like a b., 558a; The b., let loose in eastern skies, 443b; wounded b., that hath but imperfect wing, 2a
Birds b. are flown, 65a, 301a; crow thinketh her own b. fairest, 54b; God has so many singing b., 832a; Made Him b. in a moment merry, 65a; Other men catch the b., 361b; When b. shall roost, 826b
Birth *A Savior's b.!* 170b; b. and death, both of nature, 65b; b. in time added nothing to eternal b., 467a; b. Of the people of the earth, 627a; death is b., 65b; fairest things in life are death and b., 543a; forbidding b., only quicker murder, 1b; high and noble b., 435b; His b. our joy, 487a; learning, goodness, b., gifts of God, 451b; long links of death and b., 464a; narrow doors of b., 565b; nothing men more pride themselves on, than b., 544b; rais'd my b., or debas'd my

mind, 65b; save mankind by mortal b., 7b; untainted b. of Christ from Mary, 79a; Washed with fire to irradiant b., 287a
Birth-control intercourse unlawful, if conception prevented, 66a; sins of b. always mortal, 66a; To forbid birth, only quicker murder, 1b; when act not unnaturally frustrated, 66a
Birthday My b.!—what a different sound, 66b; multiply days with many years, 66b; natural b. and heavenly joys, 66b
Birthdays The b. of a rising world, 531b
Bishop allotted his proper ministrations, 433a; anoints with holy oil at baptism, 49b; appointed by bishops of province, 67b; assigns lots according to God's bidding, 67a; at ordination, presbyter blesses, b. ordains, 647a; averts judgment of last day, 69b; b. and Christ, 122b; b. is in Church, Church in b., 299b; b. is pontiff, chief of priests, 69a; b. of few words, respected, 66b; b. or presbyter shall baptize, 49b; b.'s pre-eminence, 150b; chosen by Father for episcopate, 67a; Church established in b. and clergy, 433a; condescension of divine grace creates bishop, 647b; contention over b.'s office, 66b; directs each of clergy, 69a; duty of b., judge, consecrate, offer, 69a; each bishop on throne, judge, 69b; entrusted with souls of diocese, 67b; everything suffers by translation except b., 70a; fear him as your king, 172b; feeds flock, serves as high priest, 67a; forbidden to dwell with women, 188a; forbidden to exercise secular government, 188b; forgives sins by priestly Spirit, 67a; given grace and divine Spirit, 67b; given keys of kingdom, 68b; given power to rule people, 68b; glory of Church is glory of b., 67a; has ministry of reconciliation, 68b; has power over all clergy, 69a; he is no b. who loves to rule, 68a; honor of b. and order of Church, 433a; if anyone be not with the b., 299b; Let b. be ordained by two or three bishops, 647b; Let Eucharist be valid, offered by b., 307a; let his speech show forth Spirit, 68b; looses every bond, 67a; make him holy, 69a; manages possessions of Church, 67b; may God be b.'s authority, 68b; may he ever obtain God's mercy, 68b; ministers blamelessly day and night, 67b; one altar, one b. with priests and deacons, 597b; one b. who is head of Church, 695b; ordains priests and levites, 69a; ordinary minister of confirmation, 206b; ordinary minister of ordination, 648b; Palaces belong to emperor, churches to b., 173a; parent of our souls, 68a; pontiff set visibly over Church, 130b; priests, like strings of lyre, in harmony with b., 726a; propitiates God's countenance, 67a; real distinction of rank between priest and b., 647b; regarded as Master Himself, 66b; Remember our b., preserve him to thy churches, 593a; sanctified with heavenly ointment, 68b; sent by Master to run house, 66b; shall not undertake cares of this

world, 188b; should be chosen in presence of people, 67a, 647a; should be useful to flock, 68a; strengthened by Holy Spirit, 68b; thou hast authority to forgive sins, 67b; Thy b.'s fadeless crown, 69a; thy place that of God almighty, 67b; to be b. much, to deserve, more, 68a; twice married cannot become b., 188b; universal b., 700b; whatever has his approval, pleasing to God, 67a; wherever b. appears, let people be, 122b; with undivided mind obey b. and priests, 67a, 194b; worthy to offer prayers for people, 69a; worthy to shepherd flock, 67b; you ought to love b. as your father, 172b

Bishops able to take away and grant earthly empires, 176a; all b. must make *ad limina* visits, 70a; apostles provided for succession of b., 66b; appointed with consent of Church, 66b; aristocracy of b., 117b; b. and authority of popes, 69b; b. and presbyters, specially called priests, 730b; b. and unity of Church, 133a; B., priests, deacons, must remain unmarried, 150a; By divine institution, hierarchy consists of b., priests, ministers, 190a; Church founded upon b., 433a; distinction between b., 433b; elect b. and deacons worthy of Lord, 67a; entrusted with affairs of Church, 172a; essential to organization of Church, 69b; have power of confirming and ordaining, 69a, 648b; having primacy after model of God, 433a; inherit ordinary power of apostles, 69b; in matters of faith, b. wont to judge emperors, 172b; judge men before day of judgment, 189a; jurisdiction under authority of pope, 69b; like leaders in Christ's army, 206b; may not be accused in secular courts, 188a; ministered blamelessly to flock of Christ, 66b; must examine other b., 188a; must not rashly assail kings, 172b; My honor is solid strength of my brothers, 707a; not infallible in doctrine, 70a; not vicars of Roman pontiffs, 69b, 117b; Once, no difference of style between b. and priests, 647b; one episcopate, through multitude of b., 299b; ordained by God, 67b; order of b. four-fold, 433b; ought to be nourished from revenues, 67b; over churches by divine institution, 69b; partners of His honor, 695a; pope not sovereign lord of b., but one of them, 707a; right of pope to depose b., 180b; shall be consecrated by three b., 67b; shepherds, not slave-drivers, 740b; should be accused before b., 189a; should be humble, well tested, 67a; should not devour revenues of Church, 67b; successors of the apostles, 69b, 189a, 873b; superior to priests, 69a, 648b; true doctors and teachers, 70a; truly called ordinary pastors, 69b; two classes monk should avoid, women and b., 618b; we pray also for b., 243b; you may not be judged by men, 171b

Biteth old dog b. sore, 273a

Bitter B. as wormwood, 259a; How a sweet seed a b. fruit may bear, 856a; How b. another's bread is, 318b; Sweet and b., b., sweet, 170b

Bitterness no b. in controversy, 27a

Bitters B. will purge, 263a

Blab B. it wist, and out it must, 403b

Blachernae, Our Lady of, 100b

Black B. as damning drops that fall, 20a; B. as is jet, 71a; B. but fair, 853b; b. crow thinketh own birds white, 234b; With double potence of b. and white, 490b

Blame How can I praise, and not offend, 22b; men reprehend what they cannot comprehend, 70a; those who lived Without praise or b., 601b; wish for praise when we deserve b., 714b

Blandishments b. of women, 919b

Blarney difference between b. and boloney, 70a

Blasphemy nothing worse than b., 70a; weight of b., 231b; unbelievers who impede faith by b., 57a

Blasphemed They b. God, b. their mother's womb, 238b

Bleeds My Savior b.! B.! 104b

Bless before food, b. the Maker, 278b; B. us, O Lord, and these Thy gifts, 600b; dying, b. the hand that gave blow, 349b; I b. You, I glorify You, 368a; Let us b. BVM often, 92a; Let us b. the Lord, 596a; May almighty God b. you, 595b; O lord, Who dost b. them that b., 596a; Sweet Savior! b. us ere we go, 312b; Through whom Thou dost create, sanctify, b., 593a; We praise Thee, We b. Thee, 588b

Blessed all generations shall call me b., 92a; America b. because deserves to be b., 15b; And thankfully b. and brake it, 76b; B. are they that are ambitious, 14b; *b. art thou among women,* 82a; B. art Thou Who so willed it, 90a; B. be kingdom of the Father, 587a; B. is he who expects nothing, 264a, 453a; B. is man who letteth go, 36b; *b., Who cometh in name of Lord,* 81a, 591a; everyone b. is a god, 102b; innocence and knowledge make man b., 102b; man made b. by obtaining divinity, 102b; Man never is, but always to be, blest, 445b; pleased with nothing if not b. with all, 571a

Blessed, The after Resurrection, 124b; choirs that dwell on high, 12b; some flower, In fields of heaven, 277b; little ones, Lost within light divine, 277a; Made in last promotion of the blest, 896b; O chosen band, to the great supper called, 293b; reign eternally with God, 124b; see Divine Essence, 302b; spirits in eternity, 243b; spirits of just are at rest, 247a; Those endless sabbaths b. ones see!, 785a; Where are the islands of the b.?, 415a; Where they that loved are blest, 304a; You spirits, who have thrown away, 70b

Blessedness b. and subjection of mind to God, 102b; consists in possession of truth, 102b; estate replenished with all good, 419b; everlasting b., 302a; Lot of saints, 125a

Blessed Sacrament abiding help for soul and body, 196a; adorers of Sacrament, not idolaters, 76b; angelic Bread of heaven, 75a; As Christ willed it, and spake it, 76b; At once they worship and thy food, 78a; Be a foretaste sweet to me, 75b; be Thou my sure defense, 196a; Body and Blood present, regardless of use, 76a; Body given us to keep and eat, 71b; Body we consecrate, from Virgin, 71b; bond of friendship, 71b; both Shepherd and Green Pasture, 73a; Bread and Wine, not bare elements, 70a; Bread of man today, 74b; by it we come to bear Christ, 70b; Center of rest, 77b; Choose my heart for Thy dwelling-place, 196a; Christ, adored and worshipped, 76a; Christ eaten spiritually and sacramentally, 76b; Christ's true body contained in S., 73b; confers spiritual grace, 76a; consecrated by word of Christ, 71b; Divine Coal, 195b; Divine Fire, 195b; Draw nigh, take Body of the Lord, 195b; dread presence of Thy majesty, 196a; eat and drink to participation of Spirit, 72b; *everlasting showing forth of His death,* 73b; faith alone not sufficient preparation, 76b; Faith for all defects supplying, 74a; faithful become Body of Christ, 72a; feast of the Sacrament, 72a; figure of Body and Blood in bread and wine, 70b; Flesh of God is food for me, 72a; fruit of Thy redemption, 75a; gathers peoples like corn and wine, 72b; given worship of latria, 76a; Godhead, Whom I do adore, 75a; heavenly medicine, 72a; He makes us His body in Sacrament, 72b; how well appointed His banquet, 73b; I believe that this is Thy most pure Body, 594b; I gaze in silence on the little door, 78b; I will take the Bread of Heaven, 595a; incorporates, quickens us, 73a; itself sating, of itself makes thirst, 196b; joy in harvest, 78a; judge not matter from taste, 71a; living Bread from heaven, 74b, 75a; Lo! the sacred Host we hail, 74a; Love's Captive, 198a; may be borne in processions, 76a; medicine for our wounds, 72a; memorial of Thy passion, 73b, 75a; most divine of all sacraments, 73a; my heavenly Food, 77b; no room for doubting Flesh and Blood, 71a; nourishment of faithful, 73b; O memorial of my Savior dying, 75a; O sacrament of mercy, 73a; O sacred banquet, heavenly feast!, 197b; O Thou holy Bread, Thou living Bread, 196a; O wondrous gift indeed, 74b; O'er a sign of white on the altar, 598a; Oh the mystery, passing wonder, 442b; pilgrim's hoping—leaven, 75a; received unto death and condemnation, 76b; repairs lost virtue, 76a; reservation in sacristy, 76b; S. truly contains Body, 76a; s. of altar, so well known to faithful, 485b; Sacrament of His Body and Blood, 72b; Sacrament which raises us to heaven, 71a; sacred mysteries of Thy Body and Blood, 75a; safeguard and healing remedy, 594b; sense suggests bread, faith establishes Body, 71a; spiritual Food and Drink, 70b; spiritual participation, 72b; Sweet Sacrament! we adore, 78a; Table where we communicate together, 71a; Thine aid, Thy strength, 74b; This is the Bread of Life, 195a; this wonderful Sacrament, 75a, 78a; Thou art our celestial bread, 72a; Thy pure and holy sacraments, 595b; to dogs must not be thrown, 75a; to their teeth hast prov'd Thy Deity, 77a; true presence perceived by faith, 73b; unbelievers cannot experience S., 76a; unity of body in Sacrament, 72b; we become bread of the Lord, 72b; *we being many are one body*, 73a; we handle, eat, embrace Him, 71b; we in Him and He in us, 71a; we receive Word as food, 71a; What other nation so honored as Christian people?, 197a; word of Christ consecrates this s., 597a; Yon orbed sacrament confest, 78b; you can force man to receive, but not believe, 57a

Blessed Virgin Mary above law, by singular privilege, 88b; abundant grace for overcoming sin, 86a; admire the dignity of the mother, 82b; adorned with light, makes sun her robe, 40b; after childbirth thou didst remain virgin, 24b; all generations bless thee, 90b; all-holy, immaculate, lady, 81b, 89a; all men dedicated to her immaculate heart, 91b; all-powerful, because of prayer, 97a; Almighty and all-merciable Queen, 87b; angels record thy glory, 25b; ark for tables of law, 41a; ark gilded by Holy Ghost, 100b; ark of the covenant, 84b; ark of holiness, 40b; as virgin conceived, as virgin remained, 79a; ascending, welcomed by Jesus, 41a; associated as Mother and cooperatrix, 92a; assumed into heavenly glory, 41b; be a help to helpless, 87a; Be her majesty confest, 89a; Be mine advocate in that high place, 84b; be near me as I receive Body, 88a; Be thou my life's support, 84a; bears price of our redemption, 92a; became advocate of virgin Eve, 85a; became Mother of Lord of all, 81a; begs graces from Head, 91b; Beyond all creatures, 81a; bids me love but her alone, 92b; *blessed art thou among women*, 82a; Blessed art thou, who hast carried, 79b; blessed, to have her for mediatrix, 90b; BVM and writers who describe her life, 102a; BVM does not abandon those, 87b; BVM received greater measure of grace, 86a; Blest guardian of all virgin souls, 461a; body and soul refulgent with glory, 91b; body of BVM, exempt from dissolution, 39b; bond of union for mystical body, 93a; bore Christ happily in her heart, 80b; bore Destroyer of sin, 86a; bore God and Word according to flesh, 40a, 467b; born, after Spirit like others, 80b; both espoused and immaculate, 130b; bride unbrided, 100b; bright star of day, 100a; brought forth our salvation, 166b; budding staff of Aaron, 80a; bush unburnt, 91a; by angels Mistress owned, 95b; by grace, preserved from sin, 461a; by intercession, thou deliverest our souls, 39a; by me, at my death, remain, 84a; by prayers grant rest to departed, 89a; cannot be put to confusion, 86b; carried Creator as Child, 39b; casket of God's wisdom, 79b; cause of grace and mercy here, 96a; Center, and source of endless grace, 91b; challenge to heretics, 82b; chaste and free, 91a; child-bearing, beginning of salvation, 632a; Church's unassailable tower, 100b; clothed and crowned with grace, 41b; Clothed in the Sun I see thee stand, 632b; cloud of perpetual light, 86b, 89a; combined virginity and humility, 88b; comfort to sorrowful, 87a;

common-treasure of whole world, 81a; conceived miraculously as virgin, 86a; conception effected by Holy Ghost, 50a; confirm estate of orthodox, 86b; consecrated to God, 79a; consolation of afflicted, 84b; Console me in hour of pain, 84a; contained Uncontainable, 90b; cooperated to become mother of members, 80b; cooperates in our reconcilation, 91a; co-redemptrix, 90a; Cover us with thy protection, 87b; Creator's servant and Mother, 95b; crown of virginity, 81a; crown of women, 40b; Daughter of David, 84b; daughter of thine own Son, 82b; deliver me from gates of death, 90b; deliver Those who travel, 39b; deliver us from all evil, 87b; deliver us from eternal torment, 84b; descended from Adam, 85a; deserved to be exalter forever, 82a; desired to know God, 80b; despise me not, a sinner, 82b, 89b, 98a, 98b; destroy schemes of our enemies, 87a; development of devotion to BVM, 101a; devotion to BVM built on two titles, 102a; Direct our life in tempestuous sea, 83a; dispensatrix, 90a; do not cease to pray for us, 89a; door of grace, 90b; Dreadful as a battle arrayed, 41a; dwelling of the illimitable, 81a; dwelling place of Word of God, 40b; earth's undeserved prey, 40a; effaced delinquency of Eve, 85a; eloquent men become dumb before thee, 79b; escaped pains at childbirth, 93b; excepted, when touching sin, 86a; exempt from original sin, 461a; fairest Queen, 92b; Fairest thou where all are fair, 96a; Fair lily found among the thorns, 461a; faithful should honor her with filial devotion, 102a; feast of purification, 744a; filled with confidence, I fly to thee, 89b; fill our mind with unifying light, 73a; finder of grace, 90b; flower of all woman kind, 83a; for His sake we honor her, 84a; foreshadowed by prophets, 90b; Fortress of salvation, 87a; Forth-bringer, 79b; found all Eve had wanted, 85b; found humble in sight of God, 82a; fountain of mercy, 99a; Fount of love, forever flowing, 460b; from her we received Author of life, 88b; from thee Emmanuel shows forth, 82a; full of grace and favored, 81a; furnisher of all things, 99b; garden enclosed, 86b; gate of heaven, 86b, 97b; Gate of morn, 95b; gate of safety, 100b; gate of salvation, 86b; Gather together those who belong to thee, 87a; gave birth contrary to nature, 71b; Gifts of heaven she has given, 89a; given in marriage to Creator of Marriage, 166b; Glorious Virgin, of all flowers flower, 87b; God granteth no pity Withoute thee, 96a; God has revealed very little about her, 102a; God is obedient to a woman, 82b; God vouchsafed through thee with us t'accorde, 96a; God was just your little Boy, 102a; God wills all graces come through Mary, 92a; God's spouse, 19b; golden censer that became tabernacle, 82a; Governeresse of heaven, 96a; grant victory from on high, 86b; had special gift of purity bestowed, 86a; Hail! full of grace, 90b; Hail! holy Virgin Mary—Hail!, 83b; Hail, most high, most humble one,

97a; Hail, thou, our hope, life, sweetness, 95b; Hail, thou star of ocean, 98b; handmaiden and work of His wisdom, 80a; harbor for shipwrecked, 84b; harbor of helpless, 90a; haven of refuge, 85a, 900a; have unashamed trust in her, 87a; hear my mournful litany, 83b; He hath thee crowned in royal wise, 96a; Help and relieve, thou mighty debonaire, 87b; help of Christians, 86b; Help us to conquer sin, 97b; her birth sanctified, 86a; her charity bears us up, 91a; her chastity, 92a; her conception and childbirth, 79b, 166b; Her feasts follow reason, 600b; her fecundity does not destroy virginity, 92b; her flesh brought God into world, 40b; her gate has remained shut forever, 79a; her humility, 88b; her immaculate flesh and blood, 85b; her infinite distance from Son, 101b; her intercession, 88b, 89b; her kingdom as vast as that of Son, 97b; her mercy toward needy, 99b; her most pure image, 87b; her office external, not within us, 91b; her sanctity and sanctity of saints, 92a, 102a; her Son will deny her nothing, 97a; her soul pierced with sorrow, 94a; her special glory, 81a; her virginity kept closed, 79a, 79b; her wondrous gifts and powers, 95a; He was born of her in her purity, 460a; He Who made of her, had made her, 79a; higher than heaven, 80a; high over every creature, 83a; His light, less dreadful in thee, 98b; His sole-born Daughter, 96b; holy beyond all holy ones, 100b; Holy Ghost, overshadowing thee, 82a; holy mirth Of heaven, 40b; Holy of holies, 84b; Holy Spirit descended, purifying her, 25a; honor shown to her referred to Him, 82a; hope and protection, 98a; humanity dedicated to her immaculate heart, 88a; humble pride of earth, 40b; I am too dull to praise thee, 79b; I shall keep thee from hell, 100a; Illumine all!, 91b; image of virginity, 92a; in childbirth thou didst retain virginity, 39a; In cloudy vesture stainless white, 41b; In dangers, call upon Mary, 87b; in her, all poverty and wisdom of saints, 92a; In reverence of thee and thy glory!, 91b; in thee Father was well pleased, 82a; In thee is pity, in thee tenderness, 99b; in thee Logos came down, 89a; in thee Son abode, 82a; in thee the sum Of all creation, 99b; In whom fiend no thought of sin could find, 83a; In whom God chose to wone, 83a; in whose might Word took flesh, 81b; In women's virtue life, doth begin, 25b; incarnate Love's pure dwelling, 97b; indestructible wall of kingdom, 100b; indissoluble temple, 81a; intercede for peace of world, 87a; invincible mediatrix, 95b; Ivory Tower, 84b; joy of afflicted, 84b; keep in mind examples of Mary, 82a; kept body from corruption after death, 39b; kept virginity in childbirth, 39b; Kindred to angels on high, 97b; King's daughter, 169a; Lady, thou hast such might, 91a; lamp of living light, 98b; lamp unquenchable, 81a; leads all to divine knowledge, 98b; let not her name depart from thy lips, 87b; life kept pure from all sin, 86a; life suffices for instruction of all, 92a; Lily, O Lily of Calvary hill, 92b; linked to all Trinity, 96b; look down on people who have sinned, 99a; looks on Son, 39b; loss of devotion to her, 101b; love of her and of our Lord, 101a; Magnify her, 167b, 299a; Maid yet Mother, 600a; make intercession for women vowed to God, 87a; Make us love thee, 96b; make us sharers of His glory, 91a; Make us truly to be thine, 96b; Man and God laid within her womb, 41a; mankind's glory, grace, and gifts, 40a; *Mater dolorum*, 95a; may be called mediator, 91a; may her intercession protect us, 90a; mediatrix and refuge of Christians, 90a; mercy of which she is mother, 90b; merits of BVM implore mercy for us, 99a; might of thy assistance, 87a; mild, silent little Maid like thee, 84a; ministers to men's union with God, 91a; ministered to Creator, 85b; mirror of beauty and virtue, 92a; mistress of our song, 96b; more honorable than the cherubim, 81b, 299a; most clear crystal, 83a; Mother and Virgin, 80b, 81a; mother of all Christ's members, 91b, 92b, 93a; Mother of grace, 90a; mother of Head Himself, 80b; mother of life, 39a, 40a, 90b; Mother of mine, 41a; Mother of the Lord, 79a; my body's healing, 100b; my lady most glorious and gracious, 80a; my soul's saving, 100b; mystic flower, 84b; My succour be, 87b; neglect not to walk in her footsteps, 87b; never known any was forsaken, 89b; never Let us suffer wreck, 39b; new mother of the living, 93a; Next the heavenly King, 40b; no God at all, if Mary greater, 101b; no question raised on subject of sin, 460a; none has merit such as hers, 97a; nothing can be stained where God is, 466a; nothing excluded from her dominion, 97b; nourished and carried God, 40b; O amber veil, 462b; O flower of flowers, 97b; O immaculate one, 89a; O merciful, O pious Maid, 95b; O Queen of sorrows, raise thine eyes, 94b; O sinless heart, all hail!, 88a; O thou that art so fair, 84b; O Virgin lady, 80a; obtain by her help, 87a; Of a pure and spotless Virgin, 74a; Of David's royal blood, 95a; Of eternal design the cornerstone!, 83a; Of her who is the hope of men, 600a; of number of those cleansed from sins before His birth, 460a; Of purity the spotless shrine, 83b; Of sinful man, O sinless advocate, 98b; Of the Virgin Mary mild, 75b; offered gift of virginity to God, 79b; office, one of perpetual intercession, 89b; one hope of hopeless, helper of oppressed, 98a; open to us gate of thy mercy, 86b; opened knot of Eve's disobedience, 85a; our chaste love, 40b; our defence, 84b; our home is deep in thee, 88a; our mediatrix, our advocate, 90b; Our second Eve puts on her mortal shroud, 461a; our stalwart hope by her protection, 39a; out of thee rose Sun of righteousness, 632b; overcome our foes, 90a; pardon for sinners, 84b; Parent of our Savior-brother!, 39b; pattern of life, 92a; pillar of purity, 100b; Pity sinners who before thee bow,

82b, 96a; placed not among, but over other creatures, 460b; Plead with Christ our sins to spare, 96a; Portal of bliss to man forgiven, 461a; Portal of the sky, 98b; power in distribution of graces, 92a; practice of devotion to her, 101a; pray for people, plead for clergy, 87a; pray thy Son to save our souls, 87b; prayeth For all faithful ones, 40a; precious diadem of godly sovereigns, 100b; preordained by prescient counsel of God, 90b; prerogatives hers because Mother, 84a; present prayers to your Son, 89a; prevented with special grace, 86a; proclaimed by fathers Mother of God, 81a; prompt help for those who call, 84b; protection, bulwark, 100b; protection of those who flee to thee, 98a; Pure as the snow, 462a; Pure flower of Adam's race, 97b; pure one, do thou convert me, 98a; purer than sun's splendor, 80a; Queen of heaven and earth, 92b; queen of heaven, empress of the skies, 40a; Queen of heaven enthroned, 95b; Queen of men, 40b; Queen of queens, 96b; Queen of purity divine, 96b; queen of virgins, 86a; Queen over all created things, 95b; Queen, who decks her subjects, 89b; radiance that enlighteneth mind, 98b; ravished down Spirit's flight, 91b; ray of spiritual Sun, 98b; received eternal incorruptibility, 39a; received sword of sorrow, 39b; reconcile us to thy Son, 90b; reflects beauty of chastity, 92a; refuge of Christians, 84b, 98a; refuge terrible in strength, 86b; reigns in heaven with her Son, 91b; relief for burdened, 84b; remained virgin after childbirth, 89a; rest of those who are weary, 84b; Reverence her, you married, 88b; rewards of salvation, through BVM, 88b; rod sublime *from root of Jesse*, 91a, 95b; Rose mystical, 84b; Rose of the cross, 84b; salvation of Christians, 99b; salvation of them in sorrow, 85a; satisfied debt of first mother, 85b; save me, O Lady, by thy prayers, 87a; save those thou hast chosen to rule, 86b; Save those who hope in thee, 89a; savest world by ceaseless intercession, 90a; send thy servants help from holy place, 90a; Seven lights for seven woes, 97a; She, about whose moonèd brows, 97a; she carried Him in Whom we are, 81a; she gave milk to our Bread, 81a; She is mighty to deliver, 89a; Shelter us from Satan's fraud, 83b; she ruled our Ruler, 81a; She that is heaven's Queen, 95a; she who did man's substance glorify, 83a; she whom Glory Itself chose, 80a; She with higher rank was gifted, 40a; shield us through life, 90a; shining lamp, in light passing nature, 83a; sinful soules cure, 83a; singular privilege of sanctity, 86a; sinlessness out of honor to Lord, 86a, 86b; sorrow's Mother, 94a; special glory in heaven, 86a; special privilege, 818b; *Spes infirmorum*, 95a; spotless, undefiled, incorruptible, 98a; spouse, whom Father took to Himself, 39b; sprang from root of David, 90b; staff of orthodoxy, 81a; Star of Jacob, 83b; Star of morning, 84b, 91b; star of the sea, 82b, 99a; Star that leadeth not astray, 39b;

stood before cross, 80b; Stood doleful she, 94a; strength to fearful, 87a; strengthen our God-fearing rulers, 87a, 90b; struck deep roots of humility, 91a; submitted to ordinances of law, 88b; succumbed to earthly death, 39a; suffered pains at crucifixion, 93b; sum of world's bliss, 40a; sweet Advocate, 95b; sweet fount of love, 90a; Sweet Morn! thou Parent of the Sun!, 632b; sweetest Child, how dost Thou fade, 93b; take us to thy bosom when we die, 90a; teach me to bless thy name, 95a; temple of the Holy Ghost, 40b; tent of God and Word, 100b; thee, prophets did proclaim, 81b; The moon beneath thy feet, 632b; thou art a wall, 100b; Thou art blessed and venerable, 632a; Thou art delight of angels, 84b; thou art our hopes, 87a; Thou by Him wast pre-elected, 39b; Thou comfort of us wretches, 79b; thou didst bear Creator, 82b; thou didst bring forth God, 87a; thou dost forerun the prayer, 91a; thou, flow'r of virgines art alle, 79b; thou glory of womanhood, 100a; Thou goest before in thy benignity, 91b; Thou hast borne Him Whom heavens cannot contain, 79b; thou hast borne Savior of our souls, 82a; thou hast alone destroyed all heresies, 88b; thou hast opened heavens, 86b; Thou Queen of high estate, 97b; Thou star to storm-tossed voyages dear, 461a; Thou tower against the dragon proof, 461a; thoughts pierced her as a sword, 93b; Threefold thy gift to the world, 97a; through thee, access to thy Son, 90b; through thee have we grace, 96a; Thy birth, message of joy to whole world, 632b; Thy bounty, virtue and magnificence, 91a, 91b; thy maternal prayers avail much, 98b; thy sinless breast, 97b; thy virginal body is all holy, 39b; Thy willing handmaid, 25a; Till no chance but her prayers remain, 88a; To thee I flee, confounded in errour, 87b; to whom all woeful cryen, 99b; To whom all world fleeth for sucour, 87b; Tower of David, 84b; translated Up to heaven, 40a; treasury of His providence, 79b; true position of Mary, 84a; truly celestial plant, 91a; truly Mother of God, 25a; truly she was full of grace, 79b; trusting in thee, we may not perish, 99b; Turn grief of people into joy, 87a; unassailable rampart, 87a; unceasing in prayers, 39a; Underneath her azured daïs, 683a; unfailing treasure-house of life, 100b; Unstained as virgin snow, 97b; Unto fallen people help afford, 82b; Unto thee the angels sing, 80b; untouched by husband, 79a; use thy maternal influence with Son, 98a; verily tree of life, 91a; vessel rare of God's election, 97b; Vicaire and Maistresse, 96a; Virgin became a mother, 80a; virgin before marriage, virgin in marriage, 166b; virgin ever virgin, 79a; Virgin, hail! alone the fairest! 39b; Virgin has conceived and bornèd, 78b; virgin in body and mind, 80b; Virgin is throne of the cherubim, 167b; Virgin of all virgins, 95a; virgin, thou didst bring forth, 24b, 79b, 88b; v. touched by no impurity, 80a; Virgin worthy of all praise, 90a; Virgin's spotless womb contains, 81b; virginity and wedlock honored in her, 82b; Visit thou my ailing soul, 98a; waits till earth's aid forsakes us, 88a; wall that cannot be overthrown, 90a; water gushing out of rock, 92a; we are clients of our patron, 89b; we do not know her countenance, 79a; we have you as our patron, 89a; well of mercy, 83a; We praise thee as our benefactress, 299a; we sing unto thee, we praise thee, 86b; what more chaste than she? 80a; What pleasure thee in heaven to see! 96b; Whence world's true Light born, 95b; while she defends Church, 97a; While she wept her bitter loss, 94b; White with glory of all graces, 92b; who dost bless world and sanctify, 84b; Who loveth Thee must love Thy Son, 600a; Who makest music for us to thy Son, 84b; Whose tender mercies never fail, 83b; Who turned the key to admit Love, 25b; wishes, lead all men to truth, 93a; without corruption didst bear Word, 81b; with thy protection for my armor, 87a; woman, in place of ancestor of God, 82b; womb, become temple of God, 467b; wonder, a miracle, 82b; worshipful honor of priesthood, 100b; worthy to bear fruit of salvation, 91a; worthy to go before Him, 82b; your God for Father, Spouse and Son, 96b

Blessing B. thus a world restored, 135b; Lord, dismiss us with Thy b., 103a; May Lord give you b. out of Sion, 206b; Out of God's b. into warm sun, 103a; Sweet the moments, rich in b., 233a

Blessings And turn our b. to a curse, 574a; Flowers of never fading graces, 103a; God never shuts one door but He opens two, 275b; good do not take b. as anything great, 736a; immortal dressings for worthy souls, 103a; no great b. without suffering, 103a; not temporal, but eternal, 385b; should not accept b. in silence, 59b

Blight cesspool's fetid b., 12b

Blind b. eat many a fly, 103a; b. men should judge no colors, 103b; Folk are most b. in their own cause, 103b; in country of b., the one-eyed, 103a; those willing to wax b., 103b; Where the b. headeth the b., 103b

Blindness Back to the primal gloom, 103b; limit of human b., to glory in being blind, 103a; school of darkness, 103b; spiritual and human b., 189a; Whate'er my darkness be, 240a

Bliss A good woman is man's b., 920a; BVM, sum of world's b., 40a; happy, whom He chooseth for that b.! 302a; How endless is your labyrinth of b., 903b; In the midst of misery to remember b., 603a; Jesu, King of b., 562a; Milk-soup men call domestic b., 574b; My b. is in my breast, 209a; O sudden woe, successor To worldly b.! 919b; same in subject or in king, 103a; take my chance with Socrates for b., 164b; The end is endless b., 371a

Blockhead b., ignorantly read, 103b, 667a

Blood B. is the price of heaven, 104b; b. of Christians is seed, 103b, 583a; B. of Christ, precious to Father, 104a; Drink we of the B. He shed, 442b; faith delivers through b. of Christ, 325a; Fill and satisfy me, b. unpriced, 75b; flood Of precious water, mixed with b., 230a; foemen for His b. athirst, 74b; Hail! Thou glorious and precious B., 75b; His B., offering for our sins, 484b; I see His b. upon the rose, 492b; Let the water and the b., 492a; May B. of our Lord preserve my soul, 595a; Mercy's streams in streams of blood, 233a; moulds in us a royal image, 195a; My b., 311a; O blessed be my Savior's blood, 104b; Of the B., all price exceeding, 74a; our Lord gave His B. for us, 154b; purple streams of His dear B., 104a; puts to flight devils, 195a; redeemed mankind, 231a; shedding of His immaculate b., 467a; sowing of Scripture cost much b., 61b; sprinkling of Thy b., washing away my sins, 657a; stained with that b., 307b; The glories of our b. and state, 249a; Thou didst ransom us from curse of law by Thy B., 309b; Thy spotless Body and precious B., 593b; unworthy, of hands of priesthood, 177a; very B. which flowed from His side, 311a; wash them in My b., 30b; washed the world, made heaven open, 195a; washes Church, 128b; When beauty fires b., 55a; Whose B. hath brought redemption, 35b

Bloodshed b. and ministry of altar, 104a; b. and persecution, no part of creed, 104a; Church abhors b., 103b

Blossom The world's b. smells of God, 287a

Blot b. upon a layman's coat, little seen, 730a; the art to b., 281b

Blue Eyes of most unholy b., 322b; Into the infinite b., 464a

Blundering Through sense and nonsense, 104b

Blunt B. truths more mischief than nice falsehood do, 222b

Blush Whose b. the moon beauteously mars, 97a; Young roses kindled into thought, 104b

Boar She foameth like a b., 104b

Board Fed at one only b., 198b

Boast Great b. and small roast, 105a

Boaster greatest vaunter seldom speeds, 923a; till each scared b. flies, 26b

Boasting To shun vainglory, 105a

Boasts loud b. of poor mortality, 249a

Boat b. at midnight, upon moonless sea, 2a; this creature of our hand, 105a

Body altar is a type of the b., 13b; bears imprint of sin, 191b; B. and Blood, entire in eucharist, 76a; B. and Blood, nourishment of faithful, 73b; B. and Blood, separated by cutting, 71a; b. and soul, not separated in resurr., 105b; b. is about the soul, as garment, 282a, 345b; b. of BVM, changed into incorruptibility, 39b; Body of Christ is on the altar, 13b; B. of Christ makes us partakers of eternal life, 195a; B. of Christ not destroyed by death, 71b; b. politic contains family units, 845b; B. which He assumed, 307a; bread and wine, not merely figures of B. and Blood, 310b; broken but not divided, 594a; By god's b., 248a; complete renunciation of body, 36b; corruptible b. weigheth down soul, 105a; Creator's crowning good, 105b; deliver me by Thy B. and Blood from all transgressions, 594b; dissolution of the b., 252b; Draw nigh, take B. of the Lord, 195b; earthly habitation, 105a; Eucharist is B. of Christ, 70b; ever eaten and never consumed, 594a; faithful labor to be B. of Christ, 73a; flesh is hinge of salvation for soul, 105b; frail b., which was part of me, 59b; from which issued saving fountains, 71b; grant us health of mind and b., 239b; Hail, true Body, truly born, 75b; He gave us B. to keep and eat, 71b; he will reform the b. of our lowness, 877a; hope of b., whither Head has gone, 35a; I believe that this is Thy most pure B., 594b; is anointed in baptism, 52a; Lay this b. wherever it may be, 244a; Let not reception of Thy B. turn against me, 594b; liable to punishment and death, 105a; Little, sequester'd pleasure-house, 105b; loved for soul, 236a; Man, rational soul with mortal and earthly b., 569a; May the B. of our Lord preserve my soul, 595a; May Thy B. cleave to my bowels, 595b; members of Lord's b. in Sacrament, 72b; My soul I resign to God, my b. to earth, 521a; my sure salvation, B. of the Lord, 75b; no sooner do we begin to live in dying b., 247a; One b., one spirit, one Lord, 135b; one who has difficulty with b. and soul, 106a; our b. might be said to be a prison, 105a; outer b. cleansed by water, 51b; salted meats the b. dry and bind, 263a; sanctifies those who participate, 594a; separation of b. and soul, violent, 247a; Soul and b. part like friends, 836b; soul is master, b. servant, 106a; soul is user, body is for use, 106a; State, for b. politic, not b. politic for state, 846a; State, inferior to b. politic as a whole, 846a; State, superior part in b. politic, 846a; Take we of His broken B., 442b; tenement of clay, 105b; That B. which thou gav'st, O earth, 78a; This is My b., 73b, 310b, 592a, 597a; true B., born of Virgin, 311a; Thy spotless B. and precious Blood, 593b; unity of B., bond of peace, 72b; union of soul and b. in man, 182b; unseemliness of the b., 191b; Veil'd in white to be received, 77a; very interpenetration of spirit and flesh, 247a; we become His b. in Sacrament, 72b; we being many are one b., 73a; We have to distinguish clearly between State and B. Politic, 845b; What soul loveth, not at all food for b., 278b; When head acheth, all b. is worse, 423a

Body of Christ, Mystical b. and dissidents, 123a; Body of this head is the Church, 123a; body, priestly and royal, 647b; b., which is the Church, 438b; by Spirit, body of Church sanctified and governed, 433b; Christ, living in those He has united, 166a; Christ whole is in head and in body, 128a; Church is holy, because body of Christ, 128b; Church, one vast b. in heaven and earth, 89b;

Deep mystery this, subject of meditation, 132b; Every member of Christ's body necessary to body, 173a; faithful born as members of Church, 80b; foolish, to say composed of scattered members, 132b; His body is the Church, 122b, 126a, 131a; Mary bore Head of body in flesh, 92b; Mary is bond of union for m., 93a; members dispersed throughout ages, 132a; members of His body, 93a; m. and Catholic Church, one and same, 133a; M. and Communion of Saints, 199a; m., like physical body, 132b; no expression more noble, more sublime, 132b; nor can one body be divided into pieces, 133b; one m., whose head is Christ, 132a; prayer is life of body, 89b; m., reputed to be one single person, 132a; take care you are in the B., 123a; through BVM graces pass to m., 91b; unity of mankind in truth and charity, 140a; universal Church consists of two parts, 191a; visible parts, draw life from supernatural gifts, 132b; *we, being many, are one body in Christ*, 485b

Bodies Fat wet b. go waddling by, 239b; present your b. a living sacrifice, 229b; sanctify souls and b., 441b; Though b. cannot, souls can penetrate, 360a

Bohemia I'd rather live in B., 106a

Bold as b. as brass, 48b; Fortune favors the b., 106a; Guards of the b. and free, 415a

Boldness Arrogance and b., belong to accursed of God, 724b; b., when the days are fair, 106b; Come what come would, 106b; he who naught dare undertake, 106a; Sweet is b., shyness, pain, 558a

Boloney difference between blarney and b., 70a

Bona two *summa b.*, 900a

Bonaventure, St., 106b, 196a

Bondage Christ's passion frees from b. of sin, 44a; city of confusion and house of b., 24a; O sacred state of religious b., 808b; Our b. is the price, 260b

Bonds delivered from b. of our sins, 2b; those afflicted and in b., 9b

Bone *This now is b. of my bones, flesh of my flesh,* 577a

Bones Carry my b. before you, 520b; lay my weary b. among you, 282b; Therefore did you break my b., 264b; they have numbered all my b., 657a; Think how many royal b., 623b; When rattling b. together fly, 503a

Boniface VIII, 44b, 354a

Bonny He gar'd the b. ball flee, 49a

Bonum Pax et b., 665b

Boobies B. have looked as wise, 29a

Book an irrevocable mistake, 107a; As clerics finden written in their book, 29a; Cross thee quite out of my b., 265b; God's foreknowledge is b. of life, 107b; Gold of the dead, 107a; has less value than its phrases, 107b; Like every b. I never wrote, 107a; our duty to live by one b., 107a; sitting apart in nook, with little b., 106b; The b. of God no man can write, 396b; these conquering leaves, 424a; writing b. like birth of child, 107a

Books b. of apostates, heretics, prohibited, 151b; B. which treat

of lewd subjects, prohibited, 151b; Church has right to censor, 151b; Dear, human b., 107a; Delighting to converse with b., 106b; Enchant me with your spells of art, 107a; great authors, greater than their b., 45a; happy hours employed upon my b., 107a; Man learns from two b., 803a; Men may be read, as well as b., 571a; monument of vanish'd minds, 107a; morals corrupted by reading immoral b., 151b; My b. lie closed upon the shelf, 11a; our duty to live among b., 107a; safe thing, read only Catholic b., 545a; sins scarlet, but b. were read, 107b

Boots they have greased my b. already, 521b

Boozed A man that b. of that, 278b

Border-law rough b. of heaven, 620b

Bore Christ b. us all, 597b; one who talks about himself, 107b

Boreas Die, B., And drown your ruins, 843a

Boredom dangerously infectious, 107b; man, bored without cause of b., 18a

Borgia, 107b

Born In the days ere I was b., 237a; mourn for those b. into world, 65b; those b. again through Thy grace, 670a; those b. drive out those who preceded, 65b; We are b. into world naked, 48a; we are b. in water, 49b

Borrow I come to b. what I'll never lend, 108a; Not so good to b., as lend, 108a; with thy neighbors gladly lend and b., 360a

Bosh Objecting both to kings and creeds, called B., 407a

Bosom b. of Abraham, 243b, 301b; In the b. where it lighteth, 25a; welcoming embrace of patriarchs, 244b

Bough Rest on the lower b., 453a

Bound They that are b. must obey, 642b; whatsoever is either b. or loosed on earth, 674b

Boundaries To earth's remotest b., 166b

Boundless Thou of the b. art the bound, 373b

Bourgeois completely complacent with his position, 201a; deism and atheist communism, 42b

Bridal b. chamber of His light, 229a

Bow It is better to b. than break, 930a; long b. bent, must wear weak, 108a; sweet yet cruel b. thou art, 31b; That never shot in his b., 105a

Bowed here I bow'd before Thee, 77b

Bowl The golden b. is broken, 250b; Wreath the b., 279b

Box Break the b. and shed the nard, 286b

Boy b. is born to replace father, 65b; flit not from the heavenly B., 487a; Sing lullaby, my little B., 566b

Boyhood b. is lightheaded, 11b

Boys All the b. of merry Lincoln, 48b; always more or less inaccurate, 108a; Among those girls and b., 161a

Bracelets good works, b. of Christian woman, 108a

Brain I knew the b. of Hercules, 568a; softening of heart, softening of b., 473b

Bran our b., compared with his white flour, 44b

Brass as bold as b., 48b

Brave b. man rules himself through will, 108a; Could conquer hearts so b., 208a; None but best deserve the fair, 108a; Nor think ambition wise because b., 14a; The b. man seeks not popular applause, 444a

Bravery moral b. of man, 108a; b. not mere physical courage, 108a

Bread after invocation, b. becomes Body, 162b, 310a; At morn we found the heavenly B., 78a; better half a loaf than no b., 108b; Bitter the b. of our repast, 833b; B. and Wine, not bare elements, 71a, 310b; B. of man today, 74b; b. that you store up belongs to the hungry, 154b; B. to children given, 75a; b. which Christ gave us to offer, 307a; break one B., 194b; Christ, B. which came down from heaven, 196a, 861b; Christ, Who is heavenly B., 131b; Church like scattered b., 124a; figure of B. is His Body, 70b; food of salvation, 194b; *Give us this day our daily b.,* 197b, 593b; Hail, angelic B. of heaven, 75a; Himself, the living B. from heaven, 74b, 75a; holy B. of eternal life, 592a; *If anyone eats of this b.,* 194b; *I myself am the living b.,* 194b; *I will take the B. of Heaven,* 595a; Not fresh nor old, 108b; nothing to be ashamed, earning b. by labor, 713a; O God, the B. of strength, 197b; on which side my b. is buttered, 108b; O Thou holy B., Thou living B., 196a; Paschal Victim, Paschal B., 284b; she gave milk to our B., 81a; Tasteful, well baked, 108b; that I may end as pure b. of Christ, 458a; the angels' b., 863b; This is the B. of life, 195a; Thou art our celestial b., 72a; Thus angels' B. is made, 74b; Took b. into His holy and venerable hands, 592a; which He calls His flesh, 73a; will you not take B. of life daily? 72a; Word-made-flesh, b. of nature, 74a; you became b. of Lord, 72b; you store up, belongs to hungry, 909a

Break It is better to bow than b., 930a

Breast bathe thy white b., 40b; Bearing in b. print of every dart, 31b; Be Thou the aim of every b., 36a; ere she clasps us to her b., 283a; fills her virgin breast, 25b; He lingers in b. Of our humanity, 483b; My faultless b. in furnace is, 30a; that b. of thine, 94a

Breath b. revives him, or a b. o'erthrows, 367b; By His own b., b. of life convey'd, 6a; Saw B. to breathlessness resign its b., 658b; Suck my last b., 282b; terms *b. or spirit*, 370b; The consubstantial B. of God, 440a

Breathed He b. upon disciples, saying, 2b

Bred So they believe, because they so were b., 289a

Breeze b. that may be music, 48a; there's a story in every b., 322b

Brethren b. as of one blood, 352b; Weep over me, b., friends, relatives, 500a

Breviary monument of devotion of saints, 108b

Brew As I would needs b., 279a

Bribed English statesman b., not to be b., 909a

Bridal b. robes of ardor virginal, 305a

Bride b. of Christ, 189a; b. of the Lamb, 23b; b. unbrided, 100b; chaste and pure Lady, B. of God, 98a; Glorious Agatha, now a b., 10b; what b. has more children than Holy Church? 130a

Bridegroom Behold, the B. cometh in middle of night, 896a; B. of Church is pierced with nails, 400a; Christ, B. of Church, 150a; heavenly b., 299a

Bridge living b. of My Son, 108b

Brief Be b. when you cannot be good, 939a

Bright All that's b. must fade, 550b; all things fair and b. are Thine, 373b

Brimstone burning with b. and stinking pitch, 427b

Britons brave B., foreign laws despised, 297a

Broadmindedness A man so broad to some he seem'd to be, 109a; b., and recognition one is narrow, 109a; latitudinarians and their opponents, 109a

Brocade one flutters in b., 191b

Brook Like as a b. that all night long, 689a

Broom green new b. sweepeth clean, 109a

Brother If any b. be found contumacious, 317a; I will not trust him though my b., 265b; let me not judge my b., 450a; our elder b., Christ, 305b; Sweet b., if I do not sleep, 109a

Brotherhood Charity is the bond of b., 154b; Christian solidarity of b., 257a; irrevocable assent of the whole b., 708a

Brothers B.! spare reasoning, 26b; B. we are, whatever our nationality, 143a; Christ has us as His b., 93a; Let b. avoid appearing gloomy, 497a; linsey-woolsey b., 6a

Broths b. of richest juice, 347b

Brow Hail, awful b.! hail, throny wreath! 657b; Upon her candid April b., 55b

Brown His palfrey, b. as is a berry, 446b

Brown, John, 109b

Browning, Robert, 109b

Brownson, Orestes, 109b, 221a

Brows Embrace thy radiant b., 40b

Brutality b. and refinement in adolescence, 6b

Brute Man, neither angel nor a b., 570b; The b.-tamer stands by the brutes, 608a

Bubble And now a b. burst, and now a world, 384a

Bud Giving the b. I give the flower, 638b; hope and promise of this b., 422a; showeth what fruit will follow, 109b

Builder Bright Builder of heavenly poles, 7b

Builders B. on earth by laws of land, 105a

Buildings All b. are but monuments of death, 249b; Mute monuments of man's power, 185b

Bull new papal b. every morning with *Times,* 653a

Bullying no one less given to hectoring than Hector, 110a

Bulwark all flee to thee as protection, as b., 100b; man grounded in Scripture, b. of Church, 26b

Bumper Fill the b. fair!, 279a

Burden b. of life is from ourselves, 410b; Light her yoke, her b.

sweet, 135b; Many to bear the common b. are slow, 346b

Burial ecclesiastical b. for all baptized, 110b; give me your last farewell kiss, 500a; no heavy charge for b., 110a; bodies of faithfull shall be b., 110b; if you are b. with Christ within, 52a; we are b. without inheritance, 48a

Burn better to marry, because worse to b., 573b; B. our reins and our heart, 159a; they, who love Thee not, Must b. eternally, 562a

Burns fire that kindles also b., 344b

Burnt A b. child loves the fire, 319b; B. child fire dreadeth, 344b

Bury B. her at even, 110a; to b. the dead, 155a

Burrs They cleave together like b., 343b

Bush b. unburnt, 91a; While I beat the b., 361b

Business clergy are forbidden to conduct b., 190b; Though none so busy as he, 110b

Businessman He was so stately in negotiation, 110b

Bustle b. of this world, 212a

Busy He was less b. than he seemed, 110b; None so b. as fool and knave, 110b

Butter as b. would not melt in her mouth, 456a

Buttered I know on which side my bread b., 108b

Butterfly designed to form angelic butterfly, 163b

Buy A man may b. gold too dear, 397b; b. Marcus up at price he is worth, 201b; B. then! Bid then!, 304b; b. what I'll never pay for, 108a

Buyer make yourself b. when selling, 110b

Buying b. and selling on feast days, 586a

By B. and b. never comes, 732a

Byzantine splendor of B. rite, 547a

Byzantium, 175b

C

Caesar C. is more ours than yours, 171b; C., with a senate at his heels, 318b; *render to C.,* 178b, 188b

Cage I am a darkened c., 2a

Caius, 678b

Calais you will find C. written in my heart, 521a

Calculation never made a hero, 432b

Calends hope the c., 445a

Calf Many a good cow hath an evil c., 223b

Calicem C. salutaris accipiam, 595a

Call c. upon Mary, 87b; Deaf to the universal c., 465a; *Praising, I will c. upon the Lord,* 595a

Called into God's vineyard goeth no man, but is c., 303a

Callest Thou, O Lord, c. me, 520b

Calling is there not one c. in Christ?, 131a; most important thing in life, choice of, c. 904a; worthily enter grace of Thy calling, 441b

Calls God c. those whom He deigns to call, 408a

Calm After a storm comes a c., 847b; An horrid stillness invades the ear, 111a; Not God alone in the still c. we find, 388b; straight falls the falling feather, 477b

Calvary, Mt. Blessed Lamb—on C.'s mountain, 490a; grave enactment of Thy C., 586a; Mt. C. is the academy of love, 111a; On nature's

C., 47b; O C.! C.! Mountain of love, 657b; on C., Christendom can spring, 352b; On that one holier hill than Rome, 658b; To C. with Christ we go, 846b; Upon the tree of C., 491a

Calves Change of pasture maketh fat c., 661a

Calvinist, 738a

Came I c., I saw, God conquered, 207b

Camomile Crown'd with wreaths of c., 269a

Camp weakest c., strongest school, 568b

Campagna, 477b

Campion, Blessed Edmund, 582a, 584a

Can C. something, hope, wish day come, 258b

Candle As a white c. in a holy place, 11a; From one tall c. set upon a height, 415a; Lit by the little c. of the sun, 191a; To match the c. with the sun, 111a; To set up c. before devil, 261a

Candlelight starshine and c., 111a

Candles Altar s. of earth below, 111a; when c. be out, all cats be grey, 113b

Candlestick behooves acolyte carry c., 4a

Candor To be intelligible is to be found out, 111b

Canem Qui me amat, amat et c. meum, 273a

Cannibalism artificial and even artistic, 111b

Canon authority of divine canon of Scripture, 60b; If any one saith c. of mass contains errors, 597b

Canonical books of Vulgate, c. 62b; c. age, 649a; c. authors guaranteed against error, 63b; c. title, 649a; clergy bound to recite c. hours, 267a; power of jurisdiction by c. appointment, 434a

Canonization, 793b

Canons observing c. and keeping decretals ordained, 698b; right of Roman Church to make c., 111b; venerable provisions of the c., 698b

Canossa will always remain consolation of free minds, 354a

Canterbury In England, down to C. they wend, 682b

Canticle Praise in hymn and c., 74b

Canticle of Canticles, 112a

Canticles I wept at the beauty of Your hymns and c., 546b

Canute, King, 619a

Canyon, Grand, 634a

Capital cannot do without labor, 112a, 187b; has right to just share of profits, 112a; modern world, living on its Catholic c., 867a; mutual relations between c. and labor, 287b

Capitalism false concept of right to private property, 735a; trade unions, consequence of c., 38b

Capitalist c. exploitation of workers, 319b; must respect laws of God, 112b

Caprice difference between c. and a life-long passion, 557a

Captain Christ, our c., 428a; Gabriel, c. of incorporeal hosts, 99b; O c. of the martyr host!, 847a; O C. of the wars, whence won ye so great scars?, 658b; Such c., such retinue, 598a

Captive lead c. from prison-house, 8a; Love's C., 198a; oft the abject c. doth adorn, 350b

Captivity He led c. captive, 35b

Capture whether women were married by c., 574b

Caput Omnium urbis et orbis eccle-siarum mater et c., 171a; *Urbs c. orbis,* 139b
Caravans The c. are dropping down, 540b
Cardinal Accept the red hat, 112b; by time hat came, he had no head, 112b; You have not chosen me, but I, 112b
Cardinals form senate of Roman pontiff, 113a
Card-playing let loser have his word, 112b
Care A fig for c. and a fig for woe!, 925a; all the faded family of c., 113; c.'s unthankful gloom, 146a; hasty man he wanteth never c., 422a; nor grieve too much for things beyond our c., 542b; our c. extends throughout all the churches, 698b
Careers Many girls want mission in the world, 113a
Careful regarding crowns and pounds, 113a
Carelessness appearance of c., vital in true caution, 149b
Cares clear from worldly c., 215a; Every man dangerous, who only c. for one thing, 631a; pause between the sobs of c., 59a; Shun weighty c., 423a; Unvex'd with anxious c., and void of strife!, 222b; worn with c. and age, 11b
Caresses Let me twine with you c., 683a
Carew grave of Mad C., 457b
Carlyle, Thomas, 821a
Carmel C. by the western sea, 616b
Carmelite Love-of-God eternally keep your heart a-flower, 616b
Carmelites Night is still at the Carmelites, 113a
Carnal by His death we die to c. life, 43b; c. cannot live spiritual life, 105b; faithfulness in rendering c. debt, 732a; let desire pull reason from her throne, 113a; very heathen in the c. part, 163b; vision of c. pleasure, 7a
Carnalities c. belong to carnal part of man, 113a
Carol O sing a joyous c. Unto the holy Child, 487b
Carpe c. diem religion, 497b
Carpenter By a C. mankind was created, 491b
Carrion Not, I'll not, c. comfort, despair, 258b
Carroll, Archbishop John, 101a, 585b
Cart best c. may overthrow, 113b; Set c. before horse, 447a
Carthusians, 616a
Carts well driven go along upright, 113b
Case Clear out of the c., 113b
Cases contentious or criminal c., 190b
Castle I began to think of soul as a c., 836a; no rules of architecture for c. in clouds, 336b; There shall no c. be assailed, 870b, 922b
Castles c. built in the air, 113b; Thou shalt make c. then in Spain, 277a
Casual c. depends on Providence, 373b
Casualiter Intervention c., 178a
Casuists explain away in which immutable principles put into force, 620b; Jesuits, in their capacity of c., 622a
Cat Let c. wink, let mouse run, 113b; may look on a king, 113b; would eat fish, not wet feet, 113b
Catacombs, 113b, 122a

Cata'alque Sit by my c. to dole, 251b
Catarrh Fast well and watch, 192a
Catastrophe divine c., 94b
Catechetical c. instruction of Christian people, 114a
Catechism grave responsibility of pastors, 114a; Religious paintings, c. of the ignorant, 652a
Catechumen let c. be instructed for three years, 114a
Catechumens All the c. go out!, 589b, 597b; increased in faith and understanding, 51b; stored in granary, 72b; Thy people about to be reborn, 441b; women c., 919b
Cat-foot So I crept c., 38a
Cathay Clanging up beyond C., 240b
Cathedra c. Petri, 709b; pope speaking *ex c.,* 274b, 706b
Cathedral splendid old St. Paul's, 114a; the Gothic Kingdom, 114a
Cathedrals façades of medieval c., 30a
Catherine of Sienna, St., 114b
Catholic, C. absolute and minds of men, 148a; C., but not papist, 115a; C. continuity appealed to me, 116a; C. cooperation with non-Catholics, 217a; C. political party, runs twofold risk, 654b; C. suasions result in conversion, 220b; Christian, C., as long as he lives in body, 800b; Christian is my name, C. my surname, 114b, 163a; for C., religion is whole of life, 116a; greatest thing about every a C. who, 114b; He who does not agree with Roman church, not considered C., 701a; I die like a good C., 521a; I have always been latently a C., 220b; I must be, as C. as God's Church, 265a; in communion with Orbis terrarum, 120b; loves truth of God, Church, 114b; man can be good C. in factory, 33b; may not doubt faith, 58a; means obedience to all commandments, 114b; modern world, living on its c. capital, 867a; More C. than the pope, 711a; my idea of liberal C., 644a; Pope barely C. enough for some converts, 221a; puts nothing above divine religion, 114b; rare gift to be a C., 219a; To be a C. at all, man must be orthodox, 650a; whatever done by C., 115a
Catholic Action Christ Himself laid first foundations, 115a; outside and above every political party, 115a; object, to Catholicize secular functions, 115b
Catholic Church abhors bloodshed, 103b; abiding motive of credibility, 119a; adopted Greco-Latin culture, 139b; aggregate of Christians, 191a; all are called to be members, 126b; All churches ultimately derive from great C., 738a; all men bound to embrace true Church, 119b; all things to all nations, 138b; all who are without, shall never be saved, 126b; alone intercedes for those in error, 121a; alone teaches as matters of faith, 147a; always has been C. and various heresies, 165b; ancient Church, preferable to the modern?, 136a; apostles, secondary foundation, 116b; ark to escape perishing in flood, 121b; as a general help to salvation, 128a; as infallible guide, 129a; attempered moral tone of people, 138b; authority binding on whole Church, 117a; authority in-

augurated by miracles, 116b; authority to elucidate deposit of faith, 119b; barren, before children given her, 129b; bears members of Head in spirit, 92b; began where Holy Spirit descended, 123b; began with Abel, 121b; bestrides history past two thousand years, 137a; body of Christ, endowed with supernatural life, 132a; both mother and virgin, 130b; bound together by cement of clergy, 133b; bride of Christ, 129b, 189a; bride of the Lamb, 23b; built upon facts, not opinions, 115b; by Spirit, sanctified and governed, 433b; called Catholic because extends over world, 120a; called Sion, 123b; called universal, consists of all churches, 121a; called holy, because dedicated to God, 128b; can fight, but cannot be conquered, 116b, 135a, 136b; can never grow old or obsolete, 122a; can punish unbelief of those who have received faith, 178b; cannot punish unbelief in those outside, 178b; carefully preserved monuments of wisdom, 139a; chaste, free, and Catholic, 130b; children she has begotten, 130a; Christ and C. are two in one flesh, 132a, 889b; Christ founded C. to last, 136a; Christ, living in those He has united, 166a; C. and American civilization, 142b; C. and catholicity, 121b; C. and colonization, 133a; C. and development of devotion to BVM, 101a; C. and differences of race, 138a; C. and existing ideas, 270b; C. and gates of hell, 124a; C. and gentiles, 120a; C. and history, 136a; C. and inspiration of Holy Ghost, 127a; C. and love of God, 125a; C. and private judgment, 500a; C. and religious imagery in art, 31b; C. and salvation, 121b; C. and scandals, 137a; C. and secret of its success, 136b; C. and Synagogue, 126b; C. and the churches, 134a; C. and true justice, 125a; C. and true position of Mary, 84a; C. and unity with its Head, 132b; C. of life, 131a; Church of St. Peter, 23b; city is C.; king of city is Christ, 134a, 177b; city of God, 125a; claims to judge infallibly, 118a; claims to animadvert on secular matters, 118a; communion with bishops, 299b; congregation of believers, 126b; consists principally of two parts, 123b; contains lost and saved, 116a; daily gives birth to His members, BVM, 97a; defended by BVM, 97a; determines what is true Scripture, 62a, 145b; difference between organic body and mystical body, 132a; differs from all Protestant mockeries, 115b; directive power of Church, 182a; divine messenger for whom you seek, 118b; doctrine of C. consonant with Bible, 63a; does not bring benefits of civilization, but blood, 139b; does not die, 138a; does not reject any forms of government, 255b; efficacy of baptism outside Church, 50b; either very high or very low, 122a; emancipation under Constantine, 33a; error, confuse cause of Church with civilization, 148a; established in bishop and clergy, 433a; Europe is not C., and C. is not Europe, 139b; even now is kingdom of Christ, 124b; ever held same points in same way, 119b; Every member of Christ's body, necessary to body, 173a; everywhere in heaven and on earth, 123b; exemplar is Christ, 132a; exercises only spiritual power directly, 117b; exhibiting so awful a unity, 118a; extent of its survival a mystery, 136b; faith is foundaiton of C., 124a; family of God, 727b; feeds and digests like an organism, 272b; fellowship of eternity, 123b; firm and flexible institution, 138b; form of justice, 137b; founded upon the bishops, 433a; founded upon weak man, indestructible, 136b; four marks: one, holy, catholic, lasting, 135a; fulfilment of whole creation, 140a; full realization, reserved to 'age to come,' 125b; garden, 130b; gates of hell have not prevailed, 135a, 136b; gathered before New Testament written, 62a; gathered from earth into kingdom, 124a; gathers all elements of truth, 135a; gets on by hook or crook, 220b; gives birth to peoples, 130b; glory of C., can produce saints, thinkers, 333b; glory of C. is glory of bishop, 67a; God not truly worshipped, save within C., 126a; goodly vessel, often beaten by waves, 124a; gradual emancipation from earthly influence, 181b; grain of mustard seed has grown, 121a; great sacrament, concerning Christ and C., 131a; grows under persecution, 116b; guardian of dogmas deposited with it, 273b; Guard the C. I have loved so well, 522a; Guard the company of Thy C., 596a; guards and explains divine revelation, 119b; has always venerated Mary as Mother, 92b; has a twofold work to do for mankind, 182a; has a way of growing saints, 128b; has but one ruler and one governor, 696a; has divine life which increases, 136a; has medicine of prevailing efficacy, 130a; has no part of bloodshed, 104a; has one body, many members, 126b; has possessed crown of authority, 117a; has saints and sinners, 127b; has the authority of God, 46a; has three parts, 121b; haven of eternal salvation, 123a; head is our Savior, 122b; He alone rules and governs C., 123a; He builds His C. upon one, 693a; He is Himself Church, by sacrament of body, 131b; Hers the kingdom, hers the scepter, 135b; His body is the Church, 122b; historic fact, 137a; history of C. should be called history of truth, 138a; holds to entire body of truth, 120b; holy, because body of Christ, 128b; Holy Ghost, soul of C., 126b; home after many storms, 118b; House of the Master, 66b; household of God, 172a; I believe in the holy C., 119b, 226b; I do not believe C. continually deteriorating, 136a; "idea" of C., 125a; If C. dies, world's time run, 135b; If Rome dies, other churches may order coffins, 138a; ignorant of wedlock, fertile in bearing, 130a; immediate purpose, saving of souls, 138b; importance of papacy increases, as organization of C. more complete, 702b; impossible to be just to C., 220a; impossible to escape her, 137a; incessant conflict for faith and freedom, 181b; in C., hierarchy by divine ordination, 434a; includes angels and faithful, 122b;

includes righteous, 122b; increased through invisible power of Spirit, 130b; infallible interpreter of dogma, 146a; in gilded clothing surrounded with variety, 762b; instituted for worshipping God, 123b; institution of temporal authority, 46a; in C., you are gathered into Communion of Saints, 199a; in vanguard of changing world, 32b; in view of future peace, called Jerusalem, 123b; irreconcilable enemy of despotism, 259a; irrefutable witness to divine commission, 119a; its civilizing influence, 138b; its immemorial testimony, 115b; its infallible teachings, 119a; its permanence, 135a; its power to bind and absolve, 176b; its teachings, received as His own, 119a; its true power is its own liberty, 183a; its universality, 115a; its visibility, 137a; joined visibly to pontiff set over it, 130b; joins citizen with citizen, 131b; juridical mission of Church, 119b; keeps inviolate her bridalchamber, 129b; keeps safe doctrines committed to her, 145b; kingdom on earth, 118b; kingdom of heaven, 124b; known by three particular marks, 117a; knows how to bring up a world, 140a; land flowing with milk and honey, 24a; Latin church dominates modern civilization, 138a; learns to offer herself through Him, 308a; Light her yoke, her burden sweet, 135b; like a great mountain range, 137a; like ark of Noah, 126b; like bread, becomes one mass, 124a; like Samson, C. will bury all, 135b; living organism, 272b, 548a; long sought after, tardily found, 118b; loves its neighbor, 120a; man cannot change Church or dogmas, 122a; man grounded in Scripture, bulwark of Church, 26b; many grains collected into one, 131b; many things rightly keep me in C., 116b; may not itself have sword of blood, 177a; member by baptism, 127b; member of C., at least in desire, 128a; members born after spirit of virgin, 80b; milk white hind, immortal and unchang'd, 128b; miracles worthy of great deeds, 117a; mistress and mother, 130b; moment men cease to pull against it, they feel tug, 220a; more than sum of parts, 136b; most reliable teacher of mankind, 119a; moral factory for melting raw material, 118a; mother and nurse of civilization, 140a; mother of Christians, 130a; mother of my faith, 143a; mother of unity among many, 130b, 441b; mountain, 800a; multitude of the faithful, 191a; must answer problems of reason, 16b; must have earthly and divine nature, 137b; must keep within fold those baptized, 16b; must speak to each age and nation, 270b; mysterious anticipation of kingdom, 125b; mystery, in strict theological sense of word, 125a; mystical body and C. in communion with Rome, one and same, 133a; myth of Rome's organization dies hard, 136b; name which she bears throughout world, 120b; nature of its infallibility, 129a; nature of its unity, 134b; nearer to C., farther from God, 138a; necessity of C., 118b; neither heretics nor schismatics belong to C., 429b; no man can find salvation save in C., 126a;

no one who quits Church will attain rewards, 125b; no two men enter at exactly same angle, 220a; not a cultured set, 235b; not all members, saints, 127a; not bound to any culture, 149b; not cut nor divided, 133b; not like human society, 136a; not merely human institution, 137b; not merely just or elect, 127a; not mere school of opinion for intellect, 182a; not society only, but brotherhood, 131b; not solely invisible, 137b; not solely the predestined, 127a; not taught by theologians, 411b; noted for hoary antiquity, 32b; nothing more roomy than Church of God, 127a; nuptial union of Christ and Church, 112a; one ark of salvation, 127b; one, because one in many, 134a; One central principle of unity, 134b; one C., divided by Christ into many members, 299b; one Church, founded upon rock of Peter, 135a; one C., outside which no one saved, 311a; one City under one King, 122b; One faith, one communion, one spiritual government, 134b; one God, one Christ, one Spirit, 131a; one holy catholic and apostolic Church, 126b, 132a; One in herself, not rent by schism, 134b; one vast body in heaven and earth, 89b; one who is not in C. unity, 50b; only real members profess true faith, 127b; organic and vital thing, like nation, 136b; organic constiution, immutable, 136a; outside C., everything save salvation, 126a; outside C., no salvation, 125b; partaker of divine authority, 119a; presents picture of authority and private judgment, 118a; plantation of God and beloved vineyard, 124a; possesses all truth essentially, 122a; power to define dogmas, 146b; prayer is life of Church, 89b; profession of same Christian faith, sacraments, 137a; received her mission and task for all time, 140b; republic, Whose founder and ruler Christ, 125a; right to censor books of faithful, 151b; right to teach all nations, 119b; Rock in strength, 135b; role of C. in secular civilization, 162b; saved the world, 136b; Savior does not rule C. in visible manner, 132b; she alone can offer bliss, 118b, 126a; She fear'd no danger, for she knew no sin, 128b; she, Thy wife and Church, 131a; ship of C., sailing merrily over rough water, 136a; single C. of Christ, 693a; so mysterious a vitality, 118a; social and political status of C., 182a; society supernatural and spiritual, 182a; society with common feeling, discipline, hope, 133a, 134b; society's rampart against idolatry, 458a; solid as house on massive foundations, 116b; solid rock, on which city of God is built, 174a; Son of God established society called C., 182a; sort of lucky bag, 116a; spiritual and visible, 137a; Spouse, Christ, 130a, 130b; spread abroad far and wide, 133b, 875a; standing authority in matters of faith, 117b; Stands trembling at gate of bliss, 218b; still awaits her accidental perfection, 122a; stranger in the world, 125a; teaches all the doctrines, 120a; teaches that good and bad belong to C., 127a; teaches universally one end, 120a; teachings of Church and scientific proof, 58a; temple of God, 123b; testifies to its supernatural life, 137b; that august mother, 126a; that imperishable handiwork, 138b; there is only one Church, not two, 137a; those who attack it, destroyed, 116b; those who in no wise belong to Church, 127b; Thou hast bid us hear the C., 227a; Thou hast established on earth a kingdom, 118b; three bonds of unity, 134b; threefold constitution, 117b; Thy universal family, 560b, 591b; Thy work, Thy establishment, 118b; to believe in C., is to believe in pope, 703a; to be loved needs but to be seen, 219a; To 'lose self' in a Society, 127b; traditions of C. dictated by Christ, 64a; triumph which Church celebrates over heresies, 134a; triumphing over a thousand revolutions, 118a; true and perfect society, entirely free, 181a; true Church, her origin from apostles, 116b; true kingdom for government of will, 182a; truly described as an institution, 125b; truth, after many shadows, 118b; truth shines forth from C. alone, 121a; two cities, entangled together, 124b, 125a; two parts of one Church, 124a, 191a; union of body and soul, and Church, 137b; unity in mutual connection of members, 134a; unity is preserved in source, 133b; unity, not of this earth, 135a; unity of Christians is one Man, 134a; unity of God and C., 133b; universal in time, 121b; Universality, not confined to one part of world, 148a; uses all in error, to her advancement, 120b; vast assemblage of human beings, 118a; very unlike other commonwealths, 127a; virgin in sacraments, mother in people, 130a; visible and invisible ruler, 696a; visible existence of Church as Society, 137a; visible hierarchical Church, 135a; voice, by divine assistance, infallible, 129b; warfare between C. and world, 135b; washed in His blood, 128b; watches over education of children, 291b; what He is, does not follow His members are, 128a; what she ultimately is, 125a; what world would be like, without it, 217a; when buffeted, triumphant, 125b; Where C. is, no death, 138a; where C. is, there is Spirit of God, 128a; Where Peter is, there is the C., 709a; Who has not C. for mother, cannot have God for father, 429a; Who is she that stands triumphant?, 135b; whole assembly of saints belonging to one, 123a; whole C. is one widow, 123b; whole C. possesses one and same faith, 143b; whole City of Jerusalem, 122b; whole congregation of elect, called C., 126b; wonderful mystery of Thy whole C., 797a; work of Incarnate God, 117, 129b; you prov'd her, yet she stands, 269b

Catholic Faith affirms its own divine origin, 147a; all men bound to learn, 119b; all true believers and professors, 591b; alone gives life to mankind, 174a; apostles transmitted to nations, 429b; as old as Christmas and Pentecost, 147b; as universal religion of mankind, 148b; authority of Scripture and tradition, 117a, 144a; attractive because true, 147b; comfort in tribulation, 193a; compre-

hends all religious truth, 148a, 148b; doctrine of Church, divine and unerring rule, 145b; does not admit indefinite 'seeking,' 144a; does not contradict history, 274b; door, 147b; elaborateness of C., 58a; embraces universality of things, 144b; Europe not the faith, faith not Europe, 139b; Every part of system equally certain, 270b; expansion of Christian creed and ritual, 272a; faith confessed by whole Church, 144b; f. is Europe, Europe is the f., 139b; Faith of our fathers!, 146b; fulness of truth, 144a; genuine progress, not alteration, 271a; identical with that of ancients, 145a; identity of teaching throughout, 272b; in Apostolic See, totality of Christian religion, 705b; its explicit development, 271b; manifested in Scripture and doctrine of Church, 145b; mysteries, not result of philosophical investigations, 165a; necessary to hold C., 144a, 227a; No one forced against will to embrace C., 147a, 174a, 355a, 613a; not inimical to interests of society, 146b; one faith, for all ages given, 135b; One faith, one spiritual government, 134b; only true religion, 146b; organic development of doctrine, 270b, 272a; Our religion is wise and foolish, 233a; possible to have faith and do nothing about it, 148a; quod ubique, quod semper, quod ab omnibus, 144b; refutation of heretics serves sound doctrine, 269b; Regarding substance, faith does not grow, 271b; religion Peter transmitted to Romans, 144b; revelation vs. agnosticism, 146b; some shreds discoverable in heresies, 120b; things which are for our peace, 219a; Thy glory revealed to all nations, 12a; too strict for the careless, 147b; too wide for individualists, 148a; truth that always shall prevail, 147b; truth, whose fruit is freedom, 135b; universal character of rules and doctrines, 145a; universality, antiquity, general consent, 144b; way of life and system of thought, 145a, 147b; we must trace it back to Christ, 147b; We will be true to thee till death!, 146b; what has been believed everywhere, 144b; when 'found,' is to be believed, 144a; Whosoever willeth to be saved, 227a; wind that is trumpet of liberty, 147b; With our faith, we desire no further belief, 144a; word of God, written or unwritten, 145b; You must accept whole or reject whole, 146a

Catholicism all truth contained implicitly in Christianity, 148a, 148b; as a universal religion, 122a, 148b; attractive because true, 147b; bound up with Christianity, 703a; confusing Westernism with C., 148a; deep matter, cannot take up in tea-cup, 146a; embodying every form of piety and holiness, 122b; everywhere the same, 116b; home of our race, 116b; living stream, 219b; modern C., legitimate growth, 272a; must appeal to East, 148a; no other authentic universalism than C., 148a; not mere collection of decrees and canons, 219b; not much of C. in Protestant history, 32b; primacy, bulwark of C., 696b; reconciled with true science, 147a, 761a; re-

ligion rooted in humility, 27b; seed, sown in catacombs, 116b; spirit of C., not same as Latin spirit, 771a; sum of all religions and queen, 147a

Catholicity belief in c. of Anglicanism, 24a; C., what Catholics are, 142b; Catholics and opposition to C., 115a; Church exalted in her c., 138a; frivolous arguments against C., 26b; links itself to all faculties, 147a; one of Church's securities, 121b; only divine form of religion, 537a; republicanism in politics favors C. in religion, 766a; True Catholicity, commensurate with human mind, 146a; True universalism, very reverse of eclecticism, 148b

Catholicize need of Church to C. me! 24b

Catholics C. and voice of Church in political matters, 183a; C., educated as Americans, 292b; children of Thy adoption, 51b; damned, if they do not become C., 28a; distinctions among C., because of race, 265a; forthright devotion to BVM, 101b, 102a; government of US preferable to C., 15a; I would have C. be first patriots of the land, 663b; in US, should keep to republicanism, 15a; men cease to be C. by denying universality of Church, 115a; name of C. Christians, 144b; said, C. never so good as creed, 116a; venerate St. Augustine, 44a; We are Christians and C., 147b

Catholicus Christianus mihi nomen est, C. cognomen, 163a

Cats They agreed like two c. in gutter, 264a; when candles be out, all c. be grey, 113b

Causa C. finita est, 709a

Causation chain of command, 149a; not an intuitive truth, 149a

Cause A good c. proves less in man's favor, 153b; above all others, will of God, 391b, 372b, 392a; C. causeth, 149a; draw pen in defense of bad c., 149a; everything must have a cause, 149a; God, actual and virtual c., 369a, 380a, 383b, 390a; human mind instinctively craves to know c., 419b; Judge me, O God, distinguish my c., 587a; knowledge of God, c. of other things, 383b; The c. is finished, 709a; Thou Great First C., least understood, 373b; To make our c. thine own! 491a

Causes Among all c., end holds primacy, 373b; before Your face stand c. of all things, 372b; God operates through secondary c., 21a, 373a; matrimonial c., belong to eccles. judges, 578a; our wills, included in order of c., 382b; there is for God, certain order of c., 382b; three c., final, efficient, and formal, 373a; ultimate end, first of all c., 373b

Caution appearance of carelessness, vital in true c., 149b; constant guard over actions, 4a

Cave c. of Bethlehem, 122a; contemplative life is in cave, 4b; The c. is heaven, 167b

Cavell, Edith, 318a

Cean-Salla, 254a

Cease C., then, O queens, who earthly crowns do wear, 96b, 746a

Cecilia, St., 149b

Cedar My lover is a c. tree, 564b

Cedars He that high growth on c. did bestow, 413b

Celestial Love c. desires, 258a; strong and pure c. life, 20a

Celestine V, Pope St., 753a

Cell c. of self-knowledge, 805b; With all the world for c.! 573a

Cemetery as memorial for dead, 151b; c. for all the poor, 110a

Cenobites, 618b

Censer golden c. that became tabernacle, 82a

Censers swinging c. dusk the air With perfumed prayer, 437b

Censorship applies to clergy and laymen, 152a; books of apostates, heretics, prohibited, 151b; Church's right to censor books of faithful, 151b; governmental c. of thought, 473a; We have a c. by the press, 496b

Censure dog's tooth, 152a; nature of ecclesiastical c., 117b, 178a

Censured far rather c., than praised by erring, 152a

Cent we leave world without a c., 48a

Center Catholic c. cannot admit other c., 148a; If God thy c., Be hell thy circumference, 882a

Century Better a day of strife Than a c. of sleep, 852a; fragments of a c., 252b

Cerberus, 861a

Ceremonies c. of Old Law, 68a; c., vestments, incentives to piety, 597b; superstition, to found hopes on c., 547a

Certain Catholic, more c. about fixed truths than fixed stars, 885a; Nothing more c. than death, 247b

Certainty grace gives c., reason never decided, 332a; The mysterious c.! 152b; We love c., 152a

Certitude by accumulated probabilities, 152b; C. Feeling. Joy. Peace, 395b; cooperation of God, 152b; directed to this or that particular proposition, 706a; in mathematics and in religious inquiry, 152b; mind uneasy, until it attaint c., 515a; reflex action, 152b; three conditions of c., 152b

Cervantes, 152b

Cesspool Free from cesspool's fetid blight, 12b

Celibacy Bishops, priests, deacons, must remain unmarried, 150a; clergy beget children for life which is heavenly, 151a; clergy in major orders, forbidden to marry, 150b, 151a; If a priest marry, he shall be removed, 150a; If any one saith marriage placed above virginity or c., 898a; married to a single life, 149b; mistaken c., hell, 149b; not condemnation of marriage, 150b; nowise lawful, after ordination to marry, 150b; only lectors and cantors able to marry, 150b; priest is wedded to Savior's work, 151a; priest's c., true fatherhood, 151a; *they that have wives as though they had none,* 150b

Chain no chain is stronger than weakest link, 136b; Oh! loose for us the guilty c., 28b; galling iron c. doth fall from Peter's hand, 677b

Chains freed from c. of our sins, 668a

Chair C. of Peter, 709b; grant bishop an episcopal c., 68b; He who deserts c. of Peter, 693a; Though every man may not sit in the c., 324b

Chalice C. of everlasting salvation, 592a; *I will take the c. of salvation,* 595a; there is one Flesh of

our Lord, one C., 597b; We offer Thee the c. of salvation, 590a

Chamber Catholic churches, but one bridal c., 694a

Chambers c. in the house of dreams, 277b

Champagne Adventure is the c. of life, 9a; Americans have sort of invisible c., 17b

Champion c. of the truth, 884a; makes people's wrongs his own, 153a

Champions c. of the faith, 275b

Chance His own c., no man knoweth, 153a; may win that by mischance was lost, 153a; predictions of astrology, mere c., 41b; unexpected event of concurring causes, 153a

Chances Times go by turns, c. change by course, 869b

Change As often c. from hue to hue, 153a; finds no likeness to itself in Thee, 374b; God does not c. his ways, 372b, 397b; is there some new c. in Heaven's decrees, 239a; One alone Who cannot c., 13a; Sick of this everlasting c., 374a; Something there is of pain and c., 11a; Times c. and men deteriorate, 153a; to live is to c., 153b; We cannot c. our habits in a moment, 153b; Who orderest time and c. aright, 809b; world of c. and time, 7b

Changed to be perfect is to have c. often, 153b; yet the place seemed c. and still, 448a

Chant Let me c. in sacred numbers, 489a

Chants all our c. but chaplet some decay, 253b

Chaplains Many c. chaste, but where is charity? 159a

Chaos Lo, thy dread empire, c., 153b

Character A man is seldom better than his word, 154a; crucial thing, that c. should dignify station, 846b; difficulties strengthen c., 263a; encrusted c. cannot be melted, 154a; final judgment depends on worst action, 153b; foolish, think that moods are our c., 620a; God taketh me as I am, 153b; in three sacraments, imprinted in soul, 52b, 787b; profound fascination of human c., 154a; right to one's own culture and national c., 531a; root of the matter lies in c., 154a; sacerdotal c., 23b, 648a; sacramental c. manifests Christ's c., 787a; silent old lady has power for sounding c., 154a; tested by true sentiments more than by conduct, 153b; Ye know what he hath been, 153b

Characters At death we display our true c., 154a; difficult, to enter into c. other men, 27a

Charge My c. is to preach the gospel, 190a; To flee c., and find ease, 154a; To me the wonderful c. was given, 38a

Charisma received sure c. of truth, 299b

Charitably She was so c. solicitous, 86b

Charity acquiescence of soul in contemplation, 156b; All is love's, in holy C., 156b; All is made for c., and c. for God, 156b; all mankind's concern is c., 156b; arises from inner peace, 899b; beg her by St. Charity, 20b; both means and end, 156b; brings to life those spiritually dead, 155b; brother-love, 157a; But c. and

great example gain, 317a; c. and continence, 155a; c. and decent standard of living, 157b; C. and devotion differ, 262a; c. and economics, 287b; C. is love; not all love is c., 156a; c. is owing to all, and wrongdoing to none, 132a; C. is pure gold which makes us rich, 156b; C. is the bond of brotherhood, 154b; Chastity without c., chained in hell, 159a; Christ dwells in hearts through faith quickened by c., 330a; Christian c. recognizes no property, 156a; *covers a multitude of sins,* 154a; discretion proceeds from c., 265a; Everyone must be loved equally, 154b; excels both good works and martyrdom, 154b; faith, *which worketh by c.,* 332b; for those bound to you more closely, 154b; form, mover, mother, root of virtues, 156a; foundation of peace, 154b; give to all from gifts we have received, 13a; gives peace to soul, 157a; *God is love,* 155b; good disposition of the soul, 155a; grant us an increase of faith, hope, and c., 334a; gratefully accepts dovelike eye, 152a; greater than both hope and faith, 154b; greatness of His c., 44a; He is truly great who hath great c., 156a; He who has c., far from all sin, 154b; Help thy kin, there beginneth c., 156a; holy, apostolic c., 196a; Humility is descending c., 452a; If but the world would give to love, 157a; In c., all elect been made perfect, 154b; in this life her net keeps every sort of fish, 155b; keeping c. towards God and neighbor, 214a; knows no schism, 154b; lack of c. in action, murders faith, 334a; law of c. is good and sweet, 155b, 157a; Let c. issue in good deeds, 157b; long-suffering, modest, unassuming, 157a; love of God never destroyed man's self-respect, 157b; mainstay and security of unity, 154b; much stronger than natural affection, 156b; No one commanded to distribute that which is required, 157b; not accident in God, 155b; not genuine, if words not charitable, 156b; *now there remain faith, hope, c.,* 334a; O C., my God, enkindle me! 215b; O eternal Truth, true C., 390b; organized c., scrimped and iced, 157a; over the world she draws Her cloak of c., 886a; pardoning of the unpardonable, 157b; perfection of Christian life, in c., 156a; *poured forth in their hearts by Holy Ghost,* 505b; prefer nothing to love of Christ, 155a; prefers knowledge of God to everything else, 155a; remedy of sin, 154b; renders bearable laws of slaves, 155b; role of c., in Church and State, 183b; saving work of c., 154b; school of c., 233b; sunlike in the soul, reigns c. alone, 664a; sweetness of spirit, 155a; thing both great and easy, 154b; To relieve poor; to clothe naked, 155a; Unarmed she goeth, 157a; unites us to God, 154a; very substance of God, 155b; victory of truth is c., 155a, 883b; virtue has no limits, especially c., 156a; virtue of virtues, 156a; virtues not acceptable, without c. and grace, 409b; warmed by fire of c., 6b; we cannot be certain we have c., 155b, 330a; We should love others for their own sakes, 156a; Where c. and love are, there is God, 442b; wherewith we love God, 560a; Who can express its splendor, 154a; without c. faith can be, but can profit nothing, 154b, 329b; your c., a spear, 401a

Charlemagne, 158a

Charles I, King, 158a

Charm as she would creep into your bosom, 158a; which comes from gracious politeness, 691a

Charming When men give up saying what is c., 158a

Charms C. strike sight, but merit wins, 55a; desire to please by outward c., 277b

Charon, 517b

Chase Proud Nimrod first the bloody c. began, 454b; Still with unhurrying c., 385a

Chaste And let my soul made c., 898b; BVM's virginal body all chaste, 39b; c. minds and unchaste eyes, 158b; c. wife does not have to be watched, 159a; love, my heart to c. desires shall bring, 92b; O God, gracious dweller in c. bodies, 640a; Peaceful and sober, c. was He, 205a; serve Thee with c. body, 159a; should not be proud, 215b; Spouse of those c., 159a; what more c. than she? 80a

Chastity Burn our reins and our heart with fire of Holy Ghost, 159a; C. of BVM, 92a; c. of widows and virgins, 158b; compared with martyrdom, 159a; crown of marriage, c. of procreation, 732a; does not mean we are insensible to concupiscence, 159a; Every husband exacts c. from his wife, 455a; gird yourself with cincture of c., 726b; God refuses not gift to those who ask, 150b; has three forms, 158b; He that can take it, 158b; Holiness, without c. consecrated to God, 437b; Holy virginity, better thing than conjugal c., 897b; immense advantage of c., 639a; innocency of body and soul, 159a; King of virgins and Lover of c., 159a; Let each one study own powers, 158b; Lying wrong, even to save c., 567a; of itself, charming and attractive, 158b; priesthood of c., 639b; radiance of her c., 55b; stain upon c. more dreadful than death, 158b; those who make vow of c., 150b; to love c., 158b; virgins, dedicated to God by holy c., 639b; without charity, lies chained in hell, 159a

Chaucer, Geoffrey, 159b

Cheap best is best c., 59b

Cheat to c. the Church is sacrilege, 159b

Cheater 'Tis no sin to cheat a c., 159b

Cheeks To move the c., 159b

Cheer Better one month's c., than churl's whole life, 497b

Cheerfulness always finds favor with God, 496b; always rejoice, if we keep head raised, 159b; Christian c., that modest joy, 160a; Clothe yourself with c., 496b, 602b; Rest, c., and table thinly spread, 268b

Cherubikon Hymn, 589b

Cherubim more honorable than the c., 81b, 593a; one of nine orders of angels, 18b; Virgin is throne of the c., 167b; We who mysti-

cally represent the c., 589b; which c. and seraphim do praise, 591a

Cherubs The c. sit with folded wings, 20b

Chesterton, Gilbert Keith, 160a

Chiding She not worthy of wedlock, who is worthy of c., 455a

Chief C. of all things, 378b; idea of king, implies man who is c. and shepherd, 508b

Chiesa Piu presso la c., piu lontano da Dio, 138a

Child A C. in very truth Thou seemest to me, 488a; An old knave is no c., 510b; Be a good c., and God will help you, 398a; Before C., angels sing Osanne, 87b; C. divine, 99a; c. is pledge of immortality, 161a; C. of a Virgin meek and pure, 486b; c. of weariness and woe, 77b; Creator, C. at breast, 39b; every c. likes beauty, 55a; Every Christian c. has right to instruction, 858b; Gold a royal C. proclaimeth, 298b; I am unworthy of the C., 198b; I, c. of process, 493a; Infant Jesus; Christ C., 486b; Little C. so sweet, 169b; lower animal, in form of man?, 160b; Man is declar'd almighty! God, a C.!, 468b; Many kiss the c. for the nurse's sake, 570a; My c., give Me thy heart!, 384b; mystic c. is set in these still hours, 343a; not lawful to destroy in womb, 1b; not mere creature of State, 291a; O sing a joyous carol Unto the holy C., 487b; One wept whose only c. was dead, 624b; Pleased with rattle, tickled with straw, 160b; she bears C. in her womb, 80a; spirit should become like a little c., 815b; sweetest C., how dost Thou fade, 93b; Teach, O teach us, holy C., 169a; The C. grew in wisdom, as well as in stature, 608b; The Christ-c. stood at Mary's knee, 488a; through Jesus Christ Thy beloved C., 480a; thy C. on a cross y-rent, 99b; You cannot visit c., without visiting mother, 169b; You shall not kill an unborn c., 1b; virgin with C., 79a; When thou broughtest forth that C., 39b; Who wished to become c. of man, 166a

Childbearer O glorious c., 462b

Childbearing c. of Mary and Church, 130a; she who slays is she who bears, 161b; without concupiscence, 166b

Childbirth after c. thou didst remain virgin, 24b, 39a, 79b; BVM escaped pangs of c., 39b, 79b; mother whose life is imperiled by c., 2a; mystery of thy c., 299a; writing book, like c., 107a

Childhood c. is ignorant, 11b; In c.'s feeble charms, 487b; it was a miraculous world, 161b; let your c. be like old age, 11b

Childishness I will be sorry for their c., 873b

Children adopted c. begotten by heart, 6b; All mothers worship little feet, 84a; all of us, mere children of our Father, 161a; begin by loving their parents, 161a; begotten by Church, 129b; belong to Church when baptized, 52b; born to drive out their parents, 65b; C. and fools cannot lie, 567b; c. of God, 166a; c. of renowned and noble personages, 160b; c. of the Bridegroom, 80b; c. of the holy place, 586a; c. of Thy adoption, 51b; cooperation of

God and parents in c., 160b; Eve' banished c., 95b; from their c. to spare the rod, 160b; Go, c. of swift joy and sorrow, 45a; hearts of Thy c., sincere in love for each other, 565a; human beings, being c., 571b; in mystical sense, c. of Mary, 93a; learn to creep ere they can go, 160b; No freedom so great, as that of c. of God, 353b; not gay, except now and then, 362a; One of the c. of the year, 9a; Parents bound to provide for education of c., 291a; primary end of marriage, procreation and education of c., 575b, 578b; procreation of defective c., 161a; see your c.'s c., even to third generation, 576b; that men might become c. of God, 468a; we are all c. of same mother, Mary, 93a; young c., not allowed to mix with all, 200a

Chime When I last heard their soothing c., 58b

Chip lest c. fall in your eye, 14a

Chips As merry as three c., 497a

Chivalry Ah, see the fair c. come, 582a; he loved c., 161b; Self-sacrifice and c., all come from heart, 557b; very name of horse has been given to highest mood, 162a

Choice His c. is best, 882b; should be of men approved, 9b

Choir apostolic c., 28b; bright celestial c., 258b; Form all together one c., 889b; Make of yourselves a c., 162a

Choirs admitted among c. of angels, 37a; c. of saints with greeting notes, 40a; in heavenly day, 12b; let harmonious c. proclaim, 149b; O'er angelic c. uplifted, 40a; that dwell on high, 12b; Where blissful c. imparadise their minds, 903b

Choose not c. not to be, 258b

Choosers Beggars should be no c., 56a

Chord But I struck one c. of music, 626b; silver c. in twain is snapp'd, 250b

Chords Like c. in unison they move, 890a

Chorus Every heart shall hear the c., 74b; Meetly in alternate c., 19b

Chose He c. and predestinated us, 722b

Chosen hast c. all those that love Thee, 480a; Paul, c. vessel, 664a; You have not c. me, but I have c. you, 112b

Chrism anointing before and after baptism, 49b; blend of oil and balsam, 206b; c. of salvation, 51a; fit to impart His divine Nature, 162b; holy c., blessed by bishop, 320b, 442a; oil of gladness, 51a; The c. of the light, 240b; use, in confirmation, 206b; whole Church, consecrated by unction of c., 730b

Christ-bearers You all are God-bearers, C., 888b

Christe Kyrie eleison, C. eleison, 588a

Christendom European nations, parts of wider spiritual society, 312a; new age of C., age of reconciliation, 162b; on Calvary, C. gan spring, 352b; unity from which sprang Christian Europe, 139a; word C. relates to cultural order, 162b

Christian A pagan heart, a C. soul, 164a; all his time belongs to God, 162b; attractions of C. way of life, 27b; C. ethics will not long survive C. creed, 622b; C. ideal, found difficult and left untried, 165b; C. is my name, Catholic my surname, 114b, 163a; C. name and heretics, 145a; C. order, purpose is peace, 666b; who cannot trust C. with property, 807b; C.'s God, not simply author of mathematical truths, 384b; each C., member of Church, 126b; each, member of eternal King and Priest, 730b; end of a C., greater glory of God, 728b; Faith is the beginning of a C. man, 325a; Hatred of C. name, 163a; he who perseveres to end, 163a; Joy, gigantic secret of C., 498a; keep entirely to C. food, 428b; manly C. spirit, 775b; many claim dignity of C. religion, 145a; No one is wise but the C., 163b; not his own master, 162b; one who has ruling sense of God's presence within, 163b; still a sad, good C. at her heart, 163b; To be C. the great thing, not to seem one, 163a; walks with Christ in newness of life, 52a; whatever else makes up a C. gentleman, 324b; Worship is the C. life, 929a

Christianae *testimonium animae naturaliter C.!* 834b

Christiani *Fiunt, non nascuntur C.!* 163a

Christianity affect on European civilization, 165b; all truth contained implicitly in C., 148b; alone, suited to all, 164a; as moral system made up of two elements, 164b; Away with attempts to produce mottled C., 143b; balance of beauty and severity in C., 164b; can sometimes be caught no less than taught, 319b; C. and life of soul after death, 164a; C. and meaning of human nature, 164a; C. is more than a doctrine, 166a; C. is the religion of civilization, 164b; Civil society, renovated by teachings of C., 165a; developed in westerly direction, 148a; did not believe in Judaism, but Judaism in C., 498b; difference between Catholic and Protestant view, 116a; eminently an objective religion, 928a; evangelist must prove C. true, 27b; great spiritual advantage to world, 164b; had God who knew way out of grave, 165b; has always been a learned religion, 164b; has died many times and risen again, 165b; He has a good part of C., 163b; identical with democracy, 256a; in terms of character-building, 437a; intellectual appeal of C., 164a; its fruits are negative, 164b; its lines met in eternity, 165a; living C. necessary to world, 328b; must be principle of all education, 289a; must have infallible expounder, 129a; mystery by which incarnation extends itself, 166b; never undogmatic C. professed by all, 165b; No truth can exist, external to C., 884b; not for nothing, Christian fatih spread over world, 164a; our Catholicism is bound up with our C., 703a; owes immense debt to Hellenism, 27b; prose of C., without poetry, 437a; *re-establishment of all things in Christ*, 166a; restraint on world rather than guide, 164b; spirit and letter, 164a; spirit that strives to change world, 165b; strength of C. and paganism,

163b; teaches men twin truths, 164a; truth, a quality of C., 27a; way of life *and* system of thought. 147b; When C. dies, world will die, 135b

Christianorum *Odii erga nomen C.,* 163a; *semen est sanguis C.,* 103b, 583a

Christians ablest men have been Christians, 165a; all C. priests, because members of one Priest, 730b; alone love those that hate them, 163a; blood of C. is seed, 103b; BVM, mediatrix and refuge of C., 90a, 98a; BVM salvation of C., 99b; C. are born for combat, 223a; C. are made, not born! 163a; Church of us C. 120a; flock of Christ, 66b; In C., we look not to beginnings but to endings, 163a; live in intercourse of discipline, 680b; "Look how they love one another," 163a; members of His Son, 162a; name of C. arose at Antioch, 675a; O ye proud C., weary and sad of brow, 163b; "The C. to the lion!" 544b; typical C. and love of God, 125b; We are as many as we are alleged to be, 163a; We are C., we belong to Christ, 163b

Christianus *C. mihi nomen est, Catholicus cognomen,* 163a

Christmas Ah! no eve is like C. eve! 170b; At last Thou art come, little Savior! 170a; Behold, a silly tender Babe, 168b; Christ is born! Tell forth His fame! 167b; Come, all ye faithful, 170a; first C. Day is solstice of history, 169b; God is coming here to reign, 168a; Hail, Thou ever-blessed morn! 169a; Hear, O Thou Shepherd of Israel, 166a; I saw three ships come sailing in, 168a; Light and Life to man appear, 168a; Light His way this C. night! 111a; Loud proclaim the jubilee, 167b; Love's noon in nature's night, 168b; nativity, beginning and completion of all religion, 166b; New born and newly dear, 169b; The C. stars at Bethlehem, 171a; The King is come to Israel, 169a; This day Christ is born: this day Savior appeared, 167b; this most sacred night, 170a; 'Tis C. night! 170b; Under the stars, amid the snows, 97b; We must either leave Christ out of C., 169b; we unceasingly adore that birth, 166b; When Christ our Lord was born, 170a; yearly expectation of our redemption, 169b; You cannot visit child without visiting mother, 169b

Christo *Instaurare omnia in C.,* 492b

Christopher, St., 601a

Christs Kings, were made c., 507a

Church apostolical origin gives right to rank, 433b; brighten this temple by power of Thy presence, 171a; dread throne of God on earth, 100a; every c. must agree with Roman C., 704a; full of ambitious men, 13b; 'In church with saints,' 200a; looks as if left over from earlier age, 30a; means convocation or assembly, 126b; sacred edifice, devoted to divine worship, 171b; Savior's holy home, 146a; signifies 'calling forth,' 127a; Thou heavenly, new Jerusalem, 171a; Vision of peace in prophet's dream! 171a; when consecrated, is washed, 128a; Who builds a c. to God and not to

fame, 171b; With living stones built up on high, 171a; You can force a man to enter c., 57a

Church and State civil allegiance of Christian, limited by conscience, 182a; All modern history filled with double contest, 181b; all power in Church militant, derived from supreme pontiff, 179a; Almighty has given charge of human race to two powers, 182b; American Catholics rejoice in separation, 185a; American pattern, not universally best, 183a; American society recognizes Christian conscience, 185a, 210a; antagonism, 142b; as sun is differentiated from moon, 178a; authority of Church, not inferior to civil power, 182b; belongs to our office to reprove for sin, 178a; between two powers, certain orderly connection, 182b; Bishops must not rashly assail kings, 172b; Both powers our Lord willed to bear Himself, 176b; Both swords belong to Church, 176b; Christian emperors have need of pontiffs, 174b, 175a; Christianity, constantly moulding society in its image, 181a, 182a; Church and use of force, 181b; Church differs from civil society, 182a; Church does not need assent of State, 181b; Church has twofold work to do for mankind, 182a; Church, not subject to civil power in exercise of duty, 183a; Church should not be involved in party strife, 183a; collaboration, 183b; conflict of laws, 179b, 181b; Constantine placed crown on Roman pontiff, 177a; crime, for stranger to judge servants of God, 172a; deposition of heretical rulers, 178b; differences between political and ecclesiastical powers, 176b, 178b, 180b; Do not interfere in eccles. affairs, 172a; Each in its kind is supreme, 182b; eccles. liberty and Roman Church, 177b; emperor called son of Church, 173a; Emperor, guardian of Church unity, 174a; emperor is within Church, not above Church, 172b, 173a; equal toleration of all denominations, 184a; equity of laws in America, 143a; examination of ruler belongs to consecrator, 178a; First Amendment, not piece of religious mysticism, 185a; full power in temporal as well as spiritual matters, 177b; Give to each its own, all will be well, 177b; God gave to Peter power of binding and loosing, 176a; God has established two great lights, 178a; God has given you power to judge us also, 172b; harmony of two orders, 142b, 143a, 182b; heretics, destructive both to C. and S., 432a; How can you say you have power to judge bishops?, 172a; I forbid government of kingdom to king Henry, 175b; in community which admits diversity of religious profession, 183b; in matters of faith, bishops wont to judge emperors, 172b; In matters of political welfare, temporal power obeyed before spiritual, 178b; In same city and under same king, two peoples, 177b; in supreme pontiff, fulness of pontifical and royal power, 179b; I set majesty of Caesar below God, 171b; king should promote eternal happiness, 179a; kingly power, conferred for guardianship of Church, 174a;

Kings, not exempt from jurisdiction of Church, 181b; like union of body and soul, 182b; Loyalty to God's Church and to country!, 143a; maintenance of civil law, secondary to religion, 173a; Medieval man entered State through Church, 183b; modern civilization, 'lay' or 'secular' civilization, 184a; modern man citizen, whether member of Church or not, 183b; no imperial power over things divine, 173a; no law respecting establishment of religion, 184b; no one should assume empire without consent of pope, 177a; not belong to civil power, define rights of Church, 181a; not right that man should judge gods, 172a; nothing so close to emperors as wellbeing of priesthood, 174b; Palaces belong to emperor, churches to bishop, 173a; papal dignity not derived from Caesar, 180a; political system struggles to harmonize Christianity with itself, 181a; pontiffs should make use of emperor's laws, 175a; pope, directive power over princes, 181a; pope, for spiritual good, has supreme power, 180b; pope may depose emperors, 175b; pope may release subjects from oath of fidelity, 175b; pope may seek deposition of sinful king, 179b, 180b; pope should admonish king who sins, 179b, 181a; power of giving kingdoms, to God, 173b; priest declares what conduces to beatitude, 179a; priesthood and imperial authority, ornaments of human life, 174b; priestly office is beyond the kingly, 172a; priestly power established the kingdom, 177a; priestly power has to render account for kings, 174a; priests have task of perpetual prayer, 174b; prince is minister of priestly power, 177b; prince receives sword from hand of Church, 177a; purple makes princes, not priests, 173a; religion and politics go together, 184b; Religion is above and independent of state, 181a; Salvation not assured, unless each worships true God, 172b; secular power subject to spiritual, in matters of salvation, 178b; separation, 181b, 183b; separation, not universally expedient, 143b; sovereign of territory determines religion, 180a; spiritual power has to institute earthly power, 177b; state from which religion banished, never well regulated, 845a; state has nothing to do with Church, but accept, 181a; state is not in Church, but Church is in state, 172b sword should be under sword, 179a; temporal authority should be subject to spiritual, 179a; temporal government does not owe existence to spiritual, 180a; true protection of Church, its own independence, 183a; Two cities, formed by two loves, 173a; Two guides appointed for man, 180a; two powers by which this world chiefly ruled, 174a, 177b; two swords, spiritual and temporal, 179a; unity of religion, not prerequisite for political unity, 184a; voice of Church in political matters, 183a; we exercise temporal authority on occasion, 178a; We follow whatever emperor has done without sin, 175a; When kingdom and priesthood in complete accord, 177a
Church Militant Church has three

parts, 121b, 123a; society of faithful dwelling on earth, 124a
Church Triumphant abides in bliss and helps, 123b; glorious assemblage of blessed spirits, 123b
Churches Catholic c. throughout world, one bridal chamber, 694a; c. and the Catholic Church, 134a; c. of true faith, 'cities,' 134a; even heretics and schismatics style their assemblies 'c.,' 429a; good estate of the holy c. of God, 588a; governed by bishops by divine institution, 69b; Roman c., mother and mistress of all c.s, 52a, 171a
Churl Better one month's cheer, than c.'s whole life, 497b
Cicero thou art follower of C., not Christ, 478b
Cigarette perfect type of perfect pleasure, 185a
Cinderella balance between C. and ugly sisters, 300a
Circle nature of God, c. whose center is everywhere, 386b
Circulation its c. is not of best, 296b
Circumcellions, 173b
Circumcise lips of my mouth, 747b
Circumcision mystery of c., 51b
Circumstances subject-matter, not rule of conduct, 185a
Citadel c. of contemplation, 5a
Cities churches of true faith, as 'c.,' 134a; Crowded in c. man is crushed, 185b; mystically, two cities or societies, 124b; nations, kingdoms and c. have different laws, 529a; Two c., formed by two loves, 124b, 125a, 173a
Citizen fellow c. of the angels, 569b; Medieval man became 'c.' through Church, 183b; modern man c., whether member of Church or not, 183b; No better c. than Christian mindful of duty, 185b; To train a c., to train a critic, 290b; today we need Christian c., 17a
Citizens aim of good government, union and peace of c., 615a; best poets are the worst c., 685a; cannot be forbidden associations, 38b; c. of America are her monarchs, 255b; fellow-c. of the saints, 579b; Government should be administered for welfare of c., 407a; harmony between c. and government, 257a; have power of correcting government, 405a; If c. are sane, city will be sane, 622b; legislator, whole body of c., 405a, 534a; rights, franchises, of American c., 17b; Roman Empire, rule of c., not tyrants, 778b
Citizenship Morality, very soul of good c., 185b; worthy of their American c., 265a
City Blessed c., heavenly Salem, 478b, 479a; C. is Christ's body, 123a; c. of confusion and house of bondage, 24a; c. of God, embodied in Church, 125a; c. of woe, 427a; congregation and fellowship of saints, 307b; courts of heavenly c., 302a; earthly C., love of oneself, 124b; For the c. and for the world, 710a; *Glorious things are said of thee,* 125a; happy mansion of c. above!, 303a; heavenly C., 124b, 313a; If citizens are sane, c. will be sane, 622b; involved in darkness, 427b; King and Queen of the C., 112a; lurking toys, which c. life affords, 831a; O c. on the Umbrian hills, 38a; one C. under one King, 122b; solid rock, on which c. of God is built, 174a; till Church at-

tain the celestial c., 29b; *We have not here a lasting c.,* 328b
Civil c. magistracy for human government, just, 406a
Civilization America, part of European c., 16a; Benedictines and European c., 59a; Catholic Church, source of benefits, 138b; Catholic culture does not mean universality, 139a; Christianity is the religion of c., 164b; Church and principles of Western c., 140a, 148a; Church cannot submit to particular people, 138a; Church does not bring 'benefits of c.,' 139b; Church grafts good scion upon wild stock, 140a; Church knows how to bring up a world, 140a; c. and Catholic Church, 138b, 140a, 186a; c. and culture, 235b; claim of western c. to be representative, 186a; continuous series of spiritual movements, 187a; democracy and complexity of c., 256b; fragile barriers separate c. from barbarism, 186a, 187a; ideal, back of progress and c., 396b; importance of new types of creative genius, 187a; influence of Church in Middle Ages, 139a; Latin church dominates modern c., 138a; missionary character of Western c., 187a; mother and nurse of c., 140a; one Church, divers types of Christian c., 162b; Our own civilization will pass, 140a; Religion, determining element in c., 186a; religion must not be identified with culture, 186b; return to spiritual integration of culture, 186b; saved by Catholic Church, 136b; To serve peace, to serve c., 666b; true meaning of c., 186b; unchanging law of oriental cultures, 165b; Western c. result of long process, 186b; Western culture and role of Church, 187a; word Christendom relates to cultural order, 162b
Clasp Why do you so c. me, 556b
Class Cleanse us from ire of creed or c., 523a; Each c. must receive its due share, 909b; great mistake, notion c. naturally hostile to c., 187a; great scandal, Church lost working c., 517a
Classes interests of working c. should be carefully watched over, 516b; Mr. Wells' view of c., 217b; should dwell in harmony, 187b
Classical Benedictines, pioneers of c. tradition, 59a
Classics authors who exemplify a language, 187b
Clay A house of c. for to be made, 413a; c. of humanity is a condemned c., 820b; envious weight of clay, 19b, 70b; Lord my Maker, forming me of c., 6a; Poor vessel wrought of c.!, 569b; tenement of c., 105b
Clean Be quite c. and neat, 634b; *Be ye c., you that carry,* 189b; *Create a c. heart in me, O God,* 505a; please Thee with c. heart, 159a
Cleanliness corporal c. in those that approach altar, 187b; Wash frequently thy hand, 187b
Cleanse away folly of our heart, 218b; let me c. my life with penitence, 764b; Let Thy continual pity c. and defend Church, 682b; my heart and my lips, 589a; O Lord, c. our sins, 369b; thoughts of our hearts, 586b; thy vessel, that thou mayest receive grace, 408a
Cleansed flesh is washed that soul

may be c., 105b; He c. us by immolation of His body, 176b; within and without, 745b

Cleansing 'c.' of sick soul, 689a; no c. process without destructive power, 744a

Cleave Because they c. to God, 419a; They c. together like burrs, 343b

Clemency c. of Holy Ghost, 108b; Mother of c. and love, 95b; Parent of heavenly c., 369b; prayers of Mary and c. of Master, 82b

Clement I, Pope St., 697a, 851a

Cleopatra, 585a, 637b, 906a, 925a

Clergy able to take away and grant earthly empires, 176a; All faithful owe reverence to c., 190b; assigned administration of divine mysteries, 174b; bound to recite canonical hours, 267a; bound together by cement of c., 132b; bishop has power over all c., 69a; By divine law c. distinct from laity, 190a; carry vessels of the Lord, 189b; chosen instruments of divine grace, 135a; Church is established in bishop and c., 433a; Church's ministers, like gardeners, 130b; c. and laity, 177b, 190b, 648b; corporal cleanliness in those that approach altar, 187b; devote services to divine worship, 188a; example draws others readily to piety, 189b, 190a, 190b; exempt from compulsory public services, 188a; far from c. be love of novelty!, 190a; fatal mistake, for religious to take place of secular c., 190a; forbidden to conduct business 188b, 190b; forbidden to exercise secular government, 188b; have in house only women beyond reproach, 151a, 151b, 188a; immune from military service and civil charges, 188a, 190b; in major orders, forbidden to marry, 151a; judge men before day of judgment, 189a; marriage before ordination, 150b; means all who serve in Church of Christ, 189b; must not be accused except before bishops, 189a; no harder men than men of holy Church, 159a; partners of His honor, 695a; presumption of concubinage, 151b; priests have common dignity, not uniform rank, 433a; right part of body of Christ, 191a; several degrees, 190a, 433b; should live from revenues of Church, 67b; so called because belong to lot of Lord, 189b

Clergyman bad monk makes a good c.?, 618a; dabbling in politics, 758a; often asked out to dinner, 189a

Cleric twice married cannot become c., 188b

Clerical wrong, to force anyone to embrace c. state, 649a

Clericalism, 829a

Clerics making of c., 189b; not all of divine institution, 190a; ought to lead holier life than lay people, 728b

Clerk a learned man, 727b; parish priest forgetteth that ever he was c.!, 728a

Clerks greatest c. be not the wisest men, 189b, 513a

Cleros means lot or inheritance, 189b

Climb teach him to creep, till he knows how to c., 319b

Climbed He that never c., never fell, 893a

Cloak c. of malice, 18b; in your chest belongs to naked, 154b; over

world she draws c. of charity, 886a

Clock thou wert made the clock!, 192a; To have c. with weights and chains, 448a

Clod instinctive mole Breaking the c., 564b

Cloister Show me your c., 191a; Where the green swell is in the havens dumb, 616a

Cloth cut coat after c., 6b

Clothe yourself with cheerfulness, 496b

Clothes All c. but winding-sheets for last knell, 249b; c. of women, 277b; covering for decency, 191b, 278a; desire to please by outward charms, 277b; fashion of country is the rule, 278a; God sendeth cold after c., 191b; let thy c. be plain, 191a; outward robes show soul's habiliments, 278a; We've ceased to rectify What women wear, 278a

Cloud BVM, c. of perpetual light, 89a; c. of night is passed away, 286a; has been lifted from me for ever!, 191b; little c. at tether, 477b

Clouds c. of summer kiss in flame and rain, 385a; I knew how the c. arise, 191b; The c. are backward roll'd, 36b; The snowy steeds vault upon, 191b

Clovis, King, 50b

Clues For subtle doubts had simple c., 276a

Clung C. to the mane of every whistling wind, 346a

Clusters In globèd c., 47b

Coach drawn with many horse doth easily run, 341b

Coal a-cold blow at the c., 192a; Divine C., 195b

Coast Seeing the c. clear, 792a

Coat cut coat after cloth, 6b

Cobbler The c. apron'd, the parson gown'd, 191b

Cock Every c. proud on his own dunghill, 725a; Now the shrill c. proclaims the day, 522a; O wakeful bird! proclaimer of day, 192a; sun's brave herald, 192a; symbol of good preacher, 721a; when c. crows, rise and pray, 599a; young c. croweth, 930a

Cocks As doth the c. of Ind, 153a

Cocktails have all disagreeability of disinfectant, 192a

Coelestem Panem c. accipiam, 595a

Coelestia Non eripit mortalia, Qui regna dat c., 489a

Coeli Rorate c. desuper!, 168a

Coelo terrenum quidem animal, sed c. dignum, 569a

Coena C. Domini, 442a, 597a

Coerce princes and kings chosen, to c. people from evil, 404a

Coerced no one forced to embrace Catholic faith, 58a; opinion, no one should be c., 431a

Coercion absurd to torture men into believing, 57b; Check their sins, in way to produce repentance, 173b, 431b; c. of heretics who impede faith, 57a; May only king to force conscience, be King of kings, 473a

Coessential c. and co-eternal, Spirit of God, 439a

Coeternal Almighty of Almighty, C. of Eternal, 481b; co-essential and c., 439a; consubstantial and c., 438b; The c. One!, 440a

Coetus, 137a

Coffins If Rome dies, other churches may order c., 138a

Cogitat Homo c., Deus indicat, 397a

Cognitive sense is c. faculty, 54b

Cognomen Christianus mihi nomen est, Catholicus c., 163a

Cohabitation irksome c. and divorce, 267b

Co-heir c. of grace, 455a

Co-heirs c. with Him Who is King of glory, 877b

Coin I feel no care of c., 607a; Where c. is not common, 347b

Coincidences methods by which God arranges affairs of world, 192a

Cold Fast well and watch, 192a; God sendeth c. after clothes, 191b; When I am lying c. and dead, 251b

Collaboration between Church and State, 183b

Collar priests should wear Roman c., 190a

Collect at Mass, 588b

Collecting My passion has been non-c., 192b

Cologne, 122a

Colonel not obeyed because best man, 31a

Colonization Church and c., 613a

Color Glory be to God for dappled things, 192b

Colors The c. of the dying day, 612a

Columbia C.'s true-blue sons, 830b

Combat A hard foughten field, 192b; Christians are born for c., 223a

Come C., all ye faithful, 170a; C. down, O Christ, and help me!, 492a; C., Holy Ghost, Creator, c., 670b, 682a; C., let us adore before Christ, 589a; C. what c. would, 106b; O come, O come, Emmanuel, 8b; We c. to Thee, sweet Savior, 492a; When Thou shalt c. again, 77b

Comedians women marrying c., excommunicated, 5b

Comedy amours of strumpets, 192b; sane man, can have tragedy in heart, c. in head, 798a; 'tis most hard to hit, 192b

Comely As c. as a cow in a cage, 887a

Comes He c.s! He c.s!, 94b

Cometh All c. to one, 313a; As fast as one goeth another c., 193b; Blessed is He that c. in name of Lord, 81a, 591a; He that c. now and then, 447b

Comfort All human c., vain and short, 193a; All ye who seek a c. sure, 789a; blooms on pain, 305b; BVM, c. to sorrowful, 87a; comfort all, 9b; C. in tribulation, 193a; God, c. of afflicted, 880a; greater c. shall you have of me, 584a; my consolation, to lack all human c., 193a; Sweet hope, sovereign c. of our life, 445a; Thou c. of us wretches, 79b

Comforter Dear C.! Eternal Love!, 564a; Thou art my c., 881b; Thou Who art C. and Consoler, 10a

Comforts A little thing c. us, 546a; securing honest c. of life, 38b; Withdraw Thy c., so Thou leave Thy grace, 410b

Comic all men are tragic, all men are c., 193a

Coming c. of Holy Ghost and Bible, 64b; c. of Son according to flesh, 7b; His c. against men, 8b; His c. into men, 8b; His c. to men, 8b

Comings prophets foretold two c. of Christ, 500b; three distinct c. of Lord, 8b

Command ability to enforce condition of ability to c., 529a; cause us to love that which Thou dost c., 334a; c. implies a superior, 376b; desire to c. other men, 46b; *God does not c. the impossible,* 410a; grant what Thou dost c., 215b; more ready to convince than to c., 674a; right to c., in accordance with authority of God, 46b; we were born to obey, not to c., 221a

Commanded other things c. in Gospel beside faith, 193b

Commandment *A new c. I give you,* 442b

Commandments absolute value of God's c., 47a; always cleave to Thy c., 193b, 594b; by keeping God's c., you will be powerful, 342b; c. of God not indifferent or free, 193b; God's precepts are light to loving, 193b; hearts, devoted to Thy c., 665a; If any one saith ten c. nowise appertain to Christians, 193b; make straight our ways in doing of Thy c., 490a; To fulfil God's c. daily, 808b

Commands c. of God and authority. 45b; contrary to will of God, 46b; ever meditating on Thy reasonable c., 392a; No man c., but he who has learned to obey, 642b

Commemoration *Do this for c. of me,* 309a, 647b

Commend I c. myself to blessed Lady Mary, 520a; let us c. ourselves and our life, 81b; Lord, into Thy hands I c. my spirit, 520a, 521a; We c. to Thee soul of Thy servant, 244b

Commerce application of science to c., 18a

Commingling fifty years of private and public c., 15b

Commiseration c. of our Lord, 200b

Committees Living movements do not come of c., 457a

Commixtio Huec c. et consecratio Corporis et Sanguinis, 594a

Common All is c. among us, except wives, 199a; all things for c. use of all men, 733b; Church approves devoting services to c. good, 406b; c. gift of God, 733b; c. interest always will prevail, 152b; earth c. to all men, 733b; free men governed by ruler for c. good, 404b; let everything be c. property, 615b; Many to bear the c. burden are slow, 346b; Nature created c. rights, 733b; someone to take care of what appertains to c. weal, 404b

Common Sense nothing so uncommon as c., 194a

Commons Where coin not common, c. must be scant, 347b

Commonwealth boundless c. of whole creation, 392a; human race bound together by ties, into great c., 530b; private societies part of c., 38a; cannot confer supremacy over Church, 141a

Commonwealths Church, very unlike other c., 127a; To raise up c. and ruin kings, 684b

Commune To live is to c. with God, 889a

Communicantes, 591b

Communicate c. with Church, 667b; faithful bound to c. every year, 197a

Communication by c. of properties, 482a

Communion administered to whoever will receive Him, 196b; availing plea for pardon and salvation, 196b; Behold, I approach divine c.! 196a; body-unity, 127b; Body and Blood, nourishment of faithful, 73b, 593b; Christ is ministered to me daily, 72a; communicate under species of bread only, 197a; c. of body and blood of Christ, 206a; c. of Holy Ghost, 408a; c. with bishop, 299b; daily c. increases fervor, 72a, 194b, 196b, 199a; ecclesiastical c., 127b; everlasting remedy, 595b; fasting before Eucharist, 194b; food of salvation, 194b; God, Made visible upon human face, 198b; Grace whereby soul is nourished, 72a; he who eats life cannot die, 195a; I am joined in c. with your blessedness, 694a; I am unworthy of thy Child, 198b; I approach the Physician of life, 196b; I believe that this is Thy most pure Body, 594b; I will remain in c. with Roman pontiff, 591b; I will take the Bread of Heaven, 595a; if you come clean, you come healthfully, 195a; imparts knowledge, faith, immortality, 194a; In c. we are made flesh of His flesh, 70b, 198a; In c. with glorious ever Virgin Mary, 591b; In me He dwells; in Him I live, 197b; joined in love of the fraternity, 699a; Let not c. of holy mysteries be unto judgment, 195b, 196b, 594b; Let us be What we receive, 195b; let us partake of Divine Coal, 195b; Make me sharer in thy mystic supper, 595a; makes us partakers of eternal life, 195a; May Thy Body be unto me for eternal life, 196a; May Thy Body cleave to my bowels, 595b; medicine for our wounds, 72a; moulds in us a royal image, 195a; my heart, A home for each Host, 198a; mystic Table is obtained by fasting, 337b; not necessary for little children, 197b; O sacred banquet, heavenly feast! 197b; O silence, my soul, and adore, 197b; O what could my Jesus do more, 197b; occasional abstinence, 196b; once a year as Greeks do, 195a; one bond of c., through letters, 694a: One faith, one c., 134b; only for baptized, 194a; participation in Body and Blood of Christ, 194b; proper preparation for c., 198a; receive in c. light of this Sun, 196b; reception under one species, 197a; remain in unshaken c. with one Church, 199a; remedy for soul and body, 594b; renders us terror to devil, 71b; sacrament, received unto cleansing, 195b; sacramental confession before c., 76b; Sanctification of sacramental grace, 198a; So live, that you may deserve to receive daily, 195a; soul fattens on its God, 105b; souls of faithful inebriated in Cup, 72a; spiritual and sacramental c., 199a; The can so sweet, the crust So fresh, 198a; Thou art a consuming fire to the unworthy, 196a; Thou hast appeased hunger of my soul, 196b; Thy most pure mysteries, 595a; time, wherein eternity Takes rest upon world, 198b; unworthy reception of c., 194b, 195a; we depart as lions breathing fire, 71b; what we have taken with our mouth, 595b; Where God is not, there can be no c., 198b; Where God the food, man the guest, 197b

Communion of Saints Mystical Body and C., 199a

Communism Atheist c., bourgeois deism turned round, 42b; bad Christians make c. possible, 200a; by its nature anti-religious, 199b; collaboration between c. and Christianity, impossible, 199b; c. is intrinsically wrong, 199b; Franciscan movement without balance of Church, 199a; its hatred for Christian civilization, 199b; must be replaced by true idea, 200a; no greater refutation than mother, 200a; social order which denies natural right to property, 735a

Communist doubtful, humanity passed through c. stage, 199b; revolutionary, also reactionary, 199b

Communists folly of collaboration with c., 199b; Socialists, C., uproot foundations of society, 828b

Community c. and private enterprise, 221b; Democracy, government of c. by c., 256b; ethnic c., 631b; great means intended by God, 846a; human race bound together into great commonwealth, 575a, 530b; international c., and respect for law, 531a; Nation is a c., not a society, 631b; Nation, most important c. engendered by civilized life, 631b; object of civil legislation, welfare of c., 529b; when c. becomes a nation, 631b

Companion none is like unto the mind, 865b

Companions good to have c. in misery, 612b

Companionship c. with Christ, 71b

Company Frequent not c. of immodest persons, 200a; Guard the c. of Thy Church, 596a; parents should control c. of children, 200a

Compare Do not c. one person, 200b

Comparisons C. are odious, 200a

Compass needle points faithfully o'er the dim sea, 210b

Compassion brother's misery, truly felt with miserable heart, 200b; c. of our Lord, 200b; emotion of c., 883b; great c. of BVM, 99b; no kind, we should rejoice to feel, 200b

Compassionate prefer to find nothing to need compassion, 200b

Compel Law has power to c., 529a; no part of religion, to c. religion, 354a, 871a; You do not c. man to worship, 354b

Compelled No person to be c. to embrace faith, 57a, 174a

Compendium not the man to write a c., 434b

Compensation If in one point person be aggrieved, 200b

Compete rash for shopkeeper to c. with Rothschild, 200b

Competition All c., only furious plagiarism, 201a; Free c. cannot be ruling principle, 201a; Free c., kept within limits, 287b; less productive of wealth than cooperation, 221a; When c. ceases, effort ceases, 200b

Complacency one obstacle to progress, 201a

Complain O how oft shalt thou c., 558b; "What do you c. of?" 216b

Complains He that c. or murmurs, not good Christian, 201a

Complexity c. of science and of Catholic faith, 58a

Compliment handsomest c., to call him a horse, 162a

Compliments Irish way of paying

c., 201a; Women, never disarmed by c., 572a

Compline, 201a

Composition something like giving birth to child, 107a

Compostellan C. pilgrimages, 17a

Comprehend men reprehend what they cannot c., 70a; what could fathom God were more than He, 395b

Compromise tortured by c., 635b

Compunction rather to feel c., than know its definition, 753b; two kinds of c., 764a

Comrade how long ago Since c. went with me! 201b; Let the Cross thy c. be, 232a

Comrades C. of old are we, 253a

Concealing faculty of c. thoughts in words, 367a

Conceit buy Marcus up at price he is worth, 201b; mark of the heretics, 429a

Conceits Prophane c. and feignèd fits I fly, 687b

Concentration To send someone into c. camp, 465b; unified and simple c. upon God, 213b

Conception c. of Christ and virginity of BVM, 79a; effected in Virgin by Holy Ghost, 50a; intercourse and prevention of c., 66a

Conclude from th' apparent what c. the why, 625a

Conclusion great difference, c. in abstract, c. in concrete, 201b; illogical, without ultimate assumption, 39a; No one is a martyr for a c., 582a, 760b

Conclusions c. of one generation are truths of next, 514a; reconstructing Hercules from a bone, 201b

Concord c. of earthly rulers from God, 45b; harmonious movement of several wills, 202a; peace of mankind, well-ordered c., 665a; unity, the glue of c., 133b

Concrete c. and reasoning, 751a; C. matter does not admit of demonstration, 599b; unimaginative need c. images, 202a

Concubinage presumption of c., 151a

Concubine no Christian may have c., 202a

Concubines c. do not justify concubinage, 202a; grievous sin for married men to have c., 202a

Concupiscence chastity does not mean we are insensible to c., 159a; child-bearing without c., 166b; flesh is carnal c., 229b; results of sin, ignorance, c., 412b; subordinate to reason and law of grace, 159a

Condemn not c., without careful study of case, 202a

Condemned lay down life for those c., 604a; no one c., except through merited judgment, 751b; Nor wholly stands c. nor wholly free, 22b

Condescension c. of Son, dignity of Mother, 82b; Thine unspeakable c., 491a

Condition C., circumstance, not the thing, 103a; Content thyself with thine estate, 215a

Conduct Character, tested by sentiments more than by c., 153b; Circumstances subject-matter, not rule, of c., 185a; rule for human acts is twofold, 818a; to avoid worldly c., 155a; Vulgarity, c. of other people, 904b

Confess abuse, to c. without will to be delivered, 204a; better to c.

sins than harden heart, 202b; C. faults' guilt, 719a; c. your offences in church, 202b; crown of those who C. Thy name, 205a; Daily to c. one's past sins, 203a; each should c. sin, 202a, 667b; faithful bound to c. once a year, 204b; God purifies hearts of those who c., 203a; I c. to almighty God, 587b; spare the sins of those who c. unto Thee, 822a

Confessed having first c. your offences, 307a

Confesses c. by mouth unto salvation, 640a; pardon is granted to the man who c., 764a

Confession Can anything be imagined more charitable, 204b; cleanses sinner and sanctifies righteous, 203a; c. before communion, 76b, 202b; c. of faith, 203b, 329b, 371a; c. of sins, 203b; c. of thanksgiving, 203b; external act of repentance, 202b; Full sweetly heard he c., 203b; general c. profitable, 204a; God absolves from bonds of iniquity, 203a; instituted by Lord for restoration of sinners, 202b, 203b; matter of sacrament, 668b; minister, delegate of Christ, 203a; necessary to confess all mortal sins remembered, 203b; necessary to mention circumstances of sins, 203b; of c., repentance is born, 202b; once a year, 204a; precept not satisfied by invalid c., 205a; priest assumes role of judge and doctor, 204b; priest must not ask curious questions, 204b; private c. observed from beginning, 203b; sacrilegious c. is invalid, 205a; satisfaction made, following c. of sin, 202a; second reserve against hell, 202b; secrecy of c., 204a; should be made without despair, 203a; sins can not be remitted without c. of amendment, 321a, 822a; threefold c. commended by Scriptures, 203b; where c. is, there is worship, 203a

Confessions he was qualified to hear c., 815a

Confessional Be lion in pulpit, lamb in c., 669b; Psychoanalysis is c. without safeguards of c., 739a; seal of c., inviolable, 204b; Under seal of the c., 203b

Confessionis Sub sigillo c., 203b

Confessor c. of the Lord, 205a; must never betray sinner, 204b; Saint, always ready to become a 'c.,' 794a; Saintly and prudent, modest in behavior, 205a; Thou crown that each c. boasts, 581b

Confessors why c. dwell with the great, 253a

Confidence Have c., 223a; I repose all my c. in goodness of God, 521b

Confirm duty of bishop to confirm, 69a; only fulness of priesthood can confirm, 205b

Confirmation Anoint me with heavenly grace, 207a; become son and heir of kingdom, 206a; bishop shall anoint with holy oil, 205a; bishop shall give kiss of peace, 205b; bishop shall seal him on forehead, 205b; c. of episcopal consecration, 67b; for those who would fight for Christ, 206b; I anoint thee with holy oil in God, 205a; I confirm thee with chrism of salvation, 206a; I sign thee with sign of cross, 205b, 206a, 207a; imposition of hands gives strength, 206b; In C. we believe, 788a; may Holy Ghost come down upon them, 206b; My God, accept

my heart this day, 207a; not an idle ceremony, 206b; ordinary minister is bishop, 205b, 206b; reception of holy c., 649a; sacrament of priesthood of laity, 207a; seal of gift of Holy Spirit, 205b, 206a; send forth upon them Thy sevenfold Spirit, 205b, 207a; The Lord be with you, 205b; We are enrolled by bishops, 206b

Confirmed Christ hath c. thee, 50a; Man, Thou hast c. for Thyself, 481a

Confirming bishops have power of c. and ordaining, 648b

Confirms heavinesses by which Lord tests and c. His own, 809a

Confiteor C. Deo omnipotenti, 587b

Conflict All human c. ultimately theological, 207a; c. between Church and State, 181b; Experience and c., give years to man, 319b; When soul reaches certain pitch of c., 207a

Conforming c. ourselves to what we love, 207b

Conformity c. to traditions, 207b

Confucianism, 165b

Confused modern soul c., 28a

Confusion city of c. and house of bondage, 24a; Set the world on six and seven, 207b; turned quite up so down, 207b; Woman is the c. of man, 572a

Congregation Church means c., 126b; religious c., one in which only simple vows taken, 762b; whole body of redeemed, c. and society of saints, 485a

Congress shall make no law respecting establishment of religion, 184b

Conjugal Husband and wife obliged to observe community of c. life, 580b

Connoisseurs can never be great, 415a

Conquer and yield and c. still, 424a; Could c. hearts so brave, 208a; You must either c. world or world will c. you, 925b

Conquered Christ is never c., 490b; I came, I saw, God c., 207b; Only Heaven Means crowned, not c., 349b

Conqueror All hail! dear C.! 286b; Rise—glorious C., rise, 36a; Thou c. renowned, 630a

Conquers Nothing c. except truth, 155a, 883b

Conquest King by nature and right of c., 97b; lest he should leave No kingdom unto him, 207b; pursues where courage leads way, 208a

Conquests one thing, make c., another, consolidate empire, 208a

Consanguinity impediment to marriage, 577b

Conscience aboriginal vicar of Christ, 209b; Both Americanism and Catholicism bow to sway of c., 210a; careful examination of c., before confession, 204b; Christian c. and personal liberty, 259a; Christian c., spiritual power in United States, 185a; civil allegiance of Christian, limited by conscience, 182a; c. and the Church, 118b; C. is due to yourself, reputation to neighbor, 208a; c. versus human authority, 208b, 528b; discerns sanction higher than self, 209b, 376b; enforcing c. in matters of religion, dangerous, 354b; 'freedom of c.,' 210a, 355a, 872a; good c. and

temptations, 209a; good c. is mine of wealth, 208a; good c. rejoices among adversities, 209a; has rights because it has duties, 210a, 470a; He doth bathe in bliss that hath a quiet mind, 215a; illuminated by Christ, must be guide, 210a; Immortal pow'rs the term of c. know, 209a; In matters of duty, first thoughts commonly best, 209a; inmost, ultimate Council of judgment, 608a; int'rest in her name with men below, 209a; Internal Cerberus, whose griping fangs, 861a; judgment of reason and magisterial dictate, 209b; law of right and wrong, written in our hearts, 619b; Let us beware of trifling with c., 209a; man of religious mind attends to rule of c., 376b; May only king to force c., be King of kings, 473a; mind's secret pangs, 861a; monarch in its peremptoriness, 209b; My c. is my crown, 209a; nearer, than any other means of knowledge, 209b; nothing commoner than to kill c., 210a; O honorable c., clear and chaste, 208b; O keep thy c. sensitive, 672a; obedience even to erring c., 209b; obliges in virtue of divine command, 208b; only arbiter of a Christian's actions, 259a; power to bind c., 45b; priest in its blessings and anathemas, 209b; prison of troubled c., 473a; royalty and prerogative of every man, 209a; She labored still for c. not for fees, 295b; suggests that He is our Judge, 382a; supremacy of c. and of pope, 118a, 210a; testimony of good c., 208a, 209a; The great hour of Christian c. has struck, 613a; They preached, c. did rest, 26b; ultimate asylum of soul, 210a; voice of God in man, 209a; you must leave me my c., 210a
Consciences Purify our c., O Lord, 208a; When c. to God lie bare, 535a
Conscientiam Quidquid fit contra c., 208a
Conscious God is most happy, therefore supremely c., 387b
Consciousness different levels of c., 515b
Consecrate duty of bishop to c., 69a; priests alone have power to celebrate and c., 597b
Consecrated bishop c. by imposition of hands, 68b; That which is c. to God should be honored, 788b; virginity held in honor, because c. to God, 897a; with gift of heavenly grace, 50a
Consecrates word of Christ c. sacrament, 597a
Consecratio Haec commixtio et c. Corporis et Sanguinis, 594a
Consecration altar's mystic birth, 78a; at words of priest, heavens are opened, 308b; blessing from dew of heaven, 72b; c. of bishops, 67b; effected by words of Jesus, 71b, 310b, 597a; invocation of holy Trinity, 310a; May this mixture and c. of Body and Blood, 594a; rain of divine words, 72b; Sacrament, by invisible operation of Holy Spirit, 308b; sound of a low, sweet whisper, 598a; When God comes down each day to dwell, 71a, 198a; words of c. at Mass, 592a; words of c. serve as knife, 71a
Consent enemy cannot enter save by door of our c., 861a; govern-

ment depends on c. of the people, 405a, 405b; He who is silent is supposed to c., 210a; law is established by c., 405b, 533b; Matrimonial c., 579a; members of hierarchy, not chosen by c. of people, 434a; power of rulers and c. of governed, 180b, 509a; Purity cannot be lost, without c., 745a; That which touches all, should be approved by all, 534a; with absolute internal assent and c., 24a
Consequent God's c. will and permission, 797b
Conservative Americans astonishingly c. in ideas, 18a
Conservatism Be not first by whom new are tried, 210b
Considerate we are not excused for not being c., 210b
Consideration application of mind to search for truth, 212b; Let c. begin with yourself, 601b; purifies the mind, 602a
Consistence care more for truth than c., 628b
Consolation As balm my wound to heal, 210b; benefit of Thy c., 171a; Christian's God, God of love and c., 384b; c. of afflicted, 84b; ever rejoice in His c., 439a; my c., to lack all human comfort, 193a; sweet unction of c., 602a
Consolations desire to walk to God's will through c., 281b; God's pleasure in c., 10a
Console C. me in the hour of pain, 84a
Consoled We are easily c. because easily distressed, 210b
Consoler Thou Who art Comforter and C., 10a
Consolidate one thing make conquests, another c. empire, 208a
Constancy My own betrayal in their c., 211a; too frail life of female c., 210b
Constantine I, Emperor, 33a, 177a, 211a, 871a
Constantinople, 100b, 175b, 662b, 698a, 699b, 700b, 704a
Constantinople, First Council of (381), 226b
Constantius I, Emperor, 172a
Constipated Beans cause c. tone, 53b
Constitution American C. resembles Spanish Inquisition, 15b; Catholic religion, adapted to genius of C., 184b; First Amendment to C., 184b, 185a; what king or emperor has enacted, 524b
Constitutional c. principles in England, 871b
Constitutions c. and natural law, 529b
Constrain power to c. others, from God, 406b
Consubstantial c. and coeternal, 438b; c. Breath of God, 440a; c. to the Father, 226b
Consuetudo, 236b, 237a
Consul c., king, lords over others in regard to means, 404b; was constrained his pomp to crowd, 902a
Consumed c. by flames of vice, 216a
Consummation c. of marriage presumed, until contrary proved, 579a
Consummatum C. est, 672a; marriage, said to be ratified and consummated, 578b
Contact agnosticism severs spiritual c. with God, 12a
Contagion c. of my body, 85a; that is normal in generation, 466a

Contain O God, Who dost c. all things invisibly, 171a
Contemn to c. the world, 36b
Contemplate angels c. very Source of knowledge, 22a; c. God outside, inside, above us, 213a; substance of eternity, 211b; To meditate on life and sufferings of Christ, 602a
Contemplation art prepares man for c., 33b; ascend to heights of c. by active life, 5a; bestows knowledge of things divine and human, 602a; borne up to ray of divine Darkness, 211b; by absolute withdrawal from thyself, 211b; c. and consideration contrasted, 212b; c. and meditation, 213a; c. of divine and celestial, 5b, 214a; c. of God promised as goal, 211b; dazzling obscurity of the secret silence, 211b; defined as soul's true unerring intuition, 212b; ecstasy of c., 883b; enjoyment of highest and truest Good, 211a, 211b; exhibits itself as a kind of ladder, 211b; four acts of c., 213b; grace granted only in response to longing, 212b; grade of the soul, 835a; He will not present Himself to every soul, 211a, 212b; He who would attain to life of c., 214a; history of our Lord, inexhaustible matter of c., 492a; I die because I do not die, 214b; In c., mind not at pause, but fully active, 213a; In c., Principle is sought, 212a; in some sort dead to this life, 211a, 211b; knock in prayer and it shall be opened in c., 213b; Let consideration begin with yourself, 601b; many have smothered first sparks of c., 214b; mind and will are fused into one, 213b; mind carried out of flesh, 212a; O, night more lovely than the dawn, 214b; our c. of Him, participation of His c., 396b; perfect soul desires to be rapt by c., 211a, 213a; soul set on fire with Spirit of love, 213b; strain upwards in unknowing, 211b; temptation of flesh in c., 212a; thirsting and sighing for presence of God, 213a; this new death-in-life, 214b; those who hold citadel of c., 5a; three points in c., 212b; to love things above is to mount on high, 212a; topmost height of mystic lore, 211b; unhesitating apprehension of truth, 212b; unified and simple concentration upon God, 213b; union with Him Who is above all, 211b; voice of God heard, when we rest from world, 212a
Contemplative animal cannot be c., 437b; C. prayer, deep and spiritual activity, 213b; enters God in order to be created, 214b; intuition of c., 515b; No Christian poetry by anyone not c., 690b; poet and c., 214b; ultimate perfection of c. life, 903b
Contemplatives We become c. when God discovers Himself in us, 213b
Contemplative Life aim, to mount above merely human things, 5a; C. is in a cave, 4b; foretaste of repose to come, 5a; has desirable sweetness, 214a; has reached goal, 5a; in c., contemplation of divine Light, 5b; in c., God instructs by His word, 5a; in c., we see God, 4b; makes a man perfect, 5a; marks journey's end, 4b; more meritorious than active life, 5a;

opposed to desires of flesh, 4b; reigns in self, 4b

Contempt nearer to Church, farther from God, 138a; Over-great homeliness engendereth dispraising, 215a

Contemptum amor Dei usque ad c. sui, 125a

Content In dirt and darkness hundreds stink c., 733a; See all, say nought, hold thee c., 644b; thyself with thine estate, 215a; to breathe his native air, 215a

Contention Not to love c., 746a

Contentment All earth forgot, all heaven around us, 215a

Contest toils of c. bring athletes their crowns, 879b; where c. is, there is crown, 43a

Contests crowned for c. of this world, 43a

Continence c. and divine love, 215b; C. is the daughter of faith, 899a; gift of c. owed to another, 215b; grant what Thou dost command, 215b; He that can take it, 158b; means of attaining eternal life, 215b; mountain of greater blessing of c., 216a; not a matter of our own strength, 215b; O God, Who didst subdue flames of fire, 216a; perpetual c., virginity great good, 897a; two gifts, wisdom and c., 215b; vow c. unto Christ, 216a, 640a; with spiritual weapon, we slay fleshly desires, 159a

Continuity very c. of creation, 375a

Contours c. of culture and art, 34b; invisible c. discovered from air, 34b

Contract c. under which king accepted sovereignty, 774a; Marriage, most irrevocable c., 578a

Contradict Do I c. myself? 216a

Contradiction ultimate heresy, denial of law of c., 867a

Contradictions God permits them to detach you, 216a

Contraries Nature refuseth to have c. joined, 646a

Contrast C. and oddness, from God's purpose, 216a

Contrite Make me c., keep me lowly, 170a; We c. in confession fall, 599a

Contrition c., kind of prayer, 720b; cross is instrument of c., 233b; Have mercy Thou, most gracious God! 216b; matter of sacrament, c., confession, satisfaction, 668b; O my God, I am sorry with my whole heart, 216b; repentance for sin with true grief, 667b; Spirit moves heart to c. for sins, 53a, 657a; Where prayer poured forth, sins are covered, 716a

Control desire to c. others, 46b; Who madest all and dost c., 599a

Controversial c. stronghold of Christendom, 271a; fruitless or c. discussions, 216b

Controversy Abuse, great mistake in c., 3b, 216b; c. and Catholic Church, 125b; "C. does no good," 217a; helps understanding of faith, 144b; never clear c. in sceptical age, 217a; Nothing dies harder than theological difference, 217a; superfluous or hopeless, 217a; two things to observe in c., 27a; You discharge olive-branch as if from catapult, 217a

Contumacious If any brother be found c., 317a

Convent The home is not a c., 443a

Conventional C. people who think they have no limitations, 217b; c. view ruins more lives, 217b; nothing more c. than convention of unconventionality, 217b

Conversation In c., let something be said of spiritual things, 939a; know something which others do not know, 218a; man who can dominate London dinner-table, 239b; One should be affable in c., 691a

Converse great art, to know how to c. with Jesus, 488b; in holy c. blending, 25a

Conversion accepted time, 219a; approach Church in way of reason, 219b; as vivid religious experience, 294b; attractions of Catholic art, 33b, 220b; bargain betwixt earth and heaven, 219a; blood of Christ brought c. to world, 104a; brings Eternal worlds upon its wings, 218b; burial with Christ within, 52a; Church is house with hundred gates, 220a; Church rendered fruitful with new offspring, 51b; c. of bread and wine into God's Body, 73a; c. of non-Catholics, 220b; c. of persecutors, 672b; First let a little love find entrance, 218b; I have always been latently a Catholic, 220b; like coming into port after rough sea, 219b; likened to threshing, 72b; may be offered once in lives and never again, 219a; menacing grandeur of great love affair, 220a; mystery about c., 220a; no change, intellectual or moral, 219b; no happiness comparable to c., 219b; power of example, 220a; rare gift to be a Catholic, 219a; that wonderful and singular c., 311b; they that are ours, return, 126a; threats, not way to faith, 27b; 'Tis love alone can hearts unlock, 218b; To become Catholic is not to leave off thinking, 220a; with Christ in newness of life, 52a; with difficulty do we return to Thee, 344a; workings of divine grace are secret, 220a; You must make a venture, 219b

Convert comes to Catholicism as to living stream, 219b; comes to learn, not pick and choose, 219b; c. others by what we are, 220a; 'doubtless he is very sincere,' 221a; I cannot c. men without assumptions, 27a; in a c. mourns to lose a prey, 164b; in favor with no party, 221a; it is not force that must c., 582a; pure one, do thou c. me, 98a; To c. man, necessary to enlighten him, 219a

Converted some people can be c. by reason, 147b; three states of the c., 218b; When thou art c., strengthen thy brethren, 675a

Converts difficult to acquire virtue of obedience, 221a; firm convictions as Catholics, 145b; never can distinguish between faith and emotion!, 221a; Pope barely Catholic enough for some c., 221a; raked for converts even court and stews, 221a

Convince more ready to c. than to command, 674a

Cooks vulgar dishes by c. disguis'd, 287b

Cooperated BVM c. by charity, 80b

Cooperation Catholic c. with non-Catholics, 217a; Competition less productive of wealth than c., 221a; C. is one hope of the world, 221b; c. of faithful in work of Mystical Body, 132b; c. with guidance of Holy Spirit, 15a

Co-operatrix BVM, associated as Mother and c., 92a

Coot He was as ballid as a cote, 48b

Copia great author and c. verborum, 45a

Coquetry Lesbia hath a beaming eye, 221b

Cor C. ad c. loquitur, 424b

Corda Sursum c., 591a

Co-redemptrix BVM, c., 90a

Corinthians, 697a

Cork, Ireland, 59a, 751a

Corks something to be said for c., 608b

Corn c. and wine and Eucharist, 72b; long harvest for a little c., 422a

Cornerstone Of eternal design the c., 83a

Coronation Kind as kings upon their c. day, 506b; king should swear at c., three things, 508b; right of pope to examine candidate, 177b

Corporal We should enjoy spiritual things, but use c. things, 860a

Corporations large versus small c., 221b

Corporeal God has nothing c. in substance, 386a

Corpse drunken man is living c., 280a; Like to a c., whose monument I am, 77a

Corpus C. Domini nostri custodiat animam meam, 595a; C. sumus de conscientia religionis, 133a

Corpus Christi, Feast of, 74a, 74b, 77b

Correct he does not rule who does not c., 507a; "Others, thank God, are less c. than I," 777a; those whom mildness failed to c., 22b

Corrected We will not be c. ourselves, 341a

Corrupt Human nature, not completely c., 412a

Corruption BVM kept body from c. after death, 39b; by Thy resurrection, delivered from c., 441b; c. of old creature, 166b; no c. in Thee, no stain in Thy Mother, 460a; nothing but destruction of good, 221b, 313b; theory, wealth protection against political c., 909a

Cosmas the Melodist, St., 81b

Cosmetics dissatisfaction with God's plastic skill, 221b; little powder and gauze properly disposed, 222a

Cosmic c. philosophy is constructed to fit cosmos, 759a

Cost Stop not now to count the c., 286b

Couch On my velvet c. reclining, 477b

Council, General (Oecumenical) belongs to Roman pontiff, to preside over oecumenical c., 708b; has supreme power over entire Church, 222b; I revere as Gospel, four councils, 222a, 272b; No c. called general without pope's consent, 701a; not permissible, appeal from Roman pontiff to g., 222b; unfailing guide In pope and gen'ral c., 708a

Councils, General canons of g. began in time of Constantine, 222a; decrees confirmed by Roman pontiff, 222b; have not erred in definition of faith, 129b; on them rises structure of holy Faith, 222a; Roman pontiff has authority over all councils, 222a

Councils national c., not final authority, 222a; wisdom, and c. of God, 127a

Counsel ever tell him what he ought to do, 508b; I was neither of court nor of c., 222b; more safe to hear than to give c., 9b; Nor bow thine ear from c. of sage, 149b; Three may keep c., if two be away, 813b; *whole c. of God*, 270a, 288a

Counsellor faithful servant and worthy c., 509a

Counsels evangelical c., 762b

Countenance light of Thy c. is imprinted within us, 384a

Country Anybody can be good in the c., 223a; defence, preservation, prosperity of c., 406b; God and our c.!, 143a; My c., right or wrong, 663b; Next to God is c., 663b; Nothing sweeter than one's own c., 222b; that heavenly c., 302a

Courage Conquest pursues where c. leads way, 208a; c. cool At every trifling thing!, 454b; c. to tell people twice two is four, 218a; lack of c. on part of good, 399b; physical c. not worth calling bravery, 108a; principal act of c., to endure dangers, doggedly, 223a; strong desire to live, taking form of readiness to die, 223a

Court At heaven's c., 250a; Whither the wise and great resort, 20b; c. with solemn pomp on her attends, 40a

Courteous to be rude to him was c., 223a

Courtesan Phryne had talents for mankind, 421a

Courtesy Bend thyself to temper of who ever is speaking, 939a; grace of God is in C., 223b; She is a mirror of all c., 223a

Courts civil c. shall judge criminal cases, 188b; c. of heavenly city, 302a; c. of His glory above, 41a; institution of eccles. courts, 188a; jurisdiction of eccles. c. in criminal cases, 190b; litigation before eccles. courts, 188a

Courtship dream in c., in wedlock wake, 574a, 912b

Cousin He who has the pope for a c., 710a; not permitted, to marry wife or son of uncle, 575b

Covenants four Catholic c., 223b

Covet Christians do not c. neighbor's goods, 162b

Covetous devil is ruler of c. desires, 223b, 260a; He's no way c., 223b

Covetousness O c., so hasty to submerge, 415b

Cow As comely as a c. in a cage, 887a; Many a good c. hath an evil calf, 223b; Where comes a c., there follows a woman, 921b

Cowards Passion makes us c. grow, 655b

Cowl c. hideth such a bird within, 619a

Cowley, Abraham, 26a

Crabs greatest c. be not best meat, 223b

Cradle Fling round my c., magic spells, 58b; kist the c. of our King, 168b; rocks c. of departed child, 23a

Crag wind that beats sharp c. and barren hill, 237a

Craggy c. ridge and mountain bare, 415a

Crags being damned, unto my c. ye come?, 239a; Who shall bewail the c., 304b

Crave God cannot grant as much as they can c., 342a

Create as easy to c. as to define, 254b; bring into existence without previous material, 225a; *C. a clean heart in me, O God*, 505a; greater act to restore, than to c., 752b; Through whom Thou dost c., sanctify, bless, 593a

Created all things c. for sake of His name, 70b; c. things, 224b, 390a; end for which we were c., 37a; God, known by reason through c. things, 396a; God c. all things at same time, 224a; God's knowledge of c. things, 224b; *In the beginning God c. heaven and earth*, 225a; letteth go all things c., 36b; O God, Who hast marvelously c. man, 590a, 752a; study of c. things, stepping-stone to immortal, 848a; Things mutable and also wholly c., 375a

Creates God c. of His own freewill, 225a

Creating Eternal-Absolute is ever c. new forms, 225a

Creation all things visible and invisible, 224a; angels are at peak of c., 19b; boundless commonwealth of whole c., 392a; c., a continual act, 225a, 375a; c. is Thy thought, 373b; difference between ultimate c. and gradual emergence, 224a; God fashioned all things out of nothing, 223b, 652b; God wished certain things to share in His goodness, 224b; matter has itself been made from nothing, 224a; multiplying of things, common work of Trinity, 225a; O strength and stay upholding all c., 637a; preservation involved in idea of c., 117b; twofold going forth of God, 224b; We are God's property by c. 225b; We know God by grandeur of His c., 394a; world is pregnant with things that are to come, 224b; world's c. and Christ's immolation, 43b

Creator All things suffered with C. of all things, 400a; alone knows form of angel's nature, 19a; Blest Lord, C. of the glowing light, 636a, 893b; BVM ministered to C., 85b; C. and Father of the ages, 366a; C., being uncreated, is wholly immutable, 375a; C., Child at breast, 39b; C. of all being, supremely good, 313a; *Creator of heaven and earth*, 226a; C. of the world we pray, 201a; C., one and true God, 369a; C., unto Thee we sing, 284a; C.'s servant and Mother, 95b; Father! C! Lord Most High!, 371b; God as C., 224a; God, C. and Redeemer of all the faithful, 244b; God, of all worlds C.!, 491a; illumines mind, 214a; knowledge of C. more noble than knowledge of creation, 396a; O Christ, the world's C. bright, 788b; O great C. of the sky, 824a; one true God, C. and Lord of all, 377a; Remember, O C. Lord, 167a; Thou art sweet Jesus, Thou art my C., 488a; universe proclaims it has a C., 374b

Creature Ah! who would love a c.?, 225b; corruption of old c., 166b; every being not God is God's c., 57a; every c. has place in Church, 89b; *every c. of God is good*, 57a, 399a; God maintains c. in existence, 225a; He fills every c. with benediction, 225b; *new c. in Christ*, 166b, 505a

Creatures all we are Christ's c., 352b; always need aid of His grace, 410a; BVM placed above

other c., 101b, 460b; c. and divine essence, 225b; endowed with existence by God, 319a; maintained by hand of governing agent, 224b; may be called mediators after fashion, 91a; O God, Whom all c. obey, 231a; O purest of c.! sweet Mother!, 461b; said to be in God in twofold sense, 225b; they are, because He knows them, 383a; Thou dost all c.' forms from highest patterns take, 372b

Credendi Legem c. lex statuat supplicandi, 546b

Credibility c. of Catholic faith, 58a

Credible God, infinitely visible and infinitely c., 331a

Credo C. in unum Deum, 226b, 589b

Credulity age of c. is every age, 225b

Credulous Man, naturally c., 570b

Creed America, only nation founded on c., 15b; *Apostles C.*, 226b, 227a, 227b; Christian ethics will not long survive Christian c., 622b; Cleanse us from ire of c. or class, 523a; doctrine, that one c. is as good as another, 537a; every man will make himself a c., 875b; How few have heard silver of thy c., 328b; I believe in God the Father almighty, 226a; I believe in One God, 589b; O that thy c. were sound!, 145b; Old Roman c., 226b; one and same from beginning, 226a, 269b; pestilential and deadly c., 431b; Questions put to those being baptized, 226a; said, Catholics never so good as c., 116a; Symbol of faith which Roman Church uses, 145b;

Creeds A thousand c. and battlecries, 277b; cannot determine affections, 227a; enslaved by dead c., 27b; fashionable, to stand outside c., 637a, 759a; heretical c. are dead, 27b; Popes and emperors must settle c., 583b

Creep Children learn to c. ere they can go, 160b, 319b

Cremate forbidden to c. bodies of faithful, 110b

Crept I c. cat-foot, sure and slow, 38a

Crib By the c. wherein reposing, 460b; He was true God in Bethlehem's c., 488b; Within His c. is surest ward, 487a

Cricket Merry as a c., 497a; not a c. quavered from the meadow, 814b

Crime does not hold, because every c. sin, every sin c., 820a; effective putting down of c., 526b; greatest c. is homicide, 625b; No c. rooted out once for all, 227a

Crimes public zeal to cancel private c., 227a; Successful c., 227a

Criminal jurisdiction of eccles. courts in c. cases, 188b, 190b

Criminals unprincipled c., not afraid to unleash total war, 907b

Cringingness c. of Catholics to force, 109b

Crippled c. mind, 566b

Critic generous c. fann'd the poet's fire, 228a; must be consistent in his criticism, 228a; No c.'s verdict should stand good, 228a; To train a citizen, to train a c., 290b

Criticism c. is rendering of sound reasons, 228a; c. of others, but not ourselves, 341a; dog's tooth, 152a; has become an art, 228a; Women, utter mystics in creed, cynics in c., 455b

Critics never compare Catholic

with non-Catholic, 217a; When c. disagree, 228a

Crocodile Like back of a gold-mailed saurian, 229a

Cromwell, Oliver, 229a

Crook By hook or c., 445a, 679b; Church gets on by hook or c., 220b

Crops come thronging from the ground, 843a

Cross above the C.'s trophy, 230b; adoration of c., 400b; adornment of the Church, 230a; altar, on which oblation of man's nature celebrated, 229b; Ashen c. trace on brow, 37b; At the c. her station keeping, 93b; balance of righteousness, 231b; Be mine the folly of the C., 347b; Be the C. our theme and story, 232a; Bear it with thee everywhere, 232a; Behold, wood of C. on which hung Savior, 400a; bloody sacrifice on altar of C., 309b, 486a, 489b, 586b; both a mystery and example, 230a; bright gate to Jesus' throne, 232a; BVM saw Son upon the c., 39b, 88a; By the C., death vanquished, 229a; by the C., joy is come into world, 285a, 400a; By this sign conquer, 229a; cannot be defeated, for it is defeat, 234a; cause of all the gifts of grace, 230a; Christ is laying his c. on you, 234a; Christ, offered up on gibbet of c., 75b; Come! fall before His C., 657a; Come, take thy stand beneath the C., 658a; confounds devil, 229a; C. is the crux of the matter, 234a; C. thee quite out of my book, 265b; despoiled Hades, 231b; divine school of patience, 233b; ensign of Christ's glory, 229a; Even if Thou dost endure the c., 399b; every little c. overthrows, 9a; explanation of a thousand mysteries, 233b; fair Badge of thy faith, 233a; Faithful C.! above all other, 230b; for My love thou hast nailed Me to C., 400a; gives strength to them that believe, 230a; glory of angels, 230a; glory out of shame, life out of death, 230a; Glory to Thy C., O Lord, 442a; God, ruling nations from a Tree, 230a; Hail, O C.! Brighter than all stars!, 231a; has no intrinsic virtue, 233b; honor shown to c. and Mother of God, 82a; humiliation triumphed gloriously, 229b; I cannot cast away my c., 834b; I do not ask my c. to understand, 666a; In all our actions, we make sign of c., 234a; In the c. is height of virtue, 232b; instrument of contrition, 233b; Iron c. hid in breast, 37b; its mystery, 230b; Jesus, I my c. have taken, 233a; Jesus offered Himself once only, 309b; key to everlasting life, 305b; let him take up his cross, 4b; Lord's judgment seat, 229b; marked on every faithful brow, 229a; might of kings, 230a; my hopes have always been fixed on c. of Christ, 521b; nailed to c. and pierced with spear, 399b; name which is above all names, 442b; Now shines the C.'s mystery, 230a; O clear, O wealful altar, holy cross, 232a; O C., our only hope, all hail!, 230b; O C., whereby the earth is blest, 232a; O wonderful power of the c.!, 229b; On her breast a sparkling c. she wore, 235a; On the C., the Lamb is lifted, 656a; One c. I thought so bitter, 234a; opened the gates of

Paradise, 231b; Our veneration referred to Him Who died upon it, 233b; pluck grapes of consolation from c., 486a; precious and august Tree, 231b; price of this life-giving wood, 231a; restored Adam, 229a; royal sign, 234b; sacrifice of mass, one and same with C., 309b; Salvation by the c., 231a, 232b, 797b; school of penance, 233b; See! as His altar The C. is displayed, 657b; shadow of Thy tree, 233a; sign of c. a shield, 234a; sign of c. at Gospel, 589b; source of all blessings, 230a; strength of the faithful, 230a; subdued death, 231b; suffer death upon the C., 652a; symbol of absolutely endless expansion, 234a; symbolizes true altar of prophecy, 229b; that life-bearing tree, 231b; That tremendous sacrifice, 658b; they suffer most Who have no c. at all, 234a; Thou didst draw all things unto Thee, 229b; Thou didst nail to c. sin Adam committed, 809b; thy Child on a c. y-rent, 99b; Thy C. to me unending glory, 657a; thy dread symbol, 233b; Thy Mother seeing Thee, upon the c., 93a; Thy name is honorable upon earth!, 231a; to be worshipped because of Christ, 231b; to joy in the cross of Christ, 9a; Today is suspended on tree, He that suspendeth earth, 400a; tree of life and restorer of Paradise, 231a; true ground of Christian hope, 229b; typifies the Lord, 82a, 231b; undergo ignominy of C., 655b; Upon it Life did death endure, 230a; watcher of whole world, 230a; We adore Thy C., O Lord, 230a, 285a, 400a; We have not to carry c. of others, 232b; What makes them believe is the C., 233a; when tempted, seal forehead with sign of cross, 105b, 234a; wound of demons, 230a

Crosses c. that we shape for ourselves, 232b; Do not be afraid of insults, c., death, 448b

Crow black c. thinketh her own birds white, 54b, 243b; this perennial bird, 234b

Crowds Where c. can wink; and no offence be known, 227a

Crowing c. of the prophetic bird, 678a

Crown BVM, c. of virginity, 81a; C. Him with many crowns, 490a; c. is on the Victor's brow!, 286a; c. of rejoicing, 436a; C. of most incomparable light, 40b; c. of roses and of thorns, 38a, 420a; c. of those who Confess Thy name, 205a, 581b; c. of victory promised only to contestants, 43a, 234b; C. of women, 40b; monarch's c. with fate surrounded lies, 234b; C. of conscience is my c., 209a; Our c. amid the blest, 657a; Scepter and c. Must tumble down, 249a; c. and scepter, symbols, 509b; thy bright c., 95a; Who gives the c. that lasts for aye, 298b, 489a; Who reach, lay hold on death that miss the prize, 234b;

Crowned Only Heaven Means c., not conquered, 349b; thou art c. by Christ, 43a; Why was I c. and made queen?, 100a

Crowns fate of scepters and c., 509a; If all wore c., kings would go bareheaded, 445a; imitation of c. and palms of Martyrdom, 581a; not seek to have all the c., 774b;

What are kings and c. to me?, 477b

Crows at hour when cock c., rise and pray, 599a; Our minds are like c., 608b

Crozier to c. Is joined the sword, 179b

Cruce In c. salus, 797b

Crucible our hearts and minds, tested in c. of truth, 429a

Crucified By sinners c., 97b; Christ, my c. Lord, 75b; c. One hath opened the graves, 442a; Figure c., 164a; Jesus, our Love, is c.!, 658a; let us praise Him, Who was c. for us, 399b; power of the C., 229b; To know Jesus and Him c., 488b, 602a; The lesson, and the young Man c., 492b

Crucifieth c. lusts of flesh, 36b

Crucifix I saw the C. bleeding, 235a; religion in which allowed to have c., 102a; The world is my c., 234b

Crucifixion Thou endurest the c. for all, 93a

Crucifixus Mundus mihi c. est, 234b

Cruelty c. is all perfection is, 235a; C.'s a charm In you, 235a

Crumbs c. that from its table fall, 157a

Crusade Kill them all, 235a; unending work of the Church, 235a

Crusades Dominican c., 256a

Crutch Age hath clawed me with his c., 10b

Crux Cross is the c. of the matter, 234a

Cry c. I can no more, 258b

Crying refuge of plain women, 859b; tones of infant woe, 161a

Cuckoo cuckoo, cuckoo!, 235b; sweet to hear the c. mock the spring, 235a

Cujus C. regio, illius et religio, 180a

Cultivated find beautiful meanings in beautiful things, 235b

Cultural art always product of c. period, 33a; word Christendom relates to c. order, 162b

Culture Catholic c. and believers, 139a; Church not bound to any culture, 140b; education has meant transmission of c., 292b; hard for rich in c. to enter modern church, 33b; if our culture is Greco-Latin, our religion is not, 139b; not identical with civilization, 235b; Religion, main determining element in c., 186a, 760a; right to one's own c. and national character, 531a; social c. is an organized way of life, 235b; spiritual freedom, influence on social c., 457a

Cultured Catholic Church, not a c. set, 235b

Cum Et c. spiritu tuo, 588b

Cup c. of salvation, 231a; Merry as c. could hold, 279a; water and wine, mingled in Lord's c., 597b; when Ye taste His c., 420a; wherein souls of faith, inebriated, 72a; which He taught us to offer in Eucharist, 307a

Cupid C. plague thee for thy treason!, 10b

Cupiditas Radix malorum est c., 48b

Cupidity opens door for devil's suggestion, 860a; rightly directed by the charity, 235b

Cur A gentle hound should never play the c., 273a

Cure c. of person who will not be cured, 193a

Cured What can't be c. must be endured, 295b
Curiosities Let c. alone, 236a
Curiosity c. is only vanity, 236a; knowledge for its own sake, c. 512a; Man's chief disease is c., 236a; of more value in learning than discipline, 236a; You know what a woman's c. is, 236a
Curious Men are a race c. to know, 236a
Curried short horse, soon c., 446b
Curse And turn our blessings to a c., 574a; by Him, c. made void, 90a; chain of the c. is broken, 78b; c. Of a doom unforgiving!, 254a
Cursing oftentimes c. returneth to him that curseth, 317b; the devil's Pater Noster, 236b
Customary c. law and equity, 300a
Custodians Rulers, c. of decrees of God, 784a
Custom Ancient c. has the force of law, 236b; By which people keep even kings in awe, 237a; C. is the best interpreter of laws, 237b; Follow c. of Church where you happen to be, 207b; force of eccles. c., 237b; has added to and taken away from natural law, 527a; I like to be as my fathers were, 237a; kills with feeble dint, 237a; observed as long as man can remember, 236b; rules the law, 237a; unwritten law, 237a; use of one church, not to be annulled, 874b
Customs Apostolic See makes large allowance for c., 770b; binding in one of two ways, 236b; duly written and handed down, law, 524b; Natural law, superior in dignity to c., 527a
Cycles through c. all but infinite, 20a; world has c. its course, 819a
Cynara I have been faithful to thee, C.! 556b
Cynic What is a c.? 237b
Cynics those canine philosophers, 237b
Cyprian, St., 23b, 676a

D

Da D. quod jubes: jube quod vis, 410a
Daffodil certain faith of a March d., 238a; O love-star of the unbeloved March, 237a
Daggers playing with short d., 239b
Daily D., d., sing to Mary, 89a
Dainties where d. want, 263b
Dainty Plenty is no d., 684b
Daisies drops of gold in whitening flame, 238a; that little children pull! 238a
Daisy day's-eye or else the eye-of-day, 238a; emperice and flower of flowers all, 238a
Damasus, Pope St., 144b
Dame the d. despiteful, 10b
Dames Angels with harps and alabaster d., 114a
Damn D. with faint praise, 239a
Damnably They order things so d. in hell, 428a
Damnation death eternal, called second death, 246b, 247a, 428a; delivered from eternal d., 591b; O original of our d., 368a; relegate wicked into eternal fire, 500b; rescued from eternal d., 665a; unto judgment and d., 594b
Damned, The called reprobate, 723b; City of d., 124b; d. are in abyss of Hell, 238a; ever-burning
gehenna will burn condemned, 227a, 426a; God consequently wills some to be damned, 723a; I'll be d. if I do! 28a; man is not d. unless for his evil will, 238a, 261a; one creature we know to be d., 261a; perpetual death of the d., 426b; saints see punishment of d. in hell, 427a; shall not dwell in lot of saints, 125a; state of these accurst, 238b; suffer eternal punishment with devil, 124b, 238a, 247a; their separation from life of God, 426b; their state after last judgment, 238b; those who in no wise belong to Church, 127b
Dance All be not merry that men see d., 239a; d. on the point of a needle, 19b; d. upon a jig to heav'n, 626b; Fat wet bodies go waddling by, 239b; leap into a d., 239a; lawful to d. and feast, 18a
Dances Puritan frowning on d., 745a
Dancing we should take part for sake of recreation, 239a
Dandy future belongs to the d., 239b
Danger D. well past, remembered, 239b; days are full of d., 901b; greater d. in battle, greater joy in triumph, 880b
Dangerous petition of empty hand d., 56a; playing with short daggers, 239b
Dangers In d., doubts, think of Mary, 87b, 100b; principal act of courage, to endure d., 223a; we are set in the midst of d., 239b
Dante Alighieri, 240a
Dappled Glory be to God for d. things, 192b
Dare he who naught d. undertake, 106a; Since we d. not on account of sins, 98b; To do and d., and die at need, 777a; What am I who d. to call Thee, God!, 248b
Dark In a d. night, With anxious love inflamed, 214b; The night is d., and I am far from home, 636b; The shutter'd d., the secrecy, 287a
Dark Ages Church, only thing that ever brought us out of them, 605a
Darkness A d. made of too much day, 299b; brilliance of their d., 211b; Cast away dreams of d., 7b; D. and solitude shine, for me, 836b; Farewell to d. and to sin! 240a; knowledge of God, surrounded by d., 393a; him that sitteth in d., 8a; Moses entered into d. where God was, 393a; night's blear-all black, 111a; universal d. buries all, 153b; Unto this D. which is beyond light, 394a
Darling old man's d., 574a
Dart A prey unto thy d.?, 249a; Bearing in breast the print of every d., 31b; delightful, healthgiving d., 196a; for Divine Target, 565a; O d. of love! arrow of light! 218b
Daughter d. of David, 84b; d. of thine own Son, 82b; His sole-born D., 96b; King's d., 169a; My little d. dearer than myself!, 861a; O thou undaubted d. of desires!, 258a
Daughters Which d., wives, mothers are of kings, 96b; Ye sons and d. of the King, 285b
David BVM sprang from root of D., 90b; D.'s word with Sibyl's blending! 502b; Of D.'s royal blood, 95a; O Key of D., 8a; The voice of D. singing to his harp,
690a; Tower of D., 84b; Where D.'s court shall widely rear, 440b
Dawn d. with silver-sandalled feet, 240b; Day is breaking, d. is bright, 522b; O d., at last, long look'd for day!, 240a; O rosy d.! thou dost proclaim, 402b; rosy d. which would dispel superstition, 316a; sprinkles benediction through the d., 78b; The chrism of the light, 240b; The d. is sprinkling in the east, 240a
Dawning Like the d. of morning, 8b; Now in the sun's new d. ray, 731a
Dawnists, 316a
Day A darkness made of too much d., 299b; And light'st the glow of perfect d., 809b; As fades the glowing orb of d., 894a; Before the ending of the d., 201a; Be the d. never so long, 894a; bright d. of eternity, 303a; By thy large draughts of intellectual d., 258a; d., a dedicated priest, 78b; D. delightful! d. most noted! 670b; D. is breaking, dawn is bright, 522b; D. of the King most righteous, 501b; D. of wrath and doom impending, 502a; each d. is like a year, 731b; Joy rul'd the d., and love the night, 497b; Night treads upon the heels of d., 251a; O dawn, at last, long look'd for d.!, 240a; O D., all days illuming, 522a; O Lord, Who hast brought us to beginning of this d., 731a; on that awful d., 246a; Round the d.'s dead sanctities, 312b; That d. of doom, 246a, 501b, 503a; The colors of the dying d., 612a; This d. thou shalt be with Me, 318a; Thy life is one unwearing d., 340a; 'Tis a d. with gladness mated, 40a; We joy one everlasting d., 533b; Whose d. shall never die in night, 303b
Daydreams Like the d. of melancholy men, 241a
Daylight d. divine, 41a
Days I fled Him, down the nights and d., 385a; O for the happy d. gone by, 719b; order our d. in Thy peace, 591b
Dayspring D. from on high, 167a; O Light of Light, O D. bright, 599a
Deacon bishop alone lays hands on him, 69a, 241a, 647b; duty of d. to minister at altar, baptize, preach, 242a; forbidden to exercise secular government, 188b; Grant that he may stand blameless before Thee, 242a; in Greek means minister in Latin, 242a; may marry before ordination, 150b; not ordained for priesthood, 241a; Bishops, priests, d. must remain unmarried, 150a; By divine institution, hierarchy consists of bishops, priests, ministers, 190a; charged with ministry of dispensing, 241a, 242a, 433a; elect d. worthy of Lord, 67a; example of their chastity, 241b; order of those seven, whom apostles chose, 241b; pure ministers at Thy holy altars, 241b; Send forth upon them the Holy Ghost, 241b; servants of the Church of God, 241a
Dead all who repose in Christ, 242b, 243b, 245b, 592b, 593a; as a door nail, 248a; at altar, commemoration of d., 244a; called out of the world, 245b; cannot intervene in affairs of living, 242b; care for d. and offering of

prayers, 244a; Charity brings to life those spiritually d., 155b; Church favors prayers for d., 243b, 244a; grant eternal rest to all the faithful, 244b, 246a; how art Thou numbered with the d., 93b; If thou grievest for the d., 65b; in some sort d. to this life, 211a; judge the living and the d., 28b; let perpetual light upon them shine, 243a; let us bid farewell to the departed, 245a; man must be d. before he swings, 358a; O God, Who dost rule both living and d., 244b, 541b; O lady, he is d. and gone, 242b; Oh! leave the past to bury its own d., 659a; remember me at altar of the Lord, 244a; Something was d. in each of us, 446a; souls of d. are in a place, 89a, 242b, 246b; souls of d. obtain relief through piety of living, 244a; Sweet abbey of tuneful d., 1a; first fruits of them that slept, 283b; The d. shall live, the living die, 626a; The freedom of the living d., 635b; the Immortal D., 318a; The king is d., long live the king!, 509a; They are not lost but gone before, 242b; those dear pledges, 242b; to bury the d., 155a; We commend to Thee the soul of Thy servant, 244b; Weep not the brave d.!, 242b, 254a; When I am d., I hope it may be said, 107b, 251b

Dead Sea, 264a

Deaf D. to the universal call, 465a

Dear D. God, I wish I could have been, 161a; I love thee, d., for what thou art, 921b; Well blest is he who has a d. one dead, 559a

Death absolute rest is d., 624b; After royal throne, comes d., 463b; Against d. is worth no medicine, 248a; All buildings but monuments of d., 249b; all-en-shrouding d., 243a; All d. does end, 542b; alway cruel, 247b; angel d., 41a, 252a; At d.'s final hour, call me, 75b; At d. we display our true characters, 154a; authority of life and d., 243b; avert grim d.'s unerring throes, 601b; Between d. and love, no alternative, 558b; birth and d., both of nature, 65b, 464a, 541a, 543a; BVM could not be held by d., 39a; Blind with spendor of his d., 114b; but a sharp corner, 251b; by d. did life procure, 230a; by d. trampling upon d., 35b, 90a, 285a, 588b; by d., we begin to know, 513b; By the Cross, d. has been vanquished, 229a; by woman's weakness enter'd in, 25b; celestial flight, 70b; Christ freed us from charge of death, 43b; Dead before d., 247b; d. by d. down doth He tread, 284b; D. it is to live without Thee, 542a; d.'s mildewed stair, 544a; Deliver me from everlasting d., 90b, 246a, 502a; Do not hand him over to power of enemy, 500b; doom'd to d., though fated not to die, 463b; doth with man no order keep, 248b; dread hour of d., 500a; edifice of d., 85a; *empire of d.,* 821a; end of every worldly sore, 539a; eternal, called second d., 247a; eternal Sabbath of his rest, 249b; *everlasting showing forth of His d.,* 73b; evil, only by retribution which follows, 247a; for Christ's sake, not afraid of d., 252b; From d. to life eternal, 285b; good d. does honor to whole life, 248a; good

to good, and evil to evil, 246b, 247a; Grief and d., born of sin, 415b; How life and d. in Thee Agree!, 872a; How much less strong is d. than love, 558b; How sweet is d. to those who weep, 250a; If thou fearest d., 246b, 252b; in itself is nothing, 253a; in the arms of d., 251a; I sought my d., found it in my womb, 541b; I weep and grieve when I think of d., 245a; jars horridly on nature, 247a; journey for a season, 246b; knight of the sable feather, 252a; lays his icy hand on kings, 249a; let me die a natural d., 521b; life of noise! a restless d.!, 543a; Life is coquetry Of d., 540a; life is changed, not taken away, 246a; Life is short, d. is certain, 542b; life's eventide, 74b; life's reparation, 242b; Life like a sea, 251b; makes equal high and low, 248a; man is by nature afraid of d., 252b; Mediator freed us from d., 43a; Men, not able to cure d., 301a; Merciless judgment, without appeal!, 248a; Mother of God, thou deliverest our souls, 39a; Mother of Love by death set free, 40b; My self to thee alone is known, 253a; Neither wish d., nor fear his might, 215a; not d. but repentance of sinners, 265a; Nothing more certain than d., 247b; O ancient victor, 252a; O d.! come take away, 542a; O God, Who dost not desire d. of sinners, 860a; of every man, patterned in stars, 41b; Of living d. and dying life, 563a; overthrew D., sin, Satan too, 401a; perfect life is an imitation of d., 247b; power of d. hath no avail, 442a; Public was d., 286b; quits all scores, 249b; receive at d., seal of likeness to Christ, 503a; reveals what life cannot, 543b; scent of d. is weary and sweet, 47b; separation of soul and body, 246b; shall have no more dominion over Him, 308b; sitteth in shadow of d., 8a; sleep longer than usual, 246b; So I may gain thy d., my life I'll give, 542b; soul taken up by holy angels 500b; Sudden d., only thing to dread, 253a; suffer violence of pain and d., 521b; The anchor of a love is d., 559a; The end of sin is d., 816a; the journey's end, 542b; The sanctities of life's last breath, 543a; The second d. that never dies, 428a; those in article of d., 247a; thou mighty messenger, 248a; Thou wilt not slay me, d.!, 252a; throned behind D. with a sovereignty, 374a; till d. Shall set me free to live, 296b; To absent oneself from history, is to seek d., 435a; today our Savior burst asunder gates of d., 400b; To keep d. daily before one's eyes, 247b; To love Him, life; to leave Him, d., 359a; Twixt life and d., twixt in and out, 218b; 'Twixt soul and body, a divorce, 455b; What matters d., if freedom be not dead?, 354a; Where is thy sting, O d.?, 283b; Whom neither sin could stain, nor d. hold, 467b; wins this time, 522a

Death-bed A d. has scarcely a history, 253a

Death-beds To them that on their d. rest, 283b

Deathfulness The d. and lifefulness of fire!, 490b

Deaths By all thy lives and d. of love, 258a; vulgar d. unknown to fame, 250a

Debonaire BVM, thou mighty d., 87b

Debt Dear hope! earth'd dowry, heav'n's d.!, 445b; Thy life is one long d., 233a; we should pay our d. first, 253a

Debts spendthrift never reveals all his d., 253b

Decadence To be wrong, carefully wrong, 253b

Decay All human things subject to d., 249b; all our chants but chaplet some d., 253b; How can we be given over to d.?, 245a

Deceased grant eternal rest to all faithful d., 246a

Deceit crafty serpent's cruel wile, 6a; D., weeping, spinning, God hath give To women, 920a; their loyal d., 211a; To hold with hare, and run with hound, 253b; wolf in a lamb's skin, 253b

Deceive not in human nature to d. for long, 253b; Thou canst not d., 227a, 328a

Deceived Dost thou hate to be d.?, 253b; not to wish is not to be d., 918b

Decently *no one ought to live other than becomingly,* 157b

Declaration of Independence, 15b, 16a

Decorum social d. among Catholics, 17a

Decree all things follow Thy d., 421a; d. of senate, 524a; great d. of God, 248b

Decretals observing canons and keeping d., 698b; statues of Apostolic See, 698b

Dedication d., immolation of oneself, 310a

Deed Advisement is good before the d., 739a; an end there is of every d., 395a; I have sinned exceedingly in thought, word, and d., 587b; Infer the motive from the d., 625a; of the d. the glory shall remain, 399a

Deeds by d. more than by words, 1a; distance between high words and d.!, 923a; friend in words, where d. be dead, 359a; glorious d. of Christ our King, 489a; Golden d. kept out of sight, 452a; Let charity issue in good d., 157b; my good d. Your act, my ill d. my own faults, 398b; password of our King, divine d., 435b; Thy d. undone, 283a

Deep d. forever yearning unto d., 804a; D., d.—where never care or pain, 250a

Defeat Fallen from his high estate, 254a

Defective barred from holy orders, 649a; procreation of d. children, 161a

Defects Who is free from d.?, 254a

Defectu irregulares ex d., 649a

Defence BVM, our d., 84b; d., preservation, of country, 406b; outside line of d., 271a; Sacrament, my sure d., 196a

Defend D. us from all dangers of soul and body, 793a; Let Thy continual pity d. Thy Church, 682b, 736b

Defender of marriage, 579b

Defensive no such thing as d. battle, 254b

Defensor D. vinculi, 579b

Deference d. to magnates, 504b

Define as easy to create as to d., 254b

Defined No doctrine is d. till it is violated, 274a; when doctrine considered dogmatically d., 274b

Defining doctrine regarding faith or morals, 706b

Definitio Omnis d. periculosa est, 254b

Definition Every d. is dangerous, 254b; Thou, by whom Our nothing has a d.!, 445b; Whose d. is a doubt, 218b

Definitions divine assistance enables Church to choose rightly, 272b; expression of one dogma, 270a; have grown to present shape in centuries, 270a; responsibility of council or pontiff, 274b

Degraded men, d. by industrialism, 471a

Degrees of knowledge, 511a

Dei Ad majorem D. gloriam, 367a; *Agnus D., qui tollis peccata mundi,* 594a; *Ecce Agnus D.,* 595b; *Opus D.,* 266a; *Vox populi, vox D.,* 671a

Dei Genetrix, 81a

Deific d. pathway my Love has travelled, 564b

Deification d. and love of God, 255a; men become gods by participation, 195b, 254b

Deism Atheist communism, bourgeois d. turned round, 42b

Deist Slave to no sect, 255a

Deity D. reveal'd, 77b; one and not many, 391a; Such life befits a D., 166a; Thou hast prov'd Thy D., 77a

Delay heavenly robe of d., 564b; injury, never friend, 255a; Works adjourned have many stays, 255a

Delays All d. are dangerous in war, 907a; Long demurs breed new d., 255a, 645b

Delegated d. vicegerency of authority, 699a

Deliberation acts done without full d., 33b; essential to art, 34a

Delight d. of the angels, 84b; Life not life without d., 255a; reap whole heavens of d., 553a; Youthful lordlings of d., 684a

Delights If short d. entice my heart, 585a

Delinquents Church's right to punish d., 740b

Deliver d. me from all transgressions, 594b; D. me, O Lord, from eternal death, 246a, 502a; D. us from all evils, 593b; d. us, tarry now no more, 8a; She is mighty to d., 89a

Deliverance Christ's death, cause of d., 43b

Delivered *The net is broken and we are delivered,* 24a

Delle Vigne, Pier, 423b

Delph, 448a

Democracy an achievement, always precarious, 256b, 257a; appears to many a postulate of nature, 257a; cannot separate itself from religious traditions, 183b; Catholic theology, not for or against d., 256a; Christianity identical with d., 256a; d. and brotherhood, 257a; d. and Catholic doctrine of origin of power, 255b; d. and despotism, 259b; d. and religion, 15a, 257a; doesn't give average man real power, 255b; England and America both stand for d., 16b; free market of mother-ideas, 537a; government by the people, 256b, 404a; in Catholic Church, 117b; means

government by uneducated, 256b; noblest form of government, 256b; Nor is the people's judgment always true, 739b; not arbitrament by majority, 255b; opposed to rule of mob, 256b; people educated under popular institutions, 16b; people have right to choose their rulers, 404a, 845b; People's voice is God's voice, 255a; rests on club-habit, 256a; swept Europe with Rights of Man, 256a; True d. and respect for God, 257a; under d., man enjoys greater liberty, 15a

Democracies Republics live by virtue, 766a; Two rights which d. guarantee, 257a

Democratic No one can dislike d. principle more than I, 536b; Those who teach d. charter, must believe in it, 257a

Democrats All men are d. when happy, 255b

Demon every d. is winged, 18b

Demons ashes of martyrs drive away d., 583b; D. are everywhere, 257b; intellectual without admixture of body, 260b; may rise to be men or angels, 18b; We went with ten demons, 200a

Demonstrate presuming to d. what is of faith, 26b

Demonstrated truth, d. by first principle, 883b

Demonstration Concrete matter does not admit of d., 599b; no assent, even though d., 30b; scientific d. and credibility of faith, 58a

Denial dogmatic slumber of d., 12a

Denominations right to regulate questions of eccles. discipline, 184b

Denotamur Sunt tanti quanti et d., 163a

Dentes Equi donati d. non inspiciuntur, 365b

Deny And did not Thee d., 77b

Deo D. favente, 397a; *D. gratias,* 589a; *D. optimo maximo,* 397a; *Gloria in Excelsis D.,* 588b; *Soli D. gloria,* 367b

Deo gratias Therefore we singen *Deo gratias,* 29a

Deride All fools have still an itching to d., 776b

Depart Now, Thou dost let Thy servant d. in peace!, 520b; Thou dost never d. from us, 344a

Departed All who have d. in piety and faith, 245b; endow with eternal goods him who has d., 245a; grant to souls of Thy servants d., 244b; Hail! Thou Judge of souls d.!, 483b; Mother of God grant rest to d., 89a

Departure Sweet Savior! bless us ere we go, 312b

Depose If king rules tyranically, community may d. him, 773b, 774a; Pope's power to d. princes, 141b, 701a

Deposit Christ entrusted d. of faith to Church, 119a; Church's authority to elucidate d., 119b; what was in harmony with original d., 272b

Deposition citizens have power of d., 405a; d. of sinful king by people, 179b; d. of unbelieving rulers, 178b

Depression d. and Christian cheerfulness, 160a

Depths God alone knows d. and riches of His Godhead, 383a; Out of the d. to Thee I cry, 242b

Desert divine grace and precedent

d., 445a; Nothing went unrewarded, but d., 320a; to myself a very land of want!, 261b; Wouldst thou give due d. to all?, 603b

Deserted I have d. Thee and wandered away, 261b

Deserve d. to be a bishop, 68a; if Thou shouldst render to us what we d., 603b; We win from God exactly what we d., 720b

Designer world manifests its D., 372a

Desire baptism, actual and by d., 52b, 53a; breeds d., but doth not satisfy, 96b; brim-fill'd bowls of fierce d., 258a; clothe yourself with good and holy d., 257b; d. of Thee alone, 196a; d. of the gentiles, 8a; Do not d. not to be what you are, 257b; flames of bad d., 77a, 258a, 561b; Giver of love, and beauty, and d., 490b; hearts corrupted by impure d., 861a; How larger is remembrance than d.!, 763a; love and d. contrasted, 550b; love is the root of all d., 257b, 256a; multiplied by asceticism, 37a; O Light! O Flame! the world's d., 258a; Subdue your wills, master d., 14b, 257b; The love of women's over, ended is d., 501b; To d. to love God, 257b; with fire Of unapproach'd d., 385a

Desired farther off, more d., 2a

Desires all things make young with young d., 843a; fixing all our d. on Creator, 214a; Love celestial d., 258a; Not to fulfil d. of flesh, 346a; O God, from Whom all holy d. proceed, 665a; O thou undaunted daughter of d.!, 258a; Young d. make little prease, 257b

Desiring If ever desiring, then ever praying, 257b

Despair absolute extreme of self-love, 259a; aided by agnosticism, 12a; Doubt is brother devil to D.!, 276a; Fond men, we are fixed as a still d., 448a; It takes eternity to make a man d., 259a; no hope in Divine mercy, 258b; no one calling on BVM, left to d., 87b; Not, I'll not, carrior comfort, d., 258b; pit of hell is as deep as d., 426b; Restless anxiety, forlorn d., 113a; Some perish through d., 106b; We need not d. of any man, 258b

Despise Do not d., O glorious one, 89a; highest science, truly to know and d. ourselves, 451a

Despised they wish to be humble, without being d., 473b

Despot Some races require d. to nurse, feed them, 259a

Despotism Church, enemy of d. of state, 259a; may be defined as a tired democracy, 259b

Destinies d. of humanity in America's keeping, 15a

Destiny Catholic Church and your d., 118b; doors of d., 392a; How easy 'tis when d. proves kind, 767b; In shady leaves of d., 259b; liberty in working out d., 15a; minister general, 259b; Religion is solution of problem of d., 757a; The one inexorable thing!, 259b

Destroyer D. of sin, 86a

Destruction all men to d. bring, 7b

Detail scrutinized in matters of d., 301a

Details D. are always vulgar, 259b

Deterioration I do not believe

Church has been deteriorating, 136a

Determinism Christian bound to hold acts not subject to d., 357a

Detraction He who could take d. from world, 260a

Deum Credo in unum D., 226b, 589b; Te D. laudamus, 372b

Deus Benedicat vos omnipotens D., 595b; Homo cogitat, D. indicat, 397a; Homo proponit, sed D. disponit, 397a; Sanctus, sanctus, sanctus Dominus D. Sabaoth, 591a

Development doctrines and form of d., 272a, 702b; Growth means unfolding of interior capacities, 272a

Devil able to resist d. and his temptations, 242a; An angel's witching words, 25b; blaguard the d., 261b; called god of this world, 260b; cannot lord it over servants of God, 860a; careful d. at hand with means, 819a, 826a; caught by the d.'s bait, 260a; chosen a d. to his wife, 912a; Christ overthrew might of d., 400b; conquered by same nature he deceived, 428a, 751b; Dark angel, with thine aching lust, 261a; deceived by wisdom of serpent, 347a; deliver from slavery of the enemy, 206a, 652a, 656a, 665a; d. and eternal punishment, 124b; d., and teaching of Church, 260a; dimple in the chin; a d. within, 263b; Do not hand him over to power of enemy, 500b; Don't bid the d. good-morra, 261b; empire of death, the d., 821a; enters weak in faith, 260a, 860a; every man, with him was God or d., 321b; foeman's wiles, 21a, 75b, 201b, 431b; frontiers between sense and spirit, d.'s hunting-grounds, 807a; given the d. a foul fall, 260b; go with thee down the lane, 261a; he gives himself to the d., 13a; He must needs go that the d. drives, 260b; hindered by d. from obeying God's will, 407b; I will not bear the d.'s sack, 261a; invented gambling, 362b; liar and the father of lies, 260b; Meet to set the d. on sale, 261a; more than one way of sacrificing to d., 260b; my cruel adversaire, 87b; Not even d.'s nature is evil, as nature, 314a; not lord of this world, 223b; one creature we know to be damned, 261a; rage man or d. never so much, 141b; ruler of covetous desires, 223b; Sin it were to believe the d., 260b; So long as the enemy can enter into our souls, 625a; spiritual powers of wickedness, 37b; such a monster as the d., 19b; tempts all servants of God, 260a; The d. in th'horloge, 261a; The d. is dead!, 260b; The d. is no falser than he is, 261b; The d. is no fool, 261a, 426a; The d. tempts that he may ruin, 860a; The d. with his dam, 912a; the faith is old and the d. is bold, 147a; To set up candle before d., 261a; 'twas nuts to the father of lies, 536a; will without doubt be conquered, 123a

Devils intellectual, without admixture of body, 260b; fallen angels, 19b, 260b, 313a; not so black as they are painted, 261a; repelled by sign of cross, 234b

Devoted to pious practices, 262a; to Thy name in good works, 261b

Devotion adapts itself to any shape, 262b; affection for amusements, harmful to d., 18a; certain act of the will, 261b; Charity and d. differ, 262a; consistent with state in life, 262b; Faith and d., distinct in fact, 330a; filial d. to BVM above other saints, 101a, 101b, 102a; I prefer English habits of d., 262b; Let not inward d. be visible, 262a; persevere with steadfast d., 37b; should be subordinate to doctrine, 58b; tender or deep in d., 23a; True d., nothing else than good will, 262a; we may believe without feeling d., 330a

Devotional in a drawing-room, 288a

Devotions sentiment and taste do not run with logic, 101a

Devotus Doctor D., 106b

Devout d. Soul, to whom God cometh, 197a; monastery of a d. life, 638b

Dew abundant d. of Holy Spirit, 64a; blessing from d. of heaven, 72b; d. of Thy heavenly grace, 68b, 159a; like d. on fleece, 89a; one summer evening's d., 237b; water them with d. of Thy piety, 4a; world d.-pearl'd, 192a

Dews d. of grace not in one measure fall, 302b

Diaconate protomartyr Stephen, first of that order, 242a; Savior suggested to apostles institution of d., 242a; worthy to enter ministry of d., 242a

Diadem precious d. of godly sovereigns, 100b;

Dialectic discipline ascertaining causes of things, 263a

Diamond Chaucer, I confess, is a rough d., 159b; Eyes, that displace The neighbor d., 322a

Diapason The d. closing full in man, 626a

Dice once or twice to throw the d., 362b

Dicere Orare idem est ac d., 717b

Dickens, Charles, 263a

Dictatus Papae, 175b

Diction pomp of language, tuneful d., 849a

Die always ready to d., 248b; better to d., since death comes surely, 251a; better to d. with Lord, than live without Him, 625a; Church does not d., 138a; D., driven against the wall, 324a; D. when you will, you need not wear, 250a; doom'd to death, though fated not to do, 463b; ev'ry man who lives is born to d., 542b; For Thee to live, in Thee to d., 374a; he who believes in Me, even if he d., 246a; I d. because I do not d., 214b; I d., but such a death as never ends, 542a; I d. like a good Catholic, 521a; I d. in love's delicious fire, 563a; I d. unprepared, 520b; I only cannot d., 901a; I shall d. today, and you tomorrow, 248a; in a Christian land to d., 251a; It is not hard to d. upon a throne, 543b; let him d. that is not as he was, 9a; Let me d. or live Thou in me, 542a; Live here, great heart, and love and d. and kill, 424a; love me, it was sure to d.!, 264b; My life to d. for love of Thee, 563a; Now He lives, no more to d., 285b; Oh, Lord, shall I d. at all?, 519b; rather d. for Jesus than rule earth, 490b; She can love, and she can d., 558b; take us To thy bosom when we d., 90a; They cannot wholly pass away, 243b; Those we love truly never d., 763a; thou

canst d. but once, 541b; To the good man to d. is gain, 246b

Died no one has ever d. who was not to die, 246b; She vanish'd, we can scarcely say she d., 249b; Withe Christ we d., with Christ we rose, 283b

Diem carpe d. religion, 497b

Dies She d. daily, 351b; The patient by inches d., 269a; there is nothing lives but something d., 543a

Dies D. Dominicus non est juridicus, 854a

Dieth What he d. that must he be forever, 251a

Dieu Près de l'église, loin de D., 138a

Difference no d. between men, 607b; theological d., 217a

Difficult D. thoughts, distinct from d. words, 643b; mere fact of being hard, 847b; Nothing too d. for innocent, 472a

Difficulties bend d. with gentleness and time, 364b; doubleminded find d., 263a; Ten thousand d. do not make one doubt, 263a

Digestion process of d. separates useful, 263b

Digestive roasts, d. powers increase, 263a

Dignified only man can be d., 263b, 571b

Dignities Lord, Dispenser of all d., 726b; rise from lower grade to higher d., 241b

Dignity condescension of Son, d. of Mother, 82b; freedom, realization of human d., 184a; human d. of workers, 320a; royal d. excels all others, 507b

Dignum D. et justum est, 591a; terrenum quidem animal, sed coelo d., 569a

Dignus Domine, non sum d., 595a

Dilettante versifiers and witty men, 263b

Dimple d. in the chin; a devil within, 263b

Diners cannot be long where dainties want, 263b

Dinner After good d., one can forgive anybody, 263b

Dinners Great suppers will stomach's peace impair, 263b

Dio Più presso la chiesa, più lontano da D., 138a

Diocese each d. has one bishop as head, 695b; people of d., under bishop, 67b

Diocletian, Emperor, 256a

Dipsomaniac d. and the abstainer, 279b

Direct d. and sanctify our hearts and bodies, 515b

Directive d. power of Church, 182a; pope's d. power over princes, 181a

Directors, Spiritual mere instruments to guide souls, 264a, 639b

Directs Man thinks, God d., 397a

Diriment Church has right to establish d., impediments, 579a

Dirt Poverty I love, but not d., 712b; thou art but d. and mire, 451b; to ingrovel in d. is beastly base, 334b

Disadvantage worst end of the staff, 264a

Disagreement They agreed like two cats in gutter, 264a

Disappointment Blessed is he who expects nothing, 264a; Like Dead-Sea fruits that tempt eye, 264a; why must D. all I endeavor, end?, 382a

Disapproval we could have but a nay, 264b

Discomfort d. of person who will not be comforted, 193a

Discontent first step in progress of man, 264b

Discordant harmonious echo From d. life, 287b

Discourse Sydneian showers Of sweet d., 518b

Discover To d. and to teach, distinct functions, 858b

Discoveries They make d. where they see no sun, 320a

Discovery Gigantic industry needed for d. of tiny things, 352b; Our d. of God, God's d. of us, 396b

Disciple false d., 74b; master loseth time, When d. will not hear, 858b

Discipline Catholic Church, d. of affections and passions, 689a; Christians, live in intercourse of d., 680b; Every age, its appropriate measure of d., 750a; formula of d., 633a; in school of adversity, heart forced to d. itself, 404a; law of life, law of sacrifice and d., 541a; right to regulate questions of eccles. d., 184b; school of voluntary d., mountaineering, 625a; unity of d., 133a; whatever comes from Him, method of d., 882b

Discretion Holy d., 264b; office of d. proceeds from charity, 265a; Virtues demand d., 900a; Without d., virtue becomes vice, 264b

Discrimination D. and segregations, wrong and un-American, 265a

Discussion ought to convert from error, 27a; The feast of reason, 279a

Discussions fruitless or controversial d., 216b

Disdain by expression of mind, 265a; prefer honor to d., 37a

Disease Bait thy d., 762b; common sense and leechcraft cure d., 268b; Free from d., 12b; From laws of health and sickness learn d., 601a; This d. of curiosity, 236a

Diseases first to know whence all d. start, 601a

Disfavor Cross thee quite out of my book, 265b

Disgrace In pow'r unpleased, impatient of d., 751a

Dish Salt and sugar, too much spoils d., 796b; We dipped our hands in d. together, 878b

Dishes books of Bible, d. of feast, 60a; vulgar d. by cooks disguis'd, 287b

Dismissed Go, you are d., 595b

Disobedience obstinate aversion from His laws, 819a; to legitimate authority, rebellion against God, 46b

Disordered our d. wishes and actions, 4a

Dispensation can be granted by legislator, 265b; God wonderful in d. of His works, 43b; relaxation of law, 265b; no d. from natural law, 527a; of mysteries of altar, 68b

Dispensatrix BVM, d. of graces, 90a, 92a

Dispenser property of Church belongs to pope, as principal d., 734a, 735a

Disponit Homo proponit, sed Deus d., 397a

Dispose To yield to what my Saviour shall d., 410b

Disposes Man proposes, but God d., 397a

Disposition habit is a settled d., 417b; To change d., 265b

Dispraising Over-great homeliness engendereth d., 215a

Disputes arbitrate d. on settling days, 29b

Disquisitions Faith is not built on d. vain, 327a, 875b

Dissemble To know how to d., knowledge of kings, 265b

Dissensions like small streams, are first begun, 746a

Dissent rule is far from plain, where all d., 783b

Dissidents d. and Mystical Body, 123a, 771a

Dissolution body of BVM, exempt from dissolution, 39b

Dissolved marriages d. for sake of religion, 267b

Dissonance life's d., 687a

Distil Heavens, distil your balmy showers!, 168a

Distance hair's breadth, great d., 265b

Distant d. prospects please us, 265b; So d. art Thou—yet so nigh, 374a

Distinction D. and variety in world, intended by First Cause, 892b; understand real d. and unity, 889b

Distractions Unmannerly d. come, 719b

Distressed We are easily consoled because easily d., 210b

Distrust all d. behind thee leave, 265b; I will not trust him though my brother, 265b

Disturb Let nothing d. thee, 882a

Diversity d. of religious profession, 183b

Dives I'll be D. still, 280a

Divination forbidden to keep books in which d. taught, 841b

Divine D. Nature and human beings, 21a; D., to the Divinity, 261b; draw near to d. things, 840b; He raised human, without impairing d., 467b; secular affairs one thing, d. another, 699b; task of philosophy, to inquire about the d., 680a; To err is human, to forgive d., 300b

Divine Office clergy bound to recite canonical hours, 267a; composed of words of Spirit of God, 266b; imitate on earth anthems of angels, 266a; many of laity take part in psalmody, 266b; offered to God on behalf of all Christians, 267a; part of divine tradition, 266b; prayer of mystical Body, *the eyes of the Lord in every place*, 266a; thy unwearied watch and varied round, 146a; work of God, 266a

Diviner D. feelings, kindred with the skies, 847a

Divinity angels' true divinity, 20b; d. of Christ and devotion to Mary, 101b; God alone knows depths and riches of His Godhead, 383a; God is one Divinity, 50a; He never imp31arts Himself as He is, 212a, 394a; of Jesus Christ, proved from Gospels, 483a; partaker of our mortality, partakers of His d., 466b; To be immortal is to share in D., 102b, 463a

Divinity (School) Philosophy, not concern of those who pass through D. and Greats, 681a

Divisibility d. of Church, doctrine of Anglicanism, 24a

Divorce and adultery, 267a, 267b; born of perverted morals, 267b; by destiny of death, 267a; dignity of womanhood lessened, 268a;

great evils flow from d., 268a; harm to education of children, 268a; marriages dissolved for sake of religion, 267b; now prayed for, 267a; strike with telling force At evil of d., 268a; 'Twixt soul and body, a d., 455b; women reckoned years by husbands, 268a; world is one wild d. court, 268a; wrong to leave wife who is sterile, 267a

Divorced for incompatibility of temper, 574a; man guilty of adultery if he marries d. woman, 267a

Do d. everything according to gospel, 13a; *Do this for commemoration of me,* 309a, 647b; D. well, and have well, 275a; d. what thou canst, 671b; I see much, but I say little, and d. less, 813b; It is as folk d., not as folk say, 275a; Never do anything thou cannot, 4b; To d. and dare, and die at need, 777a; To have too much to d., safer than too little, 457b; *What they say, d. ye,* 642a

Dock In d., out nettle, 880b

Docta d. ignorantia, 458a

Doctor *D. Devotus,* 106b; d. of the gentiles, 664a; fee d. for nauseous draught, 318a; Good leech is he that can himself recure, 269a; Nor without fees would attend Hippocrates, 268b; of grace, 44b; pronouncements of Augustine or any other d., 875a; There is one D., 480a; Three faces wears the d., 268b

Doctores Ecclesiae, 44b

Doctors bishops, true d. of faith, 70a; ere d. learn'd to kill, 269a; first physicians by debauch were made, 269a; God appointed doctors, 68b; of the faith, 340b; physicians, cautious grown Of other's lives, 269a

Doctrinal law of d. development, 271a

Doctrine all d. which agrees with apostolic churches, 874a; amalgam between eternal faith and temporal opinion, 270b; apostles delivered themselves with clearness, 174a; apostles transmitted teaching received from Christ, 269b; bridge and road of His d., 108b; Christianity is more than a d., 166a; committed to Church and Bible, 63a; complete and perfect in all its parts, 270b, 271a; Every part of system equally certain, 270b; grows in its explication, 271b; held more or less implicitly, 269b; infallibly interpreted by Church, 146a; keep entirely to Christian food, 428b; Let them innovate in nothing, 874a; No d. is defined till it is violated, 274a; no d. rigorously proved by historical evidence, 270a; no pow'r To coin new faith, 269b; not destroyed by progress of knowledge, 270b; of Church as unerring rule, 145b; oracle of revealed d., 23b; private opinions of saints, 874b; refutation of heretics serves sound d., 269b; *same d., in same sense and same mind,* 547b; sound faith of those that are approved, 429a; spiritual medicine for people of God, 727b; subordination of emotion and fancy to d., 58b; teaching of apostles, true gnosis, 873b; those who announce d. other than that received, 269b; truths which have not yet come before us, 57b; unity of d. and infallibility, 129a; what Catholic Church has held universally, 114b; when d. considered dogmatically defined, 274b; whether contained in Scripture, 62b

Doctrine, Development of apostolic Christianity, seen through telescope, 101a; genuine progress, not alteration of faith, 270b, 271a; idea of BVM magnified with time, 101a; in substance, one and same from beginning, 101b

Doctrines All religions have had d., 274a; and form of development, 272a; Church d., powerful weapon, 269b; expand variously according to mind, 272a; growth without change, 101a, 272b; life of d., 271b, 862b; members of one family, 146a; necessary development of Christian d., 22a; not sent into the world for nothing, 269b; principles and d. contrasted, 271b; received from apostles, 116b; require time to be comprehended, 272a

Documents historical conclusions must include more than d., 435a

Doeg, 104b

Doeth He that d. as most men do, 275a

Dog A d. will bark ere he bite, 273a; d.'s tooth, 152a; gentle hound should never play the cur, 273a; hard to make an old d. stoop, 273a; Love me, love my dog, 273a; nought good, sleeping hound to wake, 273a; poor d., not worth the whistling, 273a; Pray tell me, sir, whose d. are you?, 273b

Dogma Assumption, divinely revealed d., 41b; bigot or slave of d., 499b; complete and perfect in all its parts, 271a; further definitions as time goes on, 270a; has been fundamental principle of my religion, 274a; held more or less implicitly, 269b; I believe whole revealed d., 146a; implications of belief in Catholic d., 57b; liberty of d., 274b; live and die upon a d., 760b; only reasonable d. lives, 27b; Regarding substance, faith does not grow, 271b; same d., same meaning, same thought, 271a; Scripture and foundations of Catholic d., 60b; when doctrine considered dogmatically defined, 274b

Dogmas ancient d. thoroughly filed and polished, 271b; and science or reason, 274a; badge of heresy: unfruitful, no theology, 430a; can be reconciled with history, 274b; Catholic d., divine fact, 273b; Church does not diminish or add, 273b; deposited with Church, 273b; fettered by antiquated d., 27b; growth without change, 272b; irreformable, 129b; mere belief in d. from history, not Catholic, 270a; must be believed with divine and Catholic faith, 274b; not mere developments of latent germ, 272b; proposed by judgment of Church, 118b; responsibility of council or pontiff, 274b; Truths turn into d., 274b, 885a; whether contained in Scripture, 62b

Dogmatic Church's d. use of history, 270a; d. decisions of Apostolic See, 700b; d. faith, 324b; d. lucidity of Declaration of Independence, 15b; d. slumber of denial, 12a; 'eccles. and d. system,' 147b; Religion must be d., 274a; wind up Englishman to d. level, 297a

Dogmatism necessary to human mind, 273b

Dogmatists conscious and unconscious d., 275a; For modes of faith let graceless zealots fight, 275a

Dogs cannot exist without men, 273a; Do not give that which is holy to d., 194a; Hungry d. will eat dirty puddings, 273a; more faithful than friends, 273a; No creature more sagacious than d., 272b

Doing D., of value, 319a; Knowledge comes of d., 514b; Saying and d. are two things, 275a; We are responsible for d. what we can, 768a

Dole His d. is soon done, 847a

Doleful Stood d. she, 94a

Doll tragedy of child over broken d., 24b

Dolors On the Virgin's d. seven, 94b

Dome reverberating d., 105b

Domestic Milk-soup men call d. bliss, 574b

Domesticity Many girls have plenty to do at home, 113a

Dominate man who can d. London dinner-table, 239

Domination hypocrite, diverts government to d., 456b

Dominations one of nine orders of angels, 18b

Domine Gloria tibi, D., 589a; D., non sum dignus, 595a; Laus tibi, Domine, 589b; Miserere, D.!, 258b

Domini Coena D., 597a; Corpus D. nostri custodiat animam meam, 595a; Pax D. sit semper vobiscum, 594a; Sanguis D. nostri custodiat animam meam, 595a

Dominic, St., 615b

Dominicans, 275b

Dominicus Dies D. non est juridicus, 854a

Dominion d., device of law of nations, 46a, 178b; Unbelief, not inconsistant with d., 178b

Dominium d. politicum et regale, 405b; secular d., instituted by Church, 46a

Domino Gratias agamus, D. Deo Nostro, 591a

Dominum Habemus ad D., 591a; Laudans invocabo D., 595a; D. illuminatio mea, 536b; D. vobiscum, 588b; Sanctus, sanctus, sanctus D. Deus Sabaoth, 591a

Donation of Constantine, 175a, 175b, 177a, 211a

Donatists, 50b

Donatus, Proconsul of Africa, 173b

Done My soul! what hast thou d. for God?, 366b; Nothing d. at all, if man waited, 228a; Sooner said than d., 275a; Things d. cannot be undone, 275a; whatsoever thou wouldst not wish to be d. to thee, 397b

Doom assault of th'universal d., 248b; That day of d., 503a; The builders of their d., 261a

Door each sits still in his own d., 77b; 'Gainst her thou canst not bar d., 157a; God never shuts one d. but He opens two, 275b; of Catholic faith, 147b; Ye beg at wrong man's d., 56a

Doorkeeper At gate of monastery, let there be wise old man, 275b; O blessed d. of heaven, 674b

Doorstep Slippery the d. of great house, 275b

Doors d. of destiny, 392a

Double leading a d. life, 456b

Double-minded find difficulties, 263a

Doubt charms me no less than knowledge, 276a; D. is brother devil to Despair!, 276a; Everyone

who knows d., knows a truth, 883a; I only learned to d. at last, 276a; masses of d. that are floating about, 147a; Ten thousand difficulties do not make one d., 263a; Time trieth truth in every d., 276a; Whose definition is a d., 218b; Zeus is dead, and all the gods but D., 276a

Doubter God makes no man a slave, no d. free, 537b

Doubters future belongs to believers, not d., 58b

Doubting O d. heart!, 276a

Doubts For subtle d. had simple clues, 276a; if he d., he thinks, 275b; Who d. that he lives, 275b

Dove Blessed Spirit! D. divine!, 440a; By all the eagle in thee, all the d., 258a; Holy Ghost descending in likeness of d., 480b; Most beauteous d. with wings of gold, 461a; My d. is one, 134b; sent to view the waves' decrease, 666a

Dowry Dear hope! earth'd d., heav'n's debt!, 445b

Down D, d. proud sense!, 77b; D. in adoration falling, 74a; Stuft with d. of angels' wing, 55b

Dragon fairy-tale provides St. George to kill d., 324b

Drama danger to Christians, 276a; differences between d. and other kinds of art, 276b; fired with muses' madness, 6a; Sure there's a fate in plays, 276b; with omission of principal part, 393a;

Drawing-room devotional in a d., 288a

Draws Why He d. one, and another not, 723a

Dreadful D. as a battle arrayed, 41a

Dream d. of joy all but in vain, 277a; The d. is over, 416a

Dreamer a d. lives forever, 277b; Oh, do not let the d. die, 347b

Dreams And twenty thousand d.!, 277b; At break of day, d. are true, 277a; Cast away d. of darkness, 7b; deception of d., 276b; d. and law of God., 276b; D. are we, shadows, visions, 13a; D., who loves d.!, 827a; Enough of d.!, 277b; From all ill d. defend our eyes, 201b; grow holy put in action, 277a; mists In trance round the soul!, 277a; Oh! miserable power To d. allow'd, 277a

Dreary D.! weary! Weary! d.!, 791b

Dress fashion of country is the rule, 278a; outward robes show soul's habiliments, 278a; Singularity in d. is ridiculous, 278a; there is a kind of matronly d., 278a; We've ceased to rectify What women wear, 278a; Who is worse shod than shoemaker's wife?, 278a; whole world is under petticoat government, 278a; without affronting Christian decorum, 278a

Drill-master makes but an indifferent apostle, 614a

Drink All his occasions, to eat and d., 287b; Bacchus ever fair, ever young, 279a; bird can't fly on one wing, 280a; Blood of God is d. for me, 72a; D. deep, or taste not the Pierian spring, 532a; first drop that kilt me, 279b; Have another d., 280a; he cannot make him d., 446b; in Fleet Street, I learned to d., 279b; regard wine as drug, not a d., 279b; safest way to d., d. carelessly, 279b; sing when we d., 278b; Take and d. ye all of this, 592a; worst way to d., d. medicinally, 279b

Drinketh As deep d. the goose as the gander, 403a

Drinking Art sick from vinous surfeiting?, 278b; D. is the soldier's pleasure, 279a, 829b; Fill the bumper fair!, 279a; her jolly whistle well y-wet, 278b; immoderate d. of wine, 280a; largely sobers us again, 532a; man that boozed of that, 278b; Repeat the dose at morn, 278b; so far as d. is a sin, 279b; the flow of soul, 279a; Wreath the bowl, 279b

Drop A d., one d., 280a; first d. that kilt me, 279b

Drops D. do pierce the stubborn flint, 237a

Drought of March hath pierced the root, 29b

Drowning I am d. in a stormier sea, 492a

Drug a deadly d., 428b; Go now, and with some daring d., 762b; one man's poison, another man's d., 690b

Drum double beat Of thundering d., 280a

Drunk He that killeth a man when he is d., 625b; My mother, d. or sober, 15b

Drunken as d. as a mouse, 280a; d. man is living corpse, 280a; like d. swine, 281b

Drunkenness business of the day, 281b; premature old age, 280a; ruin of reason, 280a, 280b

Dryden, John, 281b

Dryness act done with d. of spirit, 281b

Dubious d. is unlimited, full of hope for everybody, 226a

Duchesses Of unknown d. lewd tales we tell, 799a

Due Justice, virtue that gives to each his d., 504a; To sin, not to render to God his d., 817b; To everyone should be rendered what is d. him, 281b

Duelling detestable custom of d., 281a

Dukes origin of kings and d., 844b

Dulia, 928a

Dull Be thou dull, 281a; d. prospect of a distant good, 497b; I am too d. to praise thee, 79b

Dullness Born a goddess, d. never dies, 281a

Dum D. vivimus, vivamus, 549a

Dunces wit with d. and a dunce with wits, 281a

Dung Man, sack of d., food of worms, 569a

Dunghill after d., comes Kingdom of Heaven, 463b; As spotless sun doth on the d. shine, 322a

Dutchman They who see the Flying D., 365a

Dusk Out of d. a shadow, Then, a spark, 315b

Dust A handful of d. in a shroud of shame, 251a; A heap of d. remains of thee, 281a; All is d., ashes, shadows!, 244b, 249a; Apotheosis of d., 281b; dry regardless d., 218b; Learn, O d., to obey, 451b; Remain eterne when body is but d., 901b; *Remember, man, that thou art d.,* 37b; returns to d., 244b; She that was young and fair, Fallen to d., 413a; Thou, O d., sole earthly thing, 281b; What d. we dote on, 570b; whoso doth us good turn, we write it in d., 471b

Duties Conscience has rights because it has d., 210a, 470a; human d., not empty word, 777a

Duty brave endeavor To do thy d.,

281b; conscience and sense of d., 209b; dereliction of d. involves punishment, 768a; do your d. in ninety-nine points, 281b; highest d., to respect authority, 46b; man's d. to God, before all else, 282a; The first source of d. is prudence, 738b; what we've got to do, 282a

Dwell in spirit amid heavenly things, 35b; When God comes down each day to d., 198a; Would'st thou d. in joy abounding?, 232a

Dwelling BVM, d. of the Illimitable, 39b, 81a; eternal d. in heaven, 246a; ramparts of a Godhead's d., 13b

Dwelling-place fitting d. for Holy Spirit, 860b; Look down from Thy holy d., 593b

Dwells In me He d.; in Him I live, 197b, 888a

Dyen To d. when that he is best of name, 248a

Dying All hope of never d., 299b, 623b; because I do not die, 889a; d., bless the hand that gave the blow, 349b; d. with a desire to see God, 257b; how people will know they're d., 282b; I am d. beyond my means, 253a; I am d. of a hundred good symptoms, 282b, 521b; Life is a play acted by d. men, 543a; Mere d. is too good for one, 282a; no sooner do we begin to live in d. body, 247a; only d. do not love noise of action, 217a; those whom certainty of d. afflicteth, 246a; to put off a garment, 282a

E

Each E. man for himself, 806b

Eagle By all the e. in thee, 258a; Like the young e. who has lent his plume, 282a; The e. nests near the sun, 443b; upon my e.'s wings I bore this wren, 478b; where e.'s iron wing May scarcely dare, 453a

Ear None please the fancy who offend the e., 923a

Earnest Everything, plain and easy to the earnest, 263a

Ears Come together by the e., 746a; Fields have eyes and woods have e., 323b; if their e. wasn't burnin', 403b, 807b; Let Thy merciful e. be open, 586b, 717a; Oh! open Thou mine e., 396b; Small pitchers have wide e., 282b; to do thine e. glow!, 282b

Earth abode of this earthly sojourn, 246a; bade the e. stand firm for aye, 373a; e.'s darkened place, 41b; E. to heaven it reuniteth, 168a; ere she clasps us to her breast, 283a; excluded all things of earth, 37a; foundations of e. were shaken, 400a; God Whom e., and sea, and sky, 81b; has no sorrow that Heaven cannot heal, 304a; hath no bigness at all, 414a; Heaven and e. in ashes ending!, 502b; Here on e. nothing is stable, 351b; leave dull e. behind us, 279b; O God of e. and altar, 726a; rendereth up her undeserved prey, 40a; Sweet e., we know thy dimmest mysteries, 686b; the e., the sea, 20b; this ambiguous e., 492b; This congregated ball, 282b; To earth's remotest boundaries, 166b; younger, than I am old, 11a

Earthly during this our e. pilgrimage, 560a; not to mind e. things, 425a; spiritual life is more

worthy than e., 177b; Where is e. endeavor?, 244b

Earthquake Golden E. in the east, 854b; Lord, thou hast crushed Thy tender ones, 283a

Ease He lives at e. that freely lives, 353b; Of sufferance cometh e., 851b; prodigal of e., 11b; Take mine e. in mine inn, 283a; To flee charge, and find e., 154a

East E., oh, e. of Himalay, 240b; Go thou to e., I west, 654b; Lo, in the sanctuaried e., 78b; longer e., shorter west, 283a; The e. is come, 299a

Easter All hail! dear Conqueror!, 286b; All mortal men this day rejoice, 286a; At the Lamb's high feast we sing, 284b; Behold, the night of sorrow gone, 286b; celebrated on no day save Sunday, 283a; Christ is risen from the dead, 284b; Christ is sacrificed as our Pasch, 285a; Come, ye faithful, raise the strain, 285b; controversy over date of E., 697a; death by death down doth He tread, 284b; feast of earth and heaven, 286a; Hail! Festal day!, 283b, 286a; its virtue and its might, 286a; Know ye, this is E. Day, 286b; Mary, rejoice, rejoice today!, 286a; most solemn of all solemnities, 284a; mystery of Lord's Resurrection, 283a; mystic Passover, 284b, 285a; night of E., spent in vigil, 285a; Now He lives, no more to die, 285b; O thou, the heavens' eternal King, 284a; O what a victory is Thine!, 286b; Paschal sacrifice, world's salvation, 285a; Passover of gladness!, 285a; Purge we out the ancient leaven, 286a; Rejoice and exult, O Sion, 285b; Shine, shine, O new Jerusalem, 285b; The world's blossom smells of God, 287a; This is the day which the Lord hath made, 284a; this sacred night, bright with glory or resurrection, 441b; Today the grave hast lost its sting!, 286a; Where is thy sting, O death?, 283b; With Christ we died, with Christ we rose, 283b

Eastern Church O E. Church! imperial schism, 801a; norm of celibacy, 150b

Eat All his occasions, to e. and drink, 287b; *Give them to e.,* 72a; never eat but sitting down, 287a; *Take and e. ye all of this,* 592a

Eating At meat her manners were well taught, 572b; before food, bless the Maker, 278b; He needs no more than birds, 287b; Rest, cheerfulness, and table thinly spread, 268b

Eats He who e. from the pope, dies of it!, 710a

Ebb He was at an e., 775a

Ecce E. Agnus Dei, 595b

Ecclesia Anglicana, 140b; e. abhorret a sanguine, 103b; *E. non moritur,* 138a; *foris autem ab e.,* 126a; signifies 'calling forth', 127a; *Ubi Petrus, ibi e.,* 709a

Ecclesiam extra e. nulla salus, 125b

Ecclesiarum maximus ecclesiarum instructor, 44b; *Omnium urbis et orbis e. mater et caput,* 171a

Ecclesiastical e. order subject to one person, 405a; difference between secular and e. order, 433b; Do not interfere in e. affairs, 172a; e. liberty and Roman

Church, 177b; E. power immediately from God, 180b
Echo How sweet the answer E. makes, 287b
Economic e. affairs, brought into subjection to guiding principle, 201a; E. life, inspired by Christian principles, 287b; e. motives and communists, 199b
Economics e., not vital factor in development of civilization, 186b; must conform to common good, 287b; politics and ethics, as expressions of e., 598b; restored to sanity and right order, 288a
Economy cautious dispensation of truth, 288a; national e., its end, 288a; principle of e., acted on every day, 288a
Ecstasy By all thy lives and deaths of love, 258a; Deep in grief or e., 232a; e. and will, 288b; height of love's e., 288b; never a saint but has had e., 288b; perfect soul, rapt by contemplation, 213a; thou the e. of prayers, 59a; union, rapture, transport, all one, 288b; uplifted to that vision, 211a
Ecstatic keen e. love, 20b
Ecumenical Church takes no part in 'e.' conventions, 771b; e. bishop, 700a
Eden America, E. in a wicked universe, 16a; believed to be Earth's center, 288b; Bethlehem hath opened E., 169b; in E.'s grots they lie, 243a; place of Adam's grave, 288b; To water that E., 250b
Edict constitution or e., 524b
Edification authority unto e., 129a
Educate Christian parents, to e. children as members of Church, 579b; how to e. the masses, 289a; Why do we e.?, 290a
Educated e. men can do what illiterate cannot, 289b; people must be e., 290a
Education aids Church in her mission, 290a; By e. most have been misled, 289a; All things now, to be learned at once, 289b; can never be substitute for sacraments, 292b; Catholic e. in Catholic schools, 291b; Catholic e. must recognize catholicity of truth, 290a; Catholics, trained to cope with age, 290a; child, not mere creature of State, 291a; Christianity must be principle of all e., 289a; Church concerned with all phases of e., 291b; consists in preparing man for what he must be, 292a; creed of U.S. is e., 292a; e. and actualization of Incarnation, 290a; e. and exclusion of religion, 292a, 393a; e. and modern educationists, 290b; end of marriage, procreation and e. of children, 578b; Every Christian child has right to instruction, 858b; Every e. teaches a philosophy, 393a; gentle contempt for e., 290b; if liberal e. be good, must be useful, 35a, 289b, 290a; In countries of mixed creeds, 291b; men of liberal e., 35a; tax levied to dispel mental darkness, 801b; not omnipotent, 292b; One generation forms another, 289a; Parents bound to provide for e. of children, 291a; particular place of religious and moral instruction, 289b, 291a, 393a; preparation for knowledge, 289b; religious e. and parents, 291a; subject of Christian e. is man, 291b; To exclude Church from e. of youth, fatal error, 845a; To train a citizen, to

train a critic, 290b; two inconsistent conceptions about education, 393a; University e. without theology, 864a; vastness of the word 'e.', 290b
Educationists modern e. and Catholic schools, 393a; modern e. and education, 291a
Eel as an e. by the tail, 293b
Effort God only asks you to do your best, 293b
Egere melius est minus e. quam plus habere, 361a
Egg vulgar boil an e., 293b; When on the grass a frail, crushed e. I find, 837a
Eggs newly laid, 347b; not forbidden by abstinence, 3b; ways to dress e., 293b
Eglise Près de l'é., loin de Dieu, 138a
Ego Ego te absolvo a peccatis tuis, 2b
Egypt Because I led thee out of land of E., 400b; loud timbrel o'er E.'s dark sea!, 293b; Where high the tombs of royal E. heave, 643b
Egyptian The proud E. queen, 585a
Egyptians drowning of E. prefigured baptism, 51b
Eileen Aroon, 556a, 884b
Eire Beyond the four seas of E., 910b
Elbow-room Great minds need e., 608a
Elect, The All Thy saints and e. acknowledge Thee, 792b; alone do not constitute Church, 127a; Believe that you are chosen, 797b; E. and Church, 126b; God alone knows number of e., 293b; How is it God disregards, those whom He chose?, 851a; In charity, all e. made perfect, 154b; numbered among flock of Thy e., 591b, 665a; O chosen band, to the great supper called, 293b; see Divine Essence, 302b; small flock, named 'after God's own heart', 411a; the e. Of generous love, 304b; Where souls e. abide, 243a
Election Mary, Queen by singular election, 97b; power cannot be created, save by e. and consent, 405b; vessel rare of God's e., 97b
Eleison Agios o Theos, ischyros, athanatos, e. imas, 589a; Kyrie e., Christe e., 588a
Elements e. of bread and wine in Eucharist, 71a; things primarily created in web of e., 224b
Elephant Nothing appeases enraged e. so much as little lamb, 364b; So large a trunk before, 294a
Elias Now riseth up E.' little cloud, 461a
Eligistis Non vos e. me, sed ego vos elegi, 112b
Elite difference between common people and e., 58a
Elixir vitae Beauty's e., praise, 55a
Elizabeth I, 141a, 190a, 294a
Elocution art of clothing and adorning thought, 685a
Eloquence Aristotle inferior in e. to Plato, 31a; art of saying things, 294b; e. and truth, 294a; Thou couldst a people raise, 69a
Ely Merry sang the monks who in E. fare, 619a
Elysian where the deep E. rest?, 415a
Emancipation gradual e. from

earthly influence, 181b; Roman Catholic E. Act, 141b
Embrace breaks through all ten heavens to our e., 469a; Meet and unite in sweet e.!, 197b; my enamored soul e. and kiss, 562b
Embraces chaste e. of soul's Spouse, 213a
Emergence e. of created things, 224a
Emmanuel from thee E. shows forth, 82a; O come, O come, E., 8b; true God, 81a; We must know Him by His names, E. and Jesus, 388b
Emotion hobby, never to be roused by any e., 847b; Human e. has power of influencing, 294b; truth must not be submerged by e., 58b
Emotional e. revivalist, 294b
Emotions impossible to live for ever on the heights, 294b; No human e. can be strictly attributed to God, 387b; should be servants, 294b
Emperor alleged, all things are permitted e., 173a; any mighty e., How puissant so he be, 570a; called son of the Church?, 173a earthly e., 175b; God, E. of heaven, 63b, 175b; has chief place in dignity, 174a, 395a; I will frankly call the e. lord, 550a; leads mankind to temporal happiness, 180a; makes laws which he is first to keep, 528a; must submit to those who have charge of divine things, 174b; not fitting for e. to deny freedom of speech, 355a; of Rome, appointed by God, 779a; Palaces belong to e., churches to bishop, 173a; We follow whatever e. has done without sin, 175a; We respect him as the chosen of Lord, 171b; within the Church, not above Church, 172b, 173a, 174b
Emperors conquered, under name of Christ, 120b; e. and orthodoxy of belief, 174b; good e. love freedom, bad, slavery, 355a; in matters of faith, bishops wont to judge e., 172b; in service of God and holy faith, 172b; laws command even the e., 886a; our God-fearing rulers, 87a; pope may depose e., 175b, 701a; princes of earth, 120b
Empire All e., no more than pow'r in trust, 406a; God has granted you the e., 172a; greater than e., to submit princely authority to laws, 508a; My mind to me an e. is, 607a; one thing make conquests, another consolidate e., 208a; that is the meaning of E. Day, 296b; This is the song of the e. builder, 305b
Empires failed because founded by strong men, 136b; Monarchies and e. rely on physical force, 766a; power of giving kingdoms and e., to true God, 510a
Employer duty to give every one what is just, 516b; God the great E., pays for every human deed of goodness, 604b; must never tax workers beyond strength, 516b; must respect moral dignity of laborer, 112b
Empress queen of heaven, e. of skies, 40a
Emptiness e. of complete repose, 107b
Empty man must e. himself, 629a
Emptying The e. of Himself was no loss of power, 467b

Enchant E. me with your spells of art, 107a

Encyclopedia test of good e., 395a

End Among all causes, e. holds primacy, 373b; an e. there is of every deed, 395a; as God, the e. of our going, 466b, 864a; Begin nothing without eye to th'e, 149b; best way to e. well is to begin well, 56b; Charity is both means and e., 156b; E. of all ways, 492b; e. of every episode, e. of the world, 446a; everything attains proper e., 671b; everything hath e., 395a, 497b; honor'd in his e., 493b; of good things is best, 56b; O Lord! make an end!, 521a; O Thou, our Author and our E., 445b; rather a good e. he winneth, 56a; The e. proveth everything, 395a; the future, always our e., 420a; ultimate e., first of all causes, 373b; Who had the worst e. of the staff?, 264a

Endeavor Where is earthly e.?, 244b

Ending hard beginning maketh good e., 56b; In the e. of the year, 168a

Endings In Christians we look not to beginnings but to e., 163a

Endowed few highly e. men will rescue world, 1b

Endowments e. which belong to American people, 17a

Ends All is well that e. well, 395a; God has assigned to humanity, 666b; Indifferent acts, judged by e., 395a; Joyful such e. as endless joys begin, 472a

Endurance perfection of charity, 395a; St. Paul, greatest example of patient e., 663b

Endured What can't be cured must be e., 295b

Enemy absolute monarchy, e. of the Church, 3a; Everyone is his own e., 295b; fear of the e. being removed, 652a, 665a; hands of the e., 245b; How could I know he was my e., 295b; insult of an e. can sometimes correct, 359b; make an e. of all mankind, 432b; So long as the e. can enter into our souls, 625a; The e. is glad to make you lose time, 869b; world is small, when e. is loose, 359b

Enemies Christians do good to their e., 163a; crafty e. that lie in wait, 196a; Ill fortune makes e., 359b; man cannot be too careful in choice of e., 295b; rescued from friendly hands, 271a; To pray for one's e., 297b

Enforce ability to e., condition of ability to command, 529a

Engine force of love is an e. of the soul, 214a; The unbreathing e. marks no tune, 568a

England Before whose feet the world divide, 296b; bring Thine E. back to thee!, 535b; Catholic E. restored in ecclesiastical firmament, 141b; divided into three classes, 296b; does not understand America enough, 16a; Dread thine own power!, 296a; earth, a place on which E. is found, 296b; E. and America, much alike, 16b; E. and shops, 296b; E. and survival of Catholic Church, 141b; E. look up, thy soil is stain'd with blood, 583b; E.'s excellence, fair enough for me, 296a; E.! what shall men say of thee, 296b; governed by Scotchmen, Americans, and Jews, 297b; head of Protestantism, 737a; Isn't

E.'s parting soul that nerves my tongue?, 296a; laws of E., neither better nor worse, 529b; literature of E., a living voice, 297a; O E., how hast thou forgot!, 666a; optimistic about E., 296b; O royal E.! happy child, 296a; paradise of little men and purgatory of great, 296a; party system in E., efficient machine, 407a; Pope has no temporal power in E., 141b; Protestant world in E. today, 738a; reconciled to Holy See, 141a; Religion is the least of all our trade, 756a; ruled by few immodest, 297b; Tartuffe has emigrated to E., 296b; There will never want in England men, 141a; Tyre of the west, 296a

England, Church of Anglican orders invalid, 648b; cannot call itself 'bride of the Lamb', 23b; city of confusion and house of bondage, 24a; does not possess apostolic succession, 23b; great national organ, 23b; has no power of rejecting, 272b; impossible to be Catholic in C., 220b; King, supreme head on earth, 140b; O my mother, whence is this unto thee, 23a; professes never to be in wrong, 23a; repudiated papal authority, 141a; time-honored institution, 23b; treasures accessories of Catholic worship, 23a

English E. air that was my breath, 296b; E. are a modest people, 297b; E. Church shall be free, 178a; E. Church was, E. Church was not, 142a; E. Protestantism, religion of throne, 23b; E. statesman bribed, not to be bribed, 909a; Freedom, an E. subject's sole prerogative, 353b; I prefer E. habits of devotion to foreign, 262b; something E. in repression of one's feelings, 297b; so noble a language, 297a; Than the bold E., none more fame have won, 320a; things which E. public never favors, 297a; whether God loves or hates the E., 351b

Englishman E.'s passion for ritual, 777b; greatness of England ought to make an E. humble, 663b; has instinctive veneration for law, 838a; never among under-dogs, 297b; optimistic about England, 296b; rather be an E., than belong to any other race, 297a; real reason an E. does not talk, 857b; sets up English home wherever he goes, 476b; takes for granted own superiority, 18a; takes pleasures sadly, 16b; wind up E. to dogmatic level, 297a

Englishmen as generous as they are hasty, 297a; bonds that bind E. to America, 16b; brave Britons, foreign laws despised, 297a; do not understand English system, 16b; most suspicious and touchy, 297a; Protestants, so far as not Catholic, 116b

Englishry E. shrunken, 160a

Enjoy ever seeing, ever shall e., 97a

Enjoying art of e. everybody, 263a

Enjoyment Lust, e. of one's self without reference to God, 566b

Enkindle O Charity, my God, e. me!, 215b

Enlighten reason of unbeliever, 27a; them that sit in darkness, 8a

Enlightened mystically e. by the threefold Unity, 438b

Enlightenment thought that has not been thought out, 681a

Enmity between What is of God and man, 397a; eternal e. between woman and serpent, 89b; free from all e. toward all men, 565a

Enna, Sicily, 843a

Ennoble What can e. sots, or slaves, or cowards?, 637a

Enough e. and too much, 298a; E. is e., 298a; He that knoweth when he hath e., 298a

Ensign Bright e. of the free!, 345b; E. of the people, 8a

Enslaved e. by dead creeds, 27b

Enter e. into holy of holies with pure souls, 587b

Enterprise begun of God, cannot be withstood, 479b; private e. and community, 221b

Entertain others, as if you came from other world, 636a

Entertainment five people do a thing for fun, 298a

Enthusiastic E. about existence of enthusiasm, 102a

Enthusiasts their common enthusiasm for leader, 147b

Entomb men e. themselves from night and day!, 185b

Entrance, Great, 589b

Entrance, Little, 589a

Entreaty Petition ineffectual, when barren e., 715b

Envied Better e. than pitied, 298a

Envy foul sore of e. corrupts heart, 298a; No e., no revenge, no rage, no pride, 655a; Not to give way to e., 298a; of a foreign tyrant Threateneth kings, 713b; The e., malice, and pride, 411a; to which th' ignoble mind's a slave, 298b

Eparchy bishops appointed by bishops of e., 67b

Ephesus, Ecumenical Council of, 81a

Epiclesis, 592b

Epics exceedingly mortal e. or tragedies, 689a

Epicureans E., object of pleasure, 683b

Epicurus he was E. owen son, 683b

Epileptics barred from holy orders, 649a

Epiphany day on which Savior appeared to gentiles, 298b; God revealed to gentiles by a star, 299a; its power not past, 298b; Look up, sweet Babe, 299a; make merry with water turned into wine, 299a; This day, Church joined unto heavenly Bridegroom, 299a; Thou didst appear, O Light inaccessible, 299a; wise men hasten to marriage supper of King, 299a

Episcopal e. order essential to Church, 69b; grant bishop an e. chair, 68b; ordinary and immediate e. jurisdiction, 707b; Peter, chief of e. order, 699a

Episcopate bishop chosen by Father for e., 67a; chief apostolate, preferred to any e., 676a; continue blamelessly in e., 68a; e. is one, 299b; heavy yoke of gospel, 68b; no man, who may not be called to e., 117b; part held by each severally and jointly, 133a, 299b; perfection of ministry, 68a, 727a; received by imposition of hands, 68b; succession from apostles, 299b

Episode end of every e., end of the world, 446a

Epistle at Mass, 589a

Epitome Man, e. of the world, 570a

Equal all men e. in claim to justice, 16a; by nature men e., 299b, 300a; in the dust be e. made, 249a

Equality e. and the French, 300a; e. of men before God, 300a; In Father unity, in Son e., in Holy Ghost union, 368b; Love either finds e. or makes it, 555a; official inequality, founded on unofficial e., 31a; realize e. with others, 713b

Equals amongst e. lies no last appeal, 737a; presumption, lordship over e., 845a

Equi E. donati dentes non inspiciuntur, 365b

Equity e. is nothing else than God, 300a; E. is the agreement of things, 300a; Justice differs from e., 505a; king's chief duty, to govern with e. and justice, 507b

Erin what matter, when for E. dear we fall!, 476a; who relied Upon E.'s honor and E.'s pride, 475a

Eros there Anteros with Eros, 41a; O, unknown E., What this breeze Of sudden wings, 917a

Err Every man may e., but not the whole, 129b; The most may e. as grossly as the few, 671a, 739b; To e. is human, to forgive divine, 300b, 349b

Erravi E. cum Petro, 521a

Erred I have e. with Peter, 521a

Erring e. repent and return to unity of truth, 431b

Error accepting what is false as true, 300b; all adversity and e. being destroyed, 134a, 793a; death that all e. is, 382a; devilish to remain wilfully in e., 300b; difference between heresy and e., 432a; effect of e., ultimately to promote truth, 885b; essence of e., 300b; e. of head, not of heart, 300b; every e. is erroneous, 301a; Fact and argument, tests of truth and e., 885b; hasty assumption of those in error, 38b; latitudinarian and sectarian e., 129a; *Lord, if we be in error,* 119a; may flourish for a time, 885b; Most mistaken people mean well, 301a; no authority has power to impose e., 47a; portion of divine system, instead of the whole, 146a; something to be said for every e., 301a; The natural always is from e. free, 551b

Errors All aberrations, founded on some truth, 300b; E., like straws, upon the surface flow, 300b; to confute e., 190a

Escape The birds were flown, 301a

Escapism men avoid unhappy thoughts, 301a

Espouse *I will e. thee to me in faith,* 325b

Espoused Mother of God, both maid and e., 82b

Esse Omne namque e. ex forma est, 350a

Essence angel is intelligent e., 19a; divine e. and creatures, 225b; divine e. is life, not movement, 225b; Divine E. seen by blessed, 302b, 394b; God is only immutable substance or e., 380b; God understands all things in His e., 384a, 903b; highest e., 224b; one thing, existence of thing, another, what it is, 374b; We suck out of all things kind of e., 514b

Essences e. of forms are many, 883b; e. or substances admit of accidents, 301, 380b

Established *I have e. thee above nations,* 701a

Establishment church e., settled by

law, 141b; no law respecting e. of religion, 184b

Estate Content thyself with thine e., 215a; heaven and earth, high and low e., 483a; He had his jest, and they had his e., 320a

Esteem cannot be won by flattery, 301b; E. not thyself better than others, 451a; e. of his fellows, 301b; e. of persons, amuses and contents us, 14a; man not satisfied without e. of men, 367b; noble and delicate sentiment, 301b

Eternal Amid the e. silences, 483a; E. rest grant unto them, O Lord, 767a; God, not confined in time, for He is e., 387b; How dread are Thine e. years, 340a; let e. be object of thy desire, 860a; Whose name is called the E., 167b, 390b

Eternal Life Abraham's bosom, 243b, 301b; actual knowing of truth, 301b; admitted to e. by baptism, 49a, 51a; After resurrection, we shall enjoy e., 463b, 561b; All space is its outer gate, 305b; All thy good works Shall own thee there, 402b; an everlasting home, 244b; arrows hitting the mark of beatitude, 305b; At heaven's court, 250a; attainment of God, beatitude itself, 458b; Beautiful habitations, auras of delight!, 304b; birth and death do not apply, 65b; bridal chamber of His light, 229a, 500a; call me to Thy face, 75b; chambers of rest with Abraham, 243b; Christians' future country, 680b; companionship with Christ, 71b; contemplation of God, promised as goal, 211b; courts of heavenly city, 41a, 302a; divine tabernacles, 39b; each heaven for every soul, Is paradise, 302b; end for which we were created, 37a; Endless repose, 89a, 245a, 516a; eternal consummation of all our joys, 211b; Eucharist, assurance of e., 71b; everlasting happiness, 89b, 302a; fellowship of eternity, 123b; fields of heaven, 277b; for e., many scarce move a foot, 303a; From death to life eternal, 285b; garb of immortality, 215b; gate of everlasting life, 74b, 118b, 284a; gifts of e., 813a; God has given us e. through Jesus, 70b; God's ultimate surprise, 653b; God shall be all, in all ever blest, 785a; greater than coming to be, 224a; great supper of blessed Lamb, 293b; halls of the just, 89a; happy land, 653b; happy mansion of city above!, 303a; heavenly glory, 41b; heavenly life of incorruptibility, 39b; heavenly shore, 155b, 232a; Heirs of the palace glad, 304b; heritage of angels, 71b; homesick for eternal hills, 47b, 306a; hope of future meed, 96b, 445a; I believe in *life everlasting,* 226b; In God's most holy sight, 41a, 304a; in God's vineyard, no man but is called, 303a; In the gardens of God, 41a; Jesus, Lord of life eternal, 36a; kingdom of heaven, 37a, 173b, 305b; life hereafter will be praise of God, 714b; life that will never pass away, 5a; life's procession down eternity, 251b; light divine, 41a, 229a, 245a, 277a, 303a, 500a; lot of saints, 125a, 479a; *Love* of heaven, only *way* to heaven, 304b; martyrs receive kingdom without baptism, 49b; may intercession of BVM lead us to e., 90a; men ordained to e., 765b; meritorious works proportionate to everlasting

life, 412a; more durable than fate, 305b; new life when sin shall be no more, 20a; Nobody excluded, except through own fault, 302a; no small matter, lose or gain kingdom of heaven, 303a; O Paradise! O Paradise! 304a; O world invisible, we view thee, 305a; One minute of heaven is worth them all, 304a; our fatherland, 5a, 60b; our heavenly home, 132a, 246a; our home in paradise, 246a, 500b; palm of e., 231a; partakers of this e., 463b; peace of heavenly City, 665a; possession of all joy, 96b, 246a, 500b; prize, immortality and e., 43a, 246a, 304b; rest in everlasting bliss, 245a; rewards of salvation, 7b, 88b; shining, tranquil and refreshing places, 245b; Short arm needs man to reach to heaven, 305a; short, dark passage to eternal light, 249a; Soar up, my soul, unto thy rest, 303b; sons of men made sons of Most High, 254b; souls with the saints, 245b; that heavenly country, 251a, 302a; that high place, 84b; the crown that lasts for aye, 298b; th' eternal sigh For which we bear to live, 420a; the flame-wrapped goal, 424b; The gates are pass'd, heaven is won!, 304a; the holy place, 90a; There is life for evermore, 479a; There's nothing true but Heaven, 304a; there will be degrees of dignity, 302a; *This is e., that they may know Thee,* 325b; This is the kingdom our brother built, 305b; Thou shalt reign immortally, 281b; through His side A way to paradise provide, 401a; time between death and resurrection, 246b; to desire e. with spiritual longing, 302a; to deserve everlasting life, 412a; to pass into immortal life, 303b; to reign with Christ, 252b; to this port at every step I go, 59b; visions yet to be, 464a, 521a; way to heaven, of like length and distance, 303a; we look for the life of the world to come, 226b; What a city, the New Jerusalem!, 500b; What does heaven mean for rational soul?, 303a; What is the key to everlasting life?, 305b; What joys await us there!, 421b, 479a; where all are fair, 96a; where there is no sickness, nor sadness, 245b, 479a; Where they that loved are blest, 304a; without grace, man cannot merit everlasting life, 412a; world, only peopled to people heaven, 303b; world to come is everlasting, 542b

Eterne Remain e. when body is but dust, 901b

Eternities The past, the future, two e.!, 539a

Eternity anachronism, only pedantic word for e., 33a; bright day of e., 303a; contemplate substance of e., 211b; e. and time, rightly distinguished, 435a, 869a; E. is but thought By which we think of Thee, 340a; e. is everything, this life nothing, 116a; E. is the eve of something, 844a; God is E., 383b, 387a; Homesick for harpings of e., 306a; It takes e. to make man despair, 259a; O eternal Truth, true Charity, lovely E., 390b; one persistent now, 306a; skein of e., 305b; Thine own e. is round Thee, Majesty divine!, 378a; Through the countless ages of e., 75b; Time, e.'s fountain, 869b; Time is short, e. is long, 306a,

869b; When charity shall pull up net on shore of e., 155b

Ethical confusion of aesthetic and ethical values, 9b; reconstructing e. system on basis of negation, 160a

Ethics anti-ascetic, technological system, 37a; Christian e. will not long survive Christian creed, 622b; e. and knowledge, 306b, 513b; e. of asceticism, 37a; e. of history, cannot be denominational, 434b; right living, 306b; Socrates first established e., 306b; We cannot have e. without religion, 622a

Ethiope He cometh out of E., 70a

Etiquette They're very strict on e. in hell, 428a

Eugenius III, Pope, 176b

Eugenius IV, Pope, 520b

Eunuchs e. may not become clergymen, 312a

Europe continually transformed by spiritual unrest, 165b; E. and Benedictine example, 59a; faith is E., E. is the faith, 139b; Led by my hand, he saunter'd E. round, 878b; not a political creation, 312a; not Church, and Church is not E., 139b; People talk of United States of E., 312a; western E. acquired unity and form, 187a

European America, part of E. civilization, 16a; nations, parts of wider spiritual society, 312a

Eutyches, 708a

Eucharist antidote against death, 194b; applies to us fruits of salvation, 75a, 310a; as bond of friendship, 71b; assurance of eternal life, 71b; Be zealous in observance of one E., 194b, 597b; bishop offers sweet-smelling Savor, 67a, 67b; bread and wine changed into God's Body, 70b, 73a, 162a; Bread of life, 195a; by mystical prayer, consecrated, 71b, 308b, 310b, 597a; carried up by hands of Thy holy angel, 592b; celebration of Body and Blood of the Lord, 785b; Christ contained, offered, in e., 78b; Christ eaten spiritually and really, 76b; consecrated in person of Christ, 597a, 647b; consuming fire to the unworthy, 196a; crowns all other sacraments, 306b; daily receive the E., 194b; *Do not give that which is holy to dogs,* 70b, 194a; *Do this for commemoration of me,* 309a; e. and sacrifices of Old Law, 73b, 74a, 75a; *everlasting showing forth of His death,* 73b; faith alone not sufficient preparation, 71a, 76b; fasting before E., 194b, 597a; food of salvation, 75b, 105b, 194b; Great mystery, great dignity of priests, 597b; Himself the Church, by sacrament of His body, 131b; holy mysteries, 195b, 441b, 442b, 586b, 595b; Holy things for the holy!, 593b; If gospel be true, what difficulty is there?, 306b; incorporates us in His Body, 70b, 195b; invisible operation of Holy Spirit, 310a; invocation of holy Trinity, 310a; Lasting to the end of time, 74b; let good Spirit rest upon these gifts, 586b, 590b; like threshing-floor of Lord, 72b; Lord's Table, 597a; Make me sharer in Thy mystic supper, 595a; manner of Christ's presence, 73b; many grains collected into one loaf, 131b; means thanksgiving in Latin, 308b; medicine of immortality, 194b; mystery of this water and wine, 590a, 597b; mystic feast, 729b; noblest sacrament, 306b; not

necessary for little children, 197b; O sign of unity, O bond of love, 73a; offering for Christians living and dead, 590a; offerings and services, at fixed times and seasons, 597b; one altar, one bishop, with priests and deacons, 194b, 597b; only for baptized, 70b, 194a; our daily Bread, 195b; prepared in some places every day, 597a; priests alone have power to celebrate and consecrate, 597b, 648a; real presence not confined by use, 76a; reception of both species not necessary, 197a; redemption continued during celebration of liturgy, 310a; sacrament not merely sign and virtually, but actually and really, 311a; sacrament of bread and chalice, 308b; sacrament of most holy e., 76a; sacrament of sacraments, 306b; Sacrament of the Altar, 307b, 597a; *Take and eat ye all of this,* 592a; unity of Body and Blood, 597a; we receive Godhead and Flesh conjoined, 71a, 76a; why offered to us under species, 311b

Eucharistic Sacrifice ancient sacrifices were signs, 308a; at words of priest, heavens opened, 308b; bloody and unbloody victim, one and same, 307b, 309b; break bread and offer the Eucharist, 307a; bring wine and water for e., 4a; choirs of angels are present, 308b; continues work of salvation, 310a; daily offerings of his Flesh and Blood, 150a, 307a, 308a, 308b, 310a; earthly things are united with heavenly, 308b; He is Mediator, Priest, Sacrifice, 307b; Himself the offerer and oblation, 308a; holy and most awful sacrifice, 243b; immolation of Christ, 308b, 309a; *In every place offer me a pure sacrifice,* 307a; Let souls of Christians be like altars, 310a; lips of the Church are never silent, 309b; Love lifting red hands to Overthrone, 13b; mystery of sacred oblation, 308b; no one may consecrate except priest duly ordained, 309b, 311a; not bare commemoration of Cross, 309b; not offered to martyrs, 308a; offered for living and dead, 308a, 309b; offered to holy Trinity, 88a; one Christ, offered by Christ and by us, 309a; priest imitates what Christ did, 307b; priests and faithful offer e., 309a; propitiatory sacrifice, 307b, 308a, 309b; renews in mystery, death of Only-begotten, 308b, 309a; Sacrifice goes up, in one eternal tongue, 309b; sacrifice must not be defiled, 307a; sacrifice of Christians, 307b; sacrifice of mass, one and same with Cross, 309b; spiritual sacrifice, bloodless service, 307b; through it we partake of Lord's passion, 309a; true and full sacrifice to God the Father, 307a, 307b, 308a, 309a; valid, offered by bishop, 307a; whole City, offered as sacrifice, 307b, 308a

Eva And for EVA AVE writeth, 25a, 25b

Evangelicalism broken reed, when temperature drops, 294b; conversion as vivid religious experience, 294b

Evangelii Initium sancti E. secundum, 589a

Evangelist must prove Christianity true, 27b

Evangelists Three blessed e., 494a

Eve Ah! no e. is like Christmas e.!,

170b; believed serpent, Mary believed angel, 85a; by Him, E. set free, 90a; death came through E., 79a; debt of first mother, 39b, 85b; Eternity is the e. of something, 844a; EVA's name reversing, 99a; E.'s banished children cry to thee, 95b; Mary became advocate of virgin E., 85a; Mary is new E., 93a, 461a; The faerie tale of faulty E., 20b; the way Through E. to woman!, 260b; through woman's eggement mankind was lorn, 99b

Even at e. in the wind's decline, 110a; I was heavy with the e., 312b

Evening Comes e., a tearful novice, 312b; It was e. there, 606a; When e.'s last faint beams are gone, 312b

Evensong Evermore at last they ring to e., 894a

Event Every e., type of those that follow, 434b

Eventide life's e., 74b

Events often cut the knots, 313a; seeing e. as contemporaries saw them, 435a; take place in order of Providence, 373b

Everlasting Knit in e. bands, 36a

Every E. man for himself and God for us all, 397b, 806b

Everyone his own enemy, 295b; must be loved equally, 154b

Everything All cometh to one, 313a; hath end, 395a

Everywhere God is e., 427b, 654a

Evil all e. brought by apple, 29a; as such cannot be desired, 314b; cause of e., defection of will, 313b; crime, to speak e. with truth, 313a; defect of being, 56b, 313b; deficiency of good, 313a, 314b; *deliver us from e.,* 593b; e. and freewill, 313a, 315a, 398b; e. and God's restoration of things, 314b; E. things had origin in good things, 221b, 313b, 314b; existence of e. can be a good, 313b; Fear, greater e. than e. itself, 342b; God does not will e. to be done, 315a, 392a; God foresaw good He would bring out of e., 313b, 315b, 399a; God permits e. to happen in world, 313b, 314b; good and e., like antitheses of poem, 313b; human law may tolerate e., 315b; impute e. to oneself, 315a, 399a; In this life, good never found without e., 399b; man not damned, unless for his e. will, 238a; Many a good cow hath an e. calf, 223b; Nature throws a veil over e., 313a; no being as such can be e., 399a; no one is e. by nature, 314a; not a real substance, 314b; real mystery, not in end but beginning, 315a; slave, though he be king, 399a; Take away all e., and much good would go, 314b; The world is very e., 502a; thing essentially e. cannot exist, 314b; trust God, and believe no e. lightly, 315b; whoever is e. is e. by vice, 314a

Evils Deliver us from all e., 593b; God's care, to bring good out of e., 314b; If e. come not, then our fears are vain, 315a; not anticipating e., 342a; Of two e. we should always choose less, 162a, 315a; Universal e., not cured by specifics, 315a

Evolution Adam and existence of other first parents, 316b; Church does not forbid discussion and research, 316a; development of creation like seed, 224a; I am too fat to climb a tree, 316a; no such thing as, e. of idea of God, 396a;

Out of dusk a shadow, Then, a spark, 315b; things primarily created in web of elements, 224b; Victorian secularists were 'dawnists,' 316a; world ceasing to believe in beneficence of e., 316a

Evolutionists e. and missing link, 316a

Evidence historical e., 270a

Evidences e., and mutually exclusive conclusions, 313a; e. before faith, 289b

Ex e. opere operato, 787b; E. umbris et imaginibus in veritatem, 884b; e. cathedra, 706b

Exaggerate Never e., 316b

Exaltation festival of e. of Cross, 230b

Exalted For which cause God also hath e. Him, 442b

Exalts something in humility which e. heart, 449b

Example Christianity, sometimes caught no less than taught, 319b; e. of BVM, 92a; He that giveth evil e. with contrary deed, 316b; let abbot show forth good things, 1a; One loving soul sets another on fire, 319b; Soon followeth one where multitudes begin, 341b; This noble e. to his sheep he gave, 316b

Examples E. of past times, 519a

Excelsis Gloria in E. Deo, 588b; Hosanna in e., 591a

Excess all e. is vice, 900a; E. began, and sloth sustains the trade, 269a

Excesses Two e., reason excluded, only reason allowed, 749b

Exchange God died, that kind of celestial e. might be made, 466b

Excommunication chief weapon of ecclesiastical discipline, 317b; cut off from common unity, 697a; e. and punishment, proportioned to fault, 317b; "From the Church Militant we sever thee," 317b; if a man will not repent, cut him off, 317a; let him suffer e., 317a; separation from communion, 117b; Sit anathema, 317a; those who procure abortion incur e., 2a; to be used only with circumspection, 317b

Excuse testimony of man's conscience, only complete e., 208a

Excusing do ill, and do worse in e. it, 317b

Executioner barred from holy orders, 177a, 649a

Exegesis interpretations of Scripture that are farfetched, 318a; modern methods in e., 64b; Texts explained by fasting and by prayer, 318a

Exemption tax e. of clergy, 188a

Exemplar begetting of Son, e. of all making, 370b; e. of all things, 378a

Exercise wise for cure, on e. depend, 318a; your limbs outstretch with care, 423a

Exercises discipline mind by e. of holy working, 214a; time that really matters, between religious e., 318a; We do not become perfect by multiplication of e., 624a

Exile After this our e., 95b; He made all countries where he came his own, 318b; I die an e., 318a, 504b, 520a; In Siberia's wastes No tears are shed, 318b; Long is the date of thy e., 303b; mourns in lonely e. here, 8b; smiles in e. or in chains, 414b

Exist even that I e., is Thy gift, 366b; Inasmuch as we e., we are good, 398a; that Being through

Which all e., must be one, 375b; We e. because God is good, 318b

Existence all things aware of fact of His e., 392b; as He never will not be, so He never was not, 374b; e. and God's knowledge, 319a, 383a; e. of all other things partakes of His, 376a; e. of God, 270b, 376a, 376b; God implies necessary and eternal e., 376b; God maintains creature in e., 224a, 225a, 319a; God's e. and foreknowledge, 382b; God's first effect is e., 376a; knowledge of God's e., implanted in my nature, 375a, 376a; number of lines converge towards God, 377a; one thing, e. of thing, another, what it is, 374b; right to e., 531a; three things, e., knowledge, will, 511b; We are, we know that we are, 319a, 511b

Existing world could not be known, if not e., 319a

Exists everything e. either through something or through nothing, 375b; he who questions whether God e., 376a; one Being alone e. in highest degree, 375b; to know absolutely that God e., 376a

Exomologesis, 202b

Exorcism mill of fasting and e., 72b

Expectation Mother's e. of Messias' birth, 8b

Expects Blessed be he who e. nothing, 319a, 638a

Expedients coward arts of mean e., 600b

Expense Unprofitably kept at Heaven's e., 11b

Experience A burnt child loves the fire, 319b; E. and conflict, give years to man, 319b; grim e. of days, 347b; hunger To master earth's e., 319a; Inherited E., 319b; known by e., 514b; progress, if it knows how to make capital out of e., 733a; seems better than theory, 627b; Who heeds e., trust him not, 319b

Explanation difference between stillness of mystery, and explosion of e., 759a

Exploitation capitalist e. of labor, 319b

Exploration They make discoveries where they see no sun, 320a

Expression feeling that matters, not e., 473b

Exquisites e. are going to rule, 239b

Extra e. ecclesiam nulla salus, 125b

Extravagance In squandering wealth was his peculiar art, 320a

Extreme senses can grasp nothing that is e., 321b

Extreme Unction anointing him with oil in Lord's name, 320b; confers grace, remits sin, comforts sick, 321b; for a medicine of life and salvation, 320a; for health and soundness of soul, 320a; In E. we get strength, 788a; not given to public penitents, 320b; sacrament instituted by Christ, promulgated by James, 321b; The atoning oil is spread, 321b; they have greased my boots already, 521b; unction and confession of sins, 321a

Extremist every man, with him, was God or devil, 321b

Exultation Sing to the Lord with e.!, 167b

Exultet, 441b

Eye as e. to body, so mind to soul, 835b; Better e. out than always ache, 322a; E. hath not seen, nor ear heard, 481a; Lesbia hath a

beaming e., 221b; my soul's inquiring e., 77b; No e. to watch, 215a; Paradise stood formed in her e., 322a; That searching e. of Thine, 243a; What e. sees not, heart rues not, 322a; Ye can see a mote in another man's e., 228a

Eyes all e. on him wait, 31a; Beauties in vain their pretty e. roll, 55a; blinking e. of our mind, 212a; earthly heavens, where angels joy to dwell, 322a; enfeebled with sin, 14b; E. of most unholy blue, 322b; e. of the soul, 106a, 214a; Fields have e. and woods have ears, 323b; greatest magnifying glasses in world, 892b; her e., Deep wells, 264b; Not in mine e. alone is Paradise, 653b; O sacred e., springs of living light, 322a; Such e. as may have looked from heaven, 322b; the e. of the Lord in every place, 266a; Twin flames of charity, 41b; woman's bright story Is told in her e., 322b

F

Façades f. of medieval cathedrals, 30a

Face A f. that's best By its own beauty drest, 323a; as if it had been greased, 48b; beauty of an aged f., 11a; f. of Him, who died for me, 55b, 75b, 305a, 384a; I see A Heart, a F., and a Name, 790a; Look on her f., 323b; Make good f., 323a; Man beholdeth the f., 474a; unveil'd f. of God, 20a; Why is thy f. so lit with smiles?, 36b; Wrinkled f., 10b

Faces thronged with shouting f., 30a; two f. in one hood, 323a

Fact F. and argument, tests of truth and error, 885b; reconcile theory and f., 332a; Whether our F. is F., 799b

Factions angry vociferations of warring f., 217b

Factory f.-made art bad thing, 33b

Facts depend for interpretation upon point of view, 323b; f. first, explanations afterwards, 323b; important to rely on f., 323b

Faculty By a f., we are able to do something, 417b

Faculties will, lynch-pin of f., 914a

Fade All that's bright must f., 550b; Ere you shall f., 475a; 'twas the first to f. away, 264a

Faerie The f. tale of faulty Eve, 20b

Fail Lest we fail through foeman's wile, 21a; You will f. sometimes, but not finally, 324a

Fails nothing that f. like success, 645a

Failure labor is safe, which no f. can render void, 516a; pathetic f., appeals more than success, 850b; To fear not sensible f., 324a

Faint f. for love of Thee, 196a

Faint-heartedness fault of pusillanimity and timorous mind, 324a

Fair All things swear friends to F. and Good, 219a; And all things f. and bright are Thine, 373b; Dost still hope thou shalt be f.?, 55a; Fairest thou where all are f., 96a; For Thee do I yearn, Justice, Beautiful, F., 261b; grace of God is worth a f., 324b; None but best deserve the f., 108a; O thou that art so f., 84b; she like morn is f., 623a; they who walk there are most f., 277b; What makes this earth so wondrous f.?, 633b

Fairest Both raven and ape think own young f., 54b, 160b; Fairest of women!, 2a

Fairy-tales give child idea of possible defeat of bogy, 324b

Faith Abiding f. alone wins liberty, 537b; admits us to fellowship in Divine nature, 325a; alone does not justify, 2b; arguments for f. cannot coerce unwilling, 27b; assent of Christian f., free act, 324a, 324b, 332b; assent to Christ, 57b, 333b; authority, not from miracles but God, 331a; believe f., believe *in* f., 326b; Believe that thou mayest understand, 57a, 331b; Believe that you have it, and you have it, 326b; By f., Christian soul enters into marriage with God, 325b; by which God has justified all men, 505a; Catholic f. may not be doubted, 58a; champions of the f., 275b; Christ dwells in our mind through f., 330a; confirmed by learning, 139a; discord between f. and knowledge, 331a; divine f. and human science, 58a, 270b, 330b; doctrine regarding f. or morals, 706b; door through which we enter supernatural order, 328b; evidences before f., 289b; explicit and implicit f. in mysteries, 326b, 327b; faint f., better than strong heresy, 326b; f. and acquisition of knowledge, 270b; f. and articles of creed, 325b; f. and assent to doctrine, 57b; f. and baptism, 49b; f. and belief in God, 327b; f. and certitude, 152b; f. and charity, 154b, 327a, 329b, 332b, 334a, 357a; F. and devotion, 330a; f. and hope, 329b, 330a; f. and intellect, 332b, 333a, 376a; f. and knowledge of God, 326a; f. and private inspiration, 328a; f. and reasonable proofs, 26b, 326a, 331b; f. and unbelievers, 326a; f. and understanding, 57a, 333b; f. and wisdom, 333b; f., good works and freewill, 356b; f. is a venture, 219b; F. is above senses, not contrary to them, 327a; f. is beginning, end is love, 324b, 325a; f. of ancient fathers, 271b, 704b; f. of children, 52b, 328b; f. of learned and simple, 58a, 326b; F. of our fathers! living still, 146b; foretaste of truth not yet manifested, 325b; formal motive and object of f., 145b, 326a, 326b; foundation of all virtues, 325a; foundation of Church, 124a; from which all good works flow, 325a; gift which can be given or withdrawn, 324b, 328a; *Go in peace, f. hath made thee whole,* 764b; God is the cause of f., 325b; grace believes, reason does but opine, 332a; grant us increase of f., hope, and charity, 325a, 334a; habit of mind, which begins eternal life, 325b; has two distinct meanings, 324b; Heresy, opposed to f., 430a; *I will espouse thee to me in f.,* 325b; ideology, very different from f., 457a; illogical to men of world, 39a; illuminates our minds, 325a, 327b; implicit and explicit f., 329a; In f. and hope world will disagree, 156b; infused light of habit of f., 325b, 326a, 327a, 328a; interpreted by Church, 119b; key which fits a lock, 58a, 329a; kind of knowledge, 330b; love makes f., not f. love, 330a; makes martyrs, 327b; means battles, 324b; mistake historical be-

lief for saving f., 326b; must be actual, practical, existential, 328b; must be sincere, 328a; mysteries of f. cannot all be understood by reason, 328a, 332b; no one forced to embrace Catholic f., 57a, 58a; not built on disquisitions vain, 327a, 875b; not conclusion from premises, but result of will, 327b; not lost with grace, 327a; *now there remain f., hope, charity,* 334a; *O f., thou workest miracles,* 327b; O gift of gifts! O grace of f.!, 327b; one f. for all ages given, 135b; *One Lord, one f., one baptism,* 134b, 145a; Reason is one thing, f. another, 332a, 750a, 863a; rests on divine revelations, 340b; substance of things hoped, 325a, 326b; supernatural virtue by which we believe what He has revealed, 327b; susceptible of infinite corroboration, 331a; too much f., and none, 327a; true f. cannot be deceived, 58a, 331b; true f. tested by two methods, 60b; true lights of the world, 275b; two grounds of f., 327b; under old dispensation, 51b; very essence of all religion, 327b; We like pope to be infallible in f., 152a, 695a; when necessary to confess f., 329b; without works, cannot please, 333b; without works is dead, 334a; your f., a helmet, 401a

Faith, Act of 327a

Faith, Articles of As regards substance, have not received increase, 321b, 329a; increase in number believed explicitly, 329b; like self-evident principles in philosophy, 329b; not scientifically demonstrable, 26b; things we must believe, few and plain, 327a, 329a; We believe because God reveals them, 26b

Faithful armed through Jesus, 124a; born in Church, members of Head, 80b; bound to profess faith openly, 147a; BVM perpetually intercedes for faithful, 89b; called holy, because people of God, 128b; called unto adoption, 124a, 485a, 647b; children of mother Church, 129b; Christ brings to birth, Church's faithful, 131a; Come, all ye f., 170a, 285b; consecrated to Christ by baptism and faith, 128b; distinction between f. and unbeliever, 46a, 58a; *He is Savior, especially of f.,* 43b; I have been f. to thee, Cynara!, 556b; offer eucharist by intention, 309a; owe reverence to clergy, 174b, 190b; partakers of His divine influence, 124a; plantation of God, beloved vineyard, 124a; Thou alone most f. in all things, 344a; to God and thee, 623a, 720a; we who are in Christ, 194b

Falcon dapple-dawn-drawn F., 334b

Fall all f. at times, 334b, 881a; Art thou righteous? Then fear lest thou f., 446a; Between two stools lieth the f., 162a; low they f. whose f. is from the sky, 334b; O let us f. and worship Him, 440a; Pride will have a f., 725a; To rise by others', 846b; Who climbeth highest, most dreadful is his f., 414a, 725b; without Thee, frailty of human nature cannot but f., 428b

Fall of Man Adam's f. affected his children, 186b; enormity of man's first transgression, 43a, 571b, 750a; envy of devil was reason of

man's fall, 334b, 347a; evil brought in by apple, 29a; glory which Adam lost, 229a; His doubts began with f. of man, 821b; human race fell by virgin, 85a; man fell by his own bad will, 820b; O original of our damnation, 368a; woman received venom of serpent, 85b, 99b

Fallen be kind and gentle to the f., 568b; F., but striving anew to rise, 82b; F. from his high estate, 254a

Fallere F. *fallentem non est fraus,* 159b; F., *flere, nere,* 920a

Falleth as the tree f. so must it lie, 251a; When the sky f. we shall have larks, 519a

False As f. as God is true, 334b; F. ideas, refuted by argument, 457a; f. systems of the age, 290b; My love was f., but I was firm, 344a

Falsehood defence of f. in face of truth, 38b; something is thought to be which is not, 885a

Falsehoods Blunt truths more mischief than nice f. do, 222b, 885b

Falser The devil is no f. than he is, 261a

Fame a very windy thing, 335a; all who have risen On liberty's ruins to f., 663a; blooms and dies in one short hour, 335a; In all places lives their f., 20b; noble immortality of f., 335a; not on downy plumes, f. is won, 335a; presumptuous, wish to be known by all world, 14a, 335a; To dyen when that he is best of name, 248a; To the quick brow, f. grudges her best wreath, 335a; universal desire for immortality of f., 464a; vulgar deaths unknown to f., 250a; Who builds a church to God and not to f., 171b; Your glories may survive when you are dead, 542b

Familiarity charity for all, f. not expedient, 336a; Over-great homeliness engendereth dispraising, 215a

Families f. and Mystical Body, 133a

Family body politic contains f. units, 845b; cradle of civil society, 336a; f. of God, 727b; Folded with all my f., 484b; holds from Creator right to educate, 291b; Mercifully regard prayers of Thy f., 416b; more sacred than state, 336b; new offspring of Thy f., 441b; old trinity of father, mother, child, 438a; Pour out Spirit of grace upon Thy f., 745b; sanctities that separate men from ants and bees, 336b; society, older than any state, 336a; Thy universal f., 560b, 591b; wife, as directing head of the f., 456a

Family, Holy instructed by example of Thy h., 438a; O highest Hope of mortals, 438a; O house of Nazareth the blest, 437b

Famine Devouring f., plague, and war, 249a; farmers fatten most when f. reigns, 337a

Famish fortune to fast, f. for hunger, 287a

Fanatic man who can make up his mind, servile f., 499b; Nothing to build and all things destroy, 336b

Fancies bring back Thy flocks or f., 347a; Castles built in the air, 113b, 336b; Feed your f. and your sight, 684a; My f. all be fled, 10b

Fancy f., or molding of thought,

685a; How f. throws us into perturbation!, 459a

Fantasies From nightly fears and f., 201b

Fantasy O f., that dost at time so rout, 876b

Fare The few the better f., 343b

Faren gone further and f. worse, 9a

Farewell F. again, thou lamp of light, 336b; F., f. to thee, Araby's daughters!, 336b

Farewells In lone and last f., 654a

Farmers f. and right of association, 38b; fatten most when famine reigns, 337a

Fas Divine law is called f., 523b, 524b

Fashion Be not first by whom new are tried, 337a; F. is what one wears oneself, 337a; form of ugliness we alter every six months, 337a

Fashioner BVM ministered to Fashioner, 85b

Fast do you f. on Wednesdays and Fridays, 337b; end of paschal f., 283b; fervent devotion of those who f., 338a; fortune to f., famish for hunger, 287a; Here is the f. you must keep for God, 337a; If anyone of clergy f. on Lord's Day, 337b; laity likewise shall f., 337b; In that house, as soon break neck as f., 847b; law of abstinence and f. together, 338b; No one shall taste anything at Pascha before offering, 337b; They peal a f. for me, 169a; venerable solemnity of this f., 37b

Fastidious we are f., that is, small, 415a

Fasting abolishing of oaths, more useful than f., 641a; as far as health allows, 3a; before Eucharist, 194b, 337b, 597a; better than prayer, 13a, 337a; Christian warfare with holy f., 37b; F. is a medicine, 337b; in f., almsdeeds and prayer, righteousness, 401b; law of f., 338a; mill of f. and exorcism, 72b; Subdue flesh by f. and abstinence, 338a; To love f., 338a

Fasts he who f., f. for God, 338a; Let not your f. be with hypocrites, 337b; My f. shall live like willows, 109a

Fat Change of pasture maketh f. calves, 661a; resolved to grow f. and look young till forty, 338b; She was made like a barrel, 338b; The f. is in the fire, 880b

Fatalism refuge of conscience-stricken mind, 338b

Fate commonly means necessary process apart from will of God, 339a; depends on Providence, 373b; disposition inherent in changeable, 389a; easier to command lapdog than one's own f., 339a; envious of all others' f., 247b; f. of scepters and of crowns, 509a; f., will or power of God, 339a; Man, master of his f., 339a; more durable than f., 305b; providence and f., 389a; There is no armor against f., 249a; when f. summons, monarchs must obey, 249b; Who in the night of f. must blindly steer, 339a

Fates What profits it to butt against F.?, 339a

Father, God the all of us, mere children of our F., 161a; Although no man knows F. except Son, 392b; baptize in name of F., 49a; Blessed be the kingdom of the F., 587a; BVM, spouse whom F. took to Himself, 39b; Christ in human nature, subject to F., 67a; Come, O F. of the poor, 671a; Creator and F. of the ages, 366a; Eternal F.!, 339b, 340a, 370a; F. almighty, 226b; F. and Savior Thou, of every nation, 19a; F. and the Son being One, 480b; F.! Creator! Lord Most High!, 371b; F. espoused Son to human nature, 131a; F. is my trust, 369b; F. of all! in every age, 340a; F. of faith, hope and grace, 241b; F. of heaven and earth, 372b; F. of lights, 585a, 596a; F.! the sweetest, dearest name, 340a; F.'s power, Son's wisdom, 108b; Glory be to the F., 35b; God the F. hath sealed thee, 50a; God the F. turns a school-divine, 606b; God the Son, equal with the F., 482b; holy F., physician of souls and bodies, 320b; I and the F. are one, 339a, 370b; I believe in the F. almighty, 224a, 226a; In my F.'s house there are many mansions, 302a; In the name of the F., Son, Holy Ghost, 587a; liberty to call God, F., 124a; Logos of the F., 89a; Mercy imitates the perfect F., 603b; never lacking in Word, 439a; never time when F. was, and Son was not, 339b; one F., beginning and cause of all, 339b; Our F., Who art in heaven, 593b; principle of whole Deity, 339a; Promise of the F., 36a; Son, Face of the F., 481a; supreme F. of all believers, 441b; Thee, O Christ, the F.'s splendor, 19a; Thou unbegotten God, the Sire, 368b; true Sun, His eternal F., 196b; We do not say my F., but our F., 716a; whereby we cry, Abba, Father, 1a; Who has not Church for mother, can not have God for f., 429a; Who knowest the hearts of all, 67a; who sees the Son, sees the F. also, 481a; With all His F.'s glory clad, 25a; With God the F. ever One, 28a; without Him, no man comes to F., 148b; Yet leaving not the F.'s side, 74b

Father F. in care, mother in tender heart!, 491b; man shall leave f. and cleave to wife, 577a; O God, Who hast commanded us to honor our f. and mother, 654a; pope, f. and governor of all the faithful, 702a

Fathered God Who f. me, 41b

Fatherland fount of that eternal f., 301b; letter from our f., 60b; where we are going, 492b

Fathers as such, not guaranteed against error, 63b; authority of f. not final, 340b; consensus and Catholic faith, 144b; faith of ancient f., 271b; f. and mothers of families, 518a; I like to be as my f. were, 237a; ladder by which I ascended into Church, 341a; opinions of F. who persevered in holy faith, 340a, 874b; Our f. and our guides, 415a; proclaimed Virgin Mother of God, 81a; revert to opinions of holy f., 875a; unanimous agreement of f. and Scripture, 62a; used to annotate Bible, 63b; views of our predecessors and f., 144b; we pray also for f., 243b

Fathom what could f. God were more than He, 395b

Fault born of freewill of person who deserts grace, 723a; business of finding f. is very easy, 341b; seldom we weigh neighbor in same balance with ourselves, 341a; through my most grievous f., 587b

Faultless He is lifeless that is f., 341b; Whoever thinks a f. piece to see, 341b

Faults America, with thy f., I love thee still, 14b; daily prayers make satisfaction for tiny f., 716b; Do not think of f. of others, 341b; f. of speech and of morals, 53a; Her f. and virtues lie so mix'd, 22b; let me see mine own f., 450a; They judge but half who only f. will see, 341b; unwillingness to recognize f., 805b; When God shows us f. of others, 341a; who from f. is free?, 341b

Favente Deo f., 397a

Favonius When mild F. breathes, 955b

Favor good graces of the king, 409a; guard Thy Church by Thy perpetual f., 428b

Favors A prince's f. on but few can fall, 504b

Fay By Goddes f., by Goddes f.!, 600b

Fealty pope may release subjects from oath of f., 701a

Fear A welcome f. at night, 564a; Ah f.! abortive imp of drooping mind, 342a; at least f. of hell restrain thee, 427b; At the root of all war is f., 342b; Before sinning, f. God's justice, 446a; F. God, honor the king, 176a, 343a, 773b; F. is the foundation of safety, 342a; God hath not given us spirit of f., 46b; greater evil than evil itself, 342b; If all were without f., who could restrain?, 404a, 825b; If we f. death before it comes, 252b; man cannot rule by f., 47b; no true liberty but in f. of God, 343a; spirit of holy f., 50a, 343a; The worst of passions, daily f., 554b; we f. To be we know not what, 253a; We must not f. f., 342b

Feared few would love God, unless they f., 563a; let Thy word be f. in us, 346a; Those who love to be feared, 342b

Fearest If thou f. death, 246b

Fears Adown titanic glooms of chasmèd f., 385a; F. and hopes, and hopes and f., 170b; Free from sorrows, free from f., 540b; From nightly f. and fantasies, 201b

Feast of reason, and flow of soul, 343a; f. of the Sacrament, 72a; In service o'er the mystic f. I stand, 729b; Mass must be heard on f. days of obligation, 586a; O sacred banquet, heavenly f.!, 197b; Our solemn f. let holy joys attend, 74a; Scripture is f. of wisdom, 60a; There's a f. undated, 602b; To the hall of that f. came the sinful and fair, 585a; Would you f. on delicious food?, 44b

Feather straight falls the falling f., 477b

Feathers He would fain flee, but wanteth f., 346a; See their own f. pluck'd, 282a

Features beauty lies in coincidence of f., 55a

February this time, Sacred to young and unborn, 343a

Fecundity fairy of f. of speech, 160a; f. and virginity of BVM and Church, 92b, 639a

Fed Better f. than taught, 858b

Fee f. the doctor for a nauseous draught, 318a; for a small f., 29b;

Take f. while patient is still in pain, 268b

Feeble all f. spirits naturally live in future, 659b

Feed F. by measure, 287a

Feel Unless I f., I will not believe, 333a; what did it f. like to be Out of heaven, 488a

Feeling f. that matters, not expression, 473b; Trust not to thy f., 343b

Feelings do not always lead to right conclusions, 343b

Fees Nor without f. would attend Hippocrates, 268b; She labored still for conscience not for f., 295b

Feet All mothers worship little f., 84a; all princes kiss f. of pope, 175b; f. of clay make gold of image precious, 348b; From those strong f. that followed after, 385a; He began to wash f. of His disciples, 442b; I lay a lonely heart Before Thy f., 350a; Keep thou my f., 490a; my f. that err, 493a; on the fair And silver tables of Thy f., 585a; Prostrate at her Creator's f., 94b; Star-flecked f. of Paradise, 837a; The head without the f. is nothing, 641b; They have pierced my hands and my f., 657a; thinketh f. be where head shall never come, 348b; those sacred hands and f. For me so mangled!, 657b; To kiss again the Master's f.!, 286b

Feign To know how to dissemble, knowledge of kings, 265b

Felicity F. is pure contemplation of noblest Truth, 419b

Fellow-citizen Americans respectful of their f., 15b

Fellowship Goodwill, increased by f. in faith, 403a; Poverty parteth f., we see, 713a; prayer, instrument of divine f., 720a; share in all, yet seeking all it finds, 903b; true meaning of civilization, 186b

Female God made man male and f., 131a, 572a; in sight of God, we are neither male nor f., 448b; too frail life of f. constancy, 210b; trailing robes of f. dignity, 278a

Females ferocious f. of Picasso's art, 34a

Feminine human beings, must be f. before can be masculine, 837b

Fervent f. spirit, deep and true, 789b; O with what bursts of f. praise, 78a

Fervor through f. of spirit, 36b

Festal Call the world to highest f., 36a; Hail! F. day!, 283b

Fettered f. by antiquated dogmas, 27b

Fetters No man loveth his f., 768b

Few F. though the faithful, 909a; Let thy words be f., 838b; The f. the better fare, 343b

Fiat at its f. lux, 225a

Fiction American f. known to Englishmen, 16a; best thing in English have done, 18b; Literature luxury, f. necessity, 344a; only real people, who have never existed, 343b

Fidei pugiles f., 275b

Fidelity My love was false, but I was firm, 344a; pope may release subjects from oath of f., 175b; They who wish to live in perfect f., 344a

Fides Quid est enim f., 325a

Field A hard foughten f., 192b

Fields have eyes and woods have ears, 323b; O'er earth's green f., 20a; Through the vast f. of light,

41a; Thy roots are fast within our fair f., 233b; Whose herds with milk, whose f. with bread, 215a

Fiend In whom f. no thought of sin could find, 83a; Me fro the f., and from his clawes, 232a

Fifes to hear the shrill Sweet treble of her f., 830a

Fig A f. for care and a f. for woe!, 925a; convention of the f. leaf, 809b

Fight A hard foughten field, 192b; absolution of a faithful f., 830a; alone gives us pleasure, not victory, 192b; He who flees will f. again, 738b; love that lures thee from that f., 555b; My soul with Christ join thou in f., 487a; on the side of the angels, 235a; This life, a very enjoyable f., 541a; those who dare not f. For God or right, 724b; while life lasts, to f., 777a

Fights He who f. for freedom, 354a

Figures bread and wine, not merely figures of Body and Blood, 70b, 310b; Eucharistic f. of salvation, 71a; With f. doth away, 74b

Filial f. devotion shown to BVM, 102a

Filii In nomine Patris, et F., et Spiritus Sancti, 587a

Filio Gloria Patri, et F., et Spiritui Sancto, 588a

Fill Fill up in Thy priest perfection, 68a

Find Fast bind, fast f., 344b; me a place by thee, Mother, 41a; things ere they be lost, 344b

Findeth He f. that seeks, 344b

Finding glorious f. of the Cross, 231a; Loving Thee, find Thee, love Thee, f. Thee, 564a; Still f. all, yet seeking all it finds, 903b

Fingers At my f.'s end, 344b; God laid His f. on the ivories, 251b

Finita Causa f. est, 709a

Finite all f. things are in You, 885a; art breaks through enclosure of f., 34b; f. expression made infinite, 33b

Fire All the gruel is in the f., 338b; as now on f. I am, 30b; Baptism by f., 583b; Burn our heart with f. of Holy Ghost, 159a; Burnt child f. dreadeth, 344b; burnt child loves the f., 319b; deathfulness and lifefulness of f.!, 490b; draught of liquid f., 258a; F. in the tone hand, 253b; f. is quenched by water, 22b; f. that kindles also burns, 344b; f. was no match for thee, 583a; folly, to put finger too far in f., 347b; freed from purging f., 77a; great f. returned all to the wild, 114a; His ministers a flaming f., 19b; into everlasting f., 741a; Leap out of frying pan into f., 344b; living Spring, the living F., 670b; love is like a burning f., 489a; love's all-quickening f., 493b; melted in f. of Thy love, 560a; No f. without some smoke, 344b; on f. with a great love of God, 562a; One loving soul sets another on f., 319b; save me from unquenchable f., 501b; soul on f. with Spirit of love, 213b; spark too much of heavenly f., 14b; Spirit's sacred f., 368b; Thou art a consuming f. to unworthy, 196a; tries iron, 861a; warmed by f. of charity, 6b; Washed with f. to irradiant birth, 287a; with f. Of unapproach'd desire, 385a

Fires Love is a region full of f., 554b

Firmament For the bright f. Shoots forth no flame, 824a

First Be not f. by whom the new are tried, 210b; He who would be f., let him be minister, 242a

First-born f. from the dead 467a

First-fruits For us was gathered the f., 78a

Fish All is f. that cometh to net, 345a; F. is cast away, cast in dry pools, 345a; great f. eat the small, 344b; Nother f., nor flesh, nor good red herring, 345a; Old f. and young flesh, 347b; The f. with ease into the net doth glide, 345a; When f. are soft, largest you should prize, 344b

Fisher Bless the kind f. race, 99a

Fisher, St. John, 112b

Fisherman bow before tomb of f. Peter, 675b

Fishes f. to shipping did impart Their tail the rudder, 812a; we, little f., 49a

Fishing It is ill f. before the net, 345a

Fit Quidquid f. contra conscientiam, 208a

Fiunt F., non nascuntur Christiani!, 163a

Fixed Fond men, we are f. as a still despair, 448a

Flag banner of the red and white and blue, 345b; F. of my native land, 345a; Furl that banner! True, 'tis gory, 345a; Lift up the banner red, 345b

Flagellations midnight f., 17a

Flags No f. are furled, if freedom's flag be furled, 354a; Tossing the f. of the nations to flame, 345b

Flame But when the f. is out, 22b; Lightly as a lambent f., 469a; Who shall quench the f. for me?, 502a

Flames consumed by f. of vice, 216a

Flaminian Gate Pastoral Letter "From Out the F. Gate," 141b

Flatter Poets, only fellows whom anybody will f., 685b

Flatterer friend differs from a f., 358b

Flattery A man shall win us best with f., 922a; difference between blarney and boloney, 70a; speaketh, as she would creep into your bosom, 158a; When f. sooths and ambition blinds, 345b; who defiles his tongue with adulation, 7a

Fled I f. Him, down the nights and down the days, 385a

Flee He would fain f., but wanteth feathers, 346a; To f. charge, and find ease, 154a

Fleece like dew on f., 89a

Flees He who f. will fight again, 738b

Fleet Street in F., that I learned to drink, 279b

Fleeting f. acts of man, 306a

Flemer F. of fiends out of him and her, 232b

Flesh apparel of the soul, 97a, 345b; Christ and Church are two in one f., 132a; cleansed by water of baptism, 51b; contemplative, opposed to desires of f., 4b; despise f., which passes away, 106a, 345b; f. is carnal concupiscence, 229b; F. is so newfangel, 346a; F. of God is food for me, 72a; hinge of salvation for soul, 105b; His lite for them, His f. to them, 154b, 484a; It warreth night, it warreth day, 346a; Knit is now our f. to Godhead, 36a; liberating f. by f.,

166b; Master of all f., 243b; Not to fulfil desires of f., 346a; O God of spirit and all f., 245a; Of His F. the mystery sing, 74a; Old fish and young f., 347b; one F. of our Lord, one Chalice, 597b; Pierce My f. with the nails of fear, 229b; resurrection of the f., 226a; soul is the life of the f., 345b, 835b; Subdue f. by fasting and abstinence, 3a; The fraile f., 346; *they shall be two in one f.*, 577a; virginal f. He received of Holy Ghost, 491b; we worship His flesh united with Divinity, 81a, 481a, 482a

Flies catch f. with spoonful of honey, 444a

Flight Clung to mane of every whistling wind, 346a; Which your celestial f. denied, 70b

Flock do not abandon Thy f., 28b; exalt themselves above his f., 449b; flock of bells take flight, 59a; f. of Christ, 66b, 346a, 665a; small f., named 'after God's own heart,' 411a

Flocks bring back Thy f. or fancies, 347a

Flood Whelmed the world beneath the f., 104a

Floods F. and oceans, clap your hands, 36a

Florence, Italy, 346b, 520b

Flour our bran, compared with his white f., 44b

Flower As the f. turns on her god, 555b; emperice and f. of flowers all, 238a; f. is not for the seed, but seed for f., 556a; f. of all woman kind, 83a, 87b; Of which virtue engendered is the f., 29b; Tell f. an' tree, 346b; thou mystic f., 84b; Who looks with love upon the f., 328b

Flowering F. today, tomorrow apt to fail, 54b

Flowers Agonized hopes, and ashen f.!, 416b; all the f. looked up at Him, 488a; As little f., that by chill of night, 223a; fairest f. have not the sweetest smell, 425a; my fairest thoughts, my tallest f., 363a; f. of everlasting spring, 303b; Her bosom springs with f., 602b; love I most those f. white, 238a; My eyes are f. for your tomb, 109a; O blessed babes! first f. of Christian spring, 441a; within her eyes more bright, 55b

Flown birds are f., 65a

Flute soft complaining f., 347a

Flux In f. and in reflux, 225a

Fly blind eat many a f., 103a; F., stallions, f.!, 447a; followeth the honey, 444a; I f. to thee, Mother, 89b; man is not a f., 322a; To thee, sweet fount of love, we f., 90a

Foal How can f. amble?, 447a

Foameth She f. like a boar, 104b

Fodder leave alone foreign f. of heresy, 428b

Foe banners of f., 31a; By the Cross the f. despises, 232a; homely f. all day in thy presence, 295b; I turn a late enraged f., 22b; No fatal hurt of f. she fears, 157a

Foeman All the power of the f. bind, 75b

Foemen for His blood athirst, 74b; Lest we fail through f.'s wile, 21a

Foes Hark! the f. come, 280a; round beset with foes, 1a, 74b

Foetus deliberately destroying f., murder, 1b

Fog The yellow f. came creeping down, 347a

Fold found in f. Of Thine afflicted

flock, 882a; let me be the f., 347a; one f., for that primitive flock!, 135b; one f. shepherded by all apostles, 695b; To be with mercy taken to Thy f., 484a; To fence His f. from their encroaching foes, 876a

Folded F. with all my family, 484b

Folklore mark of true f., 347a

Follow F. pleasure, and then will pleasure flee, 684a; *If anyone wishes to come after Me*, 4b

Followeth Soon f. one where multitudes begin, 341b

Folly Be mine the f. of the Cross, 347b; cleanse away f. of our heart, 218b; Folks show much f., 422b; fool who redeemed us of our f., 109b; Holy Ghost gives wisdom against f., 366b; let f. be a stranger, 901b; Shoot f. as it flies, 347b

Font regenerated in f. of baptism, 51b

Fonts all the f., from which man's heart has drawn, 240b

Food At once thy worship and thy f., 77b, 78a; before f., bless the Maker, 278b; Christ is f. for me, 72a; God gave food and drink to men, 70b; keep entirely to Christian f., 428b; lessons of Scripture, apostolic f., 72a; spiritual f. and d., 70b; What soul loveth, not all f. for body, 278b

Fool by his tongue a f. often known, 348a; f. may eke a wise man often guide, 348a; f.'s bolt is soon shot, 348a; honest man may take f.'s advice, 9b; I should be a consummate f., 24a; Never was patriot yet, but was a f., 663a; no f. to ten old f., 348a; None so busy as f. and knave, 110b; The f. is happy that he knows no more, 348a, 458b; though devil is damned, he is no damn f., 261a; To file and finish God-Almighty's f., 348b; You'll ne'er convince a f. himself is so, 348a

Foolhardy more courage to refuse than to be f., 753a

Foolish aside to toss f. things that wise men hate, 347b; If we're not f. young, we're f. old, 347b; in yourself you are exceedingly f., 123a; The f. fear death, 252b

Foolishness we are freed by f. of God, 347a

Fools Begger'd by f., 320a; cannot hold their tongue, 348a; Children and f. cannot lie, 567b; F. admire, 6b; F.! I also had my hour, 38a; God sendeth fortune to f., 566a; men are all f., 821a; more hard to conquer than persuade, 348a; rush in where angels fear to tread, 348a; world's f. were first, 452b

Football Between one f. and the next, 814a

Fops True f. help nature's work, 348b

Forbid F. us thing, 733a; God f. that I should glory, 229b

Force Church and use of f., 181b; F. is of brutes, honor is of man, 444b; F. of *juventus*, hardy as lion, 930b; f. of the feeble, 491b; In kingdom of scholars, f. is powerless, 348b; man cannot rule by fear and force, 47b; Material f., *ultima ratio* of political society, 348b; No f. the free-born spirit can constrain, 317a; rules the world, not opinion, 348b; you cannot f. man believe, 57a

Forced No one f. to embrace Catholic faith, 58a, 147a, 355a

Forehead craggy stern f., 109b

Foreign brave Britons, f. laws despised, 297a; f. ideas and customs, not encouraged, 17b

Foreigner laughs at everything, except jokes, 348b; quarrel with no man for being f., 17b

Foreigners understand foreign languages, misunderstand f., 878b

Foreknowledge God's existence and f., 382b; God's f. and our freewills, 356b; God's f. is book of life, 107b; He know beforehand all things to come in time, 383a

Foreknows God f. but does not predetermine everything, 723a

Forenoon longer f., shorter afternoon, 10a

Forerunner great F. of the morn, 494a

Foresight One good forewit, worth two afterwits, 349a

Forest I had strayed into a dark f., 10b, 922a

Foretaste Be a f. sweet to me, 75b

Fore-thought Let thy fore-wit guide thy thought, 10a

Forget F. not that I am one redeemed, 75b; 'Tis sure the hardest science to f., 565b; would forgive and did f., 349a

Forgetfulness F. of the world, 395b; out of sight, out of mind, 2a

Forget-me-not And blue f., 910b

Forgets heart that has truly lov'd never f., 555b; No true penitent f. or forgives himself, 349b

Forgive After good dinner, one can f. anybody, 263b; F. and call me back again!, 6a; F. me, Father, 216b; f. our wanderings, 603b; How easy 'tis for parents to f.!, 349a; how good God is, how ready to f., 378b; Kings can f., if rebels can but sue, 349b; My patient God, f.!, 350a; Prompt to revenge, not daring to f., 773b; Reason to rule, mercy to f., 604a; To err is human, to f. divine, 300b, 349b; to sin more than God can f., 819a; would f., and did forget, 349a

Forgiven Come to our ignorant hearts and be f., 350a; F. and forgotten, 349a; One and all to be f., 7b; Sins are f. by the Holy Ghost, 667b; sins f. in three ways, 668a

Forgiveness charity is pardoning of the unpardonable, 157b; Christ's passion, cause of f. of sins, 44a; dying, bless the hand that gave blow, 349b; F. to the injured does belong, 472a; grant me f. of my trespasses, 764a; no man holy, unless Thou grant f., 500a; Only Heaven Means crowned, not conquered, 349b

Forgives No true penitent forgets or f. himself, 349b

Forgotten Forgiven and f., 349a; Seldom seen, soon f., 350a

Fori Priviligium F., 190b

Foris f. autem ab ecclesia, 126a

Form all mutable things receive a f., 393b; everything owes its being to f., 350a; must be some eternal and immutable F., 393b; Nature, difference that gives f. to anything, 633a

Forma Omne namque esse ex f. est, 350a

Forms essences of f. are many, 883b; knowledge of things through f., 393b; Their f. and words, royal things, 20b

Fornication Let unmarried not commit f., 350a; priest who commits f. or adultery, 150a

Forsake Forsaketh sin, ere sin you f., 764b
Forsaken those seeking help of BVM, not f., 89b
Forth F., to the alien gravity, 105a
Fortitude enables us to despise inconveniences, 350b
Fortress BVM, f. of salvation, 87a
Fortuitous f. depends on Providence, 373b
Fortunate height of happiness taken from f., 9a
Fortune favors the bold, 106a; F. is stately, solemn, proud, and high, 351a; f.'s ice prefers to virtue's land, 14a; general minister Set over world's glory, 350b; Gifts of f., pass as shadow on wall, 351a; God sendeth f. to fools, 566a; goods of F.'s keeping, 48b; hath in her honey gall, 351a; he was great, e'er f. made him so, 414b; His own chance, no man knoweth, 153a; Ill f. seldom comes alone, 351b; in men has some small difference made, 191b; no sea so wavering As giddy f., 351b; Our f. rolls as from a smooth descent, 646a; Peace is better than a f., 665b; Re-bless himself in spite of f.'s day, 767b; various turns of chance below, 153a; When f. favors, 351b; when greatest found, It hastes to die, 153b; when opposite, more profitable to men, 350b; women, prone To follow f.'s favors, 920a
Forty matron grown jaded Fat, f., and fair, 853a; Thy f. hours of lonely prayer, 94b
Forum penalty in external f., 117b
Found Thou hast f. me., 410b
Foundation f. of holy Church, 674b; f. of the sky, 105b
Founder F. of angels' state, 88b
Fount everlasting f. of truth, 20a; f. of that eternal fatherland, 301b; f. perpetual of virginity, 304b; Our Shepherd, f. of living water, 400b; sweet f. of love, 90a
Fountain BVM f. of mercy, 99a; Death chill'd the fair f., 250a; F. and Author of all graces, 197a; F. of. life, that had no fount, 340a; F. of love! Thyself true God!, 440a; F. of mercy, 196b; F. of our earthly pleasure, 491b
Fountains saving f. issued from Body, 71b
Four courage to tell people twice two is f., 218a
Fox English country gentleman galloping after a f., 423b; When f. preacheth, beware your geese, 351b
Fraction Broken and distributed is the Lamb of God, 594a; The peace of the Lord be with you always, 594a
Fragrance beauty is f. of goodness, 55b
Frailty how divide the f. from the friend?, 22b; not by f. of flesh, 302a; without Thee, f. of human nature cannot but fall, 428b
Frame aids to our weakly f., 21a; Maker of this mighty f., 21b, 166b
France, 297a, 351b
Franchises f. and immunities of American citizens, 17b
Francis de Sales, St., 352a
Francis of Assisi, St., 352a, 615b, 868a
Francis Xavier, St., 352a
Franciscans, 38a, 352a, 352b
Franks F. for friends, not for neighbors, 352b
Fraternity For all we are Christ's creatures, 352b; made genuinely

present in man's personal life, 353a; terrible secret that men are men, 352b
Fratres Orate f., 590b
Fraud f. is vice of man's alone, 353a; f. of hell's black king, 7b, 83b; What force cannot effect, f. shall devise, 348b; who so gnaweth at men's conscience, 253b
Fraus Fallere fallentem non est fraus, 159b
Fray no harm done in this f., 421a
Frederick II, Emperor, 423b
Free bold and f., 415a; Bright ensign of the f.!, 345b; by nature all men are f., 353b, 405a; Canossa will always remain consolation of f. minds, 354a; Canst thou ever impose anything upon f. mind?, 317a, 353a; contradiction in two words—"f. love," 575a; f. men governed by ruler for commmon good, 404b; From sin, sense, self set f., 77b; God makes no man slave, no doubter f., 537b; Heaven set thee f., 69a; If the Son has made you f., 35a; in Jesus Christ, there is neither f. nor slave, 825b; kings rule slaves, Romans f. men, 353a; people's fitness for f. institutions, 530a; truly f., when God fashions us as good men, 505a
Freedom abridging f. of speech, 184b; Ah! F. is a noble thing, 353b; an English subject's sole prerogative, 353b; conquest of f., realization of human dignity, 184a; difference between kings and Roman emperor, 353a; essential function of authority, to safeguard f., 784b; every man should worship according to his own convictions, 354a, 354b, 871a; f. of the truthstrong mind, 778a; f. of conscience, 210a, 872a; f. of speech, 42b, 355a, 355b; f. of the living dead, 635b; f. to be heard, 257a; from chains of our sins, 668a; full liberty of thought and speech, 355b; good emperors love f., bad, slavery, 355a; Men have right to propagate true and honorable, 355b; Minds in our day, governed by respecting their f., 674a; most successful government leads to highest aim by greatest f., 407b; No f. so great, as that of children of God, 353b; O f.! once thy flame hath fled, 353b; Religious liberty, not right of being without religion, 354b; rights and power of the spirit, 354a, 457a; rulers, should be craftsmen of f., 784b; sacrosanct rights of human f., 909b; serve Thee in security and f., 134a; test of f., security enjoyed by minorities, 353b; true f. is enclos'd In circuit of the mind, 830b; What matters death, if f. be not dead?, 354a
Freely He lives at ease that f. lives, 353b
Freemen Whether slaves or f., all one in Christ, 825a
Freethinking license to take up any or no religion, 470a
Freewill aid given to weakness of human will, 412a; angel, intelligent essence with f., 19a; can man be saved by free determination of will?, 356b; Christian bound to hold acts not subject to determinism, 357a; Church has protected this noble possession, 358a; dogma of faith, 358a; evil and f., 313a; freedom of will, nothing else than volition, 357a; f. and grace, 357b, 410b, 411b; f. and responsibility

for actions, 355b; God had written, not poem, but rather play, 358a; God presses us, but does not oppress our liberty, 357b; in arbitrament of his own will, 538a; in works, in faith, 356a; included in order of causes certain to God, 356a; Justification and f., 505b; Let us not defend grace so as to do away with f., 411b; light is given you to know good and ill, 356a, 357a; man, master of his own will, 356a, 357a; man has to save his soul by choice, 538a; moved and excited by God, 357a, 357b; no galley slaves in royal vessel of divine love, 357b; not merely passive, 357b; rational soul possessed of f. and volition, 356a; shafts, feathered with f., 305b; since Adam, not lost or illusory, 357b; That our will is free, is self-evident, 358a; tragic possibilities of f., 305b; we do what we will, we will what we are able, 411b
French And how I hate the horrid F., 475a; F. of Paris, was to her unknowe, 358a; irritating thing about the F., 300a; Jack would be gentleman, he could speak F., 478a
Fresh as f. as is month of May, 599b
Fretful If f. thoughts I feel, 210b
Friar barefoot f., all in brown, 358b; The f. hooded, the monarch crown'd, 191b; There was a f., a wanton one and merry, 56a, 927b
Friars Under the feet of my f., 520a
Friday on a F. fell all this mischance, 358b
Fried F. meats do harm, 263a; Thus is he f. in his own grease, 413b
Friend A faithful f. I fain would find, 359b; called 'half of my soul,' 358b; Christ comes, all trusting as a f., 484b, 359a; flattery of a f., can pervert, 359b; how divide the frailty from the f.?, 22b; I need a f. like Thee, 789b; I want my f. to miss me, 359b; keep well thy tongue, keep f., 358b, 872b; No man f. of Jesus Christ, who is not f. to neighbor, 565b; Prove thy f. ere thou have need, 358b; sinner's dying F., 233a; To God be humble, to thy f. be kind, 360a; unfaithful to God, cannot be f. to man, 471a; What trusty treasure can countervail a f.?, 360a; Who gain'd no title, who lost no f., 846b
Friendly A fresh, a free, a f. man, 358b; kept by f. thorns More upright than a rose, 361a
Friends All things swear f. to Fair and Good, 219a; better f., when sharply divided, 16a; Delighting to converse with books or f., 106b; Even reckoning maketh long f., 664b; Heavenly f. and guides, 21a; It was not I who sought f., 360b; lay down life for our f., 565a; Many kins folk and few f., 753b; naked of friends, 1a; saints, f. of Christ, 795a; The wretched have no f., 929b; there would not be four f. in world, 403b; Where now are his relatives and f.?, 245a
Friendship A love like f., steady, 360b; all who are joined to me by f. or blood, 753b; begun in this world, will be taken up again, 360a; Charity is a love of f., 156b; courageous and divine, Must f. be, 360b; divine law intended to establish men in f. with God, 526b;

essence of f., each friend reveals himself, 360b; far above the course of nature, 59b; F. and love differ, 559a; F., of itself a holy tie, 9b; f. of poor makes us friends of kings, 712a; f.'s glance and beauty's smile, 250b; If I speak to thee in f.'s name, 922b; O f., flower of flowers, 360a; Sometimes a fragile word A f. breaks or seals, 361a; Their simple f. is a court, 20b; Three stages to perfect f. with God, 761a; 'tis the bliss of f.'s holy state, 360a; true f. only through charity, 359b; whose winning love was like a f., 59b

Frieth She frieth in her own grease, 22a

Fright nature stood recover'd of her f., 342b

Frivolity power which makes us sad about things that do not matter, 341a

Frivolous easy to be solemn, hard to be f., 830b

Frontiers Christ is extending f. of Church, 771a

Froth F. the veins of thee, 47b

Frown militant f., 109b

Frugal f. crone, whom praying priests attend, 361a

Frugality F. is a handsome income, 361a

Fruit A tree is shown by its f., 673a; always present in seed, 1b, 109b; no soil so barren but tenderness brings forth f., 840a; Plug the f. and taste the pleasure, 684a; perceive f. of Thy redemption, 75a; That blessed f., culled by other hand, 288b; The f. is Christ, not I, 328b

Fruitfulness His perfect f., 387b; inexhaustible f. of Church, 119a

Fruits every good tree maketh good f., 339a; f. of the Spirit, 262a; Like Dead-Sea f. that tempt eye, 264a; tree is known by its f., 435b

Frying pan Leap out of f. into fire, 344b

Fulfilment Mercy is the f. of justice, 604a

Full As f. as a tun, 361b

Fun And will not have the f., 42b; five people do a thing for f., 298a

Fundamentalist whatever else f. is, he is not fundamental, 361b

Funeral Bury her at even 110a; I but prepare for my own f.?, 248b; Melt in one vast f. pyre, 281b; more solace for living than aid for dead, 110a; What would shame him, would turn back f., 811a

Funereal words f. spoken, 250b

Funny Giacobbe Finelli so f., O! My!, 454a

Fur warms a monarch, warmed a bear, 361b

Furnace My faultless breast the f. is, 30a

Furnisher BVM, f. of all things, 99b

Fury Beware f. of patient man, 662a; While f.'s flame doth burn, 22b

Fuss seething f. of self-effacement, 891a

Future all feeble spirits naturally live in f., 659b; belongs to those who love, not hate, 58b; Men, not mere dung to fructify seed of f., 306a; Most men strive for present, we for f., 361b; neither f. nor past actually exists, 868b; past, f., present, all present to God, 383a; Such is; what is to be?, 724b; the f., always our end, 420a; The f. belongs to the dandy, 239b; The

past, the f., two eternities!, 539a; To improve the f., needs human care, 659a; We measure everything by standard of f., 301b

G

Gabriel, Saint, angel G.'s words, 24b; captain of incorporeal hosts, 99b; Oh, by G.'s AVE, 99a; Let G. be now His groom, 487a; sang G., rang G.!, 59a; thou didst believe words of G., 88b; thy holy joy at G.'s word, 82b

Gain g. of this world is loss of souls, 362a; Light g. makes heavy purses, 712b; Measure thy life by loss instead of g., 550b; no small g., to know your own ignorance, 458a; preach for greed of g., 48b

Gaity merry, dancing, Laughing, time, 362a

Galaxy wake of white-sailed moon, 844a

Gale wind was fair, but blew mackrel g., 915a

Galen All dreams, as in old G. I have read, 276b

Galilean through the G. night, 97b

Gall Fortune hath in her honey g., 351a

Galleon The moon was a ghostly g., 620b

Gambling Hazard is very mother of lyings, 362b; Nought lay down, nought take up, 362b; The devil invented g., 362b

Game vanity, g. of children on sands, 892a

Games lawful to play g., 18a

Gander As deep drinketh goose as g., 403a

Garb gracious g. of May, 29b

Garden g. enclosed, 86b; g. full of leaves and of flowers, 599b; My heart shall be my g., 363a

Gardener G. of the stars, 42a

Gardens In the g. of God, 41a

Garment beauty put on with g., 7a; never g. too good For Thee, 104a

Garments skirts of angels' g., 20a

Gate bright g. to Jesus' throne, 232a; But I can knock at heaven's g., 834b; g. of immortal bliss, 86b; g. of mercy, open to the faithful, 673a; G. of morn, 95b; g. of safety, 100b; g. of salvation, 86b; g. shut, virginity of BVM, 79a; golden gate to heaven, 97b; Mother of God, g. of heaven, 86b; opening the g. of heaven to man, 74b; portal of skies, 82b; Stands trembling at g. of bliss, 218b

Gatekeeper At gate of monastery, let there be wise old man, 275b

Gates BVM opens g. of heaven, 90b; deliver me from g. of death, 90b; g. of hell shall not prevail, 135a; Pass through those g. of gold, 36b; sacred g. on high, 28b; The g. are pass'd, heaven is won!, 304a; The world has narrow g. and wide, 479b; ye everlasting g., 36b

Gateway This is the g. to the promised land, 634a

Gaudeamus G. igitur, 549a

Gave the more she g. away, The more she had, 367a

Gay All thing is g. that is green, 415b; Children not g., except now and then, 362a

Gazelle I never nurs'd a dear g., 264a

Geese When fox preacheth, beware your g., 351b

Gehenna ever-burning g. will burn up condemned, 426a

Gem G. to her worth ascends, 40a

Gender G. is a much wider term than sex, 837b

General g. of heaven, 19b

Generation contagion, normal in g., 466a; g. of holy orders, 730b; g. of Son of God, 369b, 370b; One g. forms another, 289a

Generosity abundance of Thy loving kindness, 363a; He that hath talent, let him hide it not, 155a

Generous G. even to serious fault, 601b

Genetrix Dei, 81a

Genius Church has right to service of g., 532b; full use of taste, act of g., 858a; g. and imagination, not same thing, 459b; g. is, in a sort, infallible, 363b; g. must be born, never can be taught, 363a; Great wits are sure to madness near alli'd, 363a, 568a; I have nothing to declare except my g., 364a; Man, being of g., passion, intellect, 545b; mark of g., insight into subjects, 459b; men of g. usually have religious dispositions, 363b; Strange power of g., 363b; To check young g. proud career, 228a; wrapped in solitude of his own originality, 631a

Geniuses accomplished imposter, most wretched of g., 456b; Great g. have their empire, 363a

Gentiles I will call the g. Mine, 400a; O King of the g., 8a; protection of doctor of g., 664a

Gentium law of nations called jus g., 530b

Gentle A g. hound should never play the cur, 273a; anger quieted by g. word, 22b; O Thou loving, g. One, 75b

Gentleman definition of g., one who never inflicts pain, 364a; English country g. galloping after fox, 423b; Jack would be g., he could speak French, 478a; no such thing as being g. at important moments, 364b; whatever else makes up a Christian g., 324b

Gentlemen As quasimodo geniti, and g. each, 352b; God Almighty's g., 364a; honest, civil g., 364a; to-day we need Christian g., 17a

Gentleness bend difficulties with g. and time, 364b; dealt with by hands pierced, 207a; He who can preserve g. amid pains, 364b

Geography no g. for Catholic as Catholic, 122a

Geometry discovered first by Egyptians, 365a

George, St., 324b

George IV, King, 141b

German Ours is American Church, not G., Italian, 143b

Gethsemane No silence, since G., 286b

Ghost The g. of his eternity, 803a

Ghost, Holy See Holy Ghost, Paraclete

Ghostly Old sanachies with g. tale, 365a

Ghosts I do not see g., only their inherent probability, 365a

Giacobbe Finelli, 454a

Giant Theirs was the g. race before flood, 365a

Gibbon, Edward, 164b

Gibraltar, 296a

Gift as though g. could be preferable to Giver!, 366b; common g. of God, 733b; even that I exist, is Thy g., 366b; g. of language, wisdom, knowledge, 874a; It is intention which makes g., 365b; liberal education only by God's g., 35a; My good, O Lord, Thy g., 410a; O g. of gifts! O grace of faith!, 327b; O wondrous g. indeed, 74b; offer g. at altar frequently, 307a; seal of g. of Holy Spirit, 205b; Throw no g. again at giver's head, 365b

Gift-horse Never look g. in mouth, 365b

Gifts bishops offers g. of holy Church, 67a; Bless us, O Lord, and these Thy g., 600b; excellent g. of the Spirit, 874a; g. are scorn'd where givers are despis'd, 365b; g. excel virtues, 366b; g. of eternal life, 813a; g. of Holy Ghost, 900b; g. of nature, common to good and bad, 409b; g. of Thy loving kindness, 401b; give to all from g. we have received, 13a; God looks at intention of heart, rather than g., 474b; learning, goodness, birth, g. of God, 451b; one should not use God's g. to war against Him, 736a; reveive and bless these g., these offerings, 591b; richness of divine g., 437a; Take g. with a sigh, 365b; Th' eternal g. of Christ the King, 28a

Gifts of Holy Ghost g., prudence, temperance, justice, fortitude, 366b; g. of Thy seven-fold grace, 241b, 584b; Who sevenfold g. hath shed, 207a

Girl heretic g. of my soul, 227a

Girls Among those g. and boys, 161a; Many g. want a mission in world, 113a

Give all I g. is given to One, 13a; Better to g. than take, 367a; g. to all from gifts we have received, 13a; G. us our daily Bread, 197b; most men g. to be paid, 365b; whoso suffers most hath most to g., 550b

Giver as though gift could be preferable to G.!, 366b; G. of life, 85b, 793a; O won(l)rous G. of the light!, 622b

Givers gifts are scorn'd where g. are despised, 365b

Gives God to His promise g., 367a; He it is Who alone g., 171b

Glad Let us live then, and be g., 549a; rejoice with g., weep with afflicted, 155b

Gladness Farewell g.! Welcome sadness!, 791b; G., welcome! grief, begone!, 286a; have good conscience and thou shalt have g., 209a

Gladstone, W. E., 367a

Glass The g. is full, now my g. is run, 542a

Globe queen of night lays her changing g., 40b; The rattle of a g. to play withal, 925a

Gloom air of everlasting g., 427a; g. of cloudy nights, 8b; Looks of fixed g., 791b; When I sink down in g. or fear, 210b

Glooms Adown titanic g. of chasmèd fears, 385a

Gloomy Let brothers avoid appearing g., 497a

Gloria G. in Excelsis Deo, 588b; G. Patri et Filio, et Spiritui Sancto, 588a; G. tibi, Domine, 589a; Sic transit g. mundi!, 710a; Soli Deo g., 367b

Gloriam Ad majorem Dei g., 367a

Glories dear Lord God, of His g. weary, 65a; g. of our blood and state, 249a; g. which exceed all

beauty!, 211b; Vanish the g. and pomps of earth, 367b; When all the g. of the night and day, 250b; Where'er we turn, Thy g. shine, 373b; Your g. may survive when you are dead, 542b

Glorified Provided that God be g., 377b

Glorify I bless You, I g. You, 368a

Glorious more g. than hosts above, 299a

Glory All g., laud and honor To Thee, Redeemer, 652b; Be Thine the g. and be mine the shame, 219a; courts of His g. above, 41a; end of a Christian, greater g. of God, 728b; end of priest, greatest g. of God, 728b; every man must be content with g. at home, 335a; Full of g., full of wonders, 378a; G. be to the Father, Son, Holy Ghost, 284b, 519b, 588a; G. be to Thee, O Lord, 589a; G. is wont to exalt, not humble, 367a; g. of Christ, 232b; g. of Church is g. of bishop, 67a; g. of God in poverty and abundance, 775b; G. to God for all things, Amen, 519b; G. to God in the highest, 167b, 588b; Go where g. waits thee, 367b; God forbid that I should glory, 229b; God's g. and social decorum, 17a; greatest baseness of man, seeking for g., 367b; Heaven and earth are full of Thy g., 591a; holy joy is to g. in Thee, 367b; Man's deepest abasement, pursuit of g., 301b; My g. and the lifter up of my head, 124b; Naught but wind's breath is world's acclaim, 335a; no hell like declined g., 9a; O splendor of God's g. bright, 522a; sharers of His g., 91a; she whom G. itself chose, 80a; Sing His g. without measure, 74b; So g.'s thrill is o'er, 421b; special g. of Mary, 81a; The g. of Him Who moveth all that is, 377b; Thine is the g. and power, 124a; Thus passes the g. of the world!, 367a, 710a; To God alone be g., 367b; To the g. of the King, 12b; To the greater g. of God, 367a; To Thee be g. for ever more, 70b; to Thee we render g. and thanksgiving, 596a; when time shall date thy g., 10b; Who is this King of g.?, 367b; Who pants for g. finds but short repose, 367b

Gloss wit may g. and malice may obscure, 530a

Gnosis teaching of apostles, true g., 873b

Glue g. of concord, 133b

Glutton g. of words, 923a

Gluttony G., a sin, 368a; Greediness closed Paradise, 368a

Go Further than the wall he cannot g., 905b; G. in peace, faith hath made thee whole, 764b; Go, songs, ended is our brief play, 45a; G., you are dismissed, 595b; He must needs g. that devil drives, 260b; I have desired to g., 616a; To whom shall we g. if we leave thee?, 758a

Goad Folly it is to spurn against a prick, 368a

Goal contemplative life has reached g., 5a; flame-wrapped g., 424b; run toward g. of Thy promises, 808b

Goats By guileful g. to ravening wolves misled, 484a

Goblet Friend of my soul, this g. sip, 279a

God A G. does not change his

ways, 397b; abiding yet mysterious, 381b, 386b; above all, 390a; all-perfect, unchangeable Being, 56b, 619b; all things aware of His existence, 392b; alone is completely immutable, 306a, 374a; alone knows depths and riches of His Godhead, 383a; always is, nor has He been and is not, 374b; Artificer of all, 50a; attainment of G., beatitude, 102b; attribute to G. good one sees in oneself, 399a; attributes transcend our comprehension, 388a; Author of all things, 224b, 244b; author of Bible and doctrine of Church, 63a, 64a; Beauty and beautiful, same in God, 54b, 55b; beginning and end of our journey, 397a; beginning of all things, 218b; being belongs especially to G., 301a; being, encompassed with difficulty, 388a; Being, supremely good and supremely great, 375b, 378b; better known by knowing what He is not, 387a, 393b; book of G. no man can write, 396b; by nature One, by participation many, 102b; By Whom all things are directed, 39b; by Whom all things were made, 226b; can neither deceive nor be deceived, 328a; cannot be seen in His essence by human being, 394b; cannot utter what is untrue, 61b; cause of things which makes but is not made, 372b; Chief of all things, 378b; Christian's G., G. of love and consolation, 384b; common good of whole universe, 561b; conscience directs thoughts to some Being exterior, 376b; consubstantial to the Father, 226b; created things cannot be measure of G., 390a; Creator of heaven and earth, 226a; difference between knowledge of G., and love of Him!, 395a, Dispenser of orders, 241b; Emperor of heaven, 63b; Eternal-Absolute, 225a; End of all ways, 492b, 754b; everlasting fount of truth, 20a; Every man for himself and G. for us all, 397b; exemplar of all things, 378a; existence of G., as a first principle, 376b; existence can be demonstrated from effects, 376a; Father almighty, with Son and Holy Ghost, one G., 591a; Fear G., honor the king, 176a; first known from nature, afterwards by instruction, 393a; first mover is the Deity, 375a; For Thee do I yearn, Justice, Innocence, 261b; fountain of our happiness, 754b; freely gives grace to servants, 67b; Gardener of the stars, 42a; Giver of honors, 241b; gives authority to rulers, 45b; Glory to G. in the highest, 588b; G. alone is immutable, 380a; G. and our country!, 143a; G. as Creator, 224a; G.'s living is His knowing, 383b; G. is always with us, 380a; G. is, and truly is, 393b; G. is Eternity, 387a; G. is everywhere, 427b, 654a; G. is in all things, as agent, 380a; G. is infinite in all He does, 381a; G. is love, 155b, 560a; G. is not only true, but Truth Itself, 390b; G. is one, alone unbegotten, without beginning, 133b, 386a; G. is only immutable substance or essence, 380b; G. is the cause of faith, 325b; G. is the great Supreme, existing in eternity, 391a; G. is the perfect good, 399a; G. is the Prince of the Universe, 526a; G. is truly the Father, 339a;

G. is where He was, 397a; G. of Abraham, Isaac, Jacob, 384b, 395b; G. of G., 226b; G. of spirits, 243b; G. of the martyrs, 308a; G. willing, 397a; good and just, 386a; Goodness is a symbol of G., 398b; governing agent of creation, 224b; great obstacle to belief in G., 146b; Greatest Good, 57a; He alone gives, 171b; He exists more truly than He is thought, 374b; He has left His secret marks everywhere, 390a; He is, He is known, He makes other things known, 382a; HE WHO IS, principal name, 387a; His knowledge of created things, 224b; His perfect fruitfulness, 387b; Husband of the heavens, 304b; I believe in one G., 226a, 372a; G. illumines us with His light, 102b; in silence that G. is known, 396a; infinite and incomprehensible, 381a; infinitely visible and infinitely credible, 331a; Jesus is G.!, 488b; King of kings, and Lord Most High!, 21b; Knower of secrets, 241b; knowledge of G., naturally implanted in all, 394b; knowledge of G., passage from light to darkness, 393a; knowledge of Him by natural reason, 395a, 396a; law implies a lawgiver, 376b; learn about G. from conscience, 395b; Life of faithful, 66b, 345b; light that satisfies, yet never sates!, 261b; Lord of all creation, 50a; loved for Himself, 236a; made all things by His Word, 223b; made Man, that we might be made G., 466a; Maker of heaven and earth, 226b; Man proposes, but G. disposes, 397a; Man thinks, G. directs, 397a; Metaphysical proofs of G., 376b; *Moses entered into the darkness where G. was,* 393a; most hidden and most present, 379b; My G.! how wonderful Thou art, 340a; My G., my Life, my Love, 78a; names applied to G. metaphorically, 386b; nature of G., circle whose center everywhere, 386b; nature reveals its Author, 372a; never new, never old, 386b; No human emotions can be strictly attributed to G., 387b; No man hates G. without hating himself, 42b; no such thing as, evolution of idea of G., 396a; not body, but uncompounded intellectual nature, 386a; not identical with universe, 377a; nothing happens without G., 3b; O eternal Truth, true Charity, lovely Eternity, 390b; O G., Who dost contain all things invisibly, 171a; O Source of all our yearning!, 258a; O Thou, our Author and our End, 445b; omnipotent, because He can do all things possible, 388b; once mind broken to belief of Power above, 146b; one and not many, 391a; one G., to Whom name of G. belongs, 619b; one Substance, one Divinity, one Majesty, 50a; only G. is heaven to human soul, 303a; only immutable substance, 301a, 374a; only one Who has no beginning, 372a; Originator of all things, 387a; Our discovery of G., G.'s discovery of us, 396b; past all Grasp, G., 374a; *Person* in G., relation subsisting in divine nature, 378b; praise, honor and serve G., 37a; Protector of life, 66b; proved by blindness of those who seek Him not, 376b; reason implanted in

minds, reveals there is one G., 392b; Savior and Guardian, 66b; Searcher of hearts, 241b; seven great facts and doctrines concerning G., 721a; Shoreless Ocean! who shall sound Thee?, 378a; So distant art Thou—yet so nigh, 374a; so lives that He has no principle of life, 376a; sought in authority of Scriptures, 60a; source of all morality, 12a; Spirit, has nothing corporeal in substance, 386a; Substance of eternity, 211b; supreme Beauty, 54a; supreme Measure, 419a; supreme Ruler and Lord of all, 47a; supreme Truth, 64b; the Overthrone, 13b; the Principle, 212b; Thou alone art without sin, 245a; Thou art within me, and about me, 380a; Thou of the boundless art the bound, 373b; throned behind Death with a sovereignty, 374a; To discover G. is to discover oneself, 377b; To love G. in sugar, 344a; to reach G. is happiness itself, 419a; to Whom nothing is contrary, 56b; truly and absolutely simple, 391a; Unbounded, an extended Unity!, 391a; universe is too significant to be anonymous, 377a; Unless Thou wert incomprehensible, Thou wouldst not be G., 381b; very Source of knowledge, 22a; vindicate the ways of G. to man, 397a; We believe in one G., 226b; we cannot know what He is, 380b; We know G. better through grace, 395a; we worship one G. in Trinity, 227a; who knows G., increases by knowledge of G., 394a; Whom none may live and mark!, 396a; without G., no true respect for authority, 47b; word 'G.', theology in itself, 388a; world is charged with grandeur of G., 414b; yet is nothing worthily said of G., 386b; You are wholly everywhere, yet nowhere limited, 379b

God-bearer we worship thee, O G., 86b

God-bearers You all are G., Christ-bearers, 888b

Goddess Speak, g.! since 'tis thou that best canst tell, 269a

Godhead confessing the true and everlasting G., 591a; From highest heaven G. comes, 25b; God alone knows depths and riches of His G., 383a; G. here in hiding, Whom I do adore, 75a; Knit is now our flesh to G., 36a, 481a; Of the G. the grandchild, 32a; ramparts of a Godhead's dwelling, 13b

Godliness Author of all g., 753a; Keep Thy household in continual g., 261b

Godmothers there can only be g. because there is a God, 634a

Gods angels would be g., 38a; artists, like Greek gods, 35a; But the g. are dead, 276a; cannot be many G., 391a; *God stood in the synagogue of g.,* 172a; G. Bring their heaven with them, 414a; G. meet g., and justle in dark, 397b; men become g. by participation, 102b, 254b, 468a

Godward Glad thanks let us G. carry, 40a

Goeth As fast as one g. another cometh, 193b

Gold A man may buy g. too dear, 397b; All is not g. that glitters, 397b; Better than grandeur, bet-

ter than g., 857a; Charity is pure g. which makes us rich, 156b; feet of clay make g. of image precious, 348b; G., a royal Child proclaimeth, 298b; g. you have hidden belongs to the poor, 154b; golden age comes to men who forget g., 11b; hidden in ground, belongs to poor, 909a; if g. rust, what shall iron do?, 316b; I'll do with a barrel of g., 918b; The sunset-g. to find, 540a; those gates of g., 36b; undisturb'd increase Of g., which profits not, 666a; Where is g. and silver?, 244b; With locks of g. today, 239b

Golden G. deeds kept out of sight, 452a; G. towns, where g. houses are, 873a; The g. bowl is broken, 250b; The g. lure Of wealth, 909a; What more g. or august than St. Augustine?, 44b

Golden Rule, 397b, 559b

Golgotha He sits at the foot of G., 832a; The rocks and flints of G.'s way!, 233b

Good all g. men are made happy, 419b; All that is g. *in* us, is not of us, 398b; All things, g. by participation, 378a, 398a; All things swear friends to Fair and G., 219a; All things work together for g., 882b; attribute to God whatever g. one sees in oneself, 399a; Be a g. child, and God will help you, 398a; Being, supremely g. and supremely great, 378b; cause of g. things, God's goodness alone, 313b; dull prospect of a distant g., 497b; enjoyment of highest and truest G., 211a; *every creature of God is g.,* 313a, 399a; every man seeketh after his greatest g., 398a; everything in world, g. for something, 398b; Evil gotten g. never proveth well, 362a; Evil things had origin in g. things, 313b; gifts of nature, common to g. and bad, 409b; God foresaw g. He would bring our of evil, 399a; God is the perfect g., 399a; g. fish, 155b; G. is best when soonest wrought, 255a; highest g., than which there is no higher, 378a; How fatal 'tis to be too g. a king!, 714a; I deny that to be g. which hurteth, 421a; In this life, g. never found without evil, 399b; Inasmuch as we exist, we are g., 398a; lack of courage on part of g., 399b; life of g. men, living study, 777a; Love the g., pity the ill, 603b; Man understands not distance between g. and evil, 399a; Many a g. cow hath an evil calf, 223b; my g. deeds Your act, my ill deeds my own faults, 398b; My g., O Lord, Thy gift, 410a; O God, from Whom all g. things come, 776b; Peace and g., 665b; perseverance in g., gift of God, 6b; power of choosing g. and evil, within reach of all, 356a, 398b; Supreme G., worthy to be loved, 216b; testimony of g. conscience, glory of good man, 209a; To the g. man to die is gain, 246b; useful is not always g., 398b; We exist because God is g., 318b; What is evil, but privation of g.?, 313a; Whatsoever is g., g. by divine goodness, 398a

Good-bye G., dear heart, 336b

Good Friday let us behold our Life lying in the grave, 400b; noon of somber sky On Friday, 286b

Good Works active in w., unfaithful in heart, 401b; all the saints, adorned with g., 401a; All thy g. Shall own thee there, 402b; ardently loving every work of mercy, 652a; Be not proud of thy own w., 451a; can man be saved by merit of works?, 356b; cease not to adorn yourself with g., 108a; constellation Of crowns, 402b; devoted to Thy name in g., 261b; done before justification, not sins, 402a; entreaties, made sufficient by g., 401a; faith, g. and freewill, 356b; faith without works is dead, 334a; God, great Employer, pays for every human deed of goodness, 604b; Good actions must be maintained with g., 403a; g. and humility, 450a; g. and merit, 402b; How speedily prayers of people who do g., heard!, 716b; in g., just do not sin, 402a; justified by w. and not by words, 403a; Let charity issue in good deeds, 157b; Let your w. be deposits, 401a; make us ever intent upon g., 401b; Men's chief study, to do without g., 402a; meritorious w. proportionate to everlasting life, 412a; obtain by self-denial, secure by g., 535a; one spoonful of g. should no more kill the soul, 402a; open mind in holy works, 214a; password of our King, divine deeds, 435b; prayers quickly ascend, which merits of w. urge, 716a; root of all g., hope of resurrection, 768b; true bracelets of a Christian woman, 108a; vices removed by g., 5a; We do w., but God works in us the doing, 401b

Goodness Accidie, shrinking from g. of God, 3b; beauty and g. point beyond themselves, 377a; beauty is fragrance of g., 55b; cause of good things, God's g. alone, 313b, 398a; divine g., specially attributed to Holy Ghost, 440b; essence of g., in some way desirable, 398a; God wished certain things to share in His g., 224b; G. and being, really the same, 398a; G. is a symbol of God, 398b; g. itself is happiness, 419b; He wills all things in His g., 384a; I hope all my confidence in the g. of God, 521b; Natural g. comes of God, 900b; no man masters degree of g. he desires, 899b; the g. of God is everywhere, 752a, 834b; Thy g., Jesus, would I sing, 78a; Thy g. moving Thee to give each thing his grace, 372b

Goods g. of Fortune's keeping, 48b

Goodwill grace tends mightily to increase g., 403a

Goose As deep drinketh g. as gander, 403a; Little wots gosling what g. thinketh, 403a; "See man for mine!" replies pampered g., 403a

Gospel All is not g. that thou dost speak, 403a; apostles received g. from Christ, 850b; bare ministry of preaching g., 648a; by G. we seem to be with Him, 60a; cannot be understood, unless Mary mother, 92b; do everything according to g., 13a; given through our Lord, 223b; let us mull over words of g., 82a, 492a; music of g. leads us home, 62b; My charge is to preach the g., 190a; not bare promise of eternal life, 193b; of the G., not a word, 61b; reading of prophets and G., 441a; reveals disclosures behind veil, 62b; The

beginning of holy G. according to, 589a; wind that is trumpet of liberty, 147b; worthily proclaim Thy holy G., 589a; You cannot halve the g. of God's grace, 536a

Gospel at Mass, 589b

Gospels simplicity of the G., 629b; tend to view G. as mere history, 62b

Gossip all who told it added something new, 403b; If all men knew what others say of them, 403b; scandal is g. made tedious by morality, 799a

Gothic Christ prophesied whole of G., 30a; Church will probably not see G. surpassed, 29b; However my reason may go with G., 29b

Gotten Evil g. good never proveth well, 362a; Soon g., soon spent, 362a

Govern all are eligible to g., 404a; right to g. is according to jus gentium, 734a; society can not exist in which no one to g., 406b

Governance we are all subjects of God's g., 882b

Governed human life, g. by reward or punishment of law, 524b; multitude, g. through reason of one man, 404b; whole universe, g. by divine reason, 526a

Governeth No man securely g., but he who will be subject, 405a

Government aim of good g., union and peace of citizens, 615a; All empire, no more than pow'r in trust, 406a; arises from agreement and consent of subjects, 405a; begins to decay, instant it begins to govern, 407b; best form of polity, partly kingdom, aristocracy, democracy, 404a; Christianity introduced no new forms of g., 406b; Church does not reject any forms of g., 255b; contract under which king accepted sovereignty from people, 774a; democracy is noblest form of g., 256b; divine law gives power to collected body, 406a; doctrine of divine right, 407a; forms of g. derive from law of nations, 46a, 405b; God's plan of g., called eternal law, 526a; g. of souls, is art of arts, 659b; g. of US, preferable to Catholics, 15a; G. shall be upon His shoulder, 78b; harmony between citizens and g., 257a; highest duty, to respect authority, 46b; human g. should imitate divine g., 871b; institution of governing body, pertains to legislator, 405a; man is by nature a social animal, 38b, 404a, 404b, 405b; most successful g. leads to greatest freedom, 407b; nations and individuals, under moral g. of Providence, 908a; No g. can be practically perfect, 406b; people can change form of g., 405b; personal g. and impersonal g., 407a; Political power, delegated by multitude, 180b, 406a; political power derives from natural law, 180b, 406a; power, in general, comes directly from God alone, 405b; power resides immediately in whole state, 406a; religious basis of g., 407a; should be administered for welfare of citizens, 407a; supreme monarchy in temporal matters, not by divine law, 405a; temporal g. does not owe existence to spiritual, 180a; There be two kinds of kingdoms, 405b; to rule men is art of arts, science of

sciences, 403b; whole world is under petticoat g., 278a

Governments authority of g. is just, 16a; In all g. there will be defects, 406b

Governor eke Governeresse of heaven, 96a; eternal law, plan of Chief G., 526a; qualities of perfect g., 405a; takes care of what appertains to common weal, 404b

Governors obedient to our g., 45b; Princes are bound by their own laws, 528b; superiors should regard equality of their nature, 300a

Grace A little reed in the hand of g., 410b; aid given to weakness of human will, 37a, 410a, 412a; All g. to God, from Whom all graces run, 410a, 553a; aptness for g., 412b; BVM received g. above others, 81a, 85b, 86a; by which men freed from evil and do good, 408b; can be lost after baptism, 52b; Christ is principle of g., 86a, 91b; co-heir of g., 455a; dew of Thy heavenly g., 159a, 302b; difference between g., charity, devotion, 262a; divine attraction, 410b; Doctor of g., 44b; doctrine of imputation, 737b; effect of g., 411b; Every holy thought, gift of God, 408a; faith, not lost with g., 327a; faithful sealed with g., 787a; Fallen nature needs g., 412a; freely bestowed, 409a, 411b; gift of the elect, 409b; gift of Thy seven-fold g., 241b, 584b; Give what Thou bidst, and bid what Thou wilt, 198a, 410a; God does not command the impossible, 410a; God in Whom all g. doth dwell, 94b, 409b; God, said to be present more familiarly in some by g., 379b; God's g. does not operate by sin, 328a; God's g., necessary for salvation, 408a; good works merit increase of g., 402b; g. and freewill, 411b; g. and precedent desert, 445a; g. and predestination, 722b; g. believes, reason does but opine, 332a; G. not freely given, not g. at all, 408b; g. of divine assistance, 450b; g. of spiritual joys, 494a; g. of the Word, 408a; has five effects in us, 409a; has need of believing minds, 49b; heavenly gift, 50a; I dwell in g.'s court, 901a; I hope through Him for g. to live, 445b; In space cometh g., 410a; instincts of heaven, 97a; Let g. be beginning, consummation, crown, 409a; Let Thy g. always precede and follow us, 401b; life in correspondence with God, 408a; light of God's own g., 89b; love is g. itself, 554a; man cannot live justly without g., 410a, 445a; Mother of g., O Mary blest, 83b, 90a; My g. is enough for thee, 908b; Nature and g., 289b, 412b, 761a; Nature is prelude to g., 376a, 863b; Next to g., time most precious gift, 870a; no one deprived of it, save by own choice, 148b; not rendered for merits, but given oratis, 408b; Nothing has power to obtain g., as prayer, 720a; nurse of devotion, producer of tears, 409b; O Lady, door of g., 90b; perfects nature, 412b; positive reality, 409a; sanctifying g., 52a, 411b; sever'd from God and g., 6a; Spirit of g. works to restore image of God, 408b; spiritual grace conferred by Sacrament, 76a; strength to fulfil God's will, 409a, 622a; The g. of concealing a g.,

410b; theology baffled, how g. influences mind, 220b; *Thou hast found me,* 410b; unction of Holy Spirit, 128a; usually taken in three ways, 409a; We know God better through g., 395a; what would Bible profit thee without g.?, 62a; When g. of God cometh to man, 409b, 410b; whereby soul is nourished, 72a; Why He draws one, and another not, 723a; wisdom, lifeless without g., 753b; Withdraw Thy comforts, so Thou leave Thy g., 410b; without g., man cannot merit everlasting life, 412b; without Thee, we are not able to please Thee, 417a; workings of divine g. are secret, 220a

Graces BVM and distribution of g., 91b, 92a; called gratuitously, 411b; cannot be obtained without humility, 450b

Gracious we are not excused for not being g., 210b

Grade rise from lower g. to higher dignities, 241b

Gradual at Mass, 589a

Grammar God does not take pleasure in bad g., 413a; G., ground is of all, 412b; Oh, but the heavenly g. did I hold, 519a

Granary catechumens stored in g., 72b

Grandeur For g., nations have their day, 475b; world is charged with the g. of God, 414b

Granite Ground of being and g. of it, 374a

Grant God cannot g. as much as they can crave, 342a

Granted that all things salutary may be g. us, 215a

Grape Ye praise the wine, before ye taste of g., 916a

Grapes pluck g. of consolation from the cross, 486a; tumbling clusters, like swarthy g., 47b

Grasped The more 'tis g., the faster melts away, 539a

Grass The green, green g., 599b; We trample g., and prize flowers of May, 803b; While g. groweth, horse starveth, 447a

Gratia g. gratis data, 411b; *g. gratum faciens,* 411b

Gratiae Doctor g., 44b

Gratias Deo g., 589a; *G. agamus, Domino Deo Nostro,* 591a

Gratitude where is g. without a God?, 413a

Grave could not retain Mother of God, 39a; every kingdom hath a g., 413a; g. or prison Illumed by one patriot name, 663a; g. things, oldest jokes, 453b; Hell is designed for sin a g., 306a; let us behold our Life lying in g., 400b; not one dead resteth in the g., 283b; silence of the g., 464a; their second marriage-bed, 455b; Today the g. has lost its sting!, 286a; Tread lightly, she is near, 413a

Gravedigger hire of g. and price of tiles, 110a

Gravediggers ministry of g., 34a

Gravers ministry of g., 34a

Graveyard Rest in the silent acre, 413b

Gravity nothing else than natural force, 413b

Gray Young as the youngest who donned the G., 830a

Grease She frieth in her own grease, 22a, 413b

Greased they have g. my boots already, 521b

Great anxiety for show of a g. name, 629a; Being, supremely good

and supremely g., 378b; first-rate g. man, equal with other men, 415a; God, good, g., blessed, wise, 375b; G. and small have same accidents, 413b; g. man and adversity, 736a; G. men are almost always bad men, 714a; G. men, different from enlarged repetition of average, 414b; G. objects exact a venture, 444b; He is truly g. who hath g. charity, 156a; Last pageant of the little g., 543a; Let one g. man be good, 415a; Many small make a g., 413b, 880b; No pow'r can make the slave of passions g., 655a; paradise of little men and the purgatory of g., 296a; Persons and things look g. at a distance, 414b; Thou wert, O Lord! too g. for our belief, 378a; To God, most good, most g., 397a; Whither wise and g. resort, 20b

Greater How can the less the g. comprehend?, 305b

Greatest O thou, the g. and the best, 386b; The g. can but blaze and pass away, 335a

Greatness As regards His g., impossible to know Him, 392b; cannot be comprehended at once, 414b; Desire of g., god-like sin, 14b; His g. is same as His wisdom, 386b; In g. is no trust, 623b; strength and g. give ability, 419b; Thy g. hid from human eye, 77b

Greats (School) Philosophy, not concern of those who pass through Divinity and G., 681a

Grecian my heart has ever gone with G., 29b

Greece, 415a

Greed preach for g. of gain, 48b; banish g. beyond reach of scandal, 415b

Greediness closed Paradise, 368a

Greek G. and Roman republics asserted state, 14b

Greeks apologetics, discovery of G., 27b; Church and race of G., 119b

Green All thing is gay that is g., 415b; G. hills, blue from distance, 434a

Gregorian inspiration and savor of G. form, 627a

Gregory the Great (I), Pope Saint, 18b, 44b

Gregory VII, Pope St., 354a

Gregory IX, Pope, 354a

Gregory Nazianzen, Saint, 69a

Grey whether g. mare better horse or not, 446b

Greyhounds swift as birds, 454b

Grief All hath perished But g. alone, 416b; An angel's g. ill fits a penitent, 277a; Deep in g. or ecstasy, 232a; Gladness, welcome! g., begone!, 286a; G. and death, born of sin, 415b; I'll taste the luxury of woe, 416a; Joy is life's tree—g. but its leaf, 498a; Let me share thy g. divine, 93b; no greater g., than to recall happier times, 415b; Nothing speaks g. so well As to speak nothing, 416a; g., sent post, o'ertakes them on the way, 491a; See how time makes all g. decay, 416a; Sure there's a lethargy in mighty woe, 416a

Griefs Could all my bitter g. assuage, 59b; I know you: solitary g., 416b

Grieve While I in silence g., 94b; You must not g. too much, 416b; 542b

Grindstone Hold their noses to g., 637b

Ground Upon one's own sole g., 443b

Growth All g. has bound, 153b; means unfolding of interior capacities, 272a

Gruel All the g. is in the fire, 338b

Guard g. Thy Church, 428b, 522a; keep constant g. over actions, 4a

Guardian Christ, G. of our souls, 66b, 461a, 484b; Our g. spirits meet at prayer, 21b

Guardians angels given us as g., 20b

Guest Every g., received as if he were Christ, 416b; O so divine a G.!, 823b; Thou, my heavenly g., 564a; Welcome the coming, speed the parting g., 416b

Guidance importance of spiritual g., 264a

Guide having Thee for our ruler and g., 736b; Our G., our Way to heavenly rest, 36a, 417a; religious g. intelligible to all, 62b; Seek some good man who will g. you, 264a, 639b

Guilt act of sin may pass, yet g. remain, 417a; Confess faults' g., crave pardon for thy sin, 719a; g. of punishment washed away by baptism, 52a; Past innocence, past g., 564a; Wash Thou all our g. away, 491b

Guilty A g. wretch like me, 21b; O Christ, Thy g. people spare!, 792b

Guns the men behind the g.!, 830b

Gutter-snipes g. of Jerusalem, 30a

Gymnastics To elevate g., sport, to supreme scope of life, 842a

Gypsies Wild headlong creatures, 417b

Gyrovagues monks who spend whole lives wandering, 618b

H

Habemus H. ad Dominum, 591a

Habere melius est enim minus egere quam plus h., 361a

Habit A h. is a settled disposition, 417b; difference between ability and h., 417b; *in h. found as man,* 467a; h. of holy religion, 189b; law of sin is fierce force of h., 816b; one of three roads to belief, 57b

Habitations Beautiful h., auras of delight!, 304b

Habits Form small h., 417b; turn evil h. to account of virtue, 418a; We cannot change our h. in a moment, 153b

Hades prison pointed out in Gospel, h., 740b; Thou didst slay h., 400b

Haec H. commixio et consecratio Corporis et Sanguinis, 594a; *H. sunt arma militiae nostrae,* 352b

Hail All h.! dear Conqueror!, 286b; H., angelic Bread of heaven, 75a; Hail! holy Virgin Mary—Hail!, 83b; Hail, Jesus, hail! Who for my sake, 104b; H.! Mary, thou art full of grace, 25a; H., Queen of the heavens!, 461b; H., Thou ever-blessed morn!, 169a; H., Thou man's Redeemer, 36a; H., true Body, truly born, 75b

Hair beauty draws us with a single h., 418a; Her h. was a waving bronze, 264b; Long h. and short wit, 418a; Take a h. from his beard, 53b; Tomorrow silver gray, 239b; With comb and brush, cleanse teeth and h., 423a; With h. that musters, 47b

Hairs Grey h. upon my head, 10b

Half if the h. shall judge the whole, 418a

Half-penny I cannot remember saving a h., 868a

Half-truth thing from which world suffers, 418a

Half-wits H. are fleas, so little and so light, 418a

Halls h. of the just, 89a

Haloes wear their h. even in hell, 305b

Hand by no human h. installed, 35b; Dear God, though Thy all-powerful h., 421a; He sitteth on the Father's hand, 36a; His right h. brings salvation, 168a; Man of Thy right h., 481a; one whom God's hand hath touched, 23a; Sweet h.! the sweet yet cruel bow, 31b; That searching eye of Thine and chastening h., 243a; Thine unintelligible h., 283a; To offer h. to superior, impolite, 418b

Handmaid BVM, honored as Mother and H. of God, 39b, 80a; Thy willing h. heard, 25b

Hands Floods and oceans, clap your h., 36a; h. of the Man are hard and scarred, 418b; Have both their h. full, 418b; *I will wash my h. among the innocent*, 590a; Let my h. slip not the rein!, 201b; Lord, into Thy h. I commend my spirit, 520a; Many h. make light work, 924a; put yourself in His h., 882b; They have pierced my h. and my feet, 657a; Vouchsafe to consecrate and sanctify these h., 727a

Handsome I'd rather be h. than homely, 918b

Hang wretches h. that jurymen may dine, 503b

Hanged house of a man whose father was h., 573a

Hanging At Tyburn half an hour's h. endeth all, 418b

Hap No h. so hard, but may in fine amend, 497b

Haplessness Know all our h. all through, 349b

Happens nothing h. without God, 3b, 391b

Happeth It h. in one hour, 447b

Happier no greater grief, than recall h. times, 415b

Happiness all h. man can gain Is not in pleasure, 684b; attainment of God is beatitude, 102b, 419b; blessedness, estate replenished with all good, 419b; consists in possession of truth, 102b; everlasting h., 89b; false optimism, modern h., 420b; From length of life no h. can come, 539a; h. and the good, 398a, 419b; h. is the reward of virtue, 900a, 902a; My bliss is in my breast, 209a; overthrown by small occasions, 9a; shadow of things past, 420b; to reach God is h. itself, 419a; tranquil conscience and innocence produce blessed life, 208a; two kinds of h. for mortal men, 420b; Universal peace, means of securing h., 665b

Happy all good men are made h., 419b; All men are democrats when h., 255b; All would be h. at cheapest rate, 736b; Better to be h. than wise, 420a; H. is man who can cut out avarice, 48a; H. the man whose wish and care, 215a, 443a; innocence and knowledge make man blessed, 102b; knowledge and action make a man h., 511a; most h. are the most sensible, 9a; O for the h. days gone by, 719b; Whoever possesses God, is h., 419a

Harbor BVM, h. for shipwrecked,

84b, 90a; H., like the Ark of old, 230b; O happy h. of the saints, 479a

Hard Nothing so h., it does not yield to harder, 673b; policy not right, by mere fact of being h., 847b

Hard-heartedness That heart hard, which does not feel hardness, 420b

Hardened encrusted character cannot be melted, 154a

Hardy, Thomas, 420b

Hare h. has still more heart to run, 165a; I like the hunting of the h., 454b; Mad as a March h., 568a; To hold with h., and run with hound, 253b

Harem good wife, spiritual h., 921b

Hark Hark! a glad exulting throng, 8b; H., a herald voice is calling, 7b; H.! h.! my soul! angelic songs, 20a

Harlot knows not how to love, 421a; Phryne had talents for mankind, 421a

Harm act of God does injury to no one, 4a; H. done, late followeth repentance, 764b; keep us from all h., 421a

Harmed No one is h., except by himself, 421a

Harmful let Church be kept from things h., 428b; process of digestion separates useful from h., 263b

Harmonious h. echo From discordant life, 287b

Harmony cause of h., 626a; do all things in h. of God, 433a; h. of body politic, 187b; h. of Church and State, 182b; heavens revolve under guidance of h., 421b; in our life, different degrees Render sweet h., 538b; musical rhythms of h., 626a; priests, like strings of a lyre, in h. with bishop, 726a

Harms beware by other men's h., 149b; Of h. two the less is for to choose, 162a

Harp nothing save his h., 36b; Sweeping my h. of floods mine own wild ways, 686b; The h. that once through Tara's halls, 421b; Ye h. on string that giveth no melody, 421b

Harper The H. draws his golden string, 627b

Harpings Homesick for h. of eternity, 306a

Harps They throw their h. down on the floor, 20b

Harsh H. words, though pertinent, uncouth appear, 923a

Harvest Behold, we have joy in h., 78a; long h. for a little corn, 422a

Haste Folks show much folly, when things should be sped, 422b; H. maketh waste, 422a

Hasten O h., O h. to Bethlehem, 170a

Hasteth He h. well that wisely can abide, 422a

Hastily both worken well and h., 422a

Hasty The h. man never wanteth woe, 422b

Hat Mine old h. must have a new band, 422b; Set he that h. on his head?, 112b

Hate Christians alone love those that h. them, 163a; future does not belong to those who hate, 58b; H. cannot wish thee worse, 422b; Hell, where all h. one another, 428a; If h. were none, 559b; neither h. man because of his vice,

314a; O mighty house of h.!, 428a; Opposite ire and h., 476a; To h. no man, 422b

Hateful alike to God and to his foes, 715b

Hates No man h.s God without hating himself, 42b

Hatred H. of the Christian name, 163a; H. only merited, when it is *known* to be merited, 422b; Love of God and h. of man, incompatible, 559a

Hats All good h., made out of nothing, 422b

Haughty When h. power mounts high, 153b

Haunted A grey h. wind is blowing in the hall, 365a

Have Better to h. than wish, 711b; Do well, and h. well, 275a

Haven h. of refuge, 85a, 100a

Having Lest h. Him, I must have not beside, 385a

Hawking The first point of h., hold fast, 423a

Hawks With empty hands men may no h. allure, 418b

Hay When the sun shineth make h., 645b

Hazard H. is very mother of lyings, 362b

Head Better a bald h. than no h., 48b; Bow your h., proud Sicambrian, 50b; by time the hat came, he had no h., 112b; Christ, H. and exemplar of Church, 122b, 123a, 132a, 482b, 676b; error of h., not of heart, 300b; heart has reasons of which h. knows nothing, 343b; His h. was bald, 48b; our H., the Savior, 35a, 80b, 123a, 126a; Peter, visible h. of Church militant, 678a, 696a; The h. without the feet is nothing, 641b; thinketh feet be where h. shall never come, 348b; When h. acheth, all body is worse, 423a, 531b

Heads Men who assist at worship, should have h. uncovered, 928b; So many h., so many wits, 607a; Their h. be full of bees, 55b; Two h. are better than one, 607a; women should have h. covered, 928b

Heal Earth hath no sorrow, heaven cannot h., 833a; They that are whole can h. others, 423a

Healeth He hath the sore which no man h., 423a

Healing Hail! my body's h., 100b; h. power of Thine Only-begotten, 320a; h. quality of baptism, 51b

Health And h. and hope have gone, 259a; Better to hunt in fields, for h. unbought, 318a; Christ, h. of fever'd soul, 491b; From laws of h. and sickness learn disease, 601a; God's will, as much in sickness as in h., 813a; grant us h. of mind and body, 89b, 239b, 423b; H. and apostolic benediction, 709b; H., silliest word in our language, 423b; h. ought to precede labor, 289b; H.; If thou in h. wouldst stay, 187b; If thou to h. and vigor wouldst attain, 423a; no h. of soul but in cross, 232b; no more prefer h. to sickness, 37a; nor life nor h. nor riches, is your own, 711b; Take care of your h., 423b; While grace affordeth h., 607a

Healthy h. body, and a mind at ease, 857b

Hear H., O Thou Shepherd of Israel, 166a; H. the other side, 499a

Hearse cold sorrows by Thy h., 131a; Lay garland on my h. of dismal yew, 344a

Heart A h. a h., sweet Saviour, 424a; Ah! my h. is weary waiting, 600b; all the pow'rs my poor h. hath, 77a; beshrew her angry h., 22a; broken h. and God's will done, 249b, 392b; *But in my sacred h.*, 305a, 790b; children begotten by h., 6b; Christ dwells in our h., 330a; Christ had h. of a boy, 65a; Christ's h. finds an earthly heaven, 790a; *Create a clean h. in me, O God*, 505a, 589a; divine a gift as mind, 424b; does not always lead to right conclusions, 343b; error of head, not of h., 300b; Every great achievement, inspired by motives of h., 850b; fitting we should consecrate ourselves to His sacred h., 790b; full of ordure is the h. of man!, 424a; God looketh upon the h., 474a; had I but Mary's sinless h., 78a; He alone sufficient for h., Who made it, 563a; has reasons of which head knows nothing, 343b, 423a; h. of God contained in Scripture, 64a; h. of man restless until it finds rest in Thee, 559b; H. speaketh unto h., 424b; h. that has truly lov'd never forgets, 555b; h. that hath a Mother, 790b; h., whose god is God, 361a; hold both keys of Frederick's h., 423b; humanity dedicated to sacred h., 88a; I am the human h.!, 424b; I lay a lonely h. Before Thy feet, 350a; I need Thy h., sweet Jesus, 789b; I see A H., a Face, and a Name, 790a; immaculate h. of BVM, 88a, 91b; in Thy love set all mine h. a fire, 562a; infinite treasures of Thy love, 789b; Jesu, joy of every human h., 36a; Jesus Opens to you His sacred h., 789a; lack of h., 423b; lady's h. and a beggar's purse, 424a; leaps with joy at adulation, 7a; let your h. be an altar, 726b; Live here, great h., and love and die and kill, 424a; Men often mistake imagination for h., 219a; most noble of members of body, 423b; My child, give Me thy h.!, 385a; My God, accept my h. this day, 207a; My h. is love, 553b; My h. shall be my garden, 363a; my h.'s undoing, 322b; O God, to Whom every h. is open, 586b; O h. of Jesus, h. of God, 790a; O h. of Jesus, purest heart, 789b; O Lord! my h. is sick, 374a; O to that h. draw nigh, 789a; *one mind and one h.*, 615b; only h. which does not lie, 790b; Right as a Ribstone Pippin!, 424b; sacred h., symbol of infinite love, 790b; Say one word, a h. may break, 880b; Self-sacrifice and chivalry, all come from h., 557b; selfish h., 384b; She was all sentiment and tender h., 807a; softening of h., softening of brain, 473b; sometimes finds out things reason cannot, 557b; Speak from your h., 424b; sphere of woman's glories is h., 555b; That h. hard, which does not feel hardness, 420b; That h. so innocent, 789a; thrusting spear of gold into my h., 562a; To hide me in Thy sacred h., 789b; We arrive at truth also by h., 884a; wearing h. upon the sleeve, 343b; weight of fear, anchor of the h., 342a; What heav'n-entreated h. is this?, 218b; Where h. has failed, 870b, 922b;

With all my h. and soul, 564a; wounded is the wounding h., 929a
Hearth The angels of our h.!, 443b
Hearts Blessed are the h. which can bend, 537b; cleanse thoughts of our h., 54a, 462a, 586b; devoted to Thy commandments, 665a; Direct our h. in Thy tender mercy, 417a; English h. to wisdom to incline, 295b; *Father knows the h. of all*, 67a; God breaks h. to remake them, 424b; God, Searcher of h., 241b, 792b; God works in h. of men and in freewill, 408b; human h. aglow With heavenly love!, 170b; Ladies rule where h. obey, 633b; Lift up your h., 366b, 424b, 591a; live by being wounded, 424b; our h. and minds, tested in crucible of truth, 429a; Stir up our h., O Lord, 7b; 'Tis love alone can h. unlock, 218b; True Christian h. cease to lament, 769b
Heathen A very h. in the carnal part, 163b; Ignorance, mark of the h., 429a; In h. parts, 425a; Let heathen sing thy h. praise, 415a
Heaven At h.'s court, 250a; Bearing the very weight of H., 38a; Between us and hell or h., nothing but life, 539a; Blessed Sacrament raises us to h., 71a; Blood is the price of h., 104b; Cruel, each h. for every soul Is paradise, 302b; Earth has no sorrow that H. cannot heal, 304a; Earth to h. it reuniteth, 168a; feeling about h., way they ought to feel about hell, 426a; full of energetic, 426a; God's eternal clime, 7b; golden gate to h., 36b, 97b; H. and earth are full of Thy glory, 591a; H. and earth in ashes ending!, 502b; H. in earth, and God in Man, 487a; h. is mystery to us earthly creatures, 233b; h.'s home-born sons, 40a; h.'s majestic dome, 599b; H.'s offended majesty, 98b; Let h. rejoice, and earth be glad, 25a; *Love* of h., only *way* to h., 304b; men, begotten for h. and eternity, 336b; nurseries of h., 305a; One minute of h. is worth them all, 304a; only God is h. to human soul, 303a; pure heart penetrates h. and hell, 745b; reward is in h., 43a; seeming h. proves oft a damning hell, 425b; Short arm needs man to reach to h., 305a; strict to h., but wide to hell, 539a; unlearned arise and take h. by storm, 106a, 531b; What does h. mean for rational soul?, 303a; world, only peopled to people h., 303b; would be hell to irreligious man, 425b
Heavenly attain to height of h. joys, 66b; comprehend h. things, 9a, 35b; Is comen of His h. towers, 168b; Man's mind, mirror of h. sights, 607a; our Way to h. rest, 36a; partakers of Thy h. treasures, 603b; to love things h., 425a
Heavens By all the h. thou hast in Him, 258a; God bent h. and descended to earth, 468a; golden garden's bars, 42a; H., distil your balmy showers!, 168a; h. that seemed so far away, 305a; h. themselves eternal are, 385a; large book that overhangs earth, 41b; Make little h. throughout a day, 425a; opened to us by Mother of God, 86b; revolve under

guidance of harmony, 421b; Shout! ye h., with laud and praising, 167b; Whom h. cannot contain, 79b, 81a
Heavenward List to thy h. call, 37b
Heavenwards means to getting h., 292b
Hebrew H. children bearing branches, 652b
Hebrews honored for antiquity, 493a
Hectoring no one less given to h. than Hector, 110a
Hedge Where the h. is lowest, 426a
Heels Show a fair pair of h., 426a
Height On mountain's golden h., 8b; where eagle's wing May scarcely dare, 453a
Heights by charity dwell among the h., 560a; impossible to live for ever on the h., 294b
Heir h. of divine benefits, 89a; Rise, H. of fresh eternity, 286b
Heiresses All h. are beautiful, 426a
Heirs fellow-heirs of His beloved Son, 124a; h. of God by Cross, 231b; h. of salvation, 20a; H. of the palace glad, 305a; sons and h. of God, 254b
Heirship great mystery of h., 467b
Hell abyss of H., 238a, 239a; accursed shore, 238b; air of everlasting gloom, 427a; amorous drift of man's herd to h., 392a; Beholding heaven, feeling h., 425b; Between us and h. or heaven, nothing but life, 539a; brought despair to vanquished h., 283b; burning with brimstone and stinking pitch, 427b; by Him, h. led captive, 90a; city of woe, 427a; deep pit, 245b; deliver souls from pains of h., 245b; doctrine of eternal punishment, 427b; eternal fire, 94a, 501a, 741a; eternal torment, 84b; ever-burning gehenna, 227a, 426a; everlasting punishment, 246b, 500b, 741b, 750a; Everyone there has measure of pain, 426b; fear of h. restrain thee, 427b; for sin a grave, 306a; foretaste of h. in this life, 22a; fraud of hell's black king, 7b; full of the talented, 426a; *gates of h. shall not overcome*, 693a; He destroyed prisons of h., overthrew devil, 77a, 400b; Heaven would be h. to irreligious man, 425b; H. is ruled by time, 427a; If God thy center, Be h. thy circumference, 882a; If you want to understand history, study h., 435b; man buyeth h. here with pain, 425a; no h. like declined glory, 9a; nobody knows where h. is, 426b; O mighty house of hate!, 428a; pains of h., 246a; pit of h., deep as despair, 426b; place of punishment for sins, 238b, 500a; pure heart penetrates heaven and h., 745b; Relinquish all hope, ye who enter here, 427a; St. Michael h. overthrew, 19b; second death that never dies, 428a; seeming heaven proves oft damning h., 425b; strict to heaven, but wide to h., 539a; There is in h. a place Called Malebolge, 427a; They order things so damnably in h., 428a; this h. upon earth, 490b; To dread h., 426b; Where is thy victory, O h.?, 283b
Hell, Descent into fitting that Christ should descend into hell, 428a; *He descended into h.*, 226b; His resurrection from h., 592a

Hellas Bright H. lies far hence, 296a

Hellenism Christianity owes debt to H., 27b

Helmet your faith, a h., 401a

Helmsman recognized in the tempest, 895a; Savior of our souls, h. of our bodies, 484a

Help BVM, h. to helpless, 84b, 87a, 89b; divine h. we hope by, 445a; h. from on high to bring, 21a, 492a; man needs divine h., 445a; No one so rich, he does not need another's h., 428b; we need God's h. and protection, 407b

Helper h. of the oppressed, 98a; if the Lord be our protector and h., 491a, 881b

Helpfulness part of our very nature, 428b

Helping joy not in ruling men, but in h., 300a

Helps to salvation, ordered by divine decree, 128a

Hemispheres Two h. in th' equinoctial line, 25b

Hen As nice as a nun's h., 636a; He that cometh now and then, shall have fat h., 447b

Henry IV, Emperor, 176a

Henry VIII, King, 140b

Heraclius, Emperor, 100b

Herald h. of the Word, 494b

Herb Alas! no h. in any garden grows, 601b

Herbert, Lord, 250a

Herbs radish, pear, theriac, garlic, rue, 26a

Hercules, 201b, 568a, 569b

Herds Whose h. with milk, 215a

Hereafter there we shall all live on together, 65b

Heresies always has been Church, and various h., 165b; Church must hold against all h., 124b; dull h. sprawling and prostrate, 650a; expelled, as if dead branches, 135a; *For there must be also h.,* 269b; forbidden by divine and imperial laws, 429a; Lord allows and suffers these things to be, 429a; Mary, thou hast destroyed all h., 24b, 88b, 100b; not produced through little souls, 429b; shorter thing to write h., than to answer them, 430a; survive by truth they retain, 165b, 430b; triumph which Church celebrates over all h., 134a; when h. grow bold, 269b

Heresy alien and false, added later, 429a; Anglicanism's most fundamental h., 24a; as wrong to divide Church, as to fall into h., 800a; badge of h., 430a; deadly drug, 428b; difference between h. and error, 432a; even if angel from heaven should preach otherwise, 429b; faint faith, better than strong h., 326b; from Greek word meaning 'choice,' 429b; H. and schism produce no saints, 116a; initial error, urging truth at unseasonable time, 430a; leave alone foreign fodder of h., 428b; modern h. of altering soul, 837a; opposed to faith, 429b, 800b; portion of divine system, instead of whole, 146a, 430a; schism and h., distinct vices, 800a, 801a; schism grown old, 429b; severs from body of Church, 128a

Heretic Any one who pertinaciously denies truths, 432b; deviates from norm of Catholic religion, 431a, 432a; estranged from hope of eternal salvation, 125b; interprets Scripture privately, 64a;

loves his truth more than truth itself, 432b; no one who quits Church of Christ will attain rewards, 125b, 429a; outside the Church, 431b

Heretical h. creeds are dead, 27b; infamy of h. dogmas, 144b; power of popes over h. rulers, 181a

Heretics baptism given by h., true baptism, 52b; boast they do not impose yoke of believing, 430b; books of apostates, h., prohibited, 151b; brothers of Christ, according to flesh, 133a; BVM, challenge to h., 82b; Check their sins, to produce repentance, 173b, 431b; Christians shall not marry h., 580a; Church has many hidden h. in midst, 431b; Church intercedes for those in error, 121a; conceit, mark of h., 429a, 431b; conventicles of h., 121b; deny unity of faith and Church, 120a, 145a; detest St. Augustine, 44b; even h. and schismatics style assemblies churches, 120a, 429a; forbidden to administer sacraments to h., 788b; have broken visible bonds of unity, 123a; loss compensated, 126a; many claim dignity of Christian religion, 145a; neither h. nor schismatics belong to Catholic Church, 120a, 429a; No one shall pray in common with h., 800a; No person to be compelled to embrace faith, 174a, 431a; refutation, serves sound doctrine, 120b, 269b; subjected to public services, 430b; their meeting places, not churches, 144b; toleration of h., more injurious than barbarians, 429b; unbelievers may be tolerated, 871b; we desire their repentance, not death, 173b, 431a

Heritage h. of angels, 71b

Hermit religion expressed by h. or hierarchy, 122a

Hermits anchorites or h., 618b

Hero Calculation never made a h., 432b; h. perish or sparrow fall, 384a; opposition makes a h. great, 646a

Herod Why impious H., vainly fear, 298b, 368a

Heroes H. are much the same, 432b; h. of Christ, 581b

Heroism Christian h., not same as other kinds, 432b

Herring Nother fish, nor flesh, nor good red h., 345a

Hew H. not too high, 14a

Hid by Whom that which lay h., made visible, 218b; I h. from Him, 385a

Hidden He lives well that has lain well hidden, 26a; You, most h. and most present, 379b

Hierarchy all priests not of equal jurisdiction, 190a, 433a, 433b; although many priests, Peter properly rules all, 677a; among apostles, distinction of power, 433a; apostles appointed first-fruits, to be bishops and deacons, 850b; as regards order, 190a, 648a; by divine ordination instituted, 434a, 648a, 695a; Church is founded upon bishops, 433a; consists of bishops, priests, ministers, 190a, 434a; constituted in degrees of power by holy ordination, 434a; distinction between bishops, 433b; diversity of states and offices in Church, 68a, 68b, 433b; divine ministry, 849b; h. and sacraments, sole basis of unity, 135a; members, not chosen by consent or

calling of people, 434a; necessity of h., 118b; not mere developments of latent germ, 272b; on model of heavenly hierarchies, 546b; one altar, one priesthood, 704a, 692b; other degrees have been added, 190b; real distinction of rank between priest and bishop, 647b; restoration of h. in England, 141b; supreme pontificate and subordinate episcopate, 190a; ultimate goal of missionary endeavor, native h., 613b; winged h., 19b, 70b

Hierarchical apostolical origin, gives right to higher h. rank, 433b; h. constitution of Church and authoritarianism, 47a; visible h. Church, 135a

High Death makes equal h. and low, 248a; Hail, most h., most humble one!, 97a; Lord, *h. and lifted up,* 390a; To Him no h., no low, no great, no small, 387b; we yet chant the h. things of God, 377b

Highbrows Whether we are h. or lowbrows, 576b

Higher Wisdom ordained h. should look after lower, 21a

Highest Glory to God in the h., 588b; Who climbeth h., most dreadful is his fall, 414a; You, O h. and nearest, 379b

Highway path of prayer, King's h., 720a

Hill I know a wind-swept h., 814b; To climb a h. and never to descend, 553b; wind that beats sharp crag and barren h., 237a

Hills Green h., blue from distance, 434a; great h. that stormed the sky, 11a; h. look over on the south, 472a; H. peep o'er h., Alps on Alps arise, 434a, 625a; homesick for eternal h., 47b

Hilt prove faith to the h., 26b

Him By all of H. we have in thee, 258a

Himalay East, oh east of H., 240b

Himself H. is with thee now, 25a

Hind A mild white h., immortal and unchang'd, 128b; panther noblest, next the h., 22b

Hinges Back on your golden h. fly, 36b; humble souls, h. on which God moves world, 452b

Hippocrates Nor without fees would attend H., 268b

Hireling h. theory, all power for wealth, 47a

His *The Lord knoweth who are H.,* 126a

Historian Catholic h. can look difficulties in face, 136a

Historic Catholic Church, an h. fact, 137a

Historical business of h. science, show how religion has fulfilled task, 760a; h. belief and saving faith, 326b); h. conclusions must include more than documents, 435a; h. sense of Scripture, 61a; no doctrine rigorously proved by h. evidence, 270a; strict laws of thought and h. growth, 270b

History American h. unknown to most Englishmen, 16a; better written from letters, 434b; book of world, full of knowledge we need to acquire, 435a; "Canons" for writing h., 154a; Catholic Faith does not contradict h., 274b; Catholic h. contains more of Protestantism, 32b; Christ of h., 483a; Christians, towed like slaves in wake of h., 774b; Church's dogmatic use of h., 270a; collapse of our neglected h., 252b; culture and art in h., 34b; ethics of h., cannot be denominational, 434b; Everything that happens in h., serves progress of Church, 733a; Examples of past times, 519a; great writers and h. of their times, 45a; h. and Catholic Church, 136a; H. is shaped like an X, 169b; h. of our Lord, matter of contemplation, 492a; If you want to understand h., study hell, 435b; its divine purpose, 435b; last judgment, clarification of h., 503b; law of h., not to fear to speak truth, 434b; Lord and Maker of h., 482b; materialistic theory of h., 598b; Only great man can write h., 434b; Religion is the key of h., 758a; seeing events as contemporaries saw them, 435a

History, Church summing up course of ecclesiastical h., 23a; works dealing with C. must have *imprimatur,* 152a

Hoe One must not run at one's hoe, 149b

Hog Every man basteth the fat h., 775a

Holiday Time takes no h., 868b

Holiest Praise to the H. in the height, 379a

Holiness atonement and new life of h., 44a; attained, without chastity consecrated to God, 437b; BVM, ark of h., 40b; consists in doing common things with fervor, 436b; h. of authors, no guarantee against error, 63b; H. rather than peace, 436a; indwelling Holy Spirit, 436b; not all height is h., 436b; reputation of h., and evil actions, 659b; Sanctity, whereby man's mind and acts applied to God, 435b, 436a; Thine awful h., 379b; To obtain gift of h., work of *a life,* 436a; whole life conformable to that of Christ, 436a

Holiness (title) Your h. holds place of God on earth, 710a

Holy active life makes man h., 5a; Be h., for I am h., 436b; BVM, all-h. one, 89a; Church called h. because consecrated to God, 128a, 128b; Church h., because body of Christ, 128b; *Do not give that which is h. to dogs,* 194a; enter into h. of holies with pure souls, 587b; Every h. thought, gift of God, 408a; first, to be h., 435b; H. God, h. Strong One, h. Immortal One, 379a, 589a; *H., H., H., Lord God of Hosts,* 379a, 589b, 591a; h. of holies, 84b; Holy things for the holy!, 593b; no man h. in Thy sight, unless Thou grant forgiveness, 500a; One only is h., one only is Lord, 594a; Thou art h., our God, 379a; Thou only art h., 588b; We should not profane h. things, 788b; what religion needs, h. men and women, 436b; 437b;

Holy Ghost action of Holy Spirit embodied in Church, 840b; author of Bible and doctrine of Church, 63a, 64b; baptize in name of the H., 49a; bestows fulness of grace on those who believe rightly, 874a; bestow upon them the H., 189a; Blessed Spirit! Dove divine!, 371b, 440a; Burn our reins and our heart with fire of H., 159a; coeternal One!, 440a; Come, H., Creator, come, 670b, 862a; Come, O Sanctifier, bless this sacrifice, 590a; Comforter and Consoler, 10a; cooperation with guidance of

H., 15a; Descend, Spirit of the eternal King!, 671a; descending in likeness of a dove, 480b; effected conception in Virgin, 25a, 50a; effluence of God, 438a; equal adoration with Father and Son, 439a; ever rejoice in His consolation, 438b, 439a, 670b; Every truth without exception, from H., 883b; Fountain of love! Thyself true God!, 440a; fountain of wisdom, life, holiness, 439a; From Both proceeding as from One, 439a; *Gift* is His proper name, 439b; gifts of H., 366b; Glory be to the H., 35b; goodness, specially attributed to H., 440b; Heavenly King, Paraclete, Spirit of truth, 438b; Holy Paraclete, 205b, 439a, 670a, 670b; Holy Spirit, come, 440a, 671a; I believe in the H., 226a, 226b; illumination of Holy Spirit, 670a; In the name of the Father, Son, H., 587a; interpreter of divine revelation, 840b; Lifegiver and Sanctifier, 840b; living Spring, living Fire, 670b; Lord and Giver of life, 226b, 439a; Love of Sire and Son, 440a; *Love,* proper name of H., 302b, 370b, 439b; manifested Christ, 438b; moves man to belief, 53a; my protection, 369b; not inferior to Father and Son, 438b; one and same Spirit of Father and Son, 369a; proceedeth from Father and Son, 226b, 369a, 369b, 370a, 438b, 439a; Promise of the Father, 36a; *Receive the H.,* 69a, 242a, 648a, 693a, 727b; Sacrament, by invisible operation of Holy Spirit, 308b, 590b, 592b; sanctifies waters of baptism, 49b, 51b; sanctifying principle, 310b; 436b, 438b; *Send forth upon them the H.,* 241b; sending of the Holy Spirit, 242a, 670a; soul of Church, 126b, 438b; spake by the prophets, 226b; Spirit of truth, 36a, 128a; Sweet Unction and true Love!, 670b; teach faithful by light of Holy Spirit, 439a, 670a; temple of the H., 40b; terms *breath* or *spirit,* 370b; There is one H., 438b; Thy sevenfold Spirit, 205b; Treasury of good things, Bestower of life, 438b; two distinct offices of Holy Spirit, 841a; where Church is, there is Spirit, 128a; wisdom of Son, clemency of H., 108b

Holy Saturday if anyone cannot fast the two days, 337b; Lord rested in tomb, 442a; this most sacred night, 441b; You shall keep vigil all the night, 441a

Holy See (Apostolic See) alone has grown strong, 662a; anything contrary to A., not Catholic, 704b; Apostolic See, H., Chair of Peter, 709b; apostolic throne, 176a, 704a; belongs to A., to regulate liturgy, 547b; bound before others to defend faith, 694b, 698b, 705b; church of Constantinople, subject to A., 700b; consult secrets of Apostolic office, 704b; custom has been for word to be sent to us first, 693b, 697b, 698b; defines questions of faith, 705b; do honor to memory of holy apostle Peter, 697b; Does Peter's chair flatter you?, 701a; During the vacancy of the H., 709b; enemy of H. also enemy of true religion, 705b; first See is judged by no one, 703b; 709a; force of law shall belong to whatever A. has ordained, 698b, 699a, 700b, 704b; has pri-

macy by voice of Lord, 694a; has primacy over whole Church, 679a, 696a; He who deserts chair of Peter, does he still believe he is in Church?, 693a, 694b; head of Roman world, and sacred trust of apostles, 698a; I am joined in communion with your blessedness, 694a, 695a; I am moved to obedience to that S., 705b; in A., religion always preserved without spot, 705a, 705b; in relation to masses of Catholics, 702b; in this one chair unity preserved, 693b; its pre-eminence, 174b; judgment of A., than which no authority greater, 700a, 700b; let letters be written to bishop of Rome, 697b; makes large allowance for special customs, 770b; men resort to See of Peter from all quarters, 707a; monarchy of H., 117b; must approve versions of Bible, 63b; never prevailed against by false teaching, 679a; no one may appeal from this See, 698b, 700a, 701a; office of Peter, both directing power and supreme authority, 694b; one bond of communion, through intercourse of letters, 694a; one God, and Christ, one Church and one chair founded upon Peter, 692b; Only Church of Peter has always stood fast in faith, 705b; organ, mouth, head of Church, 702b; Peter continues to live in his successors, 676b, 694b, 695a, 696b; pontifical authority to rule Church and all people, 700a; rock on which Church is built, 694a; rock over which gates of hell shall never prevail, 694b; sovereignty under Lateran Treaty, 708b; They have not heritage of Peter, who have not see of Peter, 692b; We bear the burdens of all, 694a; whence flow rights of venerable communion, 698a; whence priestly unity takes its source, 704a; why should it not pass judgment on secular matters?, 176b

Holy Thursday Assist this performance of our service, 442b; day Savior celebrated pasch with disciples, 442a

Homage No h. of world they claim, 20b; when we more than human h. pay, 443a

Home angels help bring us h., 21a; dream of h., 443a; everlasting h., 244b; H. is homely though it be poor, 443a; h. is not a convent, 443a; no home within thy arms, 23a; Of youth, and h., and that sweet time, 58b; our h. in paradise, 246a; Our h., is deep in thee, 88a; sanctify h. life, 438a; This day Thou wentest h. to God, 35b

Homeliness Over-great h. engendereth disapraising, 215a

Homer, 443b

Homeward draw me h. to your heart, 107a

Homicide Parricide, more wicked than h., 852b; The greatest crime is h., 625b

Homines Tempora mutantur et h. deteriorantur, 153a

Homo H. cogitat, Deus indicat, 397a; *H. proponit, sed Deus disponit,* 397a

Honest Here lies a truly h. man, 444a; h. man may take fool's advice, 9b; h. man, noblest work of God, 444a

Honey A fly followeth the h., 444a;

Fortune hath in her h. gall, 351a; With milk and h. blest, 479a

Honor Act well your part: there all the h. lies, 281b, 444b; All do him h., 31a; All glory, laud and h. To Thee, 652b; All worldly h. now farewell, 764b; but an empty bubble, 907a; Force is of brutes, h. is of man, 444b; h. and money nearly always go together, 617b; H. is peace, 666b; love of h., zeal for virtue, 900a; no more prefer h. to disdain, 37a; paid to BVM, redounds to Him, 84a

Honorable more h., glorious than hosts above, 167b, 299a

Honored h. in his end, 493b; I have been h. and obey'd, 449b

Honors enamored of h., 445a; great matter, not to rejoice in human praise and h., 714a; h. are enthrall'd to hapless doom, 542a; h. of this world, emptiness, 444b

Hook By h. or crook, 220b, 445a, 679b; take me with Thy h., 484a

Hope And what was dead was h., 446a; BVM, our stalwart h., 39a, 98a; certain expectation of future glory, 445a; common bond of h., 133a; Cooperation is the one h. of world, 221b; cross, true ground of Christian h., 229b; Cursed, everyone who placeth h. in man, 569a; Fair h. is dead, 276a; faith and h. contrasted, 330a; grant us increase of faith, h., and charity, 334a; h., the calends, 445a; If once thy h. be anchor'd in God, 882a; inspiration of middle-aged, 446a; no love without h., no h. without love, 329b; now there remain faith, h., charity, 334a; O highest H. of mortals, 438a; Relinquish all h., ye who enter here, 427a; shall brighten days to come, 659a, 833b; springs eternal, 445b; Their endless h., to Thee that bow, 167a; we never really live, only h. to live, 420a

Hoped What can be hoped for?, 445a

Hopeless youth, h., 446a

Hopes Agonized h., and ashen flowers!, 416b; Fears and h., and h. and fears, 170b; I've seen my fondest h. decay, 264a; my h. always fixed on cross of Christ, 521b; Up vistaed h. I sped, 385a

Horace, 446a

Horizon where sea-line meets the sky, 446b

Horn All are not hunters that blow the h., 446b; drinking h. goes round, 365a

Horoscopes predictions, made by h., 41b

Horror heavy sat on every mind, 342b; my soul is filled with h., 40b

Horrors cannibals wish to sup on h., 111b

Horse A man may bring h. to water, 446b; common h., worst shod, 447a; handsomest compliment, to call him a h., 162a; only creature that weeps for man, 446b; When steed Is stole, make stable-door fast, 446b; While grass groweth, h. starveth, 447a

Horsemen White h., who ride on white horses, 582a

Horses hoofs of invisible h., 447a; like women, require soothin' word, 447a; Thunder on, you silver stallions, 447a

Hosanna angels sing Osanne, 84b, 87b; H. in excelsis, 591a; H. in the highest, 591a, 652b

Hosannas Hark! the loud h. ring, 8b; lips of children Made sweet h. ring, 652b

Hosius, Bishop, 698a

Hospitality Christian should offer h., 447b; O boundless h.!, 97a

Host Lo! the sacred H. we hail, 74a; my heart, A home for each H., 198a; O'er a sign of white on the altar, 598a; offering Himself on cross as immaculate h., 489b; Receive, O holy Father, this spotless h., 589b; Reckoners without h., must reckon twice, 447b; The God of hosts in slender H., 77a; whole world's H., 97a

Hostility indefinable as love, 297b

Hosts Holy, Lord God of H., 36a, 591a; true Body remains in consecrated H., 76a

Hot beat iron while h., 476b; H. as toast, 447b; Little pot, soon h., 712a

Hound nought good a sleeping h. to wake, 273a; swift like a h. upon the moor, 48a; To hold with hare, and run with h., 253b

Hour every sliding h., 106b; Fools! I also had my hour, 38a; my last h. is nigh, 250b; Suffered the trampling hoof of every h., 827b; Who am not sure to farm this very h.?, 248b

Hour-glass break he the hour-glass, 9a

Hours At Whose behest the h. successive move, 636a; happy h. employed upon my books, 107a; H. are golden links, 447b; Like h. at midnight passed, 827a; Thy forty h. of lonely prayer, 94b

House abiding in h. of God alway, 12b; At one small h. of Nazareth, 437b, 658b; Church, h. of Master, 66b; enter into h. of the Lord, 520a; H. without hound, 448a; In my Father's h. there are many mansions, 302a; O mighty h. of hate!, 428a; this h., as nigh heaven as my own, 303b; Three things damn a h., 448a

Household h. of God, 172a, 579b; Let your h. love you, 448a; watch over Thy h., 736b

Housekeeping care of a smallish house, 448a

Houses children that build h. of tile-shards, 26b

Howards not all the blood of all the H., 637a

Hue As often change from h. to h., 153a

Hugh by it came him sweet Sir H., 49a

Hughes, Archbishop John, 448b

Human above the flood of h. things, 159b; All h. things are subject to decay, 249b; aptness for grace, part of h. nature's estate, 412b; Before you can be saint, you have got to become h., 437b; divine Nature and h. beings, 21a; from one mass of clay, h. kind wrought, 570a; h. beings, children, 571b; h. life, governed by reward or punishment of law, 524b; h. nature, assumed by Son of God, 448b; H. nature is born of pain of woman, 638a; H. nature is h. nature, 200b; H. nature, not completely corrupt, 412a; h. nature, so capable of divine purpose, 118a; h. nature, something social, 575b; h. race fell by means of virgin, 85a; h. race knit together in mysterious membership, 186b; h. specialty of humor, 454a; It is h. to err, 300b; nothing so irrepressible,

as h. nature, 449a; O God, Who hast marvellously created h. nature, 590a; profound fascination of h. character, 154a; super-h., only place where you can find h., 855a

Humaneness religion and h., not rivals, 449b

Humanism inhuman h., 449a; two conceptions of h., 449a

Humanitarian modern h. can love all opinions, 449a

Humanitarianism hard as inhumanity, 449a; postulates of genuine h., 449a

Humanity as a whole, changeful, mystical, 571b; As long as h. lasts, can be hated, 612a; Christianity and improvement of human race, 165a; dedicated to immaculate heart of Mary, 88a; dedicated to sacred heart of Jesus, 88a; destinies of h., in America's keeping, 15a; ends God has assigned to h., 666b; future of h., 140b; He lingers in breast Of our h., 483b; human race lifted up to better things, 165a; h.'s highest destiny, 15b; May h. of Son be our help, 632b; Oh, how I love h., 475a; Who vouchsafed to share in our h., 590a

Humble gold dust of a h. life, 660b; He alone truly h., who restrains soul, 451a; h. souls, hinges on which God moves world, 452b; H. thyself in all things, 451b; they wish to be h., without being despised, 473b; When a proud man thinks he is h., 726a

Humble-minded to h., that Christ belongs, 449b

Humble-mindedness give me spirit of h., 450a

Humiliation H. is way to humility, 449b; sign that grace is in store, 450b; triumphed gloriously, 229b

Humility art of reducing ourselves to a point, 453a; attain to summit of h., 450a; Bear to be last, 452b; bed of tribulation, school of h., 880a; better to have little knowledge with h., 451b; Blessed is he that expecteth nothing, 453a; certain mystery of h., 452b; come to Christ through meekness and h., 671b; Endure undreamed h., 350a; first degree of h., obedience, 642a; grant us virtue of true humility, 450b; he is in need, who is without h., 450b; highest science, truly to know and despise ourselves, 451a; humiliation is way to h., 449b; H. is descending charity, 452a; If no h., everybody would have committed suicide, 453a; imitate Mary's h., 101a; in oneself not attractive, attractive in others, 452b; Its counterfeits abound, 452b; kiss hem of God's h., 488a; ladder of ascending actions, 450a, 451a; medicine of h., 175a; mother of salvation, 450b; O manifest infirmity, O wondrous h., 166a; old h. and the new, 453a; one of the most difficult virtues to attain, 452a; religion rooted in h., 27b, 452b; roots of humility of BVM, deep, 88b, 91a; seven degrees of h., 450a; singularly pleases God, 88b; surest sign of strength, 453b; toil of h., 883b; true h., 452a

Hummingbird From flower to flower he flies, 453b

Humor All jesting, in its nature profane, 453b; Giacobbe Finelli so funny, O! My!, 454a; human

specialty of h., 454a; If we won't brighten our h., live pleasantly, 683b; sense of h., act of laughter, 523a; Wit is lower than h., 454a
Humus Nos habebit h., 549a
Hunger fortune to fast, famish for h., 287a; h. in frost, work in heat, 923b; H. is insolent, 454a; h.'s teasing call, 287a; Men h. for Thy grace, 158a; Nevermore he knoweth h., 72a; Thou hast appeased h. of my soul, 196b
Hunt though you h. the Christian man, 165a
Hunter A mighty h., his prey was man, 454b; He knew whole of woodcraft up and down, 454a
Hunters All are not h. that blow the horn, 446b
Hunting H. a hare, Was all his fun, 454b; silly and trying business, 454b
Hunting-grounds frontiers between sense and spirit, devil's h., 807a
Huntsman that sweet H. from above, 562b
Hurry ruins saints as well as artists, 422b
Hurt More afraid than h., 342a; No fatal h. of foe she fears, 157a
Hurteth I deny that to be good which h., 421a
Hus, John, 127a
Husband A knowing wife Can always prove h. at fault, 455a; better sexes should misunderstand each other, until they marry, 455b; co-heir of grace, 455a; Every h. exacts chastity from his wife, 455a; h. and wife, 889b; H. of the heavens, 304b; make a good h., make a good wife, 455a; Thou to Thy spousal, Art H., 131a
Husbandry h. of God's Church, 271b
Husbands All women long For h. tough, 454b; H. in heaven, whose wives scold not, 455a; satisfied with their h. in flesh, 575a; women reckoned years by h., 268a
Hutch Palate, the h. of tasty lust, 198a
Hymn h. for conquering martyrs raise, 581b; I'll sing a h. to Mary, 95a; No h. worthy of Thee, 489a; Praise in h. and canticle, 74b
Hymns consolation of h., 266a; h. of thankful love and praise, 28a; I wept at the beauty of Your h., 546b; pray to God with psalms and h., 716b; To angelic h. aspire, 28b; worship Creator with h. and songs, 266a
Hyperdulia, 928a
Hypocrisy butter would not melt in her mouth, 456a; leading a double life, 456b
Hypocrite diverts government to domination, 456b; very unhappy man, 456b
Hypocrites point, like finger-posts, way They never go, 456a
Hypostases, 481b
Hypostatic grace of h. union, 482b
Hypostatically Word, h. united Himself with flesh, 481b
Hyssop For manna, thou hast returned h., 400a; Thou shalt sprinkle me with h., 587a
Hyssopo Asperges me, Domine, h., 587a

I

Ibi Ubi Petrus, i. ecclesia, 709a
Ice walking on i., 539a
Ichthys our *I.* Jesus Christ, 49a
Iconoclast not impartial, 456a

Idea Great things done by devotion to one i., 363b
Ideal Americanism, more than European i., 17a; Christian i., found difficult and left untried, 165b; only thing to be done with i., do it, 457a
Idealist To say man is i., is to say he is a man, 457a
Ideas Americans stubbornly conservative in i., 18a; Church and existing ideas, 270b; False i., refuted by argument, 457a; great i. require time to develop, 272a; I war with men on account of i., 265a; immutable types of things, eternal, 383b, 456b
Ideology very different from faith, 457a
Idiot Thinking in isolation ends in being an i., 473a
Idleness enemy of soul, 457b; Mother of vices, 457b
Idol anguish of worshipper over broken i., 24b; god endowed with attributes of Deity, 459a; yellow i. to the north of Khatmandu, 457b
Idolaters offer to idols things belonging to men, 457b
Idolatry adoration of Blessed Sacrament, not i., 76b; Church, society's rampant against idolatry, 458a; deliver pagans from worship of idols, 887a
Idols burn what you have adored!, 50b
Ignatius Loyola, St., 841a
Ignatius of Antioch, St., 23b, 697a
Ignominy undergo i. of the Cross, 655b
Ignorance blindness of i., 21b; in men, vice, 458b; I. of natural law, never excusable, 527a; 'learned i.', 458a; mark of the heathen, 429a; miserable from no cause save my i., 612a; no small gain, to know your own i., 458a; Our knowledge compared with Thine, 511b; results of sin, i., concupiscence, 412b; that divine knowledge of God through i., 394a, 609b
Ignorance, Invincible i. and salvation, 127b; no limits to invincible i., 458b
Ignorantia docta i., 458a
Ikons holy images of our Lord and our Lady to be revered, 795b
Iliad great, because life a battle, 63b
Ill Benumbing sense of i. with quiet slumbers, 826b; i. gotten, i. spent, 362a; In the rising, stifle i., 315a; my good deeds Your act, my i. deeds my own faults, 398b; They that think none i., soonest beguiled, 348a
Illegitimate barred from holy orders, 649a
Illiterate educated men can do what i. cannot, 289b
Illnesses Long i., good schools of mercy, 813a
Illuminated inwardly i., 458b
Illuminatio 'Dominus i. mea', 536b
Illumination i. and attainment to God, 102b; i. of Holy Spirit, 670a; i. of knowledge, 458b
Illumine I. all!, 91b; I. Thy Church, O Lord, 494a
Illumined we are i. by light of God, 102b
Illumines Christ i. the world, 89a; creator i. mind, 214a
Illusion American i., their country world apart, 16a; we put up with i., when we cannot get truth, 459a

Illusions every age is fed on i., 459a
Image no i. between soul and Creator, 486b; holy i., no power to hear, 459a; made Himself, way, i., pattern, 254b; Man, created to i. of God, 576a, 569a, 569b; most pure i. of BVM, 82b, 87b; prince, i. of almighty God, 3a; Son, I. of invisible God, 481a; Spirit of grace works to restore in us i. of God, 408b; We adore Thy most pure i., 656a
Imagery religious i. and Church, 31b
Images holy i. of our Lord and our Lady to be revered, 436a, 459a, 795b; honor done to them, done to prototypes, 459a; legitimate use of i., 796a; sacred relics and i., due veneration, 101b, 928a
Imagination brave man not dominated by i., 108a; genius and i., not same thing, 459b; I. in a poet, 685a, 893b; Men often mistake i. for heart, 219a; People can die of mere i., 459a; sanctify i. and senses, 16b; Starve i., feed the will, 914b; writing, depends upon force of i., 459b
Imbecility If Nietzsche had not ended in i., 473a
Imitate Him Whom thou adorest, 928a; humility of Mother of God, 88b, 101a
Imitation Bible provides pattern for i., 63b; i. of Christ, 889a
Immaculate how spotless is thy virginity, 79b; i. flesh and blood of BVM, 85b; i., glorious Lady, 593a; i. heart of BVM, 88a; i. Mother of God, 41b, 80a, 82b, 89a; nothing can be stained where God is, 466a; Oh, the rapture Of that most i. Mother, 460b; service of Thy holy and i. mysteries, 849b; Unstained as virgin snow, 97b
Immaculate Conception BVM, preserved from original sin, 460b, 461a, 462a; Conceived immaculate, 97b; I am the I., 462a; Immaculate of man's infirmities, 463a; Lo! Mary is exempt from stain of sin, 462a; O Virgin Mother of our God, 461b, 462b; our baptism, in Mary anticipated, 41b; thy birth was free from guilt, 96b; view, birth holy, but not conception, 460a; worthy habitation for Thy Son, 462a
Immanence divine transcendence and i., 380a, 390a; God, in all things by His presence, 379b, 381a; God, in all things, as an agent, 380a
Immaterial wings of your i. glory, 21a
Immaturity majority remain boys all their lives, 108a
Immeasurable art is i. translated into measurable, 34a; He is i.; Who hath made all things by measure, 387a
Immense Ruler of the dread i., 21b
Immersed soul i. in God, 288b
Immersion baptism by i., 49b, 51a
Immigrants concentration in social groups, 17b
Immoderation correct i. moderately, 614a
Immodest Frequent not company of i. persons, 200a
Immodesty Ambition is mind's i., 14a
Immolate we i. to God Body and Blood of our Lamb, 308b
Immolated for us He is i. again, 308b

Immolation dedication, i. of oneself, 310a; He cleansed us by i. of His own body, 176b; i. of Christ our Passover, 43b; I. of Isaac, 75a; knife of words of consecration, 71a

Immorality more corrupted by reading immoral books, 151b

Immortal angel has by grace i. nature, 19a; doom'd to death, though fated not to die, 463b; Holy God, holy Strong One, holy I. One, 379a, 589a; i. from the mortal, 466b; I. in its dying!, 241a; mind is subsisting form, consequently i., 836a; study of created things, stepping-stone to i., 848a; The i. could we cease to contemplate, 623b; Their noonday never knows What names i. are, 336a; To be i. is to share in Divinity, 463a; to pass into i. life, 303b

Immortality bloom of joyous i., 252a; child is a pledge of i., 161a; Christ, giver of life and i., 39a; Christianity and life of soul after death, 164a; determines all our acts and thoughts, 463b; fair i.'s perfumed nest, 286b; garb of i., 215b; Heavily Presses this i., 464a; i. of soul, 358a, 464b, 769a, 835a; i. of the thinking being, 270b; knowledge, soul survives its adventures, 446a; mortality had to be absorbed in i., 85a; our i. Flows thro' each tear, 859b; prize, i. and eternal life, 43a; promise of future i., 246a; Thou didst shed i. upon mankind by the cross, 399b; universal desire for i. of fame, 464a; world committed to some kind of belief in afterlife, 464a

Immunities rights and i. of American citizens, 17b

Immunity i. of Church, not derived from civil law, 464b

Immutable Creator, being uncreated, is wholly i., 375a; God, only i. substance or essence, 13a, 301a, 374a, 380b

Immutably God, being Who endures i., 56b

Impartial an iconoclast is not i., 456a; every man who cannot make up mind, an i. judge, 499b

Impatience anger and i. give foretaste of hell, 22a

Impediments Church may dispense from i., 577b; Church may establish i. to marriage, 577b, 579a

Impenitent No power can the i. absolve, 764b

Imperfect even imperfect being is good, 56b; so termed for want of perfection, 464b

Imperfection never attain to perfection, while we have affection for i., 672a

Imperial pope may use the i. insignia, 701a

Imperialism that is the meaning of Empire Day, 465a

Imperium sacerdotium and i., 177b

Impiety I.! of harden'd mind, 465a

Importance cherish notion of our i., 452a

Important No one, displeased at becoming i., 465a

Imposition episcopate received by i. of hands, 67b, 68b; i. of hand shall be in place of baptism, 667b; i. of hands and illumination of soul, 105b; not through laying on of my hands, 242a; virgin does not have an i. of hands, 639a

Impossibilia Nemo potest ad i. obligari, 465a

Impossibilities That God can do i., 388b

Impossible I think and think on things i., 241a; God does not command the i., 410a, 901a; No one obliged to do the i., 465a

Impostor accomplished i., most wretched of geniuses, 456b

Impoverished Begger'd by fools, whom still he found too late, 320a

Impressionism another name for final scepticism, 799b

Imprimatur Church's right to censor books of faithful, 151b

Improperia, 400b

Improvement Christianity and i. of human race, 165a; i. of workers in, 38b

Impudence good men starve for want of i., 465b

Impulses natural i. serve to wreck personality, 264b

Impulsive To be i., leads to troublesome times, 465b

Impunity child of carelessness, 465b

Impure hearts corrupted by i. desire, 861a; The i. cannot love God, 745b

Impurity In theatre, demon of i. displays pomp, 862b; Mother of God touched by no i., 80a

Imputation doctrine of i., 737b

In I. cruce salus, 797b; I. hoc signo vinces, 229a

Inaccurate majority remain i. all their lives, 108a

Incapacity modesty of mind, admitting i., 615a

Incarnate BVM bore i. Son, 39a, 81a, 82a; I. Word, 167a, 440a, 494a

Incarnated He became i. in man, 752a

Incarnation act of generous love, 8a; apostate nature linked with heavenly things, 98a; birth in time added nothing to eternal birth, 467a; Body which He assumed, 307a, 468b; body, rational soul, Deity, all in one Person, 71a, 466b, 468b; Born for us on earth below, 74a; born without defilement, 466a; chief reason, that He might lead to spiritual love, 468a; childbearing of blessed Virgin, beginning of salvation, 632a; coming of Son in the flesh, 7b; communication of properties, 482a; condescension ineffable, incomprehensible, 468a; does not cease to be God, because Man, 481a; Earth to heaven it reuniteth, 168a; extraordinary miracle, 80b, 468b, 610b; Father espoused Son to human nature, 131a; flesh belongs to divine Word as His own, 467a; for our salvation, 588b; God bent heavens, descended to earth, 468a; God of Israel entered through gate, 79a; God, seen by men, 167a; great mystery of heirship, 467b; greatness of God not cast off, 468b; He participated in our infirmities, not sins, 467b; He took upon Him form of servant, 467b; His coming to men, 8b; His earthly throne, 168a; His work on earth, 74b; History is shaped like an X, 169b; if I. a phantom, salvation a phantom also, 466a; i. of Providence capitalized, 469a; kind of celestial exchange, 466b; liberating flesh by flesh, 166b; like hook to lure devil, 467a; Lord came to seek back lost sheep, 85a; made Man, that we might be made God, 466a, 468a;

Man is God, God is man, 469a; marriage, kind of foreshadowing of i., 578b; Mary and doctrine of i., 84a; mystery by which i. extends itself, 166a, 467a, 467b; mystery of the Word made flesh, 82a, 167a, 170a; not an event but an institution, 469b; Not from necessity, but from love, 468a; ordained by God as remedy for sin, 468b; partaker of our mortality, partakers of His divinity, 466b; perfect God became perfect Man, 466a, 468a; purpose of His i., 466b, 492b; That which He was, He remaineth, 467b; thinking of i. as thing past, 469a; time raised to infinite, 469a; true faith, Godhead and manhood, 481a, 482a; union of Word and flesh in womb, 81a, 481b; unique union, 468b; what greater thing, than that God should become man?, 468a; wishing that we live by His, He died by ours, 466b; Word assumed nature of our flesh, 71a, 167a, 168a, 466b, 468b; Word suffered in flesh, was crucified, tasted death, 467a

Incense an odor of sweetness, 590a; I. doth the God disclose, 298b

Incivism heaviest stone flung at Church, 663a

Inclinations live according to reason, not i., 344a; open to supernatural inspirations, 840a; our i. are unto evil, 200a

Incline I. the ears of Thy loving kindness, 586b

Incompatible man and woman, as such, i., 574b

Incomprehensible God, infinite and i., 381a, 381b; where the I. is laid, 167b

Inconsistency T'abhor the makers, and their laws approve, 469b

Inconstancy I. of mind, beginning of all evil temptations, 860b

Incontinence stain upon chastity, 158b

Inconvenienced by afflictions, 10a

Incorporated in Christ through spiritual rebirth, 43b

Incorporation in Blessed Sacrament, 73a

Incorporeal angel is i., 19a; evident that He is i., 387a

Incorruptibility eternal i. of Mother of Christ, 39a

Increase I. and multiply, 336a, 579b

Incredible i. that i. should have been believed, 57a

Ind He cometh out of Ethiope and I., 70a

Indecision Cast off i., 881b; Such dread of sin was indolence, 470a

Independence true protection of Church, its own i., 183a

India As doth the cocks of I., 153a

Indians (American) must not be deprived of liberty, 470a

Indicat Homo cogitat, Deus i., 397a

Indifference agnosticism leads to moral i., 12a; holy i. goes beyond resignation, 470a

Indifferent i., and Catholic faith, 147b; i. heart, a ball of wax in hands of God, 470a

Indifferentism have faith, and do nothing about it, 138a; license to take up any or no religion, 470a

Indignatio I. principis mors est, 248a

Indiscretion Nothing, so like innocence as an i., 472a

Indissolubility i. of marriage, 577a, 578a, 579a

Individual assert state, to detriment of i. freedom, 14b; development of nation and i., 631b

Individualism death-dealing anarchy, 470b; flourishes in garden of Church, 129a; freed from all bonds and laws, 470b; modern i., misunderstanding, 470b

Individualists i. and Catholic faith, 148a

Individuality Each has a byway of his own, 470b; one thing worth anything, 255b; sacrifice something of i., 343b

Indolence spirit of i., 450a; Such dread of sin was i., 470a

Inductive progressive realizations of i. science, 270b

Indulgence remission of temporal punishment for sins, 471a

Indulgences Let all value i., 471a; power of conferring i., granted to Church, 470b

Indulgentiam I., absolutionem et remissionem peccatorum, 587b

Industrialism fundamental evil of i., 471a

Indwelling Christ our righteousness, by dwelling in us, 506a, 716a; God is not everywhere by i. of His grace, 379b; His coming into men, 8b; i. Holy Spirit, 436b; Thou wert with me, 54a

Infallible all confess themselves fallible, 737a; bishops not i. in doctrine, 70a; Church of Rome professes to be i., 23a; Everybody feels genius is i., 363b; i. authority, 706a; i. definitions, irreformable, 706b; i. truth, always shall prevail, 147b; Nobody can be progressive without being i., 732b; not i. acts, but acts of infallibility, 706a

Infallibility belief in i. and incarnation, 707a; Church cannot be deceived, 119a; definition of papal i., 480a; faculty or gift, 706a; from errors free, 134b; given to edification, not destruction, 129a; i. of Church, as guide, 118a, 129a; i. of Roman Church, 111b, 679a, 705b; its limitations, 129a; necessity of i. for Christianity, 129a; Only Church of Peter has always stood fast in faith, 705b; pope preserved from error in decision on faith or morals, 706b; prodigious power, sent to master evil, 129a; Roman pontiff, when he speaks ex cathedra, 706b; the whole hath a promise, 129b

Infallibly someone guessing i., 711a

Inebriated souls of faithful i. in Cup, 72a

Inequality I. of rights and power, from Author of nature, 471a; official i., essence of army, 31a; some men set over others, 300a

Inerrancy i. of writers of sacred books, 64b

Inesse t. potuit, non prodesse, 50b

Inexorable The one i. thing!, 259b

Infâme, L' Je voudrais que vous ecrasassiez l'fâme, 138a

Infamy Death's but a sure retreat from i., 444b; I wish that you would crush this infamy, 138a

Infancy Like age at play with i., 646b

Infant An I. of human years, 487a; I. Jesus; Christ Child, 486b; i. saints, 472a; Now the Maid her I. bearing, 169b; oft are heard the tones of i. woe, 161a; You shall not murder newborn infant, 1b

Infanticide no reason for condoning direct murder of innocent, 1b, 2a

Infants be as i. who do not know wickedness, 472a

Inference What is not perceived immediately, arrived at by i., 512b

Inferences Life, not long enough for religion of i., 332a

Inferior some men i. to others, 300a

Infidelity If any one saith no sin but i., 887a; unfaithful to God, cannot be friend to man, 471a

Infidelium In partibus i., 425a

Infidels salvation of man born among i., 797b

Infinite All that concerns Him is i., 81b, 492a; art provides window on i., 34b; can be comprehended by Him, 471b; dangerous, to talk glibly about i. God, 390a; finite expression made i., 33b; God is i. in all He does, 381a; God, synthesis of i. and boundary, 34b; man's soul craves i., 34b; slipshod notions about i., 689a; through cycles all but i., 20a; womb contains the I., 25a

Infinitude Wall of i., 105b

Infirmities He participated in our i., not sins, 467b; heal our i., for Thy name's sake, 369b

Infirmity look upon our i., 736b; O manifest i., O wondrous humility, 166a; old age, lengthened i., 11b

Influence if Thou Thy i. withdraw, 715a

Influencing I shrank from thought I was i. others, 471b

Ingratitude I. is soul's enemy, 47b; I.'s a weed of every clime, 471b

Inheritance He too shared common i. of flesh and blood, 481b; natural right of transmitting property by i., 471b; no share in divine i., 80a; we are buried without our i., 48a

Inhumanity Humanitarianism, hard as i., 449a

Iniquities Take away from us our i., 587b

Iniquity I have loved justice and hated i., 318a; there is no i. with God, 820b

Initium I. sancti Evangelii secundum, 589a

Injured Forgiveness to the i. does belong, 472a

Injuria Summum jus, summa i., 528a

Injuriam Actus Dei nemini facit i., 4a

Injuries Most i., happily met by indifference, 472a

Injury act of God does i. to no one, 4a

Injustice attack on organized i., 829a; does injury to sanctity of law, 472a; where most law, most i., 528a

Ink I. is black, and hath an ill smack, 472a

Inn Take mine ease in mine i., 283a; The world's an i., 542b

Innisfallen, 475a

Innocence be as infants who do not know wickedness, 472a; Came i. and she, 472a; doth slumber now, 55b; For Thee do I yearn, Justice, I., 261b; His passport is his i. and grace, 472a; i. and knowledge make man blessed, 102b; Nothing, so like i. as indiscretion, 472a; Past i., past guilt, 564a; That Thou wilt suffren i. to spill, 381b; tranquil conscience and assured i., 208a; your cruelty only proves our i., 851a

Innocency i. of body and soul, 159a

Innocent An hour sufficed for thee, Thou i.!, 483b; He's armed without, that's i. within, 444b; I will wash my hands among the i., 590a; Nothing too difficult for i., 472a

Innocent III, Pope, 354a

Innocentes Lavabo inter i., 590b

Innocents, Holy All hail, ye little martyr flowers, 441a; infant saints 472a; O blessed babes! first flowers of Christian spring, 441a; There dwell I with the babies innocent, 544b

Innovate Let them i. in nothing, but keep traditions, 874a

Innovations to which we are not committed, 472a

Innovetur Nihil i. nisi quod traditum est, 874a

Inns He knew the taverns well in every town, 472a; The i. are full; no man will yield, 168b

Inquisition Spanish I. and American Constitution, 15b; Spanish i. and Protestantism, 473a

Insane Men are so hopelessly i., 473a

Insensibility man's i. to great things, 807a

Insight angels' complete i. into objects, 22a

Insignificance feel our i., 625a

Inspiciuntur Equi donati dentes non i., 365b

Inspiration Direct our actions by Thy i., 428b; divine i. of Bible and all parts, 64a, 64b; feeling that matters, not expression, 473b; fired with the muses' madness, 6a; i. of Scripture known through Church, 62a; prevenient i. of the Holy Ghost, 505b

Inspirations sweet attractions and holy i., 562b

Installed by no human hand i., 35b

Instaurare I. omnia in Christo, 492b

Instinct How i. varies in the grov'ling swine, 473b; We know little about inner working i., 474a

Instincts all God-given i., 16b; Dipped in the i. of heaven, 97a

Institution Catholic Church, most flexible i. in world, 138b; time-honored i., of noble memories, 23b; Words of I., 592a

Institutional Religion, at all times traditional, individual, i., 758b

Institutions people's fitness for free i., 530a

Instructed i. by somebody I did not know, 292a

Instruction life of BVM, for i. of all, 92a; most profitable thing for i., history, 434a; permeated with Christian piety, 290b; religious i. of young, 290b

Instructor Maximus ecclesiarum i., 44b

Insult stiff apology, second i., 28a

Insults courage in despising i., 474a; Do not be afraid of i., 448b

Insurrection 'the sacred right of i.', 255b

Integrity i. of artist lifts man above world, 35a; i. of BVM as virgin intact, 80a

Intellect apt for the i. to know, 61b; disciplined for own sake, 289b; Divine Intellect and Its art, 31b; faith and i., 333a; has not much to do with knowledge of God, 396a; i., mind and thought, nothing apart from soul, 606b;

Man, being of genius, passion, i., 545b; most superficial of our faculties, 324a; When i. is cultivated, 608a

Intellectual angels are i. natures, 19b; By thy large draughts of i. day, 258a; Catholic Church and i. progress, 139a; i. appeal of Christianity, 164a; reaction, always found in i. advance, 888a; university modern mind, 601b

Intellectuals class capable of going quite wrong in all directions, 474a

Intelligence art is virtue of practical i., 34a; kinds of knowledge, i., science, wisdom, prudence, 512b; Too much wit, like too little, 601b

Intelligible Religion can be made i., 331a; to be i. is to be found out, 111b

Intention God looks at i. of heart, rather than gifts, 474b; i. of doing what the Church does, 52b, 788a; It is i. which makes gift, 365b

Intentions God weigheth the i., 474b; Good i. don't protect us in the least, 841b

Intercession BVM presents prayers to her Son, 25a, 88b, 89a, 90a; Hear us and plead for us, 10b; make i. for women vowed to God, 87a; Through the i. of blessed Michael, 590a

Intercessions i. for living, 593a

Intercourse deliberate frustration of act, offence, 66a; agreeable in social i., 691a; i. and health of race, 474b; nuptial commerce holy, 66a

Interest common i. always will prevail, 152b; i. is her name with men below, 209a

Interfere difficult problem, how much to i., 474b

Interior Human authority cannot legislate about i. acts, 528b; man's estate in the i. life, 494a

International i. community, and respect for law, 531a

Internationalism The international idea, 475a

Interpretation i. of Bible by modern methods, 64b; I. of Scripture according to Catholic teaching, 60b; spiritual i. of Old Testament, 61a

Interpreter Custom is the best i. of laws, 237b

Intolerance faith Which builds on heavenly cant, 164b; I pray religious i. may never take root in our land, 473a

Intoxication permanent i. of most Americans, 17b

Intrinsic i. reason, as criterion of truth, 16b

Introibo i. ad altare Dei, 587b

Introit Psalm, 588a

Intuition difference between discursive reason and i., 515a; man convinced by argument, not i., 22a

Intuitive i. vision of God, 303a

Invention glorious finding of the Cross, 231a

Invisible all things visible and i., 224a; God i. to man, by reason of eminence, 392b; O world i., we view thee, 305a; The i. things of him are clearly, 755a; things both visible and i., 120a

Invocabo Laudans i. Dominum, 595a

Invocation i. of God on waters of baptism, 49a; i. of holy Trinity, 310a

Involuntary acts more or less i., 33b; i. act may be good or bad in se, 34a

Ire Cleanse us from i. of creed or class, 523a; Opposite i. and hate, 476a; storm Of heaven's eternal i., 243b

Ireland Ah, sweet is Tipperary in the springtime, 476a; But faith like thine will never pass away, 475b; Clinging to the Old Sod, in spite of wind and weather, 896a; Erin's honor and Erin's pride, 475a; Everything about I. made for allurement, 476a; Gaels of I., men that God made mad, 476b; has conquered races, 632a; In the storied land, 475b; Island of saints, 475a; Mournful and mighty mother!, 475b; Our ever-faithful land, 662b; political conflicts are about something, 476a; They have helped to enthral a Great Land, 254a; They're neighborly in I., 635a

Ireland, Archbishop John, 17a

Irish All mourners of the world weep I., 475b; all their wars are merry, all their songs are sad, 476b; I. way of paying compliments, 201a; Ours is the American Church, not I., 143b; Who says that the I. are fighters, 476b

Irishman close to heavens because close to earth, 476b; dreams always to come back, 476b; I. he mak' me seeck!, 476a

Iron Answers the i. to the magnet's breath, 385a; beat i. while hot, 476b; Fire tries i., 861a; if gold rust, what shall i. do?, 316b; I. cross hid in breast, 37b; Sweetest Wood and Sweetest I!, 230b; When i. is hot, strike, 476b, 645b

Irregulares i. ex defectu, 649a

Irreligion no such thing really, as i., 477a

Irreligious excuses made by poor for being i., 513b

Irrepressible nothing so i., as human nature, 449a

Irritability i. in east wind, 477a

Is God i., and truly i., 393b; HE WHO IS, principal name applied to God, 387a; Whatever i., i. in its causes just, 504a

Isaac his blessing on Jacob, 72b; 'Twas with I. immolated, 75a

Ischyros Agios o Theos, i., athanatos, 41a, 589a

Islamism palpable throw-back to the Old Testament, 773a

Isle Fairest i., all isles excelling, 477a; When first I saw thy fairy i., 475a

Isolation American illusion, 16a

Israel Adonai, Leader of house of I., 8a; The King is come to I., 169a; water from rock refreshed I., 92a

Italian Ours is the American Church, not I., or Polish, 143b

Italy Ah, slavish I.! thou inn of grief!, 477a; But O the unfolding south!, 477b; country of the arts, 29b; had great architects, 30a; I flowed to I., 477b; Oh happy regions, I. and Spain, 871b; primacy of I., Christian and Catholic, 477a; recognizes sovereignty of Holy See, 708b

Ite I., missa est, 595b

Ivories God laid His fingers on the i., 251b

Ivory Her i. hands on the i. keys, 627a; I. Tower, 84b

Ivy creeping, dirty, courtly i., 477b

J

Jacinth Setting the j. bell a-swing, 56a

Jack common J. to whole flock, 478a; how J. shall have Jill, 478a

Jackass only Lord can make race horse out of j., 447b

Jacob Isaac's blessing on J., 72b; J.'s sons and daughters, 285b; ladder, J. saw in his vision, 450a; Star of J., 85b

James, Henry, 18a

January May, coupled to cold J., 573b

Jasper On a j. pavement builded, 479a

Jaundice j. of the soul, 478a

Jaundiced All looks yellow to the j. eye, 478a

Jealous bids me love but her alone, 92b; Not to be jealous, 478a

Jefferson, Thomas, 256a

Jehovah J. has triumph'd, 293b; J., Jove, or Lord!, 340a

Jerome, Saint, 44b, 99a

Jerusalem Blessed city, heavenly Salem, 478b; has fourth place after Rome, 662b; J., be converted to Lord thy God, 399b; J. the golden, 479a; means vision of peace, 123b; Shine, shine, O new J., 285b; Thou heavenly, new J., 171a; we have seen J., 541a; We will go to J., 520a; What a city, the New J.!, 500b; whole city of J., 122b; you may see good of J., 206b

Jesse Root of J., 8a, 91a, 95b

Jesting All j., in its nature profane, 453b

Jesuit Machiavellian J., 220b

Jesuits in obedience and abnegation, conspicuous, 479b; in their capacity of casuists, 622a; Puritanpapists, 480a; specific error J. called to combat, 480a

Jesus Christ Adonai and Leader of Israel, 8a; All ye who would the C. descry, 877a; All mankind in C. one man, 134a; all seasons' King and Guide, 534b; Almighty of Almighty, Co-eternal of Eternal, 481b; alone without sin, 285a; altar of life, 97b; Anointed One, 128a; Archprophet of prophets of Father, 489a; Author of life, 36a, 88b, 166b; Author of traditions of Church, 64a; Be Thou the aim of every breast, 36a; Bearer of our iniquities, 349a; became man descended from Adam, 85a; begotten and yet unbegotten, 480a; Blessed One, 84a; born of Holy Spirit and the Virgin Mary, 71b, 226a; born of the Father before all ages, 226b; Bridegroom, 80b, 299a; bridge which leads to heaven, 108b; By the authority of our Lord J., 41b; By divine nature simple; by human nature complex, 468a; by Him, hell led captive, 90a; came to fulfil law, not abolish it, 150a; captain of martyrs, 582a; Center of rest, 77b; chose time, birthplace, mother, 79a, 482b; Christ and Church, two in one flesh, 132a; C. is never conquered, 490b; C. of history, 483a; C.'s divinity, affection for His humanity, 483a; conceived by the Holy Ghost, 226a; Conqueror, 36a, 630a; consecrates Sacrament, 71b; consubstantial to the Father, 226b; Cornerstone, 8a; Creator, Child at breast, 39b; crucified under Pontius Pilate, 226a; Dayspring from on high, 167a; death merited salvation for all, 43b; desire of gentiles, 8a; Destined for world's redemption, 74a; Destroyer of sin, 86a; devotion to the Boy-Christ, 161b; divinity, and disregard of Mary, 101b; divinity, proved from Gospels, 483a; Emmanuel, 8b, 81a; end of our going, 466b, 492b; expectation of nations, 8b; Father's light and splendor Thou, 167a; fatherland where we are going, 492b; Feast of all things, 97a; flesh in flesh, God in God, 81b; for our sake became obedient unto death, 442b; foundation of Church, 116b, 125a; Founder of angels' state, 88b; Fountain, 196b, 197a, 491b; fulfils the law's command, 74a; Giver of life, 85b; God and Man, 44a, 77a, 82a, 85b, 226b, 480a, 481b; God is one, and C. is one, 133b; God of God, 226b; God, seen by men, 167a; great art, to converse with J., 488b; great Artificer divine, 81b; Great Prince of heaven!, 483a; Hail! Jesus! Hail!, 104b; has us as His brothers, 93a; having known Him, to reject Him mad crime, 492a; *He descended into hell*, 226b; He hath triumphed gloriously!, 167b; *He is Savior of all men*, 43b; He is the Vine, 486a; Head of all mankind, 43b; Head of Mystical Body, 132a; head of righteous, 122b; Head of the Church, 123a, 482b, 676b; heavenly King, 40a; heavenly Word proceeding forth, 74b; High Priest and Guardian of our souls, 484b; High Priest and universal King, 307a, 368a, 489b; High Priest, true Pontiff, 283b, 586b; His beauty, 40a; His life of woe, 74a; His three distinct comings, 8b; His threefold grace, 482b; His untainted birth, 79a; humanity dedicated to His sacred heart, 88a; I need Thee, precious J., 789b; *Ichthys*, Son of God Savior, 49a; ignorance of Scripture is not to know C., 60a; Illimitable, 81a; illumines world, 89a; in human nature, subject to Father, 67a; In Whom all joys are found, 630a; incarnate Word of God, 81a, 97b, 226b; Infant J.; Christ Child, 486b; infinite, 25b; Jesu, eternal True sublime, 205a; Jesu, joy of every human heart, 36a; Jesu, King of bliss, 562a; Jesu, salvation's Sun divine, 535a; Jesu! the very thought of Thee, 488b, 630a; Jesu, the world's Redeemer, 69a; J.! all hail, 656b; Jesus, be Thou my heavenly Food, 77b; J., behind Thy temple's veil, 789a; J., gentlest Savior, 197b; J. is God!, 488b; J.! J.!, 520b; J., King of glory, 245b; Jesus, Lord of life eternal, 36a; J., Mary, Joseph, 521b; Jesus! my Lord, my God, my All!, 78a, 521b; Jesus, my love, my Son, my God, 94a; J., our love, our Savior, 490b; Jesus, Pelican of heaven, 75a; Jesus, Redeemer of mankind, 7b, 167a; J., virgins' crown, 639b; J.! why dost Thou love me so?, 384b; judge of the living and dead, 203a, 226a; Key of David, 8a; King and Priest, 176b; King of angels, 88b; King of gentiles, 8a; King of glory, 36a, 36b, 92a; King of heavenly beauty, 230b; King of martyrs, 92a; King of virgins, 159a; King throughout all eternity, 97b; C. laid foundations of Catholic Action, 115a; Lamb of God, 77a, 588b; led captivity captive, 35b;

let us commend ourselves to Christ, 81b; Life and Virtue of the heart, 19a; Light, 7b, 86b; Little Child, 169b, 487b; Live, J., live!, 563a; lives in Church, 133a; living Bread from heaven, 74b, 131b; living spring, 168b; Logos of the Father, 89a; Lord of heaven and earth, 196b; lover of virgins, 10b; Master of His house, 66b; *Mediator between God and man*, 175a, 467a, 481a, 485a, 485b, 486a; merciful and powerful to save, 98b; Messiah triumphing, 8b; mighty Man of wonders, 286b; Monarch, 35b, 170a; Never to have known J., greatest of misfortunes, 492a; *no longer I live, but C. lives in me*, 4b; not subject to eternal law, 482b; nuptial union of C. and His Church, 112a; O Captain of the wars, 658b; O C., Thy guilty people spare!, 792b; O C., whose glory fills the heaven, 486b; O Jesu; our redemption!, 491a; O J., coeternal with the Father, 488a; O J., look on me!, 491b; O Jesus Christ, remember, 77b; O J., J.! dearest Lord!, 489a, 564a, 631a; O J., J., will it be, 251b; O J., King most wonderful, 630a; O J.! Life-spring of the soul!, 605a; O King of glory, Lord of hosts, 36a; O my Son and my God, 93a; O what could my Jesus do more, 197b; of Whose Kingdom there shall be no end, 226b; Offerer and Offering, 75b, 485b; Oh! Thou for sinners slain, 489b; one Governor of City, 122b; One holy, one Lord J., 226b, 369b; One of children of the year, 9a; one Person, Word and Man, 481a; only Son of God, 8b, 481a; Orient, Splendor of eternal Light, 8a; our Bread, 81a; our captain, 428a; our elder brother, 39b, 305b; our head, 80b, 123a; our Leader, 435b; our only Benefactor, 89a; our Passover, 43b, 284a; our Ruler, 81a; our sacrifice, 78a; Our sweet reward, 36a; Pearl of price untold, 169b; perfect God and perfect Man, 466a, 482a; Physician, 7b, 196b; prayers of Mary of great weight with Him, 82b; Prince of virgins, 166b; principle of grace, 86a; propitiation for our sins, 43b; Restorer of our race, 85b, 88b; rising Sun, 8a, 89a, 98b, 167a, 168b, 299a; Root of Jesse, 8a; royal prerogatives, 489b; Ruler and King of universe, 36a, 466a; Savior, 8b, 39a, 82a, 484a, 490b; Scepter, 8a, 449b; second Adam, 43a, 85b, 90a; sharer of our weakness, 90b; Shepherd, 28b, 73a, 74b, 166a, 484a; sits at right hand of Father, 39b, 226a; Son and Word, 13a, 467b, 480b, 482b, 485a, 491b; Spouse of Church, 112a, 159a; subject to death in our nature, 482b; suffered death for our sins, 43b; *suffered* under Pontius Pilate, 226a; sweet Huntsman from above, 562b; Sweet J.! Fount of clemency!, 371b; Sweet source divine of every good, 77b; Sweetest Jesus, Mary's Son, 75b; the Immortal Dead, 318a; the Incomprehensible, 167b; The Light of Bethlehem, 170b; This little Pilgrim, 168b; this world's ransom, 230b; *Thou art the C.*, 594b, 674b; Thou canst not deceive, 227a; Thou, deathless Life, didst come down to death, 400b; Thou knowest all, 78b;

Thou only art holy, Thou only Lord, 588b, 594a; Thou that camest to save the world, 656a; Thy Servant, 70b; Thyself, one of the Holy Trinity, 588b; Time holds the timeless One, 25a; Time, Way, and Wayfarer, 493a; to be with J., sweet paradise, 488b; to know J. and Him crucified, 75b, 488b, 602a; To restore all things in C., 492b; true God of true God, 226b; true Light Which enlightens and sanctifies world, 490a; Twin-stone of the law, 41a; two wisdoms in C., 482b; unconquered King of glory!, 247b; Uncontainable contained in BVM, 90b; unity of person, 81b; Victim, High Priest And Lamb, 75b, 235a; way by which we go, 466b, 492b; Way, Truth, and Life, 36a, 108b, 148b, 254b; we bear Christ in us by Sacrament, 70b; when Church speaks, Thou dost speak, 118b, 122b; Who was before all ages eternally, 480b; whole world's Host, 97a; Whom heavens cannot contain, 79b, 81a; Whosoever findeth J., findeth a good treasure, 488b; Wisdom and Power of God, 8a, 480b, 917b; world's Redeemer, 230b; world's true Light, 95b

Jew through the J.'s window, 49a
Jewel Spare this one j., 280a
Jews a headstrong, moody, mur'ring race, 493b; cast away from His grace, 120a; Catholic Church and J., 120b; God chose to reveal Himself to one people, 148b; God's pamper'd people, 493b; Jacob's sons and daughters, 285b; Like J. you munch, and murmur while you feed, 572b; My people, what have I done unto thee, 400a; Which J. might kiss and infidels adore, 235a; You cruel J., come work your ire, 94a
Jig dance upon a j. to heav'n, 626b
Job As poor as J., 712b; friends of J., who railed at him, 909a
Job, Book of, 63b
John I, King, 178a
John, Patriarch, 700a
John the Apostle, St., 155b; bestowed Holy Ghost, 205a; enlightened by teachings of apostle J., 494a; Rome, where J. was plunged into boiling oil, 693b
John the Baptist, St., great forerunner of the morn, 494a; herald of the Word, 494a; the Baptist J. full guiltless, 368a
Johnson, Samuel, 28a
Joined *those whom God hath j. together*, 267a, 268a, 577a; wholly j. to Thee, 559b
Jokes foreigner laughs at everything, except j., 348b; grave things, oldest j., 453b
Joking All jesting, in its nature profane, 453b
Jonson, Ben, 494a
Jordan Echoes from Judah's hills and J.'s stream, 494a; In holy J.'s purest wave, 298b; washed away sins in J., 299a
Joseph, St. A J. did betroth Them both, 872a; Chaste as the lily flower, 495b; chosen To guard the Virgin's fame, 438a; has great power with God, 495a; Man of the house, 496a; Say, what could J. see, 84a; trusty assistant in His great design, 495a; we revere him as our protector on earth, 496a; Worshipped throughout the Church, 495a

Joseph Not more did J. o'er his brethren weep, 770a

Journalism In America. j. governs for ever, 496b; nutshell truths for breakfast table, 496b

Journalist under obligation of extemporizing views, 496b

Journey among vicissitudes of j., 878a; midway the journey of this life, 10b, 922a; The world's an inn, death the j.'s end, 542b; We end our j. 'mong the dead, 248b

Jousted And j. for our faith at Tramissene, 510b

Jove but laughs at lover's perjury, 555a; If J. and heaven can violated be?, 879a; Jehovah, J., or Lord!, 340a; when J. gave us life, he gave woe, 516a

Joy After death, J. and pleasure is there none, 684a; All j. is young, and new all art, 487b; Beyond pain, j., and hope, 21b; by wood of Cross j. came into whole world, 400b; children of swift j. and tardy sorrow, 45a; Each hour brings j. before unknown, 564a; For j. is an abbreviated stair, 834a; His birth, our j., 487a; holy j. is to glory in Thee, 367b; I announce to you a great j., 709b; intensest pain and intensest j., 684b; Jesu, j. of every human heart, 36a; J. and pleasure is there none, 351b; J. is life's tree —grief but its leaf, 498a; J. is like restless day, 666a; J. is to this day pertaining, 40a; More j. in heaven is made, 216b; Mourning ruined j.'s estate, 625a; No j. so great, but runneth to an end, 351b, 497b; Now let earth with j. resound, 28b; Our j. in sorrow, 445a; Sell not thy soul for brittle j.!, 684a; small publicity of pagan, gigantic secret of Christian, 498a; soul recognizes there may be j. in pain, 684b; This Life, this Light, this Word, this J., 168b; to j. in the cross of Christ, 9a; uproarous labor by which all things live, 498b; We j. one everlasting day, 533b; where j. tastes its own eternity, 421b; Would'st thou dwell in j. abounding, 232a

Joyful J. such ends as endless joys begin, 472a

Joyfully bear patiently, if thou canst not j., 661b

Joyous let one ever be found j. in the Lord, 497a

Joys ah! how unsincere are all our j.!, 498a; grace of spiritual j., 494a; j. delusive spurn, 37b; Let thy eternal j. unto me show, 585a; Mary's j. are doubly ours, 95a; of what toys We made our j., 873a; the best Of everlasting j., 40b; those j., which they in heav'n expect, 303b

Juan, Don, 152b

Jubes Da quod j.: jubes quod vis, 410a

Jubilee Loud proclaim the j., 167b; Nature's round Makes the Silver J., 498b

Jubilees occur at various intervals, 199a

Judaism Christianity did not believe in J., but J. in Christianity, 498b

Judas And hast pointed J. out, 443a; false disciple, 74b; I kissed the face I loved so well, 878b; J. he japed with Jewen silver, 498b; like J., give Thee a kiss, 595a; received punishment of his guilt, 442a

Judge Christian j., fulfil duty of devoted father, 173b, 499a; conscience suggests that He is our J., 382a; duty of bishop to j., 69a; God alone, to j., 499a; Hail! Thou J. of souls departed!, 483b; j. living and dead, 28b, 203a; *J. me, O God, distinguish my cause,* 587a; O righteous J., 483b, 501b, 599a; our business, *not* to j., 411a; Sith Thou art rightful j., 381b; The J. is at the gate, 502a; They j. but half who only faults will see, 341b; they shall judge heavenly things, 176b; We j. all things according to divine truth, 511a; when He comes as our J., 170a

Judged by your savor will you be j., 533a; j. by God, 499a; men j. according to merits or demerits, 300a

Judges availing ourselves of terror of j. and laws, 431a; *He who j. me, is the Lord,* 701b

Judging sin of j. others, 499a

Judgment Affection bends j. to her uses, 9b; Anxiety confuses the j., 26a; cannot be pronounced, until man has run his course, 502b; decision of higher j. than my own, 23b; final j. depends on worst action, 153b; God's j., 212b; have right j. in all things, 670a; Hear the other side, 499a; Merciless j. and without appeal!, 248a; no one condemned, except through merited j., 751b; Nor is the people's j. always true, 739b; O king, love justice and j., 507b; 'Tis with our j. as with our watches, 499b; We ought not to condemn, without careful study of case, 202a

Judgment, Last bishop averts judgment of last day, 69b; Christ, will come to judge living and dead, 226a, 501a; clarification and vindication of history, 503b; Come to j., come to j., 503a; day of doom, 502a, 503a; day of wrath and vengeance, 501b; Deliver me from everlasting death on that day, 502a; dreadful day of Thy j., 242a; Each shall be rewarded according to his deeds, 500a; His coming against men, 8b; Lord shall recognize merits of each, 501a; only the last day that judges all, 503a; ratified at General J., 500b; relegate wicked into eternal fire, 500b; separation of cities, 125a; slave and master stand before Him, 500a; that day of retribution, 246a, 483b, 501a, 501b; The trumpet shall be heard on high, 626a; Thy terrible second-coming, 196a; To fear the day of j., 501a; unto j. and damnation, 594b; wax receives stamp of its identity, 503a; We are not here to j., but to give our account, 499b; when heavens and earth shall be shaken, 246a; when He comes as our Judge, 7b, 170a; When rattling bones together fly, 503a; When Thou shalt come, angelic legion round, 501b; when Thou shalt come to judge world by fire, 246a

Judgment, Particular do not let verdict of Thy j. go against him, 500a; I go before J., Who knows no favorites, 500a; Immediately after death, p., 500b

Judgment, Private belief and limitation of p., 57b; p. and authority of Church, 118a; p. and Catholic Faith, 499b, 500a; p. and interpretation of history, 270a; p. and interpretation of scripture, 270a; what one sect interprets, all sects may, 875b

Judgments j. of God, j. of men, 451a; recognize justice of all God's j., 501a; 'Tis with our j. as our watches, 805a; Trouble not yourself about human j., 766b

Judica *J. me, Deus,* 587b

Judicial J. power has two parts, 822a; Sunday, not day for j. proceedings, 854a

Juices Umbered j., and pulpèd oozes, 47b

July Through the flashing bars of J., 853a

June The fair Tanned face of J., 503b

Juniper I am J. and I am wicked, 911a

Junks j. of old Hong-Kong, 780a

Juridical human race bound together by ties, moral and j., 530b

Juris *aliqualis ratio j.,* 525b

Jurisdiction all priests not of equal j., 433b; bishop's j., unto edification, 68b; conflict of j., 181b; equal authoritative power to all apostles, 693a; exalted degree of dignity and amplitude of j., 702a; gift imparted to all, entrusted to one in particular, 676b; in matters of faith, j. belongs to clergy, 189a; j. of apostles, inherited by bishops, 69b; j. of bishops, under authority of pope, 69b; meant to spread from Peter to others, 822b; power of j. by canonical appointment, 434a; priests should make judgments regarding priests, 189a; relative j. of Church and State, 182b; *whatsoever thou shalt bind on earth,* 175b, 693a

Jury determining guilt or innocence, important, 503b

Jurymen wretches hang that j. may dine, 503b

Jus human law *j.,* 523b; *Summum j., summa injuria,* 528a

Jus *gentium,* 524a, 530b, 887a

Just actions of the j., 436a; All j. which is attuned to this, 504b; alone do not constitute Church, 127a; every j. spirit made perfect in faith, 593a; God, both good and j., 386a; in the halls of the j., 89a; spirits of j. are at rest, 247a; the j. for the unjust, 43b; Thou art indeed j., Lord, 382a; Whatever is, is in its causes j., 504a; where souls of j. repose, 89a; who believe themselves sinners, 823a

Justice all men equal in claim to j., 16a; authority with j., under and by Church, 46a; Before sinning, fear God's j., 446a; believes with heart unto j., 640a; certain rectitude of mind, 504b; Church is the form of j. 137b; commutative j., 287b; differs from equity, 300a, 505a; eternal light of j., 408a; first, maintain j., second, preserve liberty, 353a; For Thee do I yearn, J., Innocence, 261b; God fears no sops to avert His stroke, 381b; He represseth j. after thy will, 96a; Human laws, rules whereby notion of j. determined, 529b; I have loved j., therefore I die an exile, 318a, 504b, 520a; idea of service of justice, 184a; j., end of law, 3a; j. is a virtue shared by all, 504b; J. to keep, mixt with mercy, 162a; king's chief duty, to govern with equity and j., 507b; Law of charity perfects law of j., 157b; Let j. be done, though world perish, 504a; no republic, where there is no j., 765b; O king, love j. and judgment, 507b; only in Church, 125a; piety of j., first exercised towards God, 504a; retributive j., 382a; royal virtues principally two, j. and piety, 507a; rule of j. is plain, 504a; Sun of j., 8a; Thy righteousness is unto all eternity, 245a; To serve cause of peace is to serve j., 666b; Two main reasons why men fall short of j., 504b; virtue that gives to each his due, 504a; Where no true j., there can be no right, 523b

Justification grace of j. and debt of punishment, 417a; grace of j., attained by predestined, 724a; J. and freewill, 505b; no j., without prevenient inspiration of Holy Ghost, 505b; not effected by faith alone, 2b; our j., very presence of Christ, 506a; under Old Law, 51b

Justified bound to observe commandments of God, 193b; cannot avoid sin except by privilege, 86b; faith by which God has j. all men, 505a; man j., not assuredly predestinate, 724a; man not j. by his own works, 505a; men not j. by sole imputation of justice of Christ, 505b; no one truly j. by faith alone, 2b; not able to persevere without help of God, 673a; sinner j. by God moving him to righteousness, 505a

Justifies He j. us by entering into us, 506a

Justifieth it is God that j. the ungodly, 505a

Justifying He infuses j. grace, 505a; j. grace, not mere favor of God, 505b

Justinian I, Emperor, 506b

Justum Dignum et j. est, 591a

Juvenes J. dum sumus, 549a

K

Keep K. thou my feet, 490a; k. well as win, 867b

Kew Go down to K. in lilac-time, 544a

Key Catholic faith like right k., 58a; I wish I were the little k., 198a; Key of David, 8a; What is the k. to everlasting life?, 305b

Keynote taking the k. from God, 162a

Keys binding or loosing, by power of k., 69a, 675b, 699a; fingers wandered idly Over the noisy k., 626b; held both k. of Frederick's heart, 423b; I will give thee the k. of the kingdom, 675b, 693a, 822b; k. of Church, granted to apostles and successors, 68b, 311a; k. of joy's supreme domain, 677b; left to Peter, through him, to Church, 674a, 675b; Peter received specially, k. and primacy of judicial power, 677b; two k. of the Church, 822b

Kick Don't k. till you're spurred, 506a; contrary to decency, to k. anyone, 506a

Kill K. them all, 235a; Live here, great heart, and love and die and k., 424a; not lawful to slay person, 852b; seven strokes to k., 282a; Thou shalt not k., 527a

Killeth He that k. a man when he is drunk, 625b

Kin Help thy k., there beginneth charity, 156a; Many kins folk and few friends, 753b

Kind Be k. to all and severe to thyself, 506a; Christians are k.,

162b; K. as kings upon coronation day, 506b; to be k. and gentle to the fallen, 568b

Kindness K. is the word, 506b; sugar of loving k., 6b; surpass men in magnanimity and k., 568b

King A cat may look on a k., 113b; anguish of k. over ruined realm, 24b; at once our K. and angels', 88b; Bliss, same in subject or k., 103a; brightness of the eternal K., 441b; can do nothing on earth, not according to law, 533b; Christ, High Priest and universal K., 247b, 489b, 534b; co-heirs with Him Who is K. of glory, 877b; consul, k., lords over others, 404b; difference between prince and a tryant, 508a; Do law away, what is a k.?, 529b; Eternal Monarch, K. most high, 8b, 35b; Fear God, honor the k., 176a; glorious deeds of Christ our K., 489a; Great K.'s senate glorious, 28b; Had I served God as diligently as I served my k., 520b, 808a; hail Him as thy matchless K., 483b, 490a; has no peer in his realm, 45b; He is both K. and Priest, 176b; Heavenly K., Paraclete, Spirit of truth, 438b; How can I blaspheme my K., 489a; How fatal 'tis to be too good a k.!, 714a; I am a mighty K., says the Lord, 307a; idea, implies man who is chief and shepherd, 508b; If k. rules tyranically, community may depose him, 774a; if the lion knew his own strength, 509a; Jesus Christ, K. of glory, 36a, 97b, 245b, 562a; k., against pope, 24a; k. can do no wrong, 407a, 509a; k. is dead, long live the k.!, 509a; k. never dies, 508b; K. of kings, and Lord most High!, 21b; K. of virgins and Lover of chastity, 159a; K. of world, borne by unseen armies of angels, 589b; k. should promote eternal happiness, 179a; k. under law, 508a, 528b, 533b; k. who is philosopher, 691a; k.'s chief duty, to govern with equity and justice, 507b; Law is made by consent of people and ordinance of k., 533b; law makes the k., 508a; minister and vicar of God, 533b; minister of public utility, 508a; Mother of our K., 40b, 83b; never tell him what he is able to do, 508b; No k. can have political authority immediately from God, 509a; no k. where will rules, not law, 508a, 528b; O glorious K. of martyr hosts, 581b; O k., love justice and judgment, 507b; O K. of the gentiles, 8a; O Lord God, heavenly K., 588b; O mighty K. of kings, 882a; password of our K., divine deeds, 435b; represents person of state, 508a; right of pope to examine k., 177b; royal dignity excels all other earthly powers, 507b; royal virtues principally two, justice and piety, 507a; Ruler and K. of universe, 466a; said to be freed from bonds of law, to do justice, 508a; should be resplendent with virtues, 507b; should swear at coronation, three things, 508b; so called from ruling, 507a; to provide itself with k., belongs to multitude, 774a; under no one save God, 45b; victory of so great a K., 441b; Who is this K. of glory?, 36b

Kingdom after dunghill, comes K. of Heaven, 463b; beyond even the stars, 37a; Blessed be the k. of

the Father, 587a; by baptism we become children of the k., 51a; By the full k. of that final kiss, 258a; Church even now is k. of Christ, 124b; eternal and universal, 489b; every k. hath a grave, 413a; government of self-sufficient multitude, 510a; keys of k. of heaven given bishop, 68b; k. of BVM, as vast as that of Son, 97b; k. of golden deeds, 305b; k. of heaven, 136a, 173b, 839b; k. of truth and life, 489b; ministry of Christ's k., entrusted to priests, 178b; New Testament, k. of heaven, 61a; no small matter, to lose or gain k. of heaven, 303a; of Whose K. there shall be no end, 226b; plantation of God and beloved vineyard, 124a; Remember me, O Lord, in Thy k., 595a; Thy k. come; Thy will be done, 593b; Trinity, Might in one substance, K. undivided, 369b; unbaptized infants, excluded from K. of Heaven, 238b; when Mediator shall have delivered up k. to God, 485b

Kingdoms attribute power of giving k., to God, 173b, 510a; Church, and power to grant k., 176a; God, Protector of all k., 507a; grandeur, nations, k. have their day, 475b; He takes no earthly realms away, 298b; Justice taken away, what are k. but robberies?, 509b; There be two kinds of k., 405b

Kingly k. power, conferred for guardianship of Church, 174a

Kings before Whom k. shall not open lips, 8a; Bishops must not rashly assail k., 172b; By which people keep even k. in awe, 237a; can forgive, if rebels can but sue, 349b; cannot reign unless their subjects give, 858a; constituted princes by Thy disposition, 507a; Death lays his icy hand on k., 249a; difference between k. and Roman emperor, 353a; general agreement of societies, to obey k., 642a; If all wore crowns, k. would go bareheaded, 445a; If k. unquestion'd can laws destroy, 3a; Kind as k. upon their coronation day, 506b; k. are types of God, 509a; K., were made christs, 507a; not exempt from jurisdiction of Church, 181b; origin of k. and dukes, 844b; people have right supreme To make their k., 509b; princes and k. chosen, to coerce people from evil, 404a; publick pillars of the state, 509b; raise up commonwealths and ruin k., 684b; should look to interests of people, 131b; They reigned, but not by Me, 507b; types of royal and sovereign power of true Christ, 507a

Kingship glory of His k., reflected on Mother, 92a

Kiss A k., a sigh, and so away, 836b; By full kingdom of that final k., 258a; childish lips' unvalued precious brush, 510b; Every morning of your life, Kiss her, 268a; fail To win woman he forgets to k., 510a; give me your last farewell k., 500a; I saw you take his k.!, 510a; my enamored soul embrace and k., 562b; seek somewhere else a more orthodox k.?, 227a; smile or k., as he will use the art, 249a; stinging madness of one infinite k., 564b; To k. again the Master's feet!, 286b

Kiss of Peace, 510b, 589b, 594b

Knave A king may make a lord a k., 550a; Ambition makes patriot as k., 14b; An old k. is no child, 510b; none so busy as fool and k., 110b

Knaves bold k. thrive without one grain of sense, 465b; It is merry when k. meet, 510b

Knee there is no k. That knows not Thee, 630b; Upon my bended k., 77b

Kneel some k. on Lord's Day, 716a

Knell There's no music to a k., 58b

Knelt I k. to adore, 484b

Knew he k. what was what, 513a; No man could bear to live, if he k. all, 515a; He k. beforehand all things to come in time, 382b, 383a; When first I k. Thee, Thou didst raise me up, 393b

Knife smiler with k. under cloak, 878b

Knight He was a very parfit gentle k., 161b; In fifteen mortal battles he had been, 510b; K. of the sable feather, 252a; try'd adventures like this k., 19b

Knighthood k. is not in the feats of war, 161b

Knightlier a k. sort you'll never find, 601b

Knights k. of God!, 582a

Knock K. as you please, there's nobody at home, 348a; Who knows the Word, needs not k., 218b

Knot thus lovers tie their k., 2a

Know All men naturally desire to k., 513a, 513b; As regards His greatness, impossible to k. Him, 392b; be ignorant of much, if we would k. anything, 458b; by death, we begin to k., 513b; cannot be granted, God can k. more than He knows, 383b; certitude, to k. that one k.s, 152b; created mind may see God, but cannot k. all, 394b; highest science, truly to k. and despise ourselves, 451a; I am, I k., I will, 511b; if you k. not yourself, you will be without foundation, 602a; let me k. myself, let me k. Thee, 393b; many make more study to k., than to live well, 513a; master of those who k., 31a; my philosophy this, to k. Jesus and Him crucified, 602a; Never to act is never to k., 514b; possible to know but not love, 57a; Really k. what you say you k., 514a; We k., by piecemeal and accumulation, 514a; We k. God better through grace, 395a; We k. God by grandeur of His creation, 394a; we k. nothing until we k. nothing, 453a; We only k. Him in so far as we are known by Him, 396b; we wish not to k., but to talk, 236a; Wish not to k. anything, 395a

Knower Things known in k., after manner of k., 512a

Knowest Thou k. all, 78b, 384b

Knoweth As well as beggar k. his bag, 56a; *The Lord k. who are His,* 126a

Knowing believing and k. are different things, 330b; external and internal k. of angels, 21b; God's essence united to mind, principle of k., 903b; God's living is His k., 383b; k. all, and feeling nought, 456b

Knowledge An heavenly k. in my mind engrave, 339b; apprehended from things of sense, 61b; apprehension, not vision, 515a; bad things are in God's k., 383b; better to have little k. with humility,

451b; book of world, full of k. we need, 435a; BVM leads all to divine k., 98b; by stages I passed from bodies to soul, 511a; charity prefers k. of God, 155a; cognizance of temporal things, k., 515b; comes of doing, 514b; degrees of k., 511a; Demonstrative k. about God, 394b; difference between k. of God, and love of Him!, 395a; different kinds of k., 512b; discord between faith and k., 331a; divine faith distinguished from natural k. of God, 330b; divine k. of God through ignorance, 394a; Doubt charms me no less than k., 276a; education is preparation for k., 289b; end of learning is k., 514a, 515a; every k. of truth, reflection of eternal law, 526a; For God, k. contained in divine Essence, 512b; full k. and k. by faith, 330b; God's k. has no bounds, 471b; God's k. of creatures, 224b, 225b, 512b; God's k. of existence and non-existence, 383b; God's understanding, measured by eternity, 383b; healing power of k., 292a; His k. not couched in three tenses, 382b; His k. rules, 487a; human k. begins with outside of things, 888a; idea of thing known is in knower, 512b; illumine minds with light of k., 4a; in baptism we receive spirit of k., 50a; in spiritual world, 514b; Inordinate appetite of k., 513a; k. and blessedness, 102b; k. and action make a man happy, 511a; k. and existence, 319a; K. not gratis comes, 268b; k. of Divine things, wisdom, 511b; k. of God, cause of other things, 383b; k. of God, dowry of the soul, 393a; k. of God, passage from light to darkness, 393a; k. of God, reward of perfect, 301b; k. of God's essence by grace, 394b; k. of God's existence, implanted in my nature, 375a, 394b; k. of Him by natural reason, 395a; k. of intelligent beings, 512b; k. of things through forms, 393b; k. through science and k. through faith, 330b; k. which is its own end, liberal, 514b; k., without fear of God, 513a; Let k. be applied to kind of scaffolding, 511a; liberal k., apprehension of truth as beautiful, 514a; life of spirit, illumination of k., 458b; man needs a supernatural light, 888a; man's and angels' knowledge, 22a; man's k. acquired by reasoning, 22a; must precede love, 805b; natural k. of God and morality, 330b; No one has seen God in this life, as He is, 393b; not of vision, but of simple intelligence, 383b; Nothing, more excellent than k., 572a; one thing in world worth pursuing, k. of God, 396a; Our k. compared with Thine, ignorance, 511b; Our notions, never commensurate with things themselves, 514b; out of depths of ignorance to k. of God, 609b; power of viewing many things as whole, 514a; religious truth, condition of general k., 393a; right distinction between wisdom and k., 515b; science, k. of all things, 802b; shines, illumines in hidden God, three things, 382a; three things, existence, k., will, 511b; To go behind k. to criticize, impossible, 515a; To win to the k. of all, 395a; use of wisdom and k., 515b; useful and liberal k., 514a; Source of k.

itself, 22a; we do not have exact k. of Him, 380b; We suck out of all things a kind of essence, 514b

Known better k. by knowing what He is not, 393b; God, can be k. by reason through created things, 396a; God first k. from *nature,* afterwards by *instruction,* 393a; It is in silence that God is k., 396a; k. by experience, 514b; presumptuous, wish to be k. by all world, 14a, 335a; Things k. in the knower, after manner of knower, 394b, 512a, 512b; world could not be k., if not existing, 319a, 382b

Knox, Ronald A., 220b

Kosmos Only God, Who made k., can say what for, 926a

Kyrie K. eleison, Christe eleison, 588a

L

Labor capital cannot be without l., nor l. without capital, 112a, 187b; doctrine, physical l. is not in itself bad, 517a; gives workingman title to its fruits, 517a; health ought to precede l., 289b; itself is but a sorrowful song, 516b; L. is a powerful medicine, 515a; motive of work, to obtain property, 734b; mutual relations between capital and l., 287b; No l. so cheap, as that of bodily strength, 517a; nothing to be ashamed, earning bread by l., 713a; on that by which one profits little, 732a; season our l. with sacred song, 266a; serves to mortify the flesh, 516a; To l. is the lot of man below, 516a; To l. is to pray, 515b

Labora Ora et l., 718a

Laborare L. est orare, 515b

Laborer must be treated as man, 112a; should respect his own moral dignity, 112b

Laborers l. and right of association, 38b

Labors bee honored because she l., 55b; He who l. as he prays, 516a; Lingered l. come to nought, 255a

Labyrinthine down the l. ways, 385a

Lack In love is no l., 552b; Who know the l. that lurks in all, 783b

Lacking L. samite and sable, 169a

Lacks He lacks everything who, 254a

Ladder by which I ascended into Church, 341a; contemplation, as a kind of l., 211b; we must set up l. of ascending actions, 450a, 451a

Ladies rule where hearts obey, 633b

Lady, Our all-holy, immaculate, L., 81b, 593a; chaste and pure L., Bride of God, 98a; For such a l. as God's spouse, 19b; God's Mother, L. and Queen over all, 95b; Lovely L. dressed in blue, 102a; may such a L. God's Mother be, 83b; name Mary means l., 99a; Noble L.! on our race, 89a; Nor had our Lady been of heaven Queen, 29a; O l., he is dead and gone, 242b; O L., make speed To help mankind!, 461b; O L. Mary, thy bright crown, 95a; Our L. of Blachernae, 100b; Our L. of the May, 97b; Our L. of the twilight, 886a; Our L., our mediatrix, 90b; Our L. sings magnificat, 831b; Our Savior Christ and his L., 168a; save me, O L., by thy prayers, 87a; thou art so great, 91a; thy great humility, 91b

Lady Nature loves, as l. bright,

633b; To be called 'Madam,' glorious thought, 517b
Laetare Sunday, 535b
Lags Whoever l., he beats him with his oar, 517b
Laity By divine law clergy distinct from l., 177b, 190a; confirmation and priesthood of laity, 207a; Each must in his own place please God, 190b; I want l., who know their religion, 518a; If many of l. take part in psalmody, 266b; intelligent, well-instructed l., 518a; sacrament of orders distinguishes clergy from l., 648b; we do not permit l. to perform offices of priesthood, 728b
Lamb A l. before his shearers, dumb, 240b; A wolf in a l.'s skin, 253b; As a l. led out to slaughter, 442b; At the L.'s high feast we sing, 284b; Be lion in pulpit, l. in confessional, 669b; Behold the L.!, 489b, 595b; Bible, stream where lamb made, 60b; Blessed L.— on Calvary's mountain, 490a; blood of the spotless L., 229b; bride of the L., 23b; Broken and distributed is the L. of God, 594a; Christ the L. Whose Blood was shed, 284b; He is as quiet as a l., 746b; He is the true L., 284a; He was led as a L. to the slaughter, 484b; Jesus Christ, O Lord God, L. of God, 588b; L. of God! we look to Thee, 658a; L. of God, who takest away sins of world, 594a; L., Shepherd, and Savior, 93a; Lo, the Lamb, so long expected, 7b; Nothing appeases enraged elephant so much as little l., 364b; O holy sacrificed L., 77a; On the Cross, the L. is lifted, 656a; one: Victim, High Priest And L., 235a; paschal l. prefigured eucharist, 75a; See, the tender L. appears, 169a; The L. upon His throne, 490a; virgins follow L. wherever He goes, 82b; white L., that hurt was with the spear, 232b
Lambs With all the little l. that leap, 484b
Lambskin As soon goeth the young l. to market, 518b
Lame If you will walk with l. men, 518b
Lament True Christian hearts cease to l., 769b
Lamp BVM, l. unquenchable, 81a; l. of living light, 98b; O shining l., in light passing nature, 83a
Lamps behoves acolyte to light church l., 4a
Lance Son, pierced by soldier's l., 790a
Land fortune's ice prefers to virtue's l., 14a; happy l. Where they that love are blest, 653b; l. flowing with milk and honey, 24a; Raised from the sea, solid l., 373a; ruleth sky and sea and l., 36a
Lands From l. that see the sun arise, 166b; Make response, ye distant l., 36a
Lane The devil go with thee down the l., 261a
Language As writer, mastered everything except l., 849a; beautiful l. may clothe wisdom or folly, 294a; gift of l., wisdom, knowledge, 874a; inbred character of the l., 877b; pomp of l., tuneful diction, 849a; Strong l., only where chance of doing good, 887b
Languages knowledge of all l., difficult for anyone, 518b; understand foreign l., misunderstand foreigners, 878b

Langueo quia amore l., 100a
Languish No one safe, for whom all l., 54a
Languishes When head l., members have no vigor, 531b
Lap Upon my l. my Sovereign sits, 566b
Lark The l. now leaves his watery nest, 519a
Larks When the sky falleth we shall have l., 519a
Last Bear to be l., 452b; Nor yet l. to lay old aside, 210b
Late Better l. than never, 522a; He was always l. on principle, 522a; Too l. have I loved Thee, O Beauty, 54a
Lateran Basilica, Rome mother and head of all churches, 171a
Lateran Council, Fourth (1215), 204a
Lateran Palace, 175a
Lateran Treaty, 708b
Latere, legate de l., 141a
Latin barbarians ignorant of purity of L., 53a; spirit of Catholicism, same thing as L. spirit, 771a
Latin Church discipline on celibacy, 151a
Latinism confuse L. with Catholicism, 148a
Latinity abhorrence of L., 750a
Latitudinarianism Priests Thought what they pleas'd, 522a
Latitudinarians L. and opposition to latitude, 109a
Latria, 76a, 203b, 795b, 928a
Latuit Bene qui l., bene vixit, 26a
Laud All glory, l. and honor To Thee, Redeemer, 652b
Laudamus Te Deum l., 372b
Laudans L. invocabo Dominum, et, 595a
Laudanum Some fell by l., 601b
Lauds, 522a
Laugh l. is like a creed or a church, 523a
Laughed The man who l. but once, to see an ass, 503b
Laugheth He l. but from the lips forward, 523a; He l. that winneth, 917a
Laughter fills the silver land, 629b; L. and love are everywhere, 523a; l. and the love of friend, 359a
Laurel Let l. each Christian brow entwine, 104a
Laurelled L. with stole victorious, 28b
Laus L. tibi, Domine, 589b
Lavabo L. inter innocentes, 590b
Lavish For l. grants suppose a monarch tame, 523b
Law Ancient custom has the force of l., 236b, 237a, 524b; authority of prince depends on authority of l., 508a; Big fish alone escape from thee!, 530a; command of the prince, 3a; common, just, and stable precept, 525b; Custom rules the l., 237a; customary and statutory, 194a; customary l. and equity, 300b; definition of l. by its four essential parts, 525a; detects, grace alone conquers, 408a; Do l. away, what is a king?, 529b; either natural, civil, or universal, 524a; enactment of people, 524a; Englishman has instinctive veneration for l., 838a; Every l., either permits something or punishes, 524b; First fulfils the Law's command, 74a; given through Moses, 8a, 523b; God gave men l., that they might turn it into liberties, 759a; graven tables of l., 41a; highest duty, to submit to just l., 46b; human l. may not desire or approve evil,

315b; human l. may tolerate evil, 315b; human life, governed by reward or punishment of l., 524b; in most perfect l. is most perfect liberty, 354a; injustice does injury to sanctity of l., 472a; intended as concrete rule of life, 529a; king, under God and the l., 508a, 528b, 533b; l. is established by consent, 405b, 533b; L. is order in liberty, 530a; l. is so lordly and loth to maken end, 529a L. is twofold, natural and written, 523b; l. the lawyers know about, 334a; Let king attribute to l., what l. attributes to him, 528b; Let l. of prayer determine l. of belief, 546b; makes the king, 508a; Necessity has no l., 634b; net of l. is spread so wide, 530a; no king where will rules and not the l., 508a, 528b; not right exactly, but norm of right, 525b; ordinance of reason for sake of common good, 525a; precepts of l., live honorably, injure no man, render due, 523b; Right lives by l., and l. subsists by pow'r, 713b; should be honest, just, possible, 524b; State, part of body politic concerned with maintenance of l., 846a; To most, absence of l. appears freedom, 524a; Twin-stone of the l., 41a; tyrannical l. is not a l., 525a; What has pleased prince, has force of l., 194a, 523b, 533b; where most l., most injustice, 528a; written and unwritten, 194a; written l. on tables, 523b
Law, Canon does not bind unbaptized, 112a; effective guard against arbitrary power, 112a; enacted by Roman pontiffs, 111b; no priest, free to be ignorant of statutes, 698b; Roman Church and c., 111b; works dealing with c. must have imprimatur, 152a
Law, Civil ignorance of the c., sometimes permissible, 528a; injunctions of c., 538a; maintenance of c., secondary to religion, 173a; what each people or state has enacted, 524a
Law, Common laws of England not only good but best, 194a; promulgated by advice of nobles and authority of prince, 194a; unwritten law and custom in England, 193b
Law, Divine does not abrogate human law, 46a, 887a; human and divine law differ in immediate aims, 526b; law of grace, 46a; Those who violate sanctity of d., commit sacrilege, 791a
Law, Eternal all laws, are derived from e., 526a; called supreme reason, unchangeable and eternal, 525b; Laws have origin in natural, consequently e., 526a; liberty of happy who cleave to e., 537a; plan of government in Chief Governor, 526a; prescriptions of e., 538a; sole standard and rule of human liberty, 526b; Thy law is truth and truth is Thou, 525b; whole universe, governed by divine reason, 526a
Law, Human All law, directed to common wellbeing, 529a; cannot legislate about interior acts, 528b; either nature, customs, or statutes, 529b; has power to compel, 529a; law of natural reason, 46a; Laws instituted, when promulgated, 530a; leading purpose, 526b; object of civil legislation, 526b, 529b
Law, Natural as to general principles, 527b; common to all peoples, observed by instinct, 524a; con-

sists of three parts, 527a; does not vary according to time, 527b; Ignorance of the n., never excusable, 527a; imprint on us of the divine light, 525a, 527a; Laws have origin in n., 526a; no dispensation from n., 527a; not abolished by divine law, 46a; political power derives from n., 406a; superior in dignity to customs and enactments, 527a

Law, Positive application of natural law, 111b; field of p., 529a; written law, given for correction of natural law, 527b

Law, Public has to do with sacred things and magistrates, 524a

Law of Nations called *jus gentium*, 530b; exigencies of the l., 531a; forms of government derive from l., 405b; Totalitarianism robs l. of foundation, 530b

Lawgiver O Emmanuel, our King and L., 8b; law implies a l., 376b

Lawn No prelate's l., with hair-shirt lined, 607b

Lawns When the summer l. are fair, 48a

Lawrence, St., 258a

Laws All l., either divine or human, 523b; assent to l., 405b; by which Americans are governed, 17a; called just on the three counts, 525a; confirmed, when approved by those who use them, 528b; Custom is the best interpreter of l., 237b; emperor makes l. which he is first to keep, 528a; If kings unquestion'd can l. destroy, 3a; If l. of God and man are at variance, 755b; l. and arbitrary exercise of power, 112a; made for sake of body politic, 404b; Princes are bound by their own l., 528b; private l., 524b; privilege of sovereignty, giving l., 534a; should be conformable to l. of nature, 530a; that boldness of men might be checked, 524b; T'abhor the makers, and their l. approve, 469b; They who possess prince, possess the l., 714a; unjust l. do not bind, 525a

Lawsuit To go to law, and not be out of one's mind, 531a

Lawyer horrible demoralizing thing to be l., 531b; l.'s sophistry, 814a; mere sight of advocate, induces high opinion of competence, 531b

Lawyers The Utopians have no l. among them, 531b

Lay L. her in the mill-pond, 110a; Let the faithful raise the l., 168a; Most dear pause in a mellow l.!, 425a; voice of joy, eternal l., 12b

Layman blot upon a l.'s coat, little seen, 730a; l. is bound by lay ordinances, 433a, 517b; movements to Catholicize secular function l., 115b

Laymen Before the Church all l. are equal, 518a; can reach peak of holiness, 518a; Clerics ought to lead holier life than lay people, 728b; hostility to clergy, 191a; left part of body of Christ, 191a; "The l., what are they?," 518a; Theirs a spiritual priesthood, to offer spiritual sacrifices, 518a

Lazarus But fairer shone the tears of God For L., 531b

Laziness Till meat fall in your mouth, 55b

Lead L., kindly Light, amid the encircling gloom, 490a; L. me to Thy peaceful manger, 170a; L. Thou me on!, 725b; L. us, great teacher Paul, in wisdom's ways, 664a

Leader Adonai, Leader of house of Israel, 8a; our L., the Divine Word, 435b

Leaf Power that lifts the l., 157a; turn over new l., 752b

Leagues useless things, 12b

Leap L. out of frying pan into fire, 344b; Look or ye l., 149a

Learn L., O dust, to obey, 451b

Learned Ask of the l. the way, 532a; even l. find Bible difficult, 63a; 'l. ignorance,' 458a; l. minds and appeal of Christianity, 165a; Never read anything that thou mayest appear more l., 532a; reign as kings of every sliding hour, 106b; use sensible as tuning-fork for ideas, 58b; vulgar and l., 293b; With loads of l. lumber in his head, 103b; wall of division between l. and simple, 58a; world may learn by mistakes, mostly mistakes of l., 533a

Learning A little l. is a dangerous thing, 532a; Athens, home of all l., 43a; Catholics ought to be of l., followers but leaders, 532b; Church preserved monuments of ancient wisdom, 139a; end of l. is knowledge, 515a; Everybody incapable of l. has taken to teaching, 859a; fit for saints, 903b; Knowledge comes Of l. well retain'd, 513a; l. and authority of Church, 139a; not what makes us Christians, 233a; without exertion, 289b

Learns Man l. from two books, 803a

Least Who l., hath some, who most hath never all, 497b

Leave Bury her, And then l. her!, 110a; He that takes l. so oft, 336b; l. God for God, 808b; My God, wilt Thou l. me?, 395b

Leaven be converted into new l., 533a; Purge we out the ancient l., 286a

Leavened How can the lump be l., 533a

Leaves l. are many under my feet, 47b; these conquering l., 424a

Lecherous For men have ever a l. appetite, 346a

Lechery fire of l., annexed unto gluttony, 368a; Foul lust of l., behold thy due!, 566b

Lectors marriage of l. and singers permitted, 188b

Lectures British audiences do not go l. to be entertained, 533a

Lecturing boredom dangerously infectious, 107b

Lee pleasant waters of the river L., 59a

Leech Good l. is he that can himself recure, 269a; Love is the l. of life, 552a

Leechcraft common sense and l. cure disease, 268b

Leer assent with civil l., 239a

Left O what is l.—but God!, 250b

Legate l. de latere, 141a

Lege Consuetudo pro l. servatur, 237a; *Tolle l.*, 748b; *Vetustas pro l. semper habetur*, 236b

Legem L. credendi lex statuat supplicandi, 546b; *L. non habet necessitas*, 634b; *Mos regit l.*, 237a

Legis Quod principi placuit, l. habet vigorem, 533b

Legislation application of natural law to temporal business, 111b; weightier part of citizens, 534a; That which touches all, should be approved by all, 534a

Legislator Christ, Redeemer to trust, L. to obey, 752b; exists for sake of people, 404b; human l.

must attain keen sense of moral responsibility, 534a; whole body of citizens, 405a, 534a

Legitimate l. authority must proceed from God, 46b

Legitimum marriage of non-baptized, said to be legitimate (*l.*), 579a

Legs But long be thy l., short be thy life, 533b; His l. were lean, 533a

Leisure as luxury of having nothing to do, 534b; l. state, founded upon false angelism, 517a; The modern world is killing l., 534b

Leitourgia, 191a

Leitourgiai, 433a

Lend I came to borrow what I'll never l., 108a; with thy neighbors gladly l. and borrow, 360a

Lent Cross not merely for forty days, 229b; fare in L. should be austere, 535b; fast of forty days, 534b; fight against spiritual powers of wickedness, 37b; service of Christian warfare, 37b; The fast to all men known, and bound, 534b; venerable solemnity of this fast, 37b; When consciences to God lie bare, 535a

Lenten life of a monk ought to be l., 618b

Leo I, Pope St. archbishop of great and elder Rome, 707b; captain of our religion, 705a; Like a true lion (*leo*) he roared, 535b; Peter has spoken through L.!, 704b

Leo XIII, Pope, 88a, 535b

Leo I, Emperor, 174a

Leper Oh, a l. must be a terrible thing to see, 535b

Lesbia L. hath a beaming eye, 221b

Less How can the l. the greater comprehend?, 395b; It is better to want l. than to receive more, 361a; Who will do l. than they, 275a

Lessons at Mass, 589a

Lethargy Sure there's a l. in mighty woe, 416a

Letter commonally must understand spirit of l., 164a; I lack time to make it shorter, 536a

Letters History, better written from l., 434b

Leviathans Our souls shall be l. In purple seas of wine, 916b

Levites (Deacons) bound to subdue hearts to modesty, 150a; on L., their own duties are laid, 433a; ordained by bishop, 69a

Lewd Books which treat of l. subjects, prohibited, 151b; l. wife cannot be watched, 159a

Lex by *l. regia*, people bestows upon prince all its power, 533b; *Legem credendi l. statuat supplicandi*, 546b

Liar l. and the father of lies, 260b

Libel greater the truth, worse the l.!, 536a, 884a

Liberal A man so broad, to some he seemed to be, 109a; Generous even to serious fault, 601b; if l. education be good, must be useful, 290a; knowledge which is its own end, 514b; l. knowledge, 514b; l. disciplines not free unless truthful, 35a; l. education, intellect disciplined for own sake, 289b; men of l. education, 35a;

Liberalism doctrine there is no positive truth in religion, 537a; mistake of bourgeois l., 537a; properly speaking, no l. in Catholic theology, 650a; Roman pontiff ought to come to terms with l., 732b; To tolerate everything is to teach nothing, 24a; You cannot halve

the gospel of God's grace, 536a; various meanings of word, 536b
Liberals latitudinarians and their opponents, 109a
Liberating l. flesh by flesh, 166b
Liberation From sin, sense, self set free, 77b
Liberties God gave men law, that they might turn it into l., 759a; l. of English Church, 178a
Liberty A crust of bread, and l., 537b; all who have risen On l.'s ruins to fame, 663a; anarchy not l. so much as license, 18b; Christian conscience and personal l., 259a; eternal law, sole standard and rule of human l., 526b; first, maintain justice, second, preserve l., 353a; full l. of thought and speech, 355b; God's most precious gift to human nature, 353a; greater l. under popular institutions, 15a; highest of natural endowments, 538a; His love brings l., 168a; I leave you the spirit of l., 537b; idea of l. has ultimately a religious root, 538a; in most perfect law is most perfect l., 354a; individual l., 140a; larger margin of l. under democracy, 15a; Law is order in l., 530a; l. of artist, if free to create, 35a; l. of self-ruin, 18b; l. to follow will of God, 355a; love is only reconciliation of authority and l., 336a; Man must have l., 538a; no true l. but in fear of God, 343a; order of l., 666b; religious l. and First Amendment, 185a; religious l. in America, 142a; Religious l., not right of being without religion, 354b; Religious l., where coexistence of different religions admitted, 354b; universal reign of human l., 15a; widely advocated, l. of conscience, 355a
License anarchy not liberty but l., 18b; desire for rule and love of l., 46b; Liberty, if l. is kept in restraint, 538a
Licinius, Emperor, 871a
Lie as the tree falleth so must it l., 251a; Children and fools cannot l., 567b; It may be slander, but it is no l., 824b; lyen as a woman can, 920a; man not to live as he was created to live, a l., 538b; not a stone Tell where I l., 770a
Lies A liar and the father of l., 260b; bold At l. and swearing as a woman, 567b; Fine honor's stain, love's frost, mint of l., 342a; Here l. my wife: here let her lie!, 912b; On the bare earth expos'd he lies, 254a; 'twas nuts to the father of l., 536a
Life A mighty maze, not without plan, 539a; All L. death does end, 542b; All my l.'s buried here, 413b; authority of l. and death, 243b; Between us and hell or heaven, nothing but l., 539a; Blessed is he that hath a short l., 538b; BVM, mother of life, 40a; Christ, giver of l. and immortality, 39a, 400b; Christian way of l., 27b; cross on which we hang, 229b; Death reveals what l. cannot, 543b; different ways of l. in Church, 762b; every day, some new way of l., 26a; fairest things in l. are death and birth, 543a; Giver of l., eternal Lord!, 793a; God is the l. of the soul, 66b, 835b; God so lives that He has no principle of l., 376a; good death does honor to whole l., 248a; His l. for them,

His flesh to them, 484a; I am the resurrection and the l., 246a; I believe in l. everlasting, 226b; I live, yet no true l. I know, 214b; in correspondence with God, 408a; individual saves his l. by losing it, 808a; infinite Being is identical with infinite l., 374b; law of l., law of sacrifice and discipline, 541a; lay down l. for our friends, 565a; lay down l. for those condemned, 604a; l. and despair, 258b; life and victory!, 158a; l.'s miraculous germ, 411a; L.'s pleasantest three, 911b; l.'s procession down eternity, 251b; L. is a play acted by dying men, 543a; L. is but loss where death is deemed gain, 542a; L. is short, death is certain, 542b; l. is the mirror of king and slave, 540a; Light and L. to man appear, 168a; living death and dying l., 563a; Lord is my L., 522a; loses its meaning, when it loses its mystery, 628b; My God, my L., my Love, 78a; my hidden L., 77b; No l. is perfect that has not been lived, 540b; nothing but play, 161a, 392b; on l.'s happy shore, 366b; One day of l., One soul to save, 543b; perfect l. is an imitation of death, 247b; perfection of Christian l., in charity, 156a; pilgrimage in this wilderness, 301b; preciousness of His l., 44a; purpose of l. in time, 538b; secret of l. is in art, 32a; shortest l., best, 303b; Son is Way, Truth, and L., 108b; Thanks be to Thee Who gave us l., 491a; thing too glorious to be enjoyed, 541a; This day, L. dy'd, 401a; This death, it is l.'s reparation, 242b; this l., rightly called continuing trial, 650b, 736a; This L., this Light, this Word, this Joy, 168b, 373b; Thou art the resurrection and the l., 245a; To love Him, life; to leave Him, death, 359a; too important to talk about, 540b; *way, the truth and the l.,* 148b, 292a; well-spent l., only passport to heaven, 540a; Where L. was slain and Truth was slandered, 658b; Which cannot die, 382a; Who studies l., her laws more wisely sees, 601a; Worship is the Christian l., 929a
Lifeless He is l. that is faultless, 341b
Life-spring O Jesu! L. of the soul!, 605a
Lift L. up, ye princes of the sky, 36b; L. up your hearts, 591a; We l. our souls, O Lord, to Thee, 622b
Light Blest L. of saints above, 438a; Light chrism of the l., 240b; Creator of the glowing l., 636a; Crown of most incomparable l., 40b; darkness shows us worlds of l., 543b; ere created l. began, 167a; Eternal L. of faithful souls, 7b; God is L. itself, 102b, 458b; His life, our l., 487a; illumination of the true L., 170a; illumine minds with l. of knowledge, 4a; Lead, kindly L., 490a; let perpetual l. shine upon them, 243a, 246a, 767a; L. and Life to man appear, 168a; L. itself Thou art, 490b; l. of God's eternal majesty, 679a; l. of l., 226b, 469b; l. of Thine Incarnate Word, 167a; l. of Thy countenance is imprinted within us, 384a; l. that satisfies, and never sates!, 261b; O L. of L., O Dayspring bright, 522a, 599a; O Thou immortal L. divine!, 371b; place of

refreshment, l. and peace, 592b; Splendor of eternal L., 8a; Thou art, O God, the life and l., 373b; Thou art the incarnated L., 490a; true L. Which enlightens and sanctifies world, 490a; waving of angels' robes, 20a
Lightning A flash of harmless l., 453b
Lights A thousand l. their glory shed, 437b; Now that sun is setting, and evening l. kindled, 893b; L. of the world for evermore, 28b; True l. to lighten every land, 28a
Like L. will to l., 913b; No more l., than apple to oyster, 544a; people will always l. you as much as God wills, 766b
Likeness God's l. in men, compared to Hercules in marble, 569a
Lilac Go down to Kew in l.-time, 544a
Lilies Amongst the l. Thou dost feed, 639b; fairer than all l. are, 55b; Leaving the scent of l. on the air, 544a
Lily Fair l. found among the thorns, 461a; In the house of Zion's l., 488a; L., O l. of the valleys, 92b; O l. of the King! low lies thy silver wing, 544a
Limb every sap-forsaken l., 47b
Limbo Down there place is that no torments try, 544b
Limina, Ad ad limina visits of bishops to pope, 70a
Limitations Conventional people who think they have no l., 217b
Limits state does not determine l. of Church's rights, 181a
Lincoln, Abraham, 256a
Lincoln, England All the boys of merry L., 48b
Line As right as a l., 847b; more than regal l., 296a
Lineage nothing men more pride themselves on, than birth, 544b
Lingered L. labors come to nought, 255a
Link evolutionists and missing l., 316a; no chain stronger than its weakest link, 136b
Lion Be l. in pulpit, lamb in confessional, 669b; if the l. knew his own strength, 509a; Like a true l. he roared, 535b; Of all strong beasts l. bears bell, 54b; "The Christians to the l.!", 544b; Thou who didst as a l. fall asleep, 400b
Lip 'Tis not so sweet as woman's l., 279a
Lips Circumcise the l. of my mouth, 747b; Cleanse my heart and my l., 589a; l. of Church are never silent, 309b; See my l. tremble, my eyeballs roll, 282b; The l.' reasoning, 717b; These death-seal'd l., 249a
Listen L. much and speak little, 939a
Listeners hear no good of themselves, 545a
Listens He l. to good purpose, 545a; L. for thee, l. for thee, 836b
Litany Hear our mournful l., 83b, 658a
Literal l. sense of Scripture, contains no falsehood, 61a
Literary l. religion, little to be depended upon, 545a; primary duty of l. man, to have clear conceptions, 546a
Literature always anticipates life, 546a; human nature and l., 545b; L. a luxury, fiction a necessity, 344a, 546a; L. is to man, what autobiography is to individual, 545b; l. of England, a living voice,

297a; source and foundation of l., 412b; Who was ever consoled by small beer of l., 756b
Literatures On the whole, all l. are one, 545b
Little But l. things on l. wings, 880b; L. Jesus, wast Thou shy, 487b; l. souls on l. shifts rely, 600b; paradise of l. men and purgatory of great, 296a
Littleness He who stays not in l., loses greatness, 414a; Lest l. should hold me great, 347b
Liturgical ardor of l. enthusiasts, 548b; duty of Christians, to live l. life, 548a; l. laws regarding sacred music, 627b; proper approved l. books, 267a; Without heart, l. prayer becomes formal, 548b
Liturgies Great l. cannot be manufactured, 547b
Liturgy All Christian ritual derives from Christ's priesthood, 787a; all things done in holy fashion, 597b; Anglicanism prizes frame of Catholic l., 23a; belongs to Apostolic See, to regulate sacred l., 547b; Christ, all seasons' King and Guide, 534b; clothed in variety of material symbols and forms, 546b; dispensation of Christ's mysteries, 546b; diversity of usage does no harm, 51b; expresses Catholic doctrines, 145a; Follow custom of Church where you happen to be, 207b; great sacramental, 548b; grows and develops, 548a; history of kingdom of God always returning, 266b; If the psalm prays, you too pray, 739a; includes divine as well as human elements, 548a; its formative period, 548b; Let law of prayer determine law of belief, 546b; not mere ornamental ceremonial, 548a; offerings and services, at fixed times and seasons, 597b; one faith, diversity of usage, 51b; organize sacred hierachy on model of heavenly hierarchies, 546b; perpetual revolution of yearly solemnities, 266b; poetry, music, art found expression in l., 548b; prayers of Church, agelong poetry of mankind, 548b; remembrance of things done by Savior, useful to us, 548b; rule of life, laid down for Catholics, 547a; Sacred music, complimentary part of solemn l., 627a; sweet sound of Your Church's singing, 546b; system of language and rites, 547a; thy unwearied watch and varied round, 146a; what the ritual means, 548b; work of redemption, during celebration of l., 310a; worship of Church, efficacious means of achieving sanctity, 548a; worship of Mystical Body in Head and members, 547b; worthily praise Thy name, 586b
Live by Him we have been made to l., 90a; Dead to myself, I l. in Thee, 563a; For Thee to l., in Thee to die, 374a; God, Whom none may l. and mark!, 396a; great thing, to l. well, 538b; I l., yet no true life I know, 214b; king is dead, long l. the king!, 509a; Let me die or l. Thou in me, 542a; L., Jesus, l.! and let it be, 563a; L., our chaste love, 40b; l. to God, 602b; man not to l. as he was created a lie, 538b; many make more study to know, than to l. well, 513a; no great thing to l. long, 538b; no one ought to l. other than becomingly,

157b; no sooner do we begin to l., 247a, 541a; not so behaved that I should be ashamed to l., 519b; now I l., now my life is done, 542a; to l. is to change, 153b; to l. on a dunghill with Job, 543b; to l. well, know how to pray well, 717a; we never really l., only hope to l., 420a; While we l., let us l., 549a; wishing that we l. by His, He died by ours, 466b
Lived And as I l. I live, 684b; To have l. enchanted years, 540b
Livelihood anxious about supplies of this life, 215a; decent l. promoted by common effort, 38b
Lives By all thy l. and deaths of love, 258a; Christ l. in me, 4b; ev'ry man who l. is born to die, 542b; He l. well that has lain well hidden, 26a; he who l. more l. than one, 543a; not lords of our own l., 583b; Now He l., no more to die, 285b; One that l. by other's breath, 542a; Our l. unteach our doctrines we believe, 773b; there is nothing l. but something dies, 543a; two lives, active and contemplative, 5a
Living charity and decent standard of l., 157b; For small l., men run great way, 303a; God's l. is His knowing, 383b; O God, Who dost rule both l. and dead, 541b; power over l. and dead, 244b; Shall judge l. and dead, 28b; strive after happiness by l. well, 419a; The dead shall live, the l. die, 626a; things l., preferred to things not l., 374b; Weep rather the l., 254a
Load this loathsome l., 303b
Loaf better half a l. than no bread, 108b
Loan L., bargain, and commercial obligation, 110b
Lock Catholic faith like l., 58a
Locket empty l. which once contained beloved, 23a
Locks strong l. maken true, 344a; With l. of gold today, 239b
Logic Absolute proof, never be furnished by l. of words, 733a; forms by themselves, prove nothing, 549b; sentiment and taste do not run with l., 101a; While we talk l., we are unanswerable, 549b
Logos, 481b; came down like dew on fleece, 89a; divine and heavenly L., 489a; Son of God is the L. of Father, 480a; universe, created through L., 390b
Loin Près de l'église, l. de Dieu, 138a
London But L. has become, 296b; Ere L. grew too wealthy and too wise, 114a; People-pestered L., 549b; poetry, in Oxford An art, in L. a trade, 688a
Lone Lonely, unto the L. I go, 261b
Loneliness Glad for the grace of l. and yearning, 336b; In a dear rout of l., 535b; There's l. in l., 549b, 804a
Lonely I lay a l. heart Before Thy feet, 350a
Long How l., O Lord, how l., 743b
Longing hour which l. backward bends, 312b; How deeper than all l. is regret!, 763a
Long-suffering Be l. and prudent, 661a
Lontano Piu presso la chiesa, piu l. da Dio, 138a
Look L. down upon me, good and gentle Jesus, 657a; L. or ye leap, 149a; L. up, languishing soul!,

233a; thy beaming l., 36b; When Mary's l. meets thine!, 487b
Looks virtue of her lively l., 323a; Wrinkled face for l. delightful, 10b
Loose whatsoever bishop shall l., 68b
Loosed whatsoever l. on earth, 674b, 821b
Loosing authority of l., given apostles and bishops, 67a; Peter granted pontifical power of binding and l., 677a; power of binding and l., 175b; To Church, authority of binding and l. given, 677b
Loquitur Cor ad cor l., 424b
Lord Ah! dearest L.! I cannot pray, 719b; Blest L., Creator of the glowing light, 636a; Christ the L., 170a; denomination, not implying any accident in God, 374a; Giver of life, eternal L.!, 793a; God's authentic Son, our sole L., 481a; Great L. of earth and sea and sky, 487b; history of our L., inexhaustible matter of contemplation, 492a; Holy, Holy, Holy is the L. of Sabaoth, 379a; I am that L. of life, 836a; In her L. His Church rejoices, 168a; Jehovah, Jove, or L.!, 340a; King of kings, and L. most High!, 21b; L. and Master of my life, 450a; God, L. of men and angels, 63b; L. is my Life, 522a; L. of all creation, 50a, 167b; l. Of an unpurchasable word, 753a; L. of heaven and earth, 196b; L. of humankind, 550a; L. of life eternal, 36a; L. of yourself, 48a; Love, thou art absolute sole l., 554a; man in the street understood our L., 396a; O ever living L. of lords, 882a; O Jesus, Jesus! dearest L.!, 489a; O sovereign L. of nature's might, 373a; One body, one spirit, one L., 135b; One L., one faith, one baptism, 134b, 145a; One only is holy, one only is L., 594a; our redeeming L., 82b; sets His seal on all we do, 4b; supreme Ruler and L. of all, 47a; The dear L. God, of His glories weary, 65a; The L. be with you, 205b, 588b; The L. is risen from the grave, 284b; The L. knoweth who are His, 126a; to l. it over others, 300a; we acknowledge Thee to be L., 372b; Where every man would be l., 3b; Whose mercies all embrace, 25a; willing nations knew their lawful l., 550a; You are, and You are God and L. of all, 372b
Lords As l. do, when they will have their will, 745b; not l. of our own lives, 583b
Lordship presumption, l. over equals, 845a
Lore But Christes l., and His apostles twelve, 403a
Loser let the l. have his word, 112b
Losers Always to let the l. have their words, 550a
Loses No man l. Thee, unless he goes from Thee, 525b
Loseth he that l. Jesus, 488b
Loss better, little l. than long sorrow, 550b; gain of this world is l. of souls, 362a; Life is but l. where death is deemed gain, 542a; Love's the ambassador of l., 557a; Measure thy life by l. instead of gain, 550b
Losses shaken by material l., 736a
Lost Find things ere they be l., 344b; It is l. that is unsought,

804a; rotten luxury of knowing himself to be l., 259a; They are not l. but gone before, 242b

Lot To labor is the l. of man below, 516a

Lots bishop has authority assign l., 67a

Louise Madame L. sleeps well o' nights, 113a

Lourdes Appearance of BVM at L. (1858), 462a; for those who do not believe, no explanation possible, 611b; O honored cave, by Mary's smile adorned!, 462b

Love a magistrate, 554a; abridgment of all theology, 863b; Absorbed alone in l. of Thee, 77b; aching heart of l., 385a; acquiescence of soul in contemplation, 156b; All things sweet to holy l., 561b; alle thing may bind, 551b; Antony lost world for l., 555a; Between death and l., no alternative, 558b; Blessed Sacrament bond of l., 73a; brother-l., 157a; by an act of generous l., 8a; by His l., we may know God, 392b; By it laws made, marriage rites tied, 551a; cannot l. BVM too much, if we l. Him more, 101a; Canst tell me what l. is?, 557a; Carnal l., by which man loves himself, 551a; cause us to l. that which Thou dost command, 334a; Charity is l.; not all l. is charity, 156a; Christian's God, God of l., 384b; Christians alone l. those that hate them, 163a; contradiction in two words—"free l.", 575a; deep and fickle, like the sea, 558a; deific pathway my L. has travelled, 564b; difference between caprice and passion, 557a; difference between knowledge of God, and l. of Him!, 395a; end of l., 889a; every day I seem To l. Thee more and more, 392a; faint for l. of Thee, 196a; faith is beginning, end is l., 324b; few would l. God, unless they feared, 563a; First let a little l. find entrance, 218b; for ladies' l. unfit, 55a; force of l. is engine of the soul, 214a; formation of oneself on l., 37a; Friendship and l., 559a; future belongs to those who l., 58b; gift of the Holy Ghost, 551a; Giver of l., and beauty, and desire, 490b; *God is l.*, 155b, 494a, 560a; God's l. for us, not greater in heaven than now, 384a; greatness of contemplation, given to them that l., 212b; Happy man, able to l. all men alike, 565a; hate the vice and l. the man, 314a; He alone sufficient for heart, Who made it, 563a; He hath shown His perfect l., 25a; He who aspires to heavenly l., 840a; heart free, held by l. of God, 561b; heart sometimes finds out things reason cannot, 557b; His l. brings liberty, 168b; holy ardor that irradiates all, 384a; holy fires maintain l.'s heavenly life!, 455b; hope and soothfast l., 561a; How can I l. Thee as I ought?, 78a; How much less strong is death than l., 558b; I am my l.'s, He is mine, 197b; I knew His l. Who followèd, 385a; I loathe that I did l., 10b; I l. because I l., 561a; I lov'd thee with undying l., 385a; If but world would give to l., 157a; If God be Truth, and God be L., 390b; If this be l., 553b; impossible to l. unknown, 57a; In a dark night With anxious l. inflamed, 214b; In l. is

no lack, 552b; In l., respect first, ardor second, 557a; incarnate L., 97b; infinite treasures of Thy l., 789b; insists that l. shall mutual be, 551a; Jesus! why dost Thou l. me so?, 384b; Joy rul'd the day, and l. the night, 497b; King of l. needed no herald, 385b; knowledge must precede l., 805b; knows no nonage, 554a; knows no rule, 565a; Laughter and l. are everywhere, 523a; law of l. divine, 789a; let us not l. this world, 560a; Lewd l. with loss, 553a; *Look how they l. one another,* 163a; lord of terrible aspect, 551b; l. and desire contrasted, 550b; l. and faith need cultivation, 330a; l. and marriage, 559b; L. can deny nothing to l., 551a; L. is bittersweet, 554a; l. is blind all day, 551b; L. is cruel, l. is sweet, 558a; l. is grace itself, 554a; L. is life, 555b; L. is l.'s reward, 555a; l. is master where he will, 552a; L. is not blind, 558a; L. is the leech of life, 552a; l. is the root of all desire, 257b; l. is the sweetest thing on earth, 281b; L. lives by l., 552b; L.! L.! Infinite l.!, 487a; l. makes faith, not faith l., 330a; l. of Christ has gathered us together, 442; l. of Creator, in creature, 565b; l. of God and deification, 255a; L. of God and hatred of man, incompatible, 559a; l. of God and typical Christians, 125b; L. of heaven, only *way* to heaven, 304b; L. of neighbor, included in l. of God, 561a; L. one too much, thou art slave to all, 554b; l.'s a malady without a cure, 555a; L.'s great artillery, 554a; L. the good, pity the ill, 603b; L., thou art absolute sole lord, 554a; Make many acts of l., 562b; Make us l. Thee, 96b; Man has natural inclination to l. God, 562b; melted in fire of Thy l., 560a; Men always want to be woman's first l., 557a; Mt. Calvary is academy of our l., 111a; most certain sign that we l. God, 563a; My God, I l. Thee, 562a; My life to die for l. of Thee, 563a; natural for will to l., 57b; nature of l., to l. when loved, 561b; nearest road to heaven, 552a; no living in l. without suffering, 552a; no l. without hope, no hope without l., 329b; no man dies for l., but on the stage, 554b; noblest frailty of the mind, 554b; noblest thing in the world, 557b; O God, Who hast prepared for those who l., 560b; O make us l. Thee more and more, 78a; One pulse of passion, 557a; only reconciliation of authority and liberty, 336a; pour into our hearts l. of Thee, 560b; principle effect of l., unite wills, 551a; proper name of Holy Ghost, 439b; pure Mother of L., 40b; quickly inspired by beautiful woman, 54a; Real l. seeks not to possess, 557b; Self-sacrifice, chivalry, art, all come from heart, 557b; She can l., and she can die, 558b; Soft subject for siege of l., 94a; soul on fire with the Spirit of l., 213b; souls that do not love, go empty, 557b; Spirit moves heart to l. God, 53a; stays on, 551a; steadfastness of Thy l., 561a; sufficient by itself, 561a; The anchor of a l. is death, 559a; There is nothing beyond l. of God, 458b; They do not l. that do

not show their l., 552b; Those we l. truly never die, 763a; *Thou shalt l. the Lord thy God,* 527a, 671b; *Thou shalt l. thy neighbor as thyself,* 671b; Thy l.'s sweet liberty, 384b; 'Tis l. alone can hearts unlock, 218b; 'Tis there O l., they keep thy festival!, 556a; To desire to l. God, 257b; to l. all things loved of its beloved, 561b; To l. God in sugar, 344a; To l. Him, life; to leave Him, death, 359a; To l. is to wish the other's highest good, 557b; to prefer nothing to l. of Christ, 155a; true l., cleaving to the truth, 551a; trust is born of l., and l. of God, 564a; Understanding and l., two arms of soul, 887b; We are not drawn to God by iron chains, 562b; We must fear God through l., 343a; When l. ran smooth and free, 719b; Where charity and l. are, there is God, 492b; *which He had for all the saints,* 874a; Who died the Victim of pure l., 657a; with potions of oblivion kill Remorse of lost l., 427b

Loved crime, t'have l. too well, 554a; everyone who has l., 556a; God alone is to be l., 563a; He has always l. you from eternity, 384b; I will be l. but now and then, 556b; let us be l. because of Thee, 346a; Those who love to be feared, fear to be l., 342b; Too late I l. Thee, O Beauty, 54a, 559b; twofold reason why God should be l., 561a

Loveliness Each crown of l. adorns, 38a; Let your eyes drink of l. in silence, 715a; l. of skill, comes from supreme L., 54a

Lover her past her l., her future her husband, 455a; Jove but laughs at l.'s perjury, 555a; L. of men, Benefactor of our souls, 595b; O Lover of the sons of men, 6a; pulse of the patriot, soldier, or l., 421b; union of l. and thing loved, 889a; who shall give a l. any law?, 552a

Lovers always l. in the working classes, 565b; companionship of Christ produced l. of history, 564a; Love equalizes l., 565b; Poets, like l., should be bold and dare, 685a; thus l. tie their knot, 2a

Loves Every soul that l., treasurehouse, 557a; everything loves its own proper good, 561b; God l. all things that He has made, 384a; show me one who l., he will understand, 301b

Loveth He that l., void of all reason, 552b

Loving by l. God, our souls are wholly occupied with Him, 560a; heart loves God in afflictions, 10a; L. Thee, find Thee, love Thee, finding Thee, 564a; O Thou l., gentle One, 75b; Thee in and above all things, 560b

Low Death makes equal high and l., 248a; Nor are half so vile or l., 492a; To Him no high, no l., no great, no small, 387b

Lowbrows Whether we are highbrows or l., 571b

Lower l., I can find no place to stand, 445b; Wisdom ordained higher should look after l., 21a

Lowly Gave also l. mushrooms leave to grow, 413b; L. of heart, our God we pray, 731a

Loyal low and love-like, and leal, 566a

Loyalty religion grafted upon l., 23b; their loyal deceit, 211a

Lucifer L. began well, now a fiend, 56b

Luck for good l., cast an old shoe, 566a; l., and predictions of horoscopes, 41b; There's no good love without good l., 566a

Lucy, St., 566a

Lullaby Let angels sing His l., 487a; Sing l., my little Boy, 566b

Lumber With loads of learned l. in his head, 103b, 667a

Lunar on the l. world securely pry, 620a

Lunatic crippled mind, 566b

Lunatics poets and l., 473b

Lust enjoyment of one's self without reference to God, 566b, 818a; flames of unlawful passion, 159a; In which to live is death, to die is hell, 553a; principle of all sins can be called l., 818a; weight of earthly l., 85a

Lusters All l. in one purity, 97a

Lusts crucifieth l. of flesh, 36b; My l. they do me leave, 10b

Lute take this time-worn l. away, 567a; whether The voice or l. was most divine, 831b; whose leading chord is gone, 2a

Lutes fashion musical Of cadenced l., 479b

Luther, Martin, 62a, 567a

Lutheran Princes, 180a

Lux at its *fiat l.,* 225a

Lying All sin is a kind of l., 816b; sovereign remedy against l., 567b

Lyings Hazard is very mother of l., 362b

Lyre His praise my l. shall ring, 489a

M

Maccabees, Book of, 244a

Maceration penance and m., not for everyone, 623b, 668b

Machine unbreathing engine marks no tune, 568a

Machinery must be fully controlled, 37a

Mad great ones are thought m., 45a; In one word, heroically m., 104b; M. as a March hare, 568a; There is a pleasure sure In being m., 473a, 568b

Madam To be called 'M.', glorious thought, 517b

Made everything m., expressive of value, 34a; He m. thee when He might have m., 366b; Thou hast m. us for Thyself, 559b; Word, by which Thou hast m. all things, 485a

Madmen Materialists and m. never have doubts, 598b

Madness Anger, kind of temporary m., 22a; Great wits are sure to m. near allied, 363a, 568a; lies in every passion, 655b; My love's a noble m., 554b

Magi, 167a, 299a, 568b

Magic There is in stillness oft a m. power, 847a

Magisterial Thy m. ways, 814b

Magisterium living, authoritative, m. of Church, 119a, 129b; One faith, one communion, one spiritual government, 134b

Magistracy civil m. for human government, 406a

Magnanimity surpass men in m. and kindness, 568b

Magnates deference to m., 504b

Magnet The m. calls the steel, 385a

Magnificat Our lady sings m., 831b

Magnificence great riches not re-

quired for m., 32a; In thee m., 99b

Magnify M., her who is more honorable, 167b; M., my soul, her, 299a

Maid character of mistress, judged by that of m., 614a; M. yet Mother as May hath been, 600a; meek as is a m., 161b, 602a; mild, silent little M. like thee, 84a; thou, still a m., brought forth, 79b

Maiden Ah, whither shall a m. flee, 922b; I sing of a m., 83a; When the heart of a m. is stolen, 568b; wild, wild m., 47b

Maiden-mark Who thy m. protected, 39b

Maids Of all fair m. my Rosalynde is fairest, 54b

Main Street M., Heaventown, 844b

Majesty beauteous light of God's eternal m., 630b, 679a; God's m., 50a, 196a, 212b, 370a, 378a, 391a; Lord of m., 91a; O M. unspeakable!, 378a, 440a; slander of m., 878b; weight of heaven's offended m., 98b; when He cometh second time in His m., 7b

Majorem Ad m. Dei gloriam, 367a

Majority most may err as grossly as few, 739b; weakest camp, strongest school, 568b

Make We did not m. ourselves, 225b, 374b

Maker God, M. of the universe, 21b, 36a, 50a, 372a, 373a; M. of all, eternal King, 522a, 636a; M. of heaven and earth, 224a, 226b, 372a; man's own M., 6a, 80a, 83a; Son of a Virgin, M. of Thy Mother, 640b

Mala Mala mali malo mala contulit, 29a

Malady love's a m. without a cure, 555a

Malaria great deal of Roman m., 711a

Male in sight of God, neither m. nor female, 448b; *God made man m. and female,* 131a, 572a; sex more vigorous and predominant, 455b

Malebolge There is in hell a place Called M., 427a

Malice cloak of m., 18b; Much m. mingl'd with a little wit, 569a; The envy, m., and pride, 411a

Malorum Radix m. est cupiditas, 48b

Man after image of God, 244b, 356a, 569b, 576a; All-daring dust and ashes!, 249a; alone is miserable, 612b; alone is woo'd, 219a; amused by trifles, 18a; an exception, whatever else he is, 571b; Art is the signature of m., 32b; Behold the M.!, 657b; being filled with error, 300b; being of genius, passion, intellect, 545b; created to praise God, 37a; earthly animal, worthy of heaven, 569a; epitome of the world, 570a; Every m. for himself and God for us all, 397b; fall of m., 571b; fellow citizen of angels, 569b; *God made m. male and female,* 131a, 572a; He is m., who is to be m., 1b; heir of immortality, 569b; made out of slime of earth, 8b; m. and a woman, as such, incompatible, 574b; m., head of family, woman, heart, 572b; *M., Thou hast confirmed for Thyself,* 481a; master of his fate, 339a; Member of the Church, 569b; a microcosm, 739b; middle point between nothing and whole, 570b; nature is twofold, 52a; *not*

a reasoning animal, 750b; not merely evolution but revolution, 571b; not worthy of God, 570a; Poor vessel wrought of clay!, 569b; proper study of mankind, m., 571a; proposes, but God disposes, 397a; rational soul with mortal body, 569a, 835a; Remember, m., that thou art dust, 37b; social animal, 404b, 405b; superior to beasts, 300a; The ideal m.!, 571a; thinking reed, 570a; thinks, God directs, 397a; tyranization of m., 43a; What is m. in nature?, 570b

Mane m. of every whistling wind, 346a

Manger His earthly throne, 168a; where the Incomprehensible is laid, 167b

Manhood long mistled by wandring fires, 219a; Soon come, soon gone, 11a; true faith, at once Godhead and manhood, 481a

Manicheeism notion that matter is essentially evil, 517a

Mankind Adam's race, 97b, 169b; All m., in Christ one man, 43b, 134a; important place among works of God, 448b; Mary, Mother of m., 102a; Not one, but all m. in effigy, 109a, 893a; proper study of m., man, 571a; social by nature, unsocial by corruption, 449a

Manly m. Christian spirit, 775b

Manna, 75a, 284b, 400a, 572b, 913a

Manners At meat her m. were well taught withal, 572b; M. with fortunes, 731b

Manning, Cardinal, 573a

Mansion find in us m. prepared for Himself, 208a; happy m. of city above!, 303a

Mansions *In my Father's house there are many m.,* 302a

Mantle round the world a m. throw, 157a

Manual Christ, devoted Himself to m. labor, 517a

Many We are as m. as we are alleged to be, 163a

Manysidedness You cannot be everything if you are anything, 890a

Maple blood-like drip the m. leaves, 47b

Marcellinus, 173b

Marcellus, 251a, 318b

March certain faith of a M. daffodil, 238a; drought of M. hath pierced, 29b

March-bloom Look! M., 304b

Marcian, Emperor, 174a

Marcus buy M. up at price he is worth, 201b

Mare whether grey m. better horse or not, 446b

Maria M., Mother of our King, 40b

Marigold I do commend the m., 573a

Marital deliberate frustration of m. act, 66a

Mark, St., 675a

Market As soon goeth young lambskin to m., 578b; how the m. goeth, 573a

Marks three particular m. of Church, 117a

Marriage among Christians, every true m. sacrament, 575a, 578b; benedictions and ceremonies, 577b; bond, perpetual and indissoluble, 577a, 578a; chastity of m., 158b; Christian m. confers grace, 579b; Church has right to establish impediments, 577b, 579a; competency of civil power, 579a; Defender of m., 579b; dissolved by Pauline privilege, 580a; dissolved by profession of religion, 579b; efficient cause, consent of partners, 577a; end, begetting and upbringing of children, 577a, 578b; form of matrimony, 577a; governed by canon law, 579a; has God for its Author, 578b; has three blessings, 577a; husband and wife may separate from bed and board, 580b; I join you in matrimony, 576b; I, take you for my lawful wife, to have and to hold, 576b; If any one saith m. placed above virginity, 898a; *Increase and multiply*, 579b; instituted by Christ, 577b; love and m., 559b; m. of non-baptized, legitimate, 579a; mystery foreshadows union of Christ with Church, 576a, 577a, 578a; mystical m. of Church, 131a; natural right of m., 336a; no power can dissolve Christian m., 578a; not lawful for Christians to have several wives, 577b; one purpose of procreating children, 575b, 732a; ratified and consummated, cannot be dissolved, 580a; remedy for concupiscence, 578b; sacrament, signifies union of Christ with Church, 577a, 577b, 578a; servant of God N. is betrothed, 576a; servant of God N. is crowned, 576a; solemnization prohibited at certain times, 577b; Take and wear this ring, 576b; *they shall be two in one flesh*, 577a; *Those whom God has joined together*, 267a, 268a, 577a; valid m., said to be ratified, 578a; will you take N. for your lawful wife?, 576b

Marriage, Mixed Church forbids m., 580a

Marriage-bed grave, their second m., 455b

Marriages dissolved for sake of religion, 267b; Holy Scripture speaks of four m., 576b; never a compatible one, 574b; Second m., lawful, 911a

Married be m., but have no wife, 149b; begin to criticize, when they begin to admire, 455b; devotion of a m. woman, 574b; He m. the money, 618a; Let m. regard unmarried as above themselves, 897b; many holy men and women, faithful spouses, 437b; m. past redemption, 574a

Marry better sexes should misunderstand, until they m., 455b; better to m., because worse to burn, 573b; Christians shall not m. heretics, 580a; No Christian may m. deceased wife's sister, 202a; No pious Christian ought to m. twice, 580a

Marrying when will there be an end of m.?, 573b

Marsiglio of Padua, 180a

Martha, St., 580b

Martin, St., 829b

Martin V, Pope, 127a

Martyr condemned for Lord, esteemed as holy m., 580b; First victims of the m. bands, 441a; holy men, who have fought for truth, 581a; made like Christ in sufferings, 53a; No one m. for a conclusion, 327b, 582a, 760b; O captain of the m. host!, 847a; St. Agatha, Virgin and m., 10a; worthy of incorruptible crown, 580b

Martyrdom all have not the gift of m., 584a; Baptism by fire, 49b, 583b; baptism of blood, 53a; baptism of suffering, 741a; blood of Christians is seed, 583a; efficacy of m., 50b; power to remain in

flames unmoved, 629a; Reck not of racks, their torments are but toys, 58+a; She's for the Moors and m., 584a

Martyrdoms Those m. blessed, 583a

Martyrs all times are the age of m., 582a; apostles and m. pray for others, 795a; assist in healing or aiding, 242b; beautiful raiment, blood of m., 581b; blood of m. and Catholic Church, 117a; commemorated in Eucharist, 308a; companions of Christ!, 582a; confession same as if baptized, 50b; faith, that makes m., 582a; God of the m., 308a; God's true soldiers, 581b; heroes of Christ, 581b; in time of peace, 581b; King of m., 92a; knights of God!, 582a; There are two kinds of m., 581b; we multiply whenever we are mown down, 103b, 583a

Marxian m. politicians in England, 199b

Mary all graces come through M., 92a; all honor paid to M. redounds to Him, 84a; assumed into glory, 41b; blessed Mother of God, 82a; bore Christ happily in heart, 80b; bore Head of body in flesh, 92b; child of David's race, 782a; common-treasure of whole world, 81a; Daily, daily, sing to M., 89a; fulness of grace showered on M., 86a; Eve believed serpent, Mary angel, 85a; her passion, 95a; her prayers of great weight, 82b; I commend myself to blessed Lady M., 520a; I'll sing a hymn to M., 95a; In danger, in doubts, think of M., 87b; Mary, remember me!, 84b; meaning of name of M., 99a; mother of us all, 93a; new Eve, 93a; not touched of sin, 169a; our baptism, in M. anticipated, 41b; Queen by conquest, by election, 97b; richness of virginity of M., 78b; star of the sea, 99a; thou hast trampled down all heresies, 24b, 100b; true position of Mary, 84a; we are children of Mary, 93a; worked salvation of world, 90a

Mary I, Queen, 140b, 323a

Mary Magdalen, St. A lovely M., she laves earth's feet, 623a; Blessed offender!, 584b; Like M. the tearful dawn, 286b

Maryland Catholic and Episcopal in M., 585b; M., my M., 585b

Mask You cannot unmask a m., 193a

Mass *See also* Eucharist, Eucharistic Sacrifice; all things done in holy fashion, 597b; applies to us fruits of salvation, 310a; benefit to dead and living, 308a; celebrated in vulgar tongue, 597b; celebrating mystery of Lord's death, 727b; ceremonies, incentives to piety, 597b; greatest action that can be on earth, 586a; If any one saith canon contains errors, 597b; must be heard on feast days of obligation, 586a; no one may consecrate except priest, 309b, 311a; not bare commemoration of Cross, 309b; Paris is well worth a m., 585b; propitiatory sacrifice, 309b; Receive power to offer sacrifice, 727b; Sacrament, by operation of Holy Spirit, 308b; Sacrifice of the Mediator, 244a; To swear in weighty matters by m., 856a; work of redemption, continued during celebration, 310a

Masses how to educate the m., 289a; In dirt and darkness hundreds stink content, 733a; people

and 'the m.,' two distinct concepts, 845b

Master as scholar his m., 31b; Christ, M. of His house, 66b; confirms judgment of His servants, 729a; He who has not one m., has many, 598a; I admire Thee, M. of the tides, 374a; Lord and M. of my life, 450a; no art learned without m., 31b; prayers of Mary and clemency of M., 82b; Upon their Word and M. feed, 74b; When Thou art M. of the mind, 630b

Masterpieces Church has filled world with m., 33a

Masters fellow servants of servants, 825b

Mastery m. of man over himself, 37a

Mater Mater dolorum, 95a; *Omnium ecclesiarum m. et caput*, 171a

Material shaken by m. losses, 736a

Materialism other forces than those which reside in matter, 598a

Materialist m. theory of history, 598b; Nobody more parochial than m., 598b

Materialists M. and madmen never have doubts, 598b

Maternal Look thou with m. love, 40a; m. relationship of BVM, 80b; thy maternal prayers avail much, 98b

Maternity m. of BVM, 86a

Mathematical difference between artistic mind and m., 686b

Mathematicians m. go mad, poets scarcely ever do, 686b

Mathematics midway between physics and metaphysics, 598b

Matins at hour when cock crows, rise and pray, 599a; morning prayers, 266a

Matrimonial m. causes, belong to eccles. judges, 578a

Matrimony cannot be dissolved on account of adultery, 267b; form of m., inseparable union of minds, 577a; I join you in m., 576b; impediments to m., 577b; instituted by Christ the Lord, 577b

Matron Like a m. grown jaded Fat, forty, and fair, 853a

Matter Concrete m. does not admit of demonstration, 599b; has itself been made from nothing, 224a

Matters busy ourselves with m. which do not concern us, 601a

Maturity Men come to meridian, at various periods of lives, 599b

Mauvais ton neglect of cosmetics gives m., 222a

Maximo Deo optimo m., 397a

Maximus M. post apostolos ecclesiarum instructor, 44b

May as fresh as is month of M., 599b; He who will not when he m., 645b; It is the jolly month of M., 600b; maidmonth's Queen!, 600a; M. is Mary's month, 600a; Thou art the Queen of M., 97b, 600a

May-mess Look, look! a M., 304b

Maze mighty m., not without plan, 539a; tangled In the m. of sin!, 522b

Me Qui m. amat, amat et canem meum, 273a

Meals Better m. many, than one too merry, 600b

Mean coward arts of m. expedients, 600b; m. As worm, 163b; Measure is a merry m., 614a

Meanest m. have their day, 335a

Meaning Free from all m., 104b;

rest to some faint m. make pretence, 848b

Meanness m., The Savior's Cross to share?, 449b

Means Charity is both m. and end, 156b; I am dying beyond my m., 253a; If you will end, you must will m., 395a

Measurable art, immeasurable translated into m., 34a

Measure created things cannot be m. of God, 390a; Feed by m., 287a; immeasurable, Who hath made all things by m., 387a; In everything there lieth m., 601a; M. is a merry mean, 614a; M. is medicine, 278b; will of God is m. of things, 391b, 419a

Measures God alone m. reality by what He is, 867a; God m. affliction to our need, 10a

Meat abstinence from m. and drink, 3a; God never sendeth mouth but He sendeth m., 347b; greatest crabs be not best m., 223b; Look not on m., but on man, 601a; Till m. fall in your mouth, 55b

Medal m. of St. Christopher he wore, 601a

Meddleth Who m. in all thing, 601a

Meddling busy ourselves with matters which do not concern, 601a

Mediator *between God and man,* 175a, 467a, 481a, 485a; Church allows no image between soul and Creator, 486b; He is M., Priest, Sacrifice, 307b; necessary that m. should reconcile us, 757b; our M. deserved not to be punished, 43a

Mediators creatures may be called m., 91a

Mediatrix BVM, m. and refuge of Christians, 90a, 90b; rewards of salvation, through Mary, 88b; thou art an invincible m., 95b

Medici Sensus et ars m. curant, 268b

Medicine Against death is worth no m., 248a; apply m. of adequate penance, 446a; Blessed Sacrament is heavenly m., 72a; death in ambush lay in every pill, 601b; Go, take physic, 762b; greatest duty of the healing art, 601a; Labor is a powerful m., 515a; May His holy name be m. for health, 812b; Measure is m., 278b; m. of humility, 175a; m. of sin, 651b; This then must be m. for my woes, 410b

Medieval m. Christendom, sacral age, 184a; M. culture, matrix in which western type formed, 605b; M. man entered State through Church, 183b

Mediocrity those who lived Without praise or blame, 601b

Meditate in heart that which you utter with voice, 716b; To m. on life of Jesus, wisdom, 602a

Meditation contemplation and m., 213a; Let consideration begin with yourself, 601b; Seek in reading and thou shalt find in m., 213b

Meek Be m., bear adversity, 602b; m. as is a maid, 602a

Meet It is truly m. and right, 591a; m. again too late, 654b; m. as a rope for a thief, 864b; when we m. again, Some bright tomorrow, 337a

Meeting doth not m. like this make amends, 602b

Melancholy Cleanse yourself of this wicked m., 602b; should be an innocent interlude, 498a

Melchizedek *Priest after order of*

M., 307a, 484b, 486a; Thy high priest M., 592b

Melius m. est minus egere quam plus habere, 361b; *scitur m. nesciendo,* 393b

Melodies Thou art the shape of melodies, 59a

Melody m. of spheres, 626a; Swell in m. sublime, 74b

Member each Christian, m. of Church, 126b, 569b; m. of Church, in *desire,* 128a

Members BVM, clearly mother of His m., 80b; Church has one body, many m., 93a, 126b, 166b; m. of God's household, 579b; m. of His Son, 162a, 166b, 384a; only *real* m. of Church, 127b; potential and actual, 132a; we are m. of one another, 131a, 799b; what He is, does not follow His m. are, 128a

Membership condition of good and bad in Church, 127a; those who in no wise belong to Church, 127b

Memorial year by year the sad m. wreath, 763a; m. of my Savior dying, 75a

Memorials admonish us to think of those taken away, 151b

Memories long be my heart with such m. fill'd!, 603a; Waves of my thoughts and m. turn to thee, 753b

Memory And m. gild the past!, 659a; faculty of soul, 602b; love and m., 65a; sad m. of a happy story, 9a

Men All mortal m. this day rejoice, 286a; always want to be a woman's first love, 557a; begotten for heaven and eternity, 336b; but children of larger growth, 570b; circumscribed by space, 21b; God's likeness in m., 569a; heirs of salvation, 20a; may be read, as well as books, 571a; M. are m., but Man is a woman, 571b; nature of angels make m., 21b; not enough m. to go around, 565b; not mere dung to fructify seed of future, 306a; should imitate humility of BVM, 88b; whether more m. than women are saved, 293b; worry over an argument, 30b

Mencken, H. L., 256a

Mend Hard for any man all faults to m., 341b

Mental m. condition of modern world, 855a

Mercenaries m. and law of charity, 155b

Merchant This estimable m., 110b

Mercies Let your m. confess to You, 382a; The Lord, Whose m. all embrace, 25a

Merciful He is m. and powerful to save, 98b; O God, ever m. and sparing of punishment, 500b; O m., O pious Maid, 95b; virgin most m., 99a

Mercy after sinning, presume on His m., 446a; ardently loving every work of m., 652a; Blessed Sacrament, sacrament of m., 73a; BVM mother of mercy, 90b, 99a; Dost thou wish to receive m.?, 603b; flashed back from brazen gates of hell, 386a; fulfilment of justice, 604a; God granteth no pity Withoute thee, 96a; God's m., infinite, 258b, 862a; greater thing than right, 604a; Justice to keep, mixt with m., 162a; look Thou to Thine own m., 604a; Lord have m., Christ have m., 588a; May almighty God have m. upon you, 587b; Mother of God, open to us gate of m., 86b, 99b; never to despair of God's m., 386a; O God, Whose property is ever to have m., 245b; oil of m., 604a; Our misery is throne of God's m., 612b; Reason to rule, m. to forgive, 604a; Show m. to thy neighbor, 603b; thou queen of misericorde, 96a; works of m., 155a

Meredith, George, 651a

Merge To m. myself in Him, 889a

Meridian Men come to m., at various periods, 599b

Merit can man be saved by m. of works?, 356b; Catholic doctrine of m., 604b; Charms strike sight, but m. wins, 55a; consists in the virtue of love alone, 604b; Envy will m. as its shade pursue, 298a; good works and m., 402b; none has m. such as hers, 97a; Reward is what you receive, m. what you do, 604a; without grace, man cannot m. everlasting life, 412b

Merited Christ sufficiently m. salvation, 43b

Meritorious Any deliberate act done from state of grace, m., 604a; Christ's passion m. cause of salvation, 44a; m. works proportionate to everlasting life, 412a

Merits Mary! for thy m. wholly, 40a; We beseech Thee, by m. of Thy saints, 588a

Mermaid What things Done at the M.!, 923a

Merry All be not m. that men see dance, 239a; As m. as three chips, 497a; It is m. when knaves meet, 510b

Messias Great M. triumphing, 8b; Messias' speedy birth, 8b

Messenger from God's high throne, 782a

Messengers angels are m. and ministers, 19b

Met the day when first we m., 602b

Metaphors She sees a mob of m. advance, 604b

Metaphysical M. proofs of God, 376b; accentuate opposition between m. and psychological, 739b

Metaphysician Not to be a m. is no sin, 604b

Metaphysics attempt to explain things we cannot see, 604b; only thoroughly emotional thing, 605a

Metropolitan confirms episcopal consecration, 67b

Metropolitans bishops four-fold, patriarchs, archbishops, m., bishops, 433b

Michael, St. general of heaven, 19b; holy standardbearer, 245b; 605a; intercession of blessed M., 590a; Let M. stand in His defence, 487a

Microcosm Man is a m., 739b

Middle Ages age of spiritual struggle and social change, 605b; cannot be characterized as *the* Catholic culture, 605b; Church assumed many responsibilities of political society, 139a, 184a; dominant idea, strength at service of justice, 184a; inspired by Catholic spirit, 139a, 139b; unity of social body, 184a

Middle-aged Hope, inspiration of m., 446a

Midnight at m. rise and pray, 895b; in this hour, every creature hushes, 895b; Like hours at m. passed, 827a

Midway M. the journey of this life, 10b, 922a

Might God's m., 370a, 388b, 848a; great works of Thy m., 569b; m.

of BVM, 91a; M. overcometh right, 606a

Mighty *His name shall be called m.* God, 70b, 78b

Mildness whom our m failed to correct, 22b

Militant "From the Church M. we sever thee," 317b

Military please God while engaged in m. service, 606a

Militiae Haec sunt arma m. nostrae, 352b

Milk *land flowing with m. and honey,* 24a, 479a; m. products, not forbidden by abstinence, 3b

Milky Way God be thanked for the M., 844b

Mill Much water goeth by the m., 606a

Miller Every honest m. has a golden thumb, 606a

Mill-pond Lay her in the m., 110a

Mill-stone the upper m. roof'd His head, 78a

Milton, John, 606b

Milvian Bridge, Battle of, 229a

Mimes teach men tricks of adultery, 5b

Mind Ambition is m.'s immodesty, 14a; Anxiety troubles the m., 26a; as eye to body, so m. to soul, 835b; balance of the m., 607b; cannot measure its boundaries, 305b; Canst thou ever impose anything upon free m.?, 353a; Christ dwells in m. through faith, 330a; consistent in error, 301a; every clever man who cannot make up his m., 499b; eye of the m., 608a; God hateth proud and obstinate m., 190a; God, m. and source, 386a; grant us health of m. and body, 239b; human m. instinctively craves to know cause, 419b; in man, nothing better than m. and reason, 102b, 606b; inmost, ultimate Council of judgment, 608a; *Let this m. be in you,* 586b; may fix on false object, 57b; m., intellect, operations of soul, 606b; m. of archangel, in body of rhinoceros, 607b; m.'s achievement, 381a; must be persuaded, cannot be constrained, 607b; must be subject to God, 102b; natural for m. to believe, 57b; not itself measure of all things, 146b; Nothing greater than m., except God, 606b; Of all tyrannies worst, which persecutes m., 607b; *one m. and one heart,* 615b; Out of sight, out of m., 2a, 350a; Reason is the vision of the m., 749a; royal road of truth is by the m., 608b; sin can never make away with the m., 607a; Stanching, quenching ocean of a motionable m., 374a; subsisting form, consequently immortal, 836a; *The m. of the Spirit,* 876a; theological virtues join human m. to God, 900b; Thought is a kind of sight of m., 865b; 'Tis education forms the common m., 289a; uneasy, until it attains certitude, 515a; What greater work than training m., 289a; Women, represent triumph of matter over m., 572a

Mindful Be m. of Thy servants and handmaids, 591b

Minds Canossa, always consolation of free m., 354a; desire for fame tempts even noble m., 335a; differences between various kinds of m., 608a; governed by respecting their freedom, 674a; Great m. need elbow-room, 608a; hearts and m., tested in crucible of truth,

429a; monument of vanish'd m., 107a; Seek other mistress for your m., 553a; serve Him with purified m., 7b; So many heads, so many wits, 607a; Truth, discovery made by traveling m., 884a

Minister does not defile sacrament, 51b; fit to m. at Thy holy altar, 496a

Ministers angels are messengers and m., 19b; bishop m.s blamelessly, 67a; By divine institution, hierarchy of bishops, priests, m., 190a; Church's m., like gardeners, 130b; *His m. a flaming fire,* 19b

Ministry divine m., 849b; exalted work, leads to kingdom, 728b; m. and labor of His pastors, 127a; m. of angels and men, 20b, 34a; m. of the high priesthood, 68a

Minorities test of freedom, security enjoyed by m., 353b

Minority weakest camp, strongest school, 568b

Minors not bound by canon law, 112a

Minus melius est m. egere quam plus habere, 361a

Miracle anything beyond expectation of one who marvels, 608b; event inconsistent with constitution of nature, 610a; God can produce particular effects, 609b; no argument to an atheist, 610b; some m. has intervened, 680b; standing m. of this visible world, 609a; world Turned Christian, m. is born, 610a

Miracles Above nature, against nature, besides nature, 610a; attest divine origin of Christianity, 610b; authority of faith not from m. but God, 331a; can be known with certainty, 610b; external or internal, 610b; for those who believe, no explanation needed, 611b; gift of m., 411b; have confirmed holy apostolic doctrine, 609b; historical difficulties about m., 611b; I should not be Christian but for m., 608b; "impossibility" of m., 610b; m. and Catholic Church, 117a; m. and natural phenomena, 609a; m. of Scripture, not mythical, 165a, 610b; not what make us Christians, 233a; provide evidence universe is not closed system, 611b; seal of God, 609b; signs of power, 171a; signs *to them that believe not,* 610a; took them captive in net of m., 609a; Why do not m. happen nowadays?, 609a

Miraculous m. intervention of Our Lady, 100b

Mire thou art but dirt and m., 451b

Mirror BVM, m. of beauty and virtue, 92a; Clergy looked at as a m., 190a; Every saint, little looking-glass of God, 794a; living and eternal m. of God, 836a; make a m. of His hour-glass, 513b; No m. keeps its glances, 612a; Scripture like m. wherein we see progress, 60b

Mirrors so vast a store Of m., 611b

Mirth holy mirth Of heaven, 40b; indulge in reasonable m., 453b; thing too great for God to show us, His m., 498a; When m. is full and free, 153b

Misanthrope A m. I can understand, 612a

Misanthropic m. idea, one of the immortal lies, 612a

Misanthropy As long as humanity lasts, can be hated, 612a

Mischance chance may win that by m. lost, 153a

Miser m. with an eager face, 612a

Miserable Man alone is m., 612b; because they do not cleave to God, 419b; mercy, only exercised toward m., 386a; nothing m., but what is thought so, 612b

Misereatur M. vestri omnipotens, 587b

Miserere M., Domine!, 258b

Miseries soul, who has made it business to collect m., 604a

Misery brother's m. is truly felt, 200b; good to have companions in m., 612b; In the midst of m. to remember bliss, 603a; when man suffers himself, it is called m., 682b

Misreckoning M. is no payment, 664b

Missa Ite, m. est, 595b

Mission I never may know it in this life, 809a; Many girls want a m. in world, 113a; microcosm of Church as moral force, 613a; of US, to prepare world for liberty, 15a

Missionary All men and women in parish, known to m., 612b; drill-master makes but indifferent apostle, 614a; object of m. activity, bring Gospel to new races, 613b; m. character of Western civilization, 187a

Missions Church and colonization, 613a; Church grafts good scion upon wild stock, 140a; Church's aim, not domination of peoples, 613b; great hour of Christian conscience has struck, 613a; m. and culture, 140a, 613b; unequaled school for learning men, 612b; wise practice of Church, 140a

Mistaken He that is not, cannot be m., 511b; Most m. people mean well, 301a; wish to show another m., 30b

Mistakes M. are made on two counts, 614a; world may learn by m., 533a

Mistress by angels M. owned, 95b; character of m., judged by that of maid, 614a; Maistress of all the world, 96a, 98a; m. of our song, 40b

Mists m. In trance round the soul!, 277a

Mites Two m., two drops, 617b

Mixture May this m. and consecration of Body and Blood, 594a

Mob best definition of a m., 256b; deference to the m., 504b; democracy is opposed to rule of m., 256b

Mocked Scorned, m., and spurned I've been, 234a

Moderation M. is always good, except in loving God, 614a; Total abstinence, easier than m., 3a

Modern mental condition of m. world, 855a; m. world, living on its Catholic capital, 867a

Modernists collected all errors against faith, 614b

Modernism means destruction of all religion, 614b; m. and nondogmatic Christianity, 147a

Modernity m. and narrowness, 614b

Moderns road of ancient centuries, strewn with dead m., 614b

Modest Be m. in all thy words and works, 615a; English are a m.

people, 297b; The glory of a m. heart, 921b

Modesty Christian m., not enough to be so, 614b; our Redeemer loved flower of unimpaired m., 898a

Modo M. et m. non habebant modum, 732a

Mold Nature has cast men in so soft a m., 807a

Mole instinctive m. Breaking the Clod, 564b

Moment 'sacrament of the present m.', 767b

Moments One by one the m. fall, 615a; Sweet the m., rich in blessing, 233a

Monarch m.'s crown with fate surrounded lies, 617b; Eternal M., King most high, 35b; See in a manger, M. of angels, 170a; temporal m. receives authority directly from Source, 845a

Monarchical tendency to m. government in hearts of men, 615a

Monarchies M. and empires rely on physical force, 766a

Monarchs citizens of America are her m., 255b; when fate summons, m. must obey, 249b

Monarchy absolute m. in Catholic countries, 3a; advantage of m., 615a; eccles. order subject to one person, 405a; supreme m. in temporal matters, 405a

Monasteries simple Christian communal life of m., 59a

Monastery can never be merely escape from world, 617a; discipline of a m., 616a; m. of a devout life, 638b

Monastic ideals of asceticism and otherworldliness, important, 616b; m. life of Benedictines influenced Europe, 59a

Monastic Life abbot is representative of Christ, 1a; let everything be common property, 615b; life of a monk ought to be lenten, 618b; Perfection, not something you can acquire like hat, 617a; school of the Lord's service, 615b; way of God's commandments, 615b

Monasticism Benedictines leavened Europe, 59a; I do not urge you to it, 615b; not godliness, but kind of life, 615b; services to culture, 616b

Monday surfaces of soul, raw on M. mornings, 837a

Money A little wanton m., 617a; enough to last till I get to heaven, 521a; excellent rule for right use of m., 617b; I feel no care of coin, 607a; M. is power, 618a; Nothing that is God's is obtainable by m., 617a; patriotism, religion, m., three great realities, 476a

Monique 'Soeur M.', 641b

Monk bad m. makes a good clergyman?, 618a; If thou wouldst be a m., 617b; life of a m. ought to be lenten, 618b; man who has given up everything to possess everything, 619a; ought to heap up treasure in heaven, 618a; should own nothing in this world, 618a; There was a m., leader of fashions, 927b; two classes m. should avoid, 618b

Monkey Than when I was a m., 316a

Monks four kinds of m., 618b; grow old and gray in the letter, 616a; Merry sang the m. who in Ely fare, 619a; Monks! monks!

monks!, 521a; not even bodies and wills at their disposal, 618b

Monogamy based on God's original decree, 619b

Monosyllabic M. lines, stiff or languishing, 688b

Monotheism but one God, 619b

Monster Such a m. as the devil, 19b

Monsters m. and resurrection, 619b

Montes Bernardus valles, m. Benedictus amabat, 615b

Month Better one m.'s cheer, than churl's whole life, 497b

Monument at his heels a stone, 242b; m. of ancient wisdom, 23b; m. of vanish'd minds, 107a; pile became A m. to keep the name, 685a

Monuments admonish us to think of those taken away, 151b; All buildings are but m. of death, 249b

Moods foolish, think that m. are our character, 620a

Moon as sun is differentiated from m., 178a; As the full m. shining there, 853b; gentle m. grows kindly bright, 312b; Like the sweet m. at night, 41a; made of a green cheese, 620a; m. to lead And all stars to follow, 239a; Sun, moon, and stars, 20b; The m. beneath thy feet, 632b; The m. was a ghostly galleon, 620b

Moonbeams Like the breaking of m., 8b

Moonèd She, about whose m. brows, 97a

Moonlight Like m. o'er a troubled sea, 620a; m. on an April night, 55b

Moor like a hound upon the m., 48a

Moral difference in m. insight between past and present, 621b; first principle of m. life, 621a; happiness of man and sanity, depend on m. condition, 622b; human race bound together by ties, m. and juridical, 530b; integrity of m. code, 434b, 620b; m. sense of Scripture, 61a; old religionists tortured men for m. truth, 885a; state chiefly prospers through m. rule, 845b; techniques and m. idealism, 37a, 186b; there really are problems in m. conduct, 622a; violation of moral laws, punished by God, 12a

Moralists M. are unhappy people, 620b

Moralities thousand new m., 277b

Morality agree On what is pure m., 621a; as if to know much, necessary step for right m., 513b; Catholicism has no special m. of its own, 622a; Church holds it better for sun and moon to drop, 621a; confusion of art and morality, 9b; defined with reference to our last end, 817b; ethics and knowledge, 306b; first element in religion, 118b; God alone source of m., 12a; His can't be wrong whose life is in right, 275a; History, not written in interests of m., 434b; Modern m., accepting standards of one's own age, 621b; natural knowledge of God and m., 330b; right living, 306b; rough border-law of heaven, 620b; subdue to right living through laws, 404a; very soul of good citizenship, 185b

Morally no deliberate act is m. neutral, 817b

Morals works dealing with m. must have *imprimatur,* 152a; cor-

rupted by reading immoral books, 151b; doctrine regarding faith or m., 706b; Manners before m.!, 573a; triumph of mind over m., 572a

Morbidity M. and Christian cheerfulness, 160a

More better to want less than receive m., 361a; The m. the merrier, 497a

More, St. Thomas, 140b

Mores O tempora! O m.!, 700b

Moria M. pur quando vuol, 250a

Moritur Ecclesia non moritur, 138a; *Rex numquam m.,* 508b

Morn Awake, the m. will never rise, 777b; For she like m. is fair, 623a; Hail, Thou ever-blessed m.!, 169a; heavenly airs of m., 192a; m. had spread her crimson rays, 283b

Morning Forsaking now her dark and dreadful past, 623a; I like the joyous m. air, 454b; In life's happy m., 250a; Like the dawning of m., 8b; m. is a friend to the muses, 623a; Star of the m., 84b, 91b

Morrow Till the eternal m. dawn, 303b

Mors Indignatio principis m. est, 248a

Mort Le roi est m., 509a

Mortal And all we long for m.?, 623b; immortal from the m., 466b; It is generall To be mortall, 623b; What are all the petty interests of this m. life, 840a

Mortalia Non eripit m., 489a

Mortality absorbed in immortality, 85a; Death engulfs m., 251b; Didst our m. assume, 167a, 466b; loud boasts of poor m., 249a

Mortals Distracted m.! of what paltry worth, 14a

Mortification annihilated in ourselves, to live wholly to God!, 624a; better to die with Lord, than live without Him, 625a; cutting our branches, 37a; Never practise m., without counsel, 625a; penance and maceration, not for everyone, 668b; perfection, not in macerating body, 623b

Mortify better to m. the body through the spirit, 625a; Labor serves to m. flesh, 516a

Mortuus Ante obitum m., 247b

Mos M. regit legem, 237a

Moses, 223b; didst appear unto M. in burning bush, 8a; instructed concerning worship, 68a; *M. entered into darkness,* 393a

Moss The rolling stone never gathereth m., 847b

Most Who m., hath never all, 497b

Most High King of kings, and Lord Most High, 21b; Wisdom, proceeding from mouth of M., 8a

Mote Ye can see m. in another man's eye, 228a

Motes As thick as m. in the sunbeam, 854b

Mother Church, true m. of Christians, 126a, 130a; Exalt, O m. Church, today, 584b; Father in care, m. in tender heart!, 491b; give, and give again, 624b; glorious fecundity of our m., Church, 639a; I hear my m. Church proclaim, 368b, 441b; man's first mother, 39b; Mary is new m. of living, 93a, 102a; Mary, our m. by divine appointment, 91b; M. Church begets children, 130a; m. is a font and spring of life, 624b; m. of all Christ's members, 91b; M. of mercy, 95b; M. of tears!, 475b; m. of unity among many,

130b; Mournful and mighty m.!, 475b; My m., drunk or sober, 15b; no greater refutation of communism than m., 200a; No m. more indulgent but the true, 625a; O God, Who has commanded us to honor father and m., 654a; O M. Mary, flower of woman kind, 83a; of life the mother dies, 40a; Roman church, m. and mistress of all, 52a; What is a m.? Who shall answer this?, 624b; What tigress does not purr over her young, 625a; who has not Church for m., 129b, 429a; You cannot visit child, without visiting m., 169b Mother of God above law, by privilege, 81b, 88b; assumed body and soul into glory, 41b; BVM, Mother and Virgin, 81a, 82b, 98b, 591b, 593a; bore incarnate Son, 39a; Christes Mother dear, 96a; common-treasure of whole world, 81a; could not be held by death, 39a; dignity of virginity began with M., 79a; fitting M. should possess what belongs to Son, 39b; Hail! full of grace, 24b; Hail! Virgin Mother of God, 82a, 89a; holy M., ever-Virgin Mary, 588b; honor shown to her, 39b, 82a; hope and protection, 98a; I have unashamed trust in thee, 87a; If anyone does not confess BVM M., 80a, 81a; immaculate M., 80a, 460a; intercession of glorious M., 25a, 88b, 593b; Lady, M. and ever virgin, 81b, 82b, 83a; Mary fitting to be M., 80b; More honored than the cherubim, 593a; most pure M., 90a; Mother and Maiden, 83a, 91a, 639b; M. benign of our redeeming Lord, 82b; Mother Maiden and her Child, 114a; Mother most loving and merciful, 88a, 100a; mother of all Christ's members, 80b, 91b; Mother of almighty God!, 83b; Mother of Christ, of grace divine, 83b; Mother of clemency and love, 95b; Mother of grace!, 793a; Mother of Jesus!, 36b; *mother of Jesus was there*, 131a; mother of life, mother of salvation, 39a, 90b; M. of mine, 41a; Mother of my God, 95a; Mother of our King, 40b, 83b, 88b; Mother of Sun which knows no setting, 89a; Mother of the Blessed One, 84a; Mother of the Lord, 632b; Mother of the word, 89b; M., we hail thy heart, 88a; mystery of thy childbirth, 299a; name embraces whole mystery, 82a; no one has access, as His Mother, 97a; O glorious child-bearer, 462b; pray to your Son and my God, 82b; preserve thy servants from dangers, 100b; sinless M., 593a; special glory in heaven, 86a; thou didst retain thy virginity, 39a; through prayers of Mother, 196a, 490a; through thee, access to thy Son, 90b; touched by no impurity, 80a; truly M., not merely in name, 25a, 81b, 89a, 593a; turtle-dove!, 94a; we boast in thee as mediatrix, 90a; we honor her because Mother of Christ, 84a; we magnify thee, 81b, 231b; Whom world unable to contain, enclosed in thy womb, 632b; with virtues crowned, 83b
Motherhood Feast of M. of BVM, 83b, 88b
Mothering world-mothering air, 12b
Mothers above all m. shone the Mother, 84a; All m. worship little

feet, 84a; All women become like their m., 624b; fathers and m. of families, 518a; Fond m. give over your weeping, 242b
Motion All matter depends on m., 599b; angel is in perpetual m., 19a; Our nature lies in m., 624b
Motions One Who disposeth and ordereth m., 373a
Motive Infer the m. from the deed, 625a
Mould It was made of earth's m., 41a; Man, of softer m. is made, 12b; mortal m. in darkness wrapp'd, 250b
Moulds apostolic churches, m. and sources of faith, 874a
Mountain craggy ridge and m. bare, 415a; marry the m., 575a; On mountain's golden height, 8b; O tender m.-tops and delicate, 828a
Mountaineering school of stern discipline, 625a
Mountains painting m. in a mist, 42b; ramparts of Godhead's dwelling, 13b; reveal two truths, 625a
Mourn All you that weep, all you that m., 769b; O come and m. with me awhile, 658a; Sit by my catafalque to dole, 251b
Mourner Each sorrowful m. be silent!, 242b
Mourners All m. of world weep Irish, 475b; Weep not, ye m., for the dead, 242b
Mournful autumn's m. air, 48a
Mourning house of m. teaches charity and wisdom, 625a; Jesus weeps in ruins of my spring, 109a
Mouse Let cat wink, let m. run, 113b; wily m. can build his dwelling-house, 625b
Mouth from m. of Most High, 8a; God never sendeth m., 347b; m. that waters, 287a; *Our m. is open to you*, 770b; That shall not stop my m., 625b
Mouths blast of men's m., 924b
Moved everything m., is m. by another, 375a
Movement Nature, principle of m. inherent in bodies, 633a; Religion, always at root of every world m., 758a; time, proper measure of m., 306a
Movements Living m. do not come of committees, 457a
Mover first m. is the Deity, 375a
Moves Whatever m. is moved by another, 624b
Moveth glory of Him Who m. all, 377b
Much enough and too m., 298a
Mull let us m. over words of gospel, 82a
Multiply *Increase and m.*, 336a, 579b; We m. whenever we are mown down, 103b, 583a
Multitude to provide itself with king, belongs to m., 774a; welfare of m. formed into society is, 404b
Mum I will say nought but m., 813b
Mummers Grave m.!, 6a
Mundi Sic transit gloria m.!, 710a
Mundus M. mihi crucifixus est, 234b
Murder deliberately destroying foetus, murder, 1b; He that killeth man when he is drunk, 625b; husband may not m. adulterous wife, 7b; M. will out, 625b; once for all forbidden, 1b
Murmurs He that m., not good Christian, 201a
Muse Made prostitute and profligate, 688a; No m. proof against

golden shower, 688b; To m. upon the past, 69b
Muses fired with muses' madness, 6a; morning is a friend to the m., 623a
Mushrooms Gave also lowly m. leave to grow, 413b
Music abstract and personal, 33a; All curious m. but our passing bell, 249b; comforts the mind, 626a; He makes sweet m., 687b; inspiration and savor of Gregorian form, 627a; liturgical laws regarding sacred m., 627b; Make m. of the angelus!, 169a; most nigh to tears, 627a; m. of the *spears*, 626b; m.'s not immortal, 627b; m. of gospel leads us home, 62b; 'noise' poured forth in God's 'honor', 34b; There's no m. to a knell, 58b; What passion cannot m. quell?, 626a
Musician organ, where God kept stops, 627b
Mutability life's m. tends towards death, 247a; m. of mutable things, 627b; world marked with imprint of m., 380b
Mutable all m. things receive form, 393b; Things m. are wholly created, 375a
Mutantur Tempora m. et homines deteriorantur, 153a
Mute M. and magnificent, without a tear, 416a
Myrrh M. a future tomb foreshows, 298b
Myself let me know m., let me know Thee, 393b
Mysteries communion of holy m., 195b; dispensation of Christ's m., 546b; divine m. expressed in Bible, 63a; I will not reveal Thy m. to enemies, 595a; let divine m. be celebrated with joy, 441b; measured by proud according to own capacity, 628a; meditating on m., in most holy rosary, 782a; m. of Christians, older than those of Jews, 785b; m. of faith cannot all be understood by reason, 332b; m. of life, not solved by agnosticism, 12a; nature's covered m., 32a; sacred m. of Thy Body and Blood, 75a, 849b; Thy heavenly and immortal m., 595a, 595b; unchangeable m. of heavenly Truth, 211b; world is full of m., 233b
Mysterious abiding yet m., 386b; I adore Thee, because Thou art so m., 381b; If we submit everything to reason, religion will have nothing m., 756a
Mystery A secret and a m., 814a; difference between m., and explanation, 759a; Great this m., great dignity of priests, 597b; life loses its meaning, when loses m., 628b; m., doctrine unilluminated, 628a; m. of Church, 125a, 797a; m. of faith, 592a; m. of incarnation, 82a, 167a; m. of this water and wine, 590a; ordain this m. in might of Holy Spirit, 586b; The rose is a m., 41a; veil spread between this world and next, 62b
Mystic For m., important that theology should flourish, 629a; in m. contemplation leave behind senses, 211b; Make me sharer in thy m. supper, 595a; m. condition, not common condition, 628b; m. robes of chosen Aaron, 68a; thinks spiritual very close, 839b; topmost height of m. lore, 211b
Mystical m. experience, 690b; m. interpretation of Scripture, 61a; One of greatest paradoxes of m.

life, 629a; Poetic experience, distinct from m., 690a
Mystically We who m. represent the cherubim, 589b
Mysticism false m., 629b; keeps men sane, 628b; not ordinary religious experience, 628b; works dealing with m. must have *imprimatur,* 152a
Mystics have a clearer sight of ordinary mysteries, 628b; never pretend to receive new revelations, 628b
Myth Christ, not a m., 165a; work of imagination and work of art, 629b

N

Nail Dead as a door n., 248a
Nailed wicked people n. Lord of glory to Cross, 399b
Nails n. are the commandments of justice, 229b; Pierce My flesh with the n. of fear, 229b; She will not part with paring of her n., 847a
Naked N. of friends, 1a; They have left Thee n., Lord, 104a; to clothe the n., 155a; We are born into world n., 48a
Name all invoke the n. of Christ, 630a; all things created for sake of His n., 70b; anxiety for show of a great n., 629a; Blessed who cometh in n. of Lord, 81a; Confess Thy holy n., 205a; devoted to Thy n. in good works, 261b; Excessive fear of losing a good n., 766b; For very love Thy sacred n., 489a, 520a; Hatred of Christian n., 163a; *His n. shall be called mighty God,* 78b; I see A Heart, a Face, and a N., 790a; *I will call upon the n. of the Lord,* 595a; implant in our hearts the love of Thy n., 848a; In Christ's n. let us begin, 56a; In Jesus' sacred n., 602b; In the n. of the Father, Son, Holy Ghost, 587a; let not name of BVM depart from lips, 87b; May His holy n. be to them medicine for health, 812b; *my n. spreads terror among the nations,* 307a; n. to live and die for, 908a; n. of Christ, on lips of all, 629b; no other n. under heaven whereby I can be saved, 491b; understand true meaning of Thy n., 630a; We give Thee thanks for Thy holy n., 194a; which is above all names, 442b; world, filled with n. of Christ, 72b
Name of Mary, Feast of Holy, 99a
Names applied to God metaphorically, 386b; Fair king of n., 630b
Nap Let noontide sleep be brief, 631a
Napoleon, 456b, 631a
Nard Break the box and shed the n., 286b
Narrow too n. to see Church against background of cosmos, 217a
Narrow-minded Every man dangerous, who only cares for one thing, 631a; say that anybody is n., 631a
Narrowmindedness n. and broadmindedness, 109a
Nascuntur Fiunt, non n. Christiani!, 163a
Nation Church must speak to each age and n., 270b; essence of a n., relations of citizens ordered by laws, 529a; Every living n. has idea given by Providence, 631b; independent sovereign n., 838a;

know nothing of n., unless we know its history, 435a; multitude of men joined together in society, 631b; One saint will often save a n., 452b; The N. is a community, not a society, 631b
National right to one's own culture and n. character, 531a
Nationalism superficial minds lapse into heresy of speaking of national God, 747a
Nationality Brothers we are, whatever our n., 143a; has nothing in world to do with race, 632a; in its weakness, stronger than ethnology in its strength, 632a; Light of lights, cannot be quenched under bushel of n., 469b; ties formed by faith, stronger than flesh and blood, 143a
Nations all n. have the Church, 121a; And willing n. knew their lawful lord, 550a; expectation of all n., 8b; families of n., rent asunder by the wound of sin, 489b; form together community, 475a; God rules over men and n., 15a; *I have established thee above n.,* 701a; Rome conquered n., 632a
Nativity of Our Lord on the n., depends beginning and completion of all religion, 166b
Nativity of BVM birth free from guilt, 8a, 96b; Thy birth, message of joy to the whole world, 632b
Natural n. tendency of man to dwell in society, 38b; nothing can be added to n. rights, 15a; subtle man, easier to understand than n. man, 850a; supremacy of conscience, essence of n. religion, 118a; That n. to each thing, which is caused by Him, 632b; The n. always is from error free, 551b; things n., above things supernatural, 183a
Naturaliter testimonium animae n. Christianae!, 834b
Naturally *all things act as they are n. fit,* 561b
Nature All n. is but art unknown to thee, 153a; All n. is good, 633a; n. before grace, 289b; cannot hold Thee, 197b; conformity with n., formula of discipline, 673a; difference that gives form to anything, 633a; distinction between art and n., 33b; faith presupposes reason, as grace presupposes n., 376a; Fallen n. needs grace, 412a; female name we give to providence, 634a; Grace does not scrap n., but improves it, 412b, 863a; invariable uniformity in laws of n., 803a; its well-ordered motions, 373a; Let us imitate n., 633a; man master's his n. by reason, 37a; N. and grace come from same divine Author, 761a; N. is not inanimate, 633b; N. is the art of God eternal, 633a; n.'s covered mysteries, 32a; n.'s God, 255a; often deceived, grace has trust in God, 412b, 754a; reveals its Author, 372a; sin diminishes n., 412b; varies and imitates, art imitates and varies, 634a; We must not measure n. by ourselves, 633b; where less n., there more grace, 412b; wounds of n., 412b
Nature, Human knit together by common ties, 13a; positive instincts of h., 16b
Natus Et nobis Puer n. est, 168b
Naught N. shelters thee, who wilt not shelter Me, 385b
Navigators not chosen for highest birth, 65b

Nay My sacred N., 753a; we could have but a n., 264b
Nazareth At one small house of N., 658b; O house of N. the blest, 437b
Nearer nearer to Church, farther from God, 138a, 755b
Neat Be n., 634a
Nebuchadnezzar, King, 202b
Necessitas Legem non habet n., 634b
Necessity God, not bound by n. in creation, 225a, 392a; has no law, 319b; make a virtue of n., 634b; What n. proffers, n. cheapens, 634b
Neck In that house, as soon break n. as fast, 847b; my n. is very short, 634b
Necklace A duchess may ruin a duke for a diamond n., 908a
Necktie essential thing for a n. is style, 278a
Necks bent their unbending n., 100b
Need he is in n., who is without humility, 450b; I n. Thee, precious Jesus, 789b; Just because we n. Thee so, 492a
Needful Things three are n., 905b
Neediness abundance not God to me, n., 3b
Needle dance on the point of a n., 19b; To look for a n. in a meadow, 634b
Negation ethical system on basis of n., 160a; withering work of agnosticism, 12a
Negotiation He was so stately in n., 110b
Neighbor as I love myself, I love My n. for Thy sake, 564a; change n. with himself, 635a; Everyone must be loved equally, 154b; Help thy kin, there beginneth charity, 156a; He who loves his n., 560a; keeping charity towards God and n., 214a; let each be subject to n., 641b; Love of n., included in love of God, 561a; seldom we weigh n. in same balance with ourselves, 341a; Show mercy to thy n., 603b; that her n. may have life of grace, 265a; *Thou shalt love thy n. as thyself,* 671b; To love our n. in charity, 565b; We can never love n. too much, 565b
Neighborly They're n. in Ireland, 635a
Neighbors active life toils in helping n., 5a; Christians love their n., 162b; Franks for friends, not for n., 352b
Neighing importunate pawing and n., 447a
Nemo N. potest ad impossibilia obligari, 465a
Nero, 678b
Nerves Silence, best treatment for overstrained n., 635a
Nesciendo scitur melius n., 393b
Nescit Amor ordinem n., 550
Nest should bird defileth own n., 65a; I'll build n. for Thee, 564a; Of thine He made His special n.!, 84a
Nestling N. me everywhere, 12b
Nestorius, Patriarch of Constantinople, 81a, 708a
Net All is fish that cometh to n., 345a; sew up every hole in a n., 859b; *The net is broken and we are delivered,* 24a; When charity pulls up on shore or eternity the n., 155b
Netting sending Holy Ghost, n. the whole world, 670b
Neutral no deliberate act is morally n., 817b
Neutrality pray for opposite parties, 635a

Never Better late than n., 522a

New Be not first by whom n. are tried, 210b; *master of house bringeth forth n. things and old,* 613a; May the Lord put on thee the n. man, 189b; never n., never old, 386b; some n. way of life, 26a; transforming us into n. man, 131b

Newfangel Flesh is so n., 346a

Newman, Cardinal Ah, sweetest soul of all!, 635b; belief in God, and greatness of Mary, 101a, 101b; canonized at death by voice of English people, 635b; conversion, event of more than ordinary significance, 635a; Second Spring Sermon, 142a; man of rare gifts and acquirements, 635a; readiness to follow divine call, 767b

News entertain others, as if you came from other world, 636a

Newspaper much too full of things suitable to paper, 496b; Notoriety, n. fame, 638a

Newspapers Church has right to censor, 151b

Nicaea, Council of, 226b, 694b, 699b

Nice As n. as a nun's hen, 636a

Nietzsche, F. W., 473a

Nigh Draw n., take Body of the Lord, 195b; God, more n. to us than many things He made, 379b; N. and sly Wins against Fair and Square, 922a

Night Behold, Bridegroom cometh in middle of the n., 896a; Behold, the n. of sorrow gone, 286b; Brief on a flying n., 59a; But here the very noon of n., 606a; cheerless n. comes stealing on, 312b; dim shadows of the n. are waning, 522b; God hath created n., 258b; If I this n. before God's throne should stand, 492a; In a dark n. With anxious love inflamed, 214b; Joy rul'd the day, and love the n., 497b; O, guiding n., 214b; pilgrims of n., 20a; queen of n. lays her changing globe, 40b; solitude of n., favorable time for prayer, 895b; The dark n. cometh at last, 240b; The dusky veil of n. hath laid, 599a; The n. is dark, and I am far from home, 636b; The sacerdotal n., 240a; The star-usurping battlements of n., 636b; To take the veil of n., 312b

Nightingale the n. sings round it all day long, 636b

Nights I fled Him, down the n. and down the days, 385a; On the gloom of cloudy n., 8b

Nihil N. *innovetur nisi quod traditum est,* 874a

Nihilists have nothing to revolt about, 636b; Socialists, Communists, N., uproot foundations of society, 828b

Nika En tout n., 229a

Nilotic Heaving its slow length from N. slime, 229a

Nimrod Proud N. first the bloody chase began, 454b

Noah, 223b

Nobility True n. means to be a servant of Christ, 636b

Nobis Et n. Puer nauts est, 168b

Noble desire for fame tempts even n. minds, 335a

Nocturnal n. prayers, 266a

Noise Too much n. deafens us, 873a

Nomen Christianus mihi n. est, Catholicus cognomen, 163a; *Odii erga n. Christianorum,* 163a

Nomine In n. Patris, et Filii, et Spiritus Sancti, 587a

Non-being Evil, that which tends to n., 313b

Non-Catholics books of n. treating of religion, prohibited, 151b; conversion of n., 220b; difficulty of addressing n., 27a; know bark of Scripture, never pith, 63a; laws are meant to prevent you from being bad, 174a; little use in arguing against objections, 27a; may validly baptize, 50b; whose faith imperfect, 27b

Non-denominationalism fashionable, to stand outside creeds and churches, 637a

None at ninth hour, let prayer be protracted, 637b; in that hour, Christ pierced in His side, 637a

Nonsense to be hang'd for n., is the devil, 637b

Nook sitting apart in n., with little book, 106b

Noon But here the very n. of night, 606a

Norm 'h.', all such as deviate from n. of Catholic religion, 431a

Normal question, whether better to be n. or abnormal, 637b

Normality wholesome n., highest art of living, 637b

Nose If the n. of Cleopatra had been a little shorter, 637b; Many a man's tongue broke his n., 872b; moment one sits down to think, all n., 867a

Noses Hold their n. to grindstone, 637b

Nothing begins, and n. ends, 651b; Blessed be he who expects n., 638a; But n. comes from n., 600a; God fashioned all things out of n., 223b, 407b, 652b; I come from n., 464a; matter has itself been made from n., 224a; Something is better than n., 831a; we know n. until we know n., 453a; You cannot agree about n., 312a

Nothingness He rescued thee from n., 366b; man's n., insufficiency, 107b

Notions Our n., never commensurate with things themselves, 514b

Notoriety newspaper fame, 638a

Nought lay down, n. take up, 362b; Lingered labors come to n., 255a

Nourish He laid down life to n. us, 73a

Novel good n. is never a book of philosophy, 638a; study of human nature, 638a

Novelist A good n. always has a philosophy, 638a

Novelists N. are generally great liars, 638b; They find life crude and leave it raw, 638b

Novelty far from clergy be love of n.!, 190a; Let no Christian, whether philosopher or theologian embrace n., 682a; one thing public dislikes, n., 638b

Novice young probationer, And candidate of heav'n, 638b

Novices n. in the exercise of virtues, 638b

Novit Recte n. vivere, 717a

Novitiate Marriage, profession made before n., 578a

Now N., Lord, or never, 77a

Numbers Let me chant in sacred n., 489a

Nun flower of the Church, 639a; How happy is the blameless vestal's lot, 641a; kingdom of this earth I have valued as worthless, 640b; Quiet form of silent n., 641a; Received the sacred veil, 640b; She is a virgin who is married to God, 639b; There was also a nonne, a prioresse, 640b; virgin is a gift of God, oblation of parents, 639b

Nuns because of Whom you have willed to have no husbands, 640a; consecration of n., 639a; Hold fast what you have begun to be, 639a; illustrious portion of Christ's flock, 639a; religious women with solemn vows, 761a; vow of their continence, 646a; Wherever they go, let there not be less than three, 640a; women vowed to God, 87a

Nuptial n. blessing continues to grace holy matrimony, 640a; n. commerce holy, just, 66a; n. union of Christ and Church, 112a

Nurse And always keep a-hold of n., 641b; n. of infant loves, 491b

Nurseries n. of heaven, 305a

Nurture In form of Bread and Wine our n., 77a

Nut Lost with apple, won with n., 29b

Nuts 'twas n. to the father of lies, 536a, 641b

Nutshell n. truths for breakfast table, 496b

O

Oar Have an o. in every man's barge, 601a

Oars Our voices keep tune and our o. keep time, 783b

Oath I absolve all Christians from bond of o., 175b; o. may be made only in truth, 641a; pope may release subjects from o. of fealty, 701a

Oaths abolishing of o., more useful than fasting, 641a

Obedience civil allegiance of no man is unlimited, 181b; converts and virtue of o., 221a; devil does not fear austerity, but holy o., 643a; Educate youth to o. and respect, 47a; essence of all religion, authority and o., 117b; even to unworthy authorities, 46b; first degree of humility, o., 642a; in o. and abnegation, I desire Society be conspicuous, 479b; inspiration of God, 642b; no o., if power not from God, 45b; o. of Roman soldiers, 641b; o. to conscience, 643a; o. to ecclesiastical superior, 643a; O. to will of God, meritorious, 643b; prayer, without perseverance and o., 673a; right to o. from God, 46b; simple, if man recognizes God, 45b, 47a; test of sanctity, obedience to authority, 436b

Obedient Be o. to bishop, 67a, 68a; Blessed are the o., 643a; Christ for our sake became o. unto death, 442b; For who is so o. as a wife?, 455a; justice requires, subordinates should be o. to superiors, 642b

Obey general agreement of societies, to o. kings, 642a; Learn, O dust, to o., 451b; No one obliged to o. precept, unless informed, 525b; o. consistently, 643a; we must not o., if against God's will, 46b; we were born to o., not to command, 221a

Obeyed I have been honor'd and o., 449b; Let superior be o. like mother, 642a; source from which schisms have arisen, God's priest not o., 799b

Obitum Ante o. mortuus, 247b

Objections little use in arguing against o., 27a

Oblation Himself the offerer and o., 308a, 485a; Receive, O holy

Trinity, this o., 590b; sacred o. of saving Victim, 244b; Which o., do Thou bless, approve, ratify, 592a

Obligari Nemo potest ad impossibilia o., 464a

Obligations demanding rights, discharging o., 777a

Obliged No one o. to do the impossible, 465a

Oblivion And universal darkness buries all, 153b; Into the dear o. of lost things, 259a; So all his endings to o. tend, 869b; with potions of o. kill Remorse of lost love, 427b

Obscene Books which treat of o. subjects, prohibited, 151b; Do not use o. language, 643b

Obscurity He lives well that has lain well hidden, 26a; no author should be blamed for o., 643b

Obstinacy no o. like religious o., 644a

Obstinate God hateth proud and o. mind, 190a; Never be o., 644a

Obtain what they rightly ask for, 910a

Occasions immediate o. of sin, 27a, 216b

Occurs It is always the unreadable that o., 496b

Ocean Forth, to the laws of o., 105a; gales and storms of this life's o., 99a; o.'s wave-beat shore, 20a; Shoreless O.! who shall sound Thee?, 378a; Stanching, quenching o. of a motionable mind, 374a

Oceans Floods and o., clap your hands, 36a

O'Connell, Daniel, 644a

Oddness Contrast and o. come from God's purpose, 216a

Odds fight against powerful o., 646a

Odes bring Thee o. many as the sea, 489b

Odii O. erga nomen Christianorum, 163a

Odor an o. of sweetness, 249b, 590a; world, filled with o. of Christ, 72b

Odyssey O. great, because life a journey, 63b

Oecumenical council not o., not summoned by Roman pontiff, 708b; false o. concept of Church, 137b

Offence love the offender, detest the o., 644a; She hugg'd offender, forgave o., 349a

Offend care not to o., 216b; How can I praise, and not o., 22b; those set over us, 45b; whole world against us, than to o. Jesus, 488b

Offended Because I have o. Thee, 216b; God, Who art o. by sin, 668a; This hath not o. the king, 509a

Offender love the o., detest the offence, 644a; She hugg'd the o., forgave offence, 349a

Offenders number of o. hides the sin, 341b

Offer everything to Father everlasting, 644b; in union with Him let them o. up themselves, 586b; Whatever thou doest, o. it us to God, 644a

Offered Christ was o. once, 309a, 309b

Offerer both O. and Offering, 308a, 485b

Offertory at Mass, 589b

Office heresy, o. sanctifies holder, 714a; The best men for the o., 692a; To put a Catholic into o., merely because Catholic, 692a

Offices diversity of states and o. in

Church, 433b; sacred o., conferred by laying on of hands of bishop, 728b

Officials unjust treatment at the hands of o., 509a

Offspring Church rendered fruitful with o., 51b; new o. of Thy family, 441b; prevention of conception of o., 66a

Oil And so much midnight o. destroyed, 276a; anointing with holy o. at baptism, 49b; o. of gladness, 51a; takes more o. than vinegar to make good salad, 364b; The atoning o. is spread, 321b; Vials of mercy, sacring o., 321b

Ointment bishop, sanctified with heavenly o., 68b; forth her precious o. pours, 584b

Old earth is younger than I am o., 11a; fond o. man, often full of words, 11b; never new, never o., 386b; Nor yet last to lay o. aside, 210b, 337a; o. may be outrun, not outreasoned, 11b; reverence the o., love the young, 930a; too o. to study now, 62a

Older o. than dawn and sunset are, 11a

Old-fashioned settled long, ye are out of date, 26b

Olive-branch You discharge o. as if from catapult, 217a

Olives, Mount of, 36a

Olympus Ruler of O., 395a

Omnia Instaurare o. in Christo, 492b

Omnibus quod ubique, quod semper, quod ab o., 144b

Omnipotence His o. can swathe itself in infirmity, 388b

Omnipotens Benedicat vos. o. Deus, 595b

Omnipotent God called o., because He can do all things possible, 388b; Nothing happens, unless O. wills it to happen, 391b; one o. God, 226a

Omnipresence God is always with us, 380a; God is everywhere by presence of His Divinity, 379b; God is everywhere, 427b

Omnis O. definitio periculosa est, 254b

One at one, without amends, 22b; Deity, o. and not many, 391a; Father almighty, with Son and Holy Ghost, o. God, 591a; From many to make o., 889a; God is not, if He is not o., 391a; O. alone Who cannot change, 13a; O. Lord, one faith, one baptism, 134b; O. only is holy, o. only is Lord, 594a; that they may be o., as we are o., 662a

One-eyed o., king in country of blind, 103a

Oneself To discover God is to discover o., 377b

Only-begotten through Thine o. Jesus Christ, 50a

Ontological o. argument for God's existence, 375b; psychic itself belongs to domain of o., 739b

Onward O.! o.! 'neath curse and blow, 233b

Open Oh! o. Thou mine ears, 396b

Openest Who openest, and no man shutteth, 8a

Open-mindedness An open mind is often a vacant mind, 608b; object of opening the mind, 644b

Openness do in the presence of all, 4b

Opere ex o. operato, 787b

Opiate religion as 'o. of the people,' 42b, 199b

Opinion Force rules the world, not

o., 348b; holding something to be provisionally true, 644b; maintain too obstinately our own o., 739a; no one is martyr for an o., 327b; 'Tis education forms the common mind, 289a

Opinions intellectual man, full of 'views,' 645a; private o. of saints, 874b; Stiff in o., always in the wrong, 893a; To stifle the o. of citizens, 645a

Opportunist man who will never believe in anything, 645a

Opportunity He who will not when he may, may not when he will, 645b; When the iron is hot, strike, 645b; When the sun shineth make hay, 645b

Opposition from all quarters, 646a; makes a hero great, 646a

Oppress God presses us, but does not o. our liberty, 357b

Optimism all is for the best, 646a; convinced o., only reasonable philosophy, 646b

Optimo Deo o. maximo, 397a

Opus O. Dei, 266a

Oracle o. of revealed doctrine, 23b

Oramus O. te, Domine, per merita sanctorum, 588a

Orange-tree If I were yonder o., 646b

Ora O. et labora, 718a

Orare Laborare est o., 515b; O. idem est ac dicere, 717b

Orate O. fratres, 590b

Orator least pardonable fault in o., to fail in style, 849a

Orators Not o. so much with flowing words, 687b; The world runs after pulpit o., 721b

Orbi Urbi et o., 710a

Orbis Omnium urbis et o. ecclesiarum mater et caput, 171a; Quid habet o. Christianus, 44b; Securus judicat o. terrarum, 23a, 924b; Urbs caput o., 139b

Orbis Terrarum, 186a

Orchard Buried in the o., 110a; Good is an o., 647a

Ordain duty of bishop to o., 69a

Ordained Let bishop be o. by two or three bishops, 647b; priest and deacon, o. by one bishop, 647b; slaves may not be ordained without consent, 188b; when presbyter o., bishop shall lay hand upon head, 726a

Ordaining bishops have power of confirming and o., 648b

Ordains God o. bishops, 67b

Order after the o. of Melchizedek, 307a; all things have o. among themselves, 350a; arrangement of components equal and unequal, 665a; best religious o., 616b; Christian o., purpose is peace, 666b; difference between secular and eccles. o., 433b; episcopal o. essential to Church, 69b; God always preserves beauty of o., 4a; In religious o., solemn vows are taken, 762b; No part of nature acts against universal o., 633a; o., beauty of world, proclaim made by God, 372b; O. is heaven's first law, 647a; o. of those seven, whom apostles chose, 241b; o. produces agreement, 54b; o. requires, subordinates should be obedient to superiors, 642b; peace of all things, tranquillity of o., 665a; Union in distinction makes o., 54b

Orders different religious o. and congregations, 762b; final end proposed to religious o., nothing else but God, 762b; God, Dispenser of o., 241b; God established o., 68b; power of bishop and priest not same, 69a

Orders, Holy besides priesthood, there are other orders, 648a; By H. priests are made, 788a; by sacred ordination, Holy Ghost is given, 648a; character imprinted by ordination, 648a; consent or vocation of people, 648b; divine ministry, 849b; Anglican orders invalid, 23b, 648b; exercised by married man, 151a; generation of h., 730b; in New Testament, visible and external priesthood, 648a; major orders and celibacy, 151a; orders distinguishes clergy from laity, 648b; ordinary minister, consecrated bishop, 648b; presbyter blesses, bishop ordains, 647a; requirements for licit ordination, 649a; sent by ecclesiastical and canonical power, 648b; those barred from h., 649a; truly sacrament instituted by Christ, 648a

Ordinary bishops inherit o. power of apostles, 69b; conclusion that o. view is right one, 218a

Ordination bishop must be assisted by two other bishops, 648b; by sacred o., Holy Ghost is given, 189a, 648a; character imprinted by o., 648a; condescension of divine grace creates bishop, 647b; constitutes clergy in degrees of order, 434a; imposition of hands and illumination of soul, 105b; ordinary minister, consecrated bishop, 648b; o., and power to consecrate Eucharist, 647b; presbyter blesses, bishop ordains, 647a; requirements for licit o., 649a; sacred offices, conferred by laying on of hands of bishop, 728b; truly sacrament instituted by Christ, 648a

Ordinations proper celebration of o., 647a

Ordinem Amor o. nescit, 550b

Oregon School Case, 291a

Organ great national o., 23b; He was an o., where God kept the stops, 627b; Let the deep o. swell the lay, 149b; Seated one day at the o., 626b

Organism Church is a living o., 548a; feeds and digests like an o., 272b

Organization honor of bishop and order of Church, 433a; o. of Church and its success, 136b

Organizing to be powerful you must have genius for o., 784b

Orient From out its o. tabernacle drawn, 78b; O O., Splendor of eternal Light, 8a

Oriental o. rites, separated from Catholic Church, 770b; unchanging law of o. cultures, 165b

Origen, 649b

Original The more mind we have, the more o. men do we discover, 607b

Originality wrapped in solitude of his own o., 631a

Originator He Who is O. of all things, 387a

Oris O. *ratio,* 717b

Orphan By Mary's death mankind an o. is, 40a

Orphans leave us not o., 36a

Orpheus love of beautiful, like voice of O., 55a

Orthodox confirm estate of o., 86b; must be o. upon most things, 649b; To be a Catholic at all, man must be o., 650a

Orthodoxy BVM, staff of o., 81a, 101b; champion Christ's quarrel, And o.'s right!, 649b; emperors and o. of belief, 174b; Holy Ghost bestows fulness of grace on those who believe rightly, 874a; spirit of O., not same thing as Russian spirit, 771a; standard of first four oecumenical councils, 272b; that which has been rightly decreed, 174a; thinking what is right concerning God, 134a; thrilling romance of o., 649b; to preserve rule of correct faith, 705a

Our O. *Father, Who art in heaven,* 593b

Ostentation discard all empty o., 714a

Others believe better things of o., 451a; peace, if we would not busy ourselves with sayings of o., 665b

Oven No man will another in the o. seek, 650b

Over-act hard for amateur not to o., 13b

Overeating Great suppers will the stomach's peace impair, 263b; Nothing so unfitting for Christian, 650b

Overfat swine o. is cause of his own bane, 338b

Overthrone Love lifting red hands to O., 13b

Own God will know His o.!, 235a; right to o. and unbelief, 887a; We are not our o., 225b

Ownership possession with justice, only through Church, 179a

Oxford given up to 'liberalism and progress', 536b; O.'s a place where wit can never sterve, 650b; poetry, in O. An art, in London a trade, 688a; There was an O. cleric, 549b

Oyster No more like, than apple to o., 544a

P

Pace Requiescant in p., 596a

Pacificism a positive faith, 651a

Pagan apostles tamed p. breast, 26b; for dead Pan he sighed, 164a; no p. has been able to be really human, 163b; not an atheist, 651a; p. heart, a Christian soul, 164a

Paganism strength of Christianity and p., 163b

Pagans hate one another, 163a; deliver p. from worship of idols, 887a

Pageant p. of the little great, 543a

Pain Beyond p., joy, and hope, 21b; comfort blooms on p., 305b; debasing God to earthly p., 25b; For we are born in other's p., 651b; From p. to p., from woe to woe, 846b; Hate, fear and grief, the family of p., 607b; in p. the sharper sighs, 651b; Into the wind shall lightly pass the p., 399a; man buyeth hell here with so much p., 425a; medicine of sin, 651b; O, p., love's mystery, 651b; practical solution of problem of p., 684b; soul recognizes there may be joy in p., 684b; suffer the violence of p. and death, 521b; Sweet is pleasure after p., 684a; To sigh, yet feel no p., 813b; thou art oppressed with p., 451b

Pains p. of hell, 245b, 246a

Paint You only p. to live, not live to p., 652a

Painters Poets, like p., thus unskill'd to trace, 685b

Painting abstract and personal, 33a: can do for the illiterate, 651b

Paintings Religious p., catechism of the ignorant, 652a

Palace Heirs of the p. glad, 305a; Now in his p. of the west, 241a

Palate hutch of tasty lust, 198a

Palfrey His p., brown as is a berry, 446b

Palm Bless these branches of p. or olive, 652a; p. of eternal life, 231a

Palmers And p. long to seek the stranger strands, 682b

Palms And p. before my feet, 38a

Palm Sunday Hebrew children bearing branches, 652b

Pan for dead P. he sighed, 164a

Panegyric mistake, in biography, 3b

Panem P. *coelestem accipiam,* 595a

Panoply your patience, a p., 401a

Panorama p. of history, 34b

Pantheism All are but parts of one stupendous whole, 652b; God, not same with world, 377a; If any one shall say substance of God and all things, one and same, 652b; on principle incurably, nonmoral, 653a; pure mysticism, p., 653a

Pantheist pagan always has sacraments, p. has none, 651a

Pantheistic p. sentiment, never a popular sentiment, 653a

Panther fairest creature of the spotted kind, 22b

Papa, 709a

Papacy action and theory, outcome of agelong growth, 703b; anchor of safety in fierce storms, 138b; as often as questions of faith are ventilated, 704b; center of hierarchy, 133b, 138b, 433b; crown of the Catholic system, 702b; custom has been for word to be sent to us, 697b; enemy of Holy See as enemy of true religion, 705b; exhibits law of continuous organic development, 702b; I announce to you a great joy, 709b; If Rome be against me, 710a; most exalted degree of dignity and amplitude of jurisdiction, 702a; not based upon synodal or other human constitutions, 702a; one God and Christ, one Church, and one chair founded upon Peter, 692b; organ, mouth, head of the Church, 702b; Peter's power lives and authority prevails in his See, 676b; pontifical authority to rule Church and all people, 700a; principate of priesthood, 175b; rejection of primacy has driven men on to slippery course, 696b; sacred bond of union, 138b; See of prince of apostles alone has grown strong, 662a; succession of chair of Peter, 117a; supreme pontificate and subordinate episcopate, 190a; The cause is finished, 709a; The first See is judged by no one, 709a; *thou art Peter, and upon this rock I will build my Church,* 693a; Thus passes the glory of the world!, 710a; We bear the burdens of all, 694a; Where Peter is, there is the Church, 709a

Papal papal dignity not derived from Caesar, 180a; To be more p. than the pope, 710b

Papalism new papal bull every morning with *Times,* 653a

Papist Catholic, but not p., 115a; devotion to BVM, badge and sign of p., 102a; only has his writ of ease, 644b

Papistry When p. first began, 115b

Pappy P. out of the cherry-bruises, 47b

Paraclete, Holy Heavenly King, P., 205b, 438b; on twelve bright brows sits burning, 670a; Thou Spirit P., 439a; Thou who art called the P., 670b

Paradise Adam, had p. at will, 6a; brought home to p., 500b; confirmed as possessors of p., 35b; cross opened gates of p., 231b; each heaven for every soul Is p., 302b; England, p. of little men and purgatory of great, 296a; If P. be yet more fair Than earth, 653b; O P.! O P.!, 304a, 635b; our home in p., 246a; to be with Jesus, a sweet p., 488b

Paradox statement of obvious so as to make it sound untrue, 653b

Pardon BVM, p. for sinners, 84b; Confess faults' guilt, crave p. for thy sin, 719a; grant Thy faithful p. and peace, 822a; is He not more ready to p. than we to sin?, 349a; Lamb, Comes with p. from heaven, 7b; Lord, swift to p., slow to punish, 821b; p. for their sins, 244b; repentance is the price of p., 763b

Pardoning charity is p. of unpardonable, 157b

Parent bishop, parent of souls, 68a

Parents Children begin by loving their p., 161a; Christian p., to educate children as members of Church, 579b; Christians honor father and mother, 162b; cooperation of God and p. in children, 160b; How easy 'tis for p. to forgive!, 349a; O God, Who has commanded us to honor our father and mother, 654a; p. driven out by children, 65b; P. of life and love, 920b

Paris P. is well worth a mass, 585b

Parish pastor, priest upon whom p. is conferred, 660b

Parliament cannot confer supremacy over Church, 141a; Catholics permitted to sit in, 141b

Parnell, Charles Stewart, 654a

Parochialism essence of p., to assume nothing exists outside own parish, 598b

Parousia Thy terrible second-coming, 196a; when He cometh second time in majesty, 7b

Parricide more wicked than homicide, 852b

Parson A holy-minded man, the p. to a town, 727b; no one else there but priest and p., 745b; The cobbler apron'd, the p. gown'd, 191b; The p.'s cant, 814a

Parsons small offering Maketh poor p., 189b

Part Act well your p., 281b; I have done my p., 520a; one time or other we all must p., 654a; We two now p., 654a

Partakers *become p. of divine nature,* 70b; joint p. of His beloved Son, 124a

Partem *Audi alteram p.,* 499a

Partibus *In p. infidelium,* 425a

Participation in divinity makes us gods, 102b

Particles all consecrated p. contain Body, 76a

Parties Catholic vote, distributed among several p., 692a; Religion should be accounted above p., 183a

Partings The pang of all the p. gone, 654b

Parts man should hear all p. ere he judge, 499a

Party annoyance, to seem to be head of p., 471b; *Catholic* political

p., runs twofold risk, 654b; Englishmen do not understand p. system, 16b; p. system in England, efficient machine, 407a; should be majority of Catholics in all decent parties, 655a

Pasch (Pascha) Christ is sacrificed as our P., 285a, 442b; No one shall taste anything at P. before offering, 337b

Paschal At the P. Victim's feet, 285b; by this P. sacrament, 441b; new and holy Passover, 284b; P. sacrifice, world's salvation, 283b; Passover that sanctifieth all the faithful, 285a

Paschal Candle, 441b

Pass I p. away After a little while, 250b; They cannot wholly p. away, 243b

Passed foolish, merely to regret things that are p., 659b

Passing All things are p., 882a

Passion Any sudden gust of p., 655a; beard cannot be grown in p., 53b; Bid p. be at rest, 37b; by death did fame procure, 230a; By Thy p., we have been freed from passions, 441b; calling to mind the blessed p. of the same Christ, 655b, 592a; Christ's p. and debt of punishment, 44a; Christ's p. meritorious cause of salvation, 44a; Christ's p., superabundant, 44a, 752a; death of Christ and nourishment of Sacrament, 73a; difference between a caprice and a life-long p., 557a; flames of unlawful p., 159a; ignominies of the P., 43a; One pulse of p., 557a; p. of BVM, 95a; P. of Savior, 75b; Sing the trophy of His p., 229a; sorrows of P. Week, 769b; Thou wast pleased to ascend Cross in Thy flesh, 656a; Thy p. be to me a source of strength, 656b; unspeakable glory of the P.!, 229b; What p. cannot music quell?, 626a; We adore Thy p., O Christ, 400a; your ruling p., 655b

Passions Catholic Church, discipline of affections and p., 689a; Desolate p., aching hours, 416b; guide their p., whisp'ring war or peace, 687b; In men we various ruling p. find, 572a; movement of soul contrary to nature, p., 655a; No pow'r can make the slave of p. great, 655a; of ugly woman easily stirred, 54a; renunciation of body and p., 36b

Passiontide rose of His passion-tide, 95a

Passover immolation of Christ our P., 43b; mystic P., 284b

Passport His p. is his innocence and grace, 472a; well-spent life, only p. to heaven, 540a

Password p. of our King, divine deeds, 435b

Past all the p., read true, is prophecy, 659a; Examples of p. times, 519a; neither future nor p. actually exists, 868b; O that it were as it was wont to be, 582a; p., future, present, all present to God, 383a; p., life-history of human souls, 186b; Provided the p. stays decently dead, 601b; requires real courage to face the p., 659b; to break with the p. needs divine power, 659a

Pastor bishops, ordinary p. of churches, 69b; conduct of prelate should surpass people, 659b; Happy the priest who loves his p.'s lot, 660b; life of a p. sets him apart from flock, 659b

Pastoral timeliness in p. caring, 613a

Pastorate government of souls, is art of arts, 659b

Pastors God perfects the minds of those who rule, 660a; ministry and labor of His p., 127a; supernaturally enlightened p., 119b

Pasture both Shepherd and Green P., 73a, 484a; Change of p. maketh fat calves, 661a; in which sheep of Holy Church are tended, 660b

Pastures place of light, place of green p., 245a

Pater Noster, 593b; the devil's P., 236b; Pray thus three times a day, 661a

Path right p. appeared not anywhere, 10b

Pathos In blissful p., 385a; The p. of eternity, 556a

Paths Tread holy p., 719a

Patience All men commend p., 661b, 851b; cross is divine school of p., 233b; follow the example of His p., 652a; p. in restraining solicitude, 26a; P. is the companion of wisdom, 661a; p. of Thine only-begotten Son, 661a; root and guardian of all the virtues, 661a; Tribulation meriteth in p., 880a; your p., a panoply, 401a

Patient Beware the fury of a p. man, 662a; p. people, not affected by any vexation, 661a; St. Paul greatest example of p. endurance, 663b; The p. struggles, and by inches dies, 269a; to be p. without undergoing insults, 473b

Patiently bear p., if thou canst not joyfully, 661b

Patmore, Coventry, 662a

Patri Gloria P., et Filio, et Spiritui Sancto, 588a

Patriarch sleepless p. averts cataclysm, 100a

Patriarchs bishops four-fold, p., archbishops, metropolitans, bishops, 433b; God freely gives grace to p., 68a; privileges of p., established ritual, 770b; welcoming embrace of the p., 244b

Patrick, St. Hibernia's champion saint, all hail!, 662b; We revere our P.'s name, 662b

Patrimony p. of the Church, 178a

Patriot Ambition makes p. as knave, 14b; grave or prison Illumed by one p. name, 663a; If the pulse of the p., soldier, or lover, 421b; No better citizen than Christian mindful of duty, 185b

Patriotism Catholic Church commands and consecrates p., 663a; civil allegiance of Christian, limited by conscience, 182a; my country, right or wrong, 15b; Nothing sweeter than one's own country, 222b; p. and cause of God, 185b; p. and devotion to Church, 663b; p., religion, money, three great realities, 476a; taken for granted by Englishmen, 18a; We are bound to love country, 663b

Patriots I would have Catholics be first p. of the land, 663b; Rebels in Cork are p. at Madrid, 751a

Patris In nomine P., et Filii, et Spiritus Sancti, 587a

Patron BVM is patron, we are clients, 89a, 89b; Seek ye a p. to defend Your cause?, 678a

Pattern made Himself the way, image, p., 254b

Paul, St. All ye who groan, Entreat St. P., 664b; blessed apostle

P., *chosen vessel,* 694a; God established orders through P., 68b; God taught whole world by preaching of blessed P., 664a; greatest model of patient endurance, 664a; in Nero's time, P. beheaded in Rome, 678b; made worthy to sit upon one of twelve thrones, 664a; one of chiefest among saints, chosen vessel, 664a; P. and apostolic power, 129a; protection of doctor of the gentiles, 664a; when shipwrecked, 679a

Paul To rob Peter and pay P., 664b

Paul's, St. (London) St. P.'s Loomed like a bubble o'er the town, 347a; splendid old St. P.'s, 114a

Pauline Legitimate marriage, dissolved by P. privilege, 580a

Pause after a p., begin, 149b; between the sobs of cares, 59a

Pawing importunate p. and neighing, 447a

Pax P. Domini sit semper vobiscum, 594a; *P. et bonum,* 665b; *P. tecum,* 594b; *P. vobiscum,* 588b

Pay be content with your p., 906a; buy what I'll never pay for, 108a; To rob Peter and p. Paul, 664b

Payment Misreckoning is no p., 664b

Peace All rest in p. at last, 814a; Arms alone can keep p., 348b; Belligerents want p. to their own liking, 665a; BVM intercedes for p. of world, 87a; Charity, foundation of p., 154b, 157a; Christian order, purpose is p., 666b; Dispose our days in Thy p., 665a; end and aim of good government, union and p. of the citizens, 615a; give p. to the state, 582a; Give p. to Thy world, to Thy churches, 596a; grant to Thy servants p. which world cannot give, 665a; I burned for Thy p., 664b; In p. let us pray to the Lord, 588a; itself is war in masquerade, 907b; Holiness rather than p., 436a; Honor is p., 666b; make p. before sundown, 297b; May they rest in p., 596a; most disadvantageous p., better than most just war, 907b; 'My p. I send you, and I send a sword', 666b; natural to men, 651a; on earth p. to men of good will, 588b; order our days in Thy p., 591b; P. and good, 665b; P. be unto you, 588b; P. be with thee, 594b; P. I leave with you, my p. I give unto you, 594b; p. of heavenly City, 665a; p. of mankind, 665a; place of refreshment, light and p., 592b; The p. of the Lord be with you always, 594a; The purpose of all war is p., 907b; *things which are for our p.,* 219a; To serve cause of p., 666b

Peaceable Be humble and p., 488b

Peaceably Grant that course of world may be p. governed, 665a

Peaceful our times, p. under Thy protection, 665b; P. and sober, chaste was He, 205a

Peacock She is a p. in everything but beauty, 667a

Peal They p. a fast for me, 169a

Pearl Hail, Mary, p. of grace, 97b; P. of price untold, 169b; will shine in the midst of squalor, 667a; With p. dissolv'd in gold, 585a

Pearls He who would search for p. must dive below, 300b; Men should not put p. To-fore rude swine, 667a

Peasant p. traditions keep close to earth, 347a

Peccare Rex non potest p., 509a

Peccata Agnus Dei, qui tollis p. mundi, 594a; *Ego te absolvo œ peccatis tuis,* 2b

Peccati Intervention *ratione p.,* 178a

Pedant loads of learned lumber in his head, 667a

Peer p. has no authority over p., 45b

Peerage You should study P., Gerald, 18b

Peerless O p. in renown!, 847a

Pelham, John, 251a

Pelican P. of heaven, 75a

Pen denouncing angel's p., 20a; Made of quill from angel's wing, 667a

Penal not a p. law would be proposed, 872a

Penalties spiritual and temporal p., 740b

Penance according to gravity of sins, 668a; almsgiving good as p. for sin, 13a; confession required, 202b, 667b, 669a; for reconciling faithful after baptism, 668b; fruits worthy of p., required, 667b; In p., sins committed after baptism forgiven, 669b; instituted of divine right, 2b, 203b; judicial absolution pronounced by legitimate minister, 669b; keys given to loose, to bind, 669a; matter of sacrament, contrition, confession, satisfaction, 668b; ministry of reconciliation, 68b; priests, ministers of granting of Christ's grace, 203a, 668b; school of p., 233b; service man's, reward is of Power on high, 667b; Sins are forgiven by the Holy Ghost, 667b; So long as sin in world, must be p., 669b; temporal punishment to be discharged, 669b; Within Church, sins forgiven in three ways, 668a

Penances No greater perfection, because great p., 604b; purity of love with which we do them, 624a

Pencil Thy p. speaks the tongue of ev'ry land, 652a

Penitence But I'll to p. inure, 765a; let me cleanse my life with p., 764b

Penitent An angel's grief ill fits a p., 277a; Chaste Mistress, receive me a p., 98a; No true p. forgets or forgives himself, 349b

Pennies He who watches out for his p., 113a

Penny A p. can do no more than it may, 617a; He had not one p. to bless him, 617b

Pentecost apostles distributed world into parts among themselves, 677a; Church began where Holy Spirit descended, 123b; Come, Holy Ghost, Creator, come, 670b; illumination of Holy Spirit, 670a; Paraclete On twelve bright brows sits burning, 670b; sending of the Holy Spirit, 670a; There came a mighty rushing sound, 670a

People assemblage associated by right and interests, 765b; God's pamper'd p., 493b; *He will save His p. from their sins,* 460b; If by p. you understand multitude, 671a; legislator, p. or whole body of citizens, 534a; My p., what have I done unto thee?, 400a; No country deserves so well of p. as America, 255b; Nor is the p.'s judgment always true, 671a, 739b; only real p., who have never ex-

isted, 343b; p. and 'the masses', two distinct concepts, 845b; p. must be educated, 290a; p. of God's adoption, 647b; P.-pestered London, 549b; p.'s religion is ever a corrupt relivion, 757a; political power resides in multitude, 180b; Sovereignty inheres in the organic p., 838a; The p. are a many-headed beast, 671b; voice of p. is voice of God, 671a

Peoples each have peculiar needs and aspirations, 613a; P.'s voice is God's voice, 255a

Peopled world, only p. to people heaven, 303b

Perception value of existence, in powers of p., 671b

Perfect bound to observe commandments of God and Church, 193b; contemplative life makes man p., 5a; If thou wilt be p., sell thy will, 671b; In charity, all elect made p., 154b; knowledge of God, reward of p., 301b; No one is suddenly made p., 671b; p. God likewise became p. Man, 468a; p. life is an imitation of death, 247b; soul p., guided by instinct of Holy Spirit, 672a; to be p. is to have changed often, 153b

Perfected more a thing p. is, more It feels bliss, 238b

Perfection bear whole yoke of the Lord, 671b; do what thou canst, 671b; does not consist in macerating the body, 623b; doing ordinary actions well, 4b; each century calls for type of p., 17a; everything attains proper end, ultimate p., 671b; Grace is nature's p., 412b; Man's p. is to be like God, 888b; No advance on road of p., unless Christ walks beside, 672a; not something you can acquire like a hat, 617a; p. of Catholic Church, 122a; p. of Christian life, 156a, 671b; p. of the saints, 793b; supernatural p., 437a; Three stages to perfect friendship with God, 761a; ultimate p. of contemplative life, 903b; whole aim of science of Christian p., 840b; Who seeks p. in the art, 42b

Perfections God imparts p. as much as each can stand, 216a

Perfects grace p. nature, 412b

Peri One morning a P. at the gate Of Eden, 653b

Periculosa Omnis definitio p. est, 254b

Period To this dark common p., 248b

Periodicals Church has right to censor, 151b

Perish Some p. in foul seasons, 106b; They who p., p. by their own negligence, 238a; What is natural cannot wholly p., 633a

Perjury Jove but laughs at lover's p., 555a

Permanence p. of Church, 135a

Perplex surest manner to p. a man, 672a

Persecute p. for doctrine without even stating it, 672b

Persecutes Of all tyrannies, worst that which p. mind, 607b

Persecution adversity strengthens us by its suffering, 851a; anti-Christian power, could not abstain from persecution, 672b; Bodily suffering purifies souls that are good, 851a; general law of p., conversion of persecutors, 672b; never a time, when Christian does not suffer p., 672b; no part of

Creed, 104a; rage man or devil never so much, 141b; Torture us, rack us, condemn us, crush us, 851a; unbelievers who impede faith by p., 57b

Persecutions gave glorious chase To p., 672b; Lord has willed we should rejoice over p., 583b; purify Church, 672b; when p. occur, faith is crowned, 583b

Persecutors what greater miracle than conversion of, 609b

Perseverance great gift of p. unto end, 562a, 673a; never turn aside from ways of eternal life, 673a; no p., without will to persevere, 412a; p. in good, great gift of God, 6b; We cannot command final p., 673a

Persevere justified, not able to p. without help of God, 673a; p. with steadfast devotion, 37b; things being prepared for those who p., 366b

Persian A P.'s heav'n is easily made, 304a

Persistence Nothing so hard, it does not yield to harder, 673b

Person highest perfection in nature, 387b, 673b; individual substance of a rational nature, 673b; in God, relation subsisting in divine nature, 387b; same P. is God and Man, 184a, 466b; unity of p. of Christ, 81b

Persona member of Church, 127b

Personality develop p. according to individual abilities, 846a; dignity of human p., 673b; integrity of human p., 140a; lost in false universalism, 726a; natural impulses serve to wreck p., 264b; self, merged in that P., 889a; should not scandalize, 27a

Persons 'properties' of P., identical with P., 370a; Remember, world is not things, but p., 154a; two P. or Hypostases, 481b, 591a

Persuade more ready to convince than to command, 674a

Persuaded mind must be p., it cannot be constrained, 607b; We are easily p. by reasons we discover, 674a

Persuades Anything pleasant easily p., 673b

Persuasion unbelievers who impede faith by evil p., 57a

Pessimism at best an emotional half-holiday, 498b; P. is regnant, 674a; thing unfit for white man, 674a

Petavius, D., 341a

Peter To rob P. and pay Paul, 664b

Peter, St. 23b, 175b; acts in person of Catholic Church, 821b; appointed prince of apostles, visible head of Church militant, 678a; As Christ is Shepherd, is P. not shepherd?, 676a; authority of P. plenary, 69b; authority perpetuated in Roman pontiff, 69b; brought creed to Roman Church, 227a; care of whole Church, committed to blessed P., 433b, 700a; center of hierarchy, 133b; chief of apostolic band, 677a; chief of episcopal order, 699a; Church was founded upon P., 674b, 675b, 694b, 701b; continues to live in his successors, 694b; crown of Church, 116b; doorkeeper of kingdom of heaven, 674b, 676b; granted pontifical power of binding and loosing, 677a; had more authority than other apostles, 696a; head of My disci-

ples, 674b; heir of My treasures, 674b; his confession of faith, 124a; I have erred with P., 521a; *I will to thee keys of kingdom of heaven,* 675b, 693a; leader of apostles, chief herald of the Church, 674b; never called Universal Apostle, 700a; nothing conferred on apostles apart from P., 678a; office of P., both directing power and supreme authority, 694b; only P. charged with fulness of power, 701b; P., and Christ as Head of Church, 676b; P. and episcopate, 695b; Peter's power lives in his See, 676b; plays part of whole Church, 675b; primacy is given to P., 693a, 695b; prince and head of apostles, 694b; represents the Catholic Church, 675b; Savior confided to P. whole universal Church, 675b; set at head of all rulers of the Church, 676b; several things conferred upon P., apart from apostles, 678a; shepherd of the Lord's flock, 675a; source of unity, 674b; They have not heritage of P., who have not see of P., 692b; *thou art P.,* 433a, 693a; vicegerent of His love, 675a; *whatsoever thou shalt bind on earth,* 677b, 693a; *When thou art converted,* strengthen thy brethren, 675a; Where P. is, there is the Church, 709a; 'You will not live to see the days of P.', 710b

Peter's Basilica, St., Rome Beneath the apostle's crowning dome, 702a

Peter and Paul, Sts. Among the apostles princes over all, 679b; consecrated Roman church, 694a; *I can point out trophies of the apostles,* 678b; these pillars of the Church, 678b; Triumphant over death by sword and shameful cross, 679a; two crowns, golden chains, fountains, 678b

Petition cause them to ask for such things as shall please Thee, 717a; ineffectual, when barren entreaty, 715b; kind of prayer, 720b; p. Government for redress of grievances, 184b; p. of empty hand dangerous, 56a

Petitioners save me most from my p., 342a

Petri cathedra P., 709b

Petro Erravi cum P., 521a

Petrus Ubi P., ibi ecclesia, 709a

Pets House without hound, 448a

Petticoat whole world is under p. government, 278a

Phalanx p. of hostile traditions, 271a

Pharaoh Loos'd from Phar'oh's bitter yoke, 285b; The skull of P. staring at the sky, 643b

Pheasant See! from the brake the whirring p. springs, 679b

Philanthropy goodness that thou mayest do this day, do it, 679b

Philip II, King of Spain, 141a

Philip Neri, St., 23b, 635b, 680a, 781a

Philosopher A great memory does not make a p., 603a; bound to be lover of myths and poetic fables, 680b; greatest p., undone by his imagination, 459a; Let no Christian, whether p. or theologian, embrace novelty, 682a; Man existed before the p., 680a; My guide, p., and friend, 359a; not politician who is business man, but king who is p., 691a; p., at price of rejection by Christ, 1a

Philosophers astonish ordinary

men, 680a; Christians astonish p., 680a; Poets and p., alike in being big with wonder, 680b; The cynics, those canine p., 237b

Philosophic Truth and p. expression, cannot change from day to day, 682a

Philosophy Amid sons p. to him bore, 31a; called divine, 863a; called natural when nature of thing is discussed, 680b; Catholic p., a universal p., 681a; does not seek to overthrow revelation, 681b; Every education teaches a p., 393a; meditation on death, 680b; my p. this, to know Jesus and Him crucified, 602a; principles of reason, foundations of p., 863b; reward is happiness, 680b; stepping-stone to the Christian faith, 681b; truths of p. cannot be contrary to truths of faith, 863b; view, principles of scholastic p., no longer suitable, 681a; without account of supernatural revelation, 681b

Phoebus Surmounting P. in the east, 168b

Phoenix Of all chaste birds p. doth excel, 54b

Phrases splendid p. and swelling sentences, 45a

Phronema eccles. sense or p., 270a

Phryne P. had talents for mankind, 421a

Physic Go, take p., 762b; p. of the field, 601b; That which makes us have no need Of p., 762b

Physical new realists torture men for p. truth, 885a

Physician fainting world's Physician, 7b; holy Father, p. of souls and bodies, 320b; I approach the P. of life, 196b; is He not P. and we the sick, 349a; knows better than patient, what will avail, 717a; lacketh a p., 269a; *P., heal thyself,* 423a

Physicians p., cautious grown Of other's lives, 269a; The first p. by debauch were made, 269a

Physics to P. if good heed thou pay, 31b

Picasso, 34a

Picture a p. in every wave, 322b

Pictures holy p. must have *imprimatur,* 152a; unfortunate p. of God, 34b

Pie Merry as a p., 497a

Pierce O sweetest Lord Jesus, p. the marrow, 196a

Pierced They have p. my hands and my feet, 657a

Pierian Drink deep, or taste not the P. spring, 532a

Piety foundation of all the virtues, 738b; Keep Thy household in continual godliness, 261b; renunciation, only real p., 36b; royal virtues principally two, justice and p., 507a; spirit of knowledge and p., 50a; water them with dew of p., 4a; works of p., 669a

Pig buy the p. in the poke, 856b

Pilate, Pontius crucified under P., 226a

Pilgrim p.'s hoping-leaven, 75a; Stay, p.! stay!, 251a; This little P., 168b; to Rome brings back what he brought, 682b

Pilgrimage during p. in this wilderness, 301b; during this our earthly p., 560a; Ere the p. be done, 447b; Whence palmer kings once did stray To Rome, 475b

Pilgrimages Compostellan p., 17a; Then people long to go on p., 682b

Pilgrims Be Thou our guide while

p. here, 657a; lead us on our holy way!, 682a; Like p. to th' appointed place we tend, 542b; patient as p., 566a; Singing to welcome p. of night, 20a; we, but p. passing to and fro, 539a;

Pill death in ambush lay in every p., 601b

Pillar Peter, prince and head of apostles, p. of the faith, 694b; p. of purity, 100b

Pillars Kings are the publick p. of state, 509b

Pillow A p. for thee will I bring, 55b; He that on his p. lies, 765a

Pills Th' oraculous doctor's mystic pills, 762b

Pin Your heart hangeth on a joly p., 497a

Pinions Created light unfurled, to be God's p., 225a

Pious Come visit every p. mind, 440a; so devoted to p. practices, 262a

Piper There sits a p. on the hill, 915b

Pit Some very foolish influence rules the p., 276b; the deep p., 245b

Pitch burning with brimstone and stinking p., 427b

Pitchers Small p. have wide ears, 282b

Pitied Better envied than p., 298a

Pity All feel p. for those like themselves, 682b; difference between p. and misery, 682b; Let Thy continual p. cleanse and defend Thy Church, 682b; Love on p. cannot live, 554b; What wondrous p. moved Thee, 491a

Piu P. presso la chiesa, piu lontano da Dio, 138a

Pius VII, Pope, 708b

Pius XII, Pope, 88a

Place I went back to to p. I knew, 448a; p. whence we shall never pass on, 560a

Places Would to God he and you had changed p.!, 153b

Placuit Quod principi p., legis habet vigorem, 533b

Plagiarism All competition, only furious p., 201a; authors make whole plays, yet scarce write one word, 683a; theft in other poets, only victory in him, 494a

Plague Devouring famine, p., and war, 249a

Plagues If p. . . . . break not Heaven's design, 107b

Plaints Sweet Jesu, if it be Thy will, unto my p. attend, 562a

Plan final completion of God's p., 166a; interference with divine p., 216a; P. not, nor scheme—but calmly wait, 882b; Progress, time-expression of an eternal p., 186b; Thy lovely sentient human p. unplanned, 283a

Planet until they can show me some happier p., 539a

Plant BVM truly celestial plant, 91a

Plantation p. of God and beloved vineyard, 124a

Planted So faith was p., so must be restored, 479b

Platitude nothing produces such an effect as a good p., 683a

Plato Aristotle inferior in eloquence to P., 31a; As Plato or the Stagyrite, 29a; P.'s flight to God, not highest Catholic conception, 396b; P.'s ideal city, 734a

Plausible Anything will become p., 683a

Play danger to Christians, 276a;

drama, with omission of principal part, 393a; good p. for nought, work for nought, 924a; Life is a p. acted by dying men, 543a; Life, nothing but p., 329b; Life's poor p., 242b; Now p. through heaven the angel bell, 169a; Since life is but a p., 161a

Players excommunicated so long as act, 5b

Playing It be ill p. with short daggers, 239b; we should take part for sake of recreation, 239a

Plays lawful to be present at proper p., 18a; Sure there's a fate in p., 276b

Playthings And all their heavenly p. leave, 20b

Plea availing p. for pardon and salvation, 196b

Plead P. for us a pitying prayer, 96a; P. with Christ our sins to spare, 96a

Pleasantly If we won't brighten our humor, live p., 683b

Please beautiful things p. when seen, 54b; implanted, desire to p., 683b; None p. the fancy who offend the ear, 923a; p. Thee both in will and in deed, 881b; without Thee, we are not able to p. Thee, 417a

Pleased What has p. the prince, has force of law, 533b

Pleaseth He p. God whom God p., 683b; oftentimes that displeaseth Him, which p. men., 451a

Pleasing accomplish that which is p. to Thee, 392a; Nothing artificial really p., 34b

Pleasure After death, Joy and p. is there none, 684a; all happiness man can gain Is not in p., 684b; Beauty self, in Whom all p. is, 562b; Death ought to be our p., 246b; Follow p., and then will p. flee, 684a; God's good p., 10a; Joy and p. is there none, 351b; Love, hope and joy, fair p.'s smiling train, 607b; necessity, not p., compels him, 634b; Pain their aversion, p. their desire, 684b; stolen p. of one night, 533b; Sweet is p. after pain, 684a; what greater p., than scorn p., 36b; Who will, in time present, p. refrain, 683b; will withdraw men from prayer, 718b

Pleasures active life subdues p. of body, 4b; Admirers of false p., 684a; I take my p. without change, 684b; life, all chequer'd with p. and woes, 539a; loathèd p. breed displeasing pain, 542a; Repent old p., and solicit new, 765a; take p. sadly, not to say savagely, 16b

Plebiscites what the plebians alone enact, 524a

Pleni P. sunt caeli et terra, 591a

Plenitude pope possesses p. of power within Church, 701b

Plenty He that hath p. of goods shall have more, 711b; P. is no dainty, 684b

Plots From p. and treasons heav'n preserve my years, 342a; true or false, are necessary things, 684b

Plough their money is their p., 617a

Plumage Soil not thy p. With sublunary things, 854a

Plumes not on downy p., fame is won, 335a

Pluralism element of p. inherent in every true political society, 845b

Plurality where there is no p., there is unity, 369a

Plus melius est enim minus egere quam p. habere, 361a

Pneumatological concept of Church, 137b

Poaching His brethren did no p. where he went, 56a

Poe, Edgar Allen, 685a

Poem A well-made p., powerful piece of imposture, 687b

Poems P. are made by fools like me, 879b

Poesies And so my touch, to golden p. Turning love's bread, 689b

Poesy nobler flight Of p., 688a; Profaned thy heav'nly gift of p.!, 688a

Poet A double life the p. lived, 686a; A p. is not born in every race, 685a; Catholic p. should be apostle, 687a; employment of a p., 685b; enters into himself in order to create, 214b; For wine is the horse of Parnassus, 279a; horrified, had he fancied full meaning could be discerned, 689b; p. and contemplative, 214b; The generous critic fann'd the p.'s fire, 228a; The p. always treats spiritual realities as concrete, 689a; The p., great nature's own high priest, 686a

Poetess A maudlin p., 687b

Poetic P. experience, distinct from mystical experience, 690a; Should men be rated by p. rules, 688a

Poetical With Christians, p. view of things is a duty, 688b

Poetry artificiality of old pastoral p., 689b; emanates from free creativity of spirit, 690a; From me, my art, thou canst not pass away, 687a; in Oxford An art, in London a trade, 688a; Nay, what is p.? A bright-winged bird, 690a; No Christian p. worthy of name, written by anyone not contemplative, 690b; not p., prose run mad, 690b; P. is devil's wine, 687b; prosaic, always insist on p. being poetical, 689b; prose of Christianity, without p., 437a; To attempt in verse things scarce to thought assured, 865b; unlearning world's p., attaining to its prose!, 690b; used p. as medium for prose, 109b

Poets And ah, we p., I misdoubt, 684a; But p. are confin'd in narrower space, 652a; Church, most sacred and august of p., 688b; complain of moralists, 9b; From stones and poets you may know, 5b; mathematicians go mad, p. scarcely ever do, 686b; only fellows whom anybody will flatter, 685b; Pensive p. painful vigils keep, 685b; p. and lunatics, 473b; P. and philosophers, alike in being big with wonder, 680b; spoil their business with overcare, 685a; Three p., in three distant ages born, 606b; To p., Lord, Thou givest drink, 687a; We p. are creatures most absurd, 685b; whose 'works' are always collectively exhibited, 689a; will tend towards Christian orthodoxy, 686b

Poison dread p. of the serpent, 231a; heretics mingle p. with Jesus Christ, 428b; one man's p., another man's drug, 690b; p., Of things too sweet, 690b

Poisoning To assimilate blindfold, will end in p., 690b

Poisons All p. will at once undo, 26a

Pole, Cardinal, 141a, 691a

Policy forbidden to deal with matter of state or p., 480a; not right, by mere fact of being hard, 847b

Polish beat iron while hot, p. at leisure, 476b; Ours is American Church, not Italian, or P., 143b

Polite many faultlessly p. people, 28a; true, there are many very p. men, 691a

Politeness charm which comes from gracious p., 691a

Politic body p. contains family units, 845b; Cooperation of Church and body p., 184a; laws, made for sake of body p., 404b; private societies within body p., 38a; State, for body p., not body p. for state, 846a; State, superior part in body p., 846a; We have to distinguish clearly between State and Body P., 845b

Political *Catholic* p. party, runs twofold risk, 654b; Catholics should not be grouped in single party, 655a; Catholic vote, distributed among several p. parties, 692a; Christianity is constantly moulding p. society, 181a; Church can not identify her cause with p. wrong, 691b; in p. society, authority comes from below, 845b; Liberty, itself the highest p. end, 538a; Material force, *ultima ratio* of p. society, 348b; p. conditions governing Americans, 17a; P. life neigher provides our end, nor contains happiness, 691b; should be majority of Catholics in all decent p. parties, 655a; social and p. status of the Church, 182a; theory, wealth protection against p. corruption, 909a; unity of religion, not prerequisite for p. unity, 184a; world, cannot be exalted into p. perfection, 549b

Politician In friendship false, implacable in hate, 691a; opportunist p., 645a

Politicians have no politics, 692a

Politics advise Catholics to accept the political doctrines of day, 691b; Catholic Church, not party in p. of any nation, 655a; Catholics and voice of Church in political matters, 183a; Christians, content to be towed like slaves in wake of history, 774b; civil ruler dabbling in religion, 692a, 758a; hazards of p. come from nature of creature, 692a; He thinks like a Tory, talks like a Radical, 692a; men must conform either p. to religion or religion to p., 181a; more to purpose, to recall ideas of Catholic times, 691b; Politicians have no p., 692a; Priests and bishops do not dictate p. of Catholics, 692a; religion and politics go together, 184b; religion, inseparable from every act of man, 181a; Religion should be accounted above parties, 183a; The best men for the office, 692a; There is no leisure about p., 691b; *To* place and power, all public spirit tends, 691b; To put a Catholic into office, merely because Catholic, 692a; uninitiated dare to dabble in affairs of state, 691b; view, Catholic voters under influence of Church, 692a

Politicum dominium p. et regale, 405b

Polity best form of p., partly kingdom, aristocracy, democracy, 404a

Pollution That no p. we may know, 201b

Polygamy not lawful for Christians have several wives at same

time, 577b; prohibited by divine law, 577b

Pomegranate As a p., cut in twain, 625b

Pomp court with solemn p., 40a; glory in the p. of worldly things, 746a; painted p. of wooded heights, 47b; The consul was constrained his p. to crowd, 902a

Pomposity the failure of pomp, 692b

Pompous A vile conceit in p. words express'd, 692b

Pomps Vanish the glories and p. of earth in wind, 367b

Ponder On this I p., where'er I wander, 59a

Pontifex P. Maximus, 709b

Pontiff I promise obedience to Roman p., 145b; p. is chief of priests, 69a; Supreme p. and universal pope, 709b; we declare altogether necessary to be subject to Roman p., 701b

Pontifical In all his robes p. expresst, 78b; Peter granted p. power of binding and loosing, 677a; p. glory, brightness of souls, 68a; p. vestments and character of bishop, 68a

Pontificate if thou hadst never been raised to the p., 520b; supreme p., once conditions for election fulfilled, 434a

Poor A p. man may boldly sing before thieves, 712b; As p. as Job, 712b; As rich as a new shorn sheep, 712b; Be p. in folly, rich in all but sin, 775a; Defence of p. and class hatred, 187b; free of gift, as p. man of his eye, 847a; gold hidden in ground, belong to p., 909a; he is in need, who is purse-sick, 269a; He is rich enough who is p. with Christ, 775a; kingdom of heaven is kingdom of the p., 712a; p. man, rich in faith, nearer to heaven, 775b; satisfy wants of the world's p., 712a; The p. and lowly, 74b; The p. I saw at the cloister gate, 713a; To relieve the p., 155a; To desire to be p. but not inconvenienced, 713a; we are p. in ourselves, but rich in God, 395a

Pope alone deserves to be called universal, 175b; as ruler of States of Church, 178b; authority in cases of appeal, 697b; authority of Peter perpetuated in p., 69b; barely Catholic enough for some converts, 221a; Bishop of Rome, 709a; blessed p. of the city of Rome, 695a; can dispense from purely ecclesiastical regulations, 701b; can give no dispensation from divine law and natural law, 701b; captain of our religion, 705a; confirms decrees of general council, 222b; directive power over princes, 181a; father and teacher of all Christians, 696a; has full and supreme power of jurisdiction over Church, 703a; He who eats from the p., dies of it!, 710a; His name alone pronounced in all churches, 701a; his patriarchal authority, 662a; in supreme pontiff, fulness of pontifical and royal power, 179b; I promise obedience to Roman pontiff, 145b; legitimately elected, enjoys full authority, 703a; may be judged by no one, 175b; may depose emperors, 175b; may depose or absolve bishops, 701a; may dispose of kingdoms if necessary, 180b;

necessity of p., 118b; not lord of bishops, but one of them, 702a; *Papa,* 709a; pastor over Church, 700b; Peter, and Christ as Head of Church, 676b; Peter and episcopate, 695b; Peter received in special way, keys and primacy of judicial power, 677b; p. and bishops, 707a; possesses plenitude of power within Church, 701b; preserved from error of judgment in decision on faith or morals, 706b; presides over oecumenical council, 708b; property of Church belongs to P., as principal dispenser, 734a; Servant of the servants of God, 709b; successor of St. Peter, 134b, 178b; speaking *ex cathedra,* 274b; teacher of Thy universal Church, 700a; to believe in a Church, is to believe in the p., 703a; vicar of Jesus Christ, 701b; vicar of St. Peter, 695a; visible head necessary, to preserve unity in Church, 696b; you have no superior on earth, 702a; Your holiness holds place of God on earth, 710a

Popery No p.!, 710b; No union they pretend, but in non-p., 770a

Popes authority plenary, not sole, 69b; coercive power of p. over rulers, 181a; enact and submit to canons as example, 111b; have not erred in definition of faith, 129b; have primacy and authority over all churches, 695b; right of crowning emperor, 177b

Poppy flushed print in a p., 711a

Poplar when the p. trees Rustle their pale leaves, 627a

Popular Art should never try to be p., 32a

Populi Vox p., vox Dei, 671a

Port Alas! what p. can such a pilot find, 339a; How to this p. at every step I go, 59b; of his p. as meek as is a maid, 161b

Portal Heaven's P. fairest, 99a; P. of bliss to man forgiven, 461a; p. of skies, 82b, 98b

Portals Lift your p., 36b

Portent This is the p. worthy of a cry, 142a

Portion grant us to be reckoned as p. of Him, 166b; realm of nature his, who has God for p., 633a

Portrait Every p. painted with feeling, p. of artist, 711a

Possess Better to have than wish, 711b; to p. them still, all man's thought, 48b; We are not our own, 225b

Possessed What is wrongly p., not the owner's, 733b

Possesses Whoever p. God, is happy, 419a

Possessing The pleasure of p., 711b

Possession limits of private p., fixed by man's industry, 734b; p. with justice, only through Church, 179a; prestige of p. in favor, 270b; right to own according to *jus gentium,* 734a; To come to the p. of all, 395a

Possessions All that we have is but death's livery, 249b; Be not anxious about what you have, 711b; devil rules over lovers of temporal goods, 260a; easier to renounce worldly p., 712a; goods of Fortune's keeping, 48b; Man should not consider his material p. his own, 711b; p. of Church, under bishop, 67b; to God he gives p., 13a

Pot Little p., soon hot, 712a; There's no p. without bacon, 44b

Pounds careful regarding crowns and p., 113a

Poverty A glass by which to see one's truest friends, 712b; Brings one to God, 712b; glory of God in p. and abundance, 775b; height of the most sublime p., 352a; in God's sight, p. is no disgrace, 713a; no more prefer riches to p., 37a; No one should commend p. save poor, 712b; poor in goods but exalted in virtue, 352a; Possess p., 520a; P. I love, but not dirt, 712b; song, sanctitude, and p., 352a; those in bonds and p., 9b

Power absolute p. corrupts a., 714a; all p. is for mastery, 47a; all p. is for service, 47a; all p. is for wealth, 47a; all p. is from God, 180b, 526a; differences between political and eccles. p., 180b; divine law gives p. to collected body, 406a; Eccles. p. in every way immediately from God, 180b; Jesus Christ, Wisdom and P. of God, 480b; legitimate use and abuse of p., 534a; Political p., delegated by multitude to one or several, 406a; political power derives from natural law, 406a; Political p. in concrete, based on law of nations, 180b; Political p. resides immediately in whole state, 406a; p. of authorities and obedience, 45b; p. of bishops and priests not same, 69a; p. of BVM resides in prayer, 97a; p. of Father, wisdom of Son, 108b; P. to be powerful, 714a; p. to constrain others, from God, 406b; Right lives by law, and law subsists by p., 713b; royal p. can only be from God, 879a; tends to corrupt, 714a; They who possess the prince, possess the laws, 714a; three theories of p., 47a

Powerful to be p. you must have a genius for organizing, 784b; Virgin most p., 100a

Powers chiefs of p. above, 21a; fellowship with angelic p., 50a; one of nine orders of angels, 18b; royal dignity excels all other earthly p., 507b; *the powers that are, are ordained of God,* 182b; two p. by which world chiefly ruled, 174a

Practice His preaching much, but more his p. wrought, 721b; should be sustained by prayer, 717b

Praise beauty's elixir vitae, 55a; Be sparing in p., 714b; Bow down to hear the songs of p., 599a; Damn with faint p., 239a; God hates those who p. themselves, 806a; great matter, not to rejoice in human p., 714a; hearts, that once beat high for p., 421b; He does not know how to flee from p. when it abounds, 714b; His p. my lyre shall ring, 489a; Inflamed with Thy immortal p., 369b; It will but wither even as you p., 715a; P. be to Thee, O Christ, 589b; P. is pleasant, p. befitting, 605a; p. of myself, for good of neighbor, 714a; receives p., way clean window takes light, 715a; sent us back to p., who came to pray, 719a; undeserv'd is satire in disguise, 715a; We p. Thee, O God, 372b; wish for p. when we deserve blame, 714b; worthily p. Thy name, 586b

Praises come too late When man is not, 335a; her p. sing, 40b; Let our love break forth in p., 605a;

Our hearts in hymns and p. blend, 74a

Praising *P., I will call upon the Lord,* 595a; What creature From p. Thee can stay, 714b

Pray a good deal, 720b; as you can, 720b; everything for which man and Caesar can p., 171b; He knows how to live well, who knows how to p. well, 717a; If the psalm prays do you too p., 266a; lawful to p. for what is lawful to desire, 716b; Lovely Lady, Teach me how to p., 102a; Our Father, Who hast exhorted us to p., 716a; P. and work, 718a; rise from sleep at dawn, p. to God, 715b; The only way to p. is to p., 720b; those things for which we dare not p., 363a; To labor is to p., 515b; to own, while we p., that we cannot p. aright, 719b; to p. is less than to adore, 235a; To p. is the same thing as to speak, 717b; Too tired to p., I kneel, 78b; We little know the things for which we p., 718a

Prayed In single day, p. as many as hundred times, 717a

Prayer affliction will sometimes extort a short p., 718b; Alms are but vehicles of p., 13a; before all things, good to begin with p., 717a; best meditation before preaching, p., 722a; BVM has prevailing gift of p., 97a; by pure p., soul carried to God on wings, 717b; chief exercise of p., to speak to God, 719a; conformity of our will with divine will, 718b; cooperation of p. and mystical body, 132b; devout intent directed unto God, 718a; face lifted up in prayer, 266b; fasting, better than p., 13a; For p. to be effective, 718a; he may offer to Thee pure p., 36b; He that flees from p., 718b; in fasting, almsdeeds and p., righteousness consists, 401b; instrument of divine fellowship, 720a; knock in p. and it shall be opened to thee, 213b; Let law of p. determine law of belief, 546b; life of body of Church, 89b; man, by p., obtains whatever he wills, 720a; noblest and most exalted action, 720a; not necessary, set forth petitions before God, 718a; our music, 84b; Our p. ought to be short and pure, 717a; path of p., King's highway, 720a; petition, contrition, thanksgiving, three kinds of p., 720b, Physician knows better than patient, what will avail, 717a; P. is a vital act of faith, 720a; P. is conversation with God, 715b; p. is voice of man to God, 772b; raising up mind to God, 718a; revives the soul, by p. it lives, 718b; seven facts, will bring much depth into our p., 721a; The lips' reasoning, 717b; The people's p., 798b; To apply oneself frequently to p., 717a; violence we do Him, pleases God, 715b; weapon of Mother of God, 89b; We get from God exactly what we really want, 720b; Where p. poured forth, sins are covered, 716a; *Ye ask, and receive not,* 718a

Prayer-books Beads and p., toys of age, 262b; must have *imprimatur,* 152a

Prayers all shall offer p., standing, 716a; angels, summoned by your p., 20b; Besieging Thee with penetrable p., 720b; BVM presents p. to her Son, 89a; come to God with fruitless or naked p., 715b;

daily p. of faithful, satisfaction for tiny faults, 716b; equip p. with wings of fasting and almsdeeds, 401b; let odor of your p. always ascend, 726b; Offer your p. and alms, 13a; p. and praises that we pay, 69a; p. of Church, agelong poetry of mankind, 548b; quickly ascend to God, which merits of works urge, 716a; salt for food, 266a; season our labors with sacred song, 266a; souls of dead obtain relief through piety of living, 244a; We offer Thee sacrifices and p., 245b

Prays Christ p. in every soul, 720b; He p. best who does not know he is praying, 716a; He who labors as he p., 516a; the less one p., worse it goes, 720b

Preach Go and p. trifles to world, 722a; if you don't love world, don't p. to it, 722b; Nobody should p., unless commissioned, 722a; p. for nothing but greed of gain, 48b; We must meditate what we p., 722a

Preached *I have p. Apollo watered,* 130b; They argued not, but preach'd, 26b

Preacher cock, symbol of good p., 721a; Do you know how I test the value of a p.?, 721b; Vainly, p. utters word of God exteriorly, 721a; who preaches himself, 722a

Preachers ever wish to find something to smite sharply with reproof, 721b; furnish fond inventions from Scripture, 61b; ministry and labor of His p., 127a; more anxious to chide and reprove faults, 721b; peculiar way with haughty p., 721b; p. of gospel likened to oxen, 72b; should be awake in practice of good works, 721a; The world runs after pulpit orators, 721b; without fire of utterance of God, 721b; with princes of pride, p. dwelleth, 722a

Preachers, Order of (Dominicans), 275b

Preacheth When fox p., beware your geese, 351b

Preaching bare ministry of p. the gospel, 648a; best meditation before p., prayer, 722a; fewer of his own words and more of God's words, 722a; He gathers abundant fruits from his p., 722a; P. is heady wine, 722b; P., teaching, committed to the bishops, 722a

Precept Law, common, just, and stable p., 525b; No one obliged to obey p., unless informed, 525b

Precepts God's p. are light to loving, 193b; They very acts of Christ are p., 492b; weight of divine p., 212b

Precious Good and p. Jesus, 75b; In Thy wounds most p., 75b

Precipice shrink from approaching p., 149a

Predestinate man justified, not assuredly p., 724a

Predestinated He chose and p. us, that we might be so, 722b

Predestination All is thus ruled by the sight above, 259b; altercation On this vexed matter of p., 724a; Between grace and p., this difference, 722b; For how can that eternal Power be just, 724a; Incomprehensible are His judgments, 723a; p. and freewill, 356a; prescient counsel of God, 90b; purveyance, that God hath seen before, 259b; reason for p. of some, reprobation of others, 723b; relates to success of plan, 723b; That God has foreordained everything, self-evident, 724a; Why He draws one, and another not, 723a; Why should grace deliver this one and not this one?, 723a

Predestined all whom Thou dost foreknow shall be Thine, 541b; city of p., 124b; grace of justification, attained by p., 724a; no one may presume he belongs to p., 723a; number of p. is certain, 723a; preordained and directed to heaven, called p., 723b; p. and Church, 127a; p. unto evil, 724a

Predetermine God foreknows but does not p. everything, 723a

Predictions based on horoscope, mere chance, 41b

Pre-elected Thou by Him wast p., 39b

Pregnancies law of p. and birth of Christ, 80a

Pregnant let our hearts be p. by our faith in Christ, 897b

Prejudice a p. is a direction, 274b

Prelate conduct of p. should surpass people, 659b; has no authority in mortal sin, 46a; No p.'s lawn, with hair-shirt lined, 607b

Prelates p. and typical Christians, 125b

Premature praise wine before taste of grape, 714b

Premises correct p. of unbeliever, 27a

Preordained BVM, p. by prescient counsel of God, 90b

Prepared right rule, be p. for everything, 724a; to men p., delay is injury, 255a

Prerogative Conscience is royalty and p. of every man, 209a; p. which BVM has merited, 90b

Près P. de l'église, loin de Dieu, 138a

Presbyter bishop or p. shall baptize, 49b; forbidden to dwell with women, 188a; has authority only to receive holy orders, 647a; in Greek means elder in Latin, 727a; may marry before ordination, 150b; p.'s honorable position, 150b

Presbyterate Spirit common to all p., 241a

Presbyters do not possess plenitude of priestly office, 205b; one must obey p. in Church, 299b; priests of second order, 205b

Prescient p. counsel of God, 90b

Prescription possession of privilege for hundred years, 732a; p., which disposes of all heresies started later, 429a

Presence brighten this temple by power of Thy p., 171a; do in the p. of all, 4b; His invisible p., 888b; If God has stripped you of His p., 281b; *in p. of our Lord,* 436a; one who has a ruling sense of God's p., 163b; possessing feeling of His p., 281b; p. of God, 225a; Thy p. saves me from sorrow and from sin, 630a

Presence, Real As Christ willed it and spake it, 76b; Body of Christ is on the altar, 13b; Body, truly contained in sacrament, 311a; Christ's true body contained in Sacrament, 73b; denying r. is heresy, 73b; Eucharist really contains Body and Blood, 76a; here I own'd Thy presence, 77b; I believe that this is Thy most pure Body, 594b; manner of local presence in Eucharist, 73b; not as in sign, figure, or virtue, 76a; not confined to use of sacrament, 76a;

Thou to their teeth hast prov'd, 77a; true presence perceived by faith, 73b

Present hardness of heart, thinketh only of p. things, 724b; Most men strive for p., we for future, 361b; past, future, p., all p. to God, 383a; p. your bodies a living sacrifice, 229b; The past and p., only means, 420a; We believe God is p. everywhere, 266a

Presentation as Thine only-begotten Son presented in temple, 744a

Preservation p., involved in idea of creation, 117b

Preserve P., my Jesus, oh p., 198a

President p. reigns for four years, 496b

Press abridging freedom of speech or of p., 184b; In old days the rack, now the p., 496b; We have a censorship by the p., 496b

Presses God p. us, but does not oppress our liberty, 357b

Presso Piu p. la chiesa, piu lontano da Dio, 138a

Presumption Cut short p., it will aspire, 14b; devil, ready to put out men's eyes, 103b; Huntsmen push into brambles, 724b; sign of p., imagine ourselves able to handle hot coals, 724b

Presumptuous We are so p., 14a

Pretend To know how to dissemble, knowledge of kings, 265b

Pretending Tho who play at being angels, 20a

Prevent the time, days are full of danger, 901b

Prevention P. is better than cure, 724b

Prey in a convert mourns to lose a p., 164b; Where stronger on the weaker p., 12b

Price A man who knows p. of everything, 237b; Out of season, out of p., 870b

Prick Folly it is to spurn against a p., 368a

Pride about beauty, 54a; Arrogance and boldness, belong to those accursed of God, 724b; arouse Thy indignation by our p., 450b; beware even of least spice of p., 725a; broken in angels' p., 19b; But take away our p., 726a; goeth before, shame cometh after, 725a; great obstacle to faith, proud spirit, 146b; human mind, prone to p., 713b; humble p. of earth, 40b; Is there anything in history more notorious than p. of Romans?, 779b; joy and revenge of ruined p., 298a; lack of submission to God, 818a; Living on p. is windy diet, 725b; may your wisdom be without p., 11b; My p. struck out new sparkles of her own, 219a; Nothing wears like p., 726a; P. and vainglory, pack you hance, 764b; P., envy, avarice, these are the sparks, 725a; P. is the cause of alle woe, 725a; Profaned with ritual p. and state, 543a; Professions of humility, very essence of p., 452a; purple p. that laces crimson curtains of thy bed, 623a; ruled my will, 725b; secret desire to breathe different atmosphere, 726a; strives for perverse excellence, 725a; Such aim at heaven was p., 470a; that dead, silent p., 725b; The envy, malice, and p., 411a; the never failing vice of fools, 725b; The wings of swelling p., 725b; thousand objections to sin of p., 726a; Vanity, offspring of p., 892b; various kinds

of p., 725b; When haughty power mounts high, 153b; will have a fall, 725a

Priest ambassador of divine Redeemer, 730a; as pure as one who stands in heaven, 729a; assumes role of judge and doctor, 204b; Christ, High P. and Guardian of our souls, 484b; Christian p., within a Christian fane, 730a; clad in sacred vestments, Christ's vicegerent, 728a; consecrates and sanctifies, 727a; dedicated p., 78b; duty of p. to offer sacrifice, bless, govern, preach, baptize, 727a; end of p., greatest glory of God, 728b; eternal and heavenly High P., Jesus Christ, 368a; Fill up in Thy p. perfection, 68a; first he wrought, and afterward he taught, 316b; forbidden to exercise secular government, 188b; For if a p. be foul, on whom we trust, 316b; gird yourself with the cincture of chastity, 726b; Happy the p. who loves his pastor's lot, 660b; has primacy of Abel, power of Peter, unction of Christ, 728a; He is a P. after order of Melchizedek, 484b; He is both King and P., 176b; He is Mediator, P., Sacrifice, 307b; He is our true and eternal High P., 486a; If a p. marry, he shall be removed, 150a; must offer something, 484b; new P., not of law but above law, universal Advocate, 485a; no one else there but p. and parson, 745b; not just pious bachelor, 151a; O great High P., our true Pontiff, 586b; ought to be in no place where Master would not go, 728a; power to celebrate mass for the living and dead, 727b; p. and deacon, ordained by one bishop, 647b; P. and Victim are one and the same, 484b; p. God's, not martyrs', 308a; p. is wedded to Savior's work, 151a; p.'s hands handle Word of Life, 729a; real distinction of rank between p. and bishop, 647b; Receive the Holy Ghost, 727b; shall not undertake cares of this world, 188b; should give example to others of righteous life, 728a; so called from sacrificing, 727a; spot upon an alb, cannot be hid, 730a; *Thou are a P. for ever,* 307a; twice married cannot become p., 188b; who has duly received jurisdiction, 668b

Priesthood angel himself has no such dignity, 729b; *a royal p., holy multitude,* 496a, 517b; belongs to our office to reprove for sin, 178a; besides p., there are other orders, 648a; *Bestow dignity of p. upon these Thy servants,* 726b; BVM, honor of worthy p., 100b; By baptism, Christians participate in p. of Christ, 731a; conferred on designated men, 730b; confirmation and p. of laity, 207a; does not emanate from Christian community, 730a; Dread office this, 729b; in New Testament, visible and external p., 648a; no other p. apart from that one p., 133b; not transmitted by heredity, 730a; one altar, one p., 692b; Only to apostles, and their successors, granted power of p., 730a; Paraclete Himself, instituted this order, 728b; power of consecrating and offering Body, 648a; p. and desire for purity, 745a; p. and shedding of blood, 104a; p. of chastity, 639b; priestly power has

to render account for kings, 174a; requires a great soul, 729a; Sacrifice and p., conjoined, 729b; Spirit common to all presbyterate, 241a; spiritual power for dispensing sacraments, 729a; there is in Church, new, visible p., 729b; we do not permit laity to perform any offices of p., 728b; *You are a chosen race, royal p.*, 730b
Priestly all reborn in Christ, royal and p. race, 730b; body, p. and royal, 647b; first striving of p. soul, 728b; high p. Spirit, 67a; p. office, holds rank of heavenly things, 728b; What is the people itself, but p.?, 730b
Priests A city on a hill, 730a; after model of council of apostles, 433a; all Christians p., because members of one Priest, 730b; all p. not of equal jurisdiction, 433b; alone have power to celebrate and consecrate body, 597b; bishop is chief of p., 69a; bishops and presbyters, specially called p. in Church, 730b; bishops' companions and helpers, 726b; Bishops, p., deacons, must remain unmarried, 150a; bishops superior to p., 69a; bound by unbreakable law to subdue hearts, 150a; By divine institution, hierarchy consists of bishops, p., ministers, 190a; By Holy Orders p. are made, 788a; by preaching, build up the house, 727b; Clerics ought to lead holier life than lay people, 728b; consecrated as bishops' coadjutors, 727b; do not possess plenitude of priestly office, 205b; earthly angels in this life, 729b; Great is this mystery, great the dignity of p., 597b; have common dignity, not uniform rank, 433a; have received authority God has not given to angels, 729a; have task of perpetual prayer, 174b; hearts of faithful ought to be submitted to p., 174b; high p. allotted his proper ministrations, 433a; I call them My Christs, 729a; I demand purity in My ministers, 729b; let us honor the presbyters, 773b; Let your doctrine be spiritual medicine for people of God, 727b; like strings of a lyre, in harmony with bishop, 726a; minister the word of truth, 727a; offer Thee gifts and spiritual sacrifices, 727a; ordained by bishop, 69a; proclaim gospel of kingdom, 727a; purple makes princes, not p., 173a; Receive power to offer sacrifice to God, 727b; renew people through laver of regeneration, 727a; represent person of Jesus Christ before people, 730a; should wear Roman collar, 190a; source from which schisms have arisen, God's p. not obeyed, 799b; stand blameless before holy altar, 727a; They are My anointed ones, 729a; *They will be p. of God and Christ*, 730b; to p., their proper place has been assigned, 433a; true princes of the Church, 177a; upon earth, dispense things which are in heaven, 729a; with undivided mind obey bishop and p., 194b
Primacy a p. is given to Peter, 693a; bulwark, corner-stone, of Catholicism, 696b; by divine right, Peter has perpetual line of successors in p., 696b; care of whole Church, committed to blessed Peter, 700a; He builds his Church upon one, 693a; most holy church

of Rome holds leadership over churches, 695a; office of Peter, both directing power and supreme authority, 694b; Peter received in special way, keys and p. of judicial power, 677b; p. of the Apostolic See, 699a; Roman Church enjoys supreme p., 705b; *thou art Peter, and upon this rock I will build my Church*, 693a; which Peter bore among disciples, 676a
Primate bishop of apostolic see and p. of all priests, 700a
Prime O Lord, Who hast brought us to beginning of this day, 731a
Prince authority of law, 508a; difference between p. and a tyrant, 508a; image of almighty God, 3a; minister of public utility, 508a; p. is minister of priestly power, 177a; P. to her throne, 40a; said to be freed from bonds of law, to do justice, 508a; set in authority, not through knowledge of laws, 405a; Shepherd, P., with glad behavior, 74b; takes thought for all, 173b; that which pleases the p., 194a; They who possess the p., possess the laws, 714a; worthy of ruler, to acknowledge that he is bound by laws, 508a
Princely Thy Mother came From p. race, 483a
Princes Church's p., 28a; constituted p. by Thy dispostion, 507a; first duty of p., to love subjects as sons, 509a; Lift up, ye p. of the sky, 36b; Oft casteth mighty p. from their throne, 350b; p. and kings chosen, to coerce people from evil through fear, 404a; p. and subjects serve one another, 173b; P. are bound by their own laws, 528b; purple makes p., not priests, 173a; ruled by love of ruling, 173b; should not be controlled by subjects, 2b; their power from God, through consent of human wills, 180b
Princess Live, rosy p., live, 40b
Principalities one of nine orders of angels, 18b
Principates two p., 177b
Principi Quod p. placuit, legis habet vigorem, 533b
Principis Indignatio p. mors est, 248a
Principle always respectable, 731b; In contemplation, P. is sought, 212a; Man, obliged to live on p., 757a; truth, demonstrated by truth that is a first p., 883b; What is self-evident is like first p., 512b
Principles cannot be rigorously demonstrated, 731a; expel error by light of first p., 27a; p. and doctrines contrasted, 271b; p. with times, 731b; Truths and p. are divine, 884b; unproved first p. and bigotry, 64b; using correctly p., 731b
Printing scourge for sins of learned, 731b
Prioress There was also a nonne, a p., 640b
Prison All that we know who lie in gaol, 731b; body might be said to be p., 105a; Christ hath burst His p., 285b; escape from p. of self-hood, 889a; grave or p. Illumed by one patriot name, 663a; my soul in p. light, 85a; Now let the golden p. ope its gates, 743b; p. for unbelief, p. of troubled conscience, 473a
Prisoner love's patient P., 78b

Prison-house lead captive from the p., 8a
Prisons He destroyed p. of hell, overthrew devil, 400b
Privilege Legitimate marriage, dissolved by Pauline p., 580a; p. of BVM to become Mother of God, 81a; special p. to avoid all sins, 86b
Privileges Honors and p., worth nothing, 445a; may be acquired by custom, 732a; must benefit only Catholic faith, 430b; p. of churches, fixed by decrees of Nicaea, 699b; P., laws applying to individuals, 524b
Priviligium P. Fori, 190b
Prize Heaven claims right, bears p. away, 40b; p., immortality and eternal life, 43a
Prizes P. would be for legs of slowest pace, 747a
Probability p. for, doubt against, 276a
Probationer young p., And candidate of heav'n, 638b
Problem p. play means, 276b
Proceeding From both p. as from one, 439a
Procession term p. within Blessed Trinity, 370b; twofold going forth of God, 224b
Proclus, 678b
Procrastination By and by never comes, 732a; Long demurs breed new delays, 255a; Works adjourned have many stays, 645b
Procreation crown of marriage, chastity of p., 732a; dangerous when order perverted, 66a; Marriage, one purpose of procreating children, 575b; profitable to commonwealth, 66a
Procreative deliberative frustration of p. act, 66a
Prodesse inesse potuit, non prodesse, 50b
Prodigal p. of ease, 11b
Prodigious P. actions, 65b
Producers p. and right of association, 38b
Profanation Blessed Sacrament, preserved from p., 70b
Profane p. person with regard to household of God, 172a
Profession p. of faith openly, 147a
Proficiency high degree of p. leads to atrophy, 732a
Profit By right he shall no p. take, 106a; make p. out of need of another, condemned, 732b; What would Bible p. without grace?, 62a
Profitable give us those things which are p. for us, 732a
Profits labor on that by which one p. little, 732a
Profundity p. of Scriptures marvelous, 60b
Progress active life means p., 5a; Catholic Church has urged on intellectual p., 139a; Complacency is one obstacle to p., 201a; definition of man, to get on in this world, 571b; Discontent is first step in p. of man, 264b; Everything that happens in history, serves p. of Church, 733a; indicates direction, 732b; Is then religion incapable of p.?, 271a; meaningless, unless some standard, 732b; must go from easier to more difficult, 848a; p. truly such, if it knows how to make capital out of experience, 733a; properly understood, has legitimate meaning, 732b; realization of utopias, 732b; Roman pontiff ought to

come to terms with p., 732b; sacred word, 732b; time expression of eternal plan, 186b; when thing grows and remains itself, 271a; world ceasing to believe in inevitability of p., 316a; worship of mere p., 306a

Progressive Nobody can be p. without being infallible, 732b

Prohibition Forbid us thing, 733a

Proletarian one who owns nothing but power to labor, 735a

Proletarians in all countries there have been p., 735a

Proletariat Defence of p. and class hatred, 187b; In dirt and darkness hundreds stink content, 733a

Prometheus Nor is P.' vulture half so fell, 9a

Promise I read a p. there, 733a; unfailing reward of Thy p., 242a

Promised This is the gateway to the p. land, 634a

Promises faith of p., 13a; God's p., 212b; run toward goal of Thy p., 808b; Thy p. which surpass all, 560b

Promulgated Laws instituted, when they are p., 530a

Pronounce We p., declare and define, 41b

Proof Absolute p. can never be furnished by logic of words, 733a; demonstration not always able command assent, 30b; faith would have no merit if reason provided p., 331a; ultimate assumptions incapable of p., 39a

Proofs Metaphysical p. of God, 376b; p. from reason and from faith, 326a

Propaganda all art is p., 34a

Properties by communication of p., 482a

Property all things for common use of all men, 733b; beginning of usurpation, 734a; by customary law, this said to be mine, 734a; by law of nature, all things common p., 734a; Christian charity recognizes no p., 156a; Christian who cannot trust Christian with p., 807b; Church has right to acquire p., 734a; Church p. under care of bishop, 67b; earth common to all men, 733b; Every man has right to possess p. as his own, 734b; idea of p. today, 735a; let everything be common p., 615b; motive of work, to obtain p., 734b; owning of private p., 734b; p. and subjection to God, 734a; p. of Church belongs to pope, as principal dispenser, 734a; p. rights defended by associations, 38b; Redistributions of p., 199a; right of p. should remain inviolate, 734a; rights of private p., 140a; right to possess private p., derived from nature, not man, 858a; Roman pontiff, supreme dispenser of all Church p., 735a; saint, must only use what he himself needs, 794b; social order which denies natural right to p., 735a; so called from possessing rightly, 733b; That dog is mine, 734a; unbelief not incompatible with p., 734a; We are God's p. by creation, 225b; Your jurisdiction over criminal cases, not over p., 176b

Prophecies not what make us Christians, 233a; p. and Catholic Church, 117a

Prophecy all the past, read true, is p., 659a; best interpretation of p., is history of its fulfilment,

735a; His p. has fulfilled itself, 30a

Prophet not everyone who speaks in spirit, is a p., 735b; That which the p.-king of old, 230a; The p. ill sustains his holy call, 735b

Prophets appointed by God, 68b; foreshadowed BVM, 90b; for thee, p. did proclaim, 81b; God freely gives grace to p., 67b; ministry of p. and teachers, 67a; of Whom p. won Mystic visions, 8b; reading of p. and Gospel, 441a

Propitiates bishop p.s God's countenance, 67a

Propitiation Christ, p. for our sins, 43b; sacrifice of p. for common peace, 307b

Proponit Homo p., sed Deus disponit, 397a

Proportion beauty consists in due p., 54b; due p. and senses, 54b; People in ignoble circumstances, sense of p., 735b; p. and agreement make beauty, 54b; Truth lies in p., 43b

Proposes Man p., but God disposes, 397a

Prose fact man a poisoner, nothing against his p., 735b; not poetry, p. run mad, 690b; p. of Christianity, without poetry, 437a; unlearning world's poetry, attaining to its p., 690b; used poetry as medium for p., 109b

Proselytiser Catholic as p., 220b

Proskynesis, 795b

Prosper do Thou p., support, encompass them, 416b; Why do sinners' ways p.?, 382a;

Prosperity Better God beaten, than world in p., 492b; In adversity I desire p., 735b; Let no one trust a blind p., 351a; p. of some men, but very short summer day, 735b; remember it when past, 603a; There is woe in the p. of this world, 735b; There's danger in p., 602b; To love God in sugar, 344a

Prostrate P. at her Creator's feet, 94b; P. upon that holy ground, 77b

Protect stretch forth right hand of Thy majesty to p. us, 736b

Protection all flee to thee for p., 100b; anyone who hastened For shelter to BVM, 87b; any who fled to p. of BVM, 89b; defended by Thy p., 736b; honorable p. of BVM, 87b; our times, peaceful under Thy p., 665b; p. of angels' glory, 21a; p. of BVM, as armor, 87a; Safe beneath thy wing this day, 83b; We sinners crave thy sure p., 97b

Protection of Our Lady, Feast of, 87b

Protector A Helper and a P. He has become to me, 491a; God, P. of life, 66b; if the Lord be our p. and helper, 881b; O God, p. of all that trust in Thee, 736b

Protestant All churches ultimately derive from great Church, mother Church, 738a; argue pope was a Prodesan, 31a; for P., religion is a detail, 166a; I pray thee P. bear with me, 115b; P. church and theology reposes on two principles, 737b; P. churches depend on Roman Church, 738a; P. Church would lose raison d'être, if Catholic Church ceased to exist, 738a; p. countries and devotion to Mary, 101b; P. concept of invisible Church, 137b; P. protests against Catholic ornament, 32b; who still

preserves Protestantism, 738a; world in England today, 738a

Protestant Episcopal P. Church in Maryland, 585b

Protestantism absurdity of having three or four religions, 737b; active principle without doctrine, 737a; aiming at overthrow of pope, 737b; All would be happy at cheapest rate, 736b; Catholic history contains more of P., 32b; changed shape from valley to next, 737b; collection of sects, 116b; defined as exaggerated development of personal independence, 737b; doctrine without active principle, 737a; dreariest of possible religions, 24a; England is the head of P., 737a; English P., religion of throne, 23b; followers equally contented with anything else, 122a; its facts are fiction, 737a; its faith is prejudice, 737a; its formalism, 115b; its philosophy is theory, 737a; kind of parasite living upon Church, 738b; negation of divine authority of Church, 737b; never can be Christianity professed by all, 165b; no universal agreement as to what Scripture teaches, 737a; popular p., in opposition to Catholics, 737a; portion of divine system, instead of whole, 146a; Pure P., rejection of every non-spiritual element in religion, 738b; real P., assembly of elect, 116a; soul cannot be eternally satisfied with singing of hymns, 737b; viewed in its Catholic aspect, 737a

Protestants And all confess themselves are fallible, 737a; amongst equals lies no last appeal, 737a; condemn Catholic attitude towards religion, 115b; deny unity of faith and Church, 145a; hold Catholics put Mary in place of Christ, 101b; keep exhibition of faith for high days, 115b; never so real as when solemn, 116a; No union they pretend, but in non-popery, 770a; P. are Catholics gone wrong, 738a; said, P. often better than creed, 116a

Prothesis, Prayer of, 590b

Protomartyr Dared the deacon p. Earthly life for heaven, 847a; How her great p. fell, 582a

Protoplast earliest tradition of the, 372a

Prototypes honor due to them, done to, p., 459a

Proud all the p. shall be, 281a; Be not p. thy own works, 451a; bringing age upon the p., 386b; Every cock is p. on his own dunghill, 725a; God hateth p. and obstinate mind, 190a; I am very p. of my religion, 27b; O God, Who dost resist the p., 450b; p. ones of world come, 121a; Thus unlamented pass the p. away, 725b; When a p. man thinks he is humble, 726a; Yes, I am p., 714a

Prouder To kill all that he meeteth p. than he, 725a

Prove Defend faith, not p. it to hilt, 26b; forms by themselves, p. nothing, 549b; not p. what is of faith, except authority, 331b; P. thy friend ere thou have need, 358b; without assumptions no one can p. anything, 27a

Proved God p., by blindness of those who seek Him not, 376b; you p. her, yet she stands, 269b

Proveth The end p. everything, 395a

Providence All events take place in order of P., 373b; angels execute plan of p., 19b; BVM, treasury of His p., 79b; disposeth all things in their places, 153a; fountain of P., 153a; God's universal p., 21a; guides the world, 21b; His p. is not general merely, but particular and personal, 389b; If p. does not preside over human affairs, no point in religion, 754a; incarnation, idea of P. capitalized, 469a; live a rent-charge on His p., 11b; nature, female name we give to p., 634a; never repeats an effect, 6a; no one so uncivilized, who does not understand there is some P., 388b; O God, Whose p. never fails, 732a; P. and chance, 153a; p. and fate, 389a; p., and reward of good and bad, 389a; P. is the divine type itself, 389a; P. is the very divine reason itself, 389a; p. of God in contradictions, 216a; so economical, so generous!, 6a; why is it people so dispraise God's p., 388b; wont to reform depraved manners, 388b

Prudence Advisement is good before the deed, 739a; application of right reason to moral practice, 739a; come and teach us way of p., 8a; Few pay attention to p. because few possess it, 738b; great wisdom not to be rash in our doings, 739a; in baptism we receive spirit of p., 50a; kinds of knowledge, *intelligence, science, wisdom, p.,* 512b; knowledge of what is to be sought and avoided, 738b; No man is p. who is ignorant of God, 738b; The first source of duty is p., 738b; virtue of those who command, 739a

Psalm all written therein, meant to be mirror for us, 739a; If the p. prays, do you too pray, 266a, 739a; I may chant the p. and pray, 739a

Psalmody Chant we the holy p. of David, 895b; clergy have duty of p., 266a; p. and prayers said at stated hours, 266a;

Psalms all written therein, meant to be mirror, 266a; pray to God with p. and hymns, 716b

Psyche My P., bluer far are thine, 322b

Psychic p. itself belongs to domain of ontological, 739b

Psychoanalysis p. and confession, 739b; p. and confessional box, 739b

Psychoanalyst p. and the unconscious, 739a

Psychological those who accentuate opposition between metaphysical and p., 739b

Psychology Man is a microcosm, 739b

Public conditions of p. career, often misunderstood, 499b; one thing p. dislikes, novelty, 638b; p. authority and economic order, 287b; p. authority, hallowed to Christians, 46b; P. was death, 286b; P. welfare consists in sanctity of life, 435b; prince, minister of p. utility, 508a; *To* place and power, all p. spirit tends, 691b

Publications Church has right to censor, 151b

Puddings Hungry dogs will eat dirty p., 273a

Puer Et nobis P. natus est, 168b

Pugiles p. fidei, 275b

Pulp The p. so bitter, shall taste the rind?, 724b

Pulpit Be lion in p., lamb in confessional, 669b

Pulses The p. of the night, 170b

Pun you cannot pretend you have made a p., 454a

Punctuality P. is the thief of time, 522a, 739b

Punish authority of Church to p., 117b, 740b; Church cannot p. unbelief in those outside, 178b; God does not p. people for what they would have done, 860b; Lord, swift to pardon, slow to p., 821b; punish unbelief of those who have received faith, 178b

Punished When the bad are p., 740a

Punishes all can feel the God that smites, 425b

Punishment administer due p. after faults have been committed, 740b; body under p. and liable to death, 105a; Christ's passion, liberates from debt of p., 44a; doctrine of eternal p., 427b; Every age, its appropriate measure of discipline, 750a; excommunication and p., proportioned to fault, 317b; fault, evil we perform, p., evil we undergo, 341a; if every sin were now visited with manifest p., 740a; let him undergo corporal p., 317b; no such thing as humane p., 740b; O God, ever merciful and sparing of p., 500b; pain of p. without fruit of penitence, 426a; place of p. for sins, 500a; p. is the surgeon's knife, 740a; reason why everlasting p. appears hard and unjust, 750a; satisfaction for sins as to their temporal p., 669a; temporal p. for sins, 417a, 669b; The sword of heaven is not in haste to smite, 740b; Too late they believe in eternal p., 426a

Punishments by sinning I have deserved p., 216b

Purchase Ah, well! it is a p. and a prize, 304b

Pure A p. heart penetrates heaven and hell, 745b; O most p. Mary, 82a; serve Thee with a p. mind, 218b; to the p. all things are p., 209b; Yes—for a spirit, p. as hers, 745b

Purer BVM, p. than sun's splendor, 80a

Purest O p. of creatures! sweet Mother!, 461b

Purgatorial before judgment, p. fire for certain minor sins, 742a; question whether faithful are saved by sort of p. fire, 741a

Purgatory And thou shalt see those who in fire refrain, 742a; amelioration of sentence, 308a; Angels of p., receive from me, 743b; baptism at entrance of Paradise, 741a; Catholic Church has taught, there is a p., 743a; Church suffering, 121b; comes back in *bourgeois* disguise, 744a; different from hell, 741a; divine fire acts on souls, 743a; doctrine of p., supported by convictions of mankind, 744a; Ere Mercy weeps them out again, 20a; for relief from punishments, suffrages of faithful avail, 742b; freed from purging fire, 77a; frontier penance-place, 243a; guilt discharged in p., 417b; helped towards kingdom of heaven by almsgiving, 741b; Help, Lord, the souls which Thou hast made, 743b; he who is found Looking behind him, 742b; holy house of toll, 243a; If p. is a species of hell, 743a; In prison for the debt unpaid, 243a; kind of universal perpetual and progressive, p., 744a; lower than the cleansing flame, 411a; Nor is

aught suffered outside custom's scope, 742b; Now let the golden prison ope its gates, 743b; paradise of little men and p. of great, 296a; Pray for the holy souls that burn, 743a; purging fire cleansed stains, 741a; purification after death, 302b; Reformation began with revolt against p., 744a; Safe, and yet saved by fire, 243b; saved by fire, 742a; souls In prison, for the debt unpaid, 743b; souls purified by punishments of p., 742b; souls remain in places specially reserved, 246b, 741b; soul undergoes in hades some compensatory discipline, 740b; sound doctrine concerning p., 743a; temporal punishment after death, 741b; that golden palace bright, 243a; that second realm, which purifies, 742a; The fire has eaten out all blot and stain, 243a; These penal fires among, 743b

Purge P. we out the ancient leaven, 286a

Purges Christ p. friends of all that is not of Him, 564a

Purification in Church, certain things need p., 672b; Joy! joy! the mother comes, 744b; Mary, bringeth the glorious King of the new light, 744b; p. after death, 302b; p. of soul in baptism, 51b

Purified hearts have to be p. to see beauty, 54a; serve Him with p. minds, 7b; with p. mental gaze, 5a

Purifies God p. hearts of those who confess, 203a

Purify P. our consciences, O Lord, 208a; p. us from our secret vices, 218b

Puritan frowning on dances, 745a; pours righteous indignation into wrong things, 744b

Puritanism paralysis, which stiffens into Stoicism, 745a; P. was not made in Geneva, 745a; retained belief in witchcraft, 744b

Puritans A numerous host of dreaming saints succeed, 744b; killed St. George but carefully preserved dragon, 745a; Nothing to build, and all things to destroy, 744b

Purity All lusters in one p., 97a; Every soul quickened by Holy Ghost, elevated by His p., 438b; He was born of her in her purity, 460a; I demand p. in My ministers, 729b; Of p. the spotless shrine, 83b; prepares soul for love, 745b; P. of soul cannot be lost, without consent, 745a; special gift of p. conferred on BVM, 86a; To sow the seeds of perfect p., 745a; with p. unstained, found Mother of our Savior, 632a

Purple covered with derisive p., 400a; defilement of imperial p., 195a; makes princes, not priests, 173a; p. pride that laces crimson curtains of thy bed, 623a

Purpose But natheless his p. held he still, 745b; no activity is without p., 373b

Purse Do ye after him That beareth the p., 617a; yet I lost my p., 745b

Purses Light gain makes heavy p., 712b

Purse-sick He is p., 269a

Pusillanimity This fault of p. and timorous mind, 324a

Putativum invalid marriage, said to be putative (*p.*), 579a

Pyramids Where high the tombs of

royal Egypt heave, 643b; Whose might hath built the P., 516b

Pyrenees Truth on one side of P., 885b

Pyre Melt in one vast funeral p., 281b

Q

Quack empty words of boastful, lying q., 268b

Quando Moria pur q. vuol, 250a

Quanti Sunt tanti q. et denotamur, 163a

Quake she gan to q., 37b

Quarrel Come together by the ears, 746a; old Anglo-American q., 16a

Quarreling Not to love contention, 746a

Quasimodo As q. *geniti*, and gentlemen each, 352b

Queen BVM, venerated as Q. of heaven and earth, 92b; Catholicism, sum of all religions and q., 147a; Hail, holy Q., Mother of mercy, 95b; Maiden and Mother and Q., 97a; maidmonth's Q.!, 600a; Q. of men, 40b; Q. of purity divine, 96b; Q. of sorrows, 93a; Q. of Virgins, 86a; Thou Q. of high estate, 97b

Queens Cease, then, O q., who earthly crowns do wear, 96b, 746a

Queenship q. of BVM maternal, beneficent, 98a

Questions Q. are never indiscreet, 746b

Qui Q. me amat; amat et canem meum, 273a

Quia Q. amore langueo, 100a; With the q., stay content, 395a, 513a

Quick Q. as a bee, 746b

Quickened q. in the spirit, 43b

Quid Q. est enim fides, 325a; Q. *retribuam Domino*, 595a

Quidquid Q. fit contra conscientiam, 208a

Quiet He is as q. as a lamb, 746b; Then comes the q. of Christ to me, 213b

Quill pen, Made of q. from angel's wing, 667a

Quixote, Don a lean and foolish knight, 152b

Quod Q. principi placuit, legis habet vigorem, 533b

R

Race Church and differences of r., 138a; distinctions among Catholics, because of r., 265a; Nationality has nothing to do with r., 632a; *You are a chosen r., royal priesthood*, 730b; Were cripples made judges of the r., 747a

Race, Human social by nature, unsocial by corruption, 449a

Races Ireland has conquered r., 632a

Racism confine within single race, God, 747a

Rack In old days the r., not the press, 496b; Torture us, r. us, condemn us, 851a

Racked r. with your torments, 479b

Racks Reck not of r., their torments but toys, 584a

Radiance that enlighteneth the mind, 98b

Radix R. malorum est cupiditas, 48b

Rage I wrestle not with r., 22b; r. man or devil never so much, 141b

Rags One flaunts in r., 191b

Raiment beautiful r., blood of mar-

tyrs, 581b; he who bestows raiment on poor, 13a

Rain When April r. had laughed the land, 29b; When r. raineth and the goose winketh, 403a

Rainbow A mist of r. dyes, 453b; An arch of God's great temple fair, 747b; The jeweled autograph of the Most High, 747b

Raise He will know from what place to r. me up, 769a

Raised r. by thy Savior, 10b

Rampart BVM, unassailable r., 87a

Ramparts r. of a Godhead's dwelling, 13b

R_nk Dost thou wish to enjoy the first r.?, 747b; not ecclesiastical r. that makes man Christian, 747b

Ransom I receive Thee, R. of my soul, 520a; this world's r., 230b

Ransomer Jesus, the R. of man, 167a

Raphael, Saint, 486b

Rapt away from bodily senses, 211a; perfect soul, r. by contemplation, 213a

Rapture R., is irresistible, 288b; union, r., transport, all one, 288b

Rash great wisdom not to be r. in our doings, 739a; r. speech and lying, 747b

Rat If they smell a r., 747b

Ratio, 749a; *Oris r.*, 717b; *Summa r. est quae pro religione facit*, 755b

Ratiocinatio, 749a

Ratiocinative subtle r. power, divine gift, 270a

Rational God especially loves r. creatures, 384a; men whose will runs ahead of r. insight, 750b; r. grounds for their religious belief, 332a; two classes of men who can be called r., 395a; Unbelievers call themselves r., 748a

Rationalism fallacy of Victorian r., 160a; fundamental doctrine of r., 748a; heirs of r. and aceticism, 37a; owes much of its success to folly of Christians, 748a; to accept revelation and then to explain it away, 748a

Rationalist makes himself his own center, 748a

Rationalists r. and problem of Christ, 483b

Ratione Intervention r. *peccati*, 178a

Ratum valid marriage, said to be ratified (r.), 578b

Raven Both r. and ape think their own young fairest, 160b; The r.'s house is built with reeds, 748b

Raw crude things in all cause wind, 263a

Ray every r. of light and heat, 20a; Shed Thou within our hearts Thy r., 369a

Reactionary revolutionary seeks to satisfy himself he also r., 199b

Read Make effort to understand whatever you r., 848a; Men may be r., as well as books, 571a; safe thing, r. only Catholic books, 545a; Take and r., take and r., 748b

Reading fancy love of r. real study, 848b; If thou wouldst profit by thy r., 748b; much r. and conversation, 218a; Seek in r. and thou shalt find in meditation, 213b

Real Only r. people, who have never existed, 343b

Realism balance between r. and symbolism, 34b; no r. like insatiable r. of love, 749a; simply romanticism that has lost its reason, 748b

Realists Women are the only r., 749a

Realities patriotism, religion, money, three great r., 476a

Reality God alone measures r. by what He is, 867a; God, summit of all r., 762b; Mere repetition does not prove r., 611a

Realm anguish of king over ruined r., 24b

Realms He takes no earthly r. away, 298b

Reap Such as ye have sown must ye needs r., 770a

Reaper O R. of ruth, 834a

Reason all truths not from r., 332a; argument from authority based on r., 30b; difference between discursive r. and intuition, 515a; Drunkenness is ruin of r., 280a; enlighten r. of unbeliever, 27a; exalted by democratic people, 16b; faith presupposes r., as grace presupposes nature, 376a; faith would have no merit if r. provided proof, 331a; feast of r., and flow of soul, 343a; grace believes, r. does but opine, 332a; heart sometimes finds out things r. cannot, 557b; Human r., not sole arbiter of truth and falsehood, 749b; If we submit everything to r., religion will have nothing mysterious, 756a; implanted in minds, reveals there is one God, 392b; in man, like God in world, 749a; In order thus to r. back to love, 564a; in whom light of r. is darkened, 23a; intellect, most superficial of our faculties, 324a; intrinsic r., criterion of truth, 16b; Life, not long enough for religion of inferences, 332a; magnificence of faith compared with light of r.?, 332b; Make r. guide, let folly be a stranger, 901b; man excels all animals by his r., 569b; Man is but a thinking reed, 866a; not all men can give a r., 749b; not ultimate standard of faith, 332a; one of three roads to belief, 57b; practical r., concerned with practical matters, 528b; principles of r., foundations of philosophy, 863b; r. and freewill, 357a; r. and reasoning, 749h; r. and religion, 332a; reason and sense, 54b; R. is one thing and faith another, 332a; R. is the vision of the mind, 749a; Right r. leads mind to Catholic faith, 332a; role of r. to prove foundations of faith, 750a; some people can be converted by r., 147b; spark of r. cannot be extinguished, 607a; subserves faith, 863a; The feast of r., 279a; Two excesses, r. excluded, only r. allowed, 749b; unless I believe, I should not understand, 331b; weak, if dependent on authority, 45b; well known how highly Church regards human r., 750a; whole universe, governed by divine r., 526a

Reasonable no r. nature, unless endued with freewill, 357a

Reasoned old may not be outreasoned, 11b

Reasoning Brothers! spare r., 26b; by stages I passed from bodies to r. power, 511a; Clearness in argument, not indispensable to r., 750b; man is *not* a r. animal, 750b; process of r., complete in itself, and independent, 750b

Reasons eternal r. of all things of unreason and time, 372b; Every one who r., his own center, 733a; heart has its r., 343b, 423a; We are easily persuaded by r. we discover, 674a

Rebaptism of older children forbidden, 52b

Rebel Of these the false Achitophel was first, 751a

Rebellion despising authority, r. against God's will, 46b

Rebellious to keep the r. under one's hand, 568b

Rebels God's and king's r. have same good cause, 432a; Kings can forgive, if r. can but sue, 349b; R. in Cork are patriots at Madrid, 751a

Rebirth spiritual r. through Christ's death, 43b

Reborn all r. in Christ, royal and priestly race, 730b; Thy people about to be r., 441b

Rebuke Never r. anyone but with discretion, 751a

Rebuked r. publicly before all, 317a

Receive It is better to want less than to r. more, 361a; r. and bless these gifts, these offerings, 591b; R. the Holy Ghost, 69a, 242a, 648a, 693a, 727b

Receivers Where be no r., there be no thieves, 864b

Receives from us He r. what He first gave, 366b

Reckon Reckoners without host, must r. twice, 447b

Reckoning Even r. maketh long friends, 664b

Recollection With deep affection and r., 58b

Recompense Christ offered r. for sin of all, 44a; Lord gave to each different r., 442a

Reconcile Christ's passion r.'s us with God, 44a

Reconciled at one, without amends, 22b; You have offended, but still can be r., 764a

Reconcilement, r. sweet, 305a

Reconciliation atonement and man's r. with God, 44a; embraced into unity of Christ's Church, 141a; ministry of r. in word and deed, 68b; we advise r. with Church of Rome, 770b

Reconciling r. of soul, greater than r. of east to west, 751a; thy r. aid, 98b

Recreation If you have no need of r. for yourself, 751b

Recreations R. are not education, 290a

Recte R. novit vivere, 717a

Red spots are all r., rest is all grey, 296b

Redeem God chose to r. men by shame, 752b; greater act to restore, than to create, 752d; R. the nations of the earth, 166a; r. us by Thy outstretched arm, 8a

Redeemed God might have r. world by manifestation of glory, 752b; O God, Who has marvelously r. man, 752a; whole body of r., congregation and society of saints, 485a

Redeemer All glory, laud and honor To Thee, R., 652b; God, Creator and R. of all the faithful, 244b; Hail, Thou man's R., 36a; How the world's R. conquered, 230b; Jesus, Redeemer of mankind, 7b; Thine only-begotten Son as our R., 35b, 170a

Redeeming O the success of His r.!, 819b

Redemption Adam has returned to paradise, 229a; atonement, divine world-form of r., 44a; BVM associated with r. as co-operatrix, 92a; by eucharist we perceive fruit of r., 75a; Christ merited salvation

for all, 43b; Destined, for the world's r., 74a; Himself Shepherd, Pasturage, r.'s Price, 484a; His work on earth, 74b; must be applied in each case, 43b; O Jesu; our r.!, 491a; pride of man, rebuked through humility of God, 751b; redemption comes with Him, 8b; whose love Our ransom paid, 657b; yearly expectation of our r., 169b

Redemptive Christ's passion r. cause of salvation, 44a

Red Sea Egyptians drowned in R., 51b; Through the R. waters, 285b

Reed A little r. in hand of grace, 410b; Man is but a r., 570a, 866a

Re-establishment R. of all things in Christ, 166a

Refinement mingling of r. and brutality in adolescence, 6b

Reflux In flux and in r., 225a

Reform Nothing more suspicious in holy, desire to r., 437a; turn over new leaf, when you see no reason, 752b

Reformation A down-hill R. rolls apace, 736b; began with revolt against purgatory, 744a; corruption of morals, called for sweeping r., 753a; described as protest against power of pope, 737b; formidable enemy of Church, 3a; fratricidal schisms provoked by the R., 771a; movement against freedom of conscience, 210a; protest against impotence of pope, 737b

Reformed Church, not susceptible of being r. in doctrines, 129b; least deform'd, because reform'd the least, 23a; Not one R., can with another join, 770a

Reformers Both would be call'd r., 432a; cannot be trusted interpret Scripture, 62a; maintained Bible misunderstood, 62a

Refreshment place of r., light and peace, 592b; R. after pain, 243a

Refuge appeal not subterfuge, but r., 29a; BVM, r. of sinners, 85a, 98a; In Thy wounds, let me r. find, 75b; O God, our r. and strength, 753a; r. of Christians, 84b; r. terrible in strength, 86b; Thou haven of r., 100a

Refusal All price is my r., Love, 753a; him Who made the great r., 753a

Refuse more courage to r. than to be foolhardy, 753a

Refuting pleasure of r. weak arguments, 26b

Regal more than r. line, 296a

Regale dominium r., 405b

Regenerated r. in front of baptism, 51b

Regeneration atonement and man's r., 44a; Christ is sacrificed as our Pasch, 285a; effected by Holy Ghost, 50b; Souls newly born to life by Thee, 248a; washes away guilt of past, 52a; we who have put on new creature, 166b

Regenerations there are two r., 769a

Regent O R. of all rule, 882a

Regia by *lex r.*, people bestows upon prince all power, 533b

Regina R. mi, Spes infirmorum, 95a

Regio Cujus r., illius et religio, 180a

Regit Mos r. legem, 237a

Regna Qui r. dat caelestia, 489a

Regret How deeper than all longing is r.!, 763a; rather to feel

compunction, than know definition, 753b

Regulars professed regulars may not marry, 150b; those who have taken vows in an order, 761a

Reign Kings cannot r. unless their subjects give, 858a; Like good Aurelius let him r., 414b; raising man to endless r., 25b; r. in light!, 36b; to r. with Christ, 252b

Reigned *They r., but not by Me*, 507b

Reigning Where Thou art r., 19a

Rein Let my hands slip not the r.!, 201b

Reins Burn our r. and our heart, 159a

Rejoice always r., if we keep head raised, 159b; Let angelic choirs now r., 441b; R., O Virgin Mary, 24b, 88b; Rejoice, rejoice, Emmanuel, 8b; *R. thou barren that bearest not*, 129b

Rejoices In her Lord His Church r., 168a

Relatives all who are joined to me by friendship or blood, 753b; Many kins folk and few friends, 753b; Where now are his r. and friends?, 245a

Relativity nature often deceives, does not bow to her own laws, 754a

Relics good and useful to venerate r., 101b; honor paid to r., 796a; sacred r. and images, due a veneration, 928a

Relief BVM, r. for burdened, 84b

Religio Cujus regio, illius et r., 180a

Religion acts on the affections, 262b; All good comes simply and solely from r., 758a; always at root of every world movement, 758a; American invested r. in securities, 15b; as mere sentiment, mockery, 274a; as "opiate of the people," 199b; at all times more or less traditional, individual, institutional, 758b; at root of everything, 758a; can be made intelligible, 331a; *carpe diem r.*, 497b; chain of piety, from which r. received its name, 754a; Church, first tried to combine reason and r., 333a; civil ruler dabbling in r., 692a, 754a; enforcing of conscience in matters of r., dangerous, 354b; essence of all r., authority and obedience, 117b; essence of r., idea of moral Governor, 757a; existence of r., always involved theology, 864a; for sake of soul, that all r. exists, 754a; free exercise thereof, 184b; God gave men law, that they might turn it into liberties, 759a; God's demands are paramount, 116a; great central unifying force of culture, 760a; has interior acts, also external acts, 755a; I am very proud of my r., 27b; If conscience tells him certain r. is true, 758a; If r. were small enough for our intellects, 758a; If we submit everything to reason, r. will have nothing mysterious, 756a; Is then r. incapable of progress?, 271a; It is certainly no part of r. to compel r., 871a; Let r. bind us once more to one God, 754b; main determining element in culture, 186a; man can no more possess private r. than sun and moon, 759a; marriages dissolved for sake of r., 267b; meant to enforce natural code of morals, 622a; men must conform either politics to r. or r. to politics, 181a; must be dogmatic, 274a;

must not be identified with particular culture, 186b; next to r. is patriotism, 663b; no necessary mark of true r., that it is rational, 756a; no part of r., to compel r., 354a; no person shall be troubled for his r., 354b; not contrary to reason, 756a; object of r., that soul should serve God, 758b, 809a; one man's r. neither harms nor helps another man, 354a, 871a; only one absolutely true r., 146b, 148b; Our r. is wise and foolish, 233a; people's r. is ever a corrupt r., 757a; reason and r., 332a; r. and politics go together, 184b; r. and providence of God, 388b; r. and sanctity, contrasted, 755b; r. and sense of right and wrong, 118b; R. is not one department of life, 758a; R. is opiate of the people, 42b; R. is the key of history, 758a; R. is solution of problem of destiny, 757a; sanctity does not differ from r. essentially, 436a; so called, because by it we bind souls to God for divine worship, 754b; spirit and letter, 164a; spiritual loyalty, 537a; supremacy of conscience, essence of natural r., 118a; Theology, articulate r., 864a; 'The people must have a r.', 42b; True r., that by which soul is united to God, 754a; virtue by which men show God due worship and reverence, 755a; We cannot have ethics without r., 622a; When two do not agree about r., 758a; Who was ever consoled by small beer of literature, 756b; Wisdom precedes r. follows, 754a; wonderfully helpful to state, 758a; works dealing with r. must have *imprimatur*, 152a

Religione Summa ratio est quae pro r. facit, 755b

Religionists old r. tortured men for moral truth, 885a

Religions All r. have had doctrines, 274a; Catholicism, sum of all r. and queen, 147a; one principle all r. have, that there is a God, 754b

Religious absolute atheism, r. phenomenon, 42b; All r. traditions contain elements of truth, 148b; dangerous to hold faith as matter of the r. consciousness, 333a; development of r. life of man, 15a; diversity of r. profession, 183b; fatal mistake, r. to take place of secular clergy, 190a; final end proposed to r. orders, 762b; habit and tonsure contribute little, 761b; In r. society, members make profession of public vows, 762b; I pray r. intolerance may never take root in our lands, 473a; life of good r., ought to be eminent in all virtues, 761b; man who is r., is r. morning, noon, and night, 756a; many r. people are not saints, 755b; Men of r. tempers apt to hide themselves, 262b; no obstinacy like r. obstinacy, 644a; r. congregation, one in which only simple vows are taken, 762b; R. liberty, where coexistence of different religions admitted, 354b; r. life, or life of religion, 755a; r. man, only successful man, 850b; r. with simple vows, 761a; universal character of r. truth, 186b

Religious Life R. and works of perfection, 761a; Three stages to perfect friendship with God, 761a

Relinquish R. all hope, ye who enter here, 427a

Remaineth *Of that which r., give alms*, 157b

Remedies that bring salvation, 813a

Remedy become for us an everlasting r., 595b

Remember In the midst of misery to r. bliss, 603a; R. me, O Lord, in Thy kingdom, 595a

Remembrance How larger is r. than desire!, 763a; perfect r. with God and saints, 667a; What glory of r. fills, 38a

Remigius, Saint, 50b

Remission beseech Son to grant r. of evils, 98a; complete r. of sin, 308a; entire and perfect r. of sins, 668b; my Blood, shed for r. of sins, 592a; need not be despaired of, 668a; no r. of sins, outside Church, 126b, 821b; pardon for their sins, 244b; r. made, following confession of sin, 202a; r. of sins, voluntary and involuntary, 206a

Remit bishop has power to r. sins, 68b; Lord gave power to r. sins to Peter, 821b; ministers do not r. sin of their own authority, 668b

Remitted sins can not be r. without confession of amendment, 321a, 822a

Remorse A r. long and sore!, 254a; I wealthiest am when richest in r., 763a

Renaissance, 30a, 32b

Render if Thou shouldst r. to us what we deserve, 603b; *r. to Caesar*, 178b; *What shall I r. to the Lord for*, 595a

Renegadoes For r., who ne'er turn by halves, 763a

Renounce marriage, imitate the angels, 898a

Renouncement I must not think of thee, 763b

Renovated Civil society, r. by Christianity, 165a

Renown O peerless in r.!, 847a

Rent-charge live a r. on His providence, 11b

Renunciation Blessed is man who letteth go, 36b; complete r. of body, 36b; sacrifice most acceptable, 36b

Repartee Silence is the unbearable r., 814b

Repent Church ought readily to pardon children when they r., 821b

Repentance Baptize thy spotted soul in weeping dew, 765a; tears r., God is appeased, 202b; Daily to confess one's past sins, 203a; God, who desirest not death, but r. of sinners, 603b; grant me tears of r., 535a; of confession, r. is born, 202b; Remorse is easy enough, r. means love, 765b; r. for sin with true grief, 667b; r. is the price of pardon, 763b; R. is the virtue of weak minds, 765a; r. of those who do not persevere, 6b; shining doors of r., 90b; To him who remains in world, no r. too late, 764a; two kinds of compunction, 764a

Repentant may escape from snare of devil, 6b; Tear-enbalmed before he dies, 765a

Report two things necessary, good conscience and good r., 208b; When rumors increase, believe second r., 784b

Reports Not light of credit to r., 349a

Repose all who r. in Christ, 592b; Endless r., 516a; Give thou r., 636b; nothing so insupportable as

complete r., 107b; place of r., 245a; where souls of just r., 89a

Repository factory-made art of Catholic r., 33b

Reprehend r. what cannot comprehend, 70a

Repression Check their sins, to produce repentance, 173b

Representative All government r., until it begins to decay, 407b

Reprobate settled that others will not be given grace, these called r., 723b

Reprobation causality of r., unlike that of predestination, 723a; evident r. of other men, 819b; reason for predestination of some, r. of others, 723b; to permit some to fall away, r., 765b

Reprove belongs to our office to r. for sin, 178a; those whom mildness failed to correct, 22b; wish to r. with profit, 30b

Republic American r. instituted by Providence, 14b; assemblage associated by right and interests, 765b; no r., where there is no justice, 765b; Rome never was a r., 765b; Whose founder and ruler Christ, 125a

Republican r. polity of United States, 14b

Republicanism Catholicity in religion sanctions r. in politics, 766a; maintained by Catholics in US, 15a; Preferring impersonal government, called r., 407a

Republics in some soils r. will not grow, 766a; live by virtue, 766a; modern r. assert individual freedom, 14b; virtue of people is life of nation, 766a

Reputation Conscience is due to yourself, r. to neighbor, 208a, 766a; desire not the r. of the world, 766b; Excessive fear of losing a good name, 766b; He that hath an ill name is half hanged, 766b; people will always like you as much as God wills, 766b; r. and knowledge of person, 766b; sensitive to r. after death, 464a; shun things that have appearance of evil, 766a; signboard to show where virtue lodges, 766b; So long as God is served, what does it matter, 766b; Trouble not yourself about human judgments, 766b; two things necessary, good conscience and good report, 208b; woman's r., tender plant, 766a

Request Honorable r. By performance should be paid, 767a; man who asks for himself, already judged, 767a

Requiem R. aeternam dona eis, 767a

Requiescant R. in pace, 596a

Require not r. from ourselves what is not in ourselves, 767a

Requital for important works, based on management of lesser, 774b

Research enlarges limits of public prosperity, 139a

Reservation r. of consecrated Hosts, 76a, 76b

Resign in order to please Him, r. himself to Him, 767b

Resignation Blessed they who do not own will, 767a; holy indifference goes beyond r., 470a; key attitude of Christian r., 767b

Resigned r. to suffer adversities, 9a

Resolute Give me the man that with undaunted spirit, 767b; Pride at having been r., 768a

Resoluteness Through thick and thin, 767b

Resolution Every broken r. leaves mark, 768a; No one likes his own good r. noised about, 768a

Resolve firmly r. not to sin again, 216b

Resolved Must be at once r. and skilful too, 768a

Respect In love, r. first, ardor second, 557a; right to r., 531a

Respectability give society air of r., 30a

Respectful r. in the extreme, 801a

Resplendent Gather in darkness that r. One, 483b

Response Make r., ye distant lands, 36a

Responsibility freewill and r. for actions, 355b

Responsible Belief in God, unshaken foundation of r. action, 377b; We are r. for doing what we can, 768a

Responsive Bearing our r. part, 19b

Respublica R. Christiana, 184a

Rest absolute r. is death, 624b; BVM, r. of weary, 84b; break the eternal Sabbath of his r., 249b; Eternal r. grant unto them, 246a, 502a, 767a; forefathers who r. in the faith, 593a; give r. to his soul, 243b; grant r. to departed, 89a; May they r. in peace, 596a; Paradise Of everlasting r., 600a; R., cheerfulness, and table thinly spread, 268b; voice of God heard, when we r. from world, 212a; Why seekest thou r., since thou art born to labor?, 516a

Restore greater act to r., than to create, 752b; To r. all things in Christ, 492b, 797a

Restored So faith was planted, so must be r., 479b

Restorer R. of our race, 88b

Restrain If all without fear, who could r. from doing evil?, 404a, 825b

Restraint No man loveth his fetters, 768b

Resurrection After r., we shall enjoy eternal life, 463b; all shall rise again in their own sex, 769a; attain the grace of r., 655b; bodies of saints will rise again, 768b; body and soul, not separated in r., 106a; *But if He rise not?*, 769b; Christ hath risen, life reigneth, 283b; Christ is risen from the dead, 284b; Christianity had God who knew way out of grave, 165b; Faith, in the r. of the dead, 768b; grant us grace of His r., 442a; He overthrew death by His death, 285a; He shall raise bodies of all men, 500b; His r. from hell, 592a; hope of a blessed r., 246a; *I am the r. and the life*, 246a; I believe in the r. of flesh, 226a; Lord's r. signified by Eucharist, 72a; our r., anticipated in Mary, 41b; r. of body, presaged in r. of Redeemer, 751b; 'Tis the day of r., 285a; we praise and glorify Thy holy r., 400a; When rattling bones together fly, 503a; wicked arise again for punishment, 768b

Resurrections there are two r., 769a

Reticence We all keep back lots of things, 769b

Retinue Such captain, such r., 598a

Retirement Thus let me live, unseen, unknown, 770a; Walk sober off before the sprightlier age, 770a

Retreats time that really matters, between religious r., 318a; wide porch invites to still r., 146a

Retribuam Quid r. Domino, 595a

Retribution that day of r., 483b

Return with difficulty do we r. to Thee, 344a

Reunion behoves bishops to bestow upon it special attention, 772a; chief obstacle to union, confusion between culture and Church, 771a; embraced into unity of Christ's Church, 141a; How can hearts be united, where minds do not agree?, 771a; how He willed that it should be, 134b; Imitate the Good Shepherd, 770a; inconceivable, on basis of private judgment, 771b; Non-Catholics, in returning to Church, 772a; opinion, no one should be coerced into unity, 431a; outside truth, no true union ever attained, 772a; return of separated to one Church, 771b; true union, consists in unity of faith and government, 770b; we advise reconciliation with Church of Rome, 770b; work of reconciliation, only on three conditions, 771b; work of 'r.' belongs to office of Church, 772a

Reuniteth Earth to heaven it r., 168a

Revealed He r. that which it was to our profit to know, 772a; oracle of r. doctrine, 23b; premises of Christian theology, r. truths, 863a; r. truth and education, 289b; such things have been r., what I have written seems but straw, 773b; things divinely r., by word or manifestation, 394b

Reveals believe articles because God reveals them, 26b

Revel The r. in Satan's frantic train!, 277a

Revelation argument from authority based on revelation, 30b; can be made credible, 328a; Christian r., last supernatural r. world can expect, 773a; coming in of unseen world into this, 146b; completed with apostles, 773a; entire body of truth, 120b; fact of r. demonstrably true, 27a; God chose reveal Himself to one people, 148b; Holy Spirit, in Church, interpreter of divine r., 840b; man can be raised to higher than natural knowledge, 772b; marvelous disclosure through veil, 62b; new r. and mystics, 628b; not in opposition to human reason, 332b; not subject to indefinite progress, 772b; one of three roads to belief, 57b; rationalism, to accept r. and then to explain it away, 748a; revealed truth believed, because of authority of God, 330b; R. and ecclesiastical authority, 117b

Revelations Faith rests on divine r. through Scriptures, 340b; private r. of holy men, 340b

Revenge No envy, no r., no rage, no pride, 655a; Prompt to r., not daring to forgive, 773b; R. he never sought, 349a; Tit for tat, 773b

Revenues r. of Church ought to nourish bishop, 67b

Revere how r. this wondrous gift?, 78a

Reverence just and due r. for laws, 46b; Let us fear the Lord Jesus, 773b; Religion, virtue by which men show God worship and r., 755a

Revivalism broken reed, when temperature drops, 294b

Revivalist emotional r., 294b

Revolution Christian r. can succeed only by use of faith, 774b; Christian tradition, living and perpetual r., 876a; If king rules tyranically, community may depose him, 774a; Man, not merely evolution but r., 571b; You must have democracy to have a r., 256b

Revolutionary Church, essentially traditional and r., 876a; also a reactionary, 199b

Revolutionists I am very fond of r., 636b

Revolutionizing art of r. states, 774a

Revolutions The r. of men change nothing, 774b

Reward deserve to attain everlasting r., 4a; earning of r. is placed here, 43a; full r. for all good ever done, 371a; high and secret r., 211a; r. is in heaven, 36a, 43a; R. is what you receive, merit what you do, 604a; unfailing r. of Thy promise, 242a

Rewarded Each shall be r. according to his deeds, 300a, 500a

Rewarder R. of all growth in virtue, 241b

Rewards not seek to have all the crowns, 774b

Rex R. non potest peccare, 509a; R. numquam moritur, 508b

Rhetoric science of speaking well, 774b; The more r., the more mischief, 685a

Rhetorical art is a r. activity, 34a

Rhinoceros mind of archangel, in body of r., 607b

Rhyme before it was neither r. nor reason, 774b; may r., but accordeth not, 3b; To ransom one lost moment with a r., 690a

Ribstone Right as a R. Pippin!, 424b

Rich As r. as a new shorn sheep, 712b; avarice, instinct to make men r., 48b; Be poor in folly, r. in all but sin, 775a; Command the r. of this world, 711b; hard for r. to pass through eye of needle, 33b; He is r. enough who is poor with Christ, 775a; No one so r., he does not need another's help, 428b; r. in eternal wealth, 156b; riot of the r., 31a; Satan tempts by making r., not making poor, 861a; to r., she can forgive regal selfishness, 157a; we are poor in ourselves, but r. in God, 395a

Richard of St. Victor, 119a

Riches bringeth oft harm, 776a; Great r. not required for magnificence, 32a; *How hardly shall they who trust in r.,* 201a; if r. rule the roast, 783b; If you lack earthly r., 775b; It is not a sin to have r., 776a; Love, more than great richesse, 552a; no more prefer r. to poverty, 37a; what greater r. than good conscience?, 208a

Rich, Sir Richard, 140b

Riddle The glory, jest and r. of the world!, 571a

Ridicule Yet touch'd and shamed by r. alone, 776b

Ridiculous In a world where everything is r., 193a

Right As r. as a line, 847b; Assume Thy right, 36a; doctrine of divine r., 407a; For r. is r., since God is God, 777a; grant that we may think those things that are r., 776b; He can't be wrong whose life is in the r., 275a; It is truly meet and r., 591a; Law, not r. exactly, but norm of r., 525b; *Man of Thy r. hand,* 485a; mercy, greater thing than r., 604a; Might overcometh r., 606a; "Others, thank God, are less correct than I", 777a; relation between human beings in dealings with each other, 776b; r. of association, natural r., 38a; r. the day must win, 777a; r. to existence, 531a; whatever is, is r., 646b, 776b; Where no true justice, there can be no r., 523b

Righteous Art thou r.? Then fear lest thou fall, 446a; The r. wait expectant, 520a

Righteousness BVM obtained gift of r. for all, 86a; Christ our r., by dwelling in us, 506a; in fasting, almsdeeds and prayer, r. consists, 401b; life of good men, living study, 777a; O God, Whom to love above all is r., 655b

Rightly no man acts r., save by divine aid, 817a

Rights Americans generous in concession of r., 15b, 17b; By common consent, human will can institute juridical r., 529a; Conscience has r. because it has duties, 470a; demanding r., discharging our obligations, 777a; Nature created common r., 733b; nothing can be added to natural rights, 14a; R. of Man, 256a; state does not determine limits of Church's r., 181a; state must protect natural r., 38b; Two r. which democracies guarantee, 257a; universal reign of human rights, 15a

Ring Take and wear this r. as pledge of fidelity, 576b

Riot most effective r., r. of rich, 31a

Ripe Soon r., soon rotten, 777b

Rise Awake, awake, the morn will never r., 777b; bodies of saints will r. again, 768b; *But if He r. not?,* 769b; R.—glorious Conqueror, r., 36a; R., mighty Man of wonders, 286b; To r. by others' fall, 846b; when first from bed you r., 423a

Risen r. is our Christ, and with Him we, 252a; The Lord is r. from the grave, Alleluia, 284b

Rising Who doth believe, shall never miss joyful r.!, 769b

Risks generosity of heart which r. everything on God's word, 882b

Rite genius of Roman r., 547b; No one may transfer to another r. without permission, 547b; one faith, diversity of usage, 51b; universal r. of holy Church, 76a

Rites approved r. of Church, may not be contemned, 547a; few r. in place of many, 785b; form of our r., 546b; Newer r. of grace prevail, 74a; reverent service and sacred r., 34b; r. of separate churches, 117a, 770b; system of language and r., 547a; With newer r. let former ages end, 74a

Ritual All Christian r. derives from Christ's priesthood, 787a; Englishman's passion for r., 777b; increased expansion of Christian creed and r., 272a; nature's solemn r. Of changing seasons, 634a; privileges of patriarchs, or established r., 770b; Profaned with r. pride and state, 543a; what the r. means, 548b

Rituals modern people talk of needlessness of old r., 759b

River pleasant waters of the r. Lee, 59a; the fourfold r., 243a; The

onward rush of waters unconfined, 778a; What man would be wise, let him drink of r., 319b

Rivers R. are roads that move, 777b; rivers groping for the alien beach, 777b

Road I'll not reproach The r. that winds, 493a; O king, love justice and judgment, the royal r., 507b; r. of His doctrine, 108b; rolling English drunkard made the rolling English r., 778a; royal r. to faith, 23b; The r. was a ribbon of moonlight, 778a

Roads A thousand r. lead men forever to Rome, 781a; Rivers are r. that move, 777b

Roast Great boast and small r., 105a

Roasts fragrant r. digestive powers increase, 263a

Rob To r. Peter and pay Paul, 664b

Robber hands of the r. redly wear, 418b; robber's cave thinks nothing of spoils, 13b; r. theory of power, 47a

Robberies what are kingdoms but great r.?, 509b

Robe And he won the r. of Christ, 778b; heavenly r. of delay, 564a; Makes sun her r., 40b

Robes trailing r. of female dignity, 278a; waving of angels' r., 20a

Robin The r. has his silver vest incarnadined, 778b

Robin Hood Many a man speaketh of R., 105a

Rococo Art, 32b

Rock Church, founded upon r. of Peter, 135a; gracious Shepherd!, unremoving R., 484a; O r. worthy to be built upon, 674b; R. in strength, upon the R., 135b; R. of ages, rent for me, 492a; r. of St. Peter on summit enjoys pure atmosphere, 711a; r. over which gates of hell shall never prevail, 694b; solid r., on which city of God is built, 174a; The shadow of the r.!, 251a; *thou art Peter, and upon this r.,* 120a, 693a; Upon that r. I know Church is built, 694a

Rocks r. of trouble, 99a; When stubborn r. shall bow, 630b

Rod from their children to spare r., 160b; from whose tender root upsprang, 461a; Thou, R. and Blossom from a stem unstained, 640b

Roi Le r. est mort, vive le r.!, 509a

Romagna R., was not e'er Without war, 906b

Roman difference between kings and R. emperor, 353a; genius of R. rite, 547b; Greek and Roman republics asserted state, 14b; R. people, ordained to rule by nature, 779b

Romance Gliding over a sea of dreams, 780a; should never begin with sentiment, 780a; Twenty years of r., 574b; what world calls a r., 780a

Roman Church Away with jealousy of Roman preeminence, 694a; by a privilege, above the others, 121b; Catholic agrees with R., 114b; C. and Church of England, 23a; church in place of Romans, that holds primacy, 705b, 694a, 697a; development of doctrine in C., 101a; Donation of Constantine, 175a; fathers rendered Old Rome first honors, 699b; first See of apostle Peter, 675a; founded and

organized at Rome by two apostles, 704a; founded by Christ alone, 700b; from its rule, no one may dissent, 111b; guards creed in its entirety, 227a, 704a; has primacy of ordinary power over all other churches, 662b, 696a; head and hinge of all churches, 111b, 703a; head of your body, 694b, 698b; He who does not agree with R., not Catholic, 701a; In all things I desire to follow R., 874b; its more powerful pre-eminence, 704a; mother and mistress of all Christians, 52a, 662b, 707a; mother and teacher of all Churches, 145b; *mystical body of Jesus Christ,* 132b; never prevailed against by false teaching, 679a; observes canons, but not bound by them, 111b; Peter and Paul, set it above all others, 694a; plenitude of power resides in it, 121b; rock over which gates of hell shall never prevail, 694b; Symbol of faith which R. uses, 145b; The R. has never erred, 705b; thou dost soothe the heart, 145b; *trophies of those who founded this c.,* 678b; true Church of Jesus Christ, 132b; whence priestly unity takes its source, 704a; whoever separates himself from it, becomes exile, 694b; *without stain, without wrinkle,* 179b, 675a, 697a

Roman Empire all men, under sway of Rome, 172b, 779a; begotten in womb of piety, 779b; Catholicism, as religion of State, 144b; Christian empire, 507a, 779a; Church and State in R., 172b; God's providence made ready R., 779a; R., and end of world, 778b, 779a; rule of citizens, not tyrants, 778b; Thy protection for defense of Roman name, 779b

Romanesque, 30a

Romans absorbed faults of barbarians, 53a; anything in history more notorious than pride of R.?, 779b; holy nation, chosen people, 780b; O happy people, O glorious Ausonia!, 211a

Rome *ad limina* visits of bishops to R., 70a; All roads lead to R., 781a, 781b; AMOR is same word as ROMA, 149a; capital of the world, 139b, 780b, 781b; city is at center of universe, 149a; conquered nations, 632a; diverse paths lead to R., 781a; golden R., 780a; How R. her own sad sepulche appears, 781a; If R. be against me, 710a; If R. dies, other churches may order coffins, 138a; interest in R., a danger signal, 147b; Make the most of R., 781a; mighty R., St. Philip's home, 781a; mother and guardian of civilization, 781b; mystery, unfolded through centuries, 78.b; myth of R.'s organization dies hard, 136b; never was a republic, 765b; O happy R.! thou are empurpled, 780b; O happy R.! who in thy martyr princes' blood, 679a; O R. illustrious, of the world emperess!, 780b; pilgrim to R. brings back what he brought, 682b; R. and role of Peter, 677a; R. in the ages, dimmed with all her towers, 477b; so long as world shall stand, so long shall R. continue, 779a; square stones of R., 171a; The city which had taken whole world, was itself taken, 780a; The eternity of R., no mere rhetorical exaggeration, 781b; through Peter's holy See thou didst attain wider sway, 780b; two suns, R. and Constantinople, 704a; two ways, to R. and to atheism, 42a; *Urbs caput orbis*, 139b;. Walk I, today, the ways of R., 781b; was not built in one day, 781a; When at R., do as the Romans do, 207b, 780b; You may not sit in R. and strive with pope, 710b

Rood In the shadow of the r., 811a; On the r. of thy Redeemer, 232a; Sweet pledges of the saving R., 104a; To die upon the R., 445b

Roof *Lord, I am not worthy Thou shouldest enter under my r.*, 595a

Rooks When r. fly homeward and shadows fall, 213b

Root for sprung is every r., 853a; love is the r. of all desire, 257b; rod sublime *from r. of Jesse*, 8a, 91a; r. of matter lies in character, 154a

Roots Thy r. are fast within our fair fields, 233b

Rope As meet as a r. for a thief, 864b

Ropes bad manners to talk about r., 573a

Rorate R. coeli desuper!, 168a

Rosaleen My dark R.!, 475a

Rosalynde Of all fair maids my R. fairest, 54b

Rosary A set of beads, the gaudies tricked in green, 781b; life held in your hand As a r. of days, 782a; medicine which cures deal of nonsense, 782a; meditating on mysteries, in most holy r., 782a; telling his beads In penance for past misdeed, 748b

Rose A r. I marked, and might have plucked, 783a; I see His blood upon the r., 492b; kissed upon your mouth the mystic R., 783a; Love lies hidden in every r., 558a; Of all sweet flowers r. doth sweetest smell, 54b; R. mystical, 84b; R. of the cross, 84b; R. of the desert!, 782b; R. of the garden! such is woman's lot, 782b; R., thou art the sweetest flower, 782b; sweetness fresh as any r., 782b; The life of a r. is sadly fleet, 783a; The red r. whispers of passion, 783a; The r. is a mystery, 41a; the r.'s scent is bitterness To him, 783a; What would r. be worth, 782b; With Christ we died, with Christ we r., 283b

Rosebuds Sweet r. cut in dawning hours!, 441a

Rosemary The humble r., 783b

Roses crown of r. and of thorns, 38a; It seemed too late for r., 783a; weak heads ache with scent of r., 782b; scent of the r. will hang round it still, 603a; When r. fold on the hay-yard wall, 213b; Young r. kindled into thought, 104b

Rothschild rash for shopkeeper to compete with R., 200b

Rouge beauty not imparted by r., 7a

Rouge Bouquet In a wood they call the R., 830a

Rout 'Twas on a day of r. they girded me about, 658b

Rowing Our voices keep tune and our oars keep time, 783b

Royal body, priestly and r., 647b; If anyone shall resist r. power, 878b; O king, love justice and judgment, the r. road, 507b; O r. England! happy child, 296a; r. dignity excels all other early pow-

ers, 507b; r. power, can only be from God, 879a; r. prerogatives of Christ, 489b; r. virtues principally two, justice and piety, 507a; Their forms and words, r. things, 20b; Thy r. state, 197b

Royalism Preferring personal government, called r., 407a

Royalty Conscience, r. and prerogative of every man, 209a

Rude to be r. to him was courteous, 223a

Ruest Ruest on every rueful in distresse, 100a

Ruin For those whom God to r. has design'd, 568a; man, Not for fellows' ruin, but aid, 12b

Rule contravening the holy r., 317a; desire to serve, not to r., 808a; doctrine of Church as unerring r., 145b; Every r. is adapted to a certain class of things, 783b; God perfects the minds of those who r., 660a; he does not r. who does not correct, 507a; he is no bishop who loves to r., 68a; if lion knew his strength, hard to r. him, 509a; long life, secure r., faithful senate, 171b; Love knows no r., 565a; man cannot r. by fear, 47b; nothing more fortunate than r. by good, 404a; Political r., natural and necessary, to human race, 405b; rather die for Jesus than r. earth, 490b; Reason to r., mercy to forgive, 604a; right to r. according to *jus gentium*, 734a; r. is far from plain, where all dissent, 783b; r. of faith is one, 226a; r. of life, laid down for Catholics, 547a; they who pay the taxes bear the r., 858a; Thirst of r. gars great men tumble, 713b; Thou couldst not r., 69a; to lord it over others, 300a; to r. men is art of arts, science of sciences, 403b; true Christian r. and faith, 144a; Unbelief, not inconsistent with dominion, 178b; what is r. but a sad weight, 449b; when man has achieved supreme r., 404a

Ruled willing or unwilling, men must be r. by some one, 406a

Ruler chief concern of r., procure unity of peace, 404b; civil r. dabbling in religion, 692a, 758a; existence of a sovereign R., 395b; God, supreme R. and Lord of all, 47a; Great r. of the starry sky!, 636a; having Thee for our r. and guide, 736b; ideal of Christian r., 784a; just, that prince should obey his own laws, 528a; minister of public utility, 508a; multitude, governed through reason of one man, 404b; No king can have political authority immediately from God, 509a; of evil wills, the most just R., 313b; prince set in authority, not through knowledge of laws, 405a; qualities of perfect governor, 405a; represents person of the state, 508a; R. and King of the universe, 466a; r. by the ruled takes rule, 918b; R. of the dread immense, 21b; she ruled our R., 81a; takes care of what appertains to common weal, 404b; temporal monarch receives authority directly from Source, 845a; Thou r. of this earthly sphere, 369a; worthy of r., to acknowledge that he is bound by laws, 508a

Rulers authority of r., both by natural law and by divine law, 406a; believe scepters helped by BVM, 100a; consul, king, lords over others in regard to means, 404b; custodians of decrees of God, 784a; first duty of princes, to love subjects as sons, 509a; in civil communities, different r. may be chosen, 405a; ministers towards others in regard to ends, 405a; must be able to compel citizens to obedience, 406b; obedient to our r., 45b; Our earthly r. falter, 726a; our God-fearing r., 87a; princes and kings chosen, to coerce people from evil, 404a; proud ones of world, 121a; r. are chosen by all, 404a; set over us by God, 28b, 45b; should be craftsmen of freedom, 784b; superiors should regard equality of nature, 300a; their necks placed under yoke of Christ, 720b; they are happy, if they rule justly, 784a; We pray for all r., 784a; When r. disdain authority of God, 47a

Rules God r. over men and nations, 15a; In this world no one r. by mere love, 784b

Rulest Who r. all things mightily, 599a

Ruling joy not in r. men, but in helping, 300a

Rumor ever takes away from truth, 784b

Rumors Not light of credit to reports, 349a; The flying r. gather'd as they roll'd, 784b; When r. increase, believe second report, 784b

Runs Now who that r. can read it, 42a

Ruskin, John, 220b, 568a

Rust Three things that shouldn't be let r., 867b

S

Sabaoth *Holy is the Lord of S.*, 379a; *sanctus Dominus Deus S.*, 591a

Sabbath eternal S. of His rest, 249b; from word meaning rest, 442a; God rested on the seventh day, 854a; never broke the S., but for gain, 785a; observance of the S. lapsed, 442a; The S. of the tomb, 872b

Sabbaths Those endless s. the blessed ones see!, 785a

Sable Lacking samite and s., 169a

Sacerdos, 68a

Sacerdotal s. vesture of priests, 68a; The s. night, 240a

Sacerdotes, 309a

Sacerdotium s. and *imperium*, 177b

Sacerdotum, 133b

Sack bad s. that will abide no clouting, 785a; I will not bear the devil's s., 261a

Sacrament Art is beauty made a s., 33b; by this Paschal s., 441b; death of Christ, s. of salvation, 43b; Eucharist, noblest s., 306b; greatest s., Christ Himself, 548b; *great s., concerning Christ and Church*, 131a; intention of doing what Church does, 786b; outward sign, 52a; performance of act whereby some holy thing is signified, 785b; s. of divine wisdom, 726b; s. of the altar, 72b, 73b; 's. of the present moment,' 767b; signifies something in holy sense, 786a; spiritual virtue of a s., 786a

Sacramental arts became s. in character, 33a; s. character, 787a; s. grace in communion, 198a; s. power of waters of baptism, 49b; That which is consecrated to God should be honored, 788b; We should not profane holy things, 788b

Sacramentally Christ eaten s. and really, 76b

Sacraments a few rites in place of many, 785b; all Christians do not have power to administer s., 788a; all s., not necessary for every individual, 787b; apply course of salvation, 786b; by s. of new law, grace conferred through act performed, 787b; chosen instruments of divine grace, 135a, 786b, 787a; Christ is their author, 786b; Church may ordain or change what things expedient, 788a; Church's seven s., 786a, 787b; forbidden to administer s. to heretics or schismatics, 788b; form and matter, 786b; Grace in s., like effect in cause, 787a; hierarchy and s., sole basis of unity, 135a; holy and pure mysteries of altar, 68b; in three s., imprinted in soul a character, 787b; medicine of prevailing efficacy, 130a; not merely outward signs, 53a, 787b; possession of all the s., 120b; purpose of s., to help us on our way, 786b; remedies, 786b; s. of new law confer grace, 787a; s. of schismatics, 786a; separation from s., 117b; water enclosed garden of Church, 130b

Sacrifice accept the s. of praise, 590b; Be you priest and s. of God, 726b; Christ offered Himself as s., 231b, 309a; four things are to be considered in every s., 485b; He is Mediator, Priest, S., 307b; law of life, law of s. and discipline, 541a; No s. more acceptable to God, than zeal for souls, 931a; offered for the dead, 244a; Ourselves become our own best s., 791a; Paschal s., world's salvation, 283b; present your bodies a living s., 229b; renunciation, s. most acceptable, 36b; sacred sign of an invisible s., 790b; s. of cross and mass, 309b; S., so called from being 'made sacred,' 308b; That tremendous s., 658b; This is the s. of Christians, 307b, 485b; to Thee both Priest and S., 485a; true and full s. to God, 307b; true s., every work done, 791a; virtue of s. under Old Law, 51b

Sacrifice, Eucharistic See also Eucharistic Sacrifice; as often as sacrifice is offered, 72a; Brethren, pray my sacrifice may be acceptable, 590b; Christ contained, offered, in e., 78b; Come, O Sanctifier, bless this s., 590a; holy and unblemished sacrifices, 591b, 729b; in that oblation, Church is offered, 485b; in union with Him let them offer up themselves, 586b; mass takes place at time of sacrifice, 597b; May the Lord receive the sacrifice from Thy hands, 590b; of benefit to souls after death, 244b; offered only in one Catholic Church, 121a; participate in e., chief duty, 586b; pure and acceptable sacrifice, 88a; pure Victim, holy Victim, spotless Victim, 592a; Receive power to offer s. to God, 727b; signifies Lord's death, 72a; that holy and most awful s., 243b; This oblation of our service, 591b; this reasonable and unbloody sacrifice, 592b, 593a; through us He condescends day after day to be offered up, 486a; words of consecration, a knife, 71a

Sacrificed She gave him to the S., 114b

Sacrifices ancient s., signs of true sacrifice, 308a; daily s. of our tears, 308b; s. of altar or of alms, 308a; s. which we daily offer, 150a; We offer Thee s. and prayers, 245b

Sacrificial Christ's passion s. cause of salvation, 44a

Sacrilege injury done to clergy, 190b; let s., not man, be despised, 156a; Those who violate sanctity of divine law, 791a; to break into Catholic churches, 791a; to cheat the Church is s., 159b; violation of betrothal, like s., 59b

Sad Yet bide I s. and sorry, 602b

Sadden Nothing but sin should s. us, 833a

Saddle As meet as a sow to bear a s., 838b

Sadness all the s. in the sweet, 791b; Farewell gladness! Welcome s.!, 791b; great enemy of soul, s., 791b; Hence with s., 286a; in pleasing God, no grounds for s., 791b; Looks of fixed gloom, 791b; On no account give way to s., 791b; When s. shades our lonely hearts, 312b; Yet Christian s. is divine, 833b

Safe Be silent and s., 814a; by grace and mercy of God, 407b; I shall keep on the s. side, 583b; See me s. up., 248a; unwise confide causes to safe men, 149a

Safety Fear is the foundation of s., 342a; His s. must his liberty restrain, 537b; Seeing the coast clear, 792a

Sage Nor bow ear from counsel of s., 149b

Sages Before the s., 299a

Said Sooner s. than done, 275a; thing well s., wit in all languages, 519a

Sail Hoist up s. while gale doth last, 645b

Sailors Seafaring men range from one end of earth to other, 792a; watch over Thy servants in this ship, 792a

Sails With full spread s. to run before the wind, 767b

Saint Before you can be s., you have got to become human, 437b; every just spirit made perfect in faith, 593a; Every s., little looking-glass of God, 794a; hands of the s., consecrate everything they touch, 794b; I was s. of heaven by right of birth, 794a; man a s. by grace, 793b; never a s. but has had ecstasy, 288b; One is a s. only after death, 794b; One s. will often save a nation, 452b; person who has clear sight of truth, 794a; s. run mad, 793b; we declare blessed N. is a S., 793b; What s. ever won crown, without contending?, 792a; Young s., old sinner, 823a

Sainthood not negation of human life, 794b

Saintly S. and prudent, modest in behavior, 205a

Saints after Resurrection, 124b; all the s., adorned with good works, 401a; All Thy s. and elect acknowledge Thee, 792b; apostles and martyrs pray for others, 795a; assist in healing or aiding, 242b; as teeth of the Church, 792b; breviary, monument of s., 108b; by Thy s., dost enlighten all the earth, 244b; by whose merits and prayers, grant we may be defended, 591b; Catholic Church has a way of growing s., 128b; celebrate masses in honor of the s., 796a; devotions to angels and s., 796a; eagle's sight Of s. and poets, 688a; Earth's s. are those who to the last, 794a; enable us to live life of s. and angels!, 794a; even now reign with Him, 124b, 793a; fellow-citizens of the s., 579b; glory of Church, can produce s., also thinkers, 333b; good and useful to invoke s., 101b; heresy and schism produce no s., 116a; Hurry ruins s. as well as artists, 422b; images of Christ, 436a; imitating s. in life, 795b; important canon in lives of s., 793b; intercession and invocation of s., 792b, 793a, 796a; jewel which constitutes the Catholic Church, 794a; love which He had for all the s., 874a; manifest character of Christ, 129a; many religious people are not s., 755b; members conspicuous for holiness, 127b; No devotion more acceptable, than follow their virtue, 795b; offer up prayers to God for men, 796a; patrons of whole race, 795a; perfection of the s., 793b; reigning with Christ in heaven, 101b; remembering all the s., 81b; s. and true communists, 794b; sons and heirs of God, 795a; To s. honor paid, as friends of Christ, 795a; useful to have recourse to their prayers, 796a; veneration of s., 795a; We beseech Thee, by the merits of Thy s., 588a; whole body of redeemed, 485a

Salad flavor in a s. dressing, 796b; takes more oil than vinegar to make good s., 364b

Salem Blessed city, heavenly S., 478b

Salesmanship many a slip Makes for anxiety in s., 796b

Salt flesh is touched with s., 52a; S. and sugar excellent, too much spoils dish, 796b; S. will all poisons expurgate with haste, 796b; well-regulated mixture of both sugar and s., 796b

Salt-cellars S. ever should stand at the head, 796b

Salted s. meats the body dry and bind, 263a

Salus extra ecclesiam nulla s., 125b; In cruce s., 797b

Salutaris Calicem s. accipiam, 595a

Salutary that all things s. may be granted us, 215a

Salutem S. et apostolicam benedictionem, 709b

Salvation all who are without, shall never be saved, 126b; angels execute plan for human s., 21a; baptism necessary for s., 52b; bishop offers prayers for s., 69a; BVM is s. of Christians, 99b; by the cross, 797b; child-bearing Virgin, beginning of s., 632a; Christ merited s. for whole race, 43b; crowning of our s., 24b; cup of s., 231a; death of Christ, sacrament of s., 43b; each must seek own cure in Christ, 43b; God has not chosen every one to s., 219a; God's grace, necessary for s., 408a; heirs of s., 20a; He is Way, along which we journey, 486a; His work on earth, 74b; Humility, mother of s., 450b; if Incarnation phantom, s. phantom also, 466a; lay down life for s. of souls, 264b; Let no man despair of his own s., 821b; manner and time which pertains to s., 797a; my sure s., Body of the Lord, 75b; no baptism, no s., 49b; on Whom is built whole s. of mankind, 166b; outside Church, no s., 125b, 126a, 126b, 127a; recovered by virgin, 85a; rewards of s., through Mary, 88b; s. and Catholic Church, 121b; s.

and Christ as Head, 126a; s. and freewill, 356b; s. and invincible ignorance, 127b; s. and losing self in society, 127b; s. and membership in Church by desire, 128a; s. of man born among infidels and barbarians, 797b; s. of soul that was despaired of, 797a; s. of world worked by Mary, 90a; There is no expeditious road, 653b; unintellectual s., means unsaved intellect, 608b; way of s., entrance must be narrow, 615b;

Same O God, Who art ever the s., 393b

Samite Lacking s. and sable, 169a

Samson Nor S., though he were so strong, 248a

Sanachies, 365a

Sanctification faithful receive spiritual unction for s., 128a; Holy Spirit, guide of soul in s., 436b; how s. takes place in baptism, 52a

Sanctifier Come, O S., bless this sacrifice, 590a

Sanctifies heresy, office s. the holder, 714a; true Light Which enlightens and s. world, 490a; with grace of Christ, 411b

Sanctify direct and s. our hearts and bodies, 515b; S. me wholly, soul of Christ, 75a; Soul of Christ, s. me, 521b; souls and bodies, 441b; Through whom Thou dost always create, s., 593a

Sanctifying s. grace imparted in baptism, 52a

Sanction worthy of our attention, 12a

Sanctities The s. of life's last breath, 543a; Round the day's dead s., 312b; The subtle s. which dart, 510b

Sanctity can be reached by diverse ways, 437a; Clothe yourself with garment of s., 726b; does not differ from religion essentially, 436a; in Catholic Church, 128b; in cross is perfection of s., 232b; man's greatest blessing, 435b; measure saintliness by fluency, 294a; one of four prerogatives of Church, 116a; Public welfare consists in s. of life, 435b; religion and s., contrasted, 755b; s. and dignity of BVM, 86a, 89b, 92a; test of s., obedience to authority, 436b; time s. descends from cloistered life, 437a; to be in Christ, 129a

Sanctuaried Lo, in the s. east, 78b

Sanctuary children of the holy place, 586a; churches, altar of safety for those who seek s., 798a; enter into holy of holies with pure souls, 587b; Human nature is hunted, has fled into s., 855a; Priests alone allowed to remain within s., 173a; that holy ground, 77b; where grace and peace and life abound, 77b; Women may not approach altar, 13b

Sanctus *S., s., s. Dominus Deus Sabaoth,* 591a

Sands Like s. upon the great seashore, 100a; One by one the s. are flowing, 615a; Single s. have little weight, 798a; vanity, game of children on s., 892a

Sane If citizens are s., city will be s., 622b; s. man, can have tragedy in heart, comedy in head, 798a; s. man knows he has a touch of the madman, 598b

Sang Little guess'd, 'twas of thee I s., 93a

Sanguine *ecclesia abhorret a s.,* 103b

Sanguis *S. Domini nostri custodiat*

animam meam, 595a; *semen est s. Christianorum,* 103b, 583a

Sanity s. and bigotry, 65a

Sapphires Hew eyes are s. set in snow, 322a

Sarabaites, 618b

Satan overthrew Death, sin, S. too, 401a; drew Adam to death by sin, 43a; fraud of hell's black king, 7b; Grant me fro S.'s service to astart, 561b; Lucifer began well, now a fiend, 56b; now is wiser than of yore, 861a; O S., ever envious since the day, 260b; perverts cultivation of virtue, 158b; ruins souls by lust or chastity, 158b; Shelter us from S.'s fraud, 83b; The revel in S.'s frantic train!, 277a; using crafty serpent's wile, 6a

Satin Girdled with s., though God knows why, 239b

Sating itself s., of itself makes thirst, 196b

Satire If any fool is by our s. bit, 798a; S.'s my weapon, but I'm too discreet, 798b; true end of s., amendment of vices, 798a; Praise undeserv'd is s. in disguise, 715a

Satirical s. poet, check of layman on bad priests, 728a

Satisfaction by confession, s. is settled, 202b; every sinner owes God, 817b; fruits worthy of penance, required, 667b; matter of sacrament, contrition, confession, s., 668b; s. made, following confession of sin, 202a

Satisfies beauteous light that s., yet never sates!, 261b

Satisfying Christ's passion s. cause of salvation, 44a

Satyrs Gripped by s. in white and black, 239b

Savage When wild in woods, noble s. ran, 353b, 798b

Save And s. them by the barrelload, 653b; come and save man, 8a; Better spare at brim than at bottom, 798b; by ways Thou knowest s. me, 823a; *He will s. His people from their sins,* 460b; save mankind by mortal birth, 7b; Thou that camest to s. the world, 656a

Saved Believe that you are chosen to be s., 797b; can man be s. by free determination of will?, 356b; God antecedently wills all men to be s., 723a; *God will have all men to be s.,* 723a, 797a; grace, without which neither infants nor adults s., 408b; in that believeth, and is baptized, shall be s., 670b; no man s. whose salvation He does not will, 797a; whether more men than women are s., 293b; Whosoever willeth to be s., 144a, 227a

Saves as Head of mankind, Christ s., 43b

Saving Church will not admit moron not worth s., 256a; I cannot remember s. a half-penny since I was born, 868a; s. fountains of water and blood, 71b

Savior At last Thou art come, little Savior!, 170a; built of gentiles, second Church, 120a; Christ, our S. and God, 39a; does not rule Church in visible manner, 132b; God, S. and Guardian, 66b; *He is the S. of all men,* 43b; Ichthys, Jesus Christ Son of God S., 49a; Jesus, gentlest S., 197b; name Jesus means S., 490b; O blessed God, O S. sweet, 491b; O S. of mankind!, 488b; Of my S. cruci-

fied, 93b; our Head, the S., 80b; our Savior-brother!, 39b; Our S. Christ and his Lady, 168a; Praise, O Sion, praise thy S., 74b; Sacred S.! Sacred S.!, 490a; S. left high heaven to dwell, 83b; S. of all nations, 8b; S. of mankind, seated with Thee, 35b; S. of our souls, helmsman of our bodies, 484a; Sing, my tongue, the S.'s glory, 74a; Sweet S.! bless us ere we go, 312b; thou hast borne S. of our souls, 82a; We come to Thee, sweet S., 492a

Savonarola, Girolamo, 798b

Savor by your s. will you be judged, 533a

Saw I came, I s., God conquered, 207b

Say Don't s. all you'd like to s., 858a; great authors have something to s., 45a; If all men knew what others s. of them, 403b; If we s. less than we should, 939a; I see much, s. little, do less, 813b; It is as folk do, not as folk s., 275a; psychological moment when to s. nothing, 814a; S., did his sister wonder, 84a; See all, s. nought, hold thee content, 644b

Sayeth must needs be true, that every man s., 881a

Saying Grant me the power of s. things, 939a; S. and doing are two things, 275a

Sayings if we would not busy ourselves with s. of others, 665b

Scabbard stricken with the s., 856b

Scaffold Whether on the s. high, 476a

Scandal basis of every s., absolutely immoral certainty, 799a; great s. of Church lost working class, 517a; not permitted to any one to give s., 799a; s. is gossip made tedious by morality, 799a; To avoid s., 799a; Whatever opposed to will of Lord, s., 798b

Scandalize s. by occasions of sin, 27a

Scandals s. and survival of Church, 136a

Scenery To disparage s. as quite flat, 228a; where In sacred s. is shown, 13b

Scent Their s. of death, 47b

Scepter crown and s., symbols of sacred character, 509b; Hers the kingdom, hers the s., 135b; No s. theirs, but they are kings, 20b; S. and crown Must tumble down, 249a; S. of divine majesty, 449b; Scepter of house of Israel, 8a; s. of kingdoms strengthened by BVM, 90b

Scepters fate of s. and of crowns, 509a

Sceptic s. cannot say what he means, 611a; complete s. says, 'I have no right to think,' 799a

Sceptical never any clear controversy in s. age, 217a

Scepticism even more fundamental than atheism, 867a; impressionism, another name for final s., 799b; Our instinct for truth, forbids s., 799a; What matter, whether two and two be four, 799b

Sceptics future belongs to believers, not s., 58b

Schemes A thousand warring social s., 277b

Schism as wrong to divide Church, as to fall into heresy, 799b, 800a; Charity knows no s., 154b; convinced Church in s., no safety in it, 801a; cut from the Vine, 800a; heresy and s. produce no saints,

116a; heresy is a s. grown old, 429b; means, men think same but split up congregation, 800b; no s. which does not fashion for itself some heresy, 801a; O Eastern Church! imperial s., 801a; of its very nature opposed to unity, 429b, 800b; pride that bound you *in seat of scorning*, 800a; s. and heresy, distinct vices, 800a, 801a; Secede not from Church, 800a; severs man from body of Church, 128a; Why do we divide the members of Christ?, 131a; why we have separated from our brethren, 770b

Schismatic Christian cut off from Church, becomes heretic, 800b; heretic also s., converse not true, 430a; he who sets up second chair against unique chair, 693b; no one who quits Church will attain rewards, 125b, 429a; power of popes over s. rulers, 181a; rejects authority of supreme pontiff or communion, 432b; whoso separates himself from Church, 125b

Schismatics acceptance of Head, rejection of vicar, 123a; baptism of s., 50b; books of apostates, s., prohibited, 151b; brothers of Christ, according to flesh, 133a; call Church, Catholic Church, 120b; Check their sins, to produce repentance, 173b, 431b; cut themselves off from fraternal charity, 429a; do not belong to Catholic Church, 120a; even s. style their assemblies 'churches', 429a; forbidden to administer sacraments to heretics or s., 788b; have broken visible bonds of unity, 123a; laws are meant to prevent you from being bad, 174a; neither heretics not s. belong to Catholic Church, 429b; No one shall pray in common with heretics and s., 800a; s. and use of term "Catholic", 120b; severed from fabric of unity, 126a; sheep who have wandered and are lost, 50b; their wicked separation, 120a; we desire their repentance, 173b, 431a; withdrawn from body unity, 127b

Schisms fratricidal s. provoked by Reformation, 771a; source from which s. have arisen, 799b; Why are there quarrels and s. among you?, 799b

Schizophrenia s. divides soul of society, 186b

Schola value of s. as one of *loci theologici*, 341a

Scholar as s. his master, 31b; His only care was study, 801a; reading on wide range of subjects, makes s., 545a

Scholars Benedictines, s. of classical tradition, 59a; In kingdom of s., force is powerless, 348b; reign as kings of every sliding hour, 106b

Scholastic principles of s. philosophy, no longer suitable?, 681a

School district s. system, American pet, 801b; let us teach young in s., fear of God, 773b; one and one makes two, loathsome refrain, 801b; s. of penance, 233b; The free s. of America!, 802a; To tell tales out of s., 403b

Schoolhouse s. is a temple, 292a

Schoolmaster gathered their ragged classes behind friendly hedge, 802a

Schools Catholic children should not attend non-Catholic s., 291b, 802a; Church has right to estab-

lish s., 802a; Free s.! Blest is the nation they adorn, 801b; never kept people moral and religious, 293a

Science assertions of s. not necessarily true, 332b; complexity of s. and of faith, 58a; decrees of Apostolic See do not impede progress of s., 802b; enables us to deal with technique, 34a; highest s., truly to know and despise ourselves, 451a; in modern world has many uses, 803a; kinds of knowledge, *intelligence, s., wisdom, prudence*, 512b; Man learns from two books, 803a; no clash between s. and faith, 761a, 803a; Philosophy is art of arts and s. of sciences, 680b; progressive realizations of inductive s., 270b; religion suggests to s. its true conclusions, 761a; s. and atheism, 760b; s. before conscience, 289b; s. is handmaid of art, 34a; system of principles and conclusions, 802b; task hopeless, using s. to promote morality, 622a; to rule men is art of arts, s. of sciences, 403b; True s. is about things which really exist, 802b; Turn to thy s. and be wise, 238b

Sciences Church, not hostile to progress of natural s., 803a

Scientific s. demonstration and credibility of faith, 58a; s. pursuits cannot be *instrument* of ethical training, 760b

Scientism 'S.', supremacy of natural law, 803a

Scientist gives expression to his own moral principles, 803b

Scientists tend to make system substitute for God, 802b

Scitur s. melius nesciendo, 393b

Scold Husbands in heaven, whose wives s. not, 455a

Scores Death quits all s., 249b

Scorn ashes, shame and s., 30a; springs easily to vulgar-minded, 803b; We trample grass, and prize the flowers of May, 803b

Scorned S., mocked, and spurned I've been, 234a

Scourge confusion of aesthetic and moral values, 9b; s. of Thy anger, 265a

Scourges s. of sin, 750a

Scream loud s., and shriller squall, 161a

Scripture, Holy all senses built on literal sense, 61a; authority binding on whole Church, 117a; books dictated wholly by Holy Ghost, 64b; cannot be interpreted against Church, 62a; contains heart of God, 64a; contains obscure and difficult, 64b; Church determines true sense, 62a; Divine S. is feast of wisdom, 60a; expresses truth in two ways, 61b; foretells events, 61a; fulness and depth of meaning, 63a; gives counsels or commands, 61a; I accept S., according to meaning held by Church, 145b; important determine sources and forms, 64b; intimates holy truths, 61a; lessons of S., apostolic food, 72a; literal sense contains no falsehood, 61a; many points that S. leaves obscure, 875b; narrates deeds, 61a; no one has mastered every doctrine, 62b; non-Catholics know bark, not pith, 63a; not like other books, 64b; private interpretation, 64a; remains unexplored, 62b; revered for its mystery, 60a; sacred writers cannot have erred, 64b; sanction of Scripture, 23b;

set before us like mirror, 60b; single books, various dishes of feast, 60a; spiritual sense brings nothing to faith, 61a; spiritual understanding of the S., 616a; transcends every science, 61a; translation of a translation, 361b; triple sense of S., 61a; understanding, must conform to Catholic teaching, 60b; word of God, 64a; works dealing with S. must have *imprimatur*, 152a

Scriptures, Holy authority of S. leads men to believe, 60a; dew of Holy Spirit outpoured on S., 64a; epistles of Emperor of heaven, 63b; interpreted in fourfold way, 61a; its profundity is marvelous, 60b; knowledge of S. and love of flesh, 60a; more ancient than secular literature, 60a

Scruples reason why s. are a mischief, 803b

Sea boat upon moonless s., 2a; Lay her in the s., 110a; Mary, star of the s., 99a; O s., forever calling to the shore, 804a; out of the swing of the s., 616a; Raised from s., the solid land, 373a; ruleth sky and s. and land, 36a; s. before The throne is spread, 304a; s. of this life, 39b; Set in this stormy northern s., 296b; Shout in triumph, earth and s., 167b; Source and S. of man's believing, 370a; Strange s.! why is it that you never rest?, 803b; strong proxy lover, God's s., 564b; Upon the calculated s., 105a; What a s. of tears and sorrow, 94b

Sea-horses foaled of the white s., 191b

Seal baptism, a spiritual s., 50a; Lord sets s. upon all we do, 4b; receive at death, s. of likeness to Christ, 503a; s. of confessional, 204a; s. of gift of Holy Spirit, 205b; signed with s. of Holy Trinity, 500a; Under s. of the confessional, 203b

Sealed faithful s. with grace, 787a

Sea-line where s. meets the sky, 446b

Seances we've got no business there at all, 841b

Search It is lost that is unsought, 804a; s. for God, 161b

Searcheth s. all things, 918a

Seas Across what calm of tropic s., 322b

Seasickness its full gripe in none will fix, 804a

Season O, s. strange for song!, 296a; Out of s., out of price, 870b; sweet s., that bud and bloom forth brings, 842a

Seasons nature's solemn ritual Of changing s., 634a; Some perish in foul s., 106b

Sea-Star And the name of S. wearest, 39b

Seat s. of wisdom, 98b; This peaceful s. my poverty secures, 171a; your pride bound you *in s. of scorning*, 800a

Secrecy Love desires s., 554a; s. of religious men, 262b; The shutter'd dark, the s., 287a

Secret A s. and a mystery, 814a; He has left His s. marks everywhere, 390a; its place is a s., 41a; Like a s. told by angels, 8b; live to God in s., 830b; *My s. is mine*, 262a

Secreta (Secret Prayers at Mass), 591a

Secrets divine Wisdom alone can declare His s., 383a; For s. are edged tools, 804b; from Whom no s. are hidden, 586b; God, Knower of s., 241b; Men should not tell their wives S., 804a

Sect followers think differently, have different worship, 800b; Slave to no s., 255a

Sectarian latitudinarian and s. error, 129a

Sects A thousand daily s. rise up and die, 804b; cannot provide sanction of belief, 147a; frantic folly of discordant s., 133b; what one sect interprets, all s. may, 875b

Secular difference between s. and ecclesiastical order, 433b; fatal mistake, religious to take place of s. clergy, 190a; s. affairs one thing, divine another, 699b; s. civilization and new Christendom, 162b; s. power subject to spiritual, in matters of salvation, 178a

Secularism To wish to draw exact line between religion and life, 804b

Secularization complete s. of social life, modern, 760a

Securities America invested religion in s., 15b

Security serve Thee in s. and freedom, 134a

Securus S. judicat orbis terrarum, 23a, 924b

Sede S. vacante, 709b

Sedes S. apostolica, 709b

Seduce devil does not s. anyone, unless he finds him ready, 860a

See created mind may s. God, but cannot know all, 394b; I s. much, but I say little, and do less, 813b; no saint able to s. Him as He is, in mortal body, 903b; S. all, say nought, hold thee content, 644b; S., amid the winter's snow, 169a; S. me safe up, 248a; What do they not s., who s. Him?, 394a

See (Episcopal) His s. one, founded on Peter, 133b, 662a

Seed A little s., which sown in English ground, 346b; blood of Christians is s., 103b, 583a; flower is not for the s., but s. for the flower, 556a; fruit always present in s., 1b; The s. will take which in such blood is sown, 584a

Seeds s. of truth to sow, 74a

Seek s. God, and thou shalt find Him, 562b; Lord, let me s., with sturdy heart, 564a; s. and find nought, 804a; s. us, that we might s. Thee, 481a; to s. after God, to find Him, 213b

Seeking indefinite 'seeking' for faith, 144a

Seeks He findeth that s., 344b

Seeming Our transcience is only a mortal s., 447b

Seen No one has s. God in this life, as He is, 393b, 394a, 394b; Seldom s., soon forgotten, 350a; *things which are unseen, known by things s.,* 459b; What hast Thou s. in me, 384b

Sees Who s. with equal eye, as God of all, 384a

Segregations Discriminations and s., wrong and un-American, 265a

Self From sin, sense, s. set free, 77b; I'm myself but who are you?, 805a; Meekness, true knowing of man's s. as he is, 451a; My s. to thee alone is known, 253a; s. alone to be hated, 563a; S. is the Gorgon, 804b

Self-abnegation school of s., 233b

Self-approving One s. hour whole years outweighs, 805a

Self-assertion ambition, pursued not by s., 14b

Self-conceit treasures of learning with s., 451b

Self-confidence 'Tis with our judgments as our watches, 805a

Self-consciousness one realizes s. by self-differentiation, 805a

Self-contemplation God did not find satisfaction in s., 224b

Self-contempt despised in its own eyes for love of Truth, 805a

Self-control arises from fear of God, 900a; he who is striving to overcome himself, 805a

Self-criticism only sound criticism, s., 805a

Self-deception extremely easy to deceive oneself, 805b; power of an astonishing s., 805b; unwillingness to recognize faults, 805b

Self-defence S. is nature's eldest law, 805b

Self-denial Christian way of s., 27b; fortified by aid of s., 37b; *If anyone wishes to come after Me,* 4b; obtain by s., secure by good works, 535a; S. of active and contemplative life, 4b

Self-discipline Christian way of s., 27b

Self-exaltation we descend by s., ascend by humility, 450a

Self-effacement seething fuss of s., 891a

Self-evident What is s., like first principle, 512b

Self-extinction ambition must be pursued by s., 14b

Self-government civilization and development of s., 185b; s. is not anarchy, 354b

Self-hood escape from prison of s., 889a

Selfishness Each man for himself, 806b; In God there can be no s., 372a

Self-knowledge All our knowledge is ourselves to know, 806a; cell of s., 805b; Full wise is he that can himselven know, 805b; humble knowledge of thyself, surer way to God, 806a; s. of soul in contemplation, 211b; We know ourselves so little, 806a

Self-love And thou, s.! who tak'st from earth, 806a; Despair is absolute extreme of s., 259a; S. and reason to one end aspire, 684b; S. is cunning, 806a

Self-praise God hates those who praise themselves, 806a; When we but praise ourselves in other men, 806a

Self-respect love of God never destroyed man's s., 157b

Self-sacrifice Man's highest life, in s., 806b; S. and chivalry, even art, all come from heart, 557b; take care we don't sacrifice to detriment of others, 806b

Self-service Self do, self have, 806b

Self-understanding S., smilest on Thine own!, 384a

Self-will in killing our perverse s., 623b; should be poured into ocean of will of God, 806b

Sell s. him at that which he sets on himself, 201b; S. not thy soul for brittle joy!, 684a

Seller make yourself s. when buying, 110b

Semen s. est sanguis Christianorum, 103b, 583a

Semper quod ubique, quod s., quod ab omnibus, 144b

Senate Caesar, with a s. at his

heels, 318b; cardinals form s. of Roman pontiff, 113a; Great King's s. glorious, 28b; long life, secure rule, faithful s., 171b

Senatusconsultum, 524a

Send *As Father sent me, so do I s. you,* 693a; Spend, and God shall s., 939a

Sendeth God never s. mouth but He s. meat, 347b

Sense bold knaves thrive without one grain of s., 465b; But Shadwell never deviates into s., 848b; cannot perceive eucharistic presence, 73b; common s. and leechcraft cure disease, 268b; each anointed s. will see, 321b; eccles. s. or phronema, 270a; even s. sort of reason, 54b; frontiers between s. and spirit, devil's huntinggrounds, 807a; human mind needs guidance of things of s., 755a; initial knowledge of universe through s., 395b; men of s. approve, 6b; Not always kind to s., or just to wit, 276b; s. with soul be reconciled, 469a; things of s. and intellect, 61b; Through s. and nonsense, 104b; What though s. no change discerns?, 74a; without method, talks us into s., 446b

Senses delight in due proportion, 54b; in mystic contemplation leave behind s., 211b; My s. fail, but in Thy word, 78b; Where the feeble s. fail, 74a

Sensibility Man's s. to trifles, 807a

Sensible dangerous, to think oneself s., 807a; most s., impatient of all adversity, 9a

Sensuality If soul lives long enough on plane of s., 807a

Sensus S. et ars medici curant, 268b

Sentence by help of Thy grace, may he escape s. he deserves, 500a; On Whose s. all dependeth!, 502a

Sentences splendid phrases and swelling s., 45a

Sentiment s. and taste in devotion, 101a; She was all s. and tender heart, 807a

Sentimentalist essence of the s., 807a

Sentinels With s. of song, 830a

Separated return of s. to one Church, 771b

Separation American Catholics rejoice in s., 183a, 184b, 185a; for many reasons, husband and wife may separate, 580b; If woman separates from abhorrence of married state, 580b; nuptial pact, not nullified by s., 7a; 's.' between State and Church, wrongly understood, 183b; s. of Church and State, 181b; s. of Church and State, not universally expedient, 143b

Sepulchers as memorials for dead, 151b

Seraphim Fair sister of the s.!, 258a; incomparably more glorious than s., 81b; in Thy sight a s. appear, 439b; Match not thy soul against the s., 237b; one of nine orders of angels, 18b; Which angels and archangels, cherubim and s., do praise, 591a

Serapion, Bishop, 519b

Serene S. as sunset glow, 97b

Serenity breath of s. and eternity, 211a

Serfs free men and s., subject to king, 45b

Sergeant A s. at the law who paid his calls, 531a

Sergius, Patriarch, 100b
Serious grave things, oldest jokes, 453b
Seriousness test of one's s., 759b
Sermon A living s. of the truths he taught, 721b; literary point of view, in judging a s., 807b; no s. without St. Augustine, 44b; 'O the pastor'd a s. was splendid this mornin',' 807b
Sermons People don't like lay-s., even sugar-coated, 807b
Serpent crafty serpent's cruel wile, 6a; dread poison of the s., 231a; eternal enmity between woman and s., 89b; Eve had believed s., 85a; received venom of s. in heart, 85b; the trail of the s., 807b; We were deceived by wisdom of s., 347a
Servant character of mistress, judged by that of maid, 614a; Grant grace I may continue Thy s. to the end, 562a; He is Thy best s., 808b; He took upon Him form of s. without sin, 467b; Imagine thyself always to be the s. of all, 808b; look down upon Thy s., 196a; Now, Thou dost let Thy s. depart in peace!, 520b; s. of justice, 816b; s. of sin is free to sin, 816b; S. of the servants of God, 709b
Servants devil cannot lord it over s. of God, 860a; grant to us sinners, Thy s., 592b; Let us treat our s. as ourselves, 807b; S. as a class are full of complaints, 807b; S. of Christ, protected by invisible beings, 20b; s. of the Holiest, 20a; we Thy s. and Thy holy people, 592a; Where is the tumult of household s.?, 244b
Serve desire to s., not to rule, 808a; Every soul that tries to s. God knows, 809a; firm determination to s. God, 904a; good vocation, firm and constant will to s. God, 904a; Him in His sorrows and travails, 808b; object of religion, that soul should s. God, 809a; praise, honor and s. God, 37a; s. Him with purified minds, 7b; those who s. God with their hearts, 395a; We may s. God by digging with hands, 809a
Served Eighty-six years I have s. Him, 489a; Had I but s. God as I have served my king, 520b, 808a; not true, only with soul God s., 809a; whether God be s. by this means or another, 809a
Service administer high position for benefit of others, 808a; angels ever do God s. in heaven, 20b; cult of s., like many modern notions, 808a; glory of man, to remain in s. of God, 569a; good shepherd theory, all power for s., 47a; look upon all as if Christ in person, 808b; My s. with a manly zeal, 264b; O pleasant and delightful s. of God, 808b; One kind word wins more willing s., 506b; Ready s., acceptable to God, 808a; render Thee an exemplary s., 441b; school of the Lord's s., 615b; See, Lord, at Thy s., 75a; soul is chosen to s. of God, 105b; there is no sense in serving s., 808a; These are the arms of our s., 352b
Serving joy, in s. Him and belonging to Him, 377a; our happiness full, if we are s. Author of good, 497a
Servitors I tempted all his s., 211a
Servitude Ere the base laws of s. be-

gan, 353b; Hardest s. has he, 354a; prime cause of slavery, sin, 825a
Servus S. servorum Dei, 709b
Severe Be kind to all and s. to thyself, 506a
Severity balance of beauty and s. in C., 164b
Sex About s. especially men are born unbalanced, 809a; desecration of a holy instinct, 809b; Each s. desires alike, till two are one, 809a; evil of immorality in s., 809b; Gender is a much wider term than s., 837b; pretence that s. is not uniquely significant, 809b; profanation of something sacred, 809b
Sexes union of s., only for procreation, 66a
Sext (Sixth Hour), 809b
Sexual s. intercourse and conception, 66a
Shade earth's sober s., 449b
Shadow him that sitteth in s. of death, 8a; No s. can with shadowed thing compare, 810a; Out of dusk a s., Then, a spark, 315b; The s. of the rock!, 251a; Under thy s. may I lurk awhile, 810a
Shadows All is dust, ashes, s.!, 244b; Are s. not substantial things, 249a; dim s. of the night are waning, 522b; Dreams are we, s., visions, 13a; From s. and symbols to the truth, 884b; Masked by these bare s., 75a; Such lengthening s. cast, 564a; The s., all my own, 240a; When rooks fly homeward and s. fall, 213b
Shakespeare, 810a, 810b
Shall That s. be, s. be, 634b
Shallow only s. people do not judge by appearances, 29a
Shame A handful of dust in a shroud of s., 251a; Be Thine the glory and be mine the s., 219a; Honor and s. from no condition rise, 281b; In the Secret House of s., 362b; Love and s. together stood, 811a; never art so near to crime and s., 571a; Of all sweet passions s. the loveliest, 811a; Oh, what s. and desolation, 656a; Old sin, s., 818b; pride goeth before, s. cometh after, 725a; s. is as it is taken, 810b; Shun not the shelf of most deserved s., 669b; Than guilt and s. have made thee, 422b; This lot He has bequeathed to us, 752b; What would s. him, would turn back funeral, 811a
Shameful S. craving must have s. nay, 811a
Shamrock Old Erin's native s., 811a
Shandon I often think of the S. bells, 58b
Shape Never yet was s. so dread, 459b
Share capital has right to just s. of profits, 112a
Sharer He became s. of our weakness, 90b
Sharers make us s. of His glory, 91a
Sharp All thing that is s. is short, 811a
She That not impossible s., 811b, 920b
Sheaves O Binder of s., 834a
Sheds he who s. blood, may not be minister, 104a
Sheep As Jesus sought His wandering s., 580b; As rich as a new shorn s., 712b; blessed pasture in which s. of Holy Church are tended, 660b; For the lost s. that's found again, 216b; For the s. the Lamb hath bled, 285b; Good Shepherd, Who gives life for s., 484a;

He laid down life for s., 73a; Lord came to seek back lost s., 85a; schismatics are Christ's s., 50b; Where were the feeders of the s., 115b; Your s., swallow down the very men themselves, 811b
Shelley, Percy Bysshe, 811b
Shelter anyone who hastened for s. to BVM, 87b; S. us from Satan's fraud, 83b
Shelters Naught s. thee, who wilt not shelter Me, 385b
Shepherd As Christ is S., is Peter not s.?, 676a; bishop worthy to s. flock, 68a; Disarm the s., wolves the flock devour, 713b; Eternal S., Thou dost lave, 284a; Good S. laid down life for sheep, 73a, 484a; good s. theory, all power for service, 47a; gracious S.!, unremoving Rock, 484a; Hear, O Thou S. of Israel, 166a; Himself S., Pasturage, redemption's Price, 484a; idea of king, implies man who is chief and s., 508b; I met the good S., 484b; I saw the s. fold the sheep, 484b; Imitate the Good S., 770a; know Thy sheep, which knows his S.'s voice, 484a; O gracious S.! for Thy simple flock, 484a; O Lord, the eternal S., 28b; One S., by all to be own'd, 135b; Our S., fount of living water, 400b; Peter S., in body of the S., 676a; S. and Green Pasture, 73a; S. is crucified, Adam raised, 442a; S. of the Catholic Church, 484a; S., Prince, with glad behavior, 74b; this day the S. gave us, 74b; Thou art s. of sheep, prince of apostles, 677a
Shepherdess A s. of sheep, 866b; the lady of my delight, A s. of sheep, 811b
Shepherds Bishops should remember that they are s., 740b; Come we s. whose blest sight, 168b; Poor s., home-spun things, 811b; s. and kings adore in the stable, 758a; The first holy men were s., 811b
Shield be thou my support and shield, 84a; Let your baptism be your s., 401a
Shift I can s. for myself, 248a
Shifts little souls on little s. rely, 600b
Shilling To bring a s. to sixpence quickly, 617b
Shine S., s., O new Jerusalem, 285b
Shines All is not gold that s., 397b
Ship command not entrusted to high birth, 65b; More than once a s. has sunk in harbor, 812a; my s. with sails all set, 251b; s. of Church, sailing merrily over rough water, 136a
Shipping fishes to s. did impart Their tail the rudder, 812a
Ships I saw three s. a-sailing there, 168a, 856b; Like s. that have gone down at sea, 812a
Shocked time is gone for being shocked at ambition, 13b
Shocks within-doors house The s., 304b
Shod common horse, worst s., 447a; Who is worse s. than shoemaker's wife?, 278a
Shoe I wot best where wringeth me my s., 812a; The s. will hold with the sole, 812b
Shoes how hard to the feet another's s. are, 318b; Who waiteth for dead men s., 905a
Shore accursed s., 238b; heavenly s., 232a; ocean's wave-beat s., 20a; set thee on life's happy s., 366b;

What matter in what wreck we reached the s., 812a
Short Blessed is he that hath a s. life, 538b
Shortest s. life, best, 303b
Shout All night had s. of men and cry, 286b; God is gone up with a s., 35b; S. in triumph, earth and sea, 167b; S.! ye heavens, with laud and praising, 167b; There was a s. about my ears, 38a
Show This world is all a fleeting s., 304a
Showers The earth, late choked with s., 602b
Shrine In this secluded s., 896a; spotless s., 83b; Weep, weep, O Walsingham, 812b; Where you have made your s., 21b
Shrines We certainly honor their s., 581a
Shrew Every man can rule s., save he that hath her, 812b
Shrews When all s. have dined, 812b
Shroud Thou seemest in Thy sindon wrapt, 77a
Shrouds All clothes but winding-sheets for our last knell, 249b
Shuttest Who shuttest, and no man openeth, 8a
Shy Little Jesus wast Thou s., 487b
Shyness Sweet is boldness, s., pain, 558a
Siberia In S.'s wastes No tears are shed, 318b
Sic S. transit gloria mundi!, 710a
Sicambrian Bow your head, proud S., 50b
Sicilian Far the S. sea, 296a
Sick Before all things care must be taken of the s., 812b; grant that all the s. may be healed, 812b; is He not Physician and we the s., 349a; Is one of you s.? Let him send for presbyters, 320b; let s. not provoke brethren by unreasonable demands, 812b; May His holy name be medicine for health, 812b; regard Thy servant who is suffering from bodily sickness, 813a; restore his soul, which Thou hast created, 813a; to be admonished, scourge of discipline chastises them, 812b; To visit the s., 155a; we implore aid of Thy mercy, their health may be restored, 813a
Sickness From laws of health and s. learn disease, 601a; God's will, as much in s. as in health, 813a; In thee no s. may be seen, 479a; Long illnesses are good schools of mercy, 813a; Make s. itself a prayer, 813a; no more prefer health to s., 37a; Ungrateful men, why do you s. loathe, 813a
Side From thy riven s. which flowed, 492a; Hear the other s., 499a; Jesus! from out Thine open s., 656b; my refuge, Thy pierced s.!, 490a; through His s. A way to paradise provide, 401a; tide Flowing from His pierced s., 284b; Whose love-pierced, sacred s., 75b
Sides should help person see all s., 30b
Sidney, Sir Philip, 813a
Siege Soft subject for s. of love, 94a
Sigh To s., yet feel no pain, 813b
Sighs Not such sorrowful s. as men make, 813b; Send s. and groans unto thy ears, 95b
Sight earthly s. doth only please the eye, 96b; endure s. of me, alive or dead, 520b; In God's most holy s.?, 304a; out of sight, out of mind, 2a, 350a

Sigillo Sub s. confessionis, 203b
Sign at a s. from the priest, 176b; sacrament not merely s. and virtually, 311a; s. of cross a shield, 234a; thing which causes thing to enter our thoughts, 813b; when tempted, seal forehead with s. of cross, 234a
Signature Art is the s. of man, 32b
Signed S. with Cross that Jesus bore, 207a
Signo In hoc s. vinces, 229a
Signs visibly reveal s. of power, 171a
Silence best treatment for over-strained nerves, 635a; dazzling obscurity s., 211b; Elected s., sing to me, 814a; Her speech is silent, her s. speech, 838b; It is in s. that God is known, 396a; I walk down the valley of s., 814a; I will say nought but mum, 813b; Mere s. is not wisdom, 814a; psychological moment when to say nothing, 814a; S. is the unbearable repartee, 814b; s. of the grave, 464a
Silences Amid the eternal s., 483a
Silent Be s. and safe, 814a; easier to be altogether s., than not exceed in words, 813b; He who is s. is supposed to consent, 210a; The s. mouth is melodious, 815a
Silk s. and purple do not impart beauty, 7a
Silver s. chord in twin is snapp'd, 250b; Tomorrow, s. gray, 239b; Where is gold and s.?, 244b
Silvester, Pope St., 175a, 177a, 211a
Simeon, St. according to the prophecy of S., 93b; Whom S., receiving into his arms, 744b
Simon Magus O S., O lost wretches led, 815a
Simony If any bishop obtains dignity by money, 815a; pleasant absolution, for a gift, 815a
Simple Blessed are the s., 815b; God, truly and absolutely s., 391a; How blessed are the s., 815a; Love but few and s. things, 881b; s. and learned in acceptance of beliefs, 58a; S. life much comfort brings, 881b; s. require concrete examples, 58a; We are all very s., 815b
Simplicity In everything I love s., 815b; no artifice as good and desirable as s., 815b; only s. that matters, is s. of the heart, 815b; spirit should become like a little child, 815b; This admired s., 641a
Sin act of s. may pass, yet guilt remain, 417a; All s. is a kind of lying, 816b; Be of s. the double cure, 492a; becomes more scandalous, when sinner honored, 817b; better to eschew s., than to flee death, 818b; BVM excepted, when touching s., 86a; burden of sin relieved by almsgiving, 13a; by the will that we s., 913b; by thought, word, or deed, 816a; committed in ignorance, not without risk, 816a; Committing s. estranges us from Lord, 816a; consequences of s., bitter, 852a; Dame Pleasure's drugs are steep'd in s., 684a; darkness made of too much day, 299b; death of the soul, 821a; devil makes many disciples by preaching against s., 819b; difference between mortal and venial s., 820a; direct opposite of an act of virtue, 818a; disordered activity, 818a; does not hold, every crime a s., 816a; every s. a crime, 820a; escape the

snares of s., 247b; Everyone who commits s., slave of s., 816a; every s. is voluntary, 816a; fearful evil, but not incurable, 815b; forgiven by Father, Son, Holy Ghost, 50a; formal element in s., 817b; Forsaketh s., ere s. you forsake, 764b; From s., sense, self set free, 77b, 284a; God alone is without s., 815b; god-like s., 14b; God's grace does not operate by s., 328a; He participated in our infirmities, not s., 298b, 467b; Hell is designed for s. a grave, 306a; human race subject to three kinds of s., 816a; If any one saith man once justified, can s. no more, 818b; if every s. were now visited with manifest punishment, 740a, 817a; Keep us from all sin this day, 21b; law of s. is fierce force of habit, 816b; Life saved by s., is purchase dearly bought!, 472a; material element in s., 817b; medicine of s., 651b; new life when s. shall be no more, 20a; Not every s. called s. against Holy Spirit, 822b; nothing else than to neglect eternal things, 816a; number of offenders hides the s., 341b; O murdering s., 819b; O s.! how huge and heavy is thy weight, 818b; O what are the wages of s., 819a; Old s., shame, 818b; Parent of death, author of our exile, 818b; results of s., ignorance, concupiscence, 412b; servant of s. is free to s., 816b; s. diminishes nature, 412b; s. is committed in three ways, 817a; special privilege to avoid sins, 86b; The end of s. is death, 816a; There is no s. in temptation, 861a; The wreck of souls, 818b; Thou alone art without s., 245a; To be Christian, is to accept responsibility for s., 819b; to persevere long in s., work of the devil, 818a; two sides to every s., 818a; Wickedness, nothing else than withdrawal of goodness, 817b; With love of sinner and hatred of s., 823a
Sin, Mortal belongs to our office to reprove for m., 178a; conscience burdened by m., 76b; frustration of marital act, sin, 66a; m. and authority, 46a; prevention of procreation, m., 66a
Sin, Original All men sinned in Adam, 460a; BVM preserved from o., 461a, 461b; bondage unto death, 85a; by Him, curse made void, 90a; chain of the curse, 78b; consequences of the ancient trespass, 229b; corruption of old creature, 166b; defilement which inheres in origin of ordinary men, 466a; effects come through bodily birth, 43b; entire Adam, changed in body and soul for worse, 821a; fastens on whole human race, 821a; first man lost holiness and justice, wherein constituted, 821a; guilt of the original bond, 51b; Human nature, not completely corrupt, 412a; kingdom of death, 820b; O. is racial sin, not personal sin, 821a; second death, of which there is no end, 820b; sever'd from God and grace, 6a; sin of entire human race, 44a; sin of our first parent, 254b; When human nature transmitted, so is o., 821a
Sinai gavest Moses law of S., 8a
Sincere doubtless he is very s., 221a; Faith must be s., 328a
Sindon Thou seemest in Thy s. wrapt, 77a
Sinful every s. stain efface, 198a;

We commit s. act by turning to temporal attraction, 817b

Sing All things s. to me, 689b; I shall not s. again, 832b; I s. of a maiden, 83a; S. His glory, without measure, 74b; S., how the uncreated Light, 225a; S. me the men ere this, 479a; S., my tongue, the glorious battle, 230b; S., my tongue, the Savior's glory, 74a; S., s., ye angel bands, 41a; S. to the Lord with exultation!, 167b; S. we now with tuneful art, 19a; with one voice to the Father, 889b

Singer bad accompanist makes a good s., 618a

Singers marriage of lectors and s. permitted, 188b

Sings Our lady s. magnificat, 831b

Singularity Always avoids, 822b; love of s. prevail, 470b

Sinless there is none s. save Thee, 822a

Sinlessness s. of Blessed Virgin, 86a, 460a, 461a; s. of Christ, 86a

Sinned All men s. in Adam, 460a; s. exceedingly in thought, word, and deed, 587b

Sinner Art thou s., believe in His mercy, 446a; be gracious unto me a s., 823a; body of a s. is a tomb, 823a; casts himself out, 823a; Cruel, take from S. his heaven!, 305a; despise me not, a defiled s., 98a; Do not despise prayer of s., 82b; God, who desirest not death, but repentance of s., 603b; How far a s. differs from a saint, 584b; justified by God moving him to righteousness, 505a; Me, a s., in Thy blood, 75a; reject not my wretched self, a frail s., 603b; satisfaction every s. owes God, 817b; stained with wickedness in soul or body, 13a; The s.'s only stay!, 584b; To be a s., our distress, 823b; To recognize Christ in the s., 823b; what assurance s. yesterday is so today?, 823a; With love of s. and hatred of sin, 823a; Young saint, old s., 823a

Sinners all the s.' sins efface, 230b; And wicked folk reign in prosperity?, 381b; do not despise prayers of sinners, 98b; greatest s., most boring people in world, 823b; His will is that s. should suffer punishment, 797b; just, who believe themselves s., 823a; O God, Who dost not desire death of s., 860a; Oh! Thou for s. slain, 489b; Prosperous s. fare worst, 822b; show that s., great multitude, 823a; s. and holiness of Church, 128b; s. and membership in Church, 127b; S. are people who hate everything, 823b; s., of whom I am the greatest, 594b; We are s., but we do not know how great, 823b; We s. crave thy sure protection, 97b; Why do s.' ways prosper?, 382a

Sinneth no man who liveth and s. not, 245a

Sinning Before s., fear God's justice, 446a

Sins All the winter of our s., 285b; baptism and forgiveness of sins, 51a; bishop has authority forgive s., 67a, 67b, 68b; Check s., in such way as to produce repentance, 431b; Charity covers a multitude of s., 154a; Christ's passion, cause of forgiveness of s., 44a; cleansed from their s., 822a; daily prayers make satisfaction for tiny faults, 716b; forgive my s., voluntary and involuntary, 594b; freed from chains of our s., 668a; He is pro-

pitiation for s., 43b; He washes us from s., daily, 310b; human nature inclined to appraise s. by customs, 816a; If s. of man Thou scannest, 242b; judged by themselves, 395a; justly afflicted for our s., 668a; Lamb of God, who takest away s. of world, 594a; Lord gave power to remit s. to Peter, 821b; may Thy Blood be for remission of s., 196a; Men punished for sins, often visibly, always secretly, 817a; more his s., deeper his place in hell, 426b; Much hast Thou borne for s., 169a; No one s. by an act he cannot avoid, 816a; not without confession of amendment, can s. be remitted, 822a; O Lord, cleanse our s., 369b; Outside Church, no remission of s., 821b; Remember not his transgressions and s., 244a; remission of sins and martyrdom, 50b; S. are forgiven by the Holy Ghost, 667b; s. scarlet, but his books read, 107b; spare s. of those who confess unto Thee, 822a; temporal punishment for s., 417a; things deemed mere s. of thought, 817a; those to whom s. remitted, receive life everlasting, 821b; Thou who takest away the s. of the world, 588b; To hide its multitude of s., 157a; Venial s. may torment a soul like Hell, 820b; voluntary and involuntary, 245b; wash away s. of world, 75b; Where prayer poured forth, s. are covered, 716a; which we have committed in weakness, 2b; whose s. you shall forgive, 2b, 693a; Within Church, s. forgiven in three ways, 668a; you ought not to become secure about s., except on last day, 822a

Sins, Mortal all m. must be confessed, 203b; m. after baptism, must be confessed, 204b

Sins, Seven Deadly The guilt of sevenfold crimes abhorred, 584b

Sins, Venial lawful to confess v., 204a

Sion Church is called S., 123b; David's sure foundation, 479a; May Lord give you blessing out of S., 206b; Mine b. S.'s habitation, 479a; O S., adorn thy bridal chamber, 744b; O S.! open wide thy gates, 744b; Praise, O S., praise thy Savior, 74b; Rejoice and exult, O S., 285b; S. of speculation, 451a; S., that is, contemplation, 123b; S. which has been freed, 131b

Sire Thou unbegotten God, the S., 368b; Whose S. is aboriginal, 490a

Siren S. pleasant, foe to reason, 10b

Sister Fair s. of the seraphim!, 258a; my s., my spouse, a garden enclosed, 130b; our s., the death of body, 247b

Sisters religious women with simple vows, 761a

Sit Better s. still than rise and fall, 823b

Sitio for man's soul's sake; S., 836a

Six Set the world on s. and seven, 207b

Skies Into Thy native s., 36a; large volume of the s., 824a; Reflects the wonder of the s., 55b; shut in the s., 41a; what was born for the s., 250a

Skill art is deliberate s., 33b; he that hath art and s., let him share use, 155a

Skirts s. of angels' garments, 20a

Skull many a sage and learned s., 29a

Sky Above the star-illumined s., 95b; great hills that stormed the s., 11a; Great ruler of the starry s.!, 636a; low they fall whose fall is from the s., 334b; O great Creator of the s., 824a; that equal s., 273b; that little tent of blue, 824a; Today above the s. He soared, 36a; vast fields of light, 41a

Skyscrapers A thousand hollow Babels tower, 185b; Mute monuments of man's power, 185b

Slain So many hearts already she hath s., 207b

Slander It may be s., but it is no lie, 824b

Slanderer cannot succeed, 824b

Slang All s. is metaphor, 824b

Slaughter He was led as a Lamb to the s., 484b

Slave being Thy Son, becoming a S., 485a; Everyone who commits sin, s. of sin, 816a; evil is s., though he be king, 399a; God makes no man a s., no doubter free, 537b; in Jesus Christ, there is neither free nor s., 825b; Love one too much, thou art s. to all, 554b

Slave-drivers Bishops should remember that they are shepherds, not s., 740b

Slavery banished without injury to rights, 826a; bonds of s., 825a; good emperors love freedom; bad, s., 355a; He freed us from s. of sins, 131b; law of nations has imposed yoke of s., 825a; prime cause of s., sin, 825a; traffic, than which nothing more base and wicked, 826a

Slaves admonished not to despise masters, 825b; be subject to your master, 824b; Catholic Church embraces s. or free, 121b; Either be wholly s. or wholly free, 825b; kings rule s., Romans free men, 353a; no galley s. in royal vessel of divine love, 357b; s. and law of charity, 155b

Slays let it be your necessity, not choice, that s. enemy, 906a

Sleep But s. stole on me unawares, 827a; Come and release me, 827a; death's ally, oblivion of tears, 826b; falls like snowflakes, 827b; freed from bonds of s., 599a; I shall s. like a top, 826b; I s. the s. of death, 826a; The dovecote doors of s., 827a; Thy servants who repose in s. of peace, 592b

Sleeping Be thou toiling, be thou s., 232a

Sleeplessness Suffered the trampling hoof of every hour, 827b

Sleeps He s., and life's poor play, 242b

Sleeve wearing of the heart upon the s., 343b

Slime made out of s. of earth, 8b

Slip 'Tis human fate sometimes to s. and fall, 334b

Sloth S. brings in all woe, 457b

Slumber dogmatic s. of denial, 12a; Our limbs refreshed with s. now, 599a

Slumbers Benumbing sense of ill with quiet s., 826b; Cast out the s. of the soul, 599a

Small Gigantic industry needed for discovery of tiny things, 352b; Great and s. have same accidents, 413b; Many s. make a great, 413b, 880b; S. things are best, 880b

Smell The fairest flowers have not the sweetest s., 425a

Smile A scornful s. lay keen On lips, 827b; fadeless splendor of His s., 47b; friendship's glance and beauty's s., 250b; s. of an Englishman, 297b; s. of the universe, 827b

Smiles Eternal s. his emptiness betray, 827b; Piled high with bales of s. and tears, 540b; Why is thy face so lit with s., 36b

Smite iron hot, time is to s., 476b

Smiter s. that healed us, 109b

Smites all can feel the God that s., 425b

Smoke No fire without some s., 344b

Snapdragon much s. growing on walls, 827b

Snare escape from s. of devil, 6b; The devil's s., 260a

Snares Where virtue, there many s., 899a

Sneer without sneering, teach the rest to s., 239a

Sneering She was a s. woman, 828a

Sneezing absorbs faculties of soul, 828a

Snobbishness having truck with slum-and-gutter, dwellers, 828a

Snow Pure as the s., we say, 462a; S.-white the altered mountains faced the day, 828a; the s., A flock unnumbered lies, 170b; The s. lay on the ground, 170a; Unstained as virgin s., 97b

Snowflake Insculped and embossed, 828b

Soar Bade them s. and sing for His joy, 65a; S. up, my soul, unto thy rest, 303b

Sob The short thick s., loud scream, 161a

Sober Be s. and keep vigil, 502a; 'Tis a madness to be s. alone, 828b

Sociability Delighting to converse with books or friends, 106b

Social art of s. life, 890b; Belief in God, unshaken foundation of s. order, 377b; Church has mission in temporal order, 829a; common good, standard of s. justice, 287b; man is a s. animal, 404b, 405b, 575b; s. and political status of Church, 182a; s. relations, one of man's requirements, 38b

Socialism afraid of its own principles, 828b; social order which denies natural right to property, 735a

Socialist No one can be, sincere Catholic and true s., 828b

Socialists S., Communists, Nihilists, uproot foundations of society, 828b

Societies private s., natural right of man, 38a

Society can not exist in which no one to govern, 406b; Civil s., renovated by Christianity, 165a; first natural tie of human s., man and wife, 575b; give s. air of respectability, 30a; Human s., composed of unequal elements, 829a; nation, multitude of men joined together in s., 631b; natural for man to live in s., 38b, 404a; religion in mixed s., 288a; return s. to the law of His truth, 489b; schizophrenia divides soul of s., 186b; S. is a rational process, towards an ideal, 829a; state, multitude joined together by bond of s., 844b; To be in, bore; to be out of it, tragedy, 829a; to *lose self* in a Society, 127b; unity of supranational s., 530b; What s. needs, baptism of Holy Spirit, 440b;

whole body of redeemed, congregation and s. of saints, 485a

Socrates, 164b, 306b, 414b

Sod Clinging to the Old S., in spite of wind and weather, 896a

Sods The heaped-up s. upon the fire, 448a

Soft Nature has cast men in so s. a mold, 807a

Soil no s. so barren but diligent tenderness brings forth fruit, 840a; S. not thy plumage With sublunary things, 854a

Soldier brave s. who fights by my side, 227a; Drinking is the s.'s pleasure, 279a, 829b; I am a s. of Christ, 829b; If the pulse of the patriot, s., or lover, 421b; s. is proven in warfare, 895a; When falls the s. brave, 830a

Soldiers Brothers, let us be His s., 829b; glory of arms all s. know, 31a; God, of Thy s. the portion and crown, 581a; God's true s., 581b; Men of the trumpets and the drums, 830a; S. of Christ! arise, 829b; the men behind the guns!, 830b; There lie many fighting men, 830a; Those Thy old s., great and tall, 582a; Three s. sat and diced, 778b

Solemn easy to be s., hard to be frivolous, 830b; s., not so very s., 453b

Solemnity no s. compared to s. of little boy, 830b

Soli S. Deo gloria, 367b

Solicitude keeping s. in place, 26a

Solitary Sweet s. life, thou true repose, 831a

Solitude greatest saints avoided company of men, 830b; in the fort of s., 830b; live to God in secret, 830b; no true s., except interior s., 831a; only justification for life of deliberate s., 831a; Woe him that is alone, 830b

Solitudes My soul has s., 550a

Something S. is better than nothing, 831a

Solomon My lover is a fool more wise Than S., 564b; Not S., for all his wit, 248a; S.! where is thy throne?, 367b

Solus s. cum solo, 486b

Solvency s. of Catholic Church in United States, 142a

Son Above the world; below thy Son!, 97a; admire condescension of Son, 82b; All-Father's only S., 8b; *Although no man knows Father except S.*, 392b; begotten of Father before all ages, 466a; bore incarnate Son our Lord, 39a; came down from heaven for our sins, 466a; Co-equal, co-eternal S., 284a; Face of the Father, 481a; Father and the S. being One, 480b; Father could not have received name apart from S., 339b; God's authentic S., our sole Lord, 481a; God the S., equal with the Father, 482b; I believe in Jesus Christ, His only S., 480b; If the S. has made you free, 35a; Image of the invisible God, 481a; impossible, s. of these tears should perish, 859a; In the name of the Father, S., Holy Ghost, 587a; Like father, like s., 339a; living bridge of My S., 108b; one Son and God of undivided Trinity, 86b; Only-begotten S. and Word of God, 482a, 588b; reason of Father is the S. of God, 480b; sitting now at right hand of the Father, 226a; s. is not blamed for his father's wrongdoing, 818a; S. of

God, eternal Word, 466a; s. of Mary, and S. of God, 480a; Sweetest Jesus, Mary's S., 75b; Thine only-begotten S. our Redeemer, 35b, 170a; took upon Himself sins of all, 186b; Until the S. of God appear, 8b; Who loveth Thee must love Thy S., 600a; who sees S., sees the Father also, 481a; *Word,* proper name of S., 439b

Song Alleluia, s. of sweetness, 12b; And I shall spin you a s., 832a; Angels, raise the s. of triumph, 36a; heaven had wanted one immortal s., 831b; Live, mistress of our s., 40b; Singing my native s., 65a; s., sanctitude, and poverty, 65a; S. is the leap of mind, 831b; S.'s Indian summer!, 831b

Songs all their wars are merry, all their s. are sad, 476b; best of all trades, make s., 832a; Bow down to hear the s. of praise, 599a; Go, songs, ended is our brief play, 45a; He could s. make and well indite, 685a; The very best s. that ever are sung, 832a

Sonorous with voice s., 74b

Sons all heaven's own home-born s., 40a; men fear saying they are s. of God, 256a; O Lover of s. of men, 6a; s. and heirs of God, 254b; *Ye have received spirit of adoption of s.,* 1a; Ye s. and daughters of the King, 285b

Sooner S. said than done, 275a

Soonest Good is best when s. wrought, 255a

Soother Be Thou the s. of our tears, 36a

Sophia, Princess, 141b

Sophistae non verba s., 268b

Sophistry lawyer's s., 814a; Mere light s., thing I despise most, 832b

Sophists The most sophistical of all s., 832b

Sops God fears no s. to avert His stroke, 381b

Sorcery forbidden to keep books in which s. taught or commended, 841b

Sore He hath the s. which no man healeth, 423b; It is ill healing of an old s., 832b

Sorrow And counted s. gain, 635b; better, little loss than long s., 550b; BVM salvation of them in sorrow, 85a; children of swift joy and tardy s., 45a; Earth has no s. that Heaven cannot heal, 304a, 833a; every soul here s.-tossed, 833a; Half my life is full of s., 540a; her soul pierced with s., 94a; may we be delivered from s., 89b; Oh, man's capacity For spiritual s., 852a; one great s. of my life, 295b; Only by s.'s ladder shall we rise, 834a; Our joy in s., 445a; O Sower of s., 834a; Our s. is the shadow cast, 833b; Pain and s., necessary medicines, 651b; Since knowledge is but s.'s spy, 463b; S. is given us on purpose, 832b; s.'s Mother, 94a; Sure there's a lethargy in mighty woe, 416a; The darts of toil and s., 834b; this wretchid world of s., 360a; Thou didst feel nor pain nor s., 39b; thy full seas of s., 94a, 475b; To everyone, joy or s. pays respects in turn, 498a; We wedded men live in s. and care, 573b; Where there is s., there is holy ground, 833b

Sorrowing to console the s., 155a

Sorrows cold sorrows by Thy hearse, 131a; Free from s., free from fears, 540b; Make not two s. of one, 833a; Man of s., wrapt in grief, 658a; On the Virgin's dolors seven, 94b; reach God through thee, 475b; Seven lights for seven woes, 97a; s. of the BVM at the cross, 93b; The s. of the Passion week, 769b

Sorry O my God, I am s. with my whole heart, 216b; Then too late thou wilt be sorry, 10b

Soter Iesous Christos Theou Uios S., 49a

Soul according to Thy likeness, 244b; activity of the s., 302a; alight with tranquil grace within, 411a; as eye to body, so mind to s., 835b; be solicitous for s. which will never die, 106a; BVM, my soul's saving, 100b; body is about the s., as garment, 282a; cannot be saved except in flesh, 105b; difference between s. and spirit, 836a; every rational s. possessed of freewill and volition, 356a; eyes of the s., 106a, 214a; feast of reason, and flow of s., 343a; for sake of s., that all religion exists, 754a, 835a; gift of a rational s., 569a; God is the life of the s., 345b, 409b, 835a; Holy Ghost, s. of Church, 126b; Immortality, inalienable property of human s., 358a, 464b; immortal, simple in its substance, intelligent, 834b; knowledge of God, dowry of the s., 393a; life whereby we are joined unto body, called s., 835a; living and eternal mirror of God, 836a; modern heresy of altering s., 837a; more worthy than body, 177b; mysteriously purified in baptism, 52a; no health of s. but in cross, 232b; nothing but little wind and smoke?, 12a; O Life of my s., 380a; one s., many tongues, 518b; part after His image and likeness, 52a; Remember that thou hast but one s., 541b; secret rooms of the s., 440b; separation of body and s., violent, 247a; s. aspiring to God, 30a; s. is master, body servant, 106a; s. is the life of the flesh, 345b, 835b; S. of Christ, sanctify me, 521b; spirit, flesh imprisoned, 302a; sprung from the breath of God, 834b; substance, sharing in reason, fitted to rule the body, 835a; substantial form of man's nature, 837b; this world, too small for s. of man, 565b; Understanding and love, two arms of s., 887b; union of s. and body in man, 182b; We commend to Thee s. of Thy servant, 244b; What constitutes man is principally s., 837b; worthy to be spouse of Christ, 213b

Souls Come, take possession of our s., 670b; gain of this world is loss of s., 362a; government of s., is art of arts, 659b; grant Thy holy s. eternal rest, 243a; Help, Lord, the s. which Thou hast made, 243a, 743b; immediately created by God, 316a; Let s. of Christians be like altars, 310a; Pray for the holy s. that burn, 743a; remain in places specially reserved for them, 246b, 741b; sanctify s. and bodies, 441b; S. are like wax waiting for seal, 503a; spirits of just are at rest, 247a; We lift our s., O Lord, to Thee, 622b; where s. of just repose, 89a

Sound *And suddenly there came a s.*, 785b; s. so wild, 58b

Sour Sweet meat will have s. sauce,

856a; Take the sweet with the s., 856b

Source O S. of all our yearning!, 258a; S. and Sea of man's believing, 370a; S. of knowledge itself, 22a

South But O the unfolding s.!, 477b; men that live in the s. country, 843a; The hills look over on the s., 472a

Sovereign God alone is s., 838a; independent s. nation, 838a; king has no peer in his realm, 45b; saying, will of s. has force of law, 533b; s. of a territory determines religion, 180a; The doctrine of s. to states is superstition, 907b; Upon my lap my S. sits, 566b

Sovereignty concept of s. divested of all obligations, 475a; contract under which king accepted s. from people, 774a; English and political s., 838a; He has s. who acknowledges no one greater, 838a; highest privilege of s., giving laws to people, 534a; illusion, to think that there can be no s. which is not absolute, 838a; inheres in the organic people, 838a; temporal s. of popes, 708b

Sow As meet as a s. to bear a saddle, 838b

Sower O S. of sorrow, 834a

Sown Such as ye have s. must ye needs reap, 770a

Space All s. is its outer gate, 305b; circumscribed by s., 21b; In s. cometh grace, 410a; Is there on earth a s. so dear, 555a

Spade A pick-axe and a s., 413a; One must not run at one's spade, 149b

Spain a stragling road in S., 152b; Oh happy regions, Italy and S., 871b; Thou shalt make castles then in S., 277a

Spake The earl s. one thing, but thought another, 838b

Spalding, Martin John Archbishop, 109b

Spanish 'tis not S., 'tis heaven she speaks!, 838b

Spare Better s. at brim than at bottom, 798b; Ever s. and ever bare, 798b; O Christ, Thy guilty people s.!, 792b; S. to speak, s. to speed, 838b

Sparing O God, ever merciful and s. of punishment, 500b

Spark a s. too much of heavenly fire, 14b; From little s. may burst a mighty flame, 880b

Sparrow hero perish or s. fall, 384a

Speak fellow who, when he is silent, will never begin to s., 939a; If charity does not draw us to s. of ourselves, 939a; Listen much and s. little, 939a; Spare to s., she can hear, 413a; those who s. well, and do not write well, 646b; To pray is the same thing as to s., 717b

Speaking Be brief when you cannot be good, 939a; Bend thyself to temper of whomsoever is s. to thee, 939a; In s. of others, always be calm and cheerful, 838b; keeping ourselves far from gossip and evil s., 403a; not to love much s., 838b

Speaks he s. best, that hath skill to hold peace, 813b

Spear nailed to cross and pierced with s., 399b; thrusting s. of gold into my heart, 562a; white Lamb, that hurt was with the s., 232b; with a s. thou hast pierced side of

thy Savior 400b; wounded with a direful s., 230a; Your charity, a s., 401a

Specie sub s. aeternitatis, 34b, 125b

Species, Eucharistic accidents of bread and wine remain after consecration, 311b; communicate under s. of bread only, 197a; these bare shadows, 75a; veils enveloping Sacrament, 73a; why Christ's Body and Blood offered to us under s., 311b

Specifics Universal evils, not cured by s., 315a

Speculate people sitting on ground s., 18a

Speculation Americans not given to s., 18a; difficult heights of s., 106b

Speculations Of all s. the market holds forth, 201b

Sped Folks show much folly, when things should be s., 422b

Speech abridging freedom of s. or press, 184b; fairy of fecundity of s., 160a; full liberty of thought and s., 355b; many have been harmed by s., 865b; Men have right to propagate things true and honorable, 355b; organ of human society, 720a

Speed Sober s. is wisdom's leisure, 645b; Spare to speak, spare to s., 838b

Spells Fling round my cradle magic s., 58b

Spend S., and God shall send, 939a

Spendthrift s. never reveals all his debts, 253b

Spent ill gotten, ill s., 362a; Soon gotten, soon s., 362a

Spes S. informorum, 95a

Sphere Thou ruler of this earthly s., 369a; When I survey the bright Celestial s., 824a

Spheres melody of s., 626a; nine s., 626a; Our sweet reward above the s., 36a; that pure love which heavenly s. toth guide!, 551a

Sphinx All day I watch the stretch of burning sand, 659a

Sphinxes S. without secrets, 921a

Spin S., daughter Mary, s., 839b; 'They toil not, neither do they s.', 866b

Spinster tasteless dry embrace Of stale virgin, 839b

Spirit And with thy s., 205b, 588b; co-essential and co-eternal, S. of God, 439a; difference between soul and s., 836a; flesh and spirit, 105b; fruits of the S., 262a; He must have little s., who thinks s. nothing, 839b; into Thy hands I commend my s., 521a; Lord, into Thy hands I commend my s., 520a; manly Christian s., 775b; My s. longeth for Thee, 823b; primacy of the s., 837b; S. of truth, 36a; To live according to s., 124b, 840a

Spiritual art and s. pleasures, 33b; canon law affects s. welfare of faithful, 111b; Church, s. concerns of her children, 713a; germs of s. vitality, 841b; grace of s. joys, 494a; hard to put s. life on paying basis, 841a; if earthly power deviates, judged by s. power, 701b; In all conversation let something always be said of s. things, 939a; In matters of political welfare, temporal power obeyed before s., 178b; inspiring role of s. things, 162b; mystic thinks s. very close, 839b; s. freedom, influence on cial culture, 457a; s. nature man and civilization, 140a; s. re-

birth through Christ's death, 43b; sum of s. life, yielding to movements of Spirit, 840b; temporal authority should be subject to s., 179a; There are no plains in the s. life, 841b; *The s. man judges all things,* 793b; way of s. path, strewn with wrecks, 841a
Spiritualism forbidden to keep books in which divination, taught or commended, 841b
Spiritual Life by His death we are carried into s., 43b; carnal cannot live s., 105b; drawn by Him to love of things unseen, 167a; exclude all things of earth, 37a; more worthy than earthly, 177b; well-regulated vigor of s., 160a
Spirits angels s. who are sent, 19a; God of s., 243b; Our guardian s. meet at prayer, 21b; Rejoice, ye s. and angels on high, 40b; s. and powers, 21a; *Who maketh His angels s.,* 19b; world of pure s., 21a; You s.! who have thrown away, 19b, 70b
Spiritu Et cum s. tuo, 588b
Spiritually power of constraining s. and temporally, 45b
Spiritui Sancto Gloria Patri, et Filio, et s., 588a
Spiritum Sanctum Accipe S., 69a
Spiritus Sancti In nomine Patris, et Filii, et S., 587a
Spit always s. into a handkerchief, 841b
Splendor fadeless s. of His smile, 47b; O s. of God, by Whose largess I saw, 390b; O s. of God's glory bright, 522a; Splendor of eternal Light, 8a; the Father's splendor, 19a; Trumpeter sound for the s. of God!, 378a
Sport Church does not forbid s. on Sunday, 842a
Spot a s. upon an alb, cannot be hid, 730a
Spotless how s. is thy virginity, 79b
Spots man sees s. of face, when he looks in mirror, 611b
Spouse BVM, s. whom Father took, 39b; chaste embraces of soul's S., 213a; For God and for His S., 105b; He thee His Spirit for S., 96b; Him, Who is S. of perpetual virginity, 640b; I run to meet you, my S., 639b; *my sister, my s., a garden enclosed,* 130b; S. to her love those chaste, 159a; s. to her love ascends, 40a; such a lady as God's s., 19b; the King, thy S., 402b; true s. of our soul, God, 561a; wakeful sleep of the s., 213a; we share in glory of Church as s., 130b; Worthy to be called s. of Christ, 213b; your God for Father, S. and Son, 96b
Spouses many holy men and women, faithful s., 437b
Spright Eternal S.! which art in heaven, 439b
Spring coming in of second s., 142a; Eternal s., with smiling verdure here, 842b; flowers of everlasting s., 303b; Jesus weeps in the ruins of my s., 109a; O baby s., 842b; O blessed babes! first flowers of Christian s., 441a; O dying souls; behold your living s.!, 168b; our sister the s., 843a; O s.! I know thee, 842b; the coming in of a second s., 842b; The s. comes with a full heart silently, 477b; 'Tis the s. of souls today, 285b; Wedded to the heart of s., 55b; Who knows not s.?, 842b

Sprinkle Thou shalt s. me with hyssop, 587a
Spumèd S. of the wild sea-snortings, 191b
Squall loud scream, and shriller s., 161a
Squander bishops should not devour revenues, 67b
Squandering In s. wealth was his peculiar art, 320a
Squire comparing theist with English s., 165b; Fill the capacious s., 368a
Stable Here on earth nothing is s., 351b; In Bethlehem's s. born in cold, 168b; prince Jesus in the poor stable, 169a; shepherds and kings adore in the s., 758a
Staff you appeared as a true s., 80a
Stage abandoning th'ungrateful stage, 11b; no man dies for love, but on the s., 554b; representation of the world, 843b; world, great s. on which God displays wonders, 843b
Stain Whom neither sin could s., nor death hold, 467b; *without s. without wrinkle,* 675a
Stained nothing can be s. where God is, 466a
Stains outward s. washed away, inward s. blotted out, 443a
Stake ill s. That cannot stand one year, 843b; playing every day for a small s., 362b
Stallions Thunder on, you silver s., 447a
Stand If I this night before God's throne should s., 492a; ill stake That cannot s. one year, 843b; S. like tower whose summit never shakes, 223a; Wisdom! S.!, 589a
Standard We measure everything by s. of future, 301b
Star As winds that blow against a s., 834b; bright s. of day, 100a; For now is risen the bright day-star, 168a; Hail, thou s. of ocean, 98b; If thou follow but thy s., 843b; keep eyes on this s.'s shining, 99a; Mary, s. of the sea, 99a; No s. is ever lost we once have seen, 844a; S. of Jacob, ever beaming, 83b; S. of morning, 84b, 91b; they that served the stars, 167a; think past light of oldest s., 11a; Thou s. to storm-tossed voyagers dear, 461a
Star-gazing people given to s. speculate, 18a
Starlight By cloudless s. on he treads, 843b
Starry Ascending by the s. road, 35b
Stars All my s. forsake me, 240b; all the fire-folk sitting in the air!, 844a; And all the s. looked down, 488a; Bells that from night's great bell-tower hang in gold, 844a; Catholic, more certain about fixed truths than fixed s., 885a; fires of a schoolboy's rocket, 844a; Lamps of God, 111a; lights of heaven, 41a; Look at the s.! look, look up at the skies!, 844a; moon to lead And all s. to follow, 239a; movements of s. and earth, 42a; Oh, may they shine with light divine, 171a; queen of night's changing globe, 40b; Seven s. make seven glows, 97a; stains the timorous light of s., 97a; Sun, moon, and s., 20b; The Christmas s. at Bethlehem, 171a; The old Judean s. aglow, 170b; The piercing beauty of the s., 612a; The s. make no noise, 844b; The s. shone bright, 170a; they have watched since

first The world had birth, 843b; those celestial fires, 843b; When she lit her glimmering tapers, 312b; When the s. pitch the golden tents, 844a; Why are thine eyes like s. alight?, 41b; written in his s. at birth, 41b; Yet s. shall rise at last, 276a
Starshine s. and candlelight, 111a
Starve ours alone is privileg'd to s., 644b
Starward Starry amorist, s. gone, 42a
State All s. with others' ruin built, 846b; association of families, governed by supreme power, 845a; belongs to primitive essence of nation, 845a; best form of government, 404a; cannot confer supremacy over Church, 141a; community, great means intended by God, 846a; Cooperation of Church and body politic, 184a; element of pluralism inherent in every true political society, 845b; evil origin of s., 844b; exists in virtue of natural law, 38b; family is the unit of the s., 336a; freedom of individual and s., 14b; inferior to body politic as a whole, 846a; Kings are the publick pillars of the s., 509b; laws, made for sake of body politic, 404b; multitude joined together by bond of society, 844b; natural for man to live in society of many, 404a; Religion, wonderfully helpful to s., 758a; should be organic unity of real people, 845b; society of men just, only if it obeys You, 844b; s. and education of citizens, 291a; s. asserts autonomy as a political order, 185a; s., as ultimate norm of all, 747a; S., for body politic, not body politic for s., 846a; s. has nothing to do with Church, but accept, 181a; s. is not in Church, but Church in s., 172b; superior part in body politic, 846a; true view of origin and nature of s., 845a
States different ways and s. of life in Church, 762b; diversity of s. and offices in Church, 433b; within family, destiny of s. is fostered, 336a
Statesman English s. bribed, not to be bribed, 909a; S., yet friend to truth, 846b
Statesmen The privilege that s. ever claim, 691a
States of the Church patrimony of the Church, 178a; pope as ruler of the S., 178b
Station crucial thing, that character should dignify s., 846b; Graciously grant us all to gain s., 19a
Statistical In name of cautious, statistical Christ, 157a
Statuat Legem credendi lex s. supplicandi, 546b
Statutes no priest, free to be ignorant of s. of Apostolic See, 698b; s. and natural law, 529b
Stay Oh s.! oh s.!, 497b
Steam Curse wheel and s., 568a
Steed When s. Is stole, make stable-door fast, 446b
Steeds The snowy s. vault upon, 191b
Steel Piteous, sad, wise, and true as s., 344a
Steele, Sir Richard, 23a
Step one s. enough for me, 490a
Stephen, St., 241b, 242a, 582a, 847a
Steps age, with stealing s., 10b; s. of active life, 5a

Sterile It is wrong to leave wife who is s., 267a; Let us not be s., let our souls be fertile to God, 897b

Steward S., managing riches of nature, 32a

Stigma Innocence of a fault, s. of punishment, 472a

Stillness An icy s. holds, 170b; that immense and brooding s., 814b; There is in s. oft a magic power, 847a

Stinginess free of gift, as poor man of his eye, 847a; His dole is soon done, 847a; In that house, as soon break neck as fast, 847b

Stoics ancient and modern, proud of concealing their tears, 498a

Stole Laurelled with s. victorious, 28b

Stolen When steed Is s., make stable-door fast, 446b

Stoles All in s. of snowy brightness, 83b

Stomach An empty s., calling loud for food, 847b

Stone angel death did roll s. away, 41a; not a s. Tell where I lie, 770a; The rolling s. never gathereth moss, 847b

Stones From stones and poets you may know, 5b; very s. would cry out, 30a

Stools Between two s. lieth the fall, 162a

Storm After a s. comes a calm, 847b; He mounts the s., and walks upon the wind, 388b; The s. hath its rhythmical beat, 689b

Story there's a s. in every breeze, 322b

Straight As right as a line, 847b; Carts well driven go along upright, 113b; To s. and narrow gate and way, 901b

Strain The s. upraise of joy and praise, 12b

Strains the pure soul's s. sonorous, 28b

Stranger A s. on a foreign ground, 169a

Strangers By s. honor'd, and by s. mourn'd!, 318b

Straw such things have been revealed, what I have written seems but s., 773b

Strayings recall me from my s., 716b

Stream It is in vain to stop the s., 22b; only living thing can go against s., 541a; Whence flow the s. that never fail, 104a

Street down the long and silent s., 240b

Strength BVM, s. to fearful, 87a; God, s. of those who put their trust in Thee, 881b; Humility, surest sign of s., 453b; in baptism we receive spirit of s., 50a; love's s. standeth in love's sacrifice, 550b; O s. and stay upholding all creation, 637a; s. and greatness give ability, 419b; s. of Church, 135a; s. to be strong, 714a; s. to fulfil God's will, 409a; Thine aid supply, Thy s. bestow, 74b; When Thou art our s., it is s. indeed, 848a; When we feel too faint, remember Christ's s., 848a; Who in the s. of Jesus trusts, 829b

Stricken with the scabbard, 856b

Strife Better a day of s. Than a century of sleep, 852a; Unvex'd with anxious cares, and void of s.!, 222b

Strike worker has right to s., 848a

Strings Ye have many s. to the bow, 893a

Strokes seven s. to kill, 282a

Strong God, Who had made you valiant, s. and swift, 931b; Holy God, holy S. One, holy Immortal One, 379a, 589a; The protest of the weak against the s., 516b

Stronger Where s. on weaker prey, 12b

Stronghold controversial s. of Christendom, 271a

Struggle fight gives us pleasure, not victory, 192b

Strumpets debauching of virgins, amours of s., 192b

Studies prompt to do what his s. prompt him, 848a; speedy progress of s., 848a

Studious happy hours employed upon my books, 107a; reign as kings of every sliding hour, 106b

Study do not plunge immediately into ocean, 848a; so much midnight oil destroyed, 276a; s. of created things, stepping-stone to immortal, 848a; S., to mortify thy vices, 532a; What! S. until reason lost dominion, 848b

Stumble Those who s. on plain ground, 149a

Stumbleth good horse that never s., 446b

Stumbling s. blocks of world, 189a

Stupid Whenever a man does a thoroughly s. thing, 848b

Stupidity But Shadwell never deviates into sense, 848b; s. and tenderness in adolescence, 6b

Style felicitousness in choice of words, 849a; independent of wealth of material, 32a; no other s. possesses beauty of Gothic, 29b; only master of s. I ever had, Cicero, 849a

Sub *S. sigillo confessionis,* 203b

Subdeacon behoves s., to assist deacon and present chalice, 850a

Subdeacons faithfully minister at holy altars, 849b; s. not allowed carnal marriage, 150b; watchful sentinels of heavenly army in Thy sanctuary, 849b

Subintroducta, 188a

Subject let each be s. to his neighbor, 641b; necessary to be s. to Roman pontiff, 701b; we would be s. to earthly rulers, 45b

Subjection s. to rulers and will of God, 45b

Subjectivism principal barrier to acceptance of Christian revelation, 850a

Subjects princes and s. serve one another, 173b; we are all s. of God's governance, 882a

Sublime scrap of knowledge about s. things, 512a

Sublunary Soil not thy plumage With s. things, 854a

Submission Church teaches s. to authority, 131b; Our Lord makes much of s., 642b; real motive for s., lies in faith from God, 850a; s. to authority and commands of God, 45b; S. to strong, servility, 850a

Subordinates justice requires, s. should be obedient to superiors, 642b

Substance God is one Substance, 50a; God is only immutable s. or essence, 301a, 380b; essences or s. admit of accidents, 301a, 380b

Subterfuge appeal not s., but refuge, 29a

Subtle For s. doubts had simple clues, 276a; s. man, easier to understand than natural man, 850a

Succeeding S. flocks s. pastors nurs'd, 875b

Success Every great achievement, inspired by motives of heart, 850b; Failure to perform impossible task, occasion of s., 691a; pathetic failure, appeals more than s., 850b; There is nothing that fails like s., 645a

Successful religious man, only s. man, 850b; so s., no time to keep up with times, 850b

Succession regular s. of bishops, 704a; traditions preserved by continuous s., 64a

Succession, Apostolic A. and appointment of bishops, 66b; episcopal succession from time of apostles, 23b; it would take too long to set out s. of all the churches, 703b; ordination of bishops and plan of Church flows onward, 433a; roll of bishops, in due s. from apostles, 850b; s. of bishops to whom apostles entrusted Church, 873b; succession of priests, 116b, 137a; strength of Anglicanism not in A., 23b

Succour My s. be, 87b

Such S. was I, s. by nature still I am, 219a

Sue Kings can forgive, if rebels can but s., 349b

Sufficient passion of Christ more than s., 44a

Suffer able to s., unable to s., 480a; Better one s., than a nation grieve, 631b; Desire earnestly always to s. for God, 851b; s. adversities for Christ, 9a; they s. most Who have no cross at all, 234a; To s. and endure, lot of humankind, 540a, 852a

Sufferance Of s. cometh ease, 851b; S. is a sovereign virtue, 661b

Suffered All thing may be s. saving wealth, 851b; My Lord has s. as much for me, 520b; Nothing s. for God's sake, passes without merit, 851b; s. and was buried, 226b; Word s. in flesh, was crucified, tasted death, 467a

Sufferer conqueror of himself, lord of the world, 851b

Suffering adversity strengthens us by its s., 851a; Better a day of strife Than a century of sleep, 852a; Bodily s. purifies souls that are good, 851a; Christ's s. from charity, 44a; no great blessings without first s., 103a; no loss, but gain, S. with humility, 851b; One ounce of patient s., 851b; Take cross He *sends,* 851b

Sufferings of martyrs equivalent to baptism, 53a; purified and made whole by s., 321a

Suffers whoso s. most hath most to give, 550b

Sufficeth Alone God s., 882a

Sugar well-regulated mixture of both s. and salt, 796b

Suicide deprived of ecclesiastical burial, 853a; he who kills himself, a homicide, 852b; If no humility, everybody would have committed s., 453a; s., sin, 852b

Suit s. of funeral black called Sunday best, 122a

Suitor The last s. wins the maid, 853a

Sum BVM, sum of all creation, 40a, 99b

Summa *S. ratio est quae pro religione facit,* 755b

Summer In s., when soft was the sun, 853a; Like birds follow the summer, 2a; One swallow maketh not s., 853a; smiles as she passes, 853a; The s. looks out from her brazen tower, 853a; When s. took in hand the winter to assail, 853a; When the s. lawns are fair, 48a

Summits Above the s. of our souls, 21b

Summum S. jus, summa injuria, 528a

Sun Be Thou praised, above all Brother S., 853b; BVM, Makes s. her robe, 40b; Catholic church holds it better for s. and moon to drop, 621a; Christ rises like s., 89a; Jesu, salvation's S. divine, 535a; Out of God's blessing into warm s., 103a; out of thee rose S. of righteousness, 632b; rising S., 299a; S., moon, and stars, 20b; S. of grace!, 168b; Sun of justice, 8a; S. of righteousness, 167a; S. which knows no setting, 89a; true S., His eternal Father, 196b

Sunday Church does not forbid sport on S., 842a; day on which God created world, 853b; day on which Savior arose from dead, 853b; declared by Christians, 854a

Sunlight autumn's mellow s., 47b

Sunrise Golden Earthquake in the east, 854b; the great earth quaking s., 240b

Sunset his last smile e'er he slept, 241a; I reckon first the s. and dawn, 240b; Now that sun is setting, and evening lights are kindled, 893b; Serene as s. glow, 97b

Sunsets S. are quite old-fashioned, 854b

Sunshine As s., s. still, 745b; As thick as motes in the sunbeam, 854b; Blest power of s.!, 854b; To sit in s. calm and sweet, 854b

Superabundant s. recompense offered by Christ, 44a

Superficiality Popular optimism, the apotheosis of s., 646b

Superfluities S. do not hurt, 855a; s. of the world, 618a

Superior abbot should realize name of s., 1a; By nature, man made s. to beasts, 300a; command implies a s., 376b; I never have resisted voice of lawful s., 643a; Let her be cheerful in maintaining discipline, 855a; Let s. be obeyed like mother, 642a; To offer hand to s., impolite, 418b; when s. lords it over vices, rather than over brethren, 660b

Superiority by nature men not superior to each other, 300a; humility, in position of s., 450b; taken for granted by Englishmen, 18a

Superiors s. should regard equality of nature, 300a; those entrusted with guidance, obliged to animate weaker, 855a

Supernatural cherish s. spirit, 548a; control natural inclinations, open to s. inspirations, 840a; Faith, door through which we enter s. order, 328b; modern world and s., 855a; Nature is always looking for the s., 855a; super-human, only place where you can find the human, 855a; s. light, called gift of understanding, 888a; s. perfection, 437a; wonderful things above, that hang on tree of life, 840a

Supernaturally to act s., 412a

Supernature aerial perspective of s., 34b

Superstition cruellest thing in world, 955b; recurs in all ages, 955b; religion of pure good feeling, positive orgy of s., 759b; s.,

to found hopes on ceremonies, 547a

Superstitious s. practices in some religions, 58a; world left to itself, 895a

Supper, Lord's After the Lord was risen from supper, 442b; *Coena Dominica, L.,* 442a; living Bread from heaven He gave, 74b; Lord's S., unity of Body of Christ, 72b; Make me sharer in thy mystic s., 595a; On the night of that last S., 74a

Suppers From heavy s. abstain, 423a; Great s. will the stomach's peace impair, 263b

Suppliant To you the s. prayer we pour, 28b

Supplicandi Legem credendi lex statuat s., 546b

Supplicate Lord God with all humility, 717a

Supplication s. to God which pierces heaven, 310a

Support be thou my s. and shield, 84a; do Thou prosper, s., encompass them, 416b

Supports Deity s. and maintains universe, 375a

Supranational s. universalism of Catholicism, 148a

Supremacy Act of S. under Elizabeth I, 141a; State cannot confer s. over Church, 141a

Supreme God is the great S., existing in eternity, 391a; s. pontiff and universal pope, 709b; we cannot be s. over ourselves, 225b

Surfeiting Nothing so unfitting for Christian, as s., 650b; *Take heed lest hearts be overcharged with s.,* 650b

Surgery all s. is theory, 955b

Surplice habit of holy religion, 189b

Surprise gaping mouth, testified s., 955b; God's great and ultimate s., 653b

Sursum S. corda, 591a

Survival irrepressible aspiration to s., 464b

Susanna Immortal God, that savedst Susanne, 87b

Swallow One s. maketh not summer, 853a

Swallowing for ever s. things, but never throwing them up again, 532a

Swan The jealous s., against his death that singeth, 955b; The milk-white s. chants, 955b

Sway love of pleasure and love of s., 572a; O'er bright new world He gave me s., 6a

Swear not allowed to s., 641a, 856a; To s. in weighty matters by the mass, 856a

Swearing oath may be made only in truth, 641a; S. is worse than theft, 856a

Sweepeth green new broom s. clean, 109a

Sweet all the sadness in the s., 792a; All things s. to holy love, 561b; And s. is s., 856b; Dear little One! how s. thou art, 487b; S. and bitter, bitter, s., 170b; S. meat will have sour sauce, 856a; Take the s. with the sour, 856b

Sweetness all the wild s. I wak'd was thy own, 422a; I have lived too much in the s. of God, 385b; Taste Thy s., 75a; With s. fills my breast, 488b, 630a

Swelling splendid phrases and s. sentences, 45a

Swift like a hound upon the moor, 48a; To all s. things for swiftness did I sue, 346a

Swim He must needs s., 856b; learn to s. in troubled waters, 856b

Swinburne, Algernon, 849b

Swine Men should not put pearles To-fore rude s., 667a; s. overfat is cause of his own bane, 338b

Swings man must be dead before he s., 358a

Sword BVM received s. of sorrow in heart, 39b; Christ bade His followers take the s., 932a; Church and s. of blood, 177a; her thoughts pierced her as a s., 93b; He that striketh with the s., 856b; He that taketh s., worthy of perishing with s., 886a; 'My peace I send you, and I send a s.', 666b; Now at length the s. had passed, 93b; s. shall pierce thy own soul, 93b; s. should be under s., 179a; The s. of heaven is not in haste to smite, 740b; to crozier Is joined the s., 179b

Sword-blades And angry s. flashing left and right, 304b

Swords Both s. belong to Church, spiritual and material, 176b; one exercised on behalf of Church, other by Church, 179a; there are two s., spiritual and temporal, 179a

Sycamore As I sat under a s. tree, 856b

Sydneian S. showers Of sweet discourse, 518b

Symbol Catholic Church allows no s., between soul and Creator, 486b; S. of faith which Roman Church uses, 145b

Symbolical s. expression of spiritual values, 33a

Symbolism balance between realism and s., 34b

Symbols clothed in variety of material s. and forms, 546b; species of Eucharist, 73a

Sympathy motherly s. of BVM at crucifixion, 93b; Our hearts, The genuine twins of s., 890a

Sympathies With s. large enough to enfold All men, 857b

Symptoms I am dying of a hundred good s., 282b, 521b

Synagogue *God stood in the s. of gods,* 172a; that part of faithful before time of Lord, 126b

Synthesis God, s. of infinite and boundary, 689a

System 'eccles. and dogmatic s.', 147b

Systems false s. of the age, 290b

T

Tabernacle From out its orient t. drawn, 78b; I gaze in silence on the little door, 78b

Tabernacles divine t., 39b

Tabernacling God, t. with men, 30a

Table Lord's T., 597a; rise from t. and take the air, 423a; thinly spread, 268b; we depart from T. breathing fire, 71b; where we communicate together, 71a

Tables graven t. of law, 41a

Take Better to give than t., 367a; *he that can t. it,* 158b; *T. and drink ye all of this,* 592a; *T. and eat ye all of this,* 592a; *T. and read, t. and read,* 748b

Taketh God t. me as I am, 153b

Tale A good t. ill told, 857a; all who told it added something new, 403b; How many a t. their music tells, 58b; Say forth thy t., and tarry not, 857a; Scarce any t. was sooner heard than told, 784b; that fleeth far is sure to catch many new feathers, 857a; This is a fair t. of a tub, 857a

Talent He that hath t., let him hide it not, 155a; No one respects a t. that is concealed, 857b

Talented Hell is full of the t., 426a

Talents T. are distributed unevenly, 857b

Tales Refrain from listening to worldly t., 857a; t. of human things, 20b; To tell t. out of school, 403b

Talk Do not trust all who t. smoothly, 939a; feast of reason, 279a; herd, Who think too little, and who t. too much, 857b; real reason an Englishman does not t., 857b; T. to every woman as if you loved her, 857b; we wish not to know, but to t., 236a

Talkativeness as full of words as woman, 11b; Much t., sign of feeble mind, 858a

Talked For all the town t. of her, 403b

Talking t. about oneself, boring, 107b

Talks E'en wit's a burden when it t. too long, 859b

Tanti Sunt t. quanti et denotamur, 163a

Taper With waxen t. at my head, 251b

Tapers When she lit her glimmering t., 312b

Tara The harp that once through T.'s halls, 421b

Tartuffe T. has emigrated to England, 296b

Taste bad in bad t., unpardonable, 48a; full use of t., act of genius, 858a; praise wine before t. grape, 714b; Wish not to t. anything, 395a; you have tyranny of t., 274b

Taught Bachelor's wives be well t., 858b; Better fed than it, 858b; first he wrought, and afterward he t., 316b; Men must be t., as if you t. them not, 858b; through Him Thou hast t. us, 480a

Tavern guzzlers in the tavern, 200a

Taverns He knew the t. well in every town, 472a

Tax No t. more legitimate, that levied to dispel mental darkness, 801b; t. exemption of clergy, 188a

Taxation just t. by state, 858a

Taxes they who pay the t. bear the rule, 858a

Te Deum Laudamus, 340a, 372b, 858a

Te igitur, 591b

Teach better to light up than merely to shine, 213a; God didst t. multitude of gentiles by preaching of Paul, 664a; right of Church to t., 119a; t. hearts of faithful by light of Holy Ghost, 439a; T., O t. us, holy Child, 169a; Time must always ultimately t., 870b; To discover and to t., distinct functions, 858b; To tolerate everything is to t. nothing, 24a

Teacher Augustine greatest t. after apostles, 44b; t. of youth, rights of his own, 858b; The master loseth time, When disciple will not hear, 858b; witness and t. of religious truth, 23b

Teachers Brownson's vocation to teach t., 109b; Catholic t. and dogmas, 118b; ministry of prophets and t., 67a

Teaching Everybody incapable of learning has taken to t., 859a; take stand on Church's traditional t., 875a; T. of Bible and Church not

opposed, 63a; things unknown proposed as things forgot, 858b

Tear Mute and magnificent, without a t., 416a; O 'tis a t. Too true a t., 859a; our immortality Flows thro' each t., 859b

Tears Be Thou the soother of our t., 36a; Behold Thy Mother wash'd in t., 94a; daily sacrifices of our t., 308b; fair-coined soul rusting in t., 109b; gain everything, 859a; Give me t., O God, 764b; grant me t. of repentance, 535a; His t. fall from the skies, 492b; impossible, son of these t. should perish, 859a; It is only to happy that t. are a luxury, 859a; Let us haste with t. of sorrow, 7b; Man is a creature, born and nurst in it, 859a; money of whose t., 109a; music, most nigh to t., 627a; My bankrupt heart has no more t. to spend, 416a; nature is wrapt in t.!, 487a; Piled high with bales of smiles and t., 540b; shall fall like bells upon your tomb, 109a; some tell their days by flow of t., 859a; T. on my pillow—witness in vain, 859b; that trickled down our eyes, 859b; There is no cure Nor antidote but t., 765a; this wretched vale of t., 95b; those who have no t. for Time, weep in Eternity, 859b; Veiled, as with mail, in midst of t., 157a; What a sea of t. and sorrow, 94b; Where sin was hatch'd, let t. now wash the nest, 764b; Whilst I dwell in this valley of it, 251a; Your tunes are t., 441a

Technical t. processes and moral asceticism, 37a; t. processes, subordinated to ethics, 37a

Technique science enables us to deal with t., 34a; t. is good, machinery good, 37a

Techniques t. and moral idealism, 186b

Tecum Pax t., 594b

Tediousness E'en wit's a burden when it talks too long, 859b; sew up every hole in a net, 859b

Teeth In spite of his t., 873a; saints, as t. of the Church, 792b; With comb and brush, cleanse t. and hair, 423a

Teetotaler dipsomaniac and the abstainer, 279b

Telescope Put by the t.!, 803a

Tell woman would tell one anything, 11a

Temperament t., disease that afflicts amateurs, 32b

Temperance disposition which sets bounds to passions, 859b

Temperate be t., like athlete of God, 43a

Tempest in that silence we the t. fear, 111a; When the t. rages round thee, 89a

Temple BVM indissoluble t., 81a; brighten this t. by power of Thy presence, 171a; fashion their hearts to be t. of glory, 206b; Standing in t. of thy glory, 86b; t. of the Holy Ghost, 40b; The t. I would build should be all white, 928a; veil of t. rent in twain, 399b

Temples make Thy t. worthy Thee, 440a; we shall be His t., 888a

Tempora O t.! O mores!, 700b; *T. mutantur et homines deteriorantur,* 153a

Temporal Church has mission in t. order, 829a; devil rules over lovers of t. goods, 223b; Do not love things t., 448b; In matters of political welfare, t. power obeyed before spiritual, 178b; In t. law,

nothing just but from eternal law, 528a; Let t. things serve use, 860a; not all solicitude about t. affairs, forbidden, 860a; O that t. things would come to an end!, 303a; pass through things t., 736b; t. authority, instituted under Church, 46a; t. authority should be subject to spiritual, 179a; t. government does not owe existence to spiritual, 180a; t. law, may be justly changed in course of time, 528a; t. monarch receives authority from Source, 845a; We commit sinful act by turning to t. attraction, 817b; Where is the vanity of t. things?, 244b

Temporally power to constrain spiritually and t., 45b

Tempt That thou dost come to t. thy father's soul, 861a

Temptation cupidity opens door for devil's suggestion, 860a; devil cannot lord it over servants of God, 860a; enemy cannot enter save by door of our consent, 861a; ensnaring word of serpent, 85a; free our hearts from t. of evil thoughts, 860b; God does not punish people for what they would have done, 860b; hurricanes of t., 99a; *Lead us not into t.,* 408a, 593b; No man so perfect, not to have t., 860b; not be separated from Thee by t., 860a; Satan's fraud, 83b; sting of flesh, 212a; There is no sin in t., 861a; tries a just man, 861a; watchful, in beginning of t., 860b; Withstand beginning, after-remedies come too late, 860b

Temptations able to resist devil and his t., 242a; all the t. that beset us, 416b; grace to withstand the t. of devil, 861a; I am bowed down with many t., 98a; Inconstancy of mind, beginning of all evil t., 860b; Lord permits us to fail in little occasions, 861a; no order so holy, where there are not t., 860b; t. of hell cannot stain soul that does not love them, 861a; To all t. is that soul left free, 209a; we overcome great t., not by our own strength, 861a

Tempted I t. all his servitors, 211a

Tempter serpent's strength in being t., 89b

Tempts devil t. that he may ruin, 860a; God t. that he may crown, 860a; Satan t. by making rich, not making poor, 861a

Ten Commandments T. and problem plays, 276b

Tender sympathies and t. feelings, 861b

Tenderness dealt with by hands pierced, 207a; In thee is pity, in thee t., 99b; stupidity and t. in adolescence, 6b

Tenement t. of clay, 105b

Tenets T. with books, 731b

Tennyson, Alfred Lord, 861b

Tension religion and spiritual t., 207a

Tent t. of God and Word, 100b; They have struck heaven's t., 21b

Tents When the stars pitch the golden t., 844a

Terce (Third Hour), 861b

Teresa of Jesus, St. Live here, great heart, and love and die and kill, 424a; She's for the Moors and martyrdom, 584a; 'tis not Spanish, 'tis heaven she speaks!, 838b

Terrenum t. quidem animal, sed coelo dignum, 569a

Territory sovereign of t. determines religion, 180a

Terror In that most extremest t., 247b; *my name spreads t. among the nations*, 307a; O what t. in thy forethought, 247b

Testament new and eternal t., mystery of faith, 592a; nothing more due to men, than expression of last will, 914b

Testament, New belongs to those renewed by grace, 61a; Church gathered before N.T. written down, 62a; kingdom of heaven, 61a; so called because brings in new, 61a

Testament, Old must be spiritually interpreted, 61a

Testamentary apostates shall not have t. capacity, 28a

Testimonium t. animae naturaliter Christianae!, 834b

Testimony apostates disqualified from giving t., 28a; immemorial t. of Catholic Church, 115b; t. of good conscience, glory of good man, 209a; t. of man's conscience, only complete excuse, 208a

Tests heavinesses by which Lord t. and confirms His own, 809a

Text use same old t., as bold as brass, 48b

Texts T. are explained by fasting and by prayer, 318a

Thanks be to God, 275b, 519b, 589a; give t. for God's blessings, 59b; Give t. frequently to God for all benefits, 862a; give t. to God because mighty, 70b; Give t. to Him with perfect faith, 286b; Glad t. let us Godward carry, 40a; I give t. to Thee, 196b; in all places give t. unto Thee, O holy Lord, 591a; in all things give Him t., 388b; Let us give t. to the Lord, 591a; T. must I give Because seven times are not eight, 862a; we give it. for gifts conferred upon us, 862a

Thanksgiving Break forth in it., every nation!, 167b; kind of prayer, 720b; to Thee we render glory and t., 596a; when things go wrong, 862a

Theater clergy shall not witness dramatic performance, 862b; devil's own ground, 862b; In t., demon of impurity displays pomp, 862b

Theaters Altars are God's t., 13b

Theft To wrest a thing from friend is t., 159b; Your law punishes t., 864b

Theist comparing t. with English squire, 165b

Theocritus, 164a

Theodosius I, Emperor, 173a

Theologian Let no Christian, whether philosopher or t., embrace novelty, 682a; one who has mastered theology, 862b

Theologians must always return to source of divine revelation, 864a; taught by Church, 411b; t. and typical Christians, 125b

Theological All human conflict ultimately t., 207a; Nothing dies harder than t. difference, 217a

Theology angels' bread, 863b; appeal to divine authority, highest and most cogent argument, 863a; articulate religion, 864a; avails itself of human reasoning, 863a; badge of heresy: dogmas unfruitful, no t., 430a; Bonaventure, *princeps* in mystical t., 106b; Catholic t., not for or against democracy, 256a; deserves to be called highest wisdom, 863a; existence of religion, always involved t., 864a; faith, free from trammels of t., 608b; For mystic, important that t. should flourish, 629a; hath vexed me ten score times, 863b; investigation of divine knowledge, 874a; Love is the abridgement of all t., 863b; most noble of studies, 864a; Philosophy, called divine, 863a; premises of Christian t., revealed truths, 863a; principles of faith, foundations of Christian t., 863b; properly speaking, no liberalism in Catholic t., 650a; purpose of t. is threefold, 863a; remains ever fresh, 864a; science, whereby saving faith begotten, nourished, 862b; streak of agnosticism in Catholic t., 396b; teaches of God, taught by God, leads to God, 863b; t. baffled, how grace influences mind, 220b; traditional teaching of natural t., 864a; true knowledge of object of religious experience, 864a; truths of philosophy cannot be contrary to truths of faith, 863b; two kinds of t., 863a; University education without t., 864a; view, t. to be treated like philosophical sciences, 863b; word 'God', t. in itself, 388a; works dealing with t. must have *imprimatur*, 152a

Theophany (Epiphany), 299a

Theophoroi, 888b

Theophoron, 481b

Theory experience seems better than a t., 627b; None of us can go little way with t., 864b; reconcile t. and fact, almost an instinct, 332a

Theos Agios o T., ischyros, athanatos, eleison imas, 589a

Theotokos, 80a, 81a, 81b

Theou Iesous Christos T. Uios Soter, 49a

Thesis defence of t., easier than discovery of truth, 884b

Thick through t. and thin, 104b, 767b

Thief Adulterer, more grievous offender than t., 7a; As meet as a rope for a t., 864b; for no t. bears being stolen from, 864b; Like a t. that comes at midnight, 501b; My lover is a t., 564b; once a t., ever more in danger, 864b; received reward of his confession, 442a

Thieves In the midst of two t., 231b; Where be no receivers, there be no t., 864b

Things *all t. are vanity under the sun*, 534b; Remember, world is not t. but persons, 154a; T. done cannot be undone, 275a

Think herd, Who t. too little, and who talk too much, 857b; I must not t. of thee, 763b; I t. and t. on things impossible, 241a; moment one sits down to t., all nose, 867a; purpose of book of meditations, to teach you how to t., 602a

Thinker bigot or slave of dogma, t. who has thought thoroughly, 499b

Thinkers glory of Church, can produce saints, also t., 333b

Thinking harmed by t., few or none, 865b; in isolation ends in being an idiot, 473a; Man is but a t. reed, 866a; Men have power of t., that they may avoid sin, 865b; sweetest time in life in t. to be spent, 215a, 866a; To become Catholic is not to leave off t., 220a

Thinks if he doubts, he t., 275b; Man t., God directs, 397a

Thirst itself sating, of itself makes t., 196b; love and t. for Thee, 159a; My t. shall turn to springs, 109a; natural t. which is unquenchable, 864b; t. of their faith, 441b

Thirsting t. and sighing for presence of God, 213a

Thirty T. years among us dwelling, 655b

This *T. is My body*, 73b, 310b

Thomas Aquinas, St., 32a, 865a

Thomas More, Saint, 62a, 865a

Thomas of Canterbury, St., 582a, 865a

Thomism mistake to think T., house replete with philosophical convenience, 865a

Thomist no Catholicism which is T., 865b

Thorn Welcome the t., it is divinely sent, 277a

Thorns Behold the Man! who wore A crown of t., 657b; crown of roses and of t., 38a; fuel wounding t., 30a; He That is King of angels, crowned with t., 400a; heart, first to be touch'd by the t., 539a; His own resplendent t., 95a

Thought a sword, a spade, and a t., 867b; All human t. has its horizons, 867a; but one t. greater than that of universe, 866b; by t. I embrace the universe, 866a; climax of anxiety, no consecutiveness of t., 867a; creation is Thy t., 373b; earl spake one thing, but t. another, 838b; Every holy t., gift of God, 408a; full liberty of t. and speech, 355b; God, more truly t. than expressed, 374b; governmental censorship of t., 473a; He exists more truly than He is t., 374b; He must be sought beyond t., 375b; I have heard said, t. is free, 865b; I have sinned exceedingly in t., word, and deed, 587b; I shun the t. that lurks in all delight, 763b; In present day, mistiness mother of wisdom, 866b; Jesu! the very t. of Thee, 488b; kind of sight of the mind, 865b; Man's greatness lies in his power of t., 866a; nor does aspect of His mind pass from t. to t., 383a; O how the t. of God attracts, 672a; penny for your t., 865b; single t. of man, greater worth than whole world, 866a; soul's glance, 213a; strict laws of t. and historical growth, 270b; t. of God, happiness of man, 420a; Thy t. was God, which took the form of Thee, 339b; To attempt in verse things scarce to t. assured, 865b; very energy of t. keeps thee from God, 866b; What t. can think, another t. can mend, 866a

Thoughts blossom-t. that here within, 866b; Clear Thou my t., 77a; Difficult t., quite distinct from difficult words, 643b; faculty of concealing t. in words, 367a; free our hearts from temptation of evil t., 860b; Give to thy t. loftier range, 37b; Her flocks are t., 811b, 866b; I cannot conceive of a man without t., 866a; Impassioned t., high aspirations, 643a; mere chance that suggests t., 866a; my fairest t., my tallest flowers, 363a; My heart has t., 867a; Occupy your minds with good t., 865b; our t., directed to fulfilment of Thy will, 731a; second t. are best, 209a; second t. best, but not in matters of conscience, 866b; Thy frolic t. untold, 347a; to God, your very t. shout, 716b; undying t. I bear, 464a, 867a; When evil t. come into one's heart, 867b

Three T. may keep counsel, if two be away, 813b

Threshing-floor Eucharist likened to t. of Lord, 72b; scourged upon the t., 78a

Thrice T. and three times t. his name, 234b

Thrift He who watches out for his pennies, 113a; In choice of t. let honor be your gain, 867b; the really romantic thing, 867b; When t. and you fell first at a fray, 867b

Thrive hard to wife and t. both in a year, 573b; He that will t., must ask leave of wife, 912a

Throne After royal t., comes death, 463b; apostolic throne, 176a; bright gate to Jesus' t., 232a; dread t. of God on earth, 100a; English Protestantism, religion of t., 23b; Great King, from heaven's high t. descending, 168b; If I this night before God's t. should stand, 492a; It is not hard to die upon a t., 543b; living t. of Whom, 41a; stood around t. of God, 20a; To a lofty t. above, 40a; Virgin is the t. of the cherubim, 167b

Throned O ye who t. in glory dread, 28b

Thrones one of nine orders of angels, 18b

Throng Hark! a glad exulting t., 8b; I saw the t., so deeply separate, 198b

Thrush A voice peels in this end of night, 868a

Thumb Every honest miller has a golden t., 606a

Thunder Heaven's great artillery, 868a; The organ of Thy t. in the air, 586a

Thunders Mid Thine everlasting t., 378a

Tibi Gloria t., Domine, 589a; *Laus t., Domine,* 589b

Tide As the inhastening t. doth roll, 753b, 868a; Flowing from His pierced side, 284b; tarrieth no man, 645b; T. and wind stay no man's pleasure, 645b, 868a, 869a; t. of life that carries me, 753b; Until the t. doth turn, 22b

Tides I admire Thee, Master of the t., 374a

Tie Friendship, a holy t., 9b; well-tied t., 278a

Ties common t. of human nature, 13a

Tiger If man proves t. is optical illusion, 868b; kittenish and mild, 868b

Tigress What t. does not purr over her young, 625a

Tile-shards children who build houses of t., 26b

Timaeus of Plato, 372b

Time *accepted t.,* 219a; appropriate t. for each word and deed, 891a; As long as t. shall be, 6a; Behold The t. is now!, 347a; bring t. to close, as a poem's ending, 393b; cannot harm beauty, 55a; Cunning soother of all sorrow, 870a; does nothing, but is condition of all things, 870a; doth him cure, 869a; eternity and t., rightly distinguished, 435a, 869a; eternity's fountain, 869b; Fair vision of t. forever fled, 1a; Father, Who makest t. swiftly slide, 372b; God is not confined in t., 387b; God's contrivance for opportunity to know Him, 305b; God, neither began to live in t., nor endeth ever, 386a; Great acts take t., 4b; hath a taming hand, 869b; hidden root of change, 65b; holds the timeless One, 25a; Man who made t. made plenty of it, 870b; messenger of fate!, 870a; must always ultimately teach, 870b; Next to grace, most precious gift, 870a; nor t. nor life sojourns not, 869b; Now t. has fled, 11a; O sweet the t., 295b; past, most momentous part of t., 659a; present glance of God extends over all t., 383b; proper measure of movement, 306a; quickly slips, 149b; raised to the infinite, 469a; rue t. that now thou spend'st amiss, 869a; See how t. makes all grief decay, 416a; Seek not t. when t. is past, 645b; Spurns the tame laws of t. and place, 603a; steals our years away, 603a; takes no holiday, 868b; tends towards non-being, 868b; those who have no tears for T., weep in Eternity, 859b; T. and place give best advice, 870b; T. his glass sits nodding by, 870a; T. is a treasure worthy high esteem, 869a; T. is our bound no more, 252a; T. is short, eternity is long, 306a, 869b; T. is tickle, 869a; T.'s hoar wings grow young therein, 277b; T., Way, and Wayfarer, 493a; T.! where didst thou those years inter, 765a; to soul which aspires to eternity, 303b; tract of t. begins to weave, 10b; trieth truth in every doubt, 276a; very merry, dancing, Laughing, t., 362a; wears all his locks before, 645b; What are the years to t.?, 870a; What then *is* t.?, 868b; when t. shall date thy glory, 10b; Who orderest t. and change aright, 809b; wisest grieve most at loss of t., 869a

Timeless Time holds the t. One, 25a

Times go by turns, chances change by course, 869b; no time to keep up with the t., 850b; Nor is it right to say there are three t., 868b; t. telescoped, in religious art, 33a; Which cannot come again, 659a

Timidity Where heart has failed, 870b

Timiotera, 81b

Timorousness courage cool At every trifling thing!, 454b; This fault of pusillanimity and timorous mind, 324a

Tintoretto, 32b

Tiny gigantic industry needed for discovery of t. things, 352b

Tipperary Ah, sweet is T. in the springtime, 476a

'Tis ''T. I; be not afraid!', 210b

Tit T. for tat, 773b

Title canonical t., 649a; successive t., long, and dark, 870b; Who gain'd no t., who lost no friend, 846b

Toast Hot as a t., 447b

Today Happy the man who can call t. his own, 871a; In the face of the stern t., 871a; Let me get through t., 870b; Tomorrow, do thy worst, for I have liv'd t., 871a

Toil 'They t. not, neither do they spin', 866b

Toiler a t. dies in a day, 277b

Toilet t. of women, 277b

Toiling Be thou t., be thou sleeping, 232a

Tolerance Catholics bound to practical t. of other denominations, 872a; principle of 't.', 872a

Tolerate To t. everything is to teach nothing, 24a

Tolerated unbelievers may be t., 871b

Toleration each kind of religion, its place in the state, 355a; English Catholics and t., 871b; fundamental right, every man worship according to convictions, 871a; General and equal t. of all denominations, 184a; If Catholics were the 'imperial race', 872a; Mutual tolerance of religious views, product of doubt, 872a; to Christians and others, free facility to follow religion, 871a; where coexistence of different religions admitted, 354b

Tolle T. *lege, t. lege,* 748b

Tollis Agnus Dei, qui t. peccata mundi, 594a

Tomb All ye that fix your eyes upon this t., 542a; Christ raised BVM from t., 39a; dark in the silent t., 251a; My eyes are flowers for your t., 109a; Myrrh a future t. foreshows, 298b; our comeliness, within the t., 245a; Sabbath of the t., 872b; The t. is built, 250b; this cold tomb Of life, 41a; Thou hadst a virgin womb, And t., 872a; veil of the t., 250a; womb Opes on courtyard of the t., 872b; Where high the t. of royal Egypt heave, 643b

Tombstone at his heels a stone, 242b

Tomorrow I shall not fear t., 870b; T.'s falser than the former day, 445b; Who dare trust upon t., 869b

Tone having all taken the t. of God, 889b

Tongue breaketh bone, 872b; by his t. a fool is often known, 348a; Every t. proclaims thy praises, 24b; Fools cannot hold their t., 348a; Her t. is no edge tool, 872b; His t., the Spirit's two-edged sword, 872b; Hold your t., 767a; keep well thy t., keep friend, 358b; Many a man's t. broke his nose, 872b; My son, keep well thy t. and keep thy friend, 872b; no t. to wound us, 215a; Sing, my t., the glorious battle, 230b; Sing, my t., the Savior's glory, 74a; wicked t. is worse than a fiend, 872b

Tongues fiery t., 439b; Filling hearts, and t. endowing, 670b; Give t. to speak, 439a; one soul, many t., 518b; Your t. run before your wits, 872b

Tonsure, Clerical, Clerics and first t., 190a; conferring of c., 189a; habit and t. contribute little, 761b

Top-hat religion praying into a t., 122a

Torment deliver us from eternal t., 84b; Joy, heightened by contrast of t., 497a

Torments no respite or end to t., 426a; racked with your t., 479b; Reck not of racks, their t. are but toys, 584a; Who for me in t. died, 93b

Torture absurd to t. men into believing, 57b; T. us, rack us, condemn us, crush us, 851a

Tory He thinks like a T., talks like a Radical, 692a

Toryism 'springs immortal in the human breast', 537a

Totalitarianism Catholic Church, only tolerable t., 873a; idea which credits state with unlimited authority, error, 530b

Touch Lord, with Thy t. divine,

599a; Nor t. nor taste must look for more, 77b
Touches That which t. all, should be approved by all, 534a
Touto En t. nika, 229a
Tower BVM, Church's unassailable t., 100b; From the shaken t., 59a; Ivory T., 84b; Stand like t. whose summit never shakes, 223a; Thou t. against the dragon proof, 461a; T. of David, 84b
Towers High t. have been man's crime, 296a
Towns Golden t., 873a
Toys No lurking t., which city life affords, 831a; Not on her t., 103a; of what t. We made our joys, 873a
Trace no place in world but contains some t. of God, 390a
Trade He takes his life, who takes away his t., 549a; Wielding t.'s master-keys, 296a
Tradition all doctrine which agrees with apostolic churches, 874a; although many dialects, meaning of t. one and same, 873b; apostles delivered themselves with utmost clearness on certain points, 874a; apostles made over divine revelation to generation after them, 876a; apostolic t. preserved in Roman Church, 704a; Christian t., living and perpetual revolution, 876a; Church, that appeals merely to ancient written words, 876a; decree established by all bishops, 875a; divine and true, handed down from beginning, 429a; has come down to us, without addition or subtraction, 873b; In all things I desire to follow the Roman Church, 874b; In doubtful questions learn what unsuspected ancients say, 875b; living t. of Catholicism, like breath of body, 876b; Must all t. then be set aside?, 875b; number of doctrines, not in writing, 876a; not overpassing the divine t., 875a; Only that held as certain, which all have confirmed, 874b; opinions of Fathers who persevered in holy Catholic faith, 874b; order of t. handed on, 873b; Over and over again, t. turns out to be true, 435a; proper for churches, 874a; recourse to oldest churches, 873b; revert to opinions of holy fathers, 875a; Succeeding flocks succeeding pastors nurs'd, 875b; teaching of apostles, true gnosis, 873b; those at head of Church, should teach t., 874b; thoughts, principles, like breathing of Church, 876a; Thus by t. faith was planted first, 875b; t. and consensus of Fathers, 144b, 340b; t. and Scripture, 62a, 144a; t. of Church and canon of Bible, 60b; treat t. faithfully and wisely, 273b; universal t. of Fathers, 117a, 875a; We should observe everything which has been handed down, 874b; weightiest authority is Church's custom, 875a; what Catholic Church has held universally, 114b, 876a; whatever believed, has authority of Scriptures, t., usage, 875a; which has continued until now, 874a; With regard to t., two precautions to be observed, 875a; word of God, written or unwritten, 145b; youth of America, their oldest t., 15b
Traditional Church, essentially t. and revolutionary, 876a; take stand on Church's t. teaching, 875a

Traditions All religious t. contain elements of truth, 148b; derive authority from Church, 875b; dictated by Christ or Holy Ghost, 64a; I resolutely accept eccles. t., 145b; Let them innovate in nothing, but keep t., 874a; peasant t. keep close to earth, 347a; pertaining to faith and morals, 64a; phalanx of hostile t., 271a; preserved in Cath. Church by succession, 64a; received by Council of Trent, 64a; religious t. and art, 31b; to be observed in form handed down, 874b; t. of separate churches, 117a; use of one church, not to be annulled, 874b; We should not conform with human t., 876b; what other places have done well to retain, we too maintain, 874b
Traffic Jarred by sharp sounds, 185b
Tragedies exceedingly mortal epics or t., 689a; In this world, two t., 905b
Tragedy one real t. in a woman's life, 455a; sane man, can have t. in heart, comedy in head, 798a; t. of child over broken doll, 24b
Tragic all men are t., all men are comic, 193a
Tragicomedy absurd, English t., 876b
Traitor We dipped our hands in the dish together, 878b
Traitors if our religion do make us t., 583b; to hate t. and their treason love, 469b
Trambeams to-fro tender t., 111a
Trance O fantasy, that dost at time so rout, 876b; Shake off your heavy t., 239a; T. between laughters unawares, 59a; union, rapture, transport, t., all one, 288b
Tranquillity Charity gives peace to soul, 157a; quietness of heart, won by resisting our passions, 655a
Transcendence divine t. and immanence, 380a, 390a; flattened into silence in face of His t.!, 390b; misunderstand His t., 390a
Transcendent divine Being, t. end towards which all life converges, 864a; God is both t. and cause of everything, 390a
Transcendentalists essential mistakes of t., 876b
Transfiguration A wondrous sign we there behold, 877a; Upon the mount of Tabor, 877a
Transfigure our ordinary existence, 629b
Transformation worm, which never t. knows, 163b
Transformed world t., turned upside-down, 438a
Transgression enormity of man's first t., 750a
Transgressions Because of multitude of my t., 98a; deliver me by Thy Body and Blood from all t., 594b; Remember not his t. and sins, 244a
Transience Our t. is only a mortal seeming, 447b
Transient All things are passing, 882a
Transit Sic t. gloria mundi!, 710a
Translated When she was with joy t., 40a
Translation everything suffers by t. except bishop, 70a; hard to preserve in t. charm of another language, 877b; If I render word for word, result uncouth, 877b; No

literal t. can be just to original, 878a
Translator function of a t., 877b; skilled t.'s job, to keep sense, 877b
Transport union, rapture, t., all one, 288b
Transubstantiation accidents of bread and wine remain after consecration, 311b; after consecration, designated Body, 162a, 310a, 597a; bread and wine, changed into God's Body, 73a, 311a; bread and wine, not merely figures of Body and Blood, 310b; bread changed by invocation of Holy Spirit, 310b; by mystery of prayer, transformed into Flesh and Blood, 310b; change given special name of t., 73a, 310a, 311b; Church aptly uses term for conversion, 311b; difficult to imagine, but not difficult to believe, 312a; effected by words of Jesus, 70a, 71b, 310b; How can bread be Body of Christ?, 310b; So I believe and take it, 76b; why Christ's Body and Blood offered to us under species, 311b
Travel among vicissitudes of journey, protected by Thy help, 878a; men go to admire mountains, yet pass themselves by, 878a; pity, people t. in foreign countries, 878b
Traveled Led by my hand, he saunter'd Europe round, 878b
Traveler The t. sees what he sees, 878b
Travelers tiresome, those who talk of nothing but adventures, 878a
Traveling We beseech Thee for those who are t. from home, 878a
Treachery smiler with knife under cloak, 878b
Tread T. lightly, she is near, 413a
Treason Cupid plague thee for thy t., 10b; During his office t. was no crime, 879a; How safe is t. and how sacred ill, 227a; If anyone shall resist royal power, 878b; In trust is t., 881a; many forms of t., 879a; o'er the councils of the brave, 879a; slander of majesty, 878b; t. is not owned when 'tis described, 227a; What king, what crown from t.'s reach is free, 879a
Treasons From plots and t. heav'n preserve my years, 342a
Treasure Better, possession of small t. found, 879a; BVM, common-t. of whole world, 79b, 81a; For the merit of your t., 74b; Truth is t., 884a; *where thy t. is, there will thy heart be*, 478b; Whosoever findeth Jesus, findeth a good t., 488b
Treasure-house unfailing t. of life, 100b
Treasures infinite t. of Thy love, 789b; partakers of Thy heavenly t., 603b
Treasury *master of house bringeth forth new things and old*, 613a; T. of good things, Bestower of life, 438b; t. of the Church, 471a
Tree *A t. is shown by its fruit*, 673a; as the t. falleth, so must it lie, 251a; as the twig is bent the t.'s inclined, 289a; BVM verily t. of life, 91a; Deceiv'd me by the t., 6a; every good t. maketh good fruits, 339a; Fast nail'd unto a cursed t., 401a; Hast thou not eaten of the t., 254a; I will bend the t. while it is a wand, 879b; In shade of death's sad t., 94a; known by its fruits, 435b; Nor

can he well forget the t., 328b; One and only noble T.!, 230b; only God can make a t., 879b; slip from a barren t., 288b; There's no t. but has rotten wood, 879b; this painful t., 233a; Today is suspended on t., He that suspendeth earth, 400a; *t. beside running waters bearing fruit*, 532a; T. of our salvation, 842a; we honor t. as symbol of Christ, 231b; We stare at t. in infinite leisure, 759a; Who hung for us upon the T., 47b, 284b; wonderful things that hang on t. of life, 840a

Trees Aged t. do break with bending, 257b, 879b; Old t.! old t.! in your mystic gloom, 879b; pitiful t. have told me, God, of Thee, 396b; There t. for evermore bear fruit, 879b; Whose t. in Summer yield him shade, 215a; Ye cannot see the wood for the t., 879a

Tremble T. ye nations, 545a

Trent, Council of, 64a

Trespasses *forgive us our t.,* 593b, 764a

Tresses Fair t. man's imperial race insnare, 418a; these t. yellow, 10b; Wantoning With our Lady-Mother's vagrant t., 683a

Trial Is not man's life upon earth t. without intermission?, 736a; this life, rightly called one continuing t., 650b

Trials All trying things, taken as coming from hand of Lord, 880a; We must measure our t. by ourself, 880a; we profit by our t., 880a

Tribulation bed of t., school of humility, 880a; Comfort in t., 193a; meriteth in patience, 880a; prayers of those who call upon Thee in t., 880a

Tribulations All trying things, taken as coming from hand of Lord, 880a; Christians, through t., led on to perfection, 879b

Tribute my t. to American people, 15b

Trifle From little spark may burst a mighty flame, 880b

Trifles Say one word, a heart may break, 880b

Trifling courage cool At every t. thing!, 454b

Trinity, Blessed acknowledge glory of eternal T., 371a; Almighty One! almighty Trine!, 371b; BVM was linked to all T., 96b; Church is temple of t., 123b; Confess we all the Unity, 370b; Deity coequal, 371a; divine nature, identical with each of three persons, 370b; Dread T. in Unity, 369a; *essence of T. is indivisible,* 372a; everlasting, three in one, 368b; Father almighty, with Son and Holy Ghost, one God, 591a; Father is God, Son is God, Holy Spirit is God, 369a; Father is trust, Son refuge, Holy Ghost protection, 369b; Father, works of power; Son, wisdom; Holy Ghost, love, 371b; First and last of faith's receiving, 370a; godhead of Father, Son, Holy Ghost, is one, 368b; Hail day! whereon the One in Three, 854a; How can plurality consist with unity?, 370a; In Father resides unity, in Son equality, in Holy Ghost union, 368b; In nature One, in persons Three, 369b; In substance one, in persons three, 369a; invocation of holy Trinity, 310a; May my worship be pleasing unto Thee, O holy T., 596a; Might in one substance

and Kingdom undivided, 369b; More simply One, because supremely Three!, 391a; Most ancient of all mysteries!, 371b; multiplying of things, common work of T., 225a; mystically enlightened by threefold Unity, 438b; name of Father, Son, and Holy Spirit, 368a; O most holy T., have mercy upon us, 369b; O supersubstantial T., adored in Unity, 535a; O Thou immortal Light divine!, 371b; O Three in One, and One in Three, 599a; O T. of blessed light, 369a; O Unity of princely might, 369a; one divine and supreme Majesty, 370a; one God, from Whom, through Whom, and in Whom, 368b; one God, in attributes of Fatherhood, Sonship, and Procession, 369b; one Person of Father, another of Son, another of Holy Ghost, 368b; operations 'appropriated' to one Person, 372a; operations are indivisible, 371b; procession of one Person from Another, 224b; 'properties' of Persons, identical with Persons, 370a; Receive, O holy T., this oblation, 590b; sacrifice offered to holy T., 88a; signed with seal of Holy T., 500a; Son and God of undivided T., 86b; Spirit, Sire and Son the same, 368b; tabernacle of undivided T., 82a; term *procession* within B., 370b; terms *generation, father, son, word,* 370b; There yet are Persons three, 227a; Thou that instructeth Christians!, 211b; Three Persons! one Immensity, 371b; Three Selves of God, 372a; Thrice-blessed Three in One, 670b; through Whom be glory, 368a; to know It is life, and life eternal, 370a; Unity of Divine T. holds first place, 370a; very fitting to praise T., 370a; we shall adore distinction in persons, 591a; we worship one God in T., 144a, 227a, 368b; where there are no differences, there is no plurality, 369a; where there is no plurality, there is unity, 369a; which exceedeth all being, 211b; without difference or separation, 591a; worship due to the most holy T., 928a

Trinity old t., of father, mother child, 438a

Trinity College, Oxford had never been unkind to me, 827b

Trisagion, 379a

Triumph but one day for t. was allowed, 902a; Fools! I also had my hour, 38a; greater danger in battle, greater joy in t., 880b; in redeeming love, 103a; Shout in t., earth and sea, 167b; song of t., 36a; spendor of his death, 114b; which Church celebrates over heresies, 134a

Triumphed He hath triumphed gloriously!, 167b, 769b

Triumphs know nothing of war, desire t., 473b

Trivialities knowledge about t., 512a

Trojans fought for a woman, 921a

Troops Who by your glorious t. supply, 19b

Trophies *I can point out t. of the apostles,* 678b

Trophy above the Cross's t., 230b; BVM, whereby war-trophies are set up, 100b; Sing the t. of His passion, 229a

Tropic Across what calm t. seas, 322b

Tropological t. sense of Scripture, 61a

Trouble free from sin, safe from t., 593b; In dock, out nettle, 880b; no man in world without some t., 880b; rocks of t., 99a; The fat is in the fire, 880b; There's t. in every house, 881a; where comes a woman, follows t., 921b

Troubled Tossed on the waves of his t. heart, 497b

Troy such empty unrealities as T. on fire, 801b

Trumpet Let the loud t. sound, 881a; shall be heard on high, 626a; t.'s loud clangor, 881a; until the angel t. sounds, 502a; with the sound of a t., 35b; Wondrous sound the t. flingeth, 502a

Trumpets glory of arms and t., 31a

Trust Always place in God thy t., 881b; Cast off indecision, 881b; Christian who cannot t. Christian with property, 807b; generosity of heart which risks everything on God's word, 882b; God, strength of those who put their t. in Thee, 881b; I cannot fully t. to anyone, save God, 881b; I t. and find my God, 78b; I will not t. him though my brother, 265b; If God thy center, Be hell thy circumference, 882a; If once thy hope be anchor'd in God, 882a; if one will but t. God, 882b; In t. is treason, 881a; O God, protector of all that t. in Thee, 736b; On such folk, plainly, is no t., 253b; only help Of such as t. in Thee, 159a; people, how little t. is to be had in them, 882a; put yourself in His hands, 882b; So t. and rest, 882b; They cannot t. anything, they have ceased to believe in God, 342b; To t. friend, not to believe he can do no wrong, 881a; t. in BVM, 87a, 99b; t. is born of love, and love of God, 564a; T. on, to-morrow will repay, 445b; we put no t. in anything that we do, 664a; Who God possesseth In nothing is wanting, 882a; whosoever shall put his t. in Him, 385b

Trusting Nothing so bad, as not t. God, 882b

Trusts O see how Jesus t. Himself, 487b

Try t. anything once, 347b

Tube Christ not in Virgin as in t., 80a

Tuberose The t., with her silvery light, 885b

Tumult Where is the t. of household servants?, 244b

Tun As full as a t., 361b

Turn O t. to Jesus, Mother!, t., 743a; One good t. asketh another, 886a

Turk Let him kill T., not the man, 156a

Turtle-dove O Mother, t.!, 94a

Twain t. yet one, death is birth, 65b

Twig as the t. is bent the tree's inclined, 289a

Twilight Our Lady of the t., 886a; Spirit of t., through your folded wings, 886a

Twin-stone T. of the law, 41a

Two *they shall be t. in one flesh,* 577a; What matter, whether t. and t. be four, 799b

Tyburn At T. half an hour's hanging endeth all, 418b; man left to enjoy your T., 479b

Tyndale, William, 62a

Typoi, 71a

Typos, 70b

Tyrannic Beasts, subjects of t. sway, 12b

Tyrannically If king rules t., community may depose him, 774a

Tyrannies Of all t., worst that which persecutes mind, 607b

Tyrannization exile of God means t. of man, 43a

Tyranny extravagant desire for domination, 886b; Outstares the lids of large-look'd t., 249a; t. of taste, 274b

Tyrant Envy of a foreign t. Threateneth kings, 713b; he who usurps power, makes laws slaves to his will, 886b; king distinguished from t., 508a, 509b; lawful to slay t., 886a; multitude not acting unfaithfully, in deposing t., 774a; not a city lacks its t. brood, 886b; Thou t., t. jealousy, 478b; With terror doth the t. hear, 440b

Tyrants end of t. is confusion, 886b; government of t. cannot last, 886b; in Greek, same as kings in Latin, 886b; to proceed against t., action to be undertaken, 773b; worst kings who oppressed people, known as t., 886b

Tyre T. of the west, 296a

True all things t., by one primary truth, 883b; all t. and faithful ones, 40a; As false as God is t., 334b; half so t., As woman been, 572a; must needs be t., that every man sayeth, 881a; Piteous, sad, wise, and t. as steel, 344a; strong locks maken t., 344a

Trueness Their traitorous t., 211a

Truism requires real courage to say t., 881a

Truisms when they are really true, 881a

Truth All aberrations, founded on some t., 300b; All religious traditions contain elements of t., 148b; All t., belongs to us as Christians, 883a; all t. contained implicitly in Christianity, 148b; And so ye halve the t., 536a; as a light, both secret and open to all, 883a; as it exists in the intellect, 883b; authority, not a short way to t., 47a; beauty is radiance of t., 55b; better to remain silent, than speak t., ill-humoredly, 885b; care more for it. than consistence, 628b; Catholic t. is simply t., 884b; catholicity of t., 290a; champion of the t., 884a; Christ is way, t. life, 108b, 148b, 292a; Church cannot guard interests at cost of denying t., 692a; defence of thesis, easier than discovery of t., 884b; demonstrated by first principle, 883b; different sides to question, 30b; discovery made by traveling minds, 884a; discovery of t. and Scriptures, 60a; Divine t. must always be extreme, 885a; divine t., too big for this world, 885a; education liberal, according to t., 35a; elements of t., dispersed among peoples, 135a; equation of thought and thing, 883b; everlasting fount of t., 20a; Every t. without exception, from Holy Ghost, 883b; Everyone who knows doubt, knows a t., 883a; evident either in itself or through another t., 512b; evolved with man, 885a; Fact and argument, tests of t. and error, 885b; Felicity is pure contemplation of noblest T., 419b; fixed star, 885a; for knowledge of t., man needs divine help, 512b; formal motive and object of faith, 145b; From shadows and symbols to the t., 884b; God is not only true, but T. Itself, 50a, 390b; God, Whose t. is

t.'s essential, 370a; Grace is the mistress of t., 409b; greater the t., the worse the libel!, 536a, 884a; has two attributes, beauty and power, 514a; hasty assumption, before t. plain, 38b; heretic loves his t. more than t. itself, 432b; highest thing that man may keep, 884a; history of Church should be called history of t., 138a; intrinsic reason, criterion of t., 16b; Jesu, eternal T. sublime, 205a; knowledge of t. only by God's gift, 35a; knowledge of t., reflection of eternal law, 526a; law of history, not to fear to speak t., 434b; let nothing but t. issue from your mouth, 882b; lies in proportion, 434b; maid, whom men woo diversely, 885a; mind, formed by T. Itself, 213a; must be stranger than fiction, 343b; must be upheld until admitted, 47a; naked t. made known to all who are astray, 612b; new realists torture men for physical t., 885a; no other teacher of t. save You, 883a; no salvation save in t., 608b; No t. can exist, external to Christianity, 884b; nor is there any true thing, which is not true by t., 883a; Nothing conquers except t., 155a, 883b; O eternal T., true Charity, lovely Eternity, 390b; O God of t., 809b; O whole and blessed T., 380a; old religionists tortured men for moral t., 885a; on one side of Pyrenees, 885b; one and invariable, 885b; our hearts and minds, tested in crucible of t., 429a; quality of Christianity, 27a; raised to supernature by Christian t., 34b; repel from t. by fault of defender, 27a; return society to law of His t., 489b; revealed t. and education, 289b; royal road of t. is by the mind, 608b; seeds of t. to sow, 74a; seven sisters ever serving t., 883a; shines forth from Catholic Church alone, 121a; simple t. that all believe, 302a; something in moral t. and goodness, 621a; spirit is t., 128a; springs infernal in the human breast, 885a; Still is the might of t., as it has been, 884b; supreme T. cannot utter untrue, 64b; That is t. which is, 883a; Then the t. all creatures tell, 251b; there is an immutable t., 883a; those blessed strains are telling, 20a; those who do not recognize t., 27a; three states or steps of t., 883b; Thy law is t. and t. is Thou, 525b; Thy word is t., 245a; Time trieth t. in every doubt, 276a; to be loved, needs only to be seen, 884a; To utter t. from heart and mouth, 883b; too much t. stuns us, 321b, 873a; T. and philosophic expression, cannot change from day to day, 682a; t. is great, and shall prevail, 884b; T. is treasure, best tried on earth, 884a; t. of divine intellect is one, 883b; unchangeable mysteries of heavenly T., 211b; universal character of religious t., 186b; victory of t. is charity, 155a, 883b; We arrive at t., by reason, also by heart, 884a; We grope for t., 513b; We judge all things according to divine t., 511a; we put up with illusion, when we cannot get t., 459a; what in itself, and what to us, 27a; What is against t. cannot be just, 504a; Where Life was slain and T. was slandered, 658b; Which but the semblance of a falsehood

wears, 883b; which knows no change, 419a; whose fruit is freedom, 135b; will prevail in the end, 885b; witness and teacher of religious t., 23b; You hold all things in the hand of Your t., 885a

Truths all t. not from reason, 332a; authority only way to divine t., 47a; believing Catholic t. by anticipation, 57b; Blunt t. more mischief than nice falsehood do, 222b, 885b; Catholic more certain about fixed t. than fixed stars, 885a; conclusions of one generation are t. of next, 514a; divine t., beyond definition, 387b; must be believed with divine and Catholic faith, 274b; nutshell t. for breakfast table, 496b; require time to be comprehended, 272a; Too often we call t. which offend, slander, 824b; T. and principles are divine, 884b; turn into dogmas, 274b, 885a

U

Ubi U. Petrus, ibi ecclesia, 709a

Ubique quod u., quod semper, quod ab omnibus, 144b

Ugly As comely as a cow in a cage, 887a; u. woman's passions easily stirred, 54a

Uios Iesous Christos Theou U. Soter, 49a

Ulysses, 319a

Umbered U. juices, and pulped oozes, 47b

Umbrian On U. heights, in U. sky, 38a

Umbris Ex u. et imaginibus in veritatem, 884b

Unarmed U. she goeth, yet her hands, 157a

Unbaptized must not taste Eucharist, 70b; not bound by canon law, 112a; u. infants are excluded from the Kingdom of Heaven, 238b; u. persons and baptism of martyrdom, 50b

Unbegotten God is one, alone u., without beginning, 386a

Unbelief anticlericalism and rise of militant u., 473a; Church cannot punish u. in those outside, 178b; governmental efforts to suppress u., 473a; If any one saith no sin but infidelity, 887a; may deprive rulers of authority, 46a; not incompatible with right to own and rule, 887a; not inconsistent with dominion, 178b; prison for u., prison of troubled conscience, 473a; punish u. of those who have received faith, 178b; u., contrary to nature, 887a; unfaith, often chastised by tribulation, 173b; vice of u., 894a

Unbeliever correct premises of u., 27a; does not follow tradition of Catholic Church, 145a; has intercourse with the devil, 145a; u. and respect for authority, 47b

Unbelievers Begin by pitying u., 887b; brothers of Christ, according to flesh, 133a; call themselves rational, 748a; deprived of rule over faithful, 46a; may be prevented from impeding faith, 57a; occasion for u. to scoff, 26b; u. and faith, 326a; u. may be tolerated, 871b; when force may be used against u., 57a; who have not yet joined us in body, 133a

Unborn Better u. than untaught, 458b

Uncertain nothing more u. than d.'s hour, 247b

Unchanging one u. and abiding God, 306a

Unchaste u. eye is messenger of u. heart, 158b

Uncivilized kept unconquer'd and u., 297a

Unconquered kept u. and uncivilized, 297a

Uncontrolled men desire authority to live u., 46b

Unconventional No one in England under peeress can be unconventional, 217b

Unconventionality convention of u., 217b; philosophy to hink by, not rule to act by, 887b

Uncreated We acknowledge one God, u., eternal, 390b

Unction dew of heavenly ointment, 68b; faithful receive spiritual u. for sanctification, 128a; priest, has primacy of Abel, power of Peter, u. of Christ, 728a; sanctification in life-giving u., 206a; spiritual effect of u. of baptism, 49b; sweet u. of consolation, 602a

Undaunted Give me the man that with u. spirit, 767b

Undeserving u. deserve no biography, 65a

Understand All fear, none aid you, few u., 752b; believe that thou mayest u., 57a, 887b; God's act of understanding, 383b; Make effort to u. whatever you read, 848a; seek not to u. in order to believe, 57a; show me such, he will u., 301b; So vast is art, so narrow human wit, 363a; U. what thou dost not u., 887b; unless I believe, I should not u., 331b; Unless I u., I will not believe, 333a; When I say 'I u. that I am,' 319a

Understanding clear knowledge of some invisible thing, 887b; Faith assents, brings insight, 333b; Faith opens door to u., 333b; receive light of u. from above, 840a; supernatural light, called gift of u., 888a; The purest suffering carries in train, purest u., 851b; U. and love, two arms of soul, 887b; u. is the reward of faith, 57a, 887b

Understandings clever man warned me against 'u.', 888a

Understands God u. all things in His essence, 384a; if he doubts, he u. that he doubts, 275b

Understood man in the street u. our Lord, 396a

Undone As good u., as do it too soon, 275a; Things done cannot be u., 275a

Uneducated Democracy, means government by u., 256b

Unequal Human society, composed of u. elements, 829a

Unfaithful u. to God, cannot be friend to man, 471a

Unfashionable u., what other people wear, 337a

Unhappy u., a king dethroned, 509a

Unimportant men speak gravely about things not important, 453b; To feel extraordinarily u., wholesome, 452b

Union actual u. with Him, 889a; baptism and union with Christ, 51a; based on flesh and spirit of Jesus Christ, 888a; Christ, living in those He has united, 166a; do all things in u. with Jesus Christ, 105b; enter by love into u. with Life, 889b; failure of Christianity to unite all men, 165a; for the u. of all, let us pray, 588a; In Father resides unity, in Son equality, in

Holy Ghost u., 368b; In soul's u. with God, nothing is lost, 889a; intimate u., by which we commit ourselves to God, 310a; man becomes one with God, 888b; Meet and unite in sweet embrace!, 197b; ministering to men's u. with God, 91a; nuptial u. of King and Queen of City, 112a; of sexes for procreation, 66a; our u. with God, is Christ's work, 486a; self, merged in that Personality, 889a; soul seeks Word in order to yield to it, 888b; This u. of divinest love, 888b; To merge myself in Him, 889a; to which love aspires, spiritual, 889a; true u., consists in unity of faith and government, 770b; u. in distinction makes order, 54b; u. of body and spirit, obedience to bishop, 66b; u. of Christ with His Church, 577a; u. of God with Church Triumphant, 577a; u. of God with the soul, 577a; u. of lover and thing loved, 889a; u. of soul and body in man, 182b; u., rapture, transport, all one, 288b; u., which is above intelligence, 394a; u. with Him Who is above all, 211b; wedlock, mystery foreshadows u. of Christ with Church, 576a; wholly joined to Thee, 559b

Unions three u. in this world, 889b

Unions, Trade law governing t., 38b; t. and betterment of workers' conditions, 38b; t. and natural right of man, 38a; T. arose as consequence of capitalism, 38b; t. should be organized to help members, 38b

Unison sing in u. with one voice, 162a

Unite Oh, u. my heart to Thee, 170a; principle effect of love, u. wills, 551a

United all of us are u. with Christ, 93a; Every soul ought to be u. to Him, 888b; soul u. with God, feared by devil, 888b; The more a man is u. within himself, 840a; to be u. with Him, 213b

United States America is my country, 143a; American Catholics rejoice in separation, 185a; American constitution, least imperfect, 406b; American republic instituted by Providence, 14b; American society recognizes Christian conscience, 185a; America! with thy faults, I love thee still, 14b; basis on which Church can make progress, 142b; better organized than other society, 142b; Catholic blood flowed freely, 142a; Catholic Church and things American, 142b; Catholic religion, adapted to genius of Constitution, 184b; Catholics and part in Revolution, 142a; Catholics, educated as Americans, 292b; Catholics in U. should keep to republicanism, 15a; Catholic vote, distributed among several parties, 692a; Church and principles American civilization, 142b; Church left free to live, 143b; Church should keep in step, 143b; civil and religious liberty, 142a; comparative poverty of Catholic Community, 142a; Constitution, adapted to expansion of Catholic religion, 184b; country of diverse theologies and one creed, 292a; destinies of humanity in America's keeping, 15a; distinctions among Catholics, because of race, 265a; district school system, American pet, 801b; divine mission assigned

to US, 15a; equal toleration of all denominations, 184a; equity of laws in America, 143a; erroneous in America most desirable status of Church, 143b; First Amendment, not piece of religious mysticism, 185a; form of government preferable to Catholics, 15a; government provides blessings religious liberty, 142a; harmony of Church and State in U., 142b; I would have Catholics be first patriots of the land, 663b; Loyalty to God's Church and country!, 143a; master-builder of Church in U., 448b; May these U. flourish, 908a; more in accordance with needs of Catholic society, 142b; nation in which Roman Catholic faith professed, 142a; no conflict between Catholic Church and America, 143a; no law respecting establishment of religion, 184b; no man with just claim against Church, ever lost one farthing, 142a; Ours is American Church, not Irish, German, 143b; president reigns for four years, 496b; principles of Church, in harmony with Republic, 143a; principles of state, have origin in spiritual order, 184b; private and public instruction in U.S., 291a; religious as well as political destiny, 184b; right to regulate questions of eccles. discipline, 184b; seems destined for great things, 143b; 'separation' between State and Church wrongly understood, 183b; separation of Church and State, 183a; solvency of Catholic Church in U., 142a; state asserts autonomy as political order, 185a; superiority of republican U., 14b; The free school of America!, 802a; U.S. and role of Catholic Church, 143b; well-ordered Republic, 143a; why Catholic fruits worse than tree, 143a; Woe to him who would destroy harmony, 143a

Unity all adversity and error being destroyed, 134a; Awful in u., 391a; awful u. of Church, 118a; Blessed Sacrament sign of u., 73a; cannot be rent asunder, 133b; Confess we all the U., 370b; every church must agree with Roman Church, 704a; fact of missions reveals Church's faith, as Catholic u. of mankind, 613b; false oecumenical concept of Church, 137b; Form all together one chub, 889b; From many to make one, 889b; glue of concord, 133b; He who deserts chair of Peter, does he still believe he is in Church?, 693a; hierarchy and sacraments, sole basis of u., 135a; *how good it is to dwell together in u.*, 889b; how He willed that it should be one, 134b; In Father resides u., in Son equality, in Holy Ghost union, 368b; maintain stay and security of u., 154b; of body in Sacrament of altar, 72b; of faith and Church denied by heretics, 145a; one not in Catholic u., 50b; opinion, no one should be coerced into u., 431a; origin of u. should begin from one, 693a; O U. of princely might, 369a; pre-eminence of Peter, he bore figure of u. of Church, 676a; primacy is given to Peter, that u. of Church may be proclaimed, 695b; relation of all members to one head, 134a; strength of Church is her u., 135a; sun has many rays, but one light, 133b; *that they may be one, as we are one,* 662a; those who have entered into u., 889b; threefold cause, 134a; tree has many boughs, but one strength from root, 133b; true union, consists in u. of faith and government, 770b; Unbounded, an extended U.!, 391a; u. of Christians is one Man, 134a; u. of Church and episcopate, 299b; u. of Church and Head, 132b; u. of discipline, 133a; U. of Divine Trinity holds first place, 370a; u. is preserved in source, 133b; u. of faith and toleration, 184a; u. of faithful around bishop, 67a; u. of religion, not prerequisite for political u., 184a; visible head necessary, to preserve u. in Church, 696b; we are members of one another, 131a; whence priestly u. takes its source, 704a; where there is no plurality, there is u., 369a; Whoso gathers elsewhere, scatters, 133b

Universal u. cause must be applied, 43b

Universalism Authentic u. is centered, 148b; no other authentic u. than Catholicism, 148a; personality lost in false u., 726a; True u., very reverse of eclecticism, 148b

Universality U. is a contradiction in terms, 890a; U., not confined to one part of world, 148a

Universe but one thought greater than that of u., 890a; by thought I embrace the u., 866a; Christian admits that u. is manifold and miscellaneous, 598b; Deity supports and maintains u., 375a; entire u. is one dominion, 890a; entire u. pre-exists in Godhead, 890a; God is an artist, and u. is His work of art, 890a; God is the Prince of the U., 526a; God, Maker of the u., 372a; God, not identical with u., 377a; God postpones collapse of u., 926b; like seed, had all things in it on day of creation, 224a; man's, by free gift of its Maker, 372a; masterpiece of divine Providence, 149a; Miracles provide evidence u. is not closed system, 611b; plan executed through chain of command, 149a; put together with certain harmony of sounds, 421b; story of the u. is another Person's, 926b; Ultimately, faith is only key to u., 329a; u., created through Logos, 390b; u. is too significant to be anonymous, 377a; u. proclaims it has a Creator, 374b; Wonderful is this u., come from love of Creator, 890b

University practical end, training good members of society, 890b; professes to teach universal knowledge, 890b; the u. modern mind, 601b; u., an *alma mater,* not a foundry, 890b; u. training, means to a great end, 890b

Unjust u. laws do not bind, except to avoid scandal, 525a

Unkind Is Heav'n u. to man, and man alone?, 570b

Unkissed Unknown, u., 53a

Unknowing strain upwards in u., 211b

Unknown impossible to love u., 57a; u., unkissed, 53a

Unlamented Thus u. let me die, 770a

Unlawful to despise legitimate authority, 46b

Unlearned arise and take heaven by storm, 106a; u. arise, and take heaven by force, 531b

Unluckiest Three u. things to meet first thing in the morning, 566a

Unmoved Who ever dost thyself u. abide, 637a

Unpalatable prickles of an u. law, 503b

Unpardonable charity is pardoning of u., 157b; u., to be bad in bad taste, 48a

Unreadable It is always the u. that occurs, 496b

Unrighteously no man acts u., save by divine judgment, 817a

Unsatiate U. as the barren womb or grave, 342a

Unseasonable avoid u. intrusions, 891a

Unseen drawn by Him to love of things u., 167a; The things u., 103b; *things which are u., known by things seen,* 459b

Unselfishness perverse u., 891a

Unsung some u., that may be tomorrow, 45a

Untaught Better unborn than u., 458b

Untilled U. ground will bring forth thistles, 607a

Unum Credo in u. Deum, 226b

Unveil U., O Lord, and on us shine, 925b

Urban VIII, Pope, 112b

Urbi U. et orbi, 710a

Urbis Omnium u. et orbis ecclesiarum mater et caput, 171a

Urbs U. caput orbis, 139b

Usage diversity of u. does no harm, 51b; whatever believed, has authority of Scriptures, tradition, or u., 875a

Use If you have real ambitions to be of u. in world, 891a; man exclaims, "See all things for my u.!", 403a; u. of one church, not to be annulled, 874b

Useful no one so poor, not u. to fellow man, 428b; u. is not always good, 398b; u., only that of service for eternal life, 301b

Usefulness impossible to regret one's sphere of u., 891a

Usurer must be turned out of clergy, 891a

Usurpation beginning of u., 734a

Usury Let a bishop who requires u., be deprived, 891b; taking of any interest upon loan, 891b

Utilitarianism Many man acting on utilitarian principles, 891b

Utopians never enter into alliance, 12b; The U. have no lawyers among them, 531b

Utopias Progress, realization of u., 732b; weakness of all u. is this, 891b

V

Vacancy During the v. of the Holy See, 709b

Vacante Sede v., 709b

Vacuum A v. is repugnant to reason, 892a

Vain Not to speak v. words, such as move to laughter, 523a; we are so v., 14a

Vainglory man often glories more, for contempt of v., 892a; Pride and v., pack you hence, 764b; To shun v., 105a

Vale this wretched v. of tears, 95b

Valentine, St. For this was on St. V.'s Day, 892a

Valentinian I, 172b

Vales down a thousand v. I dropped, 477b

Valles Bernardus v., montes Benedictus amabat, 615b

Valley After this v. dark, heavenly light, 561b; I walk down the v. of

silence, 814a; Whilst I dwell in this v. of tears, 251a

Vanished She v., we can scarcely say she died, 249b; These are among my v. ones, 38a

Vanity *all things are v. under the sun,* 534b; amounts to sin, 817b; Curiosity is only v., 236a; desire to be known, v., 512a; game of children on sands, 892a; greatest magnifying glasses in world, man's own eyes, 892b; No gaudy skirt nor broidered belt, to gather All eyes, 892a; offspring of pride, 892b; Those who write against v., 892b; Where is the v. of temporal things?, 244b

Value A man who knows price of everything, 237b; everything made, expressive of v., 34a

Values communication of spiritual v., 33a; confusion of aesthetic and moral v., 9b; stating things in order of v., 435a

Vanquished V. in life, his death, 158a

Variability one of virtues of a woman, 921b

Variety Distinction and v. in world, intended by First Cause, 892b; *in gilded clothing surrounded with v.,* 762b

Various A man so v., that he seem'd to be, 893a

Vase you may shatter the v. if you will, 603a

Vatican City creation of V., 709a

Vaunter greatest v. seldom speeds, 923a

Veil A thin, aerial v., is drawn O'er a beauty's face, 893a; O amber v., 462b; Received the sacred v., 640b; spread between this world and next, 62b; The dusky v. of night hath laid, 599a; To take the v. of night, 312b; v. of temple rent in twain, 399b

Veiled let all women have heads v., 892b; V., as with mail, 157a

Veils enveloping Sacrament with symbols, 73a

Veneration sacred relics and images, due a v., 928a

Vengeance not cured by another v., 773b

Venom V. destroys v., 690b

Venture faith is a v. before man is Catholic, 219b; Great objects exact a v., 444b; He that never climbed, never fell, 893a; he who naught dare undertake, 106a; Not v., not have, 362a; She ne'er loved who durst not v. all, 555a; You must make a v., 219b

Verba non v. sophistae, 268b

Verdict do not let v. of Thy judgment go against him, 500a; The v. of the world is conclusive, 924b

Vermicide ferriferous v., 279b

Veronica, St. very God, is this Indeed Thy likeness, 893a

Versatility A man so various, that he seem'd to be, 893a; Ye have many strings to the bow, 893a

Verse And this unpolish'd, rugged v. I chose, 893a; great easiness of blank v., 893b; Happy who in his v. can gently steer, 688b; harsh cadence of a rugged line, 688a; liquid measures, 229a; Monosyllabic lines, stiff or languishing, 688b; The sound must seem an echo to the sense, 688b; To attempt in v. things scarce to thought assured, 865b; V. is a slow thing to create, 690a; v. versus prose, 893b; With David, v. to virtue I apply, 687b

Verses When v. like a milky torrent flow, 688a
Versifiers v. and witty men, 263b
Vesper That v. bell from afar, 58b
Vespers As fades the glowing orb of day, 894a; evening prayers, 266a; Evermore at last they ring to evensong, 894a; Joyful light of the holy glory, 893b
Vessel Afterwards too the Chosen V. went, 664b; Church a v., often beaten by waves, 124a; Cleanse thy v., that thou mayest receive grace, 408a; Paul, chosen v., 664a; rare of God's election, 97b
Vessels the v. of the Lord, 189b
Vestal How happy is the blameless v.'s lot, 894a
Vestigia Fidei some shreds discoverable in heresies, 120b
Vestments ceremonies, v., incentives to piety, 597b; v. of Old Law, 68a; worn by high priests under Old Law, 68a
Vesture In cloudy v. stainless white, 41b; nature of sacerdotal v., 68a
Vetustas V. pro lege semper habetur, 236b
Vexing Not v. thee in death, 873a
Via Media absolutely pulverized, 23a
Viaticum dying must not be deprived of v., 894a; received V. of the heavenly mystery, 894a; Receive, my brother, this Food for your journey, 894a; To crave of you v., 321b
Vicar Christ and Christ's v. Peter, 701b; king, minister and v. of God, 533b; pope, v. of Christ, 123a; Pope, v. of St. Peter, 695a; true and legitimate v. of Jesus Christ, 702a; Vicaire and Maistress, 96a; v. of Jesus Christ, 701b
Vicars bishops not v. of Roman pontiffs, 69b; Roman pontiffs, successors of Peter, v. of Jesus Christ, 695b; Thy shepherds and v., 28b
Vice assailed by v., practice of contrary virtue, 903a; condition of thing out of its proper natural bearings, 818a; consumed by flames of v., 216a; contrary to human nature, 902b; definition of v., 894b; direct opposite of virtue, 818a; hate the v. and love the man, 314a; ignorance of self, v., 894b; neither hate man because of his v., 314a; never tires men, entertaining lie, 895a; nor love v. because of the man, 314a; No v., but in shadow of some virtue, 902b; no v. so contrary to nature it obliterates traces of nature, 894b; unclean v., wallowing in depths, 14a; V. is a monster of so frightful mien, 894b; v. is contrary to nature, 894b; V. to forsake is better late than never, 894b; We act with freewill, whether to virtue or v., 356a; Where ends the virtue or begins the v., 903a; Without discretion, virtue becomes v., 264b; You do not get rid of v. by expedients, 895a
Vicegerency delegated v. of authority, 699a
Vicegerent priest, Christ's v., 728a; v. of His love, 675a
Vices correcting v. in others, 341a; four v., 894a; greatest virtues are only spendid v., 894b; Mother of v., idleness, 457b; people always brag about their v., 903a; purify us from our secret v., 218b; re-

moved by good works, 5a; v. of Church and the world, 895a; We make a ladder of our v., 894b
Vicious Virtuous and v. ev'ry man must be, 903a
Victim bloody and unbloody v., one and same, 309b; Hail! Thou saving V., offered up, 75b; Thou was to Thee both Victor and V., 485a; offer Thyself, pure and spotless V. upon altar, 586b; one: V., High Priest And Lamb, 235a; O saving V., opening wide, 74b; Our V. to become, 83b; Paschal V., Paschal Bread, 284b; pure V., holy V., spotless V., 592a; Priest and V. are one and the same, 484b; The V., the V. Behold He is here, 658a; Thyself, pure and spotless V. upon altar of cross, 486a; Who died the V. of pure love, 657a
Victor He was to Thee both V. and Victim, 485a; Today the V. o'er His foes, 286a
Victor I, Pope St., 283a, 697a
Victorian fallacy of V. rationalism, 160a; V. secularists were 'dawnists', 316a
Victories E'en victors are by v. undone, 895b
Victoriously enter v., 36b
Victory by gaining a v. over the enemy, 652a; crown of v. promised only to contestants, 234b; fight gives us pleasure, not v., 192b; grant them v. from on high, 86b; If Christ is with us, who is against us?, 895a; I thank our Lord the field is won, 895b; O what a v. is Thine?, 286b; Unless battle has preceded, cannot be v., 895a; v. and peace, gifts of God, 664b; v. in merely outward matters, 895b; v. of so great a King, 441b; v. of truth is charity, 155a; we underrate the v. of God, 453a; With Christ and for Christ, v. is certain, 895a; with cries of v. on his severed breath, 114b
Vidi V. aquam egredientem de templo, 587a
View conclusion that ordinary v. is right, 218a
Views intellectual man, full of "v.", 645a
Vigil at midnight rise and pray, 895b; Behold, the Bridegroom cometh in the middle of the night, 896a; Be sober and keep v., 502a; night of Easter, spent in v., 285a; Night v. at my heart, 252a; Now, from the slumbers of the night arising, 895b; solitude of night, favorable time for prayer, 895b; Thy forty hours of lonely prayer, 94b; You shall keep v. all the night, 441a
Vigils Pensive poets painful v. keep, 685b
Vigorem Quod principi placuit, legis habet v., 533b
Vile I am v., but Thou are holy, 170a; Nor are half so v. or low, 492a
Villages dreamy little v., 365a; The pleasant little v. that grace Irish glynns, 896a
Villainy He never yet no v. had said, 161b
Vinces In hoc signo v., 229a
Vincit Amor omnia v., 781b
Vinculi Defensor v., 579b
Vindicate v. the ways of God to man, 397a
Vine bathed every v. in such licour, 29b; He is the V., 486a
Vinegar takes more oil than v. to

make a good salad, 364b; thou hast given Me v. in My thirst, 400b
Vines branching stilly, 488a
Vineyard hanging and idling about God's v., 402a; into God's v. goeth no man, but is called, 303a; My v., thou art become to Me exceeding bitter, 400b; plantation of God and beloved v., 124a
Violence Do v. to no man, 906a; v. we do Him, pleases God, 715b
Violet In this secluded shrine, 896a; While the last v. loiters by the well, 235b
Violets Twice happy v.! that first bad birth, 896a; v., transform'd to eyes, 322b
Virgil art thou then that V., 896b; most famous and approved of all, 896b; my master, 240a
Virgin after childbirth thou didst remain v., 24b; a v. with Child, 166b; Blest guardian of all v. souls, 461a; does not have an imposition of hands, 639a; God, cannot raise v., after she has fallen, 896b; He Who dwelt in ever V., 39a; human race fell by v., rescued by v., 85a; most merciful, 99a; most powerful, 100a; my soul, no foolish v. With empty lamp, 584b; not only in body but mind, 80b; O thou Virgin, spotless, undefiled, 98a; ought not only to be so, but to be perceived so, 639a; St. Agatha, virgin and martyr, 10a; salvation recovered by v., 85a; She is a v. who is married to God, 639b; Son of a V., Maker of Thy Mother, 640b; The v. is a mother's victim, 639b; The V. Son His V. Mother left, 494a; thou abidest a v. forever, 79b; thou, still a maid, brought forth, 79b; Thou youngest v.-daughter of the skies, 896b; through soundness of faith and sanctity, 130b; to a v. grave untouch'd to go, 898b; True v. lives not but does know, 84a; v. before marriage, v. in marriage, 166b; V., hail! alone the fairest!, 39b; v. is a gift of God, oblation of parents, 639b; V. of all virgins blest!, 93b; Virgin of virgins, 89b; Virgin's spotless womb contains, 81b; virgin with Child, why do you marvel?, 79a; yet a mother in offspring, 130a
Virginal bridal robes of ardor v., 305a; v. disobedience destroyed by obedience, 85a
Virginity bestowed upon women, 79a; BVM crown of v., 81b; BVM is image of v., 92a; BVM kept v. intact, 39b; BVM offered gift of v. to God, 79b; BVM preserved v. before and after, 80a; by clean v., 83a; can be lost by thought, 897a; central idea of Christian v., to aim at divine, 898b; chastity of v., 158b; Christ chose rather to approve v., than to impose it, 897a; dignity of v. began with Mother of Lord, 79a; esteemed as more perfect than marriage, 437b; fecundity and v. of BVM and Church, 92b; fount perpetual of v., 304b; gift of holy v., 898a; gift of v., poured abundantly upon women, 897a; glad palace of v., 556a; guardian of v. is charity, 897b; had beginning from a woman, 79a; has special reward hereafter, 897a; He kept v. of BVM closed, 79b; held in honor, because consecrated to God, 897a;

He that can take it, 158b; Him, Who is Spouse of perpetual v., 640b; Holy v. and chastity, precious treasures, 898b; Holy v., better thing than conjugal chastity, 897b; Holy v. has recognized its Author, 640a; how holy and spotless is thy v.!, 79b; If any one saith marriage placed above v. or celibacy, 898a; in childbirth thou didst retain v., 39a; Let each one study own powers, 158b; Let married regard unmarried as above themselves, 897b; Let us not be sterile, let our souls be fertile to God, 897b; Neither widowhood nor v. has place, but by humility, 898b; our Redeemer loved flower of unimpaired modesty, 898a; perpetual continence, v., great good, 897a; practical method in science of divine life, 897a; Renounce marriage, imitate the angels, 898a; richness of v. of Mary, 78b; root and flower of v., crucified life, 897a; since most embrace v. while still young, 639b; stands far above marriage, 897a; to arouse desire for v., 745a; trample world by integrity of body and soul!, 897b; v. and humility combined in BVM, 88b; v. and pride, 897b; V. is a difficult virtue, 898b; V. is rule of life among angels, 898a; V. natural, marriage came after, 897a; v. of BVM, gate which was shut, 79a; v. of BVM preserved from violation, 79a; v. of BVM preserved intact, 79a; v. of Mary and Church, 130a; V., thou sayest, was all thy aid, 898a
Virgins because of Whom you have willed to have no husbands, 640a; BVM, flower of virgins all, 79b; BVM, queen of v., 86a; chastity of v., above marriage, 158b; Christ, glorious crown Of v., 159a; dedicated to God by holy chastity, 639b; follow Lamb wherever He goes, 82b; guardian and father of v., 496a; Hold fast what you have begun to be, 639a; In blessed troops they follow Thee, 639b; Jesu, the v.' crown, 639b; King of v. and Lover of chastity, 159a; more the number of v. increases, 639a; they produce v., 573b; Widows and v. shall fast often, 337b; You v., that did late despair, 665b
Virtually sacrament not merely sign and v., but actually and really, 311a
Virtue alone is happiness below, 902a; assailed by vice, practice contrary v., 903a; athlete admitted to contest of v., of 50a; can as well In cottages remain, 901b; Christian's v., only possession that cannot be conquered, 899a; comes to its strength by trial and effort, 902b; death and v., 248b; definition of v., use of gifts of God, 899a; essence of v., 900b; Everyone argues in favor of v., 901b; fortune's ice prefers to v.'s land, 14a; God does not ask the impossible, 901a; good quality of mind, whereby life is lived aright, 900a; happiness is the reward of v., 900a; has throne in soul, 899b; hath a proper dignity of her own, 899b; He who quits himself and cleaves to v., 899a; Human v., in accordance with human nature, 902b; I dwell in grace's court, Enrich'd with v.'s rights, 901a; if I v.'s rough beginning shun, 585a;

if origin rooted in pleasure, 683b; If v. be thy guide, 901a; In the cross is the height of v., 232b; inviolable and immutable, 419a; I only cannot die, 901a; I see That v. hath gone out of Me, 634a; Know and love v. while they fall!, 763a; life of v., climb from many to One, 902b; lost v. repaired by Sacrament, 76a; love of honor, zeal for v., 900a; Love v. rather than fear sin, 901b; make a v. of necessity, 634b; Mere natural v. wears away, 902a; Natural goodness comes of God, 900b; nature of v., that it should direct man to good, 900b; no man masters degree of goodness he desires, 899b; no true v., except directed towards ultimate good, 899b; No vice, but in shadow of some v., 902b; nothing else than perfect love of God, 899b; nothing takes precedence of v., 900a; observe in others, v. we have not, 899b; Oh, glorious v.!, 901a; only and highest good, 899a; ordered and measured affection, 901a; Our v. springs from freedom, 902b; Satan can pervert cultivation of v., 158b; seeks esteem of good, 900a; seldom rises through branches, 18b; Sin, direct opposite of an act of v., 818a; So good a thing is v., 899a; The power of a man's v., 901b; The whole labor of v., 902a; Thou art a queen, who dost possess entire world, 901a; To follow v. even for v.'s sake, 902a; True v. has no limits, 901b, 156a; vice, direct opposite of v., 818a; V., in price whom ancient sages had, 901a; V. is a gift from God, implanted, 900a; V. is not absence of vices, 902b; V. is perfected by art and usance, 901b; V. is what happiness deserves, 900a; We act with freewill, whether to v. or vice, 356a; Where ends the v. or begins the vice, 903a; Where v., there many snares, 899a; Without discretion, v. becomes vice, 264b; Ye were formed v. to pursue, 900b
Virtues Charity is form, root of all v., 156a; Christian v., feet and wings whereby soul moves, 902a; demand discretion, 900a; Faith, firm foundation of all v., 325a; four v. of the soul, 306b; greatest v. are only splendid vices, 894b; harvest of v., reaped from crop of insults, 474a; Her faults and v. lie so mix'd, 22b; intellectual v., good qualities rendering reason ready to know truth, 900b; moral v., perfections bringing appetites under control, 900b; multitudes of v. passed along, 902a; natural v. become supernatural, 17a; necessary to religious life, 15a; Neither faith, hope, v., acceptable without charity and grace, 409b; one of nine orders of angels, 18b; Patience, root and guardian of all the v., 661a; Piety is the foundation of all the v., 738b; practice natural and moral v., 436b; theological v. join human mind to God, 900b; three holy v. 544b; when people brag about their v., they become insufferable, 903a
Virtues, Cardinal Prudence is concerned with things, 903a
Virtues, Theological t., three, 903a
Virtuous Some of most v. men, most unhappy, 902b; v. act has

four characteristics, 900b; V. and vicious ev'ry man must be, 903a; V. living did I long relinquish, 371a
Vis Da quod jubes: jube quod v., 410a
Visibility v. of Catholic Church, 137a
Visible all things v. and invisible, 224a; God, infinitely v. and infinitely credible, 331a; things both v. and invisible, 120a; v. head necessary, to preserve unity in Church, 696b
Vision final aim of rational creatures, v. of God, 903b; desire to enjoy the v. of God, 560a; Each year but brought us nearer to the v., 903b; enjoy the v. of Him in heaven, 630b; Fair v. of time forever fled, 1a; intuitive vision of God, 303a; in v., of Him is our eternal beatitude, 486b; *Tell not the v. to any man,* 547a; The v. has flown, 416a; unregenerate children, deprived of beatific v., 238b; uplifted to that v., 211a; v. and apprehension in spiritual experience, 515a; v. of God, sea of love, 903b
Visions By thy large draughts of intellectual day, 258a; Dreams are we, shadows, v., 13a; glorious v. of the world to which I go, 521a; Mystic v. faint and dim, 8b
Visits *ad limina* v. of bishops to Rome, 70a
Vitality mysterious v. of Church, 118a
Vive Le roi est mort, v. le roi!, 509a
Vivere Recte novit v., 717a
Vivimus Dum v., vivamus, 549a
Vixit Bene qui latuit, bene v., 26a
Vobiscum Dominus v., 588b; *Pax Domini sit semper v.,* 594a; *Pax v.,* 588b
Vocation A v. lost is a prelude to a fall, 477a; best proof of true v., 904a; good v., firm and constant will to serve God, 904a; If real, will vanquish all obstacles, 904a; most important thing in life, choice of a calling, 904a
Vocations different, according to our callings, 130b; Religious v. not common, but special, 190a
Voice Hark, a herald v. is calling, 7b; needs pure intention to recognize divine v., 392b; People's v. is God's v., 255a; sing with one v. to the Father, 889b; v. of God heard, when we rest from world, 212a; v. of people is the v. of God, 671a; whether The v. or lute was most divine, 831b
Volition essential to art, 34a; every rational soul possessed of freewill and v., 356a; freedom of will is nothing else than v., 357a
Vos Benedicat v. omnipotens Deus, 595b
Vote American who does not care to v., deserves disenfranchisement, 904b; Irish-American v., intolerable anomaly, 17b; we v. as Americans, 17b
Voting casting of ballot, supreme act of citizenship, 904a
Voto baptism by desire (*in voto*), 52b, 53a
Vow deliberate and free promise made to God, 904b; made as result of fear, null, 904b; revolt against v. of marriage, 574b; those who make v. of chastity, 150b; v. continence unto Christ, 216a
Vows By paying v. to have more

v. to pay!, 904b; In religious society, members make profession of public v., 762b; No happier v. I know, 898b; Our v. are heard betimes!, 719a; Religious, persons who have taken v. in a religious society, 761a; religious with simple v., 761a; The revolt against v., 574b; v. of obedience, chastity, poverty, 762b
Vox V. populi, vox Dei, 671a
Vulgarity conduct of other people, 904b; v. there always was, 904b
Vulgate books of V., canonical, 62b
Vulture Prometheus' v., 9a
Vuol Moria pur quando v., 250a

W

Wage must be sufficient for support of family, 905a
Wager If w. were but one butterfly, 60a
Wait For evermore I w., 905a; Plan not, nor scheme—but calmly w., 882b
Waiteth Who w. for dead men shoes, 905a
Wall Antonio Sarto ees buildin' a w., 346b; BVM, w. that cannot be overthrown, 90a; Hunger pierceth stone w., 454a; of the kingdom, indestructible w., 100b
Walsingham Weep, weep, O W., 812b
Wandered I have deserted Thee and w. away, 261b
Wanderings forgive our w., 603b
Want abundance not God to me, neediness, 3b; It is better to w. less than to receive more, 361a; It is easy to w. things from the Lord, 366b; We get from God exactly what we really w., 720b; What can man w., not in God's power to give?, 905b
Wantonness wind, full of w., 37b; Your Cleopatra, Dolabella's Cleopatra, 906a
Wants getting what one w., 905b; not good to have everything one w., 353b; satisfy w. of the world's poor, 712a
War All delays are dangerous in w., 907a; At the root of all w. is fear, 342b; civil w., out of place in democracy, 255b; For w. to be just, three conditions necessary, 906b; I w. with men on account of ideas, 265a; most disadvantageous peace, better than most just w., 907b; purpose of all w. is peace, 907b; Romagna, was not e'er Without w., 906b; seldom enters but where wealth allures, 171a; sweet to those who don't know it, 906b; Triumphant leaders in the w., 28a; unjust w., one of gravest crimes, 907b; W. is the trade of kings, 907a
Wardrobe opening the purple w. in Thy side, 104a
Warfare service of Christian w., 37b
Warling young man's w., 574a
Warned Half w., half armed, 908a
Warreth It w. night, it w. day, 346a
Warrior By the Cross the w. rises, 232a; heavenly King's own w. band, 28a
Warriors W. she fires with animated sounds, 626a
Wars all their w. are merry, 476b; All w. are civil w., 907b; like mists that rise against the sun, 414b; O God, Who dost crush w., 906b

Wash He began to w. feet of His disciples, 442b; *I will w. my hands among the innocent,* 590a
Washed from stains of sin in water, 49b
Washes He w. us from sins, daily, 310b
Washing of Feet, 443a
Washington, George, 142a, 908a
Wasp Angry as a w., 22a
Waste A duchess may ruin a duke for a diamond necklace, 908a; Haste maketh w., 422a
Watch keep a continual w., 28b; w. over Thy household, 736b
Watches That marks the w. night by night, 522a; 'Tis with our judgment as with our w., 499b
Water baptize in running w., 49a; Foul w. as soon as fair will quench fire, 908b; "I don't care where w. goes, if it doesn't get into wine.", 916b; I saw w. flowing from right side of temple, 587a; man may bring horse to w., 446b; Much w. goeth by the mill, 606a; mystery of this w. and wine, 298b, 590a
Waters pleasant w. of the river Lee, 59a; sanctifying power of w. of baptism, 49b; Who bad'st the w.'s birth divide, 373a
Wave a picture in every w., 323b
Wax Souls are like w. waiting for a seal, 503a
Way as Man, the w. we are to go, 466b, 486a, 492b; attractions of Christian w., not self-evident, 27b; *Love* of heaven, only w. to heaven, 304b; One w. to hell, one w. to God, 543b; Time, W., and Wayfarer, 493a; w., image, pattern, 254b; w. of life *and* system of thought, 147b; *W., Truth, and Life,* 108b, 148b, 292a, 492b
Wayfarers spoils of w., 13b
Ways In the Church there are three w. of life, 908b; Most sure in all His w.!, 379a; only two w., to Rome and atheism, 42a; vindicate the w. of God to man, 397a; w. of Thy only-begotten Son, 7b
Weak Christ cares for you, though w., 72a; The protest of the w. against the strong, 516b; *w. things of this world hath God chosen,* 782a
Weaker The w. hath the worse, 909a
Weakness guardian of power is w., 908b
Wealth All thing may be suffered saving w., 851b; Charity, which makes us rich in eternal w., 156b; Each class must receive its due share, 909b; Nor will his w. attend him being dead, 776a; War seldom enters but where w. allures, 171a; w. of those who write ill, 45a; Well-doing is my w., 607a; what do superfluous riches profit, 48a; what greater riches than good conscience?, 208a
Wealthiest I w. am when richest in remorse, 763a
Wealthy w. and workers not intended live in conflict, 187b
Weapons Use their own w., 26b
Wear We've ceased to rectify What women w., 278a
Wearing All thing is the worse for the w., 909b
Wears Nothing w. like pride, 726a
Weary BVM, rest of w., 84b; Dreary! w.! W.! dreary!, 791b; I was w. and ill at ease, 626b
Weather After clouds black, we shall have w. clear, 909b; There's

much afoot in heaven this year, 909b
Web things primarily created in a w. of elements, 224b
Wed these, whom death again did w., 455b
Wedded We w. men live in sorrow and care, 573b
Weddeth Who w. or he be wise, 573b
Wedding No w. during Lent, 575b; *There was a w. feast,* 131a; W. is destiny, 910a
Weddings Christians, at w., shall not dance, 910a
Wedlock dream in courtship, in w. wake, 574a; fruitfulness of w., 92a; I praise w., I praise marriage, 573b; mystery foreshadows union of Christ with Church, 576a; She is not worthy of w., who is worthy of chiding, 455a
Weds Who wisely w. in his maturer years, 574a
Weed Desire of power, a vicious w., 14a; Ill w. groweth fast, 910a; worldly wither'd w., 303b
Weeds w. growing, courage to pull them up, 465a
Weep All you that w., all you that mourn, 769b; Better children w. than old men, 910a; now begin to w. when they have done, 416a; rejoice with glad but w. with afflicted, 155b; She used to w. if she but saw a mouse, 861b; those who have no tears for Time, w. in Eternity, 859b; W., living things! the mother dies, 243a; W. not for me, when I am gone, 243a; W. not the brave dead!, 254a; W. over me, brethren, friends, relatives, 500a; W., w., O Walsingham, 812b
Weeping Fond mothers give over your w., 242b; W. is the ease of woe, 910a; Whom w. wins, repentant sorrow moves, 491b
Weeps Ere Mercy w. them out again, 20a
Weight Sweetest W. is hung on thee, 230b; very w. of Heaven, 38a; w. of divine precepts, 212b
Welcome W., all wonders in one sight!, 487a
Welfare Government should be administered for w. of citizens, 407a; Public w. consists in sanctity of life, 435b; w. of God and state, 521b
Well All is w. that ends w., 395a; BVM, w. of mercy, 83a; Do w., and have w., 275a
Welldoing sow before the seeds of w., 722a; W. is my wealth, 607a
Well-dressed no man so w. as American, 18a
Well-mannered no man so w. as American, 18a
Wells spider-peopled w., 503b
Wells, H. G., 218a
Wept I have not w. with Peter, 521a; I w. not, to stone within I grew, 910a
West Go thou to east, I w., 654b; longer east, shorter w., 283a
Western claim of W. civilization to be representative, 186a
Western Church norm of celibacy, 150b
Westernism confusing W. with Catholicism, 148a
Westminster (London) Close under the Abbey of W., 660b
Westminster, First Synod of (1852), 103a, 142a
Westminster Abbey Think how many royal bones, 623b
What he knew w. was w., 513a

Wheat I am God's w., 458a, 519b, 910b

Wheel Curse w. and steam, 568a; So did I see the glorious w. roll on, 421b

Wheels Call upon the w., master, 910b

Wherefore With the *quia* stay content, 513a

Whiskeys So many beers and w. multiplied, 279b

Whisper The sound of a low, sweet w., 598a

Whistle her jolly w. well y-wet, 278b

Whistled And w. as he went, for want of thought, 910b

Whistling to keep from being afraid, 911a

White black crow thinketh her own birds w., 234b; What is w.?, 911a; With double potence of the black and w., 490b

Whitman, Walt, 256a

Whole *Go in peace, faith hath made thee w.*, 764b; They that are w. can heal others, 425a

Wicked And w. folk reign in prosperity?, 381b; arise again for punishment, 768b; contained in Church as chaff, 127a; dead members attached to living body, 127a; emboldened by cowardice of good, 399b; evil fish, 155b; I am Juniper and I am w., 911a; relegate w. into eternal fire, 500b; suffer punishment till bodies rise again, 247a

Wickedness nothing else than withdrawal of goodness, 817b; spiritual powers of w., 37b; stained with w. in soul or body, 13a

Widow A virgin w., 911b; begin courting w., before she gets home from funeral, 911b; What's world to man, when his wife's a w.?, 911b; whole Church is one w., 123b

Widowhood chastity of w., 158b; holy w., better, 911a; Neither w. nor virginity has place, but by humility, 898b

Widows chastity of w., above marriage, 158b; No crafty w. shall approach my bed, 911b; Teach w. to be prudent in faith, 911a; their calculations or thoughts, 911a

Wife A w. is the peculiar gift of heav'n, 912b; always trying to turn him into somebody else, 455b; as directing head of family, 456a; be married, but have no w., 149b; beauty, believing Christian does not require, 455a; chaste w. does not have to be watched, 159a; chosen a devil to his w., 455a; co-heir of grace, 455a; dug his w.'s grave only three feet deep, 912b; Every husband exacts chastity from his w., 455a; For who is so obedient as a w.?, 455a; good w., spiritual harem, 921b; hard to w. and thrive both in a year, 573b; husband may not murder adulterous w., 7b; Let husband manage w. like a steersman, 455a; Let woman show deference to husband, 455a; lewd w. cannot be watched, 159a; make a good husband, make a good w., 455a; *man shall leave father and cleave to w.*, 577a; No man should have secret from his w., 912b; Say, young man! if you've a w., 268a; subjection of w. to husband may vary, 456a; they both lived but one life, 455b; will you take N., here present, for your lawful w.?, 576b

Wifely This flower of w. patience, 912a

Wilde, Oscar, 890a, 912b, 913a

Wilderness during pilgrimage in this w., 30b; world, bereft Of wet and wildness, 913a

Wile crafty serpent's cruel w., 6a

Wilfulness boundless in his will!, 913a

Will All that God asks is our w., 914a; becomes strong by doing small things, 914a; Blessed they who do not their own w. on earth, 767a; brave man rules himself through w., 108a; broken heart and God's w. done, 392b; by the w. that we sin, 913b; certain, we who w. when we w., 913b; freedom of w. is nothing else than volition, 357a; God's antecedent w., 797b; God's consequent w. and permission, 797b; God's w. be done!, 521a; He acts by w., not necessity, 392a; He who makes us w. what is good, 913b; He who will not when he may, may not when he w., 645b; hindered by devil from obeying God's w., 407b; I am, I know, I w., 511b; If you w. end, you must w. means, 395a; If w. had wings, 475b; *in arbitrament of his own w.*, 538a; In His w. is perfected our peace, 665b; insupportable burden of their own w., 913b; invincibly influenced by divine grace, 412a; Liberty, liberty, from his weight of w., 827a; liberty, translation of w. into act, 537a; lynch-pin of faculties, 914a; man is not damned unless for his evil w., 238a; may fix on false object, 57b; no king where w. rules and not the law, 528b; No one may prefer own w. to w. of God, 391b; Nothing is impossible to a w. heart, 914b; our thoughts, words and works, directed to fulfilment of Thy w., 731a; please Thee both in w. and in deed, 881b; prayer, conformity of our w. with divine w., 718b; reason and w. in argument, 750b; Religion must at least touch the w., 758a, 914a; roused by Holy Spirit, 412a; Self-will should be poured into ocean of w. of God, 806b; Starve imagination, feed the w., 914b; Take from me, Lord, this tepid w., 789b; tempest of the eternal w., 237b; That one w. not another w., 645b; That our w. is free, is self-evident, 358a; theology baffled, how grace influences w., 220b; three things, existence, knowledge, w., 511b; *Thy kingdom come, Thy w. be done*, 593b; Thy w. is the sovereign measure, 914a; To hate one's own w., 913b; unable to w. what God does not w., 888b; w. of God is the measure of things, 391b; w. of God, supreme cause, 391b; w. of sovereign has force of law, 533b; w. to believe, received from God, 356b; W. w. have w., though w. woe win, 913b; With lowly love and fervent w., 312b; woefully disunited from Thy w., 604a

Wills afflicted as God wills it, 10a; fickle, unstable, billows of human w., 914a; God w. to permit evil to be done, 392a; He makes good use of evil w., 313b; He w. all things in His goodness, 384a; included in order of causes certain to God, 356a; Nothing happens, unless Omnipotent w. it to happen, 391b; our w., included in order of causes, 382b; Stir up the w. of Thy faithful people, 401b; Subdue your w., master desire, 14b;

there are two w. in us, 913a; Whatsoever God simply w., that He does, 723a; wicked w. are not from Him, 391b

Win keep well as w., 867b; to w. to the knowledge of all, 395a; We w. from God exactly what we deserve, 720b; w. to reception of divine truths, 27a

Wind Clung to the name of every whistling w., 346a; He mounts the storm, and walks upon the w., 388b; Naught but w.'s breath is world's acclaim, 335a; O what a miracle w. is this, 915a; O w., thou hast thy kingdom in the trees, 915a; Often the western w. has sung to me, 396b; The w. is blind, 915a; The w., the w. is blowing up, 915b; The w. was a torrent of darkness, 915b; Tide and w. stay no man's pleasure, 645b, 868a; West w.! I would not miss His sudden tryst, 915b; which way w. blew, 915a; w., full of wantonness, 37b; w. that is trumpet of liberty, 147b; w. was fair, but blew mackrel gale, 915a

Window art provides w. on infinite, 34b

Windows peep through w. dark and dull, 29a

Winds As w. that blow against a star, 834b; flock of w. came winging from the north, 915a; in their tricksome courses, 191b; The w. hunt up the sun, 909b; wild w. of power, 11a

Wine bring w. and water to altar, 4a; can of their wits the wise beguile, 916b; good old w. imparts a richer blood, 916a; "I don't care where water goes, if it doesn't get into w.," 916b; immoderate drinking of w., 280a; In good Falernian w., 917a; Inflaming w., pernicious to mankind, 916b; mystery of this water and w., 590a; Our souls shall be leviathans In purple seas of w., 916b; Poetry is devil's w., 687b; regard w. as drug, not a drink, 279b; taken with excess, 259a; The golden w. is drunk, 916a; To drink it with measure, 279a; Whoe'er of too much ruby w. partakes, 916a; W. is for mirth, not madness, 915b; w. is the horse of Parnassus, 279a; W. of immortal mixture, 916a; w. of life is spilled upon the sand, 492a; W. was given us of God, 915b; Ye praise the w., before ye taste of grape, 916a

Wines heavy w. The body's size increase, 916a; The taste of w., 916a

Wing one imperfect w. to soar upon, 2a

Wings O, unknown Eros? What this breeze Of sudden w., 917a; senselessly beat down w. to earth, 14a; Spread forth Thy w., 346a; w. of angels' immaterial glory, 21a

Winketh He w. with the tone eye, 917a

Winneth He laugheth that w., 917a

Winning I might put my w. in mine 'eye, 362b; no such thing as fighting on w. side, 917a

Winter But hasty w., with one blast, 917b; Die, Boreas, and drown your ruins, 843a; Four thousand w., 29a; This w. of a silent poet's heart, 687a

Wipe W. thou the blood from wounds, 95a

Wisdom BVM, handmaiden and work of His w., 80a; by which God knows all things, 383a; Child grew in w., as well as in stature, 608b; cognizance of eternal things belongs to w., 515b; difference between w. of illuminated and devout, 918a; divine W. alone can declare His secrets, 383a; Dost thou hold w. to be anything other than truth, 917b; faith and w., 333b; first task of man aspiring to w., 918a; Fruitless w. of him who has no knowledge of himself, 918a; God's w., for learning, 388b; Great are those two gifts, w. and continence, 917b; greatest w., despising world, 918a; Hail! O Christ, Word, W., Power of God, 491a; he'll never die of w., 918b; highest w., manifests hidden truths of divinity, 383a; His greatness is same as His w., 386b; His w., manifold and diverse, 383a; Holy Ghost gives w. against folly, 366b; human w. and Christian philosophy contrasted, 331b; immensity and singleness of God's w., 383a; In all created things, discern providence and w. of God, 388b; in baptism we receive spirit of w., 50a; In present day, mistiness mother of w., 866b; Jesus Christ, W. and Power of God, 480b; kinds of knowledge, *intelligence, science, w., prudence*, 512b; knowledge of Divine things may be called w., 571b; Man's little w., yours and mine, 633b; may your w. not be with pride, 11b; O W., that proceedest from mouth of Most High, 8a; Patience is the companion of w., 661a; poverty and w. of saints in BVM, 92a; power of Father, w. of Son, 108b; precedes, religion follows, 754a; right distinction between w. and knowledge, 515b; sacrament of divine w., 726b; seat of w., 98b; Sober speed is w.'s leisure, 645b; that transcendeth all, 350b; Theology deserves to be called highest w., 863a; Thou that instructeth Christians in Heavenly w.!, 211b; Thy w., with its deep on deep, 379a; To meditate on life and sufferings of Jesus Christ, w., 602a; two gifts, w. and continence, 215b; unsearchable depth of w., 394a; use of w. and knowledge, 515b; weaves itself i' the loom o' the fool, 918b; What beauty in w. of God!, 54a; which illumines minds that need it, 382a; w., and councils of God, 127a; W. is clear vision of work of God, 918a; w. is lifeless without grace, 753b; W. is the foundation, 917b; Wisdom ordained, higher should look after lower, 21a; W.! Stand!, 589a; W. and Power of God, Christ, 917b

Wisdoms There are not many w., 917b; two w. in Christ, 482b

Wise A fool may eke a w. man often guide, 348a; all that men held w., 918a; Ask, who is w.?, 918a; Be merry and be w., 497b; Better to be happy than w., 420a; Whither w. and great resort, 20b; w. men hasten to marriage supper of King, 299a; wish to be w. with impossible wisdom, 918a

Wisest greatest clerks be not the w. men, 189b, 513a; grieve most at loss of time, 869a

Wish Better to have than w., 711b; I strongly w. for what I hope, 241a; I w. I were the little key, 198a; I w. to have no wishes left, 250b; not to w. is not to be deceived, 918b

Wishers W. and woulders be no good householders, 918b

Wishes My w. are but few, 905b; our disordered w. and actions, 4a; Thy bounteous hands our w. crown, 366b; vengeance, grant foolish w., 905b

Wit A professional w., a bad character, 918b; beat your pate, and fancy w. will come, 348a; But w. is a sword, 919a; defined as justness of thought, 919a; drunkenness is very sepulture Of mannes w., 281b; E'en w.'s a burden when it talks too long, 859b; long hair and short w., 418a; Much malice mingl'd with a little w., 569a; Not always kind to sense or just to w., 276b; So vast is art, so narrow human w., 363a; Too much w., like too little, 601b; True w. is nature to advantage dress'd, 919a; Two have more w. than one, 918b; When wine were in, w. out, 279a; Whose w. in the combat as gentle as bright, 919a; W. and religion suffer'd banishment, 918b; W. is lower than humor, 454a; W. will shine, 688a

Witchcraft absolutely certain there is such a thing as w., 919a; belief in w., 745a

Within Thou wert w., and I abroad, 54a

Without *to judge them that are w.*, 178b

Witness Christians do not bear false w., 162b; required of those who believe in God, w. of God, 352b; w. and teacher of religious truth, 23b

Wits Great w. are sure to madness near alli'd, 363a, 568a; So many heads, so many w., 607a; When they were driven to their w.' end, 918; a wit with dunces and a dunce with w., 281a; Your tongues run before your w., 872b

Wive there will I w., 573b

Wives Bachelors boast how they will teach their w., 912a; But w., untried they take, 912b; Husbands in heaven, whose w. scold not, 455a; jealous folk want w. to think them so, 478a; Let us teach w. to cherish their husbands, 911b; love their w. as Lord does the Church, 575a; men, who do not boast w. bully them, 455b; more w. than one God did not create, 619b; O that w. were to their mates as kind, 912a; O w.! love tenderly husband, 455b; *they that have w. as though they had none,* 150b

Woe For ever the latter end of joy is w., 497a; From pain to pain, from w. to w., 846b; hasty man never wanteth w., 422b; her w. and w. of man, 99b; I'll taste the luxury of w., 416a; O sudden w., successor To worldly bliss!, 919b; Put off your weeds of w., 769b; Sloth brings in all w., 457b; Sure there's a lethargy in mighty w., 416a; That bank of w., 919b; This world, but thoroughfare full of w., 538b; thy dull mind, headlong cast in depths of w., 612b; Weeping is the ease of w., 910a; when Jove gave us life, he gave w., 516a; Will will have will, though will w. win, 913b

Woes life, all chequer'd with pleasures and w., 539a; Seven lights for seven w., 97a; What have his w. to do with Thee?, 570a; Who knows my heart's w., 424a

Wolf A w. in a lamb's skin, 253b; To keep the w. from the door, 919b

Wolves By guileful goats to ravening w. misled, 484a; Silence, ye w.!, 273b

Woman a softer man, 920b; A w. is a foreign land, 921a; appearance depends upon two things, 277b; as full of words as woman, 11b; bold At lies and swearing as a w., 567b; confusion of man, 572a; Death by w.'s weakness enter'd in, 25b; gateway of the devil, 919b; God is obedient to a woman, 82b; good w. is man's bliss, 920a; half so true, As w. been, 572a; holy w. should obscure beauty, 53b; Human nature is born of the pain of a w., 638a; In w.'s virtue, life doth begin, 25b; lyen as a w. can, 920a; man and w., as such, incompatible, 574b; man, head of family, w., heart, 572b; man's inseparable helpmeet, 576a; Many a w. has a past, 921a; Men always want to be a w.'s first-love, 557a; newly created w., greeted with peals of laughter, 920b; no limit to power of good w., 921a; nothing a w. so dislikes, as to have her old opinions quoted, 921b; nothing that a w. of well-balanced mind hates more, 920b; one real tragedy in w.'s life, 455a; She is not worthy of wedlock, who is worthy of chiding, 455a; sphere of w.'s glories is heart, 555b; through w., salvation restored, 85b; Trojans fought for a w., 921a; Variability, one of virtues of a w., 921b; Where comes a cow, there follows a w., 921b; where comes a w., follows trouble, 921b; who would tell her age, 11a; w. hath nine lives, 920a; W. is a thrall, 919b; W. is for mannes help y-wrought, 572a

Womanhood BVM, thou glory of w., 100a; The splendor of thy w., 922a

Womb all of us have come from w. of Mary, 93a; become temple of God, 467b; *blessed is the fruit of thy w.*, 82a; From a noble w. to spring, 74a; He whom world unable to contain, enclosed in thy w., 632a; I sought my death, found it in my w., 541b; Nature's new w., 286b; take flesh in w. of Blessed Virgin, 25a; The w. contains the Infinite, 25a; Unsatiate as the barren w. or grave, 342a; Virgin's spotless womb, 81b, 167a; When thy sacred w. He filled, 39b; w. of Mary overshadowed by grace, 87a; w. of one woman, 81a; w. Opes on courtyard of the tomb, 872b

Women All w. become like their mothers, 624b; All w. long For husbands tough, 454b; beauty of w. is the greatest snare, 919b; blandishments of w., 919b; *Blessed art thou among w.*, 82a; crown of w., 40b; dissatisfied with God's plastic skill, 221b; Fairest of women!, 2a; generally make up in heat, 921b; have a lot to bear, 921b; have more power over men because they are good, 920a; history of w., worst form of tyranny, 921a; Horses like w., require soothin' word, 447a; If w. begin to fall in disputing, 920a; In w. two almost divide the kind, 572a, 920b; Let the w. stand apart, 919b; may not approach altar, 919b; Most w. have no characters at all, 920b; never disarmed by compliments,

572a; no libel On w. clergy will not paint, 920a; nothing w. hate so much, 572b; O w.! woe to men, 920b; older, greater fools about men, 572b; Parents of life and love, 920b; prone To follow fortune's favors, 920a; represent triumph of matter over mind, 572a; shameless w., will hesitate at nothing, 811a; Sphinxes without secrets, 921a; three things in w. do not understand, 921b; two classes monk should avoid, w. and bishops, 618b; utter mystics in creed, cynics in criticism, 455b; virginity bestowed upon w., 79a; vital differences between men and w., 30b; whether more men than w. are saved, 293b; whether w. were married by capture, 574b; who have a past, 572a; W. are the only realists, 749a; W.! do not despise yourselves, 448b; "w.", God bless them!, 624b

Won defeated, who have w., 254a

Wonder especially proper to childhood, 922a; Her w. like a wind doth sing, 55b; Lost, all lost in w., 75a; O w. of surpassing might!, 25a; one of the faculties most easy to lose, 628a; Poets and philosophers, alike in being big with w., 680b; This w. lasted nine days, 922a

Wonderful God w. in dispensation of works, 43b; My God! how w. Thou art, 340a

Wonders Full of glory, full of w., 378a; Rise, mighty Man of w., 286b; Welcome, all w. in one sight!, 487a; working w. in His power and grace, 609a

Woo Ancient ladies are forc'd to w., 922b

Wood price of this life-giving w., 231a; Sweetest W. and Sweetest Iron!, 230b; Ye cannot see the w. for the trees, 879a

Woodcraft He knew whole of w. up and down, 454a

Wooded painted pomp of w. heights, 47b

Woods Fields have eyes and w. have ears, 323b; I had strayed into a dark forest, 922a

Woo'd man alone is woo'd, 219a; way a woman loves to be w., 922b

Wooes like a lover, 37b

Wooing A man shall win us best with flattery, 922a; Ah, whither shall a maiden flee, 922b; If I speak to thee in friendship's name, 922b; Nigh and sly Wins against Fair and Square, 922a; The time I've lost in w., 922b

Word A kind w. never broke a tooth, 923b; A W., a W., Thou didst utter, 25b; appropriate time for each w. and deed, 891a; appropriates to Himself attributes of humanity, 481b; bathed in new light of Thine Incarnate W., 167a; begotten of Father before all ages, 466a; BVM bore incarnate W., 81a; by the grace of the W., 408a; by which Thou hast made all things, 485a; Celestial Word, to this our earth, 7b; coeternal W., 370a; dwelling place of W. of God, 40b; Every w. man's lips have uttered, 923b; false interpreters of divine w., 60b; Father, never lacking in W., 439a; gentle w. quiets anger, 22b; God instructs us by sacred w., 5a; God made all things by His W., 223b; God's w. does not return to Him void, 269b; Hail! O Christ, W., Wisdom, Pow-

er of God, 491a; He ever possesses His own W., 482a; He's as good as his w., 923b; heavenly W. proceeding forth, 74b; hypostatically united Himself with flesh, 481b; I have sinned exceedingly in thought, w., and deed, 587b; In the beginning was the W., 597b; incarnate W., His blessed Self He lowers, 440a; known by works to be W. of the Father, 466a; let Thy w. be feared in us, 346a; lord Of an unpurchasable w., 753a; man is seldom better than his w., 154a; My King and Lord, The Incarnate W., 463a; mystery of the W. made flesh, 167a; Never have I said w. against Thee, 520a; never lacking in Spirit, 439a; never was a time when God was not W., 482a; No less flattering in her w., 922b; O only-begotten Son and W. of God, 588b; On the faithful Word attending, 25a; One ill w. axeth another, 746a; one Person, W. and Man, 481a; Only-begotten Son and W. of God, 482a; our Leader, the Divine W., 435b; power to receive divinity of W., 25a; proper name of the Son, 439b; Son and W., like essence with Father and Holy Spirit, 467b; Son of God, eternal W., 466a; soul seeks W. in order to yield to it, 288b; terms generation, father, son, w., 370b; This Life, this Light, this W., this Joy, 168b; Thy Word took flesh, 24b; Thy w. is truth, 245a; 'tis but a w. and a blow, 30b; to confess W. and flesh, 481a; To intelligent, w. is enough, 923a; took flesh in might of BVM, 91b; torture once poor w. ten thousand ways, 923a; Upon their W. and Master feed, 74b; What is w. but wind?, 922b; what w. this W. doth bring!, 168b; Who knows the w., he needs not knock, 218b; wisdom of Thy W., 231a; W. is flesh in flesh, 81b; W.-made-flesh, bread of nature, 74a; W. of God, became what we are, 465b; w. of God, written or unwritten, 145b; W. was made flesh, 71a, 168a, 481b; work of art is a w. made flesh, 34a

Words A glutton of w., 923a; Always to let the losers have their w., 550a; An angel's witching w., 25b; barren superfluity of w., 923a; Be modest in all thy w. and works, 615a; charity not genuine if w. not charitable, 156b; easier to be altogether silent, than not exceed in w., 813b; faculty of concealing thoughts in w., 367a; Fair w. make fools fain, 923a; felicitousness in choice of w., 849a; Harsh w., though pertinent, uncouth appear, 923a; heard w. that have been So nimble, 923a; hurteth not tongue to give fair w., 923a; In all His w. most wonderful, 379a; justified by works and not by w., 403a; Let thy w. be few, in the midst of many, 838b; let your w. be strong, 26b; old man, often full of w., 11b; our minds, pierced with arrows of Your w., 550b; our thoughts, w. and works, directed to fulfilment of Thy will, 731a; Such distance between high w. and deeds!, 923a; that never lie, or brag, or flatter, 627a; Too simple and too sweet for w., 939a; Who fail the w. of Christ to keep, 600a; w. of Savior effect consecration, 71b

Wordsworth, William, 923b

Work every prayer and w. may begin from Thee, 428b; good play for nought, w. for nought, 924a; hunger in frost, w. in heat, 923b; industrialism has depersonalized w., 471a; Many hands make light w., 924a; Men w. harder on that which belongs to them, 734b; motive of w., to obtain property, 734b; not only means of decent livelihood, 517b; nothing expected from w., but pay, 471a; Pray and w., 718a; season our labors with sacred song, 266a; Survey w. to be done, 149b; test of artist in excellence of w., 31b; unending w. of the Church, 235a; which redeems my many wasted days, 92b; Ye run to w. in haste, 923b

Worker betterment of w., 38b; Christ, devoted Himself to manual labor, 517a; Hail to thee, laborer!, 516b; human dignity of w., 320a; must show respect for own moral dignity, 112b

Workers employer must never tax w. beyond strength, 516b; should share in benefits which they create, 516b; trade unions and betterment of w., 38b; wealthy and w. not intended live in conflict, 187b

Working w. for gain, creditable to a man, 516b

Working-class great scandal, Church lost w., 517a; interests of w. should be carefully watched over, 516b

Workmen ministry of common w., 34a

Works author and history of his w., 45a; God wonderful in dispensation of w., 43b; great w. of Thy might, 569b; His darker w., 32a; In worldly w. degrees are three, 644b; our thoughts, words and w., directed to fulfilment of Thy will, 731a; Thy elaborate w. unwrought, 283a; W. adjourned have many stays, 255a, 645b

Works, Good See Good Works

World 'a strange w.', 926a; active life opposed to confusion of w., 4b; All the w. together not worth one soul, 925a; And now a bubble burst, and now a w., 384a; artists lifted above level of w., 35a; book of w., full of knowledge we need to acquire, 435a; bustle of this w., 212a; cause of w.'s preservation, 926b; could not exist, unless known beforehand to God, 382b; could not be known, if not existing, 319a; end of every episode, end of the w., 446a; endowed men will rescue w., 1b; fainting world's Physician, 8a; filled with name of Christ, 72b; gain of this w. is loss of souls, 362a; God made w. from nothing, 224a; great stage on which God displays wonders, 843b; How little a w. needed me, 452b; kingdom of heaven and end of w., 136a; manifests its Designer, 372a; marked with the imprint of mutability, 380b; may be divided into those who take it or leave it, 926b; only peopled to people heaven, 303b; So go'th the w., 924b; stumbling blocks of w., 189a; superfluities of the w., 618a; The w. is blind, 924b; Then place not in w. thy trust, 37b; This ordered w. which Thou hast made, 369a; This w., but thoroughfare full of woe, 538b; this w., too small for soul of man, 565b; this wretched vale of tears, 95b; those who love this w., 927a;

threefold fabrics, 81b; to contemn the w., 36b, 155a; To flee from the w., to abstain from sins, 924a; true mystery of the w., 926a; verdict of the w. is conclusive, 924b; warfare between the Church and the w., 135b; When Christianity dies, w. will die, 135b; whole w. is under petticoat government, 278a; w. is all one wild divorce court, 268a; w. is my crucifix, 234b; w. is strange, 11a; w. is very evil, 502a; w. of change and time, 7b; w. shall never exult over Church, 135b; w. transformed, turned upside-down, 438a; You must either conquer w. or w. will conquer you, 925b

Worldliness service of devil, 260b; There was a friar, 927b

Worldly Leave to the w. their world, 925a; w. wither'd weed, 303b

Worlds best of all impossible w., 926a; Three w. there are, 925b

Worm Tread a w. on the tail, 927b

Worms Have mercy on us w. of earth, 371b; how could BVM become food of w.?, 40b; Man, sack of dung, food of w., 569a; Perceive ye not that we are w., 163b; W.' food is fine end of our living, 927b

Wormwood Bitter as w., 259a; to love Him in w., 344a

Worries annoyance of many continuous w., 927b

Worse All thing is the w. for the wearing, 909b; The weaker hath the w., 909a

Worship Bethlehem has exhausted world's capacity for w., 773a; Catholicism's capacity to harmonize liturgical w., 548b; Christianity, eminently an objective religion, 928a; Church alone retains true w., 125b; due to the most holy Trinity, 928a; Follow custom of Church where you happen to be, 207b; fundamental right, every man w. according to convictions, 354a, 871a; God has no need for our w., 754b; God instructed Moses about w., 68a; Human society, bound to offer God public and social w., 928b; His w. is the result of knowledge, 754a; illicit for Catholics to take part in w. of non-Catholics, 928b; imitate Him Whom thou adorest, 928a; in divine w., necessary to make use of certain corporal acts, 755a; It is a law of man's nature, 928b; liturgy, w. of Mystical Body in Head and members, 547b; men invariably w. what they like best, 927b; Men who assist at w., should have heads uncovered, 928b; O let us fall and w. Him, 170a, 440a; Religion so called, because by it we bind souls to God for divine w., 754b; Religion, virtue by which men show God due w. and reverence, 755a; render Thee pure w., 745b; to obey in simple tranquillity, noblest w., 928a; To w. ourselves, nothing, 929a; unlawful, place forms of w. on the same footing, 354b; we w. His immaculate flesh, 482a; where confession is, there is w., 203a; women should have heads covered, 928b; w., honor and good pleasure of God, 262a; W. is the Christian life, 929a; w. Mary by imitating humility, 101a; w. of Church, efficacious means of achieving sanctity, 548a; w. of nothing is hell, 929a; You do not compel

man to w. what he does not wish, 354b

Worshipped God, to be w. by faith, hope, and love, 928a

Worshipper anguish of w. over broken idol, 24b

Worst always to choose the w., 287a; If the w. fell, 264b

Worth Not the w. of a bean, 926a

Worthy I am not w., Lord, mine eyes, 764a; *Lord, I am not w. that Thou shouldest enter under my roof*, 595a; w. of Him, 570a

Wound A nobler weapon than a w., 929a; As balm my w. to heal, 210b; My w. is great because it is so small, 929a; O royal rift, O worthy w., 929a; purple wardrobe in Thy side, 104a

Wounded The w. is the wounding heart, 929a

Wounding By w. Him Who is divine, 94a; No one heals himself by w. another, 929a

Wounds contemplate Thy five w., 657a; Hail, holy w. of Jesus!, 104a; In the five w. of Jesus dyed, 95a; In Thy w. most precious, 75b; Kneel down to kiss these w. of Thine, 657b; O cruel death, O w. most deep, 656b; On the w. to Jesus given, 94b; Thy bloody w. be made a rod, 94a; Thy crimson w., how bright, 286b; When I beheld Thy bitter w., 491b; with five w. I wounded lie, 31b; w. of Christ, 75b, 656a; w. of nature, 412b

Wrath Day of w. and doom impending, 502a; ebbing w. doth end, 22b; purple winepress of the w. of God, 929a; refrain from exciting w., 22a; To Him that hath appeas'd God's w., 286a

Wreath A w. unfading on his head, 582a; No laurel w. about my brow!, 714b; The w. of brightest myrtle wove, 929b; year by year the sad memorial w., 763a

Wreck never Let us suffer w., 39b

Wren upon my eagle's wings I bore this w., 478b

Wrestle I w. not with rage, 22b

Wrestlest thou w. in the world, 43a

Wrestling w. with (my God!) my God, 258b

Wretch A guilty w. like me, 21b; silly w. That lives in low degree, 570a

Wretched The w. have no friends, 929b

Wrinkle Smooths away a w., 279b

Write Learn to w. well, or not to w. at all, 929b; poverty of those who w. well, 45a; They who w. ill, 228a; those who speak well, and do not w. well, 646b; To w. upon all, author's sole chance, 929b; wealth of those who w. ill, 45a

Writer mastered everything except language, 849a

Writers acerbities which bite writing men, 160b; difficult for new w. to be original, 228a; great w. and history of their times, 45a; life of w., bitter business, 45a; must not heed criticism unduly, 228a

Writes When he w. well, no one w. better, 929b

Writing accompanied by poverty and contempt, 45a; by means of w., make further progress, 929b; depends upon force of imagination, 459b; last thing, know what to put first, 107a; To w. bred, 929b

Wrong Church can not identify her cause with political w., 691b; do no w., superhuman, 929b; His can't be w. whose life is in the right, 275a; king can do no w., 509a; men who do w., 929b; they ne'er pardon who have done the w., 472a; To be w., carefully w., 253b; When people agree, I feel w., 12a; When world goes w., proves Church is right, 819b

Wrong-doing charity owing to all, w. to none, 132a

Wrongs To him, who makes people's w. his own, 153a

Wrought first he w., and afterward he taught, 316b

Y

Year happeth not in seven y., 447b; In the ending of the y., 168a; That night, that y., 258b; to take spring out of y., 393a

Years down the arches of the y., 385a; For many y.!, 930a; How dread are Thine eternal y., 340a; multiply days with many y., 66b; To chasten these my later years, 94a; To have lived enchanted y., 540b; When time, who steals our y. away, 603a; When y. go by Funeral-paced, 318b; women reckoned y. by husbands, 268a

Yearning O Source of all our y.!, 258a; She would stir with y., 110a

Yearns show me one who y., 301b

Yellow All looks y. to the jaundiced eye, 478a

Yesterday Y. will not be called again, 930a; Y. with exultation, 846b

Yew Lay garland on my hearse of dismal y., 344a

Yield and y. and conquer still, 424a; It is better to bow than break, 930a; Nothing so hard, it does not y. to harder, 673b; To y. to what my Saviour shall dispose, 410b

Yoke bear whole y. of the Lord, 671b; episcopate, heavy y. of gospel, 68b; How sweet the mutual y. of man and wife, 455b; Light her y., her burden sweet, 135b; remove heavy y. of sins, 98a

Young all things made y. with y. desires, 843a; A y. man bothered, till he's married, 575a; Both raven and ape think own y. fairest, 160b; If you could influence the y., 931b; reverence the old, love the y., 930a; Say, y. man! if you've a wife, 268a; son, fine y. squire, 930a; The light y. man who was to die, 114a; The y. don't know what age is, 931b; three y. men, 216a; y. cock croweth, 930a; y. man's warling, 574a

Younger how much y. I!, 306b

Youth checked your y.'s tumultuous overflow, 931b; Educate y. to obedience, 47a; Force of *juventus*, hardy as lion, 930b; how slippery is the path of y., 930b; In life's happy morning, 250a; In y. that I thought sweet, 10b; longing for eternal recovery of y., 161b; Love is like y., he thirsts for age, 554b; Most men in years, discouragers of y., 572b; My prime of y. is but a frost of cares, 930b; My thoughtless y., wing'd with vain desires, 219a; My y. is gone, and yet I am but young, 930b; nostalgic yearning after vanished y., 161b; Not often, in our y.'s audacity, 931a; Of wanton y., repents a painful age, 149b; Of y., and home, and that sweet time, 58b; Only one y., life was still God-given!, 930b; Prime y. lasts not, 10b; Unlike the y. that all men say They prize, 543a; Y., beauty, graceful action seldom fail, 152b; Y. but lives for the hour, 931b; y., hopeless, 446a; Y. is a disease that must be borne with patiently!, 931a; y. is rash, 11b; Y., lyric, fanatical, poetic, 446a; Y. must with time decay, 884b; y. of America, their oldest tradition, 15b; Y. should watch joys, 930b; y. would be forever glad, 931a

Youths Let wilder y., whose soul is sense, 553b

Z

Zeal as for z. and quick-eyed sanc-tity, ye pass'd them by, 536a; Church has right to service of gen-ius, learning, z., 532b; ever z. be-gins its life In silent thought and fear, 932a; few catastrophes, as excess of z., 932b; Hypocritic z., no sins but those it can conceal, 456a; moved with passion, think it to be z., 932a; No sacrifice more acceptable to God than z. for souls, 931a; without knowledge, highly dangerous, 931b

Zealots For modes of faith let graceless z. fight, 275a

Zephyrinus, Pope St., 678b

Zeus Ay, Z. is dead, and all the gods but Doubt, 276a

INDEX OF SOURCES

The present work is drawn almost exclusively from Catholic sources. Unless otherwise indicated below, it may generally be assumed that this is the case.

The symbol (*) denotes that an author was not a Catholic, or if he was a Catholic, that he did not die in communion with the Church. Prefixed to a work, it indicates that the work is to be found on the Index of Prohibited Books published by the Holy See, or that the work is otherwise unreliable. The symbol (†) denotes that the opinions of the author as cited in the present work are not in accordance with normal Catholic teaching.

The dates given for Popes represent the years of their pontificate.

Abelard, Peter (1079–1142), 1, 491, 785
Acton, John Emerich Edward, Lord (1834–1902), 3, 27, 47, 112, 138, 153-154, 181, 210, 259, 270-271, 313, 328, 331, 353, 354, 406, 414, 434, 499, 538, 621, 625, 691-692, 696, 702, 714, 737, 757, 845, 871-872, 884
Adam of St. Victor (d. ca.1192), 25, 28, 39-40, 168, 232, 286, 370, 439, 605, 670, 846-847, 865
Alain de Lille (Alanus de Insulis) (ca.1120–1202), 397, 781
Alcuin (735?–804), 397, 671
Alexander VII, Pope (1655–1667), 7, 281, 368
Alexandria, Council of, 81, 467, 481, 486
Alfred, King of England (849–901), 872
Allen, William Cardinal (1532–1594), 141, 294
Alphonsa, Mother Mary (Rose Hawthorne Lathrop) (1851–1926), 833, 870
Alphonso of Liguori, St. (1696–1787), 168-169, 669
*Alsop, George (1638– ?), 585
Ambrose, St. (339?–397): *Concerning Faith (De Fide)*, 310, 386, 484, 597; *Concerning Virgins (De Virginibus)*, 80, 92, 130, 639; *Concerning Widows*, 20, 60, 158; *De Fuga*, 523, 924; *De Institutione Virginis*, 78; *De Virginitate*, 745; *Explanation of Psalm 118*, 72, 195, 260, 324-325, 481, 492, 633, 659, 741, 834; *Explanation of St. Luke*, 50, 195, 295, 408, 598, 675, 775, 796; *Explicatio Symboli ad Initiandos*, 227; *Hexaem*, 313, 345, 391, 481; *Hymns*, 28, 166, 369, 522, 599, 636, 637, 639, 809, 862, 893; *In Ps.*, 138, 172, 325, 333, 384, 386, 675, 709, 823, 881, 929; *Letters*, 4, 48, 80, 90, 172-173, 188-189, 227, 325, 354, 355, 362, 388, 455, 484-485, 528, 668, 698, 846; *On Penitence*, 320, 325, 397; *On the Duties of the Clergy*, 34, 60, 102, 137, 208, 301, 345, 361, 365, 401, 403, 471, 504, 603, 620, 633, 733, 738, 899, 917; *On the Good of Death*, 106, 246, 252; *On the Holy Spirit*,

667; *On the Incarnation*, 124, 466, 511; *On the Mysteries*, 50, 71-72, 310, 597, 785; *On the Sacraments*, 13, 43, 50, 72, 195, 310, 408, 597, 730, 753, 785, 874; *Sermons*, 20, 246; *Other works*, 102, 238, 246, 337, 356, 408, 466, 519, 716, 816, 825, 860, 899
Ancrene Riwle (13th cent.), 922
Andrew of Crete, St. (660–732), 86, 98, 100, 442, 483, 484, 488, 489, 491, 535, 764
Angelita, Sister Mary (1878–   ), 47, 78, 111, 252, 258, 281, 488, 623, 634, 690, 747, 837
Annand, Rachel (Mrs. R. A. Taylor) (1876–   ), 235
Anselm, St. (1034?–1109), 247, 319, 331, 375, 378, 380, 394, 460, 520, 560-561, 817
Anthony of Padua, St. (1195–1231), 519, 716
Antioch, Council of, 67
Antoniano, Silvio Cardinal (1542–1621), 922
Aphraates, St. (275?–345?), 480
Apostles, Twelve, Teaching of, *see* Teaching of the Twelve Apostles
Apostles' Creed, 226
Apostolic Constitutions, 49-50
Apostolic See, 709
Aquinas, St. Thomas, *see* Thomas Aquinas, St.
Arcadius, Emperor of Rome (377–408), 28
Aristides, St. (2nd cent. A.D.), 162-163, 398, 403
Arles, Council of, 5
Arnold of Citeaux (d. 1225), 235
Asterius of Amasea, St. (d. ca.410), 675
Athanasian Creed, 144, 227, 368
Athanasius, St. (295–373), 252, 407-408, 465-466
Athenagoras (2nd cent.), 390, 438, 480
Augsburg, Peace of (1555), 180
Augustine, St. (354–430): *Against Lying*, 295, 567, 634, 745, 816; *City of God*, 10, 31, 50, 54, 57, 68, 72, 107, 112, 113, 124-125, 144, 173, 237, 246-247, 307-308, 313-314, 318-319,

335, 339, 356, 362, 372, 382-383, 388-389, 391, 399, 403-404, 419, 431, 449, 466, 471, 485, 490, 501, 509-510, 511, 523, 534, 538, 541, 569, 581, 609, 624, 647, 664-665, 730, 740, 741, 754, 765-766, 769, 779, 784, 790-791, 795, 811, 817, 820, 825, 847, 852, 855, 869, 894, 896, 899, 906, 907, 917, 924, 927, 928; *Confessions,* 3, 22, 41, 54, 60, 103, 106, 164, 200, 215, 236, 244, 260, 261, 264, 268, 269, 281, 294, 301, 325, 344, 346, 358, 359, 366, 372, 374, 378, 379, 380, 382, 385, 386, 390, 393, 398, 481, 485, 511, 525, 531-532, 546, 550, 559-560, 602, 615, 627, 642, 650, 664, 682, 714, 732, 735-736, 747, 748, 769, 796-797, 801, 808, 816, 833, 844, 848, 859, 864, 868, 878, 880, 883, 885, 889, 892, 894, 913; *De Agone Christiano,* 223, 234, 260, 448, 511, 569, 675, 821, 851, 927; *De Anima et ejus origine,* 887; *De Correptione et Gratia,* 6, 399, 408, 411-412, 485, 723, 820; *De Doctrina Christiana,* 53, 154-155, 289, 318, 347, 368, 398, 566, 569, 768, 785, 792, 813, 816; *De Genesi ad Litteram,* 211, 224, 318, 379; *De Gratia et Libero Arbitrio,* 913; *De Immortalitate Animae,* 749, 802; *De Moribus Ecclesiae Catholicae,* 45, 56, 102, 130, 131-132, 301, 313, 419, 458, 569, 633, 899; *De Musica,* 625; *De Natura Boni,* 378, 380; *De Natura et Gratia,* 86, 408, 460; *De Opere Monachorum,* 848; *De Ordine,* 393; *De Just.,* 480; *De Praedestinatione Sanctorum,* 722, 797; *De Quantitate Animae,* 211, 511, 749, 754, 835; *De Spiritu et Littera,* 57, 356, 385, 408, 526; *De Trinitate,* 38, 79, 152, 211, 224, 275, 301, 329, 339, 374-375, 380, 383, 386, 391-392, 394, 438, 463, 466, 485, 511-512, 550-551, 560, 606, 609, 670, 817, 835, 862, 865; *De Utilitate Credendi,* 117, 388, 417, 430, 608-609, 754, 835; *De Vera Religione,* 120, 511, 754, 848, 883; *Enchiridion,* 56, 81, 123, 130, 221, 244, 300, 308, 313, 329, 349, 356, 369, 388, 391, 426, 481, 505, 567, 668, 716, 741, 751, 768-769, 816, 820, 821; *Letters,* 3, 35, 50, 53, 63, 72, 120-121, 126, 158, 173, 236, 238, 246, 253, 278, 333, 338, 359, 361, 379, 411, 431, 444-445, 458, 499, 538, 606, 612, 615, 618, 629-630, 640, 642, 675, 698, 714, 716, 725, 733, 751, 775, 780, 785, 792, 797, 800, 822, 823, 844, 855, 897, 906, 927, 929; *On Catechizing the Unlearned,* 11, 444, 550; *On Continence,* 566, 633, 889; *On Faith, Hope, and Charity,* 445, 619, 928; *On Free Will (De Libero Arbitrio),* 330, 350, 393, 504, 525, 528, 738, 749, 816, 859, 883, 894, 917; *On Holy Virginity,* 79, 80, 92, 216, 639-640, 897; *On John the Evangelist (Tract. in Joann.),* 57, 72-73, 128, 301, 384, 386, 493-494, 543, 560, 597, 676, 723, 786, 887; *On Patience,* 661, 852; *On the Care for the Dead,* 110, 151, 242, 244; *On the Faith and the Creed (De Fide et Symbolo),* 120, 224, 429, 438, 463, 835; *On the Good of Marriage (De Bono Conjugali),* 3, 7, 53, 158, 202, 267, 417, 474, 575-576, 732; *On the Good of Widowhood,* 215-216, 580, 911, 917; *On the Psalms,* 11,

54, 60, 65, 105, 122-123, 126, 132, 134, 203, 254, 258, 366, 381, 401, 419, 429, 490, 560, 676, 683, 714, 716, 905, 917; *Retractions,* 102, 356-357, 606, 913; *Sermons,* 6, 72-73, 79, 81, 85, 126, 130, 155, 163, 166, 195, 229, 257, 266, 300, 325, 345, 366, 394, 438, 466, 492, 495, 538, 640, 675-676, 709, 717, 721, 723, 739, 800, 835, 860, 883, 894, 897, 908; *Soliloquies,* 263, 289, 382, 393, 612, 634, 716, 883, 919; *Other works,* 4-5, 50, 66, 113, 116-17, 126, 135, 173, 208, 267, 301, 380, 386, 393, 401, 408, 411, 419, 429, 431, 456-457, 499, 504, 511, 519, 608, 632, 668, 676, 687, 694, 766, 786, 800, 887, 906, 917, 924

Aylward, Rev. J., O.P. (1813–1872), 36

Ayscough, John (1858–1928) (Pseud. of Msgr. Francis Bickerstaffe-Drew), 115, 116, 220, 221, 251, 309, 354, 659, 726, 768, 794, 803, 859

Bagshawe, Edward Gilpin Bishop (1829–1915), 462

Baker, Augustine, Ven., O.S.B. (1557–1641), 628

Baltimore, Third Plenary Council of, 190

Bangor Antiphonary, 195

Barbour, John (c.1320–1395), 353

Barclay, Alexander (1475?–1552), 83, 344, 552

Baring, Maurice (1874–1945), 6, 931

Basil, St. (c.330–379): *Against Anger,* 22; *Concerning Faith,* 324; *Discourse on Ascetical Discipline,* 618; *Homilies,* 106, 280, 909; *Letters,* 1, 266, 358, 414, 474, 568, 627-628, 691, 716, 751, 879-880; *Long Rules,* 266, 855, 894, 899; *Morals,* 45, 59, 193, 194-195, 202, 207, 216, 281, 391, 401, 447, 565, 601, 667, 774, 784, 788, 798-799, 808, 815-816, 874, 876, 891; *On Renunciation of the World,* 728, 857; *Other works,* 154

Beaumanoir, Philippe de (c.1250–1296), 236

Beaumont, Francis (1584?–1616), 239, 344, 413, 574, 623, 923

Beaumont, Sir John (1583–1627), 25, 40, 59, 106, 225, 258, 299, 303, 335, 371, 410, 414, 420, 425, 432, 444, 445, 468, 509, 513, 519, 539, 554, 655, 684, 687-688, 813, 819, 859

Bede the Venerable, St. (673?–735): *De Temporum Ratione,* 333; *Homilies,* 79, 82, 308-309, 310, 565, 677, 695, 717; *Hymns,* 494, 581, 854; *In Cantica Canticorum,* 126, 409; *In Lucam,* 130, 195, 254, 671; *Other works,* 61, 321, 432, 450, 519, 668, 695, 822, 894, 900

Bédoyère, Count Michael de la (1900–   ), 115

Bellarmine, St. Robert, *see* Robert Bellarmine, St.

Belloc, Hilaire (1870–1953): *Courtesy,* 223; *Crisis of Civilization,* 139, 186, 434-435; *Cruise of the Nona,* 256; *Economics for Helen,* 891; *Elephant,* 294; *Europe and the Faith,* 139, 779-780; *Essays of a Catholic Layman in England,* 136, 254, 533; *First and Last,* 870; *For False Heart,* 424; *Gilbert Chesterton in English Letters,* 45, 160; *Great Heresies,* 136, 165, 430, 435; *Jim,* 641;

Misc., 364; *Night,* 636; *On His Books,* 107; *On Nothing, and Kindred Subjects,* 690; *On Song,* 832; *Path to Rome,* 339, 425, 586, 625; *Song of the Pelagian Heresy,* 147, 650, 821; *Sonnets and Verse, Dedicating Ode,* 359; *South Country,* 843; *Tiger,* 868; *To Dives,* 428, 775

Benedict, St. (480–ca.547), 1, 4, 105, 155, 158, 203, 247, 266, 275, 297, 298, 302, 317, 338, 346, 386, 399, 416, 422, 426, 435, 450, 457, 478, 501, 523, 535, 560, 615, 618, 641, 642, 650, 665, 717, 740, 746, 748, 808, 812, 825, 838, 867, 883, 913, 930

Benedict XII, Pope (1334–1342), 302-303

Benedict XIV, Pope (1740–1758), 92, 579

Benedict XV, Pope (1914–1922), 47, 122, 139, 758, 777. *See also* Papal Bulls

Benedictines, Motto of, 515

Benson, Msgr. Robert Hugh (1871–1914): *An Average Man,* 13, 107, 149, 154, 201-202, 217, 219-220, 234, 276, 296, 448, 465, 477, 608, 618, 635, 735, 758, 805, 882, 889, 891; *At High Mass,* 586; *Book of the Love of Jesus, A,* 483, 720; *By What Authority?* 6, 24, 47, 129, 154, 343, 385, 424, 443, 543, 617, 631, 666, 671, 758, 882, 922; *Christ in the Church,* 56, 157, 201, 210, 234, 333, 361, 390, 484, 557, 637, 644, 684, 720, 758, 765, 806, 807, 837, 852, 885, 914; *City Set on a Hill, A,* 137, 221, 263, 272, 343, 469, 690, 808, 850; *Come Rack! Come Rope!* 55, 282, 319, 362, 392, 557, 931; *Confessions of a Convert,* 30, 157, 207, 265, 313, 328, 385, 396, 440, 643, 737, 805, 876; *Conventionalists,* 149, 282, 295, 297, 319, 344, 452, 474, 631, 637, 655, 758; *Coward,* 108, 153, 217, 557, 659, 725, 753, 867, 914; *Dawn of All,* 55, 157, 200, 255, 323, 336, 445, 477, 538, 669, 758; *Deathbed of Bloody Mary and Good Queen Bess,* 305, 543; *Friendship of Christ,* 14, 127, 262, 353, 360, 385, 392, 396, 449, 564, 565, 672, 744, 752, 758, 804, 806-807, 809, 823, 834, 841, 889; *History of Richard Raynal Solitary,* 4, 106, 198, 378, 392, 420, 515, 557, 659, 672, 809, 834, 926; *Infallibility and Tradition,* 154, 732; *Introduction to the Angelical Cardinal,* • 691; *Introduction to Lady Lovat's Life of St. Teresa,* 396, 758; *Introduction to The Mustard Tree,* 323, 750; *King's Achievement,* 210, 324, 392, 411, 416, 499, 850, 895; *Light Invisible,* 27, 200, 262, 294, 318, 328, 333, 377, 385, 396, 459, 514-515, 533, 628, 684, 750, 761, 776, 794, 807, 809, 830, 842, 850, 857; *Lord of the World,* 157, 165, 202, 221, 330, 424, 499, 557, 751; *Mirror of Shalott,* 161, 324, 328, 411, 492, 557, 620, 758, 805, 914; *Necromancers,* 194, 319, 474, 545, 621, 841, 889; *None Other Gods,* 465, 472, 732, 752, 807; *Preface to Bonds of Love,* 720, 841; *Queen's Tragedy,* 315, 820, 839, 861, 881; *Religion of the Plain Man,* 293, 396, 888; *Sanctity of the Church,* 129, 436; *Sentimentalists,* 109, 147, 154, 217, 221, 253, 263, 294, 417, 473, 637, 646, 673, 674, 720,

725, 768, 769, 815, 837, 887, 921; *Teresian Contemplations,* 791; *Winnowing,* 932

Benvenuta, Sister Mary, O.P., 653

Berengarius of Tours (ca.1000–1088), 311

Bernadette Soubirous, St. (1843–1879), 462

Bernard of Clairvaux, St. (1090?–1153) : *Ad Sororem,* 516; *Concerning Grace and Free Will,* 612; *Letters,* 4, 7, 14, 86, 155, 203, 208, 235-236, 301, 323, 331, 449, 451, 460, 524, 525-526, 632, 642, 712, 714, 736, 799, 835, 887-888, 895, 913; *Meditationes piissimae,* 569; *Memorare,* 87; *On Consideration,* 9, 13, 29, 70, 176, 208, 254, 325, 330, 370, 375, 381, 387, 415, 420, 448, 465, 516, 601-602, 644, 661, 673, 701, 707, 736, 738, 766, 767, 777, 779, 807, 887; *On the Canticle of Canticles,* 130, 212, 264, 334, 343, 378, 450, 471, 484, 488, 512, 561, 602, 604, 630, 718, 835, 888, 903, 917, 931; *On the Necessity of Loving God,* 255, 551, 561; *Sermons,* 8, 82, 86, 87, 88, 90-91, 100, 273, 468, 495, 712; *Steps of Humility,* 200, 450, 551, 883; *Other works,* 213, 295, 423, 839

Bernard of Cluny, St. (fl. 1150), 89, 479, 502

Berners, Juliana (fl. early 15th cent.?), 251

Berry, William (1902–   ), 447

Berthold of Regensburg (1210–1272), 426

Beste, John Richard Digby (1806–1885), 37, 198

Bishop, Edmund (1846–1917), 547

*Bismarck, Otto von (1815–1898), 711

Blake, Mary Elizabeth (1840–1907), 516, 861, 870

Blois, François Louis de (Blosius), Blessed, O.S.B. (1506–1566), 262, 761, 806, 840, 880

Blunt, Rev. Hugh Francis (1877–   ), 251, 543, 819

Blunt, Wilfrid Scawen (1840–1922), 237, 443, 454, 540, 543, 617, 659, 684, 686, 794, 812, 830, 928

†Bodin, Jean (1530–1596), 2-3, 534, 838, 845

Boethius, Anicius Manlius Severinus (c.480–524) : *Contra Eutychen,* 633, 673; *De Consolatione Philosophiae,* 9, 102, 153, 314, 334, 350, 353, 357, 367, 372-373, 378, 389, 398, 414, 419, 421, 458, 464, 512, 551, 603, 612, 646, 775-776, 894, 899; *De Fide Catholica,* 117, 875; *De Hebdomadibus,* 398; *De Trinitate,* 145, 350, 369

* Bohn, Henry George (1796–1884), 711

Bonaventure, St. (1221–1274), 196, 213, 232, 561, 656, 694, 698

Boniface VIII, Pope (1294–1303), 126, 132, 179, 191, 701-702

Borgia, Cesare (1475–1507), 520

Bossuet, Jacques Bénigne, Bp. of Meaux (1627–1704), 521

Bracton, Henry de (d. 1268), 45, 88, 193-194, 508, 528, 533

Bregy, Katherine (1888–   ), 424

Bridges, Madeline (Pseud. of Mary Ainge De Vere) (fl. 1870–1915), 540, 559

Bridges, Matthew (1800– ?), 36, 77, 83, 84, 86, 91, 170, 207, 233, 327, 352, 487, 489-490, 531, 657-658, 823, 854, 872

Bridgett, Rev. Thomas, C.SS.R. (1829–1899), 729-730

Britt, Matthew, O.S.B. (1877–   ), 522

Brownson, Orestes Augustus (1803–1876), 14, 17, 27, 115, 122, 142, 149, 181, 184, 219, 221, 255, 290, 292-293, 406, 518, 532, 604, 631, 635, 646, 674, 756, 772, 801, 838, 884, 885

Bulls, Papal, *see* Papal Bulls and Encyclicals

Burton, Katherine (1890–   ), 217, 807

Butler, Abbot Basil Christopher, O.S.B. (1902–   ), 125, 703, 738

Byrd, William (c.1542–1623), 826

Byzantine Rite: 81, 99, 230; *Euchologion*, 50-51, 68-69, 89, 90, 98, 195, 196, 205-206, 242, 244-245, 320-321, 500, 576, 587, 588, 589, 590, 592, 593, 594-595, 596, 726-727, 792, 850, 893; *Horologion*, 81, 82, 84, 85, 86-87, 90, 93, 98, 99, 230, 231, 244, 245, 285, 369, 370, 379, 438-439, 450, 482, 490, 502, 581-582, 637, 656, 764, 809, 822, 823, 826, 862, 896; *Menaea*, 24, 25, 39, 87, 167, 169, 231, 299, 877; *Oktoechus*, 95; *Parakletike*, 21; *Pentakostarion*, 36, 283, 284-285, 670, 764; *Triodion*, 6, 79, 81-82, 86, 98, 100, 399-400, 401, 441-442, 483-484, 488, 489, 491, 501-502, 535, 649, 764

Caesarius of Heisterbach (1180–ca.1240), 235

Cajetan, Giacomo De Vio, Cardinal, O.P. (1468–1534), 755

Callaghan, Gertrude, 110, 834

Callanan, J. J. (1795–1839), 585

Camm, Dom Bede, O.S.B. (1864–1942), 97

Campbell, Joseph (1879–   ), 11, 213, 462-463

Campbell, Robert (1814–1868), 283, 284

Campion, Blessed Edmund (1540–1581), 141, 190, 479-480, 583, 781

Camus, Jean Pierre, Bp. of Belley (1582–1652), 6, 22, 156, 232, 257, 262, 342, 343, 357, 364, 398, 410, 411, 443, 444, 452, 474, 499, 506, 537, 563, 578, 607, 624, 682, 684, 721, 724, 743, 766-767, 776, 782, 796, 807, 813, 814, 819, 824, 840, 843, 851, 885, 901, 925

Canon Law, Code of (Codex Juris Canonici) (1918): *Canon 8*, 530; *10*, 530; *12*, 112; *25*, 237; *29*, 237; *63*, 732; *80*, 265; *87*, 127; *98*, 547; *107*, 190; *108*, 190; *109*, 434; *119*, 190; *120*, 190; *121*, 190; *124*, 190, 728; *132*, 151; *133*, 151; *135*, 267; *142*, 190; *219*, 703; *222*, 708; *227-228*, 222; *230*, 113; *329*, 69; *341*, 69-70; *451*, 660; *487*, 762; *488*, 761, 762; *538*, 762; *682*, 518; *731*, 788; *737*, 52; *801*, 78; *802*, 309; *863*, 199; *870*, 669; *888*, 204; *889*, 204; *901*, 204; *906*, 204; *907*, 205; *911*, 471; *948*, 648; *951*, 648; *954*, 648-649; *971*, 649; *974*, 649; *984*, 649; *1012*, 578; *1013*, 578; *1015-1016*, 578-579; *1038*, 579; *1060*, 580; *1081*, 579; *1110*, 579; *1113*, 291; *1118*, 580; *1120*, 580; *1128*, 580; *1161*, 171; *1203*, 110; *1239*, 110; *1248*, 586; *1250*, 3; *1251*, 338; *1252*, 3, 338; *1254*, 338; *1255*, 928; *1257*, 547; *1258*, 928; *1262*, 928; *1264*, 627; *1276*, 101-102; *1277*, 796; *1307*, 904; *1316*, 641; *1322*, 119; *1323*, 274; *1324*, 430;

1325, 147, 432; *1326*, 70; *1327*, 722; *1329*, 114; *1351*, 58, 147, 613; *1372*, 291; *1374*, 802; *1375*, 802; *1379*, 802; *1384*, 151; *1385*, 152; *1386*, 152; *1499*, 734; *1518*, 735; *1556*, 703; *2214*, 740; *2350*, 853

Canons of the Holy Apostles, Ecclesiastical (4th cent.), 172, 188, 267, 312, 337, 362, 534, 647, 815, 891

Carberry, Ethna (Pseud. of Anna MacManus) (1866–1902), 350, 365, 910

Carlin, Francis (Pseud. of James F. C. MacDonnell) (1881–1945), 42, 827

Carroll, John, Archbishop (1735–1815), 101, 142, 184, 521, 908

Carthusian Order, Motto of, 234

Casimir, St. (1458–1484), 96

Cassianus, Johannes (360–435), 618

Cassiodorus, Flavius Magnus (ca.480–ca.575), 649, 717, 929

Caswall, Rev. Edward (1814–1878), 1, 7, 21, 24, 25, 28, 41, 74, 77, 78, 83, 84, 89, 90, 93, 94, 96, 104, 167, 169, 205, 240, 250, 298, 369, 371, 373, 461, 487, 491, 492, 494, 495, 582, 584, 585, 600, 605, 630, 632, 657, 664, 677, 678, 744, 789, 793, 847, 893, 922

Catherine of Siena, St. (1347–1380), 22, 108, 196-197, 264-265, 341, 349, 499, 520, 561, 604, 611, 623, 668, 702, 711, 729, 743, 805, 901

Catholic Advocate, 109

Celestine I, Pope St. (422–432), 44

Cervantes, Miguel de (1547–1616), 710

Chalcedon, Council of, 699, 704-705, 707-708

Chapman, Abbot John, O.S.B. (1865–1933), 24, 84, 101, 116, 128-129, 134, 136, 272, 315, 328, 333, 411, 452, 610-611, 720, 773, 904, 926

Charlemagne (742–814), 158, 520

Charles V, Emperor (1500–1558), 865

Charles the Bald, Emperor (823–877), 533

Chateaubriand, François Auguste René (1768–1848), 710-711

Chaucer, Geoffrey (ca.1340–1400): *An ABC*, 87, 96; *Boethius*, 364, 712; *Book of the Duchesse*, 922; *Canterbury Tales, Prologue*, 29, 48, 56, 110, 161, 203, 322, 358, 364, 446, 454, 472, 510-511, 517, 531, 533, 549, 572-573, 599, 601, 602, 606, 640, 680, 682, 683, 685, 727, 781, 801, 807, 815, 828, 848, 861, 927, 930; *Clerkes Tale*, 572, 573, 671, 745, 900, 912; *Frankeleyns Tale*, 599, 646, 661, 884; *Freres Tale*, 838; *House of Fame*, 869; *Knight's Tale*, 11, 248, 259, 295, 347, 389, 538-539, 551-552, 599, 604, 683, 718, 742, 806, 878, 920; *Legend of Good Women*, 238, 344, 365; *Man of Law's Prologue*, 529; *Man of Law's Tale*, 41-42, 87, 99-100, 223, 232, 260, 280, 381, 566, 573, 712, 919; *Maunciple's Tale*, 346, 358, 872; *Melibeus, Tale of*, 208, 215, 295, 679-680, 773, 818; *Merchant's Prologue*, 573; *Merchant's Tale*, 295, 351, 422, 455, 497, 551, 572, 812, 912; *Miller's Tale*, 459, 815, 912, 922; *Monk's Tale*, 351, 359, 804, 805; *Nonne Preestes Tale*, 358, 454, 497, 625, 724; *Pardoner's Tale*, 48, 280, 362, 368; *Parlement of Foules*, 626, 855, 892; *Persones Tale*, 317, 880;

Physicien's Tale, 764; *Prioresses' Prologue,* 91; *Reeve's Prologue,* 857; *Reeve's Tale,* 200, 278, 478, 513, 767, 828; *Roman de la Rose,* 276, 348, 359, 367, 858; *Second Nun's Prologue,* 79; *Second Nun's Tale,* 83, 84-85; *Shipman's Tale,* 617, 796, 824; *Summonour's Tale,* 280; *Treatise on the Astrolabe,* 781; *Troilus and Criseyde,* 37, 162, 207, 273, 282, 295, 322, 338, 348, 422, 445, 551-552, 599, 601, 603, 739, 813, 830, 867, 869; *Wyf of Bath's Prologue,* 280, 567, 733, 920; *Wyf of Bath's Tale,* 364, 455, 712, 854, 922

Chesterton, Cecil (1879–1918), 279
Chesterton, Gilbert Keith (1874–1936): *Alarms and Discursions,* 106, 455, 748, 803, 807; *All Is Grist,* 290, 301, 361, 454, 598, 758-759, 803; *All Things Considered,* 48, 186, 263, 279, 312, 364, 474, 499, 571, 686, 759, 830, 895; *Autobiography,* 18, 27, 102, 161, 292, 496, 644, 692, 745, 878; *Ballad of the White Horse,* 165, 476; *Ball and the Cross,* 234; *Catholic Church and Conversion,* 220, 681, 738; *Charles Dickens,* 193, 201, 256, 415, 446, 541, 748, 814, 926; *Christmas Carol,* 488; *Club of Queer Trades,* 343; *Come To Think of It,* 759; *Common Man,* 28, 65, 290, 293, 295, 347, 361, 432, 455, 523, 532-533, 565, 611, 614, 681, 691, 744-745, 759, 810, 864, 885, 919; *Defendant,* 15, 63, 453, 574-575, 844, 926; *Defense of Penny Dreadfuls,* 344, 546; *Defense of Slang,* 824; *Donkey,* 38; *Everlasting Man,* 32, 107, 110, 111, 147, 162, 163, 165, 169, 199, 234, 256, 259, 333, 336, 396, 438, 456, 541, 571, 598, 629, 689-690, 809, 819, 832, 855, 881; *Evolution,* 316; *Flying Inn,* 916; *Generally Speaking,* 17-18, 33, 35, 107, 186, 193, 275, 407; *George Bernard Shaw,* 279, 407, 476, 541, 575, 649, 659, 681; *G. F. Watts,* 418, 686, 881; *Handful of Authors,* 65, 107, 256, 290-291, 364, 454, 523, 636, 638, 651, 663, 690, 692, 749, 759, 811, 839, 890, 895, 912-913, 919; *Heretics,* 32, 136, 217-218, 274, 297, 298, 415, 420, 446, 452-453, 457, 497-498, 568, 571, 621-622, 632, 645, 672, 726, 732, 803, 804, 815, 821, 844, 885, 891, 904; *House of Christmas,* 170-171; *Miscellany of Men,* 253, 274, 297, 407, 538, 759; *Napoleon of Notting Hill,* 523, 571, 631, 775; *Orthodoxy,* 30, 58, 223, 358, 453, 455, 473, 496, 498, 558, 598, 605, 611, 628, 634, 649-650, 738, 781, 799, 832, 852, 914; *Resurrection of Rome,* 32-33, 122, 737, 759; *Robert Browning,* 228, 259, 355, 456, 572, 646, 850, 926; *The Thing: Why I Am a Catholic,* 199, 217, 256, 305, 622, 636, 739, 805, 808, 867; *Tremendous Trifles,* 9, 53, 199, 254, 256, 296, 324, 351, 365, 420, 449, 503-504, 541, 605, 759, 798, 855, 885, 902, 903; *Victorian Age in Literature,* 217, 263, 274, 294, 296, 420, 635-636, 638, 651, 674, 849, 861; *What I Saw in America,* 15-16, 228, 348-349, 857-858; *What's Wrong with the World,* 31, 165, 255-256, 268, 274, 278, 358, 407, 457, 473, 574, 616, 691, 740, 837, 850, 867-868, 891, 908, 909, 917; *Other works,* 11, 16, 17, 32,

42, 152, 256, 276, 296, 297, 300, 316, 352, 398, 449, 465, 475, 523, 541, 546, 558, 612, 625, 627, 653, 658, 726, 744, 759, 778, 783, 799, 868, 878, 910, 916-917, 921
Childe, Wilford R. (1890–   ), 114, 605
Cistercians, Motto of, 718
Clarke, Joseph I. C. (1846–1935), 233
Claudianus (Claudian) (d. 408?), 682
Clement I, Pope St. (88?–97?), 45, 66, 104, 131, 154, 190-191, 202, 215, 306, 366, 379, 401, 403, 433, 449, 480, 484, 505, 517, 538, 596, 641-642, 663-664, 667, 674, 696, 724, 763, 768, 773, 799, 806, 829, 850
Clement XI (1700–1721), 127
Clement of Alexandria (d. ca.215): *Paedogogus,* 278; *Stromateis,* 36, 350, 429, 463, 655, 715
Code of Canon Law, *see* Canon Law
Codex Theodosianus, *see* Theodosian Code
Cokain, Sir Aston (1608–1683), 813
Colonna, Egidius, *see* Egidius Colonna
*Colton, C. C. (1780?–1832), 23
Colum, Padraic (1881–   ), 201, 448, 608
Columba, St. (521-597), 501
Connelly, Mother Cornelia (Augusta Peacock) (1809–1879), 851
Connolly, Myles (1897–   ), 832
Conrad, Joseph (1857–1924), 459
Constable, Henry (1562–1613), 19, 31, 77, 92, 96-97, 207, 339, 415-416, 439, 483, 484, 545, 553, 562, 573, 584-585, 667, 679, 746, 898
Constance, Council of, 46, 180
Constantine the Great (288?–337), 188, 229, 430, 871, 914
†Constantine, Pseudo-Donation of (8th cent.), 175
Constantine I, Pope (708–715), 171-172, 709, 824-825
Constantinople, Councils of, 150, 698
Constitutions of the Holy Apostles (4th cent.), 124, 172, 243, 728
Contractus, Herman (1013–1054), 82, 95
Copernicus, Nicolaus (1473–1543), 413
Copley, Anthony (1567–1607?), 9, 334, 765, 767, 882
Corinthians, So-called Second Epistle to (2nd cent.), 13, 129, 131, 337, 763, 768, 924
Corkery, Daniel (1878–   ), 417
Corpus Juris Canonici, 210
Cosmas the Melodist, St. (d. ca.760), 81, 167, 744, 877
Council of Trent, *see* Trent, Council of
Cox, Eleanor R. (1867–1931), 544, 629
*Cram, Ralph Adams (1863–1942), 33
Crashaw, Richard (1612–1649), 40, 55, 77, 94, 97, 103, 104, 149, 168, 210, 218-219, 233, 240, 249, 258, 259, 280, 286, 299, 303, 322, 323, 348, 367, 402, 414, 416, 418, 422, 424, 444, 445, 455, 469, 487, 518, 542, 554, 558, 563, 570, 582, 584, 617, 623, 630, 638, 672, 719, 755, 762, 791, 810, 811, 836, 838, 859, 868, 872, 893, 898, 908, 910, 916, 920, 929
Custance, Olive (Lady Alfred Douglas) (1874–   ), 886
Cuthbert, Father, O.F.M.C. (1866–1939), 44
Cyprian, St. (ca.210–258): *Letters,* 67, 131,

133, 299, 307, 433, 501, 583, 596-597, 647, 674, 693, 704, 795, 799-800, 821, 924; *On Immortality,* 252, 851, 895; *On Patience,* 154; *On the Dress of Virgins,* 639; *On the Lapsed,* 203, 667; *On the Lord's Prayer,* 194, 407, 715-716; *On the Unity of the Catholic Church (De Unitate Ecclesiae),* 125, 129-130, 133, 299, 429, 693; *On Works and Alms,* 154, 401; *To Demetrianus,* 426, 764; *Other works,* 519

Cyril of Alexandria, St. (d. 444), 81

Cyril of Jerusalem, St. (ca.315–386), 49, 70-71, 120, 162, 191, 234, 243, 307, 310, 324, 380, 386, 408, 438, 466, 480, 674, 768, 815, 821

Daly, Thomas Augustine (1871–1948), 268, 278, 336-337, 345, 346-347, 453-454, 476, 535, 624, 807, 853, 868, 921-922

Damasus I, Pope Saint (366–384), 10, 675, 694

Dante Alighieri (1265–1321): *Inferno,* 9, 10, 31-32, 48, 99, 113, 200, 208, 211, 223, 238, 240, 247, 253, 255, 260, 265, 276, 302, 319, 335, 339, 346, 350, 352, 353, 415, 423, 427, 443, 465, 502, 508, 517, 545, 551, 601, 603, 634, 651, 664, 682, 725, 742, 753, 764, 767, 815, 843, 883, 896, 900, 906, 910, 919, 922; *Letters,* 537; *On Monarchy (De Monarchia),* 202, 211, 353, 404-405, 529, 532, 633, 665, 671, 750, 776, 779, 845, 875, 883, 889; *Paradiso,* 14, 61, 64, 82-83, 91, 99, 179-180, 236, 293-294, 302, 318, 326, 334, 350, 357, 370-371, 377, 381, 384, 390, 402, 415, 421, 445, 470, 499, 504, 506, 527, 538, 583, 610, 611, 619, 653, 660, 665, 677-678, 710, 722, 723-724, 740, 752, 827, 856, 863, 880, 892, 893; *Purgatorio,* 18, 25, 58, 163, 179, 196, 208, 223, 239, 312, 314, 335, 346, 357, 378, 381, 395, 398, 477, 504, 513, 544, 551, 606, 607, 683, 718, 742, 864, 865, 869, 876, 886, 924; *Vita Nuova,* 247-248, 551

D'Arcy, Rev. M. C., S.J. (1888–   ): *Death and Life,* 58, 464, 744; *Idea of God,* 186, 225, 306, 377, 396, 515, 926; *Nature of Belief,* 515, 608, 628, 739, 867; *Pain of This World,* 902

Davenant, Sir William (1606–1668), 14, 32, 107, 108, 237, 248-249, 444, 463, 497, 513, 519, 715, 777, 826, 847, 884, 918

Dawson, Christopher (1889–   ): *Christianity and the New Age,* 165-166; *Gifford Lectures,* 186-187, 235, 509, 515, 541, 548, 605, 760, 864; *Medieval Essays,* 605, 616, 703; *Religion and the Rise of Western Culture,* 457; *Understanding Europe,* 292, 312; *Other works,* 836

Descartes, René (1596–1650), 358, 376, 599, 724, 892

De Vere, Aubrey Thomas (1814–1902), 77-78, 113, 135, 237, 241, 322, 373-374, 469, 519, 555, 582, 600, 603, 658, 724, 783, 788, 791, 801, 826, 833, 842, 907, 925, 927

Didascalia Apostolorum, 67, 317, 441, 517, 580, 667

Digby, Kenelm Henry (1800–1880), 475

Dinnis, Enid (1873–1942), 20, 347, 633-634

Dionysius of Alexandria, St. (d. 265), 799

Dionysius the Carthusian (1402–1471), 569

Dionysius of Corinth, St. (2nd cent.), 678

*Dolben, Digby M. (1848–1867), 479

Dollard, Rev. James B. (1872–   ), 365, 896

Dominic, St. (1170?–1221), 520, 712

Donahoe, Daniel J. (1853–1933), 232, 368, 490, 491, 516, 602, 622, 679, 764, 789

Donnelly, Eleanor C. (1838–1917), 462

Douglas, Lord Alfred (1871–1945), 396, 415, 690, 811, 913

Douglas, Gavin (1474?–1522), 234

Downing, Prof. Eleanor (1893–   ), 41, 814

Dowson, Ernest (1867–1900), 259, 321, 543, 556, 616

Dryden, John (1631–1700): *Absolom and Achitophel,* 1, 3, 11, 14, 65-66, 104, 105, 152-153, 221, 227, 234, 281, 287, 320, 321, 341, 342, 345, 348, 349, 363, 364, 406, 493, 509, 523, 530, 549, 550, 568, 631, 637, 646, 662, 663, 671, 683, 684, 691, 692, 713-714, 744, 751, 763, 775, 776, 785, 798, 805, 819, 831, 857, 870, 879, 893, 907; *Alexandria's Feast,* 108, 153, 254, 279, 684, 829, 907; *All for Love,* 300, 418, 478, 539, 554, 570, 807, 906, 925, 929; *Annus Mirabilis,* 320, 339, 498, 620, 685, 812, 906, 914; *Astraea Redux,* 111, 279, 318, 545, 767, 879, 904; *Aurengzebe,* 253, 445, 539, 555, 930; *Britannia Rediviva,* 367, 572, 719; *Conquest of Granada,* 228, 353, 472, 646, 798; *Cymon and Iphigenia,* 55, 280, 349, 351, 811, 855, 910; *Eleonora,* 249, 360, 901-902; *Essay of Dramatic Poetry,* 494, 519, 688, 810; *Fables,* 149, 159, 276, 728; *Hind and the Panther,* 9, 12, 13, 22, 23, 128, 134, 171, 209, 219, 269, 289, 365, 417, 432, 463, 469, 478, 497, 506, 530, 537, 567, 568, 569, 584, 600, 604, 607, 624, 644, 708, 736-737, 756, 770, 783, 825, 871, 875-876, 884, 915; *Indian Emperor,* 554, 684, 765; *King Arthur,* 426, 459, 477, 907; *Mac Flecknoe,* 249, 848, 923; *Marriage à la Mode,* 555, 574; *Medal,* 110, 227, 456, 503, 913; *Ode to the Memory of Mrs. Anne Killigrew,* 249, 304, 503, 638, 688, 896; *Of Dramatic Poetry,* 655, 671, 802, 876; *Palamon and Arcite,* 444, 542, 555, 765, 911; *Religio Laici,* 318, 327, 395, 749, 804, 828, 875, 893; *Rival Ladies,* 241, 296-297, 843, 893; *Song for St. Cecilia's Day,* 280, 347, 626, 649, 881; *Spanish Friar,* 249, 277, 349, 398, 473, 550, 568, 866; *To Mr. Congreve,* 11, 363, 365, 810; *To John Dryden of Chesterton,* 48, 222, 269, 318, 685; *To Sir Godfrey Kneller,* 711, 810, 857; *Threnodia Augustalis,* 353, 416, 665; *Tyrannic Love,* 554, 685, 907; *Other works,* 3, 9, 30, 192, 228, 253, 276, 287, 298, 317, 336, 338, 340, 341, 342, 348, 349, 351, 360, 362, 397, 403, 414, 440, 443, 465, 472, 476, 478, 494, 497, 504, 509, 519, 539, 554, 555, 563, 570, 606, 646, 650, 652, 655, 665-666, 683, 685, 688, 711, 721, 724, 747, 753, 766, 773, 804, 852, 859, 871, 895, 909, 911, 912, 917, 918, 922, 929

Eadmer of Canterbury, O.S.B. (ca.1060–1124), 460
Earls, Rev. Michael, S.J. (1875–1937), 48, 616, 783
Eden, Helen Parry (1885–   ), 834
Edward I, King of England (1239–1307), 520
Egan, Maurice F. (1852–1924), 164
†Egidius Colonna (ca.1246–1316), 46, 179, 734
Eleanore, Sister Mary, C.S.C. (1890–1940), 31, 535
*Elizabeth I, Queen of England (1533–1603), 76, 141
Elliott, Rev. Walter, C.S.P. (1842–1928), 142-143, 612-613, 663
Elpis (wife of Boethius) (d. ca.493), 664, 677, 679
Elvira, Council of, 5, 150
Emory, Susan L. (1846–1917), 536, 903, 930-931
Ephesus, Council of, 81, 694
Ephraem of Syria, St. (308?–373), 80, 229, 450, 459-460, 674
Erasmus, Desiderius (1469?–1536), 26, 44, 52, 101, 103, 106, 123, 156, 160, 163, 164, 254, 262, 326, 361, 412, 444, 491, 521, 569, 583, 615-616, 623, 636, 724, 734, 795, 857, 906, 907, 918
Erigena, John Scotus (ca.810–880), 319, 902
Essex, Rev. Edwin, O.P. (1891–   ), 306, 550
Etheridge, J. St. Clair (Pseud. of Archbishop Ireland [?]), 17
Eugenius IV (1383–1447), 520
Eusebius of Caesarea (264?–349?), 119-120, 229, 283, 489, 493, 507, 583, 678, 697, 899
Everyman (Mystery Play), 248

Faber, Frederick William (1814–1863), 8, 20, 21, 36, 41, 62, 78, 88, 94-95, 100, 104, 146, 170, 197, 250, 251, 286, 304, 312, 327, 340, 366, 371, 374, 378, 379, 382, 384, 391, 392, 440, 483, 487, 488-489, 492, 495-496, 516, 535, 563, 568, 631, 653, 658, 672, 680, 719, 743, 744, 768, 777, 781, 790, 803, 819, 846, 850, 880, 910
Farley, James A. (1888–   ), 692
Farren, Robert (1909–   ), 160, 535
Field, Michael (Pseud. of Katherine Harris Bradley [1846–1914] and Edith Emma Cooper [1862–1913]), 110, 251, 763, 915
Firminus, Bishop of Trieste (6th cent.), 695
Fitzsimmon, Rev. Henry, S.J. (1566–1643), 856
Florence, Council of, 696, 742
Forrest, William (fl. 1530–1581), 573
Fortescue, Sir John (c.1394–c.1476), 194, 200, 254, 405, 529
Fortunatus, Venantius (d. c.600), 81, 90, 95, 283, 656
Fragmentum Pragense, 300
Francis, St., see Francis of Assisi, St.
Franciscan Order, Motto of, 352, 665
Francis de Sales, St. (1567–1622): Introduction to the Devout Life, 10, 18, 19, 66, 110, 156, 160, 187, 200, 204, 232, 238, 239, 260, 262, 264, 287, 360, 364, 384, 427, 452, 455,

502-503, 516, 567, 634, 643, 713, 719, 766, 775, 815, 823, 829, 840, 860, 894, 903, 911, 925; Letters to Persons in Religion, 216, 280, 303, 341, 342, 364, 410, 413, 414, 423, 451-452, 470, 558, 565, 624, 636, 643, 673, 762, 767, 774, 775, 791, 806, 808-809, 815, 833, 839, 840, 861, 869, 880, 901, 904, 927; Letters to Persons in the World, 218, 232, 248, 257, 258, 265, 288, 303, 342, 344, 360, 398, 472, 474, 537, 578, 612, 614, 634, 661, 665, 672, 719, 724, 766, 767, 804, 813, 839, 861, 925; Spiritual Conferences, 10, 156, 280, 338, 344, 360, 377, 386, 399, 465, 474, 539, 565, 570, 624, 643, 645, 672, 751, 761-762, 880, 904; Treatise on the Love of God, 10, 54, 56, 111, 156, 207, 210, 280-281, 288, 357, 470, 553-554, 562-563, 565, 638, 642, 653, 673, 719, 749, 767, 813, 863, 879, 889, 901, 913, 918; Other works, 113, 452, 521, 531
Francis of Assisi, St. (1182?–1226), 247, 352, 497, 520, 561, 569, 853
Francis Xavier, St. (1506–1552), 562
Froissart, Jean (c.1337–1410?), 434
Fulgentius, Fabius (c.480–c.550), 898
Fullerton, Lady Georgiana (1812–1885), 790

*Gambetta, Leon (1832–1882), 26
Gamble, William Miller Thomas (1875–   ), 601
Gangra, Council of, 580
Gardiner, Stephen Bishop (1483-1555), 521
Garesché, Rev. Edward, S.J. (1876–   ), 75, 582
Garth, Sir Samuel (1661–1719), 113, 208, 249-250, 265, 269, 337, 348, 398, 444, 471, 521, 574, 601, 688, 746, 842, 923
Gasparri, Pietro Cardinal (1852–1934), 157-158, 216, 500
Gasquet, Francis Aidan Cardinal (1848–1929), 711
Gelasian Sacramentary, see Sacramentaries
Gelasius I, Pope St. (492–496), 174, 429, 700
*George IV, King of England (1762–1830), 141
Germanus, St., Patriarch of Constant. (c.634–734), 39
Gerson, Jean Charlier de (1363–1429), 520, 815
Gesta Romanorum, 153
Gibbons, James Cardinal (1834–1921): Faith of Our Fathers, 14, 62-63, 104, 129, 233, 238, 459, 473, 578, 652, 692, 706, 728, 753, 757, 796; Other works, 143, 184, 185, 517
Gill, Eric Rowton (1882–1940), 33-34, 235, 292, 471, 472, 517, 571-572, 651, 663, 735, 809, 837, 907
Giltinan, Caroline (Mrs. Leo P. Harlow) (1884–   ), 198, 814-815
Glanvill, Ranulf de (d. 1190), 194
Godescalcus (Gottschalk) (10th cent.), 12
Gogarty, Oliver St. John (1878–   ), 566, 830
Goodier, Alban Archbishop, S.J. (1869–1939), 102, 135
Gower, John (d. 1408). 56, 106, 153, 162, 240, 278, 295, 344, 346, 358, 423, 425, 446, 457,

529, 550, 552, 598, 612, 661, 712, 725, 818, 865, 870, 918, 922, 924
Graham, Dom Aelred, O.S.B. (1907–), 200, 458, 548-549, 622
Grand Coutumier de Normandie (13th cent.), 236
Gratian (d. c.1179), *Decretum,* 111, 524, 527, 528, 619, 734
Gratian, Emperor of Rome (375–383), 188
Gray, John (1866–1934), 564
Greek Anthology, 100
Gregorian Sacramentary, *see* Sacramentaries
Gregory I, Pope St. (Gregory the Great) (590–604): *Dialogues,* 308, 367, 394, 426, 742, 764; *Homilies,* 5, 18-19, 73, 155, 159, 214, 252, 331, 379, 446, 492, 476, 497, 581, 661, 668, 711, 817, 931; *Hymns,* 369, 373, 490, 522, 534, 584, 599, 824, 854, 893, 895; *Letters,* 44, 51, 63-64, 175, 222, 267, 353, 662, 700, 707, 822, 825; *Morals,* 5, 22, 43, 51, 60-61, 63, 121, 126, 134, 155, 211-212, 214, 218, 224, 247, 266, 298, 299-300, 342, 366, 377, 379, 389, 418, 450, 473, 721, 722, 736, 740, 777, 791, 805, 808, 817, 835, 851, 899, 908; *Pastoral Care,* 13, 45, 189, 300, 302, 404, 450, 456, 473, 659-660, 661, 713, 714, 721, 733, 812, 817, 825; *Other works,* 149, 504, 531, 651, 665, 709, 717, 924
Gregory VII, Pope St. (1073–1085), 114, 130, 175-176, 318, 520, 700-701, 705, 844-845
Gregory of Nazianzen, St. (c.330–390), 71, 80, 374, 403, 466, 501, 704, 729, 929
Gregory of Nyssa, St. (d. 394?), 393, 639, 741, 892, 896-897
Gregory of Tours, St. (538–594), 50
Gregory the Great, *see* Gregory I, Pope St.
Griffin, Gerald (1803–1840), 98, 556, 603, 623, 884-885
Griffiths, Dom Bede, O.S.B. (1906–), 122, 135, 140, 148, 377, 396–397, 565, 617, 809, 819
Grimald, Nicholas (1519–1562), 360, 399, 549, 901, 912
Guiney, Louise Imogen (1861–1920), 26, 103, 109, 192, 259, 324, 359, 423, 424, 447, 488, 914

Habington, William (1605–1654), 19, 70, 248, 306, 413, 494, 502, 553, 633, 688, 714-715, 765, 824, 843
Hadrian IV, Pope (1154–1159), 825
Hall, Msgr. Louis (1844–1911), 679
Hamilton, William (1704–1754), 465, 806
Hawes, Stephen (1475–1530), 161-162
Hawker, Robert Stephen (1803–1875), 103, 739, 855
Hayes, Rev. James M. (1875–), 457
Hayes, Patrick Joseph Cardinal (1867–1938), 448
Hecker, Rev. Isaac Thomas, C.S.P. (1819–1888), 14-15, 16, 142, 147, 190, 225, 315, 390, 410, 436, 440, 480, 624, 672, 737, 757, 766, 840-841, 876
Héloise (d. c.1164), 520
Henry IV, King of France (1553–1610), 175-176, 585

*Henry VIII, King of England (1491–1547), 140, 521
Henry, Msgr. Hugh Thomas (1862–), 74, 75, 94, 437, 440, 858
Henryson, Robert (1425–1506), 297, 905, 908
Heywood, Jasper, S.J. (1535–1598), 149, 286, 644
Heywood, John (c.1494–c.1578), 6, 9, 10, 14, 22, 29, 48, 49, 53, 54, 55, 56, 58, 59, 65, 103, 104, 105, 106, 108, 109, 112, 113, 138, 149, 153, 154, 158, 160, 189, 191, 192, 193, 222, 223, 228, 236, 239, 248, 253, 261, 263, 264, 265, 269, 273, 275, 276, 278, 279, 282, 283, 287, 293, 295, 298, 301, 313, 322, 323, 324, 334, 335, 338, 341, 342, 343, 344, 345, 346, 347, 348, 349, 350, 351, 358, 361, 362, 365, 367, 368, 397, 403, 410, 413, 415, 416, 418, 420, 421, 422, 423, 424, 425, 426, 443, 445, 446, 447, 454, 455, 456, 457, 458, 472, 478, 497, 499, 510, 518, 519, 522, 533, 549, 550, 552, 566, 567, 568, 573-574, 600, 601, 606, 607, 614, 617, 620, 625, 634, 636, 637, 642, 645, 650, 659, 661, 664, 683-684, 711, 712-713, 714, 725, 728, 746, 749, 753, 766, 768, 773, 775, 776, 777, 781, 783, 785, 798, 804, 806, 811, 812, 813, 823, 824, 826, 831, 832, 838, 839, 843, 847, 851, 853, 856, 857, 858, 864, 865, 867, 869, 872, 879, 880-881, 886, 887, 893, 894, 905, 908, 909-910, 912, 913-914, 915-916, 917, 918, 919-920, 922-925, 927, 929, 930
Hickey, Emily H. H. (1845–1924), 623, 715, 720
Hilary of Poitiers, St. (c.315–367), 71, 125-126, 131, 133-134, 368, 390, 481, 622, 670, 674-675, 764
Hildebert of Lavardin (or Tours) (c.1056–1133), 370, 479
Hilton, Walter (d. 1395), 156, 213, 303, 409, 630, 712, 773, 797, 820, 839, 888
Hinkson, Katherine Tynan (1861–1931), 30, 38, 65, 113, 154, 192, 201, 217, 222, 235, 251, 282, 424, 443, 447, 476, 496, 503, 507, 531, 565, 572, 635, 647, 806, 819, 843, 850, 855, 921, 931
Hippo, Council of, 597
Hippolytus, St. (ca.160–235), 5, 67, 70, 110, 114, 194, 205, 226, 234, 241, 337, 350, 501, 510, 599, 637, 639, 647, 715, 726, 809, 849, 861, 874, 892-893, 895, 919
Hoccleve, Thomas (c.1368–c.1450), 255, 444, 749
Holland, Hugh (1563–1633), 810
Holy Office, Decrees and Instructions of, 128, 136, 147, 227, 272, 274, 483, 703, 771-772, 773, 803, 885
†Honorius of Augsburg (or Autun) (fl. 1106–1135), 177
Honorius, Emperor of Rome (395–423), 189
Hopkins, Rev. Gerard Manley, S.J. (1844–1889): *Ad Mariam,* 600; *Barnfloor and Winepress,* 78; *Beginning of the End,* 416; *Blessed Virgin Compared to the Air We Breathe,* 12; *Candle Indoors,* 111; *Carrion Comfort,* 258; *Easter,* 286; *God's Grandeur,* 414, 440; *Habit of Perfection,* 198, 814; *Heaven Haven,* 616; *Inversnaid,* 913;

Loss of the Eurydice, 792; *No worst, there is none*, 542; *Pied Beauty*, 192; *Rosa Mystica*, 41; *Starlight Night*, 304, 844; *Silver Jubilee*, 498; *Thou Art Indeed Just, Lord*, 382; *Windhover*, 334; *Wreck of the Deutschland*, 374; *Transl.*, 75
Hormisdas, Pope St. (514–523), 705
Hosius, Bishop of Cordoba (c.255–c.358), 172
Houselander, Caryll (1901–1954), 548
Howard, Henry, Earl of Surrey (1517–1547), 54, 111, 215, 239, 552, 569, 842, 853
Howard, Bl. Philip (1557–1595), 159, 656
Hügel, Friedrich, Baron von (1852–1925), 458, 653, 720-721, 758, 841
Hugh of Fleury, O.S.B. (d. ca.1120), 176
Hugh of Lincoln, St. (d. 1200), 48-49
†Hugh of St. Victor (d. 1141), 177, 191
Hughes, John Joseph Archbishop (1797–1864), 122, 137, 142, 184, 644, 691
Hughes, Rev. Philip (1895–   ), 629
Hunter-Blair, Abbot Oswald, O.S.B. (1853–   ), 82
*Hus, John (1369?–1415), 127, 180
Husenbeth, Rev. Frederick Charles (1796–1872), 169, 789
Hymns and Sacred Verse: *See especially* Adam of St. Victor, Bernard of Cluny, (Matthew) Bridges, Byzantine Rite, Caswall, Faber, Fortunatus, Gregory I, Hilary of Poitiers, Neale, Newman, Prudentius, Roman Rite, Southwell, etc.
Hymns for the Year, 216, 327, 445, 563

Ignatius of Antioch, St. (d. ca.110), 519; *Letter to the Ephesians*, 66, 105, 162, 194, 324, 480, 673, 726, 888, 889; *Letter to the Magnesians*, 67, 433, 498, 533, 888; *Letter to the Philadelphians*, 596; *Letter to Polycarp*, 43, 158, 401, 575; *Letter to the Romans*, 458, 490, 583, 697, 910; *Letter to the Smyrneans*, 67, 122, 307; *Letter to the Trallians*, 241, 428
Ignatius of Loyola, St. (1491–1556), 37, 204, 479, 641, 739
Imelda, Sister Mary (Wallace) (S.L.) (1884–   ), 627
Innocent I, Pope St. (401–417), 205, 320, 698, 704, 780
Innocent III, Pope (1198–1216), 121, 177-178, 275, 309, 368, 491, 671, 695, 701
Innocent VI, Pope (1352–1362), 75
Ireland, John Archbishop (1838–1918), 15, 17, 31, 65, 143, 185, 210, 217, 255, 265, 365, 530, 613, 663, 692, 766, 801-802, 904
Irenaeus, St. (c.125–c.202), 85, 128, 143, 223-224, 299, 307, 356, 372, 392, 465, 569, 606, 703-704, 873
Iris, Scharmel (1889–   ), 711
Irnerius (ca.1055–ca.1130), 505
Isidore of Seville, St. (ca.560–636): *Etymologies*, 19, 42, 51-52, 53, 61, 64, 69, 123, 126, 189, 206, 214, 222, 236, 242, 263, 272-273, 285, 306, 308, 365, 412, 421, 429, 433, 434, 442, 446, 507, 518, 523-524, 530, 581, 597, 625-626, 631, 680, 717, 727, 733, 754, 774, 786, 844, 854, 863, 886, 903; *On the Offices of*

the Church, 51, 730-731; *On the Supreme Good*, 5, 817; *Sentences*, 61, 404, 528, 825
Ivo of Chartres, St. (ca.1040–1116), 177

Jacopone da Todi (d. 1306), 93, 460
*James I, King of England (1566–1625), 480
†James of Viterbo (Giacomo Capoccio) (d. 1308), 179
Jeanne d'Arc, St. (1412–1431), 351, 398, 520
*Jean of Jandun (fl. 1327), 180
Jerome, St. (347–419?), 26, 31, 44, 60, 68, 78-79, 86, 108, 158, 159, 163, 265, 282, 294, 359, 365, 372, 458, 478, 528, 550, 573, 614, 634, 667, 672, 675, 694, 712, 747, 766, 775, 779, 780, 792, 795, 800, 807, 816, 823, 838, 874, 877, 896, 897, 927, 930
Joachim of Flora (d. 1202), 36
John XXII, Pope (1316–1334), 180, 433, 696
John, King of England (1167?–1216), 178
John III (John Sobieski), King of Poland (1624–1696), 207
John of Avila, Bl. (1500–1569), 862
John Baptist de la Salle, St. (1651–1719), 22, 134, 159, 160, 191, 278, 298, 418, 506, 637, 638, 776, 841, 862, 878
John Chrysostom, St. (347–407): *Homilies*, 7, 10, 29, 55, 65, 70, 71, 195, 246, 253, 280, 282, 289, 313, 342, 415, 421, 423, 463, 474, 497, 515, 522, 583, 603, 625, 641, 678, 716, 729, 735, 740, 747, 775, 800, 810, 816, 822, 828, 832, 853, 856, 899, 909, 915, 919; *Other works*, 159, 222, 283, 307, 337, 421, 519, 675, 728-729, 865, 897
John of Damascus, St. (ca.675–749): *Exposition of the Orthodox Faith*, 19, 21, 25, 52, 73, 79, 82, 85, 90, 93, 95, 145, 224, 231, 254, 310-311, 334, 357, 369-370, 375, 381, 387, 391, 394, 439, 467-468, 481-482, 491, 609, 718, 723, 764, 772, 795, 797, 817, 835, 875, 898, 900; *Other works*, 39, 84, 89, 99, 195, 245, 339, 680, 898; *Hymns*, 25, 82, 89, 99, 245, 285, 500
John of Paris (d. 1306), 117, 179, 405, 510, 695-696, 702, 729
John of Ruysbroeck, Blessed (1293–1381), 395, 836
John of Salisbury (ca.1115–1180): *Policraticus*, 5-6, 7, 54, 56, 177, 268, 276, 300, 301, 376, 383, 435-436, 453, 454, 498, 508, 545, 645, 680, 683, 691, 732, 736, 754, 783, 879, 886, 900, 911, 918
John of the Cross, St. (1542–1591), 201, 213, 214, 232, 264, 288, 395, 399, 402, 565, 671, 718, 851, 866, 880, 888
Johnson, Lionel (1867–1901): *Ash Wednesday*, 37; *Before the Cloister*, 833; *Burden of Easter Vigil*, 769; *By the Station of King Charles at Charing Cross*, 158; *Cadgwith*, 99; *Christmas*, 169; *Dark Angel*, 261, 428; *Darkness*, 720; *De Amicitia*, 494; *Descant upon the Litany of Loretto*, 84; *Dream of Youth*, 20; *Flos florum*, 92; *Friends*, 794; *In England*, 296; *In Falmouth Harbor*, 635; *Ireland*, 475, 929; *Laleham*, 543, 909; *Mastery*, 452; *Men of Assisi*, 38; *Our Lady of the May*, 97; *Oxford Nights*, 107, 827; *Parnell*, 476, 654; *Post Liminium*,

659; *Precept of Silence,* 416; *Sursum Corda,* 424; *Te Martyrum Candidatus,* 582-583; *To Certain Friends,* 360; *To Leo XIII,* 535; *To Weep Irish,* 475; *Visions,* 261, 305, 428, 743; *Winchester,* 540
Joseph of the Studium, St. (d. 883), 36
Jonas of Orleans (d. ca.843), 507
Julianus Pomerius (fl. ca.500), 5, 214, 325, 560
Julius I, Pope St. (337–352), 697
Justinian I, Byzantine Emperor (483–565), 174, 266, 523, 533
Justin Martyr, St. (ca.100–ca.165), 307, 355, 435, 500, 583, 645, 680, 853-854, 883, 926-927
Juvencus (fl. 330), 780

Kaye-Smith, Sheila (1887–   ), 220, 533
Kelly, Blanche Mary (1881–   ), 814
Kempis, Thomas a, *see* Thomas a Kempis, St.
Kilmer, Aline (1888–1941), 342, 448, 763
Kilmer, Joyce (1886–1918), 305, 354, 715, 778, 830, 832, 834, 844, 873, 879
King, Eleanor Hamilton (1840–1920), 550, 827
Kinsman, Frederick Joseph (1868–1944), 24
Knox, Msgr. Ronald A. (1888–   ), 109, 116, 148, 169, 217, 377, 498, 522, 608, 611, 622, 653, 679, 690, 703, 767, 773, 777, 799, 926

Lactantius, Lucius Caelius (ca.260–340), 5, 7, 66, 125, 192, 267, 388, 615, 673, 685, 687, 754, 824
La Farge, John (1835–1910), 849, 858
La Farge, Rev. John, S.J. (1880–   ), 151, 611
Lanfranc (d. 1089), 855
Langland, William (ca.1332–ca.1400), 6, 156, 159, 248, 278, 339, 352, 412, 498, 516, 529, 531, 550, 552, 566, 604, 661, 690, 714, 722, 746, 749, 810, 836, 853, 863, 864, 884, 905, 923
Lanspergius (John Justus of Landsberg) (1489–1539), 882
Laodicea, Council of, 13, 575, 580, 800, 855, 862, 910
Lateran Basilica, Inscription, 171
Lateran Council, 208, 311
Lateran Treaty, 708-709
Lathrop, George Parsons (1851–1898), 157, 626, 908
Lay Folks' Mass Book (13th cent.), 585
*Lea, Henry Charles (1825–1909), 138
Leander of Seville, St. (ca.534–600), 61
Ledwidge, Francis (1891–1917), 503
*Lee, Nathaniel (1653?–1692), 397
Leeson, Jane Elizabeth (1807–1882), 285
Leo I, Pope St. (440–461): *Dogmatic Epistle to Flavian,* 467, 481; *Letters,* 150, 174, 408, 433, 647, 695, 698, 705, 707-708, 770; *Sermons,* 35, 166, 229-230, 298, 467, 486, 546, 676-677, 695, 705, 707, 779, 780
Leo X, Pope (1513–1521), 222, 425, 710; *see also* Papal Bulls and Encyclicals
Leo XIII, Pope (1878–1903), 17, 18, 38, 43, 46-47, 63, 64, 69, 106, 112, 119, 132, 134, 137, 138, 139, 143, 151, 157, 165, 182-183, 185, 186, 187, 223, 255, 267-268, 290, 315, 336,

355-356, 358, 371-372, 390, 399, 406, 406-407, 428, 434, 440, 471, 492, 516, 526, 528, 530, 532, 535, 538, 540, 547, 578, 614, 617, 643, 648, 663, 678, 681, 707, 713, 714, 720, 721, 732, 734, 748, 757, 770-771, 774, 790, 826, 828, 841, 845, 852, 858, 864, 865, 905; *Hymns,* 437, 438; *see also* Papal Bulls and Encyclicals
Leonine Sacramentary, *see* Sacramentaries
Leslie, Sir Shane (1885–   ), 192, 687
Liturgical Sources, *see* separate entries under Byzantine Rite; Roman Rite; Sacramentaries; *see also* Hymns and Sacred Verse
Lodge, Thomas, (1558?–1625), 10, 14, 54, 261, 295, 322, 351, 542, 553, 602, 684, 713, 775, 782, 792, 831, 856, 867, 869, 901
Lombard, Peter, *see* Peter Lombard
*Longfellow, H. W. (1807–1882), 882
Louis IX, St., King of France (1226–1270), 520, 736, 862
Lucifer of Cagliari (d. 370), 172
Luis de Granada, Ven., O.P. (1504–1588), 11, 160
Lunn, Sir Arnold (1884–   ), 27, 42, 116, 136, 147, 160, 217, 220, 294, 316, 319, 333, 343, 483, 499-500, 547, 598, 608, 611, 622, 625, 651, 722, 748, 777, 803, 850, 867, 872
Lydgate, John (ca.1370–c.1450), 48, 70, 103, 159, 239, 248, 253, 260, 269, 278-279, 280, 323, 348, 351, 413, 414, 457, 476, 552, 573, 617, 667, 764, 770, 782, 894, 918, 927, 930
Lyons, Council of, 705

McCarthy, Denis Florence (1817–1882), 416, 460, 476, 600, 730
MacDonagh, Thomas (1878–1916), 558, 911
McDougall, Alan G. (1895–   ), 21, 495, 731, 782, 877
McGee, Thomas D'Arcy (1825–1868), 475, 748
Mackenzie, Sir Compton (1883–   ), 237-238
MacManus, Seumas (1869–   ), 31, 48, 223, 261, 275, 279-280, 297, 418, 447, 448, 506, 518, 566, 573, 575, 618, 682, 745, 802, 805, 811, 812, 815, 844, 853, 857, 867, 870, 872, 879, 881, 911, 912, 918, 921, 923, 931
McNabb, Rev. Vincent, O.P. (1868–1943), 12, 33, 35, 37, 47, 55, 79, 86, 98, 100, 407, 469, 614, 622, 722, 784
Madeleva, Sister M., C.S.C. (1887–   ), 11, 25, 171, 252, 479, 564, 926
Mahony, Rev. Francis Sylvester (Father Prout) (1804–1866), 58-59
Manegold of Lautenbach (fl. 1080), 507-508
Mangan, James Clarence (1803–1849), 254, 318, 367, 475, 671, 685, 831
Manning, Henry Edward Cardinal (1802–1892): *Eternal Priesthood,* 69, 183, 198, 266, 436, 457, 660, 720, 721-722, 728, 730, 752, 870; *Other works,* 129, 181-182, 207, 477, 635, 737, 781, 872, 884
Mannyng, Robert (fl. 1288–1338), 920
Maritain, Jacques (1882–   ): *Art and Poetry,* 9, 790, 794; *Art and Scolasticism,* 33; *Freedom in the Modern World,* 37, 42,

162, 183, 380, 390, 432, 435, 437, 449, 613, 654-655, 673, 733, 774; *Man and the State*, 183-184, 257, 537, 620, 631-632, 838, 845-846; *Range of Reason*, 34, 42, 162, 328, 352-353, 464, 690; *Things That Are Not Caesar's*, 139-140, 148-149, 354, 390, 643, 750, 771, 838, 865; *Three Reformers*, 470

*Marsiglio of Padua (d. c.1342), 180, 405, 534

Martin V, Pope (1417–1431), 46, 127

Martin, Gregory (ca.1539–1582), 115

Martindale, Rev. C. C., S.J. (1879–   ), 116, 488

Mary I, Queen of England (1516–1558), 140-141, 521

Mary, Queen of Scots (1542–1587), 521

Maryland Toleration Act, 354

Massinger, Philip (1583–1640), 249

Maxims, 4, 138, 236-237, 465, 508, 534, 755, 854

Maximus the Confessor, St. (ca.580–662), 155, 394, 458, 559, 560, 565, 618, 717, 899-900

Maynard, Theodore (1890–   ), 16, 17, 27-28, 296, 558, 612, 650, 738, 832, 917

Merton, Thomas (Rev. M. Louis, O.C.S.O.) (1915–   ): *Ascent to Truth*, 12, 329, 390, 411, 622; *Canticle for the Blessed Virgin*, 843; *Figures from an Apocalypse*, 328-329; *In April When Our Land Last Died*, 252; *Living Bread*, 166, 503, 629; *Poetry and the Contemplative Life*, 34, 548, 690; *Seeds of Contemplation*, 92, 102, 213-214, 228, 259, 329, 342, 372, 381, 396, 422, 428, 435, 437, 453, 503, 602, 608, 617, 618, 629, 687, 713, 715, 721, 726, 774, 794, 819, 823, 831, 841, 876, 889, 902, 903-904, 929; *Seven Storey Mountain*, 35, 109, 426, 837, 928; *Sign of Jonas*, 30; *Waters of Siloe*, 59, 616-617, 619, 762

Methodius of Olympus, St. (d. 311), 639

Metrophanes of Smyrna, St. (d. ca.910), 370

Meynell, Alice (1847–1922): *Advent Meditations*, 9; *At Night*, 827; *Beyond Knowledge*, 819; *Builders of Ruins*, 783; *Chimes*, 59; *Christ in the Universe*, 492; *Crucifixion*, 852; *Easter Nights*, 286-287; *First Snow*, 828, 873; *Fold*, 347; *Garden*, 363, 867; *General Communion*, 198; *I Am the Way*, 493; *In Autumn*, 47; *In Early Spring*, 686, 843; *In February*, 343; *Intimations of Mortality*, 623; *Lady Poverty*, 713; *Laughter*, 523; *Launch*, 105; *Letter from a Girl to Her Old Age*, 11; *Lord, I Owe Thee a Death*, 907; *Lover Urges the Better Thrift*, 556; *Maternity*, 624; *Messina*, 283; *Modern Mother*, 510; *Moon to the Sun*, 853; *Nurse Edith Cavell*, 317-318; *Parentage*, 161; *Poet of One Mood*, 686; *Poet to the Birds*, 666, 831; *Rainy Summer*, 909; *Reflections in Ireland*, 476; *Regrets*, 753; *Renouncement*, 556, 763, 827; *Rhythm of Life*, 420; *Rivers Unknown to Song*, 777-778; *Roaring Frost*, 915; *Robert Browning*, 643; *St. Catherine of Siena*, 114; *San Lorenzo's Mother*, 13; *Shepherdess*, 811, 866; *Soeur Monique*, 152, 277, 626-627, 641, 782; *Song of Derivations*, 464, 867; *Spring in the Alban Hills*, 477; *Song of the Night at Daybreak*, 240; *Summer in England*, 907; *Thoughts in Separation*, 21; *Threshing Machine*, 568; *Thrush Before Dawn*, 868; *To a Daisy*, 238; *To Any Poet*, 251; *To O—— Of Her Dark Eyes*, 322-323; *To One Poem in a Silent Time*, 687; *To Silence*, 814; *To Sleep*, 827; *To the Beloved*, 59, 425, 814, 836; *To the Body*, 608; *To the Mother of Christ, Son of Man*, 483; *To Tintoretto in Venice*, 32; *Treasure*, 540; *Two Boyhoods*, 240, 923; *Unexpected Peril*, 543; *Unlinked*, 687; *Unmasked Festival*, 602; *Unto Us a Son Is Given*, 169, 487; *Via, et Veritas, et Vita*, 493; *Veni Creator*, 349-350; *Visiting Sea*, 549, 804, 868; *Voice of a Bird*, 678; *Watershed*, 477; *West Wind in Winter*, 915; *Why Wilt Thou Chide*, 753; *Wind Is Blind*, 915; *Wind of Clear Weather in England*, 915; *Young Neophyte*, 638; *Your Own Fair Youth*, 612

Meynell, Wilfred (1852–1948), 484

Michelangelo Buonarroti (1475–1564), 521

Michael (VIII) Palaeologus, Byzantine Emperor (1224–1282), 705

Miller, J. Corson (1883–   ), 540, 783

Miriam, Sister, R.S.M. (1886–   ), 55, 234, 295, 328, 361, 559, 832, 834, 889

Modestus of Jerusalem, St. (d. 634), 39

Moore, Thomas (1779–1852), 2, 11, 13, 20, 29, 37, 58, 66, 104, 164, 201, 208, 210, 215, 221, 227, 228, 239, 241, 250, 264, 269, 276, 277, 279, 282, 287, 293, 300, 304, 322, 327, 336, 353, 359, 360, 363, 367, 416, 421-422, 424, 425, 443, 452, 456, 459, 475, 477, 497, 510, 532, 536, 537, 539, 543, 549, 550, 555, 566-567, 568, 602, 603, 620, 621, 626, 629, 634, 636, 641, 646, 653, 654, 659, 663, 666, 667, 691, 715, 719, 735, 745, 751, 763, 782, 783, 806, 807, 810, 811, 812, 813, 831, 833, 836, 843-844, 853, 854, 879, 884, 885-886, 890, 918, 919, 922, 929

More, St. Thomas, *see* Thomas More, St.

Mowle, Peter (16th cent.), 869

Mulholland, Rosa (Lady Gilbert) (1841–1921), 358

Murray, Rev. John Courtney, S.J. (1904–   ), 125, 183, 185, 257, 473, 613, 829

National Catholic Alumni Federation, 140

*Neale, John Mason (1818–1866), 8, 12, 19, 25, 28, 35, 36, 74, 81, 166, 167, 168, 195, 201, 232, 242, 247, 283, 285, 286, 298, 369, 442, 478, 479, 488, 494, 501, 502, 534, 566, 581, 584, 599, 639, 656, 670, 682, 809, 824, 842, 854, 877

Neocaesarea, Council of, 150

Newman, John Henry Cardinal (1801–1890): *Apologia pro Vita Sua*, 4, 23, 42, 101, 108, 118, 121, 129, 146, 152, 153, 201, 209, 219, 253, 263, 269, 274, 276, 288, 297, 300-301, 311-312, 332, 360, 376, 388, 414, 423, 427, 430, 457, 471, 486, 536, 621, 720, 756, 768, 796, 804, 820, 827, 839, 888; *Development of Christian Doctrine*, 62, 117-118, 129, 146, 153, 271-272, 274, 306, 432, 643, 737, 869;

Difficulties of Anglicans, 115-116, 118, 209-210, 269-270, 327, 470, 731; *Discourses to Mixed Congregations,* 146, 165, 219, 327, 332, 376-377, 381, 388, 414, 492, 582, 638, 745, 757; *Discussions and Arguments,* 259, 274, 289, 296, 301, 332, 348, 434, 458, 545, 549, 756-757, 760-761, 802, 838, 895; *Dream of Gerontius,* 20, 503, 571, 743, 866; *Essays Critical and Historical,* 221, 262, 389, 469, 628, 688-689, 724, 737, 748, 756, 864, 866; *Grammar of Assent,* 27, 57, 62, 145-146, 152, 164-165, 208, 209, 315, 382, 395, 514, 546, 549, 706, 731, 733, 750, 751, 756, 768, 772, 849, 852; *Historical Sketches,* 12, 55, 164, 185, 209, 289, 363, 388, 544, 784; *Historical Studies,* 27, 584, 616, 902; *Idea of a University,* 29, 45, 108, 185-186, 187, 228, 289-290, 293, 297, 319, 332, 364, 398, 452, 459, 496, 514, 545-546, 599, 608, 619, 645, 672, 680-681, 690, 706, 761, 792, 848, 856, 858, 864, 866, 885, 890; *Lead, Kindly Light,* 636; *Letters,* 3, 24, 29, 89, 91, 101, 146, 210, 217, 219, 262, 270, 327, 330, 340-341, 490, 506, 536-537, 608, 643, 703, 706, 711, 714, 757, 794, 801, 849, 862, 928; *Meditations and Devotions,* 97, 118-119, 381, 809; *Oxford University Sermons,* 1, 39, 57, 108-109, 146, 164, 185, 217, 273, 327, 330, 333, 338, 430, 444, 672, 681, 748, 749, 750, 756, 882, 891; *Parochial and Plain Sermons,* 20, 156-157, 163, 225, 253, 263, 281, 304, 330, 360, 376, 420, 423, 436, 513, 633, 643, 651, 719, 756, 819, 823, 852, 882, 923, 925; *Present Position of Catholics in England,* 23-24, 64, 582, 610, 683, 737, 791, 876, 885, 929; *Sermons,* 23, 103, 118, 135, 142, 164, 349, 389, 448, 842, 925, 928; *Other works,* 26, 30, 62, 69, 107, 149, 153, 161, 169, 191, 210, 219, 228, 243, 250-251, 254, 296, 304, 323, 379, 399, 415, 424, 436, 449, 470, 493, 514, 518, 536, 537, 542, 563, 581, 586, 599-600, 603, 607-608, 610, 621, 628, 633, 638, 720, 725, 729, 743, 793, 794, 798, 803, 819, 833, 847, 862, 866, 869, 876, 877, 884, 909, 914, 918, 925, 932

Nicaea, Council of, 31, 67, 188, 317, 662, 716, 795, 891, 894

Niceno-Constantinopolitan Creed, 119, 224, 226, 372

Nicephorus I, Byzantine Emperor (d. 811), 352

Niceta of Remesiana, St. (d. ca.402), 199, 372, 485-486, 858, 875

Nicholas I, Pope St. (858–867), 175, 700, 709

Nicholas of Cusa, Cardinal (1401?–1464), 405

Noyes, Alfred (1880–), 239, 277, 345, 378, 446, 544, 558, 620, 627, 778, 780, 886, 907, 915, 926

Oakeley, Canon Frederick (1802–1880), 170

O'Brien, Edward Joseph Harrington (1890–1941), 55

O'Connell, Daniel (1775–1847), 115

O'Connell, William Henry Cardinal (1859–1944), 112, 777, 848

Odo of Cluny, St. (ca.879–943), 584

O'Donnell, Rev. Charles L., C.S.C. (1884–1934), 191, 306, 464, 564, 627

O'Hagan, Justice John (1822–1890), 75

O'Hagan, Thomas Baron (1812–1885), 97

O'Malley, Charles J. (1857–1910), 689

Optatus of Mileve, St. (d. ca.366), 13, 172, 693-694

Orchard, Rev. W. E. (1877–), 147-148, 220, 738, 744, 873

Origen (185?–254?), 18, 92, 260, 356, 386, 398, 740-741, 856, 874, 924

O'Reilly, J. B. (1844–1890), 106, 157, 264, 276, 277, 319, 359, 365, 444, 506, 559, 608, 666, 763, 783, 814

O'Riordan, Conal (1874–1948), 421

O'Sheel, Shaemas (1886–), 29, 277, 324

Pacianus of Barcelona, St. (d. ca.390), 114, 163

Pallen, Condé B. (1858–1929), 251-252, 345, 453, 463

Palumbella, Callisto (18th cent.), 94

Papal Bulls and Encyclicals:
  Benedict XII (1334–1342), *Benedictus Deus* (1336), 302-303
  Benedict XV (1914–1922), *Ad Beatissimi Apostolorum* (1914), 47, 758; *Pacem Dei Munus Pulcherrimum* (1920), 139
  Boniface VIII (1294–1302), *Clericis Laicos* (13th cent.), 191; *Unam Sanctam* (1302), 126, 132, 179, 701-702
  Clement XI (1700–1721), *Unigenitus* (1713), 127
  John XXII (1316–1364), *Licet Iuxta Doctrinam* (1327), 180, 433
  Leo X (1513–1521), *Pastor Aeternus* (1516), 222
  Leo XIII (1878–1903), *Aeterni Patris* (1879), 43, 390, 681, 864, 865; *Annum Sacrum* (1899), 790; *Ap. Const. Officiorum ac Munerum* (1897), 63, 151, 841; *Apostolicae Curae* (1896), 648; *Arcanum Divinae Sapientiae* (1880), 267-268, 578, 757; *Diuturnum* (1881), 406-407; *Divinus Illius Magistri* (1897), 291-292, 372, 440, 794, 858; *Exeunte Jam Anno* (1888), 720; *Graves de Communi* (1901), 157, 428, 528; *Immortale Dei* (1885), 18, 46, 138, 182-183, 355, 407, 540, 643, 714, 774, 845; *Inscrutabili* (1878), 138, 186, 681; *Libertas Praestantissimum* (1888), 46, 119, 139, 255, 315, 355, 358, 406-407, 526, 528, 530, 538, 748, 757; *Longinque Oceani* (1895), 143, 183, 532; *Militantis Ecclesiae* (1897), 290; *Praeclara Gratulationis* (1894), 770-771; *Providentissimus Deus* (1893), 63, 64, 721; *Quod Apostolici Muneris* (1878), 471, 734, 828; *Rerum Novarum* (1891), 38, 157, 165, 187, 336, 516, 540, 617, 713, 732, 734, 828, 845, 852, 858, 905; *Sapientiae Christianae* (1890), 46-47, 183, 185, 223, 336, 399, 663; *Satis Cognitum* (1896), 69, 119, 132, 134, 137, 678, 707; *Tametsi*

(1900), 492; *Testem Benevolentiae* (1899), 17, 139, 547, 614, 771

Paul III (1534–1549), *Sublimis* (1537), 470

Pius II (1458–1464), *Execrabilis* (1460), 708

Pius IV (1559–1565), *Injunctum Nobis* (1564), 145

Pius IX (1846–1876), *Singulari Quadam* (1854), 127; *Ineffabilis Deus* (1854), 461-462

Pius X (1903–1914), *Ad Diem Illum* (1904), 93; *E Supremi Apostolatus Cathedra* (1903), 492; *Lamentabili* (1907), 136, 147, 227, 272, 274, 483, 703, 773, 803, 885; *Motu Proprio* (1903), 627; *Pascendi Dominici* (1907), 183, 190, 614

Pius XI (1922–1939), *Ad Catholici Sacerdotii* (1935), 928; *Ad Salutem* (1930), 44; *Caritate Christi Compulsi* (1932), 377, 669, 721; *Casti Connubii* (1930), 2, 66, 161, 336, 456, 559, 572, 579, 622; *Divini Redemptoris* (1937), 199; *Lux Veritatis* (1904), 93; *Mit Brennender Sorge* (1937), 747; *Mortalium Animos* (1928), 132, 706-7, 771; *Non Abbiamo Bisogno* (1931), 115; *Quadragesimo Anno* (1931), 201, 221, 287-288, 319-320, 471-2, 517, 828-829, 905, 909; *Quas Primas* (1925), 489

Pius XII (1939–   ), *Auspicia Quaedam* (1948), 88; *De Motione Oecumenica* (1949), 771-772; *Divino Afflante Spiritu* (1943), 64; *Evangelii Praecones* (1951), 140, 613-614; *Humani Generis* (1950), 119, 133, 316, 682, 750, 773, 864; *Mediator Dei* (1947), 34, 310, 548-549, 586, 730, 731; *Menti Nostrae* (1950), 151, 728; *Munificentissimus Deus* (1950), 41; *Mystici Corporis* (1943), 119, 123, 127-128, 132-133, 137, 199, 518, 628; *Sancta Virginitas* (1954), 159, 437, 898-899; *Sertum Laetitiae* (1939), 38; *Summi Pontificatus* (1939), 449, 489, 530, 534

Sixtus V (1589–1590), *Triumphantes Jerusalem*, 106

Pascal, Blaise (1623–1662), **Pensées:* 12, 14, 18, 20, 30, 42, 57, 65, 107, 138, 152, 164, 192, 204, 210, 216, 219, 229, 233, 236, 249, 253, 276, 294, 300, 301, 306, 315, 317, 321, 327, 332, 335, 338, 348, 353, 362, 363, 367, 376, 384, 395, 403, 413-414, 420, 423, 424, 444, 452, 459, 463, 473, 504, 509, 531, 536, 539, 546, 547, 563, 566, 568, 570, 601, 603, 607, 610, 612, 621, 624, 633, 634, 637, 646-647, 674, 680, 683, 734, 749, 753-754, 755-756, 767, 774, 777, 793, 799, 805, 806, 807, 814, 823, 824, 828, 849, 866, 873, 884, 885, 886, 887, 892, 901, 904, 906, 918, 925

Patmore, Coventry (1823–1896): *Amelia,* 413; *Angel in the House,* 55, 276, 456, 556, 572, 839, 920-921, 922; *Auras of Delight,* 304; *Azalea,* 654; *By the Sea,* 540; *Child's Purchase,* 92-93; *Crest and Gulf,* 392; *Deliciae Sapientiae De Amore,* 304-305, 385, 556, 585; *De Natura Deorum,* 510, 556, 612; *Epigram,* 510; *Farewell,* 654; *Faint Yet Pursuing,* 862; *Let Be,* 436; *L'Allegro,* 59; *Magna Est Veritas,* 884; *Memoirs,* 807, 819; *Olympus,* 574; *Pain,* 651; *Peace,* 666, 830; *Principle in Art,* 29-30, 32, 45, 218, 228, 436; *Regina Coeli,* 84; *Religio Poetae,* 57-58, 331, 363, 459, 532, 547, 556, 559, 574, 604-605, 686, 689, 794, 920; *Remembered Grace,* 411; *Revelation,* 925; *Rod, Root and the Flower,* 469, 757; *St. Valentine's Day,* 842; *Tired Memory,* 277; *To His Wife,* 522; *To the Body,* 105; *To the Unknown Eros,* 296, 803, 917; *Toys,* 873; *Tristitia,* 427; *Victory in Defeat,* 255, 349; *Other works,* 147, 556

Patrick, St. (ca.385–461), 388, 717

Paulinus of Aquileia, St. (726–802), 677, 679, 780

Paul III, Pope (1534–1549), *see* Papal Bulls and Encyclicals

Paulus Diaconus (ca.720–799), 494

Pepler, Hilary Douglas (1878–1951), 334

Peter of Blois, Bl. (ca.1135–ca.1203), 728

Peter Chrysologus, St. (d. 450), 695, 726

Peter Damian, St. (988–1072), 232, 247, 302, 898

Peter Lombard (ca.1100–ca.1160), 786

Peter the Venerable (ca.1092–1156), 44, 167-168

Petrarch, Francesco (1304–1374), 248

Philip II, King of Spain (1527–1598), 521

Philip Neri, St. (1515–1595), 870

Phillips, Charles Joseph (1880–1934), 631

Piatt, John J. (1835–1917), 335-336, 443

Pise, Rev. C. C. (1801–1866), 149, 345

Pius II, Pope (1458–1464), *see* Papal Bulls and Encyclicals

Pius IV, Pope (1559–1565), *see* Papal Bulls and Encyclicals

Pius VI, Pope (1775–1799), 578

Pius IX, Pope (1846–1876): *Syllabus of Errors,* 46, 118, 127, 129, 146, 165, 181, 222, 274, 332, 377, 464, 472, 530, 598, 681, 708, 732, 734, 737, 749-750, 757, 772, 777, 802, 845, 863; *Sayings,* 522, 672; *see also* Papal Bulls and Encyclicals

Pius X, Pope St. (1903–1914), 187, 300, 829; *see also* Papal Bulls and Encyclicals

Pius XI, Pope (1922–1939), *see* Papal Bulls and Encyclicals

Pius XII, Pope (1939–   ), 34, 38, 47, 58, 92, 93, 97-98, 137, 140, 256-257, 288, 380, 407, 437, 449, 465, 470, 474-475, 517, 518, 531, 605-606, 613, 645, 666, 733, 735, 739, 781, 803, 804, 829, 837-838, 842, 846, 872, 890, 907, 909; *see also* Papal Bulls and Encyclicals

Plunkett, Joseph M. (1887–1916), 492, 834

Polycarp, St. (ca.70–156?), 154, 368, 489, 583, 629, 911

Pomerius, Julianus, *see* Julianus Pomerius

Pope, Alexander (1688–1744): *Dunciad,* 6, 153, 273, 281, 457, 477, 604, 685, 731, 785, 878; *Elegy to the Memory of an Unfortunate Lady,* 281, 318, 413, 725; *Eloisa to Abelard,* 242, 282, 565, 570, 629, 641, 644,

765, 894; *Epistle to Dr. Arbuthnot,* 239, 348, 687, 690, 827; *Essay on Criticism,* 6, 103, 210, 222, 228, 297, 298, 300, 337, 341, 348, 349, 363, 434, 446, 478, 499, 532, 625, 626, 633, 667, 672, 685, 688, 692, 715, 725, 776, 805, 806, 858, 885, 919; *Essay on Man,* 14, 38, 103, 107, 153, 156, 161, 191, 229, 255, 262, 273, 275, 281, 298, 318, 322, 335, 347, 348, 359, 361, 384, 387-388, 389, 397, 403, 406, 414, 420, 425, 432, 444, 445, 458, 473-474, 532, 537, 539, 542, 570-571, 601, 607, 633, 635, 637, 646, 647, 652, 655, 680, 684, 715, 752, 776, 777, 805-806, 809, 893, 894, 902, 903; *First Epistle of the First Book of Horace,* 282, 335, 444, 607, 671, 733, 793; *First Epistle of the Second Book of Horace,* 280, 367, 606, 685, 739, 810, 831; *First Satire of the Second Book of Horace,* 279, 343, 798; *January and May,* 574, 839, 910, 911, 912; *Letters,* 263, 264, 273, 319, 364, 572, 635, 638, 654, 685, 688, 784, 892, 919; *Moral Essays,* 171, 289, 361, 368, 397, 506, 521, 571, 572, 625, 626, 655, 731, 781, 861, 920; *Ode to Solitude,* 215, 443, 770; *Rape of the Lock,* 55, 235, 323, 418, 503, 828; *Second Epistle of the Second Book of Horace,* 293, 606, 770; *Temple of Fame,* 403, 784, 799, 902; *Translation of Homer,* 32, 250, 416, 454, 472, 516, 878, 916; *Wife of Bath,* 574, 580, 912; *Windsor Forest,* 413, 454, 679; *Other works,* 45, 161, 163, 242, 273, 282, 340, 348, 373, 421, 537, 626, 714, 776, 798, 814, 846, 881, 872

Postgate, Venerable Nicholas (1596–1679), 491

Potter, Rev. Thomas Joseph (1828–1873), 36, 167, 495, 677, 893

Pounde, Thomas, S.J. (1539–1614), 582, 584

Prideaux, Thomas (ca.1525–ca.1592), 349

Probyn, May, 169

Procter, Adelaide Anne (1825–1864), 11, 88, 197-198, 258, 276, 277, 287, 349, 384-385, 416, 445, 447, 540, 555, 615, 626, 659, 666, 690, 704, 790, 833, 844, 870-871, 880, 882, 923

Prosper of Aquitaine, St. (d. ca.463), 408, 546, 717

Prout, Father, *see* Mahony, Francis Sylvester

Proverbs, 29, 44, 159, 203, 263, 295, 434, 446, 448; *see also* Heywood, John

Prudentius, Aurelius Clemens (348–413), 72, 229, 242, 298, 428, 440, 441, 483, 489, 522, 636, 779, 877

Pseudo-Dionysius (the Areopagite) (ca.5th cent.), 73, 211, 306, 394, 546, 551, 717

Quirk, Rev. Charles J., S.J. (1889–   ), 834

Rabanus Maurus, Bl. (776–856), 19, 440, 605, 670, 793

Rabelais, François (ca.1490–1553), 710

Raccolta, 104

Randall, James R. (1839–1908), 250, 251, 585, 778, 884

Rawes, Rev. Henry Augustus (1826–1885), 207

Remigius, St. (ca.437–ca.533), 50

Repplier, Agnes (1858–1945), 15, 48, 225-226, 292, 367, 434, 435, 472, 646, 659, 841

Ricchini, Rev. Augustine (18th cent.), 782

Richard of St. Victor (d. 1173), 213, 561

Richelieu, Armand Jean du Plessis, Cardinal de (1585–1642), 265, 521

Rickaby, Rev. Joseph, S.J. (1845–1932), 41, 604, 681, 865

Robert Bellarmine, St. (1542–1621), 21, 40, 117, 137, 180, 405-406, 509, 585, 615, 710

Robinson, Henry Morton (1898–   ), 234, 794

Roche, James J. (1847–1908), 32, 251, 281, 418, 530, 537, 777, 826, 908, 918

Roman Rite: *Breviary,* 7-8, 19, 21, 24, 28, 35, 36, 39, 69, 73, 74, 79, 81, 82, 87, 90, 93, 94, 95-96, 98-99, 104, 166, 167, 171, 201, 205, 230, 231, 240, 283, 284, 298, 299, 369, 373, 399, 400, 437, 438, 440, 441, 442, 461, 462, 467, 486, 494, 495, 515-516, 522, 534, 535, 581, 582, 584, 585, 599, 605, 630, 632, 637, 639, 640, 655-656, 664, 670, 677, 679, 731, 782, 788-789, 792, 793, 809, 824, 854, 858, 862, 877, 893-894, 895, 922; *Missal,* 2, 7, 20-21, 24-25, 28, 35, 37, 43, 51, 74, 75, 88-89, 93-94, 121, 134, 145, 159, 167, 169-170, 171, 196, 208, 216, 230-231, 239, 244, 245-246, 258, 261, 265, 284, 285, 299, 338, 339, 358, 363, 371, 392, 400, 401, 409, 417, 421, 428, 431, 433, 438, 439, 441, 442-443, 450, 462, 486, 489, 493, 494, 496, 502, 507, 535, 541, 560, 576, 586, 589-596, 603, 630, 632, 652, 654, 655, 657, 661, 664, 665, 668, 670, 671, 679, 682, 700, 717, 732, 736, 744, 751, 753, 767, 776, 782, 789-790, 792, 793, 797, 808, 812-813, 822, 848, 860, 862, 877, 878, 880, 881, 887, 906, 910; *Pontifical,* 4, 68, 69, 189, 205, 206, 241, 242, 640, 726, 727, 945-950; *Ritual,* 2, 51, 244, 246, 321, 500, 502, 576, 600, 894; *Sarum Missal,* 443

Romanus the Melodist, St. (6th cent.), 169, 399, 501

Rome, Councils of, 150, 202, 575, 675, 694

Rooney, John J. (1866–1934), 305, 778, 830

Rufinus (d. 395), 79, 339, 387, 467, 481, 527

Ruysbroeck, Bl. John, *see* John of Ruysbroeck

Ryan, Abram Joseph (1839–1886), 170, 198, 345, 498, 582, 598, 654, 686, 777, 781, 782, 790, 791, 803-804, 814, 830, 833, 852, 857, 859, 879

Sacramentaries: *Gelasian,* 7, 66, 87, 90, 99, 203, 215, 218, 231, 244, 283, 673, 677, 730; *Gregorian,* 39, 231, 507, 603-604, 700; *Leo-nine,* 35, 166, 218, 302, 325, 416-417, 425, 497, 560, 565, 603, 678-679, 745, 779; *S. of Serapion,* 9-10, 50, 67-68, 243-244, 320, 784, 812, 878

Salisbury, John of, *see* John of Salisbury

Salerno, School of, 12, 26, 53, 108, 187, 192, 263, 268, 278, 287, 344, 347, 423, 601, 631, 796, 804, 908, 916

Santeuil, Jean de (1630–1697), 25, 40-41, 632, 744, 847

Sardica, Council of, 693, 697-698

Sarum Missal, 443

*Savonarola, Girolamo, O.P. (1452-1498), 216, 317, 520, 710

Scannell, Canon, 312

Secundinus, St. (Sechnall) (c.372-457), 662

Sedulius, Caelius (5th cent.), 166, 298, 489

Sedulius Scotus (fl. 840), 507

Sergius I, Pope (687-701), 535

Seton, Mother Elizabeth Ann (1774-1821), 521

Sheed, Francis Joseph (1897-   ), 107

Sheen, Fulton John Bishop (1895-   ), 28, 42, 43, 70, 200, 259, 426, 565, 739, 823, 841

Shepherd of Hermas (2nd cent.), 257, 260, 337, 342-343, 472, 496, 602, 661, 775, 832, 860, 881, 882-883, 894, 899

Sherburne, Sir Edward (1618-1702), 209, 401, 585, 861

Shirley, James (1596-1666), 58, 107, 249, 436, 665, 765, 836

Shorter, Dora Sigerson (1870-1918), 915

Sili, Louise Morgan, 564

Simeon Stylites the Younger, St. (521-597), 196

Sinnott, Rev. (19th cent.), 662

Siricius, Pope St. (384-399), 59, 150, 694, 698

Sixtus V, Pope (1585-1590), 106

Skelton, John (1460-1529), 160, 260, 273, 403, 478, 513, 623, 625, 747, 869, 873, 912, 924, 930

Smaragdus (d. 840), 507

Southwell, Bl. Robert (1561?-1595): *Assumption of Our Lady*, 40; *Burning Babe*, 30, 486; *Child My Choyse*, 359, 487; *Content and Rich*, 22, 209, 351, 607, 725, 846, 901, 905; *Death of Our Lady*, 40; *Flight into Egypt*, 441; *Fortune's Falsehood*, 351; *Great and Small*, 413; *I Die Alive*, 542; *Lewd Love is Loss*, 345, 410, 425, 552-553, 810; *Life is But Loss*, 539, 542; *Look Home*, 607, 866; *Loss in Delay*, 10, 237, 255, 257, 315, 645, 798, 868, 870, 879; *Love's Servile Lot*, 553; *Man's Civil War*, 684; *Man to the Wound in Christ's Side*, 929; *Mary Magdalen's Complaint*, 542; *Nativity of Christ*, 168, 366; *New Haven, New War*, 487-488; *Of the Blessed Sacrament of the Altar*, 77; *Preparative to Prayer*, 718-719; *St. Peter's Complaint*, 192, 322, 341, 342, 410, 472, 491, 669, 687, 763, 764-765, 818, 826, 833, 903, 920, 923; *Scorn Not the Least*, 803; *Seek Flowers of Heaven*, 303; *Sin's Heavy Load*, 818; *Time Goes by Turns*, 153, 351, 497, 869; *To the Christian Reader*, 901; *Upon the Image of Death*, 248; *Verses Prefixed to Short Rules of Good Life*, 718; *Virgin Mary's Conception*, 461; *Virgin Mary to Christ*, 94; *Virgin's Salutation*, 25

Sozomen (5th cent.), 173

Spalding, John L. Archbishop (1840-1916), 514, 663

Spellman, Francis Joseph Cardinal (1889-   ), 624

Stanyhurst, Richard (1547-1618), 371

Stephen I, Pope St. (254-257), 874

Stephen of Tournai (1128-1203), 177, 527

*Sterling, George (1896-1926), 240, 643, 636, 931

Stoddard, Charles W. (1843-1909), 59, 413

Strahan, Speer (1898-   ), 713

Stuart, Henry Longan (1875-1928), 769

Suarez, Francisco, S.J. (1548-1617), 181, 406, 509, 525, 529, 774

Sullivan, Timothy Daniel (1827-1914), 476

Sulpicius Severus (c.360-420), 829

Supreme Court of the U.S., 291

Syllabus of Errors, *see* Pius IX, Pope

Sylvester I, Pope St. (314-335), 709

Tabb, John Banister (1845-1909), 47, 65, 103, 157, 170, 239, 240, 243, 253, 261, 286, 305, 312, 315, 336, 453, 464, 540, 555, 620, 634, 685, 689, 743, 804, 811, 826-827, 866, 867, 896

Tauler, John, O.P. (1300-1361), 889

Teaching of the Twelve Apostles (Didache), 1, 3, 13, 49, 67, 70, 124, 194, 202, 307, 337, 368, 397, 422, 456, 559, 643, 661, 671, 735, 824

Teresa of Jesus, St. (1515-1582): *Autobiography*, 200, 257, 288, 562, 566, 811, 859, 920; *Maxims*, 4, 38, 200, 262, 315, 316, 341, 389, 451, 495, 506, 523, 541, 562, 607, 615, 644, 645, 751, 808, 822, 838-839, 851, 882; *Poems*, 214, 562, 882, 888-889; *Other works*, 236, 521, 617, 642, 718, 836

*Tertullian, Quintus Septimus (ca.150-ca.230): *Against Marcion*, 356, 391, 393; *Apology (Apologeticum)*, 1, 18, 26, 80, 103, 133, 158, 163, 171, 199, 227, 267, 294, 313, 397, 422, 544, 550, 583, 617, 683, 715, 778, 784, 834, 851; *De Spectaculis*, 5, 36, 246, 372, 500-501, 862; *De Praescriptione Haereticorum*, 143-144, 163, 429, 693, 850-851, 873-874; *Soul's Testimony*, 60, 246, 252, 257, 463, 518, 619, 680, 834; *To His Wife*, 158, 215, 573, 575, 634; *To Scapula*, 163, 354, 779, 871; *Treatise on the Soul*, 740, 815, 834; *Women's Dress*, 18, 53, 192, 221-222, 277, 342, 367, 455, 614, 683, 911, 919; *Other works*, 49, *85, *105-106, 202, *226, *234, *267, *573, *619, *674, 692, *697, *738, 763

Thayer, Mary Dixon, (1897-   ), 102, 161, 558

Theoctistus of the Studium (d. ca.890), 784

Theodore of the Studium, St. (d. ca.826), 502, 649

Theodosius I, Emperor of Rome (346-395), 28

Theodosian Code (Codex Theodosianus), 144, 188, 189, 429, 430-431, 699, 791, 798, 878

Theophanes, St. (759-815), 6

Theresa of Jesus, *see* Teresa of Jesus, St.

Thérèse of Lisieux, St. (1873-1897), 295

Thewlis, Venerable John (d. 1616), 769

Thomas a Becket, St. (1117-1170), 520

Thomas a Kempis (1379?-1471): *Imitation of Christ*, 2, 9, 36-37, 56, 61-62, 75-76, 156, 193, 197, 209, 232, 236, 303, 315, 317, 331, 336, 341, 343, 344, 367, 397, 398, 405, 409-410, 412, 427, 436, 451, 474, 488, 513, 516, 532,

552, 597, 619, 628, 629, 642, 654, 655, 661, 665, 712, 714, 724, 728, 739, 745, 748, 753, 761, 766, 776, 793, 797, 805, 806, 808, 813, 815, 818, 830, 840, 851, 860-861, 880, 881, 918, 923, 932; *Other works,* 106, 451, 516, 602, 881

Thomas Aquinas, St. (1225–1274): *Against the Errors of the Greeks,* 331, 387, 877-878; *Commentary on the Ethics,* 620, 691, 802; *Commentary on the Metaphysics,* 387, 549, 680, 890; *Commentary on the Sentences,* 21, 45-46, 52, 73, 130-131, 178, 196, 325, 370, 383, 468, 515, 604, 607, 609, 668, 754, 817, 820, 863; *Compendium of Theology,* 43, 314, 334, 370, 376, 468, 482, 718, 903; *Concerning Reasons of Faith,* 26, 311, 482; *Contra Gentes (Gentiles),* 19, 31, 43-44, 203, 206, 216, 225, 302, 325, 373, 387, 390, 394, 399, 417, 419, 538, 569, 668, 723, 769, 786, 822, 863; *Disputations Concerning Evil,* 3, 314, 341, 412, 725, 817-818, 821, 860; *Disputations Concerning Potency,* 225, 373, 609-610, 633; *Disputations Concerning Truth,* 57, 145, 193, 208, 306, 325, 326, 411, 525, 604, 607, 614, 673, 723, 787, 797; *Exposition of the Apostles' Creed,* 116, 121, 126, 128, 134, 135, 325, 609, 705; *Exposition of the De Divinis Nominibus,* 54, 224-225, 314, 381, 390, 512, 802, 890; *Exposition of the De Trinitate,* 598, 731, 802, 863; *Governance of Rulers,* 178-179, 404, 508, 615, 773-774, 845, 886; *Quodlibets,* 2, 61, 293, 384, 409, 412, 420, 701, 722, 875; *Sermons,* 73, 92, 576-577; *Summa Theologica,* 22, 26, 30, 31, 43-44, 46, 53, 54, 57, 61, 73, 82, 86, 91, 111-112, 129, 132, 134, 145, 156, 178, 203, 213, 223, 225, 258, 260, 261, 271, 306, 309, 311, 326, 329, 330, 331, 333, 340, 357, 366, 373, 374, 376, 380, 383-384, 387, 388, 392, 394-395, 398, 404, 409, 412, 417, 427, 428, 429-430, 432, 433, 436, 439, 457-458, 460, 468, 482, 486, 492-493, 502, 504, 505, 512-513, 517-518, 525, 526, 527, 528-529, 530, 533-534, 551, 561, 569, 577, 604, 610, 621, 624, 633, 642, 647, 671, 673, 711, 718, 723, 734, 752, 755, 765, 772, 787, 800-801, 818, 820, 859-860, 863, 871, 877, 883, 887, 888, 890, 892, 900, 902, 906, 913, 924; *Other works,* 52, 74-75, 85, 117, 131, 149, 155-156, 196, 260, 306, 330, 331, 357, 370, 387, 389, 412, 426-427, 436, 445, 468, 504, 520, 561, 577, 739, 749, 754-755, 761, 773, 786, 823, 831, 835-836, 848, 900, 903

Thomas More, St. (1478–1535): *Confutation of Tyndale,* 402, 523, 857; *Dialogue of Comfort,* 46, 62, 193, 303, 335, 425, 446, 539, 880, 905; *Meditations and Devotions,* 326, 718, 865; *Utopia,* 12-13, 273, 303, 531, 811; *Other works,* 11, 26, 60, 62, 103, 112, 140, 160, 207, 248, 260, 279, 303, 315, 316, 323, 324, 326, 335, 348, 351, 402, 410, 430, 471, 508-509, 513, 529, 531, 543-544, 552, 561-562, 567, 617, 620, 634, 696, 706, 712, 725, 735, 774, 776, 810, 848, 857, 859, 895, 920, 924

Thomas of Celano, O.F.M. (c.1200–1255), 483, 502, 729

Thompson, Francis (1859–1907): *Absence,* 654; *Assumpta Maria,* 41; *Briona Nolte,* 625; *Captain of Song,* 662; *Carmen Genesis,* 225, 926; *Carrier Song,* 2, 21, 95, 305, 831; *Contemplations,* 5; *Corymbus for Autumn,* 47, 853; *Daisy,* 472, 651, 654, 783, 791-792; *Dead Astronomer: Stephen Perry, S.J.,* 42, 97; *Dread of Height,* 334; *Dream Tryst,* 277; *Echo of Victor Hugo,* 870; *Envoy,* 45, 833, 856; *Ex Ore Infantum,* 487-488; *Fair Inconstant,* 55; *Gilded Gold,* 278, 544; *Grace of the Way,* 305; *Heaven and Earth,* 185; *Heaven and Hell,* 425; *Her Portrait,* 251, 519, 623, 837, 923; *Hound of Heaven,* 191, 211, 283, 312, 346, 385, 620, 683, 724, 870; *In No Strange Land,* 305; *Judgment in Heaven,* 540, 620, 653, 686; *Lilium Regis,* 544; *Lion and the Child,* 556; *Making of Viola,* 839; *May Burden,* 600; *Mistress of Vision,* 240; *Misc.,* 914; *Ode After Easter,* 287, 420, 659, 843; *Ode for the Diamond Jubilee of Queen Victoria,* 296, 827; *Ode to the Setting Sun,* 65, 95, 233, 253, 543, 623, 747, 854; *Orient Ode,* 78, 131, 396, 490, 510; *Passion of Mary,* 41, 95; *Past Thinking of Solomon,* 872; *Poppy,* 497, 556, 711; *Scala Jacobi Portaque Eburnea,* 837; *Shelley,* 109; *Sister Songs,* 229, 283, 386, 472, 510, 559, 620, 658, 686, 689, 827, 843, 918; *Song of the Hours,* 191, 447-448, 844, 854, 869; *To a Child Heard Repeating Her Mother's Verses,* 844; *To a Snowflake,* 828; *To Daisies,* 238; *To My Godchild,* 305; *To Olivia,* 557; *To Stars,* 844; *To the Dead Cardinal of Westminster,* 540, 573; *To the English Martyrs,* 354, 865; *Veteran of Heaven,* 658; *Whereto Art Thou Come?,* 885

Tichborne, Chidiock (d. 1586), 541-542, 930

Toledo, Council of, 878-879

Tours, Council of, 103

Tregian, Frances (1548–1608), 336, 882

Trent, Council of: *Catechism,* 116, 121, 123-124, 127, 128, 134, 309, 331, 432, 696, 702; *Creed of Pope Pius IV,* 145; *Session 3,* 62; *4,* 64; *5,* 461, 821; *6,* 2, 86, 193, 315, 327, 357, 402, 410, 417, 424, 505-506, 673, 724, 752, 818, 822, 887, 901; *7,* 52, 206, 547, 787-788; *13,* 76, 197, 311, 740; *14,* 2, 202, 203-204, 321, 668-669; *21,* 197, 788; *22,* 189-190, 309, 597-598, 796; *23,* 69, 434, 577, 648, 729; *24,* 150, 267, 577, 578, 579, 580, 898; *25,* 281, 317, 459, 470, 743, 796

Tynan, Katharine, *see* Hinkson, Katharine Tynan

*Tyrrell, Rev. George (1861–1909), 138

Ullathorne, William Bernard Archbishop (1806–1889), 4, 26, 157, 160, 213, 233, 332-333, 380, 410, 452, 458, 646, 662, 720, 775, 782, 791, 836, 840, 852, 857, 892, 902, 914, 925

United States, Constitution of the, 184

Urban V, Pope (1362–1370), 865

Urban VIII, Pope (1623–1644), 112, 710

Valens I, Emperor of Rome (328–379), 188
Valentinian II, Emperor of Rome (d. 392), 28, 188
Valentinian III, Emperor of Rome (419–455), 699
Vann, Rev. Gerald, O.P. (1906–   ), 161, 207, 437, 534, 628, 837, 922, 929
Vatican Council, 58, 64, 119, 274, 327-328, 330, 332, 377, 396, 598, 610, 652-653, 678, 696, 703, 706, 707, 750, 772
Vaux, Thomas, 2nd Baron Vaux of Harroden (1510–1556), 10, 215, 413, 541, 813, 865-866
Verstegan, Richard (1565–1620), 513, 566, 570, 714, 830-831, 869, 901
Victorinus, Caius Marius (fl. 361), 288
Vincent of Beauvais (ca.1190–ca.1264), 572, 712
Vincent of Lerins, St. (d. ca.450), 60, 81, 114, 144-5, 269, 271, 273, 340, 429, 649, 874-875
*Virgil, Publius Virgilus Maro (70–19 B.C.), 397
Vladimir I, St. (980–1015), 547
*Voltaire, François Marie Arouet de (1694–1778), 138

Walpole, Blessed Henry, S.J. (1558–1595), 479, 583-584, 764
Walsh, Thomas (1871–1928), 859
Walworth, Rev. Clarence Alphonsus, C.S.P. (1820–1900), 13, 235
Ward, Rev. Leo Richard, C.S.C. (1893–   ), 198
Ward, Wilfrid Philip (1856–1916), 635
Ward, William George (1812–1882), 607, 653
Warham, William Archbishop (1450–1532), 521
*Washington, George (1732–1799), 142
Watkin, Edward Ingram (1888–   ), 34, 148, 745
Waugh, Evelyn (1903–   ), 297

Wells, Blessed Swithin (d. 1591), 656
Westminster Hymnal, 487
Wilde, Oscar (1854–1900) : Ballad of Reading Gaol, 362, 446, 543, 731, 824; Burden of Itys, 235, 237, 627; Critic as Artist, 12, 109, 907; Decay of Lying, 32, 343, 496, 546, 567, 638, 849, 854, 859, 923; English Renaissance, 32, 35, 55, 297; Ideal Husband, 236, 337, 455, 572, 683, 746, 780, 904, 912; Importance of Being Earnest, 456, 612; Lady Windemere's Fan, 11, 12, 111, 158, 237, 472, 540, 573, 574, 692, 799, 859, 905, 921; Picture of Dorian Gray, 29, 185, 223, 228, 235, 259, 295, 296, 319, 348, 422, 522, 557, 572, 574, 614, 621, 667, 711, 739, 750, 780, 814, 848, 867, 921, 926; Soul of Man Under Socialism, The, 32, 496, 638, 732; Woman of No Importance, 11, 15, 18, 161, 239, 263, 264, 278, 364, 423, 424, 478, 557, 571, 574, 624, 799, 829, 857, 921; Other works, 4, 9, 56, 240, 253, 296, 337, 346, 347, 364, 413, 434, 492, 540, 557, 620, 625, 627, 687, 735, 833, 926
William I, King of England (William the Conqueror) (1027?–1087), 520
William of St. Thierry, Abbot (ca.1085–1148), 426, 888
Williams, Michael (1878–1950), 235, 885
Wippo (Wipo) (fl. 1041), 285, 295
Wiseman, Nicholas Patrick Stephen Cardinal (1802–1865) : Lectures, 23, 145, 706, 708, 735; Other works, 141, 660, 702
Wolsey, Thomas Cardinal (1472?–1530), 282, 520-521, 808
*Wyclif, John (ca.1328–1384), 46
Wyse, Rev. John (1825–1898), 95

Ximénes de Cisneros, Francisco Cardinal (1436–1517), 520

Young, William (19th cent.), 135, 197, 251

CORRIGENDA

Present reading	Page	Correct reading
Caswell	83b	Caswall
Sermon	91a	*Sermones*
quod ubique	144b	(quod ubique
Donation	175a, b	False Donation
Glanvill . . . (13th cent.)	194a	Glanvill . . . (12th cent.)
prevented as . . . com- municating from	194b	prevented, as . . . com- municating, from
When rocks fly	213b	When rooks fly
Sermon	258b	*Sermones*
St. John Chrysostom	285b	St. John of Damascus
hast	286a	has
man . . . assumed	290a	man assumed
Soli Deo Gloria	367b	(Soli Deo Gloria)
℣ Because	400b	℟ Because
Session 6, Canon 2	410a	Session 6, ch. II
Session 6, ch. II	410a	Session 6, Canon 2
Gelasian	442b	Gallican
informities	463a	infirmities
'Sublimis Deus'	470a	'Sublimus Deus' (June 4, 1537)
(Collect Gregorian	494a	Collect. (Gregorian
Lauterbach	508a	Lautenbach
Méaux	521b	Meaux
(5th to 8th cent.)	last line, 593b	(ca. 5th cent.)
(5th to 8th cent.)	fifth line, 594a	(4th cent.)
feast	600b	feasts
St. Thomas a Kempis	797b	Thomas a Kempis